C0-ATR-836

PROVERBS, SENTENCES,
AND
PROVERBIAL PHRASES

From English Writings Mainly Before 1500

PROVERBS, SENTENCES, AND PROVERBIAL PHRASES

From English Writings Mainly Before 1500

by BARTLETT JERE WHITING
with the collaboration of
HELEN WESCOTT WHITING

THE BELKNAP PRESS
of HARVARD UNIVERSITY PRESS
Cambridge, Massachusetts

1968

Distributed in Great Britain by Oxford University Press, London

Library of Congress Catalog Card Number 67-22874

Burton L. Stratton, Typographer

Printed in the United States of America

To

FRANCIS PEABODY MAGOUN, JR.

HAMILTON MARTIN SMYSER

ARCHER TAYLOR

our friends for more than forty years

PREFACE

When the preparation of a book has taken far too many years, the author not infrequently refers to the extraordinary complexity of his task, and to a heavy load of teaching and the other academic burdens which have hindered his research. Though these excuses might perhaps be as true in this case as in many others, candor requires the confession that this book would have been done long since save for indolence and procrastination, qualities which slow scholarship to the same degree that they make life tolerable. In recent years indolence and procrastination have been tempered, if that is the word, by my collaborator, and at this point it is proper to state her share in this book other than as a catalyst. After I had made the first typed copy of the manuscript, she did the major part of verifying the quotations and references. She then typed and proofread the final copy, including the index, and read the galley and page proofs with me. She is not responsible for the contents as such, but to her is largely due whatever accuracy and consistency the book possesses.

To list the names of all those who have given me information and advice through the years would be beyond my memory's grasp and, in any event, the result would read like a directory and necrology of scholars. George Lyman Kittredge, my faculty adviser from my freshman year through graduate school, fostered my interest in proverbs. When he encouraged me, in 1923 or thereabouts, to begin collecting for this book, he remarked, more wisely than I knew, that it might well take many years. My other friends who remember having helped me will know that I am grateful and will forgive me for not listing them in either alphabetical or chronological order.

I am deeply indebted to the John Simon Guggenheim Foundation for making me a Fellow in 1961, and to Harvard University for grants from the Joseph H. Clark Bequest. The Harvard University Press has my profound thanks for its willingness to produce so handsomely a volume not inevitably destined for the best-seller lists. Here I am happy to single out Mrs. Edward T. Wilcox, who is, in the proper sense of the word, the gossip of this book.

My greatest debt, which is both institutional and human, is to the collections and staff of the Harvard College Library, in or near which my research has been done. It contains in one form or another all but a dozen or so of the books which I consulted and these it secured for me on interlibrary loan. In the third edition (1661) of the *Compleat Angler* (p. 118) Isaac Walton quotes Dr. Boteler (?William Butler) as having said of strawberries, "Doubtlesse God cou'd have made a better berry, but doubtlesse God never did." If Walton's taste and conscience let him substitute recreation for berry and angling for strawberry, I may be allowed to put our library in the place of both.

B.J.W.

Cambridge, Massachusetts
July 1968

INTRODUCTION

SOURCES

In assembling the quotations of which this book consists an effort was made to read, sometimes more than once, everything of a literary nature written before 1500, and many things hardly literary in character, which have survived and are available. I have not attempted, save occasionally, to survey unpublished manuscript materials. Ideally this should have been done, but, aside from the inevitable postponement of a work already too long in gestation, the nature of the unprinted texts, mainly religious and didactic, suggests that they would do little more than increase the examples of sentences,[1] especially those of Biblical origin. I have made grateful use of the following bibliographical books, identified by short titles if included in my own bibliography: Brown-Robbins; Arthur H. Heusinkveld and E. J. Bashe, *A Bibliographical Guide to Old English* (Iowa City, 1931); MED: *Plan and Bibliography* (Ann Arbor, 1954); NED: *Bibliography* (Oxford, 1933); Robbins-Cutler; Lena L. Tucker and A. R. Benham, *A Bibliography of Fifteenth Century Literature* (Seattle, 1928); John E. Wells, *A Manual of the Writings in Middle English, 1050–1400* (New Haven, 1916) and Supplements; Samuel K. Workman, *Fifteenth Century Translations as an Influence on English Prose* (Princeton, 1940). Of these my greatest debt is to Brown-Robbins, Robbins-Cutler, and the bibliography for the MED, since without them I should lack what little confidence I have in the inclusiveness of my search.

In addition to things clearly or inferentially composed before 1500, I have drawn upon writings later than 1500 by a number of authors born twenty years or so before the turn of the century. These include Alexander Barclay, Lord Berners, Gavin Douglas, William Dunbar, Stephen Hawes, Sir Thomas More, John Skelton, and Thomas Watson. Finally, I have included the sayings preserved by John Heywood (c1497–1578) in his various writings. Heywood[2] is the first great collector of English proverbs,

[1] Despite its usual modern meaning, sentence now seems to me preferable to *sententia*, frequently used, or to the more cumbersome, though less ambiguous, sententious remark. The NED defines Sentence (4) as "A quoted saying of some eminent person, an apophthegm. Also, a pithy or pointed saying, an aphorism, maxim. *Obs.*" Obsolete or not, the definition is comprehensive and no medievalist should fear the obsolete.

[2] For a full discussion of Heywood's *Dialogue*, see the introduction to Rudolph E. Habenicht's edition (University of California Publications, English Studies, 25, Berkeley, 1963). Heywood used relatively few proverbs in his plays (see Whiting *Drama*, p. 181); and in *The Spider and the Fly*, where proverbs are frequent, he recast them freely.

drawn on by subsequent men of letters and makers of dictionaries alike, and his work stands as a dividing line, however thin and artificial, between the earlier and later stock of English proverbs. Anyone who turns the pages of the present volume will be struck by the number of familiar sayings which seem to appear for the first time in Heywood. An examination of the standard dictionaries of English proverbs, notably Tilley's, will show that many of the proverbs in Heywood, though not found before 1500, were recorded by sixteenth-century writers before Heywood. The temptation, therefore, to regard Heywood uncritically as the originator of this or that proverb should be resisted. That he did invent some is likely enough, since it would be an impulse hard to resist, especially in the *Dialogue*, but that he did it often is contrary to the evidence, if only because so many sayings in Heywood are found only once or twice before him, thus showing the importance of the chance survival of a text or two.[3] One thing is certain, however: if Heywood did invent a saying it was accepted without question by later collectors.

CONTENTS

Any discussion of the contents of a collection of medieval proverbs must begin with a statement of the obvious fact that, no matter how popular a saying may appear, it comes to us at one remove or more from popular usage. The medieval proverbs which survive do so only because they were written down by educated men, none of them collectors from the field. In most cases the sayings were incorporated in literary works by authors who did not hesitate to make changes suggested by context, application, and meter. We sometimes forget that Heywood's *Dialogue* and *Epigrams* are poems, although Heywood's standards of prosody are such as to let him use proverbs without too drastic changes for rhyme or rhythm's sake. What we have in most quotations is the proverb, not as an author may have heard or read it, but in the form which suited his immediate convenience or whim.

Those who edit collections of proverbial material are impelled by a tradition, dating at least from Erasmus, to furnish definitions of their wares. The results have rarely satisfied either the editors or those readers who chose to be concerned. One reason for this discomfort lies in the miscellaneous nature of the sayings which, at least since Erasmus, are brought together in most collections. We do not find solely proverbs, whether or not designated as popular, but in addition things which must be given

[3] Habenicht (p. 73) is, perhaps, too generous when he says that Heywood includes enough proverbs "without known sources to suggest strongly that he was the most original proverb maker of modern times."

other names if the word "proverb" is to carry even the slightest precision of meaning. It might be better, indeed, to attempt no exact definition of proverb but to rely rather on the common and received understanding of what is likely to be found in a book called a Dictionary of Proverbs or the like. As an old hand at collecting, quoting, paraphrasing, and attempting definitions of proverbs,[4] I am inclined to feel that there is little gain in going over the old ground once more, especially since no simple definition, or even series of simple definitions, is likely to fit everything found in a comprehensive collection. A Middle English author remarked, and the statement is not without grandeur, that "Aristotle wrote a thousand books." Aristotle also gave what Synesius called the first Greek definition of proverbs, which he said were those portions of man's early philosophy which had survived because of brevity and cleverness. We could indeed do worse than accept this definition to a point by agreeing that proverbs are ordered combinations of words, of whatever origin or age, which survived for a time because of brevity and cleverness. Even here we must be liberal in our interpretation of brevity and cleverness. In another place Aristotle says that proverbs are "metaphors from species to species." He illustrates his statement by saying that when a man receives injury rather than an expected profit, he may compare himself to the Carpathian and the hare, but he does not trouble to tell the presumably well-known story of the Carpathian and the hare.[5]

If Aristotle was the first Greek to advance a definition he was far from the last, Greek or other, to do so. For a selection of later definitions, most less satisfactory than Aristotle's if only because longer and therefore more confusing, I refer to the article already mentioned. Here I shall attempt, without any comforting hope of success, to approach the problem by discussing the contents of this book, which does not differ markedly from similar volumes. Our title calls for the inclusion of proverbs, popular in the sense that they were originally passed on by word of mouth, sentences, literary in the sense that they were originally passed on by writing, and proverbial phrases, which are even less easy to describe than are the other two. One might say that proverbs and sentences are statements which convey a more or less obvious moral or lesson, and that proverbial phrases particularize a person or situation without pointing an obvious lesson. The distinction between proverbs and sentences, however, is often

[4] My first, most elaborate, and most confident effort appeared in *Harvard Studies and Notes in Philology and Literature* 14(1932), 273–307. To my mingled gratification and embarrassment portions of this are still quoted from time to time, with or without approval. A more modest discussion, owing much to Archer Taylor, introduces our *Dictionary of American Proverbs,* but even this attempt at reasonable discrimination did not please all our reviewers.

[5] For references, see the article cited in note 4 above.

narrow indeed, and some proverbial phrases are sufficiently wise. The threefold division is, in fact, an excuse rather than an explanation.

There are several means by which the compiler of a book such as this satisfies himself that a particular saying is a proverb. In many cases an author labels a proverb as such. He may call it a proverb, a byword, an (old) saw, or he may introduce it with such words as: "men say," "it is known from old," "sooth is said," "I have heard say," "as say these clerks." We must observe that there is nothing to prevent an author from calling something a proverb which has not previously been so regarded or which may even be his own invention. Nevertheless, if something is called a proverb in the fourteenth century, it is unwise for someone in the twentieth century to disagree. Too much writing has disappeared, too little speech was ever put into writing, for us to suppose a first recording to be necessarily a first occurrence.

In the medieval period there are a number of collections, some quite extensive, of English proverbs, each accompanied by one or more Latin versions. The evidence suggests that these collections were educational tools, that the vernacular proverbs are original, and that the Latin versions are models for translation or paraphrase by students, or are examples of students' efforts.[6] Several of the collections show interrelation and derivation and certain of the proverbs are never, or rarely, found outside the collections. There are also a number of poems which consist largely of proverbs. Some of these, such as *Proverbis of Wysdom* and *Fyrst thou sal,* are no more than dogged accumulations of proverbs united by little other than meter and occasional rough associationism. The authors felt free to indulge in line and couplet fillers, and their proverbs are frequently no more than loose moral and religious statements, if "statement" is not sometimes too precise a word. Here, too, there are interrelations, but these poems have not been closely studied as a group. In addition, there are poems, such as the *Proverbs of Hendyng* and the *Good Wife* poems,[7] especially *How the Good Wyfe Wold a Pylgremage,* where proverbs have a structural function. One need only look at the surviving versions of *Hendyng* to see the degree to which scribal editors added, deleted, and substituted proverbs.

Every compiler of a collection of proverbs relies on the judgment of his predecessors.[8] If a saying has been included by a previous editor, no

[6] For a fuller account of these collections, the earliest of which is from the late Old English period, see *Franciplegius: Medieval and Linguistic Studies in Honor of Francis Peabody Magoun, Jr.,* ed. Jess B. Bessinger, Jr., and Robert P. Creed (New York, 1965), 274–7.

[7] See Mustanoja in the bibliography.

[8] I am, for example, greatly indebted to Apperson, MED, NED, *Oxford,* Skeat, and Tilley, as well as to those who have studied the proverbs in particular authors, and to editors who have enriched their notes with parallels to the proverbs found in their texts.

matter when that editor lived or what his qualifications may have been, the temptation is overwhelming to retain the saying. Authority is a mighty bulwark and, conversely, there is a natural reluctance to invite the question, If X and Y and Z considered this saying worthy of inclusion in a collection of proverbs, what are your grounds for omitting it, other, of course, than ignorance or negligence? We must face the likelihood that when collectors draw mechanically upon earlier compilations, and in English this has been customary since Bacon rifled Heywood's *Dialogue* (and also Erasmus and others) for his *Promus,*[9] a not inconsiderable number of sayings become what may be called dictionary proverbs; that is, though they are repeated from collection to collection, they are no longer found in literary or popular use.[10] Proverbs that may be dictionary proverbs will be readily recognized from lack of currency. In regard to them we are not much worse off than as regards other proverbs in one respect: until the time of the modern field collector we cannot assert with even partial assurance that a proverb was current among the people at a particular time or even that it was genuinely popular in origin.[11] That a proverb becomes obsolete does not mean that it was not once a proverb. We are at the mercy of our sources and the further back we go the less ample and reliable our sources are. For myself, if comprehensive and competent collectors, such as Apperson, the editors of the *Oxford Dictionary,* and Tilley, enter something as a proverb, then I include it here, even if I find it only once in my sources. Perhaps I should particularly mention that if a saying of Biblical origin has appeared in the collections I have ordinarily entered it, even though I have found it only in direct translations from the Bible.

Finally, the collector relies on his own judgment without regard to precedent. Most people feel able to identify a proverb, and this confidence is strengthened by familiarity. There comes to be a sense of recognition,

[9] The *Promus,* to be sure, was not printed until 1883, and then as an anti-Stratfordian piece. The English proverbs in Jan Gruter's *Florilegium Ethicopoliticum* seem to come in the main from Heywood; see Archer Taylor, *Proverbia Britannica,* Washington University Studies, XI(1924), Humanistic Studies, 2, 410–1. William Camden, in his turn, took over Gruter's proverbs for the *Remaines concerning Britane* (1614) (Taylor, 411–2), as did James Howell for *ΠΑΡΟΙΜΟΓΡΑΦΙΑ, Proverbs, or Old Sayed Sawes and Adages* (1659), which is the third part of his *Lexicon Tetraglotton* (1660). Howell also drew upon Heywood independently, so to speak, and even quoted three pages from the *Dialogue,* for once with due acknowledgment (Taylor, p. 412; Habenicht [as in note 2 above], p. 28). Howell, by the by, concluded his work with "Divers Centuries of New Sayings, which may serve for Proverbs to Posterity." Anyone who thinks that familiarity with genuine proverbs, purloined or not, leads to convincing imitations has only to read Howell to be disillusioned.

[10] See below, pp. xiv–xv.

[11] Field collectors, finding it not as easy to ask an informant to recite proverbs as to sing songs or tell tales, resort to prepared lists, a method which may produce mixed results; see Whiting *NC,* pp. 347–8.

a pricking of the thumbs, which says that a statement is proverbial. The revelation is not infallible, nor is it always immediate, since it frequently comes only with the second or third appearance of a phrase when the earlier examples are gone beyond recall. Occasionally, then, proverbial means what the editor chooses it to mean, neither more nor less. Such considered or, if one prefers, snap judgments are inevitable and in limited numbers excusable, though one would be suspicious of a collection entitled *Proverbs Newly Identified*. Like other compilers I have been guided by instinct, but not, I trust, to an excessive degree.

The preceding paragraphs have ostensibly dealt with proverbs but, so far as clear-cut definitions go, they apply to sentences as well. We may make a distinction between the two, as I once did, by saying that a proverb is an expression which owes its birth to the people and testifies to its origin in form and phrase,[12] whereas a sentence is a piece of wisdom which has not crystallized into specific current form and which anyone feels free to rephrase to suit himself.[13] We can further say that the language of proverbs is concrete, that of sentences abstract, and that there is more likely to be a second level of meaning in proverbs than in sentences. Medieval writers, however, did not give heed to such definitions and distinctions, and they used the same words and phrases for what we regard as proverbs and for what, once we have set up the two categories, we can only consider sentences. The Wife of Bath on one occasion (*CT* III[D] 659–60) uses "proverbs" to describe sentences of Biblical origin and "old saw" for a popular proverb.[14] A poet felt as free to recast a proverb as to rephrase a sentence and, though the observation about language is generally sound, some popular proverbs are abstract and some sentences are concrete. Many Middle English works are translations, and what is clearly a proverb in the original language may seem anything but popular in translation or paraphrase.[15]

Modern definitions, useful as they may be, cannot be methodically applied to the earlier period, nor do generalizations from later centuries hold. For example, Tilley, in the Foreword to his *Dictionary* (p. vii), writes as follows: "In the main, those proverbs which are illustrated by a considerable number of examples are the people's proverbs, the popular proverbs. Conversely, foreign and learned proverbs often show only a few

[12] See p. 302 of the article cited in note 4 above for an expanded version of this definition.

[13] See p. 306 of the same article.

[14] Indeed, where Chaucer applies the word "proverb" to particular sayings, we would be likely to call nineteen of them sentences and no more than five proverbs.

[15] See "Proverbs in Certain Middle English Romances in Relation to their French Sources," *Harvard Studies and Notes in Philology and Literature* 15(1933) 75–126. The many quotations in this volume from Caxton's translations afford further evidence.

examples in literature. For instance, under M80, *A blind man can judge no colors,* there is an example from Erasmus, fifteen examples in all from proverb collections, and just one from literature. The strong vitality of the English proverbs is shown by their frequency outside the collections." The statement is reasonable and the evidence persuasive, yet, if we look at this foreign, learned proverb, M50 in the present volume, we find nine examples from literature, two of them after 1500, one from a collection before 1500,[16] and two from Heywood. Tilley could almost as well have cited his P646, *Be it better, be it worse, do after him that bears the purse,* where he finds two examples from literature and ten from collections. The present volume (P441) shows three examples before Heywood, all from collections. Of the two sayings, the first is from Latin and abstract rather than concrete, while the second is, so far as we know, native English, and is concrete rather than abstract. Thus we see that Tilley's generalization is stood on its head. Nor does it gain support from Apperson (pp. 29, 54) and *Oxford* (pp. 25, 51), who give additional examples: of the first, three from literature (one each from the seventeenth, eighteenth, and twentieth centuries)[17] and one from a seventeenth-century collection, and of the second, two from literature (one each from the seventeenth and nineteenth centuries)[18] and one from an eighteenth-century collection. Neither saying is in Taylor and Whiting, and I have noted no modern instances of either, though it would be strange if authors of an antiquarian turn did not use them occasionally. With all proper diffidence, and remembering that there are fewer sources for the earlier period, these examples permit us to say that a learned origin, foreign or native, cannot be securely inferred from the number of times a saying is used, that sentences are more apt to be paraphrased and adapted, and that obsolescence is no respecter of origins. Two examples do not make a rule, any more than one swallow makes a summer,[19] and other instances might be made to yield other conclusions. In the field of popular and sententious widsom,

[16] There are more and larger collections from after 1500 than before, but that fact is of no great significance here.

[17] Another example, and by far the most artful adaptation of the saying, is in Henry Fielding's *Tom Jones* (bk. vi, ch. 1): "To treat of the Effects of Love to you, must be as absurd as to discourse on Colours to a Man born blind; since possibly your Idea of Love may be as absurd as that which we are told such blind Man once entertained of the Colour Red (ed. 1750: Scarlet); that Colour seemed to him very much like the Sound of a Trumpet; and Love probably may, in your Opinion, very greatly resemble a Dish of Soup, or a Sir-loin of Roast-beef."

[18] The second of these is from Sir Walter Scott, who commonly borrowed proverbs from printed sources.

[19] Here is a saying of classical origin, but concrete rather than abstract, rarely found other than in its fixed form, probably thought of as a popular proverb, and yet relatively uncommon in modern literary use.

definitions and generalizations are harmless exercises in ingenuity and fallibility, but they belong, if anywhere, in an introduction and should not be permitted to limit the scope and usefulness of a collection. Mr. Kittredge was fond of quoting from a freshman of long ago who wrote, "This casts a dark light on the subject," and that remark is an appropriate epigraph for this and most similar discussions.

Although the term proverbial phrase is an admitted catch-all, some of the groups of sayings commonly thought of as under the designation may be isolated. Comparisons, such as As busy as a bee (B165), As lean as a rake (R23), or As right (*also* crooked) as a ram's horn (R26, 27), and similes, such as To foam like a boar (B397), To die like a dog (D321), or To eat like a horse (H532), make up perhaps the largest number.[20] Many of these phrases are popular and have long been recognized as such, but many others are clearly literary in origin and some peculiar to a single author. One may observe, for instance, Lydgate's fondness for figures involving tigers (T284–97), and other authors are as positive in their preferences. Once one begins to collect such figures of speech it is difficult either to stop or to discriminate too closely, and I have included more examples than are to be found in most earlier collections. In the aggregate they illustrate a common, if not too admirable, trick of style. Another large group are what may be called expressions of worthlessness or contempt, such as the entries under bean (B82–93), cress (C546–9), flea (F260–3), not always to be distinguished from fly (F339–45), and straw (S804–15). These phrases, for the greater part, seem popular, but here too we must allow for the inventiveness of authors. A large group of phrases use place names to suggest inclusiveness or distance, such as Between Orkneys and Ind (O52) or From (any place, or simply hence) to Rome (R182). All collections contain some of these idioms, but I have been more hospitable to them than have most of my predecessors. Other phrases are based on various activities of animals and human beings at work and at play, such as To bend one's bow (B480), To chew on the bridle (B533), To stand on the ice (I4), To knit a knot (K97), To drive in the nail (N8), To hold the plow (P275), To lead (rule) the ring (R138), One's rock (distaff) is spun (R163), To fall with one's own sweng (S950). Still others, such as To look as the devil looks over Lincoln (D212) or Leicestershire full of beans (L192), may be called local sayings, and are far less common in the early period than later.[21] Another small group includes personal names, such as Jenken and Julian (J23), John Thomson's man (J53), Kit has lost her keys (K70), or As

[20] For a large collection of modern examples from California, see Taylor *Comparisons*, with its learned and far-reaching introduction.

[21] See G. F. Northall, *English Folk-Rhymes* (London, 1892).

wise as Tom (Jack) a thumb (T362), where the identity of the individual, if the name ever represented other than a type, and frequently the precise meaning of the phrase are lost. To dissect the proverbial phrase further would not clarify it more, and perhaps we may simply say that what is not clearly a proverb or a sentence is a proverbial phrase.

In sum and in repetition, this book is a collection of sayings, some popular and others not, some guides for conduct and some descriptive and idiomatic phrases. That readers will disagree with the propriety of some entries—and it would be odd almost to a proverb if there were not disagreement—will not disturb me to the degree that I shall be troubled when I learn of the omissions which I must have made. What is in a book can be ignored, what is not there can be neither weighed nor used.

TREATMENT OF QUOTATIONS

The men responsible for the pages from which most of the quotations in this book are taken, the men who stand between the manuscripts and the reader, range from fifteenth-century printers to twentieth-century editors. Their texts, taken all in all, exhibit nearly every variety of whimsicality, ignorance, carelessness, and conscientious scholarship. In consequence, I have tried to introduce, though probably not without exception or omission, certain conventions likely to aid the user of the book.

All quotations begin with a capital letter, and the first letter of every line of verse is capitalized. The passages from Old English are otherwise given unaltered and the following changes are found only in the later quotations. Modern usage is followed with regard to *i* and *j*, *u* and *v*. All symbols for *and* are replaced by that word and neither here nor elsewhere is the expansion of contractions indicated. Thorn and eth, and their various equivalents, are replaced by *th*. The yogh, also varied in form by scribes, printers, and editors, is represented by the letters for the sounds which seem to be intended, usually *g*, *gh*, or *y*. Some of these changes produce words whose appearance will disturb, if not revolt, textual purists, and no one is likely to deny that quotations from the *Ormulum*, odd enough unaltered, look odder still without the protective glamor of double thorns and double yoghs. Indeed, out of a nostalgia which may seem frivolous, two words have been left as Holt printed them. Finally, where marks of punctuation are absent or sporadic, I have tried to supply the minimum necessary for understanding, and I have occasionally altered editorial punctuation which seems misleading. Perhaps I have done too little pointing and have left the reader too free to follow Lord Timothy Dexter's injunction to salt and pepper to suit himself.

DATING

Few users of this volume will need to be reminded that the dates attached to the quotations are almost all approximate and frequently questionable. Dates of literary composition are at best kittle cattle, to use the Scots proverbial phrase, not the least so in the centuries with which we are concerned. Even when we are reasonably confident of the life span of an author, such as Chaucer, his individual works can rarely be fixed in time. All too few dated their own works as did the author of *Ayenbite* and, on occasion, Lydgate. Nevertheless, a collection of this kind would be confusing indeed if not arranged "on historical principles," and so I have dated in accord with the best available guides. No one, so far as I know, has ventured to compile a list of Old English writings with even approximate dates of composition. Authorities differ so widely as to the dates of the surviving manuscripts, themselves often at far removes from the author, that the task may be hopeless as well as dangerous. Here I have tried to follow the most plausible suggestions, whether traditional or lately hatched.

For the Middle English period I have adopted, unless oversight intervened, the dates of composition established for the MED (see *Plan and Bibliography*, p. 18). I have, however, systematically omitted the question marks which the MED properly affixes to many dates, on the ground that such cautions have little significance for the present book. Many works, especially short anonymous poems, from the second half of the fifteenth century are not included in the MED. Here I have depended on the Bibliography to the NED, statements by editors or commentators, and, where all else failed, on what is little better than the old rule of New England, "by guess and by gorry." Thus, I have been perhaps too free with c1450, a1475, c1475, a1500 and c1500. Advice as to dating early printed books has been given me by Miss Katherine Pantzer, the editor of the late William A. Jackson's forthcoming revision of the *Short Title Catalogue*. What I have hoped to achieve is that the chronological sequence from the first quotation of any saying to the last be substantially correct, even if individual dates may be uncertain or wrong. In any case, the dates help the searching eye to separate the quotations.

ENTRY FORMS

The entry forms in this volume are in general similar to those in Tilley. There is a lemma, or standard form, for each entry. Wherever feasible the lemma gives the usual wording of common sayings, but it will be noted that the early phrasings are not always those which were later to become fixed. Authors, indeed, reworded sayings so frequently that the lemma, even with important variations included in parentheses, cannot always reproduce the modifications presented in the quotations. In such cases the word (*varied*) follows the lemma and warns the reader to check the lemma against the quotations. The lemmas for Old English sayings are given in modern English, but here, and throughout, obsolete words are frequently retained in the spellings favored by the NED and are accompanied by translations.

The lemmas indicate the various forms of the more recurrent comparisons when the phrase is not quoted in full throughout the entry. As dead as stone (S759), for example, may appear thus, or As dead as a stone, As dead as any stone, or As dead as the stone. The lemma will read As dead as (a, any, the) stone. In the body of the entry the bibliographical reference will be followed by a, or any, or the, as the case may be.

Where sayings, usually comparisons or similes, are found only once and cannot be matched in later collections, they are brought together under a lemma for the earliest quotation (see A83 and A145). This arrangement has obvious disadvantages but seems preferable to the multiplication of short entries. In addition to economy of space, it serves to isolate the sayings most likely to be peculiar to a single author.

The alphabetical arrangement is based on a key word in each saying. Ordinarily the word chosen is the first important noun, but, where there is no suitable noun, the first important verb serves, and in the rare cases where there is neither noun nor verb of importance some other significant part of speech is used. Parasyntactic forms of comparisons follow the full form, thus Snow-white after As white as snow, and share the same number (S437). Homonyms are separated, as, if the number of entries warrants, are substantive, verbal, and adjectival uses of the same word. Unlike Tilley, I have not distinguished between the singular and plural of nouns. All sayings which come under a single key word are grouped by the first words of the lemmas, except that articles are ignored. I could wish that there were fewer sayings under such neutral words as man and thing, and the reader cannot be expected to realize the degree to which I have limited these categories.

Each lemma has a number which consists of the appropriate letter of the alphabet followed by a numeral. Thus, we have A1 to A260, and then B1 and so on.

All quotations are dated, although the dates are often far from precise (see the remarks under "Dating" above). A bibliographical reference without quotation indicates that the particular example is identical, save perhaps for spelling, with the lemma.

With few exceptions (Y11 is a notable case), all occurrences which I have noted have been entered.[22] Tilley, on the contrary, sometimes prints only a selection and gives at the end of the entry the number of occurrences which he has omitted. This expedient, to be sure, saves space, but an example will suggest that it can be detrimental. Tilley, it will be remembered (see p. xv above), uses *A blind man can judge no colors* to contrast the evidence afforded by sayings in collections with that in works of literature. As good a parallel as the one I chose would have been *The blind eat many a fly* (Tilley B451), a saying which, so far as we can tell, is native English and painfully concrete. Here Tilley has an example from Skelton and fourteen from collections, whereas in this volume (B348) there are four examples from literature, including Skelton, and three from collections before Heywood. Apperson (pp. 55–6) and *Oxford* (p. 50) add one example from the sixteenth century and two from the seventeenth. Tilley, however, indicates that he has omitted twenty occurrences, and we are left to wonder which of these are from literature and which from collections. The space saved is negligible in proportion, and even if there is little apparent utility in multiplying instances of As red as a rose (R199) and As white as snow (S437) and As still as stone (S772), it is better to have them than to leave the rare but interested reader to guess at their spread in chronology and literary use.

After the quotations, references are given to works[23] in which later examples of the saying are to be found or, nearly as significant, which show that the saying has not been recorded after the period with which we are concerned. With few exceptions, I have not attempted to cover continental collections, although books which I cite frequently refer to foreign parallels. As it stands, material is made available to trace the history of many sayings in later English and American usage. Finally, cross-references, by entry numbers, are given to comparable sayings within the collection. References of this kind are easy to multiply and I have not attempted to compete with the Index.

Until the computer, itself already proverbial, takes over proverbs, no arrangement can satisfy everyone, least of all its maker, and I can only say to this book what Chaucer said to his *Troilus*, "That thow be understonde, God I biseche!"

[22] Some discretion has been exercised in the case of foreign works which appear in several English translations. Thus, I have not entered similes from every translation of the Psalms, or sentences from every version of the *Distichs of Cato*, or every saying from Caxton's *Royal Book*, since Friar Loren's *Somme* was represented earlier by the *Ayenbite of Inwit* and *Vices and Virtues*.

[23] Perhaps I should apologize for the frequency with which my own name appears in this connection. That it is not from sheer exhibitionism is suggested, to me at least, by the fact that, if examples had been cited from Old French sources, four more titles would have been added.

BIBLIOGRAPHICAL REFERENCES

The list below is a short-title finding list for this volume and has, unlike the bibliography for the MED, no independent value. Only enough bibliographical detail is given to enable the user to locate the source; it has seemed pointless to indicate whether an early print has been read from an original or from microfilm, but published facsimiles are identified. Works quoted no more than two or three times are not entered; for these adequate references are supplied in the text.

AB: Altenglische Bibliothek, ed. E. Kölbing, Heilbronn, Leipzig, 1883–90.

Adam Davy (c1308): *Adam Davy's 5 Dreams about Edward II,* ed. F. J. Furnivall, EETS 69, 1878.

Additional MS. 37075 (a1500): *BM Additional MS. 37075, ff. 70a–71a,* ed. B. J. Whiting in *Franciplegius: Mediaeval and Linguistic Studies in Honor of Francis P. Magoun, Jr.,* ed. J. B. Bessinger, Jr., and R. P. Creed, New York, 1965, 274–89.

Aelfric *Heptateuch* (c1000): *The Old English Version of the Heptateuch,* ed. S. J. Crawford, EETS 160, 1922.

Aelfric *Homilies* (c1000): *The Sermones Catholici, or Homilies of Aelfric,* ed. Benjamin Thorpe, 2 vols., Aelfric Society, London, 1843–6.

Aelfric *Judith* (c1000): in Assmann, 102–16.

Aelfric *Lives* (c1000): *Aelfric's Lives of Saints,* ed. W. W. Skeat, EETS 76, 82, 94, 114, 1881–1900.

Aelfric *Pastoral Letters* (c1000): *Die Hirtenbriefe Aelfrics,* ed. Bernhard Fehr, *BAP* 9, Hamburg, 1914.

Against Adultery (a1500): in Horstmann *Legenden 1881,* 368–70.

Agnus (a1450): *Agnus Castus, a Middle English Herbal,* ed. Gösta Brodin, Essays and Studies on English Language and Literature 6, Upsala, 1950.

AJP: American Journal of Philology 1(1880)—.

Alas! what rulythe (a1500): in *Report on the Manuscripts of Lord Middleton,* Historical Manuscripts Commission, 1911, 267–8.

Alcock *Mons* (1496): John Alcock, *Mons perfeccionis, otherwyse in englysshe the hyll of perfeccion,* W. de Worde, 1496.

Alcock *Sermo pro episcopo* (a1500): *In die Innocencium, Sermo pro episcopo puerorum,* W. de Worde, [?1496].

Alexander A (c1350): *The Gests of King Alexander of Macedon,* ed. Francis P. Magoun, Jr., Cambridge, Mass., 1929, 121–70.

Alexander B (c1350): as above, 171–216.

Alexander C (a1400 [*Ashmole*], a1500 [*Dublin*]): *The Wars of Alexander,* ed. W. W. Skeat, EETS ES 47, 1886. (All quotations are from *Ashmole* unless *Dublin* is specified.)

Alexander Buik (c1400): *The Buik of Alexander,* ed. R. L. Graeme Ritchie, 4 vols., paged continuously, STS, 1921–9.

Alexander-Cassamus (a1500): *Editio Princeps des mittelenglischen Cassamus (Alexanderfragmentes) der Universitätsbibliothek Cambridge,* ed. Karl Rosskopf, Erlangen, 1911.

Alexius (c1400): *The Life of St. Alexius* in Adam Davy, 19–79.

Alfred *Augustine* (a900): *König Alfreds des Grossen Bearbeitung der Soliloquien des Augustinus,* ed. W. Endter, *BAP* 11, Hamburg, 1922.

Alfred *Boethius* (897): *King Alfred's Old English Version of Boethius, De Consolatione Philosophiae,* ed. Walter J. Sedgefield, Oxford, 1899.

Alfred *Gregory* (a900): *King Alfred's West-Saxon Version of Gregory's Pastoral Care,* ed. Henry Sweet, EETS 45, 50, 1871–2.

Alfred *Lays of Boethius* (a900): in Alfred *Boethius,* 151–204.

Alfred *Orosius* (a900): *King Alfred's Orosius,* ed. Henry Sweet, EETS 79, 1883.

Alisaunder (a1300): *Kyng Alisaunder,* ed. G. V. Smithers, 2 vols., EETS 227, 237, 1952–7. (The text is in vol. I, which is cited without volume number.)

Allen *R. Rolle* (v.d.): *English Writings of Richard Rolle,* ed. Hope Emily Allen, Oxford, 1931.

Alphabet (c1450): *An Alphabet of Tales,* ed. Mary M. Banks, EETS 126–7, 1904–5.

Alysoun (c1325): in Brown *Lyrics XIII,* 138–9.

Amadace (a1400): *Ireland Blackburne MS.* in John Robson, *Three Early English Metrical Romances,* CS 18, 1842, 27–56; (a1500): *Advocates MS. 19.3.1* in Henry Weber, *Metrical Romances of the Thirteenth, Fourteenth, and Fifteenth Centuries,* 3 vols., Edinburgh, 1810, III, 243–75.

Amis (c1300): *Amis and Amiloun,* ed. MacEdward Leach, EETS 203, 1937.

Amours: F. J. Amours, ed., *Scottish Alliterative Poems in Riming Stanzas,* STS, 1892–7.

Ancrene (a1200): *Ancrene Wisse, edited from MS. Corpus Christi College Cambridge 402* by J. R. R. Tolkien, EETS 249, 1962.

Ancrene (GC) (a1300): *The English Text of the Ancrene Riwle, edited from Gonville and Caius College MS. 234/120* by R. M. Wilson, EETS 229, 1954.

Ancrene (Merton) (a1350): *The Latin Text of the Ancrene Riwle, edited from Merton College MS. 44* by Charlotte D'Evelyn, EETS 216, 1944.

Ancrene (Nero) (a1250): *The English Text of the Ancrene Riwle, edited from Cotton MS. Nero A.XIV* by Mabel Day, EETS 225, 1952.

Ancrene (Recluse) (a1400): *The Recluse,* ed. Joel Påhlsson, Lund, 1918.

Ancrene (Royal) (a1500): *The English Text of the Ancrene Riwle, edited from British Museum MS. Royal 8 C.1* by A. C. Baugh, EETS 232, 1956.

Ancrene (Trinity) (a1300): *The French Text of the Ancrene Riwle, edited from Trinity College Cambridge MS. R.14.7* by W. H. Trethewey, EETS 240, 1958.

Ancrene (Vitellius) (a1300): *The French Text of the Ancrene Riwle, edited from British Museum MS. Cotton Vitellius F vii* by J. A. Herbert, EETS 219, 1944.

Anglo-Saxon Charms (v.d.): Godfrid Storms, *Anglo-Saxon Magic,* 's-Gravenhage, 1948.

Annot (c1325): *Annot and Johon* in Brown *Lyrics XIII,* 136–8.

Apocalypse (c1350): *An English Fourteenth Century Apocalypse Version with a Prose Commentary,* ed. Elis Fridner, Lund Studies in English 29, 1961.

Apology (c1400): *An Apology for Lollard Doctrines,* ed. James H. Todd, CS 20, 1842.

Apperson: G. L. Apperson, *English Proverbs and Proverbial Phrases: A Historical Dictionary,* London, 1929.

Archiv: Archiv für das Studium der neueren Sprachen und Literaturen 1(1846)—.

Arderne *Fistula* (c1425): John Arderne, *Treatises of Fistula in Ano,* ed. D'Arcy Power, EETS 139, 1910.

Arthour and M.[1] (a1300): *Arthour and Merlin, nach der Auchinleck-HS.*, ed. Eugen Kölbing, *AB* 4, Leipzig, 1890.

Arthour and M.[2] (a1425 [*Lincoln's Inn*], a1500 [*Douce*]): *Arthour and Merlin* (the later version), as above, 275–370.

Arthour and M.[3] (c1500): *Merline* in *Percy Folio Manuscript*, I, 422–96.

Arthur (a1400): ed. F. J. Furnivall, EETS 2, 1864.

Arundel Vulgaria (c1495): *A Fifteenth Century School Book from a Manuscript in the British Museum* (*MS. Arundel 249*), ed. William Nelson, Oxford, 1956.

Ashby: George Ashby's *Poems*, ed. Mary Bateson, EETS ES 76, 1899.

Ashby *Dicta* (a1475): *Dicta et opiniones diversorum philosophorum*, as above, 42–100.

Ashby *Policy* (a1471): *Active Policy of a Prince*, as above, 12–41.

Ashby *Prisoner* (1463): *A Prisoner's Reflections*, as above, 1–12.

Ashmole: Elias Ashmole, *Theatrum Chemicum Britannicum*, London, 1652.

ASMP: The Anglo-Saxon Minor Poems, ed. Elliott V. K. Dobbie, *ASPR*, VI, 1942.

Asneth (a1475): *The Storie of Asneth*, ed. H. N. MacCracken, *JEGP* 9(1910), 224–64.

ASPR: The Anglo-Saxon Poetic Records, ed. George P. Krapp, 6 vols., New York, 1931–42.

Assembly (a1500): *The Assembly of Ladies* in Skeat *Chaucerian*, 380–404.

Assembly of Gods (a1475): [John Lydgate], *The Assembly of Gods*, ed. Oscar L. Triggs, Chicago, 1895; EETS ES 69, 1896.

Assmann: Bruno Assmann, ed., *Angelsächsische Homilien und Heiligenleben*, *BAP* 3, 1889.

Athelston (a1400): ed. A. McI. Trounce, EETS 224, 1951.

Audelay (a1450): *The Poems of John Audelay*, ed. Ella K. Whiting, EETS 184, 1931.

Avowynge (c1425): *The Avowynge of King Arther* in John Robson, *Three Early English Metrical Romances*, CS 18, 1842, 57–93.

Awntyrs (a1400): *The Awntyrs off Arthure at the Terne Wathelyne* in Amours, 116–71.

Ayenbite (1340): *Dan Michel's Ayenbite of Inwyt*, ed. Richard Morris, EETS 23, 1866.

Banester *Guiscardo* (a1475): *Early English Versions of the Tales of Guiscardo and Ghismonda*, ed. Herbert G. Wright, EETS 205, 1937, 2–37.

Bannatyne (v.d.): *The Bannatyne Manuscript*, ed. W. Tod Ritchie, 4 vols., STS, 1928–34.

BAP: Bibliothek der angelsächsischen Prosa, ed. C. W. M. Grein *et al.*, 1872—.

Barbour *Bruce* (c1375): *The Bruce . . . Compiled by Master John Barbour*, ed. W. W. Skeat, 2 vols., STS, 1894.

Barclay *Castell* (1506): *The Castell of Labour*, translated from the French of Pierre Gringore by Alexander Barclay . . . with an Introduction by A. W. Pollard, RC 143, 1905.

Barclay *Eclogues* (c1515): *The Eclogues of Alexander Barclay*, ed. Beatrice White, EETS 175, 1928.

Barclay *Mirrour* (c1523): *The Mirrour of Good Maners*, reprinted from the edition of 1570, Spenser Society, 1885.

Barclay *St. George* (1515): *The Life of St. George*, ed. William Nelson, EETS 230, 1955.

Barclay *Ship* (1509): *The Ship of Fools*, ed. T. H. Jamieson, 2 vols., Edinburgh, 1874.

Barlam (1438): *Barlaam und Josaphat*, ed. C. Horstmann, Programm . . . des . . . Gymnasiums zu Sagan, Sagan, 1877.

Barlam and Josaphat (*Northern*) (1438): in Horstmann *Altenglische Legenden 1875*, 226–40.

Barlam and Josaphat (*South English Legendary*) (a1450): as above, 113–48.

Barlam and Josaphat (*Vernon*) (1438): as above, 215–25.

Bartholomaeus-Trevisa (a1398[1495]): *Bartholomeus de proprietatibus rerum*, tr. John de Trevisa, W. de Worde, 1495.

Basterfeld (a1500): in Horstmann *Legenden 1881*, 367–8.

Basyn (a1500): *The Tale of the Basyn* in Hazlitt *EPP*, III, 44–53.

Becket I (c1300): *The Life and Martyrdom of Thomas Beket*, ed. William H. Black, PS 19, 1845.

Becket II (c1300): *Die ME. Thomas Beket-legende des Gloucesterlegendars*, ed. Hermann Thiemke, Palaestra 131, Berlin, 1919.

Becket III (a1500): "The Legend of the Saracen Princess" in Paul A. Brown, *The Development of the Legend of Thomas Becket*, Philadelphia, 1930, 262–8.

Bede (a900): *The Old English Version of Bede's Ecclesiastical History of the English People*, ed. Thomas Miller, Part I, EETS 95–6, 1890–91.

Beowulf (c735): *Beowulf and the Fight at Finnsburg*, ed. Fr. Klaeber, 3d ed., Boston, 1936.

Bernardus *De cura* (a1500): *Bernardus de cura rei famuliaris*, ed. J. R. Lumby, EETS 42, 1870.

Berners *Arthur* (a1533): John Bourchier, Lord Berners, *The History of the Valiant Knight, Arthur of Little Britain*, ed. E. V. Utterson, London, 1814.

Berners *Castell* (a1533): *The Castell of love, translated out of Spanyshe into Englysshe, by John Bowrchier, knyght, lorde Bernes*, R. Wyer, London, c1552.

Berners *Froissart* (1523 [vols. 1–3], 1525 [vols. 4–6]): *The Chronicle of Froissart, Translated out of French by Sir John Bourchier, Lord Berners, Annis 1523–25*, with an Introduction by W. P. Ker, 6 vols., Tudor Translations, London, 1901–3.

Berners *Golden Boke* (1532): José M. Gálvez, *Guevara in England, nebst Neudruck von Lord Berners' "Golden Boke of Marcus Aurelius,"* Palaestra 109, Berlin, 1916.

Berners *Huon* (a1533): *The Boke of Duke Huon of Burdeux done into English by Sir John Bourchier, Lord Berners*, ed. S. L. Lee, EETS ES 40, 41, 43, 50, 1882–7.

?Berners *Boke of St. Albans* (1486): Dame Juliana Berners, *The Boke of Saint Albans*, with an Introduction by William Blades, London, 1899.

Beryn (c1400): *The Tale of Beryn*, ed. F. J. Furnivall and W. G. Stone, Chaucer Society, 1887; EETS ES 105, 1909.

Bestiary (a1250): in Morris *Old English Miscellany*, 1–25.

Betson *Treatyse* (c1500): Thomas Betson (?Betton), *A ryght profytable treatyse*, W. de Worde, c1500; facsimile, Cambridge, 1905.

Beves (c1300 [*Auchinleck*], a1500 [*M* (*Chetham*)]): *The Romance of Sir Beves of Hamtoun*, ed. Eugen Kölbing, EETS ES 46, 48, 65, 1885–94.

Blickling Homilies (c970): ed. R. Morris, EETS 58, 63, 73, 1874–80.

Body and Soul (c1330 [*Auchinleck*], c1300 [*Laud*], c1390 [*Vernon*], a1450 [*Digby*]): *The Desputisoun Bitwen the Bodi and the Soule*, ed. Wilhelm Linow, *EB* 1, 1889. (*Auchinleck* is quoted without designation, *Laud* as *L*, *Vernon* as *V*, and *Digby* as *D*.)

Body and Soul (*Royal*) (a1450): *A disputeson betwen the body and the sowle*, ed. H. Varnhagen, *Anglia* 2(1878–9), 229–44.

Böddeker: K. Böddeker, ed., *Altenglische Dichtungen des MS. Harl. 2253,* Berlin, 1878.

Boke of Curtasye (*Sloane*) (a1450): in Furnivall *Babees Book,* 299–327.

Boke of Noblesse (c1451): ed. John G. Nichols, RC 77, 1860.

Bokenham (1447): Osbern Bokenham, *Legendys of Hooly Wummen,* ed. Mary S. Serjeantson, EETS 206, 1938.

Bokenham *Mappula* (a1447): *Mappula Angliae,* ed. C. Horstmann, *ESt* 10(1887), 1–34. (Drawn from Higden's *Polychronicon.*)

Bonaventura *Meditations* (a1325): *Meditations on the Supper of Our Lord,* ed. J. M. Cowper, EETS 60, 1875.

Bonum Est (a1400): *Bonum Est Confiteri Domino* in *Qui Habitat,* 51–92.

Bowers *Three Middle English Religious Poems:* R. H. Bowers, ed., *Three Middle English Religious Poems,* University of Florida Monographs, Humanities, 12, 1963.

Bozon *Contes* (a1400): *Les Contes Moralisés de Nicole Bozon,* ed. Lucy T. Smith and Paul Meyer, SATF, 1889.

?Bradshaw *Radegunde* (c1500): ?Henry Bradshaw, *The Lyfe of Saynt Radegunde,* ed. F. Brittain, Cambridge, 1926.

Bradshaw *St. Werburge* (1513): Henry Bradshaw, *The Life of Saint Werburge of Chester,* ed. C. Horstmann, EETS 88, 1887.

?Brampton *Psalms* (1414): *A Paraphrase on the Seven Penitential Psalms in English Verse, Supposed to have been Written by Thomas Brampton,* ed. W. H. Black, PS 5, 1842.

Brinton *Sermons* (v.d.): *The Sermons of Thomas Brinton, Bishop of Rochester* (*1373–1389*), ed. Sister Mary A. Devlin, 2 vols., CS, 3d Series, 85–6, 1954.

Brotanek: Rudolf Brotanek, ed., *Mittelenglische Dichtunge aus der Handschrift 432 des Trinity College in Dublin,* Halle, 1940.

Brown *Lyrics XV:* Carleton Brown, ed., *Religious Lyrics of the XVth Century,* Oxford, 1939.

Brown *Lyrics XIV: Religious Lyrics of the XIVth Century,* 2d ed. rev. G. V. Smithers, Oxford, 1952.

Brown *Lyrics XIII: English Lyrics of the XIIIth Century,* Oxford, 1932.

Brown *Register: A Register of Middle English Religious and Didactic Verse,* 2 vols., Oxford, 1916–20.

Brown-Robbins: Carleton Brown and Rossell H. Robbins, *The Index of Middle English Verse,* Index Society, New York, 1943.

Brut (c1400 and v.d.): *The Brut or the Chronicles of England,* ed. Friedrich W. D. Brie, EETS 131, 136, 1906–8.

Burgh *Cato* (a1440): "Die Burghsche Cato-Paraphrase," ed. Max Förster, *Archiv* 115(1905), 298–323, 116(1906), 25–40.

Burial and Resurrection (c1485): in *Digby Plays,* 171–226.

Canticum de Creatione (1375): ed. C. Horstmann, *Anglia* 1(1877–8), 303–31.

Capgrave *Chronicle* (a1464): John Capgrave, *The Chronicle of England,* ed. Francis C. Hingeston, RS 1, 1858.

Capgrave, *Katharine* (c1450): *The Life of St. Katharine of Alexandria,* ed. C. Horstmann and F. J. Furnivall, EETS 100, 1893.

Capgrave *Lives* (c1450): *Lives of St. Augustine and St. Gilbert,* ed. J. J. Munro, EETS 140, 1910.

Capgrave *Solace* (c1450): *Ye Solace of Pilgrimes,* ed. C. A. Mills, London, 1911.

Carl (a1445): *Sir Gawain and the Carl of Carlisle,* ed. Auvo Kurvinen, Annales Academiae Scientiarum Fennicae B 71.2, Helsinki, 1951.

Carpenter's Tools (a1500): *The Debate of the Carpenters Tools* in Hazlitt *EPP*, I, 79–90.

Castel of Love (c1390): in *Vernon*, I, 355–406.

Castelford (a1350): Thomas Castelford, *Chronicle*, ed. (in part) Frank Behre, Göteborgs Högskolas Årsskrift 46.2, 1940.

Castle (a1450): *The Castell of Perseverance* in *Macro Plays*, 77–186.

Catholicon Anglicum (1483): ed. S. J. H. Herrtage, EETS 75, 1881.

Cato (*Copenhagen*) (a1400): *Distichs of Cato*, Copenhagen Royal Library MS. Thott in-folio 306. (Printed in part by A. Brusendorff in K. Malone and M. B. Ruud, *Studies in English Philology: A Miscellany in Honor of Frederick Klaeber*, Minneapolis, 1929, 320–39; but all quotations are taken from a photostat of the manuscript.)

Cato (*Rawlinson*) (a1475): "Eine nordenglische Cato-Version," ed. Max Förster, *ESt* 36(1906), 4–55, odd pages.

Cato (*Sidney*) (c1450): as above, even pages.

Cato (*Vernon*) (c1390): in *Vernon*, II, 553–609.

Caxton *Aesop* (1484): *The Fables of Aesop as first printed by William Caxton in 1484*, ed. Joseph Jacobs, 2 vols., London, 1889. (The text is in vol. II.)

Caxton *Arte and Crafte* (1490): *A lityll treatise . . . of the arte and crafte to knowe well to dye*, 1490.

Caxton *Aymon* (c1489): *The Right Plesaunt and Goodly Historie of the Foure Sonnes of Aymon*, ed. Octavia Richardson, EETS ES 44–5, 1884–5.

Caxton *Blanchardyn* (c1489): *Blanchardyn and Eglantine*, ed. Leon Kellner, EETS ES 58, 1890.

Caxton *Book of Good Manners* (1487): *Book of good maners* (1487), Pynson, 1494.

Caxton *Cato* (1483): [*Distichs of*] *Cathon*, 1483. Translation of a French prose version.

Caxton *Charles* (1485): *The Lyf of the Noble and Crysten Prynce, Charles the Grete*, ed. S. J. H. Herrtage, EETS 36–7, 1881.

Caxton *Chesse* (1474): *Game and Playe of the Chesse*, ed. William E. A. Axon, London, 1883.

Caxton *Chronicles* (1480): *Cronycles of Englonde* (1480), 1482.

Caxton *Curial* (1484): *The Curial made by maystere Alain Charretier*, ed. F. J. Furnivall, EETS ES 54, 1888.

Caxton *Curtesye* (c1477): *Book of Curtesye*, ed. F. J. Furnivall, EETS ES 3, 1868.

Caxton *Dialogues* (c1483): *Dialogues in French and English*, ed. Henry Bradley, EETS ES 79, 1900.

Caxton *Doctrinal* (1489): *The Doctrinal of Sapyence*, Westminster, 1489.

Caxton *Eneydos* (1490): ed. W. T. Culley and F. J. Furnivall, EETS ES 57, 1890.

Caxton *Fayttes* (1489): *The Book of Fayttes of Armes and of Chyvalrye*, ed. A. T. P. Byles, EETS 189, 1932(1937).

Caxton *Godeffroy* (1481): *Godeffroy of Boloyne*, ed. Mary N. Colvin, EETS ES 64, 1893.

Caxton *Golden Legende* (1483): *The Golden Legende* (1483), [W. de Worde], 1493.

Caxton *Jason* (c1477): *The History of Jason*, ed. John Munro, EETS ES 111, 1913.

Caxton *Mirror* (1481): *Mirrour of the World*, ed. Oliver H. Prior, EETS ES 110, 1913.

Caxton *Ordre of Chyvalry* (1484): *The Book of the Ordre of Chyvalry*, ed. A. T. P. Byles, EETS 168, 1926.

Caxton *Ovyde* (1480): *Ovyde Hys Booke of Methamorphose, Books X-XV*, ed. Stephen Gaselee and H. F. B. Brett-Smith, Oxford, 1924.

Caxton *Paris* (1485): *Paris and Vienne*, ed. MacEdward Leach, EETS 234, 1957.

Caxton *Recuyell* (1471): *The Recuyell of the Historyes of Troye,* ed. H. Oskar Sommer, 2 vols., London, 1894.

Caxton *Reynard* (1481): *The History of Reynard the Fox,* ed. Edward Arber, English Scholar's Library 1, London, 1878.

Caxton *Royal Book* (1484): *The ryal book or a book for a kyng,* 1484.

Caxton *St. Winifred* (c1485): ed. C. Horstmann, *Anglia* 3(1880), 295–313.

Cely Papers (v.d.): ed. Henry E. Malden, CS, 3d Series, 1, 1900.

Charles of Orleans (c1440): *The English Poems of Charles of Orleans,* ed. Robert Steele, 2 vols., EETS 215, 220, 1941, 1946.

Chastising (c1400): *The Chastising of God's Children and the Treatise of Perfection of the Sons of God,* ed. Joyce Bazire and Eric Colledge, Oxford, 1957.

Chaucer: *The Works of Geoffrey Chaucer,* ed. F. N. Robinson, 2d ed., Boston, 1957. (Page references in the following entries are to this edition.)

Chaucer *ABC* (c1370): *An A B C,* 524–6.

?Chaucer *Against Women Unconstant* (c1370): 540.

Chaucer *Anel.* (c1375): *Anelida and Arcite,* 304–8.

Chaucer *Astr.* (1391): *A Treatise on the Astrolabe,* 545–63.

Chaucer *BD* (1369): *The Book of the Duchess,* 267–79.

Chaucer *Boece* (c1380): 320–84.

Chaucer *Bukton* (c1396): *Lenvoy de Chaucer a Bukton,* 539.

Chaucer *CT* (v.d.): *The Canterbury Tales,* 17–265.

Chaucer *Fortune* (c1390): 535–6.

Chaucer *Gentilesse* (c1380): 536.

Chaucer *HF* (c1380): *The House of Fame,* 282–302.

Chaucer *Lady* (c1370): *A Complaint to his Lady,* 528–9.

Chaucer *LGW* (c1386[Prol. F], c1395[Prol. G]): *The Legend of Good Women,* 482–518.

Chaucer *Mars* (c1385): *The Complaint of Mars,* 529–33.

?Chaucer *Merciles Beaute* (c1390): 542.

Chaucer *PF* (c1380): *The Parliament of Fowls,* 310–8.

Chaucer *Pity* (c1370): *The Complaint unto Pity,* 526–8.

?Chaucer *Proverbs* (c1390): 543.

Chaucer *Purse* (1399): *The Complaint of Chaucer to his Purse,* 539–40.

?Chaucer *Rom. A* (a1400): *The Romaunt of the Rose, Fragment A,* 565–81.

Chaucer *Rosemounde* (c1380): *To Rosemounde,* 533.

Chaucer *Scogan* (c1393): *Lenvoy de Chaucer a Scogan,* 538–9.

Chaucer *Stedfastnesse* (c1390): *Lak of Stedfastnesse,* 537.

Chaucer *TC* (c1385): *Troilus and Criseyde,* 389–479.

Chaucer *Truth* (c1390): 536.

Chauliac (a1425): *The Middle English Translation of Guy de Chauliac's Anatomy,* ed. Björn Wallner, Lunds Universitets Årsskrift, N.F., Avd. 1, 56.5, Lund, 1964.

Chaunce (c1450): "The Chance of the Dice," ed. Eleanor P. Hammond, *ESt* 59(1925), 1–16.

Chester Plays (a1425): ed. H. Deimling and Dr. G. W. Matthews, EETS ES 62, 115, 1893, 1916.

Chestre *Launfal* (a1400): Thomas Chestre, *Sir Launfal,* ed. A. J. Bliss, London, 1960.

Chevelere (a1400): *The Romance of the Chevelere Assigne,* ed. Henry H. Gibbs, EETS ES 6, 1868.

Child: Francis J. Child, ed., *The English and Scottish Popular Ballads,* 5 vols., Boston, 1882–98.

Child (a1400): *The Child of Bristowe* in Horstmann *Legenden 1881,* 315–21.

Chronicle (c1325): *An Anonymous Short English Metrical Chronicle,* ed. Ewald Zettl, EETS 196, 1935.

Chronicle of London (c1443 and v.d.): *A Chronicle of London from 1089 to 1483,* [ed. Nicolas H. Nicolas and Edward Tyrrell], London, 1827.

Chronicles of London (v.d.): ed. Charles L. Kingsford, Oxford, 1905.

Claudian *Stilicho* (1445): "Eine mittelenglische Claudian-Übersetzung," ed. Ewald Flügel, *Anglia* 28(1905), 255–99.

Cleanness (c1380): *Purity,* ed. Robert J. Menner, Yale Studies in English 61, New Haven, 1920.

Cleansing (a1400): *The Cleansing of Man's Soul,* ed. Charles L. Regan, unpublished Harvard dissertation, 1963.

Cleges (c1400): *Sir Cleges* in McKnight, 38–59.

Cloud (a1400): *The Cloud of Unknowing,* ed. Phyllis Hodgson, EETS 218, 1944.

Cock (c1500): *Cock Lorell's Bote,* ed. E. F. Rimbault, PS 9, 1843.

Cockayne: T. Oswald Cockayne, ed., *Leechdoms, Wortcunning, and Starcraft of Early England,* 3 vols., RS, 1864–6.

Colkelbie (a1500): *Colkelbie Sow* in *Bannatyne,* IV, 279–308.

Colyn Blowbol (a1500): *Colyn Blowbols Testament* in Hazlitt *EPP,* I, 92–109.

Complaint against Hope (c1450): ed. Kenneth G. Wilson, University of Michigan Contributions in Modern Philology 21, 1957.

Consail and Teiching (c1450): *The Consail and Teiching at the Vys Man Gaif his Sone* in Girvan, 66–79.

Consilia Isidori (c1400): in *Yorkshire Writers,* II, 367–74.

Contemplacioun (c1480): *The Contemplacioun of Synnaris* in *The Asloan Manuscript,* ed. W. A. Craigie, 2 vols., STS, 1923–5, II, 187–241.

Conversion (c1485): *The Conversion of St. Paul* in *Digby Plays,* 27–52.

Copland *Apolyn* (1510): Robert Copland, *The Romance of Kynge Apollyn of Thyre,* reproduced in facsimile by Edmund W. Ashbee, London, 1870.

Copland *Helyas* (1512): *The History of Helyas Knight of the Swan* [with an introduction by Robert Hoe], Grolier Club, New York, 1901.

Corneus (a1500): *Syre Corneus,* ed. Hermann Hedenus, Erlangen, 1904.

Court of Love (a1500): in Skeat *Chaucerian,* 409–47.

Court of Sapience (c1475): ed. Robert Spindler, Beiträge zur englischen Philologie 6, Leipzig, 1927.

Coventry Plays (a1500): *Two Coventry Corpus Christi Plays,* ed. Hardin Craig, EETS ES 87, 1902(1957).

CS: Camden Society, Publications, London, 1838—.

Cursor (a1325 [*C(otton Vesp.)*], a1400 [*F(airfax), G(öttingen), T(rinity)*]): *Cursor Mundi,* ed. Richard Morris, 3 vols., EETS 57, 59, 62, 66, 68, 99, 101, 1874–93. (When the versions are in virtual agreement, *C* is quoted without designation.)

Dame Sirith (a1400): in McKnight, 1–20.

Daw Topias (1402): *The Reply of Friar Daw Topias* in Wright *Political Poems,* II, 39–114.

De Claris Mulieribus (c1450): *Die mittelenglische Umdichtung von Boccaccios De Claris Mulieribus,* ed. Gustav Schleich, Palaestra 144, Leipzig, 1924.

De Clerico (c1325): *De Clerico et Puella* in Brown *Lyrics XIII,* 152–4.

De Miraculo Beate Marie (a1440): in Horstmann *Legenden 1881,* 503–4.

Death and Life (a1450): *Death and Liffe,* ed. Israel Gollancz, Select Early English Poems 5, London, 1930.

Defence (1459): "A Defence of the Proscription of the Yorkists in 1459," ed. J. P. Gilson, *English Historical Review* 26(1911), 512–23.

Defensor *Liber* (a1050): Defensor's *Liber Scintillarum, with an Interlinear Anglo-Saxon Version,* ed. E. W. Rhodes, EETS 93, 1889.

Degare (c1330): *Sire Degarre,* ed. Gustav Schleich, Heidelberg, 1929.

Degrevant (c1440 [*Thornton*], a1500 [*Cambridge*]): *Sir Degrevant,* ed. Karl Luick, Wiener Beiträge zur englischen Philologie 47, 1917.

Deonise (a1400): *Deonise Hid Divinite,* ed. Phyllis Hodgson, EETS 231, 1955.

Desert (a1450): "The Desert of Religion," ed. Walter Hübner, *Archiv* 126(1911), 58–74.

Destruction of Troy (a1400): *The Gest Hystoriale of the Destruction of Troy,* ed. G. A. Panton and David Donaldson, EETS 39, 56, 1869–74.

Dicts (1450 [*Scrope*], a1460 [*Helmingham*]): *The Dicts and Sayings of the Philosophers: The Translations made by Stephen Scrope, William Worcester and an Anonymous Translator,* ed. Curt F. Bühler, EETS 211, 1941. (Quotations are from *Scrope* unless identified as from *Helmingham.*)

Digby Plays: ed. F. J. Furnivall, EETS ES 70, 1896.

Disciplina Clericalis (a1500): *Peter Alphonse's Disciplina Clericalis,* ed. W. H. Hulme, Western Reserve Studies 1.5, Cleveland, 1919.

Discrecioun of Stirings (a1400): *A Pistle of Discrecioun of Stirings* in *Deonise,* 62–77.

Discrescyon of Spirites (a1400): *A Tretis of Discrescyon of Spirites* in *Deonise,* 80–93.

DOST: *A Dictionary of the Older Scottish Tongue from the Twelfth Century to the End of the Seventeenth,* ed. Sir William A. Craigie, Chicago, 1931—.

Douce MS. 52 (c1450): "Die mittelenglische Sprichwörtersammlung in Douce 52," ed. Max Förster, *Festschrift zum XII. Allgemeinen Deutschen Neuphilologentage in München, Pfingsten 1906,* Erlangen, 1906, 40–60. (In large part identical with *Rylands MS. 364.*)

Douglas *Aeneid* (1513): *Virgil's Aeneid, Translated into Scottish Verse by Gavin Douglas,* ed. David F. C. Coldwell, 4 vols., STS, 1957–64. (Text is in vols. II, III, IV.)

Douglas *Palice* (1501): *The Palice of Honour* in *The Poetical Works of Gavin Douglas,* ed. John Small, 4 vols., Edinburgh, 1874, I, 1–81.

Drury (c1434): "John Drury and His English Writings," ed. Sanford B. Meech, *Speculum* 9(1934), 70–83.

Dunbar (v.d.): *The Poems of William Dunbar,* ed. W. M. Mackenzie, Edinburgh, 1932.

Durham Proverbs (c1025): *The Durham Proverbs . . . from Durham Cathedral MS. B. III. 32,* ed. O. Arngart, Lunds Universitets Årsskrift, N.F., Avd. 1, 52.2, Lund, 1956.

Dyboski: Roman Dyboski, ed., *Songs, Carols, and other Miscellaneous Poems from the Balliol MS. 354, Richard Hill's Commonplace-Book,* EETS ES 101, 1907.

EB: Erlanger Beiträge zur englischen Philologie, ed. H. Varnhagen, Erlanger, 1889–1904.

Ecclesiastical Institutes (c1000): in Benjamin Thorpe, *Ancient Laws and Institutes of England,* 2 vols., London, 1840, II, 394–442.

Edward of York *Master* (c1410): Edward, Second Duke of York, *The Master of Game,* ed. W. A. and F. Baillie-Grohman, London, 1904.

Edward the Confessor (c1350): *The Middle English Verse Life of Edward the Confessor,* ed. Grace E. Moore, Philadelphia, 1942.

Edward the Confessor Prose I (c1450): as above, 75–106.

Edward the Confessor Prose II (c1450): as above, 108–30.

EETS: Early English Text Society, Original Series, 1864—.

EETS ES: Early English Text Society, Extra Series, 1867–1920.

Eger (a1500): *Eger and Grime,* ed. James R. Caldwell, Harvard Studies in Comparative Literature 9, Cambridge, Mass., 1933.
Eglamour (a1400): *Sir Eglamour,* ed. Gustav Schleich, Palaestra 53, Berlin, 1906.
Eight Goodly Questions (a1500): in *Poetical Works of Geoffrey Chaucer,* ed. Robert Bell, 4 vols., London, 1880, IV, 421–3.
XI Pains (a1300): *The XI Pains of Hell* in Morris *Old English Miscellany,* 147–55.
ELH: [*A Journal of English Literary History*], Baltimore, 1(1934)—.
Elucidarium (c1400): *Die mittelenglische Version des Elucidariums des Honorius Augustodunensis,* ed. F. Schmitt, Burghausen a.s., 1909.
Emaré (c1400): *The Romance of Emaré,* ed. Edith Rickert, EETS ES 99, 1906.
English Chronicle (a1471): *An English Chronicle of the Reigns of Richard II, Henry IV, Henry V, and Henry VI,* ed. John S. Davies, CS 64, 1856.
English Conquest (a1500, a1525 [*Dublin*]): *The English Conquest of Ireland,* ed. F. J. Furnivall, EETS 107, 1896.
Epistle of Othea (c1450): *The Epistle of Othea to Hector,* ed. James D. Gordon, Philadelphia, 1942.
Erthe (a1325): *The Middle English Poem, Erthe upon Erthe, Printed from Twenty-four Manuscripts,* ed. Hilda M. R. Murray, EETS 141, 1911.
ESt: Englische Studien, Heilbronn, Leipzig, 1(1877)–76(1944).
Evangelie (c1300): "The Middle English Evangelie," ed. Gertrude H. Campbell, *PMLA* 30(1915), 529–613.
Everyman (c1500): ed. W. W. Greg, Materialien zur Kunde des älteren englischen Dramas 24, Louvain, 1909.
Exeter Book: ed. George P. Krapp and E. V. K. Dobbie, *ASPR,* III, 1936.
Eye and Heart (a1500): ed. Eleanor P. Hammond, *Anglia* 34(1911), 235–65.
Fabyan (c1500): Robert Fabyan, *The New Chronicles of England and France* (1516), ed. Henry Ellis, London, 1811.
Femina (c1400): ed. William A. Wright, RC 152, 1909.
Ferumbras (c1380): *Sir Ferumbras,* ed. S. J. Herrtage, EETS ES 34, 1879.
Firumbras (a1400): *Firumbras and Otuel and Roland,* ed. Mary I. O'Sullivan, EETS 198, 1935.
Fisher *English Works* (v.d.): *The English Works of John Fisher,* ed. John E. B. Mayor, EETS ES 27, 1876.
Fisher *Henry VII* (1509): *Sermon . . . the body beynge present of . . . Henry the .vij.,* as above, 268–88.
Fisher *Treatyse* (1509): *Treatyse concernynge the fruytful saynges of Davyd the kynge,* as above, 1–267.
Fisher *Wayes* (a1535): *The Wayes to perfect Religion,* as above, 364–428.
Fitzjames *Sermo* (1495): Richard Fitzjames, *Sermo die lune in ebdomada Pasche,* facsimile, Cambridge, 1907.
Five Dogs of London (1456): in Robbins *Historical Poems,* 189–90.
Flemish Insurrection (a1325): "Song on the Flemish Insurrection" in Böddeker, 116–21.
Florence (c1400): *Le Bone Florence of Rome,* ed. Wilhelm Vietor, Marburg, 1893.
Floris (*Auchinleck*) (c1330): *Floris and Blancheflour,* ed. A. B. Taylor, Oxford, 1927.
Floris (c1250 [*Cambridge*], a1300 [*Cotton Vitellius*], a1400 [*Trentham*]): *King Horn, Floriz and Blauncheflur, The Assumption of our Lady,* first ed. (1866) J. R. Lumby, re-ed. G. H. McKnight, EETS 14, 1901, 71–110.
Foly of Fulys (c1450): *The Foly of Fulys and the Thewis of Wysmen* in Girvan, 52–65.
Forme of Cury (a1399): ed. Samuel Pegge, London, 1780.

Fortescue *Dialogue* (a1475): *Dialogue Between Understanding and Faith* in *The Works of Sir John Fortescue,* ed. Thomas (Fortescue), Lord Clermont, 2 vols., London, 1869, I, 483–90.

Fortune alas alas (a1500): "A litell Tretys by wey of compleint ageins ffortune," ed. Eleanor P. Hammond, *Anglia* 32(1909), 481–90.

Foundation of St. Bartholomew's (c1425): *The Book of the Foundation of St. Bartholomew's Church in London,* ed. Norman Moore, EETS 163, 1923.

Fraternity (a1500): "A Fraternity of Drinkers," ed. A. C. Baugh in *Philologica: The Malone Anniversary Studies,* Baltimore, 1949, 200–7.

French and Hale: Walter H. French and C. B. Hale, edd., *Middle English Metrical Romances,* New York, 1930.

Furnivall *Babees Book:* F. J. Furnivall, ed., *The Babees Book, etc.,* EETS 32, 1868(1894).

Furnivall *Early English Poems* (v.d.): *Early English Poems and Lives of Saints,* Philological Society, Berlin, 1862.

Furnivall *Hymns* (v.d.): *Hymns to the Virgin and Christ,* EETS 24, 1867.

Fyftene Joyes (1509): *The fyftene Joyes of maryage,* W. de Worde, 1509.

Fyrst thou sal (c1450): "Me. Disticha (aus Hs. Add. 37049)," ed. Karl Brunner, *Archiv* 159(1931), 86–92. (In part identical with *Proverbis of Wysdom.*)

Gamelyn (c1350): *The Tale of Gamelyn* in *The Complete Works of Geoffrey Chaucer,* ed. W. W. Skeat, 7 vols., Oxford, 1894–7, IV, 645–67.

Gast of Gy (a1400): ed. Gustav Schleich, Palaestra 1, Berlin, 1898.

Generydes A (a1450): *A Royal Historie of the Excellent Knight Generides,* ed. F. J. Furnivall, RC 85, 1865.

Generydes B (a1450): *Generydes, A Romance in Seven-line Stanzas,* ed. W. A. Wright, EETS 55, 70, 1873–8.

Genesis and Exodus (c1250): *The Story of Genesis and Exodus,* ed. Richard Morris, EETS 7, 1865.

Gesta (a1450): *The Early English Versions of the Gesta Romanorum,* ed. S. J. H. Herrtage, EETS ES 33, 1879(1962).

Giraldus *Opera: Giraldi Cambrensis Opera,* ed. J. S. Brewer *et al.,* RS, 8 vols., 1861–91.

Girvan: R. Girvan, ed., *Ratis Raving and Other Early Scots Poems on Morals,* STS, 1939.

God man and the devel (c1390): *A dispitison bitwene a god man and the devel* in *Vernon,* I, 329–54.

God of hefne that sittest (a1450): "A Sermon on the Lord's Prayer," ed. Frank A. Patterson, *JEGP* 15(1916), 406–18.

God that all this world (a1422): in *Chronicle of London,* 216–33.

Golagros (c1475): *The Knightly Tale of Golagros and Gawane* in Amours, 1–46.

Good Wife (c1350 [*E*], c1425 [*H*], c1450 [*L*], a1500 [*A*, ?*N* (printed 1597)], c1500 [*T*]): *The Good Wife Taught her Daughter* in Mustanoja, 158–72, 197–221.

Good Wyfe Wold (a1475): *The Good Wyfe Wold a Pylgremage* in Mustanoja, 173–5.

Governance of Lordschipes (a1425): in Steele *Secreta Secretorum,* 41–118.

Governayle (1489): (*A*) *tretyse that is cleped Governayle of helthe,* Caxton, 1489; facsimile by W. Blades, 1858.

Gower *CA* (a1393): John Gower, *Confessio Amantis* in *The Complete Works of John Gower,* ed. G. C. Macaulay, 4 vols., Oxford, 1899–1902, vols. II, III.

Gower *Peace* (c1400): *To King Henry the Fourth, In Praise of Peace,* as above, III, 481–92.

Gowther (c1400): *Sir Gowther,* ed. Karl Breul, Oppeln, 1886.

Greene *Carols:* Richard L. Greene, ed., *The Early English Carols*, Oxford, 1935. (Citations are to Greene's numbers and stanzas, except for the Appendix, to which page references are given.)

Gregorius (c1330 [*Auchinleck*], c1350 [*C(leopatra)*], c1390 [*Vernon*], a1500 [*R(awlinson)*]): *Die mittelenglische Gregorius-legende,* ed. Carl Keller, Heidelberg, 1914. (Ordinarily *Vernon* is quoted without designation.)

Gregory *Chronicle* (c1475): William Gregory, *Chronicle of London* in *The Historical Collections of a Citizen of London,* ed. James Gairdner, CS, N.S. 17, 1876, 57–239.

Grene Knight (a1500): in *Percy Folio Manuscript,* II, 56–77.

Grete ferly (a1400): "Of tho flode of tho world," in *Yorkshire Writers,* II, 67–70.

Guiscardo (c1485): in Banester *Guiscardo,* 38–98.

Guy[1] (c1300 [*Advocates*], c1475 [*Caius*]): *The Romance of Guy of Warwick,* ed. Julius Zupitza, EETS ES 42, 49, 59, 1883–91. (When *A* and *C* do not differ, *A* is quoted without designation.)

Guy[2] (a1475): *The Romance of Guy of Warwick: The Second or 15th-century Version,* ed. Julius Zupitza, EETS ES 25–6, 1875–6.

Guy[3] (a1400): A fragment of *Guy of Warwick* (*BM Sloane MS. 1044*), ed. Julius Zupitza, *Sitzungsberichte der phil.-hist. Classe der Kaiserlichen Akademie der Wissenschaften* (Vienna) 74(1873), 623–9.

Guy[4] (a1500): *Guy of Warwick, nach Coplands Druck,* ed. Gustav Schleich, Palaestra 139, Leipzig, 1923.

Guy[5] (a1400): A fragment of *Guy of Warwick* (*BM Additional MS. 14408*) in W. B. D. D. Turnbull, ed., *The Romances of Guy of Warwick and Rembrun his Son,* Abbotsford Club 18, Edinburgh, 1840, xxviii–xlii.

Guylforde *Pylgrymage* (1506): *The Pylgrymage of Sir Richard Guylforde to the Holy Land, A.D. 1506,* ed. Henry Ellis, CS 51, 1851.

Hali Meidenhad (c1200): ed. F. J. Furnivall, EETS 18 (revised), 1922.

Halliwell *Early English Miscellanies:* J. O. Halliwell, ed., *Early English Miscellanies in Prose and Verse,* Warton Club 2, London, 1855.

Halliwell *Selection:* J. O. Halliwell, ed., *A Selection from the Minor Poems of Dan John Lydgate,* PS 2, 1840.

Hardyng (1464): *The Chronicle of John Hardyng,* ed. Henry Ellis, London, 1812.

Harley MS. 3362 (c1470): *BM Harley MS. 3362,* ff. 2a–5a, 7b, 9a, 17a, 18a. English and Latin proverbs, printed (in part) in *Retrospective Review,* 2(1854), 309, and (in part) by Max Förster in *Anglia* 42(1918), 199–203. (Where there is no reference to a printed source the quotations are from a photostat of the MS.)

Havelok (c1300): *The Lay of Havelok the Dane,* ed. W. W. Skeat, 2d ed. rev. K. Sisam, Oxford, 1939(1915).

Hawes *Comforte* (1511): Stephen Hawes, *The comforte of lovers,* W. de Worde, ?1515.

Hawes *Convercyon* (1509): *The convercyon of swerers,* W. de Worde, 1509.

Hawes *Example* (1504): *The Example of vertu,* W. de Worde, [?1509].

Hawes *Pastime* (1506): *The Pastime of Pleasure,* ed. W. E. Mead, EETS 173, 1928.

Hay *Alexander* (c1450): *The Taymouth Castle Manuscript of Sir Gilbert Hay's "Buik of King Alexander the Conquerour,"* ed. Albert Herrmann, Wissenschaftliche Beilage zum Jahresbericht der Zwölften Städtischen Realschule zu Berlin, Programm 128, Berlin, 1898.

Hay *Governaunce* (1456): Sir Gilbert Hay, *The Buke of the Governaunce of Princis* in Hay *Prose Manuscript,* II, 71–165.

Hay *Knychthede* (1456): *The Buke of the Order of Knychthede* in Hay *Prose Manuscript,* II, 1–70.

Hay *Law* (1456): *The Buke of the Law of Armys* in Hay *Prose Manuscript,* I.

Hay *Prose Manuscript: Gilbert of the Haye's Prose Manuscript* (*A.D. 1456*), ed. J. H. Stevenson, 2 vols., STS, 1901–14.

Hazlitt *EPP:* W. Carew Hazlitt, ed., *Remains of the Early Popular Poetry of England,* 4 vols., Library of Old Authors, London, 1864–6.

Hendyng C (a1325): "Zu den Sprichwörtern Hending's" (*Cambridge Univ. Libr., Gg.I.1*), ed. H. Varnhagen, *Anglia* 4(1881), 182–91.

Hendyng H (c1325): (*Harley 2253*) in Böddeker, 287–300.

Hendyng O (c1250): (*Oxford Bodl., Digby 86*), ed. Varnhagen, as above, 191–200.

Henley *Husbandry* (a1300): *Walter of Henley's Husbandry,* ed. Elizabeth Lamond, London, 1890.

Henryson (c1475): *The Poems and Fables of Robert Henryson,* ed. H. H. Wood, 2d ed., Edinburgh, 1958.

Hermit (a1375): "The Eremyte and the Outelawe," ed. Max Kaluza, *ESt* 14(1890), 165–82.

Heuser: W. Heuser, ed., *Die Kildare-Gedichte: Die ältesten mittelenglischen Denkmäler in anglo-irischer Überlieferung,* Bonner Beiträge zur Anglistik 14, 1904.

Heywood *BS* (v.d.): John Heywood, *Ballads and Songs* in Heywood *Works,* 250–74.

Heywood *D* (1546, 1549): *A dialogue conteynyng the number of the effectuall proverbes in the Englishe tounge* in Heywood *Works,* 18–101.

Heywood *E* (1555, 1556, 1560, 1562): *Epigrammes* in Heywood *Works,* 104–248.

Heywood *Four PP* (c1545): *The playe called the foure PP,* W. Myddylton, c1545.

?Heywood *Gentylnes* (c1525): K. W. Cameron, *Authorship and Sources of "Gentleness and Nobility,"* Raleigh, N.C., 1941, 93–128.

Heywood *Johan* (1533): *A Mery play betwene Johan Johan the husbande, Tyb his wyfe, and syr Johan the preest,* W. Rastell, 1533.

Heywood *Love* (1534): *A Play of Love,* W. Rastell, 1534.

Heywood *Pardoner* (1533): *A Mery play betwene the pardoner and the frere, the curate and neybour Pratte,* W. Rastell, 1533.

Heywood *Spider* (1556): *The Spider and the Flie,* ed. A. W. Ward, Spenser Society, N.S. 6, 1894.

Heywood *Weather* (1533): *The Play of the Wether,* W. Rastell, 1533.

Heywood *Wit* (c1525): *A Dialogue on Wit and Folly,* ed. F. W. Fairholt, PS 20, 1846.

Heywood *Works:* John Heywood, *Works* (1562) *and Miscellaneous Short Poems,* ed. Burton A. Milligan, Illinois Studies in Language and Literature 41, 1956.

Hichecoke *This Worlde* (a1500): "Hichecoke's This worlde is but a vanyte," ed. R. H. Bowers, *MLN* 67(1952), 331–3.

Higden-Trevisa (a1387): *Polychronicon Ranulphi Higden Monachi Cestrensis; together with the English Translations of John Trevisa and of an unknown Writer of the Fifteenth Century,* ed. C. Babington and J. R. Lumby, 9 vols., RS, 1865–86.

Higden-Anon. (a1425): as above. (The anonymous translation is quoted or cited only when there is some significant variation from Trevisa.)

Hill (a1500): Proverbs from Richard Hill's Commonplace-Book, in *Balliol MS. 354,* in Dyboski, 128–41.

Hilton *Scale* (1395[1494]): Walter Hilton, *Scala perfecconis,* W. de Worde, 1494.

Hoccleve: Thomas Hoccleve, *Works,* ed. F. J. Furnivall (I, III) and Israel Gollancz (II), EETS ES 61, 72, 73, 1892, 1897, 1925 (for 1897). (Page references in the following entries are to this edition.)

Hoccleve *Compleint* (c1422): I, 95–110.
?Hoccleve *De Guilleville Poems* (1413): III, xxiii–lxii.
Hoccleve *Dialog* (c1422): *Dialogus cum Amico,* I, 110–39.
Hoccleve *Jereslaus's Wife* (c1422): I, 140–78.
Hoccleve *Jonathas* (c1425): I, 215–42.
Hoccleve *Lerne to Die* (c1422): *How to Lerne to Die,* I, 178–215.
Hoccleve *Letter of Cupid* (1402): I, 72–91.
Hoccleve *Male Regle* (1406): *La Male Regle,* I, 25–39.
Hoccleve *Regement* (c1412): *The Regement of Princes,* III, 1–197.
Holland *Howlat* (c1450): Richard Holland, *The Buke of the Howlat* in Amours, 47–81.
Horman *Vulgaria* (1519): William Horman, *Vulgaria,* ed. M. R. James, RC 184, 1926.
Horn (c1225): *King Horn,* ed. Joseph Hall, Oxford, 1901.
Horn Childe (c1330): as above, 179–92.
Horstmann *Altenglische Legenden 1875* (v.d.): Carl Horstmann, ed., *Altenglische Legenden,* Paderborn, 1875.
Horstmann *Legenden 1881* (v.d.): *Altenglische Legenden: Neue Folge,* Heilbronn, 1881.
Horstmann *Sammlung* (v.d.): *Sammlung altenglischer Legenden,* Heilbronn, 1878.
How a Merchant (c1475): *How a Merchande dyd hys wyfe betray,* ed. E. Kölbing, *ESt* 7(1884), 118–25.
How the Wyse Man (c1450 [*Lamb.*], a1500 [*Camb., Harl.*]): *How the Wyse Man Taught hys Sone,* ed. Rudolph Fischer, *EB* 2, 1889.
How to Hear Mass (a1400): in *Vernon,* II, 493–511.
Hunterian Mus. MS. 230 (a1500): in John Young and P. H. Aitken, *A Catalogue of the Manuscripts in the Library of the Hunterian Museum in the University of Glasgow,* Glasgow, 1908, 174–5.
Hunting of the Hare (a1500): *The Hunttyng of the Hare* in Henry Weber, ed., *Metrical Romances of the Thirteenth, Fourteenth, and Fifteenth Centuries,* 3 vols., Edinburgh, 1810, III, 279–90.
I Repent (c1325): *I Repent of Blaming Women* in Brown *Lyrics XIII,* 141–3.
Idley (c1450): *Peter Idley's Instructions to his Son,* ed. Charlotte D'Evelyn, Modern Language Association, Monograph Series 6, Boston, 1935. (Book ii [pp. 109 ff.] draws upon R. Mannyng's *Handlyng Synne.*)
Imitatione (*1*) (a1500): *The Earliest English Translation of the First Three Books of the De Imitatione Christi,* ed. John K. Ingram, EETS ES 63, 1893, 1–150.
Imitation (2) (1502): *William Atkynson's Translation of the First Three Books of the De Imitatione Christi,* as above, 153–258.
Instructions for Christians (c1100): "Instructions for Christians, A Poem in Old English," ed. James L. Rosier, *Anglia* 82(1964), 4–22.
Inter Diabolus et Virgo (a1500): in F. J. Furnivall, "Three Middle English Poems," *ESt* 23(1896–7), 444–5.
Interludium de clerico et puella (a1300): in McKnight, 21–4.
Ipomadon A (a1400): *A Good Tale of Ipomadon* in *Ipomedon in drei englischen Bearbeitungen,* ed. Eugen Kölbing, Breslau, 1889, 3–253.
Ipomadon B (a1425): *The Lyfe of Ipomydon,* as above, 257–319.
Ipomadon C (c1460): *The Prose Ipomedon,* as above, 323–58.
Irlande *Meroure* (1490): Johannes de Irlandia, *The Meroure of Wyssdome,* ed. Charles Macpherson and F. Quinn, 2 vols., STS, 1926, 1965.
Isumbras (a1350): *Sir Ysumbras,* ed. Gustav Schleich, Palaestra 15, Berlin, 1901.
Ives: D. V. Ives, "The Proverbs in the *Ancren Riwle,*" *MLR* 29(1934), 257–66.
Jacob and Joseph (a1300): *Iacob and Iosep,* ed. Arthur S. Napier, Oxford, 1916.

Jacob's Well (c1450): ed. Arthur Brandeis, EETS 115, 1900. (Part I only, which prints less than half the text.)

Jak and his Stepdame (a1500): ed. J. Zupitza, *Archiv* 90(1893), 57–82.

Janson: Horst W. Janson, *Apes and Ape Lore in the Middle Ages and the Renaissance,* London, 1952.

Jeaste (a1500): *The Jeaste of Syr Gawayne* in *Syr Gawayne,* ed. Frederic Madden, Bannatyne Club 61, London, 1839, 206–23.

JEGP: Journal of English and Germanic Philology (vols. 1–4 appeared as *Journal of Germanic Philology*), Urbana, Ill., 1(1897)—.

Jente: Richard Jente, ed., *Proverbia Communia,* Indiana University Publications, Folklore Series, 4, Bloomington, 1947.

John the Reeve (a1461): in *Percy Folio Manuscript,* II, 550–94.

Joseph (c1350): *Joseph of Arimathie,* ed. W. W. Skeat, EETS 44, 1871.

Julian *Revelations* (a1400): *Revelations of Divine Love Shewed to . . . Julian of Norwich,* ed. (and modernized) Roger Hudleston, London, 1927.

Junius MS (v.d.): *The Junius Manuscript,* ed. George P. Krapp, *ASPR,* I, 1931.

Kail (v.d.): J. Kail, ed., *Twenty-Six Political and other Poems (including "Petty Job"),* EETS 124, 1904.

Kalender (1506): *The Kalender of Shepherdes,* ed. H. Oskar Sommer, London, 1892.

Kay *Siege* (c1483): John Kay (Caius), *The Siege of Rhodes* [London, ?Lettou and Machlinia, c1483].

Kempe (a1438): *The Book of Margery Kempe,* ed. Sanford B. Meech and Hope E. Allen, EETS 212, 1940.

Kennedy (a1500): *The Poems of Walter Kennedy,* ed. J. Schipper, Denkschriften der Kaiserlichen Akademie der Wissenschaften, phil-hist. Classe, 48, Vienna, 1902.

Ker *Catalogue:* N. R. Ker, *Catalogue of Manuscripts Containing Anglo-Saxon,* Oxford, 1957.

King Edward (a1400): *King Edward and the Shepherd* in French and Hale, 949–85.

King Hart (c1500): in *The Poetical Works of Gavin Douglas,* ed. John Small, 4 vols., Edinburgh, 1874, I, 85–120.

Kingis Quair (a1437): ed. W. M. Mackenzie, London, 1939.

Kneuer: Karl Kneuer, ed., *Die Sprichwörter Hendyngs,* Weilheim, 1901.

Knight of Curtesy (a1500): *The Knight of Curtesy and the Fair Lady of Faguell,* ed. Elizabeth McCausland, Smith College Studies in Modern Languages 4.1, 1922.

Knighton (v.d.): *Chronicon Henrici Knighton,* ed. Joseph R. Lumby, 2 vols., RS, 1889–95.

Knyghthode and Bataile (c1458): ed. R. Dyboski and Z. M. Arend, EETS 201, 1936.

La Tour-Landry (c1450): *The Book of the Knight of La Tour-Landry,* ed. Thomas Wright, EETS 33, rev. ed., 1906.

Ladder (c1450): *A Ladder of Foure Ronges* in *Deonise,* 100–17.

Lady Bessy (c1500): *The Most Pleasant Song of Lady Bessy,* ed. J. O. Halliwell, PS 20, 1847.

Lambeth Homilies (a1225): in Richard Morris, *Old English Homilies . . . First Series,* EETS 29, 34, 1867–8, 3–159.

Lambeth Prose Legends (a1500): *Prose Legends from Lambeth MS. 432,* ed. C. Horstmann, *Anglia* 3(1880), 320–60.

Lambewell (a1500): *Sir Lambewell* in *Percy Folio Manuscript,* I, 142–64.

Lamentation of Mary Magdalene (c1475): in *Poetical Works of Geoffrey Chaucer,* ed. Robert Bell, 4 vols., London, 1880, IV, 395–415.

Lamwell (a1500): *Sir Lamwell* in *Percy Folio Manuscript,* I, 521–35.

Lancelot (c1500): *Lancelot of the Laik*, ed. Margaret M. Gray, STS, 1912.
Landavall (a1475): in Chestre *Launfal*, 105–28.
Lanfranc (a1400): *Lanfrank's "Science of Cirurgie,"* ed. Robert v. Fleischhacker, EETS 102, 1894.
Lanterne (a1415): *The Lanterne of Light*, ed. Lilian M. Swinburn, EETS 151, 1917.
Lapidaries (v.d.): *English Mediaeval Lapidaries*, ed. Joan Evans and Mary S. Serjeantson, EETS 190, 1933.
Laud Troy (c1400): *The Laud Troy Book*, ed. J. Ernst Wülfing, EETS 121–2, 1902–3.
Lavynham (a1400): Richard Lavynham, *A Litil Tretys on the Seven Deadly Sins*, ed. J. P. W. M. van Zutphen, Rome, 1956.
Lawman (a1200 [*A: Caligula*], c1300 [*B: Otho*]): *Laȝamons Brut*, ed. Frederic Madden, 3 vols., London, 1847. (When the manuscripts are in virtual agreement, or when *B* is wanting, *A* is quoted without designation.)
Lay Folks' Catechism (c1400): ed. T. F. Simmons and H. E. Nolloth, EETS 118, 1901.
Lay of Sorrow (a1500): *"The Lay of Sorrow* and *The Lufaris Complaynt,"* ed. Kenneth G. Wilson, *Speculum* 29(1954), 716–9.
Le Morte A. (a1400): *Le Morte Arthur*, ed. J. Douglas Bruce, EETS ES 88, 1903.
Lean: Vincent S. Lean, *Lean's Collectanea*, 4 vols. in 5, Bristol, 1902–4.
Leconfield Proverbs (a1500): "Die Proverbs von Lekenfield und Wresil (Yorks)," ed. Ewald Flügel, *Anglia* 14(1891–2), 471–97.
Leechbook (c1450): *A Leechbook or Collection of Medical Recipes of the Fifteenth Century*, ed. Warren R. Dawson, London, 1934.
Legat *Sermon* (c1400–25): Hugo Legat's *Sermon* in *Three Middle English Sermons*, 1–21.
Legend of Mary (a1330): in Horstmann *Legenden 1881*, 499–502.
Leversege (1465): "The Vision of Edmunde Leversegge," *Notes and Queries for Somerset and Dorset* 9(1905), 22–35.
Libeaus (c1350): *Libeaus Desconus*, ed. Max Kaluza, *AB* 5, Leipzig, 1890.
Libelle (1436): *The Libelle of Englyshe Polycye*, ed. George Warner, London, 1926.
Liber Cure Cocorum (a1475): ed. Richard Morris, Philological Society, Berlin, 1862.
Lichfield *Complaint* (a1447): "The Complaint of God to Sinful Man and the Answer of Man, by William Lichfield," ed. Edv. Borgström, *Anglia* 34(1911), 498–525.
Liebermann: F. Liebermann, *Die Gesetze der Angelsachsen*, 3 vols., Halle, 1898–1916.
Lither lok Sermon (a1300): in C. Brown, "Texts and the Man," *Bulletin of the Modern Humanities Research Association* 2(1928), 104–5.
Lord that is (a1450): in *Legends of the Holy Rood*, ed. Richard Morris, EETS 46, 1871, 210–21.
Love *Mirrour* (a1400): Nicholas Love, *The Mirrour of the Blessed Lyf of Jesu Christ*, ed. Lawrence F. Powell, Oxford, 1908.
Lovelich *Grail* (c1410): Henry Lovelich, *The History of the Holy Grail*, ed. F. J. Furnivall, EETS ES 20, 24, 28, 30, 95, 1874–1905.
Lovelich *Merlin* (c1410): *Merlin*, ed. Ernst A. Kock, EETS ES 93, 112, 185, 1904–32.
Loveliest Lady (c1325): *The Loveliest Lady in Land* in Brown *Lyrics XIII*, 148–50.
Lovely Song of Wisdom (a1500): "Cantus cuiusdam sapientis: A lovely song of wisdom," ed. Karl Brunner, *Archiv* 164(1933), 192–9. (Identical in part with *Proverbs of Salamon*.)
Lover's Mass (c1450): ed. Eleanor P. Hammond, *JEGP* 7(1908), 95–104.
Ludus Coventriae (a1475): *Ludus Coventriae or the Plaie called Corpus Christi*, ed. K. S. Block, EETS ES 120, 1922.
Lufaris Complaynt (a1500): in *Lay of Sorrow*, 719–23.

Lumby *Bernardus de Cura* (a1500): J. R. Lumby, ed., *Bernardus de cura rei famuliaris, with some Early Scottish Prophecies, etc.*, EETS 42, 1870.

Lumby *Ratis Raving:* J. R. Lumby, ed., *Ratis Raving and other Moral and Religious Pieces*, EETS 43, 1870.

?Lydgate *Compleynt* (c1430): in Lydgate *Temple*, 59–67.

Lydgate *Dance* (c1430): *The Dance of Death*, ed. Florence Warren and Beatrice White, EETS 181, 1931.

Lydgate *Fall* (a1439): *Fall of Princes*, ed. Henry Bergen, EETS ES 121–4, 1924–7.

Lydgate *Life* (a1422): *Life of Our Lady*, ed. Joseph A. Lauritis, R. A. Klinefelter, V. F. Gallagher, Duquesne Studies, Philological Series, 2, Pittsburgh, 1961.

Lydgate *Miracles of St. Edmund* (c1445): in Horstmann *Legenden 1881*, 440–5.

Lydgate *MP* (v.d.): *The Minor Poems of John Lydgate*, ed. Henry N. MacCracken, EETS ES 107, 192, 1911, 1934.

Lydgate *Pilgrimage* (a1430): *The Pilgrimage of the Life of Man*, ed. F. J. Furnivall and K. B. Locock, EETS ES 77, 83, 92, 1899–1904.

Lydgate *Reson* (c1408): *Reson and Sensuallyte*, ed. Ernst Sieper, EETS ES 84, 89, 1901–3.

Lydgate *St. Albon* (1439): *S. Albon und Amphabel*, ed. C. Horstmann in *Festschrift zu dem funfzigjährigen Jubiläum der Königstädtischen Realschule*, Berlin, 1882, 103–95.

Lydgate *St. Edmund* (c1433): *St. Edmund and St. Fremund* in Horstmann *Legenden 1881*, 376–440.

Lydgate *St. Giles* (a1449): in Horstmann *Legenden 1881*, 371–5.

Lydgate *Serpent* (1422): *The Serpent of Division*, ed. H. MacCracken, London, 1911.

Lydgate *Temple* (1420): *Temple of Glas*, ed. J. Schick, EETS ES 60, 1891.

Lydgate *Thebes* (c1421): *Siege of Thebes*, ed. Axel Erdmann and Eilert Ekwall, EETS ES 108, 125, 1911, 1930.

Lydgate *Troy* (a1420): *Troy Book*, ed. Henry Bergen, EETS ES 97, 103, 106, 126, 1906–35.

Lydgate and Benedict Burgh *Secrees* (a1449): *Secrees of old Philisoffres*, ed. Robert Steele, EETS ES 66, 1894. (Burgh's part professedly begins with line 1492.)

Lyfe of Joseph (c1502): *The Lyfe of Joseph of Armathia* in *Joseph*, 37–52.

Lyfe of Roberte (c1500): *The Lyfe of Roberte the Devyll* in Hazlitt *EPP*, I, 217–63.

Macer (a1450): *A Middle English Translation of Macer Floridus de Viribus Herbarum*, ed. Gösta Frisk, Essays and Studies on English Language and Literature 3, Upsala, 1949.

McKnight: George H. McKnight, ed., *Middle English Humorous Tales in Verse*, Boston, 1913.

Macro Plays: ed. F. J. Furnivall and A. W. Pollard, EETS ES 91, 1904.

Malory (a1470): *The Works of Sir Thomas Malory*, ed. Eugène Vinaver, 3 vols., Oxford, 1947.

Man have mynd (a1500): in *Pieces from the Makculloch and the Gray MSS.*, ed. George Stevenson, STS, 1918, 54–6.

Mandeville *Travels* (c1400): ed. P. Hamelius, EETS 153, 1919.

Mandeville (*Egerton*) (a1425): *The Buke of John Maundevill from the . . . Egerton MS. 1982 in the British Museum*, ed. George F. Warner, RC 119, 1889.

Mankind (c1475): in *Macro Plays*, 1–34.

Manly-Rickert: John M. Manly and Edith Rickert, edd., *The Text of the Canterbury Tales*, 8 vols., Chicago, 1940.

Mannyng *Chronicle A* (a1338): *The Story of England by Robert Manning of Brunne*, ed. F. J. Furnivall, RS, 2 vols., 1887.

Mannyng *Chronicle B* (a1338): *Peter Langtoft's Chronicle* (*as illustrated and improv'd by Robert of Brunne*), ed. Thomas Hearne, 2 vols., Oxford, 1725; reprinted in *The Works of Thomas Hearne,* III, IV, London, 1810.

Mannyng *Handlyng* (c1303): *Robert of Brunne's Handlyng Synne,* ed. F. J. Furnivall, EETS 119, 123, 1901-3.

Marriage (a1500): *The Marriage of Sir Gawaine* in *Percy Folio Manuscript,* I, 103–18.

Mary and the Cross (c1390): *Disputation between Mary and the Cross* in *Vernon,* II, 612–26.

Mary Magdalene (*Digby*) (c1485): in *Digby Plays,* 55–136.

Maximian (a1300): *Le Regret de Maximian* in Brown *Lyrics XIII,* 92–100.

Mayden, Modur, and comely Qween (c1390): in *Vernon,* I, 121–31.

MED: *Middle English Dictionary,* ed. H. Kurath and S. M. Kuhn, Ann Arbor, Michigan, 1952—.

Meditations (a1400): *Meditations on the Life and Passion of Christ,* ed. Charlotte D'Evelyn, EETS 158, 1921.

Medwall *Fulgens* (c1497): Henry Medwall, *Fulgens and Lucres,* ed. Seymour de Ricci, Henry E. Huntington Facsimile Reprints 1, New York, 1920.

Medwall *Nature* (a1500): Tudor Facsimile Texts, 1908.

Medytacyons of saynt Bernarde (1495): W. de Worde, 1496.

Meidan Maregrete (a1300): in Horstmann *Legenden 1881,* 489–98.

Melayne (a1400): *The Sege off Melayne and The Romance of Duke Rowlande and Sir Otuell of Spayne,* ed. Sidney J. Herrtage, EETS ES 35, 1880.

Melusine (c1500): ed. A. K. Donald, EETS ES 68, 1895.

Mergarete (a1475): in Horstmann *Legenden 1881,* 236–41.

Merita Missae (a1500): in *Lay Folks Mass Book,* ed. Thomas F. Simmons, EETS 71, 1879, 148–54.

Merlin (c1450): *Merlin or the Early History of King Arthur,* ed. Henry B. Wheatley, EETS 10, 21, 36, 112, 1865–99.

Metham (1449): *Amoryus and Cleopes* in *The Works of John Metham,* ed. Hardin Craig, EETS 132, 1916.

Metrical Paraphrase OT (a1425): *A Middle English Metrical Paraphrase of the Old Testament,* lines 1–6000, ed. Herbert Kalén, Göteborgs Högskolas Årsskrift 28.5, 1923; ll. 6001–9624, ed. Urban Ohlander, Gothenburg Studies in English 5, Stockholm, 1955; ll. 9625–14088, as above, 11, 1961; ll. 14089–18372 (end), as above, 16, 1963.

Middle English Sermons (c1415): *Middle English Sermons . . . from British Museum MS. Royal 18 B. xxiii,* ed. Woodburn O. Ross, EETS 209, 1940.

Miller of Abington (a1500): *A Mery Jest of the Mylner of Abyngton* in Hazlitt *EPP,* III, 98–118.

Minot (a1352): *The Poems of Laurence Minot,* ed. Joseph Hall, 3d ed., Oxford, 1914.

Miracles of Our Lady (c1390): in *Vernon,* I, 138–67.

Mirk *Festial* (a1415): *Mirk's Festial: A Collection of Homilies by Johannes Mirkus,* ed. Theodor Erbe, EETS ES 96, 1905.

Mirk *Instructions* (a1425): *Instructions for Parish Priests,* ed. Edward Peacock, EETS 31, 1868, rev. ed., 1902.

Miroure of Mans Salvacionne (a1500): ed. A. H. Huth, RC 118, 1888.

Misyn *Fire* (1435): Richard Misyn, *The Fire of Love and the Mending of Life . . . Englisht from . . . Richard Rolle,* ed. Ralph Harvey, EETS 106, 1896, 1–104.

Misyn *Mending* (1434): as above, 105–31.

MLN: Modern Language Notes, Baltimore, 1(1886)—.

MLR: Modern Language Review, Cambridge, 1(1905)—.

Moder of gresse (a1400): Robert M. Garrett, "Middle English Rimed Medical Treatise," *Anglia* 34(1911), 163–93.

Monk of Evesham (c1485): *The Revelation to the Monk of Evesham,* ed. Edward Arber, English Reprints 18, London, 1869.

More *Answer* (1533): *The answer to the first part of the poysoned booke* in More *Workes,* 1035–1138.

More *Apologye* (1533): *The Apologye of Syr Thomas More, Knyght,* ed. Arthur I. Taft, EETS 180, 1930.

More *Comforte* (1534): *A dyalogue of comforte agaynste tribulacyon* in More *Workes,* 1139–1264.

More *Confutacion* (1532 [bks. i–iii, 339–522], 1533 [bks. iv–ix, 522–832]): *The Confutacion of Tyndales Aunswere* in More *Workes,* 339–832.

More *Correspondence* (v.d.): *The Corespondence of Sir Thomas More,* ed. Elizabeth F. Rogers, Princeton, 1947.

More *Debellacyon* (1533): *The Debellacyon of Salem and Bizance* in More *Workes,* 929–1034.

More *Early Poems* (c1503): in More *Workes,* [1–16].

More *Heresyes* (1528): *A Dialogue concernynge heresyes* in More *Workes,* 105–288.

More *Passion* (1534): *A treatice upon the passion of Chryste* in More *Workes,* 1270–1349.

More *Picus* (c1505): *The life of John Picus* in More *Workes,* 1–34.

More *Richard* (1513): *The history of king Richard the thirde* in More *Workes,* 35–71.

More *Supplicacion* (1529): *The supplicacion of soules* in More *Workes,* 288–339.

More *Treatyce* (1522): *A Treatyce . . . uppon these wordes of holye Scrypture, Memorare novissima* in More *Workes,* 72–102.

More *Workes: The workes of Sir Thomas More . . . wrytten by him in the Englysh tonge,* London, 1557.

Morris *Old English Miscellany:* Richard Morris, ed., *An Old English Miscellany,* EETS 49, 1872.

Morte Arthure (a1400): ed. Erik Björkman, Alt- und mittelenglishche Texte 9, Heidelberg, 1915.

Morton: James Morton, ed., *The Ancrene Riwle,* CS 57, 1853.

MP: Modern Philology, Chicago, 1(1903)—.

Mum (c1405): *Mum and the Sothsegger,* ed. Mabel Day and Robert Steele, EETS 199, 1936.

Mustanoja: Tauno F. Mustanoja, ed., *The Good Wife Taught her Daughter, The Good Wyfe Wold a Pylgremage, The Thewis of Gud Women,* Annales Academiae Scientiarum Fennicae 61, Helsinki, 1948.

Myne awen dere (a1450): "Myne awen dere sone," ed. Tauno F. Mustanoja, *Neuphilologische Mitteilungen* 49(1948), 145–93.

Myrour of lewed men (c1425): in *Vernon,* I, 407–42.

Myroure of oure Ladye (c1450): ed. John H. Blunt, EETS ES 19, 1873.

Napier: Arthur Napier, ed., *Wulfstan: Sammlung der ihm zugeschriebenen Homilien,* Sammlung englischer Denkmäler 4, Berlin, 1883.

NED: *A New English Dictionary on Historical Principles,* 13 vols. (with *Supplement*), Oxford, 1884–1933.

Nevill *Castell* (1518): William Nevill, *The Castell of Pleasure,* ed. Roberta D. Cornelius, EETS 179, 1930.

Newton (c1500): "The Poems of Humfrey Newton," ed. R. H. Robbins, *PMLA* 65(1950), 249–81.

Nicodemus (a1350 [*Galba*], a1425 [*Additional*], c1450 [*Sion*]): *The Gospel of Nico-*

demus in *The Middle-English Harrowing of Hell and Gospel of Nicodemus,* ed. William H. Hulme, EETS ES 100, 1907.

Nominale (c1350): *Nominale sive Verbale,* ed. W. W. Skeat, *Transactions of the Philological Society,* 1906, 3*–26*.

Northern Homily Cycle (*Edin. Coll. Phys.*) (c1300): *English Metrical Homilies from Manuscripts of the Fourteenth Century,* ed. John Small, Edinburgh, 1862.

Northern Homily Cycle Narrationes (*Vernon*) (c1390): "Die Evangelien-geschichten der Homiliensammlung des MS. Vernon," ed. C. Horstmann, *Archiv* 57(1877), 241–316.

Northern Passion (v.d.): ed. Frances A. Foster, 2 vols., EETS 145, 147, 1913–6.

Northern Verse Psalter (a1400): *Anglo-Saxon and Early English Psalter,* ed. J. Stevenson, 2 vols., Surtees Society 16, 19, 1843–7.

Norton *Ordinall* (c1477): Thomas Norton, *The Ordinall of Alchimy* in Ashmole, 1–106.

Now late me thought (a1500): "De Arte Lacrimandi," ed. Robert M. Garrett, *Anglia* 32(1909), 269–94.

NQ: Notes and Queries, 1st Series, 1(1849–50)—.

Nut Brown Maid (a1500): in *Percy Folio Manuscript,* III, 174–86.

O Man more (a1500): in *Rawlinson MS. C 813,* 393–5.

O thou most noble (1487): "The Mayor of Waterford's Letter" in *The Popular Songs of Ireland,* ed. T. Crofton Croker, London, 1839, 318–31.

Octavian (c1350 [*NL*], a1375 [*S*], a1500 [*NC*]): ed. Gregor Sarrazin, *AB* 3, 1885.

Odo of Cheriton (a1250): *Eudes de Cheriton et ses Dérivés* in Léopold Hervieux, *Les Fabulistes Latins,* IV, Paris, 1896.

Of Clene Maydenhod (c1390): in *Vernon,* II, 464–8.

Of the seven Ages (c1450): ed. E. C. York, *MLN* 72(1957), 484–5.

Old English Cato (c900): in Warner, 3–7.

Old English Martyrology (a900): *An Old English Martyrology,* ed. George Herzfeld, EETS 116, 1900.

Old English Nicodemus (c1000): "The Old English Version of the Gospel of Nicodemus," ed. W. H. Hulme, *PMLA* 13(1898), 457–541.

Orcherd (c1425): *The Orcherd of Syon,* ed. Phyllis Hodgson and Gabriel M. Liegey, EETS 258, 1966 (vol. I, text only).

Orfeo (c1330 [*Auchinleck*], a1500 [*Harley*]): *Sir Orfeo,* ed. A. J. Bliss, Oxford, 1954. (Unless otherwise designated, all quotations are from *Auchinleck.*)

Orm (c1200): *The Ormulum,* ed. Robert Holt, 2 vols., Oxford, 1878.

Orologium (a1400): "Orologium Sapientiae, or The Seven Poyntes of Trewe Wisdom," ed. C. Horstmann, *Anglia* 10(1887), 323–89.

Otuel (c1330): in *Rouland,* 65–116.

Otuel and Roland (a1325): in *Firumbras,* 59–146.

Owayne Miles (*Auchinleck*) (c1300): ed. Eugen Kölbing, *ESt* 1(1877), 98–112.

Owayne Miles (*Brome*) (c1450): in Smith *Common-place Book,* 82–106.

Owayne Miles (*Cotton Caligula*) (c1450): ed. Eugen Kölbing, *ESt* 1(1877), 113–21.

Owl (c1250 [*Cambridge*], a1300 [*Jesus*]): *The Owl and the Nightingale,* ed. J. W. H. Atkins, Cambridge, 1922. (Unless otherwise designated, all quotations are from *Cambridge.*)

Owst *Literature:* G. R. Owst, *Literature and Pulpit in Medieval England,* Cambridge, 1933.

Oxford: The Oxford Dictionary of English Proverbs, ed. W. G. Smith and Janet E. Heseltine, 2d ed. by Sir Paul Harvey, Oxford, 1948.

Page *Siege* (c1420): John Page, *Siege of Rouen,* ed. Herbert Huscher, Kölner anglistische Arbeiten 1, Leipzig, 1927.

Palladius (1440): *The Middle-English Translation of Palladius De Re Rustica,* ed. Mark Liddell, Berlin, 1896.

Papelard Priest (a1349): "Middle English Lyrics," ed. A. H. Smith, *London Mediaeval Studies* 2(1951), 42–5.

Paris Psalter (1–50) (c900): *Libri Psalmorum Versio Antiqua Latina: cum Paraphrasi Anglo-Saxonica,* ed. Benjamin Thorpe, Oxford, 1835.

Paris Psalter (51–150) (c900): *The Paris Psalter and the Meters of Boethius,* ed. George P. Krapp, *ASPR,* V, New York, 1932.

Parker Chronicle (v.d.): *Two of the Saxon Chronicles,* ed. Charles Plummer and J. Earle, 2 vols., Oxford, 1892–9.

Parker *Dives* (a1470): Henry Parker, *Dives and Pauper,* W. de Worde, 1496.

Parliament of Birds (c1430): ed. Eleanor P. Hammond, *JEGP,* 7(1908), 105–9.

Partenay (a1500): *The Romans of Partenay or of Lusignen,* ed. W. W. Skeat, EETS 22, 1866(1899).

Partonope (a1450): *The Middle-English Versions of Partonope of Blois,* ed. A. Trampe Bödtker, EETS ES 109, 1912. (Unless otherwise designated, all quotations are from *BM Additional MS. 35288.*)

Partonope S (c1455): Fragment of a shorter version, as above, 481–8.

Passe forth (a1456): "Balade Moral of Gode Counseyle," in Gower *CA,* II, clxxiii–iv.

Paston (v.d.): *The Paston Letters,* ed. James Gairdner, 6 vols., London, 1904.

Patience (c1380): ed. Israel Gollancz, 2d ed., London, 1924.

Paues (c1400; c1425 [Acts]): Anna C. Paues, ed., *A Fourteenth Century English Biblical Version,* Cambridge, 1904.

Pauline Epistles (a1400): *The Pauline Epistles Contained in MS. Parker 32, Corpus Christi College, Cambridge,* ed. Margaret J. Powell, EETS ES 116, 1916.

Pearl (c1380): ed. E. V. Gordon, Oxford, 1953.

Pecock *Donet* (c1445): Reginald Pecock, *The Donet,* ed. Elsie V. Hitchcock, EETS 156, 1921.

Pecock *Faith* (c1456): *Book of Faith,* ed. J. L. Morison, Glasgow, 1909.

Pecock *Folewer* (c1454): *The Folewer to the Donet,* ed. Elsie V. Hitchcock, EETS 164, 1924.

Pecock *Repressor* (c1449): *The Repressor of Over Much Blaming of the Clergy,* ed. Churchill Babington, 2 vols., RS, 1860.

Pecock *Reule* (c1443): *The Reule of Crysten Religioun,* ed. William C. Greet, EETS 171, 1927.

Peniworth (c1330): *A Peniworth of Witte,* ed. E. Kölbing, *ESt* 7(1884), 111–7.

Pepysian Gospel (c1400): *The Pepysian Gospel Harmony,* ed. Margery Goates, EETS 157, 1922.

Perceval (a1400): *Sir Perceval of Gales,* ed. J. Campion and F. Holthausen, Alt- und mittelenglische Texte 5, Heidelberg, 1913.

Percy Folio Manuscript: Bishop Percy's Folio Manuscript, ed. John W. Hales and F. J. Furnivall, 3 vols. with a supplementary volume (here cited as IV), London, 1867–8.

Perry *English Prose Treatises:* George G. Perry, ed., *English Prose Treatises of Richard Rolle de Hampole,* EETS 20, 1866(1921).

Perry *Religious Pieces: Religious Pieces in Prose and Verse . . . from Robert Thornton's MS.,* EETS 26, 1867(1914).

Person: Henry A. Person, ed., *Cambridge Middle English Lyrics,* Seattle, Washington, 1962.

Peterborough Chronicle (v.d.): as *Parker Chronicle* above.
Phoenix Homily (a1000): in Warner, 146–8.
Pierce (c1395): *Pierce the Ploughmans Crede,* ed. W. W. Skeat, EETS 30, 1867, rev. ed., 1873.
Piers (a1376 [*A*], c1378 [*B*], a1387 [*C*]): *The Vision of William Concerning Piers the Plowman,* ed. W. W. Skeat, 2 vols., Oxford, 1886(1924).
Piers of Fullham (a1500): in Hazlitt *EPP,* II, 1–15.
Pilgrimage LM (c1450): *The Pilgrimage of the Lyf of the Manhode,* ed. William A. Wright, RC 91, 1869.
Pistle of Preier (a1400): in *Deonise,* 48–59.
Plowman's Tale (c1400): in Skeat *Chaucerian,* 147–90.
Plumpton Correspondence (v.d.): ed. Thomas Stapleton, CS 4, 1839.
PMLA: [*Publications of the Modern Language Association of America*], Baltimore, Menasha, Wisc., 1(1884)—.
Poema Morale (c1175): *Das frühmittelenglische "Poema Morale,"* ed. Hans Marcus, Palaestra 194, Leipzig, 1934.
Pol. Rel. and Love Poems: Political, Religious, and Love Poems, ed. F. J. Furnivall, EETS 15, 1866, rev. ed., 1903.
Ponthus (c1450): "King Ponthus and the Fair Sidone," ed. F. J. Mather, Jr., *PMLA* 12(1897), 1–150.
PQ: Philological Quarterly, Iowa City, 1(1922)—.
Praise of Women (c1330): "Die Quelle des mittelenglischen Gedichtes 'Lob der Frauen,'" ed. F. Holthausen, *Archiv* 108(1902), 288–301.
Pricke (a1400): *The Pricke of Conscience,* ed. Richard Morris, Philological Society, Berlin, 1863.
Prikke of love (c1390): *The Spore of Love* in *Vernon,* I, 268–97.
Primer (c1400): *The Prymer, or Lay Folks' Prayer Book,* ed. Henry Littlehales, EETS 105, 1895.
Prohemy of a Mariage (c1475): in Halliwell *Selection,* 27–46.
Promptorium (a1475): *The Promptorium Parvulorum,* ed. A. L. Mayhew, EETS ES 102, 1908.
Proper tretyse (c1500): "Further Marginalia from a Copy of Bartholomaeus Anglicus," ed. J. G. Milne and Elizabeth Sweeting, *MLR* 40(1945), 244–5.
Proprium Sanctorum (c1350): ed. C. Horstmann, *Archiv* 81(1888), 83–114, 299–321.
Prose Alexander (c1440): *The Prose Life of Alexander, from the Thornton MS.,* ed. J. S. Westlake, EETS 143, 1913.
Prose Psalter (c1350): *The Earliest Complete English Prose Psalter,* ed. Karl D. Bülbring, EETS 97, 1891.
Proverbes of diverse profetes (c1390): in *Vernon,* II, 522–53.
Proverbis of Wysdom (a1400): ed. Julius Zupitza (from *Bodl. 14525*), *Archiv* 90(1893), 241–68. (In part identical with *Fyrst thou sal.*)
Proverbis of Wysdom (II) (a1400): "Die Sprichwörter Hendings und die Proverbis of Wysdom," ed. G. Schleich (from *Bodl. 1851*), *Anglia* 51(1927), 221–4. (Quoted only when differing from above.)
Proverbs of Alfred (c1250 [*T(rinity)*], a1300 [*J(esus)*]: *The Proverbs of Alfred,* ed. O. S. A. Arngart, 2 vols., Skrifter Utgivna av Kungliga Humanistiska Vetenskapssamfundet i Lund 32, 1942–55. (Text is in vol. II.)
Proverbs of Good Counsel (c1450): in F. J. Furnivall, *Queene Elizabethes Achademy,* EETS ES 8, 1869, 68–70.
Proverbs of Salamon (a1500): ed. Karl Brunner, *Archiv* 161(1932), 194–5, 164(1933), 178–91. (Identical in part with *Lovely Song of Wisdom.*)

PS: Percy Society, Publications, London, 1840–52.
Psalterium b. Mariae (c1390): in *Vernon,* I, 49–105.
Pseudo-Alcuin (a1000): "Übersetzung von Alcuin's *De Virtutibus et Vitiis Liber,"* ed. B. Assmann, *Anglia* 11(1889), 371-91.
Quare (a1500): *The Quare of Jelusy* in *Miscellany Volume,* STS, 1933, 195–212.
Quatrefoil (a1400): *The Quatrefoil of Love,* ed. Israel Gollancz and Magdalene M. Weale, EETS 195, 1935.
Quatuor Sermones (1483): *Quatuor Sermones, reprinted from the first edition printed by William Caxton at Westminister,* RC 111, 1883.
Qui Habitat (a1400): *An Exposition of Qui Habitat and Bonum Est in English,* ed. Björn Wallner, Lund Studies in English 23, 1954.
Quixley *Ballades* (a1450): "Quixley's Ballades Royal," ed. Henry N. MacCracken, *Yorkshire Archaeological Journal* 20(1909), 33–50.
Ragman Roll (a1500): in Hazlitt *EPP,* I, 68–78.
Ratis (c1450): *Ratis Raving* in Girvan, 1–51.
Rauf (c1475): *The Taill of Rauf Coilyear* in Amours, 82–114.
Rawlinson MS. C 813 (v.d.): "The Songs in Manuscript Rawlinson C. 813," ed. Frederick M. Padelford, *Anglia* 31(1908), 309–97.
Rawlinson MS. D 328 (c1475): "A Collection of Proverbs in Rawlinson MS. D 328," ed. Sanford B. Meech, *MP* 38(1940), 113–32.
Rawlinson Troye (c1450): *The Sege of Troye,* ed. Nathaniel E. Griffin, *PMLA* 22(1907), 157–200.
RC: Roxburghe Club, Publications, London, 1814—.
Regius Psalter (c1000): *Der altenglische Regius-Psalter,* ed. Fritz Roeder, Studien zur englischen Philologie 18, Halle, 1904.
Reinbrun (c1300): *Reinbrun, Gij sone of Warwike* in *Guy*[1], 631–74.
Rel. Ant.: Reliquiae Antiquae, ed. Thomas Wright and J. O. Halliwell, 2 vols., London, 1845.
Remedie of Love (a1500): in Chaucer, *Workes,* ed. John Stow, London, 1561, cccxxi[v]–cccxxiiii[v].
Remors (c1500): *The remors of conscyence,* W. de Worde, [?1532].
RES: Review of English Studies, London, 1(1925)—.
Richard (a1300): *Der mittelenglische Versroman über Richard Löwenherz,* ed. Karl Brunner, Wiener Beiträge zur englischen Philologie 42, 1913.
Ripley *Compound* (1471): George Ripley, *The Compound of Alchymie* in Ashmole, 107–93.
Rivers *Cordyal* (1479): Anthony Woodville, Earl Rivers, *The Cordyal,* ed. J. A. Mulders, Nijmegen, [1962].
Rivers *Dictes* (1477): *Dictes and Sayings of the Philosophers,* Caxton, 1477; facsimile, Detroit, The Cranbrook Press, 1901.
Rivers *Morale Proverbes* (1478): *The morale proverbes of Cristyne,* Caxton, 1478.
Robbins: Rossell H. Robbins, ed., *Secular Lyrics of the XIVth and XVth Centuries,* 2d ed., Oxford, 1955.
Robbins *Historical Poems: Historical Poems of the XIVth and XVth Centuries,* New York, 1959.
Robbins-Cutler: Rossell H. Robbins and John L. Cutler, edd., *Supplement to the Index of Middle English Verse,* Lexington, Kentucky, 1965.
Robert (c1390): *Roberd of Cisyle,* ed. Richard Nuck, Berlin, 1887.
Robert of Gloucester (c1300): *The Metrical Chronicle of Robert of Gloucester,* ed. William A. Wright, 2 vols., RS, 1887.
Robert the Devil (1502): *The Lyf of . . . Roberte the Devyll,* W. de Worde, [?1502].

Roland (c1400): *Fragment of the Song of Roland* in *Melayne,* 107–36.
Rolle *Meditatio* (a1349): Richard Rolle, *Meditatio de Passione Domini,* ed. Harald Lindkvist, Skrifter Utgifna af Kungliga Humanistiska Vetenskaps-Samfundet i Uppsala 19.3, 1917.
Rolle *Mending* (a1500): *Richard Rolle of Hampole's Mending of Life from the Fifteenth Century Worcester Cathedral Manuscript F. 172,* ed. W. H. Hulme, Western Reserve Studies 1.4, Cleveland, 1918.
Rolle *Psalter* (c1340): *The Psalter or Psalms of David . . . with a Translation and Exposition in English by Richard Rolle of Hampole,* ed. Henry R. Bramley, Oxford, 1884.
Romaunt (a1400): *The Romaunt of the Rose,* Fragments B and C in Chaucer (Robinson), 581–637.
?Ros *La Belle Dame* (a1500): ?Sir Richard Ros, *La Belle Dame Sans Mercy* in Skeat *Chaucerian,* 299–326.
Rote or Myrour (a1496): *The rote or myrour of consolacyon and conforte,* W. de Worde, 1499 (1496).
Rouland (c1330): *Rouland and Vernagu* in *The Taill of Rauf Coilyear . . . with the Fragments of Roland and Vernagu and Otuel,* ed. S. J. H. Herrtage, EETS ES 39, 1882, 37–61.
Rowlande (a1400): *The Romance of Duke Rowlande and of Sir Ottuell of Spayne* in *Melayne,* 55–104.
RS: Rolls Series; Rerum Britannicarum Medii Aevi Scriptores, or Chronicles and Memorials of Great Britain and Ireland during the Middle Ages, London, 1858–96.
Rule of St. Benet (*1*) (a1425): *Three Middle-English Versions of the Rule of St. Benet,* ed. Ernst A. Kock, EETS 120, 1902, 1–47.
Rule of St. Benet (*2*) (a1450): as above, 48–118.
Rule of St. Benet (*3*) (1491): as above, 119–40.
Russell *Boke* (a1475): John Russell, *The Boke of Nurture Folowyng Englondis gise* in Furnivall *Babees Book,* 117–99.
Ryght as small flodes (a1500): *A Treatise of a Galaunt* in Hazlitt *EPP,* III, 151–60.
Rylands MS. 394 (c1450): "A Medieval Collection of Latin and English Proverbs and Riddles, from the Rylands Latin MS. 394," ed. W. A. Pantin, *Bulletin of the John Rylands Library, Manchester* 14(1930), 81–114. (In large part identical with *Douce MS. 52.*)
Ryman (c1490): "Die Gedichte des Franziskaners Jakob Ryman," ed. Julius Zupitza, *Archiv* 89(1892), 167–338.
St. Agatha (c1375): in Horstmann *Legenden 1881,* 45–8.
St. Alexius (c1300): in Horstmann *Legenden 1881,* 174–88.
St. Anne (*1*) (c1400): *The Middle English Stanzaic Versions of the Life of Saint Anne,* ed. Roscoe E. Parker, EETS 174, 1928, 1–89.
St. Anne (*2*) (c1475): as above, 90–109.
St. Anne (*3*) (c1500): as above, 110–26.
St. Anthony (a1425): ed. C. Horstmann, *Anglia* 4(1881), 116–38.
St. Bartholomew (c1375): in Horstmann *Legenden 1881,* 119–23.
St. Birgitta (c1475): *The Revelations of Saint Birgitta,* ed. William P. Cumming, EETS 178, 1929.
St. Catherine (c1375): in Horstmann *Legenden 1881,* 165–73.
St. Christopher (c1440): in Horstmann *Legenden 1881,* 454–66.
St. Cuthbert (c1450): *The Life of St. Cuthbert in English Verse,* ed. James T. Fowler, Surtees Society 87, 1891.

St. Editha (a1450): *S. Editha sive Chronicon Vilodunense im Wiltshire Dialekt,* ed. C. Horstmann, Heilbronn, 1883.

St. Elizabeth of Spalbeck (c1425): ed. C. Horstmann, *Anglia* 8(1885), 107–18.

St. Erkenwald (c1386): ed. Henry L. Savage, Yale Studies in English 72, New Haven, 1926.

St. Etheldreda (a1450): in Horstmann *Legenden 1881,* 282–307.

St. Juliana (c1200): *The Liflade ant te Passiun of Seinte Juliene,* ed. S. R. T. O. d'Ardenne, Liége and Paris, 1936; EETS 248, 1961.

St. Kateryne (a1500): in Horstmann *Legenden 1881,* 260–4.

St. Katherin of Senis (c1493): "The lyf of saint Katherin of Senis," ed. C. Horstmann, *Archiv* 76(1886), 33–112, 265–314, 353–91.

St. Katherine (c1330): in Horstmann *Legenden 1881,* 242–59.

St. Katherine (Gibbs) (a1450): *The Life and Martyrdom of Saint Katherine of Alexandria,* ed. A. G. H. Gibbs, RC 112, 1884.

St. Katherine of Sienna (c1425): "Ueber S. Katerina of Senis," ed. C. Horstmann, *Anglia* 8(1885), 184–96.

St. Katherine (Royal) (c1200): *The Life of Saint Katherine, from the Royal MS. 17 A. xxvii,* ed. Eugen Einenkel, EETS 80, 1884.

St. Margarete (a1500): *The lyfe of saynte Margarete,* Robert Redman, [?1530].

St. Marherete (a1225): *Seinte Marherete, the Meiden ant Martyr,* ed. Frances M. Mack, EETS 193, 1934(1958).

St. Mary Oignies (c1425): ed. C. Horstmann, *Anglia* 8(1885), 134–84.

St. Matthew (c1375): in Horstmann *Legenden 1881,* 131–7.

St. Mergrete (c1330): in Horstmann *Legenden 1881,* 225–35.

St. Peter and St. Paul (c1375): in Horstmann *Legenden 1881,* 62–81.

St. Robert (a1425): *The Metrical Life of St. Robert of Knaresborough,* ed. Joyce Bazire, EETS 228, 1953.

Salamon sat and sayde (a1500): ed. Karl Brunner, *Anglia* 54(1930), 291.

Salisbury Psalter (c1100): ed. Celia and Kenneth Sisam, EETS 242, 1959.

Salomon and Marcolphus (1492): *The Dialogue or Communing Between the Wise King Salomon and Marcolphus,* ed. E. Gordon Duff, London, 1892.

Salutacioun to ure lady (c1390): in *Vernon,* I, 134–7.

Sandison: Helen E. Sandison, *The Chanson d'Aventure in Middle English,* Bryn Mawr College Monographs 12, 1913.

SATF: Société des Anciens Textes Français, Publications, Paris, 1875—.

Satirical Description (c1460): *A Satirical Description of his Lady* in Halliwell *Selection,* 199–205.

Sawles Warde (c1200): ed. R. M. Wilson, Leeds School of English Language, Texts and Monographs 3, 1938.

Sayings of St. Bernard (c1325): *Sayings of St. Bernard: Man's Three Foes* in *Vernon,* II, 511–22.

Schleich: G. Schleich, "Die Sprichwörter Hendings und die Proverbis of Wysdom," *Anglia* 51(1927), 220–77.

Scottish Legends (a1400): *Legends of the Saints in the Scottish Dialect,* ed. W. M. Metcalfe, 3 vols., STS, 1888–96.

Scottish Troy (c1400): *Barbour's des schottischen Nationaldichters Legendensammlung nebst den Fragmenten seines Trojanerkrieges,* ed. C. Horstmann, 2 vols., Heilbronn, 1881–2, II, 218–304.

Scrope *Epistle* (c1440): Stephen Scrope, *The Epistle of Othea to Hector . . . Translated from the French of Christine de Pisan,* ed. George F. Warner, RC 141, 1904.

Secrete of Secretes (c1450): in Steele *Secreta Secretorum*, 3–39.

Seege of Troye (a1350 [*Egerton*], a1425 [*Lincoln's Inn*], c1450 [*Arundel*], a1475 [*Harley*]): *The Seege or Batayle of Troye*, ed. Mary E. Barnicle, EETS 172, 1927. (*Egerton* is cited without designation.)

Seldom seen (a1390): in *Vernon*, II, 715–8.

Sellyng *Evidens* (a1456): ed. Albert C. Baugh in "Richard Sellyng," *Essays and Studies in Honor of Carleton Brown*, New York, 1940, 176–81.

Sen that Eine (a1500): in *The Maitland Quarto Manuscript*, ed. W. A. Craigie, STS, 1920, 103–7.

Serlo: "The Proverbs of Serlo of Wilton," ed. A. C. Friend, *Mediaeval Studies* 16(1954), 179–218.

Serve thy god (c1450): "Kleinere Dichtungen der Handschrift Harley 3810," ed. R. Jordan, *ESt* 41(1909–10), 261–2.

Seven Sages A (c1330): *The Seven Sages of Rome* (*Southern Version*), ed. Karl Brunner, EETS 191, 1933.

Seven Sages B (a1450): *The Seven Sages, in English Verse*, ed. Thomas Wright, PS 16, 1845.

Seven Sages C (a1350): *The Seven Sages of Rome*, ed. Killis Campbell, Boston, 1907.

Seven Sages D (c1400): *The Buke of the Sevyne Sagis* in *The Asloan Manuscript*, ed. W. A. Craigie, 2 vols., STS, 1923–5, II, 1–88.

Seven Wise Masters (1493): *The History of the Seven Wise Masters of Rome*, ed. George L. Gomme, Chap-books and Folk-Lore Tracts, 1st Series, 2, London, 1885.

Shillingford (v.d.): *Letters and Papers of John Shillingford*, ed. Stuart A. Moore, CS, N.S. 2, 1871.

Shirley *Death of James* (a1456): John Shirley, *The Dethe of the Kynge of Scotis*, Miscellanea Scotica 2.3, 1818.

Shoreham *Poems* (a1333): *The Poems of William of Shoreham*, ed. M. Konrath, EETS ES 86, 1902.

Siege of Jerusalem (a1400): ed. E. Kölbing and Mabel Day, EETS 188, 1932.

Singer: Samuel Singer, *Sprichwörter des Mittelalters*, 3 vols., Bern, 1944–7.

Sir Gawain (c1390): *Sir Gawain and the Green Knight*, ed. J. R. R. Tolkien and E. V. Gordon, Oxford, 1925(1936).

Skeat: Walter W. Skeat, *Early English Proverbs*, Oxford, 1910. (References are to the numbers given to the proverbs.)

Skeat *Chaucerian:* Walter W. Skeat, ed., *Chaucerian and Other Pieces: Being a Supplement to the Complete Works of Geoffrey Chaucer*, Oxford, 1897.

Skelton (v.d.): *The Poetical Works of John Skelton*, ed. Alexander Dyce, 2 vols., London, 1843.

Skelton *Magnificence* (c1516): ed. Robert L. Ramsay, EETS ES 98, 1908.

Slaughter (*Digby*) (c1485): *Slaughter of the Innocents* in *Digby Plays*, 1–23.

Sloane MS. 747 (c1490): *BM Sloane MS. 747*, f. 66a. (English proverbs, printed in part by M. Förster, *Anglia* 42[1918], 203–4.)

Smaller Vernon Collection (c1350): in Horstmann *Sammlung*, 3–97.

Smith: Charles G. Smith, *Shakespeare's Proverb Lore: His Use of the Sententiae of Leonard Culman and Publilius Syrus*, Cambridge, Mass., 1963.

Smith (c1500): *The Tale of the Smyth and his Dame* in Horstmann *Legenden 1881*, 322–8.

Smith *Common-place Book:* Lucy T. Smith, ed., *A Common-place Book of the Fifteenth Century . . . Printed from the Original Manuscript at Brome Hall, Suffolk*, London, 1886.

South English Legendary (c1300): edited from *Corpus Christi College Cambridge MS. 145 and British Museum MS. Harley 2277 . . .* by Charlotte D'Evelyn and Anna J. Mill, 3 vols., EETS 235–6, 244, 1956, 1959.

South English Legendary (Bodley) (a1450): "Des Ms. Bodl. 779, jüngere Zusatzlegenden zur südlichen Legendensammlung," ed. C. Horstmann, *Archiv* 82(1889), 307–53, 369–422.

South English Legendary (Laud) (c1300): *The Early South-English Legendary*, ed. C. Horstmann, EETS 87, 1887.

South English Legendary: OT History (c1280): in Adam Davy, 82–90, 96–8.

Southern Passion (c1280): ed. Beatrice D. Brown, EETS 169, 1927.

Sowdone (c1400): *The Romaunce of the Sowdone of Babylone and of Ferumbras his Sone*, ed. Emil Hausknecht, EETS ES 38, 1881.

SP: Studies in Philology, Chapel Hill, N.C., 1(1906)—.

Spalding *Katherine* (a1450): "Ein mittelenglischer Katharinenhymnus von Richard Spalding," ed. F. Holthausen, *Anglia* 60(1936), 150–64.

Speculum Christiani (1) (a1400): ed. Gustaf Holmstedt, EETS 182, 1933, odd pages.

Speculum Christiani (2) (c1450): as above, even pages.

Speculum Gy (c1300): *Speculum Gy de Warewyke*, ed. Georgiana L. Morrill, EETS ES 75, 1898.

Speculum Misericordie (c1455): ed. R. H. Robbins, *PMLA* 54(1939), 935–66.

Speculum Sacerdotale (c1425): ed. Edward H. Weatherly, EETS 200, 1936.

Spiritus Guydonis (c1400): in *Yorkshire Writers*, II, 292–333.

Squire (a1500): *The Squyr of Lowe Degre*, ed. William E. Mead, Boston, 1904.

Stanbridge *Vulgaria* (1508[1519]): *The Vulgaria of John Stanbridge and the Vulgaria of Robert Whittinton*, ed. Beatrice White, EETS 187, 1932, 1–30.

Stanzaic Life (a1400): *A Stanzaic Life of Christ*, ed. Frances A. Foster, EETS 166, 1926.

Stations (a1500): *The Stasyons of Jerusalem* in Horstmann *Legenden 1881*, 355–66.

STC: A Short-Title Catalogue of Books Printed in England, Scotland, and Ireland . . . 1475–1640, ed. A. W. Pollard and G. R. Redgrave, London, 1926.

Steele *Secreta Secretorum:* Robert Steele, ed., *Three Prose Versions of the Secreta Secretorum*, EETS ES 74, 1898.

Stevens *Music:* John Stevens, *Music and Poetry in the Early Tudor Court*, London, 1961.

Stevenson: Burton Stevenson, *The Home Book of Quotations*, 9th ed., New York, 1958.

Stockholm Prose Recipes (c1450): *Aus mittelenglischen Medizintexten: Die Prosarezepte des Stockholmer Miszellankodex X.90*, ed. Gottfried Müller, Kölner anglistische Arbeiten 10, Leipzig, 1929.

Stodye of Wysdome (a1400): *A Tretyse of the Stodye of Wysdome* in *Deonise*, 12–46.

Stonor Letters (v.d.): *The Stonor Letters and Papers, 1290–1483*, ed. Charles L. Kingsford, 2 vols., CS, 3d Series, 29–30, 1919.

STS: Scottish Text Society, Publications, Edinburgh, 1884—.

?Suffolk (c1450): Henry N. MacCracken, "An English Friend of Charles of Orléans," *PMLA* 26(1911), 142–80.

Susan (c1400): *Pistill of Susan* in Amours, 172–87.

Svartengren: T. Hilding Svartengren, *Intensifying Similes in English*, Lund, 1918.

Symon *Lesson* (c1475): *Symon's Lesson of Wysedome* in Furnivall *Babees Book*, 399–402.

Take Good Heed (c1460): in Robbins *Historical Poems*, 206–7.

Tale of the Lady Prioress (a1500): in Halliwell *Selection*, 107–17.

Talk of Ten Wives (a1475): in F. J. Furnivall, ed., *Jyl of Breyntfords Testament*, privately printed, London, 1871, 29–33.

Talkyng (c1390): *A Talkyng of the Love of God,* ed. Cecilia M. Westra, 's-Gravenhage, 1950.
Tars (c1390 [*Auchinleck*], c1390 [*Vernon*]): *The King of Tars,* ed. F. Krause, *ESt* 11(1887–8), 1–62. (Except in cases of significant variation *Auchinleck* is cited without designation.)
Taylor *Comparisons:* Archer Taylor, *Proverbial Comparisons and Similes from California,* Folklore Studies 3, Berkeley, Cal., 1954.
Taylor *Proverb:* Archer Taylor, *The Proverb,* Cambridge, Mass., 1931 (reprint, Hatboro, Pa., 1962).
Taylor and Whiting: Archer Taylor and B. J. Whiting, *Dictionary of American Proverbs and Proverbial Phrases, 1820–1880,* Cambridge, Mass., 1958.
Templum Domini (a1425): in Roberta D. Cornelius, *The Figurative Castle,* Bryn Mawr, Pa., 1930, 91–112.
Terens (c1520): *Terens in englysh,* [?Paris, c1530].
Theophilus (a1500): "Eine neue mittelenglische Version der Theophilus-sage," ed. W. Heuser, *ESt* 32(1903), 1–23.
Ther ne is dangyer (1484): in Caxton *Curial,* 19.
Thewis (c1475): *The Thewis off Gud Women* in Mustanoja, 176–96.
Tho oure lord god (a1400): in *Sixth Report of the Royal Commission on Historical Manuscripts,* London, 1877, Appendix, 319–20.
Thomas de Hales (a1300): *Love Ron* in Brown *Lyrics XIII,* 68–74.
Thomas of Erceldoune (c1400): *The Romance and Prophecies of Thomas of Erceldoune,* ed. James A. H. Murray, EETS 61, 1875.
Thre Ages (a1400): *The Parlement of the Thre Ages,* ed. Israel Gollancz, Select Early English Poems 2, London, 1915.
Thre Prestis (a1500): *The Thre Prestis of Peblis,* ed. T. D. Robb, STS, 1920.
Three Kings (c1400): *The Three Kings of Cologne,* ed. C. Horstmann, EETS 85, 1886.
Three Kings' Sons (c1500): ed. F. J. Furnivall, EETS ES 67, 1895.
Three Middle English Sermons (a1450): *Three Middle English Sermons from the Worcester Chapter Manuscript F.10,* ed. D. M. Grisdale, Leeds School of English Language, Texts and Monographs 5, 1939.
Three Old English Prose Texts (v.d.): *Three Old English Prose Texts in MS. Cotton Vitellius A xv,* ed. Stanley Rypins, EETS 161, 1924.
Tilley: Morris P. Tilley, *A Dictionary of the Proverbs in England in the Sixteenth and Seventeenth Centuries,* Ann Arbor, Michigan, 1950.
Times of Edward II (c1330): "Poem of the Evil Times of Edward II" in Wright *Political Songs,* 323–45.
Times of Edward II (*Bodley*) (c1330): "On The Evil Times of Edward II: A New Version from MS. Bodley 48," ed. T. W. Ross, *Anglia* 75(1957), 173–93.
Times of Edward II (*Peterhouse*) (c1330): *A Poem on the Times of Edward II,* ed. C. Hardwick, PS 28, 1849.
Tiptoft *Tullius* (a1470): John Tiptoft, Earl of Worcester, *Tullius de Amicicia,* Caxton, 1481.
Titus (a1400): *Titus and Vespasian, or, The Destruction of Jerusalem,* ed. J. A. Herbert, RC 146, 1905.
To you beholders (c1460): in Brotanek, 48–9.
Torrent (a1400): *Torrent of Portyngale,* ed. E. Adam, EETS ES 51, 1887.
Tottenham (a1500): *The Tournament of Tottenham* in French and Hale, 990–8.
Toulouse (c1400): *The Erl of Tolous and the Emperes of Almayn,* ed. Gustav Lüdtke, Sammlung englischer Denkmäler in kritischen Ausgaben 3, Berlin, 1881.
Towneley Plays (a1460): ed. George England and A. W. Pollard, EETS ES 71, 1897.
Treatise of Perfection (c1400): in *Chastising,* 229–58.

Tree (a1475): *A devout treatyse called the Tree and xii. frutes of the holy goost,* ed. J. J. Vaissier, Groningen, 1960.

Tretyse of Love (1493): ed. John H. Fisher, EETS 223, 1951.

Trevet (c1450): *Nicholas Trevet's Chronicle: An Early Fifteenth-century English Translation,* ed. William V. Whitehead (unpublished Harvard dissertation, 1960).

Trevisa *Dialogus* (a1402): John Trevisa, *Dialogus inter Militem et Clericum,* ed. Aaron J. Perry, EETS 167, 1925.

Triamour (c1400 [*Cambridge*], a1500 [*Percy*]): *Syr Tryamowre,* ed. Anna J. E. Schmidt, Utrecht, 1937. (*Cambridge* is cited without designation.)

Trinity College Homilies (a1200): *Old English Homilies of the Twelfth Century,* ed. Richard Morris, EETS 53, 1873.

Trinity MS. 0.2.45 (a1300): "Frühmittelenglische Sprichwörter," ed. Max Förster, *ESt* 31(1902), 5–9.

Tristrem (a1300): *Sir Tristrem* in *Die nordische und die englische Version der Tristansage,* ed. Eugen Kölbing, 2 vols., Heilbronn, 1878–82, II.

Tulle of Olde Age (1481): ed. Heinz Susebach, Studien zur englischen Philologie 75, Halle, 1933.

Tundale (c1400): *Tundale, Das mittelenglische Gedicht über die Vision des Tundalus,* ed. Albrecht Wagner, Halle, 1893.

Turke (a1500): *The Turke and Gowin* in *Percy Folio Manuscript,* I, 88–102.

Twelfth-century Homilies (c1175): *Twelfth-century Homilies in MS. Bodley 343,* ed. A. O. Belfour, EETS 137, 1909.

Two Apocrypha (a1000): *Two Apocrypha in Old English Homilies,* ed. Rudolph Willard, Beiträge zur englischen Philologie 30, 1935.

Usk (c1385): Thomas Usk, *The Testament of Love* in Skeat *Chaucerian,* 1–145.

Vercelli Book: The Vercelli Book, ed. George P. Krapp, *ASPR,* II, 1932.

Vercelli Homilies (a1000): *Die Vercelli-Homilien,* ed. Max Förster, *BAP* 12, Hamburg, 1932. (Part I only.)

Vernon: The Minor Poems of the Vernon MS., ed. Carl Horstmann and F. J. Furnivall, EETS 98, 117, 1892, 1901.

Vespasian Psalter (c850): in Henry Sweet, ed., *The Oldest English Texts,* EETS 83, 1885, 188–401.

Vices and Virtues (c1400): *The Book of Vices and Virtues,* ed. W. Nelson Francis, EETS 217, 1942.

Vices and Virtues (*Stowe*) (c1200): ed. F. Holthausen, EETS 89, 159, 1888, 1921.

Vision of Philibert (a1475): in Halliwell *Early English Miscellanies,* 12–39.

Vulgaria quedam abs Terencio (1483): W. de Machlinia, 1483.

Wærferth *Gregory* (a893): *Bischofs Wærferth von Worcester Übersetzung der Dialoge Gregors des Grossen,* ed. Hans Hecht, *BAP* 5, Leipzig, 1900.

Wall Verses at Launceston Priory (a1450): ed. R. H. Robbins, *Archiv* 200(1963), 338–43.

Wallace (c1470): *The Actis and Deidis of . . . Schir William Wallace,* ed. James Moir, STS, 1885–9.

Walter *Spectacle* (c1520): Wyllyam Walter, *The spectacle of lovers,* W. de Worde, [c1520].

Walther: Hans Walther, *Proverbia Sententiaeque Latinitatis Medii Aevi, Lateinische Sprichwörter und Sentenzen des Mittelalters,* Carmina Medii Aevi Posterioris Latina 2.1–5, Göttingen, 1963–7.

Walton *Boethius* (1410): *Boethius: De Consolatione Philosophiae, Translated by John Walton, Canon of Oseney,* ed. Mark Science, EETS 170, 1927.

Warkworth (a1500): John Warkworth, *A Chronicle of the First Thirteen Years of the Reign of Edward the Fourth,* ed. J. O. Halliwell, CS 10, 1839.

Warner: Rubie D-N. Warner, ed., *Early English Homilies from the Twelfth Century MS. Vesp. D. XIV,* EETS 152, 1917.

Waterhouse: Osborn Waterhouse, ed., *The Non-Cycle Mystery Plays, together with the Croxton Play of the Sacrament and the Pride of Life,* EETS ES 104, 1909.

Watson *Oliver* (1518): Henry Watson, *The History of Oliver of Castile,* ed. Robert E. Graves, RC 136, 1898.

Watson *Ship* (1509): *The shyppe of fooles,* W. de Worde, 1509.

Watson *Valentine* (c1505): *Valentine and Orson,* ed. Arthur Dickson, EETS 204, 1937.

Way of Woman's Love (c1325): in Brown *Lyrics XIII,* 162–3.

WBible (c1395): *The Holy Bible . . . by John Wycliffe and his Followers,* ed. Josiah Forshall and Frederic Madden, 4 vols., Oxford, 1850. (Quotations are ordinarily from the second version, unless the first version is indicated by the date a1382.)

Weddynge (c1450): *The Weddynge of Sir Gawen and Dame Ragnell* in *Sources and Analogues of Chaucer's Canterbury Tales,* ed. W. F. Bryan and Germaine Dempster, Chicago, 1941, 242–64.

Wheatley MS.: The Wheatley Manuscript: A Collection of Middle English Verse and Prose Contained in a MS. now in the British Museum, Add. MSS. 39574, ed. Mabel Day, EETS 155, 1921.

When the son (c1450): "How a Lover Praiseth his Lady," ed. Eleanor P. Hammond, *MP* 21(1923–4), 379–95.

Whiting *Ballad:* B. J. Whiting, "Proverbial Material in the Popular Ballad," *Journal of American Folklore* 47(1934), 22–44.

Whiting *Devil:* "The Devil and Hell in Current English Literary Idiom," *Harvard Studies and Notes in Philology and Literature* 20(1938), 201–47.

Whiting *Drama: Proverbs in the Earlier English Drama,* Harvard Studies in Comparative Literature 14, Cambridge, Mass., 1938.

Whiting *Froissart:* "Proverbs in the Writings of Jean Froissart," *Speculum* 10(1935), 291–321.

Whiting *NC:* "Proverbs and Proverbial Sayings" in N. I. White and Paull F. Baum, edd., *The Frank C. Brown Collection of North Carolina Folklore,* Durham, N.C., I(1952), 331–501.

Whiting *Scots* I, II: "Proverbs and Proverbial Sayings from Scottish Writings before 1600," *Mediaeval Studies* 11(1949), 123–205, 13(1951), 87–164.

Whittinton *Vulgaria* (1520): as Stanbridge *Vulgaria,* 33–128.

Why I Can't (c1475): *Why I Can't Be a Nun* in Furnivall *Early English Poems,* 138–48.

Wife Lapped (c1500): *A merry Jeste of a Shrewde and Curste Wyfe lapped in Morrelles skin* in Hazlitt *EPP,* IV, 179–226.

William (a1375): *The Romance of William of Palerne,* ed. W. W. Skeat, EETS ES 1, 1867.

Winner (c1353): *A Good Short Debate Between Winner and Waster,* ed. Israel Gollancz, 2d ed., Oxford, 1930.

Wisdom (c1475): *A Morality of Wisdom, Who is Christ* in *Macro Plays,* 35–73.

Wohunge of Ure Laverd (c1225): in Richard Morris, *Old English Homilies . . . First Series,* EETS 29, 34, 1867–8, 269–87.

Wold God that men (a1500): in Thomas Wright, *Songs and Carols,* PS 23, 1847, 9–10.

Wright *Political Poems:* Thomas Wright, ed., *Political Poems and Songs . . . from the Accession of Edward III to that of Richard III,* 2 vols, RS, 1859–61.

Wright *Political Songs: The Political Songs of England from the Reign of John to that of Edward II,* CS, 1839.

WSG (c1000): *West Saxon Gospels: Matthew (1904), Mark (1905), Luke (1906), John (1904),* ed. James W. Bright, 4 vols., Boston, 1904–6.

Wulfstan *Homilies* (a1023): *The Homilies of Wulfstan,* ed. Dorothy Bethurum, Oxford, 1957.

Wyclif *EW* (v.d.): *The English Works of Wyclif, Hitherto Unprinted,* ed. F. D. Matthew, EETS 74, 1880. (Many titles, as the dates indicate, are no longer ascribed to Wyclif.)

Wyclif *Sermons* (a1425): in Wyclif *SEW,* I, II.

Wyclif *SEW* (v.d.): *Select English Works of John Wyclif,* ed. Thomas Arnold, 3 vols., Oxford, 1869–71. (See note to Wyclif *EW.*)

Wyntoun (c1420): *The Original Chronicle of Andrew of Wyntoun,* ed. F. J. Amours, 6 vols., STS, 1903–14. (Wyntoun states that he took over the verses between viii 2965 and ix 1120 [V 370–VI 357] from an anonymous chronicler; see I xxxix, xc ff., and esp. xciii f.)

Ye that are comons (a1500): in Robbins *Historical Poems,* 233–5.

Yonge *Governaunce* (1422): James Yonge, *The Governaunce of Prynces* in Steele *Secreta Secretorum,* 121–248.

York Plays (a1450): ed. Lucy Toulmin Smith, Oxford, 1885.

Yorkshire Writers (v.d.): *Yorkshire Writers: Richard Rolle of Hampole . . . and his Followers,* ed. Carl Horstmann, 2 vols., London, 1895–6.

Young Children's Book (a1500): in Furnivall *Babees Book,* 17–25.

Ywain (a1350): *Ywain and Gawain,* ed. Albert B. Friedman and Norman T. Harrington, EETS 254, 1964.

PROVERBS, SENTENCES,
AND
PROVERBIAL PHRASES

A1 To know not **A** from the windmill
1402 *Daw Topias* 57[13–4]: I know not an a From the wynd-mylne. Apperson 1; *Oxford* 346.

A2 **A**,B,C
a1400 Julian *Revelation* 145[6–8]: I have teaching with me as it were the beginning of an ABC, 234[5–6]: He willeth that we have knowing here as it were in an ABC. **c1420** Wyntoun IV 149.231–2: Sa mony abbayis foundit he As letteris ar in the Abbece (*var.* ABC). **c1475** Henryson *Robene* 151.17–8: At luvis lair gife thow will leir, Tak thair ane a b c. **1490** Irlande *Meroure* 14.12–3: The meroure of wissdome or A.B.C. of cristianite. **1523** Skelton *Garlande* I 420.1475–6: In ryming and raylyng with hym for to mell, For drede that he lerne them there A,B,C, to spell. Taylor and Whiting 1.

A3 **A** per se
c1475 Henryson *Testament* 107.78–9: O, fair Creisseid, the flour and A per se Of Troy and Grece. **a1500** *The Merchant and his Son* in Hazlitt *EPP* I 135.39: Thow schalt be an a-persey. **a1500** *Partenay* 45.1148: She was A woman A-per-se, alon. **a1500** *Thre Prestis* 24.356: In all the science sevyne he was an A per C, 46.1066. **1501** Douglas *Palice* 36.9: Chauceir, as *a per se* sans peir. **1501** ?Dunbar *To the City of London* 177.1. **a1513** ?Dunbar *Manere of the Crying* 174.133. **1513** Douglas *Aeneid* II 3.8. **1519** Horman *Vulgaria* 275[12]. **1533** Heywood *Weather* A3^{r}[35]: Some saye I am I perse I. Apperson 1; Tilley A275; Whiting *Drama* 333:379, *Scots* I 130.

A4 To bring an **Abbey** to a grange
a1440 Burgh *Cato* 32.1126: Somtyme was an abbey, ther is now a graunge. **c1450** Idley 127.1170–1: Ffor like as an abbeye is brought to a graunge, So all thyng was turned out of kynde. **a1475** *Vision of Philibert* 26[20–1]: And nowe that abbay is torned to a grange, Farewel thi frenschype, thi kechyne is cold. **c1522** Skelton *Colyn* I 327.420–1: Turne monasteris into water milles, Of an abbay ye make a graunge. Apperson 1; *Oxford* 65; Tilley A3. See **H8, T546.**

A5 He is not wise that **Abides** where he is not needed
c1250 *Owl* 42.465–6: Vor he nis nother yep ne wis, That longe abid thar him nod nis. See **C447.**

A6 He that **Abides** well has not lost
a1393 Gower *CA* II 271.1656–8: Ne haste noght thin oghne sorwe, Mi Sone, and tak this in thi witt, He hath noght lost that wel abitt, II 349.1776–7: And therof, Sone, I wol thee rede, Abyd, and haste noght to faste. See **H171.**

A7 Those that **Abide** long may walk wrong at last
c1450 Capgrave *Katharine* 135.909–10: Thenke (on) other that have abeden longe, And at the laste thei have walked wronge. See **D157.**

A8 To him that **Abides** shall betide well
c1450 *Douce MS.52* 45.19: Who-so wyl abyde, He schal wel be-tyde. **c1450** *Rylands MS.394* 97.7^{v}.5. See **B318.**

A9 In **Abiding** great harm may fall
a1420 Lydgate *Troy* I 319.6097–8: For in abydyng and in swiche delaies Gret harme may falle. See **D157.**

A10 In **Abiding** is found remedy
1420 Lydgate *Temple* 45.1089–92: For in abiding, of wo and al affray—Whoso can suffre—is founden remedie, And for the best ful oft is made delay, Er men be heled of hir maladie. See **S866.**

A11 In **Abiding** lies hope
c1450 Capgrave *Katharine* 93.224: And in a-bydyng men seyn there lyeth hope.

A12 In long **Abiding** is little prow (*benefit*)
c1450 Capgrave *Katharine* 93.248: In longe a-bydynge is ful litel prow.

A13 To fall **Aboard** with
a1400 Wyclif *Sermons* I 294[14–5]: Thes men that now dremen an accident withouten suget mai falle aborde with these foolis. MED abord 1(d); NED Aboard 2d.

A14 As old as **Abraham's** mother
c1450 Idley 163.248: And she bee as oolde as Abrahaums modir.

A15 In **Abraham's** bosom (*varied*)
a893 Wærferth *Gregory* 310.8–9: He wæs boren fram Godes englum and aseted in Abrahames bearme. **c1000** *Larspel* in Napier 238.6–7: And sceal beon seo gode sawel on Abrahames fæðmum. **c1000** *WSG* Luke xvi 22: On Abrahames greadan. **c1300** *Southern Legendary Life of Jesus* in C. Horstmann *Leben Jesu, ein Fragment* (Münster, 1873) 36.162–3. **c1303** Mannyng *Handlyng* 215.6653–8: Abrahams bosum ys a dwellyng That holy men have yn restyng, That to Ihesu, Goddys sone, cam, That flesshe and blode yn Mary nam. Abrahams bosum ys a stede, men telle, Betwyxe paradys and helle. **a1387** *Piers* C ix 283: In Abrahammes lappe. **a1393** Gower *CA* III 194.1023: In Habrahammes barm on hyh. **c1395** *WBible* Luke xvi 22: The begger diede, and was borun of aungels in to Abraham bosum. **a1398**(1495): Bartholomaeus-Trevisa B3ᵛ[2.4–5]. **a1400** *Pricke* 83–4.3059–61. **a1400** Wyclif *Sermons* I 2[17]. **c1400** *Pepysian Gospel* 64.23–4: In Abrahames barme. **c1400** *Primer* 70[13–4]. **1402** *Daw Topias* 99[8]. **a1415** Mirk *Festial* 274.2. **a1425** *Chester Plays* I 205.10–2: Wend I mott the same way, that Abraham went, the sooth to say, and in his bosome be. **a1450** *Lessouns* in Kail 119.382. **c1450** Idley 194.2122–3, 2138. **1483** Caxton *Golden Legende* 286ʳ (*by error* 285ʳ) [1.39]. **1490** Irlande *Meroure* 115.18–9. **a1500** *Miroure of Mans Salvacionne* 18 *gloss:* The Lymbe was the free prisonne in hell, called Abraham bosme in whilk were haly faders and othere of the ald lawe that shuld be redemyd be crist, 100[5]. **1522** More *Treatyce* 91 A[14–5], **1529** *Supplicacion* 317 G[1–2], **1534** *Comforte* 1157 A[5]: That ryche mans bosome, 1159 DE: And rest in Abraham that welthi rich mans bosome. *Oxford* 1; Taylor and Whiting 2; Tilley A8.

A16 **Absence** drives one from the heart
c1385 Chaucer *TC* iv 427: Absence of hire shal dryve hire out of herte. See **E213, S307.**

A17 Long **Absence** causes division (is a shrew)
a1439 Lydgate *Fall* III 911.3140: Long abscence causeth devisioun. **a1500** *Piers of Fullham* 13.290–1: And therfor it is said in wordes few, How that long absence is a sherew, 317: In such caas absence is a sherew, 14.351. Apperson 1; Tilley A9.

A18 As fair as **Absolon** (*varied*)
a1200 Lawman III 153.28816–7: That was the faireste mon: With uten Adam and Absolon. **a1300** *Maximian* 92.16–7: He wes feirest mon Withhouten apselon. **a1300** Thomas de Hales 70.83: And al so veyr as absalon. **c1303** Mannyng *Handlyng* 142.4208: Who was feyrer than Absolon? **c1390** *Of clene Maydenhod* 465.18: That weore so feir as Absolon. **a1395** *WBible* II Kings xiv 25: Sotheli no man in al Israel was so fair as Absolon. **a1400** *Pricke* 240.8926–7, cf. 243.9023. **c1415** *Middle English Sermons* 68.8. **a1449** Lydgate *Thoroughfare* in *MP* II 824.61. **a1450** *Song of Mortality* in Brown *Lyrics XIV* 96.14. **c1450** Idley 172.836: Whoo more beautevous than feire Absolon? **1456** Hay *Law* 65.9. **c1475** Henryson *Fables* 98.2842: Wer I als fair as Jolie Absolon. **1479** Rivers *Cordyal* 9.24. **1493** *Tretyse of Love* 81.6: The beaute of absolon. **a1500** Kennedy 26.19. **a1500** *Miroure of Mans Salvacionne* 145[18]. **a1500** *Salamon sat and sayde* 291.26. **1509** Watson *Ship* B8ᵛ[14], Gg2ᵛ[8]. **a1513** Dunbar *Of Manis Mortalitie* 149.12. Whiting *Scots* I 130.

A19 **Abundance** is better than necessity
1509 Watson *Ship* A2ʳ[4–6] (*The first of two A signatures*): Knowynge that Melius est habundare quod deficere. It is better to have haboundaunce of dyvers thynges than to have necessyte.

A20 Great **Abundance** often makes an evil conclusion
c1475 Henryson *Fables* 16.377–8: Grit aboundance and blind prosperitie Oftymes makis ane evill conclusioun. Cf. *Oxford* 1.

A21 He that is not born to **Abundance** is not of gentle blood
c1485 *Guiscardo* 80.726–8: Seying it is a proverbe sufficient and kinde: "He that ys nat born to habundance of good, But nedy for povert, ys nat (of) gentyll blood." See **G43.**

A22 Of the **Abundance** of the heart the mouth speaks
c1000 *WSG* Matthew xii 34: Soþlice of þære heortan willan se muþ spicþ. **c1200** *Vices and*

Virtues (*Stowe*) 101.8: Of that the herte is full, tharof spekth the muth. **1340** *Ayenbite* 203–4: Vor be the mochelhede of the herte: the mouth spekth thet zayth our lhord ine his spelle. **c1385** Usk 35.27–8: Sodeynly in their mouthes procedeth the habundaunce of the herte, and wordes as stones out-throwe. **c1390** Chaucer *CT* X[I] 627: For after the habundance of the herte speketh the mouth ful ofte. **c1395** *WBible* Matthew xii 34: For the mouth spekith of plente of the herte. **a1400** *Gast of Gy* 50.830–3 (cf. *Spiritus Guydonis* 309[12–4]). **c1400** *Consilia Isidori* 371[5]. **c1400** *Vices and Virtues* 225.20–1: For of grete plente of herte the mouth speketh. **a1470** Parker *Dives* E8ᵛ[1.28–30]: The mouth, sayth he, speketh of suche thynges wherof it is plente in the herte. **1483** Caxton *Cato* H6ᵛ[8–9], I1ᵛ[13–4]: For it is sayd comynly, **1484** *Royal Book* R2ᵛ[21]. **c1485** *Conversion* 48.563: Of the hartes habundans the tunge makyth locucion. **1492** *Salomon and Marcolphus* 12[1]. **1533** More *Confutacion* 713 G[2–4], *Debellacyon* 965 E[5–6]. Taylor and Whiting 2; Tilley A13.

A23 No (good) **Accord** where every man would be a lord
a1500 *Salamon seyth* in Person 52.1–4: Salamon seyth ther is none accorde Ther every man wuld be a lord. Wher every man is plesyd with his degre Ther is both pece and unyte. **1546** Heywood *D* 78.7–8: Tys sayde, there is no good accorde, Where every man would be a Lorde, **1556** *Spider* 194[6–7]: It is and hath ben said: thers no good accorde: In place where as every knave will be a lorde. *Oxford* 2; Tilley A15. See **G476, J6.**

A24 There may be no **Accord** 'tween truth and fraud
a1449 Lydgate *Fabules* in *MP* II 574.230–1: And phylosophers by wrytyng bere recorde, Twene trowthe and fraude may be non acorde.

A25 **Ace** may resist sice (*six*)
c1458 *Knyghthode and Bataile* 59.1612–4: And if thin ooste is ace, and his is syis, What so thei sey, covertly by prudence, Dispose the to make resistence. MED as (b). See **M801.**

A26 Not reprehend an **Ace**
1440 Palladius 19.15–6: That of his woord, his werk, entent or mood Noon invident may reprehende an ace.

A27 Not worth an **Ace**
1513 Douglas *Aeneid* IV 192.14: Quhat is weill said thai love not worth ane ace. Whiting *Scots* I 130.

A28 To set at an **Ace**
a1425 *Piers* C ix 166 (*var.*): And sette peers at an ase.

A29 To set on an **Ace** (*i.e.*, risk at dice)
a1513 Dunbar *Advice to Spend* 147.27: That his auld thrift settis on ane es.

A30 The spear (sword) of **Achilles**
c1395 Chaucer *CT* V[F] 239–40: And of Achilles with his queynte spere, For he koude with it bothe heele and dere. **a1449** Lydgate *Complaint* in *MP* II 382.25–8: Achilles swerde the egge was kervy(n)g, The plat therof was softe and recureabile; Wownded of the egge was mortall yn werkyng, The fatall plate was medycynabill. *Oxford* 612; Tilley S731; Whiting *Scots* I 130. See **F253.**

A31 **Acquaintance** of lordship is dear bought
c1450 *Proverbs* in *Rel. Ant.* I 205[9–10]: Aqueyntanse of lordschip wyll y noght, For furste or laste dere hit woll be bowght. Apperson 2.

A32 Between this and **Acre**
1485 Caxton *Charles* 167.1–2: Thys is the strongest cyte that is bytwene thys and Acres.

A33 He sits high that deals out **Acres**
c1250 *Hendyng O* 198.39: Heye he sit, that akeres deleth. Kneuer 71; *Oxford* 593; Schleich 267; Singer III 135; Tilley A25.

A34 From **Adam** to this time
a1375 *William* 117.3614: Feller saw never frek from adam to this time.

A35 The old **Adam**
c1375 Barbour *Bruce* II 34.250: Fra vem of ald Adammis syne. **c1395** *WBible* Prologue (I 40[30]): Wynne of old Adam. **a1396**(1494) Hilton *Scale* H4ʳ[13]: The old Adam. **a1400** *Meditations* 33.1253–4: Now is for olde Adamis gylt Newe Adam with wrong y-spylt. **a1500** Kennedy 73.1142: Lif fell in dede for luf of ald Adam. *Oxford* 2; Taylor and Whiting 3; Tilley A29; Whiting *Scots* I 130.

A36 To live **Adam's** eld (*age*)
a1300 *Richard* 401.6299–300: And gaff hym the cyte to welde, Though he levyd Adammis elde.

A37 We are all come from **Adam** and Eve
a1396(1494) Hilton *Scale* H2ᵛ[26]: For all come we of adam and eve. **a1400** Wyclif *Sermons* I 32[31]: We came alle of Adam and Eve. **a1450** *Declaryng* in Kail 81.57–8: Though thou be of gentyl blod, Thenk all com of Adam and Eve. **c1485** *Guiscardo* 80.743–9: Furst when oure modyr Eve brought forth Abell and Caym, Who

cowde prefer hymself of byrth or of lynage, And of theym tweyne infauntes, who cowde a tytyll claym In gentyll blood, in noblenes, or in hygh parage? That tyme was no dyfference betwyxt gentylman and page, But every man was fayne to put hym in devour Hys lyvyng for to gete with swetyng and gret labour. **1486** ?Berners *Book of St. Albans* A1^r[27–8]: A bonde man or a churle wyll say all we be cummyn of adam. **c1497** Medwall *Fulgens* F5^v[6–7]. **a1513** Dunbar *To the King* 42.38. **1523** Berners *Froissart* III 224[28–30]: We be all come fro one father and one mother, Adam and Eve: wherby can they say or shewe that they be gretter lordes than we be? **c1525** ?Heywood *Gentylnes* 108.489–90, 517–8. Whiting *Scots* I 130. See **C263, 538, F81.**

A38 When **Adam** delved and Eve span who was then the gentleman?
1374 Brinton *Sermons* I 154[1]: Cum vanga quadam tellurem foderat Adam *et cetera,* 195[29]. **1381** *Balliol MS.354,* f.200b in Brown-Robbins 3922: Whan adam delffid and eve span, Who was than a gentilman? **c1390** *Of Women cometh this Worldes Weal* in Brown *Lyrics XIV* 177.97–102: For God and Mon wer fer a-twinne Whon he made Monkuynde of Séé-flod. I wolde wite, whon that Eve gon spinne, Bi whom that youre gentrie stod? Hou be-come ye godes kinne But barelych thorw the wommones blod? **a1393** Gower *CA* II 361.2222–6: And forto loke on other side Hou that a gentil man is bore, Adam, which alle was tofore With Eve his wif, as of hem tuo, Al was aliche gentil tho. **a1450** *Song of Mortality* in Brown *Lyrics XIV* 96.1–2: When adam delf and eve span, spir, if thou wil spede, Whare was than the pride of man that now merres his mede? **c1450** Greene *Carols* 336 (refrain): Now bething the, gentilman, How Adam dalf and Eve sp(an). **c1470** *Harley MS.3362* f.5a (*the English in a later hand*): Cum vanga quadam tellurem foderit Adam Et Eva neus fuerat, quis generosus erat. Whan Adam dalf and Eve span, Who was then a gentleman? **a1475** *Ludus Coventriae* 29.415: Ye (*Adam*) must delve and I (*Eve*) xal spynne. **c1475** *Rawlinson MS. D 328* 121.50: Whanne Adam dalfe and Eve spanne, ho was tho a gentelman? **a1500** Hill 131.25. **c1525** ?Heywood *Gentylnes* 108.485–8: For when Adam dolf and Eve span, Who was then a gentylman? But then cam the churl and gederyd good, And ther began furst the gentyll blood. **1556** Heywood *Spider* 197[19–21]: For thei finde in booke: This demaund written. When Adam dolve and Eve span, Who was in those golden daies, a gentleman? Apperson 2; Jente 778; *Oxford* 2–3; Taylor and Whiting 4; Tilley A30.

A39 As **Adamant** draws iron
a1400 ?Chaucer *Rom.* A 1182–4: Right as an adamaunt, iwys, Can drawen to hym sotylly The iren that is leid therby.

A40 As hard as **Adamant**
c1200 *Hali Meidenhad* 52.546: Ha is heardre iheortet then adamantines stan. **1340** *Ayenbite* 187[23–4]: Hy byeth harde ase an aymont. **a1410** Love *Mirrour* 202[26]: That harde herte . . . harder than the adamaunde. **c1450** *Pilgrimage LM* 85[28–9]: He is as hard as adamaunt. **1484** Caxton *Royal Book* P2^v[21]. **1509** Barclay *Ship* II 127[3]: Mollyfy your hertis that ar harde as adamant. **a1535** Fisher *Sermon . . . upon a good Friday* in *English Works* 403.17–8: Hys hart be harder then any . . . Adamant stone. Svartengren 260; Taylor and Whiting 4. See **D227.**

A41 As strong as any **Adamant**
1483 Caxton *Golden Legende* 177^r[2.25]: He was strenger thenne ony adamant. Cf. Taylor and Whiting 4.

Adder, see **Serpent**

A42 **Adder** (Serpent) in the bosom
c1395 Chaucer *CT* IV[E] 1786: Lyk to the naddre in bosom sly untrewe. **1481** Caxton *Godeffroy* 66.34–5: But they, lyke as the serpent that prycketh or styngeth hym that kepeth hym warme in his bosomme. **1534** More *Comforte* 1200 B[1–5]: It is a thing right hard . . . to kepe a serpent in thy bosome, and yet be safe fro stinging. *Oxford* 600–1.

A43 As speckled as an **Adder**
a1398(1495) Bartholomaeus-Trevisa P3^r[1.11–2]: The stalke therof is specklyd as an Adder.

A44 As wise (wary) as **Adders** (serpents) and as simple as doves
a900 Alfred *Gregory* 237.20–1: Beo ge swa ware sua sua nædran and sua bilwite sua culfran. **c1000** *WSG* Matthew x 16: Beoþ eornustlice gleawe swa næddran, and bylwite swa culfran. **a1050** Defensor *Liber* 85[16–7]: Drihten segð on godspelle: beoð eornostlice snotere swa næddran and anfealde swa culfran. **a1200** *Trinity College Homilies* 195[16]: Giepe alse the neddre. **c1395** *WBible* Matthew x 16: Therfor be ye sligh as serpentis, and symple as dowves. **a1400** Wyclif *Sermons* I 200[17–9]: Christ seith . . . loke ye be prudent as neddris, and symple as

dowves, 201[5]. **c1425** *Speculum Sacerdotale* 239.25: He was symple as the dowve, wyse as the serpent. **1533** More *Confutacion* 763 A[8–10]: If wee be not onely simple as doves, but also prudent and wise as serpentes. Cf. Tilley M1162. See **D361, 380.**

A45 To dread one as an **Adder** (*etc.*) (A number of single quotations are brought together here) **a900** Alfred *Augustine* 37.12–3: Ic hyt hondrede swa þare nædram (*bite*). **c1000** Aelfric *Lives* II 380.58: And þa mædena onscunode (*hated*) swa swa man deþ næddran. **a1393** Gower *CA* III 55.3966–7: Al specheles and on the gras Sche glod forth as an Addre doth. **a1400** *Alexander C* 247.4757: And he be-held on that hend and hissis as a neddire. **a1450** *Myne awen dere* 158.279–80: Fra hys fletynge thou kepe the thus As fra the nedder that is venemus.

A46 To flee as from an **Adder** (*varied*) **c1000** ?Aelfric *Lives* II 22.318–9: Sona þu flihst fram me on þi gemete swilc man næddran fleo. **c1400** *Lay Folks' Catechism* 89.1306: As fro the Neddyrys face fonde to fle synne.

A47 To sting (stang) like an **Adder** **1456** Hay *Law* 30.18: Thai stang as ane edder. **a1513** Dunbar *Of the Changes of Lyfe* 141.9: This day it stangis lyk ane edder. Whiting *Scots* I 131.

A48 He that thinks to **Advance** himself often does himself damage (*varied*) **c1505** Watson *Valentine* 80.22–3: But suche weneth to avaunce hymself that oftentymes dothe his owne dommage. **1525** Berners *Froissart* VI 307[7–8]: Often tymes a man thynketh to be avaunced, and is pulled backe. See **S193.**

A49 **Adventure** (*fortune, luck*) gives victory more often than does force **1489** Caxton *Fayttes* 100.8–9: Adventure gyveth often vyctory more than doeth force. See **H101, M801.**

A50 **Adventure** may often avail **c1420** Wyntoun III 63.794–6: Awenture oft may awaile, And prowes pynys al perille, And eftyr hope hart hapnys qwhylle (*var.* And efter hope happinnis quhile).

A51 **Adventure** never abides in one point **a1439** Lydgate *Fall* I 302.3644: Nat in o poynt a-bit noon aventure. See **C141.**

A52 The **Adventure** of the world is wonderful **1481** Caxton *Reynard* 61[15–7]: The aventure of the world is wonderly, It goth otherwhyle by wenyng: Many one weneth to have a thing whiche he muste forgoo.

A53 Some goodly **Adventure** is shaped sometime to every wight, *etc.* (*varied*) **c1385** Chaucer *TC* ii 281–7: For to every wight som goodly aventure Som tyme is shape, if he it kan receyven; But if that he wol take of it no cure, Whan that it commeth, but wilfully it weyven, Lo neyther cas ne fortune hym deceyven, But ryght his verray slouthe and wrecchednesse; And swich a wight is for to blame, I gesse. **c1503** More *Early Poems* [2] CD: And men had sworne, Some man is borne, To have a lucky howre. Cf. Tilley T283. See **F540, G359, T312, W275.**

A54 Whatever stands on **Adventure** is uncertain **a1393** Gower *CA* III 166.7817–20: For what thing stant on aventure, That can no worldes creature Telle in certein hou it schal wende, Til he therof mai sen an ende. See **H98.**

A55 By **Adventuring** a little one may assay what will come of the whole **1519** Horman *Vulgaria* 396[3]: By adventerynge of a lytell let us assaye what wyl come of the hole. See **H40.**

A56 **Adversity** tests friends **c1390** *Proverbes of diverse profetes* 539.261–4: Yif thou falle in adversite, Thou shal fynde and wite, parde, Of whom thou wendest a frend have had, Then wole to the be enemy sad. Smith 2. Cf. Tilley A42, 43. See **F634, 667, P417.**

A57 He is wise that can be patient in **Adversity** **1504** Hawes *Example* Cc1^{r}[6–7]: For evermore right wyse is he That can be pacyent in adversyte. Smith 4. Cf. Tilley P106.

A58 He that takes not **Advice** is born in an evil hour **1485** Caxton *Charles* 61.28–9: For he that taketh not advys is borne in an evyl houre. See **C470.**

A59 **Advise** well before you speak **c1450** *Fyrst thou sal* 91.169: Avyse the wele or thou speke.

A60 **Advise** you well whatever you say **a1400** *Proverbis of Wysdom* 244.24: What sum ever thou say, avyse the wele, 246.117–8: A-vyse the well, what ever thu say, And have few wordis, I the pray. **c1450** *Fyrst thou sal* 88.32. **a1500** *Think Before You Speak* in Brown *Lyrics XV* 280–2.8: Whate ever thow sey, A-vyse the welle, 16, 24, *etc.* Cf. *Oxford* 469; Tilley A44, 45.

A61 He that is evil **Advised** oft has pain
1483 Caxton *Cato* H4ʳ[5–6]: Therfore saith the comyn proverbe that evyl advysed hath ofte payne.

A62 **Advisement** is good
c1385 Chaucer *TC* ii 343: Avysement is good byfore the nede. **a1450** *Generydes A* 151.4870: Oft avisement mich goode dooth. **c1450** *Alle that well* in *MLN* 70(1955) 251.53–4: For wete it wel, bothe elde and yunge, Vysement is good in al thyng. **a1500** *Ghostly Battle* in *Yorkshire Writers* II 422–3: Also what-so-ever thow doo, thynke or speke, that hit be do with goode avysement, and wysely to thynke on the begynnyng and on the endyng. Cf. *Oxford* 250; Tilley I34. See **M335, T18, W167.**

A63 Some speak of **Affairs** who know not how they go
c1505 Watson *Valentine* 239.27–8: Suche speaketh of the affayres that can not tel howe they go. See **R156.**

A64 More **Afraid** than hurt
c1400 *Sowdone* 49.1709–10: For of all thinge thou arte aferde, Yet arte thou neyther hurte ner take. **1533** More *Apologye* 178[32]: Wers afrayed then hurte. **1546** Heywood *D* 25.35: And be more fraid then hurt. Apperson 426–7; *Oxford* 432; Taylor and Whiting 147; Tilley A55.

A65 To find no **After-char** (*return*)
a1325 *Cursor* III 1254.21921–2: Qua-sum be-for will noght be-warr, He sal find than nan efter-char (*T* yeyn char). See **G5.**

A66 **Afterclap**
c1330 *Times of Edward II* (*Bodley*) 191.346: And seththe on the riche cam the after-clap.

A67 Beware of an **Afterclap** (*varied*)
1375 *Canticum de Creatione* 314.476–7: Ther fore sondred shel they be Ffor drede of after clap. **c1412** Hoccleve *Regement* 32.855–6: That after-clap, in my mynde so deepe Y-fycched is, *Balade* I 63.20: And I so sore ay dreede an aftir clap, **c1422** *Lerne to Die* 187.243: Of thaftirclap insighte had no man lasse. **1469** Paston V 12[9–10]: Thynk of after clappes and have provysion in all your work. **a1475** *Turne up hur halter* in *Rel. Ant.* I 77[17]: But yet be war of after clappys. **1496** *Jhesus be your spede* in Mary D. Harris ed. *The Coventry Leet Book* (EETS 135, 1908) 577[22–4]: Both erly and late, Kepe well your pate For after-clappys. **a1500** Hill 139.6: And bere the evyn for drede of after-clappes. **a1500** *Landsdowne MS.762* in *Rel. Ant.* I 289[3]: Be ware of after clappes. **a1500** *Theophilus* 13.50[4–5]: In chaffaring of mys happe Witnesse is good for after clappe. **c1503** More *Early Poems* [14] D[1]: But for all that beware of after clappes. **1518** Watson *Oliver* F3ᵛ[16–8]: Olyver . . . sayd unto hym as evyll avysed of afterclaps. **1556** Heywood *E* 108.6.7: Touche not to muche for feare of after claps. *Oxford* 43–4; Taylor and Whiting 4; Tilley A57; Whiting *Drama* 222, 267, *Scots* I 131.

A68 Think of the **After-tale** (*reckoning*)
a1500 Greene *Carols* 388.6: Thynke well on the after-tayll. MED after- prefix 2m; NED Tail sb.[2] IV 4.

A69 It is good for **Age** to set a governail (*rule*) and youth sue (*follow*) it
c1412 Hoccleve *Regement* 178.4962–3: Goode is that age sette a governayle, And youthe it sue: thus may al avayle. See **C452.**

A70 Old **Age** serves for the counsel (*varied*)
a1393 Gower *CA* III 351.4137: Old age for the conseil serveth. **a1420** Lydgate *Troy* I 126.3852–3: For wit of hem that be ronne in age, Is more than force with-oute experience. Jente 181. Cf. Smith 6. See **M252, 255.**

A71 Not worth an **Aglet** (*tag*) of a blue point
1533 More *Confutacion* 675 H[8–9]: It is not al worth an aglet of a good blewe poynte. Apperson 458:29; Tilley P456. Cf. Whiting *Drama* 333:376. See **P285.**

A72 **Aid** after the field
a1500 *MS. Marginalia* in Hoccleve I 185, n.3: Post bellum auxilium: Ayde after the felde is alredy faught. Alfred Henderson *Latin Proverbs and Quotations* (London, 1869) 334. See **C51, L168, 178.**

A73 To shoot from (*miss*) one's **Aim**
c1380 *Patience* 17.128: So that schomely to schort he schote of his ame. Tilley A85.

A74 As vain (*empty*) as **Air**
c1390 *Talkyng* 18.5: More veyn then is the eir. Cf. Tilley A90.

A75 If the **Air** is disturbed one day, it will be fair another
c1450 *Foly of Fulys* 57.207–9: Thocht a day strublyt be the are, Aneuthir eftir cummys faire, Quhill were, quhill bettir, as cummys the cass. See **S798.**

A76 Ill **Air** slays sooner than the sword
c1450 *Ratis* 5.167–8: Trow weil the philosophuris word, Than (*for* That) sonar slais ill air na suord. *Oxford* 314; Tilley A93.

A77 To know no more than blind **Alan** of the moon
a1508 Dunbar *Testament* 72.11–2: Nescimus quando vel qua sorte, Na blind Allane wait of the mone. Whiting *Scots* I 131.

A78 **Ale** makes many a man to run over the fallows
a1500 Greene *Carols* 423.6: Ale mak many a mane to ryne over the falows, Ale mak many a mane to swere by God and Al-Halows, And ale mak many a mane to hang upon the galows.

A79 There is no good **Ale** for sale in hell
1555 Heywood *E* 149.16.3: Wherby sins in hell no good ale is to sel.

A80 To mend as sour **Ale** in summer
1546 Heywood *D* 91–2.44–5: Than wolde ye mend . . . as sowre ale mendth in summer. Jente 411; *Oxford* 419; Tilley A106.

A81 The **Ale-house** is known by the ale-stake
1509 Barclay *Ship* I 38[15–6]: By the ale stake knowe we the ale hous, And every Inne is knowen by the sygne. See **G35.**

A82 **Alexander** might rather put Darius from his throne than Diogenes from virtue
a1387 Higden-Trevisa III 309–11: There come that by-sawe that he myghte lightloker putte Darius out of his trone and out of his kyngdom than Dyogenes out of the state of vertue. **a1425** Higden-Anon. III 309–11: Whereof a proverbe was spronge, that kynge Alexander myghte putte rather kynge Darius from his realme then Diogenes from vertu.

A83 As mickle (*great*) as **Alexander** (*etc.*) (A number of single quotations are brought together here)
a1400 *Pricke* 241.8968: Als mykelle als was Alexander the gret kyng. **c1400** *Plowman's Tale* 157.335: And ben as proude as Alexaunder. **c1450** Idley 172.837: Whoo more victorious than Alisaundre ony tyme beforn? **a1500** *Croxton Sacrament* in Waterhouse 68.352: And strenger than Alexander, that all the wor(l)de ded gett.

A84 As rich as **Alexander**
c1303 Mannyng *Handlyng* 142.4209–10: Who was rycher yn every thyng Than Alaxandre the ryche kyng? **a1500** Kennedy 26.20: Richer in grace than Alexander the Gret.

A85 To appeal from **Alexander** drunk to Alexander sober
1529 More *Supplicacion* 331 E[1–4]: As the knight of kyng Alexander appealed from Alexander to Alexander, from Alexander the drunke, to Alexander the sober. *Oxford* 12: Philip; Tilley P252.

A86 **All** are not holy that heave (*lift*) their hands to heaven
c1475 Henryson *Fables* 80.2325: All ar not halie that heifis thair handis to hevin. Whiting *Scots* I 190. Cf. Apperson 5: All are not saints; Jente 625, 792; Tilley A116.

A87 **All** are not abed that shall have ill rest
1509 Barclay *Ship* I 13[21]: All are nat in bed whiche shall have yll rest. **1546** Heywood *D* 88.272: All be not a bedde, that shall have yll rest. Apperson 5; *Oxford* 1; Tilley A114.

A88 **All** are not merry whom men see dance
c1430 Lydgate *Dance* 50.392: Al ben not meri whiche that men seen daunce, 62.511–2: But many a man yif I shal not tarie Ofte daunceth bot no thynge of herte. Apperson 415; *Oxford* 421; Tilley D23. See **D8.**

A89 **All** are not sound that pass by the way
a1500 *O man more* 394.46: All be not sownde that passe by the wey.

A90 **All** are not true that speak fair
c1350 *Good Wife E* 162.69: For al is noght trewe that faire speket, **c1450** *L* 199.82–3: For alle men ben not trewe That kunne fair her wordis schewe. **a1500** *O man more* 393.10: All is nott truste that spekes full faire. *Oxford* 228; Tilley A112. See **S580.**

A91 **All** covet all lose
c1300 Robert of Gloucester I 455.6253: Ofte wo so coveiteth al al leseth ywis. **a1438** Kempe 60.12–3: And for thei wold han al thei lost al. **a1439** Lydgate *Fall* II 333.145–7: Men seyn off old, who that coveitith all, At onset hour suchon shal nat chese, But al his gadryng attonys he shal lese, II 654.2481: Who al coveiteth, sumtyme al doth leese, III 728.1993–5: Who al coveiteth, ye shal undirstond, He al forgoth, ful weel afferme I dar, At unset hour, wheroff ech man be war, **a1449** *Fabules* in *MP* II 598.932–4: An olde proverbe hathe bene sayd, and shall, Towchynge the vyce of grete covetyce—Who all covetythe offt he losythe all, 599.948: Who all covetythe, faylyth offt in fere. **c1450** Idley 90.574: Ffor who woll all coveite all shall loose. **c1450** *Ratis* 39.1380–1: And quhen thow yarnis al to have, Than beis thow left and al the lave. **c1450** *Rylands MS.394* 95.19: Tout covet tout perde, Alle coveyteth alle lesith. **c1475** Henryson *Fables* 75.2189–90: He that of ressoun can not be content, Bot covetis all, is abill all to

tyne. **1481** Caxton *Reynard* 95[34–5]: It falleth ofte who that wold have all leseth alle, **1484** *Aesop* 245[18–20]: For by cause that he supposeth to wynne al he leseth all that he hath. **a1500** Hill 129.39: He that all coweitith, often all lesith. **1509** Barclay *Ship* I 13[25]: He oft all lesys that coveytes all to have. **1523** Berners *Froissart* II 287[29–30]: It is an olde sayenge, He that all coveteth al leseth, **1525** IV 200[19]. **1546** Heywood *D* 97.231: All covet all leese, **1555** *E* 161.94, 194.278: He woulde all have and naught forgo, no, He may all forgo and naught have so. Apperson 5, 290; Jente 270; *Oxford* 7; Smith 43; Tilley A192, 194; Whiting *Scots* I 153. See **A104, G340, M707, 774, 780.**

A92 **All** is but a vanity
c1395 *WBible* Ecclesiastes xii 8: The vanyte of vanytees, and alle thingis ben vanyte. **c1475** *Mankind* 28.760: "Vanitas vanitatum," all ys but a vanyte. **1509** Fisher *Henry VII* 285.9: Vanyte of vanytees and all is but vanyte. Tilley A152. See **W664.**

A93 **All** is corruptible
a1400 *Romaunt B* 4856: For bycause al is corrumpable.

A93.1 **All** is for the best
c1390 Chaucer *CT* I[A] 4176: But yet, nafors, al sal be for the beste, **c1395** III[D] 1496: Al is for the beste, IV[E] 1161: And for oure beste is al his governaunce, V[F] 885–6: I woot wel clerkes wol seyn as hem leste, By argumentz, that al is for the beste. **a1400** Wyclif *Sermons* I 320–1: And so, as many men seien, alle thingis comen for the beste; for alle comen for Goddis ordenance, and so thei comen for God himsilf; and so alle thingis that comen fallen for the beste thing that mai be. Burton Stevenson *Home Book of Proverbs, Maxims and Familiar Phrases* (New York, 1948) 173.2; Taylor and Whiting 26.

A94 **All** is good that helps
1528 More *Heresyes* 197 G[14–5]: *Hogni aiuto e bono,* al is good that helpeth.

A95 **All** is lost that is given to a churl, *etc.*
1509 Barclay *Ship* II 182[24]–183[4]: But all is lost that thou dost gyve to fynde Four sortis of people: the first is a vylayne Or chorle, for agayne thou shalt hym prove unkynde, The seconde a childe, for his forgetfull mynde Expellyth kyndnes, the thirde a man in age, The fourth a woman varyable as the wynde, Beynge of hir love unstable and volage.

A96 **All** is not lost that lies in peril
c1500 *Melusine* 147.25–6: All is not yet lost that lyeth in parell. Tilley A148.

A97 **All** lies and bleeds
1546 Heywood *D* 73.100: Advyse ye well, for here dooth al ly and bleede, **1555** *E* 184.209: Here lithe all and bleadth, all, thats fals and foolish. Tilley A159.

A98 **All** must be as God will have it
a1533 Berners *Arthur* 129[15–6]: All must be as God wyll have it. See **G269.**

A99 **All** that comes comes by necessity
c1385 Chaucer *TC* iv 958: For al that comth, comth by necessitee, 1048–50: By which resoun men may wel yse That thilke thynges that in erthe falle, That by necessite they comen alle. See **N160.**

A100 **All** that is amiss may be amended
a1450 *Generydes B* 210.6592: All that is amys . . . may be amend.

A101 Dispraise not **All** though one have offended
a1500 *Right best beloved* in *Rawlinson MS. C 813* 396.43–4: Itt is a trewe proverbe and off olde antiquite: Dispraise nott all, thoughe one have offended. See **L14.**

A102 He speaks of **All** and considers not half
1533 Heywood *Weather* C2v[39]: Thou spekest of all and consyderest not halfe.

A103 He that despises **All** displeases all
c1390 Chaucer *CT* VII 1070[B 2260]: "He that al despiseth, al displeseth," as seith the book.

A104 He that shoots at **All** may lose all
1556 Heywood *Spider* 426[27]: Shooting at all, I have lost all quight. See **A91.**

A105 He that wins shall take **All**
c1330 *Degare* 88.482: He, that winneth, al sschal take.

A106 Leave **All** and find all
a1500 *Imitatione* (*1*) 107.15: Leve all and thou shalt finde all. **1502** *Imitatione* (*2*) 226.34: Forsake all thynges for god, and thou shalt fynde all thinges. See **G96, L233.**

A107 One may not know **All** or have all
1483 Caxton *Cato* I8v[31–3]: Therfore saith the proverbe that one may not al knowe, nor one may not have all, For none is parfyghte in no scyence.

A108 Trust not **All,** though you trust in part
a1500 *O man more* 394.22: Trust nott all, thoughe thou trust in perte.

A109 Win **All** or lose all
a1338 Mannyng *Chronicle A* I 124.3533: Other al to wynne, or al to lese, 295.8411–2, 442.12634,

II 481.13878. **c1450** *Merlin* II 366[21]: For owther I will all gete or all lese, 598[15–6]: Ffor this day be ye come all for to lese or all for to wynne.

A110 (From here) to **Almaigne**
c1300 *Guy*[1] 146 A 2482: Was non wiser in-to Almayne.

A111 An **Almond** for (a) parrot
c1522 Skelton *Speke* II 4.50: An almon now for Parrot, dilycatly drest. Apperson 483; *Oxford* 9; Tilley A220.

A112 A blanched **Almond** is no bean
c1516 Skelton *Magnificence* 13.381: A blaunched almonde is no bene.

A113 It were **Alms** to wring one by the ear
c1497 Medwall *Fulgens* E1v[16]: It were almys to wrynge me by the eare. Apperson 9; Tilley A225.

A114 As clear as any **Amber**
c1440 *Revelation* in *Yorkshire Writers* I 389[43]: That fyre . . . was als clere as any ambir.

A115 To cast (*etc.*) **Ambs-ace**
a1250 *Harrowing of Hell*, ed. W. H. Hulme (EETS ES 100, 1907) 10.97–8: Stille, stille, satanas! The is fallen aunbesas. **c1300** *Becket I* 22.450: Thu ert icome therto to late: thu hast icast ambezas. **c1300** Robert of Gloucester I 86.1182: Ac he caste ambesas tho he to londe com. **c1300** *South English Legendary* I 39.72: That the quene wolde habbe iheved, ac hure vel ambes as, 196.494, 282.103, II 625.450. **c1300** *South English Legendary* (*Laud*) 233.497. **c1390** Chaucer *CT* II[B] 124–5: Youre bagges been nat fild with ambes as, But with sys cynk, that renneth for youre chaunce. **a1400** *Tho oure lord god* 319[60]. **a1437** Lydgate *That Now is Hay* in *MP* II 812.102: Nowe sise, nowe synke, nowe ambbes aas, **a1449** *Doublenesse* in *MP* II 441.75–8: With sis and synke they kan avaunce, And than by revolucion They sette a felle conclusion Of ambesase, *Order* in *MP* II 451.57–60: And he also that halt hym-selff wys, Wich in werkyng hath noon experience, Whos chaunce goth nouther on synk nor sis, With ambes-as encreseth his dyspence. MED ambes-as; NED Ambs-ace.

A116 To shine like **Amel** (*enamel*)
c1350 *Libeaus* 118.2098–100: Hir body and hir winge Schine in alle thinge, As amall gay and geld. See **F214.**

A117 He may soon **Amend,** for he cannot appair (*become worse*)
1555 Heywood *E* 163.106: He may soone amend, for he can not apeyre. Apperson 10; *Oxford* 10; Tilley A237.

A118 He that is not **Amended** by others cannot amend others
a1387 Higden-Trevisa V 29[1–2]: Other men beeth nought amended by hym that is nought amendid by other men. (Ascribed to Ptolemaeus: Qui per alios non corrigitur, alii per eum non corrigentur.) See **M170.**

A119 **Amorets** (*love-knots*) (may) be as well in black mourning as in bright burnet (*cloth*)
a1400 *Romaunt B* 4755–6: And eke as wel be amourettes In mournyng blak, as bright burnettes. Tilley L519. Cf. *Oxford* 390–1.

A120 As fixed as an **Anchor**
a1449 Lydgate *De Profundis* in *MP* I 82.117: Fyx as an anker stable in hys creaunce.

A121 To be like an **Anchor**
c1340 Rolle *Psalter* 52 (15.2): The whilk hope is as ankere in stremys of this warld.

A122 To weigh **Anchor**
1546 Heywood *D* 34.35: I will streight weie anker. NED Weigh, vb.[1] 5b.

A123 **Angels** (*gold coins*) work wonders
1509 Barclay *Ship* I 25[19–21]: But nowe a dayes he shall have his intent That hath most golde, and so it is befall That aungels worke wonders in westmynster hall. Cf. *Oxford* 468, 609; Tilley A242, 027.

A124 As bright as **Angel**
1503 Dunbar *Thrissil* 109.50–1: The purpour sone . . . In orient bricht as angell did appeir. Whiting *Scots* I 131.

A125 As fair as a(n) **Angel**
c1475 *Wisdom* 40.159: Fayer as a angell, of hewyn the ayer. **a1533** Berners *Arthur* 442[31–2]: He semed to be as fayre as an aungel descended from heaven. Svartengren 214. Cf. Taylor and Whiting 6.

A126 To glitter like **Angels**
c1375 Barbour *Bruce* I 196.233–4: Maid thame glitterand, as thai war lik Till angellis he, of (hewinis) rik.

A127 To shine like **Angels**
c1375 Barbour *Bruce* I 315.425–6: The Yngliss men, in othir party, That richt as angelis schane brichtly. **1513** Bradshaw *St. Werburge* 68.1790: Shynynge lyke angels. Whiting *Scots* I 131–2.

A128 To sing like an **Angel**
c1390 Chaucer *CT* I[A] 1055: And as an aungel hevenysshly she soong, VII 3291–2[B4481–2]:

For trewely, ye have as myrie a stevene As any aungel hath that is in hevene. **a1393** Gower *CA* III 407.779–82: Singende he harpeth forth withal, That as a vois celestial Hem thoghte it souneth in here Ere, As thogh that he an Angel were, 431.1671. **a1400** ?Chaucer *Rom. A* 671–2: They songe her song as faire and wel As angels don espirituel. Whiting *Drama* 303:5.

A129 After **Anger** game (*mirth*)
c1385 Chaucer *TC* iv 1562–3: And if so be that pees heere-after take, As alday happeth after anger game. See **W697.**

A130 He that blames **Another** often seeks his own shame
a1393 Gower *CA* II 146.579–80: For who so wol an other blame, He secheth ofte his oghne schame.

A131 He that loves **Another** better than himself dies for thirst at the fountain
1509 Watson *Ship* N4r[6–8]: For it is a comon proverbe that he the whiche loveth another better than hymselfe, deyeth for thurste at the fountayne. See **F381.**

A132 A soft **Answer** (fair words, *etc.*) breaks (slakes) ire (wrath)
a1050 Defensor *Liber* 205[2–3]: Answaru liþe tobrycð yrre; spæc stið awecð hatheortnysse. **c1350** *Good Wife* E 160.27: Fare wordes wrath slaketz. **c1395** *WBible* Proverbs xv 1: A soft answere brekith ire; an hard word reisith woodnesse. **a1450** *Declaryng* in Kail 83.132: For fayre speche doth wraththe breke. **1450** *Dicts* 38.13: A soft worde puttithe a-way grete ennoy. **c1450** *Fyrst thou sal* 88.17–8: A soft worde swages ire, Suffer and hafe thi desyre. **c1450** *Good Wife* L 198.33–4: A fair worde and a meeke Dooth wraththe slake. **c1450** Idley 84.190–1: A softe worde swageth Ire And causeth grete rest, it is no nay. **1454** *Mazer inscription* in *Archaeologia* 50(1887) 188: Soft words swageth fyre (*for* ire); Suffyr and have thi desyre. **1483** *Quatuor Sermones* 31[9]: Soft speche . . . slakyth wreth. **1493** *Tretyse of Love* 94.16–7: For Salamon sayth, "Fayre answere refreyneth Ire." Apperson 200; *Oxford* 602; Tilley W822. Cf. Jente 368.

A133 An **Anthony** pig
c1425 *Brut* II 385.22–4: And there come to hym an Antony pygge, and folowed the ost al that way tyl thay come tylle a grete wasch. **c1430** *Brut* in C. L. Kingsford *English Historical Literature in the Fifteenth Century* (Oxford, 1913) 305[35–6]: And as thei reden ther come to hem an antony pigge, and he folowid the hoste. **c1450** *Alphabet* I 215.15–6: Ther come in-to the howse unto thaim a swyne of Saynt Antons. **a1475** *Good Wyfe Wold* 173.8: And rene thou not fro hous to house lyke an Antyny gryce. **1519** Horman *Vulgaria* 16[3]: I have behest a pygge to saynt Anthony. **1533** Heywood *Johan* A1r[6–7]: But she wyll go a gaddynge very myche Lyke an Anthony pyg with an olde wyche. Apperson 11; MED Anton(y); NED Anthony; *Oxford* 556; Tilley S35; Whiting *Scots* II 120.

A134 (From here) to **Antioch**
c1300 *Guy*[1] 96.1705–6: Ther nis knight that so miche preysed be Unto Antiage (C: Antioche) that riche cite.

A135 From **Anwick** (Lincolnshire) to Aungey (?Angers)
c1516 Skelton *Magnificence* 35.1121–2: There is not a better dogge for hogges Not from Anwyke unto Aungey.

A136 An **Ape** does as he sees others do
a1400 *Discrecioun of Stirings* 68.8–9: Men sein comonly that ape doth as he other seeth. Janson 287 ff.

A137 An **Ape's** tail (*i.e.*, nothing)
1471 Ripley *Compound* 158[3–4]: For they shall have as much by ther *Phylosophy*, As they of the tayle of an Ape can take. **c1495** *Arundel Vulgaria* 54.232: I doubte not but er he depart thei shall make hym as clen from it as an ape fro tailys. Tilley A268, M1095.

A138 The **Ape** thinks her own babes beauteous
1533 More *Apologye* 1[6–8]: Isopes ape, that thought her own babes so beutuouse, and so farre passyng in all goodly feature and favour. Janson 41; Tilley A270.

A139 As crabbed as the **Ape**
1509 Watson *Ship* Dd7r[3–4]: With pervers hertes, crabbed as the ape. Cf. Whiting *Scots* I 132: angry.

A140 As drunk as an **Ape**
a1500 *Colyn Blowbol* 104.280: Such as wilbe as drongen as an ape. Apperson 167; Svartengren 206–7; Tilley A265.

A141 As harmless as a she **Ape**
a1500 *I have a lady* in Person 39.32: That as a she ape she ys harmelesse. **1546** Heywood *D* 39.134: But she can no more harme than can a she ape. Tilley M149.

A142 As piled (*bald*) as an **Ape**

c1390 Chaucer *CT* I[A] 3935: As piled as an ape was his skulle. Cf. Svartengren 254.

A143 As tut-mouthed (*with protruding lips*) as an **Ape**
a1513 Dunbar *Of ane Blak-moir* 66.6: Scho is tute mowitt lyk ane aep.

A144 The higher an **Ape** climbs the more his hinder parts appear
c1395 *WBible* Proverbs iii 35, *gloss:* For thanne the filthe of her foli aperith more, as the filthe of the hyndrere partis of an ape aperith more, whanne he stieth an high. Apperson 12–3; Janson 38; *Oxford* 295; Tilley A271. See **C571.**

A145 To be cutted (*mutilated, ?castrated*) like an **Ape** (*etc.*) (A number of single quotations are brought together here)
a1300 *Alisaunder* 243.4337: He shal be cutted als an ape. **c1380** Chaucer *HF* 1212: And countrefete hem as an ape. **a1450** *York Plays* 258.107: He lokis lurkand like an nape. **c1450** Idley 82.96: Use not to scorne and mocke as an Ape, 118.659: They plukke hym, they pulle hym, they tumble hym as an ape.

A146 To be like an **Ape** tied with a clog
1450 *Death of the Duke of Suffolk* in Wright *Political Poems* II 232[3–4]: Jac Napes wolde one the see a maryner to ben, With his cloge and his cheyn, to seke more tresour. **a1450** *Boke of Curtasye* (*Sloane*) 302.108: Thou art lyke an ape teyghed with a clogge. *Oxford* 322; Tilley J10.

A147 To drink wine **Ape**
c1390 Chaucer *CT* IX[H] 44–5: I trowe that ye dronken han wyn ape, And that is whan men pleyen with a straw. **a1420** Lydgate *Troy* I 309.5779: And with a strawe playeth like an ape. **1509** Barclay *Ship* I 96[20]: Some are Ape dronke full of lawghter and of toyes. Janson 246–53; MED ape 3(b); *Oxford* 12.

A148 To make an **Ape** of someone
c1387-95 Chaucer *CT* I[A] 706: He made the person and the peple his apes, **c1390** 3389: And thus she maketh Absolon hire ape, **c1395** VIII [G]1313: Right as hym liste, the preest he made his ape! **a1533** Heywood *Johan* B3[r][5]: To make her husband her ape. NED Ape 4; Tilley A273; Whiting *Scots* I 132.

A149 To mow like an **Ape**
c1380 Chaucer *HF* 1805–6: This soun was so ful of japes, As ever mowes were in apes. **c1485** *Slaughter* (*Digby*) 12.296: And make them to lye and mowe like an ape. **a1450** *Boke of Curtasye* (*Sloane*) 301.59–60: An apys mow men sayne he makes, That brede and flesshe in hys cheke bakes. Tilley M1030.

A150 To put an **Ape** in someone's hood
c1390 Chaucer *CT* VII 440–1[B1630–1]: The monk putte in the mannes hood an ape, and in his wyves eek, by Seint Austyn! MED ape 2(b); NED Ape 4.

A151 By **Appearance** men should give judgement
1525 Berners *Froissart* VI 44[21–2]: By apparaunce men shulde gyve judgement. Cf. *Oxford* 328: Never judge; Taylor and Whiting 7. See **F1.**

A152 False **Appearance** does harm
c1380 Chaucer *HF* 265–6: Allas! what harm doth apparence, Whan hit is fals in existence! **a1400** *Romaunt C* 7465–8: But shalt thou never of apparence Sen conclude good consequence In non argument, ywis, If existens al fayled is. **a1439** Lydgate *Fall* I 69.2517: But, o allas! what harm doth apparence, **a1449** *Cok* in *MP* II 814.36–7: But what is wers than shynyng apparence, Whan it is prevyd ffals in existence? See **S146, 147.**

A153 Two **Appetites** uneath (*hardly*) accord
1513 Douglas *Aeneid* II 193.17: Twa appetitis oneth accordis with othir. Whiting *Scots* I 132.

A154 A wicked **Appetite** comes before sickness
c1390 Chaucer *Fortune* 55: Wikke appetyt comth ay before syknesse. See **G167.**

A155 An **Apple** may be fair without and bad within (*varied*)
a1225 *Lambeth Homilies* 25[26–7]: And bith al swa is an eppel iheoweth, he bith with-uten feire and frakel with-innen. **c1250** *Proverbs of Alfred* 108 T 334–40: Moni appel is wid-uten grene, Brit on beme, and bittere widinnen; So his moni wimmon In hire faire bure, Schene under schete, and thocke hie is in an stondes wile, **a1300** 109 J 334–9: Mony appel is bryht with-ute, And bitter withinne; So is mony wymmon On hyre fader bure Schene under schete And theyh heo is schendful. **1340** *Ayenbite* 229[23–5]: Ase thet frut ne is naght guod, thagh hit by wel vayr with-oute, huanne hit is vorroted and wermethe. **c1395** Chaucer *CT* VIII[G] 964–5: Ne every appul that is fair at eye Ne is nat good, what so men clappe or crye. **c1408** Lydgate *Reson* 103.3915–8: Of trees ther ben eke many paire That ber applys gret and faire, Delytable in shewyng, But wonder bitter in tastyng. **c1475** *Prohemy of a Mariage* 43[22–3]: Appeles and peres that semen very

gode, Ful ofte tyme are roten by the core. **a1500** *O man more* 393.9: Every fair apple thou maye nott counte is good. **a1500** *Clerk and the Nightingale II* in Robbins 177.23–6: Clerk, be a appyl thou myght se—Sownd with-owtte and grene, And in the core rotyd be: So faryth a woman, I wene. **c1515** Barclay *Eclogues* 168.772: A pleasaunt apple is oft corrupt within. MED appel 4; *Oxford* 187; Skeat 284; Tilley A300, F29. See **C308, G365, S342, 365, W278, 425, 511.**

A156 The **Apple** (ball) of one's eye
897 Alfred *Boethius* 133.12–3: Hi scilde swa geornlice swa (swa) man deð þone æppel on his eagan. **c900** *Paris Psalter* 31 (16.8): Geheald me . . . and beorh me, swa swa man byrhð þam æplum on his eagum mid his bræwum. **c1340** Rolle *Psalter* 56 (16.9): Kepe me as the appile of the eghe, 515 (Song of Moses [II] 14). **c1350** *Prose Psalter* 16 (16.9). **c1395** *WBible* Deuteronomy xxxii 10, Psalms xvi 8, Proverbs vii 2, Ecclesiasticus xvii 18, xxix 16, Zechariah ii 8. **a1400** *Northern Verse Psalter* I 39 (16.8). **c1450** *Jacob's Well* 250.16–7: Kepyn hym as the bal of his eyghe. **1493** *Tretyse of Love* 63–4: For whan this blessyd bodi was borne of his moder, he was more tender than is the apple of the eye. MED appel 6(a); Taylor and Whiting 8; Tilley A290. See **E221.**

A157 (**Apples,** eggs and nuts you may eat after sluts)
a1529 Skelton *Elynour* I 109.436–8: Another sorte of sluttes, Some brought walnuttes, Some apples, some peres. Apperson 13; *Oxford* 12; Tilley A296.

A158 As round as an **Apple**
c1300 *South English Legendary* II 415.407: As appel the eorthe is round. **c1325** *Maid of Ribbesdale* in Böddeker 157.58–9: Hyre tyttes aren anunder bis As apples tuo of parays. **c1398** W. Paris *Cristine* in Horstmann *Sammlung* 189.441–2: Hire paps were als rounde ywys(s)e As an appille, thate growes in felde. **a1400** ?Chaucer *Rom. A* 819: As round as appil was his face. **c1410** Lovelich *Merlin* II 412.15395–7: Hire pappes . . . hard and rownde . . . As two smale apples. **c1440** *Liber de Diversis Medicinis,* ed. Margaret S. Ogden (EETS 207, 1938) 75. 26–7: Wynd it rounde as any appill. **c1450** *Merlin* II 227[15–6]. **1481** Caxton *Mirror* 61[20–1], **1485** *Charles* 90.24–5: Hir pappes were reysed after the facyon of ij apples, 198.20–1: Ij pappes . . . rounde, and somewhat enhaunced lyke ij rounde apples. **a1500** *With humble hert* in *Archiv* 131(1913) 62.106. **1506** *Kalender* 122.8. Svartengren 279; Taylor and Whiting 8; Whiting *NC* 362.

A159 As sweet as **Apples**
c1390 Chaucer *CT* I[A] 3261–2: Hir mouth was sweete as . . . hoord of apples leyd in hey or heeth.

A160 Better an **Apple** given than eaten
c1250 *Hendyng O* 195–6.25: Betere is appel iyeven, then al ieten, **a1325** *C* 184.14: Betir is one appil iyevin, than twein iyetin. **a1500** *Additional MS.37075* 277.9: Better be appylys yevyn than etyn. Apperson 13; Kneuer 30; MED appel 4; *Oxford* 37; Schleich 254–5; Singer III 128–9; Skeat 74; Tilley A292; Walther III 929.22229e. See **F691, P86.**

A161 Lost with an **Apple** and won with a nut
1546 Heywood *D* 36.33: She is lost with an apple, and woon with a nut. Apperson 14; *Oxford* 387; Tilley A295.

A162 The more **Apples** the tree bears the more the tree bows
c1450 *Pilgrimage LM* 4–5: The mo appelen the tre bereth the more she boweth to the folk.

A163 Never a good **Apple** on a sour stock
a1387 *Piers* C xi 206–7: For god seith hit hymself, "shal nevere good appel Thorw no sotel science on sour stock growe." MED appel 4; *Oxford* 250.

A164 No more like than an **Apple** to an oyster
1533 More *Confutacion* 724 C[7–8]: No more lyke then an apple to an oyster, *Apologye* 39[35–6]: Mych lesse lyke . . . then is an apple lyke unto an oyster. Apperson 13; *Oxford* 13; Tilley A291.

A165 Not set a rotten **Apple**
1485 Caxton *Charles* 109.28–9: He setteth nomore by the than of . . . a roten apple, **c1489** *Aymon* II 442.10–2: I shall not sette a rotyn appull for all the power of Charlemagne. Apperson 458; *Oxford* 549.

A166 Not worth an (rotten) **Apple**
a1400 *Romaunt B* 4532: Ne worth an appel for to lowe. **c1489** Caxton *Aymon* II 544.31–2: The sones of a traytour whiche ben not worthe a roten apple. *Oxford* 549.

A167 One rotten **Apple** rots the sound
1340 *Ayenbite* 205[23–4]: A roted eppel amang the holen: maketh rotie the yzounde yef he is longe ther amang. **c1390** Chaucer *CT* I[A] 4405–7: Of a proverbe that seith this same word,

"Wel bet is roten appul out of hoord Than that it rotie al the remenaunt." **c1400** *Vices and Virtues* 227.11–2: An appel that is roten and lith longe amonge other maketh the other rotee. **1484** Caxton *Royal Book* R3v[21–3]: An appel roten yt it be emonge the sounde and hole, corrupteth the good apples, yf it lye longe emonge them. Apperson 13; MED appel 4; *Oxford* 549; Skeat 239; Tilley A294. See **C559, H291, L289, S217, 280, 351, T201.**

A168 A sour **Apple** when hot shits out all it knows
c1450 *Rylands MS.394* 106.19.25–7: A sowre appul when it is hoote Shytes out alle that he woote. Omne quod est in se calidum pomum cacat acre. Walther III 586.19852.

A169 Though the **Apple** trendles (*rolls*) never so far it shows whence it came
c1000 *Cotton Faustina MS. A x* in *Anglia* 1(1878) 285: Se æppel næfre þæs feorr ne trenddeð, he cyð hwanon he com. Pomum licet ab arbore igitur unde revolvitur tamen providit, unde nascitur. **c1250** *Owl* 14.135–8: Thegh appel trendli fro(m) thon trowe, Thar he and other mid growe, Thegh he bo thar-from bi-cume, He cuth wel whonene he is icume. **a1400** Bozon *Contes* 23[15–6]: Trendle the appel nevere so fer, he conyes fro what tree he cam (*var.* hit kytes wethin hit comes), 206[4–6]. Robbins-Cutler 3799.6; Eric G. Stanley ed. *The Owl and the Nightingale* (London, 1960) 107. Cf. Jente 299; Taylor and Whiting 8. See **B581, K30, 32, M82, P199, T94.**

A170 To spare neither the **Apple** nor the colk (*core*)
c1400 *Laud Troy* I 266.9008–11: But then come thedir kyng Odemon Out of Troye with mechel ffolk, He spared neyther the appul ne the colk, Un-til he come to (the) Melle. MED colk 1(a): "to do all one can."

A171 He that **Approves** (*helps*) other men often wastes his own
a1500 Henley *Husbandry* 42[33–4]: For the wiseman seith he that approvith to other men often tymes he wastithe his owne. Cf. French text (p. 2[27–8]): Hom dyst en reprover ke de loyns se purveyt de pres sen joyst. MED ap(p)rouen 2(a).

A172 As uncertain as **April**
a1440 Burgh *Cato* 320.714–5: This woorldis welthe, ebbynge and flowyng ay At no certeyn, as is wantoun Aprile. Stevenson 93.13, 15, 18.

A173 As wholesome (sweet) as the **April** shower
c1408 Lydgate *Reson* 165.6310–1: For holsom as the Aprile shour Fallyng on the erbes newe. **1504** Hawes *Example* Aa4v[19]: More sweter fer than the Aprell shour. *Oxford* 13.

A174 In **April** the cuckoo can sing her song by rote
1562 Heywood *E* 246.95.3–4: In Apryll the Koocoo can syng hir song by rote, In June out of tune she can not syng a note. Apperson 127; Tilley A309. See **C600.**

A175 To have passed many an **April** and many a May
a1400 *Romaunt B* 3978–9: For many an Aprill and many a May We han passed. See Robinson's note, p. 877.

A176 To hold **April** from rain
c1375 Chaucer *Anel.* 309–10: I myghte as wel holde Aperill fro reyn, As holde yow, to make yow be stidfast.

A177 A blind **Archer** (*Cupid*) by chance gives many a mortal wound
a1439 Lydgate *Fall* I 197.6992–3: As a blynd archer with arwes sharp(e) grounde Off aven-ture yeveth many a mortal wounde. See **M36.**

A178 A blind **Archer** (*Cupid*) may hurt his friend rather than his foe
a1405 Lydgate *Black Knight* in *MP* II 401–2.461–7: And who that is an archer, and ys blynde, Marketh nothing, but sheteth by wenynge; And for that he hath no discrecion, With-oute avise he let his arowe goo, For lak of syght and also of resoun, In his shetyng hit happeth oft(e) soo, To hurt his frende rathir then his foo.

A179 He is a good **Archer** that never fails to hit the mark
a1430 Lydgate *Pilgrimage* 321.11776–8: He ys an archer good Wych ffaylleth nat hym-sylff taquyte, Alway the marke for to smyte, 325.11915–6: An Archer eke, in thynne and thykke, Faylleth somtyme off the prykke. See **M45.**

A180 **Argus** and his eyes
c1385 Chaucer *TC* iv 1459: Youre fader is in sleght as Argus eyed. **a1387** Higden-Trevisa II 171[18–24]. **c1395** Chaucer *CT* III[D] 358–60: Thogh thou preye Argus with his hundred yen To be my warde-cors, as he kan best, In feith, he shal nat kepe me but me lest, IV[E] 2111–3: Lo, Argus, which that hadde an hondred yen, For al that evere he koude poure or pryen, Yet

was he blent. **c1408** Lydgate *Reson* 12.422–4: That Argus . . . With hys hundred eyen bryght The noumbre of hem nat tel(le) myght, **a1430** *Pilgrimage* 167.6358–61: Intellect or entendement, Wych hath Eyen . . . As manye (or an hundryd mo) As hadde Argus of yore agoon, **c1433** *St. Edmund* 381.242: Eyes as Argus, **a1439** *Fall* I 11.383, 221.803, **1439** *St. Albon* 114.191. **c1440** Charles of Orleans 147.4373–4: That passyng hard hit is such on aspien Though hit were Argus with his hundrid eyene. **a1447** Bokenham *Mappula* 33[6–7]. **a1449** Lydgate *Exposition* in *MP* I 64.143: But her my symplesse, with Argus nat cleer eied. **c1450** *Pilgrimage LM* 117[25–6]. **1520** Whittinton *Vulgaria* 85.22: Havynge moo eyes than Argus. MED Argus; NED Argus 1; *Oxford* 184; Taylor and Whiting 9; Tilley E254.

A181 As black as (any) **Arnement** (*ink*)
a1300 *Alisaunder* 341.6408: Eighen hij han so arnement. **c1330** *Seven Sages A* 132.2765–6: A garnement, Ase blak ase ani arnement. See **I43.**

A182 The **Arrow** often hits the shooter
a1500 Hill 129.27: Often times the arow hitteth the shoter. Apperson 16; Tilley A324. See **D22.**

A183 An **Arrow** that is shot must be fended off or fled (*varied*)
a1338 Mannyng *Chronicle A* I 407.11639–40: An arewe that ys schoten, ye se, Eyther bihoves hit men fendit or fle. **c1450** *Merlin* II 641 [19–20]: For he that seeth the arow comynge he ought to blenche that he be not smyten. See **S845.**

A184 As piercing as **Arrows**
1484 Caxton *Royal Book* F7ᵛ[23–4]: Tongues . . . more percyng than arowes.

A185 As sharp as an **Arrow**
a1400 *Seven Penitential Psalms* in *Wheatley MS.* 44.607–8: In this world (is) noon so scharp arowe As was the turment. Taylor and Whiting 9.

A186 As swift (swiftly) as an **Arrow**
a800 *Riming Poem* in *Exeter Book* 168.72: þonne flanhred dæg. **1340** *Ayenbite* 66[10–2]: The tonge . . . more zuyfter thanne arwe vlyinde. **a1387** Higden-Trevisa I 65[18–9]: As swiftliche as an arwe to a manis sight. **c1395** Chaucer *CT* IVE 1672–3: Thanne shal youre soule up to hevene skippe Swifter than dooth an arwe out of a bowe. **a1398**(1495) Bartholomaeus-Trevisa Gg3ᵛ[2.1–2]: Tigris is the moost swyftest beste in flyght as it were an arow. **c1400** *Vices and Virtues* 64.2–3. **a1475** *Mergarete* 239.393: And some are suyfter than an arow. **1503** Dunbar *Thrissil* 110.84: Quhilk did furth swirk als swift as ony arrow. **1513** Douglas *Aeneid* III 246.82: Als swyft as . . . feddyrrit arrow fleys. Taylor and Whiting 9; Tilley A322; Whiting *Scots* I 132.

A187 This **Arrow** came never out of your own bow
a1500 Hill 129.30: This arow cwmmeth newer owt of thin own bow. Apperson 16; *Oxford* 55; Tilley B511.

A188 To glide like an **Arrow** (from the bow)
a1300 *Arthour and M.*[1] 167.5920: So aruwe of bowe ich forth glod. **1513** Douglas *Aeneid* II 207.159: As a fleand arrow to land glaid. See **F288.**

A189 To pierce like an **Arrow**
c1440 Scrope *Epistle* 56[6]: An evil kepte tong . . . perchith as an arwe.

A190 To run like an **Arrow**
c1385 Chaucer *TC* iv 1548–9: And thow, Symois, that as an arwe clere Thorugh Troie rennest. **a1398**(1495) Bartholomaeus-Trevisa C5ᵛ[1.27–9]: For he (*the Tigris*) rennyth streyghtly and sharply as it were an arowe. Cf. Apperson 605; Taylor and Whiting 9; Tilley A321. See **Q7.**

A191 To shoot like an **Arrow** from a bow
c1300 *South English Legendary* II 706.257: And as an arwe schet of a bowe that bodi schet ther inne.

A192 To spring like an **Arrow** from a bow
a1300 *Alisaunder* 289.5530: Als arewe of bowe forth he sprang.

A193 **Arse** over head
c1400 *St. Anne(1)* 71.2721: Thai welterd all ars over hede. See **H323.**

A194 As a man wipes his **Arse** he does nothing else
1492 *Salomon and Marcolphus* 8[4–5]: As a man wypyth his ars he doth nothing ellys.

A195 As true as one's **Arse** makes music
c1420 Wyntoun IV 142.173–4: I trow he dois na mare sic thing Than myn eris can musik sing. **c1450** *Alphabet* I 26.8–9: It is als trew at Genulphus duse meracles as it is at myne ars syngis. Whiting *Scots* I 132.

A196 A naked **Arse** cannot be robbed
1492 *Salomon and Marcolphus* 9[20]: A nakyd ars no man kan robbe or dispoyle. See **B528.**

A197 An open **Arse** has no lord
1492 *Salomon and Marcolphus* 10[4–5]: An opyn arse hath no lord.

A198 To gape and grin like the **Arse** of a squirting hen
a1500 *Colyn Blowbol* 104.284–5: And they whiche also both gape and gren Like the (ars) of a squirtyng hen.

A199 The **Artificer** talks of his craft
a1449 Lydgate *World* in *MP* II 844.17: Off his crafft talkyth the artificeer.

A200 Sudden **Ascending** suddenly declines
a1439 Lydgate *Fall* II 552.2910: Sodeyn ascendyng doth sodenli declyne. See **C296.**

A201 To fall like an **Ash** (tree)
a1338 Mannyng *Chronicle A* I 435.12437–8: When he fel, he gaf a lasche As wyth a blast had falle an asche.

A202 As cold as **Ashes**
c1385 Chaucer *CT* I[A] 1301–2: So woodly that he lyk was to biholde The . . . asshen . . . colde. **a1405** Lydgate *Black Knight* in *MP* II 392. 232: Now colde as asshes dede, **a1420** *Troy* II 522.4439–40: That Troilus wexe in hir herte as colde, With-oute fire as ben these asshes olde, III 671.3641. **1479** Rivers *Cordyal* 35.7: I wex colde as asshes. MED asshe n.(2) 3.

A203 As dead as **Ashes**
c1385 Chaucer *CT* I[A] 1301–2: So woodly that he lyk was to biholde The . . . asshen dede, **c1386** *LGW* 2649: Ded wex hire hew, and lyk an ash to sene, **c1390** *CT* VI[C] 209: And with a face deed as asshen colde. **a1405** Lydgate *Black Knight* in *MP* II 392.222: The dedely face lyke asshes in shynyng, **a1420** *Troy* I 191.1644: But of hewe as any asche deed, II 514.4167: And he of colour liche to ashes dede. **c1477** Caxton *Jason* 156.1: He . . . becam . . . dede as asshes. MED asshe n.(2) 3.

A204 As faint as **Ashes**
c1400 *Alle owr mischevis* in *PMLA* 54(1939) 385.14–5: Ffor owr kynde is fer more feynt Than askis ben qwan fyr is qweynt.

A205 As pale as **Ashes**
c1385 Chaucer *CT* I[A] 1364: His hewe falow and pale as asshen colde. **a1387** Higden-Trevisa I 123[6]: Pale as asshes. **a1450** *Generydes A* 223.7248. **a1450** *Partonope* 257.6654: His Coloure is lyke the pale asshe, 292.7401: And now is pale as asshen dede, 421.10166. **c1477** Caxton *Jason* 156.1, **1490** *Eneydos* 110.18–9. **c1499** Skelton *Bowge* I 41.293. **a1500** *Alexander-Cassamus* 67.373. **1525** Berners *Froissart* IV 142[9]. Apperson 482; MED asshe n.(2) 3; Svartengren 235–6; Taylor and Whiting 10; Tilley A339.

A206 As wan as **Ashes**
a1450 *Partonope* 421.10165–6: Chonged hir fressh colour rede Into . . . wanne as asshes dede. **a1500** *Court of Love* 435.996: With colour slain, and wan as assh(es) pale.

A207 I proud and you proud, who shall bear the **Ashes** out?
1549 Heywood *D* 38.104: I proud, and thou proud, who shall beare thashes out. Apperson 604; *Oxford* 312; Tilley A341.

A208 To be like **Ashes**
c1375 Chaucer *Anel.* 173: Other colour then asshen hath she noon. **1471** Caxton *Recuyell* I 23.20–1: His face was lyke unto asshen.

A209 The treasure of **Asia**
c1390 *Of clene Maydenhod* 468,115: And al the tresour of Asye. See **G295.**

A210 As dizzy (fell, deaf) as any **Ask** (*lizard*)
c1420 Wyntoun III 150.1974 (*var.*): Mar dessy than ony ask, 1980: Mare fell than ony ask, 151.1974: Mar def than ony as(k).

A211 **Ask** and have
c1495 *Arundel Vulgaria* 72.302: Aske and have. Tilley A343.

A212 He that **Asks** receives
c1000 *WSG* Luke xi 10: Ælc þara se bitt onfehð; and se ðe secð, he fint. **c1395** *WBible* Luke xi 10: For ech that axith, takith, and he that sekith, fyndith. Cf. Tilley S213. See **S136.**

A213 To **Ask** for what never was is a fool asking
a1300 *Tristrem* 38.1360–4: To aski that never no wes, It is a fole askeing Bi kinde: It is a selli thing, For no man may it finde!

A214 He that **Asks** foolishly must be warned (*denied*) hastily
a1400 *Romaunt B* 2603–4: Whoso askith folily, He mot be warned hastily.

A215 A busy **Asker** shall speed (*succeed*)
a1513 Dunbar *Dream* 129.81–2: Ane besy askar soonner sall he speid Na sall twa besy servandis out of dreid.

A216 To quake (*etc.*) like an **Aspen** leaf
c1385 Chaucer *TC* iii 1200: Right as an aspes leef she gan to quake, **c1386** *LGW* 2648: And quok as doth the lef of aspe grene, **c1395** *CT* III[D] 1667: That lyk an aspen leef he quook for ire. **a1400** *Ipomadon A* 192.6727, 196.6871: As an aspenleff she shoke. **c1400** *Brut* I 75.35–6: And than shal tremble the lande . . . as an aspe lef. **c1412** Hoccleve *Regement* 71.1954: With hert as tremblyng as the leef of aspe. **a1425**

Nicod.(1) (Add.) 1772 (from MED). **a1449** Lydgate *See Myche* in *MP* II 800.9: Movynge and clappyng lyke the leffe of aspe. **1449** Metham 61.1654–5: Than evyn as an espys lef doth schake Ayens the wynd, ryght so than dyd he. **c1475** *Mankind* 27.727: My body tirtrymmelyth as the aspen leffe. Apperson 18; MED aspe 2(a); *Oxford* 15; Svartengren 382–3; Taylor and Whiting 10; Tilley L140. See **L146.**

A217 **Aspy** (*find out*) before you speak
a1400 *Proverbis of Wysdom* 245.61: A-spye well, ore thou speke.

A218 As dull as an **Ass**
c1200 Orm I 128.3714–5: Withth mannkinn thatt wass stunnt, and dill, And skillæs swa summ asse. **c1405** *Mum* 36.294: As dul as an asse. **c1412** Hoccleve *Regement* 139.3864: I am as . . . dulle as is an asse. **1422** Yonge *Governaunce* 212.5–6. **a1439** Lydgate *Fall* III 676.52, **1439** *St. Albon* 157.1727: O folysshe asses dull of discretion. **a1500** *Court of Love* 422.477: And not to wander lich a dulled ass. **a1500** *O man more* 395.53. **1509** *Fyftene Joyes* D2^v[15]: For he as harde and dull is as an asse. **1509** Watson *Ship* II^r[7]. **1513** Douglas *Aeneid* II 151.158: Or forto drowp lyke a fordullyt ass. **c1516** Skelton *Magnificence* 43.1386: They drove me to lernynge lyke a dull asse. MED asse 1(c); Tilley A348; Whiting *Drama* 304.10.

A219 As free born as a wild **Ass**
c1422 Hoccleve *Lerne to Die* 187.242: But heeld my self free born as a wylde asse.

A220 As lewd (*ignorant*) as an **Ass**
c1400 *Beryn* 77.2538: I wer lewder then an asse. **c1412** Hoccleve *Regement* 139.3864: I am as lewed . . . as is an asse, **1415** *Oldcastle* III 19.352. **c1415** *Middle English Sermons* 196.31–2.

A221 As naked as an **Ass**
c1516 Skelton *Magnificence* 59.1893: Nowe hath he ryght nought, naked as an asse.

A222 As rude as an **Ass**
a1449 ?Lydgate *Evil Marriage* in *MP* II 458.62: She makith hir husbond rude as a dul asse. **1456** Hay *Governaunce* 157.23: Sum man rude as ane as.

A223 As slow as an **Ass**
c1300 *South English Legendary* II 424.666: Slou as an asse.

A224 An **Ass** in a lion's skin
1484 Caxton *Aesop* 219–20: The fourthe fable is of the asse and of the skynne of the Lyon. *Oxford* 16; Tilley A351.

A225 A crowned **Ass** is more to be dreaded than a lion
a1439 Lydgate *Fall* I 206.237–8: Men sholde off resoun dreede a leoun lasse Than the reudnesse off a crownyd asse, II 546.2677–9, **a1449** *Look* in *MP* II 767.69–70: As asse, up reysed unto the roial see Off a leoun, knowith nat day fro nyht, *Mesure* in *MP* II 773.33–4: A crownyd asse rude, that can no goode, That wylle play a countarffetyd lyon. See **K60.**

A226 He seeks for the **Ass** he sits on
c1450 *Pilgrimage LM* 81[16–7]: Thou art lich him that sit on his asse and yit seecheth it over al. *Oxford* 403: mare; Whiting *NC* 427: horse.

A227 Like an **Ass** to the harp
c1380 Chaucer *Boece* i pr. 4.2–3: Artow like an asse to the harpe? **c1385** *TC* i 731–5; Or artow lik an asse to the harpe, That hereth sown whan men the strynges plye, But in his mynde of that no melodie May sinken hym to gladen, for that he So dul ys of his bestialite? **a1410** Lydgate *Churl* in *MP* II 480.274–5: To heeryn a wisdam thyn eris ben half deeff, Lik an asse that listeth on a harpe, 482–3.339–40: I told hym mad that bryngith foorth an harpe, Ther-on to teche a rude, for-dullid asse. **1410** Walton *Boethius* 29[13–4]. **1509** Barclay *Ship* II 257[14]: The swete Cymball is no pleasour to an asse. **1509** Watson *Ship* Dd4^v[1–2]: These fooles here wyll do also well as the asse playenge on the cymbales. Apperson 18–9; MED asse 1(c); *Oxford* 16, 608: sow; Tilley A366. See **F402, 074, S972.**

A228 Shear **Ass** and scrape ass, *etc.*
c1250 *Hendyng O* 199.44: Sher asse and shrap asse, ne bringest thou nevere asse to gode rodehorse. Kneuer 61–2; Schleich 276; Singer III 141. Cf. Apperson 19: Ass's head; *Oxford* 693; Tilley A370. See **O71.**

A229 To be like an **Ass**
c1380 Chaucer *Boece* iv pr. 3.119: He lyveth as an asse. **1436** *Libelle* 5.83: He that seyth nay in wytte is lyche an asse. **a1475** *Asneth* 227.19–20: And as able ys the asse to danielis dremys, As the cukkou with crochetis ony countour to close. Whiting *Ballad* 26.

A230 Where **Asses** get lordships there is seldom good rule
1481 Caxton *Reynard* 87[5–6]: Where as asses geten lordshippis there men see selde good rewle. See **C271.**

A231 Without **Assay** (*trial*) no man is virtuous

a1449 Lydgate *Fabules* in *MP* II 506.609: Withouten assay no man is vertuous. See **W484.**

A232 **Assay** (*test*) and so approve
1449 Metham 148.14–5: Fyrste asay this tretys and so appreve yt, quod Jon Metham. Cf. *Oxford* 675. See **M270, P429.**

A233 He seldom **Aswinds** (*perishes*) who thinks of (trusts to) himself
a1200 Lawman II 328.17940–1: For selde he aswint, The to him seolve thencheth (B: tresteth).

A234 **Attemperance** holds the mean
c1390 Chaucer *CT* X[I] 833; Attemperaunce, that holdeth the meene in alle thynges. See **M454.**

A235 To dance **Attendance**
c1522 Skelton *Why Come* II 46.625–6: And, syr, ye must daunce attendaunce, And take pacient sufferaunce. **1555** Heywood *E* 191.257: He daunceth attendance. Apperson 134; *Oxford* 128; Tilley A392.

A236 A little **Atter** (*poison*) makes much sweet bitter
a1225 *Lambeth Homilies* 23[19]: A lutel ater bitteret muchel swete. Apperson 504; *Oxford* 509; Skeat 2. See **G12.**

A237 To cast out as **Atter**
c1000 *Corpus Christi Homily* in Assmann 146.46: Of eowrum gebeorscipe awurpað eall swa attor. Cf. Tilley P459. See **V18.**

A238 Speak not where there is no **Audience**
c1390 Chaucer *CT* VII 1047[B2237]: For Salomon seith: "Ther as thou ne mayst have noon audience, enforce thee nat to speke," 2800–2 [B3990–2]: For certeinly, as that thise clerkes seyn, Whereas a man may have noon audience, Noght helpeth it to tellen his sentence. **c1395** *WBible* Ecclesiasticus xxxii 6: Where heryng is not, schede thou not out a word.

A239 **Aught** (*property*) is good in need
a1500 *Carpenter's Tools* 84.127–8: Ffore, and a man have ought before, When he has nede, it is gode store. Cf. Tilley A395.

A240 **Aught** is not the treasure of our elders, but the loan of God
a1300 *Proverbs of Alfred* 87 J 142–3: Ayhte nys non ildre istreon (T: eldere stren) Ac hit is godnes lone. See **G334.**

A241 Where **Aught** is hidden, there is armth (*poverty*) enough
a1250 *Proverbs of Alfred* 114 T 412–3: For ther hachte is hid, Ther is armthe inoch.

A242 To be more gracious than **Augustus** and better than Trajan
a1387 Higden-Trevisa V 13[13–5]: That yit in oure tyme me prayeth in plesynge of princes, "More gracious mote thou be than evere was Augustus, and bettre than Traianus." Latin: Felicior sis Augusto, meliorque Trajano.

A243 **(A)vail** que vail
c1375 Barbour *Bruce* I 213.147: Thai wald defend, avalye que valye. **c1408** Lydgate *Reson* 55.2087: Vaylle or wher yt vaylle nought. **a1500** *Partenay* 96.2672: Vail that vail might. **1513** Douglas *Aeneid* III 5.167: Vail que vailye, 171.86, 282.129. NED Vail v.[1] 2d; Whiting *Scots* I 133, II 147.

A244 An **Avaunter** (*boaster*) and a liar are all one
c1385 Chaucer *TC* iii 309: Avauntour and a lyere, al is on. **1480** Caxton *Ovyde* 46[2–3]: Be not . . . a vauntour ne lyar. **a1500** *Court of Love* 442.1240–2: Thus hath Avaunter blowen every-where Al that he knowith, and more, a thousand-fold; His auncetrye of kin was to Lière. Apperson 58; *Oxford* 685; Skeat 175; Tilley V19.

A245 **Avows** are common to all, but the hardest part lies in the achieving
c1400 *Alexander Buik* III 262.5477–9: The avowis ar to all men common, Bot yit, or all the play be done, The hardest lyis at the escheving. See **B414.**

A246 **Awe** (and) law
a1415 *Lanterne* 70.9–10: Youre awe is lawe, who dar seie naye? 95.15–6: Hir owene children waxen wilde and wantoune and wole nothir take awe ne lawe. MED aue 3(e).

A247 **Aweless,** lawless
c1450 *Rylands MS.394* 99.11: Awghles, lawles. See **W493.**

A248 As boring (piercing) as an **Awl**
1340 *Ayenbite* 66[10–2]: A feloun thet heth the tonge . . . more boryinde thanne zouteres eles. **c1400** *Vices and Virtues* 64.2–4: Than ben here tonges . . . more persynge than an al. **1484** Caxton *Royal Book* F7[v][23–4].

A249 As meet as **Ax** to helve
c1450 Capgrave *Katharine* 19.45–6: Al his noble werkys on to pees and love Were made as mete as ex on-to helve. See **A254.**

A250 The **Ax** is an informer, not a thief
a700 *Laws of Ine* in Liebermann I 108.43[E]: Seo æsc bið melda, nalles ðeof (*Earlier in the*

same law: Forþamþe fyr bið þeof). Liebermann II 287, *s.v.* Anzeiger. See **R219.**

A251 To hang up one's **Ax** (hatchet)
c1250 *Owl* 56.658: Hong up thin ax! nu thu might fare! **c1300** Robert of Gloucester II 767.11770–1: He mighte segge wan he com, lute ich abbe iwonne, Ich mai honge up min ax, febliche ich abbe agonne. **c1300** *South English Legendary* II 482.156: Hi mighte honge up here axe, for lute hi hadde iwonne. **a1325** *Sir Simon Fraser* in Böddeker 134.230–1: Tprot, scot, for thi strif! Hang up thyn hachet ant thi knyf. **c1390** *Sir Gawain* 15.477: Now sir, heng up thyn ax, that hatz innogh hewen. **c1422** Hoccleve *Dialog* 136.736: Hange up his hachet and sette him adoun. **c1450** *How mankinde dooth* in Furnivall *Hymns* 69.346: Hange up thin hachet and take thi reste. **a1500** Hill 129.25: Whan thow hast well don, hange wp thi hachet, 132.46. **1546** Heywood *D* 43.87: I have hangd up my hatchet, **1555** *E* 172.147. Apperson 289; *Oxford* 275–6; Tilley H209.

A252 To hold the **Ax** by the helve
a1450 *Castle* 153.2571–2: Resun wyl excusyn us alle: He helde the ex be the helve. MED ax(e) n.(1) 2(b): "to be in control."

A253 To put the **Ax** at the root (*varied*)
c1000 *WSG* Matthew iii 10: Eallunga ys seo æx to ðæra treowa wurtrumum asett. **c1200** Orm I 351.10063–4: Thatt axe shollde tha beon sett Rihht att te treowwess rote. **c1250** *Hendyng O* 200.47[4–6]: For ofte wen mon wenez best Lif and hele, ro and rest, The ax is at the rote. **a1325** M. Kildare *Swet Jesus* in Heuser 82[24–9]: Riche man bethenche the, . . . Thou ne art bot a brotil tre . . . The ax is at the rote. **c1395** *WBible* Matthew iii 10: The ax is put to the roote of the tree. **c1425** *Orcherd* 301.17–8: The axe of my rightwiisnesse is sett at the roote of thi tree. MED ax(e) n.(1) 2(b).

A254 To put the **Ax** in the helve
c1410 Lovelich *Grail* II 363.410: But yit Cowde he not putten the Ex In the helve. MED ax(e) n.(1) 2(b): "to solve a problem." See **A249.**

A255 To send the **Ax** after the helve
1546 Heywood *D* 97.220: For here I send thaxe after the helve awaie. Apperson 632: Throw; *Oxford* 291: Helve; Tilley A411.

Ay, see **Egg**

A256 Better is an **Ay** (*egg*) with este (*pleasure*) than an ox with chest (*strife*)
c1250 *Hendyng O* 194.16: Betere is on ey with heste, then on oxe with cheste. Apperson 41; Kneuer 33–5; Schleich 257; Singer III 131; Tilley E67. See **M700.**

A257 I can bring you from the **Ay** but not from the kind (*nature*)
a1250 Odo of Cheriton 181[10]: Of (eie) hi the brothte, of athele hi ne mythte (*Vars.* Of a ey hi ye brohte, of kynde i ne myche *and* Of on egge y the broughght, bytt of thy kynde y maye noghght); hoc est: De ovo te eduxi; de natura non potui. Cf. Tilley N50. See **K26.**

A258 Not give an **Ay**
c1400 *Sowdone* 80.2793: But thay with-in gafe not an Eye.

A259 Not worth an **Ay**
a1300 *Tristrem* 85.3167: This lond nis worth an ay. **a1338** Mannyng *Chronicle B* I 181[8]. **a1400** *Rowlande* 62.221–2. **a1475** *Talk of Ten Wives* 33[15]: He is not worth a nay. **a1500** *Thre Prestis* 47.1078: It is nocht worth ane eg into his sicht. **c1503** More *Early Poems* [12] A[7]: And all not worth an egge. Apperson 458:36; Tilley E95.

A260 As blue as **Azure**
a1400 Julian *Revelations* 137[8]: The colour of his cloth was blue as azure. **1481** Caxton *Mirror* 118[11]: And the heven as blew as Azure.

B

B1 To know not a **B** from a bull's foot
c1400-25 Legat *Sermon* 8.36–9: But tis peple that tis prechith, thow they vownd a bole-fot writen in hir book, trust it wel ther-to, thei wolde tel it forth, and tat is for no-thing ellus but wantyng of wit and of discreciun. **1402** *Daw Topias* 57[13–5]: I know not . . . A b from a bole fote, 84[6]: I knowe a b fro a bole fote. Apperson 21; *Oxford* 346; Taylor and Whiting 12: Buffalo's foot. Cf. Tilley B1.

B2 As still as a **Babe**
a1500 *Stations* 358.159: And he ley as a babe stylle.

B3 **Bachelors'** wives and maids' children are well taught
1546 Heywood *D* 78.16: Bachelers wives, and maides children be well tought. Apperson 21; *Oxford* 18; Tilley B10. Cf. Taylor and Whiting 13. See **B12, K66.**

B4 One's **Back** is broad enough
a1470 Malory II 757.28–9: I may beare well the blame for my bak ys brode inowghe. Apperson 21; *Oxford* 18; Tilley B13.

B5 To claw one's **Back** (*i.e.,* to flatter)
c1390 Chaucer *CT* I[A] 4326: For joye him thoughte he clawed him on the bak. **c1395** *Pierce* 14.365: Whou they (curry) kinges and her back claweth. **a1475** *Turne up hur halter* in *Rel. Ant.* I 77[16]: Thanke me, women, I claw your bakkis. **c1500** Greene *Carols* 379.9: Covetyse so swetly there bakes dothe clawe, 419 B 19: And c(l)awthe (*?beat*) her servantes abowte the bake, Yff to here they outhe had sayd. **1509** Barclay *Ship* I 105[22]: His maysters backe he must oft shrape and clawe, 211[27–8]: All folysshe mockers I purpos to repreve, Clawe he his backe that felyth ytche or greve. **1546** Heywood *D* 36.49–50: I clawd hir by the backe in waie of a charme, To do me, not the more good, but the lesse harme. *Oxford* 96; Tilley B17. See **H67.**

B6 To give (the) **Back**
a1325 *Cursor* I 152.2499: The five gave bak to wine a-way, 258.4390: The mantel left, he gafe the bak. **a1400** *Destruction of Troy* 308.9474: Thai were boun to gyffe bake, and the bent leve. **c1420** Wyntoun VI 57.4523: Tuk hail the flicht, and gaf the bak. **c1425** *Avowynge* 92[14–5]: And there mete hor sege brake, And gerut hom to giffe us the bake. **1513** Douglas *Aeneid* III 33.32: Sum gave the bak, takand the flycht gude speid, 221.39, 253.11, 254.28, 272.106, IV 5.139, 46.52, 47.75, 59.109, 94.104, 107.44, 119.66, 125.107, 153.130. MED bak 6(c); NED Back sb.[1] 24c.

B7 Not to know whether one goes **Backward** or forward
1457 Paston III 116[12–4]: My maister can not know wheder he go backward or forward till thys be doon, 117[10–1]: My maister shall nevere know whethyr he goth bakward or forward. Cf. NED Backward 5b.

B8 As fat as any **Bacon**
c1450 *Way to Jerusalem* in S. Purchas *Hakluytus Posthumus or Purchas his Pilgrimes* (Glasgow, 1905) VII 536[2]: And faat as any Bacon. Svartengren 183.

B9 **Bag** and baggage
1556 Heywood *Spider* 97[20]: At crevis, and windowes, with bag and baggage, 355[2]. Taylor and Whiting 14.

B10 To have a **Bag** full of wiles
a1450 *Gesta* 371[19]: I have xviij^{en} (wiles) and a bage full moo. NED Bag 17: tricks.

B11 The greater **Bailiff** the sorer his pain

1509 Barclay *Ship* II 279[18]: The greatter Baylyf the sorer is his payne.

Bairn, see **Child**

B12 The **Bairn** is eath (*easy*) to busk (*dress*) that is unborn
c1475 Henryson *Fables* 62.1764: The barne is eith to busk that is unborne. See **B3.**

B13 **Bairns** often make an ill ending for fault of chastising
c1450 *Consail and Teiching* 78.421–2: For fault of frendis chaistisinge Garris barnis oft mak ill endinge. See **Y1**

B14 Young **Bairns** learn at old men's schools
c1500 *King Hart* 109.12: And barnis young suld lerne at auld mennis sculis. Whiting *Scots* I 134. See **C347, D298, S216.**

B15 "I fear we part not yet," quoth the **Baker** to the pillory (*varied*)
a1325 *Hail seint Michael* in Heuser 157[13–6]: Hail be ye bakers with yur lovis smale . . . To the fair pillori, ich rede ye tak hede. **1546** Heywood *D* 63.58–9: I feare we parte not yeet, Quoth the baker to the pylorie. Apperson 23; *Oxford* 20; Tilley L171.

B16, (As) unsure as a **Balance**
1509 Barclay *Ship* I 32[11]: Nowe up nowe downe unsure as a Balaunce.

B17 To hang in the **Balance**
c1380 Chaucer *Womanly Noblesse* 18: Considryng eke how I hange in balaunce, **a1400** *Romaunt B* 5321: This love so hangeth in balaunce. **a1420** Lydgate *Troy* III 720.5348–9: And yit I stonde of lif in iupartie, With-oute refut hanginge in ballaunce. **a1437** *Kingis Quair* 76.111[3]: Bot now thy mater so in balance hangith. **a1439** Lydgate *Fall* I 86.3123–4: Al ertheli blisse dependith in a weer, In a ballaunce onevenli hangyng. **a1500** *His Mistress* in Robbins 155.10. *MED* hongen 8(d).

B18 After **Bale** comes boot
c1250 *Floris* 110.821: Hu after bale hem com bote. **c1350** *Gamelyn* 660.631: After bale cometh boote thurgh grace of god almight. **a1400** *Alexander C* 242.4620: For eftir . . . bale blis us aperis. **c1400** *Beryn* 118.3956: So aftir bale comyth bote. **a1425** *Chester Plays* II 431.113–4: After Bale Boot thou bringes, And after Teene tyde Tydinges. **a1450** *Generydes A* 14.434: But aftre bale ther may come bote, 104.3328. **c1455** *Speculum Misericordie* 943.106: Ffore after bale ther comyht bote. **c1475** *Rawlinson MS. D 328* 120.41: After bale (*MS.* bate) comyth bote. Apperson 60; *Oxford* 21. See **B22, 463.**

B19 **Bale** will blin (*cease*) (*varied*)
a1400 *Alexander C* 228.4160: As, be the bale nevir so breme it blynnes at the last. **a1425** *Metrical Paraphrase OT* 28.6603–4: And in no poynt he is to prays That can not byde his bale to blyn. **a1500** *Eger* H 283.1619–22: In world there is no bale nor bliss, Or whatsoever that it is, But at the last it will overgang, Suppose that many think it lang. See **D340, M587, S798, W430.**

B20 Be blithe in **Bale,** for that is (the) best remedy
c1475 Henryson *Fables* 21.521: Be blyith in baill, ffor that is best remeid.

B21 He that begins to brew **Bale** may confound himself
a1338 Mannyng *Chronicle A* I 411.11763–6: So may bytide, then schal hym rewe That he bigan this bale to brewe; and hit bytydes many stoundes, That who so bygynneth, hym self confoundes. See **P232.**

B22 When **Bale** is highest boot is nighest (*varied*)
c1225 *Wohunge of Ure Laverd* 277[13]: Bote ther the bale was alre meast, swa was te bote nehest. **c1250** *Hendyng O* 193.13: There the bale is mest, there is the bote nest. **c1250** *Owl* 58.685–8: For Aluered seide of olde quide, An yut hit nis of horte islide: "Wone the bale is alre-hecst, Thonne is the bote alrenecst," 60.697–700. **c1300** *South English Lengendary* II 662.1573–4: Thare it was soth for wanne a man is in mest sor and teone Thanne is oure Loverd is help next. **c1385** Usk 81.142–4: Lo, an olde proverbe aleged by many wyse: —"Whan bale is greetest, than is bote a nye-bore." **c1390** *Talkyng* 38.13–4: For whon the bale was most, Then was the bote next. **a1400** *Cursor* I 280 F 4775–6. **a1400** *Firumbras* 15.423: Whenne bale ys aldermest, bote ys ful hende. **a1400** *Proverbis of Wysdom* 244.14: When bale is most, bote is nexte. **a1450** Audelay 212.44: When bale is hyest then bot may be. **c1450** *Chaunce* 10.200–1: For when that most ys nede Than boote ys next. **c1450** *Douce MS.52* 52.91. **c1450** *Fyrst thou sal* 90.129–30. **c1450** *Rylands MS.394* 102.10. **a1475** Russell *Boke* 119.32. **a1500** *Almyghty god* in *Anglia* 3(1880) 547.190: Wher bale ys moste, bote ys heste. **a1500** Hichecoke *This Worlde* 333.43–4. **1546** Heywood *D* 55.4: When bale is hekst, boote is next, **1555** *E* 196.287. Apperson 60; Jente 7; Kneuer 35–6; *Oxford* 21; Schleich 256; Singer III 130; Skeat 83; Tilley B59; Whiting *Ballad* 23, *Drama* 193. See **B18, M313.**

B23 As hard as **Baleen** (*whalebone*)
a1350 *Seege of Troye* 97.1216–7: That al hard bycom his skyn Als eny balayn . . . to hewe in.

B24 As round as a **Ball**
c1300 *South English Legendary* (*Laud*) 318.654: The eorthe a-midde the grete se ase a luy(te) bal is round. **a1400** *Cursor* I 38 F 521: His heved ys rouned as a balle. **a1400** Julian *Revelations* 12[15]. **c1450** Capgrave *Katharine* 169.1461: Hir moder fel doun as round as ony balle, 334.2244. **a1500** *Beauty of his Mistress II* in Robbins 124.18: With pappes rounde as any ball. **a1500** *Leconfield Proverbs* 495[5]: The worlde is rounde lyke a ball. Taylor *Comparisons* 69; Tilley B61; Whiting *NC* 365, *Scots* I 134.

B25 To chulle (*kick*) as a **Ball** (*etc.*) (A number of single quotations are brought together here)
a1400 *Grete ferly* 67.16–7: And chulles hym as men don a balle That is casten fro hande to hande. **c1400** *Laud Troy* I 272.9217–8: He and his smot at him alle, As men smeten atte balle. **a1475** *Assembly of Gods* 17.557: Walewyng with hys wawes and tomblyng as a ball. **a1500** *Beves* 48 M 799–800: Men myght se over all Hedys cirlyng as a ball. **a1500** *Octavian* (*NC*) 140.1271–2: That the hedde fro the body wente, As hyt were a balle. **c1515** Barclay *Eclogues* 177.1065: Weake is thy promis revolving as a ball.

B26 To have the **Ball**
c1400 *Beryn* 78.2580: They shull be behynd, and wee shul have the ball.

B27 To lose the **Ball** in the (one's) hood
a1300 *Alisaunder* 345.6470–1: Ac arst many of his knighttes gode Loren the balles in the hode. **a1300** *Arthour and M.*[1] 14.393–4: Mani hert forles his blod And mani the bal up in the hod. **a1300** *Richard* 313.4551–2: Men off armes the swerdes out breyde, Balles out off hoodes soone thei pleyde. **a1325** *Otuel and Roland* 110.1648–9: That thay ne lore in that tyde, The balles in here hod. **c1330** *Tars* 62.1216–7: He schuld for-lesse that ich day, The hal (*for* bal) up in the hode. **c1400** *Beryn* 115.3860: And as they wold nat lese the ball within hir hood. **a1460** *Towneley Plays* 20.388: I shrew thi ball under thi hode. **a1475** *Seege of Troye* 196 H 1378kl: And many on les the hert blode, And many on the ballis in the hode. **a1500** *Gest of Robyn Hode* in Child III 74.364[1–2]: That he ne shall lese his hede, That is the best ball in his hode. MED bal 4; NED Ball 8.

B28 To play **Ball** under foot
a1449 Lydgate *Look* in *MP* II 768.117: Lat fals presumpcioun pley bal undir foote.

B29 To roll like a **Ball**
c1385 Chaucer *CT* I[A] 2614: He rolleth under foot as dooth a bal. **a1437** *Kingis Quair* 94.172[2]: That fro my quhele be rollit as a ball. Whiting *NC* 365.

B30 To strike the **Ball** under the line
1549 Heywood *D* 51.340: Thou hast striken the ball, under the lyne. Apperson 24; *Oxford* 626; Tilley B62.

B31 To trendle (*roll*) like a **Ball**
a1300 *Richard* 313.4534: That the hed trendelyd off as a bal. **c1400** *Laud Troy* I 176.5954: Sche . . . trendeles as doth a bal.

B32 To turn like a **Ball**
c1390 Chaucer *Truth* 9: In trust of hir that turneth as a bal. **c1390** *Ever More Thank God of All* in Brown *Lyrics XIV* 158.30: Reches tornyth as a ball. **a1400** *Proverbis of Wysdom* 244.33: The world turnythe, as a ball. **c1400** *Laud Troy* I 176.5954. **a1420** Lydgate *Troy* I 56.1506, 202.2027. **a1425** *Deceit II* in Robbins 100.2. **c1430** *Parliament of Birds* 109[24]: In love to turne as a bal. **a1439** Lydgate *Fall* I 14.487, 201.43, III 953.1210: The wheel of Fortune tourneth as a ball, **a1449** *Consulo* in *MP* II 753.84: Lyke sondry wedrys which turnyd as a ball, **a1449** *Look* in *MP* II 766.45. **c1460** *Take Good Heed* in Robbins *Historical Poems* 207.28: To your foos that be turnyng ever as a balle. **a1500** *Leconfield Proverbs* 485[39]. **1504** Hawes *Example* Aa5^{v}[23]: Alway turnynge lyke to a ball. **1509** Barclay *Ship* I 187[16], 269[17]. **1555** Heywood *E* 157.68.7: Turnd round as a ball. MED bal 1(a).

B33 To be but **Ball Play**
a1200 *Ancrene* 95.22–4: Al the wa of this world is ievenet to helle, alre leaste pine al nis bute bal plohe, 112.1–2: I the forme yeres nis bute balplohe. MED bal 3(b).

B34 As sweet as **Balm**
a1405 Lydgate *Black Knight* in *MP* II 383.26–7: The dewe . . . as eny baume suete, **a1449** *Procession* in *MP* I 39.106: With goostely fumys as any bawme so swoote. **a1450** *Cometh nere ye folkes* in *Transactions of the Lancashire and Cheshire Antiquarian Society* 10(1892) 73.82: Swettur thanne bawme is thy swete lycore. **a1475** *Ludus Coventriae* 58.18: That xal be swettere than bawmys breth, 147.47. **a1500** *Beauty of his Mistress III* in Robbins 126.5. **a1500** Kennedy 42.359. **1509** Barclay *Ship* II

221[22]: Some shyne without: and as swete bawme they smell. Svartengren 307.

B35 Low **Banks** soon overflow
c1500 Greene *Carols* 348.1: Banckes that lawe buthe sone overflowe.

B36 To bear the **Banner**
c1400 *Of Clerks Possessioners* in Wyclif *EW* 130[7–8]: Thes mendynauntis beren the baner for sutilte. See **B230, F316.**

B37 To be the **Bar** or beam in someone's eye
1556 Heywood *Spider* 329[3–4]: Ye are the principall bar: Or beame, in their iyes. See **M710.**

B38 To leap over the **Bar**
c1515 Barclay *Eclogues* 8.255–6: Thou wadest nowe to farre, Thy selfe forgetting thou leapest over the barre.

B39 As several as a **Barber's** chair
1528 More *Heresyes* 230 G[10–1]: They bee yet as severall as a barbers chayre, and never take but one at once. Apperson 25; *Oxford* 105; Tilley B73, 74.

B40 Some dear bought **Bargains** would be sold good cheap
1549 Heywood *D* 32.37: Som bargains deere bought, good cheape wold be sold. *Oxford* 22; Tilley B81.

B41 Such **Bargains** are bitter that have a bare end
a1400 *Destruction of Troy* 82.2502: Soche bargens are bytter, that hafe a bare end.

B42 To buy a **Bargain** dearly
a1352 Minot 23.64: All thaire bargan dere thai boght. **c1375** *St. Bartholomew* 123.358: This bargan sal ful dere be boghte. **a1425** *Christ's Testament* in *Vernon* II 640.104. **a1450** *York Plays* 49.126: This bargan sall be bought. **1520** Whittinton *Vulgaria* 100.13–4: That bargen shall he bye full dere or we have done. MED bargain 3.

B43 One cannot both **Bargain** and buy all in one day
1525 Berners *Froissart* V 119[21–2]: We muste one tyme bargayne, and another tyme bye; we can nat both bargayne and bye all in one day. See **C168.**

B44 To **Bark** before one does offence
a1420 Lydgate *Troy* III 803.1063: He (*Cerberus*) berketh first or he do offence. Cf. Whiting *NC* 365. See **S576.**

B45 To hill (*cover, conceal*) as the **Bark** the tree
a1350 *Ywain* 21.741–2: Als the bark hilles the tre, Right so sal my ring do the. Cf. *Oxford* 444: Near; Tilley B83.

B46 **Barking** of hounds may not (do) damage
a1430 Lydgate *Pilgrimage* 209.7473–6: And off me thys wysdam lere, Berkyng off houndys for to here, Yt may to the, by good suffraunce, Nouther damage nor do grevaunce. Jente 746; Tilley B85. See **C636, H561.**

B47 To have a **Barley-hat** on one's head
a1500 *Colyn Blowbol* 105.293–4: They that be manly in dronkenesse for to fyte, Whan one ther hede is sett a barly-hate. NED Barley B 2, Barley-cap, Barley-hood.

B48 An old **Barn** would be underset (*supported*)
c1516 Skelton *Magnificence* 15.454: An olde barne wolde be underset.

B49 To burn one's **Barn** to kill the flies
c1400 *Beryn* 72.2349–54: But I fare like the man, that, for to swele his vlyes He stert in-to the bern, and aftir stre he hies, And goith a-bout the wallis with a brennyng wase, Tyll it was atte last, that the leem and blase Entryd in-to the Chynys, wher the whete was, And kissid so the evese, that brent was al the plase. Apperson 72; *Oxford* 69; Taylor and Whiting 17; Tilley H752 (all *mice*).

B50 To thrash in (*a woman's*) **Barn**
a1500 *Ragman Roll* 72.53: And whoo so lyst may thressyn in youre berne. Apperson 627.

B51 As broad as a **Barn Door**
a1400 *Alexander C* 250.4852: A blason as a berne-dure that all the body schildis. **c1545** Heywood *Four PP* D3^{v}[6]: Bendynge hys browes, as brode as barne durres. Taylor *Comparisons* 16: big; Tilley B93.

B52 After **Barrat** (*trouble*) or bale bliss appears
a1400 *Alexander C* 242.4620: Eftir baret or bale blis us aperis. See **B325, J61.**

B53 As great as a **Barrel**
c1477 Caxton *Jason* 177.13–4: And (*the dead*) were as grete as barellis. **c1500** *Melusine* 297.4–5: The tayll as grete and thykk as a barell. Taylor *Comparisons* 16; Whiting *Drama* 304:16, *NC* 366 (all *big*).

B54 Neither **Barrel** better herring
1500 *Harley MS.2321* in *Rel. Ant.* I 207[1]: Neyther barrell better herring. **1546** Heywood *D* 101.41: In neither barrell better hearyng. Apperson 27; *Oxford* 24; Tilley B94.

B55 To be made like a **Barrel**
c1450 *Weddynge* 248.242: And lyke a barelle she was made.

B56 As mortal as a **Basilisk**
1512 Copland *Helyas* B3r[20–1]: Matabrune began to caste an eye on her by a false and cursed regarde more mortell than of a Baselyske. MED basilisk; Tilley B99.

B57 As big (great) as a **Basin**
1465 Leversege 24[11]: Gret eyn as they had byn ij basons. **a1533** Berners *Huon* 381.28–9: .II. eyen bygger then .ii. basyns ful of brynnyngs fyre, 427.18: His eyen as great as a basyn.

B58 As broad as a **Basin**
a1225 *St. Marherete* 20.25–6: His twa ehnen . . . brade ase bascins. **a1500** *Arthour and M.*[2] 344.1106: With eyghen brod (*var.* bryghes of eyghne) as a basyn cleer. See **S68.**

B59 As clear as a **Basin**
a1300 *Arthour and M.*[1] 44.1490: The eighen so a bacine cler. **a1425** *Arthour and M.*[2] 344.1576. **c1500** *Arthour and M.*[3] I 468.1499.

B60 As yellow as a **Basin**
a1400 ?Chaucer *Rom. A* 539–40: Hir heer was as yelowe of hewe As ony basyn scoured newe.

B61 As bare as a **Bast** (*?mat*)
a1400 *Alexander C* 70.1339: Als bare as a bast. **a1400** *Destruction of Troy* 155.4773: Till all was bare as a bast (see Notes 500). MED bast n.(1) 2(b).

B62 As dry as a **Bast** (*rope*)
a1430 Lydgate *Pilgrimage* 399.14777: Dreye as a bast, voyde off blood. MED bast n.(1) 2(a).

B63 A **Bastard** (baby) of Beelzebub's kin (bower)
a1376 *Piers* A ii 100: A bastard i-boren of Belsabubbes kunne. **1546** Heywood *D* 67.59: Ye be a baby of Belsabubs bowre. Apperson 34; *Oxford* 18; Tilley B7. See **D203.**

B64 **Battle** (War) without head is not well (*varied*)
a1338 Mannyng *Chronicle B* I 2[20]: For werre withouten hede is not wele, we fynde. **c1410** Lovelich *Merlin* I 174.6583–4: Here mown ye se that bataille With-owten hed may not be. **c1450** *Merlin* I 92[20–1]: Now maist thow se that peple ne a-vaile not in bataile with-oute a gode lorde. See **H257, 362.**

B65 **Battles** are ever in doubt (*varied*)
c1395 *WBible* II Kings xi 25: For the bifallyng (*var.* happe) of batel is dyverse, and swerd wastith now this man, now that man. **c1400** *Laud Troy* I 58.1941–3: But for batayles ben evere in doute, And er that it be brought aboute, No man wote who schapis the better, II 336–7.11420–2: Hap of ffyght is no certayn; No man wot how it schal schape, Who schal dye and who schal skape. **a1420** Lydgate *Troy* II 467.2537–40: Sith dotous ever is the fyn of fyght—Now up, now doun, now dirke, and after bright: For no wyght may ben ay victorious In pes nor werre, nor ylyche eurous. **c1420** Wyntoun II 245.1377: Syn werde (*var.* ure) of batail (is) dowttousse. **c1421** Lydgate *Thebes* 151.3659–60: For yif it be darreyned be batayłle, who tresteth most may ful likly faille. **1489** Caxton *Fayttes* 84.18–9: Al dedes of batayIle ben doon at alaventure, wherfore noon ought trust therto, 87.8–9: The falles and the adventures of the bataylles ben wondrefull and merveyllous, For hyt happeth at suche a tyme as god wylle helpe that one partye and nought that other. **a1500** *English Conquest* 25[13–4]: The adventure of bataill ben ofte doutfull and mych uncertayn, 147.23: The unsure adventures of fyght And of battaylle. **1513** Douglas *Aeneid* III 217.3: And quhou the chance of batale yeid al wrang, IV 78.105–6: Behald the chance of batale variabill, Persave of weir the fykkill ward onstabill. Smith 321; Tilley C223; Whiting *Drama* 281, *Scots* I 135. See **C157, F139, 533, W39.**

B66 In **Battle** (war) no error may be amended
1340 *Ayenbite* 83[22–5]: Vor ase zayth the boc of the art of knyghthod in othre quereles huanne me mysnymth hou thet hit by vounde myd amendement. Ac errour ine batayle ne may naght by amended vor hi is anon awreke. **c1400** *Vices and Virtues* 82.6–10. **c1420** Wyntoun V 415.3531–6: And Caton sayis, on othir thynge Men may oft mak a mendynge Qwhen men trespassis; bot in feicht, Qwhen men rewllit ar noucht richt, Men sal (it) noucht weil mende agayne, For in the nek folowis the payne. **c1458** *Knyghthode and Bataile* 16.411–3: Caton the Wise seith: where as men erre In other thinge, it may be wel amended; But emendatioun is noon in werre. **1489** Caxton *Fayttes* 22.11–4: For Cathon saith that of alle thynges the faultes may be amended, sauf such that be doon in bataylles, of the whyche the payne ensieweth anone the faulte. Cf. *Oxford* 692; Tilley W43.

B67 Of **Battle** (war) the final end is peace (*varied*)
c1400 Gower *Peace* III 483.66: For of bataile the final ende is pees. **1401** *Treuth, reste, and pes* in Kail 12.88: And ende of batayle begynneth

pes. **1436** *Libelle* 55.1090: The ende of bataile is pease sikerlye. **c1470** *Wallace* 222.1315–8: Thus wysmen has ws kend, Ay efftir wer pees is the finall end. Quharfor ye suld off your gret malice ces; The end off wer is cheryte and pes. **1484** Caxton *Aesop* 43[5–6]: For after grete werre cometh good pees. **c1500** *God Governs* in Brown *Lyrics XV* 88.68–70: For after werr comyth pes and rest And often, for the gretter adverssite, After-ward the gretter prossperite. *Oxford* 692; Tilley W55; Whiting *Scots* II 149. See **W37.**

B68 There is hard **Battle** where kin and friends battle
a1470 Malory III 1084.4–6: For hit ys an olde-seyde sawe, "there ys harde batayle thereas kynne and frendys doth batayle ayther ayenst other."

B69 Not give a **Bauble**
c1400 *Laud Troy* I 186.6315–6: Thanne strok to Ector alle that rabel, But he yaff nought ther-of a babel.

B70 To wear (bear) a **Bauble**
1508(1519) Stanbridge *Vulgaria* 15.21: For his folysshenes he may were a bable. **c1522** Skelton *Speke* II 21.422: He make(th) them to bere babylles. See **F394.**

B71 As bold as blind **Bayard** (*varied*)
c1380 *Cleanness* 34.886: That thay blustered as blynde as Bayard watz ever. **1384** Wyclif *Church and her Members* in *SEW* III 356[29–31]: And sith thes popis ben not hardy as blynde Bayard, thei moten seie that thei speken ofte with God, that techith hem that it mut be thus, and so thes popis mai not erre. **a1393** Gower *CA* III 202.1280–4: Bot as Baiard the blinde stede, Til he falle in the dich amidde, He goth ther noman wole him bidde; He stant so ferforth out of reule, Ther is no wit that mai him reule. **c1395** Chaucer *CT* VIII[G] 1413–6: Ye been as boold as is Bayard the blynde, That blondreth forth, and peril casteth noon. He is as boold to renne agayn a stoon As for to goon bisides in the weye. **c1400–25** Legat *Sermon* 7.29–30: For, aftur the comen sawe, ther is non so bolde as is blind bayard. **a1420** Lydgate *Troy* I 280.4731–2: But ben as bolde as Baiard is, the blynde, That cast no peril what wey(e) that he fynde, III 873.3506–7: For blind Baiard cast pereil of no thing, Til he stumble myddes of the lake, **a1439** *Fall* II 636.1828–9: Ther hasti deemyng so bestial is and dull, On blynde Baiard thei braiden at a pull, **c1440** *Debate* in *MP* II 549.234–5: Whan the famous worthi Duke of Clarence Rood on Baiard with his eyen blynde. **1449** Metham 9.237–8: But trwth ys seyd, blynd Bayard of no dowts doth purvey, Tyl he hath fallyn in the myd wey. **a1450** Audelay 44.952: Bot al blustyrne furth unblest as bayard the blynd, 46.993, 145.381: I bluster forth as Bayard blynd. **a1450** *Tottenham* 993.92: May i mete with Bernard, on Bayard the blynde. **c1450** *When the son* 390.235–6: As bayard the blynd trottyng on the Ise, When he is down ye japen merely. **c1454** Pecock *Folewer* 33.36–34.1: Thou schalt as oft go undir bigilyngis as baiard goith undir the cartis thillyngis, or ellis thus, thou schalt be as oft bigilid as bayard gooth undir the carte to be thillid. **a1456** *Of alle the crafftes* in *MLN* 19(1904) 37[11]: Bothe *Rudd* and *Goore* and eke *Bayard* the blynde. **1471** Caxton *Recuyell* I 4.21–3: And began boldly to renne forth as blynde bayard in thys presente werke. **1478** Stonor *Letters* II 54–5: I shall do lyke blynde byar, that is to s . . . (*MS. defective*). **1528** More *Heresyes* 244 A[13–4]: The harme that may growe by suche blynde bayardes. **a1529** Skelton *Garnesche* I 123.101: Bolde bayarde, ye are to blynde. **1532** More *Confutacion* 500 C[5–6]: Bee bolde upon it lyke blynde bayarde, **1534** *Comforte* 1142 FG: So foolish to putte their lyves in suche lewde and unlearned blynde bayardes handes. **1546** Heywood *D* 32.50: Who so bolde as blynde Bayard is, **1555** *E* 162.101. Apperson 28; MED baiard n.(1) (c); NED Bayard sb.[1] 2c, 3; *Oxford* 54; Skeat 288; Svartengren 112; Tilley B112; Whiting *Drama* 304:17, *Scots* I 135. See **M654.**

B72 Beat not **Bayard** for birth or for brend (*a brindle horse*)
a1450 Audelay 14.118–23: What was Abel the worse thagh Kayme his borne broder Were cursid for his covetyse . . . Loke ye bete not Bayard for bryd ne fore brend. MED birth 5, brend. (Do not punish Bayard for something not his fault.)

B73 To lead **Bayard** from (keep B. in) his stable
c1400 *Beryn* 96.3183–4: Fful trewe is that byword, "a man to servesabill Ledith offt(e) beyard from his owne stabill." **1546** Heywood *D* 56.30–1: Their landlorde came to their house to take a stresse For rent, to have kept Bayard in the stable. Apperson 28; *Oxford* 330; Tilley B111.

B74 **Be** as be may (is no banning)
c1386 Chaucer *LGW* 1145: Be as be may, I take of it no cure, 1852, **c1390** *CT* VII 2129[B3319]: Be as be may, I wol hire noght accusen. **c1400**

Beryn 102.3389. **1406** Hoccleve *Male Regle* 34.289: Be as be may, no more of this as now. **a1450** *Seven Sages B* 19.543: And by than as hit may. **a1470** Malory I 294.20. **c1475** *Mankind* 22.577. **1523** Skelton *Garlande* I 417.1415: But yet for all that, be as be may, **a1529** *Elynour* I 103.261: Be that as be maye. **1546** Heywood *D* 60.62: Be as be maie is no bannyng, **1555** *E* 190.252. Apperson 28; *Oxford* 25; Tilley B65.

B75 Better not to **Be** than not to be well
c1450 *Douce MS.52* 46.24: Hit is better not to be; than not to well be. Prestat non esse, quam non feliciter esse. **c1450** *Rylands MS.394* 97.28: Then to not well be. Walther III 928.22229a.

B76 Holy **Bead** (*prayer*) breaks a bond that the right hand may not
a1350 *Magdalen MS.27* in H. O. Coxe *Catalogue Codicum MSS.* (Oxford, 1852) II ii 18: Holy Bede breket bond, That ne mai, the rith hond.

B77 To unfold a **Bead-roll**
1546 Heywood *D* 80.3: But now am I forst, a bead roule to unfolde.

B78 As bright as **Beams**
a1400 *Northern Verse Psalter* I 165 (50.20): And bigged be thai, bright als bem, 199 (64.2): And to the, bright als bem, II 67 (115.19). **a1450** *Three Middle English Sermons* 43.713–4: Eghen . . . as brith as bemis of the sunne. MED bem 7(f).

B79 To shine like **Beams**
a1400 *Ipomadon A* 123.4267: Hit shone as beymes bryghte.

B80 Dear of (*at*) a bored **Bean**
1513 Douglas *Aeneid* II 151.155: Haldand opynyon deyr of a boryt beyn. DOST Bene.

B81 A **Bean** in a monk's hood
1546 Heywood *D* 79.56: And she must syt like a beane in a moonkes hood, **1555** *E* 177.177: A beane in a monkes whood, very good, Here is the beane, but where is the whood. Apperson 29; *Oxford* 25; Tilley B117.

B82 Not avail a **Bean**
1413 ?Hoccleve *De Guilleville Poems* lii 39: And alle my witte availeth not a beane. **a1440** Burgh *Cato* 318.608: To reden hem availeth not a been.

B83 Not base (*lower*) a **Bean**
a1400 *Alexander C* 148.2567: Yit was the berne noght a bene baist of his wordis.

B84 Not bid a **Bean**
a1375 *William* 151.4754: I ne bidde nought a bene worth.

B85 Not count a **Bean**
c1385 Chaucer *TC* v 363: God helpe me so, I counte hem nought a bene! **a1390** *Seldom sene* 716.43–4: Sum tyme thei counted nought a Bene Beo al ffraunce. **c1390** ?Chaucer *Merciles Beaute* 29: I counte him not a bene, 39. **a1400** *Piers* B iii 141 [*var.* from MED bene (1) 2(b)]: She counteth noght a bene. **c1450** Capgrave *Katharine* 386.1468: Thi witte counte I not worth a beene.

B86 Not give a **Bean**
c1300 *Beves* 36.744: Thar of ne yef he nought a bene. **c1330** *Floris* (*Auchinlech*) 55.878. **a1400** *Romaunt C* 6464. **c1400** *Laud Troy* II 515.17505–6: I yeve right not of alle his tene, Not the value of a bene.

B87 Not praise a (three) **Bean(s)**
c1395 Chaucer *CT* IV[E] 1854: She preyseth nat his pleyyng worth a bene. **c1450** *Pilgrimage LM* 84[12–3, *var.* from p. 248, *s.v.* verres]: I preyse not thi woordes ne thi dedes at thre benes. **1509** *Fyftene Joyes* E6r[29]: For she his dede not prayseth worthe a bene.

B88 Not reck a **Bean**
c1390 Chaucer *CT* I[A]: 3772: This Absolon ne roghte nat a bene, II[B] 94: I recche noght a bene, VII 2814[B4004]. **c1412** Hoccleve *Regement* 86.2383: Be his day kept, he rekketh nat a bene.

B89 Not set a **Bean**
a1450 *York Plays* 296.105: And saie hym a borowed bene sette I noght be hym. **a1513** Dunbar *General Satyre* 152.28: That all the lawis ar not sett by ane bene, *Of Luve* 103.57–8.

B90 Not tell (*count*) a **Bean**
c1330 *Times of Edward II* (*Bodley*) 180.96: Noman tellet be trewthe more than of a bene. **a1400** *Floris* 96.760: Of his lyf tolde he not a beene.

B91 Not the better of a **Bean**
c1405 *Mum* 17.151: And not the better of a bene.

B92 Not worth a **Bean**
c1300 Robert of Gloucester II 703.10223: Lete abbe ir franchise and al nas wurth a bene. **c1300** *South English Legendary* I 132.102: Al nis worth a bene, 134.154, 240.64. **c1350** *Times of Edward II* (*Peterhouse*) 22[6–7]: Ther is no rych man that dredeth God The worth of a bene. **c1385** Chaucer *TC* iii 1167: Swiche argumentes ne ben naught worth a beene, **c1395** *CT* IV[E] 1263. **a1387** Higden-Trevisa V 337[18–9]: He

were of false byleve that trowede that that argument were worth a bene. **a1400** *Ipomadon A* 178.6238. **1410** Walton *Boethius* 116[16], 299[21]. **a1450** *Pety Job* in Kail 131.333. **a1460** *Towneley Plays* 274.527. **c1499** Skelton *Bowge* I 34.95. **a1500** *Court of Love* 430.796. **a1508** Dunbar *Tretis* 88.128: And may nought beit worth a bene in bed of my mystirs, **a1513** *Twa Cummeris* 84.23. **1546** Heywood *D* 40.189: Beggyng of hir booteth not the woorth of a beane, **1555** *E* 167.128(2).3. Apperson 456; Tilley B118; Whiting *Drama* 334:392, *Scots* I 135.

B93 To lay (*wager*) a **Bean**
c1378 *Piers* B xi 165: "Lawe with-outen love," quod Troianus, "leye there a bene."

B94 To take a **Bean** for a pease
a1393 Gower *CA* III 67.4408–9: He wol ayeinward take a bene, Ther he hath lent the smale pese. Apperson 487; *Oxford* 492. Cf. Tilley B116.

Bear, sb.

B95 As black as a **Bear**
c1330 *Seven Sages A* 132 B[2–3]: He made a garment for hym As blak as any beres skyn. **c1350** *Libeaus* 76 (*var.* 1368): He was blake as any bere. **a1420** Lydgate *Troy* I 367.7801: Of skyn was blak . . . as eny bere. **c1425** *Avowynge* 59[2]: And ther-to, blake as a bere.

B96 As boistous (*rough*) as a **Bear** (*etc.*) (A number of single quotations are brought together here)
c1400 *Plowman's Tale* 151.139: As boystous as is bere at bay. **a1425** *Bodley MS.95* f.41 in Owst *Literature* 312: He is blind as a bere. **a1425** *Governance of Lordschipes* 104.11: Wayk and sleuthful as Bere. **c1450** Capgrave *Katharine* 379.1244: Venemous in anger was he as a bere. **1456** Hay *Governaunce* 157.20: Lythir and hevy, suere (*slothful*) as a bere. **1480** Caxton *Ovyde* 131[13–4]: More cruel than a beer new fawned. **c1515** Barclay *Eclogues* 27.800: This tiran is feller then a bere. Cf. Taylor *Comparisons* 30–1; Taylor and Whiting 19.

B97 As fouly (*ugly*) as a **Bear**
a1400 *Morte Arthure* 32.1089: And the flesche in his fortethe fowly as a bere. MED fouli (b). Cf. Whiting *NC* 366: ugly.

B98 As handsomely as a **Bear** picks mussels
1546 Heywood *D* 27–8: Eche of his jointes against other justles, As handsomly as a beare picketh muscles. Apperson 29; *Oxford* 26; Tilley B126.

B99 As rough as (a, any) **Bear**(s)
a1300 *Alisaunder* 301.5760: And wymmen as beres rowe, 323.6114: Rugh hij waren als a bere, 331.6251, 337.6358: Als beres (L bores) hij been rughye. **a1400** *Alexander C* 227.4126: And roghe as a bere. **a1420** Lydgate *Troy* I 367.7801: Of skyn was . . . rowe as eny bere. **1481** Caxton *Mirror* 84[29–30]: Men and wymmen alle naked and also Rowhe as beeres, **c1489** *Aymon* I 117.21–2: They were as roughe as beres that ben famysshed. **c1505** Watson *Valentine* 38.19: He was also rough as a beere, 96.2. **a1529** Skelton *Garnesche* I 117.23: Hys basnet routh as a bere. **a1533** Berners *Huon* 489.29. Whiting *NC* 366.

B100 As slow as a **Bear**
1422 Yonge *Governaunce* 212.4–5: Slow as a bere. **c1450** *Secrete of Secretes* 35.20–1: Hevy and slowe as a bere.

B101 The **Bear** thinks one thing, but his leader thinks another (*varied*)
c1385 Chaucer *TC* iv 1453–4: For thus men seyth, "that on thenketh the beere, But al another thenketh his ledere." **c1450** *Rylands MS.394* 109.24: The berewarde and the bere thenken not alle on. Apperson 30; *Oxford* 477; Tilley H667.

B102 Like a **Bear** to the stake
a1400 *Lamentacio sancti Anselmi* in *Leeds Studies in English* 3(1934) 35.173–5: Thow schalt stande as bere at stake, Ffor sorwe to swelle and nevere to swage, Thow schalt be beytyd as a bere. **a1400** Wyclif *Sermons* II 337[3–4]: And thus it is a foule thing to be led as a bere to a stake. **a1410** Lydgate *Churl* in *MP* II 474.131–2: And hath no fredam . . . To gon at large, but as a bere at stake. **c1450** *Chaunce* 15.354: Ye be to thryve as lothe as bere to stake. **c1500** *Lancelot* 100.3384–6: As at the stok the bere Snybbyth the hardy houndis that are ken, So farith he. **1509** Watson *Ship* Bb2r[8]: Bynde the as a bere unto a stake. **1546** Heywood *D* 34.33–4: I shall nedes this viage make, With as good will as a beare goth to the stake. Apperson 30; *Oxford* 26; Tilley B127. See **S664.**

B103 Like a (she-) **Bear** whose whelps have been ravished
c1395 *WBible* Proverbs xvii 12: It spedith more to meete a femal bere, whanne the whelpis ben ravyschid, than a fool tristynge to hym silf in his foli, Hosea xiii 8: Y as a femal bere, whanne the whelps ben ravyschid, schal mete hem. **a1450** *Gesta* 366[19–20]: As a bere whos whelpes are taken awaye, that of grete Ire spareth no

beste. **1479** Rivers *Cordyal* 83.1–3: I shal come ageynst them as a she bere whiche hath lost her whelpes. See **L367, T293.**

B104 To be baited as a **Bear**
c1400 *Plowman's Tale* 167.648: He shal be baited as a bere. **1522** Skelton *Why Come* II 36.304: He bayteth them lyke a bere.

B105 To bind **Bears**
c1390 *Think on Yesterday* in Brown *Lyrics XIV* 144.53–4: Ne non so stif to stunte ne stare, Ne non so bold Beores to bynde. **c1420** Wyntoun VI 341.989–90: Lettande that he sulde beris bynde, And he mycht on feylde the Scottis fynde. **c1440** Lydgate *Debate* in *MP* II 562.548–50: Som man is strong, hardi as a Leoun To bynde Beeris or Booris to oppresse, Wher-as anothir hath gret discrecioun. **1464** Hardyng 74[21]: Then canne a lorde, though he may beres bynde. **a1475** *Ludus Coventriae* 326.1607: With mede men may bynde berys. **a1513** ?Dunbar *Manere of the Crying* 170.7–8: That with the strenth of my hand Beres may bynd. **1523** Skelton *Howe the Douty Duke* II 74.208–9: And full of waste wynde, Howe ye wyll beres bynde. MED ber(e) n.(1) 1(d); Tilley B134; Whiting *Drama* 335:402, *Scots* I 136.

B106 To roar like a **Bear**
a1375 *Octavian*(S) 54.1739: That he ne rorede as a bere. **c1380** Chaucer *HF* 1589: That they gonne as beres rore. **a1393** Gower *CA* II 134.160. **c1395** *WBible* Isaiah lix 11. **a1400** *Stanzaic Life* 328.9708: And as beeres romeon(?). **a1500** *Gregorius* 115 R 292: That he gan roren as a bere. Whiting *Ballad* 26.

B107 To sweep (*drive together*) as **Bear** does sheep (*etc.*) (A number of single quotations are brought together here)
a1300 *Richard* 438.7005–6: And with hys ax doun he sweepe Off the Sarezynys as bere doth scheepe. **c1330** *Gregorius* 115 A 620: That he groned (*V* grunte) as a bere. **a1400** *Ipomadon A* 9.208: Here I lye as bere in denne, 169.5902: As bere ay was he boune, 230.8062: As a bere. **c1400** *Laud Troy* I 236.8013: Thei blew and cried—as wilde bere brayes. **c1500** *Lancelot* 98.3331: He farith as . . . o beyre. **1509** Watson *Ship* Dd5^r^[31]: Slepynge lyke beres. **c1515** Barclay *Eclogues* 140.17: Hobled as a beare.

Bear, vb.

B108 **Bear** with those who bear with you
1546 Heywood *D* 89.37: Beare with them, that beare with you. Apperson 30; Tilley B136.

B109 To **Bear** one well
c1450 *Douce MS.52* 48.44: Thow hast bore the welle. Tu bene gessisti seu te bene nunc habuisti. **c1450** *Rylands MS.394* 97.8^v^.13.

B110 A bare **Beard** will soon be shaved
a1475 *Good Rule* in Brown *Lyrics XV* 265.49–50: A bare berde wyl sone be shave Ther no here is lefte Aboute (*Rel. Ant.* I 75[2]: Ther as ys but lyttyl here abut). Apperson 23–4; MED berd n.(1) 4b; *Oxford* 20.

B111 Long **Beard**(s) heartless, *etc.*
c1400 *Brut* I 249.31–2: Longe berde hertles, peyntede Hode witles, Gay cote graceles, maketh Engl(i)sshemen thriftles. **c1500** Fabyan 440[3–6]: Long beerdys hartles, Paynted hoodys wytles, Gay cotis graceles Makyth Englande thryfteles. Apperson 378; *Oxford* 380; Tilley B145.

B112 Maugre (*despite*) one's **Beard**
a1350 *Ywain* 21.783: Here sal thou be mawgre thaire berd. **a1420** Lydgate *Troy* II 426.1084: Despit his berd, and maugre his power. **c1440** Charles of Orleans 130.3877: Maugre thi berd. MED berd n.(1) 4a(d); NED Beard le; Whiting *Drama* 334:394.

B113 To bay at one's **Beard**
a1450 *York Plays* 323.88: Late bryng hym to barre, and at his berde sall we baye.

B114 To be in one's **Beard**
c1450 *Gest of Robyn Hode* in Child III 60.91[1]: "Thou arte ever in my berde," sayd the abbot. NED Beard le.

B115 To cast (put) in one's **Beard**
a1440 Burgh *Cato* 320.721–2: Wedde nat a wiffe for hir inheritaunce, For she wol caste it wel oft in thy berde. **1464** Paston IV 91[4–5]: Thi (*They*) putt my kynne in my berd, seyinge, I am come of lordys. MED berd n.(1) 4a(c); NED Beard le.

B116 To make one's **Beard**
c1380 Chaucer *HF* 689–91: And moo berdys in two houres Withoute rasour or sisoures Ymad, then greynes be of sondes, **c1390** *CT* I[A] 4096–7: Yet kan a millere make a clerkes berd, For al his art, **c1395** III[D] 361. **c1400** *Beryn* 15.436: But who is, that a womman coud nat make his berd, 16.485: I trow my berd be made, 20.622: For makeing of his berd. **c1425** Hoccleve *Jonathas* 231.433. **c1450** *Duke of Suffolk* in Wright *Political Poems* II 225[15]. **c1450** Idley 87.409: Ffor he woll softly make thy berde. **c1450** *Ponthus* 97.30. **a1460** *Towneley Plays*

171.188–9: Might I thaym have spyde, I had made thaym a berd. **a1475** *Assembly of Gods* 49.1657: That he made her beerdyd on the new gete. **a1500** *Piers of Fullham* 4.46–7: Thus berdes byn made al day full feele Wyth anglers. **1525** Berners *Froissart* IV 113–4: Joselyn, that shall make youre beerdes without any rasoure. MED berd n.(1) 4a(b); NED Beard le.

B117 To meet (*etc.*) in the **Beard**
a1338 Mannyng *Chronicle B* 207[16]: The cuntre sone he fond in his berd redy ran. **a1352** Minot 14.95–6: When that he trowed no harm him till, And keped him in the berde. **c1380** *Ferumbras* 98.3066: The(y) mette hem in the berde. **c1385** Chaucer *TC* iv 41–2: And in the berd, withouten lenger lette, Hire fomen in the feld anon hem mette. **c1390** *God man and devel* 339.394–5: Alle men of the thenne schule be fert That bifore wolde mis-seye the in thi bert. **a1400** *De Pseudo-Freris* in Wyclif *EW* 297[19–20]: Shulden reprove hem in here beerd. **c1400** *Laud Troy* I 41.1383–4: And kepe him evene in the berd, For he was nought of him aferd. **c1412** Hoccleve *Regement* 148.4100–1: Largesse wolde he with shelde and spere Even in thi berde. **a1420** Lydgate *Troy* I 324.6283–4: Proudly in the berde With hem to mete were no thing a-ferde, 373.8005, II 409.514–5: But liche a knyght, evene a-forn his berd, He gan prese in, 427.1138, 429.1203, 441.1627, 468.2580, 493.3449–50, III 683.4044: And gan to hurtle with him in the berde, **c1421** *Thebes* 160.3906. **c1477** Caxton *Jason* 106.18–9: He cam and put him tofore the berde of the knight Fletheris. **c1500** *Lancelot* 102.3469. MED berd n.(1) 4a(c); NED Beard le.

B118 To shake one by the **Beard**
c1330 *Times of Edward II* (*Bodley*) 178.36: Yif symony myghte mete hym with, he wold schak hym be the berd, 191.342. **a1352** Minot 11.28–30: The right aire of that cuntre Es cumen, with all his knightes fre: To shac him by the berd. **a1500** *Degrevant* (*Cambridge*): 55.835: I shal schak hym by the berd. See **B286.**

B119 To shave one's **Beard**
a1400 *Firumbras* 3.18–9: They lystyn her gode scharp Swerdys And leydyn on the sarsyns and schoven here berdys. **c1412** Hoccleve *Regement* 156.4339–40: His sonnes and his doughtres both, I mene, Hir berdes shaved he right smothe and clene. **1418** *Man, be warre* in Kail 62.53: Er drede and repref thy berd shave. Whiting *Drama* 362:832.

B120 To turn again (*back*) the **Beard**
c1330 *Otuel* 108.1464–6: Traitours tourneth ayein the berd, Tourneth ayein alle with me, And we wole make the freinche fle. MED berd n.(1) 4a(b).

B121 To wipe from one's **Beard**
c1400 *Beryn* 110.3658: Ffor I can wipe(n) al this ple cleen(e) from yeur berd.

B122 In good **Bearing** begins worship
c1350 *Good Wife E* 158.17: In thi god beringe biginnet thi wrschipe, **a1500** *N* 210.19–20: For after thy bering, So shall thy name spring. Apperson 257; *Oxford* 250.

B123 To bere (*roar*) like a **Bear Whelp**
a1390 *Mary and the Cross* 619.277: Beerynge as a Beore whelp.

B124 As blind as a **Beast**
a1426 *Metrical Paraphrase OT* 51.15591: I byde here blynd as best in bale. **c1480** *Contemplacioun* 227.1171: Blynd as brutale best Irressonable. **1509** Barclay *Ship* II 145[14]: We labour here for deth as bestis blynde, 189[26].

B125 As brain-wood (*mad*) as **Beasts** (*etc.*) (A number of single quotations are brought together here)
a1376 *Piers* A x 61: And ben brayn-wode as beestes, so heore blod waxeth. **c1390** *Body and Soul* 78 V 199: But as a beest doumbe and daft. **c1390** Chaucer *CT* I[A] 4107: Wery and weet, as beest is in the reyn. **a1393** Gower *CA* II 249.861–2: And thanne he scheweth his tempeste Mor sodein than the wilde beste. **a1400** *Morte Arthure* 4.107: And brynge the bouxsomly as a beste, 122.4147: Bot ever bouxum as beste, blethely to wyrke. **c1400** *Laud Troy* I 269.9139–40: Ther were thikkere aboute him men Then bestis In somer liggis In fen. **a1450** *Rule of St. Benet* (2) 76.1021: Now als a best meke sal I be. **c1450** *Jacob's Well* 290.23: Sytten stylle as a beeste. **c1475** *Wisdom* 40.158: Fowll as a best, be felynge of synne. **1483** Caxton *Golden Legende* 390v[2.10]: Alle naked as a beest. **a1513** Dunbar *Maner of Passing* 168.47: And syne sit doun abasit as ane beist.

B126 As cruel as a **Beast**
a1393 Gower *CA* III 101.5677: O mor cruel than eny beste. **1513** Bradshaw *St. Werburge* 48.1187: More cruell than a beest.

B127 As wild as a **Beast**
a1325 *Cursor* III 1210 CGT 21151–2: Thar mad he wit his sermon mild Mek the men als beistes wild. **a1393** Gower *CA* III 58.4080–1: Ther was

no beste which goth oute More wylde than sche semeth ther. **a1500** ?Ros *La Belle Dame* 326.845: Wild as a beest, naked, without refute.

B128 As wood (*insane*) as a **Beast**
a1400 *Morte Arthure* 113.3837: That wode alls a wylde beste he wente at the gayneste. **c1400** *Laud Troy* II 348.11811–2: But Priamus . . . As wood was as a best savage.

B129 Every **Beast** loves its like (*varied*)
1340 *Ayenbite* 145[18–9]: Mochil is grat scele thet we to-gidere lovie, vor ech best ase zayth salomouns loveth his anliche. **c1395** *WBible* Ecclesiasticus xiii 19: Ech beest loveth *a beeste* lijk it silf; so and ech man *owith to love* his neighbore. **c1400** *Vices and Virtues* 143.34–5: Every beste loveth his owne liknesse, as Salamon seith. **a1439** Lydgate *Fall* I 117.4229–30: Everi beeste and everi creature Loveth his semblable, off kyndli riht, I gesse. MED alich. See **E171, F574, L272.**

B130 A good **Beast** (mild bitch) may have ill whelps
1509 Barclay *Ship* I 52[11–4]: But this forsothe oft tymes fynde I true That of a good beste, yl whelpes may weshewe. In lyke wyse of a Moder that is bothe chast and goode Often is brought forth a ful ungracious Brode. **1509** Watson *Ship* B7ʳ[1–2]: Oftentymes a mylde bytche bryngeth forth shrewed whelpes.

B131 A scabbed **Beast** hates the horse-comb
c1450 *Pilgrimage LM* 114[10–1]: For riht as a scabbed beste hateth hors comb . . . riht so hate i techinge. See **G7, H231, 505.**

B132 To abide like a **Beast**
c1350 *Libeaus* 92.1652–3: And beldly ther abide, As bestes brought to bay. **1485** Caxton *Charles* 192.2–3: He abode there deed lyke a beest. **a1500** Basterfeld 368.73: There I abyde as best in stalle.

B133 To be like **Beasts** in lechery (*varied*)
a1300 *Alisaunder* 335.6296–7: And beeth comen in luxure As ben bestes in pasture. **a1393** Gower *CA* II 69.1240–1: Noght as a man bot as a beste, Which goth upon his lustes wilde, III 440.2025: And take lust as doth a beste. **c1412** Hoccleve *Regement* 58.1602–3: But some folke, as beestes Hire luste ay folwen. **c1420** Wyntoun III 339.1795–7: That alkyn kynde of lechory He oyssit als commonlly As he a best but wit had beyn. **a1450** Quixley *Ballades* 42.98: Newe love seketh, as that he were a beste. **1509** Barclay *Ship* I 113[28]: Their owne sensualyte ensuynge as a beest, II 260[17]: But lyke to unresonable bestis in vylenes.

B134 To be worse than a **Beast**
a1393 Gower *CA* II 296.2598: Whan he is worse than a beste. **1439** Lydgate *St. Albon* 157.1725: Worse than beastis, o voyde of all reason. **c1500** *Everyman* 4.49: They wyll be cume moche worse than bestes.

B135 To beat one as a **Beast**
a1500 *Our Lady's Imprecation* in Brown *Lyrics XV* 20.62: And lete yow bete hym as a beest. **1523** Berners *Froissart* I 411[15–6]: And were beate downe lyke beestes.

B136 To chase as **Beasts**
a1350 Castelford 117.22908: Tham als bestes for to enchace. **1525** Berners *Froissart* V 454[9–10]: And were chased lyke beastes.

B137 To die like **Beasts**
a1393 Gower *CA* II 293.2476: Lich to these othre bestes die. **c1420** Wyntoun III 53.654: The tothir as bestis thar deande.

B138 To drive like (as) **Beast(s)**
c1400 *Laud Troy* II 436.14795–6: He droff doun alle that come him by, As doth bestes that ben hungry. **a1470** Malory III 1216.5–6: For I am dryvyn therto as beste tylle a bay.

B139 To flee like a **Beast**
a1300 *Alisaunder* 139.2474: And fleeth als a beeste wilde. **a1420** Lydgate *Troy* II 442.1651: Lik as bestis that fled fro the deth.

B140 To go like a **Beast**
c1300 *South English Legendary* II 613.76: And yeode aboute as a best that ne couthe no wisdom. **c1470** *Wallace* 309.399–400: Lik a wyld best that war fra reson rent, As wytlace wy in to the ost he went.

B141 To have no more rest than a **Beast**
c1300 *Havelok* 35.943–4: Wolde he nevere haven rest, More than he were a best. **c1475** *Guy*[1] 411 C 7492–3: Of all the nyght had she no reste, No more than had a wylde beste.

B142 To live like (a) **Beast(s)**
a1387 Higden-Trevisa I 371[9–10]: Thilke wicked men, that levede as bestes. **a1393** Gower *CA* III 334.3491–2: And lived worse than a beste. **c1395** Chaucer *CT* IV[E] 1281–2: They lyve but as . . . a beest, In libertee. **c1400** *Plowman's Tale* 164.528: But liven wors than witles beestes. **c1400** *Vices and Virtues* 81.1. **a1450** Audelay 89.226–7: Bot leven after here flesschele lust As bestis don, unresnabele. **c1450**

De Claris Mulieribus 79.1556–7: And lyvyde harde of necessyte, Wylde as bestys. **c1450** *Ratis* 41.1460. **c1475** *Guy*[1] 617 C 10899–900. **1481** Caxton *Godeffroy* 31.9: And lyved so out of rule as beestis, **c1489** *Aymon* II 466.26–7. **1509** Barclay *Ship* I 72[20]: Lyvyth as a best of conscyence cruell. **1525** Berners *Froissart* IV 240[22], VI 155[5–6]: They lyve but grosely and rudely like unto beestes.

B143 To roar like **Beasts**
c1375 Barbour *Bruce* I 97.418: Rycht as bestis can rair and cry. **a1425** *Metrical Paraphrase OT* 18.14404: And als rude bestes oft thei rare.

B144 To run about like a **Beast**
a1393 Gower *CA* II 134.161–3: And as it were a wilde beste, The whom no reson mihte areste, He ran Ethna the hell a-boute. **a1450** *Partonope* 317.7909: As a wylde beste he renneth a-boute.

B145 To slay as **Beasts**
c1400 *Laud Troy* II 406.13800: And sclow hem as thei hadde ben bestes. **a1439** Lydgate *Fall* II 624.1417: Slayn lik beestis. **1489** Caxton *Fayttes* 95.1: They ben slayne as bestes, **c1489** *Aymon* I 82.9–10: For they slewe the one thother, as domm bestes, II 346.14–5: But slew eche other as thicke as bestes, 350.32.

B146 To sleep like a **Beast** (*etc.*) (A number of single quotations are brought together here)
c1330 *Degare* 111.855: That al night as a beste sleptest. **a1350** *Ywain* 45.1653–4: Obout he welk in the forest, Als it wore a wilde beste. **c1390** *Body and Soul* 82 V 268: And bouwen as a bounden beeste. **a1400** *Pricke* 17.599: And fares als an unresonabel beste. **a1400** *Siege of Jerusalem* 77.1304: And as a beste quelled (*killed*). **c1400** *Beryn* 77.2544: His meyne were a-stonyd, and starid forth as bestis. **c1400** *Laud Troy* I 310.10513: He rolled his eyen as best ramage, II 372.12621–2: Thei folwed hem with bryght swordis, As bestis gone be-fore the herdis, 378.12833: Thei wepe and crye as bestes braye. **a1450** *Gesta* 387[29]: And sate still on his horse, as a beste. **a1450** *York Plays* 348.342: For he is boune (*bound*) as beeste in bande. **c1450** *Alphabet* II 336.14: Faght as he had bene a wude beste. **c1450** Idley 166.452: And closed as a beste kepte in a foolde. **c1470** *Wallace* 154.457: The peple beryt (*roared*) lyk wyld bestis in that tyd. **c1489** Caxton *Aymon* I 234.1–2: Ye speke well like a beste. **a1500** *Partenay* 17.272: He is A more foole then Any mute best. **1509** Barclay *Ship* I 93[25]: And there as bestes to stryve. **1525** Berners *Froissart* V 191[20–1]: They lepte in one upon another lyke beestes, without ordre or reason.

B147 To stand like a **Beast**
a1350 *Ywain* 8.274: Bot als a beste than stode he still. **a1376** *Piers* A iv 143: And stooden as bestes. **c1395** Chaucer *CT* III[D] 1034: This knyght ne stood nat still as doth a best. **a1450** *Gesta* 290[7].

B148 A wild **Beast** a man may meek (*tame*), a woman's answer is never to seek (*varied*)
a1500 *Hunterian Mus. MS. 230* 175: A weld best a man may meyke, A Womans answer is never for to seyke, quod Rychard Wylloughbe. **c1500** *Royal MS. 12 E xvi*, f.34b in Robbins-Cutler 106.5: A wyld beest a man may tame, A womanes tunge will never be lame. **c1500** *Sidney Sussex College Cambridge MS. 99* in M. R. James *Catalogue* (Cambridge, 1895) 115: All wylde beasts a man may tame, But a womanes tongue will never be lame. All wilde beasts a man may make Meeke, But a womanes aunswer ys never to seeke. Tilley W670.

B149 He is sore **Beaten** that dares not weep
a1400 *Ipomadon A* 36.1174–5: On thynge ys, yf he take kepe: Sore is he bett, that darre not wepe. *Oxford* 559: Sair dung bairn; Tilley B41.

B150 **Beauty** (Fairness) and chastity seldom accord (*varied*)
a1400 *Scottish Legends* II 100.52–4: And chast, perles of farnes, Thocht men seldine thai twa se In a yung persone to be, 215.19–22: An uthyre thing als is sene, That gud acorde seldine has ben Betwene farnes and chastyte, In quhat persone that thai be. **a1450** *Partonope* 303.7635–7: For comynly it is not sene they be Herborowed to-gedre now in oon plase, Beaute and chastite. **1480** Caxton *Ovyde* 64[2–5]: Ye be wel nyce yf ye wene lyve Chaste and have so moche beaulte. A woman may not be fayre and Chaste, yf nature lye not, the one or that other she muste leve, 65[29–31]. **1513** Douglas *Aeneid* II 152.200: Quhat of bewte, quhar honeste lyis ded? **c1520** Walter *Spectacle* B3ᵛ[13]: Beaute and wysedome seldome dothe agre. *Oxford* 28; Tilley B163; Whiting *Scots* II 158.

B151 **Beauty** and folly go together
1532 Berners *Golden Boke* 246.4225: For beautie and foly alway gothe to gyther. Tilley B164.

B152 **Beauty** without bounty is never good (*varied*)
a1387 *Piers* C xviii 163–4: *Beaute saunz bounte*, blessed was hit nevere, Ne kynde *saunz cortesie* in no contreye preysed. **a1393** Gower *CA* III 18.2594–5: Nature sette in hire at ones Beaute with bounte so besein. **a1405** Lydgate *Floure* in *MP* II 416–7.215–21: But my lady is so avysee

That, bountie and beautie bothe in her demeyne, She maketh bountie alway soverayne. This is to meane, bountie gothe afore, Lad by prudence, and hath the soveraynte, And beautie foloweth, ruled by her lore, That she ne fende her in no degre. **c1420** Wyntoun V 262.1489–90: Scho wes waill plesand of bewte; Men suld hir love for hir bounte. **c1422** Hoccleve *Jereslaus's Wife* 140.8–9: And for that beautee in womman, allone Withouten bontee, is nat commendable. **c1440** Charles of Orleans 140.4175–6: And make in thee a privy moon That pite lakkith in bewte. **a1450** Audelay 208.25: Beute is noght without bonte. **c1450** *Merlin* II 227[12–3]: And yef she hadde grete bewte ther-to she hadde as moche bounte. **c1450** *Ratis* 37.1300–1: Sen bewte may nocht duel alway, Be sykire of bownte gyf thou may. Apperson 32; Tilley B174; Whiting *Scots* I 136. See **G371.**

B153 Misused **Beauty** often does ill
a1400 *Scottish Legends* II 215.17–8: Thar-for mysoysit beute Dois Il ofte, men ma se.

B154 No worldly **Beauty** can always last (*varied*)
a1439 Lydgate *Fall* II 587.70: No worldli beute in erthe may alway laste. **c1450** *Ratis* 19.665–7: Fore bewte lestis bot a quhill, And yet oft-tyme It prowys Ill. Baith fals, fell, fainte and faikyne. Whiting *Scots* I 136. Cf. Apperson 31; *Oxford* 28; Tilley B165. See **W671.**

B155 "Too late aware," quod **Beauty,** when it passed (*varied*)
c1385 Chaucer *TC* ii 397–8: Lat this proverbe a loore unto yow be: "To late ywar, quod beaute, whan it paste." **a1393** Gower *CA* II 339.1421–2: Bot now, allas, to late war That I ne hadde him loved ar. Skeat 160. See **L90.**

B156 A **Beck** is as good as a dieugarde
1546 Heywood *D* 40.187–8: And thus with a becke as good as a dieu gard, She flang fro me. Apperson 32; *Oxford* 28; Tilley B181.

B157 To bring one in a **Beck** (*i.e.,* to deceive)
c1400 *Laud Troy* II 525.17826–7: Loke that thow us no-thyng glos And brynge us slely In a bek. NED Beck sb.[2], 2; Tilley B182.

B158 Loath to **Bed** and loath from bed, so one shall know the slow (*sluggard*)
c1450 *Douce MS.52* 49.59: Lothe to bedde and lothe fro bedde, me schall know the slow. **c1450** *Rylands MS.394* 99.16: And so the slowe sone me shall knowe. Apperson 579: Sluggard; *Oxford* 598; Tilley B192, S547.

B159 To dance in **Bed**
c1400 *Why Poor Priests have no Benefice* in Wyclif *EW* 246[25–6]: And yif it be for daunsynge in bedde, so moche the worse.

B160 To lie in **Bed** till the meat falls in one's mouth
1549 Heywood *D* 33.29–30: Tyll meate fall in your mouth, will ye ly in bed, Or sit styll. *Oxford* 364.

B161 To make one go to **Bed** at noon
1546 Heywood *D* 86.221: It seemth ye wolde make me go to bed at noone. *Oxford* 242; Tilley B197.

B162 As bright as a **Bee** (*ring*)
a1300 *Tristrem* 60.2171: With Ysonde bright so beighe. **c1350** *Octavian* (*NL*) 123.921: That maydene brighte als goldene bey. **a1400** *Le Morte A.* 79.2625: Wythe pomelles bryghte as goldis beghe. MED bei 4.

B163 As blind as a **Bee**
a1400 *Siege of Jerusalem* 1.14: Blyndfelled hym as a be (cf. note, p. 91). **c1500** *Smith* 325.286: Almost I am as blynde as a be. Svartengren 173.

B164 As blithe as any **Bee**
a1450 *Castle* 104.901: Beth now blythe as any be. Whiting *Scots* I 137.

B165 As busy as a **Bee**
c1380 Chaucer *CT* VIII[G] 195: Lo, lyk a bisy bee, withouten gile, **c1395** IV[E] 2422–3: For ay as bisy as bees Been they, us sely men for to deceyve. **a1400** *Scottish Legends* II 371. 98–9: For cecil as besy be Ententifly servit has the. **c1405** *Mum* 56.989: The bee in his bisynes, 57.1051. **a1425** *St. Anthony* 117.22–4: And so, as a bese bee, wlde he never turne home agayn untyll-tyme he had fone a holy man. **c1475** Henryson *Fables* 71.2046: I think to work als besie as ane Be. **1513** Douglas *Aeneid* IV 142.58: The bissy beys. Apperson 73, 74; *Oxford* 71; Svartengren 126; Taylor and Whiting 22; Tilley B202; Whiting *Scots* I 137.

B166 As quick as a **Bee**
c1500 *Wife Lapped* 196.395: And then came the mother as quick as a bee. **1546** Heywood *D* 34.38: And home agayne hytherward quicke as a bee. Apperson 518; Tilley B203.

B167 As thick as **Bees**
a1300 *XI Pains* 148.39–40: Thickure hi hongeth ther over al, Than don been in wynterstal. **a1300** *Richard* 438.7003–4: They gunnen on hym as thykke to ffleen, As out off the hyve doth the been. **c1385** Chaucer *TC* ii 193–4: For nevere yet so thikke a swarm of been Ne fleigh, as Grekes fro hym gonne fleen, iv 1356: Alday as

thikke as been fleen from an hyve. **c1400** *Laud Troy* I 186.6294–6: Ther bees sat nevere so thikke on hyve . . . That he ne scles oure men. **a1420** Lydgate *Troy* I 326.6375: As thikke as swarme of ben, II 546.5247: Thikke as swarm of ben. **c1440** *St. Christopher* 464.873–5: For alle thaire arows hange in the ayre, Als thike als leves dose on trees Or ells that thay were swarmes of beese. **1509** Barclay *Ship* I 13[10–1]: Other as thycke doth rowe In theyr small botes, as Bees about a hyve. **a1513** Dunbar *Devillis Inquest* 79.107: Solistand wer as beis thik. Taylor and Whiting 22–3; Tilley B210; Whiting *Drama* 305:21.

B168 As wise as a **Bee**
1456 Hay *Governaunce* 157.26–7: Sum man wys as a bee.

B169 A **Bee** draws honey from bitter herbs
a1450 *Partonope* 2.51–3: The fly wyche ys callud the bee, Hys hony he draweth be hys kynde Off bytter erbes. Tilley B205.

B170 A **Bee** gives honey and stings
a900 *Homeletic Fragment* in *Vercelli Book* 60.18–23: Ænlice beoð, Swa þa beon berað buta ætsomne Arlicne anleofan, ond ætterne tægel Hafoð on hindan, hunig on muðe, Wynsume wist. Hwilum wundiað Sare mid stinge, þonne se sæl cymeð. **a1420** Lydgate *Troy* III 717.5218–9: And as a be, that stingeth with the tonge Whan he hath shad oute his hony sote. **a1449** Lydgate and Burgh *Secrees* 22.679: A bee yevith hony and styngeth with the tayl. **c1450** *Myroure of oure Ladye* 128[2–3]: A bee gyveth hony and styngeth. **a1456** *Passe forth* clxxiv 25–8: Fawvel fareth even right as doth a bee; Hony mowthed, ful of swetnesse is she, But loke behinde and ware thee from hir stonge, Thow shalt have hurt yf thou play with her longe. Apperson 33; *Oxford* 29; Tilley B211; Whiting *Drama* 149.

B171 A dead **Bee** makes no honey
1492 *Salomon and Marcolphus* 11[5–6]: A dede bee makyth no hony. Apperson 32; *Oxford* 132; Tilley B206.

B172 Not worth a **Bee**
a1338 Mannyng *Chronicle A* II 466.13436: And Romayns ar nought worth a be!

B173 Those that drive **Bees** lick their fingers
1492 *Salomon and Marcolphus* 7[12–3]: That beys dryve lykke faste theyre fyngres.

B174 To breed (big [*dwell*]) as **Bees** in the bike (*nest*)
a1460 *Towneley Plays* 391.147: Wormes shall in you brede as bees dos in the byke. **a1500** *Thre Prestis* 29.513–4: With that his wounds war fillit ful of fleis As ever in byke thair biggit onie beis.

B175 To drone like a **Bee**
a1513 Dunbar *Of Discretioun in Asking* 32.8: And he that dronis ay as ane bee. Whiting *Ballad* 26: hum.

B176 To murmur (*etc.*) like a swarm of **Bees**
c1395 Chaucer *CT* V[F] 204: They murmureden as dooth a swarm of been. **a1420** Lydgate *Troy* II 442.1660–1: As a swarme of been, The Grekis flokmel fled, 548.5330. **c1440** Charles of Orleans 7.193–4: But even liche as hit were a swarme of bene So gan ther thoughtis to me multiply. **a1500** *Beves* 72 M 1279–80: Aboute Beves than can they dryve, As Bees done aboute an hyve. Taylor and Whiting 23; Whiting *Drama* 305:21.

B177 To swarm (*etc.*) like **Bees**
a1300 *Richard* 372.5793–4: As bees swarmen abowte the hyves, The Crystene-men in afftyr dryves. **c1300** *Beves* 71.1407–8: So faste hii gonne aboute him scheve, Ase don ben aboute the heve, cf. 74.43–4. **c1350** *Libeaus* 68 *var.* 1217–8: As bene abowte an hyve Of him ran the blod. **c1395** Chaucer *CT* III[D] 1693: Right so as bees out swarmen from an hyve. **a1500** *Court of Love* 410.59–60: And thiderward, as bees, At last I sey the peple gan pursue. **a1508** Dunbar *Flyting* 11.217: The boyis as beis owt thrawis. Taylor and Whiting 23; Whiting *Scots* I 127. See **S937.**

B178 **Beef** has bones, eggs have shells, but ale has nothing else
a1500 Greene *Carols* 422 A 2.5: Bryng us in no befe, for ther is many bonys, But bryng us in good ale, for that goth downe at onys . . . Bryng us in no eggys, for ther ar many schelles, But bryng us in good ale, and gyfe us noth(y)ng ellys. **a1529** Skelton *Elynour* I 107.277–81: And blessed her wyth a cup Of newe ale in cornes; Ales founde therin no thornes, But supped it up at ones, She founde therin no bones. Apperson 75: Buy(7); *Oxford* 74; Tilley L52. See **B446.**

B179 As foul as **Beelzebub**
c1450 *Weddynge* 251.345: Thowghe she were as foulle as Belsabub.

B180 As blind as a **Beetle**
a1378 *Piers* C (ed. W. W. Skeat, EETS 54, 1873 [1859]) xviii 38 (*var.*): He was blynd as a betil. **a1450** *St. Editha* 81.3632: Bot as bleynde as a betulle they weron evermore. Apperson 54:12;

Oxford 50; Svartengren 171–2; Taylor and Whiting 24; Tilley B219.

B180a Beetle-blind
1532 More *Confutacion* 397 C[15]: So beetle blynded, 1533 579 F[14–5]: We be not yet so betle blynd, 580 A[11, 14], D[13], F[5], 581 A[8], 582 A[6–8]: Till either some blind bettle, or some holy bumble bee come flye in at their mouthes. **1556** Heywood *Spider* 4[11], 90[5], 142[14]: I were a beaste of beetill heded blindenes, 390[28].

B181 As dull as a **Beetle**
1520 Whittinton *Vulgaria* 36.17–8: As dull as a betle. Obtusa qualis est pistillus (*pestle*). Apperson 170; *Oxford* 161; Tilley B220.

B182 With a **Beetle** be he smitten who gives his son all his things
a1300 *Royal MS. 8. E xvii* in Brown *Register* I 362: Wyht suylc a betel be he smyten, That al the werld hyt mote wyten, That gyfht his sone al his thing, And goht hym self a beggyn. **a1375** John of Bromyard *Summa* in T. Wright *Selection of Latin Stories*(PS 8[1842]) 221: Wit this betel the smieth, And alle the worle thit wite, That thevt the ungunde alle this thing, And goht him selve a beggyng. **a1400** *Trinity MS. 0 9. 38* in Furnivall *Babees Book* 35: With thys bytel be he smete, that alle the worle mote hyt wete, That yevyt hys goode to hys kynne and goth hym sylfe A beggyng. **c1415** *Middle English Sermons* 90.35–8: With this betull be he smytte, That all the world well it witt, That yeveth the unkeend all is thinge, And goyth hym-selfe on beggynge. **c1450** *Rylands MS.394* 105.31–2, 1–2: With a betull be he smeton, That alle the world may it weton, That yeves his childe alle his thynge, And gooth hym selfe abegynge. *NQ* 4 III (1869) 526, 589; Tilley G308.

B183 A **Beggar's** appetite is always fresh
a1449 Lydgate *Cok* in *MP* II 817.141: A beggers appetight is alwey ffressh and good. Cf. Apperson 34: beggar's purse; *Oxford* 31: Beggar's scrip; Tilley B242.

B184 A **Beggar** should not go away for warning once
1471 Caxton *Recuyell* I 116.6–8: But he remembrid that a beggar shold not go away for ones warnyng.

B185 Beggars should be no choosers
1546 Heywood *D* 40.170: Beggers should be no choosers, **1555** *E* 149.18. Apperson 34; *Oxford* 31; Taylor and Whiting 24; Tilley B247.

B186 Nothing worse than a **Beggar** (poor man) who has domination (*varied*)
a1439 Lydgate *Fall* II 651.2369–75: Nothyng mor cruel, nor nothyng more vengable, Nor mor hasti to execucioun, Nor mor deynous, nor mor untretable, Than whan a beggere hath domynacioun: A curre mor froward than a strong leoun. And semblabli, non so gret cruelte As whan a wrech is set in dignite, III 1004.3025–8: Whan beggers rise to domynacioun, Is non so dreedful execucioun Of cruelte, yif it be weel souht, Than of such oon that cam up of nouht, **c1440** *Debate* in *MP* II 564.601–3: A parlious clymbyng whan beggerrs up arise To hih estat—merk this in your mynde—Bi fals prerogatives ther neihbours to despise, **a1449** *Look* in *MP* II 767.65–8: Reyse up a beggere that cam up of nouht, Set in a chayer of wordly dignite. Whan fals presumpcioun is entryd in his thouht, Hath cleene forgete his stat of poverte, *World* in *MP* II 844–5.20–3: A beggere sett in a chayer of degree, Hym silff not knowyng in sovereyn dignite, If this teerme to hym were appliable, Clene forgetith his consanguinite. **a1500** *English Conquest* 113.32–4: For ther is nothynge so bolde ne so kene, as is that man that is of noght come, whan he is an-hey broght, and unkyndely sette in Maystry. **1523** Berners *Froissart* I 264[6–7]: Poore men first mounteth up, and unhappy men sleeth them at the ende, **1525** V 5–6: It is sene, a poore man mounted into gret estate and in favoure with his mayster, often tymes corrupteth and distroyeth the people and the realme. Cf. Apperson 35; *Oxford* 30–1; Taylor and Whiting 24; Tilley B238. See **C271, W714.**

B187 One **Beggar** is woe that another goes into the town (by the door)
c1450 *Douce MS.52* 49.66: On begger is wo, that anothir in to the towne goth. **c1450** *Rylands MS.394* 100.12. **1520** Whittinton *Vulgaria* 71.28–9: But it is comenly sayd, every begger is woo that ony other shold by the dore go. Apperson 35; *Oxford* 30; Tilley B237. See **D318, K82.**

B188 To bind a **Beggar** is folly
a1500 *Hunterian Mus. MS. 230* 175: Yt is folly to byend a begare (*so* Robbins-Cutler 1628.8), Yff it be wyell soyghtt, Whanne it is provyd that he have Ryghtt noghtt. Cf. Tilley B226.

B189 To know as well as a **Beggar** knows his bag
1546 Heywood *D* 48.219–20: And my selfe knowth him . . . Even as well as the begger knowth his bag. *Oxford* 30; Tilley B234.

B190 To be brought to **Beggar-staff**
c1510 *Plumpton Correspondence* 199[33]: We are brought to begger staffe. NED Beggar 8.

B191 At the **Beginning** put the remedy (*varied*)
a1420 Lydgate *Troy* I 369.7873–4: Wherfore, at the gynnyng The remedie is put of every thing. **1422** Yonge *Governaunce* 161.33–5: The grete Poet Ovydie Sayth, Pryncipijs obsta, "Wytstonde the begynnynge," ffor lyghtyre is a fressh wounde to hele, than a festrid, 164.14. Ovid *Remedia Amoris* 91–2. Cf. Tilley B263; Whiting *Drama* 247.

B192 At the **Beginning** the way is longest
c1415 *Middle English Sermons* 148.15–6: And men sey, "At the begynnynge the vey is lengest."

B193 The **Beginning** is more than half the work (*varied*)
c1415 *Middle English Sermons* 148.16–7: And the wise man seth that halfe he hath don that well begynneth is werke. **c1495** *Arundel Vulgaria* 21.82: It was a noble sayng of Aristotle: Begynnynge is more than halfe the worke. Horace *Epistles* I 2.40: Dimidium facti qui coepit habet. Apperson 674; *Oxford* 700; Tilley B254; Whiting *Drama* 165, *NC* 369, *Scots* I 137: Begin (2).

B194 The **Beginning** of wisdom is the fear of God (*varied*)
c900 *Paris Psalter* 95 (110.7): þæt byð secga gehwam syntru on frymðe, þæt he godes egesan gleawe healde. **a1000** *Pseudo-Alcuin De Virtutibus* 388.434: Godes ege is se frume wisedom. **c1000** *Regius Psalter* 214 (110.10): Fruma wisdomes (is) ege (Hlafordes). **a1050** Defensor *Liber* 64[16]: Salomon sæde angynn wisdomes ege drihtnes. **c1100** *Salisbury Psalter* 236 (110.10). **c1300** *Speculum Gy* 40.883–4: Initium sapientiae, timor domini: "Drede of god in alle thing Off wisdom is the beginning." **c1350** *Prose Psalter* 139 (110.9). **c1395** *WBible* Psalms cx 10: The bigynnyng of wisdom is the drede of the Lord, Proverbs ix 10. **c1400** *Treatise of Perfection* 238.29–30: Salomoun in the proverbes says: Drede of god is the begynnynge of wisdome. **c1412** Hoccleve *Regement* 175.4852: Begynnynge of wisdom is, god to drede, **c1422** *Lerne to Die* 209.840: Begynnynge of wisdam is dreede of god. **a1425** *Contemplations* in *Yorkshire Writers* II 76[21]: I Rede that the drede of god is begynnynge of wysedom. **c1450** *Serve thy god* 262.25–6: Ffor the begynnyng of wysdom is for to drede goddys ryghtwysnes.

B195 A **Beginning** that is not virtuous is followed by a contagious end
a1420 Lydgate *Troy* I 119.3619–20: For her gynnyng was nat vertuous, An ende folweth ful contagious.

B196 **Beginning** without end avails as a flowered tree where the fruit fails
a1500 *Colkelbie* 280.25–6: Ffor begynnyng without end quhat availis Bot lyk a tre flureist quhair the fruct falis. See **T104.**

B197 A blissful **Beginning** is one that has a fair issue (*varied*)
a1400 *Destruction of Troy* 75.2256–7: A Proverbe: A blisfull begynnyng may boldly be said, That ffolow to the fer end and hath a faire yssue. **a1500** *Partenay* 34.789–90: Se here a noble gynnyng in presence! God yif that the ende therof be ful good!

B198 Every **Beginning** is hard
c1475 *Rawlinson MS. D 328* 126.86: Every begynnyng hys harde. **c1495** *Arundel Vulgaria* 21.82: For the begynnynge of every thynge is the hardiste. Tilley B256.

B199 An evil **Beginning** has a foul ending (*varied*)
c1300 *Becket* II 114.1459–60: Therfore god for righte wreche uvel ginnyng (*Becket I* 73.1439: ending) me doth sende, And ic doute for my wrecche gult, that worse schal beo the ende. **a1415** Mirk *Festial* 120.10–1: Then, for hyt ys oft sene, all evell begynnyng hathe a foule endyng. **a1439** Lydgate *Fall* I 325.4465–6: A fals begynnyng, auctours determyne, Shal be processe come onto ruyne, III 864.1468: His gynyng cursid, hadde a cursid fyn, 886.2241: Ther gynnyng cursid hadde a wengable fyn. **c1475** Gregory *Chronicle* 191–2: But welle I wote that every ylle begynnynge moste comynly hathe an ylle endyng, and every goode begynnyng hathe the wery goode endyng. *Proverbium: —Felix principium finem facit esse beatum.* Apperson 193; Tilley B261. See **C119, F695, 700, T180.**

B200 A fair **Beginning** may have a foul end
c1410 Lovelich *Grail* I 168.769–70: For there say nevere Man So fayr A begynneng As hadde kyng Tholome, ne so fow(l) An Endyng. **a1420** Lydgate *Troy* I 209.2242–4: For though a gynnyng have his appetite, Yet in the ende, pleynly this no fable, Ther may thing folwe, whiche is nat commendable. **1471** Caxton *Recuyell* I 220.8–9: The begynnyng is fayr but the end is fowle. See **C403, E131, F498, G20, 281, M188.**

B201 A ferly (*wonderful*) **Beginning** often flecches (*gives way*) at the end (*varied*)
c1300 *South English Legendary* (*Laud*) 413.378: Ase ofte verlich bi-guynninge: flechchez atthen

ende. **c1385** Chaucer *TC* ii 791: Ful sharp bygynnyng breketh ofte at ende. See **B197.**

B202 A fortunate **Beginning** that causes strife is worthless
a1420 Lydgate *Troy* I 209.2245–6: For what is worthe a gynnyng fortunat, That causeth after strif and gret debat?

B203 A good **Beginning** is spilled (*spoiled*) with a bad ending
a1475 *Tree* 119.11–2: Many . . . spille here good by gynnyng with a bad endyng. Cf. Whiting *Drama* 151.

B204 A good **Beginning** makes a good end(ing)
c1300 *South English Legendary* I 216.67–8: This was atte verste me thingth a god begynnynge, Ther after was the betere hope to come to god endynge. **c1325** *Hendyng H* 288.13: God beginning maketh god endyng. **c1375** Barbour *Bruce* I 121.263–6: For gude begynnyng and hardy, And it be followit vittely, May ger oftsiss unlikly thing Cum to full (conabill) endyng. **a1419** *Letter* in *MLR* 22(1927) 75[7–8]: Make a good end of that they han well bygonne. **a1449** Lydgate *Haste* in *MP* II 764.155–7: A goode begynnynge requireth a good issue, A good preamble a good conclusyon, For vertuous lyff vertuous gwerdon. **a1450** *Partonope* 438.10820–1: Thes wordes ye seyn full trew they be, Thing wele ended is wele be-gonne. **c1450** *Douce MS.52* 55.122: Of a gode begynnyng comyth a gode endyng. **c1450** *Rylands MS.394* 105.18.26. **a1471** Ashby *Policy* 38.824–5: And your matiers shall have goode begynnyng, And consequently come to goode endyng, **a1475** *Dicta* 93.1105–6: So of goode begynnyng is goode endyng, And of shreudenesse comethe Il concludying. **c1475** Gregory *Chronicle* (see **B199** above). **c1475** *Rawlinson MS. D 328* 117.1.2: A good be-gynnyng makyth a god ende. **a1500** *Additional MS. 37075* 277.1. **a1500** Hill 129.42. **1546** Heywood *D* 37.71: Of a good begynnyng comth a good end, **1555** *E* 171.141. Apperson 257, 674; Kneuer 16–7; *Oxford* 250; Schleich 247; Singer III 24–5; Skeat 67; Taylor and Whiting 24; Tilley B259; Whiting *Drama* 127, *Scots* I 137. See **L94, T200, W646.**

B205 A harsh (hard, ill) **Beginning** has a good end(ing)
c1420 Wyntoun VI 267.27–8: Thus eftyr a royde harsh begynnynge Hapnyt a fast and gud endynge. **c1450** Trevet 241.19–20 [f.49a, col. 2]: In trust and hopyng that thys harde begynnyng God woll convey hit to a full good endyng. **1546** Heywood *D* 25.21: And a hard beginnyng makth a good endyng, 90.74: And tourne his yll begynnyng to a good ende, **1555** *E* 150.21: Of a harde beginning, comth a good endyng. Apperson 284; *Oxford* 250; Tilley B260.

B206 It is as good to lose at the **Beginning** as in the end
1478 *Cely Papers* 11[1–2]: It ys as good for to lese in the begeyng as in the ende.

B207 No good **Beginning** without a good end(ing)
c1000 Aelfric *Homilies* I 56[25–7]: Forðan ðe ne bið nan anginn herigendlic butan godre geendunge. **1422** Yonge *Governaunce* 157.11–2: For wyth-out a good ende, lytill is worth a good begynnynge. **1504** Hawes *Example* Ccl^v[27]: Wo worth begynnynge without good ende. Cf. Jente 140.

B208 Such **Beginning** such end
1546 Heywood *D* 94.130: Such beginnyng suche ende we all daie see. Apperson 607; *Oxford* 31; Tilley B262.

B209 What has a **Beginning** must have an ending
c1410 Lovelich *Merlin* I 108.4037–8: There nas nevere thyng that hadde begynneng, But of necescite it moste haven endyng. **c1450** *Merlin* I 54[34–5]: Ther is no-thynge that hath begynnynge, but it moste have endynge.

B210 A wise **Beginning** is praised by the end
a1420 Lydgate *Troy* I 131.4024: Wis begynnyng is preysed be the ende. See **P39.**

B211 He that has once been **Beguiled** ought to keep him from the same
1484 Caxton *Aesop* 203[9–11]: And therfore he that hath ben ones begyled by somme other ought to kepe hym wel fro the same. Apperson 468. See **C201.**

B212 A **Beguiler** will ever beguile others
1484 Caxton *Aesop* 58[4–5]: For a begyler wylle ever begyle other.

B213 To defraud the **Beguiler** is no fraud
c1450 *Alphabet* I 167.27–8: Fallere fallentem non est fraus. **1474** Caxton *Chesse* 116[8–9]: Hit Is sayd in proverbe to defraude the beguylar is no fraud, **1484** *Aesop* 50[4–5]: For as men saye it is meryte to begyle the begylers. Tilley D182; Walther II 19.8746. See **F610, G487, M114, V34.**

B214 **Behest** (Hote, Promise) is debt
a1338 Mannyng *Chronicle B* II 284[8–10]: Hote is dette thing, ther treuth has maistrie . . . Your hote salle be holden, als dette in that manere, [23]: For your hote is dette als to me. **c1390** Chaucer *CT* II[B] 41: Biheste is dette.

c1412 Hoccleve *Regement* 64.1772: And of a trewe man, be-heste is dette. **c1450** Idley 89.488: I calle never suche a promyse to be a dette. **c1477** Caxton *Jason* 183.12–3: I have promised hit and promis is dew. **a1500** *Lovely Song of Wisdom* 196.21.2: For of a trewe mane byheste es dett. **a1500** *Young Children's Book* 19.49: Fore every promys, it is dette. **c1500** *Everyman* 10.248: Promyse is duyte, 28.821: Wyll you breke promyse that is dette? Apperson 513; Jente 460; *Oxford* 520; Skeat 241; Tilley P603; Whiting *Drama* 92, 93, 258. See **C483, H378.**

B215 Fair **Behests** (Promises, Words) make fools (sots) fain (*varied*)
c1325 *De Clerico* 153.24: Feir biheste maketh mony mon al is serewes mythe. **a1338** Mannyng *Chronicle A* I 175.4979–80: Ffor y have herd seye fele sythe, That faire byhestes maketh foles blithe. **a1449** Lydgate *Amor* in *MP* II 748.97–8: The faire behestis maken foolis gladde, Fye on the werk whan hestis ben contrayre, *Fabules* in *MP* II 594.825–6: As it fallythe at preffe, offt(e) sithe, Fayr behestes makythe foles oftetyme blythe. **a1470** Parker *Dives* X7v[1.6–7]: For fayre byhestes make sottes blythe. **1471** Ripley *Compound* 157[14]: And so fayre promys makyth folys fayne. **a1475** *Vision of Philibert* 25[19]: Fayre promese ofte makyth foollis fayne. **c1475** *Rawlinson MS. D 328* 118.11: A fere beheyste makyt a fole gladde. **a1500** Hill 128.11: Faire behestis makith folis fain. **a1500** *Lovely Song of Wisdom* 196.20.4. **a1500** Warkwork 20[15]: Fayre wordes and promyses makes fooles fayne. **c1500** *Everyman* 14.379. **c1500** *Lady Bessy* 2[23]. **1503** *Plumpton Correspondence* 176[15]: Your frinds trowes ye beleve fayr words and fayr heightes. **1546** *Heywood D* 73.117: Let faire woordes make fooles fayne, **1555** *E* 178.180. Apperson 200; Jente 610; MED bihest 1b (b); *Oxford* 188; Tilley W794; Whiting *Ballad* 23, *Scots* II 160. See **H470.**

B216 Trust to no **Behest**
c1460 *To you beholders* 48.18: And trust to no behest. **a1500** Hichecoke *This Worlde* 333.38: Yn many beheste ys litell truste.

B217 She that cannot **Behight** (*promise*) small may she do
c1425 Hoccleve *Jonathas* 226.302–3: Smal may shee do that can nat wel byheete, Thogh nat parfourmed be swich a promesse. Cf. Apperson 506: He is poor indeed that can promise nothing; *Oxford* 511; Tilley N261.

B218 He that should go **Behind** many times goes before
a1393 Gower *CA* II 348.1737–9: And thus I finde That he that scholde go behinde, Goth many a time ferr tofore.

B219 **Belief** has the mastery and reason is under
a1471 *English Chronicle* 77[3–4]: Fle reasoune, and folow the woundre, For beleve hathe the maystry and reasone ys under.

B220 **Believe** it not till you see it
c1330 *Seven Sages A* 197.486: I leve hyt not tyll y hyt see. Tilley B268. Cf. Whiting *Drama* 112.

B221 **Believe** not all you hear (*varied*)
a1250 *Proverbs of Alfred* 106 C 325–8: Ne gin thu nefre lev(en) Alle mannes speche. Ne alle the thinge That tu (herest) singe. **c1280** *South English Legendary: OT History* 84.94: Ne al that thou herest, ne leve thou noughth: yif thou wilt wel fare. **a1393** Gower *CA* II 64.1062–3: On other half, men scholde noght To lihtly lieve al that thei hiere, 143.471: Sche lieveth noght al that sche hiereth. **1438** *Barlam and Josaphat* (*Northern*) 232.521: Ne trow noght all that thou heres say. **a1450** *Barlam and Josaphat* (*South English Legendary*) 124.353–4: Ne leve thu never alle thing that thu myght here, For men lyeth ofte moche, whan they speke I fere. **a1450** *Myne awen dere* 165.509–10: Whare-evere thou commes amange thy perys, Thou trowe noght all thynge that thou herys. **a1484** Caxton *Aesop* 37[1–2]: It is not good to byleve all suche thynges as men may here. **a1500** *Disciplina Clericalis* 47–8: Beleeve nor trust nat to every man. Apperson 36; *Oxford* 32. See **H617, M115, 310, 749, S487.**

B222 **Believe** well and have well
1546 Heywood *D* 91.31: Beleve well, and have well, men say. Apperson 36; *Oxford* 32; Tilley B265.

B223 He that **Believes** each man seldom does well
a1200 Lawman I 342.8017–8: Yif thu ilevest ælcne mon, Selde thu sælt wel don. Apperson 36; Jente 317; *Oxford* 32; Skeat 6.

B223.1 **Believing** often deceives its master
a1533 Berners *Huon* 149.22–3: But often tymis belevynge desseyveth his mayster.

B224 As blithe as a **Bell**
c1470 *Wallace* 24.223: Compleyne also, yhe birdis, blyth as bellis. **c1475** Henryson *Fables*

83.2421: The Tod lap on land, als blyith as ony bell. NED Blithe A 2.

B225 As blue as a **Bell** (*?a flower name*) (*etc.*) (A number of single quotations are brought together here)
a1400 *Moder of gresse* 182.727: His flour is blew like to a belle. **c1420** Page *Siege* 200.1279–80: With that they cryde alle "newelle," Also schyrle as any belle. **a1425** *Somer Soneday* in *Rel. Ant.* II 7[10–1]: Kenettes questede to quelle, Al so breme (*loud*) so any belle. **a1450** *Castle* 184.3592: Thou devyle bold as a belle. **c1450** Greene *Carols* 452.10: Sone my wombe began te swelle A(s) greth (*great*) as a belle. **a1475** *Liber Cure Cocorum* 39[20]: As tome (*empty, light*) as belle hit wille hit make.

B226 As round as a **Bell**
c1400 *Beryn* 84.2784–5: The tre I told to-fore, that round as any bell Berith bowe and braunce. **1402** *Daw Topias* 69[21–2]. **a1460** *Spurious Chaucerian line* in Manly-Rickert VI 495–6: Stif and round as ony belle. **c1460** *Satirical Description* 200[4]: Here jowys been rownde as . . . bele. **1471** Ripley *Compound* 134[19]: Round as any Bell.

B227 As sweet as **Bell**
1501 Douglas *Palice* 20.25: Voices sweit as bell. Whiting *Ballad* 26.

B228 A **Bell** without clapper is without sound
a1393 Gower *CA* II 310.346–7: Withoute soun as doth the belle, Which hath no claper forto chyme.

B229 No need to hang a **Bell** on a bitch's tail
c1250 *Hendyng O* 199.42: Tharf the nevere houngen belle on bicchetaille. Kneuer 60–1; Schleich 275–6; Singer III 141.

B230 To bear the **Bell**
c1303 Mannyng *Handlyng* 144.4274: Yn alle sloghnesse he bereth the bel. **c1385** Chaucer *TC* iii 198–9: And lat se which of yow shal bere the belle, To speke of love aright! **a1400** *Ipomadon A* 137.4782: Of bounte berethe the bell, 169.5893. **c1400** *Thomas of Erceldoune* 12.219. **c1408** Lydgate *Reson* 52.1946: Of beaute for to bere the belle, **a1420** *Troy* I 32.716, II 552.5470: That to-forn alle bare a-weie the belle. **a1450** *York Plays* 228.195. **c1450** *Epistle of Othea* 10.4, 68.20. **c1450** Greene *Carols* 30.1. **c1450** Idley 184.1557. **c1450** *Weddynge* 257.595. **1456** *Princes most excellent* in Mary D. Harris ed. *The Coventry Leet Book* (EETS 135, 1908) II 289[22]: I, Alexander, that for chyvalry berith the balle (*rime:*principall). **a1460** *Towneley Plays* 106.186, 172.197. **1464** *God Amend* in Robbins *Historical Poems* 198.42. **1464** Hardyng 39[11], 143[32]. **a1471** Ashby *Policy* 33.645, **a1475** *Dicta* 64.488. **a1475** *Ludus Coventriae* 151.5, 178.2. **a1475** *Talk of Ten Wives* 29[12]. **a1500** *Basyn* 47.80. **a1500** *O man beholde* in *JEGP* 35(1936) 253[8]. **a1500** *Power of the Purse* in Robbins 56.26. **c1500** *Wife Lapped* 190.246. **c1516** Skelton *Magnificence* 47.1498, **1523** *Howe the Douty Duke* II 73.183: We bear away the bell, **a1529** *Garnesche* I 127.27. **1546** Heywood *D* 39.130: For beautie and stature she beareth the bell, **1556** *Spider* 176[25]: Yet doth that glossie web beare the bell awaie, 286[18]. Apperson 30; *Oxford* 32; Skeat 173; Tilley B275; Whiting *Drama* 334:393, *Scots* I 138. See **B36, 372, C576, F316, L71.**

B231 To burn like a **Bell**
a1400 *Awntyrs* 131.188: I burne als a belle. **a1425** *St. Robert* 52.349: I sall gar bryn yowe als a belle.

B232 To hang the **Bell** about the cat's neck
c1378 *Piers* B Prol. 168–70 (cf. 146–81; C i 165–95): To bugge a belle of brasse or of brighte sylver, And knitten on a colere for owre comune profit, And hangen it up-on the cattes hals. **1388** *On the Times* in Wright *Political Poems* I 274[3–4]: The cattys nec to bylle *Hic et hic ligare veretur.* **1509** Barclay *Ship* II 254[4]: About the Cattis necke suche men a bell doth tye (*From the woodcut and probably unrelated*). **c1522** Skelton *Colyn* I 317.163–5: And loth to hang the bell Aboute the cattes necke, For drede to have a checke. **1546** Heywood *D* 48.241: And I will hang the bell about the cats necke, **1555** *E* 191.255: Who shall ty the bell about the cats necke how, Not I (quoth the mouse) for a thing that I know. Apperson 88; P. F. Baum in *MLN* 34(1919)462–70; *Oxford* 32; Taylor and Whiting 60; Tilley B277.

B233 To have one's **Bell** rung
1381 John Ball in Knighton II 139[28–9]: Jon Balle gretyth you wele alle and doth yowe to understande, he hath rungen youre belle. **c1385** Chaucer *TC* v 1062: Thorughout the world my belle shall be ronge! **a1393** Gower *CA* II 176–7.1727–9: How Perse after his false tunge Hath so thenvious belle runge, That he hath slain his oghne brother, 238.452: And ek so lowde his belle is runge. **a1405** Lydgate *Black Knight* in *MP* II 393.262: And Fals-report so loude ronge the belle. **a1450** *Partonope* 236.6139–40: And thes wemmen had wel I-ronge

Here belle, wyche was hevy to here, 345.8514–6: Wrake in no wise myght for-bere Hir susters sothes algate to telle, She thought she wolde rynge hir belle. **1513** Douglas *Aeneid* II 3.10: Wyde quhar our all rung is thyne hevynly bell, 22: Presume to write quhar thy sweit bell is rung, IV 191.128. Whiting *Scots* I 138. See **H485.**

B234 To ring like a **Bell**
c1385 Chaucer *TC* ii 1615: He rong hem out a proces lik a belle, **c1390** *CT* VI[C] 331: And rynge it out as round as gooth a belle. **c1440** *Degrevant* 78.1207–8: With twa trompets of the beste, That range als a belle. Whiting *Drama* 305:25, *Scots* I 138.

B235 To ring the (one's black) **Bell(s)**
c1412 Hoccleve *Regement* 70.1929–30: Thei stryven who best rynge shal the belle Of fals plesance. **1506** Hawes *Pastime* 135.3544–5: Her name was alyson that loved nought elles But ever more to rynge her blacke belles (Note 238: "The allusion is not entirely clear, but almost certainly obscene.").

B236 To speak like a **Bell** (*etc.*) (A number of single quotations are brought together here)
a1300 *Alisaunder* 181.3226: He spaak with tunge als a belle. **a1393** Gower *CA* II 100.2390–1: Ther mai nothing his tunge daunte, That he ne clappeth as a Belle, III 73.4640: And clappe it out as doth a belle. **c1400** *Thomas of Erceldoune* 2.31: The wodewale beryde (*resounded*) als a belle. **a1450** *Partonope* 15.533: The hornes sownen as any belle, 420–1.10137–9: Therfore all men that be so light of tonge That as a grete bell that longe is ronge Noyse her lesynges.

Belly, see **Womb**

B237 The **Belly** cries out every day
1519 Horman *Vulgaria* 47[24]: The bely wyll nat let one day skape unserved: but he wyll crye out. Cf. Apperson 37: My belly cries cupboard; *Oxford* 33; Tilley B301.

B238 Better fill the **Belly** than the eye
1474 Caxton *Chesse* 131[8–9]: And therfore hit is sayd in proverbe, hit is better to fylle the bely than the eye. **1522** More *Treatyce* 95 D[11–2]: So farforth that men commonly say, it wer better fil his (*a glutton's*) bely than his eye. Apperson 43; *Oxford* 39; Tilley G146.

B239 A fasting **Belly** may never be merry
a1500 Hill 131.22: A fastyng bely may never be mery. Apperson 204; Tilley B292.

B240 Hill (?Hold) **Belly** fill
c1525 ?Heywood *Gentylnes* 105.426–7: There is no joy nor pleasure in this world here, But hyll bely fyll and make good chere. Tilley B298.

B241 To wish something in another's **Belly**
c1495 *Arundel Vulgaria* 80.335: I wolde thei (*shoes*) were hole in his bely, so gode me helpe, that first shapyde them. Tilley B299; Whiting *Scots* I 138.

B242 When the **Belly** is full the bones would be at rest (*varied*)
a1450 *Three Middle English Sermons* 31.313–4: Vor whan his beli is so vul o mete and drynke that a may no mor, a-non he is sluggi, a-non he is slepi. **c1450** *Jacob's Well* 141.22: Thi bely seyth he is full, and muste take a reste. **c1475** *Mankind* 22.581: I xall slepe, full my bely, and he were my brother. **1492** *Salomon and Marcolphus* 10[27–8]: The wretchyd wombe is full, go we now to bedde. **a1500** *Basyn* 45.39: But when the baly was full, lye downe and wynke. **a1500** Medwall *Nature* G1ᵛ[31–3]: And whan I am well fed, Than get I me to a soft bed My body to repose. **a1500** Hill 129.36: Whan the beli is fwll, the bonis wold hawe rest. **c1515** Barclay *Eclogues* 51.13: When full is the wombe the bones would have rest, 28: A full bely asketh a bed full of rest, **c1523** *Mirrour* 59[28]: And when belly full is, the bones would have rest. **1546** Heywood *D* 62.2. Apperson 38; *Oxford* 33; Tilley B303. See **D396, M477, T257, V11, W368.**

B243 When the **Belly** is full the goad of lust is excited
a900 Alfred *Gregory* 309.15–6: þonne sio womb bið full and aðened, ðonne bið aweaht se anga ðære wrænnesse. Cf. Apperson 38: When the belly is full the mind is amongst the maids; Jente 5; *Oxford* 33; Tilley B304. See **B429, C125, M469, S752, V12, W553.**

B244 To be (play) **Belly-blind**
a1400 *Alexander C* 275.5648: That brynt in bely-blind night as bright as the son. **c1475** Henryson *Fables* 81.2383: Thow playis bellie blind. MED beli 1(c); NED Belly-blind; Whiting *Drama* 305:26.

B245 To have a **Belly-full**
c1475 *Mankind* 23.632: Of murder and manslawter I have my bely fyll. **1483** Caxton *Golden Legende* 162ᵛ[2.30–1]: The werkemen dranke her bely full. **1533** Heywood *Pardoner* B1ʳ[42]: Therfore preche hardely thy bely full. NED Belly-ful; Taylor and Whiting 25; Tilley B306. See **F143.**

B246 To be **Belly-naked**
c1395 Chaucer *CT* IVE 1326: And saugh him al allone, bely-naked. **a1400** *Alexander C* 227.4125: Thare fand thai bernys and bridis and all bale-nakid. **a1500** *Basyn* 51.163: And ran to hir maistrys all baly naked. MED beli 1(c); NED Belly 16a.

B247 The **Beloved** is longed for most
c1025 *Durham Proverbs* 11.9: Æfter leofan menn langað swiðost. Post amabilem hominem durissime tedet.

B248 As bright (*clear*) as a **Beme** (*trumpet*)
a1100 *Phoenix Homily* 147.23: His stemne is swa briht swa beme.

B249 To be a **Bench-whistler**
a1449 Lydgate *Order* in *MP* II 455.176[H]: Al suche benche-whistelers, God lete hem never the. **1555** Heywood *E* 173.153: Thou art a benchwhistler, a shryll whystlyng wenche. But how long hast thou whistled in the kynges benche. Apperson 38; NED Bench-whistler; Tilley B307.

B250 To give one a **Benedicite**
c1300 *Guy*[1] 310 A 5744–5: And yaf him swiche benedicite That he brak his nek. **c1400** *Laud Troy* I 200.6793–4: Ye yaff him suche a benedicite, That he fel dede open the ble. MED benedicite n. 2(b).

B251 Not worth a **Bent** (*piece of grass*)
a1436 *Spurious Chaucerian line* in Manly-Rickert VI 204–5: Your testament is no wurth a bent.

B252 To know the **Bent** of one's bow
a1426 Lydgate *Mumming at Hertford* in *MP* II 680.198: We knowe to weel the bent of Jackys bowe. **c1434** Drury 83.27: Fela, i knowe the bynd of thyn bowe wil i-now. **c1450** Idley 88.438: Thow shalt never kenne the bent of his bowe. **1546** Heywood *D* 47.188: Though I, havyng the bent of your uncles bow, 1555 *E* 189.244. Apperson 38; *Oxford* 34; Tilley B313.

B253 To bow like a **Bercelet** (*hound*)
a1400 *Destruction of Troy* 73.2196: Ger hom bowe as a berslet. **a1500** *Alexander C* 29 Dublin 786*: Was never barslett in band more buxum to hys lord.

B254 **Bernard** is made a monk
c1395 *WBible* I Kings xix 24 *gloss:* This (*i.e.* wher and Saul among profetis) is seide of him, in whom sum devocioun apperith sudeynly at an our, as whanne a man of dissolute liyf schewith ony signe of devocioun, it is seide of him, Bernard is maad a munk, so and thanne it was seid of sich man, wher and Saul among profetis, as if he seide thilke devocioun is transitorie and at an our, and is not stidefast.

B255 **Bernard** the monk saw not all
c1386 Chaucer *LGW* F 16: Bernard the monk ne saugh nat all. R. M. Smith in *MLN* 61(1946) 38–44, 62(1947)190–1, 432; *Oxford* 34.

B256 To know as **Bernard** knew his shield
1473 Paston V 198[13–5]: Master Lacy . . . knowyth my seyde proctor theer, as he seythe, as weell as Bernard knewe his sheeld.

B257 As black as a **Berry**
a1400 ?Chaucer *Rom. A* 928: And blak as bery. **a1470** Malory II 910.5: Blacker than ony beré, 915.35, 934.30–1: Horse and man all black as a beré, 962.27–8: blacker than a byry. Svartengren 245.

B258 As bright as a **Berry**
c1450 *Song of Scorn* in Robbins 163.4: As brith as bery broune.

B259 As brown as a **Berry**
c1387-95 Chaucer *CT* I[A] 207: His palfrey was as broun as is a berye, **c1390** I[A] 4368: Broun as a berye. **1513** Douglas *Aeneid* IV 67.27: Of cullour soyr, and sumdeill broun as berry. Apperson 70; Svartengren 252–3; Tilley B314; Whiting *Scots* I 138.

B259a **Berry-brown**
c1353 *Winner* 91: Berry-brown was his berde. **a1475** *Golagros* 19.551: Bery broune wes the blonk. Cf. **c1500** *Fox and the Goose* in Robbins 43.20: E-mange the beryis browne. Taylor and Whiting 26; Whiting *Ballad* 26, *Scots* I 138.

B260 From **Berwick** to Dover (Kent, Ware)
a1338 Mannyng *Chronicle B* I 120[17–8]: Than the riche and pouere, and alle comonly, For (fro) Berwick to Dovere held hir for lady, II 305[7]: That if alle Inglond fro Berwik unto Kent. **c1387-95** Chaucer *CT* I[A] 692–3: But of his craft, fro Berwyk into Ware, Ne was ther swich another pardoner. Apperson 38–9; *Oxford* 34–5; Tilley B315. See **C45, D369, T545.**

B261 As bright as **Beryl**
c1325 *Annot* 136.1: Ichot a burde . . . ase beryl so bryht. **c1380** *Cleanness* 43.1132: Wel bryghter then the beryl other browden perles. **c1440** *Degrevant* 36.530–1: A lady wyghte, Thare es no beralle so brighte. **c1445** Lydgate *Miracles of St. Edmund* 442.165. **a1475** *Ludus Coventriae* 374.46. **c1485** *Slaughter* (*Digby*) 21.506. **a1500**

Against Adultery 370.146: And als bryght as any ber(i)alle. **c1500** *Smith* 328.530. Whiting *Scots* I 139.

B262 As clean (*pure*) as **Beryl**
c1380 *Cleanness* 23.554: As the beryl bornyst byhovez be clene.

B263 As clear as **Beryl**
a1405 Lydgate *Black Knight* in *MP* II 384.37: Water clere as berel. **c1410** Lovelich *Grail* I 222.265–6: And so Cler be-Cam that Tre withal, As Evere dyde ony berylle. **a1422** Lydgate *Life* 501.1018–9: In a closet more clere than . . . any byrell bryght to be-holde, **a1439** *Fall* I 284.2987: Watris, as any berell cleer. **c1450** *Chaunce* 5.24. Svartengren 361; Whiting *Scots* I 139.

B264 As round as **Beryl**
a1410 Lydgate *Churl* in *MP* II 470.55–6: The burbly wawis in ther up boylyng Round as berel, ther bemys out shewyng.

B265 The **Best** is behind
c1500 Skelton *Comely Coystrowne* I 17.68: The best is behynde. **a1525** *Robin Hood and the Potter* in Child V 111.30: Her es more, and affter ys to saye, The best ys beheynde. **1555** Heywood *E* 170.137: The best is behynde, the woorst is before. Apperson 40; *Oxford* 35; Tilley B318. See **F493, W684.**

B266 The **Best** is best cheap
1546 Heywood *D* 83.119: The best is best cheape. Apperson 39–40; *Oxford* 35; Tilley B319.

B267 Choose (Keep to) the **Best**
c1390 Chaucer *CT* VII 1208[B2398]: And in alle thise thynges thou shalt chese the beste, and weyve alle othere thynges. **1509** Barclay *Ship* I 11[5]: Rede gode and bad, and kepe the to the best.

B268 Deem the **Best** till the truth be tried out
a1400 *Jug inscription* (*British Museum*) in Joan Evans *English Art 1307–1461* (Oxford, 1949) 90[5–6]: Deme the best in every dowt Til the trowthe be tryed out. **c1450** *Harley MS.3810* in *Rel. Ant.* I 92[9–10]: Deme the best of every doute, Tyl the truthe be tryed out, 205[5–6]. **c1450** *Bodley MS.11951* in Furnivall *Babees Book* 332.16–7. **c1450** *Serve thy god* 262.33–4: Deme the best of every dome, Tyl the truthe be tryed out. **c1475** Gregory *Chronicle* 217[25–6]: God knowythe, but every man deme the best tylle the trought be tryde owte. **a1500** *See Much* in Brown *Lyrics XV* 280.31: Loke were thu art yn dowt, and deme the (beste). **a1500** *Think Before you Speak* in Brown *Lyrics XV* 281.35–6: Deme the beste of every dede Tyll trowth have serchyd truly the roote. **1528** More *Heresyes* 105 G[6–7]: It is therfore well done to deme the beste. Apperson 141. Brown-Robbins 3087; Robbins-Cutler 675.5; Tilley B324. See **J77.**

B269 Who does **Best** has best meed
a1325 *Sarmun* in Heuser 95.212: Wo best mai do, best is his mede.

B270 Who does **Best** has least thank
a1393 Gower *CA* III 9.2264–5: For ofte a man mai se this yit, That who best doth, lest thonk schal have.

B271 Who has done **Best** does right well
a1450 *Partonope* 429.10472: Who so hath do beste dothe right wele.

B272 Who says the **Best** shall never repent
a1449 Lydgate *Say the Best* in *MP* II 795.1–2: Who seith the best shal never repent, A vertu callid of full grete reverens, 796–9.43, 59, 67, *etc.—varied refrain.*

B273 A good **Be Still** is worth a groat
a1449 Lydgate *Cok* in *MP* II 815.67–8: And theron was sowyd this scripture, "A good be still is weel wourth a groote," 817.136, 153, 818.171–2: A good be stille with discreet sci-lence, For a good grote may not wel be bought. **1546** Heywood *D* 73.98: A good be still is woorth a grote. Apperson 256; *Oxford* 36; Tilley B329. See **S77.**

B274 Better **Betimes** than too late
a1420 Lydgate *Troy* I 46.1188: But bet it is by-tymes than to late. **1523** Berners *Froissart* III 90[18–9]: It is better to be advysed betyme than to late. Apperson 43: Better early. See **T211.**

B275 The **Better** you are the better besee (*take care of*) yourself
c1250 *Hendyng O* 193.14: So the bet the be, So the bet the bise. **c1250** *Owl* 106–8.1269–72: Forthi seide Alfred swithe wel, And his worde was Goddspel, That evereuch man, the bet him beo, Eaver the bet he hine beseo. **c1450** *Douce MS.52* 53.105: The better thou be The bettur (the) be-se. **c1450** *Rylands MS.394* 103.17.19. Kneuer 31–3; Schleich 256–7; Singer III 130; Skeat 81. See **E32, S671.**

B276 Love your **Better** (*varied*)
a1400 *Proverbis of Wysdom* 245.69–70: Love all way thy better and grugge nott agen thy gretter. **c1450** *Fyrst thou sal* 89.75–6: Worschyp ay thi bettyr And grotche not agayn thi gretter. **c1450**

Ponthus 145.19–20: He that wolle soffre of his bettre and of his grettre, he overcomes hym. **a1500** *Sone, I schal* in Furnivall *Babees Book* 34.12: Unto thi betere evermore thou bowe. See **B485, P345.**

B277 Seldom comes the **Better**
a1247 Odo of Cheriton 179[1]: Selde cumet se betere. **a1325** Odo (*Additional MS. 11579*) in T. Wright ed., *Selection of Latin Stories* (PS 8, 1842) 50[14]: Selde comet the lattere the betere. **a1500** *Douce MS.101* in Odo of Cheriton, *as above,* n.[1]: Sylden ys the latur prophete the bettur. **c1515** Barclay *Eclogues* 17.551–2: When the good is gone (my mate this is the case), Seldome the better reentreth in the place. **1519** Horman *Vulgaria* 434[1]: It is comynly sayd: that selde cometh the better. **1546** Heywood *D* 25.23, **1555** *E* 164.110.4, 111.1. Apperson 556–7; *Oxford* 572; Tilley B332.

B278 What is **Better** than well?
c1390 Chaucer *CT* I[A] 3370: What wol ye bet than weel? **c1395** VIII[G] 1283.

B279 To brew a sorry (lither [*bad*]) **Beverage**
a1300 *Richard* 307.4393: A sory beverage there was browen! **c1300** Robert of Gloucester I 45.621: So that a luther beverage to hare biofthe (*var.* byhofe) hii browe. See **B529.**

B280 As great as a **Bible**
1515 Barclay *St. George* 67.1592: A myghty volume moche gretter than a byble.

B281 As true as the **Bible**
c1400 *Toulouse* 244.552(*var.*): As trew as byble. **a1430** Lydgate *Pilgrimage* 282.10283: Trewe as any byble. See **G399, P48.**

B282 To have more letters than a **Bible**
c1450 Idley 176.1109: I trowe more letter than is in a bible.

B283 The **Bigger** eats the bean
1546 Heywood *D* 73.107: Alwaie the bygger eateth the beane. Apperson 29; Tilley B345.

B284 To be **Bill** under wing (*varied*)
a1393 Gower *CA* III 126.6525–6: What he mai gete of his Michinge, It is al bile under the winge. **a1450** *Seven Sages B* 75.2195–7: And whende hyt were soth that ho sayed, And bylle undyr wynge layede, And toke rest tyl hyt was daye (*literal*). **1546** Heywood *D* 73.113: If he chide, kepe you byll under wyng muet. MED bile n. (1) 1(b); *Oxford* 44; Skeat 134; Tilley B348.

B285 To couch down one's **Bill**
a1393 Gower *CA* II 374.2710–1: If he (*the somnolent man*) mai couche a doun his bile, He hath al wowed what him list. MED bile n. (1) 1(b).

B286 To shake one by the **Bills**
c1380 Chaucer *HF* 868: That he may shake hem be the biles. MED bile n. (1) 1(b). See **B118.**

B287 Fast **Bind** fast find
1546 Heywood *D* 23.28: Fast binde fast finde, **1555** *E* 195.283. Apperson 204; *Oxford* 192; Taylor and Whiting 27; Tilley B352; Whiting *Drama* 100. See **F149.**

B288 He that **Binds** well can unbind well
1484 Caxton *Aesop* 135[22–3]: For who that wel byndeth well can he unbynd. See **B287.**

Bird, see **Fowl**

B289 As blithe as **Bird** on bough
a1330 *Legend of Mary* 501.154: Icham blither than brid on bough. **a1400** *Melayne* 30.921: And als blythe als birde one boughe. **a1450** *Seven Sages B* 103.3035. Taylor and Whiting 27; Tilley B359; Whiting *Ballad* 26, *NC* 370. See **F564.**

B290 As blithe as **Bird** on brier
a1352 Minot 25.128: That are was blith als brid on brere. **c1400** *Seven Sages D* 57.1797. **a1450** *Ave Gloriosa* in Brown *Lyrics XV* 38.13: Als blith as bird on brer. **a1475** *Sinner's Lament* in Anne L. Leonard *Zwei mittelenglische Geschichten aus der Hölle* (Zürich, 1891) 17.42. **c1475** Henryson *Fables* 101.2941. Tilley B359; Whiting *Scots* I 139.

B291 As gentle and jolly as **Bird** on rice ([*twig*], bough)
c1330 *Orfeo* 27.305: Gentil and jolif as brid on ris. **a1400** Chestre *Launfal* 79.931: Gentyll, jolyf as bryd on bowe. **a1475** *Landavall* 125.433: Jentyll and jolyff as birde on bowgh.

B292 As glad as **Bird** of day
c1330 *Degare* 117–8. 967–8(*var.*): And shee was gladde to see that syghtt As ever was byrde of the daye lyght. **c1395** Chaucer *CT* VIII[G] 1342: Was nevere brid gladder agayn the day. See **F566.**

B293 As jolly as **Bird** in May
a1393 Gower *CA* II 109.2703–4: Mor jolif than the brid in Maii He makth him evere freissh and gay. Cf. Tilley B358.

B294 As light as **Bird** on bough (brier)
a1450 *York Plays* 213.388: I am als light as birde on bowe. **a1500** Basterfeld 367.45: Than

was I lyght as byrd on brere. **c1500** *Occupations of the Months* in Robbins 62.5: I am as lyght as byrde in bowe. Svartengren 297. See **F567.**

B295 As meek as **Bird** in cage (*etc.*) (A number of single quotations are brought together here)
c1303 Mannyng *Handlyng* 136.4004: As meke as bryd yn kage. **a1400** *Firumbras* 20.575–6: Was never bryd on morw so redy to flyght, Ne half so wod as roulond was to fyght. **c1400** *Beryn* 27.814: Ffor his hert was evir mery, ryght as the somer bridd. **a1500** *As I fared thorow* in Dyboski 89.41: And man were hayll as birde on bowgh. **a1500** *To his Mistress* in Robbins 204.5: Then was I glade as bryde on brer. **c1500** *From a Caitiff* in Robbins 198.28: In grene growand as bird on brere. **c1500** *King Hart* 85.8: And als so blyth as bird in symmer schene.

B296 As merry as **Bird** on bough, *etc.*
c1410 Lovelich *Merlin* II 336.12586: And also merye as bryd on bowh. **c1450** Greene *Carols* 28 (*refrain*): Man be merie as bryd on berie. **c1450** Idley 178.1200: And that shall make the murie as a birde on a boughe. **c1475** *Wisdom* 56.626. **a1500** *Alexander-Cassamus* 73.497–8: There is no bryde yn Erth meryere yn his cage Than he ys yn that presoun. **c1500** Greene *Carols* p. 320 i[1]: And than I am mery ofte As any byrde on brere. Tilley B359; Whiting *Ballad* 26. See **F568.**

B297 A **Bird** could not come in (fly out) without being seen
a1523 Berners *Froissart* II 237[18–9]: They were so straitly watched . . . that a byrde coud nat come out of the castell without spyeng, III 348[10–2]: A byrde coude scant have flyen into the towne, but that some of the host shulde have sene her, it was so set rounde about. Margaret Erskine *The Family at Tammerton* (New York, 1966) 205: He had that place sewed up so tightly that I doubt if even a fly could have left.

B298 A **Bird** does not change its nest for small occasion
c1515 Barclay *Eclogues* 144.136: For small occasion a birde not chaungeth nest. Cf. Apperson 187: Every bird likes its own nest; *Oxford* 45; Tilley B385; Whiting *NC* 371:17.

B299 The **Bird** flies so oft about the glue (*birdlime*) that he loses his feathers
c1440 Scrope *Epistle of Othea* 109[7–8]: The birde that flieth so ofte abowte the glewe that he lesyth his feddris. MED brid 1c(d). See **B623.**

B300 A **Bird** in a cage desires its liberty
c1390 Chaucer *CT* IX[H] 163–74: Taak any bryd, and put it in a cage . . . His libertee this brid desireth ay. Cf. Tilley B361.

B301 A **Bird** in the hand is better than two in the wood (*varied*)
c1450 Capgrave *Katharine* 93–5.250–2: It is more sekyr a byrd in your fest Than to have three in the sky a-bove, And more profytable to youre be-hove. **c1470** *Harley MS.3362* f.4a in *Retrospective* 309[29]: Betyr ys a byrd in the hond, than tweye in the wode. **c1475** *Rawlinson MS. D 328* 119.27: Hyt ys better a byrd yn hon than iiij with-owyt. **a1500** *Additional MS.37075* 278.17: Better (*MS.* beeter) ys the byrd yn hond than ij in the wodde. **a1500** Hill 128.6: A birde in hond is better than thre in the wode. **1509** Barclay *Ship* II 74[3–4]: Better have one birde sure within thy wall Or fast in a Cage than twenty score without. **c1525** Heywood *Wit* 24[19–20]: An old proverb makythe with thys, whyche I tak good, Better one byrd in hand then ten in the wood, [22–5], 26[19–20], **1546** *D* 46.181: Better one byrde in hande than ten in the wood, **1555** *E* 152.40. Apperson 48; *Oxford* 44–5; Taylor and Whiting 27; Tilley B363; Whiting *Drama* 155, 221, *Scots* I 139.

B302 The **Bird** is not praised for its fair feathers
a1500 *Additional MS.37075* 278.23: No man prysyth the byrde for hys fayre federys. Cf. Tilley F153, 163.

B303 The **Birds** are flown
1546 Heywood *D* 56.40: For er the next daie the birdes were flowne eche one, **1555** *E* 194.280. Apperson 49; *Oxford* 45; Taylor and Whiting 29; Tilley B364; Whiting *Ballad* 35, *Drama* 291. See **N87.**

B304 The **Birds** of heaven shall bear thy voice (*varied*)
c1395 *WBible* Ecclesiastes x 20: For the briddis of hevene schulen bere thi vois, and he that hath pennys, schal telle the sentence. **1546** Heywood *D* 74.140–2: I did lately heere, . . . By one byrd, that in mine eare was late chauntyng. Apperson 48; *Oxford* 45; Taylor and Whiting 27; Tilley B374. See **S123.**

B305 The good **Bird** afaites (*trains*) itself
c1489 Caxton *Blanchardyn* 14.6–8: For it is sayde in comyn langage, that the goode byrde affeyteth hirself. See **B316.**

B306 It is a foul **Bird** that fouls its own nest (*varied*)
c1250 *Owl* 10.98–100: Tharbi men segget a vorbisne: “Dahet habbe that ilke best That fuleth his owe nest.” **c1390** *Of Women cometh this*

Worldes Weal in Brown *Lyrics XIV* 176.73–4: I holde that Brid muche to blame That defouleth his owne nest. **a1400** Bozon *Contes* (Latin) 205[30–1]: Hyt ys a fowle brydde that fylyth hys owne neste. **1402** Hoccleve *Letter of Cupid* 80.183–6: An olde proverbe seyde ys in englyssh: men seyn "that brid or foule ys dyshonest, What that he be and holden ful chirlyssh, That useth to defoule his oune neste." **c1450** Capgrave *Katharine* 391.1593–4: It is neyther wurshipful ne honest On-to mankeende to foule soo his nest. **c1450** Idley 82.89: It is an unclene birde defouleth his neste. **1509** Barclay *Ship* I 173[7]: It is a lewde byrde that fyleth his owne nest. **a1513** Dunbar *In Prais of Wemen* 83.23: That fowll his nest he fylis. **a1529** Skelton *Garnesche* I 125.195–8: Rede and lerne ye may, How olde proverbys say, That byrd ys nat honest That fylythe hys owne nest. **1533** More *Confutacion* 685 B[2–4]: Then shall ye see for lacke of other shift this fayre egle byrde foule befile hys nest. **1546** Heywood *D* 75.163: It is a foule byrd, that fyleth his owne nest. Apperson 323; Jente 677; *Oxford* 314; Taylor and Whiting 28; Tilley B377; Whiting *Ballad* 23, *Scots* I 139.

B307 Like a **Bird** in a cage
c1400 *Laud Troy* II 486.16503: And thow him holdis as brid In cage. **c1450** Idley 179.1271: Keepe hym cloos as a birde an a cage. **1513** Douglas *Aeneid* IV 187.16–7: My muse sal now be cleyn contemplatyve, And solitar, as doith the byrd in cage. **1525** Berners *Froissart* VI 367[18–9]: The kyng than myght have slayne hym . . . as easely as a byrde in a cage, **a1533** *Huon* 207.21–2: These frenchemen are as a byrde beynge in a cage. Whiting *Scots* I 140.

B308 Not a **Bird** to be taken by chaff
1481 Caxton *Reynard* 110[25–6]: I am no byrde to be locked ne take by chaf, I know wel ynowh good corn. Apperson 49; *Oxford* 85; Taylor and Whiting 29; Tilley B396. See **D320.**

B309 One **Bird** can chastise itself by another (*varied*)
a1450 Quixley *Ballades* 48.309: O brid by a nother can hym chastie, 316, 323. **1509** Barclay *Ship* I 204[24–5]: For if one byrde be onys tane in a snare, The other avoyde as fast as they may flee. See **C161, M170.**

B310 To be latched (*caught*) like a **Bird** in snare
a1325 *Flemish Insurrection* 119.83: Hue were laht by the net, so bryd is in snare. Cf. Whiting *Drama* 306:29.

B311 To fly like a **Bird**
c1410 Lovelich *Grail* IV 262.765: And lyk As tweyne briddes they Comen fleynge, 277.4–5: As swyftly as Evere brid gan to fle It drof the vessel forth. **1484** Caxton *Royal Book* G2ʳ[4–5]: Moche faster fledde fro us than byrdes fleyng. **c1515** Barclay *Eclogues* 107.27–8: But start fro my bed, as lightly was I prest, Almoste as a birde out flyeth from her nest.

B312 To keep close as a **Bird** in a bush (*etc.*) (A number of single quotations are brought together here)
a1393 Gower *CA* II 264.1412–3: Bot as a bridd which were in Mue Withinne a buissh sche kepte hire clos. **c1400** *Laud Troy* I 171.5803–4: A Thousand knyghtes alle at ones Fel on Ector as bryddes in grones (*snares; MS.:* groves). **c1450** Idley 189.1867: And laye stille in his bedde as birde in his neste. **c1450** *Merlin* I 183[34–5]: We shall be take as a bridde in a nette. **a1533** Berners *Huon* 475.21–2: They fledde before hym as the byrde dothe before the hauke.

B313 To live as a **Bird**
a1338 Mannyng *Chronicle B* I 153[24]: Dame Jone kept hir dere, thei lyved als birde in cage. **c1395** Chaucer *CT* IV[E] 1281–2: They lyve but as a bryd . . . In libertee. **a1400** Wyclif *Sermons* I 194[20–1]: Lyvynge comun lyf as briddis, and taken noon heede to worldeli goodis.

B314 To ride like **Birds** seeking their prey
1525 Berners *Froissart* V 235[27–8]: These sayd Almayns rode alwayes covertly, lyke byrdes flyeng in the ayre sekyng for their praye. Cf. Whiting *NC* 370: All birds of prey are silent.

B315 We shall catch **Birds** to-morrow
1546 Heywood *D* 89.46: Than we shall catche byrds to morow, **1556** *Spider* 122[27–8]: Be ye there againe (quoth the flie), by my fay, We shall catch byrdes to morow: and flies to day. Apperson 49; *Oxford* 84; Tilley B398.

B316 A well engorged (*fed*) **Bird** keeps well its nest
c1515 Barclay *Eclogues* 51.27: A birde well ingorged kepes well her nest. See **B305.**

B317 As clean (bare) as a **Bird's Arse**
c1475 *Mankind* 18.482: Yt ys as clen as a byrdis ars. **1528** More *Heresyes* 238 B[11–2]: As bare as a byrdes arse. **1546** Heywood *D* 90.60. Apperson 25; Svartengren 254; Tilley B391. Cf. Taylor *Comparisons* 58; Whiting *NC* 431: Jaybird.

B318 He has **Birr** (*wind*) who may bide (it)
a1325 *Hendyng C* 183–4.10: Birre haved, that

wele bide mai. Kneuer 23–5; Schleich 268; Singer III 135–6. See **A8, T303, W264.**

B319 As poor (bare) as the **Bishop** of Chester
a1475 *Herkyn to my tale* in *Rel. Ant.* I 81[4]: Then wax I as pore as tho byschop of Chestur, *Herkons to my tale* 85[4]: I wolde I were as bare as the beschope of Chester! Apperson 25.

B320 A **Bishop** that speaks not is made a porter
1492 *Salomon and Marcolphus* 7[24–5]: A bisshop that spekyth not is made a porter of a gate.

B321 As bollen (*swollen*) as a **Bit** (*leather bottle*)
c1300 *Body and Soul* 37 L 212: That list ther bollen as a bite.

B322 To bridle with a rough **Bit**
1555 Heywood *E* 159.80: I wyll brydell the with rough byt, wyfe.

B323 The **Bitch** bites ill though she bark still (*varied*)
a1250 *Proverbs of Alfred* 132 T 616–21: The bicche bitit ille, Thau he berke stille; So deit the lusninde luthere mon Ofte then he dar-it don Thau he be with-uten stille, He bit with-innin hille. **a1430** Lydgate *Pilgrimage* 408.15150–2: I kan byte also be-hynde With my sharpe tooth fful wel, And yet ne berke neveradel. Apperson 157; Jente 746; *Oxford* 23; Skeat 43; Tilley D503. See **D309.**

B324 To drink the **Bitter** with the sweet
a1393 Gower *CA* II 82.1708–10: He drinkth the bitre with the swete, He medleth sorwe with likynge, And liveth, as who seith, deyinge. See **R220, S945.**

B325 After **Bitterness** comes sweetness
a1200 *Ancrene* 191.13–4: Efter bitternesse kimeth swetnesse. See **B52, E161, 175, F295, 502, H178, J61, L2, 70, P8, S298, 507, T484, W146, 287.**

B326 As true as **Black** is blue
1513 Skelton *Against the Scottes* I 182.17–9: That is as trew As blacke is blew And grene is gray.

B327 **Black** will take no other hue
1546 Heywood *D* 93.86: Blacke will take none other hew. Apperson 53; *Oxford* 49; Tilley B436.

B328 In **Black** and white (white and black)
c1385 Chaucer *TC* ii 1320: Have here a light, and loke on al this blake. **a1439** Lydgate *Fall* I 13.465: Havyng no colours but onli whit and blak, III 1015.3399–400: Nor othir colours this processe tenlumyne, Sauff whyte and blak, 1016.3441, **1439** *St. Albon* 112.99: I have no colours but only blacke and whyte. **a1449** Lydgate and Burgh *Secrees* 11.337–8: I have no Colour but Oonly Chalk and sable, To peynte or portreye. Apperson 53; *Oxford* 47; Taylor and Whiting 30; Tilley B439.

B329 To beat **Black** and blue
a1460 *Towneley Plays* 247.126: Bett hym blak and bloo. *Oxford* 27. Cf. Taylor and Whiting 30.

B330 To make **Black** white (white black)
a1393 Gower III 292.2187–8: Of feigned wordes make him wene That blak is whyt and blew is grene. **a1430** Lydgate *Pilgrimage* 389.14394: And preve also that whyht ys blak. **c1450** *Foly of Fulys* 56.155: Thai luf nocht to mak of blak quhyt. **1480** Caxton *Ovyde* 49[17–8]: He had taughte his sone make of blak whyte and of whyte black. **a1500** *Mischance Reigns* in Wright *Political Poems* II 240[9–10]: Wyght ys blak, as many men seye, And blak ys wyght, but summe men sey nay. **1525** Berners *Froissart* V 8[8–11]: He was so blynded with this duke . . . that if he had sayd, Sir, this is whyte, though it had ben blacke, the kyng wolde nat have sayd the contrayre. **1528** More *Heresyes* 170 A[8–9]: They woulde all tell me that a thynge were white which I see my self is black, **1532** *Confutacion* 403 A[3–5]: We woulde at his word take white for blacke, and blacke for whyte, **1534** *Comforte* 1151 E[4–5]: Wher white is called blacke, and right is called wronge. *Oxford* 48, 705; Taylor and Whiting 30; Tilley B440, 441; Whiting *Drama* 335:406, *Scots* I 140.

B331 What compare is between **Black** and white? (*varied*)
1513 Douglas *Aeneid* II 3.27: Or quhat compar is betwix blak and quhyte. **1533** More *Confutacion* 672 A[4–5]: As unlike as are whyte and blacke. Tilley B438. See **J32.**

B332 **Blackbeard** or whitebeard
1450 Paston II 152[12–4]: Then they shall be quyt by Blackberd or Whyteberd; that ys to sey, by God or the Devyll. MED blak adj. 1(e).

B333 Not set a **Blackberry**
c1412 Hoccleve *Regement* 170.4715: He settith noght therby a blakberie.

B334 To go **Blackberrying**
c1390 Chaucer *CT* VI[C] 405–6: I rekke nevere, whan that they been beryed, Though that hir soules goon a-blakeberyed! MED a-blak(e)-beried Cf. Taylor and Whiting 31. See **S527.**

B335 As fat as a **Bladder**

c1395 *Pierce* 9.222: With a face as fast as a full bledder.

B336 As full as a **Bladder** of wind
c1200 *Vices and Virtues* (*Stowe*) 73.18–9: For here modinesse, hwarof here herte is swa full swa is bladdre of winde.

B337 A **Bladder** full of wind is laid low by a needle's point (*varied*)
a1200 *Ancrene* 145.7–9: A bleddre ibollen of wind ne deveth nawt in to theose halwende weattres, Ah a nelde prichunge warpeth al the windut. **c1380** Chaucer *CT* VIII[G] 438–41: For every mortal mannes power nys But lyk a bladdre ful of wynd, ywys. For with a nedles poynt, whan it is blowe, May al the boost of it be leyd ful lowe. **1483** Caxton *Golden Legende* 365^{r-v}: Thy powre . . . is lyke a bladder ful of wynde, whyche wyth the pryckyng of a nedyll ys anone gon awey and come to nought.

B338 To swell like a **Bladder**
a1430 Lydgate *Pilgrimage* 382–3.14143–4: That, lyk a bladder, in ech cost, I wex swolle with ther bost. Cf. Whiting *Scots* I 140.

B339 As white as **Blanchflower**
c1400 *Laud Troy* II 452.15350–1: Pollexene, That is whitter then Blauncheflour. See **F308.**

B340 Not set a **Blas** (*breath*)
c1420 Wyntoun IV 282.2024: A blase I set nocht by yow baith.

B341 To blow a cold **Blast**
a1460 *Towneley Plays* 127.344: Els blawes a cold blast! See **W309.**

B342 As breme (*fierce*) as **Blaze**
c1385 Chaucer *TC* iv 184: As breme as blase of straw iset on-fire.

B343 As bright as a **Blaze** of fire
c1300 *Havelok* 46.1253–4: Al so briht, al so shir So it were a blase of fir. **a1400** *Scottish Legends* I 264.295–6: Scho aperit til hyr in gret Ire, And visage as bles of fyre. **c1485** *Mary Magdalene* (*Digby*) 91.967: As bryth as fyr'ys blase.

B344 To shine like a **Blaze**
c1000 *Dioskorides* in Cockayne I 300[22–3]: þeos wyrt . . . scineð on nihte swa blæse.

B345 As black as **Bleck** (*ink*)
a1400 *Ipomadon A* 176.6156: Blake as any bleche (*so MS.*) hys face. MED blacche (a). See **I43.**

B346 The **Blessing** of the heathen gods: a short life and evil ending
a1500 *Beves* 70 M 1217–8: They (*heathen gods*) geve the theire blessynge, That is shorte liffe and evill endyng.

B347 To give a **Blessing** in a clout
1546 Heywood *D* 96.186: Ye can geve me your blessyng in a clout. Apperson 254: God-fathers; *Oxford* 248; Tilley G277.

B348 The **Blind** eat many a fly
c1450 *Fyrst thou sal* 90.120: Many a flee etes the blynde. **c1490** *Sloane MS.747* f.66a: The blynde etyth many a flye. **a1500** *Additional MS.37075* 277.3. **a1500** *Scorn of Women* in Robbins 224–5.7, 14, *etc.* (*refrain*). **c1500** *Trials of Old Men in Love* in Robbins 164.8. **c1500** *Of their nature* in Stow *Chaucer* (1561) CCCXLI^{v}[2.14]: Beware alwaye the blind eateth many flye, [2.20–1]: But whether that the blind eate flesh or fish, I pray God kepe the fly out of my dishe. **1528** Skelton *Replycacion* I 213.151–2: But, as the man sayes, The blynde eteth many a flye, cf. 216.244, 252. **1546** Heywood *D* 77.231: The blynde eate many flies, **1555** *E* 175.165, 191.259. Apperson 55–6; *Oxford* 50; Tilley B451; Whiting *Drama* 50, *Scots* I 141. See **F338.**

B349 If the **Blind** bearing the lame stumble, both shall fall
c1385 Usk 72.92–3: (If) the blynde in bering of the lame ginne stomble, bothe shulde falle. **a1500** *O man more* 394.40: The lame man dothe the blynde man lede.

B350 If the **Blind** lead the blind they both fall into the ditch
a900 Alfred *Gregory* 29.7–8: Gif se blinda ðone blindan læt, hi feallað begen on ænne pytt. **c1000** Aelfric *Homilies* II 320[13–5]: Be ðam cwæð se Hælend to his discipulum, "Gif se blinda man bið oðres blindan latteow, þonne befeallað hi begen on sumum blindum seaðe," *Pastoral Letters* 15.65, 130.173. **c1000** *WSG* Matthew xv 14: Se blinda gyf he blindne læt, hig feallað begen on ænne pytt, Luke vi 39. **a1023** Wulfstan *Institutes of Polity* in Napier 276.9–10: Hu mæig bli(n)d man oþerne lædan. **c1200** *Vices and Virtues* (*Stowe*) 127.10: The blinde latt thane blinde. **a1300** *Alisaunder* 265.4742: And wers may blynde blynde siweye. **c1300** *Body and Soul* 49 L 367–8: Ac hwanne the blinde lat the blinde, In dike he fallen bothe two. **a1393** Gower *CA* II 231.179–81: And as the blinde an other ledeth And til thei falle nothing dredeth, Riht so thei hadde non insihte. **c1395** *WBible* Matthew xv 14: And if a blynd man lede a blynd man, bothe fallen doun in to the diche, Luke vi 39. **a1400** *Ancrene* (*Recluse*)

162.33–163.1: As god seith in the gosspell, whan the blinde ledeth the blinde, bothe fallen in the diche. **a1400** Wyclif *Sermons* I 73[28–9]: Lake, 160[11–2], 210[11–2], 305[11–2], II 25[13–4]: But now foolis and sinful men lede other foolis into the diche. **c1400** *Elucidarium* 27[1–2], 31[29–30]: That the blynde ledith the blinde, that al cristendom is nygh fallen into the diche of eendeles dampnacioun. **c1400** *How Men ought to Obey Prelates* in Wyclif *EW* 32[14–5]: Lake. **c1400** *Of Curatis* in Wyclif *EW* 153[1–2]. **c1400** *Of Prelates* in Wyclif *EW* 88[32–3]: Thus blynde anticristis prelatis leden blynde lordis . . . to helle. **c1400** *Satan and his Priests* in Wyclif *EW* 266[25–6]: Lake of synne. **c1400** *Seven Deadly Sins* in Wyclif *SEW* III 133[19–20]. **c1400** *Why Poor Priests Have No Benefices* in Wyclif *EW* 248[15–6]. **c1415** *Middle English Sermons* 139.33–5. **a1425** Mirk *Instructions* 1.1–3. **c1425** *Orcherd* 267.6–7. **c1450** *Speculum Christiani* (2) 172.25–6. **a1475** *Corruption of the Times* in Wright *Political Poems* II 235–7.8, 16, *etc.* (*refrain*): Ffor now the bysom ledys the blynde. **c1500** *Smith* 323.73–5: For, and two blynd men together go, Full oft they fall bothe two—It must nedes be so. **1506** Barclay *Castell* C8^{v}[1–2]: Whan one blynde ledeth another, lyghtly Often they bothe fall in the pytte, **1509** *Ship* I 203[5–6]: A blynde man hym ledyth that also hath no syght, So both in the dyche fallyth. **1509** Fisher *Treatyse* 124.12–3. **1509** Watson *Ship* K2^{r}[26–9]: One blynde man can not love another, but dyffameth eche other, and somtyme the one ledeth the other in an evyll waye and falleth bothe in the dytche and all bycause that they have no guyde. **a1513** Dunbar *Maner of Passing* 168.34–5: Thow ma rycht weill in thi mynde consydder That ane blynde man is led furth be ane uther. **c1516** Skelton *Magnificence* 57.1824: I sawe a losell lede a lurden, and they were bothe blynde. **1546** Heywood D 72.59: Where the blynd leadth the blynd, both fall in the dike. Apperson 56; *Oxford* 51; Taylor and Whiting 33; Tilley B452; Whiting *Drama* 101, *Scots* I 140.

B351 All worldly **Bliss** is mixed with bitterness
a1439 Lydgate *Fall* I 59.2161: Al worldli blisse is meynt with bittirnesse. See **J59.**

B352 **Bliss** that comes after woe is full sweet
a1300 *Jacob and Joseph* 18.533: The blisse is ful swete that cometh after wo. See **S944.**

B353 As blunt as a **Block**
1533 More *Confutacion* 682 F[14]: As blont as a blocke. Cf. Tilley B453.

B354 To fall like a **Block**
c1400 *Cleges* 55.451–2: He gafe the stewerd sych a stroke, That he fell doune lyke a bloke.

B355 To lay a **Block** in another's way
1533 More *Confutacion* 539 C[9–12]: Men might . . . laye a blocke or twayne in hys waye, that woulde breake hys shinnes ere he lepte over it. **1546** Heywood *D* 74.144: I have . . . mo blockes in his waie to laie. Tilley B454.

B356 As black (swart) as a **Bloman** (*Ethiopian*)
a1200 *Ancrene* 121.21: Blac ase blamon. **a1225** *St. Marherete* 24.21–2: Muche deale blackre then eaver eani blamon. **c1300** *South English Legendary* (*Laud*) 372.176: Swarttore thane evere ani bloughman.

B357 As bright as **Blood** (on snow)
a1300 *Tristrem* 38.1354–5: A brid bright thei ches As blood opon snoweing. **c1390** *Salutacioun to ure lady* 135.35: Heil brihtor then the blod on snowe. **c1410** Lovelich *Merlin* II 412.15401–2: And as bryht coloured forto se As dropes of blod in snow. **a1450** *Castle* 87.356: Ther Criste syttyht, bryth as blode.

B358 As red as (any) **Blood**
a1200 Lawman II 243.15940: The other ræd alse blod. **a1300** *Richard* 94.306: A stede rede as blode, 95.333, 106.557. **a1300** *Tristrem* 37.1299–1300: Riche sail thai drewe, White and red so blod. **c1303** Mannyng *Handlyng* 318.10203, 319.10229. **c1308** Adam Davy 15.140. **a1325** *Cursor* II 574.9999: It es rede als ani blod, III 1286.22497: ani. **a1325** *Owayne Miles* (*Auchinleck*) 104.90[3]. **c1330** *Degare* 99.662. **1381** *Ancient Cookery* in *Forme of Cury* 101[20]: any. **a1387** Higden-Trevisa I 123[7]. **c1387–95** Chaucer *CT* I[A] 635. **a1398**(1495) Bartholomaeus-Trevisa C3^{v}[1.32–3), Q2^{r}[2.6], 115^{r}[1.6]. **a1400** *Floris* 91.622. **c1400** *Brut* I 72.31–2, 204.16–7: eny. **c1400** *Florence* 14.387. **c1400** *Laud Troy* I 145.4901–2: any, 214.7272: any, II 402.13646–7: any. **c1400** Mandeville *Travels* 141.17–8. **c1400** *Roland* 131.859–60. **c1410** Lovelich *Grail* II 292.510: any, 360.287: any, 362.375, 365.462, 381.464–5: ony, *Merlin* II 238.8952, III 455.16993: any. **a1415** Mirk *Festial* 132.1. **c1415** *Middle English Sermons* 217.13: anny. **c1420** Wyntoun II 22.119: As blude als rede, IV 381.783–4: And the mone als reide was seyn, Bludlyk as it al blude had beyn. **a1422** Lydgate *Life* 529.1401: any. **a1425** *Ipomadon B* 314.2182: any. **c1433** Lydgate *St. Edmund* 410.786. **a1450** *South English Legendary* (*Bodley*) 381.29. **1464** Hardyng 217[1–2]. **a1470** Malory II 988.8, 990.18–9. **a1471** *English Chroni-*

cle 63[5–6]. **1471** Ripley *Compound* 162[20]. **c1477** Norton *Ordinall* 90[17]. **1483** Caxton *Golden Legende* 139v[1.27–8], 427r[1.14–5]: ony. **a1500** *Croxton Sacrament* in Waterhouse 76.594. **a1500** *Eger* 275.1501: any. **a1500** *Partenay* 113.3213. **a1500** *Right noble Lord* in Ashmole 392[3]: As red as blood as Gold it were. **a1500** *Take Erth of Erth* in Ashmole 270[7–8]. **c1500** Greene *Carols* 78.3. **c1500** *King Hart* 110.18. **c1500** *Lady Bessy* 33[19]: any. **c1515** Barclay *Eclogues* 217.981. Apperson 526; *Oxford* 535; Taylor and Whiting 33; Tilley B455; Whiting *Drama* 306:31, *Scots* I 141.

B358a Blood-red
c1000 Apuleius in Cockayne I 242[15]: Sanguineus, þæt is blodread. **a1100** *Phoenix Homily* 147.11: His fet synden blodreade. **c1300** Robert of Gloucester I 465.6390: A robe . . . of blod red scarlet, II 614.8611. **c1300** *South English Legendary (Laud)* 254.475. **c1308** Adam Davy 13.63. **a1350** (MED a1333) *Quis est iste* in Brown *Lyrics XIV* 28.2. **a1382** *WBible* Isaiah i 18: Thei weren red as blod red silc, **c1395:** Though youre synnes ben as blood reed. **a1400** *Alexander C* 270.5472. **a1400** *Meditations* 12.422, 35.1310: (bl)od-red lilie. **a1400** *Perceval* 20.606, 36.1101. **c1400** *Alexander Buik* III 248.5023. **c1420** Wyntoun II 69.779–80. **c1440** *Revelation* in *Yorkshire Writers* I 389[42]. **a1445** *Carl* 152.563. **a1470** Malory I 321.14–5. **a1500** *Gowther* 154.467(*var.*). **c1500** Greene *Carols* 321.4. **1501** Douglas *Palice* 7.14, **1513** *Aeneid* III 175.40. MED blod-red; NED Blood-red; Taylor and Whiting 33; Whiting *Ballad* 26.

B359 Blood draws to blood
a1420 Lydgate *Troy* II 454.2071–2: For naturelly blod wil ay of kynde Draw un-to blod, wher he may it fynde. Cf. Taylor and Whiting 33: Blood is thicker than water. See **L272, S293.**

B360 Blood (*kin*) may suffer blood to be hungry, but blood may not see blood bleed
c1378 *Piers* B xviii 392–3: For blode may suffre blode bothe hungry and akale, Ac blode may nought se blode blede, but hym rewe. Apperson 439: Need; *Oxford* 570: See him; Tilley S201; Whiting *Scots* I 175: Friend.

B361 Blood will have blood
c1395 *WBible* Genesis ix 6: Who evere schedith out mannus blood, his blood schal be sched. **a1439** Lydgate *Fall* I 199.7048–9: As riht requereth, bi unwar violence, Blood shad for blood is fynal recompence, 309.3897–9, II 353.886: Blood shad for blood, **a1449** *Fabula* in *MP* II 512.802: Blood wil have wreche, that wrongfully is spent. *Oxford* 52; Taylor and Whiting 33; Tilley B458; Whiting *Drama* 263, 281, 284, 291, *Scots* I 141.

B362 Churlish **Blood** seldom recures (*gets*) to be gentle
a1439 Lydgate *Fall* II 559.3156–7: For cherlissh blood seelde doth recure To be gentil be weie of his nature. See **C270.**

B363 Even **Blood,** even good, even age makes meetly (*fitting*) marriage
a1450 Audelay 4.83–5: Evan of blood, evan good, evan of age, Fore love to-geder thus cum thai schalde, Fore thes makus metely maryage, 209.14–6. Apperson 366: Like; *Oxford* 368; Tilley B465. See **C401, L551, M175, Y33.**

B364 Gentle **Blood** loves gentle drink
a1500 *Best tre* in Dyboski 106.81–2: Gentill blode loveth gentill drynk, Nam simile amat simile. See **L272.**

B365 There is no **Blood** in a stockfish
1555 Heywood *E* 184.209: Thou never sawst bloud bleed out of a stockfish. Cf. Apperson 56; *Oxford* 694; Taylor and Whiting 34; Tilley B466, W107.

B366 To fry in one's **Blood**
c1395 *WBible* Song of Solomon v 6 *gloss:* Therfor it is seid of a man left in turment, he is fried in his blood. See **G443.**

B367 To love as one's **Blood**
c1300 *Beves* 77.1468: That i lovede ase min hertte blode. **c1300** *South English Legendary* I 110.9: The quene lovede hure owe sone as echman deth is blod. See **B569, L252.**

B368 True **Blood** may not lie
c1489 Caxton *Aymon* I 248.25: But as men sayen, "true blood may not lye."

B369 Unkind **Blood** comes of unkind blood (*varied*)
c1303 Mannyng *Handlyng* 42.1168: Of unkynde cumth unkynde blode. **a1420** Lydgate *Troy* I 147.132–3: A man for litel wil strive with his brother; Blood is unkynde, whiche gretly is to drede.

B370 To hang like a **Blood-pudding**
a1400 *Ipomadon A* 176.6151–2: Every lype, I dar avowe, Hyngyth lyke a blode puddynge!

B371 As bright as **Bloom**
a1350 *Isumbras* 20.251–2: Hir lyre es als . . . bryghte als blome on tree. **c1390** *Gregorius* 26.203: Ther lai the ladi briht so blom, 116.900: briht so the blome. **c1400** *Florence* 24.686.

B372 To bear the **Bloom**
a1338 Mannyng *Chronicle A* I 146.4166: Of alle knyghtes he bar the blome, 367.10512: That he over hym ne bar the blome, *B* II 322[20]. See **B36, 230, F316.**

B373 To welk (*wither*) like a **Bloom**
a1400 *Northern Verse Psalter* II 11 (102.15): Man his daies ere als hai, Als blome of felde sal he welyen (*for* welken) awa. See **F328.**

B374 As bright as **Blossom**
a1425 *Somer Soneday* in *Rel. Ant.* II 8[29]: Bryght as the blostme, with browes i-bente. **a1450** Audelay 204.29: Breghter then the blossum that blomyth on the hill. **a1500** *Lambewell* I 147.83. **c1500** Newton 264.25. **c1500** *Smith* 328.526. Whiting *Scots* I 141. See **F302.**

B375 As bright as **Blossom** on bough
c1390 *Gregorius* 136.1047: The ladi bright so blosme on bouh. **a1400** *Athelston* 76.290: As bryght as blosme on bowgh. **a1460** *Towneley Plays* 162.70–1: An angell to me drogh, As blossom bright on bogh.

B376 As bright as **Blossom** on brier
c1350 *Libeaus* 36.623–4: A maide y-clipped in arme, As bright as blosme on brere. **c1390** *Gregorius* 6.47: A douhter briht so blosme on brere, 34.286. **a1400** *Athelston* 69.72. **a1400** Chestre *Launfal* 79.934. **a1400** *Le Morte A.* 23.724, 27.835. **a1450** *Castle* 174.3247: Bryther thanne blossum on brere. **a1450** *York Plays* 220.20. **a1475** *Landavall* 125.431. **a1500** *Octavian* (*NC*) 66.40–1. **c1500** Newton 269 xiii 6. **c1500** *Smith* 324.214.

B377 As bright as **Blossom** on broom
c1350 *Gregorius* 116 C 728: The lady bright so blosme on brom (R the brom).

B378 (As) bright as **Blossom** on the spray
1523 Skelton *Garlande* I 417.1412: Her ble was bryght as blossom on the spray.

B379 As bright as **Blossom** on tree
c1390 *Gregorius* 54.432: That er was briht so blosme on treo. **c1400** *Toulouse* 234.332–3.

B380 As comfortable (*pleasing*) as **Blossom** on brier
a1500 *Beauty of his Mistress III* in Robbins 127.17: Your chere ys as comfortable as blossome on brere.

B381 As red as **Blossom** on brier
c1330 *Tars* 33.14: With rode red so blosme on brere. **a1400** *Le Morte A.* 6.179–80: Hyr Rode was rede as blossom on brere, Or floure that springith in the feld. **c1400** *Gowther* 136.35. **a1475** *Seege of Troye* 201 H 1582f.

B382 As sweet as **Blossom** on tree (brier)
a1400 *Meditations* 51.1921–2: He goth awey fro me, Swetter than is the blosme on tre. **a1500** *Coventry Plays* 46.399: Swetter than eyver wasse blossum on brere! See **F307.**

B383 As white as **Blossom** on tree, *etc.*
c1330 *Gregorius* 41 A 58: To hir that was white so blosme on tre, 55 A 166, **c1350** 138 C 875: The lady white so blosme on bow. **c1350** *Octavian* (*NL*) 67.40–1: He byhelde hir faire lyre, Was whyte so blossome on the brere. **c1390** Chaucer *CT* I[A] 3323–4: And therupon he hadde a gay surplys As whit as is the blosme upon the rys. **c1400** *Triamour* 62.628: Sche was whyte os blossom on flowre. **a1508** Dunbar *Goldyn Targe* 114.51: A saill, als quhite as blossum upon spray. Whiting *Scots* I 141. See **F308.**

B384 **Blue** (Inde, Azure) is true (*varied*)
a1325 *Cursor* II 574.9991–3: The midward heu that is of Ind . . . That es takening of al sothfast. **c1370** ?Chaucer *Against Women Unconstant* 7, 14, 21: In stede of blew, thus may ye were al grene. **c1375** Chaucer *Anel.* 329–32: Your figure Before me stont, clad in asure, To profren eft a newe asure For to be trewe, **c1385** *TC* iii 885: This blewe ryng. **c1385** Usk 92.34–6: This jewel, closed in a blewe shel, (by) excellence of coloures sheweth vertue from within, 45–7: Kyndely heven, whan mery weder is a-lofte, apereth in mannes eye of coloure in blewe, stedfastnesse in pees betokening within and without. **c1395** Chaucer *CT* V[F] 644–5: And covered it with veluettes blewe, In signe of trouthe that is in wommen sene. **a1420** Lydgate *Troy* I 74.2090: Whos (*women's*) blewe is lightly died in-to grene, 218.2577: Now stable as blew, **c1433** *St. Edmund* 416.117: The saphir blewh his hevenly stabilnesse, **a1439** *Fall* I 182.6445–7: She wered coloures off many dyvers hewe, In stede off bleu, which stedfast is and cleene; She loved chaunges off many dyvers greene (cf. *MP* II 444.75–7), III 676.43–4: Hir habit was of manyfold colours: Wachet bleuh of feyned stedfastnesse, **1439** *St. Albon* 122.666: The felde of Asure betokneth stedfastnes. **c1440** Charles of Orleans 39.1153–4: The coloure blew Which hewe in love is callid stedfastnes, 161.4807: For as for blew y clothe therin myn hert. **a1449** Lydgate *Fabula* in *MP* II 493.195–6: Of stable blew is her bothen hewe To shewe that too in love wer nevir so trewe. **c1450** Holland *Howlat*

62.430–1: In the takinnyng of treuth and constance kend, The colour of asure, ane hevinliche hewe. **c1450** ?Suffolk *What shal I say* 166.21–2: My colour shal be blewe, That folke may know of my stedfast lyvyng. **a1500** *Assembly* 383.83: Her colours blewe, al that she had upon, 384.116: Al your felawes and ye must come in blew. **a1500** *Court of Love* 415–6.246–8: Lo! yonder folk . . . that knele in blew, They were the colour ay, and ever shall, In sign they were, and ever will be trew. **a1500** *Love Longing* in Robbins 217.89–90: My tombe ytt schalbe blewe In tokyne that I was trewe. **a1500** *Squire* 12.205–6: Then shall ye were a shelde of blewe, In token (that) ye shall be trewe. Apperson 648; *Oxford* 672; Taylor and Whiting 34; Tilley T542; Whiting *Scots* I 141. See **G452.**

B385 At the first (sudden) **Blush**
c1454 Pecock *Folewer* 39.12: At the first bluysch, **c1456** *Faith* 206[22–3]: At the first blusch of reding of hem, tho bokis apperiden not to be such. **a1500** Medwall *Nature* G2v[40–1]: I shuld not ly At the fyrst blushe. **1519** Horman *Vulgaria* 132[19–20]: He speketh or writteth better and more comelye: at a soden blusshe: than with avisement. MED blish 2; NED Blush sb. 2.

B386 After the **Boar** the leech and after the hart the bier
c1410 Edward of York *Master* 15[13–5]: Therfore men seyn in olde sawes, aftir the boor the leche, and aftere the hert the boor (*for* bere).

B387 As abelgen (*enraged*) as a **Boar**
a1200 Lawman I 72.1696–9: Brutus wes onbolgen Swa bith tha wilde bær, Wenne hundes hine bistondeth I thon wode-londe, II 469.21261–4: Al wæs the king abolgen, Swa bith the wilde bar, Thene he i than mæste, Monie (swyn) imeteth, III 217.30319–23: And he iwræth abolgen Wunder ane swithe, Swa bith a bar wilde, Thenne he bith in holte Bistoden mid hunden.

B388 As anbursten (*angered*) as a **Boar** (*etc.*)
(A number of single quotations are brought together here)
a1200 Lawman III 25.25831–2: And he anbursten agon, Swulc (hit) weore a wilde bar. **a1325** *Song of the Husbandman* in Böddeker 104.51: Cometh the maister budel, brust (*enraged*) ase a bore. **a1400** *Ipomadon A* 176.6148: Blake brysteld as a bore, 6176: Blakkere more then a bore, 237.8324: As gryme as any bare (*MS.* bore). **a1400** *Siege of Jerusalem* 44.781: Than wroth as a wode bore he wendeth his bridul. **a1450** *Partonope* 82.2655–7: Agysor . . . thatt as a bore . . . ys ravennous, 86.2752: As fers ynne batyl as eny bore, 144.4041.

B389 As bold as (a, any) **Boar**
c1350 *Libeaus* 76.1362: Beld as wilde bore. **c1375** Barbour *Bruce* I 36.233: And barownys that war bauld as bar. **a1400** *Susan* 182.226: a. **a1400** *Le Morte A.* 8.229. **a1400** *Torrent* 55.1576: eny. **c1400** *Florence* 21.602: any, 54.1593: any. Whiting *Scots* I 142.

B390 As breme (*fierce*) as (a, any) **Boar**
a1325 *Cursor* I 286.4899: The sargantz that ware brem als bare. **a1350** *Isumbras* 13.168 (*var.*): And watirs breme als bare. **c1375** *St. Peter and St. Paul* 69.403: any. **c1380** *Ferumbras* 22.545: And bente hym brymly as a bor. **a1400** *Amadace (I)* 33[20]. **a1400** *Eglamour* 46.685: any. **a1400** *Ipomadon A* 105.3652: any, 184.6432, 211.7405: any, 220.7705–6: any, 223.7826: any. **a1400** *Le Morte A.* 8.229, 9.266: Breme as Any wilde bore, 30.951: any, 47.1600, 62.2101: any, 66.2214: any, 78.2606: any, 98.3248–9: Mordred . . . Made hym breme As Any bore at bay. **a1400** *Melayne* 31.948, 969, 40.1236. **a1400** *Rowlande* 60.166, 80.802, 93.1237, 98.1396: any. **c1400** *Gowther* 139.108 (*var.*). **c1400** *Laud Troy* I 309.10480: any. **c1440** *Degrevant* 80.1255–6: a. **c1450** Holland *Howlat* 73.775: a. **a1470** Malory III 1193.6–7: ony. **a1475** *Golagros* 25.733, 28.822: ane. **a1500** *Eger H* 275.1506: any. **a1500** *Turke* I 92.36. **c1500** *Wife Lapped* 214.847: a. **a1513** Dunbar *Of the Passioun* 157.58: Als brim as ony baris woid. **1513** Skelton *Against the Scottes* I 187.161: Your beard so brym as bore at bay. Tilley B482; Whiting *Scots* I 142.

B391 As keen (*savage*) as a **Boar**
a750 *Riddles* in *Exeter Book* 200.18: Ond eofore eom æghwær cenra. **c1400** *Triamore* 67.834: As kene as ony bore.

B392 As wood (*mad*) as (a, any) **Boar**
c1375 *St. Katherine* in Horstmann *Legenden 1881* 171.558: That was als wode als a wild bare. **a1400** *Destruction of Troy* 211.6523: And as wode as a wild bore wan on his horse, 219.6813: As wode in his wit as a wild bore. **a1400** *Ipomadon A* 228.8013: He was as wode as any bore, 229.8032: Thowe thow were wode as bore. **a1420** Lydgate *Troy* II 547.5297–8: As wood As boor, III 686.4158–9: As wood As any . . . boor. **a1450** *Partonope* 151.4226–7: Kynge Sornegowre That wode ys as a wylde bore. Whiting *Scots* I 142.

B393 To come like a **Boar**
c1300 Lawman B II 250.16093–6: Uther sal habbe one sone, That sal ut of Cornwale come,

Alse hit were a wilde bor, Ibrustled mid stele. **a1338** Mannyng *Chronicle A* 290.8267–8: Uter sone schal com fro Cornewaille, As a fyghtyng bor in bataille. **a1500** *Amadace* (*A*) 250.171: He come lyke a breme bare.

B394 To defend oneself like the (a) **Boar**
1340 *Ayenbite* 69[11–2]: Hi ham defendeth ase the bor. **c1400** *Vices and Virtues* 67.4: Thei defenden hem-self as a boor. **c1450** *Merlin* II 210[5–6]: But deffended hem on fote as wilde bores. **1484** Caxton *Royal Book* C8[r][4]. **a1500** *Partenay* 77.2105: As A wyld boor deffendyd hym at ende.

B395 To fare like a **Boar**
c1330 *Tars* 35 A 98: Also a wilde bore he ferd. **a1420** Lydgate *Troy* II 465.2468–9: In her fight thei fare Like . . . bores in her rage, III 605.1429: As wylde boris, evene so thei fare. **c1500** *Lancelot* 98.3331: He farith as . . . o beyre. **a1533** Berners *Huon* 122.23: He faryd lyke a wyld bore in the wood, 291.9–10. Whiting *Scots* I 142.

B396 To fight like a **Boar**
a1200 Lawman I 320.7502–3: I-seyen heo Julius Cesar Fæhte al swa a wilde bar. **a1338** Mannyng *Chronicle A* I 433.12397–8: Then was he woder then he was or, Ffightyng als a wylde bor. **c1385** Chaucer *CT* I[A] 1699: That foughten breme, as it were bores two. **c1440** *Degrevant* 110.1713: The knyght had foghtene als a bare. **a1470** Malory I 209.27–9: Sir Borce and Sir Birell . . . fought as two boorys that myght no farther passe. **a1475** *Guy*[2] 96.3370: He faght, as a wylde bore. **c1489** Caxton *Aymon* I 113.33–5: Reynawde fought soo sore, that never . . . bore foughte soo strongly agenste ony other best. Whiting *Scots* I 142.

B397 To foam like a **Boar**
c1300 Robert of Gloucester I 297.4233: He vemde and grunte and stod ayen as it were a strong bor. **c1380** *Ferumbras* 29.699: That the fom of hure mouth out spronge, so doth out of the bore. **a1420** Lydgate *Troy* III 638.2541: Armed hym, fomynge as a boor. **c1450** *Edward the Confessor Prose I* 102[27–8]: She vomyd at the mouthe lyke a boore and she gnast hir tethe to-geder mervelously. **c1475** Henryson *Testament* 111.192–3: And at his mouth ane bullar stude of fome Lyke to ane Bair quhetting his Tuskis kene. **1483** Caxton *Golden Legende* 164[v][2.43]: Fomyng lyke a bore, 312[r][1.42]: Foomyd at mouth lyke a bore. **a1500** *Beves* 181 M 3594. **a1500** *Triamour* (*P*) II 122.1203. **c1500** *Lyfe of Roberte* 233.357: And lyke a boore at the mouth he dyd fome. **1546** Heywood *D* 53.405, **1556** *Spider* 264[5]. *Oxford* 212; Tilley B484; Whiting *Drama* 306:33, *Scots* I 142.

B398 To grent (*gnash the teeth*) like a **Boar** (*etc.*) (A number of single quotations are brought together here)
a1300 *Alisaunder* 305.5837: That he grented als a bore. **c1300** *Havelok* 61.1866–7: But dursten he newhen him no more Thanne he bor . . . wore. **c1330** *Rouland* 54.629–30: Vernagu rout (*snored*) thore, As a wild bore. **c1380** *Ferumbras* 64.1877: His brest he bend up as a bor. **c1387** *De Officio Pastorali* in Wyclif *EW* 425[24–6]: Lyve . . . as boris in sty. **c1395** Chaucer *CT* III[D] 1829: He groneth lyk oure boor, lith in oure sty. **a1400** *Morte Arthure* 124.4214: Bot yitt he byddys as a bore, and brymly he strykes. **c1400** *Alexander Buik* I 90.2852–3: And oft he turned appartly, Richt as it war ane baittit bair. **c1405** *Mum* 71.1531: Thus thay blowe as a bore. **a1420** Lydgate *Troy* II 427.1142–3: Lik . . . a wylde bore, Gan Troyens assaille. **a1450** *Partonope* 446.11120–1: Now as wode bores . . . Partonope and the soudan gan go. **c1450** *Merlin* II 194[19–20]: He pursude . . . as fiercely as a wilde boor. **a1470** Malory I 309.23–4: Trasyng, traversyng, and foynyng, rasyng and hurlyng lyke two borys, 323.11–2, II 843.26–7: And than they cam togydyrs egirly as two wylde borys, III 1057.19–20: Foynyng togydir with their swerdis as hit were wylde boorys, 1070.19–20: Se yondir ys a company of good knyghtes, and they holde them togydirs as borys that were chaced with doggis. **a1500** *Beves* 160 M 3107: Some lay bledynge as a bore. **c1500** *Lyfe of Roberte* 238.483: So lyke a bore he threwe up hys headde. **a1507** Dunbar *Dance* 120.33: He brandeist lyk a beir. **1523** Berners *Froissart* III 394[27]: Thrustyng with their speares and shulders lyke wylde bores.

B399 To hurtle together like **Boars**
a1470 Malory II 486.25–6: They hurteled togydirs as wylde borys, 718.30: Hurtelynge togydyrs lyke two borys, 829.6–7.

B400 To leap like a **Boar**
c1300 *Guy*[1] 160 A 2738: Als a wilde bore he lepe him to, 528 A 173.2.

B401 To look like a **Boar**
c1395 Chaucer *CT* III[D] 2160–1: He looked as it were a wilde boor; He grynte with his teeth, so was he wrooth. **a1400** *Siege of Jerusalem* 30.543: An hey breydeth the brond, and as a bore loketh.

B402 To run like a **Boar**
a1420 Lydgate *Troy* I 255.3857–8: Thei ran I-fere . . . Liche . . . this boris wylde. **1519** Horman *Vulgaria* 193[32]: He came runnynge upon me lyke a wylde bore. Whiting *Scots* I 142.

B403 To rush together like two **Boars**
a1470 Malory I 298.30: So they russhed togydyrs lyke two borys, 415.21, II 640.22–3, 641.3–4.

B404 To scum (*foam*) like a **Boar**
c1380 *Ferumbras* 121.3887–8: For angre . . . A skuntede (*for* skumede [NED Scum v. 5b]) als a bore. **1485** Caxton *Charles* 156.11–2: And began to scumme at the mouth lyke a bore enchaffed.

B405 To smite like a **Boar**
c1385 Chaucer *CT* I[A] 1658: As wilde bores gonne they to smyte. **c1450** *Merlin* II 461[4–5]: He smote a-monge hem Irous as a wilde boor.

B406 To stand like a **Boar**
c1421 Lydgate *Thebes* 91.2200: And liche a boor stondyng at his diffence, **1439** *St. Albon* 141.849–50: Agaynst hym so obstynate they stode Lyke wylde boores . . . in theyr rage. **a1533** Berners *Huon* 515.21–2: He stode at a baye lyke a wylde bore bayted with houndis.

B407 To whet like a **Boar**
a1420 Lydgate *Troy* II 543.5141: Or liche a bore that his tusshes whette (*he behaved*). **a1460** *Towneley Plays* 175.318: I mon whett lyke a bore. **1502** *Robert the Devil* B1ᵛ[29–30]: Whetted his teeth lyke a bore.

B408 As bare as a **Board**
c1405 *Mum* 58.1070: As bare as a bord.

B409 (As) hard as a **Board**
1483 Caxton *Golden Legende* 361ʳ[2.13]: Hard as a borde. Svartengren 259.

B410 As plain as a **Board**
a1475 *The Flower and the Leaf* in Skeat *Chaucerian* 363.58–9: That every braunch and leef grew by mesure, Plain as a bord, of on height, by and by.

B411 As stiff as a (any) **Board**
c1300 *South English Legendary* II 503.337: As stif as eni bord hire honden bicome anon. **1483** Caxton *Golden Legende* 361ʳ[2.13]: Styff . . . as a borde. **1513** Douglas *Aeneid* II 215.78. **c1515** Barclay *Eclogues* 7.236. Taylor and Whiting 35; Tilley B485.

B412 A poor **Board** may be enriched with cheerful will
c1477 Caxton *Curtesye* 27.258–9: The poete saith hou that a poure borde Men may enriche with cheerful will and worde. Apperson 257; Svartengren 263; Tilley G338. See **M700.**

B413 **Boast** and deignous (*haughty*) pride often mishappen
a1338 Mannyng *Chronicle B* II 289[5–6]: Boste and deignouse pride and ille avisement Mishapnes oftentide, and dos many be schent. See **P385.**

B414 Great **Boast** and small roast
1546 Heywood *D* 46.177: Great bost and small roste. Apperson 270; *Oxford* 263; Tilley B488. See **A245, B419.**

B415 Great **Boast** at the board and little in the field
c1500 Fabyan 196[31–2]: It is nat syttyng for a knyght to make great boste at the borde, and to do lytell in felde. See **C516, F659, M367, S581, T49, W617.**

B416 There is more **Boast** in a pot of wine than in a carcass of Saint Martin
c1350 *Ywain* 13.468–70: It es sene, now es efter mete: Mare boste es in a pot of wyne Than in a karcas of Saynt Martyne. See note, p. 110.

B417 To make great **Boast** and do little
1474 Caxton *Chesse* 70[23–5]: They have their tonges redy for to make grete boost and doo lityll. They ben large in promysynges and small gyvers. Cf. Apperson 270: Great braggers; Tilley B591. See **B414, H371, P409, 411, S396.**

B418 He **Boasts** little who travels widely
c1025 *Durham Proverbs* 15.46: Hwon gelpeð se þe wide siþað. (D)e calamitate iactitantes qui de longe itineribus. See note, p. 18.

B419 **Boasters** promise Rome and Jerusalem, but the deed is behind
c1300 *South English Legendary* I 334.221–2: For suche beoth lo this bostares that bloweth mon of winde And bihoteth Rome and Jerusalem ac the dede is bihinde. See **B414, 417.**

B420 By **Boasting** men may know fools
c1450 *How the Wyse Man* 40.124: Bi boostynge men mowe foolis knowe. See **F401.**

B421 Hardy is the **Boat** that strives against the barge
a1449 Lydgate *Fabules* in *MP* II 588.640: Hardy is the bote that stryvith agenst the barge. See **C553, P319.**

B422 The little **Boat** will drench (*sink*) when it is over-fraught (*overloaded*)
a1440 Burgh *Cato* 25.854–5: Men seen al day: the litell boot and barge Wol drench a-non, whan it is over-freiht. See **C16, S249, T118, W6.**

B423 To beshit the **Boat** (*i.e.*, make oneself unwelcome)
1472 Paston V 147[1–3]: My modyr takyng hys part, so I have almost beshet the bote, as for my modyrs house. See **R151.**

B424 **Bodies** on earth are ruled by the planets above
c1464 Capgrave *Chronicle* 10[14–6]: For this is a comoun proverbe at the philosopheris, that the bodies in erd be mech reuled after the planetis above.

B425 Dead **Bodies** are easy to keep (*guard*)
1525 Berners *Froissart* IV 200[13]: The deed bodyes are easy to be kept. Whiting *Froissart* 298:61. Cf. Tilley M510.

B426 The delicately fed **Body** makes an unchaste bed
1522 More *Treatyse* 97 B[1–2]: The body dilicately fed, maketh as the rumour saith, an unchast bed. See **C125.**

B427 He that keeps his **Body** saves a good castle
c1450 Idley 95.868: A good castell saveth he that his body kepeth. See note, p. 218 and **C72.**

B428 He that keeps not his **Body** keeps nothing
1523 Berners *Froissart* III 416[24–5]: He that kepeth natte his body, kepeth nothyng.

B429 When the **Body** is full the tongue is ready to speak amiss
c1390 *Proverbes of diverse profetes* 547.383–4: Whon the bodi I-fuld is, The tonge is redi to speke amis. See **B243.**

B430 Where the **Body** is there are the eagles gathered
a983 Wæferth *Gregory* 295.21–2: Swa hwider se lichama byþ, þider beoð gesomnode þa earnas. **c1000** *WSG* Matthew xxiv 28: Swa hwær swa hold byð, þæder beoð earnas gegaderude, Luke xvii 37: se lichama. **c1395** *WBible* Matthew xxiv 28: Where ever the bodi schal be, also the eglis schulen be gaderid thidur, Luke xvii 37. Apperson 81: carcase; *Oxford* 78; Taylor and Whiting 56; Tilley C73. See **R44.**

B431 More **Bold** than wise
1534 Heywood *Love* D4[r][19–20]: Ye seme more bolde Then wyse. Apperson 426; Tilley B506.

B432 As right (upright) as a **Bolt**
a1000 *Phoenix Homily* 146.30: þær ælc treow swa riht swa bolt. **c1390** Chaucer *CT* I[A] 3264: Upright as a bolt. **1556** Heywood *Spider* 159[13]: Standing formoste, and as a bolte uprighte, 235[14]. MED bolt 1(a).

B432a **Bolt** upright
c1390 Chaucer *CT* I[A] 4266: The milleres doghter bolt upright, VII 316[B1506]: Have hire in his armes bolt upright. **1440** *Palladius* 58.967. **a1450** *South English Legendary* (*Bodley*) 322.524: Thy nekke bolt upryght. **c1450** *Chaunce* 12.241: Ffor bolteupryght ageyn the walle ye stonde. **1555** Heywood *E* 139. 100.4. MED bolt-upright; NED Bolt, adv.; Taylor and Whiting 36; Whiting *Drama* 306:35.

B433 He that draws three **Bolts** in one bow shall shoot too high or too low
1509 Barclay *Ship* I 104[13–4]: (He) that draweth thre boltis atons in one bowe At one marke shall shote to hye or to lowe. See **B617, 084.**

B434 One's **Bolt** is shot
c1475 *Mankind* 29.775: My bolte ys schott. *Oxford* 585; Tilley B512. See **F408, S274.**

B435 To bring one's **Bolt** to stand in the butt
1546 Heywood *D* 47.188–9: Though I . . . Can no way bryng your bolte in the but to stand.

B436 To buy a **Bolt**
c1303 Mannyng *Handlyng* 262.8299–302: A kaynard and an olde folte, That thryfte hath loste, and boghte a bolte, He shal become(n) a dyssour, And telleth how he was a lecchour. MED bolt 1(b).

B437 To shoot a featherless **Bolt**
c1400 *Beryn* 55.1764: To shete a fethirles bolt, al-most as good me were.

B438 As true as any **Bond**
1369 Chaucer *BD* 933–5: Ne lasse flaterynge in hir word, That purely hir symple record Was founde as trewe as any bond. Cf. Apperson 306: An honest man's; *Oxford* 300; Taylor and Whiting 413; Tilley M458.

B439 To bind when no **Bond** will help
a1393 Gower *CA* II 325.894–5: Whanne helpe may no maner bond, Thanne ate ferste wolde he binde. See **S697.**

B440 As bare as any **Bone**
a1325 *Erthe* 22.87–8: Til the be made frome the erthe, As bare as any bon. Apperson 25; MED bar 3a(a).

B441 As bright as **Bone**
a1300 *Maximian* 99.242: Maidenes so bright so

bon. **a1500** *On a dere day* in Dyboski 85.114: Pray we that byrde so bright as bon. See **R229.**

B442 As clean as (any) **Bone**
c1390 *This World* in Brown *Lyrics XIV* 161.29–30: Sum are for-yete clene as bon A-mong alle maner nacions. **a1393** Gower *CA* III 50.3805–6: Into his bath he wente anon And wyssh him clene as eny bon.

B443 As white as **Bone**
c1385 Chaucer *TC* ii 926: An egle, fethered whit as bon. **c1400** *Alexander Buik* IV 398 *cont.* 9769: Upone ane stede als quhyte as bane. **c1450** Capgrave *Katharine* 63.770. Whiting *Scots* I 143. See **I68, W203.**

B444 The nearer the **Bone** the sweeter the flesh
a1398(1495) Bartholomaeus-Trevisa Kk3ᵛ[1.26–32]: And therfore it is that ever the nerer the boon the swetter is the flesshe: for the bones ben malyncolyk colde and drye: and flesshe in his kynde is sangweyne and swete: And soo there is sourenesse and swetnesse medlyd and for that the more lykynge. Apperson 438; Jente 801; *Oxford* 445; Tilley B520. See **P208.**

B445 Not give a **Bone**
c1400 *Laud Troy* I 249.8446: I yeve not of the a bone!

B446 To choke with the **Bones** of buttered beer
1532 More *Confutacion* 423 C[4–6]: Tindal standeth in daunger of choking . . . with the bones of buttred beere. See **B178.**

B447 To find (give one) a **Bone** to gnaw
c1440 Charles of Orleans 172.5134: It myght wel happe yow fynde a bon to gnaw. **1556** Heywood *Spider* 316[27–8]: He giveth us now a bone, Of pittie: and pollisie, to gnaw upon. Apperson 59–60; *Oxford* 55; Tilley B522.

B448 To find no **Bones** in something
1459 Paston III 145[7]: He . . . fond that tyme no bonys in the matere, 195–6: But they were so bold they were not aferd, for they fownde no bonys to sey in her verdyte. MED bon n. (1) lc(c).

B449 To fret (prick) to the bare **Bone**
c1250 *Hendyng O* 198.35[4–6]: Betere is the holde loverd then the newe, That the wole frete and gnawe To the bare bon. **a1400** ?Chaucer *Rom. A* 1056–60: These losengeris hem preyse, and smylen, . . . And aftirward they prikke and poynten The folk right to the bare boon, Bihynde her bak whan they ben goon.

B450 To gnaw on one's own **Bone**
a1449 Lydgate *Look* in *MP* II 769.127: Lat everey man gnawe on his owne boon. Apperson 189. Cf. *Oxford* 241: Gnaw the bone; Tilley B516.

B451 To pill (*rob*) to the hard (bare) **Bones**
a1529 Skelton *Boke of Three Fooles* I 205[21–2]: Fle frome the foolisshe women, that pylleth the lovers unto the harde bones. **1534** More *Comforte* 1212 D[15–6]: He pilleth them with taxes and tallages unto the bare bones.

B452 To shove (put) a **Bone** in one's hood
a1500 Greene *Carols* 401 B 5: Some of them be trewe of love Beneth the gerdell but nat above, And in a hode a bone can chove. **a1500** *Piers of Fullham* 15.359–61: That can make and put a bone In the hoodis of their hosbondes, Whan they be goon fer oute of londe. **1555** Heywood *E* 179.187.2–3: And I wishe (quoth she) a bone in your whood. Wyshe that bone away (said he) tis not good. Tilley B524. See **H483.**

B453 **Bongre** malgre (Malgre bongre)
c1400 *Vices and Virtues* 77.25: Maugre bongre. **c1450** *Pilgrimage LM* 154[14–5]: Thi god he shal be boongre mawgree. **1480** Caxton *Ovyde* 72[37]: Bongre malgre. MED bon-gre. See **W277.**

B454 As open as a **Book**
a1415 *Lanterne* 134.34–5: Her owene conscience as open as a book in the whiche thei schal rede her owene dampnacioun. Taylor and Whiting 37.5.

B455 As true as **Book** or bell
c1400 *Toulouse* 244.551–2: Y schall heyl hyt day and nyght, As trew as bok or bell.

B456 **Book,** bell and (*rarely*) candle
c1300 *Guy*[1] 430 A 62.2–3: Have he Cristes curs and mine With boke and eke with belle. **c1330** *Praise of Women* 291.60: He schal be curssed with boke and belle. **c1330** *Seven Sages* A 85.1913 (*var.*): I swor the by boke and bell. **a1350** *Ywain* 81.3023: So þus the do, by bel and boke. **a1393** Gower *CA* III 139.6979–82: Sacrilegge . . . Which rifleth bothe bok and belle. **a1400** *Athelston* 71.148–50: That wole I nought, For al the gold that evere was wrought—Be masse-book and belle, 88.681: I swere bothe be book and belle, 91.792. **a1400** *Awntyrs* 118.30: That borne was in borgoyne, by boke and by belle. **a1400** *Cursor* II 979 G 17109–10: Curced in kirc than sal thai be Wid candil, boke, and bel, III 1432 F 25038: Cursed he is with boke and belle. **a1400** *Le Morte A.* 91.3018: Than he hym cursyd with boke And belle. **a1400** *Or Crist into cloudes* in *PMLA* 70(1953) 218.43:

He sware sadly on othe be boke and be belle. **a1400** *Quartrefoil* 2.33: Scho blyssede his body with buke and with belle. **a1400** *Scottish Legends* I 343.114: But ony aythe one bel ore buke. **c1400** *Beryn* 33.1017: And swore be book and bell. **c1400** *Laud Troy* I 207.7013: He swar here deth by bok and belle, II 501.17009: But by him that schope book and belle, 518.17599–601: And ther made thei alle her othes By boke and belle and holy clothes That longed to her sacrament. **c1400** *Plowman's Tale* 186.1241: Thou shalt be cursed with boke and bell. **c1400** *St. Anne (1)* 37.1401: Curst be he with brek (*so MS.*) and bell. **c1400** *Toulouse* 227.190: Y swere by boke and by bell. **c1408** Lydgate *Reson* 174.6635: He cursed hem with book and belle. **c1420** Wyntoun V 103.3018–21: Schir Wịlyam Besat gert for thi His chaplayne in his chapel Denownsse, cursse withe buk and bel, Al tha that had part. **a1445** *Carl* 136.341: That well was hym, be bocke and belle. **a1450** *York Plays* 108.180: By bukes and belles. **a1461** *John the Reeve* 574.407: Swere to me by booke and bell. **a1470** Malory III 1228.6–7: I shall curse you with booke, belle and candyll. **c1475** Gregory *Chronicle* 115[32–3]: He was cursyde in every chyrche in London, whithe boke, belle, and candelle. **a1500** Greene *Carols* 456.1: He made me to swere be bel and boke. Apperson 37; *Oxford* 32; Taylor and Whiting 25; Tilley B276; Whiting *Drama* 340:489, *Scots* I 138.

B457 Old **Books** make young wits wise
1464 Hardyng 32[8]: Old bokes maketh young wittes wise. See **F128.**

B458 To be out of one's **Book** (letters, papers)
c1395 Chaucer *CT* III[D] 1363–4: I shal for thy sake Do striken hire out of oure lettres blake. **c1450** *Develis Perlament* in Furnivall *Hymns* 47.192: He is oute of oure bookis, and we out of his. **a1500** *Partenay* 164.4735: For of his paupires strike oute plain be ye! **1549** Heywood *D* 53.387: And I . . . crosse the quyte out of my booke. Tilley B534.

Boot (1)

B459 As black as a **Boot**
1438 *Barlam and Josaphat (Vernon)* 221.503: That on was whit, that othur blac as a Boote. William Gore *The Mystery of the Painted Nude* (New York, 1938) 52; Svartengren 242.

B460 Not set an old **Boot**
c1422 Hoccleve *Lerne to Die* 190.312–3: Nat so moche as by an old boote or cokir Sette y ther-by.

B461 To shine like a greased **Boot**
a1529 Skelton *Garnesche* I 118.5: (Your) lothesum lere to loke on, lyke a gresyd bote dothe schyne.

Boot (2)

B462 Better that **Boot** (*remedy*) bring down bale than that bale be beaten and boot never the better
a1376 *Piers* A iv 79–80: Hit is betere that boote bale a-doun bringe Then bale be beten and boote never the better. MED bote n. (1) 2(e).

B463 To be (brew) **Boot** of bale
a1450 *Castle* 90.445: Thou schalt be my bote of bale, 116.1313: Brewe thee bote of bale, 162.2864: Sum bote of bale thou me brewe. **c1516** Skelton *Magnificence* 64.2070: She is the bote of all my bale. See **B18.**

B464 Not worth a **Bore** (*hole*)
c1390 *Prikke of love* 276.310–2: Other menne goodnes setteth luit, Thou seist hit is not worth a Bore, So that thin may seme the more.

B465 As alone as one was **Born**
c1385 Chaucer *TC* iv 298: Allone as I was born, *CT* I[A] 1633: And on his hors, allone as he was born, **c1395** III[D] 885: Allone as he was born.

B466 As naked (bare) as one was **Born**
a1300 *Lither lok Sermon* 105[5]: To bedde gon as nakid so thu were (borin). **a1300** *Richard* 192.2073–4: And also naked syxty score As they were of theyr moders bore. **c1300** *Havelok* 64.1949. **c1300** *Northern Homily Cycle (Edin. Coll. Phys.)* 142[18]. **c1300** *South English Legendary* I 20.42. **c1303** Mannyng *Handlyng* 185.5697. **a1325** *Cursor* II 980 CG 17121. **a1350** *Isumbras* 8.100. **c1350** *Libeaus* 119.2119–20: But sche stod al naked, As god hadde her maked, 122.2167–8: But sche stod me before Naked, as sche was bore. **a1350** *Ywain* 64.2382. **c1375** *St. Thomas* in Horstmann *Legenden 1881* 23.202–3: And did the appostel on tham to stand With bare fete, als he was born. **c1398** W. Paris *Cristine* in Horstmann *Sammlung* 185.156. **c1400** *Brut* II 301.4. **a1400** *Firumbras* 55.1736. **a1400** *Scottish Legends* I 253.155, II 473.1077. **c1400** *Beryn* 67.2192: He wosshid, nakid as he was bore, he had(de) be in Room. **c1420** Wyntoun V 231.1039. **a1425** *I thank thee, lord* in Richard Morris *Legends of the Holy Rood* (EETS 46, 1871) 194.164. **a1425** *Meditation on the Passion* in *Yorkshire Writers* I 114[13–4]. **c1440** *St. Christopher* 464.818. **a1456** Shirley *Death of James* 26[14–5]: He was nalid nakynd, as he was first borne of

his modir. **c1495** *Arundel Vulgaria* 3.7: I lepe oute off my bede as nakyde as ever I was borne. **a1500** *Jack and his Stepdame* 80.384. **a1500** *Squire* 31.673. **c1505** Watson *Valentine* 101.20–1. **1515** Barclay *St. George* 98.2452: Hys quene he spolyd all bare as she was borne. **a1533** Berners *Huon* 158.13, 169.7. *Oxford* 442; Taylor and Whiting 38; Tilley B137; Whiting *Scots* I 143. See **M721.**

B467 It is qued (*evil*) to **Borrow** and worse ever to sorrow
a1300 *Alisaunder* 71.1241–2: Qued it is mychel to borowe, And wers it is ever to sorowe. Cf. Apperson 61: He that goes a-borrowing; *Oxford* 248; Tilley B545. See **S625.**

B468 Not so good to **Borrow** as to be able to lend
1546 Heywood *D* 37.72: Not so good to borowe, as be able to lend. Apperson 455; *Oxford* 57; Tilley B543.

B469 To creep into one's **Bosom**
1546 Heywood *D* 35.17: She speaketh as she would creepe into your bosome. Tilley B546.

B470 Not worth a **Bottle** (*bundle*) of hay
c1489 Caxton *Aymon* II 450.19: Ye be not worthe a botelle of heye.

B471 To bring the **Bottom** out of the bag
1399 *Ther is a busch* in Wright *Political Poems* I 363[7–9]: The grete bagge, that is so mykille, Hit schal be kettord, and maked litelle; The bothom is ny ought. **1546** Heywood *D* 98.5–6: And in small tyme he brought the world so about, That he brought the bottome of the bag cleane out. Apperson 61; Tilley B550.

B472 As brittle as a rotten **Bough**
a1425 *Deceit II* in Robbins 100.3: (B)rotylle at assay lyke the rotyn bowe.

B473 He who is **Bound** must bow (*varied*)
a1200 Lawman I 45.1051–2: Ah heo mot nede beien, The mon the ibunden bith, **c1300** *B*: Ac he mot neode, The man that his in bende. **a1393** Gower *CA* II 145.540: For who is bounden, he mot bowe. **a1460** *Towneley Plays* 118.80–1: Wo is hym that is bun, Ffor he must abyde. **1546** Heywood *D* 72.86: They that are bound must obaie. Apperson 62; *Oxford* 58; Tilley B354.

B474 **Bounteth** (*gift*) asks reward
a1450 *York Plays* 122.116–8: For I have herde declared Of connyng clerkis and clene, That bountith askis (*MS.* aftir) rewarde. See **G74.**

B475 It is a good **Bourd** (*jest*) to drink of a gourd
a1460 *Towneley Plays* 115.481–3: It is an old by-worde, It is a good bowrde, For to drynk of a gowrde. Apperson 62, 257.

B476 To teach one to chant both **Bourdon** (*bass*) and mean (*tenor*)
c1400 *Laud Troy* I 195.6597–600: And thow this batayle efft haunte, I schal the teche for to chaunte, I schal the teche bothe burdoun and mene, Ne be thow nevere so wroth ne wrene.

Bow, sb.

B477 As the **Bow** was bent
c1370 Chaucer *ABC* 29–31: Were now the bowe bent in swich maneere As it was first, of justice and of ire, The rightful God nolde of no mercy heere. MED benden v. (1) 1(b).

B478 A bent **Bow** becomes slack (*varied*)
a1475 *Assembly of Gods* 37.1243–4: The bende of your bowe Begynneth to slake. **a1475** *Good Rule* in Brown *Lyrics XV* 265.63–4: To myche bende wyl breke the bowe, Whan the game is alther beste. **c1475** Henryson *Fables* 3.22–3: Forther mair, ane Bow that is ay bent Worthis unsmart, and dullis on the string. **1549** Heywood *D* 45.121: But a bow long bent, at length must ware weake. Apperson 62; Jente 104; *Oxford* 59; Tilley B561; Whiting *Scots* I 143. See **C425.**

B479 To be bent like a **Bow**
c1450 *When the son* 391.316: The browys smale cercled and bent lyke a bowe.

B480 To bend one's **Bow**
a1475 *Ludus Coventriae* 47.140: Alas that evyr this bowe was bent.

B481 To bend one's **Bow** but shoot not
1404 *Lerne say wele* in Kail 16.57–60: Though a man holynes preche, He sheteth noght, but bent his bowe; But he lyve as he teche, He nys not trusty for to trowe. See **L463.**

B482 To have one's **Bow** bent after the French guise
a1475 *Ludus Coventriae* 110.54–6: All men may me now dyspyse And seyn olde cokwold thi bow is bent Newly now after the frensche gyse.

B483 To unbend one's **Bow**
a1393 Gower *CA* II 89.1966–8: Thanne was I furthest ate laste, And as a foll my bowe unbende, Whan al was failed that I wende.

a1439 Lydgate *Fall* I 80.2915–6: And mercy thanne hath unbent the bowe Off his fell ire. **a1500** *Proverbs of Salamon* 190.85.7–8: Than helle were empty and faste loken And bowe of goddys wrath unbente.

Bow, vb.

B484 Better **Bow** than break (*varied*)
c1385 Chaucer *TC* i 257–8: The yerde is bet that bowen wole and wynde Than that that brest. **a1393** Gower *CA* II 69.1247–8: And is that selve of whom men speke, Which wol noght bowe er that he breke, 242–3.620–1. **a1400** *Ipomadon A* 68.2335–6: For mekyll I preyse that wande, That brekes not and will well bowe. **a1400** *Proverbis of Wysdom* 245.58: Better is to bow, then to brest. **c1400-25** Legat *Sermon* 7.8–9: These maner of men, that tus have lever breke and to-berste than bowe and bende. **c1405** *Mum* 72.1553: Bowe ere thou breste. **1413** *God save the kyng* in Kail 54.133. **c1450** *Fyrst thou sal* 88.46, 91.180. **c1450** Idley 82.88: Ffor better is the tree that bowe than breste. **a1475** *Tree* 62.12–3: A tree that is drye will rather brek than bowe. **c1475** Henryson *Fables* 69.1998: To bow at bidding, and byde not quhill thow brest. **a1500** *Proverbs of Salamon* 189.77.3: Pryde wole breste or he bende. **a1500** ?Ros *La Belle Dame* 314.491–2: For worse it is to breke than bowe, certayn, And better bowe than fal to sodaynly. **a1500** *Sone, y schal thee schewe* in Furnivall *Babees Book* 34.16. **1546** Heywood *D* 34.50, **1555** *E* 173.155. Apperson 42; *Oxford* 39; Skeat 149; Tilley B566, 636; Whiting *Scots* I 143. See **T460.**

B485 He that will not **Bow** in skill (*with reason*) is unwise
a1338 Mannyng *Chronicle B* I 9[2]: He that wille not bowe in skille, I hold him unwis. See **B276.**

B486 It is evil to **Bow** (*control*) that which will not be true
a1250 *Proverbs of Alfred* 110 T 355–6: Ac thoch hit is ivel to bewen That tre ben ne ville.

B487 Where you must needs **Bow,** be meek
a1400 *Romaunt B* 1939: Be meke, where thou must nedis bow.

B488 As round as a **Bowl**
1481 Caxton *Mirror* 102[6]: As rounde as a bowle. Whiting *Drama* 306:37.

B489 To lack but a **Bowl** and a besom (*broom*) of being an honest man
1520 Whittinton *Vulgaria* 96.3–4: Ye behave you lyke an honest man, ye lak but a bolle and a besom. Cf. Apperson 305–6; *Oxford* 300; Tilley M183.

B490 To throw one **Bowl** for another
1484 Caxton *Aesop* 290[26–7]: And therfore I threwe to the one bole for another. (To pay one back in his own coin, though neither MED or NED has *bole* for *bowl.*)

B491 As pale as **Box** (*tree*)
c1385 Chaucer *CT* I[A] 1301–2: So woodly that he lyk was to biholde The boxtree, **c1386** *LGW* 866: And pale as box she was. Svartengren 236.

B492 To be in a wrong **Box**
1546 Heywood *D* 92.68: And therby in the wrong boxe to thryve ye weare, **1556** *Spider* 394[10]: Thou art in a wrong boxe. Apperson 715; *Oxford* 735–6; Tilley B575.

B493 Of a shrewd (*bad*) **Boy** comes a good man
c1475 *Rawlinson MS. D 328* 123.67: Of a scrod boey comyt a god man. *Oxford* 444; Tilley B580.

B494 To play the old **Boy**
a1500 Medwall *Nature* D1^{v}[10–1]: He that wold lordshyp enjoy And playe ever styll the old boy.

B495 As sweet as **Bragget** (*drink*)
c1390 Chaucer *CT* I[A] 3261: Hir mouth was sweete as bragot.

B496 As sharp as **Bramble**
a1430 Lydgate *Pilgrimage* 420.15595–6: Mor sharp . . . Than brembel, 421.15658–9: Ffor, I have mor sharpnesse Than outher brambel, bussh or brere. **c1450** *Pilgrimage LM* 133[33]: More sharp than brambere.

B497 As sweet as **Bramble** flower
c1390 Chaucer *CT* VII 746–7[B1936–7]: And sweete as is the brembul flour That bereth the rede hepe.

B498 To fade like the **Brambleberry**
a1500 Greene *Carols* 415.3: Me thynk this wor(l)d is wonder wery And fadyth as the brymbyll bery.

B499 To bolt (sift) to the **Bran**
c1390 Chaucer *CT* VII 3240[B4430]: But I ne kan nat bulte it to the bren. **1533** More *Apologye* 2[3–4]: Syfted to the uttermost flake of branne. MED bran 2, bulten v. (1) 1(b).

B500 As fresh as **Branch** in May
c1385 Chaucer *TC* v 844: This Diomede, as fressh as braunche in May. *Oxford* 225.

B501 To quake like a **Branch**
c1386 Chaucer *LGW* 2680–1: She rist hire up, and dredfully she quaketh, As doth the braunche that Zepherus shaketh.

B502 As black as (any) **Brand**
a1300 *Alisaunder* 321 M 359: So blake they were as eny bronde, 321.6110–1: The selve men of the londe Weren blake so colowzy (*var.* cole) bronde, 331.6249–50: colowy bronde. **c1350** *Libeaus* 92.1658–9.

B503 As hot as the **Brand**
a1300 *XI Pains* 154.253–4: On heom is mony yrene beond, That is hatture thene the brond.

B504 As red as (a) **Brand**
c1330 *Rouland* 41.145 (Stars) as red as brond that brent. **a1533** Berners *Huon* 140.11–2: His eyen more redder and brynnynge then a bronde of fyre, 343.13: He became as reed as a bronde of fyre.

B505 Este (*pleasant*) are one's own **Brands** (*varied*)
c1250 *Hendyng O* 194.16: Este ben owene brondes, C 185.19: gledes. **c1450** *Douce MS.52* 48.54: Hit is mery a man to syt by his owne fyre. **c1450** *Rylands MS.394* 98.23. Apperson 186, 305; Jente 336; Kneuer 33–5; *Oxford* 482; Schleich 257; Singer III 131; Skeat 75. Cf. Smith 181. See **H420, O76, T139.**

B506 Take away the **Brands** (wood) to quench the fire (*varied*)
c1382 Wyclif *De Pontificium* in *SEW* III 242[11–2]: And so it were a medicyne, that men that han power drow awey thes bronndes that norischeth this fire. **a1400** *Stanzaic Life* 363.10669–72: And ryght As fir clekket is Quen the brondes ben tan Away, So is the Holy Gost I-wis In mon quen charite is Abatet ay. **a1400** Wyclif *Sermons* I 387[10–1]: Take awei thes brondis yif thou wole quenche the fier. **a1422** Lydgate *Life* 413.1453–4: For the fyre, may no while brenne Aftur the brondes, ben taken awaye. **a1425** *Daily Work* in *Yorkshire Writers* I 150[34–5]: The wise man sais: "If thou wil abate the flawme: abate the brandis." **a1440** Burgh *Cato* 314.460: With drawe the brond, the fier shal eek discrees. **c1450** Capgrave *Katharine* 81.29–32: And as we see, the more is leyd to brenne The grettere fyer ther is, it is no dowte; Ffor drawe a-wei the shides fro it thenne, Soone wil the fyre be quenched and be oute. **c1450** *Speculum Christiani* (2) 228.7–8: For the fire is not so grete bo(t) it muste faile if the brondes be wyth-drawen. **1456** Hay *Law* 161.35–6: For quhen men takis the brandis fra the grete fyre, it slokis the sonar. **a1470** Parker *Dives* M2[r][2.35–8]: For the wyse man sayth, whan the wood is withdrawe, the fyre abateth and is quenched. **1532** Berners *Golden Boke* 237.3940–1: Whan ye take the wood fro the fire, it leveth brennyng. See **P327.**

B507 To be like burning **Brands**
a1300 *Alisaunder* 299.5715: Eighen he had so brennyng bronde. **c1400** *Laud Troy* I 228.7730: His eyen were lyke to brennande brondes.

B508 To blaze like a **Brand**
a1425 *Nicodemus* (*Additional*) 31.126: All of fyne golde blasand as brande.

B509 To burn like a **Brand**
c1350 *Apocalypse* 64.10: Brennande as a bronde. **c1395** *WBible* Ecclesiasticus xlviii 1: His word brente as a brond. **1402** *Daw Topias* 53[7]. **c1410** Lovelich *Grail* IV 219.170: Eche brenneng as brond so bryht. **a1425** *Chester Plays* II 425.690: That burne shall as a Brand.

B510 To startle and sparkle like a **Brand**
c1516 Skelton *Magnificence* 24.741: I make them to startyll and sparkyll lyke a bronde.

B511 As hard as any **Brass**
c1300 *Beves* 125.2676: His sides wer hard ase eni bras, 132.16. **a1325** *Cursor* II 342.5903: The king(s) hert wex herd as bras. **c1330** *Degare* 79.352 (*var.*): And harder than any brass. MED bras 2(b).

B512 As sure as **Bread** is made of flour
a1500 *Medicines* in Brown *Lyrics XV* 276.93: As siker as bred is made off flowre.

B513 He is worthy to eat **Bread** of bran who feeds his foe with flour
1419 *Remembraunce* in Kail 70.49–50: Hit is worthy, he ete bred of bran, That with floure his foo will fede. MED bran 2. See **C153, M63.**

B514 He that gives **Bread** to another man's hound shall have no thanks
1492 *Salomon and Marcolphus* 8[12–4]: He that gevyth bred to an othre manys hownde shall have no thanke.

B515 He would have better **Bread** than is made of wheat
1546 Heywood *D* 83.117–8: Lyke one of fond fancy so fyne and so neate, That would have better bread than is made of wheate. Apperson 42; *Oxford* 39; Tilley B622.

B516 To ask for **Bread** and be given a stone
c1000 *WSG* Matthew vii 9: Hwylc man is of eow, gyf his sunu hyne bit hlafes, sylst þu him

stan? **c1395** *WBible* Matthew vii 9: What man of you is, that if his sone axe hym breed, whethir he wole take hym a stoon? **c1443** Pecock *Reule* 442[7–9]: Who of you askith his fadir breed, whether he schal yeve him a stoon? *Oxford* 15.

B517 To bake bitter **Bread**
a1450 *Castle* 124.1593: To bakyn thee a byttyr bred. See **B566, D397.**

B518 To bake one's **Bread** in a tankard
a1500 *How the Plowman* in Hazlitt *EPP* I 214.141: Theyr brede was baken in a tankarde. Cf. Whiting *Drama* 335:404.

B519 To bake one's **Bread** in his cheek
a1450 *Boke of Curtasye* (*Sloane*) 301.59–60: An apys mow men sayne he makes, That brede and flesshe in hys cheke bakes. MED baken 4(d).

B520 To eat no more **Bread** (*varied*)
c1400 *Laud Troy* I 129.4348–50: Schuld thei nevere have eten brede, . . . Ne hadde not come the duke Nestor, 153.5168–70: Nadde his armes the strenger bene, Ne scholde he nevere have spoken word, Ne bred eten at no bord, 185.6279–80: He set a strok upon his heved, That he ete no more bred, 200.6776, 317.10741–2. **c1400** *Sowdone* 19.649–50: Shal he never more ete brede, All traitours evel mot thai fare, 85.2954. **c1400** *Toulouse* 250.680–1: Certys, and my lord hyt wyst, Etyn were all our bredd. **a1450** *Generydes A* 96.3067–8: I shuld for Anazaree be awreke, And elles brede mot I never breke, 221.7173–4. **a1450** *York Plays* 368.289–90: Mi lorde I schall lenghe so ther liffe, That tho brothelles schall never bite brede. **a1475** *Ludus Coventriae* 33.155: He xal here after nevyr ete brede. **a1500** *Turke* 100.260–1: With-out thou wilt agree unto our law, Eatein is all thy bread. See **C583.**

B521 To have one's **Bread** baked
a1352 Minot 32.51: For Philyp the Valaise had he (*for* his) brede baken. **c1380** *Ferumbras* 23.577: For evere my bred had be bake, myn lyf dawes had be tynt, 95.2986: Wel sone hur bred was y-bake, hure lif-dawes wern ago. MED bred n. (1) 5(b); NED Bake v. 6.

B522 Whoso eats dry **Bread** with pleasure needs no meat
a1500 *MS. Marginalia* in Hoccleve I 193, n. 2: Socrates 30. Who-so eateth drie breade with pleasure, the same nedethe no meate to hit; and to whome no maner of drinke comethe a-misse, the same requireth none other cuppe but soche as ys redye in the waye.

B523 Not to be a **Breakfast** for one
c1500 *Melusine* 279.22–5: Yf they were here alle rosted or soden, and yf it were custome to ete suche flesshe, they were not to the regarde of our peple suffysaunt for a brekfast. Whiting *Drama* 336:417. See **D251.**

B524 To go forth as a **Breath**
c1400 *Elucidarium* 2[22]: He gooth forth as a breeth.

B525 To spill (*waste*) **Breath**
c1300 *South English Legendary* I 56.53: Thou spillest breth, 63.37, 240.41, II 363.154. Tilley B642. See **W329.**

B526 The **Brede** (*breadth*) of a straw (hair)
a1300 *Richard* 121.781: A strawes brede thycke and more. **c1300** *South English Legendary* II 555.138: You neschal failli of youre met noght a strawes brede. **a1350** *Nicodemus* (*Galba*) 32.163–4: Whas hevid so heldes brede of ane hare, Hardily hag of his hand. **a1400** *Awntyrs* 160.584–5: He wanted noghte to be slayne The brede of ane hare. **a1450** *York Plays* 328.243: If you barnes bowe the brede of an hare. **a1475** *Guy*[2] 234.8149: Nother flewe a strawe brede. **1533** Heywood *Weather* C1[v][8]: The tre removyth no here bred from hys place, **1562** *E* 162.101.18: Not the breade of one heare. Taylor and Whiting 167; Tilley H28, 29; Whiting *Scots* I 183.

B527 In **Brede** nor length
c1410 Lovelich *Grail* I 144.916: That entren he ne Myhte In brede ne lengthe, II 346.226–7: For the Ademaunt hath no More strengthe Ayens the Eyr, In brede ne lengthe. MED brede n.(2) 5c: not in any way.

B528 To beg a **Breech** of a bare-arsed man
1546 Heywood *D* 33.5–6: There is nothyng more vayne . . . Than to beg a breeche of a bare arst man. Apperson 66: Breeke; Jente 172; *Oxford* 642: Taking; Tilley B644. See **A196.**

B529 As one **Brews** let him drink (bake) (*varied*)
1264 *Song of Lewes* in Brown *Lyrics XIII* 131.11: Let him habbe ase he brew, bale to dryng. **a1325** *Cursor* I 170.2848: Suilk als thai brued now ha thai dronken. **a1325** *Hendyng C* 185.17: First sour brewit, sit sour drinkit. **c1330** *Seven Sages A* 63.1483–4: Thou schalt suffre kare and howe, And drinke that thou hast ibrowe, 190 E 3531: Thou shalt drynke as thou haste browyn. **c1378** *Piers* B xviii 361–2: The bitternesse that thow hast browe, brouke it thi-selven, That art doctour of deth, drynke that thow madest. **a1393**

Gower *CA* II 270.1626–7: And who so wicked Ale breweth, Fulofte he mot the werse drinke. **a1445** *Carl* 124.160: Suche as he brewythe, seche schall he drenke, 125 B 121–3: Such as hee bakes, such shall hee brew; Such as hee shapes, such shall hee sew; Such as he breweth, such shall he drinke. **a1450** *Castle* 171.3163: As he hath browyn, lete hym drynke, 174.3275: Lete hym drynke as he brewyth, 175.3300–1: As he hathe browne and bake, Trewthe wyl that he drynke. **a1450** *Generydes A* 53.1722. **a1450** *South English Legendary* (*Bodley*) 416.97–8: And ther he fond the drinke, I-wis, so ich trowe, That he hadde to him-self ther-by-fore I-browe! **a1450** *The declaryng* in Kail 81.80: Lete fooles drynke that they dede brewe. **c1450** *Consail and Teiching* 67.45–6: Syne in that breth oft-tyme thai brew, Quhilk eftirward ful sare thai rew. **c1450** *Douce MS.52* 52.97: So brewe, so drynke. **c1450** *Rylands MS.394* 103.16v.11. **c1450** *Warning to King Henry* in Wright *Political Poems* II 230[36]: Let hem drynk as they hanne brewe. **a1460** *Towneley Plays* 132.501–2: Bot we must drynk as we brew, And that is bot reson. **a1500** *Eger* (*H*) 327.2384. **a1500** *To yow, mastres* in *Rawlinson MS. C. 813* 382.5: God sende yow drynke suche as ye brewe. **c1500** Greene *Carols* 346.1,2,3,4: Elles must we drynk as we brewe. **c1505** Watson *Valentine* 226:31–2: Suche drynke as you have brewed I shall make you drynke at thys houre (*literal*). **1546** Heywood *D* 31.28: As I woulde needes brewe, so must I needes drynke. Apperson 67; Kneuer 31–3; *Oxford* 64; Schleich 256–7; Singer III 130–1; Skeat 123; Tilley B654; Whiting *Ballad* 23, *Drama* 194, 228, *Scots* I 143–4. See **B279.**

B530 Tender **Brewis** (*sopped bread*) is wholesome for feeble stomachs
a1449 Lydgate *Order* in *MP* II 450.33–40: Off this fraternyte (*backbiters*) there is mo than oon Proverbe seyd in old language: Tendre broweys skalt with a mary-boon, For feble stomakys is holsom in potage; The mary is good, the boon doth but damage. In symulacyoun ys ffals duplycyte, Who leveth the mary braideth on dotage, And cheseth the boon, God let hym never the. Apperson 671: Weak food.

B531 As simple (blithe) as **Bride** in bower
a1400 ?Chaucer *Rom. A* 1014: Hir chere was symple as byrde in bour. **c1475** *Golagros* 13.351: Blith and bousom that berne as byrd in hir bour.

B532 Break not the **Bridge** that you passed
c1340 Rolle *Psalter* 337 (93.1): Breke noght the brygge that thou passid. Cf. Archer Taylor *The Proverb and An Index to The Proverb* (Hatboro, Pa., 1962) Index 17.

B533 To chew (bite) on the **Bridle**
a1393 Gower *CA* II 270.1629–31: Betre is upon the bridel chiewe Thanne if he felle and overthrewe, The hors and stikede in the Myr, III 192.929–30: And as who seith, upon the bridel I chiewe. **1400** *Love god and drede* in Kail 3.85–6: The brydell with teeth thay byte That of god taken non hede. **c1515** Barclay *Eclogues* 83.822: Smelling those dishes they bite upon the bridle. **1546** Heywood *D* 88.6: To have made hir chew on the brydell one fit. Apperson 68; *Oxford* 46–7; Tilley B670; Whiting *Drama* 335:405.

B534 To give one the **Bridle**
c1395 Chaucer *CT* III[D] 813: He yaf me al the bridel in myn hond. **1546** Heywood *D* 88.8: I gave hir the brydell at begynnyng. Tilley B671; Whiting *Drama* 346:573.

B535 To hold (by) the **Bridle**
c1375 Chaucer *Anel.* 183–4: His newe lady holdeth him so narowe Up by the bridil, at the staves ende. **a1439** Lydgate *Fall* II 417.3157: And bisynesse off labour heeld the bridill.

B536 To lead with a **Bridle**
c1400 Paues 32 (James 3.2): He may with a brydul leden al the body aboute. MED bridel 1b.

B537 To let the **Bridle** go
1532 Berners *Golden Boke* 232.3673–4: And their bridell lette go at libertie.

B538 To rule the **Bridle**
1532 Berners *Golden Boke* 160.1610: Letteth vice rule the bridle.

B539 To run on (with) the **Bridle**
1509 Fisher *Treatyse* 77.23–4: Rennynge on his owne brydell. **c1516** Skelton *Magnificence* 66.2136: They set theyr chyldren to rynne on the brydyll. **a1525** Berners *Froissart* VI 74[37]: But have suffred hym to rynne on the bridell. **1528** More *Heresyes* 153 E[6], **1529** *Supplicacion* 326 E[15–6]. **a1546** Heywood *D* 88.9–10: And now she taketh the brydell in the teeth, And runth away with it.

B540 To set a **Bridle** on one's tongue
a1460 *Dicts* (*Helmingham*) 19.14: And settith a bridell on his tunge.

B541 To take the **Bridle** with (in) one's teeth
c1300 *Body and Soul* 39 L 227–8: With thi teth

the bridel though laught (*took*), Though dist al that i the forbed. **a1400** *Romaunt B* 3299–300: Tak with thy teeth the bridel faste, To daunte thyn herte. **1509** *Fyftene Joyes* C7v[21]: Fast with my tethe I toke the brydell so. **1523** Berners *Froissart* III 308[22–3]: Nowe it is tyme to take bridell in the tethe. **1528** More *Heresyes* 150 B[1–3]: Thei take the bridle in the teth, and renne foorth lyke an hedstrong horse. **1532** Berners *Golden Boke* 140.965–6. **1546** Heywood *D* 88.9. Cf. *Oxford* 641: bit; Taylor and Whiting 30; Tilley B424.

B542 As rough as a **Brier**
a1460 *Towneley Plays* 119.101: As rugh as a brere. Apperson 539.

B543 As sharp as (any) **Brier**
c1395 Chaucer *CT* IV[E] 1825: Lyk to the skyn of houndfyssh, sharp as brere. **a1425** *St. Robert* 55.436: Was never sharper . . . brere. **c1500** *King Hart* 105.28: The rute is bitter, scharp as ony breir. Svartengren 256; Whiting *NC* 376, *Scots* I 144.

B544 In the **Briers**
c1450 Idley 124.1033: That maketh maidens stomble and falle in the breris. **1520** Whittinton *Vulgaria* 98.14–5: That leves a man stykkynge in the breres. **1556** Heywood *Spider* 362[8]: Leaving flies in the briers. Apperson 358: Leave; *Oxford* 359: Leave; Tilley B673; Whiting *Drama* 336:419, *Scots* I 144.

B545 Not worth a crooked **Brier**
a1400 *Romaunt C* 6191: It is not worth a croked brere.

B546 To sting worse than **Briers**
a1449 Lydgate and Burgh *Secrees* 28.885: They stynge wers than brerys.

B547 To be like the **Brier-flower**
c1380 *Cleanness* 31.791: Of ble as the brere-flor where so the bare schew(e)d.

B548 Better spare at **Brim** (brink) than at bottom
1546 Heywood *D* 71.43: Better spare at brym than at bottem, **1555** *E* 136.88.7–8: Not at bottom but at brynke, Better foresee than forthinke. Apperson 45; *Oxford* 41; Tilley B674.

B549 To leave the **Brim** to wade to the bottom
1556 Heywood *Spider* 420[2]: Leaving the brim: to the botum to wade.

B550 To **Bring** but (*out*) what is brought in
c1420 Wyntoun IV 73.5070: Scho can brynge but (*var.* owt) that is broucht in. Cf. Whiting *Scots* I 145: But.

B551 As sharp as any **Bristles**
c1400 *Laud Troy* II 324.11005: Thow (*Death*) art scharp as any bristeles.

B552 Not worth the **Bristle** (brust) of a swine
c1300 *Guy*[1] 212 A 3679–80: Thou sest Mahoun ne Apolin Be nought worth the brestel of a swin. **c1330** *Rouland* 61.860–1: No Jubiter, no apolin, No is worth the brust of a swin. **c1330** *Tars* 52.796–7: Mahoun no Apolin Is nought worth the brostle of a swin.

B553 To have brows like **Bristles**
a1375 *Octavian* (S) 30.932: Hys browys, as brystelys of a swyn. **a1460** *Towneley Plays* 119.102: She is browyd lyke a brystyll.

B554 Between **Britain** and Constantinople
a1300 *Arthour and M.*[1] 266.9741–2: Bitvene Breteine and Costentinenoble No worth another knight so noble.

B555 From hence to the **Britain Sea**
a1475 *Guy*[2] 15.522: From hens to the see of Bretayne.

B556 **Britons** are boasters (*varied*)
a1300 Lawman III 51.26449–52: Bruttus beoth bolde, Ac hii beoth onwreast itold, For evere hii yelp makieth, Hire mansipe his the lasse. **c1300** Robert of Gloucester I 299.4266: And that bote yelpinge and bost mid brutons nothing nas. **a1338** Mannyng *Chronicle A* I 442.12651–2: "Bretons," he saide, "ar bot avaunturs, And manace mikel at rebours." **a1350** Castelford 98.22411–2: He saide britons in everilke place Habundes in rosing and manace. **a1400** *Morte Arthure* 40.1348: Evere ware thes Bretouns braggers of olde, 41.1393–4: Yone are bolde bosturs, that syche bale wyrkez; It befell hym full foule, that tham so fyrste namede. **c1450** *Merlin* II 652[9–10]: And seide that Bretouns coude well manece but at the dedes thei were but esy. **a1470** Malory I 207.24–7: Thes Englyshe Bretouns be braggars of kynde, for ye may see how they boste and bragge as they durste bete all the worlde, 207.11–2(*Caxton's text*): These Bretons ben ful of pryde and boost and they bragge as though they bare up alle the worlde. See **F615.**

B557 To hide like **Brocks** (*badgers*)
a1200 Lawman II 110.12816–7: Inne eorthe and inne stockes, Heo hudeden heom alse brockes.

B558 To look like a **Brock** in a band
a1450 *York Plays* 258.117–8: He lokis like a brokke, Were he in a bande for to bayte.

B559 To stink like a **Brock**
a1350 *Ywain* 3.97–8: It es ful semeli, als me think, A brok omang men forto stynk. **a1529** Skelton *Garnesche* I 128.55: Sche seyd your brethe stank lyke a broke. Apperson 69; *Oxford* 621; Svartengren 309; Tilley B679; Whiting *Drama* 307:41, *Scots* I 144.

B560 As black as burnt **Brods** (*?thorns*)
a1300 *Guy*[1] 430 A 62.10: As blac he is as brodes brend.

B561 To go to **Brood** (*breeding*) but (*without*) nest
c1250 *Owl* 116.1385–6: An swo heo doth, for heo beoth wode The bute nest goth to brode. (To fornicate, of a woman.)

B562 No **Brook** too little to seek the sea
897 Alfred *Boethius* 53.5: Nis nan to ðæs lytel æwylm þæt he þa sæ ne (ge)sece. Cf. *Oxford* 544: Rivers run, quote 1608: Tilley R140. See **F289.**

B563 A new **Broom** sweeps clean
1546 Heywood *D* 61.82: The greene new brome sweepth cleene, **1555** *E* 156.67. Apperson 443; Jente 549; *Oxford* 450; Taylor and Whiting 44; Tilley B682; Whiting *Drama* 230.

B564 When **Broom** bears apples and hemlock honey
a1500 *Wold God that men* 10[4–6]: Whan brome wylle appelles bere, And humloke hony in feere, Than sek rest in lond. **c1520** Walter *Spectacle* C3[v][22–3]: When brome bere apples or homlockes hony, Than trust the wordes of women. Robbins-Cutler 3928.3. See **G421.**

B565 When the **Broom** blows the groom woos (*varied*)
a1300 *Trinity MS. 0.2.45* 5[1]: Whanne bloweth the brom, thanne wogeth the grom; Whanne bloweth the furs, thanne wogeth he wurs. **a1500** *Harley MS. 1002* in *RES* NS 2(1951)119: When the clot klyngueth and the cucko synguth and the brome sprynguth, then his tyme a yongelyng for to go a wowyng. *Oxford* 260: Gorse.

B566 To brew a wicked **Broth**
a1400 *Laud Troy* I 272.9242: A wicked brotthe thei ther brewe. See **B517, D397.**

B567 It is good for **Brothers** to won yfere (*live together*)
c1300 *South English Legendary* (*Laud*) 179.19: Guod it is and murie: brethren to wonie i-fere!

B568 Not trust him though he were one's **Brother**
1549 Heywood *D* 50.286: I will not trust him though he were my brother. Apperson 649.

B569 To love one like an own **Brother**
c1000 Aelfric *Homilies* I 268[4]: And þeah ðone man lufigan swa swa agenne broðor. **c1300** *Lay-Folks Mass-Book*, ed. T. F. Simmons (EETS 71, 1879) 54.564–5: So that ilk mon love wele othere, As he were his owne brothere. **c1420** Wyntoun V 34.2051–2: For thy thai were ay till other Als speciall as brother to brother. Taylor and Whiting 44. See **B367, L252.**

B570 Woe to the **Brother** who beswikes (*betrays*) the other
a1200 Lawman I 190.4451–3: The saeg wes itreouwe: Wa wurthe a thon brother, The biswiketh thene other.

B571 To shend (*spoil*) the **Browet** (*broth*) and cast the crock amid the coals
c1405 *Mum* 8.51–2: That shente all the browet, And cast adoun the crokk the colys amyd. See **F71, G484.**

B572 Maugre one's **Bryn** (*eyebrows*)
a1338 Mannyng *Chronicle B* II 237[20]: And maugre bothe his bryn was fayn to com to grith.

B573 As wild as a **Buck**
1509 Barclay *Ship* I 63[18]: More wylde and wanton than . . . buk, 297[19]: More wyldly wandrynge than . . . bucke. Apperson 686; Tilley B692; Whiting *NC* 376.

B574 To blow the **Buck**'s horn
c1390 Chaucer *CT* I[A] 3386–7: She loveth so this hende Nicholas That Absolon may blowe the bukkes horn. **a1449** Lydgate *Amor* in *MP* II 746.55: In al suche case love blowith the bukkis horn, *Fabules* in *MP* II 594.824: The wolffe made hym blow the bokk(e)s horne, *Look* in *MP* II 768.107: Som can dissymele and blowe the bukkys horn (*deceive another*), *Servant* in *MP* II 428.19–20: I blewe alwey the bukkes horne, So unhappy was my chaunce. MED bukke 1b; *Oxford* 53; Skeat 204. See **H489.**

B575 Like **Buckets** in a well
a1300 *Fox and Wolf* in McKnight 28.73–6: Tuo boketes ther he founde, That other wende to the grounde, That wen me shulde that on opwinde, That other wolde adoun winde. **c1385** Chaucer *CT* I[A] 1533: Now up, now doun, as boket in a welle. **1484** Caxton *Aesop* 278[8–22]: Two bokettys were there of whiche as the one came upward the other wente dounward . . . For thus hit is of the world, For when one cometh doune the other goth upward. **1555** Heywood *E*

164.110: As fast as one goth, an other cumth in ure. Twoo buckets in a well, come and go sure, **1556** *Spider* 287[1]: Two buckets in a well, thone up and tother downe. Apperson 70; *Oxford* 67; Skeat 218; Tilley B695; Whiting *Scots* I 144. See **O45.**

B576 To play **Buckhood**
a1475 *Promptorium* 357: Pleyyn bukhyde: angulo. **c1475** Henryson *Fables* 14.333: Quhylis wald he wink, and play with hir buk heid, 36.970: He playit bukhude behind, ffra beist to beist. DOST Buk-hid; MED buk-hide: "A game; blindman's buff; ?hide-and-seek;" Whiting *Scots* I 144.

B577 To come to **Buckle** and bare thong
1546 Heywood *D* 90.55–6: That little and little he decaied so long Tyll he at length came to buckle and bare thong. Apperson 71; *Oxford* 67; Tilley B696.

B578 As broad as a **Buckler**
c1387-95 Chaucer *CT* I[A] 470–1: An hat As brood as is a bokeler. Svartengren 286.

B579 **Bucklersbury** electuary (merchant)
c1435 Lydgate *Letter to Gloucester* in *MP* II 666.41–3: Nat sugre-plate, maad by thappotecarye, Plate of briht metal, yevith a mery soun, In Boklerys-bury is noon such letuary. **1520** Whittinton *Vulgaria* 50.17–20: Thy company and thou, that can bothe forge and lye be two mete marchauntes to utter ware in buklersbury. Tu et tibi consocius, qui et fabricare et mentiri nostis: inter pharmacapolas ad antidota vendenda, maxime estis idonei. See note, p. 135.

B580 **Buds** (*bribes*) bear bernes (*men*) through
c1475 Henryson *Fables* 80.2322: Seis thow not Buddis beiris Bernis throw? Whiting *Scots* I 177. Cf. Apperson 67, 245; *Oxford* 64, 237; Tilley B658, G108. See **G64, M496.**

B581 The **Bud** has tarage (*flavor*) from the root (*varied*)
a1430 Lydgate *Pilgrimage* 261.9462–6: The bud hath tarage off the roote, Lyk as an appyl or a pere, Thogh yt be born, nevere so fere, Yt savoureth (whan that al ys do,) Off the Tre that yt kam fro. **c1450** Capgrave *Katharine* 153.1216–8: And in oure philosophie, I hope, thus is it founde That naturally the braunche oute of the rote Shal take his savour, be it soure be it swote. See **A169, K30.**

B582 Not praise at a **Bud**
c1450 *Pilgrimage LM* 61[7–8]: Preyseth it nouht at a bodde, 128[6–7]: Here wittes i preyse not at a budde. (French [229, 230]: ne la prise ung bouton.)

B583 As bright as **Bugle** (*a blue flower*)
c1460 *Satirical Description* 199[4]: As bryght as bugyl. NED Bugle sb.[2].

B584 Hasty **Building** cannot be sure
1532 Berners *Golden Boke* 398.10050: For all buyldynge hastely made can not be sure.

B585 As fierce as a **Bull**
1480 Caxton *Ovyde* 131[9]: More fyers than a Bulle.

B586 As great as a **Bull**
c1300 *Guy*[1] 374 A 7157: His nek is greter than a bole. **a1500** *Partenay* 106.2988: Which was All so gret As A bole his hede. Cf. NED Bole[1].

B587 As strong as a **Bull**
c1450 *Secrete of Secretes* 35.24: Strong as a bole. Svartengren 392; Taylor and Whiting 46; Tilley B713.

B588 To bell (*roar*) like a **Bull** (*etc.*) (A number of single quotations are brought together here)
a1375 *William* 66.1891: Bellyng as a bole that burnes wold spille. **a1420** Lydgate *Troy* II 465.2468–70: In her fight thei fare Like . . . sterne bolis, whan thei ben savage. **a1470** Malory I 267.11: Than they hurteled togedyrs as two wylde bullys, II 474.19: And lyke too bullis they laysshed togydirs. **1490** Caxton *Eneydos* 162.4–5: And approched eche other ryght harde, lyke two bulles. **a1513** Dunbar *Complaint to the King* 5.27: That ladis may bait him lyk a buill.

B589 To cry like **Bulls**
c1400 *Laud Troy* I 198.6704: Thei cried . . . as boles rore. **a1420** Lydgate *Troy* II 555.5546: Liche wylde bolis thei gan crye. **c1450** *Merlin* II 552[20]: He fledde cryinge and brayinge as a bole.

B590 To roar like a **Bull**
c1300 *Havelok* 82.2438–40: That he rorede als a bole That wore parred in an hole With dogges forto bite and beite. **a1420** Lydgate *Troy* II 555.5546: Liche wylde bolis thei gan . . . rore. **1513** Bradshaw *St. Werburge* 50.1233: He rored . . . lyke a wylde bull. Taylor and Whiting 46; Tilley B715.

B591 To yell like **Bulls**
c1400 *Laud Troy* I 198.6704: Thei . . . yelled as boles rore. **1513** Bradshaw *St. Werburge* 50.1233: He . . . yelled lyke a wylde bull.

B592 As bright as **Bullace** (*a wild plum*) **c1460** *Satirical Description* 199[4]: As bryght as . . . bolace. Svartengren 225; Whiting *NC* 377.

B593 As wood (*mad*) as a wild **Bullock** **1455** Paston III 39[17–8]: Howard was as wode as a wilde bullok.

B594 As rugged as **Burs** **c1545** Heywood *Four PP* D3ᵛ[7]: Shakynge hys eares, as ruged as burres.

B595 To cleave (together) like **Burs** **a1300** *Arthour and M.*[1] 231.8279–80: To gider thai cleved in that werre, So with other doth the burre. **a1400** *Bonum Est* 75.7–8: Thei cleven alle to-geder as burres don. **c1515** Barclay *Eclogues* 85.872: Together they cleave more fast then do burres. **1546** Heywood *D* 76.207: They cleave together like burs. Apperson 102; *Oxford* 97; Tilley B723; Whiting *Drama* 307:43, *Scots* I 144.

B596 To join as **Bur** to bur **c1523** Barclay *Mirrour* 78[22]: Testie foes joyned as burre to burre.

B597 To stick like a **Bur** **1534** Heywood *Love* C1ʳ[14–5]: Her owne tale lyke a bur Stack to her owne back. Apperson 601–2; Taylor and Whiting 48; Tilley B723, 724.

B598 An easy **Burden** breaks no bones **c1450** Idley 91.620: And an easi burthen breketh noo boonys.

B599 Light **Burden** far heavy **1546** Heywood *D* 97.217: Light burdeine far heavy, **1555** *E* 164.113. Apperson 364; Jente 454; *Oxford* 367; Tilley B727.

B600 To lay the **Burden** on another's back **c1515** Barclay *Eclogues* 52.54–8: "So mens common gise Is alway to lay the burthen or the sacke (Which them sore grieveth) upon some other backe." "Nothing is truer then is this of thee sayde, It is a true proverbe, and pretyly convayde." Tilley B728.

B601 Too long **Burden** makes weary bones **1463** *Stonor Letters* I 62[4]: To long burthyn makyth wery bonys.

B602 **Burgess'** bairns thrive not to the third heir **a1500** *Thre Prestis* 6–8.93–5: To you I have ane questioun to Declare, Quhy burgess barnis thryffid nocht to the thrid aire, Bot castis away it that thar eldaris wan, 12.173, 182, 16.248. Whiting *Scots* I 144–5. See **G333.**

B603 From **Burrian** to Berwick **c1450** Holland *Howlat* 77.895–6: That no bird was him lyke, Fro Burone to Berwike.

B604 One beats the **Bush** and another takes the bird (*varied*) **a1393** Gower *CA* II 194.2355–6: And takth the bridd to his beyete, Wher othre men the buisshes bete. **a1400** *Ipomadon A* 172.6019–22: For oftyne tymes has bytydde And sayd off long tyme agoone, That on the bushe bettes one, A nothere man hathe the bryde. **a1439** Lydgate *Fall* I 144.5127–8: Oon bet the busshe, another hath the sparwe, And alle the birdis in his possessioun. **a1450** *Generydes B* 144.4523–4: Butt as it hath be sayde full long agoo, Some bete the bussh and some the byrdes take. **c1450** *Douce MS.52* 47.36: On betyth the buske, a-nother hathe (the) brydde. **1472** Paston V 142[6–7]: We bette the busschysse and have the losse and the disworschuppe and ether men have the byrds. **c1470** *Harley MS.3362* f.4b in *Retrospective* 309[30]: Sum man bet the buschys, another hath the bryddys. **a1475** *Ludus Coventriae* 111.81–3: Here may all men this proverbe trow, That many a man doth bete the bow, Another man hath the brydde. **c1475** *Rawlinson MS. D 328* 118.16: On betyt the broscus, a-nother hath the bordys. **1546** Heywood *D* 23.34–5: And while I at length debate and beate the bushe, There shall steppe in other men, and catche the burdes. Apperson 31; *Oxford* 28; Taylor and Whiting 48; Tilley B740; Whiting *Scots* I 145. See **D147, F418.**

B605 To be like **Bushes** **a1350** *Ywain* 8.261: His browes war like litel buskes. **c1390** *Sir Gawain* 6.182: A much berd as a busk over his brest henges. **a1425** *Chester Plays* I 153.509: His beard like a buske of breeres.

B606 To burn like a dry **Bush** **c1410** Lovelich *Grail* IV 219.177–8: And that as lihtly he brende there As a drye busch whanne it is On fere.

B607 To lay a **Bush** before the gap (*varied*) **c1400** *Beryn* 55.1789: He leyith a bussh to-fore the gap. **1529** More *Supplicacion* 328 A[14–6]: We have stopped them that gap al ready with suche a bush of thornes, as will pricke theyr handes. MED bush n. (1) 3(a). Cf. Tilley G28. See **G32, 33.**

B608 To wend about the **Bush** (*varied*) **c1475** Henryson *Fables* 69.1996: About the busk with wayis thocht thow wend. **1520** Whittinton *Vulgaria* 35.12–3: A longe betynge about the busshe and losse of tyme. **c1520** *Terens* B3r[16–7]: Thou must furst sue to The old mans frendys, ells Abowt the bush dost thow go (*i.e. lose your desire*). Apperson 31; *Oxford* 27; Taylor and Whiting 48; Tilley B742; Whiting *Scots* I 145.

B609 Under the **Bush** one must abide fair weather
c1250 *Hendyng O* 194.17: Ounder buskes me shal fair weder abide, **a1325** *C* 185–6.20: Under bousse man scal wedir abide. **c1450** Greene *Carols* 338.4: Under the busch ye shul tempeste Abyde tyl hit be over goo. **a1500** *Sloane MS.747* f.66a: Under the busshe yt ys gode fayre weder to abyde. Apperson 73, 658; *Oxford* 18; Skeat 82.

B610 As round as a **Bushel**
c1545 Heywood *Four PP* D3v[8]: Rolynge his yes as rounde as two bushels.

B611 A **Bushel** of March dust is worth a king's ransom
1533 Heywood *Weather* C2r[7–8]: And now to mynde there is one olde proverbe come: One bushell of march dust is worth a kinges raunsome. Apperson 400; *Oxford* 407; Tilley B743.

B612 In a **Bushel** of weening (*surmising*) is not a handful of cunning
c1477 Norton *Ordinall* 22[5–6]: An old Proverbe, *In a Bushell of weeninge, Is not found one handfull of Cunninge.* **a1500** Hill 131.32: In a busshell of wynnynge, ys not a hondfull of cunnyng. Apperson 73; NED Weening 1; Tilley B744. (Both Apperson and Tilley read *winning.*)

B613 In little **Business** stands great rest
c1390 Chaucer *Truth* 10: Gret reste stant in litel besinesse. **a1400** *Proverbis of Wysdom* 245.57: In lytyll besynesse stondythe grete rest. **c1450** *Fyrst thou sal* 90.127. **1458** Paston III 124[11–2]: Youre fadye sayde: In lityl bysynes lyeth muche reste. **1523** Skelton *Garlande* I 417.1410: With litell besynes standith moche rest. Tilley B751. See **R118.**

B614 One **Business** begets another
1528 More *Heresyes* 105 B[4–5]: It is an olde said saw, that one busynes begetteth and bryngeth forth another. Apperson 469; Tilley B753.

B615 The **Butcher** shows his flesh fairly (*to advantage*), for he would sell it
a1475 *Good Wyfe Wold* 174.29–30: Seyd hit ys full ryve, "The bocher schewyth feyr his flesche, For he wold sell hit full blythe."

B616 To tail (*hew*) (*etc.*) as the **Butcher** does
a1300 *Alisaunder* 107.1883–4: Hem to pieces thai gonne talle, So bocher that hog upon his stalle, 159.2827–8: He hem to-hiwe by fyve, by sex, So the bocher dooth the oxe. **c1330** *Body and Soul* 50.407–8: Ye ladde me bi your enprise, As the bucher (L: bothelere, D: belwether, *Royal* 239:344: shepherde) doth the schepe.

B617 He hits the **Butt** very late that bends many bows
1509 Watson *Ship* E3v[18–9]: He hytteth the butte veray late that bendeth many bowes. See **B433.**

B618 As sure as if it were sealed with **Butter**
1546 Heywood *D* 88.267–8: Every promise that thou therin dost utter, Is as sure as it were sealed with butter, **1555** *E* 165.120. Apperson 555; *Oxford* 632; Tilley B769.

B619 It is not all **Butter** that the cow shits
1546 Heywood *D* 95.145–6: But against gaie glosers, this rude text recites, It is not all butter, that the coow shites. *Oxford* 72; Tilley B775.

B620 No **Butter** will cleave to his bread
1546 Heywood *D* 88.265: But there will no butter cleave on my breade. Apperson 74; *Oxford* 72; Tilley B778.

B621 To look as if **Butter** would not melt in one's mouth
1546 Heywood *D* 38.120: She lookth as butter wolde not melte in hir mouth. Apperson 74–5; *Oxford* 136; Taylor and Whiting 49–50; Tilley B774.

B622 As foul as a **Butterfly**
1456 Hay *Governaunce* 157.27: Ane othir fule as a buterflee.

B623 The **Butterfly** and the candle (*varied*)
1340 *Ayenbite* 206[16–7]: Zuo long vliyth the vlindre (*moth*) aboute the candle thet hi bernth. **a1398**(1495) Bartholomaeus-Trevisa B3r[1.1–5]: (*A gnat*) drawyth towarde lyghte and gladly he seeth lyghte, and soo unwarly he fallyth in to a candyll, other in to the fyre, And for covetyse for to se lyght he brennyth hymselfe ofte, dd1v[2.25–30]: And Papia sayth that butterflyes be smalle fleenge beestys that come by nyghte whan lighte is kyndlyd in candels, and laboureth to quenche the lyghte of the candyls, and so thei be brent in the fyre of the candylles. **c1400** *Vices and Virtues* 228.5–6: And so longe fleiyheth the botrefliye a-boute a brennyng candel that at the last he falleth ther-ynne and brenneth. **c1440** Charles of Orleans 201.5988–90: But as the moth doth bi the candil fyre Kan not eschewe the flawmys en-

combraunce But fleth abowt ay brennyng nere and nere. **c1440** Scrope *Epistle* 109[3–7]: To this Seynt Austyn seith that he that is not besy to eschewe inconveniencees is leche a b(u)tyrflye that turnyth so ofte abowte the fyre of the lampe that he birneth his wenges and thanne is drowned in the oyle. **c1450** *Epistle of Othea* 139.19–24 (*as Scrope*). **1484** Caxton *Royal Book* R4r[19–21]: And the gnat fleeth so longe at the flamme of the candell, that atte laste it brenneth. Owst *Literature* 43; *Oxford* 212; Taylor and Whiting 251; Tilley F394. See **B299.**

B624 (Not) but a **Butterfly**
c1390 Hilton *Mixed Life* (*Vernon*) in *Yorkshire Writers* I 288[14]: What is al the pompe of this world in richesse or jolyte but a boturflye?

B625 Not give (worth, set) a **Butterfly**
a1300 *Richard* 216.2515–6 (*var.*): Ffor Kyng R. and his galyes We wolde nought geve twoo boterflyes. **c1390** Chaucer *CT* VII 2790[B3980]: Swich talkyng is nat worth a boterflye, **c1395** IV[E] 2303–4: I sette right noght, of al the vileynye That ye of wommen write, a boterflye! Whiting *Drama* 336:426:

B626 To fare like a **Butterfly** on a lime-twig
1532 More *Confutacion* 480 H[8–10]: He fareth lyke a butter flye fallen on a lime twigge, which the more it striveth and flotereth, ever the faster it hangeth.

B627 To hawk for a **Butterfly**
c1516 Skelton *Magnificence* 19.575: He hawketh, me thynke, for a butterflye. Apperson 291; Tilley H231.

B628 To wander like **Butterflies**
c1477 Norton *Ordinall* 93[8]: Let such like Butterflies wander and passe. MED buter-flie 1(c).

B629 To have one's **Buttock** pricked with a thorn
c1500 *Lyfe of Roberte* 242.597: I trowe youre buttocke be prycked with a thorne.

B630 Not give a **Button**
a1300 *Richard* 433.6903–4 (*var.*): For thy lyfe and thy barons He wyll not gyve two botouns. Taylor and Whiting 50.

B631 Not praise a **Button**
1340 *Ayenbite* 86[27]: Hi ne prayseth the wordle bote ane botoun. **c1450** *Merlin* II 486[33–4]: I preise not at a boton . . . the speche.

B632 Not set a **Button**
c1400 *Beryn* 111.3696: That set of hym selff the store of a boton. **c1420** Wyntoun IV 293.2142: I set noucht thar by a buton. **c1450** *Merlin* II 527[16–7]: I wolde not sette at a boton what oon seide. **1519** Horman *Vulgaria* 36[28]. **a1533** Berners *Huon* 649.28. Whiting *Scots* I 146.

B633 Not the value of a **Button**
c1400 *Brut* I 199.1–2: Ne forto have of me as miche helpe as the value of a botoun.

B634 Not vail (avail) a **Button**
a1300 *Tristrem* II 40.1448: It no vailed o botoun. **c1300** *Beves* 47.1003–4: Hauberk ne scheld ne actoun Ne vailede him nought worth a botoun. **c1400** *Alexander Buik* I 33.1045–6: Sa that nouther scheld nor blassone Availlit him of ane buttoune. **c1408** Lydgate *Reson* 95.3593–4: Avaylle may, me lyst nat glose, Nat the boton of A rose. **c1475** *Guy*[1] 131 C 2216: His shelde availled him not a botoun. *Oxford* 72; Whiting *Scots* I 146.

B635 Not worth a **Button**
c1300 *Guy*[1] A 2216: His scheld nas nought worth a botoun, 346 A 6459–60: He carf the brini that newe was, Nought worth a botoun it nas. **c1390** *Proverbes of diverse profetes* 526.73: Hit nis not worth an old Botoun. **a1430** Lydgate *Pilgrimage* 325.11942: Yt ys nat worth a smal botoun. **1532** More *Confutacion* 355 D[1]. Apperson 456; *Oxford* 72; Taylor and Whiting 50; Tilley B782; Whiting *Scots* I 146.

B636 He **Buys** dearly who bids (*asks*)
1340 *Ayenbite* 194[24–6]: And this is thet me zayth ine atwytinge. "Dyere ha bayth: thet byt," 198[1]: Thet to mo(c)he bayth thet byt. **c1400** *Vices and Virtues* 214.30–3: For, as Senek seith, nothing is so dere bought as that that a man hath bi biddyng, and that is the proverbe that men seyn. "Dere he bieth that asketh." **1484** Caxton *Royal Book* Q5v[28]: The proverbe saith that it is over dere bought that is demaunded.

B637 To **Buy** and sell (be bought and sold)
c1325 *Flemish Insurrection* 116.3: Hou the flemmysshe men bohten hem ant solde. **c1330** *Rouland* 60.837–8: Smite ich eft on sithe, Thi liif is bought and seld. **a1393** Gower *CA* II 212.3059–61: The Chapmen of such mercerie With fraude and with Supplantarie So manye scholden beie and selle. **a1400** *Torrent* 75.2165–6: To wend over the see fome, There god was bought and sold. **a1425** *Metrical Paraphrase OT* 88.12530–2: The werkes that god here wyll have wroyght . . . Aw nawder to be sold ne boyght. **a1450** Audelay 3.78–9: Nou yif a

woman maryd schal be, Anoon sche schal be boght and sold, 4.107: He wold here sell that he had boght, 209.8–9. **a1450** *Generydes A* 187.6039: His live was nigh boght and sold. **a1450** *Generydes B* 133.4170: This galy lith not here to by ne selle (*?literal*). **a1450** *York Plays* 420.449: Thus schall the sothe be bought and solde. **c1450** *How mankinde dooth* in Furnivall *Hymns* 59.23: He is bought and soolde. **c1450** Idley 85.293: By hym many Regions be bought and solde. **1485** R. Holinshed *Chronicles* (London, 1808) III 444[41]: For Dikon thy maister is bought and sold. **c1497** Medwall *Fulgens* B5r[30]: I tell you the mater is bought and solde. **c1516** Skelton *Magnificence* 49.1576: Why, was not for money Troy bothe bought and solde? 80.2543: To day in surety, to morowe bought and solde, **1522** *Why Come* II 32.169: I drede we are bought and solde. **c1525** Heywood *Wit* 18[18]: By and sell! **1546** *D* 35.20: You to bye and sell, **1556** *Spider* 32[16]: When many a flie, to harme was bought and solde. Apperson 61; *Oxford* 58; Tilley B787; Whiting *Scots* I 146. See **G100, S458.**

B638 To be a blind **Buzzard**
c1378 *Piers* B 266: I rede eche a blynde bosarde do bote to hymselve. **c1383** Wyclif *Vita Sacerdotum* in *SEW* III 238[5]: Thes blynde bosardes. **c1400** *Office of Curates* in Wyclif *EW* 157[9]. **1402** *Daw Topias* 98[5–6]: But of other thou blundyrst as a blynde buserde. **a1425** *Of Mynystris* in Wyclif *SEW* II 412[37]: Thes blynde bussardis. Apperson 54–5; MED busard 1 (c); Skeat 111; Svartengren 172; Taylor and Whiting 50–1; Tilley B792.

B639 To be hurt with the **Bygirdle** (*purse*)
a1200 *Ancrene* 67.11–2: Thench as the prisun walde the the other hurte sare with the bigurdel. See **P302, 448.**

B640 Strange **Bypaths** often do great offence
a1449 Lydgate *Freond* in *MP* II 757.60–2: Straunge bypathes doone offt gret offence, Til unkouthe folke that fayle experience Unto what parte that pathe dothe hem lede.

C

C1 Render unto **Caesar** the things which are Caesar's
c1000 *WSG* Matthew xxii 21: Agyfað þam Casere þa þing þe ðæs Casyres synt, and Gode þa ðing þe Godes synt. **c1384** *WBible* Matthew xxii 21: Therfore yelde yee to Cesar (**c1395:** the emperoure) tho thinges that ben Cesaris (**c1395:** the emperouris) and to God tho thingis that ben of God. *Oxford* 538; Tilley C9.

C2 As plat (*flat*) as a **Cake**
c1410 Lovelich *Merlin* III 492.18401: That Stylle he lay as plat a kake. Cf. Apperson 218: flat; *Oxford* 209; Taylor and Whiting 275: pancake; Tilley P39.

C3 A crooked **Cake** makes a strong womb (*stomach*)
c1450 *Douce MS.52* 57.142: A crokyd cake makyth a stronge wombe. Tortula curvata dat viscera fortificata. MED croked 1(f): "Irregular in shape; ?coarse."

C4 Not count a **Cake**
a1450 *Myn awen dere* 167.580: Than thai counte the noght a cake. **c1475** *Golagros* 4.103: Thi schore compt I noght ane caik. Whiting *Scots* I 146.

C5 To eat one's **Cake** and have it
1546 Heywood *D* 96.181: Wolde ye bothe eate your cake, and have your cake? Apperson 178; *Oxford* 167; Taylor and Whiting 52–3; Tilley C15.

C6 Hence to **Calais**
c1497 Medwall *Fulgens* D1r[25]: There ys no man hens to cales. **a1513** Dunbar *Complaint to the King* 5.6: I sall him knawin mak hyne to Calis.

C7 When the **Calends** of January fall on Thursday, there should be plenty of good(s) and peace
a1470 Parker *Dives* E2v[1.14–8]: In the yere of our lorde a thousande and four hondred, the kalendas of Januarye felle on the thursdaye whan, as they saye, sholde falle plente of all good and peas also. Apperson 331.

C8 As wise as a **Calf**
1533 Heywood *Weather* C2v[40]: Thou arte wyse as a calfe. **1533** More *Apologye* 65[34]: As wyfe (*for* wyse) as a calf. See **W29.**

C9 It is not all for the **Calf** that the cow lows
c1330 *Times of Edward II* 332.183–5: Hit nis noht al for the calf the kow louweth, Ac hit is for the grene gras that in the medewe grouweth So god. Apperson 118; *Oxford* 50.

C10 To dread as **Calf** does bear (*etc.*) (A number of single quotations are brought together here)
a1300 *Alisaunder* 103.1819–20: Men dreden hym, on uche half, So chalf the bere. **c1390** Chaucer *CT* I[A] 3259–60: Therto she koude skippe and make game, As any . . . calf folwynge his dame. **c1400** *Laud Troy* I 135.4571–2: He cleff the body even In halff, As it hadde ben a cloven calff.

C11 To kill the fatted **Calf**
c1000 *WSG* Luke xv 23: And bringað an fætt styric and ofsleað. **c1395** *WBible* Luke xv 23: And brynge ye a fat calf, and sleye. *Oxford* 334.

C12 After a **Calm** follows sudden rage (look for a storm)
a1420 Lydgate *Troy* III 710.4992: After the calm folweth sodeyn rage. **1534** More *Lewys the lost lover* in *Workes* 1432 D[8]: Ever after thy calme, loke I for a storm. Apperson 604; *Oxford* 4; Taylor and Whiting 54; Tilley C24. See **S119.**

C13 As hard as for a **Camel** to pass through the eye of a needle
c1000 *WSG* Matthew xix 24: Eaðelicre byð þam olfende to ganne þurh nædle eage, þonne se welega on heofona rice ga, Mark x 25: nædle þyrel, Luke xviii 25. **a1050** Defensor *Liber* 177[9–10]: Eþelicur ys olfend þurh þyrel nædle þurhfaran þænne weligne ingan on rice heofena. **c1200** *Vices and Virtues* (*Stowe*) 69.7–9: Ne mai na more . . . the riche mann cumen in to hevene riche, thanne mai the olvende cumen thurh the naedle eighen. **c1350** *The Mirror of Saint Edmund* in Perry *Religious Pieces* 31.12–4: And of tham Jhesu saise in the gospelle that "lyghtere it ware a camelle to passe thurghe a nedill eghe, than the riche to com in-to the blysse of heven!" **c1390** *Mirror of St. Edmund* in *Yorkshire Writers* I 251[6–7]: Hit weore lihtore to a chamaile gon thorw the eighe of an nedele, then the riche entre in to the joye of hevene. **c1395** *WBible* Matthew xix 24: It is lighter a camel to passe thorou a needlis ighe, thanne a riche man to entre in to the kyngdom of hevens, Mark x 25, Luke xviii 25. **c1400** *Pepysian Gospel* 68.22–5: And tho seide Jesus to hem that who so hym affieth in his richesse ne may nomore entren with inne the blisse of hevene than a camel may thorough a nedel hole. **c1450** *Pilgrimage LM* 3[24–5]: The riche mighte not entre there no more than a camele miht passe thoruh the eye of a nedele, 153[23–5]. **c1450** *Speculum Christiani* (2) 222.5–6: Not so wicked man, not so schalt thou entre. The nedel ee or the hole of it is streyte and receyvez not such packes. **a1470** Parker *Dives* A3ʳ[1.39–2.1]: It is more easy, sayd he, a Camele to passe thrugh nedels eye than the riche man to entre in the kyngdome of hevens. **1495** Fitzjames *Sermo* E5ʳ[9–10]: Full harde it is a ryche man to entre the kyngdom of heven. **1522** More *Treatyce* 92 E[17–20]: Our saviour Christ said it were as harde for the riche manne to come into heaven, as a great cable or a Camel to go through a nedles eye, **1532** *Frith* in *Workes* 839 B[10–5], **1534** *Comforte* 1204 BC: It is more easy for a Camell (or as some saye) for *Camelus* so signifyeth in the Greke tonge, for a gret cable rope, to goe thorowe a nedles eye, then for a ryche manne to enter into the kingdome of god, DE. *Oxford* 447; Taylor and Whiting 54; Tilley C26.

C14 As strong as a **Camel**
c1395 Chaucer *CT* IV[E] 1196: Syn ye be strong as is a greet camaille. **1506** *Kalender* 148.8: Stronge and myghty as the camel.

C15 It becomes him as it becomes a **Camel** or bear to dance
1533 More *Answer* 1115 H[9–11]: It as properlye becommeth the manne to taunte, as it becommeth a Camel or a beare to daunce. Tilley C30.

C16 A man may overload a strong **Camel**
c1523 Barclay *Mirrour* 25[30]: A man may overlode a mightie strong camell. See **B422, S249, T118, W6.**

C17 As crooked as a **Cammock** (*crooked stick*)
a1529 Skelton *Garnesche* I 117.30: Crokyd as a camoke. Apperson 122; Tilley C33; Whiting *Scots* I 146–7. See **T470.**

C18 As right (*straight*) as a crooked **Cammock**
1522 Skelton *Why Come* II 30.114: As right as a cammocke croked. See **R27.**

C19 As bright as **Candle**
a1300 *Arthour and M.*[1] 92.3203–4: Wild fer, That brent bright so candel cler.

C20 As burning as a **Candle**
a1533 Berners *Huon* 103.5: Eyen brynynge lyke a candell.

C21 As clear as any **Candle**
a1400 *Romaunt B* 3199–200: Hir eyen twoo were cleer and light As ony candell that brenneth bright. **a1400** *Scottish Legends* I 4.109: In-to the nycht as candil clere.

C22 As upright as a **Candle**
1546 Heywood *D* 60.31–2: Upright as a candle standth in a socket, Stoode she that daie. Tilley C38.

C23 He that worst may must hold the **Candle**
c1450 *Complaint Against Hope* 20.39: And how I moote forthe the candel holde (cf. note, p. 46). **a1500** *Coventry Plays* 47.457–8: And now he thatt ma worst of all The candyll ys lyke to holde. **1546** Heywood *D* 63.47: Who that woorst maie, shall holde the candell. Apperson 713; *Oxford* 733; Tilley C40.

C24 One **Candle** can light many (*varied*)
c1350 *Alexander B* 180.233–6: Of a torche that is tend tak an ensample: That though ludus of the lem lihtede an hundred, Hit scholde nouht lesen his liht no the latur brenne While the weke and the waxe unwasted lasteth. **1369** Chaucer *BD* 963–5: That she was lyk to torche bryght That every man may take of lyght Ynogh, and hyt hath never the lesse, **c1395** *CT* III[D] 333–5: He is to greet a nygard that wolde werne A man to lighte a candle at his lanterne; He shal have never the lasse light, pardee.

c1395 *WBible* Numbers xi 17 *gloss:* As yif many candlis weren lightid by o candil and yit that candil hath never the lesse light. **a1400** *Alexander C* 230.4231-2: For many lightis of a light is lightid othire-quile, And yit the light at tham lightis is lightid as before. **c1425** *Orcherd* 246.2-3. **c1440** *Prose Alexander* 78.4-6: The whilk I may prove bi this simylitud—I suppose a man hadd in his hand a lyght candill, many other candills may be lyghted thare at, and it lose na-thynge of his lyghte. Tilley C45. See **W491.**

C25 To set a **Candle** before the devil
1461 Paston IV 12[20-1]: For it is a comon proverbe, "A man must sumtyme set a candel befor the Devyle." **1520** Whittinton *Vulgaria* 107.3-4: Thou art aboute to please a shrewe (I have espyed) as a man that offereth a candell to the devyll. **1546** Heywood *D* 36.47-8: Thought it not evyll To sette up a candle before the devyll, **1555** *E* 152.37. Apperson 79; Jente 493; *Oxford* 298; Tilley C42.

C26 To shine like **Candles**
a1398(1495) Bartholomaeus-Trevisa h7ʳ[1.8]: Theyr eyen shyne as candelles.

C27 When all **Candles** are out all cats are gray
1561 Heywood *D* 27.39-40: When all candels be out, all cats be grey, All thinges are then of one colour, as who say. Apperson 85; Jente 126; *Oxford* 86; Tilley C50. See **F557.**

C28 To fly out like **Candlelight**
a1400 *Ipomadon A* 227.7982-3: So hard they hewe on helmus bright, The fyre flew oute as candyll lyght.

C29 To shine like **Candlelight**
c1380 *Ferumbras* 83.2544: Thay schyne ther in tal that house, so doth the candelight. **c1400** *Triamour* 64.728: That felde schon as candull lyght.

C30 **Candlemas Day**
1523 Skelton *Garlande* I 418.1439-45: With Marione clarione, sol, lucerne, *Graund juir,* of this Frenshe proverbe olde, How men were wonte for to discerne By candelmes day what wedder shuld holde; But Marione clarione was caught with a colde colde, *anglice* a cokwolde, And all overcast with cloudis unkynde, This goodly fowre with stormis was untwynde. Apperson 79; Le Roux de Lincy *Le Livre des Proverbes Français* (2 vols., Paris, 1842) I 64-5; *Oxford* 76-7; Tilley C52.

C31 My **Cap** is better at ease than my head
1546 Heywood *D* 87.242: My cap is better at ease then my hed, **1555** *E* 155.64: Thy cappe is better at ease then thy hed. Apperson 81; *Oxford* 78; Tilley C65.

C32 To set one's **Cap** (houve [*cap*] (*i.e.,* deceive, pay back)
c1387-95 Chaucer *CT* I[A] 586: And yet this Manciple sette hir aller cappe, **c1390** 3143: How that a clerk hath set the wrightes cappe, 3911: Thogh I answere, and somdeel sette his howve.

C33 As swift as **Caprets** (*roes*)
c1395 *WBible* I Paralipomenon (Chronicles) xii 8: Thei weren swift as capretis in hillis.

C34 Such **Captain** such retinue
a1393 Gower *CA* II 291.2421: Such Capitein such retenue. Apperson 366-7; *Oxford* 78. See **C192, L455, M408, P403.**

C35 As clear as **Carbuncle**
c1390 *A salutacioun to ure lady* 137.105-6: Charbokel never so cler schone As ye schyne in cristes see. **c1516** Skelton *Magnificence* 49.1556: Her eyen relucent as carbuncle so clere.

C36 To outface with a **Card** of ten
a1499 Skelton *Bowge* I 42.314-5: Fyrste pycke a quarell, and fall oute with hym then, And soo outface hym with a carde of ten. Apperson 476; *Oxford* 481; Tilley C75.

Care, sb.

C37 He has **Care** that keeps children
c1425 *Good Wife H* 171.172: Care he hath that childryn schall kepe. Apperson 96:4. Cf. *Oxford* 92; Tilley C330.

C38 Keep you from **Care** and bless you from the mare (*goblin*)
c1450 *Douce MS.52* 46.26: Kepe the fro care, And blesse the fro the mare. See **M375.**

C39 The least **Care** of nine
1533 Heywood *Johan* B1ʳ[19]: That is the lest care I have of nyne. Whiting *Drama* 352:678.

C40 They are worthy to have **Care** who will not be aware by others
a1300 *Alisaunder* 169.3025-6: Hii ben worthi to habben care That nylleth ben by othere yware. See **C161, M170.**

C41 To borrow **Care**
c1370 Chaucer *Lady* 10: Ther nedeth me no care for to borwe. Cf. Taylor and Whiting 382: Trouble.

C42 To have no **Care** for the plow
a1393 Gower *CA* II 274.1792–4: Of yonge men the lusti route Were of this tale glad ynowh, Ther was no care for the plowh.

Care, vb.

C43 To **Care** (*sorrow*) gains nothing
c1330 *Gregorius* 55 A 169–70: No helpeth it no thing to care, Y not no gayneth (V: For hit geyneth) it the nought. Cf. Apperson 82: Care is no cure; *Oxford* 78; Tilley C83. See **M729.**

C44 To lie in **Carebed**
a1300 *Tristrem* 32.1123–4: Thre yer in carebed lay Tristrem. **c1390** *Northern Homily Cycle Narrationes* (*Vernon*) 299.36: In Care bed he lay so longe. **a1400** *Perceval* 34.1062: The kyng to carebedd es gane. MED care n. (1) 2(b); NED Care sb.[1] 6; Whiting *Ballad* 35.

C45 From **Carlisle** (in)to Kent
c1350 *Libeaus* 92.1661–2: Nas non so queinte of gin From Carlile into Kent. **a1450** *Castle* 83.201. **1523** Skelton *Garlande* I 369.196: Yet they ryde and rinne from Carlyll to Kente. See **B260.**

C46 Merry **Carlisle**
a1445 *Carl* 158.652: In the towne of mery Carelyle. **a1500** *Lambewell* 144.4: He sojourned in merry Carlile. **a1500** *Marriage* I 105.1, 107.20. **c1500** *Adam Bell* in Child *Ballads* III 25–7.66, 68, 77, 96.

C47 As sweet as **Carp**
a1430 Lydgate *Pilgrimage* 414.15365: Swettere than . . . karp.

C48 An ill **Carpenter** makes many chips
a1533 Berners *Arthur* 367[13–4]: The knight is an yll carpenter, for he maketh many chyppes. Cf. Tilley C93.

C49 Such **Carpenter** such chips (*varied*)
a1533 Berners *Arthur* 319[25–6]: I se wel he is a good carpenter, for he hath made here a fayre syght of chyppes. **1546** Heywood *D* 83.101: Suche carpenters, such chips. Apperson 607; Jente 369; *Oxford* 79; Tilley C94.

C50 To hew like the **Carpenter**
a1300 *Arthour and M.*[1] 247.8837–8: Ich knight hewe on his per, On schide so doth the carpenter. **c1410** Lovelich *Merlin* II 383.14312–4: Swich a noyse . . . As of alle the world the carponteris In wodes hadde hewen stowt and fers. **a1533** Berners *Arthur* 474[27–8]: He did cutte so among his enemies as a carpenter doth hewe chyppes out of a gret tree.

C51 All too late when the **Cart** (bier, wain, death, poverty) is at the gate (*varied*)
a1300 *Lither lok Sermon* 105[35–6]: Ak god itot thanne is to late, Thanne is te carte atte gate. **a1300** *Proprietates Mortis* in Brown *Lyrics XIII* 130.13–4: Al to late, al to late, Wanne the bere ys ate gate. **c1300** *Body and Soul* 55 L 441–4: Nay, bodi, nough is to late, For to preighe and to preche, Nou the wayn is ate yate, And thi tonge hath leid the (*A* lorn his) speche. **a1325** *Hendyng C* 190–1.46: "Al to late, al to late, Wan the deth is at the gate" Quod Marcol. **c1350** *Proprium Sanctorum* 302.335–6: To do penaunce hit is ful late Whon the deth is at the yate. **a1393** Gower *CA* III 162.7667–9: Bot that is spoken al to late, For thanne is poverte ate gate And takth him evene be the slieve. **a1400** *All to Late* in *Pol. Rel. and Love Poems* 250.7: Al to late, al to late, then is te wayne atte yate. **a1400** *Pricke* 55.2000–1: When the dede es at the yhate, Than es he warned over late. **c1420** Wyntoun II 58.633–4: And to ask mercy is to lait Quhen the wayne is at the yet. **c1450** *Douce MS.52* 52.93: Alle to late, alle to late, When deth is come to yate. **c1450** *Rylands MS.394* 102.19: weyne. **a1500** *Thre Prestis* 51.1231–2: Than is over lait, allace, havand sik let, Quhan deiths cart will stand befoir the get. Kneuer 48–9; Schleich 268–9; Singer III 136–7. See **A72, L168, 178, M484, S45.**

C52 The best **Cart** may overthrow (*varied*)
c1450 Idley 93.754–6: A man may so overcharge bothe cart and wayne That it woll breke and all overthrowe, And moche harme therof may happe to growe. **1549** Heywood *D* 45.149: The best cart maie overthrowe. Apperson 83; *Oxford* 35; Tilley C101. See **W6.**

C53 **Cart** and plow bear up clergy and chivalry
a1430 Lydgate *Pilgrimage* 311.11400–1: Carte and plowh, they ber up al The clergye and the chevalrye.

C54 A greased **Cart** goes more easily
c1450 Idley 90.544: A Carte goith more easily whan he is greesed. See note, p. 216.

C55 The long **Cart** often has a heavy carriage (*burden*)
c1475 *Prohemy of a Mariage* 28[8]: The long cart offte hath hevy cariage.

C56 (To be able) to drive a **Cart** between
1556 Heywood *Spider* 119[19]: Betwene whiche: and thy case thou maist drive a carte.

C57 To be cast at **Cart's** arse

1549 Heywood *D* 33.23: I am cast at carts ars. Apperson 83–4; *Oxford* 81; Tilley C106.

C58 To be cast in a **Cart**
c1450 Idley 179.1258: He cowde not calle to mercie—he was cast in wanhopis carte.

C59 To overthrow a **Cart** in the mire
a1393 Gower *CA* II 183.1974–6: So that his carte amidd the Myr, Be that I have his conseil knowe, Fulofte sithe I overthrowe. MED cart 1(b).

C60 To set the **Cart** before the horse
1520 Whittinton *Vulgaria* 36.2–3: That teycher setteth the cart before the horse that preferreth imitacyon before preceptes. **1528** More *Heresyes* 154 C[5–7]: We woulde go make the carte to drawe the horse, **1533** *Apologye* 126[1]: Set the carte before the horse. Apperson 83; *Oxford* 80; Taylor and Whiting 56; Tilley C103. See **S873.**

C61 To shove at the **Cart**
c1422 Hoccleve *Dialog* 132.617: Now, good freend shove at the cart, I yow preye. **1471** Paston V 110[34–5]: Yff ye be cleer owt off Doctor Aleyn danger, kepe yow ther, and her afftr ye maye schoffe as well at hys carte.

C62 "Draw to thee!" quoth the **Carter**
c1250 *Owl* 100.1186: "Drah to the!" cwath the cartare. E. G. Stanley ed. *The Owl and the Nightingale* (Edinburgh, 1960) 134 (not taken as a Wellerism).

C63 From **Carthage** to Ind, *etc.*
a1430 Lydgate *Pilgrimage* 205.7305–6: That, from cartage in-to Inde, Men myghte nat a bettre fynde, **c1440** *Debate* in *MP* II 565.648–9: Natur his giftis doth dyversly devide, Whoos power lastith from Cartage into Fryse, **a1449** *So as the Crabbe Goth Forward* in *MP* II 467.42: Frome Cartage to Constaunce.

C64 As common as the **Cartway** (way)
a1376 *Piers* A iii 127: As comuyn as the cart-wei to knaves and to alle, **c1378** B iii 131: to eche a knave that walketh. **1402** *Daw Topias* 110[12–3]: And maken hem als comoun As the cart weye. **1464** Hardyng 175[27–8]: Amonge them was comon as (the) carte waye, Ryot, robbery, oppressyon, nyght and daye. **a1470** Parker *Dives* A1^r[2.31–2]: As comon as the cartewaye. **c1475** *Wisdom* 57.655: Lust ys now comun as the way. Apperson 109; Tilley C109, H457. See **S831.**

C65 As open as the **Cartway**
c1415 *Middle English Sermons* 102.14–5: And the moste prevey place is as opone to hyme as is the carte veye.

C66 A dry **Cart-wheel** cries the loudest
c1450 *Jacob's Well* 260.26–7: As a carte-qweel, drye and ungrecyd, cryeth lowdest of othere qwelys. Cf. Tilley W287. See **W207.**

C67 The **Case** is altered
a1500 *Nut Brown Maid* 184.196: The case is altered now. Apperson 83; *Oxford* 80; Taylor and Whiting 57; Tilley C111.

C68 Hasty **Case** requires short redress
c1421 Lydgate *Thebes* 152.3691–2: And hasty cas, as folk seyn that be wys, Redresse requereth by ful short avys.

C69 On new **Case** lies new advice (*varied*)
c1385 Chaucer *TC* iv 416: And upon newe cas lith newe avys, **c1390** *CT* VII 1225[B2415]: For the lawe seith that "upon thynges that newely bityden bihoveth newe conseil." **a1500** *English Conquest* 111.7–9: The kynges messangers . . . upon new adventures toke new consail. Cf. Taylor and Whiting 70.

C70 Better a **Castle** of bones than of stones
?c1350 R. Holinshed *Chronicles* (1577, London, 1818) VI 256–7: I remember the proverbe "Better a castell of bones than of stones." Where . . . valiant men are prest to helpe us, never will I . . . cumber my selfe with dead walles. *Oxford* 37. See **W27.**

C71 A **Castle** that speaks and a woman that hears will both be gotten
a1500 Warkworth 27[18–25]: For ther is a proverbe and a seyenge, that *a castelle that spekythe, and a womane that wille here, thei wille be gotene bothe:* for menne that bene in a castelle of warr, that wille speke and entrete withe ther enemyes, the conclusione therof (is) the losynge of the castelle; and a womanne that wille here foly spokyne unto hyre, if sche assent noght at one tyme, sche wille at another. And so this proverbe was prevede trewe by the seide Erle of Oxenforde. Apperson 84; *Oxford* 96; Tilley C122; Whiting *Scots* I 156: Damsel.

C72 He keeps a fair **Castle** that keeps well his mouth
c1390 *God man and the devel* 340.440–1: Her-of is I-writen a word that is couth: "He kepeth a feir castel that kepeth wel his Mouth." Apperson 337. See **B427.**

C73 No **Castle** so strong but will be won at last
c1408 Lydgate *Reson* 181.6919–21: And castel ys ther non so stronge, The sege ther-at may be

so longe That at the last yt wil be wonne. See **C79, 163, F501.**

C74 No **Castle** so strong that hunger will not win **a1338** Mannyng *Chronicle A* I 180.5115–24: Ther ys no castel so strong idight, That honger ne wynneth wythouten fight; Wythouten wepen or armour, Honger yeldeth castel and tour. God castel dredes no power, Emperour, kyng, ne kayser, Ne other help me have at nede; Bot of honger ys al the drede. Ther force hath mad manye assayes, Honger hit wynnes byn fewe dayes. See **H637, 640.**

C75 Of a little **Castle** comes a greater **a1533** Berners *Huon* 258.5–6: I have herd say that often tymes of a little castell cometh a greater. See **L402.**

C76 Though a **Castle** be well manned a man may creep in at a single hole **a1225** *Lambeth Homilies* 23[19–21]: And thah an castel be wel bemoned mid monne and mid wepne, and ther beo analpi holh that an mon mei crepan in, nis hit all unnet?

C77 To make **Castles** in Spain **a1400** *Romaunt B* 2573–4: Thou shalt make castels thanne in Spayne, And dreme of joye. **c1477** Caxton *Jason* 25.6: And after he began to make castellis in Spaygne as lovers doo. Apperson 84; Stuart A. Gallacher in *Journal of American Folklore* 76(1963) 324–9; A. Morel-Fatio in *Mélanges offerts à M. Emile Picot* (Paris, 1913) I 335–42; *Oxford* 82; Taylor and Whiting 57; Tilley C125.

C78 As trusty as a **Castle Wall** **a1338** Mannyng *Chronicle A* I 178.5077–8: Ffor eche man tok a tre to stal, As tristi as a castel wal.

C79 A **Castle Wall** long assailed may not be kept (*varied*) **c1395** Chaucer *CT* III[D] 263–4: Thou seyst men may nat kepe a castel wal, It may so longe assailled been over al. **c1450** *Epistle of Othea* 141.8–9: Who put all hys tryste in a castell wall, A grett foole at long tyme prove hym-selfe he schall. See **C73, 163, F501, T131, W507.**

C80 As a **Cat** plays with a mouse (*varied*) **1340** *Ayenbite* 179[32–4]: The dyevel playth ofte mid the zeneyere ase deth the cat mid the mous thanne he his heth ynome and hvanne he heth mid hire longe yplayd: thanne he his eth. **c1390** Chaucer *CT* I[A] 3346–7: I dar wel seyn, if she hadde been a mous, And he a cat, he wolde hire hente anon. **c1390** *Truth is Best* in Brown *Lyrics XIV* 170.71: We schul him hunte as Cat doth mys. **c1400** *Vices and Virtues* 183.24–6: And thus the devel pleieth ofte with the synful, right as the catt with the mous whan he hath y-take here. For whan he hath longe y-pleied, he eteth here. **a1450** *Castle* 105.954–5: I schal hym bynde In hell, as Catte dothe the mows. **1484** Caxton *Royal Book* O6ᵛ[25–6]: The devyl playeth ofte with the synnar, lyke as the catte doth with the mous. **a1500** *Colyn Blowbol* 105.288–9: And be as nyce in a mannys hous, As is a catt playing with a mous. **c1500** *Wife Lapped* 200.493–4: Even as the cat was wonte with the mouse To play, forsoth even so did he. Apperson 85; Taylor and Whiting 61; Tilley C127; Whiting *Drama* 307:56.

C81 As a **Cat** plays with (turns with) a straw **a1398**(1495) Bartholomaeus-Trevisa ee6ᵛ[1.35–9]: And he (*a cat*) is a full lecherouse beest in youthe: swyfte, plyaunt and mery, and lepyth and resyth on all thynge that is tofore him. And is led by a strawe and playeth therwyth. **c1400** *Beryn* 98.3244: And turne round a-boute, as a Cat doith with a strawe. **c1456** Pecock *Faith* 229[15–7]: Now trowe this, now trowe the reverse, like as a man kan with a strawe turne a katte, now hidir, now thidir.

C82 As blind as a **Cat** **1533** More *Confutacion* 647 D[2–3]: As starcke blinde as a catte.

C83 As clean as **Cats** had licked him **c1450** *Douce MS.52* 50.73: He is as clene as cattus hadde lykkyd hym. **c1450** *Rylands MS.394* 100.19.

C84 As piled (*hairy*) and singed as any **Cat** **a1430** Lydgate *Pilgrimage* 371.13703: Pyled and seynt as any kaat.

C85 As stone-still as two **Cats** **c1400** *Laud Troy* I 200.6788: Thei lay ston-stille as two cattes. Taylor and Whiting 59: still; Whiting *Drama* 307:56.

C86 A **Cat** falls on its feet **a1398**(1495) Bartholomaeus-Trevisa ee6ᵛ[2.16–7]: And (*a cat*) falleth on his owne fete whan he fallyth out of hye place. **1519** Horman *Vulgaria* 434[31–2]: Cattes and dogges whan they shal fall from hye so nymbleth therself: that they wyl pitch upon their fete. Apperson 86; *Oxford* 82; Taylor and Whiting 58; Tilley C153.

C87 The **Cat** fiddles the mouse a dance **c1490** *Sloane MS.747* 204.18: The catte fydylt the mowse a daunce. Cf. Apperson 87: The cat invites the mouse to a feast; Whiting *NC* 377: Bug (5).

C88 A **Cat** may look at a king
1546 Heywood *D* 74.154: A cat maie looke on a king, **1555** *E* 165.117. Apperson 85; *Oxford* 83; Taylor and Whiting 58; Tilley C141.

C89 The **Cat** often mouses after her mother (*varied*)
a1300 *Proverbs of Alfred* 111 J 357–8: For ofte museth the kat After hire moder. **1546** Heywood *D* 43.89: Cat after kynde good mouse hunt. Apperson 86; Jente 143; *Oxford* 82; Skeat 41; Tilley C136; Whiting *Drama* 49. See **D25, M720.**

C90 A **Cat** that has a good skin shall be flayed
1492 *Salomon and Marcolphus* 6[18–9]: A catte that hath a good skyn shal be flayne.

C91 The **Cat,** the rat, and Lovell our dog rule all England under a hog
a1500 Fabyan 672[26–7]: The catte, the ratte, and Lovell our dogge, Rulyth all Englande under a hogge. Apperson 87–8; *Oxford* 83–4; Tilley C143.

C92 The **Cat** winked when her eye was out
1528 More *Heresyes* 241 A[11–3]: But yet as weomen saye, somewhat it was alway that the cat winked whan her eye was oute. **1546** Heywood *D* 66.20–1: But somewhat it is, I see, when the cat wynkth, And bothe hir eyne out. Apperson 88; *Oxford* 84; Tilley C174.

C93 The **Cat** would eat fish but would not wet its feet
a1300 *Trinity MS.0.2.45* 7(11): Cat lufat visch, ac he nele his feth wete. **c1380** Chaucer *HF* 1783–5: For ye be lyke the sweynte cat That wolde have fissh; but wostow what? He wolde nothing wete his clowes. **a1393** Gower *CA* II 331.1108–11: And as a cat wolde ete fisshes Withoute wetinge of his cles, So wolde he do, bot natheles He faileth ofte of that he wolde. **c1395** *Pierce* 15.405: Thou woldest not weten thy fote and woldest fich kacchen. **c1395** *WBible* Proverbs xiii 4 *gloss:* He is liyk the cat that wolde ete fisch, netheles he eschewith to putte his feet in to the water. **c1450** *Rylands MS.394* 93.13: The catt wolle fyssh ete, but she wol not her fote wete. **c1470** *Harley MS.3362* f.5a in *Retrospective* 309[33] and Förster 202.14: The cat wold ete (*rest lacking*). **a1475** Henryson *Fables* 70.2001: I (*the fox*) can nocht fische, ffor weiting off my feit. **c1475** *Rawlinson MS. D 328* 121.51: The catte wol hete fyse bute a wol not chyth (*sic*) the water. **a1500** *Harley MS.2321* in *Rel. Ant.* I 207[3]: The cat doth love the fishe, but she will not wett her foote. **1549** Heywood *D* 45.125: The cat would eate fyshe, and would not wet her feete, **1555** *E* 191.258. Apperson 88; *Oxford* 84; Skeat 209; Tilley C144; Whiting *Scots* I 147.

C94 Clim! clam! **Cat** leap over dam
a1400 Bozon *Contes* 145[7–8]: Clym! clam! cat lep over dam (Tache! tache! vuyle vivre en pache), 212[13–4]. MED cat 1(b).

C95 Let no man buy a **Cat** unless he sees the clivers (*claws*)
a1300 *Trinity MS.0.2.45* 7(10): Ne bigge no man cat, bute he iseo the clifres. Nullus emat catum, nisi viderit unguipedatum. Quem scio saccatum, fallor si comparo catum. Stultus saccatum reputor si comparo catum. Walther III 468.19068a. See **C102, P187.**

C96 Let the **Cat** wink
c1443 Pecock *Reule* 402[8–10]: And summe othere eldre (*children*) whanne thei desiren and asken to be leid in bed to slepe, thei seie, "lete the cat wynke," or sum othere inpertynent resoun. **c1522** Skelton *Colyn* I 328.458–9: But swete ypocras ye drynke, With, Let the cat wynke! **a1529** *Elynour* I 105.305–6: But drynke, styll drynke, And let the cat wynke. **1546** Heywood *D* 66.22: Let the cat winke, and leat the mouse ronne, **1555** *E* 186.222. Apperson 86; *Oxford* 84; Tilley C152.

C97 Now sits the **Cat** thereas . . .
a1470 *Harley MS.3362* f.4a: Now syt the cat theras . . . Iam catus resedet ubi iam matrona sedebat. Walther II 624.10324.

C98 One cannot give the **Cat** so much but that she will wag her tail
1492 *Salomon and Marcolphus* 12[13–5]: Men kan not geve the katte so moche but that she woll hyr tayle wagge.

C99 A singed **Cat** dwells at home
c1395 Chaucer *CT* III[D] 348–54: Thou seydest this, that I was lyk a cat; For whoso wolde senge a cattes skyn, Thanne wolde the cat wel dwellen in his in; And if the cattes skyn be slyk and gay, She wol nat dwelle in house half a day, But forth she wole, er any day be dawed, To shewe hir skyn, and goon a-caterwawed. **a1398**(1495) Bartholomaeus-Trevisa ee6^{v}[2.22–6]: And whan he (*a cat*) hath a fayre skynne he is as it were prowde therof, and gooth faste abowte, And whan his skynne is brente thenne he bydeth at home.

C100 The tame **Cat** burns oft its skin, but not the wild cat

1340 *Ayenbite* 230[4–5]: The privé cat bezength ofte his scin and zuo ne deth naght the wylde cat. **c1400** *Vices and Virtues* 254.30–2: The tame catt brenneth ofte his fel, and so doth not the wilde catt. **1484** Caxton *Royal Book* S8r[10–1]: The catte brenneth ofte hyr skynne and so dooth not the wylde catte.

C101 To agree like two **Cats** in a gutter
1546 Heywood *D* 61.98: They two agreed like two cats in a gutter. Apperson 653; *Oxford* 6; Tilley C185.

C102 To buy a **Cat** in the sack
c1400 *De Blasphemia* in Wyclif *SEW* III 422[18]: To bye a catte in tho sakke is bot litel charge. Tilley C170. Cf. Jente 82. See **C95, P187.**

C103 To fall like a **Cat**
c1400 *Laud Troy* I 181.6137–8: That he fel to the grounde as a cat, Wel even upon his ketil-hat, 261.8842: That thei fel doun as dede cattis.

C104 To kew (*mew*) like a **Cat**
a1450 *Castle* 169.3118: Thow thou kewe as a kat.

C105 To see like a **Cat** in the night
a1300 *Alisaunder* 281.5266: By nighth als a catt hii seeth. Whiting *NC* 382.

C106 To teach one how the **Cat** sneezes (*i.e.*, put in one's place, bully)
a1500 *Basyn* 45.30–1: Eche taught hym ever among, how the katte did snese, Right at his owne wille.

C107 To turn the **Cat** in the pan
1383 ?Wyclif *Grete Sentence* in *SEW* III 332[7–9]: And bi here suteltes turnen the cat in the panne, and tarien pore men in here right. **1546** Heywood *D* 82.55: To tourne the cat in the pan. Apperson 89; *Oxford* 677; Skeat 298; Tilley C172; Whiting *Drama* 368:916.

C108 Well wot the **Cat** whose beard he licks (*varied*)
a1300 *Trinity MS.0.2.45* 7(8): Wel wot hure cat, whas berd he lickat. Murelegus bene scit, cuius barbam lambere suescit. **a1325** *Hendyng* C 189.40: Wel wote badde (*cat*) wose berde he lickith. **c1450** *Douce MS.52* 50.78: Welle wotes the catte, whoos berde he lykkys. **c1450** *Rylands MS.394* 100.32. **c1470** *Harley MS.3362* f.4b in *Retrospective* 309[31] and Förster 203.16: Wel wot the cat whas berd he (*no more*). Murilegus bene scit, quorum gernobada lambit. **c1490** *Sloane MS.747* 204.20: Wel wote the cat, whose berde he lykd. **1492** *Salomon and Marcolphus* 9[14–5]: The catte seeth wele whoos berde she lycke shall. **1523** Skelton *Garlande* I 418.1438: And wele wotith the cat whos berde she likkith. **1549** Heywood *D* 98.246: The cat knowth whose lips she lickth well enough. Apperson 87; Kneuer 50–1; *Oxford* 83; Schleich 270–1; Singer III 138; Tilley C140; Walther II 1017.15749–50.

C109 Who shall find a **Cat** true in keeping milk? (*varied*)
1492 *Salomon and Marcolphus* 6[22–3]: Who shal fynde a catte trewe in kepyng mylke? **a1533** Berners *Arthur* 66–7: Wysdome is greate if the cat never touched mylke; as much to say as, whan love toucheth, wysedome is than oftentymes overcome. Cf. Apperson 87: That cat is out of kind; *Oxford* 83; Tilley C167. See **P328.**

C110 Not avail a **Cat's Tail**
1481 Caxton *Reynard* 50[13–4]: It sholde not avaylle me a cattes tayl.

C111 **Catch** and hold
1546 Heywood *D* 23.28: Than catche and holde while I may. Apperson 89.

C112 **Catch** that catch may
a1393 Gower *CA* III 358–9.4420–2: And whan thei come were anon Among thebreus, was non insihte, Bot cacche who that cacche myhte. **c1395** Chaucer *CT* III[D] 76: Cacche whoso may, who renneth best lat see. **c1503** More *Early Poems* [12] B[5]: Catch who so may. **c1516** Skelton *Magnificence* 55.1750: They catche that catche may, kepe and holde fast, **1522** *Why Come* II 28.48. **1555** Heywood *E* 197.293. Apperson 89; *Oxford* 85; Tilley C189.

C113 To go a **Caterwauling**
c1395 Chaucer *CT* III[D] 354: To shewe hir skyn, and goon a-caterwawed. **1532** More *Confutacion* 342 A[9–10]: They maye runne out a caterwawing, and so wow and wedde. **1533** Heywood *Johan* A2r[40]: She shall repent to go a catter wawlyng, **1546** *D* 74.155: My cat gothe a catterwawyng. Tilley C192.

C114 **Cattle** (*property*) comes and goes
c1330 *Times of Edward II* (*Peterhouse*) 16[23–4]: Forsothe catel cometh and goth As wederis don in lyde (*March*). **a1400** *Trust Not* in *Pol. Rel. and Love Poems* 263.3–4: Worldes catel passet sone That wacset and wansit rit as te mone. **a1500** *Salamon sat and sayde* 291.35: Catel cummys and catel gase ryth as dos the fflode. See **F108, G330, 334, R119, T101, 161, 449, W671.**

C115 The more **Cattle** man has the more his heart craves (*varied*)

c1300 *Northern Homily Cycle* (*Edin. Coll. Phys.*) 143[17–8]: That the mar catel that man haves, The mar and mare his hert craves. **1484** Caxton *Aesop* 106[5–7]: For the myserable avarycious the more goodes that they have the more they desyr to have. **1509** Barclay *Ship* I 158[12]: The more that they have (the more they thynke they lacke), **c1523** *Mirrour* 64[49]: The moo they receyve, alway they gape for moo. Tilley M1144. Cf. Whiting *Drama* 123. See **M53, W713.**

C116 To brew a **Caudle** for one's head (*i.e.*, defeat him)
a1533 Berners *Arthur* 94[29]: By that tyme my brother hathe brewed a caudel for his heed.

C117 When I am dead make me a **Caudle**
c1300 Robert of Gloucester II 766.11767: As me seith wan ich am ded make me a caudel. **c1350** Serlo 216.103: Than ich am dede mak me kaudel. Apperson 138; *Oxford* 132; Tilley C196.

C118 **Cause** causes
1546 Heywood *D* 34.55–6: Cause causeth . . . and as cause causeth mee, So will I doo. Tilley C198.

C119 **Causes** badly begun are seldom brought to good end
c1390 Chaucer *CT* VII 1404[B2594]: The Book of Decrees seith, "Seelden, or with greet peyne, been causes ybroght to good ende whanne they been baddely bigonne." See **B199.**

C120 He that is angry without a **Cause** shall be made at one without amends
1508(1519) Stanbridge *Vulgaria* 23.21: Yf thou be angry with me without a cause, thou shall be made at one without a mendes. **1546** Heywood *D* 69.109–10: He . . . that will be angry without cause, Must be at one, without amendes. Apperson 11; *Oxford* 11; Tilley C200.

C121 Let the **Cause** cease and the effect will cease (*varied*)
c1385 Chaucer *TC* ii 483: But cesse cause, ay cesseth maladie. **c1412** Hoccleve *Regement* 60.1660: Styntynge the cause, the effect styntith eek (*margin:* cessante causa). **a1415** *Lanterne* 83.16–8: As the philosophur seith "Cessante causa, cessabit officialis," whanne the cause cesith, the spede therof schal cese. **c1415** *Middle English Sermons* 86.21–3: As the Philosop(h)ur seyth: "Cessante causa, cessat effectus—cessynge the cause, cessynge the effecte." **c1485** *Guiscardo* 46.136–7: For when the cause ys shent, The effect therof shall sone fade and fall. Apperson 617:10; *Oxford* 86; Tilley C202; Whiting *Scots* I 147.

C122 To fish a **Cause**
c1385 Chaucer *TC* iii 1162: As he that nedes most a cause fisshe. **c1400** *Seven Sages D* 32.990: To fische a causs heir or thare. NED Fish v.[1] 7.

C123 As sweet as **Cense** (*incense*)
a1450 *Castle* 137.2026: So come paramourys, swetter thanne sens. **1513** Douglas *Aeneid* III 94.28: Flowris sweit as sens, IV 68.44.

C124 As stable as any (a) **Center**
c1395 Chaucer *CT* V[F] 22: Of his corage as any centre stable. **c1421** Lydgate *Thebes* 72.1724: But pleyn and hool as a Centre stable, **a1422** *Life* 289.598: And evere Ilyche, as any centre stable, **a1439** *Fall* II 509.1310, 1439 *St. Albon* 143.935, **a1449** *Fabula* in *MP* II 486.7, *Secrees* 37.1163–4: A kynges promys shulde be Just and stable, As a Centre stonde in 0 degre, **c1475** *Aesop* (*Harl.*) in *Anglia* 9(1886) 3.38: Stable as a centre on a grounde of trowth.

C125 (Without **Ceres** and Bacchus Venus grows cold)
a1050 Defensor *Liber* 87[9]: Butan clænum hlafe ond wine acolað (venus) (*translating* Sine cerere et libero friget venus). **c1380** Chaucer *PF* 275–7: And Bachus, god of wyn, sat hire besyde, And Ceres next, that doth of hunger boote, And, as I seyde, amyddes lay Cypride, **c1385** *TC* v 208: He corseth Ceres, Bacus, and Cipride. **c1412** Hoccleve *Regement* 140.3890–2: And do to Bachus and Venus homage; Ffor non of hem two can be wel from othir, Thei love as vel as doth sustir and brothir. **c1475** *Thewis* 180.73–4: Fore metis and drinkis delycyus Causis lichory, men sais thus. **1483** *Vulgaria quedam abs Terencio* O2[v][14–7]: This is a trew saynge that men say comenly: whyth oute mete and drynk bodily lust coleth or abateth . . . Sine venere et libero friget venus. **1484** Caxton *Royal Book* S3[v][28–9]: For overmoche mete and drynke alyghteth the fyre of lecherye. **1509** Barclay *Ship* I 94[1–3]: Dronkennes and wretchyd glotony . . . Engendreth the rote of cursed Lechery. *Oxford* 86–7, 416; Tilley C211; Whiting *Ballad* 37. See **B243, 426, D395, G168, L228, W359, 553.**

C126 Though one is **Chafed** (*heated, angered*) let it cool
a1400 *Proverbis of Wysdom* (*II*) 223.73: Thow thou be chaufed, let it kele.

C127 As light as **Chaff**

c1200 Orm II 11.10534: That . . . wass lihht all allse chaff. Svartengren 298.

C128 He that sows **Chaff** shall mow poorly
1492 *Salomon and Marcolphus* 7[3–4]: He that sowyth chaf shal porely mowe. See **S542.**

C129 To be blown like **Chaff** by the wind
1497 Laurentius Wade *Beket* in *ESt* 3(1880) 432.827–8: As chaff blowne away by course off the wynde, Soo forsoke the bisshoppys owr blissede Thomas here. Whiting *Scots* I 148.

C130 Praise your **Chaffer** (*wares*) like (*according to*) the market
a1449 Lydgate *Consulo* in *MP* II 751.23: Lyke the market so preyse thy chaffare. Cf. Jente 693. See **L68.**

C131 To gnaw one's own **Chain**
c1385 Chaucer *TC* i 509: Now artow hent, now gnaw thin owen cheyne!

C132 As like as **Chalk** to coals
1533 More *Confutacion* 674 F[8–9]: No more like together, then is chalke to coles. Tilley C216.

C133 As white as **Chalk**
c1395 Chaucer *CT* V[F] 409: Amydde a tree, for drye as whit as chalk. **a1400** *Destruction of Troy* 99.3047: Hir chekes full choise, as the chalke white, 201.6201. **c1410** Lovelich *Grail* II 315.241–2: And the bon, As whit it lay Lik as doth Chalk In the Clay. **a1437** *Kingis Quair* 95.177[3]: A turtur quhite as calk. **c1450** *Jacob's Well* 3.5. **c1455** *Partonope S* 485.183. MED chalk 2; Taylor and Whiting 63–4.

C133a Chalk-white
c1390 *Sir Gawain* 25.798: Chalkwhyt chymnees, 30.958. **a1400** *Alexander C* 15.468: Hire chere at was chalke-quyte as any chaffe worthis, 84.1562, 86.1584. **a1400** *Morte Arthure* 31.1026: A chargour of chalke-whytt sylver, 40.1363, 62.2116, 67.2268, 75.2522, 90.3039, 96.3266, 98.3328, 107.3648: A chalke-whitte mayden. **a1437** *Kingis Quair* 89.157[3]. **c1440** *Degrevant* 96.1506: Chalked whyte (**a1500** *Cambridge:* chalkwhyghth) als the mylke. NED Chalk-white.

C134 Chalk and cheese
a1393 Gower *CA* II 16.416: Lo, how thei feignen chalk for chese, 193.2346–7: And thus folofte chalk for chese He changeth with ful litel cost. **1528** More *Heresyes* 241 H[15–7]: Many . . . that can perceive chalke fro chese well ynough. **1546** Heywood *D* 68.82: As a lyke to compare in taste, chalke and chese. Apperson 90; *Oxford* 87; Taylor and Whiting 64; Tilley C218; Whiting *Drama* 337:445.

C135 The **Chameleon** lives on air and changes color
1340 *Ayenbite* 62[30–2]: The lyeghere . . . is ase the gamelos thet leveth by the eyr and naght ne heth ine his roppes bote wynd, and heth ech manere colour thet ne heth non his oghen. **c1400** Mandeville *Travels* 193.5–11: And ther ben also in that contree manye camles, that is a lytill best as a Goot that is wylde and he lyveth be the eyr and eteth nought ne drynketh nought. **c1400** *Vices and Virtues* 60.28–31: And right so doth the lighere, and therfore he fareth as a butre-flye, that lyveth bi the aier and hath no thing in hire guttes but wynd, and at every colour that sche seth sche chaungeth hire owne. **c1450** *Jacob's Well* 151.16–8: A lyere is lykenyd to a bryd clepyd gamaltan. This bryd lyveth be the eyre, and hath no-thyng in hym but wynde. He wyl chaungyn hym to alle colourys that he seeth. *Oxford* 377. See **P272, W477.**

C136 The **Chameleon** may change to all colors save red and white
c1400 Mandeville *Travels* 193.5–11: Many camles that is a lytill best as a Goot . . . And he may chaunge him in to all maner coloures that him list, saf only in to red and white. Tilley C222.

C137 To change like a **Chameleon**
a1393 Gower *CA* II 109.2696–701: Anon his olde guise change He wole and falle therupon, Lich unto the Camelion, Which upon every sondri hewe That he beholt he moste newe His colour. MED camelioun (a); Tilley C221.

C138 Chance comes in many manners
c1303 Mannyng *Handlyng* 98.2774: For chaunce comth (*var.* chaunsis comyn) on many manere.

C139 Chance may fall which no man weened (*expected*)
c1390 *Northern Homily Cycle Narrationes* (*Vernon*) 297.26: Ffor chaunce mai falle that no man wende. See **M241.**

C140 Provide for hard **Chances** which afterwards may assail
c1523 Barclay *Mirrour* 20[26]: Provide for harde chaunces which after may assayle.

C141 There is no **Chance** but may turn
1525 Berners *Froissart* VI 220[4–5]: There is no chaunce but maye tourne. See **A51.**

C142 Change is no robbery
1546 Heywood *D* 68.78: Chaunge be no robbry, **1555** *E* 177.179: is no. Apperson 199: Fair; *Oxford* 182: Exchange; Taylor and Whiting 123; Tilley C228.

C143 **Change** of pasture makes fat calves
1546 Heywood *D* 67.43: Chaunge of pasture makth fat calves. Apperson 91; *Oxford* 88; Tilley C230. See **C145.**

C144 **Changes** are sweet
1508 Dunbar *Tretis* 86.53: Changeis ar sueit. Tilley C229; Whiting *Scots* I 148.

C145 **Changing** of country does not change courage
1480 Caxton *Ovyde* 10[35–6]: For it is sayd that for chaungynge of contre the corage is not chaunged and nomore shal myne. (Not from Ovid.) See **C143.**

C146 To sing **Chantepleure**
c1375 Chaucer *Anel.* 320–1: I fare as doth the song of *Chaunte-pleure;* For now I pleyne, and now I pleye. **1428** Lydgate *Complaint for My Lady of Gloucester* in *MP* II 612.96: They song lyche to the Chaunteplure, **a1430** *Pilgrimage* 2.30–1: Ffor sche is lyke to the chaunteplure; Wo after Joye and after song wepyng, **a1439** *Fall* I 59.2159–60: It is nat lik onto the chaunteplure, Gynnyng with joie, eendyng in wrechidnesse, III 675.8–9: She braideth ever on the chaunteplure: Now song, now wepyng, 1022.3623, **a1449** *Servant* in *MP* II 429.63–4: That I may singe the Chaunteplure As man forsake in every place, *They that no While Endure* in *MP* II 819.22.

C147 To serve the **Chapel** and let the church stand
c1330 *Times of Edward II* 327.78: And thus theih serven the chapele, and laten the churche stonde. (Of priests who leave their parishes to hunt and whore.)

C148 To deliver the **Chaplet** (*i.e.,* to pass the buck)
c1500 *Three Kings' Sons* 24.39–25.1: The kyng of Scottes . . . thought that everich of the kynges aforesaid had delyverd to hym the Chapelet.

C149 He is a foolish **Chapman** who buys horse or ox and looks only at the head
a1200 *Ancrene* 108.12–4: Ant nis he fol chapmon the hwen he wule buggen hors other oxe, yef he nule bihalden bute that heaved ane?

C150 This **Char** (*job*) is heaved (*?done*)
a1450 *Seven Sages B* 88.2603: This char hys heved. (A widow [of Ephesus] has just knocked out her late husband's teeth and is about to hang him up.) Apperson 91; *Oxford* 88; Tilley C241.

C151 To lay more **Charges** on one's back than he may bear away
c1420 Wyntoun III 305.1327–8: Mar chargis on his bak to lay Than he mycht lichtly bere away. NED Back, sb.[1] 2c, quote 1588. See **F56.**

C152 **Charity** becomes cold (*varied*)
c1000 *WSG* Matthew xxiv 12: And for þam þe unryhtwisnys rixað, manegra lufu acolaþ. **c1395** *WBible* Matthew xxiv 12: And for wickidnesse schal be plentevouse, the charite of manye schal wexe coold. **a1425** *Vae Octuplex* in Wyclif *SEW* II 385[31]: But charite is now coold. **1513** Bradshaw *St. Werburge* 136.166: Charite was colde. **c1522** Skelton *Speke* II 24.493: Cheryte so colde. **1533** More *Confutacion* 566 C[2–3]: Charity waxeth cold many a winter after. Apperson 106: Cold; *Oxford* 101: Cold; Taylor and Whiting 65; Tilley C253.

C153 **Charity** begins with oneself
c1400 *Of Prelates* in Wyclif *EW* 78[21–2]: Whanne charite schuld bigyne at hem-self. **c1415** *Middle English Sermons* 256.1: Sith, than, every charite begynneth of hym-selfe. **c1425** *Orcherd* 43.16. **1483** Caxton *Cato* C7r[19–20]: The charite ought to begynne at thy self, E2v[14–5]: Charyte begynneth at hym self. **1509** Barclay *Ship* I 277[22–4]: For perfyte love and also charite Begynneth with hym selfe for to be charitable And than to other after his degre. **1509** Watson *Ship* N3v[4–5]: For charyte well ordeyned ought to begynne at hymselfe. Apperson 91–2; *Oxford* 88; Skeat 299; Taylor and Whiting 65; Tilley C251. See **B513, M63, 172, O55, S43, 524, Z1.**

C154 **Charity** has no brother
c1400 Gower *Peace* III 489.266: And in this wise hath charite no brother.

C155 **Charity** heles (*covers*) all sins
c1395 *WBible* Proverbs x 12: Charite hilith alle synnes, I Peter iv 8: For charite coverith the multitude of synnes. **a1400** Paues 23 (I Peter iv 8): For charite heleth the mul(ti)tude of synnes. **c1450** *Speculum Christiani* (2) 214.23–4: As it is seyde: cheryte coverez the multitude of synnes. **1534** More *Comforte* 1168 H[1–2]. *Oxford* 88; Tilley L503.

C156 To have no **Charter** of one's life
c1450 *Fyrst thou sal* 91.175–6: Thou has no chartyr of thi lyfe, Cawse no debate ne make no stryfe.

C157 While (*sometimes*) one **Chases** and while he is chased
c1400 *Alexander Buik* II 177.2754: Quhyle men

chaissis and quhyll chaissit is. See **B65, V8, 32, W39.**

C158 If you are not **Chaste** be privy
c1303 Mannyng *Handlyng* 263.8315–6: The apostle seyth thys autoryte, "Gyf thou be nat chaste, be thou pryve." Apperson 92; *Oxford* 89; Tilley L381.

C159 Evil **Chasting** (*rebuke*) will wend (*turn*) to folly
c1300 *South English Legendary* (*Laud*) 414.394: For of(te) vuel chastingue to folie wolie wiende.

C160 He is wise that will **Chastise** himself
a1400 *Romaunt B* 3239: He is wis, that wol hymsilf chastise. Cf. Apperson 283: Happy is he; *Oxford* 277; Tilley C255.

C161 To **Chastise** oneself by others
a1300 *Alisaunder* 15.240–1: Me wondreth that men ne beeth a-gaste, And that somme hem by othere ne chasteth. **1340** *Ayenbite* 156[29–30]: Vor me kan zigge: thet zofte he him chasteth, thet be othren him chasteth. **c1400** *Vices and Virtues* 155.30–1: For men beth woned to seye, "Softe is he chastied that bi an other chastieth hymself." **1456** *Five Dogs of London* 190 e: Ffelix quem faciunt aliena pericula cautum. **c1475** Henryson *Fables* 38.1033: *as in 1456.* **1477** Rivers *Dictes* 71[18–9]: He is right happy that can chastyse him self, taking exemple by other. **1484** Caxton *Aesop* 117[1–3]: Fayre doctryne taketh he in hym self that chastyseth hym by the perylle of other, 117–8: And therfor he is wel happy that taketh ensample by the dommage of other. Jente 424; Walther II 47–8. See **B309, C40, E197, F116, 449, L247, M170, 581, 585, S428, W47, 391.**

C162 Whoso will not be **Chastised** by others shall (be) overthrown
a1300 *Alisaunder* 171.3035–6: Who so ne wil by other hym chaste, Overthrowe he shal in haste.

C163 She may not abide in **Chastity** that is assailed upon every side
c1395 Chaucer *CT* III[D] 255–6: She may no while in chastitee abyde, That is assailled upon ech a syde. See **C73, 79.**

C164 **Chatting** to chiding is not worth a chewet (*?jackdaw*)
a1546 Heywood *D* 73.114: Chatting to chiding is not woorth a chuet. Apperson 92; *Oxford* 89; Tilley C256.

C165 Be not where there is **Chaveling** (*squabbling*) and chest (*strife*)
c1250 *Owl* 28.293–7: At sume sithe herde (I) telle Hu Alvred sede on his spelle: "Loke that thu ne bo thare Thar chavling both and cheste yare, Lat sottes chide and vorth thu go." See **S91.**

C166 Light **Cheap** (*bargain*) yields litherly (*badly*)
c1250 *Hendyng O* 196–7.30: Lightte chepes luthere foryeldeth, **a1325** *C* 188.31: Lith chepe lither forweldeth, **c1325** *H* 297.232: Lyht chep luthere yeldes. **c1450** *Rylands MS.394* 103.19: Lythe chepe, lythur foryeldys. **a1460** *Towneley Plays* 121.170–1: And men say "lyght chepe Letherly for-yeldys." Apperson 364; Kneuer 43; *Oxford* 367; Schleich 265; Singer III 135; Tilley C258.

C167 What is good **Cheap** may be dear, and dear good cheap also
c1390 *Cato* (*Vernon*) 571.225–6: That is good chep may beo dere, And deore good chep also. *Oxford* 251.

C168 **Cheap** (*bargain*) before you buy
c1497 Medwall *Fulgens* C4v[20–1]: Fyrst ye shall Chepe or ever you by. Cf. *Oxford* 449: Never cheapen. See **B43, H550.**

C169 To say (play, *etc.*) **Checkmate**
1338 Mannyng *Chronicle A* I 300.8554: The Payens we al mat wyth that chekke. **c1385** Chaucer *TC* ii 754: Shal noon housbonde seyn to me "chek mat!". **c1390** *Robert* 43.184: With o draught he was chekmat. **c1390** *Talkyng* 38.3–4: With a poynt of chekmat comen me with inne. **c1400** *Sowdone* 8.266: Thai helde hem selfe Chek-mate, 84.2926: And felle alle chek-mate. **c1408** Lydgate *Reson* 128.4896: To tel, how that I was chek mate. **1419** *A remembraunce* in Kail 72.108: Ne delivere chekkys, er that he be mat. **a1420** Lydgate *Troy* I 199.1894: For in swiche pley unwarly cometh chek-mate, III 637.2494, 813.1406. **c1422** Hoccleve *Lerne to Die* 184.161: Al that lyf berith with hir chek is maat. **a1430** Lydgate *Pilgrimage* 172.6541: Thanne of Folye, he chek maat, 234.8440: Un-to hym to seyn "chek maat," 247.8948: Dysarmyd, nakyd, and chek-maat, 276.10064, 409.15206, 647.24160, **c1430** *Dance* 56.459, **a1437** *That now is Hay* in *MP* II 810.45: "Chekemate to beawtye," seyth rymplyd age, **a1439** *Fall* I 6.182, 21.762, 42.1526, 282.2933: Hath a fals joie to shewen hir chekmatis, II 330.52: I stood chekmaat for feer, 340.399, 587.67, III 923.170: Lik a woman that wer with wo chekmaat, **c1445** *Miracles of St. Edmund* 441.84, **a1449** *Fabules* in *MP* II 504.551. **a1450** Audelay 21.319: After chec fore

the roke, ware fore the mate. **a1450** *Generydes A* 241.7796–7: Ye sey unto this knight chek, And I sey chekmate to you (*literal*), 7801: With you he will play chek mate (*figurative*). **a1450** *Generydes B* 152–3.4777–80: "What tyme is now to play Atte Chesse?" quod he, "Thu byddest thy felaw chese, I understonde; Butt for certeyn I saye chek mate to the, Kyng Auferius is here withynne the land." **a1450** *Gesta* 71[30–1]: Than is hit to the man chekmate. **a1450** *Partonope* 316.7889: And your love hathe made hym chek-mate. **c1450** Capgrave *Katharine* 395.1733. **c1450** Idley 84.208: Remembre the draught of chek mate. **c1450** *Pilgrimage LM* 96[23]: Thou shalt make him chek and maat, 200[17]: She mowe seye to thee chek and maat. **a1461** *John the Reeve* 589.792–3: Hee vayled neither hatt nor hood, But stood with him checkmate. **a1475** *Good Rule* in Brown *Lyrics XV* 266.81–2: He that is bothe chek and mate It is ful hevy to restore. **c1475** *Guy*[1] 35 C 597. **c1480** *Contemplacioun* 217.832. **c1490** Ryman 240.11[2]: Therfore with us thou playest chekmate. **c1497** Medwall *Fulgens* F3[r][24]. **a1500** *A Ballad* in *Rel. Ant.* I 28[28]. **a1500** *Farewell* in Brown *Lyrics XV* 236.12. **a1500** *Fortune alas alas* 488.110. **a1500** Greene *Carols* 401 A 6, B 3. **a1500** Medwall *Nature* B4[r][11]: But that reason may have a chek mate, H2[r][20]: I have gyven hym a chek mate. **a1500** *Proverbs of Salamon* 185.55.8. **a1500** *The Seven Names of a Prison* in *Rel. Ant.* I 271[25]: A mane above is sone under by a draght of chekmate. **a1500** *Vanitas* in Brown *Lyrics XV* 239.33: Yit in a whyle thu schall be cheke-mate. **c1500** Greene *Carols* 408.14: When on his cheke he ys chekmate. **c1500** Skelton *Deedmans Hed* I 19.29–30: Oure days be datyd, To be chekmatyd. **c1500** *Smith* 324.119–20: Thou maye se by hyr chere That she is chekmate. **1504** Hawes *Example* Cc2[v][7]: In a gloryous chaumbre without chekmate, Ee8[r][5], **1506** *Pastime* 173.4603. **a1513** Dunbar *Rewl of Anis Self* 75.21. **1513** Bradshaw *St. Werburge* 58.1470: Whan dethe with his darte sayth to us chekemate. **1513** Skelton *Against the Scottes* I 186.128: Lost is your game, ye are checkmate, **c1516** *Magnificence* 11.307: I wyll not use you to play with me checke mate. **1520** Whittinton *Vulgaria* 104.22: He gaf hym noo lesse than a dosen chekmates or they had done. **1522** Skelton *Colyn* I 350.1014–5, *Speke* II 10.201, *Howe the Douty Duke* II 79.386, **a1529** *Garnesche* I 118–9.7: Be ware yet of chek mate, 14, 21, 28, 35, 42. MED chek-mat; NED Checkmate; Tilley C262; Whiting *Drama* 337:449, *Scots* I 148. See **M417.**

C170 To **Checkmate** someone
a1375 *Octavian* (S) 55.1745–6: Ther was many an hethen hounde, That thay chekmatyde. **1501** Douglas *Palice* 37.22: How may ane fule your hie honour chekmait?

C171 **Cheek** by cheek
a1338 Mannyng *Chronicle B* I 223[26]: So often away he wan, and umwhile cheke bi cheke. **a1533** Berners *Arthur* 352[11–2]: And soo rode togyther cheke by cheke tyl they came to theyr tentes, *Huon* 188.33–189.1: Rydynge cheke by cheke by kynge yvoryn. Apperson 92; Tilley C263.

C172 Maugre one's **Cheeks**
a1376 *Piers* A iv 37: Maugre hire chekes, vii 146: Maugre thi chekes, **c1378** B vi 41: Maugre Medes chekes, xiv 4. **c1380** *Patience* 15.54: Maugres my chekes. **a1400** *Alexander C* 96. 1747: Malegreve his chekis, 162.2782. **a1400** *Laud Troy* I 149.5029, II 404.13734. **c1405** *Mum* 64.1300: Malgre his chekes. **a1450** *Death and Life* 11.316: Mauger his cheekes.

C173 Between **Cheer** and thought a great division
a1420 Lydgate *Troy* I 114.3468–9: And thus ther was a gret divisioun A-twexe his chere and menyng of his thought.

C174 Good **Cheer** by countenance but not with hearts
a1470 Malory II 803.30–2: Aythir made other goode chere as by countenaunce, but nothynge wyth there hartes. See **F2, 6, H271, L376, M755, S138, 589.**

C175 Good **Cheer** is best sauce at table
a1500 Hill 131.31: In a thyn table, good chere is best sawse. Walther II 491.12099. Cf. Tilley C264, 266.

C176 Good **Cheer,** not many dainties, make a feast
a1449 Lydgate *Fabules* in *MP* II 581.433–4: As men seyen and reporte, at the leste, Nat many deyntees, but good chere maketh a feste. Cf. Apperson 92: A cheerful look; *Oxford* 251: When good cheer, 700: Welcome is; Tilley C266. See **M700.**

C177 Under fair **Cheer** poison is often hid
a1439 Lydgate *Fall* II 547.2709: Under fair cheer is ofte hid fals poisoun. See **G12, H433, 440, P289, S871, V19.**

C178 Better **Cheese** and bread than great dainty with anger
c1515 Barclay *Eclogues* 88–9.951–4: Better is it

with chese and bread one to fill, Then with a great dayntie, with anger and ill will, Or a small handfull with rest and sure pleasaunce, Then twenty dishes with wrathfull countenaunce. See **M700.**

C179 You see no green **Cheese** but your teeth must water
1546 Heywood *D* 97.232–3: Ye may see no greene cheese But your teeth must water. Apperson 274; *Oxford* 266; Tilley C275.

C180 As red as (any) **Cherry**
a1400 *Le Morte A.* 121.3956; With Roddys feyre and Rede as chery. **c1400** *Florence* 59.1761: Of the wyne redd as cherye. **a1450** *Lord that is* 217.219: Dropes rede as ripe cherrees. **a1500** *Squire* 33.713: Your ruddy read as any chery. Apperson 526; *Oxford* 535; Taylor and Whiting 66; Tilley C277; Whiting *Drama* 307:59.

C181 As ruddy as the **Cherry**
c1516 Skelton *Magnificence* 49.1558: Her lusty lyppes ruddy as the chery.

C182 As thick as **Cherries**
c1400 *Laud Troy* I 259.8778–9: Ther nis no tre so thikke of chiries As Gregeis ligge aboute him couched.

C183 **Cherry-ripe**
a1500 Greene *Carols* 401.B 4: And some of theym (*women*) be chiry-ripe. NED Cherry 10.

C184 Not chare (*?care for*) the value of a **Cherry**
a1400 *Chevelere* 17.329: I charde not thy croyse . . . the valwe of a cherye. Apperson 456.

C185 Not set a **Cherry**
a1513 Dunbar *Ane his awin Ennemy* 2.22: And sett nocht by this warld a chirry, *Of Covetyce* 142.42. Whiting *Scots* I 148.

C186 To be like a **Cherry**
1447 Bokenham 13.451: Hyr chyry chekys. **a1500** *The Beauty of his Mistress II* in Robbins 124.13: Hur lyppes ar lyke unto cherye. **c1500** Newton 270.26: Youre chek like a chere. Whiting *Ballad* 26.

C187 Not give a **Cherry-stone** (*varied*)
c1300 *Guy*[1] 552 A 203.7: Therof yive y nought a chirston. **a1400** *Ipomadon A* 99.3439–40: They sett all othur off worthynes But at a chery stone. **c1400** *Alexander Buik* I 4.106: He prysis him nocht worth a chirrie-stane. NED Cherry-stone.

C188 From hence to **Chester**
1546 Heywood *D* 41.12: Not a more gagglyng gander hense to Chester.

C189 As tender as a **Chick**
a1400 ?Chaucer *Rom. A* 541: Hir flesh (as) tendre as is a chike. Apperson 622; Svartengren 66; Tilley C287.

C190 To creep like **Chickens** under the dame's wing (*etc.*) (A number of single quotations are brought together here)
a1325 Bonaventura *Meditations* (*1*) 10.285–6: Behold the dyscyplys, yn here wendyng, As chekenes crepyn undyr the dame wyng. **c1420** Wyntoun V 431.3778–9: He gert feil fal doun til his fet Sprewlande, as thai chekynnys war. **a1430** Lydgate *Pilgrimage* 346.12727–8: I was take up in-to lyte, As a chykne off a kyte. **c1477** Caxton *Jason* 29.26–7: And breke thy necke as the necke of a cheken. **1532** Berners *Golden Boke* 426.10944–5: Ill may the chekyn truste the kyte, or the lambes the wolves.

C191 After **Chiding** came raps
1519 Horman *Vulgaria* 328[19]: After chydynge came rappis. Iurgantium ira pervenit ad manus. Cf. Taylor and Whiting 412: A word and a blow.

C192 A good **Chieftain** makes good men
a1400 *Scottish Legends* II 89.708–9: And be assay men ma wele kene That gud chiften makis (gud) men. Cf. Tilley C70. See **C34, L455, M408, P403.**

Child, see **Bairn**

C193 As buxom (*obedient*) as a **Child**
a1450 *Rule of St. Benet* (*2*) 111.2268: Of bering bowsum os a child.

C194 As chaste as a **Child**
a1430 *St. John* in Horstmann *Legenden 1881* 468.61: Chaste as a childe.

C195 As meek as a **Child**
a1338 Mannyng *Chronicle A* I 132.3753: And also meke was as a child. **c1440** ?Nassington *Speculum Vitae* in *ESt* 7(1884) 470.135–6: Thei schulde become bothe meke and myld And debonere, os ony chylde. **a1450** *Castle* 141.2128: Whanne he stod meker thanne a chylde. **c1475** *Golagros* 13.350: And he is maid on mold meik as ane child. Svartengren 63.

C196 As merry as a **Child**
c1400 *Laud Troy* I 164.5548–51: So mery was nevere . . . no child playing with his top, As Ayax was.

C197 As mild as a **Child**

1340 *Ayenbite* 98[33]: Become milde ase a child. **a1450** *Desert* 60.53–4: Men that ar mylde And debonere als a chylde.

C198 As naked as a **Child**
c1400 *Sowdone* 90.3159: Make him naked as a Childe.

C199 Better a young **Child** weep than an old man
c1450 *Douce MS.52* 53.103: Better is a yong chylde wepe than an olde man. **c1450** *Rylands MS.394* 103.12. **c1475** *Rawlinson MS. D 328* 123.61: Hit ys better to se a chyld wepe than a man. **1546** Heywood *D* 44.116: Better children weepe then olde men, **1555** *E* 154.51. Apperson 42; Jente 129; *Oxford* 39; Tilley C326. See **M295.**

C200 Better is a **Child** unborn than unbeaten (*varied*)
c1250 *Proverbs of Alfred* 98 T 243–4: For betere is child unboren Thenne unbeten (J: unbuhsum). **c1250** *Hendyng O* 191.4: For betere were child ounboren, then ounbeten. **c1303** Mannyng *Handlyng* 161.4855–6: Better were the chylde unbore Than fayle chastysyng and syththen lore. **c1350** *Good Wife E* 170.161–2: Betere were child unbore Than techingeles forlore, **c1425** *H* 172.208: Better wer a childe unborn than untaught. **c1450** *Douce MS.52* 54.106: Better is a chylde unborne then unlerned. **c1450** Idley 180.1275–6: Better were the childe to be unborn Than unchastised and set in no governaunce. **c1450** *Rylands MS.394* 104.23. **a1475** *Assembly of Gods* 39.1308–9: For bettyr were a chylde to be unbore, Then let hyt have the wyll and for ever be lore. **c1475** *Rawlinson MS. D 328* 118.18: Better ys a chyld on-bore then on-taughth. **c1475** Symon *Lesson* 399.4–6: Old men yn proverbe sayde by old tyme "A child were beter to be unbore Than to be untaught, and so be lore." **1495** Fitzjames *Sermo* G3[r][7–9]: A comyn proverbe it is and a wyse (that better is a chylde unborn than untaught). **a1500** Hill 129.37: Better it is to be wnborne than wntawght. **1520** Whittinton *Vulgaria* 109.29–30: For it is comenly sayd, it is better a chylde unborne than untaught. **1546** Heywood *D* 37.57: Better unborne then untought, I have heard saie, **1555** *E* 172.146. Apperson 46; Kneuer 18–9; *Oxford* 42–3; Schleich 249; Singer III 125–6: Skeat 42; Tilley U1. See **Y1.**

C201 A burnt **Child** dreads the fire (*varied*)
c1250 *Hendyng O* 199.43: Brend child fuir fordredeth. **a1325** *Cursor* II 418.7223–4: Sare man aght to dred the brand That brint him forwit in his hand. **1340** *Ayenbite* 116[1–2]: The ybernde ver dret. **c1395** Chaucer *CT* VIII[G] 1407–8: O! fy, for shame! they that han been brent, Allas! kan they nat flee the fires heete? **a1400** *Romaunt B* 1819–20: "For evermore gladly," as I rede, "Brent child of fir hath myche drede." **c1400** *Beryn* 4.78: Brennyd Cat dredith feir. **1406** Hoccleve *Male Regle* 37.390: The fyr, men seyn, he dreedith that is brent. **a1410** Lydgate *Churl* in *MP* II 476.178: For brent child dredith fyer. **c1412** Hoccleve *Regement* 86.2382: He that is brent, men seyn, dredith the fire. **c1450** *Douce MS.52* 48.52: Brende chylde fyre dredis. **c1450** *Rylands MS.394* 98.11. **c1470** *Harley MS.3362* f.2b in *Retrospective* 309[16]: Onys y-brend ever dret feer. **c1470** *Wallace* 88.456: A brynt child mayr sayr the fyr will dreid. **1484** Caxton *Royal Book* K3[r] [6–7]: Brent chylde fyre dredeth. **c1515** Barclay *Eclogues* 70.512: For children brent still after drede the fire. **1546** Heywood *D* 62.6: And burnt childe fyre dredth. Apperson 73; Jente 777; Kneuer 36–7; *Oxford* 70; Schleich 260; Singer III 132; Taylor and Whiting 68; Tilley C297; Whiting *Scots* I 133. See **B211, H53, M160, S253, W87.**

C202 A **Child** first creeps and afterward goes (*walks*)
c1443 Pecock *Reule* 376[27–8]: And right as a babe firste he bigynnyth to crepe, aftirward to go. **c1450** *Douce MS.52* 55.116: Fyrst the chylde crepyth and after gooth. **c1450** *Rylands MS.394* 104.18.10. **a1460** *Towneley Plays* 103.100: Ffyrst must us crepe and sythen go. **c1515** Barclay *Eclogues* 2.53–4: Like as these children do, Which first use to creepe, and afterwarde to go. **1546** Heywood *D* 47.197: Children learne to creepe er they can learne to go, **1555** *E* 154.54: Children must learne to creepe ere thay can go. Apperson 214–5; *Oxford* 92, 204; Tilley C332. See **C205, K34.**

C203 A **Child** is easily wroth and easily saught (*appeased*) (*varied*)
a1415 Mirk *Festial* 26.18–20: Scho bethoght hur how that chyldern don no vengeans, but lightly ben saght, thogh thay ben wrothe. **a1449** Lydgate *Stans Puer* in *MP* II 743.80–4: To childer longeth nat to be vengable, Sone mevyd and sone fforgevyng; And as it is remembrid by old writyng, Wratthe of children sone is overgoon, Withe an appell partyes be maad at oon. **c1450** *Ratis* 49.1728–31: And as of Child of yhong manere Wil Change fantasiis seire, For lytil blytht, for lytil wraithe, For lytil leif, for lytil laithe. **a1500** *Disciplina*

Clericalis 51–2: The kyng whiche is . . . light to wrath as a chield. See **F412, W547.**

C204 A **Child** loves an apple more than a castle (*varied*)
1340 *Ayenbite* 208[31–2]: He nele the yave pere ne eppel, ase me deth ane childe. **1348** Rolle *Form* in Allen *Rolle* 113.164–5: Barnes, that lufes mare an appel than a castel. **a1398** (1495) Bartholomaeus-Trevisa m5ᵛ[2.2–3]: And they (*children*) love an apple more than golde. **c1400** *Vices and Virtues* 231.7–8: For he wole not paie the with an appel or a peere, as doth a child. **1484** Caxton *Royal Book* H1ʳ[24–6]: Suche people been lyke a chylde that loveth better an apple or a myrrour than a royame, R5ᵛ[17–8]: He (*God*) wyl not appease the wyth an appel or with a pere, as a chylde.

C205 A **Child** must choose children's gear
a1400 *Alexander C* 98.1773: For ai a child mot him chese to childire geris. See **C202.**

C206 A **Child's** bird and a knave's wife have great sorrow (*varied*)
a1400 *Lambeth MS.120* in M. R. James and C. Jenkins *Catalogue* (Cambridge, 1930) 199: Foure leden an il lyf: Huntys hors hors (*sic*), an knavis wyef, Cherlys cherl, and chyldys bryd, Michil soruyn ys hem be tyd. **a1410** Lydgate *Churl* in *MP* II 484.372–5: Un-to purpoos this proverbe is ful riff, Rad and reportid bi oold remembraunce: A childis (*var.* chorles) brid, and a knaves wyff Have oft(e) sithe gret sorwe and myschaunce. **1523** Skelton *Garlande* I 419.1451–2: But who may have a more ungracyous lyfe Than a chyldis birde and a knavis wyfe? Apperson 95; M. R. James *Descriptive Catalogue . . . Corpus Christi College Cambridge* (Cambridge, 1909) I 192; *Oxford* 91; Tilley C320. See **C261, V37.**

C207 A **Child's** love is lost for an apple
1483 Caxton *Cato* G5ʳ[26–7]: The chylde (for for an apple one leseth his love). Cf. Tilley A295. See **L561, M297.**

C208 **Child's** pig and father's flitch
c1450 *Douce MS.52* 54.113: Childe is pigge and fader is the flicche. **c1450** *Rylands MS.394* 104.21: Cheeldes pygge and faderis flyche. Apperson 95; *Oxford* 91; Tilley C321.

C209 A **Child** should love and trust his mother best
a1450 *Partonope* 186.4962–6: My ffayre sone, ye wotte well thys, In alle thys worlde a-lyve ther nys Thynge that better loved shulde be, Ne trusted neyther, as thynketh me, Then of a chylde shulde be the moder. Stevenson 1627:4: A boy's best friend is his mother. See **C211.**

C210 A **Child** taught young will be the better when old (*varied*)
a1300 *Proverbs of Alfred* 97 J 225–32: If hit so bi-tydeth That thu bern ibidest The hwile hit is lutel, Ler him mon-thewes; Thanne hit is wexynde Hit schal wende ther-to The betere hit schal iwurthe Ever buven eorthe. **a1300** *Arthour and M.*[1] 3.9–16: Childer, that ben to boke ysett, In age hem is miche the bett, For thai mo witen and se Miche of godes privete, Hem to kepe and to ware Fram sinne and fram warldes care, And wele ysen, yif thai willen, That hem no tharf never spillen. **c1320** *Bodley MS.2305* f.9a in Andrew G. Little *Studies in English Franciscan History* (Manchester, 1917) 151: Chastez your children whil thei be yonge, Of werk, of dede, of speche, of tonge, Ffor if ye lete hem be to bolde, He wil yowe greve whan thei ben olde. See **Y27, 32.**

C211 A **Child** that has lost his mother, his help is behind
c1300 *Becket I* 9.162: For child that hath his moder ilore, his help is moche bi hynde. See **C209.**

C212 The **Child** that the mother blesses is often eased
c1425 Hoccleve *Jonathas* 231.440–1: The chyld whom that the modir usith blesse, Fful often sythe is esid in distresse.

C213 A **Child** trows what men say is sooth
c1450 *Jacob's Well* 245.15: As a yung chyld trowyth it sooth that men sayn.

C214 Give your **Child** when he will crave and your whelp while it will have and you shall have a foul child and a fair hound
c1303 Mannyng *Handlyng* 231–2.7237–42: For, thus seyth the olde man Yn a proverbe that he can, "Gyve thy chylde when he wyl krave, And thy whelp whyl hyt wyl have, Than mayst thou make yn a stounde A foule chylde and a feyre hounde." Apperson 95; *Oxford* 237; Skeat 98; Tilley C304.

C215 If your **Child** is not afeared give him enough of the yard (*rod*)
c1390 *Proverbes of diverse profetes* 537–8.233–6: Yif thi child be not a-fert, Gif him i-nouh of the yerd; Thou schalt him so make a good mon With-outen brekynge of eny bon. See **Y1.**

C216 Lief (*dear*) **Child** behoves (*needs*) lore (*varied*)

c1250 *Hendyng O* 191.4: Lef child bihoveth lore, And evere the levere the more, **a1325** *C* 182.3: Lothe childe behovid lore, And leve childe som del more, **c1325** *H* 289.37: Luef child lore byhoveth. **c1350** *Good Wife E* 168.155: Lef child lore bihoveth. **c1378** *Piers* B v 37–8: My syre seyde so to me, and so did my dame, That the levere childe the more lore bihoveth. **c1450** *Douce MS.52* 53.100: Lefe chylde lore be-hoveth. **c1450** *Good Wife L* 202.182–3: Leve child byhoveth loore, And evere lever the more. **c1450** *Rylands MS.394* 103.30. **a1475** *Good Wyfe Wold* 173.5–6: Seyd hit ys full yore That lothe chylde lore behowyyt, and leve chylde moche more. **c1475** Symon *Lesson* 402.87–8: For, as the wyse man sayth and prevyth, A leve chyld, lore he be-hovyth. Apperson 139; Kneuer 18–9; Schleich 249; Singer III 125.

C217 Of a **Child** and (a) drunken man truth was tried
c1425 *St. Mary Oignies* 154.8: Atte laste treuthe was tryed oute of a childe and dronken man. *Oxford* 92; Tilley C328. See **C229.**

C218 Oft men kiss the **Child** for the nurse's sake
c1470 *Harley MS.3362* f.2a in *Retrospective* 309[3] and Förster 199.3: Ofte me kessyt the chil (*rest lacking*). Osculor hunc ore puerum nutricis amore. **c1475** *Rawlinson MS. D 328* 125.83: Ffor the love off the nursse the chyld ys y-chest. **1546** Heywood *D* 86.214: Many kisse the childe for the nurses sake. Apperson 343; Jente 578; *Oxford* 340; Tilley C312. See **L37, P27.**

C219 Seely (*good*) **Child** is soon learned.
a1300 *Trinity MS. 0.2.45* 9 (18): I-seli child is sone ilered. **c1300** *South English Legendary* II 615.158: For sely child is sone ilered. **a1325** *Hendyng C* 183.6: Seli childe is sone ilerid, And unselinis nevir aferid, **c1325** *H* 290.69: *first part only.* **c1390** Chaucer *CT* VII 512[B 1702]: For sely child wol alday soone leere. **c1450** *Consail and Teiching* 69.121: Fore sely barnis are eith to leire. **c1450** *Rylands MS.394* 104.26: Sely chylde, sone lerned. Apperson 257, 519; Kneuer 64; *Oxford* 590; Schleich 269; Singer III 137; Skeat 245; Tilley B44.

C220 To be **Child's** game (play)
a1300 *The Cloisterer's Lament* in *Rel. Ant.* I 292[38]: It is but childes game that thu witz David dayles. **c1400** *Vices and Virtues* 141.34–5: Al hym thenketh is but childes playe amydde the strete. **1438** *Barlaam* 7.24: Thou hast made a childes play. **c1493** *St. Katherin of Senis* 307.17: (It) is but a chyldys game in comparison. **c1522** Skelton *Colyn* I 322.301–2: Of symony, men say, But a chyldes play. Taylor and Whiting 68.

C221 To be no **Child's** game (play)
a1325 *Otuel and Roland* 74.489: Ne was ther no chyldys game. **c1330** *Gregorius* 115 A 612: Ther no was no childes playe (*R* gamen). **c1350** *Octavian NL* 121.878: Was thore no childes playe, 124.1038, 125.950. **c1350** *Libeaus* 37.641. **c1395** Chaucer *CT* IV[E] 1530–1: I warne yow wel, it is no childes pley To take a wyf. **a1400** *Le Morte A.* 10.304: By-twene them was no chi(l)dis play, 67.2245. **1449** Metham 44.1194–5: For yt ys no chyldys pleyng To fyght with sqwyche a devyl. **a1450** *Tottenham* 995.154: I wot it ys no chylder-game whan thay togedyr met. **a1500** *Imitatione* (*1*) 107.18–9: This is not . . . children pley. Tilley C324; Whiting *Drama* 338:452, *Scots* I 134.

C222 To rock like a **Child** in a cradle
c1350 *Libeaus* 95.1711–2: Set and rokked in his sadell, As a child doth in a cradell.

C223 To weep like a **Child**
c1390 Chaucer *CT* I[A] 3759: And weep as dooth a child that is ybete. **a1470** Malory I 358.19–20: And ever he wepte as he had bene a chylde.

C224 Well he stands that strenes (*begets*) a good **Child**
c1300 *Havelok* 101.2983: Him stondes wel that god child strenes. *Oxford* 700; Skeat 57.

C225 Well is the **Child** that may thrive (be his father what he be)
c1350 *Good Wife E* 170.168: Wel is the child that thrive mai. **a1450** *South English Legendary* (*Bodley*) 331.5–6: And that men seth wel ofte: also thinketh me, Therfore wel is the child that may I-the, be fadir what he be. See **F73.**

C226 What a **Child** takes in youth he has a smell of in age
1520 Whittinton *Vulgaria* 110.9–11: It is evydent to every man: that a chyld taketh in youthe (be it good or bad) comenly in age he hath a smell therof. See **C375, 524, L248, M308, S240, Y32.**

C227 Who sees a **Child** sees nothing
1487 Caxton *Book of Good Manners* F8^r[29–30]: For as the comyn proverbe saith, how (*for* who) seeth a chylde seeth no thyng. (*I.e.*, from the child one cannot judge the man.)

C228 A wise **Child** is father's bliss
a1300 *Proverbs of Alfred* 97 J 224: Wis child is fader blisse. Apperson 696.

C229 **Children** and fools cannot lie
1546 Heywood *D* 48.217: Men say also, children and fooles can not ly. Apperson 96; *Oxford* 92; Tilley C328. See **C217.**

C230 **Children** are often unlike their elders
c1395 Chaucer *CT* IV[E] 155–6: For God it woot, that children ofte been Unlyk hir worthy eldres hem bifore.

C231 **Children** have quickest wits when fasting
c1495 *Arundel Vulgaria* 39.163: It is a comyn saynge that Children have most quyke wyttes when they be fastynge, but I fynde the contrary.

C232 He may surely swim that is held up by the **Chin**
1471 Ripley *Compound* 156[17–8]: But he they say may surely swym in dyche, Whych ys upholden by the chyn. **c1475** *Rawlinson MS. D 328* 119.25: He may the better suwe that ys holdde up by the schyn. **a1500** Hill 129.47: He mai lightli swim, that is hold wp by the chin. **1546** Heywood *D* 26.21: He must needes swym, that is holde up by the chyn. Apperson 614–5; *Oxford* 636; Tilley C349.

C233 To swear by one's **Chin**
a1200 Lawman II 363.18764: And swor bu his chinne. **1265** *Song of Lewes* in Brown *Lyrics XIII* 132.30: Sire simond de mountfort hath suore bi ys chyn.

C234 As merry as three **Chips**
1546 Heywood *D* 30.42: So playde these twayne, as mery as three chipps. Apperson 414; *Oxford* 420; Tilley C356.

C235 He that hews over high **Chips** (*spoons, spale*) fall in his eye (*varied*)
a1338 Mannyng *Chronicle B* I 91[15–6]: In Wyndesouere is he leved, sorow than is his pyne, That he wis over his heved, the chip falles in his ine, II 330[10]: It fallis in his iye, that hewes over hie, with the Walays. **c1385** Usk 38–9.19–21: For commenly it is spoken, and for an olde proverbe it is leged: "He that heweth to hye, with chippes he may lese his sight." **a1393** Gower *CA* II 88.1917–8: Fulofte he heweth up so hihe, That chippes fallen in his yhe. **a1400** *Eglamour* 5.70–2: Mayster, the man, that hewes over-hey, The chyppis (*vars.* spones, spaile) fallis in his eye; Thus fallis it ay-whare. **c1405** *Mum* 69.1473–4: And who-so hewe over heede, though his hoode be on, The spones wol springe oute and spare not the eye. **a1420** Lydgate *Troy* I 48.1230–2: And it is not holsom a man to hewe Aboven his hed, whan it is overe highe, List the chippis wil fallen in his eye. **a1425** *Neither too Humble* in Brown *Lyrics XV* 286.17–20: Ther-for loke that thow be scley, Ffor no thyng hew thow tow hey, Last they falle don in-to thy ey, The spones that Above they be. **c1433** Lydgate *St. Edmund* 414.5–7: And I am ferful above myn hed to hewe, Lyst froward chippis of presumpcioun Sholde blynde myn eyen in ther fallyng doun. **c1440** *Prose Alexander* 36.10–2: And tharefore es thare a commone proverbe: that "wha sa hewes to hie, the chippes will falle in his egh." **a1449** Lydgate *Fabules* in *MP* II 572.168: Me lyst nat hewe chyppes above myn hede. **c1450** *Douce MS.52* 55.128: Who-so hewyth to hye, There falle chippis in his ye. **c1450** *Rylands MS.394* 107.21^{v}.6. **1492** *Salomon and Marcolphus* 7[14–6]: As ye smyte wyth an axe in an hard tre, beware that the chippes falle not in youre ye. **a1500** Hill 129.48: Clime not to hie, lest chipis fall in thin eie, 132.38: He that heweth to hye, the chippis will fall in his ye. **c1500** Greene *Carols* 348.3: To hew abow thy hedde, hit is but vanite, Lest in thy yee ther falle a chyppe. **1546** Heywood *D* 84.134: Hewe not to hye, lest the chips fall in thine iye. Apperson 300; *Oxford* 293–4: Tilley C354, 357; Whiting *Scots* I 188. See **H221.**

C236 Not differ a **Chip**
1556 Heywood *Spider* 176[24]: Thei differ not a chip.

C237 Not worth a **Chip**
1546 Heywood *D* 94.140: His gaine is not woorth a chip. Apperson 456:5.

C238 As cold as **Chisel**
c1390 *Gregorius* 52.428: As cold as chisel under led.

C239 **Choice** is good in most things
1560 Heywood *E* 214.48.1: Choice is good in most things, folke say.

C240 A choking **Choke-plum**
1556 Heywood *Spider* 162[1–2]: The spiders tale . . . semth a choking choke plum Against flies. See **O93.**

C241 **Choose** and crave not, quod Carter
a1500 *MS. Marginalia* in Hoccleve I 201, n. 1: Choos and Crave not, quod Carter.

C242 To **Chop** and change
a1438 Kempe 127.24–5: Thu gevist the to bying

and sellyng, choppyng and chongyng. **c1450** Idley 210.432: Thei chop and change and mak marchandysse. **c1475** *Wisdom* 56.642: Choppe and chonge with symonye. **1519** Horman *Vulgaria* 335[12–3]: Choppyng and chaungynge, 340[13–4, 21–2]. *Oxford* 94; Tilley C363; Whiting *Scots* I 149.

C243 The **Chough** is wood (*insane*)
c1395 Chaucer *CT* III[D] 231–3: A wys wyf shal, if that she kan hir good, Bere hym on honde that the cow is wood, And take witnesse of hir owene mayde. **a1450** *Partonope* 424. 10282: I have bore you on honde the cowe was wode. **a1500** Medwall *Nature* A4ʳ[4]: Or bere hym on hand the kow ys wood. **1546** Heywood *D* 81.27 (*apparently misunderstood*). See Robinson *Chaucer* 699 (note).

C244 To chitter (chatter) like a **Chough**
c1405 *Mum* 37.345: So chiding and chatering (as choghe) were he ever. **1402** *Daw Topias* (*Jack*) 40[7]: Or chyterynge as chowghes. See **J19.**

C245 To say **Christ** (God) sain (*bless*) as when men sneeze
a1456 *Hit is no right* in *MLN* 19(1904) 38[15]: Yit might I seyne cryst seeyne, as whan men sneese. **1483** Caxton *Golden Legende* 25ʳ[2.34–9]: In this manere somtyme snesing they deyed. So whan ony persone was herd snesing, anone they that were by sayd to him, god helpe you, or, crist helpe you: and yet endureth the custome. *Oxford* 226: Friend at; Tilley G178.

C246 If **Christmas** on the Sunday be a troublous winter you shall see
a1500 *Song* in M. A. Denham *Collection of Proverbs and Popular Sayings* (PS 20, 1847) 69[1–3]: Yf Crystmas day on the Sonday be, A trobolus wynter ye shall see, Medlyd with waters stronge. Apperson 99.

C247 To turn **Christmas** into Lent
a1500 *Lay of Sorrow* 716.17: My cristenmess Is turnit In to lent. See **G369.**

C248 Who that makes in **Christmas** a dog to his larder, *etc.*
c1417 *Lansdowne MS.762* in *Rel. Ant.* I 233[21–4]: Who that maketh in Cristemas a dogge to his larder, And in Marche a sowe to his gardyner, And in Maye a fole of a wise mannes councell, He shall never have good larder, faire gardeyn, nor wele kepte councell. **1486** ?Berners *Boke of St. Albans* F5ᵛ. Apperson 162.

C249 As bright as **Chrysolite**
1513 Douglas *Aeneid* IV 68.37: Crysp haris, brycht as chrisolyte.

C250 The **Church** is no hare (wild cat), it will abide
1340 *Ayenbite* 51[2–3]: The cherche nys non hare, hy abyt me wel. **c1400** *Vices and Virtues* 47.23–4: I mot slepe, for the chirche is noon hare; he wole abide me wel. **a1450** *Pride of Life* in Waterhouse 102.425–6: Nay churc nis no wyl coot (*MS.* cot), Hit wol abid ther. **c1450** *Jacob's Well* 141.22–3: The cherche is non hare, there men leve it they may fynde it. **c1450** *Lincoln Cath. Lib. MS. A 6.2* f.68b in Owst *Literature* 44–5: But there is many that carythe not for the preste, ne for the chyrche. For thei wil sey—"it is no wilde catt, ne it wyll not flee." And so thei sett not by the chyrche, ne by the kepers there-of. **1484** Caxton *Royal Book* E7ᵛ[17]: The chirche is non hare, he wyl not flee awaye. Tilley C376.

C251 The nearer the **Church** the farther from God
c1303 Mannyng *Handlyng* 290.9241–2: Tharfor men seye, an weyl ys trowed, "The nere the cherche, the fyrther fro God." **c1450** *Douce MS.52* 45.15: The nere the chyrche, the fer fro Crist. **c1450** Idley 210.395–6: But the nerer the chyrch the ffarther from God—Yt ys a proverbe. **c1450** *Rylands MS.394* 96.4. **c1475** *Rawlinson MS. D 328* 126.87: The nyer the cherche the ferder fowre good. **a1500** *Additional MS.37075* 277.7: The nerer the chyrch the further fro God. **a1500** Hill 130.12. **1546** Heywood *D* 33.15: The nere to the churche, the ferther from God, **1555** *E* 174.157. Apperson 438; *Oxford* 445; Skeat 100; Tilley C380. Cf. Jente 798.

C252 To pill (*rob*) the **Church** to lead (mend) the choir
c1515 Barclay *Eclogues* 47.1268: Some pill the Churche, therewith to leade the quere, **c1523** *Mirrour* 30[31]: Uncover not the Church, therwith to mende the quere. Apperson 658; *Oxford* 545; Tilley K101.

C253 Who goes to **Church** against his will comes home accursed
c1450 *Douce MS.52* 46.21: Who-so goth to chirch agenst his will, he comyth home acursyd. **c1450** *Rylands MS.394* 97.12–3.

C254 He that will not willingly go into the **Church Door** shall unwillingly be led into hell door
a900 Bede 442.21–3: þonne him gelomp ðæt

sume men gewuniað cweðan: Se ðe ne wile cirican duru wilsumlice geeadmoded ingongan, se sceal nede in helle duru unwillsumlice geniþerad gelæded beon.

C255 Be the **Churl** never so hard he shall quake ere he pass Lizard (Point, Cornwall)
1456 *The Itineraries of William Wey* (RC 76, 1857) 155[4–9]: Prima pars Anglie percepta et visa a nautis nostris vocatur Browsam Rokke; . . . quinta, Lizarda, de qua communiter dicitur, Be the chorel nevyr so hard, He shall quwake by the berde ar he passe Lyzarde.

C256 A **Churl** does a churl's deed
c1395 Chaucer *CT* III[D] 2206: I seye, a cherl hath doon a cherles dede.

C257 The **Churl** gave a doom which came to him(self) after
c1405 *Mum* 39.421–2: For as hit is y-seide by eldryn dawes, "The churle yafe a dome whiche came by hym aftre." See **D342.**

C258 A **Churl** is deemed by his deed
a1400 *Romaunt B* 2200: A cherl is demed by his dede. MED dede 7. See **V35.**

C259 A **Churl** is the better for pilching and peeling, *etc.*
a1200 *Ancrene* 46.2–4: For eaver me schal thene cheorl peolkin and pilien, for he is as the within the spruteth ut the betere that me hine croppeth ofte, **a1400** (*Recluse*) 37.23–4: Yt fareth by the Cherle as by the wythye, the more men croppen it, the more it wexeth, **a1500** (*Royal*) 12.27–9: For ever men shal pluke and pile the chorle, For he fareth as doth the wytheg that springeth and spredeth the better that men croppen it oft.

C260 A **Churl** of birth hates gentle blood
c1440 Lydgate *Debate* in *MP* II 564.598: A cherl of berthe hatith gentil blood. Cf. Tilley M743.

C261 A **Churl's** churl is often woebegone (*varied*)
a1410 Lydgate *Churl* in *MP* II 279–80: For it was seyd of ffolkis yoore a-goon, A cherlis cherl (*vars.* wyfe, brid) ful oft is woo-bigoon, 484.361: Whoo serveth a cherl hath many a carful day, 371: A cherlis cherl (*var.* byrde) is alwey woobegon. Apperson 100. See **C206, V37.**

C262 A **Churl** would that each man were the same
a1410 Lydgate *Churl* in *MP* II 474.140: But who is a cherl wold eche man were the same. See **F409.**

C263 **Churls** spring from such seeds as lords
c1390 Chaucer *CT* X[I] 761–2: Thynk eek that of swich seed as cherles spryngen, of swich seed spryngen lordes. As wel may the cherl be saved as the lord. The same deeth that taketh the cherl, swich deeth taketh the lord. Wherfore I rede, do right so with thy cherl, as thou woldest that thy lord dide with thee, if thou were in his plit. See **A37, F81, K43.**

C264 Claw a **Churl** by the arse and he shits in one's hand
1546 Heywood *D* 83.97: Claw a churle by thars, and he shyteth in my hand. Apperson 100; Tilley C386.

C265 For a **Churl** to reign is contrary to nature
a1449 Lydgate *Look* in *MP* II 767.60: A cherl to regne is contrary to nature.

C266 Give a **Churl** rule and he will not be sufficed (*satisfied*)
a1470 Malory II 712.23–4: And as ever hit is an olde sawe, "Gyeff a chorle rule and thereby he woll nat be suffysed." Apperson 100. See **C271.**

C267 It is evil (*hard*) to know **Churls** in charnel
c1378 *Piers* B vi 50–1: For in charnel atte chirche, cherles ben yvel to knowe, Or a knighte fram a knave there. See **E22, K43, L448.**

C268 It is the **Churl's** kind to be courteous to him whom he dreads
a1450 *Partonope* 113–4.3375–80: For thus ys ever chorles kynde: He thatt he dredythe, schalle hym fynde Curteyse, esy, and debonowre, Tyll thatt he may have tyme and leysowr Hys master to do summe fowle despyte; Hys kendenes ther-wythe he wolle aquyte.

C269 Of a **Churl** can come nought but poison and filth
c1489 Caxton *Blanchardyn* 173.17–20: For men sayen that "of a kerle may nought come but poyson and fylth, that maketh the place to stynke where he haunteth ynne." Apperson 100.

C270 Of **Churls,** both man and wife, can depart no good fruit
c1489 Caxton *Blanchardyn* 173.12–4: And therfore I saye that "of churles, both man and wyff, can departe noo goode fruyte." Apperson 100. See **B362.**

C271 To give a **Churl** domination is bad (*varied*)
a1439 Lydgate *Fall* III 695.778–80: What thyng mor cruel in comparisoun Or mor vengable off will and nat off riht, Than whan a cherl

hath domynacioun, **a1449** *Mesure* in *MP* II 773.35–6: And he allso that is a cherll of blode Brought up of naght unto dominacioun (*is bad*). **a1450** *Partonope* 110.3303–5: Butte sethen (of) a chorle I turned the name In-to an Erle, no wonder thow schame In the yende be my re-warde. **1509** Barclay *Ship* II 8[23–4]: For the frenche man sayth in his langage, No thynge is wors than a churle made a state, 98 [21–2]: For make a carle a lorde, and without any fable In his inwarde maners one man styll shall he be, 319[27–8]: No erthly thynge makes more de-bate Than a vyle chorle come to a state. See **A230, B186, C266, P428, W714.**

C272 To stand and strive with a **Churl** has little avail
a1430 Lydgate *Pilgrimage* 301.10994–5: Ffor, wyth a cherl to stonde and stryve, Yt wolde nat but lyte avaylle.

C273 Like a **Cipher** in algorism (*arithmetic*)
c1385 Usk 72.82–4: Although a sypher in au-grim have no might in significacion of it-selve, yet he yeveth power in significacion to other. **c1405** *Mum* 25.53–4: Than satte summe as siphre doth in awgrym, That noteth a place and no thing availith. **c1425** *Crafte* in Robert Steele *The Earliest Arithmetics in English* (EETS ES 118, 1922) 5.17: A cifre is no figure sig-nificatyf. **c1440** Charles of Orleans 69.2042–3: Me thynkith right as a syphir now y serve That nombre makith and is him silf noon. **c1500** *Heartless Mistress* in Robbins 140.12: And I lyke a syphyr syt yow by. **a1513** Dunbar *To the King* 28.20: Bot ay as syphir set amang thame. Ap-person 100; *Oxford* 95; Skeat 126; Taylor and Whiting 70; Tilley C391.

C274 As round as a **Circle**
a1400 Lanfranc 111.15: But al the heed is round as a sercle. **c1450** Capgrave *Katharine* 80.35: Here cours, thei sey, as sercle it is rownd. See **C402.**

C275 A **City** on a mountain may not be hid
c1000 *WSG* Matthew v 14: Ne mæg seo ceaster beon behyd þe byð uppan munt aset. **c1395** *WBible* Matthew v 14: A citee set on an hil may not be hid. **1418** *Man, be warre* in Kail 61.17–8: On a mowntayne, a sete may not be hyd, Ne lordis werkis in no degre. **1533** More *Confutacion* 830 B[8–9]: That cytie can not be hyd that is set upon an hill. See **T122.**

C276 Like the **Clapper** of a mill that will not be still
1340 *Ayenbite* 58[13–5]: Thet byeth ase the cleper of the melle thet ne may him naght hyealde stille. **c1400** *Vices and Virtues* 55.32–3: And faren right as the clappe of a water mylle, that cannot stynte. **c1450** *Jacob's Well* 148.24–5: The first is outrage in here woordys as a clapp of a melle, that nevere wyll be stylle.

C277 **Clatterers** love no peace
1523 Skelton *Garlande* I 371.241: Make noyse enoughe, for claterars love no peas.

C278 To suck one's **Claws** with the bear
c1515 Barclay *Eclogues* 6.192: Save onely to sucke our clawes with the Beare.

C279 To **Claw** where it does not itch
1509 Barclay *Ship* II 256[17–8]: Let hym nat grutche but kepe hym coy and styll And clawe were it itchyth, **c1515** *Eclogues* 44.1191–2: It would make one clawe where as it doth not itche To see one live poore because he would dye riche, 143.99–100: But Codrus I clawe oft where it doth not itche, To see ten beggers and halfe a dosen riche. **1533** More *Confutacion* 629 A[2–3]: It would make you claw your head, and yet should ye feele none itche at all. **1546** Heywood *D* 87.239: Thou makest me claw where it itcheth not. Apperson 554–5; Jente 710; *Oxford* 567; Tilley M49; Whiting *Drama* 234.

C280 As clean as **Clay**
a1450 *Castle* 99.736: Clenner clothyd thanne any clay.

C281 As cold as **Clay**
a1475 *Ludus Coventriae* 213.115: Ffor who my hert is colde as clay. Apperson 106; Tilley C406; Whiting *Ballad* 26–7, *NC* 384.

C282 As dry as **Clay**
c1400 *Laud Troy* I 19.632: And make trees drye as clay. **a1475** *Ludus Coventriae* 143.255: Myne hand is ded and drye as claye.

C283 As heavy as **Clay**
a1325 Bonaventura *Meditations* 12.357: Here yen were slepy and hevy as clay.

C284 As pale as **Clay**
c1380 *Ferumbras* 3.81: He wax so pal so clay. Apperson 482; Tilley C406.

C285 As soft as **Clay**
a1430 Hoccleve *Roundel* II 37.5: Hir bowgy cheekes been as softe as clay.

C286 To cling (*wither*) like **Clay**
a1300 *A Song of Sorrow* in Brown *Lyrics XIII*

122.17: Thei clungin so the cley. **a1325** *Elde* in Heuser 170.1[9–10]: Eld wol(d) keld And cling so the clai. **a1325** Kildare *Swet Jesus* in Heuser 81.2[5]: Al we beth iclung so clai. **a1400** *In Alisaundre* in Horstmann *Sammlung* 178.388: I clynge as cleygh, Icaught in care. **a1475** *Ludus Coventriae* 48.164: My hert doth clynge and cleve as clay. See **C300.**

C287 To do away (*etc.*) like **Clay** (fen, loam)
c1000 *Regius Psalter* 29 (17.43): Swa swa fen stræta ic dilȝe hy. **c1100** *Salisbury Psalter* 97 (17.43): fen. **c1350** *Prose Psalter* 20 (17[18].46): Y shal don hem o-way as lome of the stretes. **c1395** *WBible* Psalms xvii 43: Y schal do hem awei, as the cley of stretis. **a1400** *Northern Verse Psalter* I 49 (17.43): fen of gates. **a1400** *Scottish Legends* II 411.144–6: And the gret state and dignite I refuse and forsakis ay, As undire my fet I do clay. **c1450** *St. Cuthbert* 146.4953: As clay of ways I sall thaim struye.

C288 Not give (count) a **Cleat** (*wedge*)
a1350 *Octavian (NL)* 115.779: Ne gyffe i noghte a clide (*MS.* chide). **a1390** *Seldom seen* 717.54: Of al ffraunce yaf nought a clete. **1410** *With god of love* in Kail 38.110: Ne counte his gynnyng at o clete. MED clet (b); NED Cleat 2.

C289 To dwell in one's **Cleping** (*calling*)
c1395 *WBible* I Corinthians vii 20: Ech man in what clepyng he is clepid, in that dwelle he. **c1400** Paues 63 (I Corinthians vii 20): And eferiche man in the clepynge that he is ycleped, duelle he stille to-fore God. Tilley C23.

C290 To be put to one's **Clergy**
1546 Heywood *D* 69.101: She chopth logyke, to put me to my clargy. NED Clergy 5.

C291 The greatest **Clerks** are not the wisest men
c1390 Chaucer *CT* I[A] 4054–5: "The gretteste clerkes been noght wisest men," As whilom to the wolf thus spak the mare. **c1454** Pecock *Folewer* 57.29: Grettist clerkis ben not wisist men, 37, 58.38–59.1, 60.4, 12 (*Pecock denies the saying's truth*), 61.5–9: Therfore rathir over litil and over neischli y have write ayens this unwiisdom, this vice and synne, and ayens the users therof, than over mych or over scharpli, Namenlich for that y have not herde othire men speke or write eny thing worth ayens this so greet defaut. **c1475** Henryson *Fables* 39.1064. **1476** Paston V 250[6–7]: Grettest clerkys are nott alweye wysest men. **1481** Caxton *Reynard* 63[19–20]: It is true that I long syth have redde and herde that the beste clerkes ben not wysest men, **1484** *Aesop* 128–9 (*the fable but not the proverb*). **1487** *O thou most noble* 330[3–4]: In such cases they saie, now and then, The best clearkes be not the wysest men. **1520** Whittinton *Vulgaria* 60.3–4: It is comenly sayd, the greatest clerkes be not all the wysest men of the worlde. **1546** Heywood *D* 71.54, **1555** *E* 183.206. Apperson 273; Jente 288; *Oxford* 97; Skeat 233; Tilley C409; Whiting *Scots* I 149. See **C513, W393.**

C292 They are not all **Clerks** that have short tippets
1481 Caxton *Mirror* 167[26–7]: Ffor they be not alle clerkes that have short typettis. See **H2.**

C293 Wise **Clerks** converted from wicked works are strongest faithed
c1385 Chaucer *TC* i 1002–8: Ensample why, se now thise wise clerkes, That erren aldermost ayeyn a lawe, And ben converted from hire wikked werkes Thorugh grace of God that list hem to hym drawe, Thanne arn they folk that han moost God in awe, And strengest feythed ben, I undirstonde, And konne an errowr alderbest withstonde.

C294 To fall like a **Clew** of thread
c1400 *Laud Troy* I 200.6774–5: That of his hors fel that kynge, As it were a clew of thred.

C295 He that never **Climbed** never fell
a1513 Dunbar *Of Content* 145.29: Gif we not clym we tak no fall. **1546** Heywood *D* 55.10: He that never climbde, never fell, **1555** *E* 192.262. Apperson 102; *Oxford* 449; Tilley C412.

C296 The higher one **Climbs** the deeper his fall (*varied*)
c1340 Rolle *Psalter* 134 (36.21): Swa ill men, the heghere thai klymbe in honurs and riches, the soner thai dye, and the deppere thai ere in hell. **a1400** *Proverbis of Wysdom* 244.34: Clemme nott to hygh, lest thou fall. **a1410** Lydgate *Churl* in *MP* II 477.208–10: Wordly desires stond al in aventure, And whoo disireth to clymbe to hih a-loftt, Bi sodeyn torn, felith often his fal unsoftt, **a1420** *Troy* I 34.784: Who clymbeth hyghe may not falle softe, **c1430** *Dance* 16.133: Hi(e) clymbyng up (a f)alle hathe for his mede, 24.208: No wight is sure that clymbeth over hye, 70.597: Who clymbeth hyest somme-tyme shal dessende, **a1437** *That Now is Hay* in *MP* II 813.126: Who clymbeth hyest gothe ofte base, **a1439** *Fall* I 94.3435–6: Who clymbeth hiest, his fal is lowest doun; A mene estat is best, 173.6117–8: But ay the hiere ther

clymbyng is att all, Allas, the sorere is ther onhappi fall, III 683.293–4: I eschewe to clymbe to hih aloffte, List for presumpcioun I sholde nat fall(e) softe, 884.2192: Hih clymbyng up hath ofte an unwar fall, 942.824: Who clymbeth hiest, most pereilous is his fall, 953.1211: Sodeyn clymbyng axeth a sodeyn fall, 1001.2930: Swich sodeyn clymbyng axeth a sodeyn fall, **c1440** *Debate* in *MP* II 565.634: Whoo clymbith hihest most dreedful is his fall. **c1440** *Prose Alexander* 36.8–10: For wha so ever clymbez hier, than his fete may wynn to sum halde, he sall falle onane down to the grounde. **a1449** Lydgate *Consulo* in *MP* II 752.66: Clymb nat to hih, thus biddith Socrates. **1449** Metham 14.371–2: For he that hyest in that leddere dothe clyme Deppest in-to wo fallyth, qwan he hat(h) lost hys pray. **c1470** *Harley MS. 3362* f.2b: He that clymbith hey (*rest lacking*), f.18a: The hyere that a man styghyt the sorrer he fallyth. **a1475** *Ludus Coventriae* 356.32: Whoso clyme over hie he hath a foule fall. **c1475** Henryson *Fables* 89.2614: Nor clym so hie, quhill he fall of the ledder. **c1475** *Wisdom* 50.444: Who clymyt hye, hys fall gret ys. **c1475** *Yutte Y se but fewe* in *English Studies* 41(1960) 198.5–8: Or that thu clyme bethenke the thrye: Thu schalte downe falle, therfore do weele. Have thu mynde howe thu moste dye; Be ware lest that Fortune turne hur whele. **c1499** Skelton *Bowge* I 31.26–8: But of reproche surely he maye not mys, That clymmeth hyer than he may fotynge have; What and he slyde downe, who shall hym save? **a1500** *Consideryng effectually* in Person 45.61–2: My fraylte me commandyd not for clymme so hye, Lest I beyng there sodaynly fall hem fro. **a1500** *Man Begins* in Brown *Lyrics XV* 237.5: Quho hiest clymbis most sud(danly descendis). **c1500** Greene *Carols* 348.1: The hyere men clemmeth the sorere ys the falle. **c1503** More *Early Poems* [15] B[8]: None falleth farre, but he that climbeth hye. **1509** Barclay *Ship* I 140[12–4]: For this is dayly sene, and ever shall, That he that coveytys hye to clym aloft If he hap to fall, his fall can nat be soft, 189[10]: For who that hye clymmeth his fall can nat be soft, II 320[27–8]: For who that clymmes by stately pryde, For grevous wyndes can nat abyde. **1509** Fisher *Treatyse* 159.22–3: The hyer that a man be in honour the greter is his fall. **1511** Hawes *Comforte* A4r[17]: Clymbe not to fast, lest sodeynly ye slyde. **1513** Bradshaw *St. Werburge* 40.931: Who clymbeth to hye often hath a fall. **1513** Douglas *Aeneid* III 169.16: Clym nevir our hie, nor yit to law thou lycht. **1520** Whittinton *Vulgaria* 77.14–5: The hyer a man ascendeth the more nede he hath to loke about hym: for yf he fayle of hold or slyppe the greter is his fall. Apperson 102, 607; Jente 803; *Oxford* 282; Smith 152; Tilley C414, F131; Whiting *Drama* 135, 196, 300, *Scots* I 149–50. See **A200, D156, E113, 143, 150, F505, 531, H279, L445, M724, 727, P380, R144, S355.**

C297 A **Cloak** for the rain
c1515 Barclay *Eclogues* 140.5: This lustie Codrus was cloked for the rayne (*literal*). **c1516** Skelton *Magnificence* 20.609: Ye, for your wyt is cloked for the rayne. **1546** Heywood *D* 74.137: What cloke for the rayne so ever ye bryng mee. Apperson 102; *Oxford* 98; Tilley C417.

C298 He that casts away his **Cloak** in showers shall never thee (*thrive*)
a1449 Lydgate *Order* in *MP* II 451.49–56: In the book of prudent Cypryan Wich callid is "a gardeyn of fflours," He seith . . . he that casteth his cloke a wey in shours, Out of the tempest whan he may ffle . . . On of the nombre that schall never the.

C299 Not worth a **Clod**
a1513 Dunbar *Of Discretioun in Taking* 36.39: Sic justice is not worth ane clod. DOST Clod, n. 1.

C300 To cling (*etc.*) like (a) **Clot** in (of) clay
a1325 *Erthe* 15.23: Out of this erthe in-to the erthe, there to clinge as a clot of clay. **c1330** *Praise of Women* 292.73–4: That doth his hert(e) rise on hy, So clot, that lith in clay yclong so sore. **c1400** *Laud Troy* I 312.10602: He felde hem doun as clottis of clay, II 504.17133–4: And sche fel ded and stille lay Among hir horses as clot of clay. Whiting *Drama* 308:62. See **C286.**

C301 As lithy (*flexible*) as **Cloth**
c1000 *Larspell* in Napier 234.21–2: And heo bið swa liðig swa clað.

C302 As pale as **Cloth**
c1489 Caxton *Aymon* II 419.7–8: And becam pale as a white cloth for the grete wrathe that he had. Taylor and Whiting 72; Tilley C446.

C303 As near as any **Cloth**
a1500 *For Old Acquaintance Sake* in Robbins 134.13–4: Witt locces (*locks*) of love I am besette, That syttes me nere then anny clothe. See **S255.**

C304 Better to lack (lose) **Cloth** than loaf (bread)
c1475 *Rawlinson MS. D 328* 119.21: Hyt ys beter to lake the clothe than the love. Melius

est vere mappa quam pane carere. **a1500** Hill 129.51: Better it is, to lese cloth than brede. Apperson 44; MED cloth 7; Tilley C427; Walther II 855.14610.

C305 The **Cloth** is of another hue
c1450 *Develis Perlament* in Furnivall *Hymns* 42.23–4: We ben bigilid alle with oure lyst, The clooth is al of anothir hew. MED cloth 7; Whiting *Scots* I 150.

C306 Falsely woven **Cloth** may keep no fresh colors
a1449 Lydgate *Fabules* in *MP* II 579.368: Clothe falsly woven may kepe no fresshe colours.

C307 It is a bad **Cloth** that will take no color
1546 Heywood *D* 93.88: It is a bad clothe that will take no colour. Apperson 22; *Oxford* 19; Tilley C431.

C308 One may not always know the **Cloth** though the color shines freshly
a1430 Lydgate *Pilgrimage* 408.15170–1: Men ne knowe alway cloth, Thogh the colour fresshly shynes. See **A155.**

C309 To cut it out of broad **Cloth**
c1516 Skelton *Magnificence* 6.145–6: It were a shame, to God I make an othe, Without I myght cut it out of the brode clothe. Cf. Taylor and Whiting 72: whole; Tilley C433.

C310 Under a white **Cloth** moths are often hid
1492 *Salomon and Marcolphus* 7[1–2]: Undre a whyte cloth often are hyd mothys.

C311 Let him that is afraid of his **Clothes** dance naked
c1385 Usk 23.85–6: He that is aferd of his clothes, let him daunce naked! See **T298.**

C312 **Clothing** cannot make a man be good
c1515 Barclay *Eclogues* 201.558–60: It is not clothing can make a man be good. Better is in ragges pure living innocent Then a soule defiled in sumptuous garment. See **H446, P149.**

C313 Fair **Clothing** amends a man
a1400 *Romaunt B* 2255–8: Mayntene thysilf aftir thi rent, Of robe and eke of garnement; For many sithe fair clothyng A man amendith in myche thyng. Taylor and Whiting 73.

C314 Worldly **Clothing** does a man much worship
a1450 *Three Middle English Sermons* 62–3.405–7: Syn the sest wel that worldliche clothyn maad of her or o wlle of unresonable bestes doth a man so miche worschepe e this world.

C315 After misty (black) **Clouds** a clear sun (clear weather)
c1400 *Beryn* 118.3955: Aftir mysty cloudis there comyth a cler sonne. **c1450** Idley 91.658: Ffeire wedir is shewed after clowdes dym. **1546** Heywood *D* 46.172: After cloudes blacke, we shall have weather cleere, **1555** *E* 152.38: After clouds blacke, we shall have wether cleere: And after wether cleere, we shall have cloudes blake: Now whot, now colde, now fayre, now foule appeere: As wether cleerth or cloudth, so must men take. Apperson 103; *Oxford* 4; Skeat 154; Tilley C442. Cf. Whiting *Drama* 186. See **D41, M592, 686, R11.**

C316 As far as the **Cloud**
c1385 Chaucer *TC* iii 433–4: From every wight as fer as is the cloude He was. See **E20.**

C317 As high as a **Cloud**
a1460 *Towneley Plays* 375.263: Hir hede as hy as a clowde.

C318 To be under a **Cloud**
c1500 *Lady Bessy* 18[9–10]: He said, we must come under a cloud, We must never trusted bee, 79[5–6]: Then came he under a clowde, That some tyme in England was full hee. *Oxford* 98; Tilley C441.

C319 To i-wite (*go*) like a **Cloud**
c970 *Blickling Homilies* 59[19–20]: Ealle þa gewitað swa swa wolcn. **c1395** *WBible* Job xxx 15: Myn helpe passide awei as a cloude.

C320 To magnify one above the **Clouds**
c1400 *Three Things* in Wyclif *EW* 186[2–3]: And magnyfien hem above the cloudis. See **S687.**

C321 A little **Clout** may (make) loathly a large piece
c1200 *Ancrene* 131.1–2: For a lute clut mei ladlechin swithe a muchel hal pece, **a1400** (*Recluse*) 125.33–4: For a litel clout may make a foule spott. Ives 264:12.

C322 Not worth a **Clout**
a1475 Russell *Boke* 135.296: Be not rasche ne recheles, it is not worth a clowt.

C323 To be carved as through a woolen **Clout**
a1300 *Alisaunder* 249.4451–2: That the spere carf thorough-out As thorough a wollene clout.

C324 As black as (a, any) **Coal**
c1225 *Horn* 35 C 589–90: Thar he tok his gode fole Also blak so eny cole. **c1300** *Beves* 81.1548: eni. **c1303** Mannyng *Handlyng* 52.1449: In-to the watyr, blak as kole. **a1325** *Cursor* III

1287.22489: And worth (T wexe) all (T as) blac sum (T as) ani cole. **a1325** *XV Signa* in Heuser 101.42, 102.66: the. **a1375** *Octavian* (S) 26.796, 27.840, 43.1352. **c1375** *St. Bartholomew* 120.86: His hare es crisp and als cole blac, 122.305: any. **c1380** *Ferumbras* 80.2437, 115.3660. **c1385** Chaucer *CT* I[A] 2692: any. **a1393** Gower *CA* III 116.6204: eny. **c1395** *WBible* Lamentations iv 8: The face of hem was maad blackere than coolis. **a1400** *Alexander C* 20.606: a. **c1400** *Laud Troy* II 477.16203. **c1410** Lovelich *Grail* II 362.377: ony. **a1415** Mirk *Festial* 56.15: a. **a1430** Lydgate *Pilgrimage* 384.14213. **c1440** *Revelation* in *Yorkshire Writers* I 389[29–30]: any. **a1450** *Castle* 140.2117. **a1450** *Generydes A* 106.3406, 112.3588, *B* 62.1942, 67.2076. **a1450** *Partonope* 138.3918. **c1450** Capgrave *Katharine* 63.770. **c1450** *Epistle of Othea* 78.21–2. **c1450** La Tour-Landry 29.5. **c1450** *Merlin* II 665[20]: eny. **c1450** *Northern Passion* 206–7 A CGg 1770: any. **c1450** Trevet 345.22–3 (f.71a, col. 2): a. **a1460** *Towneley Plays* 5.136: any. **1465** Leversege 23[13]: any. **a1470** Malory II 988.8: ony. **a1475** *Assembly of Gods* 57.1952: a. **1483** Caxton *Golden Legende* 159[v][2.43–4]. **1483** *Vulgaria quedam abs Terencio* Q1[r][8]: a. **c1489** Caxton *Aymon* I 60.19: a, 209.15–7: a, 314.23–4: a, **1489** *Doctrinal* E2[r][13]: a. **a1500** *Guy*[4] 121.3863: any, 179.5913: any. **a1533** Berners *Arthur* 159[17–8]: any, *Huon* 147.20: a. Apperson 51; Svartengren 243–4; Taylor and Whiting 73; Tilley C458; Whiting *Drama* 308:65, *Scots* I 150.

C324a Coal-black
c1250 *Owl* 8.75: Thin eghene both col-blake. **a1300** *Richard* 92.273–4: All togyder coleblacke Was his horse. **c1375** *St. Anastasia* in Horstmann *Legenden 1881* 26.94. **c1380** *Ferumbras* 34.807. **c1385** Chaucer *CT* I[A] 2142, **c1390** I[A] 3240. **a1393** Gower *CA* II 248.808. **a1400** *Ipomadon A* 71.2417. **c1400** *Gowther* 151.410 (*var.*). **c1440** Lydgate *Debate* in *MP* II 543.87. **a1450** *Generydes A* 175.5629–30. **a1450** *Partonope* 74.2447, 336.8313. **1513** Douglas *Aeneid* IV 106.22. MED col-blak; NED Coal-black; Whiting *Ballad* 27.

C325 As dark as the Coal
c1390 Chaucer *CT* I[A] 3731: Derk was the nyght . . . as the cole. Svartengren 238.

C326 As hasty as Coals
c1450 *Pilgrimage LM* 134[14]: I am more hastyf than coles.

C327 As hot as the (a) Coal
a1349 *A Song of Love* in Brown *Lyrics XIV* 102.13: Lufe es hatter then the cole. **c1375** *All Souls* in Horstmann *Legenden 1881* 149.232–3: And of his finger fell doun a drope In (the) maister hand, hate als a cole. Apperson 315; Tilley 462; Whiting *Ballad* 27, *NC* 385. See **G142.**

C328 As murk as any Coal
a1450 *Northern Passion* 206 CDd 1770: The sunne wax myrk as any cole.

C329 As red as (a) Coal(s)
c1350 *Libeaus* 36.620 (*var.*): As red as ffyerye cole. **a1405** Lydgate *Black Knight* in *MP* II 392.234: Now as coles red. **1471** Caxton *Recuyell* II 567.30: a. **c1505** Watson *Valentine* 140.19–20: More redder than a flambinge cole. **a1533** Berners *Huon* 489.27–8: His eyne more redder then .ii. brynynge coles, 754.20–1: He waxed as reed as a brenninge coole. Whiting *NC* 385. See **G143.**

C330 As swart as (any) Coal
a1000 *Two Apocrypha* 38 C[19–20]: Sweart swa col. **c1000** *Læce Boc* in Cockayne II 332[19]: Swa sweart swa col. **c1300** *Guy*[1] 374 A 7158: His bodi is swarter than ani cole.

C330a Coal-swart
a1000 *Vercelli Homilies* 101.325: He bið coll-sweart.

C331 Not worth a Coal
c1400 *Laud Troy* I 226.7674: Off on that is not worth a cole.

C332 To be colored as (the) Coal
a1200 Lawman II 318.17700–1: Iblaecched he haefede his licame, Swulc ismitte of cole. **c1380** *Cleanness* 19.456: He (*a raven*) watz colored as the cole.

C333 To bear no Coals
1522 Skelton *Why Come* II 34.240: Wyll ye bere no coles? Tilley C464.

C334 To blow at the Coal
1485 Caxton *Charles* 119.11: Ye can wel playe and blowe atte cole. **a1500** Hill 129.52: He that hath nede, mwst blowe at the cole. **1522** Skelton *Why Come* II 29.81: We may blowe at the cole, **1523** *Garlande* I 386.610: Brainles blenkardis that blow at the cole. **1546** Heywood *D* 40.184: Leat them that be a colde blowe at the cole. Apperson 57; *Oxford* 101: Cold; Tilley C460, 465. See **F199, G146.**

C335 To burn like (a, any) Coal
c1390 *Northern Homily Cycle Narrationes* (*Vernon*) 310.37: Mi tonge brenneth as a Cole. **a1398**(1495) Bartholomaeus-Trevisa r7[r][1.23]: It

brennyth as a cole. **a1400** *Scottish Legends* I 221.458: Brynt as thai colis ware. **a1400** Wyclif *Sermons* I 155[7]: Bi siche love men brennen as coolis. **c1400** *Laud Troy* II 418.14194: He brende In yre as any cole. **a1500** *The Stacyons of Rome* in *Pol. Rel. and Love Poems* 169.767: Hit brent as helle cole. See **G147.**

C336 To glister like **Coals**
a1400 *Siege of Jerusalem* 73.1252 (*var.*): That glystered as coles. See **G149.**

C337 To ruckle (*heap, etc.*) **Coals** of fire on one's head
a1200 *Ancrene* 207.16–7: Thus thu schalt, seith Salomon, rukelin on his heaved bearninde gleden. **c1378** *Piers* B xiii 144: Cast coals (**a1387** C: hote coles) on his hed, and al kynde speche. **c1395** *WBible* Proverbs xxv 22: For thou schalt gadere togidere coolis on his heed, Romans xii 20: For thou doynge this thing schalt gidere togidere colis on his heed (*Gloss: colis:* that is, the heete of charyte, ether of the Holy Goost, ether the brennyng heete of penaunce, *on his heed:* that is, soule). **a1400** *Pauline Epistles* 38 (Romans xii 20): For thou doande that, thou schalt hepe the colys of fyre; *that is to seye the hete of charite* up on his hed. **c1400** Paues 55 (Romans xii 20): For doynge these thinges thou schalt gedere to-geder coles of fuyr up-on his hed. *Oxford* 99; Taylor and Whiting 74; Tilley C468.

C338 To sparkle like a **Coal**
1485 Caxton *Charles* 26.31–2: Eyen . . . sparklyng lyke a cole.

C339 The **Coast** is (not) clear
c1522 Skelton *Colyn* I 359.1259: Tyll the cost be clere. **1546** Heywood *D* 90.69: All was not cleere in the coste. *Oxford* 99; Taylor and Whiting 74; Tilley C469; Whiting *Ballad* 35.

C340 A Kendal (*green cloth*) **Coat** and a russet hood never agree
a1500 *O man more* 393.12–4: A kendall cote and a russett hoode, Faire speche and dedes contrarye, Two faces in on hoode, doo never agree.

C341 To be in someone's **Coat**
1520 Whittinton *Vulgaria* 98.3–4: Yf thu were in my coote thu woldes have lytle luste to scoffe. Tilley C473. Cf. Taylor and Whiting 328: Shoe(4).

C342 To cut one's **Coat** after one's cloth
1546 Heywood *D* 58–9: I shall Cut my cote after my cloth. Apperson 131; *Oxford* 126; Taylor and Whiting 74–5; Tilley C472; Whiting *Scots* I 150.

C343 To pay one on the **Coat**
a1460 *Towneley Plays* 175.326: I shall pay thaym on the cote.

C344 To **Cobble** and clout
1528 Skelton *Replycacion* I 216.222–3: Ye cobble and ye clout Holy Scripture so about. Cf. Apperson 104; *Oxford* 99.

C345 To destroy as one destroys **Cobweb**
a1387 Higden-Trevisa VII 343[3–4]: Lanfranc . . . destroyede the castes of the myghti men as who destroyeth copweb.

C346 As red as a **Cock**
c1450 La Tour-Landry 168.12–3: And was reed as a cok, and had a good lyvynge colour. Taylor and Whiting 75; Tilley T611.

C347 As the **Cock** crows so the chicken learns (*varied*)
c1450 *Douce MS.52* 48.43: As the cocke croweth, so the chekyn lernyth. **c1450** Idley 102.1287–8: I sey no thyng but as myn auctor techeth: Ever the yonge cok croweth as the olde precheth. **c1450** *Rylands MS.394* 97.11 **1509** Barclay *Ship* I 235[28]: The yonge Cok lerneth to crowe hye of the olde. **1546** Heywood *D* 35.12: The yonge cocke croweth, as he the olde heereth. Apperson 719; *Oxford* 100; Taylor and Whiting 75; Tilley C491; Whiting *Scots* I 151. See **B14, D298, S216.**

C348 A **Cock** among hens takes what comes next to hand
a1393 Gower *CA* III 390.159–63: Bot as a cock among the Hennes, . . . Riht so can he nomore good, Bot takth what thing comth next to honde.

C349 The **Cock** has low shoes
a1449 Lydgate *Cok* in *MP* II 813–8.7–8: An old proverbe groundid on sapience Alle goo we still, the Cok hath lowe shoon, 16, 24, *etc.* (*refrain*). Apperson 5: All go; MED cok n. (1) 5(a).

C350 A **Cock** (cur, wight) is keen (*bold*) on his own mixen (dunghill)
a1200 *Ancrene* 74.14: As me seith that curre is kene on his ahne mixne, **a1250** (*Nero*) 62.18: coc. **a1387** Higden-Trevisa VII 5[16–7]: For, as Seneca seith, a cok is most myghty on his dongehille. **a1400** *Ancrene* (*Recluse*) 63.18–9: As Men seien on englisch, Cok is kene on his owen dunge hyll. **a1430** Lydgate *Pilgrimage* 276.10046–50: And yt ys sayd off ffolkys Sage, And a proverbe wryte off old, How that every whyht ys bold Up-on hys owne (erly and late), At the dongel at hys gate. **c1450** *Pilgrimage LM* 96[14–5]: Eche wight is strong on his owen dung hep and tristeth to his cuntree. **1546** Heywood *D* 42.30:

Every cocke is proude on his owne dunghill, **1555** *E* 189.242. Apperson 105; Jente 313; *Oxford* 100; Skeat 22; Tilley C486. See **C474, 567, F570, M207, R45.**

C351 A **Cock** were a fair fowl were he not often seen (*varied*)
c1450 *Douce MS.52* 47.39: A cock were a feyre fowle, nere he where ofte i-seyn. **c1450** *Rylands MS.394* 97.2: A cok were a feyre foule ner' he ofte seen. **1528** More *Heresyes* 132 BC: No more mervailous is a koko than a cock, though the one be sene but in somer and the other all the yere. MED cok n. (1) 5(a). See **D48, L208, P270, T109.**

C352 Many an old **Cock** maintains his flock but all our eggs come from the young cock
c1475 *Prohemy of a Mariage* 29[12–4]: Many a cok is olde On the dungehil and mayntenethe al his flokke, But alle oure eyren comen of the yong cokke. MED ei n. (1) 6.

C353 To cast to (at) the **Cock**
c1422 Hoccleve *Complaint* 109.386: Farwell my sorow, I caste it to the cok. **a1499** Lydgate *Testament* in *MP* I 353.651–2: My pater noster, my crede, or my beleve, Cast atte cok, lo, this was my maner. **1474** Paston *V* 207[19–20]: Whedyr it shalbe necessary for me to come up to London hastyly or not, or ellys kast all at the Kok. MED casten 3(c), cok n. (1) 5(b).

C354 To cry **Cock**
a1508 Dunbar *Flyting* 12.248: Cry cok, or I sall quell the. **1513** Douglas *Aeneid* IV 4.120: And by consent cry cok, thy ded is dycht. Whiting *Scots* I 151. See **C534, 534.1, 536.**

C355 To hop like **Cocks** in a croft (*cultivated field*)
a1460 *Towneley Plays* 239.354–5: We must hop and dawnse As cokys in a croft.

C356 To set **Cock** (*spigot*) on the hoop
1519 Horman *Vulgaria* 436[23–4]: He setteth al thynges at cocke in the hope. Omnia in fortunæ casibus ponit. **1534** More *Comforte* 1177 E[4–5]: Sette cocke a hoope, and fyll in all the cuppes at ones. **1546** Heywood *D* 70.23: He maketh havok, and setteth cocke on the hoope, **1556** *Spider* 298[17]: To set cocke on hope and run on heade. Apperson 105; *Oxford* 100; Tilley C493; Whiting *Drama* 338:460.

C357 To wear a **Cock's-comb**
1522 Skelton *Why Come* II 64.1232: Ye may weare a cockes come. **1546** Heywood *D* 72.78: Except ye bryng him to weare a cocks comb at ende. NED Cock's-comb 2.

C358 To be **Cock-sure**
a1500 Medwall *Nature* C3[r][29]: The mater ys cok sure. **1522** Skelton *Why Come* II 35.279: He maketh himselfe cock sure. NED Cock-sure.

C359 To play **Cock Wat**
c1516 Skelton *Magnificence* 37.1192: What canest thou do but play Cocke Wat?

C360 Not set a **Cocker** (*?leggings, ?boot*)
c1422 Hoccleve *Lerne to Die* 190.312–3: Nat so moche as by an old boote or cokir Sette y ther-by.

C361 **Cockle** and cȯrn (*contrasted*)
c1390 Chaucer *CT* II[B] 1182–3: He wolde sowen som difficulte, Or springen cokkel in our clene corn. **a1393** Gower *CA* II 453.1881–3: To sowe cokkel with the corn, So that the tilthe is nyh forlorn, Which Crist sew ferst his oghne hond. **c1405** *Mum* 29.62: Right as the cockil cometh fourth ere the corne ripe. **a1449** Lydgate *Ryght as a Rammes Horne* in *MP* II 464.53–4: Eretikes han loste here frowardenesse, Wedid the cokle from the pure corne, *St. Austin* in *MP* I 205.387–8: Nor so darnel growe nor multeplye, Nor no fals Cokkly be medlyd with good corn, *Sey the Best* in *MP* II 796.48: Among good greyn no cockill sow. **c1450** Idley 180.1277–8: Remeve hastelie the cokkill fro the corn, Ffor if it growe and seede it doith grevaunce. **1528** More *Heresyes* 248 C[13]: Some cokle among the corn. *Oxford* 608; Tilley C497, 659. See **C429, D19, 20.**

C362 Not worth a **Cod** (*seed pod*)
a1338 Mannyng *Chronicle B* II 289[26]: I telle not worthe a cod, for alle thi faire is faynt.

C363 **Coin** exalts man more than cunning
c1515 Barclay *Eclogues* 187.170: How coyne more than cunning exalteth every man.

C364 Where **Coin** is not common commons must be scant
1546 Heywood *D* 59.2: Where coine is not common, commons must be scant. Apperson 106; *Oxford* 101; Tilley C508.

C365 After great **Cold** comes great heat
a1400 *Proverbis of Wysdom* 245.49: After grete cold comythe grete hete. **c1450** *Fyrst thou sal* 88.41: See **H305.**

C366 Who has no **Cold** has no dainty (*pleasure*) of heat
a1500 ?Ros *La Belle Dame* 310.353–4: Who hath no cold, of hete hath no deyntè, The toon for the tother asked is expresse. See **W231.**

C367 To play **Cole-prophet**

1546 Heywood *D* 33.19–20: Ye plaie coleprophet . . . who takth in hande, To knowe his answere before he do his errande, **1562** *E* 244.89: Thy prophesy poysonly to the pricke goth: Coleprophet and cole poyson thou art both. Apperson 107; NED Cole-prophet; Tilley C510.

C368 **Coll** under canstick (*candlestick*)
1546 Heywood *D* 36.31–2: Coll under canstyk, she can plaie on bothe handes, Dissimulacion well she understandes. Apperson 107; *Oxford* 102; Tilley C512.

C369 After a **Collar** comes a rope
a1461 *John the Reeve* 590.814–6: Fful oft I have heard tell That after a coller comes a rope; I shall be hanged by the throate. *Oxford* 4; Tilley C513.

C370 To have many **Collars** on
1470 Paston V 74[15–6]: I have many collars on, as I shall tell yow when I come. MED coler 4(b); NED Collar 8.

C371 As black as a **Collier's** sack
a1430 Lydgate *Pilgrimage* 134.5126–7: Swych wer foul and blake of syht Lyche to a colyers sak. Cf. NED Collier 3, quote 1732.

C372 The **Collier** of Croydon
c1515 Barclay *Eclogues* 34.965: And as in Croidon I heard the Collier preache. See note, p. 233.

C373 •It is a dear **Collop** that is cut out of one's own flesh
1546 Heywood *D* 40.162–3: It is a deere colup That is cut out of thowne fleshe. Apperson 139–40; *Oxford* 133; Tilley C517.

C374 Under **Color** of kissing is much old hate
c1385 Usk 16.58–9: But often under colour of kissinge is mokel old hate privély closed and kept. See **E96.**

C375 All that a young **Colt** is taught he will hold
1340 *Ayenbite* 220[21–3]: Vor ase me zayth. "Huo that tekth colte endaunture: hyalde hit wyle therhuyle hit ilest." **c1400** *Vices and Virtues* 200.5–7: As the proverbe seith: "Al that men techeth a colt whan men schal tame hym and daunty, he wole holde as longe as he lasteth," 244.20–3: For as men seith that techeth a colte in dauntyng tyme, that is whan he cometh first to honde, right as thou wolte have hym for evere-more after, the whiles he lasteth. See **C226.**

C376 Of a ragged **Colt** comes a good horse
c1450 *Douce MS.52* 53.104: Of a ragged colte comes a gode hors. **c1450** *Rylands MS.394* 103.17.15. **c1475** *Rawlinson MS. D 328* 121.43. **a1500** Hill 128.10. **1520** Whittinton *Vulgaria* 108.22: Many a ragged colt proved to (be) a good horse. **1546** Heywood *D* 43.83: For of a ragged colte there comth a good horse. Apperson 520; *Oxford* 530; Tilley C522. See **C515.**

C377 To have a **Colt's** tooth
c1390 Chaucer *CT* I[A] 3888: And yet ik have alwey a coltes tooth, **c1395** III[D] 602: But yet I hadde alwey a coltes tooth. Apperson 107–8; *Oxford* 102–3; Skeat 229; Tilley C525; B. J. Whiting in *Mediaeval Studies in Honor of J. D. M. Ford,* ed. U. T. Holmes, Jr. and A. J. Denomy (Cambridge, Mass., 1948) 321–31.

C378 To leap about like **Colts** (*etc.*) (A number of single quotations are brought together here.)
c1300 *Guy*[1] 308 A 5709–10: Than lopen about hem the Lombars As wicked coltes out of haras. **c1390** Chaucer *CT* I[A] 3263: Wynsynge she was, as is a joly colt, 3282: And she sproong as a colt dooth in the trave. **c1405** *Mum* 61.1185: And kiketh faste as a colte that casteth downe hymsilf. **a1450** *Castle* 161.2814: As kene koltys thow they kynse (?*wince*).

C379 What is good for a **Colt** is not good for a stallion
c1450 *Pilgrimage LM* 71[23–4]: For that that is good for a colt is not good for a staloun.

C380 As one **Comes** so shall he pass
a1513 Dunbar *Of Manis Mortalitie* 149.4: For as thow come sa sall thow pas. See **F392, G182, W395.**

C381 He **Comes** not too late for whom any good is shaped
c1450 *Douce MS.52* 50.71: He comys not to late, That any gode is y-shape. Non mora fit dura, bona cui sunt ulla futura. **c1450** *Rylands MS.394* 100.13. Walther III 327.18064.

C382 He that **Comes** first has his bills read first
a1500 *Assembly* 399.575–8: And upon that was mad an ordinaunce, They that cam first, hir billes shuld be red. Ful gentelly than sayd Perseveraunce, "Resoun it wold that they were sonest sped." Cf. Apperson 214: First come; *Oxford* 204; Taylor and Whiting 77; Tilley C530. See **M558.**

C383 He that **Comes** last makes all fast
1555 Heywood *E* 183.202: He that cumth last make all fast. Apperson 108; *Oxford* 351.

C384 Lightly **Come** lightly go (spend)
c1390 Chaucer *CT* VI[C] 781: And lightly as it comth, so wol we spende. **a1420** Lydgate *Troy* I 277.4635: Lightly it cam and lightly went a-way. **a1475** Fortescue *Dialogue* I 489[19]: For thyng that lightly cometh, lightly goeth. **a1500** *Carpenter's Tools* 80.27–8: Wyte thou wele it schall be so, That lyghtly cum, schall lyghtly go. **a1500** *Lay of Sorrow* 718.137: That as It cummyth as sone away It goth. **a1500** *Thre Prestis* 16.223: Tharfor that lychtly cummis will lichtly ga. **1546** Heywood *D* 94.112: Light come, light go, **1555** *E* 169.132. Apperson 365; Jente 466; *Oxford* 367; Skeat 261; Taylor and Whiting 77: Easy; Tilley C533; Whiting *Scots* I 151. See **F638, G52, I26, W284.**

C385 **Comers** and goers bring all to nought
a1325 *BM Additional MS.33956* f.100b in *Catalogue of Additions, 1888–93* 139[1–2]: Comers and goers bryngeth hym al to naghte.

C386 After **Comfort** keen cares
a1513 Dunbar *Of the Changes of Lyfe* 141.17: Nixt efter comfort cairis kein.

C387 Cold **Comfort**
c1380 *Patience* 22.264: Lorde, colde watz his cumfort and his care huge! *Oxford* 102; Tilley C542.

C388 Ill **Coming** to the end of a shot (*reckoning*) and beginning of a fray
1546 Heywood *D* 82.69–70: And it is yll commyng, I have heard say, To thend of a shot, and beginnyng of a fray. *Oxford* 39; Tilley C548.

C389 The ten **Commandments** (*i.e.*, fingernails)
c1545 Heywood *Four PP* E1v[17]: Thy wyfes .x. commaundementes may serch thy .v. wittes. Apperson 622; *Oxford* 105; Taylor and Whiting 78; Tilley C553.

C390 The **Commendation** of the people is sometimes false
c1390 Chaucer *CT* X[I] 473: Certes, the commendacioun of the peple is somtyme ful fals and ful brotel for to triste; this day they preyse, tomorwe they blame.

C391 In a **Commonalty** is no certainty (*varied*)
a1471 Ashby *Policy* 40.870–1: Put no ful truste in the Comonalte, Thai be ever wavering in variance. **1523** Berners *Froissart* I 403[16–8]: He alwayes sayd that in a comynalte, ther was never no certentie, but finally shame, rebuke, and dyshonour. See **C392, M104.**

C392 In the **Commons** no man may trust (*varied*)
c1375 Barbour *Bruce* I 46.500–2: Sa fayris (it) ay commounly; In commownys may nane affy, Bot he that may thar warand be. **a1420** Lydgate *Troy* III 710.4993–4: To-day thei love (and) to-morwe hate, To trust a comoun lasteth by no date, 722.5411–2: Of the comowns, whiche in thinges newe Rejoyshen ay, after though thei rewe, **a1439** *Fall* II 390.2203: In trust off comouns is no perseveraunce, 410.2921–3: Loo, what it is in comouns to assure! Stormy off herte, onseur off ther corage, That seelde or never ther frenship doth endure, 447.4231–2: The comoun peeple, which stant in noun certeyne, With everi wynd turnyng up-so-doun, 490.621–3: The comouns hertis were turnid up-so-doun, Whos love is lik, preved at assay, A blase of fyr, now briht and now away, 636.1818–24: Lik a blase for a w(h)ile liht, Which sheweth (ful) cleer and is nevir aftir seyn, Or lik a sonne for a moment briht, Unwarli shroudid with a cloude of reyn, Riht so the wyndi favour bloweth in veyn, May resemble for a mutabilite, Of them that doon for any comounte. **1464** Hardyng 108[13–4]: As comons would ever yet of olde and newe, Eche yere their kyng to chaunge and renewe. Whiting *Scots* I 151. Cf. Jente 235. See **C391, P134, W422.**

C393 A **Commonty** is hard to appease
1523 Berners *Froissart* III 196[25–6]: Ye have harde often tymes recorded howe it is a harde warke to apease a commontie whan they be styrred.

C394 **Company** shortens the way
a1500 *Coventry Plays* 59.825–6: For you have eyver lovid cumpany, For yt dothe schorttun well youre wey. Apperson 257: Good company; Tilley C566. See **C398, T36.**

C395 Draw to such **Company** as you would be like (*varied*)
a1325 *Cursor* I 10.45–6: For be the thyng man drawes till Men schal him k(n)aw for god or ill. **a1400** *Speculum Christiani (1)* 107.3–4: Anothir is fle fro wikkid companie, for suche as a man drawis him to suche schal he be or wors. **a1450** *Myne awen dere* 175.835–6: Swylke company thou drawe (*MS.* drawe noght) to As thyselfe thynke for to do. **c1450** *Consail and Teiching* 66.9–12: Fore be thar cumpany men may knaw To gud or Ill quhethir at thai draw; Fore syk inclynacione and syk wyll Syk cumpany evir drawis tyll. **1477** Rivers *Dictes* 23[32–4]: Acompanye the with good people and thou shalt be on of hem; acompany the with badde and thou shalt be on of thoos. **1509** Barclay *Ship* II

35[27–8]: For eche man is reputyd of the same sort As is the company wherto he doth resort. **a1513** Dunbar *Rewl of Anis Self* 75.28: Sic art thow callit as is thy cumpany. Jente 127; *Oxford* 588: Sike a man; Taylor and Whiting 78, 233–4; Tilley M248, 382; Whiting *Scots* I 151. See **C396, L570.**

C396 Good **Company** makes good men and ill company makes ill
c1450 *Consail and Teiching* 66.5–6: Gud cumpany gud men makis, And of the Ill oft men ill takis. Cf. Smith 31; Tilley M536. See **C395.**

C397 It is better to be alone than in the **Company** of evil people
1450 *Dicts* 6.9–11: Bettir . . . to be aloone than to be in company and felawschip of eville peple. **1477** Rivers *Dictes* 9[20–2]: It is better a man . . . to be a lone than to be acompayned with evill people. Apperson 41–2; *Oxford* 38; Tilley C570.

C398 It is merry to have **Company**
a1450 *Partonope* 391.9468–70: With all myn herte I am gladde nowe That I have overtaken you. For mery it is to have company. See **C394, T36.**

C399 Who does after **Company** lives the better in rest
c1400 *Beryn* 6.162: Ffor who doith after company, may lyve the bet in rest. Cf. Taylor and Whiting 310: Rome.

C400 **Comparisons** are odious
c1440 Lydgate *Debate* in *MP* II 561.526: Odious of old been all co(m)parisouns, **a1449** *Amor* in *MP* II 745.15: Make no comparisoun, wayte on the tyde. **1456** Hay *Law* 282.11: Comparisoun is odious. **a1500** *Colkelbie* 281.58: Without odius crewale comparisoun. **1528** More *Heresyes* 225 B[13–4]: Saving the comparisons be odious. Apperson 110; *Oxford* 106; Smith 32; Taylor and Whiting 78; Tilley C576; Whiting *Scots* I 151.

C401 Where there is no **Comparison** (*equality*) lust and liking fall
c1400 *Beryn* 54.1753–4: Wher is noon comparisoun, of what thing so it be, Lust and likeing fallith there. See **B363, L551, M175, Y33.**

C402 As round as (a) **Compass** (*circle*)
c1408 Lydgate *Reson* 42.1573–4: A chapelet As compas rounde, 73.2732. **a1511** Guylforde *Pylgrymage* 58[19]: That stonde in the see rounde as a compas. See **C274.**

C403 An evil **Conclusion** may follow a good syllogism
a1400 *Romaunt B* 4456–9: For many tymes, whanne she wole make A full good silogisme, I dreede That aftirward ther shal in deede Folwe an evell conclusioun. See **B200.**

C404 By **Concord** small things multiply
c1412 Hoccleve *Regement* 187.5195–7: By concorde, smale thinges multiplien; And by discorde, hate, ire, and rancour, Perysshen thinges grete, and wast and dyen. Whiting *Scots* I 151. Cf. Tilley U11.

C405 **Concords** soon taken are good
1471 Caxton *Recuyell* II 651.12–4: Therfore saie men in a proverbe, that the concordes or peas sone taken ben good.

C406 One ill **Condition** defaces all the good
1546 Heywood *D* 80.69–70: With many condicions good, one that is yll, Defaceth the flowre of all, and dooth all spyll. Tilley C585. See **A167.**

C407 To gush like a **Conduit**
a1439 Lydgate *Fall* I 154.5482: Lich a conduit gusshed out the blood.

C408 A **Conscience** room (*large*) on which to turn eight oxen and a wain
a1513 Dunbar *Of the Warldis Instabilitie* 30.41–3: Kirkmen so halie ar and gude, That on thair conscience, rowme and rude, May turne aucht oxin and ane wane. Cf. *Oxford* 548: Room to swing, quote a1679; Tilley C603a, W888, quote 1617.

C408.1 To have a spiced **Conscience**
c1387-95 Chaucer *CT* I[A] 525–6: He waited after no pompe and reverence, Ne maked him a spiced conscience, **c1395** III[D] 434–5: Ye sholde been al pacient and meke, And han a sweete spiced conscience. D. Biggins in *English Studies* 47(1966) 169–80; Tilley S746.

C409 Whose **Conscience** is (en)cumbered and is not clean, of other men's deeds the worst will he ween (deem)
c1450 *Fyrst thou sal* 90.143–4: Whos conscience is incombyrd and is not clene Of other mens dedes the warst he wil wene. **c1450** *Proverbs* in *Rel. Ant.* I 205[1–2]: Whos conscience is combred and stondith nott clene, Of anothir manis dedis the wursse woll he deme. **a1500** *Salamon seyth* in Person 52.5–6. Apperson 112; *Oxford* 107; Tilley C611.

C410 Hence to **Constantine** (Algeria)

1555 Heywood *E* 169.130(2).3: That could and wolde, reache hence to Constantine.

C411 Hence to **Constantinople**
a1500 *Partenay* 157.4516–7: To constantinoble fro-thens is no faill, Ne myght ymage finde with it to compare.

C412 Be you **Content,** of more have you no need
a1513 Dunbar *Rewl of Anis Self* 75.19: Be thow content, of mair thow hes no neid. Cf. Tilley C623.

C413 He ought to be **Content** who need not flatter nor borrow
1477 Rivers *Dictes* 58[14–6]: Than some axed him of howe moche goode a man ought to be content, and he answered to havė so moche as he neded, nat to flatre nor borowe of other. Apperson 112; *Oxford* 108; Tilley N89.

C414 **Contraries** cure contraries (*varied*)
c1390 Chaucer *CT* VII 1276–7[B2466–7]: And as touchynge the proposicioun which that the phisiciens encreesceden in this caas, this is to seyn, that in maladies that oon contrarie is warisshed by another contrarie, 1282[B2472]: And thanne have I cured oon contrarie by another. **a1398**(1495) Bartholomaeus-Trevisa o5v[2.10–1]: And soo we hele contraryes with contraryes. **a1400** Lanfranc 257.2–3: And summen han now newe rulis: that with contrariis contrarie thinges schulen be curid. **a1400** *Scottish Legends* I 167.589–91: And of his Il had sic persawyne That throu contrare contrare thynge Is helpyne ofte. **c1400** *Seven Sages D* 35.1104: Contrare suld be helit with contrare. **a1425** Mirk *Instructions* 48.1553–4: Countur wyth countur ys I-huled ofte, When they be leyde to-gedur softe. **c1450** Idley 94.773: Contrarie by her contraries ofte have cure. **c1450** Trevet 146.36 (f. 30b, col. 1): Contrary thynges be ofte heled by contraryous thynges. **a1500** Medwall *Nature* E3v[9]: Quia contraria contrariis curantur, H4r[9–10]: So that the contrary in all maner of wyse Must hele hys contrary, as physyk doth devyse.

C415 Of two **Contraries** is one lore (learning)
c1385 Chaucer *TC* i 645: Sith thus of two contraries is o lore. **a1400** *Of Faith* in Wyclif *EW* 350[22]: Sith philosopheres seyn that contraries han oon lore. **a1500** Medwall *Nature* H4r[39–41]: Of .ii. contrarys there ys but one lernyng, That ys to say, whan thou knowyst well that on, The other contrary ys knowen anon. See **E166.**

C416 A **Cony** covers her head and weens all is well
1533 More *Confutacion* 588 D[13–5]: As doth a conye that covereth her hed, and weneth all were well when all her loynes be open. Cf. *Oxford* 478: Ostrich; Tilley O83.

C417 To run like **Conies**
a1500 *Stations* 361.399–400: And than ranne we ferre and nere As conys doth to ther covere.

C418 He is an evil **Cook** that cannot lick his own lips (*varied*)
1508(1519) Stanbridge *Vulgaria* 27.37: He is an evyll coke that can not lycke his owne lyppes. **1546** Heywood *D* 90.67: A poore cooke that maie not licke his owne fyngers. Apperson 323; *Oxford* 109; Tilley C636.

C419 As bald as a **Coot**
a1325 *Le Traité de Walter de Bibbesworth,* ed. Annie Owen (Paris, 1929) 117.782 A: A balled cote. **a1420** Lydgate *Troy* I 278.4673: And yit he was ballid as a cote. **a1508** Skelton *Phyllyp* I 63.410–1: And also the mad coote, With a balde face to toote. **1534** Heywood *Love* C2r[23]: Thou blynde, balde cote, **1546** *D* 27.49: Balde as a coote. Apperson 24; *Oxford* 20; Tilley C645.

C420 As pilled (*bald*) as a **Coot**
1528 More *Heresyes* 238 B[10–1]: As pilled as a coote.

C421 A mad **Coot**
a1508 Skelton *Phyllyp* I 63.410: And also the mad coote. Cf. *Oxford* 720; Taylor and Whiting 80; Tilley W561.

C422 To play **Cop-out**
a1508 *Freiris of Berwik* in Dunbar 191.387: The Freiris playit cop owt. **a1513** Dunbar *Quhone Mony Benefices Vakit* 27.13: Ane thristis, ane uther playis cop out. **1513** Douglas *Aeneid* II 63.92: I wil nocht say that ilkman playt cop owt. DOST Cop, 1b; Whiting *Scots* I 152.

C423 As red as **Coral**
c1390 Chaucer *CT* VII 2859[B4049]: His coomb was redder than the fyn coral. Svartengren 247.

C424 A **Cord** is a good thing, but not knit to a man's throat
c1380 Wyclif *De Papa* in *EW* 476[3–6]: And a coorde is a good thing, and faste knytting therwith is good bothe to man and to beeste in plasis where it wolde do good; but knytte this coorde to mannus throte and it myghte soone strangle this man. See note, pp. 534–5.

C425 The **Cord** which is always bent sometimes breaks
1487 Caxton *Book of Good Manners* F1r[11–2]: The corde whiche is allewaye bente or stratched somtyme breketh. Cf. Tilley B561. See **B478.**

C426 As hard as a **Core**
a1500 *Croxton Sacrament* in Waterhouse 79.679: That styckyth at my hart as hard as a core. NED Core sb.[1] 1b.

C427 As thick as **Corn** when it is sown
c1400 *Laud Troy* I 186.6295–6: Ne corn In lond is thikker sawen, That he ne scles oure men, II 383.12995–6: The Peple lay as thikke as . . . the corn whan it was sawe.

C428 **Corn** (grain) and chaff (weed) (*variously contrasted*)
c1200 Orm I 49.1482–3: And siththenn winndwesst tu thin corn, And fra the chaff itt shaedesst, 51.1531–2, II 9.10482–5: Himm shollde brinngenn inn hiss hannd Hies winndell forr to winndwenn, And forr to clennsenn himm hiss corn, And fra the chaff to shaedenn. **a1300** *Pembroke College Cambridge Library MS.265* in M. R. James *Catalogue* (Cambridge, 1905) 244[9]: The korn fro chaf is departud. **a1325** *Cursor* III 1444.25248–9: Corn sal fra the caf be clene, The gode sal fra the wic be draun. **1340** *Ayenbite* 62[22–4]: The lyeyere is amang the men . . . ase thet chef amang the corn, 137[27–8]: Vor he y-zizth more ynogh of chef thanne of corn. **c1340** Rolle *Psalter* 159 (43.7): We sall drife thaim fra us, as cafe fra corne. **c1390** Chaucer *CT* II[B] 701–2: Me list nat of the chaf, ne of the stree, Maken so long a tale as of the corn. **a1393** Gower *CA* II 28.844–5: The chaf is take for the corn, As forto speke of Romes myht, 187.2127: And bringe chaf and take corn, 347.1709–10: It were a schort beyete To winne chaf and lese whete. **c1400** *Vices and Virtues* 60.20–1: The lyyere fareth as a fals peny among the goode and as chaf doth among the corn, 136.9: And seeth wel more chaf than corn. **c1408** Lydgate *Reson* 167.6387–8: That wel ys him that kan beforn The chaffe dessever fro the corn, **a1420** *Troy* I 5.150–1: Of the dede the verreie trewe corn, So as it fil severid from the chaf, **c1421** *Thebes* 3–4.55–6: Voyding the Chaf sothly for to seyn, Enlumynyng the trewe piked greyn, **1426** *Title and Pedigree* in *MP* II 620.278: The chaf to voide and take the true corne, **a1430** *Pilgrimage* 268.9755: Leff the chaff, and tak the corn, **1431** *Defence* in *MP* I 33.82–3: Wherfor I rede the greyn and purid corne Thow cherissh wel, and lay the chaff aside, **c1433** *St. Edmund* 414.1011–2: Off the trouthe gadren out the corn And voide the chaff of prolixite, **a1439** *Fall* I 2.24: Out of old chaff trie out ful cleene corn, II 471.5107–8: So of that lynage he hath the weed upshorn, Fond among alle no greyn of good(e) corn, III 924.199: With litil greyn your chaff ye can abuse, 1012.3297: Voideth the weed, of vertu tak the corn, **1439** *St. Albon* 127.21: Good graine from chaf was discerned. **1447** Bokenham 2.46–7: Who is so nyce that wil good corn Awey caste for it growyth in chaf? **a1449** Lydgate *De Profundis* in *MP* I 78.24: Voyde the chaff, and gadryn out the corn. **a1449** Lydgate and Burgh *Secrees* 23.734: As undir Chaaf is Closyd pure Corn. **a1475** *Assembly of Gods* 60.2070–1: Take therof the best and let the worst be—Try out the corne clene from the chaff. **a1475** *Ludus Coventriae* 193.170–1: Corne that is good man kepe it ful clene, Chaff that is sympyl is sett wul nere at nought. **c1475** *Mankind* 2.43: The corn xall be savyde, the chaffe xall be brente, 3.46, 55. **1481** Caxton *Mirror* 48[20–1]: Alle in lyke wyse shal it be of them that leve the good grayn for the chaff, **1484** *Royal Book* F6r[1–2]: The chaffe emonge the corne, L7r[28]: For he fyndeth more chaffe than grayn, R6v[13–4]: As grete dyfference as bytwene the chaffe and the corne. **a1496** *Rote or Myrour* B7v[17–8]: The purgynge of the corn fro the chafe. **c1500** Greene *Carols* 116.1: Oute of the chaffe was pured this corne. **1506** *Kalender* 169.16: And the chaffe fro the corne clene out to trye. MED chaf 4(c); Whiting *Drama* 339:469, *Scots* I 148, 152. Cf. *Oxford* 110: In much corn; Tilley C659. See **D374, F693, S824, W205.**

C429 **Corn** seldom grows without some weeds
c1421 Lydgate *Thebes* 183.4558–9: For seelde in feldys groweth eny corn But yif some wede spryng up ther-among. See **C361.**

C430 His **Corn** (provender) pricks him
c1385 Chaucer *TC* i 218–9: As proude Bayard gynneth for to skippe Out of the weye, so pryketh hym his corn. **1546** Heywood *D* 44.98–9: For whan provander prickt them a little tyne, They did as thy wife and thou did, **1555** *E* 188.236: His provender prickth him. Apperson 515; *Oxford* 522; Tilley C665, P615. Cf. Taylor and Whiting 268: Oats.

C431 Many small **Corns** make a mickle load for a horse
a1400 *Pricke* 93.3417–21: And tharfor the poet on this wyse says: *De minimis granis fit Maxima summa caballo.* "Als of many smale cornes es

made Til a hors bak a mykel lade." **a1415** Mirk *Festial* 100.31–3: For ryght as a man may wyth mony smal cornys overcharche a strong hors. Walther I 621–2. See **D413, L402, S559.**

C432 No good **Corn** may grow of froward (*bad*) seed
a1439 Lydgate *Fall* II 588.116: Of froward seed may growe no good(e) corn. Apperson 325: Ill seed.

C433 Out of good **Corn** men may weed darnel (*a weed*)
a1439 Lydgate *Fall* I 190.6732: Out off good corn men may sum darnel weede. Apperson 460: No wheat. Cf. *Oxford* 110: In much corn; Tilley C659.

C434 To be more than **Corns** in granges
c1380 Chaucer *HF* 697–8: And eke of loves moo eschaunges Then ever cornes were in graunges.

C435 To buy (sell) **Corn** in grass
c1400 *Vices and Virtues* 32.9: Summe bien the corn in gras, or wyn whan it bloweth. **a1500** *Proverbs of Salamon* 195.6.6: He doyth but selle hys corne on gresse. Whiting *NC* 38. Cf. Tilley C656.

C436 To fly about as **Corn** when it is sown
c1300 *South English Legendary* (*Laud*) 98.230: That the peces a-boute flowen ase corn hwane man it sev (*for* sew).

C437 To meng (*mix*) **Corn** with drawk (*a weed*) and darnel (*a weed*)
c1475 *Mankind* 20.530: I xall menge hys corne with drawk and with durnell.

C438 To sift as one does **Corn** or bran
a1325 *Cursor* II 888.15523–4: He wil the sift nu if he mai, As man dos corn or bran (G: corn in barn).

C439 To sow **Corn** in the sea-sand
c1522 Skelton *Speke* II 17.342: To sowe corne in the see sande, ther wyll no crope growe. Tilley S87. See **G441.**

C440 To sway down (fall) as **Corn** before the scythe
a1400 *Alexander C* 222.3970–1: Thai swey doun as swiftly tha swart men of ynde, As evire did corne in a croft be-fore a kene sithe. **c1440** *Prose Alexander* 72.3–4: Bot the Indienes fell thikfalde in the batell as corne dose in the felde be-fore the sythe.

C441 Beware of **Corners**
1509 Barclay *Ship* I 170[1–2]: Beware of corners, do nat your erys aply To pleasaunt wordes.

C442 In a **Corner**
a1395 *WBible* Deeds (Acts) xxvi 26: For nether in a cornere was ought of these thingis don. **c1475** *Mankind* 24.637: Ye, ande hys fayer wyff halsyde in a cornere. **c1545** Heywood *Four PP* B1ʳ[2]: Have ye nat a wanton in a corner?

C443 In the **Corner** of a cartwheel
a1387 *Piers* C xvi 161–2: And bere hit (*Patience*) in thy bosom abowte wher thou wendest, In the corner of a cart-whel with a crowe croune. MED corner n. (1) 8(d): "a jocular phrase of obscure significance."

C444 To creep in every **Corner** of one's great bag
1131 *Peterborough Chronicle* I 262[4–7]: Her him trucode ealle his mycele craftes. Nu him be hofed þat he crape in his mycele codde in ælc hyrne, gif þær wære hure an unwreste wrenc þat he mihte get beswicen anes Crist and eall Cristene folc.

C445 The **Corser** (*horse-dealer*) has his palfrey dight (*made ready*)
a1475 *Good Wyfe Wold* 173.24: The corsser hathe his palfrey dyght all reydy for to sell. See note, p. 233.

C446 The more **Cost** the less avail
1401 *Treuth, reste, and pes* in Kail 12.91: The more cost, the lesse avayle. Cf. Apperson 426: More cost.

C447 Come not to **Council** but if you are cleped (*called*) (*varied*)
c1390 *Cato* (*Vernon*) 557.51–2: Never to counseyl that thou come, But gif thou cleped be eke. **a1400** *Alexander C* 38.832: And I to consaile un-callid I can noght thar-on. **a1400** *Cato* (*Copenhagen*) 324[23–4]: Prese nought the To counseil til thou clepid be. **a1440** Burgh *Cato* 304.17–9: And be thow never to smert To here mennys counsell; but kepe the thens, Till thow be clepyd. **a1449** Lydgate *Order* in *MP* II 451.46: Cometh to counsail or he callyd be, 453.122. **c1450** *Foly of Fulys* 62.359–60: Thai cum wncallyt to consaill, And syne thai can na-thing consaill. **c1450** *Go way, Fore that* in Lumby *Ratis Raving* 9.14: To consell cum thow nocht wncald. **1451** Paston II 246[13–4]: And I told hym it was no curtese to medyll hym in a mater butt if he wer callyd to councell. **1483** Caxton *Cato* B4ᵛ[32–3]: Thou oughtest not to goo to no counceyl before that thou be called therto. **a1500** Lydgate *Stans Puer* (*expanded version*) in F. J. Furnivall ed. *Queene Elizabethes Achademy* (EETS ES 8, 1869) 61.167:

Com not to counsell bot if thou be callyd. **a1500** *Young Children's Book* 19.55: Un-callyd go thou to no counselle. *Oxford* 103; Tilley C678; Whiting *Scots* I 152. See **A5, G486, O20, S167.**

C448 Better take **Counsel** at first than repent too late
c1450 *Epistle of Othea* 81.8–9: Better is at the fyrst, concell for to take, Then after to repent, when hytt is to late. See **F439, R84.**

C449 **Counsel** is most useful
c900 *Maxims* in *Exeter Book* 160.118: Ræd biþ nyttost.

C450 The **Counsel** of a wise man helps mickle
a1350 Castelford 68.21607–10: Consaile of A man that es wise Helpes mikel in speding for to rise. Wise mannes consail ful mikel spedes Esplait (*success*) to haf, quhen comes to dedes. Smith 39.

C451 The **Counsel** of many wise men is better than that of one man
c1400 *Spiritus Guydonis* 294[13–4]: The counseil of mony wyse men is beter then the counseil of o mon al-one. Cf. *Gast of Guy* 6.99–102.

C452 The **Counsel** of young men is sometimes good, but that of the old commonly better
1450 *Dicts* 136.4–5: The counsaile of yonge men somtyme is good, bot that of the olde is comonly better. See **A69, M252.**

C453 **Counsel** passes all things to him who thinks to be a king
a1393 Gower *CA* III 443.2109–10: For conseil passeth alle thing To him which thenkth to ben a king.

C454 **Counsel** will out
a1420 Lydgate *Troy* III 709.4951–4: But soth is seid of ful yore a-goon Of olde wyse, that counseil is ther noon In al this wor(l)d so prively y-cast That it wil oute, platly, at the last. See **E23, M806.**

C455 Good **Counsel** is good for him that will do after it
1481 Caxton *Reynard* 75[8–9]: Good counseyl is good for hym that wil doo ther after.

C456 Good **Counsel** is good to hear
a1393 Gower *CA* II 8.156: For good consail is good to hiere. Cf. Jente 644.

C457 Good **Counsel** is good to lere (*learn*)
c1380 *Ferumbras* 77.2354: God counsail is god to lere.

C458 Good **Counsel** wants when it is needed most
c1390 Chaucer *CT* VII 1048[B2238]: "I see wel," quod this wise man, "that the commune proverbe is sooth, that 'good conseil wanteth whan it is moost nede.'" Apperson 115.

C459 He that cannot hide **Counsel** may not fail of woe (*varied*)
a1393 Gower *CA* II 245.727–30: For who that can no conseil hyde, He mai noght faile of wo beside, Which schal befalle er he it wite, As I finde in the bokes write. **a1450** *Myne awen dere* 162.401–4: Better it is still to hald Than efter rewe when it is talde, And therfore, sone, everemore hafe doute Baldly to tell thy counsell oute.

C460 He that follows the **Counsel** of his foe must burst or bend
a1500 *Proverbs of Salamon* 179.18.5–6: He muste nedys breste or bende That foloweth the counsell of hys foo.

C461 If you are happy keep your own **Counsel**
a1500 Hill 133.18: Yf thow be happy, kepe thyn own cownsayle.

C462 If you may not hide your own **Counsel,** how dare you pray another to keep it? (*varied*)
c1390 Chaucer *CT* VII 1147[B2337]: For Seneca seith: "If so be that thou ne mayst nat thyn owene conseil hyde, how darstou prayen any oother wight thy conseil secrely to kepe?" **a1450** *Myne awen dere* 161.397–8: How soulde he thy counsaill hele That thyne awen hart can noght consele? **1450** *Dicts* 98.14–5: If thou maist not kepe thine owne counsail, muche les may he kepe (it) to whomme thou telles it. **c1450** Idley 86.344–5: How shold thow my counceill heele That thyn owne not kepe can? **a1475** Ashby *Dicta* 78.776–7: He that can not kepe his owne secretnesse, How shold a nother kepe it in sadnesse? **1477** Rivers *Dictes* 51[1–2]: And said if thou can not kepe thyn own secretes, moche lesse woll he kepe hit to whom thou hast told hit to. **a1500** *I saw ane rob* in *Bannatyne* II 207.41–2: A man that will his awin counsale discure, How suld ane uthir man it keip. **1509** Barclay *Ship* I 246[6–7]: For howe wylt thou thynke that another man Can kepe thy counsell syns thou thy selfe ne can. Apperson 115; *Oxford* 112; Tilley C682; Whiting *Scots* I 152.

C463 If you show your **Counsel** to every man some shall deceive you
a1500 *Att my begynnyng* in *Rawlinson MS. C 813* 323.11–2: Yff thou showe thy counsell to every man, Some shall disceyve the, thou wottes nott when.

C464 It is more sure to take **Counsel** than to give
a1500 *Imitatione (1)* 10.20–2: I have herde ofte tymes that it is more sure to here and to take counseile than to yeve counseile.

C465 Take no **Counsel** of a fool
c1390 Chaucer *CT* VII 1173[B2363]: For Salomon seith, "Taak no conseil of a fool." **c1395** *WBible* Ecclesiasticus viii 20: Have thou not councel with foolis. Tilley C697. See **F425.**

C466 Tell not your **Counsel** to a fool
c1280 *King Solomon's Book* in Adam Davy 83.55: To fool ne to non uncouth man thi conseil (thou) ne telle. MED fol. 4b(d).

C467 Tell not your **Counsel** to your foe
a1450 *Myne awen dere* 157.268–72: Tell nevere thy counsell till thy fa, No do nevere efter his counsaill All if he sware it soulde the vaill. All that he says, trowe thou it wele, Is for thy skathe evere ilke a dele. See **F366, S512.**

C468 Tell not your privy **Counsel** to him that it may not avail
c1450 *Fyrst thou sal* 88.15–6: Tel not thi prevy counsell To hym that may it noght avayle. See **F384.**

C469 To cry one's **Counsel** at the cross (*varied*)
c1400-25 Legat *Sermon* 7–8.33–4: For God is for-bed that i schulde crie ate cros al that ever i schulde finde writen e mi book. **c1415** *Middle English Sermons* 102.23–4: God hereth hem as lithly as thoo that thei were cried at the crosse. **a1450** *Partonope* 306.7679–80: I hadde as lefe my counseylle crye In London atte crosse in Chepe. **a1500** *Counsels* in Brown *Lyrics XV* 284.38: Ner (let) thy councell at the crosse be cryde. **c1500** Skelton *Dyvers Balettys* I 24.36: It can be no counsell that is cryed at the cros. **1556** Heywood *Spider* 293[20–1]: But sins ye will have counsell cride at the crosse, I wyll disclose. *Oxford* 121; Tilley C841; Whiting *NC* 471: Secrets.

C470 Work all by **Counsel** and you shall not rue (*varied*)
a1050 Defensor *Liber* 200[12]: Butan geþeahte naht þu do, and æfter dæde þu na dædbetst. **a1338** Mannyng *Chronicle A* II 539.15551–2: "Conseil," seid Cadwalyn, "he schuld take; Als conseil gaf, so schulde men make." **1340** *Ayenbite* 159[2–4]: Ine an othre stede zayth he (*Solomon*). "Do be red al thet thou dest, and efterward hit ne ssel the vorthenche." **c1380** *Ferumbras* 77.2344: Ho that ne wol bi conseil dan, som tyme hym schal mone. **c1390** Chaucer *CT* I[A] 3529–30: For thus seith Salomon, that was ful trewe, "Werk al by conseil, and thou shalt nat rewe," VII 1003[B2193]: Salomon seith: "Werk alle thy thynges by conseil, and thou shalt never repente." **c1390** *Proverbes of diverse profetes* 546.357–60: With-outen counseil do no gret thing; Aftur that dede thou schal have good knowing That gode counseyl dude the profyte, With-outen whuche thou scholdest had lyte. **c1395** Chaucer *CT* IV[E] 1483–6: To weyven fro the word of Salomon. This word seyde he unto us everychon: "Wirk alle thyng by conseil," thus seyde he, "And thanne shaltow nat repente thee." **c1395** *WBible* Ecclesiasticus xxxii 24: Sone, do thou no thing with out councel; and aftir the dede thou schalt not repente. **a1400** *Benjamin Minor* in *Yorkshire Writers* I 170[34–5]: Forwy he that dus all thyng with consaile, hym sall newere forthynk it. **c1400** *Vices and Virtues* 158.4–5: (*Solomon*) seith, "Do bi counseil al that thou dost, and whan al is ydo thou schalt not repente the," 188.28–9: Ne do no thing withoute good counseil, and after the dede thou schalt not repente the. **1406** Hoccleve *Male Regle* 28.85–6: To doon as that Salomon wroot and mente, That redde men by conseil for to werke. **c1408** Lydgate *Reson* 109.4150–2: For who wil nat by counsayl werk(e), Ful ofte sith to his reprefe Falleth in sorowe, and meschefe, 110.4197–9: And by recorde of thise clerkys Counsayl is good in al(le) werkys, As storyes telle mo than oon, 111.4223–6: By which example to hys avayl Ech man werke by counsayl, And take on him non empryse Without(e) consayl of the wyse. **c1422** Hoccleve *Dialog* 124.391: And Salomon bit aftir conseil do, 126.451–2. **a1425** *Rule of St. Benet (1)* 8.4–6: Als haly writ bidis: "Omnia fac cum consilio—Alle thing do wid cunsale, and eftir the dede sal the noht mis-like." **c1440** *Prose Alexander* 13.36–7: Bot alde men wirkes all by consaile and by witte. **a1450** *Myne awen dere* 167–8.587–8: Do nothinge withouten counsell, And thou sall nevere of gode ende fayle. **c1450** *Foly of Fulys* 59.251: All thing thai wyrk with wyss consaill. **c1450** Idley 84.239–40: Werke be counceill, as seith the wyse, And thou shalt not lightly the repent. **a1471** Ashby *Policy* 22.281: The wiseman saithe do all thinge with counseil. **1484** Caxton *Royal Book* N3r[21–3]: He (*Solomon*) sayth also in another place, Doo by good counceyll alle that thou shalte doo. And thenne thou shalte not repente the, O8v[28–30]. **1491** *Rule of St. Benet (3)* 120.23–5: Accordynge to scripture that seyth: "Doo all thynges wyth counseyle and thou shall not repente after." **1492** *Salomon*

and Marcolphus 13[11-2]: Do alle thynges by counsell and thou shalt not aftre forthinke it. **1523** Berners *Froissart* III 217[31-3]: Worke by counsayle, and ye shall alweys be so well counsayled, that every man shall prayse you. Curt F. Bühler in *Speculum* 24(1949) 410-2; Whiting *Drama* 136, 284, *Scots* I 152. See **A58, M176, 302.**

C471 Wray (*reveal*) not your privy **Counsel**
c1450 *Fyrst thou sal* 90.123: Thi prevy cownsel do thou not wrye.

C472 **Counselling** is no commandment
c1395 Chaucer *CT* III[D] 67: But conseillyng is no comandement. **c1395** *WBible* I Corinthians vii 25: But of virgyns Y have no comaundement of God; but Y gyve counseil. **c1449** Pecock *Repressor* II 316[3-4]: An ensaumpling of counseil and not of comaundement. Apperson 115; *Oxford* 112; Tilley C681; Whiting *Scots* I 152.

C473 The **Counselling** of women is either too dear or too little of price
c1390 Chaucer *CT* VII 1096[B2286]: Eek som men han seyd that the conseillynge of wommen is outher to deere, or elles to litel of pris.

C474 He that defends himself in his own **Country** has a prerogative
a1420 Lydgate *Troy* I 333.6598-600: For he is sothe hath a prerogatyf And a-vauntage, that in his contre Hym silfe diffendith. See **C350.**

C475 The more **Countrymen** the worse
c1450 *Douce MS.52* 55.123: The mo cuntremen, the worse. **c1450** *Rylands MS.394* 105.5. **c1470** *Harley MS. 3362* f.2b in *Retrospective* 309[19]. Jente 462.

C476 **Courage** is best for those who must suffer great misery
a800 *Guthlac* in *Exeter Book* 87.1348-9: Ellen biþ selast þam þe oftost sceal Dreogan dryhtenbealu. Cf. Smith 40, 41.

C477 A noble **Courage** cannot lie
c1505 Watson *Valentine* 103.29-30: For it is commonly sayde that a noble courage can not lye. Cf. Tilley H316.

C478 Furthest from **Court,** greatest with the lord
a1449 Lydgate *Tyed* in *MP* II 832.19: Furthest fro court, grettest with the lorde.

C479 He that dwells always in one **Court** shall con (*learn*) little good (*varied*)
a1400 *Ipomadon A* 9.220-3: The wyse man and the boke seys: In a cowrte who so dwell alweys, Full littill good shall he con, 10.268-70: In a courtte who ay soioyrons so And se the maner of no moo, Of no mo they can. **c1460** *Ipomadon C* 324.37-8: For the wise man saith, he was never wele taght man of a court ne of oo scole. See **S90.**

C480 In **Court** a man must sail after every wind
c1515 Barclay *Eclogues* 97.1145-6: In court must a man sayle after every winde, Himselfe conforming to every mans minde. See **W317.**

C481 Neither of **Court** nor of council
1546 Heywood *D* 52.364: I was neyther of court nor of counsayle made. Apperson 116; *Oxford* 113; Tilley C727.

C482 Young **Courtiers** oft are beggars in their age
c1515 Barclay *Eclogues* 93.1055-6: And an olde Proverbe is sayde by men moste sage, That oft yonge courters be beggers in their age. Apperson 116-7; *Oxford* 738; Tilley C737.

C483 **Covenant** is avenant (*honorable*)
c1450 *Douce MS.52* 53.102: Covenaunt is avenaunt. **c1450** *Rylands MS.394* 103.7. See **B214.**

C484 Fast **Covenant** makes easy ending
c1450 *Rylands MS.394* 105.21: Faste convenaunt makes hesye endynge.

C485 A foolish **Covenant** ought not to be held
c1500 Fabyan 234[40]: A nyce folysshe covenaunte ought nat to be holden. See **O13, T197.**

C486 Hence to **Coventry**
1533 Heywood *Johan* A3r[6]: That is the most bawde hens to Coventre.

C487 A meet **Cover** for such a cup
1532 More *Confutacion* 342 E[6-7]: A verye mete cover for suche a cuppe. Tilley C742, 906.

C488 None **Covet** more than those who have enough
c1430 Lydgate *Dance* 44.336: No(ne) more coveite than thei that have ynow. See **G449, W713.**

C489 **Covetise** is mother of poverty (*varied*)
a1387 Higden-Trevisa III 475[11]: Covetise is moder of povert. **c1395** Chaucer *CT* III[D] 1187-90: He that coveiteth is a povre wight, For he wolde han that is nat in his myght; But he that noght hath, ne coveiteth have, Is

riche, although ye holde hym but a knave. Apperson 117–8; Whiting *Scots* I 153. See **C494.**

C490 Covetise is natural to the old (*varied*) **c1385** Chaucer *TC* iv 1368–9: My fader, as ye knowen wel, parde, Is old, and elde is ful of coveytise, **c1390** *CT* I[A] 3883–5: Foure gleedes han we, which I shal devyse,—Avauntyng, liyng, anger, coveitise; Thise foure sparkles longen unto eelde. **a1400** Wyclif *Sermons* I 411[8–9]: And coveitise of worldli goodis lastith ever with him (*man*). **c1415** *Middle English Sermons* 210.2–3: For be a man never so old, he is as freshe in covetyse as is the yongest man in a countree. **a1450** *Castle* 80.92–5: Hard a man is in age, and Covetouse be kynde; Whanne all other synnys man hath for-sake, Evere the more that he hath, the more he is in his mynde To gader and to gete good with woo and with wrake, 151.2502–3: Com on, olde man! it is no reprefe That Coveytyse be thee lefe. **a1450** *Gesta* 47[17–9]: And therfore seith Seneca, *Cum omnia peccata senescunt, sola cupiditas iuvenescit,* This is to sey, When all vices wexith old, oonly Covetise wexith yong, that is to sey, in an old man, 127 (*Second Version*) [8–9]. **c1450** *How mankinde dooth* in Furnivall *Hymns* 74.519–20: Quod Coveitise, "age hath me highte; Suget to me he dooth him binde." **c1450** *Ratis* 39.1376–9: Bot ay the eldar that thow bee, The mar the vyce (*Covetise*) encoverys the, And makis the bot a kepar knawin Quhar thow suld lord be of thin awin. **c1450** *Speculum Christiani* (2) 66.24–6: When other vices wexen olde wyth us, oonly covetyse wexes yonge in olde men. **a1470** Parker *Dives* A6[r][1.24–30]: Covetyse reygneth moost in olde folke. . . . Pryde is fyrste in youthe, covetyse last in age, Z3[r][1.14–7]: For in olde folke whan al other temptacyons cesse, than is temptacyon of covetyse of the eye and of worldely good moost brennynge. **c1475** *Wisdom* 53.532–3: So to covetyse he xall wende, For that enduryth to the last ende. **a1500** Medwall *Nature* D4[v][8–10]: Mary, whan hys hed waxeth hore Than shalbe good season To folow covetyse and hys way. **c1500** Greene *Carols* 350.4: Whan' all thynges fall away, Than covetyse begyneth to play. **1532** Berners *Golden Boke* 288.5612–3: The olde man lyveth and dieth with covetise, 352.7658–9: The disordinate covetise of the olde persons. **1534** More *Passion* 1297 G[8–12]: But covetice canne nothynge gette awaye. For the more full, the more greedye, and the elder the more nygarde, and the rycher the more needye. Apperson 118; *Oxford* 592; Tilley M568, S479; Whiting *Scots* I 133: Avarice. See **F596.**

C491 Covetise (Avarice) is the root (mother, ground) of all evils **a900** Alfred *Gregory* 73.2–3: Ælces yfeles wyrttruma wære ðæt mon wilnode hwelcre gitsunge. **c1000** Aelfric *Homilies* I 256[17]: Ac seo gytsung is ealra yfelra ðinga wyrtruma, II 410[2–3]: Seo grædignys is, swa swa se apostol Paulus cwæð, wyrtruma ælces yfeles, 462[9], *Lives* I 356.280–1: Se þridda leahter is avaritia, þæt is seo yfele gitsung, And seo is wyrtruma ælcere wohnysse. **a1023** Wulfstan *Homilies* 203.74–6: Se apostol cwæð: *Radix omnium malorum est cupiditas.* Gitsung is wyrtruma, he cwæð, æghwylces yfeles. **a1050** Defensor *Liber* 110[6–7]: Paulus se apostol sæde, wyrtruma ys soðlice ealra yfela grædignyss. **c1175** *Twelfth Century Homilies* 134.9–10: Theo graedignesse is, swa swa the apostolus Paulus saede, rotae of ylc ufel. **a1200** *Ancrene* 105–6.1–2: Al is gisceunge and rote of deadlich sunne. **a1225** *Lambeth Homilies* (Aelfric) 103[14–5]: *Avaricia,* thet is theo ufele gitsunge; heo is more of elchere wohnesse. **1340** *Ayenbite* 34[18–20]: The zenne of avarice and of covaytyse thet is rote of alle kveade, ase zayth zaynte paul. **c1340** Rolle *Psalter* 144 (38.10): Avarice . . . is rote of all synnes. **c1350** *Smaller Vernon Collection* 16.507–8: Of alle maner uvel the rote Is avarice iclept and ihote. **a1384** Wyclif *Ten Commandments* in *SEW* III 90[8–10]: And herfore, seith Seynt Paul, that the roote of all yvelis is wickide coveitise in a mannys soule. **c1390** Chaucer *CT* VI[C] 334: *Radix malorum est Cupiditas,* 426, VII 1130[B2320]: For the Apostle seith that coveitise is roote of alle harmes, 1840 [B3030], X[I] 739. **c1395** *WBible* I Timothy vi 10: For the rote of alle yvelis is coveytise. **a1400** *Destruction of Troy* 383.11774–5: Covetous . . . That rote is and rankist of all the rif syns. **a1400** Lavynham 6.27–8. **a1400** *Pauline Epistles* 219 (I Timothy vi 10). **a1400** Wyclif *Sermons* II 334[1–2]: Poul biddith at the first that Cristen men coveite not yvel thingis, bi yvel desires, for this is rote of othir synnes. **c1400** *De Apostasia* in Wyclif *SEW* III 433[14–5]. **c1400** *Order of Priesthood* in Wyclif *EW* 173[14–5]: Covetise . . . ground of alle synnes, as poul seith. **c1400** Paues 115 (I Timothy vi 10). **c1400** *Scottish Troy* 240.395–7: Inne the which dame Averyce Fastenede hyre rotes at devyce, That moder is of alkyne wice. **c1400** *Vices and Virtues* 30.6–7. **a1410** Love *Mirrour* 139[1–2]: Depe covetise that is the foulest vice and roote and cause of many other vices. **c1412** Hoccleve *Regement* 170.4733–4: This makith covetise or Avarice Roote of al harmes, fo to conscience. **a1415** *Lanterne* 128.16–7. **a1420** Lydgate *Troy* I 22.356–7: Covetise, Grounde and rote of wo and al meschaunce, III 735.5863–4, 736.5879–80: This false werme, moder and norice Of al meschef and of every vice. **a1425** *Contemplations* in *Yorkshire Writers* II 80[36–7]: I rede where that the synne of covetyse is in a man, that man is made subgect to all other vyces, 81[1–2]. **a1425** Higden-Anon. Cont. VIII 455[27]: This sede was avarice, the roote of alle synne, 505[44–5]: O thou covetyse, moder of vices. **1435** Misyn *Fire* 5.7. **a1439** Lydgate *Fall* II 448.4277, 454.4476–7. **c1440** Scrope *Epistle of Othea* 106[2–4]. **c1449** Pecock *Repressor* II 555[8–12]: But so it is, that love to money (and namelich greet love to money) is worthi to be forborn, as experience weel schewith, for that it is moder of passing myche yvel, and, as Poul seith, it is "the roote of al yvel." **a1450** *Castle* 150.2454–7: Ther is no dysese nor debate Thorwe this wyde werld so rounde, Tyde nor tyme, erly nor late, But yet Coveytyse is the grounde. **c1450** *Consail and Teiching* 73.261. **c1450** *Epistle of Othea* 136.13–4. **c1450** *Jacob's Well* 118.12–3, 119.30–1. **c1450** *Ratis* 36.1252–3: Cowatice That is modir of ilk wyce. **c1450** *Speculum Christiani* (2) 66.6. **1456** Hay *Knychthede* 57.32–3: It (*Avarice*) is rute of all wikkitnesse, *Law* 27.34–5. **a1470** Parker *Dives* A1r[2.25–8]: For covetyse of richesses more than is nedefull to a man for to have is rote of all evylles, a4r[2.13–5]: Sayth saynt Poule that covetyse is rote of all maner wyckednesse, Q5v[1.32–3], X7v[1.24], Z2r[2.20–1]: It is rote and begynnyng of every evyll. **1471** Caxton *Recuyell* II 662.7: Avaryce is moder of all vyces, **1474** *Chesse* 110[27–8]: Seneque reherceth in the book of the cryes of women that avarice is the foundement of alle vices, **1483** *Cato* B8r[33]: Avarice is cause and the roote of alle synnes, *Golden Legende* 117v (*by error* 118) [2.20–1], **1484** *Ordre of Chyvalry* 100.15–6: Avaryce . . . whiche is moder and rote of all evyls and of treson, *Royal Book* D6v[26–8], N1r (*by error* 4)[20–1]: The covetyses of the world, whyche is the rote of alle vyces. **1490** Irlande *Meroure* 53.27. **a1500** *Compleint* in *Findern Anthology* PMLA 69(1954) 640[*between* 7 *and* 8]. **a1507** Dunbar *The Dance* 121.55–6. **1509** Watson *Ship* M3v[7]: Avaryce, moder of all evylles. **a1529** Skelton *Boke of Three Fooles* I 201[4]: Avaryce, mother of all evylles. **a1533** Berners *Castell* L4v[4–5]. **1533** More *Confutacion* 544 B[14–5]. Apperson 117–8; Taylor and Whiting 230; Tilley C746; Whiting *Drama* 123, *Scots* I 153. See **E176.**

C492 **Covetise** never rests
a1338 Mannyng *Chronicle* A I 92.2571–2: Bot Covetyse that nevere restes, Venym amonges men hit kestes.

C493 Through **Covetise** some lose goods and life
c1470 *Wallace* 126.521: Throuch cowatys sum losis gud and lyff.

C494 He that is **Covetous** is poor
1450 *Dicts* 38.1–2: If thou be covetouse, thou schalt be pore. See **C489.**

C495 Over **Covetous** was never good
1481 Caxton *Reynard* 95[35]: Over covetous was never good. *Oxford* 115.

C496 As bald as a **Cow**
a1400 *Hunting of the Hare* 287.187: Sym, that was balyd lyke a kow.

C497 As great as a **Cow**
c1350 *Libeaus* 74.1344 c–d (*var.*): He is also grete, As is a . . . kowe.

C498 As rough as a **Cow**
a1300 *Alisaunder* 311.5946: He was rughher than any ku.

C499 A **Cow** in a cage
c1405 *Mum* 20.260–2: For it fallith as well to fodis of xxiiij yeris, Or yonge men of yistirday to geve good redis, As becometh a kow to hoppe in a cage! **a1475** *Asneth* 227.14–5: Hit ys not fetis for to see a cowe in a cage, Ye desire to make a fool of my lordis ape. **1546** Heywood *D* 60.45–6: She is in this mariage As comely as is a cowe in a cage. Apperson 118; *Oxford* 104; Tilley C747.

C500 He that feeds his **Cow** well eats often of the milk
1492 *Salomon and Marcolphus* 7[19–20]: He that fedyth well is cowe etyth often of the mylke.

C501 It becomes one as well as a **Cow** to bear a saddle
c1450 *Chaunce* 12.258–9: Now trewly yow becometh al your gere As wel as Cowe a sadel to bere. Apperson 118; *Oxford* 28; Tilley C758; Whiting *Ballad* 35. See **D311.**

C502 Many a good **Cow** brings forth a sorry (evil) calf
1520 Whittinton *Vulgaria* 72.18–9: It is comenly

sayd: many a good kowe bryngeth forthe a sory calfe. **1546** Heywood *D* 39.141: But many a good coowe hath an evill caulfe. Apperson 119; *Oxford* 251; Tilley C761.

C503 To hip (*hop*) like a **Cow**
a1400 *Pricke* 43.1539: And some gas hypand als a ka.

C504 To ear (*plow*) with another's **Cow** Calf (quey [*heifer*])
c1395 *WBible* Judges xiv 18: If ye hadden not erid in my cow calf, *that is, my wiif,* ye hadden not founde my proposicioun. **c1420** Wyntoun II 286.221–6: "Had nocht your telche (*var.* tilche) bene wrocht With my quhy, yit had ye nocht Fundin my propositioun;" As quha say of this hid ressoune, "My wif has tald it yow but faill, And kepit yow out of tinsaill." *Oxford* 508; Tilley H395; Whiting *Scots* I 187–8. See **P274.**

C505 Whoso bulls my **Cow** the calf is ever mine
1304 Ralph of Hengham in *Essays in Medieval History Presented to T. F. Tout,* ed. A. G. Little and F. M. Powicke (Manchester, 1925) 196, n. 3: Et tunc dixit Hengham: Wo so boleth myn kyn, ewerc (*for* ewere) is the calf myn. MED bolen; Tilley C765.

C506 At good need a **Coward** cowers behind
a1300 *Alisaunder* 115.2053: At gode nede coward behynde coureth.

C507 By one **Coward** a whole work is sometimes left and lost
c1500 *Melusine* 140.30–1: For by one only Cowarde and feynted herte is sometyme lefte and loste al a hoole werke.

C508 A **Coward** never has fair love
1480 Caxton *Ovyde* 47[19–20]: Therfore it is sayde comunely that a Coward hath never fayre love.

C509 A **Coward** will never show mercy
a1470 Malory III 1114.26–7: Than woll a cowarde never shew mercy. Apperson 120; *Oxford* 116; Tilley C778. See **M91.**

C510 The veriest **Coward** that ever pissed
1508(1519) Stanbridge *Vulgaria* 22.21: He is the veryest cowherde that ever pyst. Imbellissimus est omnibus. Tilley K120.

C511 As sour as the **Crab** (*apple*)
a1475 *Tree* 97.18: The mydill is soure as the crabbe. *Oxford* 606: wer; Tilley C783; Whiting *NC* 388: Crabapple.

C512 As the **Crab** goes forward (*i.e.,* not at all)
a1449 Lydgate *So as the Crabbe* in *MP* II 466–7.8: So as the crabbe gothe forward, 16, 24, 32, 40, 48, 467.56: Howe that the crabbe goothe bakward. **1533** More *Confutacion* 632 F[14–5]: For lo thus creepeth he forward lyke a crabbe.

C513 The greatest **Crabs** are not all the best meat
1546 Heywood *D* 50.294: But the greattest crabs be not all the best meate. Apperson 120; *Oxford* 117; Tilley C786. See **C291.**

C514 One **Crab** blames another for her backward pace
a1225 *Lambeth Homilies* 51[30–5]: Crabbe is an manere of fissce in there sea. This fis is of swulc cunde thet ever se he mare strengthdeth him to sw(i)mminde mid the watere, se he mare swimmeth abac. And the alde crabbe seide to the yunge, hwi ne swimmest thu forthwarth in there sea alse other fisses doth, and heo seide, Leofe moder, swim thu foren me and tech me hu ic scal swimmen forthward. **1509** Barclay *Ship* I 203[8]: One crab blamys another for hir bacwarde pace, 237[15–6]: The yonge crab bacwarde doth crepe or go As doth the olde, none can hir cours redres. Cf. Apperson 154; *Oxford* 148; Tilley D394. See **D281, F359, P397.**

C515 A sour **Crabtree** has a fair bud
a1500 *O man more* 393.11: A sowre crabtre hathe a faire budde. See **C376.**

C516 The greatest **Crackers** (*boasters*) are not the boldest men
1509 Barclay *Ship* I 198[14]: For greattest crakers ar nat ay boldest men, **c1523** *Mirrour* 76[18]: For the greatest crakers are not the boldest men. Apperson 272; Tilley B489; Whiting *Drama* 231. See **B46, 415, C636.**

C517 All **Crafts** (*tricks*) are coldly rewarded
c1025 *Durham Proverbs* 14.38: Cræfta gehwilc byþ cealde forgolden. (O)mne ingenium accerbior rependitur.

C518 As great a **Craft** is keep well as win (*varied*)
c1385 Chaucer *TC* iii 1633–4: For also seur as reed is every fir, As gret a craft is kepe wel as wynne. **a1387** Higden-Trevisa I 235[1–3]: That this is lasse maistrie, to wynne and to conquere, than it is to kepe and to save that that is conquered and i-wonne. **1464** Hardyng 422[24]: For lighter bee thei for to wynne, then holde.

Oxford 332; Skeat 185. Cf. Apperson 337: Keep(4); Tilley K12. See **H412, K3.**

C519 **Craft** is all
c1395 Chaucer *CT* IV[E] 2016: For craft is al, whoso that do it kan.

C520 **Craft** is better than idleness
1483 Caxton *Cato* D6r[14–5]: For it is sayd comynly that crafte is bettre than the ydelnesse.

C521 **Craft** is better than the sparhawk
1483 Caxton *Cato* H6v[1–2]: It is sayd in a comyn proverbe that crafte is better than the sparhawke.

C522 **Craft** is better than wealth
c900 *Old English Cato* 4.16–7: Cræft byð betre þone æht.

C523 **Craft** may attain to such thing as seems impossible by nature
a1439 Lydgate *Fall* II 392.2264–5: Yit crafft in cas to such thyng mai atteyne, Which bi nature semeth an inpossible.

C524 He is blessed that learned a good **Craft** in his youth
a1325 *Hendyng C* 182.4: He is iblessid oso goddis mowthe, That god craft lernit in is yougthe. Kneuer 19–20; Schleich 250; Singer III 126. See **C226, Y32.**

C525 One's first **Craft** is left with one
1369 Chaucer *BD* 791–2: I ches love to my firste craft; Therefore hit ys with me laft. See **S240.**

C526 Sometime it is a **Craft** to flee from thing which in effect one hunts (*varied*)
c1385 Chaucer *TC* i 747–8: Ek som tyme it is a craft to seme fle Fro thyng whych in effect men hunte faste. **1549** Heywood *D* 43.69–70: Folowe pleasure, and then will pleasure flee, Flee pleasure, and pleasure will folowe thee. Apperson 222; *Oxford* 213; Tilley L479; Whiting *Drama* 276. See **L487, T162.**

C527 There is good **Craft** in daubing
?1454 Paston II 300[13–4]: And seyth to her that ther is gode crafte in dawbyng. Apperson 121; *Oxford* 117; Tilley C803.

C528 To be of one **Craft** but not of one kind
1533 Heywood *Weather* C1r[17]: We be of one crafte but not of one kynde.

C529 Who swears by **Craft** is by craft forsworn
a1420 Lydgate *Troy* III 744.6144: Who swereth by craft is by craft forsworn. See **G491.**

C530 Without **Craft** nothing is well behaved
c1516 Skelton *Magnificence* 42.1350: Without crafte nothynge is well behavyd.

C531 As still as a **Crag**
a1400 *Scottish Legends* II 394.255–6: For unsterit scho stud stil As a crag, to byd godis wil.

C532 To seek the **Crammels** (*crumbs*) in the rissoles (*an entrée made with crumbs*) (*i.e.,* to waste time)
1340 *Ayenbite* 253[9–10]: The bysye other the malancolien they byeth ylich than thet zekth the crammeles ine the russoles, other than thet zekth thet vel ine the aye other thane knotte ine the resse.

C533 To take **Cranes** flying
c1500 *Melusine* 79.23–5: He weneth as me semeth to take the cranes flighing (*French:* les grues en vollant), by my feith he shall well fayll and mysse of that he hath said.

C534 To cry **Crauch**
c1508 Dunbar *Flyting* 12.245: Cry crauch, thow art our sett. See **C354, 536.**

C534.1 To yeie (*cry*, say) **Cravant**
a1200 *Ancrene* 149.25: Buheth him as he bit and yeieth cravant, cravant, **a1400** (*Recluse*) 137.29–30: And lithe adoun and leteth hym up and seith cravant. **c1400** *Robartes MS.* in *Neuphilologische Mitteilungen* 67(1966) 63.17–8: That we may venquysch our enmy, And gar him flee and "cravat" cry. See **C354.**

C535 Shameful **Craving** must have shameful nay
1549 Heywood *D* 46.154: Shamfull cravyng . . . must have shamefull naie. Apperson 560–1; *Oxford* 578; Tilley C808.

C536 To cry **Creak**
1523 Skelton *Howe the Douty Duke* II 77.300–1: Gyve it up, and cry creke, Lyke an huddypeke. Tilley C810; Whiting *Drama* 340:485. See **C354, 534, 534.1.**

C537 As sweet as **Cream**
a1415 Mirk *Festial* 233.1: Be glad and blyth, swete as creme. Svartengren 63.

C538 Each **Creature** was made of one matter
a1449 Lydgate *Look* in *MP* II 767.58: Of o mateer was maad ech creature. See **A37.**

C539 Hasty **Credence** causes great hindering (*varied*)
a1410 Lydgate *Churl* in *MP* II 477.201: Hasty credence hath causid gret hyndryng, 481.302–5: Tauht I the nat this wisdam in sentence: To every tale brouht to the of newe, Nat hastily yeve ther-to credence, Into tyme thou knowe that is were trewe? 482.321–2: Thou shuldist nat, aftir my sentence, To every tale yeve to hasty

credence, **a1439** *Fall* I 134.4810–1: Hasti credence is roote off al errour, A froward stepmooder off al good counsail.

C540 As long as a man may say two **Creeds**
c1450 F. Heinrich ed. *Ein mittelenglisches Medizinbuch* (Halle, 1896) 107[7–8]: Thenne let the pacient use ther of a sponfulle at ones and holde in his mowth as longe as a man may sey ii Credys. MED crede n. (2) (b). See **P50.**

C541 As sooth (sicker, true) as the **Creed**
a1300 *On Serving Christ* in Morris *Old English Miscellany* 91.16: Leve we this for sayn, soth al so the crede. **a1393** Gower *CA* III 26.2912: And also siker as the crede. **c1395** Chaucer *CT* VIII[G] 1047: Bileveth this as siker as your Crede. **a1439** Lydgate *Fall* II 608.836: This stori, trewe as is the creede. **c1440** Charles of Orleans 37.1097: This is as trewe as crede. **a1450** *Castle* 142.2166: Take it sothe, as mes crede (*mass-creed*). **a1500** *To yow, mastres* in *Rawlinson MS. C 813* 383.28: Thys ys as trew as ys your crede. **c1503** More *Early Poems* [16] C[10]: Them to beleve, as surely as your crede. **1513** Douglas *Aeneid* III 253.15: Suyth as is the creid. **c1516** Skelton *Magnificence* 8.218: All that ye say is as trewe as the crede. Svartengren 355; Tilley C819; Whiting *Drama* 308:76, *Scots* I 154. See **B281, G399, P48.**

C542 To believe as one's **Creed**
c1450 Capgrave *Katharine* 333.2237: Be caught be nature, leve this as youre creede. Whiting *Drama* 308:76, *Scots* I 154.

C543 To can (*know*) more than the **Creed**
c1385 Chaucer *TC* v 89–90: As he that koude more than the crede In swich a craft. MED crede n. (2) (b).

C544 To ken (*teach*) one his **Creed**
a1352 Minot 27.4: Sir Edward sall ken yow yowre crede, 32.38, 35.14. MED crede n. (2) (b).

C545 To sing such a **Creed**
a1393 Gower *CA* II 239.478–9: For er I sunge such a crede, I hadde levere to be lewed. MED crede n. (2) (b).

C546 Not count (at) a **Cress**
c1385 Usk 25.133: Is nought to counte at a cresse, 125.44–5: Of al thy good service she compteth nat a cresse. **c1400** *Piers* A iii 137 in Skeat's EETS edition I 35 n.: Heo countith hit not at a cresse. **c1440** *Degrevant* 14.206: I cownt hym noghte at a cresse. **a1508** Dunbar *Flyting* 9.129: Na man comptis the ane kers.

C547 Not dread (*etc.*) a **Cress** (A number of single quotations are brought together here)
c1380 *Ferumbras* 168.5441–2: The Amerel ne dredeth hym noght . . . the value of a kerse. **c1380** *Pearl* 13.343: For anger gaynes the not a cresse. **c1400** *Beryn* 31.971: This vaylith nat a karse. **a1425** *St. Robert* 67.818: Never yytt yt newed (*yielded*) to now a cresse.

C548 Not set a **Cress**
c1390 Chaucer *CT* I[A] 3756: Of paramours he sette nat a kers. **a1420** *Spurious Chaucerian line* in Manly-Rickert VII 4: I sette not be hem a kers.

C549 Not worth a **Cress**
c1378 *Piers* B x 17: Wisdome and witte now is nought worth a carse. **c1385** Usk 73.109: Trewly their might is not worth a cresse. **a1393** Gower *CA* II 242.588: And so to me nys worth a kerse, 270.1652. Apperson 456; *Oxford* 118, 124; Skeat 227.

C550 As merry as a **Cricket**
1509 *Fyftene Joyes* E5^{v}[18]: And as mery as it were a crykket. **1546** Heywood *D* 42.27: Mery as a cricket. Apperson 413; *Oxford* 420; Taylor and Whiting 84; Tilley C825.

C551 A **Cripple** should not mock others for not going upright
a1439 Lydgate *Fall* III 787.444–5: Shame for a crepil, to stonde that hath no miht, To rebuke othir for thei go nat upriht! *Oxford* 428; Tilley C827.

C552 As dry as **Critons** (*cracklings*)
c1395 *WBible* Psalms ci 4: My boonus han dried up as critouns. **c1400** *Primer* 41[5–6]: My bones drieden up as critouns.

C553 The **Crock** should not strive with the wall
c1390 Chaucer *Truth* 12: Stryve not, as doth the crokke with the wal. **a1430** Lydgate *Pilgrimage* 390.14459–60: Hard ys to sporne ageyn an hal, Or a crokke a-geyn a wal. See **B421, P319, W20.**

C554 As coy as a **Crocker's** (*potter's*) mare
1546 Heywood *D* 60.34: She was to them, as koy as a crokers mare. Apperson 120; *Oxford* 116; Tilley C833. (Tilley seems to take *croker* as a proper name.)

C555 **Crocodile** tears
c1100 *Wonders of the East* in *Three Old English Prose Texts* 62.2–3: þan hy (*a race called "donestre"*) hine (*a victim*) fretað ealne buton þon heafd(e) ond þonne sittað and wepað ofer þam heafde. **a1398**(1495) Bartholomaeus-Trevisa cc3^{v}[1.10–4]: Phisiologus sayth that yf the coco-

dryll fyndyth a man . . . he sleeth hym yf he maye, and thenne he wepyth upon hym, and swolowyth hym at the laste. **c1400** Mandeville *Travels* 192.22–3: Theise serpentes slen men and thei eten hem wepynge. *Oxford* 118; Taylor and Whiting 85; Tilley C831; Whiting *Drama* 309:79.

C556 The treasure of **Croesus**
a1393 Gower *CA* III 75.4730–4: The tresor of Cresus And al the gold Octovien, Forth with the richesse Yndien Of Perles and of riche stones Were al togedre myn at ones. Cf. Apperson 530; *Oxford* 540; Taylor and Whiting 85; Tilley C832; Whiting *Scots* I 154.

C557 In the **Crook(ing)** (*crescent*) of the moon
c1400 *Beryn* 13.398: Ffor he met with his love, in crokeing of the moon. **c1430** *Brut* II 427.25–8: And all the cheveteynys, with the soudiourys, were taken, and led to the Cite of Paris in the croke of the mone, they myght sey; for of hem ther scapid but a fewe on lyve, 441.13–5: So that they (*the defeated Scots*) may say wele "In the croke of the mone went thei thidre warde, And in the wilde wanyende come thei homewarde." **1435** *Chronicles of London* (Julius B II) 75[22–4]. **1435** *Great Chronicle of London*, ed. A. H. Thomas and I. D. Thornley (London, 1938) 132[23–5]. **c1443** *Chronicle of London* 109[11–3], 122[23–7]: And so myghte he wel sey, that in the crook of the mone com he thedirwarde, and in the wylde wanyande wente homward: *With reste and pees, A man schal best encrees.* MED crok 6(a). See **W36.**

C558 The **Crop** stands under the root
a1393 Gower *CA* II 7.118: Now stant the crop under the rote. See **H92, 548.**

C559 One **Crop** of a turd mars a pot of pottage
1546 Heywood *D* 80.66: One crop of a tourd marrth a pot of potage. *Oxford* 317; Tilley W240. See **A167.**

C560 **Cross** (crouch [*cross*]) nor (and) pile
a1393 Gower *CA* II 141.390–1: Whos tunge neither pyl ne crouche Mai hyre. **c1435** Lydgate *Letter to Gloucester* in *MP* II 667.59–60: Of cros nor pyl ther is no reclus, Preent nor impressioun in al thy (*a purse's*) seyntuarye. **a1440** Burgh *Cato* 320.718: Sume man ther is, that hathe nouthir cros ne pile. **c1450** *The Summum Bonum* in Brown *Lyrics XV* 291.12: For here-In of al wynnyng lyth crosse and pile. **c1475** *Wisdom* 63.862–3: With the crose and the pyll I xall wrye yt, That ther xall never man dyscrey yt. **a1500** *Mischance Reigns* in Wright *Political Poems* II 240[22]: Cross and pyle standen in balaunce. Apperson 123; *Oxford* 119–20; Tilley C835; Whiting *Scots* I 154. See **D191.**

C561 To make a **Cross** on a gate (*i.e.*, not to return)
1549 Heywood *D* 53.386: And now will I make a crosse on this gate, **1555** *E* 196.289. Apperson 123; *Oxford* 119; Tilley C842.

C562 To make one a **Cross** of the same wood
c1395 Chaucer *CT* III[D] 484: I made hym of the same wode a croce.

C563 As black as a **Crow's** bill
1471 Ripley *Compound* 149[6]: Powder blacke as a Crowes byll. **a1500** *Ancient Scottish Prophecy, No. 1* in Bernardus *De cura* 18.6: In a clowde als blak as the bill of A crawe.

C564 As black as a **Crow's** feathers
a1500 *Court of Love* 437.1060: His berd as blak as fethers of the crow.

C565 As black as any (a) **Crow**
c1330 *Horn Childe* 191.1049: With foules blac as ani crawe. **c1385** Chaucer *CT* I[A] 2692: As blak he lay as any . . . crowe. **1513** Douglas *Aeneid* III 19.7. **1534** More *Comforte* 1249 H[4–5]: He is no blacker then a crowe. Apperson 51; *Oxford* 47; Taylor and Whiting 85; Tilley C844; Whiting *Scots* I 154.

C566 As swart (*black*) as any **Crow**
c1300 Robert of Gloucester II 697.10049: So swart so eni crowe amorwe is fot was.

C567 The **Crow** defends her nest well against the falcon
1471 Caxton *Recuyell* II 557.16–8: For ye may take ensample of the crowe that otherwhyle deffendeth well her neste agayn the fawcion. See **C350, R45.**

C568 The **Crow** thinks her own birds white (fairest)
1513 Douglas *Aeneid* III 171.77–8: Yit, by my self, I fynd this proverb perfyte, "The blak craw thinkis hyr awin byrdis quhite." **1533** More *Apologye* 1[8–9]: The crow that accompted her own byrdes the fayrest of all the fowles that flew. **1546** Heywood *D* 67.35: The crow thinkth hir owne birdes fairest in the wood. Apperson 124; *Oxford* 120; Taylor and Whiting 85–6; Tilley C851; Whiting *Scots* I 154.

C569 The **Crow** weens that he is the fairest bird of all
1481 Caxton *Mirror* 103[7–8]: The crowe weneth that he is the fairest birde of alle other, and the beste syngyng. Cf. Tilley K40. See **M579.**

C570 Evil **Crows** bring forth evil birds
1529 More *Supplicacion* 306 G[9–10]: Lest evill crowes bringe you forth evill byrdes. *Oxford* 180.

C571 Flys the **Crow** never so far the arse ay follows
c1315 *Gonville and Caius College Cambridge MS.* in *Law Quarterly Review* 37(1921) 311 (*Speculum* 18[1943] 431, n. 5): Ne flye the Crowe never so fer ay folweth hers, the tail. Tilley C858. See **A144.**

C572 To have a **Crow** to pull (pluck)
a1460 *Towneley Plays* 18.311: We have a craw to pull. **1509** Barclay *Ship* II 8[16]: He that hir weddyth, hath a crowe to pull. **1522** Skelton *Speke* II 19.389: Whyche of yow fyrste dare boldlye plucke the crowe, **a1529** *Garnesche* I 127.48: Ye pressyd pertely to pluk a crow. **1546** Heywood *D* 75.160: If he leave it not, we have a crow to pul. Apperson 124; *Oxford* 120; Tilley C855; Whiting *Drama* 359:782, *Scots* I 154–5.

C573 To have the (black) **Crow** bite one
c1422 Hoccleve *Dialog* 139.810: But I your freend be, byte me the crowe! **c1460** *Satirical Description* 204[21]: The blak crowe moote yow byght. Whiting *Ballad* 35.

C574 To say the **Crow** is white
c1450 Idley 88.439: Though he seie with the that white is the crowe. **c1497** Medwall *Fulgens* A4v[14–5]: Ye, goth the worlde so now a day That a man must say the crow is white. **a1500** *Court of Love* 421.430–1: Sey as she seith, than shalt thou not be shent, The crow is whyte. **1509** Barclay *Ship* II 212[13–4]: That if theyr mayster say that the crowe is whyte, They say the same, and have therin delyte. **1513** Douglas *Aeneid* II 107.26–7: Quhat wenys thou, frend, the craw be worthyn quhite, Supposs the holkis be all ourgrowyn thi face? **1528** More *Heresyes* 207 BC: Thei can have no more holde than if thei would say the crowe were white. **1546** Heywood *D* 73.116: Were not you as good than to say, the crow is whight, **1555** *E* 177.175. Apperson 124–5; *Oxford* 120; Tilley C853; Whiting *Drama* 340:483, *Scots* I 154.

C575 From the **Crown** to the toe
c1300 *Havelok* 61.1847: Fro the croune til the to. Apperson 125; Tilley C864. See **F468, H215, T421.**

C576 To bear the **Crown**
c1475 Henryson *Fables* 19.464: Off craftie crawing he micht beir the Croun. See **B36, 372, F316.**

C577 To have one's **Crown** shaved
c1400 *Laud Troy* I 76.2549–50: But sat alle stille everychon, As who hadde schaven hem a croun.

C578 Till **Crow's-feet** grow under one's eyes
c1385 Chaucer *TC* ii 402–3: So longe mote ye lyve, and alle proude, Til crowes feet be growen under youre yë. Taylor and Whiting 86; Tilley C865.

C579 Between this and **Croydon**
c1515 Barclay *Eclogues* 29.843: He hath no felowe betwene this and Croydon.

C580 To mince as **Crumbs** of bread
c1450 *St. Cuthbert* 197.6757–8: All northumbirlande provynce He thoght as croms of brede to mynce.

C581 To take one's **Crumbs**
1474 Paston V 211[8–11]: But, God thanke yow, I toke so my crommys whyls I was wyth yow, that I felyd my sylfe by the weye that God and ye hade made me stronger than I wenyd that I had ben. Apperson 493: Pick up; *Oxford* 498; Taylor and Whiting 86; Tilley C868.

C582 As dry as a **Crust**
a1398(1495) Bartholomaeus-Trevisa p3r[2.3]: And is drye as a crouste.

C583 He never bought **Crust** again
c1330 *Otuel* 93.953–4: And anawe of nubie he smot, That nevere eft crouste he ne bot. See **B520.**

C584 The more **Crust** the less crumb
c1450 *Rylands MS.394* 94.18: The more cruste the lasse cromme. NED Crumb 3, quote 1726.

C585 Much **Cry** and little wool
a1475 Sir John Fortescue *The Governance of England,* ed. Charles Plummer (Oxford, 1885) 132[26–8]: And so his hyghnes shall have theroff, but as hadd the man that sherid is hogge, muche crye and litil woll. Apperson 428, 432; *Oxford* 263–4; Taylor and Whiting 86; Tilley C871.

C586 When men have well **Cried** then they will round (*whisper*)
c1385 Chaucer *TC* iv 587: For whan men han wel cryd, than wol they rowne.

C587 As bright as (any, the) **Crystal**(-stone)
c1300 *South English Legendary* (*Laud*) 312.456: And Maketh hire schyne a-boute brightore thane ani cristal. **a1325** *Cursor* III 1246.21783–4: Was na cristal was als bright, Na sa scene to mans sight (T lighte). **a1393** Gower *CA* II 337.1321–2 (*MS.*A): The beaute of hire face schon Wel

bryhtere than the Cristall ston. **c1395** *WBible* Numbers xi 7: *Whiit and bright as cristal.* **c1350** *Gregorius* 168 C 1094: Bright and clere so cristal stone. **c1408** Lydgate *Reson* 12.436: Bryghter than . . . cristal. **c1485** *Slaughter* (*Digby*) 21.506: Brighter than . . . clere cristall. **c1500** Greene *Carols* 240.5: Whan Mary, as bryght as crystall ston. Whiting *NC* 389.

C588 As clean as (any) **Crystal**
a1100 *Phoenix Homily* 147.10: His eagene twa . . . synden swa claene swa cristal. **a1400** *Siege of Jerusalem* 6.102: As clene as clef, ther cristalle sprynges. **a1400** Wyclif *Sermons* II 310[25–6]: And thei ben of clene lyf, as cristal is clene withouten motis. **c1400** *Plowman's Tale* 158.346. **a1410** Lydgate *Churl* in *MP* II 470.54: Lich silver stremys, as any cristal cleene. **a1415** Mirk *Festial* 107.16: any. **a1450** *York Plays* 35.5: His Aungell cleere, as cristall clene. **a1460** *Towneley Plays* 95.308: She is as clene as cristall clyfe. **a1475** *Ludus Coventriae* 375.47: As crystall clene it clensyth you clere. **c1475** *Golagros* 17.478: The sone, as cristall sa cleyne. **a1500** *I Have Now Set* in Brown *Lyrics XV* 74.17: Beyng as clene as clere crystall. **a1500** *Take Erth of Erth* in Ashmole 274[25]. **1501** Douglas *Palice* 54.22: Water as of the cristall clene. Whiting *Scots* I 155.

C588a Crystal-clean
c1408 Lydgate *Reson* 129.4927: The water was so cristal clene, **a1449** *My Lady Dere* in *MP* II 422.68: Ryvers crystal clene.

C589 As clear as (the, any) **Crystal**(-stone)
a1350 *Ywain* 25.900: Hir yghen clere als es cristall. **c1350** *Apocalypse* 195.1, 196.4. **c1390** *Mayden, Modur, and comely Qween* 123.112: Heil clerore then the Cristal-ston. **a1398**(1495) Bartholomaeus-Trevisa t4^{r}[2.42]. **a1400** *Alexander C* 146.2541, 263.5280: Was nevir na cristall so clere as was tha clere strandis. **a1400** *Ancrene* (*Recluse*) 197.8–9: A clere flode as Cristal, 22–3. **a1400** *Cursor* I 30 F 376, III 1354 F 23688: ani. **a1400** *Destruction of Troy* 100.3063–4: The slote of hir slegh brest . . . As any cristall clere, 431.13183: the. **a1400** *Pricke* 172.6349, 173.6396–7: And be made als clere and fayre and clene, Als any cristal that here es sene, 204.7577–8. **a1400** *Scottish Legends* II 319.541. **a1405** Lydgate *Black Knight* in *MP* II 384.37, **c1408** *Reson* 4.123–4: And the wellys thanne appere As cristal or quyk sylver clere, 100.3808–9: Ben cler, ageyn the sonne bryght, As any cristall to be-holde. **c1410** Lovelich *Grail* I 222.265–6: And so Cler be-Cam that Tre withal, As Evere dyde ony . . . Cristal. **a1415** Mirk *Festial* 107.10–1. **a1420** Lydgate *Troy* III 580.588–9: Terys . . . as any cristal clere, **a1422** *Life* 510.1137–9: A well . . . To loke upon as any cristal clere. **a1425** *London Lapidary* in *Lapidaries* 31[17–8], cf. 51[18–9]. **a1439** Lydgate *Fall* III 858.1257. **c1440** *Degrevant* 36.530–2: A lady wyghte, Thare es . . . Na cristalle so clere. **c1440** *Prose Alexander* 99.36: any. **a1449** Lydgate *Ave* in *MP* I 300.26, *Fifteen Joys* in *MP* I 260.4, *Testament* in *MP* I 343.379: ony. **a1450** *Three Middle English Sermons* 43.713–4: ani, 44.729: ani. **a1450** *York Plays* 308.24. **c1450** Greene *Carols* 190.5. **c1450** *Myroure of oure Ladye* 288[27], 304[22]. **a1460** *Towneley Plays* 269.361. **c1460** *The Coronation I* in Brown *Lyrics XV* 68.13: the, *The Coronation II* in Brown *Lyrics XV* 71.58: Hire Colour as Cleer as Cristal bryght. **a1475** *Asneth* 231.101. **a1475** *Assembly of Gods* 47.1603: any. **a1500** *The Beauty of his Mistress II* in Robbins 124.16: With eyes clere as crystall stoune. **a1500** *The Beauty of his Mistress III* in Robbins 127.25: Your throte as clere as crystall stone. **a1500** *High Empress* in Brown *Lyrics XV* 27.8. **a1500** *Partenay* 19.337–8. **a1500** *Take Erth of Erth* in Ashmole 269[8–9]: Water of the Wood: Cleere as Chrystall schynyng bryght. **a1504** Hawes *Example* Aa4^{v}[2], Ee5^{r}[24]. **a1506** Barclay *Castell* G8^{v}[19], **1509** *Ship* II 290[14]. **1513** Bradshaw *St. Werburge* 35.773: the, 159.815: the, 195.1906: the. **1515** Barclay *St. George* 17.185. **1520** Whittinton *Vulgaria* 36.27. **c1523** Barclay *Mirrour* 14[19]. **a1525** Berners *Froissart* VI 161[12]. Apperson 101; Svartengren 361–2; Taylor and Whiting 86; Tilley C875; Whiting *Drama* 309:78, *Scots* I 155.

C589a Crystal-clear
a1439 Lydgate *Fall* I 181.6402: Watir cristal cleer, **1439** *St. Albon* 118.444: A bath of water cristall-clere. **c1500** *Everyman* 31.898: Thy rekenynge is crystall clere.

C590 As hard as **Crystal**
a1398(1495) Bartholomaeus-Trevisa t4^{v}[1.7]: It is harde as cristall.

C591 As sheen as **Crystal**
1439 Lydgate *St. Albon* 141.866: Lyke perles rounde as any christall shene.

C592 As white as **Crystal**
1465 Leversege 27[21]: Whyght as crystall. **a1500** *I love on lovyd* in *Rawlinson MS. C 813* 857.19. **1509** Watson *Ship* Ee3^{r}[7]: Smocke more whyter than the crystal. **a1533** Berners *Huon* 426.16.

C593 To be like **Crystal**(-stone) (*varied*)
c1325 *Loveliest Lady* 149.30: Hire loveliche chere as cristal. **a1400** *Eglamour* 56.834: Hir eghne als cristalle-stane. **c1405** *Mum* 29.63: With a cleer colour, as cristal hit semeth. **a1420** Lydgate *Troy* I 33.744–5: Watrys . . . That sprange lyche cristal in the colde welle. **c1440** *Prose Alexander* 91.7: Of clere water as cristalle. **c1475** Henryson *Testament* 111.176: As Cristall wer his Ene. **a1490** Caxton *Eneydos* 16.29: Slewe a white bulle as crystall. **a1500** *Court of Love* 426.655: With yen as cristall. Whiting *Scots* I 155.

C594 To shine like (the, any) **Crystal**
a1325 *Ipotis* in Smith *Common-place Book* 27.65: The iii hevyne schynyth as Crystall. **c1330** *Orfeo* 32.357–8: Al the ut-mast wal Was clere and schine as cristal. **c1380** Chaucer *Rosemounde* 3: For as the cristal glorious ye shyne. **c1395** *WBible* Apocalypse xxii 1. **a1398**(1495) Bartholomaeus-Trevisa K5ʳ[1.15]. **a1400** *Cursor* I 31 GT 376. **a1400** *Torrent* 9.227–8: Presyos stonys, Schynyng ase crystall clere. **c1410** Lovelich *Merlin* III 477.17815–6: Helmes . . . Schyneng as bryht as ony cristal. **a1420** Lydgate *Troy* I 49.1267–8, **1420** *Temple* 1–2.21–2: Again the sonne that shone . . . As eny cristal. **a1450** *Generydes A* 7.176: That shoone as clere as doth cristall. **c1450** Idley 132.1473. **a1470** Malory II 750.33: Hys shylde that shone lyke ony crystall. **c1500** ?Bradshaw *Radegunde* 8[7].

C595 A **Cuckold** has no gall (*varied*)
a1439 Lydgate *Fall* I 294.3367: And summe afferme how such folk (*cuckolds*) ha(ve) no gall. **a1500** *Corneus* 4.95–6: Cokwold was kyng Arthour, Ne galle non he hade, 107, 8.204: For cokwoldes have no galle. **a1500** *Piers of Fullham* 14.338–9: And into suche myscheyf falle That he unware hath lost his galle. **a1508** Skelton *Phyllyp* I 65.469–77: The storke also, That maketh his nest, In chymneyes to rest; Within those walles No broken galles May there abyde Of cokoldry syde, Or els phylosophy Maketh a great lye. See **D364.**

C596 A **Cuckold** will not drown
a1500 *Piers of Fullham* 14.337–47: That many a man hath had an horn, And into suche myscheyf falle That he unware hath lost his galle, To make hym sure that he not drowne, Nor with sodeyn wawes sowne, Whiche, as clerkys determyne, Is right a perfyte medicyne, Both on ffreshe water and on see, That folke shall not drowned be: I mene hosbondes yong and old That beren the name of cokwold.

C597 To set a **Cuckold** on the high bench
a1475 *Ludus Coventriae* 127.95–6: And feetly with help sche can consent To set A cokewold on the hye benche.

C598 To wear a **Cuckold Hood** (hat)
c1460 *Ipomadon C* 351.29–30: And I had wold, par aventure the king might have wered a cukwold hoode. **a1500** *Corneus* 7.185–6: And now he is a cokwold fyne To were a cokwoldes hate.

C599 To dance in the **Cuckold Row**
a1500 *Corneus* 7.196–7: Lordynges, all now may ye know, That i may dance in the cokwold row. *Roxburghe Ballads*, ed. W. Chapell and J. W. Ebsworth (9 vols., Hertford, 1871–99) III 382.51–2: And think our little babes divine Were got in Cuckolds Row, IX clxv °[32]: We (*Cuckolds*) needs must be brothers, for we dwell in a row.

C600 The **Cuckoo** can sing but one lay (song)
a1410 Lydgate *Churl* in *MP* II 483.344–7: And semblably in Aprill and in May, Whan gentil briddis make most melodie, The cookkow syngen can but o lay, In othir tymes she hath no fantasye, **a1430** *Pilgrimage* 388–9.14382–4: I resemble the Cookkoow, Wych up-on o lay halt so long, And kan synge noon other song. Apperson 128; *Oxford* 63; Tilley C894; Whiting *Drama* 272, *Scots* I 181: Gowk. See **A174, S479, 933.**

C601 The **Cuckoo** sings only of himself
1340 *Ayenbite* 22[7–8]: The yelpere is the cockou thet ne kan naght zinge bote of himselve, 59[20–1]. **c1380** Chaucer *PF* 498–9: The cokkow . . . So cryede . . . "kokkow!" **c1400** *Vices and Virtues* 17.27–8: For the avauntor fareth as a cokkow, that can no song but of hymself, 57.1–2: Thei faren as a cokkow, that can synge of no thing but of hymself. **c1450** *Jacob's Well* 149.13: Thei fare as the cuccuke, that syngyth but of him-self, 263.25–6: Thou faryst as cuckow, that evere syngeth his owen name. **c1450** *Pilgrimage LM* 118[24–5]: The kockow that can nouht singe and jangle but of him self. **a1484** Caxton *Royal Book* C7ʳ[24–6]: He that avanteth hym is lyke unto the cuckow that can synge noo thynge but of hym self, F4ʳ[19–20]. **a1500** *Discourse* in *RES* 24(1948) 8[39]: Syngyng ay as a cockow, that can synge noon other songe but of hym self. MED cokkou 1(b).

C602 The **Cuckoo** sings through the year
a1500 *Piers of Fullham* 15.352–4: Ffor thorow the yere som folkys lyvyng Have herd the cockoo

freshe synge In contreyes many mo than one. Apperson 128; *Oxford* 123; Tilley C891.

C603 **Cuckoos** and cuckolds (*varied*)
c1385 Chaucer *CT* I[A] 1928–30: Jalousye, That wered of yelewe gooldes a gerland, And a cukkow sittynge on his hand, **c1390** IX[H] 243: This crowe sang "Cokkow! cokkow! cokkow!" **c1400** *Femina* 61[13–4]: Song of kokkow in somer we have To preyse that take we non hede. **c1497** Medwall *Fulgens* E3v[29–33]: By cokkis bonis for it was a kocko, And man say amonge He that throwyth stone or stycke At suche a byrde he is lycke To synge that byrdes songe. **1509** Barclay *Ship* I 298[26–8]: So that whyle he after the owle doth go Fedynge the Couko, his wyfe hir tyme doth watche Receyvynge another whose egges she doth hatche, **c1515** *Eclogues* 191.267–8: Then was no cucko betwene the east and west To lay wrong egges within a straunge nest. **a1529** Skelton *Garnesche* I 126.4: Ye syng allway the kukkowe songe. See **N111.**

C604 To chew the **Cud**
c1395 *WBible* Hosea vii 14: Thei chewiden code on wheete, and wyn. Apperson 94; *Oxford* 91; Taylor and Whiting 87; Tilley C896.

C605 Not set a **Cue** (*half farthing*)
c1515 Barclay *Eclogues* 1.14: Men by their writing scantly set a qu. NED Cue sb.[1] 2.

C606 Not worth a **Cue**
c1516 Skelton *Magnificence* 2.36: Lyberte was not worthe a cue, **1522** *Why Come* II 34.231–2: Small newes the true is, That be worth ii. kues. **c1523** Barclay *Mirrour* 16[26]: All these . . . are scantly worth a kue.

C607 To have something thrust in one's **Cule** (*arse*)
a1300 *Richard* 176.1831–2: For all your boost and your orguyl, Men shall threste in your cuyle. MED cul n. (1).

Culver, see **Dove**

C608 As mild as a **Culver** (*dove*)
c1200 Orm II 21.10836–7: Birrth wurrthenn milde, and soffte, and meoc, And aeddmod allse cullfre.

C609 As tame as a **Culver**
1422 Yonge *Governaunce* 212.2: Pryve and tame as a culvere.

C610 To quake like a **Culver** smitten by the eagle
c1386 Chaucer *LGW* 2317–9: And quok for fere, pale and pitously . . . as the culver, that of the egle is smiten.

C611 **Cunning** has no foe
c1499 Skelton *Bowge* I 47.447–8: Connynge hath no foo Save hym that nought can, Scrypture sayth soo.

C612 **Cunning** is a sicker stage
a1500 *In a chambre* in Sandison 120.46–7: Connyng is syker stage, And service is no sykyrnesse.

C613 **Cunning** is flower of all treasure
c1450 *Proverbs of Good Counsel* 69.51: For of all Tresure, Conny(n)ge ys flowur.

C614 **Cunning** is no burden
c1450 *Alle that well* in *MLN* 70(1955) 251.36: Kunny(n)g is non byrdeyn. **1520** Whittinton *Vulgaria* 40.18–9: Connynge (be it never so moche) semeth no burden to hym that hath hit. Apperson 129, 347; *Oxford* 123; Tilley C899.

C615 **Cunning** surmounts all earthly treasure
c1499 Skelton *Bowge* I 36.153–4: Loo, what it is a man to have connynge! All erthly tresoure it is surmountynge. See **H435, Q5.**

C616 Hasty **Cunning** soon waxes dry
a1475 *Tree* 16.2–3: Thou shuldist every day lerne right litel, for hasty kunnyng wexith sone drye.

C617 To have scant the **Cunning** of a snite (*snipe*)
c1515 Barclay *Eclogues* 165.682: Though they have scantly the cunning of a snite.

C618 Who will be **Cunning** must sue (*follow*) the cunning
c1477 Caxton *Curtesye* 51.504: Who wil be connyng he muste the connyng sewe. See **W398.**

C619 A drunken **Cunt** has no porter
1522 More *Treatyce* 97 B[2–10]: Men are wont to write a short rydle on the wal, that D.C. hath no. P. Rede ye this rydle I canot: but I have hard say, that it touche(t)h the redines that woman hath to fleshly filth, if she fal in dronkenes. And if ye fynde one that can declare it, thoughe it be no greate authoritie, yet have I heard saye that it is very true. Tilley C901. See **R92, W494.**

C620 Give your **Cunt** to ?cony (*?sweetheart*) and crave after(?ward) wedding
a1325 *Hendyng C* 190.42: Yeve thi cunte to cunnig, And crave affetir wedding. Kneuer 51–2; Schleich 271–2; Singer III 138.

C621 As merry as **Cup** and can
1546 Heywood *D* 66.43: Mery we were as cup and can could holde. Apperson 129; *Oxford* 124; Tilley C903.

C622 The **Cup** abyes (*pays for*) the default of supper
c1300 *South English Legendary* I 131.76–8: As me seith alday, the coppe abuth the defaute of soper, And be(o) he ihandled wel ynou, as hom thincth it is right Atte faillynge of the soper to drinke forte midnight. See **D398.**

C623 Fill a **Cup** (of ale) at the beginning of a tale (before we fight)
c1300 *Havelok* 1.13–4: At the biginning of ure tale, Fil me a cuppe of ful god ale. **c1300** *Beves* 194.4107–8: Ac er than we be-ginne fighte, Ful us the koppe anon righte. **c1515** Barclay *Eclogues* 169.811–2: I pray thee Codrus (my whey is weake and thin) Lende me thy bottell to drinke or I begin. Cf. Chaucer *CT* VI[C] 321–8.

C624 Let go the **Cup**
a1376 *Piers* A v 188: Ther was laughwhing and lotering and "let go the cuppe." *Oxford* 123.

C625 To bear the **Cup** even
1473 Paston V 201[7–9]: He wolde also doo, as ye wolde have hym nowe, ber the cuppe evyn, as What-calle-ye-hym seyde to Aslake. Apperson 83: carry; Tilley C907.

C626 To carp (*prate, boast*) with the **Cup** (*i.e.*, boast over their drinks)
a1400 *Morte Arthure* 81.2749–50: The kreuelleste knyghttes of the kynges chambyre That kane carpe with the coppe knyghtly wordes.

C627 To drink of a **Cup** (*varied*)
a1300 *Richard* 439.7023–4: And thoo that wolden have come uppe, They drank off Kyng Richardis cuppe (*were killed*). **c1390** *Gregorius* 12.97–8: Heo Corven bothe with o knyf And of o Coppe dronken same. **c1440** *Prose Alexander* 40.16–7: We schulde all perische at anes and all drynke of a coppe. **a1533** Berners *Arthur* 505[5]: They dranke of the same cup (*were paid back*). Tilley C908.

C628 To drink without **Cup**
c1395 Chaucer *CT* V[F] 942: Withouten coppe he drank al his penaunce. **c1400** *Beryn* 11.306: Ffor such was his fortune, he drank with-out the cupp, 15.460: He shall drynk for kittis love with-out(e) cup or pot. **a1450** *Chronicle of London* 122[14–6]: And pryncypally to the toun of Poperynge and of Belle, where Haukyns (*the defeated and slain Flemish*) drank be note withoughte cuppe. **a1500** *Now late me thought* 278[23]: Allas he (*the buffeted Jesus*) dranke withoute cope. Whiting *Drama* 342:509.

C629 To kiss the **Cup**
a1400 *Cloud* 108.7: For men wil kysse the cuppe, for wine is ther-in. **c1412** Hoccleve *Regement* 137.3813–5: More is preysinge And honurable, a man compleyne of thrist, Than dronken be, whan he the cuppe hath kist. **a1450** *Partonope* 195.5181–2: He kyssed the cuppe, but never a delle Ther-of he dronke. **a1450** *York Plays* 257.80: This cuppe saverly for to kisse. **a1500** *Carpenter's Tools* 88.234: Therefore the cope ons I wylle kys. **c1503** More *Early Poems* [1] C[5–7]: And an olde trot, Than can god wot, Nothyng but kysse the cup. *Oxford* 340; Tilley C909.

C630 To sit between the **Cup** and the wall
1513 Bradshaw *St. Werburge* 11.53: Some to syt bytwene the cuppe and the wall.

C631 To take the **Cup** as it comes
c1353 *Winner* 448: Take the cup as it comes, the case as it falls.

C632 A well filled **Cup** never made a wise man
c1475 *Rawlinson MS. D 328* 124.71: Well y-fyllyd cup makyt never wyse man. See **W360.**

C633 When the **Cup** is fullest bear it fairest
c1025 *Durham Proverbs* 15.42: Swa fulre fæt swa hit mann sceal fægror beran. Vas quantum plen(i)or tantum moderatius ambulandum. **c1325** *Hendyng H* 293.125: When the coppe is follest, thenne ber hire feyrest. Apperson 129, 241; Kneuer 25–8; *Oxford* 123, 230; Schleich 250–1; Singer III 127; Tilley C910. Cf. Taylor and Whiting 87.

C634 **Cupid** (Love) is blind
c1380 Chaucer *HF* 137–8: Daun Cupido, Hir blynde sone, 617: Hys blynde nevew Cupido, **c1385** *CT* I[A] 1965: And blynd he (*Cupido*) was, as it is often seene, *TC* iii 1808: Thy blynde and wynged sone ek, daun Cupide, **c1386** *LGW* F 237–8: And al be that men seyn that blynd ys he, Algate me thoghte that he myghte se. **a1393** Gower *CA* II 36.47: For love is blind and may noght se, 103.2490–1: Bot sche which kepth the blinde whel, Venus, 230.159–60: As he is blind himself, riht so He makth his client blind also, 265.1465, 348.1732–3, 440.1417, III 176.349, 359: This blinde Boteler, 179.453–4: boteler, 443.2104: love, 2130–1: For love, which that blind was evere, Makth alle his servantz blinde also, 447.2268, 462.2794: This blinde god. **c1395** Chaucer *CT* IV[E] 1598:

love. **a1400** *Discrecioun of Stirings* 72.25–6: That is to sey, in love that is blinde to many thinges and seeth bot that o thing that it sekith. **a1400** *Romaunt B* 3703: The God of Love, blynde as stoon. **c1400** ?Clanvowe *Cuckoo and the Nightingale* in Skeat *Chaucerian* 355.201–2: Love. **a1405** Lydgate *Black Knight* in *MP* II 401.453–4: O God of Love! unto the I crie, And to thy blende double deyte, *Floure* in *MP* II 418.264, **c1408** *Reson* 141.5381: But is as blynde as stok or ston, **a1420** *Troy* I 8.266, 308.5730–1, III 768.6955, **1420** *Temple* 36.855. **a1437** *Kingis Quair* 71.94[3]. **a1430** Lydgate *Pilgrimage* 226.8135–6, **a1439** *Fall* I 155.5532, 197.6986–7: Poetis seyn he is blynd to been a juge. He is depeynt(e) lich a blynd archer, 327.4555. **c1440** Charles of Orleans 219.6523: So blynd is love and wenyth othir be. **a1450** *Partonope* 437.10796: That may not be; in this case love is blynde. **c1450** Capgrave *Katharine* 274.404, 304.1337: Thou loved ful weel blynde Venus and Cupide. **c1450** Idley 101.1182–3: Loo, how love is blynde and may not see And so he weneth that all othir be. **1474** Caxton *Chesse* 39[10–2]: For theophrast saith that alle love is blynde, ther love is ther can not ryght Jugement by guyen, For alle love is blynde. **c1475** Henryson *Testament* 109.134–5: O fals Cupide . . . And thy Mother, of lufe the blind Goddes, 115.282–3. **a1500** *Court of Love* 410.53. **a1500** *Sen that Eine* 105.70. **c1500** Fabyan 61[21–2], 197[34–5]. **1504** Hawes *Example* Ee7r[15]: Love. **1509** Barclay *Ship* I 80[4], II 298[3]. **1509** Watson *Ship* Ee4v[19–20]. **1513** Bradshaw *St. Werburge* 39.890. **1513** Douglas *Aeneid* II 147.3. **1518** Nevill *Castell* 90.391. **c1523** Barclay *Mirrour* 57[29], [40]: blinde Venus. Apperson 384; MED blind, adj. 1(c); *Oxford* 389; Erwin Panofsky *Studies in Iconology* (New York, 1962) vii–viii, 95–128; Taylor and Whiting 230; Tilley L506; Whiting *Drama* 251, 288, 289, 296, *Scots* I 155, 204.

C635 To be **Cupshotten**
a1338 Mannyng *Chronicle A* I 265.759–60: Als they were best in gladyng, and wel cuppeschoten. **1468** Paston IV 306[14]: A lytel copschotyn, but yit he is no brawler. **1528** More *Heresyes* 153 E[7]: Be cup shotten. **1546** Heywood *D* 41.16: He was . . . somwhat cupshotten.

C636 A **Cur** that bays bremely (*fiercely*) bites never the faster (*varied*)
a1400 *Alexander C* 100.1804–5: At ilka cote a kene curre as he the chache wald; Bot as bremely as he baies he bites nevir the fastir. **c1440** *Prose Alexander* 22.20–3: Wate ye noghte wele that hundes, that berkes mekill, bytes men noghte so sone, als does hundes that commes on men wit-outten berkynge. **c1450** *How mankinde dooth* in Furnivall *Hymns* 77.619–20: Though my fleissche berke, he schal not bitee, From his lustis y wole him tye. Apperson 157; *Oxford* 23; Tilley B85; Whiting *NC* 396. See **B46, 415, H561.**

C637 **Curs** and ravens beat all others away from carrion
c1515 Barclay *Eclogues* 165.673–5: Like as when curres light on a carion, Or stinking ravens fed with corruption: These two all other away do beate and chace.

C638 **Curs** fight with each other but show all their might against a stranger
c1515 Barclay *Eclogues* 85.871–4: They fare like to curres . . . Though eche one with other ofte chide, braule and fight, Agaynst a poor stranger they shewe all their might. See **D335.**

C639 To grin and gnar (*snarl*) like a butcher's **Cur**
c1523 Barclay *Mirrour* 78[24]: Grinning and gnarring as doth a butchers curre.

C640 No man can **Curse** another and protect himself (from the effect)
c1000 Aelfric *Homilies* II 36[2–3]: Ne mæg nan man oðerne wyrian, and him sylfum gebeorgan. Cf. Taylor and Whiting 88:6. See **D342, P232.**

C641 To miss the **Cushion**
c1522 Skelton *Colyn* I 349.997–8: And whan he weneth to syt, Yet may he mysse the quysshon. **1546** Heywood *D* 97.227: Ye myst the cushin, for all your hast to it. Apperson 419; *Oxford* 427; Tilley C928.

C642 To set one beside the **Cushion**
1546 Heywood *D* 97.228: And I maie set you besyde the cushyn yit. Apperson 39; *Oxford* 35; Tilley C929.

C643 **Custom** gives jurisdiction
1456 Hay *Law* 252.10–1: For the law sais that custum gevis oft tyme jurisdictioun.

C644 **Custom** is overcome with custom
a1500 *Imitatione* (*1*) 26.30–1: Custume is overcome with custume. **1502** *Imitatione* (*2*) 170.14–5: For evyll custome may be overcome by good custome.

C645 **Custom** is stronger (harder) to break than nature
1450 *Dicts* 274.31–2: Costome is (strenger) to breke thanne nature. **1477** Rivers *Dictes* 111[24]:

Custume is harder to breke than nature. See **T129.**

C646 Custom (Usage) is the second kind (*nature*) (*varied*)
a1387 Higden-Trevisa VII 339[21]: Costome is the secounde fro kynde. **a1393** Gower *CA* III 185.663–4: For in Phisique this I finde, Usage is the seconde kinde, *var.:* Usage is the seconde kinde In love als wel as other weie. **c1420** Wyntoun V 201.659–60: For thi haldis clerkis be thar saw That custum is the tothir law. **1422** Yonge *Governaunce* 238.7–8: For as ypocras Sayth, "Costome is the seconde nature or kynde." **a1447** Bokenham *Mappula* 33–4: And the wolde (*old*) proverbe seithe: custome and use is a nother nature or kynde. **a1450** *Myne awen dere* 177.879–82: For custome is of propyr kynde: Trowth makes a man inclynde Owther till gude or till ill, Whether that he hase used hym till (*To exchange* custome *and* Trowth *would improve the sense*). **c1450** La Tour-Landry 9.16–7: Usage makithe custume, 116.22–3: And all comithe but of usaunce and custume. **1456** Hay *Governaunce* 126.22–3: Usage is ane othir nature the quhilk is perilous to change. **c1480** *Contemplacioun* 197.289–90: The secund natur Is callit conswetud Quhilk lichtly levis nocht the ald usage. **1509** Barclay *Ship* I 164[6–7]: Whan costome and use is tourned to nature It is right harde to leve, **c1523** *Mirrour* 24[15]: When custome and use is tourned to nature. Apperson 130; *Oxford* 125; Tilley C932, U22; Whiting *Scots* I 155.

C647 Custom makes law
1382 Wyclif *Seven Werkys of Mercy Bodyly* in *SEW* III 175[34]: Sithen custom makis lawe.

C648 Custom passes all things
1450 *Dicts* 114.5–6: Custome passithe alle thingis. See **U8.**

C649 Custom taken in tender age is hard to part
a1430 Lydgate *Pilgrimage* 324.11889–92: Ffor custoom take in tendre age, (As seyn thys olde ffolkys sage,) Wyth-oute labour (thys no nay,) Ys ful hard to parte away. See **S240.**

C650 Custom takes no new guises
1509 Watson *Ship* H3^{v}–H4^{r}: Be it good or evyll, custome taketh no newe gyses.

C651 Custom will dere (*harm*)
a1475 *Ludus Coventriae* 54.97–8: It may gendyr custom in the, By-ware of custom ffor he wyl dere.

C652 Evil **Custom** is hard to blin (*leave off*) (*varied*)
a1425 *Christ's own Complaint* in *Pol. Rel. and Love Poems* 226.572: Yvel custum is ful hard to blynne. **c1425** Arderne *Fistula* 55.29–31: Ffor John Damascen seith "It is hevy for to chaunge noying custom, and most if it be olde." Cf. Smith 50.

C653 Old **Custom** is hard to put away (break)
a1422 Lydgate *Life* 661.341–3: For olde custome is harde to putte away, And usage grevythe folkes full sore To do a-way that thei have kepte of yore. **a1500** *Imitatione* (*1*) 16.25–6: Olde custom is harde to breke. **1502** *Imitatione* (*2*) 163.37–8: It is harde to leve a custom of longe continuaunce. See **M361.**

C654 Not set two Doncaster **Cuts** (*?bob-tailed horses, ?geldings*)
c1516 Skelton *Magnificence* 10.293: I set not by the worlde two Dauncaster cuttys. Apperson 162; NED Cut sb.[2] 28.

C655 To call one **Cut** (*?bob-tail*)
a1500 Medwall *Nature* B1^{v}[11–2]: Yf thou se hym not take hys owne way, Call me cut when thou metest me a nother day. Tilley C940; Whiting *Drama* 337:432.

C656 To keep one's **Cut**
c1400 *Beryn* 41.1309–10: Now kepe thy Cut, Beryn; for thow shalt have a fit Somwhat of the world, to lern(e) better witt, 56.1805: Kepe thy Cut nowe, Beryn! for thow art in the case. **c1422** Hoccleve *Dialog* 138.788–9: Thow shalt be bisy ynow, I undirtake, Thy kut to keepe. **a1475** *Ludus Coventriae* 205.151–2: We xal the tecche with carys colde A lytyl bettyr to kepe thi kutte (*a Pharisee to the woman taken in adultery*). MED cut n. (2) 2(b): "to put up with one's lot; know one's position."

C657 To say **"Cut"**
c1400 *Beryn* 41.1288: And lepe out of the Chambir, as who seyd "cut!" MED cut *interj.*

C658 As sweet as **Cypress**
c1485 *Mary Magdalene* (*Digby*) 132.2047: Swetter than . . . cypresse.

D

D1 Most **Dainty** (*delicacy*) comes behind
a1475 *Liber Cure Cocorum* 55[21–2]: And most dayntè, come behynde: Thys is a rewle mad in kynde. Milton *At a Vacation Exercise in the College* (1628) 14: The daintiest dishes shall be served up last.

D2 As bright as a **Daisy**
c1250 *Harley MS.3376* f.16^v in Ker *Catalogue* 313[6]: Brihture then the daisei him thet me longgeth. **a1300** *Alisaunder* 406 L 6230–1: My make Blassameye Al so bryght as daies eyghe.

D3 As white as the **Daisy**
c1387-95 Chaucer *CT* I[A] 332: Whit was his berd as is the dayesye.

D4 Of one **Damage** to make twain
1525 Berners *Froissart* V 226[12–3]: It is none honour . . . to make of one yvell dommage twayne. See **S513.**

D5 Our **Dame** is often about our halfpenny
c1450 *Rylands MS.394* 96.28*: Ofte is owre dame aboute our halfpenye. Sepe recordatur oboli michi que dominatur.

D6 Your **Dame** was swived (japed) ere you were born
c1420 Wyntoun V 301.2048: Thi dame was swywit or thou was borne. **c1470** *Wallace* 115.154: Thi deme has beyne japyt or thow was born. Cf. Tilley M1196: If your mother had not lost her virginity you would not have been born.

D7 From **Dan** to Beersheba
c1395 *WBible* Judges xx 1: Fro Dan til to Bersabee, I Kings iii 20, II Kings xvii 11, III Kings iv 25, I Paralipomenon xxi 2: Fro Bersabe til to Dan. *Oxford* 128; Taylor and Whiting 90.

D8 Does he **Dance** merrily who is mirthless?
c1380 Chaucer *PF* 592–3: Daunseth he murye that is myrtheles? Who shulde recche of that is recheles? *Oxford* 421. See **A88.**

D9 That **Dance** is done
a1450 *York Plays* 81.225: That daunce is done, 149.96. **a1460** *Towneley Plays* 72.238: Ffy on hym! nay, nay, that dawnce is done.

D10 To be brought (caught) in a **Dance**
a1450 *Partonope* 192.5087: Thus ys he broghte in the devellys dawnce, 330.8163–4: But God may ordeyn here-after that ye In loves daunse caught may be. **c1500** *Alone, alone* in Stevens *Music* 342.3[6–8]: My hert ys braught Full low forfought Yn lovys daunce. **c1500** *Sore I Sigh* in Robbins 154.9: Thys am I brought in-to lovers dawnce. **1509** Barclay *Ship* I 42[12]: And whan they ar onys into my daunce brought.

D11 To break (off) the **Dance**
1513 More *Richard* 53 D[8–10]: He had departed . . . and broken all the daunce.

D12 To lead someone a **Dance**
1476 Paston V 263[20–2]: He roode so welle he ledde uss a dawnce faster than alle we cowde weell folowe. **a1500** Skelton *Kynge Edwarde* I 2.29: She toke me by the hand and led me a daunce.

D13 To learn (*teach*) someone a new **Dance**
a1352 Minot 14.14: Thare lered Inglis men tham a new daunce. **a1475** *Assembly of Gods* 29.957: Yet I trow I shall lerne hem a new daunce.

D14 To set someone last upon a **Dance**
a1405 Lydgate *Black Knight* in *MP* II 397.355: For (he) him set last upon a daunce.

D15 After **Danger** comes grace
a1513 Dunbar *Complaint to the King* 41.75: Bot eftir danger cumis grace.

D16 Before **Danger** imagine all dangers
c1523 Barclay *Mirrour* 13[25]: Thou muste before daunger imagine daungers all. See **D18, F495, S47.**

D17 To be in one's **Danger** and debt
1461 Paston III 286[25–6]: I am gretly yn your danger and dette for my pension. Tilley M451.

D18 Where **Danger** is it is great wisdom to provide before
c1475 Henryson *Fables* 61.1738–40: Quhair danger is, or perrell appeirand, It is grit wisedome to provyde befoir, It is devoyd, ffor dreid it hurt yow moir. See **D16.**

D19 Never utter (*sell*) **Darnel** with good corn
a1449 Lydgate *Cok* in *MP* II 814.19: Uttre nevir no darnel with good corn. See **C361.**

D20 To take the **Darnel** and cast corn from the sheaf
a1449 Lydgate *Say the Best* in *MP* II 795.10: Take the darnel and cast corn fro the sheffe. See **C361.**

D21 As sharp as a **Dart**
a1398(1495) Bartholomaeus-Trevisa T8r[1.25]: Sharpe as dartes. **c1410** Lovelich *Grail* I 141.779: But that schowr was As scharpe As A dart. **1509** Barclay *Ship* II 4[1]: Theyr cruell tunge is sharper than a dart. Svartengren 256.

D22 One's **Dart** oft returns to his own reproof
1509 Barclay *Ship* I 55[14]: His darte oft retourneth to his own reprefe, 213[2]: And his owne dartis retourne to hym agayne. See **A182, D342, E180, F374, 555, G490, M84, 200, 289, P232, S345, 848.**

D23 To drive like **Darts**
1509 Barclay *Ship* I 54[12]: Somtyme his wordes as dartis he doth dryve.

D24 Not dread a **Date**
c1400 *Alexander Buik* IV 411.10191: Thy mannace dreid I nocht ane dait.

D25 The naughty **Daughter** learns of the bawdy dame
1509 Barclay *Ship* I 56[14]: Than shal the noughty doughter lerne of the bawdy dame. See **C89, M720.**

D26 As holy (*etc.*) as **David**
1340 *Ayenbite* 204[13–5]: Non ne wes . . . milder thanne david. **c1390** Chaucer *CT* X[I] 955: But he be . . . hoolier than David. **c1400** *Vices and Virtues* 226.1: Non holier than David. **c1410** *Mirror of Sinners* in *Yorkshire Writers* II 437[11–2]: Thou schalt be . . . moore waar than Davyd. **1484** Caxton *Royal Book* R3r[7]: More holy than davyd, **1489** *Doctrinal* 14v[13–4]: holy, K3v[14–5]: holy. **a1513** Dunbar *Of Manis Mortalitie* 149.12: Meik David.

D27 As wise as a **Daw**
c1525 ?Heywood *Gentylnes* 122.983: Then fare ye well, as wyse as two dawys. Svartengren 51.

D28 To cough one a **Daw** (fool)
c1516 Skelton *Magnificence* 34.1061: What! thou wylte coughe me a dawe for forty pens? 1065: A, I trowe ye shall coughe me a fole. Tilley F508.

D29 To speak like a **Daw**
c1516 Skelton *Magnificence* 43.1379: Ye speke lyke a dawe.

D30 After an evil **Day** to have a merry night
c1475 *Rauf* 86.135: Efter ane evill day to have ane mirrie nicht. Cf. Apperson 22: Bad day; *Oxford* 19; Tilley D87.

D31 After the **Day** comes the night (*varied*)
a1449 Lydgate *God* in *MP* I 29.77–8: When day is passyd, the dirke nyght Closith al the wourld with his blak weede. **a1500** *English Conquest* 51.8–9: Aftyr the bryght day, comyth the nyght. **1506** Hawes *Pastime* 208.5478: After the day there cometh the derke nyght. **1509** Barclay *Ship* II 319[22]: After the day cometh the nyght.

D32 All the **Days** of poor men are wick(ed)
c1390 Chaucer *CT* II[B] 117–8: Yet of the wise man take this sentence: "Alle the dayes of povre men been wikke." **c1395** *WBible* Proverbs xv 15: Alle the daies of a pore man ben yvele.

D33 As bright as (the, any) **Day**
a1300 *Thrush* in Brown *Lyrics XIII* 105.124–6: Hy beth brighttore ounder shawe Then the day wenne hit dawe In longe someres tide. **a1300** *Tristrem* 80.2971: To Ysonde bright so day. **c1300** *Havelok* 22.588–9: She saw ther-inne a liht ful shir, Also briht so it were day, 69–70.2093–5: A mikel liht In the bour (ther) Havelok lay, Also briht so it were day. **c1390** Chaucer *CT* I[A] 3310: Hir forheed shoon as bright as any day. **c1390** *Gregorius* 34.289. **c1390** *Mayden, Modur, and comely Qween* 124.121. **a1400** *Meditations* 21.783: Jhesu so bright as spryng of day. **c1400** *Thomas of Erceldoune* 3.43: any. **c1400** *Tundale* 85.1475: Sone wex hit bryght as the day. **a1422** Lydgate *Life* 613.368, 667.421. **a1450** *Partonope* 19.691. **a1450** *York Plays* 443.326, 491.4: That berde is brighter than the daye. **a1500** Greene *Carols*

150 ABD (*refrain*), C (*refrain*): any. **a1500** *Orfeo* 30 H 338: ony. **a1500** *She Sang* in Brown *Lyrics XV* 7[2]: ony. **1509** Barclay *Ship* II 274[25]: Shynynge as bryght as is the sonny day, **1515** *St. George* 78.1904: the. Svartengren 226; Taylor and Whiting 92; Tilley D55; Whiting *Drama* 309:89. See **D67.**

D34 As clear as the **Day**
c1460 W. Huchens *Hymn to the Virgin* in *Pol. Rel. and Love Poems* 291.3: Aurora bryght, clere as the day. Apperson 101; Svartengren 363; Taylor and Whiting 92; Tilley D56.

D35 As doughty as the **Day** is fair (bright)
a1200 Lawman I 292.6845–6: Tha iwarth he swa duhti Swa the dæi feire (B: brihte).

D36 As light as **Day**
a1400 *Orologium* 334.39: Hit lihtete as the daye with joye. **a1400** *Scottish Legends* II 363.198: That licht as day ves the presone. **c1400** Mandeville *Travels* 158.4: It is als light as day. Taylor and Whiting 92.

D37 As like (asunder) as **Day** and night
a1437 *Kingis Quair* 76.109[5–7]: Als like ye bene as day is to the nyght, Or sekcloth is unto fyne cremesye, Or doken foule onto the fresche dayesye. **c1458** *Knyghthode and Bataile* 6.141–2: Thei are asondir As day and nyght.

D38 As ruddy as **Day**
1445 Claudian *Stilicho* 281.280: Whos cheke as rody as day.

D39 As sicker as (any) **Day**
a1450 *Partonope* 40.1512: For also syker as any daye, 177.4778: Off hys knyghtes, as syker as day, 199.5264, 424.10292: any. Taylor and Whiting 92: sure.

D40 Be the **Day** never so long ever comes evensong (*varied*)
a1393 Gower *CA* III 182.578–9: Bot hou so that the dai be long, The derke nyht comth ate laste. **a1400** *Merton College Oxford MS.248*, f.146b in Robbins-Cutler 2284.8: Ne bee the day nevere so longe, evere comethe evensong. **1506** Hawes *Pastime* 208.5479–80: For though the day be never so longe At last the belles ryngeth to evensonge. **1508**(1519) Stanbridge *Vulgaria* 18.36: Be the daye never so longe at last cometh evensonge. **1546** Heywood *D* 84.141–2: Yet is he sure be the daie never so long, Evermore at laste they ryng to evensong, **1556** *Spider* 396[6–7]: In the daie most long here past, Yet they (evermore) ring to evensong at last. Apperson 136; *Oxford* 131, 382; Tilley D59.

D41 A bright **Day** is oft seen after a great rain
c1450 *Lover's Mass* 101[26–7]: Ffor ofte sythe men ha seyn A ful bryght day after gret reyn. Cf. Tilley R8. See **C315, R11.**

D42 **Day-couth** (*-clear*)
a1000 *Judgement Day* in *ASMP* 59.40: þæt hit ne sy dægcuð, þæt þæt dihle wæs.

D43 The **Day** is come that he fasted the even for
1470 Paston V 90[26–31]: The daye is comen that he fastyd the evyn for, as an holye yonge monke fastyd mor than all the covent, aftr that for hys holynesse and fastyng hopyd to be abbott, whyche afterwarde was abbott; than lefte he hys abstynens, seyng, "The daye was come that he fast the evyn for."

D44 The **Day** is short, the work is long
c1400 *Beryn* 109.3631: The day is short, the work is long. Apperson 136; *Oxford* 130. See **L245.**

D45 The **Day** of doom (*varied*)
a1500 *English Conquest* 139.34–5: Thay grauntyth . . . the Englysh pepil fully the maystry, a lytel ar the day of Dome. **1532** More *Confutacion* 412 H[3–4]: From tyme to time al dayes even to the day of dome. **1546** Heywood *D* 86.222–3: The daie of doome shall be doone, Er thou go to bed at noone or night for mee. Cf. Whiting *Scots* I 160. See **D346.**

D46 A **Day's** respite is worth much
c1489 Caxton *Aymon* II 429.17–8: I have ofte herde saye that a day respyte is worthe moche. **a1533** Berners *Huon* 128.11–2: It is a commen sayeng, one day of respyte is worth .c. yere. Cf. Apperson 469: One day of respite.

D47 **Days** that have no rest pass lightly
c1477 Caxton *Jason* 86.3–4: The dayes that have no reste passe lightly.

D48 Every **Day** like to other is common thing (and) seldom praised
c1450 La Tour-Landry 142.5–6: For every day lyke to other is thinge comune, it is selden praised (*car chose commune n'est point prisée*). See **C351, T109.**

D49 Farewell my good **Days**
a1470 Malory II 823.32–3: And but yf that ye helpe me now, farewell my good dayes forever! **a1475** *Ludus Coventriae* 296.733: Hese good days thei xul be past. **1546** Heywood *D* 63.52: Then farewell my good daies, they wyll be soone gon. Apperson 204; Tilley D115.

D50 Happy be that **Day** that ordains merry years
c1425 Arderne *Fistula* 7.34–5: And in another place it is seid, "happy or blessid be, that day that ordeyneth mery yeres."

D51 He that comes every **Day** shall have a cockney (*egg*)
1549 Heywood *D* 53.390–1: He that comth every daie, shall have a cocknaie. He that comth now and then, shall have a fatte hen. Apperson 108; Tilley D77.

D52 It suffices to the **Day** its own malice
c1000 *WSG* Matthews vi 34: Æghwlyc dæg hæfð genoh on hys agenum ymbhogan. **c1395** *WBible* Matthew vi 34: For it suffisith to the dai his owen malice. *Oxford* 629.

D53 Never to see fair **Day** more
a1533 Berners *Huon* 91.27–8: Thou shalt newer se fayre day more, 122.11, 306.10, 638.15.

D54 No **Day** is like another
a1300 *Alisaunder* 375.6985: Nys no day other ylyk. Skeat 64.

D55 One **Day** is ofttimes better than a whole year
1481 Caxton *Reynard* 66[6–7]: Oftymes one day is better than somtyme an hole year. Apperson 469; *Oxford* 130; Tilley D83.

D56 One **Day** often brings what all the year may not (*varied*)
a1250 *Rawlinson MS. C 641* in *Zeitschrift für französische Sprache und Litteratur* 21(1899) 3.5: On dai bringth thet al ier ne mai. **c1385** Chaucer *CT* I[A] 1668–9: Yet somtyme it shal fallen on a day That falleth nat eft withinne a thousand yeer. **c1450** *Douce MS.52* 44.4: Oft bryngeth on day, That all the yere not may. **c1450** *Rylands MS.394* 95.1. **c1475** *Rawlinson MS. D 328* 122.56: Hyt fortynyt yn a day that fortunyt not yn a yere (*MS.* here). **a1500** Hill 128.20: Hit fallith in a dai, that fallith not all the iere after. Apperson 283; Jente 347; *Oxford* 87; Skeat 221; Tilley H741. See **H598, Y10.**

D57 One knows not what **Day** shall fall (*happen to*) him to-morrow
c1425 *Governance of Lordschipes* 57.34–5: Ffor thou woot noght what day to-morwe sal falle the.

D58 A shining **Day** is oft meint (*mixed*) with rain
a1439 Lydgate *Fall* III 967.1706: A shynyng day is ofte meynt with reyn. See **J59.**

D59 To awend (*turn*) **Day** to night and night to day
c1000 *Sermo* in Napier 297.27–9: Ge syttað ealle niht and drincað oð leohtne dæg and swa awendað dæg to nihte and niht to dæge. **c1330** *Times of Edward II* 336.290: Hii kunnen of the faire day make the derke niht.

D60 To come a **Day** after the fair
1546 Heywood *D* 32.53: But a daie after the fayre, comth this remors. Apperson 136; *Oxford* 130; Taylor and Whiting 93; Tilley D112.

D61 To see **Day** at a little hole
c1440 Charles of Orleans 205.6121: But at a litille hole day mowe we see. **1546** Heywood *D* 38.92: I see daie at this little hole. Apperson 136–7; *Oxford* 569; Tilley D99. See **H414.**

D62 To shine like the bright **Day**
a1470 Malory II 548.25–6: For the moone shone as the bryght day. See **D68.**

D63 To steal a **Day** from Lent
c1300 *South English Legendary* I 123.45–6: Me thincth he were a queinte man bote he couthe gramerie That ssolde stele a day of Leinte, seggeth gif ich lie.

D64 To wit (*know*) not whether it was **Day** or night
c1280 *Southern Passion* 41.1144: And ffor drede nuste whather hit was day or night. **a1300** *Arthour and M.*[1] 251.9011–2: That he sat astoned up right And nist, whether it was dai or night. **a1300** *Richard* 100.423–4: And for that stroke that hym was gyven He ne wyst whether it was daye or even. **c1400** *Triamour* 65.763–5. **c1410** Lovelich *Merlin* III 673.25339–40: For So sore he fyl, the sothe to say, That he ne wyste whether hit was nyht or day. **c1450** *Merlin* II 367[11]: He wiste not whether it was nyght or day, 391[23–4]: nyght or day, 459[21–2]: nyght or day, 476[13–4]: day or nyght, 496[29–30]: nyght or day. See **H542.**

D65 Upon a glad **Day** have unware (*unexpected*) woe in mind
c1390 Chaucer *CT* II[B] 426–7: Upon thy glade day have in thy mynde The unwar wo or harm that comth bihynde.

D66 Who may not play one **Day** in a week may think his thrift is far to seek
c1545 Heywood *Four PP* B2[r][5–6]: Who may nat play one day in a weke, May thynke hys thryfte is farre to seke.

D67 As bright as **Daylight**
c1250 *Of One That Is* in Brown *Lyrics XIII* 24.3:

Brightore then the dai-is light. **c1325** *De Clerico* 152.2: Heo is briht so daies-liht. See **D33.**

D68 To shine like the **Daylight**
a1450 *Partonope* 220.5802–3: A-none, and ther-In a candell bryghte, That shonne as the day lyghte. See **D62.**

D69 As bright as the **Day-star**
1422 Yonge *Governaunce* 167.34–5: More bryghtyr Shynynge than the day-sterre.

D70 To shine like a **Day-star**
1483 Caxton *Golden Legende* 311v[1.5–6]: To shyne lyke as a day sterre.

D71 The **Dead** has few friends (*varied*)
c1250 *Proverbs of Alfred* 120–2 T 485–6: For fewe frend we sculen finden Thanne we henne funden. **a1303** Mannyng *Handlyng* 203.6300: For the dede hath few(e) frendys. **c1325** *Hendyng H* 299.288: Ffrendles ys the dede. **a1450** *Myne awen dere* 150.46: For sothe it is, deede has no frende. **1456** Hay *Law* 245.21–3: Quhen a lord is dede he gettis few frendis, and lyfand men gettis ay frendis. **a1470** Parker *Dives* Y4r[1.33–4]: Be a man deed, he fyndeth fewe frendes. **a1500** Greene *Carols* 366.6: And thynke wyll dede man have no frond. Apperson 138; Kneuer 58; *Oxford* 227; Schleich 273; Singer III 139–40; Skeat 93; Tilley M591. See **D85.**

D72 The **Dead** is forgotten (out of mind)
c1400 *Laud Troy* II 325.11013–6: Be he nevere so strong ne bold, He is for-geten and nought of told, When he is ded and hennes past; In erthe is none that evere may last. **c1450** *Fyrst thou sal* 91.185: The ded is oute of mynde. Cf. Jente 405. See **D77, E213, S307.**

D73 The **Dead's** counsel is soon overwent (*passed over*)
a1338 Mannyng *Chronicle A* I 274.7999–800: Bot thei dide nought his comandement; The dedes conseyl ys sone overwent. See **E201.**

D74 To be nought but (*except when*) **Dead**
c1250 *Owl* 96.1137–8: Thi lif is evre luther and qued, Thu nar(t) noght bute ded. Cf. Apperson 494: Like a pig, he'll do no good alive; *Oxford* 637: Swine; Tilley M1005; Whiting *NC* 391. See **W472.**

D75 Who is so **Deaf** as he that will not hear?
1546 Heywood *D* 91.41–2: Who is so deafe, or so blynde, as is hee, That wilfully will nother here nor see? **1555** *E* 163.103: Who is so deafe, as he that will not heare. Apperson 139; *Oxford* 132–3; Taylor and Whiting 32–3; Tilley H295.

D76 Not worth a **Deal** (*bit*)
c1475 *Prohemy of a Mariage* 31[4]: It is not worthe a dele. MED del n. (2) 4; NED Deal sb.[1] 5b.

D77 After **Death** no memory abides
a1422 Lydgate *Life* 616.414–5: Eke after dethe a-bydyth no memorye, For ay with dethe comyth for-yetylnesse. See **D72.**

D78 Against **Death** there is no defence (*varied*)
a1325 *Otuel and Roland* 138.2539: There nys no bote of mannys deth. **c1330** *Orfeo* 46.552: It nis (*var.* Ther is) no bot of mannes deth. **c1412** Hoccleve *Regement* 2.32–3: Deth, fro which no wight lyvyng Defendyn hym may, 193.5366–7: What myght his force availle A-gayn the deth? no thing, sanz faille. **c1421** Lydgate *Thebes* 27.591–2: But for they segh hevynesse and thoght Ageynes deth vayleth lit or noght, **c1430** *Dance* 55.480: For a-geyns deth is fynaly no boote, **a1439** *Fall* I 168.5977: But, o allas, ageyn deth is no boone! **a1450** *Castle* 160.2793: A-geyns me (*Death*) may no man stonde. **a1470** Malory III 1251.13–4: But ayenste deth may no man rebell. **a1475** *Ludus Coventriae* 221.357: Ageyn deth is no resystens. **c1475** Henryson *Fables* 30.792: Aganis deith may na man mak defence, *Thre Deid Pollis* 206.36. **c1500** ?Bradshaw *Radegunde* 44[10]: But agayne deth may be no remedy. **a1525** Berners *Froissart* V 60[14–5]: Agaynst dethe none may stryve. Apperson 527; *English and Germanic Studies* 2(1948–9) 39; *Oxford* 537; Tilley R69.

D79 As bitter as **Death**
a1475 *Tree* 139.5: Lust is bitterrer than deth, as salomon seith.

D80 As dumb as **Death**
c1378 *Piers* B x 137: And as doumbe as deth. Apperson 571: silent; *Oxford* 589; Taylor and Whiting 95.

D81 As sicker as **Death**
a1450 *Partonope* 273.6999: As siker as dethe, with-outen nay. Apperson 611: sure; Smith 56; Taylor and Whiting 95; Tilley D136.

D82 As sooth as **Death**
c1380 Chaucer *HF* 502: But this as sooth as deth, certeyn. Cf. Taylor and Whiting 95.

D83 As still as **Death**
a1400 *Meditations* 39.1466: And lay stille a(s) deth in swoun. **c1450** *Myroure of oure Ladye* 30[32]: And lay styll as dede. Taylor and Whiting 95.

D84 As strong as the **Death**
c1300 *Guy*[1] 168 A 2912: That venim is strong so the deth. Svartengren 391.

D85 **Death** and poverty seldom have friends
a1400 *Scottish Legends* II 79.343–4: For ded and poverte seldine quhen Has frend, that we suld kene. **c1415** *Middle English Sermons* 86.19–21: Ther-fore it is a proverbe that muche peple have seid, that dethe and poverte hath few (*MS.* new) frendes. Tilley P468. See **D71.**

D86 **Death** and poverty will not be hidden
1492 *Salomon and Marcolphus* 9[5–6]: The deth nor povertye wyll not be hyd.

D87 **Death** can be a friend to no wight
a1475 *Ludus Coventriae* 219.277: Deth to no wyht can be a frende.

D88 **Death** can (*knows*) no courtesy
a1475 *Ludus Coventriae* 177.259–62: All men dwellyng upon the grownde Be-ware of me (*Death*), be myn councel, Ffor feynt felachep in me is fownde, I kan no curtesy as I yow tel.

D89 **Death** dreads no man
c1500 *Everyman* 6.115–6: I am dethe that no man dredeth, For every man I rest and none spareth.

D90 **Death** falls on the feyest (*most fated*)
c1475 Henryson *Fables* 62.1767: Deith on the fayest fall. See **M88.**

D91 **Death** for death
a1420 Lydgate *Troy* II 485.3146–7: For right requereth, and also good resoun, That deth for deth is skilful guerdonynge, 505.3853–4: For right requereth, with-outen any drede, Deth for deth, for his final mede, **a1439** *Fall* I 309.3913: Deth quit for deth; loo, heer his fynal meede, II 471.5116: Deth quit with deth, and rage with rage. Whiting *Drama* 281.

D92 **Death** gives no warning
c1500 *Everyman* 7.132: I may saye deth geveth no warnynge.

D93 **Death** hangs in his nose
1519 Horman *Vulgaria* 60[7–8]: Deth hangeth in his nose, or he is at dethis dore.

D94 **Death** is an end of every worldly sore (*varied*)
c1385 Chaucer *CT* I[A] 2849: Deeth is an ende of every worldly soore. **a1439** Lydgate *Fall* I 166.5892: For off al werre deth is the fyn parde, III 708.1261: Men seen how deth is fyn of al myscheeff. Smith 53.

D95 **Death** is better than shameful life
c735 *Beowulf* 2890–1: Deað bið sella Eorla gehwylcum þonne edwitlif. See **D104, 239.**

D96 **Death** is certain but not the time (*varied*)
c735 *Beowulf* 3062–5: Wundur hwar þonne Eorl ellenrof ende gefere Lifgesceafta, þonne leng ne mæg Mon mid his (ma)gum meduseld buan. **a900** Bede 210.17–8: Forðon him cuð forðfor toweard wære ond ungewiis seo tid þære ilcan forðfore. **c1000** *Halwendlic lar* in Napier 135.18–20: And uton geþencan, þæt us ys uncuð seo tid and se dæg, þe we sceolon þas lænan woruld forlæton. **a1200** *Ancrene* 76.6: Death, that we beoth siker of, and unsiker hwenne. **c1250** *Proverbs of Alfred* 90 T 165–72: Wot no mon the time Wanne he sal henne rimen (J turne), Ne no mon then hende, Wen he sal henne wenden. Drittin hit one wot, Domis lovird, Wenne we ure lif Letin scullen. **c1275** *Old Kentish Sermons* in Morris *Old English Miscellany* 36[3–5]: For al so seid thet holi writ thet non ne wot thane dai of his diathe. For Man mai longe lives wene and ofte him legheth se wrench. **a1300** *Sinners Beware!* in Morris *Old English Miscellany* 78.190–2: For nes non that wiste Bute him seolve criste, Hwenne his ende-day were. **a1300** *Three Sorrowful Tidings* in Brown *Lyrics XIII* 18: Thru tidigge us cumet iche dei—Ful wel leve me his may: On, We sulle honne; Thath other, we nite wanne; The thridde his of muchel kare,—We nite fwider we sulle fare, 19: Wanne ich thenche thinges thre Ne mai nevre blithe be: That on is ich sal awe, That other is ich ne wot wilk day. That thridde is mi meste kare, I ne woth nevre wuder i sal fare. **c1300** *Speculum Gy* 23.491–2: For siker noman wite ne may, Whanne shal ben his ending day. **a1325** *Cursor* III 1357.23732–3: Es na thing certainer than dede, Ne uncertainer than es that tide. **1372** *Advocates MS.18.7.21* (John Grimestone), f.87b in Robbins-Cutler 3100.5: Siker to dele to alle men, To tellen of is time novere no man kan. **c1390** *God man and the devel* 335.239–40: The thridde thing is that I thenke, that I schal wende henne Out of this world, but wot I never whenne. **c1395** Chaucer *CT* IV[E] 124–6: And al so certein as we knowe echoon That we shul deye, as uncerteyn we alle Been of that day whan deeth shal on us falle. **a1400** *Mortality* in *Pol. Rel. and Love Poems* 263.4: Deye we ssulin sikerliche; bot god wot wanne and were. **a1400** *Seven Penitential Psalms* in *Wheatley MS.* 29.245–6: I wote wel I mote hennys wende, Bot whedir and when I can not say. **a1400** *Thre Ages* 292–4: And now es dethe

at my dore that I drede moste; I ne wot wiche daye, ne when, ne whate tyme he comes, Ne whedir-wardes, ne whare, ne whatte to do aftire, 635–6: Ne noghte es sekire to youre-selfe in certayne bot dethe, And he es so uncertayne that sodaynly he comes. **a1400** *Three Certainties* in *Pol. Rel. and Love Poems* 250: Hit beoth threo tymes on tho day That sothe to witen me mai: That on ys, that i shal henne, That other, that y not whenne; That thridde is my moste care, That y not whider i shal fare. **a1400** Wyclif *Sermons* I 252[8–10]: For, as it is ofte seid, deeth is the thridde thing that God wole have unknowun to man, for he shulde ever be redi. **c1409** *A good makynge* in Kail 34.97–8: Man, thou wost wel thou shalt dyghe; What deth, ne where, thou nost whenne. **c1415** *Middle English Sermons* 276.30–6: For foure thinges in tyme of dyinge oweth grettely to be drad. First thou shalt die and yitt thou wot never when; the secound, thou shalt die bot thou wotys not where; the thirde, thou shalt die, thou wotyst not how, whethur of chaunse of infirmite othur by age or othur veys; and the fourte most dredefull ys, thou wat never where thou shalt becom aftur thi dethe. **c1422** Hoccleve *Dialog* 117.210: For deathe comethe, wot ther no wyght whan. **a1425** *Chester Plays* I 117.327: Sith I must dye I wot not what daye. **a1425** *Daily Work* in *Yorkshire Writers* I 146[1]: Deade that we are siker of and wate noght when. **a1450** *Gesta* 304[14]–305[1]: And therfore saide a certayne saynt, in vitis patrum, this in verse, Sunt tria que vere Me faciunt sepe dolere Est primum durum, Quoniam scio me moriturum; Est magis addendo Moriar, set nescio quando, Inde magis flebo, Quia nescio quo remanebo. This is to say, Thre thinges ben, in fay, That makith me to sorowe all way: On is that I shalle henne; An othir, I not never when; The thirde is my most care, I wot not whethir I shall fare. Secundum illud in vitas patrum, Ther ben iij. thingis that I drede; On is, that I shall passe; another is, I not when, and come afor the dome; The third is, I not whedir the sentence shall go for me or agenst me. **a1450** *Knowe thy self* in Kail 103.57: Thenke thou shalt dye, and nost whenne. **c1450** *Douce MS.52* 51.83: Sore I syke and well I may For thre thyngis, that comyn ay. The fyrst is: I schall hen; The secunde: I not never when; The thrydde is most care: I not nere, whidur I schall fare. **c1450** *How the Wyse Man* 42.145–8: And deeth is evere, as y trowe, The moost certeyn thing that is; And no thing so uncerteyn to knowe, As is the tyme of deeth, ywis. **c1450** Idley 105.1435: Thow hast no sertente of the houre of Dethe. **c1450** *Rylands MS.394* 101.1–3. **1458** Paston III 124[14–6]: And ther knoweth no man how soon God woll clepe hym, and therfor it is good for every creature to be redy. **c1475** Henryson *Fables* 102.2967–8: For deith will the assay, Thow wait not quhen—evin, morrow or midday, *Thre Deid Pollis* 205.12–4: The hour of deth and place Is uncertane, Quhilk Is referrit to the hie god allane; Heirfoir haif mynd of deth, that thow mon dy. **1484** *Ther ne is dangyer* 19.19: Ne than the deth nothyng more certayn. **1495** *Meditacyons of saynt Bernarde* B3^{r}[10–1]: For deth is sure and undowted: but the houre of deth is prevy and unknowen. **a1500** *Ancrene* (*Royal*) 37.1–2: Deth that we are sekyr of, bot we wot not w(h)en, ny where, ny how we shal dye. **a1500** *Epitaph in Pakefield Church, Suffolk*, in *The East Anglian* 2(1864–6) 321: Al schul we hen, Whedir ne when May no man ken, But god above. **a1500** Greene *Carols* 370.3: Whan I schal dey, I know no day; What countre or place I cannot sey; 371.3: Whan I shal deye I ame not suere, In what countre or in what howere. **a1500** *Harley MS.2321* in *Rel. Ant.* I 208[9–10]: When thou hast gathered all that thou may, Thou shalt departe, and knowest not what day. **a1500** Hill 141.13–8: Whan I thynk on thingis thre, Well carefull may I be: One is, that I shall henne; an other is, I wot not when. Off the thirde is my most care, For I shall dwell I wot not wher. **a1500** *Jesu, Mercy* in Brown *Lyrics XV* 227.171–2: Thou kepe me, lord, I schal dy, And wote nevere wher, whou, ne when. **a1500** *Man Begins* in Brown *Lyrics XV* 237.3: The deth certane, the houre unseker(nes). **a1500** *Timor Mortis* in *MLR* 28(1933) 236[25–8]: Ther is no thyng that ever God made More certeyn to us than oure dethe is, But more uncerteyne thyng none is yhadd Than the ourre off dethe to us, ywysse. **c1500** Greene *Carols* 376.6: Thou shalt dy thou wote not whan, Nor thou wotest where. **c1500** *Proper tretyse* 244[35–6]: Thynk on thy endyng as nye as thou can: Thou knowyst not how, where, nor whan. **1506** Barclay *Castell* E5^{v}–6^{r}: From deth we can us not refrayne The daye and houre is uncertayne, **1509** *Ship* I 154[23]: The deth is sure, the houre is uncertayne, II 114[5–7]: No thynge we muse On deth . . . Whiche sure shall come, though tyme be varyable. **1525** Berners *Froissart* V 108[6–7]: It is sayd, and it is of trouthe, that there is nothyng more certayne than dethe. *Oxford* 456; Tilley N311, 316; Whiting *Drama* 299. See **D241, M144.**

D97 Death is common to all (*varied*)

a1325 *Otuel and Roland* 119.1916–8: By the Ensampyl, who mowe se That no man schall hys deth fle For none skynnes nede. **a1338** Mannyng *Chronicle A* I 318.9077–8: Of deth may non the bale bete, The sorewe nedly byhoveth men lete. **c1350** *Royal MS. 8 E xvii* f.109 in George F. Warner and J. P. Gilson *Catalogue* I (1921) 259.25: Riche and pouere, yong and eld, There whiles thou havest thi wil a weld, Sek thi sowle bote: Ofte wan man weneth best Lif and hale, tho and rest, Deth is at his fote. **c1375** Barbour *Bruce* II 177.167–70: Lordingis, . . . swa is it gane With me, that thar is nocht bot ane, That is, the ded, withouten dreid, That ilk man mon thole on neid. **c1390** Chaucer *CT* VII 1613[B2803]: For deeth is the ende of every man as in this present lyf. **c1390** *Gregorius* 10.87–8: Everi mon to dethe schal dryve And eft up risen atte dome. **a1400** *Ten Stages* in *Pol. Rel. and Love Poems* 267.8: For det is comun, that wil the take. **a1420** Lydgate *Troy* III 689.4281–3: The fatal hour, hard for to remewe, Of cruel deth, which no man may eschewe Nor in this lyfe finally eskape. **a1450** *Gesta* 151[6]: Dethe, that sparithe no man, 366[18–9]. **c1450** Idley 133.1574–6: Deeth at laste that all thyng taketh When age cometh and nature faileth—Of all erthly thyng an ende he maketh. **c1450** *Pilgrimage LM* 206[13–4]: This thing is al commune to eche man and womman. **a1470** Malory II 867.12: For of dethe we be syker. **a1475** *Ludus Coventriae* 214.130: Ffor deth is dew to every man. **c1475** *Wisdom* 64.880: Dethe, to every creature certen ys. **c1477** Caxton *Jason* 162.1–2: Ther was nothing so certayn for every creature as the deth. **c1500** Fabyan 90[47]: Deth whiche sparith no creatour. **c1500** *O mortall man* in *Studia Neophilologica* 26(1953) 64.78: Dethe wyll no man spare. **1509** Barclay *Ship* I 154[24]: Deth is generall to every creature, 265[5]: Deth all thynge drawyth. *Oxford* 7–8; Smith 52; Tilley D142; Whiting *Scots* I 157. See **D243, K49.**

D98 Death is common to old and young (*varied*) **a1300** *Alisaunder* 52 L 912–3: Nis in this world so siker thyng So is deth to olde and yyng. **1481** *Tulle of Olde Age* 71[14–5]: Deth is comon to all ages. **1509** Barclay *Ship* II 172[26–7]: Yet deth dayly steleth slyely on the: doutles Both yonge and olde must go the same passage. *Oxford* 464. See **M41, 385, S209.**

D99 Death makes all things (a)like **1474** Caxton *Chesse* 80[30–1]: Deth maketh alle thynge lyke and putteth alle to an ende. See **K49.**

D100 Death takes feeble and strong **a1500** *Partenay* 61.1607: Tho feble and stronge dethe takyth expresse, 208.6066: But deth sparith noght tho feble ne stronge, 211.6149–53: For noght man may do gain mortal deth, lo! The feble and strong takith she ech hour; Non hir escapith As by no labour, Be it king, or pope, or lordes of landes, All most nedis passe truly by hyr handes.

D101 Death takes high and low (*varied*) **c1385** Chaucer *CT* I[A] 3030: He moot be deed, the kyng as shal a page, **c1390** II[B] 1142–4: For deeth, that taketh of heigh and logh his rente, Whan passed was a yeer, evene as I gesse, Out of this world this kyng Alla he hente. **a1393** Gower *CA* II 96.2247–51: For al schal deie and al schal passe, Als well a Leoun as an asse, Als well a beggere as a lord, Towardes deth in on acord Thei schullen stonde, 361–2.2246–9: Althogh ther be diverse weie To deth, yit is ther bot on ende, To which that every man schal wende, Als wel the beggere as the lord. **a1425** *Metrical Paraphrase OT* 102.9281–2: And ded, (he) wyst wele, wold not glose, Ne take reward to knyght ne knave. **a1430** Lydgate *Pilgrimage* 663.24761–4: The which (as I wel telle can) Is common to every man. Ther may no man, of no degre, Hygh nor lowh, his power fle, **a1439** *Fall* III 721.1751: Deth spareth nouther hih blood nor hih lynages, **c1440** *Debate* in *MP* II 564.612–3: Tweene riche and poore what is the difference, Whan deth approchith in any creature, **a1449** *Tyed with a Lyne* in *MP* II 834.66: Both high and lough shal go on dethis daunce. **c1450** *Pride of Life* in Waterhouse 94.203–6: Yet thogh thou be kinge Nede schalt have ende; Deth overcomith al thinge Hou-so-ever we wende. **a1460** *Towneley Plays* 390.111–8: Ther is none so styf on stede, Ne none so prowde in prese, Ne none so dughty in his dede, Ne none so dere on deese, No kyng, no knyght, no Wight in wede, Ffrom dede have maide hym seese, Ne flesh he was wonte to fede, It shall be Wormes mese. **1509** Barclay *Ship* I 130[28]: For dethe is lyke to hye and lowde (*for* lowe) degre. *Oxford* 7–8; Smith 54; Tilley D143; Whiting *Drama* 291. See **K49, P298, R111.**

D102 Death, Weird or Fortune are not to be blamed **1445** *He michti Makar* in Felix J. H. Skene *Historians of Scotland* (Edinburgh, 1877) VII 387[9–10]: Quhat proffyt is it, with fortoun for to flyt? Deed, weird na fortoun ar nocht for to wyt. Cf. Smith 1.

D103 If **Death** would receive meed (*bribe*) many would overbid others (*varied*)
a1400 *Proverbis of Wysdom* (*II*) 224.89–90: Yif dethe wolde resayve mede, Many wolde other overbede. **c1500** *Everyman* 7.127–9: For and I (*Death*) wolde receyve geftes great All the worlde I myght gete; All my custome is clene contrary. Tilley D149.

D104 A noble **Death** is better than a vile domination
1450 *Dicts* 250.4–5: A noble dethe is better than a vile dominacioun. **1477** Rivers *Dictes* 99[6–7]. See **D95, 239.**

D105 One may not die but such **Death** as God has ordained
c1450 *Merlin* II 521[4–6]: We be alle in aventure, ne we may not deye but on soche deth as god hath us ordeyned.

D106 One's **Death** (destiny) was shaped before his shirt (*varied*)
c1385 Chaucer *CT* I[A] 1566: That shapen was my deeth erst than my sherte, *TC* iii 733–4: O fatal sustren, which, er any cloth Me shapen was, my destine me sponne, **c1386** *LGW* 2629–30: Syn fyrst that day that shapen was my sherte, Or by the fatal systren had my dom. **a1405** Lydgate *Black Knight* in *MP* II 402.487–9: Er I was borne, my destanye was sponne By Parcas sustren, to sle me if they conne, For they my dethe shopen or my shert. **c1440** Charles of Orleans 112.3345–6: Fortune hath cast me to myschef Which shapen had my death tofore my shert. **a1450** *Partonope* 47.1716: Hyt was me shape or then my serke. **1490** Irlande *Meroure* II 141.1–3: It was his destany and he mycht be na maner evade it, for it was ordand for him . . . or evir cot or goune was schapin for him.

D107 To be at **Death's** door
1515 Barclay *St. George* 41.822: As she that was at dethes dore or brynke. **1519** Horman *Vulgaria* 56[3]: He is at dethis dore, 60[7–8]. *Oxford* 134; Tilley D162. See **P231.**

D108 To drink **Death's** drink
c1200 Orm I 45.1373–4: Thaer Cristess menniscnesse Drannc daethess drinnch o rodetreo. **a1250** *Death's Wither-Clench* in Brown *Lyrics XIII* 15.7–8: Nis king ne Quene That ne sel drinke of deth-is drench.

D109 To drink of **Death's** flood
a1200 *Trinity College Homilies* 111[29–30]: He ferde fro hevene to helle, he dranc of dethes flode. MED flod 6(d).

D110 To flee as from the **Death**
c1400 *Laud Troy* I 135.4575: Thei fled fro him as fro the ded.

D111 To hate as (any) **Death**
a1387 Higden-Trevisa I 159[20]: For hym he hateth as deth. **c1400** *Brut* I 128.18: And hatede synne as deth, 253.11–2: eny.

D112 Unexpected **Death** often comes to the man so foolish as not to fear (know) his Lord
a750 *Seafarer* in *Exeter Book* 146.106: Dol biþ se þe him his dryhten ne ondrædeþ; cymeð him se deað unþinged. **a900** *Maxims* in *Exeter Book* 157.35: Dol bið se þe his dryhten nat, to þæs oft cymeð deað unþinged.

D113 **Debt** must be quit (paid)
c1420 Wyntoun II 7.65–6: For all honest det suld be Quyt with possibilite. **c1475** *Prohemy of a Mariage* 42[27–8]: And wel ye wote by holy chirches lawe, Dette must be payd by othe, sothe is this sawe.

D114 Not to die in one's **Debt**
a1450 *Partonope* 409–10.9868–9: The white shelde thinketh not to dey At this tyme in the soudans dette. **a1460** *Towneley Plays* 285.195: I shall not dy in youre dett! **c1500** *Cock* 1[9]: She shyll not dye in his dette. **1508**(1519) Stanbridge *Vulgaria* 20.9. **a1529** Skelton *Garnesche* I 125.173. Tilley D165.

D115 Not to dwell in one's **Debt** (*varied*)
c1400 *Laud Troy* I 151.5111–2: He wolde not longe dwelle In here dette, He sclow doun right alle that he mette, II 500–1.16998–9: Iff any (*warrior*) lefft In other det, Thei thenke hit schal be wel quyt.

D116 To pay the **Debt** to nature (of death)
a1333 Shoreham *Poems* 2.25: And his dethes dette yelde. **c1375** Barbour *Bruce* II 146.209–10: That hym worthit neyd to pay the det That na man for till pay may let. **c1400** *Seven Sages D* 1.10–2: Quhen the empryce, his moder deire, Throw det of natur this lyf left, As all that levis mon leif heir eft. **a1420** Lydgate *Troy* III 867.3310–1: And after that, she fil in-to seknesse, And hir dette yalde un-to nature, **a1449** *Guy* in *MP* II 523.185: Paide his dette of deth on-to nature, 538.566: Hath yolde hir dette, by deth, un-to nature. **1464** Hardyng 183[18–20]: But in the yere, as Bede hath saied and wryte, That every manne his debte to kynd paye mote: Kyng Ine dyed. **c1470** *Wallace* 25.251: He has payit at he aw. **1479** Rivers *Cordyal* 8.1–2: Also by the comune lawe of nature, every man muste

paye his mortal tribute, 141.2–3: Whenne thou shalt paye unto our lorde thy dette of naturale dethe. **1490** Caxton *Arte and Crafte* A1^{v}[17–8]: It (*death*) is the payment of the dette of nature. **a1500** *Craft of Dying* in *Yorkshire Writers* II 407[31–4]: Deth is nothing els but a . . . payinge of dette of naturall dutee. **c1500** Fabyan 388[18]: Whiche, unto deth, hath payde his dette due. Apperson 140; Taylor and Whiting 96; Tilley D168.

D117 Yield to all man (their) **Debt**
c1395 *WBible* Romans xiii 7: Therfor yelde ye to alle men dettis. Tilley D634.

D118 Of an evil **Debtor** men nim (*take*) oats for wheat
a1200 *Ancrene* 161.1: Me nimeth ed uvel dettur aten for hweate. **a1400** *Twelve Profits* (*Royal*) in *Yorkshire Writers* II 55[30–1]: For as men comunely saien: "Of an yvel dettoure men taken roghe ootes for wheete." **a1500** *Twelve Profits* (*Rawlinson*) in *Yorkshire Writers* II 401[39–40]: For it is communly seid: "of an evyll payer men receyveth otis for whete." Jente 770; *Oxford* 134; Tilley D173.

D119 **Deceit** deceives and shall be deceived
a1439 Lydgate *Fall* I 324.4432: Deceit deceyveth and shal be deceyved. See **C529, G491.**

D120 **Deceit,** weeping, spinning God has given to women (*varied*)
c1395 Chaucer *CT* III[D] 401–2: Deceite, wepyng, spynnyng God hath yive To wommen kyndely, whil that they may lyve. **a1500** *Court of Love* 424.541–2: That they be bound by nature to disceive, And spinne, and wepe, and sugre strewe on gall. **a1500** *Scorn of Women* in Robbins 225.29–34: Women of kinde have condicions thre: The furst ys they be full of deseyte; To spynne also ys theyre propurte; And wemen have a wondyrfull conseyte: Ffor they can wepe oft, and all ys as teyte, And ever when they lyst, the teere ys in the ey. **c1520** Walter *Spectacle* C3^{v}[24–7]: That nature hathe gyven theym no man can deny, It is theyr proprytees to be full of dysceytfulnes, To wepe and spynne, and hyde no secretnes, To lye and flatter. Apperson 140; *Oxford* 726; Skeat 267; Tilley W716. See **W537.**

D121 One **Deceit** brings out another
c1520 *Terens* C6^{r}[21]: One dysseit an other doth out bryng. Tilley D174.

D122 He that will **Deceive** a man will first speak fair to him
a1415 Mirk *Festial* 112.11–2: For thylk that wyll fyrst dessayve a man, thay woll fyrst speke fayre to hym. See **M196, S618, W581.**

D123 Who may sooner **Deceive** another than he in whom men conceive no malice?
a1439 Lydgate *Fall* I 108.3898–9: But who may soner a-nother man deceyve, Than he in whom no malice men conceyve? See **E97.**

D124 By praiseworthy **Deeds** one may be sure to do well in every nation
c735 *Beowulf* 24–5: Lofdædum sceal In mægþa gehwære man geþeon.

D125 A **Deed** done before is ready at need
c1350 *Good Wife E* 166.117–8: Redi is ate nede Bifor don dede.

D126 A **Deed** done before speeds another
c1350 *Good Wife E* 166.124–5: Bifore don dede Another spedet, **a1500** *N* 213.131–2: Before done deede Another may speede.

D127 A **Deed** well done quemes (*pleases*) the heart
c1425 *Good Wife H* 167.131: A dede wele don herte it whemyth. Apperson 141.

D128 Deem not my **Deeds,** though yours be nought
c1450 *Cambridge MS. Ii. iii.26* in *Rel. Ant.* I 205[3–4]: Deme nott my dedis, thogh thyne be noght; Say whate thow wilte, knowyst nott my thowght.

D129 Evil **Deeds** come to an evil end
1525 Berners *Froissart* IV 215[27]: Ever yvell dedes come to an yvell ende. See **D137, W647.**

D130 A good **Deed** done through prayer is bought and sold too dear
a1400 *Romaunt C* 5234–6: For good dede, don thurgh praiere, Is sold and bought to deere, iwys, To hert that of gret valour is. See Robinson's note, p. 879.

D131 He is gentle that does gentle **Deeds**
c1395 Chaucer *CT* III[D] 1168–70: Reedeth Senek, and redeth eek Boece; Ther shul ye seen expres that it no drede is That he is gentil that dooth gentil dedis. Jente 401; MED dede 7; *Oxford* 235; Smith 60.

D132 Ilk (*every*) good **Deed** helps (an)other
1513 Douglas *Aeneid* III 171.86: Ilk gode deid helpis other.

D133 Let the **Deeds** accord with the hest (*promise*)
a1420 Lydgate *Troy* I 88.2559: So that your dede acorde with your heste. See **W642, 645.**

D134 No **Deed** so dern (*secret*) that it sometime shall be seen
c1330 *Gregorius* 129 A 709–10: Ther nis non so dern dede That sum tyme it schal be sene. See **M806.**

D135 To be more wise (better advised) after the **Deed**
a1387 Higden-Trevisa II 169[8–10]: The men beeth . . . to fore the dede blondrynge and hasty, and more wys after the dede. **a1447** Bokenham *Mappula* 32[27–9]: And aforne that they schuln oughte doo, inportune they byn and fulle hardy, But aftir the dede bettir avysid and more avesy; and therfore they lyghtly willyn forsake that they hane be-gunne. Cf. Tilly E192.

D136 A true **Deed** is better than a false word
c1300 *South English Legendary* I 334.220: Betere is triwe dede thanne fals word.

D137 Ungracious **Deeds** cannot escape an ill ending
a1500 *Eger P* 282.1089–90: Thus ungracious deeds without mending Can never Scape without an ill endinge. See **D129, W647.**

D138 When **Deed** is done it is too late
a1475 *Good Wyfe Wold* 175.60: When dede ys doun, hit ys to lat. Apperson 625; *Oxford* 154. See **D287.**

D139 When the **Deed** is done it is time to take sage counsel
a1533 Berners *Arthur* 23[16–7]: For whan the dede is done, than it is tyme to take counsayle both sage and secret. (Of illicit sexual intercourse.)

D140 Who is untrue of **Deeds** it shall rue him sorely
a1300 *Alisaunder* 399.7360–1: Who-so is of dedes untrewe, Ofte it shal hym sore rewe. Apperson 647:14; Skeat 66.

D141 **Deem** (Judge) not that you be not deemed (judged)
c1000 *WSG* Matthew vii 1: Nellen ge deman, þæt ge ne syn fordemede, Luke vi 37: Nelle ge deman, and ge ne beoð demede. **c1395** *WBible* Matthew vii 1 : Nyle ye deme, that ye be nat demyd, Luke vi 37: Nyle ye deme, and ye schulen not be demed. **1509** Barclay *Ship* I 155[18]: Juge nat another, and thou shalt nat jugyd be. **1509** Watson *Ship* H1^{r}[3–4]: Juge not but yf that ye wyl be juged. *Oxford* 328.

D142 He can never **Deem** well that does evil
a1500 Hichecoke *This Worlde* 333.35–6: This proverbe is true and full sothe, He kan never wele deme that evyll dothe. See **I62.**

D143 He that soon **Deems** soon shall repent
c1390 Chaucer *CT* VII 1030[B2220]: For the commune proverbe seith thus: "He that soone deemeth, soone shal repente," 1135[B2325]. Apperson 288: Haste; *Oxford* 604: Soon; Skeat 248. See **D344, N136.**

D144 None so bold to **Deem** as he that is blent (*blinded*)
a1420 Lydgate *Troy* III 873.3504–5: For to deme ther is noon so bolde, As he that is blent with unkonnyng.

D145 **Deeming** sets many men's wits in err(or)
a1500 *Salamon seyth* in Person 52.9–10: Demyng and musyng over ferre Meny mennys wyttys it settisse yn erre.

D146 The mickle **Deer** hene (*oppress*) the little
a1200 *Trinity College Homilies* 211[3–4]: And alse the michele deor heneth the little and bi hem libbeth on the wilderne. See **F232, G444.**

D147 One slays the **Deer** whose part is none of the venison
a1439 Lydgate *Fall* I 144.5125–6: Oon sleth the deer with an hokid arwe, Whos part is non yit off the venysoun. See **B604, F418.**

D148 To be beset like a **Deer** in a net
a1325 *Otuel and Roland* 141.2637–8: Tho turpyn was by-set, As a der in the net. **c1350** *Libeaus* 66.1186–7: But sone he was besette, As deer is in a nette.

D149 To to-dreve (*disperse*) (*etc.*) like **Deer** to wood (A number of single quotations are brought together here)
c1000 Aelfric *Lives* II 90.356: And judas hi to-dræfde swa swa deor to wuda. **a1200** Lawman II 111.12828–9: Heo leopen ut of than wuden, Swulc hit deor weoren. **c1250** *A Springtide Song* in Brown *Lyrics XIII* 110.58–60: He was to-drawe, So dur islawe In chace. **a1300** *Alisaunder* 137.2435–7: So hij weren a-cowarded alle That hij ferden so dere in halle, And floteden so fyre in felde, 209.3736–7: There hij holdeth hem to-gidre, So flok of dere in thondre-wedre. **a1300** *Arthour and M.*[1] 196.6999–7000: Urn and stirten ther and her, For houndes so doth the wilde der. **c1400** *Laud Troy* I 210.7134: But sat stille as dere on the land, 268.9107–8: He drow hem doun, as men doth dere In wilde wodis to lordis lardere. **c1440** *Degrevant* 24.339–40: Als the dere in the dene To dede he thame dyghtis. **a1500** *Eger P* 242.652: He spowted forward as he had beene a deere.

D150 For **Default** of a good man they set a shrew on (the) bench (*varied*) c1450 *Douce MS.52* 54.110: For defawte of a goode man me settus a shrew on benche. **c1450** *Rylands MS.394* 104.17ᵛ.10. **c1475** Henryson *Want of Wyse Men* 189–191.8, 16, *etc.* (*refrain*): Sen want of wyse men makis fulis to sit on binkis. *Oxford* 691; Tilley W30; Whiting *Scots* II 156.

D151 Where there is **Default** of good heads there is default in body and foot
1525 Berners *Froissart* V 182[4–7]: Where there is defaulte of good heedes, there must nedes be defaulte in the body and in the fote: and he that hath no foote can do nothynge that is worthe. See **H214, 223, 232, 252, 254.**

D152 What is **Deferred** is not auferred (*removed*)
1493 *Seven Wise Masters* 60[15]: For that is dyfferred, it is not therfore auferred. NED Aufer, quote 1631: That is not auferred which is but deferred.

D153 In **Deferring** is oft great damage
a1420 Lydgate *Troy* I 180.1239–40: For in differryng is ofte gret damage, To werke in tyme is double avauntage. See **D157.**

D154 Black **Deformity** is no fault with Moors
c1515 Barclay *Eclogues* 205.679–80: No fault with Moriens is blacke difformitie, Because all the sort like of that favour be.

D155 Avaunt never of your **Degree**
a1500 *Leconfield Proverbs* 487[17–20]: This proverbe lerne of me, Avaunt nevyr of thy degree, If thoue have a goode properte Let other men comend and prayse the. See **M173, P351.**

D156 The higher **Degree** the sorer the fall
c1200 *Hali Meidenhad* 18.181–2: Ah se thu herre stondest, beo sarre offeaaret to fallen, for, se herre degre, se the fal is wurse. **c1400** *Apology* 38[14]: For ai the heiar degre, the sarrar is the falle. **a1425** Mirk *Instructions* 44.1415–6: The herre that a mon ys in degre, the sarrer forsothe falleth he. See **C296, M216.**

D157 **Delay** is dangerous (*varied*)
a1300 *Ancrene* (*Trinity*) 80.25–6: Li delai est mout perilious. **a1450** *Gesta* 253[28–9]: For delaynge of tyme may be hadde wickyd werke. **?1461** Paston IV 9[3]: Quia mora trahit periculum. **1463** *Plumpton Correspondence* 9[7–8]: And for Gods sake performe it (*quia mora trahitt periculum*). **1523** Berners *Froissart* III 337[12–4]: If one shulde enterprise a great mater, it shulde nat be long delayed, for in the delay the enemyes take advyce to their advauntage. Apperson 141–2; *Oxford* 136; Taylor and Whiting 96–7; Tilley D195; Whiting *Drama* 148, *Scots* I 157. See **A7, 9, D153, 450, L384, M419, P145, S390, T44, 148.**

D158 He that dines with **Delight** must sup with Poverty
c1516 Skelton *Magnificence* 61.1965–6: He dynyd with Delyte, with Poverte he must sup.

D159 A foolish **Demand** behooves a foolish answer
1484 Caxton *Aesop* 175[19–20]: For to folysshe demaunde behoveth a folysshe ansuere. Apperson 225:32. Cf. Tilley Q10. See **F391.**

D160 From **Denmark** unto Ind
c1395 Chaucer *CT* III[D] 823–4: God helpe me so, I was to hym as kynde As any wyf from Denmark unto Ynde.

D161 Better **Depart** betimes than tarry too long
a1533 Berners *Huon* 322.9–10: It is better departe betymes than to tary to longe.

D162 **Departing** (parting) of dear friends is a noyous (*painful*) thing (*varied*)
a1400 *Scottish Legends* II 41.1419–20: For it is a full noyus thing Of dere frendis the departynge. **a1500** *Eger P* 326.1341–2: Parting is a privye payne, But old friends cannott be called againe! **c1500** *Everyman* 12.302: I wyll remembre that partynge is mournynge. **c1515** Barclay *Eclogues* 139.823–4: Departing is a payne, But mirth reneweth when lovers mete againe. Tilley P82.

D163 Southern **Dere** (*harm*) goes northward and northern war to the south is hard
a1338 Mannyng *Chronicle A* I 100–1.2813–24: Bot contek and covetyse Out of the north wyl alwey ryse, Ffor thus men seide by elde dawe, And yit hit is a comun sawe: "Southerne der gos Northward, And Northerne werre to the south ys hard; Bot northern der and southern werre, Non dredeth, other they come nought nerre; Bot northerne (werre) that ys the doute, And southern der the north dos loute." In Brennes tyme, als ye may here, Hit ferde in thys ilke manere. See **N124.**

D164 **Desert** and reward are oft far odd
1546 Heywood *D* 51.332: Desert and rewarde be oft tymes thynges far od. Apperson 142; *Oxford* 137; Tilley D206.

D165 Such **Desert** such payment
a1533 Berners *Arthur* 321[1]: Of suche deserte, suche payment. Cf. Tilley D207. See **H185, W190.**

D166 **Deserve** and desire
a1500 *MS. Marginalia* in Hoccleve I 183 n. 2: Some desarve or they desyer, and yett they

lacke that they Requyre; Some desyre or they desarve, and yett the(y) gayne whylle other starve, Quod Carter. Apperson 215: First deserve; *Oxford* 205; Tilley D208.

D167 The **Desire** of a kingdom knows no kindred
1513 More *Richard* 51 F[8–10]: We have also had experience that the desire of a kingdome knoweth no kinred.

D168 **Despair** gives hardiment (*courage*)
c1420 Wyntoun V 409.3452–8: Bot I haf herd oft tymys say That dispayr giffis hardyment; For qwhen (men) trowis in thar entent That thai can set for thaim na rede, Bot anerly mon bide the dede, To wenge thar ded thai tak thaim wil, And swa takis hardyment thaim til. Apperson 142; *Oxford* 137; Tilley D216.

D169 One cannot flee his **Destiny** (*varied*)
a1393 Gower *CA* II 207.2860: Mai noman fle that schal betide. **c1400** *Laud Troy* I 311.10549–50: But sicurly he myght not fle On no manere his destane. **a1420** Lydgate *Troy* III 860.3050–1: Sith it is hard destyne to eschewe, As seyn tho folke in ther oppinioun, **c1421** *Thebes* 52–3.1233–4: But thing in soth that destine hath shape, Her in this world ful hard is to eskape. **a1456** Shirley *Death of James* 13[18–21]: And thus, as hit is said by the old wise fadirs, many years or we were borne, what thyng that destyned to a person, be hit late be hit sone, at the last ever hit cumyth. **a1460** *Towneley Plays* 119.84: What that destany dryfys, it shuld so be. *Oxford* 212: Flying; Tilley F83. See **S190, T167, W164.**

D170 If **Deuce Ace** cannot, and sice cinque will not, quartre trey must pay for all
a1500 Hill 134.3–4: "Dews-ays" non possunt, "syse-sinke," sed solvere nolunt; Omnibus est notum, "quatur-trey" solvere totum. Apperson 576; *Oxford* 594; Tilley S496.

D171 More by a **Deuce Ace**
a1500 Medwall *Nature* C4^r[11–3]: I shall bryng that hart of hys To be more howt (*haughty*) than yt ys By a dewys ase.

D172 To be of **Deuce Ace** (?*lucky*)
1481 Caxton *Reynard* 47[33–4]: He was a pylgrym of deux aas. NED Deuce[1] 5.

D173 As angry as the **Devil**
c1400 *Brut* I 268.23–4: And angry as the Devel ageynes ham that wer of the Kyngus Conseil, 33: The Mortyme(r), as a Devel for wrath.

D174 As drunken as the **Devil**
c1380 *Cleanness* 56.1500: Tyl he be dronkken as the devel, and dotes ther he syttes. Apperson 167–8; Svartengren 194.

D175 As false as the **Devil**
1546 Heywood *D* 75.191: And the devill is no falser then is he. Tilley D218. See **F132.**

D176 As fell as any **Devil**
c1375 Barbour *Bruce* II 47.539*–40*: He wes mair fell Than wes ony devill in hell.

D177 As foul as the **Devil**
c1380 Chaucer *HF* 1637–8: Tok out his blake trumpe of bras, That fouler than the devel was, See **F133.**

D178 As grisly as the **Devil**
a1300 *Alisaunder* 284.5362: And als the devel hii were griseliche.

D179 As like as the **Devil** and St. Austin
1513 Douglas *Aeneid* II 7.143: Ne na mair lyke than the devill and Sanct Austyne. Cf. *Oxford* 433: Lawrence.

D180 As strong as the **Devil**
c1400 *Sowdone* 29.1006: Some horible and stronge as devel of helle. **1490** Caxton *Eneydos* 150.2: Thoughe he were as stronge as the devyll.

D181 The **Devil** and his dam
c1350 *Libeaus* 107 *var.* 1920^g–h^: Though the devil and his dame Come with his brothir in same. **a1450** *York Plays* 300.237: What the devyll and his dame schall y now doo? **c1500** *Wife Lapped* 210.743: Ryde to the Devell and to his dame. **1549** Heywood *D* 87.227: The divell with his dam, hath more rest in hell, **1556** *E* 121.36.6–7: I can not wed the divell . . . For I have wedded his dam before, 122.40.14: I go not an ynche from the divell or his dam, *Spider* 37[17]: Is it the divell? or is it our dame? **1560** *E* 210.26.4: The divell will come in, when the divels damme goth out, **1562** 236.46.1–2: When was the devils dam create, tholde withred jade? The next leape yere after wedding was first made. Apperson 145; Jente 161; *Oxford* 138; Tilley D225; Whiting *Ballad* 35, *Drama* 340:497, *Scots* I 158.

D182 The **Devil** finds work for the idle (*varied*)
a1200 *Ancrene* 216.10–2: As sein Jerome leareth, ne beo ye neaver . . . idel, for anan rihtes the feond beot hire his werc. **1340** *Ayenbite* 31[21–2]: Vor huanne the dyevel vynt thane man ydel, he hine deth to worke. **c1380** Chaucer *CT* VIII[G] 7: Lest that the feend thurgh ydelnesse us hente, **c1390** *CT* VII 1595[B2785]: And therfore seith Seint Jerome, "Dooth somme goode dedes that the devel, which is oure enemy, ne

fynde yow nat unocupied." **c1400** *Chastising* 211.4–5: Therfor seint jerom seith: Do alwei sum goode, that the devel fynde the never unoccupied. **c1400** *Vices and Virtues* 27.6–8: For whan a man is ydele and the devel fyndeth hym ydel, he him setteth a-swithe to werke, 228.12–5: For whan the enemy, that is the devel, ne abideth not whan he fyndeth a man or a womman ydele and slowghe to do good; he putteth hem anon to worche in his werkes, cf. 24–7. **a1425** *Daily Work* in *Yorkshire Writers* I 139[6–7]: When the fend fyndis man idel: he puttis in his hert foule thoughtis of fleshli filth, or other folys. **a1475** *Tree* 16.4–5: Loke . . . that the fende fynde the not ydel. **c1475** *Wisdom* 48.393–6: Ye fonnyde fathers, founders of foly, Ut "quid hic statis tota die ociosi?" Ye wyll p(er)yse or ye that aspye, The dewyll hath acumberyde yow expres. **1484** Caxton *Royal Book* D5r[15–6]: For whan the devyl fyndeth a man ydle he putteth hym anone in his werkys, R4r[28–30]: For the devyl whyche slepeth not, whan he fyndeth a man ydle and slowe to do wel, put hym self to laboure and maketh hym falle lyghtly in to synne. **1519** Horman *Vulgaria* 40[5]: The devylle is redy to tempte hym that is ydell. Apperson 148:84; *Oxford* 139, 312; Taylor and Whiting 318; Tilley B594; Whiting *Devil* 210:19, *Scots* I 158.

D183 The **Devil** go with you down the lane
1549 Heywood *D* 85.184: I pray God the devel go with the, downe the lane. Apperson 143:13; *Oxford* 139; Tilley D236.

D184 The **Devil** has cast a bone
c1400 *Seven Deadly Sins* in Wyclif *SEC* III 133[22–3]: And so tho fend haves cast a boon, and made these honndes to feght; and by a bal of talow lettis hom to berke. **a1475** *Assembly of Gods* 53.1805–6: Whyche causyd hym among hem to cast in a boon, That found theym gnawyng ynough everychoon. **1546** Heywood *D* 64.72–3: The divell hath cast a bone . . . to set stryfe Betweene you. Apperson 146:52; *Oxford* 55, 139; Tilley B518, D237.

D185 The **Devil** in a band
a1460 *Towneley Plays* 129.407–8: Then may we be here the dewill in a bande, Syr gyle.

D186 The **Devil** is a liar and the father of lies
c1000 Aelfric *Homilies* I 170[4–6]: Se deofol . . . is fæder ælcere leasunge. **c1000** *WSG* John viii 44: For þam þe he is leas and his fæder eac. **a1200** *Ancrene* 44.17: The deovel is leas and leasunge feader. **1340** *Ayenbite* 62[24–6]: The lyeghere is ylich the dyevle, thet is his vader, ase god zayth ine his spelle. Vor he is lyeghere and vader of leasinges. **c1395** *WBible* Job xvi 9 *gloss:* The devel, which is a liere, and the fadir of leesing, John viii 44: For he is a liere, and fadir of it. **c1400** *Of Dominions* in Wyclif *EW* 291[1]: The fend is fadir of lesyngis. **c1400** *Satan and his Priests* in Wyclif *EW* 268[29–30], 270[14–5]. **c1400** *Vices and Virtues* 60.21–3: The devel . . . as God seith in the gospel . . . is lighere and fadre of lesynges. **c1415** *Middle English Sermons* 101.4–6: The fendes childe, that is fadur of all liers—"Quia diabolus est mendax et pater eius." **a1425** *De Sacramento Altaris* in Wyclif *EW* 357[27]. **c1425** *Orcherd* 72.31–2, 98.14–5. **c1438** Kempe 243.26: The Devyl, fadyr of lesyngys. **a1484** Caxton *Royal Book* F6r[2–4]. **a1500** *Craft of Dying* in *Yorkshire Writers* II 409[12–3]. **a1500** *Craft of Deyng* (*Cambridge MS.*) in Lumby *Ratis Raving* 3.60–1. Whiting *Devil* 210:24.

D187 The **Devil** is dead
c1400 *Brut* I 248.13–4: And communeliche Englisshemen saide amongus ham that the devel was dede. **a1475** *Ludus Coventriae* 324.1536–7: Be the deth the devyl deyd We were of hym so sore Atreyd. **c1475** *Mankind* 22.586: Qwyst! pesse! the Devll ys dede! **c1500** Greene *Carols* 473.3: The devyll is dede. **c1522** Skelton *Colyn* I 312.36–7: The devyll, they say, is dede, The devell is dede. **1546** Heywood *D* 92.57, **1555** *E* 161.98. Apperson 146; *Oxford* 140; Tilley D244. See **D202.**

D188 The **Devil** is not dead
a1200 *Ancrene* 176.21: The deovel nis nawt dead, that wite ha, thah he slepe. See **D202.**

D189 The **Devil** is not so black as he is painted
1534 More *Comforte* 1249 H[1–3]: Some saye in sport, and thinke in earnest: The devill is not so blacke as he is paynted. Apperson 147; *Oxford* 141; Taylor and Whiting 99; Tilley D255; Whiting *Devil* 207–8.

D190 The **Devil** made a souter (*cobbler*) a shipman (*varied*)
c1390 Chaucer *CT* I[A] 3903–4: The devel made a reve for to preche, Or of a soutere a shipman or a leche. **1533** More *Confutacion* 790 H[16–7]: The proverbe of Apelles, *Ne sutor ultra crepidam.* *Oxford* 607; Tilley D257; Whiting *Scots* II 128.

D191 The **Devil** may hop (dance) in a pouch (purse)
c1412 Hoccleve *Regement* 25.684–5: The feend, men seyn, may hoppen in a pouche Whan that no croys there-inne may a-pere. **c1475** *Mankind*

18.481: The devll may daunce in my purse for ony peny. **c1495** *Arundel Vulgaria* 89.373: And yet the devyll may daunce in ther purse for eny crose or quoyn is in it. **c1499** Skelton *Bowge* I 44.363–4: And his pouche, The devyll myghte daunce therin for ony crowche. Apperson 147; *Oxford* 139; Tilley D233. See **C560.**

D192 The **Devil** owed him a shame (debt)
c1400 *Laud Troy* I 101.3410–1: Loke, what schame the devel him augthte, That to himself hath suche bale brewed. **a1425** *Chester Plays* I 190.93–6: If we hym may take or get, The Devill ought hym debte, And so he shall be quit, Such Mastrees for to make. **1533** More *Confutacion* 727 H[10–2]: (He) prayd me to forgeve him the one lye, in which the devil he sayde, ought hym a shame. Apperson 147; Tilley D261.

D193 The **Devil** makes war where he sees peace
1523 Berners *Froissart* III 73[15–8]: For ye knowe, or els ye have herde say of the wyse sages, howe the Devyll subtellytiseth night and day to make warre, where as he seythe peace, and seketh lytell and lytell how he may come to his ungraycyous entent.

D194 The **Devil** to pay
a1500 *Tutivillus* in *Rel. Ant.* I 257[4–5]: Beit wer be at tome for ay, Than her to serve the devil to pay. Apperson 148; *Oxford* 142; Taylor and Whiting 99; Tilley D268; Whiting *Devil* 217:57.

D195 "Ecce *etc.*," said the **Devil** to the friars
c1475 *Mankind* 12.318: "Ecce quam bonum et quam Jocundum," quod the devll to the frerys.

D196 Farewell, the **Devil** is up!
c1475 *Wisdom* 52.518: "Farewell," quod I, "the devyll ys wppe!"

D197 Go to the **Devil** and say I bade!
a1460 *Towneley Plays* 12.94: Go to the dwill, and say I bad!

D198 Go to the **Devil** or forth to Kent
c1440 Charles of Orleans 202.6028–9: And go they to the deville or forth to kent Kare not for them. Notes (II 38) suggest a reference to Kentish longtails, and that "the devil" and "Kent" are the same. Cf. Tilley K16.

D199 He must needs go that the **Devil** drives
a1475 *Assembly of Gods* 2.21: He must nedys go that the devell dryves. **1523** Skelton *Garlande* I 418.1434: Nedes must he rin that the devyll dryvith. **1533** Heywood *Johan* A4v[21–2]: There is a proverbe whiche trewe nowe preveth, He must nedes go that the dyvell dryveth. **1533** More *Confutacion* 557 D[1–2]: He must needes go, whom the dyvel dryveth. **1546** Heywood *D* 81.41: He must needes go, whom the divel dooth drive, **1556** *Spider* 230[22]: But forth he must (they say) that the devill doth drive. Apperson 440; *Oxford* 447; Taylor and Whiting 260; Tilley D278; Whiting *Devil* 209:15, *Drama* 137.

D200 In the **Devil's** date (date of the devil)
a1376 *Piers* A ii 81: In the date of the devel the deede was a-selet. **a1475** *Assembly of Gods* 13.425: Ys hit thus! . . . what in the devyllys date! **c1499** Skelton *Bowge* I 44.375: Ay, quod he, in the devylles date, 47.455: Lete theym go lowse theym, in the devylles date! **c1516** *Magnificence* 30.944, 67.2172, **c1522** *Speke* II 22.439: And the date of the Devyll dothe shrewlye accord. *Oxford* 130.

D201 Not worth the **Devil's** dirt
1402 *Daw Topias* (*Jack*) 73[9–11]: Thes soluciones Ben not worthe The devellis dirt.

D202 Seldom lies the **Devil** dead by the gate (*road*) (in a dike)
a1460 *Towneley Plays* 123.229: Seldom lyys the dewyll dede by the gate. **c1475** Henryson *Fables* 72.2063: Heir lyis the Devyl . . . deid in ane dyke. Apperson 144:33; *Oxford* 572; Tilley D293. See **D187, 188.**

D203 To be the **Devil's** chick
c1380 *Ferumbras* 135.4331–2: He semeth ful wel the devels chyke, Y-sprong of the pyt of helle. See **B63.**

D204 To bear the **Devil's** sack
c1516 Skelton *Magnificence* 23.721: Thus can I lerne you, Syrs, to bere the devyls sacke. **1546** Heywood *D* 77.247–8: I will not beare the divels sacke, by saint Audry, For concelyng suspicion of their baudry. Tilley D318.

D205 To cast the **Devil** from the cliff
1484 Caxton *Aesop* 177–8: Moder, I am soo grete a clerke that I can cast the devylle fro the clyf.

D206 To dread someone (*etc.*) like the **Devil** (A number of single quotations are brought together here)
c1375 Barbour *Bruce* II 46.533: Thai dred him as the devill of hell. **c1400** *Florence* 67.1991: Hyppyng (*limping*) on two stavys lyke the devyll. **c1400** *Laud Troy* I 259.8795–6: Achilles come thenne ffast ridande As a devel with foule semblande, II 419.14223: He fferde as it were a devel of helle. **c1400** *Sowdone* 84.2948: She

grenned like a develle of helle. **a1460** *Towneley Plays* 17.283: It stank like the dwill in hell.

D207 To dwell in the **Devil's** arse
a1400 *Romaunt C* 7575–6: For thou shalt for this synne dwelle Right in the devels ers of helle. Cf. Chaucer *CT* III[D] 1675–99; G. L. Kittredge in *Harvard Studies and Notes in Philology and Literature* 1(1892) 21.

D208 To flee as the **Devil** from holy water
c1500 *Lyfe of Roberte* 226.174: They dyd flee fro hym, as the devyll fro holy water. Apperson 143:7; *Oxford* 141; Tilley D220; Whiting *Devil* 203:1.

D209 To give the **Devil** the one to carry away (fetch) the other
1533 Heywood *Johan* A3^{v}[8]: I wold gyve the dyvell the tone to cary away the tother, *Weather* D2^{r}[16]: The devyll shall have the tone to fet the tother. Tilley D298.

D210 To hate like the **Devil**
a1500 Fabyan 299[4]: Those that they hatyd as the devyll. Whiting *Devil* 213. See **F135.**

D211 To have the **Devil** at one's elbow
1534 More *Passion* 1315 C[2–6]: We may well thyncke that the devyll is than even besy aboute us, and not as it is commenly sayde at our elbowe, but, even at our very harte. NED Elbow 4a, quote 1698; Tilley D294, quote 1666.

D212 To look as the **Devil** looks over Lincoln
1546 Heywood *D* 92.55–6: Than wolde ye looke over me, with stomake swolne, Like as the divel lookt over Lincolne. Apperson 143:5; *Oxford* 141; Tilley D277. See **D308.**

D213 To look like a **Devil**
c1400 *Laud Troy* I 148.5022: Ector tho loked as a devele. Whiting *Devil* 213.

D214 To murmur (patter) the **Devil's** paternoster
c1390 Chaucer *CT* X[I] 506–8: Servauntz . . . wol . . . seyn harm, and grucche, and murmure prively for verray despit; whiche wordes men clepen the develes *Pater noster,* though so be that the devel ne hadde nevere *Pater noster,* but that lewed folk yeven it swich a name. **a1475** *Promptorium* 210: Gronyn, or grutchyn privyly, quod dicitur the devylis pater noster. **1484** Caxton *Royal Book* F8^{v}[21–2]: He grutcheth ayenst god, and syngeth the devyls pater noster. **1546** Heywood *D* 49.255: Pattryng the divels Pater noster to hir selfe. Apperson 149–50; *Oxford* 490; Tilley D315.

D215 To play the **Devil** in the horologe
1519 Horman *Vulgaria* 334[7]: Some for a tryfull play the devyll in the orlege. Aliqui in nugis tragedias agunt. **1546** Heywood *D* 68.90: Here is the divell in thorologe, **1555** *E* 170.136. Apperson 150:106; *Oxford* 505; Tilley D302.

D216 (To resemble) the **Devil** in a cloud
a1529 Skelton *Garnesche* I 119.25: The facyoun of your fysnamy the devyl in a clowde.

D217 To sail in the **Devil's** barge
a1500 *Quare* 199.176–7: Lat thame go saile all in the Devillis barge, And quhethir thay flete or in to hell synk.

D218 A (*on,* in) (the) **Devil Way**
c1200 *St. Juliana* 65.705–6 (cf. p. 147): In alre diche deofle wei ne mahte nawt letten. **c1300** *South English Legendary* I 152.123: He wende forth adevelwei, 244.62: And wende forth adevelwey bothe fleiss and bon, 260.391: Nou an alle develwey, 264.510: And wende in the develes weie, 274.281, 327.367: He wende an alle develwei, 340.383: And the devel yeode adeolwei, II 399.79, 465.56, 476.373: Deide and wende adevelewey, 379, 550.222. **c1303** Mannyng *Handlyng* 28.767: Ye shul go a deveyl weye, 343.11073. **a1325** M. Kildare *Swet Jesus* in Heuser 83.9[3]. **c1330** *On the King's Breaking* in Wright *Political Songs* 254[2]. **a1375** *William* 68.1978: Where dwelle ye, a devel wai. **c1390** Chaucer *CT* I[A] 3134: Tel on, a devel wey! **c1395** III[D] 2242: Lat hym go honge hymself a devel weye! **a1400** *Firumbras* 22.651–2: That sarsin ded fyl uppon the playn And hys soule a-devylway, gyf y durst it sayn, 34.1035–6. **c1400** *Seven Sages D* 46.1444. **c1422** Hoccleve *Jereslaus's Wife* 148.236–7: And foorth on devel way Rood this tirant. **a1440** *De Miraculo Beate Marie* 503.29. **a1445** *Carl* 135 B 261. **a1450** *York Plays* 37.52: Daunce in the devilway, 88.354, 130.121, 269.398, 306.407, 313.188. **c1450** *Seege of Troye* 33 A 405: "Ffey a devel way," tho sayd he. **a1460** *Towneley Plays* 12.89: Or sit downe in the dwill way, 22.449. **a1475** *Assembly of Gods* 39.1317. **a1475** *Ludus Coventriae* 296.728: Cast hym down here in the devyl way. **c1475** *Mankind* 6.153: Go we hens, a devll wey! 19.514. **a1500** *Degrevant* 53 (*Cambridge*) 791–2: Go and glad thi gest, In all the devyl way! **c1522** Skelton *Colyn* I 336.672: Come downe, in the devyll way! **1523** *Garlande* I 386.635: Of a dysour, a devyl way, grew a jentilman, *Howe the Douty Duke* II 77.330–1: Sir Dunkan, in the

devill waye, Be well ware what ye say. MED a devel-wei; NED Devil 19; Whiting *Drama* 341:499, *Scots* I 158.

D219 A (*on*, in) (the) twenty **Devil Way**
c1330 *Seven Sages A* 104.2287–8: And bad hir go that ilche dai On alder twenti devel wai. **c1386** Chaucer *LGW* 2177: A twenty devel-wey the wynd hym dryve! **c1390** *CT* I[A] 3713: And lat me slepe, a twenty devel wey, 4257: And forth he goth, a twenty devel way. **c1390** *Northern Homily Cycle Narrationes* (*Vernon*) 303.355–6: He (*a devil*) wente a wey Al on twenti devele wey. **c1395** Chaucer *CT* VIII[G] 782. **c1421** Lydgate *Thebes* 9.162: Shet youre portoos, a twenty develway. **a1425** *Chester Plays* I 56.219–20, II 416.452. **a1426** Lydgate *Mumming at Hertford* in *MP* II 678.106. **a1437** *Kingis Quair* 61.56[7]: And bid thame mend, in the twenty devil way. **c1440** *Degrevant* 52.791–2: Thou lett me noght of my rest, In twentty develle way! **c1450** Greene *Carols* 403.4: A twenty devele name, let hem goo! **a1460** *Towneley Plays* 21.439: Com downe in twenty dwill way, 155.465, 210.200. **a1475** *Ludus Coventriae* 205.143. **c1500** *Be pes* in Stevens *Music* 339.1[4]: Leff werke a twenty-a-devell away! **c1500** Greene *Carols* 408.4: In the twente devyls way, Who bade the geve my gud away. **1509** *Fyftene Joyes* D4ᵛ[26]: I tolde you late in twenty devylles waye. **1513** Douglas *Aeneid* II 10.260. **1519** Horman *Vulgaria* 422[9]. **1533** Heywood *Pardoner* B2ᵛ[1]: Dryve hym hence . . . in the .xx. devyll waye.

D220 **Devotion** of ten mark(s)
a1400 Wyclif *Sermons* I 291[25–6]: And preestis taken her ordris for devocioun of ten mark.

D221 As tender (*etc.*) as **Dew** (A number of single quotations are brought together here)
a1400 ?Chaucer *Rom. A* 1013: Hir flesh was tendre as dew of flour. **a1400** Chestre *Launfal* 70.608: And as lyght as dew he leyde hem doune. **c1440** *St. Christopher* 464.840–1: And als so softe to my lykynge Als dewe es in a may mornynge. **c1450** *The Maiden Makeles* in Brown *Lyrics XV* 119.3–4: He cam also stylle ther his moder was As dew in aprylle, that fallyt on the gras, 6, 8.

D222 To drop like **Dew**
a1400 *Destruction of Troy* 78.2367–8: That (*sweat*) stremys from hym straght, and stert uppon the erthe, And dropis as dew or a danke rayne. **a1450** *Dispute Between Mary and the Cross* in Richard Morris *Legends of the Holy Rood* (EETS 46, 1871) 199.55–6: The blood ran on my briddes bak, Droppynge as dewe on ryssche. **a1450** *The lord that is* 217.199: The blood droppyd as dew on ryssche.

D223 To go away (*etc.*) like **Dew** (A number of single quotations are brought together here.)
a1325 M. Kildare *Swet Jesus* in Heuser 81.2[1–2]: This world is love is gon awai, So dew on grasse in somer is dai. **a1400** *Amadace I* 55[8]: He glode a-way as dew in towne (**a1500** *A* 275.761: as dew in son). **a1400** *Destruction of Troy* 260.7997: That the droupes, as a dew, dankit (*wet*) his fas. **a1400** *Morte Arthure* 10.312–3: No more dowtte the dynte of theire derfe wapyns Than the dewe that es daunke, when that it doun falles. **1439** Lydgate *St. Albon* 183.1264: Faded away as dewe on sommer floures, **1449** *Procession* in *MP* I 38.95: To make his grace as golde dewe doune to fleete. **a1500** *Man have mind* 56.68–9: Bot all our drivis (*passes away*) as dew bedene That one the bery bidis bene.

D224 As oft as **Dewdrops** are wet
c1325 *Way of Woman's Love* 163.29–30: Ase fele sythe and oft As dewes dropes beth weete.

D225 As bright as **Diamonds**
c1470 *Wallace* 295.1930: Cler aspre eyn, lik dyamondis brycht. Taylor and Whiting 101.

D226 As clear as **Diamond**
c1500 *O beauteuous braunche* in *Anglia* 72(1954) 402.12: Tha(n) dyamond more clere. Svartengren 362.

D227 As hard as (the, a) **Diamond**
a1400 *Romaunt B* 4385: Have herte as hard as dyamaunt. **c1400** *Vices and Virtues* 192.30: Thei ben as harde as the diamaunt. **c1408** Lydgate *Reson* 181.6913, **a1449** *Fabula* in *MP* II 512.785: the. **c1450** *Pilgrimage LM* 85[29–30]. **1480** Caxton *Ovyde* 67[6]: Myn herte were harder than a Dyamond, 160[5]: a. Taylor and Whiting 101. See **A40.**

D228 As splendent as a **Diamond**
c1500 *The Beauty of his Mistress III* in Robbins 127.43–4: Splendant In bewtye as a dyamond most precyouse In syght.

D229 As stable as a **Diamond**
1439 Lydgate *St. Albon* 178.954: His herte stronge, stable as dyamant.

D230 As steadfast as a **Diamond**
c1408 Lydgate *Reson* 180.6892–3: For stydfast as a dyamaunt That breketh nat but with gootys blood. See **D233.**

D231 A **Diamond** does not shine until it is polished
1471 Caxton *Recuyell* I 183.20–1: The dyamond shyneth not tyl hit be pollisshyd.

D232 A **Diamond** in dung is not fair
c1523 Barclay *Mirrour* 27[27–8]: A Diamant in donge is not fayre to beholde, It loseth the beaŭtie except it be in golde. See **S59.**

D233 A **Diamond** will not be broken
1439 Lydgate *St. Albon* 146.1108: Lyke a dyamande, he wolde not be broke. See **D230.**

D234 As fair as **Diana**
a1300 *Alisaunder* 407.7505: Also fair as was Dyane.

D235 As smooth as a **Die**
1556 Heywood *E* 116.27.6: Thy way, both faire and smooth as a dye is. NED Die sb.[1] 2f; Tilley D325.

D236 As square as **Dice**
a1475 *Liber Cure Cocorum* 38[27]: Square as dises thou shalt hit make, 45[12–3]: After cut crust of bred I kenne, Sware as dyse.

D237 Not dere (*harm*) a **Dice**
a1400 *Destruction of Troy* 28.808: Ne never dere hym a dyse with no dede efte. **a1400** *Siege of Jerusalem* 46.804: That alle dere noght a dyȝs (*vars.* dyce, dyte, dissh). MED de ld; NED Die sb.[1] 3b.

D238 Better to **Die** than live ever in woe
a1439 Lydgate *Fall* I 233.1224–5: And it was said sithe(n) ful yore ago, Bet is to deie than ever to lyve in wo. Smith 58.

D239 Better to **Die** with honor than live in shame (*varied*)
a1200 Lawman I 248–9.5832–5: For leovere us is here Mid manscipe to fallen, Thanne we heonne i-funde farren, Ure frenden to scare (B: s(h)onde). **a1300** *Alisaunder* 173.3065–6: More honoure is faire to sterve Than in servage vilely serve. **a1300** *Arthour and M.*[1] 68.2359–60: For he hadde lever dye in fight, Than schond tholi and unright, 256.9197–8: Better is, to sterve worthschipliche, Than long to liven schandfulliche. **c1300** Robert of Gloucester I 241.3417–8: And levere al so me is Vor to deye myd honour than libbe in ssame ywys. **c1330** *Horn Childe* 181.166–7: Better manly to be slayn, Than long to live in sorwe and pain. **c1350** *Joseph* 17.495–6: Betere hit were douhtilyche to dighen on or oune, Then with schendschupe to schone and us a-bak drawe. **a1375** *William* 126.3900–1: And more mensk it is manliche to deie, Than for to fle couwar(d)li for ought that mai falle. **c1410** Lovelich *Merlin* III 444.16593–6: For mochel more worschepe for us hit were Oure defendaunt to deyen here Thanne schamfully to ben sewed and slayn Or uppon hape taken and browht agayn, 503.18819–21: For bettere hit were us uppon hem deye Thanne longe this lyf to lyven, in feye, In povert, mischef, and disherited also. **a1420** Lydgate *Troy* I 86.2494–5: For every man schulde be rather fayn To dye in honour, than lyven as a wreche, **c1421** *Thebes* 169.4123–5: And better it wer to every werreyour Manly to deye with worship and honour, Than lik a coward with the lyf endure. **a1450** *Partonope* 112.3554–6: I hadde lever a thowsand folde For to dye thenne for to be schamed. **c1450** *Merlin* II 235[20–2]: Ffor better is a gode ende and to dye with honour, than longe to endure and after all lese, and than dye with dishonour, 273[25–6]: Ffor better it is to dye with honoure than dye olde and pore and disherited, 329[11]: Hadde I lever to dye with worship than lyve with shame, 334[26–8], 439[33–4]. **c1450** *Rawlinson Troye* 178.22–3: Ffor y had lever ende and die with worshipp then endure and leve in repreve and shame. **a1460** *Dicts* (*Helmingham*) 163.22–3: It is bettir to deye worshipfully than for to lefe in shame. **1464** Hardyng 125[32–3]: For better is with honour for to dye, Then with (lyf ay) ashamed for to be. **a1470** Malory I 144.16–7: I had levir to dye with honour than to lyve with shame, 409.27–8. **a1475** *Guy*[2] 60.2099–2100: Hyt ys bettur slayn to be, Then cowardely awey to flee, 120.4203–4: Bettur hyt ys to wende wyth honowre, Then to dwelle here wyth grete dolowre, 140.4897–8: For lothe he was for to flee: He had wele levyr slayne bee. **c1475** *Guy*[1] 125 C 2119–20: Better it is to dye manly Than to flee with shame and vilanye, 133 C 2241–2: For better it is manly dede bee Than with shame awey to flee. **1477** Rivers *Dictes* 47[24]: Better it is worshipfull deth than shamefulle life, 53[34–5]: Thou dost evyl to flee from the honourable deth to the shamefull lyff, 70[21–2]. **1483** Caxton *Golden Legende* 224[r][2.26–8]: We had lever deye wyth our lord chastely, than lyve synfully, **1485** *Charles* 125.7–8, **c1489** *Aymon* I 204.27–8, 232.24–6, **1490** *Eneydos* 10.17–8: For a thynge more noble is to dye than vylanously to be subdued. **1509** Barclay *Ship* I 173[21]: Better is to dye chast: than longe to lyve in shame, **c1523** *Mirrour* 41[36]. **1525** Berners *Froissart* V 190[7–8], **1532** *Golden Boke* 251.4404–5. Skeat 62; Smith 55; Tilley H576; Whiting *Drama* 39, 296. See **D95, 104, F140.**

D240 Learn to **Die** and then you shall know how to live
c1400 *Vices and Virtues* 68.22–3: Lerne to dye, and than schalt thou kunne lyve.

D241 One **Dies** when he least wenes (*expects*)
a1500 *Salamon sat and sayde* 291.33: And qwen he lest wenys he dyes in myd warde. See **D96.**

D242 We **Die** but once (*varied*)
a1400 *Torrent* 36.993: A man schall But onnys Dyee. **a1450** *York Plays* 414.338: We dye but onys. **a1460** *Towneley Plays* 320.481. **1481** Caxton *Reynard* 33[3]. **1506** Barclay *Castell* A8v[6]: I sholde dye no more but ones. **1523** Berners *Froissart* I 31[21–2]: But sayd he hadde but one dethe to dye, the whiche was in the will of God. *Oxford* 400–1; Taylor and Whiting 102; Tilley M219.

D243 We must all **Die** (*varied*)
c735 *Beowulf* 1004–8: Ac gesecan sceal sawlberendra Nyde genydde, ... gearwe stowe, þær his lichoma legerbedde fæst Swefeþ æfter symle, 1386–7: Ure æghwylc sceal ende gebidan Worolde lifes, 2590–1: Swa sceal æghwylc mon Alætan lændagas. **a1350** *Seven Sages C* 97.2846: Al sal we dy bath ald and ying. **c1385** Chaucer *CT* I[A] 3034: Thanne may I seyn that al this thyng moot deye. **c1392** *In Wenlok* in *Publications of the Bedfordshire Historical Record Society* 5(1920) 108[16]: Deye mot I ned ones. **c1395** Chaucer *CT* IV[E] 38: Alle shul we dye. **c1420** Wyntoun III 269.821–2: Syne in the flux hym hapnyt to de, For thar is nane that case may fle. **a1425** *Metrical Paraphrase OT* 33.6796: Then dyed, as erthly men bus all. **c1430** Lydgate *Dance* 8.80: Adames children alle thei mosten deie, **a1439** *Fall* I 95.3452–8: Erthe is the eende off everi maner man; For the riche with gret possessioun Deieth as soone, as I reherse can, As doth the poore in tribulacioun: For deth ne maketh no dyvisioun Bi synguler favour, but twen bothe iliche, Off the porest and hym that is most riche, **a1449** *Tyed with a Lyne* in *MP* II 834.78–9: Nothyng more sure than al men shal deye, Late men aforne make theyr ordynaunce. **c1470** *Wallace* 187.173: Rycht suth it is that anys we mon de. **1474** Caxton *Chesse* 80[17–8]: For ther is no man that lyveth but he must nedes dye, **c1489** *Aymon* I 231.16–7: For ones we must deye wythoute faylle. **a1500** *Knight of Curtesy* 16.444: At the last we all must dye. **c1500** *Three Kings' Sons* 146.7: There is nobody, be he olde or yonge, but ones shall dy. **1506** Barclay *Castell* E6r[3–4]: For this is a thynge moost certayne That fyrst or last we must nedes dye. **a1508** Dunbar *Testament* 72.9–10: Cum nichill sit certius morte, We mon all de, quhen we haif done. **1509** Barclay *Ship* I 153[13]: We knowe that we all must have an ende, II 125[13]: We all must die. **1509** Watson *Ship* S8v[27]: Ones muste we deye, none excepte. **a1533** Berners *Huon* 206.30: We be all made to dye. *Oxford* 7–8; Smith 67; Tilley M505; Walther I 309.2678; Whiting *Drama* 39, 262, *Scots* I 159. See **D97, K49.**

D244 A great **Difference** between gold (wool) and gossamer
a1445 Lydgate *Horns Away* in *MP* II 662.5: Tween gold and gossomer is greet dyfference, **a1449** *Order* in *MP* II 451.63–4: Tween wolle and gossomer is a gret difference, Stuf for a chapman that is nat lyk to the, 454.138: And gadreth gossomer to pakke it for wolle. MED gos-somer (b).

D245 (There is) **Difference** between staring and stark-blind
1546 Heywood *D* 84.137–8: The difference betwene staryng and starke blynde, The wise man at all tymes to folow can fynde. Apperson 152; *Oxford* 145; Tilley D334.

D246 There is no **Difference** between a liar and a great teller of tidings
1450 *Dicts* 96.6–7: Ther is no difference bi-twene a lier and a grete teller of tidingis. **1477** Rivers *Dictes* 48[13–4]: Ther is noo difference bitwix a grete teller of tydingis and a lyer. See **S251, W593.**

D247 To be in the **Dike** (*ditch*)
a1460 *Towneley Plays* 103.93: Poore men ar in the dyke and oft tyme mars. **1546** Heywood *D* 22.7: Then my beautifull mariage lithe in the dike. See **D266, L24, M573.**

D248 First **Dine** and after go to mass
a1449 Lydgate *Ryme* in *MP* II 794.75: First to dyne, and after go to messe.

D249 **Dinners** cannot be long where dainties want
1546 Heywood *D* 59.1: Diners can not be long, where deinties want. Apperson 153; *Oxford* 146; Tilley D344.

D250 He that comes late to **Dinner** has least part in the meat
1492 *Salomon and Marcolphus* 12[15–6]: He that late comyth to dyner, his parte is leest in the mete.

D251 Not to be half a **Dinner** for someone
c1375 Barbour *Bruce* II 9.187–8: Bot thai ar

nocht, withouten wer, Half-deill ane dyner till us here! See **B523.**

D252 **Discord** is worse than sword or pestilence
a1420 Lydgate *Troy* III 696.4515–6: For wher Discord holdeth residence, It is wel wers than swerd or pestilence!

D253 Where **Discord** is there may no quarrel prove (*succeed*)
a1420 Lydgate *Troy* I 201.1960–2: Wher is discorde, ther may no querel preve; For on that part wher hertis be nat oon, Victorie may in no wyse goon.

D254 **Discretion** is the mother of all virtues
c1500 *Lancelot* 57.1916–7: Discreccioune sall mak the diversitee, Wich clepith the moder of al vertewis. Cf. Taylor and Whiting 103.

D255 To be **Disguised** (*drunk*)
1562 Heywood *E* 211.34.5: Three cuppes full at once shall ofte dysgyse thee. *Oxford* 147; Tilley D362.

D256 All her **Dishes** are chafing dishes
1562 Heywood *E* 235.38: Wyfe, all thy dishes be chaffyng disshes plast: For thou chafest at sight of every dishe thou hast. Apperson 154; Tilley D377.

D257 Better a small **Dish** with joy than divers dainties with murmur
c1515 Barclay *Eclogues* 157.469–70: Better one small dish with joy and heart liking Then divers daynties with murmure and grutching. See **M614, 700, P329.**

D258 A **Dish** for a king
c1495 *Arundel Vulgaria* 7.22: A disch for a kynge. Shakespeare *Winter's Tale* iv.3.8: For a quart of ale is a dish for a king; *Sing a song of sixpence* in Iona and Peter Opie *Oxford Dictionary of Nursery Rhymes* (Oxford, 1951) 394.

D259 To break a **Dish** (*?create a disturbance*)
1546 Heywood *D* 48.239: I maie breake a dishe there.

D260 To give up one's **Dish**
c1400 *Laud Troy* I 264.8956–9: Hadde he laste longe In his wode geris, Achilles hadde yeven up his dische, Hadde he never eten flesche ne fische He myght not the strokes susteyne.

D261 To have full **Dishes** of woulds and of wishes
a1393 Gower *CA* III 192.922–4: Bot yit is noght mi feste al plein, Bot al of woldes and of wisshes, Therof have I my full disshes. See **W403.**

D262 Who is far from his **Dish** (good) is nigh his harm
c1450 *Douce MS.52* 45.12: Who is ferre from his disshe, is nyhgh his harme. **c1450** *Rylands MS.394* 96.10. **1546** Heywood *D* 92.52: A man far from his good, is nye his harme, **1555** *E* 168.130. *Oxford* 401: Man far from; Tilley M232.

D263 He **Dispraises** himself that dispraises all others
1450 *Dicts* 262.16–7: He dispreisethe him-selfe that in preising him dispreisethe alle other.

D264 If one **Dispraises** himself he pleases no man
1492 *Salomon and Marcolphus* 7[10–1]: Yf I shulde myself dyspreyse, no man shall I please.

D265 **Dissention** begins by another, reconciling by oneself
c1390 Chaucer *CT* VII 1691[B2881]: For the wise man seith "The dissensioun bigynneth by another man, and the reconsilyng bygynneth by thyself." Cf. Taylor and Whiting 389.

D266 To cast (someone) in the **Ditch**
c1499 Skelton *Bowge* I 34.115: Whome she hateth, she casteth in the dyche. See **D247, L24, M573.**

D267 As common as **Ditch-water**
c1450 Idley 203.2725: To dele with them that are commun as water in a dyche.

D268 As digne (*haughty*) as **Ditch-water**
c1390 Chaucer *CT* I[A] 3964: She was as digne as water in a dich. **c1395** *Pierce* 14.375: They ben digne as dich water, that dogges in bayteth. Apperson 153.

D269 As light (*simple*) as **Ditch-water**
c1425 *Crafte* in Robert Steele *The Earliest Arithmetics in English* (EETS ES 118, 1922) 18.8–10: Then worch forth in the other figurys till thou come to the ende, for it is lyght as dyche water. NED Ditch-water.

D270 **Diversity** (*discrimination*) is required between like things
c1385 Chaucer *TC* iii 404–6: Wyde-wher is wist How that ther is diversite requered Bytwixen thynges like, as I have lered. **c1385** Usk 22.45–6: For this is sothe: betwixe two thinges liche, ofte dyversitè is required.

D271 There is a **Diversity** between having riches and riches having you
c1515 Barclay *Eclogues* 41.1133–4: There is diversitie Betwene to have riches, and riches to have thee. Cf. Tilley R113.

D272 Better it be **Done** than wish it had been done
1546 Heywood *D* 77.257: Better it be doone than wishe it had bene doone. Tilley D417.

D273 **Do** as others do
c1400 *Beryn* 37.1151: But "doith as othir doith." **1546** Heywood *D* 63.27–8: He that dooth as most men doo, Shalbe least wondred on. Apperson 154–5. Cf. Whiting *Drama* 79. See **M101.**

D274 **Do** as you would be done to
a900 *Laws of Alfred* in Liebermann I 44.49.5 (E): Ond þæt ge willen, þæt oðre men eow ne don, ne doð ge ðæt oþrum monnum. **c1000** *Be rihtan cristendome* in Napier 144.1–2: And riht is, þæt manna gehwylc oðrum beoda þæt riht, þæt he wille, þæt man him beode. **c1000** *Corpus Christi Homily* in Assmann 139.39–43: þy cweð se hælend on his godspelle . . . Don ge oðrum mannum ælc ðara þinga, þe ge willan, þæt hy eow don. **c1000** *Ecclesiastical Institutes* II 410[32]: Hwæt ge willen þæt eow oðre men don, do ge hiom þæt ylce. **c1000** *WSG* Luke vi 31: And swa ge wyllað þæt eow men don, doþ him gelice. **c1300** *Northern Homily Cycle* (*Edin. Coll. Phys.*) 51[5–6]: That es at say, if man till nehbor do, That he wald he did him to. **c1340** Rolle *Psalter* 351 (100.4): That is, that was myspayand to be done til me, .i. wild noght do it til my neghbure. **a1393** Gower *CA* II 218.3274–9: And ek he tok a remembrance How he that made lawe of kinde Wolde every man to lawe binde, And bad a man, such as he wolde Toward himself, riht such he scholde Toward an other don also. **c1395** *WBible* Luke vi 31: And as ye wolen that men do to you, do ye also to hem in liik maner. **a1400** *Clergy May Not Hold Property* in Wyclif *EW* 387[8–9]: Alle thinges that ye wollen that other men done to yow, do ye to hem. **1400** *Love god, and drede* in Kail 4.115–6: As thou wolde men dede for the, Do thou so liche eche man have hisse. **c1400** Mandeville *Travels* 196.3–4: For wee don to noman other wise than wee desiren that men don to us. **1404** *Lerne say wele* in Kail 22.243–4: Do no wrong ne (no) debate, But as thou wolde men dede by the. **c1408** Lydgate *Reson* 23.838–40. **a1425** *Cursor* III 1535 CG 27722–3. **c1440** Charles of Orleans 188.5612–4. **c1440** Scrope *Epistle of Othea* 86[24–5]: Hermes seith, "Do not to thi felawe that the which thou woldyst not were done to the." **a1450** Audelay 29.543, 48.60. **a1450** *Boke of Curtasye* (*Sloane*) 304.175–6: To another man do no more amys Then thou woldys be don of hym and hys. **a1450** *Rule of St. Benet* (2) 114.2368–70. **1450** *Dicts* 104.23–4, 156.23–4: Ne do to noon other man that that thou woldist not have doon to the. **c1450** *Epistle of Othea* 116.6–7. **c1450** *Good Wife L* 201.153. **c1450** *Ratis* 10.337–8: Bot that thow pres to do, my sone, Rycht as thou wald to the war done. **1456** Hay *Law* 163.31–2, 173.4–6, 225.18–20. **a1470** Malory III 1114.27–8: And allwayes a good man woll do ever to another man as he wolde be done to hymselff. **1477** Rivers *Dictes* 12[11–2], 67[32–3]. **1483** *Quatuor Sermones* 25[24–5]: Doo right and reson to hym . . . as thou woldest he dyd to the. **1484** Caxton *Aesop* 49[1–3], 288[1–3], 291[2–4], *Royal Book* M4v[6–8]. **1491** *Rule of St. Benet* (3) 139.14–7. **1495** Fitzjames *Sermo* C4r[19–22]. **1509** Barclay *Ship* II 39[13–4]: For thou oughtest nat do to any creature That thynge whiche thou of hym wolde nat endure. **1509** Fisher *Treatyse* 225.2: Even as ye do to other, so shall ye be done to. **1509** Watson *Ship* Q3r[17–8]. **1513** Douglas *Aeneid* II 17.501, III 169.13. **c1523** Barclay *Mirrour* 9[6–7]: For drede of correction not presuming to do, But like as him selfe would gladly be done to, 34[44], 69[49]: Then deale as thou woldest that men should dele with thee. **1532** More *Confutacion* 463 E[8–9]. **1534** Heywood *Love* C2v[34]. *Oxford* 148; Taylor and Whiting 104; Tilley D395; Whiting *Drama* 285, *Scots* I 159. See **J79, M284, 467.**

D275 **Do** ever well while you have space
c1450 *Fyrst thou sal* 91.177–8: Do ever wele whils thou has space, If thou wyll thou may hafe grace. See **M59.**

D276 **Do** or die
c1470 *Wallace* 67.593: Her is no chos, bot owdir do or de, 76.63, 297.12. **c1475** Henryson *Fables* 99.2886: And quhen scho saw thair wes bot do or de. **c1475** *Thewis* 192.263: Than is thar nocht bot do ore dee. Taylor and Whiting 104; Whiting *Scots* I 159.

D277 **Do** well and dread no man
c1450 *Bühler MS.21* in *Studies in Medieval Literature in Honor of Albert C. Baugh*, ed. MacEdward Leach (Philadelphia, 1961) 286[5]: Do wel and dred nought. **c1450** *Fyrst thou sal* 89.73–4: Do thou wele and drede no man, For trewthe to kepe is best thou can, 105–6: Do thou ay wele and drede no man, And say not al that thou can. **c1450** *Proverbes of Good Counsel* 68.9–10: The beste wysdom that I Can, Ys to doe well, and drede no man. **c1500** Greene *Carols* 354 (*refrain*): Do well, and drede no man, 387 (*refrain*). *Oxford* 149. Cf. Jente 247.

D278 **Do** well and have well

c1375 Barbour *Bruce* I 297.643: Giff he weill dois, let hym veill ta. **c1378** *Piers* B vii 113–4: But "Dowel, and have wel, and god shal have thi sowle, And do yvel, and have yvel." **a1425** *Chester Plays* I 43.581–4: Wottes thou not well that for thy deed, If thou doe well, thou may have meede; If thou doe fowle, fowle for to spede, And sicker therof to be? **c1450** *Douce MS.52* 47.32. **a1475** Ashby *Dicta* 67.545–6: It is a comon sawe, he that doth wele, Shal have it by goode lawe, Reason and skyle. **c1483** Caxton *Dialogues* 47.38: Who doth well shall well have. **a1500** Hill 130.8: Do well whill thou art here and thou shalt have well els wher. **1506** Barclay *Castell* G2[r][2]: If thou well do thou shalte well fynde. **1546** Heywood *D* 91.32. Apperson 155; Jente 245; *Oxford* 149; Tilley D398.

D279 He that **Does** as he can, blame him no man
c1450 *Douce MS.52* 44.1: He that doth as (he) can, Blame hym no man. **c1450** *Rylands MS.394* 95.5.1.

D280 He that **Does** well recks not who sees it
1474 Caxton *Chesse* 144[12–4]: And therfore it is sayd in a comyn proverbe, he that well doth reccheth not who seeth hit.

D281 It is as one **Does** and not as he says (*varied*)
1523 Berners *Froissart* III 260[28–9]: It is sayd moost comenly, If it be as he dothe, it is as he saythe, **a1533** *Huon* 327.16–7: Ye may say your pleasure, but in the doynge is all the mater. **1546** Heywood *D* 77.234: But it is as folke dooe, and not as folke saie. Apperson 154; *Oxford* 148; Tilley D394; Whiting *NC* 395. See **C514, W642.**

D282 Let us gladly **Do** as we teach
c1030 *Laws of Cnut* in Liebermann I 300.20 (G): Uton don eac georne, swa we gyt læran wyllað. See **D289, L107, 463.**

D283 None **Does** so well but some may amend it
1509 Barclay *Ship* II 287[17]: None doth so well but some may it amende. See **M233.**

D284 So **Does** that so may
c1450 *Douce MS.52* 54.111: So does, that so may. **c1450** *Rylands MS.394* 104.16.

D285 We must **Do** as we may when we may not do as we would
c1520 *Terens* C6[v][22–3]: As it is comenly told, We must do as we may when we may not as we wold.

D286 Well worth almost **Done**
c1450 *Douce MS.52* 47.34: Welle worth allemoost done. Res bene laudatur, cum ferme perficatur.

D287 What is **Done** may not be undone (*varied*)
a1300 *Richard* 122.807–8: Sere, let be that thought! Now it is don it helpes nought. **1369** Chaucer *BD* 708: For that ys doon ys not to come, **c1380** *HF* 361: But that is don, is not to done. **c1440** Charles of Orleans 133.3974: But hit is doon not undoon now. **c1450** *Ponthus* 107.1–2: The thynges that be doone may not be undoone. **a1470** Malory II 745.32–3: And a thynge, sir, be done, hit can nat be undone. **a1500** Medwall *Nature* H3[v][5]: A thyng don can not be called agayn. **c1500** *Melusine* 333.5–6: This that is doo may be none otherwyse. **1523** Berners *Froissart* III 17[25]: But sithe it is done it can nat be undone agayne. **1546** Heywood *D* 37.83: Thinges doone can not be undoone, **1556** *Spider* 342[22]: This thing once done, can never be undoone. Apperson 468, 625; *Oxford* 154; Robbins-Cutler 3897.5; Smith 74; Taylor and Whiting 104; Tilley T200; Whiting *Drama* 41, 50, 78, *Scots* I 159. See **D138, H134, K96, P45, T198.**

D288 In **Dock** out nettle (*varied*)
c1385 Chaucer *TC* iv 461: Nettle in, dok out, now this, now that, Pandare. **c1385** Usk 13.166–7: I have not played raket, "nettil in, docke out," and with the wethercocke waved. **1533** More *Confutacion* 809 D[3–4]: Thus playe in and out, like, in docke out netle. **1546** Heywood *D* 62.104. Apperson 326; *Oxford* 318; Skeat 187; Tilley D421–2.

D289 His **Doctrine** was according to his works
c1450 Capgrave *Lives* 69.7–8: The man tawt no-thing but that he ded, for in al his lyf his doctrine was accordyng to his werkys, **a1464** *Chronicle* 70[8–9]: Ther went a proverb of him (*Origen*) in that lond,—"His doctrine was lich his lyf." See **D282, E127, L107, 463.**

D290 Daw (*fool*) **Doddypoll**
1402 *Daw Topias* (*Jack*) 99[7–8]: And yit, Dawe Dotypolle. **c1425** Hoccleve *Jonathas* 217.49: O lewde dotepol straw for his wit! **a1460** *Towneley Plays* 173.231: Ffy, dotty-pols. Apperson 156; NED Doddypoll; *Oxford* 358; Tilley D429.

D291 As dumb and deaf as a doted (*stupid*) **Doe**
a1425 *Chester Plays* II 288.195: Dumbe and deafe as a doted doe.

D292 As dunned (*dun*) as a **Doe**
a1400 *Eglamour* 18.260–1: Twa gud grewhoundis: Are donnede als any doo.

D293 As swift as the (a) **Doe**
a1425 *Chester Plays* I 202.434: For I am swifter then is the doe. **a1475** *Mergarete* 239.390: Som are swyfter than a do.

D294 As wild and wanton as (a) **Doe**
1509 Barclay *Ship* I 63[18]: More wylde and wanton than . . . do. Whiting *Ballad* 27.

D295 To dance like any (a) **Doe**
c1380 *Pearl* 13.345: For thogh thou daunce as any do. **a1450** *Castle* 82.188: I dawnse doun, as a doo, be dalys ful derne.

D296 To go like a **Doe**
1436 *Libelle* 15.292: They wente lyke as a doo.

D297 To trip like a **Doe**
a1500 *Coventry Plays* 28.816: And then wyll I for fayne trypp lyke a doe. Tilley D431.

Dog, see **Hound**

D298 After the old **Dog** the young whelp barks
a1471 Ashby *Policy* 32.615: Aftur the oolde dogge the yonge whelpe barkes. Apperson 158:19. See **B14, C347, S216.**

D299 As chaste as (a) **Dog** at bitchwatch
1519 Horman *Vulgaria* 104[16]: He is as chaste as dogge at bytchewatche.

D300 As dear as a **Dog** that lies in a ditch
c1380 *Cleanness* 65.1791–2: That watz do doghty that day and drank of the vessayl; Now is a dogge also dere that in a dych lygges.

D301 As fast as a **Dog** will lick a dish
1546 Heywood *D* 80.22: She will lie as fast as a dogge will licke a dishe. Apperson 362; *Oxford* 192; Tilley D478.

D302 As foul as a **Dog** (hound)
c1390 *Talkyng* 14.17–8: Whi nam I hunted with hem foule as a dogge. **a1500** *Becket III* 264.91: Ne that sche scholde among cristis men fouler than a hound helden be.

D303 (As low as) a **Dog** for the bow
c1395 Chaucer *CT* III[D] 1369–71: For in this world nys dogge for the bowe That kan an hurt deer from an hool yknowe Bet than this somnour knew a sly lecchour, IV[E] 2013–4: And eek to Januarie he gooth as lowe As evere dide a dogge for the bowe. **a1420** Lydgate *Troy* I 95.2801–2: That thei (*old women*) in love alle the sleightes knowe; And sche was made as dogge for the bowe. MED boue n. (1) 1(d); Tilley D437.

D304 As weary as **Dog** of the bow
c1515 Barclay *Eclogues* 82.800: Till thou be all (?as) wery as dogge of the bowe. Whiting *Drama* 271, 310:95. Cf. Taylor and Whiting 105–6.

D305 At every **Dog's** bark seem not to awake
1546 Heywood *D* 73.104: At every dogs barke, seeme not to awake. Apperson 158; *Oxford* 152; Tilley D525; Whiting *Scots* I 160.

D306 A **Dog** has a day
1546 Heywood *D* 47.185: A dog hath a daie. Apperson 159; *Oxford* 151; Taylor and Whiting 106; Tilley D464; Whiting *Drama* 43, 131.

D307 The **Dog** is in the well
c1325 *A levedy a(n)d my love* in *Rel. Ant.* II 19[2]: The doge is in the welle. MED dogge 3; Tilley D504.

D308 The **Dog** looks over toward Lincoln and little sees thereof
c1383 Wyclif *Vita Sacerdotum* in *SEW* III 236[32–5]: Somme men seyn that pouder of temporale godes makes these freris to owverloke tho lawe of hor God, as dogge lokes ofer towarde Lincolne, and litel sees theroff. See **D212.**

D309 A (gentle) **Dog** (hound) will bark (snarl) ere he bite
c1450 *Consail and Teiching* 70.162: For gentill hund gyrnis or he byt. **1549** Heywood *D* 87.233: A dog will barke er he bite. Apperson 158:29; *Oxford* 152; Tilley D461. See **B323.**

D310 Hungry **Dogs** will eat dirty puddings
1546 Heywood *D* 27.52: Hungry dogges will eate durty puddyngs. Apperson 319; *Oxford* 310–1; Taylor and Whiting 106; Tilley D538.

D311 It becomes not a **Dog** to bear a saddle
1492 *Salomon and Marcolphus* 12[20–1]: It becomyth not a dogge to bere a sadyll. See **C501.**

D312 It is a poor **Dog** that is not worth the whistling
1546 Heywood *D* 52.365–6: And it is . . . A poore dogge, that is not woorth the whystlyng. Apperson 160; *Oxford* 510; Tilley D488.

D313 It is hard to make an old **Dog** stoop
1549 Heywood *D* 87.235: But it is harde to make an olde dog stoupe. Apperson 160; Jente 576; *Oxford* 645: Teach; Tilley D489. See **H513, 570, T129.**

D314 Not help more than a **Dog** whelp
c1400 *Laud Troy* I 293.9925–6: At this nede may he not helpe No more then may a dogge whelpe.

D315 Not praise (worth) a rotten **Dog**

c1500 *Melusine* 285.36–286.1: Nother thou nor thy god I preyse not a rotyn dogge.

D316 An old **Dog** bites sore
1546 Heywood *D* 78.23–5: It is saide of olde, an olde dog byteth sore. But by God, tholde bitche biteth sorer and more. And not with teeth (she hath none) but with hir toung. Apperson 157–8; *Oxford* 470; Tilley D499.

D317 A quick (*live*) **Dog** (hound) is better than a dead lion
c1390 *Proverbes of diverse profetes* 534.189–92: Better is a quik and an hol hounde Then a ded lyon liggyng in grounde, And better is povert with godnes Then richesse with wikkednes. **c1390** *Think on Yesterday* in Brown *Lyrics XIV* 145.73–8: Salamon seide in his poysi, He holdeth wel betere with an hounde That is lykyng and Joly, And of seknesse hol and sounde, Then be a Leon, though he ly Cold and ded uppon the grounde. **c1395** *WBible* Ecclesiastes ix 4: Betere is a quik dogge than a deed lioun. Apperson 376; *Oxford* 378; Taylor and Whiting 105; Tilley D495. See **F445.**

D318 To accord like **Dogs** in a market
c1449 Pecock *Repressor* I 85–6: And men schulden accorde to gidere in keping her service to God, as doggis doon in a market, whanne ech of hem terith otheris coot. Cf. Tilley T643. See **B187.**

D319 To be unable to give a **Dog** a loaf
1546 Heywood *D* 83.112–3: Whiche shall bryng us shortly to be unable, To geve a dog a loaf, as I have oft saide. Cf. Tilley P193.

D320 To beguile an old **Dog**
c1475 Henryson *Fables* 70.2009: It is ane auld Dog, doutles, that thow begylis. Whiting *Scots* I 160. Cf. Jente 417. See **B308.**

D321 To die like a **Dog** (hound)
c1300 *Beves* 74.12: To juge a knyght to houndys dedd, cf. 72 M 1252: a doggis dede. **c1350** *Octavian (NL)* 113.731: Als dogges thane salle thay dy. **a1393** Gower *CA* II 180.1858: That lich an hound he scholde die, 212.3037: Thi deth was to the houndes like. **a1400** *Siege of Jerusalem* 44.782: Yif ye as dogges wol dey. **a1425** *Lollard Chronicle of the Papacy JEGP* 41(1942) 182.216: Thu schalt die as a dogge, 192.531. **a1464** Capgrave *Chronicle* 169[28]. **c1475** *Ludus Coventriae* 203.112: But he xal dye lyke a dogge whelpe. **1481** Caxton *Godeffroy* 203.38–9: Dyeng and languysshyng for hongre lyke as other houndes. *Oxford* 144; Taylor and Whiting 107; Tilley D509; Whiting *Scots* I 159–60.

D322 To draw one forth as a **Dog**
a1400 *Destruction of Troy* 65.1970: And drawen as a dog and to dethe broght. **c1450** Capgrave *Katharine* 343.177: Drawe hem foorth as doggis on-to the place.

D323 To drive one as **Dog** (out of mill-house)
c1300 *Havelok* 65.1966–7: And drive hem ut, thei he weren crus, So dogges ut of milne-hous. **a1325** *On Consistory Courts* in Böddeker 112.82: Ase dogge y am dryve.

D324 To fare like **Dogs** in a poke
a1400 *De Pseudo-Freris* in Wyclif *EW* 319[6–8]: And thus thei faren ofte as don doggis in a poke; oon drawith forth an-other agen. **a1400** Wyclif *Sermons* II 358[2–5]: For than shulde pees be in the Chirche withouten strif of doggis in a poke. Anticrist hath put diverse doggis in the poke of his obedience; and thei grutchen agens this, for it is so unkyndely. Apperson 161:84; Skeat 301. See **P190.**

D325 To gape like **Dogs** for a bone
1503 More *Early Poems* [11] D[3]: And gape therefore, as dogges doe for the bone. **1509** Barclay *Ship* II 93[23]: Gapynge as it were dogges for a bone.

D326 To have as much pity as a **Dog**
a1500 *Cock* 2[30]: He had as moche pyte as a dogge.

D327 To help a **Dog** over a stile
1546 Heywood *D* 48.248–9: As good a deede, As it is to helpe a dogge over a style. Apperson 349; *Oxford* 291; Tilley D479.

D328 To howl like a **Dog**
a1438 Kempe 105.23: Sche howlyd as it (had) ben a dogge. **a1533** Berners *Huon* 205.30–1: The paynyms . . . cryenge and howlyng lyke dogges.

D329 To lie (in field, *etc.*) like a **Dog** (hound) (*varied*)
c1300 *Havelok* 63.1921–2: Ilc on other wirwed lay Als it were dogges that weren henged. **c1330** *Praise of Women* 296.227–9: And as a dogge in feld to ly, Wolves and houndes to don his masse Bi night. **c1385** Chaucer *TC* iv 626: Shulle in a strete as dogges liggen dede. **c1400** *Laud Troy* II 362.12290: And ligge In dikes as dede houndes. **c1420** Wyntoun III 263.729–30: And outhe the erde but sepulture As a doge lay that emperoure.

D330 To live like a **Dog** (hound)
a1376 *Piers* A v 98: Thus I live loveles, lyk a luther dogge. **c1390** *Psalterium b. Mariae* 78.652: Princis lyvynge as dogges. **a1500** *How the Plowman* in Hazlitt *EPP* I 211.48: Or elles thou

lyvest as an hounde. Taylor and Whiting 107–8; Whiting *Drama* 342:504.

D331 To shoot on one like **Dog** on bear (*etc.*) (A number of single quotations are brought together here)
c1300 *Havelok* 60.1838–9: And shoten on him, so don on bere Dogges, that wolden him to-tere. **a1325** *Cursor* II 784.13658–9: Wit this thai scott (F: shotte; T: huntid) him als a dog Right ute o thair synagog. **c1395** *Pierce* 14.357: And deleth in devynitie as dogges doth bones. **c1420** Wyntoun III 479–81.3748–9: Rufyn, me thynk the Lyk a keyn (*var.* bund) doge that ay bayis (*var.* brayis). **1460** Paston III 241[25–6]: The false chayler that kepeth me entretethe me worse thanne it weere a dogge. **c1500** *Lyfe of Roberte* 236.449–50: Yt was hys pleasure to eate fleshe on the frydaye; A dogge dyd faste as well as he. **c1500** *Wife Lapped* 214.848: And like a dog she rated him than. **1509** Barclay *Ship* I 182[11]: Narrynge (*snarling*) with thyselfe lyke as a dogge doth barke. **1523** Berners *Froissart* III 374[19–20]: Spared no more to slee them than they had ben dogges, 395[22–3], **a1533** *Arthur* 475[19–20]: They . . . bet them downe lyke dogges, *Huon* 488.7–8: Thou lyest worse than a dogge.

D332 Two **Dogs** are stronger to take a wolf than a dog alone
1483 Caxton *Cato* D8^{v}[11–2]: For two dogges be stronger for to take a wulf thenne one dogge allone. See **T548.**

D333 Two **Dogs** on one bone were overmuch (*varied*)
c1500 *Lady of Pite* in *MLR* 49(1954) 292.56: Ffor hit were overmoche, ii dogges on o boon. **a1500** *To Yow, Mastres* in *Rawlinson MS. C 813* 382.6–8: For lyttle rest ys ther or non, By exsperyense, as ytt doethe shewe, Hwer many dogges be att on bone, 16, 24, *etc.* Tilley D544. See **L108.**

D334 Two **Dogs** (hounds) strive for a bone and the third (a kite) carries it away
c1385 Chaucer *CT* I[A] 1177–80: We stryve as dide the houndes for the boon; They foughte al day, and yet hir part was noon. Ther cam a kyte, whil that they were so wrothe, And baar awey the boon bitwixe hem bothe. **1534** More *Comforte* 1141 CD: And now strive there twayne for us, our Lorde send the grace, that the third dog cary not away the bone from them both. Apperson 653–4; *Oxford* 679; Tilley D545; Whiting *Drama* 271.

D335 (When) **Dogs** brawl at the door all set on the sorry hound
a1500 *Colkelbie* 286.135–6: Ffor brawle doggis at the dure All settis on the sory hound. See **C638.**

D336 No more trust than in a **Dog's Tail**
a1464 Capgrave *Chronicle* 281[11–2]: It was no more trost to the Pope writing than to a dogge tail (*var.* to a dogge's tail waggyng).

D337 **Dole** (*grief*) may make no amending
c1420 Wyntoun VI 166.5829–30: Bot dule mycht mak nane amending As of his deid, 167.6025–6: Bot playnt, na duyl, na yit menynge Micht helpe noucht. Whiting *Scots* I 160. See **G455, L52, M729, R81, S514.**

D338 **Dole** should be overpassed where there is no remedy
a1500 *Partenay* 29.657–8: A man shold shortly the dole overpas, When remedy non may be in the cas. See **D341.**

D339 His **Dole** (*act of charity*) is soon done
1546 Heywood *D* 47.208: His dole is soone doone.

D340 There is no **Dole** but is forgotten
c1505 Watson *Valentine* 37.3–4: For there is no dole but that it is forgotten by processe. See **B19, S517, 798.**

D341 Where there is great **Dole** without redeeming, to name it is but eking of pain
c1470 *Wallace* 116.195–6: Quhar gret dulle is, bot rademyng agayne, Newyn off it is bot ekyng of payne. See **D338.**

D342 **Doom** (cursing) returns to one's own door (*varied*)
c1175 *Poema Morale* 178.124: Er deth and dom come to his dure, he mai him sore adreden. **a1300** *Proverbs of Alfred* 79 J 80–1: And everuyches monnes dom, To his owere dure churreth. **c1300** *Casus de Jordano de Vavasore* in *Bracton de Legibus et Consuetudinibus Angliæ*, ed. G. E. Woodbine (New Haven, 1915) I 83.n^{2}: Et unde senex dixit, "Oft owen dome ac (*for* at) owen durre charreth." **c1390** Chaucer *CT* X[I] 620: And ofte tyme swich cursynge wrongfully retorneth agayn to hym that curseth, as a bryd that retorneth agayn to his owene nest. **c1400** *Of Dominion* in Wyclif *EW* 288[11–2]: Drede we nought this thondir (*of curses*), for it turneth agen and cursith the welle that it come fro. Apperson 130; *Oxford* 124–5; Taylor and Whiting 88; Tilley C924. See **D22, F49, H374, J79, S345, T448, W610.**

D343 **Doom** (*judgment*) spares not clerk nor knight
c1300 *Havelok* 95.2812–3: Lokes that ye demen him riht, For dom ne spareth clerk ne kniht.

D344 Hasty **Dooms** are oft meint (*mixed*) with wrong (*varied*)
c1408 Lydgate *Reson* 88.3319–20: And hasty domys ever among Ben oft(e) sithe meynt with wrong, **a1422** *Life* 629.594–5: For sodem dom meynt with ignoraunce, Hathe a long tayle sewyng of repentaunce. See **D143, N136.**

D345 A just **Doom** accepts (*favors*) no person
c1395 *WBible* Exodus xxiii 3 *gloss:* For just doom accepteth no person. See **G216.**

D346 Till **Doomsday**
c1200 Orm II 262.17681–2: Off all thatt follc thatt fra thiss dayy Till Domess dayy shall wurrthenn. **a1300** *Alisaunder* 331.6235–6: That nevere in-tyl domesday There ne shal shippe out passe. **a1338** Mannyng *Chronicle* A I 306.8734: That hit myght laste til Domesday. MED domes-dai 1(b); NED Doomsday 1b. See **D45.**

D347 As dumb as a **Door**
a1376 *Piers* A xi 94: And as doumbe as a dore. **a1450** *York Plays* 322.65: Bot domme as a dore gon he dwell. Apperson 170.

D348 At a wrong **Door**
1546 Heywood *D* 24.55: Ye deale this dole (quoth I) out at a wrong dur, **1555** *E* 158.75: Thou begst at wrong doore. Apperson 162: Dole. See **M292.**

D349 Here is the **Door,** here (there) is the way
c1475 *Mankind* 6.154: Here ys the dore, her ys the wey! **1546** Heywood *D* 46.167: Here is the doore, and there is the wey. Apperson 299; *Oxford* 154; Tilley D556.

D350 To adventure to the **Door**
c1350 *Gamelyn* 661.666: I wil auntre to the dore that I hadde mete. W. W. Skeat *Complete Works of Geoffrey Chaucer* V(1894) 487: "Spoken proverbially, there being no door in the wood."

D351 To go from **Door** to midden (*i.e.,* ?a slight distance, ?from good to bad)
a1460 *Towneley Plays* 34.375–6: I will not, for thi bydyng, Go from doore to mydyng.

D352 As dead (dumb) as a **Doornail** (doortree)
a1375 *William* 29.628: I am ded as dore-nail, 110.3396. **a1376** *Piers* A i 161: And ded as a dore-nayl, **c1378** B i 185: dore-tre. **a1400** *Alexander C* 246.4747: Dom as a dore-nayle and defe was he bathe. **a1400** *Siege of Jerusalem* 62.1074. **a1400** *Three Ages* 65. **c1405** *Mum* 75.1646. **1533** More *Debellacyon* 1014 B[15–6]: As dead as ever was dore nayle. Apperson 137; *Oxford* 131; Skeat 105; Taylor and Whiting 109–10; Tilley D567.

D353 To sleep like a **Dormouse**
c1450 Idley 95.866–7: Be stronge in herte, bow not as a wande, Or as a dormoyse that al day slepeth. **1523** Skelton *Garlande* I 411.1248: *Dormiat in pace,* lyke a dormows! Svartengren 169; Tilley D568; Whiting *NC* 400.

D354 As drunk as a **Dossil** (*spigot*)
a1450 *Three Middle English Sermons* 32.344–5: Ate laste cumth hom as drunke as a dosel. Cf. Chaucer *CT* III[D] 1931.

D355 He is a **Dote** (*fool*) who says all his will when he should be still
a1300 *Proverbs of Alfred* 119 J 461–3: For-thi ich holde him for (a) dote, That sayth al his wille, Thanne he scholde beon stille. See **F444.**

D356 Of one **Doubt** (*fear*) to make twain
1509 Barclay *Ship* I 167[12]: And of one doute, thou fole, thou makest twayne. See **S513.**

Dove, see **Culver**

D357 As chaste as a **Dove**
c1450 *Secrete of Secretes* 35.18: Chaste as a dowve.

D358 As edmod (*humble*) as **Dove**
a1200 *Trinity College Homilies* 49[25]: Buth admode alse duve.

D359 As meek as (the, any, a) **Dove**
c1300 *Passion of St. Paul* in Horstmann *Legenden 1881* 77.48: For meke he was als the doufe is. **a1400** Wyclif *Sermons* I 78[14]: Mekenesse of the dowfe. **c1408** Lydgate *Reson* 141.5368: Symple and as dovwe meke, 157.5987: Of porte as any dowve meke. **1512** Copland *Helyas* A7ʳ[19–20]: She is meke as a douve. **a1533** Berners *Arthur* 62[22]: As meke as a dove. Taylor and Whiting 110. Cf. Tilley D573.

D360 As seemly and demure as a **Dove**
a1470 Malory II 854.19: Semely and demure as a dove.

D361 As simple as (a) **Dove**
a1400 ?Chaucer *Rom. A* 1219: And she was symple as dowve on tree. **c1400** *Pepysian Gospel* 30.15: Symple as a douve. **c1425** *St. Mary Oignies* 138.3: a. **1456** Hay *Law* 30.17: a. **1483** Caxton *Golden Legende* 44ᵛ[1.30]: a. Tilley D572. See **A44.**

D362 As sweet as **Dove**'s eye
a1325 *Cursor* II 538.9361: Als douves eie hir lok es suete.

D363 As white as a **Dove**
c1440 *Prose Alexander* 107.33: Grete fewles white als doufes. **1492** *Salomon and Marcolphus* 12[5]: Is she whyte as a dove. Whiting *NC* 400.

D364 The **Dove** (culver) is without (has no) gall
c1000 Aelfric *Homilies* I 584[34–5]: Culfre is bilewiten nyten, and fram geallan biternysse ælfremed, II 44[23–5]: We rædað on bocum be ðære culfran gecynde, þæt heo is . . . buton geallan, 46[3]: Seo culfre is buton geallan. **a1200** *Ancrene* 151.27: Habbe culvre cunde, that is with ute galle. **c1200** Orm I 41.1258–9: Forr cullfre iss milde, and meoc, and swet, And all withthutenn galle, cf. 1252–3. **a1250** *Bestiary* 25.789: (*The dove*) ne haveth in hire no galle. **c1340** Rolle *Psalter* 497 (Song of Hezekiah 7): .I. sall thynke as dofe, that is, mekly, withouten gall of yre and wickidnes. **a1398**(1495) Bartholomaeus-Trevisa k3v[1.23–6]: And some fowles have galles pryvely hydde in a gutte. As culvours or douves and water crowes and swallowes, A8r[2.4–5]: A culuovre hathe no galle. **a1400** *A Jhū thow sched thi blode* in *MLR* 35(1940) 324.79–80: Jhū thu sofred mekell kare, It semid well thou had na gall. **a1400** *Stanzaic Life* 328.9699: In hyr wontes galle, 9709–10: The secund kynde the dowfe has, Ho has no bytternes of galle. **c1408** Lydgate *Reson* 178.6796–7: They be so ful of pacience, And as a dowve they ha no galle, **a1422** *Life* 654.240–3: But like a dove . . . Wantynge also the galle of envye, **a1449** *Ryme* in *MP* II 793.33: To have a galle, and be clepid a douffe. **1456** Hay *Law* 30.17: Thai war symple as a dow but gall. **1483** Caxton *Golden Legende* 31r[1–2]: The douve . . . hath noo galle, 93r[2.14–5]: The douve . . . is . . . symple and wythout galle. **a1500** *Miroure of Mans Salvacionne* 163[16]: Swete doufe without galle. Tilley D574; Whiting *Ballad* 35. See **C595.**

D365 To beck (*nod*) like a **Dove**
c1390 Chaucer *CT* VI[C] 396–7: And est and west upon the peple I bekke, As dooth a dowve sittynge on a berne.

D366 To kiss like **Doves**
a1400 ?Chaucer *Rom. A* 1297–8: But men myght seen hem kisse there, As it two yonge dowves were.

D367 To mourn like (a) **Dove**
a1400 *Stanzaic Life* 328.9707: We mournen as dowfe ay. Cf. Whiting *NC* 400: mournful.

D368 As full of holes as a **Dovehouse**
c1475 *Wisdom* 72.1110: My body full of holys, as a dove-hows.

D369 From **Dover** to Durham (Humber)
a1338 Mannyng *Chronicle B* II 301[22]: Tho banerettis ilkone fro Dover to Durham ware. **a1500** *Piers of Fullham* 10.226: Ffor all the leches from dovyr and unto humbre. See **B260, T545.**

D370 None so cunning between **Dover** and Calais
a1500 *Croxton Sacrament* in Waterhouse 73.509–12: For, now ye ar cum, I dare well saye Betwyn Dovyr and Calyce the ryght wey Dwelleth non so cunnyng, by my fey, In my judgyment.

D371 To make **Downs** and dales and do marvels
1340 *Ayenbite* 59[23–4]: Ich wille maki the helles and the danes. **c1400** *Vices and Virtues* 57.4–5: I wole make dounes and dales and do mervailes. (A boast.)

D372 **Draff** (*swill*) is good enough for swine
c1525 ?Heywood *Gentylnes* 121.932: Drafte is good inough for swyne. Apperson 163; *Oxford* 156; Tilley D580.

D373 **Draff** is my errand but drink I will
c1475 *Rawlinson MS. D 328* 122.53: Draffe ys my erante but drynke y woll. **1546** Heywood *D* 42.39–40: Iwys I know, or any more be tolde, That draffe is your errand, but drinke ye wolde. Apperson 164; *Oxford* 156; Tilley D581.

D374 To write the **Draff** (*chaff*) of stories and forget the corn
c1395 Chaucer *LGW* G 311–2: But yit, I seye, what eyleth the to wryte The draf of storyes and forgete the corn? See **C428.**

D375 Why should one sow **Draff** when he may sow wheat?
c1390 Chaucer *CT* X[I] 35–6: Why sholde I sowen draf out of my fest, Whan I may sowen whete, if that me lest?

D376 To lie like a **Draffsack**
c1390 Chaucer *CT* I[A] 4206: And I lye as a draf-sak in my bed.

D377 As fierce as a **Dragon**
a1508 Dunbar *Tretis* 93.342: That I to flyte wes als fers as a fell dragoun. Whiting *Scots* I 161.

D378 As full of venom as any **Dragon**
a1400 *Firumbras* 26.760: And ful of venym as any dragoun.

D379 As wood (*mad*) as **Dragon**

a1338 Mannyng *Chronicle A* II 478.13795–8: Was nevere . . . dragoun . . . That was so wod, beste to byte, As Wawayn was.

D380 To be both **Dragons** and doves
a1508 Dunbar *Tretis* 91.263: Be dragonis baith and dowis ay in double forme. See **A44.**

D381 To fight (*etc.*) like a **Dragon** (A number of single quotations are brought together here)
a1338 Mannyng *Chronicle B* I 183[16]: And fauht as a dragon. **c1400** *Laud Troy* I 153.5191: He strok (*went*) forth as a dragoun. **c1500** *Lyfe of Roberte* 237.482: And rode oute of the wodde, lyke a wylde dragon.

D382 As derf (*bold*) as the **Drake** (*dragon*)
a1400 *Le Morte A.* 78.2607: And derfe of drede as is the drake.

D383 To burn like a **Drake**
c1330 *Tars* 43 A 428–9: Develen thre, And ich brent as a drake, **c1390** 43 V 401–2: Develes thre, Al brennyng as a drake.

D384 To drive (*rush*) in as a **Drake**
a1450 *Castle* 83.197: As devyl dowty, in draf as a drake.

D385 **Dread** first found (*invented*) gods
c1385 Chaucer *TC* iv 1408: Eke drede fond first goddes, I suppose. **a1464** Capgrave *Chronicle* 22[5–9]: This witnesseth the Poete (*?Petronius*), where he seith,—"Primos in orbe Deos fecit inesse timor." Thus he meneth,—"The first goddis that were, thei come in be dreed." See Robinson's note, p. 831. Walther III 952.22396.

D386 **Dread** opens the ears
c1340 Rolle *Psalter* 228 (65.15): For drede oppyns the eren.

D387 **Dreams** are false (*varied*)
a1376 *Piers* A viii 135–6: Bote Catoun construweth hit nay an canonistres bothe, And siggen bi hem-selven *sompnia ne cures,* **a1387** C x 302–3: Ac men setten nat by songewarie, men seen hit ofte faile, Caton counteth hit at nouht and canonistres at lasse. **c1385** Chaucer *TC* v 1276–7: Have I nat seyd er this, That dremes many a maner man bigile? **c1390** *CT* VII 2940–1[B4130–1]: Lo Catoun, which that was so wys a man, Seyde he nat thus, "Ne do no fors of dremes?" **a1400** *Cato* (*Copenhagen*) A7v[13]: To metynggis truste thou no kyn thyng. **a1440** Burgh *Cato* 318.599: Dreede no dremys, so seithe Deutronomy. **c1450** *Epistle of Othea* 117.21: To trust myche in dremes is ful gret abusioun. **1501** Douglas *Palice* 48.22: Cry out on dremis, quhilks are not worth ane mite. **1532** Berners *Golden Boke* 353.7690–1: I saye beleve not in dreames, **a1533** *Huon* 521.23: Gyve no fayth nor credence to dremes. Jente 296, 532; Tilley D587. See **S952.**

D388 **Dreams** are true (*varied*)
c1405 *Mum* 52.874–5: For dreme is no dwele by Danyel-is wordes, Though Caton of the contrarye carpe in his bokes. cf. 65.1309ff. **c1440** Charles of Orleans 159.4739–42: And alle be hit that sum folkis say To truste on dremys nys but trifille play, Yet oon may mete the dreme wel yn his sevyn (*for* sweven) As aftirward that shalle bifalle him evyn.

D389 To drink a lither (*evil*) **Drench** (*drink*) (*i.e.,* have ill fortune)
c1300 Robert of Gloucester II 858.296: And evere whanne hi come hii dronke of luthere drenche. **a1500** *Melusine* 308.21–2: For ye shal drynk therfore of an evyl drynk. See **D397.**

D390 He that will keep from **Drenching** (*drowning*) keep from the brink (*shore*)
c1400 *Seven Deadly Sins* in Wyclif *SEW* III 158[20–1]: Ffor he that wil kepe hym fro drenchyng of water, kepe hym fro the brynke for to be siker. Cf. Tilley D623.

D391 The **Dretching** (*prolonging*) of one sin draws in another
c1390 Chaucer *CT* X[I] 1000: And eek the drecchynge of o synne draweth in another.

D392 Evil **Drifts** (*plots*) drive to nought
1513 More *Richard* 39 B[7–8]: Ever at length evil driftes dreve to nought, **1534** *Comforte* 1162 D[12–3]: One subtil drifte driveth an other to nought.

Drink, sb.

D393 A bitter **Drink** heals a fever (*varied*)
c1385 Chaucer *TC* iii 1212–6: O, sooth is seyd, that heled for to be As of a fevre, or other gret siknesse, Men moste drynke, as men may ofte se, Ful bittre drynke; and for to han gladnesse, Men drynken ofte peyne and gret distresse. **a1440** Burgh *Cato* 32.1121–2: For fisik seithe, my child, I the ensure: A bittir drynk the sharpe sekenesse may cure. *Oxford* 47; Tilley M558, P327.

D394 He in whom **Drink** has domination can keep no secret (*varied*)
c1390 Chaucer *CT* VI[C] 560–1: In whom that drynke hath dominacioun He kan no conseil kepe, it is no drede. **a1420** Lydgate *Troy* I 309. 5746–7: For w(h)er as wyn hath domynacioun, No secrenesse may be kepte in mewe. **c1450**

Secrete of Secretes 36.16–7: Make nevir thi messangere of man that is dronkelew, for bi him shalle be seid and told alle that he knowith. *Oxford* 6. See **C632, D425, W360.**

D395 Hot **Drinks** cause fleshly insurrection
a1500 Medwall *Nature* G2r[1–2]: For hote drynkys and delycate refeccyon Causeth flesshely insurreccyon. See **C125.**

D396 Much **Drink** and labor will have rest
c1395 Chaucer *CT* V[F] 347–9: The norice of digestioun, the sleep, Gan on hem wynke and bad hem taken keep That muchel drynke and labour wolde han reste. See **B242.**

D397 To brew someone a **Drink** of woe
a1300 *Richard* 408.6439–40: Anon i wole to hem goo, And brewe hem a drynke of woo. See **B517, 566, D389, 405.**

D398 What is **Drink** without meat?
a1460 *Towneley Plays* 106.194: What is drynk withoute mete? Cf. Tilley H292. See **C622.**

D399 While one wastes **Drink** the drink wastes him
c1523 Barclay *Mirrour* 62[22]: While thou wasteth drinke the drinke wasteth thee. Tilley H292.

Drink, vb.

D400 **Drink** but when you are dry
1513 Douglas *Aeneid* II 149.99: Hant no surfat, drynk bot quhen thou art dry, IV 190.88: Nane ar compellit drynk not bot thai have thryst. Cf. Tilley F147.

D401 **Drink** hot and swallow hot
c1450 *Rylands MS.394* 104.20: Drynke hoot and swolow hoot. Apperson 315: Hot sup; *Oxford* 307; Tilley S997.

D402 **Drink** less and go home by light
c1250 *Hendyng O* 195.24: Drink eft lasse, and go bi lightte hom. Apperson 165; Kneuer 44–5; *Oxford* 157; Schleich 263–4; Singer III 134; Skeat 94.

D403 The more some **Drink** the more they wax dry
1509 Barclay *Ship* I 51[17]: The more that some drynke: the more they wax drye. **1532** Berners *Golden Boke* 332.7009: The more I dranke, the more thyrst I hadde. Apperson 186–7; *Oxford* 177; Tilley D625; Whiting *Scots* I 161. See **M432.**

D404 To **Drink** on the morrow asks drunkenness over even
c1400 *Seven Deadly Sins* in Wyclif *SEW* III 156–7: As glotouns of drinke wil drinke in the morowe, and that, as thei seyn, askes dronkenes owver even.

D405 To **Drink** woe (misease, *etc.*)
c1380 Chaucer *HF* 1879–80: For what I drye, or what I thynke, I wil myselven al hyt drynke, **c1385** *TC* ii 784: Oure wrecche is this, oure owen wo to drynke, iii 1035: But goodly drynketh up al his distresse. **a1400** *Romaunt C* 6807: Such folk drinken gret mysese. MED drinken 2(b). See **D397, S941.**

D406 You have **Drunken** more than you have bled
c1516 Skelton *Magnificence* 9.260: Me semeth that ye have dronken more than ye have bled. Tilley D608.

D407 **Drones** love rest well
c1450 Capgrave *Katharine* 262.21: We sey not of hem but "dranes love weel reste."

D408 To be like a **Drone**
1127 *Peterborough Chronicle* I 258[11–3]: And þær he wunede eall riht swa drane doð on hive. Eall þæt þa beon dragen toward swa frett þa drane and dragað fraward. **1408** Vegetius(1) 10b: Thogh a coward be used to armes . . . Forsothe he is but as a drane in an hyve, and devoureth and etith out the hony (from MED hive). **a1449** Lydgate *Cok* in *MP* II 817.121: Foo unto hevys and enemy is the drane. **a1456** Sellyng *Evidens* 177.24: Thoo wanne I nought, but wastide as a draane.

D409 As many as **Drops** in the sea
c1395 *WBible* Ecclesiasticus xviii 8: The noumbre of the daies of men . . . ben arettid as the dropis of the watir of the see. **1490** Caxton *Arte and Crafte* A3r[8–10]: As many . . . as there ben dropes of water and smalle gravell in the see. **1498** *Doctrynall of deth* (London, de Worde, 1532) B3v[25–6]: As many synnes as there are droppes of water in the see, or cornes of sonde in the worlde. **a1500** *Craft of Deyng* (*Cambridge MS.*) in Lumby *Ratis Raving* 3.82–3. **a1500** *Craft of Dying* in *Yorkshire Writers* II 409[47]. Whiting *Scots* I 161. See **W58.**

D410 As small as **Drops** of rain
a1500 *To the, maist peirlas* in Frank A. Patterson *Middle English Penitential Lyric* (New York, 1911) 90.21–2: Bot also smal as droppis of rane Wan wormys so schill sall al to schow ws.

D411 As thick as **Drops** of rain
a1500 *O dere God, pereles* in Dyboski 52.21–2:

But, as thyke as dropis of rayn, Shall wormes all to-chew(e) us. See **H13, R12.**

D412 Little **Drops** thirl (*pierce*) the flint on which they often fall (*varied*)
a1200 *Ancrene* 114.21–4: Seith job theose wordes, lapides excavant aque et allivione paulatim terra consumitur, lutle dropen thurlith the flint the ofte falleth thron. **c1385** Usk 135.101–2: So ofte falleth the lethy water on the harde rocke, til it have thorow persed it. **c1395** *WBible* Job xiv 19: Watris maken stoonys holowe, and the erthe is wastid litil and litil bi waischyng awey of watir. **a1398**(1495) Bartholomaeus-Trevisa P8^r[1.17–8]: As droppyng of reynes percith a stone. **a1400** Wyclif *Sermons* II 351[1–2]: For the droppe persith the stone not bi oones, but by longe lastinge. **c1400** *Orologium* 336.2–3: For what is softere thanne water, or harder thanne stone? And yit by ofte fallynge and smytynge of water the stone is persede. **c1408** Lydgate *Reson* 181.6917–8: Water that droppeth ever in oon Myneth ful depe in-to A stoon, **a1439** *Fall* I 202–3.106–12: The rounde dropis off the smothe reyn, Which that discende and falle from aloffte On stonys harde, at eye as it is seyn, Perceth ther hardnesse with ther fallyng offte, Al-be in touchyng, water is but soffte, The percyng causid be force nor puissaunce, But off fallyng be long contynuaunce. **c1440** Charles of Orleans 184.5501–2: For men may se the tendir drope of rayne Perse the stoon in fallyng quantite. **c1477** Caxton *Jason* 26.21–3: How well the stone is myned and holowed by contynuell droppyng of water. Apperson 112; *Oxford* 107–8; Skeat 10; Taylor and Whiting 111; Tilley D618; Whiting *Drama* 141, 249, *Scots* II 151. See **R22, S780, W69.**

D413 Of a **Drop** waxes a much (*great*) flood
a1250 *Ancrene* (*Nero*) 32.35–6: And of a drope waxeth amu-che flod and adrencheth the soule. **c1440** *Our daily work* in *Yorkshire Writers* I 317[9–10]: Of a drope and a drope, waxes a mekill flode that drownnes the saule. Cf. Tilley D617. See **C431, L402, S559.**

D414 To distill down like dewy **Drops**
a1449 Lydgate *St. Giles* 373.158–9: Thy wounde open, thy blood distillyng doun As dewy droopys ageyn the sonne sheene.

D415 As dry as **Dross**
a1450 *Castle* 125.1607: Al thi doynge, as dros is drye.

D416 After **Drought** comes dry
c1450 *Douce MS.52* 57.145: After drowyth comyth drye.

D417 After **Drought** comes rain
a1449 Lydgate *Doublenesse* in *MP* II 440.37: After grete drought ther cometh a reyne. **a1500** *Cotton Vespasian MS. A xxv* in *Rel. Ant.* I 323: After droght commyth rayne; After plesur commethe payne; But yet it contynyth nyt so. For after rayne, Commyth drought agayne, And joye after payne and woo. **a1513** Dunbar *All Erdly Joy* 146.19: Wes nevir sic drowth bot anis come rane. **c1516** Skelton *Magnificence* 2.12–3: Howe after a drought there fallyth a showre of rayne, And after a hete oft cometh a stormy colde. Apperson 3; Jente 538; Tilley D621; Whiting *Scots* I 161. See **D426.**

D418 **Drought** never makes dearth of corn
1533 Heywood *Weather* C2[19–20]: And it is sayd, syns afore we were borne, That drought doth never make derth of corne. Apperson 166; *Oxford* 159; Tilley D622.

D419 He that is **Drowned** may no man hang
1506 Barclay *Castell* A8^r[15–6]: This is a worde sayde overall, He that is drowned may no man hange. Apperson 60; *Oxford* 56–7; Taylor and Whiting 39; Tilley B139.

D420 **Drunkenness** breaks what wisdom touches
c1425 Arderne *Fistula* 4.27–9: As seith a wise man, "Ebrietas frangit quicquid sapiencia tangit;" "Dronkenes breketh what-so wisdom toucheth." Walther I 860.6874.

D421 **Drunkenness** excuses no vice
c1485 *Monk of Evesham* 47[2–3]: And as a certen wyse man seith dronkinnes excusith no vise. See **M103, S694.**

D422 **Drunkenness** exiles wit
1464 Hardyng 73[1–3]: Dronkennes . . . exiled witte out of his brayn doubteles. Cf. Smith 76. See **W360.**

D423 Though **Drunkenness** be forbidden, one shall not always be drinkless (*varied*)
c1385 Chaucer *TC* ii 716–8: For though a man forbede drokenesse, He naught forbet that every creature Be drynkeles for alwey. **c1385** Usk 132.144–5: For though dronkennesse be forboden, men shul not alway ben drinklesse. Cf. Burton Stevenson *Home Book of Proverbs, Maxims and Familiar Phrases* (New York, 1948) 635.9.

D424 Where **Drunkenness** is guide each virtue is set aside
a1430 Lydgate *Pilgrimage* 353.13021–2: Ffor, wher dronkeness ys guyde, Ech vertu ys set asyde.

D425 Where **Drunkenness** reigns there is nothing secret (*varied*)
c1000 Aelfric *Homilies* I 604[25–6]: Salomon cwæð, "Ne bið nan ðing digle þær ðær druncennys rixað." **a1325** *Cursor* II 418.7229–30: Or drunkennes oft mai bitide Dos man his consail to un-hide. **c1390** Chaucer *CT* II[B] 776–7: Ther dronkenesse regneth in any route, Ther is no conseil hyd, withouten doute, VI[C] 558–61: For dronkenesse is verray sepulture Of mannes wit and his discrecioun. In whom that drynke hath dominacioun He kan no conseil kepe, it is no drede, VII 1193–4[B2383–4]: Thou shalt also eschue the conseiling of folk that been dronkelewe, for they ne kan no conseil hyde. For Salomon seith, "Ther is no privetee ther as regneth dronkenesse." **c1395** *WBible* Proverbs xxxi 4: A! Lamuel, nyle thou give wyn to kingis; for no pryvete is, where drunkenesse regneth. **a1425** *Cursor* III 1545 CG 27886: It (*drunkenness*) mase oft kounsail to be talde. Apperson 168; *Oxford* 602; Skeat 244. Cf. Smith 46. See **D394, W360.**

D426 After **Dry** comes wet and after wet comes dry
c1475 *Rawlinson MS. D 328* 123.62: After dry comyth wete and after wete comyth dry. See **D417.**

D427 Drink but with the **Duck**
a1376 *Piers* A v 58: Drinken bote with the doke and dynen but ones. Apperson 165; *Oxford* 157. See **W353.**

D428 To draw aside as **Duck** from falcon
c1378 *Piers* B xvii 61–2: Ac whan he hadde sighte of that segge, a-syde he gan hym drawe, Dredfully, by this day! as duk doth fram the faucoun.

D429 To milk **Ducks**
a1500 Greene *Carols* 413.3: "Wher hast thou be, thow sory ladde?" "Milked dukkes, my moder badde." (Teacher and tardy schoolboy.) Cf. Whiting *NC* 417: Grandmother.

D430 To swim as does the **Duck** after the drake
c1390 Chaucer *CT* I [A] 3575–6: Thanne shaltou swymme as myrie, I undertake, As dooth the whyte doke after hire drake.

D431 Like a **Duke?** Like a duck
1546 Heywood *D* 87–8.258–60: Then every daie to fare lyke a duke with thee. Lyke a duke, lyke a duck (quoth she) thou shalt fare, Except thou wilt spare, more than thou dost yet spare. *Oxford* 368; Tilley D636.

D432 To be at **Dulcarnon**
c1385 Chaucer *TC* iii 930–1: I am, til God me bettre mynde sende, At dulcarnoun, right at my wittes ende. Apperson 170; *Oxford* 161; Tilley D638.

D433 To drink **Dumb-seed**
c1405 *Mum* 51.839: And hath y-drunke dumseede, and dar not be seye. MED domb 7(b).

D434 **Dun** is in the mire
c1390 Chaucer *CT* IX[H] 5: And seyde, "Sires, what! Dun is in the myre!" **c1412** Hoccleve *Regement* 86.2384. **c1450** Capgrave *Katharine* 143.1046–7: Ffor as wyth me, dun is in the myre, She hath me stoyned and brought me to a bay. **c1450** *Duke of Suffolk* in Wright *Political Poems* II 224[9]: And alle gooth bacwarde, and Donne is in the myre. **a1460** *Towneley Plays* 373.204–5: Bot if this draght be well drawen don is in the myre. **1523** Skelton *Garlande* I 418.1433: Dun is in the myre, dame, reche me my spur. Apperson 170; *Oxford* 161–2; Skeat 289; Tilley D643.

D435 As dead as the **Dung**
a1425 *Chester Plays* II 435.235: Why were I not dead as is the donge?

D436 As foul as any **Dung**
c1390 *Hou a man schal lyve parfytly* in *Vernon* I 225.127–8: As to thi bodi : foulore hit is Then ever was eny donge.

D437 The **Dung** of a calf does not stink long
1492 *Salomon and Marcolphus* 8[15–6]: The dung of a calf stynkyth not longe.

D438 To forsee (*despise*) as **Dung**
897 Alfred *Boethius* 104.8–9: Ac licgað forsewe(ne) swa (swa) miox under fletune. **c1000** Aelfric *Lives* I 38.241: Middan-eardlice lustas swa swa meox forseah, 198.37–8: And heo þæt eall forseah On meoxes gelicnysse þe lið under fotum. **1447** Bokenham 100.3637: And rychesse as dung she dede despyse, 113.4125–6: And ful precyous ornamentys wyth hym he broht, Wych of Anneys as dung were set at noht, 280.10299–300: I as dung now despyse Al temporal thingis. Svartengren 140.

D439 As vile as a **Dunghill**
c1390 *Mirror of St. Edmund* in *Yorkshire Writers* I 242[1]: Thou art vilore then a dongehul.

D440 The **Dunmow** flitch
a1376 *Piers* A x 188–90: Thaugh thei don hem to Donmowe, but the devel helpe To folewen aftur the flucchen, fecche thei hit nevere; Bote yif thei bothe ben forswore, that bacoun thei

tyne. **c1395** Chaucer *CT* III[D] 217–8: The bacon was nat fet for hem, I trowe, That som men han in Essex at Dunmowe. **a1426** Lydgate *Mumming at Hertford* in *MP* II 680.186–7: I trowe the bakoun was never of hem fette, Awaye at Dounmowe in the Pryorye. **c1450** Idley 143.2197–2217: I can fynde no man now that will enquere The perfite weies unto Dumnowe, Ffor they repent them withyn a yere And many withyn a weke, as somme trowe. That causeth the waies be roughe and overgrowe That no man may fynde path ne gappe—The world is turned into anothir shappe. Beif and moten woll serve well ynowe, And to goo so ferre for a litell bacon flycche, And hath longe hanged and is resty and toughe, And the waye, I telle you, is comerous and thicke— . . . It were petie allsoo thabbey shold be oppressed With many comers to that straunge place; Or her bacon in ony wyse shold be lessed—God kepe you all fro suche a trespaace! And graunt eche wedded man such a grace To abide at hom with a groyne or a chappe, Till the worlde be turned into anothir shappe. Apperson 171; *Oxford* 210; C. L. Shaver in *MLN* 50(1935) 322–5; Tilley F375; Whiting *Drama* 342:515.

D441 As plain as **Dunstable** highway
1546 Heywood *D* 73.119: For were ye as plaine as dunstable hy waie. Apperson 171; *Oxford* 162; Tilley D646.

D442 As innumerable as the **Dust** of earth
a1395 *WBible* II Paralipomenon i 9: Thi greet puple, which is so unnoumbrable as the dust of erthe. Svartengren 398.

D443 Like **Dust** (powder) in the wind
c900 *Paris Psalter* 1 (1.5): Ac hi beoð duste gelicran, þonne hit wind toblæwð, 38 (17.40): Ic hi todælde swa smæle, and swa swa duste beforan winde, and hi adilgode swa swa deð dust on here-stræτum, 78 (34.6): Syn hi tostencte, swa swa dust beforan winde. **c1000** *Regius Psalter* 1 (1.4): Swa arlease swa swa dust þæt awyprð wind of ansyne eorðan, 29 (17.43), 59 (34.5). **c1100** *Salisbury Psalter* 97 (17.43), 121 (34.5). **a1300** *Arthour and M.*[1] 137.4843–4: That he tok, he al torof, So dust in winde and aboute drof. **c1340** Rolle *Psalter* 511 (Prayer of Habakkuk 21): Cumys . . . to waste me, as dust bifor the wynd. **c1350** *Prose Psalter* 1 (1.5): The wicked . . . as a poudre, that the wynde casteth fram the face of therthe, 20 (18.46): Y shal littelel (*for* d) hem as poudre to-fore the face of the wynde, 39 (34.6). **c1395** *WBible* Psalms i 4: Thei ben as dust, which the wynd castith awei fro the face of erthe, xvii 43: And y schal al to-breke hem, as dust bifor the face of wynd, xxxiv 5. **a1400** *Firumbras* 51.1585–6: That were woundyd and slayn and to grounde throwe, As poudre that were brent and with wynde y-blowe. **a1400** *Northern Verse Psalter* I 49 (17.43): And I sal gnide als duste bi-for wind likam. **1447** Bokenham 178.6509–10: Yet shul thei rote and a-wey pace As doth dust beforn the wyndys face? **a1450** *St. Katherine* (*Gibbs*) 26[19–20]: The . . . ornamentes . . . that schal be as pouder be fore the wynd. **c1450** Idley 145.2339: It woll waast away as dust with the wynde.

D444 To bear **Dust** (powder) in the wind
a1200 *Ancrene* 144.16–9: The is umben withuten hire to gederin gode theawes, he bereth dust i the wind, as sein gregoire seith, Qui sine humilitate virtutes congregat, quasi qui in vento pulverem portat. **c1300** *Speculum Gy* 31.669–72: Hit fareth bi swiche, as we finde, As who-so bereth poudre in grete winde; For, bere he nevere so muche, Hit fleth awey ful lihtliche. **a1450** *Gesta* 42[3]: As men berith poudir in the wynde. See **F265.**

D445 To drive **Dust** in someone's eyes
a1500 *A Ballad* in *Rel. Ant.* I 28[11]: Yet for to dryve the dowste yn hys eye. Apperson 172; *Oxford* 162; Taylor and Whiting 114; Tilley D650.

D446 To shake (*etc.*) the **Dust** from one's feet
c1000 *WSG* Matthew x 14: Asceacaþ þæt dust of eowrum fotum, Mark vi 11, Luke ix 5, x 11. **c1384** *WBible* Matthew x 14: Smytith awey the dust fro youre feet, **c1395** Mark vi 11: Schake awei the powdir fro youre feet, Luke ix 5, x 11: We wipen of ayens you the poudir that cleved to us of youre citee, Deeds of Apostles xiii 51: And thei schoken awei in to hem the duste (**c1384:** powdir) of her feet. **c1400** *Pepysian Gospel* 30.8–10: (Hii) schulden wypen the dust under her feete upon her heveden in witnessynge that hii ne hadden nothing of heren. **1533** Heywood *Pardoner* A1^{v}[14–5]: At suche a house tary ye no more, And from your shoes scrape away the dust. *Oxford* 578; Taylor and Whiting 113–4.

D447 To todeal (*divide*) as small as **Dust**
897 Alfred *Boethius* 28.21–2: þeah ðu hi smale todæle swa dust.

D448 It may (be)fall a **Dwarf** to outray (*vanquish*) a giant
a1439 Lydgate *Fall* II 343.531–2: But it may

falle a dwery in his riht Toutraie a geaunt, for al his grete myht. Apperson 172.

D449 Like a **Dwarf** (child) sitting on a giant's neck
c1277 L. Thorndike *Liber de Similitudinibus et Exemplis* in *Speculum* 32(1957) 791 n. 76: Nota sumus sicut nani super humeros gygantum. **a1387** Higden-Trevisa I 15[7–8]: As a dwerf sittynge on a geauntis nekke. **a1425** Chauliac 2–4: Fforsothe we bene children in the nekke of a gygant, ffor we may see what-so-ever the gygant may se and somwhat more. Apperson 172; *Oxford* 163; Tilley D659.

D450 **Dwelling** (*delay*) has oft wrought scathe (*harm*)
c1300 *Havelok* 49.1352: Dwelling haveth ofte scathe wrouht. Apperson 141–2; *Oxford* 136; Skeat 179. See **D157, T44.**

E

Eagle, see **Erne**

E1 The **Eagle's** eye pierces the sun (*varied*)
a1398(1495) Bartholomaeus-Trevisa A3^v[2.15–8]: (*The Eagle is*) most sharpe in acte and dede of seenge and beholdynge the sonne in roundenesse of his cercle, wythoute ony blemysshynge of eyen. **c1408** Lydgate *Reson* 171.6528–30: I mene the foule most Royal Which hath fethres grey and donne And perceth eke the shene sonne, **c1425** *Ballade on a New Year's Gift* in *MP* II 649.8–9: This staately bridde doothe ful heghe soore, Percyng the beemys of the heghe sonne, **c1440** *Debate* in *MP* II 540.21: Themperiall Egle pershyng the sonne bemys, **a1449** *Cok* in *MP* II 815.81–3: The royall egle . . . Whoos eyen been so cleer and so bryght, Off nature he perce may the sunne, *Look* in *MP* II 765.18–9: Which with his look percith the fervent sonne, The Egle. **a1450** *Three Middle English Sermons* 58.261–4: For as seith Isider in his ethimologiis, libro 12, capitulo 7°, the egle . . . wile also loke openliche o the sunne whan a schynez clerest and never twynkle with his eyen. **c1450** *Alphabet* II 274.24–5: For as the egle emang all birdis fleis hyest and seis nexte the son. **c1450** Holland *Howlat* 58.318: (Ernes) Perses the sone with thar sicht, selcouth to herd. **1533** More *Confutacion* 580 F[7–8]: Tindales owne sharpe egle eyen. Tilley E3; Whiting *Drama* 311:106, *Scots* I 161.

E2 An **Eagle** wreaks him (*avenges himself*) on a fly
a1500 *Court of Love* 428.702–3: She saw an egle wreke him on a fly, And pluk his wing, and eke him, in his game. Cf. Apperson 173: The eagle does not catch flies; *Oxford* 163; Tilley E1.

E3 He that has **Ears** let him hear
c1395 *WBible* Apocalypse ii 7: He that hath eeris, here he. Tilley E25.

E4 In at one **Ear** and out at the other
c1385 Chaucer *TC* iv 434: Oon ere it herde, at tothir out it wente. **a1400** *Romaunt B* 5151–2: For all yede out at oon ere That in that other she dide lere. **c1415** *Middle English Sermons* 166.22–3: But itt commeth in at the on ere and goyth oute at the othur. **a1420** Lydgate *Troy* III 608.1533: For thorugh his eris it passed as a soun. **c1450** *Lambeth Prose Legends* 356.8–10: Now everichone lesseth bothe thayre eris, that the tone lat not go out all that the tother taketh in. **a1475** *Assembly of Gods* 58.1996–9: I herde what they seyde. But neverthelese my wyt ys so thynne, And also of Deth I was so afrayed, That hit ys oute where hyt went ynne. **a1483** Caxton *Cato* B1^v[26–7]: For that that entryth in to one of theyr eerys yssueth out ageyn by theyr other eere. **c1500** *Lyfe of Roberte* 229.249: All one wyth hym: in at the one eare and out at the other. **1546** Heywood *D* 93.92: Went in at the tone eare, and out at the tother, **1555** *E* 160.89. Apperson 469–70; *Oxford* 318; Tilley E12.

E5 It seems more to use the **Ears** than the tongue
c1425 Arderne *Fistula* 6.36–7: For a wise man seith, "It semeth more to use the eres than the tunge."

E6 One has two **Ears** and one mouth and should hear half more than speak
1450 *Dicts* 72.7–10: And he sawe oon that spake somuche that noon might make him be stille; to whome he saide: freende, he said, thou hast ii eris and thow hast bot oo mouthe, wherefore thou shuldist bi the halfe more hire than speke. **1483** Caxton *Cato* C7^v[25–7]: Sayde Socrates

to a man that spake overmoche, here me, sayd he, thou that hast but one mowthe and two eerys by nature oughtest to here twyes so moch as that thou spekest. Apperson 473–4; *Oxford* 679; Tilley N44. See **H265.**

E7 Over the **Ears** in love
1534 Heywood *Love* B4ᵛ[44]: Quyte over the eares in love. Cf. Apperson 660; *Oxford* 684.

E8 To be in every man's **Ear**
c1400 *Roland* 120.455: It was in every manys ere, and not to seche.

E9 To be led by the **Ear**
a1500 Medwall *Nature* D1ʳ[14]: And not to be led by the ere. **c1516** Skelton *Magnificence* 23.712: I can fede forth a fole and lede hym by the eyre. Cf. Taylor and Whiting 264: Nose (6).

E10 To be over the hard **Ears**
1534 More *Comforte* 1156 C[8–10]: Plounge hym into the poole of penaunce over the harde eares. Whiting *Drama* 343:517.

E11 To be worth one's **Ears**
a1376 *Piers* A Prol. 75: Weore the bisschop i-blesset and worth bothe his eres. **a1460** *Towneley Plays* 171.165: Had ye bene woth youre eres thus had thay not gone.

E12 To have one's **Ears** glow (tingle)
c1385 Chaucer *TC* ii 1021–2: And we shal speek of the somwhat, I trowe, Whan thow art gon, to don thyn eris glowe! **c1400** *Laud Troy* I 190.6451: A Ector, thin ere aught to glowe. **1519** Horman *Vulgaria* 434[15]: Myn earis tyngled at that tale. Non æquis auribus id audiebam. **1546** Heywood *D* 60.37–8: I suppose that daie hir eares might well glow, For all the towne talkt of hir hy and low, **1555** *E* 190.250: Thyne eares may glowe, lets see whether they glow John. I lye: thyne eares can not glowe for thou hast non. Apperson 173; *Oxford* 164; Taylor and Whiting 115; Tilley E14.

E13 To lie (*etc.*) by the **Ears**
1519 Horman *Vulgaria* 198[5]: They were redy to fyght or lye by the earis. **1533** Heywood *Johan* B4ᵛ[24]: Here they fyght by the erys a whyle, **1546** *D* 62.101: Together by the eares they come, **1556** *Spider* 231[9–10]: He setth them all . . . together by the eares. Apperson 76; *Oxford* 576; Taylor and Whiting 115; Tilley E23; Whiting *Drama* 343:518, *Scots* I 162.

E14 To make (*etc.*) a deaf **Ear**
a1396(1494) Hilton *Scale* M3ᵛ (*by error* K3ᵛ) [31]: And make deef ere to hem, as though thu herde hem not. **a1400** *Scottish Legends* II 101.92: And til hym len a def ere ay. **c1450** *Merlin* II 261[34–5]: And the carll leide to the deef ere. **c1493** *St. Katherin of Senis* 305.7–8: To alle suche counseylles of sowle-hele he gaf a deef ere. **1533** More *Debellacyon* 1016 F[9–10]: Whereto thys man geveth a deafe eare alway. Tilley E13.

E15 To tickle one in the **Ear**
a1500 Medwall *Nature* A4ʳ[3–5]: But yf Reason tykyll hym in the ere, Or bere hym on hand the kow ys wood, He shall never be able to do erthly good.

E16 Where **Ears** are there are causes, where women are there are words
1492 *Salomon and Marcolphus* 6[5–6]: Were erys are there are causes, where women be there are wordys. Tilley W686. See **W497.**

E17 **Early** up and never the nearer
1546 Heywood *D* 21.33–4: And than their timely weddyng doth clere appere, That they were earely up, and never the nere. Apperson 173; *Oxford* 164; Tilley E27.

E18 To make **Earnest** of game (*varied*)
c1390 Chaucer *CT* I[A] 3186: And eek men shal nat maken ernest of game. **a1393** Gower *CA* II 246.733–4: Thogh it beginne on pure game, Fulofte it torneth into grame, III 199.1178–9: Bot afterward al thilke game Was into wofull ernest torned. **c1450** *Edward the Confessor Prose I* 90[28]: But at the laste ther game was turnyd in-to ernest. **c1475** Henryson *Fables* 29.770–1: Me think na man may speik ane word in play, Bot now on dayis in ernist it is tane. Taylor and Whiting 413:8.

E19 As broad as the **Earth**
a1000 *Vercelli Homilies* 130.220–1: His miht is . . . bradre þonne eorðe.

E20 As far as **Earth** from heaven
a1393 Gower *CA* II 38.105–6: For I was further fro my love Than Erthe is fro the hevene above. See **C316.**

E21 As pale as the **Earth**
a1470 Malory I 281.33–4: He was passyng paale as the erthe for bledynge.

E22 **Earth** (Dust, Ashes) must to earth (dust) (*varied*)
a893 Wærferth *Gregory* 264.23–4: Of eorðan hi wæron gewordene and to eorðan eft gelice beoþ gehworfene. **c970** *Blickling Homilies* 123[9–10]: þu eart eorðe . . . and þu scealt on eorþan

gangan and eft to eorðan weorðan. **c1000** Aelfric *Homilies* I 18[17–8]: þu eart of eorðan genumen, and þu awenst to eorðan. þu eart dust, and ðu awentst to duste, 300[8–9]. **a1023** Wulfstan *Homilies* 225.8–10: Of eorðan gewurdan ærest geworhte þa ðe we ealle of coman, and to eorðan we sculan ealle geweorðan. **a1023** ?Wulfstan *Adam se æreste man* in Napier 5.12–4: (*as above*). **c1050** *St. Mildryð* in *Archiv* 132(1914) 334.24–6: Wæs heo swyðe gemyngi, þæt we ealle of twam mannum comon, and of eorðan lame ge-sceapene and gewrohte wæron, and to þam eft ge-wurðan sceolan. **c1303** Mannyng *Handlyng* 274.8695–700: The lorde that made of erthe, erles, Of the same erthe made he cherles; Erles myght, and lordes stut, As cherles shal yn erthe be put; Erles, cherles, alle at ones, Shal none knowe youre, fro oure bones. **c1395** *WBible* Genesis iii 19: For thou art dust, and thou schalt turne agen in to dust, Ecclesiastes xii 7: And dust turne agen in to his erthe, wherof it was. **c1410** *Mirror of Sinners* in *Yorkshire Writers* II 437[43–4]: Of eerthe thow weere i.-maad, and in to eerthe thou schalt turne. **c1440** Lydgate *Debate* in *MP* II 565.636–7: Hih and low wer maad of oo mateer; Of erthe we cam, to erthe we shal a-geyn. **a1450** *In the ceson* in *Archiv* 167(1935) 33.22[3–4]: For asses thou was afore this instaunce, And asses sal thou be after for certayne. **c1450** *Jacob's Well* 195.32–196.1: Thou were asschys, thou art asschys, thou schalt ben asschys! **1483** *Quatuor Sermones* 26[14–6]: Thou art a man of erthe . . . and of the erthe thou lyvest And to the erthe thou shalt turne ageyn. **1483** ?Skelton *Kynge Edwarde* I 2.13–4: I slepe now in molde, as is naturall That erth unto erth hath his reverture. **a1500** *Man have mynd* 54.4: For erd til erd Is ordanit ay. Apperson 174; Tilley E30.

E23 The **Earth** will discover secrets
a1420 Lydgate *Troy* III 709.4955–60: For the peple which that is rual Seith that secres, whiche be nat kouthe at al, The erthe wil, as thei make mynde, Discuren hen of his owne kynde, And of nature up casten and disclose The thing that men ar wont in it to close. See **C454, M806.**

E24 Merry to be low upon **Earth** (rather) than in high houses
c1500 Greene *Carols* 348.2: A-law upon the yerthe ys merey to be Then in hey howsys other grete toures. See **E150, G479, K77, R191, S457.**

E25 To lick the **Earth**
c900 *Paris Psalter* 30 (71.9): And his feondas foldan liccigeað. **c1000** *Regius Psalter* 130 (71.9). **c1100** *Salisbury Psalter* 172 (71.9). **c1340** Rolle *Psalter* 254 (71.9): His ennimies sal licke the earthe. **c1350** *Prose Psalter* 86 (71.9). **c1395** *WBible* Psalms lxxi 9: Hise enemyes schulen licke the erthe. **a1400** *Northern Verse Psalter* I 231 (71.9): And his faas the erthe sal licke. **1435** Misyn *Fire* 24.26–8. *Oxford* 340: Kiss the dust; Taylor and Whiting 113: Bite the dust; Tilley D651. See **G430.**

E26 To lie like an **Earth-clot**
c1400 *Laud Troy* I 201.6819–20: Thei lay stonstille In that plot, As it hadde ben an erthe-clot.

E27 **Ease** (Opportunity, Leisure) makes (a) thief
c1200 *Hali Meidenhad* 22.230: Me seith that eise maketh theof. **a1300** *Ancrene* (*Trinity*) 223.9: Eise si com lem dit, si fet souvent larron. **a1387** Higden-Trevisa VII 379[2–3]: I see wel that ese maketh the to synne. **a1425** Higden-Anon. VII 379[4–5]: Me thenke that oportunite makethe a thefe. **c1450** *Douce MS.52* 47.35: Ese makyth thefe. **1480** Caxton *Ovyde* 65[5–6]: Hit is sayde comunely that the layzir maketh the theef. Apperson 475; Jente 614; *Oxford* 164, 478; Tilley O71. See **W426.**

E28 (He is at **Ease** that) has enough (and can say ho!)
a1450 *Myne awen dere* 162.421: And hase ynogh and can saye "ho." **a1470** Parker *Dives* A1r[2.37–9]: It is an olde proverbe. He is well atte ease that hath ynough and can saye ho. **c1475** *Wisdom* 54.565–6: Farewll, consyens! I know not yow; I am at eas, hade I inow. **c1500** Greene *Carols* 350 (*refrain*): Forsothe, I hold hym well and withowt woo That hath ynowgh and can say "Whoo!" **1549** Heywood *D* 84.126: He that knoweth whan he hath enough, is no foole. Apperson 174; *Oxford* 718; Tilley E36, 163. See **E116, H398.**

E29 He is at **Ease** that seldom thanks (*varied*)
c1350 *Good Wife E* 164.94: At ese he is that selde thonket, **c1425** *H* 165.98: At ese he is that seldam thankith, **c1450** *L* 201.140–1: He hath eese at weelde That thanketh God feele and seelde, **a1500** *N* 213.110–1: For oft at ease he is That loves peace I wis.

E30 He lives at **Ease** that owes no debt
a1500 *Good Wife A* 220.161–2: At es he lyves that awe no dette; It is no les, withouten lette.

E31 He may not have all his **Ease** that shall thrive

c1425 *Good Wife H* 169.154: All his ese may he nought have that thryve schall, **c1500** *T* 208.153–4: All ease may nat fall To hym that thryve shall. Apperson 174.

E32 He that is at **Ease** let him keep himself therein
1471 Caxton *Recuyell* II 516.9–10: He that is well at his ese late hym kepe hym there in. See **B275, F423, S297.**

E33 To take one's **Ease** in his inn
1546 Heywood *D* 26.20: And take mine ease in mine in, **1555** *E* 151.26: thine. Apperson 618; *Oxford* 640; Tilley E42.

E34 The longer **East** the shorter west
1546 Heywood *D* 58.35–6: And therby men have gest, Alwaie the longer east the shorter west. Apperson 379; *Oxford* 382; Tilley E45.

E35 He that will in **East Cheap** eat a goose so fat, *etc.*
a1500 *Trinity College Cambridge MS. 599* in M. R. James *Catalogue* II (Cambridge, 1901) 73: He that wyll in Eschepe ete a goose so fat, With harpe, pype, and song, He must slepe in Newgate on a mat, Be the nyght never so long. Secundum Aristotilem. Apperson 174.

E36 **Eat,** drink (and make merry) for we shall die to-morrow
c1395 *WBible* Isaiah xxii 13: Ete we, and drynke we, for we schulen die to morewe, I Corinthians xv 32. **a1396**(1494) Hilton *Scale* L2r[20–2]: And therfore they saye: Ete we, drynke we: and make we mery here, for of this life we be syker. **a1400** *Pauline Epistles* I Corinthians xv 32. **1492** *Salomon and Marcolphus* 10[23–4]: Lete us ete and drinke, we shall alle deye. **1495** *Medytacyons of saynt Bernarde* B2v[1]: Ete, dranke, and made mery. **c1505** Watson *Valentine* 102.30–1: Lordes ete and drynke and make good chere, for to morowe shall be youre laste daye. Taylor and Whiting 116.

E37 **Eat** to live, not live to eat
a1387 Higden-Trevisa III 281[13–5]: Socrates seide that meny men wil leve forto ete and drynke, and that they wolde ete and drynke and (that) forto lyve. **1422** Yonge *Governaunce* 237.33–4: Ypocras answarid, "Fayre sone, I wolde ette forto lyfe, and not lyfe to ette." **a1425** *Governance of Lordschipes* 67.25–6. **1456** Hay *Governaunce* 117.2–4: To quham he (*Ypocras*) ansuerde agayne, sayand that he ete in entent to lyve lang, and lyvit nocht in entent till ete. **1487** Caxton *Book of Good Manners* B7v[1]: (*Socrates said that*) people ought not lyve for to ete, but to ete for to lyve. **1489** *Governayle* B5r[5–8]: Men that have goode understondyng etyn for they wolde lyve, but they that goon by fleshelynes wolden lyve for to ete and contrary to nature. **a1500** *MS. Marginalia* in Hoccleve I 196 n.5: Non vivas ut edas; sed edas. ut vivere possis. Lyve not as a glutton, styll for to eate, But fede to maintayne lyfe by thie meate. **1522** More *Treatyce* 101 AB: Where as . . . we shoulde eate but for to live, these glotons . . . wold not wish to live and it were not for to eate. Apperson 176; *Oxford* 167; Tilley E50; Walther I 870.6952.

E38 That which I **Ate** (spent), that I had, *etc.*
c1300 *Pembroke College Cambridge MS. 32* f.153a in M. R. James *Catalogue* (Cambridge, 1905) 35: That ich et, that ich hadde; That ich gaf, that ich habbe; That ich ay held, that i nabbe. **a1400** *Royal MS. 17 B xvii* f.2b in Brown *Register* I 364: That I hete and that I drinke, that may I ha(ve); That I lene fals men, long I may hit c(rave); That I dele for my soule, that may I fynde; That I leeve my secatours, that is long by(hynde). **a1500** *Epitaph at St. Albans* reproduced in *The Beauties of England and Wales* (London, 1808) VII 100: Lo, al that ever j spent, sum time had j; Al that j gaf in god intent, that now have j; That j neyther gaf ne lent that now abie j; that j kept til j went that lost y. Apperson 595; Brown-Robbins 3275; C. F. Bühler in *Renaissance News* 8(1955) 10–1; *Oxford* 613; Robbins-Cutler 1924.3; Tilley S742. See **M59, S623.**

E39 After an **Ebb** a flood (*varied*)
a1407 Henry Scogan *Moral Balade* in Skeat *Chaucerian* 242.142–3: Knowe ye nat, by reson That, after an ebbe, ther cometh a flood ful rage? **c1412** Hoccleve *Regement* 25.668–9: (He) with-drow the flood Of welthe, and at grounde ebbe sette he me. **a1439** Lydgate *Fall* I 171.6079: Ebbe afftir flowe maketh no delay, **a1449** *Pageant* in *MP* II 738.117: An ebbe of povert next floodys of richesse, *Tyed with a Lyne* in *MP* II 834.60: Ebbe after floode of al prosperite. **c1450** Idley 104.1410: Ever an ebbe cometh after a floode. **1506** Hawes *Pastime* 174.4652: After an ebbe there cometh a flowynge tyde. **1546** Heywood *D* 48.222: He was at an ebbe, though he be now a flote. Tilley F378. See **F295, 300.**

E40 He that is at an **Ebb** in Newgate shall ere long be afloat at Tyburn
1555 Heywood *E* 154.56: Thou art at an ebbe in Newgate, thou hast wrong. But thou shalt

be a flote at Tyburne ere long. Apperson 443; *Oxford* 394; Tilley E56.

E41 A low **Ebb** comes after a high flood
c1450 Idley 93.740: A low ebbe cometh after a hyee floode. Tilley F381. See **P424.**

E42 To fare like **Ebb** and flood
a1475 *As I cam by a forrest syde* in Sandison 114.21: Hit fars be the as ebb and flod. **a1500** *Theophilus* 7.13[2]: This world farith as ebbe and flode. See **G330, S111.**

E43 As fresh as an **Eel**
a1460 *Towneley Plays* 127.356: As fresh as an eyll. Apperson 235; Whiting *Scots* I 162.

E44 As slick as an **Eel**
1534 Heywood *Love* E2r[27]: And coryd tyll he be slyke as an ele. Tilley E60.

E45 As slipper as an **Eel**
c1412 Hoccleve *Regement* 72.1985: Mi wit is also slipir as an eel, **c1422** *Lerne to Die* 205.726: Worldly trust is as slipir as an eel. **c1440** *Daily Work* in *Yorkshire Writers* I 311[29–30]. **c1450** *Epistle of Othea* 83.16: A rakell tong glydeth slypper as an eele. **a1475** *Assembly of Gods* 31.1026. **a1500** *Piers of Fullham* 2.7. **1555** Heywood *E* 195.285(1).2: But slyper as an eeles tayle is the holde of it. Apperson 579; *Oxford* 597; Taylor and Whiting 117; Tilley E60.

E46 To culpon (*cut up*) someone like an **Eel**
c1400 *Laud Troy* I 185.6255: He culpunte him as he were an ele.

E47 To glide like an **Eel**
c1440 Scrope *Epistle* 56[6]: An evil kepte tong glydith as an ele.

E48 To hold an **Eel** by the tail (*varied*)
c1395 *WBible* Job *Prologue* I 671[1–3]: As if thou woldest an eel or laumprun holde with streite hondis, how myche strengerli thou thristis, so myche the sunnere it shal sliden awey. **c1440** *Daily Work* in *Yorkshire Writers* I 311[35–6]: Sodanly thay fra thame glyde als a sleper eele mene haldes by the tayle. **c1450** *Epistle of Othea* 113.12: And yett is hyt feble hold on a slipper eele. **c1450** John of Fordun *Scotichronicon* (Edinburgh, 1759) II 376[9]: Als sikir for to hald as a water eeil. **1483** Caxton *Cato* C8r[13–5]: Men say comynly that he is a fole that promysseth for to gyve the ele whiche he holdeth onely but by the tayle, whyche may lightly escape fro hym. **1523** Skelton *Garlande* I 382.501: A slipper holde the taile is of an ele. **1546** Heywood *D* 36.43–4: Her promise . . . Is as sure to holde as an ele by the tayle. Apperson 179; *Oxford* 298; Taylor and Whiting 117; Tilley E61. See **G470.**

E49 Great **Effect** may be written in little place
c1385 Chaucer *TC* v 1629: Ek gret effect men write in place lite. Cf. Tilley M1284. See **M328, 783.**

Egg, see **Ay**

E50 As full as an **Egg** is of oatmeal (mustard)
1520 Whittinton *Vulgaria* 96.7–8: Ye be as ful of good maner as an egge is of oote mele. **1533** More *Confutacion* 582 D[1–2]: As full of reason as an egge full of mustarde. *Oxford* 230; Tilley M622.

E51 It is far to bid hait (*hurry up*) to an **Egg** ere it go (*walk*)
a1460 *Towneley Plays* 105.150–1: It is far to byd hyte To an eg or it go. See **K34.**

E52 Not noy (*annoy*) an **Egg**
a1400 *Alexander C* 22.676: It sall the noy noght a neg nane of his thoghtis.

E53 Not win an **Egg**
a1500 *Thre Prestis* 16.245: He can nocht wirk be craft to wyn ane eg.

E54 To come in with one's five **Eggs**
1533 More *Confutacion* 626 (*by error* 560) D[12–3]: Wherin he came forth per dy with his five egges. **1546** Heywood *D* 60.41: In came a thyrde, with his .v. egges, **1555** *E* 192.261. Apperson 180; *Oxford* 104; Tilley E92.

E55 Not set an **Egg-shell**
1481 Caxton *Reynard* 110[20]: Thou woldest not sette by me an egge shelle.

E56 To reave (*spoil*) **Egypt** (the Egyptians)
c1000 Aelfric *Heptateuch* Exodus iii 22: And reafiaþ Egypte. **a1382** *WBible* Exodus iii 22: And ye shulen spoyle Egipte. **a1425** *Foundation of St. Bartholomew's* 33.14–5: Moyses . . . that fyrst taught us to spoyle the egipcians. **1534** More *Passion* 1295 G[15]: Spoyled the Egipcians. *Oxford* 615.

E57 As bitter as **Eisell** (*vinegar*)
a1450 *Pety Job* in Kail 135.441: My syn ys bytter than eysell. **c1450** Idley 168.570: A bitter stomake as eysell.

E58 To assay above **Ela**
a1508 Skelton *Phyllyp* I 66.486–7: He hath well assayde To solfe above ela. *Letters of Robert Carter, 1720–1727,* ed. Louis B. Wright (San Marino, California, 1940) 80: Your next paragraph is a note above Elah, sure. You were . . . looking

upon me as one of your dependents and inferiors. NED Ela.

E59 **Eld** (*age*) is a selcouth (*strange*) thing, *etc.* **a1325** *Cursor* I 212.3589–94: Eild es thou a selcut thing, That al it gerns that er ying; Quhen thai it have thai are unfayn, And wald ha youthed than again; Than wald thai be als thai war ar, Bot sua it mai be never mare.

E60 **Eld** is crabbed
c1400 *Alexander Buik* II 156.2081–2: Bot of eld it is the richt For to be crabed day and nicht. NED Crabbed 1b.

E61 In **Eld** is wisdom and usage (*varied*)
c1385 Chaucer *CT* I[A] 2447–8: As sooth is seyd, elde hath greet avantage; In elde is bothe wysdom and usage. **a1400** *Scottish Legends* II 103.142: For in elde suld wit be socht. See **M118.**

E62 In **Eld** it must bite that does so young
a1400 *Titus* 206.4580: On elde most it byte, that soo doth yonge. See **T222.**

E63 As sweet as the **Elder** (*i.e.*, not sweet)
a1500 *The Lover's Mocking Reply* in Robbins 221.35: With brethe as swete as ys the Elder tre.

E64 As fierce as an **Elephant**
a1400 *Alexander C* 220.3922: Fere fersere than an olifant.

E65 As strong (stark) as (an, the) **Elephant**(**s**)
a1300 *Alisaunder* 351.6595: And als an olyfaunt he is strong. **1340** *Ayenbite* 84[22]: Maketh man . . . strang ase olyfont. **c1400** *Vices and Virtues* 83.6: Strong as the olifaunt. **1456** Hay *Governaunce* 157.25: Sum man stark as ane elephant. **1471** Caxton *Recuyell* I 157.22: olifantes, II 410.30–1: olyphantes, **1484** *Royal Book* H1^{v}[3]: an. **1509** Watson *Ship* S8^{r}[26]: the. Taylor *Comparisons* 78.

E66 To make an **Elephant** of a gnat
1533 More *Debellacyon* 1025 G[5–6]: Making in some of them an elephant of a gnatte. *Oxford* 211: Fly; Tilley F398.

E67 As tough as any **Elm**
c1499 Skelton *Bowge* I 35.129: Favoure we have tougher than ony elme.

E68 As white as **Elp's** (*elephant's*) bone
c1330 *St. Katherine* 248 A 281: Hir body . . . that er was white so alpes bon. See **I68, W203.**

E69 As green as (an, any, the) **Emerald**
c1380 Chaucer *PF* 174–5: Ech in his kynde, of colour fresh and greene As emeraude. **c1410** Lovelich *Grail* II 365.465: As Grene As An Emeraude it was there, 416.385–7. **a1470** Malory II 990.19: ony. **c1522** Skelton *Speke* II 2.18: My fedders freshe as is the emrawde grene. **1556** Heywood *E* 120.34.3: the, *Spider* 365[2]: the. Taylor and Whiting 119.

E70 The **Emerald** of chastity may not be recovered
a1439 Lydgate *Fall* II 367.1405–7: For it is said and hath be said ful yore, The emeraud greene off parfit chastite, Stole onys away may nat recurid be. See **K94, M20, N13.**

E71 As thick as **Emmets** (*ants*)
c1300 Robert of Gloucester I 436.5984–5: Tho thikce hii come that thet lond overal hii gonne fulle As thikke as ameten crepeth in an amete hulle.

E72 As wise as an **Emmet**
1456 Hay *Governaunce* 157.26–7: Sum man wys as . . . ane emot. Cf. Taylor *Comparisons* 65: provident.

End, sb.

E73 All that is begun untimely has no perfect **End**
897 Alfred *Boethius* 12.5–6: Forðon eall þæt mon untiidlice ongynð næfð hit no æltæwne ende.

E74 **End** and beginning oft accord
c1523 Barclay *Mirrour* 24[6]: Oft ende and beginning accordeth without fayle.

E75 The **End** crowns
1509 Watson *Ship* Dd1^{r}[25]: For the ende crowneth. Apperson 182; *Oxford* 171; Smith 79; Tilley E116.

E76 The **End** gives corn
c1523 Barclay *Mirrour* 37[35]: For well he considereth that thende geveth corne.

E77 The **End** is oft variable from the (be)ginning (*varied*)
a1420 Lydgate *Troy* I 335.6674–5: And from the gynnyng ofte variable The ende is seyn. **c1440** *Prose Alexander* 50.18–9: For ofte tymes we see that the lattere end of a man discordes wit the firste.

E78 The **End** is the strength of every tale
c1385 Chaucer *TC* ii 260: Sithen th'ende is every tales strengthe.

E79 An **End** of an old song
1522 Skelton *Why Come* II 29.85–6: An end of an olde song, Do ryght and do no wronge. Apperson 587; *Oxford* 171; Tilley E126.

E80 The **End** of bliss is sorrow (*varied*)
a1350 *Magdalen Oxford MS.27* in H. O. Coxe *Catalogus Codicum MSS.* (Oxford, 1852) II ii 18: The ende of lagthre is woth, and the ende of bliz is sorege, for wende fwer thu wende, so reges is tin ende. **c1385** Chaucer *TC* iv 836: The ende of blisse ay sorwe it occupieth, **c1390** *CT* VII 3205[B4395]: For evere the latter ende of joye is wo. **c1395** *WBible* Proverbs xiv 13: Morenyng ocupieth the laste thingis of joye. **a1400** *Sermon Against Miracle-Plays* in *Rel. Ant.* II 54[10–1]: The wise man seith, "The ende of myrthis is sorowe, and ofte youre lawghyng shal be medelid with sorowe." **a1420** Lydgate *Troy* I 220.2620–1: And thus of good ay the fyn is wo, Namly of hem that so pynche and spare. **1487** *O thou most noble* 321[2]: The end is woe that first begon with game. **a1496** *Rote or Myrour* B4v[25–8]: As Salomon sayth . . . The ende of wordely joye is occupyed with wepynge and sorowe. **a1500** *English Conquest* 51.7: The end of every gladnes is Sorrow. **1506** Hawes *Pastime* 208.5476–7: The ende of Ioye and all prosperyte Is dethe at last. Skeat 193. See **J58, S145.**

E81 The **End** proves (*etc.*) everything (*varied*)
a1393 Gower *CA* III 231.2383: An ende proveth every thing. **1402** *Daw Topias* 89[5–6]: Loke that every werke is knowen, Plenili bi his eende. **a1450** Quixley *Ballads* 43.120: The ende scheweth al the sore aventure, 127, 134. **a1475** Ashby *Dicta* 45.55–6: The ende shall showe every thinge as it is, Truly justly, or els falsly iwys. **1478** Rivers *Morale Proverbes* [8.7]: Thende dooth shewe every werk as hit is. **1509** Barclay *Ship* II 318[19]: Eche thynge is provyd at the ende. **1534** Heywood *Love* D2v[9]: Who shall wynne the ende, the ende at ende shall try. Apperson 182; *Oxford* 171; Tilley E116; Whiting *Drama* 40, 103, 222, 299. See **E85, P39, 413, T90.**

E82 Ever at the **End** wrong will wend (have woe)
a1300 *Arthour and M.*[1] 56.1895–8: Men seyt, yere and other to Wrong wil an hond go, And ever at the nende Wrong wil wende. **a1300** Henley *Husbandry* 4[11–3]: Kar hom dit en englyse: On yeer other to wro(n)ge wylle on honde go. Ant evere aten hende wrong wile wende. **a1400** *Proverbis of Wysdom* 244.29: Ever att end wrong wyll wend. **c1450** *Fyrst thou sal* 88.33: Ever at the ende wrong wil out wende. **a1500** Hichecoke *This Worlde* 333.33–4: A yere or a wronge will onne goo, And ever at the hynde wronge will have woo. Robbins-Cutler 2698.

E83 If the **End** is well all is well (*varied*)
1381 *Jack Carter* in Knighton II 139[10–11]: For if the ende be wele, than is alle wele. **a1450** Audelay 94.397: Fore al is good that good end, 123.364: Fore al is good that hath good end, 224.38. **1456** Hay *Law* 88.15–6: Quhen the end is gude of a thing, all is callit gude. **c1500** Greene *Carols* 408 (*refrain*): "Alas," sayd the gudman, "this ys an hevy lyff!" And "All ys well that endyth well," said the gud wyff. **1515** Barclay *St. George* 102.2571: Whan the ende is good than all is fortunate. **1546** Heywood *D* 37.70: All is well that endes well, **1555** *E* 176.171. Apperson 6–7; Jente 436, cf. 641; *Oxford* 701; Taylor and Whiting 6; Tilley A154. See **E92.**

E84 Look at (think on) the **End** (ending) (*varied*)
c1280 *South English Legendary: OT History* 83.50: In everych dede that thou doost: thine endynge have in mynde. **c1300** *Royal MS.8 E xvii* in A. Chr. Thorn *Les Proverbes de Bon Enseignement de Nicole de Bozon* (Lund, 1921) 9.20: Er yu do eny thing thenk one the ending. **c1303** Mannyng *Handlyng* 169.5133–4: And gyf thou bygynne any thyng, Thenk what shal be the endyng. **a1325** *Cursor* I 256.4379–80: For qua bigin wil ani thing He aght to thinc on the ending. **1340** *Ayenbite* 150[32–3]: Thet is thet the wyse zayth, "Of al thet thou sselt beginne: loke thane ende and to huet heavede thou sselt come." **c1380** Chaucer *Boece* II pr. i 85–6: But wisdom loketh and mesureth the ende of thynges. **a1393** Gower *CA* II 275.1811–4: He bad hem, if thei wolde winne, They scholden se, er thei beginne, Here ende, and sette here ferste entente, That thei hem after ne repente. **a1400** *Destruction of Troy* 74.2245–7: Hit is no counsell to encline, ne to calle wise, Ne not holsom, I hope, that hedis to the first, And for-sees not the fer end, what may falle after. **c1400** *Beryn* 55.1787–9: But nowe a word of philosophy, that fallith to my mynde, "Who take hede of the begynnyng, what fal shal of the ende, He leyith a bussh to-fore the gap, ther fortune wold in ryde." **c1400** *Laud Troy* I 69–70.2337–42: I have herd say and red in boke, That a wis man schal not loke Afftir a thing that is atte begynnyng, But evere-more afftir the endyng; For many thynges begynnes wele And in the ende fares amys every dele. **c1400** *Vices and Virtues* 149.20–2: And that is that that the wise seith: In al that thou bigynnyst, take goode hede of the ende and to what thou myght brynge it at the laste. **c1410** *Mirror of Sinners* in *Yorkshire Writers* II 438[16–8]: For alle wise men awaiten as bisily to the eende of every thyng, as to the

bigynnyng, and rathere moore. **a1420** Lydgate *Troy* I 208–9.2232–4: And prudently consyderen in your herte Al, only nat the gynnyng but the ende, And the myddes, II 485.3162–4: For to a wysman, only is nat dewe To se the gynnynge and the ende noght, But bothe attonis peisen in his thought. **a1450** *Gesta* 39[20]: Bihold wele the ende. **a1450** *Myne awen dere* 174.783–6: If thou will welth and worschep wynne, What thynge in erthe at thou begynne, Avisemente firste I reede thou take What manere of ende that it will make, 799–800: Avyse the, sone, before thy dede And evere till the endynge take hede. **a1450** *Partonope* 438.10814–8: Of all your labour now cometh the fyne, Ye have wele be-gonne, with-oute faile, But all that certeyn may litell avayle, As sey thes olde men, but if the ende Be wele parfouremed in the same kynde. **c1450** *Alphabet* I 108.17–8: Evur at the begynyng umthynk the whatt will com of the endyng. **c1450** *Douce MS. 52.* 55.126: Whenne thou bygynnys a thyng, thenke on the endynge. **c1450** *Epistle of Othea* 75.6: In the begynnyng take hede of the eend, 76.6. **c1450** *Fyrst thou sal* 87.7–8: T(h)ynke on the ende or thou begyn And it sal the kepe fro trobil and syn, 90.137–8. **c1450** Idley 88.446–7: Er thou take on hand ony grete emprise, Undir-stonde the begynnyng and thende. **c1450** *Jacob's Well* 4.14–5: Lokyth in the begynnyng of every werk that ye do, how it schal be perfourmyd, and what schall be the ende! **c1450** *Pilgrimage LM* 20[15–6]: For of hem that wil taketh men seen nouht allwey the eende. **c1450** *Rawlinson Troye* 187.22–3: Hit wer gode to thenk on the ende. **c1450** *Rylands MS.394* 106.1. **c1450** *Serve thy god* 262.35–6: Thinke on the ende, or thou begyn, And thou schalt never be thral to syn. **1456** Hay *Law* 88.13–5: Oure autouris philoso-phouris sais that in all thingis men lukis to the end. **a1470** Parker *Dives* Y2^r^[1.20–1]: In the begynnynge of every dede, thynke on the ende. **a1471** Ashby *Policy* 39.828–9: In al your maters, er ye begynne, Thenke what ende wol be the conclusion. **1471** Caxton *Recuyell* II 519.1–5: Considere in this empryse not onely the begyn-nyng but also the myddell and the ende . . . ffor otherwhyle lityll prouffyten some thynges well begonne that come unto an evyll ende. **c1475** Henryson *Fables* 62.1760: Off everilk thing behald the fynall end, 65.1864–6: Grit fule is he, that hes na thing in thocht Bot thing present, and efter quhat may fall, Nor off the end hes na memoriall. **c1475** *Rawlinson MS. D 328* 120.36: What-so-ever thu do be-holde the ynde. **1477** Rivers *Dictes* 9[16–7]: The lokyng upon the ende of the worke, yf it be good, yeveth hope to the begynnyng. **1484** Caxton *Aesop* 34[19–20]: For he dothe prudently and wysely whiche taketh good hede to the ende, 195[1–4]: He whiche is wyse and sage ought fyrst to loke and behold the ende or he begyn-neth the werke or dede, 196[10–2]: Therfore he whiche is wyse yf he wysely wylle governe hym self ought to take ever good hede to the ende of his werke, *Royal Book* M6^v^[23–4]: In al that thou begynnest, beholde the ende. **a1500** *Craft of Lovers* in Stow's *Chaucer* CCCXLI^r^[2.12]: At your beginning think on the terminacion. **a1500** Hichecoke *This Worlde* 332.13: Er thu begynn, thynke of the ende. **a1500** Hill 131.30: Whan thow doste any thynge, think on the ende. **a1500** *Imitatione (1)* 32.31: In all thinges beholde the ende. **a1500** *Leconfield Proverbs* 486[14]: Evyr more remembr the ende. **a1500** *Proverbs of Salamon* 182.38.1: Thenke on the ende or thou begynne. **a1500** *Salamon seyth* in Person 52.21–2: Be never thrall un to synne And thynke on the ende or thou be gynne. **a1500** *Think Before You Speak* in Brown *Lyrics XV* 281.23: Man, yn the begynnynge thenk on the eynde. **c1500** *Everyman* 3.10–1: Man in the begynnynge Loke well and take good hede to the endynge. **1502** *Imitatione* (2) 174.1: In all thy labours beholde the ende, 178.26–7: Ever remembre the ende of every thynge that thou begynnest. **1504** Hawes *Example* Bb4^v^[2]: Thynke on the ende or thou begynne. **1509** Bar-clay *Ship* I 30[28]: Beware the ende, 89[6–7]: For he that is wyse wyll no thynge assay With-out he knowe howe he well ende it may, II 140[22]: Beware the ende for that oft payth for all. **1509** Fisher *Henry VII* 270.10–1: Expectan-dus est finis. The ende is to be abyden and loked upon. **1525** Berners *Froissart* IV 387[34–6]: For who soo ever enterprysed to doo a thynge, ought to regarde what ende may come therof. **c1525** Heywood *Wit* 7–8: But that wytt whych bostythe the full of his wynnyng, As thowghff he knewe th'end of thing at begynnyng, That wytt schall schow wyttles ympedyment. **a1533** Berners *Arthur* 358[27–9]: Whan one begynneth a mater, it is great wysdome to regarde and beholde what ende it wyl come untoo. **1555** Heywood *E* 192.267: He knowth none ende of his good, marke his wynnyng, He knowth of his good none ende, nor begynnyng, **1556** *Spider* 235[26–8]: This common saying: before thou ought begin, have an iye to the ende, 240[7]: Ere thou ought begin, have an eie to the ende, 246[3–4]: Ere we ought begin . . . have an Iye to the ende, 251[8–9]: Ere anie wight ought begin, Have an Iye to thend, 255[16–7]: Ere thou ought begin: have an iye to the ende, 258[22–3]: This sage saying, the wyfe have saide and saie, Have an iye to the ende, ere thou ought begin, 261[18–9]: In this begoon to scan, Before the end, what thend maie be, 266[2]: Vew thend of all, ere the beginning be woon, 270[28]: At their . . . beginning, to have iye to thend, 276[23]: Ere ought begin: have iye to thend. Apperson 397:60; Robbins-Cutler 4049.3; Smith 78; Tilley E125, 128; Whiting *Drama* 72, 81, 93, 133, *Scots* I 162. See **H245.**

E85 Praise at the **End**
a1300 *Tristrem* 13.406–7: Of thing, that is him dere, Ich man preise at ende! **a1400** *Gast of Gy* 96.1665–6 (cf. *Spiritus Guydonis* 326[3–4]): For mans lyfe es to prayse na thing, Bot if he may have gud endyng. **1471** Caxton *Recuyell* II 492.12–5: For all the loange and preysynge is in the ende. Who that begynneth a werke wherof the begynnyng is fayre and the ende fowle, all is loste. **c1523** Barclay *Mirrour* 24[21]: Remember that all thinges are praysed at good ende, 37[36]: And nought can be surely praysed before the ende. See **E81, 158, H363, L254, P39, S715, T125.**

E86 Seen in **End** seen in all
c1250 *Hendyng O* 197.31: Sene hon hende, sene on al. Kneuer 59; Schleich 274; Singer III 140.

E87 Take heed to your **End** (*i.e.*, death) (*varied*)
a1325 *Sarmun* in Heuser 94.167: Takith gode hede, men, to yur end. **a1400** *Alexander C* 182.3094–5: Heves noght your hert up to highe, take hede to your end; It limps noght all-way the last to licken with the first, 196.3297–8: Loke to thine ende, For die the bose, quen all is done and ay thi day scortis. **a1400** *Proverbis of Wysdom* 246.87–8: Where ever thou be, have god yn mynd And al way thynk on thyn end. **c1440** *Prose Alexander* 55.36–7: Bot alway thynke on thy laste ende, 65.33: And tharefore take hede to thi laste ende. **a1450** *Castle* 186.3647–9: To save you fro synnynge, Evyr at the begynnynge Thynke on youre last endynge! **1450** *Dicts* 122.17–8: He is unhappy that is handelinge in his malice and that thinkithe not on his eende. **c1450** *Fyrst thou sal* 89.69–70: What ever thou do hafe god in mynde And thinke ymonge on thi last ende. **a1500** *Additional MS.37075* 277.6: What thu doyst thynk on the endyng day. **a1500** *Gostly Batayle* in *Yorkshire Writers* II 428[43–4]: Salomone seyth: "In alle thy werkes thynke one thy ende, ande thou shalt never doo syne." **a1500** *Harley MS.4294* in *Rel. Ant.* I 316[1–2]: Man, remember thy end, And thou shalt never be shend. **a1500** *MS. Marginalia* in Hoccleve I 181 n. 3: Before thou pretend any evill in thy harte, Remember the end when thow shalt departe, quod Carter. **c1500** *O mortall man* in *Studia Neophilologica* 26(1953) 64.74: Consyder thyne ende, and consydyr whether thou shalte goe. Tilley E125.

E88 To care which **End** goes before
c1497 Medwall *Fulgens* C1ʳ[26]: For he carith not whiche ende goth before. Tilley E130.

E89 To have the worse **End** (of the staff)
a1387 Higden-Trevisa II 29[4–7]: That yere men of that side schal have the worse ende and be overcome, and men of the other side schal have the better ende and be at here above. **a1500** *Coventry Plays* 49.502–5: Yea, he thatt hatth soche on on hym to crawe He schal be sure, asse God me sawe, Eyver the worse yend of the staff to have, Att the lattur yend. **1546** Heywood *D* 64.3: Who had the wurs ende of the staffe? Apperson 715: wrong; *Oxford* 171; Tilley E132; Whiting *Drama* 343:528, *Scots* I 163.

E90 Who serves not to the **End** loses his reward
1484 Caxton *Royal Book* D6ʳ⁻ᵛ: And it is sayd comynlye, who that serveth and serveth not to thende, loseth hys rewarde. See **P371, S163, T104.**

End, vb.

E91 He **Ends** not well who does wickedly
a1471 Ashby *Policy* 17.140: He endithe not wele that wykkidly dothe.

E92 Well is him that may **End** well
a1325 *Hendyng C* 182.1: Wel is him that wel ende mai. Kneuer 16–7; *Oxford* 701; Schleich 247; Singer III 124–5. See **E83.**

E93 Wrothly (*badly*) **Ends** who lither (*wickedly*) does
a1325 *Hendyng C* 190.45: Wrothelich endit that lithir doth. Kneuer 52–3; Schleich 272; Singer III 138. See **W571.**

E94 A foul **Ending** falls from false living
c1420 Wyntoun III 283.1023–4: For thar hym fel a foule endynge For his fals and his il liffynge. Whiting *Scots* I 163.

E95 An **Enemy**'s mouth seld says well
1481 Caxton *Reynard* 7[22–3]: It is a comyn proverbe, An Enemyes mouth saith seeld wel. Apperson 182; Jente 766; *Oxford* 172; Tilley E144.

E96 Eschew reconciled **Enemies**

c1390 Chaucer *CT* VII 1182[B2372]: And eek thou shalt eschue the conseillyng of thyne olde enemys that been reconsiled. Apperson 183; *Oxford* 525; Tilley H373. See **C374, E100, F662.**

E97 A familiar **Enemy** (foe) is the worst (*varied*) **897** Alfred *Boethius* 67.22–4: Hwylc is wirsa wol oððe ænegum men mare daru þonne he hæbbe on his geferrædenne and on his neaweste feond on freondes anlicnesse? **a1200** *Ancrene* 52.8–10: For na feondschipe nis se uvel as is fals freondschipe; feond the thuncheth freond is sweoke over alle. **a1300** *Alisaunder* 265.4719: From pryvees may noma(n) hym warie. **c1300** *Body and Soul* 41 L 241–4: Ho may more trayson do Or is loverd betere engine, Than he that al is trist is to, In and ought (*A:* And is with him) as oune hyn? **c1300** *Guy*[1] 184 A 3167–8: Non no may so wele tresoun do So may he that his trust is to. **c1300** Robert of Gloucester I 105.1454–5: Ther was tricherie inou vor no mon ne mai bet do Gile another than thulke that he truste mest to. **c1300** *South English Legendary* (*Laud*) 348.105–6: For noman ne may to other sonere tricherie do Thane thilke that is him evere neigh and that he trist mest to. **a1325** *Cursor* II 418.7231–4: That oft in faand man findes sua, Man priveest es mast man faa, Ne thare es nan so gret mai greif Als traitur dern and prive theif. **a1350** *Ancrene* (*Merton*) 28.22–3: Boecius: Nulla pestis peior quam familiaris inimicus. **c1375** Barbour *Bruce* I 131.529–30: And nane may treson do titar than he That man in trowis l(e)awte. **c1380** Chaucer *Boece* III pr. v 68–70: And what pestilence is more myghty for to anoye a wyght than a famylier enemy? **c1385** *TC* v 1266–7: But who may bet bigile, yf hym lyste, Than he on whom men weneth best to triste? **c1385** Usk 72.107–8: Nothing is werse, ne more mighty for to anoy than is a familier enemy. **a1393** Gower *CA* II 202.2674–7: These olde Philosophres wise Thei writen upon thilke while, That he mai best a man beguile In whom the man hath most credence. **c1395** Chaucer *CT* IV[E] 1784–94: O famulier foo, that his servyce bedeth! O servant traytour, false hoomly hewe . . . God graunte thee thyn hoomly fo t'espye! For in this world nys worse pestilence Than hoomly foo al day in thy presence. **c1395** *WBible* Ecclesiasticus xxxvii 1 *gloss:* No pestilence is myghtiere to anoye, than is an homely enemye. **a1400** *Arthur* 17.543–4: Who may best bygyle a man But such as he tryst upan? **a1400** *Romaunt B* 3931–2: For he may best, in every cost, Disceyve, that men tristen most. **a1400** *Scottish Legends* II 328.849–52: For is nane, I undir-ta, Sa paytener, na sa fellone fa, As is mast hamely, gyf that he Vil wikit man or tratour be. **a1400** Wyclif *Sermons* I 140[6]: For homely enemyes ben the worste. **c1400** *Brut* I 216.32–217.2: Wel may now a man see by him that no man may desceyve another, rathere than he that he most trust oppon. **1410** Walton *Boethius* 151[11–2]: A more parelous meschief is there none Than is thi foo with the famuliere. **a1420** Lydgate *Troy* III 696.4517–8: For what is worse, outher fer or nere, Than a foo that is famyler? **a1425** *Metrical Paraphrase OT* 57.7645–6: Ffor none may bettur a man betray Then he in whom his hert (is trist). **a1439** Lydgate *Fall* I 182.6455–9: Damage i(n) erthe is non so grevous, As an enmy which that is secre, Nor pestilence non so pereilous As falsnesse where he is preve, And speciali in femynyte. **a1450** *Myne awen dere* 155.197–9: Bot he that thou tristis mykell in And in thy nede will fra the twyn, He that is maste enmy of all. **a1450** *Partonope* 110–1.3316–8: There-fore me seythe an olde sawe: He to home a man dothe tryste, Ever may dyseve hym beste, *R:* He to whom a man dothe truste Evermore may defende him beste. **1456** Hay *Law* 187.28–9: For the law sais that we have nane samekle a fa, na sa evill a pestilence as a familier inymy. **c1470** *Wallace* 5.111–2: Is nayne in warld, at scaithis ma do mar, Than weile trastyt in borne familiar. **c1480** Caxton *Ovyde* 118[30–2]: For ofte he is deceyveth by hym on whome he moste sette in his affyance and trusteth. A man may never kepe hym wel fro a traytre, **1481** *Reynard* 81[24–6]: He or they to whomme a man trusteth moost is ofte by hym or them deceyvyd, **1483** *Cato* A4v[26–8]: For it is sayd comunely that there is none soo evyl an enemye as he that sheweth hym a frende by fyction. **1495** *Medytacyons of saynt Bernarde* E2r[15–6]: For an enmye of housholde noyeth moost. **a1500** Hill 130.14: In whom I trust most, sonnest me deseyvith. **a1500** *Thre Prestis* 49.1143–4: Me to begyle quha hes mair craft and gin Than thay in quhome my traist ay maist is in? **c1505** Watson *Valentine* 14.19–21: Now there is not a worse enemy than he which is famylyer in a house whan he casteth hym for to doo evyl. **1513** Douglas *Aeneid* IV 3.88: Thir fays famyliar beyn full quaynt to knaw. **c1523** Barclay *Mirrour* 26[43–4]: A counterfayted frende with paynted spech ornate, By false fayned favour disceyveth worst of all. **1532** Berners *Golden Boke* 312.6361–2: These myschevous people are our homely and familiar enmies. Apperson 713; *Oxford* 37–8, 465; Tilley D181, P243. See **D123, F4, 45, 365, 669, 673, I49, T494, V15.**

E98 Give **Enemies** leisure to flee
c1420 Wyntoun V 409.3459–64: Tharfor said Scipio, that was wisse, That men sulde gif thar innymys Laysar to fle, that war straytly Stade, for swa (sulde men) lichtly Ourcum (thaim); for qwha to the flicht Hym settis, tynys bathe hart and mycht. Whiting *Scots* I 163. Cf. Apperson 67: To make a bridge of gold; *Oxford* 249; Smith 34; Tilley B665.

E99 There is no little **Enemy** (*varied*)
c1390 Chaucer *CT* VII 1324[B2514]: Senek seith: "A man that is well avysed, he dredeth his leste enemy." **1450** *Dicts* 136.11–2: Noise not thyne ennymye for litille though he (be) litille, for he may noy the more than thou thinkist, 162.12–3: Thou shuldist think that the febelist of alle thyne enmyes is myghtier than thou. **c1450** *Consail and Teiching* 75.331–2: Lat nocht lichtly of a lytill fa, For gret men war desavit swa. **c1450** Idley 96.904–6: Therfore holsom it is wherever thou goo Thyn enemyes to drede in every place, Not oonly the grete, but the smale alsoo. **a1475** Ashby *Dicta* 57.323–4: Repute never oon enemye litel, For he may hurt you more bi his malice, 66.526–7: Youre leest enemy, Repute ye strenger Than your selfe in his fals Iniquite. **1483** Caxton *Cato* I6v[25–6]: It is sayd comynly that ther is no lytel frende nor none lytelle enemye, **1484** *Aesop* 194[16–8]: For there is none soo lytyl but that somtyme he may lette and avenge hym self. **a1500** *Colkelbie* 296.477–80: To contempt a small fo, Quhill he haith grace to ryd or go At liberty and fredome, I hold it is no wisdome. **c1500** *Melusine* 113.1–2: Dyspreyse not your enmyes though they be litel, 191.2–3: Despyse never none enemy, thaugh he be lytel, 197.23: For there nys none litel enmy. **1525** Berners *Froissart* V 403[32–4]: He is nat wise that feareth nat his ennemyes, thoughe they be never so fewe. Jente 651; *Oxford* 172; Tilley E142, M389. See **M784.**

E100 Trust never an (old) **Enemy** (*varied*)
c1390 Chaucer *CT* VII 1183[B2373]: The book seith that "no wight retourneth saufly into the grace of his olde enemy." **a1400** *Proverbis of Wysdom* 244.21: Trust never in thyn enmy. **c1450** *Fyrst thou sal* 91.165: Trest never thine old enmy. **c1450** *Go way, Fore that* in Lumby *Ratis Raving* 9.21: Thi enemys auld trow never In. **1525** Berners *Froissart* IV 196[40]: For ther is no trust in a mannes enemy. *Oxford* 673; Smith 16; Whiting *Scots* I 163. See **E96, F364.**

E101 From **England** to Almaigne
1533 More *Confutacion* 736 B[4–6]: From the hither end of England to the ferther ende of Almaine.

E102 Merry **England**
c1300 Robert of Gloucester I 1 (*var.* 1): Engelond his ryght a merye lond. **c1325** *Chronicle* 25.605: In Engelond that is so me(r)y. **a1400** *Cursor* I 9 G 8: Meri ingland, 21 G 235. **a1470** Malory I 209.13: Oure noble knyghtes of mery Ingelonde. **a1500** *Becket III* 263.58: Engelond is a meri cuntre. NED Merry 1b; *Oxford* 420.

E103 To speak plain **English**
a1439 Lydgate *Fall* I 294.3360: To speke pleyn Inglissh, made hym a cokold. **a1438** Kempe 113.4–5: Thu lyest falsly, in pleyn Englysch. Tilley E152.

E104 **Englishmen** and Gascons are naturally covetous
1523 Berners *Froissart* II 164[2–3]: Englysshmen and Gascons naturally are covetouse.

E105 **Englishmen** are born under the domination of the moon
1490 Caxton *Eneydos* 2.20–3: For we englysshe men ben borne under the domynacyon of the mone, whiche is never stedfaste but ever waverynge, wexynge one season and waneth and dyscreaseth another season.

E106 **Englishmen** are changeable
a1500 Alcock *Sermo pro episcopo* B3r[2.2–7]: A faythfull conclusyon to all wyse straungers, That Englysshmen be as chaungable in theyr maners and wyttes as they be in outwarde garmentes. See **E111.**

E107 **Englishmen** are envious
c1303 Mannyng *Handlyng* 141.4165–6: We Englys men theron shulde thynke, That envye us nat blynk. **1523** Berners *Froissart* I 31[16–7]: These Inglisshemen most commonly have ever great envy at straungers, III 417[7–9]: Englysshmen are right envyouse of the welthe of other, and alwayes hath ben, **1525** IV 67[10–2]: The Scottes somewhat resembled the Englysshemen, because they be envyous over strangers. See **F617.**

E108 (**Englishmen** in fashion) are the apes of every nation
c1450 Idley 159.28: We be called the verri aapes of every nacion. Tilley E153.

E109 Englishmen (Kentishmen) have tails (*varied*)
a1200 Lawman III 184–7.29543–600: (The story of St. Augustine at Dorchester [B: Rochester]). **a1300** *Richard* 117.69–70 (*var.*): The kyng named hym kyng by name, And cleped hym (*Richard*) taylarde, and seid hym shame, 173.1775–6: And he answered, he helde no wardes Of the Englysshe taylardes, 176.1830: Go hom, dogges, with your tayle, 179.1877–8: And shote to them with arblast, The tayled dogges (*var.*: doggetayles) for to agast, 180.1886, 184.1958–60: Slee downe righte the Frensshe cowarde, And ken them in batayl That ye have no tayl, 187.2006, 194–5.2124–6, 196.2158, 416.6585–6: But see, lord, withouten ffayle, Fro his body kyttes the tayle, 417.6599: Kyng R. with hys grete tayle. **c1300** Robert of Gloucester II 821.1–10: (St. Augustine at Rochester). **a1338** Mannyng *Chronicle A* II 528.15209–12: Ffor they wyth tailles the godeman schamed, Ffor tailles al Englische kynde ys blamed; In manie sere londes seyd, Of tho tailles we have umbreyde, *Chronicle B* I 158[26]: And what haf I to do with Inglis tayled kyng? **a1350** *Rel. Ant.* II 230–7: (A Latin satire against Rochester). **c1400** *Brut* I 97.4–16: (St. Augustine at Rochester). **c1438** Kempe 236.29–30: Thei clepyd hir Englisch sterte (*tail*) and spokyn many lewyd wordys un-to hir. **c1471** *Recovery of the Throne* in Wright *Political Poems* II 279[16]: Thay (*Kentishmen*) vanysshyd away as thayre tayles had be brente. **1483** Caxton *Golden Legende* 139v[1]: (St. Augustine at Rochester). **a1508** Dunbar *Flyting* 9.125: And he that dang Sanct Augustine with ane rumple. **c1513** Skelton *Viltissimus Scotus Dundas Allegat Caudas Contra Angligenas* 193.7–10: This Dundas, This Scottishe as, He rymes and railes That Englishmen have tailes, 29–31: Dundas of Galaway With thy versyfyeng rayles How they have tayles. Apperson 338; Alan M. Cohn in *PMLA* 77(1962) 343; Ch. -V. Langlois in *Revue Historique* 52(1893) 309–11; F. Liebermann in *Archiv* 104(1900) 124–5; *Oxford* 333; L. M. C. Randall in *Art Bulletin* 42(1960) 25–38; Tilley K17.

E110 Englishmen love gift
a1300 *Richard* 265.3375: Men saye, Englysschemen love gyffte.

E111 Nothing pleases **Englishmen** for any term
a1470 Malory III 1229.13–4: Alas! thys ys a greate defaughte of us Englysshemen, for there may no thynge us please no terme. See **E106.**

E112 When **English(men)** see their advantage they forget the virtue of truces
c1420 Wyntoun VI 413.2599–604: It is of Inglis nacioune The comon kynd conditioune Off trewis the wertu to foreyet, Quhen thai wil thaim fore wynnyng set, And rekles of gude faithe to be, Quhare thai can thare awantage se.

E113 He that **Enhances** himself too high declines the lower (*varied*)
a1400 *Alexander C* 158.2714: He that enhansis him to heghe the heldire (*Dublin:* lawer) he declynes. **1484** Caxton *Aesop* 247[1–3]: He that over moche enhaunceth hym self sooner than he wold, he falleth doune. See **C296.**

E114 The **Enmity** of a wise man is better than the friendship of a fool
a1500 *Disciplina Clericalis* 19[8–9]: Bettir is the enymite of a wiseman than the friendship of a foole.

E115 Enough is as good as a feast
a1470 Malory I 246.10–1: For inowghe is as good as a feste. **a1475** *Assembly of Gods* 59.2035: As good is ynowgh as a gret feste. **1546** Heywood *D* 101.60: Enough is as good as a feast, **1555** *E* 182.200. Apperson 184–5; *Oxford* 174; Taylor and Whiting 121; Tilley E158; Whiting *Drama* 120, 192, *Scots* I 163.

E116 Enough is enough (*varied*)
c1395 Chaucer *CT* III[D] 336: Have thou ynogh, thee thar nat pleyne thee. **1546** Heywood *D* 101.58: Enough is enough. Apperson 185; *Oxford* 174; Taylor and Whiting 121; Tilley E159. See **E28, 126.**

E117 Enough is not half full
1513 Douglas *Aeneid* III 119.89: Enewch is nocht halff fyll. Whiting *Scots* I 163.

E118 Enough often comes to the man that todraws (*?spends*)
a1350 Castelford 3.19791–2: Anogh, es sene and saide in saghes, Ofte comes unto that man to draghes. See **G261, L83.**

E119 Enough should suffice
1480 Caxton *Ovyde* 89[27–8]: Ynough myghte have suffysed hym. See **S868.**

E120 He has **Enough** that can hold him content
a1477 Caxton *Curtesye* 25.231: He hath ynough that can holde hym content. **1509** Barclay *Ship* II 104[20–1]: Thus is that man both wyse and excellent That with ynoughe can holde hym selfe content. **a1513** Dunbar *Of Content* 144–5.5, 10, *etc.* (*refrain*): He hes anewch that is content.

Oxford 175; Tilley E162. See **F462, L394, 403, P294, S867.**

E121 He has **Enough** that has bread enough
c1378 *Piers* B vii 86: He hath ynough that hath bred ynough, though he have nought elles: *Satis dives est, qui non indiget pane. Oxford* 541.

E122 He that has **Enough** to help himself and will not, I shall not
a1400 Bozon *Contes* 44[28–9]: He that hadd inou to help him self wital, Sithen he ne wold, I ne wile ne I ne schal. Cf. Taylor and Whiting 154:3.

E123 No one sings "**Enough,** enough"
a1450 *Castle* 158.2720–1: "I-now, I-now," hadde nevere space; That ful songe was nevere songe, 169.3116: For thou seydyst nevere "I-now I-now." See **M788.**

E124 Not to have **Enough** till one's mouth is full of clay
a1450 *Castle* 155.2638–9: Mankynde seyth he hath never I-nowe, Tyl his mowthe be ful of clay. Apperson 185; *Oxford* 175; Tilley E166. See **M290.**

E125 There is not **Enough** where nought leaves (*remains*)
c1450 *Douce MS.52* 56.133: There is noughht i-now, there nought levys. **c1450** *Rylands MS.394* 107.26. *Oxford* 175; Tilley E168.

E126 What need to have more than **Enough?**
c1440 Charles of Orleans 4.99: What nede is hit to have more then y-nough? **c1475** Henryson *Fables* 16.375–6: Quha hes aneuch, of na mair hes he neid, Thocht it be littill into quantatie. **a1500** *How the Wise Man* 34.178: More then ynogh thou nevyr coveyte. **c1515** Barclay *Eclogues* 83.820: When man hath inough what nedeth him have more? See **E116, W713.**

E127 An **Ensample** (*example*) in doing is more than in teaching
a1415 Mirk *Festial* 216.18–20: Then saythe Seynt Austeyn that an ensampull yn doyng ys mor commendabull then ys techyng other prechyng. Apperson 194; *Oxford* 181; Taylor and Whiting 122; Tilley E213. See **D289.**

E128 **Entermete** (*meddle*) not too much
a1400 *Proverbis of Wysdom* 245.63: To mekyll not thow auntermete. See **F432.**

E129 Better to flee than to abide a foolish **Enterprise** (*varied*)
c1500 *Melusine* 288.16–7: Oftyme it is said that bettre is to flee, than to abyde a folyssh enterpryse. **1523** Berners *Froissart* II 497[7]: And of a folysshe enterprice cometh no good. Tilley D79.

E130 Rash **Enterprises** oft bring to ruin
c1515 Barclay *Eclogues* 168.779: Rashe enterprises oft bringeth to ruine.

E131 The **Entry** glad, the end trouble and sorrow
a1439 Lydgate *Fall* III 751.2842: The entre glad; the eende trouble and sorwe. See **B200, W41.**

E132 Proud **Entry** foul end
a1400 *Destruction of Troy* 74.2248–50: What proffet any prowes with a prowde entre, To begyn any goode, on a ground febill, And fortune it faile, and have a fowle ende?

E133 Better be **Envied** than pitied
1546 Heywood *D* 42.48: Better be envied than pitied, folke sey. Apperson 42; *Oxford* 38; Tilley E177.

E134 **Envy** is green
c1450 *Epistle of Othea* 38.7–8: Off Envye that sche in the have no hold, Wyche colour qwhyte into green can chaung, 16–8: Sche had hyr syster herce in envyose scorne and became . . . greene ffor verrey pure envy. See **I70.**

E135 **Envy** is the lavender (*laundress*) of the court
c1386 Chaucer *LGW* F 358: Envie ys lavendere of the court alway. **a1393** Gower *CA* II 213.3095–7: Senec witnesseth openly How that Envie proprely Is of the Court the comun wenche.

E136 **Envy** may not die
c1450 *Ponthus* 32.11–2: Bot envye that may not dye comes aftre upon theym, 66.21. **a1523** Berners *Froissart* I 42[23–5]: Envy . . . which never dyed in Inglande, and also it reigneth and wyl reigne in dyvers other countres (Whiting *Froissart* 313:293: On dist ensi que envie ne poet morir en Engleterre), III 417[6–7]: There is a comune proverbe, the whiche is true, and that is, howe envy never dyeth. Apperson 185; *Oxford* 175; Tilley E172.

E137 **Envy** never has rest
c1505 Watson *Valentine* 67.5–6: But envye is of suche nature that it hathe never reste. See **H270.**

E138 Old **Envy** makes new distance (*quarrel*)
a1475 *Good Rule* in *Rel. Ant.* I 74[34]: For old envy makyth newe dystayns.

E139 Better **Ere** (*early*) than too late

a1250 *Ancrene* (*Nero*) 153.23: Betere is er then to lete. Apperson 43; Skeat 27.

E140 As white as **Ermine**
c1450 *When the son* 392.324: Whitter of hir self then ermyn.

Erne, see **Eagle**

E141 As fous (*eager*) as **Erne** (*eagle*) in flight
a1325 *Cursor* II 1034.18060: Was never ern sa fus (FT: fresh) o flight.

E142 As swift as the (an) **Erne**(s)
a1200 *Ancrene* 100.24: Ure witheriwines swiftre then earnes. **a1300** *Meidan Maregrete* 495.210: Ic com thider sone, swift as an erne. **c1395** *WBible* II Kings i 23: Thei weren swiftere than eglis, Jeremiah iv 13, Lamentacions iv 19: Oure pursueris weren swiftere than the eglis of hevene. **a1400** *Stanzaic Life* 270.7993–4: But as an erne he went Swiftely thenne out of our sight. **c1490** Ryman 256.7: As egles, swifte of fete. Svartengren 378; Whiting *Scots* I 161.

E143 Though the **Erne** fly highest he must come down to the low earth
a1400 *Scottish Legends* I 123.495–8: For thocht the eyrne fle heyeste, And the sone seis clerlyaste, Yet mon of fors he cum done To the law yherd, and ther sujorne. See **C296.**

E144 To fly like an **Erne**
a1300 *Jacob and Joseph* 17.519: For nou me thuncheth that ich mai flen as an ern. **a1393** Gower *CA* III 250.630–2: For as an Egle with his winges Fleth above alle that men finde, So doth this science (*Astronomy*) in his kinde. **c1395** *WBible* Habakkuk i 8: Thei schulen fle as an egle hastynge to ete.

E145 An **Error** not repressed is half sustained
1459 *Defence* 516[13]: Hit is rehersed in scriptures autentique that an erroure not repressed is halfve susteyned.

E146 **Eschewing** is the only remedy
c1380 Chaucer *PF* 140: Th'eschewing is only the remedye! Apperson 20; Skeat 136.

E147 Sometimes is **Esne's** (*serf's*) time, sometimes (an) other's
c900 *Old English Cato* 4.33–4: Swa man on ealden bigspellan cwyðð, "Hwilen byð esnes tid, hwilen oðres."

E148 High **Estate** and humility are seldom seen in one person
a1400 *Scottish Legends* II 146.761–2: And hey estate and humylyte In a persone seldine se we. Cf. Chaucer *TC* ii 167–8.

E149 In high **Estate** is no assurance
c1423 Lydgate *Serpent* 54.5: In highe estate is none assurance, **a1439** *Fall* III 754.2947: In hih estat is litil sekirnesse. See **M216, R191.**

E150 A mean **Estate** is better than high climbing
1478 Rivers *Morale Proverbes* [7.21–2]: A meene estat is better to entende Than hygh climmyng, lest that oon sone descende. See **C296, E24, K77.**

E151 Spend after your **Estate**
a1400 *Proverbis of Wysdom* 245.80: And spend after thyn estate. **c1450** *Fyrst thou sal* 89.66.

E152 With **Este** (*dainty food*) one may overquat (*glut*) himself
c1250 *Owl* 32–4.353–7: Mid este thu the might overquatie, And overfulle maketh wlatie; And evrich mureghthe mai agon Yif me hit halt evre forth in on, Bute one, that is Godes riche.

E153 The **Ethiopian** (Blueman) cannot change his skin (*varied*)
a1387 Higden-Trevisa VI 377[19]–79[1]: But for the Blewman (*Lat.* Aethiops) chaungeth nought lightliche his skyn. **c1395** *WBible* Jeremiah xiii 23: If a man of Ethiopie mai chaunge his skyn, ether a pard mai chaunge hise dyversitees. **c1500** Fabyan 217[4]: But lyke as the man of Inde, at no tyme, chaungeth his coloure. Apperson 53; *Oxford* 693; Taylor and Whiting 121–2; Tilley E186, L206; Whiting *Drama* 41. See **K26.**

E154 To trow (*believe*) as the **Evangel**
a1400 *Romaunt B* 5453: And trowe hem as the Evangile. See **G401.**

E155 The **Eve** accords nothing with the morrow
a1439 Lydgate *Fall* III 751.2840–1: That day began with joie and gret gladnesse; The eve nothyng accordyng with the morwe. See **M694.**

E156 To have a part of **Eve's** smock
c1330 *Seven Sages A* 100.2196–200: And had a wif was queint and fair, But sche was fikel under hir lok, And hadde a parti of Eve smok. And manie ben yit of hire kinne, That ben al bilapped ther inne. MED Eve.

E157 After **Even** (night) comes day
a1500 *Imitatione* (*1*) 49.31: After evene cometh day. **1502** *Imitatione* (*2*) 186.32–3: After the night the day.

E158 At **Even** praise (hery [*praise*]) the (fair) day
c1250 *Hendyng O* 197.33: At even me shal preisen the feire dai, **a1325** *C* 188.34: At eve

man scal the dai heri. **1381** *Jack Carter* in Knighton II 139[10]: For at the even men heryth the day. **c1420** Wyntoun III 37.415–6: For at the ewyn, or eftyr, ay Men prisis ay the fayr day, 36.417–8 (*var.*): For at the evin of the faire day Men prysis it, the suth to say. **a1439** Lydgate *Fall* III 976.2024: The faire day men do preise at eve, 2032, 977.2040. **c1450** *Douce MS.52* 45.10: At evene prayse the fayre day. **c1450** *Rylands MS.394* 96.30. **1481** Caxton *Reynard* 75[7–8]: Me ought not preyse to(o) moche the daye tyl even be come. Apperson 509–10; Kneuer 67–8; *Oxford* 515; Schleich 265; Singer III 135; Tilley D100; Whiting *Scots* I 156. Cf. Jente 640. See **E81, 85, F543, H363, L254, M270, P39, S715, T125.**

E159 **Even** red, morn fair, *etc.*
c1000 *WSG* Matthew xvi 2–3: On æfen ge cweðaþ, To morgen hyt byþ smylte weder; þes heofon ys read. And on morgen ge cweþað, To dæg hyt byð hreoh weder; þeos lyft scinð unwederlice, Luke xii 54–5: Þonne ge geseoð þa lyfte cumende on westdæle, sona ge cweðað, Storm cymð; and hit swa byð. And þonne ge geseoð suðan blawan, ge secgað, þæt (*hæte*) is towerd, and hit byð. **c1395** *WBible* Matthew xvi 2–3: Whanne the eventid is comun, ye seien, It schal be clere, for hevene is rodi; and the morewtid, To dai tempest, for hevene schyneth heveli, Luke xii 54: Whanne ye seen a cloude risynge fro the sunne goynge doun, anoon ye seien, Reyn cometh; and so it is don. And whanne ye seen the south blowynge, ye seien, That heete schal be; and it is don. **c1454** Pecock *Folewer* 54.19–21: We trowen that this day schal be a reyny day for that his morownyng was reed, or that to morow schal be a fayre day for that his eventide is reed. Apperson 186, 526–7; *Oxford* 176–7, 595; Taylor and Whiting 122; Tilley E191, M1175, 1178, S515.

E160 **Evensong** and morrowsong are not all one (*varied*)
c1387-95 Chaucer *CT* I[A] 830–1: If even-song and morwe-song accorde, Lat se now who shal telle the firste tale. **c1450** *Rylands MS.394* 94.21: Even songe and morn songe beth not both on. **c1475** *Rawlinson MS. D 328* 123.66: Hef song and moro hys not hall hone. **?1505** *Answer of William Roper* in James Raine ed. *Volume of English Miscellanies* (Surtees Society 85,1890) 31[24–5]: And then we sayd, and he walde be the saym man att morne as he hys at hevyn, we wald tayk thaym. Cf. *Oxford* 177.

E161 A merry **Eventide** follows a sorry morrowtide
1502 *Imitatione* (2) 169.25: A mery eventyde foloweth a sory morow tyde. See **B325, E175, F295, M695.**

E162 For **Evermore** and longer too
c1475 Henryson *Fables* 12.278–9: "Ye, dame" (quod scho), "how lang will this lest?" "For evermair, I wait, and langer to."

E162.1 **Everything** attains its guerdon (*reward*) like as it is
a1420 Lydgate *Troy* III 658.3217–8: For every thing, platly for to seyne, Like as it is, his guerdoun doth atteyne.

E163 **Everything** follows its nature
a1449 Lydgate *Fabules* in *MP* II 573.187: Thus every thyng foloweth hys nature.

E164 **Everything** (All thing) has a (be)ginning
c1385 Chaucer *TC* ii 671–2: For every thyng, a gynnyng hath it nede Er al be wrought, withowten any drede. **c1450** Capgrave *Katharine* 217.762: All thing that is made, be-gynnyng must have. **c1475** *Rawlinson MS. D 328* 126.86: Every thynge hath a begynnyng. **a1500** Hill 128.12: All thing hath a begining. **1533** More *Confutacion* 831 E[6–7]: Every thyng muste nedes have a begynnyng. **c1500** *Melusine* 304.21–2: In every thing most be bygynnyng, tofore the ende commeth. Apperson 8; *Oxford* 180; Skeat 163; Tilley B257; Whiting *Drama* 242, 244. See **T166.**

E165 **Everything** here does change and vary
a1437 Lydgate *That Now is Hay* in *MP* II 812.123: Every thynge here dothe chaunge and varye.

E166 **Everything** is declared by its contrary
c1385 Chaucer *TC* i 637: By his contrarie is every thyng declared. See **C415.**

E167 **Everything** is wist (*known*) though it be covered with the mist
c1380 Chaucer *HF* 351–2: O, soth ys, every thing ys wyst, Though hit be kevered with the myst. Cf. Jente 695. See **M806.**

E168 **Everything** loses its goodhead (*goodness*) with unmethe (*excess*)
c1250 *Owl* 32.349–52: Vor hit is soth, Alured hit seide, And me hit mai ine boke rede: "evrich thing mai losen his godhede Mid unmethe and mid overdede." See **E200.**

E169 **Everything** must have its course (turn)
1523 Berners *Froissart* III 289[39]: Every thyng

must have his course, **1525** V 100[33], VI 346[14]: Every thynge muste have his tourne.

E170 **Everything** of (the) world is vain
a1393 Gower *CA* II 20.560: For every worldes thing is vein. See **W664.**

E171 **Everything** seeks its semblable
c1500 *Three Kings' Sons* 74.16: Thus everi thinge sekith his semblable. See **B129, F574, L272.**

E172 **Everything** shows in the tasting
a1300 *Alisaunder* 227.4038–41: It is ywrite that every thing hym-self sheweth in the tastyng. So it is of lewed and clerk—Hym-self sheweth in his werk. Apperson 514: Proof; *Oxford* 520; Skeat 63.

E173 **Everything** takes a tarage (*quality*) from whence it comes
a1410 Lydgate *Churl* in *MP* II 483.348–50: Thus every thyng, as clerkes specifie, Frute on trees, and folk of every age, Fro whens thei cam, (thei taken) a tarage. See **T94.**

E174 **Everything** which is not eternal ages
a1000 *Latin-English Proverbs* in *ASMP* 109.6: Æghwæt forealdað þæs þe ece ne byð. Senescunt omnia que eterna non sunt. **c1000** *Royal MS. 2 B. v* in *Anglia* 2(1879) 374: Æȝhwæt ealdað þæs, þe ece ne byð. Senescunt quæ eterna non sunt.

E175 After **Evil** comes good
a1200 Lawman I 153.3608–9: After uvele cumeth god Wel is him the hit habbe mot (*B*: Wel his him the hit bide mot). See **B325, E161, F295.**

E176 All **Evil** is in delight of money
1450 *Dicts* 42.19–20: Alle evil is in delite of money. See **C491.**

E177 Better to be still than to speak **Evil**
1512 Copland *Helyas* A6v[17–8]: It is better to be styl than to speke evyll. See **S732.**

E178 **Evil** shall have that evil will deserve
c1390 Chaucer *CT* VII 632[B1822]: Yvele shal have that yvele wol deserve. Apperson 194; Skeat 247; Tilley S277.

E179 **Evil** that may betide should be dreaded
a1500 *Good Wife N* 215.189–90: For evill that may betide A man before should dread.

E180 The **Evil** that one works falls upon himself (*varied*)
c1300 Lawman II 458.21007–10: Heore yeolp and hire game, Ful ham (A: Ilomp heom) seolve to grame: So doth wel iware, The man that uvel wircheth (*A*: the mon the swa ibereth). **1484** Caxton *Aesop* 7[13–5]: For he that thynketh evyll ageynst good the evil whiche he thynketh shall ones falle upon hym self, 66[3–4]: For he that sercheth evylle evyll cometh to hym, 207[1–3]: Now the evyl which men wysshe to other cometh to hym whiche wyssheth hit, 266[1–3]: Ofte it happeth that the evyll whiche is procured to other cometh to hym whiche procureth it. See **D22, F374, P232.**

E181 From **Evil** to worse, as the cook to a baker
1492 *Salomon and Marcolphus* 11[16–7]: From evyll into worse, as the cooke to a bakere.

E182 He that can (*knows*) **Evil** is held wise
c1390 *Proverbes of diverse profetes* 551.429–32: He that con evel is holde wys and worth, Symplesse and wit ne mowe not forth; The lufthalf is put uppon the riht, And wrong for wynnyng ovur right hath miht.

E183 He that deals with **Evil** must take heed
c1400 *Roland* 114.249: He must tak hed that with evyll delithe.

E184 He that does **Evil** hates the light (*varied*)
c1000 *WSG* John iii 20: Ælc ðara þe yfele deð hatað þæt leoht, and he ne cymþ to leohte, þæt his weorc ne syn gerihtlæhte. **c1200** Orm II 229.16740–5: Forr wha sitt iss thatt ifell doth, He shunethth lihht and leme, And fleth to cumenn to the lihht, Thatt he ne wurrthe taeledd Thurrh tha thatt sen hiss fule lasst And hiss unnclene dede, 240.17058–9: And off, thatt he thatt ifell doth Ayy hatethth lihht and leme. **c1250** *Owl* 22.229–30: Vor evrich thing that schuniet right Hit luveth thuster and hatiet light. **c1395** *WBible* Proverbs i 20 *gloss:* For he that doith yvele, hatith light, and he cometh not to the light, lest hise werkis ben repreved, John iii 20. **c1475** Henryson *Fables* 10.203: For comonly sic pykeris luffis not lycht, 79.2294: Lowrence come lourand, for he lufit never licht. **1480** Caxton *Ovyde* 109[22–3]: For bryghtnes and lyght is not good for theves and malfactours. **1501** Douglas *Palice* 81.25: Thift lovis licht but lite. **1509** Barclay *Ship* I 298[7]: Yll doers alway hate the lyght. Apperson 155:26; Jente 209; *Oxford* 150, 315; Tilley I26; Whiting *Scots* II 110: Picker. See **T75.**

E185 He that does **Evil** tharf (*need*) not expect well (*varied*)
c1390 Chaucer *CT* I[A] 4319–20: And therfore this proverbe is seyd ful sooth, "Him thar nat wene wel that yvele dooth." **1492** *Salomon and Marcolphus* 9[16–7]: He that doth evyll and hopyth good, is disceyvyd in thayme bothe.

a1500 *Proverbs of Salamon* 186.63–8: Who so doyth evell not wele thar wene. Apperson 194, 291; *Oxford* 150; Skeat 236; Tilley E199.

E186 He that lives **Evil(ly)** shall end evil(ly)
a1387 *Piers* C x 291: Bote he that uvel lyveth, uvel shal ende. See **S978.**

E187 He works **Evil** that works with hasty will
a1400 *Ancrene* (*Recluse*) 77.13–4: Yvel wircheth the man oither the womman that wircheth with hasty wille. See **H162.**

E188 If you are ashamed to speak **Evil** be more ashamed to do it
a1500 *MS. Marginalia* in Hoccleve I 199 n. 1: Yf thow be ashamed to speeke evell, be more ashamed to doe the same.

E189 Neither laugh (at) nor scorn the **Evil** of other men
1484 Caxton *Aesop* 48[12–4]: And therfore men sayen comynly that of the evylle of other men ought not to lawhe ne scorne.

E190 None that purpose **Evil** work well
c1395 *WBible* Ecclesiasticus xxxvii 3 *gloss:* Noon that purposith yvel, worchith wel.

E191 Of a little **Evil** well may come a greater
1484 Caxton *Aesop* 48[1–2]: Of a lytyl evylle may wel come a gretter. See **S559.**

E192 Of **Evil** comes war (*worse*), of war comes worst of all
c1475 Henryson *Fables* 30.805–6: Off evill cummis war, off war cummis werst of all. Whiting *Scots* I 164.

E193 Of two **Evils** (harms, ills) choose the least (*varied*)
c1385 Chaucer *TC* ii 470: Of harmes two, the lesse is for to chese. **a1393** Gower *CA* II 421.714–6: For this thou myht wel understonde, That where a man schal nedes lese, The leste harme is forto chese. **c1400** *Laud Troy* II 511.17343–4: For-whi I say: better hit is Off two harmes to chose the les. **c1410** Lovelich *Merlin* I 156.5865–6: For of tweyne badde it is good to take The bettere, and it not forsake. **a1420** Lydgate *Troy* III 702.4708: Of tweyne harmys the lasse for to chese, 718.5275–9: As in proverbe it hath be seied of yore, That yif a man be constreyned sore, And may not fle, to fallen in a treyne, Lete hym chese the lasse harme of tweyne, And the gretter prudently eschewe, **c1433** *St. Edmund* 406.538–9: And of too harmys at so streiht a prykke It were wisdam to chese the lasse wykke. **c1445** Pecock *Donet* 58.30–2: Weie wel and knowe rightli whiche of the ii yvelis is the grettir, that the lasse yvel be take and receivid forto lacke the grettir. **a1450** *Gesta* 10[4–5]: Sire, hit is wreten, that of too Evelis the lasse Evill is to be chosyn. **c1450** *Merlin* I 82[11–2]: For of two evelles it is gode to take the lesse. **c1453** Pecock *Folewer* 130.3–4: In a perplexite bitwixe ii yvelis, the lasse yvel is to be chosen, 132.33–5, 138.22–4, 219.22–4. **1456** Hay *Law* 86.21–2, 203.21–3: The wryttin law sais that quhen twa evillis concurris togeder, than suld wis men tak the leste evill of the twa. **1461** Paston IV 12[22–3]: Yet of ii. harmys the leste is to be take, **1465** *IV* 149[26]: For of ii. hurtes the grettyst ys best to be eschewyd. **1471** Caxton *Recuyell* I 120.25–6, II 652.16: Men ought of two evyll thynges chese the lasse ylle, **1474** *Chesse* 130[5–6], **1484** *Aesop* 248[1–4]: Of two evyls men ought ever to eschewe and flee the worst of both yf ony of them may be eschewed, [16–9]: And therfore he is ful of wysedome and of prudence who of two grete evyls may and can escape the grettest of bothe, **1485** *Paris* 39.16–7: But it byhoveth to eschewe of two evyls the werse, **1489** *Fayttes* 240.8–9: Soo ought to be chosen of thees two evyll the best. **1493**(1671) *Seven Wise Masters* 12[9–10]. **c1500** *Melusine* 237.34–5. **c1515** Barclay *Eclogues* 202.587–8: Of two evils perdie To chose the least ill is none iniquitie. **1518** Watson *Oliver* N2r[6–7]: Of two evylles it is the beste to eschewe the worste. **1519** Horman *Vulgaria* 415[31]: harmes. **1546** Heywood *D* 26.16: yls, **1555** *E* 184.211: Ils, **1556** *Spider* 292[23–4]: Wise flies saie (and have) Of two inconveniences, the worst eschew. Apperson 654; *Oxford* 181; Taylor and Whiting 122; Tilley E207; Whiting *Drama* 155, 257, *Scots* I 164. See **F387, G357, I16, T152, W111.**

E194 Often happens **Evil** for a good turn
c1489 Caxton *Aymon* I 265.13–5: The proverbe may well be reherced for a trouth, that sayth "Often happeth evill for a good torne." Apperson 463; Tilley E204.

E195 To yield (render) **Evil** for good
c1395 *WBible* I Kings (I Samuel) xxv 21: He hath yolde to me yvel for good. **1484** Caxton *Aesop* 134[1–2]: Men ought not to rendre evylle for good. Tilley E204.

E196 To wink on the **Ewe** and worry the lamb
1546 Heywood *D* 36.27: She can wynke on the yew, and wery the lam. Apperson 694.

E197 Better to take **Example** by others than others by him

1477 Rivers *Dictes* 107[16–7]: It is bettir to take exemple by other, than other to take yt by hym. See **C161, M170, W47.**

E198 By ill **Example**(s) souls are slain (good spill [*perish*])
a1425 *Metrical Paraphrase OT* 27.10359–60: By yll exempyls oft tyme is sene Ffull mony sawlys with syns slayn. **c1515** Barclay *Eclogues* 209.796: By ill example good are in doubt to spill.

E199 Both **Excess** and default smack (*taste of*) vices
a1400 *Epistola* in *Yorkshire Writers* II 62[5]: Both excesse and defaute smakes vices: as clerkis saien. See **E203, I40.**

E200 Flee **Excess**
c1450 *Consail and Teiching* 75.329: Fle excess in al kind of thinge. See **E168.**

E201 **Executors** are not to be trusted
a1450 Audelay 13.88–9: Then is he a traytour Fore he trustys to his secatour, 84.99: And trost not to thi secatoure, 92.346–7: Ensampil be other se thou may, Be ware ye sekators. **a1500** Greene *Carols* 382: Have in mynd, in mynd, in mynd, Secuters be oft onekynd. Cf. Tilley W700. See **D73, M59.**

E202 **Experience** and art may profit more than hardiness in battle
c1412 Hoccleve *Regement* 144.3984–90: Experience and art in a bataille, Of the prudent knyght more may profite, Than hardinesse or force may availle Of him that therof knoweth noght or lite. Hardinesse, in effecte, nat worth a myte Is to victorious conclusioun, But with hym medle art, wit, and resoun. See **L381.**

E203 **Extremity** is a vice (*varied*)
a1393 Gower *CA* III 161.7641–3: Betwen the tuo extremites Of vice stant the propretes Of vertu. **1456** Hay *Law* 118.22–3: In everilk extremitee thare is vice and na vertu. **c1523** Barclay *Mirrour* 61[13]: Extremitie in all thing is very ill fitting. Apperson 188; *Oxford* 177; Tilley E224. See **E199, I40.**

E204 Before an **Eye** may open or wink
a1400 *Pricke* 135.4969–70: And that in als short whyle als hert may thynk, Or mans eghe may open or wynk. See **T547.**

E205 Better **Eye** out than always ache
1546 Heywood *D* 32.48: Better eye out then alwaie ake, **1555** *E* 149.17. Apperson 43; *Oxford* 39; Tilley E226. See **F151, P9.**

E206 Better is **Eye** sore than all blind
c1250 *Hendyng O* 192.9: Betere is heye sor, then al blind. Apperson 195; Jente 116; Kneuer 22; *Oxford* 39; Schleich 252; Singer III 127; Skeat 71.

E207 Ever is the **Eye** to the wood lea (?*lee*) wherin is that I love (*varied*)
a1200 *Ancrene* 52.3: Ah eaver is the ehe to the wude lehe, **a1250** (*Nero*) 42.16–7: Auh ever is the eie to the wude leie therinne is thet ich luvie. **c1350** Serlo 215.98: Evir is min eye i the wode leie. **a1460** *Dicts* (*Helmingham*) 135.22–3: The yghe of the lover is knowe by the lokynge upon that that he loveth. Ives 258:3; Tilley E233. See **H278, L558, N39, S506, T386, W450.**

E208 An **Eye** for an eye and a tooth for a tooth
c1000 *WSG* Matthew v 38: Ge gehyrdon þæt gecweden wæs, Eage for eage, and toð for teð. **a1325** *Cursor* II 388.6701: Ei for ei, and toth for toht. **c1395** *WBible* Exodus xxi 24: He schal yelde . . . iye for iye, tooth for tooth, Matthew v 38: Ye han herd that it hath be seid, Ighe for ighe, and tothe for tothe. **c1400** Paues 207 (Matthew v 38). MED eie n. (1) 7b.

E209 The **Eye** is a thief
a1393 Gower *CA* II 44.319–20: So that an yhe is as a thief To love, and doth ful gret meschief. Cf. Apperson 196: shrew; *Oxford* 183; Tilley E229.

E210 The **Eye** is not fulfilled with sight nor the ear with hearing
a1500 *Imitatione* (*1*) 3.4–6: Have mynde ofte tymes of that proverbe, that the eye is not fulfilled with the sight nor the ere with heringe. **1502** *Imitatione* (*2*) 154.14–5: Nother our iye is sufficyently satisfyed with seinge, ne our eris with herynge.

E211 The **Eye** is the messenger of folly
c1485 *Conversion* 48.571–2: Oculus est nuncius peccati,—That the Iey ys ever the messenger of foly. Walther III 565.19711c.

E212 The **Eyes** are more greedy than the sack (*varied*)
a1430 Lydgate *Pilgrimage* 351.12916–8: And yet myn Eyn be mor gredy, Mor desyrous to do gret wast Than ys my sak outher my tast. **c1450** *Pilgrimage LM* 157[29–30]: The eyen ben more unmesurable than the sak is either long or brod. **c1495** *Arundel Vulgaria* 10.39: For how moch soever be servede them at the table their ey is never fyllyde. Cf. Apperson 195: His eye is bigger than his belly; *Oxford* 183; Tilley E261.

E213 Far from **Eye** far from heart
c1250 *Hendyng O* 194.18: Fer from eye, fer from herte. **c1450** *Merlin* II 693[8–10]: Trewe is the proverbe that the wise man seith that "who is fer from his iye is soone for-yeten." **c1450** *Rylands MS.394* 102.18. **1472** Paston V 154[11–2]. **c1475** *Rawlinson MS. D 328* 119.19: Ffyr frwo the he ys fyr frwo the hert. **c1477** Caxton *Jason* 83.38–9: Men saye communely That ferre ys from the eye, Is ferre from the herte, 127.33–4: Who is fer fro the eye fro the herte recueleth. **a1500** *Eye and Heart* 261.718–9: That who sumever that is fer from the ey Is fer from the hert. Apperson 196:19, 476; Kneuer 39–40; *Oxford* 190–1; Schleich 258; Singer III 132; Skeat 226; Tilley S438. See **A16, D72, E216, L536, S130, 307.**

E214 He is blind in both **Eyes** that does not see into the heart
c1025 *Durham Proverbs* 12.17: Blind byþ bam eagum se þe breostum ne starat. Cecus duobus oculis qui pectore non cernit. See **M226.**

E215 Maugre (For both) one's **Eyes**
c1385 Chaucer *CT* I[A] 1796: Maugree hir eyen two, **c1395** III[D] 315: Maugree thyne yen. **c1386** *St. Erkenwald* 12.194: I may not bot boghe to thi bone for bothe myne eghen. **a1400** *Morte Arthure* 13.426, 37.1238. **a1450** *Pride of Life* in Waterhouse 94.193–4: I schal lyve ever mo For bothe two thin eye.

E216 That which the **Eye** sees not the heart rues not (*varied*)
a1200 Serlo 189.12: That einen ne sen, herte ne reut. **c1250** *Hendyng O* 194.19: That eye ne seeth, herte ne reweth. **a1325** *Cursor* I 264.4507–8: For lang was said, and yeit sua bes, "Hert sun for-gettes that ne ei seis," **a1400** *G:* Sone hert forgetis that eyen ses. **c1475** *Thewis* 188.190: At e nocht seis, hart nocht yarnis. **a1489** Caxton *Doctrinal* H4ʳ[12–3]: The wyse man saith that thyng whiche the eyen see not the herte coveyteth not. **a1500** *Eye and Heart* 261.726–8: For this tale is ful trewe, That folkis say that women callid are, That the ey seith the hert doith rewe. **a1500** *Harley MS. 2321* in *Rel. Ant.* I 207[4]: That which the eye seeth not, the hart doth not rue. **a1546** Heywood *D* 81.40. Apperson 196; Jente 165; Kneuer 64–5; *Oxford* 183; Schleich 259; Singer III 132; Tilley E247. See **E213, S130, 307.**

E217 To blear one's **Eyes**
a1300 *Richard* 282.3735–6: Youre Sawdon is nought so slye So queyntyly to blere myn yghe. **c1330** *Seven Sages A* 155 E 3037: Blereyd were bothe his yee, 199.608. **c1330** *Times of Edward II* 333.223: Anon he wole beginne to blere the wives eighe. **c1350** *Libeaus* 85.1523. **c1353** *Winner* 278. **a1375** *Octavian* (S) 39.1217, 44.1387–8: For to blere the soudanes ye, Queynte lesynges he gan to lye. **a1376** *Piers* A Prol. 71. **c1380** *Ferumbras* 20.507. **c1390** Chaucer *CT* I[A] 3865: With bleryng of a proud milleres ye, 4049: Yet shal I blere hir ye, IX[H] 252: For al thy waityng, blered is thyn ye. **a1400** *Cursor* III 1118 F 19526. **a1400** *De Pseudo-Freris* in Wyclif *EW* 316[16–7]. **a1400** *Ipomadon A* 54.1834–5. **a1400** *Romaunt B* 3911–2: Leccherie hath clombe so hye That almoost blered is myn ye. **c1400** *Beryn* 15.445. **c1400** *De Blasphemia* in Wyclif *SEW* III 420[23]. **1402** Hoccleve *Letter of Cupid* 76.105. **a1420** Lydgate *Troy* I 144.20. **c1420** Wyntoun II 243.1356. **a1425** *Ipomadon B* 294.1420. **a1430** Lydgate *Pilgrimage* 407.15106. **1436** *Libelle* 19.350. **a1440** Burgh *Cato* 309.229. **a1449** Lydgate *Ale-Seller* in *MP* II 430.27. **1449** Metham 73.1980. **a1450** *Seven Sages B* 48.1404, 67.1969, 77.2261, 100.2952. **a1471** Ashby *Policy* 39.857. **a1475** *Ludus Coventriae* 91.283: Blere myn ey and pyke out a mote. **c1475** Henryson *Fables* 71.2041. **c1485** *Mary Magdalene (Digby)* 92.985. **a1500** *Against the Friars* in Wright *Political Poems* II 250[7]. **a1500** Medwall *Nature* D4ʳ[11]. **a1500** *Remedie of Love* CCCXXIIʳ[1.25]. **a1500** *To yow, mastres* in *Rawlinson MS. C 813* 383.35. **c1500** Skelton *My darlyng dere* I 23.28. **1506** Barclay *Castell* E2ʳ[14]. **a1508** Dunbar *Testament* 73.79, *Tretis* 91.277. **c1516** Skelton *Magnificence* 12.354, **c1522** *Colyn* I 337.686. **1532** More *Confutacion* 391 D[3], 393 F[6], 404 A[7–8], 647 D[1], 653 A[2], 792 D[17–8]. **1546** Heywood *D* 23.29: For feare mine eie be blerde, **1556** *E* 109.10.37: To blynd or bleare blunt eies, *Spider* 392[25]. MED bleren v. (1) 2; NED Blear v.[1] 3; Whiting *Drama* 335:408, *Scots* I 165.

E218 To blend (*blind*) one's **Eyes**
a1393 Gower *CA* III 72.4594: Blente in such wise hir lady yhe.

E219 To have clear **Eyes** and cannot see (*varied*)
1406 Hoccleve *Male Regle* 28.97–8: Who-so cleer yen hath, and can nat see, Ful smal, of ye, availlith the office. **c1430** Lydgate *Dance* 52.408: Somme have feyre yghen that seen never a dele. **a1450** *Myn awen dere* 169.622: Thou has brade eghen and may noght see.

E220 To have one's **Eye** in his arse and his heel (finger) after

a1376 *Piers* A xi 79–80: For alle that wilneth to wite the weyes of god almihti, I wolde his eghe weore in his ers and his heele (B fynger) aftur.

E221 To love as one's own **Eye** (*varied*)
c1400 *Seven Sages D* 39.1214: His stewart that was his ane E. **a1519** Horman *Vulgaria* 171[14]: I love the as myn owne yen. Amo te oculitus. See **A156.**

E222 To put out one's **Eye** with one's own weapon
c1458 *Knyghthode and Bataile* 47.1277–8: Ne go thei not amonge us, lest espyes With wepon of our owne out putte our eyis. See **S652.**

E223 To say black is his **Eye**
c1412 Hoccleve *Regement* 102.2822–3: The riche and myghty man, thogh he trespace, No man seith ones that blak is his eye. **1519** Horman *Vulgaria* 356[21–2]: In the kyngis letters is made playne mencion that no man shall sey blacke in (*for* is) myn yie. Nequis ilum mihi molestus sit. Apperson 52; *Oxford* 48; Tilley E252.

E224 To wink with one **Eye** and look with the other
1549 Heywood *D* 50.285: He winkth with the tone eie, and lokth with the tother. Apperson 694; *Oxford* 715; Tilley E241.

E225 Troubled **Eyes** have no clear sight (*varied*)
c1390 Chaucer *CT* VII 1700–1[B2890–1]: They that been wrothe witen nat wel what they don, ne what they seyn. Therfore the prophete seith that "troubled eyen han no cleer sighte." **c1450** *Pilgrimage LM* 176[13–4]: With purblynde eyen and thwartinge may not be hool lookinge. *Oxford* 325; Skeat 252.

E226 The unwhole (*diseased*) **Eye** shuns the sun's bright leam (*ray*)
c1200 Orm I 327.9393–6: Yiff thatt tin eghe iss all unnhal Withthinnenn o the sene, Itt shunethth, thatt tu wast te sellf, The sunness brihhte leome.

E227 To be an **Eyesore**
1546 Heywood *D* 27.37: To take lacke of beautie but as an eye sore, **1555** *E* 152.35: It is but an eie sore, but an eye sore, fye That eye sore is as yll as any sore eye. Tilley E273.

F

F1 Deem not after the **Face**
c1395 *WBible* John vii 24: Nile ye deme aftir the face, but deme ye a rightful doom. Apperson 13: Appearances; *Oxford* 328; Taylor and Whiting 7; Tilley A285. See **A151, M167, 342.**

F2 The **Face** may fail to be the heart's token
c1475 Henryson *Fables* 97.2837: The face may faill to be the hartis takin. See **C174, H248, 271, L166, W495.**

F3 The **Face** of treason is black within and white without
a1400 *Romaunt C* 7332–3: That hadde of tresoun al his face Ryght blak withynne, and whit withoute. See **W425.**

F4 He that makes the fairest **Face** shall soonest deceive
c1495 *Arundel Vulgaria* 50.215: For he that maketh the fairest face and spekith the fairest wordes shall sonest deceyve the. See **E97.**

F5 In the **Face** faith, in the tail fraud
a1420 Lydgate *Troy* I 239.3314: Feyth in hir face and fraude ay in the tail. See **S96.**

F6 In the **Face** peace, in the heart war
a1420 Lydgate *Troy* III 743.6132: Pes in the face, but in the herte werre. Cf. *Oxford* 186: A fair face and a foul heart; Tilley F3. See **H271.**

F7 To follow one's **Face**
c1380 *Cleanness* 37–8.977–8: Loth and tho lulywhit, his lefly two deghter, Ay folwed here face, bifore her bothe yghen. Apperson 222: nose; *Oxford* 213; Tilley N230.

F8 To have a double **Face** (visage)
a1393 Gower *CA* Pr. 130: And lawe hath take hire double face. **1402** Hoccleve *Letter of Cupid* 76.94: Suche as (they) ben with a double visage. **1410** Walton *Boethius* 64[3–4]: Attaynt that blynde goddes hast thou take With double face of doutfull aventure. **c1412** Hoccleve *Regement* 50.1367: That sche a-boute baar dowble visage. **a1449** Lydgate *Servant* in *MP* II 429.70: Your nature hathe so double a face. **c1450** Idley 146.2390: Make good countenauns and beere a double face. **a1500** *The Clerk and the Husbandman* in Robbins 181.29: Women can schaw a dowbull face. **1506** Hawes *Pastime* 120.3109: Aha quod fortune with the faces twayne. **1513** Dunbar *Of the Warldis Instabilitie* 29.10: The figurit speich with faceis tua. See **F12, 13, 516, W641.**

F9 To have one's **Face** shorn against the wool
1546 Heywood *D* 46.173–4: What should your face thus agayne the woll be shorne For one fall? **1555** *E* 173.152: Thy face is shorne ageynst the wull. Apperson 4; *Oxford* 579; Tilley F14.

F10 To make (bear, set) a good **Face**
a1387 Higden-Trevisa VII 25[13]: And made good face to the eorle and semblant. **a1420** Lydgate *Troy* I 269.4366: Make ther good face and glad in port the feine. **c1489** Caxton *Aymon* I 227.4: And bere oute a good face as long as we ben alyve. **1555** Heywood *E* 163.108: I did set a good face on the matter. Apperson 258; *Oxford* 252; Tilley F17.

F11 To wash one's **Face** in an ale clout
1549 Heywood *D* 38.101–2: As sober as she seemth, fewe daies come about But she will once wasshe hir face in an ale clout. Apperson 668; *Oxford* 693; Tilley F19.

F12 Trust not him that has two **Faces** and two tongues
1484 Caxton *Aesop* 104[6–7]: Therfore men must not truste in hym that hath two faces and two tongues. See **F8, T381.**

F13 Two **Faces** (visages) in one hood
a1439 Lydgate *Fall* II 560.3160: Out of oon hood(e) shewe facis tweyne, III 891.2429: Out of oon hood(e) shewe too visages, 894.2553, 911.3142, **a1449** *Ballade per Antiphrasim* in *MP* II 432.1: Undir your hood is but oo contenaunce, *Exposition* in *MP* I 69.272: God lovyd never two facys in oon hood, *Freond* in *MP* II 758.107, *Mesure* in *MP* II 775.76: Can nat shewe in one hoode two visages, *Order* in *MP* II 450.21, 455.178: Whiche in oon hode can shewe a double face. **a1449** Lydgate and Burgh *Secrees* 22.676. **c1450** Idley 85.291. **c1460** *Take Good Heed* 206.21: Nor two fases in a hode is never to tryst. **a1475** *Hit is ful harde* in *MLN* 55(1940) 566.2: Double visage loketh oute of every hood. **c1475** Henryson *Against Haisty Credence* 216.53–4: Within ane hude he hes ane dowbill face, Ane bludy tung, undir a fair pretence. **c1475** *Wisdom* 59.721: Jorowur, in on hoode berith to facis. **c1499** Skelton *Bowge* I 46.428. **a1500** Hill 130.4: He hath II faces under on hode. **c1500** Greene *Carols* 346.3: Another thynge, ser, merke we well: "Two faces in on hode, a fayre castell." **1506** Hawes *Pastime* 117.3036. **c1516** Skelton *Magnificence* 23.710. **1528** More *Heresyes* 271 G[14–6]. **1546** Heywood *D* 35.16: None better to beare two faces in one hood, **1555** *E* 158.74. Apperson 654; *Oxford* 679; Taylor and Whiting 126; Tilley F20; Whiting *Drama* 368:920. See **F8, H242.**

F14 At (In) the new **Fair**
a1376 *Piers* A v 170–1: Thenne Clement the cobelere caste of his cloke, And atte newe feire he leyde hire to sulle. **c1400** *Seven Deadly Sins* in Wyclif *SEW* III 167[7–8]: Hit is seide that mony comynes wil chaffere in tho new feyre, and thus chaunge hor wyfes and lye in avoutrie. **a1450** Audelay 36.728–9: Ye curatis, fore your covetys ye castun in the new fayre The churches that ye byn chosun to be Godus ordenauns. Skeat *Piers* II 92, note.

F15 The **Fair** is done
c1350 *Gamelyn* 652.270: For sothe at this tyme this feire is y-doon. Apperson 201.

F16 The **Fair** lasts all the year
1546 Heywood *D* 63.57: The fayre lasteth all the yere, we be new kneet, **1555** *E* 155.63. Apperson 201; *Oxford* 186; Tilley F26.

F17 **Fair** and soft (Soft and fair) (men go far) (*varied*)
c1385 Chaucer *TC* v 347: God woot, they take it wisly, faire, and softe. **a1393** Gower *CA* II 42.232: He seide to me softe and faire, 128.3415–6: It takth ayein, bot softe and faire, If eny thing stond in contraire, 243.652: softe and faire, 329.1058–9: faire and softe, III 199.1195–6: faire and softe, 254.786: softe and faire, 321.3234*: softe and faire. **a1400** *Destruction of Troy* 312.9588: Soght to the Citie softly and faire. **c1400** *Beryn* 35.1080: And taughte hym feir and sofft, 83.2746. **c1412** Hoccleve *Regement* 86.2376–7. **c1415** Mirk *Festial* 240.8–9: Forto bryng hym ageyne to hys place, soft and fayre, wythout any harme or deses. **c1440** Scrope *Epistle of Othea* 68[19–20]. **a1450** *Generydes B* 48.1497: They toke hym uppe and layde hym soft and fayr. **c1450** *Douce MS.52* 48.50: Fayre and softe me ferre gose. **c1450** *How the Wyse Man* 39.103–4: But softe and faire a man may tame Bothe herte and hynde, bucke and do. **c1450** Idley 91.619: Softe men farre goo, this is an olde loore. **c1450** *Pilgrimage LM* 71[7–9]: For softe men fer goth (.) Soonere is the mule ofte times at seynt james that goth roundliche than is thilke that smiteth and sporeth his hors. **c1450** *Rylands MS.394* 98.1. **a1460** *Towneley Plays* 234.211: All soft may men go far, 285.209: Ffare and softly, sir, and say not to far. **1481** Caxton *Godeffroy* 79.33, **c1489** *Aymon* I 229.16, 270.26–7, *Blanchardyn* 17.17–8. **c1495** *Arundel Vulgaria* 80.335: Fare faire and softly with thiselfe. **c1497** Medwall *Fulgens* D3r[5]: Soft and fayre, myne arme is sore. **a1500** *Coventry Plays* 50.551: For soft and essele men goo far. **c1500** *Melusine* 283.26–8. **a1513** Dunbar *Bewty* 106.70–1. **c1522** Skelton *Colyn* I 349.988. **a1533** Berners *Arthur* 488[16]. Apperson 585; *Oxford* 185–6; Taylor and Whiting 127; Tilley S601; Whiting *Drama* 364:858, *Scots* II 127.

F18 **Faith** has a fair name, but falsehood fares better
a1508 Dunbar *Tretis* 95.460: Faith has a fair name, bot falsheid faris bettir.

F19 **Faith** is seldom seen in thraldom
1449 Metham 2.30: And feyth in thraldam ys selde seyn.

F20 To throw a **Falchion** (*sword*) at a fly
c1303 Mannyng *Handlyng* 338.10915–8: Kowardyse hyt ys, and foule maystry, To throwe a faucoun at every flye; Of flyes men mow hem weyl spourge, And throwe to hem naght but scourge. (Fr. Pur chescune musche oscir, Ne treiez espé, cum funt il.) Skeat 102 (*in error*). Cf. Whiting *Scots* I 165.

F21 All one a **Falcon** and a kite, *etc.*
a1400 Lydgate *Churl* in *MP* II 483.358–60: All oon to the a ffaucoun and a kyte, As good an

oule as a popyngay, A donghyl doke, as deynte as a snyte. Cf. Tilley K114.

F22 As clear as **Falcon**
1485 Caxton *Charles* 90.15: Hyr eyen clere as fawcon mued.

F23 As fain as **Falcon** would fly (of flight)
c1400 *Roland* 134.978–9: Was never faucon fayn . . . Then this prince was fo . . . (*MS.* torn). **a1425** *Chester Plays* I 194.205–6: But fayne wold I fight my fill, As fayne as fawcon wold flye. **c1440** *Degrevant* 100.1555–6: Was never fawcone of flyght Sa fayne als thay ware. See **F562.**

F24 As fair as a **Falcon**
a1350 *Seven Sages C* 5.122: With eghen faire als a faukoun.

F25 As fresh as (the) **Falcon** (to the flight)
a1300 *Richard* 203.2287–8: Than was Rycharde fresshe to fyght As ever was fawkon (*var.* foule) to the flyght. **c1300** *Beves* 36.735–6: Thanne was he ase fresch to fight, So was the faukoun to the flight. **c1385** Chaucer *TC* iii 1783–4: Ful ofte his lady from hire wyndow down, As fressh as faukoun comen out of muwe. **a1400** *Alexander C* 263.5257: Scho was so faire and so fresche as faucon hire semed. **c1485** *Mary Magdalene* (*Digby*) 90.942: I have a favorows fode, and fresse as the fakown. See **F564, H194.**

F26 As gentle as (a) **Falcon**
1523 Skelton *Garlande* I 402.1006–7: Jentill as fawcoun Or hawke of the towre, 1021–2, 1036–7. **1562** Heywood *E* 245.91.1: Thy wyfe is as gentle as a falcon. Apperson 243; MED faucoun 1(b); Tilley F35. See **G48.**

F27 As gray as a **Falcon**
a1400 ?Chaucer *Rom. A* 546: Hir yen grey as is a faucoun.

F28 As light as **Falcon** of flight
a1500 *Eger H* 335.2519–20: For both their hearts they were so light, As ever Falcon was of flight. See **F567.**

F29 As like as any **Falcon** is (to) another
a1300 *Alisaunder* 416 L 6407–8: Hit is the yliche, leove brothir So any faukon is anothir.

F30 As prest (*active*) of flight as **Falcon** to his prey
a1500 *From a Departing Lover* in Robbins 199.37–8: Now And y were as prest of flyght As ever was faucoun tyl his pray.

F31 As swift as **Falcon**
a1508 Dunbar *Goldyn Targe* 114.53–4: Quhilk tendit to the land full lustily, As falcoune swift desyrouse of hir pray. Whiting *Scots* I 165.

F32 To be reclaimed like a **Falcon** (*etc.*) (A number of single quotations are brought together here)
a1338 Mannyng *Chronicle B* I 72[11]: Morkar recleymed es, as es the faukon fre. **a1393** Gower *CA* III 283.1842–3: And as the gentil faucon soreth, He fleth, that noman him reclameth. **c1400** *Alexander Buik* I 60.1903–5: As falcone that wald have fude ful fain Come lansand to the lure agane, Sa come the douchty duke to the fecht. **c1400** *Laud Troy* I 219.7434–6: That saw Ector aboute rayle, As faucoun flees afftir drake, A-mong Gregeis gret murdir make, 235.7964–5: Ector evere aboute rayled, As faucoun doth opon his pray, II 396.13427: Thei to-gedur as ffaucouns fflyes. **c1450** *Merlin* I 135[8–9]: Thei smote in a-monge hem as faucouns amonge starlinges. **a1470** Malory I 197.1–2: The dredfull dragon . . . come in the wynde lyke a faucon.

F33 To fare like a **Falcon**
a1513 Dunbar *Birth of Antichrist* 71.25: And as ane falcone fair fro eist to west. Whiting *Scots* I 165.

F34 To know a **Falcon** from a crow
1522 Skelton *Why Come* II 50.771–3: And graunt him grace to know The faucon from the crow, The wolfe from the lam.

F35 To let a **Falcon** fare
a1500 *Tottenham* 993.88–90: He gyrd so hys gray mere That sche lete a faucon-fare At the rereward. MED faucoun 3.

F36 To look like a **Falcon**
c1330 *Seven Sages A* 4 B 102: He loked lustely as a ffawcon. **c1380** *Ferumbras* 41.1074: And lokede so the facoun.

F37 To make a **Falcon** (sparrowhawk) of a buzzard
a1300 *Alisaunder* 171.3043–6: Niltou nevere, late ne skete, A goshauk maken of a kete, Ne faukon maken of bosard, Ne hardy knighth make (of) coward. **a1400** *Romaunt B* 4031–3: This have I herd ofte in seiyng, That man (ne) may, for no dauntyng, Make a sperhauk of a bosard. Apperson 593; *Oxford* 341: Kite. See **G397, W566.**

F38 As jolly and jocund as the **Falconer**
a1500 *Lambewell* 160.512: Jolly and Jocund as the faulconer.

F39 After a foul **Fall** comes shame

a1400 *Stodye of Wysdome* 40.15–6: For after a foule fal and a faylyng cometh sone schame.

F40 He that never had **Fall** goes full whole
a1420 Lydgate *Troy* III 873.3502: He goth ful hool that never had(de) fal! Cf. Jente 233.

F41 To **Fall** in and not to fall out
1546 Heywood *D* 41.21: I cam to fall in, and not to fall out.

F42 The **False** and (the) covetous are soon accorded
c1422 Hoccleve *Jereslaus's Wife* 160.575–6: Fful sooth is seid, the fals and coveitous Been soone accordid. See **R60.**

F43 The **False** think nothing as do the true
c1375 Chaucer *Anel.* 105: But nothing thinketh the fals as doth the trewe. Skeat 142. See **W259.**

F44 To be **False** and speak fair
a1450 *Myne awen dere* 154.171–2: The use is now in ilke a lande For to be fals and fayre spekand. See **F50, S583.**

F45 (Beware of) **Falsehood** in fellowship
a1471 Ashby *Policy* 26.408: Be wele ware of falsehode in felawship. **a1500** *Clerk and the Husbandman* in Robbins 180.11–2: Ffalse-hode in felychype wole the be-tray, Yefe thou to women gyf credens. **1555** Heywood *E* 183.208: There is falshed in felowship. Apperson 202; *Oxford* 189; Smith 110; Tilley F41; Whiting *Drama* 232. See **E97.**

F46 **Falsehood** and truth are ever at debate
a1450 *Generydes B* 166–7.5220–1: Ffull ofte it hath be seide, and trew it is, Ffalshede and trougth is ever atte debate.

F47 **Falsehood** (is) the mother of every vice
1501 Douglas *Palice* 67.15: Out on all falsheid, the mother of everie vice.

F48 **Falsehood** shall not avail against truth
c1421 Lydgate *Thebes* 86.2077–8: For this the fyn, falshede shal not availe, Ageynes trouth in feeld to hold batayle.

F49 **Falsehood** will rebound to where it rose
a1420 Lydgate *Troy* III 725.5494–6: For falshede ay wil ageyn rebounde Where it roos first, to his original Resorte ageyn, right as doth a bal. See **D342.**

F50 To feign **Falsehood** under fair words (*varied*)
a1400 *Destruction of Troy* 9.253: Ne the ffalshed he faynit under faire wordes, 34.994: And faynet ay faire wordes under felle thoghtes, 374.11489–90: He thoght his falshed to feyne, undur faire wordes, And his cautels to colour under coynt speche. See **F44, S583, W581.**

F51 **Falseness** (falsehood, falset) comes to an evil end (*varied*)
c1330 *Seven Sages A* 191 E 3546–7: And clerkys tellyd in hyr wretynge Of falssenys comythe evylle endynge, 191 B 3803–4: In what Contrey that man doth wende, Ever falshede hath evyll ende. **a1375** *Octavian* (S) 61.1957–8: Thus clerkys seyth yn her wrytynge, That falsnesse cometh to evel endynge. **c1375** Barbour *Bruce* II 28–9.122–3: Bot I trow falsat evirmar Sall have unfair and evill ending, 34.244–5: Bot sekirly falsat and gyle Sall evir have an evill ending. **a1400** *Torrent* 75.2153–4: Falshode wyll have a foule end, And wyll have evermore. **c1400** *Florence* 73.2176–81: For thy schulde men and women als Them be thynke or they be false Hyt makyth so fowle an ende,—Be hyt nevyr so slylylye caste Yyt hyt schamyth the maystyr at the laste In what londe that evyr they lende. **a1420** Lydgate *Troy* I 19.246–9: That al falshed draweth to an ende: For thoughe it bide and last a yer or two, The ende in soth schal be sorwe and wo Of alle that ben false and envious. **c1450** *Consail and Teiching* 70.172: And falsat sal nevir mak fare end. **c1475** Henryson *Fables* 23.568: For falset failyeis ay at the latter end, 69.1997: Falset will failye ay at the latter end. **a1500** *Beves* 213 M 4231–2: Hit is sothe, with oute lesyng: Of falshede comyth never good ending. *Oxford* 189; Whiting *Drama* 96, *Scots* I 165–6. See **Q8.**

F52 Who uses **Falseness** shall be quit with falseness
a1439 Lydgate *Fall* III 917.3373–4: Who useth falsnesse, ful weel afferme I dar, shal with falsnesse be quit or he be war. See **B213, F491, 610, G487, V34.**

F53 **Falset** is a feigned friend
a1500 *Eger H* 299.1903–4: Falset is ay a fained friend, And it cometh ay at the last end.

F54 As broad as a **Fan** (*winnowing basket* [*NED*]; *modern sense* [*MED*])
c1390 Chaucer *CT* I[A] 3314–5: Crul was his heer . . . And strouted as a fanne large and brode. **a1445** *Carl* 130.254–5: Over his brest his lockus lay As brod as anny fane. **a1450** *Tottenham* 992.66: A harrow brod as a fanne.

F55 **Fancy** may bolt bran and make one take it (as) flour
1546 Heywood *D* 67.61: Fancy may boult bran,

and make ye take it floure. Apperson 203; *Oxford* 190; Tilley F54. See **F299.**

F56 He that overlades himself shall not bear his **Fardel** (*bundle*) far
1483 Caxton *Cato* I3ʳ[23–4]: It is sayd comynly that who overladyth hym self shall not bere ferre his fardell. See **C151, O64.**

F57 To see one's **Fare** (*food*)
1546 Heywood *D* 52.382: Ye see your fare (sayd she) set your hert at rest, **1555** *E* 197.298: Ye see your fare, a very straunge fare to see, A blynde man may see our fare as well as wee. Tilley F57.

F58 **Far-fetched** and dear bought (is good for ladies) (*varied*)
a1400 *Romaunt B* 2738–9: A man loveth more tendirly The thyng that he hath bought most dere. **c1450** *Douce MS.52* 44.7: Ferre fet and dere i-bowght is good for ladys. **c1450** *Rylands MS.394* 96.18. **c1470** *Harley MS.3362* f.2b: Thyng fer y-browt ys wel ylovyd. **a1500** Hill 132.45: A thynge ferre fett, is good for ladyes. **c1516** Skelton *Magnificence* 15.455: It is moche worthe that is ferre fet, **c1522** *Speke* II 7.131: Deyntes for dammoysels, chaffer far fet, **a1529** *Elynour* I 106.334: It was dere that was farre fet. **1546** Heywood *D* 48.236–7: Dere bought and far fet Are deinties for Ladies, **1556** *Spider* 198[5]: But with disshes deinty: fer fet and dere bought. Apperson 203; Jente 174; *Oxford* 133; Tilley D12; Whiting *Drama* 140, *Scots* I 166. See **L519, M307, N163, T155.**

F59 He that is afraid of every **Fart** must go far to piss
1546 Heywood *D* 74.129–30: They that will be afraid of every farte, Must go far to pisse. Tilley F67. See **T298.**

F60 Not give a **Fart**
1556 Heywood *E* 138.96.6: What would I geve trowest thou? what? not a fart. Whiting *Drama* 344:540, *Scots* I 166.

F61 Not set a **Fart**
a1460 *Towneley Plays* 19.369: Bi all men set I not a fart. **c1497** Medwall *Fulgens* E4ᵛ[26]: He settyth not by hym selfe a fart. Whiting *Drama* 344:540.

F62 Not worth a **Fart**
c1390 *God man and the devel* 336.269–70: Now is non worth a fart, But he bere a baselart. **a1400** *Tho oure lord god* 320[8]: Elles it nere naught worth a fart. **a1425** *Chester Plays* I 95.234: Thy speach is not worth a fart. **a1450** *Castle* 143.2209: Al myn Enmyte is not worth a fart. Whiting *Ballad* 35, *Drama* 344:540. See **P152.**

F63 To get a **Fart** of a dead man
1546 Heywood *D* 47.207–8: I shall geat a fart of a dead man as soone As a farthyng of him. Tilley F63.

F64 Not further a **Farthing**
a1400 *Destruction of Troy* 288.8884: Ne never fortherit me a ferthing to fylsy my goodes.

F65 Not worth a **Farthing**
c1350 *Libeaus* 13.196–8: This child . . . Is nought worth a ferthing. **a1400** *Firumbras* 7–8.161–2: Thus was the theves craft . . . nought worth a ferthyng. **a1425** *Arthour and M.*[2] 282.139–40: Moyne, oure kyng, Is nought wourth a ferthyng. **a1450** *Generydes A* 154.4929–30. **c1475** *Mankind* 25.688: That jakett xall not be worth a ferthynge. **1520** Whittinton *Vulgaria* 93.6–7. Apperson 456; *Oxford* 60; Tilley F71.

F66 To fail (*lack*) two **Farthings** of a halfpenny
c1475 *Mankind* 18.473: By the masse, I fayll ii farthyngis of an halpeny.

F67 To think one's **Farthing** good silver
1546 Heywood *D* 38.107: She thinkth her farthyng good sylver, **1555** *E* 189.241. Apperson 204; *Oxford* 651; Tilley P194.

F68 As light as a **Fas** (*fringe, tassel*)
1513 Douglas *Aeneid* II 215.84: Pasys thar weght als lychtly as a fass. DOST Fas 2.

F69 Not worth a **Fas**
c1475 Henryson *Want of Wyse Men* 190.47: Sik gouvernance I call noucht worth a fasse. **1513** Douglas *Aeneid* II 151.156: Says nocht your sentens thus, skant worth a fass. DOST Fas 2; NED Fas 2; Whiting *Scots* I 166.

F70 The plain **Fashion** is best
1555 Heywood *E* 182.201: The playne fashin is best. Apperson 500; *Oxford* 504; Tilley F75.

F71 The **Fat** is in the fire
1546 Heywood *D* 22.11: The fat is in the fire, **1555** *E* 189.243. Apperson 205; *Oxford* 193; Taylor and Whiting 127–8; Tilley F79. See **B571, G484.**

F72 To fleet (*skim*) the **Fat** from one's beard
1546 Heywood *D* 23.30: And therby the fat cleane flit fro my berde, **1556** *Spider* 196[7]: Ye will flit the fat from their beardes. *Oxford* 193; Tilley F80.

F73 Be the **Father** what he be, well is the child to (that may) thee (*prosper*)
c1450 *Douce MS.52* 55.121: Be the fadur what he be, Welle is the chylde to the. **c1450** *Rylands MS.394* 105.19: Be the fader what may be, well is the childe that may thee. See **C225, F76.**

F74 The **Father** punishes most tenderly the child he loves most dear
c1500 ?Bradshaw *Radegunde* 42[16–7]: The childe whome the father loveth most dere He doth most punysshe tenderly in fere. See **Y1.**

F75 The **Father** sought never his son in the oven but if he had been therein himself (*varied*)
1493 *Seven Wise Masters* 40[19–22]: But it appereth by a comyn proverbe, he that is defectyfe or culpable hymselfe in a synne, he jugeth every man to be in the same, or elles that fader soughte never his sone in the oven: but yf he had ben therin hymselfe. **1546** Heywood *D* 86.202–3: No man will an other in the oven seeke, Except that him selfe have beene there before. Apperson 477; *Oxford* 456; Tilley W353.

F76 The **Father** to the bough, the son to the logh (*place, stead*) (plow)
1223 *Bracton's Note Book*, ed. F. W. Maitland (London, 1887) III 501[12–3]: Unde dicitur Anglice fader to the bowe, the sune to the lowe. **a1293** *Consuetudines Cantiae* (*Royal MS.9 A ii 33*) in George F. Warner and J. P. Gilson *Catalogue* I(1921) 279: Sey vader to the bogh and sey sone to the logh, in *Statutes of the Realm* I(1810) 223 n. 13: The fader to the boughe, and the son to the plogh. Apperson 206; *Oxford* 194; Tilley F84; *Victoria History of the County of Kent* III(1932) 325. See **F73.**

F77 The **Fathers** have eaten a sour grape and the teeth of sons shall be astonied (*dulled*) (set on edge)
c1395 *WBible* Jeremiah xxxi 29–30: In tho daies thei schulen no more seie, The fadres eeten a sour grape, and the teeth of sones weren astonyed; but ech man schal die in his wickidnesse, ech man that etith a sour grape, hise teeth schulen be astonyed, Ezekiel xviii 2: This proverbe . . . Fadres eetin a bittir grape and the teeth of sonnes ben an egge (**a1382:** wexen on egge) *ether astonyed.* Tilley F98. See **S463.**

F78 He that will not hear his **Father** or mother it shall not avail him
a1475 *Guy*[2] 34.1187–9: He, that wyll not hys fadur here, Nodur the cowncell of hys modur dere, Hyt schall hym nothynge avayle. **a1500** *Guy*[4] 53.1481–4: But he, that wyll not doe in skyll His fathers and his mothers wyll, Some shame shall hym betyde, Whether so he go and ryde. See **F82, S352.**

F79 No one may be so subject as to **Father** and mother
c1505 Watson *Valentine* 171.23–4: It is sayde oftentymes that never one maye be soo subjecte as to father and mother.

F80 Such **Father** such son (*varied*)
c1340 Rolle *Psalter* 342 (94.10): Ill sunnys folous ill fadirs. **c1378** *Piers* B ii 27: And Mede is manered after hym (*her father*) righte as kynde axeth; *Qualis pater, talis filius; bona arbor bonum fructum facit.* **c1386** Chaucer *LGW* 2446–51: And lyk his fader of face and of stature, And fals of love; it com hym of nature, As doth the fox Renard, the foxes sone, Of kynde he coude his olde faders wone, Withoute lore, as can a drake swimme Whan hit is caught and caryed to the brymme. **a1400** *The Song of Moses* in Wyclif *SEW* III 38[23–4]: Untrewe fadris geten often tymes untrewe sones, for whanne a child is norischid among vices, how schulde he be unfilid? **c1450** *Myroure of oure Ladye* 280[23]: So ys the father knowen by the sonne. **c1475** *Rawlinson MS. D 328* 124.68: Sygge fader sygge sonne. **1509** Barclay *Ship* I 49[1]: The son oft foloweth the faders behavour, 236[15–8]: An olde proverbe hath longe agone be sayde That oft the sone in maners lyke wyll be Unto the Father, and in lyke wyse the mayde Or doughter, unto the mother wyll agre. Apperson 366; Jente 421; *Oxford* 194; Taylor and Whiting 128; Tilley F92. See **L385, M720.**

F81 We all come from one **Father** and mother
897 Alfred *Boethius* 68.30–1: Ælc mon wat þat ealle men of anum fæder comon and of anre meder, 69.17–9: Hwæt, ealle men hæfdon gelicne fruman, forþan hi ealle comon of anum fæder and of anre meder, and ealle hi beoð git gelice acennede, *Lays of Boethius* 174–5.1–6. **c1450** *Ponthus* 87.34: We be all comen of oon fadre and modre. See **A37, C263.**

F82 Who that will not leve (*believe*) his **Father** shall leve his stepfather (*varied*)
c1300 *Guy*[1] 90 A 1591–4: For often ichave herd it say, And y me self it sigge may, "Who that nil nought leve his fader, He schel leve his stef-fader." **a1500** Hill 128.16: He that will not be warned bi his owne fader, he shall be warned bi his stepfader. **1509** Barclay *Ship* I 203[13–4]: But who that of his moders doctryne hath disdayne: Shall by his stepdame endure wo care

and payne, [18–21]: And who that nat foloweth the commaundement Of his fader . . . May fortune after . . . Obey that stranger, whom he nat gladly wolde. **1509** Watson *Ship* K2^{r-v}: (They) that wyl not folowe the good ensygnementes . . . of theyr moders . . . shall have a stepmoder harde and cruell. **1546** Heywood *D* 93.94–5: He that will not be ruled by his owne dame, Shall be ruled by his stepdame. Apperson 292; Jente 258; *Oxford* 552; Tilley D19. See **F78.**

F83 Whom the **Father** loves the mother hates
c1495 *Arundel Vulgaria* 17.68: But it hapenyth many tymes, as menn say, whom the father loveth, the mother hateth.

F84 He has but one **Fault,** he is nought
1546 Heywood *D* 45.148: He hath . . . but one faute, he is nought. Apperson 206; *Oxford* 194–5; Tilley F108.

F85 To curry **Favel** (*a fallow horse*) (*varied*)
c1330 *Peniworth* 117.329–30: Thus sche stroked his here and made it tough, And conraid fauvel wele ynough. **a1400** *Grete ferly* 68.109–10: Therfore lite may now with lordis duelle But thoo that kon conraye fawenelle. **a1400** *Proverbis of Wysdom* 246.91–2: Who so wyll in cowrt dwell, Nedis most he cory favell, (*II*) 223.80: famelle. **c1400** *Beryn* 12.362: As thoughe she had lernyd cury favel, of som old(e) ffrere. **1404** *Lerne say wele* in Kail 20.190: Thou corayest ffavel, and stelest his hay. **c1412** Hoccleve *Regement* 190. 5281–2: But he hyde The trouth, and can currey favel. **a1450** Audelay 24.394: Loke thou core not favele ne be no flaterer, 46.1005–6: Fore favel with his fayre wordis and his flateryng, He wyl preche the pepul apert hem for to pay. **a1456** *Passe forth* clxxiv 22: Pley not with pecus ne ffawvel to thy feere. **c1475** Gregory *Chronicle* 213[33–4]: Men of worschyppe that wylle not glose nor cory favyl for no parcyallyte. **c1475** *How a Merchant* 123.204: There sche currayed favell well. **c1515** Barclay *Eclogues* 29.826: Flatterers and lyers, curriers of fafell. **c1516** Skelton *Magnificence* 24.727: My tonge is with Favell forked and tyned. **1520** Whittinton *Vulgaria* 83.11: To cory favell craftely. **c1523** Barclay *Mirrour* 72[48]: With none curry favour. **1549** Heywood *D* 71.35: They can currifavell, and make faire wether. *Oxford* 163; Taylor and Whiting 128; Tilley C724; Whiting *Scots* I 166.

F86 **Favor** does great ease
c1475 Gregory *Chronicle* 237[27–8]: But favyr at sum tyme dothe grete ese.

F87 **Favor** is fostered more than right
a1420 Lydgate *Troy* I 9.297: For favour only is fostered more than ryght.

F88 As faint as a **Fawn**
a1400 *Seven Penitential Psalms* in *Wheatley MS.* 54.830: He was feynt as fowen in frith.

F89 **Fay** (*promise*) without fait (*act*) is feebler than nought
a1376 *Piers* A i 160–1: That fay withouten fait is febelore then nought, . . . but the deede folewe. MED dede 7. See **W642.**

F90 He that is **Feared** does ever well
1523 Berners *Froissart* III 292[18]: He dothe ever well that is feared.

F91 Make not too many **Feasts**
a1400 *Proverbis of Wysdom* 245.73: Make not to many festis. **c1450** *Fyrst thou sal* 89.77.

F92 Never **Feast** but it must have an end
c1500 *Three Kings' Sons* 197.21–2: But there was nevir ffeste in this worlde but onys it must have an ende. See **T87.**

F93 As fele (*many*) as **Feathers** upon fowls
c1380 Chaucer *HF* 1381–2: For as feele eyen hadde she As fetheres upon foules be.

F94 As light as a **Feather**
1509 Watson *Ship* C2^{v}[16]: Other ben as lyght as a fether. **a1533** Berners *Huon* 510.14–5: As lyghtly as thoughe it had bene but a fether. **1560** Heywood *E* 207.13.1: Nothyng is lighter then a feather. Apperson 364; *Oxford* 366; Taylor and Whiting 129; Tilley F150; Whiting *Drama* 311:112, *Scots* I 166.

F95 As soon as a **Feather** should enter an anvil
c1450 *Pilgrimage LM* 85[27–8]: A fethere shulde as soone entre in to an anevelte as woordes shulden entren in him or profiten.

F96 (Not) account at a **Feather**
c1378 *Piers* B xix 410: Or that acounted Conscience at a cokkes fether or an hennes.

F97 Not grieve a **Feather**
c1400 *Laud Troy* I 203.6882: Hit greved not him of a feder.

F98 Not prevail the weight of a **Feather**
c1525 ?Heywood *Gentylnes* 123.1005–7: Arguments . . . Do not prevayle the weyght of a fether.

F99 Not worth a **Feather**
1533 More *Apologye* 162[23]: Not worth a fether.

F100 She may not bear a **Feather** but she must breathe

1546 Heywood *D* 38.105–6: She maie not beare a fether, but she must breath, She maketh so much of hir peynted sheath. Tilley F159.

F101 To hang together like **Feathers** in the wind
c1516 Skelton *Magnificence* 57.1818: Thy wordes hange togyder as fethers in the wynde, **c1522** *Speke* II 14.294–5: Knakkes, That hang togedyr as fethyrs in the wynde. Tilley F162.

F102 To lime one's **Feathers**
c1385 Chaucer *TC* i 353: For love bigan his fetheres so to lyme. NED Lime v.[1] 3.

F103 To play with a **Feather**
c1350 *Smaller Vernon Collection* 53.754–6: And lost faste his moneye, Atte laste he lost al togedere And leve hedde to pley with a fedre.

F104 To pull (pluck) one's **Feathers**
c1385 Chaucer *TC* v 1541–7: Fortune . . . Gan pulle awey the fetheres brighte of Troie Fro day to day, til they ben bare of joie. **1415** Hoccleve *Oldcastle* I 16.257–8: Some of thy fetheres were plukkid late, And mo shuln be. **a1439** Lydgate *Fall* II 503.1067–8: Fortune gan . . . Of his prosperite the fethris for to pull. NED Feather 1b.

F105 To turn like a **Feather** in the wind
1510 Copland *Apolyn* 22[18–20]: Fortune . . . ever tornyng and varyenge as a feder in the wynde. Cf. Tilley F162.

F106 To wear a **Feather**
1533 Heywood *Johan* A2ʳ]25]: I fere she wyll make me weare a fether. See **H483.**

F107 Better **Fed** than taught
c1495 *Arundel Vulgaria* 13.52: Ye may say I lake curtesy, and better fedde than taught. **1546** Heywood *D* 37.58: But ye be better fed then taught farre awaie, **1555** *E* 152.42. Apperson 43; *Oxford* 39; Tilley F174.

F108 **Fee** (*wealth*) is transitory under lift (*heaven*)
a800 Cynewulf *Elene* in *Vercelli Book* 101.1269–70: F(eoh) æghwam bið Læne undere lyfte. See **C114, W671.**

F109 To be felled like **Fee** (*cattle*) in fold
a1425 *Metrical Paraphrase OT* 115.4002: Sone ware thei feld os fee in fold.

F110 The **Feeble** are ever beneath
c1300 Robert of Gloucester I 374.5142–3: Ac the feble is evere binethe, vor hii that abbeth mighte Mid strengthe bringeth ofte that wowe to the righte. See **W131.**

F111 The **Feeling** of a man's heel may not be likened to the heart
a1393 Gower *CA* III 444.2154–5: The fielinge of a mannes Hiele Mai noght be likned to the Herte.

F112 He is as fierce that flays the **Fell** (*skin*) as he that holds the foot
a1400 *Siege of Jerusalem* 57.987–8: For as fers is the freke atte ferr ende, That of fleis the fel as he that foot holdeth.

F113 To seek the **Fell** (straw, hair) in the egg
1340 *Ayenbite* 253[9-11]: The bysye other the malancolien that byeth ylich . . . than thet zekth thet vel ine the aye. **c1400** *Vices and Virtues* 280.30–1: That faren as he that secheth the strawe in an egge. **1484** Caxton *Royal Book* U4ʳ[9–10]: He that secheth heer in the egge or under the hyde. See *Vices and Virtues*, note, p. 315.

F114 Ask my **Fellow** whether I be a thief
1546 Heywood *D* 76.206: To axe my felow whether I be a theefe, **1555** *E* 156.65, **1556** *Spider* 387[13–4]: This trithe trewth like in preefe, As to axe my felow, whether I be a theefe. Apperson 18; *Oxford* 15; Tilley F177.

F115 He is no **Fellow** (*friend*) that will have all
c1400 *Sowdone* 78.2716: He is no felowe, that wole have alle.

F116 He should beware that sees his **Fellow** spurn
1501 Douglas *Palice* 29.27–30.1: For by exempilis oft I hard tofoir He suld bewar that seis his fellow spurne. See **C161, W47.**

F117 Never call your **Fellow** knave nor your brother whoreson
1533 Heywood *Weather* B4ʳ[25–6]: You shulde never call Your felow knave, nor your brother horeson.

F118 Who serves a **Felon** is evil quit
a1400 *Romaunt B* 3146: Who serveth a feloun is yvel quit. See **T67.**

F119 There is no **Felony** that women cannot think
c1300 *South English Legendary* I 283.110: For me seith ther nis no felonie that womman ne can thenche. See **W545.**

F120 As foul as the (a) **Fen**
c1300 *Northern Homily Cycle* (*Edin. Coll. Phys.*) 111[10]: And mas thaim fouler thanne the Fen. **a1508** Dunbar *Flyting* 8.84: Far fowlar than ane fen. Whiting *Scots* I 167.

F121 To be defouled as a **Fen** (turd) in the way **c1395** *WBible* Ecclesiasticus ix 10: Ech womman which is an hoore . . . schal be defoulid as a fen (*vars.* thost, toord) in the weie. MED fen (2).

F122 To fall as **Fen** (*mud*) from foot **c1325** *Loveliest Lady* 150.74: Er then thou falle ase fen of fote.

F123 He is no true **Fere** (*friend*) that will not scot (*share*) in lure (*loss*) as in beget (*gain*) **c1225** *On Ureisun* in R. Morris *Old English Homilies . . . First Series* (EETS 29, 34, 1867–8) 187[7–8]: Nis na trewe ifere the nule naut scottin in the lure ase in the bigete.

F124 To draw the **Fescue** (*straw*) (*i.e.*, delay matters) **1471** Caxton *Recuyell* I 97.20–1: We shall not long drawe the festue. See **S818.**

F125 To be infect with the **Fever-lurden** (*laziness*) **a1500** *Colyn Blowbol* 93.24–5: I trow he was infecte certeyn With the faitour, or the fever lordeyn. Apperson 209; *Oxford* 588; Tilley F197.

F126 Better go betimes with a **Few** than tarry for many and go too late **1532** Berners *Golden Boke* 184.2162–3: For better it were with a fewe to go betymes, than to tary for many and goo to late.

F127 **Field** has eyes and wood ears (*varied*) **a1300** *Trinity MS. O. 2. 45* 8.15: Veld haved hege, and wude haved heare. Campus habet lumen et habet nemus auris acumen. **c1385** Chaucer *CT* I[A] 1521–2: But sooth is seyd, go sithen many yeres, That "feeld hath eyen and the wode hath eres." **a1400** *King Edward* 959.268: Wode has erys, fylde has sight. **c1470** *Harley MS.3362* f.4a in *Retrospective Review* 309[28] and Förster 202.15: Feld hath eye, wode hath ere. Visum campus habet, nemus aurem, consilium nox. **c1500** *Lady Bessy* 47[25]: Feilde hath eyne and wodde hath eares. **1518** Watson *Oliver* F3v[1]: The feldes hathe syght and every wood hathe sowne. **1546** Heywood *D* 74.150: But feelds have eies, and woodes have eares. Apperson 210; *Oxford* 199–200; Skeat 216; Tilley F209; Walther I 260.2272–3a.

F128 Out of old **Fields** comes all the new corn (*varied*) **c1380** Chaucer *PF* 22–3: For out of old feldes, as men seyth, Cometh al this newe corn from yer to yere. **c1433** Lydgate *St. Edmund* 418.239–40: As newe greyn out off feeldis olde And leves greene growe out off trees gray. **1464** Hardyng 22[34–5]: As in olde feldes, cornes freshe and grene grewe, So of olde bookes cometh our cunnyng newe, 32[3]: As out of olde feldes newe corne groweth eche yere. **a1475** *Mumming of the Seven Philosophers* in Robbins 111.22–3: Ffor oute of olde feldes, as men sayth, Cometh all these new cornes from yere to yere. Apperson 467. See **B457, G494.**

F129 That **Field** is not worthy to till that may not yield the seed again **a1325** *Cursor* III 1362.23851–2: Hyt is not worthy (FG: Il worth[i]) to tille that feld That noght again the sede mai yeild.

F130 Farewell **Fieldfare** **c1380** Chaucer *PF* 364: The frosty feldefare, **c1385** *TC* iii 861: The harm is don, and fare-wel feldefare! **a1400** *Romaunt B* 5507–10: But seyn in voice of flaterie, That now apperith her folye, Overall where so they fare, And synge, "Go, farewel, feldefare." **a1449** Lydgate *Servant* in *MP* II 429.55–6: And sange "Go farewell feldfare," As man forsake in every place. Apperson 204; *Oxford* 191; Skeat 180; Whiting *Scots* I 167.

F131 As black as (the) **Fiend(s)** **a1400** ?Chaucer *Rom. A* 973–4: For shaft and ende, soth for to telle, Were also blak as fend in helle. **c1450** *Jacob's Well* 11.1: He turnyd al blak lyche the feend. **a1500** *Court of Love* 442.1221: He loked blak as fendes doth in hell. *Oxford* 47–8.

F132 As false as **Fiends** **c1400** *Plowman's Tale* 164.536: All such ben falser than ben fendes. See **D175.**

F133 As foul as any **Fiend** **c1475** *Wisdom* 65.908: Thys ys fowler than ony fende. See **D177.**

F134 To flee as from the **Fiend** **a1513** Dunbar *To the King* 1.23: Fra it as fra the Feynd thay fle.

F135 To hate someone like **Fiends** **a1300** *Alisaunder* 259.4647: That evere hateden hem so fendes. See **D210.**

F136 A **Fig** for (it) **a1500** *Court of Love* 427.685: A fig for all her chastitee! Taylor and Whiting 131–2; Tilley F210; Whiting *Drama* 344:553, *Scots* I 167.

F137 Not worth a **Fig** **a1450** *Barlam and Josaphat* (*South English Legendary*) 140.974: Ffor this ilke resoun nys nought worth afyge. **1528** More *Heresyes* 241

G[3–4]: Those reasons bee not woorth a figge. Apperson 456; *Oxford* 200; Taylor and Whiting 132; Tilley F211.

F138 To further never a **Fig**
a1400 *Destruction of Troy* 398.12206: He fortherit never a fyge with his fight yet.

F139 He that first begets (*gains*) in **Fight** after(ward) loses
a1200 Lawman II 448.20771–6: And of(t) hit ilempeth A veole cunne theoden, Ther gode cnihtes Cumeth to sturne fihte, That heo ærest bigiteth After heo hit leoseth. See **B65, F533, V8, W39.**

F140 In **Fight** is mensk (*honor*) and in flight shame
c1420 Wyntoun VI 209.6559: In feicht is mensk, and schoym in flicht (*var.* To fecht is mensk and schame to fle). See **D239.**

F141 Well **Fights** that well (fast) flees
c1250 *Hendyng O* 193.10: Wel fight, that wel fleth. **c1250** *Owl* 18.176: "Wel fight that wel fliht" seith the wise. **a1450** *Gesta* 374[20–1]: For it is an olde sawe, he feghtith wele that fleith faste. **c1470** *Wallace* 189.247–8: The flearis than with erll Patrik relefd To fecht agayn. Apperson 211; Kneuer 22–3; *Oxford* 200–1; Schleich 252–3; Singer III 127; Skeat 72; Taylor and Whiting 132; Tilley D79. See **F282, 428.**

F142 Well **Fights** that well speaks
c1250 *Owl* 90.1072–4: "Wel fight that wel specth," seith in the songe. Of hire tunge ho nom red: "Wel fight that wel specth" seide Alvred. Apperson 593; *Oxford* 612.

F143 To have one's **Fill** of fight(ing)
c1375 Barbour *Bruce* I 296.626: Thai sall thar fill haf of fechtyng. **a1400** *Eglamour* 37.556–8: Throwe the helpe of God, by it was nyghte, The geant had his fill of fyghte—The boke says: sum dele mare. **c1420** Wyntoun VI 211–2.6610–1: Thow may find (percas) thy fill of fechting. **a1470** Malory II 581.14–5: Mesemyth ye have nyghe youre fylle of fyghtynge. Tilley F215. See **B245.**

F144 Not worth a **Fille** (*the plant chervil*)
a1300 *Seinte Margarete* in *Seinte Marherete,* ed. Oswald Cockayne (EETS 13, 1866) 28.146: For thu ne might mid al thi mighte anuye hire worth a fille. **c1300** *Pilate* in Furnivall *Early English Poems* 113.87: And ne yaf noght worth a fille. **c1300** Robert of Gloucester I 194.2722: And thou nart noght worth a fille, 439.6018. **c1300** *South English Legendary* I 18.70: And youre nis worth a ville, 105.576, 296.146, 317.54, II 570.142, 638.848, 641.946, 700.88. **c1330** *Owayne Miles* (*Egerton*) in Horstmann *Altenglische Legenden 1875* 202.572: Hit nas not worth afille. MED fille n. (2) 2.

F145 **Filth** and eld (*age*) are great wardens upon chastity
c1395 Chaucer *CT* III[D] 1215–6: For filthe and eelde, also moot I thee, Been grete wardeyns upon chastitee.

F146 Like **Filth** overstrewn with flowers
1369 Chaucer *BD* 628–9: She is the monstres hed ywrien, As fylthe over-ystrawed with floures.

F147 To put out one's **Fins**
1461 Paston III 252–3: He and alle his olde felaweship put owt their fynnes, and arn ryght flygge (*?ready for action*) and mery. MED fin n. 1(c).

F148 To pull a **Finch**
c1387–95 Chaucer *CT* I[A] 652: Ful prively a fynch eek koude he pulle. G. L. Kittredge in *MP* 7(1910) 475–7; MED finch b: "To do something with cunning."

F149 He may well **Find** that hides
a1450 *Seven Sages B* 68.1981: He may wel fynde that hyde hym selven. Apperson 300; *Oxford* 294; Tilley H453. See **B287.**

F150 At one's **Finger's** end
1533 More *Confutacion* 707 B[6–8]: The feeling fayth of hys false harte they must nedes feele at theyr owne fingers end. Apperson 212; *Oxford* 202; Tilley F245.

F151 Better is **Finger** off than ache ever
a1200 *Ancrene* 184.24–5: For betere is finger offe then he ake eaver. Apperson 41; *Oxford* 37; Tilley F225. See **E205.**

F152 Each **Finger** is a thumb
1534 More *Passion* 1299 C[10–1]: Every fynger shalbe a thombe. **1546** Heywood *D* 70.26: Whan he should get ought, eche fynger is a thumbe. Apperson 212; *Oxford* 202; Tilley F233.

F153 The second **Finger** is named Lickpot
a1398(1495) Bartholomaeus-Trevisa i3^{v}[1.1–7]: The seconde (*finger*) . . . is namyd Likpot, and also the techer. For wyth hym we grete and shewe and teche all thynge. The thyrde is the mydle fingre and hyght Impudicus also. **a1475** *Promptorium* 263: Lykpote ffinger: *Index.* **a1483** *Catholicon Anglicum* 217[2]: A Lykpotte (Lykpot fyngyr A); *index, demonstrarius.* **a1500** *Ilke a fynger* in *Catholicon Anglicum* 131 n. 3[3–4]:

The next (*to the little*) fynger hat *leche man*, for quen a leche dos oght, With that fynger he tastes all thyng howe that hit is wroght. **a1500** *Pictorial Vocabulary* in Thomas Wright and R. P. Wülcker *Anglo-Saxon and Old English Vocabularies* I(1884) 752.36: *Hic index* . . . a lykpot. NED Lickpot.

F154 To have a lime **Finger**
c1499 Skelton *Bowge* I 49.509: Lyghte lyme fynger, he toke none other wage. **1546** Heywood *D* 38.98: And wyll be lyme fyngerd I feare. Apperson 212; *Oxford* 202; Tilley F236. See **L433.**

F155 To put (set) **Finger** in the eye
1477 Shillingford 19[29]: Germyn putte his fynger yn his ye and wepte. **1534** Heywood *Love* C1r[7]: But streyght way she set the fynger in the eye. Tilley F229.

F156 To put one's **Finger** in a hole
1546 Heywood *D* 77.239–40: But me thinkth your counsell weith in the whole, To make me put my fynger in a hole. Tilley F472. Cf. Whiting *NC* 407:4.

F157 To put one's **Finger** in the fire
1546 Heywood *D* 64.75–6: Or to put my finger to far in the fyre, Betweene you. Apperson 213; *Oxford* 526; Tilley F230.

F158 To see through one's **Fingers** (*i.e.*, to deceive)
1481 Caxton *Reynard* 65[20] And teche men see thurgh their fyngres. Cf. Tilley F243; Whiting *Scots* I 167.

F159 To suck out of one's **Fingers'** ends
1546 Heywood *D* 52.360: I sucke not this out of my owne fingers eends. Apperson 607; *Oxford* 628–9; Tilley F244; Whiting *Drama* 345:555.

F160 With a wet **Finger**
1519 Horman *Vulgaria* 280[7]: I wyll helpe all thy besines with a wete fynger. Hanc molestiam declinabo ne sicco adhuc digito. **1528** More *Heresyes* 178 G[5–6]: They should sone shew you the churche with a wete finger. **1546** Heywood *D* 95.170–1: Naie (quoth he) with a wet fynger ye can fet, As muche as maie easyly all this matter ease. Apperson 677; *Oxford* 702–3; Tilley F234.

F161 As angry as **Fire**
1509 *Fyftene Joyes* F (*for* G) 1v[2]: Whiche is as angrye as the brennynge fyre. Cf. Taylor and Whiting 134:mad.

F162 As bright as (the, any) **Fire**
a1425 *Arthour and M.*[2] 346.1607–8: And sparklede abowte bryght, As doth the fuyr from thondur lyght. **a1400** *Cursor* III 1247 G 21786: The bridil schane bright als fire. **a1430** Lydgate *Pilgrimage* 75.2806. **a1450** Greene *Carols* 27.2. **a1450** *Three Middle English Sermons* 39.578–9: That brente as brith as ani veir. **c1450** Greene *Carols* 28.3. **a1460** *Towneley Plays* 149.287. **a1470** Malory II 1029.25–6: ony. **1483** Caxton *Golden Legende* 144 (*by error* 145)v[2.38–9]. **1515** Barclay *St. George* 42.834. Tilley F248.

F163 As burning as (a, the, any) **Fire**
1340 *Ayenbite* 203[28]: Berninde ase ver. **c1390** *Miracles of Our Lady* 156.40: His leg was brennyng as a fuir. **a1400** *Salutation to Jesus* in Brown *Lyrics XIV* 106.11: Thi luf es byrnand als the fyre. **a1400** *Scottish Legends* II 59.415. **c1400** *Alexius* 42.461–2. **c1400** *Ilka Man* in *Yorkshire Writers* II 286.344. **c1400** *Tundale* 8.147, 30.523–4, 49.867–8: His ene were brode in his hede And all brennand as fyre rede. **c1410** Lovelich *Grail* II 182.311–2: And bothe his Eyen . . . Also Cleer brennenge As Ony Fere, 209.439: For his vesage As brenneng Fyr it was, III 42.107–8: And his Eyen brenneng In his hed As thowh it were flawmes of fir so Red. **a1415** Mirk *Festial* 85.25–6. **a1420** Lydgate *Troy* II 418.797: the. **c1420** Wyntoun II 249.1438: the. **a1445** *Carl* 131 B 181. **a1475** *Guy*[2] 110.3860: And hys eyen, as fyre, brennyng. **c1485** *Guiscardo* 54.277: the. **1513** Douglas *Aeneid* II 23.1, IV 45.11–2: And as the fyre all byrnand schayn the feildis Of brycht armour.

F164 As clear as (any) **Fire**
a1430 Lydgate *Pilgrimage* 10.358–9: Havyng a swerd, fflawmyng as cler As any ffyr. **1483** Caxton *Golden Legende* 407r[2.19]: Face clere as fyre.

F165 As fell as (the, any) **Fire**
c1390 *Sir Gawain* 26.847: Felle face as the fyre. **a1400** *Alexander C* 252.4922: With fell face as the fire and ferly faire schapen. **c1400** *Alexander Buik* IV 396.9714: Thare men micht se the fecht fell as fyre. **a1425** *Metrical Paraphrase OT* 61.7804, 70.2378, 80.8508. **a1500** *Northern Passion* 93 H 922ab: And when the jews thir wordes herd, Ffel als any fire thai ferd. **1522** Skelton *Why Come* II 34.246: any.

F166 As fervent as (the, any) **Fire**
c1475 *Court of Sapience* 160.893: Pees, fervent as the fere. **c1475** *Why I Can't* 138.7: For they were as forfent as ony fyre. **1513** Bradshaw *St. Werburge* 48.1187: the. **1515** Barclay *St. George*

65.1530: Theyr malyce kendlynge moche ferventer than fyre.

F167 As fierce as (any, the) **Fire**
a1450 *Generydes A* 124.3928: And therto as fers as any fire. **c1470** *Wallace* 38.165: Thair cheyff chyftan feryt als fers as fyr, 205.767: ony, 268.1050: With cruell strakis, that flawmyt fers as fyr, 290.1772. **c1475** *Golagros* 32.945: Alse ferse as the fyre. **c1475** Henryson *Testament* 111.185: ony. **a1513** Dunbar *Fenyeit Freir* 69.79–80: The sparhalk to the spring him sped, Als fers as fyre of flynt. Whiting *Scots* I 167–8.

F168 As flaming (inflaming) as **Fire**
c1303 Mannyng *Handlyng* 226.7025–6: Atyre . . . flammyng as fyre. **1483** Caxton *Golden Legende* 244ʳ[2.20–1]: Eyen flammyng as hoot fyre. **1513** Douglas *Aeneid* II 166.45: His mynd inflambyng as fyre. Whiting *Drama* 312:115.

F169 As hasty as (the) **Fire**
c1400 *Florence* 3.73: He waxe hasty as the fyre. **c1477** Norton *Ordinall* 92[29]: Some now be onward as hasty as fier.

F170 As hot as (any, the) **Fire**
a1375 *William* 37.907: As hot as ani fure. **c1380** Chaucer *PF* 246: Sykes hoote as fyr. **c1390** *Talkyng* 18.5–6: Hattore . . . then is the fuir that brenneth. **a1393** Gower *CA* III 172.209–10: the, 409.846: eny. **c1395** *WBible* Hosea vii 6: He was maad hoot, as the fier of flawme. **a1400** *De amico ad amicam* in E. K. Chambers and F. Sidgwick *Early English Lyrics* (London, 1907) 16.40–1: Vostre amour en moun qoer Brenneth hote as doth the fyr. **a1405** Lydgate *Black Knight* in *MP* II 392.232, **a1420** *Troy* I 205.2126, II 466.2501: any, III 581.606: any, 851.2739: any, **c1421** *Thebes* 27.607: eny. **a1425** *Chester Plays* I 89 *var.* 6. **a1425** *Governance of Lordschipes* 72.21. **1435** Misyn *Fire* 103.17: Hattar then fire is this mervellus heet. **a1439** Lydgate *Fall* II 360.1149. **a1450** *Gesta* 46[28]. **c1450** Idley 86.314: ony, 127.1165, 165.381: the. **c1475** *Guy*[1] 31 C 511. **c1475** *Prohemy of a Mariage* 35[18]. **c1485** *Guiscardo* 56.322. **a1500** *Characteristics of Counties* in *Rel. Ant.* I 269[23]: Kent, as hot as fir. **a1500** *Guy*[4] 25.494. **a1500** *Remedie of Love* CCCXXIIIʳ[2.34]. **a1509** Barclay *Ship* II 316[12]. **1509** *Fyftene Joyes* E5ᵛ[32]. **1513** Bradshaw *St. Werburge* 49.1217: the. **1513** Douglas *Aeneid* II 81.38, 124.30, 218.67, III 31.92, 91.85, 175.26, 176.74, 184.74, 246.117, 272.102: any, IV 31.2, 52.135, 76.10, 80.44, 98.37, 131.96, 168.104. Apperson 315; Taylor and Whiting 134; Tilley F247; Whiting *Scots* I 168.

F170a **Fire-hot**
a800 Cynewulf *Elene* in *Vercelli Book* 92.936: Fyrhat lufu. **c1000** *Vercelli Homily* 9 in *Festschrift für Lorenz Morsbach* (Halle, 1913) 116.1: Ælc þara eȝena is fyre hat.

F171 As red as (any, the) **Fire**
c1280 *Southern Passion* 66.1797: His lokyng and his fface was as red so eny ffur is. **a1300** *Alisaunder* 19.297: Mars was swithe reed fere lyche. **a1300** *Arthour and M.*[1] 43.1456: That other is red, so fer is lem, 44.1489: That on was red so the fer. **c1300** Robert of Gloucester I 225.3179: A dragon as red ase fur. **a1325** *XV Signa* in Heuser 102.70: Worth as rede, as hit wer fire. **c1350** *Joseph* 9.259–60: the. **c1385** Chaucer *CT* I[A] 2164: Rubyes rede as fyr sparklynge, *TC* iii 1633: For also seur as reed is every fir. **a1400** *Eglamour* 52 (*var. after*) 774: Hys hed as fyre was reed. **c1400** *Laud Troy* I 228.7733: any. **c1400** *Pepysian Gospel* 102.10. **c1410** Lovelich *Grail* II 310.39, 313.147–8: Cloth so Red, Him thowhte it brenneng fer In that sted, 314.188–9: Wondirfully Red In that plas, As Owt Of the Forneys Comen flawmes of fire. **a1420** Lydgate *Troy* I 281.4769: Whos berd and her, reed as flawme of fire, 367.7807. **c1420** Wyntoun II 23.125. **a1425** *Arthour and M.*[2] 343.1544, 1074, 344.1575, 1105: eny. **a1450** *Partonope* 392.9503–4. **a1470** Malory II 1029.25–6: ony. **1485** Caxton *Charles* 151.3–4: And on that other syde as rede as fyre enflammed, 176.1–2: Hyr eyen were rede as brennyng fyre. **c1485** *Mary Magdalene* (*Digby*) 60.153: ony. **c1489** Caxton *Aymon* I 27.6: ony. **c1500** *Arthour and M.*[3] 468.1498. **1506** Barclay *Castell* A4ᵛ[16]. **a1533** Berners *Huon* 374.29: With eyen redder then fyer. Apperson 526; Taylor and Whiting 134; Tilley F248; Whiting *Scots* I 168.

F171a **Fire-red**
c1300 *South English Legendary* I 324.282: That he was al fur red. **a1382** *WBible* Leviticus xiv 49: Fier reed silk, 51, 52. **c1387-95** Chaucer *CT* I[A] 624: That hadde a fyre-reed cherubynnes face.

F172 As sharp as **Fire**
897 Alfred *Boethius* 127.16–7: Buton he hæbbe swa scearp andgit swaðær fyr. **c1400** *Plowman's Tale* 150.91: The Griffon shewed as sharp as fyre. **1515** Barclay *St. George* 88.2161: (Winds) more sharpe than fyre flame.

F173 As sparkling as (the) **Fire**
a1400 *Romaunt B* 3136: His eyes reed sparclyng as the fyr glowe. **c1400** Mandeville *Travels*

187.25–6: Eyen that ben . . . sparklynge as fuyre. **a1533** Berners *Arthur* 511[11]: Eyen sparkelyng as fyre.

F174 As startling (*prancing*) (*etc.*) as the **Fire** (A number of single quotations are brought together here)
c1385 Chaucer *CT* I[A] 1502: He on a courser, startlynge as the fir, **c1386** *LGW* 1204. **a1437** *Kingis Quair* 58.46[4]: And grete balas lemyng as the fyre. **a1450** *Myne awen dere* 171–2.715–6: A grete lorde that is full of yre Is perilous as any fyre. **c1450** *St. Cuthbert* 20.689–90: And, mewre in face, that semely sire Was gliterand as brynnand fire. **c1475** Henryson *Orpheus* 133.122: Ene glowand as fyre. **a1500** *Alexander C* 27 Dublin 750*: He hed so ferdfull a face as ony fyre lokez. **a1500** *Power of the Purse* in Robbins 56.10: Rydest out of cuntre as wyld as eny fyer. **a1500** *Yonge and olde* in *ESt* 41(1909–10) 263.17–8: On the fryday As lyght As fyre God to moyses A-pered in syght. **1513** Douglas *Aeneid* IV 53.6: In breithfull stoundis rasyt brym as fyre, 132.129: Dire, wikkit as fyre.

F175 As swift as **Fire**
1513 Douglas *Aeneid* II 163.49: Rynnyng swyft as fyre. Whiting *Scots* I 168.

F176 As thick as **Fire** of (*from*) the thunder-dint
a1300 *Richard* 219.2562–4 (*var.*): Flones and quarelles ffleyth betwene Also thykke, withouten stynt, As fuyre of the thondyr-dynt.

F177 As twinkling as the **Fire**
a1437 *Kingis Quair* 45.1[2]: The rody sterres twynklyng as the fyre. Whiting *Scots* I 169.

F178 As wood (*mad*) as (the, any) (wild) **Fire**
a1400 *Destruction of Troy* 41.1217: Alse wode of his wit as the wild ffyre. **a1400** *Firumbras* 12.298: Syr Roulond calyd nemes as wod as any fyre, 49.1537: any, 51.1600: any. **c1470** *Wallace* 348.492: Thocht thow war wod as fyr.

F179 Better a small **Fire** to warm than a great fire to harm
c1515 Barclay *Eclogues* 39.1067–8: Then better is small fire one easyly to warme, Then is a great fire to do one hurte or harme. Apperson 41; *Oxford* 37; Tilley F249.

F180 **Fire** afonds (*tests,* proves) hard iron
a1050 Defensor *Liber* 106[2–3]: Swa swa fyr afandað isen heard, ealswa win heortan ofermodigra þreað. **c1395** *WBible* Ecclesiasticus xxxi 31: Fier preveth hard irun. See **G298, M522, S327, 410.**

F181 **Fire** and pride no man may hide
c1375 Barbour *Bruce* I 86.119–24: For men sais (oft), that fire, na pryd, But discoveryng, may no man hyd. The pomp of pryde ay furth shawis, Or ellis the gret bost that it blawis; And thair may no man fire sa covir, (Bot) low or reyk sall it discovir. Apperson 213. See **F194.**

F182 **Fire** and tinder (*etc.*) are perilous (*varied*)
a893 Wærferth *Gregory* 276.20–2: "Aga la, wif, onweg fram me! Nu gyt is cwic sum spearca, Ac anim þæt ceaf onweg!" (*An old man, who had become a priest, speaks to his old wife when she approaches his deathbed.*) **c1303** Mannyng *Handlyng* 252.7923–4: But of wymmen hyt ys grete wundyr, Hyt fareth with hem as fyre and tundyr. **c1330** *Four Foes* in Brown *Lyrics XIV* 33.50–2: Is non so war no so wight That he no felles him in fight, As fire dos in tunder. **a1393** Gower *CA* II 164.1274–6: And lich the fyr which tunder hente, In such a rage, as seith the bok, His Moder sodeinliche he tok, III 100.5623–6: And fyr, whan it to tow aprocheth, To him anon the strengthe acrocheth, Til with his hete it be devoured, The tow ne mai noght be socoured. **c1395** Chaucer *CT* III[D] 89–90: For peril is bothe fyr and tow t'assemble: Ye knowe what this ensample may resemble. **c1450** La Tour-Landry 25.5–6: It will make her do and thenke the worse, as it were to putte fere in flexe. **c1458** *Knyghthode and Bataile* 6.142–3: And as fier wasteth tundir, So Sathanas his flok. **a1475** *Good Wyfe Wold* 174.40: Feyr and towe ileyde togedor, kyndoll hit woll, be resson. **1483** Caxton *Golden Legende* 177v[1.8–9]: Lyke as fyre put in strawe or in towhe wasteth it. **c1500** Betson *Treatyse* C3r[13–7]: Ther is no thynge more peryllous to a man than is a woman and to a woman no thynge more contagyous than is a man, for eyther of them is chaff and eyther is fyre. **c1523** Barclay *Mirrour* 56[48–9]: Cont(*for* j)oyne not fire to flaxe, the one hote, the other drye, It harde is to kepe both, flaming sodaynly. **1532** Berners *Golden Boke* 236.3924: For of necessitie the drie flaxe will brenne in the fire. **1534** More *Comforte* 1200 B[1–4]: It is a thing right hard . . . to put flexe unto fyre, and yet kepe them fro burning. **1546** Heywood *D* 77.242: In my house to lay fyre and tow together. Apperson 213; *Oxford* 202, 203; Skeat 262; Taylor and Whiting 134; Tilley F268, 278.

F183 **Fire** and water will not kindle
c1460 *Take Good Heed* 206.19–20: Ffor fyre and water to-gider in kyndeling be brought, It passeth mannes power. See **W83.**

F184 **Fire** is quenched in its own smoke

a1475 *Tree* 78.20–1: Lete it be quenchid as fere in his owne smoke.

F185 **Fire** is raked (*covered up*) in old ashes
c1390 Chaucer *CT* I[A] 3882: Yet in oure asshen olde is fyre yreke. **a1420** Lydgate *Troy* I 146. 79–81: For litel fire under asches reke So may be kyndled that it wil oute breke In-to swyche flawme, men may it nat apese, **a1449** *Exposition* in *MP* I 60.11–2: In aysshis olde a lytel ffer there ys Wich yeveth no light nor clernesse at a neede. **c1450** *Fyrst thou sal* 91.179: In old askes may fyer be rake. Jente 261; MED asshe 3. See **G154.**

F186 **Fire** makes rusty lead bright
c1450 Capgrave *Katharine* 348.306–7: Ffor right as fyre maketh the rusty leed Bryght and shene, so made the fyre these men.

F187 **Fire** of spoons (*chips*) and love of grooms (*boys*) soon will be at an end
a1475 *Good Wyfe Wold* 174.42: A fyr of sponys and lowe of gromys ful soun woll be att an ende. Apperson 385; *Oxford* 391; Tilley L526. See **H554, L484.**

F188 In **Fire** and water is great peril
a1400 *Proverbis of Wysdom* 245.44: In fyre and watere is grete perell. Cf. *Oxford* 203: Fire and water have no mercy; Tilley F254.

F189 Like **Fire** in flint
c1470 *Wallace* 158.574: As fyr on flynt it feyrryt thaim betweyne. **c1475** Henryson *Fables* 14.328: And till her hole scho went as fyre on flint. Whiting *Scots* I 168.

F190 Like **Fire** of (out of, from) flint
c1300 *Amis* 56.1321–2: Sir Amiloun, as fer of flint, With wretthe anon to him he wint. **c1338** Mannyng *Chronicle A* I 300.8543–4: Wyth swerdes of werre double dyntes, The sparkles fleye as fir of flyntes. **a1400** *Siege of Jerusalem* 30.530: As fur out of flynt ston ferde hem bytwene, 65.1122: That fur out flowe as of flynt stonys (*var.* it dooth of flyntes). **c1400** *Alexander Buik* II 236.4635–6: Dyntis, That kest fyre as man dois flyntis, 243.4867: Togidder thay straik as fyre of flint. **c1440** *Degrevant* 88.1381–2: The frek als fyre of the flynt In his armes he hir hent. **a1450** Spalding *Katherine* 152.i.13–4. **c1470** *Wallace* 178.1216: Als fersly fled as fyr dois off the flynt, 259.746: out off. **a1475** *Guy*[2] 83.2898: That the fyre flewe owt, as hyt dothe of flynte. **a1475** *Ludus Coventriae* 287.469: Brennyng in flamys as fyre out of flynt. **c1475** *Golagros* 23.676: out of, 26.758: As fyre that fleis fra the flynt, thay fechtin sa fast, 29.857: out of, 33.978: out of. **c1475** Henryson *Fables* 22.552. MED flint 2(b); Whiting *Scots* I 167–8.

F191 A little **Fire** is acquenched with a puff, a great fire waxes with wind
a1200 *Ancrene* 66.14–5: Lute fur wes ther that a puf acwencte, for thear as muche fur is, hit waxeth with winde, **a1400** (*Recluse*) 51.31–2: And men seien often by ensample there that mychel fyre is, it wexeth with the wynde more and more, **a1500** (*Royal*) 31.26–8: Litel fire is sone blowen owte with a litel wynde, But gret fire is incresed by gret wynde. Cf. *Oxford* 373: Little wind.

F192 Make no **Fire,** raise no smoke
1546 Heywood *D* 74.136: Make no fyre, reyse no smoke. Apperson 214; *Oxford* 203; Tilley F275.

F193 The nearer the **Fire** the hotter
c1385 Chaucer *TC* i 448–50: And ay the ner he was, the more he brende. For ay the ner the fir, the hotter is,—This, trowe I, knoweth al this compaignye. **a1400** *Romaunt B* 2477–8: Whereso (thou) comest in ony coost, Who is next fyr, he brenneth moost. Jente 802; *Oxford* 203; Tilley F281; Whiting *Scots* I 167.

F194 No **Fire** without some smoke (*varied*)
c1375 Barbour *Bruce* I 86.123–4: And thair may no man fire sa covir, (Bot) low or reyk sall it discovir. **c1390** Chaucer *CT* VII 1185[B2375]: "It may nat be," seith he (*Seneca*), "that where greet fyr hath longe tyme endured, that ther ne dwelleth som vapour of warmnesse." **c1422** Hoccleve *Dialog* 134.683: Wher no fyr maad is may no smoke aryse. **a1449** Lydgate *Fabula* in *MP* II 488.68: Withoute smoke fire ne may nat brenne. **c1450** *Douce MS.52* 48.51: Where no fyre, is no smoke. **c1450** *Jacob's Well* 154.10–1: And as after fyir comyth smoke, so after ire and stryif comyth contek and chydyng. **c1450** *Rylands MS.394* 98.7: Where is no fyre ther is no smoke. **c1470** *Harley MS.3362* f.4a: Wher no feer ys ybere, no smoke arysyth. **a1500** *Eight Goodly Questions* 422[23]: No fire make, and then no smoke woll arise. **a1500** *Remedie of Love* CCCXXIIII^{v}[1.47]: Kindle no fire, no smoke woll arise. **1546** Heywood *D* 74.135: There is no fyre without some smoke. Apperson 582; *Oxford* 454, 458; Taylor and Whiting 340; Tilley F282, S569. See **F181, R77.1.**

F195 (A) perilous **Fire** that breeds in the bedstraw
c1395 Chaucer *CT* IV[E] 1783: O perilous fyr, that in the bedstraw bredeth! *Oxford* 129.

F196 Soft **Fire** makes sweet malt
a1500 Hill 128.22: A softe fire makith swete malte. **1546** Heywood *D* 21.30: Soft fire maketh sweete malte, **1555** *E* 149.16. Apperson 585; *Oxford* 602; Tilley F280; Whiting *Drama* 143, 214.

F197 To be like **Fire**
a1325 *Cursor* II 996 CG 17372: And his cher lik was slaght o(f) fire, **a1400** FT: And his semblaunt like to ffyr. **a1400** *Titus* 37.787: Hem thoght his lokyng was as a fyre. **a1500** *Partenay* 47.1195: As shinyng fire his visage semynge be.

F198 To bear **Fire** in one hand and water in the other (*varied*)
c1300 *Northern Homily Cycle* (*Edin. Coll. Phys.*) 37[13–6]: That es at say, thir glotherers That in thair an hand fir beres, In the tother water ber thai, Als lawed men er won to say. **a1420** Lydgate *Troy* III 710.4987–91: On swiche folke, platly, is no trist, That fire and water holden in her fist, Beinge with bothe y-liche indifferent, Now hoot, now colde;—liche as there entent Of newe changeth. **c1450** Idley 87.398–9: To please both parteis is his desire, Beere in bothe handis water and fire. **1484** Caxton *Aesop* 242[1–3]: Men ought to beware and kepe hym self from hym whiche bereth both fyre and water. **a1500** *To yow mastres* in *Rawlinson MS. C 813* 383.9: Ye beyre bothe fyre and watter also. **c1516** Skelton *Magnificence* 23.711: Water in the one hande and fyre in the other. **1546** Heywood *D* 36.25: Fyre in the tone hande, and water in the tother. Apperson 213–4; *Oxford* 79; Tilley F267.

F199 To blow at the **Fire**
c1440 Rolle *Two Ways* in Perry *English Prose Treatises* 33[3–6]: Bot habyde and suffire a while, and go blawe at the fyre, that es, firste do thi werkes, and go than allane to thi prayers. Apperson 57. See **C334, G146.**

F200 To burn like (a, any, the) **Fire**
a1325 *Cursor* III 1538.27771: That brennes mans mede als fire (F: That he brennis as a fire). **c1350** *Good Wife E* 164.91: Ne bren thou noght so fir. **c1385** Chaucer *TC* iii 425: But Troilus, though as the fir he brende, **c1386** *LGW* 1750–1: Desyr That in his herte brende as any fyr. **a1393** Gower *CA* III 88.5211–2: the. **c1395** *WBible* Ecclesiasticus ix 9: Covetise brenneth an high as fier, ix 11. **a1400** *Eglamour* 46.685 (*var.*). **a1400** *Northern Verse Psalter* II 71 (117.12). **a1400** *Romaunt B* 2548: ony. **a1400** *Scottish Legends* I 323.929, II 138.493, 160.285. **c1400** *Alexander Buik* I 47.1481–2: ony, IV 431.10825–6: ony. **c1400** ?Clanvowe *Cuckoo and the Nightingale* in Skeat *Chaucerian* 355.193. **c1400** *Laud Troy* I 47.1573: the, 132.4482: any. **1401** *Treuth, reste, and pes* in Kail 11.62: Hit brenneth breme as fyre in gres. **a1425** *Chester Plays* I 191.134: the. **a1450** *Death and Life* 6.165: H(er) eyes farden as the fyer that in the furnace burnes. **c1450** Holland *Howlat* 61.418: the. **c1450** *Ratis* 24.825–6. **c1470** *Wallace* 301.143. **c1485** *Guiscardo* 42.66: the. **a1500** *Lamwell* 525.151: the. **1504** Hawes *Example* Ee7ᵛ[4]: It brenneth hote lyke fyre. **1513** Bradshaw *St. Werburge* 39.893: the. Whiting *Drama* 312:115, *Scots* I 168.

F201 To come to fetch **Fire**
c1385 Chaucer *TC* v 484–5: Pandare answerde, "Be we comen hider To fecchen fir, and rennen hom ayein?" Apperson 109; *Oxford* 198; Tilley F283.

F202 To drive like **Fire**
a1400 *Firumbras* 14.384: And with that come claryoun, dryvand as fere. Taylor and Whiting 134.

F203 To fare as (a) **Fire**
a1350 Castelford 128.23193: He bade tham fight and far als fire. **c1390** *Each Man* in Brown *Lyrics XIV* 140.30: Hit fareth as a fuir of heth. **a1460** *Towneley Plays* 169.101: With-in I fare as fyre.

F204 To flee (*etc.*) as from **Fire** (A number of single quotations are brought together here)
a800 *Parker Chronicle* I 14[4–5]: þa Walas flugon þa Englan swa fyr, *Cotton Domitian* (ed. B. Thorpe, 1861) I 23[13–4]: þa Wealas flugon þa Englen swa man flucð fyr. **c1300** Robert of Gloucester I 311.4416: Vor to awreke is uncle deth as fur is herte tende (*kindled*). **a1400** *Destruction of Troy* 125.3857–8: The here of that hathell was huet as the fire, Bothe o berde and above all of bright rede, 297.9153: All hatnet his hert, as a hote fyre. **a1400** *Ipomadon A* 223.7835–6: The sparkels frome the helmes flowe As fer, that lemys in lowe. **c1400** *Scottish Troy* 275.1671–3: Throw a blynde fulische desyre That thare hartis as birnand fyre Ameved. **c1410** Lovelich *Grail* I 134.543: And Owt he sprang As fyr Offe brond. **1481** Caxton *Reynard* 56[16–7]: His eyen glymmerd as fyre, **c1489** *Aymon* II 435.23: For grete wrathe he loked as fire. **a1500** *Guy*[4] 96.2999: Eskeldarde came pricking as fyre. **a1500** *Peterborough Lapidary* in *Lapidaries* 71[8]: A stone red shinyng as brennyng fire. **1509** Barclay *Ship* II 5[23]: Hir wrath in hete passyth hote fyre.

F205 To glide away like **Fire**
a1300 *Alisaunder* 241.4316: He glyt away so dooth the fure (*so MS.*). Whiting *Scots* I 168.

F206 To glow like **Fire**
a1450 *Seven Sages B* 91.2687–8: And dyde oppon hym a wondir tyre, Alle hyt glowyd as fyere. Whiting *Drama* 312:115.

F207 To (in)flame like **Fire**
a1400 *Destruction of Troy* 64.1958: His een flamnet as the fyre with a felle loke, 180.5532. **a1400** *Scottish Legends* I 16.314: Enflammyt agannis hym as fyre, 168.630: a, 201.387: ony, II 140.549: Fore he wes flammyt as of fyre. **a1485** Caxton *Charles* 167.21–2: Eyen al enflammed lyke fyre. Whiting *Drama* 312:115, *Scots* I 168, 169.

F208 To lay **Fire** in one's bosom
a1500 *Remedie of Love* CCCXXIII[r][1.41–7]: Maie a man, thinkest, hide and safe laie Fire in his bosome, without empairement And brenning of his clothes, or whider he may Walke on hotte coles, his feete not brente, As who saieth naie, and whereby is mente This foresaied proverbe and similitude, But that thou ridde the, plainly to denude. Cf. Tilley M1233. See **S334.**

F209 To pass (fare, go) through **Fire** and water
c900 *Paris Psalter* 19 (65.11): We þuruh fyr farað and þuruh floda þrym. **c1000** *Regius Psalter* 116 (65.11): We foron þurh fyr and wæter. **c1100** *Salisbury Psalter* 161 (65.12). **c1340** Rolle *Psalter* 227 (65.11): We passid thurgh fire and watire. **c1350** *Prose Psalter* 76 (65.11): We passed by fur and water. **c1382** *WBible* Psalms lxv 12: Wee passiden thurgh fyr and watir. **a1396**(1494) Hilton *Scale* N7[v][6–9]: For thyse soules are thus called fro synne and thus righted, or elles on other manner lyke by dyvers assayenge, bothe thorugh fyre and water. **a1500** *Imitatione* (*1*) 29.17–8: Thou must go throghe fyre and water. **1502** *Imitatione* (2) 171.36–7. Apperson 214; *Oxford* 202; Taylor and Whiting 134; Tilley F285.

F210 To play with **Fire**
c1300 *South English Legendary* II 401.138: An hard puf him was blowe agen to teche him pleie with fure (*literal*). *Oxford* 505; Tilley F286.

F211 To rake in the **Fire**
a1449 Lydgate *Fabula* in *MP* II 498.358–9: Yff loves ffevere do yow ouht to quake, Telle me the soth and rake nat in the fyre.

F212 To sleep still while others blow the **Fire** (*i.e.*, stir things up)
c1495 *Arundel Vulgaria* 84.351: For while other men blouth the fyre, I slepe styll.

F213 When the **Fire** is clean blown out where shall we go dine?
a1475 *Good Rule* in Brown *Lyrics XV* 265.55–6: Whan the fere is clene blowen oute Where shal we go dyne thanne?

F214 As white as the **Fire-amel** (*enamel*)
a1437 *Kingis Quair* 58.48[1]: About hir nek, quhite as the fyre amaille. See **A116.**

F215 As hot as the **Fire-brand**
c1450 Idley 129.1310: She was as hoote as the fire brande.

F216 As inflamed as a **Fire-brand**
a1533 Berners *Huon* 165.9–10: He was more inflamed than a byrnynge fyer brond.

F217 To glow like a **Fire-brand**
a1350 *Seven Sages C* 106.3111–2: With brade tonges and bright glowand, Als it war a firebrand.

F218 As fervent as **Fire-flaught** (*lightning flash*)
a1507 Dunbar *Dance* 121.63: As fyreflawcht maist fervent.

F219 To ride like a **Fire-flaught**
c1400 *Alexander Buik* IV 354.8359–60: The ane agane the uther rade As fyreflaucht that is fell to feill.

F220 Not worth a **Fire-stick**
c1300 *Havelok* 36.966: Was it nouht worth a fir-sticke.

Fish, sb.

F221 All is **Fish** that comes to net
c1522 Skelton *Colyn* I 347.935: All is fysshe that cometh to net. **1523** Berners *Froissart* III 376[22–3]: All was fysshe that came to net. **1546** Heywood *D* 49.262. Apperson 6; *Oxford* 207; Taylor and Whiting 134; Tilley A136.

F222 As dumb as the **Fish**
a1449 Lydgate and Burgh *Secrees* 73.2310: Dowmbe as the ffyssh. Apperson 434: mute; *Oxford* 440; Svartengren 178; Tilley F300; Whiting *Scots* I 169.

F223 As fere (*sound*) as a **Fish**
a1325 *Cursor* II 470.8175: That als a fische thou made me fere. **a1400** *Alexander C* 232.4281–2: Us mistris nevire na medcyne for malidy on erthe, Bot ay . . . as fere a(s) fisch quen he plays. Apperson 682; Skeat 47. See **F228, P172, 195, T485.**

F224 As fresh as **Fish**
a1400 *Alexander C* 232.4282: Bot ay as fresche . . . a(s) fisch.

F225 As full as **Fish**

c1475 Henryson *Fables* 101.2946: Now full as (fysche) (*vars.* fitche, pease).

F226 As naked as **Fish**
a1400 *Grete ferly* 69.138: And as fisshis thai are naked of grace and of vertuus.

F227 As thick as **Fish** in a net
c1450 *Alphabet* II 395.9: Thai war als thykk as it had bene fyssh in a nett.

F228 As whole as (a, any) **Fish**
c1410 Lovelich *Grail* II 201.153–4: And his Arm be-Cam As hol Anon As was fisch that bar A bon. **a1415** Mirk *Festial* 110.20: He was hole as a fyssh, 141.18–9, 182.4: any, 265.6: a **1486** ?Berners *Boke of St. Albans* A5r[10]: And she shall be hoole as a fysh. Apperson 682; Tilley F301. See **F223, P172, 195, T485.**

F228a Fish-whole
c1200 *St. Juliana* 53.569–71: Heo ase fischhal as thah ha nefde nowher hurtes ifelet. **a1400** *Alexander C* 148.2575: As fast was he fysche-hale. **a1400** *Chevelere* 18.353. **a1400** *Morte Arthure* 80.2709. **a1425** *Mandeville* (*Egerton*) 52.7. **c1450** *Alphabet* II 269.15.

F229 Fish is cast away that is cast in dry pools
1549 Heywood *D* 45.118: Fishe is caste awaie that is cast in drie pooles. Apperson 215; *Oxford* 206; Tilley F307.

F230 The **Fish** is taken by the bait (*varied*)
c1000 Aelfric *Homilies* I 216[9–12]: þa getimode ðam reðan deofle swa swa deð þam grædigan fisce, þe gesihð þæt æs, and ne gesihð þone angel ðe on ðam æse sticað. **c1000** *Passio Beatae Margaretae* in Assmann 172.71–2: Ic eam befangan . . . eall swa fisc on hoce. **a1225** *St. Marherete* 8.9: Ase fisc a-hon on hoke. **a1325** *Cursor* II 968.16931–2: And als the fisch right wit the bait Apon the hok es tan. **c1390** *Castel of Love* 384.1127–30: Ac he was caught and over-comen, As fisch that is with hok I-nomen, That whon the worm he swoleweth a last He is bi the hok I-tighed fast. **c1390** *Luytel Sarmoun* in *Vernon* II 477.41–8: Ne miht thou seo, synful Mon, So doth the ffisschere with his hok: Hou he teseth on the Bank A brodly breyd I the Brok; Cometh the ffisch and fongeth hit, So wrothly wrieth on the Crok, The ffisch is be-wyled thorw the worm—So wo is the ffisch that he hit tok. **c1395** *WBible* Ecclesiastes ix 12: But as fischis ben takun with an hook, and as briddis ben takun with a snare, so men ben takun in yvel tyme, whanne it cometh sudeynli on hem. **c1425** *Myrour of lewed men* 425.603–4: Then the fend him to the dede as for his prison toke, And choked on the godhede as fisch dos on the hoke. **a1439** Lydgate *Fall* I 110.3968–9: As is a fissh with bait off fals plesaunce, The hook nat seyn, to brynge hym to myschaunce. **c1450** Idley 84.230–1: Lyeng at al howres in awayte As a fysshe doith after his baite, 96.894–5: As a fysshe full ofte by a swete baite Is lost clierely from his grete pleasaunse. **c1450** La Tour-Landry 59.3–5: And as the wyse saieth, the dethe lyeth under the delites, as the fysshe that takithe his bayte upon an hoke. **a1475** *Asneth* 256.710–1: For as the fyssh by the hook ys take by distresse, So ys beaute drow me to hym by vertuus provydence. Apperson 216:18; *Oxford* 205; Tilley F306; Whiting *Drama* 253, 312:116. See **H455.**

F231 Great **Fish** are taken in the net, small fish escape
c1450 *Jacob's Well* 80.20–2: Grete fyssches are takyn in the nett, and slayn; smale fyssches scapyn through the nett into the watyr, and lyven, 239.5–7: Smale lytell fyssches skyppyn thrugh the maskys of a nett in-to the watyr, and lyven, grete fyssches hange stille in the nett, and arn dede. **1509** Barclay *Ship* I 191[6–8]: For whan the Net is throwen into the se The great fysshe ar taken and the pryncipall Where as the small escapyth quyte and fre. See **L106.**

F232 The great **Fish** eat the small (*varied*)
a1200 *Trinity College Homilies* 179[1–2]: Eft-sone the more fishes in the se eten the lasse. **a1300** *Alisaunder* 329.6192–5: He seigh the ikeres (*nicors*) woniynge And the fisshes lotyinge Hou every other gan mete, And the more the lesse gan frete. **c1300** *Northern Homily Cycle* (*Edin. Coll. Phys.*) 136[2–4]: And gret fisches etes the smale. For riche men of this werd etes, That pouer wit thair travail getes. **a1400** Wyclif *Sermons* I 70[3–4]: And the more fishes swele-wen the lasse. **a1415** *Lanterne* 46.2–3: But as the greet fisches eeten the smale, so mighti riche men of this world devouren the pore to her bare boon. **c1440** Lydgate *Debate* in *MP* II 564.592: Of grettest fissh devourid been the smale, **a1449** *Fabules* in *MP* II 575.239–40: Grete pykes, that swymme in large stewes, Smaller fysshe most felly they devour, 588.638–9: By examples, in stwes long and large, Of grete fissh devoured bien the smale. **a1450** *Castle* 161.2821: The grete fyschys ete the smale. **a1450** *Pride of Life* in Waterhouse 100.361–2: Thai farit as fiscis in a pol The gret eteit the smal. **1509** Barclay *Ship* I 101[1]: The wolfe etis the shepe, the great fysshe the small, **c1515** *Eclogues* 120.357–8: But this hath bene sene forsooth and

ever shall, That the greater fishe devoureth up the small. Apperson 271; *Oxford* 264; Tilley F311. See **D146, G444, W473.**

F233 Like a **Fish** out of water (*varied*)
a1376 *Piers* A xi 204–7: Whanne fisshes faile the flood or the fresshe watir, Thei dighe for the droughte whanne thei dreighe lengen; Right so be religioun it roileth and stervith, That out of covent and cloistre coveiten to libben. **c1378** ?Purvey *De Officio Pastorali* in Wyclif *EW* 449[27–9]: For as they seyn that groundiden thes cloystris, thes men myghten no more dwell out ther-of than fishes myghte dwelle out of water. **c1385** Chaucer *TC* iv 765: How sholde a fissh withouten water dure? **c1387–95** *CT* I[A] 179–80: Ne that a monk, whan he is recchelees, Is likned til a fissh that is waterlees. **a1393** Gower *CA* III 356.4321–3: And wax so ferforth womannyssh, That ayein kinde, as if a fissh Abide wolde upon the lond. **a1400** Wyclif *Sermons* II 15[29–30]: And how thei weren out of ther cloistre as fishis withouten water. **c1425** *Orcherd* 283.18–22. **a1449** Lydgate *My Lady Dere* in *MP* II 422.65–70: What is a fisshe out of the see, For alle his scales silver sheene, But ded anoon, as men may se? Or in ryvers crystal clene, Pyke, bathe, or tenche with ffynnes grene, Out of the water whane they appere? **1483** Caxton *Golden Legende* 74v[2.6–12]: For lyke as fysshes that have ben longe in the water, whan they come in to drye londe thei muste deye. In lyke wyse the monkes that goon out of theyr clostre . . . they muste nedes lese theyr holynesse, **1489** *Doctrinal* K5r[28–9]: An holy man sayth, that lyke as a fysshe may not lyve out of the water, nomore may a monke lyve spiryrituelly out of hys cloistre. **1496** Alcock *Mons* C5v[16–9]: Saynt Anthony sayth, ryght as a fysshe maye not lyve wythout water but in shorte tyme is deed, Ryght so a monke beynge wythout his celle is dede in the syghte of god. **a1500** *Ffrere gastkyn* in *Anglia* 12(1889) 269[7–8]: A fysche to lyve all ways yn lond, Quid vero mirabilius. Apperson 216; *Oxford* 206–7; Taylor and Whiting 135; Tilley F318; Whiting *Drama* 223.

F234 More than **Fish** (which) swim
a1300 *XI Pains* 149.63–4: Mo saulen tholieth ther swich wo Thene fysses swimme.

F235 Neither **Fish** nor flesh nor good red herring
1546 Heywood *D* 36.45: She is nother fyshe nor fleshe, nor good red hearyng. Apperson 219–20; *Oxford* 206; Taylor and Whiting 136; Tilley F319.

F236 Old **Fish** and young flesh (are best)
c1395 Chaucer *CT* IV[E] 1418–20: "Oold fissh and yong flessh wolde I have ful fayn. Bet is," quod he, "a pyk than a pykerel, And bet than old boef is the tendre veel." **1546** Heywood *D* 67.42: Olde fish and yong flesh . . . dooth men best feede. Apperson 467; *Oxford* 470; Tilley F369.

F237 To be (be)set (taken) as **Fish** in a net
c1350 *Libeaus* 66.1186–7(*var.*): But sone he was besette, As fisch is in a nette. **c1420** Wyntoun V 409.3449–50: Swa that it semyt thai war set Amange thar fais, as fische in net. **a1425** *Metrical Paraphrase OT* 27.6570: Bot be tane os a fysch in A nett. **1523** Berners *Froissart* I 133[19–20]: The ii. erles fell in the handes of their ennemies, lyke fysshes in a net. Whiting *Scots* I 169.

F238 To love something (*etc.*) more than **Fish** the flood (A number of single quotations are brought together here)
c1400 *Alexander Buik* III 333.7751–2: The folk that hardy was and gude, That better luffit fecht than fisch the flude. **c1400** *Laud Troy* I 193.6529–30: As ffische is dreven to the bayte, So waytes he him at som defaute. **a1450** *Castle* 87.353–4: Werldis wele, be strete and stye, Faylyth and fadyth, as fysch in flode.

F239 When **Fish** fly in the air
c1477 Caxton *Jason* 44.34–6: Certes that shal not be unto the tyme that the fysshes flee in the ayer. And that the byrdes swymme in the water.

Fish, vb.

F240 To **Fish** fairly
c1385 Chaucer *TC* ii 328: Than have ye fisshed fayre! **1402** Hoccleve *Letter of Cupid* 76.100–1: Thow fisshest fayre: she that the hath fired, Ys fals and inconstant. See **F675.**

F241 To **Fish** in another place
a1533 Berners *Arthur* 56[2–3]: The emperoure maye goo fysshe in an other place, for here he hath well fayled.

F242 **Fishers** trouble the waters
1509 Fisher *Treatyse* 78.34–9.1: Lyke as fysshers do whan they be aboute to cause fysshe to come in to theyr nettes or other engyns, they trouble the waters to make them avoyde and flee from theyr wonte places. Apperson 217; *Oxford* 206, 207–8; Taylor and Whiting 395; Tilley F334; Whiting *Scots* II 151.

F243 To be deceived in one's **Fist** (*i.e.*, cheated)

c1390 *Charity is no longer Cheer* in Brown *Lyrics XIV* 170.15: He schal be deceyved in his fist.

F244 To whistle in one's **Fist**
c1450 *Complaint Against Hope* 14.13: Now may I wistle in my fyste. Cf. Tilley W313.

F245 Misspend not **Five,** flee seven, keep well ten and come to heaven
a1400 *Proverbis of Wysdom* 247.157–8: Myspend we nott fyve, and fle we seven, Kepe we wel .x and com to heven. **a1500** *Bodley MS. Rawlinson F 32* in Robbins 253: Myspend we nott fyve, and fle we seven; Kepe wel x, And come to Heven. **a1500** *Cambridge University MS. Ee 4.37* in Robbins 80: Kepe well x And flee fro vii; Rule well v And come to hevyn. **a1500** Hill 140.1–2: Kepe well X and flee from sevyn; Spende well V, and cum to hevyn. *Athenæum* (1893) I 81: Keep ten [the Commandments], Flee seven [the seven deadly sins], Use well five [the five senses], And win heaven (*from the writer's memory*). Brown-Robbins 1817.

F246 To fare like a **Flag** (*rush*) when it folds (*bends*)
a1450 Audelay 220.85: My hert fare(s) fore freght as flagge when hit foldus.

F247 To wag like a **Flag** with the wind
c1400 *Laud Troy* I 264.8969–70: Ector saw Achilles wagge As with the wynd doth the flagge.

F248 The **Flame** of love is the hotter for not being seen
1472 *Stonor Letters* I 126[36–8]: Though the fflame of the ffyre of love may not breke oute so that it may be seyn, yet the hete of love in yt self is never the les, but rather hooter in yt self.

F249 **Flame-red**
a1382 *WBible* Isaiah i 18: If youre synnes weren as flaume red silc.

F250 To burn like **Flame** of fire
a1449 Lydgate *Exposition* in *MP* I 65.147: Though charite in us brente as flawme of fyre.

F251 To fare like **Flame** of fire
a1350 Castelford 130.23225–6: On thar famen that bataile fars So flame of fire that na thing spars.

F252 To shine like the **Flame** of fire
a1470 Parker *Dives* L5ʳ[1.19–20]: His face shone and glymered as the flame of fyre.

F253 **Flat** and edge
c1385 Chaucer *TC* iv 927: Beth rather to hym cause of flat than egge. **a1449** Lydgate *Look* in *MP* II 771.205–7: Lat nat your swerd be whet to do vengaunce, Twen flat and egge thouh shapnesse tokne liht, The flat of mercy preent in your remembraunce. See **A30.**

F254 He that can **Flatter** has all things after his pleasure
1509 Watson *Ship* Bb6ʳ[12–5]: For it is a comyn sayenge, He the whiche can flatter, hathe all thynges after his pleasure, And he that sayeth trouth, shall have his hede broken. Cf. Tilley T562.

F255 **Flattery** flowers (*prospers*) truth plores (*weeps*)
1373 Brinton *Sermons* I 113[28–9]: Flatrie flourith, treuthe plourith. Cf. Tilley T562.

F256 To smoke like burned **Flax**
a1400 Wyclif *Sermons* II 189[13–4]: Preestis of the chirche, that smokiden bi pride as brent flex.

F257 Not give a **Flax-beat** (*?an instrument to beat flax, ?a blow struck in beating flax*)
c1400 *Laud Troy* I 157.5315–6: But he yaff not a flax-bete Off alle her bost. MED bete n. (3), flex 2(c).

F258 A **Flea** does not spare kings
a1398(1495) Bartholomaeus-Trevisa ff4ᵛ[1.36–8]: And (*a flea*) sparyth not kynges, but a lytell flee greveth them yf he touche theyr flesshe.

F259 A **Flea** in one's ear
a1430 Lydgate *Pilgrimage* 264.9574–8: And your wordys everychon Ben so unkouth and merveyllous, And to my wyt so daungerous, That they faren, whan I hem here, As a flee were in myn Ere. **c1440** Charles of Orleans 105.3141: For in myn ere may noon suche fleis crepe. **c1450** *Pilgrimage LM* 91[17]: And manye oothere grete wundres whiche ben fleen in myne eres. **1546** Heywood *D* 45.136: He standth now as he had a flea in his eare, **1556** *Spider* 384[26]: As everie flie had had a flea in his eare. Apperson 219; *Oxford* 209; Taylor and Whiting 138; Tilley F354.

F260 Not count a **Flea**
c1475 Henryson *Fables* 82.2402: His dart Oxin I compt thame not ane fle. Whiting *Scots* I 169. See **F341.**

F261 Not grieve a **Flea**
1501 Douglas *Palice* 73.11–2: Yow had nouther force nor micht, Curage nor will for to have grevit ane fla.

F262 Not set (half) a **Flea**
c1420 Wyntoun III 60.771: And set nocht by my lif a fle. **1501** Douglas *Palice* 29.3: Yit of my deith I set not half ane fle. See **F344.**

F263 Not worth a **Flea**
c1475 Henryson *Fables* 71.2045: He is not worth ane fle, 78.2286. **1509** *Fyftene Joyes* D1^r[16]: For it was nothynge worth a symple fle. **a1513** Dunbar *How Sall I Governe Me* 25.33: My freindis ar not worthe ane fle. **a1533** More *Confutacion* 526 G[7]: Not woorth a flee. Apperson 456; Tilley F353; Whiting *Scots* I 170. See **F345.**

F264 To be slain like **Fleas**
1523 Berners *Froissart* III 234[10]: They shulde be slayne lyke flees.

F265 To keep **Fleas** (or wild hares) in an open lease (*pasture*) (*varied*)
c1395 *WBible* I Kings xxvi 20: For the kyng of Israel yede out, that he seke a quike fle, as a partrich is pursuede in hillis. **a1500** Medwall *Nature* G2^v[32–4]: I had lever kepe as many flese Or wyld hares in an opyn lese As undertake that. **1509** Barclay *Ship* I 166[3–4]: As great fole, as is that wytles wratche That wolde kepe flees under the son fervent. See **D444.**

F266 No more than a **Flea-biting** (*varied*)
a1396(1494) Hilton *Scale* D4^v[7–9]: For the felynge of thyse temptacions fyleth the soule nomore than yf they herde a hound berke or a flee byte. **a1475** *Tree* 81.15: Suffre bakbiteris as thou must suffre the bityng of a flee. **1534** More *Comforte* 1262 E[9–11]: All that they all can dooe, can be but a fle byting, in comparison of the myschief that he goeth about. **1546** Heywood *D* 64.69: And but a fleabytyng to that did ensew, **1555** *E* 181.195: Tis but a fleabityng. Taylor and Whiting 138; Tilley F355; Whiting *Drama* 345:559. See **F354.**

F267 A **Fleer** gets a follower
c1475 Henryson *Fables* 88.2576: Ane flear gettis ane follower commounly.

F268 **Fleet** (*float*) or sink (*varied*)
c1370 Chaucer *Pity* 110: Ye rekke not whether I flete or synke, **c1375** *Anel.* 182: Him rekketh never wher she flete or synke, **c1380** *PF* 7: Nat wot I wel wher that I flete or synke, **c1385** *CT* I[A] 2397: Ne reccheth nevere wher I synke or fleete. **a1393** Gower *CA* II 270.1628: Betre is to flete than to sincke. **a1415** *Lanterne* 106.4–5: Thei charge not whethir thei synk or swyme. **c1450** Capgrave *Katharine* 95.276: Whiche may see men fleete and also hem synke. **a1475** *Turne up hur halter* in *Rel. Ant.* I 76[37]: Whedyr she ever flete or synke. **a1500** *Court of Love* 417.311: And let it sink or flete. **a1500** *Fortune alas alas* 487.84: I myght for him (chese to) synke or saile. **a1509** Barclay *Ship* I 278[21]: No man shall moche force whether he flete or synke. **c1516** Skelton *Magnificence* 9.254: Here is none forsyth whether you flete or synke. **c1523** Barclay *Mirrour* 28[49]: Caring for none other whether they flete or sinke. **a1534** Heywood *Love* E3^r[26]: Sinke women or swim, **1546** *D* 92.73: Feelde ware might sinke or swym, while ye had eny. Apperson 574; *Oxford* 592; Taylor and Whiting 335; Tilley S485; Whiting *Drama* 363:840.

F269 A **Flent**(?) will make a slide(?)
a1475 *Good Wyfe Wold* 174.53–4: A flent wol make a slyde. So goth the frendles thorowe the toun; no man bydyth hym abyde. (No help in MED or NED.)

F270 (As small as) **Flesh** to (the) pot
c1400 *Laud Troy* I 171.5807: Ector him hew as fflesch to pot, II 505.17137–8: For he ne lefft not of hir a spot That he ne hit hewe as flesch to pot. **a1438** Kempe 15.27–8: He had levar ben hewyn as smal as flesch to the pott, 142.13, 204.27–8: Hakkyd as smal as flesche to the potte. **c1450** G. R. Owst, "A 15th Century Manuscript in St. Albans Abbey," *St. Albans and Hertfordshire Architectural and Archaeological Society: Transactions* (1924) 57[29–30]: Thei alto hackiden her yong children, whanne thei weren newe cristened, as fleisch to the pot. **a1460** *Towneley Plays* 169.98–9: Ffor if ye do, I clefe You small as flesh to pott. **a1500** *Partenay* 82.2272–3: Tham all to-chapped And kerve in pecis sad, As men don the flesh uppon the stal had. **a1500** *Squire* 24.447–8: But loke thou hew hym al so small, As flesshe whan it to potte shall. Tilley F361. See **W688.**

F271 Each (every, all) **Flesh** is hay (grass)
c1395 *WBible* I Peter i 24: For ech fleisch is hey, and al the glorie of it is as flour of hey; the hei driede up, and his flour felde doun. **c1400** Paues 19 (I Peter i 24): For eferich flesch is gras, 214 (*Bodley Douce MS.250*): For al flesch is but as muke or hey. **a1500** *Imitatione* (*1*) 47.31–2: Every flesshe is grasse. **1502** *Imitatione* (*2*) 185.18–9: Every man lyvynge in a mortall body, sayth our lorde, is resembled to hay. Taylor and Whiting 138–9; Tilley F359.

F272 The **Flesh** is frail (unstable, sick)
c1000 *WSG* Matthew xxvi 41: And þæt flæsc ys untrum. **c1384** *WBible* Matthew xxvi 41: Bote the flesh (is) seik *or unstable.* **a1393** Gower *CA* III 394.288–9: Bot whanne a man hath welthe

at wille, The fleissh is frele and falleth ofte. **a1425** *Chester Plays* II 351.517: Flesh is frayle and fallinge aye. **a1450** *Descryvyng* in Kail 68.126: He waxeth syk, for flesch is frele. **c1450** *How mankinde dooth* in Furnivall *Hymns* 74.521: Fleissch is freele. Tilley F363. See **S635.**

F273 It is hard to take out of the **Flesh** what is bred in the bone (*varied*)
a1470 Malory II 550.14–5: Harde hit ys to take oute off the fleysshe that ys bredde in the boone. **1481** Caxton *Reynard* 29[5–6]: That whiche clevid by the bone myght not out of the flesshe, 40[20–1]: He is borne to robbe stele and to lye, this clevid to his bones and can not be had out of the flessh. **a1500** Bernardus *De Cura* 3.61–2: For in sertane Owt of the flesche wyl nocht brede in the bane. **1546** Heywood *D* 89.18: It will not out of the fleshe that is bred in the bone. Apperson 66; *Oxford* 63; Taylor and Whiting 37; Tilley F365; Whiting *Scots* I 142. See **S505.**

F274 Wholesome **Flesh** often corrupts in an unwholesome pot
1532 Berners *Golden Boke* 237.3949–50: Oftentymes some holsome fleshe for meate corrupteth in an unholsome potte.

F275 To mend as the **Fletcher** (*arrow maker*) does his bolt
1546 Heywood *D* 91.44: Than wolde ye mend, as the fletcher mends his bolte. Apperson 412; *Oxford* 419; Tilley F370.

F276 As fair as the **Fleur-de-lis**
c1390 *Salutacioun to ure lady* 136.68: Heil fayrore then the flour delys. See **F304, L276.**

F277 As fresh as the **Fleur-de-lis**
c1380 *Pearl* 8.195: Quen that frech as flor-de-lys. **a1460** *Towneley Plays* 203.258: Floure more fresh then floure de lyce! **a1500** *Alexander-Cassamus* 68.389: Damyselle . . . as fresh as flour-de-lys. See **F306, L277.**

F278 As white as the **Fleur-de-lis**
c1387-95 Chaucer *CT* I[A] 238: His nekke whit was as the flour-de-lys. **1485** Caxton *Charles* 90.19: Hyr chekys . . . whyt as the flour de lys, 151.3. See **F308, L279, 285.**

F279 To fade like **Fleur-de-lis**
c1450 Greene *Carols* 368.2: Myn fleych xal fadyn as flour-de-lys. See **F317.**

F280 Not worth a **Flick** (MED ?, NED *light blow*)
1447 Bokenham 81.2957: Thy craft . . . is not worth a flykke!

F281 **Flight** is the best fight against lechery
a1470 Parker *Dives* P4v[1.8–9]: For ayenst lecherye flyght is best fyght.

F282 Witty **Flight** is sign of no coward
c1440 Charles of Orleans 130.3876: For witty flight is signe of no coward. See **F141, 428.**

F283 As dry as a **Flint**
1533 Heywood *Weather* B3v[32]: Myldams as drye as a flynt.

F283.1 As fierce as **Flint**
1513 Douglas *Aeneid* III 256.102: As he on cace was fleand ferss as flynt, IV 47.92: And lansys up on hycht als fers as flynt. Whiting *Scots* I 170.

F284 As hard as (the, any, a) **Flint**
a750 *Riddles* in *Exeter Book* 202.78: Flinte ic eom heardre. **a800** *Christ* in *Exeter Book* 36.1187–8: Modblinde men . . . Flintum heardran. **c1000** *Larspell* in Napier 234.20–1: And heo bið swa heard swa . . . flint. **a1300** *Tristrem* 41.1451–2: The devel dragouns hide Was hard so ani flint. **c1300** *Beves* 38.792: eni. **c1330** *Body and Soul* 30.98: Thou were harder than the flint. **a1350** *Seege of Troye* 106.1352: And his skyn was as hard as flynt, 116.1465: eny, 137.1721: eny. **a1398**(1495) Bartholomaeus-Trevisa gg3r[1.3]. **a1400** *Perceval* 66.2058: the. **a1400** *Scottish Legends* II 21.707. **1439** Lydgate *St. Albon* 182.1192. **a1475** *Tree* 116.15–6: the. **a1500** *Eger H* 233.838: the. **c1500** *Lover's Farewell* in Robbins 213.128. **a1535** Fisher *Sermon . . . upon a good Friday* in *English Works* 403.17: Hys hart be harder then any flynte stone. Apperson 284; *Oxford* 278; Taylor and Whiting 139; Tilley S878; Whiting *Drama* 312:120, *Scots* I 170.

F285 **Flint-gray**
a750 *Riddles* in *Exeter Book* 181.19: Flintgrægne flod.

F286 To flay the **Flint**
a1393 Gower *CA* III 74.4691–5: He takth, he kepth, he halt, he bint, That lihtere is to fle the flint Than gete of him in hard or neisshe Only the value of a reysshe Of good in helpinge of an other. Apperson 576; Jente 58; *Oxford* 209; Taylor and Whiting 139; Tilley F373.

F287 As belive (*quickly*) as **Flo** (*arrow*)
c1300 *South English Legendary* (*Laud*) 475.464–5: His schip bi-gan to go So blive . . . a(s) . . . flo.

F288 To go as the **Flo** flies from the bow

a1300 *Alisaunder* 45.783–4: He it untyed and lete gon So of bowe fleigheth the flon. See **A188.**

F289 All **Floods** (streams) enter the sea and the sea overflows not (*varied*)
c1395 *WBible* Ecclesiastes i 7: Alle floodis entren in to the see, and the see fletith not over *the markis set of God.* **c1450** *Jacob's Well* 304.2–4: Thin herte is lyche the see-gravel and sande, that sokyth in, and drynketh in, all waterys, and yit the see is nevere full. **c1515** Barclay *Eclogues* 45.1217: Likewise as streames unto the sea do glide. Jente 51; Tilley R140, S181. See **B562.**

F290 As unstable as a **Flood**
1509 Barclay *Ship* I 190[28]: Unstable as a flode.

F291 To fade like a **Flood**
a1450 *Castle* 102.837–8: I schal thee lere of werldlys lay, That fadyth as a flode.

F292 To fare like (a) wild **Flood**
1381 *Jack Trewman* in Knighton II 139[24]: Synne fareth as wilde flode.

F293 To flow like (a) **Flood**
c1390 *Psalterium b. Mariae* 92.984: Of grace, flowynge as flood.

F294 To run like a **Flood**
a900 *Old English Martyrology* 148.13–4: þæt blod arn of þære ylcan stowe swa flod. **a1300** *Arthour and M.*[1] 162.5757–8: Ther was sched so michel blod, That it ran as a flod, 188.6707–8: Of hem ran as michel blod, So in river, when it is flod, 226.8089–90: And eke ther ourne stremes of blod, Al so it were a wel gret flod, 259.9301–2: That in the cuntre ran hethen blod, So in the river doth the flod. Whiting *Scots* I 170.

F295 When the **Flood** of woe is passed the ebb of joy must follow
a1420 Lydgate *Troy* I 157.455–6: As whan the flood of wo is overpassed, The ebbe of Joye folwen most in haste. See **B325, E39, 161, 175, F300.**

F296 As fallow as the **Floor**
a1460 *Towneley Plays* 117.13: Ffor the tylthe of oure landys lyys falow as the floore.

F297 More than **Flother** (*flakes*) in the snow
a1300 *XI Pains* 149.73–4: Mo saules tholieth ther sucche wowe Thane be flothre in the snowe.

F298 As pure as **Flour** taken from the bran
c1450 Idley 82.103–4: Be as pure as floure taken fro the brann In all thy clothyng.

F299 The **Flour** is gone, now sell the bran (*varied*)
c1395 Chaucer *CT* III[D] 477–8: The flour is goon, ther is namoore to telle; The bren, as I best kan, now moste I selle. **1484** Caxton *Royal Book* R6v[13–4]: As grete dyfference as is bytwene . . . the brenne and the floure of whete. MED bran 2. See **F55.**

F300 After a **Flow** an ebb
a1420 Lydgate *Troy* I 202.2013: After a flowe, an ebbe folweth ay, 219.2594–6: For ay after the flowe, Of nature, right as it is dewe, Folwyng the mone the(r) mote an ebbe sewe. Apperson 220; *Oxford* 211; Tilley F378. See **E39, F295.**

F301 Among fair **Flowers** grows many a weed
a1500 *O man more* 394.39: For amonges faire flowres grewethe many a wede. See **G34, H354.**

F302 As bright as (any, the) **Flower**
a1300 *Jacob and Joseph* 5.147–8: Mani fair bour, . . . bright so eni flour. **c1330** *Gregorius* 131 A 721: The levedi at hom so bright so flour. **c1400** *Alexander Buik* I 28.881: With vapnis that war bricht as flour. **a1475** *Landavall* 22.71. **a1500** *Lamwell* 524.81: the. Taylor and Whiting 140. See **B374.**

F303 As clear as the (any) **Flower**
a1400 *Scottish Legends* I 438.419–20: Sittand with facis mare clere Thane the floure of a rosere. **1493** *Treatyse of Love* 30.33: Your colour that was more cleer thane ony flour.

F304 As fair as (the) **Flower(s)**
c1300 *Havelok* 56.1719: That is so fayr so flour on tre, 99.2917. **c1303** Mannyng *Handlyng* 121.3502: That have here wurdys feyre as flours, **a1338** *Chronicle* B I 212[1]: Isabelle fair as floure. **a1375** *St. Andrew* in Horstmann *Legenden 1881* 9.404: Him thoght hir faire als floure in felde. **c1375** *St. John* in Horstmann *Legenden 1881* 37.237: A while ye sall be faire als floures. **c1386** Chaucer *LGW* 2425–6: Ligurges doughter, fayrer on to sene Than is the flour ageyn the bryghte sonne. **a1400** *Eglamour* 47.704–5: Cristabelle . . . Es faire als flour one filde. **a1400** *Ipomadon A* 6.111: That fayre as flowre in felde. **a1400** *Meditations* 32.1197–8: Alas, the beaute of his childhode, Ffairer than the flour that spryngeth brode. **a1400** *Torrent* 2.31 (*note*): The kyng hathe a dowghttyr feyer ase flowyr. **a1422** Lydgate *Life* 474.640: A greyn of David, fayrer then floure in may. **c1455** *Partonope* S 482.34: That fayir was as flowr on hille. **a1460** *Towneley Plays* 268.323–4: Thi face with blode is red, Was fare as floure in feylde. **c1475** *Golagros* 13.352: Fayr of fell and of face as flour unfild. Svartengren 221. See **F276, L276.**

F305 As flitting (*etc.*) as **Flowers** (A number of single quotations are brought together here)
c1385 Usk 76.102–3: How passinge is the beautee of flesshly bodyes, more flittinge than movable floures of sommer! **a1400** *Responcio* in E. K. Chambers and F. Sidgwick *Early English Lyrics* (London, 1907) 18.23: I were as light as the flour. **c1400** *Alle owr mischevis* in *PMLA* 54(1939) 385.10–1: Ffor we ben feyntere than the flowr That with the wynd fadith his colowr. **c1450** *Owayne Miles* (*Cotton Caligula*) 118.407–8: And also develes on eche a syde, As thykke as flowres yn someres tyde. **a1500** Greene *Carols* 456.3: We made as mery as flowres in May. **a1500** *Lambewell* 147.97–8: Her bewtie passeth us as far As betweene the flower and the steale (*stalk*).

F306 As fresh as (any) **Flower(s)** (in May)
a1393 Gower *CA* III 188.767–8: He seth hire face of such colour, That freisshere is than eny flour. **c1408** Lydgate *Reson* 32.1167: More fresh of hewe than may flours. **a1508** Dunbar *Tretis* 87.87: But als fresche of his forme as flouris in May, *Goldyn Targe* 114.58–9: Ladyes . . . Als fresch as flouris that in May up spredis. **c1522** Skelton *Colyn* I 347.945: Fresshe as flours in May. Apperson 235; *Oxford* 225; Tilley F389. See **F277, L277.**

F307 As sweet as any (the) **Flower(s)**
a1300 Thomas de Hales 72.151: Thu art swetture thane eny flur. **a1500** *Guy*[4] 224.7463–4: Out of his mouth came a savour Also sweete as any flower. **c1500** Newton 269.7: Ye are swetter then the flores to me most swete. **1506** Hawes *Pastime* 20.397. Svartengren 308. See **B382.**

F308 As white as (the, any) **Flower**
c1225 *Horn* 3 C 15: He was whit so the flur. **a1300** *Richard* 87.138: Off that lady whyt so flour, 328.4891: the. **c1300** *Reinbrun* 665.103.10. **a1325** *Otuel and Roland* 124.2079. **c1330** *Seven Sages A* 142 E 2909. **a1350** *Seege of Troye* 63.781. **a1350** *Seven Sages C* 112.3282. **a1350** *Ywain* 39.1421. **c1350** *Libeaus* 83.1489. **a1375** *Octavian* (S) 3.39–40, 51.1610: eny. **c1375** Barbour *Bruce* I 196.232. **a1400** ?Chaucer *Rom. A* 356. **a1400** Chestre *Launfal* 60.261, 64.387, 73.742. **a1400** *Eglamour* 11.145 (*var.*), 13.184, 54.806, 57.851 (*var.*), 58.866, 62.922, 81.1214. **a1400** *Torrent* 17.456–7: A whyt sted, As whyt as the flowyr in med. **c1400** *Alexander Buik* I 24.756, 39.1214. **c1400** *Emaré* 23.728–9: He wax the fayrest chyld onlyfe, Whyte as flour on hylle, 30.946. **c1400** *Florence* 7.194, 46.1343, 69.2048. **c1400** *Gowther* 150.374. **c1400** *Toulouse* 245.576 (*var.*). **a1425** *Of alle the joyus* in Bowers *Three Middle English Religious Poems* 35.89. **a1425** *Seege of Troye* 132 LH 1671. **c1455** *Partonope* S 483.83: Whittere thanne is the flowr in feyld. **a1475** *Guy*[2] 2.55: Whyte sche was, as felde flowre. **a1475** *Landavall* 28.351. **1480** Caxton *Ovyde* 130[38]: More whyte than the floure of Lygoustre or of Lylye. **a1500** *Beves* 24 M 397. **a1500** *Feast of All Saints* in *Archiv* 79(1887) 437.211: floures. **a1500** *Knight of Curtesy* 4.97: any. **1513** Douglas *Aeneid* III 115.90. **a1533** Berners *Huon* 549.405: Her skynne was as whyte as ye floure in the mede. See **B339, 383, F278, L279, 285.**

F309 By the **Flowers** the fruits are known
1532 Berners *Golden Boke* 263.4782: By the floures the fruites are knowen. See **G417, I25, T465.**

F310 The fairest **Flower** in one's garland
1472 Paston V 142[18–9]: Yf we lesse that, we lesse the fayereste flower of owr garlond. **1546** Heywood *D* 89.37–9: She is scand, Not onely the fairest floure in your garland, But also she is all the faire flowers thereof. *Oxford* 188; Tilley F387.

F311 The **Flower** of chivalry
a1475 *Guy*[2] 139.4845: Of chevalre he hathe the flowre. **c1500** *Lady Bessy* 21[24]: They be the flower of chivalry. Whiting *Ballad* 35.

F312 The **Flower** of the frying-pan
c1397 Medwall *Fulgens* D2[v][20]: Com forthe, the flowre of the frying pane. Tilley F385.

F313 A **Flower** proceeds out of the rough spine (*thorn*)
a1422 Lydgate *Life* 529.1410–1: And oute of hem even Ilyke procede As dothe a floure oute of the rough spyne. See **R206.**

F314 Some fresh **Flowers** grow on thistles
a1439 Lydgate *Fall* II 397.2467–8: And summe floures, ful fressh off apparense, Growe on thistles rouh(e), sharp and keene.

F315 Some fresh (golden) **Flowers** have a bitter root
a1439 Lydgate *Fall* I 111.4000: Summe fressh(e) floures han a ful bittir roote, **a1449** *Look* in *MP* II 768.114: Som goldene floures have a bittir roote.

F316 To bear the **Flower**
c1400 *Beryn* 111.3694: Ffor of the world(e) wyde the dayis he bare the floure. **a1439** Lydgate *Fall* I 162.5760: For he off fairnesse bar awei the flour. **a1450** *York Plays* 495.130. **a1475**

Guy[2] 24.814. **a1500** *Guy*[4] 13.89. **c1500** Fabyan 294[2.28]: To bere of all the flowre. **1519** Horman *Vulgaria* 404[23]: He bere away the floure and laude of that game. **a1529** Skelton *Garnesche* I 124.149. MED flour n. (1) 4(b). See **B36, 230.**

F317 To fade like (a, the) **Flower(s)**
c1390 *Think on Yesterday* in Brown *Lyrics XIV* 144.43: That heo ne schal fade as a flour. **a1400** *Alexander C* 50.1007: For be the floure never sa fresche it fadis at the last. **a1415** Mirk *Festial* 283.34: Thys world, that ys fals and fadyth as a flowre. **a1420** Lydgate *Troy* I 202.2008–9: And sodeynly, as a somer flour, He can his honour maken for to fade. **1422** Yonge *Governaunce* 153.30: And as flouris shall fade. **a1439** Lydgate *Fall* I 172.6086: a, **a1449** *Benedic* in *MP* I 4–5.106–8: A mannys dayes beon but welked hay, Or lyke a floure ful feyre and fresshe to se Which in feelde faadethe and gothe awey, *Epistle* in *MP* I 17.114. **a1450** *Castle* 166.3001: a. **c1475** Henryson *Orpheus* 69.90–1: Lyk till a flour that plesandly will spring, Quhilk fadis sone, and endis with murnyng. **1479** Rivers *Cordyal* 35.18: a. **a1490** Ryman 220.5: But, as a floure, shalt fade away, 255.4: a, 266.3: a. **a1500** *O dere God, pereles* in Dyboski 52.10: the. **c1500** *Everyman* 3.17–8: Bothe strengthe, pleasure, and beaute Wyll vade from the as floure in maye. **a1513** Dunbar *Of Manis Mortalitie* 150.25–6: Thy youth Sall feid as dois the somer flouris. Taylor and Whiting 140; Tilley F386; Whiting *Scots* I 171. See **F279.**

F318 To fail like the **Flower**
1340 *Ayenbite* 81[10–1]: Hit fayleth and valouweth ase thet flour of the velde. **a1400** *Pricke* 20.695: That son fayles and fades, als dos the flour. **c1400** *Vices and Virtues* 79.30–1: Fairenesse is schort, that soone faileth and widereth as the flour. **a1422** Lydgate *Life* 268.308: Whose beaute fayleth as floure in frosty mede. **1484** Caxton *Royal Book* G7^v[9–11]: It is sone faylled and anone passed . . . as the flour of the felde or of the medowe.

F319 To fall like (a, the) **Flower**
c1325 *Man Must Fight Three Foes* in Brown *Lyrics XIII* 136.63: We falleth so flour when hit is frore. **1410** Walton *Boethius* 159[11–2]: So smart it is, so lightly wil it fayle, And fallen dounright as a somer floure. **a1425** *Chester Plays* II 430.85: the. **a1450** Audelay 83.36–7: Fore ale this wordle honor Schal fal and fade as doth a floure, 165.24–5. **a1500** Greene *Carols* 366.1: a. **a1500** *Imitatione (1)* 47.32: All his glory shal falle as the floure of grasse. **1502** *Imitatione (2)* 185.19–20: All his bodely pleasure shall sone fade and fall, as doth the floures in the medowe.

F320 To fallow (*wither*) like (a) **Flower**
c1325 *An Old Man's Prayer* in Brown *Lyrics XIV* 6.90: Y falewe as flour y-let forthfare. **a1500** *To the, maist peirlas* in Frank A. Patterson *Middle English Penitential Lyric* (New York, 1911) 89.10: Sall fallou and faid as dois a flour.

F321 To fare like (the, a) **Flower**
a1300 *Alisaunder* 241.4314–5: It fareth with man so dooth with floure—Bot a stirte ne may it dure. **c1375** *Song of Love* in Brown *Lyrics XIV* 104.57: Bot fleschly lufe sal fare as dose the flowre in may. **c1400** *Love* in Furnival *Hymns* 25.113–4: But al fleischli love schal fare As dooth the flouris of may. **a1450** Audelay 19.252–3: For al har lordchip and here londys hit farys as a floure; This day hit ys fresche, tomorrow hit is fadyng, 22.324–5.

F322 To flourish like a **Flower**
a1400 *Meditations* 3.93–4: The world that was welked for elde, Fflorscheth ageyn as flour in felde. **c1450** Idley 111.148: His frealte floresshed as floure in Maii.

F323 To glide away (*etc.*) like (a) **Flower** (A number of single quotations are brought together here)
a1300 *Alisaunder* 3.7–8: Somme for the lyves drede That glyt away so floure in mede. **c1395** *WBible* Psalms cii 15: He bithoughte that we ben dust, a man is as hey; his dai schal flowre out so as a flour of the feeld. **a1400** *Meditations* 16.595–6: Ffor shame his hew chaunged anon As doth the flour whan somer is gon. **a1400** *Rowlande* 70.503–4: Thaire armours hewenn laye in the felde, Als floures that strewede were. **c1400** *Alle owr mischevis* in *PMLA* 54(1939) 385.17: We welkin as flour on wintris day. **a1425** *Chester Plays* II 415.414–7: And as the flowrs new springes, Falleth, fadeth, and hings, So thy joy now it raignes, That shall from thee be rafte, 432.145: My flesh that as flower can flee.

F324 To go out like (a) **Flower(s)**
c1382 *WBible* Job xiv 2: That as a flour goth out, and is totreden. **a1450** *Lessouns* in Kail 113.177: Man geth out as don floures.

F325 To know the **Flower** among the weeds
a1400 *Orologium* 334.10: So that thou mayhte knowe the flowres amonge the wedes.

F326 To pass like (the, a) **Flower**

a1300 *Alisaunder* 427.7827–8: And thise maidenes, with rody faas, Passen sone als floure in gras. **c1385** Chaucer *TC* v 1841: This world, that passeth soone as floures faire. **c1395** *WBible* James i 10: For as the flour of gras (**c1384:**hay) he schal passe. **a1400** *Meditations* 21.761–2: Ryght as the flour fair in felde Passeth hethen and weyketh for elde. **a1430** Lydgate *Pilgrimage* 2.41: It al schal passe as doth a somer flour. **1469** *Epitaph* in John Weever *Ancient Funerall Monuments* (London, 1631) 406: As flowers in feeld thus passyth lif. **1523** Skelton *Garlande* I 361.9: How all thynge passyth as doth the somer flower. See **M220.**

F327 To waste away like a summer **Flower**
a1420 Lydgate *Troy* III 874.3568: Wastyng a-way as doth a somer flour, **a1439** *Fall* II 586.58–9: Al beute shal waste a-wey and fade Like somer flours.

F328 To wither like a **Flower**
a1500 *Leconfield Proverbs* 480[22]: It widderithe away lyke a floure. **a1535** Fisher *Wayes* 376.32–5: Goodlinesse of other men, which lyke a flower to day is fresh and lustie, and to morrowe . . . is withered and vanisheth away. See **B373.**

F329 As flat-mouthed as a **Fluke** (*flatfish*)
a1400 *Morte Arthure* 32.1088: Flatt-mowthede as a fluke, 82.2779: Floke-mowthede schrewe. NED Fluke sb.[1] lb.

F330 As drunk-light (?drunkelew [*drunk*]) as a **Fly**
a1500 *Colyn Blowbol* 104.273: Ffor than they ben as dronke-lyight as a flye.

F331 As light as (a) **Fly**
1509 Barclay *Ship* II 290[21–2]: My pleasaunt pace Is lyght as fle. Apperson 364; *Oxford* 366; Tilley F392.

F332 As superfluous as **Flies**
c1382 Wyclif *Petition to the King* in *SEW* III 514[3–4]: Sich privat sectes shulde be superflue and waste, as flies lyvinge in the eyr.

F333 As thick as **Flies**
1489 Caxton *Fayttes* 152.11: Strokes of crosbowes thykker than flyes. Taylor and Whiting 140.

F334 Dear enough a **Fly**
1533 Heywood *Pardoner* B2[r][39]: And tell you fables, dere inoughe a flye.

F335 **Flies** follow (the) honey
c1390 Chaucer *CT* X[I] 441: Thilke manere of folk been the flyes that folwen the hony, or elles the houndes that folwen the careyne. **c1412** Hoccleve *Regement* 111.3062–4: Senek, by hem that folweden Nero, Seith thus, "a fflye folweth the honye; The wolf, careyn." **c1425** *St. Mary Oignies* 137.14–5: Flyes folowe hony, wolves the caryone, and theves hir praye, not the man. *Oxford* 211.

F336 A **Fly** and a friar will fall in every dish
c1395 Chaucer *CT* III[D] 834–6: A frere wol entremette hym everemo. Lo, goode men, a flye and eek a frere Wol falle in every dyssh and eek mateere. **a1500** *Carmina Jocosa* in *Rel. Ant.* I 91[1–6]: Flen, flyys, and freris populum domini male cædunt, . . . Destrue per terras breris, flen, flyyes, and freris. Flen, flyyes, and freris, foul falle hem thys fyften yeris, For non that her ys lovit flen, flyyes, ne freris. Apperson 220; *Oxford* 211. Cf. Selwyn G. Champion *Racial Proverbs* (New York, 1938) 294:121: Flies and priests can enter every where (Slovenian).

F337 Hungry **Fly** bites sore
c1250 *Hendyng O* 197–8.35: Houngri flei bit sore. **1546** Heywood *D* 92.54: Hungry flies byte sore, **1555** *E* 159.84. Apperson 319; Jente 396; Kneuer 59–60; *Oxford* 311; Schleich 274–5; Singer III 140; Tilley F402.

F338 (If) **Flies** follow you, you swallow enough
a1325 *Heil seint Michel* in Heuser 157[10]: Fleiis yow folowithe, ye swolowith ynow. See **B348.**

F339 Never avail a **Fly**
1534 More *Comforte* 1143 B[9]: Can never availe a flye.

F340 Not care a **Fly**
1509 *Fyftene Joyes* G5[v][30–1]: I Care not therof a . . . fly.

F341 Not count a **Fly**
c1390 Chaucer *CT* I[A] 4192: I counte hym nat a flye. **a1400** *Piers B* (*Trinity*) in T. Wright *Vision and Creed of Piers Ploughman* (2nd ed. 1856) II 433.1428–9: Conscience and his counseil He counted at a flye. MED flie n. (1) 4(a). See **F260.**

F342 Not dread more than a **Fly**
c1380 *Ferumbras* 16.437: Hym dredeth nothyng of Olyver no more than of a flye.

F343 Not give two **Flies**
a1300 *Richard* 216.2515–6: Ffor Kyng R. and hys galyes We wolde nought geve twoo (*vars.* thre, twenty) fflyes. Whiting *Drama* 345:561.

F344 Not set a **Fly**
1447 Bokenham 106.3875–6: Of dygnyte, Wych dacyan hym hycht, he set not a flye. **c1516** Skelton *Magnificence* 14.412: I set not by hym a fly, 53.1710, 59.1889, **1523** *Howe the Douty Duke* II 72.161–2. **1533** More *Debellacyon* 967 B[21]: Never after to set a flye. Whiting *Drama* 345:561. See **F262.**

F345 Not worth a **Fly**
a1300 *Richard* 262.12(*var.*): Of my purchas ne getest thugh no wurth a flye! **c1300** Robert of Gloucester II 629.8814–5: Wat was thi strengthe wurth and thi chivalerie Tho thou lore grace of god, ywis, noght wurth a flye. **a1352** Minot 2.24. **c1380** Chaucer *PF* 501: Al this nys not worth a flye! **c1380** *Ferumbras* 153.4930, 181.5840. **c1390** Chaucer *CT* VII 170–1[B1360–1]: As helpe me God, he is noght worth at al In no degree the value of a flye, **c1395** V[F] 1131–2, VIII[G] 1150. **c1400** *Alexius* 65.990. **c1400** *Beryn* 99.3278. **c1412** Hoccleve *Regement* 23.613: By that sette I naght the worth of a flye. **c1450** Capgrave *Katharine* 308.1449. **1513** Skelton *Against the Scottes* I 185.104, **c1516** *Magnificence* 16.470, **1522** *Why Come* II 31.145. **c1525** ?Heywood *Gentylnes* 99.208–9. **1532** More *Confutacion* 369 E[10–1], 634–5, 765 E[9–10]. Apperson 456–7; *Oxford* 211; Tilley F396; Whiting *Drama* 345:561. See **F263.**

F346 To be fleyed (*frightened*) by a **Fly**
a1400 *Morte Arthure* 72.2441: Thou will be flayede for a flye, that on thy flesche lyghttes. Cf. Whiting *Drama* 345:562.

F347 To be latched (*caught*) as **Flies** in lime (*birdlime*)
a1300 *Alisaunder* 25.419–20: Er she be laughtte in her folye So in the lyme is the fleighe.

F348 To come as **Flies** to (a) sore
c1200 *Vices and Virtues* (*Stowe*) 89.32–3: Al dai thar cumeth to thohtes, al swo doth flighen to sare. See note, p. 186.

F349 To eat a **Fly**
a1415 *Lanterne* 11.8–9: Thei seien this man (*a Lollard*) hath eten a fliye, that gyveth him lore of Goddis lawe. See **G176.**

F350 To fly down (*i.e.,* die) like **Flies**
a1338 Mannyng *Chronicle B* II 305[23]: Als fleihes doun thei fleih, ten thousand at ones.

F351 To gape as one would catch **Flies**
a1400 *Cloud* 105.20–1: Thei have it in costume to sitte gapyng as thei wolde kacche flies. Cf. Apperson 102: A close mouth catches no flies; *Oxford* 98; Tilley M1247.

F352 To know not a **Fly** in the milk
c1450 *Pilgrimage LM* 80[30–1]: If i kneewe not a flye in mylk whan thou toldest it me i hadde gret wrong. MED flie n. (1) 4(b): "(not) to perceive the obvious."

F353 To take (keep) **Flies** and butterflies with children
c1425 *St. Mary Oignies* 149.6–7: Whethere wil (ye) folowe and take flyes and flyand botirflyes with childer. **c1450** *Alphabet* 518.22–4: For God, what seke ye ther? Will ye go kepp butterflies as barnys duse?

F354 No more than a **Fly-bite(ing)**
a1350 *Ywain* 3.93–4: Na mare manes me thi flyt Than it war a flies byt. **c1400** *Laud Troy* I 184.6239–40: He yaff no more of his smytyng Then of a fflyes bytyng. See **F266.**

F355 Not worth (weigh) a **Fly Tail**
1534 Heywood *Love* D1r[33]: No ayde . . . worth tayle of a fly, **1556** *Spider* 98[8]: This tale weith not a flie taile.

F356 Not set a **Fly Wing**
a1460 *Towneley Plays* 231.94: He settys not a fle wyng bi sir cesar.

F357 As rugged (*shaggy*) as a **Foal**
a1500 *Guy*[4] 121.3864: His body rugged as any fole, 180.5914: Rugged as a rough fole. Apperson 540; Svartengren 230.

F358 As tattered (*shaggy*) as a (feltered [*matted*]) **Foal**
c1375 *St. Bartholomew* 122.305–6: A fende . . . tatered als a filterd fole. **a1400** *Pricke* 43.1537: Som gas tatird als tatird foles. **a1460** *Towneley Plays* 5.137: And ugly, tatyrd as a foyll.

F359 How can the **Foal** amble if the horse and mare trot?
1549 Heywood *D* 44.93: How can the fole amble, if the hors and mare trot? Apperson 221; *Oxford* 212; Tilley F408. See **C514.**

F360 As fresh as any (the) **Foam**
a1400 *Alexander C* 274.5604: Of fethir fresch as any fame as ere thir fedill dowfis. **a1400** *Destruction of Troy* 100.3079: Ffresshe and of fyne hew as the fome clere.

F361 As white as (the, any) **Foam**
c1325 *Chronicle* 4.75–6(*var.*): Thi lemman, That ys wyttore then the fom. **c1385** Chaucer *CT* I[A] 1659: That frothen whit as foom for ire wood. **a1400** *Eglamour* 2.26: That was a dogheter, white als fame, 42.637, 45.680(*var.*), 60.892(*var.*). **a1400** *Rowlande* 85.967. **a1400** *Scottish Legends* I 444.105: Fare and quhyt, as

vatir fame. **c1400** *Emaré* 16.497, 26.818. **c1400** *Toulouse* 228.199(*var.*) **c1440** *Degrevant* 38.562: Scho es white als the fame (*var.* seys ffame), 90.1402: Whytte als the see-fame. **a1500** *Eger H* 327.2371: And Ladies quyet as any fame. Taylor and Whiting 141; Whiting *Scots* I 171.

F362 To be like the sea **Foam**
a1350 *Isumbras* 20.251: Hir lyre es als the see fome.

F363 Give your **Foe** a foul name
a1200 *Ancrene* 163.26: Yef thi fa a ful nome. MED foul, adj. 6. See Taylor and Whiting 106: Dog (29).

F364 He that will trow (*trust*) his **Foe** shall sometime rue
c1375 Barbour *Bruce* I 40.326–7: Now I persawe, he that will trew His fa, it sall him sum tyme rew. See **E100, F367.**

F365 An open **Foe** is better than a feigned friend
a1500 *Thre Prestis* 49.1147–8: Now weil I se, and that I underta, Than feinyeit freind better is open fa. Apperson 221; *Oxford* 37–8; Tilley F410; Whiting *Drama* 151. See **E97.**

F366 Tell never your **Foe** that your foot sleeps (aches)
c1250 *Hendyng O* 193.12: Tele thou nevere thi fo that thi fot slepeth (**c1325** *H* 291.93: aketh). **c1475** *Rawlinson MS. D 328* 118.12: Tell nevere thy foo that thy fote slepith. Apperson 442; Kneuer 29; *Oxford* 646; Schleich 253; Singer III 128; Skeat 73; Tilley F412. See **C467, S512.**

F367 Trust not too much in the favor of your **Foes**
c1460 *Take Good Heed* 209.13: Trust not to moche in the favour of youre foos. See **F364.**

F368 To have no more **Foison** (*strength*) than the lamb against the lion
a1338 Mannyng *Chronicle A* I 56.1591–2: The other alle had no foysoun Than had the lomb ageyn the lyoun.

F369 All **Folk** shall not thrive at once
c1450 *Chaunce* 5.6–7: This worldes course I have herd sey ful ryve Ys that alle folke shall not at ones thryve.

F370 Diverse **Folk** say (deem) diversely
c1390 Chaucer *CT* I[A] 3857: Diverse folk diversely they seyde, **c1395** V[F] 202: Diverse folk diversely they demed. Cf. Whiting *Scots* I 171. See **H230, M202.**

F371 **Folk** call on the horse that will carry
1546 Heywood *D* 51.330: Folke call on the horse that will cary alwey. Apperson 312:20, 314:65; *Oxford* 710; Tilley F414.

F372 **Folk** that have no head or lord can do little good
c1489 Caxton *Aymon* II 501.15–6: Ye wote well that folke that have noo hede nor noo lorde can doo but lityll goode. See **H257, M217.**

F373 Irous (*angry*) **Folk** are to be forborne.
c1450 *Pilgrimage LM* 26[13]: For irowse folk ben to forbere.

F374 Many **Folk** think to do many things the hurt therof lights on their own necks
a1533 Berners *Arthur* 270[11–2]: But many folkes thynke to do many thynges, the whyche the hurte therof lyghteth on theyr owne neckes. See **D22, E180, P232.**

F375 Old **Folks** can (*know*) much
c1395 Chaucer *CT* III[D] 1004: Thise olde folk kan muchel thyng. See **M255, S60.**

F376 Young **Folk** are seldom wise
c1412 Hoccleve *Regement* 6.147: And ful seelde is, that yong folk wyse been.

F377 **Folly** heaped upon folly grieves God
a1400 Wyclif *Sermons* I 389[5–6]: For folie hepid upon folie greveth God.

F378 **Folly** is no sapience
a1500 *Colkelbie* 294.424–5: Be this ye may weill ken That foly is no sapience.

F379 **Folly** shall be found in many words
c1395 *WBible* Ecclesiastes v 2: Foli schal be founden in many wordis. See **W593.**

F380 **Folly** to begin and more folly to continue
1525 Berners *Froissart* IV 319[36–7]: Foly it was to begyn, and more foly to contynewe. See **F383.**

F381 Great **Folly** to take heed to another and not to one's own need
1478 Rivers *Morale Proverbes* [6.5–6]: Grete folye is in him that taketh hede Upon other, and not to his owen nede. Apperson 696–7. See **A131, N85.**

F382 He that begins the **Folly** should repent
c1450 *Merlin* II 498[16]: He that be-gan the foly it is reson that he repent.

F383 It is better to leave **Folly** than to maintain it
c1477 Caxton *Jason* 116.27–9: For as it is said communly, hit is better to leve folie thenne to mayntene folie. Apperson 46. See **F380.**

F384 It is **Folly** to give counsel to folk that will do but folly
a1325 *Cursor* I 108.1743–4: For it es foli give consail to The folk that wil but foli do. See **C468.**

F385 It is no **Folly** to change counsel when the thing is changed
c1390 Chaucer *CT* VII 1065[B2255]: For I seye that it is no folie to chaunge conseil whan the thyng is chaunged. Cf. Taylor and Whiting 70: Circumstance.

F386 Many for **Folly** fordo (*ruin*) themselves
c1425 *Good Wife H* 171.166: Many for folye hemself fordooth.

F387 To do one **Folly** and flee a greater is wisdom
a1338 Mannyng *Chronicle A* I 170.4837–42: A folye to do, and fle a wel more, Men haldes that wysdam and lore; To do a folye, yut were hit skyl, Ffort(o) lyvere a man fro more peryl; And god hit were to suffre a wo, Ffor to venge hym of hys fo. See **E193.**

F388 To feign **Folly** while (*sometimes*) is wit (wisdom)
c1375 Barbour *Bruce* I 15.343–4: And Catone sayis ws, in his wryt, "To fenyhe foly quhile is wyt." **c1390** *Cato* (*Vernon*) 582.353–6: Ffeyne the fol, thei thou be wys, Ther fooles aren beodeene; A Mon to feynen him on that wyse Is wismon, als I wene. **a1400** *Cato* (*Copenhagen*) A6^v[19–20]: It is grete wisdom sothly, When it is tyme, to feyne foly. **a1430** Lydate *Pilgrimage* 54.2009–10: Yt ys wysdom, ryht, and no wrong, To feyne foly evere a-mong. **c1450** *Pilgrimage LM* 13–4: It is gret wysdom what any man saye sum time to feyne folye. Smith 112. Cf. *Oxford* 716: It is wisdom. See **M346, 350, W378.**

F389 To find the **Folly** that one seeks (fraists [*seeks*])
a1350 *Ywain* 13.456: I fand the folies that I soght. **c1390** *Sir Gawain* 11.324: And as thou foly hatz frayst, fynde the behoves. **c1450** *Merlin* II 572[33–4]: And seth ye folye have sought, folie have ye founden.

F390 Where **Food** fails is faint strength
a1400 *Siege of Jerusalem* 50.877–8: For ther as fayleth the fode ther is feynt strengthe, And ther as hunger is hote, hertes ben feble. See **H645.**

F391 Answer a **Fool** according to his folly
c1300 *South English Legendary* (*Laud*) 494.188: Ffor-sothe thou axest as a fol, and swich ansuere me schul the yive. **c1395** Chaucer *CT* IV[E] 1655–6: Justinus, which that hated his folye, Answerde anon right in his japerye. **c1395** *WBible* Proverbs xxvi 4–5: Answere thou not to a fool bi his foli, lest thou be maad liik hym. Answere thou a fool bi his fooli, lest he seme to him silf to be wiis. **1492** *Salomon and Marcolphus* 30[9–10]: It is to be answeryd to a fole aftyr his folysshnes. Apperson 225; Tilley F442. See **D159.**

F392 Come a **Fool** and go a fool (*varied*)
c1300 *South English Legendary* I 125.122: Ac a fol thi sulf hider thou come and a fol thou sselt hom wende. **1509** Barclay *Ship* I 145[26–8]: And at the last retournyth home agayne More ignorant, blynder and gretter folys Than they were whan they firste wente to the scolys, 177[18–9]: But whan theyr journey they homwarde must addres As folys unware, [27–8]: When he departyd, If that he were a sote Agayne anone he comyth in the same mynde and cote, II 88[28]: Sende a fole forth and so comys he agayne. Apperson 228:91; Jente 217; *Oxford* 216; Tilley F460; Whiting *Scots* I 172. See **C380, F460, G182, H424, W395, 413.**

F393 A **Fool** abides not till he hang
c1450 *Pilgrimage LM* 155[31–2]: But sooth it is that the folk seyn, The fool abideth nouht til he honge.

F394 A **Fool** and his bauble (*varied*)
a1400 *Ancrene* (*Recluse*) 121.16–7: A more fole than he that bereth a Babyl. **c1450** *Douce MS.52* 54.109: A fole sholde never have a babull in hande. **c1450** *Epistle of Othea* 143.23: Wysedam pleseth not a fool so well as is bable. **c1450** *Rylands MS.394* 104.17^v.7. **a1500** Hill 130.9: A fole will not geve his babill for the Towr of London. **1509** Barclay *Ship* I 256[6–7]: For it is oft sayd of men both yonge and olde A fole wyll nat gyve his Babyll for any golde, II 276[13–4]: For it is sayde, and provyd true and verytable That folys hath no pleasour but onely in they(r) bable, **c1515** *Eclogues* 151.326: The foole in his bable hath pleasure for to toy. **c1520** *Terens* C2^r[26]: Therfore I may have a folis bable wythall. **c1523** Barclay *Mirrour* 60[33]: Fooles rejoyce in their bable. Apperson 224:22, 227:81; *Oxford* 155, 216, 218; Tilley F476, 509, 511, 548; Whiting *Drama* 117. See **B70.**

F395 The **Fool** can find no wit but what he has of kind (*nature*)
a1450 *Partonope* 2.46–9: The fole of byrth can no wytte ffynde But that he hath by taste of

kynde. Of alle that under heven ys The wyse taketh wysdam I-wys.

F396 The **Fool** can hele (*hide*) nothing but he wray (*declare*) it out
c1280 *South English Legendary: OT History* 84.80: For the fool ne can hele nothing bot he it out wrie. Cf. Whiting *Drama* 45.

F397 A **Fool** cannot be still
c1380 Chaucer *PF* 574: But soth is seyd, "a fol can not be stille." Apperson 227:65; *Oxford* 217: foolish; Skeat 139.

F398 A **Fool** dreads not his enemies
a1400 *Twelve Profits* in *Yorkshire Writers* II 46[21–2]: These are tho (*flattering*) enmyes of whilk (tho) comune proverbe tellis: "ffoole ne drede(s) (tham) noght." **1525** Berners *Froissart* IV 313[36–7]: He is but a foole that fereth not his enemyes. Cf. Jente 474.

F399 A **Fool** is fain of gift and a wise man beweeps it
c1450 *Rylands MS.394* 100.1: Foole fayne ys of gefte and wyse man it be wepys.

F400 A **Fool** is known by his laughing
c1390 *Proverbes of diverse profetes* 534.179–80: The fol is knowen bi his lauhwhing, And the wyse bi his sad beryng. **1422** Yonge *Governaunce* 141.17–9: This provyth Sothe by this wers Per multum risum, potes cognoscere Stultum. Anglice. "By ofte laghynge thow mayste know a fole." **a1500** *How the Wyse Man* 30.68: For folys byn by laghyng knowe. Apperson 224:20; Tilley F462. See **F415.**

F401 A **Fool** is known by his tongue (*varied*)
a1420 Lydgate *Troy* I 345.7022: For be his tonge a fole is ofte knowe. **c1450** *Epistle of Othea* 82.26–7: Ffor thu meyst lerne in wyse mennes scole That, by mykle talkyng, thu schalt know a foole. **a1460** *Dicts* (*Helmingham*) 97.19–20: A man maye knowe a foole by his moche language. **c1523** Barclay *Mirrour* 73[25]: And a foole is knowen by speche negligent. Apperson 224:18, 226:43; Tilley F465. See **B420, M260, W578.**

F402 A **Fool** is like a mole which hears and understands not
c1440 Scrope *Epistle to Othea* 40[22–3]: A foole is leche a molle, the which heryth and understondyth not. **c1450** *Epistle of Othea* 49.19–20. See **A227.**

F403 The **Fool** loves nothing but his folly (*varied*)
c1280 *South English Legendary: OT History* 83.56: For the fool, bot his foly nothing ne loveth wel. **c1395** *Remonstrance against Romish Corruptions*, ed. J. Forshall (London, 1851) 77–8: And it is seid in Proverbis, *No thing no but fooli, pleesith a fool.* **c1395** *WBible* Proverbs xv 21: Folie is joye to a fool. **c1475** *The hart lovyt* in Smith *Common-place Book* 11[3]: The fowlle lovyt hys folly, the wysseman lovyt hys skyll.

F404 A **Fool** may give a wise man counsel (*varied*)
a1350 *Ywain* 40.1477–8: Bot yit a fole that litel kan, May wele cownsail another man. **c1385** Chaucer *TC* i 630: A fool may ek a wisman ofte gide. **a1400** *Cato* (*Fairfax*) in *Cursor* III 1669.48: Of fole leris wise. **a1400** *King John and the Bishop* in *PMLA* 46(1931) 1029.76–7: My lord (quod he) you have red it That a foule may teach a wysman wyt. **a1450** Audelay 46.1012–3: For at a fole ye ma(y) lere, Yif ye wil take hede. **a1450** *Partonope* 2.53–8: And the wyse can ffynde In folys tales sum-tyme wysdame. Ther-fore fulle ofte the wyse manne Wolle here the fole and eke the wyse, Where-thorowe he can the better devyse To drawe wysdam oute of ffoly, 321.7981–3: Yite is an olde proverbe seide is all day: Of a fole a wyse man may Take witte, this is withouten drede. **c1450** *Epistle of Othea* 131.20–1: For sum-tyme it fortuneth the foole teche the wyse man. **c1460** *Ipomadon C* 351.44–5: For a fole among wise men oft doos mich eas! **a1500** *Merita Missæ* 148.9–10: For sumtym is A folle as good to here As the word of A freer. Apperson 223:12; *Oxford* 214; Skeat 150; Taylor and Whiting 142; Tilley F469. See **M340, 345.**

F405 A **Fool** never believes till he feels sore
c1489 Caxton *Aymon* II 485.26: For a fole never byleveth tyll he fele sore. Apperson 223:10. See **F416.**

F406 A **Fool** never wot (*knows*) where he shall strike but ever lays on thick
a1400 *Ipomadon A* 196.6885–7: A fooll wott never, where he shall stryke, But ever more lay on thyke, Where he may lyghttly hytte.

F407 A **Fool's** bell is soon rung
a1400 *Romaunt B* 5263–5: For every wis man, out of drede, Can kepe his tunge til he se nede; And fooles can not holde her tunge; A fooles belle is soone runge. Apperson 224:23; *Oxford* 216; Skeat 139.

F408 A **Fool's** (sot's, woman's) bolt is soon shot (*varied*) c1250 *Hendyng O* 192.7: Sottes bolt is sone isotten, *C* 184.12: Fole is. **a1300** *Proverbs of Alfred* 119 J 460: And sottes bolt is sone ischote. **c1300** *Beves* 56.1191–2: Men saith . . . in olde riote, That wimmannes bolt is sone schote. **c1300** *South English Legendary* II 535.54: A fol womman as thu ert, youre bolt is sone ischote. **c1330** *Seven Sages A* 39.979–82: Hit is not hale To leve stepmoderes tale, For here bolt is sone ischote, More to harm than to note. **a1350** *Seven Sages C* 25–6.751–4. **a1350** *Ywain* 58.2168: For fole bolt es sone shot. **a1400** *Proverbis of Wysdom* 246.113: A fole is bolt is sone i-shote. **a1449** Lydgate *Say the Best* in *MP* II 796.50–1: A foole hath redy bent his bow To shete his bolt, till he repent. **a1450** *Myne awen dere* 175.819–20: For oftetymes thou hard saye, "A foles bolt sone schotte awaye." **c1450** *Fyrst thou sal* 89.89. **a1470** Parker *Dives* A1v[1.19–20]: But it is a comon proverbe, A foles bolte is soone shotte. **a1475** *Good Wyfe Wold* 174.48: A follys bolt ys son ischot, and dothe but lyttyll good. **c1475** *Mankind* 29.775: How say ye, ser? my bolte ys schott. **c1475** *Rawlinson MS. D 328* 121.49. **1509** Barclay *Ship* I 108[21]: And lyghtly his folysshe bolt shall be shot out. **a1522** More *Treatyce* 73 B[8–9]: We presume to shoote our folish bolte. **1546** Heywood *D* 65.10, **1555** *E* 179.185, 189.244.2: What bolts shootst thou from that bow, fooles bolts I trow. Apperson 224:24; Kneuer 28–9; *Oxford* 216; Schleich 251; Singer III 127; Tilley F515; Whiting *Drama* 267, *Scots* I 172. See **B434.**

F409 A **Fool's** chief pleasure is to have all others like him
1509 Barclay *Ship* II 236[13–4]: That a Fole hath chefe pleasour and confort To have all other lyke hym of the same sort, 307[19]: A fole in felawes, hath pleasour and delyte. See **C262.**

F410 A **Fool's** errand may not speed (*prosper*)
1400 *Love god, and drede* in Kail 2.46: And fooles erande may not spede. Taylor and Whiting 142.

F411 A **Fool's** paradise
1462 Paston IV 49[34–5]: I wold not be in a folis paradyce. **c1477** Norton *Ordinall* 28[12]: For lewde hope is fooles Paradice. **c1503** More *Early Poems* [14] C[7]: Put the and kepe the in a fooles paradise. **1519** Horman *Vulgaria* 334[32]: He hath set his lorde in a folys paradyse. Apperson 225:29; *Oxford* 216; Tilley F523; Whiting *Drama* 345:564.

F412 A **Fool's** rage lasts but a throw (*instant*)
a1420 Lydgate *Troy* I 345.7021: The rage of folis that last but a throwe. Cf. Whiting *Drama* 119. See **C203.**

F413 A **Fool's** tongue is the key of his secrets
1450 *Dicts* 166.13–4: A fooles tunge is the key of his secretes. **1477** Rivers *Dictes* 72[7]: The tongue of a foole is the key of his secret. Cf. Apperson 224:27.

F414 A **Fool's** word is not to trow (*trust*)
a1400 *Romaunt B* 4531–2: A foolis word is nought to trowe, Ne worth an appel for to lowe.

F415 The **Fool** turns his thought to laughter
a1425 *Rule of St. Benet (1)* 14.32–3: The fool turnes hys thoght intil laghter, and helpis noht. See **F400.**

F416 **Fools** fear never a thing till they take the acolee (*blow*)
c1450 *Merlin* 570[3–4]: And ther-fore is seide a proverbe, that foles love (*error for* fear) never a thinge till he take the a-coole. H. Oskar Sommer *Le Roman de Merlin* (London, 1894) 405.41–2: Et por ce dist on encore en reprovier que fols ne crient devant quil prent lacolee. See **F405.**

F417 **Fools** hasten so much that they repent after
1481 Caxton *Reynard* 110[7–9]: Men fynde many fooles that in hete hasten hem so moche that after they repente hem and thenne it is to(o) late. Tilley F518. See **H158, 159.**

F418 **Fools** lade (*bale*) pools, wise men eat the fish
c1450 *Utter thy langage* in Furnivall *Babees Book* 332.12–3: Folus lade polys; wisemenn ete the fysshe; Wisemenn hath in ther hondis ofte that folys after wysshe. Apperson 226:52; *Oxford* 218; Tilley F538. See **B604, D147.**

F419 **Fools** oft take resin for frankincense
c1450 *Epistle of Othea* 136.18: Fools take rosen ofte for frankensense.

F420 Found a **Fool,** left a fool
c1450 *Alphabet* I 133.3: And therfor as I fand the a fule, so will I lefe the.

F421 He is a **Fool** that agrees to the counsel of a child
a1533 Berners *Huon* 97.31–2: He is a fole that agreeth to the counsell of a chyld.

F422 He is a **Fool** that begins anything without provision
1509 Barclay *Ship* I 75[5–7]: A fole forsoth is he And to be lawghed to derysyon, That ought begynneth without provysyon.

F423 He is a **Fool** that cannot hold himself content when he is at ease
1519 Horman *Vulgaria* 104[1–2]: He is a foole that can nat holde hym selfe content whan he is well at ease. Apperson 226:58; Tilley E163. See **E32.**

F424 He is a **Fool** that casts away his old water ere he have new
c1475 *Rawlinson MS. D 328* 121.44: He ys a fole that castith a-way his olde water or he have new. *Oxford* 81; Tilley W90. See **O27, T132, 157.**

F425 He is a **Fool** that deals with fools
a1400 *Thre Ages* 263–4: I seghe wele samples bene sothe that sayde bene (ful) yore: Fole es that with foles delys: flyte we no lengare. Apperson 227:70, 76; Whiting *Scots* I 172. See **C465, F442.**

F426 He is a **Fool** that discovers his counsel to his wife
c1421 Lydgate *Thebes* 118.2869–70: A fool he was to Jupard his lif Forto discure his counsel to his wif. See **W242.**

F426.1 He is a **Fool** that falls at debate with wealth
c1516 Skelton *Magnificence* 1.5: A fole is he with Welth that fallyth at debate. Tilley F452, quote 1573.

F427 He is a **Fool** that falls into reasoning with his master
c1475 Henryson *Fables* 70.2014–5: Bot now I se he is ane fule perfay That with his maister fallis in ressoning. See **S160.**

F428 He is a **Fool** that fights while flitting (*flight*) may help
c1353 *Winner* 154–5: I holde hym bot a fole that fightis whils flyttynge may helpe, When he hase founden his frende that fayled hym never. See **F141, 282.**

F429 He is a **Fool** that goes at large and makes himself thrall (*varied*)
a1410 Lydgate *Churl* in *MP* II 480.272–3: He is a fool at all That goth at large, and makith hymsilf thrall. **a1475** *Good Wyfe Wold* 175.57: He is a foll that wyll be bonde whyll he mey forber.

F430 He is a **Fool** that intends to increase the light of the sun with small brands of fire
1509 Barclay *Ship* I 149[1–4]: He is a fole . . . Whiche with small brondes of fyre . . . Entendyth . . . Of the shynynge sonne for to encrease the lyght. See **W80.**

F431 He is a **Fool** that leaves the better and chooses the worse
c1400 *Five Questions of Love* in Wyclif *SEW* III 184[19–20]: He is a miche fool that leeveth the bettere and chesith the werse.

F432 He is a **Fool** that meddles of craft he has not learned
c1450 *Pilgrimage LM* 122[10]: He is a fool that medleth him of craft that he hath not lerned. See **E128, M403, R54.**

F433 He is a **Fool** that puts his trust in a thief
a1533 Berners *Huon* 706.26–8: It is sayd in a comen proverbe that a man is taken for a foole that putteth his trust in a thefe.

F434 He is a **Fool** that takes a charge that does (*makes*) him fall
a1500 *Guy*[4] 23.437–8: For holden he is a foole of all, That taketh a charge, that doth him fall.

F435 He is a **Fool** (sot) that takes more than he may wield
a1200 Lawman I 278.6513–6: For the mon is muchel sot The nimeth to him seolven Mare thonne he maghen walden, He sael halden rather. **c1300** *Guy*[1] 26.453–4: For a fole he schal him held That taketh more than he may weld. Apperson 268; *Oxford* 262.

F436 He is a **Fool** that thinks mickle and speaks more
c1330 *Horn Childe* 190.971–2: Michel he thought and more he speke, For fole men schuld him hold. See **M791, T207.**

F437 He is a **Fool** that will forget himself
c1385 Chaucer *TC* v 97–8: I have herd seyd ek tymes twyes twelve, "He is a fool that wole foryete hymselve." Apperson 227:71; *Oxford* 215; Skeat 201; Tilley F480.

F438 He is a **Fool** that will not do what may prow (*benefit*) him
a1325 *Cursor* III 1513.27126–7: And es he for a fule to trou, That will noght do that mai him prou.

F439 He is a **Fool** that will not gladly hear counsel in time
c1475 Henryson *Fables* 65.1862–3: Grit fule is he, that will not glaidlie heir Counsall in tyme, quhill it availl him nocht. Whiting *Scots* I 152. See **C448.**

F440 He is a **Fool** that with one hound (in)tends to take two hares
1509 Barclay *Ship* I 103[1–3]: A fool he is and

voyde of reason Whiche with one hounde tendyth to take Two harys in one instant.

F441 If a **Fool** say nothing men ween (*think*) him wise (*varied*)
c1390 *Proverbes of diverse profetes* 548.385–8: A fol yif he speke no thing, Men wene he beo wys in doyng; Whon he bi-gynneth to Jangle fast, Then men knowen wel his cast. **c1395** *WBible* Proverbs xvii 28: Also a foole, if he is stille, schal be gessid a wiis man. **c1523** Barclay *Mirrour* 73[27]: If a foole were able to kepe him in scilence He should be reputed a man of sapience. Smith 114; Tilley F531. See **P156.**

F442 It behooves that he be a **Fool** that loves the fellowred (*company*) of fools
1340 *Ayenbite* 205[31–2]: Vor huo thet loveth velawrede of fol: hit behoveth that he by fol. **c1400** *Vices and Virtues* 227.19–20: For who-so loveth companye of fooles, it bihoveth hym to be a fool. See **F425.**

F443 It falls to a **Fool** to show folly and (to) a wise man to suffer his words (*varied*)
a1400 *Destruction of Troy* 165.5080–1: Ffor it falles to a fole his foly to shew, And a wise man witterly his wordes to suffer. **1471** Caxton *Recuyell* II 561.12–4: Hit was the nature of a fole to shewe folye, And to a wyse man to suffre hit. See **F453.**

F444 Men may ken (*know*) a **Fool** by folly (*foolish*) words
c1303 Mannyng *Handlyng* 105.2967–8: By foly wurdys mow men a fole kenne; Thurgh blast of mouthe the fyre wyl brenne. See **D355.**

F445 The most **Fool** is wiser than he that was buried yesterday
c1390 *Think on Yesterday* in Brown *Lyrics XIV* 145.81–4: The moste fool, I herde respounde, Is wysore while he lyve may, Then he that hedde a thousend pounde And was buried yuster-day. See **D317.**

F446 A natural **Fool** in a house alone will make shift or chevisance (*provision*) for himself
1506 Barclay *Castell* A3v[2–4]: An olde proverbe came in me subvenaunce, A naturall foole in a house alone Wyl make for hymself shyft or chevysaunce. (Not in Gringoire)

F447 None so much a **Fool** but he may find his fellow
c1450 *Merlin* II 572[34–6]: Therfore may ye seye verily that ther nys noon so moche a fole but he may finde his felowe. Cf. Tilley F493. See **G382, M64.**

F448 Oft fails the **Fool's** thought (*varied*)
c1375 Barbour *Bruce* I 24.582: Bot oft failyeis the fulis thocht, 272.21. **c1385** Chaucer *TC* i 217: But alday faileth thing that fooles wenden. **c1385** Usk 77.122: Thus al-day fayleth thinges that fooles wend. **c1420** Wyntoun IV 343.241: But oft failyeis fulys thoucht. **c1430** Lydgate *Dance* 72.608: For moche faileth of thynge that foles thynke. **1484** Caxton *Aesop*, ed. R. T. Lenaghan (Cambridge, Mass., 1967) 218[12–3]: Therfore it is sayd ofte, that moche lacketh he of that that a fole thynketh or weneth. **a1533** Berners *Huon* 714.2–3: It is an olde sayenge that many thynges remayneth of such folysshe thoughtes. Apperson 227:67; *Oxford* 422; Skeat 148; Tilley A129. See **F451, H467, M785, T491, W263.**

F449 One **Fool** (friar) cannot be ware by another
c1385 Chaucer *TC* i 202–3: O veray fooles, nyce and blynde be ye! Ther nys nat oon kan war by other be. **c1475** Gregory *Chronicle* 230[20]: But one fryer couthe not be ware by a nother. See **C161, W47.**

F450 Strive not with **Fools**
c1450 La Tour-Landry 22.5: For folke shulde not strive with foles. Cf. Whiting *Drama* 54: With fooles it is follie to vary.

F451 That (which) the **Fool** thinks ofttimes comes to folly
c1500 *Melusine* 254–5: But that the fole thinketh oftymes commeth to foly. Tilley A129. See **F448.**

F452 There is no **Fool** to the old fool
1546 Heywood *D* 63.36: But there is no foole to the olde foole, **1555** *E* 177.176. Apperson 228:104; *Oxford* 216; Taylor and Whiting 142; Tilley F506. Cf. Jente 120.

F453 Though a **Fool** will not leave his folly, a wise man must suffer patiently
a1420 Lydgate *Troy* I 344–5.7004–6: For though a fool his foly wil nat leve To presume to speke unkonnyngly, A wys man moste suffre paciently. See **F443.**

F454 Though you bray a **Fool** in a mortar, you may not drive his folly from him
a900 Alfred *Gregory* 265.25–267.2: Salomonnes cwide . . . þeah ðu portige ðone dysegan on pilan, swa mon corn deð mid piilstæfe, ne meaht ðu his dysi him from adrifan. **c1395** *WBible* Proverbs xxvii 22: Though thu beetist a fool in a morter, as with a pestel smytynge above dried barli; his foli schal not be don

awei fro him. Apperson 225:34; NED Bray v.[2] 16; Tilley F447.

F455 To be not such a **Fool** as one seems
a1500 *Thre Prestis* 30.528: And said he was not sik a fuil as he semes, 33.638: Ye ar not sik ane fule as ye let yow. *Oxford* 214: looks.

F456 To have a **Fool's** hood
1509 Barclay *Ship* I 36[13–4]: For his Foles Hode his iyen so sore doth blynde That Pryde expelleth his lynage from his mynde, 38[1]: Come nere disgysed foles: receyve your Foles Hode, [14]: To kepe you from the rayne, ye shall have a foles hode. *Oxford* 303; Tilley H585.

F457 To play the **Fool** without a visor (*mask*)
c1516 Skelton *Magnificence* 37.1178: Thou can play the fole without a vyser. Cf. *Oxford* 505.

F458 To sing a **Fool** a mass
c1385 Chaucer *TC* iii 88: Or was to bold, to synge a fool a masse. **a1410** Lydgate *Churl* in *MP* II 483.341: And mad is he that syngith a fool a mass. MED fole (*foal*) 1b.

F459 Who may be a **Fool,** but if he love?
c1385 Chaucer *CT* I[A] 1799: Who may been a fool, but if he love? MED fol 4c. Cf. Smith 190; Tilley L558.

F460 Who sends a **Fool** abides a fool
1340 *Ayenbite* 211[27–8]: Vor ase me zayth communliche, huo thet fol zent: fol abyt. **c1400** *Vices and Virtues* 234.20–1: For as men seith, "Who-so a fool sendeth, a fool abideth" (*var.* a fool he abydeth). **c1450** *Salisbury Cath. Libr. MS.103* in Owst *Literature* 44[6]: Ffor it is seyd, "He that fool sendyth, fool abydeth." *Oxford* 574; Tilley F488. See **F392.**

F461 Won (*dwell*) not with **Fools** if you will learn good
c1280 *South English Legendary: OT History* 82.25: With the fole ne wone thou nought, yif thou wilt good lerne.

F462 **Foolhardiness** is never content with enough
1519 Horman *Vulgaria* 396[5]: Fole hardynes is never content with ynoughe. See **E120.**

F463 **Fool-haste** does no advantage (*varied*)
a1393 Gower *CA* II 271.1680–2: Folhaste doth non avantage, Bot ofte it set a man behinde In cause of love, 276.1861: Folhaste is cause of mochel wo. **c1400** *Scottish Troy* 275.1680–2: For quhilk It happinnis oft, god wate, And is richt suth withoutine dreid That of fule haist cummis no speid. *Oxford* 282; Whiting *Scots* I 185. Cf. Tilley F518. See **H166.**

F464 Better go on **Foot** than ride (a) wicked horse
c1325 *De Clerico* 152.12: The is bettere on fote gon, then wycked hors to ryde.

F465 The **Foot** is not the head (*varied*)
a1393 Gower *CA* II 430.1038–41: And thus the nyce reverence Of foles, whan that he was ded, The fot hath torned to the hed, And clepen him god of nature. **a1430** Lydgate *Pilgrimage* 311.11373–6: Thanne al ylyche (yiff thow tok hed) The ffoot as good as ys the hed; A knave also, by hys werkyng, Sholde ben Egal wyth the kyng. **1546** Heywood *D* 72.61–2: Folke show much foly, when things should be sped. To ren to the foote, that maie go to the hed. Apperson 222; Tilley F562.

F466 The **Foot** which spurns in the way often has overthrown its head
a1393 Gower *CA* III 443.2102–3: The fot which in the weie sporneth Fulofte his heved hath overthrowe.

F467 Four swift **Feet** are better than two hands
1451 Paston II 221[12–4]: And he remembered Wyndhams manhood, that iiii. swyft fete were better than ii. hands, and he toke his hors with the spores. Cf. Whiting *Scots* I 172.

F468 From the **Foot** to the crown
a1425 *Metrical Paraphrase OT* 96.17240: Clense all hyr cors fro fote to crown. **a1500** *Merchant and his Son* in Hazlitt *EPP* I 137.72: Fro the fote up to the crowne. See **C575, T421.**

F469 A ganging (*going*) **Foot** ay gets food
a1425 *Cursor* III 1569 CG 28939: For gangand fote ay getes fode. *Oxford* 248; Tilley F565.

F470 One's **Feet** are as good as his head
1555 Heywood *E* 195.282: He hath set in foote, thynges by wyt to be sped, His foote shall dooe servyce as good as his hed.

F471 To have a good **Foot** to dance on (*i.e.,* a new argument)
1481 Caxton *Reynard* 80[24–5]: I have now a good foot to daunse on.

F472 To have but seven **Feet** of earth (*varied*)
a1325 *Erthe* 32.21–2: When erth has gotyn erth alle that he maye, He schal have but seven fote at his last daye. **c1330** *Body and Soul* 30.89–92: Thou that never in alle thi live Of this warldes mock mightest be sad, Now schaltow have at al thi sithe Bot seven fet, unnethe that. **a1450** *Song of Mortality* in Brown *Lyrics XIV* 97.19–20: Of erth aght that the was raght thou sal not have, I hete, Bot seven fote ther-in to rote, and

thi wyndyng-schete. **c1450** *Ponthus* 146.25–7: And ye shall have noo more of the erthe, save oonly your lenghte, as the pouere shall have. **1509** Watson *Ship* Ff8ᵛ[27–8]: After that you are deed, mondayne popes, you shall have but seven fote of erthe. **a1533** Berners *Arthur* 95[13]: He taketh no more of the erth but his owne length (*of one knocked to the ground*). Apperson 575: Six feet; *Oxford* 593; Tilley F582.

F473 To have no quick **Foot** to go
c1449 Pecock *Repressor* I 221[32–3]: The iiiᵉ. argument hath no quyk foot for to go.

F474 To have one **Foot** in the grave
1483 Caxton *Cato* I1ʳ[23–4]: Yf he had one foote in his grave. **1509** Barclay *Ship* I 44[14]: Thy grave is open thy one fote in the pyt. **1522** More *Treatyce* 94 E[1–2]: The tone fote almost in the grave already. Apperson 470; *Oxford* 476; Taylor and Whiting 143; Tilley M346.

F475 To have too many **Feet** in bed
1546 Heywood *D* 82.73: Here is, sens thou camst, to many feete a bed. See **T140.**

F476 To hold one's **Foot** near the fire (*i.e.*, go into danger)
c1500 *Three Kings' Sons* 29.2–5: Have ye drede . . . that y dar not holde my fote nere the fire.

F477 To know no more than one's **Foot**
c1300 *South English Legendary* I 208.126: Nostou namore thanne thi vot, upe God al it is. See **L161.**

F478 To look so high that one forgets his **Feet**
1509 Barclay *Ship* I 187[15]: Suche lokys so hye that they forget theyr fete. See **P74.**

F479 To ride but on one's **Foot**
c1400 *Plowman's Tale* 180.1032: Hir faders ryde not but on hir fete. Cf. Taylor and Whiting 324: Shank's mare. See **H512.**

F480 To set one's **Foot** on another's neck
c1400 *Beryn* 81.2656: So hard(e) settith he his fote in every mannys nek.

F481 To stand on one's own **Feet**
c1400 *Beryn* 40.1254: Thow shalt, for me, hereaftir stond on thyn owne fete.

F482 To ween (*think*) one's **Feet** are where his head came not yet (*varied*)
c1340 Rolle *Psalter* 22 (6.4): As some foles does that wenes thaire fete are thare whare thaire heved come noght yit. **1549** Heywood *D* 45.143: He thinkth his feete be, where his head shall never come. Apperson 229; *Oxford* 651; Tilley F577.

F483 When a man treads draw your **Feet** to yourself
1492 *Salomon and Marcolphus* 11[10–1]: Whan a man tredyth drawe to you youre fete.

F484 When the **Foot** warms then the shoe harms (*varied*)
c1450 *Rylands MS.394* 94.5: When the foote warmes than the sho harmys. **c1470** *Harley MS.3362* f.2b in *Retrospective* 309[15]: Whan the scho harmt, the fot war . . . **c1475** *Rawlinson MS. D 328* 122.54: When the wote (*sic*) warmyd than the scho harmyd. **a1500** Hill 128.21: While the fote warmith, the sho harmith. **1546** Heywood *D* 63.26: While the leg warmeth, the boote harmeth. Apperson 359; *Oxford* 361; Tilley L188.

F485 As great as a **Football**
c1450 *Alphabet* I 84.30–1: Als grete as a futeball. Taylor and Whiting 143: big.

F486 To be shaped like a **Football**
a1430 Hoccleve *Roundel* II 38.19: Hir comly body shape as a footbal.

F487 To chulle (*kick*) as a **Football**
a1400 Wyclif *Sermons* II 280[6–7]: And now thei clouten ther shone with censuris, as who shulde chulle a foot-balle.

F488 To go like a **Football**
c1350 *Octavian* (*NL*) 141.1243–4: That the heved fro the body went, Als it were a foteballe.

F489 **Force** constrains
c1505 Watson *Valentine* 149.8: The force constrayneth. Whiting *Drama* 200. See **M534.**

F490 **Force** is no good right
a1338 Mannyng *Chronicle A* I 408.11659–60: And force, ye wite wel, ys no god right But pruyde out of mesure myght. See **N166.**

F491 It is leeful (*legal*) to off-shove (put off) **Force** with force
c1390 Chaucer *CT* I[A] 3912: For leveful is with force force of-showve. **c1433** Lydgate *St. Edmund* 407.570: Force to put of with force, is good lawe. Skeat 230. Cf. Smith 344. See **B213, F52, 610, G487, 491, M535, O56, V34.**

F492 When **Force** cannot help subtlety must avail
1523 Berners *Froissart* I 176[12–3]: Whane force can nat helpe, subtylte and craft must avayle.

Apperson 607; *Oxford* 628; Tilley S952. See **L381, M801.**

F493 The **Foremost** is always behind
1369 Chaucer *BD* 890: The formest was alway behynde. *Oxford* 35. See **B265.**

F494 The longer **Forenoon** the shorter afternoon
1546 Heywood *D* 58.34: The longer forenoone the shorter after noone. Apperson 379; *Oxford* 382; Tilley F592.

F495 A **Foresight** is worth treasure
c1500 *Lyfe of Roberte* 219.39: A foresight, sayeth Salomon, ys worthe treasoure. See **D16.**

F496 One good **Forewit** is worth two afterwits
1546 Heywood *D* 31.23: Yet is one good forewit woorth two after wits. Apperson 470; *Oxford* 220; Tilley F595.

F497 **Forgive** and forget
a1250 *Ancrene* (*Nero*) 55.6–7: Al thet sore were voryi-ten and foryiven vor glednesse. **c1378** *Piers* B xvii 242: Bothe foryive and foryete, and yet bidde for us. **c1422** Hoccleve *Dialog* 134.671–2: In hir repreef, mochil thyng haast thow write, That they nat foryeve have ne foryite. **a1470** Malory I 396.11–2: And all was forgyffyn and forgetyn. **1519** Horman *Vulgaria* 179[24]: Let this be for gyven and forget. **1529** More *Supplicacion* 315 H[2]. **1546** Heywood *D* 65.26: Forgeven and forgotten, 91.11, **1556** *E* 136.88.2, *Spider* 358[20]. Apperson 230; *Oxford* 220; Taylor and Whiting 144; Tilley F597; Whiting *Scots* I 172.

F498 The **Forme** (*beginning*) seldom folds to (*matches*) the finish
c1390 *Sir Gawain* 16.498–9: A yere yernes ful yerne, and yeldes never lyke, The forme to the fynisment foldes ful selden. See **B200.**

F499 To be neither the **Former** nor the last
a1200 *Ancrene* 46.24–5: Nart tu nawt te ane i this this thing the forme ne the leaste. *Oxford* 204: first; Tilley F295.

F500 Once **Forsworn** ever forlorn
1344 *Year Books of the Reign of King Edward the Third, Years XVIII and XIX*, ed. Luke O. Pike (RS, 1905) 291: Ones forsworne, evere forlorne. See **M87.**

F501 A **Fort** which many assail must needs be sure
1534 Heywood *BS* 251.51–2: Wee see a forte hadde neede bee sure, Which many doth assault. See **C73, 79, W507.**

F502 After adverse **Fortune** prosperity shines
c1523 Barclay *Mirrour* 45[28]: After advers fortune shineth prosperitie. See **B325.**

F503 After hard **Fortune** ease succeeds again
c1523 Barclay *Mirrour* 26[8]: As after harde fortune succedeth ease agayne.

F504 Best not to strive against **Fortune's** balance
c1412 Hoccleve *Regement* 3.59–63: Best is I stryve nat Agayne the pays of fortunes balaunce; Ffor wele I wote that hir brotel constaunce, A wyght no while suffer can sojourne In a plyt.

F505 Better to suffer and abide **Fortune** than hastily to climb and suddenly to slide (*varied*)
a1450 *Fairfax MS.16* in F. J. Furnivall *Parallel-Text Edition of Chaucer's Minor Poems* (Chaucer Society 21) 425: Better is to suffre and fortune abyde, And (*for* Than) hastely to clymbe and sodeynly to slyde. **c1450** *Fyrst thou sal* 89.101–2: Better it is to suffer and abyde Than hastely to chym (*for* clym) and sodanly to slyde. **c1450** *Rules for Conduct* in Smith *Common-place Book* 14[3–4]: Better yt ys to suffer and fortyn to a-byd, Than hey for to clyme and sodenly for to slyde. **c1450** *Tuta paupertas* in Person 53.60[3–4]: Therfor with surenes yt is better in povertie tabide Then hastily to be Riche and sodaynly to slyde. **a1500** *St. George's Chapel, Windsor, MS. E.I.I.*, f.95b in *The Library*, 4th series, 13(1933) 74: Bettur it is for tyme to abyd, then lietely to clym and sodenly to slyde. **a1500** *Who so off welth* in Dyboski 139.9–10: Better yt ys to suffre, and fortune to abyde, Than hastely to clyme, and sodeynly to slyde. **1511** Hawes *Comforte* C5r[5]: Clymbe not to fast, but yet fortune abyde. Robbins-Cutler 512.8. Cf. Smith 119. See **C296.**

F506 **Fortune** and her wheel (*varied*)
c1200 *Hali Meidenhad* 40.429: Thus this worldes hweol warpeth ham abuten. **a1325** *Cursor* III 1356 CGT 23719–20: Dame fortune turnes than hir quele And castes us dun until a wele. **a1338** Mannyng *Chronicle A* I 179.5103–6: But Dame ffortune had turned her whel Donward til wo, that er was wel; Ffor tho that aboven were wond to be, Donward theym now turneth sche. **1340** *Ayenbite* 24[22–5]: Vor huanne the lheuedi of hap heth hire huewel y-went to the manne and arered and yzet to the heghthe of hare huewel ase (the) melle to the wynde, 76[28–31]: The guodes of fortune (hap) and the leuedy fortune went hare huewel eche daye and benymth and yefth and went thet is above benethe, 181[19–20]: Efter thise . . . comth . . . dame fortune mid al hare huewel. **c1375** Barbour

Bruce I 347.651*–658: For twa contraris, yhe may wit wele, Set agane othir on a quhele; Quhen ane is hye, the tothir is law, And gif it fall that fortoune thraw The quheill about, it that on hicht Was ere, (on force) it most doune lycht; And it, that wondir lawch wer ere, Mon lowp on loft on the contrere. **c1376** Brinton *Sermons* I 10[9–11]: rota fortune, 99[21–4], II 354[11–3]. **c1385** Chaucer *CT* I[A] 925–6: Thanked be Fortune and hire false wheel, That noon estaat assureth to be weel, *TC* i 138–40: And thus Fortune on lofte, And under eft, gan hem to whielen bothe Aftir hir course, 837–40, iv 1–7. **c1385** Usk 34.3. **c1390** Chaucer *CT* VII 2397–8[B3587–8], 2445–6[B3635–6]. **a1393** Gower *CA* II 8.138–9: After the tornynge of the whiel, Which blinde fortune overthroweth, 20.561, 107.2624–5: And thus the whiel is al miswent, The which fortune hath upon honde, 137.241–3, 163.1226–7, 179.1822–3: Bot the blinde whiel, Which torneth ofte er men be war, 257.1136–8, III 156.7445–6, 175.292–3: Bot so fortune upon hire whiel On hih me deigneth noght to sette, 298.2393–6, 433.1736–8: Fro this day forth fortune hath sworn To sette him upward on the whiel; So goth the world, now wo, now wel. **a1400** *Alexander* C 104.1850–3: For sen we riden on the rime and on the ringe seten Of the qwele of Fortoun, the quene that swiftly changis, Ofte pas we in povert fra plente of gudis, Fra mirthe in-to mournyng, fra mournyng in-to Joye. **a1400** *Awntyrs* 137.270–2: False fortune in fyghte, That wondirfulle whele wryghte, Mase lordis lawe for to lyghte. **a1400** *Destruction of Troy* 447.13676–83. **a1400** *Fortune's Wheel* in *Pol. Rel. and Love Poems* 266.1–4. **a1400** *Morte Arthure* 100.3388: Abowte scho whirles the whele and whirles me undire. **a1400** *Pricke* 36.1273–9. **a1400** *Tho whele of fortune* in *Yorkshire Writers* II 70–1. **c1400** *Beryn* 31.943–6: Save the whele of ffortune, that no man may withstonde; Ffor every man on lyve, ther-on he is gond: O spoke she turnyd Bakward, right atte highe noon, All a-geyn Berinus, 39.1234, 67.2196–8. **c1400** *Vices and Virtues* 75.7–10, 185.21–2. **c1408** Lydgate *Reson* 37.1358–60: For fortune doth hir (*Juno's*) lust obey, The gerful lady with hir whel, That blynd is and seth never a del, **a1420** *Troy* I 72.2046, II 401.200–1, 451.1981. **c1422** Hoccleve *Dialog* 119.264–6: Thogh a man this day sitte hye on the wheel, To morwe he may be tryced from his sete; This hath be seen often among the grete. **c1423** Lydgate *Serpent* 56.1–3: Of custome hit fallith that when the blynde goddesse of variawnce Dame fortune hathe enhansed a man hieste upon hir whele, with a sodeyne sweihe sche plungeth hym down, 65.20–3, 66.25–6. **a1425** Higden-Anon.Cont. VIII 512[46–7]. **a1430** Lydgate *Pilgrimage* 519–25.19470–667, **c1430** *Compleynt* 63–4.362–80, *Dance* 2.15–6. **a1437** *Kingis Quair* 47.9, 90–4.159–172. **a1437** Lydgate *That Now is Hay* in *MP* II 810.35. **c1440** Charles of Orleans 66.1951–2. **c1440** *Prose Alexander* 23.22–6. **1447** Bokenham 228.8380–3: Lowe of byrth, by fortune set hye Up-on hyre whele, wych ay unstable And vertyble ys and ful mutable, Nevyr stondyng styl but evere turnyng, 241.8886–8. **a1449** Lydgate *Benedictus* in *MP* I 9.65, *Fabula* in *MP* II 503.519–20, *God* in *MP* I 28.41–8, *Thoroughfare* in *MP* II 826.130–3: Deth . . . castith downe princes from Fortunes wheele, As hir spokes rounde about(e) goo. **1449** Metham 15.388–9, 54.1472–3. **a1450** *For lac of sighte* in *Archiv* 127(1911) 326–7: Fortunes whele so felly with me pleyth. **a1450** *Knowe thy self* in Kail 101.11–2. **a1450** *Myne awen dere* 178–9.932–8. **a1450** *Partonope* 38.1411–2: Blessyd be fortune that wyth hys whele Hath alle my sorowe turned to wele, 159.4389–91: Lo, thus ffortune can turne hur dyse Nowe up, nowe downe; here whele ys unstabelle. On her ys no truste; she ys so varyabelle, 161.4428–9, 379.9226–8. **a1450** *Thorow-owt a pales* in Dyboski 95.21. **c1450** *Against Death* in Brown *Lyrics XV* 246.5–7. **c1450** Capgrave *Katharine* 69.868–70. **c1450** *De Claris Mulieribus* 55.1131–2. **c1450** *Epistle of Othea* 104.21, 113.19–21: Wherto accordyth the philosophre Socrates seyyng: The wheel of fortune is lyke a ingyne made to take fysche. **c1450** *How mankinde dooth* in Furnivall *Hymns* 73.493: Now y am undre Fortunes whele. **c1450** Idley 146.2350. **c1450** *Pilgrimage LM* 182[26–7]. **c1451** *Boke of Noblesse* 48[28–9]. **1456** Hay *Law* 65.10–2. **c1460** *Take Good Heed* 206.29. **1463** Ashby *Prisoner* 8.222. **a1467** *Musyng uppon the mutabilite* in *Rawlinson MS. C 813* 325–6. **a1470** Malory III 1201.14–5: But fortune ys so varyaunte, and the wheele so mutable, that there ys no constaunte abydynge. **c1470** *Wallace* 113.89–104. **a1475** *Assembly of Gods* 10.316–9. **c1475** Henryson *Fables* 82.2418–9: Thus fairis it off Fortoun: As ane cummis up, scho quheillis ane uther doun, *Orpheus* 144.484–8, *Testament* 124.550. **c1475** *Yutt Y se but fewe* in *English Studies* 41(1960) 197–8. **1480** Caxton *Ovyde* 98[13]: Thus goth Fortune by hys varyable whele rennynge and tornynge, **1483** *Cato* D1^{v}[12–3]: The whele of fortune waxeth and waneth as dothe the mone, **1484** *Aesop* 67[2–3], 68[3–4], *Royal Book* D1^{r-v}, G5^{r}[11–4], O7^{v}[8]. **c1485** *Guiscardo*

50.212–4, 60.376–8: O fortune inconstaunt . . . Hyt semeth thow art nat able to rule thy whele! **c1485** *Mary Magdalene* (*Digby*) 66.312. **1487** *O thou most noble* 319[9]. **a1500** *Ancient Scottish Prophecy, No. 2* in Bernadus *De Cura* 32.12–3. **a1500** *Court of Love* 439.1133–4. **a1500** *Fortune* in Brown *Lyrics XV* 262.6, 13, 20. **a1500** Hill 139.7–8: Fortune ys varyant, ay tornyng her whele, He ys wyse that ys ware or he harm fele. **a1500** *Lufaris Complaynt* 720.48, 721.84–6. **a1500** *Proverbs of Salamon* 184.48.1–8. **a1500** *Timor mortis* in *MLR* 28(1933) 235[5–10]. **a1500** *Vanitas* in Brown *Lyrics XV* 240.50–1. **a1500** *Who so off welth* in Dyboski 139.7. **c1500** *Melusine* 298.20–2. **c1500** *So put yn fere* in Stevens *Music* 345.2[5]. **c1500** *O ye all that* in *Anglia* 72(1954) 404.8. **1501** Douglas *Palice* 8.26–9.4. **c1503** More *Early Poems* [12] D[7–9]: That may set once his hande uppon her whele, He holdeth faste; but upwarde as he stieth, She whippeth her whele about, and there he lyeth. **1509** Barclay *Ship* I 186[1–4], 187[16]. **1509** Watson *Ship* F8^r[5–8], I1^v[7–13], I2^r[1–2]. **a1511** Hawes *Comforte* B1^r[22]. **a1513** Dunbar *Best to be Blyth* 143.7, 12, *Birth of Antichrist* 70.14. **c1516** Skelton *Magnificence* 63.2022–30. **1525** Berners *Froissart* V 318[6–10], 392–3, VI 84[2–3], 90[9–11], **1532** *Golden Boke* 318.6548–8: Fortune hath tourned her whele. Apperson 231; S. C. Chew in *ELH* 6(1939) 83–113; *Oxford* 221; Howard R. Patch *The Goddess Fortuna in Mediaeval Literature* (Cambridge, Mass., 1927); Taylor and Whiting 144; Tilley F617, S768; Whiting *Drama* 84, 87, 238, 239, 243, 252, 253, 265, 287, 288, 289, *Scots* I 173.

F507 Fortune assails many a man when he best weens (*thinks*) to stand
a1449 Lydgate *Fabula* in *MP* II 508.666–7: How many a man hath Fortune assayled, With sleihte i-cast, whan he best wende ha stonde. See **F531, S669.**

F508 Fortune can both smile and frown
c1516 Skelton *Magnificence* 79.2524: Sodenly thus Fortune can bothe smyle and frowne. Whiting *Drama* 236. Cf. Smith 115.

F509 Fortune can dissolve the wealth of every creature
c1412 Hoccleve *Regement* 2.15–8: Bysily in my mynde I gan revolve The welthe onsure of everye creature, How lightly that ffortune it can dissolve, Whan that hir lyst that it no lenger dure.

F510 Fortune changes not her chance
a1449 Lydgate *So as the Crabbe Goth Forward* in *MP* II 466.12: Fortune chaungethe not hir chaunse.

F511 Fortune comes into many a place
a1500 *Beauty of his Mistress II* in Robbins 125.38–40: I have harde men say In towne and strette, How fortune cummethe yn-to many a place—And with good fortune I trust to mete.

F512 Fortune enhances one and casts down another (*varied*)
1480 Caxton *Ovyde* 120[32–3]: Thus fortune enhaunceth that one and casteth doun another, **1489** *Fayttes* 286.22–3: Fortune enhaunceth men atte her owne plaisire. Whiting *Drama* 137. See **F534, O45.**

F513 Fortune envies that men live at ease
a1420 Lydgate *Troy* I 33.750–2: But the ordre of Fortunys myght Hath evere envy that men lyve in ese, Whos cours enhasteth unwarly to dissesse.

F514 Fortune fails at the most need
c1378 *Piers* B xi 28: Thou shalt fynde Fortune the faille at thi moste nede.

F515 Fortune fails oft
a1400 *Cato* (*Copenhagen*) B3^v[10]: Ffor fortune faylyth ofte and doth but were.

F516 Fortune has a double face (*varied*)
a1420 Lydgate *Troy* I 78.2251: Fortune with hir double face, **a1430** *Pilgrimage* 1.19. **c1440** Charles of Orleans 72.2128–30: The sotilnes Of seytfulle fortune with hir dowbil chere That doth eche game so torne and ovyrdresse. **a1449** Lydgate *Mydsomer Rose* in *MP* II 782.44–6: Fortune is double, *Thoroughfare* in *MP* II 823.19–20. **a1449** Lydgate and Burgh *Secrees* 39.1209: Ffortune braydeth ay On doubylnesse. **c1500** Skelton *Dyvers Balettys* I 26.11: Ware yet, I rede you, of Fortunes dowble cast. Whiting *Drama* 137. See **F8.**

F517 Fortune has gall in her honey
c1390 Chaucer *CT* VII 2347[B3537]: But ay Fortune hath in hire hony galle. See **G12, H433.**

F518 Fortune has governance of all things
c1450 *Chaunce* 5.15: Syth fortune hathe of alle thynge governaunce.

F519 Fortune (Ure, Adventure, God) helps hardy man (the bold)
c1375 Barbour *Bruce* I 136.15–7: Certis, I may weill se That it is all gret certante. That ure helpis ay hardy men. **c1385** Chaucer *TC* iv 600–2: Thenk ek Fortune, as wel thiselven woost, Helpeth hardy man to his enprise, And weyveth

wrecches for hire cowardise. **a1393** Gower *CA* III 371.4902–3: Fortune unto the bolde Is favorable forto helpe. **a1439** Lydgate *Fall* II 671.3071: And Fortune, which helpeth hardi man. **c1470** *Wallace* 217.1139–41: A hardy man, that is lykly with all, Gret fawour will off fortoun till him fall, Anent wemen is seyne in mony place. **1481** Caxton *Reynard* 66[5–6]: Who that is hardy th(e) aventure helpeth hym. **1483** *Vulgaria quedam abs Terencio* Q3r[3]: Fortune helpeth bolde men or hardy men. **a1518** Nevill *Castell* 92.432: God alwayes helpeth bolde men and fortune also. Apperson 231; *Oxford* 221; Skeat 189; Taylor and Whiting 144; Tilley F601; Whiting *Scots* I 172–3. See **G214, H96, L510, M317, U3, W185.**

F520 Fortune is a mother to some, a stepmother to others
c1515 Barclay *Eclogues* 186.153–4: Fortune to them is like a mother dere, As a stepmother she doth to us appeare. **1532** Berners *Golden Boke* 321.6642–3: Fortune . . . whiche is thy unjuste stepmother. Apperson 231; *Oxford* 221; Tilley F609. See **S720.**

F521 Fortune is blind
a1475 *Cato* (*Rawlinson*) 41.474–5: Say thou noght, that fortune is blynd, But blame thi-self, thou art by-hynd. *Oxford* 221; Tilley F604.

F522 Fortune is both white and black
a1450 Quixley *Ballades* 48.317–21: To som that in fortune will hem affie, Sche is bothe white and blak, now frend, now foo: Now lyve in joye, now in purgatorie, Withouten rest, withouten rewle: se, lo! How sche tourneth the face hir sutoure fro.

F523 Fortune is changeable (*varied*)
a1338 Mannyng *Chronicle A* I 88.2449–53: Lady ffortune, thou art chaungable; O day art thou nevere stable; No man may of the affye, Thou turnes hym doun that er was heye; That now ys doun, upward thou turnes. **c1375** Barbour *Bruce* I 346–7.632–5: Lo! quhat falding in fortoune is, That quhile apon a man will smyle, And prik him syne ane othir quhile! In na tyme stabilly can sche stande. **c1385** Chaucer *CT* I[A] 1242: Fortune is chaungeable. **a1393** Gower *CA* II 20.563: Fortune stant no while stille, III 402.585–9: Fortune hath evere be muable And mai no while stonde stable: For now it hiheth, now it loweth, Now stant upriht, now overthroweth, Now full of blisse and now of bale, 440.2013. **c1395** Chaucer *CT* IV[E] 2057: O sodeyn hap! o thou Fortune unstable! **a1400** *Alexander C* 104.1855–7: Quen we suppose in oure sele to sit althir heist, Than fondis furth dame Fortoun to the flode-gatis, Drawes up the damme-borde and drenchis us evire. **c1408** Lydgate *Reson* 2.47–8: After this Fortune sone, Which ofter changeth as the mone. **1410** Walton *Boethius* 67[9–10]: For when fortune stondeth in stabilite, The name of fortune may no lenger leste. **c1412** Hoccleve *Regement* 42.1139–41. **1414** ?Brampton *Psalms* 17[14]: As fortune chaungyth, so muste we. **a1420** Lydgate *Troy* I 42.1066: Fortune that is variable, 48.1236, 144.1–2, 202.2020: As fortune, whiche that chaungeth ofte, II 512.4077 ff., III 689.4274 ff., 785.417 ff., 874.3546 ff. **c1420** Wyntoun V 419.3610–2: Bot Forton, withe hir fals changynge, That ay warrayis prosperite, Suffer it othir wayis to be. **a1422** Lydgate *St. Bernard* in *MP* I 208.55: Fortunys troubly varyaunce, **a1430** *Pilgrimage* 576.21609: Ffortune is nowncerteyn. **a1440** Burgh *Cato* 27.943: For fortune is moodir of changeabilnesse, 31.1079: Fortune is unstable, 314.4578: Fortune chaungethe ofte withynne an hour. **a1449** Lydgate *Fabula* in *MP* II 503.503: For verray stonyng of Fortunys fikylnesse, 504.545, *Mumming at London* in *MP* II 682.1–10: Loo here this lady that yee may see, Lady of mutabilytee, Which that called is Fortune, For seelde in oon she doothe contune. For as shee hathe a double face, Right so every houre and space She chaungethe hir condycyouns, Ay ful of transmutacyouns. Lyche as the Romans of the Roose Descryvethe hir, *Pageant of Knowledge* in *MP* II 733.256, 738.113, *Prayer* in *MP* I 21.21–2, *St. Denis* in *MP* I 128.35–6, *Thoroughfare* in *MP* II 825.108, *World* in *MP* II 844.3: On flittyng fortune I gan me remembre. **c1450** Idley 161.156–7, 171.773–7, 184.1566. **c1450** ?Suffolk *Not far fro marche* 168.22–5. **a1460** *Towneley Plays* 291.379–85. **c1470** *Wallace* 52.145: Fals fortoun changis fast, 53.152. **1471** Caxton *Recuyell* II 412.16 ff. **c1475** Henryson *Fables* 57.1604–7, *Testament* 121.469: Fortoun is fikkill, quhen scho beginnis and steiris. **a1483** Kay *Siege* [40.12–3]: Fortune was so mervayllously instable. **a1483** Caxton *Cato* D1v[7]: Fortune holdeth hyr never in one poynte. **c1485** *Guiscardo* 78.696. **1489** Caxton *Fayttes* 14.26–8. **a1500** *Findern Anthology* in *PMLA* 69(1954) 639–40.1–7, 20–1, 26–8. **a1500** *Lufaris Complaynt* 722.118–23. **a1500** *Ragman Roll* 70.15–21. **a1500** *Sweet Enslavement* in Robbins 131.12. **a1508** Skelton *Phyllyp* I 62.366–7: Of fortune this the chaunce Standeth on varyaunce. **a1509** Barclay *Ship* I 126[6–7]: And in thy welthe to this saynge intende That fortune ever hath an incertayne ende, 190[26]: Fortune is

full of changes and mutabylyte, 269[17], II 250[3–4]. **a1509** Watson *Ship* I2v[14–6]. **1513** Douglas *Aeneid* IV 34.121–4. **c1515** Barclay *Eclogues* 27.796. **c1516** Skelton *Magnificence* 67.2156–7, **1523** *Garlande* I 362.11: How oftyn fortune varyeth in a howre. **c1523** Barclay *Mirrour* 26[5]. **1525** Berners *Froissart* V 54[7], 147[37], 152[37–8], 224[7]: Fortune is alwayes chaungeable, VI 77[33–4], 89[11–2], **1532** *Golden Boke* 319.6585. **1556** Heywood *Spider* 424[21]: Fickill fortune will never leave her old cast. Apperson 231; *Oxford* 221; Smith 116; Tilley F606; Whiting *Drama* 37, 41, 124, 135, 137, 238, 239, 253, 265, 291, 302, *Scots* I 173. See **H98, M164, W184.**

F524 **Fortune** is common to every wight
c1380 Chaucer *HF* 1547–8: Ryght as her suster, dame Fortune, Ys wont to serven in comune, **c1385** *TC* i 843–53: Woost thow nat wel that Fortune is comune To everi manere wight in som degree? And yet thow hast this comfort, lo, parde, That, as hire joies moten overgon, So mote hire sorwes passen everechon. For if hire whiel stynte any thyng to torne, Than cessed she Fortune anon to be. Now, sith hire whiel by no way may sojourne, What woostow if hire mutabilite Right as thyselven list, wol don by the, Or that she be naught fer fro thyn helpynge? iv 391–2: Ne trust no wight to fynden in Fortune Ay propretee; hire yiftes ben comune.

F525 **Fortune** is contrary (and perverse)
1422 Lydgate *Serpent* 51.16: Fortune, whiche is ay contrary and pervers, **a1449** *Thoroughfare* in *MP* II 826.116: But for al that fortune was yit contrayre.

F526 **Fortune** is false
a1400 *Scottish Legends* II 83.493–5: Allace! fortune, thu art ful fals, That quhylum smylit apon me, And now has left me in this degre. **c1412** Hoccleve *Regement* 49–51.1352–93. **1428** Lydgate *Complaint for My Lady of Gloucester* in *MP* II 609.23, **c1440** *Debate* in *MP* II 565.642: Fortune is fals, hir sonne is meynte with reyn. **c1470** *Wallace* 85.365–6. Whiting *Drama* 291.

F527 **Fortune** is first friend and sith (*then*) foe
c1390 Chaucer *CT* VII 2723[B3913]: Fortune was first freend, and sitthe foo.

F528 **Fortune** is mother of all tribulation
1518 Watson *Oliver* R2r[28–9]: Fortune . . . is moder of all trybulacyon.

F529 **Fortune** is (not) my foe
c1378 *Piers* B xi 60: And thanne was Fortune my foo. **c1385** Chaucer *TC* i 837: For wel fynde I that Fortune is my fo. **c1390** *Deo Gracias II* in Brown *Lyrics XIV* 138.21–2: Yif fortune wolde be so my fo From me to turne hir freoly faas. **a1393** Gower *CA* II 393.3408: For nou fortune is thus mi fo. **c1400** *Beryn* 43.1365, 61.1995. **c1450** ?Suffolk *Walkyng allon* 163.5. **c1475** *Why I Can't* 139.55. **c1485** *Slaughter* (*Digby*) 3.60: Ffortune I fynde that she is not my ffoo. **a1533** Berners *Castell* D1r[5–6]: Fortune is rather myne enemye. Whiting *Scots* I 173.

F530 **Fortune** is uncertain to all mortal folk
c1380 Chaucer *Boece* I pr. iv 232: Fortune, that is uncerteyn to alle mortel folk.

F531 **Fortune** makes a man rathest (*soonest*) to fall when he is most on height
a1393 Gower *CA* III 208.1509–12: Bot fortune is of such a sleyhte, That whan a man is most on heyhte, Sche makth him rathest forto falle: Ther wot noman what schal befalle. See **C296, F507.**

F532 **Fortune** meddles (*mixes*) her joys with bitterness
c1500 Fabyan 91[16–7]: Dame fortune is accustomed to medle hir joyes of this world with some bitternesse. Cf. Apperson 231: Fortune rarely brings; Whiting *Drama* 287. See **J59.**

F533 The **Fortune** of fighters (*etc.*) is uncertain (*varied*)
a1400 *Destruction of Troy* 58.1751–2: But the fortune of feghters may be fell chaunse, And siker were to sit and solas us here. **c1450** *Merlin* I 184[27–8]: Some tyme he wan, and many tymes he loste, as is the fortune of werre. **1489** Caxton *Fayttes* 64.8–9: The fortune of the vyctorye can not be knowen of afore, 100.9–11: Impossyble it is to Jugge to the certeyn the ende of the bataylle of whiche fortune dysposeth, **1490** *Eneydos* 98.21–2: The fortune of ba(ta)ylle is doubtouse. **c1500** Fabyan 451[24–5]: Dyverse fortunys fell and chauncys of warre. **1523** Berners *Froissart* II 488[17–8]: The fortunes of warre be ryght peryllous, **a1533** *Arthur* 91[12–3]: It was but the fortune of that play (*tourney*). Smith 321; Taylor and Whiting 144–5; Whiting *Drama* 271. See **B65, F139, M192, W39, 183.**

F534 **Fortune** reverses high men and raises small
1480 Caxton *Ovyde* 89[28–31]: But fortune, that reverseth and throweth doun hye men And reyseth smale and lowe men, brought hyme to hys dysconfyture. . . . He trusted overmoch in fortune. See **F512, T128.**

F535 **Fortune** seems truest when she will beguile (*varied*)
c1385 Chaucer *TC* iv 2–3: Fortune, That semeth trewest whan she wol bygyle. **c1385** Usk 34.4–5: For certes, Fortune sheweth her fayrest, whan she thinketh to begyle. **a1500** *Leconfield Proverbs* 480[25–6]: Esperaunce in fortune when she smylithe. Nay, beware, for she begilethe. **a1500** *Lufaris Complaynt* 720.41–2: Bot quhen fortune semys most trewe and stable, Than to begyle a wicht scho is most hable.

F536 **Fortune** turns her back
a1400 *Scottish Legends* II 78.301–4: And forton, that wont wes quhile As teyndir frend on hyme (to) smyle, Turnyt hyr bak on hym wrathly, And hyme dissawit sudandly. **a1437** *Kingis Quair* 46.6[3]: Fortune the bak hym turnyt.

F537 **Fortune** will have her course
a1420 Lydgate *Troy* I 239.3307–8: But Fortune wil have hir cours alwey, Whos purpos holt, who seyth ye or nay.

F538 Good **Fortune** oft flowers with good wit
a1437 *Kingis Quair* 83.133[5]: And oft gud fortune flourith with gude wit.

F539 The good or evil **Fortune** of a man's life is in the good or evil choosing of his friend or his wife
a1500 *MS. Marginalia* in Hoccleve I 200 n. 1: The good or evell fortune of all a mans lyffe, Ys in the good or evell chowsinge of his frend or his wiffe. Tilley M467.

F540 He that avoids **Fortune** when she ministers shall not embrace her when he has need
a1420 Lydgate *Troy* II 452.2007–12: Yif he refuse his hap of wilfulnes, Fortune avoidynge thorugh unkynd(e)nes Whan sche mynstreth to hym of hir grace: Another tyme he schal hir nat embrace, Whan he hath nede to hir helpe at al, To socour hym or he cacche a fal. See **A53, G359, W275.**

F541 He that has evil **Fortune,** men speak the worse therof (*varied*)
1523 Berners *Froissart* III 325[21–2]: It is an olde sayng, He that hath any yvell fortune, men wyll speke the worst therof, **1525** VI 90[2–4]: It is sayde in an olde proverbe: He that hath mysfortune, every man offereth hym wronge. Smith 121; Tilley M559; Whiting *Froissart* 298:59. See **H141.**

F542 In **Fortune**'s favor no man can be sure
1523 Skelton *Garlande* I 416.1402–3: In fortunis favour ever to endure, No man lyvyng, he sayth, can be sure.

F543 One should not prize his **Fortune** until his last day
c1420 Wyntoun III 37.411–4: Withe slichtis swa suppose yhe slyde, Yhour lattyr day yit mon yhe byde; Befor that day on nakyn wysse Yhe sulde your forton happy prysse. See **E158.**

F544 Smiling **Fortune** deceives under (a) pall
c1523 Barclay *Mirrour* 26[47]: Right so fortune smiling disceaveth under pall.

F545 To fight with **Fortune** is no wit
a1513 Dunbar *Of Discretioun in Asking* 33.44: To fecht with fortoun is no wit.

F546 Trust not in **Fortune** (*varied*)
a1325 *Lady Fortune* in Brown *Lyrics XIV* 56: The levedi fortune is bothe frend and fo, Of pore che makit riche, of riche pore also, Che turnes wo al into wele, and wele al into wo, No triste no man to this wele, the whel it turnet so. **c1390** Chaucer *CT* VII 2136[B3326]: Lo, who may truste on Fortune any throwe? 2723–5[B3913–5]: Fortune was first freend, and sitthe foo. No man ne truste upon hire favour longe, But have hire in awayt for everemoo, 2762–5[B3952–5]. **c1400** *Laud Troy* I 174–5.5909–18. **c1412** Hoccleve *Regement* 172.4778: Naght in fortune truste, or by hir sette. **a1420** Lydgate *Troy* I 198.1862 ff., III 791.630 ff., **a1430** *Pilgrimage* 370.13643–4: Lat no man trusten on ffortune, Wych selde, in on, lyst to contune. **a1440** Burgh *Cato* 307.170–6. **c1440** Charles of Orleans 88.2615–6: Als truste not fortune with her chere covert Which wolle flatir to brynge thee fresshe in smert. **c1440** Scrope *Epistle* 84[10–3]: In Fortune, that grete myghty godesse, Trist not to mych, ne in hyre promyse; For in a lytell space she chaungeth, And the hyest ofte overthroweth. **c1450** *Epistle of Othea* 113.6. **c1450** Idley 91.603–30, 145.2341. **a1500** *Leconfield Proverbs* 485[11–2]. **a1500** *Lufaris Complaynt* 720.43–5. **a1500** *Partenay* 17.269–73. **a1500** *Who Trusteth Fortune* in Brown *Lyrics XV* 260.2: Who trustith fortune sonnest hath a fall. **c1500** *Melusine* 215.23–6. **a1509** Barclay *Ship* I 124[1–2], 125[13–4], **c1515** *Eclogues* 37–8.1039–40, 177.1068–70.

F547 What **Fortune** will have shall be had
c1500 *Fortune Will Have her Way* in Brown *Lyrics XV* 259.5–7: What fortune will have, it schal be had Who-so-ever will say nay; Therfor lete it passe, and be not sad.

F548 When **Fortune** lists to flee no man may withhold her course
c1390 Chaucer *CT* VII 1995–6[B3185–6]: For

certein, whan that Fortune list to flee, Ther may no man the cours of hire withholde.

F549 Who prides him in **Fortune's** goods is a full great fool
c1390 Chaucer *CT* X[I] 471: Certes also, whoso prideth hym in the goodes of fortune, he is a ful greet fool; for som tyme is a man a greet lord by the morwe, that is a caytyf and a wrecche er it be nyght. See **M688.**

F550 Hence **Forty Pence,** Jack Noble is a-bed
a1500 Medwall *Nature* F2^r[42–3]: She opened a wyndow and put forth her hed, Hens .xl.d. quod she, Jak noble ys a bed. Apperson 204; *Oxford* 191; Tilley F618.

F551 No longer **Foster** (*provider*) no longer leman (*sweetheart*)
c1412 Hoccleve *Regement* 60.1661: Ne lenger forster, no lenger lemman. **1546** Heywood *D* 96.200–1: I saie to suche (said she) no longer foster, No longer lemman. Apperson 448–9; MED forster 2; *Oxford* 454; Tilley F714.

F552 As heavy as a **Fother** (*weight*)
c1300 *Guy*[1] 208.3598: His stroke was hevi so a fother.

F553 Not count a **Fother**
1513 Douglas *Aeneid* III 228.159: I compt not of thir paygane goddis a fudder.

F554 To fall (down) as a **Fother**
c1380 *Ferumbras* 27.641 (*original draft*): Every strok that thou me raught falleth doun as a fother, 172.5549: Wyth strokes that fullen as a fother thay laid doun Sarazyns ech on other.

F555 To have the **Fother** fall on one's own head (in his own neck)
a1300 *Richard* 171.1739–40: For many man weneth to greve other, and on his heed (*var.* in his owne nek) falleth the fother. **c1410** Lovelich *Merlin* I 122.4590: Atte laste on him-self falleth the fothyr. See **D22, N43, P232.**

F556 To lay on like a **Fother**
c1400 *Laud Troy* II 501.17001–2: So betis and lais echon on other Stalworth strokes as a ffother.

F557 As good is the **Foul** as the fair in the dark
c1525 ?Heywood *Gentylnes* 121.930–1: Tote, man, for all sych venereall werk As good is the foule as the fayre in the derk. **1546** Heywood *D* 27.38: The fayre and the foule, by darke are lyke store. *Oxford* 326: Joan; Tilley J57. See **C27.**

F558 He that has imene (*dealings with*) the **Foul** never comes from it clean
c1250 *Owl* 28.299–302: And yet Alvred seide an other side A word that is isprunge wide: "That wit the fule haveth imene, Ne cumeth he never from him cleine." *Oxford* 222; Skeat 31. See **P236.**

F559 To shine like **Fouldre** (*lightning*)
a1500 *Miroure of Mans Salvacionne* 112[21]: His face like foudre shynyng.

F560 To run like a **Foumart** (*polecat*) after hens
c1400 *Laud Troy* I 49.1657–8: Hercules rides overal and rennes—As a fulmard doth afftir the hennes, II 479.16279–80.

Fowl, see **Bird**

F561 As fain as **Fowl** of day (*varied*)
c1250 *Genesis and Exodus* 1.15–6: Cristene men ogen ben so fagen So fueles arn quan he it sen dagen. **c1330** *Horn Childe* 188.754–6: And than was Horn as fain o fight, As is the foule of the light, When it ginneth dawe. **c1350** *Octavian* (*NL*) 139.1203–4: That als fayne bene for to fyghte, Als fowle es of dayes lyghte. **a1376** *Piers* A xi 109: Than was I as fayn as foul on feir morwen, B xi 153: Of faire morwe, C xii 103: Of fair morwenynge. **c1385** Chaucer *CT* I[A] 2437: As fayn as fowel is of the brighte sonne, **c1390** VII 51[B1241]: As fowel is fayn whan that the sonne up riseth. **a1400** *Alexander C* 130.2264: And thai als fayne . . . as fowell of the day (*Dublin:* is on morne). **a1400** *Siege of Jerusalem* 58.1009: Fayn as the foul of day was the freke thanne. **a1500** *Octavian* (*NC*) 138.1231–2: That also fayne are of fyght, As fowle of day aftur nyght. Apperson 232; *Oxford* 222; Skeat 223.

F562 As fain as **Fowl** of flight (that flies)
c1330 *Degare* 117–8.967–8(*var.*): Sche was fayn off that syghtt As ys the fowle of hys flyghtt. **c1405** *Mum* 15.97: As fayne (as) the foule that flieth on the skyes. See **F23.**

F563 As fain as **Fowl** of May
c1385 *TC* v 425: For was ther nevere fowel so fayn of May.

F564 As fous (*eager*) as **Fowl** to flight (*etc.*). (A number of single quotations are brought together here)
c1330 *Otuel* 114.1673–4: Thei were also fous to fight, As evere was a foul to flight. **a1350** *Ywain* 18.629–30: And sone he saw cumand a knight Als fast so the fowl in flyght. **a1400** *Le Morte A.* 46.1576–7: Than was Syr mador Also blythe As foule of day after the nyght. **c1400** *Roland* 136.1032: As freche to fight as foulis stout.

c1450 *Chronicles of London* 121[13–4]: Syr William bowsere, as foule in fright (frith [*woodland*]), Preste he ther was upon his pray. **1481** Caxton *Mirror* 73[26–7]: And is more delyverer to goo than is fowle to flee. **1513** Douglas *Aeneid* II 14.375–6: Als ryfe . . . As evir fowlis plungit in laik or puyll. See **B289, F25.**

F565 As glad as **Fowl** in flight
c1485 *Conversion* 40.332: I am ryght glad as foule on flyte.

F566 As glad as **Fowl** of day, *etc.*
c1300 *Beves* 7.148–9: Gladder icham for that sawe, Than the fouel, whan hit ginneth dawe. **c1350** *Octavian* (*NL*) 91.490–2: Als blythe were thay thane of that syghte, Als es the fowelles, whene it es lighte, Of the dayes gleme. **c1385** Chaucer *Mars* 1: Gladeth, ye foules, of the morowe gray, **c1390** *CT* VII 38[B1228]: But was as glad therof as fowel of day. **a1445** *Carl* 153–5 B 449–50: They were as glad of that lady bright As ever was fowle of the daylyght. **c1450** Idley 111.146: The monke was as gladde as foule of day, 113.293. **1465** Leversege 25[4]: And as a fowle is glad of sprynging of the day. **a1500** *Octovian* (*NC*) 90.487–9: As glad they were of that syght, As fowlys be of day lyght And of the sonne leme. **a1500** *Tale of the Lady Prioress* 111[21]: Sir John was as glad of thys as ever was fowle of daye. Apperson 232; *Oxford* 222; Tilley F624. See **B292.**

F567 As light as **Fowl** to fly, *etc.*
a1325 *Cursor* III 1350.23621: Thir sal be light als fuxul to flei. **a1350** *Ywain* 35–6.1303–4: Him thoght that he was als lyght, Als a fowl es to the flyght. **c1420** Wyntoun II 69.783–4: And of speide he is mare licht Than ony foule is apon flicht. **a1430** Lydgate *Pilgrimage* 260.9417–8: And off nature to be mor lyht Than any ffoul that ffleth in flyht. See **B294, F28.**

F568 As merry as **Fowl** on rice (*branch*)
c1400 *Laud Troy* I 271.9186–7: Ther was no foule so merye on ris, Then Troilus was. See **B296.**

F569 As swith (*swift*) as **Fowl** flies (in flight)
a1200 Lawman II 473.21355–6: Neh al swa swi(the), Swa the fughel in fligheth. **a1300** *Richard* 223.2631–2: That the galey yede also swyfte, As ony foule by the lyfte. **c1380** *Ferumbras* 121.3863: And forth he renneth al so swyft, As foul that fleth on the lift. **c1387–95** Chaucer *CT* I[A] 190: Grehoundes he hadde as swift as fowel in flight. **c1400** *Alexander Buik* I 15.462–3: On bausand that, I underta, Is suifter than is foull of flicht. **1480** Caxton *Ovyde* 23[6]: Ranne as swyftly as two fowles flee. **1513** Douglas *Aeneid* IV 54.52: Flaw furth swyft as fowle up towart hevyn. Whiting *Scots* I 174.

F570 Every **Fowl** is froward (*hard*) to be daunted in its own nest
a1420 Lydgate *Troy* I 333.6611–2: As every foule is froward to arest, For to be daunted in his owne nest. See **C350.**

F571 Fair **Fowls** are oft found faint and frough (*frail*)
c1475 *Rauf* 99.523: Oft fair foullis ar fundin faynt, and als freuch. See **T119.**

F572 The fairest **Fowl** engenders the foulest
c1378 *Piers* B xii 238: The fairest foule foulest engendreth. MED foul 10. (The peacock)

F573 Farrest **Fowls** have fairest feathers
a1513 Dunbar *To the King* 42.21: Ay fairast feddiris hes farrest foulis. *Oxford* 190; Tilley F625; Whiting *Scots* I 174.

F574 **Fowls** come to their like
a1382 *WBible* Ecclesiasticus xxvii 10: Foules to the lic to them comen togidere (**c1395:** Volatilis comen togidere to *briddis* liik hem silf). Taylor and Whiting 28. See **B129, E171, L272.**

F575 No **Fowl** eats another of its kind
1340 *Ayenbite* 185[31–3]: Vor ase zayth the boc thet spekth of kende of bestes, "no voghel ne eth of othren yef he is of his kende." **c1400** *Vices and Virtues* 190.32–191.1: For as the boke that speketh of kynde of beestes seith, non foule wole ete of a-nother foule that is of his kynde. **1484** Caxton *Royal Book* P1ᵛ[25–8]: For as the book sayth whyche speketh of the nature of bestes: No byrde eteth another byrde of his owne nature, Ne a beest also eteth not another beest of his owne nature. Cf. Taylor and Whiting 106:25.

F576 More than **Fowls** (under heaven)
a1300 *XI Pains* 148.31–2: In mo pyne he schal beo Than foweles under heovene fleo, 149.63–4: Mo saulen tholieth ther swich wo Thene . . . fueles go, 154.245–6.

F577 To be fanged (*caught*) like a **Fowl** in the fowler's grin (*snare*) (*etc.*) (A number of single quotations are brought together here)
a1225 *St. Marherete* 8.8–9: And ase the fuhel the is ivon in thes fuheleres grune. **a1300** *Alisaunder* 199.3550: And ben yshett so foule in cage. **a1300** *Arthour and M.*[1] 59.2007–8: Uterpendragon made joie than, So doth the

foule, when it dawy gan. **a1325** Bonaventura *Meditations* (*1*) 16.505: They cryed on hym, as foules on owle. **a1325** *Cursor* III 1573.29081–2: Mani man in forme daus Perist was als fuxl in lime. **c1350** *Octavian* (*NL*) 149.1357: He sprent als any fowle of flyghte. **c1375** Barbour *Bruce* I 169.188: Tharfor he slepit as foul on twist. **c1380** *Ferumbras* 132.4243: A knyght, Prykyng so doth the foul on flyght. **c1390** *Thre messagers* in *Vernon* II 445.97–8: Such men ben ofte al-one I-let To pleye as the foul in the lift. **a1400** *Pricke* 191.7071–5: Alle that pomp . . . Es passed oway . . . als foghel fleghand in the ayre als wynd. **a1400** *Laud Troy* I 158.5348: He ffelde hem ded as foules of snowe. **a1450** *Song of Mortality* in Brown *Lyrics XIV* 96.6: To travel here whils we are fere, als fouls to the flight. **a1500** *Miroure of Mans Salvacionne* 34[16]: Thi son wham we abide and seke als foghil the day. **a1500** *Octavian* (*NC*) 148.1385: He sprange, as fowle dothe yn flyght. See **N115.**

F578 To flee as small **Fowls** do afore the falcon
a1533 Berners *Arthur* 90[11–2]: All fledde before hym as the smal fowles dooth afore the fawcon. Whiting *Scots* I 173.

F579 To fly like **Fowls**
c1300 *Guy*[1] 170 A 2932: Opon her stedes as foule thai fleth. **1340** *Ayenbite* 71[13–4]: Al hit ywent well rathre thanne . . . voghel vlyinde. **a1400** *Siege of Jerusalem* 17.310: Flowen, as the foule doth, that faucoun wolde strike. **c1408** Lydgate *Reson* 183.7006–8: Fleeth with-out(e) more lettyng With swyfter wynges and more ryght Than dooth any foule of flyght. MED flien 1(b).

F580 To ride as a **Fowl** may fly
a1300 *Alisaunder* 113.1983: And rideth swithe so foule may flen. **c1380** *Ferumbras* 123.3921: And ryde after as foul on flight.

F581 To run like a **Fowl** that flies
c1400 *Laud Troy* I 194.6579: And he ran forth as foule that flyes. **c1410** Lovelich *Merlin* III 632.23778: And gan forto rennen as fowl with flyht. **a1475** *Guy*[2] 294.10253–4: Hys hors . . . That ranne as faste, as fowle, that flyeth. **1513** Douglas *Aeneid* IV 108.96: On horssis that semyt ryn as fowle dois fle.

F582 The **Fowler's** melody beguiles the birds (*varied*)
c1385 Usk 55.54–5: Lo! the bird is begyled with the mery voice of the foulers whistel. **c1390** *Cato* (*Vernon*) 570.219–20: The foulere chaccheth briddes feole With swete melodye. **a1398**(1495) Bartholomaeus-Trevisa h7[v][1.3–7]: Ofte by swete noys the fouler bringeth theym (*birds*) to grynnes and snares, as the poete sayth: The pype syngyth swetly whyle the fouler dysceyvyth the byrde, oo1[v][1.9–12]: Pypyng begyleth byrdes and foules Therfore it is sayd, The pype syngeth swete whyle the fouler be-gyleth the byrde. **a1400** *Cato* (*Copenhagen*) A4[r][3–4]: For the pipe chauntyth merely the whyle, When men the briddys willyn begyle. **a1410** Lydgate *Churl* in *MP* II 476.185–6: The quaile-pipe can most falsly calle, Til the quaile undir the nett doth creepe. **a1437** *Kingis Quair* 83.135[1–5]: For as the fouler quhistlith in his throte Diversly, to counterfete the brid, And feynis mony a suete and strange note Till sche be fast lokin his net amyd That in the busk for his desate is hid. **a1440** Burgh *Cato* 309.238–9: The whistlyng fouler maketh mery song, And yit briddis bigilethe he a-mong. **c1450** *Cato* (*Sidney*) 16.163–4: For the pipe chaunteth merili, the while The fouler the briddis wil begile. **c1470** *Wallace* 225–6.1421–3: Syn plesand wordis off you and ladyis fayr, As quha suld dryff the byrdis till a swar With the small pype, for it most fresche will call. **1483** Caxton *Cato* D5[v][2–4]. **a1500** *Piers of Fullham* 5.94–7: *Ffistula dulce canit volucrem dum decipit Auceps* Ffull swetely sowneth the pype and syngeth, Whyll the fowler with hys deseyttes bryngeth The gentyll fowles in to hys false crafte. *Oxford* 222.

F583 If the **Fowler** shows his gins (*traps*) he will never attain birds
a1430 Lydgate *Pilgrimage* 405.15032–8: Yiff the fowlere ay in dede Shewede his gynnes and hys snarys . . . Bryddes, ffor al his grete peyne, Ther-to wolde never atteyne. **c1450** *Pilgrimage LM* 216[26–9]: He who that wole desceyve briddes he may not sette the wacches in the thikke ther thei ben ne in the pathes For if thei seyen a wacche there anoon thei wolden flee.

F584 Trust not a blear-eyed **Fowler** though he weep
a1410 Lydgate *Churl* in *MP* II 476.187–9: A blereyde fowler trust nat, thouh he weepe, Eschew his thombe, of wepyng take non heed, That smale briddis can nype bi the hed.

F585 As deceivable as **Foxes** (*varied*)
a1415 *Lanterne* 111.11: Descyvable as foxis. **a1439** Lydgate *Fall* II 629.1609: And be deceit a fox for subtilite.

F586 As fell as a **Fox**
a1450 *Castle* 97.672: I am feller thanne a fox.

F587 As fickle as a **Fox**
a1500 *Virtues Exiled* in Brown *Lyrics XV* 269.13: Ffraus is fykyll as a fox.

F588 As malicious as a **Fox**
a1449 Lydgate and Burgh *Secrees* 73.2301: (He is) lyk the ffox malicious. MED fox 5.

F589 As red as any **Fox**
c1387-95 Chaucer *CT* I[A] 552: His berd as any . . . fox was reed. *Oxford* 535; Svartengren 247; Whiting *NC* 411.

F590 As sly as the **Fox**
a1393 Gower *CA* II 212.3033: Thin entre lich the fox was slyh. Taylor and Whiting 145.

F591 As wily as a **Fox**
c1450 John of Fordun *Scotichronicon* (Edinburgh, 1759) II 376[8]: Mare wily than a fox. **1479** Rivers *Cordyal* 56.26: Wylyer than foxes. Tilley F629.

F592 Ay runs the **Fox** as long as he has foot
c1475 Henryson *Fables* 31.826–7: Now find I weill this proverb trew . . . "Ay rinnis the ffoxe, als lang as he fute hais." **a1507** Dunbar *Epetaphe* 66.45–8: Wyvis thus makis mokkis Spynnand on rokkis; "Ay rynnis the fox Quhill he fute hais." *Oxford* 382; Tilley F627; Whiting *Scots* I 174.

F593 The **Fox** can fage (*flatter*) when it would attain its prey
1471 Ripley *Compound* 159[13–4]: For than the Fox can fagg and fayne When he would faynyst hys prey attayne.

F594 The **Fox** feigns dead till the birds come to his tongue
c1400 *Of Clerks Possessioners* in Wyclif *EW* 123[21–2]: The fox feyneth hym dede til briddis comen to his tounge, and thanne he schewith hym on lyve.

F595 The **Fox** is as wily as the hare
c1495 *Arundel Vulgaria* 59.256: It is an olde proverbe, "as wyly is the foxe as the hare," the which in myn opinion cannot be alway true, for wher the foxe was iii dais in the scole, the hare sportyde hym in the feldes takynge no thought for the kynges sylver. (Note p. 97, recognizes neither proverb nor fable.)

F596 The **Fox** may change his skin but not his will
a1387 Higden-Trevisa IV 423[10–3]: Oon Buculus an olde man cride in despite of Vaspacianus, and seide, "The fox may chaunge his skyn, but nought his wille; ffor Vaspacianus his covetise was nevere the lasse for the passinge of his age." Apperson 233:25; *Oxford* 223; Tilley W616. See **C490.**

F597 The **Fox** said the raisins are sour
1484 Caxton *Aesop* 100–1: A foxe . . . sayd these raysyns ben sowre and yf I had some I wold not ete them. **c1503** More *Early Poems* [10] BC: Thus lyke the fox they fare once forsoke, The pleasaunt grapes, and gan for to defy them, Because he lept and yet could not come by them. Apperson 268; *Oxford* 262; Taylor and Whiting 158–9; Tilley F642.

F598 The **Fox** will be an anchor (*hermit*) (for he begins to preach)
c1500 *Lyfe of Roberte* 242.595: Will youe see, fellowes? the fox wylbe an anker. **1502** *Robert the Devil* C1[v][4–5]: Nowe, syrs, take hede, the foxe wyll be an aunker, for he begynneth to preche. Cf. *Oxford* 224: At length the fox turns monk; Tilley F640.

F599 If the **Fox** do evil men say worse by him
a1400 *Ancrene* (*Recluse*) 53.21–2: And yif the fox do yvel, yutt men sayen wers by hym. MED fox 5.

F600 To ask (have) no more of the **Fox** than the skin
c1515 Barclay *Eclogues* 94.1074: I aske of the foxe no farther then the skin. **1546** Heywood *D* 96.183–4: And be a man never so greedy to wyn, He can have no more of the foxe but the skyn, **1555** *E* 165.119, **1556** *Spider* 277[16]. Apperson 234:37; *Oxford* 457; Tilley M1163. See **M682.**

F601 To fall as flat as **Fox**
c1485 *Mary Magdalene* (*Digby*) 82.730: As flat as fox, I falle before your face.

F602 To flee like **Fox** to hole
c1400 *Laud Troy* I 181.6117: Thei ffle fro him as ffox to hole.

F603 To flit (*go*) like a **Fox**
a1450 *Castle* 105.936: Envye flet as a fox, and folwyth on faste.

F604 When the **Fox** fulls (is full) then he flays (pulls) the geese
c1450 *Douce MS.52* 57.146: When the fox fulles, then fleys he the gese. **c1450** *Rylands MS.394* 108.25.1: Aucas excoriat vulpes cum se saciavit. **c1470** *Harley MS.3362* f.2b in *Retrospective* 309[21]: Whan the vox ys ful, he pullyth gees. Walther I 189.1669, 1671. See **S753.**

F605 When the **Fox** preaches keep well your geese (let the geese beware)
a1450 *Castle* 101.804: Ya! whanne the fox prechyth, kepe wel yore gees. **a1460** *Towneley Plays* 12.84: Let furth youre geyse, the fox will preche. **c1475** *Rawlinson MS. D 328* 125.84: When the wox prechyth be-ware the gese. **a1500** *National Library of Wales Peniarth MS.356* p. 195 in Robbins-Cutler 4034.3: Wen the fox prechys kep wyll the ges. **1546** Heywood *D* 84.154: Whan the fox preacheth, then beware your geese, **1555** *E* 175.166. Apperson 234:35; *Oxford* 223; Taylor and Whiting 145; Tilley F656; Whiting *Drama* 245, 272.

F606 He that takes the **Frame** (*profit*) shall have part of sin and shame
c1303 Mannyng *Handlyng* 148.4419–20: But as he taketh therof the frame, He shal have parte of synne and shame.

F607 To be out of **Frame**
c1500 Fabyan 564[1–2]: Townes . . . were farre out of frame. **1533** More *Confutacion* 650 C[11–2]: The worlde beyng farther oute of frame. NED Frame 5.

F608 Betwixt this and **France**
a1450 *Generydes A* 144.4624–6: Treulie betwix this and Fraunce, . . . Is such a knight. **c1450** Capgrave *Katharine* 286.775: There is noon swiche be-twyxe this and frauns.

F609 **Fraud** fears falsehood
c1515 Barclay *Eclogues* 191.274: Fraude feareth falshode, suspecting oft in vayne.

F610 **Fraud** quit with fraud (*varied*)
a1439 Lydgate *Fall* I 324.4436: Fraude quit with fraude is guerdoun covenable, II 499.935: Fraude ay with fraude resceyveth his guerdoun, III 886.2271: Fraude for fraude; deceit is quit with gile, **a1449** *Fabules* in *MP* II 584.521: Where fraud ys usid, fraude mot rebounde, 525: Who useth fraude, with fraude shalbe quyt. **1515** Barclay *St. George* 92.2286: And frawde agay(n)st fraude. See **B213, F52, 491, G487, 491, M114, V34.**

F611 **Fraud** will out at last
a1420 Lydgate *Troy* III 725.5497–8: For, who for fraude evere doth him caste, Truste right wel, it wil out at the laste. See **M806.**

F612 **Freedom** is a noble thing (*varied*)
c1375 Barbour *Bruce* I 10.225: A! fredome is a nobel thing! **a1410** Lydgate *Churl* in *MP* II 484.376–8: Whoo hath freedam, hath al suffisaunce, Better is freedam with litel in gladnesse, Than to be thral in al wordly richesse, **a1439** *Fall* III 896.2591–7: Tresour of tresours, yf it be weel souht, Is vertuous fredam with large liberte; . . . For it transcendith and hath the sovereynte Above al richessis that been in erthe founde, A man at large freeli to stonde unbounde. **1484** Caxton *Aesop* 32[2–4]: For fredome and lyberte is better than ony gold or sylver, 33[24–6]: For lyberte shold not be wel sold for alle the gold and sylver of all the world, 90[1–2]: Lyberte or freedome is a moche swete thynge, 91[10–2]: There is no rychesse gretter than lybe(r)te for lyberte is better than alle the gold of the world. *Oxford* 225; Tilley F668.

F613 Who loses his **Freedom** loses all
a1410 Lydgate *Churl* in *MP* II 472.94–5: I remembre a proverbe seid of old, "Who lesith his fredam, in soth, he lesith all." Apperson 235; *Oxford* 386. See **L227.**

F614 The more it **Freezes** the more it binds (?meaning)
1492 *Salomon and Marcolphus* 13[10–1]: The more it fryseth the more it byndeth.

F615 The **French** can boast well
a1325 *Otuel and Roland* 63.133–7: The frenche konne yelpe wel,—Fful evyl mote they thryve! Ffaynte men they gonne a-gaste, And off here dedys thay best unwraste, Suche maystrye to kythe. **c1330** *Otuel* 73.266–8: Thine freinsche knightes kune yelpe wel, And whan thei beth to werre ibrought, Thanne be thei right nought. See **B556.**

F616 Spell (Speak) **French** and construe art and you shall seld come to your part
c1450 *Douce MS.52* 48.45: Spele Frenssh and construe art, And thou schalt selde com to thy part. **c1450** *Rylands MS.394* 97–8.23–6: Speke frensche . . . Gallica sillabica, logicalia construe dicta, Et propriam partem pertinges raro per artem. MED construen 5(a): "?to engage in scholarship or learning, ?practice courtly manners;" Walther II 214.10147a.

F617 **Frenchmen** sin in lechery, Englishmen in envy
c1303 Mannyng *Handlyng* 140.4149–52: A forbyseyn ys tolde thys, Seyd on Frenshe men and on Englys, "That Frenshe men synne in lecherye, And Englys men yn envye." Apperson 235. See **E107.**

F618 **Frenzy,** jealousy and heresy never die (*varied*)

1528 Skelton *Replycacion* I 223.406–8: For be ye wele assured, That frensy nor jelousy Nor heresy wyll never dye. **a1546** Heywood *D* 80.9–10: Fransy, heresy, and jelousy are three, That men say hardly or never cured bee. Apperson 235; *Oxford* 225; Tilley F672.

F619 As mute as a gray **Friar**
a1500 Medwall *Nature* C1r[23]: As mewet as yt were a gray frere.

F620 Two **Friars** and a fox make three shrews, *etc.* (*varied*)
c1450 *Douce MS.52* 57.147: Thre freris and thre fox maken thre shrewys; and ever berus the fox the box of alle gode thewys. **c1450** *Rylands MS.394* 109.4–7: Two frereus and a fox maken thre shrewes And ever bereth the fox the box of alle goode thewes. Una, duo fratres, vulpes, pravos faciunt tres. Pixidis ast morum gestrix erit ipsa bonorum. **c1470** *Harley MS.3362* f.2b: Tre frerys and a vox (*no more*). Walther V 460.32125b.

F621 Now **Friday** shines and now it rains fast
c1385 Chaucer *CT* I[A] 1534–5: Right as the Friday, soothly for to telle, Now it shyneth, now it reyneth faste. Apperson 236–7.

F622 Seld is the **Friday** all the week alike
c1385 Chaucer *CT* I[A] 1539: Selde is the Friday al the wowke ylike. Apperson 237; *Oxford* 226; Skeat 219.

F623 To have fele (*many*) **Fridays** in one's forehead
c1475 *Prohemy of a Mariage* 32[10]: In thi forehed fele fridayes this no fage. Cf. Apperson 236: Friday look; *Oxford* 226; Tilley F681.

F624 All are not **Friends** that men deem (so)
a1440 Burgh *Cato* 30.1038: For all be nat freendis that men demethe. Cf. Apperson 238:11; Tilley A112.

F625 Assay (prove, *etc.*) your **Friend** ere you have need
c1390 *Fy on a faint Friend* in Brown *Lyrics XIV* 156.37–40: Or thou have nede, thi frendes a-tast, Whuche be stif and whuche wol bende, And ther thou fynde bouwynde or bast—And ever fy on a feynt frende! **a1400** *Proverbis of Wysdom* 244.30: Ore thow have nede, assay thy frend. **a1449** Lydgate *Amor* in *MP* II 747.85–6: Pref thy friende afore, and thou shalt se Whom thou maist trust, thy journay for to spede. **a1450** Audelay 26.452–3: Assay thi frynd or thou have nede And of his answere take good hede. **a1450** *Myne awen dere* 173.758: Or thou hafe nede, thy frende thou prove. **c1450** *Fyrst thou sal* 88.34: Our thou hafe nede assay thy freet frende. **1474** Caxton *Chesse* 99[6–8]: And hit appertayneth and behoveth a man to assaye and preve his frende er he have nede. **c1475** *Rawlinson MS. D 328* 119.23: A-say thy frynd ar thow haw nede. **a1477** Rivers *Dictes* 15[7–8]: Enforce your self to winne frendis and than first preve them, ar ye put to moch truste in them. **a1500** *Faythfull frende* in [Joseph Haslewood] *The Book Containing the Treatises of Hawking* (London, 1810) E5v[30–1]: Therfore I rede you . . . To assaye your frendes or ye have nede. **a1500** *Additional MS.37075* 278.12: Asay thi frende er thu have nede. **a1500** *Gest of Robyn Hode* in Child III 62.112[3–4]: For it is good to assay a frende Or that a man have nede. **a1500** Greene *Carols* 389 *refrain and last line:* Man, be ware and wyse indede, And asay thi frend or thou hast nede. **a1500** Hill 132.34: Assay thy frend or thow have nede. **a1504** Hawes *Example* Cc1r[8–9]; Prove thy frende in a mater fayned, Or thou have nede. **1546** Heywood *D* 54.443: Prove thy freende er thou have neede, **1555** *E* 151.27. Apperson 515, 651; *Oxford* 522; Smith 306; Tilley F718; Whiting *Ballad* 24. See **F658, K101, L580, M58, 270, P429.**

F626 Before men know their **Friend** they must eat together many bushels of salt (*varied*)
a1470 Tiptoft *Tullius* C3v[1–4]: And sothe it is that is said, how men maye ete many busshellis of salt or they parfyte and accomplysshe theyr dutee of frendship. **c1495** *Arundel Vulgaria* 44.192: As Cicero saith, men must ete togedre many bushels of salt before they know their frendes. Cicero *De Amicitia* xix 67; Apperson 73; *Oxford* 30; Tilley F685.

F627 Better is a **Friend** unknown than known
?1468 Paston IV 294[13–4]: And ye knowe welle, maistras, better ys afrende unknow then knowen.

F628 Better is the **Friend** that pricks than the flatterer that oints (*anoints, "butters"*)
c1450 La Tour-Landry 123.29–30: Beter is the frende that prikithe, thanne the flatour that oynteth. See **W692.**

F629 Better to have **Friends** enough than to be a friendless king
a1440 Burgh *Cato* 313.394–5: Freendis inowe to have is bettir thyng Than is freendles a man to been a kyng.

F630 Every **Friend** has need of his friend
1483 Caxton *Cato* B4v[30–1]: For every frende hath nede of hys frende.

F631 A faithful **Friend** is the most worth of all good things
a1500 *MS. Marginalia* in Hoccleve I 171 n. 1: Of all good thinges the worlde brought forth, A faithefulle frend ys thinge moste worthe.

F632 A **Friend** avails either far or near, but the nearer is the more useful
c1025 *Durham Proverbs* 10.2: Freond deah feor ge neah, byð near nyttra. Amicus tam prope quam longe bonus est.

F633 A **Friend** in court is better than penny in purse
a1400 *Romaunt B* 5541–2: For freend in court ay better is Than peny in purs, certis. **c1470** *Harley MS.3362* f.4a: Betyr ys a frend in coort (*no more*). **c1495** *Arundel Vulgaria* 47.202: Men say it is better to have a frende otherwhils in courte than a peny in pursse. **a1500** Hill 131.29: Better is a frend in cowrte, than a peny (in) my purse. **1509** Barclay *Ship* I 70[29]: Better is a frende in courte than a peny in purse. Apperson 237; *Oxford* 227; Tilley F687.

F634 A **Friend** in need (*varied*)
c1025 *Durham Proverbs* 10.3: Æt þearfe man sceal freonda cunnian. Amicus in necessitate probandus est. **c1250** *Proverbs of Alfred* 133 T 640: A sug fere the his help in nod. **a1300** *Alisaunder* 211.3759: Now shal Ich wite who is my frende. **c1303** Mannyng *Handlyng* 80.2251: At nede shul men prove here frendys. **a1325** *Cursor* II 768.13389: In nede than sal thai find us freind. **a1338** Mannyng *Chronicle A* I 243.6933–4: And hit ys also worldes honur, At nede ther frendes for to socour. **1340** *Ayenbite* 186[21–2]: Vor ate niede me yzizth huet vrend is. **c1378** *Piers* B xv 173: For a frende that fyndeth hym failled hym nevere at nede. **c1380** *Ferumbras* 8.230: Ne schal no man bet prove is frende bot a-say hem on his nede. **c1390** *Cato* (*Vernon*) 599.535–6: Beter leche knowe I non Then trewe frend is at neode. **c1390** Chaucer *CT* VII 1306–7[B2496–7]: For Catoun seith: "If thou hast nede of help, axe it of thy freendes; for ther nys noon so good a phisicien as thy trewe freend." **a1393** Gower *CA* II 274.1772: And soghten frendes ate nede, III 80.4912–4: Thus hiere I many a man compleigne, That nou on daies thou schalt finde At nede fewe frendes kinde. **a1400** *Cato* (*Copenhagen*) B3ʳ[11–2]: Ffor noon wil trustyer helpe at nede Than trewe frendis, as y kan rede. **a1400** Chestre *Launfal* 69.580: Gyfre kedde he was good at nede. **a1400** *Romaunt B* 5551–3: For Ynfortune makith anoon To knowe thy freendis fro thy foon, By experience, right as it is. **a1400** *Titus* 98.2146–8: Per fay, Jacob I shal the save When tyme cometh thou art in nede; Than ogh men frenshep to shewe in dede. **c1400** *Alexander Buik* II 206.3659–60: For quha is gude freind in laute, At ane myster men may se. **c1400** *Vices and Virtues* 201.11–2: For at the nede schal a man see who is his frend, 232.3–5: For as men were woned to seie, "At the moste nede men were woned to seche here frendes." **c1410** Lovelich *Grail* I 123.161–2: But Evere At Nede A man May se What men that welen his Frendes be. **c1415** *Middle English Sermons* 86.15–7: He seyth that this is a frende and a felowe at the borde, but he shall not dwell in the tyme of nede. **a1439** Lydgate *Fall* III 824.39: At a streiht neede fewe freendis men do fynde, 911.3139: At a streiht neede fewe freendis abidyng. **a1440** Burgh *Cato* 27.932–3: For whan all othir ben ful ferr to seche, The feitheful knowe freende kan beste be thi leche. **c1440** Charles of Orleans 129.3859: At nede the frendis preven what thei be. **a1449** Lydgate *Amor* in *MP* II 747.69–70: Love may go pley, and his dogge hey shake, For any friend he fyn(dith) at strayt nede, *Fabula* in *MP* II 507.642: He thouhte, he wolde preeve his freend at neede, *A Freond at Neode* in *MP* II 755–9.8, 16, 24, *etc.*: Ful weele is him that fyndethe a freonde at neede, *Order* in *MP* II 452.93: And he that hoteth, and faileth his frend at nede. **a1450** *Gesta* 131[6–9]: And therefore seithe the wise man, *Est amicus meus, et non permanebit in tempore necessitatis,* This is to seye, ther is a frende at the table or at the mete borde, the wiche wolle not or shal not abide in tyme of nede. **a1450** *Love that god loveth* in Kail 78.173–4: Though trewe love have lityl to spende, Evere he fyndeth a frend at nede. **a1450** *Myne awen dere* 156.245–6: A frende is mare worthe in a nede Than all the gude that thou may bede, 173.753–5: For swilke a frende is to sette by In tyme of nede tendirly Will with the stande in ill and gude. **1450** *Dicts* 70.32–72.2: And thei askid him whenne he knewe his frendis; and he aunswered: in necessitee, for in prosperitee everi man is a frende. **c1450** *Foly of Fulys* 64.438: And falyeis evir thar frend at neid. **1455** Paston III 15[16–7]: At suche a tyme a man may knowe hese frendes and hese fooes asonder, **1460** 205[12–4]: A very frende at nede experience will schewe be deede, as wele as be autorite of Aristotle in the Etiques that he made of moralite. **a1475** Ashby *Dicta* 67.561: A Freende is knowen in necessite. **a1475** *Ludus Coventriae* 321.1430–1: Such a frende fyndyst thou nevyr none To help the at thi

nede. **1477** Rivers *Dictes* 39[13–5]: One asked him whan he shulde knowe his frende? He sayd in necessite, for in prosperite every man is frendely, 116[35–6]: He ys thy verray frende that in thy necessite offerith hym self and alle his goodes unto the. **1484** Caxton *Aesop* 88[19–20]: For a trewe frend is oftyme better at a nede than a Royalme, 251[16–7]: The philosopher saith that the very and trewe frend is fond in the xtreme nede, *Royal Book* B1v[16–7]: In the tyme of adversyte and of poverte the veray frende is proved, M5v[13–4]: At nede is seen who is a frende, P6v[21], **1485** *Charles* 48.13–5: The comyn proverbe sayth: "At nede a man knoweth hys frende," **c1489** *Aymon* II 433.33–4: But it is sayd, that at the nede the frende is knowen. **c1495** *Arundel Vulgaria* 44.193: A man shall knowe his frende best in adversite, ffor than all flaterers lyghtly departith. **a1500** *Disciplina Clericalis* 15[17–8]: Many friendis bien nombred in prosperitee but a fewe in necessite. **a1500** *Miroure of Mans Salvacionne* 17[27]: A trewe freend sall be knawen in grete adversitee. **a1500** *Thre Prestis* 45.1027–8: The tother twa his freindis war indeid, As he thocht quhen that he had ony neid, 49.1151–2: Now is over lait to preif my freind in deid, Quhan that I have sik mister and sik neid. **c1500** *Everyman* 10.229: Than be you a good frende at nede, 29.854: Thou shalt fynde me a god frende at nede. **c1500** *Fortune Will Have Her Way* in Brown *Lyrics XV* 259.2: Frendys be feer and feynte at nede. **1525** Berners *Froissart* V 120[10]: At a pynch a frende is knowen, **a1533** *Arthur* 191[20–1]: Whan nede cometh, than is the frende knowen, 322[2]: Whan nede is, than a frende is proved, 505[26]: Ever at nede a man shal know his frend. **1546** Heywood *D* 54.444: A freende is never knowen tyll a man have neede, **1555** *E* 190.247. Apperson 237–8; Jente 430; *Oxford* 227; 497; Smith 2; Taylor and Whiting 146; Tilley F693, 694; Whiting *Drama* 135, 148, *Scots* I 175. See **F659, 672, N46, 74, P338.**

F635 A **Friend** may become a foe (*varied*)
c1250 *Proverbs of Alfred* 102–4 T 298–309: Wurthu nevere so wod, Ne so desi of thi mod, Thad evere sige thi frend Al that the likit, Ne alle the thonkes That thu thoch(t) havist; For ofte sibbie men Foken hem bitwenen, And ef(t) it so bilimpit Lo(th)e that ye wurthen, Thanne wot thi fend Thad her viste thi frend. **a1400** *Proverbis of Wysdom* 246.97–8: Tel no man, what thou wilt do: That now is frend, may be fo. **c1450** *Consail and Teiching* 72.213–8: Thi secret consail nevir wndo Bot neid or fors dryv the thar-to, For thow may tell It till a frend Quhilk eftyr may be unkend And chang his love and be thi fa; Thow art unsikir quhen It is swa. **c1450** Idley 86.349–50: And so behave the in langage ever moo, That thou be not ferde if thy frende be thi foo. **a1500** Hichecoke *This Worlde* 333.41–2: Tell no man wat thu wilte doo, That now is thi frynde mai be thi foo. **a1500** *Lansdowne MS.* in *Rel. Ant.* I 288–9: To thy frende thowe lovest moste Loke thowe tell not alle thy worste, Whatesoever behappes; For whane thy frende ys thy foo, He wolle tece alle and more too, Be ware of after clappes. **1509** Barclay *Ship* I 200[13–4]: He that is nowe thy frende may after be thy fo; Warne nat thy ennemy of that that thou wylt do, 246[25–7]: Ne to thy frende shewe nat thy mynde also, For if that he after become thy fo, As often hapneth, than myght he the bewry. **a1513** Dunbar *Rewl of Anis Self* 75.12: Ane freind may be thy fo as fortoun steiris.

F636 The **Friend** that does me no good and the enemy that does me no damage are all one
a1449 Lydgate *Freond* in *MP* II 758.105–6: Alle one to me that freonde that dothe no gode, And that enemye that dothe me no damage. Tilley F409.

F637 **Friends** fail fleers
1513 More *Richard* 55 A[12–3]: Frendes fayle fleers. Apperson 238: flyers; *Oxford* 228; Tilley F737.

F638 **Friends** lightly taken are lightly left again
1532 Berners *Golden Boke* 134.787–135.788: Frendes lyghtly taken, are lyghtly lefte agayne. See **C384.**

F639 **Friends** may not always be yfere (*together*)
c1385 Chaucer *TC* v 342–3: For wel thou woost, my leve brother deere, That alwey frendes may nat ben yfeere. **c1390** *Against My Will* in Brown *Lyrics XIV* 134.20: And frendes are not ay I-fere. **c1433** Lydgate *St. Edmund* 386.541–2: But it was seid sithe go many a yeer: That freendis alwey maynot been infeer, **1439** *St. Albon* 139.706–8: It is a by-worde and a full olde sawe, Whiche hath be sayd syth gone many a yere: Frendes alway may not ben in fere. *Oxford* 228.

F640 A great **Friend** is Plato, but a greater friend is truth (*varied*)
a1425 Chauliac 22.5–6: For Socrates or plato is frend, but sothfastnes or treuthe is more frend. **c1454** Pecock *Folewer* 152.12–3: (Aristotle) seide: "A great freend is plato, but a gretter freend is trouth." Walther I 113.962.

F641 He comes soon again that finds no **Friend**
a1500 *Additional MS.37075* 277.11: He comyth sone ayene that fyndyth no frende. See **G182.**

F642 He is a good **Friend** that does good
1477 Rivers *Dictes* 48[33–5]: He is a good frende that doth the good and a myghty frende that defendeth the from harme. Apperson 238:21; Tilley F706.

F643 He is a slack **Friend** that promises and is long in fulfilling
1532 Berners *Golden Boke* 300.5993–301.5994: The Grekes saye: that he that promyseth and is longe in fulfyllynge, is but a slacke frende. See **G80.**

F644 He is a true **Friend** that loves me for my love and not for my good (*property*)
a1500 Hill 131.20: He ys a trew frend, that loveth me for my love and not for my good. Apperson 647.

F645 He is no good **Friend** that hides deceit toward another
c1025 *Durham Proverbs* 13.26: Ne byð þæt fele freond se þe oþrum facn heleð. Non erit fidelis amicus qui mala celat imminens.

F646 He is no traist (*true*) **Friend** that is a foe for nought
a1500 *Salamon sat and sayde* 291.10: He was never my trayst frend that was my fa for noght.

F647 He is not wise that leaves his **Friend** for any good, *etc.*
c1475 *Guy*[1] 583 C 10408–15: He ys not wyse, be myn hood, That levyth hys frend for any good, Hys hownd other hys hawke so dere, Hys horse other hys good squyer: Though he myght not quyte the fyrst day, Yet do hym not awey; For are the VII yere wynne he may All his costage in on daye.

F648 He that helps his **Friend** does himself freme (*benefit*)
a1200 Lawman I 29.674–5: He deth him selva freoma (*B*: mansipe) Tha helpeth his freondene.

F649 Kiss and be (good) **Friend**
a1338 Mannyng *Chronicle B* I 64[22]: And kisse and be gode frende in luf and in a wille. **c1400** *Toulouse* 273.1187: We schall kyss and be god frend. **a1415** Mirk *Festial* 124.20–1: And kys and be frendes, 186.24–5. **1419** *A Remembraunce* in Kail 69.13: Make hem kyssen and be frende. **c1450** Holland *Howlat* 76.843–4: Thai forthocht that thai faucht, Kissit samyn and saucht. **a1450** *How Man's Flesh* in Kail 92.111: That y and my soule be frendis and kisse. **a1450** *Partonope* 185.4929–30: Eche man ys kyste and other frynde, And eche ys shapen to hys cuntre. **a1470** Malory I 410.33: And kyssed togydir and made frendys for ever. Apperson 343; *Oxford* 339–40; Tilley F753.

F650 Leave not an old **Friend** for a new (*varied*)
c1280 *South English Legendary: OT History* 83:36: Thine olde frende that thou fonded haste, bileve thou for no newe. **c1350** Serlo 216.102: Ne let naut thin olde frende for the newe. **c1395** *WBible* Ecclesiasticus ix 14: Forsake thou not an eld frend; for a newe frend schal not be liik hym. **a1440** Burgh *Cato* 310.268–70: Chaunge nat thi freende, that thou knowest of old, For any newe in trost, that thou shalt fynde Bettir than he. **1445** Claudian *Stilicho* 261.44: Ne to caste aside thin olde frende for fyndyng of a newe. **a1450** *Myne awen dere* 164.470–1: I warne the that thou nevere forsake Thyne alde frende for another newe. **1483** Caxton *Cato* D7^{v}[20–2]: Men oughte to love more the olde frende approved, thenne the newe frende whiche is not approved nor assayed. See **N97, O27.**

F651 Liefer (*more gladly*) lose the lesser **Friend** than the great
1464 Paston IV 107[18–9]: He seide lever he hadde lose the lesser frende than the greete frende.

F652 Make not your **Friend** your foe
a1425 *Chester Plays* II 310.712: Make not thy frend thy foe! **a1500** *Harley MS.116* in *Rel. Ant.* I 316[8–9]: I made of my frend my foo, I will beware I do no more soo. **a1500** Hichecocke *This Worlde* 332.9: Of thi frynde make not thi foo. Apperson 321; *Oxford* 227.

F653 My **Friend** borrowed money and I have lost my friend and my money
1474 Caxton *Chesse* 112–3: And herof speketh Domas the philosopher and sayth that my frende borowed money of me And I have lost my frende and my money attones. Apperson 360; *Oxford* 361; Tilley F725. See **F666, G341.**

F654 One may write to his **Friends**, *etc.*
1555 Heywood *E* 183.205: Ye may write to your freendes that ye are in helth: Who may write to his freendes that he is in welth. Apperson 715; Tilley F743.

F655 One should hold a **Friend** in every way
c900 *Maxims* in *Exeter Book* 161.144: Wel mon sceal wine healdan on wega gehwylcum.

F656 One true **Friend** should prove another

1532 Berners *Golden Boke* 298.5916: One true frende shulde prove an other.

F657 Praise not a **Friend** till you have proved him
a1500 *Disciplina Clericalis* 15[1–2]: Ne praise thow nat a friend til thow have proved hym. See **L580.**

F658 Prove your **Friends** ere you trust them
1450 *Dicts* 18.6–7: Enforce you to gete freendis, bot first prove theym or ye trust to greetly. Smith 306; Tilley T595. See **F625.**

F659 Some are **Friends** at board who are behind at need (*varied*)
c1280 *South English Legendary: OT History* 83.31: For summe ben at thi borde thi frende, ac at thi nede bihynde. **1483** Caxton *Cato* I1v[33–5]: For many one be founden whiche are onely frendes at the table, that is to saye, atte dyner and souper, and not in adversyte. See **B415, F634, M367, T49, W617.**

F660 There is none so evil beloved but he has some **Friend**
a1450 *Gesta* 418[1–2]: For there is non so Evyll be-lovyd but he hathe some Frende.

F661 A true **Friend** is a great help
1481 Caxton *Reynard* 68[20]: A triew frende is a grete helpe. Smith 124.

F662 Trust not a new **Friend** made of an old foe
1513 More *Richard* 40 G[2–5]: None of us I beleve is so unwise, oversone to truste a newe frende made of an olde foe. Cf. Tilley H373. See **C374, E96, 100.**

F663 A trusty **Friend** is hard to find (*varied*)
c1450 *Proverbs of Good Counsel* 70.58: A tr(u)sty frende ys hard to fynde. **a1475** *Good Wyfe Wold* 174.50: A trusty frende ys good ifonde, whoso mey hyme reche. **a1500** *Att my begynnyng* in *Rawlinson MS. C 813* 323.7: A trustye frende ys harde to fynde. **c1500** *Proper tretyse* 244[15]: A trusty freynd ys hard to fyend. *Oxford* 188: Faithful; Smith 126.

F664 Undernim (*reprove*) your **Friend** if you see him misdo
c1280 *South English Legendary: OT History* 84.73–4: Undernyme thi frend yif thou seest hym mysdo; Yif he is a fool or thi foo, ne do thou noughth so.

F665 When **Friends** meet (there) is joy and pleasance
a1449 Lydgate *Fabules* in *MP* II 582.452: When frendis mete, ys joy and plesaunce. Cf. Apperson 415: Merry; *Oxford* 421; Tilley F750, 758; Whiting *Scots* I 175. See **H46.**

F666 When I lent I was a **Friend** (*varied*)
a1400 *Proverbis of Wysdom* 247–8.161–6: I wold lene, but I ne thare: I have be dissevyd, I wyll be ware. When I lent, I had a frend; But, when I askyd, he was unkynd: So off my frend I made my fo; There fore I will no more do so. **1474** Caxton *Chesse* 112[18–21]: And also hit is said in reproche whan I leve (*for* lene) I am thy frend and whan I axe I am thy enemye as wo saith god at the lenynge and the devyll at rendrynge. **a1500** *Harley MS.941* in *Rel. Ant.* I 259: I wold lene but I ne dare, I have lant I will bewarre; When y lant y had a frynd, When y hym asked he was unkynd: Thus of my frynd y made my foo, Therefore darre I lene no moo. I pray yo of your gentilnesse Report for no unkyndnesse. **a1500** *Harley MS.2321* in *Rel. Ant.* I 208[1–2]: When I lent I was a frend, When I asked I was unkinde. Jente 453; *Oxford* 361; Tilley F723; Whiting *Scots* I 199. See **F653, G341.**

F667 When one has **Friends** through Fortune, mishap will make them enemies
c1380 Chaucer *Boece* iii pr. 5.66–8: Certes swiche folk as weleful fortune maketh frendes, contraryous fortune maketh hem enemys, **c1390** *CT* VII 2244–6[B3434–6]: For what man that hath freendes thurgh Fortune, Mishap wol maken hem enemys, I gesse; This proverbe is ful sooth and ful commune. Apperson 238; *Oxford* 426; Skeat 254; Smith 121, 127. See **A56.**

F668 Your eld (*old*) **Friend** is best treasure
c1280 *South English Legendary: OT History* 83.32: Best tresore is thine elde frende, that men on erthe may fynde. Archer Taylor "An Old Friend is the Best Friend" in *Romance Philology* 9(1955) 201–5.

F669 Feigned **Friendship** is enmity
1414 ?Brampton *Psalms* 17[6–7]: For frendschyp feyned is enemyte: Folys ben favouryd all here fylle. See **E97, F673.**

F670 **Friendship** is more than cattle (*property*)
a1400 *Romaunt B* 5540: Frendshipp is more than is catell. Smith 130; Whiting *Drama* 229.

F671 **Friendship** may not hang by the wind or for fair eyes
1475 Paston V 230[12–4]: Frendship may not hang by the wynde, nor for faire eyne, but causis must be shewid.

F672 The **Friendship** soon sinks that flees its friend in adversity
a1500 *Fortune alas alas* 487.87–9: The soth is said, such frendship sone doth synke, That from his frend fleeth in adversite, And will not (bide) but in prosperite. See **F634, P338.**

F673 No **Friendship** so perilous as feigned friendlihood
a1439 Lydgate *Fall* I 111.4003–4: And under a shadwe off feyned freendliheed, Ther is no frenship so pereilous for to dreed. See **E97, F669.**

F674 To find (feel) no **Friendship**
c1470 *Wallace* 66.577–8: Feill of thaim ma na freyndschip with him fand; Fyfteyn that day he schot to dede of his hand, 67.612: On athir side no frendschip was to feill, 76.62: feill. See **G368, L554.**

F675 To fish well and catch a **Frog** (*varied*)
c1503 More *Early Poems* [15] D[4–7]: Lo in this ponde be fyshe and frogges both, Cast in your nette: but be you liefe or lothe, Holde you content as fortune lyst assyne: For it is your owne fishyng and not myne. **1546** Heywood *D* 42.51: He hath well fysht and caught a frog. Apperson 217; Jente 750; *Oxford* 205; Tilley F767; Whiting *Scots* I 175. See **F240.**

F676 To hang like a **Frog**
c1400 *Laud Troy* I 317.10752: The duke hanged as a frogge. (The duke had been split from head to crotch.)

F677 To slay like **Frogs**
c1400 *Laud Troy* II 376.12756: And sclayn oure men as frogges.

F678 To brustle (*sizzle*) like a monk's **Froise** (*pancake*)
a1393 Gower *CA* II 375.2731–3: He routeth with a slepi noise, And brustleth as a monkes froise, Whanne it is throwe into the Panne.

F679 As cold as **Frost**
c1385 Chaucer *TC* i 523–4: But also cold in love towardes the Thi lady is, as frost in wynter moone, v 535: As frost, hym thoughte, his herte gan to colde, **c1386** *LGW* 2683: As cold as any frost now waxeth she. **c1430** ?Lydgate *Compleynt* 66.526–7: And now as cold, with-oute drede, As frost is in the wynter mone. **c1450** *Jacob's Well* 284.16: Make the in dreed cold as frost.

F680 As false as **Frost** in May (*etc.*) (A number of single quotations are brought together here)
a1325 *Sir Simon Fraser* in Böddeker 127.42–3: Fals wes here foreward, so forst is in may, That sonne from the southward wypeth a way. **a1415** *Lanterne* 9.10–1: But stille thei lien harde congelid as froost. **1440** Palladius 108.621: To make hem hoor as frost. **1533** More *Apologye* 181[32]: As gret a dyfference as bytwene frost and fyre.

F681 They must hunger in **Frost** that will not work in heat
1549 Heywood *D* 45.126: They must hunger in frost, that will not woorke in heete. Apperson 318; *Oxford* 310; Tilley F772; Whiting *Scots* I 175.

F682 To freeze like **Frost**
c1425 Hoccleve *Jonathas* 227.320: But that myn herte as the cold frost may freese.

F683 To pass like **Froth** on the face of water
c1395 *WBible* Hosea x 7: Samarie made his kyng to passe, as froth on the face of water.

F684 They must be **Frowards** (*brave warriors* [MED]) that deal with evil frekes (*men*)
c1400 *Roland* 110-1.132–3: They must be Frowardis that delithe with evyll frekis Or he shall have evyll sped at the last end.

F685 Evil **Fruit** witnesses evil root
a1400 *Of Confession* in Wyclif *EW* 331[18]: With yvel frute witnessith yvel rote. Apperson 607.

F686 The **Fruit** can renew the root's virtue
a1420 Lydgate *Troy* I 3.98: The rotys vertu thus can the frute renewe. MED fruit 3(b).

F687 The **Fruit** (*essential part*) of every tale is to be said
c1390 Chaucer *CT* II[B] 706: The fruyt of every tale is for to seye.

F688 **Fruit** seldom falls but if it be ripe
a1475 *Vision of Philibert* 25[5]: The frut fallyt syld, but yeyf hit be rype.

F689 Good **Fruit** seldom comes of evil seed
a1023 ?Wulfstan *Larspel* in Napier 243.17: Seldan cymð god wæstm of yfelum sæde.

F690 Hasty **Fruits** have no long residence (*life*)
a1449 Lydgate *Haste* in *MP* II 761.65–8: At prime-tens, men seen hit wel at ye, Hasty ffrutus have no longe resydens, Ryght feyre outward the coore doth putrifye, Dayly perceyvyd of olde experyence. See **F694, R142.**

F691 If you will be whole let all **Fruit** be
c1450 *Douce MS.52* 47.37: Yf thou wylle hole be, lete all frute be. See **A160, P86.**

F692 One seldom sees the **Fruit** and the flower together

1532 Berners *Golden Boke* 333.7040–2: Seldomme we see the fruyte and the flowre to gyther: for whan the one is rype and in season, the other is cleane gone and avoyded.

F693 Take the **Fruit** and let the chaff be still
c1390 Chaucer *CT* VII 3443[B4633]: Taketh the fruyt, and lat the chaf be stille. See **C428.**

F694 There is no **Fruit** that is soon ripe and dures (*lasts*) long
1519 Horman *Vulgaria* 284[8]: There is no fruyte: that is soone rype and dureth longe. See **F690, R142.**

F695 The **Frume** (*beginning*) was unhende (*bad*) and so was the end
a1200 Lawman II 130.13265–6: The frume wes unhende And al swa wes the ænde. See **B199.**

F696 Out of the **Frying-pan** (water) into the fire
c1515 Barclay *Eclogues* 10.336: Out of the water thou leapest into the fyre. **1528** More *Heresyes* 179 F[4–5]: Than lepe they lyke a flounder out of a frying panne into the fyre. **1546** Heywood *D* 76.214–5: But as the flounder doothe, Leape out of the friyng pan into the fyre. Apperson 240; *Oxford* 230; Taylor and Whiting 147–8; Tilley F784.

F697 Little knows the **Full** what ails the hungry (*varied*)
c1450 *Douce MS.52* 54.115: Lytyl wote the full, what the hungry aylys. **c1450** *Rylands MS.394* 104.2. **a1475** *Boke of Curtesy* in *ESt* 9(1885) 59.17–8: For the full wombe, wythowtte fayle, Whot lytull what the emty ayle. **c1475** *Rawlinson MS. D 328* 121.45: Lytill wote the full what the hongre eylyth. **1478** Rivers *Morale Proverbes* [3.7–8]: He that is fed and hath his hertis luste, What peigne the hungry hath, he wole not truste. **1546** Heywood *D* 40.190: Littell knoweth the fat sow, what the leane dooth meane. Apperson 591; *Oxford* 374; Tilley S676. See **G101, H149, 646, W551.**

F698 To pass like a **Fume**
1484 Caxton *Royal Book* G7v[9–10]: It is . . . anone passed as a fume.

F699 To vanish away like a **Fume**
1483 Caxton *Golden Legende* 279r[1.28–9]: He vanysshed awaye as a fumee or smoke. See **R77, S414.**

F700 If the **Fundament** (*foundation*) is false the work must needs fall
a1450 Audelay 21-2.320–1: For yif the fondment be false the werke most nede falle Withyn a lyty(l) stounde. See **B199.**

F701 Not worth a **Funk** (*spark*)
a1338 Mannyng *Chronicle B* I 172[25–6]: Now of this olde monk and this new kyng, That was not worth a fonk. MED fonke b.

F702 The **Fur** is not all like the sleeves
1492 *Salomon and Marcolphus* 6–7: It standyth wryten, that the furre is not all lyke the slevys.

F703 As great as a **Furnace** (*etc.*) (A number of single quotations are brought together here)
c1387–95 Chaucer *CT* I[A] 559: His mouth as greet was as a greet forneys. **a1420** Lydgate *Troy* I 367.7804–5: Whos eyen were spark(e)ling as bright As a fourneis with his rede levene. **1483** *Quatuor Sermones* 28[19–20]: That day, sayth malachy, shal brene as hote as a furneys of fyre.

F704 To steam (*glow*) like a **Furnace**
c1387–95 Chaucer *CT* I[A] 201–2: His eyen stepe, and rollynge in his heed, That stemed as a forneys of a leed.

F705 As fierce as any **Fury** of hell
c1503 More *Early Poems* [11] C[1]: And looketh as fierce as any fury of hell.

G

G1 As close and covert as **Gabriel's** horn
c1450 Idley 125.1054–5: They (*wives*) be as cloos and covert as the horn of Gabriell That will not be herde but from hevene to hell. Cf. Taylor and Whiting 149.

G2 Till **Gabriel** blow his horn (*varied*)
a1400 *Clergy May Not Properly Hold Property* in Wyclif *EW* 382[27–8]: And I wote wel that gabriel schal blow his horne or thai han prevyd the mynor. **1522** More *Treatyce* 101 C[5–7]: Now shall they fal in the bed, and fro thence laid and lefte in the mire, til Gabriell blowe them up, **1533** *Apologye* 98[21–2]: And slepe shall they saye tyll Gabryels trumpe awake them. Apperson 242; *Oxford* 231; Tilley G1.

G3 Many (a) **Gadling** (*fellow*) is goodly on horse and unworth in wike (*duty*)
c1250 *Proverbs of Alfred* 108–10 T 341–4: Swo is moni gadeling Godelike on horse Wlanc (*C:* bold) on werwe (*C:* bi glede) And unwurth (*J:* uvel) on wike (*CJ:* at neode). Cf. Notes pp. 175–6. See **H107, 421.**

G4 Light **Gains** make heavy purses
1546 Heywood *D* 47.196: Light gaynes make heavy purses, **1555** *E* 173.150: Lyght geynes make heavy purses. Lyght losses make heavy curses. Apperson 364; *Oxford* 367; Tilley G7. Cf. Jente 54.

G5 Too late comes **Gainchare** (*repentance, means of return*) (*varied*)
c1325 *Defence* in Brown *Lyrics XIII* 147.35–6: To late cometh the geynchar, When love ou hath ybounde. **c1390** *Thre messagers* in *Vernon* II 444.43–4: Ffor ther nis no geyn-char, Whon Aventures cometh to turnement. NED Gainchare. See **A65, H9.**

G6 As sweet as **Galingale**
a1400 *Floris* 73.119–20: Galyngale ne lycorys Is not so soote as hur love is.

Gall (1)

G7 To claw (*etc.*) one on the **Gall** (*sore*) (*varied*)
c1395 Chaucer *CT* III[D] 939–41: For trewely ther is noon of us alle, If any wight wol clawe us on the galle, That we nel kike, for he seith us sooth. **c1400** *Beryn* 37.1150–1: Yet "touch no man the galle," It is my pleyn counsell, 107.3564: Howe Geffrey had I-steryd, that went so nyghe the gall. **c1405** *Mum* 49–50.770–1: For thou has rubbid on the rote of the rede galle And eeke y-serchid the sore and sought alle the woundz. **a1439** Lydgate *Fall* III 924.200–1: On your diffautis ye list nat for to bide: The galle touchid, al that ye set aside. **c1516** Skelton *Magnificence* 39.1232–4: I kyndell in her suche a lyther sparke That rubbed she must be on the gall Bytwene the tappet and the wall, **1522** *Why Come* II 27.25: Not rubbe you on the gall, **1523** *Garlande* I 365.97: Savynge he rubbid sum upon the gall. **1546** Heywood *D* 75.177: Where your wurds now do but rub him on the gall. Apperson 540; *Oxford* 550; Tilley G12; Whiting *Drama* 361:809, *Scots* I 176. See **B131, H505.**

Gall (2)

G8 As bitter as (the, any) **Gall**
c1225 *Wohunge of Ure Laverd* 283[17]: Galle that is thing bittrest. **a1300** *Alisaunder* 275.5064: Ac there was never galle so bitter. **c1303** Mannyng *Handlyng* 53.1470: In-to the watyr bytterer than galle. **a1325** *Flemish Insurrection* 119.99: Ther hi habbeth dronke bittrere then the galle. **c1325** *Prayer of Penitence* in Brown *Lyrics XIII* 156.12: the. **c1330** *Jesu that for us* in *ESt* 9(1885–6) 43.25. **c1343** Rolle *Ego* in Allen

R. Rolle 64.102: the, **a1349** *Commandment* in Allen *R. Rolle* 75.64: the. **c1380** *Cleanness* 39.1022: the. **c1385** Chaucer *TC* iv 1135–7: Tho woful teeris . . . As bittre weren . . . For peyne, as is . . . galle. **a1393** Gower *CA* III 176.341: the. **a1400** *Benjamin Minor* in *Yorkshire Writers* I 162.46: tho, 171[42]: Bitter os gall forbi hony. **a1400** *In One is All* in Brown *Lyrics XV* 83.46: the. **a1400** *Stodye of Wysdome* 44.16. **a1400** *Ye Flour of hour gerland* in *Archiv* 87(1891) 432.8[2]: Hour joye es byterrer than es any galle. **c1408** Lydgate *Reson* 104.3945, **a1420** *Troy* I 379.8226, III 771.7089. **a1425** *Christ's Own Complaint* in *Pol. Rel. and Love Poems* 227.617. **a1425** *Northern Passion* 20 A 172: the. **c1425** *Orcherd* 52.31. **a1430** Lydgate *Pilgrimage* 404.14976: any. **a1438** Kempe 137.25–6: Sche must voydyn that was in hir stomak as bittyr as it had ben galle. **a1439** Lydgate *Fall* III 867.1597, **a1449** *See Myche* in *MP* II 800.10. **a1450** *Castle* 147.2342. **a1450** *Desert* 61.177. **a1450** *Pety Job* in Kail 135.441. **c1450** Idley 117.609, 122.899, 168.570: A bitter stomake as . . . gall, 189,1834. **c1450** *Myroure of oure Ladye* 224[22]. **c1450** *Three Kings of Cologne* in *Archiv* 129(1912) 65.701. **a1475** *Guy* [2] 81.2824: (t)he. **a1475** *Ludus Coventriae* 220.323. **a1475** *St. Birgitte* 60.27: the. **c1475** Henryson *Fables* 24.609. **c1485** *Mary Magdalene* (*Digby*) 92.997: ony. **1487** *O thou most noble* 330[9]. **a1500** *Medicines* in Brown *Lyrics XV* 274.40: He is more bitter than venyn or gall. **a1500** *Remedie of Love* CCCXXII^{v}[1.21]: any. **a1500** *Throwe a towne* in Sandison 122.42: the. **1504** Hawes *Example* Aa5^{v}[26]. **a1508** Skelton *Phyllyp* I 79.917. **1509** Barclay *Ship* I 217[3]. **1509** Watson *Ship* Bb4^{v} [9–10]. Apperson 50; Taylor and Whiting 149; Tilley G11; Whiting *Scots* I 176.

G9 As fell as **Gall**
c1515 Barclay *Eclogues* 83.823: Anger fell as gall.

G10 As green as (any) **Gall**
c1400 *Plowman's Tale* 152.162: With glitterand gown as grene as gall. **a1500** *Grace of the holy goste* in *Anglia* 3(1880) 536.118: And become grene as any galle.

G11 As sour as **Gall**
c1475 Henryson *Fables* 15.345: Thy gansell sour as gall. **a1509** Barclay *Ship* II 304[17]: Thou first art swete, at last more soure than gall.

G12 **Gall** and honey (sugar)
c1390 *Of clene maydenhod* 466.61–2: No more is no thing to him I-lyche Then Galle is to the hony-streme. **a1420** Lydgate *Troy* I 8.277–8: With sugred wordes under hony soote, His galle is hidde lowe by the rote, 18.218: Galle in his breste and sugre in his face, 26.516: Nor how to galle with hony he was lured, III 749.6321–4: And now the galle of conspirac(i)oun, That under sugre of symulacioun Hath so longe closid ben and hidde, In dede is now execut and kyd, **a1439** *Fall* I 111.4001: And lothsum gall can sugre eek undermyne, 217.655: Which galle and hony (togedir) doun distille, **a1449** *Fabula* in *MP* II 490.127–8: But, as to them, that han i-tastyd galle, Mor aggreable is the hoony soote, *Look* in *MP* II 768.111: Galle undir sugre hath doubyl bittirnesse, *Say the Best* in *MP* II 795.11: Sugurat gall with aureat eloquens, *Servant* in *MP* II 429.71–2: Whos galle ay newe dothe infect The sugre of men in every place. **a1449** Lydgate and Burgh *Secrees* 28.882: And sugryd galle honyed with Collusyoun. **a1475** *Tree* 118.15–6: A litel galle makith bitter a gret quantite of hony. **a1500** *Scorn of Women* in Robbins 224.19: Theyre gall ys hyd undyr a sugryd wede. **a1513** Dunbar *Of Content* 145.17: With gall in hart and huny in hals. Skeat 255. See **A236, C177, F517, H433, P289, V19.**

G13 To have one's **Gall** forburst (burst)
a1450 *Castle* 163.2901: For-brostyn, I trowe, be hys galle. **a1460** *Towneley Plays* 175.301: Bot I kyll hym and his I wote I brast my gall, 276.288–9: That he shall soyn yelde the gast, Ffor brestyn is his gall. Taylor and Whiting 149.

G14 As grease-grown (*fat*) as a **Galt** (*boar*)
a1400 *Morte Arthure* 33.1101: Gresse-growen as a galte.

G15 To groan like a **Galt**
a1400 *Alexander C* 246.4743: Umquile he groned as a galt.

G16 Each good **Game** is good (*well*) played
c1300 *Cayphas* in *Rel. Ant.* II 241[31–2]: A wel sooth sawe sothlich ys seyd, Ech god game ys god y-pleyd.

G17 **Game** and wisdom are good together
a1220 Giraldus *Descriptio Kambriae* in *Opera* VI 188[6]: God is to gedere gamen and wisdom (Latin, n. 3: Bona est una cum jocunditate sapientia).

G18 **Game** goes in the womb (*belly*)
a1300 *South English Legendary* II 510–1.573–5: Tho he hadde ynome our Loverdes flesh he sat longe in thoghte, And al laghinge an Englisch

thuse wordes forth broghte: Me saith game goth a wombe, and ich sigge game goth an hurte. Robbins-Cutler 2140.5.

G19 **Game** is good while it lasts, but it fares like the wind's blast
a1300 *Alisaunder* 15.235–9: Gamen is good whiles it wil last, Ac it fareth so wyndes blast— The werldelich man, and lesse and maast, Here leve there-inne so wel waast. Whan it is beest to thee henne it wil haste.

G20 **Games** gladly begun may have a heavy end
c1390 *Sir Gawain* 16.495–6: Gawan wats glad to begynne those gomnes in halle, Bot thagh the ende be hevy, haf ye no wonder. See **B200.**

G21 Half in **Game** and half in earnest
1468 Paston IV 305[28–9]: Halff in game and halff in ernest. NED Game 2a. See **S641.**

G22 How the **Game** goes, *etc.*
a1300 *Alisaunder* 61.1045–6: The gamen ne geth noughth al by lyne—There summe leigheth and summe whyne. **a1330** *Times of Edward II* 331.180: Alle wite ye, gode men, hu the gamen goth. **a1350** *Seven Sages C* 53.1553: When he wist how the gamin ferd. **c1375** Barbour *Bruce* I 163.36: Bot othir wayis the gammyn yude, 284.319: That (how) sa evir the gammyn ga. **a1393** Gower *CA* II 227.44–5: That how so that the game goth With othre men, I am noght glad. **c1420** Wyntoun III 41.487: Bot or the gamyn was al gane, V 219.918: Swa sal noucht al the gamyn gange. **c1430** ?Lydgate *Compleynt* 66.569: And pleynely thus the game hathe go. **c1450** Greene *Carols* 403.2: His herte is colde, Howsoevere the game go. **c1450** Idley 87.371: Thow shalt knowe how the game shall goo. **a1460** *Towneley Plays* 130.427: Bot how so the gam gose, 371.139: How so the gam crokys. **a1470** Malory III 1054.20–1: For howsomever the game goth, there was treson amonge us. **a1475** *Assembly of Gods* 13.426: I see well howe the game gooth. **c1489** Caxton *Aymon* I 239.28–9: And cared not how the game sholde goo, 270.6: How somever the game gooth, 315.26–7. **a1500** *Jeaste* 209.78–9: Whan they come, youe shall here tell Howe the game shall goo. **1501** Douglas *Palice* 28.3: The game gais uther gait. See **G137.**

G23 To begin the **Game**
1534 More *Comforte* 1222 B[10]: Here beganne nowe the game.

G24 To can (*know*) a **Game** worth two of that
a1400 *King Edward* 964.420: I con a game worthe thei twoo. Apperson 645: Trick; *Oxford* 670; Tilley T518; Taylor and Whiting 382.

G25 To find **Game** in one's hood
c1380 Chaucer *HF* 1809–10: And for to lawghe as they were wod, Such game fonde they in her hod, **c1385** *TC* ii 1109–10: Loke alwey that ye fynde Game in myn hood. **a1500** *Ragman Roll* 78.208: I rede that this game ende in your hood. MED game 6(b). See **J15.**

G26 When **Game** (*etc.*) is best, is best to leave (*varied*)
a1393 Gower *CA* III 477.3086–7*: In his proverbe seith the wise, Whan game is best, is best to leve. **a1400** *Proverbis of Wysdom* 245.50: When game is best, is tyme to lete, 64: In thy most lust is gwod to lete. **a1400** *Scottish Legends* I 54.885–6: For-thi quhen the play best is, Best is to lefe than I-wyse. **c1450** *Douce MS.52* 49.58: When game is best, Hit is tyme to rest. **c1450** *Fyrst thou sal* 88.42: When the gain is at the beste gode is to lete. **c1450** Idley 82.86: And leve thy pleye whan it is beste. **c1450** *Rylands MS.394* 99.7. **c1475** *Rawlinson MS. D 328* 120.40: When the game is best yt ys tyme to rest. Jente 20; *Oxford* 359; Tilley P399; Whiting *Scots* II 111.

G27 As wise as a **Gander**
1509 Barclay *Ship* I 179[10]: Shall home come agayne as wyse as a gander. Apperson 696; *Oxford* 716; Whiting *Drama* 314:137.

G28 To have as great devotion as a **Gander**
1509 Barclay *Ship* I 221[20–1]: Before the auters he to and fro doth wander With evyn as great devocyon as a gander.

G29 As swift as **Ganyie** (*arrow*)
1513 Douglas *Aeneid* III 246.82: Als swyft as ganye . . . fleys.

G30 To pierce like any **Ganyie**
a1513 Dunbar *On his Heid-Ake* 3.4: Perseing my brow as ony ganyie.

G31 He that **Gapes** till he be fed may famish for hunger
1549 Heywood *D* 33.30–1: He that gapeth till he be fed, Maie fortune to fast and famishe for honger. Apperson 243; *Oxford* 233; Tilley G31.

G32 To stop **Gaps** with rushes
1549 Heywood *D* 95.157: Ye will (quoth she) as soone stop gaps with rushes. Apperson 604; *Oxford* 623; Tilley G29. See **B607.**

G33 To stop two **Gaps** with one bush
1549 Heywood *D* 95.156: I will learne, to stop

two gaps with one bushe. Apperson 604; *Oxford* 623; Tilley G30. See **B607.**

G34 There is no **Garden** so full of fresh flowers but there are some weeds
a1449 Lydgate *Look* in *MP* II 769.145–6: There is no gardeyn so ful of fressh flouris, But that ther been among som weedys seene. Apperson 448; *Oxford* 233; Tilley G37. See **F301, H354.**

G35 An ivy **Garland** at a tavern door is a false token but there be good wine
c1475 *Why I Can't* 147.358–60: A fayre garlond of yve grene Whyche hangeth at a taverne dore, Hyt ys a false token as I wene, But yf there be wyne gode and sewer. See **A81, T47, W354.**

G36 What needs an ivy **Garland** to show a wineless tavern?
1436 *Libelle* 31.598–9: What nedeth a garlande whyche is made of ivye Shewe a taverne wynelesse?

G37 **Garlic** makes a man sleep
1508(1519) Stanbridge *Vulgaria* 15.4: Garlyke maketh a man to slepe. Apperson 243: Garlic makes a man wink; *Oxford* 233; Tilley G40.

G38 To pull **Garlic** (Pilgarlic)
c1400 *Beryn* 5.122–3: And yee shull here howe the Tapster made the Pardoner pull Garlik al the longe nyghte. **1483** *Catholicon Anglicum* 279: To Pille garleke; *vellicare.* **c1483** Caxton *Dialogues* 27.7: I shall not, I pylle the gharlyk. **1522** Skelton *Why Come* II 30.106: They may garlycke pyll, **a1529** *Garnesche* I 122.68: Your pyllyd garleke hed. Apperson 495; Tilley P324.

G39 To be driven to the **Gate**
a1338 Mannyng *Chronicle A* I 169.4830: Nede me dryveth until the gate. MED gate n. (1) 2e.

G40 Win the **Gate** and lightly have all the place after
1506 *Kalender* 71.28–30: So when enmys wyll take a castell, yf they wynne the gate they woll lyghtly have all the place after. Cf. Whiting *Scots* I 164: Entry. See **K69.**

G41 Tell it not in **Gath**
c1395 *WBible* II Kings (II Samuel) i 20: Nyle ye telle in Geth, nether tell ye in the weilottis of Ascolon. *Oxford* 233.

G42 To shine like a **Gem**
a800 *Phoenix* in *Exeter Book* 102.299–300: And þæt nebb lixeð Swa . . . gim. **a1400** *Scottish Legends* II 11.380: Yone man that schenis as a geme.

G43 **Gentilesse** is old richesse
c1395 Chaucer *CT* III[D] 1109–10: Ye speken of swich gentillesse As is descended out of old richesse. Apperson 307: Honour; *Oxford* 302; Tilley G60. See **A21.**

G44 **Gentle** must be won with gentilesse
c1440 Charles of Orleans 5.140: For gentille must be wonne with gentiles.

G45 A **Gentleman** says the best that he can
a1450 *Wall Verses at Launceston Priory* 342: Hit falleth to a gentil man To say the best that he can Of every man in his absence And say him soth in his presence. **c1450** *Utter thy langage* in Furnivall *Babees Book* 332.18–9: It is the properte of A gentilmann To say the beste that he cann. **a1478** *Sayings Printed by Caxton* in Skeat *Chaucerian* 450.7–10: Hit falleth to every gentilman To saye the best that he can In (every) mannes absence, And the soth in his presence.

G46 He may be called a **Gentleman** who can (*knows*) virtue and fair having (*manners*)
c1420 Wyntoun III 153.2003–4: He may be callit a gentil man, That wertu and fayr haffyne can. See **M57.**

G47 Farewell, gentle **Geoffrey**
c1475 *Mankind* 6.155: Farwell, jentyll Jaffrey! **1546** Heywood *D* 46.168: Farewell, gentill Geffrey. Apperson 204; *Oxford* 191; Tilley G81; Whiting *Drama* 344:538.

G48 As gentle as (a) **Gerfalcon**
c1475 *Guy*[1] 7 C 75–7: Gentil she was and as demure As girfauk, or fawkon to lure, That oute of muwe were drawe. See **F26.**

G49 As just as **German's** lips
1546 Heywood *D* 63.33–4: Just (quoth she) As Jermans lips. Apperson 244–5; *Oxford* 329; Tilley G87.

G50 A Christmas **Gestening** (*entertainment*) is quit at unset steven (*unappointed time, unexpectedly*)
c1460 *Take Good Heed* 207.39–40: Ffor a cristmas gestenyng, as clerkis rede, At on-set stevyn is quyt, in dede. See **M210.**

G51 Evil (Ill) **Gotten** worse (ill) spent
c1450 Capgrave *Solace* 38[12–3]: Because it was wrongfully gote it had the lesse grace for to be weel spent. **a1500** *Harley MS.2321* in *Rel. Ant.* I 208[5]: Evill gotten, wors spent. **1546** Heywood *D* 79.42: Yll gotten yll spent, **1555** *E* 166.126. Apperson 193–4; Jente 598; *Oxford* 315–6; Tilley G90. See **L467.**

G52 Soon **Gotten** soon spent
1546 Heywood *D* 79.42: Soone gotten soone spent. Apperson 588; *Oxford* 604; Tilley G91. See **C384, W284.**

G53 What one may not **Get** that would he have
c1375 Chaucer *Anel.* 203: For what he may not gete, that wolde he have.

G54 As pale as a **Ghost**
c1387-95 Chaucer *CT* I[A] 205: He was nat pale as a forpyned goost. Svartengren 234; Taylor and Whiting 151.

G55 To give up the **Ghost**
a900 *Old English Martyrology* 218.29: Ond hyre gast ageaf. **c1000** Aelfric *Homilies* I 430[19–20]: And mid þysum worde he ageaf his gast, *Lives* I 254.255: And heora gastas ageafon. **c1000** *WSG* Matthew xxvii 50: And asende hys gast. **c1300** *South English Legendary* I 67.148: That he(o) almest yaf the gost, 100.432: He was al upe the pointe thane gost forto yelde. **1384** Rolle *Form* in Allen *R. Rolle* 101.166–7: Als thou war redy to gyf the gast. **c1350** *Smaller Vernon Collection* 43.119–20. **1375** *Canticum de Creatione* 323.858. **c1375** Barbour *Bruce* II 146.214: As gud Cristyn the gast he gaf. **c1395** *WBible* Matthew xxvii 50: And gaf up the goost. Taylor and Whiting 152.

G56 To look like a **Ghost**
a1500 Medwall *Nature* G2ʳ[36]: Ye loke now as yt were a gost.

G57 As mickle as a **Giant**
c1400 *Laud Troy* I 217.7367: He was mechel as a geaunt. Whiting *NC* 414: big.

G58 As stable as a **Giant**
a1449 Lydgate *Fabules* in *MP* II 569.94: Stable as a geaunt.

G59 As stark as **Giants**
a1513 Dunbar *To the Quene* 60.21: Sum thocht tham selffis stark, lyk gyandis.

G60 **Giants** were on earth in those days
c1395 *WBible* Genesis vi 4: Sotheli giauntis weren on erthe in tho daies. *Oxford* 236.

G61 To be called to **Gib's** feast
1534 Heywood *Love* D2ʳ[3]: That eche kys of her mouth called you to gybbes fest. NED Gib sb.[1] 3.

G62 As free of **Gift** as a poor man of his eye
1546 Heywood *D* 47.206: As free of gyft, as a poore man of his eie. Apperson 235; *Oxford* 225; Tilley G96.

G63 Every **Gift** looks backward
c1025 *Durham Proverbs* 13.28: Gyfena gehwilc unde(r)bæc besihþ. Omnia dona retrorsum respiciunt.

G64 The **Gift** of a man alarges (*increases*) his way
c1395 *WBible* Proverbs xviii 16: The gift of a man alargith his weie. *Oxford* 237. See **B580, L80, M496.**

G65 The **Gift** unasked is far more to prize
c1420 Wyntoun VI 243.7031–2: And unaskyt he gaf oftsyis; The gift was the fer mar to prysse.

G66 **Gifts** blind the eyes of wise men (judges)
a900 *Laws of Alfred* in Liebermann I 40.46(E): Ne onfoh ðu næfre medsceattum, forðon hie ablendað ful oft wisra monna geðoht and hiora word onwendað. **c900** *Old English Cato* 7.32–3: Ne nym þu medsceattes, for heo ablændeð wisra manna geðancas and wændeð rihtwisra word. **c1000** Aelfric *Heptateuch* Deuteronomy xvi 19: For ðam medsceattas ablendað wisra manna geðancas and awendaþ rihtwisnessa word. **a1050** Defensor *Liber* 154[8–9]. **c1280** *South English Legendary: OT History* 84.75: Riche giftes and presents maken thise Juges blynde. **a1325** *Cursor* II 1000.17453–4: Quen giftes han for-don the sight, Qua mai than folu the reul o right. **c1395** *WBible* Exodus xxiii 8: Take thou not giftis, that blynden also prudent men, and destryen the wordys of just men, Deuteronomy xvi 19: For whi giftis blynden the iyen of wise men, Ecclesiasticus xx 31: Presentis and giftis blynden the iyen of jugis. **c1422** Hoccleve *Jereslaus's Wife* 176–7: Wher-of it is writen thus: "Yiftes or meede blynden the Juges yen." **a1450** *Gesta* 321[7]: This is to say, yiftis blyndith the yen of jugis. Tilley B659, G105. See **G82, 88.**

G67 **Gifts** can incline great hearts
a1420 Lydgate *Troy* III 734.5817: And yiftes grete hertis can encline.

G68 **Gifts** gar (*make*) crooked matters even
c1475 Henryson *Fables* 80.2323: And giftis garris crukit materis hald ffull evin. See **N149.**

G69 **Gifts** mar many (a) man
a1460 *Towneley Plays* 242.439: Bot gyftys marres many man.

G70 **Gifts** may do mickle
a1400 *Ipomadon A* 194.6806: I se well, gyftes may mekyll doo.

G71 The **Gifts** of Fortune are borrowed ware **c1503** More *Early Poems* [15] B[10]: The gyftes of fortune count them borowed ware.

G72 **Gifts** should not be asked again **1483** *Quatuor Sermones* 50[26–7]: And shall not be askyd ageyn, as gyftes of comyn wymmen and Jogelers. Cf. Taylor and Whiting 199: Indian giver.

G73 He despises a great **Gift** that knows not himself **1492** *Salomon and Marcolphus* 11[14–5]: He dyspyseth a great gifte that knowyth not hym self. See **K100.**

G74 He is bound that takes **Gift** **c1350** *Good Wife E* 162.75: Bunden is that giftes takitz. **a1450** *Myne awen dere* 156.223–4: The grete gifte he gifys the Will make the bonde whare thou was fre. Apperson 62; Tilley G104. Cf. Smith 135. See **B474, G77.**

G75 He loses **Gifts** that makes them to an ingrate **c1025** *Durham Proverbs* 14.35: Leana forleosaþ se þe lyþran deð. Premio caret qui beneficium ingrato prestet.

G76 He that gives a **Gift** by time (*early*) his thank is the more (*varied*) **c1386** Chaucer *LGW* F 451–2: For whoso yeveth a yifte, or dooth a grace, Do it by tyme, his thank ys wel the more. **c1412** Hoccleve *Regement* 168.4668–9: Yeve it (*a gift*) as blyve, his thank is wel the more; This vouche I on holy scriptures lore. **a1420** Lydgate *Troy* I 120.3639–40: For thing parformed in his due date More vertu hath than whan it commeth late, **c1433** *St. Edmund* 395.1044–6: For of such giftes that callid been roial Men seyn, with prynces who that hath to doone, A gifte is doublid whan it is yove soone. **a1440** Burgh *Cato* 26.894: For thyng yoven be tyme is yoven twise. **a1450** *Myne awen dere* 153.144: For he that dose betyme, he dose twyse. **a1471** Ashby *Policy* 28.497–8: Therfore some thinges oons by tyme doon Ben worthe twyes other thing overgoon. **1483** Caxton *Cato* D5r[33]: It is sayd who gyveth sone gyveth twyes. Apperson 246:11; *Oxford* 239–40; Skeat 210; Tilley G125; Walther I 232.2032–4. See **T45.**

G77 He that takes **Gifts** sells his freedom **c1390** *Proverbes of diverse profetes* 528.101–4: Ffreo he is to do man riht That yift ne present taketh of no wiht; He that yiftes (taketh) without decert, His freodam he sulleth and leoseth apert. Tilley G104. See **G74.**

G78 He was full wise that first gave **Gift** (meed) **a1300** *Tristrem* 19.626–7: He was ful wise, y say, That first yave yift in land. **c1300** *Havelok* 53.1635: He was ful wis that first yaf mede. **a1393** Gower *CA* III 75.4719–22: For thus men sein, in every nede He was wys that ferst made mede; For where as mede mai noght spede, I not what helpeth other dede, 77.4798–9: So was he wys that ferst yaf mede, For mede kepeth love in house. **c1420** Wyntoun VI 199.6450: Qwha giffis sic giftis he is richt wysse. Apperson 697; *Oxford* 719.

G79 Little **Gift** draws much love **c1450** *Consail and Teiching* 76.364: Fore lytill gift drawis mekil luf.

G80 A little **Gift** without behest (*promise*) is more dear than a great thing of behest **c1390** *Proverbes of diverse profetes* 547.373–6: Mon holdeth a luite yift more dere With-outen be-heste with gode chere, Then he wolde of a gret thinge Of bi-heste with long tariinge. See **F643.**

G81 Little **Gifts** make friend of foe **a1300** Lawman I 329 B 7715–6: Of mannes fo maki frend, With lutell yiftes. See **L82.**

G82 Noble **Gifts** bring right to wough (*wrong*) (*varied*) **c1300** *South English Legendary* II 647.1124–5: Noble yiftes and giuwe(l)s with hom also hy nome For therwith me may the righte bringe to wou. **a1450** *Myne awen dere* 172.727–31: And thou be maister or justice For to gif dome in grete assyce, To take giftes I the forbede, For ofte will a man for mede Torne righte to wrange and wrange to ryghte. See **G66, 88, 296, M494, N149.**

G83 Praise not the **Gift** but the will **a1450** *Myne awen dere* 175.812: Prays noght the gifte, bot all the will. See **W267.**

G84 That **Gift** is held more dear which is given with glad cheer **a1400** *Romaunt B* 2383–6: For men that yift holde more dere, That yeven is with gladsome chere. That yift nought to preisen is, That man yeveth maugre his. See **L23.**

G85 Throw no **Gift** at the giver's head **1546** Heywood *D* 47.199: Throw no gyft agayne at the gevers head, 1555 *E* 155.58. Apperson 246; *Oxford* 656; Tilley G101.

G86 What is freer than **Gift?** **1451** Paston II 256[12]: And askyd here Wat was freer than gyfte. **c1475** Henryson *Fables*

78.2268: And is thair oucht (sayis thou) frear than gift? **a1500** *New Year's Morning* in *Pol. Rel. and Love Poems* 67.24–5: Men sei that no thinge is so free as gyfte, And to take it ayene y were fulle to blame. Apperson 235; *Oxford* 463; Tilley G103.

G87 With **Gift(s)** a man may make friends (*varied*)
a1393 Gower *CA* III 163.7726: With yifte a man mai frendes make. **a1533** Berners *Arthur* 361[31–4]: Give ye gyftes largely to these noble knightes, . . . the which shal make you to be beloved of every body; . . . there is noo sweter thynge than largely to gyve.

G88 With **Gifts** men may overgo (*overcome, bribe*) good wise men
c1350 *Good Wife E* 162.73: Gode wise men with yiftes men mai overgon. See **G66, 82, M322.**

G89 As sweet as the **Gillyflower**
a1500 *Beauty of his Mistress III* in Robbins 127.18: And your-selfe as swete as ys the gely-floure.

G90 To give up the **Girdle**
a1400 *Alexander C* 6.181: Bot gefe thaim up the girdill. Apperson 247; Tilley G117.

G91 To hang at one's **Girdle**
1456 Paston III 69[3–5]: So wold Jesus, one of yow iii., or som suche othyr yn your stede, myght hang at hys gyrdyll dayly to aunsuer hys materes.

Give, sb.

G92 Mickle **Give** (*gift*) ofdraws (*attracts*) love
a1200 *Ancrene* 197.27–8: Muchel yeove of-draheth luve.

Give, vb.

G93 Better to **Give** than to take
a1393 Gower *CA* III 163.7725: Betre is to yive than to take. **c1395** *WBible* Acts xx 35: It is more blesful to gyve, than to resseyve. **a1470** Parker *Dives* A2r[1.2–5]: Cryste Jhesus sayd thus . . . It is, he sayth, more blysfull to gyve than to take. **1546** Heywood *D* 27.34: Thus better to geve then take, **1555** *E* 148.11: Better give then take. Apperson 43; *Oxford* 40; Smith 136; Tilley G119.

G94 **Give** and take
1519 Horman *Vulgaria* 98[31]: A man muste somtyme gyve and somtyme take. *Oxford* 238; Taylor and Whiting 152–3; Tilley G121; Whiting *Drama* 196, 229.

G95 **Give** me and I thee and so may (shall) we friends be
a1400 *Six Things in Prayer* in *Yorkshire Writers* I 302[17–8]: Thane by-twix us may be fulfillide that one ynglysche es sayd: Gyff thou me and I the, and so may we frendis be! **c1450** *Douce MS.52* 44.3: Yefe me and I the, And so schul we frendus be. **c1450** *Rylands MS.394* 95.20. Jente 366.

G96 He that **Gives** not what he loves has not what he desires
1340 *Ayenbite* 77[33–4]: He thet ne yefth thet he loveth: he ne nymth thet he wylneth. **c1400** *Vices and Virtues* 76.12–3: As men seyn in olde tyme: "Who-so gyveth nought that he loveth, ne hath not that he desyreth." **1484** Caxton *Royal Book* G5v[16–8]: It is trouthe that is comunelye sayd, who that gyveth not that whyche he loveth, he taketh not whiche he desyreth. See **A106, L233.**

G97 He that will not **Give** shall not take
a1393 Gower *CA* III 77.4788–9: What man that scars is of his good And wol noght yive, he schal noght take. Whiting *Scots* I 177.

G98 One may **Give** what were better got
a1325 *Hendyng C* 184.14: Soche, man, thou misth yevin that betir were getin, Quod Marcol. Kneuer 30; Schleich 254–5; Singer III 128–9.

G99 They that **Give** are ever welcome
a1533 Berners *Huon* 235.28–9: It is a sayenge that they that gyve are ever welcome. Apperson 247. See **H52.**

G100 To **Give** and sell someone
a1500 *Clerk and the Nightingale I* in Robbins 173.24: She may me gif and sell. See **B637.**

G101 The **Glad** and the sorry sing not all one song
1492 *Salomon and Marcolphus* 13[8–9]: They synge not al oon songe, the glad and the sory. See **F697, H149, W551.**

G102 All earthly **Gladness** finishes with woe
1513 Douglas *Aeneid* II 65.20–1: Heir verifeit is that proverbe teching so, "All erdly glaidness fynysith with wo." See **J58, W671.**

G103 All worldly **Gladness** is meddled (*mingled*) with grievance
a1439 Lydgate *Fall* I 57.2049: Al worldli gladnesse is medlid with grevaunce. See **B351, J59.**

G104 The **Gladness** of one is rage to another
a1420 Lydgate *Troy* I 168.835: Gladnes of on is to another rage. (In games of chance.) Cf.

Tilley M483: One man's meat. See **G329, H653, M30, 486, O42.**

G105 To have **Gladness** men often drink pain and great distress
c1385 Chaucer *TC* iii 1215–6: For to han gladnesse, Men drynken ofte peyne and gret distresse. Apperson 50.

G106 As sharp as a **Glaive** (*sword*)
1477 Rivers *Dictes* 25[23]: An evil tonge was sharper than a glayve. **a1500** *Court of Love* 424.544: And whet their tong as sharp as . . . gleyve.

G107 To glow like **Glaives** on gleed (*fire*)
c1475 *Golagros* 19.558: As glavis glowand on gleid, grymly thai ride.

G108 As bright as (the, any) **Glass**
c1000 Aelfric *Homilies* II 518[9–10]: His lic . . . beorhtre ðonne glæs, *Lives* II 304.1378–9. **c1225** *Horn* 3 C 14: He was bright so the glas. **c1300** *Beves* 66.167–8: The cite of Damasce, That shon as bryght as glas, 132.15: Hys eyen were bryghte as any glas. **c1330** *Degare* 79.353 (*var.*): eny. **c1330** *Seven Sages A* 150 E 3068: any. **a1338** Mannyng *Chronicle B* I 95[20]. **c1385** Chaucer *CT* I[A] 1958: any. **a1398**(1495) Bartholomaeus-Trevisa G4r[1.36–7]: The glasy humour is clene and pure and bryghte as glasse. **a1400** *Torrent* 20.552–4: On the tayle an hed ther wase, That byrnyd Bryght as anny glase, In fyer whan yt was dyght. **c1400** *Laud Troy* I 162.5474: any. **c1408** Lydgate *Reson* 12.436. **1410** Walton *Boethius* 59[19–20]: The wawes than that were . . . bright Lyk as the glas or as the someres day. **a1439** Lydgate *Fall* III 924.208: Brotil glas sheweth brihter than doth steel. **c1440** Charles of Orleans 157.4669. **c1450** Capgrave *Katharine* 225.900. **c1450** *Edward the Confessor Prose I* 101[36]. **c1450** *How mankinde dooth* in Furnivall *Hymns* 67.297. **c1450** *Northern Passion* 160 A 411*: any. **c1450** *Owayne Miles* (*Cotton Caligula*) 118.465. **a1475** *Assembly of Gods* 9.276. **a1475** *Guy*² 4.132: ane. **c1475** *Guy*¹ 591 C 10537: any. **1483** Caxton *Golden Legende* 200v[1.9–10], 311v[2.29]. **a1500** *Beves* 128 M 2427. **c1500** Newton 270.25. Svartengren 224; Tilley G135.

G109 As britchel (*brittle, etc.*) as (any, the) **Glass**
a1200 *Ancrene* 86.13–4: This bruchele vetles bruchel as is eani gles, 27–8. **c1400** *Vices and Virtues* 80.32–3: That is bruteler and febler than is the glas. **a1420** Lydgate *Troy* III 797.854: Brotel as glas, pretendinge outward stel, **a1449** *Testament* in *MP* I 344.397: Lyke brotel glasse, not stable nor like stell. **a1460** *Towneley Plays* 120.121: And brekyll as glas. **1471** Ripley *Compound* 184[15]: Then brotyll wyll thy *Ferment* as any glas be. **c1475** Henryson *Testament* 125.569: Brukkill as glas. **1506** Hawes *Pastime* 204.5364: Of his wanton youthe brytle as the glasse. Apperson 68; Svartengren 265; Taylor and Whiting 153; Tilley G134; Whiting *Drama* 314:140, *Scots* I 177.

G110 As clean as **Glass**
c1425 *St. Mary Oignies* 156.16: Clenner than glas. **c1450** Idley 120.751: His consciens was clensed as clene as glas. **a1460** *Towneley Plays* 221.542–3: As cleyn . . . As . . . shynand glas. **1479** Rivers *Cordyal* 123.12. Whiting *Scots* I 177.

G111 As clear as (the, any) **Glass**
c1350 *Apocalypse* 120.2: A Cee clere as glas, 121.3, 192.21, 193.7. **c1380** Chaucer *Boece* I m. vii 5–6: The wawes, that whilom weren clere as glas, **c1390** *CT* II[B] 194–5. **c1390** *Christenemon and a Jew* in *Vernon* II 485.42: Seththe cler as the glas. **a1400** *Ancrene* (*Recluse*) 196.11–2, 25–6. **1410** Walton *Boethius* 59[19–20]: the. **a1422** Lydgate *Life* 501.1018. **c1450** *De Claris Mulieribus* 36.724. **c1450** *How mankinde dooth* in Furnivall *Hymns* 67.297. **1481** Caxton *Reynard* 11[14–5]: Polyshed as clere as ony glas. Svartengren 362; Taylor *Comparisons* 26; Tilley G135; Whiting *Drama* 314:140, *NC* 414.

G112 As frail as **Glass**
1436 *Libelle* 30.579–80: But wee be frayle as glasse And also bretyll. **c1475** Henryson *Want of Wise Men* 190.45: Gude faith is flemyt, worthin fraellar than glas.

G113 As gray as (any) **Glass** (*of eyes only*)
a1300 *Maximian* 100.266: Min heien so grei so glas. **a1350** *Isumbras* 20.247(*var.*): His eyen are gray as any glasse. **c1350** *Libeaus* 53.943. **c1387-95** Chaucer *CT* I[A] 152, **c1390** I[A] 3974. **c1400** *Toulouse* 235.343: any. **a1500** *Beauty of his Mistress III* in Robbins 126.14: With your rollyng eyes whyche ar as glasse clere (*MS.:* grey). **c1500** Newton 270.25. Svartengren 236; Whiting *Drama* 314:140.

G114 As green as (any) **Glass**
a1325 *Otuel and Roland* 68.291: The helm was grene as glas. **a1400** *Eglamour* 52. *var. after* 774: Hys wynges were grene as any glas. **1481** Caxton *Reynard* 82[28]: The thirde colour was grene lyke glas. Whiting *Ballad* 27.

G115 As pure as **Glass**
a1405 Lydgate *Black Knight* in *MP* II 386.78:

The water pure as glas. **c1450** *Edward the Confessor Prose I* 101[36]. **c1502** *Lyfe of Joseph* 49.387–8: Whan the nightyngale Wrestes out her notes musycall as pure as glas.

G116 As slidder (*slippery*) as any **Glass**
c1303 Mannyng *Handlyng* 172.5259–60: The plank . . . Was as sledyr as any glas. Cf. Taylor and Whiting 153: slippery.

G117 As sliding (*perishable*) as **Glass** (*etc.*) (A number of single quotations are brought together here)
a900 *Old English Martyrology* 150.6–7: þeos mennisce tyddernes bið swa slidende swa þæt glæs. **a1338** Mannyng *Chronicle A* I 74.2081: Sabren hit highte, as whit as glas. **1340** *Ayenbite* 82[13–4]: Thet more is . . . fyeble thanne gles. **c1380** *Pearl* 37.1025: The stretes of golde as glasse al bare. **c1450** *Owayne Miles* (*Brome*) 98.414: Yt wos glyddyr as ony glass, (*Cotton Caligula*) 118.413–4: A brygge ther was, Ffor sothe kener then ony glasse. **a1475** *Assembly of Gods* 19.614: Formyd lyke a dragon, scalyd harde as glas.

G118 As smooth as any **Glass**
c1200 *St. Katherine* (*Royal*) 82.1660–1: Isliket and ismaket As eni gles smethest. **c1400** *Laud Troy* I 281.9521–2: Every a ston of Marbil was As smethe as any glas. Apperson 582; Taylor and Whiting 153; Tilley G136; Whiting *Ballad* 27.

G119 It is not all true that (ap)pears in **Glass**
a1500 *Clerk and the Husbandman* in Robbins 181.28: Hyt ys nat all tru that peryth in glasse!

G120 To gleam like the (any) **Glass**
a1400 *Destruction of Troy* 127.3943: (*Eyes*) glemyt as the glasse. **a1445** *Carl* 154.607: The wallys glemyd as any glasse. **a1475** *Alas that any kyndeman* in *Rel. Ant.* I 77[4]: And yet he glemyd as any glas.

G121 To glisten (*glitter*) like **Glass**
c800 *Rune Poem* in *ASMP* 28.30: Glisnaþ glæshluttur.

G122 To glister (*glitter*) like **Glass**
a1529 Skelton *Elynour* I 110.482: Her face glystryng lyke glas, *Garnesche* I 117.37: Your ien glyster as glasse.

G123 To glitter like **Glass**
a1400 *Morte Arthure* 91.3097: All gleterand as glase undire grene hyllys. **a1425** *Metrical Paraphrase OT* 12.6056: And brygh glyterand as any glas. **c1470** *Wallace* 142.78: Baith hilt and hand all glitterand lik the glas. Whiting *Scots* I 178.

G124 To shine like (the, any, a) **Glass**
a1300 *Alisaunder* 426 L 6547: Theo ladies schynen so the glas. **c1300** *Beves* 125.2675: His wingges schonn so the glas. **c1380** Chaucer *HF* 1289: That shoone ful lyghter than a glas. **c1380** *Pearl* 37.1018: O jasporye, as glas that glysnande schon. **c1387–95** Chaucer *CT* I[A] 198: His heed was balled, that shoon as any glas. **a1425** *Metrical Paraphrase OT* 33.1082: And (gart) hi(r) face to schyn os glasse. **c1450** Idley 91.604. **a1460** *Towneley Plays* 281.82–3: any. **a1475** *Vision of Philibert* 33[12]: the. **1480** Caxton *Ovyde* 130[41]. **c1499** Skelton *Bowge* I 43.353: His face shone lyke a glas. **1501** Douglas *Palice* 50.14: the. Whiting *Scots* I 178.

G125 To to-burst like brickle (*brittle*) **Glass** (*etc.*) (A number of single quotations are brought together here)
c1200 *St. Katherine* (*Royal*) 100.2002–3: Toburston and tobreken As thah hit were bruchel gles. **c1380** *Pearl* 40.1106: On golden gates that glent as glasse. **a1400** *Torrent* 16.426: Yt (*a sword*) ys ase glemyrryng ase the glase. **1447** Bokenham 19.689: An huge dragoun, glasteryng as glas. **c1485** *Mary Magdalene* (*Digby*) 91.969: They brast as ony glase.

G126 Who that beholds in the **Glass** well he sees himself, *etc.*
1484 Caxton *Aesop* 56[5–10]: For men sayn comynly who that beholdeth in the glas well he seeth hym self. And who seeth hym self wel he knoweth hym self, And who that knowith hym self lytel he preyseth hym self, And who that preyseth hym self lytyll he is ful wyse and sage. See **K100.**

G127 As bright as **Gleam**
c1308 Adam Davy 12.27–8: Hii wexen out so brighth so glem That shyneth of the sonne-bem.

G128 As red as any **Gleam**
c1500 *Arthour and M.*[3] 467.1467: The other red as any gleame.

G129 To glent (*shine*) like **Gleam**
a1400 *Le Morte A.* 106.3493: And sythe, as gleme, A-way it glente.

G130 To glide like the (a) **Gleam**
a1450 *York Plays* 135.272: Als the gleme in the glasse gladly thow glade. **c1480** *Contemplacioun* 232.1295–6: As thingis transitore and nocht perpetuale And of the sone gois glyding as a gleme.

G131 To glisten like (the) **Gleam**
a1225 *St. Marherete* 20.31–2: The glisnede ase gleam deth. **a1400** *Destruction of Troy* 100.3066–7: With a necke . . . Glissonand as the glemes that glenttes of the snaw, 357–8.10970–1: All thaire colouris by corse were of cleane white, As the glyssenond glemes that glenttes on the sknowe.

G132 To glitter like the **Gleam**
a1450 *York Plays* 308.20: And myne eyne thei glittir like the gleme in the glasse.

G133 To go like a **Gleam**
c1390 *Each Man* in Brown *Lyrics XIV* 140.28: Riht as a glentand glem hit geth.

G134 To go **Gleaning** before the cart has carried
1549 Heywood *D* 44.113: Thou goest a glenyng er the cart have caried. Apperson 248; *Oxford* 240; Tilley G140.

G135 As gray as the **Glede** (*kite*)
c1380 *Cleanness* 62.1696: And al wat gray as the glede.

G136 As greedy as a **Glede**
c1500 *King Hart* 98.27: Desyr, als gredie as ane glede. Svartengren 182.

G137 The **Glee** (*affair*) is gone other ways
c1375 Barbour *Bruce* I 235.701: Bot othir wayis all yeid the gle, II 31.176: Bot othir wayis the gle is gane. NED Glee lc. See **G22.**

G138 To play another **Glee** (*game*)
a1450 *South English Legendary* (*Bodley*) 350.130: And ic him wol teche to pleye an other gle.

G139 As burning as (the, any) **Gleed** (*coal*)
a1400 *Child* 318.244: His faders soule brennynge as glede. **a1420** Lydgate *Troy* I 344.6997: Of hasty Ire brennyng as the glede, 379.8223: Brennyng of Ire as the fyry glede, III 641.2630: the, **c1421** *Thebes* 70.1667: the, **a1430** *Pilgrimage* 73.2717–8: the, 89.3351–2: Hyr Eyen . . . Brennyng bryht as any glede, **a1439** *Fall* I 226.949: any, **a1449** *Exposition* in *MP* I 62.74: The foure wheelys, brennyng briht as gleede, *Letabundus* in *MP* I 49.22: the.

G140 As fervent as the **Gleed**
a1449 Lydgate *St. Edmund* in *MP* I 127.94: Brennyng in charite, fervent as the gleede.

G141 As fierce as any **Gleed**
1513 Douglas *Aeneid* IV 38.1: Turnus . . . als fers as ony gleid.

G142 As hot as (the, any) **Gleed**
a1300 *What Love Is Like* in Brown *Lyrics XIII* 108.11: Love is hardi and hot as glouinde glede. **c1385** Chaucer *TC* iv 337: A thousand sikes, hotter than the gleede. **a1405** Lydgate *Black Knight* in *MP* II 392.231: And hote as glede now sodenly I suete, **a1420** *Troy* I 35.796: To make hem brenne, hoot as any glede, III 590.909: any, 634.2403–4: any. **c1430** ?Lydgate *Compleynt* 66.525: Now hattere, than the verray glede. **a1475** *Guy*[2] 8.261–2: any. **a1500** *Lufaris Complaynt* 721.100. **1513** Douglas *Aeneid* II 159.35. Whiting *Scots* I 178. See **C327.**

G143 As red as (any, a, the) **Gleed**
c1300 *Horn* 28 L 505–6: Sette him on a stede, Red so eny glede. **c1330** *Seven Sages A* 133 F 2775–6: And tongys theryn also redd, As hyt were a brennyng gledd. **c1378** *Piers* B ii 12: any. **c1385** Chaucer *CT* I[A] 1997: any, **c1386** *LGW* F 235: Twoo firy dartes, as the gledes rede. **c1390** *Castel of Love* 403.1543–4: eny. **a1400** *Athelston* 84.572: ony, 91.782: ony. **1406** Hoccleve *Male Regle* 30.159: the. **c1500** *Smith* 324.182: a. Apperson 526: fire; Svartengren 249. See **C329.**

G143a **Gleed-red**
c1200 *Sawles Warde* (*Bodley*) 10.77–8: An unrude raketehe gledread of fure, 16.136: Hare eawles gledreade.

G144 To be colored like the **Gleed**
c1390 Chaucer *CT* VII 2384[B3574]: Caught with the lymrod coloured as the gleede. **a1420** Lydgate *Troy* I 1.11: Of colour schewyng lyche the fyry glede.

G145 To blaze like a **Gleed**
c1350 *Alexander A* 148.729: And bright blased his blee as a brend glede.

G146 To blow at the **Gleed**
c1380 *Ferumbras* 74.2230: We have a game in this contray: to blowen atte glede. Apperson 57; *Oxford* 101. See **C334, F199.**

G147 To burn like a (the, any) **Gleed**
a1393 Gower *CA* II 227.39–40: So that I brenne as doth a glede For Wrathe. **a1400** *Morte Arthure* 4.116–7: Egh(e)n, That full brymly for breth brynte as the gledys. **a1420** Lydgate *Troy* I 73.2056: Al-be for hym I brenne as doth the glede, 208.2221: the, 235.3168: the, 310.5811: any. **a1475** *Seege of Troye* 168 H 162r: ony. **a1500** *Guy*[4] 25.495: any. Whiting *Scots* I 178. See **C335.**

G148 To gleam like **Gleeds**
a1400 *Awntyrs* 147.393: He and his gambesouns glomede als gledys.

G149 To glister (*glitter*) like the **Gleed**
c1380 *Ferumbras* 138.4437–8: Ys eghene depe, And glystryd as the glede. Whiting *Ballad* 27. See **C336.**

G150 To glitter like the **Gleed**
a1400 *Siege of Jerusalem* 23.415: Hit glitered as gled (*var.* red) fur, ful of gold riche. Svartengren 227; Whiting *Scots* I 178.

G151 To glore (*shine*) like any **Gleed**
c1375 *St. Bartholomew* 122.311: His eghen glored als any glede. Whiting *Scots* I 178.

G152 To glow like (a, any, the) **Gleed**
a1387 *Piers* C xx 189: So that the holy gost gloweth bote as a glede. **a1400** *Siege of Jerusalem* 73.1251–2: With perles and peritotes, alle the place ferde As glowande gledfur that on gold st(r)iketh. **1400** *Love god, and drede* in Kail 4.110: Er his soule glowe as glede. **1410** Walton *Boethius* 126[12]: In all thyn herte glowen as a glede. **1414** *Dede is worchyng* in Kail 56.14: When it is hot, and gloweth as glede. **a1425** *Somer Soneday* in *Rel. Ant.* II 8[18]: a. **a1445** *Carl* 128.236–7: a. **c1450** *Pilgrimage LM* 23[31]: Hire eyen glowynge as gleedes. **a1508** Dunbar *Tretis* 87.108: That as a glemand gleyd glowis my chaftis. **1513** Douglas *Aeneid* II 74.55: Hir eyn glowit as ony gleid for ire, III 164.5: the. **a1529** Skelton *Garnesche* I 117.37: a. Whiting *Scots* I 178.

G153 To spring over like (a) **Gleed**
a1338 Mannyng *Chronicle B* II 295[14]: Was no cheyne so hie, that he ne sprong over als glede.

G154 Wry (*cover*) the **Gleed** and hotter is the fire (*varied*)
c1385 Chaucer *TC* ii 538–9: And wel the hotter ben the gledes rede, That men hem wrien with asshen pale and dede. **c1385** Usk 133.38–9: Wel the hoter is the fyr that with asshen is overleyn. **c1386** Chaucer *LGW* 735–6: As, wry the glede, and hotter is the fyr; Forbede a love, and it is ten so wod. **1420** Lydgate *Temple* 15.359–62: Me to complein, god wot, I am not boold, Unto no wight, nor a woord unfold Of al my peyne, allas the hard(e) stond! That hatter brenne that closid is my wounde. Apperson 214; *Oxford* 203; Skeat 162; Tilley F264, 265. See **F185.**

G155 To go like a **Gleeman's** bitch
a1376 *Piers* A v 197–9: Thenne gon he for to go lyk a gleo-monnes bicche, Sum tyme asyde and sum tyme arere, As hose leith lynes to lacche with foules. Apperson 166.

G156 All worldly **Glory** is transitory
1422 Lydgate *Serpent* 54.5: All worldely glori is transtori. **1456** Hay *Law* 46.33: Et sic transit gloria mundi. **a1500** *Imitatione* (*1*) 6.10–1: Hou sone passith the glory of this worlde! Stevenson 782:3. Cf. Whiting *Scots* I 178. See **W671.**

G157 **Glory** (?*fame*) is best
c900 *Maxims* in *Exeter Book* 159.80: Dom biþ selast. See **H448.**

G158 **Glory** (*praise*) noys (*harms*) many
1480 Caxton *Ovyde* 49[22]: But glorye noyeth many. See **H450.**

G159 Not praise (for) a **Glove**
c1250 *Hendyng O* 192.6[4]: Ne preise ich the nouht for a glove.

G160 Not set at a **Glove**
c1450 *Pilgrimage LM* 180[25–7]: I hatte jolyfnesse the lyghte . . . that sette nouht alle daungeres at a gloove.

G161 Not the mountance (*value*) of a **Glove**
a1500 *Alexander-Cassamus* 54.70–1: No man hath Joye of me, As towchyng love, the mow(n)taunce of my glove.

G162 Not worth a **Glove**
a1325 *Cursor* III 1509.26991: Bot til unskil noght worth a glove. **a1400** *Athelston* 82.492–4: I schal nought leve on thy lond Wurth the gloves on thy hond, To begge ne to borwe.

G163 As nesh (*soft*) as **Glue**
a1475 *Crafte of Lymnynge of Bokys* in *Early English Miscellanies* (Warton Club, 1855) 82[25–6]: Sethe hit to hit be as nesshe as glew.

G164 The **Glutton** says (to his stomach) "Though thou burst, this good morsel shall be eaten"
1340 *Ayenbite* 56[9-11]: Ac the tonge the lyckestre him ansuereth: and zayth, "Thagh thou ssoldest to-cleve: ich nelle naght lete askapie this mes." **c1400** *Vices and Virtues* 53.18–9: Than answereth the glotouns tonge and seith, "theigh thou breste, this good mossel schal be ete." Cf. Apperson 37: Better belly burst; *Oxford* 38; Tilley B291.

G165 None sighs so sore as the **Glutton** that may (eat) no more
a1500 Hill 129.46: Non sigheth so sore as the gloton that mai no more. Apperson 248; Tilley G144.

G166 **Gluttony** is the mother of all vices
1474 Caxton *Chesse* 131[9–10]: And lucan sayth that glotonye is the moder of alle vices.

G167 Gluttony (Excess, Repletion) slays more than sword (knife) (*varied*)
c1400 *Seven Deadly Sins* in Wyclif *SEW* III 158–9: Ffor, as clerkes seyn comynly, glotorie slees mo men then dos swerde. **1406** Hoccleve *Male Regle* 28.111–2: But .xx.[ti] wynter past continuelly, Excesse at borde hath leyd his knyf with me. **c1410** Edward of York *Master* 8[22–4]: For as Ypocras telleth, ful repleccions of metes sleeth moo men that (*for* than) eny swerde or knyfe. **a1415** *Lanterne* 45.18–9: Certis excesse of mete and drink sleeth many moo than doith the swerid. **a1430** Lydgate *Pilgrimage* 351.12926–8: Excesse and superfluyte Slen mo men, nyh and ffere, Than outher swerd, dagger or spere. **a1450** *Castle* 125.1620: For gloton kyllyth with-owtyn knyf. **1483** Caxton *Cato* F8v[2–4]: The mowth . . . sleeth more folke than the swerde in bataylles. **1509** Barclay *Ship* II 266[5–7]: Mo dye By glotony . . . Than by hunger, knyfe, or deth naturall. **1522** More *Treatyce* 100 H[7–10]: There should be found (as Salomon saith) mo dead of the cup and the kechen, than of the dente of sworde. Apperson 248; *Oxford* 241; Tilley G148. See **A154, K89, M142.**

G168 Gluttony wakens lechery (*varied*)
c1200 Orm II 50.11653–8: Forr gluterrnesse wacceneþþ all Galnessess laþe strenncþe, And all þe flaeshess kaggerrleʒʒc And alle fule lusstess Biginnenn þaere and springenn ut Off gluterrnessess rote, 70.12222–3: Forr all þe flaeshess fule lusst Wacceneþþ þurrh glutterrnesse. **a1333** Shoreham *Poems* 95.273–6: Her hys for-bode glotenye, So ich the by-hote; For hyt norysseth lecherye, Ase fer, the brondes hote, 112.381–4: Ac glotonye entycyth To lecherye her, Ase that hy norysseth Hote brondes thet fere. **c1395** *WBible* Ecclesiastes vii 3 *gloss:* Wherynne the synne of gloteny is ofte doon, and the synne of leccherie sueth ofte. **a1400** *Proverbis of Wysdom* 246.121–2: Be well ware of glotenye; For hit engendrithe lechery. **c1412** Hoccleve *Regement* 137.3804–5: Glotonye is ful plesant to the fende, To leccherie redy path is sche. **a1430** Lydgate *Pilgrimage* 355.13063–6: And for that I am glotonye, I dar trewly specefye How Venus (yt ys no ffayl) Evere me sueth at the tayl, **a1439** *Fall* III 681.235–6: The vice of glotenye, Which is norice unto lecherie. **a1450** *Castle* 144.2258–60: In meselynge glotonye, With goode metis and drynkys trye, I norche my syster Lecherye. **1474** Caxton *Chesse* 131[22–3]: And thus the vice of glotonye provoketh lecherye. **1509** Barclay *Ship* II 328[12–3]: The greattest part to glotony inclyne Whiche is the rote of Venus insolence. See **B426, C125, L228, W359, 553.**

G169 To be taken in one's **Gnare** (*snare*)
c1350 *Prose Psalter* 9 (9.16): In the gnares (*var.* grynnes) that the folk hid, is her fote taken. See **P232, S427.**

G170 As manly as a **Gnat**
a1500 *Colyn Blowbol* 105.295: Than arn they as manly as a ganat. Cf. Whiting *Drama* 314:143.

G171 As thick as **Gnats**
a1300 *Arthour and M.*[1] 255.9161–2: Gavelokes, also thicke flowe So gnattes, ichil avowe.

G172 Not set a **Gnat**
c1516 Skelton *Magnificence* 53.1704–5: I wolde not set a gnat By Magnyfycence.

G173 Not the mountance (*value*) of a **Gnat**
c1390 Chaucer *CT* IX[H] 254–5: Noght worth to thee, as in comparisoun, The montance of a gnat.

G174 Not work as much as a **Gnat**
c1395 Chaucer *CT* III[D] 346–7: After thy text, ne after thy rubriche, I wol nat wirche as muchel as a gnat.

G175 Not worth a **Gnat**
c1400 *Plowman's Tale* 161.459: Such maters be nat worth a gnat. Apperson 457; Tilley G149.

G176 To eat a **Gnat**
c1516 Skelton *Magnificence* 38.1193: He wyll make the ete a gnat. See **F349.**

G177 To starve (*die*) like a **Gnat**
c1385 Chaucer *TC* iv 595: Than sterve here as a gnat, withouten wounde.

G178 To strain at a **Gnat** and swallow a camel (*varied*)
a900 Alfred *Gregory* 439.23–5: Be ðæm wæs gecweden on ðæm godspelle to Fariseum ðæt hi wiðbleowen ðære fleogan, and forswulgun ðone olfend. **c1000** *WSG* Matthew xxiii 24: La blindan latteowas, ge drehnigeað þone gnætt aweg, and drincað þone olfynd. **a1200** *Ancrene* 9.1–2: The siheth the gneat and swolheth the flehe, 10.1–2. **c1384** Wyclif *Church and her Members* in *SEW* III 350[19–21]: And this errour reproveth Crist in Phariseis, that siyen the gnat and swolowen the camele, for thei chargen lesse more harm. **c1395** *WBible* Matthew xxiii 24: Blynde lederis, clensinge a gnatte, but swolewynge a camel. **a1400** *Ancrene*

(*Recluse*) 4.19–20: The gnatte foloweth the flesche, that is to saye Many maken mychel strengthe there lest is, 5.26: The gnat sweloweth the flee. **a1400** Wyclif *Sermons* I 76[14–5]: And thus freris, as Pharisees, clensen the gnatte and swolewen the camel. **c1400** *Apology* 45[23–4]: Blind foolis, clensing forth the knatt, but swelowyng the camely. **c1400** *Of Prelates* in Wyclif *EW* 100[12–4]: Swolwynge the grete cameile al hool and siynge or clensynge a litel gnatte. **c1400** *Order of Priesthood* in Wyclif *EW* 172[21–2]: Clensynge the gnatte and swolwynge the g(r)ete camaile alhool. *Oxford* 624; Taylor and Whiting 153–4; Tilley G150.

G179 He may evil **Go** that is near lame
a1475 *Ludus Coventriae* 90.238: He may Evyl go that is ner lame. Apperson 325: Ill run; Tilley R208. See **R235.**

G180 He that cannot **Go** before must come behind
c1450 *Douce MS.52* 52.92: Who-so may not go byfore, com by-hynde. **c1450** *Rylands MS.394* 102.13. **c1475** *Rawlinson MS. D 328* 117.5: He that may not goo be-fore moste goye be-hind. **a1500** *Additional MS.37075* 278.15: Who so may not go byfore, lett goe byhynd. **a1500** *Coventry Plays* 58.804–5: That man thatt canot goo before Nedis must cum behynd. Tilley G156.

G181 The more (further) one **Goes** the further behind
a1449 Lydgate *Tyed with a lyne* in *MP* II 832.1–2: The more I go, the further I am behynde: The more behynd, the nere the weyes end. **c1450** *A Balade by Squire Halsham* in Brown *Lyrics XV* 263.8–9 (see note p. 344): The more I goo the ferther I am behinde, The ferther behinde the ner my wayes ende. **1477** Rivers *Dictes* 119[4–6]: He that goth owte of his weye, the more he goth, the ferther he is behinde. **1528** More *Heresyes* 177 AB: Than have we well walked after the balade. The further I goo the more behynde, **1533** *Confutacion* 648 H[10-1]: An old english balad that beginneth The farther I go the more behynd. **c1545** Heywood *Four PP* E3v[28]: The farther they seke hym the farther behynde hym, **1546** *D* 89.34: The further ye go, the further behynde, **1555** *E* 160.90. Apperson 241; *Oxford* 231; Tilley G151. See **H172.**

G182 Soon I **Go**, soon I come
c1475 *Rawlinson MS. D 328* 120.31: Sony y go, sony y cum. Cum ito cum curso sum qui veni. See **C380, F641.**

G183 To **Go** further and fare worse
1546 Heywood *D* 67.57: And might have gone further, and have faren wurs. Apperson 250; *Oxford* 241; Taylor and Whiting 154; Tilley G160.

G184 As foul as a **Goat**
a800 *Christ* in *Exeter Book* 37.1230–1: Swa fule swa gæt, Unsyfre folc.

G185 As rammish (*rank*) as a **Goat**
c1408 Lydgate *Reson* 89.3378: Rammysh taraged as a goot.

G186 Each **Goat** halts on her own sore
c1450 *Rylands MS.394* 94.1: Eche gote halteth on her awghne sore. See **S266.**

G187 A **Goat** is no wiser for its fair beard
1484 Caxton *Aesop* 196[5–6]: O mayster goote yf thow haddest be wel wyse with thy fayre berde. Apperson 250; Tilley G169.

G188 To hate more than **Goat** does knife
a1300 *Interludium de clerico et puella* 21.21: Yu hates me mar than gayt dos chnief. **c1450** *Pilgrimage LM* 84[24]: She hateth it more than the goot the knyf.

G189 To stink like a **Goat**
c1395 Chaucer *CT* VIII[G] 886: For al the world they stynken as a goot. *Oxford* 621; Whiting *NC* 415.

G190 To go for **Goat-wool**
1513 Douglas *Aeneid* III 118.48: Sum glasteris and thai gang at, and all for gait woll. NED Goat 4c; Tilley G170.

G191 All goes but **God's** will
c1325 *Winter Song* in Brown *Lyrics XIV* 10.8–10: That moni mon seith soth hit ys: "Al goth bote godes wille, Alle we shule deye thah us like ylle."

G192 As false as **God** is true
c1400 *Beryn* 79.2591: Thoughe it be as fals a thing, as God hym-selff is trewe. **1546** Heywood *D* 81.23: She is of trouth as fals, as God is trew. Apperson 202; Tilley G173.

G193 As sicker (*sure*) as **God** is God
c1400 *Lay Folks' Catechism* 57.878: Also sykyr as god ys god, 882–3.

G194 As sicker as **God** is in heaven
c1400 *Vices and Virtues* 319[22]: As siker as god is in hevene. **c1415** *Middle English Sermons* 108.10–1: As sicur as God is in heven. **c1475** *Mankind* 24.653: As sekyr as Gode ys in hewyn, so yt ys! Apperson 647: true; *Oxford* 672; Taylor and Whiting 154; Tilley G175.

G195 As sicker as of **God's** cope (*i.e.*, not sure at all)
c1400 *Beryn* 15.453: But therof he shall be sikir as of goddis cope.

G196 As sooth as **God** is king
c1395 Chaucer *CT* IV[E] 1267: As sooth as God is kyng. *Oxford* 604.

G197 As sooth (sure) as **God** is true
c1390 Chaucer *CT* II[B] 169: And al this voys was sooth, as God is trewe. **a1533** Berners *Castell* H4r[15]: As sure as God is true.

G198 Be not inquisitive of **God's** privity (*varied*)
c1390 *Cato* (*Vernon*) 577.289–90: Enquere not of privites Of God ne eke of hevene. **c1390** Chaucer *CT* I[A] 3163–4: An housbonde shal nat ben inquisityf Of Goddes pryvetee, nor of his wyf, 3454: Men sholde nat knowe of Goddes pryvetee, 3558: I wol nat tellen Goddes pryvetee. **a1400** *Cato* (*Copenhagen*) A5v[5]: Enquere nought of goddis privyte. **a1400** *Gast of Gy* 109.1891–4: It falles noght unto me To tell noght of godes prevete; It es na question us unto, What so his will es for to do. **c1420** Wyntoun III 33–5.375–8: For the thyngis that ar to be To wit ar Goddis prewate; For thi tharof the certane Is nane can tel bot God allan. See **G255.**

G199 Give for **God** and God shall send
1509 Barclay *Ship* I 31[28]: Gyve for god, and god shall sende at all houres. Cf. *Oxford* 238: Give; Tilley G247: Spend. See **G242, 261, 273.**

G200 **God** amend defaults (all)
1469 Paston V 60[28]: God amend defowts. **c1522** Skelton *Speke* II 17.352–3: God amend all, That all amend may!

G201 **God** and his saints laugh at lovers' oaths
a1500 ?Ros *La Belle Dame* 311.375–7: Ful sikerly, ye (*lovers*) wene your othes laste No lenger than the wordes ben ago! And god, and eke his sayntes, laughe also. Apperson 334–5: Jove; *Oxford* 328; Smith 220; Tilley J82. See **L527, 578.**

G202 **God** asks things in measure
c1400 *Seven Deadly Sins* in Wyclif *SEW* III 159[23]: God Almyghty askes thing in mesure.

G203 **God** bless the brewer
c1515 Barclay *Eclogues* 78.703: God blesse the brewer, well cooled is my throte. Apperson 5; *Oxford* 64; Tilley B450.

G204 **God** does not give one man every thing
c1515 Barclay *Eclogues* 140.30: For God not geveth to one man every thing.

G205 **God** forgave his death
c1385 Chaucer *TC* iii 1577: God foryaf his deth. **a1400** *Amadace I* 35[28]: Thenke that Gode for-gave his dede. **c1489** Caxton *Aymon* I 48.7–8: Have remembraunce that god forgaffe his dethe to Longys. **a1500** *Amadace A* 253.235: Forgyf, seyd Sir Amadas, God forgyfes the deyd. **1525** Berners *Froissart* VI 166[35–7]: Christ . . . pardoned his dethe. **1556** Heywood *Spider* 131[12]: I forgeve even as god forgave. Whiting *Ballad* 37.

G206 **God** gives (to the rich) and may take away
a900 *Maxims* in *Exeter Book* 162.155–6: Mæg god syllan Eadgum æhte and eft niman. **c1395** *WBible* Job i 21: The Lord yaf, the Lord took awei. **a1425** *Metrical Paraphrase OT* 17.14373–6: God gyf(es) us here certayn To weld both wyld and tame And takes yt agayn. **a1450** Audelay 211.15: Thus God He geves and takys away. **1454** Paston II 318[3–4]: Oon Lord above giffeth and takith as hym plesith. Jente 353. See **T319.**

G207 **God** has a good plow
c1425 *Avowynge* 81[30–2]: Sir, God hase a gude plughe, He may send us alle enughe, Qwy schuld we spare? (Said by a lavish spender.)

G208 **God** has done his part: she has a good face
1556 Heywood *Spider* 4[17]: God hath done his part; she hath a good face. Apperson 251; Tilley G188.

G209 **God** have mercy, horse
1546 Heywood *D* 81.38: God have mercy hors. Apperson 254; *Oxford* 247–8; Tilley G276.

G210 **God** help and have all
c1450 *Douce MS.52* 45.9: Helpe God and have alle. **c1450** *Rylands MS.394* 96.28. **c1475** *Rawlinson MS. D 328* 120.35: God helpe and have all. **a1500** *Additional MS.37075* 278.20: Gode helpe and have alle. Cf. *Oxford* 283: Have God; Tilley G229.

G211 **God** helps his man (*varied*)
c1300 *Havelok* 56.1712–3: Loke nou, hu God helpen kan O mani wise wif and man. **c1410** Lovelich *Merlin* III 424.15828: Weteth wel that God wil not foryeten his manne. **c1425** *Avowynge* 91[25]: Yette God helpus ay his man. **a1449** Lydgate *Guy* in *MP* II 529.342: God faileth never His frend on see nor lond. **c1470** *Wallace* 30.378: God helpis his man. **c1505** Watson *Valentine* 38.3: God . . . never forgeteth his frendes, 211.30–1, 309.30: God . . . forgetteth not his good frendes at nede, **1518** *Oliver* P1r-

[5–6]: Oure lorde the whiche never forgeteth his frendes at theyr nede. **a1533** Berners *Huon* 91.2: God . . . never forgettyth his frendes, 170.2. See **G248, H308.**

G212 God is a good fellow
1533 More *Confutacion* 657 A[10]: God is a good felowe. Apperson 252: man; *Oxford* 244; Tilley G195; Whiting *Drama* 346:579.

G213 God is a righteous man—and so is his dame
a1500 *Gest of Robyn Hode* in Child III 68.240[3–4]: For God is holde a ryghtwys man, And so is his dame. Apperson 252: man; Jente 111; *Oxford* 244; Tilley G195.

G214 God is ever ready to help a bold courage (*varied*)
a800 *Andreas* in *Vercelli Book* 15.458–60: Forþan ic eow to soðe secgan wille, þæt næfre forlæteð lifgende god Eorl on eorþan, gif his ellen deah. **1515** Barclay *St. George* 43.863: God ever is redy to helpe a bolde courage. Cf. Smith 140; Tilley F601. See **F519, H96, L510.**

G215 God is good to dread (*varied*)
a1400 *Proverbis of Wysdom* 244.3–4: The fyrst proverbe to begynne, Drede god and fle fro synne, 247.137–8: Love god and fle fro synne, And so may thow hevyn wynne, (*II*) 222.39–40: God is good for-to drede. Vertue must have mede. **c1450** *Fyrst thou sal* 88.43–4: God is gode al way to drede Of vertewe has thou moste nede.

G216 God is no accepter (*respecter*) of persons
c1395 *WBible* Deeds of Apostles x 34: God is no acceptor of persoones. **1479** Rivers *Cordyal* 8.12: Now truly ther shal be none excepcion of persones, 82.3–4: Our lord shal juge justely and shal except no persone. **a1500** *St. Jerome* in *Anglia* 3(1880) 338.29–30: God is not acceptoure of parsonys. **1509** Fisher *Treatyse* 72.29: God is none accepter of persones. Cf. Tilley L505. See **D345.**

G217 God is no botcher
1546 Heywood *D* 60.59–60: God is no botcher . . . He shapeth all partes, as eche part maie fytte other, **1555** *E* 155.62. Apperson 252; *Oxford* 244; Tilley G199.

G218 God is where he was
1546 Heywood *D* 55.7: Take no thought in no case, God is where he was, **1555** *E* 190.245. Apperson 252; *Oxford* 244; Tilley G202.

G219 God keep me from my friends, I may well keep me from my enemies
1450 *Dicts* 262.17–21: And oon praid God that he wolde kepe him from his freendes . . . bicause that I may wele kepe me from myne ennemye in whom I truste not, bot noot from my freende in whome I truste. **1477** Rivers *Dictes* 106[11–6]. Apperson 239:29; *Oxford* 136; Tilley F739. See **E97.**

G220 God keep the moon from the wolves
1484 Caxton *Aesop* 54[11–2]: God kepe and preserve the mone for (*for* fro) the wolves, 115[19–20]: For god kepe the mone fro the wulves.

G221 God loves a clean soul and a merry
c1475 *Wisdom* 51.494: God lowyt a clene sowll and a mery.

G222 God loves a glad giver
c1395 *WBible* II Corinthians ix 7: For God loveth a glad gyvere. **a1400** *Cleansing* 190.21–2 (f.125v): Oure Lord lovith a glad gever. **a1400** *Pauline Epistles* II Corinthians ix 7: For a glad gifar lufys god. **1522** More *Treatyce* 75 C[14–5].

G223 God made marriage in paradise
c1390 Chaucer *CT* X[I] 883: For God made mariage in paradys, 918. Cf. Apperson 404: Marriages; *Oxford* 409; Taylor and Whiting 230; Tilley M688.

G224 God may fordo (*undo*) destiny
a1470 Malory I 119.31: But God may well fordo desteny.

G225 God may help all thing(s)
c1375 Barbour *Bruce* I 262.614: Now help thame god that all thing may. Cf. Smith 139.

G226 God may send a fortune to a poor squire as well as to a great lord
1523 Berners *Froissart* I 315[13–5]: For as well God may sende by his grace suche a fortune to fall to a poore squyer, as to a great lorde.

G227 God never sends mouth but he sends meat
1546 Heywood *D* 25.20: God never sendth mouth, but he sendeth meat. Apperson 252; *Oxford* 245; Taylor and Whiting 154; Tilley G207. See **L249.**

G228 God's foison (*plenty*)
c1300 *Speculum Gy* 43.994–5: And anon god putte his fuisoun Up-on hire mele. **c1303** Mannyng *Handlyng* 188–9.5805–6: And God shal gyve the hys blessyng, And foysyn. **c1390** Chaucer *CT* I[A] 3165–6: So he may fynde Goddes foyson there, Of the remenant nedeth nat enquere, II[B] 504: God sente his foyson at hir grete neede. **a1425** *Metrical Paraphrase OT*

78.12200: For goddes fuson sal thore be fun. **a1475** *Ludus Coventriae* 81.267: Goddys foyson is evyr to his servauntys. **c1475** *Mankind* 13.323: I prey Gode sende yt hys fusyon!

G229 **God's** grace is better than armor
a1300 *Arthour and M.*[1] 206.7358–60: With ous schal be godes gras: His grace is better in to afie, Than armour other compeinie. See **G413.**

G230 **God's** grace is worth a fair (*varied*)
a1415 Mirk *Festial* 86.19–20: Ye have a comyn sayng among you, and sayn that Godys grace ys worth a new fayre. **c1450** *Douce MS.52* 47.41: The grace of God is better then .III. feyrys. **c1450** *Rylands MS.394* 97.7: thre chepynges. **1546** Heywood *D* 55.6: Alwaie the grace of God is woorth a fayre. Apperson 253; *Oxford* 261; Tilley G394. See **G413.**

G231 **God's** help is ever near
a1400 *Amadace I* 42[20–1]: For God may bothe mon falle and rise, For his helpe is evyr more nere, **a1500** A 260.414–5: A man may falle and yette ryse, Goddes helpe his ay nere!

G232 **God** sees through every bore ([*hole*], each miss, all)
1400 *Love god, and drede* in Kail 4.95: Ffor god seeth thurgh every bore, 103: Ffor god seeth thurgh eche mysse. **c1523** Barclay *Mirrour* 25[45]: Note that God seeth all.

G233 **God** send an irous man little might
c1395 Chaucer *CT* III[D] 2014: An irous man, God sende hym litel myght!

G234 **God** sends a shrewd (wild) cow short horns
a1500 *Eight Goodly Questions* 423[24–5]: He thinketh not how men have saied beforne, God sendeth a shrewd cow a short horne. **1509** Barclay *Ship* I 182[6]: To a wylde cowe god doth short hornys sende. **1546** Heywood *D* 39.125: God sendth a shrewd coow short hornes. Apperson 118; *Oxford* 125; Tilley G217; Whiting *Scots* I 178.

G235 **God** sends cold after clothes
1546 Heywood *D* 25.24: God sendth colde after clothes. Apperson 253; *Oxford* 246; Tilley G218.

G236 **God** sends fortune to fools
1546 Heywood *D* 79.36: That they saie as ofte, God sendeth fortune to fooles, **1555** *E* 166.124. Apperson 253; *Oxford* 246; Tilley G220.

G237 **God** sends the cow, but not by the horn (*varied*)
a1400 *Cloud* 57.9–10: For thei sey that God sendeth the kow, bot not by the horne. **c1450** *Ladder* 106.28–30: And so as ho sayth: "He gevyth the oxe by the horne," that is, whan he not callid offeryth his grace. *Oxford* 243–4.

G238 **God** set (all) upon seven
1400 *Susan* 183.264: Bothe the sonne and the see thou (*God*) sette uppon sevene. **a1460** *Towneley Plays* 115.486–7: My son that I neven, Rewarde you this day as he sett all on seven, 140.737–8: The fader of heven god omnypotent, That sett all on seven. **c1475** *Golagros* 35.1045: I swere be suthfast God, that settis all on sevin!

G239 **God** speed the plow
c1400 *Trinity College Cambridge MS.594* f.iiib in M. R. James *Catalogue* (Cambridge, 1901) II 64: God spede the plough and sende us korne I now. **c1450** *Merthe of alle* in *Anglia* 36(1912) 104.12: God spede the plowe al day, 24: all-way. **1472** Paston V 147[12–3]: God sped the plowghe. **a1500** *God spede the Plough* in *Pierce* 68–71.7–8: Than to an husbond I sed this sawe, "I pray to God, spede wele the plough," 16, 24, *etc.* Apperson 594–5; *Oxford* 612; Tilley G223.

G240 **God** stint all strife
1546 Heywood *D* 89.50: I can no more herin, but god stint all stryfe. *Oxford* 246; Tilley G225.

G241 **God** takes me as I am and not as I was
1546 Heywood *D* 91.19: God taketh me as I am, and not as I was.

G242 **God** will send
c1475 *Wisdom* 62.827–8: I hoope of a goode yer, For ever I trost God wyll send. See **G199, 261, 273.**

G243 **God** will send time to provide for time
1546 Heywood *D* 55.22–3: God will sende Tyme to provyde for tyme. *Oxford* 247; Tilley G228.

G244 **God** will stand with the right
a1500 *Lady Bessy* 8[19]: For God will stand ever with the right.

G245 **God** wot (knows) all
c1390 Chaucer *CT* VII 113[B1303]: God woot al. **1504** W. Cornish *Tretyse* in *Archiv* 120(1908) 426.138: But God knowthe alle; so dothe not kyng Hary.

G246 He is rich to whom **God** will send weal
a1393 Gower *CA* III 12.2400–1: He is riche and wel bego, To whom that god wole sende wele.

G247 He that lists to please **God,** let his neighbor live in ease (*varied*)
c1420 *Mazer inscription* in *Archaeologia*

50(1887) 149: Hoe so lustythe god to plese, let hys neyghbore lyve in ese. **a1500** Hichecoke *This Worlde* 333.47–8: Yf thu wilte thi Lorde plece: Helpe thi nebur yn his disece.

G248 He thrives well that **God** loves (?loves God)
c1350 *Good Wife E* 158.5–6: Wel thrivet That God lovet, **c1450** *L* 197.5–6: He muste neede weel thrive That liveth weel al his lyve. Apperson 631; *Oxford* 656. See **G211.**

G249 He would spend **God's** cope (*i.e.,* a large amount) if he had it
1520 Whittinton *Vulgaria* 58.18: He wolde spende goddes coope yf he had it. NED Cope sb.[3]; Tilley G271.

G250 Help yourself and **God** will help
c1475 *Rawlinson MS. D 328* 122.52: Helpe thy sylfe and god wol helpe, 123.65. **1509** Barclay *Ship* I 226[20–1]: So unto god for helpe they cry and call, But they them selfe wyll helpe no thynge at all. Jente 690; Taylor and Whiting 154.

G251 Here is **God** in the ambry (*cupboard*)
1546 Heywood *D* 68.89: Here is God in thambrie, **1555** *E* 170.135: There is god in thalmery, a well playde part. Apperson 252; Tilley G249.

G252 If **God** is for us, who is against us?
c1395 *WBible* Romans viii 31: If God for us, who is ayens us? **a1400** *Pauline Epistles* Romans viii 31: If god be for us, who schal be ageyn us? **c1400** Paues 53 (Romans 8.31): Yif God is with ous, who is ayeyns ous? **c1438** Kempe 227.12–4: Owr Lord seyd a-geyn, "Yf I be wyth the, ho schal ben a-geyns the?" 227.24–5. **1509** Fisher *Treatyse* 89.20–1: If almyghty god be with us, who may saye or do ayenst us? **1534** More *Comforte* 1147 F[1–2]: If God be wyth us, saieth saint Paul, who can stand against us? Tilley G238.

G253 It is not good to strive with **God**
c1390 *Ever more Thank God of All* in Brown *Lyrics XIV* 159.68: Hit is not gode with god to strywe. **a1400** *Eglamour* 88.1311: With God may na man stryve.

G254 I-worth (*happen*) what i-worth (*may happen*) i-worth **God's** will
a1200 Lawman III 297.32240–1: Iwurthe thet iwurthe, Iwurthe Godes wille. **c1250** *Proverbs of Alfred* 124 T 503–5: Sei thu aten-ende, Wrthe thad iwurthe, Iwurthe godes wille. Skeat 15. Cf. Tilley A161.

G255 Let **God** and me alone
c1415 *Middle English Sermons* 68.32–5: When on chalouns you, than it is a comon seyinge of the pepull, "Ye latt God and me a-lone." Thei thenke hem-selfe so wurthy that thei will not be corecte of no man. See **G198.**

G256 Out of **God's** blessing into the warm sun
1546 Heywood *D* 71.57–8: Ye runne Out of gods blessing into the warme sunne. Apperson 476; *Oxford* 480; Tilley G272. See **S175.**

G257 Please **God** and love him and doubt (*fear*) nothing
1513 Bradshaw *St. Werburge* 95.2589–90: Ofttymes to her covent she had a comyn sayenge: "Please god and love hym and doubte ye nothynge."

G258 Run **God,** run devil
c1522 Skelton *Colyn* I 358.1224: Renne God, renne devyll, *Speke* II 22.438: Ryn God, rynne Devyll. See **S286.**

G259 Serve **God** devoutly, *etc.* (*varied*)
c1450 *Fyrst thou sal* 91.161–2: Ryse up arely, seryf god devoutly, The warld as nede is besyly, 187–8: Go to the mette appetytly And ryse yp temperatly. **c1450** *Serve thy god* 261.1–4: Serve thy god trwly, And the world bysely, Ete thy mete merely, So schalt thou lyve in hele. **a1475** *Porkington MS.10* in *Neuphilologische Mitteilungen* 54(1952) 59–60: Aryse erlly, And serve God dewoutly, Go by the way sadly, Ansswer the peppull demurly, Go to thy mete appetently, And to thy sopper soborly, And arys temparatly, And (go) to thy bede meryly, And be therin jocondlye, And slepe sourly. **c1475** *Rawlinson MS. D 328* 122.60: Serve god herteli And the werke be sely. Ete the mete merely. Thanke god hertely, Yeffe thu leve porely; He may mende hys layse Withowte eny grese. **a1500** *Magdalene College Camb. MS.13* f.2a in M. R. James *Catalogue* (Cambridge, 1909) 26[16–20]: If thou wylte lyve purelye, Then speke and answere demurelye, Sarve god dewlye, And do thy werke trulye, And so shall thu wynne heven surelye. **a1500** Hill 141.5–12: Serve God truly And the world besily; Ete thy mete meryly, And ever leve in rest! Thank God highly; Thowgh he visit the porely, He may amend it lygthly, Whan hym lykethe beste. Cf. Apperson 173: Early to bed; *Oxford* 164; Taylor and Whiting 21; Tilley B184. See **R143, S89.**

G260 Since (the time that) **God** was born
c1390 *Who says the Sooth* in Brown *Lyrics XIV* 154.61–2: Seththe the tyme that god was boren, This world was never so untrewe. **c1475** *Wis-*

dom 57.682–3: Ther wer never so moche reynande Seth Gode was bore.

G261 Spend and **God** shall send
a1400 Greene *Carols* p. 429: Spende and God schal sende; Spare and ermore care. **c1450** *Douce MS.52* 45.16: Spende, and God wyl sende; Spare, and evere bare. **c1450** *Rylands MS.394* 96.7.12. **c1500** Greene *Carols* 419 A 9: For we will spend Till God more send. **1546** Heywood *D* 71.45: Spend, and god shall send . . . saith tholde ballet. Apperson 595; *Oxford* 613; Tilley G247. See **E118, G199, 242, L80, 83.**

G262 Thank **God** for whatever he sends
a1449 Lydgate *Look* in *MP* II 769.142: What evyr God sent, thank hym with al thy myght.

G263 There is **God** when all is done
1546 Heywood *D* 30.43: Ye there was God (quoth he) when all is doone. *Oxford* 246; Tilley G250.

G264 Though **God** suffers long, at the last he smites (*varied*)
a1300 *Trinity College Cambridge MS.323* f.46a in M. R. James *Catalogue* (Cambridge, 1900) I 444: Godis wreche late arecheit, An wonne he smit, ful sore he hit. **c1300** *South English Legendary* I 251.127–8: Oure Loverd soffreth awile is fon here ayen him fighte; Attelaste he smit wel harde wanne he cudde is mighte. **a1415** Mirk *Festial* 88.2–4: For thagh he abyde long, at the last, he woll smyte suche that woll not amende hom; and when he smytyth, he smytyth sore, 142.18–9: Ye mou segh, thogh God abyde longe, how sore he smytythe at the last. **c1422** Hoccleve *Complaint* 99.113: He suffrith longe (but) at the laste he smit, *Jereslaus's Wife* 164.699–700: Lo, thogh god him to wreke a whyle abyde, The fals and wikkid, qwytith he sum tyde. **1509** Hawes *Convercyon* A3r[13]: I maye take vengeaunce, thoughe I tary longe. Jente 358; Tilley G224. Cf. Whiting *Scots* I 179:7.

G265 To attempt (*tempt*) **God** over much is not wisdom
a1470 Malory I 246.11–2: For to attemte God overmuche I holde hit not wysedom.

G266 To be **God**'s apes
c1385 Chaucer *TC* i 912–3: And seyd that Loves servantz everichone Of nycete ben verray Goddes apes. **1513** Douglas *Aeneid* II 147.21: And your trew servandis sylly goddis apys, III 1.11: Ye verray goddis apis! NED Ape 4; Whiting *Scots* I 179. Cf. Tilley D247.

G267 To be one of those to whom **God** bade ho (*stop*)
1546 Heywood *D* 49.271: She is one of them, to whom God bad who, **1555** *E* 173.154. Apperson 250; Tilley G264.

G268 To climb to **God** on a short tree
c1440 *Lyarde* in *Rel. Ant.* II 288[7–10]: And als I come hamewarde, another I mette With a rape abowte his nekke to the gebette. Other sayntis gett thay none, therfor thay wille noghte thee, And therfore thay clyme alle to God one a schorte tree. MED climben 3(e). Cf. Tilley H353.

G269 To **God** nothing is impossible (*varied*)
c1000 *WSG* Mark x 27: Ealle þing mid Gode synt eaðelice, Luke i 37: For þam nis ælc word mid Gode unmihtelic, xviii 27: Gode synt mihtelice þa ðing þe mannum synt unmihtelice. **a1023** Wulfstan *Homilies* 151.146–7: He mæg ful georne witan hit þæt hit wæs Gode yðdæde þa he hit swa gedon habban wolde. **c1395** *WBible* Mark x 27: For alle thingis ben possible anentis God, Luke i 37: For every word schal not be impossible anentis God, xviii 27: Tho thingis that ben impossible anentis men, ben possible anentis God. **a1400** *Scottish Legends* II 11.373–4: For to god as we ma se Nathing may inpossible be, 306.83–4. **c1420** Wyntoun II 17.62–3: To God that we mai nocht defend, Sen na thing is that he na may. **a1425** *Chester Plays* I 106.39–40: But nothing to Gods might and mayne Impossible is, 208.77–8: For to that highe comlye kinge Impossible is no thinge. **c1425** *St. Katherine of Sienna* 186.15: Hee . . . to whome no thinge is impossibil. **c1438** Kempe 223.26–7: Sche wiste wel to God was nothyng impossibyl. **1439** Lydgate *St. Albon* 173.699. **c1450** Idley 91.634. **a1460** *Towneley Plays* 112.373–4: Nothyng is inpossybyll Sothly, that god wyll. **a1470** Parker *Dives* A3r[2.5–6]: To God alle thynge is possyble. **a1475** *Ludus Coventriae* 359.120. **c1493** *St. Katherin of Senis* 266.9–10. **a1500** *Coventry Plays* 4.87. **c1502** *Lyfe of Joseph* 47.320. **1512** Copland *Helyas* D3v[9–10]: There as god lyst to werke nothynge abydeth impossyble to his dyvyne wyll. **1518** Watson *Oliver* E4r[21–2]. **1534** More *Comforte* 1204 E[6–7]: For unto God . . . all thynges are possible. Jente 355; Taylor and Whiting 154; Tilley N300. See **A98, G276.**

G270 To make **God** a beard of straw
1484 Caxton *Aesop* 116[1–2]: The ypocrytes maken to god a berd of strawe.

G271 To take such as **God** sends (*varied*)
a1450 *Gesta* 411[29–30]: For goddis love ye are welcome to me; and take such as god sendith. **a1450** *Myne awen dere* 162.419–20: That man is mykell to commende That haldes hym payed, whatevere God sende. **c1450** *Foly of Fulys* 57.206: Thai tak in thank at god wyl send. **a1470** Malory III 1169.24: All ys wellcom that God sendyth us. **1477** Rivers *Dictes* 102[21–2]: Men ought to receyve merily all that God sendeth hem. Whiting *Drama* 114, 226, *Scots* I 179. Cf. Tilley A138, M285.

G272 To teach one how **God's** grame (*anger*) came to town
c1330 *Seven Sages A* 126.2691–4: No, sire, sche saide, thi swerd me reche And ich him schal, with min hond, teche Hou godes grame com to toune, Right amide ward his croune. (A widow is about to mutilate her husband's corpse.)

G273 To wish after "**God** me send"
a1393 Gower *CA* II 301.10–1: And so he wol his time borwe, And wissheth after "God me sende." Cf. *Oxford* 364: We must not lie; Tilley D388. See **G242.**

G274 What **God** does he does anon (*at once*)
c1500 *Melusine* 203.22–3: Wel sayth he trouth that sayth "that god doth he doth anoone."

G275 When **God** is dead
a1500 *Clerk and the Nightingale II* in Robbins 178.51: They (*women*) schul be god wan god is dede.

G276 Where **God** will help is none helpless (nothing will fail) (*varied*)
c1250 *Genesis and Exodus* 92.3232: Thor god wile is non helpeles. **a1300** *Alisaunder* 81.1407–8: Ac sooth it is, cayser ne kyng Ne may ayeins Goddes helpyng. **a1300** *Jacob and Joseph* 3.62: That oure Loverd wole habben ido mai no man binime. **c1300** *Havelok* 24.647–8: Soth is, that men seyth and suereth: "Ther God wile helpen, nouht ne dereth." **c1300** *South English Legendary* (*Laud*) 400.259–60: Loverd, muche is thi mighte and that thou cuddest there—For that thou i-saved habbe wolt nothing ne schal fur-pere. **c1300** *South English Legendary* I 195.438: Thing that God wol habbe ywest ne ssel nothing sle. **a1325** *Cursor* I 236.3995–6: For man that thou (*God*) will help in nede Thar him never na derfnes drede, 4007–8: For qua godds help es wit-all Ful siker mai he wend over all (T: But who so god helpe wol May savely go at the fol). **a1340** *Ayenbite* 166[16–7]: And huam thet god wile helpe: no thing him ne may derie. **a1350** *Edward the Confessor* 9.246: As ho-so hath god to helpe him thar the lasse agaste. **c1375** Barbour *Bruce* I 19.456: Bot quhar god helpys, quhat may withstand? 280.203. **a1393** Gower *CA* II 149.693–4: Bot what the hihe god wol spare It mai for no peril misfare, III 13.2426: Bot wel is him whom god wol helpe, 417.1160: That God wol save mai noght spille. **a1400** *Cursor* II 432 F 7502: Ther god wille help doute is na nede. **a1400** *Firumbras* 38.1171: But ther our Lord woll helpe, ne dar no man doute. **a1400** *Melayne* 50.1543: Bot there god will helpe ther es no lett. **c1400** *Brut* I 91.4–5: But al thing that God wil have done, moste bene done. **c1400** *Vices and Virtues* 166.24–5. **a1425** *Metrical Paraphrase OT* 48.1591–2: Loe, how sone god hath socur sent; That he wyll save, be savyd thei sall. **a1450** Quixley *Ballades* 47.288: Noon is siker that god hath not in warde, 295, 302. **c1450** *Edward the Confessor Prose II* 112[14–5]: But hym nedeth the lesse to feer, that hath god to his defensour. **c1450** *Merlin* II 524[25–6]: And ther-fore is seide a proverbe, that god will have saved, no man may distroye. **c1450** *Ponthus* 19.28: Whome Gode wolle have keped, shal be keped. **1484** Caxton *Royal Book* N7v[12–3]: Whome god wyl ayde and helpe, none may noye ne greve, **c1489** *Blanchardyn* 155.4–6: For men sayen comynly, that he whome god wyll have kept, may not be peryshed. **a1500** *Imitatione* (*1*) 42.12–3: For him that he (*God*) wol helpe, no mannys overthwartnes shal mowe noye. **1502** *Imitatione* (*2*) 181.10–1: And loke, to whom so ever god putteth furth his hande to helpe, ther can no adversite hurte hym. **c1505** Watson *Valentine* 244.12–3: Who that god wyl helpe none can hurte them. **a1533** Berners *Huon* 82.26–7: Who that god wyll ayde no man can hurt, 256.25–6: That god wyl ayde no man can lette, 480.24–6: It is a comune proverbe sayde, whome that god wyll ayde no man can hurte, 489.20–1: He that oure lorde Jesu chryste wyll have savyd can not peryse, 638.31–2: Often tymes it is sayde that god wyll have savyd can not be perysshed, 664.1–2: Whom god wyll ayde can not be perysshed. Apperson 251–2, 292; *Oxford* 246; Skeat 50; Tilley G263. See **G269.**

G277 Where **God** wills there it rains
1492 *Salomon and Marcolphus* 16[2–3]: I have herde it and I knowe well that where god woll there reynyth it. Apperson 254; *Oxford* 247; Tilley G256.

G278 Who hopes in **God's** help his help cannot start (*depart*)

1546 Heywood *D* 25.37: Who hopeth in Gods helpe, his helpe can not starte. Apperson 254; NED Start 4e; Tilley G275.

G279 Both bade me **God-speed,** but none bade me welcome
1546 Heywood *D* 35.10: Bothe bad me god speede, but none bad me welcome. Tilley G279.

G280 To gape as a **Gogmagog**
a1450 *Castle* 135.1942: I gape as a Gogmagog whanne I gynne to gase. MED Gogmagog (c).

G281 A glad **Going Out** oft brings forth a sorrowful coming home
a1500 *Imitatione* (*1*) 25.28–9: A glad goinge oute ofte tymes bringith furthe a sorful comyng home. **1502** *Imitatione* (*2*) 169.24–5: It is oftymes sene that a glad goinge out folowith a sory returnynge. See **B200.**

G282 All is not **Gold** that shines (*varied*)
c1200 *Hali Meidenhad* 10.97: Nis hit nower neh gold al ther ter schineth. **c1250** *Hendyng O* 200.46: Hit nis nout al gold, that shineth. **c1380** Chaucer *HF* 272: Hyt is not al gold that glareth. **c1385** Usk 54–5.47–8: For every glittring thing is nat gold. **c1395** Chaucer *CT* VIII[G] 962–3: But al thyng which that shineth as the gold Nis nat gold, as that I have herd it told. **a1400** Wyclif *Sermons* I 224[2–4]: And so men hav taught comunli that men shulden not holde al gold that shyneth as gold, for many thingis ben fourboshid ful falseli. **a1410** Lydgate *Churl* in *MP* II 481.306: All is nat gold that shewith goldissh hewe. **1422** Yonge *Governaunce* 156.23: Hit is not al golde that Shynyth as golde. **a1439** Lydgate *Fall* II 547.2707–8: Al is nat gold, to speke in pleyn langage, That shynith briht, 553.2944: Al is nat gold that shyneth briht, III 911.3160: Al is nat gold that is cleer shynyng, **a1449** *Amor* in *MP* II 747.77: Al nys nat golde that shyneth bright, *Mydsomer Rose* in *MP* II 781.12: Al is nat gold that outward shewith bright, *World* in *MP* II 847.93: Al is not goold which shynyth cleer and bryght. **c1475** *Prohemy of a Mariage* 43[21]: Sithe not is golde al that as golde dothe shyne. **a1500** *Additional MS.37075* 277.4: Hyt ys not gold that shynyth as gold. **a1500** Hill 129.26: It is not all gold that glareth. **a1500** *O man more* 393.8: All is nott golde that shynes full clere. **a1500** *Scorn of Women* in Robbins 224.18: "All ys nat gold that shynyth!" Men, take hede. **a1500** *Thre Prestis* 49.1150: And weil I wait al is not gold that glitters. **a1508** Dunbar *Tretis* 89.202: He had the glemyng of gold, and wes bot glase fundin. **1546** Heywood *D* 38.122: All is not golde that glisters by tolde tales. Apperson 6; Jente 623; Kneuer 62–4; *Oxford* 249; Schleich 276–7; Singer III 141–2; Skeat 206; Taylor and Whiting 154–5; Tilley A146; Whiting *Drama* 122, 134, 215, *Scots* I 179. See **S755, T96.**

G283 All that you ween **Gold** i-worth (*turns*) to maslin (*brass*)
c1200 *Hali Meidenhad* 10.88: Al is thet tu wendest golt, iwurthe to meastling.

G284 As bright as (any, the) **Gold**
a900 *Solomon and Saturn* in *ASMP* 48.488: Oðer bið golde glædra. **c1275** *Kentish Sermons* in Morris *Old English Miscellany* 27[33–5]: Si gode beleave licht and is bricht ine tho herte of tho gode Manne ase gold. **a1300** *Alisaunder* 292 M 69: The thre shynyd as bryght as gold. **c1300** *Owayne Miles* (*Auchinleck*) 110.181: ani. **c1330** *Owayne Miles* (*Egerton*) in Horstmann *Altenglische Legenden 1875* 202.550: And brightere than ani gold. **c1385** Chaucer *CT* I[A] 2141: any. **a1400** *Destruction of Troy* 99.3034: Bright as the brent gold enbowet thai were. **a1437** *Kingis Quair* 58.47[1], 88.152[4]: ony. **a1439** Lydgate *Fall* I 69.2528–9. **1447** Bokenham 208.7645: Whos wengys bryhter glastryd than gold. **c1450** Greene *Carols* 124 A 2. **c1455** *Partonope* S 484.137. **a1500** Medwall *Nature* C2v[15–6]: Yt (*hair*) cryspeth and shyneth as bryght As any pyrled gold. **1513** Douglas *Aeneid* IV 70.112, 168.131: Abufe the schynand sternys, as gold brycht. Taylor and Whiting 155; Whiting *Scots* I 179. See **G322.**

G284a Gold-bright
c800 *Order of the World* in *Exeter Book* 165.78: Goldtorht sunne. **a900** *Old English Martyrology* 92.10: Mid goldebeorhtum hreglum.

G285 As clean as **Gold**
a1023 Wulfstan *Homilies* 130.34–6: Ær we beon æfre ælcere synne swa clæne amerede swa æfre anig gold mæg clænost amerod weorðan. **c1340** Rolle *Psalter* 110 (30.25): That is clen as purged gold, **a1349** *Commandment* in Allen *R. Rolle* 80.242–3: Als clene as the golde that es proved in the fournes. **a1400** *Pricke* 87.3201: Unto thai be als clene als gold fyned. Whiting *Scots* I 179.

G286 As clear as (any) **Gold**
c1330 *Owayne Miles* (*Egerton*) in Horstmann *Altenglische Legenden 1875* 202.549–50: More cler . . . than ani gold. **1435** Misyn *Fire* 97.16: Makes us clerar then golde. **c1477** Caxton *Jason* 127.34: Myrro is clere a(s) golde.

G287 As gay as (the) **Gold**
a1425 *Chester Plays* I 12.83: That us hath made

gaier then gould. **a1450** *York Plays* 124.19–20: Than glorius gulles that gayer (is) than golde in price. **c1450** Holland *Howlat* 48.28: With girss gaye as the gold.

G288 As gilt as **Gold** (*etc.*) (A number of single quotations are brought together here)
a1400 *Cursor* III 1528 F 27603: And with-oute gilt as golde. **c1400** *Alexander Buik* II 166.2398: Hir hare that to fyne gold is feir. **c1408** Lydgate *Reson* 129.4928: And as gold the gravel shene, **1439** *St. Albon* 126.895: A boke compyled, rycher than golde in coffers. **c1450** Idley 117.596: To thy undirstondyng as sure as the goolde. **c1470** *Wallace* 24.212: For thou till hir was fer derer than gold. **c1500** *Lover's Farewell* in Robbins 213.130: Ffarewell gloriouse as gold y-grave.

G289 As glittering as **Gold**
c1000 Aelfric *Lives* I 110.338: Glitiniende swa swa gold. **a1325** *Erthe* 6.14: He that gose appone erthe gleterande as golde. **a1450** *O ye al whilk* in *Archiv* 167(1935) 27[15]: Thogh gleteryng thou be as byrnysched gold bright. **a1461** *John the Reeve* 568.261: Glitering as gold itt were. **1513** Bradshaw *St. Werburge* 61.1579: Glyterynge as . . . the beten golde. See **G324.**

G290 As precious as **Gold**
a1439 Lydgate *Fall* I 151.5398: The which(e) wern mor precious than gold. Whiting *Drama* 314:146.

G291 As pure as **Gold**
c1340 Rolle *Psalter* 246 (69.4): He cumes pure out as gold. **a1449** Lydgate *Doublenesse* in *MP* II 442.99: To ben as pure as golde y-fyned. Whiting *NC* 416.

G292 As red as **Gold**
a1398(1495) Bartholomaeus-Trevisa xl^{r-v}: The mone is red as golde. **a1500** *Knight of Curtesy* 13.343: The comely heare as golde so rede. See **G323.**

G293 As shining as (any, the) **Gold**
c1303 Mannyng *Handlyng* 226.7025–6: Atyre, Shynyng as golde. **1383** *Grete Sentence* in Wyclif *SEW* III 275[22–3]: Schynyng to God betre than doth ony gold to men. **c1395** Chaucer *CT* III[D] 304: For his crispe heer, shynynge as gold so fyn. **a1400** *Le Morte A.* 31.973. **a1400** *Pricke* 240.8907: Alle schynand als gold bryght burnyst. **a1400** *Scottish Legends* II 204.19. **c1400** *Tundale* 116.2025–6. **a1415** Mirk *Festial* 144.6–7. **1438** *Barlam and Josaphat* (*Vernon*) 224.685–6. **a1450** *What that phebus* in Sandison 123.1. **c1450** *Seege of Troye* 5 A 38: A toppe schyny(n)g ryght as golde. **a1475** *Book of Quinte Essence*, ed. F. J. Furnivall (EETS 16, 1866[1889]) 12.30–1. **1485** Caxton *Charles* 90.13: Hyr heyre was shynyng as the fyne gold, 198.16. **1506** Hawes *Pastime* 80.2035–6: Her heer was downe so clerely shynynge Lyke to the golde late puryfyed with fyre. **1509** Barclay *Ship* II 297[20]: Thy here . . . shynynge as golde bryght, **1515** *St. George* 23.355: His heer shynynge as golde moste fyne and pure. **c1520** Walter *Spectacle* $A2^r$[6]: the. Tilley G280.

G294 As yellow as (any, the) **Gold**
a1300 *Alisaunder* 273.4980: Here hii habben yelewe so golde, 345.6485–6: Her here her clothing is, Also yelewe as any golde. **c1385** Chaucer *CT* I[A] 2141: With nayles yelewe . . . as any gold. **a1400** *Alexander C* 20.607: As any yare yeten gold yalow was the tothire (*eye*). **a1449** Lydgate *My Lady Dere* in *MP* II 421.35: Yolowe as golde clere. **1490** Caxton *Eneydos* 60.32–4. **a1500** *Catalogue of Delights* in Robbins 120.19: Her heer is yelou as the gold. **c1505** Watson *Valentine* 85.1–3: the fyne golde, 140.18: fine, **1509** *Ship* $M1^r$[13–4]: fyne, $Ee3^r$[4]. **1523** Skelton *Garlande* I 373.289: the, **a1529** *Boke of Three Fooles* I 204[21–2]: fine. Apperson 717; Taylor and Whiting 155; Tilley G280; Whiting *Ballad* 27, 28. See **G325.**

G295 For (Not for) all the **Gold** (good) of Carthage (Ind, France, Arabia, Rome, Galilee, Spain, in the Rhine, Christianity, in the world)
a1300 *Alisaunder* 53.903–4: For al the golde of Cartage Nolde he take othere gage. **a1300** *Richard* 271.3526–8: That hym hadde levere have ben at home, . . . Thenne al the good that was in Ynde. **a1300** *Tristrem* 79.2900–1: For alle the golde of Ynde Ybroken no schal it be. **c1375** Barbour *Bruce* I 11.239–40: And suld think fredome mar to pryss Than all the gold in warld that is. **c1380** *Ferumbras* 12.359: Thou noldest profry me to fight, for al that gold of fraunce, 109.3462: fraunce. **c1390** *Of Clene Maydenhod* 468.113: Thaugh al the gold of Arabye. **a1393** Gower *CA* II 229.100: For al the gold that is in Rome. **a1400** ?Chaucer *Rom. A* 1093: Worth all the gold in Rome and Frise. **c1400** *Laud Troy* I 159.5399: For al the gold of Galilee, 216.7314: For alle the gode of Jerusalem, II 417.14151: For al the gold of hethen Spayne, 512.17387: For alle the good of hethen Spayne. **c1440** *Degrevant* 36.541–2: Me ware lever that scho war myne Than alle the golde in the ryne (*C:* Reyne). **a1470** Malory II 699.11–3: For I had lever . . . than all the golde betwyxte this and Rome I had bene there.

c1489 Caxton *Aymon* I 170.22: For all the golde of spayne, 274.27–9: spayne. **a1500** *Grace of the holy goste* in *Anglia* 3(1880) 538.197: hens to Rome. **c1500** *Lady Bessy* 8[24]: For all the gold in Christantye, 10[8], 23[10], 25[13], 36[26], 37[16]. **c1505** Watson *Valentine* 213.3: Fraunce. **1532** Berners *Golden Boke* 213.3075–7: in the worlde, **a1533** *Arthur* 343[31–3]: of the worlde, 460[19–20]: of the world, 494[20–1]: of the world, *Huon* 302.11–2: In the worlde, 322.32–323.1: in the worlde, 369.6–7: of the worlde, 622.15–6: in the worlde. See **A209.**

G296 **Gold** and silver overcome all (the) world
1123 *Peterborough Chronicle* I 252[29–30]: Ac þet ofer com Rome þet ofer cumeð eall weoruld, þet is gold and seolvre. **1525** Berners *Froissart* VI 255[3]: There is nothynge but it is overcome with golde and sylver. See **G82, M490, 624, 633, Q9.**

G297 **Gold** (the noble) is a cordial
c1387-95 Chaucer *CT* I[A] 443: For gold in phisik is a cordial. **c1435** Lydgate *Letter to Gloucester* in *MP* II 666.44: Gold is a cordial, gladdest confeccioun (*in a begging letter*). **c1450** Idley 100.1133–4: And also a cordiall is the glorius noble, He is so pure, so precious, and so noble.

G298 **Gold** is afonded (*tried, etc.*) in (the) fire (furnace) (*varied*)
c1000 Aelfric *Homilies* I 6[2–3]: Swa swa gold bið on fyre afandod, 268[14–5]: Swa swa man afandað gold on fyre, swa afandað God þæs mannes mod on mislicum fandungum. **c1340** *Ayenbite* 106[26–7]: Verst he his wypeth and clensethi ase deth thet ver (thet) clenzeth and fineth thet gold. **c1340** Rolle *Psalter* 326 (88.45): Thi wreth, that is, rightwis pyne, brennys as fire, that purges gold and wastis stra, 431 (118.140): And purgis my hert, as fournas gold. **c1395** *WBible* Job xxiii 10: He schal preve me as gold, that passith thorough fier, Wisdom iii 6: He prevede hem as gold in a furneis, Isaiah i 25 *gloss:* As gold and silver is purgid fro al filthe bi the fier, I Peter i 7: That the prevyng of youre feith be myche more preciouse than gold, that is prevyd bi fier. **a1400** *Allemighty god* in *Yorkshire Writers* II 38.175–6: Til thai be clensid clene ther-by, as gold is founden in fire meltande. **a1400** *Twelve Profits* (*Royal*) in *Yorkshire Writers* II 49[32–3]: He proved hom as gold in tho herthe. **c1400** *Remedy* in *Yorkshire Writers* II 107[3–5]: As the gold is pured and purged by the fyre . . . so is a man by temptacyon proved for good, 109[24–6]. **c1400** *Vices and Virtues* 105.8–9, 167.22–3: No more than the gold may be fyned with-oute fier. **1420** Lydgate *Temple* 49.1191–3, **a1422** *Life* 415.1483: As gold in fyre is fynyde be assay. **c1422** Hoccleve *Complaint* 108.358–9: Gold purgyd is thou seyst, in the furneis, For the fyner and clenner it shall be. **a1435** Misyn *Fire* 59.29–30. **c1449** Pecock *Repressor* I 99[12–4]: Right as good trewe gold, the more it suffrith the fier, the more cleerli he is seen to be trewe gold. **a1450** *Three Middle English Sermons* 59.295–8: Gold, as seith clerkes, it wil gladliche take no corupcion . . . and, thei it be cast e the ver, it will onliche purifie and clense it-self and nawth brene. **c1450** *Consail and Teiching* 77.399–400. **a1460** *Dicts* (*Helmingham*) 167.30–1. **a1475** Ashby *Dicta* 86.951–2. **1477** Rivers *Dictes* 72[19–20]. **1484** Caxton *Royal Book* G3v[5–6]. **c1485** *Monk of Evesham* 72[16]: Clensyd as gold ys in a fornes. **c1495** *Arundel Vulgaria* 44.191: Likewyse as golde is provyde by fyre, so is a trusty frende knowne in trouble, 192. **a1500** *Imitatione* (*1*) 14.34–15.1, 19.18–9. **a1500** *Life of Holy Job* in *Archiv* 126(1911) 369.134: Lyke as the filth from fyne golde tryed ys by fyre. **a1500** *Norwich Creation B* in Waterhouse 17.128. **a1500** *Twelve Profits of Anger* in *PMLA* 53(1938) 83.14[3–8]: Ffor as the fyre the golde from drosse may fyne, That ys moost precyous metall and dere, And as the fyle the yren from ruste maketh shyne, And as the flayle from chaffe beteth cornes sere, And as the pressour from grapes presseth the wyne, So clensyth anger the soule and maketh yt clere. **a1500** *Twelve Profits* (*Rawlinson*) in *Yorkshire Writers* II 395[36–7]. **1502** *Imitatione* (*2*) 162.25–6, 165.39–40. Tilley G284, T337, 448; Whiting *Drama* 314:146, *Scots* I 180. See **F180, M522, S327, 410.**

G299 **Gold** is good and learning is much better
1506 *Kalender* 169.8–9: Caton the grete clarke some tyme sayd so, Howe golde is good and lernynge moche better.

G300 **Gold** is the metal whereby love is attained
1523 Berners *Froissart* I 26[5–7]: Golde . . . is the metall wherby love is attaygned both of gentylemen and of pore souldiours.

G301 **Gold** may be gone but worship is ay new
c1470 *Wallace* 209.888: Gold may be gayn, bot worschip is ay new. See **N12.**

G302 **Gold** may speed in every need
a1438 Kempe 59.15: Gold . . . whech may spede in every nede.

G303 **Gold** passes lead (other metals)
c1300 *Becket* I 51.1031–2: For gold ne passeth noght in bounte so moche leode, iwis, As digneté of preosthod passeth the lewed man that is. **1471** Caxton *Recuyell* II 456.2–4: Lyke as the gold passith all other maner metallis semblably he passith all other werkis of nature.

G304 If **Gold** rust, what shall iron do?
c1387-95 Chaucer *CT* I[A] 500–2: That if gold ruste, what shal iren do? For if a preest be foul, on whom we truste, No wonder is a lewed man to ruste.

G305 The more **Gold** a man has the more he covets
a1400 *Alexander C* 245.4688–90: I se na godlaik in gold bot grefe to the saule, For the fastir it fallis on a freke the fastir he covettis. **c1440** *Prose Alexander* 88.1: For ay the mare that a man hase thare-offe, the mare he covetes. Smith 210. See **M675.**

G306 No **Gold** so bright but that it will draw rust from that which is rusted
a1200 *Ancrene* 83.22–4: Beo neaver se briht or, Metal, gold, seolver, Irn, stel, that hit ne schal drahe rust of an other that is irustet, for hwon that ha longe liggen togedere.

G307 Though the **Gold** be now so red, yet it is given for bread
a1500 *Additional MS.37075* 278.13: Thow the gold be now so rede, gyt yt ys gevyn for brede.

G308 To be better than **Gold** (in coffer)
c1412 Hoccleve *Regement* 74.2040: Whos sentence is wel bette than gold in cofre. **c1502** *Lyfe of Joseph* 39.80: For thy grace, I have spyed, is better than golde.

G309 To be like **Gold** (*varied*)
1369 Chaucer *BD* 858: Me thoghte most lyk gold hyt (*hair*) was, **c1390** *CT* VII 2864[B4054]: And lyk the burned gold was his colour. **a1400** *Destruction of Troy* 99.3021: The here of hir hede, huyt as the gold, 122.3757: Crispe herit was the kyng, colouret as gold. **c1400** *Alexander Buik* IV 437.10995: With hair as gold. **a1420** Lydgate *Troy* I 287.4985: Lik gold hir tressis. **c1475** Henryson *Testament* 112.222: Quhyte hair as gold. **a1500** *Court of Love* 430.780: Her here as gold. **1501** Douglas *Palice* 19.12: Hir hair as gold . . . was hewit. Whiting *Scots* I 180. See **G327.**

G310 To gleam like **Gold**
c1475 *Golagros* 2.21: And uthir glemyt as gold and gowlis so gay. **c1475** Henryson *Fables* 32.868: The ground wes grene, and als as gold it glemis.

G311 To glisten like **Gold** (*etc.*) (A number of single quotations are brought together here)
c1325 *In a fryht* in Böddeker 159.3: Heo glystnede ase gold when hit glemede. **a1400** *Destruction of Troy* 297.9135: The faire heris of that fre flammet of gold. **a1500** *Miroure of Mans Salvacionne* 31[26]: Brynnyng als gold in fyre.

G312 To glister (*glitter*) like **Gold**
a1500 *Grene Knight* 68.278: His geere glistered as gold. **1509** Barclay *Ship* II 297[20]: Thy here glystrynge . . . as golde bryght. Whiting *Ballad* 28, *Drama* 314:146.

G313 To glitter like **Gold**
c1455 *Partonope S* 484.147: As gold a-bowte hit gleterede bryght. Whiting *NC* 416, *Scots* I 179.

G314 To leam (*shine*) like **Gold**
a1400 *Destruction of Troy* 16.459: And his lookes full lovely lemond as gold. **a1400** *Torrent* 11.290–1: In to the hale sche hym lad, That lemyred ase gold bryght.

G315 To shine like (the, any) **Gold**
a1000 *Old English Holy Rood* in Richard Morris *Legends of the Holy Rood* (EETS 46, 1871) 15[34–5]: And þær ætywedon þa nægles and on þare eorþan scinan and blican swa þæt seloste gold. **c1300** *St. Alexius* 187.580: That brighte schane als duse the golde. **c1330** *Owayne Miles* (*Egerton*) in Horstmann *Altenglische Legenden 1875* 200.507: The yat schinede brighte, gold as it were. **c1350** *Libeaus* 118 (*vars.*) 2098–2100: Hir body and hir winge Schine in alle thinge As it were betyn (gletering) gold. **c1380** Chaucer *HF* 1386–7: Hir heer, that oundy was and crips, As burned gold hyt shoon to see. **c1380** *Pearl* 7.165–6: As glysnande golde that man con schere, So schon that schene, 8.213: As schorne golde schyr her fax thenne schon. **a1387** Higden-Trevisa I 413[24]: For he schyneth as gold ful brighte. **c1390** Chaucer *CT* I[A] 3314: the, **c1395** V[F] 1247: Shoon as the burned gold with stremes brighte. **a1400** *Destruction of Troy* 126.3900: And in sighkyng it shone as the shyre golde. **a1400** *Ipomadon A* 70.2401: gold ycore. **a1400** *Pricke* 72.2632: And thar be fyned als gold that shynes clere. **a1400** *Stanzaic Life* 22.661: As gold hit shone. **c1400** *Florence* 52.1545: Golde redd. **c1400** *Thomas of Erceldoune* 4.63: clere golde. **a1420** Lydgate *Troy* I 215.2460: any, **a1422** *Life* 353.602, 493.899: His stole that lyke to golde doth shine, **a1449** *Testament* in *MP* I

331.37. **c1450** Hay *Alexander* 7[9]. **c1450** *Speculum Christiani* (2) 50.14–5. **a1470** Malory I 196.15: the. **a1475** *St. Birgitta* 74.22–3. **a1475** *Seege of Troye* 198 H 1443st. **1480** Caxton *Ovyde* 4[12–3]: More shynyng than fyn golde enameld, 21[27–8]. **a1500** *Court of Love* 412.138: gold so fyne, 426.654. **c1505** Watson *Valentine* 81.17–8: the. **a1508** *Freiris of Berwik* in Dunbar 186.140: the reid gold. Whiting *Drama* 314:146, *Scots* I 180. See **G328.**

G316 What is **Gold** but stone but if a wise man has it?
a1300 *Proverbs of Alfred* 83 J 108–9: For hwat is gold bute ston, Bute if hit haveth wismon?

G317 When I woo, **Gold** in my glove
c1450 *Douce MS.52* 55.120: When I wowe, golde in my glove; When I have, that I wylle, Goddys grame to thy bylle. Cum procor, est aurum cirothecis undique staurum; Velle meo facto, maledicta gratia sit tibi rostro. **c1450** *Rylands MS.394* 105.18.26–7: In my glove inowe . . . on thy bylle.

G318 Who has no **Gold** his treasure is soon spent
a1449 Lydgate *Cok* in *MP* II 817.133: Whoo hath no goold his tresoure soone (is) spent. See **G343.**

G319 As galliard (*gay*) as **Goldfinch**
c1390 Chaucer *CT* I[A] 4367: Gaillard he was as goldfynch in the shawe.

G320 As glad as any **Goldfinch**
c1400 *Beryn* 16.476: As glad as eny goldfynch.

G321 To leap like a **Goldfinch** on the hedge
a1300 *Alisaunder* 45.781–2: Ac Alisaundre lep on his rygge So a golfynche dooth on the hegge.

G322 As bright as **Gold Wire**
a1410 Lydgate *Churl* in *MP* II 471.59: With sonnyssh fetheris brihter than gold wer, **a1420** *Troy* I 280.4742: Bounde in a tresse, brighter thanne golde were, **1420** *Temple* 11.271–2. **a1425** *Metrical Paraphrase OT* 80.8504: Like to gold wyre so was it bryght. **c1505** Watson *Valentine* 159.18–9. See **G284.**

G323 As glistening as **Gold Wire** (*etc.*) (A number of single quotations are brought together here)
c1350 *Alexander A* 127.179–80: Long loveliche tresses Glisiande as gold-wire. **a1420** Lydgate *Troy* III 752.6424: With here to-rent, as any gold wyr shene. **a1425** *Metrical Paraphrase OT* 58.1979–80: The berdes of them wer gylt Like unto the gold wyre (*var.* unto rede gold). **c1450** *Weddynge* 261.743: Her her was to her knees as red as gold wyre. See **G292.**

G324 As glittering as **Gold Wire**
c1475 Henryson *Testament* 111.177: As goldin wyre sa glitterand was his hair. **a1508** Dunbar *Tretis* 85.19: So glitterit as the gold wer thair glorius gilt tressis. Whiting *Scots* I 180. See **G289.**

G325 As yellow as **Gold Wire**
a1400 *Susan* 219.192–3: Hir here was yolow as wyre Of gold fynyd with fyre. **a1420** Lydgate *Troy* I 284.4902: With lokkis yelwe lik gold were of colour. See **G294.**

G326 To be crisped (*curled*) like **Gold Wire**
a1420 Lydgate *Troy* I 71.1977: His sonnysshe here, crisped liche gold wyre.

G327 To be like **Gold Wire**
a1200 Lawman I 300.7048: His hæd wes swulc swa beoth gold wir (*B:* That [hadde] heer so gold wir). **c1300** Robert of Gloucester II 816.270: His her was ase goldwyr. **a1420** Lydgate *Troy* II 513.4124–5: Hir her . . . Like to gold wyr, III 580.590: Hir heer also, resemblynge to gold wyre. **a1437** *Kingis Quair* 45.1[4]: Rynsid hir tressis like the goldin wyre. **a1450** *York Plays* 308.21–2: And the hore that hillis my heed Is even like to the golde wyre. **a1500** *Beves* 24 M 400: With her long as gold wire on the grene. **a1533** Berners *Huon* 776.10: His heere lyke gold wyre. See **G309.**

G328 To shine like (the, any) **Gold Wire**
c1350 *Libeaus* 53.938–9: The her schon on hir heed, As gold wire schineth bright. **a1400** Chestre *Launfal* 61.298: Her here schon as gold wyre, 79.938–9: The her schon upon her hed As gold wyre that schynyth bryght. **a1420** Lydgate *Troy* I 72.2042. **a1445** *Carl* 140.418. **a1475** *Assembly of Gods* 12.373: Whoos long here shone as wyre of goold bryght. **a1475** *Landavall* 109.111, 125.436–7. **a1475** *Seege of Troye* 181 H 788d. **c1500** *Lady Bessy* 9[9]: the. **c1500** Newton 270.15: Youre here hit shynes as any gold wire. **1513** Douglas *Aeneid* III 162.41: the brycht gold wyre. See **G315.**

G329 What grieves one **Gome** (*man*) glads another
c1353 *Winner* 391: For if it greves one gome, it gladdes another. See **G104, H653, M486, O42.**

Good(s), sb. (1) property, *etc.* (Note the presence of word plays between the senses of **Good** [1] and **Good** [2])

G330 All worldly **Good** fares as ebb and flood

a1325 *Ipotis* in Smith *Common-place Book* 31.193–4: Yt faryt be all thys wardly good, As be and ebbe and be a flood. **1438** *Barlam and Josaphat* (*Northern*) 235.695–6: This werldely gude, That ebbes and flowes here als the flode. See **C114, E42, G338, W671.**

G331 Be not sorry for loss of worldly **Good**
c1450 Idley 185.1611–3: Beith not sorie for losse of worldlie goodis; They com by fortune whiche is transtorie, Now heere, now ther, as ebbis and flodes.

G332 Deal with no **Good** that is misgot (evil begot)
a1400 *Proverbis of Wysdom* 246.114: Dele with no gwode, that is mysgote. **c1450** *Fyrst thou sal* 89.90: Dele with no godes evyl begot. Cf. Tilley G301.

G333 Evil-gotten **Goods** thrive not to the third heir (*varied*)
c1303 Mannyng *Handlyng* 295.9435–6: Here mayst thou se, evyl-wunne thyng, With eyre shal never make gode endyng, 296.9469–72: Unneth lasteth aght that men bye With that ys wunne with marchaundye; Yn erytage nat long hyt vayleth, The thred eyre leseth, that outher travayleth, 9477–8: For thys men se, and seye alday, "The thred eyre selleth alle away." **a1425** *Bird with Four Feathers* in Brown *Lyrics XIV* 214.207–8: Men seith, good gete untrewly, The thridde heire broke it may. **a1450** *Castle* 80.103: And his (*the covetous man's*) eyr aftyrward comyth evere be-hynde. **1464** Hardyng 18[17–23]: For when Henry the fourth first was crouned, Many a wyseman sayd then full commenly, The third heyre shuld not joyse, but be uncrouned, And deposed of all regalitee. To this reason they dyd there wittes applye, Of evill gotton good the third should not enjoyse, (Of longe agone it hath bene a commen voyse). **a1470** Parker *Dives* X5[r][1.28–31]: For it is a comon proverbe De male quesistis vix gaudet tercius heres. Of evyl goten good the thyrde heyre unneth hath Joye, X8[v][1.2–3]: Of evyl goten good unneth Joyed the thyrde heyre. **1474** Caxton *Chesse* 145[12–3]: For of evyll gooten good the thyrde heyr shall never rejoyce. **c1475** *Political Retrospect* in Wright *Political Poems* II 268[19–20]: Scripture saithe heritage holdyn wrongfully Schal never cheve ne with the thred heyre remayne. **1484** Caxton *Aesop* 238[18–9]: For of the thynge wrongfully and evylle goten the thyrd heyre shalle never be p(o)ssessour of hit, **1489** *Fayttes* 233.15–7: Be ye in certeyne that noo good evyl goten can be longe possessed nor kept of hym that geteth hit nor of his heyres. **a1500** *Proverbs of Salamon* 187.69.3–4: The londe that ys geten mys The thrydde heyre rejoiseth yt noght. **1509** Barclay *Ship* I 30[6–7]: For that which he getteth and kepeth wrongfully His heyre often wasteth moche more unthryftely. **1513** More *Richard* 67 C[10–1]: The thinge evill gotten is never well kept. Apperson 324; *Oxford* 315; Skeat 101; Tilley G305; Walther I 620.5081. See **B602, G336, 342, L467, M44.**

G334 **Good** is but a lent loan
a1400 *Amadace I* 42[22–3]: For gud his butte a lante lone, Sum tyme men (have) hit, sum tyme none. **a1460** *Towneley Plays* 13.116–7: Yis, all the good thou has in wone Of godis grace is bot a lone. **c1475** *How a Merchant* 120.115–6: Gode ys but a lante lone, Some tyme men have hyt and some tyme none. **a1500** *Amadace A* 261.416–7: Gud is bot a lant lone, Sumtyme hasse a man oght, sumtyme non. Whiting *Ballad* 37: gear. See **A240, C114, F108.**

G335 **Good** that was gotten in many a day may slip away in short time
a1475 *Mumming of the Seven Philosophers* in Robbins 111.41–2: Ffor in short tyme the good may slyp away That was gotyn in many a sondry day. See **H602.**

G336 **Goods** falsely gotten seldom come to good end (never prove well)
c1523 Barclay *Mirrour* 80[28]: For goodes falsly gotten come seldome to good ende. **1546** Heywood *D* 52.352: Evill gotten good never proveth well. Apperson 324; *Oxford* 315; Smith 86; Tilley G301; Whiting *Scots* I 180. See **G333, 342, M586, R114, W371.**

G337 The **Goods** of friends ought to be common
1450 *Dicts* 52.5–6: The goodes of freendes ought to be comune. **1477** Rivers *Dictes* 31[17]: The goodis of frendes ought to be comyn. Apperson 10.

G338 The **Goods** of this world are variable
1483 Caxton *Cato* G4[r]]27–8]: The goodes of thys worlde been varyable, now one is ryche, and now poure. See **G330, W671.**

G339 The greater **Good** forlorn (*lost*), the less might
1410 Walton *Boethius* 224[2]: The gretter good forlorne, the lesse myght.

G340 He that desires other men's **Goods** oft loses his own
1484 Caxton *Aesop* 10[1–3]: He that desyreth

to have other mens goodes oft he loseth his owne good. See **A91.**

G341 I had my **Good** and my friend, *etc.*
a1500 *Silver and Friend* in Robbins 81: I had my good and my ffrend, I lent my good To my ffrend, I askyd my good Of my ffrend, I lost my good and my ffrend. I made of my ffrend my ffoo: I will be war I do no more soo. Robbins, notes 254–5; Brown-Robbins 1297. See **F653, 666, M27.**

G342 Ill-gotten **Good** shall be gone
a1425 *St. Robert* 67.830: Yll gytten gode, men says ytt sall be gane. See **G333, 336, N166.**

G343 Little **Good** soon spent
1555 Heywood *E* 176.169.2: Lyttle good, soone spended. Apperson 371; *Oxford* 373; Tilley G299. See **G318.**

G344 The more **Good** that a man has the better he is
c1400 *Seven Deadly Sins* in Wyclif *SEW* III 126[20–2]: Ffor hit is seide comynly, that evere tho more gode that a man haves, evere tho better he is, and tho more to telle by. See **M769.**

G345 Such **Goods** as are gathered with sin are lost with sorrow
a1500 Warkworth 26[6–7]: Suche goodes as were gaderide with synne, were loste with sorwe. See **R120.**

G346 Suffice to your **Good**
c1390 Chaucer *Truth* 2: Suffyce unto thy good, though it be smal. **a1393** Gower *CA* III 163.7735–9: Senec conseileth in this wise, And seith, "Bot if thi good suffise Unto the liking of thi wille, Withdrawh thi lust and hold the stille, And be to thi good sufficant."

G347 Who has no **Good** can (do) no good
c1412 Hoccleve *Regement* 45.1233–4: I have herd men seyn, Who-so no good hath, that he can no good. **a1475** *Landavall* 106.26: Who hath no good, goode can he none. See **L392.**

G348 Who has no **Good** is far from his friends
c1412 Hoccleve *Regement* 35.957: Who no good hath, is fer his frendes fro. See **P295, 301, 335.**

Good, sb. (2), virtue, benefit, *etc.*

G349 **Good** comes of good and ill ofttime of ill
c1450 *Consail and Teiching* 66.17–8: Fore of the gud the gud ay cummys, And of the Ill oft-tyme Ill sum ys.

G350 **Good** is current and lasts with God
c900 *Maxims* in *Exeter Book* 161.120: God bið genge, and wiþ god lenge.

G351 He that can (*knows*) no **Good,** who shall warn him if he never thrive?
a1500 Hill 129.38: He that no good can nor non will lern, If he newer thriwe, who shall him warne?

G352 He that thinks to begin **Good** let him make a beginning with himself
a1000 Aethelwold *Edgar* in Cockayne III 438[31–2]: Hit eac swa on bocum awritan is. Se þe god beginnan þence, he þæt angin on him sylfum astelle. See **M113.**

G353 How shall one do **Good** to another who can do no good to himself?
1484 Caxton *Aesop* 92[1–3]: How shalle one do ony good to another, the whiche can doo no good to his owne self? See **P150, T50.**

G354 Little **Good** comes of gathering where wretched avarice burns
a1500 *Colkelbie* 282–3.19–24: For in old proverbe we sing, Cumis littill gud of gaddering Quhair wrechit awerice birnis, Hyding hurdis in to hirnis And knawis nevir quhome till. *Oxford* 373; Whiting *Scots* I 176.

G355 No **Good** may befall him who thinks ill
a1500 ?Ros *La Belle Dame* 311.397: Who thinketh il, no good may him befal. *Oxford* 314. See **S197.**

G356 No man may have **Good** but he buy it
a1400 *Romaunt B* 2737–9: May no man have good, but he it by. A man loveth more tendirly The thyng that he hath bought most dere. *Oxford* 278: Hard to come. See **L519, W420.**

G357 Of two **Good**(s) choose the better
c1350 *Mirror of Saint Edmund* in Perry *Religious Pieces* 29.36–30.1: And of twa gude, chese the bettire and leffe the lesse gude. **a1400** Wyclif *Sermons* I 296[21–2]: For he synneth hugeli that of two goodis chesith the worse. **1456** Hay *Law* 86.21–2: A man suld betuix twa gudis ches the best. **1483** *Quatuor Sermones* 26[3–4]: And of two good to chese the bettir. See **E193, W111.**

G358 One gets no **Good** but if he bid or pray
a1450 Audelay 26.454–5: Thou getyst no good withoutyn drede Bot yif thou byd or pray. See **M276.**

G359 When **Good** comes it ought not to be refused
1484 Caxton *Aesop* 163–4: Whan somme good cometh to somme it ought not to be reffused For it maye not ben recoverd as men wyll. See **A53, F540, W275.**

G360 Who sets not by **Good** shall set by sorrow

1480 Caxton *Ovyde* 45[17–8]: Hit is a comyn proverbe, and trouthe it is. Who that setteth nought by good shalle sette by sorowe.

Good, adj.

G361 For **Good** and all
1519 Horman *Vulgaria* 299[9]: We begen a newe counte for good and all. Apperson 255–6; Tilley G325.

G362 It is **Good** to be sure
a1500 Medwall *Nature* F2v[15]: It ys good to be sure ever more.

G363 It is **Good** to be ware
1478 *Stonor Letters* II 53[20]: It is good to be ware.

G364 It must needs be **Good** that causes so many good deeds
c1385 Usk 79.72–3: Nedes mot it be good, that causeth so many good dedes. Apperson 263.

G365 Not all is **Good** that is fair
c1300 *South English Legendary* II 693.40: Hyt nys noght al god that is vayr. See **A155.**

G366 To have as **Good** as one brings
a1533 Berners *Arthur* 67[20]: Ye shall have as good as ye brynge.

G367 He often says "Have **Good Day**" that is loath to take his leave (*varied*)
a1393 Gower *CA* II 377.2814–5: Bot he seith often, "Have good day," That loth is forto take his leve. **a1500** *Mostyn MS.129* in *Historical Manuscripts Commission: Report on Manuscripts in the Welsh Language* I(1898) 65: Loth to depart byds oft fare well. **c1500** Greene *Carols* 141.6: But oftyntymys I have hard say That he is loth to pert away That oftyn byddyth, "Have gud day!"

G368 There was no **"Good Day"** but fell strokes
a1420 Lydgate *Troy* I 327.6381–2: Ther was no "gooday," nor no saluyng, But strokis felle. See **F674, L554.**

G369 My **Good Friday** is better than your Pace (*Easter*)
c1375 Henryson *Fables* 11.248: My gude friday is better nor your pace. See **C247.**

G370 Greedy is the **Goodless**
c1250 *Hendyng O* 196.26: Gredi is the goedles. Apperson 273; Kneuer 30; *Oxford* 266; Schleich 255; Singer III 129.

G371 **Goodness** is better than beauty
c1500 *Melusine* 135.2–3: Goodnes and bounte is betre than fayrenes and beaulte. (French, in footnote, Bonte vault mieulx que beaulté.) See **B152.**

G372 "Beware" quoth the **Goodwife,** when she smote off her husband's head
c1475 *Mankind* 23.611: "Be-ware," quod the goode wyff, when sche smot of here husbondis hede: "be-ware!"

G373 Where the **Goodwife** is master the goodman may be sorry
c1475 *Mankind* 8.195: Wher the goode wyff ys master, the goode-man may be sory.

G374 As deep drinks the **Goose** as the gander
1549 Heywood *D* 85.162: But as deepe drinketh the goose, as the gander. Apperson 265; *Oxford* 135; Tilley G345.

G375 As gray as **Goose** (*etc.*) (A number of single quotations are brought together here)
c1390 Chaucer *CT* I[A] 3317: His rode was reed, his eyen greye as goos, **c1395** IV[E] 2275: So that ye men shul been as lewed as gees. **c1400** *Laud Troy* I 219.7428–9: Thei dyed thikkere then men dryves gece To chepyngtoun for to selle. **c1450** *Alphabet* I 19.14: Mad as a guse.

G376 As wise as wild **Geese**
1528 More *Heresyes* 179 F[8–9]: All as wise as wilde geese. Apperson 696; *Oxford* 716; Tilley G348.

G377 As witless as a wild **Goose**
a1529 Skelton *Garnesche* I 118.18: As wytles as a wylde goos. **1533** More *Answer* 1079 A[4–5]: His witlesse writing maketh men weene he were a wilde gose. Tilley G348; Whiting *Drama* 315:147.

G378 The **Goose** is good, the gansel (*garlic sauce*) sour as gall
c1475 Henryson *Fables* 15.345: Thy guse is gude, thy gansell sour as gall. Tilley G350. See **G388.**

G379 The **Goose** is over the moon
1533 More *Confutacion* 812 F[6–8]: They were so farre inspired with the spirit of the buttery that the goose was over the mone. Cf. Taylor and Whiting 156:5.

G380 He that turns the **Goose,** by right should have the neck
a1500 Hill 131.21: He that torneth the gose, by right shuld have the nekke. Apperson 266; Tilley G355.

G381 Not to dare go for the **Goose** that blows (*hisses*) (*varied*)
1340 *Ayenbite* 32[10–1]: And to the childe that

ne dar naght guo his way vor the guos thet blauth. **c1400** *Vices and Virtues* 27.30–1: And the child that dar nought goo in the weie for the boones that wistleth with the wynde (see note p. 294). **1484** Caxton *Royal Book* d5v[9–10]: The chylde that dare not goo in the waye for gaglyng and syflyng of the ghees. **a1500** *Tudor Crosse Rowe* in *JEGP* 58(1959) 249.11–2: G for gyklard and lawer (*sic*) with her one Eye, The hyssyng of gander made hym ron a-way. Cf. Taylor and Whiting 37; Tilley B481.

G382 There is no **Goose** (dove) so gray that will be without a make (*mate*) (*varied*)
c1395 Chaucer *CT* III[D] 269–70: Ne noon so grey goos gooth ther in the lake As, seistow, wol been withoute make. **1513** Douglas *Aeneid* II 148.53: The snaw quhyte dow oft to the gray maik will. *Oxford* 259; Skeat 264; Tilley G362. See **F447, M64.**

G383 To eat of the **Goose** that grazes on one's grave
1509 Barclay *Ship* II 170[6–7]: For suche as they moste gladly dede wolde have Etyth of that gose that graseth on theyr grave. Apperson 266:16; *Oxford* 166; Taylor and Whiting 156; Tilley G353.

G384 To gangle (*jangle*) like a **Goose**
c1450 Idley 210.416: Gangle as a gosse and Jangyll as a Jey.

G385 To have as good a mind as has a **Goose** on a spit
1506 Barclay *Castell* E4v[7–8]: I had in me as good a mynde As hath a gose upon a spete. (French [p. 71]: Eut en luy autant de propos Que ung oyseau qui est sur la branche.)

G386 To kill the **Goose** that lays the golden eggs
a1400 *Alexander C* 42.893–4: For sais your lord, the lefe hen that laide hir first (*Dublin:* frist, Latin: ova aurea) egg, Hire bodi now with barante is barely consumed. **1484** Caxton *Aesop* 245[3–10]: A man whiche had a goos that leyd every day an egge of golde . . . and slewe her. Apperson 266; *Oxford* 334; Taylor and Whiting 156; Tilley G363.

G387 To know a **Goose** from a swan
c1516 Skelton *Magnificence* 10.298–9: In faythe, els had I gone to longe to scole, But yf I coulde knowe a gose from a swanne. Cf. Apperson 265; Tilley G369.

G388 To sell a fat **Goose** for little, but the garlic cost many shillings
c1400 *Of Prelates* in Wyclif *EW* 82[32–3]: Thei sillen a faat goos for litel or nought, but the garlek costith many shillyngis. Apperson 266. See **G378.**

G389 To shoe the **Goose** (gosling)
1415 Hoccleve *Oldcastle* I 19.337: Yee medle of al thyng, yee moot shoo the goose. **1435** *Whalley* (*Lancashire*) *misericord* in Francis Bond *Wood Carvings in English Churches* I (Oxford, 1910) 186: Whoso melles of wat men does, Let hym cum hier and sho the ghos. **c1475** *Why I Can't* 144.251–4: For whoso chateryt lyke a py And tellethe alle that he herethe and seethe, He schall be put owte of company, And scho the gose, thus wysdum us lereth. **1546** Heywood *D* 65.37: Who medleth in all thyng, maie shooe the goslyng, **1555** *E* 182.199. Apperson 411; *Oxford* 417, 582; Taylor and Whiting 156; Tilley G354; Whiting *Drama* 362:835.

G390 To stagger like a **Goose**
c1434 Drury 82.13–4: This man hath drunkyn hese leggis a-sonder and stagert as a goose. Iste homo eviravit tibias suas in potando.

G391 To steal a **Goose** and stick down a feather
a1546 Heywood *D* 52.350–1: As dyd the pure penitent that stale a goose And stack downe a fether, **1555** *E* 175.164. Apperson 601; *Oxford* 619; Tilley G365.

G392 To totter like **Geese**
c1400 *Laud Troy* I 286–7.9720–1: Thei sat toterynge as it were gece—What for the strokes and the hete.

G393 To wit (*know*) no more than a **Goose**
c1330 *Times of Edward II* 333.222: Thouh he wite no more than a gos wheither he wole live or die.

G394 As great as a **Goose Egg**
c1395 *Pierce* 9.225: As greet as a gos eye growen all of grece. Apperson 265.

G395 As open as a **Goose Eye**
a1500 Medwall *Nature* E4v[9–10]: Nay, all ys open that they do there, As open as a gose eye. Apperson 265; Tilley G371.

G396 Not give a **Goose Wing**
c1378 *Piers* B iv 36: Thei ne gyveth noughte of god one gose wynge.

G397 A **Goshawk** and a crow
a1449 Lydgate *Cok* in *MP* II 815.79: A ffresh comparisoun, a goshawk and a crowe. See **F37.**

G398 As sooth as (the) **Gospel**
c1303 Mannyng *Handlyng* 283.9010: Ys as soth as the gospel. **c1325** *Chronicle* 75.1236: For it is sothe as godspel. **a1338** Mannyng *Chronicle B* I 123[14]: the. **c1350** *Smaller Vernon Collection* 18.646. **c1390** *Psalterium b. Mariae* 84.796. **a1450** *Partonope* 49.1760: the. **a1500** *On England's Commercial Policy* in Wright *Political Poems* II 282[12]: The wiche ys soth as gospelle of the masse. *Oxford* 672.

G399 As true as (the, any) **Gospel**
c1410 Lovelich *Merlin* III 562.21086: Which is as trewe as the gospelle. **a1440** Burgh *Cato* 305.68: This is as gospell trewe, 313.406: For this is as trewe as gospel douteles. **a1477** Caxton *Curtesye* 51.503: This . . . is as the gospel trewe, **1481** *Reynard* 71[29]: the. **c1497** Medwall *Fulgens* C5v[21]: the. **a1500** *As dyvers doctours* in *Lay Folks Mass Book*, ed. T. F. Simmons (EETS 71, 1879) 368[38]. **a1500** *Christ's Resurrection* in *Archiv* 79(1887) 447.600–1: the trew. **a1500** *O man more* 394.28: the. **a1500** *Ten Commandments* in Robbins 165.17: the. **c1500** Greene *Carols* 408.1: the. **c1500** *Miracle of B.V.* in *PMLA* 38(1923) 377.74: ony. **c1505** More *Picus* 9 E[9–10]: As trew as the gospell of seint John. **1509** Barclay *Ship* I 100[11]: the, **c1515** *Eclogues* 21.637: the. **1523** Skelton *Howe the Douty Duke* II 68.4–5: the. **1532** More *Confutacion* 404 D[3–4]: the. **1556** Heywood *Spider* 250[25]. Apperson 647; *Oxford* 672; Taylor and Whiting 157; Tilley G378; Whiting *Drama* 315:148. See **B281, C541.**

G400 **Gospel** in one's mouth
1546 Heywood *D* 63.53: Gospell in thy mouth (quoth he) this strife to breake. Tilley G379.

G401 To be (Not to be) **Gospel**
c1250 *Owl* 106.1269–70: Forthi seide Alfred swithe wel, And his worde was Goddspel. **a1338** Mannyng *Chronicle A* I 330.9441–2: Al that evere Merlyn teld, As gospel the kyng hit held. **c1385** Chaucer *TC* v 1265: That every word was gospel that ye seyde. **c1385** Usk 54.37–8: And wenene al be gospel the promise of your behestes. **c1395** Chaucer *LGW* G 326: Al ne is nat gospel that is to yow pleyned. **a1400** *Romaunt C* 7607–8: All is not gospel, out of doute, That men seyn in the town aboute. **a1400** Wyclif *Sermons* II 213[26]: For men seyen that prestis wordis shulden be as the gospel. **c1400** *Brut* I 74.24–5: His worde shal bene gospelle. **c1400** *De Blasphemia* in Wyclif *SEW* III 407[34]: That al holy Chirche shulde trowe hit as gospel. **a1438** Kempe 202.35–6: Now Gospel mote it ben in yowr mowth. **a1450** *Seven Sages B* 67.1957–8: And wende hit were al gospel That the clerkys dyden hym to wite. **a1500** *Clerk and the Husbandman* in Robbins 181.27: Thow wenis that thai be in the gospell. **1546** Heywood *D* 63.54: All is not gospell that thou doest speake. Apperson 267; *Oxford* 260; Tilley A147. See **E154.**

G402 As light as any **Gossamer**
c1435 Lydgate *Letter to Gloucester* in *MP* II 666.26: As any gossomer the countirpeys was liht. Svartengren 297.

G403 As smooth as **Gossamer**
a1430 Lydgate *Pilgrimage* 303.11078: Smothe as gossomer in the hayr.

G404 To be but **Gossamer**
a1400 *Morte Arthure* 79.2687: For this (*wound*) es bot gosesomere, and gyffen on erles.

G405 To gird (*rush*) out like a **Gote** (*stream*)
c1400 *Laud Troy* I 201.6817: The blod gerd out, as were a gote.

G406 The fools of **Gotham**
a1460 *Towneley Plays* 106.180: Sagh I never none so fare bot the foles of gotham. Apperson 267; *Oxford* 716–7; Tilley M636.

G407 He may not **Govern** many (people) that cannot govern himself
1450 *Dicts* 122.5: He may not governe muche peple that can not governe him-silf. **1477** Rivers *Dictes* 61[8–9]: He that can not nor wil governe him self is not able to governe many other. *Oxford* 105; Tilley C552. See **L443, M228, 402, 407.**

G408 Where a **Governor** is not the people shall fall (*varied*)
c1395 *WBible* Proverbs xi 14: Where a governour is not, the puple schal falle. **a1400** *Alexander C* 223.4007–8: Wete ye wele . . . be werrayours laghes, that quen the governoure is gane than is the gomes wastid. **c1440** *Prose Alexander* 72.29–31: Wate ye noghte wele that thare na governour es the folke are sparpled be-lyfe als schepe that ere wit-owtten ane hirde. **a1533** Berners *Arthur* 496[27–8]: For people without a governour are halfe discomfyted. See **H253, 257.**

G409 He is not well arrayed that is clothed with another's **Gown**
1484 Caxton *Aesop* 220[22–5]: For as men sayn comynly he is not wel arayed nor wel appoynted whiche is clothed with others gowne.

G410 **Grace** fails commonly where (there) is division
c1400 *Beryn* 87.2894: And grace faylith comynlych, wher is dyvisioun.

G411 **Grace** grows after governance
a1425 *Trinity Coll. Cambridge MS.602* in M. R. James *Catalogue* (Cambridge, 1901) II 95: Grace growith aftir governance. **a1475** *Good Rule* in Brown *Lyrics XV* 263.9–10: Al is for defaute of grace That god grucchyth oure governaunce. **a1500** *Beauty of his Mistress II* in Robbins 125.37: Yett throughe governance growethe grace. Apperson 267.

G412 **Grace** never grew of wretched avarice
a1500 *Colkelbie* 304.6: Of wrechit awarice grew nevir grace.

G413 The **Grace** of God (is great enough)
c1378 *Piers* B ix 176: And thanne gete ye the grace of god and good ynogh to lyve with. **c1380** *Pearl* 24.660: And the grace of god is gret innogh. Apperson 253; *Oxford* 261; Tilley G393. See **G229, 230.**

G414 **Grace** passes gold
c1425 *And ye will please* in Person 25.16–9: Grace passeth gollde And precyous stoon, And god schalbe god When goolde ys goon. **a1500** *Salamon seyth* in Person 53.29–30.

G415 Out-take (*except*) **Grace** all thing shall pass
a1400 *Proverbis of Wysdom* 244.28: Owte take grace all thyng shal passe. *Oxford* 261.

G416 To graff (*graft*) a green **Graff** on a rotten root
1549 Heywood *D* 53.415: Than graffe we a greene graffe on a rotten roote.

G417 As the **Grain** is in the grape (grass) (so) grows the fruit
a1400 *Alexander C* 140.2425–6: And ye at wickid ere within ay wickidly ye thinke; For as the grayne is in the grape (*Dublin:* of the grase) growis the frutis. See **F309.**

G418 Of a small **Grain** the earth engenders great trunks
1481 *Tulle of Olde Age* 53[8–12]: Ffor of a smale grayne of a figge or of a litle smale pepyn or kernell of a roysyn or of a smale corne of whete or of ony othir seedys or of som smale wandes and braunchis the erthe engendreth grete tronkes and grete trees and bowes. See **K12, O7.**

G419 Of good **Grain** grows good wheat
a1449 Lydgate *St. Austin* in *MP* I 193.17: Of good greyn sowe growith up good wheete.

G420 One **Grain** of pepper smarts more than a sack full of wheat
c1500 *Melusine* 128.19–21: Yet one grayne of peper alone smertith more on mans tonge than doth a sacke full of whette. Tilley G400.

G421 One cannot gather **Grapes** from thorns (*varied*)
c1000 Aelfric *Homilies* II 406[2–3]: Hwa gaderað æfre winberian of ðornum, oþþe fic-æppla of bremelum? **c1000** *WSG* Matthew vii 16: Cwyst þu gaderað man winberian of þornum, oððe ficæppla of þyrncinum? Luke vi 44: Ne hig of þornum ficæppla ne gaderiaþ, ne winberian on gorste ne nimað. **c1385** Usk 128.4–7: For if thou desyre grapes, thou goest not to the hasel; ne, for to fecchen roses, thou sekest not on okes; and if thou shalt have hony-soukels thou levest the frute of the soure docke. **c1395** *WBible* Matthew vii 16: Whether men gaderen grapis of thornes, or figus of breris? Luke vi 44: And men gaderen not figus of thornes, nethir men gederen a grape of a buysche of breris. **a1400** Wyclif *Sermons* I 21[1–3]: Goddis word, that men gederen not of thornes grapis . . . ne gidere not figis of breris. **c1450** Capgrave *Katharine* 284.695: Who seketh grapes oute of the brere? Tilley G411. See **N94, T223.**

G422 As green as (the, any) **Grass**
c1200 *Hali Meidenhad* 48.514–5: Thi rudie neb schal leanin, ant ase gres grenin (*become green*). **a1300** *Meidan Maregrete* 494.172: He wert ase grene so gres ine someres tide. **1375** *Canticum de Creatione* 307.201: As gras hire body was grene. **a1387** Higden-Trevisa I 123[8]: Grene as gras. **c1390** *Sir Gawain* 8.235: the. **a1398**(1495) Bartholomaeus-Trevisa M2^{v}[1.12–3]. **a1400** *Eglamour* 52 (*var. after* 774): Hys wynges were grene as any gras. **c1410** Lovelich *Grail* II 376.283–4: As grene . . . As . . . Gras In ony Mede. **a1415** Mirk *Festial* 67.17. **a1425** *Life of Adam and Eve* in *Wheatley MS.* 83.12. **a1470** Malory II 990.35–991.1: ony. **a1475** *Assembly of Gods* 11.334: Grene as any gresse in the somertyde. **a1475** *Mergarete* 238.303–4: A dragone . . . That was of colour as grasse grene. **a1475** *Tree* 140.2. **a1500** *As I fared thorow* in Dyboski 89.38. **a1500** *I have a lady* in Person 39.10: any. **a1500** *Inter Diabolus et Virgo* 444.17–445.37: What ys grenner than ys the wode? . . . Gras ys grenner than ys the wode. **c1500** *King Hart* 97.6. **c1505** Watson *Valentine* 140.18–9: More greaner than the grasse in May. **a1508** Dunbar

Tretis 85.24: Thair mantillis grein war as the gress that grew in May sessoun. Apperson 273–4; Taylor and Whiting 159; Tilley G412; Whiting *Scots* I 181.

G422a Grass-green
a1300 *Alisaunder* 19.299: Mercurye he made gres-grene. **c1325** *Early English Receipts* in *Archaeological Journal* 1 (1844) 65[7]: Vorte make grasgrene. **c1405** *Mum* 53.879. **a1500** *Eger P* 202.291. **a1500** *St. Margarete* B3r[12].

G423 As swith (*quickly*) as **Grass** falls from the scythe (*etc.*) (A number of single quotations are brought together here)
a1300 *Richard* 431.6857–8: And slowen Sarezynes also swythe As gres fallith fro the sythe. **c1300** *South English Legendary* (*Laud*) 187.106: So ful of sweordes pointes i-pighte ase Mede is ful of gras. **c1325** *Way of Woman's Love* 163.29–31: Ase fele syth and oft . . . Ase . . . grases sour ant suete. **a1400** *Ipomadon A* 134.4665–6: And as oftyne tymes thou her grette, As gresses ther be groande. **a1400** *Seven Penitential Psalms* in *Wheatley MS.* 46.634: And I wexide drye as dooth the gras. **a1500** *Marriage* 118.200: I am glad as grasse wold be of raine.

G424 As thick as **Grass**
c1380 Chaucer *HF* 1350–3: And they were set as thik of nouchis . . . As grasses growen in a mede. **c1380** *Ferumbras* 102.3220: The Sarasyns . . . come as thykke as gras.

G425 **Grass** seldom waxes in the path (*varied*)
c1350 *Nominale* 12*.362: Sylden waxus gres in the path. **c1400** *Beryn* 44.1403: The gras shuld growe on pament, or I hym home bryng. Apperson 269; *Oxford* 262; Tilley G415.

G426 More than **Grass** that grows
c1395 Chaucer *CT* III[D] 773–4: And therwithal he knew of mo proverbes Than in this world ther growen gras or herbes. **a1500** *The Beauty of his Mistress II* in Robbins 126.51: And as monye moo as gressys grewe. **a1508** Dunbar *Flyting* 11.195–6: Ma wormis hes thow beschittin Nor thair is gers on grund. Whiting *Scots* I 181.

G427 Not dread a **Grass**
c1400 *Laud Troy* I 291.9876: Thei dredde not the Troyens a gras.

G428 Not give a **Grass**
a1450 *Castle* 142.2170: Thou thou speke evyl, I ne yeve a gres.

G429 Sweet **Grass** makes good hay
a1500 *O man more* 394.47: Swete gresse makes good haye.

G430 To bite the **Grass**
a1300 *Arthour and M.*[1] 199.7106–7: And sexten thousinde to grounde slowe; Mani mouthe the gres bot. See **E25.**

G431 To dry like **Grass**
1414 ?Brampton *Psalms* 32[20]: As gres in medewe I drye and dwyne.

G432 To fallow (*fade*) like meadow **Grass**
a1300 Thomas de Hales 68.15–6: Under molde hi liggeth colde And faleweth so doth medewe gres.

G433 To fare like **Grass** growing on a chimney
1450 *Dicts* 24.11–3: The goodnes of oon ignoraunt man or unkonnyng man farith as gresse growing on a chimney (**a1460** [*Helmingham*] 25.11: lyke the herbes that growen upon dongehilles). Cf. Tilley G414: Grass grows not in hot ovens.

G434 To lie down like **Grass** that men mow
c1300 Robert of Gloucester I 382.5253: The gode knightes leye adoun as gras that me doth mowe. Cf. Whiting *Drama* 315:150.

G435 To wallow (*wither*) as does the **Grass**
a1450 *Bodley MS.1619* in *ESt* 10(1887) 248.634: I welowide, as doith the gras.

G436 What was green **Grass** is now welked (*withered*) hay (*varied*)
a1393 Gower *CA* III 452.2436–7: That which was whilom grene gras, Is welked hey at time now. **a1400** *Northern Verse Psalter* I 303 (89.6): It wites als gresse areli at dai, Areli blomes and fares awai; At even doun es it broght, Un-lastes, and welkes, and gas to noght. **a1425** *Complaynt of Criste* in *Pol. Rel. and Love Poems* 202.191–2: Furst A man growys As A gras, And Aftyr-warde welkythe as flowre or hay, 203.187–8. **a1447** Lichfield *Complaint* 509.55–6: Ffyrst a man growyth as grasse, And after welkyth as flourys or haye. **a1500** *Good Counsel* in *Bannatyne* II 145.11: Ffor of grene gress sone cumis wallowit hay. See **H212.**

G437 While the **Grass** grows the horse starves (*varied*)
c1450 Capgrave *Katharine* 95.253–4: The grey hors, whil his gres groweth, May sterve for hunger, thus seyth the proverbe. **c1450** *Douce MS.52* 45.20: While the grasse growes, the goode hors sterves. **c1450** *Rylands MS.394* 97.8. **c1475** *Rawlinson MS. D 328* 120.38: Whyle the

grasse growyth the horsse stervyth. **a1500** *Harley MS.2321* in *Rel. Ant.* I 208[12]: While the grasse growes the steede starves. **a1500** Hill 128.2: While the grasse grwith, the hors sterwith, 132.43. **1513** Douglas *Aeneid* III 118.45: Sum grenys quhil the gyrss grow for his gray meir. **1546** Heywood *D* 46.180: While the grasse groweth the horse sterveth. Apperson 269; Jente 26; *Oxford* 262; Tilley G423; Whiting *Drama* 256, *Scots* I 181–2. See **S504.**

G438 Who has dread of every **Grass** let him beware to walk in any mead
c1412 Hoccleve *Regement* 68.1887–8: Men seyn, who-so of every grace hath drede, Let hym beware to walk in any mede. *Oxford* 196; Tilley G416. See **T298.**

G439 **Grass Time** is done, my fodder is now forage
c1390 Chaucer *CT* I[A] 3868: Gras tyme is doon, my fodder is now forage.

G440 **Grass Widow**
1528 More *Heresyes* 230 G[8–9]: Then had wives bene in his tyme litle better than grasse widowes be nowe. NED Grass widow.

G441 To sow in **Gravel** (*varied*)
1447 Bokenham 50.1845–51.1846: Or betythe the wynde, or in gravel doth sowe, Or eryth the bank were nought wyl growe. **c1450** *De Claris Mulieribus* 91.1791–2: Leste that I eyre the bareyn se-banke And gete me more of laboure than of thanke. **c1522** Skelton *Speke* II 17.342: To sowe corne in the see sande, ther wyll no crope growe. Apperson 503; *Oxford* 508; Tilley S87, 184. See **C439.**

G442 As hard as **Gravel-stones**
c1450 *Jacob's Well* 281.26: Harde as gravell-stonys, 282.8.

G443 To fry in one's own **Grease** (*sometimes literally*)
a1300 *Richard* 309.4436–7: Thenne as wrehches in hous to brenne, And ffrye in oure owne gres! **c1395** Chaucer *CT* III[D] 487–8: That in his owene grece I made hym frye For angre, and for verray jalousye. **c1400** *Laud Troy* I 273.9278: Many on swalt (*died*) In his owne gres. **1420** Lydgate *Temple* 14 *var.* 3c.1: Thus is he fryed in his owene gres. **c1450** Capgrave *Katharine* 343.165–6: These renegates that we may see Ffrye in her grees (*burned alive*)! **1546** Heywood *D* 53.407: She fryeth i hir owne grease. Apperson 269–70; *Oxford* 230; Skeat 269; Tilley G433; Whiting *Ballad* 36. See **B366.**

G444 The **Great** eat the small
1506 Barclay *Castell* E2ʳ[9–10]: Every daye well mayst thou se That the grete doth ete the small. See **D146, F232.**

G445 He that takes **Great** or small takes a charge
a1393 Gower *CA* III 163.7727–9: Bot who that takth or gret or smal, He takth a charge forth withal, And stant noght fre til it be quit.

G446 Two **Great** (men) may not (be) in one sack (*i.e.*, agree)
c1412 Hoccleve *Regement* 182.5049: Men say two grete may nat in o sak.

G447 The **Greater** you are the lower look you be
c1485 *Conversion* 48.550: The gretter thou art, the lower loke thu be; Bere the never the hyer for thi degre. See **H280.**

G448 Hethen (*hence*) into (between this and) **Greece**
c1380 *Pearl* 9.231: No gladder gome hethen into Grece. **1555** Heywood *E* 182.199.3: No goose neede go barfote betwene this and Greese.

G449 **Greediness** is never full (*varied*)
c1200 Orm I 356.10215–20: Forr hellepitt niss naefre full, Ne gredignesse nowwtherr. Forr whase itt iss thatt gredig iss To winnenn erthlic ahhte, Ayy alls he mare and mare gett Ayy lisste himm affterr mare. **a1400** *Romaunt B* 5719–20: Such gredynesse hym assaylith That whanne he most hath, most he failith. See **C488, M53.**

G450 To burn like **Greekish Fire**
c1477 Caxton *Jason* 136.26: Her eyen sparklyng and brennyng as fyre Grekyssh. NED Fire 8b, Greekish 4.

G451 **Greeks'** gifts are not without deceit
1513 Douglas *Aeneid* II 67.57–8: Or gif ye traist ony Grekis gyftis be Withowt dissait, falshed and subtelte. *Oxford* 196.

G452 **Green** for falseness (change)
c1395 Chaucer *CT* V[F] 646–7: And al withoute, the mewe is peynted grene, In which were peynted alle thise false fowles. **a1420** Lydgate *Troy* I 218.2577: Chaunging now as grene, **a1439** *Fall* III 676.46: Meynt with liht greene for chaung and doubilnesse. See **B384.**

G453 Rootless **Green** must soon die (*varied*)
c1385 Chaucer *TC* iv 769–70: For which ful ofte a by-word here I seye, That "rooteles moot grene soone deye." **a1393** Gower *CA* II 373.2680–3: For lich unto the greene tree, If that men toke

his rote aweie, Riht so myn herte scholde deie, If that mi love be withdrawe. Apperson 538; *Oxford* 458; Skeat 192; Whiting *Scots* II 145:7.

G454 To think to go upon the fair **Green** when one falls in the mire
a1393 Gower *CA* II 54.681–3: He wolde make a wornman wene To gon upon the faire grene, Whan that sche falleth in the Mir.

G455 **Greeting** (*weeping*) helps not (*varied*)
c1300 *Havelok* 7.166–7: And seyde, "that greting helpeth nouht, For al to dede am ich brouht." **c1410** Lovelich *Merlin* II 319.11939–40: And therfore nethyr with wepyng ne with mone We mown not helpen that is to done. **c1450** *Merlin* I 174[1–3]: And therfore I sey wepinge, ne makynge of sorowe, ne may us not a-vaile; but wemen shull wepe. See **D337, L52, M729.**

G456 As sharp as **Greisiler** (*gooseberry bush*)
c1450 *Pilgrimage LM* 133[33]: More sharp than . . . greisiler.

G457 As fresh as **Greyhound** to hare
c1300 *Reinbrun* 662.93.2–3: Ase fresch a was to fight Ase grehonde to hare.

G458 As glad as **Greyhound** let off leash
a1375 *Octavian* (*S*) 25.767–8: As glad, as grehond ylete of lese, Florent was than.

G459 As swift as a **Greyhound**
a1420 Lydgate *Troy* I 384.8371: Swift as a grehond that renneth oute of lees. **1485** Caxton *Charles* 79.15–6: An hors as swyft as a grehounde, 151.1–2. Svartengren 377.

G460 A **Greyhound** should be headed like a snake, *etc.*
1486 ?Berners *Boke of St. Albans* F4v[16–9]: The propreteis of a goode Grehound. A Grehounde shulde be heded like a Snake, and necked like a Drake. Foted like a Kat. Tayled like a Rat. Syded lyke a Teme. Chyned like a Beme. Apperson 274–5; Tilley S283.

G461 To chase as a **Greyhound** does the hare (fox)
c1400 *Sowdone* 89.3119–20: The Cristen hem chased to and fro, As a grehounde dothe the hare. **1422** Yonge *Governaunce* 174.10–1: Scipion hym chased as a grefhound dothe the Fox.

G462 To fail as does the **Greyhound** of the hare
a1425 *Arthour and M.*[2] 350.1695–6: Yet may thow faile of al thy fare, As doth the grehound of the hare. **c1500** *Arthour and M.*[3] 472.1609: hound.

G463 To fare as **Greyhounds** do with hares
a1300 *Richard* 340.5109–10: And that Rycharde with theyr folke fares As grehoundes do with hares. **a1470** Malory I 222.6–7: They fared with the Romaynes as grayhoundis doth with harys.

G464 To smite (thrust) among the press as **Greyhound** (out of leash)
a1300 *Arthour and M.*[1] 252.9027–8: And smiten hem amid the pres, So grehound doth out of les, 254.9125–6, 267.9759–60. **a1300** *Richard* 183.1933–4: As greyhoundes stryken out of lese Kynge Rycharde threste amonge the prese. **a1338** Mannyng *Chronicle B* I 189[7–8]: On ther first eschel he smot in fulle hastif, And thorgh tham ilka del, als grehound or mastif.

G465 To spare as **Greyhound** does the hare (*etc.*) (A number of single quotations are brought together here)
c1350 *Libeaus* 91.1636–8: The porter nold nought spare, As greyhound doth the hare, To ham he ran full whate. **c1390** *Talkyng* 60.22: I lepe on him raply as grehound on herte. **a1400** *Morte Arthure* 32.1075: He grennede as a grewhounde. **a1400** Wyclif *Sermons* II 359[23–4]: And thus thes prelatis suen apostlis as grehoundis suen an hare. **c1402** *Daw Topias* (*Jack*) 95[19–20]: Dawe, ye folowen Crist, As greyhounde doth the hare. **c1500** *Cock* 2[12]: And pulde as it had been grehondes at a hare. See **H584.**

G466 To groan like a **Grice** (*pig*)
a1475 *Ludus Coventriae* 149.95: The gredy devyl xal grone grysly as a gryse.

G467 To sleep like a **Grice**
a1300 *Jacob and Joseph* 1.11–2: To fullen oure wombe hit is lutel pris, And seththe ligge slepe, such hit were a gris. See **H408, S970.**

G468 He is not wise that does so that his **Grief** is more
a1393 Gower *CA* III 153.7348–9: He is noght wys that fint him grieved, And doth so that his grief be more. See **S193.**

G469 To look like a **Griffin**
c1385 Chaucer *CT* I[A] 2133: And lik a grifphon looked he aboute.

G470 It is slippery to **Grip** where there is no hold
c1450 *Royal MS. 17 D xviii* f.lb in G. F. Warner and J. P. Gilson *Catalogue of Western MSS. in the Old Royal and King's Collections* II (1921) 256: Slyppur is to grype on whome is no holde. See **E48.**

G471 Good is **Grith** (*peace*) and good is frith (*peace*)
a1200 Lawman II 626–7.24957–64: For god is grith and god is frith. The freoliche ther haldeth with, And godd sulf hit makede, Thurh his godd-cunde; For grith maketh godne mon Gode workes wurchen, For alle monnen bith tha bet, That lond bith tha murgre. Skeat 14.

G472 Patient **Grizel**
c1395 Chaucer *CT* IV[E] 1177: Grisilde is deed, and eek hire pacience. **a1437** Lydgate *That Now Is Hay* in *MP* II 811.59–60: And Gresylde . . . and all her pacience, **a1439** *Fall* I 10.348: And off Grisildis parfit pacience, **a1449** *Ballade* in *MP* II 379.9, 426.42, 431.36, 436.87, 437.98, 843.108. **c1450** *Chaunce* 11.206: Now spronge ys newe Grisildes pacience. **a1500** Greene *Carols* 399.5: For they be of the condicion of curtes Gryzell. **1501** Douglas *Palice* 23.22: The onlie patient wife Gressillida. **c1520** Walter *Spectacle* C2r[18–9]: Who can expresse the wyfely pacyence Of Grysell. *Oxford* 490; Tilley G456; Whiting *Scots* I 182.

G473 Old **Grizzle** (*horse, gray haired old man*)
a1393 Gower *CA* III 451.2403–7: For loves lust and lockes hore In chambre acorden nevere-more, And thogh thou feigne a yong corage, It scheweth wel be the visage That olde grisel is no fole. **c1393** Chaucer *Scogan* 34–5: But wel I wot, thow wolt answere and saye: "Lo, olde Grisel lyst to ryme and playe!" **c1412** Hoccleve *Regement* 15.400–1: Of me thus wold thou thinke:—This olde dotyd Grisel holte him wyse. See **M690.**

G474 Not (scant) worth a (good gray) **Groat**
1469 Paston V 33[1]: I was not woorthe a groote withowt yow. **1509** Barclay *Ship* I 159[14]: Their wyt skant worth a grote. **1546** Heywood *D* 48.221: And I knew him, not woorth a good grey grote. Apperson 457; *Oxford* 268; Tilley G458.

G475 To hang a **Groin** (*i.e.*, hang back, complain)
1546 Heywood *D* 78.4–5: As evermore like a hog hangeth the groyne, On hir husbande, except he be hir slave. *Oxford* 368; Tilley A384.

G476 Where **Grooms** and the goodmen are all alike great, woe worth the wones (*houses*)
c1405 *Mum* 5.65–7: For, as it is said by elderne dawis, "Ther gromes and the goodmen beth all eliche grette, Woll wo beth the wones and all that woneth ther-in." *Oxford* 268; Skeat 125. See **A23.**

G477 As though one were waxed (*grown*, crept) out of the **Ground**
a1300 *Richard* 419.6629–30: Ffor it fferde, thar no man axe, As they out off the ground were waxe. **c1395** Chaucer *CT* V[F] 1613–5: Sire, I releesse thee thy thousand pound, As thou right now were cropen out of the ground, Ne nevere er now ne haddest knowen me. See **S785.**

G478 The **Ground** (land) that bears wicked weeds bears wholesome herbs (*varied*)
c1385 Chaucer *TC* i 946–52: For thilke grownd that bereth the wedes wikke Bereth ek thise holsom herbes, as ful ofte Next the foule netle, rough and thikke, The rose waxeth swoote and smothe and softe; And next the valeye is the hil o-lofte; And next the derke nyght the glade morwe; And also joie is next the fyn of sorwe. **a1387** Higden-Trevisa VI 461[19–22]: And as the same lond bereth evel herbes and good, as the netle groweth somtyme next the rose, so of the same mylde Edmond com Edwyn the worste and Edgar the beste (Latin [p. 460]: Et sicut eadem terra bonas et malas herbas nutrit, et urtici quandoque proxima est rosa, *etc.*). Skeat 154; Whiting *Scots* II 104.

G479 He that lies on the **Ground** is surer (*varied*)
1509 Barclay *Ship* I 32[8–10]: He that is symple, and on the grounde doth lye And that can be content with ynoughe or suffisaunce Is surer by moche than he that lyeth on hye, **c1523** *Mirrour* 25[8]: He slepeth most surely which is nearest the grounde, 46[3]: A man on grounde resting can not much lower fall. Apperson 363; *Oxford* 365; Tilley G464. See **E24, S457.**

G480 To build on brotel (*brittle*) **Ground** and find brotelness
c1395 Chaucer *CT* IV[E] 1279–80: On brotel ground they buylde, and brotelnesse They fynde, whan they wene sikernesse.

G481 To get no **Ground** of one
1478 Paston V 321[34–5]: He holdeth hys own that thay gayt no grownd of hym. NED Get 5c.

G482 To think the **Ground** bears one not
1546 Heywood *D* 37.66–7: These lovers in dotage Thinke the ground beare them not, but wed of corage. Tilley G466.

G483 When the **Ground** is clear the work is all the clearer
c1523 Barclay *Mirrour* 7[49]: For when the grounde is clere, the worke is clerer all.

G484 To cast the **Gruel** in the fire

c1385 Chaucer *TC* iii 711: Or casten al the gruwel in the fire. Apperson 205; *Oxford* 193. See **B571, F71.**

G485 If you love your **Guest,** at his coming feed his beast
c1470 *Harley MS.3362* f.3a: The comyng of thy gest, yyf thou lowe feed hy's best.

G486 An unboden (*unbidden*) **Guest** not (*knows not*) where he shall sit.
c1450 *Douce MS.52* 48.53: Unbodun gest not, where he shall sytte. **c1450** *Rylands MS.394* 98.18. **a1500** *Additional MS.37075* 278.27: He that ys not bedyn he not wher to sytte. **1546** Heywood *D* 33.22: An unbydden geast knoweth not where to syt. Apperson 658; Jente 268; *Oxford* 682; Tilley G476. See **C447.**

G487 **Guile** shall be guiled with guile
a1400 *Cato* (*Copenhagen*) A3^v[24]: So gyle wyth gyle shal gylyd be. See **B213, F52, 491, 610, G491, M114, V34.**

G488 **Guile** under the gore (*cloak, cover*)
a1393 Gower *CA* III 103.5730: So was ther guile under the gore. See notes, III 505.

G489 It is not gradely (*well*) gotten where **Guile** is the root
c1378 *Piers* B xviii 289: It is noughte graythely geten there gyle is the rote.

G490 One's **Guile** descends upon his own head
a1393 Gower *CA* III 71.4578–9: Yit ate laste here oghne guile Upon here oghne hed descendeth. See **D22, P232.**

G491 The **Guiler** is beguiled (*varied*)
c1378 *Piers* B xviii 336–7: The olde lawe graunteth, That gylours be begiled and that is gode resoun, 358: And gyle is bigyled and in his gyle fallen, **a1387** C xxi 166: And by-gyle the gylour and that is a good sleithe. *Ars ut artem falleret.* **c1390** Chaucer *CT* I[A] 4321: A gylour shal hymself bigyled be. **a1393** Gower *CA* III 204.1379–81: For often he that wol beguile Is guiled with the same guile, And thus the guilour is beguiled. **a1400** *Romaunt B* 5759: Bigiled is the giler than, *C* 6822–4: But I, that were my symple cloth, Robbe bothe robbed and robbours And gile giled and gilours. **c1410** Lovelich *Merlin* I 122.4589–90: Ho that often desireth to be-gylen anothyr, Atte laste on him-self falleth the fothyr. **a1425** *St. Robert* 61.623–4: Here may thou se He that begyles, begylde sall be. **c1450** *Merlin* I 63[16–7]: It falleth often to hem that wolden begile, that thei be-giled hem-self. **1484** Caxton *Aesop* 50[16–7]: He that begyleth other is oftyme begyled hym self, 268[3–5]: For ofte hit happeth that he whiche supposeth to begyle somme other is hym self begyled, 309[8–11]: And thus whanne a begyler is begyled he receyved the sallary or payement whiche he ought to have. Apperson 275–6; Jente 351; Skeat 237; Tilley D179; Walther I 158.1379. See **D119, F52, 491, 610, G487, M114, R154, S92, 94, 857, T444, 447, V34.**

G492 He that is **Guilty** deems all things be spoken of him (*varied*)
c1390 *Cato* (*Vernon*) 567.179–80: The wikked mon weneth that alle men Have him in heore thouht. **c1395** Chaucer *CT* VIII[G] 688–9: For Catoun seith that he that gilty is Demeth alle thyng be spoke of hym, ywis. **a1400** *Cato* (*Copenhagen*) A3^r[18–9]: For he that is gilty Levyth alle men spekyn of hym. **a1440** Burgh *Cato* 307.168–9: But to the suspect of harme it semeth Men speke of hym; he noon othir demyth. **c1450** *Chaunce* 15.370–1: Who gilty is so seythe Catoun the wise Demeth loo they my maners now dispise. **a1475** *Cato* (*Rawlinson*) 13.122–3: The gylty supposeth in every toun Men speken of hym, when thei roun. **1483** Caxton *Cato* D1^r[23–4]: He whiche is gylty and ful of vyces and of synnes wenyth that al that men say in secrete is of his fayte or dede. **1509** Barclay *Ship* II 256[24–5]: He that is gylty thynketh all that is sayde Is spokyn of hym, and touchynge his offence. Cf. Apperson 111: guilty conscience; *Oxford* 269; Smith 101; Tilley C606. See **M326, S84, 290.**

G493 He is wise that does after the common **Guise**
a1500 Medwall *Nature* B4^v[9–10]: For every man clepyth hym wyse That doth after the comen gyse. See **R184.**

G494 There is no new **Guise** that is not old (*varied*)
c1385 Chaucer *CT* I[A] 2125: Ther is no newe gyse that it nas old. **c1450** *Complaint Against Hope* 20.36: Ffor ever is the oolde the newe. **c1515** Barclay *Eclogues* 179.1114: All that newe falleth of olde time hath bene sene. *Oxford* 464; Skeat 222. See **F128, T146.**

G495 To run like **Gutters**
a1400 *Siege of Jerusalem* 31.560: And goutes fram gold wede as goteres they runne.

H

H1 **Hab** or nab
1546 Heywood *D* 23.40: Hab or nab. Apperson 277; *Oxford* 270; Tilley H479.

H2 The **Habit** does not make the monk (*varied*)
a1200 *Ancrene* 10.8–9: Unwise . . . weneth that ordre sitte i the curtel, 17–9: Herin is religiun, nawt i the wide hod ne i the blake cape, ne i the hwite rochet ne i the greie cuvel. **1340** *Ayenbite* 165[31–3]: Vor the clothinge ne maketh naght thane monek, ne the armes thane knyght: ac the guode herte and the dedes of prouesse. **c1380** Wyclif *De Papa* in *EW* 467[25–6]: For crounne and cloth maken no prest. **c1385** Usk 91.121–2: For habit maketh no monk; ne weringe of gilte spurres maketh no knight. **a1400** *Romaunt C* 6192: Abit ne makith neithir monk ne frere. **c1400** *Vices and Virtues* 166.1–2: For the abite maketh not a monke ne the armes a knyght. **1402** *Daw Topias* 68[15–8]: And, Jacke, no more than the sadil Makith thin hors a mere, No more makith oure abitis Monkes ne freris. **1402** *Jack Upland* in Skeat *Chaucerian* 192.44: Maketh youre habit you men of religion, or no? **c1450** *Pilgrimage LM* 128[1–2]: Men knowen nouht . . . folk bi the clothinge. **a1470** Malory I 63.26–30: Worthynes and good tacchis and also good dedis is nat only in araymente, but manhode and worship (ys hyd) within a mannes person; and many a worshipfull knyght ys nat knowen unto all peple. And therefore worship and hardynesse ys nat in araymente, III 1300. **1484** Caxton *Ordre of Chyvalry* 55.10–1: For under many a fayr habyte hath ben ofte vyle courage ful of barate and of wyckednesse, *Royal Book* N7r[21–2]: For the habyte maketh not the monke, ne the armes the knyght. **a1500** *Imitatione (1)* 19.10–1: If thou wolt lede a religiose life, habite and tonsure litel availith. **1510** Copland *Apolyn* 27[7–8]: The habyte maketh not the relygyous man. Apperson 308; *Oxford* 116; Tilley H586; Whiting *Ballad* 24. See **C292.**

H3 Under vile **Habit** lurks oft a proud heart
a1500 *Miroure of Mans Salvacionne* 53[1]: Ffor undere fulle vile habit lurkes oft ane hert als proude. See **H376, L539, M267, P92, 330, R226, V46.**

H4 By small **Hackneys** men chastise great coursers
1464 Hardyng 419[6]: By small hackeneys greate coursers men chastice. See **W211.**

H5 A little **Hackney** is meet for a little man
c1515 Barclay *Eclogues* 45.1225: For a litle man mete is a small hakney.

H6 To labor like a **Hackney**
a1500 Medwall *Nature* F4v[18–9]: Your body laboreth as doth an hakney That bareth the burdon every day.

H7 Not worth a **Haddock**
1546 Heywood *D* 99.36: Till they both were not woorth a haddocke. Apperson 457; *Oxford* 270; Tilley H4.

H8 To bring **Haddock** to paddock (*frog, toad*)
1546 Heywood *D* 99.35: And thus had he brought haddocke to paddocke. Apperson 277; *Oxford* 65; Tilley H5. See **A4.**

H9 Beware of **Had-I-wist** (*varied*)
a1393 Gower *CA* II 87.1887–8: Upon his fortune and his grace Comth "Hadde I wist" fulofte aplace, 143.473: And is al war of "hadde I wist," 309.302–5: For many a vice, as seith the clerk, Ther hongen upon Slowthes lappe Of suche as make a man mishappe, To pleigne and telle of hadde I wist, 325.898–9: Thanne is he war, and seith at ende, "Ha, wolde god I

hadde knowe!" **a1400** *Abuses of the Age II* in Robbins *Historical Poems* 145.30–1: For yif we abide fort "hadde y wyst," Thanne is al to late. **a1400** *Arthur* 17.545–6: Ther ys no man wel nye, y tryste, That can be waar of hadde wyste. **a1400** *Child* 317.155. **a1400** *Proverbis of Wysdom* 246.90. **c1400** *Beryn* 72.2348: But nowe it is to late to speke of had-I-wist. **1404** *Lerne say wele* in Kail 22.229: His last ende is had-y-wist. **a1450** Audelay 208.1–2. **c1450** *Complaint Against Hope* 14.16: That I so yonge shal syng of hadywiste. **c1450** *Douce MS.52* 53.98: And kepe the welle fro "Had I wyst." **c1450** *Epistle of Othea* 81.6: Had y wyst byfore, thus schold hyt not have be, 113.6–7: Trust not on fortune, called the grett goddes; Ffor ofte sche conveyth many to haddy-wyste, 140.7. **c1450** *God Send Us Patience* in Brown *Lyrics XV* 234.40–1: And therfor ben we y-ware to late— Than may we synge of had-y-wyste. **c1450** *How mankinde dooth* in Furnivall *Hymns* 73.497–8: What helpith . . . Thi wissching And thin hadde-y-wist. **c1450** Idley 82.84, 191.2002. **c1450** *Proverbs of Good Counsel* 69.56. **c1450** *Rylands MS.394* 103.16^{v}.16. **a1460** *Towneley Plays* 119.93: "Had I wyst" is a thyng it servys of noght. **c1460** *Take Good Heed* 206.22: Beth wele war be-fore, and thenk of "had I wyst." **a1471** Ripley *Compound* 153[19]: And thus for (*had I wyst*) they suffer losse and wo. **a1475** *Good Rule* in Brown *Lyrics XV* 264.35, 41–4: But had-I-wyst comyth ever to late Whan ther lackyth bothe lok and ky; What nede is it to spare the yate, Ther no thyng is lefte in the wey? **a1475** *Good Wyfe Wold* 175.60. **a1475** *Turne up hur halter* in *Rel. Ant.* I 77[25]. **c1475** *Mankind* 25.678: I xulde have don bettur, hade I wyst. **c1475** *Prohemy of a Mariage* 28[11]: Thanne is to late to sey, if I had wiste. **c1475** *Thewis* 183.101: Than "had I wittyn" will thai say. **c1477** Norton *Ordinall* 75[32]. **1483** ?Skelton *Kynge Edwarde* I 3.40: Example to thynke on Had I wyst. **a1500** *Against Hasty Marriage I* in Robbins 37.5: Ffor "had y wyst" commeth to late for to lowse yt. **a1500** *Att my begynnyng* in *Rawlinson MS. C 813* 323.5, 8: For hadde-i-wyste commethe ever by-hynde. **a1500** Basterfeld 367.35: Than was to late off "had I wyste." **a1500** Greene *Carols* 344.5: And lok thou thynk well of "had-I-wyst." **a1500** Hichecoke *This Worlde* 332.12. **a1500** *Lamentacio Peccatoris* in Horstmann *Legenden 1881* 529.28–9: And all ys tornyd to "adywyst." Had y wyst, yt wyll not bee. **a1500** *Leconfield Proverbs* 486[6]. **a1500** *New Year's Morning* in *Pol. Rel. and Love Poems* 66.17–8: And as towcheing to this olde worlde called "hadywiste," Unto my lives ende ful y Deffie. **a1500** *Piers of Fullham* 11.252: An hundreth men ben harmed with had i wyste. **a1500** *Proverbs of Salamon* 194.2.6: And hadde ywyste stondyth faste by. **a1500** *Sone, y schal thee schewe* in Furnivall *Babees Book* 34.20. **a1500** *Think Before You Speak* in Brown *Lyrics XV* 281.43–4: Haddywyst comyth ever to late Whan lewyd woordis beth owte y-spronge. **a1500** *Urbanitatis* in Furnivall *Babees Book* 15.72: And kepe the welle from hadde-y-wiste. **c1500** Greene *Carols* 346.1. **c1500** *Proper tretyse* 244[13]. **c1516** Skelton *Magnificence* 7.211, 44.1395. **1520** Whittinton *Vulgaria* 94.28. **1546** Heywood *D* 21.32, **1555** *E* 191.256. Apperson 277; NED Had-I-wist; *Oxford* 270; Tilley H8, 9, 10; Whiting *Drama* 162, 257, *Scots* I 182. Cf. Jente 2. See **G5.**

H10 To be loose in the **Haft**
c1330 *Times of Edward II* 339.361–2: Unnethe is nu eny man that can eny craft, That he nis a party los in the haft. **c1450** Idley 90.558–9: Thow shalt fynde hem loois in the hafte, But thou paie freely or thou goo, 115.435–6: Thow shalt fynde the fende full loose in the hafte If he may have the undre his dominacioun. Apperson 381; NED Haft sb.[1] 1b; Tilley H472. Cf. *Oxford* 385: hilts.

H11 To have other **Hafts** in hand
a1450 *York Plays* 158.75–6: Sone, hense away! I wolde thou wente, For othir haftis in hande have we. MED haft (b).

H12 As sharp as **Hail**
c1410 Lovelich *Grail* II 290.456: As scharpe as storm Of hail therto. Svartengren 256; Whiting *Scots* I 182.

H13 As thick as (the, any) **Hail(-stones)**
a1200 Lawman II 100.12578–9: Swa thicke wes heore væræ (*arrows' flight*) Swulc hit haghel wærun. **a1300** *Richard* 199.2201–2: And shotte quarelles, and eke flone, As thycke as the hayle-stone, 219.2562–4: Flones and quarelles ffleys betwene Also thykke, withouten stynt, As hayl afftyr thondyr-dynt, 244 *var.* 2969–70: He gaderede his folk togedere, As thykke as haile falles in wedere. **a1338** Mannyng *Chronicle A* II 470.13550–2: So thykke atones gon they fleye,— Also thikke . . . al so hail that stormes blew. **c1386** Chaucer *LGW* 655: For strokes, whiche that wente as thikke as hayl. **a1400** *Siege of Jerusalem* 33.597–8: The fals Jewes in the felde fallen so thicke As hail froward heven, hepe over other. **c1400** *Alexander Buik* I 52.1648–9. **a1425** *Arthour and M.*[2] 305.600: As thikke as hayl in

thondur lyght. **c1450** *Merlin* 214[19–20]. **c1470** *Wallace* 323.857: The derff schot, draiff as thik as a haill schour. **a1475** *Seege of Troye* 187 H 1065kl: And eke ffloon As thyke as ony hayle ston. **1481** Caxton *Godeffroy* 108.36–7: They shotte so thycke upon our peple that there was never . . . hayl so like, **1485** *Charles* 191.28–9. **a1500** *Quare* 197.102–3: ony. **c1500** *Arthour and M.*[3] 440.575. **c1500** *Lady Bessy* 40[26–7]: any. **c1500** *Lancelot* 25.840. **c1500** *Melusine* 165.27–8: hayle stones. **1509** Barclay *Ship* II 193[6], 297[26]: With precious stones beset as thycke as hayle. **1513** Douglas *Aeneid* II 139.132, III 275.12: haill schour, IV 95.157–8: The fell tempest of dartis schote and flanys, So thik as ony schour of scharp hailstanys. **a1533** Berners *Huon* 714.11–3: The shot flewe so thycke of both partyes that it semed to be . . . hayle. Apperson 623; Taylor and Whiting 166; Tilley H11; Whiting *Scots* I 182, 183. See **D411, R12.**

H14 To fall like **Hail** (*etc.*) (A number of single quotations are brought together here)
a1200 Lawman II 183.14516–7: Heo comen to hirede, Alse haghel the valleth, 437.20503–4: Tha halden hit (*for* heo) to sæ, Swa hahghel deh from wolcne (*B:* Also the hawel that falleth), 531.22714–6: Al hit to him bæh, Riche men and pouere, Swa the haghel valleth. **a1300** *Alisaunder* 125.2206–7: So on the shyngel lithe the haile Every knighth so liith on other. **a1300** *Arthour and M.*[1] 165.5873–4: Arthour smot on hem, saunfaile, So on the singel dothe the haile. **c1400** *Alexander Buik* I 10.311–2: As in grit wynd dois haill and snaw, Sa come thay on but dreid or aw. **c1458** *Knyghthode and Bataile* 105.2876–7: The storm of shot as hail So rayketh on. **a1533** Berners *Arthur* 143[23–4]: The tyles and stones flew all about the hous lyke hayle.

H15 To fling like **Hail** (*varied*)
a1300 *Alisaunder* 319.6074–5: Bothe parties flungen togedres, So dooth the hayl with the wedres. **a1300** *Arthour and M.*[1] 222.7931–2: On the sexten .m. thai com flinge, So hail doth on the singel.

H16 To be **Hail Fellow**
1519 Horman *Vulgaria* 216[26–7]: He waxed hayle folowe with hym. Latin: Ut cum eo ex aequo viveret. Apperson 277; *Oxford* 270; Taylor and Whiting 130; Tilley H14, 15.

H17 To hop like **Hailstones** (*varied*)
a1400 *Perceval* 38.1190–2: Made the Sarazenes hede-bones Hoppe, als dose hayle-stones, A-bowtte one the gres. **c1400** *Florence* 22.640–1: Hedys hopped undur hors fete As hayle stones done in the strete.

H18 As black as any (a, an) **Hair**
a1325 *Cursor* III 1288.22510: Dune (FGT: Dim) and blak sum (FT: as) ani (F: a) hair. **a1500** *Miroure of Mans Salvacionne* 153[6]: The sonne blakke als an hayre.

H19 As fele (*many*) as **Hairs** on beasts
c1380 Chaucer *HF* 1388–90: She Had also fele upstondyng eres And tonges, as on bestes heres. See **H24.**

H20 A **Hair** in one's neck
c1450 *Consail and Teiching* 71.199–200: Think one the har is in thi nek, And be weil war quhome of thou spek. *Oxford* 271.

H21 A **Hair** of the dog that bit one (All examples but last are literal)
c1450 *Leechbook* 54.130: (Ffor bytynge of an hownd): take town cresses and piliall riall and seith it in water and giff hym to drynke, and ley of the houndis her therto, if thou may have it. **c1450** *Stockholm Prose Recipes* 103.20–26: Gyf a wood hownd hawe betyn ony man . . . take the same howndis her, and leye it to the sor; and it schall holyn anon, for this hath ben prewyd. **a1500** George Henslow *Medical Works of the Fourteenth Century* (London, 1899) 19.2–4: And yif thou miste have of the hundys here, ley hit ther-to, and hit schal hele hit (*dog-bite*), 116.9–10: And ley on the bytyng of the hondys here, if thou may have it. **1546** Heywood *D* 54.428: I pray the leat me and my felow have A heare of the dog that bote us last night. Apperson 278; O. v. Hovorka and A. Kronfeld *Vergleichende Volksmedizin* (2 vols., Stuttgart, 1908–9) II 423; *Oxford* 271; Taylor and Whiting 166; Tilley H23.

H22 His **Hair** grows through his hood (hat)
a1450 *Wall Verses at Launceston Priory* 342: Whoso loveth wel to fare, Ever spende and never spare, Bot he have the more good, His heer wol growe thurgh his hood. **c1450** *Egerton MS.1995* f.64b in Robbins-Cutler 1014.5: Gret huntyng by ryvers and wode, Makythe a manys here to growe thorowe hys hoode. **1457** *Libeaus* 128 (*end of MS.* N): He that lovyth welle to fare, Ever to spend and never spare, But he have the more good, His here wol grow throw his hood. Quod More. **c1499** Skelton *Bowge* I 43.350: His here was growen thorowe his hat. **c1500** Greene *Carols* 410.14: Hys here shall grow thorow his hode. **c1515** Barclay *Eclogues* 5.146: At divers holes his heare grewe through his hode. **1546** Heywood *D* 71.34: That will make his heare grow through his hood, **1555** *E* 172.149. Apperson 278; *Oxford* 270–1; Tilley H17; Whiting *Drama* 347:600.

H23 Long **Hair** and short wit (*varied*)
c1425 *Speculum Sacerdotale* 122.1–3: And we clippe the heeres that we mowe have wittis of oure hedes redy and spedy for to serve God. **1549** Heywood *D* 85.157: Thy tales . . . shew long heare, and short wit. Apperson 278; *Oxford* 70–1; Tilley B736. Cf. Taylor and Whiting 167:13. See **W410.**

H24 More than **Hairs** on one's head
1465 Paston IV 137[33–4]: More men then Dabeney hadde herys on hys hede. Svartengren 395; Tilley H30. See **H19.**

H25 Not care a **Hair**
1481 Caxton *Reynard* 60[11–2]: I carre not for the beste of them an heer. **1509** Barclay *Ship* I 31[10]: Thou carest nat a here.

H26 Not count a **Hair**
c1400 *Alexander Buik* II 182.2895: I compt nocht all thare schore ane hare. **a1445** *Carl* 124.156: I count hym not worthe an har. Taylor and Whiting 167: care.

H27 Not give a **Hair**
c1475 *Guy*[1] 469 C 8316: Ne yave I not an here.

H28 Not help a **Hair**'s end
c1378 *Piers* B x 334: Helpeth nought to heveneward one heres ende.

H29 Not prize a **Hair**
c1400 *Alexander Buik* III 308.6961: All that he prysit nocht ane hare.

H30 Not trespass the value of a **Hair**
1481 Caxton *Reynard* 29[29–30]: He had not trespaced to ony man the value of an heer.

H31 Not worth a **Hair**
c1250 *Owl* 130.1550: That nis wurth one of hire heare. **1509** Barclay *Ship* I 177[12]: Skantly worth a here. Apperson 457; *Oxford* 270; Tilley H19; Whiting *Scots* I 183.

H32 Take a **Hair** from his beard
1546 Heywood *D* 81.48: Take a heare from his beard, and marke this conceite. Tilley H22.

H33 To be destroyed both **Hair** and hide
c1450 *St. Cuthbert* 200.6860: Thai were destroyed, bath hare and hyde. Cf. Taylor and Whiting 183.

H34 To love one's least **Hair** more than another's body
a1425 *Arthour and M.*[2] 368.2402–4: Merlyn loved well Uther, The least heere, that was on his crowne, Then all the body of Pendragon. **c1500** *Arthour and M.*[3] 493.2288–90. Cf. Tilley W549. See **T357.**

H35 To multiply above the **Hairs** of one's head
c1340 Rolle *Psalter* 238 (68.5): Multiplide thai ere aboven the hares of my heved. Svartengren 395.

H36 To turn against the **Hair**
c1385 Usk *Testament* 58.22: But ayenst the heer it turneth. Apperson 4; *Oxford* 5; Tilley H18.

H37 Not worthy a **Hake**
c1400 *Laud Troy* I 231.7848: Ye bene not alle worthi an hake.

H38 Welcome **Hake** (*?idle fellow*) and make (*mate*)
c1522 Skelton *Colyn* I 320.250–2: Howe some synge *Laetabundus* At every ale stake, With, welcome hake and make! NED Hake sb.[5].

H39 **Half** a loaf is better than no bread
1546 Heywood *D* 47.200: For better is halfe a lofe than no bread. Apperson 278; *Oxford* 271; Taylor and Whiting 167–8; Tilley H36.

H40 The **Half** shows what the whole means (*varied*)
1461 Paston IV 12[15]: For a man may her by the halfe qwat the hole menyth. **a1500** *Proverbs of Salamon* 178.13.7–8: That knowyth be the halfe word what the hole ment He can see where resone rydes. **1546** Heywood *D* 57.29–30: Thats just, if the halfe shall judge the whole (quoth I) But yet here the whole, the whole wholly to try, 86.217: This halfe shewth, what the hole meaneth. Apperson 279; NED Halfword, quote 1581; *Oxford* 271; Tilley H44. See **A55, L390.**

H41 He that has **Half** needs will have all
1509 Barclay *Ship* I 101[3]: He that hath halfe nedes wyll have all.

H42 A **Halfpenny** is as good saved as lost
c1525 ?Heywood *Gentylnes* 105.413: A halpeny is as well savid as lost.

H43 Not the better of a **Halfpenny**
1532 More *Confutacion* 476 C[12–3]: Not the better of an half-peny.

H44 Not worth a **Halfpenny**
1489 Caxton *Doctrinal* K3r[6–7]: Saynt Jherome seyth that a monke whyche hath evyl entencyon to proprete is not worth a halfpeny. NED Halfpenny 4b.

H45 As nice as a **Halfpennyworth** of silver spoons
1546 Heywood *D* 98.252–3: Yet was she nowe, sodeinly waxen as nyse As it had bene a halporth of silver spoones. Apperson 444; Tilley H52.

H46 It is merry in **Hall** when beards waw (*wag*) all
a1300 *Alisaunder* 67.1163–4: Mery swithe it is in halle Whan that berdes waweth alle. **c1475** *Rawlinson MS. D 328* 120.37: Hyt is mery in hall when berdys waggyth all. **1546** Heywood *D* 82.76: It is mery in halle, when berds wag all, **1555** *E* 147.2.1. Apperson 414; *Oxford* 420–1; Tilley H55. See **F665.**

H47 **Hall Benches** are slidder (*slippery*)
c1475 Henryson *Fables* 89.2608: Bewar in welth, for Hall benkis ar rycht slidder. **a1500** *Thre Prestis* 32.614: For wit thow weil Hal binks ar ay slidder. *Oxford* 272; Tilley B355; Whiting *Scots* I 183. See **L461.**

H48 The **Halt** comes ever behind
c1450 *Rylands MS.394* 93.26: The halte comys ever be hynde, 27: The halte and the blind, ever ben be hynde. Jente 243.

H49 Knit (Turn) up her **Halter** and let her go!
c1450 Greene *Carols* 403.1: Knet up the heltre, and let here goo. **a1500** *Clerk and the Husbandman* in Robbins 180–1.16, 32, *etc.* (*varied refrain*): Bot turne up hyr haltur and let hyr goe! **a1500** *Turne up hur halter* in *Rel. Ant.* I 75–7 [8, 16, *etc.*] (*varied refrain*): Turne up hur halster and let hur go. MED halter n. (1) 2.

H50 It is hard **Halting** before a cripple (*varied*)
c1385 Chaucer *TC* iv 1457–8: It is ful hard to halten unespied Byfore a crepel, for he kan the craft. **a1415** Hoccleve *Balade* I 50.41–3: I warne thee that it shal be ful hard For thee and me to halte on any syde, But he espie us. **1481** Caxton *Reynard* 65[38–9]: Ye knowe the state of the world in suche wyse as noman may halte tofore you. **1523** Berners *Froissart* III 213[32–3]: It is hard haltynge before lordes and theyr counsayles, for they se clerely. **1546** Heywood *D* 76.195: It is harde haltyng before a creeple ye wot. Apperson 280; *Oxford* 272; Skeat 196; Tilley H60.

H51 As bare as one's **Hand**
c1420 Page *Siege* 139.88: And made hyt as bare as my hende. Cf. Apperson 25; Tilley B18.

H52 The bringing **Hand** is ever welcome
a1400 *Cursor* III 1421 G 24819–20: Welcum was his presand and he, Als bringand hand es wont to be (other *MSS.*: Als bringand wont was [ay is, es] to be). See **G99.**

H53 Burnt **Hand** dreads fire
a1500 Hill 129.45: Brente hond fire dredith. See **C201.**

H54 From **Hand** to mouth
a1500 Henley *Husbandry* 43[3]: Then they can none other shifte, but fro the hande to the mowthe. **1522** More *Treatyce* 88 G[11]: They that live fro hande to mouthe. Apperson 280; *Oxford* 376; Taylor and Whiting 170; Tilley H98.

H55 The **Hand** follows the heart
c1340 Rolle *Psalter* 204 (57.2): The hand folous the hert.

H56 The **Hand** is hurt that bourds (*plays*) with the bear
a1456 *Passe forth* clxxiv.24: The hande is hurt that bourdeth with the bere.

H57 The **Hand** that is foul may not do away another man's filth
1340 *Ayenbite* 237[23–5]: Vor ase zayth saynt gregorie, "the hand thet is voul and behorewed ne may othremanne velthe do away." **c1400** *Vices and Virtues* 263.15–7: For, as seynt Gregori seith, the honde that is foul and unclene ne may not do awey the unclennesse of anothere. MED foul, adj. 6.

H58 The **Hands** that are used in the fire fear not the kettle
1492 *Salomon and Marcolphus* 9[21–2]: Thandys that are usyd in the fyre, fere not the ketyll.

H59 He that has good **Hands** must needs have good customs
1532 Berners *Golden Boke* 195.2498–9: It hath ben an old saying: He that hathe good handes, muste nedes have good customes.

H60 Hooked **Hands** make a man to lose his head
c1250 *Proverbs of Alfred* 114 T 391–2: And hokede honden make then mon is hewit to lesen. See **L433.**

H61 Let not your left **Hand** know what your right hand does
c1000 *WSG* Matthew vi 3: Soþlice þonne þu ælmessan do, nyte þin wynstre hwæt do þin swyþre. **c1395** *WBible* Matthew vi 3; Whanne thou doist almes, knowe not thi left hond what thi right hond doith. Tilley H79.

H62 Many **Hands** make light work
c1300 *Beves* 156.3352: Mani hondes maketh light werk! **c1350** *Good Wife E* 166.130–1: The werk is the sonere idon that hat many honden. Many honden maken light werk. **1402** *Daw Topias* 106[20–1]: Yit many hondis togider Maken light werk. **c1450** *Douce MS.52* 50.70: Many hondys makyn lyghth worke. **c1450** *Good*

Wife L 200.110–1: For manye handis and wight Make an hevy worke light. **c1450** *Rylands MS.394* 100.100. **c1470** *Harley MS.3362* f.9a: Many handis makyth lyth werk. **1481** Caxton *Godeffroy* 101.6. **a1500** Hill 128.24. **a1500** *Landsdowne MS.762* in *Rel. Ant.* I 290[1]. **c1500** *Good Wife T* 206.105–6: Many hondys and smert Makyn lyght werke. **1546** Heywood *D* 70.30, **1555** *E* 193.270, **1556** *Spider* 234[14]: The old proverbe sayth, manie hands make light wark. Apperson 399; *Oxford* 405; Taylor and Whiting 169; Tilley H119.

H63 No **Hand** is so sure that it can always make good
c1515 Barclay *Eclogues* 78.700: No hand is so sure that can alway make good. See **S671.**

H64 To be wise after the **Hand**
a1393 Gower *CA* II 325.893: Thanne is he wys after the hond. Cf. Tilley E192, M368.

H65 To bear one (wrong) on (in) **Hand**
c1300 *Guy*[1] 536 A 184.6: That he berth him an hond. **c1300** *South English Legendary* II 639.909: Other he the wole bere an hond that thou ert is traitour, 911. **c1325** *As I stod on a day* in *Rel. Ant.* II 19[18]: Sche bar me fast on hond, that I began to rave. **c1385** Chaucer *TC* iv 1404: Makynge his sort, and beren hym on honde. **a1387** Higden-Trevisa I 11–3, VIII 115[7–8], [13]. **c1395** Chaucer *CT* III[D] 226, 232, 393. **c1400** *Satan and his Children* in Wyclif *EW* 214[15]. **1402** *Daw Topias* 107[1–2]. **1402** Hoccleve *Letter of Cupid* 83.274. **1402** *Jack Upland* in Skeat *Chaucerian* 195.153: Why berest thou god in honde, and sclaundrest him. **1410** Walton *Boethius* 170[10]: And wiche ben fals that beren wrong on honde. **1413** ?Hoccleve *De Guilleville Poems* III lvii 189. **1436** *Libelle* 32.624. **c1437** *Brut* II 577.14–5: And bare hym on hond that he was a spy. **a1438** Kempe 107.16, 145.2. **c1445** Pecock *Donet* 43.18–9, 157.32. **1447** Bokenham 61.2204: That he it us bere on hande styfly. **c1449** Paston II 110[19]. **c1449** Pecock *Repressor* I 151[6–7, 10–1], 154[32], 155[6–7], 253[26], 275[9, 12], II 339[9, 12], 417[12], 442[17]. **a1450** *Generydes A* 59.1904, 94.2985, 273.8857: For wrong ye bere him on hond. **a1450** *Generydes B* 89.2780: Ye bere me wrong in hand. **a1450** *Partonope* 307.7699–700, 424.10282. **c1450** Idley 131.1388, 151.2702. **c1450** *Jacob's Well* 295.4–5. **c1450** *Merlin* I 9[18–9]. **c1454** Pecock *Folewer* 77.33–4, 114.9. **1460** Paston III 210[20], **1461** III 291[8], 298[18]. **a1464** Capgrave *Chronicle* 258[4–5], 269[9–11]: Tho men that were counted rich were bore on hand that thei had consented to the tretouris. **1464** Paston IV 94[4–5], **1469** V 27[8], **1470** V 78–9. **c1475** *Guy*[1] 531 C 9511: For that ye beryth hym wrong on hand. **1479** *Cely Papers* 24[5–6]. **1481** Caxton *Godeffroy* 259.17, *Mirror* 113[27–8]: And yf they be charged and born wrongly on honde without reson, *Reynard* 61[27], 69[26], 94[22], 115[8], **1483** *Golden Legende* 172^r[1.6], **c1489** *Blanchardyn* 75.10–1. **1489** Paston VI 121[20]. **c1497** Medwall *Fulgens* D5^v[32], **a1500** *Nature* A4^r[4], H2^r[21]. **c1500** Fabyan 557[5]. **c1500** *God Governs* in Brown *Lyrics XV* 87.45: For wreth or Envy falsly borne on hond. **1513** Douglas *Aeneid* IV 21.86, 167.76. **c1516** Skelton *Magnificence* 12.352. **1519** Horman *Vulgaria* 119[1], 170[5]: He is my countre man: as he bereth me an hande. Latin: Uti mihi vult persuasum, 279[11–2], 302[18]: I prey you lette no man be blamed for this false berynge an hande. **1522** Skelton *Why Come* II 40.449. **1523** Berners *Froissart* I 74[9], III 490[33–4]. **1528** More *Heresyes* 108 F[4–5]: Many thinges borne wronge in hande, 109 D[3], E[3–4], [9], 121 F[2], 207 A[11–2], 234 A[14–5], **1529** *Supplicacion* 294 E[13], 330 D[9–10], **1532** *Confutacion* 348 G[1–2], 351 C[15], 382 H[15], 408 A[6], 413 C[13], 438 H[4], 500 F[1], 634 H[10–1], 711 (*by error* 611) A[1], 765 G[14], 787 D[19]. **a1533** Berners *Huon* 422.29–30. **1533** More *Apologye* 33[4], 35[6], 63[15], 192[29], **1534** *Comforte* 1177 D[12]. **1556** Heywood *E* 124.45.3: To beare a man in hand. E. H. Duncan in *Tennessee Studies in Literature* 11(1966) 19–33; MED beren v.(1) 13 (g, h, i); Tilley H94; Whiting *Drama* 334:392a, *Scots* I 184.

H66 To bless with the left **Hand** (*varied*)
a1450 *Gesta* 285[4]: And yafe the stiwarde hire blessing with the lefte hond. **c1475** *Mankind* 19.515: I blysse yow with my lyfte honde: foull yow befall! **1511** Hawes *Comforte* C5^r[24–5]: But me to bere, I trowe, they lost a lyppe, For the lyfte hande extendyd my Journaye. MED blessen 5; Tilley L578.

H67 To claw one's **Hand**
c1515 Barclay *Eclogues* 114.187: Calling him master, and oft clawe his hand. See **B5.**

H68 To depart (*part*) on even **Hands**
a1470 Malory I 318.7: And there they departed on evyn hondis, II 461.13–4.

H69 To grope (lime, grease) one's **Hands**
a1387 Higden-Trevisa VII 7[11–2]: Elsinus ordeyned hym advoketes, and groped here hondes, (Anon.: Yiffenge grete yiftes to his

advocates) and gat slyliche a maundmente. **c1500** Fabyan 675[15]: That wolde thy hande with golde of gyftes lyme. **1509** Watson *Ship* Gg3v[12]: And that theyr handes be greced. **c1516** Skelton *Magnificence* 15.432: Wyth golde and grotes they grese my hande. Apperson 270; Tilley M397; Whiting *Drama* 347:593. See **J72.**

H70 To have both **Hands** full
c1450 *Merlin* II 515[26–7]: We shull have bothe handes full. **a1470** Malory I 422.23–5: But whan thou metyste with sir Trystrames thou shalt have bothe thy hondys full, II 597.31: They shall have bothe there hondys full, III 1219.18–9. Taylor and Whiting 170; Tilley H114.

H71 To have the better **Hand**
a1470 Malory II 973.21–2: And I may have the bettir honde. **a1475** *Guy*² 22.747–8: Ther was no justyng in that londe, But Guy had the bettur honde. **a1483** Kay *Siege* [47.12]: They hadde the better hand. **a1533** Berners *Arthur* 101[18–9].

H72 To have the higher **Hand**
c1200 *St. Katherine* (*Royal*) 36.756–7: Yef ha mahen on me The herre hond habben. **c1200** *Vices and Virtues* (*Stowe*) 127.20: Hie hafden the heighere hand over me. **c1250** *Genesis and Exodus* 96.3392: Hadde hegere hond, and timede wel. **a1300** *Richard* 348.5281: And who that haves the heyere hand. **c1325** *Chronicle* 69.267–8. **a1338** Mannyng *Chronicle A* I 75.2103, II 572.16508. **a1350** *Ywain* 59.2200, 87.3260. **a1375** *William* 45.1178. **c1380** *Ferumbras* 23.566, 28.669, 127.4058. **a1387** Higden-Trevisa VII 125[18]. **c1387-95** Chaucer *CT* I[A] 399: If that he faught, and hadde the hyer hond. **a1393** Gower *CA* III 178.404. **a1396**(1494) Hilton *Scale* P5v[31–2]. **a1400** *Alexander C* 38.810. **a1400** *Cursor* II 402 T 6956. **a1400** *Destruction of Troy* 38.1102, 238.7362: Thaim happynt not the herhond to have of hor fos, 259.7983, 311.9571. **c1400** *Sowdone* 92.3232. **a1420** Lydgate *Troy* III 606.1448–9, **a1426** *Mumming at Hertford* in *MP* II 679.144, **a1439** *Fall* I 83.3042–3. **c1450** Capgrave *Katharine* 73.929. **a1450** *Merlin* I 175[17–8]. **c1458** *Knyghthode and Bataile* 59.1618–9. **a1470** Malory II 969.24–5. **a1475** *Promptorium* 279[44]. **c1475** *Guy*¹ 496 C 8821. **c1495** *Arundel Vulgaria* 65.276. **a1500** *Guy*⁴ 107.3360. **1519** Horman *Vulgaria* 97[31], 307[22–3], 370[3, 15], 375[7], 376[24, 32], 378[5], 380[17], 388[29], 392[9], 408[5].

H73 To have the over **Hand**
a1200 Lawman I 55.1290: Ah Brutus hefde tha overe hond, 65.1520–1: Whether ich mage the ufere (*B* overe) hond Habben of than kinge, 105.2484, II 345.18324–5. **c1200** Orm I 189.5460–1: Forr whase winneth th oferrhannd and sige off lathe gastess, II 42.11421–2, 44.11481–2, 236.16965. **c1300** Robert of Gloucester I 131.1840: And tho he adde thun over hond, 207.2913, 375.5152. **a1325** *Cursor* I 152.2508: Fra thai had geten the over-hand, II 402.6956, III 1272.22234. **a1338** Mannyng *Chronicle A* II 533.15375–6: The Englische . . . The over hand hadde. **a1350** Castelford 41.20854: And ever thai wan and had overhande, 82.21975–6, 134.23347. **c1375** Barbour *Bruce* I 256.452: Till thai had gottyn the ovir hand. **a1400** *Morte Arthure* 126.4299–300. **c1420** Wyntoun V 413.3513, VI 121.5415, 150.5609–10, 335.910. **a1425** *Metrical Paraphrase OT* 69.2363, 120.13710. **c1440** *Prose Alexander* 13.16–7, 25.10. **a1447** Bokenham *Mappula* 32[19–20]. **a1450** *Generydes B* 96.2996. **c1450** *Consail and Teiching* 75.342: Qwhar thow has ourhand ore maistry. **c1450** *De Claris Mulieribus* 80.1599. **c1450** *Edward the Confessor Prose II* 120[14]. **1456** Hay *Governaunce* 152.31. **c1471** *Arrival of Edward IV*, ed. John Bruce CS I (1838) 12[21], 34[7–8]. **1481** Caxton *Reynard* 92[29–30, 32]. **a1500** *Beves* 195 M 3893. **a1500** *English Conquest* 51.10–1, 87.19–20, 107.2–3, 119.22–3: He had the over-hande . . . he loste the over-hand. **a1500** Medwall *Nature* A4v[32], B4r[15]. **c1500** *Three Kings' Sons* 142.21–2. **1513** Douglas *Aeneid* III 124.69, 267.61, IV 92.38, 148.38, 152.61, 168.114: Beand victour with the ovir-hand. **1519** Horman *Vulgaria* 324[13]. **a1525** *English Conquest* 34.6, 144.9. **a1533** Berners *Arthur* 119[1–2], *Huon* 302.25. Whiting *Drama* 356:745, *Scots* I 184.

H74 To have the upper **Hand**
1481 *Tulle of Olde Age* 79[16–9]: Marcus Attilius . . . overcame and had the uppirhande and victorye of the men of Cartage. **c1500** Fabyan 93[31–2]: He . . . hath gotten . . . the . . . upper hande, 661[21–2]. **1525** Berners *Froissart* V 147[26–7], **a1533** *Huon* 502.9–10. **1533** Heywood *Pardoner* B4v[27]. Taylor and Whiting 169; Tilley H95; Whiting *Drama* 369:926, *Scots* I 184.

H75 To hold one in (on) **Hand**
a1325 *Cursor* II 938.16428: Bot wald tham hald in hand. **1369** Chaucer *BD* 1019: Hyr lust to holde no wyght in honde, **c1380** *HF* 692: And eke moo holdynge in hondes, **c1385** *CT* V[F] 1371, *TC* iii 773. **a1420** Lydgate *Troy* I 246.3550: Of nature thei can hym holde on honde, II 534.4841: With delaies she hilde hym forthe on honde.

c1440 Charles of Orleans 205.6111. **a1500** *Ragman Roll* 77.193. **c1505** More *Picus* 5 E[1–2]: We will holde the reder no lenger in hand. Whiting *Scots* I 184.

H76 To know as well as one's **Hand**
1481 Caxton *Reynard* 89[39–40]: He knewe al the tokenes of the uryne as wel as his honde.

H77 To offer with **Hand** but not with heart
c1375 *St. Katherine* in Horstmann *Legenden 1881* 165.74: Thai offerd with hand, bot noght with hert. See **M755.**

H78 To play on both **Hands**
1546 Heywood *D* 36.31: She can plaie on bothe handes, **1556** *Spider* 265[14]: How he pleyth on both handes: as Juglers do oft. Apperson 500; Tilley H115; Whiting *Drama* 359:780.

H79 To put one's **Hand** between the bark and the tree
1546 Heywood *D* 64.73–4: But it were foly for mee, To put my hande betweene the barke and the tree. Apperson 26; *Oxford* 23; Tilley H88.

H80 To put one's **Hand** into a blind bag of snakes and eels
1528 More *Heresyes* 165 E[6–12]: I have herde my father meryly say every man is at the choyce of his wife, that ye shold put your hande in to a blynde bagge full of snakes and eles together, .vii. snakes for one ele, ye wold I wene reken it a perillous choice to take up one at adventure. *Oxford* 527; Tilley H89; Whiting *Scots* I 154: Creel. See **S154.**

H81 To put to a helping **Hand**
a1500 *Imitatione (1)* 115.31–2: It is sone amendid, whan it pleasith the to put to an helping honde. Tilley H97.

H82 To set one's **Hand** on his halfpenny
1546 Heywood *D* 28.17: So harde is your hande set on your halfpeny, **1555** *E* 153.44: Thy hand is on thy halfepeny. Apperson 281; *Oxford* 273; Tilley H315.

H83 To set (put) one's **Hand** to the plow
a900 Alfred *Gregory* 403.1–2: Hit is awrieten on ðæm godspelle ðæt nan mon ne scyle don his hond to ðære sylg and hawian underbæc. **c1000** *WSG* Luke ix 62: Nan man þe hys hand asett on hys sulh, and on bæc besyhð, nys andfenge Godes rice. **c1395** *WBible* Luke ix 62: No man that puttith his hoond to the plough, and biholdynge bacward, is able to the rewme of God. **c1400** *Pepysian Gospel* 21.11–2. **a1430** Lydgate *Pilgrimage* 644.24031: I sette myn hand unto the plough, **a1449** *Testament* in *MP* I 354.670–1: Entryng this tyme into relygioun, Onto the plowe I put forth myne hond. Whiting *Scots* I 184.

H84 To slay (do, make) out of **Hand**
c1390 *Sir Gawain* 70.2285: Dele to me my destiné, and do hit out of honde. **c1500** Fabyan 599[1–2]: They slewe hym there out of hande. **a1533** Berners *Arthur* 183[10]: Sle them out of hand. **1546** Heywood *D* 20.44: For one of them thinke I to make out of hande, 23.40, 26.48. NED Hand 33.

H85 To spit on (in) one's **Hands** and take better hold
1534 More *Comforte* 1242 E[1–3]: And hardly spet well on youre handes and take good holde. **1546** Heywood *D* 69.108: Naie, I will spyt in my handes, and take better holde. Apperson 596; *Oxford* 614; Tilley H120–1.

H86 To take what comes to **Hand**
a1393 Gower *CA* III 390.162–3: Riht so can he nomore good, Bot takth what thing comth next to honde.

H87 To wash one's **Hands** (of a thing)
c1000 *WSG* Matthew xxvii 24: þa genam he wæter and þwoh hys handa beforan þam folce, and cwæð, Unscyldig ic eom fram þyses rihtwisan blode. **c1395** *WBible* Matthew xxvii 24: Pilat . . . took watir, and waischide hise hondis . . . and seide, Y am giltles of the blood of this rightful man. **1465** Paston IV 156[7–8]: Yf he do oght therin, he doyth it closely, as he ys wont to doo, and wayshyth hys hondys ther of as Pylate dyde. Taylor and Whiting 170; Tilley H122.

H88 Who limes (*smears with bird-lime*) his **Hands** they must be the more unclean
a1393 Gower *CA* II 146.574–7: For who so wole his handes lime, Thei mosten be the more unclene; For many a mote schal be sene, That wolde noght cleve elles there. See **P236.**

H89 With empty **Hands** men may toll (reclaim, lure, allure) no hawks
c1378 *Piers* B v 438–9: For I have and have hadde some dele haukes maneres, I nam noughte lured with love but there ligge aughte under the thombe. **c1390** Chaucer *CT* I[A] 4134: With empty hand men may na haukes tulle. **a1393** Gower *CA* III 75.4723–5: Fulofte he faileth of his game That wol with ydel hand reclame His hauk, as many a nyce doth. **c1395** Chaucer *CT* III[D] 415: With empty hand men may none haukes lure. **a1449** Lydgate *Consulo* in *MP* II 750.15: With empty hand men may noon haukys

lure. **c1450** Idley 90.545–6: In olde proverbe it is saide, whiche is sure, With empty hande men may no hawkes lure. **1472** Paston V 162[19–20]: For as moche as men may nott lure none hawkes with empty handys. **c1475** Henryson *Fables* 80.2335: With emptie hand na man suld Halkis lure. **1549** Heywood *D* 71.32: With emptie handes men maie no haukes allure. Apperson 291; Jente 512; *Oxford* 170; Skeat 235; Tilley H111; Whiting *Scots* I 183–4.

H90 A **Handful** of yards (*sticks*) are arveth (*hard*) to break
a1200 *Ancrene* 129.12–4: An hondful of yerden beoth earveth to breoken hwil ha beoth togederes; euchan itweamet, lihtliche bersteth, **a1400** (*Recluse*) 125.5–6: An hondeful of yerdes while hii ben to giders hii nyllen noughth breken. See **T241, V47.**

H91 To be fangen (*taken, etc.*) **Hand-habend** (*with* [*the thing stolen*] *in hand*)
a935 *Laws of Aethelstan* in Liebermann I 150.1[H]: Ærest þæt mon ne sparige nænne þeof þe æt hæbbendre honda gefongen sy, 166 Prol. 2[H]. **c1250** *Floris* 105.667–70: Hit is right thuregh alle thing, Felons inome hond habbing, For to suffre Jugement Bithute ansuere other acupement. **a1300** *Alisaunder* 235.4197: Thou art ynome honde-habbynde. **c1300** *South English Legendary* I 336.267: For hi were inome hond habbinge. **c1330** *Seven Sages A* 26.677–8: And who is founde hond habbing, Hit nis non nede of witnessing, **a1350** *C* 25.749–50, 53.1563–4: Now have I tane the hand-haveing; Thou may deny it for nothing. MED hond-having; NED Hand-habend. Cf. Taylor and Whiting 305: Red-handed; Whiting *Scots* II 116.

H92 To make a **Handmaid** a (over her) lady
c1395 *WBible* Ecclesiasticus x 32 *gloss:* For of the handmayde he makith a ladi, and ayenward, and this is most unrightful. **a1450** *Three Middle English Sermons* 73.748–9: Thus is a vowl abusiun and a vowl errour e kende, that te handmayde schal thus ha lordschipe over hir owne lady. See **C558, H548, S158, T188.**

H93 Have **Handsel** (*payment*) for the mare!
a1500 *Robin Hood and the Potter* in Child III 111.32[4]: Haffe hansell ffor the mare! Whiting *Ballad* 36.

H94 Less than a **Handworm's** (*itchmite's*) hipbone
c1150 *Anglo-Saxon Charms* 154.12: And miccli lesse alswa anes handwurmes hupeban.

H95 (First) **Hanged** and then indicted
1556 Heywood *Spider* 222[5]: That he should streight be hangd, and then endited. See **L593.**

Hap, sb.

H96 **Hap** (*luck, fortune*) helps hardy man
c1386 Chaucer *LGW* 1773: Hap helpeth hardy man alday. **1513** Douglas *Aeneid* III 248.175: Hap helpis hardy man. Skeat 189; Whiting *Scots* I 184. See **F519, G214, L510.**

H97 **Hap** is hard, *etc.*
a1500 Hill 140.111: Happe is harde, grace hath no pere, Fortune is a nyggard, and frendship is dere.

H98 **Hap** is unstable and unsteadfast
a1387 Higden-Trevisa I 139[14–6]: And whan they mette to gidres hap was unstable and unstedefast; ones with that oon side, and eft with that other. See **A54, F523, M164.**

H99 The **Haps** over man's head are hung with a tender thread
a1393 Gower *CA* III 208.1513–4: The happes over mannes hed Ben honged with a tendre thred. See **S979, T244.**

H100 If **Hap** help not hope is hindered
c1500 *Digby MS.230* in Lydgate *Troy* IV 29[23–4]: If happ helpe not Hope is hindered.

H101 More by **Hap** than strength
c1475 Gregory *Chronicle* 202[15]: And by happe more thenne strengythe that innocent recoveryd. See **A49.**

H102 Some have **Hap** and some hang
c1250 *Hendyng O* 195.21: Som haveth happe, and sum hongeth bi, **a1325** *C* 188.32: Wi, one havit happe, an othir hangith tharbi. Kneuer 66–7; Schleich 262; Singer III 133. Cf. Apperson 587; Jente 273; *Oxford* 277; Tilley H136.

H103 With **Hap** and halfpenny and a lamb's skin
a1500 *Thre Prestis* 12.183–4: Becauss thar faderis purely can begyn With hap and halfpenny and a lam skyn. Apperson 283; *Oxford* 277; Tilley H135, 610; Whiting *Scots* I 185.

H104 Without good **Hap** there may no wit suffice
c1503 More *Early Poems* [10] B[4–5]; Without good happe there may no wit suffise, Better is to be fortunate than wyse. See **H106.**

Hap, vb.

H105 **Hap** what hap may
c1408 Lydgate *Reson* 124.4735: But happe what ever happe may. **c1489** Caxton *Aymon* II

332.2–3: I care not . . . hap as it hap wyll. **a1500** Medwall *Nature* C3[r][21]: Hap what hap may. Apperson 283; Tilley C529; Whiting *Drama* 347:604.

H106 Better to be **Happy** (*lucky*) than wise
1546 Heywood *D* 79.32: They would saie, better to be happie then wise, **1555** *E* 166.123, **1556** *Spider* 103[2–3]: But I coulde not be: both happie and wice, This proverbe proveth this a fooles decre. Apperson 45; *Oxford* 38; Tilley H140. See **H104.**

H107 At the **Hard** (*test, adversity*) one may find who goes before, who lies behind
c1250 *Owl* 46.527–8: At than harde me mai avinde (W)o geth forth, wo lith bihinde. See **G3.**

H108 **Hard** for hard is good enough
a1325 *Song on the Times* in Heuser 138.23[8]: Hard for hard is gode ynowgh.

H109 **Hardiment** (*boldness*) taken suddenly may gar (*cause*) unlikely things to come to fair endings
c1375 Barbour *Bruce* I 232.632–5: Lo! how hardyment tane suddanly, And drivin syne till end scharply, May ger oft-siss unlikly thyngis Cum to richt fair and gud endingis.

H110 As brainless as a March **Hare**
a1500 *Colyn Blowbol* 105.303: And be as braynles as a Marshe hare.

H111 As dreadful (*timid*) as a (the) **Hare**
a1425 *Governance of Lordschipes* 104.7–8: Dredful as a hare. **a1449** Lydgate and Burgh *Secrees* 73.2297: Dreedful as the hare. Cf. Svartengren 114; Tilley H147: fearful.

H112 As light as the **Hare** (*etc.*) (A number of single quotations are brought together here)
a1325 *Flemish Insurrection* 119.81: This frenshe come to flaundres so liht so the hare. **1422** Yonge *Governaunce* 211.39–212.1: Feynte as an hare. **c1450** *Secrete of Secretes* 35.16–7: (*A man is*) fferd as an hare. **1456** Hay *Governaunce* 157.16: Rad and coward as a hare. **c1475** Henryson *Fables* 77.2242: The Husband than woxe angrie as ane hair. **a1529** Skelton *Elynour* I 99.112: As wyse as an hare!

H113 As mazed (*crazed*) as a March **Hare**
1523 Skelton *Garlande* I 386.632: Masid as a marche hare.

H114 As merry as a March **Hare**
c1516 Skelton *Magnificence* 30.922: As mery as a Marche hare.

H115 As swift as the **Hare**
c1380 *Ferumbras* 120.3829: The dromedary ys swifter than the hare, 121.3859: And renneth swyfter than the hare. Whiting *NC* 420, *Scots* I 185.

H116 As wood (*mad*) as any (an, a) (March) **Hare**
c1350 *Smaller Vernon Collection* 94.81: And ros up wod as eny hare. **c1395** Chaucer *CT* III[D] 1327: For thogh this Somonour wood were as an hare. **1440** Palladius 88.36–8: Yet in this mone is forto sowe tares And not in Marche, lest they enoye thi bestis; Thi oxon myght be wood therof as haris. **a1450** *Partonope* 319.7934: There he renneth wode as any hare. **c1485** *St. Erasmus* in Horstmann *Sammlung* 199.81: Than was this tyrant as wode as an hare. **c1497** Medwall *Fulgens* G2[r][6]: As made as an hare. **a1500** *St. Walstan* in *Norfolk Archæology* 19(1914–6) 258[22]: A Lunaticke man, mad as any hare. **1528** Skelton *Replycacion* I 210.35: I saye, thou madde Marche hare, **a1529** *Ware the Hauke* I 158.104–5: But lyke a Marche harum, His braynes were so *parum.* **1529** More *Supplicacion* 299 H[3–4]: As mad not as a march hare, but as a madde dogge. **1546** Heywood *D* 76.224: As mad as a marche hare, **1555** *E* 161.95, **1562** *E* 230.4.4: Yet hast thou the marche hares mad propertee. Apperson 389; *Oxford* 396; Taylor and Whiting 171–2; Tilley H148.

H117 The **Hare** is squat!
c1516 Skelton *Magnificence* 41.1300: So how, I say, the hare is squat!

H118 The **Hare** went (to) the market to sell scarlet, *etc.*
c1475 *Rawlinson MS. D 328* 124.76: The hare wente the markyth scharlyt forto syll; The grehoun stode hym be-fore mony for to tell. Latin: Fforum lepus petabat lutum ad vendendum; Ante stabant leporarii nummos numerando.

H119 **Hares** and hearthstones
a1350 *Ercyldoun's Prophecy* in *Rel. Ant.* I 30[6]: Hwan hares kendleth (*give birth*) in hertth-stanes. **c1353** *Winner* 14: And hares appon herthe-stones schall hurcle (*crouch*) in hire fourme. **c1400** *Thomas of Erceldoune* xviii [4]: When hares kendles othe herston. **a1500** *The Mone in the mornyng* in *Rel. Ant.* I 84[12]: The hare and harthestone hurtuld to-geydur. MED hurkelen.

H120 There (Here) goes the **Hare** away
a1500 Medwall *Nature* G2[r][24]: There went the hare away. **1522** Skelton *Why Come* II 30.117: There went the hare away. **1546** Hey-

wood *D* 77.227: And here gothe the hare awaie, **1555** *E* 166.121: There, **1556** *Spider* 123[7]: here. Apperson 286; *Oxford* 279; Tilley H157. Cf. Whiting *Drama* 258.

H121 To be chased like **Hare**(s)
a1338 Mannyng *Chronicle B* I 210[5]: About thei gan him chace, and hunted him als hayre. **a1400** *Morte Arthure* 43.1444: We hafe bene chased to daye and chullede as hares. **a1470** Malory I 210.10–1: Thes Romaynes this day have chaced us as wylde harys.

H122 To be like a **Hare**
c1400 *Brut* I 75.22: A cowarde as an here. **c1450** *Merlin* I 162[1–2]: Alle other be but as hares as in comparison to hym.

H123 To droop and dare (*be afraid*) as the **Hare** for the hounds (*etc.*) (A number of single quotations are brought together here)
a1300 *An Orison of Penitence* in Brown *Lyrics XIII* 125.44–6: To drupe and dar We athe wel mare, Alse for the hondis doyt the har. **c1390** Chaucer *CT* VII 103–5[B1293–5]: Thise wedded men, that lye and dare As in a fourme sit a wery hare, Were al forstraught with houndes grete and smale. **a1393** Gower *CA* II 374.2720: Awey he skulketh as an hare. **c1400** *Beryn* 73.2390: Beryn turnyd, as an hare, and gan to renne blyve. **c1400** *Thomas of Erceldoune* xix[6]: When a scot ne may hym hude ase hare in forme. **a1420** Lydgate *Troy* I 247.3602: Thou wentist out as hare among (the) houndis, **a1449** *Testament* in *MP* I 354.668: Wilfull, rekles, made stertyng as a hare. **a1475** *Ludus Coventriae* 202.80: The hare fro the fforme we xal a-rere. **1513** Douglas *Aeneid* IV 126.171–2: And alss feill syss went turnyng heir and thar, Lyke as befor the hund wiskis the hair.

H124 To flee like (the, an) **Hare**(s)
a1393 Gower *CA* III 341.3776: Thei fledde, as doth the wylde Hare. **c1400** *Laud Troy* I 184.6230: Thei fled fro him as hares fro the hounde, 207.7009. **c1408** Lydgate *Reson* 92.3493–4: And fle from hir in every part, As doth an hare the lyppart. **c1450** *Ponthus* 85.20–1: So they fled all afor hym, as doos the hayres afor the grehoundes. **a1500** *Partenay* 53.1388–9: That . . . doth fle . . . (As) hare fro grohund. Whiting *Drama* 316:159, *Scots* I 185.

H125 To hunt a **Hare** with a tabor (*varied*)
c1405 *Mum* 5.58–9: Men myghtten as well have hun(t)yd an hare with a tabre As aske ony mendis for that thei mysdede. **a1449** Lydgate *Cok* in *MP* II 817.122: Men with a tabour may lyghtly cacche an hare. **1520** Whittinton *Vulgaria* 89.2–3: I have as greate appetyte to my booke to daye as an hare to a tabre. **1546** Heywood *D* 33.17–8: And yet shall we catche a hare with a taber, As soone as catche ought of them, and rather, **1556** *Spider* 148[27]: And thant shall with a tabor take a wat. Apperson 286; Jente 533; *Oxford* 311; Skeat 124; Tilley H160.

H126 To look as though one would find a **Hare**
c1390 Chaucer *CT* VII 696–7[B1886–7]: Thou lookest as thou woldest fynde an hare, For evere upon the ground I se thee stare. Cf. Joseph S. Fletcher *Dead Men's Money* (New York, 1920) p. 65: He was a . . . man that you might occasionally see in Berwick streets, walking very fast with his eyes on the ground, as if, as the youngsters say, he was seeking sixpences.

H127 To run like (the, an) **Hare**
c1380 *Ferumbras* 115.3661–2: Ne saw he nevere be-fore that day . . . hare so renne a-way, So dude that jantail fole. **1502** *Robert the Devil* B3^r[28–9]: They ranne away from hym lyke the hare frome the houndes. **a1518** Nevill *Castell* 79.95–6: Lyke to an hare she ranne in haste, He folowed lyke a grehounde.

H128 To set the **Hare's** head against the goose's giblet
1546 Heywood *D* 69.98: Set the hares head against the goose jeblet, **1556** *Spider* 203[23–4]: Wherin let us be content: To set the hares head, against the goose jeblet. Apperson 287; *Oxford* 279; Tilley H161.

H129 To start a **Hare**
1473 Paston V 179[12–4]: Raff Blaundrehasset wer a name to styrte an hare . . . it myght per case styrt xx^{ti} harys at onys. **1556** Heywood *Spider* 166[10]: How we both: betwene both parts: can the hare starte.

H130 To wit where the **Hare** walks
c1405 *Mum* 60.1144–6: Whenne thay witen wel y-now where the hare walketh, Thay leden men the long waye and love-dayes breken And maken moppes wel myry with thaire madde tales.

H131 Who hunts most the **Hares** most shall he find of them
c1410 Edward of York *Master* 12–3: And therfore men sayn in olde sawes, who so hunteth most the hares moost (s)hal he fynde of hem, *for Phebus Erle of Foys, the good huntere, seith that* whanne ther bene few hares in a Countre

thei shul be hunted and slayn, for the hares of othere contre about shul come in that marche.

H132 Of a **Harlot's** love think you not sure
a1500 *O man more* 394.48–9: Of a harlottes love thynke the nott sure, She lovethe for money and nott for plesur(e).

H133 Better be still than to speak **Harm**
a1400 *Romaunt C* 7511–2: For it is better stylle be Than for to speken harm, parde! Cf. Whiting *Drama* 132. See **T366.**

H134 **Harm** done is done, whoso may rue it (*varied*)
c1385 Chaucer *TC* ii 789: But harm ydoon is doon, whoso it rewe. **a1420** Lydgate *Troy* I 199.1895–6: And harme y-done to late is to amende, Whos fyn is ofte other than thei wende, 248.3621: For harme y-don to late is to compleine, **a1439** *Fall* I 183.6494: Whan harm is doon, ful hard is to recure, II 354.915: Harm doon, to late folweth repentaunce. Apperson 528; *Oxford* 539. See **D287, M729, R84, 86, T198.**

H135 He is happy that amends a **Harm** hastily
a1400 *Destruction of Troy* 366.11216–9: Hit is said oft-sithes, and for sothe holdyn, He is happy, that a harme hastely amendes, Or any perties have pyne, or put unto dethe, Or be travailed with tene, or tyne of there goodes.

H136 He that will seek **Harm** shall find harm
1481 Caxton *Reynard* 50[17–8]: Yf he wil seche harm he shal fynde harme. Apperson 287; *Oxford* 280; Tilley H167.

H137 Less **Harm** to deceive than to be deceived
a1400 *Romaunt B* 4840–2: But men this thenken evermore, That lasse harm is, so mote I the, Deceyve them than deceyved be.

H138 One must hold to his **Harm(s)**
a1375 *William* 128.3987–8: That we have wrongli wrought, nowe is it wel sene; We mot holde to oure harmes, it helpes nought elles. **a1425** *Chester Plays* I 144.302: But I must needes hold the harm that I have.

H139 Seldom comes one **Harm** and no more (*varied*)
a1300 *Alisaunder* 72 L 1275–6: Men tellen in old mone The qued comuth nowher al one. **c1390** *Northern Homily Cycle Narrationes* (*Vernon*) 265.363: But ofte cometh care uppe care. **a1400** *Ipomadon A* 48.1623–4: Come never sorow be it one, But there come mo full gryme. **a1450** *Partonope* 210.5542: For efter won evylle comythe mony mo. **c1450** *Douce MS.52* 45.11: Seldun comyth on harme and no mo. **c1450** *Rylands MS.394* 96.6^{v}4. **a1500** *English Conquest* 49.23–4: Hit ys oft founde, Selde befallyth one Harme that more ne comyth aftyr, 69.15–7: As y fynd ofte, good adventures comyn ofte Slowely and aloon, but mysadventures ne comyth never more al-oon. **c1500** Fabyan 622[30]: Thus one mischief ensued upon an other. **1509** Barclay *Ship* II 251[5–7]: For wyse men sayth, and oft it fallyth so, As it is wryten and sayd of many one, That one myshap fortuneth never alone. **1509** Watson *Ship* Dd3^{r} [12–4]: The prudentes saye a comyn proverbe. If there come yll, it is never alone and by our faute encreaseth more. **1532** Berners *Golden Boke* 202.2736–7: For commonly one unhappynes chaunceth not, but an other foloweth, 430. 11087–8: Of one travayle cometh infinite travayles to man. Apperson 419; *Oxford* 426–7; Smith 204; Taylor and Whiting 246; Tilley M1012; Whiting *Scots* II 99.

H140 To make two **Harms** of one (*varied*)
a1415 Mirk *Festial* 120.27–8: And soo make two harmes of on. **1418** *Man, be warre* in Kail 62.38: For a penyworth of harm, tak not two. **a1470** Malory II 1002.32: And better ys one harm than twayne. **c1489** Caxton *Aymon* I 246.26–7: Men sayen comynly that it is better to doo one harme than two. See **S513.**

H141 Who has **Harm** and scathe every man will put more to (it)
1481 Caxton *Reynard* 16[11–2]: Who hath harme and scathe every man wil be ther at and put more to. Cf. Whiting *NC* 441:27. See **F541, M89, 312.**

H142 To hang like a **Harp**
a1450 *Castle* 143.2224: That myn hed hangyth as an harpe.

H143 Have among you, blind **Harpers**
1546 Heywood *D* 82.64: Have among you blynd harpers. Apperson 290; *Oxford* 283; Tilley H176.

H144 Out of **Harre** (*joint, order*)
a1300 *Cloisterer's Lament* in *Rel. Ant.* I 292[25]: I horle at the notes and heve hem al of herre. **a1327** *For thar wer thai* in Wright *Political Songs* 318.726–7: Wer never dogges there Hurled out of herre. **a1393** Gower *CA* II 257.1148–9: Thus, for I stonde in such a wer, I am, as who seith, out of herre, 411.346: Wherof this world stant out of herre, III 200.1237, 208.1518: And sette his welthe al out of herre, 275.1576–7, 328.3302–3, 335.3542,

c1400 *Peace* III 486.185. a1449 Lydgate *Testament* in *MP* I 344.398: Fer out of harre, wilde of condicioun. a1450 *York Plays* 286.378, 324.136. c1450 Capgrave *Katharine* 63.758: Some hadde the bether and some were of herre (*var.* And sum had the werr), 111.530, 133.891. c1450 Idley 136.1751. a1460 *Towneley Plays* 234.210. c1516 Skelton *Magnificence* 65.2095. MED herre n. (1) 1(d); NED Harre 3. Cf. Tilley J75.

H145 As fierce as a **Hart**
1422 Yonge *Governaunce* 212.1: Fierse as an harte.

H146 As light as **Harts**
a1396(1494) Hilton *Scale* T4v[18–20]: Jhesu makyth soules lighte as hertes that sterten fro therthe over busshes and breres.

H147 As swift as **Hart(s)**
a1375 *Octavian* (*S*) 45.1417: Hyt ys swyfter than hert. **a1387** Higden-Trevisa I 159[4]: And beeth swifter than hertes. **a1449** Lydgate *Haste* in *MP* II 762.82: More swyft of cours than . . . hert. Whiting *Scots* I 185.

H148 As wild as a **Hart**
a1449 Lydgate *Testament* in *MP* I 342.350: Wylde as an herte. **c1450** Idley 90.591: As wilde as a herte. Cf. Apperson 686: buck; Tilley B692.

H149 The **Hart** which goes free on the laund (*glade*) not (*knows not*) what ails an ox
a1393 Gower *CA* III 444.2160–1: The hert which fre goth on the launde Not of an Oxe what him eileth. See **F697, W551.**

H150 To be hunted like a **Hart** at bay
c1450 *How mankinde dooth* in Furnivall *Hymns* 70.401: Thus y am huntid as an herte to a-bay.

H151 To flee like the **Hart** tofore the lion
a1300 *Alisaunder* 129.2271–2: That folk tofore hym fleigh, certe, Tofore the lyoun so dooth the herte.

H152 To leap like a **Hart**
c1000 Aelfric *Homilies* II 16[18–9]: þonne hleapð se healta swa swa heort.

H153 To run like a **Hart**
c1380 *Ferumbras* 115.3661–2: Ne saw he nevere be-fore that day Hert . . . so renne a-way, So dude that jantail fole. **1471** Caxton *Recuyell* I 317.26–7: He cam rennyng as lightly and also swyftely as the herte rennyth in the valeye, II 461.17–9. Whiting *Drama* 316:161.

H154 **Harvest** ears, thick of hearing
1546 Heywood *D* 91.39: You had on your harvest eares, thicke of hearyng. Apperson 287; *Oxford* 280; Tilley H186.

H155 One's **Harvest** is in (*i.e.*, it's all up)
c1405 *Mum* 5.79: That, but if God helpe, youre hervest is ynne.

H156 To make a long **Harvest** for a little corn
1549 Heywood *D* 55.1–2: Ye have . . . Made a long harvest for a little corne. Apperson 288; *Oxford* 381; Tilley H184.

Haste, sb.

H157 All **Haste** is odious
a1449 Lydgate *Haste* in *MP* II 759.1: Alle haste is odious.

H158 Do not that thing in **Haste** to repent after
a1533 Berners *Castell* F3v[22–3]: He shuld not do that thyng in haste, wherby to repent hym after. See **F417, H159, W542.**

H159 Great **Haste** leads repentance after it (*varied*)
1450 *Dicts* 266.22–3: Grete haast ledith repentaunce after him. **1477** Rivers *Dictes* 53[2]: Hastynesse engendreth repentaunce. **1509** *Fyftene Joyes* G6v[10–1]: Suche thynge somtyme a man may do in haste, That afterwarde he shall repent the waste. Apperson 288; Tilley H191. See **F417, H158, R32, 67, 90.**

H160 **Haste** and wisdom are things far odd
1546 Heywood *D* 21.42: Than seeth he hast and wisdome thinges far od. Apperson 288; *Oxford* 280; Tilley W523. See **M449.**

H161 **Haste** is meddled (*mixed*) ay with mischief
a1420 Lydgate *Troy* I 345.7032: And hast is ay medlid with meschefe.

H162 **Haste** makes waste
1534 Heywood *Love* D1v[10]: Hast, wast, **1546** *D* 21.28: Hast maketh waste, **1555** *E* 149.15. Apperson 288; *Oxford* 281; Tilley H189; Whiting *Drama* 122, 223, *NC* 420. See **E187, M97, 99.**

H163 He that can (*knows*) but **Haste** can not of hap (*luck*)
a1437 *Kingis Quair* 82–3.133[3–4]: For he that can bot haste, Can noght of hap, the wis man it writ.

H164 An ill **Haste** is not good
a1533 Berners *Huon* 320.25–6: It is a saynge that an yll haste is not good. Apperson 448.

H165 In **Haste** no waste
a1500 Medwall *Nature* C2v[41–3]: I begate the

horson in bast, It was done all in hast, Ye may se there was no wast.

H166 In wicked **Haste** is no profit (speed)
c1390 Chaucer *CT* VII 1054[B2244]: In wikked haste is no profit, X[I] 1003: For wikked haste dooth no profit. **a1449** Lydgate *Haste* in *MP* II 764.145: In wykkyd haste was never founde speede. *Oxford* 281. See **F463.**

H167 More **Haste** than good speed
1513 More *Richard* 41 E[2–3]: In greate haste, not in good speede. **1546** Heywood *D* 32.61: In more haste than good speede. *Oxford* 433; Tilley H197. See **S621.**

H168 The more **Haste** the worse (less) speed
c1450 *Douce MS.52* 51.86: The more hast, the worse spede. **c1450** *Rylands MS.394* 102.4. **1519** Horman *Vulgaria* 434[29]. **1546** Heywood *D* 21.44: The more haste the lesse speede, **1556** *Spider* 124[17]: Yet might that change bring smal good spede: in great haste. Apperson 427; Jente 372; *Oxford* 281; Smith 149; Taylor and Whiting 173; Tilley H198. See **P1, R33, 238, W652.**

H169 No **Haste** but good
1546 Heywood *D* 97.225: No hast but good. Apperson 448; *Oxford* 280–1; Tilley H199.

H170 Of a little **Haste** comes oft great mischief
c1450 *Epistle of Othea* 65.13–4: And for as myche that of a lytle hast comyth ofte grett myscheff.

Haste, vb.

H171 He **Hastes** well that wisely can abide
c1385 Chaucer *TC* i 956: He hasteth wel that wisely kan abyde, **c1390** *CT* VII 1054[B2244]: The proverbe seith, "He hasteth wel that wisely kan abyde." **c1440** Lydgate *Debate* in *MP* II 565.650: He lastith (*var.* hastith) weel that wisly can a-byde, **a1449** *Haste* in *MP* II 759–64.8, 16, 24, *etc.* (*slightly varied refrain*): He hastuth weele that wysely can abyde. Apperson 288; *Oxford* 398; Skeat 155. See **A6.**

H172 To **Haste** and be ever behind
a1393 Gower *CA* II 309.290: I haste and evere I am behinde. See **G181.**

H173 To be none of the **Hastings**
1546 Heywood *D* 51.343–4: Toward your woorkyng . . . ye make such tastinges, As approve you to be none of the hastinges. Apperson 288–9; *Oxford* 281; Tilley H203.

H174 Be neither too **Hasty** nor too slow
c1450 *Fyrst thou sal* 89.107–8: Be nowther to hasty ne to slawe, Fle not to hye ne crep not to lawe.

H175 My old **Hat** must have a new band
1546 Heywood *D* 60.49: And now mine olde hat must have a new band. Tilley H205.

H176 To know no more than one's old **Hat**
c1385 Chaucer *TC* iii 320: Ne knewe hem more than myn olde hat! MED hat la(c).

H177 It is good to have a **Hatch** before the door
1546 Heywood *D* 43.66: It is good to have a hatche before the durre. Apperson 289; *Oxford* 282; Tilley H207.

H178 After **Hate** comes love (*varied*)
a1200 Lawman I 355.8319–24: For ofte hit is ilumpen, Inne feole leoden, Thet æfter muchele hatinge Hehghe men heom luvede, And æfter muchel weorld-scome Wurth-scipe wurhten, **c1300** *B* 8319–24: For hofte hit his b(i)-valle In wel fale leode, That after hate Cometh love, And after worliche same Worsipe hi-lome. **a1338** Mannyng *Chronicle A* I 171.4865–6: After hate, love wyl be, And after schame, worschip men se. **a1450** *Generydes A* 291.9409–10: Oft men seyne, "aftre hate strong Grete love fele folk among." **1471** Caxton *Recuyell* II 473.13–4: Ofte tymes men seyth that after grete hate cometh grete love. See **B325.**

H179 Old hoarded **Hate** makes wrath rise
1400 *Love god, and drede* in Kail 6.165: Old horded hate maketh wratthe to rise. See **H181.**

H180 There is never great **Hate** but where first was as much love
1532 Berners *Golden Boke* 425.10912–3: There is never gret hate, but where as moch love was fyrst. Apperson 273; *Oxford* 265; Tilley H210.

H181 Old **Hatred** bears a new death (kindles new envy)
c1400 *Alexander Buik* III 299.6660–1: And auld hatrent, as men sais, Beris ane new deid alvais. **a1439** Lydgate *Fall* III 735.2266: Of old hatreede to kyndle newe envie. See **H179.**

H182 **Hauntise** (*companionship*) makes love
1471 Caxton *Recuyell* I 183.24: Hauntyse maketh love.

H183 The more **Havande** (*wealth*) the more feeble of heart
c1353 *Winner* 323: The more havande that he hath, the more of hert feble. MED haven la(g).

H184 Better to **Have** than wish
a1450 *Barlam and Josaphat* (*South English Legendary*) 125.422: Beter Is have than weche.

1546 Heywood *D* 67.30 Better to have then wishe, **1555** *E* 193.272. Apperson 46; *Oxford* 42; Tilley H214. See **H411.**

H185 One shall **Have** as he has wrought (done)
c1300 *Worldes blis ne last* in Brown *Lyrics XIII* 82.64: Thu shalt haven as thu havest wrokt. **c1450** *Owayne Miles* (*Cotton Caligula*) 116.285: As thu hast don, so shalte thu have. MED haven 7c (f). See **D165, M39, W190.**

H186 That (which) we cannot **Have** we must forgo
a1500 Medwall *Nature* F2^{v}[9–10]: That we can not have we must forgo, There ys none other remedy.

H187 Who that **Had** (?would have) that he has not would (?should) do that he does not
1546 Heywood *D* 96.175–6: Ye (quoth she) who had that he hath not, woulde Doo that he dooth not, as olde men have tolde. Apperson 277; *Oxford* 283; Tilley H216.

H188 Never a **Haw** the higher
a1400 *Alexander C* 118.2097: Was nevire the heghare of a hawe his hert full of pride.

H189 Not avail three (an) **Haw(s)**
c1385 Chaucer *TC* iv 1398: Or calkulyng, avayleth nought thre hawes. **c1390** *Alexius* (*Vernon*) 76.581: And that avayled not worth an haue. **1410** Walton *Boethius* 66[3]: Thi labour all availeth not an hawe.

H190 Not give a(n) **Haw**
a1300 *Meidan Maregrete* 491.70: Of alle thine mitte ne yeved ho word an hawe. **a1325** *Otuel and Roland* 88.952: Off hem y ne yeve nought an hawe. **c1330** *Otuel* 71.192: And yaf nought of hem alle an hawe. **c1330** *St. Margaret* 227.78: Of thi pouste no yiveth sche nought an hawe. **c1400** *Laud Troy* II 412.14001: But he yaff not ther-of an hawe, 496.16834. **a1450** *Castle* 91.481. **a1475** *Ludus Coventriae* 29.22, 272.13. **a1500** *Christ's Resurrection* (*Ashmole*) in *Archiv* 79(1887) 442.80.

H191 Not grieve a **Haw** (*etc.*) (A number of single quotations are brought together here)
c1300 *South English Legendary* I 56.66: It ne grevede noght an hawe. **c1325** *God that al this myhtes* in Brown *Lyrics XIII* 157.28: Crist ne stod me never hawe. **c1440** *When adam dalfe* (*Thornton*) in *Yorkshire Writers* I 368.32: Ne latyne ne lawe may helpe an hawe. **a1450** *Castle* 112.1169: Thou I nevere faste, I rekke (not) an hawe.

H192 Not set a **Haw**
c1385 Usk 33.100: Of thy misaventure sette they nat an hawe. **c1395** Chaucer *CT* III[D] 659–60: But al for noght, I sette noght an hawe Of his proverbes n'of his olde sawe. **1402** *Daw Topias* 47[20–1]: And Cristis bitter passioun Ye sette not at an hawe. **1406** Hoccleve *Male Regle* I 37.380: For by hem two, he settith nat [an] hawe. **a1450** *Partonope* 107.3244. **a1450** *St. Editha* 73.3286: Ny set by non of hem an hawe. **a1475** Russell *Boke* 124.99.

H193 Not worth an **Haw**
a1300 *Arthour and M.*[1] 202.7224: No telle y you nought worth an hawe. **c1300** *Passion of St. Paul* in Horstmann *Legenden 1881* 77.71: His resoune es noght worthe a hawe. **c1300** Robert of Gloucester II 722.10767. **c1300** *South English Legendary* I 131.82, 329.52. **c1385** Chaucer *TC* iii 854: Nay, swiche abodes ben nought worth an hawe. **c1385** Usk 51.71–2. **c1390** *Castel of Love* 368.505. **c1390** *God man and the devel* 336.282. **c1390** *Northern Homily Cycle Narrationes* (*Vernon*) 299.25. **c1400** *Laud Troy* II 388.13174. **c1400** *Plowman's Tale* 156.304. **c1412** Hoccleve *Balade* I 67.20, *Regement* 176.4886. **a1420** Lydgate *Troy* I 260.4043. **c1450** *Epistle of Othea* 82.25. **c1460** *Ipomadon C* 353.50–354.1. **a1475** *Good Rule* in Brown *Lyrics XV* 266.88. **a1475** *Ludus Coventriae* 179.27. **c1497** Medwall *Fulgens* C5^{r}[25–6]. **a1500** Basterfeld 368.95. **a1500** *Piers of Fullham* 10.224. **a1500** *Theophilus* 21.96[5]. **1509** Barclay *Ship* I 72[10]: Byenges and sellynges scant worth a hawe. **c1516** Skelton *Magnificence* 65.2089, **c1522** *Speke* II 23.471. Apperson 457; *Oxford* 283; Tilley H221.

H194 As fresh as the **Hawk**
c1350 *Joseph* 19.595: Also fresch as the hauk, freschore that tyme. See **F25.**

H195 As hende (*comely*) as **Hawk** in chete (*cabin*, frith [*wood*], hall)
c1325 *I Repent* 141.28: And are al hende ase hauk in chete. **c1330** *Praise of Women* 291.59: Hende in halle as hauke in frith. **c1380** *Pearl* 7.184: I stod as hende as hawk in halle.

H196 As hooked as a **Hawk's** beak
a1529 Skelton *Garnesche* I 117.40: Howkyd as a hawkys beke, lyke Syr Topyas.

H197 As hook-nebbed as a **Hawk**
a1400 *Morte Arthure* 32.1082: Huke-nebbyde as a hawke.

H198 As ready as any (a) **Hawk** to lure (that is lured)
c1395 Chaucer *CT* III[D] 1338–40: This false theef, this somonour, quod the Frere, Hadde

alwey bawdes redy to his hond, As any hauk to lure in Engelond. **c1450** Idley 142.2143–4: We be as redy as an hauke that is lured To every-thyng that they wolle to us bede. See **L589.**

H199 A **Hawk** comes unto lure when a kite will not come nigh
c1475 *Prohemy of a Mariage* 29[3–4]: I say an hauke comethe oftyn unto lure, Whan that a kyte atal wol not come nyghe. Cf. Apperson 82: A carrion kite will never make good hawk; *Oxford* 341; Tilley K114. See **H203.**

H200 **Hawk** that has tint (*lost*) its prey is eath (*easy*) to reclaim
a1325 *Cursor* I 210.3529–30: For hauk es eth, als i here say, To reclayme that has tint his pray. Apperson 290.

H201 To go like a **Hawk** that flies (*etc.*) (A number of single quotations are brought together here)
c1300 *Guy*[1] 192 A 3336: As hauk that fleythe his hors gan gon. **a1393** Gower *CA* II 108.2671–3: Ther is a vice of Prides lore, Which lich an hauk whan he wol sore, Fleith upon heihte in his delices, III 145–6.7070–2: And thus he loketh on the fleissh, Riht as an hauk which hath a sihte Upon the foul, ther he schal lihte. **c1400** *Laud Troy* I 190.6444–5: Ye scholde sitte and wake nyghtes, As hauke on perche that sittes in mewe. **a1450** *Castle* 91.460: As a hawke, I hoppe in my hende hale.

H202 Ware the **Hawk**
a1529 Skelton *Ware the Hauke* I 163.245, 164.259, 269, 278, 165.289, 299, 312, 166.322. *Oxford* 692; Tilley H227.

H203 Wild **Hawks** are reclaimed rather (*sooner*) than hens
1464 Hardyng 420 *var.*[14]: Wilde haukes to hande than hennys rather been reclaymed. See **H199.**

H204 As hoar as a **Hawthorn**
c1378 *Piers* B xvi 173: As hore as a hawethorne and Abraham he highte.

H205 As dried (dry) as **Hay**
c1000 *Regius Psalter* 64 (36.2): Swa swa heg hrædlice hy adrugiað. **c1100** *Salisbury Psalter* 124 (36.2): Swa hig snellice adrugað. **c1340** Rolle *Psalter* 354 (101.12): .I. dryed as hay. **c1350** *Prose Psalter* 42 (36.2): Hii shul drien hastilich as hay. **c1395** *WBible* Psalms xxxvi 2: Thei schulen wexe drie swiftli as hey, ci 12: Y wexede drie as hei, Isaiah li 12: The sone of man, that schal wexe drie so as hei. **a1398**(1495) Bartholomaeus-Trevisa Q1ʳ[2.32–7]. **a1400** *Northern Verse Psalter* I 111 (36.2), II 7 (101.12). **c1400** *Primer* 41[18]. **c1450** *Pilgrimage LM* 206[16]. **1479** Rivers *Cordyal* 18.6–7. **1509** Fisher *Treatyse* 148.4, 151.2, 162.16. Svartengren 300.

H206 Make **Hay** while the sun shines
1509 Barclay *Ship* II 46[4–7]: Who that in July whyle Phebus is shynynge About his hay is nat besy labourynge And other thynges whiche ar for his avayle Shall in the wynter his negligence bewayle. **1546** Heywood *D* 22.17: Whan the sunne shinth make hay. Apperson 291; *Oxford* 398–9; Taylor and Whiting 175; Tilley H235. Cf. Whiting *Drama* 111.

H207 To fade like **Hay**
a1450 *Ancrene* (*Royal*) 40.7–8: How frely they ben, and fadyng as is hay. **a1500** Greene *Carols* 366.1: And man xalt fade as dose hay, 378.9: As hey thei schall fayd and well away.

H208 To spring up like **Hay**
c900 *Paris Psalter* 255 (91.6): Heap synnigra hige onlic. **c1000** *Regius Psalter* 174 (91.8): þonne upaspringað synfulle swa swa hyg. **c1100** *Salisbury Psalter* 207 (91.8). **c1350** *Prose Psalter* 114 (91.7): Whan synyers ben born as hay multipliand. **c1395** *WBible* Psalms xci 8: Whanne synneris comen forth, as hey.

H209 To vanish like **Hay**
1435 Misyn *Fire* 41.10–1: Ilk fleschly beute is as hay lightly vanischand.

H210 To wax old like **Hay**
c1395 *WBible* Ecclesiasticus xiv 18: Ech man schal wexe eld as hey.

H211 To wither like **Hay**
c1405 *Wyt and Wille* in Kail 22.5: Right as hay, they mon widre. **1509** Fisher *Treatyse* 148.10: Wydred as hey, 162.16, 23. **a1529** Skelton *Elynour* I 97.62: Wyddered lyke hay. Whiting *Scots* I 186.

H212 What now is **Hay** sometime was grass
a1437 Lydgate *That Now Is Hay* in *MP* II 809–13.8, 16, 24, *etc.*: That now is heye some tyme was grase. See **G436.**

H213 To sing of **Hazelwood**
1402 *Daw Topias* 79[6–7]: For the which y trowe thou maist Of hasilwode singe. MED hasel 2(b). Cf. Chaucer *TC* iii 890, v 505, 1174–5.

H214 As the **Head** needs the other limbs so the limbs need the head
c1000 Aelfric *Homilies* I 274[7–8]: Ealswa wel

behofað þæt heafod þæra oðera lima, swa swa ða lima behofiað þæs heafdes. See **D151.**

H215 From **Head** to heel
c1400 *St. Anne (1)* 52.2006–7: Our lamed childe es now hale Ffro hys hede to hys hele. **a1425** *Metrical Paraphrase OT* 58.15855–6: Ffor he has rent and ryches ryfe And hape and hele fro hed to heyle. MED hed 1b(a); NED Head 44; Tilley T436. See **C575, F468, T421.**

H216 A good **Head** does comfort to its meiny (*household*) (*varied*)
a1425 *Of Mynystris* in Wyclif *SEW* II 397[6–8]: For as a good heed doith confort to the meyne of this heed, so a foul, abbominable heed doith disconfort to his meyne. **a1430** Lydgate *Pilgrimage* 12.420–3: And sythen he that was her hed Suffrede peynys, deth, and woo, The membrys wolde endure also, And ffolwe ther hed on al thyng. See **H360.**

H217 He has no **Head** that will not defend it
c1300 *Arthour and M.*[1] 257.9214: He nath non heved, that nil it defende.

H218 He that has a **Head** of verre (*glass*), ware (*keep*) him from cast of stones
c1385 Chaucer *TC* ii 867–8: And forthi, who that hath an hed of verre, Fro cast of stones war hym in the werre! *Oxford* 285; Skeat 166; Tilley H789.

H219 A **Head** dow not (*is not able to*) stand forout (*without*) members
a1500 *Thre Prestis* 8.105–8: Ane hed Dow nocht on body stand allane Fforowt memberis to be of mycht and mane Ffor to wphald the body and the hed, And sekerly to gar It stand in steid.

H220 The **Head** should not disdain the foot
c1421 Lydgate *Thebes* 13.262–5: And ageyn kynde it is out of doute, That eny hed be recorde of the wyse, Shuld the foot of disdeyn despyse Which bereth hym up.

H221 Hew not over your **Head** (too high)
1402 *Daw Topias (Jack)* 99[1–2]: Yit, Dawe, thou hewist hye, And puttist thi mouthe in heven. **a1449** Lydgate and Burgh *Secrees* 15.459: Yit wer me loth Ovir myn hed to hewe. **c1450** Capgrave *Katharine* 145.1081–2: Hewe not so hye but if ye may it holde, Desyre no thyng that may not goten be. **c1450** *Fyrst thou sal* 91.172: Over thi hede loke never thou hewe. **c1450** *Proverbs of Good Counsel* 68.21: Over thi hed loke thowe never hewe. **c1456** Pecock *Faith* 202[22–5]: For y wote weel thei hewen above her heedis, and weenen that thei han more and clerer sight in kunnyng, thanne thei han. **a1500** *Salamon seyth* in Person 52.23: Over thy hed loke thou never hew. See **C235.**

H222 His **Head** is to his heels
a1425 *Chester Plays* I 153.513–4: Hartles is he nowe, For aye to his heeles his head is. Cf. *Oxford* 287: His heart is in his heels; Tilley H314. See **H295.**

H223 If the **Head** is hurt the hand will appair (*impair*)
c1405 *Mum* 69.1472: For and thy heede be hurte thy (honde) wol apeire. See **D151.**

H224 In spite of one's **Head**
a1475 *Ludus Coventriae* 368.359: And makyn alle this merthe in spyth of oure hed.

H225 Maugre one's **Head**
a1300 *Alisaunder* 304 M 223: And mawgre the hedes of them all. **c1330** *Degare* 93.564: He sschal adoune maugre his hed. **c1350** *Libeaus* 54.972: Maugre thin heved hore. **1369** Chaucer *BD* 1201: Mawgree my hed, **c1385** *CT* I[A] 1169, 2618, *Mars* 220, **c1386** *LGW* 2326, **c1390** *CT* II[B] 104, VII 3412[B4602], X[I] 974. **c1390** *Sir Gawain* 48.1565. **c1395** Chaucer *CT* III[D] 887. **c1400** *Alexander Buik* II 173.2610. **c1400** *Brut* I 278.27. **c1400** Mandeville *Travels* 15.12. **c1410** Lovelich *Merlin* II 376.14067. **a1420** Lydgate *Troy* III 720.5341. **c1440** Charles of Orleans 45.1325. **c1449** Pecock *Repressor* I 52[18]. **a1450** *Partonope* 378.9197, 439.10862, 447.11143. **a1450** *St. Editha* 65.2881. **c1450** Capgrave *Katharine* 280.583, *Lives* 15.7. **1463** Ashby 9.270. **a1470** Malory I 115.6–7, 258.2, 284.26, 303.19, 304.2, II 566.35, 594.27, 695.3, 825.26, 889.27, 997.32–3, III 1168.12, 1200.33–1.1, 1229.35–30.1. **1471** *Stonor Letters* I 118[9, 13]. **a1475** *Ludus Coventriae* 134.327. **a1500** *To his Mistress* in Robbins 190.6. **c1500** *Lyfe of Roberte* 254.896. **1513** Douglas *Aeneid* II 168.129, IV 173.57. **1546** Heywood *D* 56.42. MED hed 2a(b); NED Head 60, Maugre B 2; Whiting *Scots* I 186.

H226 Mickle (great) **Head** little wit
c1475 *Mankind* 3.47: Yowur wytt ys lytyll, yowur hede ys mekyll. **1562** Heywood *E* 238.56: Thy head is great, and yet seemth that head but thin: Without here without, and without wit within. Apperson 271; *Oxford* 422; Tilley H245; Whiting *NC* 421.

H227 The more wise **Heads** in any matter the better
c1450 Capgrave *Katharine* 137.958–9: For the moo wyse heedes ther be In ony mater, the

better it is, as thenketh me. Cf. Taylor and Whiting 177: Two heads. See **H250, W409.**

H228 One **Head** of hearts makes realms sure
a1420 Lydgate *Troy* I 201. 1965–6: On hed of hertis maketh rewmys sure, Divisioun causeth discounfeture.

H229 A scald (*scabby*) **Head** may be covered and not seen
a1500 Greene *Carols* 407.7: A scald hed maye be coveryd and not sene.

H230 So many **Heads** so many wits (*varied*)
c1395 Chaucer *CT* V[F] 203: As many heddes, as manye wittes ther been. **c1503** More *Early Poems* [12] B[1]: Lo thus ye see divers heddes, divers wittes. **1509** Watson *Ship* A2^r[12–4 (*the first of two A signatures*)]: Therence sayth. Tot capita tot sensus, also many heedes also many opynyons. **1513** Douglas *Aeneid* II 193.16: Quhou mony hedis als feil consatis beyn. **1528** More *Heresyes* 179 F[7–8]: As many heades as many wittes. **1546** Heywood *D* 23.44: So many heds so many wits, **1555** *E* 148.8, **1556** *Spider* 230[15]. Apperson 586; Jente 46; *Oxford* 406, 418; Skeat 279; Tilley H279. See **F370, M202, T63.**

H231 (A) sore **Head** (hates) a comb (*varied*)
c1450 *Pilgrimage LM* 114[11]: (A) sor hed (hates) a comb, 154[4]: A soor hed maketh no joye of a good comb. Apperson 552: Scabby; *Oxford* 564; Tilley H264. See **B131.**

H232 There the **Head** is gone the members fail
c1410 Lovelich *Grail* I 168.767–8: So that it semeth there the hed is Gon, The Membres Fayllen thanne Everichon. See **D151, H252, 257, 362.**

H233 There the **Head** is unwhole (*ill*) all the limbs are idle (*useless*)
a900 Alfred *Gregory* 129.7–8: Sua eac ðær ðæt heafod bið unhal eall ða limu bioð idelu. See **H272, 301.**

H234 To bear a **Head**
a1500 Medwall *Nature* G3^r[5]: I fere no man that bereth an hed. Whiting *Drama* 348:615.

H235 To break my **Head** and give me a houve (*cap*, plaster)
a1449 Lydgate *Ryme without Accord* in *MP* II 793.35: To breke myn hede, and yeve me an houffe. **1546** Heywood *D* 95.610: To breake my heade, and than geve me a plaster. Apperson 65; *Oxford* 62; Tilley H269.

H236 To cast ones' **Heads** together
c1516 Skelton *Magnificence* 19.566: Nay, let us our heddes togyder cast. Taylor and Whiting 177; Tilley H280.

H237 To claw a sorry man's **Head**
c1400 *Beryn* 41.1308: Ffor tho gan he to glow(e) (*for* claw) first a sory mannys hede. MED clauen 1(a).

H238 To give one's **Head** for nought
a1500 Medwall *Nature* C2^r[14–5]: A well drawen man ys he and a well taught That wyll not gyve hys hed for nought. Apperson 247; *Oxford* 239; Tilley H252.

H239 To have a **Head** full of bees
1513 Douglas *Aeneid* III 120.120: Quhat bern be thou in bed, with hed full of beys. **1549** Heywood *D* 55.28: Their hartes full heavy, their heades be full of bees. Apperson 33:9; *Oxford* 29, 284; Tilley H255; Whiting *Drama* 334:395, *Scots* I 137.

H240 To have a hoar **Head** and a green tail
c1390 Chaucer *CT* I[A] 3877–9: For in oure wyl ther stiketh evere a nayl, To have an hoor heed and a grene tayl, As hath a leek. **1532** Berners *Golden Boke* 339.7249–50: The old lecherous lover is as a swyne with a white heed and a grene taylle. Apperson 681–2; *Oxford* 297, cf. 267; Tilley L177.

H241 To have his **Head** under your girdle
1546 Heywood *D* 75.176: Then have ye his head fast under your gyrdell, **1555** *E* 178.183: He hath thy hed under his gyrdell. Apperson 293; *Oxford* 285; Tilley H248.

H242 To have two (three) **Heads** in one hood
a1400 *Romaunt C* 7385–6: That they had ofte, for the nones, Two heedes in oon hood at ones. **c1433** Lydgate *St. Edmund* 406.557: (He) Hatid too heedis closid in oon hood. **a1500** *Royal MS. 17 A xvi* f.3 in Brown-Robbins 1626: It is a wonder, be the rode, Whan too hedys loke in a hood. **1523** Berners *Froissart* I 262[20–1]: They began to murmure, and began to ron togyder thre heedes in one hood. Apperson 654; *Oxford* 679. See **F13.**

H243 To lie in one's **Head**
a1450 *Gesta* 284[10]: He lyeth in his hed. **1460** Paston III 210[28]: He lyeth falsly in hise hede. See **T414.**

H244 To perceive neither the **Head** nor the tail
1533 More *Debellacyon* 933 E[7–9]: He maketh as though Salem coulde neither perceive the hed nor the taile. Taylor and Whiting 176; Tilley H258; Whiting *Drama* 348:614. See **T9.**

H245 To see only the **Head** and not the end
a1420 Lydgate *Troy* I 197.1843–4: Namly, whan thei to a purpos wende Only of hed, and se nat to the ende. See **E84.**

H246 To to-shrape (*scratch*) someone's **Head**
c1200 *St. Katherine* (*Royal*) 56.1184–5: And schrenchte (*cheat*) then alde deovel And Teschrapet his heaved.

H247 To varnish one's **Head** (visage, pate)
c1390 Chaucer *CT* I[A] 4149: Wel hath this millere vernysshed his heed. **a1449** Lydgate *Jak Hare* in *MP* II 446.27: Ful pale dronken, weell vernysshed of visage, 447.65: And whan thou hast weel vernyssht thi pate. Cf. NED Wash v. 5c.

H248 To weep in one's **Head** and not in one's heart
a1200 Lawman II 145.13625–8: Swithe he gon to wepen, And særiliche siken, Ah hit wes an hafde And noht an his heorte. See **F2.**

H249 Too many **Heads** are a great loss to a realm
1525 Berners *Froissart* V 24[20–1]: It was a great losse to a realme whan there be many heedes and chefe governours. Cf. Taylor and Whiting 79; Tilley C642.

H250 Two **Heads** are better than one
1546 Heywood *D* 35.74: For two heddes are better then one, **1556** *E* 137.93.1. Apperson 655; *Oxford* 680; Taylor and Whiting 177; Tilley H281. See **H227, T549.**

H251 When the **Head** has no disease all the members are the sounder
1509 Barclay *Ship* II 324[22–3]: Whan that the hede hath no diseas nor payne Than all the membres greatly the sounder be. See **H258.**

H252 When the **Head** is fallen all the members are accumbered (*oppressed*)
a1300 *Alisaunder* 445.8018–9: Whan the heved is yfalle, Acumbred ben the membres alle. See **D151, H232, 362.**

H253 When the **Head** (lord) is fled the meiny is in much how (*sorrow*, woe)
a1300 *Alisaunder* 249.4469–70: And whan the hede (*L* lord) is yflowe The maynee is in mychel howe (*L* wo). See **G408, H257.**

H254 When the **Head** is sick, the limbs ache (*varied*)
a1200 *Ancrene* 184.16–7: Ah nis euch lim sar with sorhe of the heaved? **c1400** Gower *Peace* III 489.260: Of that the heved is siek, the limes aken. **c1405** *Mum* 49.763–4: For there the heede aketh alle the lymes after Pynen. **1471** Caxton *Recuyell* I 35.17–8: Wher the heed is seke or evyll the membres may not be hoole ner good, 44.29–30: Whan the heed aketh alle the other membres suffren payne. **a1500** *Ye that are comons* 235.63: For ef the hede be syke, the body es natt well. **1525** Berners *Froissart* V 18[27–9]: Ye have herde often tymes sayde, that if the heed be sicke, all the membres can nat be well, VI 90[33–4]: For whan the heed is sicke the body canne have no joye. **1533** Heywood *Weather* D4ᵛ[11–2]: As longe as heddes from temperaunce be deferd, So longe the bodyes in dystemperaunce be, **1546** *D* 87.244: For whan the head aketh, all the bodie is the wurs. Apperson 293; Jente 33; *Oxford* 284; Tilley H275; Whiting *Scots* I 186. See **D151, L287.**

H255 When the **Head** is unwraste (*evil*) the help (heap [*host*]) is the worse
a1200 Lawman II 259.16307–8: Thenne that hæfd is unwræst The hælp (*B* heop) is thæ wurse.

H256 Where the **Head** is sick there is no law
1492 *Salomon and Marcolphus* 22[5–6]: Where as the hede is seke and evyll at ease, there is no lawe. Cf. Tilley H275.

H257 Where (there) is no **Head** all things (are) decayed
c1545 Heywood *Four PP* B4ʳ[20]: All thynge decayed where is no hedde. See **B64, F372, G408, H253, L60.**

H258 The **Heal** (*health*) of the head helps all the members
a1400 *Alexander C* 148.2552: For ay the hele of the hede helpis all the menbris. See **H251.**

H259 It is ill **Healing** of an old sore
1546 Heywood *D* 88.16: And it is yll healyng of an olde sore. Apperson 324; *Oxford* 286; Tilley H283. See **S502.**

H260 The **Health** of love must be found where the wound was taken
a1400 *Romaunt B* 1965–6: The helthe of love mot be founde Where as they token first her wounde. *Oxford* 571.

H261 **Health** of soul is better than gold (*varied*)
c1395 *WBible* Ecclesiasticus xxx 15: The helthe of soule is in the hoolynesse of rightfulnesse, and it is betere than ony gold and silver. **1484** *Ther ne is dangyer* 19.17: Ne ther is no rychesshe but in helthe. Apperson 294; *Oxford* 286; Tilley H288, 289.

H262 As good is he that **Hears** and understands not as he that hunts and takes not
c1450 La Tour-Landry 7.19–21: As the wise man saithe, "as good is he that herithe and understondithe not, as he that huntithe and takithe not," 17.30–3: For there is an olde proverbe that saithe, "asmoche is he worthe that huntithe and takithe not as he that herithe and understondith not."

H263 Be swift to **Hear** but slow to speak (*varied*)
c1395 *WBible* James i 19: Be ech man swift to here, but slow to speke, and slow to wraththe. **c1450** *Serve thy god* 262.31–2: Be swyfte to here and slow to speke, Late to wrath and lothe to (wreke). Apperson 614.

H264 **Hear** and see and say nought, *etc.* (*varied*)
a1400 *Proverbis of Wysdom* 246.95–6: Hyre and se, and say nowght, Be ware and wyse, and lye nought, 99–100: Hyre and se, and be styll: Suffere and have thy will, 119–20: Hyre and se, and say but lyte, And use nott fore to chyde, 247.127: Hyre and se, say and do the best, (*II*) 224.87–8: Here and se and be styll; Thou may the sunner have thi wille. **a1449** Lydgate *Cok* in *MP* II 818.169: Here all thyng and kepe thy pacience. **a1450** *Gesta* 175[14–6]: Seithe the cokke, "her, and see, and sey nowte, thenne thu maiste have alle thi wille." **c1450** Idley 82.59: Tell never the more though thou moche hire. **c1450** *Proverbs of Good Counsel* 69.52–3: Yf thou wylte leve in peas and Reste, Here, and see, and sey the beste. **c1470** *Harley MS.3362* f.2a in *Retrospective* 309[2] and Förster 199.2: Here ye and sey nawt. **1474** *Stonor Letters* I 149[7]: I here muche and sey no thyng. **c1475** *Why I Can't* 143.213–4: And so I was tawght whan I was yong, To here and se, and sey not alle. **a1477** Caxton *Curtesye* 15.137–9: Thenne do my childe as techeth you the wyse, . . . Here and see, ande be stylle in every prees. **c1499** Skelton *Bowge* I 38.211–2: The soveraynst thynge that ony man maye have, Is lytyll to saye, and moche to here and see. **a1500** Greene *Carols* 343.1: (Her) and see, and sey not all, 6, 344.3: Whatsoever be in thi thought, Her and se, and sey ryght nought, 345.2. **a1500** *Squire* 10.159–60: If ever ye wyll come to your wyll, Here and se, and holde you styll, 23.428. **a1500** *Think Before You Speak* in Brown *Lyrics XV* 282.45–6: The kocke seyth wysly on hys songe, "Hyre and see and hold the stylle!" **a1500** *Throwe a towne* in Sandison 121.4, 12, 20, *etc.* (*varied refrain*): Hyre, and se, and sey not all. **a1500** *Young Children's Book* 23.101: Here and se, and sey thou nought. **c1500** *Proper tretyse* 244[9–10]: Yff thou wylt lyve in peace and rest, Here and se and saye the best. **1506** Hawes *Pastime* 160.4259: Bothe here and se and than holde you styll. **1509** Barclay *Ship* I 200[19–21]: For oft is sayde, and true it is certayne That they that wyll lyve in quyetnes and rest Must here and se and hasty wordes refrayne. Apperson 374:18; *Oxford* 286–7, 376; Robbins-Cutler 3081; Tilley M1274, 1277, N275, P140. See **M316, 789, S611, T205, W379.**

H265 Love to **Hear** more than to say
c1400 *Consilia Isidori* 373[14]: Love more to here than to seye. See **E6.**

H266 Who **Hears** oft and speaks seld wins the field
1556 Heywood *E* 114.20.21–4: Who hereth oft, And speaketh seeld, Be witte alofte, He wynth the feeld.

H267 If there are no **Hearers** there shall be no rounders (*tattlers*)
a1475 *Tree* 79.17: Yif ther be none hereris ther shal no rowneris be. Apperson 294; *Oxford* 287; Tilley H297.

H268 As free as **Heart** might think or tongue tell
1513 Bradshaw *St. Werburge* 176.1329–31: The place that tyme was made as fre As the sayd erle was in his castell, Or as hert myght thynke or tonge myght tell.

H269 Boldest **Hearts** are nearest death
c1515 Barclay *Eclogues* 163.628: But boldest heartes be nerest death certayne, 169.805–6: Alas, bolde heartes be nerest death in warre, When out of daunger cowardes stande a farre.

H270 An envious **Heart** frets itself (oft does smart)
c1350 *Good Wife E* 164.87–8: Envious herte Himsilf fret, **c1500** *T* 207.125–6: An envyous hert Oft doth smert. Apperson 185. See **E137.**

H271 A felonious **Heart** under a friendly face
a1439 Lydgate *Fall* II 566.3403: With felenous herte under a freendli face. See **C174, F2, 6.**

H272 Fro (*When*) the **Heart** is discomfited the body is not worth a mite
c1375 Barbour *Bruce* I 58.197–8: And fra the hart be discumfyt, The body is nocht worth a myt, 305.187–8. See **H233, 301.**

H273 Gentle **Heart** kithes (*shows*) gentilesse (*varied*)
c1395 Chaucer *CT* V[F] 483: For gentil herte kitheth gentillesse. **a1508** Dunbar *Tretis* 92.316: For never bot in a gentill hert is generit ony

ruth, **a1513** *Quhone he list to Feyne* 100.41: Nor out of gentill hart is fundin petie. See **P243.**

H274 A good **Heart** cannot lie
c1489 Caxton *Aymon* I 288.2–3: For a good herte can not lye whan it cometh to a nede. *Oxford* 252, cf. 357: Leal. Cf. Tilley H303.

H275 A hardy **Heart** is hard to supprise (*overcome*)
c1475 Henryson *Fables* 73.2109: Ane hardie hart is hard for to suppryis.

H276 The **Heart** knows the bitterness of its soul
c1395 *WBible* Proverbs xiv 10: The herte that knowith the bittirnesse of his soule. *Oxford* 287.

H277 A **Heart** of stone (iron, steel) would melt (*varied*)
c1200 *Hali Meidenhad* 22.228–9: Stani were his heorte yef ha ne mealte i teares. **c1375** *St. Agatha* 46.51–2: Hard iren might we better melt Than hir hert. **c1385** Chaucer *TC* iii 114: It myghte han mad an herte of stoon to rewe, **c1386** *LGW* 1841–2: Al hadde folkes hertes ben of stones, Hyt myght have maked hem upon hir rewe. **a1400** *Le Morte A.* 19.588–91: There is no lady of flesshe ne bone In this world so thryve or thro, Thoughe hyr herte were stele or stone, That might hyr love hald hym fro. **a1400** *Scottish Legends* I 447.227–8: Quhay that saw It, and pyte had nane, His (hart) was hardare than the stane. **a1410** Love *Mirrour* 230[11–3]: But thou fynde thyn herte melte in to sorwful compassioun suppose fully and halde that thou haste to harde a stonye herte. **1410** Walton *Boethius* 80[8]: For that most scheend a verry herte o(f) stele. **a1420** Lydgate *Troy* I 261.4076: An hert of stel ne myght it not endure, II 542.5093: He wolde enclyne his harde herte of stele, 554.5548: An herte of stele myght it not sustene, III 673.3714–6: Whiche wold(e) meve to compassioun . . . Any herte though it were made of stel. **a1425** *Hayle, bote of bale* in *Wheatley MS.* 9.121: Hert of ston, wilt thow nought melt? **a1439** Lydgate *Fall* I 196.6935: What herte off steel coude doon to hym damage, II 504.1116–8: No man hadde so harde a stonen herte, That miht of riht his eyen keepen drie, To seen the processe of his tormentrie. **a1450** *Partonope* 309.7731–2: That though hir herte were made of stele, No wonder it was though it did melte, 349.8608: Though youre herte be now as stele. **a1475** *Ludus Coventriae* 268.1054–5: A hert hard as ston how mayst thou lest Whan these sorweful tydyngys Are the told. **1481** Caxton *Reynard* 63[11–2]: An herte of stone myght have pyte on me. **c1485** *Burial and Resurrection* 176–7. 152–3: To have seyn hir, a harte of stone, For ruthe wald have relente, 211.1204: Stony hartes of flint thou wald tham have mevid, 212–3. 1241–2: Yf my harte wer of flinte, I have caus to wepe. **c1500** *King Hart* 89.8–9: The grundin dairtis scharp, and bricht to se, Wald mak ane hart of flint to fald and fle. **c1500** *Lover's Farewell* in Robbins 210.27–8: Y-wys ye wold upon me rewe—Though your hert wer made of steell! **a1513** Dunbar *In Secreit Place* 54.40: Your musing waild perse ane harte of stane. Taylor and Whiting 178, 179; Tilley H311; Whiting *Drama* 348:617, *Scots* I 187. See **H535, J40.**

H278 **Heart** on the hoard and hands on the sore
c1475 Henryson *Orpheus* 142.408–10: "Now find I weill this proverb trew," quod he, "'Hart on the hurd, and handis on the soir; Quhair Luve gois, on forss mone turne the E.'" Cf. Apperson 639: tongue; *Oxford* 663; Tilley S648, T404. See **E207, T386.**

H279 A high **Heart** may dread a fall
a1450 *Generydes A* 53.1713–4: Min hert so high set have I, A fall I drede to have therby! See **C296.**

H280 The higher that you are, the lower be your **Heart**
a1400 *Proverbis of Wysdom* 244.41–2: Ever, the hygher that thou art, Ever the lowere be thy hert. **c1450** *Serve thy god* 262.29–30. Apperson 187. See **G447.**

H281 In **Heart** (hird [*retinue*], earth) is not to hide
c1300 *Amis* 22.501: In herd (*var.* hert) is nought to hide. **c1300** *Guy*[1] 398 A 20.9: In herd is nought to hide. **a1325** *Otuel and Roland* 79.649: In hert ys nought to huyde. **c1330** *Horn Childe* 179.39: In herd is nought to hide, 57, 181.189, 183.396, 187.669, 729. **a1400** Chestre *Launfal* 54.57: In herte ys naght to hyde. **a1400** *Ipomadon A* 72.2479, 76.2608: erthe, 113.3918, 138.4803: erthe, 206.7241: erthe. **c1400** *Emaré* 4.120, 31.996. **c1400** *Gowther* 142.189 (*var.*). **c1400** *Triamour* 84.1629, 86.1704. **c1440** *Degrevant* 14.196: In hert (*C* herde), 72.1104: hert (*C* herd), 86.1340: hert (*C* herd). See **L169.**

H282 In spite of one's **Heart**
a1533 Berners *Arthur* 61[11]: In the spyte of thi herte, 87[34–5].

H283 In the **Heart** is the hoard of ilk man's word

a1350 *Ywain* 5.147–8: And in the hert thare es the horde And knawing of ilk mans worde.

H284 Maugre one's **Heart**
c1485 *Slaughter* (*Digby*) 5.94: Maugre ther hertes. Whiting *Drama* 348:616. Cf. Tilley S764.

H285 No troubled **Heart** but sometime rejoices again
1525 Berners *Froissart* VI 77[34]: Nor herte troubled, but somtyme agayne rejoyceth. See **S511.**

H286 Noble **Heart** is hard to overcome
c1375 Barbour *Bruce* I 175–6.352–4: Now may we cleirly se, That nobill hert, quhar-evir it be, Is hard till ourcum throu mastry.

H287 A noble **Heart** may not suffer shame
1481 Caxton *Godeffroy* 166.18–9: But that a noble herte maye not suffre shame.

H288 Noble **Heart** will have no doubleness (*duplicity*)
c1500 *Lancelot* 37.1256: For noble hart wil have no dowbilness.

H289 Of foul **Heart** comes foul thought
c1303 Mannyng *Handlyng* 262.8289: Of foule herte cumth foule thoght.

H290 Of wicked **Heart** comes wicked will
c1400 *Alexander Buik* III 298.6639: Of wicked hart cumis wicked will.

H291 One faint **Heart** may discourage two dozen good men
1525 Berners *Froissart* IV 188[4–5]: One faynt harte may dyscourage two dosyn of good men. See **A167.**

H292 One's **Heart** is full high when his eye is full low
1546 Heywood *D* 39.139: Her herte is full hie, when her eye is full low. See **W495.**

H293 Pluck up your **Heart**
a1500 Medwall *Nature* A2r[43]: Pluck up thyn harte and holde thyn hed upryght. Tilley H323.

H294 A Proud **Heart** in a beggar's breast (*i.e.*, does not fit)
a1449 Lydgate *Ryme* in *MP* II 793.41: A prowde hert in a beggers brest. Apperson 515; *Oxford* 521, cf. 348; Tilley H324. See **L450, 452.**

H295 To have one's **Heart** in his hose
a1460 *Towneley Plays* 113.424: Thy hart is in thy hose. **1522** Skelton *Why Come* II 35.286: Their hertes be in thyr hose. **1546** Heywood *D* 47.184: Your hert is in your hose all in dispaire, **1555** *E* 154.53. Apperson 294–5; *Oxford* 287–8; Tilley H314; Whiting *Drama* 348:618. See **H222.**

H296 To set at one's **Heart** what another sets at his heel
1546 Heywood *D* 44.109–10: Nor will (I) not holde the now: nor suche foly feele, To set at my hert that thou settest at thy heele, **1555** *E* 153.49: Shall I set at my hart, that thou settst at thy heele? Apperson 295; *Oxford* 355; Tilley H317; Whiting *Scots* I 187: Heel.

H297 To take **Heart** of grace
c1520 *Terens* C4v[5]: I take hart agrace. **1546** Heywood *D* 88.13: She takth such hert of grace, **1555** *E* 160.92: Thou takest hart of grasse wyfe, not hart of grace, Cum grasse, cum grace, syr, we grase both in one place. Apperson 295; *Oxford* 288; Taylor and Whiting 179; Tilley H332; Whiting *Drama* 348:617.

H298 A true **Heart** will not ply (*submit*) for any menace
a1400 *Romaunt B* 4389–90: A trewe herte wole not plie For no manace that it may drye.

H299 When the **Heart** is full of pride the tongue is full of boast
1520 Whittinton *Vulgaria* 77.2–3: Whan the herte is full of pryde the tongue is full of boost and braggynge.

H300 Where **Heart** is failed there shall no castle be assailed
a1393 Gower *CA* III 128.6573–4: Bot as men sein, wher herte is failed, Ther schal no castell ben assailed. Apperson 198; *Oxford* 185.

H301 Where **Hearts** fail the lave (*rest*) of limbs (a)vails little
c1400 *Alexander Buik* II 136.1421–4: It semis weill quhair hartis failyeis, The laif of lymmes lytle vailyeis; And quha hes hart hardy and gude, Strenth him doubilles in mane and mude. Cf. *Oxford* 661: Tine heart; Tilley G54. See **H233, 272.**

H302 Where the **Heart** is, there the body is abandoned
a1533 Berners *Arthur* 436[18–9]: Where as the hert is, there is the body habandoned, for the body enclyneth to the herte. See **T240.**

H303 Who has the **Heart** is lady (lord) of the body (*varied*)
1369 Chaucer *BD* 1152–4: She was lady Of the body; she had the herte, And who hath that, may not asterte. **a1400** *Romaunt B* 1792–5: But it bihovede nedes me To don right as myn

herte bad. For evere the body must be lad Aftir the herte, in wele and woo, 2084–5: For of the body he is full lord That hath the herte in his tresor.

H304 Who sings merry that sings not of the **Heart?**
a1410 Lydgate *Churl* in *MP* II 473.112: Who syngith mery, that syngith nat of herte?

H305 After great **Heat** comes cold: let no man cast his pilch (*cloak*) away
c1390 ?Chaucer *Proverbs* 1–4: What shul thise clothes thus manyfold, Lo! this hote somers day?—After greet heet cometh cold; No man caste his pilche away. *Oxford* 9: Although. See **C365.**

H306 As high as **Heaven** (heaven high)
a750 *Riddles* in *Exeter Book* 242.94.2: Hyrre þonne heofon. **c1408** Lydgate *Reson* 12.425: An in hir coroune, high as hevene. **1546** Heywood *D* 66.45: And she for hir parte, made us cheere heaven hye. Svartengren 285; Taylor *Comparisons* 48: sky; Whiting *NC* 422.

H307 As if **Heaven** would fall
a1200 Lawman III 94.27454–5: To-somne heo heolden, Swulc (*B:* ase) heovene wolde vallen. **c1390** Chaucer *CT* VII 3401[B4591]: It semed as that hevene sholde falle.

H308 From **Heaven** comes help
c1475 *St. Anne* (2) 91.29: Ffrom heven cometh helpe ys an old proverbe. See **G211.**

H309 From **Heaven** intill (*to*) hell
c1440 *Degrevant* 78.1211–2: He was the stowteste geste Ffra hevene intille helle. Whiting *Drama* 349:619.

H310 In **Heaven** are large leasows (*pastures*)
a1200 *Ancrene* 51.26–7: As me seith, pleien in heovene large lesewen, **a1250** (*Nero*) 41.20: Ase me seith ine heovene is large leswe.

H311 It is fair in **Heaven**
a1400 *Stodye of Wysdome* 26.2: We seyen that it is feyre in heven. Note (p. 132): "Not in the Latin."

H312 To go to **Heaven** as a bucket into a well (*i.e.,* in the opposite direction)
c1400 *Plowman's Tale* 156.297–8: They folowe Christ that shedde his blood To heven, as bucket in-to the well. **a1415** *Lanterne* 54.18–9: For it draweth hem toward hevene as bocket in to welle. **c1450** Idley 186.1687: As a boket to the welle to hevene they goo.

H313 Until **Heaven** falls
a1415 *Lanterne* 89.11–2: Ye schal not grounde your viciouse sweryng til that hevene be fallen.

H314 When **Heaven** (the sky) falls we shall catch many larks (*varied*)
c1450 Idley 178.1181: We shall kacche many larkis whan hevene doith falle. **c1475** *Rawlinson MS. D 328* 120.34: Yf heva(n) falle meny lerkys schall be take. **a1500** Hill 128.7: And hewin fall, we shall hawe mani larkis. **1533** More *Debellacyon* 1022 BC: This good man shall see the skye fall first and catche larkes ere it happen. **1546** Heywood *D* 25.32: When the sky falth we shall have larks, **1556** *Spider* 269[7]: But when the skie falth we shall have larks. Apperson 576; *Oxford* 595; Tilley S517. Cf. Jente 737.

H315 The **Heaviest** shall weigh most
1481 Caxton *Reynard* 75[3–4]: Yet shal the hevyest weye moste. Jente 704.

H315.1 Be not too pensive (*sad*) for any **Heaviness**
1420 Lydgate *Temple* 49.1175: And (be) nought to pensif for non hevynes.

H316 Too **Heavy** or too hot
a1393 Gower *CA* III 128.6599–601: So that I fiele and wel I wot, Al is to hevy and to hot To sette on hond withoute leve. **c1395** Chaucer *CT* III[D] 1435–6: I spare nat to taken, God it woot, But if it be to hevy or to hoot. **1523** Berners *Froissart* II 146[20–1]: Left nothyng untaken, without it were to hote, to colde, or to hevy. **1546** Heywood *D* 56.48–9: They might convey thinges, Suche as were neither to heavie nor to whot. Apperson 639–40; *Oxford* 26; Skeat 273; Tilley N322.

H317 As hardy as **Hector**
1432 Lydgate *Ballade* in *MP* II 627.66: Hardy as Hector, **a1439** *Fall* III 901.2799: As Ector hardi. **1525** Berners *Froissart* V 219[26]: He wente ever forwarde lyke a hardy Hector.

H318 As strong as **Hector**
a1500 Kennedy 26.18: Stranger than Hectour. Whiting *Drama* 316:165, *Scots* I 187.

H319 A **Hedge** is not without briers
c1390 *Charity* in Brown *Lyrics XIV* 171.21–2: Such Men may not ben with-oute, No more then hecgh with-outen Brere.

H320 The **Hedge** sits (*stands*) that deals (*divides*) acres (*fields*)
1130 *Peterborough Chronicle* 261[12]: Oc man seið to biworde, hæge sitteð þa aceres dæleth. Apperson 296.

H321 To bear it out even to the hard **Hedge** (*i.e.*, to the very end)
c1503 More *Early Poems* [2] E[15–7]: With visage stout, He bare it out, Even unto the harde hedge.

H322 Where the **Hedge** is lowest men overskip (may soonest over)
c1500 Greene *Carols* 348.3: Where the hegge ys lawest men dothe over-skyppe. **1546** Heywood *D* 73.109: Where the hedge is lowest, men maie soonest over. Apperson 296; Jente 158; *Oxford* 357; Tilley H364.

H323 **Heel**(s) over head
c1380 *Patience* 23.271: Ay hele over hed, hourlande aboute. **c1475** Henryson *Fables* 89.2601: Quhill sum man tit thair heillis over thair heid. Taylor and Whiting 180. See **A193.**

H324 To can (*know*) no more than one's (left) **Heel**
a1387 Higden-Trevisa II 161[12–3]: Now children of gramer scole conneth na more Frensche than can hir lift heele. **a1500** *Tale of the Lady Prioress* 108[1–2]: Dyverse mene fawttes wylle fele, That knowethe no more then doythe my hele.

H325 To fight with one's **Heels**
c1475 Gregory *Chronicle* 198[13–7]: The Erle of Wyltschyre . . . fought manly with the helys, for he was a feryd of lesynge of beute. MED hele n. (3) 1(c).

H326 Make not your **Heir** your executor (*varied*)
c1303 Mannyng *Handlyng* 43.1181–3: Ne be thou nevere yn swych errour To make thyn eyr thy secutour, Ne thy sekutoure thy fysycyene. **c1390** *Proverbes of diverse profetes* 537.219–22: Ffor love ne nouther for honour Mak not thin heir thin executour, Ne mak thin heir no ficiscian, In hope to live ever hol man. **a1450** *Myn awen dere* 150.32: Lat nevere thyne are thy sectur be, 151.52: Make nevere thyne are thy medecynere. **c1450** Idley 128.1228–30: And Senec counceilleth in all maner of wyse That thou never sett the in suche erroure To make thyn heire to be thyn exectoure, 1237, 1242–4, 1251, 1256–8. *Oxford* 216.

H327 One knows not who shall be his **Heir**
a1450 *Castle* 80.105: Man knowe not who schal be his eyr, and governe his good, cf. 163.2905–8.

H328 Seldom does any **Heir** help his brother
c1350 *Gamelyn* 646.40: Selde ye see ony eyr helpen his brother.

H329 As black as (the) **Hell**
a1400 *Alexander C* 18.562: And blake as the hell. **1513** Douglas *Aeneid* III 137.154: A laithly smok he yiskis blak as hell. Apperson 51; Tilley H397; Whiting *Devil* 230, *Scots* I 188.

H330 As dark as (any) **Hell**
c1400 *Laud Troy* I 214.7241: Hit was as derk as helle. **c1400** *Thomas of Erceldoune* 11.171: Wher hit was derk as any hell. Svartengren 237; Tilley H397; Whiting *Devil* 231.

H331 As hard as **Hell**
c1375 *Song of the Love* in Brown *Lyrics XIV* 104.48: Luf es hard as hell. **c1395** *WBible* Song of Songs viii 6: Envy is hard as helle. **a1425** *Chester Plays* II 430.77–8: The paynes that I have long in bee, As hard as hell.

H332 As murk as **Hell**
a1400 *Pricke* 29.1025: Elles war this world myrk als helle.

H333 That which is once in **Hell** comes out never (*varied*)
c1378 *Piers* B xviii 148–9: For that is ones in helle, out cometh it nevere; Job the prophete, patriarke, reproveth thi sawes, *Quia in inferno nulla est redempcio.* **c1395** *WBible* Job vii 9: He that goith doun to helle, schal not stie. **a1475** *Ludus Coventriae* 226.47–8: Be this tyxt of holde remembryd to myn intencion Quia in inferno nulla est redempcio. Apperson 297:7; *Oxford* 536–7.

H334 They that are in **Hell** ween (*think*) there is no other heaven
1546 Heywood *D* 49.278: They that be in hell, wene there is none other heven. Apperson 297; *Oxford* 290; Tilley H410.

H335 As cruel as **Hell-fire**
a1400 *Stanzaic Life* 358.10530: As helle fir cruell.

H336 As feer (*fierce*) as **Hell-fire**
a1400 *Stanzaic Life* 358.10530: As helle fir . . . fere.

H337 As dark as **Hell-pit**
1369 Chaucer *BD* 170–1: This cave was also as derk As helle-pit overal aboute.

H338 He that needs **Help** must crave his help
a1393 Gower *CA* III 447.2245–6: Whom nedeth help, he mot his helpe crave, Or helpeles he shal his nede spille. See **M276.**

H339 **Help** me and I shall help you
a1400 ?Wyclif *Of Confession* in *EW* 334[27–8]:

As if oon seid to anothur "helpe me, here, and I shul helpe thee." See **K1.**

H340 If one **Helps** not himself no other will **1525** Berners *Froissart* VI 354[36–8]: If ye entende nat to helpe yourselfe . . . none other wyll, 356[25–6]: If ye wyll nat helpe yourselfe, who shulde helpe you. Cf. *Oxford* 291; Taylor and Whiting 154: God (3); Tilley H412.

H341 He would eat the **Hen** and all her chickens **1478** Paston VI 2[25–6]: Wherffor men sey ffowle off hym, and that he wolde ete the henne and alle hyr chekynnys.

H342 The **Hen** is lief (*dear*) when she lays, loath when she says "cluck" **a1450** *Cotton Faustina MS. B vi* in J. O. Halliwell *Dictionary of Archaic and Provincial Words* (9th ed. London, 1878) I 256: Leef henne wen ho leith, Looth wen ho clok seith. MED clok. Cf. Whiting *Drama* 19.

H343 The **Hen** lays and cackles and the chough comes and reaves her of her eggs **a1200** *Ancrene* 36.18–20: The hen hwen ha haveth ileid ne con bute cakelin, ah hwet biyet ha throf? Kimeth the kaue ananriht and reaveth hire hire eairen. Apperson 298:13. See **H375, P178.**

H344 A **Hen** may hold a man in (*save him*) a cow **c1475** Henryson *Fables* 80.2324: Suntymis ane hen haldis ane man in ane Kow. See **L206, P123, 250.**

H345 Not give a pulled (*plucked*) **Hen** **c1387-95** Chaucer *CT* I[A] 177: He yaf nat of that text a pulled hen.

H346 Not help a halting **Hen** **1513** Douglas *Aeneid* III 228.160: Quhais power may nocht help a haltand hen.

H347 Not worth a (pulled) **Hen** **c1395** Chaucer *CT* III[D] 1112: Swich arrogance is nat worth an hen. **a1400** *Romaunt C* 6856: Her astat is not worth an hen. **c1458** *Knyghthode and Bataile* 26.673: a pulled hen. **a1508** Dunbar *Tretis* 91.269. **a1509** Barclay *Ship* I 198[13]: At the profe is skantly worth a hen. Apperson 457; Tilley H426; Whiting *Scots* I 188.

H348 To be (strong) hearted like a **Hen** **1522** Skelton *Why Come* II 35.273: Stronge herted lyke an hen, **c1522** *Colyn* I 317.168–9: How be it they are good men, Moche herted lyke an hen.

H349 **Hen-heart(ed)** **a1450** *York Plays* 326.198: A! henne-harte! ill happe mot you hente. **1522** Skelton *Why Come* II 32.165: Lyke henherted cokoldes. NED Henheart, -hearted.

H350 To scald one like a **Hen** (*etc.*) (A number of single quotations are brought together here) **a1300** *Meidan Maregrete* 496.234–5: Wellinde laumpes letet on hire renne, From the necke to the to, scalden ir as an henne! **c1400** *Laud Troy* I 198.6720: Thei fle fro him, as hen doth fro the fox. **c1450** *Ponthus* 69.29–30: For he keped theym, as the hen did hir byrdes undre hir weng. Whiting *Scots* I 188.

H351 (To write) as a **Hen** scrapes (*scratches*) **a1500** *Colyn Blowbol* 96.99–100: For on booke he skrapith like an hen, That no man may his letters know nor se. Whiting *NC* 424. Cf. M. M. Mathews *Dictionary of Americanisms* (Chicago, 1951) Hen 9.

H352 As sweet as **Hencam** (?) **c1500** *Cock* 3[9]: For as swete was theyr brethe as henkam.

H353 What with **Hepe** (*pruning-knife*), what with crook **a1393** Gower *CA* III 25.2872–3: So what with hepe and what with crok Thei make here maister ofte winne. See **H458.**

H354 Among sweet **Herbs** oft grow stinking weeds **1509** Barclay *Ship* II 41[20]: For amonge swete herbys oft growyth stynkynge wedes. Cf. Whiting *Drama* 247. See **F301, G34.**

H355 Eat no **Herbs** that you do not know **1450** *Dicts* 86.3: Ne ete noon erbis that thow knowist not.

H356 He that fully knows the **Herb** may safely lay it to his eye **c1380** Chaucer *HF* 289–91: Therfore I wol seye a proverbe, That "he that fully knoweth th'erbe May saufly leye hyt to his ye." **c1385** Usk 56.114–5: Eke an herbe proved may safely to smertande sores ben layd. Apperson 397–8; A. C. Baugh "Chaucer and the Panthère d'Amours" in *Britannica: Festschrift für H. M. Flasdieck* (Heidelberg, 1960) 59–61; Skeat 86–7.

H357 To pass like an **Herb** **c1395** *WBible* Psalms lxxxix 6: Eerli passe he, as an eerbe, eerli florische he, and passe.

H358 As strong as **Hercules** **a1449** Lydgate *Mesure is Tresour* in *MP* II 780.137: Strong as Herculees of manhood and of myght. Whiting *Drama* 316:168, *NC* 424.

H359 To beat as **Herds** do on weary beasts
c1400 *Laud Troy* I 270.9162–3: And beten on hem, as don herdes On weri bestis that drow In the plow.

H360 All the **Here** (*army*) is bold when the leader is bold
c1025 *Durham Proverbs* 13.31: Eall here byþ hwæt þonne se lateow byþ hwæt. Omnis exercitus quando dux est alacer. See **H216.**

H361 Who that is **Here** knows where he shall be another year?
a1500 Greene *Carols* 121 *refrain:* Who wot nowe that ys here Where he schall be anoder yere? See **T350.**

H362 If the **Heretoga** (*captain*) errs then is all the here (*army*) idle (*varied*)
a900 Alfred *Gregory* 129.8–9: Sua eac bið se here eal idel, ðonne he on oðer folc winnan sceal, gif se heretoga dwolað. **1003** *Peterborough Chronicle* 135[15–6]: þonne se heretoga wacað þonne bið eall se here swiðe gehindred. Fr. Klaeber "An Old English Proverb" *JEGP* 5(1903–5) 529. See **B64, H232, 252, 257, 551.**

H363 Praise the **Heretoga's** might, but when he has won the victory
c1000 Aelfric *Homilies* II 560[23–4]: Hera þæs heretogan mihte, ac swaðeah þonne he sige begytt. See **E81, 158, P39, S715.**

H364 To give up one's **Heritage** for a dishful of pottage
c1420 Wyntoun II 159.205–8: Than Esaw for outtyn let, For hungir that he was in set, For a disful of potage Gaf up alhail his heretage. Tilley B403. See **R130.**

H365 As much as a shotten (*spawned*) **Herring** has shrimps in her tail
1533 More *Confutacion* 626 (*by error* 560) E[12–4]: Yet hathe the man as much shame in his face, as a shotten hering hath shrimpes in her taile.

H366 As thick as **Herrings** fleet (*swim*)
c1400 *Laud Troy* I 198.6699–700: Eche man on other schetis, As thikke as heryng fletis, II 418.14204–5: Thei falle thikkere than heryng fletes In-myddes the se In here scole. NED Herring 2; Svartengren 396.

H367 Not worth a (red) **Herring**
a1300 Thomas de Hales 70.85–6: Al were sone his prute a-gon, Hit nere on ende wrth on heryng. **c1450** *Pilgrimage LM* 68[3]: Hise sheeldes weren nevere woorth to him a red hering. Apperson 457; Whiting *NC* 424.

H368 To lie bound as **Herring** in mease (*measure*)
a1425 *Al es bot a fantum* in *Yorkshire Writers* II 458.32: When thou lyes bonden als hering dos in maies. Cf. Tilley H445.

H368.1 Not lose a **Herring-cob** (*-head*)
1440 Capgrave *St. Norbert* 1582: We lose not in this hous a heryng-cobbe. From MED hering 2.

H369 Not harm a **Herring-tail**
c1400 *Laud Troy* II 512.17398–401: I did nevere be nyght ne day Anythyng a-geyn Gregays . . . That harmed hem a heryng-tayle.

H370 Behight (*promise*) not too many **Hests** (*promises*)
a1400 *Proverbis of Wysdom* 245.74: Behight nott to many hestis. Notes p. 257.

H371 **Hest** without gift is not to prize
a1400 *Romaunt B* 4475–6: And heeste certeyn, in no wise, Withoute yift, is not to prise. See **P411.**

H372 When **Hest** and deed vary they do a great contrary
a1400 *Romaunt B* 4477–8: Whanne heest and deede asunder varie, They doon (me have) a gret contrarie. See **W642.**

H373 **Hething** (*shame*) have the hathel (*man*) who thinks harm
c1353 *Winner* 67–8: And alle was it one sawe, appon Ynglysse tonge, "Hethyng have the hathell that any harme thynkes." See **S197.**

H374 **Hething** is hamald (*home-grown*)
a1400 *Morte Arthure* 54.1843: For hethynge es hame-hold, have it who so will(e). M. M. Banks in *Modern Language Quarterly* (London) 6(1903) 66: "Curses come home to roost." See **D342.**

H375 **Hide** and have, publish (*make public*) and have not
c1450 *Douce MS.52* 55.125: Hyde and have; publysshe and nouhght have. **c1450** *Rylands MS.394* 106.6. See **H343.**

H376 Safest **Hiding** is underneath humblest clothing
a1400 *Romaunt C* 6147–8: And certeynly, sikerest hidyng Is undirnethe humblest clothing. See **H3.**

H377 Who will be **High** he shall be low
a1450 *Thorow-owt a pales* in Dyboski 95.19–20: Therfor the gospell seyth full well: "Who will be high, he shall be low." **a1500** *Carpenter's*

Tools 85.169–70: Therefore I schall telle the a saw, Who so wold be hyghe he schall be law. See **C296, M216.**

H378 All **Hights** (*promises*) should be held
c1475 Henryson *Fables* 78.2276: All hechtis suld haldin be! See **B214.**

H379 What you **Hight** (*promise*) see you hold
c1450 *Go way, Fore that* in Lumby *Ratis Raving* 9.16: Quhar thow hechtys, se thow hald.

H380 As fix (*fixed*) as a great **Hill** of stone
c1433 Lydgate *St. Edmund* 437.1351: Yt stood as fyx as a gret hill off ston.

H381 As high as a **Hill**
1513 Douglas *Aeneid* II 26.21: Heich as a hill the jaw of watir brak.

H382 As still as a **Hill**
c1300 *South English Legendary* II 570.126: Evere heo lai stille as an hul.

H383 Behave (Live) on the **Hill** as one would in the hall
1509 Barclay *Ship* II 266[27–8]: It is an olde saynge that man ought of dutye Behave hym on hyll, lyke as he wolde in hall, **c1523** *Mirrour* 25[43–5]: Live thou upon hill as thou would live in hall, What thou wouldest not do in open company, That do thou not alone. Apperson 302; *Oxford* 149; Tilley H462. See **H384.**

H384 Fart on **Hills** and fart where you would not (in hall)
c1425 Arderne *Fistula* 5.15–8: It is seyde, "Pede super colles pedes ubi pedere nolle." "Ffart upon hilles and thou shalt fart whar thou wolde noght agayn thi willes." **c1450** *Rylands MS.394* 103.18: Fart on hyll and fart yn halle. Vivas monticola ceu vis in principis aula, 21: Fart on hyll, and fart ther thu nylle. Pede super colles, pedes ubi pedere nolles. Walther III 772.21130b. See **H383.**

H385 High **Hill** suffers many showers
c1500 Greene *Carols* 348.2: Hill that buth hye sufferith many showres. Cf. Whiting *Drama* 300, *Scots* I 189. See **R191.**

H386 The higher **Hill**, men shall the farther see
1515 Barclay *St. George* 59.1316: The hyer hylle man shall the farther se.

H387 The higher the **Hill** (mountain) the more the wind thereon
a1200 *Ancrene* 92.24–5: For se the hul is herre, se the wind is mare thron. **c1400** *Chastising* 97.15–6: The higher that a mounteyn is, there is the gretter wynd. Apperson 689; *Oxford* 265; Skeat 23. See **P247, R191, T435, 462, W302, 344.**

H388 A **Hill** made a dreadful noise and a mouse was born (*varied*)
a1393 Gower *CA* III 335–6.3554–73: I rede whilom that an hell . . . A wonder dredful noise made; . . . And ate laste it was a Mous, The which was bore. **1533** More *Debellacyon* 930 A[9–10], F[6–11]: And when these gret hilles had thus travailed longe . . . one was brought a bedde, with sore labour at last delivered of a dead mouse. Apperson 430; *Oxford* 436; Tilley M1215.

H389 As swift as (the) **Hind**
a1375 *Octavian* (S) 45.1417: Hyt ys swyfter than . . . hynde. **a1449** Lydgate *Haste* in *MP* II 762.82: More swyft of cours than . . . hynde. **1509** Watson *Ship* A4ᵛ[25–6] (*the first of two A signatures*): Go rennynge more swyfter than the hynde.

H390 To be to-frushed (*broken to pieces*) as the **Hind** is by the lion
a1300 *Alisaunder* 107.1887–8: Hii weren tofrussht from foot to croun, So the hynde is of the lyoun.

H391 Not give a **Hip**
c1330 *Seven Sages A* 116.2522: Of hem ne yive i nowt an hepe. NED Hip sb.².

H392 To catch (have) one on the **Hip**
c1400 *Beryn* 55.1780–1: Beryn he had I-caughte Somwhat oppon the hipp. **1546** Heywood *D* 75.175: Then have ye him on the hyp. Apperson 474; *Oxford* 296; Taylor and Whiting 183–4; Tilley H474; Whiting *Drama* 349:624.

H393 To quit one his **Hire** (*varied*)
a1350 *Ywain* 71.2639: And sone quit to tham thaire hire. **a1425** *Metrical Paraphrase OT* 9.9703–4: Tho thre so had ther hyre in hy, Aftur ther werkes ware worthy wrake. **c1500** *Lyfe of Roberte* 243.624: I have payde my men theyr hyre (*killed them*). See **W3.**

H394 As full as a **Hive** of honey
c1390 Chaucer *CT* I[A] 4372–3: He was as ful of love and paramour As is the hyve ful of hony sweete.

H395 As full as **Hives** of bees
c1450 Capgrave *Katharine* 269.255: The Innes arn ful as hyves of been.

H396 As great as a **Hive**
c1350 *Libeaus* 74.1341: His heed greet as an hive.

H397 To swarm like a **Hive**
1380 *Cleanness* 11.223: Hurled into hell-hole as the hyve swarmez.

H398 Without (To say, make, bid, *etc.*) **Ho** (*cessation, halt*)
c1385 Chaucer *TC* ii 1083: But that was endeles, withouten hoo. **c1390** *Deo Gracias II* in Brown *Lyrics XIV* 139.36: For in myn hond ther stod non ho. **a1400** *Scottish Legends* II 330.910: Come on hastely but ony haw. **a1400** *Seven Penitential Psalms* in *Wheatley MS.* 40.511: Bot, whanne we sees and can sey "hoo!" **1400** *Love god, and drede* in Kail 4.109: Er he fele het, y rede say hoo. **1418** *Man, be warre* in Kail 62.54: Asese of covetys and say hoo. **c1420** Wyntoun IV 239.1375: This bischope said, and thar made ho. **c1422** Hoccleve *Dialog* 111.26–7: Yf thou be wyse of that matter hoo, Reherse thow it not. **a1437** *Kingis Quair* 89.157[5]. **c1450** *Chaunce* 13.277: To spekyn goode your tonge seyde never hoo. **c1450** *How mankinde dooth* in Furnivall *Hymns* 67.294. **a1456** Shirley *Table* in E. P. Hammond *English Verse Between Chaucer and Surrey* (Durham, N.C., 1927) 195.33. **a1470** Malory I 36.30–1. **c1470** *Wallace* 26.265, 123.406. **a1500** *Complaint* in Skeat *Complete Works of Geoffrey Chaucer* (Oxford, 1897) IV xxix 16–7. **1513** Douglas *Aeneid* II 152.182: and cry ho! III 129.38. **c1523** Barclay *Mirrour* 64[48]: The sacke without bottome which never can say hoo. **1546** Heywood *D* 49.271: She is one of them, to whom God bad who. Apperson 303; NED Ho int.[2] B; *Oxford* 480; Tilley H477; Whiting *Scots* I 189. See **E28, M792.**

H399 **Hoard** has hate
c1390 Chaucer *Truth* 3–4: For hord hath hate, and climbing tikelnesse, Prees hath envye, and wele blent overal.

H400 There is many a **Hocket** (*trick*) in amours
a1300 *Alisaunder* 375.6990–1: Many hokett is in amoures! Stedfast seldom ben lecchoures.

H401 To play at the **Hoddypeak** (*?to make a fool of oneself*)
c1516 Skelton *Magnificence* 37.1162: Can he play well at the hoddypeke?

H402 In **Hodymoke** (*?concealment*)
a1425 Mirk *Instructions* 59.1919: Huyde hyt not in hodymoke. See **H628.**

Hog, see **Pig, Sow, Swine**

H403 Every man bastes the fat **Hog**, *etc.* (*varied*)
1509 Barclay *Ship* I 100[26]: The fat pygge is baast, the lene cony is brent. **1546** Heywood *D* 54.447–8: Every man basteth the fat hog we see, But the leane shall burne er he basted bee, **1555** *E* 196.286. Apperson 188; *Oxford* 24; Tilley H487. See **H537, S959.**

H404 To be bristled as **Hogs** (*etc.*) (A number of single quotations are brought together here)
a1300 *Alisaunder* 301.5761: Bristled hii weren as hogges. **c1400** *Laud Troy* I 317.10750–1: On bothe the sides his hors he felle, As he hadde ben a cloven hogge. **c1400** *Sowdone* 28.958: And sle hem down as hogges. **c1400** *Of Prelates* in Wyclif *EW* 96[16–8]: Til thei heten and drynkyne her legges and hondes out of myght, and here hevyd out of wytt and ben as dede hogges. **a1470** Malory I 339.17–8: You kepte my son in the kychyn and fedde hym lyke an hogge. **c1489** Caxton *Aymon* II 420.17–8: The frenshemen . . . entred in to the dyches as hogges doon in a myre, 426.1–2: They felle where thei wente, musselinge in the grounde as hogges.

H405 To lie like a **Hog** in a sty (the mire)
c1400 *Laud Troy* II 469.15921: And ligge not ther as an hog In sty. **a1415** *Lanterne* 117.31–2: To liee in grooti placis as an hogge in the myre. Whiting *Drama* 316:171. See **S966.**

H406 To peg (*?stuff*) one like a peny (*?penned*) **Hog**
a1400 *Alexander C* 232.4278: To pegge us as a peny hoge. NED Peg 6.

H407 To rout (*snore*) like a **Hog**
1546 Heywood *D* 41.193: A sleepe . . . routyng lyke a hog. *Oxford* 550; Tilley H497. See **S968.**

H408 To sleep like **Hogs**
c1400 *Satan and his Children* in Wyclif *EW* 216[32]: Fallen in lecherie and slepen as hooggis. Apperson 577: pig; Taylor and Whiting 185; Whiting *Drama* 316:171. See **G467, S970.**

H409 To couch a **Hog's Head** (*i.e.*, lie down to sleep)
1546 Heywood *D* 64.88: I will couche a hogs hed. NED Couch vb.[1] le, Hogshead 3; *Oxford* 111; Tilley H504.

H410 As foul is he that **Holds** as he that fos (*seizes*)
c1303 Mannyng *Handlyng* 243.7627–8: And yyt men sey, as men gos, As foule ys he that halt, as he that fos (*var.* flos). (By taking *fos* as an unusual form of *fon*, we get something like The receiver is as bad as the thief.) See **R60, T73.**

H411 Better **Hold** than crave
c1450 *Consail and Teiching* 69.140: It is far bettir hald na craif. **a1460** *Towneley Plays* 13.142–3: And it is better hold that I have Then go from doore to doore and crave. Cf. Tilley K9, H510; Whiting *Scots* I 190. See **H184.**

H412 **Hold** fast when you have it
1546 Heywood *D* 40.177: Hold fast whan ye have

it, **1555** *E* 197.294: Holde fast when ye have it, if it be not thyne, Holde fast and run fast when thou hast it freend myne. Apperson 304; Jente 234, 361; *Oxford* 298; Tilley H513. See **C518, K3.**

H413 Who may **Hold** that (a thing that) will away?
c1385 Chaucer *TC* iv 1628: For who may holde a thing that wol awey? **c1450** *Fortune in Life* in Smith *Common-place Book* 17.56: For no man can hold that wyll a-wey. **c1465** *Stonor Letters* I 70[17]: Ther may no man hold that woll awaye. **a1470** Malory I 402.11–2: Therfore wete you well, there may no man holde that woll away. **a1475** *Turne up hur halter* in *Rel. Ant.* I 75[3]: Ho may hold that wyll away? **a1513** Dunbar *Meditatioun* 26.27: Quhy wald thow hald that will away? **1546** Heywood *D* 79.40: Who maie holde that will awaie. Apperson 682; *Oxford* 299; Tilley H515; Whiting *Scots* I 189–90.

H414 Through (At) a little **Hole** a man may see his friend
c1450 *Douce MS.52* 56.130: Thorowgh a litul hole a man may se his frende. **c1450** *Rylands MS.394* 107.16. **a1500** Hill 132.50: At a lytill hole, a man may se his frende. See **D61.**

H415 To look at a wrong **Hole**
a1450 *Gesta* 161[15–6]: Thow lokist at a wronge hole; thy wordes bethe in wast.

H416 Between **Holland** and Arderne
1481 Caxton *Reynard* 9[22–3]: The fayrest hennes that were bytwene holland and arderne.

H417 Never to lie but when the **Holly** grows green
a1508 Dunbar *Testament* 73.63–4: Qui nunquam fabricat mendacia, Bot quhen the holyne growis grene. Apperson 305; Whiting *Scots* I 190.

H418 To be like the **Holly** flower
a1500 *Catalogue of Delights* in Robbins 121.37–8: Her nek is like the holly flour Replete with all swete odour.

H419 Court **Holy Water**
1519 Horman *Vulgaria* 333[33]: I have many feyre promessis and halywater of court. Apperson 116; *Oxford* 113–4; Tilley H532.

H420 **Home** is homely
1546 Heywood *D* 25.28: And home is homely, though it be poore in syght, **1555** *E* 148.10. Apperson 305; *Oxford* 300; Taylor and Whiting 186; Tilley H534. See **B505.**

H421 Many one bears him bold at **Home** who dares do full simply if he come out
a1450 *Generydes A* 172.5521–2: Many oon bereth him bold at home, Dar doo ful simplie if he out come. See **G3.**

H422 One's long **Home** (house, bold, bower)
a800 Cynewulf *Fates* in *Vercelli Book* 53.92–3: þonne ic sceal langne ham, Eardwic uncuð, ana gesecan. **a1300** *Alisaunder* 43.748–9: A pytt he dude sone make, And broughth hym in his longe hous. **c1300** *South English Legendary (Laud)* 463.38: And to heore longue home broughten heom ful sone. **c1303** Mannyng *Handlyng* 273.8653–4, 289.9194. **a1325** *Erthe* 3.64: Er erthe go to erthe, bild thi long bold. **c1325** *Body and Soul* in Böddeker 243.233–4. **c1390** *Love Holy Church* in Brown *Lyrics XIV* 189.22: To bringe us to ur longe bour. **a1400** *Scottish Legends* I 2.32. **a1415** Mirk *Festial* 295.8. **c1420** Wyntoun V 119.3242. **a1425** *Al es bot a fantum* in *Yorkshire Writers* II 458.54. **c1440** *Daily Work* in *Yorkshire Writers* I 317[43]. **c1450** *Against Death* in Brown *Lyrics XV* 247.35. **1513** Douglas *Aeneid* III 14.149: First se that hym to hys lang hame thou have. Apperson 379; *Oxford* 381; Taylor and Whiting 186; Tilley H533; Whiting *Scots* I 190.

H423 To pay one **Home**
1546 Heywood *D* 31.24: This paith me home lo, and full my foly hits.

H424 Welcome **Home** as wise as you went
c1545 Heywood *Four PP* A2^r[31]: Yet welcome home as wyse as ye wente. Tilley F460. See **F392.**

H425 Who loves to won (*dwell*) at **Home** can (*knows*) little good (*varied*)
a1400 *Ipomadon A* 9.211–2: Who lovys ay at home to wonne, Lyttill gode shall he conn. **c1400** *Vices and Virtues* 70.30–1: And he that nevere yede fro home can no good. Cf. *Oxford* 300: Home-keeping.

H426 Over great **Homeliness** (familiarity) engenders dispraising (*varied*)
c1390 Chaucer *CT* VII 1686[B2876]: For right as men seyn that "over-greet hoomlynesse engendreth dispreisynge," so fareth it by to greet humylitee or mekenesse. **c1425** Arderne *Fistula* 5.23–4: Ffor after wise men, Over moche homelynes bredeth dispisyng. **a1425** *Governance of Lordschipes* 56.15–7: Ffor over mekyl familiarite among the poepyl brynges in despyt and contempt of worschipe. **c1449** Pecock *Repressor* I 184[9–10]: Overmyche homelines

with a thing gendrith dispising toward the same thing. **a1450** *Myne awen dere* 167.569–74: Gyf thou be man of grete power And hase under the servauntes sere, Owre-hamely to thame be thou noghte, For in that vise and thay be broghte, It will gare thayme thy state despyse And set the les be thy servise. **1450** *Dicts* 130.32–3: It longith not to a grete lorde to be famulier conversaunt with his peple; thei shalle praise him the lesse. **c1450** *Foly of Fulys* 58.225–6: For our-hamly to folk lawly Causis disspising comonly. **c1450** *Ladder* 113.4–6: For it is sayde in Olde Englisshe: "Overe mych felaship makith otherwhile men to be dispised." **c1450** *Secrete of Secretes* 13.1–2: For bi ovyr moche homelynes he shalle be the lasse honourid. **1456** Hay *Governaunce* 93.11–3: For our mekle syk hamelynes engenderis lychtlines and vilipensioun of princis, and nurisis and engenderis dispite and lesse honour, *Law* 302.31–2: For ony thing that commouns seis our oft thai pris all the lesse. **a1475** *Good Wyfe Wold* 174.32: Over-homly ys not best, men mey dem aryght. **c1500** *Lancelot* 51.1698–1700: For, as the most philosephur can duclar, To mych to oyss familiaritee Contempnyng bryngith one to hie dugre. **a1500** *Imitatione (1)* 9.24–5: Charite is to be had to all men, but familiarite is not expedient. **1502** *Imitatione* (2) 158.43–159.1. **1519** Horman *Vulgaria* 275[25]: The oft presens of a man abrode in syght maketh hym naught set by. **c1520** Walter *Spectacle* D1r[26]: To moche famylyaryte dysdayne dothe engendre. Apperson 203; *Oxford* 190; Skeat 251; Taylor and Whiting 127; Tilley F46; Whiting *Drama* 156. See **H632.**

H427 Homer sleeps sometimes
a1387 Higden-Trevisa V 57[6–8]: He may take hede that the grete Homerus slepeth somtyme, for in a long work it is laweful to slepe som tyme. **1533** More *Apologye* 2[32–4]: The wryter have as Horace sayth of Homere, here and there some tyme fallen in a litle slomber. Apperson 305; *Oxford* 300; Tilley H536.

H428 As dulcet (*sweet*) as **Honey**
a1475 *Tree* 97.18: The ende is doucete as hony.

H429 As smolt (*calm, smooth*) as **Honey**
a1000 *De Sancto Johanne* in *ESt* 8(1885) 477.9–10: Thonne flowaeth seo welle swa faegere and swa smoltlice swa hunig.

H430 As sweet as **Honey** (and the honeycomb)
c900 *Paris Psalter* 112 (118.103): Hit is halwende, hunige mycle And beobreade betere and swetre. **a1000** *Pseudo-Alcuin* 375.91–2: Swettre byð mines muðes gomen þinre spæce, þone hunig oððe beobread. **c1000** Aelfric *Homilies* II 136[30]: And on swæcce swettran þonne beona hunig. **c1000** *Regius Psalter* 31 (18.11): Swetran ofer hunig and beobread. **c1100** *Salisbury Psalter* 99 (18.11), 251 (118.103). **c1300** *South English Legendary* I 318.82: So swete so eny hony. **a1325** *Cursor* I 12 CF 75–6: Hir luve . . . That suetter es than hony o bike. **c1340** Rolle *Psalter* 70 (18.11): Swetter aboven huny and huny kambe, 426 (118.103), **1348** *Form* in Allen *R. Rolle* 106.49. **c1350** *Apocalypse* 78.10. **c1350** *Prose Psalter* 21 (18.11), 151 (118.103) **c1390** *Talkyng* 26.17. **c1395** *WBible* Judges xiv 18: What is swettere than hony, Psalms xviii 11, cxviii 103, Ecclesiasticus xxiv 27, xlix 2, Apocalypse x 9. **a1396**(1494) Hilton *Scale* R6r[22–5]: Thyn holy wordes . . . are swetter to my chekes . . . than honey is to my mouthe. **a1400** *Alexander C* 218.3855: Was nevir na hony in na hyve undire heven swettir. **a1400** *Meditations* 29.1093. **a1400** *Northern Verse Psalter* I 53 (18.11), II 93 (118.103). **c1400** *Primer* 4[2]. **c1400** *Seven Sages D* 22.691. **c1415** *Middle English Sermons* 12.33–13.1. **c1420** Wyntoun II 285.216. **1435** Misyn *Fire* 55.6–7, 81.9. **1447** Bokenham 64.2326–8, 114.4172–3. **a1450** *The lord that is* 218.249–50. **1450** *Dicts* 8.4. **c1450** Capgrave *Lives* 24.22: Thes holy letteris, whech be swete as hony. **c1450** Idley 113.303. **c1450** *Myroure of oure Ladye* 128 [2], 286[17, 18, 23, 25–6]. **c1450** *St. Cuthbert* 43. 1454. **a1475** *St. Birgitta* 39.6. **c1475** *Court of Sapience* 165.1035. **c1475** Henryson *Fables* 27.700: Hennis ar sa honie sweit, *Orpheus* 130.39. **c1475** *Mankind* 9.218. **1481** *Tulle of Olde Age* 30[9]: A langage swetter than hony. **c1485** *Mary Magdalene (Digby)* 58.94. **a1500** *Beauty of his Mistress III* in Robbins 126.15: Lyppes as swete as honye, 127.23–4. **a1500** *Imitatione* (*1*) 145.7–8. **a1500** *Miracle of B. V. (Egerton)* in PMLA 38(1923) 321.20. **a1500** *Remedie of Love* CCCXXIIv[1.18]: The lips of a strumpet been sweter than honie. **1502** *Imitatione* (2) 254.36–7. **1509** Fisher *Treatyse* 227.23–4. **a1513** Dunbar *In Secreit Place* 54.15. **a1535** Fisher *Sermon . . . upon a good Friday* in *English Works* 388.18–9. Apperson 614; *Oxford* 635; Taylor and Whiting 187; Tilley H544; Whiting *Drama* 316:173, *Scots* I 190. See **H442.**

H430a Honey-sweet
c1000 Aelfric *Homilies* II 118[22]: Mid hunigswettre þrotan. **c1390** *Talkyng* 60.15: Hony swet. **c1395** Chaucer *CT* IVE 1396: That is in mariage hony-sweete. **1413** ?Hoccleve *De Guilleville Poems* xxvi 98. **a1422** Lydgate *Life* 601.199.

a1450 *Ancrene* (*Royal*) 16.33–4. **a1450** Audelay 95.4. **c1475** *Court of Sapience* 178 *var.* [3]. **c1475** Henryson *Fables* 14.315. **a1500** *With humble hert* in *Archiv* 131(1913) 62.83. **1509** Barclay *Ship* II 290[23]. **1513** Douglas *Aeneid* II 181.27. MED honi-swete; NED Honey-sweet.

H431 Hard to lick **Honey** out of a marble stone
c1435 Lydgate *Letter to Gloucester* in *MP* II 666.33–4: Harde to likke hony out of a marbil stoon, For ther is nouthir licour nor moisture. Cf. Apperson 56: Blood; *Oxford* 694: Water; Tilley B466, W107.

H432 He that handles **Honey** shall lick his fingers
1481 Caxton *Reynard* 63–4: How shold ony man handle hony, but yf he lycked his fyngres. Apperson 307; Tilley H549.

H433 **Honey** and gall (poison, venom) (*varied*)
a1325 *Cursor* III 1472.25729: Hony thai bede and gif us gall. **c1390** *Marie Moder* in *Vernon* II 459.295–6: As Hony and galle to-gedre brought; Swete and Bitter a-cordeth nought. **a1400** *Lamentacio sancti Anselmi* in *Leeds Studies in English* 3 (1934) 35.195–6: A carful chaungyng men may calle To chaungyn hony for bittir galle. **a1400** *Meditations* 11.392: And under hony venym is dight. **1406** Hoccleve *Male Regle* 27.79–80: As he that nat betwixt hony and gall Can juge ne the werre fro the pees, **c1412** *Regement* 27.721: Hire hony wordys tornen me to galle, 183.5085–7: Many a hony worde and many a kus Ther is; but wayte on the conclusioun, And pryve galle all turnyth up-so-doun, 195.5416: The hony takith, and levyth the gal, **c1425** *Jonathas* 217.41: That hony first yaf and now yeveth galle. **a1439** Lydgate *Fall* II 428.3576–7: A bait of hony, shad out a pryme face, With mortall venym hid undir to manace. **c1450** Idley 87.403: That undir hony he hideth galle. **c1499** Skelton *Bowge* I 35.131: But under hony ofte tyme lyeth bytter gall. **a1500** *Court of Love* 437.1040: But under hony gall. **a1500** *Disciplina Clericalis* 57[21–2]: Forsoth thow etest no hony without venym. **1506** Hawes *Pastime* 178.4751–2: For the blynde love dooth perceyve ryght nought That under hony the poyson is wrought. **c1515** Barclay *Eclogues* 70.518: I thought it hony, I see nowe it is gall. **1532** More *Confutacion* 422 H[6–7]: Turnyng all honye into poyson, 427 B[10–1]: With a little honey he myngleth so muche poyson. Apperson 306, 307; *Oxford* 301; Taylor and Whiting 187; Tilley H556, 561; Whiting *Drama* 237, *Scots* I 190. See **C177, F517, G12, H440, S948.**

H434 **Honey** is more sweet if mouths have first tasted wick (*nasty*) savors (*varied*)
897 Alfred *Boethius* 52.2–4: Ælcum men þincð huniges biobread þy weorodra gif he hwene ær biteres onbirigð, *Lays of Boethius* 169.8–11. **c1380** Chaucer *Boece* III m. i 5–6: Hony is the more swete, if mouthes han first tasted savours that ben wykke, **c1385** *TC* iii 1219–20: And now swetnesse semeth more swete, That bitternesse assaied was byforn. **1410** Walton *Boethius* 127[11–2]: And hony is the swetter for to fele To hym that hath som bitter thing in taaste. See **L519.**.

H435 **Honey** is sweet but cunning is sweeter
1506 *Kalender* 169.7: Hony is swete but conynge is swetter. See **C615.**

H436 **Honey** shed out, sharp-tailed (stung after) as a bee
a1439 Lydgate *Fall* II 432.3706–7: Plesaunce in speche, and undir that falsheed, Hony shad out, sharp tailled lik a bee, III 932.486: Shad hony first, stang aftir as doon beene. Cf. Apperson 307: Honey is sweet but the bee stings; *Oxford* 301; Tilley H553.

H437 Much **Honey** engleims (*surfeits*) the maw (*stomach*) (*varied*)
c1378 *Piers* B xv 56: The man that moche hony eteth, his mawe it engleymeth. **c1390** Chaucer *CT* VII 1416–7[B2606–7]: And Salomon seith, "If thou hast founden hony, ete of it that suffiseth; for if thou ete of it out of mesure, thou shalt spewe." **c1395** *WBible* Proverbs xxv 27: As it is not good to hym that etith myche hony. *Oxford* 301; Skeat 250; Tilley H560.

H438 Of **Honey** and gall in love there is store
a1500 *Magdalene College Cambridge MS. F.4.19* in M. R. James *Catalogue* (Cambridge, 1909) 46[9–13]: Ibi mel ubi fel, Of honny and galle In Love ther is store, The honny is smale, But the galle is more. Tilley H557. Cf. Walther II 850.14574.

H439 To lick **Honey** from thorns (*varied*)
c1200 *Hali Meidenhad* 10.95: Ha lickith honi of thornes. **a1225** *Lambeth Homilies* 185[17–9]: Nis nan blisse sothes inan thing thet is utewith, thet ne beo to bitter aboht, thet et huni ther in beoth liked of thornes. **c1250** *Hendyng O* 195.22: Al to dere is bouht honi, That mon shal liken of thornes. **a1300** *This World's Bliss* in Brown *Lyrics XIII* 79.35–6: Thu lickest huni of thorn iwis, That seist thi love o werldos blis, 81.35–6. **c1390** *Talkyng* 4.29–30: Nis no blisse otewith, that hit nis to deore a bought, As hony that me likketh on prikkynde thornes. **a1393**

Gower *CA* III 192.927–8: And thus, as I have seid aforn, I licke hony on the thorn. **c1450** *Douce MS.52* 50.79: Hit is harde to lykke hony fro the thorne, 51.80: Dere is the hony bought, That on thornes is sought. **c1450** *Rylands MS.394* 100.3, 7. **a1500** *Additional MS.37075* 277.10: Hyt ys harde to lyke hony of thornys. Apperson 307; Jente 683; Kneuer 43–4; *Oxford* 301; Schleich 262; Singer III 133; Tilley H554.

H440 Under soot (*sweet*) **Honey** covert bitterness
a1439 Lydgate *Fall* I 322.4373: Under soote hony, covert bittirnesse. See **H433.**

H441 As delicious as any **Honeycombs**
a1450 *Three Middle English Sermons* 43.715–6: Lippis . . . as delicius as ani honikombis.

H442 As sweet as the **Honeycomb**
a750 *Riddles* in *Exeter Book* 202.58–9: Ic eom on goman gena swetra þonne þu beobread blende mid hunige. **a893** Wærferth *Gregory* 71.26–8: Hit him wæs swa wynsum, swa he hæfde beobreades swetnysse on his muþe. **c1390** *Of clene Maydenhod* 467.101–2: Non hony-Com that renneth on streme Was never yut so swete wrouht. **a1400** *Meditations* 49.1847–8: The swete lomb, Swetter than the hony-comb. **a1415** *Lanterne* 63.3. **a1500** *With humble hert* in *Archiv* 131(1913) 62.83: More hony-swete than ever was the hony-combe. See **H430.**

H443 It is yet but **Honeymoon**
1546 Heywood *D* 30.44: Abyde (quoth I) it was yet but hony moone. Apperson 307; Tilley H563.

H444 As thick as **Honeysuckles**
a1400 *Laud Troy* I 159.5381–3: Ther lay aboute him hondes and knokeles, As thikke as any honysocles, That In somer stondes In grene medes.

H445 **Honor** and ease may not be together
1464 Hardyng 181[16]: For honour and ease together maye not been. Apperson 307: are seldom bedfellows; *Oxford* 302; Tilley H568. See **M139.**

H446 **Honor** is not given for clothes
a1450 *Foly of Fulys* 55.115–6: He honoris na man for riches, For honore is nocht gevyne for claithis. Whiting *Scots* I 190. See **C312, P149.**

H447 **Honor** is worth more than gold or silver
1484 Caxton *Ordre of Chyvalry* 50.13–4: For honour is more worth than gold or sylver withoute ony comparyson. Jente 333. Cf. Whiting *Drama* 260. See **N12.**

H448 **Honor** surmounts all things
a1533 Berners *Arthur* 25[27]: Honour surmounteth all thinges. See **G157.**

H449 Who may have **Honor** and ease for nought?
a1500 *Thre Prestis* 28.482: Honour and eis, sir, quha may have for nocht?

H450 Worldly **Honor** is deceivable
1480 Caxton *Ovyde* 120[33–5]: Wherfore one oughte not to sette his cure and glorye in worldly honoure. For it is over deceyvable. And in short tyme is faylled and goon. See **G158.**

H451 Be hende (*courteous*) of (*with*) your **Hood**
a1400 *Proverbis of Wysdom* 245.71–2: Off thywho (*so MS.*) all way be hend, And to thy self be trew frend, (*II*) 222–3.57–8: Of thin hood alwey be hende, And to thi self be trew frende! **c1450** *Fyrst thou sal* 89.63–4: Of thi hode be thou hende And specially to thi frende.

H452 To be shaped (given) a **Hood** (*i.e.,* deceived; often cuckolded)
a1426 Lydgate *Mumming at Hertford* in *MP* II 676.54: With suche a metyerde she hathe shape him an hoode. **a1506** Hawes *Pastime* 134.3519: She gave her husbande many a furde hode. **1509** Barclay *Ship* I 168[5–7]: It is best remedy For hym that gladly wolde escape the hode Nat to be Jelous, [21]: With a hode shall he unwars be overdect, 169[6]: And with theyr hodes whiche they them selfe purchace, [10]: So that the wyfe must nedes gyve them a hode, 236[13–4]: If the wyfe knowe, in mynde she wyll be wroth Without he have a hode of the same cloth.

H453 To wear (go with) a threadbare (riven [*torn*]) **Hood**
c1450 Idley 93.739: It (*war*) woll make hym weere a threedbare hoode. **a1460** *Towneley Plays* 13.140–1: Ffor had I giffen away my goode, Then myght I go with a ryffen hood. See **S379.**

H454 To wear a parted **Hoof**
a1500 *O man more* 394.43: Manye on weres a perted hoofe.

H455 The **Hook** is hid under the bait
a1439 Lydgate *Fall* II 567.3449–50: Which cast hir baitis and anglis of plesaunce, An hook hid undir of vengable cruelte. **1509** Barclay *Ship* I 240[17–8]: The hoke of deth is hyd under the bayte Of folysshe lust. See **F230.**

H456 Set no **Hook** (*scythe*) in other men's ripe (*harvest*)
a1387 Higden-Trevisa VIII 183–5: Thou hast

no leve to sette thyn hook in other men ripe. **a1425** Higden-Anon. VIII 183–5: Hit is not lawefull to the to put a sythe into the corne of other men. Apperson 570.

H457 To lay (cast) out **Hook** and line
c1385 Chaucer *TC* v 777: To fisshen hire, he leyde out hook and lyne. **a1420** Lydgate *Troy* II 424.1015: And him to treyne leide out hoke and laas, 516.4208–9, III 731–2.5738–9: Ful craftely he leyde oute hoke and lyne, With lusty bait of fals(e) covetyse, **c1421** *Thebes* 70.1670–1: By sotyl craft leyd oute lyne and hokes, The Jalous folk to traysshen and begyle, **a1439** *Fall* II 458.4601: Hym to be-tra(i)sshe she cast out hook and lyne, III 689.549: And Marius, leid out hook and lyne, **a1449** *Fabula* in *MP* II 510.740–1: He wolde, that deth had leyd hook and lyne Tacacchyd hym into his bittir las. **a1533** Berners *Arthur* 309[28–30]: For yf a woman be mynded to cast forthe her hokes and lynes to take ony man therwith, it is very harde to scape out of theyr daunger.

H458 With (By) **Hook** or crook
1383 Wyclif *Grete Sentence* in *SEW* III 331[32–3]: And compellen men to bie alle this with hok or crok. **c1400** *Why Poor Priests* in Wyclif *EW* 250[31]: With hook or with crok. **c1445** Pecock *Donet* 140.25–9: As prechers ben woned to wrynge oute of a worde alle maters whiche to hem liken, bi wrasting of sillablis and of lettris and bi hookis and crokis of lettris, which conteynyng is litil worþ. **c1520** *Terens* A7[r][16]: By hoke or croke. **c1522** Skelton *Colyn* I 359.1240: By hoke ne by croke. Apperson 308–9; *Oxford* 303; Taylor and Whiting 187; Tilley H588; Whiting *Drama* 349:631, *Scots* I 190. See **H353.**

H459 Not (a)vail a **Hop**
c1400 *Laud Troy* I 164.5537: Here armes vayled not an hoppe.

H460 Between **Hope** and dread man shall lead his life rightly
a1400 *Suo sit fairhed* in *Rel. Ant.* I 160[3–4]: Bituene hope and drede Schal man his lif right lede.

H461 Folly (*foolish*) **Hope** deceives many a man
c1430 Lydgate *Dance* 16.128: For foli hope deceyveth many a man. See **H467, 469.**

H462 He that lives upon good **Hope** should beware
1519 Horman *Vulgaria* 433[3]: He lyveth upon good hope: but let hym beware: lest it deceve hym.

H463 **Hope** helps the careful (*sorrowful*) mind
a1500 *MS. Marginalia* in Hoccleve I 155 n.[1]: Of alle thinges that I can fynde, Hope dothe help the carefull mynd, quod Carter. Cf. Apperson 310: Hope helpeth; Smith 155. See **H475.**

H464 **Hope** in, hope out! thus can you feed fools
c1450 *Complaint against Hope* 40.120: Hope in, hope out! thus kane ye foles fede!

H465 **Hope** is hard there hap (*luck*) is foe
a1400 *Harley MS.2316* in *Rel. Ant.* II 120[37–40]: Hope is hard ther hap is foo; Hap wile helpen ther hope is froo; Unhap at nede is werdes wo, God sende him hap that wolde wel do. Cf. Whiting *Drama* 299.

H466 **Hope** leaves not a man (*varied*)
a1400 *Cato (Copenhagen)* A7[r][23–4]: Ffor hoope is of so goode nature, It leevyth no man whyle he may dure. **a1440** Burgh *Cato* 317.563: Hope leveth nat a man, thouh man leve the brethe. **c1450** *Ratis* 17.573: Gud hop left nevir hire frend at the last. **1519** Horman *Vulgaria* 17[27]: In al chauncis hope is the last companion remaynyng.

H467 The **Hope** of a fool may of-blench (*deceive*)
c1300 *Guy*[1] 316 A 5856: Hope of fole may of-blenche. See **F448, H461, 469, 477.**

H468 **Hope** of long life guiles many a good wife
c1325 *Hendyng H* 299.304: Hope of long lyf gyleth mony god wyf. Apperson 309; *Oxford* 303; Schleich 268–9; Singer III 136–7. See **M204.**

H469 **Hope** oft makes blenches (*plays tricks*) on a foolish man
c1300 *Havelok* 12.307: Hope maketh fol man ofte blenkes. Apperson 309; MED blench 1(b); *Oxford* 303. See **H461, 467, 477.**

H470 **Hope's** fair behest (*promise*) deceives fele (*many*)
a1400 *Romaunt B* 4446–8: Hir (*Hope's*) faire biheeste disceyveth feele; For she wole byhote, sikirly, And failen aftir outrely. See **B215.**

H471 **Hope** shall pay wretches their wage
a1500 ?Ros *La Belle Dame* 320.683–4: And in the ende, ye shal knowe for certayn, That hope shal pay the wrecches for their wage!

H472 **Hope** well and serve well and that shall save you
c1385 Usk 81.144–5: Hope wel and serve wel; and that shal thee save, with thy good bileve.

H473 **Hope** which is delayed torments the soul

c1395 *WBible* Proverbs xiii 12: Hope which is dilaied (**a1382:** deferrid) turmentith the soule. Apperson 309; *Oxford* 303; Tilley H600; Whiting *Drama* 185.

H474 If it were not for **Hope** no lover would live
a1400 *Romaunt B* 2778: Nere hope, ther shulde no lover lyve.

H475 If it were not for **Hope** the heart would break (burst) (*varied*)
a1200 *Ancrene* 43.6: As me seith, yef hope nere, heorte to breke. **a1300** *Tristrem* 10.272–5: And held his hert in an, That wise: It brast thurch blod and ban, Yif hope no ware to rise. **c1395** Chaucer *CT* VIII[G] 869–70: For sorwe of which almoost we wexen wood, But that good hope crepeth in oure herte. **a1400** *Pricke* 196. 7266: And men says, warn hope ware it (*heart*) suld brest. **a1450** *Gesta* 228[6–7]: If hope wer not, hert shulde breke, 230[6]: But yf hope wer, herte shulde breste, (*second version*) [8–9]: Were not hope stedfast, hert ofte sithes wold brest. **c1450** *Complaint against Hope* 22.45–6: And thane seyne these wise folkes alle, That ne wer hope, hert shulde breste. **c1450** *Douce MS.52* 55.127: Hope ne were, Hert brostun were. **c1450** *Rylands MS.394* 107.21ᵛ.1. **c1470** *Harley MS.3362* f.4a: Yyf hope nere hert wolde toberste. **a1500** *Ghostly Battle* in *Yorkshire Writers* II 428[34–5]: Ther ys an olde proverbe that, ne hope were, herte wolde breste. **a1500** Hill 129.40: Ner hope harte wold breste. **c1500** Newton 271.8: Were not good hope, oure hertes wold berst, 272.16, 20, 28. Apperson 309–10; *Oxford* 304; Tilley H605; Whiting *Scots* I 191. See **H463.**

H476 In good **Hope** sickerness (*assurance*) sometimes lies
c1450 Capgrave *Katharine* 223.854: Ffor in good hope lygth somtyme sekyrnesse.

H477 Lewd (*foolish*) **Hope** is fools' Paradise
c1477 Norton *Ordinall* 28[12]: *For lewde hope is fooles Paradice.* See **H461, 467, 469.**

H478 A small **Hop-o'-my-thumb**
1546 Heywood *D* 41.25: It is a small hop on my thombe. Apperson 309; Tilley H613; Whiting *Drama* 317:175.

H479 As hoar as **Horehound**
a1425 *Somer Soneday* in *Rel. Ant.* II 9[20]: And I beheld on hadde an heved hor als horhowne.

H480 As crumped (*crooked*) as a **Horn**
c1408 Lydgate *Reson* 48.1800: Cromped ageyn, as is an horn.

H481 As hard as (any, an) **Horn**
a1350 *Seege of Troye* 97.1216–7: That al hard bycom his skyn Als eny . . . horn to hewe yn. **a1398**(1495) Bartholomaeus-Trevisa cc7ᵛ[2.18]: Harde as an horne. **a1475** *Assembly of Gods* 19.618: any. **a1508** Dunbar *Flyting* 11.212: Hard as horn. Apperson 284–5; Tilley H621.

H482 As loud as a (the) **Horn**
a1450 *Gesta* 46[32–3]: She cried, and seid with a vois, as hit had be an horne. **a1500** *Inter Diabolus et Virgo* 444.12: What ys loder than ys the horne? 445.32. Apperson 383; Tilley H615; Whiting *NC* 426.

H483 **Horns** of cuckoldry (*varied*)
a1400 *Romaunt B* 4250: With hornepipes of Cornewaile. **a1439** Lydgate *Fall* I 294.3360–7: To speke pleyn Inglissh, made hym a cokold. Alas, I was nat avysid weel biforn, Oncunnyngli to speke such language; I sholde ha said, how that he hadde an horn, Or souht sum tee(r)me with a fair visage Texcuse my rudnesse off this gret outrage, As in sum land Cornodo men them call, And summe afferme how such folk ha(ve) no gall. **a1449** ?Lydgate *Evil Marriage* in *MP* II 459.78–81: And if (so be) he be no spere-man good, Hit may well hap he shall have an horn, A large bone to stuff wythall his hood, A mowe be-hynde, and fayned chere beforn. **a1460** *Towneley Plays* 135.600–1: Sagh I never in a credyll A hornyd lad or now. **c1475** *Wisdom* 60.760–1: Yowur (*adulterous women*) mynstrell an hornepype mete, That fowle ys in hym-selff, but to the erys swete. **a1500** Greene *Carols* 407.7: But the hod of a— syr, ye wott what I mene—Wych with too hornys infeckyd was and smytten, By surgery to be helyd it is forbyddyn, For thei have such an yssue abow the cheke. **a1500** *Miller of Abington* 118.477–9: Wherefore he did beare an horne, For steeling of this meale onlie, His wife and doughter were laine by. **a1500** *Piers of Fullham* 14.336–7: Whiche hath cawsed here to forn That many a man hath had an horn. **a1500** *Ryght as small flodes* 155.95–6: For in wastynge and vanyte men reken not what is lorne For wyfe and for woman for to were the horne (*perhaps female headgear*). **a1500** *Tudor Crosse Rowe* in *JEGP* 58(1959) 249.7: D for danyell the dastard was dubled in hys hornes. **c1515** Barclay *Eclogues* 191.265: No horned kiddes were living at that time. **1532** Berners *Golden Boke* 407.10339–40: With a horne on

my heed, a common cuckolde. **1533** Heywood *Weather* A4v[40]: For womens hornes sounde more in a mannys nose, B1r[16]: But who maketh al these hornes, your self or your wife? [28]: I thynke his name is mayster horner, **1555** *E* 172.149.2: Or dooth thy heare perse through thy whood, lyke a horne. Apperson 310–1; NED Horn 7; *Oxford* 304; Taylor and Whiting 188; Tilley H622–6; Whiting *Drama* 349:633, 362:837, *Scots* I 191. See **B452, F106.**

H484 One can never make a good lilting **Horn** of a pig's tail
c1450 *Chaunce* 15.355–6: But sothe ys seyde that man shal never make Of pigges tayle a goode lyltinge horne to blowe. Apperson 495:28; *Oxford* 304; Tilley H619. See **L6, S316.**

H485 One's **Horn** is blown
c1386 Chaucer *LGW* 1383: Have at thee, Jason! now thyn horn is blowe! **a1450** Audelay 13.77–8: Fore here cursid covetyse Here horne is e-blaw. **a1460** *Towneley Plays* 375.249–50: Mi name is tutivillus, My horne is blawen. **a1500** *Lay of Sorrow* 718.120: So wyde Is blawin youre horn. See **B233.**

H486 Simnel **Horns** (*cake, bun*) bear no thorns
a1400 *Trinity College Cambridge MS.1109* 55 in M. R. James *Catalogue* (Cambridge, 1902) III 91: Simenel hornes ber none thornes, Alleluya. **c1470** *Harley MS.3362* f.3a in *Retrospective* 309[25] (*English only*): Krakenel hornys havyth non . . . Non sunt artochopi pungentes cornua spini. MED crak(e)nel; NED Cracknel, Simnel; Walther III 390.18528.

H487 To be put to the **Horn**
a1500 Kennedy 30.91: Put to the horn, exilit fra Goddis face. NED Horn 14; Whiting *Scots* I 191.

H488 To bear a **Horn** and blow it not
a1393 Gower *CA* III 126.6523–4: And berth an horn and noght ne bloweth, For noman of his conseil knoweth. **c1450** *Rylands MS.394* 93.29: He is wyse and well tawght, that berys a horn and blowes it nowght. **c1475** *Rawlinson MS. D 328* 121.48: He ys wyse and wel y-taght that beryth a horne and blow hym noghth. **a1500** Greene *Carols* 344 *refrain:* I hold hym wyse and wel itaught Can bar an horn and blow it naught. **a1500** *St. George's Chapel, Windsor, MS. E.I.I.* f.95b in *The Library,* 4th series, 13(1933) 74: He is wise and wele tawght that can bere an horne and blow it not. Apperson 310; *Oxford* 697; Robbins-Cutler 3172.5; Tilley H618.

H489 To blow in a **Horn**
c1421 Lydgate *Thebes* 75.1790–1: But lete his brother blowen in an horn, Wher that hym lyst or pypen in a red. MED blouen v. (1) 4(c). See **B574.**

H490 To blow one's **Horn**
c1500 Fabyan 259[27–8]: After he had lewdely blowed his horne.

H491 To draw (shrink) in one's **Horns**
a1300 *Richard* 287.3863–4: And gynne to drawe in here hornes As a snayl among the thornes. **c1385** Chaucer *TC* i 300: He was tho glad his hornes in to shrinke. **a1420** Lydgate *Troy* I 77.2199: And causeth Love hornys for to schrynke, **a1422** *Life* 415.1474–5: The trouthe, may no while dare Hornes shrynke, ne hyde hym in his neste. **a1425** *Of Mynystris* in Wyclif *SEW* II 403[9–10]: And many men . . . drawun in her hornes for thes apostates. **a1430** Lydgate *Pilgrimage* 49.1835–7: Lych hornys of a lytell snayl, Wych serve for noon avayl, But for a lytel strawh wyl shrynke, **a1439** *Fall* I 190. 6723–4: And who is knowe ontrewe in his cuntre, Shrynkith his hornis whan men speke of falshedde. **c1450** *Pilgrimage LM* 12[21–2]: Thine hornes ben of a snayl that hyden hem for a straw anoon as thei have felt it. **1483** *Quatuor Sermones* 31[14–5]: Drawe in thyn hornys of pryde as a snayle when he is touchyd. Apperson 164; *Oxford* 156; Taylor and Whiting 189; Tilley H620; Whiting *Drama* 359:783.

H492 To dress one's **Horns** high (out)
c1440 Lydgate *Debate* in *MP* II 562.554–5: No man presume so hih his hornes dresse, For no prerogatiff his neihbour despise, **a1449** *Ryght as a Rammes Horne* in *MP* II 463.36: Nor Dissymulynge owte his hornes dresse.

H493 To enhance the **Horn**
c1395 *WBible* Psalms *Prol.* II 738[20]: An other the hornene trumpe enhauncende, Psalms lxxiv 5: Nyle ye enhaunce the horn, Ecclesiasticus xlvii 13: Crist . . . enhaunside his horn with outen ende. MED enhauncen 4a.

H494 To give one a **Horn** (*i.e.,* deceive, but not cuckold)
c1440 Charles of Orleans 62.1829–30: Hit were thi shame to geve me thus an horne Make not of me thus light a noforsyng, 205.6112: And pratily then to gyve hem so an horne, 216.6430: I am to ware of thee to were an horne. **a1500** *Court of Love* 446.1390: This folissh dove will give us all an horn.

H495 As meek as a **Hornet**

a1500 *I have a lady* in Person 39.33: And as an hornet (she is) meke and pytelesse.

H496 To run (be) **Horn-wood** (*-mad*)
a1450 *Partonope* 314.7845: Horne-wode he renneth for your sake. **1546** Heywood *D* 99.26: She was (as they say) horne wood. *Oxford* 304; Tilley H628.

H497 As big as any **Horse**
a1533 Berners *Huon* 426.1-2: This byrd . . . was bygger than any hors. Taylor *Comparisons* 16; Taylor and Whiting 190; Whiting *Drama* 317:176.

H498 As great as a **Horse**
a1425 *Mandeville* (*Egerton*) 50.11-2: Grete lumppes . . . als grete as a hors.

H499 As high as any **Horse**
a1533 Berners *Huon* 374.13-4: A . . . serpent heyer then any hors, 28-9.

H500 As holy as a **Horse**
1528 More *Heresyes* 136 H[9-10]: As pore and as haulting as his hors, and as holy to, **1534** *Comforte* 1226 H[2-3]: Everye man woulde faine seme as holye as an horse. Apperson 312; Tilley H629.

H501 As shortly as a **Horse** will lick its ear
1546 Heywood *D* 94.123-4: Ye will get it againe . . . I feare, As shortly as a horse will licke his eare. Apperson 312; *Oxford* 585; Tilley H630.

H502 The common **Horse** is worst shod
1546 Heywood *D* 51.331: But evermore the common horse is woorst shod. Apperson 313; *Oxford* 105; Tilley H637.

H503 Ever longer the worse looks the blind **Horse**
c1275 *Ancrene* (*Cleopatra*) in Morton 98 n.c: Se lengre se wurse lokede blind hors. **c1450** *Douce MS.52* 45.18: Ever lenger, the wors lokys the blynde hors. **c1450** *Rylands MS.394* 96.1. Ives 263:7; *Oxford* 50. See **L430.**

H504 A galled **Horse** will wince for noise of saddles
a1449 Lydgate *Look* in *MP* II 771.181-2: A gallyd hors wyl wyncen in a stable, For noyse of sadlys, hevy outhir liht.

H505 A galled **Horse** will wince when he is touched (*varied*)
c1382 Wyclif *Lincolniensis* in *SEW* III 231[9-10]: As a horse unrubbed, that haves a sore back, wynses when he is oght touched or rubbed on his rugge. **a1439** Lydgate *Fall* I 190.6721-2: A gallid hors, the sooth yff ye list see, Who touchith hym, boweth his bak for dreede. **1483** *Quatuor Sermones* 27[18]: A gallyd horse that is touchyd on the sore wynseth and wryeth. **1546** Heywood *D* 86.211: I rub the gald hors backe till he winche, **1555** *E* 171.140: Rub a galde horse on the backe and he wyll kycke. Apperson 242; *Oxford* 550; Skeat 297; Tilley H700; Whiting *Drama* 230, *Scots* I 191. See **B131, G7.**

H506 A gentle **Horse** with a soft bit will turn of its own wit
c1500 Greene *Carols* 379.8: A gentyll horse with a softe bytte Woll torne on the ryght hond of hys owne wytt. Cf. Tilley H643.

H507 A groaning **Horse** and a groaning wife never fail their master
1546 Heywood *D* 66.5-6: A gronyng horse, and a gronyng wife, Never fayle their maister. Apperson 275; *Oxford* 268; Tilley H649.

H508 He is free of his **Horse** that has none
c1250 *Hendyng O* 196.29: He is fre of hors, that non ne haveth. Apperson 312:33; Kneuer 40-3; *Oxford* 225; Schleich 264-5; Singer III 134-5.

H509 He must not care for his **Horse** that would run down a stag
c1025 *Durham Proverbs* 15.41: Ne sceall se for horse murnan se þe wile heort ofærnan. Non debet equo parcere qui vult cervum pervertere.

H510 He that had best (good) **Horse** held him best saved (got best away)
a1375 *William* 48.1273: And he that hadde best hors than held him best saved. **c1375** Barbour *Bruce* I 218.278-9: The remanand war fleand ay, Quha had gud horse, gat best avay! See **R239.**

H511 He that has no **Horse** may ride on a staff (*varied*)
c1325 *An Old Man's Prayer* in Brown *Lyrics XIV* 4.34: A staf ys nou my stede. **a1400** *Cleges* 47.247-52: Syr clegys than a staff he toke; He had no hors, so seyth the boke, To ryde hys jorneye, Nether sted ne palferey, Bot a staff was his hakney, As maner in poverte. **a1400** *In this werd* in *MLR* 7(1912) 151[5-8]: Wylum haved I fere and flicke, God hors on to ride; Nou hys min hors a wrechyd sticke That stondit be my seyde. **a1449** Lydgate *Cok* in *MP* II 817.137: Whoo hath noon hors, on a staff may ryde. *Oxford* 305. Cf. Taylor and Whiting 324.

H512 He that has no **Horse** must go on foot
1492 *Salomon and Marcolphus* 11[21-2]: It standeth wryten in a boke, he that hath no horse muste go on fote. See **F479.**

H513 A **Horse** that ever trotted is hard to make amble (*varied*)
c1400 *Beryn* 31.939-40: As hors that evir trottid, trewlich I yew tell, It were hard for to make hym, aftir to ambill well. **a1450** *South English Legendary* (*Bodley*) 346.16-8: For who-so wille lerny gode yong he mot by-ginne; Comeliche an englich, Ich wot, me seyth forthy, Fol hard it is to teche an old hors aumbly. **1459** *Defence* 522[6-7]: It were as harde to make hem tru as for to make an olde trotetere to amble. Cf. Tilley F408. See **D313, T129.**

H514 A **Horse** with four feet may stumble
a1439 Lydgate *Fall* III 1015.3386: An hors with foure feet may stoumble among and slydre. Apperson 311; *Oxford* 305-6; Tilley H663.

H515 It is a good **Horse** that never stumbles
1546 Heywood *D* 32.54-5: Though it be a good hors That never stumbleth, **1555** *E* 163.104. Apperson 312-3; *Oxford* 253; Taylor and Whiting 191; Tilley H670; Whiting *Drama* 227.

H516 It would make a **Horse** break his halter
1546 Heywood *D* 61.77-8: And to thinke wherfore they bothe put both in ure, It wolde have made a hors breake his halter sure. Apperson 313; *Oxford* 305; Tilley H673.

H517 It would make a **Horse** weep
a1500 *Colyn Blowbol* 93.22: An hors wold wepe to se the sorow he maide. Cf. Taylor and Whiting 191: laugh. See **H535.**

H518 Look not a given **Horse** in the teeth (mouth)
1508(1519) Stanbridge *Vulgaria* 27.18: A gyven hors may not (be) loked in the tethe. **1546** Heywood *D* 27.44: No man ought to looke a geven hors in the mouth. Apperson 245-6; Jente 480; *Oxford* 236-7; Taylor and Whiting 191; Tilley H678.

H519 Many a blind **Horse** draws well in the cart
a1500 *O man more* 394.19: Many a blynde horse drawethe well in the carte.

H520 Never prick a free (*willing*) **Horse**
1477 Paston V 294[19-20]: It shall never neede to prykk nor threte a free horse. Apperson 311:5, 312:27; Jente 510; *Oxford* 616; Tilley H638.

H521 A proud **Horse** that will not bear its own provender
1546 Heywood *D* 98.250: A proude horse that will not beare his own provander. Apperson 515; *Oxford* 521; Tilley H683.

H522 Recover the **Horse** or lose the saddle too
1549 Heywood *D* 95.151-2: This will I doo, Recover the hors, or leese the saddle too. Apperson 688: Win; *Oxford* 711; Tilley H639.

H523 A scabbed **Horse** seeks its like
1492 *Salomon and Marcolphus* 11[12-3]: Where a skabbyd horse is he sekyth his lyke and eyther of thaym gnappyth othre. See **L272.**

H524 A scald (scabbed) **Horse** is good enough for a scabbed (scald) squire
1546 Heywood *D* 49.282: A scald hors is good inough for a scabde squyer, **1555** *E* 174.161: A scabde horse is good enough, for a scalde squyre. Apperson 552; *Oxford* 564; Tilley H690.

H525 A short **Horse** is soon curried (wiped)
c1450 *Douce MS.52* 45.17: Short hors is son i-curryed. **c1450** *Rylands MS.394* 96.15. **c1475** *Rawlinson MS. D 328* 117.4: A schorte horse ys son wypyd. **c1490** *Sloane MS.747* 204.21. **a1500** Hill 128.8. **1546** Heywood *D* 35.5, **1555** *E* 153.45. Apperson 567; *Oxford* 584; Taylor and Whiting 190; Tilley H691. Cf. Jente 346.

H526 To be drawn with wild **Horses**
c1380 *Ferumbras* 181.5827-8: Wyth wilde hors mot y beo drawe, Bot y wolde her right fawe A lyme of me for-gon. **a1475** *Guy*[2] 235-6.8212-4: Arste wyll y be drawyn wyth horsys stronge, Then evyr y schulde in soche a nede Yelde me unto soche a quede. **1523** Berners *Froissart* II 255[32-4]: He was so true, that to be drawen with wylde horses, he wolde never consent to any shame. MED hors 2(e); Taylor and Whiting 192.

H527 To be hired like a **Horse** from day to day
1402 Hoccleve *Letter of Cupid* 76.102-3: She, for the rode of folke ys so desired, And as an hors fro day to day ys hired. Cf. NED Hackney 2.

H528 To be pricked like a **Horse** that goes in the plow
a1325 Bonaventura *Meditations* (*1*) 18.567-8: They punged hym furthe thurgh every slogh, As an hors ys prykked that goth yn plogh.

H529 To bere (*roar*) like a bagged **Horse** (*stallion*)
a1507 Dunbar *Dance* 122.79-80: Lichery . . . Come berand lyk a bagit hors.

H530 To bite and plain (whine [*whinny*]) like a **Horse**

c1375 Chaucer *Anel.* 157: Ryght as an hors, that can both bite and pleyne, **c1395** *CT* III[D] 386: For as an hors I koude byte and whyne. **a1430** Lydgate *Pilgrimage* 555.20828: Lych an hors she gan to wyne. **a1460** *Towneley Plays* 30.229: Thou can both byte and whyne.

H531 To call a **Horse** a horse
1533 More *Apologye* 46[18–20]: Theyr nature is so playne, and theyr utteraunce so rude, that they can not call an horse but an horse. Cf. Tilley D508, S699.

H532 To eat like a **Horse**
1469 Paston V 22[11]: I eete lyek a horse. Taylor *Comparisons* 49; Taylor and Whiting 192; Whiting *NC* 427.

H533 To fnort (*snort, snore*) like a **Horse** in sleep
c1390 Chaucer *CT* I[A] 4163: That as an hors he fnorteth in his sleep. *Oxford* 550: Routing.

H534 To run as swiftly as a **Horse**
1471 Caxton *Recuyell* II 365.23–4: Hercules that ran also swiftely as an hors, 480.8–9. Cf. Whiting *Scots* I 191.

H535 To touch a **Horse**'s heart
1562 Heywood *E* 237.49.3–4: Then are ye so tart and tough, That your taunts would touche a hors hart most rough. See **H277, 517.**

H536 Trust not to a **Horse's** foot, a hound's tooth or a woman's faith
c1450 John of Fordun *Scotichronicon* (Edinburgh, 1759) II 377: Till horsis fote thou never traist, Till hondis tooth, no womans faith. Apperson 314:69; *Oxford* 673; Tilley H711.

H537 What man has **Horse** men give him horse
a1393 Gower *CA* III 163.7719: What man hath hors men yive him hors. See **H403.**

H538 When an ambling blind **Horse** begins to stumble he casts himself down
a1400 Wyclif *Sermons* II 352[17–9]: For an aumblynge blynd hors, whanne he bigynneth to stumble, he lastith in his stumblynge til he cast himsilf doun.

H539 Where the **Horse** wallows some hairs fall (are lost)
c1475 *Rawlinson MS. D 328* 125.77: Ther the hors whallyt ther sum herris fallyt. **a1500** Hill 129.33: Whan the hors waloweth, som heris be loste. Apperson 314:71; *Oxford* 305; Tilley H704.

H540 While the **Horse** kicks (be)ware he smite you not
c1450 *Douce MS.52* 46.23: While the hors kykys, war that he the ne smyte. **c1450** *Rylands MS.394* 97.24.

H541 Who may water that **Horse** which will not drink? (*varied*)
c1175 *Lambeth Homilies* 9[35–6]: A, hwa is thet mei thet hors wectrien the him self nule drinken? **1546** Heywood *D* 43.80–1: A man maie well bring a horse to the water, But he can not make him drinke without he will, **1555** *E* 154.50: . . . leade a horse . . . without he list. Apperson 314; *Oxford* 356; Skeat 1; Taylor and Whiting 191; Tilley H682, M262.

H542 To know not whether one is on **Horseback** or on foot
a1470 Malory II 647.5–7: And than was he so enamered uppon her that he wyst nat whether he were on horseback other on foote. Kathleen M. Knight *Valse Macabre* (New York, 1952) 93: They don't know whether they're afoot or on horse back. See **D64.**

H543 A **Horse-dung** stopped (*stuffed*) full of cloves will savor sweetly
a1500 *O man more* 394.41–2: A horse donge stopped full of clovez Wyll saver swetly at a manys nose.

H544 To suck blood like a **Horse-leech**
a1430 Lydgate *Pilgrimage* 401.14874–6: That dryeth and sowketh up my blood. . . . Evene lyk an horse leche.

H545 As high as two **Horse-loaves**
1546 Heywood *D* 36.38: As high as twoo horse loves hir person is. Apperson 301; NED Horse-loaf; *Oxford* 294; Tilley H721.

H546 As hot as **Horse-piss**
c1515 Barclay *Eclogues* 75.631: Or hote as horse pis. Svartengren 311.

H547 The shorter the **Hose** the longer ?leashes (lainers [*thongs*]) (*varied*)
c1470 *Harley MS.3362* f.2b in *Retrospective* 309[11] and Förster 201.9: Schorte hosin behowyth longe (*thonges*). Ad curtas caligas ligulas decet addere longas. **a1475** *Rawlinson MS. D 328* 119.24: The scherter the hose the lynger lessys. **a1500** *Additional MS.37075* 278.16: The schorter hosyn the longer laynerys. Walther I 41.343.

H548 (To put the) **Hose** above the shoe
a1393 Gower *CA* III 355.4303–7: To sen a man fro his astat Thurgh his sotie effeminat, And leve that a man schal do, It is as Hose above the Scho, To man which oghte noght ben used. See **C558, H92.**

H549 To wear a **Hose** upon one's head
c1395 Chaucer *CT* VIII[G] 724–6: Ther I was wont to be right fressh and gay Of clothyng and of oother good array, Now may I were an hose upon myn heed. Cf. Apperson 394: A man is a man though he have but a hose on his head; *Oxford* 402; Tilley M244.

H550 He that reckons without his **Host** reckons twice (*varied*)
c1489 Caxton *Blanchardyn* 202.5–7: But it ys sayd in comyn that "who soever rekeneth wythoute his hoste, he rekeneth twys for ones." **a1533** Berners *Arthur* 422[35–6]: It is an olde sawe, he that reckeneth withoute his hoost must reken twise. **1546** Heywood *D* 32.44: But reckners without their host must recken twyce, **1555** *E* 152.36: Recknyng without thine hoste thou must recken twyse. Apperson 525–6; *Oxford* 535; Taylor and Whiting 193; Tilley H726; Whiting *Scots* I 191–2. See **C168.**

H551 A **Host** without a chief seldom attains to good effect
1478 Rivers *Morale Proverbes* [5.3–4]: An hoost withouten a chief for capitaine Is selden seen to good effect attaine. See **H232, 362.**

H552 **Hot** cools, white soils, dear becomes hateful, light darkens (*varied*)
a800 *Riming Poem* in *Exeter Book* 168.67: Searohwit solaþ, sumurhat colað. **c1000** *Cotton Faustina MS. A x (F)* in *ASMP* 109.1–4: Hat acolað, hwit asolað, Leof alaðaþ, leoht aðystrað. Ardor frigesscit, nitor squalescit, Amor abolescit, lux obtenebrescit. **c1000** *Royal MS. 2 B. V* in *Anglia* 2(1879) 374.3. **c1250** *Owl* 108.1275–80: Nis (nout) so hot that hit nacoleth, Ne noght so hwit that hit ne soleth, Ne noght so leof that hit ne alotheth, Ne noght so glad that hit ne awrotheth: Ac eavereeu(c)h thing that eche nis, Agon schal, and al this worldes blis. **a1393** Gower *CA* III 464.2857: That erst was hete is thanne chele. **a1425** *Al es bot a fantum* in *Yorkshire Writers* II 457.11: Be ye never so hate yit may it kele. **a1500** *Clerk and the Nightingale I* in Robbins 173.19: That now is hot shalbe cole. See **L484.**

H553 Men deem him **Hot** whom men see sweat
c1385 Chaucer *TC* ii 1533: For hym men demen hoot that men seen swete.

H554 Soon **Hot** soon cold
a1449 Lydgate and Burgh *Secrees* 60.1872: Soone hoot, soone Coold. **a1470** Malory III 1120.2: Sone hote sone colde. **a1500** *Nut Brown Maid* 181.127–8: Itt is told of old, "soone hott, soone cold, And soe is a woman." **1546** Heywood *D* 89.36. Apperson 588; *Oxford* 604; Tilley H732; Whiting *Drama* 140. See **F187, H633, L484.**

H555 To make neither **Hot** nor cold
1481 Caxton *Godeffroy* 125.16–8: Nevertheles he was that made neyther hoot ne cold ne kept not the peple but at theyr wyll.

Hound, see **Dog**

H556 As covetous (avarous) as (a) **Hound**
c1000 *Larspell* in Napier 241.6–7: And þu wære swa gifre swa hund, and þu næfre nære full þe ma. **c1400** *Plowman's Tale* 159.385–6: To catche catell as covytous As hound, that for hunger woll yall. **a1425** *Governance of Lordschipes* 104.8: Averous as hounde. **a1449** Lydgate and Burgh *Secrees* 73.2298: As a hound Coveytous. Apperson 273: Greedy; Tilley D434.

H557 As hende (*polite*) as (a) **Hound**
c1350 *Alexander A* 167.1179: Ne hownde to his hous-lorde so hende to queme. **a1400** *Alexander C* 16.494: And laide as hendly as a hunde his hede in hire arme.

H558 As hende as **Hound** is in kitchen
c1378 *Piers* B v 261: I am holden . . . as hende as hounde is in kychyne. Apperson 158:18; *Oxford* 292; Skeat 109. Cf. Jente 673; Tilley D462. See **H596.**

H559 As hungry as a **Hound**
c1475 Henryson *Fables* 101.2946: Now hungris as ane Hound. Apperson 318: dog; *Oxford* 310; Svartengren 181; Taylor and Whiting 105.

H560 As vile as a **Hound** (*etc.*) (A number of single quotations are brought together here)
c1300 *South English Legendary* II 612.65: He(o) ssolde . . . vylore than an hound be(o). **c1350** *Smaller Vernon Collection* 23.962: Thou art unschomefast as an hound. **c1425** *ABC Poem* in *Pol. Rel. and Love Poems* 273.66–7: Tho iewys, egre as ony hounde, Threwyn hus body to the grounde. **c1433** Lydgate *St. Edmund* 433.1135: The offycerys, ravynous lik houndis. **1515** Barclay *St. George* 86.2119: And crept to the knyght meke as symple hounde.

H561 The feeblest **Hounds** bark most
a1387 Higden-Trevisa III 427[5–7]: (*Alexander said*) hit is the manere of the feblest houndes for to berke most, and evere the lasse myght they haveth they berketh the fastere. Apperson 157:2; *Oxford* 23; Smith 72. See **B46, C636.**

H562 Have **Hound** as gossip and a staff in your other hand

a1200 W. Map *De Nugis Curialium*, ed. M. R. James (Oxford, 1914) 211-2: Proverbium Anglicum de seruis est, *Have hund to godsib, ant stent* (*?for stang, sting*) *in thir oder hond*, quod est, Canem suscipe compatrem, et altera manu baculum. **a1300** *Trinity MS. O.2.45* 8(14): Nim hund to godsep and anne staf in thire hond. Quisquis fungetur cane compatre, virga paretur.

H563 **Hound** and cat kiss, (but they) are not the better friends
a1300 *Trinity MS. O.2.45* 7(9): Hund and cat kissat, ne beoth hi no the bet ifrund. Nunquam pace rate sociatur cum cane cata. Si catulo catus det basia, non fit amatus. Apperson 87:45; *Oxford* 82.

H564 **Hound** eats what hen (*poor*) man speles (*saves*)
a1300 *Trinity MS. O.2.45* 6(6): Hund eet, that hen man spelat. Sepe vorat gnarus canis id quod servat avarus. MED hen adj. Cf. *Oxford* 86: Cats eat what hussies spare; Tilley C181.

H565 The **Hound** in the manger (*varied*)
a1393 Gower *CA* II 132.84-7: Thogh it be noght the houndes kinde To ete chaf, yit wol he werne An Oxe which comth to the berne, Therof to taken eny fode. **a1430** Lydgate *Pilgrimage* 468.1747-8: Ffor I resemble un-to that hound Wych lyggeth in a stak off hay, Groynynge al the longe day, Wyl suffre no beste ther-to to gon, And yet hym sylff wyl ete noon. **c1450** *Pilgrimage LM* 142[12-5]: But i am lich the hound that lyth on the hep of hey to which if any sette hand he abayeth and berketh and cryeth al be it that he ete noon ther of. Apperson 160-1; *Oxford* 151; Taylor and Whiting 106; Tilley D513.

H566 A **Hound** is one's best friend
a1450 *Gesta* 46[17-8]: The best frend that I have in this world is my hounde. Whiting *NC* 396:5.

H567 The **Hound** (dog) returns to his vomit (and the sow to her wallowing) (*varied*)
a900 Alfred *Gregory* 419.26-8: Be ðæm is awriten ðæt se hund wille etan ðæt he ær aspaw, and sio sugu hi wille sylian on hire sole æfterðæmðe hio aðwægen bið. **c1000** Aelfric *Homilies* II 602[25-6]: He bið þam hunde gelic, þe spiwð and eft ett þæt þæt he ær aspaw, *Lives* I 272.163-4. **c1000** *Vitas Patrum* in Assmann 201.194-5: And he sæde, þæt wære gelicost, þe hund eft hwyrfde to his spiwðan. **c1000** *Pseudo-Alcuin* 385.356-8: Hit wære gelicost þan þe se hund wære eft gecerred to his spywðen and eft fræte þæt ilca, þæt he ær speaw. **a1175** *Twelfth-century Homilies* 52.7-8: Ilice getheawod tham hunde the aet thaet he aer speaw. **c1175** *Lambeth Homilies* 25[4-5]: Thenne hafest the thes hundes lage the nu speoweth and ef(t) hit fret, and bith muchele fulre thene he wes earthon. **a1325** *Cursor* III 1503.26782-3: That thai thaim to thair filthes fest, Als hund to that he for-wit kest. **c1350** *Apocalypse* 201.13-4: As the hounde dooth casteth that he hath eten and whan he is of hungred gooth ayein therto. **c1383** Purvey *Leaven of Pharisees* in Wyclif *EW* 25[19]: Thei turnen to synne as an hound to his spuyng. **c1390** Chaucer *CT* X[I] 138: The hound that retourneth to eten his spewyng. **c1390** *Hail, Mary!* in *Vernon* I 58.191-2: Torn thenne a-yein not to vomyt, As hound that hath eten bones. **c1395** *WBible* Judges ii 16 *gloss:* But aftirwarde thei turneden ayen to her spewing, Proverbs xxiii 35 *gloss,* xxvi 11: As a dogge that turneth ayen to his spuyng; so is an unprudent man, that rehersith his fooli, II Peter ii 22: For thilke very proverb bifelde to hem, The hound turnede ayen to his castyng, and a sowe is waischun in walwyng in fenne. **a1398**(1495) Bartholomaeus-Trevisa bb7r[2.29-33]: He (*the dog*) is to . . . glotonous: and etyth therfore ofte careyne . . . and castyth it up: but afterward whan he is an hungryd he taketh ayen that that he caste up in fowle manere. **a1400** *Ancrene* (*Recluse*) 198.26-8. **a1400** *Romaunt C* 7285-6: He is the hound, shame is to seyn, That to his castyng goth ageyn. **c1400** Paues 27 (II Peter ii 22), 220 (*Bodley Douce MS.250*). **c1400** *Why Poor Priests Have no Benefices* in Wyclif *EW* 253[19-20]. **a1425** *St. Robert* 47.163-4: Als a hounde that kastes out of his kytte And ay turnes and takys eft hys vomytte. **a1450** *Gesta* 278[13-4]. **c1450** Trevet 234.15-7 (f.47b, col.2): He was lyke an hounde in soo moche as hee after . . . wolde returne agayne to hys foule synne. **1483** Caxton *Golden Legende* 291v[2.12-4]. **c1485** *Monk of Evesham* 84[12]. **1509** Fisher *Treatyse* 85.33-5: Lyke a dogge that tourneth agayne to his vomyte, or a sowe ones waltred in the cley wyll retourne to that fylthy place. **1532** More *Confutacion* 346 D[9-10]: Lyke a dogge returning to hys vomite. *Oxford* 152; Taylor and Whiting 106-7; Tilley D455, 458; Whiting *Scots* I 160. See **S962.**

H568 **Hound** will in where he finds it open
a1250 *Ancrene* (*Nero*) 26.3-4: Hund wule in blitheliche hwar se he i vint hit open, **a1400** (*Recluse*) 25.8-9: For men seien abywoorde the

hounde wil in there he fyndeth open. Apperson 158:22; Ives 262:3; *Oxford* 478; Tilley D564.

H569 It is not good to wake a sleeping **Hound** (cat) (*varied*)
c1385 Chaucer *TC* iii 764: It is nought good a slepyng hound to wake, **c1395** *CT* V[F] 1472: "Ye, wyf," quod he, "lat slepen that is stille." **a1402** Trevisa *Dialogus* 19.10–2: Miles: Ye stireth me and wakith me as hit were of my sleep, and makith me speke other wise than y thought. Clericus: Lete the hound wake and berke (*var.:* Miles: Ye awake the slepynge dogge *etc.*). **c1405** *Mum* 76.1703: Hit is no wisedame forto wake Warrok while he sl(epeth). **a1425** Higden-Anon. Cont. VIII 488[8–9]: Where men of Fraunce hadde experience that hit was perellous to wake an olde dogge from slepe. **c1450** Idley 86.326: Awake not hym that is asleepe. **1509** *Fyftene Joyes* H4[v][8]: For he awaked hath the slepynge catte. **1546** Heywood *D* 41.194: It is evyll wakyng of a sleepyng dog, **1555** *E* 151.30: ill wakyng. Apperson 578; *Oxford* 362, 689; Tilley W7; Whiting *NC* 398:40.

H570 It is too late to lead an old **Hound** in a band
1492 *Salomon and Marcolphus* 11[23–4]: It is to late an olde hounde in a bande to lede. Cf. Taylor and Whiting 105:6. See **D313.**

H571 A mad **Hound** cares for neither friend or foe (bites his own master)
897 Alfred *Boethius* 111.17–8: Se . . . ne myrnð nauþer ne friend ne fiend þe ma þe wedende hund, *Lays of Boethius* 192.17–8: Ac he reðig-mod ræst on gehwilcne, wede hunde wuhta gelicost. **1340** *Ayenbite* 70[3–5]: Thise byeth ase wode houndes, thet biteth and ne knaweth naght hare lhord. **c1400** *Vices and Virtues* 67.34–5: Thilke fareth as a wod hound, that biteth and knoweth not his owne maister. Apperson 161:79; *Oxford* 396. See **M90.**

H572 The more **Hounds** the worse lap (*liquid dog food*)
c1450 *Rylands MS.394* 94.12: The mo houndes the werse lape. Quo numerus maior lingentium lucio peior. NED Lap sb.[2].

H573 Not worthy (for) **Hounds** to dwell in
c1400 Mandeville *Travels* 83.10: The contree is not worthi houndes to duell inne. Cf. Taylor and Whiting 85: Crow(1).

H574 To be hanged like **Hounds**
c1470 *Wallace* 148.270: As bestiall houndis hangit our a tre. Taylor and Whiting 107. See **T552.**

H575 To be harled (*pushed, dragged*) like **Hounds**
c1280 *Southern Passion* 50.1385: Ffor hi beoth y-harled her and ther, as houndes ffoule ynow.

H576 To be worse than a (any) **Hound**
a1300 *Richard* 257.3263: He is wurs than an hound! **a1325** *Otuel and Roland* 73.465: And thou worse than ony hounde. **a1325** *Ten Commandments* in Heuser 114.13: eni. **c1330** *Seven Sages A* 64.1513: an, **a1350** *C* 56.1649: ani. **a1450** *Partonope* 211.5580: ony. **a1475** *Ludus Coventriae* 67.126: an. **a1500** *Guy*[4] 110.3491: houndes.

H577 To chase as **Hound** does the hare (harts)
a1338 Mannyng *Chronicle A* I 271.7706: And chased hem as hound doth the hare. **a1400** *Melayne* 50.1558–9: And thus thay chase tham here and thare, Als the howndes dose the hare. **a1400** *Siege of Jerusalem* 33.595 (*var.*). **c1400** *Laud Troy* I 189.6420: He chases us as hound doth hares. **c1410** Lovelich *Grail* IV 293.614: As faste as the howndes hertes don chas.

H578 To couch (*crouch*) like a **Hound**
c1440 *Prose Alexander* 9.7–8: And righte as a honde will couche when his maister biddes hym, so dide he till Alexander. Whiting *Drama* 310:95.

H579 To do no more reverence to one than to a **Hound**
c1400 *Brut* I 240.26–7: For men dede him no more reverence than me wolde do unto an hunde.

H580 To doubt (*fear*) not the valure (*worth*) of an old dead **Hound**
1485 Caxton *Charles* 110.32–3: For I doubte the not the valure of an olde dede hounde and drowned. See **H590.**

H581 To drive as **Hound** does the hart (hare)
a1200 Lawman III 65.26760–2: Tha gon he to riden Aefne al swa swithe, Swa hund thene heort driveth. **a1375** *Octavian* (S) 48.1529–30: The soudan drof hem yn the feld, As hond doth the hare.

H582 To follow as **Hound** does hare (*etc.*) (A number of single quotations are brought together here)
c1300 *Havelok* 66.1994: He folwede hem so hund dos hare. **a1325** *Cursor* II 968.16129–30: And werid him on his aun bit, Als hund es on a ban. **c1330** *Horn Childe* 181.206–7: The yrise folk about him yode, As hondes do to bare. **c1400** *Satan and his Children* in Wyclif *EW*

216[33]: And fightten as woode houndis. **c1400** *Laud Troy* I 219.7437–8: He made hem fle for drede a-ferd, As hound dos dere of his herd. **a1430** Lydgate *Pilgrimage* 349.12862–3: I trace affter, as doth an hound, To ffynde the ffwet wher mete ys good. **a1450** *Castle* 105.923–4: Walkyn and wende Hyghe over holtis, as hound aftyr hare. **a1450** *Generydes A* 161.5143–4: As an hound that wold bite, Semblaunce he made forto smite. **c1450** *Seege of Troye* 115 A 1449–50: And wan ector had that wonde, He grevyd as hyt wer an honde. **a1500** *Beves* 30 M 512: That they lay gronyng as an hound.

H583 To gnaw (and bite) like a **Hound**
c1400 *Laud Troy* II 547.18576: And as an hound hem gnow and bot. **c1515** Barclay *Eclogues* 82.805: On it faste gnawing as houndes ravenous.

H584 To grin like a **Hound**
a1325 *Otuel and Roland* 94.1144: He grenned as an howunde, 105.1495. **a1350** Castelford 91.22222: Griseli and als A hunde he grinde. **a1500** *Beves* 48 M 6: That they lay grennynge lyke an hounde. See **G465.**

H585 To hate one like a **Hound**
a1300 *Beves* 93.1848: For he hateth hem ase hounde. **c1375** *St. Catherine* 167.226: For als a hund all thai hir hated. **c1400** *Why Poor Priests Have no Benefice* in Wyclif *EW* 250[16–7]. **a1425** *Metrical Paraphrase OT* 77.8367. **a1508** Dunbar *Tretis* 91.273: I hatit him like a hund. Whiting *Scots* I 192.

H586 To hold with the **Hound** (fox) and run with the hare (*varied*)
a1449 Lydgate *They That No While Endure* in *MP* II 821.33: Ner he that holdeth bothe with hounde and hare. **c1450** *Duke of Suffolk* in Wright *Political Poems* II 224[5]: Sum of yow holdith with the Fox, and rennythe hare. **c1450** *Jacob's Well* 263.19–20: Thou hast a crokyd tunge heldyng wyth hownd and wyth hare. **1546** Heywood *D* 36.24: To holde with the hare, and run with the hound, **1555** *E* 158.72, **1556** *Spider* 152[17]. Apperson 541; *Oxford* 553; Tilley H158. See **S631.**

H587 To hoot (spit, halloo) on one as he had been a **Hound**
a1325 *Cursor* II 904.15833–4: Thai huited (*F:* spitte, *T:* halowed) on him viliker Than he had ben a hund.

H588 To hunt as **Hound** does the hare (werewolf)
a1325 *Song of the Husbandman* in Böddeker 104.56–7: That me us honteth as hound deth the hare. He us honteth ase hound hare doht on hulle. **a1352** Minot 28.21: He sall you hunt als hund dose hare. **a1375** *William* 124.3835–6: I wold him hunte as hard as ever hounde in erthe Honted eny werwolf. **a1425** *Arthour and M.*[2] 295.414: But hunted them, as hound doth hare. **c1500** *Arthour and M.*[3] 434.397. Whiting *Scots* I 192.

H589 To ride (and run) as (a) **Hound**(s) (upon their prey)
c1400 *Laud Troy* I 168.5676–7: Among the Troyens he rode and ran, As hundes doth upon his pray. **c1475** *Guy*[1] 485 C 8560: To Gye rode as an hounde.

H590 To set no more by one than of an old dead **Hound**
1485 Caxton *Charles* 109.28–9: He setteth nomore by the than of an olde hounde dede. See **H580.**

H591 To spurn one as a **Hound**
a1500 *Stations* 358.158: With ther fete thei spurned (him) as a hunde, 164: Spurne ye his body as a hounde.

H592 To stink like the (a, any) **Hound** (*varied*)
a1300 *XI Pains* 150.123: And stinketh fulre thane the hund. **a1325** *Owayne Miles* (*Auchinleck*) 106.116.4: It stank fouler than ani hounde. **c1325** *Body and Soul* in Böddeker 238.71: Stynken worse then any hound. **a1400** *Ancrene* (*Recluse*) 33.31–2: For oure mouth stynketh upon hym fouler than any roten dogge, 99.30: For her mouth stinketh fouler tofore god than any roten dogge. **a1400** *Firumbras* 11.277: an. **a1415** Mirk *Festial* 192.21–2: The whech choynus stonk as a pulled honde. **1438** *Barlam and Josaphat* (*Vernon*) 220.388: an. **a1460** *Towneley Plays* 391.146: And stynke as dog in dyke. **a1475** *Guy*[2] 111.3888: Hyt stanke as a pyllyd howinde. **a1500** *Stations* 366.809–10: And had lyghe stynkynge in the grond, A hundreht parte wers than a hunde. **a1513** Dunbar *Of a Dance* 61.48: He stinckett lyk a tyk. Whiting *Drama* 310:95, *Scots* II 147.

H593 To strangle **Hounds** with a lump of tallow
a1400 Wyclif *Sermons* I 247[12–3]: But the fend hath stranglid these houndis with talwe, that thei mai not berke. **c1400** *De Apostasia* in Wyclif *SEW* III 440[5–7]: For a lumpe of talowe stranglith the houndis, and lettith hem bothe to berke and to byte.

H594 To take a (strange) **Hound** (dog) by the ears

c1390 Chaucer *CT* VII 1543[B2733]: For right as he that taketh a straunge hound by the eris is outherwhile biten with the hound. **c1395** *WBible* Proverbs xxvi 17: As he that takith a dogge bi the eeris. *Oxford* 722: Wolf; Tilley W603.

H595 When the **Hound** shits he barks not
1492 *Salomon and Marcolphus* 10[26–7]: So whan the hownde shytyth he berkyth noth.

H596 While the **Hound** gnaws bone yfere (*fellow*) wills he none (*varied*)
a1300 *Trinity MS. O. 2.45* 8(16): Wil the hund gnagth bon, ifere nele he non. Dum canis os rodit, sociari pluribus odit. **c1415** *Middle English Sermons* 89.15–6: For when the hounde knawithe the bone, than of felishippe kepeth he none. **c1470** *Harley MS.3362* f.5a in *Retrospective* 309[33] and Förster 202.13: Whyl the dogge gnaweth (*bone, cumpanion wold he have non*). Apperson 162; *Oxford* 151; Tilley D518; Walther I 799.6445. See **H558.**

H597 As harsh as a **Hound-fish**
a1400 *Morte Arthure* 32.1084: Harske as a hunde-fisch.

H598 It happens in an **Hour** that happens not in seven years (*varied*)
1525 Berners *Froissart* IV 298[10–2]: For a case may fall in an houre or in a daye that peradventure shall not fall agayne in an hundreth dayes. **1546** Heywood *D* 48.230: It hapth in one houre, that hapth not in .vii. yere, **1555** *E* 151.31, **1556** *Spider* 260[11]: Hit hapth on one houre, that before never hapt, 268[25]: Hap hapth in one houre, as hath hapt in no houres. Apperson 283; *Oxford* 87; Tilley H741. See **D56, Y10.**

H599 One dies when his **Hour** comes
a1533 Berners *Huon* 285.4–5: Have no doute of me that I shal dye tyll myn houre be come. See **M246.**

H600 One **Hour** makes past labor happy
1515 Barclay *St. George* 102.2572: One hour makyth happy all the labour past.

H601 One may catch in an **Hour** what will savor full sour as long as he lives
a1460 *Towneley Plays* 119.97–8: Ffor thou may cach in an owre That shall (savour) fulle sowre As long as thou lyffys. See **L274, M148, 642.**

H602 To lose in an **Hour** what one might labor for the long year (*varied*)
a1393 Gower *CA* II 327.969–71: For in an houre He lest al that he mai laboure The longe yer. **1523** Berners *Froissart* II 58[16–7]: You myght lese more in a daye, than we have wonne in twenty yere. See **G335.**

H603 As great as a **House**
c1000 Aelfric *Lives* II 104.566: Ylp is ormæte nyten mare þonne sum hus. **a1300** *Alisaunder* 280.5235–6: Hii maden fyres vertuous Fyve hundreth, uche gret als an hous. Taylor *Comparisons* 16: big.

H604 Better to hold a poor **House** than lie in prison in fetters of gold
a1500 *MS. Marginalia* in Hoccleve I 218 n.[1]: Therefore better yt were, a pouer house to holde, Then to lye in preason in fetteres of golde. Robbins-Cutler 512.5. See **M237.**

H605 Buy no **House** before you know your neighbor
a1500 *Disciplina Clericalis* 39[30–1]: Ne bie thou non house bifore that thow knowe thi neighburgh.

H606 He that will build a **House** securely must not set it on the highest hill
897 Alfred *Boethius* 26.23–4: Se þe wille fæst hus timbrian ne sceal he hit no settan up on ðone hehstan cnoll, *Lays of Boethius* 159.4–6: He ne herde þæt on heane munt Monna ænig meahte asettan Healle hroffæste. **a1470** Parker *Dives* A2^{v}[2.17–9]: The hous that standeth hyghe on a hylle is in more tempest than the one in the valaye. See **W344.**

H607 He that will keep a good **House** must ofttimes break a sleep
a1500 *Good Wife N* 215.182–3: He that woll a good house keepe Must ofte-times breake a sleepe. NED Break 29a. See **H610.**

H608 The **House** is surest when the doors are barred
1509 Barclay *Ship* I 110[20]: Also the hous is surest whan the dorys be barryde. See **S697.**

H609 The **Houses** of laborers stand longest
c1025 *Durham Proverbs* 14.33: Tilige(nd)ra hus lencgest standath. (I)nstanter laborantium diutissime stat domus. See **R191.**

H610 It behooves him to do mickle that will look to a good **House**
a1500 *Good Wife N* 214.147–8: Mikell him behoves to doe A good house that will looke to. Apperson 316:10. See **H607.**

H611 Seldom is the **House** poor there God is steward
c1350 *Good Wife E* 158.11: Selde is the hous pouere wher God is stiward. Apperson 251–2.

H612 They reck not whose **House** burns so they may warm them by the coals
1481 Caxton *Reynard* 78[24–6]: They retche not whos(e) hows brenneth, so that they warme them by the coles. Apperson 72:5; *Oxford* 534; Tilley H763.

H613 To be shifted out of **House** and home
1519 Horman *Vulgaria* 422[26]: I am shyft out of house and home at my fathers.

H614 To eat one out of **House** (*varied*)
a1460 *Towneley Plays* 124.245: I were eten outt of howse and harbar. **1469** Paston V 22[11–2]: I eete lyek a horse, of purpose to eete yow owte at the dorys. **1483** *Vulgaria quedam abs Terencio* O7r[9]: They shall soone ete the out of house. **1509** Barclay *Ship* II 93[17]: And ete theyr mayster out of hous. Apperson 177; NED Door 6; *Oxford* 166; Taylor and Whiting 194; Tilley H784.

H615 To mend one **House** and (im)pair another
1546 Heywood *D* 90.52: I will now mend this house, and payre an other, **1555** *E* 159.81. Tilley H774.

H616 When a **House** is fired it is too late to treat of the sparkle that caused it (*varied*)
c1385 Chaucer *TC* iii 856–9: For whan a chaumbre afire is, or an halle, Wel more nede is, it sodeynly rescowe Than to dispute and axe amonges alle How this candele in the strawe is falle. **a1420** Lydgate *Troy* I 369.7870–3: For thow(gh) that men with hornys blowe and pipe Whan an hous is fired in his hete, Of the sparkle to late is to trete That causid al. See **T324.**

H617 Whoso builds his **House** after every man, it shall stand acrook
c1450 *Douce MS.52* 46.25: Who-so byldeth after every man his howse, hit schall stonde a-croke. **c1450** *Rylands MS.394* 97.30. Cf. Tilley D593. See **B221, M115.**

H618 Whoso that builds his **House** all of sallows (*willows*), *etc.*
c1395 Chaucer *CT* III[D] 654–8: Thanne wolde he seye right thus, withouten doute: "Whoso that buyldeth his hous al of salwes, And priketh his blynde hors over the falwes, And suffreth his wyf to go seken halwes, Is worthy to been hanged on the galwes!" **c1417** *Lansdowne MS.762* in *Rel. Ant.* I 233: Who that byldeth his howse all of salos, And prikketh a blynde horsse over the folowes, And suffereth his wif to seke many halos, God sende hym the blisse of everlasting galos! **1486** ?Berners *Boke of St. Albans* F5v. Apperson 71; *Oxford* 68.

H619 The better the **Household** the nobler the guests
c1025 *Durham Proverbs* 13.27: Swa cystigran hiwan swa cynnigran gystas. Tam honestos hospites quam suscipientes esse oportet. See note p. 17.

H620 Full woeful is the **Household** that wants a woman
a1460 *Towneley Plays* 129.420–1: Ffull wofull is the householde That wantys a woman. *Oxford* 722.

H621 To be up in the **House-roof**
1546 Heywood *D* 71.48: He is at three woordes up in the house roufe. Apperson 317; *Oxford* 309; Tilley H797, W783.

H622 A clean-fingered **Housewife** and an idle
1546 Heywood *D* 38.97: A cleane fingred huswyfe, and an ydell, men saie. Apperson 101; Tilley H798.

H623 To make one a **Houve** (*cap*) above a caul (*netted cap*)
c1385 Chaucer *TC* iii 775–6: And maken hym an howve above a calle, I meene, as love another in this while. MED calle 1(b); NED Houve.

H624 To make one a **Houve** of glass (*varied*)
c1300 *Body and Soul* 49 L 374: And madest me an houve of glas. **c1378** *Piers* B xx 171: And thei gyven hym agayne a glasen houve. **c1385** Chaucer *TC* v 469: Fortune his howve entended bet to glaze! **a1400** *Scottish Legends* II 278.227–8: Thu did nocht ellis, I se now, Bot to god mad a clasine how. **a1425** *Celestin* in *Anglia* 1(1877–8) 82.626–7: Coveitise me taughte, fals it was, Thou madeste me an houve of glas. **a1500** *Clerk and the Nightingale II* in Robbins 179.81–2: And sche schal make a glasyn cappe, And to skorn lawth the. NED Houve.

H625 **Howe** (?*prudence*) binds wisdom
c1250 *Hendyng O* 192.6: Howe bind wisdom, *C* 184.11: Hou bind wis man. Kneuer 25–8; Schleich 250–1; Singer III 126–7.

H626 To flee like a **Howlat** chased with crows
a1508 Dunbar *Flyting* 11.219: Than fleis thow lyk ane howlat chest with crawis.

H627 In **Hudder-mudder**
1461 Paston III 289–90: He and hys wyfe and other have blaveryd here of my kynred in hedermoder. **c1522** Skelton *Colyn* I 313–4.69–70: For in hoder moder The Churche is put in faute. NED Hudder-mudder.

H628 In **Hugger-mugger**
c1516 Skelton *Magnificence* 13.387: As men dare

speke it hugger mugger. **1528** More *Heresyes* 184 B[14–5]: Not alway whispered in hukermoker, 281 C[8–9]: They . . . teache in hucker mucker, **1532** *Confutacion* 341 D[13]: Kepte in hucker mucker, 355 G[16–7]. **1556** Heywood *Spider* 46[6]: Then here (in hucker mucker) me to murder. NED Hugger-mugger; *Oxford* 309; Tilley H805; Whiting *Drama* 350:639. See **H402.**

H629 That would I see, quod blind **Hugh**
1533 Heywood *Pardoner* B3r[34]: Mary, that wolde I se, quod blynde hew. Apperson 55; *Oxford* 570; Tilley G84. See **M51.**

H630 By **Hums** and ha's
1469 Paston V 21[12–3]: He wold have gotyn it aweye by humys and by hays, but I wold not so be answeryd. NED Hum sb.[1] 2a.

H631 Hence to **Humber**
a1450 *Partonope* 136.3881–2: For the marchandys hynnes to Humbere The valewe ther-off cowthe not nummbere.

H632 Too much **Humbleness** makes people over bold
a1475 Ashby *Dicta* 76.748–9: For to meche humblesse, used of olde, Make the meche people to be over bolde. See **H426.**

H633 Hot **Humor** (*?affection*) that is parted will sooner wax cold
c1400 *Seven Deadly Sins* in Wyclif *SEW* III 131[3–4]: Ffor hote humoure that is partid wil souner waxe colde. See **E216, H554, S307.**

H634 What one wins in the **Hundred** he loses in the shire (*varied*)
1520 Whittinton *Vulgaria* 93.10–1: What so ever thou wynnes in the shyre thou shall lese it in the hondreth. **1546** Heywood *D* 92.76: What ye wan in the hundred ye lost in the sheere. Apperson 317; *Oxford* 387; Tilley H809.

H635 Full hard is **Hunger** in hale (*healthy*) maw
a1400 *Scottish Legends* I 169.653–4: Fore It is sad in elderys saw: "Ful harde is hungyre in hale maw." **c1420** Wyntoun II 159.199–200: For hym thoucht that ane hard thraw, Hungyr than in til hail maw. Tilley H816; Whiting *Scots* I 192.

H636 He can have you who calls for you, said the man who saw **Hunger** going away
c1025 *Durham Proverbs* 15.45: Age þe se þe æfter cige, cwæþ se þe geseah hungor of tune faran. Te habe(a)t qui te vocet, ait qui famem vidit abeuntem.

H637 **Hunger** breaks the stone wall (*varied*)
c1420 Page *Siege* 164.602: Ffor hunger brekythe the stone walle. **c1450** *Douce MS.52* 46.28: Hungur brekyth stone and walle. **a1500** *Guy*[4] 19.295–6: But I have heard say—and yet I shall —That hunger breaketh a stone-wall. **1546** Heywood *D* 55.19: Hunger perseth stone wall, **1556** *Spider* 253[12]: Manie say oft, honger perseth the stone wall. Apperson 317–8; *Oxford* 310; Taylor and Whiting 195–6; Tilley H811.

H638 **Hunger** chases the wolf out of the wood
1483 Caxton *Cato* B6v[4–5]: For thus as hunger chaceth the wolfe out of the wode, thus sobrete chaseth the devyl fro the man. Apperson 318; Jente 391; *Oxford* 310; Tilley H812.

H639 **Hunger** drops out of his nose
1546 Heywood *D* 49.265: Hunger droppeth even out of bothe their noses, **1555** *E* 180.192: Hunger droppeth out of his nose. Apperson 318; *Oxford* 310; Tilley H813.

H640 **Hunger** fights within and may overcome without iron
1489 Caxton *Fayttes* 62.7–8: For honger fighteth within forth and may over come wythout yron, 101.2–3: Grete wisedom it is to constrayne hys enemye more by honger than by yron, 128.1–2. See **C74, H645.**

H641 **Hunger** has no skill (*discrimination*)
c1515 Barclay *Eclogues* 81.760: Or (*butter*) worse then thy chese, but hunger hath no skill.

H642 **Hunger** is the best sauce (*varied*)
a1375 *William* 66.1181–3: Thei ete at here ese as thei might thanne, Boute salt other sauce or any semli drynk, Hunger hadde hem hold. **c1375** Barbour *Bruce* I 71.539–41: And thai eyt it with full gud will, That soucht (nane othir) salss thar-till Bot appetyt, that oft men takys. **a1376** *Piers* A vii 248–9: Ete not, ich hote the, til hunger the take, And sende the sum of his sauce to saver the the betere. **c1390** Chaucer *CT* VII 2834[B4024]: Of poynaunt sauce hir neded never a deel. **a1500** *Ancrene* (*Royal*) 19.16–7: Let hunger provok thin appetit and no lustynes, 21–3: Hungor and salte ar sause god ynogh to an hole man for any mete, as Seyn Bernard seys. **a1500** *MS. Marginalia* in Hoccleve I 189 n. 5: Socrates: The best sauce in the worlde for meats is to be hungrye. **c1515** Barclay *Eclogues* 80.743: Make hunger thy sause be thou never so nice, **c1523** *Mirrour* 61[22]: Let hunger be thy sauce thy meates to season. Apperson 318; *Oxford* 310; Skeat 127; Smith 156; Taylor and Whiting 195; Tilley H819; Whiting *Scots* I 132: Appetite. See **M473, S63.**

H643 **Hunger** makes hard beans (bones) sweet (soft)
c1450 *Douce MS.52* 46.29: Hungur makyth harde benys swete. **c1475** *Rawlinson MS. D 328* 123.63: Hungger makyth arde benis honi suete. **a1500** *Additional MS.37075* 278.24: Honger makyth hard bens hony swete. **a1500** Hill 133.55: Hungre maketh harde bones softe. **1549** Heywood *D* 40.173: Hunger makth hard beanes sweete. Apperson 318; Jente 389; *Oxford* 310; Tilley H822; Walther I 849.6804. See **S753.**

H644 **Hunger** passes kind (*nature*) and love
c1420 Page *Siege* 160.521: But hunger passyth kynde and love. **c1430** *Brut* II 401.21–2: And we may preve by that pepull there, that houngir passithe kyndenesse and eke love.

H645 There **Hunger** is hot, hearts are feeble
a1400 *Destruction of Troy* 168.5171: And there hongur is hote, hertis ben febill. See **F390, H640.**

H646 The **Hungry** and the full sing not one song
1492 *Salomon and Marcolphus* 10[22–3]: The hungery and the fulle synge not oon songe. Cf. Tilley B290, S676. See **F697, W551.**

H647 The **Hungry** dies as well as the full fed
1492 *Salomon and Marcolphus* 10[24–5]: The hungery dyeth as wele as the full fedd.

H648 A **Hunter's** mass
c1400 *Order of Priesthood* in Wyclif *EW* 168[5–6]: And blabren out matynys and masse as hunteris with-outen devocion. NED Hunter 5d.

H649 To hunt as **Hunter** does the hare
a1325 *Pers of Birmingham* in Heuser 162.9[5–6]: With streinth to hunt ham ute, As hunter doth the hare.

H650 To set out spears like a **Hurcheon** (*hedgehog*)
c1375 Barbour *Bruce* I 312.353–4: That, as ane hyrcheoune, all his rout Gert set out speris all about. NED Hurcheon.

H651 To have one on the **Hurdle**
1546 Heywood *D* 75.175: Then have ye him on the hyp, or on the hyrdell. NED Hurdle 1c.

H652 He that has a privy **Hurt** is loath to have an outward shame
a1470 Malory I 396.15–6: For he that hath a prevy hurte is loth to have a shame outewarde.

H653 The **Hurt** of one makes the other happy
c1475 Henryson *Fables* 39.1065: The hurt off ane happie the uther makis. See **G104, 329, M486, O42.**

H654 A little **Hurt** in the eye derves (*troubles*) more than a mickle in the heel
a1200 *Ancrene* 61.3–4: Alutel hurt i then ehe derveth mare then deth a muchel i the hele, for the flesch is deaddre, **a1500** (*Royal*) 23.9–10: As a litel hurt in the egh greves more then a grete stroke on the bake.

H655 Such **Husband** such wife
1474 Caxton *Chesse* 35[7]: Suche husbond suche wyf. See **W239.**

I

I1 As cold as (any) **Ice**
c1300 *Guy*[1] 30.515: That y wex cold as ise. **c1300** *Owayne Miles (Auchinleck)* 105.93[4]: And cold it was as ani ise. **c1330** *Owayne Miles (Ashmole)* in Horstmann *Altenglische Legenden 1875* 165.378: Caldore was then eny is. **a1393** Gower *CA* III 173.245–6: Ne frosen ys upon the wal More inly cold than I am al. **a1405** Lydgate *Black Knight* in *MP* II 392.234. **c1440** *Revelation* in *Yorkshire Writers* I 387[22]: any. **a1450** *Generydes A* 237.7683–4. **a1450** *Love that god loveth* in Kail 73.24. **c1450** La Tour-Landry 188.26–7: ony. **1481** Caxton *Mirror* 112[28], *Reynard* 37[26–7]. **a1500** *Ghostly Battle* in *Yorkshire Writers* II 432[20–1]: any. **a1500** *Peterborough Lapidary* in *Lapidaries* 92[27]: anny. **c1515** Barclay *Eclogues* 110.97. Apperson 106; Taylor and Whiting 197; Tilley I2; Whiting *Scots* I 192.

I1a **Ice-cold**
a750 *Seafarer* in *Exeter Book* 143.14: Iscealdne sæ, 19. **c897** Alfred *Lays of Boethius* 197.3: Iscalde sæ. Taylor and Whiting 197; Whiting *Ballad* 28.

I2 He was never wise that went on the **Ice**
c1450 *Douce MS.52* 48.46: He was never wyse, That went on the yse. Cf. Whiting *Scots* I 192.

I3 To melt away like **Ice** of winter
c1395 *WBible* Wisdom xvi 29: The hope of an unkynde man schal melte awei as iys of wyntir, and schal perische as superflu watir.

I4 To stand on the **Ice**
c1412 Hoccleve *Regement* 33.907–9: Be war, rede I! thou standist on the ys: It hath ben seen, as weleful and as wys As thou, han slide.

I5 To vanish like the **Ice**
1509 Barclay *Ship* I 282[21]: Theyr hope vanyssheth as doth the . . . yce.

I6 **Idleness** is the nurse (mother, gate) of the vices (evils, sins) (*varied*)
a1050 Defensor *Liber* 89[7–9]: Idelnysse soðlice underþeodde raþe galscype undersmyhð æmtigne galnys raþe ofþrycð. **a1200** *Ancrene* 216.16: Of idelnesse awakeneth muchel flesches fondunge. **a1200** Lawman II 624–5.24911–22: For idelnesse is luther On ælchere theode, For idelnesse maketh mon His monscipe leose; Ydelnesse maketh cnihte For-leosen his irihte; Idelnesse græitheth Feole uvele craften; Idelnesse maketh leosen Feole thusend monnen; Thurh etheliche (?ideliche) dede Lute men wel spedeth. **c1300** Robert of Gloucester I 282.4022–4: Vor wanne men beth al ydel that er batailes soghte, Hor ydelnesse hom ssal bringe to sunne of lecherye, To taverne and to sleuthe and to hasardrie. **a1338** Mannyng *Chronicle A* I 405.11565–70: Ffor Idelnesse norischeth but ivel; Temptacion of flesche and of the devel; Idelnesse maketh man ful slow, And doth prowesse falle right low; Idelnesse norischeth lecherye, And doth us tente to such folye. **c1340** *Ayenbite* 206[24–6]: Thanne the writinge zayth thet idelnesse . . . is maystresse of moche quead. **c1380** Chaucer *CT* VIII[G] 1–3: The ministre and the norice unto vices, Which that men clepe in Englissh ydelnesse, That porter of the gate is of delices, **c1390** VII 1589[B2779]: For Salomon seith that "ydelnesse techeth a man to do manye yveles," X[I] 714: Thanne comth ydelnesse, that is the yate of alle harmes. An ydel man is lyk to a place that hath no walles; the develes may entre on every syde, or sheten at hym at discovert, by temptacion on every syde. **a1393** Gower *CA* II 330.1086–9: Ther is yit on, which Ydelnesse Is cleped, and is the Norrice In mannes kynde of every vice, Which secheth eases manyfold, III 357–8.4384–6: And worldes ese, as it is told, Be weie of kinde is the norrice Of every lust which toucheth vice.

c1395 *WBible* II Kings xi 1 *gloss:* For the poete seith, If thou takist away idilnessis, the craftis of coveitise, that is, of leccherie, perischiden, Ecclesiasticus xxxiii 29: Idilnesse hath taughte miche malice. **a1400** *Scottish Legends* I 1.1–5: Catone sais, that suthfaste thing is, That Idilnes giffis nourysingis To vicis. Tharefor, quha-sa wil be Vertuise suld Idilnes fle, As sais "the romance of the rose," II 313.311–2: And welth had and Idilnes, That drew hyme in-to wantones. **c1400** *Lay Folks' Catechism* 95.1389–91: For ydylnesse . . . is witte wyssynge and wey to al maner synnes and vices. **c1410** Edward of York *Master* 6[36]: Ydelnesse is foundement of alle vices and of synnes. **c1420** Wyntoun IV 151.263–4: That thai sulde noucht for idilnes Fal in til ewil thowlesnes. **1422** Yonge *Governaunce* 158.3–5: For holy write sayth Ociositas inimica est anime, et radyx viciorum, That is to say, "Idylnysse is the enemy of the Sowle, and rote of vicis." **a1425** *Daily Work* in *Yorkshire Writers* I 139[5]: Idelnesse is norice til all vices. **a1439** Lydgate *Fall* I 131.4685–6: Idilnesse, Mooder off vicis, 263–4.2249–51: Moodir off vices, callid idilnesse, Which off custum ech vertu set aside In ech acourt wher she is maistresse, 271.2520: Fond idilnesse mooder off vices alle, 2527, II 358. 1058–60: Idilnesse, . . . For she off vices is a cheeff maistresse, III 794.696–7: And ground of al, as cheef(e) porteresse, Texile vertu was froward idilnesse. **c1440** *Daily Work* in *Yorkshire Writers* I 314[9]: Ydilnes es a vyce that wyrkes mekill evyll, for it nuresche to all that evyll es. **c1440** Scrope *Epistle of Othea* 71[2–3]: And Arystotle seith that ydilnes ledyth a man to all inconveniences, 77[31–2]: And a wyse man seith, "Idilnes engendyrth idylnes (*for* ignorance) and errour." **a1449** Lydgate *Dietary* in *MP* II 706.140–1: Slombryng ydilnesse, Which of al vices is cheeff port(e)resse, *Epistle* in *MP* I 18.132: That moder of vyces is wilful ydelnesse, *Fabules* in *MP* II 571.135: Vyces all procede of idelnesse. **1450** *Dicts* 290.19–20: Idelnes engenderithe ignoraunce, and ignoraunce errour. **c1450** Capgrave *Lives* 55.29: Ydilnesse, whech is step-modir of all vertu. **c1450** *Epistle of Othea* 99.8–9: Therfor seyth aristotle: Ydelnes bryngeth in all inconveniences. **1471** Caxton *Recuyell* I 4.3–4: Ydlenes whyche is moder and nourysshar of vyces, II 503.1: In eschewyng of ydlenes moder of all vices. **a1475** *Tree* 147.14–5: Ydilnes . . . is the yate of all vices and namly of carnel vices. **c1475** *Rawlinson MS. D 328* 125.82: Off all y-dellys commyt hall myscheffe. Omne malum pertulit ociositas e pro ocio devenit omne malum. **c1475** *St. Anne* (2) 92.60–1: Ffor idylnes ys nought in no degre, The moder of vyce ys, I am in suerte. **c1475** *Thewis* 184.120: Fore mekill ill cummys of ydilnes. **1483** Caxton *Cato* C2ᵛ[23–4]: Slouthfulnesse whiche is moder and nourice of alle synnes, G2ᵛ[1–2]: Ydlenesse and slouthfulnesse, moder of al synnes. **1483** *Quatuor Sermones* 35[27–8]: Fle ydelnesse for it is enemye of cristen sowlis, stepmoder to goodnes . . . and the key of all vyces. **c1483** Caxton *Dialogues* 3.12–3: Flee ydlenes, smal and grete, For all vices springen therof, **1484** *Royal Book* C2ʳ[4]: Flee ydlenes whyche is cause of alle evyl, R4ʳ⁻ᵛ: Ydlenesse . . . is maystresse of many evylles. **1491** *Rule of St. Benet* (3) 121.29–30: Idylnesse, the norisshe of al synnes. **c1497** Medwall *Fulgens* F5ᵛ[22]: Idelnes the causer of syn. **a1500** *Leconfield Proverbs* 482[35]: Idilnes whiche in youthe is moder of all vice. **a1500** Medwall *Nature* I2ʳ[11–3]: Idelnes . . . ys the very moder and maysters of syn. **c1500** Betson *Treatyse* C2ʳ[20–1]: Beware of ydelnes the whiche is moder of all synne and unclennesse. **c1500** ?Bradshaw *Radegunde* 4[14–5]: Ydelnesse Whiche to all vyce is rote and maistresse. **c1500** *Lyfe of Roberte* 262.1136: Idlenes to myscheif many a one doth brynge. **c1500** *Passetyme* in Stevens *Music* 344.2[5–7]: Idelnes Ys cheff mastres Of vices all. **1506** Barclay *Castell* A2ʳ[6]: Idelnes moder of all adversyte. **a1507** Dunbar *Dance* 122.81: And Ydilnes did him (*Lechery*) leid. **1509** Barclay *Ship* I 18[7–8]: Ydilnes whyche (as saint Bernard sayth) is moder of al vices. **1509** Hawes *Convercyon* A2ʳ[20–1]: For ydlenesse, the grete moder of synne, Every vyce is redy to lette ynne. **a1520** Whittinton *Vulgaria* 41.6: Idelnes . . . is the nourysshe of all vyces. **c1520** Walter *Spectacle* A1ᵛ[1]: Ydelnesse is rote of all vyces. **c1525** ?Heywood *Gentylnes* 121.942–3: Idylnes, Whych is the moder of vyce and wretchydnes. **1532** Berners *Golden Boke* 243.4141–3: Ydelnesse . . . whiche openeth the gate to all vyces, **a1533** *Arthur* iii[5–6]: Ydelnesse is reputed to be the moder of al vices. **1533** Heywood *Weather* D1ᵛ[26–7]: Lest vyce myght enter on every syde, Whyche hath fre entre where ydylnesse doth reyne. Apperson 322; *Oxford* 313; Smith 157; Taylor and Whiting 198; Tilley I13; Whiting *Drama* 104, 135, 157, 247, *Scots* I 192–3. See **O14, S392.**

I7 Rather ill occupied than in **Idleness**
1556 Heywood *E* 129.60.6–7: That in thee, er idelnesse shalbe spied, Thou wilt yet rather be ill occupied. Cf. Tilley I7, 8. See O15.

I8 **Ignorance** is fountain and mother of all evils
1483 Caxton *Cato* I2ʳ[12]: Ignoraunce is fontayne

and moder of alle evyls. Cf. *Oxford* 313; Tilley I18.

I9 **Ignorance** shall excuse (no man)
c1412 Hoccleve *Regement* 92.2549: Excuse schal hym naght his ignorance. *Oxford* 314; Tilley I19.

I10 Cast (*plan*) not to wreak (*avenge*) all **Ill**
c1450 *Fyrst thou sal* 91.170: Caste the not al yll to wreke. See **W718.**

I11 He that can (*knows*) **Ill** might as well learn goodness
1509 Barclay *Ship* I 47[7]: He that can yll as well myght lerne goodnes.

I12 If one does **Ill** evil shall he speed
a1400 *How to hear Mass* 498.206: Yif thou do ille, uvel schalt thou spede.

I13 **Ill** speaks ill
1435 Misyn *Fire* 35.26: Yll treuly yll spekis. Cf. Apperson 326: Ill will; Whiting *Drama* 84.

I14 Some may better suffer **Ill** seven years than weal a half year
a1500 *Proverbs of Salamon* 195.5.7–8: Some vii yeere suffur may bettur ylle Than halfe yeere weele as he dyd before.

I15 They that think no **Ill** are soonest beguiled
1546 Heywood *D* 77.250: For they that thinke none yll, are soonest begylde. Smith 286; Tilley T221.

I16 To suffer a less **Ill** to let (*prevent*) a more mischief (*varied*)
a1425 *Metrical Paraphrase OT* 23.10221–4: Syr, yt is wysdom, And wys men hath bene lefe To suffer A lese yll (*var.* evyl) com And (*var.* to) lett (a) more myschefe, 61.11557–8: Suffer sall we A lese harme forto lett a more. See **E193.**

I17 We may do much **Ill** ere we do much worse
1549 Heywood *D* 48.246: We maie doo much ill, er we doo much wars. Apperson 155:21; *Oxford* 149; Tilley I25.

I18 **Ill-will** makes the worst of everything
c1515 Barclay *Eclogues* 108.36: For ill will maketh the worst of every thing. Cf. Apperson 326; *Oxford* 317; Tilley I41.

I19 As dry as an **Image**
1480 Caxton *Ovyde* 26[18–9]: She was Drye and lene as an ymage. Taylor and Whiting 198.

I20 As dumb as an **Image**
a1430 Lydgate *Pilgrimage* 376.13902–3: Ffor they be dowmb in ther spekyng, As an ymage wrouht off Tre or ston.

I21 As stable as an **Image**
c1500 *O beauteous braunche* in *Anglia* 72(1954) 402.20: But stable as an Ymage.

I22 As stark (*stiff*) as an **Image**
c1425 *St. Elizabeth of Spalbek* 108.2–3: Alle starke as an ymage of tree or stoon, 111.44: Alle starke as an ymage.

I23 As still as an **Image**
a1400 *Romaunt B* 2408: Styl as an ymage of tree.

I24 A good **Imp** (*shoot*) brings forth good fruit
a1533 Berners *Huon* 12.7–9: I have harde say that a good Impe bryngethe forth good freute. See **T465.**

I25 An **Imp** savors ever of its root
1464 Hardyng 181[6–10]: (Or what kynd of) ympe in gardein or in frith Ymped is, in stocke fro whence it came It savourith ever, and (is) nothyng to blame; For of his rote frome whiche he dooth out spryng, He must ever tast and savour in eatyng. See **F309.**

I26 Light **Impressions** are lightly ready to the flight
c1385 Chaucer *TC* ii 1238–9: For-whi men seith, "impressiounes lighte Ful lightly ben ay redy to the flighte." Apperson 326, 365, 588; *Oxford* 367, 604. See **C384.**

I27 As sweet as (any) **Incense**
a1500 *Imitatione* (*1*) 135.9–10: Smelling muche swetter than eny soot encence. **c1500** Betson *Treatyse* B6v[18–9]: Grutche not ayenst adversyte, but take it as swete as encence. **1502** *Imitatione* (2) 247.39–40: Gyvynge a more swete odour unto thy goodnes than incense by fyer.

I28 As good is an **Inch** as an ell
1546 Heywood *D* 95.166–7: As good is an inche As an ell. Apperson 327; *Oxford* 319; Tilley I47.

I29 For each **Inch** to quit (*return*) a span
a1500 *Good Counsel* in *Bannatyne* II 145.7: And for ilk inche he will the quyt a span, 21.

I30 An **Inch** breaks no square
1555 Heywood *E* 147.4: An inche breakth no square. Apperson 65; *Oxford* 319; Tilley I54.

I31 Of an **Inch** to make a large span (an ell)
a1393 Gower *CA* II 66.1112–3: And of an ynche a large spanne Be colour of the pees thei made. **c1450** Capgrave *Katharine* 129.819: Ye shal not make an elne of an unch.

I32 To set more by an **Inch** of one's will than an ell of his thrift (*varied*)

1520 Whittinton *Vulgaria* 91.34–5: Many a man setteth more by an ynche of his wyl than an ell of his thryfte. **1546** Heywood *D* 95.163–4: Ye liked then better an ynche of your wyll Than an ell of your thrift. *Oxford* 319; Tilley I50.

I33 When I gave you an **Inch** you took an ell (*varied*)
1534 More *Passion* 1305 AB: He . . . never gyveth halfe an ynch of pleasure, withoute an whole elle of payne. **1546** Heywood *D* 95.168: For whan I gave you an ynche, ye tooke an ell. Apperson 327; *Oxford* 238; Taylor and Whiting 198; Tilley I49.

I34 By one **Inconvenience** another is chastised
1489 Caxton *Fayttes* 254.38–255.2: A comon proverbe that sayth that by an inconvenyent is chastysed another inconvenient, also by the same hurt is another hurt repayred.

I35 From hence to **Ind** (*India*) (*varied*)
a1300 *Richard* 165.1641–2: Hennes to the lond off Ynde, Betere thenne schalt thou non fynde, 265.3391 (*var.*): The best to Inde att this tyme. **c1300** *Beves* 61.1276: Though he be bi-yende Ynde! **c1300** *Guy*[1] 450 A 88.4: From henne to Ynde that cite. **c1300** *Havelok* 40.1085: Thouh y souhte hethen in-to Ynde. **c1300** *Reinbrun* 639.24.7: Betwene this and the lond of Ynde. **a1350** *Seven Sages C* 78.2274: Thar es none swilk fra hethin to Ynde, 100.2943: For to seke fra hethin till Ynde. **1369** Chaucer *BD* 888–9: To gete her love no ner nas he That woned at hom, than he in Ynde, **c1390** *CT* VI[C] 721–2: For I ne kan nat fynde A man, though that I walked into Ynde. **a1400** ?Chaucer *Rom. A* 624: Although he sought oon in-tyl Ynde. **c1400** *Laud Troy* I 76.2559–60: A ffebler herte schulde ye not ffynde Thow ye sought henne into Inde. **c1408** Lydgate *Reson* 63.2362: Thogh men soughten in-to ynde. **a1450** *Partonope* 239. 6208–9: A ffeyrer, a semylyer shall no man fynde, Thowe a man soghte to the grette Ynde, 470.11906–7. **c1450** *Chaunce* 8.129: In al this worlde un to the gretter ynde. **a1500** *Assembly* 395.482–3: As I suppose, fro this countrey til Inde, Another suche it were right fer to finde! **a1513** Dunbar *Of Content* 144.6: Quho had all riches unto Ynd. Whiting *Scots* I 193.

I36 From **Ind** to the Oxlyane
a1400 *Ipomadon A* 8.181–2: As worthy a corte she holdes an, As ys fro Ynde to the Oxlyane (*French:* Orient).

I37 As black as **Inde** (*indigo*)
a1425 *St. Robert* 55.434: Thre men blakker than ynd. **a1470** Malory I 31.28–9: Than he com on so faste that his felyship semed as blak as inde.

I38 As blue as (blee [*color*] of) **Inde**
a1300 *Alisaunder* 281.5263: Her visages ben blew so ynde. **c1380** *Pearl* 3.76: Of bolles as blwe as ble of Ynde. **c1400** Mandeville *Travels* 31.5.

I38a **Inde-blue**
a1450 *Agnus* 130.14–5: The lef of this herbe is ynde blew. **c1516** Skelton *Magnificence* 49.1553: The streynes of her vaynes as asure inde blewe.

I39 The **Indignation** of a prince is death
1475 *Stonor Letters* I 156[19–20]: The indyngnacion of a prince ys dethe. **1486** ?Berners *Boke of St. Albans* F5[r]: The secunde is thindignacion of a prince—Quia indignacion regis vel principis mors est. See **T124.**

I40 All **Infirmity** comes of too much or too little
a1449 Lydgate *Dietary* in *MP* II 704.77–80: Off mykil or litel cometh al infirmyte, Attween thes too for lak of governaunce, Dryve out a mene, excesse or scarsete, Set thi botaill upon temperaunce. See **E199, 203, M454.**

I41 The worst **Infortune** is to remember past prosperity (*varied*)
c1385 Chaucer *TC* iii 1625–8: For of fortunes sharpe adversitee The worste kynde of infortune is this, A man to han ben in prosperitee, And it remembren, whan it passed is. **1556** Heywood *Spider* 33[17–8]: Of pleasure past, remembraunce doth alwaie The pinche of present payne, right much augment. Smith 203; Tilley M1010.

I42 **Ingratitude** is the worst of all vices
a1439 Lydgate *Fall* III 718.1651–2: For of al vicis, shortli to conclude, Werst of alle is ingratitude. Smith 158; Tilley I66.

I43 As black as **Ink**
c1515 Barclay *Eclogues* 143.96: At every tempest they be as blacke as inke. **a1533** Berners *Arthur* 476[13–4]: Thei are as blacke as ony ynke. Apperson 51; Taylor and Whiting 200; Tilley I73. See **A181, B345.**

I43a **Ink-black**
1546 Heywood *D* 68.77: Ynke blacke . . . face.

I44 **Ink** is all black and has an ill smack
1546 Heywood *D* 68.68: Inke is all blacke And hath an ill smacke, No man will it drinke nor eate, 74: Blacke inke is as yll meate, as blacke pepper is good. Tilley I74. See **P139, S440.**

I45 To keep some **Ink** in one's pen
a1500 *Piers of Fullham* 10.230–1: Kepe alwey sum ynke in thy pene To wryte with all thynges that bere charge. Apperson 327; Tilley I75.

I46 To get an **Inkling**
1546 Heywood *D* 90.72–3: Or that by gesse had got an inklyng Of hir hoord. Tilley I79.

I47 Whoso comes late to his **Inn** shall early forthink (*be displeased*)
c1450 *Douce MS.52* 48.48: Who-so comyth late to his in, schall erly forthynke. **c1450** *Rylands MS.394* 98.5: to hynne. Jente 339; *Oxford* 351.

I48 To be high in the **Instep**
1546 Heywood *D* 47.209: He is . . . hy in thinstep, **1555** *E* 188.233. Apperson 301; *Oxford* 294; Taylor and Whiting 200; Tilley I84.

I49 A false **Intent** under a fair pretence has caused many an innocent to die
c1475 Henryson *Fables* 100.2918–9: Ane fals Intent under ane fair pretence Hes causit mony Innocent for to de. See **E97.**

I50 The **Intent** gives every good deed its right name
c1450 *Myroure of oure Ladye* 60[9–10]: For thentente gyveth every good dede hys ryght name. See **W267.**

I51 The **Intent** is all
c1385 Chaucer *TC* v 1630: Th' entente is al. **c1412** Hoccleve *Regement* 58.1596: The entente is al. See **W267.**

I52 He that cannot refrain his **Ire** has no power over his wit
1477 Rivers *Dictes* 22[2–3]: He that can not refrayne his ire hath no power ovir his witte. Apperson 10; Tilley A246. See **I62, W703.**

I53 He that girds (*strikes*) with great **Ire** often shoots into shame
a1400 *Destruction of Troy* 69.2070–4: Thow se not that sothely said ys of olde, And oft happes to hit qwo so hede tas:—"He that girdis with grete yre his grem for to venge, Ofte shapis hym to shote into shame ferre, With hoge harmes to have, and his hert sarre." (*The passage in which this appears is labelled "A Proverbe," but eleven lines before the quotation.*) Cf. Smith 8. See **S193, W706.**

I54 **Ire** distroubles (*disturbs*) the thought
a1400 *Scottish Legends* II 448.213–6: For Ire distroblis sa the thocht, That suthfastly deyme ma it nocht, Thocht he war nevire sa wyse a kyng, As cattowne sais in his teching. **c1450** *Cato* (*Sidney*) 22.245–6: For ire disturbleth so thi thout, That sein the sothe wel mai it nout. **a1500** *Ancrene* (*Royal*) 30.28–9: A man that is malyciously wroth is for the tyme half wode, and as caton seith *Ira impedit animam, &.* See **I62, W704, 705.**

I55 As hard as **Iron**
c1000 Aelfric *Lives* I 294.165: Seo heofen bið swa heard eow swa isen. **c1330** *Degare* 80.362: His hide was hard so iren wrout. **c1408** Lydgate *Reson* 32.1189: Harder than Iren. **a1425** *Complaynt of Criste* in *Pol. Rel. and Love Poems* 220.451, 221.489. **a1430** Lydgate *Pilgrimage* 113.4275–6. **a1447** Litchfield *Complaint* 525.525. **1481** Caxton *Godeffroy* 152.3–4. **a1533** Berners *Huon* 98.8. Svartengren 260; Taylor and Whiting 200–1.

I56 As strong as **Iron**
a1300 *Alisaunder* 327.6166–7: A clay hii habbeth, in verrayment, Strong so yrne. **a1450** *Three Middle English Sermons* 76.850: As strong and as durable as any orn (*Latin:* ferrea). **1484** Caxton *Royal Book* N8[r][25]. **1513** Douglas *Aeneid* III 41.211. Svartengren 391.

I57 (The) **Iron** passed through his soul
c850 *Vespasian Psalter* 338 (104.18): Iren ðorhleorde sawle his. **c1340** Rolle *Psalter* 368 (104.17): Yryn passid thorgh his saule. **c1395** *WBible* Psalms civ 18: Irun passide by his soule. *Oxford* 321; Tilley I90.

I58 **Iron** sharpens (whets, files) iron
a1050 Defensor *Liber* 205[3–4]: Isen mid isene byð gescryrped, and mann scyrpð ansyne freond(es) his. **c1395** *WBible* Proverbs xxvii 17: Yrun is whettid bi irun; and a man whettith the face of his frend. **a1475** Fortescue *Dialogue* I 486[13–4]: For as oon iren fyleth another, so a synner chastiseth his semblable. Tilley I91a.

I59 **Iron** (steel) that lies still gathers rust (*varied*)
a1200 *Ancrene* 216.18–9: Irn that lith stille gedereth sone rust. **1489** *Governayle* A7[r][3–4]: Soo iron and ech metall rustyth when it restyth. **c1515** Barclay *Eclogues* 168.769: For lacke of using as stele or yron rust. Tilley I91.

I60 Smite while the **Iron** is hot (*varied*)
c1385 Chaucer *TC* ii 1275–6: Pandare, which that stood hire faste by, Felte iren hoot, and he bygan to smyte, **c1390** *CT* VII 1036[B2226]: Right so as, whil that iren is hoot, men sholden smyte. **c1412** Hoccleve *Regement* 73.2015–6: I took corage, and whiles it was hoot, Un-to my lord the prince thus I wroot (*perhaps not the same*). **a1420** Lydgate *Troy* I 319.6110–2:

The Iren hoot, tyme is for to smyte; And nat abide til that it be colde: For nouther thanne it plie wil nor folde. **c1475** *Court of Sapience* 153.719–20: The blessyd son than knew hys fadyrs wyll, Felt iren hoote and thought tyme for to smyte. **c1489** Caxton *Aymon* I 136.7–8: Ye knowe well That whan the yron is well hoote, hit werketh the better. **c1500** *Melusine* 211.21–2: Whan the yron is hoot it moste be wrought and forged. **1546** Heywood *D* 23.20: Whan thyron is hot strike, **1555** *E* 192.268. Apperson 605–6; Jente 25; *Oxford* 626; Smith 279; Taylor and Whiting 201; Tilley I94; Whiting *Drama* 230, 244, *Scots* I 193.

I61 While the **Iron** is in the wound no plaster may make it sound
a1400 *Cursor* III 1507 F 26924–5: And quilis that irene is in wounde, Is plaster nane mai make hit sounde. See **L172.**

I62 He that is **Irous** and wroth may not deem well
c1390 Chaucer *CT* VII 1125[B2315]: He that is irous and wrooth, he ne may nat wel deme. See **D142, I52, 54, W701.**

I63 "Is" shall turn to "was"
a1400 *Proverbis of Wysdom* 244.27: That now is, shall turne to "was." **c1450** *Fyrst thou sal* 88.49–50: That now is sal turne to was, Ontaken grace al thinge sal pas. See **T301.**

I64 All **Isles** are ill and the "Syciliens" worst of all
1532 Berners *Golden Boke* 377.9353–5: For there is an ancient proverbe that sayth, lyghtly all these ylles ar yl, and the Syciliens worste of all.

I65 **Itch** and ease can no man please
1546 Heywood *D* 67.51: An olde saide sawe, itche and ease, can no man please. Apperson 328; *Oxford* 321–2; Tilley I106.

I66 He that in **Itching** will forbear no scratching must bear the smarting (*varied*)
a1200 *Ancrene* 123.25–6: Hwil the yicchunge least, hit thuncheth god to gnuddin, ah threfter me feleth hit bitterliche smeorten. **1549** Heywood *D* 39.154–6: And he Whom in itching no scratchyng will forbere, He must beare the smartyng that shall folow there. Apperson 328; *Oxford* 172; Tilley I105.

I67 As ruddy as eld (*old*) **Ivory**
c1395 *WBible* Lamentations iv 7: Rodier than elde yver, feirere than safire. *AV:* more ruddie . . . than rubies.

I68 As white as (plain, bone of) **Ivory**
c1380 *Pearl* 7.178: Hyr vysayge whyt as playn yvore. **a1398**(1495) Bartholomaeus-Trevisa L5ᵛ[2.34]: But is whyte nyghe as yvourye. **c1408** Lydgate *Reson* 46.1717: Hys tethe eke white as evory, **a1422** *Life* 493.908–9: And like yvoury that comes fro so fer, His tethe shall be evyn smothe and white. **1445** Claudian *Stilicho* 281.280: Whos toothe was white as boone of Ivore. **a1533** Berners *Arthur* 381[13–4]. Apperson 680; Taylor and Whiting 201; Tilley I109; Whiting *Scots* I 193–4. See **B443, E68, W203.**

I69 To be like **Ivory**
a1325 *Cursor* II 538.9360: And ilk toth es als ywori.

I70 As green as **Ivy(-leaf)**
c1440 Scrope *Epistle* 31[4–5]: Fle ever the fals godes envie, That made Aglaros grennere than ivie, [12]: And grene as ivy leffe. See **E134.**

I71 Not worth an **Ivy-leaf**
a1393 Gower *CA* II 317.586: That al nys worth an yvy lef. Apperson 458; *Oxford* 322.

I72 To pipe in (with) an **Ivy-leaf**
c1385 Chaucer *CT* I[A] 1837–8: That oon of you, al be hym looth or lief, He moot go pipen in an yvy leef, *TC* v 1432–3: But Troilus, thow maist now, est or west, Pipe in an ivy lef, if that the lest! **c1385** Usk 134.50: He may pype with an yvè-lefe; his frute is fayled. **a1400** *Clergy May not Hold Property* in Wyclif *EW* 372[31–3]: The seculer party may go pipe with an yvy lefe for eny lordeschipis that the clerkis will yeve hem agen. **a1410** Lydgate *Churl* in *MP* II 480.276: Thou maist go pypen in a ivy leeff. Apperson 497; *Oxford* 501; Tilley I110.

J

J1 Jack a Thromm's bible
a1475 *Burlesques* in *Rel. Ant.* I 84[2–5]: And therto acordes too worthi prechers, Jack a Throme and Jone Brest-Bale; these men seyd in the bibull that an ill drynker is unpossibull hevone to wynne. **c1516** Skelton *Magnificence* 45.1427: Ye, of Jacke a Thrommys bybyll can ye make a glose, **1523** *Garlande* I 370.208–9: Or reche hym a stole, To syt hym upon, and rede Jacke a thrummis bybille. See **T362.**

J2 Jack and Jill
a1460 *Towneley Plays* 33.336: Sir, for Jak nor for gill will I turne my face. **a1475** *Boke of Curtesy* in *ESt* 9(1885) 62.90: And jangyll neydur wyth Jack ne Jyll. **a1475** *Ludus Coventriae* 314.1237: Thow ther come both jakke and gylle. **c1522** Skelton *Colyn* I 323.323–4: What care they though Gil sweate, Or Jacke of the Noke, 344.857: Bothe Gyll and Jacke at Noke. *Oxford* 322. Cf. Tilley J66. See **J23.**

J3 Jack of Dover (Paris)
c1390 Chaucer *CT* I[A] 4347–8: And many a Jakke of Dovere hastow soold That hath been twies hoot and twies coold. **1533** More *Confutacion* 675 EF: And served you wyth a Jak of Paris, an evyl pye twyse baken. Apperson 163; *Oxford* 323; Tilley J20.

J4 Jack of the Vale
c1516 Skelton *Magnificence* 9.258: Or ellys some jangelynge Jacke of the Vale.

J5 Jack out of office
1546 Heywood *D* 65.13: And Jack out of office she maie bid me walke, **1555** *E* 186.221: He is jacke out of office. Apperson 330; *Oxford* 323; Tilley J23.

J6 Jack Robin is as good as John at the Noke
c1475 Gregory *Chronicle* 190[17–9]: Save only they kepte (no) ordyr among them, for als good was Jacke Robyn as John at the Noke. Cf. *Oxford* 326; Tilley J66. See **A23.**

J7 Jack shall have Jill
c1516 Skelton *Magnificence* 10.286–7: What avayleth Lordshyp, yourselfe for to kyll With care and with thought howe Jacke shall have Gyl? **1546** Heywood *D* 64.2: Al is wel. Jack shall have gill, **1555** *E* 149.12: All shalbe well. Apperson 329; *Oxford* 322–3; Taylor and Whiting 202; Tilley A164.

J8 Jack with the bush
c1515 Barclay *Eclogues* 87.920: Then Jacke with the bush shal taunt thee with a chek. Note p. 245 suggests "Jack in office."

J9 Jack would be a gentleman (if he could speak French)
c1500 Skelton *Comely Coystrowne* I 15.14: Lo, Jak wold be a jentylman, 16.42: For Jak wold be a jentylman, that late was a grome. **1549** Heywood *D* 45.142: Jacke would be a gentleman if he could speake frenche. Apperson 330–1; *Oxford* 324; Tilley J4.

J10 No more power than **Jack** Hare
c1475 Gregory *Chronicle* 233[24–7]: He . . . sayde that no pryste had noo more pouer to hyre confessyon thenn Jacke Hare.

J11 To be common **Jack** to all
1546 Heywood *D* 51.328: I have bene common Jacke to all that hole flocke. Apperson 110; Tilley J7.

J12 To play **Jack** the hare
a1449 Lydgate *Servant* in *MP* II 429.53–4: And thus I pleyde Jacke the Haare And gane to hoppe a newe trace. (Spent money to no purpose, made a fool of one's self.)

J13 Little **Jangling** causes much rest
c1390 Chaucer *CT* IX[H] 349–50: The Flemyng

seith, and lerne it if thee leste, That litel janglyng causeth muchel reste. Apperson 372; J. Grauls and J. F. Vanderheijden "Two Flemish Proverbs in Chaucer's *Canterbury Tales*," *Revue Belge de Philologie et d'Histoire* 13(1934) 745–9; *Oxford* 374; Skeat 290. See **M482.**

J14 **January** and May
c1395 Chaucer *CT* IV[E] 1693–5: That she, this mayden, which that Mayus highte, . . . Shal wedded be unto this Januarie. **1420** Lydgate *Temple* 7.184–5: For it ne sit not unto fressh(e) May Forto be coupled to oold(e) Januari. **a1437** *Kingis Quair* 76.110[2]: Eke Januarye is (un)like to May. Apperson 332, 408; *Oxford* 413; Taylor and Whiting 203; Tilley M768; Whiting *Scots* I 194.

J15 To blow a **Jape** in one's hood
c1385 Usk 89.49–50: Thus goth he begyled of that he sought; in his hode men may blowe a jape. MED blouen v.(1) 7(c). See **G25.**

J16 To jet like a **Jasp**(?)
a1529 Skelton *Garnesche* I 118.17: Lusty Garnysche, lyke a lowse, ye jet full lyke a jaspe. Notes II 182: "Does it mean—wasp?"

J17 As jolly as the (any, a) **Jay**
c1325 *Loveliest Lady* 149.39: Gentil, jolif so the Jay. **c1390** Chaucer *CT* I[A] 4154: As any jay she light was and jolyf. **c1400** *Tundale* 116 (*var.* after 2020): The joly jay. **a1475** *Ludus Coventriae* 154.77: I am jolyere than the jay. **a1500** *Lambewell* 160.512–3: Jolly and Jocund as . . . the Jay that sitts on a bough. **c1516** Skelton *Magnificence* 15.465: And jet it joly as a jay.

J18 A **Jay** may chatter in a golden cage, *etc.*
a1439 Lydgate *Fall* II 554.2953–4: A jay may chatre in a goldene cage, Yit ever sum tech mut folwe of his lynage. See **K30.**

J19 To chatter like (the, a) **Jay(s)**
c1385 Usk 2.29–31: How shulde than a Frenche man born suche termes conne jumpere in his mater, but as the jay chatereth English? **c1395** Chaucer *CT* VIII[G] 1397: They mowe wel chiteren (*vars.* chatteryn, clater, jangle) as doon thise jayes. **a1415** *Lanterne* 56.21–2: Redars . . . janglen her lessouns as jaies chatiren in the cage. **a1440** Burgh *Cato* 306.116: Such jayissh (*Latin:* verbosos) folk. **a1475** *Ludus Coventriae* 353.19: Thei chateryn . . . As they jays were. **a1500** Medwall *Nature* B1^{v}[38]: That other (chatreth) lyke a jay. See **C244, J21.**

J20 To clatter like a **Jay**
a1470 Malory II 805.15: And in his slepe he talked and claterde as a jay.

J21 To jangle like a **Jay**
c1353 *Winner* 26: Fro he can jangle als a jaye. **c1390** Chaucer *CT* II[B] 774: Thou janglest as a jay. **a1400** *Ipomadon A* 180.6312. **c1400** *Plowman's Tale* 172.791. **1402** *Daw Topias* (*Jack*) 104[17], 109[7]: Thou jangelyng jay. **1413** Hoccleve *Balade* I 40.37. **a1430** Lydgate *Pilgrimage* 389.14414. **a1450** *York Plays* 357.265. **c1450** Capgrave *Katharine* 336.2322. **c1450** Holland *Howlat* 74.789: The jangland Ja. **c1450** Idley 210.416. **a1475** Russell *Boke* 119.36. **a1500** ?Ros *La Belle Dame* 322.744. **a1500** *Squire* 7.51. **a1508** Skelton *Phyllyp* I 63.396: The janglynge jay, 90.1269: Of some janglynge jayes. See **J19.**

J22 **Jealousy** is love (*varied*)
c1385 Chaucer *TC* iii 1023–6: Folk now usen To seyn right thus, "Ye, jalousie is love!" And wolde a busshel venym al excusen, For that o greyn of love is on it shove. **c1450** La Tour-Landry 24.19–21: For the wise man saithe that jelosye is a gret ensaumple of love, for he that lovith me not, rechithe not whedir y do well or evell. **a1500** *Quare* 207.436–7: And quhareof long it hath bene said or this, That of hote lufe ay cummith Jelousye.

J23 **Jenken** and Julian
a1500 *London Lickpenny* in *Anglia* 20(1897–8) 416.94: Some sange of Jenken and Julian, to get them selvs mede. *Oxford* 322: Jack. See **J2.**

J24 To differ as far as **Jericho** and Jersey
1556 Heywood *Spider* 171[6–7]: Cause of woorship due to both differ as far, As Jerico and Jersei, in joining jar.

J25 From **Jersey** to Jewry
1556 Heywood *Spider* 369[3]: All my frendes from Jersey to Jurie.

J26 From **Jerusalem** to Burgundy
a1400 ?Chaucer *Rom. A* 554–5: Fro Jerusalem unto Burgoyne Ther nys a fairer nekke, iwys.

J27 He that has once been at **Jerusalem** may lie by authority
1533 More *Confutacion* 726 GH: Menne saye that he which hath been once at Hierusalem maye lye by authoritie, because he shalbe sure seldome to meete anye manne that hath bee there. Cf. Tilley M567, T476. See **P18, R185.**

J28 Thence to **Jerusalem**
1556 Heywood *E* 117.28.32: I thinke thence to Jerusalem.

J29 As black as (any) **Jet**
a1400 *Of erbis* in *Anglia* 18(1895–6) 323.636: Blac polyssyd as geet it is. **a1420** Lydgate *Troy*

I 173.987: Blak as is get, **a1430** *Pilgrimage* 384. 14213. **1440** Palladius 151.697. **a1500** Greene *Carols* 446.3. **1504** Hawes *Example* Ee5[r][23]: Marble, blacke as the gette, **1506** *Pastime* 134.3500: And every tothe as blacke as ony gete. **1560** Heywood *E* 209.23.2. Apperson 51; Taylor and Whiting 204; Tilley J49; Whiting *Scots* I 194.

J29a Jet-black
c1477 Caxton *Curtesye* 7.44: Youre naylis loke they be not gety (*var.* geet) blake. Taylor and Whiting 204.

J30 As bright as **Jet**
c1450 Capgrave *Solace* 50[2–3]: A blak ston polchid as brith as geet.

J31 As white as any **Jet**
c1460 *Satirical Description* 201[1]: Hire teeth been whight as ony jete.

J32 No more like than **Jet** and crystal
a1475 Banester *Guiscardo* 4.49: No more lyke to theme then gete to cristall. See **B331, J35.**

J33 To be hued like **Jet**
a1500 *Ragman Roll* 76.161: O fayr lady, hewyd as ys the gett.

J34 To glister like **Jet**
a1430 Hoccleve *Roundel* II 37–8.4: And as the Jeet hir yen glistren ay, 10, 16, 24.

J35 To put no difference between **Jet** and beryl (crystal)
c1485 *Guiscardo* 70.551: Hyt semeth ye put no dyfference betwene get and berall (*Statelie Tragedie:* christall). See **J32.**

J36 To shine like (the, any) **Jet**
c1390 Chaucer *CT* VII 2861[B4051]: His byle was blak, and as the jeet it shoon. **a1420** Lydgate *Troy* I 277.4645: Whos her was blak, schynyng as doth get. **a1450** *Generydes A* 175.5630–1: And ther-to he shoon As any gete ayeinst the light.

J37 Jawed like a **Jetty**
a1529 Skelton *Elynour* I 96.38: Jawed lyke a jetty.

J38 As false as a (any) **Jew**
1460 *Jack Cade's Proclamation* in James Gairdner *Three Fifteenth-century Chronicles* (CS NS 28, 1880) 97[1]: He is falser than a Jewe or Sarasyn. **a1500** *When men motyth* in *Archiv* 135(1916) 300.8[4]: But all ben false as any jewe.

J39 As vile as a **Jew**
c1325 *Prayer of Penitence* in Brown *Lyrics XIII* 157.29: Ich holde me vilore then a gyw.

J40 It would make a **Jew** rue
a1508 Skelton *Phyllyp* I 61.335–7: And it were a Jewe, It wolde make one rew, To se my sorow new. See **H277.**

J41 Not to deal so with a **Jew**
c1499 Skelton *Bowge* I 47.462: I coude not dele so with a Jew! Cf. Apperson 660: I will use you like a Jew; *Oxford* 684; Tilley J52.

J42 To be worse than a **Jew**
c1326 *Prayer of Penitence* in Brown *Lyrics XIII* 159.29: I holde me wel worse than a jewe. **a1330** *Times of Edward II* (*Bodley*) 189.276: And in this we beth worse than J(e)w or Sarsyn. **1502** *Robert the Devil* C3[v][15]: (I) am wors than a Jewe.

J43 To have no more pity than a **Jew**
c1500 *Lyfe of Roberte* 233.355: For pittye had he no more than a Jue.

J44 Many well counterfeited **Jewels** make the true mistrusted
1513 More *Richard* 67 E[6–8]: As many well counterfaited jewels make the true mistrusted.

J45 As patient as **Job** (*varied*)
c1395 Chaucer *CT* III[D] 436: Sith ye so preche of Jobes pacience. **a1425** *Governance of Lordschipes* 41.18: The pacience of Job. **1509** Barclay *Ship* I 113[4]: As Job als pacyent. **1509** Watson *Ship* B8[v][13]: Also pacyent as Job. *Oxford* 490; Taylor and Whiting 205; Tilley J59.

J46 As poor as **Job**
a1338 Mannyng *Chronicle B* II 323[16]: Als bare was his toure as Job the pouere man. **a1393** Gower *CA* III 15.2505: As povere as Job. **a1400** Wyclif *Sermons* I 407[8–9]: As beggeris and theves ben ofte porer than Joob was. **c1415** *Middle English Sermons* 200.28–9: And be-com as poure as ever was Job. **c1475** Henryson *Fables* 101.2944. **a1500** *Salamon sat and sayde* 291.18: War a man als pouer as jop. **1506** Barclay *Castell* H4[r][18]. Apperson 505; *Oxford* 510; Svartengren 342; Taylor and Whiting 204; Tilley J60; Whiting *Drama* 318:187: bare.

J47 **Job**'s comforter
c1395 *WBible* Job xvi 1–2: Joob answeride, and seide . . . alle ye ben hevy coumfortouris. Apperson 333; *Oxford* 326; Tilley J62.

J48 Come hither **John,** my man
1473 Paston V 187[12–3]: And so I am as he that seythe "Come hyddr John, my man." (The writer does not know what to do.)

J49 **John** Blunt
1508 Dunbar *Tretis* 88.142–3: For all the buddis (*bribes*) of Johne Blunt, quhen he abone clymis, Me think the baid (*wait*) deir abroucht, sa bawch (*feeble*) ar his werkis. *Oxford* 326; Whiting *Scots* I 194.

J50 **John** Drawlatch
1546 Heywood *D* 89.44: To make me John drawlache, or such a snekebill. Apperson 333–4; *Oxford* 327; Tilley J68.

J51 **John,** John, pick a bone
c1475 *Rawlinson MS. D 328* 119.28: Jon Jon pyke a bone to-morrow thu schall pyke none. Johannes johannes opica qui cras os non opicabis nullum.

J52 **John** Long the carrier
1549 Heywood *D* 46.151–2: But for my rewarde, let him be no longer tarier, I will send it him by John Longe the carier. Apperson 334; *Oxford* 327; Tilley J71.

J53 **John** (?Joan) Thomson's man
a1513 Dunbar *To the King* 38–9.4: God gif ye war Johne Thomsounis man! 8, 12, *etc. Oxford* 327; Tilley J73; Whiting *Scots* I 194.

J54 To be out of **Joint**
1415 Hoccleve *Oldcastle* I 14.200: For thow haast been out of joynt al to longe. NED Joint 2; Tilley J75.

J55 As sweet as **Jonathan**
c1303 Mannyng *Handlyng* 142.4211: Who was swetter than Jonatas?

J56 From hence to **Jordan**
a1400 *Ipomadon A* 93.3214–5: A better stede non ther es From hethen to flem Jurdanne.

J57 Not worth a **Jot**
a1500 *Think Before You Speak* in Brown *Lyrics XV* 281.39: Boost ne brage ys worth a Joote. NED Jot sb.[1].

J58 After **Joy** comes woe (*varied*)
c1390 Chaucer *CT* VII 3205[B4395]: For evere the latter ende of joye is wo. **a1393** Gower *CA* II 407.193–4: For every joie bodily Schal ende in wo, III 215.1781: Which endeth al his joie in wo, 360.4461–3: It is a sori lust to lyke, Whos ende makth a man to syke And torneth joies into sorwe. **a1400** *Destruction of Troy* 388.11881–2: Hit is said oftsythes with sere men of elde, The last Joy of joly men Joynys with sorow. **c1400** *Scottish Troy* 247.671–2: For it is nought new certanly Llast Joye that sorow occupye. **a1420** Lydgate *Troy* II 516.4230: For ay the fyn, allas! of Joie is sorwe, III 746.6222–4: But soth is seid, that ay the fyn of Joye Wo occupieth, as men ful ofte se, **c1421** *Thebes* 122.2958: Joye at the gynnyng, the ende is wrechednesse, **c1430** *Dance* 12.64: How that al joye endeth yn hevynesse. **a1456** Sellyng *Evidens* 177.47: For of this worldes eonde the Joye is woo. **1471** Caxton *Recuyell* II 665.15–6: But the custome of fortune is suche that grete joye endeth in tristres and in sorowe. **c1475** Henryson *Fables* 13.290–1: Yit efter joy oftymes cummis cair, And troubill efter grit prosperitie, *Prais of Aige* 186.26: Of erdly joy ay sorow is the end. **a1500** *Court of Love* 420.407: For to moche joye hath oft a wofull end. **a1513** Dunbar *Wowing* 53.50–1: Quhen men dois fleit in joy maist far, Sone cumis wo, or thay be war, *Of the Changes of Lyfe* 141.19: Nixt efter joy aye cumis sorrow, *All Erdly Joy* 145–6.4: All erdly joy returnis in pane, 8, 12, *etc.* **1513** Douglas *Aeneid* II 153.220–1: By the wil I repeyt this verss agane. "Temporal joy endis wyth wo and pane." Apperson 3; *Oxford* 328; Whiting *Scots* I 194–5. See **E80, G102, J61, P255, 263, 265, T302.**

J59 Every **Joy** is meddled (*mixed*) with its pain (*varied*)
c1477 Norton *Ordinall* 35[6]: But that every Joy is medled with his paine. **c1509** *Fyftene Joyes* A2[v][29]: All worldly Joye medled with bytternes. **1525** Berners *Froissart* VI 77[35]: None that is joyfull, but somtyme is sorie and troubled. Cf. Apperson 448: No joy without annoy; *Oxford* 328; Smith 160; Tilley J85. See **B351, D58, F532, G103, M583, S137, 516, 947, V28.**

J60 If one has **Joy** one moment he shall have twain of sorrow for it
a1529 Skelton *Boke of Three Fooles* I 205[9–10]: Yf you have joye one only momente, thou shalt have twayne of sorow for it.

J61 **Joy** after woe and woe after gladness (*varied*)
c1385 Chaucer *CT* I[A] 2839–41: That knew this worldes transmutacioun, . . . Joye after wo, and wo after gladnesse. **c1385** Usk 82.180: Trewly, next the ende of sorowe anon entreth joy. **c1390** Chaucer *CT* II[B] 421–4: O sodeyn wo, that evere art successour To worldly blisse, spreynd with bitternesse! The ende of the joye of oure worldly labour! Wo occupieth the fyn of oure gladnesse. **a1420** Lydgate *Troy* I 157.471–2: For ay the fyn of wo Mote be gladnes whan that sorwe is go, **1420** *Temple* 17.397: And joy awakith whan wo is put to flight, 411: Thus ever joy is ende and fine of paine. **a1425** *Metri-*

cal Paraphrase OT 27.6591: For aftur wo all sall be well. **1440** Palladius 22.111-2: And aftir woo, To joy, and aftir nyght, to sey good morow. **a1470** Malory I 436.4-6: And bade her be of goode comforte, for she sholde have joy aftir sorow. **a1506** Hawes *Pastime* 75.1927: Joye cometh after whan the payne is paste, 148.3915: Joy cometh after whan the sorowe is past, 175.4678: Joye cometh after whan the payne is gone, 182.4867: The thyrde was Joye after grete hevynes, **1511** *Comforte* A4r[11]: Joye cometh after, whan the payne is gone. Skeat 154, 225; Whiting *Scots* II 157. See **B52, 325, J58, P269, S973, W133.**

J62 Little **Joy** is soon done
a1500 Greene *Carols* 382.1: Lytyll joye ys son done, 2, 3, 4.

J63 None has perfect **Joy** if it come not of love
1484 Caxton *Royal Book* H6r[20-2]: Lyke as sayth the proverbe. That none hath parfyght Joye yf it come not of love.

J64 Oft in **Joy** there comes adversity
a1439 Lydgate *Fall* I 97.3517: But offte in joie ther cometh adversite.

J65 To fly for **Joy**
c1410 Lovelich *Grail* III 184.570: So that for Joye hem thowhte they flye. MED flien 1b.

J66 As bad as **Judas**
a1500 *Partenay* 117.3337: I here more wurse then Judas the synnour.

J67 As false as **Judas**
c1400 *Beryn* 71.2314: And they been falsher then Judas, 99.3282: He was as fals as Judas, that set(te) Criste at sale.

J68 A **Judas** kiss (*varied*)
c1000 *WSG* Luke xxii 48: þa cwæð se Hælend, Judas, mannes Sunu þu mid cosse sylst? **a1250** *Ancrene* (*Nero*) 86.1-2: Hit is iudases cos. **c1300** *South English Legendary* I 112.76: And custe him Judas is cos and ther with him slou. **c1395** *WBible* Luke xxii 48: And Jhesus seide to hym, Judas, with a coss thou bytrayest mannys sone. **a1400** Lavynham 11.31-2: With a iudas kesse schewith a love y fayned. **c1412** Hoccleve *Regement* 183.5081-2: The kus of Judas is now wide sprad, Tokenes of pees ben, but smal love is had. **a1449** Lydgate *Order* in *MP* II 455.187: Can kiss with Judas and kit a mans purs. **c1450** *Jacob's Well* 92.12: At the laste thou acordyst wyth Judas kus. **c1475** Gregory *Chronicle* 203[27-9]: They hadde made love days as Judas made whythe a cosse with Cryste for they cyste ovyr the mane. **a1500** *Ballad* in *Rel. Ant.* I 29[12-3]. **a1500** *Clerk and the Nightingale I* in Robbins 175.77-80: Kysse of women wyrkyth wo with synne mony folde; Judas kissed god also and to the jewes he hym solde. **1509** Watson *Ship* Q8r[26-8]. **c1523** Barclay *Mirrour* 75[35]. **a1533** Berners *Huon* 52.6-8: The kysse that he gave hym was lyke to the kysse that Judas gave to our lorde god. Apperson 335; *Oxford* 328; Tilley J92.

J69 **Judas** sleeps not
1461 Paston III 284[20]: For on the adversaire parte Judas slepith not.

J70 To draw in **Judas'** yoke not Christ's
c1340 Rolle *Psalter* 390 (108.10): Thai draw in judas yok, not in cristis, as thei sey.

Judge, sb.

J71 After the **Judge** so his ministers
c1395 *WBible* Ecclesiasticus x 2: Aftir the juge of the puple, so and hise mynystris; and what maner man is the governour of the citee, siche ben also men dwellinge ther ynne. See **K56, L455, M408, P135, 403.**

J72 He that anoints the **Judge's** hands often makes his ass lean
1492 *Salomon and Marcolphus* 7[26-7]: He that is wonte to anointe the juges handes oftyn tymes he makyth his asse lene. See **H69.**

J73 He that weeps afore a **Judge** loses his tears
1492 *Salomon and Marcolphus* 8[27-8]: He that wepyth afore a juge lesyth his terys.

J74 Ill **Judges** so judged
1509 Barclay *Ship* I 27[19]: Ill Judges so juged.

J75 That **Judge** is wise that understands a matter soon and judges at leisure
c1390 Chaucer *CT* VII 1031[B2221]: And eek men seyn that thilke juge is wys that soone understondeth a matiere and juggeth by leyser. *Oxford* 328; Tilley J95.

J76 When a **Judge** is wood (*insane*) it is hard to treat before him without loss of blood
c1421 Lydgate *Thebes* 151.3663-4: For hard it is whan a Juge is wood, To tret aforn him with-out loos of blood.

Judge, vb.

J77 **Judge** not before you know
c1385 Usk 26.41-2: After the sawes of the wyse, "thou shalt not juge ne deme toforn thou knowe." Apperson 141: Deem. See **B268, N137, P42, S406.**

J78 Who gives hasty **Judgment** must be the first to repent
a1450 *Partonope* 414.9974–6: I have herde sey, and other mo, That who so yeveth hasty Jugement Moste be the first that shall repent. Apperson 335. Cf. Tilley J97.

J79 Who judges with wrong shall fang (*receive*) the same **Judgment**
a1350 *Ywain* 71.2641–2: Wha juges men with wrang, The same jugement sal thai fang. See **D274, 342.**

J80 To know how **Judicare** came into the creed
a1300 *Cloisterer's Lament* in *Rel. Ant.* I 292[18]: Now wot i qwou *judicare* was set in the crede. **1402** *Daw Topias* 58[17–8]: But, good Jak, herdist thou evere How *judicare* cam into crede? **a1460** *Towneley Plays* 247.128: How "Judicare" comys in crede shall we teche, or we go. **a1500** *For thi self* in *Archiv* 86(1891) 387[1–2]: For thi self, man, thou may see, How judicare come in crede, [10, 18: Syn], 388[6, 14, 22]. **a1500** Greene *Carols* 406.5: He schal know how "judicare" cam in the Cred. **1546** Heywood *D* 32.61–2: I am taught to know . . . How *Judicare* came into the Creede. Tilley J98; F. L. Utley in *Mediaeval Studies* 8(1946) 303–9.

J81 To mell (*mix*) **Justice** with mercy (*varied*)
1456 Hay *Law* 299.7–8: For that is a kingis propre condicioun, to ay justice with merci melle. **1506** Hawes *Pastime* 129.3372: Justyce to kepe myxte with mercy amonge, 131.3424: And eke syr Justyce and syr myserycorde. Whiting *Drama* 96. Cf. *Oxford* 419.

K

K1 **Ka** (*claw*) me ka thee
1549 Heywood *D* 51.321: Ka me, ka the. Apperson 337; *Oxford* 329; Tilley K1. See **H339.**

K2 Not worth a sour **Kale-stock**
1522 Skelton *Why Come* II 38.352: Nor worth a sowre calstocke. Cf. Whiting *Scots* I 195.

K3 More light (*easy*) to **Keep** than to make
c1400 Gower *Peace* III 487.218: More light it is to kepe than to make. See **C518, H412.**

K4 Who **Keeps** him(self) surest slides soonest
a1500 *Colkelbie* 302.209: Quho that surest dois keip him sonest dois slyd. See **S669.**

K5 In **Keeping** of richesse is thought and woe
c1412 Hoccleve *Regement* 10.239–40: I have herd seyn, in kepyng of richesse Is thoght and wo, and besy a-wayte al-way. Cf. Tilley R108.

K6 No **Kemp** (*champion*) born that someone may not stoop (*bring*) to ground
a1200 Lawman III 30.25945–50: And ich the wule suggen, Thurh sothe mine worden: Næs nan kempen iboren Of naver nare burden, That mon ne mæi mid strenthe Stupen hine to grunde. See **M64.**

K7 To couch like **Kennets** (*small dogs*)
a1400 *Morte Arthure* 4.122: Cowchide as kenetez before the kynge selvyn.

K8 Between this place and **Kent**
c1515 Barclay *Eclogues* 159.541: Some shalt thou finde betwene this place and Kent.

K9 From **Kent** to Northumberland
a1300 *Arthour and M.*[1] 65.2235: Fram Kent to North-Humber lond.

K10 Here or in **Kent**
c1490 Ryman 240.10: Come thou no more here nor in Kent. Cf. Apperson 338: Kent and Christendom; *Oxford* 332–3; Tilley K16.

K11 To be born in **Kent**
c1450 Idley 131.1425–6: And thoughe myn Englysshe be symple to your entent, Have me excused—I was born in Kent. **1471** Caxton *Recuyell* I 4.27–30: I . . . was born and lerned myn englissh in kente in the weeld where I doubte not is spoken as brode and rude englissh as in ony place of englond. **a1500** *How the Plowman Learned his Paternoster* in Hazlitt *EPP* I 214.147–8: He was patched, torne, and all to rente; It semed by his langage he was borne in Kente. Idley 3.

K12 Of a little **Kernel** comes a mickle tree
c1000 Aelfric *Homilies* I 236[16–7]: Men geseoð oft þæt of anum lytlum cyrnele cymð micel treow. Taylor and Whiting 268: Oak; Tilley S211. See **G418, O7.**

K13 As green as any **Kex** (*stem of a plant*)
a1300 *Alisaunder* 322 M 362: And her bodyes were grene as eny kexe.

K14 As light as a **Kex**
1556 Heywood *E* 124.47.7: Ye make my hert lyght as a kyx. Svartengren 298. Cf. Tilley K22; Whiting *Drama* 318:195.

K15 (Not) count a **Kex**
c1400 *Laud Troy* I 202.6860: He countes hem as thei were a kex.

K16 As cold as (any, a) **Key**
a1393 Gower *CA* III 173.244–6: For certes ther was nevere keie Ne frosen ys upon the wal More inly cold than I am al, 462.2816–7: Tok out mor cold than eny keie An oignement. **a1450** Audelay 220.81–2: Bot soche a carful k(ny)l to his hert coldis, So doth . . . the kye, that knoc kelddus. **1501** Douglas *Palice* 26.25: Hart cald as a key. **1546** Heywood *D* 61.88: Cold as a kay. Apperson 106; *Oxford* 101; Tilley K23; Whiting *Scots* I 195.

K16a Key-cold
1528 More *Heresyes* 185 E[11]: Cay colde as thei be, **1534** *Comforte* 1143 E[8–9]: To waxe . . . key cold, 1234 A[3]: kaye cold, 1236 F[9], 1260 H[3–4]. NED Key-cold.

K17 Not all **Keys** hang at one wife's (man's) girdle
c1450 *Rylands MS.394* 94.27: Not all keyes hongen atte oo wyves gyrdell. **c1475** *Rawlinson MS. D 328* 121.42: All keyes hangeth not by on-ys gyrdyl. **a1500** Hill 129.50: All the keis hange not bi on mannis girdill. **1546** Heywood *D* 47.191: The kays hang not all by one mans gyrdell, **1555** *E* 188.235. Apperson 339; Jente 286; *Oxford* 333; Tilley K29.

K18 Your **Key** is meet (*fit*) for every lock
c1500 Skelton *Womanhod* I 20.22–3: Youre key is mete for every lok, Youre key is commen and hangyth owte. Apperson 339; Tilley K27.

K19 As cant (*lively*) as any **Kid**
c1475 Henryson *Fables* 14.331: Quhylis up, quhylis doun, als cant as ony kid.

K20 As playing as young **Kids**
1480 Caxton *Ovyde* 130[41]: More playeng and deduysyng than yong kyddes.

K21 To skip like any **Kid**
c1390 Chaucer *CT* I[A] 3259–60: Therto she koude skippe and make game, As any kyde.

K22 When the **Kid** runs men may see its arse
1492 *Salomon and Marcolphus* 6[10]: Whan the kydde rennyth, men may se his ars. Cf. Apperson 12–3: The higher the ape goes; *Oxford* 295; Tilley A271.

K23 To reek like a **Kiln**
c1425 *Avowynge* 64[23–4]: As kylne other kechine; Thus rudely he rekes.

K24 Far from thy **Kin** cast thee, *etc.*
c1417 *Lansdowne MS.762* in *Rel. Ant.* I 233: Far from thy kyn cast the, Wreth not thy neighber next the, In a good corne countrey rest the, And sit downe, Robyn, and rest the. **1486** ?Berners *Boke of St. Albans* F5[v]: Fer from thy kynnysmen keste the, Wrath not thy neighborys next the, In a goode corne cuntre threste the, And sitte downe, Robyn, and rest the. Apperson 203. See **K63.**

K25 He that mans him with his **Kin,** *etc.*
1486 ?Berners *Boke of St. Albans* F5[v]: Who that mannyth hym with his kynne, And closith his croofte wyth cheritrees, Shall have many hegges brokynne, And also full lyttyll goode servyes. Robbins-Cutler 4106.5. See **K63.**

K26 It is difficult to change one's own **Kind** (*nature*)
1484 Caxton *Aesop* 98[12–3]: Hit is moche dyffycyle and hard to chaunge his owne kynd. See **A257, E153.**

K27 **Kind** covets ay its law
c1450 *St. Cuthbert* 8.271–2: Bot sene it is in ald sawe, That kynde coveyts ay his lawe. See **L103.**

K28 **Kind** fails not at need
a1387 Higden-Trevisa I 415[13–6]: In bookes ye may rede, That kynde failleth not at nede; Whanne no man hadde craft in mynde, Than of craft halp God and kynde. See **K31.**

K29 **Kind** follows (to) kind (*varied*)
a1387 *Piers* C xi 243–4: For god seide ensample of such manere isshue, That kynde folweth kynde and contrarieth nevere. **1471** Ripley *Compound* 130[3]: For kynd to kynde hath appetyble inclynacyon. See **K33, L272.**

K30 **Kind** may not flee from its stock
a1439 Lydgate *Fall* I 206.243–5: For from his stok kynde may nat fle; Ech thyng resortith, how ferr ever it go, To the nature which that it cam fro. See **A169, J18, K32, M82.**

K31 **Kind** often works what seems impossible to the leech
a1400 Lanfranc 173.16: For ofte tyme kinde worchith, that that semeth unpossible to the leche. See **K28, 38, N30.**

K32 **Kind** will ay appear like itself
a1449 Lydgate *Vertu* in *MP* II 836.46: For lyk hymsilf kynd wyl ay appere. See **K30.**

K33 **Kind** will be friend
c1350 *Joseph* 16.488: For evere the kuynde wol be frend for ought that mai bi-falle. See **K29.**

K34 **Kind** (Blood) will creep where it may not go
c1450 *Douce MS.52* 51.85: Kynde crepus, ther hit may no go. **c1450** *Rylands MS.394* 101.4. **a1460** *Towneley Plays* 135.591–2: I trow, kynde will crepe Where it may not go. **c1475** *Rauf* 86.126: "Now is anis," said the Coilyear, "kynd aucht to creip." **1481** Caxton *Reynard* 70[34]: For blood must krepe where it can not goo. **a1500** *Att my begynnyng* in *Rawlinson MS. C 813* 324.39–40: Kynde will crepe wher itt may nott goo And shewe itt-selffe whens itt came fro. **a1500** *Beauty of his Mistress II* in Robbins 125.47–8: For hereafter ye shall knowe Wher kynde can-not goo, ytt wyll crepe. **c1500** *Everyman* 12.316: For kynde wyll crepe where it may

not go. **a1546** Heywood *D* 43.90: Kinde will creepe where it maie not go. Apperson 385–6; Jente 621; *Oxford* 336; Tilley K49. See **C202, E51.**

K35 Kind will give blood
c1300 *Southern Legendary Life of Jesus* in C. Horstmann *Leben Jesu, ein Fragment* (Münster, 1873) 34.122–3: Ake natheles he thoughte on kuynd hede, that Man hath to is childe, And that kuynde blod it wole yive.

K36 Kind will have its course
c1400 *Beryn* 4.86: Ffor "kynde woll have his cours," though men the contrary swer. Apperson 437; *Oxford* 444; Smith 213. See **L542.**

K37 Kind will spring out
a1400 *Perceval* 12.354–6: Scho wiste wele by that thynge That the kynde wolde oute sprynge For thynge that be moughte.

K38 Where **Kind** fails cunning can do boot (*remedy*)
a1439 Lydgate *Fall* I 185.6543: Wher Kynde faileth, cunnyng can do boote. See **K31.**

K39 As rich as the **King**
a1500 *Inter Diabolus et Virgo* 444.20: What ys recher than ys the kynge? 445.40: Jhesus ys recher than ys the kynge. Taylor and Whiting 208; Tilley C832.

K40 Better the **King** halt than the kingdom
a900 Alfred *Orosius* 96.27–31: Læcedemonie . . . him to gielpword hæfdon þæt him leofre wære þæt hie hæfdon healtre cyning þonne healt rice.

K41 If a **King** forvay (*go astray*) the common people often have abought (*paid for*) the king's sin
a1393 Gower *CA* III 345.3928–31: If so be that a king forsveie, Fulofte er this it hath be sein, The comun poeple is overlein And hath the kinges Senne aboght. MED forveien.

K42 (A **King**) is above his laws
1460 *Jack Cade's Proclamation* in James Gairdner *Three Fifteenth-century Chronicles* (CS NS 28, 1880) 94[14–6]: They sey that owre sovereyn lorde is above his lawys to his pleysewr . . . The contrary is trew. Cf. Tilley K61. See **K45.**

K43 A **King** is born as naked as a laborer
c1485 *Guiscardo* 80.741–2: For as nakyd ys a kyng born, I undyrstand, As ys the laborer that hath nedyr house ne land. See **C263, 267, L448.**

K44 The **King** is lord of this (*English*) language
1391 Chaucer *Astrolabe* Prol. 56–7: And preie God save the king, that is lord of this langage. Apperson 342; *Oxford* 338; Tilley K80.

K45 A **King** may be above his laws in mercy
1515 Barclay *St. George* 33.609: A kynge in mercy may be above his lawes. Cf. Tilley M898. See **K42.**

K46 King or kaiser
1546 Heywood *D* 56.38: And thus, kyng or keyser must have set them quight. Tilley K56.

K47 A **King's** ransom
c1470 *Wallace* 22.150: Mycht thai hawe payit the ransoune of a king, 138.904: Than off pur gold a kingis gret ransoune. NED Ransom 2.

K48 A **King's** word must stand (*varied*)
a1200 Lawman II 574.23727–8: For hit bicumeth kinge That his word stonde. **a1393** Gower *CA* II 127.3368–9: And this wot every worthi lif, A kinges word it mot ben holde. **c1395** Chaucer *CT* IV[E] 2315: I am a kyng, it sit me noght to lye. **a1449** Lydgate and Burgh *Secrees* 37.1167: Woord of a kyng mut stonde in 0 degre. **1456** Hay *Law* 242.32–3: A kingis word suld stand and nocht be frustrit, as Sanct David sais. **c1460** *Ipomadon C* 352.29–30: And asked the king, if the graunt of a kinges mouth shuld not be hold ferme and stable and the king said yea. **c1475** Henryson *Fables* 77.2251: Yone Carllis word, as he wer King, sall stand, 79.2289: I may say, and ganesay, I am na King. **1492** *Salomon and Marcolphus* 8[19]: A kynges worde shulde be unchaungeable or stedfaste. **a1500** *Orfeo* 40 H 429: A kyng-is worde most nede be holde. **a1500** *Thre Prestis* 43.953–4: It fallis to na King To brek his vow or yit his oblissing. **c1500** *Lancelot* 50.1671–2: O kingis word shuld be o kingis bonde, And said It is, a kingis word shuld stond. **1509** Fisher *Treatyse* 230.25–7: It is a comyn proverbe. Verbum regis stet oportet. A kynges worde must stande. Apperson 342; Tilley K83; Whiting *Scots* II 160:5.

K49 A **King** shall die as well as a knave
a1500 *Fortune alas alas* 488.108–9: Aswele a kyng as a knafe shal dye, Ne wetyng wher ne whan, erly or late. See **D97, 101, 243, R111.**

K50 A **King** should not be a lion in peace nor a hare in war (*varied*)
c1330 *Times of Edward II* 334.252: And nu ben theih liouns in halle, and hares in the feld. **a1338** Mannyng *Chronicle A* I 182.5181–4: Hit falleth no kyng to felon res, As lyon in the tyme of pees, Ne in tyme of werre for to dare, Ne to fle for drede, as doth the hare. See **L38.**

K51 A **King** that strives with his (*subjects*) may not speed well
a1338 Mannyng *Chronicle B* II 293[23–4]: A kyng that strives with hise, he may not wele spede, Whore so he restis or rives he lyves ay in drede.

K52 A **King** to-day and to-morrow he dies
a1050 Defensor *Liber* 202[8]: Swa eac cyning to dæg ys and to morgen he swelt. **c1395** *WBible* Ecclesiasticus x 12: So and a king is to dai, and to morewe he schal die. See **T351.**

K53 **King** wilful, doomsman (*judge*) nimming (*taking bribes*), etc. (*varied*)
c1000 *De XII Abusivis Secundum Disputationem Sancti Cipriani Martyris* in Rubie D-N. Warner *Early English Homilies from the Twelfth Century MS. Vesp. D. XIV* (EETS 152, 1917) 11–6: Nu synd twelf abusiva . . . *Duodecim abusiva sunt seculi . . . Senex sine religione. Adolescens sine obedientia. Dives sine elemosina. Femina sine pudicitia. . . . Pauper superbus. Rex iniquus. Episcopus negligens. Plebs sine disciplina. Populus sine lege* (11.10–6). . . . Se ealde mann þe byð buten æwfæstnysse (11.32). . . . Se junge mann beo buten gehersumnysse (12.7–8). . . . Se welige mann beo buten ælmesdæden (12.16). . . . þe wif beo unseodefull (12.38). . . . Se þearefe beo modig (14.9). . . . Se cyng beo unrihtwis (14.26). . . . Se biscop beo gemeleas (15.16). . . . þæt folc beo buten steore (15.32). . . . þæt folc beo buten æ (16.7). **c1250** *Ten Abuses* in Morris *Old English Miscellany* 184: Hwan thu sixst on leode King that is wilful, And domesman niminde, Preost that is wilde, Bischop slou, Old mon lechur, Yunch man liegher, Wimmon schomeles, Child un-theaid, Thral un-buxsum, Atheling britheling, Lond with-ute laghe, Al so seide bede: Wo there theode. **a1300** *Cotton Cleopatra MS. C vi* in *Rel. Ant.* II 15: King conseilles, Bissop loreles, Wumman schameles, Hold-man lechur, Jongman trichur, Of alle mine live Ne sau I worse five. **a1300** *Gonville and Caius College Cambridge MS.365* in M. R. James *Catalogue* II(1908) 415: Theys bet the thre that god for les: Holdman Gytles, Yongman recheles, Womman sameles. **a1300** *Harley MS.913* in Heuser 184: Bissop lorles, Kyng redeles, Yung man rechles, Old man witles, Womman ssamles—I swer bi heven kyng: Thos beth five lither thing. **a1300** *Ipswich MS.6* in *Proceedings of the Suffolk Institute of Archaeology and Natural History* 22 (1934–6) 94: Ailredus rex. Wanne king is radles and led bissop loreles and eldman witles and jungman recheles and winman scameles, wanne thralles sullen thriven, and adelinges duinen, wanne child is king, and cherlessune bissop, wanne gold sal speken and gume sal suien: thanne sal engelong to same gon. Whanne child is king, and cherl bissop and thral alderman, thanne is the folc wo. **a1300** *Trinity College Cambridge MS.108* in M. R. James *Catalogue* I(1900) 131: (?Ald man) witles, Yung man recheles, Wyman ssameles, Betere ham were lifles. Aluredus King. **a1400** *Graham MS.* f.123a in *Sixth Report of the Royal Commission on Historical Manuscripts* (1877) Appendix 320 [51–5]: Kyng of lond redles, Bysschope wytles, yongchilde gyeles, yong man rechcles, Oldman careles, Proutman goldles, Womman schameles, Strongman skoleles, Povereman loveles, hem were betere be lyfles. **a1400** Ridgewell Church in V. Pritchard *English Medieval Graffiti* (Cambridge, 1967) 75–6: A yong rewler, wytles, A pore man spendar, haveles, A ryche man thif, nedeles, An old man lecher, lwveles, A woman rebolde, sameless. **c1450** *Rawlinson MS.32* in *Rel. Ant.* II 316[3–8]: A yong man a rewler, recheles; A olde man a lechowr, loweles; A pore man a waster, haveles; A riche man a thefe, nedeles; A womman a rebawde, shameles. These v. shalle never thrif blameles. **c1500** *Bannatyne* III 43–4.11–5: A yong man chiftane witless, A pure man spendar getles, A auld man trechor trewtless, A woman lowpar landless, Be sacnt Jeill, sall nevir ane of thir so weill (Cf. II 324. 1–3). **c1500** *Series* in Brown *Lyrics XV* 269–70. 1–17: Ther ben iii poyntis of myscheff . . . Pore men proude that lytyl han, . . . A Ryche man thef is a-nodyr, . . . Olde man lechere is the iiide. Apperson 719; Pseudo-Cyprianus *De XII Abusivis Saeculi*, ed. Siegmund Hellmann (Texte und Untersuchungen zur Geschichte der altchristlichen Literatur 34[1909]); *Oxford* 471; Whiting *Scots* II 163.

K54 New **King** new case
a1425 *Metrical Paraphrase OT* 12.9822: Of a new kyng A new comyn case. See **L453.**

K55 One shall not do a **King** to death
a1300 *Richard* 130.957–8: But now it is ordeyned soo, Men schal no kyng to deth doo.

K56 Such **King** such people (*varied*)
a1475 Ashby *Dicta* 60.393: Suche as the kynge is, suche bene al other, 65.504: As the kyng is, suche bene al in his cure. **1485** Caxton *Charles* 22.15: For suche as is the Kyng suche is the Royame. See **J71, L455, M408, P135, 403.**

K57 There is no **King** where there is no law

1492 *Salomon and Marcolphus* 14[9–10]: I shall alweyes saye, There is no king were no lawe is.

K58 To live like a **King**
a1410 Lydgate *Churl* in *MP* II 481.291: To have lived lik a kyng. Tilley P592; Whiting *Drama* 318:192. See **L457.**

K59 To speak as lordly as a **King**
c1390 Chaucer *CT* I[A] 3900: He gan to speke as lordly as a kyng.

K60 An unlettered **King** is like a horned (crowned) ass
1422 Yonge *Governaunce* 150.18–9: For he sayth, that a kynge unletterid, is lyke an hornyd asse. **a1533** Berners *Huon* 730.19–21: Comonly it is said that a kyng without letter or conynge is compared to an asse crowned. Apperson 341; Tilley K69; Whiting *Scots* I 195. See **A225, L442.**

K61 An unwise **King** is but an ape in the house roof
c1400 *Apology* 89[28]: As Bernard seith, A kynge unwise is but a nape in the house rofe. Cf. Tilley K69; Whiting *Scots* I 195.

K62 Each **Kingdom** divided against itself will be cast down (*varied*)
c1000 *WSG* Matthew xii 25: Ælc rice þe byð twyræde on him sylfum byþ toworpen; and ælc ceaster oððe hus þe byð wiþerweard ongen hyt sylf, hyt ne stent, Mark iii 24–5, Luke xi 17. **a1050** Defensor *Liber* 133–4: Drihten segð on godspelle ælc rice todæled ongean hit byð toworpen, and ælc ceaster oþþe hus todæled ongean hit sylf, hit ne stynt. **c1395** *WBible* Matthew xii 25: Eche kingdom departid ayens it silf, schal be desolatid, and eche cite, or hous, departid ayens it self, schal not stonde, Mark iii 24–5, Luke xi 17. **a1439** Lydgate *Fall* I 105–6.3822: Kyngdamys devyded may no while endure, 3829, 3836, 3843, III 996.2732–4: This verray soth: wher is dyvysioun, Be witnesse and record of scripture, May no kyngdam nor cite long endure. Tilley K89. See **R55.**

K63 Many **Kinsfolk** and few friends
1546 Heywood *D* 54.440: Many kynsfolke and few freends, some folke saie, **1555** *E* 190.246. Apperson 399; *Oxford* 406; Tilley K97. See **K24, 25.**

K64-5 **Kinsmen's** goods must be shared
c1025 *Durham Proverbs* 11.13: Gemæne sceal maga feoh. Commune peccunia propinquorum. See **M145.**

K66 **Kirkmen** were ay gentle to their wives
1501 Douglas *Palice* 73.9: For kirkmen war ay gentill to thair wyifis. Cf. Tilley B10, W357. See **B3.**

K67 Near is my **Kirtle** but nearer is my smock (*varied*)
1461 Paston III 251[9]: Nere is my kyrtyl, but nerre is my smok. **c1505** Watson *Valentine* 79.22–3: Your shyrte is more nerer your body than your gowne. **1546** Heywood *D* 40.158: Though ny be my kyrtell, yet nere is my smocke. Apperson 437; Jente 522; *Oxford* 444; Tilley P250.

K68 **Kiss** ere you sleep, *etc.*
a1500 *Gonville and Caius College Cambridge MS.249* in M. R. James *Catalogue* (Cambridge, 1907) I 300: Kysse or thow sclepe, Luk or thow lepe, Suppe or thow dyppe. See **L435.**

K69 **Kissing** is earnest of the remenant (*varied*)
a1400 *Romaunt B* 3677–80: For whoso kyssynge may attayne, Of loves payne hath (soth to sayne) The beste and most avenaunt, And ernest of the remenaunt. **c1450** La Tour-Landry 185.13–5: The kyssynge is nyghe parente and Cosyn unto the fowle faytte or dede. **1480** Caxton *Ovyde* 46[30–1]: Thou mayst gete suche a kysse, thou shalt wel mowe atteyn to the surplus. Apperson 344; Tilley K107. See **G40.**

K70 **Kit** has lost her keys
1533 More *Apologye* 102[1–2]: Lost them of lykelyhed as some good kytte leseth her kayes. *Oxford* 341; Tilley K109.

K71 To reek like (a) **Kitchen**
c1425 *Avowynge* 64[23–4]: As . . . kechine; Thus rudely he rekes.

K72 As dead as a **Kite**
c1400 *Laud Troy* I 156.5274: He lay ther ded as a kyte.

K73 As fair and white as a **Kite's** foot
a1529 Skelton *Elynour* I 108.424–5: As fayre and as whyte As the fote of a kyte.

K74 As yellow as a **Kite's** feet (*varied*)
1509 Barclay *Ship* I 287[10–1]: Thoughe he be yelowe as kyte Is of hir fete. **1534** More *Comforte* 1149 H[12–4]: And beutyfieth her faire fell wyth the couloure of a kites clawe. Apperson 717; *Oxford* 737; Svartengren 252; Tilley K115.

K75 A **Kite** may not fly with royal eagles
a1439 Lydgate *Fall* II 554.2952: With roial egles a kite may nat flee.

K76 He was never a good **Knape** (*lad*) who had his dame at the gate
c1450 *Douce MS.52* 56.132: Was he never gode knappe, that hadde his dame at the yate. **c1450** *Rylands MS.394* 107.23: Nemo bonus servus, foribus qui matre potitur. Walther III 79.16317b.

K77 He that is destined to be a **Knave** lives in more surety than does a lord
a1450 *Partonope* 379.9231–4: Lytell ought a man to make a-vaunte Of wordly prosperite or therof Joye have, For he that is destyned to be a knave, Lyveth more in suerte then dothe a lorde. See **E24, 150.**

K78 It is merry when **Knaves** meet
c1500 *Cock* 14[28]: But mery it is whan knaves done mete. **1549** Heywood *D* 46.157: Some saie also it is mery when knaves meete. Apperson 415; *Oxford* 421; Tilley K143.

K79 A **Knave** has broke(n) a lad
c1477 Caxton *Curtesye* 47.475–6: And yf ought breke somme tunges that be bade Wil mocke and saie a knave hath broke a lad.

K80 The more **Knaves** the worse company
1549 Heywood *D* 46.158: But the mo knaves the woorse company to greete. Apperson 427; *Oxford* 342; Tilley K146.

K81 An old **Knave** is no child (babe)
1528 More *Heresyes* 242 A[4–5]: An olde knave is no chylde. **1546** Heywood *D* 64.82, **1555** *E* 172.148: babe. Apperson 464; *Oxford* 471; Tilley K132.

K82 One **Knave** disdains another
1533 Heywood *Pardoner* B4ʳ[10]: One knave dysdaynes another. Tilley K134. See **B187, L220.**

K83 Two false **Knaves** need no broker
1546 Heywood *D* 46.156: Two false knaves neede no broker, men say, **1555** *E* 154.52. *Oxford* 117; Tilley K147.

K84 Walk, **Knave,** walk
1546 Heywood *D* 68.84–5: Walke drab walke. Nay (quoth she) walke knave walke. Saieth that terme. Apperson 665; *Oxford* 690; Tilley K140.

K85 To be laid under **Knee**
c1250 *Hendyng O* 196.29[5–6]: Thenne is the fredom al foryeten, And leid ounder kne.

K86 As keen as (any) **Knife**
a1425 *Metrical Paraphrase OT* 24.775: Qwer for hyr care was kene os knyfe, 17.6212: Hyr care was kene as any knyfe. **a1450** *York Plays* 45.7: My cares aren keen as knyffe, 52.223. Taylor and Whiting 210.

K87 As sharp as **Knife**
a1400 *Seven Penitential Psalms* in *Wheatley MS.* 53.811: For synne is scharp as knyves oord, *Bodley MS.1619* in *ESt* 10 (1887) 252.811: as knyf or sword. **c1410** Lovelich *Grail* II 409–10.159–60: As scharpe And trenchaunt they were As Evere was knyf. **a1440** Burgh *Cato* 306.102: With sharper tonge than is . . . knyffe. **1509** Barclay *Ship* II 6[19]. **1509** *Fyftene Joyes* I8ᵛ[15]. Whiting *NC* 433.

K88 Bourd (*jest*) not too far with a sharp **Knife**
a1500 *O man more* 394.32: And bowrde nott to farre with a sharpe knyffe. See **S977.**

K89 No more perilous **Knife** than a superfluous morsel
c1450 *Pilgrimage LM* 157[33]: Ther is noon more perilowse knyf than is a superflue morselle. See **G167.**

K90 To eat one's **Knife**
c1497 Medwall *Fulgens* D3ᵛ[27–8]: Nay, I had lever she had etyn my knyfe, I utterly forsake her. Cf. Tilley K158.

K91 To kill (slay, be slain, be wounded) without **Knife**
c1300 *Amis* 65.1561–3: So wicked and schrewed was his wiif, Sche brac his hert with-outen kniif, With wordes harde and kene. **a1450** *Castle* 111.1127–8: Kyll hym a-non, with-owtyn knyve, And speke hym sum schame were thou go, 125.1620: For gloton kyllyth with-owtyn knyf. **a1450** *Partonope* 210.5534–6: Yeffe ye thus departe fro me, And breke your beheste, ye shulle se Ye shulle me sle wyth-owten knyffe. **a1475** *Ludus Coventriae* 28.401: I sclow my self with-owtyn knyff. **c1485** *Conversion* 48.555: It consumyth natur, the body sleyth with-owt knyf. **a1500** Basterfeld 367.30: I scleughe myselve with-outene knyffe. **a1500** *Ten Commandments of Love* in Robbins 167.68: And wounded lyeth without knife or darte. See **R167.**

K92 What should he give that licks his **Knife?**
a1400 *Romaunt C* 6502: What shulde he yeve that likketh his knyf? Apperson 246:10; *Oxford* 238; Tilley L345.

K93 A **Knight** of the common hall
a1508 Skelton *Phyllyp* I 70.645–8: Some say she was lyght, And made her husband knyght Of the comyne hall, That cuckoldes men call.

K94 **Knights** once shamed never recover
a1470 Malory I 218.3: For knyghtes ons shamed recoverys hit never (1–2 [Caxton's text]: For

ones shamed maye never be recoverd). See **E70, M20, N13.**

K95 A manly **Knight's** prowess is proved most in mischief
a1420 Lydgate *Troy* I 270.4392–4: For in proverbe it hath ben said ful yore, That the prowes of a manly knyght Is preved most in meschef.

K96 After the **Knot** (is knit) it helps not to bewail
c1475 *Prohemy of a Mariage* 28[10]: After the knot it helpeth nat to bewail. Cf. Tilley K167. See **D287, M729.**

K97 To knit a **Knot**
c1405 *Mum* 34.240: And knytte there a knotte and construed no ferther, 47.693: But thenne he knittith a knotte. **a1450** *York Plays* 229.233–4: But Judas, a knott for to knytt, Wilte thou to this comenaunt accorde? **a1460** *Towneley Plays* 59.106–8: Loke ye do it well in wrytt, And theron a knott knytt, Ffor it is prophecy. **c1475** *Prohemy of a Mariage* 35[6]: At last the knot is knyt. NED Knit la.

K98 To seek (find) a **Knot** in the (a) rush
1340 *Ayenbite* 253[9–12]: The bysye other the malancolien thet byeth ylich than thet zekth . . . thane knotte ine the resse. **c1400** *Vices and Virtues* 280.29–31: As many sotile men and curious and malencolious don, that faren as he that secheth . . . a knot on the rissche. **1533** More *Confutacion* 778 G[4–5]: Thys wer but finding of a knot in a rushe. Apperson 345; NED Knot sb.[1] 14b; *Oxford* 343; Tilley K168.

K99 First **Know** and after love
1471 Caxton *Recuyell* I 183.16: Hyt behoveth fyrst to knowe and after that to love. See **L580.**

K100 **Know** thyself
a1387 Higden-Trevisa I 241[7]: Knowe thy self. **c1390** Chaucer *CT* VII 2139[B3329]: Ful wys is he that kan hymselven knowe! **c1390** *Each Man* in Brown *Lyrics XIV* 139–42.12: For uche mon oughte himself to knowe, 24, 36, *etc.* **a1393** Gower *CA* III 298.2389: Bot know thiself, what so befalle. **1400** *Love god, and drede* in Kail 1.8: Man, knowe thy self, love god, and drede, 16, *etc.* **c1405** *Man, know thy self* in Kail 27.8: Man, knowe thy self, and lerne to dye! **a1415** Mirk *Festial* 116.22–3: Sayng thus: "Anothe selitos;" that is to say: "Know thyselfe." **1422** Lydgate *Serpent* 54.11–3: In greke this worde Nothis politos, whiche is as mochill to seyne in owre englische tonge as knowe thiselfe. **1422** Yonge *Governaunce* 154.35–6: Saynge in gru, Notisclotos, that is to Say, have knowynge of thy-Selfe. **a1425** *Metrical Paraphrase OT* 19.14447: Man, knaw thi selfe ryght sone! **a1439** Lydgate *Fall* II 489.568–70: *Gnotos Eolitos* in Greek he sholde seyn, Which in our tunge pleynli doth expresse, "Knowe thi-silff." **a1450** *Knowe thy self* in Kail 101.9: What thou art, knowe thy self wel. **c1450** *Jacob's Well* 276.25. **c1450** *Speculum Christiani* (2) 122.7–8: Bernardus: Stody thou and knowe thi-selfe. **a1475** Ashby *Dicta* 79.813–4: To knowe hymself is a vertuous thing, First to godward and to the world also. **1481** Caxton *Reynard* 73[23–4]. **a1500** *Therfor be thyn* in Dyboski 82–3: 8, 16, *etc.* **c1516** Skelton *Magnificence* 59.1888. *Oxford* 344, 718; Smith 167; Tilley K175. See **G73, 126, M135.**

K101 **Know** (well) ere you knit (too fast) (*varied*)
a1400 *Proverbis of Wysdom* 244.39–40: Know well, ore thou knyt to fast; Fore ofte rape rewythe at last, 245.55–6: Know well, ore thou knytt: Then wyll men prayse thy wytt. **c1450** *Fyrst thou sal* 89.61–2. **c1450** Idley 136.1725: Therfore knowe or ye knytte, it may availle. **a1500** *Against Hasty Marriage I* in Robbins 37.1–4: Know or thow knytte; Prove or thow preyse yt. Gyf thou know or thou knyt, than mayst thou Abate; And gyf thou knyt er thou knowe, Than yt ys to late. Ther-fore Avyse the er thou the knot knytte. **a1500** Hill 139.11–2: Know or thou knyte, and then thou mayst slake, Yff thou knyte or thou know, than yt ys to late. **a1500** *Man, be war* in T. Wright *Songs and Carols* (PS 23, 1848) 34[1–2]: Man, be war, er thou knyte the fast, Oftyn ran rewth at the last. **a1500** *MS. Marginalia* in Hoccleve I 124 n.[1]: Know er thow knyt, and then thow mayst slake; If thou knyt er thow know, then hytt is to late, 156 n.[2], 228 n.[9]. *Oxford* 344. See **F625, P429, T204.**

L

L1 **Lab** (*tell-tale*) it wist (*knew*) and out it must
c1470 *Harley MS.3362* f.2b in *Retrospective* 309[8] and Förster 201.8: Labbe hyt whyste, and owt yt muste. Consilium sciunt blas et celare nequunt. **1562** Heywood *D* 35.22: Looke what she knowth, blab it wist, and out it must. Apperson 51; *Oxford* 47; Tilley B433; Walther I 372.3185. Cf. Chaucer *TC* iii 299–300: Proverbes kanst thiself ynowe and woost, Ayeins that vice, for to ben a labbe.

L2 After **Labor** is time of quiet
1413 ?Hoccleve *De Guilleville Poems* xxxv 20: And aftir laboure, tyme is of quiete. See **B325.**

L3 After sore **Labor** sweet rest is delectable
c1515 Barclay *Eclogues* 107.1: After sore labour sweete rest is delectable.

L4 All **Labor** is light to a lover
1434 Misyn *Mending* 123.30: All labyr is lyght to a lufar. **a1500** Rolle *Mending* 49[32–3]: Al maner of labour is light to a lovier. See **L529.**

L5 Every **Labor(er)** must have rest (*varied*)
c1395 Chaucer *CT* IV[E] 1862–3: For every labour somtyme moot han reste, Or elles longe may he nat endure, V[F] 349: Muchel drynke and labour wolde han reste. See **T441.**

L6 Great **Labor** to make a straight javelin of a crabbed (*crooked*) tree
c1523 Barclay *Mirrour* 24[8]: To make a streyght Javelin of a crabbed tree, Theron must great labour . . . be layde. See **H484, S316.**

L7 Incessant **Labor** overcomes all things
1509 Fisher *Treatyse* 147.8-11: It is wryten. Labor improbus omnia vincit. Incessaunt laboure by the waye of intercessyon overcometh all thynges. Tilley L5.

L8 It is great **Labor** to get gear, fear to conserve it, and more anger to lose it
a1500 *Colkelbie* 283.25–7: Gret laubor is to get geir And to conserve it Is feir And moir angir is to leiss.

L9 No **Labor** is a thing of shame
a1500 *MS. Marginalia* in Hoccleve I 192 n.[2]: So(crates) 21. No kinde of Labore is a thing of shame, But ydelnes evermore worthie of blame, 205 n.[3].

L10 One profits by **Labor** and wastes by idleness
1489 Caxton *Fayttes* 99.10–1: A man proffyteth by labour and by ydlenes he wasteth.

L11 To have one's **Labor** (travail, work) in vain (idle, waste)
a1338 Mannyng *Chronicle A* I 135.3840: Bot his travaille was al in veyn. **c1375** Barbour *Bruce* I 164.50: And vast no mair travale in vayn. **c1385** Usk 7.69–70: I wot wel al my labour were in ydel, 90.109: Thy traveyle is in ydel. **a1393** Gower *CA* III 54.3926, 400.527. **c1395** *WBible* Leviticus xxvi 20: travel. **a1400** *Ipomadon A* 159.5547: travayle. **a1400** Lanfranc 270.16: traveile in idil. **1402** Hoccleve *Letter of Cupid* 81.220: travayle and labour. **a1410** Lydgate *Churl* in *MP* II 482.329. **1410** Walton *Boethius* 97[1]. **c1412** Hoccleve *Regement* 14.367: ydel, 104.2889: Your labour shal naght ydel be, ne veyne, 119.3311: waast. **a1420** Lydgate *Troy* III 865.3222, 872.3486. **c1422** Hoccleve *Dialog* 125.436, *Jereslaus's Wife* 162.630, 170.868: ydil was and veyn. **a1425** *Metrical Paraphrase OT* 108.13283: werke. **c1425** *Orcherd* 268.31–2. **a1430** Lydgate *Pilgrimage* 138.5277, 301.11016, 333.12224, **a1439** *Fall* I 168.5951, III 679.150, 750.2828. **a1445** *Carl* 122.128. **1447** Bokenham 74.2684, 88.3227. **a1450** *Generydes B* 131.4102. **a1450** *Of the seven Ages* 485[38]. **a1450** *York Plays* 182.125: travayle. **c1450** ?Suffolk *What shall I say* 166.19. **a1454** Paston II 296[4]. **a1470** Malory I 377.13–4, III 1213.25–6:

Hyt ys waste laboure now to sew to myne uncle. **c1470** *Wallace* 69.682: travaill, 145.166: trawaill. **c1475** Henryson *Testament* 124.565. **1493** *Seven Wise Masters* 134[26]. **c1493** *Saint Katherin of Senis* 60.24. **a1500** *Assembly* 402.668. **a1500** *Nut Brown Maid* 174.4, 177[8]. **a1500** *Piers of Fullham* 12.278. **a1500** *Triamour* (*P*) II 105.731. **a1500** *Timor Mortis* in *MLR* 28(1933) 236[44]. **c1500** Fabyan 322[11], 400[29], 413[19–20]: travayle, 470[21–2]. **c1500** *Smith* 328.503. **1501** *Plumpton Correspondence* 158[8]. **c1503** More *Early Poems* [10] C[3]. **1504** Hawes *Example* Bb3v[14]. **1513** Bradshaw *St. Werburge* 41.952, 164.976. **a1518** Nevill *Castell* 79.97: waste. **a1533** Berners *Arthur* 257[31]: wast. **1533** More *Debellacyon* 1026 H[6–7]. NED Labour 1b. See **V1.**

L12 You shall never **Labor** younger
1562 Heywood *D* 34.32: Set forward, ye shall never labour yonger. *Oxford* 347; Tilley Y36.

L13 Not give a threaden **Lace**
c1400 *Laud Troy* I 246.8351–2: I yeve not a threden lace Off thyn evel wil.

Lack, sb.

L14 For **Lack** (*fault*) of one all are not to blame
a1420 Lydgate *Troy* II 521.4387: For lak of oon, alle are nought to blame. See **A101.**

L15 **Lack** of forewit is cause of care
a1500 *Salamon seyth* in Person 52.17–8: In every place wher y gan fare Lacke of forwytte is cause of care. See **L435.**

L16 No **Lack** to lack a wife
1546 Heywood *D* 101.56: No lacke to lacke a wife. Apperson 448; *Oxford* 347; Tilley L18.

Lack, vb.

L17 **Lack** (*blame*) not where you have loved (*praised*)
c1450 *Consail and Teiching* 76.373–4: Lak nocht quhar thow has lovit mekile, Fore men wyll say thow art our-fekile. **1456** Hay *Law* 30.15–6: And reprovandly lak that thai before had lovit. See **L562, P353.**

L18 A **Lad** (*low fellow*) to wed a lady is an inconvenient (*misfortune*)
1513 Bradshaw *St. Werburge* 43.1014–5: By a proverbe auncyent "A lad to wedde a lady is an inconvenyent."

L19 (A) **Lady** of fair dighting (*gay apparel*) is arbalest to the tower
1340 *Ayenbite* 47[19–21]: Vor ase zayth the vorbisne, "levedi of vaire dightinge is arblast to the tour." **c1400** *Vices and Virtues* 44.4–5: For men seyn in olde proverbes, "Ladies of riche and gay apparail is arwblast of tour" (296 *French:* Dame de bel atour est arbalaste a tour). **1484** Caxton *Royal Book* E6r[3–4]: For thus, as sayth the proverbe, dame dacor (?dator) is the arblast to the tour. MED arblast 2(b): A crossbow drawn by a winch mechanism.

L20 As light as **Lait** (*lightning*)
c1390 *Sir Gawain* 7.199: He loked as layt so lyght.

L21 To shine like **Lait**
c1175 *Lambeth Homilies* 43[8]: And heore ethem scean swa deth the leit a-monge thunre.

L22 As white as (any) **Lake** (*linen*)
c1300 *Guy*[1] 520 A 162.6: As white as . . . lake. **c1408** Lydgate *Reson* 104.3941: Sommtyme white as cloth of lake. **1447** Bokenham 69.2526, 200.7345: ony. **c1450** *As softe as syghes* in *Archiv* 127(1911) 324.14. **a1450** *Castle* 132.1849. **a1500** *Eger H* 225.723, 241.981, 333.2497, 335.2511, 345.2687. Whiting *Scots* I 196.

L23 A little **Lake** (*gift*) that comes from good will is lief (*dear*) to God
c1175 *Poema Morale* 174.73–4: Litel loc is gode lief thet cumth of gode iwille, And ethlete muchel iyeve thanne si hierte is ille. See **G84.**

L24 To lie in the **Lake** (*ditch*)
a1500 *Thre Prestis* 20.283–4: The theif full weile he will him self ourby Quhen the lele man in the lak will ly. See **D247, 266, M573.**

L25 As amiable as a **Lamb**
1479 Rivers *Cordyal* 82.23–4: Crist that . . . is now amyable . . . as a lambe. **1512** Copland *Helyas* A7r[19–20]: She is . . . amyable as a lambe.

L26 As blissful as a **Lamb** (*etc.*) (A number of single quotations are brought together here)
1422 Yonge *Governaunce* 212.3–4: Blesful as a lambe. **a1439** Lydgate *Fall* III 677.67: Now as a lamb tretable and benigne. **c1450** *Merlin* II 640[2–3]: Thow shalt be as wery ther-of as the lambe is of the wolf. **1456** Hay *Governaunce* 157.18: Sum suete as a lam.

L27 As chaste as a **Lamb**
a1398(1495) Bartholomaeus-Trevisa N8v[2.23–4]: It makyth men chaste as a lombe. Tilley L33.

L28 As gentle as a **Lamb**
a1533 Berners *Arthur* 85[27]: Gentyl as a lambe. *Oxford* 234; Taylor and Whiting 212; Tilley L34.

L29 As humble as a **Lamb**

c1515 Barclay *Eclogues* 197.446: Humble as a lambe, and called was Abell. Whiting *Drama* 318:197.

L30 As low as a **Lamb**
c1350 *Alexander A* 167.1178: Was nere lambe in no londe lower of chere. **1372** *Song of the Nativity* in Brown *Lyrics XIV* 77.63–4: Sithen, loveliche as a lomb, He put himself in here puwer. **a1376** *Piers* A vi 43: He is as louh as a lomb, ix 77, **c1378** B xx 36. **c1450** *Secrete of Secretes* 35.19. Apperson 519: Quiet; *Oxford* 234: Gentle.

L31 As meek as (a, any) **Lamb(s)**
c1225 *Wohunge of Ure Laverd* 273[34]: And tu, mi leve jhesu, for thi mikle meknesse to lamb was evenet. **c1300** *Speculum Gy* 13.260: Meke as a lomb, ful of pite. **c1340** Rolle *Psalter* 400 (113.4): Goed men that ere innocentis and meke as lambis. **c1350** *Seven Sages C* 34.1012: a. **c1375** *St. Cecelia* in Horstmann *Legenden 1881* 161.139–40: Now meke to the has scho made him Als a lamb. **c1380** Chaucer *CT* VIII[G] 199: As meke as evere was any lomb, to yow. **c1380** *Pearl* 30.815: As meke as lomp. **c1390** *Talkyng* 50.31–2: So meke as hit weore a lomb. **a1400** *Scottish Legends* I 337.1433, II 371.103: a. **c1400** *Brut* I 74.25: a. **a1410** Love *Mirrour* 233[15–6]: He as a meke and most pacient lambe. **a1410** *Prophecy* in Minot 108.150: a, 154, 157: a. **a1425** *St. Robert* 62.666. **1439** Lydgate *St. Albon* 142.884: a, **a1449** *Quis Dabit* in *MP* I 326.59: a, *Testament* in *MP* I 361.857. **a1450** *Three Middle English Sermons* 46.810–1: ani. **c1450** *Alphabet* I 118.4: a, II 270.18: a. **c1450** *Bothe yonge and oolde* in Furnivall *Hymns* 32.5: ony. **a1460** *Towneley Plays* 327.52: a. **1465** Leversege 28[23–4]: a. **a1475** *Ludus Coventriae* 274.90: A. **1479** Rivers *Cordyal* 82.23–4: a. **1483** Caxton *Golden Legende* 170v[2.3]: a, 192r[2.1]: lambes. **1483** *Vulgaria quedam abs Terencio* P7v[18–9]: a. **a1500** *Coventry Plays* 71.7–8: And after, mekely as a lamb, Upon the crose there dyd he dye. **a1500** Greene *Carols* 399.2: a. **a1500** *Think Before you Speak* in Brown *Lyrics XV* 282.62: As lome be meke. **1509** Hawes *Convercyon* A3r[13]: a. **a1533** Berners *Arthur* 85[27]: a. *Oxford* 234; Taylor and Whiting 213; Tilley L34; Whiting *Drama* 318:197, *Scots* I 196. See **S204.**

L32 As mild as (a) **Lamb**
c1300 *South English Legendary* I 349.33: And bicom as milde as a lomb, (*Laud*) 62.299: And for it (*a lamb*) is with-oute felonie and milde ase ihesu crist, 491.54: Als a lomb he is now mylde. **c1390** *Talkyng* 50.31–2. **a1410** *Prophecy* in Minot 108.157: a. **a1425** *St. Robert* 62.666: Als . . . mylde als lamme thai was. Apperson 416; *Oxford* 234; Taylor and Whiting 213; Tilley L34. See **S205.**

L33 As simple as a (the) **Lamb**
1422 Yonge *Governaunce* 212.3–4: Sympill . . . as a lambe. **a1425** *Governance of Lordschipes* 104.10–1. **a1449** Lydgate and Burgh *Secrees* 73.2301: the.

L34 As soft as a **Lamb**
a1425 *Governance of Lordschipes* 104.10–1: Softe as lombe. **c1500** *Cock* 1[4]. **1512** Copland *Helyas* A7r[19–20].

L35 As still as a **Lamb**
a1400 *Meditations* 38.1419: Writ hou he stod as lomb so stille. **a1439** Lydgate *Fall* I 196.6934: Stille as a lamb. **a1500** *Guy*[4] 122.3896. **c1500** *St. Anne (3)* 114.108. **1520** Whittinton *Vulgaria* 99.35. *Oxford* 234; Tilley L34; Whiting *Drama* 318:197.

L36 As tame as a **Lamb**
c1421 Lydgate *Thebes* I 158.3847: And lik a lombe was this Tygre tame, **c1433** *St. Edmund* 412.868: There was no lamb more tame. **c1450** *Jacob's Well* 268.23. **1483** Caxton *Golden Legende* 170v[2.2–3]. **1502** *Robert the Devil* C5v[23]. **a1513** Dunbar *To the Quene* 59.17: Ar now maid tame lyk ony lammis. Taylor and Whiting 213; Whiting *Scots* I 196. See **S211.**

L37 He that kisses the **Lamb** loves the sheep
1492 *Salomon and Marcolphus* 12[23]: He that kyssyth the lambe lovyth the shepe. See **C218, P27.**

L38 A **Lamb** (Lion) here and a lion (lamb) there (*varied*)
a1200 *Ancrene* 157.10: Lomb her, liun ther. **c1300** Robert of Gloucester I 96.1320–2: The prinse he sede other king nis to preisi noght, That in time of worre as a lomb is bothe mek and milde, And in time of pes as leon bothe cruel and wilde. **c1385** Usk 24.121–2: Lyons in the felde and lambes in chambre; egles at assaute and maydens in halle. **a1400** *Orologium* 347.31: The lambe is turnede in to a lyone. **a1420** Lydgate *Troy* I 18.216: In porte a lambe, in herte a lyoun fel, **c1433** *St. Edmund* 390.785: In pes lik lambes, in werre lik leouns, **a1439** *Fall* II 430.3650: In werre a leoun, and a lamb in pes, **1439** *St. Albon* 120.515: As a lambe in chambre, in bataile a lion. **a1450** *Gesta* 42[20–1]: In the feld he was a lyon, and in halle he was a lambe. **a1450** *Partonope* 425.10306–8: The

lorde above, merveyles can wele done, That can herborowe so in oo persone A lyons herte and a lambes also. **c1450** Capgrave *Katharine* 17.8: A lomb to the meke, a leon to the proude. **c1450** *Jacob's Well* 268.23–4: It makyth the tame as a lambe, there wretthe made the first ferse and wylde as a lyoun. **a1464** Capgrave *Chronicle* 145[12–3]: The Kyng of Frauns in face schewid himself a lomb, and in work a leon. **1464** Hardyng 98[24–6]: He had also a lambishe pacience, To here all pleyntes mekely with sobernes, A lyons chere in felde, 148[12–3]: As a lyon in felde was moste douteous, In house a lambe of mercy ever replete. **a1500** *Merita Missae* 153.174–5: They fare in chyrche as a lyone strong, And meke in feld as any lomb. Apperson 348–9; Taylor and Whiting 212; Tilley L311; Whiting *Scots* I 196. See **K50, L329, M10, 751.**

L39 The **Lamb** is not used to play the lion
a1439 Lydgate *Fall* II 545.2628–30: For of antiquite The lamb nat used to pleie the leoun, Nor no meek dowve envied the faucoun.

L40 Outward **Lambs** and inward wolves
a1400 *Romaunt C* 7013–6: Outward, lambren semen we, Fulle of goodnesse and of pitee, And inward we, withouten fable, Ben gredy wolves ravysable.

L41 To be bestepped (*attacked*) like a **Lamb** with wed (*mad*) wolves (*etc.*) (A number of single quotations are brought together here)
a1225 *St. Marherete* 8.7–8: Bistepped and bistonden ase lomb with wedde wulves. **a1300** *Alisaunder* 129.2280: And roof hym thorough als a lombe, 135.2390: And thorough hym thirleth so a lombe. **a1325** Bonaventura *Meditations* 16.484: And he, as a meke lambe, aftyr hem come. **c1370** Chaucer *ABC* 172: Right soo thi Sone list, as a lamb, to deye, **c1386** *LGW* 2317–8: And quok for fere, pale and pitously, Ryght as the lamb that of the wolf is biten. **c1390** *Charter of the Abbey* in *Yorkshire Writers* I 359–60: Crist wente as mekeliche to his hongynge as a lomb doth to his scherynge. **c1390** Chaucer *CT* I[A] 3704: I moorne as dooth a lambe after the tete. **c1390** *Lamentacioun* in *Vernon* I 307.229–30: I seigh nevere my sone chaungen hewe, But evere in on, as lomb I-lyche. **a1393** Gower *CA* III 373.4983–5: That lich a Lomb whanne it is sesed In wolves mouth, so was desesed Lucrece. **c1395** Chaucer *CT* IV[E] 538: And as a lamb she sitteth meke and stille. **1415** Hoccleve *Oldcastle* I 10.54: But, as a lamb, to holy chirche obeide. **a1426** Higden-Anon. Cont. VIII 457[18–20]: The kynge . . . apperede amonge theym as a lambe amonge wulfes. **1439** Lydgate *St. Albon* 135.497: Lyke a meke lambe, myne herte dyd agryse, 146.1112–3: Than was he put under governance Of the juge, as a lambe amonge houndes, 151.1448: Lyke a lambe monges wolfes all torent. **1493** *Tretyse of Love* 45.24: He was broughte forth thus as a lambe. **1555** Heywood *E* 148.6.5: Oh how like lambes, man and wyfe here agree, **1556** 120.33.3: Agreede lyke lams together dyvers yeres.

L42 To be led like a **Lamb** to death (knife, sacrifice)
c1300 *Evangelie* 601.1480–1: I am ledde opon that wise, As a meke lombe to sacrifice. **c1300** Robert of Gloucester I 468.6447: That so ver as milde lomb to dethe ylad were. **a1400** *Meditations* 14.499–500: Thou art led as lamb to knyf That goth so stille and maketh no stryf. **c1425** *Speculum Sacerdotale* 107.36: Ladde to be crucified as a lombe unto sacrifice. **a1450** Audelay 55.7–8: And as a lomb and ennosent, To be lad to sacrefyce. **a1475** *Woefully Arrayed* in Brown *Lyrics XV* 157.17: Like a lambe led unto sacrefise.

L43 To flee as **Lambs** do from the wolf
a1533 Berners *Arthur* 181[9–10]: Al fledde before hym, as lambes doth fro the wolfe. Whiting *Drama* 318:197. See **S221.**

L44 To follow like a **Lamb**
a1410 Love *Mirrour* 228[9]: He folwed hem as an innocent lambe. **a1450** *St. Katherine* (*Gibbs*) 16[4]: As a debonayr lombe folewed this oold Adrian. **c1489** Caxton *Blanchardyn* 106.26–8: They folowed after at the backe of hym, as the yonge lambe do the sheep. See **S222.**

L45 To look like (a) **Lamb**(s)
c1378 *Piers* B xv 200: Loketh as lambren and semen lyf-holy. **a1450** *York Plays* 281.273: He lokis like a lambe. **1546** Heywood *D* 92.58: I looke lyke a lambe in all your woordes to mee, **1556** *Spider* 197[16]: Flies looking like lams: spiders lyke lions looke.

L46 To look like **Lambs** and live as wolves
a1387 *Piers* C xvii 270: And as lambes thei loken and lyven as wolves. See **W474.**

L47 To seek after a **Lamb** and find a lion
c1450 Idley 143.2194: To seke after a lambe and fynde a leoun. See **L50.**

L48 To send as **Lambs** betwixt wolves
c1000 *WSG* Luke x 3: Nu ic eow sende swa

swa lamb betwux wulfas. **c1395** *WBible* Luke x 3: Y sende you as lambren among wolves.

L49 To stand like a **Lamb**
a1325 *Cursor* II 918.16063: Bifor tham jesus stode als a lambe, III 1376.24067. **c1390** Chaucer *CT* II[B] 617–8: For as the lomb toward his deeth is broght, So stant this innocent. See **S230.**

L50 Whilom a **Lamb,** now turned to a tiger
c1500 Fabyan 114[47–8]: This man that whylome was a lambe, was now turnyd to a tygre. See **L47.**

L51 To lap in a **Lambskin**
1546 Heywood *D* 79.59–60: She must obey those lambs, or els a lambs skyn, Ye will provyde for hir, to lap her in. Apperson 349; Tilley L40.

L52 To **Lament** does not avail
c1485 *Conversion* 45.475–6: Yt doyth not avayl us thus to lament, But lett us provyd for remedy shortlye. See **D337, G455, M729.**

L53 As bright as **Lamp**
a1325 *Cursor* III 1220.21311: The first o thaim als lamp es bright.

L54 To leam (*shine*) like (a) **Lamp**
a1508 Dunbar *Goldyn Targe* 113.30: That all the lake as lamp did leme of licht. Whiting *Scots* I 196.

L55 To shine like a **Lamp**
a1400 *Destruction of Troy* 158.4849: With a lyve of lewte, that as a laump shynes. Whiting *Scots* I 196.

L56 To wound like a **Lance**
c1475 *Mankind* 30.808: Yowur crymynose compleynt wondyth my hert as a lance.

L57 As stable as **Land**
a1400 Wyclif *Sermons* I 92[20]: Other men weren stable as lond.

L58 Each **Land** is own country to the strong
c1300 *South English Legendary* II 660.1528: Ech lond is . . . owe contreie to the stronge. Tilley M426.

L59 It is evil won **Land** to have while living and then hell at one's end
c1475 *Rauf* 112.918–20: That is full evill wyn land To have quhill thow ar levand, Sine at thine end hell.

L60 A **Land** headless (lordless, without a king) is in sorrow and dread (*varied*)
a1338 Mannyng *Chronicle A* I 232.6617–8: A lond hedles in tyme of nede, Over al thanne ys sorewe and drede. **c1410** Lovelich *Merlin* I 175.6601–2: What vaylleth the Lond that is lordles, Whanne hit hath nede rankewr to ses, 181.6839–40: For a lond with-owten governour May not enduren ayens ony schowr. **c1450** Capgrave *Katharine* 67.848: What is a lond whan it hath non hed? **c1450** *Merlin* I 92[27–8]: Thow shalt knowe well what a londe is worth that is with-outen a kynge, 95–6: And a londe withoute a lorde a-vaileth litill. See **H257, M217.**

L61 On fat **Land** grow foulest weeds
a1387 *Piers* C xiii 224: On fat londe and ful of donge foulest wedes groweth. Apperson 39:16; *Oxford* 193; Skeat 120.

L62 To be large (*generous*) of other men's **Land**
c1375 Barbour *Bruce* I 277.146–8: And larg(e)ly emang his men The landis of Scotland delt he then. Of othir mennis landis large wes he. Whiting *Scots* I 197. See **T217.**

L63 What is a **Land** where men are none? (*varied*)
a1393 Gower *CA* III 307.2695: What is a lond wher men ben none? **a1400** *Cursor* III 1358 F(L)T 23765–6: That lond is esy for to wynne That no man is to kepe it in, 1359 G 23765–6: Eth es for to win wind (*for* with) here, The land that nan is bote to were.

L64 To meet at **Land's End**
1549 Heywood *D* 85.166: Thou gossepst at home, to meete me at landes ende. Apperson 350; *Oxford* 349; Tilley L62.

L65 (Be)ware of hempen **Lane**
c1412 Hoccleve *Regement* 17.453–5: Me thynkyth this a verray inductif Unto stelthe; ware hem of hempen lane! Ffor stelthe is medid with a chekelew bane. NED Hempen 1b.

L66 Large (*blatant*) **Language** causes repentance
a1449 Lydgate *Cok* in *MP* II 817.154: Large language causith repentaunce.

L67 Mickle **Language** (*much talk*) may not all be faultless
c1477 Caxton *Curtesye* 14.136: Mekell langage may not all fautless be. See **M184, 203, 669, 773, S587, 590, 608, T37, 453, W593.**

L68 Utter your **Language** like the audience
a1449 Lydgate *Consulo* in *MP* II 750–3.8: Lyke the audience so uttir thy language, 16, 24, 32, 48, 56, 96. See **C130, T58.**

L69 A **Languet** (*latchet*) to tie up one's hose (*i.e.*, a blow)
a1460 *Towneley Plays* 29.224–5: Take the ther a langett To tye up thi hose!

L70 After **Languor** (*suffering*) lee (*peace*)
a1425 *Chester Plays* II 432.141–2: Pearles Prince of most Posty That after Langour sendeth Lee. See **B325, P8.**

L71 To bear the **Lantern**
c1412 Hoccleve *Regement* 23.615–6: That went on pylgrymage to taverne, Which be-for unthrift berith the lanterne. **a1500** *On England's Commercial Policy* in Wright *Political Poems* II 283[12]: Of alle the remes in the worlde this beryth the lanterne. NED Lantern 1c. See **B230.**

L72 To have eyes like **Lanterns**
a1400 *Alexander C* 267.5398: That light lemand eghen as lanterns he had. **c1440** *Prose Alexander* 102.36: And his eghne lyke twa lanternes.

L73 To hide one's **Lantern** (candle) under a bushel
a900 Alfred *Gregory* 43.2–3: Crist on his godspelle cuæð: Ne scyle nan mon blæcern ælan under mittan. **c1000** *WSG* Matthew v 15: Ne hi ne ælað hyra leohfæt, and hit under cyfe settað, ac ofer candelstæf þæt hit onlihte eallum þe on þam huse synt, Mark iv 21: Cwyst þu cymð ðæt leohtfæt þæt hit beo under bydene asett, oððe under bedde? Wite geare þæt hit sy ofer candelstæf asett, Luke viii 16. **c1390** Chaucer *CT* X[I] 1036: Ne men lighte nat a lanterne and put it under a busshel, but men sette it on a candle-stikke to yeve light to the men in the hous. **c1395** *WBible* Matthew v 15: Ne me teendith not a lanterne, and puttith it undur a busschel, but on a candilstike, that it gyve light to alle that ben in the hous, Mark iv 21, Luke viii 16, xi 33. **a1396**(1494) Hilton *Scale* E5r[2–4]: There is no man that lyghteth a lanterne for to sette it under a busshell but upon a candelstycke. **a1400** Wyclif *Sermons* I 270[13]: For bi this prestis ben hid under the bushel, 271[22–3]: That man puttith his lanterne in hidd place or undir a bushel. **c1400** Paues 205 (Matthew v 15): Nor men lyghte not a lanterne and putte it undir a buschel. **c1433** Lydgate *St. Edmund* 396.1089–92: Who can or may keepe cloos or hide A cleer lanterne whan that it is lyht, On a chaundelabre whan it doth abide; Or of the sonne difface the bemys bryht? **a1450** *Lernyng* in Kail 100–1.155–8: Youre prechyng shal be candel light, Nought under worldly buschel hyd, But on a candel-styke on hight; Nought under a chiste, under a lyd. **c1450** Capgrave *Lives* 93.1–2: He (*God*) is not wone to lyte a lanterne and hide it undyr a buschell, 136.10–1. **1487** *O thou most noble* 329[5–7]. **1528** More *Heresyes* 184 C[3–4]. *Oxford* 294; Taylor and Whiting 220; Tilley L275.

L74 To illumine like **Lanterns**
c1470 *Wallace* 371.1255: Lyk till lawntryns it illumynyt so cler. Whiting *Scots* I 197.

L75 To leam (*shine*) like a **Lantern**
c1325 *Loveliest Lady* 148.21–2: Hire lure lumes liht Ase a launterne anyht.

L76 To look like a **Lantern**
a1376 *Piers* A vii 164: He lokede lyk a lanterne al his lyf after. Skeat 110.

L77 As lean as **Lantern-horns**
a1400 *Siege of Jerusalem* 67.1146: Som lene on to loke as la(n)terne-hornes.

L78 To have something (someone) by the **Lap**
1413 ?Hoccleve *De Guilleville Poems* xxxvii.10–1: I wend, in sothfastnesse, Have had for evere Joye be the lappe. **c1422** Hoccleve *Dialog* 127.490: Now have I god, me thynkith, by the lappe.

L79 The false **Lapwing** (*varied*)
c1380 Chaucer *PF* 347: The false lapwynge, ful of trecherye. **a1393** Gower *CA* III 111.6045–7: And yit unto this dai men seith, A lappewincke hath lore his feith And is the brid falseste of alle. **c1400** *Plowman's Tale* 189.1339: And lapwinges, that wel conneth ly. **a1500** *Piers of Fullham* 14.328–30: Lappewynkes playnly, it is no fable, In their hertes ben so unstable, Whether they ben old or yong of age. Cf. Apperson 350; *Oxford* 350; Tilley L68.

L80 He that begins with **Largess** fails not to speed (*succeed*)
a1420 Lydgate *Troy* I 330.6496–9: For who that can with larges first be-gynne, Ne failleth nat after wel to spede Thorugh help of men, whan that he hath nede: For love folweth fredam comounly. See **G64, 261, M638.**

L81 **Largess** is worth little there wisdom wants
c1225 *Wohunge of Ure Laverd* 271[26–7]: Bote largesce is lutel wurth ther wisdom wontes.

L82 **Largess** stints all manner of strife
c1516 Skelton *Magnificence* 13.367: For Largesse stynteth all maner of stryfe. See **G81.**

L83 The more **Largess** gives away the more God sends her
a1400 ?Chaucer *Rom. A* 1155–60: Not Avarice,

the foule caytyf, Was half to gripe so ententyf, As Largesse is to yeve and spende; And God ynough alwey hir sende, So that the more she yaf awey The more, ywys, she hadde alwey. See **E118, G261.**

L84 To flee as the **Lark** does the sparhawk
c1380 *Ferumbras* 87.2679–80: And floghe thanne out of is way . . . So doth the larke on someres day, The sperhauk that is in flighte, 173.5555–6: Al-so floghe the Sarzyens Roland . . . So sperhauk doth the larke. **1485** Caxton *Charles* 193.31–3: For there was never larke fledde more ferfully tofore the sperhawke than the sarasyns fledde tofore rolland, **c1489** *Blanchardyn* 63.18–9: The whiche his enmyes fledde, as the larke doth the sperhauke. **a1500** *Partenay* 53.1388: That As A larke fro A hauke doth fle. **1525** Berners *Froissart* IV 360[8–9]: And fled before them as the larke dothe before the hawke.

L85 To rise or (*before*) the **Lark**
a1439 Lydgate *Fall* III 713.1428: In the dawenyng roos up or the larke. Apperson 533; *Oxford* 28; Taylor and Whiting 214; Tilley B186.

L86 Not reck a **Last** (*trace*)
a1400 *Scottish Legends* II 207.102–3: Rekis nocht a laste Hou foule ore unfaire we be. NED Last sb.[1] 1.

L87 What may ever **Last?**
c1380 Chaucer *HF* 1147: But men seyn, "What may ever laste?" *Oxford* 252: Good gear, 732: World. See **T87.**

L88 Evil **Late** (*behavior,* lake [*play*]) evil name
c1350 *Good Wife E* 160.44: Evil lat, evil name, **c1425** *H* 161.48: Evell lak, evell name.

L89 Better **Late** than never
c1330 *Gregorius* 146 A 835: Better is lat than never blinne. **a1387** Higden-Trevisa III 279[15–6]: And seide that it was bettre to lerne that crafte late than lerne it nevere. **c1395** Chaucer *CT* VIII[G] 1410: For bet than nevere is late. **a1400** *Ancrene* (*Recluse*) 160.24: Ac bettere is late than never Austin seith. **c1435** ?Lydgate *Dance* (*Lansdowne*) 61.440: Bettir late than nevyr to do good deede. **1448** Shillingford 36[8]. **c1450** *Douce MS.52* 56.140. **c1450** *Rylands MS.394* 108.24.1. **a1475** *Assembly of Gods* 36.1204: He seyde Vyce to forsake ys bettyr late then never. **c1475** *Rawlinson MS. D 328* 122.55: Beter latte to thri than never. **1483** Caxton *Cato* G1[r][21–2]. **a1500** Hill 129.43. **1529** More *Supplicacion* 336 G[3–4]: Sith that late is better than never, **1534** *Comforte* 1216 AB. **1546** Heywood *D* 37.85, **1555** *E* 198.300. Apperson 44; *Oxford* 40; Smith 169; Taylor and Whiting 215; Tilley L85. See **T211.**

L90 **Lateware** receives no good at the dole (*distribution*)
a1393 Gower *CA* II 308.250–3: Bot Slowthe mai no profit winne, Bot he mai singe in his karole How Latewar cam to the Dole, Wher he no good receive mihte. See **B155.**

L91 He **Laughs** that wins
1546 Heywood *D* 26.22: He laugth that wynth, **1555** *E* 187.229: They laugh that win. Apperson 352; *Oxford* 352; Taylor and Whiting 215; Tilley L93; Whiting *Drama* 264.

L92 (He) that now **Laughs** oft may weep
a1500 *Clerk and the Nightingale I* in Robbins 173.20: That now lawgh oft may wepe.

L93 As green as (the, any) **Laurel**
c1395 Chaucer *CT* IV[E] 1464–6: I feele me nowhere hoor but on myn heed; Myn herte and alle my lymes been as grene As laurer thurgh the yeer is for to sene. **a1405** Lydgate *Floure* in *MP* II 417.238: Fayrest in our tonge, as the laurer grene. **c1500** *Lancelot* 3.82: A birde, that was as ony lawrare gren. Cf. Tilley L95.

L94 All the **Lave** (*rest*) good and so good end
c1420 Wyntoun VI 257.1–6: *Omnis consummacionis* I saw that ende, The prophet said, lik to commende: Al the laif gud, and sa gud ende, In al statis I that commende. Al the laif gud, and sa gud fyne, Makis al the sowme gud, said Hendyne. See **B204.**

L95 **Lave** (*remnant*) in the rock (*distaff*) is no thief
a1400 Bozon *Contes* 117[15–23]: Ils ne veolent pas aver le noun des larons, sicom l'em dit jadys de un peigneresce en suth pays, de un femme qe fust apellé *Leve in thi rokke,* qe fust sotil en le mester de peigneresce, mès nul oeveraigne prendreit de homme ne de femme qu ele ne prendreit e en portereit graund partie de la leyne, ja tant ne lui fust doné pur son servise, dont de lui sourdi un tiel parlance: *Leve in thi rokke ne is no thef, Take other mannez wulle is hire to lef.*

L96 As sweet as any **Lavender** seeds
a1500 *Beauty of his Mistress III* in Robbins 127.18–20: And your-selfe as swete as ys . . . any lavender sedes strawen yn a coofer To smell.

L97 **Law** can do nothing without good (*property*)
a1475 *Hit is ful harde* in *MLN* 55(1940) 566.5:

Lawe can do no thyng withouten good. See **L110.**

L98 **Law** goes as it is favored
1455 Paston III 22[7–8]: For nowadays ye know well that law goeth as it is favored. See **L100.**

L99 The **Law** goes by no lanes
c1400 *Beryn* 101.3358–9: The lawe goith by no lanys, But hold(ith) forth the streyt wey, even as doith a lyne. See **T512.**

L100 The **Law** is ended as folk are friended
1556 Heywood *Spider* 123[13–4]: Yet sum say, sumtime, that the law is eended, In sum case, in sum place: as folke are freended. Apperson 396:46; *Oxford* 402; Tilley M63. See **L98.**

L101 The **Law** is not to hide
c1330 *Horn Childe* 186.618: The lawe is nought to hide.

L102 **Law** lies in lordship (*varied*)
c1405 *Mum* 73.1583–4: For lawe lieth muche in lordship sith loyaute was exiled, And poure men pleyntes penylees a-bateth. **c1415** *Middle English Sermons* 238.39–239.1: For trewly lawe goys as lordshipp biddeth hym. See **M534.**

L103 **Law** of kind (*nature*) is free
a1439 Lydgate *Fall* II 361.1170: Afferme also, how lawe of Kynde is fre. See **K27.**

L104 The **Law** of Medes and Persians
c1395 *WBible* Daniel vi 12: The word is soth bi the decree of Medeis and Perseis, which it is not leveful to breke, 15: Wite thou, kyng, that it is the lawe of Medeis and of Perseis, that it is not leveful that ony decree be chaungid, which the kyng ordeyneth. *Oxford* 353; Tilley L113.

L105 **Laws** are forlorn (*lost*) in war time
c1300 Robert of Gloucester I 392–3.5389–91: Vor they me segge that lawes beth in worre tyme vorlore. Nas it noght so bi is daye, vor thei he in worre werre, Lawes he made right-volore and strengore than er were. Cf. Tilley D624.

L106 **Laws** are like lop-webs (*cobwebs*) which take small flies and let great flies go
c1412 Hoccleve *Regement* 102.2815–21: Smal tendirnesse is had now of our lawes; Ffor if so be that oon of the grete wattes A dede do, which that a-geyn the lawe is, No thyng at al he punysshid for that is; Right as lop-webbys, flyes smale and gnattes Taken, and suffre grete flyes go, Ffor al this worlde, lawe is now rewlyd so. **1534** More *Comforte* 1226 E[7–14]: The lawes . . . shall they make as an olde Philosopher saide to be muche lyke unto cobwebbes, in whych the lyttle Knattes, and Flyes stycke styll and hange fast, but the great humble Bees breake them and fly quite thorowe. Apperson 353; *Oxford* 354; Tilley L116. See **F231, T71.**

L107 Such **Law** as a man gives another he should use himself (*varied*)
c1390 Chaucer *CT* II[B] 43–5: For swich lawe as a man yeveth another wight, He sholde hymselven usen it, by right; Thus wole oure text. **a1500** Warkworth 13[6–8]: And so the Erle of Worcetre was juged be suche lawe as he dyde to other menne. Apperson 392; *Oxford* 353; Skeat 101; Tilley L118. See **D282, L463.**

L108 To hold no better **Law** than the hound with his fellow
a1300 *Arthour and M.*[1] 17.491–2: And held no better lawe, Than the hounde with his felawe, **a1500** *Arthour and M.*[2] 296.493–6. Cf. Tilley D462. See **D333.**

L109 Where **Law** lacks error grows
a1393 Gower *CA* II 19.511–2: Wher lawe lacketh, errour groweth, He is noght wys who that ne troweth.

L110 Who will have **Law** must have money
c1475 *Wisdom* 57.669: Wo wyll have law, must have monye. Tilley L125. See **L97.**

L111 Wrong **Laws** make short lords
1464 Hardyng 186[16–8]: A proverbe is of olde was (which) wysemen kend, That wronge lawes (make ever) shorte lordes, Whiche wysemen (yet) remembre, and recordes. *Oxford* 736.

L112 From **Lawdian** (?Lothian) to London
c1475 Henryson *Sum Practysis* 159.61: Thair is nocht sic ane lechecraft fra lawdian to lundin.

L113 As sweet as the **Lawn**
a1500 Kennedy 42.362: Bot with that face mair sueiter than the lawn. DOST *s.v.* Laun, suggests *quhiter* for *sueiter*, or *balm* for *lawn*. Cf. Whiting *Ballad* 28: White.

L114 He that will sell **Lawn** before he can fold it shall repent before he have sold it
1546 Heywood *D* 32.35–6: He that will sell lawne before he can folde it, He shall repent him before he have solde it. Apperson 353; *Oxford* 573; Tilley L121.

L115 As blae (*livid*) as **Lead**
a1325 *Cursor* II 466.8073: Bla als led thai war. **c1440** *St. Christopher* 460.525: His body wexe als bla als lede.

L116 As black as (any) **Lead**
c1303 Mannyng *Handlyng* 365.11727–8: Thys Ananyas fyl dowun dede, As, blak, as any lede. **a1325** *Cursor* II 466.8073: Blac . . . als led thai war. **c1440** *St. Christopher* 464.827.

L117 As blo (*blackish blue*) as (any) **Lead**
c1400 *Thomas of Erceldoune* 8.136: Hyr body als blo as ony lede (*var.* beten leed). **a1425** *Metrical Paraphrase OT* 128.18365: So lay he bolnand, blo als led. **a1438** Kempe 69.34–5: Sche wex as blo as any leed, 105.20–1: (*She*) wex al blew and al blo as it had ben colowr of leed. **a1460** *Towneley Plays* 268.327. **a1475** *Guy*[2] 134.4667: any. **a1490** Ripley *Mistery* in Ashmole 383[12]: any. **1493** *Tretyse of Love* 31.7–9: The fayr colour of your lyppys ys now becum as blo as led that had be gretly betyn. **c1522** Skelton *Speke* II 21.428: Wanne, bloo as lede.

L118 As blue as (any) **Lead**
c1410 Lovelich *Merlin* I 179.6764: Al-thowgh he seme as blw as led. **a1437** *Kingis Quair* 88.153[2]: With bakkis blewe as lede. **a1438** Kempe 140.23: Than wex sche al blew as it had ben leed. **1449** Metham 56.1512: ony. **a1508** Skelton *Phyllyp* I 53.61.

L119 As cold as (any) **Lead**
c1390 *Mary and the Cross* 620.303: Heore hertes were colde as lumpyng led. **1449** Metham 61.1650: Hys hert gan cold . . . wax as ony led. **c1450** Idley 209.342: The prest hart waxyd colde . . . as lede. **1509** Barclay *Ship* I 296[4]. Svartengren 313; Whiting *Scots* I 197.

L120 As dowf (*dull*) as (any) **Lead**
1513 Douglas *Aeneid* II 219.95: Harland hys wery lymmys dolf as led, IV 28.102: Full cald of curage, dolf as ony led, 31.189: the led.

L121 As dull as **Lead**
a1500 *As I fared thorow* in Dyboski 89.29: This makyth my hart as dull as lede. **c1522** Skelton *Speke* II 23.459. Svartengren 53.

L122 As haw (*blue*) as (the) **Lead**
c1475 Henryson *Testament* 114.257: Haw as the Leid. **1501** Douglas *Palice* 19.27: Dartis haw as leid. Whiting *Scots* I 198.

L123 As heavy as (the, any, a piece of, a clob of, lump of) **Lead**
a750 *Riddles* in *Exeter Book* 202.74–5: Hefigere ic eom . . . þonne . . . unlytel leades clympre. **a1325** *Maximion* in Böddeker 247.82: Myn herte is hevy so led, 250.151, 253.251. **a1338** Mannyng *Chronicle A* I 317.9069–70, *B* I 38[6], II 252[1]. **c1340** Rolle *Psalter* 505 (Song of Moses [I] 11). **a1350** *Alexius* (*1*) (*Laud 108*) 66.444: Hevy so any led. **c1375** *St. Cristina* in Horstmann *Legenden 1881* 95.253. **c1380** *Ferumbras* 130.4171–2. **c1390** *Alexius* (*Vernon*) 66.443–4: He fel a-doun to the grounde As hevi as the led. **c1390** *Lamentacioun* in *Vernon* I 324: *var.* after 624. **c1390** *Verses on the Earthquake of 1382* in Brown *Lyrics XIV* 188.69. **c1395** *WBible* Ecclesiasticus xxii 17: What schal be maad hevyere than leed? **a1400** *Alle-mighty god* in *Yorkshire Writers* II 43.564. **a1400** *Amadace I* 30[6]. **a1400** *Esto Memor Mortis* in Brown *Lyrics XIV* 240.26: any. **a1400** *Ipomadon A* 44.1474, 50.1687. **a1400** *Le Morte A*. 29.905: Any, 114.3738: Any. **a1400** *Northern Verse Psalter* I 31 (12.4 *var.*). **a1400** *Scottish Legends* I 473.530. **c1400** *St. Anne* (*1*) 21.771. **c1400** *Gowther* 155.492. **c1400** *Laud Troy* II 338.11478: the. **c1400** *Plowman's Tale* 152.159–60: A staf of golde, and perrey, lo! As hevy as it were mad of leed. **c1412** Hoccleve *Regement* 140.3882: He vexith hevy as a peece of leed. **1414** ?Brampton *Psalms* 13[19]: My synnes ben hevy as hevy leed. **c1422** Hoccleve *Lerne to Die* 203.655: And my look ful dym and hevy as leed. **a1425** *Hayle, bote of bale* in *Wheatley MS.* 8.62: Never no leede so hevy was, 12.205: the. **a1425** *Metrical Paraphrase OT* 48.7337, 12.9806, 106. 13177. **a1430** Lydgate *Pilgrimage* 375.13854, 618.23160–1: as a clobbe of leed, 650.24259–60. **c1430** ?Lydgate *Compleynt* 61.182: ony. **a1449** Lydgate *Fabula* in *MP* II 510.738. **1449** Metham 61.1650: ony. **a1450** *Castle* 164.2924: any. **a1450** *Generydes A* 159.5102: any. **a1450** *Partonope* 409.9865–6: The soudan hoveth as hevy as lede, The tothe-ache I trow be in his hede, 438.10805. **a1450** *York Plays* 103.15, 139.20–1, 166.297: any, 241.21: any, 367.262. **c1450** Capgrave *Katharine* 67.850, 103.411: ony, 356.549: the, 364.784, 379.1238: oony, 392.1620: ony, 394.1685. **c1450** Idley 84.217: ony, 128.1226, 209.342. **c1450** *Jacob's Well* 141.27. **c1450** *Northern Passion* 54 CIi 533, A 533: any. **a1460** *Towneley Plays* 42.82, 346.210, 389.71: any. **c1470** *Wallace* 27.309. **a1475** Banester *Guiscardo* 30.518. **a1475** *Guy*[2] 168.5877, 306.10646: the. **a1475** *Ludus Coventriae* 13.421, 160.273: as lympe of leede, 317.1332. **1481** Caxton *Reynard* 37[26], **1483** *Golden Legende* 195[r][2.3]. **c1485** *Burial and Resurrection* 179.225, 192.617. **c1485** *Mary Magdalene* (*Digby*) 64.272. **a1500** *Coventry Plays* 64.1015: any. **a1500** *Now late me thought* 279[30]. **1523** Skelton *Garlande* I 426.3. Apperson 296; Taylor and Whiting 216; Tilley L134; Whiting *Ballad* 28, *Drama* 319:201.

L124 As hot as any **Lead** (*cauldron*)
c1450 Idley 135.1656: He loovith hir as hoote as ony leede.

L125 As low as **Lead**
a1425 *Metrical Paraphrase OT* 73.2314: To lyght them that lay low os led, 34.14977. **a1475** *Court of Sapience* 213.2306: They are but erthe, and brought (as) lowe as lede.

L126 As pale as (any, beaten) **Lead**
a1400 *In Alisaundre* in Horstmann *Sammlung* 180.521: Hire face was pale as eny leed. **1449** Metham 72.1969: ony. **a1500** *Chaucers Dreme* in Speght *Chaucer* 357v[2.38]: any. **a1500** *Squire* 42 P 150: as beaten leade. **c1500** *Lady Bessy* 9[8]. **1506** Hawes *Pastime* 76.1958: ony, 216.5619: ony. **1515** Barclay *St. George* 84.2066, 85.2094. Tilley L135; Whiting *Scots* I 198.

L127 As red as burning **Lead**
c1350 *Seven Sages A* 133 E 2788–9: And the tonge also there on rede, As evyr was brennynge lede.

L128 As sad (*heavy*) as the **Lead**
a1513 Dunbar *Dream* 128.20: Sad as the leid. NED Sad A 7, quote c1638.

L129 As wan as (the, any) **Lead**
c1325 *When I think* in Brown *Lyrics XIII* 151.13: Mi soule is won so is the led. **c1395** Chaucer *CT* VIII[G] 728: Now is it wan and of a leden hewe. **a1398**(1495) Bartholomaeus-Trevisa v4v[2.31–2]: Pale in colour other wanne as leed. **c1420** Page *Siege* 198.1231–2: With wan color as the lede (*vars.* as any lede; wan as lede), Not lyke to lyve but unto dede. **c1450** *Brut* II 420.30. **a1460** *Towneley Plays* 391.146. **a1500** *Orfeo* 10 Harley 106: ony. **a1513** Dunbar *Dream* 128.25: Hir hew was wan and wallowed as the leid. **1520** Whittinton *Vulgaria* 36.29. Tilley L135.

L130 **Lead** and gold (*varied*)
c1300 *South English Legendary* II 644.1037–8: For led nepasseth noght so muche in bounte as gold iwis, For the dignete of preost herre thanne lewed is. **a1325** *Cursor* III 1362.23861–2: Hu mai he be him-selven hald That cheses him the led for gold, **a1400** FT: That chesyth lede And levyth the gold. **1534** Heywood *Love* B3v[23]: No greater dyfference betwene lede and golde. Whiting *Drama* 319:201.

L131 To be like **Lead**
a1400 *Morte Arthure* 116.3954: His lippis like to the lede, and his lire falowede. **c1400** *Thomas of Erceldoune* (*Thornton*) 8.136: And all hir body lyke the lede, (*Lansdowne*) 9.136: And all hir body as betyn lede. **a1420** Lydgate *Troy* III 608.1526: Of colour like to lede, **a1430** *Pilgrimage* 346.12756: Hyr fface colouryd was lyk led. **a1450** *Death and Life* 6.170: And her lere like the lead that latelye was beaten. **c1475** Henryson *Orpheus* 140.351: Hir Lilly lyre wes lyk unto the leid, *Testament* 110.155: His lyre was lyke the Leid. **c1500** Greene *Carols* 420.5: Ye loke lyke lede, 462.3: Lyke lede hys colore was. **1509** Barclay *Ship* II 115[20–1]: With colour . . . Somtyme as lede. **1513** Douglas *Aeneid* III 23.52: This ryver collorit as the led.

L132 To have no **Lead** on one's heels
c1475 *Mankind* 21.548: I promes yow I have no lede on my helys. Tilley L136; Whiting *Drama* 352:675.

L133 To sink like (a plumb of) **Lead**
a1400 *Thy Joy be in the love of Jesus* in Brown *Lyrics XIV* 108.11: Syn synkes as lede. **c1410** Lovelich *Grail* III 113.289–90: Into the water they sonken . . . As thowgh it hadde ben . . . led. **a1500** *Stations* 365.769: Bot synkys done, as a plombe of lede.

L134 To wallow (*fade*) like **Lead**
c1475 *Thewis* 185.132: And vallowit on the morn as lede. Whiting *Scots* I 198.

L135 To weigh like any **Lead**
c1475 *Mankind* 25.692: Yt weys as ony lede.

L136 As fele (*many*) as **Leaves** on trees (*varied*)
c1380 Chaucer *HF* 1945–7: And eke this hous hath of entrees As fele as of leves ben in trees In somer, whan they grene been. **a1508** Dunbar *Flyting* 11.195–6: Ma wormis hes thow beschittin Nor thair is . . . leif on lind. Cf. Taylor and Whiting 216.

L137 As green as (a) **Leaf**
c1475 Henryson *Testament* 113.238: Now grene as leif. **1525** Berners *Froissart* IV 448–9: The duke . . . waxed pale and grene as a lefe.

L138 As light as **Leaf**
c1390 *Think on Yesterday* in Brown *Lyrics XIV* 143.13: This day, as leef we may be liht.

L139 As light as **Leaf** (up)on lind
c1325 *In may hit murgeth* in Brown *Lyrics XIII* 146.3: Ant lef is lyht on lynde. **c1378** *Piers* B i 154: Was nevere leef upon lynde lighter ther-after. **c1395** Chaucer *CT* IV[E] 1211: Be ay of chiere as light as leef on lynde. **a1450** *Castle* 184.3595–6. **a1450** *Partonope* 27.990. **c1450** *Chaunce* 8.104. **c1450** *Robin Hood and the Monk*

in Child III 100.76. **c1475** *Golagros* 10–1.289–90: Yit sall be licht as leif of the lynd lest, That welteris doun with the wynd, sa waverand it is. **a1500** *Ryght as small flodes* 157.138. Apperson 368; Tilley L139; Whiting *Scots* I 198. See **L295.**

L140 As light as **Leaf** on (a) tree
a1400 *Rowlande* 86.996: He was lyghte als lefe one tree. **a1450** *York Plays* 444.346: Nowe am I light as leyf on tree. **a1460** *Towneley Plays* 127.357–8: As lyght I me feyll As leyfe on a tre, 325.623. **c1475** Henryson *Robene* 153.65–6: Robene on his wayis went, Als licht as leif of tre. Whiting *Scots* I 198.

L141 As lithy (*pliable*) as a **Leaf**
a1400 *Siege of Jerusalem* 59.1027–8 (*var.*): That the fyngres and feet, fustes and joyntes, Weryn lethy as a leef and lost han her strengthe.

L142 As swift as **Leaf** on lind
a1450 *Pride of Life* in Waterhouse 96.263–4: Qwher is Mirth my messager, Swifte so lefe on lynde.

L143 As thick as **Leaves** (*varied*)
a1300 *XI Pains* 154.241–2: Ther-inne goth soulen thikkur inouh Than leves fallen of the bouh. **c1300** Robert of Gloucester I 93.1287–8: That folc vel doun vorwounded and aslawe in either side As thicke as leves doth of tren ayen winteres tide. **c1400** *Laud Troy* I 287.9737–8: As thik as leve on the tre He sles hem doun by two or thre. **c1440** *St. Christopher* 464.873–4: For alle thaire arows hange in the ayre, Als thike als leves dose on trees. Taylor and Whiting 216.

L144 To fall like (a, the) **Leaf** (leaves)
c1300 Robert of Gloucester I 310.4401: That folc vel to grounde aslawe as leves doth of tre. **c1395** *WBible* Isaiah lxiv 6: And alle we fellen doun as a leef, and our wickidnessis as wynd han take awei us. **a1400** *Responcio* in E. K. Chambers and F. Sidgwick *Early English Lyrics* (London, 1907) 19.26: I falle so doth the lef on the tree. **c1400** *Laud Troy* I 316.10707–8: Thei falle afftir him as doth the leves In wynter-tyme that growes on greves. **1414** ?Brampton *Psalms* 30[10]: I falle as doth the leef on tre.

L145 To fallow (*fade*) like the **Leaf** (*etc.*) (A number of single quotations are brought together here)
c1325 *De Clerico* 152.3: Al y falewe so doth the lef in somer when hit is grene. **c1390** *Of clene Maydenhod* 466.40: Hit wol to-dryve as lef on bouh. **c1395** *WBible* Proverbs xi 28: But just men schulen burjowne as a greene leef. **c1400** *Laud Troy* I 264.8965–8: On every a side Achilles schakes . . . As levis wagges with the wynde. **a1450** *Partonope* 40.1484–7: Here herte wyth-in her body fferde Lyke as the leffe dothe on a tre, When hyt ys blowe, as thou may see, Wyth hydowesse wynde and tempaste grette. **c1500** *O lady myne* in *Anglia* 72(1954) 411.122: And never fro yow to meve as lefe wyth wynde.

L146 To quake like (the, any, a) **Leaf** (leaves) (on tree, lind)
a1400 *Meditations* 7.225–6: With that woys the fend gan quake As doth the lef when wyndis wake, 50.1913–4: Thei gonne to quake, As doth the lef whan wyndes wake, 57.2181: Thei quaked as dede the lef on tre. **a1400** *Quatrefoil* 14.418: Qwakande als lefe appon tree. **a1410** *Prophecy* in Minot 110.239–40: Than sall all Ingland quakeand be, Als leves that hinges on the espe tre. **c1410** Lovelich *Grail* II 346.215–7: That It ne qwakede and schok Also As dide Ony lef uppon A tre That with the wynd Mevede sekerle. **a1450** *Partonope* 371.9067–8: That as a lefe With wynde yshake, so quoke hir brethe. **a1460** *Towneley Plays* 365.360: Mi flesh it quakys as lefe on lynde. **a1475** *Guy*[2] 339.11808: All y qwake as leef on tre. Whiting *Scots* I 198. See **A216.**

L147 To tremble like (a, the) **Leaf** (on tree, on aspen tree)
a1400 *Quatrefoil* 14.418: Trembland . . . als lefe appon tree. **1413** ?Hoccleve *De Guilleville Poems* lvii 179: But tremble as doth a leef upon a tree. **c1440** Charles of Orleans 89.2637: With hert tremblyng as leef of aspen tre. **1471** Caxton *Recuyell* I 278.20–2: The moste hardy . . . tremblid for fere as a leef on a tree, II 380.11–2: And tremblyng as the leef on the tree they durst not abide. Whiting *Scots* I 198. See **A216.**

L148 To turn the **Leaf**
1480 Caxton *Ovyde* 5[18–9]: Now I wil torn my muse on that other side of the leef and synge a songe. **1546** Heywood *D* 69.105: She will tourne the leafe. Apperson 652; *Oxford* 676; Taylor and Whiting 217; Tilley L146.

L149 But (*without*) **Lealty** all other virtues are not worth a flea
c1475 Henryson *Fables* 78.2285–6: For it is said in Proverb: "But lawte All uther vertewis ar nocht worth ane fle." Apperson 456:12.

L150 In **Lealty** there is no lack
a1500 *Eger H* 299.1908: And in lawtie there is no lack. See **L508.**

L151 **Lealty** is kend (*made known*) at the last

c1450 *Consail and Teiching* 70.171: For atte last lawte is kend.

L152 **Lealty** is the fairest thing
c1450 *Ratis* 17.565–6: Quhen ilke thing cumis to the lycht Than lawte fairest is in sicht.

L153 **Lealty** is to love (*praise*)
c1375 Barbour *Bruce* I 16.365–74: Leaute to luff is gretumly; Throuch leaute liffis men rychtwisly: With a wertu (of) leaute A man may yeit sufficyand be: And but leawte may nane haiff price, Quhethir he be wycht or he be wyss; For quhar it failyeys, na wertu May be off price, na off valu, To mak a man sa gud, that he May symply gud man callyt be.

L154 As bright as any **Leam** (*flame*)
a1300 *Meidan Maregrete* 491.53: Maidan Maregrete, britt so eni leme, 494.161. **c1330** *St. Margaret* 229.134.

L155 To low (*glow*) as **Leam**
a1400 *Alexander C* 8.226: The lede lawid in hire lofe as leme dose of gledis.

L156 He that may **Learn** and hold fast shall be wise at the last
a1475 *Guy*[2] 1.15–6: He, that myght lerne and holde faste, He schulde wexe wyse at the laste.

L157 **Learn** or be lewd (*ignorant*)
c1450 Idley 81.36: But thow lerne thow shalt be lewde. **c1477** Caxton *Curtesye* 4.21: Who wolle not lere, nedely must be lewid. **a1500** *Lytylle Childrenes Lytil Boke* (*Harley MS.541*) in Furnivall *Babees Book* 24[109–10]: Lerne or be lewde, quod Whytyng. **a1529** Skelton *Garnesche* I 130.127: Lerne or be lewde.

L158 He that wot (*knows*) **Least** oft says most
c1175 *Poema Morale* 177.112: Se thet lest wot seith ofte mest, and se thet al wot, is stille.

L159 As heavy as **Leather**
a1425 *Metrical Paraphrase OT* 12.9806: Hyr hert was hevy os lether.

L160 As tough as **Leather**
a1300 *Alisaunder* 327 M 415–6: Clay they have in that lande As towghe as leder. Apperson 642; Taylor and Whiting 401; Tilley L166.

L161 To look in the **Leather** of one's left boot
c1380 *Cleanness* 58.1580–1: And alle that loked on that letter as lewed thay were, As thay had loked in the lether of my lyft bote. See **F477.**

L162 To shine like barked (*tanned*) **Leather**
a1449 Lydgate *Jak Hare* in *MP* II 446.30: As barkyd leder his fface ys schynyng.

L163 Better **Leave** than lack
1546 Heywood *D* 26.12: Better leave then lacke. Apperson 44; *Oxford* 40; Tilley L172.

L164 He that will thrive must ask **Leave** of his wife (*varied*)
a1500 *Basyn* 45.21–3: Hit is an olde seid saw, I swere be seynt Tyve; Hit shal be at the wyves will if the husbonde thryve, Bothe within and with(o)wte. **a1500** Greene *Carols* 410.13: For hym that cast hym for to thryve, He must aske leve of his wyff. **1549** Heywood *D* 45.127: He that will thrive must aske leave of his wife. Apperson 631; *Oxford* 656; Tilley L169.

L165 **Leave** is light
1546 Heywood *D* 37.56: Ye might have knokt er ye came in, leave is light, **1555** *E* 169.134. Apperson 357; *Oxford* 359; Tilley L170.

L166 To lie with one's **Leches** (*looks*)
a1200 Lawman II 148.13703–4: Mid his lechen he gon lighen, His heorte wes ful blithe. See **F2.**

L167 **Lechery** is no sin (*varied*)
c1303 Mannyng *Handlyng* 22.593: Lechery ys but lyght synne. **c1378** *Piers* B iii 57–8: Who may scape the sklaundre the skathe is sone amended; It is a synne of the sevene sonnest relessed. **a1439** Lydgate *Fall* II 361.1181–3: Reherse these storyes for excusacioun Off ther errour, therbi a pris to wynne, As tofor God lecheri wer no synne. **c1450** Idley 200.2555: As tofore God lecherie were noo synne (*from Fall*). **c1475** *Mankind* 26.699: There arn but sex dedly synnys: lechery ys non. **1533** More *Confutacion* 705 AB: For never was there with us so great a lechour, that ever woulde preache that lecherye was no sinne. Whiting *Scots* II 125. See **L478.**

L168 The **Lectuary** (*remedy*) comes all too late when men carry the corpse to the grave
c1385 Chaucer *TC* v 741–2: But al to late comth the letuarie, Whan men the cors unto the grave carie. *Oxford* 4. Cf. Apperson 3; Tilley D133. See **A72, C51, L178, M484, S45.**

L169 In **Lede** (*people*) is not to lain (*conceal*)
a1300 *Richard* 82.24 (*var.*): In Lede is nought to leyn. **a1400** *Awntyrs* 123.83: In lede es noghte to layne. **c1450** Holland *Howlat* 56.267: Mony allegiance leile, in leid nocht to layne it, 76.852. See **H281.**

L170 He is a good **Leech** that can recure himself
c1430 Lydgate *Dance* 54.424: Good leche is he

that can hym self recure. Apperson 261; Tilley P262.

L171 Leech, heal thyself
c1000 *WSG* Luke iv 23: Eala, læce, gehæl ðe sylfne. **c1395** *WBible* Luke iv 23: Leeche, heele thi silf. **c1400** *Elucidarium* 29[16]: Blynde leches, heeleth first youre silf. **c1412** Hoccleve *Regement* 7.162–3: Cure, good man! ya, thow arte a fayre leche! Cure thi self. **c1425** *Orcherd* 282.19–20. **c1449** Pecock *Repressor* I 3[23]. **1450** *Dicts* 84.1: And whan the leche may not hele him-silf, how shulde he hele other, 156.6–8: Thou shalte fare as a seke leche, the whiche canne not hele him-silf and enforcethe him to hele othir that hathe the same sikenes. **1477** Rivers *Dictes* 34[1–2], 44[35–6], 67[16–7]: Thou shalt be as the leche that is seke and can not hele him self. **1484** Caxton *Aesop* 221[18–9]: For the leche whiche wylle hele somme other ought fyrste to hele hym self. Apperson 492; *Oxford* 497; Tilley P267. See **S43.**

L172 A **Leech** may do no cure while the iron sticks in the wound
c1175 *Lambeth Homilies* 23[14–5]: Hu mei the leche the lechnien, tha hwile thet iren sticat in thine wunde? See **I61.**

L173 A **Leech** may not heal a wound unless the sick man show it to him (*varied*)
c1000 *Pseudo-Alcuin* 384.331–2: Hwu mæig se læce gehælen þa wunde, þe se untrume scuneð, þæt he him eowie? **a1050** Defensor *Liber* 38[9–10]: Ambrosius sæde ne na soðlice him gegearcian miht læcedom þæs þe ys wund digle. **1340** *Ayenbite* 174[27–9]: And thervore zayth boeice the wyse thet "yef thou wilt thet the leche the hele: hit be-hoveth thet thou onwri thine wonde." **c1380** Chaucer *Boece* I pr. iv 4–6: Yif thou abidest after help of thi leche, the byhoveth discovre thy wownde, **c1385** *TC* i 857–8: For whoso list have helyng of his leche, To hym byhoveth first unwre his wownde. **c1390** *Who says the Sooth* in Brown *Lyrics XIV* 153.38–40: For let a man be sore I-wounde, Hou schulde a leche this mon releeve, But yif he mighte ronsake the wounde? **a1400** *Cursor* III 1498 F 26598–9: For mai na leche save na wounde, Bot hit ware sene un-to the grounde. **c1400** *Vices and Virtues* 176.18–9: Ne the leche ne may not hele a wounde but he see openliche al the wounde. **1410** Walton *Boethius* 29[15–8]. **c1412** Hoccleve *Regement* 10.260–3: Ryght so, if the list have a remedye Of thyn annoy that prikketh the so smerte, The verray cause of thin hyd maladye Thou most discover, and telle oute al thin herte. **1420** Lydgate *Temple* 38.913–7: For who that wil of his preve peine Fulli be cured, his life to help and save, He most mekeli oute of his hertis grave Discure his wound, and shew it to his lech, Or ellis deie for defaute of speche. **1450** *Dicts* 58.33–60.1: A leche may nott hele a sike man bot if he telle him the trouthe of his sikenes. **a1475** Ashby *Dicta* 90.1052–4: And hidithe to his leche the verite . . . He must slee hymselfe. **1480** Caxton *Ovyde* 14[29–32]: In al the worlde is no master ne Physycyen so subtyl that can gyve a covenable medecyn ne plastre, but yf the pacyent gyf hym knowlege of his payn and gryef, **1484** *Royal Book* O4r[15–6]: The Surgyen ne myght hele the sore but yf he sawe the wounde. **a1500** *Disciplina Clericalis* 31[24–7]: How moche a sike man hidith and takith awey the knowlache of his infirmyte from his leche, so moche more grevous and sharp shal his grevaunce and sikenes be. **c1500** *Lancelot* 4.105–6: For long ore he be fonde, Holl of his leich, that schewith not his vound. See **M25, S503.**

L174 The **Leech** pines (*pains*) the wound that it may be healed
c1175 *Twelfth Century Homilies* 38.22–3: All swa ðe læce deþ ðe læcnæð þene mon—þe pinæð on þa wundæ ðæt heo wurðæ ihæled.

L175 The three (best) **Leeches:** a glad heart, a temperate diet and take no thought (*varied*)
a1449 Lydgate *Dietary* in *MP* II 704.61–4: Ther be thre lechees consarve a mannys myht, First *a glad hert,* he carith lite or nouht, *Temperat* diet, holsom for every wiht, And best of all, for no thyng *take no thouht.* **1520** Whittinton *Vulgaria* 43.11–3: To refresshe the mynde with myrthe, exercyse the body with labour, and to use temperate dyet be the chefest phisicyons for a student. Cf. Apperson 156; *Oxford* 497–8; Tilley D427. See **M131, 214, 514.**

L176 To be one's last (To need no other) **Leech**
c1380 *Ferumbras* 86.2660: A kulde hem doun afforn him ther and was hure last leche. **c1400** *Gowther* 159.605–6: Thei fell to tho ground and rosse not yytte, Nor lokyd aftur no leyche. **a1425** *Arthour and M.*[2] 370.2455–6: For all, that he might ever reach, Trulye, they need noe other leech. **a1440** *De Miraculo Beate Marie* 504.77–8: The frere had nedid none other leche Bot sone he hade bene slayne. **a1450** *Generydes A* 40.1275–6: On him I shal take such wreche, Shal him never nede noo leche, *B* 180.5657–8: He smote Gusare so harde uppon the cheke, That

leche craft hym nede non other seeke. **a1475** *Guy*[2] 65.2270–2: Ther was none, that he wold spare, Nor none, that he myght reche, That had nede of odur leche. **a1533** Berners *Huon* 122.24–6: Whom so ever he towchyde with a full stroke, had no nede after of any surgyon, 230.23–4, 299.2–3, 377.30–1. See **S46.**

L177 To be one's **Leech** (*i.e.*, to befriend)
a1475 *Good Wyfe Wold* 174.51: Yefe anny fortun fall amysse, then mey he be thy leche.

L178 While men go after a **Leech** the body is buried
c1385 Usk 134.79: While men gon after a leche, the body is buryed. Apperson 679. See **A72, C51, L168.**

L179 The **Leechdom** (*remedy*) is vain which may not heal the sick
c1000 Aelfric *Homilies* I 60[33–4]: Ydel bið se læcedom þe ne mæg ðone untruman gehælan.

L180 As green as (a, any) **Leek**
a1398(1495) Bartholomaeus-Trevisa L7ᵛ[2.1–2]: A stone grene as a leke, JJ4ᵛ[1.20–1]: a. **a1400** ?Chaucer *Rom. A* 212: ony. **a1500** *Peterborough Lapidary* 83[4]: Grene as lyk, 117[15]. Apperson 273; *Oxford* 266; Taylor and Whiting 217; Tilley L176.

L181 As lithy (*pliable*) as a **Leek** (*etc.*) (A number of single quotations are brought together here)
a1400 *Siege of Jerusalem* 59.1027–8: That the fyngres and feet, fustes and joyntes Was lythy as a leke and lost han her strengthe, 67.1146 (*var.*): And some was lene on to loke as a leke. **1402** *Daw Topias* 43[20]: As lewid as a leke. **a1450** *Generydes A* 237.7683–4: To his face she leid hir cheke, She felt it cold as . . . leke.

L182 Dear enough a **Leek**
c1300 *Times of Edward II* 333.228: Hit shal be dere on (*Peterhouse* 19[15]: y-now) a lek, whan hit is al i-wrouht. **c1395** Chaucer *CT* VIII[G] 795: And othere swiche, deere ynough a leek.

L183 Not give a **Leek**
c1380 Chaucer *HF* 1708–9: And seyden they yeven noght a lek For fame. **a1400** *Scottish Legends* II 198.777: Na gyfis nocht of the a leke. **c1400** *Laud Troy* I 197.6664.

L184 Not tell (*count*) a **Leek** (*etc.*) (A number of single quotations are brought together here)
a1338 Mannyng *Chronicle B* I 161[14]: It was not told a leke, that non of his thien led. **a1400** *Romaunt B* 4830: Sich love I preise not at a lek, 5374: Men wole not sette by hym a lek, 5730: And though they die, they sette not a lek. **c1400** *Laud Troy* II 404.13733: His myght vayled him not of two lekes. **a1460** *Towneley Plays* 5.129: Now, therof a leke what rekys us? **c1471** *Recovery of the Throne* in Wright *Political Poems* II 278[5]: Thay were not of thayre entent the nere of a leke. **1555** Heywood *E* 178.182(2).4: I weene not the value of a good greene leeke.

L185 Not worth a (one) **Leek**
c1300 *Northern Homily Cycle* (*Edin. Coll. Phys.*) 54[10]: Thi vayage es noht worthe a leke. **a1338** Mannyng *Chronicle A* I 442.12654: Ther dedes ar nought worth a leke, II 457.13182, *B* I 204[13]. **a1375** *Octavian* (S) 38.1205. **c1395** Chaucer *CT* IV[E] 1350: That every man that halt hym worth a leek. **a1400** *Alexander C* 230.4228: And your lare of a leke suld nevire the les worth. **c1400** *Sowdone* 50.1726. **c1412** Hoccleve *Regement* 60.1662, 127.3517, **c1422** *Complaint* 100.143: They wold(en) not have holde it worthe a leke. **a1430** Lydgate *Pilgrimage* 111.4198: Yet al yt ys nat worth a lek, 306.11197, 407.15099. **c1450** Capgrave *Katharine* 55.628, 111.535. **c1450** *Epistle of Othea* 140.3. **c1450** Greene *Carols* 417.1. **a1460** *Spurious Chaucerian line* in Manly-Rickert VI 493. **a1460** *Towneley Plays* 17.285: This is not worth oone leke. **1464** Hardyng 397[23]. **a1500** *Piers of Fullham* 2.16. **c1500** *King Hart* 119.20: ane. **c1522** Skelton *Colyn* I 318.183. **c1523** Barclay *Mirrour* 71[33]. Apperson 457; *Oxford* 360; Tilley 066; Whiting *Drama* 352:679, *Scots* I 199.

L186 Not worth a **Leek's** blade
a1400 *Child* 315.7–8: The beste song that ever was made Ys not worth a lekys blade. **c1440** Scrope *Epistle* 10[1]: The all were not worthe a leke blade.

L187 Not worth a **Leek's** clove
c1300 *Guy*[1] 210 A 3643–4: Bodi and soule no nought ther-of No is nought worth a lekes clof.

L188 Set her upon a **Leeland** and bid the devil fetch her
a1449 ?Lydgate *Evil Marriage* in *MP* II 461 (*var.*): Than, yf she than wyll be no better, Set her upon a lelande, and bydde the devyll fet her.

L189 A **Leg** of a lark is better than the body of a kite
1546 Heywood *D* 25.26–7: For a leg of a larke Is better than is the body of a kyght. Apperson 350; *Oxford* 360; Tilley L186.

L190 Long be your **Legs** and short be your life
1562 Heywood *D* 85.158: But long be thy legs,

and short be thy lyfe. Apperson 378; *Oxford* 380; Tilley L192.

L191 To set out one's better **Leg**
a1500 Medwall *Nature* C3r[36]: Set out the better leg, I warne the. *Oxford* 35; Taylor and Whiting 218; Tilley F570.

L192 **Leicestershire** full of beans
a1500 *Characteristics of Counties* in *Rel. Ant.* I 269[39]: Leicesterschir, full of benys. Apperson 359; *Oxford* 578; Tilley M372.

L193 By **Leisure** men pass many a mile
1420 Lydgate *Temple* 17.393: For men bi laiser passen meny a myle.

L194 **Leisure** overcomes those whom will may not
c1400 *Consilia Isidori* 368[42]: Ofte-tyme leyser (*Lat.* assiduitas) hath overcome whom wylle myghte not.

L195 To repent at **Leisure**
c1505 Watson *Valentine* 46.22–3: One may do an evil thinge, wherby he may repent him all at leyser. Cf. Tilley H191.

L196 When **Leisure** is more listening (*?attention*) is better
c1350 *Joseph* 6.164: Whon ure leyser is more ure lustnynge is bettre.

L197 As bright as **Lampning** (*?for* levening [*lightning*])
a1325 *Cursor* II 986.108 *–9 *: His lokyng was als bright Os is the rede lempninge.

L198 Not worth a **Lence** (*?pin*)
c1450 Holland *Howlat* 68.606: Of lokis nor lynx mycht louss worth a lence. DOST Lence.

L199 Who is not holy in **Lent** or busy in harvest is not likely to thrive
c1434 Drury 76.3–4: For after the proverbe of old men, ho (so) is not holy in Lente or besi in hervest is not lykly to thryve.

L200 As stout as a **Leopard**
c1375 Barbour *Bruce* II 1.1–2: The erll of Carrik, schir Eduard, That stowtar wes than ane libbard, 46.524: Stoutar he maid than a libard. **a1500** *Guy*[4] 209.6946: Prowde and stoute as a leoparde.

L201 As swift as a **Leopard** (*etc.*) (A number of single quotations are brought together here)
c1300 *Guy*[1] 330 A 6123–6: In alle the world is so swift a best, Libard no ro, in no forest, No dromedarie no is ther non So swithe goand so is he on, 534.181.7–8: Douk Berard Prout and stern as a lipard. **a1338** Mannyng *Chronicle A* II 478.13795–8: Was nevere lubard ne lyoun, Ne wilde wolf ne dragoun, That was so wod, beste to byte, As Wawayn was Romayns to smyte. **c1350** *Libeaus* 93.1672–3: He rod to the felde ward, Light as a libard. **c1400** *Laud Troy* I 223.7562: Strong and yrus as any lyparde. **c1450** *Pilgrimage LM* 115[11]: Feers i am thanne as Leopard. **c1505** Watson *Valentine* 114.17–8: He was more fyerser than a Leoparde. **a1475** *Guy*[2] 145.5058: Felle he was, as a lybarte.

L202 To be like a **Leopard**
c1400 *Sowdone* 63.2191–2: This geaunte hade a body longe And hede, like an libarde, 2198. **a1470** Malory II 734.21–3: Kynge Arthure lykened . . . sir Palomydes . . . unto a wood lybarde.

L203 To come like a **Leopard**
c1330 *Seven Sages A* 67.1570: And he com als a leopard.

L204 To lead like a **Leopard**
c1400 *Laud Troy* I 180.6095–6: Achilles led the formast warde, As is als it were a lyparde.

L205 To run like a **Leopard**
c1400 *Laud Troy* I 43.1432: He ran thedur as a lyparde.

L206 Better for the **Less** to quit (*save*) the more
c1400 *Beryn* 69.2254: Ffor better is, then lese all, the las the more quyt. See **H344.**

L207 For the **Less** to lose (leave, forgo) the more
a1393 Gower *CA* III 77.4777–9: For often times of scarsnesse It hath be sen, that for the lesse Is lost the more. **c1450** *Douce MS.52* 50.75: For the lesse me lefus the more. **c1450** *Rylands MS.394* 93.3: It is no wysemanys lore to take the las and leve the more, 100.23: me lysed. **c1450** *Seege of Troye* 118 A 1493–4: As men haf y-sayd her-by-fore—Ffor the lasse men lesyth the more. **a1475** *Guy*[2] 289.10043–4: In proverbe hyt ys seyde full yare: Mony for the lesse forgoyth the mare. **1523** Berners *Froissart* III 46[38]: And douted leest he shulde lese the more for the lesse, 321[10], **1525** IV 65[29–30].

L208 One lets (*thinks*) **Less** of the thing that one has often
a1200 *Ancrene* 210.23: Me let leasse of the thing that me haveth ofte, **a1250** (*Nero*) 188.1: Me let lesse deinte to thinge thet me haveth ofte. See **C351.**

L209 To have (no) **Letters** of life
c1376 *Piers* A xii 86: We han letteres of Lyf,

he shal his lyf tyne, **c1378** B x 89: For we have no lettre of owre lyf, how longe it shal dure. *Oxford* 455; Tilley M327.

L210 **Leve** (*believe*) none better than yourself (*varied*)
c1350 *Good Wife E* 168.143: Lef non betere than thisilf, **c1450** *L* 200.127: And trust noon bettir than thisilf for no fair speche, **c1500** *T* 208.167–8: For who that loveth hymsylf best Most may lyve in rest. Apperson 649:11.

L211 As bright as (any, the) **Levin** (*lightning*)
a1330 *Legend of Mary* 499.4: (He w)as brighter than ani leven. **c1330** *St. Margaret* 227.65: Than maiden Mergrete, bright so ani leven. **c1408** Lydgate *Reson* 134.5118: Brighter than the firy levene. **a1438** Kempe 8.22–3: ony. **a1449** Lydgate *Praise of Peace* in *MP* II 788.82: *Caritas* in love brente briht as levene. **c1450** Capgrave *Katharine* 300.1194: As bright he semed as it were the levene. **c1485** *Mary Magdalene* (*Digby*) 132.2043: the. **a1500** *Miracles of B. V.* (*Egerton*) in PMLA 38(1923) 321.29: the. **1513** Douglas *Aeneid* III 154.170: Brycht as fyry levyn. See **L266.**

L212 As flaming as any **Levin** (*etc.*) (A number of single quotations are brought together here)
a1420 Lydgate *Troy* III 695.4458: As any levene so flawmynge is thi light, **1439** *St. Albon* 182.1195: Fervent in fyry ire as any leven. **1513** Douglas *Aeneid* III 251.94: Forcy as fyry levin, IV 54.51: This Tarchon, ardent as the fyry levyn.

L213 As light as (the, any) **Levin**
c1375 *St. Stephen* in Horstmann *Legenden 1881* 33.437: Thai kest up fire ligh als the levyn. **a1400** *Le Morte A.* 100.3308: They lemyd lyght As Any levyn, 109.3586: Any. **a1400** *Melayne* 4.112: Ane angele lyghte als leven. **a1425** *Metrical Paraphrase OT* 58.7693. **a1450** *Castle* 104.893, 181.3499: the. **a1450** *York Plays* 479.175: the.

L214 As swift as **Levin**
a1439 Lydgate *Fall* III 731.2114: His conquest was swifft as . . . levene. Apperson 518. See **L269.**

L215 To leam (*shine*) like the **Levin**
c1425 *Avowynge* 89[19–20]: And there come fliand a gunne, And lemet as the levyn.

L216 To shine like **Levin**
c1300 *Guy*[1] 522 A 166.8–9: And alle the pleynes ther-of it schon As it were light of leven.

L217 To shoot out like **Levin**
a1338 Mannyng *Chronicle B* I 174[4]: It affraied the Sarazins, as leven the fire out schete.

L218 To burn like a **Leye** (*flame*)
c1350 *Alexander B* 193.555: That in his licamus lust as a lie brente.

L219 To lance up like any **Leye**
a1450 *Castle* 145.2290–1: I make a fer in mans towte, That launcyth up as any leye.

L220 A **Liar** hates his fellow
1450 *Dicts* 140.18–9: Men seeithe ever a lier hatithe his felawe, and oo thef takithe a-nother and will his distruccion. See **K82.**

L221 A **Liar** is like a false (bad) penny among the good
1340 *Ayenbite* 62[22–3]: The lyeghere is amang the men ase the valse peny amang the guode. **c1400** *Vices and Virtues* 60.20–1: The lyghere fareth as a fals peny among the goode. **c1450** *Jacob's Well* 151.14–5: A lyere faryth as a badde peny amonge gode.

L222 A **Liar** is not believed (*varied*)
1477 Rivers *Dictes* 97[10–1]: The reward of a lyar is that he be not bilevid of that he rehersseth. **1484** Caxton *Aesop* 205[1–4]: He whiche is acustomed to make lesynges, how be it that he saye trouthe, Yet men byleve hym not, [20–1]: For men bileve not lyghtly hym whiche is knowen for a lyer.

L223 There are more **Liars** than leeches
a1376 *Piers* A vii 260: Ther beoth mo lyghers then leches.

L224 **Liberty** makes many a man blind
c1516 Skelton *Magnificence* 3.52: Lyberte makyth many a man blynde.

L225 **Liberty** may sometimes be too large
c1516 Skelton *Magnificence* 2.37: Lyberte may somtyme be to large. Cf. *Oxford* 665: Too much; Smith 174; Tilley L225.

L226 **Liberty** without rule is not worth a straw
c1516 Skelton *Magnificence* 43.1378: Yet Lyberte without rule is not worth a strawe.

L227 To lose **Liberty** is a pain
1472 Paston V 139[17]: Remembyr what peyn it is a man to loese lyberte. See **F613.**

L228 **Lickerousness** engenders fleshly lust
a1430 Lydgate *Pilgrimage* 354.13039–42: Ffor lykerousnesse Off welfare, and gret excesse, Engendre and cause naturelly Fflesshly lust and lechery. See **C125, G168.**

L229 As sweet as **Licorice**
a1300 *Alisaunder* 27.427–8: His love is also swete, iwys, So . . . lycorys. **c1390** Chaucer *CT* I[A] 3206–7: And he hymself as sweete as is the

roote Of lycorys. **a1400** *Floris* 73.119–20: Lycorys Is not so soote as hur love is. **c1450** *Northern Passion* 14 CIi 120a. **c1450** *Owayne Miles (Auchinleck)* 108.148[6]. **a1500** *Beauty of his Mistress III* in Robbins 126.5. **a1500** *Gracious and Gay* in Robbins 144.7. **c1500** Newton 270.21.

L230 Well **Lied** well said
1556 Heywood *Spider* 196[22]: Well lide: well saide.

L231 What first was **Lief** (*dear*) is made loath
a1500 *Piers of Fullham* 13.294–5: And thus full oft the game goth, That first was lief it makith loth.

L232 Where once is **Lief** let never be loath
c1450 *Rylands MS.394* 94.3ᵛ.18: Ther onys is lefe, lett never be lothe. See **L562.**

L233 Who will have **Lief** he lief must let (*give up*) (*varied*)
c1100 *Instructions for Christians* 14.104–5: Ac gif þu nelt naht leofes gesyllan, Ne miht þu na gebicgan þæt ðe best licað. **c1385** Chaucer *TC* iv 1585: Ek "whoso wol han lief, he lief moot lete." Apperson 459: Nought (4). See **A106, G96, M211, S141, T330, W255.**

L234 As dear as **Life**
c1250 *Genesis and Exodus* 99.3483: His word gu wurthe digere al-so lif. **1513** Douglas *Aeneid* II 156.64: To thi systir derrar than hir awyn lyve. See **L246.**

L235 As lief (*dear*) as one's own **Life**
a1200 Lawman I 124.2935–6: Heo wes hire fader al swa leof, Swa his aghene lif, 126.2978: Theou aert leovere thene mi lif, 148.3480–1: That ich ham wes swa leof, Levere thenne hire aghe lif, *B* That ich ham was so leof, Ase hire oghen lif, 211.4946–7, II 137.13439–40, 158.13923–4, 177.14375–6, 269.16561, 360.18698–9. See **L252, M136.**

L236 As sicker (*certain*) as the **Life**
a1393 Gower *CA* III 225.2163–4: And seith, "So siker as the lif, A god hath leie be thi wif." Svartengren 355: sure.

L237 A good **Life** a good death (end) (*varied*)
1450 *Dicts* 94.9–10: He that lyveth good lif schalle die good dethe. **c1450** La Tour-Landry 194.26–8: And, as men say communely, of honest and good lyf cometh ever a good ende. **a1500** *Good Wife N* 211.40: Good life ends wele. **1509** Barclay *Ship* I 65[11]: And his godly lyfe a godly ende shal fynde. Apperson 260; *Oxford* 253–4, cf. 366; Tilley L391.

L238 Good **Life** wins well
c1350 *Good Wife E* 160.32: God life wel winneth, **c1450** *L* 198.40–1: For he that in good liif renneth, Ful ofte weel he wynneth, **c1500** *T* 204.38: Good lyfe reneweth and well wynneth.

L239 **Life** is better than gold or good
a1420 Lydgate *Troy* III 718.5285: The lyf is bet than gold or any good.

L240 **Life** is but a breath
c1400 *But thou say Sooth* in Brown *Lyrics XIV* 206.53: Thenke thi lyf is but a breth. Whiting *Drama* 163. See **L242.**

L241 **Life** is but a dream and death wakes it
1532 Berners *Golden Boke* 332.7020–1: Lyfe is but a dreame, and deathe waketh it. See **M165.**

L242 **Life** is but as a wind-blast
a1400 *Pricke* 54.1943: For his lyf is noght bot als a wynd blast. **a1450** *Gesta* 358[4–5]: What is the lyf of man or of any best but a litell wynde? See **L240.**

L243 **Life** is like a flower, *etc.*
a1450 *Gesta* 235[2–5]: For the lyf of man is likenid nowe to a flour, nowe to hete or warmnes, and nowe to a fleinge shadowe . . . and nowe to an arowe shote to a marke.

L244 **Life** is often lost soonest when it is held dearest
a1023 Wulfstan *Homilies* 226.12–4: Eala, lytel is se fyrst þyses lifes, and lyðre is, þæt we lufiað and on wuniað, and for oft hit wyrð raðost forloren þonne hit wære leofost gehealdan.

L245 **Life** is short, craft (science) is long
c1380 Chaucer *PF* 1: The lyf so short, the craft so long to lerne. **a1425** Chauliac 24.3: Life is short, crafte forsothe is long. **c1477** Norton *Ordinall* 87[14–5]: Whereof said *Maria* Sister of *Aron, Lyfe is short, and Science is full long.* Apperson 16; MED craft n. (1) 3(b); *Oxford* 14; Skeat 135; Tilley A332. Cf. Taylor and Whiting 220:10. See **D44.**

L246 **Life** is sweet
c1380 *Patience* 18.156: For be monnes lode never so luther, the lyf is ay swete. **a1393** Gower *CA* II 453.1861: The lif is suete. **a1450** *York Plays* 65.279: Lyff is full swete. **1532** Berners *Golden Boke* 258.4617–8: Whan lyfe was at the swetest. **1556** Heywood *Spider* 368[24]: Life was sweete, death was sowre. Apperson 363; *Oxford* 366; Taylor and Whiting 220; Tilley L254; Whiting *Ballad* 38. See **L234.**

L247 The **Life** of other men is our shower (*example*) (*varied*)

a1300 *Alisaunder* 3.17–8: For Caton seith, the gode techer, Othere mannes liif is oure shewer. **a1393** Gower *CA* III 393.256: And every man is othres lore. See **C161, M170, W47.**

L248 The **Life** one uses in youth shall be kept in age
c1450 La Tour-Landry 9.34–5: For suche lyff as ye will contynue, use you to in youre youthe, ye shal be by youre flesshe constreined to kepe in youre age. See **C226, Y32.**

L249 **Life** was never lent but livelihood was shaped
c1378 *Piers* B xiv 39: For lente nevere was lyf but lyflode were shapen. Apperson 252; *Oxford* 245. See **G227.**

L250 Of evil **Life** comes evil ending (*varied*)
a1300 *Alisaunder* 27.455–6: Yhereth now hou selcouthe (*L* sunful) liif Cometh to shame, sorough, and striif, 45.751–2: Sooth it is, upe al thing, Of yvel liif yvel endyng. **a1415** Mirk *Festial* 56.20–1: Thus who so lyveth a fowle lyfe, he may be sure of a foule ende. **a1439** Lydgate *Fall* III 842.663: Vicious lyff kometh alwey to myschaunce. **c1450** La Tour-Landry 72.3–4: For gladly evell lyff hathe evell ende. Apperson 193; *Oxford* 316; Smith 178; Tilley L247. See **L406, 412.**

L251 This wretched **Life** is but as a maze
c1445 ?Lydgate *Kalendare* in *MP* I 364.35: For this wrecchid lyfe is but as a mase.

L252 To love one as his **Life** (*varied*)
a1200 Lawman I 211.4953: And he heo leovede alse his lif, II 146.13644: And iluved hine swa mi lif, *B* 355.18572. **a1300** *Interludium de clerico et puella* 21.20: Y luf the mar than mi lif. **a1300** *Jacob and Joseph* 7.195: The quene lovede Josep ase hir owe lif, 15.433. **c1300** *Havelok* 13.349, 54.1662–3, 56.1707. **c1300** *Guy*[1] 264.4605–6: Min owhen wiif, That y loved more than mi liif. **a1325** *Cursor* III 1334.23336. **c1325** *Chronicle* 69.296. **c1330** *Degare* 57.23. **c1330** *Orfeo* 12.123–4. **c1330** *Otuel* 72.251–2. **c1330** *Peniworth* 113.13. **c1330** *Seven Sages A* 9.256, 118.2556, B 2653: more than, 142 E 2897, B 2926: better than, 159 E 3099, B 3228. **a1338** Mannyng *Chronicle A* I 82.2294, *B* I 83[23]. **a1350** *Seege of Troye* 63.795, 109.1363. **a1350** *Seven Sages C* 11.317–8, 96.2814: more than, 132.3932. **a1350** *Ywain* 44.1624: better than, 62.2292, 106.4012. **c1350** *Octavian* (*N*) 101.641, 119.823. **c1350** *Smaller Vernon Collection* 37.137–8. **c1353** *Winner* 430. **1372** *Song of the Blessed Virgin* in Brown *Lyrics XIV* 79.32. **a1375** *William* 163.5150: miin owne. **c1380** Chaucer *HF* 175–6, **c1390** *CT* I[A] 3221–2: moore than, II[B] 535: right as, 625: right as, IX[H] 139–40: moore than. **c1390** *Gregorius* 12.96: his owne. **c1390** *Northern Homily Cycle Narrationes* (*Vernon*) 274.6. **a1393** Gower *CA* II 150.749–51: her oghne, 380.2930–1: hire oghne hertes, III 93.5386–7: His oghne hertes, 98.5558, 107.5885–7, 113.6119–21. **c1395** Chaucer *CT* V[F] 816: hire hertes, 1093: his owene hertes. **c1395** *WBible* I Kings xviii 1: his owne soule (**c1382** liif), xx 17. **a1400** *Athelston* 69.74. **a1400** Chestre *Launfal* 71.654. **a1400** *Cursor* II 750 F 13050: mare than. **a1400** *Floris* 90.602. **a1400** *Northern Verse Psalter* II 83 (118.47). **a1400** *Scottish Legends* I 384.383–4, II 93.836–7. **c1400** *Alexius* (*Laud 622*) 26.147. **c1400** *Beryn* 5.112: his owne, 36.1112: his owne. **c1400** *Brut* I 41.22–3: As miche as. **c1400** *Laud Troy* I 91.3071–2, II 409.13890: more than, 452.15347–8: more than. **c1400** *Toulouse* 241.481–2: his owne. **a1425** *Alexius* (*Laud 463*) 72.536 (*Trinity:* more than). **a1425** *Metrical Paraphrase OT* 53.7529: lely as. **a1450** *Gesta* 48[9–10] (second version): as mych as. **a1450** *Northern Passion* 218 CDd *var.* 1846. **a1450** *Partonope* 5.156, 14.495: hys owne. **a1450** *St. Editha* 38.1690. **a1450** *St. Etheldreda* 286.159: his owne. **a1450** *Seven Sages B* 1.10, 46.1334: hire owen, 73.2144: hys ouen, 97.2867, 112.3312. **a1450** *York Plays* 58.63. **a1460** *Towneley Plays* 56.141–2. **1464** Hardyng 17[9]. **a1470** Malory II 867.1: well as. **a1475** *Guy*[2] 310.10775–6. **a1475** *Landavall* 113.200. **c1475** *Brome Abraham* in Waterhouse 39.81. **c1475** *How a Merchant* 118.8: trewly as. **c1477** Caxton *Jason* 119.4–5: better thenne. **a1500** *Clerk and the Nightingale I* in Robbins 174.61. **a1500** *Colkelbie* 298.69. **a1500** *Good Knight* in Horstmann *Legenden 1881* 329.23. **a1500** *Grene Knight* II 60.44: deerlye as. **a1500** *Orfeo* 34.376. **c1500** *Letter* in Robbins 192.23: evyn as. **c1500** *Lyfe of Roberte* 253.890. **c1500** Newton 260.14. **c1505** Watson *Valentine* 17.35. **1508**(1519) Stanbridge *Vulgaria* 16.5. **1518** Watson *Oliver* S4v[26]. Svartengren 136; Whiting *Drama* 319:206, *Scots* I 200. See **B367, L235, S526.**

L253 What is **Life** where living is extinct?
1546 Heywood *D* 91.26: What is lyfe? Where livyng is extinct cleere. Apperson 364; Tilley L268.

L254 When the **Life** of man ends then is time to commend him
c1420 Wyntoun III 37.417–8: And qwhen the

lif of man tays ende Than is tyme hym to commende. See **E85.**

L255 He is **Lifeless** that is faultless
1546 Heywood *D* 45.147: He is liveles, that is fautles, olde folkes thought. Apperson 364; *Oxford* 366; Tilley L270. See **M235.**

L256 As high as the **Lift** (*sky*)
a1513 ?Dunbar *Manere of the Crying* 171.50: Hir heid wan heiar than the lift. Whiting *Drama* 319:207.

L257 As light as the **Lift**
c1200 *Vices and Virtues* (*Stowe*) 95.19–20: And hie is liht alswo the left. Cf. Tilley A90.

L258 As bright as any **Light**
c1300 *South English Legendary* I 20.26: Brightore than eny light that evere an eorthe schon. **a1400** *O Gloriosa* in Brown *Lyrics XIV* 54.10: Brightore thow art than eny light.

L259 As clear as (any) **Light**
a1387 Higden-Trevisa I 411[10]: That is knowe as clere as light. **c1450** *Alphabet* II 261.7: Clerar than any light. Whiting *Drama* 319:208.

L260 **Light** is not good for sick folks' eyes (*varied*)
c1385 Chaucer *TC* iii 1136–7: This light, nor I, ne serven here of nought. Light is nought good for sike folkes yen! **a1400** *Orologium* 338.23–4: Ffor the liht is noyes and grevous to seke eyene, and is confortable and likynge to clene and clere eyene. Apperson 588–9; *Oxford* 367; Tilley L274.

L261 The **Light** of day is more grateful because of the horrid darkness of the night (*varied*)
897 Alfred *Boethius* 52.6–7: And þancwyrðre bið eac þas dæges leoht for þære egeslican þiostro þære nihte. **1420** Lydgate *Temple* 17.400–1: And folk also rejossh(e) more of light, That thei with derknes were waped and amate. See **L383.**

L262 To leam (*shine*) like a **Light**
c1350 *Joseph* 22.687: Heom thoughte he leomede as liht al on a lowe.

L263 To shine like **Light**
c1000 Aelfric *Homilies* II 518[11–2]: His andwlita scean swiðor þonne leoht.

L264 To stand in one's (own) **Light**
c1390 Chaucer *CT* I[A] 3394–6: For though that Absolon be wood or wrooth, By cause that he fer was from hire sight, This nye Nicholas stood in his light. **a1393** Gower *CA* II 251.919–20: I wolde thanne do my myht So forto stonden in here lyht. **a1440** Burgh *Cato* 321.737: For than thou stondist foule in thyne owne liht. **a1475** *Mumming of the Seven Philosophers* in Robbins 111.31–3: Ffor than ye stand foule in your owne lyght, And whoso doth, hymsylf shall foule a-dere With shame. **c1499** Skelton *Bowge* I 42.305: It is lyke he wyll stonde in our lyghte, **1523** *Garlande* 392.755: How daungerous it were to stande in his lyght. **1532** More *Confutacion* 355 E[1–2]: To stande not a lyttle in his owne lyght, 520 (*by error* 502) A[2–3]: There wyll stande styll in his lyghte the wordes of the apostle, **1533** *Apologye* 1[1–3]: Stand . . . in myne owne lyghte, **1534** *Passion* 1272 D[14–5]: That standeth in her own light. **1546** Heywood *D* 67.55: Ye stand in your owne light. Apperson 599–600; *Oxford* 618; Taylor and Whiting 220–1; Tilley L276; Whiting *Scots* I 200.

L265 To vanish away as **Light** that is burned out
a1500 *Alexander-Cassamus* 62.262–3: For plesaunt thowghtis vanche awey as lyghte That is brent owt.

L266 As bright as **Lightning**
a1420 Lydgate *Troy* I 367.7804–6: Whos eyen were spark(e)ling as bright As . . . the lightnyng that cometh doun fro hevene. See **L211.**

L267 As burning as **Lightning**
c1410 Lovelich *Grail* II 290.461–2: And Also brennenge . . . As lyghteneng that to-fore the thondir doth fle.

L268 As quick as **Lightning**
c1300 *South English Legendary* II 473.300: Ac quic hi doth as lightinge thurf purgatorie gon. Apperson 518; Taylor and Whiting 221.

L269 As swift as **Lightning**
c1410 Lovelich *Grail* II 290.451–2: As swift they weren In alle thing As to-forn the thondir is the lyhgtenyng. Svartengren 380; Taylor and Whiting 221; Tilley L279. See **L214.**

L270 To be like **Lightning**
c1000 *Old English Nicodemus* 484.9: His ansyn wæs swylce ligræsc, 492.14–5. Whiting *Drama* 319:209.

L271 As bitter as **Lign-aloes**
c1385 Chaucer *TC* iv 1135–7: Tho woful teeris that they leten falle As bittre weren, out of teris kynde, For peyne, as is ligne aloes.

L272 **Like** to like (*varied*)
c1300 *South English Legendary* II 694.66: Vor ech thyng loveth hys ilyk, so seyth the bok ywis. **c1350** *Alexander B* 213.1041: For wel

lovus every lud that liche is him tille. **a1400** *Cleansing* 14.19–20 (f.9v): Ffor resonabely a creature sekith him to whom he is lyke. **a1400** *Scottish Legends* I 23.543: For lyk to lyk accordis wele, 226.133–4: And in proverbe I haf hard say That lyk to lyk drawis ay. **a1400** *Stanzaic Life* 234.6913–6: Ffor ofte tyme a mon may se And is uset communely, Thing that is like withe like wol be And to hit coveite kyndely. **c1400** *Consilia Isidori* 370[40–1]: For lyke to lyke ys woned to be joyned. **c1440** *Prose Alexander* 88.2–3: For comonly a man luffes hym that es lyke till hym selfen. **1447** Bokenham 45.1639–42: Lyche to lyche evere doth applie, As scheep to scheep and man to man, Pertryche to pertryche and swan to swan So vertu to vertu is agreable. **a1449** Lydgate *Fabula* in *MP* II 489.78–84: For lich of lich is serchyd and enqueerid: To merthe longith to fynden out gladnesse, And wo can weepe, thouh he be nat leryd, And dool eek drawith unto drerynesse; Honour is weddyd unto worthynesse. Unto his semblable thus every thyng can drawe, And nothyng bynde hem but natur by hir lawe. **1450** *Dicts* 292.5–6: (For) everi thinge rejoyseth him with his liknes, the good with the good and the yvel with the ivel. **c1450** Capgrave *Katharine* 153.1219–20: Fferthermore yet seyn oure bookis thus: "That every liche his lyche shal desyre." **c1450** *Proverbs of Good Counsel* 70.74–5: As for this proverbe dothe specify, "Lyke wyll to lyke in eche company." **1456** Hay *Law* 77.24–7: Like lufis lyke, and lyke drawis to like, and lyke joyis with the lyke, Quia similis similem sibi querit, et omne simile applaudit de suo simili. **a1470** Malory II 527.5–7: For evermore a good knyght woll favoure another, and lyke woll draw to lyke. **a1470** Tiptoft *Tullius* A8r[5–7]: What so ever it be in the nature of thynges, or in all the world, whiche hath a naturell movyng, desireth his lyke, and fleeth his contrarye. **c1475** *Thewis* 182.118: Lyk drawys to lyk ay comonly. **c1477** Caxton *Jason* 121.2: And that it is so that every like loveth his semblable, **1484** *Royal Book* B6v[4–5]: Naturelly al thynges lyke and semblable love eche other. **1492** *Salomon and Marcolphus* 11[11–2]: Everything chesyth his lyke. **a1500** *Att my begynning* in *Rawlinson MS. C 813* 323.24: Similis similem sibi querit. **a1500** Hill 131.23: Hit is, and ever shall be: a like will drawe to like. **1504** Hawes *Example* Dd4r[28]: For lyke hath lyke his operacyon. **1509** Barclay *Ship* II 35[5]: For lyke wyll have lyke, [20–1]: For it is a proverbe, and an olde sayd sawe That in every place lyke to lyke wyll drawe, **c1523** *Mirrour* 27[21]: For like unto like will, or ought so by prudence. **a1535** Fisher *Wayes* 377.3–4: Lyke alway doeth covet like. **1546** Heywood *D* 25.23: Like will to like, **1556** *Spider* 230[3]: Like sort to like, **1562** *E* 244.90.1. Apperson 367–8; Jente 365, 374, 380; *Oxford* 368–9; Smith 180; Taylor and Whiting 222; Tilley L286; Whiting *Drama* 127, 128, *Scots* I 200. See **B129, 359, 364, E171, F574, H523, K29, L570, M93, 175, 250, 344, R91, T100, 115, W716, Y37.**

L273 It is sweet **Liking** to love and to be loved again
c1420 Wyntoun II 299.397–400: It is suet likyn and na payn To luf and to be luffit agane; Bot for luff yheylde fenyheynge It is to leil hart ay trowynge. See **L506, 514, 543, 574, 576.**

L274 Short **Liking** shall be long bought
a1475 *Ludus Coventriae* 28.398: Schort lykyng xal be longe bought. Apperson 567. See **H601, M642.**

L275 **Lill** for lall
c1405 *Mum* 66.1357: And pleyen lille for lalle with many leude (kitte). **c1420** Wyntoun II 289.263: And to qwhit hym lil for lall (*var.* law). Apperson 368; NED Lill for loll.

L276 As fair as the **Lily** (*etc.*) (A number of single quotations are brought together here)
c1385 Chaucer *CT* I[A] 1035–6: That Emelye, that fairer was to sene Than is the lylie upon his stalke grene. **a1400** *Meditations* 1.16: And lyk the lilye maud ful clene, 3.101: Hit is as the lilye dilicyous, 46.1751: Wher is his face as lilie cler. Svartengren 221:fair. See **F276, 304.**

L277 As fresh as (the) **Lily** (lilies)
a1420 Lydgate *Troy* I 256.3921–2: That whilom was frescher for to sene Than the lillye on his stalke grene, III 580.585–6: Hir natif colour, as fresche to the sight As is . . . the lillye whight, 683.4075–7: That verrayly ther was no lylye flour . . . Of whitnes fressher on to sene, **a1449** *Mydsomer Rose* in *MP* II 784.104: Fressher than lilies. **a1450** Audelay 157.61–2: Ryght as the lele is freschist in hew, Haile! beute passeth as maydyns clene. See **F277, 306.**

L278 As sweet as **Lily**
a1400 *Meditations* 29.1081–2: Jhesu is swetter of savour Than . . . lilie or any other flour. **1501** Douglas *Palice* 10.18: A Quene, as lyllie sweit of swair. Svartengren 308. See **L284.**

L279 As white as (the, any) **Lily** (in May)
c1000 Aelfric *Lives* II 362.114–5: Cyne-helmas . . . snaw-hwite swa swa lilie. **a1250** *On God*

Ureisun in Brown *Lyrics XIII* 4.53: Heo beoth . . . so hwit so the lilie. **a1300** *Jacob and Joseph* 5.147–8: Mani feir bour, Whit so eni lilie. **c1300** *Guy*[1] 520 A 162.6: As white as lilii. **a1350** *Isumbras* 20.252 (*var.*): She is as white als any lyle of blee. **c1350** *Joseph* 19.563: Bothe Armure and hors al (whit) as the lilye. **c1385** Chaucer *CT* I[A] 2178: An egle tame, as any lilye whyt. **a1400** *Alexander C* 220.3902. **a1400** ?Chaucer *Rom. A* 1015–6. **a1400** Chestre *Launfal* 61.292: Sche was as whyt as lylye yn May. **a1400** Julian *Revelations* 192[24]. **1447** Bokenham 120.4393–4. **c1450** *When the son* 390.273: White as lyly when he ys yn hys delyte. **a1475** *Landavall* 109.105: in May. **a1475** *Ludus Coventriae* 90.243: This yerde as lely whyte. **1481** Caxton *Mirror* 113[20]: the. **a1500** *Craft of Lovers* in Stow *Chaucer* CCCXLI[r][29]: the. **a1500** *Miracles of B.V.* in *PMLA* 38(1923) 366.21–2. **a1500** *O my lady dere* in *Rawlinson MS. C 813* 331.121: any. **1506** Hawes *Pastime* 146.3861: ony, 198.5229: ony, **1511** *Comforte* C2[v][1]: ony. **1513** Bradshaw *St. Werburge* 122.3390: the. **a1533** Berners *Arthur* 56[15–6]: the. Apperson 680; Taylor and Whiting 223; Tilley L296; Whiting *Scots* I 200. See **F278, 308, L285.**

L279a **Lily-white**
c1325 *Annot* 137.12: With lilye-white leres. **c1325** *Lady, Have Ruth on Me* in Brown *Lyrics XIII* 140.31. **c1350** *Alexander A* 128.195. **c1380** *Cleanness* 37.977. **c1390** *Prayer* in *Vernon* II 739.130. **a1400** *Susan* 173.16. **a1422** Lydgate *Life* 297.711. **1447** Bokenham 13.449. **a1450** *Partonope* 194.5160. **c1458** *Knyghthode and Bataile* 37.996. **a1475** *Ludus Coventriae* 145.304. **c1500** ?Bradshaw *Radegunde* 51[11]. **c1500** Greene *Carols* 432.1.2. **1513** Douglas *Aeneid* II 16.447, 24.37. **c1516** Skelton *Magnificence* 49.1555. **a1533** Berners *Arthur* 51[18], *Huon* 627.12–3. **1533** More *Apologye* 114[7]. Taylor and Whiting 223; Whiting *Drama* 320:210, *Scots* I 200.

L280 A **Lily** among thorns (*varied*)
c1395 *WBible* Song of Solomon ii 2: As a lilie among thornes, so is my frendesse among doughtris. **a1439** Lydgate *Fall* I 111.4009–11: But offte tyme men may beholde and see That lelies growe among these netlis thikke, And flourdelis amyd these weedie wikke. **a1475** *Tree* 161.20–162.1: Virginite . . . growith among wordly puple as dothe the lilie amonge thornis, for like as a lilie amonge thornis growith up right with oute horting so doth chast virginite amonges wordly puple, thus seith salomon. Cf. Tilley F384, M1344.

L281 To be like (the) **Lily**
a1350 *Ywain* 67.2510: And the mayden with lely lire. **a1400** *Meditations* 17.639: And his body so lylye-lyk. **a1400** *Rowlande* 74.619: Als lely like was hir coloure. **c1400** *Gowther* 136.34: To the lyly was likened that lady clere. **a1450** *York Plays* 96.97: This lady is to the lilly lyke. **c1450** *How mankinde dooth* in Furnivall *Hymns* 67.298: Mi lire as lillye and roose of hewe. **c1450** *St. Cuthbert* 43.1453: In whitnes lily. **c1455** *Partonope S* 482.39: As lelye leef sche hadde the lyire. **a1460** *Towneley Plays* 391.145: Youre lyre the lylly lyke. **a1500** *Beauty of his Mistress III* in Robbins 127.21: Your necke lyke the lyllye. Whiting *Scots* I 201.

L282 To shine like (the) **Lily**
c1390 *Northern Homily Cycle Narrationes* (*Vernon*) 300.41–2: Hire colour, That schyned as lilie. **a1400** *Destruction of Troy* 99.3023: The shede thurghe the shyre here shone as the lilly.

L283 As pure as **Lily-flower**
c1490 Ryman 187.3[4]: As pure as lilly floure.

L284 As sweet as **Lily-flower**
c1475 *Lamentation of Mary Magdalene* 414[35]: Sweeter than lilly flour. See **L278.**

L285 As white as (any, a, the) **Lily-flower**
c1300 *Horn* 2 L 15: So whit so eny lilye flour. **a1350** *Song of Five Joys* in Brown *Lyrics XIV* 44.12: Levedi, quite als leli floure. **c1350** *Octavian* (*NL*) 147.1335. **c1390** Chaucer *CT* VII 867[B2057]: As whit as a lilye flour, 2863 [B4053]: His nayles whitter than the lylye flour. **a1400** *Athelston* 69.70. **a1400** *Le Morte A.* 90.2994. **a1400** *Torrent* 57.1638–9. **c1400** *Emaré* 3.66, 7.205. **c1400** *Florence* 31.901, 35.1024, 52.1538. **c1400** *Gowther* 150.374 (*var.*). **c1400** *Triamour* 66.793–4. **1439** Lydgate *St. Albon* 182.1188: any. **a1450** *Gesta* 392[9]. **a1450** *St. Etheldreda* 301.842: ony. **c1450** *Seege of Troye* 132 A 1671. **c1455** *Partonope S* 482.67: the. **a1475** *Guy*[2] 136.4754. **a1475** *Landavall* 107.61. **c1475** Henryson *Testament* 118.373. **a1500** Greene *Carols* 145 *refrain.* **a1500** *Guy*[4] 13.76. **a1500** *Joy thu virgyn* in C. Everleigh Woodruff *A XV Century Guide-Book* (London, 1933) 80[13]. Whiting *Ballad* 28, 29. See **F278, 308, L279.**

L286 As white as **Lily-spring** (*-sprig*)
a1400 *Meditations* 25.939: In a cote whit so lilie-spryng.

L287 If one **Limb** is unhealthy all the others suffer
c1000 Aelfric *Homilies* I 274[8–9]: Gif an lim bið untrum, ealle ða oðre þrowiað mid þam anum. **a1400** *Cloud* 60.22–3: For right as if a lyme of oure body felith sore, alle the tother lymes ben pined and disesid therfore. **1533** More *Confutacion* 789 E[7–10]: For as saynct Paule sayeth, If one membre taketh hurte, all the members bee greved therewyth. See **H254.**

L288 The many **Limbs** of the body all obey one head
c1000 Aelfric *Homilies* I 272[25–6]: We habbað on anum lichaman manega lima, and hi ealle anum heafde gehyrsumiað.

L289 The rotted **Limb** shends (*harms*) the whole
1340 *Ayenbite* 148[9]: Vor the leme vorroted ssolde ssende the hole. **c1400** *Vices and Virtues* 146.25–6: For the roten membres schulde schende the hole. Cf. Tilley E246. See **A167.**

L290 To have no **Limb** (lith) without lack
c1330 *Body and Soul* 56.468: Nas no lim withouten lak. **a1393** Gower *CA* II 81.1691: Sche hath no lith withoute a lak.

L291 As tough as any **Lime** (*mortar*)
a1399 *Forme of Cury* 77[16]: Tyl it be towh as eny lyme.

L292 To lie in the **Lime** (*bird-lime*)
c1450 Holland *Howlat* 80.969: Tharfor I ly in the lyme, lympit, lathast. Whiting *Scots* I 201.

L293 To be **Lime-fingered**
c1303 Mannyng *Handlyng* 76.2137: Tho that have here handys as lyme. **c1499** Skelton *Bowge* I 49.509: Lyghte lyme fynger, he toke none other wage. **1546** Heywood *D* 38.98: And wyll be lyme fyngerd I feare. Apperson 212; *Oxford* 202; Tilley F236.

L294 As gentle as the **Lind**
a1500 *Croxton Sacrament* in Waterhouse 67.309: Now, Jason, as jentyll as ever was the lynde.

L295 As light as (the) **Lind**
c1350 *Joseph* 19.585: Ther nas no lynde so liht as thise two leodes. **a1450** *Pety Job* in Kail 133.395: Than were I glad, and lyght as lynde. **a1460** *Towneley Plays* 97.368. **c1499** Skelton *Bowge* I 39.231. **a1513** ?Dunbar *Manere of the Crying* 171.16: the. **1513** Douglas *Aeneid* III 234.57. Whiting *Drama* 320:212, *Scots* I 201. See **L139.**

L296 As aright as (a) **Line**
1340 *Ayenbite* 153[22–3]: Huanne me geth vorth onlepiliche and a-right ase line. **1484** Caxton *Royal Book* M8r[23]: Whan one goeth forth aryght as a lyne. See **L300.**

L297 As egal (*equal*) as a **Line**
1439 Lydgate *St. Albon* 120.538: Stande egall as a lyne.

L298 As even as (any, a) **Line**
a1338 Mannyng *Chronicle A* I 164.4695: Evene as lyne the wynd gan dryve, *B* I 150[16]. **c1400** *Beryn* 34.1070: And drawe hym to his ffeleshipp as even as a lyne, 101.3359: But hold(ith) forth the streyt wey, even as doith a lyne. **c1400** *Sowdone* 64.2237: That wente as even as eny lyne. **a1420** Lydgate *Troy* I 365.7709: any. **c1420** Wyntoun II 75.864: a. **a1450** *York Plays* 328.245: a. **a1500** *Court of Love* 430.785. Whiting *Scots* I 201.

L299 As plain as (a) **Line**
a1420 Lydgate *Troy* I 160.546: Of walles old, was made pleyn as lyne, **c1421** *Thebes* 190.4638–9: And with the soyle made pleyn as a lyne, To wyldernesse turnyd and desert.

L300 As right as (a, any) **Line**
c1385 Chaucer *TC* iii 228: To Troilus tho com, as lyne right. **c1400** *Vices and Virtues* 152.21–2: Whan a man goth forth evenliche as right as a lyne, 158.13–4: a. **c1408** Lydgate *Reson* 11.399: Hys eye up-cast ryght as lyne, 60.2248: any, 74.2774: Ryght as lyne and no thing wronge, **a1420** *Troy* I 30.636: any, 133.4075: Towardis the Grekis, as eny lyne righte, 163.653, 173.1012, 216.2491: a, 328.6435: any, 337.6729: as any lyne right, II 419.844, 430.1242, 440.1596: any, III 830.2031: any, 856.2912–3: any, **c1421** *Thebes* 90.2167: eny, **a1422** *Life* 594.101–2: any, **a1430** *Pilgrimage* 45.1705: any, 86.3237: any, 321.11771, **1430** *St. Margarete* in *MP* I 181.228: eny, **a1439** *Fall* I 276.2685: any, III 804.1053: any, 858.1251: a, **1439** *St. Albon* 131.238: any, 160.1930: any, **c1445** *Kalendare* in *MP* I 373.271: a, **a1449** *Fifteen Ooes* in *MP* I 241.99, *Testament* in *MP* I 346.451. **1501** Douglas *Palice* 32.26. **1546** Heywood *D* 44.97: Thou folowest their steppes as right as a lyne. Apperson 531; Whiting *Drama* 320:213, *Scots* I 201. See **L296.**

L300a **Line-right**
a1420 Lydgate *Troy* I 111.3365: And lyne right a-geyn the wormes hed, 349.7150–1: Cesar discendid was Doun lyne right, 384.8370, 387.8507, II 417.762–3, 422.937–8, III 575.396, 635.2434, 639.2566–7, 686.4174, **c1421** *Thebes* 33.750, **a1422** *Life* 601.209, **a1430** *Pilgrimage*

320.11751, 321.11758, 581.21779, **c1433** *St. Edmund* 423.569. NED Line-right.

L301 As straight as (a, any) **Line**
c1385 Chaucer *TC* ii 1461–2: But to his neces hous, as streyght as lyne, He com, **1391** *Astr.* ii 26.21–2: And the almycanteras in her Astrelabyes ben streight as a lyne. **c1412** Hoccleve *Regement* 113.3134: Thidir wil I goo, streght as any lyne. **a1420** Lydgate *Troy* I 337.6739: any. **c1422** Hoccleve *Lerne to Die* 204.692: To purgatorie y shal as streight as lyne. **a1425** *Templum Domini* 101.384: a. **a1437** *Kingis Quair* 88.151[4]: ony. **a1440** Burgh *Cato* 311.335: any. **c1450** Idley 169.664: a. **c1450** *When the son* 393.365: a. **a1475** *Flower and the Leaf* in Skeat *Chaucerian* 362.29: a. **a1500** *Court of Love* 412.137. **a1500** *Partenay* 173.5026. **c1503** More *Early Poems* [2] E[3–4]: a. Apperson 604–5; *Oxford* 624; Taylor and Whiting 223; Tilley L303; Whiting *Scots* I 201.

L302 As upright as a (any) **Line**
a1405 Lydgate *Black Knight* in *MP* II 385.67: The cedres high, upryght as a lyne, **c1408** *Reson* 72–3.2730–1: And evene upryght As any lyne, **a1420** *Troy* II 557.5638.

L303 To draw the (in one) **Line**
1455 Paston III 32[22–3]: And sworn that he shal be rewled, and draw the lyne with theym. **1546** Heywood *D* 82.87: We drew both in one line.

L304 To pluck the **Lining** from a bowl, *etc.*
a1449 Lydgate *Jak Hare* in *MP* II 445–8: 8: Wich of a bolle can plukke out the lynyng, 16: tancard, 24: pecher, 32, 40: pot, 48: cuppe, 56, 64, 72: pott, 80: cuppe.

L305 As bold(ly) as (any, a) **Lion**
a1325 *Otuel and Roland* 138.2524: And bolder thanne any lyon. **a1398**(1495) Bartholomaeus-Trevisa X6r[2.31]: The lyon bold and hardi. **a1420** Lydgate *Troy* I 76.2168: Bolde and hardy, liche a fers lyoun. **c1489** Caxton *Aymon* I 239.27–8: All boldly as a lyon. Apperson 59; Svartengren 113; Taylor and Whiting 223–4; Whiting *Scots* I 201.

L306 As breme (*fierce*) as **Lion**
1464 Hardyng 86[1]: As . . . bryme as lyon Marmerike. Whiting *Scots* I 201.

L307 As courageous(ly) as (a) **Lion(s)**
a1400 *Firumbras* 21.605: Corajous as a lyoun. **1485** Caxton *Charles* 120.17: (They) goon corageously as lyons. **c1505** Watson *Valentine* 114.17–8: He was . . . more courageous than a lyon. Taylor and Whiting 224.

L308 As cruel as (a) **Lion(s)**
a1338 Mannyng *Chronicle B* I 44[22]: That was S. Edmunde, cruelle als a leon. **c1386** Chaucer *LGW* 627: With stoute Romeyns, crewel as lyoun. **a1420** Lydgate *Troy* III 603.1365: And as cruel as a wood lyoun, 763.6787–8: More cruel . . . than . . . lyoun. **c1425** *Speculum Sacerdotale* 13.2: He beynge of a wronge cruel kynde, as a lyon. **a1430** Lydgate *Pilgrimage* 41.1530: Cruel as be lyouns. **c1450** *Pilgrimage LM* 10[6]. **a1500** Kennedy 46.456: O man, mair cruell, than ever wes wild lioun. **1523** Berners *Froissart* I 379[33]: a. Whiting *Scots* I 201.

L309 As eager(ly) (*fierce[ly]*) as (a, any) **Lion(s)**
a1300 *Richard* 431.6856: Ffaughte, egre as lyouns. **a1350** *Isumbras* 35.452 (*var.*): He was egur os a lyon full ryght. **c1350** *Libeaus* 17.262–4, 31.530–1, 38.670–1: a. **a1375** *Octavian* (S) 34.1079–80. **c1380** *Ferumbras* 22.554: He beholdeth oppon Olyver egrelich as lyoun. **a1400** *Firumbras* 4.39: eny, 26.758: any, 764: any. **c1400** *Roland* 133.935: A. **a1425** *Seege of Troye* 90 L 1137: any. **a1470** Malory I 111.22: lyons. **a1500** *Guy*[4] 99.3092: any.

L310 As fell as (the, a) **Lion(s)**
a1300 *Alisaunder* 113.1989–90: Alisaundre . . . fel so lyoun. **a1338** Mannyng *Chronicle A* II 533.15375–7: The Englische . . . fel als the lyoun, Monk ne clerk wolde they non spare. **c1350** *Libeaus* 94.1698: With fell herte as lioun. **c1375** *St. Cecilia* in Horstmann *Legenden 1881* 161.135–6: a. **a1400** *Meditations* 15.525–6: But feller than the lioun wod Thou were. **a1400** Wyclif *Sermons* I 408[128]: a. **c1410** Lovelich *Merlin* III 628.23636: Ryht as a lyown he wax . . . felle. **c1450** *Pilgrimage LM* 10[6]. **c1500** *Melusine* 200.34–5: lyons. Whiting *Scots* I 201.

L311 As fierce as (a, any) **Lion(s)**
c1300 *Body and Soul* 25 L 20: As a lyun fers. **c1375** *St. Cecilia* in Horstmann *Legenden 1881* 161.136: That als a lion was fers. **c1380** *Ferumbras* 69.2073: A knyght as fers as any lyoun, 85.2633–4: any, 106.3366: any. **c1385** Chaucer *CT* I[A] 1598: As fiers as leon pulled out his swerd. **a1400** *Meditations* 25.929: a. **a1400** *Rowlande* 69.470: any. **c1400** *Sowdone* 26.879: a. **c1410** Lovelich *Merlin* III 628.23636: Ryht as a lyown he wax feers, 631.23734: ony. **a1420** Lydgate *Troy* I 195.1752: Beying as fers as a wood lyoun, II 430.1252–3. **a1422** *God that all this world* 222[31]. **a1430** Lydgate *Pilgrimage* 41.1530: lyouns, **c1433** *St. Edmund* 410.772:

liouns. **c1450** *Jacob's Well* 268.23–4: a. **c1460** *Ipomadon C* 347.11: a. **a1470** Malory I 32.31: a. **c1470** *Wallace* 21.113: a. **1480** Caxton *Ovyde* 98[7]: a, **1481** *Mirror* 84[6]: lyons. **c1485** *Slaughter (Digby)* 10.231–2: Ffor thei be as fers as a lyon in a cage Whan thei are broken ought to reve men of ther lives. **c1489** Caxton *Aymon* II 343.1: a. **a1500** *Disciplina Clericalis* 51–2: a. **a1500** *Guy*[4] 75.2249–50: any. **1513** Douglas *Aeneid* IV 76.13: Fers as a wild lyoun. **1523** Berners *Froissart* III 86[1]: a, **1525** IV 188[21–2]: a, **1533** *Arthur* 512[13]: He was as fyerse of harte as a raged lyon. Taylor and Whiting 224; Tilley L308; Whiting *Scots* I 201.

L312 As fresh as any **Lion**(s)
a1475 *Guy*[2] 232.8077–8: The barons, That frescher were, then any lyons. **a1500** *Eger H* 245.1035: And was as fresh as any lyon. Whiting *Scots* I 201–2.

L313 As furious as **Lion**(s)
a1420 Lydgate *Troy* II 546.5246: More furious than . . . lyoun. **1485** Caxton *Charles* 141.14–5: The frensshe men, furyous . . . as lyons. Whiting *Scots* I 202.

L314 As hardy as (any, the, a) **Lion**(s)
a1200 *Ancrene* 141.9: Beoth eaver ayein him hardi ase liun. **1340** *Ayenbite* 84[22]: Maketh man hardi ase lyoun, 164[15]. **c1380** *Ferumbras* 75.2280: And of the chambre out thay paste, as hardy as any lyouns. **c1385** Chaucer *TC* v 830: Yong, fressh, strong, and hardy as lyoun. **c1395** *WBible* II Kings xxiii 20 (*translator's addition*): Twei knghtis hardi as liouns. **c1400** *Vices and Virtues* 83.5–6: the, 164.18: a. **a1420** Lydgate *Troy* I 283.4865: a, III 717.5239: lyouns, 796.818, **c1421** *Thebes* 79.1888, **a1422** *Life* 579.306. **1422** Yonge *Governaunce* 211.39: a. **a1425** *Governance of Lordschipes* 104.7: a. **a1430** Lydgate *Pilgrimage* 211.7560: lyouns, **a1439** *Fall* II 594.325, 598.459, III 676.58, 843.714, 878.1964, 900.2761: leouns, **1439** *St. Albon* 142.892: a, **c1440** *Debate* in *MP* II 562.548: a, *Fabules* in *MP* II 569.93: a, *Pageant of Knowledge* in *MP* II 734.274: a, *They that no while endure* in *MP* II 819.25: a, 820.1: a. **a1449** Lydgate and Burgh *Secrees* 73.2297. **c1450** *Secrete of Secretes* 35.16: a. **1456** Hay *Governaunce* 157.15, *Law* 60.12–3, 169.18: a. **1484** Caxton *Royal Book* H1ᵛ[2–3]: a, N7ᵛ[23]: a. **1506** *Kalender* 148.1: the. **1525** Berners *Froissart* IV 188[21–2]: a. Apperson 59; *Oxford* 54; Whiting *Scots* I 202.

L315 As keen (*fierce*) as **Lion**
a1300 *Alisaunder* 75.1315: Kyng Alisaunder, so lyoun kene. Whiting *Scots* I 202.

L316 As light as (a) **Lion**
a1375 *William* 125.3862: Light as a lyoun he leide on al a-boute. **a1400** *Siege of Jerusalem* 43.762: Light as a lyoun, wer loused out of cheyne. **c1400** *Roland* 135.986: Was never lione mor light of hert. Whiting *Scots* I 202.

L317 As proud as (a) **Lion**(s)
c1300 *Body and Soul* 25 L 20: As a lyun . . . proud. **a1415** *Lanterne* 111.11: Proude as lyouns. **c1450** *Alphabet* II 270.16–7: a. **c1460** *Ipomadon C* 347.11: a. **1464** Hardyng 86[1]. **c1489** Caxton *Aymon* II 392.7–8: They ranne the one upon thother as proudly as it had ben two lions. **1502** *Robert the Devil* C4ᵛ[26]: a.

L318 As rampant as (a) **Lion**(s)
a1338 Mannyng *Chronicle B* II 242[4]: That the Walsh men slouh raumpand as leouns. **c1390** *Mary and the Cross* 623.418: The devel stod lyk a lyon raumpaunt. **a1393** Gower *CA* III 303.2573: And goth rampende as a leoun. **c1400** *Laud Troy* II 418.14197: As lyoun rampyng forth he went. **c1421** Lydgate *Thebes* 91.2197: a. **a1425** *St. Anthony* 119.4–5: a. **1456** Hay *Law* 169.18: a. **a1470** Malory I 224.18–9: And raumped downe lyke a lyon many senatours noble. **c1475** Henryson *Orpheus* 133.121: a. Whiting *Scots* I 202–3.

L319 As real (*regal*) as a **Lion** (*etc.*) (A number of single quotations are brought together here)
c1386 Chaucer *LGW* 1605: And of his lok as real as a leoun, **c1390** *CT* VII 1915–6[B3105–6]: But if that I Be lik a wilde leoun, fool-hardy. **c1410** Lovelich *Grail* I 126.259–60: For so wilde Rasyng was nevere lyown As they thanne Isswed Owt of that town. **a1450** *Partonope* 82.2655–7: Agysor . . . Thatt as a . . . lyon . . . ys ravennous. **1471** Caxton *Recuyell* I 157.22: Hard as lyons, II 637.18: And ran out all araged as a lyon. **c1485** *Mary Magdalene (Digby)* 91.944: I am lofty as the lyon. **c1489** Caxton *Aymon* I 230.21–2: Sore an-angred as lyons. **c1490** Ryman 256.7: As myghty . . . as lyons.

L320 As sicker (*firm*) as (the) **Lion**
1340 *Ayenbite* 166[26–7]: He maketh him ziker ase lyoun. **c1400** *Vices and Virtues* 167.1: He maketh (hym) as siker as the lyon.

L321 As stark (*strong*) as a (the) **Lion**
c1420 Wyntoun II 285.215: Qwhat than the lion is starkar? **1456** Hay *Law* 169.18: Stark . . . as a lyoun.

L322 As stern as any (a) **Lion**
c1300 *Guy*[1] 180 A 3124: Sterner than ani lyoun. **c1300** *Reinbrun* 660.88.10–1: Thei he wer te bataile boun Ase sterne als eni lyoun, 672. 124.1–2. **c1300** *Speculum Gy* 13.262: a. **1432** Lydgate *Henry VI's Triumphal Entry* in *MP* II 633.75: a, **a1439** *Fall* II 359.1096–7: Lik a leoun, ful sterne off look and face, With his leffł hand my throte he dede enbrace. **a1475** *Seege of Troye* 203 H 1610cd: Also sterne he is in fyght As a lyon out rages on heyght. **a1500** *Beves* 47 M 772: any.

L323 As stout (*proud, fierce*) as a **Lion**
c1475 *Guy*[1] 535 C 9586–7: Duke berrard As stowte as a lyon. Apperson 59.

L324 As strong as (a) **Lion(s)**
c1395 *WBible* Judges xiv 18: What is strengere than a lioun? II Kings i 23: *Thei weren* . . . strongere than liouns. **c1490** Ryman 256.7[5]: As . . . stronge as lyons. Taylor and Whiting 224.

L325 As vengeable as (any) **Lion(s)**
1439 Lydgate *St. Albon* 166.276–7: Vengeable as lyons Of innocentes to shede the christen blode. **1502** *Robert the Devil* E5[v][8]: More vengeable than ony lyon.

L326 As wild as (the, a) **Lion**
a1325 *Maximion* in Böddeker 253.263: Wildore then the leo. **a1400** *Destruction of Troy* 122.3746: Wode in his wrathe, wild as a lion, 171.5257: a. **a1439** Lydgate *Fall* III 711.1369. **c1450** *Jacob's Well* 268.24: a.

L327 As wood (*mad*) as (any, a) **Lion(s)**
a1325 *Otuel and Roland* 75.532: And wode as eny lyoun. **a1338** Mannyng *Chronicle A* II 478.13795–8: Was nevere . . . lyoun . . . That was so wod, beste to byte, As Wawayn was. **a1350** *Seege of Troye* 91.1137: And he wexe wood as Lyoun, 116.1476. **a1393** Gower *CA* III 101.5684: And he than as a Lyon wod. **a1400** *Alexander C* 188.3167: a. **a1400** *Destruction of Troy* 123.3810: a, 191.5877: Une wode of his wit as a wild lyon, 207.6405: Wode for the wap, as a wild lyon. **c1400** *Brut* I 224.26–7: a. **a1420** Lydgate *Troy* I 192.1652: Lik a lyon, so wood . . . was he, II 433.1351, III 601.1271, 666.3494, 686.4158–9, 765.6852, 844.2522: any, **c1421** *Thebes* 160.3904, **a1439** *Fall* II 542.2525, **a1449** *Fifteen Ooes* in *MP* I 242.130: lyowns. **c1450** *Alphabet* I 118.3: a. **a1470** Malory I 30.29: a, II 527.18–9: Than sir Launcelot rode here and there as wode as a lyon that faughted hys fylle. **1485** Caxton *Charles* 141.14–5: lyons. Whiting *Scots* I 202.

L328 As wroth as any (a) **Lion**
a1350 *Seege of Troye* 117.1476: He woxe wroth as eny lyoun. **a1400** *Destruction of Troy* 61.1861: And wrothe at his wordes as a wode lion. **a1420** Lydgate *Troy* I 192.1652: a, III 639.2547–8. **c1450** *Merlin* I 159[23–4]: a. **c1489** Caxton *Aymon* II 343.1: a.

L329 Be not a **Lion** in your house
c1395 Chaucer *CT* III[D] 1989: Withinne thyn hous ne be thou no leon. **c1395** *WBible* Ecclesiasticus iv 35: Nyle thou be as a lioun in thin hous, turnynge upsedoun thi meneals. **c1450** *Foly of Fulys* 57.196: To ramp as lyone in thar houss. **c1450** Idley 102.1296: Be not in thy hous as a lyon wylde. See **L38.**

L330 A **Lion** in the way
c1395 *WBible* Proverbs xxii 13: A slow man schal seie, A lioun is without-forth; Y schal be slayn in the myddis of the stretis, xxvi 13: A slow man seith, A lioun is in the weie, a liounnesse is in the foot pathis. **a1500** *Leconfield Proverbs* 484[29–30]: The ydyll saithe oute of his house he dar not go Ffor the lyon is in the way, Salamon writithe so. *Oxford* 370; Taylor and Whiting 224; Tilley L312; Whiting *Scots* I 201. See **W476.**

L331 (A) **Lion(s)** of Cotswold
c1437 *Brut* II 582.25: Come rennyng on hym fersli, as lyons of Cotteswold. **a1500** Medwall *Nature* G3[r][8–9]: Ye are wont to be as bold As yt were a lyon of cottyswold. **1546** Heywood *D* 53.406: For she is as fierce, as a Lyon of Cotsolde. Apperson 115; *Oxford* 111; Tilley L323; Whiting *Drama* 339:473.

L332 The **Lion**'s mouth
c1395 *WBible* Psalms xxi 22: Make thou me saaf fro the mouth of a lion, II Timothy iv 17: Y am delyveride fro the mouth of the lioun. **a1400** *Pauline Epistles* II Timothy iv 17: I am delyveryd of the mouth of the lyoun. *Oxford* 273, 370.

L333 Of a **Lion** to make a lamb (*varied*)
c1380 Chaucer *CT* VIII[G] 197–9: For thilke spouse that she took but now Ful lyk a fiers leoun, she sendeth heere, As meke as evere was any lomb, to yow! **a1400** *Scottish Legends* II 371.101–3: For hyme, that scho als fellone Til spouse (tuk) as a woud lyone, Mek as a lame scho has the send. **a1425** *St. Robert* 56.476: Of a lyon makys a lambe. **1447** Bokenham 206. 7586–8: For, lo, hyr husbond whom she dede take, As fers fyrst as a voyde lyoun, As a lamb she hath maad to the buxum. **1483** Caxton *Golden Legende* 364[v][1.35–7]: The spouse whom

she hath taken whiche was lyke a wood lyon: She hath sente hym hyther lyke as a meke lambe, **1489** *Doctrinal* C3r[31–2]: He whyche was to fore fiers as a lyon was softe and debonayre as a lombe. See **W461.**

L334 To assail like a **Lion**
a1420 Lydgate *Troy* I 139.4281–5: Hercules . . . Liche a lyoun, wood and dispitous . . . Gan of newe hem of Troye assaile. **c1450** Trevet 96.16–7 (f. 19b col. 2): Assayled . . . as a lyon. **a1475** *Guy*[2] 238.8295–6: And assayled Gyowne, As he were a lyone.

L335 To be like (a) **Lion(s)** (*varied*)
c1000 Aelfric *Lives* II 84.282: He wearð þa leon gelic on his gewinnum and dædum. **a1300** *Richard* 198.2193–4: Than answered Kynge Rycharde, In dede lyon, in thought lybarde. **c1300** *Havelok* 51.1866–7: But dursten he newhen him no more Thanne he . . . leun wore. **c1385** Chaucer *CT* I[A] 1773–5: Fy Upon a lord that wol have no mercy, But been a leon, bothe in word and dede, 2630–3: Ne in Belmarye ther nys so fel leon, That hunted is, or for his hunger wood, Ne of his praye desireth so the blood, As Palamon to sleen his foo Arcite. **a1393** Gower *CA* II 200.2590–2: Lich to the Leoun in his rage, Fro whom that alle bestes fle, Such was the knyht in his degre, 212.3034–5: Thi regne also with pride on hih Was lich the Leon in his rage, III 335.3536–8: For thanne he mote, as it befalleth, Of his knyhthode as a Leon Be to the poeple a championn, 380.5240: Riht as a Leon in his rage. **a1400** *Morte Arthure* 115.3922: Londis als a lyon with lordliche knyghtes. **a1420** Lydgate *Troy* I 282.4832: And to his enmyes lyk a fers lyoun, II 466.2516: As wode lyouns, with mortal chere and face, 496.3544: For liche a lyoun al that day he wrought, 525.4548–9: And, lik a lyoun in his cruelte, He made hem tourne, III 603.1354: Liche a lyoun whetted with woodnes, 644.2722: Lik a lyoun toke of hem noon hede, **c1421** *Thebes* 57.1356: In her fury lik . . . lyouns, **1422** *Serpent* 58.4: Liche a lion not dismaied nor aferde. **a1425** *Chester Plays* I 96.251–2: And as a lion in his weale, Christ shalbe haunsed hye. **a1430** Lydgate *Pilgrimage* 378. 13985–6: And off hyr look . . . She was lyk to a ffers lyoun, 383.14160: Off contenaunce lyk a lyoun, **a1449** *Guy* in *MP* II 517.18–9: To Denmark pryncis . . . Lyk woode lyouns, void of all pite. **a1470** Malory II 734.21–2: Kynge Arthure lykened sir Trystram . . . unto a wood lyon. **c1470** *Wallace* 39.173: His corage grew in ire as a lyoune. **1485** Caxton *Charles* 26.31–2: He had the eyen like a lyon. **a1500** *Degrevant* 69 C 1057: He ys a lyoun in feld. **a1500** *Eger H* 275.1512: As wood lyons they wrought that time. **a1500** *Guy*[4] 51.1395–6: Guy answered him on hye As egre lyon with hart hardy. **c1500** *Lancelot* 94.3171–2: Thar he begynyth in his ferss curag Of armys, as o lyoune in his rag. **c1500** *Melusine* 113.10–1: Have an herte as a fyers Lyon ayenst your enemyes. **1513** Douglas *Aeneid* III 217(*chapter verse*): Lyke a wod lyoun past within the town. **1523** Berners *Froissart* I 172[11–2]: He and his wyfe, who had both the hertes of a lyon, 185[8–9]: His wyfe, who had . . . the hert of a lyon, 220[10]: She had the harte of a lyon, **a1533** *Arthur* 504[11–2]: They layde on with theyr swordes like two wyld lions. Whiting *Drama* 320:214, *Scots* I 201.

L336 To bear oneself (heart) like a **Lion**
a1338 Mannyng *Chronicle A* I 237.6753: Til us ye bere yow as lyouns. **c1350** *Libeaus* 100. 1792–3: Ther nis erl ne baroun, That bereth herte as lioun. **c1400** *Alexander Buik* I 22.670: His hede he bair as ane lyoun. **a1420** Lydgate *Troy* I 352.7276: And as a lioun bern hym in his fight. **1481** *Tulle of Olde Age* 83[12–3]: Bare hym so vigorously as a lyon in bataile.

L337 To bray like a **Lion**
c1477 Caxton *Jason* 52.6–7: And there (he) brayed as a lyon. Whiting *Scots* I 202.

L338 To break out (loose) like a **Lion**
a1420 Lydgate *Troy* III 780.258: And oute he brak like a wode lyoun. **c1489** Caxton *Blanchardyn* 88.32–4: Blanchardyn, lyke as . . . a lyon that is broken loos from his boundes Heved upward his swerde.

L339 To come like a **Lion**
c1400 *Laud Troy* I 147.4973: Ector come as a lyoun. **a1420** Lydgate *Troy* III 629.2333: Cam myghty Troylus lyk a wod lyoun. **a1470** Malory II 622.19. **1485** Caxton *Charles* 75.17: Olyver came as a lyon hungry ayenst fyerabras. **a1500** *Eger P* 274.989–90: But Gray steele came on Sir Grime Like a lyon in his woodest time.

L340 To defend oneself like a **Lion**
a1338 Mannyng *Chronicle* A I 424.12111–2: The bere assailled the dragoun, And he defended hym as a lyoun. **c1400** *Alexander Buik* III 249.5053. **a1475** *Guy*[2] 54.1890, 97.3379, 140.4895. **a1475** *Seege of Troye* 189 H 1127.

L341 To devour like a **Lion**
a1430 Lydgate *Pilgrimage* 516.19327–31: I go and serche, day and nyght, With alle my fforce, with al my myght, Lyche a ravenous lyoun,

Ffor to devoure, up and doun, Alle ffolkys. **c1477** Caxton *Jason* 20.11–2: We shal put hem to deth al so lightly as the lyon devoureth the lambe with his teth and clawes.

L342 To enter (in) like (a) **Lion(s)**
c1420 Lydgate *Troy* I 134.4118: Whiche entred (in) liche a wood lyoun. **c1440** *Prose Alexander* 42.22–3: The macedoynes . . . as wode lyouns ere enterde oure landez. **1485** Caxton *Charles* 234.6: As a lyon entred in to the bataylle.

L343 To fall on someone like **Lions**
a1420 Lydgate *Troy* II 453.2054–5: Everyche on other lik . . . lyons Be-gan to falle, **1439** *St. Albon* 181.1131–3: The paynyms lyke . . . lyons, . . . Fyllen upon the martyr.

L344 To fare like (a) **Lion(s)**
a1300 *Richard* 274.3610: As a wood lyoun he ffarde, 340.5108: The Crystene ferden as lyouns. **c1300** *Guy*[1] 484 A 132.4, 485 C 8545–6. **a1350** *Seege of Troye* 111.1403–4: As a wood lyoun ferde he That hadde fasted dayes three. **c1375** *St. Catherine* 171.594. **c1375** *St. James* in Horstmann *Legenden 1881* 98.104. **c1380** *Ferumbras* 26.627: As twey lyons thay furde right, That wolde slen his preye, 76.2293–4: For Al so furde this xii barons by that foule hepe, Also wolde so many lyouns among so many schepe. **a1400** *Destruction of Troy* 41.1209, 323.9888–9: Dyomede . . . Ffore with his fos as a fuerse lyon. **a1400** *Pricke* 61.2224–5. **a1400** *Rowlande* 60.173: a. **c1410** Lovelich *Merlin* III 618.23250: For as a lyowm he ferde in trawnce. **a1420** Lydgate *Troy* II 543.5138–40: That like . . . a lyoun wood, That wer deprived newly of his praye, Right so firde he, **1422** *Serpent* 51.17–8. **a1425** *Seege of Troye* 136 L 1738–9. **1449** Metham 61.1660–1: That as a lyoun wode for ire, ryht so he faryd Nygh owte off hys mend. **a1450** *Partonope* 398.9615, 409.9850, 432.10577–8: As a lyon that wode was he ferde, That hongry was and lakked his pray, 443.11009. **c1460** *Ipomadon C* 342.47–8: And, as the boke sais, right as a feers lion among othre bestes, so fore he with all. **a1470** Malory II 738.11: a, 760.16–7: He fared as hit had bene an hungry lyon. **c1500** *Lancelot* 98.3331: o. Whiting *Scots* I 202.

L345 To fight like (a, the) **Lion(s)**
a1300 *Alisaunder* 205.3661–2: The barouns Foughtten so don the lyouns, 309.5876: For als a wode lyoun he faughth. **a1300** *Arthour and M.*[1] 54.1855–6: And ther faught sir Uterpendragon, As he were a wode lyoun. **a1300** *Richard* 441.7062 (var.). **c1300** *Guy*[1] 208.3599–600. **a1325** *Otuel and Roland* 115.1810–1: So fast tho he gan to fyght, As hyt were a wylde lyoun. **a1338** Mannyng *Chronicle B* I 183[15]: a wilde. **c1350** *Libeaus* 113.2029–30: a. **a1375** *Octavian* (S) 36.1133–4. **c1385** Chaucer *CT* I[A] 1656: In his fightyng were a wood leon. **a1400** *Guy*[5] xxxvii[19]. **c1400** *Alexander Buik* II 234.4558: ane. **c1400** *Laud Troy* I 159.5368. **a1425** *Arthour and M.*[2] 359.1947–8. **a1439** Lydgate *Fall* II 535.2270. **a1450** *Partonope* 361. 8845–6. **1464** Hardyng 393[27–8]: The regent was there that daye, a lion, And faught in armes. **a1470** Malory I 33.34: a. **1475** *Boke of Noblesse* 46[24–5]: a. **c1475** *Golagros* 33.961: As lyoune, for falt of fude, faught on the fold. **c1489** Caxton *Aymon* I 113.33–5: Reynawde fought soo sore, that never lyon . . . foughte soo strongly agenste ony other best. **a1500** *Eger H* 281.1584. **a1500** *Eye and Heart* 259.676. **a1500** *Guy*[4] 70.2075: Guy fought agayne as egre lion. **a1500** *Triamour* (*P*) II 108.823: a feirce. **c1500** *Arthour and M.*[3] I 479.1836–7. Taylor and Whiting 224; Whiting *Scots* I 202.

L346 To find something dear (*difficult*) as the **Lion** does the bear
a1300 *Arthour and M.*[1] 211.7517–8: The cristen fond the hethen dere, So the lioun doth the bere.

L347 To go like (the, a) **Lion(s)**
c1200 *Sawles Warde* 18.163–4: The unwhiht with his ferd ase liun iburst geath abuten ure hus. **c1300** Robert of Gloucester I 447.6142: As leon hardi ynou he wende aboute wide. **c1325** *Charter of Christ A* in Mary C. Spalding *Middle English Charters of Christ* (Bryn Mawr, Pa., 1914) 24.65–6: He fand me gangand in the way Als the lyon gase to his pray. **c1395** *WBible* I Peter v 8: The devel, as a rorynge lioun goith aboute, sechinge whom he schal devoure. **a1450** *Partonope* 446.11120–1: Now as . . . lyons two Partonope and the soudan gan go. **c1500** *Lancelot* 32.1095: Lyk to o lyone in to the feld he gais.

L348 To grim (*be angry*) like a greedy **Lion** (*etc.*) (A number of single quotations are brought together here)
c1000 Aelfric *Lives* I 242.62: þa grimetede se wælhreowa swa swa grædig leo, II 166.138–9: We yrsiað Swa swa leo. **a1200** Lawman I 174.4084–5: He liththe (*goes*) geon theos leoden, Sulch hit an liun were. **a1300** *Arthour and M.*[1] 223.7971–2: And dasched hem amid the pres, So lyoun doth on dere in gres, 268.9781–2:

Thus her and tar he leyd adoun, So it were a wode lyoun. **a1300** *Tristrem* II 40.1444–5: As a lothely lioun, that bataile, (*he*) wald abide. **c1300** *Guy*[1] 80 A 1429–30: Als a lyoun he heyed him fast, That his prey wold have on hast, 228 A 3959–60: Bifor the soudan com Gyoun, And him biheld als a lyoun, 232 A 4053–4: Gyoun That him wered als a lyoun, 296 A 5340: Therwith he him werd as a lyoun. **a1350** Castelford 136.23385–8: Thai fledde him al so men wer won To fle fra ane cruelle lion, Quam grete hunger makes to sek Qwat beste so comes to him to clek. **c1390** *Visions of seynt poul* in *Vernon* I 253.63–4: Of hem tok I (?thei) no more kep But as a Lyun doth of a schep. **a1400** *Destruction of Troy* 189.5810: Launsit, as a lyoun, 358.10985: And as a lion on the laund launchit aboute. **a1400** *Discrescyon of Spirites* 82.17–8: He thenkith himself for to rise . . . as a lyon rennyng felly, for to asaile the seeknes of oure sely soules. **a1400** *Pricke* 79.2907–8: Grysly devels agayn it raumpande, Als wode lyons to wayt thair pray. **c1400** *Alexander Buik* II 221.4140: For he berit as ane lyoun in rage. **a1420** Lydgate *Troy* II 416.749–50: But lik a lyoun in his hungri rage Issed oute, 418.796: Discendid is lik a wode lyoun, 438.1539–40: Lyk a lyoun, with a sterne face, Evere in oon so gan hem to enchase, 542.5102–3: So indurat, and hertid as lyoun He was alweie, III 604.1394: For lyke lyouns thei gan hem enchase, 808.1252: Liche a lioun his fomen gan oppresse. **c1422** Hoccleve *Lerne to Die* 202.645–6: In hidles, in awayt as a Leoun He hath leyn. **1449** Metham 34.904: Had noght Amoryus hym qwyt as a fers lyon. **a1450** *St. Katherine* (*Gibbs*) 53[8–9]: The tyraunt as a ranpynge lyon grynted wyth hys teeth. **c1450** *Merlin* II 196[18–9]: But disparbled a-brode fro hym as from a wode lyon in rage, 663[1–2]: He spronge in a-monge the Romaynes as a wood lyon a-monge wilde bestes. **a1470** Malory II 812.10–1: And anone they laysshed togydyrs as egirly as hit had bene two lyons, 906.33–5: And one of thos three shold passe hys fadir as much as the lyon passith the lybarde, both of strength and of hardines. **c1489** Caxton *Aymon* II 413.1–2: All swellynge wyth angre as a fiersfull lion. **a1500** *Partenay* 53.1369: Men hym doubted As thai wold A lion. **1513** Douglas *Aeneid* III 263.8: Than, as wod lyon, ruschit he in the fight.

L349 To leap like (a) **Lion**(**s**)
a1200 Lawman I 62.1462–3: And towardes Numbert he leop, Swilc hit an leon weora, II 58.11570–1: Tha lep mi fader up, Swulc hit an liun weore, 127.13201–2: And an voten leop, Swulc hit an liun weore, 216.15298–9: He to than cheorle leop, Swulc hit a liun weoren, 267.16493–4, 276.16709–10, 380.19168–9, 469.21269–70, 481 *B* 21561–2, 622.24847–8, III 70.26894–5. **a1375** *William* 47.1231: Latherly as a lyoun he lepes in-to the prese. **a1450** *Castle* 105.938: I lepe as a lyon. **a1500** *Alexius* (*Cotton*) 68.353–4: She com Forthe with A raply rese, As A lyon lept oute of A lees. **a1500** *Beves* 204 M 4070: Up he lepud as a lyon. Whiting *Scots* I 202.

L350 To let (*behave*) like a **Lion**
a1400 *Alexander C* 20.612: And as a lyon he lete quen he loude romys. **a1400** *Morte Arthure* 113.3831: Letande alls a lyon, he lawnches them thorowe.

L351 To look like a **Lion**
c1330 *Tars* 35 A 105: And loked as a lyoun. **c1350** *Gamelyn* 648.125: He loked as a wilde lyoun. **c1378** *Piers* B xiii 302: And as a lyon on to loke and lordeliche of speche, xv 198: And as a lyoun he loketh. **c1385** Chaucer *CT* I[A] 2171: And as a leon he his lookyng caste, **c1390** VII 3179[B4369]: He looketh as it were a grym leoun. **c1390** *Tars* 35 V 105: He lokede as a wylde lyon. **c1395** Chaucer *CT* III[D] 429: For thogh he looked as a wood leon. **a1400** *Morte Arthure* 4.119, 5.139: By lukynge, withowttyn lesse, a lyon the semys. Whiting *Ballad* 29.

L352 To meet like (a) **Lion**(**s**)
c1300 *Guy*[1] 289 A 5094: And he mett with hem als a lyoun. **a1439** Lydgate *Fall* I 103.3732–3: And how the brethre mette a-mong the pres, Lich too . . . leouns.

L353 To play the **Lion**
c1385 Chaucer *TC* i 1074: And in the feld he pleyde the leoun. **a1420** Lydgate *Troy* II 423.976: For thilke day (the) lyoun pleyed he, 450.1950, 548.5325–7, **c1421** *Thebes* 172.4200, **c1433** *St. Edmund* 403.381, **1439** *St. Albon* 120.518, 555, **c1440** *Debate* in *MP* II 541.52, 548.222. Whiting *Scots* I 202.

L354 To prick (*go rapidly*) as a **Lion**
c1410 Lovelich *Grail* III 195.142: Amonges hem he prekede As A fers lyown, *Merlin* II 294.11025: But into that pres prekede as a wood lyown.

L355 To rage like a **Lion**
1509 Barclay *Ship* II 209[11]: Lyke to a Lyon in dedes he shall rage. Whiting *Scots* I 202.

L356 To range like (a) **Lion**(**s**)
a1420 Lydgate *Troy* I 140.4312–3: And lyche a

lyoun rengyng on the playn Bar downe and slowe, 381.8263–5: Lik a ferse lyoun Among(es) Troyens renging up and doun Ulixes went, **a1439** *Fall* II 499.946–7: Tirauntis . . . regnyng lik wood leouns.

L357 To ride like any (a) **Lion**
a1420 Lydgate *Troy* III 577.467–8: As eny lyoun stronge, With his swerd gan riden hem amonge. **a1500** *Eger P* 244.663–4: He rydeth feircely out of the towne As he were a wild Lyon.

L358 To roar like (a) **Lion(s)**
c1395 *WBible* Jeremiah li 38: Thei schulen rore togedire as liouns, Ezekiel xxii 25: As a lioun roringe and takinge prei, thei devouriden men, Hosea xi 10: He schal rore as a lioun. **c1400** *Laud Troy* II 419.14243: As a lyoun rores, to him he cried. **1471** Caxton *Recuyell* II 332.27–8: He began to rore as an olde lyon.

L359 To run like (a) **Lion(s)**
c1400 *Laud Troy* I 320.10843–6: Achilles than to Ector rennes,—As lyoun doth out of her dennes, When thei are hungred, afftir bestes That thei se walke In wilde forestes. **a1420** Lydgate *Troy* I 255.3857–8: Thei ran I-fere . . . Liche wode liouns, II 446.1790: lyouns, 477.2877–8: lyons, III 600.1260: a. **a1470** Malory I 29.7: a. **1471** Caxton *Recuyell* II 432.17–8: lyons. **c1475** *Guy*[1] 123 C 2072: a. **c1500** *Melusine* 202.24: a. **a1533** Berners *Arthur* 184[24]: a.

L360 To slay like (a, the) **Lion**
a1338 Mannyng *Chronicle A* II 482.13889–91: As the lyon for hunger snacches And sleth the best that he first lacches, So ferd Arthur wyth ilkon. **c1400** *Laud Troy* I 43.1433–4: And sclow Gregeis here and there As a lyon fers and fere, 259.8776–7: To scle the Gregais wold he not ses, As hongre lyoun bestes vories, 309.10473–4: And sclow his men—as lyoun bestis That is for-hungred In wilde forestis. **a1420** Lydgate *Troy* I 138.4244–6: Whom Pollux hath, lyche a ferse lyoun . . . slawen, III 637.2484–5: And like a wood lyoun He slow that day of hem many oon.

L361 To smite like (the, a) **Lion(s)**
a1300 *Arthour and M.*[1] 265.9673–4: These four smot on hem, certes, So the lyoun doth on the hertes. **c1300** *Guy*[1] 130 A 2223–4: Aither semed a lyoun of mode, So hard thai smiten with swordes gode. **c1300** *Reinbrun* 650.59.4–5: Togedres thai smite, with-outen faile, Ase sterne lyouns in bataile. **a1338** Mannyng *Chronicle A* II 495.14273–4: Byfore hym dide bere his dragoun, Moddred to smyte as a lyoun. **c1450** *Merlin* II 238–9: He smote a-monge the saisnes so fiercely as a wode lyon.

L362 To start up like (a) **Lion**
a1300 *Arthour and M.*[1] 253.9082–4: Adragein anon up stirt . . . So it were a wode lyoun. **c1395** Chaucer *CT* III[D] 794: And he up stirte as dooth a wood leoun, 2152. **a1400** *Firumbras* 51.1613: Fful sone charlys stert up as a lyoun. **a1500** *Guy*[4] 91.2790: Up he start as eger lyon, 197.6516: an, 219.7303: an.

L363 To sue (*pursue*) like a **Lion**
a1420 Lydgate *Troy* I 384.8386–7: He gan aftir sewe In his chaas, as a wood lyoun. **a1500** *Guy*[4] 144.4673: Heraude him sued as an eger lyon.

L364 Who painted the **Lion?**
c1395 Chaucer *CT* III[D] 692: Who peyntede the leon, tel me who? **1484** Caxton *Aesop* 121[1–15]. **c1500** Fabyan 262[47]: Quis pinxit leonem.

L365 As enraged as a **Lioness**
1480 Caxton *Ovyde* 122[35]: She was more enraged than a lyonesse.

L366 As stubborn as a **Lioness**
c1395 Chaucer *CT* III[D] 637: Stibourn I was as is a leonesse.

L367 Like a **Lioness** whose whelps have been taken from her
a1400 *Scottish Legends* I 453.436–8: Out of wyt for wa scho ferd, As a lyones come ful thra, That men had tane the quhelpis fra. See **B103, T293.**

L368 To fare like a **Lioness**
a1420 Lydgate *Troy* III 678.3902–3: Or like, in soth, to a lyounesse, That day she ferde.

L369 To start forth like a **Lioness**
c1390 *Alexius* (*Vernon*) 68.470–1: Heo sturte forth in haste i-wis, As A lyonesse.

L370 He can ill pipe that lacks his upper **Lip**
1546 Heywood *D* 94.139: He can yll pype, that lackth his upper lyp. *Oxford* 501; Tilley L324, cf. P348.

L371 **Lips** are the worst part by which men sin against God
a1400 Wyclif *Sermons* II 187[14]: For lippis ben the worste part bi which men synnen agens God. See **W635.**

L372 Such **Lips** such lettuce
1546 Heywood *D* 83.102: Suche lips, such lettice. Apperson 366; *Oxford* 371; Tilley L326; Whiting *Drama* 131, *Scots* I 203.

L373 To laugh but from the **Lips** forward
1532 More *Confutacion* 432 F[2–3]: He laugheth but from the lyppes forwarde. Tilley T423.

L374 To make a **Lip**
1529 More *Supplicacion* 294 F[6]: Ye make a lippe, and thinke it so mad. NED Lip 2.

L375 To scald one's **Lips**
1513 Douglas *Aeneid* II 10.256–9: Perfyte symylitudis and exemplis all Quharin Virgill beris the palm of lawd, Caxtoun, for dreid thai suld hys lyppis scald, Durst nevir twich. Apperson 552: Scald; *Oxford* 564; Tilley L328.

L376 With **Lips** not heart (*varied*)
c1340 Rolle *Psalter* 16 (4.5): The whilk loves god with thaire lippis, bot thaire hert is fere fra him, 78 (21.6): For thi thai spake with lippes, noght in thaire hert, 208 (58.8): Bot now in mykill prechynge in lippis noght in dede, *Ten Commandments* in Perry *English Prose Treatises* 11.5–6: When we honour God with oure lyppys, and oure hertys erre ferre fra Hym. **a1400** *Cleansing* 201.11–2 (f.132[v]): A praiere that is seide or bode oonly with the lippes and not with the hert is not fructuous, 206.6–8 (f.135[v]). **c1400** *Lay Folks' Catechism* 43.662–4: For they worschipe hym with here lyppis and not with here hertys. **c1425** *Orcherd* 403.28–9. **c1450** *Speculum Christiani* (2) 190.7–8: This peple worschipen me wyth lyppes, bot the herte of hem is fer fro me, 30–1: Ysidorus: A fervente prayer is not of lippes bot of hertes. **1529** More *Supplicacion* 336 E[13–4]: It lyeth but in the lippes, and never came nere the hert. See **C174, M755, S79, T383, W631.**

L377 Your **Lips** hang in your eye (light)
c1516 Skelton *Magnificence* 33.1050: Tusshe! thy lyppes hange in thyne eye. **1546** Heywood *D* 67.54: Your lips hang in your light. Apperson 369–70; *Oxford* 371; Tilley L330.

L378 **Lip-labor**
1528 More *Heresyes* 116 C[10–3]: Whiche kinde of prayer these . . . heritiques nowe cal lippe labour in mockage. NED Lip-labour; Taylor and Whiting 225; Whiting *Drama* 353:686. Cf. Tilley L331.

L379 The **Liquor** is semblable to the vessel
c1523 Barclay *Mirrour* 54[17]: Men judgeth the licour to the vessell semblable.

L380 To distill like **Liquor** out of an alembic
c1385 Chaucer *TC* iv 519–20: This Troylus in teris gan distille, As licour out of a lambic ful faste.

L381 Better is **List** (*cunning*) than lither (*evil*) strength (*varied*)
a1200 *Ancrene* 138.18–9: Betere is wis liste then luther strengthe. **a1200** Lawman II 297.17209–13: Hit wes yare iquethen, That betere is liste (*B* sleahthe) Thene ufel stren(g)the, For mid liste (*B* slehthe) me mai ihalden That strengthe ne mai iwalden. **c1200** *St. Katherine* (*Royal*) 58.1233–4: With meokelec and liste, Nawt with luther strencthe, cf. 71.1516–9. **a1220** Giraldus *Descriptio Kambriae* in *Opera* VI 188[8–9]: Betere is . . . liste thene lither streingthe. **a1400** *Benjamin Minor* in *Yorkshire Writers* I 170[35]: Ffor better liste then lythere strenght. **a1400** *Cloud* 87.6–7: Bot wirche more with a list then with any lither strengthe. **a1400** *Pistle of Preier* 58.2. **a1400** *Stodye of Wysdome* 41.4. **1481** Caxton *Reynard* 104.1: The connyng goth to fore strengthe, **1484** *Aesop* 240[1–2]: Better is crafte and subtylte than force. **1515** Barclay *St. George* 63.1469–70: For many tymes it provyd is at length That craft and gyle subduyth myght and strength. Apperson 43; Tilley P462. See **E202, F492, M281, 801, O51, Q5, S833, 858.**

L382 **Lith** (*help*) and selthe (*success*) are fellows
c1300 *Havelok* 49.1338: Lith and selthe felawes are. Apperson 174, 327; *Oxford* 372.

L383 By **Lither** (*bad*) men know the good
c1378 *Piers* B x 435: For bi lyther men knoweth the gode. See **L261, T110, W231.**

L384 **Liting** (*delay*) is selcouth (*wonderfully*) ill
a1400 *Cursor* III 1499 F 26631: For liting is ful selcouth ille. See **D157.**

L385 The **Litter** is like to the sire and dam
1549 Heywood *D* 44.92: The litter is lyke to the syre and the damme. *Oxford* 372; Tilley L337. See **F80, M720.**

L386 Better a **Little** gotten with right than much with wrong (*varied*)
a1250 *Yc ou rede ye sitten stille* in *SP* 28(1931) 598.107–8: Betere is lutel wid riste igete Thene wid wronge muchel imeten. **a1395** *WBible* Proverbs xvi 8: Betere is a litel with rightfulnesse than many fruytis with wickidnesse. **a1400** *Northern Verse Psalter* I 113 (36.16): Better is litel to right, with wele, Over richesses of sinful fele. Tilley L360.

L387 Better a **Little** sure than much in fear and doubt
1509 Barclay *Ship* II 74[2]: And better a lytell sure than moche in fere and dout. See **M700.**

L388 Better to have a **Little** with ease than much with malease
a1300 *Alisaunder* 399.7358–9: Better is litel to habbe in ayse Than mychel aghghtte in malayse.

Apperson 371; *Oxford* 375; Tilley L350. See **M700.**

L389 Better to have **Little** with worship than much with shendship (*shame*)
c1300 *Guy*[1] 254.4445–6: Lever ich hadde litel with worthschipe Than michel with schenschipe.

L390 By the **Little** men should beware of the more
a1470 Parker *Dives* C8^r^[2.25–6]: That by the lytyll men sholde beware of the more. See **H40.**

L391 Good to fast a **Little** and have full saulee (*amount of food*) at supper
c1450 *Pilgrimage LM* 4[3–4]: And good it were to faste a litel for to have ful saulee at the sopere.

L392 He that can (do) **Little** has soon done
a1325 *Nego* in Wright *Political Songs* 211[11–2]: For whoso can lite, hath sone i-do, Anone he drawith to *nego*. See **G347.**

L393 He that gives me **Little** is on (*favorably disposed to*) my life (*varied*)
c1250 *Hendyng O* 196.27: He that me luitel yefth, he me lif on. **c1450** *Douce MS.52* 44.2: He that a lytul me yevyth, to me wyllyth longe lyffe. **c1450** *Rylands MS.394* 95.10: He that yeveth me alitel wol my lyfe. Apperson 247; Kneuer 31; *Oxford* 239; Schleich 255–6; Singer III 129–30; Skeat 80. Cf. Jente 224.

L394 He that has **Little** and can be content is better at ease than he that is rich and always cares for more
c1495 *Arundel Vulgaria* 59.253: He that hath but litell and can be content is better at ease than he that is riche and alwaye careth for more. See **E120, L403, S867.**

L395 He that has **Little** or nought is rich
1483 Caxton *Cato* E7^v^[13–4]: The proverbe sayth that he whiche hath lytel, or as nought, is ryche. Cf. Taylor and Whiting 265: Blessed be nothing. See **N140.**

L396 **Little** and little the cat eats the bacon (flesh, flitch)
c1450 *Rylands MS.394* 94.30: Lytell and lytell the catt eteth the bakon. **c1475** *Rawlinson MS. D 328* 122.59: A lytel and a lytel the cate etuthe the flesch. Murilegus parvan paulatim devorat unam. **a1500** Hill 130.16: A litill and a litill, the cat etith up the bacon fliche. **1546** Heywood *D* 84.144: Yet littell and littell the cat eateth the flickell. Apperson 87; *Oxford* 82; Tilley L353.

L397 A **Little** in the morning, nothing at noon, and a light supper makes to live long
a1500 *Harley MS.2321* in *Rel. Ant.* I 208: A little in the morninge, nothing at noone, And a light supper doth make to live longe. Apperson 371; Tilley L356.

L398 **Little** may help there much behooves (*is needed*)
c1450 *Douce MS.52* 52.94: Lytyll may helpe, there myche be-hoveth. **c1450** *Rylands MS.394* 103.16.15. Cf. Taylor and Whiting 225.

L399 **Little** said, soon amended, *etc.*
1555 Heywood *E* 176.169: Lyttle sayde, soone amended. Lyttle good, soone spended. Lyttle charge, soone attended. Lyttle wyt, soone ended. Apperson 372–3; Jente 151; *Oxford* 374; Tilley L358.

L400 Much yern (*very active*) brings **Little** home
c1450 Greene *Carols* 418.3: Myche yerne bryngth lytel hom.

L401 Of a **Little** one gives a little
c1450 *Douce MS.52* 45.14: Of a litul me yevyth a litul. Apperson 372; Tilley L363.

L402 Of **Little** waxes mickle
a1200 *Ancrene* 32.11–2: Thus ofte, as me seith, of lutel muchel waxeth, 153.25–7: The cwene seide ful soth the with a strea ontende alle hire wanes: thet muchel kimeth of lutel, **a1400** (*Recluse*) 140.4–5: A lefdi seide a spark broughth al hir hous on brennyng and so it fareth ofte of litel cometh mychel. **a1500** *Colkelbie* 296.475–6: Ye may consave be this twich That oft of littill cumis mich. Apperson 398: Many; Jente 760; *Oxford* 404; Skeat 292; Tilley L362; Whiting *Scots* I 203. See **C75, 431, D412, S559.**

L403 To have **Little** and be content is worship, *etc.*
1450 *Dicts* 106.8–10: To have litille and to be content is worshup, and to have muche and not content, it is shame. See **L394.**

L404 Where **Little** is promised there is little lying
c900 *Old English Cato* 3.26: þær lyt gehaten byð, þær byð lyt leane (*var.* lygena).

L405 He that **Lives** (loves God) best prays best
c1400 *Order of Priesthood* in Wyclif *EW* 169[8]: For who lyveth best preieth best, 173[23–4]: That man that loveth best god preieth best.

L406 He that **Lives** cursedly may be sicker to end dolefully
a1415 Mirk *Festial* 194.28–9: Thus whoso lyvyth

cursydly, he may be sykur forto ende dolfully. Apperson 374:17; *Oxford* 378; Tilley L392. See **L250, 412.**

L407 He that **Lives** longest shall suffer most woe
c1430 Lydgate *Dance* 70.584: Who lengest leveth moste shal suffre wo. Apperson 374:9. Cf. Jente 423.

L408 He that **Lives** well shall die well (*varied*)
c1412 Hoccleve *Regement* 104.2870: Ffor who so lyveth wel, wel shal he dye. **c1430** Lydgate *Dance* 38.296: Who lyveth a-right mote nedes dye wele. **1477** Rivers *Dictes* 47[23]: He that liveth wele shal die wele. **c1500** *Lyfe of Roberte* 262.1129: He that lyveth well here, no evyll death shall dye. **1506** Barclay *Castell* E5r[2]: For who well lyveth well doth ende. **1506** *Kalender* 169.26: He that levyth well maye not dye amys. **1509** Barclay *Ship* II 316[26]: Who justly lyveth justly also shall ende. Apperson 376; Tilley L391.

L409 To **Live** as one learns (*teaches*)
a1376 *Piers* A v 36: And libben as ye lereth us, we wolen love ou the betere. Apperson 509; *Oxford* 514–5. See **L463, P347.**

L410 We **Live** as we may, not as we would
1483 *Vulgaria quedam abs Terencio* Q7v[4]: We live as we may, not as we wold.

L411 We no sooner begin to **Live** than we begin to die
c1340 Rolle *Psalter* 496 (Song of Hezekiah 5): For na sonere bigyn we to life than we bigyn to dye. Cf. Chaucer *CT* I[A] 3891–2.

L412 A cursed **Living** asks a cursed ending (*varied*)
a1415 Mirk *Festial* 120.13–4: For as Seynt Austyn sayth: "A cursyd lyvyng before, askythe a cursyd endyng aftyr," 194.22: Thus algatys a curset lyfuyng schewythe a fowle ende. **a1439** Lydgate *Fall* III 961.1483–4: Ther fals lyvyng Of riht requereth to have an evel eendyng. See **L250, 406.**

L413 Better be oft **Loaded** than overloaded
c1000 *Royal MS.2 B.v* in *Anglia* 2(1878–9) 373: Selre byth oft feðre þænne oferfeðre. Meliora plura quam gravia honera fiunt. **c1025** *Durham Proverbs* 14.37: Betere byþ oft feðre þonne oferfeðre. Meliora plura quam gravia honera fiunt. See **O64.**

L414 **Loaves** and fishes
c1000 *WSG* John vi 9–26: Her is an cnapa þe hæfþ fif berene hlafas and twegen fixas . . . ge æton of ðam hlafon, and synt fulle. **c1395** *WBible* John vi 9–26: A child is here, that hath fyve barli looves and twei fischis . . . ye eten of louves, and weren fillid. Apperson 376; *Oxford* 378; Tilley L401.

L415 Seldom comes **Loan** laughing home
c1250 *Hendyng O* 194–5.20: Selden cometh lone lauinde homward. **c1450** *Douce MS.52* 51.82: Seldun comyth lone laughyng home. **c1450** *Rylands MS.394* 101.13. Apperson 376, 556; Jente 132, 364; Kneuer 37–8; *Oxford* 572; Schleich 260–1; Singer III 132–3; Skeat 84; Tilley L402; Whiting *Scots* I 203.

L416 Ever the **Loath** shall have the land
c1475 *Rawlinson MS. D 328* 125.78: Ever the lothe schall have the land. De ffuraci speres erit hosus sepeus eres. Walther I 619.5068.

L417 Seldom erndes (*intercedes*, ends) well the **Loath**, and seldom pleads well the wroth
c1250 *Owl* 80.942–4: For hit seide the king Alfred: "Sel(d)e endeth wel the lothe, An selde plaideth wel the wrothe." **a1400** *Additional MS. 35116* f.24b in *Études Anglaises* 7(1954) 14: Selde erendez wel the lothe, And selde pledez wel the wrothe. *Oxford* 572; Skeat 33; Eric R. Stanley ed. *Owl and the Nightingale* (London, 1960) 126.

L418 What is **Loath** is loath to hear
a1325 *Cursor* III 1362 CG 23833–4: For said it es for gain mani rathe, Lathe es to here that man es lathe, **a1400** F: For saide hit is gane mani yere That man lovis noght: lath is to here.

L419 Strong **Locks** make true men of those that would steal
a1393 Gower *CA* III 129.6631–3: For this proverbe is evere newe, That stronge lokes maken trewe Of hem that wolden stele and pyke. See **L421.**

L420 To have under **Lock** and key
c1250 *Owl* 132.1557: He hire bilu(k)th mid keie and loke. **a1393** Gower *CA* III 129.6621–3: Which under lock and under keie . . . Hath al the Tresor underfonge. **a1439** Lydgate *Fall* I 137.4886: The brond reservyng under lok and keie. Apperson 376–7; Tilley L407.

L421 Trusty **Locks** make true servants
c1450 *Douce MS.52* 56.138: Tristy lockes make true servauntes. See **L419.**

L422 Under yellow **Locks** are hidden foul scabs
c1515 Barclay *Eclogues* 11.357–8: Oft under yelowe lockes Be hid foule scabbes and fearefull French pockes.

L423 To be ten miles beyond the **Lodestar**
c1450 Idley 85.279–80: He is beyonde hymsilf so farre, Ten myle beyonde the loode sterre!

L424 To chop **Logic**
c1522 Skelton *Colyn* I 331.530: Suche logyke men wyll chop. **1528** More *Heresyes* 153 E[8–9]: And chop logicke with her maistres. **1528** Skelton *Replycacion* I 212.118–9: When ye logyke chopped, And in the pulpete hopped. **1546** Heywood *D* 69.101: She chopth logyke, **1556** *Spider* 187[5–6]: To chop logike ech with other in rude reasoning, 198[17]: And take upon him in chop logik lawse. Apperson 97–8; *Oxford* 94; Tilley L412; Whiting *Drama* 338:453.

L425 Between **London** and Hull
1509 Barclay *Ship* I 12[28]: Than is none holde wyser bytwene London and Hul.

L426 (From here) unto **London**
a1425 *Chester Plays* II 293.327–8: No ladd unto London Such law can him leere.

L427 From **London** to great Ind
c1450 Idley 143.2182: It might fortune not fro London to grete Ynde.

L428 From **London** to Louth
a1425 *Chester Plays* I 159.651–2: From London to Louth, Such an other shepherd I wot not where is.

L429 **London** lickpenny
a1500 *London Lickpenny* in *Anglia* 20(1897–8) 418.111: For well london lykke peny for ones and eye. Apperson 377; *Oxford* 379; Tilley L228.

L430 The **Longer** the worse
a1023 Wulfstan *Homilies* 117.23–4: Forðam þeos woruld is fram dæge to dæge a swa leng swa wyrse, 123.14: Hit is on worulde a swa leng swa wyrse, 137.47. **1402** *Letter* in *Review of English Studies* 8(1932) 262[4]: Ever lenger the wers. Cf. Jente 423; Tilley D71. See **H503.**

L431 As long as **Longius**
1528 More *Heresyes* 162 H[11–3]: If he be as longe as Longyus, and have an hye harte and trust upon his owne witte.

L432 **Longly** or short(ly)
a1338 Mannyng *Chronicle B* I 222[11]: To say longly or schorte, alle armes bare. Cf. Apperson 378; *Oxford* 380; Taylor and Whiting 227; Tilley L419.

L433 To have **Loofs** (*palms*) like bird-lime
1513 Douglas *Aeneid* III 119.71: Na labour list thai luk till, thar luffis ar byrd lyme. NED Bird-lime b. See **F154, H60.**

Look, sb.

L434 Lither (*evil*) **Look** and twinkling are tokens of horeling (*adultress*)
a1300 *Lither lok Sermon* 104–5: Lither lok and tuingling, Tiheng and tikeling, Opin brest and singing, Theise mid-outin lesing, Arin toknes of horeling. Apperson 666: Wanton.

Look, vb.

L435 First **Look** and afterward leap (*varied*)
c1450 *Douce MS.52* 57.150: First loke and aftirward lepe; Avyse the welle, or thow speke. **a1500** *National Library of Wales Peniarth MS.356* p.196 in Robbins-Cutler 1941.5: Loke or thu speke (*for* lepe), And thynke or thu speke. **1520** Whittinton *Vulgaria* 44.19: It is wysdom to loke before what maye fal here after. **1546** Heywood *D* 22.56: To looke or ye leape, **1555** *E* 148.5. Apperson 380; *Oxford* 383; Taylor and Whiting 228; Tilley L429; Whiting *Drama* 129, 139, *Scots* I 203. See **K68, L15, S127, W424.**

L436 He that **Looks** before and not behind may find harm
a1393 Gower *CA* III 153.7350–2: For who that loketh al tofore And wol noght se what is behinde, He mai fulofte hise harmes finde. See **S96.**

L437 To **Look** as if one would eat one
1508(1519) Stanbridge *Vulgaria* 29.13: Thou lokst on me as thou wolde ete me. Cf. Tilley L438.

L438 A lowly **Looking** and a purse makes fools
a1475 *Good Wyfe Wold* 175.58: A lowely lokynge and a porse makys follys her and ther. See note, p. 234.

L439 As stable as the **Loop** (*sapphire*)
a1449 Lydgate *Our Lady* in *MP* I 258.93: Stable as the lowpe. NED Loop sb.^{4} 2.

L439.1 As free as a **Lord**
c1425 *Orcherd* 339.21: He hath maad hym fre as a lord. Whiting *Scots* I 204.

L440 Beware how you play with **Lords**
c1395 Chaucer *CT* III[D] 2074: Beth war, therfore, with lordes how ye pleye. Cf. Tilley C279.

L441 Beware of **Lords'** promises
1450 Paston II 159[6]: *Circumspecte agatis,* and be war of lordis promysses. See **W374.**

L442 Each is not lettered that now is made a **Lord**
1509 Barclay *Ship* I 21[15]: Eche is nat lettred that nowe is made a lorde. See **K60.**

L443 He cannot be a good **Lord** that was not a theow (*servant*)
c1100 *Instructions for Christians* 17.235–7: Næfre ic ne gehyrde þæt wurde laford god Eft on ylde, se ðe ær ne was Gode oððe monnum on iugoð þeowa. Tilley S237. See **G407, M228, 402, 407, S856.**

L444 He is **Lord** of Fortune that will not reck of her
c1385 Chaucer *TC* iv 1587–9: And thynk that lord is he Of Fortune ay, that naught wole of hire recche; And she ne daunteth no wight but a wrecche. See **M100.**

L445 The higher that a **Lord** is raised the more perilous the overthrow
c1440 Scrope *Epistle* 110[22–3]: Therfor Tholome seith, "The hyer that a lorde be raysed the perylouser is the ovyrthrowe." **c1450** *Epistle of Othea* 141.16–7: For tholome seyth: The hyer a lord is lyfte up, the gretter and more perilous is hys fall. See **C296.**

L446 If the **Lord** bids slay (flee), the steward bids flee (slay)
a1400 Bozon *Contes* 12[10–1]: For yif the loverd bidd sle, the stiward biddes fle (*var.* If the loverd biddes flo, the stiward biddes slo, cf. 198[25]).

L447 A **Lord** a niggard is a shame
c1516 Skelton *Magnificence* 13.387–8: As men dare speke it hugger mugger: "A lorde a negarde, it is a shame." See **M120, S628.**

L448 **Lord** and knave are all one when they are born and when they die
a1393 Gower *CA* II 407.201–2: For lord and knave al is o weie, Whan thei be bore and whan thei deie. See **C267, K43, L451, P298.**

L449 A **Lord** beloved of his citizens may not be vanquished
c1390 Chaucer *CT* VII 1339–40[B2529–30]: For thus seith Tullius, that "ther is a manere garnysoun that no man may venquysse ne disconfite, and that is a lord to be biloved of his citezeins and of his peple." *Oxford* 628.

L450 A **Lord's** heart and a purse that peises (*weighs*) light (do not agree)
a1449 Lydgate *Look* in *MP* II 768.102: A lordis herte, a purs that peiseth liht. Apperson 382. See **H294.**

L451 A **Lord's** siege (*excrement*) and rural men's ordure savor alike
c1515 Barclay *Eclogues* 91.1015–6: But yet the lordes siege and rurall mens ordure Be like of savour for all their meates pure. See **L448.**

L452 A **Lord's** stomach and a beggars's purse accord ill (*varied*)
c1515 Barclay *Eclogues* 181.21–2: But a lordes stomake and a beggers pouche Full ill accordeth. **1546** Heywood *D* 38.117–8: There is nothing in this worlde that agreeth wurs, Then dooeth a Ladies hert and a beggers purs, **1555** *E* 153.47: There is nothing in this world that agreeth wurse, Then doth a lordes harte and a beggers purse. Apperson 382; *Oxford* 348; Tilley H324. See **H294.**

L453 New **Lords** new law(s)
a1450 *St. Editha* 96.4312–3: Willyham Conquerour was made here kyng, And made newe lordus and eke new lawe. **1483** Caxton *Golden Legende* 310ʳ[1.34–5]: We have a newe kynge, newe lawes. Apperson 444; *Oxford* 451; Taylor and Whiting 229; Tilley L446. See **K54.**

L454 No **Lord** no law
c1450 Capgrave *Katharine* 121.688: Where is no lord, there is no lawe, men say.

L455 Such **Lord** such meiny (*servants*) (*varied*)
1340 *Ayenbite* 235[24–5]: Vor to zuiche lhorde zuich maine. **c1400** *Vices and Virtues* 200.18: For men seyn, "Suche lord, alle suche meyne," 261.14–5: For al suche lord, al suche meyne. **a1450** *Myne awen dere* 159.321: For swilke servaundes, swilke is the lorde. **a1450** *South English Legendary* (*Bodley*) 410.63: Wikked was the lord: and wikkid ek the meyne! **c1450** *Salisbury Cath. Lib. MS.103* f.102ᵇ in Owst *Literature* 43[25]: It is an olde sawe, Swych lord, swyche meyne. **1450** *Dicts* 142.33: After the lord, the meynye disportith, **a1460** (*Helmingham*) 143.36: An evel lorde, an evel meyne. **1484** Caxton *Royal Book* P6ʳ[29]: It is comynly sayd, suche lord such meyne. See **C34, 192, J71, K56, M408, P403.**

L456 Those that rob openly are called **Lords** and those that rob privily are called thieves
1532 Berners *Golden Boke* 397.10024–6: Nowe adayes in Italye they that robbe openly are called lordes: and they that robbe prively are called theves. See **T68.**

L457 To live (fare) like (a) **Lord**(s)
c1390 *Tarry not till To-morrow* in Brown *Lyrics XIV* 194.9: Thou leod that lives as lord in londe. **c1425** *Metrical Paraphrase OT* 121.18143: Thou sall lyf als a lord. **a1460** *Towneley Plays* 377.307: Thise laddys thai leven as lordys riall. **c1475** Henryson *Fables* 10.221: For quhylis I fair alsweill as ony Lord. **1519** Horman *Vulgaria* 50[32]: He ledeth a lordis lyfe. Mollem et feriatam vitam agit. See **K58.**

L458 Under great **Lords** men have (take) great strokes
a1400 *Proverbis of Wysdom* 246.107: Under grete lordis men have gret strokis. **c1450** *Fyrst thou sal* 89.87: Undyr gret lords men takes gret strokes. **a1500** Hichecoke *This Worlde* 332.21.

L459 What is a **Lord** without his meiny?
c1412 Hoccleve *Regement* 18.463: What is a lord withouten his meynee? **c1450** Capgrave *Katharine* 73.936–7: What is a lord but if he have mene? What is a peple but if he have a lord?

L460 Fie on **Lordship** when liberty is gone
a1410 Lydgate *Churl* in *MP* II 473.110: Fy on lordship whan liberte is gon!

L461 In **Lordship** is no sickerness
c1390 Chaucer *CT* VII 2239–40[B3429–30]: Lordynges, ensample heerby may ye take How that in lordshipe is no sikernesse. See **H47.**

L462 When **Lordship** fails good fellowship avails
1456 *Five Dogs of London* 189a: Whan lordschype fayleth, gode felowschipe awayleth.

L463 Such **Lore** such life
a1387 Higden-Trevisa V 55[8–9]: Hit was a proverbe of hym (*Origen*), "Suche as was his lore, suche was his lyf." See **B481, D282, 289, L107, 409, P358, 360, 361, 397.**

L464 Better to **Lose** than win wrongfully
c1515 Barclay *Eclogues* 168.777: Better is to lose then wrongfully to winne.

L465 As good **Lost** as found
1546 Heywood *D* 39.140: A gest as good lost as founde, for all this show. Apperson 383; *Oxford* 386; Tilley L454.

L466 It is **Lost** that is unsought
c1385 Chaucer *TC* i 809: And lost, that is unsought. **1546** Heywood *D* 48.233: It is lost that is unsought. Apperson 383; *Oxford* 387; Tilley L455. See **U5.**

L467 It is right that it be evil **Lost** that is evil won
1481 Caxton *Reynard* 8[28–9]: Male quesisti et male perdidisti, hit is ryght that it be evil loste that is evil wonne. Apperson 193–4; *Oxford* 315–6; Tilley G90. See **G51, 333.**

L468 What is **Lost** cannot be recovered
1525 Berners *Froissart* VI 99[35–6]: That is loste canne nat be recovered. Cf. Tilley L456.

L469 Who **Loses** himself has won little
a1393 Gower *CA* III 231.2381–2: Bot lich to wolle is evele sponne, Who lest himself hath litel wonne.

L470 Let **Losers** have their words
1533 More *Debellacyon* 1018 F[4–6]: Hit is an olde curtesye at the cardes perdy, to let the leser have hys wordes. **1546** Heywood *D* 79.53–4: And where reason and custome (they say) afoords, Alwaie to let the loosers have their woords, **1555** *E* 166.125. Apperson 383; *Oxford* 386; Tilley L458.

L471 Better a little **Loss** than a long sorrow
c1378 *Piers* B Prol. 195: For better is a litel losse than a longe sorwe. *Oxford* 37. See **P9.**

L472 Of one **Loss** three (twain)
1473 Paston V 192[11–2]: Iff I have one losse I am lyffe (?like) therfor to have three. **1509** Barclay *Ship* II 70[24]: So of one losse oft tymes make they twayne. See **S513.**

L473 A **Louse** could not wander (*walk*) on that threadbare tabard
a1376 *Piers* A v 111–3: In a toren tabart of twelve wynter age; But yif a lous couthe lepe, I con hit not i-leve Heo scholde wandre on that walk, hit was so thred-bare. Apperson 383; Tilley L469.

L474 Not give a **Louse**
a1450 *Castle* 92.491–2: This werldys wysdom yevyth no(t) a louse Of God, 100.772–3: Loke thou yeve not a lous Of the day that thou schalt deye. Tilley L472.

L475 Not worth a **Louse**
c1380 *Ferumbras* 16.439: Him semede it nas noght worth a lous. **c1490** Ryman 239.2: But stynking fisshe not worthe a lowce. **c1497** Medwall *Fulgens* C5r[16]. Apperson 457:23; Tilley L472; Whiting *Drama* 353:693.

L476 He must needs **Lout** (stoop) that dare do no other
c1300 *Body and Soul* 43 L 303–4: Thorfore most i nede loute (*A:* stoupe), So doth that non other dar.

Love, sb.

L477 Against **Love** ('s strength) may no wight be (*varied*)
a1393 Gower *CA* II 235.344–6: For it sit every man to have Reward to love and to his miht, Ayein whos strengthe mai no wiht. **1480** Caxton *Ovyde* 159[38–9]: Who is he tha(t) ayenst love hath ony strengthe. **a1533** Berners *Arthur* 282[16]: Ayenst love no man can be. See **L518, M224.**

L478 Alas! that (ever) **Love** is sin
c1395 Chaucer *CT* III[D] 614: Allas! allas! that evere love was synne! **c1400** *Beryn* 3.48: Allas! that love ys syn! See **L167.**

L479 As good **Love** comes as goes
a1475 *Turne up hur halter* in *Rel. Ant.* I 77[34]: As gode love wol come as go. **c1475** Henryson *Fables* 21.512: The proverb sayis, "als gude lufe cummis as gais." *Oxford* 389; Tilley L475; Whiting *Scots* I 204.

L480 For **Love** or gold
a1300 *Alisaunder* 416.6405–6: This othir yeir tho thow noldest To me come for love no for golde. Taylor and Whiting 229.

L481 Hearty **Love** loves not many words
1519 Horman *Vulgaria* 179[22–3]: Harty love loveth nat many wordis. Sincerus amor linguae assertationem indignatur. See **W543.**

L482 Hot (hasty) **Love** does not hold long
c1475 *Lett lowe to lowe* in *Anglia* 73(1956) 300[17–20]: Qwer-as hasty lowe ys qwiche some wyl decever, Lowe thatt ys hott qwiche contenews never, Mutable lowe cannott in-Dever, Bott stedffast lowe qwiche Reman(es ever). **c1500** Newton 263.16: Hit was so hote and so hasty hit myght not longe hold. Cf. Tilley L488.

L483 Hot **Love** does not reign
a1500 *How shall y plece* in *Archiv* 106(1901) 274[13]: Hote love doth not Rayne.

L484 Hot **Love** soon cold (*varied*)
c1390 Chaucer *CT* I[A] 3754: His hoote love was coold and al yqueynt. **c1450** Idley 100.1147–8: As in olde proverbe is playnly tolde: Hoote love and newe sone wexeth colde. **a1470** Malory III 1120.1–2: And ryght so faryth the love nowadayes, sone hote sone colde. **a1490** *Fickle Mistress* in Robbins 138.33–4: Love ys strange in all degre, Summtyme hoyt and sumtyme colde. **a1500** *Guy*[4] 26–7.555–8: For love is hote, and love is colde, And love maketh a man both young and olde; But true love is good to have, Though it be of a poore knave. **c1500** Fabyan 89[23]: Often it happeneth that hote love is soone colde. **1546** Heywood *D* 21.36: Hotte love, soone colde. Apperson 315; *Oxford* 307; Tilley L483; Whiting *Drama* 142, *Scots* I 204. See **F187, H552, 554, L546.**

L485 Hot **Love** will often sour
a1300 *Alisaunder* 375.6992: Hote love often after wil soure.

L486 Hotter **Love** colder care
c1390 *Mary and the Cross* 622.361–2: The hattore love, the caldore care, Whon frendes fynde heore fruit defoyled.

L487 If you flee **Love** it shall flee you
a1400 *Romaunt B* 4783–4: If thou fle it (*Love*), it shal flee thee; Folowe it, and folowen shal it thee. See **C526, T120, 162, W549.**

L488 If you win **Love** in an hour you may lose it in three or four
1534 Heywood *Love* B4v[9–11]: And drede, this bad angell, sware bloud and bones, That if I wan your love all in one howre, I sholde lose it all agayne in thre or fowre.

L489 In great **Love** is great mourning
a1300 *Alisaunder* 227.4060–1: In mychel love is grete mournynge; In mychel nede is grete thankynge.

L490 In great **Love** is sometimes sorrow and sometimes bliss
a1450 *Generydes A* 302.9771–3: And, ye know, in grete love is Som tyme sorow, somtyme blis, Som tyme yvel, som tyme goodnes.

L491 It is hard to start from **Love** and death
c1450 Idley 101.1196–7: It is harde fro love and deth to sterte—They goo so inwardly unto the herte. See **L523.**

L492 Let never your **Love** be on a hill
a1500 *Counsels* in Brown *Lyrics XV* 284.37–8: Lette nevere thy luffe be on an hylle, Ner thy councell at the crosse be cryde.

L493 Lose not the **Love** of your friend for a little
a1500 *Good Wife N* 214.168–9: Loose not the love of thy frind, For a litle that thou mighst spend.

L494 Louken (*shut up*) **Love** at the end will kithe (*be made known*)
a1325 *Cursor* I 252.4275–6: For qua thar-for be wrath or blith Luken luve (GT: Prive love) at the end wil kith. Skeat 45. Cf. Apperson 384: Love and a cough; *Oxford* 388; Tilley L490. See **M806.**

L495 **Love** and lordship will have no fellowship
c1385 Chaucer *CT* I[A] 1623–6: O Cupide, out of alle charitee! O regne, that wolt no felawe have with thee! Ful sooth is seyd that love ne lordshipe Wol noght, his thankes, have no felaweship. **a1393** Gower *CA* II 194.2365–7: And is his propre be the lawe, Which thing that axeth no felawe, If love holde his covenant. **a1439** Lydgate *Fall* III 734.2220–3: Unto purpos was saide ful yore agon, How that love nouther

hih lordshippe,—Preeff hath be maad in many mo than oon,—Nouther of hem wolde have no felashipe. Apperson 384; *Oxford* 388; Skeat 220; Tilley L495; Whiting *Scots* I 204–5. See **L501.**

L496 Love at first sight
c1385 Chaucer *TC* ii 667–9: This was a sodeyn love; how myght it be That she so lightly loved Troilus, Right for the firste syghte, ye, parde? **1532** Berners *Golden Boke* 240.4059–60: All this love caused, one onely syght. *Oxford* 388–9; Taylor and Whiting 229–30; Tilley L426.

L497 Love binds
a1200 *Ancrene* 208.10: Me seith that luve bindeth. **c1385** Chaucer *TC* i 236–8: For evere it was, and evere it shal byfalle, That Love is he that alle thing may bynde, For may no man fordon the lawe of kynde. **1493** *Tretyse of Love* 5.14: Men sey that love byndeth.

L498 Love brings to sorrow
a1400 *Ipomadon A* 36.1192–4: It ys full swete, to enter in love, But ay more and more it brynges above To sorowe, and that I se. See **L504.**

L499 Love can espy (find out) all
c1386 Chaucer *LGW* 742: But what is that that love can nat espye, **c1395** *CT* IV[E] 2126–7: What sleighte is it, thogh it be long and hoot, That Love nyl fynde it out on som manere?

L500 Love can find a remedy for every sore
c1485 *Guiscardo* 54.295–6: Tyll at the last that love, to whom nothyng ys hyd, The whyche for every sore can fynde a remedy.

L501 Love can (*knows*) no friendship
a1449 Lydgate *Fabula* in *MP* II 495.255: Love can no frenship, I se weel, in no coost. Tilley L549. See **L495.**

L502 Love changes oft
a1400 *Romaunt B* 4353–7: It is of Love, as of Fortune, That chaungeth ofte, and nyl contune; Which whilom wol on folk smyle, And glowmbe on hem another while; Now, freend, now foo, (thow) shalt hir feel. Cf. Tilley L488.

L503 Love dares anything
a1393 Gower *CA* III 201.1261–6: Who dar do thing which love ne dar? To love is every lawe unwar, Bot to the lawes of his heste The fissch, the foul, the man, the beste Of al the worldes kinde louteth. For love is he which nothing douteth.

L504 Love ends in woe
c1385 Chaucer *TC* iv 834: Endeth thanne love in wo? Ye, or men lieth! See **L498.**

L505 Love follows freedom (*generosity*)
a1420 Lydgate *Troy* I 330.6499: For love folweth fredam comounly. See **L515.**

L506 Love for love is skillful guerdoning (*reasonable reward*) (*varied*)
c1385 Chaucer *TC* ii 392: As love for love is skilful guerdonynge. **a1500** ?Ros *La Belle Dame* 312.434–6: Also in you is lost, to my seming, Al curtesy, which of resoun wold say That love for love were lawful deserving. See **L273, 514.**

L507 Love for riches is attaint (*infected*) when poverty comes
a1500 *Guy*[4] 27.559–60: Love for richesse is false and feynte; When povertie commeth, it is atteynte. Cf. Tilley P531. See **P334, 343.**

L508 Love has no lack (*varied*)
a1400 *Ipomadon A* 88.3018–20: But sothe ys sayd in olde sawe, Whedur that ever love will drawe, Lake no lettyng mase. **a1415** Mirk *Festial* 165.29: For love hathe no lake. **c1450** *In Praise of Brunettes* in Robbins 30.3: Ther y love ther ys no lac. **1506** Hawes *Pastime* 151.4021: Where that is love there can be no lacke. **1546** Heywood *D* 24.14: In love is no lacke, **1555** *E* 148.9. Apperson 384:3; *Oxford* 390; Tilley L485; Whiting *Scots* I 204. See **L150.**

L509 Love has no law
a1449 Lydgate *Virtues* in *MP* I 108.481: Poetys seyen howe love hath no law. Apperson 385:22; *Oxford* 390; Tilley L508. See **L579, 592.**

L510 Love helps the hardy
1480 Caxton *Ovyde* 47[17–8]: Love helpeth the hardy. See **F519, G214, H96.**

L511 Love hurts no man
1471 Caxton *Recuyell* I 181.18–9: Men saye that love hurteth no man.

L512 Love is a great mastery
a1470 Malory II 740.8–9: And well I wote that love is a grete maystry. See **L544.**

L513 Love is a woeful bliss
a1393 Gower *CA* III 110.5993–5: And seith love is a wofull blisse, A wisdom which can noman wisse, A lusti fievere, a wounde softe. Cf. Smith 185; Tilley L505a.

L514 Love is bought for love
a1450 *Love that god loveth* in Kail 76.123–4: Of alle that may be bought and sold, Love for love is evenest boughte. Apperson 385:21; *Oxford* 390. See **L273, 506, 543.**

L515 **Love** is faint when gifts fail
a1400 *Proverbis of Wysdom* 244.17–8: Gefe, where gyftis may avayle: Love is faynt, when gyftis faile. Robbins-Cutler 908.8. See **L505, 526.**

L516 **Love** is free
c1385 Chaucer *CT* I[A] 1606: What, verray fool, thynk wel that love is free. **a1393** Gower *CA* II 56.752: To love is every herte fre, 88.1929–30: I seie in excusinge of me, To alle men that love is fre. **c1395** Chaucer *CT* V[F] 767: Love is a thyng as any spirit free. **a1400** *Romaunt B* 3432: For wel wot ye that love is free. **c1450** Idley 99.1098: Thus love is at large and to every thyng free, 136.1733: Ffor love is free and will not be constreyned. **a1470** Malory II 781.22: For love is fre for all men, III 1097.25–7: And with many knyghtes love ys fre in hymselffe, and never woll be bonde; for where he ys bonden he lowsith hymselff. *Oxford* 390; Whiting *Ballad* 24.

L517 **Love** is full of dread (*varied*)
c1385 Chaucer *TC* iv 1644–5: For I am evere agast, forwhy men rede That love is thyng ay ful of bisy drede. **a1393** Gower *CA* III 52.3850–2: For love is everemore in doute, If that it be wisly governed Of hem that ben of love lerned, 112.6059: Men sein that every love hath drede. **1506** Barclay *Castell* D2^r[14–8]: This proverbe that I the lere Kepe it in thy remembraunce: Love goth never without fere. Fere without love may ryght well be, We fere without love them that us menasez (*French* p. 59.1615: Amour ne va jamais sans crainte). Apperson 384–5; *Oxford* 390; Skeat 200; Tilley L507.

L518 **Love** is master (lord)
a1393 Gower *CA* II 36.34–5: It hath and schal ben everemor That love is maister wher he wile, III 71.4556: For love is lord in every place. See **L477, 538, 540.**

L519 **Love** is more (sweet) that is bought with woe (dear bought)
1420 Lydgate *Temple* 52.1255–6: And therfor of yow t(w)oo Shal love be more, that it was bought with wo. **c1475** *Court of Sapience* 158.852: Eke love ys more swete, that ys dere bought. **c1500** Newton 269.16: Ffor lof is the swetter the der that it is boght. See **F58, G356, H434, M307, W376, 420.**

L520 **Love** is more than gold
c1421 Lydgate *Thebes* 112.2716: For love is more than gold or gret richesse.

L521 **Love** is not in heart as in mouth
a1300 *Love is blisse* in Brown *Lyrics XIII* 209[7–8]: Love is sewed as it were kouth And is nout in herte als in mouth. See **M755.**

L522 **Love** is not old as when it is new
c1395 Chaucer *CT* IV[E] 855–7: But sooth is seyde—algate I fynde it trewe, For in effect it preeved is on me—Love is noght oold as whan that it is newe. Cf. Whiting *Ballad* 38: Love is bonnie. See **L524, 537.**

L523 **Love** is stalworth (strong, forcy) as death
c1340 Rolle *Psalter* 297 (79.19): Says the wys man, that luf is stalworth as ded, **1348** *Forme* in Allen *R. Rolle* 111.112–4: For luf es stalworth als the dede . . . and hard als hell, **a1349** *Commandement* in Allen *R. Rolle* 74.46–7: In this degre es lufe stalworth as dede and hard as hell. **c1375** *Song of Love* in Brown *Lyrics XIV* 104.48: For luf es stalworth as the dede. **c1395** *WBible* Song of Songs viii 6: For love is strong as deth. **a1400** Rolle *Encomium* in Perry *English Prose Treatises* 2.1: For luf es strange als dede. **a1400** Wyclif *Sermons* I 155[3]: stronge. **1435** Misyn *Fire* 22.36–7: In the cantikyls it is sayd: "lufe als dede is strange, And lufe is hard as hell." **1439** Lydgate *St. Albon* 140.785: stronge, 177.938–9: stronge. **a1475** *Tree* 46.18: Charite is strong as deth as salomon seith. **c1475** Henryson *Annunciation* 199.1: Forcy as deith Is likand lufe. See **L491.**

L524 **Love** is sweet at first and sour at last (*varied*)
a1393 Gower *CA* III 391.190–4: For al such time of love is lore, And lich unto the bitterswete; For thogh it thenke a man ferst swete, He schal wel fielen ate laste That it is sour and may noght laste. **c1410** Lovelich *Merlin* III 571.21419–20: A joye, a joye et amours Et sen issent a dolours. **c1450** *Merlin* II 310[12–4]: Saf that thei seiden in refreite of hir songe, "Vraiement comencent amours en joye, et fynissent en dolours." **c1500** *King Hart* 113.9–10: This drink wes sweit ye fand in Venus tun! Sone eftir this it sal be staill and soure. *Oxford* 390; Tilley L513; Whiting *Scots* I 205. See **L522, 537.**

L525 **Love** is vendable
a1400 *Romaunt B* 5804: For love is overall vendable. See **L548.**

L526 **Love** lasts as long as the money endures
1474 Caxton *Chesse* 97[17–20]: And herof men saye a comyn proverbe in england that love lasteth as longe as the money endureth and whan the money faylleth than there is no love. Apperson 385; *Oxford* 390; Tilley P531. See **L515.**

L527 Love laughs when men are forsworn
a1500 *Piers of Fullham* 14.326–7: Ffor men have seyn here to foryn, That love laughet when men be for sworn. Cf. Apperson 334: Jove; *Oxford* 328; Tilley J82. See **G201, L578.**

L528 Love leads the ring
c1343 Rolle *Ego* in Allen *R. Rolle* 68.237: Bot suth than es it sayde that lufe ledes the ryng.

L529 Love makes every work appear easy
a1535 Fisher *Wayes* 364.12–4: Love maketh everie worke appeare easie and pleasaunt, though it be ryghte displeasaunt of it selfe. Cf. Tilley L523. See **L4.**

L530 Love makes low things high
a1400 *Stanzaic Life* 356.10489–92: Also luf makes loghe thyng hegh, Be mony wayes mon may se, As men that ben grete lordis negh, Who-so is lufd, on hegh gos he.

L531 Love makes the villain (*churl*) courteous, *etc.* (*varied*)
a1393 Gower *CA* II 363.2296–304: For evere yit it hath be so, That love honeste in sondri weie Profiteth, for it doth awei The vice, and as the bokes sein, It makth curteis of the vilein, And to the couard hardiesce It yifth, so that verrai prouesse Is caused upon loves reule To him that can manhode reule. **a1450** *Partonope* 162.4453–7: Lowe, thys can love wyth-owte ffayle Make eche man hys mastere use: Knyghtes shame to refuse, Clerkes to love well clergye, And ladyes to cheresse curtesy. Cf. Tilley L521.

L532 The **Love** of ladies causes pain to lovers and death to horses
c1500 *Melusine* 56.8–10: Ye have longe syn herd say how somtyme the love of ladyes causeth peyne and traveyll to the amerous lovers, and deth to horses.

L533 Love puts reason away (*varied*)
a1393 Gower *CA* II 64.1051–2: For Love put reson aweie And can noght se the righte weie, III 390.153–4: For love, which is unbesein Of alle reson, as men sein. **1509** Barclay *Ship* I 81[15]: For he that loveth is voyde of all reason. *Oxford* 390; Tilley L517; Whiting *Scots* I 205. Cf. Apperson 384:7.

L534 Love's law is out of rule
a1393 Gower *CA* II 35.18: For loves lawe is out of reule. *Oxford* 390.

L535 Love's old dance
c1385 Chaucer *TC* ii 1106–7: "How ferforth be ye put in loves daunce?" "By God," quod he, "I hoppe alwey behynde!", iii 694–5: But Pandarus, that wel koude ech a deel The olde daunce, **c1387-95** *CT* I[A] 475–6: Of remedies of love she knew per chaunce, For she koude of that art the old daunce, **c1390** VI[C] 79: And knowen wel ynough the olde daunce. **a1400** *Romaunt B* 4300: For she knew all the olde daunce. **1472** *Stonor Letters* I 126[35]: Every thyng that longeth to love's daunce. **a1500** *Alexander-Cassamus* 58.166: How long I have perseveryd thus in love daunce, 60.214–5: She lyst not to lere Recclesly to hoppe forth yn lovys daunce. Randle Cotgrave *Dictionarie of the French and English Tongues* (London, 1611) *s.v.* Danse: Elle scait assez de la vieille danse. She knowes well enough what belongs to the Game; she hath bin a hackster, a twigger, a good one, in her time; MED connen 3 (a), daunce 4a.

L536 Love stands in no certain(ty) of (*for*) folk that are seldom seen
a1500 *Piers of Fullham* 13.296–7: Ffor love stant in no certeyn Of folke that ben seldom sayn. See **E213, S130, 307.**

L537 (**Love**) that began soft has a smart ending
a1325 *Cursor* I 10.58: (*Love*) that soft began has endyng smart. See **L522, 524.**

L538 (**Love**) will be lord and sire
c1380 Chaucer *PF* 12: There rede I wel he (*Love*) wol be lord and syre. See **L518.**

L539 Love will be set under rags as well as (under) rich rochet (*linen garment*)
a1400 *Romaunt B* 4753–4: For also wel wol love be set Under ragges, as riche rochet. Cf. Apperson 385: Love lives in cottages; *Oxford* 390–1; Tilley L519. See **H3.**

L540 Love will daunt both king and knight
a1400 *Ipomadon A* 209–10.7346–54: Love is so mekyll off myghte, That it will daunte bothe kyng and knyght, Erle and bold barowne; They, that wyseste is of witte, Fro tyme they be takyne wyth it, Hit takythe fro them there reasowne. Love may save, love may spille. Love may do, what that he will, And turne all up and downe. Cf. Apperson 384: Love is above King. See **L477, 518, 538, 545.**

L541 Love will find a way
a1393 Gower *CA* II 263.1362–6: Who loveth wel, it mai noght misse, And namely whan ther be tuo Of on acord, how so it go, Bot if that thei som weie finde; For love is evere of such a kinde. Apperson 386; *Oxford* 392; Tilley L531.

L542 Love will have its course

a1450 *Generydes B* 29.896: Ffor love will have his course for eny thing. See **K36.**

L543 **Love** will (is paid with) love
c1386 Chaucer *LGW* 1187: Love wol love, for nothing wol it wonde. **1532** Berners *Golden Boke* 166.1576–7: It is an olde proverbe of Pythagoras: Love is payd with other love, 429.11043: For love onely is payed with love agayne. *Oxford* 292: Herb, cf. 389: Love begets love. See **L273, 506, 514.**

L544 **Love** will not be constrained by mastery
c1395 Chaucer *CT* V[F] 764–6: Love wol nat been constreyned by maistrye. Whan maistrie comth, the God of Love anon Beteth his wynges, and farewel, he is gon! *Oxford* 389; Tilley L499. Cf. Smith 188. See **L512.**

L545 **Love** will not be daunted
a1400 *Ipomadon A* 25.800–2: All othere thynges men daunte may, But, sertenly, be no waye Love wille not be daunte! See **L540.**

L546 Mad **Love** lasts but a while
c1520 Walter *Spectacle* A4^v[21]: For suche madde love lasteth but a whyle. See **L484.**

L547 The new **Love** chases out the old
c1385 Chaucer *TC* iv 414–5: And ek, as writ Zanzis, that was ful wys, "The newe love out chaceth ofte the olde," 421–4: For also seur as day comth after nyght, The newe love, labour, or oother wo, Or elles selde seynge of a wight, Don olde affecciouns alle over-go. *Oxford* 441; Skeat 186; Tilley L538. See **N6, T141.**

L548 One may cheap (*bargain for*) **Love** with cattle (*property*)
c1390 *Talkyng* 30.17–8: For everiwher mai men with catel love chepen. See **L525.**

L549 Show **Love** to win love
c1523 Barclay *Mirrour* 74[14]: Shewe thou love to win love in worde, heart and dede. Apperson 385:27; Tilley L515.

L550 There are no foul **Loves** (*varied*)
a1400 *Orologium* 337.25–8: Also hit falleth oft-sithes that that thinge that summe menne demene fowle and unsemelye in him that thei love not, othere, that lovene him, presene and comende that selfe thinge as feyre and comelye. **c1505** Watson *Valentine* 101.27–9: It is sayde commonly that there is no foule loves whan the hartes geveth them therto. Apperson 449, cf. 385:33; Jente 340; *Oxford* 389; Taylor and Whiting 230; Tilley L545.

L551 There is no perfect **Love** where there is no equality
1532 Berners *Golden Boke* 175.1862–3: There is no parfite love, where is no egalitie betwene the lovers. Smith 129; Tilley F761. See **B363, C401, M175, Y33.**

L552 Through **Love** every law is broken
c1385 Chaucer *TC* iv 618: Thorugh love is broken al day every lawe. *Oxford* 390.

L553 To be full (true) of **Love** beneath the girdle but not above
a1500 *Characteristics of Counties* in *Rel. Ant.* I 269[35–6]: Northampton, full of love, Beneath the girdel, and not above. **a1500** Greene *Carols* 401. B 5: Some of them be treue of love Beneth the gerdell but nat above. Cf. Tilley W520.

L554 To have little (no) **Love** (*varied*)
c1300 *Guy*[1] 130.2213–4: Al togider thai gun smite; Semblant of love thai kidde bot lite, 466 A 108.12: Of love was ther no speche, 482 A 130.5. **a1350** *Ywain* 18.633–4: To speke of lufe na time was thare, For aither hated uther ful sare, 94.3530: Litel luf was tham bi-twene. **c1350** *Libeaus* 113.2027–8: Faste he gan to fight; Of love ther nas no word. **c1400** *Laud Troy* I 183.6198: Litel love was be-twene hem two. **c1410** Lovelich *Merlin* III 443.16536: Ther was a signe of lytel love, 605.22738. **a1450** *Generydes A* 181.5809–10: There began bataile strong, For litle love was hem among, 188. 6057–8: He smote the king on the helm above A stroke that was not for noo love, *B* 194. 6089–90: Betwix them twayne it was noo tyme to trete, All maner love and frenshippe was forgete. **c1450** *Merlin* II 657[24]: And these hem chaced that cowde hem not love. **c1475** *Guy*[1] 345 C 6413–4: Whan he theim had overe-take, Contenaunce of love he did noon make. See **F674, G368.**

L555 True **Love** (en)dures in (the) heart
a1300 *Alisaunder* 114.2043: Treowe love in heorte durith.

L556 True **Love** never failed man
a1400 *Romaunt B* 4587: For trewe Love ne failide never man.

L557 True **Love** will never stain
c1520 Walter *Spectacle* B1^r[4]: Trewe love wyll never stayne. Cf. Tilley T543.

L558 Where **Love** is there is the eye
a1396(1494) Hilton *Scale* H4^v[9–10]: For where the love is there is the eye, and where the likynge is there is moost the herte thynkynge. **a1400** *Ancrene* (*Recluse*) 38.28–30: Auris zelo audit omnia, ubi amor ibi oculus. Salomon seith, the jelous ere hereth al thing, there as

is love, there is his eighe. **c1425** *St. Mary Oignies* 146.15: Where love is, there is the eye. **a1450** *God of hefne, that sittest* 414.394–5: Ffor wyse men siggeth and sleyre, War is thi love thar is thin eyre. Tilley E233. See **E207.**

L559 Where there is little **Love** there is little trust
c1500 Greene *Carols* 346.1: Wher is lytyll love, ther is lytill tryste.

L560 Where true **Love** is it shows
c1450 *Epistle of Othea* 50.7: Where trew love is, hytt scheweth; hyt wyl nott feyne.

L561 Win **Love** with a pear and lose it for a pin
c1516 Skelton *Magnificence* 32.1016–7: With a pere my love you may wynne, And ye may lese it for a pynne. See **C207.**

Love, vb.

L562 First to **Love** (*praise*) and then to lack (*blame*) is a shame (*varied*)
c1390 *Cato* (*Vernon*) 602.561–4: Thing that thou hast ones preised Be-fore the folk over al, Blame hit not ther-afturward, Beo hit gret or smal. **c1408** Lydgate *Reson* 123.4678–83: The noble sentence of Caton, Which comaundeth, thus I mene, A man to preysen in A mene, Both in high and low degre, And by no superfluyte, Lyst after be no lak y-founde. **a1440** Burgh *Cato* 29.1011–3: And iff hit happe the in audience An thyng to preyse, be war, that thou ne blame It eft ageyn riht in the same presence. **c1450** *Cato* (*Sidney*) 46.551–4: Thou preise no thing to speciali, But thou it know al fulli; For drede, that no lacchenes the take, That thou ne love, that thou did lake. **c1475** *Rauf* 85.87: For first to lofe and syne to lak, Peter! it is schame. Whiting *Scots* I 205. See **L17, 232, P353.**

L563 He **Loves** little that hates for nought
c1440 Charles of Orleans 205.6122–3: He lovith lite als may y wel avise That hatith for nought. Tilley L347, O16.

L564 He **Loves** me well that tells me for my good
1496 *The cyte is bond* in Mary D. Harris ed. *The Coventry Leet Book* (EETS 135, 1908) II 578[17]: He luffeth me well that telleth me for my goode. See **L566.**

L565 He that **Loves** leally forgets late
a1325 *Cursor* I 264.4509–10: Bot i dar sai, and god it wat, "Qua leli luves for-gettes lat (F for-getis noght). **c1380** Chaucer *PF between* 679 *and* 680 *some MSS.:* Qui bien aime a tard oublie (Robinson 796). **a1400** *Cursor* I 265 T 4509–10: But I dar saye god woot ever Who so truly doth foryeteth he nover. **c1430** *Parliament of Birds* 106[30]: Qui bien ayme tard oublye. Skeat 141.

L566 He that **Loves** well chastises well
1484 Caxton *Aesop* 85[10–1]: For he that well loveth, wel he chastyseth, 211[10–1]. Tilley L564. See **L564, Y1.**

L567 If you **Love** him that loves you not you lose your love
1492 *Salomon and Marcolphus* 9[27]: If thou love hym that lovyth not the thou lesyth thyn love.

L568 **Love** me little and long (*varied*)
a1500 *How shall y plece* in *Archiv* 106(1901) 274[13]: Love me lytyll and longe. **1546** Heywood *D* 63.62: Love me little, love me long. Apperson 386; *Oxford* 391; Tilley L559.

L569 **Love** me love my hound (dog)
a1500 *Jak and his Stepdame* 81. *var.:* In olde termys it is fownd He, that lovythe me, lovythe my hound And my servaunt also. **1546** Heywood *D* 93.100: Love me, love my dog, **1555** *E* 159.85. Apperson 386–7; *Oxford* 391; Taylor and Whiting 240; Tilley D496. See **L573.**

L570 Such as you **Love** such are you like
c1450 *Consail and Teiching* 66.26: Syk as thow lufis, syk art thow lyk. See **C395, L272.**

L571 There I **Love** there I hold
a1393 Gower *CA* II 15.388–9: And thus the riht hath no defence, Bot ther I love, ther I holde.

L572 What one **Loves** not another does
1546 Heywood *D* 62.21: That one loveth not, an other doth, which hath sped. *Oxford* 392; Tilley M810.

L573 Whoso **Loves** me loves mine
c1300 *Speculum Gy* 17.339–40: For men seith soth, by wit(te) myne: "Whoso loveth me, he loveth myne." See **L569.**

L574 **Lovers** desire to have loving
c1400 *Alexander Buik* III 259.5366: For lovers desyres to have loving. See **L273, 576.**

L575 **Lovers** live by looks
c1440 Charles of Orleans 104.3126–7: Parde folk sayne that lovers lyve by lokis And bi wisshis and othir wanton thought. Smith 186; Tilley L501. See **M109.**

L576 **Lovers** live by love as larks live by leeks
1546 Heywood *D* 37.64: Lovers live by love, ye as larkes live by leekes. Apperson 387; *Oxford* 393; Tilley L569. See **L273, 574.**

L577 No **Lover** has his ease
c1385 Chaucer *Mars* 208: But he be fals, no lover hath his ese.

L578 Though a **Lover** be found unstable, the forfeit is pardonable
a1450 *Partonope* 239.6214–5: All-thowe a lover be fownde unstabell, Yette ys the forfette Pardonabell. See **G201, L527.**

L579 Who shall give (a) **Lover**(s) law?
c1380 Chaucer *Boece* III m. xii 52–5: But what is he that may yeven a lawe to loverys? Love is a grettere lawe and a strengere to hymself (*thanne any lawe that men may yyven*), **c1385** *CT* I[A] 1163–6: Wostow nat wel the olde clerkes sawe, That "who shal yeve a lovere any lawe?" Love is a gretter lawe, by my pan, Than may be yeve to any erthely man. **1410** Walton *Boethius* 209[9–10]: Bot who to lovers may a lawe make, For love is rather to hym-self a lawe! **a1439** Lydgate *Fall* I 163.5801–3: But it is seid(e) sithen gon ful yore, Ther may no lawe lovers weel constreyne, So inportable is ther dedli peyne. **a1450** *Partonope* 354.8709–10: Therfore this is a full olde sawe: Who may give to a lovere lawe? **1532** Berners *Golden Boke* 242.4104–6: Do you not knowe that the goddis made a lawe over al thingis except on lovers, bycause they may not abyde it? Apperson 387. See **L509, 592.**

L580 Be scarce of your **Loving** (*praise*) till it come to proving
a1400 *Cato* (*Fairfax*) in *Cursor* III 1672.211–3: Be scarske of thi loving Til hit come to proving Of thi gode frende. Apperson 515; *Oxford* 522. See **F625, 657, K99.**

L581 As bright as the **Low** (*flame*)
c1420 Wyntoun III 433.3107–8: That is a stern withe blessis schyre, Bricht as the law of a fyre.

L582 As hot as the **Low**
a1400 *Destruction of Troy* 17.494: In a longyng of love as the lowe hote.

L583 To heat (*etc.*) like a **Low**
a1400 *Destruction of Troy* 68.2054: That his harme, as a hote low, het hym with in, 180. 5532: His Ene flammet as . . . a fuerse low, 250.7723: His Ene levenaund with light as a low fyn.

L584 To stand like a **Low** (*hill*)
c1300 *Havelok* 55.1699: Tho stod Havelok als a lowe.

L585 As bright as **Lucifer**
c1502 *Lyfe of Joseph* 50.422: Bryghter than lucyfer in his resplendence. **a1508** Dunbar *Goldyn Targe* 114.81: Wyth bemys blith, bricht as Lucifera.

L586 As low as **Lucifer**
c1400 *Plowman's Tale* 151.119: As lowe as Lucifer such shal fall, 124. **a1529** Skelton *Garnesche* I 127.28: Lothsum as Lucifer lowest in helle.

L587 As proud as **Lucifer**
c1390 *Talkyng* 18.26: His pruide passeth lucifer. **c1400** *Plowman's Tale* 159.381: They ben as proude as Lucifer, 173.833. **c1400** *Office of Curates* in Wyclif *EW* 156[26]: As proude of here veyn kunnynge as lucifer. **a1425** Higden-Anon. Cont. VIII 484[36–7]: The seide duke of Yrlonde enhawnced in pride lyke Lucifer. **a1450** *Partonope* 404.9740. **1509** Barclay *Ship* II 59[21]. Apperson 514; *Oxford* 521; Taylor and Whiting 230–1; Tilley L572.

L588 To shine like **Lucifer**
1513 Bradshaw *St. Werburge* 69.1816: As Lucyfer shynynge.

L589 To reclaim (bring) to (the) **Lure**
c1390 Chaucer *CT* IX[H] 71–2: Another day he wole, peraventure, Reclayme thee and brynge thee to lure. **c1430** Lydgate *Dance* 24.207: For to accounte ye shul be browght to lure, **a1439** *Fall* I 60.2166: Fortune koude recleyme hem to hir lure. **a1500** *Lover and the Advocate of Venus* in Robbins 171.78: Wel nowe ye be recleymed to the lure, 85–6. **a1500** ?Ros *La Belle Dame* 319.634: They be so wel reclaymed to the lure. See **H198.**

L590 In worldly **Lust** is little trust
a1420 Lydgate *Troy* III 874.3563–4: In al worldly lust, Who loke aright, is but litel trust.

L591 Let **Lust** overgo (*conquer*) and it will like (*please*) you
a1200 *Ancrene* 64.14: Let lust overgan and hit te wule likin, 123.4–5. **c1250** *Hendyng O* 192.8: Let lust overgon, and eft hit shal the liken. **a1400** *Ancrene* (*Recluse*) 49.29: Lete lust overgoo and eft it wil the lyke, as the versifiour seith, 119.7–8. Apperson 502; Kneuer 21–2; Schleich 251–2.

L592 **Lust** of love exceeds law
a1393 Gower *CA* III 393.262–3: Bot forto loke

of time go, Hou lust of love excedeth lawe. See **L509, 579.**

L593 **Lydford** law
c1405 *Mum* 16–7.145–7: Now, be the lawe of Lydfford in londe (and) in water Thilke lewde ladde oughte evyll to thryve, That hongith on his hippis more than he wynneth. Apperson 388; *Oxford* 364; Tilley L590. See **H95, S88.**

L594 To buy the **Lye** and drink not of the wine
a1393 Gower *CA* II 250.894–5: And thus fuloften have I boght The lie, and drank noght of the wyn.

L595 From this town to (On this side) **Lynn**
a1460 *Towneley Plays* 283.154–5: I am the most shrew in all myn kyn, That is from this towne unto lyn. **a1500** *Fraternity* 202[5]: None suche a thyssyd lyn.

L596 A **Lynx** can see through (pierce) (a) stone wall(s)
c1385 Usk 76.103–4: And if thyne eyen weren as good as the lynx, that may seen thorow many stone walles. **a1400** *Pricke* 16–7.575–7: And cler eghen and als bright Als has a best that men Lynx calles, That may se thurgh thik stane walles. **a1449** Lydgate *Look* in *MP* II 766.42: The Lynx with lookyng percith a stoon wal. **1484** Caxton *Royal Book* G7v[4–5]: Who myght see as clere as a beest that is callyd a lynx, whyche seeth thorugh oute a walle.

M

M1 Madge (Margery) (the) good cow
c1425 Hoccleve *Jonathas* 217.38–40: Lest wommen un-to Magge, the good kow, Me likne and thus seye "o, beholde and see The double man." **1546** Heywood *D* 87.249–50: Margery good coowe . . . gave a good meele, But than she cast it downe again with hir heele. Apperson 403; *Oxford* 115; Tilley M661.

M2 To draw as the **Magnet** does iron
1447 Bokenham 13.459–60: He had more seyn wych his herte drow As the magnet doth iryn.

M3 As black as **Mahound** (*Mohammed*)
a1350 *Seege of Troye* 107.1350: His body was blak as Mahoun.

M4 As courteous(ly) as a (any) **Maid**
c1390 Chaucer *CT* VII 444–5[B1635–6]: He sayde, As curteisly as it had been a mayde. **a1400** *Arthur* 2.41: As courteys as any Mayde. **c1477** Caxton *Jason* 75.9–10: The yong knight whiche was fayr and curtois as a mayde.

M5 As coy (*quiet*) as a **Maid**
c1386 Chaucer *LGW* 1548: And Jason is as coy as is a mayde, **c1395** *CT* IV[E] 2–3: Ye ryde as coy . . . as dooth a mayde Were newe spoused, sittynge at the bord.

M6 As meek(ly) as (a) **Maid(en)** (may)
c1387–95 Chaucer *CT* I[A] 69: And of his port as meeke as is a mayde, **c1390** I[A] 3202: And lyk a mayden meke for to see. **a1400** *Destruction of Troy* 6.130: As meke as a Mayden, and mery of his wordis, 122.3745: Meke as a maiden, mery with all, 126.3892: But ay meke as a maydon, and mylde of his speche. **c1400** *Cleges* 38.21: Meke as meyd was he. **c1408** Lydgate *Reson* 96.3650. **a1430** *St. John* in Horstmann *Legenden 1881* 468.57: Thou was methe and meke, as maydene for mylde. **a1445** *Carl* 114.4: He was as meke as mayde in bour. **c1450** Capgrave *Katharine* 19.37, 161.1334: Lete mekenesse dwelle with suche a freshe may. **c1450** Idley 102.1298: But (be) meke and gentill as a mayde childe, 137.1821: Meke as a maye. **1456** *Princes most excellent* in Mary D. Harris ed. *Coventry Leet Book* (EETS 135, 1908) II 288[16]: Mekely as a maydyn my langage wyll I make. **c1470** *Wallace* 295.1937:a. Whiting *Scots* II 94.

M7 As shamefast as a **Maid**
a1500 *English Conquest* 27[1–2]: A man . . . shamefaste as a mayd.

M8 As still as a (any) **Maid**
c1395 Chaucer *CT* IV[E] 2–3: Ye ryde as . . . stille as dooth a mayde Were newe spoused, sittynge at the bord. **a1425** Mirk *Instructions* 24.783: But syt thou stylle as any mayde. **1509** *Fyftene Joyes* E4(*for* 3)[r][5]: As styll he is and muet as a mayde. Svartengren 177:mute.

M9 As sweet as any **Maid**
a1500 *Partenay* 214.6242: He is more suetter then is any maide.

M10 A **Maid** in hall, a lion in the field
1464 Hardyng 334[10–2]: As a mayde in halle of gentilnesse, And in all other places sonne to rethorike, And in the felde a lyon Marmorike. See **L38.**

M11 A **Maid** should be seen and not heard
a1415 Mirk *Festial* 230.1–2: For hyt ys an old Englysch sawe: "A mayde schuld be seen, but not herd." Apperson 96:10, 391; *Oxford* 92–3; Taylor and Whiting 68; Tilley M45.

M12 There are (no) more **Maids** than Malkin
1546 Heywood *D* 43.62: There was no mo maydes but malkyn tho, **1555** *E* 174.159: There be mo maydes then Malkyn. Apperson 427; *Oxford* 397; Tilley M39.

M13 As bashful as a **Maiden**

c1500 *Three Kings' Sons* 23.8: As basshfull as a mayden. Svartengren 67.

M14 As pure as a **Maiden**
a1500 Medwall *Nature* B2ᵛ[23]: Gyltles of syn and as a mayden pure.

M15 As sober as a **Maiden**
a1400 *Alexander C* 231.4266: And thar-to suffirand oure-selfe and sobire as a mayden.

M16 **Maidens** are lovely and nothing sicker (*secure*) (*varied*)
c1425 *Good Wife H* 171.184: Maydenys ben lovelich and nothing sekir, **c1450** *L* 202.189–90: Maydens ben fair and amyable, But of her love ful unstable, **c1500** *T* 209.194–5: Maydonys be lovely, But to kepe they be untrusty.

M17 **Maidens** move (*change*) their minds
a1400 *Destruction of Troy* 324.9950–1: Oft ho waixet hir wit and hir wille chaunget, And mevyt hir mynd, as maydons done yet. Cf. Tilley W673, 674.

M18 **Maidens** should laugh softly that men hear them not
a1500 *Good Wife N* 211.47–8: Maydens should laugh softlye That men here not they bee. See note, p. 231.

M19 What has become of those mild **Maidens**?
a1500 *Devyce proves* in *Bannatyne* IV 34.6–7: Quhair ar becum thir madynis myld as mude? Of thir wyvis ar non now fundin gude. Whiting *Scots* II 94.

M20 **Maidenhead** (Virginity) once lost can never be found (*varied*)
c1200 *Hali Meidenhad* 14.131–2: Meithhad is thet tresor, thet, beo hit eanes forloren, ne bith hit neaver ifunden. **c1390** Chaucer *CT* II[B] 29–31: It wol nat come agayn, withouten drede, Namoore than wole Malkynes maydenhede, Whan she hath lost it in hir wantownesse, X[I] 871: For certes, namoore may maydenhede be restoored than an arm that is smyten fro the body may retourne agayn to wexe. **a1393** Gower *CA* III 100.5646–9: And thus this tirant there Beraft hire such thing as men sein Mai neveremor be yolde ayein, And that was the virginite, 116.6208–11: To kepe hire maidenhede whit . . . That no lif mai restore ayein. **a1439** Lydgate *Fall* II 367.1399–1400: Nor never in story nouther rad nor seyn, That maidenhed lost recurid was ageyn. **a1470** Malory II 961.14–5: And shall lose hir virginité which she shall never gete agayne. See **E70, K94, N13, T186.**

M21 **Maidenhood** without the love of God is like a lamp without oil (*varied*)
1340 *Ayenbite* 233[4–5]: Vor maydenhod wythoute the love of god is ase the lompe wythoute oyle. **a1376** *Piers* A i 162–3: Chastite withouten charite . . . Is as lewed as a laumpe that no liht is inne. **c1400** *Vices and Virtues* 257.35–258.2: For virginite with-oute the love of God is right as the laumpe with-oute oile. Skeat 43–4.

M22 Not avail the value of a **Mail** (*half-pence*)
c1421 Lydgate *Thebes* 167.4075–6: For nouther force nor manhode may availle In swiche meschief the valewe of a maylle.

M23 **Maintainers** are partners of the sinning
1436 *Libelle* 33.651: But maynteners ar parteners of the synnynge. See **T70, 74.**

M24 **Make** and (or) mar
1469 Paston V 41[15–6]: For thys mater is to all usse eyther makyng or marryng. **a1475** *Assembly of Gods* 17.556: And so dyd Neptunus, that dothe bothe make and marre. **c1497** Medwall *Fulgens* B2ʳ[16]: The mariage utterly to mare or to make. **c1516** Skelton *Magnificence* 33.1037–9: All that I make forthwith I marre; . . . I make on the one day, and I marre on the other, **1522** *Why Come* II 49.730: To make all or to mar. **c1545** Heywood *Four PP* B1ᵛ[17]: For when they wolde make it, ofte tymes marre it, **1555** *E* 152.39: Make or mar, **1556** *Spider* 113[13–4]: or, 219[10]: to make or to mar. *Oxford* 399; Tilley M48.

M25 If one hides his **Malady** there can be no medicine
a1393 Gower *CA* II 40.164–7: Sche seide, "Tell thi maladie: What is thi Sor of which thou pleignest? Ne hyd it noght, for if thou feignest, I can do the no medicine." See **L173, S503.**

M26 The **Malice** of a woman passes the malice of a man
c1395 *WBible* Ecclesiasticus xxv 17 *gloss:* So the malice of a womman passith al the malice of a man, 26: Al malice is schort on the malice of a womman; the parte of synner is falle on hir. See **W545.**

M27 Some get **Malice** for the good they lend
1509 Barclay *Ship* I 134[13–4]: Yet some get malyce for that gode that they len And where they lent twenty gladly taketh ten. See **G341.**

M28 **Malt** is above wheat with him
1546 Heywood *D* 41.17–8: Sixe daies in the weeke beside the market daie. Malt is above wheate

with him, market men saie, **1562** *E* 245.94.7–8: Looke where so ever malte is above wheate. There in shotte ever drinke is above meate. Apperson 393; *Oxford* 400; Tilley M58.

M29 To live the age of **Malvern Hills**
c1495 *Arundel Vulgaria* 37.156: For and yf I lyff the age of malvornn hyllys I shall yelde hym a foole styll. Cf. Apperson 393, 466:11; Taylor and Whiting 183.

M30 All **Men** are not of one condition
c1450 La Tour-Landry 176–7: For al men ben not on one condycion, ne of one manere; for that thynge whiche pleseth to one is dyspleasyng to the other. See **G104.**

M31 All **Men** are not true
a1500 Hill 129.28: It is comenly said, that all men be not trew. Tilley M503.

M32 All **Men** flee the death (*varied*)
c1375 Barbour *Bruce* I 211.90: For all men fleis the ded richt fayn. **1525** Berners *Froissart* V 432[20]: Every man is lothe to dye. See **D110.**

M33 All **Men** that speak of the fire of love know not what it is
a1396(1494) Hilton *Scale* C5ᵛ[26–7]: Al men that speke of the fire of love knowen not wel what it is. See **R156.**

M34 Although a **Man** is wise yet the wisdom of twelve is more
a1393 Gower *CA* II 8–9.157–8: Althogh a man be wys himselve, Yit is the wisdom more of tuelve.

M35 Another **Man's** arse is a murk mirror (*varied*)
c1475 Henryson *Sum Practysis* 160.90: It is ane mirk mirrour Ane uthir manis erss. **1513** Douglas *Aeneid* III 121.135: To me is myrk myrrour ilk mannys menyng. Whiting *Scots* I 132. Cf. Tilley M991. See **M226, 580.**

M36 As a blind **Man** casts his staff (*varied*)
c1384 Wyclif *Church and her Members* in *SEW* III 349[22–4]: And sith thei witen not who is beterid by entryng into thes ordris, thei doon as a blynd man castith his staf, to brynge ony to ther ordre. **a1393** Gower *CA* II 416.534–7: Therof the Jelous takth non hiede, Bot as a man to love unkinde, He cast his staf, as doth the blinde, And fint defaulte where is non. **a1400** Wyclif *Sermons* II 230[33–4]: And yf it sue ony tyme, it fallith as a blynd man castith his staf. **c1450** *Rylands MS.394* 95.25–6: So kastis the blynde man his staffe, So smytis he that may not see. **a1470** Parker *Dives* C8ᵛ[2.1–3]: Somtyme they happen to saye suche trouthes as the blynde man caste the staf. **1546** Heywood *D* 96.189–90: Ye cast and conjecture this muche like in show, As the blind man casts his staffe, or shootes the crow. Apperson 54:8; *Oxford* 51; Serlo 186.2; Tilley M74. Cf. Whiting *Drama* 255. See **A177.**

M37 As a blind **Man** starts a hare
c1380 Chaucer *HF* 680–1: That ben betyd, no man wot why, But as a blynd man stert an hare. Apperson 54:7, 286:8; Jente 343; *Oxford* 51; Skeat 208; Tilley M81.

M38 As **Man** lives longer his doom becomes stronger
a1300 *Trinity College Cambridge MS. 323* f.46a in M. R. James *Catalogue* (Cambridge, 1900) I 444: Eveir asse mon livit lengore, So is dom iwrt strengore.

M39 As **Men** deserve they receive their guerdon (*varied*)
a1449 Lydgate *Fabules* in *MP* II 578.344: As men deserve, they receve theyr guerdon, 579.367: As men deserve, reporte yeveth theym theyr lawde. **c1450** *Bi a forest* in Furnivall *Hymns* 96.21: As y deserve, so schal y have. See **H185.**

M40 As sicker as **Men** eat bread
a1500 *Medicines* in Brown *Lyrics XV* 274.59: And els, as seker as men etyth brede.

M41 As soon dies a young **Man** as an old (*varied*)
c1430 Lydgate *Dance* 70.592: As sone dyeth a yonge man as an olde. **a1440** Burgh *Cato* 31.1097: And as the old so deye the yonge a-monge. **a1450** *Gesta* 364[10]: Alse sone deyeth the yong as the olde. **c1450** *Alphabet* I 148.18–9: Als sone dyes a yong man as ane olde man. **1483** Caxton *Cato* D1ᵛ[23–4]: For assone deyeth yonge as olde, I6ᵛ[6], **1489** *Doctrinal* L7ʳ[3–4]. Apperson 588; Whiting *Drama* 184. See **D98, M204, 385, S209.**

M42 As soon is the great **Man** slain as the little man
c1390 Chaucer *CT* VII 1666–7[B2856–7]: And by cause that in batailles fallen manye perils, and happeth outher while that as soone is the grete man slayn as the litel man. See **K49.**

M43 The avaricious **Man** lacks the good that he has as well as that he has not
c1395 *WBible* Prefatory Epistles of St. Jerome I 75[1–3]: For it is an old sothsawe, to the avarouse man as well lackith the good that he hath, as that he hath not. **1489** Caxton *Doctrinal* G8ʳ[14–6]: For the scripture saith that al

so wel lacketh to the riche avaricious that whiche he hathe, as that whiche he hath not. Smith 201.

M44 The avaricious **Man's** heir wastes his property
c735 *Beowulf* 1753–7: Hit on endestæf eft gelimpeð, þæt se lichoma læne gedreoseð, Fæge gefealleð; fehð oþer to, Se þe unmurnlice madmas dæleþ, Eorles ærgestreon, egesan ne gymeð. See **G333.**

M45 Be a **Man** never so good yet may he have a fall
a1470 Malory II 516.3–4: Here may a man preve, be he never so good yet may he have a falle. See **A179, S671.**

M46 Because the blind **Man** halts he thinks all men do the same
c1515 Barclay *Eclogues* 158.509–10: Because the blinde man halteth and is lame, In minde he thinketh that all men do the same.

M47 Best for a **Man** to apply (himself to) the business that he can (*knows*)
c1503 More *Early Poems* [1] AB: Wyse man alway, Affyrme and say, That best is for a man Diligently For to apply The business that he can, And in no wyse, To enterpryse An other faculte, For he that wyll, and can no skyll, Is never lyke to the. Cf. Tilley C480. See **R54.**

M48 Better be an old **Man's** darling than a young man's warling
1546 Heywood *D* 82.82–3: It is better to be An olde mans derlyng, then a yong mans werlyng. Apperson 464; NED Warling; *Oxford* 38; Tilley M444–5.

M49 Better is one **Man** dead than all folk lost (two)
c1300 *Cayphas* in *Rel. Ant.* II 241[22–4]: Hit com to sothe that ich tho seyde, Betere hit were that o man deyde, Than al volk were y-lore. **a1400** *Ipomadon A* 129.4485: For better is oo man dede, then tow.

M50 The blind **Man** cannot judge in hues (deems no colors) (*varied*)
c1385 Chaucer *TC* ii 21: A blynd man kan nat juggen wel in hewis. **a1393** Gower *CA* III 15.2489–90: The blinde man no colour demeth, But al is on, riht as him semeth. (*Margin:* Cecus non judicat de coloribus.) **c1412** Hoccleve *Regement* 36.994: The blynde man of coloures al wrong deemeth (*Margin:* Cecus non judica [de coloribus; et nota hic de scriptoribus]). **c1425** *Orcherd* 330.19–20: A blynd man . . . lacketh light to deeme colouris. **c1450** *Rylands MS.394* 93.31: Blynde men demyn no colouris. **1479** Rivers *Cordyal* 122.3–4: I am as oon born blinde that disputeth in colours. **c1480** *Contemplacioun* 234.1368: As blynd men blunderand of colouris to dispute. **c1500** *King Hart* 109.18: To by richt blew, that nevir ane hew had sene! **1528** More *Heresyes* 134 D–H: (A feigned miracle is exposed when a man who claimed to have been born blind could suddenly distinguish colors), **1534** *Comforte* 1259 BC: Those . . . are yet in a maner as farre therefro, as the borne blynd man, fro the right ymaginacion of colours. **1546** Heywood *D* 77.229: But blinde men should judge no colours, **1555** *E* 166.122. Apperson 54; *Oxford* 51; Skeat 157; Tilley M80; Whiting *Scots* I 140. See **M132.**

M51 A blind **Man** may see (that)
1562 Heywood *E* 197.298: A blynde man may see our fare as well as wee. Tilley M82. See **H629.**

M52 A covetous **Man** has no rest
1450 *Dicts* 272.6–7: A covetous man hathe noo reste, ne a covetous man may not be riche.

M53 A covetous **Man** never has enough (*varied*)
c1433 Lydgate *St. Edmund* 429.898–900; With covetise he was so set affyre, . . . The mor he gadred, the mor he doth desire, **a1439** *Fall* II 433.3732–3: Ther may no tresour ther dropesie weel staunche; The mor thei drynke the mor thei thruste in deede. **a1450** *Castle* 92.504–6: He muste nedys, ovyr al thynge, Evere-more be covetowse: Non est in mundo dives, qui dicit "habundo." **a1470** Parker *Dives* A4^{r}[2.9–10]: For as I sayd Ecclesiastes the .v. ca. The nygarde hath never ynough. **c1515** Barclay *Eclogues* 48.1288: For covetous with coyne be never saciate. Tilley M88, N163; Whiting *Drama* 242, 247, *Scots* II 153. See **C115, G449, W713.**

M54 Dead **Men** in ground may be afeared of you
c1350 *Libeaus* 14. *var.* 216^{h-i} : Theo dede men in grounde Of the aferd may beo. Cf. Tilley M436.

M55 Dead **Men** often times make peace
a1533 Berners *Arthur* 387[24–5]: Oftentymes deed men maketh peas.

M56 Dead **Men** tell no tales
a1470 Malory II 465.24–5: And som of the beste of hem (*dead men*) woll telle no talys. Apperson 138; *Oxford* 132; Taylor and Whiting 234:8; Tilley M511.

M57 Deem no **Man** gentle but only by his deeds
a1439 Lydgate *Fall* III 709.1294–5: In hih(e) berthe, mene, or louh kynreede, Deeme no man gentil, but onli bi his deede. See **G46.**

M58 Deem no **Man** till you know him
a1449 Lydgate *Say the Best* in *MP* II 796.47: And deme no man till thou him know. See **F625, M270.**

M59 Do, **Man,** for yourself while you have space (*varied*)
c1380 Brinton *Sermons* II 486[13–6]: Sed post mortem quid erit de cumulis per tales naballes et nigardos iniustissime congregatis? Certe per uxores, heredes, et executores deprimentur et ineorum usus proprios redigerentur. Dic quomodo, et sic farwel Jacke, et cetera. **1435** *Epitaph* in Thomas F. Ravenshaw *Antiente Epitaphes* (London, 1878) 9[9–12]: Man, yt behoveth ofte to have in mynde, that thow gevest with thyn honde, that shalt Thow fynde, Ffor women ben slowfull and chyldren beth unkynde, Executors beth covetous and kepe all that they fynde. **a1450** Audelay 19.257–9: Do fore youreself or ye gone; Trust not to an other mon Ellus med of God get ye non. **a1450** *Castle* 166.2996–7: Now, good men, takythe example at me! Do for youre self, whyl ye han spase! **c1450** *Lambeth MS.259* in M. R. James and C. Jenkins *Descriptive Catalogue* (Cambridge, 1930–2) 405: Do sum gode, man, in the lyve qwell thu hast the mynd; Thi chylder woll forgete the sone, the wyf woll wax unkynd. Ffor yf thu well not wen thu may, thay well breng the be hend. Exsecutorys bene full covytus, tha take all at tha fynd. **c1450** *Tile at Great Malvern* in M. R. James *Abbeys* (London, 1926) 78: Thenke, man, thi life Mai not ever endure. That thou dost thi self Of that thou art sure, But that thou kepist Unto thi sectur cure, And ever hit availe thee, Hit is but aventure. **1489** Caxton *Doctrinal* G8v[21–2]: Whylles that ye be maister and owner, doo for your self. **c1490** Ryman 254.7: Do for thy self, while thou art here; For, whenne thou art layde in thy grave, Though that thy soule did brenne in fere, Yet frendes fewe thenne shuldest thou have: They that to the shulde be moost dere, Wille sey, of thyne nothing they have. **a1500** *Colkelbie* 304.254–6: Spend with wirchep and spair nocht godis gud How littill wat thow ane udir tyme quho may Bruk thy wyfe and baggis eftir thy day. **a1500** *Harley MS.3038* in *Rel. Ant.* I 314: Do mon for thiselffe, Wyl thou art alyve; For he that dose after thu dethe, God let him never thryve. *Quod Tucket.* Da tua, dum tua sunt. Post mortem tunc tua non sunt. Wyse mon if thou art, of thi god Take part or thou hense wynde; For if thou leve thi part in thi secaturs ward, Thi part non part at last end. Too secuturs and an overseere make thre theves. **a1500** *Hunterian Mus. MS.230* 175: Man on the molde, have this in mynde, That thowe Soyth here, that salt thou fynd. Wemen ben laches, And chyldren on kynd, Servirs cum after and Tak qwat they fynd. **a1500** *Man, be war* in T. Wright *Songs and Carols* (PS 23, 1848) 34[9–12]: Man, have this in thi mynd, What thow doest with thyn hond, that shal thou fynd. Wyves be rekeles, chyldren be onkynd, Excecuturs be covetys and hold that thei fynd. **c1500** *Epitaph* in John Weever *Ancient Funerall Monuments* (London, 1631) 413: Man, the behovyth oft to have this in mynd, That thou geveth wyth thin hond that sall thow fynd, For wydowes be sloful, and chyldren beth unkynd, Executors be covetos, and kep al that they fynd. Apperson 155, 654, 698:47; Robbins-Cutler 1820; Tilley M422, W700; Walther I 591.4861. See **D275, E38, 201.**

M60 A drunken **Man** is likened to a wood (*mad*) man
a1450 *Myne awen dere* 177.889–90: A dronken man, I tell the this, Till a wode man likenyd is.

M61 Each **Man** chooses like (*after*) his opinion
a1449 Lydgate *Fabules* in *MP* II 573.200: Yche man cheseth lyke hys opinion.

M62 Each **Man** follows his condition
a1439 Lydgate *Fall* I 133.4770: And ech man folweth his condicioun. See **M70.**

M63 Each **Man** had liefer do better to himself than to another
c1520 *Terens* B4v[14–6]: The comen proverbe is a trew sayng, That ych man had lever to hym self do better, Than to an other. (Omnes sibi melius esse male quam alteri.) Walther III 596.19922. See **B513, C153, M73, N85.**

M64 Each **Man** meets his match (*varied*)
c1400 *Beryn* 4.83: Lo! howe the clowdis worchyn, ech man to mete his mach! **a1475** *Seege of Troye* 203 H 1612gh: Ther is noman soo stronge of kynde But he may his make fynde. (The *Beryn* quote seems to mean: Jack has his Jill.) See **F447, G382, K6, M416.**

M65 Each **Man** must have a beginning, for the fair lasts but a while
c1450 Idley 151.2687–90: Somme lye also as chepmen do for wynnyng; Many a true man they sligelie begile. Eche man, they sey, must

have a begynnyng, Ffor the feire lasteth but a while.

M66 Each **Man** must speak for himself
c1300 *South English Legendary* II 627.526: Echman mot speke for him sulve. See **M73.**

M67 Each **Man** rejoices to do such thing to which he is disposed
a1439 Lydgate *Fall* II 434.3786–7: Ech man rejoyssheth (this sentence is nat glosid) To doon swich thyng to whiche he (is) disposid. See **M75, 121.**

M68 An envious **Man** waxes lean
c1470 *Harley MS.3362* f.2b in *Retrospective* 309[20]: A envyows man wexit lene. Apperson 185; Smith 81; Tilley M96.

M69 Every false **Man** has a make (*mate*)
1402 Hoccleve *Letter of Cupid* 74.57–8: And for that every fals man hath a make, (As un-to every wight is lyght to knowe). See **T73.**

M70 Every **Man** after his manner (fashion)
c1522 Skelton *Speke* II 6.92–3: Every man after his maner of wayes, *Pawbe une aruer,* so the Welche man sayes. **1546** Heywood *D* 48.228: Every man after his fassion. Apperson 191; *Oxford* 179; Tilley M100. Skelton Notes II 341: "Either *Paub un arver,* Every one his manner, or *Paub yn ei arver,* Every one in his manner." See **M62, 74.**

M71 Every **Man** as he loves, quoth the goodman, when he kissed his cow
1546 Heywood *D* 60.54–5: And in this case every man as he loveth Quoth the good man, whan that he kyst his coowe. Apperson 191–2; *Oxford* 178; Taylor and Whiting 235; Tilley M101, 103; Whiting *Drama* 214–5.

M72 Every **Man** can rule a shrew, save he that has her
1546 Heywood *D* 78.18: Every man can rule a shrewe, save he that hath her. Apperson 568; *Oxford* 551; Tilley M106.

M73 Every (Each) **Man** for himself (*varied*)
c1385 Chaucer *CT* I[A] 1181–2: And therfore, at the kynges court, my brother, Ech man for hymself, ther is noon oother. **1478** Paston V 322[32]: For ther is every man for hym selff. **1513** Douglas *Aeneid* IV 113.125: Every man for hym self, as he best mycht. **c1515** Barclay *Eclogues* 36.1009: Eche man for him selfe, and the frende (?fiend) for all. **c1520** *Terens* C3^r^[4–5]: Every man Is for hym self. **1546** Heywood *D* 96.203: Every man for him selfe, and god for us all, **1555** *E* 161.96. Apperson 189; *Oxford* 178; Taylor and Whiting 234–5; Tilley M112, 113; Whiting *Drama* 114. See **M66, 116.**

M74 Every **Man** has his guise
1483 *Vulgaria quedam abs Terencio* Q3^v^[8]: Every man hat(h) his guyse. See **M70.**

M75 Every **Man** is lightly (*easily*) inclined to his own desire
c1390 Chaucer *CT* VII 1283[B2473]: How lightly is every man enclined to his owene desir and to his owene plesaunce! *Oxford 32:* Believe what. See **M67, 121.**

M76 Every **Man** is woe when he shall forgo (*lose*) a good friend
c1300 *Guy*[1] 230.4003–4: Everich man is swithe wo When he schal a gode frende for-go.

M77 Every **Man** may not have his list (*desire*)
a1400 *Proverbis of Wysdom* 246.89: Every man may not have his lyst.

M78 Every **Man** may not sit in the chair
1546 Heywood *D* 55.5: Every man may not syt in the chayre. Apperson 7; *Oxford* 8; Tilley M107.

M79 Every **Man** shall (*must*) bear his own works
a1393 Gower *CA* II 18.491–2: For every man hise oghne werkes Schal bere.

M80 Every **Man** shall do divers gins (*tricks*) to slay his foe (*varied*)
a1300 *Alisaunder* 225.4010–1: Every man to slen his foo Dyvers gynne so shal do. **c1300** *Guy*[1] 301 A 5531–2: Man schal ben awreken of his fo In what maner he may com to, 350 A 6555–6: Ich man schal his might don, For to awreke him of his fon. **a1475** *Guy*[2] 149.5217–8: Man schulde preve in all wyse To venge them on ther enmyse. **1523** Berners *Froissart* II 41[27–8]: For alwayes by right of armes a man ought to greve his ennemy, **1525** V 3–4: A man ought to take his ennemy whersoever he fynde hym.

M81 Every **Man** should feed the good (*varied*)
a1300 *Alisaunder* 65.1127–8: Wel is the moder that may forth fede Childe that helpeth hire at nede. **c1300** *Havelok* 55.1693: Wel is him that god man fedes. **a1350** *Isumbras* 50.635–6: And sayd: My palmere es strange enoghe: He is worthi to fede. **c1400** *Alexander Buik* I 82.2597–9: To nureis gude men and worthy Men sould thame preis ay idantly, For it is proffeit and honour, 100.3151–2: It is gude thing, suthlie, To nurris gude men and wourthy. **c1450** *Merlin* I 26[2–3]: He (that) ought doth for a gode man, lesith not his traveyle. **a1500** *Guy*[4] 217.7229–30:

Every man should the good feede: They may ever helpe at neede. *Oxford* 700.

M82 Every **Man** shows by his works whose child he is
c1382 Wyclif *De Pontificum* in *SEW* III 249[18–20]: Ffor every man . . . and specially prelatis, schewen bi her werkis whos children thei beth. See **A169, K30, T465.**

M83 Every wise **Man** dreads his enemy
c1390 Chaucer *CT* VII 1316[B2506]: For every wys man dredeth his enemy.

M84 An evil **Man** will take vengeance and on himself falls the scathe (*harm*)
c1390 *Northern Homily Cycle Narrationes* (*Vernon*) 312.235–8: That ofte we seo falle such chaunce Ther an uvel mon wol take venjaunce Of mon with whom he is wrathe, And on him self falleth al the scathe. Cf. Tilley M89. See **D22.**

M85 Fele (*many*) **Men** may pass where they find no peril, *etc.*
c1470 *Wallace* 246.335–6: Feill men may pass, quhar thai fynd na parell; Rycht few may kep, quhar nayn is to assaill.

M86 For a **Man** to strive with a stronger man than himself is a woodness (*madness*), *etc.*
c1390 Chaucer *CT* VII 1481–3[B2671–3]: Forthermoore, ye knowen wel that after the comune sawe, "it is a woodnesse a man to stryve with a strenger or a moore myghty man than he is hymself; and for to stryve with a man of evene strengthe, that is to seyn, with as strong a man as he is, it is peril; and for to stryve with a weyker man, it is folie." Seneca *De Ira* ii 34.1 (*Moral Essays,* trans. John W. Basore, Loeb Classical Library, I[1928] 242).

M87 A forsworn **Man** shall never have manship (*courage*) long (never speed)
c1300 Lawman I 177 B 4148–9: Ne mai nevere for-swore man, Mansipe leng oghe. **c1300** *Amis* 48.1102: And forsworn man schal never spede. See **F500.**

M88 The fous (*ready* [*for death*]) **Man** must go, the fey man die
c900 *Maxims* in *Exeter Book* 157.27: Fus sceall feran, fæge sweltan. See **D90.**

M89 The friendless **Man** is loath for his misfortunes
a800 *Fortunes of Men* in *Exeter Book* 154.31–2: Lað bið æghwær Fore his wonsceaftum wineleas hæle. See **H141, M312.**

M90 Give not a **Man** in frenzy a sword or knife (*varied*)
a1400 Wyclif *Sermons* I 26[11–2]: For what man wolde bi resoun, kepyng a man in frenesie, gyve him a swerd or a knyf bi which he wolde slee himsilf? **1422** Yonge *Governaunce* 167.36–8: The Powere of a prynce that is not ryghtfull demenyt, ys lykenyd to a sharpe Swerde in a wodemanys honde. **1522** Skelton *Why Come* II 44.575–81: Now frantick, now starke wode. Shulde this man of suche mode Rule the swerde of myght, How can he do ryght? For he wyll as sone smyght His frende as his fo: A proverbe longe ago. **1546** Heywood *D* 88.12: Ill puttyng a nakt swoord in a mad mans hande. Apperson 325; *Oxford* 442; Smith 324; Tilley L156, P669; Whiting *Drama* 118. See **H571.**

M91 A good **Man** is never in danger but when he is in the danger of a coward
a1470 Malory III 1126.4–6: But hyt ys an olde-seyde saw: "A good man ys never in daungere but whan he ys in the daungere of a cowhard." Apperson 260; Tilley M150. See **C509.**

M92 A good **Man** makes a good wife
c1450 Idley 102.1246: Ever a good man maketh a good wyffe. **1492** *Salomon and Marcolphus* 12[25–6]: Of a good man cometh a good wyf. Apperson 259; *Oxford* 253; Tilley H831.

M93 Good **Men** draw together and every fool to his fellow
a1400 *Titus* 208–9.4625–8: As in proverbes (*var.* the prophecye) it is ytolde, Bothe of zonge and of oolde, The gode men togedre thei drawe, And every fool (*var.* shrew) to his felawe. See **L272.**

M94 Great **Men** for taking are set full famous at the Session and poor takers are hanged high
a1513 Dunbar *Of Discretioun in Taking* 36.46–8: Grit men for taking and oppressioun Ar sett full famous at the Sessioun, And peur takaris ar hangit hie. See **T68.**

M95 A guilty **Man** behooves (*needs*) mercy
c1025 *Durham Proverbs* 13.24: Forworht mann friþes behofað. Reus propitiatione indiget.

M96 Happy **Man** happy dole
1546 Heywood *D* 23.54: Happy man happy dole, **1555** *E* 195.284, **1556** *Spider* 102[28]. Apperson 284; *Oxford* 277; Tilley M158.

M97 Hasty **Man** wants (lacks, fails) never care (sorrow, woe)
c1385 Chaucer *TC* iv 1567–8: Beth naught to hastif in this hoote fare; For hastif man ne

wanteth nevere care. **a1400** *Proverbis of Wysdom* 246.125–6: Hasty man lackythe no sorow: But he have to day, he shal to morow. **a1449** Lydgate *Haste* in *MP* II 759.9: The hasti man ffayleth never woo. **1449** Metham 36.966–7: But trwe that proverbe than prevyd so, That overhasty man wantyd never woo. **c1450** *Epistle of Othea* 78.10: For an hasty man wanteth never woo. **c1450** Greene *Carols* 338.1 *and refrain:* Sith hasty man lakked never woo. **c1450** Idley 84.238: Ffor an hasty man wanteth never woo. **a1475** Banester *Guiscardo* 34.559–60: Vherfor it hath be spokyn aforne agoo: "Ane hasty creature (*var.* man) never wanteth woo." **c1475** *Rawlinson MS. D 328* 117.7: A hasty man lackyth never owye. **c1477** Norton *Ordinall* 30[30]: That a hasty man shall never faile of woe. **c1485** *Guiscardo* 66.482–3: Remembre the proverbe, seying of long ago: "A cruell hasty man wanteth never wo." **c1495** *Arundel Vulgaria* 60.257: My father warnyde me . . . sayng many a tyme that comyn poynt, "an hasty man lakkith never wo." **a1500** *Counsels* in Brown *Lyrics XV* 283.17–8: I have harde sungone wyth a harpe, That haste men sholde wante no woo. **a1500** Hill 129.41: Hasti man lakkith newer woo. **c1500** *Order of Shoting* in *Retrospective Review* 1(1853) 206[5–6]: Ye have hard say, and I have hard the same, An hasty man ful sildam wanteth wo. **1546** Heywood *D* 21.46: The hasty man never wanteth wo, **1555** *E* 147.3.1. Apperson 289; *Oxford* 282; Tilley M159; Whiting *Scots* II 94. See **H162.**

M98 Hasty **Men** are oft outrayed (*vanquished*) when their tongues are too prest (*prompt*)
c1390 *Suffer in Time* in Brown *Lyrics XIV* 202.65–6: Hasti men ben ofte outrayede Whon heore tonges ben to preste.

M99 Hasty **Men** soon slain
a1500 *How shall y plece* in *Archiv* 106(1901) 274[12]: An old seyd saw, hasty men sone slayn. See **H162, M146.**

M100 He is highest among **Men** who recks never who has the world in hand
a1387 Higden-Trevisa V 27[13–5]: Among his (*Ptoleomaeus'*) proverbis . . . He is higheste among men that reccheth nevere who hath the world on honde. **c1395** Chaucer *CT* III[D] 324–7: The wise astrologien, Daun Ptholome, That seith this proverbe in his Almageste: "Of alle men his wysdom is the hyeste That rekketh nevere who hath the world in honde." *Oxford* 535; Skeat 265. See **L444.**

M101 He that does what no **Man** does all men wonder on him
c1350 *Smaller Vernon Collection* 48.400–4: A proverbe that he (*St. Bernard*) riht wel couthe, He wolde sey on this manere, As ye mowe nouthe ihere: "He that doth that doth no man, On him wondreth uche mon than." Qui hoc facit quod nemo, mirantur omnes. **a1387** Higden-Trevisa VIII 19[4–6]: That proverbe is ofte had in his (*Bernard's*) mouth and alwey in his herte, "Alle men wondreth of hym that doth as noon other dooth." **1483** Caxton *Golden Legende* 239v[1–2]: He (*Bernard*) hadde in his herte alwaye this proverbe and ofte sayde it, who doth that noman doth alle men wondre on hym. Apperson 395:35. Cf. Tilley M511. See **D273.**

M102 He that goes with wise **Men** shall be wise
c1395 *WBible* Proverbs xiii 20: He that goith with wiis men, schal be wiis; the freend of foolis schal be maad liik hem. Jente 230.

M103 He that kills a **Man** when he is drunk shall be hanged when he is sober
1549 Heywood *D* 39.153–4: He that kylth a man, whan he is dronke . . . Shalbe hangd when he is sobre. Apperson 340; *Oxford* 335; Tilley M175. See **D421, S374, 694.**

M104 He that serves a common **Man** serves by short process of time
a1456 Shirley *Death of James* 9[12–3]: He that serveth a comon mane, he serveth by short procese of tyme. (The speaker had incorrectly thought to have the support of his fellow nobles.) See **C391.**

M105 He that will kill a **Man** for a mess of mustard will kill ten for a custard
1555 Heywood *E* 183.207: He will kill a man for a messe of mustard He will kill ten men then for a custard. Tilley M180.

M106 He was a **Man:** let him go
c1450 Greene *Carols* 392.5: And quan I have non in myn purs, Peny bet ne peny wers, Of me thei holdyn but lytil fors: "He was a man; let hym goo."

M107 Holy **Men** should deem angels
c1000 Aelfric *Lives* II 294.1213–4: þæt se cwyde mihte beon on Martine ge-fylled þæt halige menn sceolon englum deman. Cf. Chaucer *TC* ii 894–5.

M108 A hundred **Men** may see a man yet not one know his will
a1400 *Ipomadon A* 16.489–90: A hundyrd men may a man se, Yet wott not one his wille.

M109 Hungry **Men** may not live on looks
c1475 Henryson *Fables* 6.104: For houngrie men may not leve on lukis. Cf. Apperson 394:7. See **L575.**

M110 The idle **Man** excuses him in winter because of the great cold, *etc.*
c1390 Chaucer *CT* VII 1593[B2783]: For ther is a versifiour seith that "the ydel man excuseth hym in wynter by cause of the grete coold, and in somer by enchesoun of the greete heete." **c1395** *WBible* Proverbs xx 4: A slow man nolde ere for coold; therfor he schal begge in somer, and me schal not gyve to hym.

M111 If a wise **Man** provides (for) what is to come, it grieves him the less
c1495 *Arundel Vulgaria* 45.194: A wise mann, yf he do provyde what is to cum, it must nedys greve hym the lesse when it comyth to hym. See **M305, W49.**

M112 If every **Man** knew how brittle his shinbones were, he would never leap where he might go (*walk*)
c1450 *Douce MS.52* 56.134: Wyst every man, how bretell were his shen-bon, Wolde he never lepe, there he myhght gon. **c1450** *Rylands MS.394* 107.22.5–6: ever any man . . . Nolde.

M113 If every **Man** mend one, all shall be mended
1528 More *Heresyes* 233 D[2–7]: So would I fayne that every man would wene ther were but one man naught in al the hole world, and that that one wer himselfe. And that he would therupon goe about to mend the one, and thus wold al ware well. **1555** Heywood *E* 147.1.1: If every man mende one, all shall be mended. Apperson 190; *Oxford* 178; Tilley M196. See **G352.**

M114 (If) the **Man** that is false trusts his friends they beguile him
a1338 Mannyng *Chronicle B* II 329[17–9]: Selcouthly he endis the man that is fals, If he trest on his frendes, thei begile him als Begiled is William. Cf. Tilley M300. See **B213, F52, 491, 610, G491, V34.**

M115 If you believe each **Man** you will seldom do well (*varied*)
a1200 Lawman I 342.8015–8: Ful soh (*B* soth) seide the seg (*B* man) The theos saghe talde: Yif thu ilevest aelcne mon, Selde thu sælt wel don. **c1390** *Proverbes of diverse profetes* 531.143–4: Hose leeveth uche monnes seying, Whon othur laughwhen, he schal make murning. Apperson 36; Jente 317; *Oxford* 32; Skeat 6. See **B221, H617, T490, W629.**

M116 Ilk **Man** is most holden (*bound*) to save himself
c1340 Rolle *Psalter* 432 (118.145): For ilk man is maste haldyn to safe him selfe. See **M63, 73.**

M117 In old **Men** is children's wit (will) (*varied*)
c1390 *Cato* (*Vernon*) 600.541–2: In old mon is childes wit, Soth thou schalt hit fynde. **a1400** *Cato* (*Copenhagen*) B3v[7–8]: Ffor in olde men ofte tymys is seene Childryn wit, with outyn wene. **a1400** *Cato* (*Fairfax*) in *Cursor* III 1671.166–8: For wisest and mast of maine Ginin childis witte a-gaine, Quen thai ar un-welde. **a1440** Burgh *Cato* 28.967–8: Whan age cometh, this is sothe certeyn, A man begynneth to ben a chyld a-geyn. **c1450** *Ratis* 48.1684–5: And quhill (*old men*) hass appetyt and wyll As fallis wantone childyr tyll. **1484** Caxton *Royal Book* U7v[13–6]: And the scripture sayth that a chylde of an hondred yere shal be cursyd. That is to say, that he that is of grete age and lyveth as a chylde shal be cursyd. **1509** Watson *Ship* G2r[8–10]: It happyneth oftentymes that olde and auncyente men become chyldysshe agayne. Apperson 464–5; *Oxford* 472; Smith 25; Taylor and Whiting 68; Tilley M570; Whiting *Scots* II 106. See **M256.**

M118 In old **Men** is sapience and in long time prudence
c1390 Chaucer *CT* VII 1164[B2354]: For the book seith that "in olde men is the sapience, and in longe tyme the prudence." **c1395** *WBible* Job xx 12: Wisdom is in elde men, and prudence is in myche tyme. Jente 181; *Oxford* 3. Cf. Whiting *Drama* 131. See **E61.**

M119 In other **Men's** houses be not bold
c1450 *Fyrst thou sal* 91.168: In other mens hows be not so bold.

M120 In rich **Men** who are sparing worship is away
c1400 *Alexander Buik* III 309.6992–3: Bot worship is away, I wis, In ryche men that sparand is! See **L447, S628.**

M121 It is eath (*easy*) to till (*entice*) a **Man** to do his will (*varied*)
a1400 *Scottish Legends* II 103.159–60: For eth is a man to til To do it that is his wil. **c1500** *Three Kings' Sons* 7.38–9: Gladly everi man meveth his maister of suche matiers as moost may please hym. Whiting *Scots* II 95. See **M67, 75, T24, 126, 174.**

M122 It is hard for a **Man** to mend all faults
1546 Heywood *D* 45.146: But harde is for any man all fautes to mende. *Oxford* 7; Tilley M200.

M123 It is hard to depart (*separate*) a **Man** from his own will
a1438 Kempe 45.28–9: Her mayst thow se how hard it is to departyn a man fro hys owyn wyl. See **W519.**

M124 It is hard to please all **Men** (folk, parties) (*varied*)
c1475 ?Lydgate *So as the Crabbe* in *MP* II 467.54 (*var.*): To please al folk it is ful hard. **1475** Paston V 231[22–3]: Yt is nomor but that he can not plese all partys. **a1500** *Additional MS.37075* 278.22: There may no man all men ples. Nemo potest vere cunctim perfecta placere. **a1500** Hill 132.49: Ther may no man all men please. Nemo potest vere cunctis omnino placere. **a1500** *Imitatione* (*1*) 111.32–3: And to plese all men is not possible. **1502** *Imitatione* (*2*) 230.8–9: But to satysfye all men it is impossyble. **1523** Skelton *Garlande* I 412.1259: Hard it is to please all men. Apperson 285, 449; *Oxford* 506: parties; Tilley P88, cf. M526. Cf. Walther I 900.7164, III 89.16395; Whiting *Drama* 156. See **P133.**

M125 (It is) meet that a **Man** be at his own bridal
1546 Heywood *D* 28.40: Meete, that a man be at his owne brydale. Apperson 396; *Oxford* 400; Tilley M201.

M126 It speeds (*helps*) a **Man** to be drunk once in a month
c1400 *Seven Deadly Sins* in Wyclif *SEW* III 161[1–2]: And if thou sey that hit spedes a man to be dronken ones in a moneth, for myche gode comes therof. *Schola Salernitana . . . ex recensione Zachariæ Sylvii* (Rotterdam, 1667) 136: Si quis semel in mense inebrietur: quo videlicet per ebrietatem vomitus excitetur; Burton Stevenson *Home Book of Proverbs, Maxims and Familiar Phrases* (New York, 1948) 637.7.

M127 A large (*generous*) **Man** has thirled (*pierced*) hands
a1200 *Ancrene* 203.1–2: For swa me seith bi large mon the ne con nawt edhalden, that he haveth the honden, as mine beoth, ithurlet. Ives 265:15.

M128 A leal **Man** is not taken at half a tale
c1475 Henryson *Fables* 79.2288: Ane leill man is not tane at halff ane taill. Whiting *Scots* II 138.

M129 A lither (*bad*) **Man** shall be saved through goodness of a woman
c1300 *South English Legendary* II 530.449–50: For me saith a lither man schal isaved beo Thurf godnisse of a god womman.

M130 Little **Man,** long man, red man (*varied*)
c1250 *Proverbs of Alfred* 133–4 T 646–69: The luttele mon he his so rei, Ne mai non him wonin nei; So word he wole him-selven ten, That is lovird maister he wolde ben, Bute he mote himselven pruden: He wole maken fule luden. He wole grennen cocken and chiden; And hewere faren mid unluden. Yif thu me wld ileven Ne mai me never him quemen. The lonke mon is lethe-bei, Selde comid is herte rei. He havit stoni herte; No-thing him ne smerteth. Bi ford dayes he is aferd Of sticke and ston in huge werd. Yif he fallit in the fen He thetit ut after men. Yif he slit in-to a dige, He is ded witerliche. The rede mon he is a quet, For he wole the thin iwil red. He is cocker thef and horeling Scolde of wrechedome he is king. **c1400** *Brut* I 217.12–3: Ay is in the rede of somme evel shrede. **a1450** *Boke of Curtasye* (*Sloane*) 308.307–10: In no kyn house that rede mon is, Ne womon of tho same colour y-wys, Take never thy Innes for no kyn nede, For those be folke that ar to drede. **c1470** *Harley MS.3362* f.17a: The longe man ys zeld wys, the schort myld zeld ys. The whyth ys ful of cowardys, the red ful of feloni ys. To the blak draw thy knyf, with the brown led thy lyf. Apperson 527; *Oxford* 536, 584; Tilley M155, 395; Whiting *Scots* II 96:19.

M131 Longer lives a glad **Man** than a sorry (*varied*)
c1390 *God man and the devel* 347.705: Lengor liveth a glad mon then a sori. **c1450** *Douce MS.52* 49.57: As long levyth a mery man as a sory. **c1450** *Rylands MS.394* 99.10.12. Apperson 414; *Oxford* 381; Tilley M71; Whiting *Drama* 113, 226. See **L175, M214, 514.**

M132 A **Man** born blind (cannot) play well at chess (paint or write)
a1449 Lydgate *Ryme* in *MP* II 794.74: A blynde borne man to pley wele at chesse. **c1477** Norton *Ordinall* 16[19–22]: For it were a wonderous thing and queinte, A man that never had sight to peinte. How shoulde a borne blinde Man be sure To write or make good Portrature. See **M50.**

M133 **Man** does as he is when he may do as he will
c1025 *Durham Proverbs* 11.14: Man deþ swa he byþ þonne he mot swa he wile. Homo facit sicut fit quando potest sicut vult. **c1150** N. Longchamps (Wireker) *Contra Curiales* in Thomas Wright *Anglo-Latin Satirical Poets . . . of the Twelfth Century* (RS I[1872]) 201[32–4]: Quod Anglico proverbio dicitur, "Cum licet homini

quod libet, tunc demum qualis fuerit prodet." **a1325** *Hendyng C* 185.18: Wan man mai done als he wille, Than doth he als he is. **1340** *Ayenbite* 26[17–9]: Ne sselt thou nevre y-wyte huet man ys: alhuet he ys ther he wyle by. **a1400** *Proverbis of Wysdom* 248.167–8: When man hath, what his wyll is, Then shewyth he, what he is. **c1450** *Bodley MS.15426* f.55a in Brown-Robbins 3990: When man hath what wyll is, Then shewyth he what he is. Kneuer 50; Schleich 270; Singer III 137; Tilley A402.

M134 A **Man** has but one life
c1390 *Northern Homily Cycle Narrationes* (*Vernon*) 305.27: I have, he seide, lyf but on. **a1400** *Firumbras* 27.798: Ne hath eche man but o lyffe, selle ye hyt dere!

M135 A **Man** has knowledge of all thing save of himself
a1393 Gower *CA* III 209.1567–8: Men sein, a man hath knowleching Save of himself of alle thing. *Margin:* Bernardus. Plures plura sciunt et seipsos nesciunt, 229.2313–4: Thou knewe alle othre mennes chance And of thiself hast ignorance. See **K100.**

M136 As **Man** has nothing so lief (*dear*) as his life
c1385 Usk 86.105–6: Pardy, a man hath nothing so leef as his lyf. See **L235.**

M137 A **Man** in peril of drowning catches whatsoever comes next to hand
1534 More *Comforte* 1144 D (*by error* C) [9–16]: Fareth lyke a man that in peril of drowning catcheth whatsoever cometh nexte to hande, and that holdeth he fast be it never so simple a sticke, but then that helpeth him not: for that sticke he draweth down under the water with him, and there lie they drowned both together. Apperson 166; *Oxford* 159; Taylor and Whiting 233; Tilley M92.

M138 **Man** in the moon
c1325 *Man in the Moon* in Brown *Lyrics XIII* 160.1: Mon in the mone stond and strit. **c1385** Chaucer *TC* i 1023–4: Quod Pandarus, "Thow hast a ful gret care Lest that the cherl may falle out of the moone!" **a1449** Lydgate *Fabules* in *MP* II 572.166–7: Deme how the cherle came furst in the mone: Of suche mysteryes I take but lytell hede. **c1449** Pecock *Repressor* I 155[23–6]: As is this opinioun, that a man which stale sumtyme a birthan of thornis was sett in to the moone, there forto abide for evere. **c1475** Henryson *Testament* 114.261–3: And on hir breist ane Churle paintit full evin, Beirand ane bunche of Thornis on his bak, Quhilk for his thift micht clim na nar the hevin. **a1500** *Ancient Scottish Prophecy No. 1* in Lumby *Bernardus de Cura* 21.123: Qwhen the man and (?in) the mone is most in his mycht. **c1522** Skelton *Speke* II 15.307–8: For Jerico and Jerssey shall mete togethyr assone As he to exployte the man owte of the mone. **1528** More *Heresyes* 154 E[10–3]: A good olde ydolater, that never hadde herde . . . of other god then only the man in the mone. **1533** Heywood *Pardoner* B3v[27]: But he wolde here no more than the man in the mone. **1533** More *Confutacion* 542 G[1–2]: Where is no more colour to speake therof then of the man in the mone. **1562** Heywood *E* 233.27.4: Wee say (not the woman) the man in the moone. Apperson 424; *Oxford* 95, 401; Taylor and Whiting 236–7; Tilley M240.

M139 A **Man** in war may not have all pleasance
c1470 *Wallace* 96.710: A man in wer may nocht all plesance haiff. See **H445.**

M140 **Man** is born to labor as the (a) bird to flight
a1393 Gower *CA* II 364.2340–4: The noble wise Salomon, Which hadde of every thing insihte, Seith, "As the briddes to the flihte Ben made, so man is bore to labour." **c1395** *WBible* Job v 7: A man is borun to labour, and a brid to flight. **a1400** *Pricke* 16.542–3: He (*Job*) says, "man es born to travaile right Als a foul es to the flight." **c1400** *Lay Folks' Catechism* 95.1386–7: And therfore we be kendly born to swynke, as the foul is born to fle kendly. **a1402** Trevisa *Dialogus* 71.19–20: Hooly Writ . . . seith: "Man is y-bore to travail and a foul to flight." **a1450** *Song of Mortality* in Brown *Lyrics XIV* 96.5–6: Born ar we, als salomon us hyght, To travel here whils we ar fere, als fouls to the flight. MED flight n. (2) 2(b).

M141 A **Man** is changeable
c1340 Rolle *Psalter* 90 (24.15): A man is chawngabile. See **M647, W526.**

M142 **Man** is oft murderer of his own body by immoderate diet
1515 Barclay *St. George* 58.1294–5: By immoderate dyet: exces and glotony Man oft is mordrer of his owne body. Cf. Tilley M304. See **G167.**

M143 A **Man** (lord) is worth as much as his land is worth (as he has)
1340 *Ayenbite* 90[7–9]: This thi-zelf the myght yzy by skele thet hyer bevore me heth yzed. Zuo moche is worth the man: ase is worth his

land. **c1400** *Vices and Virtues* 88.20–2: An olde resoun that me seith: "As moche as a man hath, so moche is he worth." **c1410** Edward of York *Master* 9[15–7]: For men saiden in olde sawes, so moche is a lord worth as he can make his londis availe. *French (in footnote)*: Tant vaut seigneur tant vaut sa gent et sa terre. **1484** Caxton *Royal Book* H4v[5–7]: Thynke on this proverbe whiche is comunely sayd. As moche is a man worth as his londe is of value, H5r[5–6]. *Oxford* 402.

M144 A **Man** knows not his end
c1395 *WBible* Ecclesiastes ix 12: A man knowith not his ende. See **D96.**

M145 A **Man** may be bold over his kin
c1500 *Everyman* 13.326: For over his kynne a man may be bolde. See **K64.**

M146 A **Man** may be too hasty to come to his enemy
a1533 Berners *Arthur* 214[16–7]: A man may be anone to hasty to come to his enemye. See **M99.**

M147 A **Man** may buy gold too dear
1546 Heywood *D* 83.120: A man may by gold to deere. Apperson 75; *Oxford* 73; Tilley M257.

M148 A **Man** may call with the beck of a finger what he cannot put away with both hands
1520 Whittinton *Vulgaria* 94.24–5: A man may call unto hym with the bekke of a fynger that he can not put away with bothe handes. See **H601.**

M149 A **Man** may contend, God gives victory (*varied*)
c1515 Barclay *Eclogues* 168.780: A man may contende, God geveth victory. **a1533** Berners *Huon* 753.27–8: Men maketh batayles and god gyveth the victory. See **M162, 218.**

M150 A **Man** may handle his dog so that he may make him bite him
1562 Heywood *D* 87.236–7: A man maie handle his dog so, That he maie make him byte him, though he would not. Tilley M258.

M151 A **Man** may love his house well though he ride not on the ridge
1546 Heywood *D* 66.17–8: A man may love his house well, Though he ryde not on the rydge, I have heard tell. Apperson 395; *Oxford* 389; Tilley M266. See **S214.**

M152 A **Man** may not always abide in one place
1523 Berners *Froissart* I 255–6: But alwayes a man may nat abyde in one place.

M153 A **Man** may not put to his eye the salve with which he healed his heel
c1385 Usk 22.44–5: And so may nat a man alway putte to his eye the salve that he heled with his hele.

M154 A **Man** may (not) sin with his wife and (nor) hurt himself with his knife (*varied*)
1340 *Ayenbite* 48[25–7]: And mid oghene zuorde man may him-zelve sle. Alsuo may be mid his oghene wyve zeneye dyedliche. **c1390** Chaucer *CT* X[I] 859: And for that many man weneth that he may nat synne, for no likerousnesse that he dooth with his wyf, certes, that opinion is fals. God woot, a man may sleen hymself with his owene knyf, and make hymselve dronken of his owene tonne, **c1395** IV[E] 1839–40: A man may do no synne with his wyf, Ne hurte hymselven with his owene knyf. **c1400** *Vices and Virtues* 45.8–10: For a man may slen hymself with his owne swerd, and also a man may do dedly synne with his owne wif. **a1449** Lydgate *Order* in *MP* II 453.131: And woundeth hymself with his owne knyf. **c1450** *Jacob's Well* 161.21–3: For As a man may sle him-self, wyth his owne knyif, So he may synne dedly, wyth his owne wyif. **1483** *Quatuor Sermones* 36[24–5]: For as thou mayst slee thy self wyth thyn oune swerde right so thou mayst wyth thyn oune wyf. **1484** Caxton *Royal Book* E6v[8–9]: A man may sle hym self wyth his owen swerde. So a man may synne dedely with his owne wyf, **1489** *Doctrinal* I6v[6–7]: A man may slee hym self wyth hys owne swerd or knyf. Tilley F479.

M155 A **Man** may not wive and thrive all in one year (*varied*)
a1349 *Papelard Priest* 45.90: I may noust wyne (*for* wyve) and thrive al in a yere. **a1460** *Towneley Plays* 103.96–9: It is sayde full ryfe, "A man may not wyfe And also thryfe, And all in a yere." **c1497** Medwall *Fulgens* C5r[11]: I may not wed and thryve all to gether. **a1500** *Jesus College Cambridge MS.22* in M. R. James *Catalogue* (London, 1895) 24. Will still to wiffe woulde leade me, But wit would ytt a rede me Of wyving to be were; Inne Will to Will in wivinge, Or elles farewell all thryving, Awoue ytt well I dere. **c1500** Greene *Carols* 410.13: For hym that cast hym for to thryve, He must aske leve of hys wyff. **1546** Heywood *D* 45.129: It is harde to wive and thryve bothe in a yere. Apperson 631, 701; *Oxford* 721; Tilley Y12. See **S133.**

M156 A **Man** may so long be nourished bv venom that he weens it wholesome meat c1384 ?Purvey *Fifty Heresies* in Wyclif *SEW* III 389[6–7]: As men seyn, a mon may so long be norischid litel and litel by venym, that he wenes hit be holsum meete and gode.

M157 A **Man** may stoop times enough when he shall (*must*) tine (*lose*) the crown (of his head) (*varied*)
c1378 *Piers* B xi 35: A man may stoupe tymes ynow whan he shal tyne the croune. **c1385** Chaucer *TC* iv 1105–6: A man may al bytyme his nekke beede Whan it shal of, and sorwen at the nede. **c1475** Henryson *Fables* 62.1766–7: The nek to stoup, quhen it the straik sall get, Is sone aneuch. *Oxford* 623; Tilley T305.

M158 A **Man** must be a fool, or young or old
c1385 Chaucer *CT* I[A] 1811–2: But all moot ben assayed, hoot and coold; A man moot ben a fool, or yong or oold.

M159 A **Man** of small stature oft rescues a lord of high honor
c1475 Henryson *Fables* 54.1499–1500: For oft is sene ane man off small stature Reskewit hes ane Lord off hie honoure. Whiting *Scots* II 95. Cf. Tilley W182. See **M483, S44, T113.**

M160 A **Man** ought to dread the brand that burnt him in his hand
a1325 *Cursor* II 418.7223–4: Sare man aght to dred the brand, That brint him forwit in his hand. See **C201.**

M161 A **Man** ought to seignory (*rule*) over riches and not serve them
1474 Caxton *Chesse* 111[29–32]: And therfore hit is sayd in proverbe that a man ought to seignorye over the riches and not for to serve hit and yf thou canst dewly use thy rychesse than she is thy chamberyer. Cf. Tilley R113.

M162 **Man** proposes and God disposes
c1378 *Piers* B xi 36–7: "*Homo proponit,*" quod a poete and Plato he hyght, "And *deus disponit,*" quod he, "lat god done his wille," xx 34: *Homo proponit et deus disponit.* **a1439** Lydgate *Fall* I 292.3291–4: A man off malice may a thyng purpose Bi a maner froward provydence; But God a-bove can graciousli dispose Ageyn such malice to make resistence. **a1450** *Goodly Balade* in Skeat *Chaucerian* 406.43–5: *Je vouldray:*—but (the) grete(e) god disposeth And maketh casuel by his providence Such thing as mannes frele wit purposeth. **c1470** *Harley MS.3362* f.2b in *Retrospective* 309[18]: A man purposyt, God dysposyt. **c1471** *Gaudete justi* in *Archiv* 130 (1913) 310.33–5: Homo proponit, oftymes in veyn, But deus disponit, The boke telleth pleyn. Quy serra serra. **a1500** *Imitatione* (*1*) 22.5: Ffor man purposith and god disposith. **c1500** *Melusine* 265.11–2: But as the wyse man saith "the fole proposeth and god dysposeth." **1502** *Imitatione* (*2*) 167.1–2: For man entendeth, but god disposeth. **1509** Fisher *Treatyse* 222.20–1: It is a comyn proverbe. Homo proponit et deus disponit. Man purposeth and god dysposeth. **1509** Watson *Ship* F9r[20–2]: For it is a comyn proverbe all aboute, man dothe purpose and god dothe dyspose, Ff7r[24–6]: For as it is sayd comynly all aboute, the man purposeth and god dysposeth. **1513** Bradshaw *St. Werburge* 40.930: Tho man prepose god dysposed all. Apperson 397; *Oxford* 403; Taylor and Whiting 235; Tilley M298; Walther II 346.11102. See **M149, 218.**

M163 A **Man's** adventure (*chance*) shall betide him at last
c1330 *Gregorius* 97 A 489–92: Mani man wendeth (*var.* walken) fer and wide, Moche may heren and sen among, Atte last him schal bitide His aventour be it never so strong. See **M239, 243.**

M164 A **Man's** hap (*luck*) is not ay (*ever the same*)
c1425 *Avowynge* 71[6–8]: A mon's happe is notte ay, Is none so sekur of a say, Butte he may harmes hente. See **F523, H98.**

M165 **Man's** life is but a shade
a1325 *Sarmun* in Heuser 93.153–4: Man is lif nis bot a schade, Nou he is and nou he nis. See **L241.**

M166 A **Man's** wit is never understood till at a great need
c1500 *Three Kings' Sons* 127.1–2: It is alwey saide that a mannys witte ys nevir undirstond til at a grete nede. See **W536.**

M167 A **Man** shall be known by his deeds and not by his looks (*varied*)
c1422 Hoccleve *Complaint* 102.202–3: Man by his dedes and not by his lokes, Shall knowne be, as it is writen in bokes. **c1475** Henryson *Fables* 97.2838–9: Thairfoir I find this Scripture in all place: Thow suld not Juge ane man efter his face. See **F1, M342.**

M168 A **Man** shall (*ought to*) have good will
c1300 *Havelok* 23.600: For man shal god wille have. *Oxford* 257.

M169 A **Man** shall love his friend by measure and not hate his enemy overmuch
1481 Caxton *Reynard* 75[4–5]: A man shal love

his frende by mesure and not his enemye hate overmoche. Tilley T309.

M170 A **Man** should be chastised by another (*varied*)
a1338 Mannyng *Chronicle B* II 289[19]: Allas! non with other chastised yit wille be. **c1375** Barbour *Bruce* I 6.121–2: And wyss men sayis he is happy, That be othir will him chasty. **c1420** Wyntoun V 171.209–12: Qwha will be othir hym self chasty, Happy may he be callyt for thi; Wysse men sayis he is happy, That can tak sampil at othir hym by. **a1449** Lydgate *Examples* in *MP* II 445.101–2: But who-so listeth not by othir hym-silf chastice, Othir woll by hym, whan he shall it rewe. **1436** *Libelle* 25.480–1: Therefore beware, I can no better wylle, Yf grace it woll, of other mennys perylle, 99 (*var.*) [7–12]: A proverbe saithe that is ful oolde And in many langages tolde, That signe hit ys and demonstracion And of grace a grete probacion Whan men be waar of theyr infelicitie Be other mennes dedys, what so they be. **a1450** *Castle* 155.2616–8: I lete a man no bettyr thanne a best, For no man can be war be other Tyl he hathe al ful spunne. **c1450** Idley 150.2624–5: Who will not be ware by othir mennes correccioun, Othir men by hym shal be chastised. **c1470** *Harley MS.3362* f.2a in *Retrospective* 309[6]: and Förster 200.6: He ys an happy man, that ys war be anothyr mannys dedys. *Est felix culpa quem castigat aliena.* **c1475** Gregory *Chronicle* 230[20]: But one fryer couthe not be ware by a nother. **1477** Rivers *Dictes* 86[33–5]: And said a man that is not to be correctid by other men, may surly correcte them of their faultes, **1478** *Morale Proverbes* [2.23–4]: He is happy that can exemple take Of his neighburgh, seing him sorwes make. **1483** Caxton *Golden Legende* 334v[1.17–8]: He is blessyd that can beware by other mennes harmes. **a1500** *MS. Marginalia* in Hoccleve I 224 n.[2]: *Felix quem faciunt aliena pericula cautum:* Fortunate is he who hathe the happe To bewarre by an-other mannes clappe. **1509** *Fyftene Joyes* A6v[6]: There is not one by other can be ware. **1511** Hawes *Comforte* C5v[11–3]: But evermore it is an olde sayd sawe, Examples past dooth theche one to withdrawe Frome all suche perylles. **1513** Douglas *Aeneid* II 149.90–1: Thar beyn bot few exempil takis of othir, Bot wilfully fallys in the fyre. **1549** Heywood *D* 51.337: It is good to beware by other mens harmes, **1556** *Spider* 374[1]: Wyse ants are warnd: by other ants harmes (ants say). *Oxford* 43; Tilley M612, 615; Walther II 47.8952. See **A118, B309, C40, 161, E197, L247, M581, 585, W47, 391, 719.**

M171 A **Man** should blame or commend as he finds
c1449 Pecock *Repressor* I 48[11–3]: The oolde wiis proverbe, *A man schulde blame or commende as he fyndeth.* Apperson 109.

M172 A **Man** should keep from the blind and give to his kin
1461 Paston IV 12–3: And it is a comon proverbe, "A man xuld kepe fro the blynde and gevyt to is kyn." Apperson 395. See **C153.**

M173 **Man** should not praise nor blame himself
c1300 *South English Legendary* II 534–5.43–5: For in his boc the wise man Catoun saith also That man neschal him silve preise ne blame nothemo For so doth foles that beoth idreight with veyne glorie and prute. **c1390** *Cato* (*Vernon*) 581.345–6: Preise no mon him-selven, Ne blame him-self also. **a1400** *Cato* (*Copenhagen*) A6v[9–10]: Loke thou noo preisyng of thy selfe make, Ne yit thy selfe thou shulde nough(t) lacke. **a1440** Burgh *Cato* 315.494–5: Thi silfe also looke that thou nat preise Ne dispreise, but lette othir men allone. **c1450** *Rylands MS.394* 99.20: Preyse not thi selfe ne lak not thy nowgh werk. Whiting *Drama* 242. Cf. Apperson 396; Tilley A26, M476. See **D155, P351.**

M174 A **Man** should not trust on a broke(n) sword, *etc.*
1460 Paston III 213–4: Et est commune et vulgare dictum: "A man schuld not trusty on a broke swerd, ne on a fool, ne on a chylde, ne on a dobyl man, ne on a drunke man."

M175 **Man** should wed his similitude
c1390 Chaucer *CT* I[A] 3227–8: He knew nat Catoun, for his wit was rude, That bad man sholde wedde his simylitude. Smith 193. See **B363, C401, L272, 551, M254, Y33.**

M176 A **Man** should work ever by sapience
a1500 *O man more* 394.20–1: For as I have redde in Seneca sentence: A man shulde worke ever by sapience. See **C470.**

M177 A **Man** that bears him stout when he should bow, if in chance he lout (*stoop*) he finds foes enow
a1338 Mannyng *Chronicle B* II 296.13–4: A man that beris him stoute, whan he suld bowe, In chance if that he loute, he findes foos inowe. Cf. Tilley M194, 235.

M178 A **Man** that goes upon plain ground has nothing to stumble at
1471 Caxton *Recuyell* II 516.11–2: A man that goth upon playn ground hath no thynge to stomble at.

M179 A **Man** that has a wart above his shin shall need none of his kin
a1500 *National Library of Wales Peniarth MS.356* p. 297 in Robbins-Cutler 69.5: A mon that hathe a wart abowne his schin, he schall never need non of hys kyn.

M180 The **Man** that has little is soon loathed
a1200 Lawman I 129–30.3057–8: For sone heo bith ilagheth The mon the lutel ah (*B* For sone hi beoth lothe, The men the lutel ogheth), 147.3463–5: For heo me seiden alre sohust (*B* sothest) That he bithe unworth and lah, The mon the litul ah. See **P295.**

M181 The **Man** that in his youth learns yerne (*eagerly*) may be in eld a wenlich (*excellent*) lorthew (*teacher*)
a1300 *Proverbs of Alfred* 81 J °96–°101: The mon the on his youhthe Yeorne leorneth Wit and wisdom And i-writen reden He may beon on elde Wenliche lortheu. *Oxford* 358. See **M407, Y32.**

M182 A **Man** that is weary is half overcome
1489 Caxton *Fayttes* 63.28–9: For a man that is wery is half over come.

M183 The **Man** that long enjoys life must endure pleasure and pain
c735 *Beowulf* 1060–2: Fela sceal gebidan Leofes ond laþes se þe longe her On ðyssum windagum worolde bruceð.

M184 **Man** that tells many things, some must needs be false
c1390 *Cato* (*Vernon*) 582.363–4: Mon that telleth mony thinges, Ffals most nede sum beo. See **L67, W593.**

M185 A **Man** that weds a wife when he winks (*has his eyes shut*), it is a wonder but he stare afterwards
a1500 *Trials of Marriage* in Robbins 37.3–4: A man that wedyth a wyfe whan he wynkyth, But he star afterward, wonder me thynkyth!

M186 A **Man** without reason is worse than blind
c1450 *Consail and Teiching* 71.194: Fore man but resone is ver na blind. **a1500** Medwall *Nature* E1ᵛ[26]: Man wythout reson ys but blynde.

M187 A **Man** wot when he goes, but he wot not when he comes
c1450 *Douce MS.52* 49.56: A man wote, when he goes; but he wote not, when he comys. **c1450** *Rylands MS.394* 98.27: but he not when. **c1470** *Harley MS.3362* f.4a: A man wot whan he goth, But he not whan he comyth.

M188 Many (a) **Man** begins well and ends with much unsele (*misery*)
c1390 *Northern Homily Cycle Narrationes* (*Vernon*) 308.117–8: Ffor mony men bi ginneth wel, And endeth with ful muchel uncel. See **B200.**

M189 Many (a) **Man** does much evil all his unthanks (*unwillingly*)
a1200 Lawman I 353.8279–82: Whilen hit wes iseid Inne soth spelle, That moni mon deth muchel uvel, Al his unthankes. Skeat 7.

M190 Many (a) **Man** for aught (*property*) hastes (*succeeds*) evilly
c1250 *Proverbs of Alfred* 100 T 270–5: For moni mon for achte Ivele ihasted, And ofte mon on faire Fokel chesed. Wo is him that ivel wif Brinhit to is cotlif. See **M191.**

M191 Many (a) **Man** for land wives to shond (*disgrace*)
c1325 *Hendyng H* 299.280: Monimon for londe wyveth to shonde. Apperson 398; Kneuer 57–8; *Oxford* 404–5; Schleich 273; Singer III 139; Skeat 92. See **M190.**

M192 Many a **Man** has been taken and then delivered again
c1400 *Alexander Buik* II 152.1949–50: For mony ane man hes bene tane And syne delyverit weill agane. See **F533.**

M193 Many (a) **Man** is slipper (*unreliable*) of tongue
a1475 *Ludus Coventriae* 93.346–7: And as we redyn in old sage Many man is sclepyr of tonge.

M194 Many (a) **Man** sings that wife home brings; wist he what he brought he might weep
a1300 *Proverbs of Alfred* 101 J 280–3: Monymon singeth That wif hom bryngeth; Wiste he hwat he brouhte, Wepen he myhte. **c1325** *Hendyng H* 293.133–8: Monimon syngeth When he hom bringeth Is yonge wyf; Wyste whet he broghte, Wepen he mohte Er syth his lyf. Apperson 398; Kneuer 53–5; *Oxford* 404; Skeat 78. For Low German versions, see *Anglia* 3(1880) 370 and *Jahrbuch des Vereins für niederdeutsche Sprachforschung* 14(1888) 134.51, 144.46.

M195 Many a **Man** speaks of marriage that wot no more of it than does my page
c1395 Chaucer *CT* IVE 1443–4: Ther speketh many a man of mariage That woot namoore of it than woot my page. See **R156.**

M196 Many (a) **Man** speaks to me fair(ly) that had leifer break my head than help me over a stile (*varied*)
c1450 Greene *Carols* 384.5: Many man, fayre to me he spekyt, And he wyste hym wel bewreke; He hadde we(l) levere myn hed tobreke Thann help me over a style. **c1460** *Take Good Heed* 206.2–4: Ffor som that speke ful fayre, thei wolde your evil spede; Though thei pere in your presence with a fayre face, And her tunge chaunged, the hert is as it was. **1471** Paston V 127[2–3]: Therefore be ware of symulacion, for thei wull speke ryht fayr to you that wuld ye ferd right evyll. See **D122, S512, 618, W581.**

M197 Many (a) **Man** (that) calls another a fool is twice so much a fool
a1400 *Ipomadon A* 184.6436–40: But ofte is sayd be men of skole, Many man callys another a foole, Well sought yff it wore, Hym selff in suche a chaunce myghte be, He is twys so moche foule as hee.

M198 Many (a) **Man** threats and speaks that were better to be stone still
a1352 Minot 5.31–2: Bot many man thretes and spekes ful ill That sum tyme war better to be stane still.

M199 Many (a **Man**) weens to do well that does all to wonder (*evil*)
a1200 *Ancrene* 39.6–7: Moni weneth to do wel, the deth al to wundre (*Nero:* cweade). **c1450** *Rylands MS.394* 93.22: Many on wenys to do well, and don alle to wede.

M200 Many a **Man** weens to put his enemy to rebuke and oft it falls on himself
a1470 Malory I 69.2–3: For many a man wenyth to put hys enemy to a rebuke, and ofte hit fallith on hymselff. See **D22, P232, S193.**

M201 Many (a) **Man** weens, what he tharf (*needs*) not to ween, to have a friend
a1300 *Proverbs of Alfred* 107 J 317–22: Monymon weneth That he weny ne tharf, Freond that he habbe, Thar me him vayre bi-hat; Seyth him vayre bi-vore, And frakele bi-hynde.

M202 Many **Men** many minds (*varied*)
c900 *Maxims* in *Exeter Book* 162.167: Swa monige beoþ men ofer eorþan, swa beoþ modgeþoncas. **a1325** *Cursor* III 1483 C 26067: O (*Of*) sere men sere opinion. **c1390** Chaucer *CT* II[B] 211: Diverse men diverse thynges seyden, **c1395** IVE 1469–70: Diverse men diversely hym tolde Of mariage manye ensamples olde. **a1400** *Cato* (*Copenhagen*) A3[r][4]: For feele men feele thyngys wil say. **a1400** *Scottish Legends* I 235.468: For syndry men sais thingis sere. **a1425** Mirk *Instructions* 47.1536: For mony men fulle dyvers ar. **1456** Hay *Law* 79.1–3: Thare is a decretale in the lawis canoun, the quhilk sais, that Als mony men, als mony divers willis is in this warld. **c1475** *Lett lowe to lowe* in *Anglia* 73(1956) 300[13–6]: Dyvers lows divers dysposicians, Dyvers men divers condosconys, Dyvers wemen dyvers tucyions, Divers promysys and Repromcycians. **1483** *Vulgaria quedam abs Terencio* Q3[v][8]: Many men many opinyons. **1525** Berners *Froissart* V 105[9–10]: Men spake therof in dyvers maners, every man after his owne opynion. Apperson 586; *Oxford* 406; Taylor and Whiting 235; Tilley M583; Whiting *Drama* 136, 245. See **F370, H230.**

M203 Many **Men** speak many things and therefore little faith is to be given
a1500 *Imitatione* (*1*) 111.31–2: Many men spekith many thinges, and therfore litel feithe is to be yoven. **1502** *Imitatione* (*2*) 230.7–8: Many folke say many thynges and therfore lytle feyth is to be gyven. See **L67.**

M204 Many (Young) **Men** ween, what they need not ween, long life (*varied*)
c1000 *Be rihtan Cristendome* in Napier 147.23–6: þa geongan men hopiað, þæt hi moton lange on þissere worulde libban, ac se hopa hi bepæcð and beswicð, þonne him leofost wære, þæt hi lybban moston. **c1250** *Death's Wither-Clench* in Brown *Lyrics XIII* 15.1–2: Man mei longe him lives wene, Ac oft him liyet the wreinch. **c1250** *Hendyng O* 200.47: Mani man weneth that he wene ne tharf, longe to liven and him lieth the wrench. **c1250** *Proverbs of Alfred* 88 T 153–60: Monimon wenit That he wenen ne tharf Longes livis, Ac him scal leghen that wrench, For thanne he is lif Alre beste trowen, Thenne sal he letin Lif his oghene. **c1275** *Kentish Sermons* in Morris *Old English Miscellany* 36[4–5]: For Man mai longe lives wene and ofte him legheth se wrench. **c1325** *Hendyng H* 299.304: Hope of long lyf gyleth mony god wyf. **a1333** Shoreham *Poems* 2.27–8: Yet meni yong man weneth longe leve, And leveth wel litle wyle. **1340** *Ayenbite* 129–30: And thervore zayth the guode man, "Man may longe his lyves wene and ofte him lyegheth his wrench,

ase vayr weder went in-to rene and verliche maketh his blench. The ne is nother king ne kuene thet ne ssel drinke of deathes drench. Man thervore the bethench er thou valle of thi bench thi zenne aquench." **c1400** *Vices and Virtues* 183.15–7: The ferthe thing is hope of long lif, as the devel seith hem, "thu art yong; thou schalt lyve longe." Kneuer 48–9; *Oxford* 303; Schleich 268–9; Singer III 136–7. See **H468, M41, 385.**

M205 Men are blind in their own case (*varied*)
c1422 Hoccleve *Complaint* 101.169–71: And there-with-all I thowght(e) thus anon: "Men in theyr owne case bene blynd alday, As I have hard say many a day agon." **1474** Caxton *Chesse* 39[17–9]: For every man is lasse avysed and worse in is owne feet and cause than in an other mans. **1546** Heywood *D* 77.230: And folk oft tymes ar most blind in their owne cause. Apperson 55; *Oxford* 50; Tilley M540. See **M244.**

M206 Men can make fair words enough till they have their lust
a1450 *Partonope* 230.6017–8: For fayre wordes men can make I-nowe, tyll they have here luste. See **P326.**

M207 Men in their own country shall oft speed (*succeed*) though (?) they be less
c1400 *Laud Troy* I 112.3779–80: For offte men In theire owne contre Scholde spede ȝow (?thow [*though*]), ther were less then we. See **C350, F570, R45.**

M208 Men love of proper kind newfangleness
c1395 Chaucer *CT* V[F] 610–1: Men loven of propre kynde newefangelnesse, As briddes doon that men in cages fede. See **N28, T142.**

M209 Men may be overwise in many matters
c1450 Capgrave *Katharine* 129.844: In many maters men may ben overe-wyse!

M210 Men (Friends) may meet at unset steven (*time*)
c1350 *Smaller Vernon Collection* 34.548–9: Thulke were frendes of long tyme met, Theos weoren unknowen, and no stevene set. **c1385** Chaucer *CT* I[A] 1523–4: It is ful fair a man to bere hym evene, For al day meeteth men at unset stevene. **c1390** *Make Amends* in Brown *Lyrics XIV* 199.81–3: Loke thou bere the feir and even, Thaugh thou be lord, Bayli, othur Meire, For ofte men meten at un-set steven. **a1400** *Eglamour* 86.1273–5: It es sothe sayd, by God of heven, That ofte metis men at un-sett stevyn; For sothe, sa did thay thare! **a1400** *Proverbis of Wysdom* 244.26: Att unsett steven men may mete. **a1420** Lydgate *Troy* I 76.2163–5: And this contek, in ernes and no game, Juparted was betwixe Love and Schame, Metyng to-gidre ther at un-set stevene. **c1450** Idley 162.197–8: And at unset steven this gentilmen met With this galaunt undir a forest side, 166.439: And at unsette tyme they mette at a gate. **a1461** *John the Reeve* 561.92: Oft men meete att unsett steven. **a1500** *Counsels* in Brown *Lyrics XV* 284.52: Ffor ofte mene mete at un-sette stevene. **a1500** *Guy*[4] 68.1997: Nowe we be mette at unsette steven. Skeat 217; Whiting *Ballad* 24, *Scots* II 95–6. See **G50.**

M211 Men must suffer to have better
c1489 Caxton *Blanchardyn* 68.24–5: Men must suffre for better to have. See **L233.**

M212 Men of war are not good companiers with ladies and gentlewomen
c1500 *Three Kings' Sons* 36.19–20: It is a comon seyyng that men of warre be not good companyers with ladies and gentilwomen.

M213 Men ought not to put at their feet that which they hold with their hands
1483 Caxton *Cato* F7[r][13–5]: For the comyn proverbe sayth that men oughte never to put at theyr feet that whyche they holde wyth theyr handes, I7[v][22–4]: Therfore sayth the proverbe that one ought not to sette and putte at his feet that which he holdeth in his handes.

M214 Men should make merry while they may
c1400 *Alexander Buik* II 244.4879–80: Men suld mak mirrie quhill thay mocht, For dis-cumfort availyeis nocht! See **L175, M131, 514.**

M215 Men should speed to help them that have great need (*varied*)
c1300 *Guy*[1] 108 A 1909–10: Hem to help men schul spede That to help han gret nede. **1484** Caxton *Royal Book* R6[r][10–1]: For as it is woned to be sayd, unto the moost nede ought one alleweye to renne.

M216 Men that are in high estate ofttimes come to low degree
c1440 *Prose Alexander* 9.33–5: For men sees ofte tymes men that ere in heghe astate com to lawe degree, and men that ere in lawe de-gree, come till heghe astate. See **D156, E149, H377.**

M217 Men without a lord are as sheep with-out a shepherd
a1533 Berners *Huon* 747.19–20: For men with-out a lorde are as shepe without a sheparde. See **F372, H257, L60.**

M218 Men work and Fortune judges
a1533 Berners *Castell* F4v[15–7]: Thou knowyst that men workyth, and fortune judgith. See **M149, 162.**

M219 Mishearing **Men** bewray (*malign*) me
c1250 *Hendyng O* 198.38: Misherinde men he me biwreien. Kneuer 60; Schleich 275; Singer III 140–1.

M220 Mortal **Man** shall pass away as a flower turns to hay
c1490 Ryman 266.3[5–7]: Seint James seith: "As a floure newe By hete of sonne turneth to hay, So mortall man shall passe away." See **F326.**

M221 The much (*great*) **Men** should not blame the little
c1500 *Heartless Mistress* in Robbins 140.17–8: Ffor Caton redeth in verses by ryme, The moche men shuld nat the lytyll blame.

M222 No **Man** but himself knows what sticks him
c1200 *Hali Meidenhad* 10.97–8: Nat thah na mon bute ham seolfen hwet ham sticheth ofte. Cf. Tilley M129. See **G186, S266.**

M223 No **Man** can be in every place at once
1509 Barclay *Ship* I 160[21]: Syns no man can be atonys in every place. *Oxford* 454–5; Tilley M221.

M224 No **Man** can escape love (*varied*)
c1385 Chaucer *TC* i 241–2: Men reden nat that folk han gretter wit Than they that han be most with love ynome, 976–9: For this have I herd seyd of wyse lered, Was nevere man or womman yet bigete That was unapt to suffren loves hete, Celestial, or elles love of kynde. **a1393** Gower *CA* II 5.75–6: Of love, which doth many a wonder And many a wys man hath put under, 47–8.440–4: For so wys man was nevere non, Bot if he wel his yhe kepe And take of fol delit no kepe, That he with lust nys ofte nome, Thurgh strengthe of love and overcome, 57.769–72: It is and hath ben evere yit, That so strong is no mannes wit, Which thurgh beaute ne mai be drawe To love, 258.1194–5: Love is of so gret a miht, His lawe mai noman refuse, 263.1355–7: To folwe thilke lore and suie Which nevere man yit miht eschuie; And that was love. **a1400** *Ipomadon A* 25.806–8: Who entrys in to lovys scolys, The wyseste is holdyn moste foolys, Fro that they have graunte. Tilley L496, 529, 531. See **L477.**

M225 No **Man** can know his ure (*fate*)
a1440 Burgh *Cato* 320.720: No man can know his ure.

M226 No **Man** can look into another's breast
1528 More *Heresyes* 105 G[5–6]: Sith no man can loke into an others breste. See **E214, M35.**

M227 No **Man** can serve two lords (masters)
a900 Alfred *Gregory* 129.23–4: Ne mæg nan mon twam hlafordum hieran. **c1000** Aelfric *Homilies* II 460[22–5]: Drihten cwæð . . . "Ne mæg nan man twam hlafordum samod ðeowian; oððe he ðone ænne hatað and ðone oðerne lufað, oððe he hine to ðam anum geðeot and ðone oðerne forsihð," *Lives* I 378.219–20: And ure drihten cwæð þæt man gecwæman ne mæg Twam hlafordum æt-somne, þæt he ne forseo þone oðerne. **c1000** *Sermo* in Napier 298.4–8: And swa man mot oðrum twegra hyran, gode ælmihtigum and his beboda healdan, oððe þan earman deofle anrædlice fyljan; forþan nis na ma hlafordinga on worulde, þonne twegen, god ælmihtig and deofol. **c1000** *WSG* Matthew vi 24: Ne mæg nan man twam hlafordum þeowian; oððe he soðlice ænne hatað and oðerne lufað, oððe he bið anum gehyrsum and oðrum ungehyrsum. Ne magon ge Gode þeowian and woruldwelan, Luke xvi 13. **c1225** *Cotton Vespasian Homilies* in R. Morris *Old English Homilies . . . First Series* (EETS 29, 34, 1867–8) 241[28–9]: *Nemo potest duobus dominis servire.* Nan ne mai twan hlaforde the wransehte bien samod thowie. **c1300** *South English Legendary* II 384.11: He understod wel that me nemighte twei loverdes servi noght. **a1325** *Cursor* III 1504.26816–7: For mai naman wit quem to winn To serve at ans laverds tuin. **c1330** *Times of Edward II* 325.43–4: But everi man may wel i-wite, who so take yeme, That no man may wel serve tweie lordes to queme. **a1393** Gower *CA* II 28.860–2: For Crist himself makth knowleching That noman may togedre serve God and the world. **c1395** *WBible* Matthew vi 24: No man may serve tweyn lordis, for ethir he schal hate the toon, and love the tother; ethir he shal susteyne the toon, and dispise the tothir. Ye moun not serve God and richessis, Luke xvi 13. **a1400** *Ancrene* (*Recluse*) 48.6–7: Nemo potest duobus dominis servire, &c. Noman seith oure lorde may serve two lordes to queme, 94.8–9. **a1400** *Pricke* 31.1104–5: He says "na man may serve rightly Twa lordes to-gedir, that er contrary." **a1400** Wyclif *Sermons* I 36[11]: First seith Crist . . . that no man may wel serve two fulle lordes. **c1409** *Good makynge* in Kail 32.30: Thou mayst not serve two lordis to pay.

1411 *Good steryng* in Kail 45.149–50: Ye may not serve two lordis to plese, Ffede fatte shep in greceles lese. **c1425** *Orcherd* 294.16–7. **a1449** Lydgate *Ryme* in *MP* II 792.9–10: A man that usith to serve lordis twayne, The whiche holdith contrary to oone oppynioun. **a1450** Audelay 37.745–6: Who may serve two lordis and bothe to here pay, That is, this wyckyd word and God to plesyng? **a1450** *South English Legendary (Bodley)* 317.255–6: Ffor noman ne may servy: I-fere lordus two, Yif that hy ben witherward, and paye hem alle bo. **c1450** *Speculum Christiani (2)* 18.2–4: No man may serven two lordes contrarie, for other he schal hate on and love another, or he schal draw to that on and despise that other. **1474** Paston V 209[3–4]: Quia duobus dominis nemo potest servire. **c1477** Caxton *Jason* 57.29–30: For no man may wel serve two maistres, for that one corumpeth that other, **1483** *Golden Legende* 106r[2.10–1]: Ther may noman serve two lordes whiche ben contrarye to other, **1484** *Aesop* 70[1–3]: None maye do no good to two lordes at ones whiche ben contrary one to that other, [20–2]: And therfore he that wylle serve two lordes contrary one to other may-not be good ne trewe. **1509** Barclay *Ship* I 103[4–7]: Rightso is he (*a fool*) that wolde undertake Hym to two lordes servaunt to make For whether, that he be lefe or lothe The one he shall displease, or els bothe, 104[6–7]: He that togyder wyll two maysters serve Shall one displease and nat his love deserve. **1509** Watson *Ship* E3r[12–3]: For one can not two maysters serve At ones, E3v[1–5]. **1523** Berners *Froissart* II 150[9–10]: He coude nat acquyte hymselfe trewely to serve two lordes. **1534** More *Comforte* 1228 G[3–4]: No manne may serve twoo Lordes at once. Apperson 449; *Oxford* 455; Taylor and Whiting 239; Tilley G253, M322; Whiting *Scots* I 203–4. See **W115, 119.**

M228 No **Man** commands surely but he that has learned to obey
a1500 *Imitatione (1)* 24.14–5: No man surely comaundith but he that hath lerned to obeye. **1502** *Imitatione (2)* 168.21–2: And none that surely commaundeth but they that be redy to be obedyent. See **G407, M402, 407, S856, T50.**

M229 No **Man** dies without heir
1401 *Treuth, reste, and pes* in Kail 13.123: Withouten heire dyeth no man. Cf. Tilley L54.

M230 No **Man** has all
c1515 Barclay *Eclogues* 149.268: No man hath all, this thing is true doubtlesse.

M231 No **Man** has too many friends
c1025 *Durham Proverbs* 10.4: Nafað ænig mann freonda to feala. Amicos plures nemo habet.

M232 No **Man** holds the plow so well that he does not balk (*leave a ridge unplowed*) otherwhile (*at times*)
a1393 Gower *CA* II 240.514–5: Bot so wel halt noman the plowh That he ne balketh otherwhile. See **M235.**

M233 No **Man** is so hardy that another is not also
a1400 *Perceval* 47.1451–2: Es there no man so hardy, That ne a-nothir es alswa. Tilley M343. See **D283.**

M234 No **Man** is so wise that one may not beswike (*deceive*) him
a1200 Lawman I 32.753–4: Nis nawer nan so wis mon, That me ne mai bi-swiken, **c1300** II *B* 211.15182–3: Ac thar nis no man so wis, That me ne mai bi-swike. Apperson 450, 698:48; *Oxford* 718; Tilley M344.

M235 No **Man** is without fault (sin) (*varied*)
a900 Alfred *Gregory* 145.14–5: Forðæm nan man nis ðe eallunga sua libban mæge ðæt (he) hwilum ne agylte. **c900** *Old English Cato* 3.19: Geðænc þu þæt nan man nis lehterleas. **c1000** *Larspell* in Napier 233.23–4: Ne bið þeah næfre nan man leahterleas ne synleas ealra þinga. **c1300** *South English Legendary* II 413.344: Thulke man nas nevere ibore that among ne dude wou. **c1340** Rolle *Psalter* 144 (38.11): For naman is withouten syn, 423 (118.87): For nane is sa parfite man in erth, that he ne has outher fallyn, or bene in poynte to fall. **a1400** *Bonum Est* 51.4: No mon mai liven in this lyf that he ne schal sinne sum-tyme. **c1450** Hay *Alexander* 23[2.13]: Thair is na man vithe out sum falt may vret. **c1450** *Ponthus* 105.15: Ther is noo body bot that he has sume tache. **1509** Fisher *Treatyse* 23.28–9: No creature lyveth that never dyde amysse, 33.32: I praye you who lyveth that never synned, *Henry VII* 286.23–4: Noo man that lyveth here can be assured not to fall. **1509** Watson *Ship* Ff7r[13–5]: For there is none but that he may fayle somtyme and yf he be never so cunnynge nor wyse. Apperson 189; Jente 545; *Oxford* 178; Smith 98; Tilley M116; Whiting *Scots* II 95:9. See **L255, M232, T144.**

M236 No **Man** knows bliss that never endured woe (*varied*)
a1200 *Trinity College Homilies* 33[2]: Ne wot no man hwat blisse is, the navre wowe ne bod. **c1385** Chaucer *TC* i 640–1: Ne no man may

ben inly glad, I trowe, That nevere was in sorwe or som destresse. See **W255.**

M237 No **Man** loves his fetters, be they made of gold
1549 Heywood *D* 32.38: No man loveth his fetters, be they made of gold. Apperson 387:13; *Oxford* 393; Tilley M338. See **H604.**

M238 No **Man** may always have prosperity
c1395 Chaucer *CT* IV[E] 810: No man may alwey han prosperitee.

M239 No **Man** may (do) against (refuse his fatal) chance
a1300 *Arthour and M.*[1] 32.1041–2: Man, wele wot, that ani gode kan, Ogain chaunce no may no man. **a1420** Lydgate *Troy* III 740.6005: For no man may his fatal chaunce refuse. **a1425** *Arthour and M.*[2] 326.1101–2, 941–2. **c1500** *Arthour and M.*[3] I 455.1054–5. See **M163, 243.**

M240 No **Man** may have perfect bliss in earth and also in heaven
c1395 Chaucer *CT* IV[E] 1637–9: I have . . . herd seyd, ful yoore ago, Ther may no man han parfite blisses two,—This is to seye, in erthe and eek in hevene.

M241 No **Man** may have that high cunning to know what shall befall
c1400 *Beryn* 11.307–8: Ne no man of us alle May have that highe connyng, to know what shal be-falle. See **C139.**

M242 No **Man** may live so right(ly) that (he) has power to flee death
a1338 Mannyng *Chronicle B* II 339[16–8]: May no man lyve so right, no so wele him yeme, No so stalworth be, ne so douhtį of dede, That has powere to fle the dede that is to drede.

M243 No **Man** may withsay his hap (*fortune*)
a1393 Gower *CA* II 252.978: Ther mai noman his happ withsein. See **M163, 239.**

M244 No **Man** ought to be judge in his own cause (*varied*)
c1449 Pecock *Repressor* II 381[17]: Noman oughte be juge in his owne cause which he hath anentis his neighbour. **1456** Hay *Law* 257.18–9: For the lawe civile sais, that na man suld be juge in his awin cause. **c1456** Pecock *Faith* 196–7: Thanne makist thou thi silf juge in thin owne cause, and forto so do it is over myche perilose in maters of lasse charge than these ben. *Oxford* 328; Smith 162; Tilley M341. See **M205.**

M245 No **Man's** chance is always fortunate
1420 Lydgate *Temple* 17.402: Non manis chaunce is alwai fortunate.

M246 No **Man** shall die ere his day
c1425 *Avowynge* 90[1–4]: Then owre feloys con say, Schalle nomon dee or his day, Butte he cast him selfe a-way, Throghhe wontyng of witte. Taylor and Whiting 236:28. See **H599.**

M247 No **Man** travails to wit things that he wot
c1380 Chaucer *Boece* V m. iii 24–6: As who seith, nay; for no man ne travaileth for to witen thingis that he wot.

M248 No manly **Man** will cast all perils
1519 Horman *Vulgaria* 286[13]: No manly man wyll caste all parell. Nemo fortis omnia pericula metitur. See **T298.**

M249 No need forbid a **Man** that may not stand to run
c1450 *Burgeys, thou haste* in *PQ* 35(1956) 95.53–4: It is none nede forbeden hastely A man to renne whiche that may not stonde.

M250 None knows so well a worthy **Man** as he that is worthy
c1500 *Lancelot* 51.1707–8: For ther is non that knowith so wel, I-wyss, O worthy man as he that worthi Is. See **L272.**

M251 Of all mister **Men** (*tradesmen*) most they hang thieves
c1325 *Hendyng H* 298.264: Of alle mester men mest me hongeth theves. Apperson 624; Kneuer 57; *Oxford* 418; Schleich 272; Singer III 139.

M252 Of old **Men** ask counsel (*varied*)
1450 *Dicts* 134.1: Aske gladly counsaile of olde men. **c1450** John of Fordun *Scotichronicon* (Edinburgh, 1759) II 344: Kingis state giff thou will lede, Till ald mennis consall tak gude hede. Jente 181. See **A70, C452, M255.**

M253 Of wise young **Men** old fools come many times
1532 Berners *Golden Boke* 157.1518: Many tymes of wyse yonge men cometh olde foles. See **S19.**

M254 An old **Man** and a may (*maid*) may not accord (*varied*)
a1425 *Chester Plays* I 110.125–6: Well I wist an old man and a may Might not accord by no way, 145–9: God let never an old man Take him a yonge woman . . . For accord there may be none. **a1475** *Ludus Coventriae* 88.182: It is a straunge thynge An old man to take a yonge wyff, 91.278–9: And old man may nevyr thryff With a yonge wyff. **a1500** *Coventry Plays*

5.133–5: All olde men, insampull take be me—How I am be-gylid here may you see!—To wed soo yong a chyld. Whiting *Scots* II 106. See **M175, Y33.**

M255 Old **Men** can wis (*guide*) and rede
a1425 *Arthour and M.*[2] 361.2056: For old men can thee wishe and reede. **c1500** *Arthour and M.*[3] I 482.1943. See **F375, M252.**

M256 Old **Men** dote
a1400 *Cato* (*Fairfax*) in *Cursor* III 1671.163–5: If thou be wise in thi thoght, Loke atte thou skorne noght Doted man in elde. **a1500** *Additional MS.37075* 277.5: Hyt ys a comyn sawe that old men dotyth. Est vulgare dictum quod senes desipiscunt. See **M117.**

M257 One **Man** alone knows not all policy
1509 Barclay *Ship* I 58[19]: One man alone knowys nat all polycye.

M258 One **Man** alone may not purchase (*obtain*) all
a1449 Lydgate *Fabules* in *MP* II 599.949–50: One man allone may not all purchase, Nor in armys all the worlde enbrace. Cf. Jente 325; Tilley M315, 353.

M259 One **Man** breaks what another makes
c1430 Lydgate *Dance* 20.175–6: But ofte hit happeth In conclusioun That oo man breketh that another made. Cf. Tilley H102.

M260 One may know a wise **Man** by (his) hearkening and holding his tongue
1477 Rivers *Dictes* 48[23–5]: One may knowe a wyse man by harkenyng and holding his tunge and a man may knowe a fole by his moche clatering. Cf. *Oxford* 718; Tilley M606. See **F401, W587.**

M261 One ought ever greet a wise **Man** worthily
a1200 Lawman II 518.22427–8: For aevere me aehte wisne mon Wurthliche igreten. Skeat 10.

M262 One ought to rise soon before an old **Man** (*varied*)
c1250 *Proverbs of Alfred* 131 T 590–4: Yif thu on benche sitthest, And thu then bevir hore sixst The bi-foren stonden, Buch the from thi sete, And bide hine sone ther-to. **c1395** *WBible* Leviticus xix 32: Rise thou bifor an hoor heed, and onoure thou the persoone of an eld man. **1481** *Tulle of Olde Age* 65[11–2]: Men ought to rise sone anone before the old man and bowe them in obeyng hym. Jente 182.

M263 A one-eyed **Man** is well sighted when among blind men
1522 Skelton *Why Come* II 43.529–32: But have ye nat harde this, How an one eyed man is Well syghted when He is amonge blynde men? Apperson 342; *Oxford* 338; Taylor and Whiting 209.

M264 Other **Men's** good (*property*) is sweet
a1393 Gower *CA* III 113.6118: For other mennes good is swete. See **W71.**

M264.1 Play with no angry **Man**
c1390 Chaucer *CT* VI[C] 958–9: I wol no lenger pleye With thee, ne with noon oother angry man.

M265 A poor **Man** is not set by, a rich man shall be worshipped (*varied*)
c1460 *Ipomadon C* 353.49–354.1: So it faires: a poer man for his povert is noght set by, bot a richman, thogh he be noght worth an haw, he shal be worshipped for his riches! **a1500** *Proverbs of Salamon* 188.71.1–6: At a pore mannes resone ys sett no prys Thogh no man can amenden hyt, But they seyne, lo, the foole ys nys, He weneth he passeth all mennes wytt; A ryche mannes worde ys holden wys Thogh hyt be halfe with foly knytt. Apperson 506:30. Cf. Jente 434. See **M274, 671, P297, 436, R110.**

M266 A poor **Man** (beggar) may sing before thieves
c1380 Chaucer *Boece* II pr. v 182–5: As who seith, a pore man that bereth no rychesse on hym by the weie may boldely synge byforn theves, for he hath nat whereof to be robbed. **a1387** Higden-Trevisa I 413[3–6]: The poete seith a sawe of preef, The foot man lereth synge to fore the theef, And is wel bolder on his way Than the horsman riche and gay. **c1395** Chaucer *CT* III[D] 1191–4: Verray poverte, it syngeth proprely; Juvenal seith of poverte myrily: "The povre man, whan he goth by the weye, Bifore the theves he may synge and pleye." **a1400** Wyclif *Sermons* II 364[21–2]: For it is seid comounli that a wey-goer, whan he is voide, singith sure bi the theef, and money makith him drede more. **1410** Walton *Boethius* 100[19–20]: Haddest thou be povere, it hadde be for thi prow, Before the theef thou mightest have gone and songe. **a1439** Lydgate *Fall* I 174.6171: And tofor thevys he merili doth synge, II 344–5.582–5: The poore man affor the theeff doth synge Under the wodis with fresh notis shrille; The riche man, ful feerful of robbynge, Quakyng for dreed(e), rideth foorth ful stille. **1546** Heywood *D* 55.14: The begger maie syng before the theefe, 17, **1555**

E 158.73, **1556** *Spider* 411[1]: Begger flies: before theevis flies maie sing (we saie). Apperson 35, 573; Jente 172; *Oxford* 30; Tilley B229. See **P43, W717.**

M267 A poor **Man** proud is bad (*varied*)
a900 Alfred *Gregory* 183.13–4: Se earma upahafena. **c1000** Aelfric *Lives* I 292.123: Eft bið swiðe þwyrlic þæt ðearfa beo modig. **a1225** *Lambeth Homilies* 113[30–1]: (Th)e ehtuthe untheau is thet the wrecche mon beo modi. **c1395** *WBible* Ecclesiasticus xxv 3–4: My soule hatide thre spicis, and Y am greved greetli to the soule of hem, a pore man proud, and a riche man liere, and an eld man a fool and unwitti. **1434** Misyn *Mending* 110.26: Qwhat is wars then a poyr man prowed. **a1439** Lydgate *Fall* I 28.992: And with povert pride hath an interesse, **a1449** *Look* in *MP* II 768.98: A poore man proud is nat comendable. **c1450** Idley 99.1086–7: And thre thyngis he seith be odible: A pouere man proud and hye of port. **a1475** *Good Rule* in Brown *Lyrics XV* 265.52: And is not ellys but pore and proude. **a1475** *Ludus Coventriae* 227.75: Thow poverte be chef; lete pride ther be present. **1484** *Ther ne is dangyer* 19.2: Ne pride but of a poure man enryched. **1493** *Seven Wise Masters* 41[6–8]: Have in mynde what the wyse man sayth. A poore man proude, A ryche man a lyer, An olde man a fole god hatyth. **a1500** Rolle *Mending* 34[36–7]: What thyng is worse than a prowde poore man? **c1500** *Series* in Brown *Lyrics XV* 270.5–6: Pore men proude that lytyl han, That wolden beryt owte as riche men goo. **1523** Skelton *Howe the Douty Duke* II 72.144: Proude and poore of state. **1532** Berners *Golden Boke* 387.9699: The proude pore folkes. **1562** Heywood *E* 244.85.2: Poore Peter oft as proude, as Peter the riche. Apperson 506; *Oxford* 510; Taylor and Whiting 291; Tilley P474. See **H3, P110, 379, 395.**

M268 Poor **Men** have no souls
1555 Heywood *E* 175.167: Poore men have no soules. Apperson 506; *Oxford* 511; Tilley M577.

M269 Poor **Men's** money (purse) is fast knit (*shut up*)
c1450 *Douce MS.52* 55.118: Powre mennys mony is fast i-knytt. **c1450** *Rylands MS.394* 104.14: purs.

M270 Praise no **Man** till you have (as)sayed him
a1500 *Additional MS.37075* 278.14: Preys no man tyll thow have sayd hym. See **A232, E158, F625, M58.**

M271 The rich **Man** is bond and servant to the penny and the devil
1483 Caxton *Golden Legende* 58ᵛ[2.18–21]: For the ryche man adverse is bonde and servaunt to the peny and to the devyll: Amator pecunie servus est mammone.

M272 A rich **Man** is held wise (*varied*)
c1390 Chaucer *CT* VII 1–2[B1201–2]: A marchant whilom dwelled at Seint-Denys, That riche was, for which men helde hym wys. **a1500** *Salamon sat and sayde* 291.28–9: He is haldyn wyce He that has and gode may gete, ben he never sa nyce. See **M265, 671, R108.**

M273 The rich **Man** seldom has good counsel but he have it of himself
c1390 Chaucer *CT* VII 1153[B2343]: Men seyn that the riche man hath seeld good conseil, but if he have it of hymself.

M274 Rich **Men** are believed, poor men are reproved
c1450 *Fyrst thou sal* 90.153–4: The ryche men ar belefyd, The pore men are reprefyd. See **M265, 671, P436.**

M275 A scald (*scabby*) **Man's** head is lief (*easy*) to be broke
c1450 *Douce MS.52* 48.47: A scalde mannys hede is lefe to breke. **c1470** *Harley MS.3362* f.2a in *Retrospective* 309[4] and Förster 199.4: A scallyd mannys hed ys good to be broke. Frangitur ex facili caput infantis glabriosi. **a1500** Hill 130.10: A skalde man-is hede is sone brokyn. **1546** Heywood *D* 66.47: A scalde head is soone broken, **1562** *E* 238.55.6: So even as soone is a scald mans head broken. *Oxford* 564; Tilley H265; Walther II 184.9926.

M276 Seldom gets a dumb **Man** land (*varied*)
a1200 Serlo 196.31: Selden gifis men dumb man land. **a1393** Gower *CA* II 71.1293: For specheles may noman spede, III 179.446–9: He was no fol that ferst so radde, For selden get a domb man lond: Tak that proverbe, and understond That wordes ben of vertu grete. **1406** Hoccleve *Male Regle* 38.433: The proverbe is "the doumb man, no lond getith." **c1450** *Douce MS.52* 50.72: Seldun getes the dom man gode. **c1450** *Rylands MS.394* 100.15. **a1500** *Rawlinson MS. A 273* f.96 in *Zeitschrift für französische Sprache und Litteratur* 21(1899) 2.13: Seld men gyfth a dumbe man lond. Raro datur muto libera terra puto. **a1513** Dunbar *Of Discretioun in Asking* 32.26–7: Nocht neidfull is men sowld be dum: Na thing is gottin but wordis sum. **1555** Heywood *E* 194.275.2: Doome men wyn nought in deede.

Apperson 170; *Oxford* 161; Tilley F418; Whiting *Scots* II 94–5, 160:6. See **A215, G358, H338, S554.**

M277 A shamed **Man** must walk in shadow, a pure man in the light
c900 *Maxims* in *Exeter Book* 159.66: Sceomiande man sceal in sceade hweorfan, scir in leohte geriseð.

M278 Shend (*harm*, despise) no unkouth (*unknown*, unked) **Man**
a1350 *Ywain* 79.2943–4: For soth, ye er unhende An unkouth man so forto shende. **a1500** *Beves* 18 M 315: Thou sholdiste none unkyd man dispise!

M279 A simple **Man's** counsel may prevail (*varied*)
a1450 *Generydes B* 39.1209–11: And oftentymes it hath be sene expresse, In grete materys, withouten eny fayle, A sympill mannys councell may prevayle. **1464** Hardyng 74[18–21]: For oftymes a symple manne to sight More wysedome hath in his insight, And better reason canne in his braynes fynde, Then canne a lorde, though he may beres bynde.

M280 Singing **Man** seldom weeps
c1350 *Nominale* 6*.128: Syngynge man silden weputh.

M281 A sly **Man** is better than a strong man
c1395 *WBible* Proverbs xvi 32: A pacient man is betere than a stronge man. **a1400** *Stodye of Wysdome* 41.3–5: For betir is a sley man than a strong man, ye, and betyr is list then lither strengthe. And a sley man spekith of victories. See **L381, M801.**

M282 Smite no **Man** without a cause
c1450 *Rylands MS.394* 105.7: Smyte we no man with ought acause.

M283 Some **Man** may steal a horse better than some other stand and look on
1546 Heywood *D* 92.62–3: Some man maie steale a hors better Than some other may stande and looke upone, **1555** *E* 176.173. Apperson 601; *Oxford* 619; Tilley H692.

M284 Such as **Men** begin toward others oft shall they find
a1393 Gower *CA* II 145–6.566–9: And ofte swich as men beginne Towardes othre, swich thei finde, That set hem ofte fer behinde, Whan that thei wene be before. See **D274, P232.**

M285 Ten **Men** in a little throw (*while*) may be brought to ground
a1325 *Otuel and Roland* 126.2158–60: Men seyeth in old sawe, That ten men in a lytel thrawe Mowe be brought to grownd.

M286 That **Man** is poor that has no friend
a1450 *Myne awen dere* 179.943–4: And thus men says withowten ende, "That man is poer that has no frende."

M287 That **Man** is worthy to bear blame (be lame) that hews off his own foot
a1500 *Proverbs of Salamon* 194.4.7–8: That man ys worthy to bere blame Hys owne foote doyth ofheweee. **a1500** *Lovely song of wisdom* 194.9[7–8]: He es wele worthy for to be lame His ownne fete that will offhewe.

M288 There are few **Men** liberal of promise but they will break some or all
1478 Rivers *Morale Proverbes* [5.5–6]: Fewe men there be of promys liberalle, But some of hem thay wol breke or elles alle.

M289 Those who desire another **Man's** death advance their own
a1533 Berners *Huon* 315.33–316.1: Often tymes they that desyre another mans deth avaunseth there owne. See **D22, P232.**

M290 Till **Man** is at death's door he never says he has enough
a1450 *Castle* 101.813–4: Tyl man be dyth in dethys dow, He seyth nevere he hath I-now. See **E124**

M291 To be a good (noble) **Man** (knight) of his hands
c1450 *Merlin* I 141[9]: And a gode knyght shall he be of his honde. **a1470** Malory I 158.33: He is a passyng good man of his hondis, 416.28–9: noble knyght, II 692.27–8: noble knyght, 717.24: noble knyghtes. **a1533** Berners *Arthur* 62[24]: good knight, 369[7–8]: He is a ryghte fayre knight . . . and of his handes suche as ye may se. Apperson 619–20; Tilley M163; Whiting *Drama* 353:699.

M292 To beg at a wrong **Man's** door
1546 Heywood *D* 33.4: Ye beg at a wrong mans dur. Tilley D376. See **D348.**

M293 To fare like a **Man** that says he would (have) no silver, and looks away and takes a noble
1456 Paston III 102[17–9]: He farith as a man wole sey he wold noo silvere, and lokith awaywardes and takith a noble.

M294 To have a dead **Man's** head in one's dish
1546 Heywood *D* 82–3.89–90: For I never meete

the at fleshe nor at fishe, But I have sure a deade mans head in my dishe. Tilley W336.

M295 To see old **Men** weep is great ruth
a1425 *Seege of Troye* 156 L 2000–1: Theo kyng weopte for theo mukil untrewthe; To seo olde men weope hit is gret rewthe. Tilley C326; Whiting *Ballad* 37. See **C199.**

M296 A too hardy **Man** is oft (a) fool
a1300 *Alisaunder* 309.5894–6: Tohardy man wel ofte is fole! So had the kyng yben neigh, Ac God h(y)m sent help from heigh.

M297 Traist (*trust*) not to rich **Men's** hightings (*promises*), *etc.*
a1500 *Salamon sat and sayde* 291.7–9: Tyl riche men hetynges trayst thou ryth noght, And of womannis wepynges charge thou never noght, A chyldis love is sone done for a thynges of noght. See **C207, W374.**

M298 A true **Man** will not hide his visage
c1450 Idley 159.41–2: And it hath be said longe in oolde usage: A true man woll not hide his visage.

M299 True **Men** (come) in at doors, thieves in at windows
1556 Heywood *Spider* 97[6–7]: This is tholde use alwaie: all the worlde knowes, Trew men in at doores, theeves in at windowes. See **W349.**

M300 Two envious **Men** shall not both ride upon an ass
1484 Caxton *Aesop* 86[18–9]: Ne two envyous men shal not both ryde upon an asse. Cf. Tilley T638.

M301 Two **Men** bear a feather
1546 Heywood *D* 51.347–8: If your meete mate and you meete together, Than shall we see two men beare a fether. Tilley M592.

M302 Unadvised **Men** are reputed fools
a1475 Ashby *Dicta* 59.385: Unavised men, foles bene repute. See **C470.**

M303 Uncouth (*unknown*) **Man** oft can give good counsel
c1300 *Guy*[1] 504 A 144.10–1: For ofte it falleth uncouthe man That gode counseyle give can, 503–5.9062–3: For hyt fallyth well to straunge men Eyther other wysdom to ken.

M304 The unwise **Man** and the forweaned (*spoiled*) child have but one law
a1200 *Trinity College Homilies* 41[23–5]: The unwise man and forwened child habbeth bothe on lage, for that hie habben willeth bothe here wil.

M305 A warned **Man** may live
a1500 *Norwich Creation A* in Waterhouse 9.36: A warned man may live: who can yt denye. See **M111, W49.**

M306 What a gelded **Man** has that he gives to his neighbors
1492 *Salomon and Marcolphus* 11[3]: That a geldyd man hath that gevyth he to his neigborwes.

M307 What a **Man** gets easily is not so dearworth (*precious*) as that which is gotten with difficulty (*varied*)
c1000 Aelfric *Homilies* I 248[29–30]: Swa hwæt swa man eaðelice begyt, þæt ne bið na swa deorwyrðe swa þæt þæt earfoðlice bið begyten. **c1477** Caxton *Jason* 46.32–4: For the thyng that is goten by grete travayle and long requestes is moche more worth and better kept, thenne that is goten lightly. See **F58, L519.**

M308 What a **Man** learned in youth will hold best in his eld (*varied*)
c1410 Edward of York *Master* 69[12–4]: And also men sayn that a man lernyd in yougth wil it hald best in his eelde. **1484** Caxton *Royal Book* S3[r][25–6]: For it is sayd, that which is lerned in yougthe is mayntened in age. Tilley Y42. See **C226, Y32.**

M309 What all **Men** say is not lies (*varied*)
a1400 *Scottish Legends* II 105.205–6: For I fynd suthfastnes, That al men sais, is nocht les. **a1470** Malory I 444.9: Hit may nat be false that all men sey. **c1475** *Rawlinson MS. D 328* 118.8: Hit ys cominly truye that all men sayth. **1520** Whittinton *Vulgaria* 72.22: It is lyke to be true that every man sayth. **c1523** Barclay *Mirrour* 52[8]: It nedes muste be true which every man doth say. **1546** Heywood *D* 48.216: It must needes be true, that every man sayth, **1555** *E* 174.158. Apperson 647; *Oxford* 672; Tilley M204. Cf. Whiting *Scots* II 145. See **M802, R234, S487, V52.**

M310 What all **Men** say need not be truth (*varied*)
c1450 La Tour-Landry 199.4–5: It is no nede that al that men sayn be trouthe. **1562** Heywood *E* 245.95.2: But all is not alway: as all men do say. See **B221, S487.**

M311 What profit to a blind **Man** of a bright sunbeam (lantern)?
c1000 Aelfric *Lives* I 106.275: Hwæt fremað þam blindan seo beorhta sun-beam? **c1475** *Prohemy of a Mariage* 44[25–8]: To be wedded, but, frende, I trowe that ye Have no more nede

to suche fragilite In this youre age, if ye wel disceme, Than hathe a blynde man of a brihte lanterne.

M312 When a **Man** is brought to mischief he has few friends
a1430 Lydgate *Pilgrimage* 369.13624–6: Whan a man ys to mescheff brouht, And falle in-to adversyte, Fful fewe frendys than hath he. See **H141, M89.**

M313 When a **Man** is in most sorrow then is our Lord's help next
c1300 *Becket II* 123.1585–6: Ther hit is soth, wen a mon is in mest sorwe and tene, Thenne is our lordes help next, as hit was tho isene. See **B22.**

M314 When a **Man** weens to be most sure then is he near his danger
c1500 *Three Kings' Sons* 58.12–3: Alas, fortune! whan a man weneth to be moost sure, than is he nere his daungere. See **S669.**

M315 When every **Man** has his part, the king has the least
c1330 *Times of Edward II* 338.332: Whan everi man hath his part, the king hath the leste.

M316 When every **Man** has said, do you the best
c1400 *Roland* 111.160: When every man hathe said, do ye the best. See **H264.**

M317 When **Man** assists God works not for nought
c1515 Barclay *Eclogues* 190.254: When man assisteth God worketh not for nought. Cf. Taylor and Whiting 154. See **F519.**

M318 When **Men** are merriest death says "checkmate"
a1500 *Fortune alas alas* 488.110: When men be meriest alday deth seith chek mate.

M319 When old **Men** may not do then will they speak
c1390 Chaucer *CT* I[A] 3881: For whan we (*old men*) may nat doon, than wol we speke.

M320 When two noble **Men** encounter one must have the worse
a1470 Malory II 535.13–5: And whan two noble men encountir, nedis muste the tone have the worse, lyke as God wyll suffir at that tyme. **a1500** *Eger H* 283.1607–10: So wight in world was never none, But where two meets them alone, And departs without company, But one must win the victorie.

M321 Where a **Man** is jealous there is a cuckold in that house
c1303 Mannyng *Handlyng* 68.1893–4: Men sey, ther a man ys gelous, That ther ys a kokewolde at (*var.* at that) hous. **c1450** Idley 141.2076–7: Ffor it is said wher that a man is gelous A verri cokewold dwelleth in that hous.

M322 Where is the **Man** that may not be overgone (*overcome*) with meed (*gift*)?
a1200 Lawman I 329.7711–2. Whaer is the ilke mon That me ne maei mid mede over-gan? *B:* Ware his nou the ilke man That ne may mid mede beo over-come? Cf. Taylor and Whiting 235:16; Tilley B659. See **G88, M491.**

M323 Where see you any rich dead **Man?**
a1500 Greene *Carols* 366.2: Qw(e)re se ye ony rych dede man?

M324 While a **Man** has ought, company will go with him till he be brought to nought
a1500 *Salamon sat and sayde* 291.5–6: Qwyllys a man haves owth Cumpany wil with him go til he be broght to noght.

M325 Who waits for dead **Men's** shoes shall go long barefoot
1549 Heywood *D* 53.416: Who waitth for dead mens shoen, shall go long barefoote. Apperson 138; *Oxford* 132; Taylor and Whiting 234; Tilley M619; Whiting *Drama* 221.

M326 A wicked **Man** flees when no man pursues
c1395 *WBible* Proverbs xxviii 1: A wickid man fleeth, whanne no man pursueth. **1492** *Salomon and Marcolphus* 6[9]: The wykkyd man fleyth, no man folwyng. Tilley W333. See **G492, S290.**

M327 A wight (*strong*) **Man** wanted never and (*if*) he were wise
c1475 Henryson *Fables* 73.2108: Ane wicht man wantit never, and he wer wyis. *Oxford* 708–9; Tilley M418; Whiting *Scots* II 94.

M328 The wise **Man** can belock (*lock up*) fele (*much*) with few words
c1250 *Proverbs of Alfred* 118 T 458–9: The wise mon mid fewe word Can fele biluken. *Oxford* 199; Tilley W799. See **E49, W587.**

M329-30 A wise **Man** has delight in wisdom, a fool has despite of doctrine
a1449 Lydgate *Fabules* in *MP* II 572.181–2: For as a wyseman in wysdom hathe delyte, Ryght so a foole of doctrine hathe dyspyte.

M331 A wise **Man** may easily know a saying and also say it
c1025 *Durham Proverbs* 12.16: Eaðe (wis) man

mæg witan spell and eac secgan. (P)rudenti facile clausum insinuatur.

M332 A wise **Man** needs no teaching
a1533 Berners *Arthur* 415[9–10]: A wyse man nedeth no teching.

M333 A wise **Man** never yet stood on my feet
c1422 Hoccleve *Complaint* 104.252: There nevar stode yet wyse man on my fete.

M334 Wise **Man** of rede, wise man of deed
c1300 *Havelok* 7.180: Wis man of red, wis man of dede. MED dede 7.

M335 A wise **Man's** tongue trips without advisement
1509 Barclay *Ship* I 108[28]: For a wyse mannys tunge, without advysement trypes. See **A62.**

M336 A wise **Man** sees peril long before it comes
1509 Barclay *Ship* I 76[14]: A wyse man seyth peryll longe before it come.

M337 A wise **Man** should not be too frightened or too fain
a800 *Wanderer* in *Exeter Book* 135.65–8: Wita sceal geþyldig, Ne sceal no to hatheort ne to hrædwyrde, . . . Ne to forht ne to fægen. **c1025** *Durham Proverbs* 12.23: Ne sceal man to ær forht ne to ær fægen. Ne(c) cito pavidus nec ilico arrigens qui esse debet.

M338 The wise **Man** that dreads harms eschews harms
c1390 Chaucer *CT* VII 1320–1[B2510–1]: For Senec seith that "the wise man that dredeth harmes, eschueth harmes, ne he ne falleth into perils that perils eschueth." See **W49.**

M339 The wise **Man** will hear wisdom, the fool draws near to folly
a1325 *Cursor* I 10.27–8: The wisman wil o wisdom here, The foul hym draghus to foly nere.

M340 Wise **Men** are often ware by fools
c1385 Chaucer *TC* i 635: Thus often wise men ben war by foolys. **a1439** Lydgate *Fall* I 146.5200–1: For it is tauht in scoolis, That wise men been alday war be foolis. Whiting *Drama* 155. See **F404, M345, W400.**

M341 Wise **Men** ay overcome fools
a1475 *Assembly of Gods* 49.1660–3: Oft ys hit seene, with sobre contenaunce, That wys men fooles overcome ay, Turnyng as hem lyst and all her varyaunce, Chaunge from ernest in to mery play. Cf. Whiting *Drama* 183.

M342 Wise **Men** deem not things after what they seem
a1393 Gower *CA* II 255.1073–5: Forthi the wise men ne demen The thinges after that thei semen, Bot after that thei knowe and finde. See **F1, M167.**

M343 Wise **Men** doubt and dread the worst
a1500 Medwall *Nature* H1r[8–9]: How be yt that I dout and drede The wurst, as wyse men do.

M344 Wise **Men** draw to the wise and fools to the fools' guise
a1400 *Titus* 101.2223–4: For wise men drawen to the wise, And foles to the foles gyse. See **L272.**

M345 Wise **Men** have knowledge of (*from*) fools
c1450 *Consail and Teiching* 77.401–2: Wysmen of fulys has rycht knawlege As in a meroure thar wysage. See **F404, M340, W401.**

M346 Wise **Men** oft do mad deeds
c1516 Skelton *Magnificence* 10.302: But ofte tymes have I sene wyse men do mad dedys. See **F388, M350.**

M347 Wise **Men's** ettling (*aim*) comes not ay to that ending that they think
c1375 Barbour *Bruce* I 24.583–5: And wyss mennys etling Cummys nocht ay to that ending That thai think it sall cum to, 272.22–3: And wiss menis etling cumis nocht Till sic end as thai weyn alwayis. Whiting *Scots* II 156.

M348 Wise **Men** should dread their enemies
a1420 Wyntoun V 407.3412–4: Wysse men sulde dreide thar innymysse; For lychtlynes and succudry Drawis in defoulle (*var.* defoulling) commonly.

M349 Wise **Men** should have fools in captivity (*varied*)
c1525 ?Heywood *Gentylnes* 95.80–1: For reason wyll ever it shuld so be Wyse men to have folys in captyvyte, 125.1093–4: For it is Almyghty Goddys purveaunce Wyse men of folys to have the governaunce.

M350 The wiser **Man** the better can he bourd (*jest*)
a1500 *Thre Prestis* 29.492: The wyser man the better can he bourd. Apperson 696; *Oxford* 455, 718; Tilley M321, 428; Whiting *Scots* II 156. See **F388, M346, W378.**

M351 Work as a wise **Man** and change your will
a1400 *Destruction of Troy* 20.576: Wirkes as a

wise man, and your wille chaunge. Cf. Apperson 696:14; Tilley M420.

M352 You are never the nearer a wise **Man** for him
1484 Paston VI 79[16–7]: For ye har never the nerer a wysse man for hym.

M353 A young **Man** without pain (*effort*) is worth little
a1533 Berners *Arthur* 37[11]: For a yonge man withoute payne is litle worth.

M354 Young **Men** may tweon (*doubt*) whether they may live, but the old certainly know death (*varied*)
a1225 *Lambeth Homilies* 109[14–6]: Yunge monnan mei tweonian hwether hi moten alibban, ac the alde mei him witan iwis thone deth. **1522** More *Treatyse* 79 F[11–3]: A yonge man may die soone, and an olde manne cannot live long, **1534** *Comforte* 1139 G[10–2]: For as we well wot, that a young man may dye soone: so be we very sure that an olde man cannot live long, 1172 E[11–3]: As the younge man may happe sometime to dye sone, so the old man can never live long. Apperson 720; Jente 122; *Oxford* 739; Taylor and Whiting 236; Tilley M609.

M355 Young **Men's** wives may not be taught and old men's wives are good for nought
a1500 *Harley MS.3835* in Henry Littlehales *Prymer or Lay Folks' Prayer Book* (EETS 109, 1897) II xlix: If thow art young then mary not ekit: If thou art old thou hast more wite. For young mens wifes (may n)ot be taught, And olde mens wifes be good for naught.

M356 Young **Men** that take to arms should speak little
c1400 *Alexander Buik* II 125.556–8: Speke softer and be not sa bald! For young men that to armes tais Sould lytill speke, how ever it gais.

M357 Young **Men** that take wives hastily oft repent it
a1400 *Ipomadon A* 145.5041–3: Yonge men ofte, I saye, for thy, That takes them wyffes so hastly, Repentes it sithe full ill! Taylor and Whiting 172:3. See **R67.**

M358 **Manhood** is not worth but (*unless*) it is meddled (*mixed*) with wisdom
a1470 Malory II 700.19–20: For manhode is nat worth but yf hit be medled with wysdome.

M359 The best **Manner** to flee is to depart by time
c1489 Caxton *Blanchardyn* 203.20–2: He putte hym self to flyght, for hym thought the best manere for to flee was for to departe by tyme.

M360 Evil **Manners** follow an evil complexion (*temperament*)
a1400 Lanfranc 8.9: Evyle maners but folowen the liiknes of an yvele complexioun. See **W265.**

M361 It is hard to forbear a wont (*accustomed*) **Manner**
c1420 Wyntoun IV 61.4875–6: Syn it was harde for to forbere, As clerkis (*var.* commone) sayis, a wont manere. See **C653.**

M362 **Manners** and clothing make a man (*varied*)
a1400 *Proverbis of Wysdom* 245.59: Ever maner and clothyng makyth man. **c1450** *Consail and Teiching* 71.185–6: For maner makis man of valour And bringis a man to gret honor. **c1450** *Douce MS.52* 50.77: Maner makys man. **c1450** *Fyrst thou sal* 88.47: Maners and clothyng makes man. **c1450** Idley 82.102: Ffor clothyng ofte maketh man. **c1450** *Rylands MS.394* 100.30. **a1475** *Hit is ful harde* in *MLN* 55(1940) 566.13–4: And thou be poure do alle that thou canne To use goode maners for maner maket(h) man. **c1477** Caxton *Curtesye* 24.238: Remembre well that maner maketh man. **a1500** *Att my begynning* in *Rawlinson MS.813* 323.25: Grace and manerz make a man. **a1500** Hichecoke *This Worlde* 332.6: Maners and clothe man doth make. **a1500** *Poem on . . . Masonry* in James O. Halliwell *Early History of Freemasonry in England* (London, 1840) 36.726: Gode maneres maken a mon. **a1500** *Urbanitatis* in Furnivall *Babees Book* 14.34: Nurtur and good maners maketh man. **1509** Barclay *Ship* I 282[3–4]: For an olde proverbe true and verytable Sayth that good lyfe and maners makyth man. **1513** Bradshaw *St. Werburge* 131.6–7: By a proverbe, certan, "Good maners and conynge maken a man." **1520** Whittinton *Vulgaria* 115.8–9: For maners (as they say) maketh man. Apperson 13, 398; *Oxford* 12, 404, 466; Taylor and Whiting 72–3; Tilley A283, G391, M629, 827. See **M628.**

M363 There is **Manner** in all things
c1477 Caxton *Jason* 46.37: But ther is in all thinge manere. See **M464.**

M364 To have seen more good **Manners** than one has borne away
1520 Whittinton *Vulgaria* 95.19–20: Good syr, it semeth ye have seen more good maners than ye have borne awaye. Apperson 260; *Oxford* 343; Tilley M631.

M365 **Many** are called and few are chosen

a800 *Guthlac* in *Exeter Book* 51.59: He (*God*) fela findeð, fea beoð gecorene. **c1000** Aelfric *Homilies* I 532[16–7]: Fela sind gecigede and feawa gecorene, II 82[3–4]. **c1000** *WSG* Matthew xx 16: Soþlice manega synt geclypede, and feawa gecorene, xxii 14: gelaþode. **c1275** *Kentish Sermons* in *Old English Miscellany* 34[11–2]: Fele bieth i-clepede, ac feaue bieth i-cornée. **c1340** Rolle *Psalter* 62 (17.19): For many ere cald and fa chosen, 385 (106.38). **c1395** *WBible* Matthew xx 16: For many ben clepid, but fewe ben chosun, xxii 14. Taylor and Whiting 237.

M366 **Many** may do more than one alone
1481 Caxton *Reynard* 25[4–5]: Ffor many maye doo more than one allone. See **O35.**

M367 **Many** speak boldly that will not suffer at time of need
c991 *Maldon* in *ASMP* 12.198–201: Swa him Offa on dæg ær asæde On þam meþelstede, þa he gemot hæfde, þæt þær modiglice manega spræcon þe eft æt þearfe þolian noldon, 13.212–5. See **B415, F659, S581, T49, W617.**

M368 As cold as **Marble** (stone)
a1300 *Wyt is thi nachede brest* in *Medium Ævum* 4(1935) 104[4]: Thine zedes hongen colde al so the marbre ston. **a1325** *Christ on the Cross* in Heuser 128.9: His lendin so hangith as cold as marbre stone. **a1420** Lydgate *Troy* III 671.3633: As marbil cold. **1474** Caxton *Chesse* 110[3–4]: Colde . . . as marbill. **a1500** *Eye and Heart* 244.195: The erthe as colde as marble semed me. Taylor and Whiting 237.

M369 As gray as **Marble**
a1400 *Moder of gresse* 177.519: And gray als marbylle.

M370 As hard as **Marble** (stone)
c1300 *Reinbrun* 655.74.11–2: He is so hard to hewe upon Ase marbel. **c1425** *Orcherd* 49.25: As hard as ony marbil stoon. **1474** Caxton *Chesse* 110[3–4]: Harde as marbill. **a1500** ?Ros *La Belle Dame* 321.717: O marble herte, and yet more hard, pardè. **1509** Barclay *Ship* II 131[19]: Our hertis harder than . . . marbell stone. Taylor and Whiting 237.

M371 As stiff as **Marble** stones
c1515 Barclay *Eclogues* 171.878: Like marble stones his handes be as stiffe.

M372 Seld mosses the **Marble** (stone) that men oft tread (*varied*)
a1376 *Piers* A x 100–1: I have lerned how lewede men han lered heore children, That selde mosseth the marbelston that men ofte treden. **a1475** *Good Wyfe Wold* 173.12: Syldon mossyth the ston that oftyn ys tornnyd and wende. **1546** Heywood *D* 42.36: The rollyng stone never gatherth mosse. Apperson 537; *Oxford* 547; Taylor and Whiting 355; Tilley S885.

M373 **March** (weather) is unstable (*varied*)
c1430 ?Lydgate *Compleynt* 63.297–311: O Marche, I may ful wel warye, . . . Wondurful, and ay unstable, Right dyvers and varyable: Now canst thow Reyne, now shyne . . . Ful seeld in oon thou doost abyde. **a1449** Lydgate *Freond* in *MP* II 758.93–4: Gerisshe, stormisshe of entencion, Liche march weder, let noman take hede, *Mydsomer Rose* in *MP* II 783.62–3: As gery March his stoundys doth discloose, Now reyn, now storm, now Phebus bright and cleere, *Testament* in *MP* I 342.351–2: Stormyssh as Marche, with chaunges ful sodeyne, After cleer shynyng to turne and make it reyne. Cf. Apperson 401; *Oxford* 407; Taylor and Whiting 238; Tilley M643.

M374 **Marcolf** to sit in Solomon's see (*chair*)
c1440 Lydgate *Debate* in *MP* II 564.604–8: Fals supplantyng clymbyng up of foolis, Unto chaires of wordly dygnyte, Lak of discrecioun sett jobbardis upon stoolis, Which hath distroied many a comounte: Marcolff to sitt in Salamon-is see. Cf. Robert J. Menner *The Poetical Dialogues of Solomon and Saturn* (New York, 1941) 26–35.

M375 Away the **Mare**
c1450 Idley 114.379: Ne crieng among chepmen, "away the mare!" **c1516** Skelton *Magnificence* 41.1326: Nowe then goo we hens. Away the mare! **a1529** *Elynour* I 98.108–10: But drynke tyll they stare And brynge themselfe bare, With, Now away the mare. Apperson 20; Tilley M646; Whiting *Drama* 334:383. See **C38.**

M376 The gray **Mare** is the better horse
1528 More *Heresyes* 215 H[12–3]: Whether the gray mare may be the better horse or not. **1546** Heywood *D* 69.100: The grey mare is the better hors. Apperson 274; *Oxford* 267; Taylor and Whiting 238; Tilley M647; Whiting *Drama* 140.

M377 My old **Mare** would have a new crupper
1546 Heywood *D* 60.48: What, mine olde mare woulde have a new crouper. Apperson 465; *Oxford* 471; Tilley M651.

M378 This (?Thus) bites the **Mare** by the thumb
1546 Heywood *D* 79.61: This biteth the mare by the thumbe, as they sey. Apperson 50; *Oxford* 47; Tilley M654.

M379 To be mouthed like a **Mare**
a1300 *Alisaunder* 323.6115: Hii weren mouthed als a mere.

M380 To fill one's maw like a **Mare** at a mow
a1400 *Alexander C* 237.4434: Than as a Mare at a moghe youre mawis ye fill.

M381 To shoe the mockish **Mare**
c1522 Skelton *Colyn* I 318.180–1: For let se who that dare Sho the mockysshe mare. *Oxford* 583; Tilley M655.

M382 Better **Marked** (*noted*) than mint (*aimed*)
c1400 *Beryn* 15.434: Ffor offt is more better I-merkid then I-mynt.

M383 To bring some one to five **Marks**
a1400 Wyclif *Sermons* I 370[14–6]: And thus synne concludith men moost of al thing that mai be; for it bringith man to fyve markis more noyousli than other skilis. See **S244.**

M384 Adieu **Market** and welcome green woods!
c1470 *Wallace* 149.296: Adew market, and welcum woddis greyne! See **W559.**

M385 One finds at the **Market** more skins of calves than of kine
1483 Caxton *Cato* D1ᵛ[24–5]: Men fynde at the markette hows moo skynnes of calves than of kyen. Cf. Tilley L39. See **D98, M41, 204, S209.**

M386 One knows how the **Market** goes by the market men
1546 Heywood *D* 47.213–4: Men know . . . How the market goth by the market men. Apperson 403; *Oxford* 343; Tilley M676.

M387 To make **Market**
a1400 *Alexander C* 14.420–1: Amon his awen god in armes with his qwene, And make with hire market as (he) a man were. Cf. Apperson 403; Tilley M672.

M388 By **Marriage** many things are appeased
a1533 Berners *Arthur* 387[25]: By maryage many thynges are appeased. See **W699.**

M389 **Marriage** is an adventurous balance
a1450 Quixley *Ballades* 42.90–1: For sayde it is, "aventurous balance Is mariage."

M390 As soon pick **Marrow** out of a mattock
1520 Whittinton *Vulgaria* 91.27–9: A man myght as soone pyke mary out of a mattok as dryve .iii. good latyn wordes out of your fortop. Cf. Taylor and Whiting 34:12.

M391 **Martin** ape
a1300 *Alisaunder* 343.6452–5: Rugh hii ben also hounde, From the hevede to the grounde; Visages after martyn ape—Folk it is wel yvel yshape. **c1395** *WBible* Isaiah xxxiv 14 *gloss:* Martynapis ben liyk apis, and ben (long) tailid. NED Martin²; note to *Alisaunder* II 143.

M392 To clatter like **Masons** battering on stones
c1400 *Laud Troy* I 225.7623–4: A thousand swerdes aboute him clatered As Masons hadde on stones batered.

M393 To lay on like **Masons** on the stone
a1300 *Alisaunder* 133.2365–6: On other half hii leggeth on, So the mason on the ston, 399–401.7378–9: Aither othere legeth on, Als the mason on the ston.

M394 At **Mass** and meat
c1450 *Foly of Fulys* 64.453: With wnrest baith at mes and met. Cf. *Oxford* 416; Tilley M825.

M395 **Mass** nor matins
1528 More *Heresyes* 145 H[6–12]: Men say sometyme . . . it maketh no matter they saye, ye maye beginne agayne and mende it, for it is nother masse nor mattyns. *Oxford* 412; Tilley M708.

M396 As long as a **Mast**
c1390 Chaucer *CT* I[A] 3264: Long as a mast.

M397 As stiff as any **Mast**
c1390 *Mary and the Cross* 622.385: Thou stod stif as eny mast.

M398 As straight as any (the) **Mast**
1480 Caxton *Ovyde* 130[40]: More strayt than eny maste is in a shipp. **a1500** *Court of Love* 411.88: But Phebus bemes, streight as is the mast.

M399 As strong as (a) **Mast**
a1325 *Erthe* 34.59: Erthe up-on erth is stronge as a mast. **c1465** Rotheley *Halfe in dede sclepe* in *PQ* 5(1926) 333.110: a. **a1513** Dunbar *Sowtar* 124.27: He wer strang as mast.

M400 To stand (up) like a **Mast**
c1300 *Havelok* 36.986: Havelok stod over hem als a mast. **a1460** *Towneley Plays* 265.232: It standys up lyke a mast.

M401 A good **Master** makes a good disciple
c1500 Fabyan 551[39]: A good master maketh a good dyssyple. Cf. Tilley M721, 723.

M402 It becomes him evil to be a **Master** that cannot order himself
1520 Whittinton *Vulgaria* 56.29–30: It becometh hym evyll to be a mayster upon servauntes that can not ordre hymselfe. See **G407, M228, 407, S142.**

M403 It is evil thinking to be **Master** of the craft that one can (*knows*) nothing of
c1505 Watson *Valentine* 187.6–8: But it is sayde commonly that it is evyll thinking to be mayster of the crafte that they can nothyng of. See **F432, R54.**

M404 The **Master** loses his time when the disciple will not hear
a1400 *Romaunt B* 2149–52: The maister lesith his tyme to lere, Whanne the disciple wol not here. It is but veyn on hym to swynke, That on his lernyng wol not thinke.

M405 The **Master** of the heart may be master of the good
a1393 Gower *CA* III 76.4764–5: Ther sche is maister of the herte, Sche mot be maister of the good.

M406 (Most) **Master** wears no breech
a1500 Greene *Carols* 407 (*refrain*): The most mayster of the hows weryth no brych. **1546** Heywood *D* 64.4: Shall the maister weare a breeche, or none? **1555** *E* 181.196: The master weareth no breeche. Apperson 66; *Oxford* 697; Taylor and Whiting 42; Tilley M727.

M407 One may not be **Master** without he have first been a disciple
1484 Caxton *Aesop* 176[1–2]: One maye not be mayster without he have be fyrste a disciple, 179[6–7]: For none ought to say hym self mayster withoute that he have fyrst studyed. See **G407, M181, 228, 402, S856, T50.**

M408 Such **Master** such servant
c1505 Watson *Valentine* 317.37–8: For suche mayster suche servaunt. **a1533** Berners *Huon* 232.17–8: Such as the mayster was so was the servaunt. Apperson 366–7, 646; *Oxford* 412, 671; Taylor and Whiting 239; Tilley M723; Whiting *Drama* 129, *Scots* II 97. See **C34, 192, J71, K56, L455, P135, 403.**

M409 To marry the **Master's** daughter (*i.e.*, to be birched)
1520 Whittinton *Vulgaria* 87.29–30: I maryed my maysters doughter to daye, full soore agayn my wyll.

M410 Too early **Master** the sooner knave (*varied*)
a1400 *Proverbis of Wysdom* 244.38: To erly mayster, the sonner knave, (*II*) 221.22: To erlyche mayster, the lenger knave. **c1450** *Douce MS.52* 50.68: Erly mayster, longe knave. **c1450** *Rylands MS.394* 100.17. *Oxford* 164; Tilley M712.

M411 Who will be **Master** must be servant to pity
a1393 Gower *CA* II 219.3299–300: And seith, "Who that woll maister be, He mot be servant to pite." See **P243.**

M412 It is no **Mastery** for a lord to damn a man without answer
c1386 Chaucer *LGW* F 400–1: For, syr, yt is no maistrye for a lord To dampne a man without answere of word. See **P42.**

M413 **Mastery** (Strength) mows the meadow down
c1420 Wyntoun III 314.1498–1500: Bot it is said in commone sawis That mastry mawis the medow doune ay, And sa fell heire, the suth to say. **c1450** *Douce MS.52* 54.108: Strenhgth mowes downe the medow. **c1450** *Rylands MS.394* 104.5: *omits* downe. *Oxford* 413; Louise W. Stone "Une proverbe du moyen age: Force paist le pré," *Zeitschrift für romanische Philologie* 73(1957) 145–59; Tilley M741; Whiting *Scots* II 97.

M414 One may have **Mastery** of others if he have seigniory of his own flesh
c1300 *Becket I* 13.261–2: For he thoghte he mighte wel of othere habbe maistrie, If he hadde of his owe flesch thurfout seignurye. See **R231.**

M415 Not worth a **Mat**(?)
c1390 *This World* in Brown *Lyrics XIV* 161.43: Monnes miht nis worth a Mat.

M416 To find (meet with) one's **Match**
c1300 *South English Legendary* I 339.364: The ssrewe fond is macche tho. **a1470** Malory II 687.30: And there shalt thou fynde thy matche. **c1475** Henryson *Fables* 87.2555: For all your mowis ye met anis with your matche. Apperson 411; Tilley M745. See **M64.**

M417 To give one a blind **Mate**
1556 Heywood *Spider* 68[14]: To geve him this blinde mate. See **C169.**

M418 **Matters** of great weight are not concluded at the first time
1525 Berners *Froissart* V 169–70: But maters of so great a weyght are nat lyghtly concluded at the first tyme. Tilley M757.

M419 When a **Matter** is begun it would not be prolonged
1525 Berners *Froissart* V 85[15]: Whan a mater is begon, it wolde nat be prolonged. See **D157.**

M420 As gross as a **Maul**

1520 Whittinton *Vulgaria* 60.19: He hath a heed as grose as a malle.

M421 Maugre one's **Maw**
1463 Ashby *Prisoner* 9.270: Maugre . . . his maw.

M422 As fresh as (the month of) **May**
c1385 Chaucer *CT* I[A] 1037: And fressher than the May with floures newe, **c1387-95** I[A] 92: He was as fressh as is the month of May, **c1395** V[F] 281: And been a feestlych man as fressh as May, 927-8: That fressher was and jolyer of array, As to my doom, than is the month of May. **a1420** Lydgate *Troy* II 409.518-9: As fresche be-seyn as May is with his flouris, The ladies then ascendid of the toun. **c1475** Henryson *Thre Deid Pollis* 205.17: O wantone yowth, als fresche as lusty may. Tilley M763; Whiting *Scots* II 97. Cf. Apperson 235-6; *Oxford* 225.

M423 **May** (is) the month of gladness
a1420 Lydgate *Troy* I 49.1293: And May was com, the monyth of gladnes. Apperson 414-5; *Oxford* 413; Tilley M1106.

M424 **May** surmounts other months
a1393 Gower *CA* III 60.4172-4: And lich unto the freisshe Maii, Whan passed ben the colde schoures, Riht so recovereth he his floures, 132.6736-9: That lich unto the fresshe Maii, Which othre monthes of the yeer Surmonteth, so withoute pier Was of this Maiden the feture. **1420** Lydgate *Temple* 10-1.250-64: A ladi . . . (who) . . . as Mai hath the sovereinte Of evere moneth . . . Surmounteth al.

M425 Who that **May** not as they would, will as they may
1546 Heywood *D* 72.85: Who that maie not as they wolde, will as they maie. Apperson 409; Tilley M769.

Mead (1)

M426 As fresh as a **Mead**
a1500 *Alexander-Cassamus* 52.25-6: This mayd(e) fre, Of roshes and floures as fresh as ys (a) mede.

M427 As full as **Mead** of grass
c1300 *South English Legendary* I 28.112: As fol of swerdes pointes as mede is of gras.

M428 As green as a **Mead**
c1450 *Merlin* I 163[12]: As grene as a mede.

M429 To be embroidered like a **Mead**
c1387-95 Chaucer *CT* I[A] 89-90: Embrouded was he, as it were a meede Al ful of fresshe floures, whyte and reede.

Mead (2)

M430 As mild as **Mead**
a1400 *Alexander C* 249.4824: Was nevir no mede . . . so mild undire heven. **a1500** *Devyce proves* in *Bannatyne* IV 34.6: Quhair are becum thir madynis myld as mude? **a1500** *Eger H* 343.2655: And your two maidens myld as mood. Whiting *Scots* II 97.

M431 As sweet as (the, any) **Mead**
c1350 *Proprium Sanctorum* 84.118: That made ure Meole swetter then mede. **c1390** Chaucer *CT* I[A] 3261: Hir mouth was sweete as . . . the meeth. **c1390** *Talkyng* 26.17-8: Swettore art thou then . . . Meode. **a1450** *Castle* 100.776: Thou art swetter thanne mede. **a1450** *York Plays* 424.89: Thi love is swetter thanne the mede. **c1450** *Owayne Miles* (*Auchinleck*) 108.149[2]: The water is swetter than ani mede. **a1460** *Towneley Plays* 341.111. Whiting *Scots* II 97. See **M525.**

M432 Sometimes after **Mead** men are most thirsty
c1025 *Durham Proverbs* 11.8: Hwilum æfter medo menn mæst geþyrsted. Post medum maxime sitit. See **D403.**

Meal (1)

M433 One must have much **Meal** to stop every man's mouth
1509 Barclay *Ship* I 208[17]: One must have moche mele, to stoppe eche mannys mouth. Apperson 604; Jente 218; *Oxford* 623.

Meal (2)

M434 Better are many **Meals** than a merry night (one too merry)
c1353 *Winner* 364-5: Bot one(s) I herd in a haule of a herdmans tong,—Better were meles many than a mery nyghte. **1546** Heywood *D* 86.192: Better are meales many, than one to mery. Apperson 41; *Oxford* 38; Tilley M788.

M435 Two hungry **Meals** make the third a glutton
1546 Heywood *D* 54.421: And two hongry meales make the thyrd a glutten. Apperson 655; *Oxford* 414; Tilley M789.

M436 To be a **Mealmouth**
1546 Heywood *D* 35.18-20: And when the meale mouth hath woon the bottome Of your stomake, than will the pickthanke it tell To your most enmies. NED Mealmouth, Mealy-mouthed; Tilley M791.

M437 By fair **Means** or foul

a1511 Guylforde *Pylgrymage* 63[19]: By fayre meanes or foule. **1525** Berners *Froissart* IV 46[7–8]: He wolde have her, outher by fayre meanes or by foule. Taylor and Whiting 240. Cf. Tilley M794.

M438 In a good **Mean** men longest may endure
a1439 Lydgate *Fall* II 491–2.644: In a good mene men lengest may endure, 651, 658, *etc.*

M439 Keep (thee) in a **Mean** (*varied*)
c1408 Lydgate *Reson* 166.6339–42: In every thing to kepe a Mene, To refuse and voyde clene Of excesse all surplusage Aftir doctrine of the sage, **a1420** *Troy* II 401.211: But late prudence kepe the in a mene. **a1475** *Tree* 134.18–20: Of the mesure of etyng and drinkyng it is ful hard forto yif a certeyn rewle but thus that thou kepe a good mene be twene to moche and to litel. Whiting *Scots* II 97. See **M458, W117.**

M440 Let the **Mean** suffice
1406 Hoccleve *Male Regle* 36.353–6: Who-so, passynge mesure, desyrith, (As that witnessen olde Clerkes wyse,) Him self encombrith ofte sythe, and myrith; And for-thy let the mene thee souffyse.

M441 **Mean** and measure are lauded in all thing(s)
c1523 Barclay *Mirrour* 61[14]: But meane and measure is lauded in all thing. See **M444.**

M442 **Mean** is a treasure
a1500 *Leconfield Proverbs* 483[33]: An olde proverbe it is meane is a treasure. See **M461.**

M443 **Mean** is a virtue
c1386 Chaucer *LGW* F 165–6: For vertu is the mene, As Etik seith. **a1400** *Romaunt C* 6527–8: The mene is cleped suffisaunce; Ther lyth of vertu the aboundaunce. **c1475** *Magnificencia Ecclesie* in *PMLA* 24(1909) 692[24–5]: Ffor *virtus in medio consistit,* yef this text be derke, Lo in the mene ys vertu. **a1500** *Leconfield Proverbs* 486[10]: Meane is a vertu of greate price. See **V45.**

M444 A **Mean** is good in all thing(s)
c1408 Lydgate *Reson* 110.4194: A mean ys good in alle thing. See **M441.**

M445 A **Mean** is measure
1515 Barclay *St. George* 58.1284: A meane is mesure, **c1523** *Mirrour* 33[11]: A fayre meane is measure in all thing commendable. See **M454.**

M446 The **Mean** is (the) best
a1396(1494) Hilton *Scale* C4v[5–6]: It is good to kepe descrecion for the meane is the best. **a1439** Lydgate *Fall* II 344.554: A mene is best, with good(e) governaunce, **a1449** *Fabules* in *MP* II 599.951–2: A meane is best withe good governaunce, To them that be content withe suffisaunce. **c1450** Idley 146.2356–7: Betwene poverte and grete habundaunce Meane is the beste, to be content with suffisaunce. **1477** Rivers *Dictes* 109[25]: In all thinges the meane is best. **c1500** Greene *Carols* 348 (*refrain*): In every state, in every degre, The mene ys beste, as semeth me. Smith 195; Tilley M793. See **M456.**

M447 The **Mean** is the merry part
1556 Heywood *Spider* 426[28]: The meane is the merie part: being soong right. See **M454.**

M448 A measurable **Mean** is best
c1450 *ABC of Aristotle* in *Queene Elizabethes Achademy,* ed. F. J. Furnivall (EETS ES 8, 1869) 67.21: A mesurable mene is best for us all. Apperson 410.

M449 To be too hasty is no good **Mean**
1525 Berners *Froissart* V 21[13–4]: To be to hasty is no good meane. See **H160.**

M450 To serve one with the same **Mease** (*measure*)
c1505 Watson *Valentine* 51.12–3: He . . . thought to serve him with the same mese. See **M465.**

M451 Be content with **Measure**
a1440 Burgh *Cato* 31.1087: Withe mesure be content. See **N138.**

M452 He that loves **Measure** and skill oft has his will
c1350 *Good Wife E* 162.56–7: That mesure loveth and skil Ofte hath his wil. Apperson 409.

M453 **Measure** is a merry meal
a1400 *Proverbis of Wysdom* (*II*) 222.33–4: Mesure is a mery mele, After syknes cometh hele. **c1450** *Fyrst thou sal* 88.59–60. See **S917.**

M454 **Measure** is a merry mean (*varied*)
c1405 *Mum* 11.139: But mesure is a meri mene, though men moche yerne. **a1450** Audelay 184.26: Then mesuere hit is a mery mene. **a1475** Russell *Boke* 124.107: Mesure is a mery meene whan god is not displesed. **a1475** *Tree* 128.14–6: What is maner in good living; but mesure that no thing be had to moche ne to litell but in a scarce mene. **1483** *Quatuor Sermones* 26[30–1]: The seventh vertue is mesure, whiche is a mene betwene to moche and to lytel. **1509** Barclay *Ship* I 188[18]: A mery thynge is mesure and easy to sustayne. **c1516**

Skelton *Magnificence* 7.188: For Measure is a meane, nother to hy nor to lawe, 13.380: Yet Mesure is a mery mene. **c1523** Barclay *Mirrour* 25[28]: But measure is meane. **1534** More *Comforte* 1184 D[17]: Measure is a mery meane. **1546** Heywood *D* 84.135: Measure is a mery meane, **1555** *E* 167.128. Apperson 409; *Oxford* 415; Skeat 25; Tilley M804. See **A234, I40, M445, 447, W117.**

M455 **Measure** is an excellent virtue
1509 Barclay *Ship* I 185[4]: Gydynge hym by mesure a vertue excellent. See **V45.**

M456 **Measure** (I-met) is best
a1200 *Ancrene* 148.23: Euch thing thah me mei overdon, best is eaver mete. **a1425** *Measure* in Brown *Lyrics XV* 286–7.8: Mesure is best of all thynge, 16, 24. **1509** Barclay *Ship* I 189[5]: Content the with measure (therfore) for it is best. *Oxford* 415. See **M446.**

M457 **Measure** is good
c1412 Hoccleve *Regement* 49.1335: Mesure is good; let hir the gye and lede. Jente 469.

M458 **Measure** is good in all meat
1481 Caxton *Reynard* 14[39]: Mesure is good in alle mete. See **M439.**

M459 **Measure** is medicine (*varied*)
a1376 *Piers* A i 33: Mesure is medicine, thauh thou muche yeorne. **1549** Heywood *D* 84.127: Feed by measure, and defie the phisicion. Apperson 409; *Oxford* 415; Skeat 25.

M460 **Measure** is meed
c1400 *Lay Folks' Catechism* 87.1293: For mesure ys mede to us in al that we do.

M461 **Measure** is treasure
a1440 Burgh *Cato* 315.505: The olde sawe seithe: Mesur is tresure. **a1449** Lydgate *Mesure is Tresour* in *MP* II 776.1: Men wryte of oold how mesour is tresour. **c1450** *Douce MS.52* 51.81. **c1450** *Rules for Conduct* in Smith *Common-place Book* 14[1-2]: Man in merthe, hath meser in mynd, For meser ys treser whan merthe ys behynd. **c1450** *Rylands MS.394* 101.9. **a1475** *Mumming of the Seven Philosophers* in Robbins 111.40: The olde (*saw*) ys that "mesure ys tresure." **c1475** *Mankind* 9.230. **a1500** *Compleint un-to dame fortune* in *PMLA* 69(1954) 640.22: as men doon seye. **a1500** *Mostyn MS.129* in *Historical Manuscripts Commission Report on Manuscripts in the Welsh Language* I(1898) 65: Be not two nigarde nor be not two ffree, Ffor measure is treasure in every degree. **c1516** Skelton *Magnificence* 5.125, **c1522** *Speke* II 4.64. Apperson 409–10; Jente 469; *Oxford* 415; Tilley M805. See **M442, W383.**

M462 **Measure** restrains by reason
c1390 Chaucer *CT* X[I] 834: Mesure also, that restreyneth by resoun.

M463 Over **Measure** is not cunning (*wise*)
c1303 Mannyng *Handlyng* 113.3232: But over mesure ys nat cunnaunt. See **O63.**

M464 There is **Measure** in all things (*varied*)
a1325 *Cursor* III 1582.29404–5: For in alkin thing o dede Aght man mesure wit him lede. **c1385** Chaucer *TC* ii 715: In every thyng, I woot, there lith mesure. **c1390** *God man and the devel* 353.923: And Mesure in alle thyng. **c1425** Arderne *Fistula* 4.31–5: Ffor the wise man seith, "Sicut ad omne quod est mensuram ponere prodest, Sic sine mensura deperit omne quod est:" "As it profiteth to putte mesure to al thing that is, So without mesure perissheth all thing that is." **a1430** Lydgate *Pilgrimage* 43.1598: Mesure ys good in every thyng, 603. 22609–10: Every thyng (I the ensure) To governe it by mesure, **a1449** *Mesure is Tresour* in *MP* II 776.8 (*varied refrain*): Alle thyng is weel so it in mesure be. **c1450** *Fyrst thou sal* 90.128: In al thinge is mesure ay the beste. **a1500** *Miroure of Mans Salvacionne* 16[31]: Mesure be dette to kepe in evry thing. **1509** Barclay *Ship* I 97[4]: In eche thynge ought to be had measure, II 266[1]: But in every thynge is ordre and mesure, **c1523** *Mirrour* 61[2]: In all thinges measure is counted commendable. Apperson 410; *Oxford* 415; Smith 196; Tilley M806; Whiting *Drama* 135. See **M363.**

M465 To quit with the same **Measure** that one borrows
a1460 *Towneley Plays* 11.51–2: With the same mesure and weght That I boro will I qwite. See **M450.**

M466 Where **Measure** is there is no lacking
1506 Hawes *Pastime* 100.2591: Where that is mesure there is no lackynge.

M467 With what **Measure** you mete it shall be measured unto you (*varied*)
c1000 *WSG* Matthew vii 2: On ðam ylcan gemete þe ge metaþ, eow byþ gemeten. **c1395** *WBible* Matthew vii 2: In what mesure ye meten, it schal be meten agen to you. **a1400** *Destruction of Troy* 378.11615–8: But god, that all giltis godely beholdis, And wrangis in his wrathe writhis to ground, Oft-sithes in the same settis to fall A man with that mesure he metis till another. **c1400** *Consilia Isidori* 373[45–6]:

By what mesure thou mesureste, yt schalle be mesured agen to the. **c1415** *Middle English Sermons* 43.30–2: Than the same mesure that thou metiste to thi neyghboure, the same mesure shall be meton to the, 102.37–103.3. **a1439** Lydgate *Fall* III 918.3379–81: For short conclusioun biddith men take heede, Thei shal resceyve ageynward suich mesour As thei mesure unto their neih(e)bour. **c1505** More *Picus* 13 C[5–6]: It is written: In what measure that ye mete, it shalbe mette you agayn. **1509** Barclay *Ship* I 27[1–3]: Loke in what Balance, what weyght and what mesure Thou servest other, for thou shalt served be With the same after this lyfe, I the ensure. **1556** Heywood *Spider* 427[21]: Our mesure mette to other, shal to us be mottun. Tilley M801; Whiting *Drama* 291. See **D274, M495.**

M468 After **Meat** dishes are rife (*plentiful*)
c1450 *Douce MS.52* 45.8: After mete disshes ben rybe (*for* ryve). Crebrescunt vacui certe post prandia disci. **c1450** *Rylands MS.394* 96.23: ryve. **c1475** *Rawlinson MS. D 328* 119.29: ryffe. Walther I 426.3626.

M469 After **Meat** play arises
a1300 *Alisaunder* 193.3439: After mete ariseth pleie. Cf. Apperson 411: When meat is in anger is out; Tilley M846. See **B243.**

M470 All **Meats** to be eaten, all maids to be wed
1546 Heywood *D* 62.22: All meats to be eaten, and all maides to be wed. Apperson 7; *Oxford* 7; Tilley M850.

M471 Make merry at **Meat**
a1400 *Proverbis of Wysdom* 245.75: Make mery at mete. **c1450** Capgrave *Lives* 70.2: At mete was he myri. Apperson 414; *Oxford* 420; Tilley M815. Cf. Whiting *Scots* II 98.

M472 **Meat** lains (*conceals*) many (a) lack
c1425 *Avowynge* 92[13–4]: Mete laynes mony lakke, And there mete hor sege brake.

M473 **Meat** savors better to the hungry than to the full
a1400 *Twelve Profits (Royal)* in *Yorkshire Writers* II 57[5–6]: As tho meete savers better to tho hungrye then to tho ful, **a1500** (*Rawlinson*) 403[13]: As mete savereth more to an hungry man than to an unhungrye man. Cf. Whiting *Drama* 115. See **H642.**

M474 The **Meat** you eat is well set (*invested*)
c1300 *Havelok* 33.907: Wel is set the mete thu etes. Apperson 674.

M475 Show me not (Look not on) the **Meat** but show me (look on) the man
1459 Paston III 145[18–9]: Schew me not the mete, schew me the man. **1534** Heywood *Love* D4^r^[11–2]: This proverbe answereth you playne, Loke not on the meat, but loke on the man, **1546** *D* 67.47: Looke not on the meate, but looke on the man. Apperson 410; *Oxford* 415: Measure; Tilley M838.

M476 Sweet **Meat** has sharp (sour) sauce
a1500 *Colyn Blowbol* 98.130–1: Ffor of right, and as old bookes doon trete, Sharpe sawce was ordeigned for swete mete. **1509** *Fyftene Joyes* A8^r^[28]: For with the swete mete the sauces soure. **c1522** Skelton *Colyn* I 328.450: Yet swete meate hath soure sauce, 330.483–5: For els, as I sayd before, After *gloria, laus,* May come a soure sauce. **1546** Heywood *D* 32.46: Sweete meate will have sowre sawce, **1555** *E* 181.197. Apperson 614; *Oxford* 635; Tilley M839; Whiting *Drama* 199. See **S64, 942.**

M477 Those that have much **Meat** must have much sleep
c1450 Capgrave *Lives* 71.15–6: Thei that have mech mete must have mech slep. See **B242.**

M478 To do one more good than **Meat** or drink
c1495 *Arundel Vulgaria* 15.59: It doth me more goode then mete or drynke, 45.195: I am suer ther wyl nother mete nother drynke do me goode but if I here from the. Cf. Apperson 410; Tilley M842.

M479 To seek fat **Meat** in (a) hound's nest
a1400 *Romaunt C* 6503–4: It is but foly to entremete, To seke in houndes nest fat mete. Cf. Tilley B777.

M480 What helps it to have **Meat** where drink lacks?
a1393 Gower *CA* II 347.1718–9: What helpeth it a man have mete, Wher drinke lacketh on the bord?

M481 **Meddle** no further than you have to do
a1500 Medwall *Nature* A4^r^[14]: And medyll the no further than thou hast to do. Tilley M854.

M482 Little **Meddling** makes much rest (*varied*)
a1400 *Proverbis of Wysdom* 247.128: Lytyll medlyng makythe mych rest. **a1449** Lydgate *See Myche* in *MP* II 801.29: Lytell medelynge causeth quiete and rest (cf. Brown *Lyrics XV* 280.29: mellyng). **1504** Hawes *Example* Bb4^r^ [6–7]: Who lytell medeleth is best at ease, For well were he that all myght please. **1546**

Heywood *D* 64.78: Of little medlyng cometh great reste. Apperson 372; Jente 458; *Oxford* 374; Tilley M858. See **J13.**

M483 A little **Medicine** does away a great evil (*varied*)
a1450 *Barlam and Josaphat* (*South English Legendary*) 133.723: As lytil medesyne gret evil doth a wey. **1483** Caxton *Golden Legende* 395r[1.17–8]: A lytyll medecyne ofte delyvereth a grete languor. See **M159, S44, T113, 203.**

M484 **Medicine** avails not when the sick is dead (*varied*)
a1420 Lydgate *Troy* I 119.3626–7: For evene liche as a medicine Availeth nat, whan the seke is ded, **1439** *St. Albon* 114.201–3: To late amonge is made a medicine Whan that a sore wexith ded and corrumpable, For lacke of surgiens is waxen incurable. **c1450** Capgrave *Katharine* 115.582–4: Ffor medecyn comyth overe-late Whan that the man is deed and hens I-goo And wyth his freendis boorn oute at the gate. **c1505** More *Picus* 24 A[3–4]: To late commeth the medicine, if thou let the sore, By long continuaunce encrease more and more. See **A72, C51, L168, 178, M488.**

M485 The **Medicines** that soonest heal are bitter
1477 Rivers *Dictes* 101[6–7]: The medicines that sonest heleth people aren bittre and of evyll savour. See **M487.**

M486 Some **Medicine** is for Peter that is not good for Paul
a1400 Lanfranc 331.24–6: For sum medicyne is for peter that is not good for poul, for the diversite of complexioun. Cf. Tilley M483. See **G104, 329, H653, O42.**

M487 A strong **Medicine** answers to a strong sickness
c1425 Arderne *Fistula* 7.31–2: A strong medicyne answerith to a strong sekenes. Cf. Taylor and Whiting 103. See **M485.**

M488 There is no **Medicine** against death
c1430 Lydgate *Dance* 54.432: A-gens dethe is worth no medicyne. Apperson 527; *Oxford* 537. See **M484.**

M489 To take one's **Medicine**
1520 Whittinton *Vulgaria* 97.30–1: Take thy medicyne (though it be somwhat bytter) with a good wyll, it wyll worke to thy ease at lenght. Taylor and Whiting 241.

M490 **Meed** does most in every quest
a1475 *Ludus Coventriae* 326.1604–7: Ffor mede doth most in every qwest, And mede is mayster bothe est and west, Now trewly, serys, I hold this best, With mede men may bynde berys. See **G296.**

M491 **Meed** is strong
a1393 Gower *CA* III 78.4846–7: Bot for men sein that mede is strong, It was wel seene at thilke tyde. See **M322.**

M492 **Meed** is the devil
c1303 Mannyng *Handlyng* 263.8330: Men sey ofte "mede ys the devyl."

M493 **Meed** may speed (*succeed*) rather than truth
a1400 *Proverbis of Wysdom* 246.93–4: Mede may spede, and that is ruth, That mede shall spede rather, than trewthe. **c1450** *Fyrst thou sal* 89.81–2: Men may say and that is rewthe That mede sal spede rather than trewthe.

M494 Through great **Meed** right is brought into wrong
c1280 *South English Legendary: OT History* 83.52: For oft the righth, thorough gret mede is in-to wrong y-broughth. See **G82, M630.**

M495 To have one's **Meed** like his desert (*varied*)
c1421 Lydgate *Thebes* 86.2072: Lik thi desert thow shalt have thy mede, **a1439** *Fall* III 918.3376: As men disserve, suich shal be ther meede. **1504** Hawes *Example* Aa5r[25]: After thy desert shall be thy mede. **1509** Watson *Ship* B2r[11–2]: Where after his deserte he shall have mede, Yf he have done well he shall ryght well spede. See **M467.**

M496 With **Meed** men may fare over water
a1200 *Trinity College Homilies* 41[20]: Mid mede man mai over water faren. See **B580, G64.**

M497 Whoso flits (*fights*) or turns again (*attacks*) he begins the **Mellay**
a1350 *Ywain* 14.503–5: And als, madame, men says sertayne That, wo so flites or turnes ogayne, He bygins al the melle. (Chretien *Yvain*, ed. W. Foerster [Halle, 1887] 25.641–3: Que cil ne fet pas la meslee, Qui fiert la premiere colee, Ainz la fet cil qui se revange.)

M498 He that **Menaces** is in great fear (*varied*)
c1500 *Melusine* 279.34–6: But oft he that menaceth is somtyme in grete fer and drede hym self, and aftirward overthrawen. **c1505** Watson *Valentine* 242.23–4: For it is sayd comonly that suche menaceth that have great drede.

M499 He that **Menaces** most has cause to fare feebly
a1400 *Ipomadon A* 158.5511–3: He that moste ys manasand, Hym selff hathe cause, I understond, Febly yf he fare!

M500 Good **Mending** and short ending
a1460 *Towneley Plays* 102.78–9: And send theym good mendyng With a short endyng. A. C. Cawley *Wakefield Pageants in the Towneley Cycle* (Manchester, 1958) xxix. Cf. *Oxford* 419; Tilley M874.

M501 He is a **Merchant** without money or ware
1555 Heywood *E* 179.186: He is a marchaunt without money or ware. Apperson 413; Tilley M883.

M502 He that knew what would be dear, need be a **Merchant** but one year
1546 Heywood *D* 19.7–8: Who so that knew, what wolde be deere, Should neede be a marchant but one yeere. Apperson 413; *Oxford* 344; Tilley M887.

M503 A **Merchant** may not endure ay in prosperity (*varied*)
c1385 Usk 135.97–9: A marchaunt that for ones lesinge in the see no more to aventure thinketh, he shal never with aventure come to richesse. **c1395** Chaucer *CT* VIII[G] 947–50: A marchant, pardee, may nat ay endure, Trusteth me wel, in his prosperitee. Somtyme his good is drowned in the see, And somtyme comth it sauf unto the londe. Tilley M880.

M504 A **Merchant** of eelskins
1533 More *Confutacion* 742 A[4–6]: He shaved his beard and went like a merchant of eeles skinnes. **1546** Heywood *D* 71.39–40: If he holde on a while, as he begins, We shall see him prove a marchaunt of eele skins. Apperson 412–3; *Oxford* 419; Tilley M882.

M505 **Merchants** live poorly to die rich
1532 Berners *Golden Boke* 348.7543: The marchantis live porely to die ryche.

M506 He is worthy to have **Mercy** that will crave mercy (*varied*)
a1338 Mannyng *Chronicle A* I 304.8675–8: Wel ys worthy, mercy to have, That mekely mercy wyl crave. Agayn mercy who-so ys grym, God wyl have no mercy of hym. **a1350** *Ywain* 87.3273–4: And by scill sal he mercy have, What man so mekely wil it crave, 106.4003–4: And what man so wil mercy crave, By Goddes law he sal it have. **a1475** *Ludus Coventriae* 201.38: Who so Aske mercy he xal have grace. **c1475** *Mankind* 32.856: Aske mercy, and hawe. **c1500** *Everyman* 20.570: Aske god mercy and he wyll graunte truely. **a1533** Berners *Huon* 719.2–5: I have often tymes hard say that he that humbleth hymselfe and cryethe for marcy reason then requereth that he shulde have marcy graunted hym. See **M538.**

M507 **Mercy** passes all thing(s)
c1390 *Mercy Passes all Things* in Brown *Lyrics XIV* 125–131.12 (*refrain*): How Merci passeth alle thinge. **a1450** *Castle* 168.3064: But mercy pase alle thynge, 171.3153: Mercy pasyt mannys mysdede. Whiting *Drama* 91.

M508 **Mercy** passes right
c1385 Chaucer *CT* I[A] 3089: For gentil mercy oghte to passen right, *TC* iii 1282: Here may men seen that mercy passeth right. **c1385** Usk 105.137: Mercy bothe right and lawe passeth. **a1422** Lydgate *Life* 340.425: But undir hope, that mercy passith Right. Jente 373; *Oxford* 419; Skeat 184. See **P242.**

M509 To make **Mercy** go afore might
a1449 Lydgate *Fabula* in *MP* II 514.843: And made mercy to goon afforn his myht.

M510 Whoso will have **Mercy** must be merciful
c1000 *WSG* Matthew v 7: Eadige synt þa mildheortan, for þam þe hi mildheortnysse begytað. **c1395** *WBible* Matthew v 7: Blessid ben merciful men, for thei schulen gete merci. **a1500** *Hunterian Mus. MS.230* 175: A man wythe owtt mercy mercy schall mys, He schall have mercy that mercy full is. **1513** Bradshaw *St. Werburge* 100.2750–2: Who-so wyll have mercy Must be mercyable as in proverbe wryten is; Who is without mercy of mercy shall mys. Tilley M895.

M511 To have no more **Merit** than Malkin of her maidenhead (*varied*)
a1376 *Piers* A i 157–8: Ye nave no more merit in masse ne in houres Then Malkyn of hire maydenhod that no mon desyreth. **a1387** Higden-Trevisa VII 355[4–7]: A wise man wolde wene that eorle Roger hadde as moche mede of that he was a monk, as Malkyn of here maydenhood, that no man wolde have, and nought a deel more. Apperson 427; *Oxford* 400.

M512 To sing merrier (sweeter) than the **Mermaid(s)**
c1390 Chaucer *CT* VII 3270[B4460]: Soong murier than the mermayde in the see. **a1430** Lydgate *Pilgrimage* 396.14689–90: My song ys swettere, hem tagree, Than off meremaydenys in the se. **a1533** Berners *Huon* 190.18–20: The vyall made so swete a swonde that it semed

to be the mermaydes of the see. Whiting *Scots* II 98.

M513 Be **Merry** though you are hard betided (*in trouble*)
a1400 *Proverbis of Wysdom* 246.105–6: Be thou mery, thow thou be hard betid; Fore goddis mercy thou must abyde.

M514 Good to be **Merry** and wise
c1497 Medwall *Fulgens* G3r[1–2]: Ye, thou art a maister mery man, Thou shall be wyse, I wot nere whan. **1534** More *Comforte* 1161 G[3–4]: It were good to make sure and to be mery, so that he be wyse therwith. **1546** Heywood *D* 21.38: Good to be mery and wise, **1555** *E* 151.33. Apperson 413; *Oxford* 420; Taylor and Whiting 241; Tilley G324; Whiting *Drama* 144, 231. See **L175, M131, 214.**

M515 **Merry-go-down**
c1500 Greene *Carols* 419 A 4: I know a drawght of mery-go-down (*wine*). Apperson 414; NED Merry-go-down; Tilley M900.

M516 A corby **Messenger**
a1325 *Cursor* I 116.1889–92: For-thi men sais on messager That lengs lang to bring answare, He mai be cald, with right resun, An of messagers corbun (GT ravyns), 198.3332–3: Licknes to corbin (FGT raven) had he nan! Sa welworth suilk a messager. **c1380** *Cleanness* 19.456: Corbyal untrwe. **c1450** Holland *Howlat* 75.812–4: How Corby messinger . . . with sorowe now syngis; Thow ischit out of Noyes ark, and to the erd wan, Taryit as a tratour, and brocht na tythingis. **c1475** Henryson *Fables* 43.1160–2: Schir Corbie Ravin wes maid Apparitour . . . The charge hes tane, and on the letteris bure. *Oxford* 109–10; Tilley M903; Whiting *Scots* I 152.

M517 A **Messenger** shall not be beaten or bound (have no harm)
c1450 *Douce MS.52* 49.67: The(r) schall no man bete ne bynde a messyng (*for* messynger). Non decet artare, qui mittitur, aut religare. **c1450** *Ponthus* 21.32–4: Ye shall goo save and sure —for a messynger shall have noon harme, bot if he require dedes of armes. **c1450** *Rylands MS.394* 100.14: messanger. Walther III 244.17470. Cf. *Oxford* 421; Tilley M905.

M518 To come before the **Messenger** (*i.e.*, without warning)
1546 Heywood *D* 42.34: To come on us before the messenger thus. Tilley M904.

M519 As tough as **Metal**
a1349 Rolle *Meditatio* (*Upps.*) 43.10–1: Make me towghe as metal.

M520 As true as any **Metal** that is new forged
c1385 Chaucer *Mars* 200–1: For thogh so be that lovers be as trewe As any metal that is forged newe. Svartengren 11.

M521 To melt like **Metal**
a1450 *Partonope* 371.9048: His herte as metalle then gan melte.

M522 To purge (prove) like **Metal** in the fire (furnace)
c1400 *Remedy* in *Yorkshire Writers* II 110[34–5]: To pourge and pure goddes specyall lovers as the metall is in the fyre. **c1450** Capgrave *Lives* 95.17–8: Thus was the blessid man proved as metal in the fornays. See **F180, G298, S327, 410.**

M523 True **Metal** requires no alloy
a1449 Lydgate *Horns Away* in *MP* II 662.6: Trewe metall requeryth noon allay.

M524 Short **Meters** do great pleasance
a1449 Lydgate *St. Gyle* in *MP* I 162.36: For short metris do gladly gret plesaunce. See **P408.**

M525 As sweet as (the) **Meth** (*mead*)
c1390 Chaucer *CT* I[A] 3261: Hir mouth was sweete as . . . the meeth. **c1390** *Talkyng* 26.17–8: Swettore art thou then . . . Meth. **c1450** Idley 113.303: Whos grace is swetter than . . . methe. See **M431.**

M526 As long living (old) as **Methuselah**
a1400 *Pricke* 241.8952–3: Ilkane moght als lang be lyfand thare, Als Matussale namely dyd here. **1509** Watson *Ship* H2r[17]: Also olde as ever was matheusale. Taylor and Whiting 242; Tilley M908.

M527 To go as smooth(ly) as a **Mew** (?*gull*)
c1450 Idley 116.512: Then he will goo as smothe as a mewe.

Mickle, sb., see **Much**

M528 As bright as **Midday**
c1340 Rolle *Psalter* 331 (90.6): Makis him to seme bryght as mydday.

M529 After dark **Midnight** the mirthful morrow
a1513 Dunbar *Of the Changes of Lyfe* 141.18: Nixt dirk mednycht the mirthefull morrow. See **N108.**

M530 As dark as **Midnight**
c1400 *Thomas of Erceldoune* 10.171: Whare it was dirke als mydnyght myrke. **a1450** Audelay 158.90: Bot darker then the myrke mydnyght. Taylor and Whiting 242.

M531 As murk as (any, the) **Midnight**
a1400 *Alexander C* 225.4077: As mirke as any mydnight quen the mone failes. **a1400** *Destruction of Troy* 120.3688–9: The hevyn in hast hepit with cloudis, Wex merke as the mydnight, 150.4628: the. **a1400** *Scottish Legends* I 243. 154–5: Thai put in presone the gud man sone, Quhare in merknes, as mydnycht. **a1450** *Death and Life* 14.406: That was ever merke as midnight.

M532 As still as **Midnight**
1513 More *Richard* 64 D[6–7]: Al was as styl as the midnight. Taylor and Whiting 242.

M533 Do after **Might** and not after will
a1500 *Salamon sat and sayde* 291.15: Ffor the behowys do efter myth and noght eftyr wyll.

M534 **Might** is (overcomes) right (*varied*)
c1330 *On the King's Breaking his Confirmation of Magna Charta* in Wright *Political Songs* 254[13–8]: For might is riht, Liht is night, And fiht is fliht. For miht is riht, the lond is laweles; For niht is liht, the lond is loreles; For fiht is fliht, the lond is nameles. **1381** *Jack Milner* in Knighton II 139[2–6]: With ryght and with myght, with skyl and with wylle, lat myght helpe ryght, and skyl go before wille and ryght before myght, than goth oure mylne aryght. And if myght go before ryght, and wylle before skylle; than is oure mylne mys adyght. **1381** *John Ball* in Knighton II 139[29–30]: Nowe ryght and myght, wylle and skylle. **a1393** Gower *CA* III 2.2021–2: For wher that such on is of myht, His will schal stonde in stede of riht. **a1400** *Four Proverbs* in *Pol. Rel. and Love Poems* 251: Mithgh is Rithgh; lithgh is nithgh; Fithgh is flithgh. **a1400** *Saw* in Joseph Ritson *Pieces of Ancient Popular Poetry* (London, 1791) 58: Ther ys leythe reythe and meythe, Meythe overset reythe for the defawte of leythe, Bot and reythe methe com to leythe, Scholder never meythe overset reythe. **a1475** Fortescue *Dialogue* I 490[16]: But strength maykyth right after his owne opynyoun. **1546** Heywood *D* 73.115: Might overcomth right, **1555** *E* 172.145, 190.248.2: Where althynge is there ryght is lost by myght. Apperson 416; Brown-Robbins 1857; Jente 22; *Oxford* 423; Robbins-Cutler 2167; Taylor and Whiting 242; Tilley M922; Whiting *Drama* 254. See **F489, L102, M630, T169, 180.**

M535 **Might** shall be withstood with might
a1393 Gower *CA* II 210.2983: That miht with miht schal be withstonde. See **F491.**

M536 To have no more **Might** than drops of rain in the sea
1340 *Ayenbite* 84[18–21]: Naght ne habbeth more of myghte . . . thanne ther byeth dropen of rayn ine the ze. **c1400** *Vices and Virtues* 83.4–5: Al hath no more myght than dropes of reyn haven in the see. Cf. Tilley D613, W88.

M537 (With) **Might** (main) and main (might)
a900 *Anglo-Saxon Charms* 158.14: Eorþe þe onbere eallum hire mihtum and mægenum. **a1300** *Thrush* in Brown *Lyrics XIII* 104.89: That ihesu crist yaf might and main. **c1300** *Body and Soul (L)* 63.579: And kesten it with myght and mayn. **c1350** *Als y yod* in T. Wright *Langtoft* (RS 47, 1868) II 454[22]: And so mikel of mithe and mayne. **a1400** *Or Crist into cloudes* in *PMLA* 70(1955) 222.111: With myght and with mayne thou carpe of thi crede. **a1400** *Stanzaic Life* 32.932: Merveiles to meve with mayn and myght, 35.1051: Jewes haden never myght ne mayn. **c1400** *Tundale* 26.467. **c1420** Page *Siege* 145.208. **c1420** Wyntoun II 83.964, III 331.1678. **a1425** *Chester Plays* I 106.39, 203.462, 211.163: I have mayne and mighte, 214.247, II 307.650: Marrs my mynd, mayne and might, 308.669: mayne and might, 339.204: mayn and might. **a1425** *Metrical Paraphrase OT* 143.5011, 13.6089, 51.7455: Then dyde he all his mayn and myght, 60.7777, 59.11509. **a1450** *Death and Life* 15.442. **a1450** *Myne awen dere* 155.208. **a1450** *St. Editha* 98.4412: With alle herre mayne and alle herre myght. **a1450** Spalding *Katherine* 158 xiv 12. **c1450** *St. Cuthbert* 134.4565, 175.6014, 179.6145. **c1455** *Speculum Misericordie* 942.65. **1483** Skelton *Dethe* I 9.89. **a1500** *Coventry Plays* 62.943, 66.1081. **a1500** *Croxton Sacrament* in Waterhouse 71.432: Now set on, felouse, with mayne and might. **a1500** *O glorius lady* in Rolf Kaiser *Medieval English* (Berlin, 1961) 509.47. **a1500** *Revelations of Methodius* in *PMLA* 33(1918) 165.329, 168.464, 173.626. **a1500** *Thre Prestis* 8.106. **a1500** *Trust in my luf* in *Anglia* 83(1965) 45[4]: And you to menske with mayn and meght. **c1500** *Lady Bessy* 8[14]: He will come with main and might. **a1508** Skelton *Phyllyp* I 91.1297. **1513** Bradshaw *St. Werburge* 25.474: And cruelly to slee by power mayne and myght. Taylor and Whiting 242–3; Tilley M923.

M538 Who bids (for) **Milce** (*mercy*) may have it
c1300 Lawman II B 281.16829–32: Evere hit was, and yet hit his, Alse us wel bi-hoveth, That wo milce biddeth, That he hit maghe habbe. See **M506.**

M539 As sweet as **Mildew** (*honey-dew*)
c1225 *Wohunge of ure Laverd* 269[2–3]: Swetter is munegunge of the then mildeu o muthe.

M540 A Scottish **Mile**
c1450 *Merlin* II 197[3–4]: Thei were but two scottish myle fro the town.

M541 To have but a **Mile** to midsummer
1460 *In the day of faste* in *English Chronicle* 92[25]: Tho bestys that thys wroughte to mydsomer have but a myle. *Oxford* 423. Cf. Tilley M1117.

M542 A Welsh **Mile**
c1450 *Merlin* II 247[35–6]: All the contrey was of hem covered the length of a walshe myle, 509[17]: Thei hadde riden half a walsh myle. *Oxford* 702; Tilley M925.

M543 As mild as **Milk**
a1400 *Alexander C* 249.4824: Was nevir . . . no milke so mild undire heven. Taylor and Whiting 243.

M544 As sweet as (any) **Milk**
a1300 *Alisaunder* 26 L 427–8: His love is al so swete y wis So ever is mylk. **c1330** *St. Margaret* 229.136: Me thenke this paines swetter than ani milkes rem, cf. 493.128. **c1390** *Talkyng* 26.17: Swettore art thou then . . . Milk in Mouthe. **1447** Bokenham 114.4172–3. **a1475** *Tree* 97.17–8. **a1500** *St. Katheryne* 262.188: And (*torture*) swettur than ony mylke. Svartengren 307; Taylor and Whiting 243.

M545 As white as (any, the) **Milk**
c1000 Aelfric *Homilies* II 518[9–11]: His lic . . . hwittre ðonne meoloc, *Lives* II 304.1378–9. **c1000** *Wonders of the East* in *Three Old English Prose Texts* 62.11–3: Hy beoð swa on lichoman swa hwite swa meolc. **a1300** *Alisaunder* 11.175: A mule also whyte so mylk, 59.1031, 292 M 66: Whyt as melke withouten fayle. **a1300** *Richard* 84.68: Also whyte as ony mylk, 98.387, 134.1036: ony. **c1300** *Beves* 55.1157, 189.3769–70: eny. **c1300** *South English Legendary* I 234.400: eny. **c1300** *South English Legendary* (*Laud*) 85.80, 350.187: eni, 402.321: So ȝwhiiht schininde so eni milk the bodies hole and sounde. **a1325** *Cursor* II 468 CF 8120: Als milk thair hide be-com sa quite, 596 CG 10380. **c1330** *Horn Childe* 182. 296. **c1330** *Orfeo* 14.146. **a1338** Mannyng *Chronicle B* II 334[21]. **a1350** *Ywain* 23.819, 83.3106: any. **c1350** *Libeaus* 16.248. **c1390** *Gregorius* 102.807: the. **c1395** *WBible* Genesis xlix 12. **a1399** *Forme of Cury* 41[3]: eny. **a1400** *And Martha keped* in Horstmann *Sammlung* 165.185. **a1400** ?Chaucer *Rom. A* 1196. **a1400** *Destruction of Troy* 129.3985: as the mylke white. **a1400** *Firumbras* 35.1055–6. **a1400** *Floris* 79.366. **a1400** *Ipomadon A* 70.2384: anny, 84.2898: anny, 184.6454. **a1400** *Moder of gresse* 173.337: any, 175.422: any. **a1400** *Laud Troy* II 457.15507. **a1415** Mirk *Festial* 158.19, 162.33, 232.5: any. **a1425** *Ipomadon B* 274.645: any. **a1430** Lydgate *Pilgrimage* 579.21725: any, **1430** *St. Margarete* in *MP* I 188.414, **a1439** *Fall* I 73.2670, **1439** *St. Albon* 136.536, 173.694: The blody streme as mylke ranne all whyte. **c1440** *Degrevant* 96.1505–6: the. **a1450** *Generydes A* 10.286. **a1450** *Partonope* 66.2238: eny, 136.3864: eny. **c1450** Capgrave *Katharine* 63.773: the. **c1450** *Leechbook* 202.647. **a1475** *Guy*[2] 12.389–90: any, 16.537. **a1475** *Seege of Troye* 199 H 1530h. **a1475** *Talk of Ten Wives* 31[22]: ony. **c1475** Henryson *Fables* 49.1349. **a1500** *Catalogue of Delights* in Robbins 121.27: any. **a1500** *Eger H* 201.323: the. **a1500** *Grene Knight* II 73.397–8: any. **a1500** *Guy*[4] 35.843–4. **a1500** Medwall *Nature* D2[r][39]: any. **a1500** *O my lady dere* in *Rawlinson MS. C 813* 332.126. **a1500** *Octavian* (*NC*) 104.718: any. **a1500** *South English Legendary: Miracles B. V.* (*Harley*) in *PMLA* 38(1923) 320.18: eni. **c1500** *King Hart* 110.10. **c1500** *Lady Bessy* 47[11]. **1506** Hawes *Pastime* 64.1592, 146.3866: the, 202.5315: the. **a1508** Skelton *Phyllyp* I 57.213, 85.1120: the, **1523** *Garlande* I 393.797. Apperson 680–1; Taylor and Whiting 243; Tilley M931; Whiting *Drama* 320:225, *Scots* II 98.

M545a Milk-white
a1050 *Old English Prudentius Glosses at Boulogne-sur-Mer*, ed. Herbert D. Meritt (Stanford Studies in Language and Literature 16, 1959) 11.100: Of meolchwyttre, 71.683: Meolchwitum. **a1200** Lawman II 243.15938: The oder is milc-whit. **c1300** *Guy*[1] 48 A 823: A gerfauk that is milke white. **a1325** *Chronicle* 23.563. **c1330** *Degare* 106.787 (*var.*). **c1330** *Horn Childe* 191.1044. **c1330** *Peniworth* 117.353. **c1350** *Libeaus* 9.132, 53.944. **a1375** *Octavian* (*S*) 53.1679. **a1400** *Alexander C* 82.1498, 86.1579, 216.3776, 240.4533, 269.5468. **a1400** *Amadace I* 42[7], 50[14]. **a1400** *Morte Arthure* 67.2287. **a1400** *Scottish Legends* I 181.50, II 47.23, 476.1172. **c1400** *Gowther* 158.563. **a1415** Mirk *Festial* 202.2, 25. **c1425** *Brut* II 347.16. **c1433** Lydgate *St. Edmund* 427.771, **1439** *Fall* III 921.94, **1439** *St. Albon* 175.818–9, **c1440** *Debate* in *MP* II 543.89. **1445** Claudian *Stilicho* 293.409. **1449** Metham 59.1600. **a1500** *Amadace A* 260.404, 269.617. **a1500** *Court of Love* 430.787. **a1500** *Eger P* 204.311. **a1500** *Guy*[4] 35.845.

c1500 *King Hart* 91.6. **1501** Douglas *Palice* 10.17, 52.20, **1513** *Aeneid* II 49.97, 115.103, 130.73, 223.39, III 80.189, 127.35, 146.39, 163.74, 199.142, 238.42, IV 87.12. **1546** Heywood *D* 68.76: A milke snow white . . . skyn. MED diademen 4; Taylor and Whiting 243; Whiting *Scots* II 98.

M546 As white as **Milk's** foam
c1380 *Ferumbras* 124.3955–6: An hert . . . As wyt ase melkys fom, 182.5879.

M547 As white as **Milk's** ream (*cream*)
a1300 *Arthour and M.*[1] 43.1455: That on is white so milkes rem. **a1425** *Arthour and M.*[2] 343.1543, 1073. **c1500** *Arthour and M.*[3] I 467.1466.

M548 As white as morn (morn's, morrow's) **Milk**
c1325 *Maid of Ribbesdale* in Böddeker 158.77: Whittore then the moren mylk. **c1387–95** Chaucer *CT* I[A] 357–8: An anlaas and a gipser al of silk Heeng at his girdel, whit as morne milk, **c1390** I[A] 3236: A barmclooth eek as whit as morne milk. **c1450** *Richard* 84.68 (*var.*): Also whyte as any mornes mylk. **c1522** Skelton *Colyn* I 323.317: Whyte as morowes (*MS.* marys) mylke.

M549 **Milk** (Honey) and honey (milk)
c1000 Aelfric *Heptateuch* Exodus iii 8: On þæt land þe þe flewð meolce and hunie, Numbers xvi 13: Of ðam lande þe weol meolce and hunige. **c1395** *WBible* Exodus iii 8: A lond that flowith with milk and hony, Numbers xvi 14: The lond that flowith with streemys of mylk and hony, Ezekiel xx 6: The lond flowynge with mylk and hony. **a1422** Lydgate *Life* 556.1179–80: The londe also of promyssyon, That mylke and hony bothe in-fere shedyth. **c1493** *Saint Katherin of Senis* 307.15–6: The rebellyon of holy chirche was that tyme in comparyson of this scisme but hony and mylke. **a1500** *English Conquest* 103.26–8: His spech, as hit were honny and mylke out of the mouth, but ever hit was medlid with wenym at the Ende. **1534** More *Comforte* 1161 H[3–4]: The land of beheste that floweth mylk and honey. *Oxford* 423.

M550 **Milk-warm**
c1450 *Leechbook* 72.187: Till it be mylke warme.

M551 To be like **Milk**
a1449 Lydgate *Ballade per Antiphrasim* in *MP* II 432.14: Moost like to mylk of you is necke and chyne. **a1460** *Towneley Plays* 377.324: Youre twyfyls youre nek abowte as mylke. Whiting *Scots* II 98.

M552 From **Mill** and from cheaping (*market*) . . . men bring tidings
a1200 *Ancrene* 48.17–9: Swa that me seith i bisahe. From mulne and from chepinge, from smiththe and from ancre hus, me tidinge bringeth. Apperson 416; Ives 263:6.

M553 A **Mill** that grinds not is worth as much as an oven that bakes not
c1450 *Ponthus* 6.31–2: For men sayn in scorn, that as mytch is a mylne worthe that gryndyth not as an oven that baketh not.

M554 One's **Mill** has ground its last grist (*i.e.*, to be near death)
c1450 *How mankinde dooth* in Furnivall *Hymns* 74.504: Thi mylle hath grounde thi laste griste. MED grist n. (1) (b).

M555 To be like a **Mill** without (a) sluice
1340 *Ayenbite* 255[8–13]: Zome volk . . . byeth ase the melle wythoute scluse, thet alne-way went be the yernynge of the wetere. Vor hi habbeth ase vele wordes ase ther comth of weter to the melle. **c1400** *Vices and Virtues* 282.37–283.2: (Men) that fareth as a mille without scluse, that evere goth as the watre renneth, for thei have so many wordes as the mylle hath watre.

M556 To clack like a **Mill**
c1450 Idley 82.50: Lete thy tonge not clakke as a mille. Whiting *Scots* II 98. Cf. Whiting *Drama* 285.

M557 To clap like a **Mill**
c1390 Chaucer *CT* X[I] 406: Janglynge is whan a man speketh to muche biforn folk, and clappeth as a mille, and taketh no keep what he seith, **c1395** IV[E] 1200: Ay clappeth as a mille, I yow counsaille. **c1412** Hoccleve *Regement* 7.171: Thou art as ful of clap as is a mylle. **a1426** Lydgate *Mumming at Hertford* in *MP* II 680.177: It longethe to us to clappen as a mylle. Cf. *Oxford* 664: Tongue. See **W92.**

M558 Whoso comes to **Mill** first grinds first
c1395 Chaucer *CT* III[D] 389: Whoso that first to mille comth, first grynt. **1475** Paston V 229[3–4]: For who comyth fyrst to the mylle, fyrst must grynd. Apperson 214; S. B. Ek *Den som kommer först till kvarns,* Scripta Minora Regiae Societatis Humaniorum Litterarum Lundensis, 1963–4:1; Jente 240; *Oxford* 204; Skeat 266; Tilley M941. See **C382.**

M559 (An honest **Miller**) has a thumb of gold
c1387–95 Chaucer *CT* I[A] 562–3: Wel koude he stelen corn and tollen thries; And yet he

hadde a thombe of gold, pardee. **c1500** *Cock* 3[20–1]: A myller dustypoll than dyde come, A Joly felowe with a golden thome. Apperson 417; *Oxford* 424; Tilley M953.

M560 A **Miller** is a thief (*varied*)
c1387-95 Chaucer *CT* I[A] 562: Wel koude he stelen corn, **c1390** I[A] 3939: A theef he was for sothe of corn and mele. **c1483** Caxton *Dialogues* 36.27–34: Gherard the myllar, After that men saye, Steleth the half Of corn or of mele Of them that to hym Brynge to grynde. The half he steleth not, But a lytyll of every sack. **c1500** *Cock* 3[23–4]: Many sayd that he with reprefe Of all craftes was nexte a thefe. **1509** Barclay *Ship* II 307[2]: With Myllers and bakers that weyght and mesure hate. **1532** Berners *Golden Boke* 186.2234–7: And there was an ancient lawe that a myller, a smyth, a baker, or a poynt maker, myght not be a Senatour, bycause men of the sayd occupations were commonly taken with deceytes and gyles. **1533** Heywood *Weather* B4ᵛ[29]: Who wolde be a myller? As good be a thefe. Apperson 417; *Oxford* 424; Tilley M955; Whiting *Scots* II 99.

M561 A **Miller** tolls more than once (*varied*)
c1387-95 Chaucer *CT* I[A] 562: Wel koude he . . . tollen thries. **c1450** *When the son* 388.167: Myllers that tyllyth not twyes yn a myle. **a1475** *Assembly of Gods* 21.698: Double tollyng myllers. Apperson 417:4; *Oxford* 633: Sure; Tilley M958.

M562 A **Millpost** thwitten (*whittled*) to (compared to) a pudding-prick
1528 More *Heresyes* 236 H[5–6]: Here was a gret post wel thwyted to a pudding pricke. **1546** Heywood *D* 100.2–3: For here is a myll post Thwytten to a puddyng pricke, **1556** *Spider* 142[20–1]: Shulde set forth that righte, mighte in conclusion quicke, Thwighte that myll poste of righte to a poding pricke, 269[21]: Pooding prikes they, mylposts we, comparde are, **1562** *E* 232.19.3–4: Good deedes by good wyll had, differ there brother. A pooddyng pricke is one, a mylpost is an other. Apperson 418; *Oxford* 657; Tilley M964.

M563 As great as any **Millstone**
c1400 *Beryn* 2.35: As grete as eny mylstone, upward gon they stert.

M564 Better stir a **Millstone** than her
c1375 *St. Agatha* 46.49–50: We might better stir A milne-stone than we may hir. See **M726, R161, S792, W24.**

M565 To lay a **Millstone** in (*on*) one's neck
c1000 *WSG* Matthew xviii 6: Betere him ys þæt an cwyrnstan si to hys swyran gecnytt, and si besenced on sæs grund, Mark ix 42, Luke xvii 2. **c1395** *WBible* Matthew xviii 6: It spedith to hym that a mylnstoon of assis be hangid in his necke, and he be drenchid in the depnesse of the see, Mark ix 41, Luke xvii 2. **1509** Barclay *Ship* I 105[27]: For than layth malyce a mylstone in his necke. Taylor and Whiting 244.

M566 To see far in a **Millstone**
1546 Heywood *D* 37.75–6: She thought . . . she had seene far in a milstone, Whan she gat a husbande, **1555** *E* 155.57: Thou seest far in a mylstone. Apperson 556; *Oxford* 425; Taylor and Whiting 245; Tilley M965.

M567 To weigh heavier than a **Millstone**
c1477 Caxton *Jason* 83.13–4: A requeste that weyeth more hevier on my herte than mylne stone shold on my heed.

M568 As quick as a man's **Mind**
c1300 *South English Legendary* II 418.502: And mai be(o) nouthe here and ther as quik as a mannes munde. See **T232.**

M569 Out of **Mind** the less told of
a1450 *Of the sacrament* in Kail 104.30: Out of mynde, the lasse of tolde. See **S307.**

M570 A wicked **Mind** with words fair and sly
c1475 Henryson *Fables* 100.2913: Ane wickit mynd with wordis fair and sle. See **M755, W631.**

M571 **Mine** and thine make discord (*varied*)
c1330 *Song on the Times* in Wright *Political Songs* 252[4]: Myn ant thyn duo sunt, qui frangunt plebis amorem. **c1390** *Proverbes of diverse profetes* 540.277–80: Yif twey wordes never hedde be mad, Everi mon good pes might ha had; Myn and thyn, heore either word Bi-twene mony men maketh discord. **a1470** Parker *Dives* X7ʳ[1.15–21]: For nyghe all the debate in this worlde is for myne and thyne. And therfore sayd a phylsopher . . . Put out of this worlde two wordes, myne and thyne, and all the worlde shall be in peas. Whiting *Scots* II 99. Cf. *Oxford* 422; Taylor and Whiting 242; Tilley M910.

M572 As wise as **Minerva**
1369 Chaucer *BD* 1072: Or ben as wis as Mynerva.

M573 In the **Mire**
a1352 Minot 29.71: Has left us ligand in the mire. **a1449** Lydgate *See Myche* in *MP* II 800–1.24–5: O worde myse spoken may bringe the in the myre. So depe, in sothe, tyll thow ther

in be drent. **c1450** Capgrave *Katharine* 133.880. **c1450** Idley 86.315. **c1490** Ryman 240.12. **c1500** *King Hart* 119.27: For he hes left his maister in the myre. **c1500** *O mortall man* in *Studia Neophilologica* 26(1963) 63.41: Lyke a man in a fury thow doste caste in the myre. **1513** Douglas *Aeneid* III 65.156: Full laith to leif our wark swa in the myre. **1522** Skelton *Why Come* II 34.248, **c1522** *Colyn* I 352.1071–2: Or els in the myre They saye they wyll you cast. **1533** More *Answer* 1117 D[4]: I have set hym here so fast in the mire, *Confutacion* 608 A[6–7], 614 D[5–6]. **1546** Heywood *D* 64.76: And lay my credence in the myre. Tilley M989; Whiting *Scots* II 99. See **D247, 266, L24.**

M574 To despise as **Mire**
c1450 Capgrave *Katharine* 153.1223: Or ellis youre herte despiseth joye as myre.

M575 As bright as a **Mirror**
a1398(1495) Bartholomaeus-Trevisa S8ʳ[1.4]: Bryght as a myrrour.

M576 As clear as a **Mirror**
a1398(1495) Bartholomaeus-Trevisa JJ1ʳ[1.7–8]: Clere as a myrrour. Whiting *NC* 445.

M577 A false **Mirror** oft deceives a man's look
a1475 *Assembly of Gods* 51.1727: Oft a false myrrour deceyveth a mannys look.

M578 Look in your **Mirror** and deem no other wight
a1449 Lydgate *Look in thy Merour* in *MP* II 765–72.8: Look in thy merour and deeme noon othir wiht (*refrain*).

M579 None so foul does in a **Mirror** pry but she is fair in her own eye
a1420 Lydgate *Troy* I 221.2679–80: For non so foule doth in a myrour prye, That sche is feir in hir owne eye. See **C569.**

M580 One's **Mirror** may be the devil's arse
a1529 Skelton *Garnesche* I 126.18: They (*for* Thy) myrrour may be the devyllys ars. See **M35.**

M581 To make a **Mirror** of the falling of another (*varied*)
a1439 Lydgate *Fall* II 432.3715: Lat othris fallyng a merour to you bee. **c1450** *Pilgrimage LM* 137[5–6]: For of the mischef of an oother eche may make a mirrowr for him self. Cf. Tilley M448. See **C161, M170, W47.**

M582 Every **Mirth** may last so long that it will list unwrast (*please poorly*)
a1250 *Owl* 32.341–4: Evrich murghthe mai so longe ileste That ho shal liki wel unwreste: Vor harpe, and pipe, and fugheles (song) Misliketh, yif hit is to long. See **P408.**

M583 **Mirth** and heaviness are ever intermeddled
a1449 Lydgate *Fabula* in *MP* II 509.694: Evir entirmedlyd is merthe and hevynesse. See **J59.**

M584 It is a great **Mischance** to let a fool have governance
c1380 Chaucer *HF* 957–9: Loo, ys it not a gret myschaunce To lete a fool han governaunce Of thing that he can not demeyne?

M585 **Mischance** of one should be another's lore
1501 Douglas *Palice* 30.2: Mischance of ane, suld be ane utheris loir. See **C161, M170.**

M586 Great **Mischief** follows ill winning
c1450 *Ratis* 4.108: Gret mischef folowis ill vynyng. See **G336.**

M587 **Mischief** may not always last
c1420 Wyntoun VI 39.4295: For myscheiff may noucht lest alwayis. See **B19, S798, W430.**

M588 **Misery** may be mother where one beggar begs of another
1546 Heywood *D* 99.41–2: But as men saie, misery maie be mother, Where one begger is dryven to beg of an other. Apperson 418–9; *Oxford* 426; Tilley M1007.

M589 Of a **Mishap** sometimes comes a good turn
1519 Horman *Vulgaria* 396[7]: Somtyme of a myshappe cometh a good turne. See **T150.**

M590 **Misreckoning** is no payment
1555 Heywood *E* 185.215: Mysrecknyng is no paiment, **1556** *Spider* 74[7]. Apperson 419; Jente 518; *Oxford* 427; Tilley M1014.

M591 One **Misrule** brings in another
a1439 Lydgate *Fall* III 747.2694–5: Thus everi surfet englued is to othir, And o mysreule bryngeth in anothir. See **S333.**

M592 After **Mists** Phoebus shines bright
a1449 Lydgate *Guy* in *MP* II 520.84: And affter mystys Phebus schyneth bright. See **C315.**

M593 As dark as **Mist**
a1450 *South English Legendary* (*Bodley*) 337.41: Bokus so derk as myste (*rime* myghte).

M594 To go away like the **Mist**
a1325 *Seven Sins* in Heuser 124.92: Hit went awei, so doth the miste.

M595 To mete (*measure*) the **Mist** (on Malvern Hills)
a1376 *Piers* A Prol. 88–9: Thow mihtest beter meten the myst on Malverne hulles, Then geten a mom of heore mouth til moneye weore schewed. **c1405** *Mum* 17.171–2: Ther is as moche good witte in swyche gomes nollis, As thou shuldist mete of a myst fro morwe to even.

M596 Dear enough a **Mite**
c1385 Chaucer *TC* iv 684: And with hire tales, deere ynough a myte, **c1386** *LGW* 741: It nas nat sene, deere ynogh a myte. **1406** Hoccleve *Male Regle* 33.269: Al-thogh that they a myte be to deere. **a1420** Lydgate *Troy* I 147.130.

M597 Not (a)mend a **Mite**
a1375 *William* 145.4543: So that non might a-mend a mite worth, i wene, 160.5030, 161.5069, 169.5347–8: It amende ne might, Nought that fel to swiche a fest forsothe, half a mite. **c1380** *Pearl* 13.351: Thy mendez mountez not a myte. **c1420** Wyntoun III 291.1146. **a1450** *York Plays* 303.322. **c1475** *Golagros* 36.1069. Whiting *Scots* II 99.

M598 Not ask a **Mite**
c1420 Wyntoun VI 213.6626: I sall nocht ask thairof ane myt.

M599 Not (a)vail a **Mite**
c1378 *Piers* B xx 177–8: Surgerye ne fisyke May noughte a myte availle. **a1400** *Romaunt B* 5762: Hymsilf it availeth not a myte. **a1440** Burgh *Cato* 306.117. **c1440** Charles of Orleans 135.4029: For othir thing hit vaylith not a myte. **c1440** Lydgate *Debate* in *MP* II 547.187. **c1475** Henryson *Fables* 52.1448: Sall not availl ane myte. Whiting *Scots* II 99.

M600 Not care a **Mite**
c1485 *Slaughter* (*Digby*) 6.142: I care not a myght. Tilley M1026; Whiting *Scots* II 99.

M601 Not change a **Mite**
a1475 *Assembly of Gods* 53.1814: Be hyt ryght or wrong, he changeth nat a myte.

M602 Not count a **Mite**
a1475 *Assembly of Gods* 47.1606–7: Count I no more To that in comparyson valewyng then a myte. **c1475** Henryson *Want of Wyse Men* 191.53: Thay compt nocht cursing a myte. **1513** Douglas *Aeneid* II 107.19: I compt it nevir a myte. Tilley M1026; Whiting *Scots* II 99.

M603 Not force (*care*) the worth of a **Mite**
1534 Heywood *Love* B2v[41]: I forse for no man the worth of a myte. Tilley M1026.

M604 Not give a **Mite**
c1380 *Ferumbras* 55.1579: Y nolde noght gyve a myte. **a1400** *Romaunt C* 7550: He yeveth nat now therof a myte (*French* Il n'i donrait pas une escorce De chesne). **c1412** Hoccleve *Regement* 56.1535. **a1450** *Castle* 84.247. **a1475** Banester *Guiscardo* 30.490.

M605 Not hinder a **Mite**
c1422 Hoccleve *Dialog* 128.509: And pardee, freend that may nat hyndre a myte.

M606 Not praise a (poor) **Mite**
c1395 *Pierce* 10.267: Y preise nought thi preching but as a pure myte. **a1400** *Alexander Buik* I 56.1176–7: That thay prysit nocht worth ane myte Thair strenth nor yit thair chevalry. **c1408** Lydgate *Reson* 118.4497.

M607 Not reck a **Mite**
c1375 Chaucer *Anel.* 269: Alas! ye rekke not a myte, **c1385** *Mars* 126, **c1395** *CT* VIII[G] 698. **a1420** Lydgate *Troy* II 548.5319. Whiting *Scots* II 99.

M608 Not set a **Mite**
c1385 Chaucer *TC* iii 832–3: And if to lese his joie he sette a myte, Than semeth it that joie is worth ful lite, 900: I nolde setten at his sorwe a myte. **c1385** Usk 55.68: Al sette ye at a myte whan your hert tourneth. **a1420** Lydgate *Troy* I 97.2892. **c1420** Wyntoun IV 335.152. **c1422** Hoccleve *Jereslaus's Wife* 148.225. **a1425** *Metrical Paraphrase OT* 11.14171–2: He suld not sett be the The mountynance of a myte. **c1440** Charles of Orleans 142.4252. **1522** Skelton *Why Come* II 47.674, **1523** *Howe the Douty Duke* II 73.165–6. Whiting *Drama* 354:714.

M609 Not the value of a **Mite**
a1420 Lydgate *Troy* I 191.1620: Nat the valu, I suppose, of a myte.

M610 Not weigh half a **Mite**
a1450 *Lord that is* 216.180–1: Thi hert weyeth not half a myte Ageyn the lif that lastith ay.

M611 Not worth a (three) **Mite(s)**
a1375 *William* 70.2017: Never to weld of worldes merthe the worth of a mite, 151.4736: I wold nowt wilne a mite worth. **c1375** Barbour *Bruce* I 58.198: The body is nocht worth a myt, 305.188. **a1376** *Piers* A viii 54: Schal no devel at his deth-day deren him worth a myte. **c1380** Chaucer *CT* VIII[G] 511: For in effect they been nat worth a myte, **c1385** I[A] 1558, **c1395** III[D] 1961, VIII[G] 633. **a1400** *Alexander C* 236.4426. **c1412** Hoccleve *Regement* 36.976–7, 144.3988–9. **c1420** Wyntoun III 305.1322, V

197.596: That custum is noucht worthe thre mytis. **c1422** Hoccleve *Dialog* 122.334, *Lerne to Die* 197.523. **c1440** Charles of Orleans 52.1524: Mi wordis alle nar worthi to him a myte, 153.4564. **c1450** Holland *Howlat* 49.72. **1471** Ripley *Compound* 190[26]. **c1500** Greene *Carols* 379.2. **1501** Douglas *Palice* 48.22, 81.26, **1513** *Aeneid* II 15.424. **c1525** Heywood *Wit* 3[6]. Tilley M1026; Whiting *Scots* II 100.

M612 He that **Mocks** shall be mocked (*varied*)
c1475 *Rawlinson MS. D 328* 125.81: He that mokyt schall noght be owyn mokyt. Qui me deridet non inde risus abibit. **1483** Caxton *Cato* G3r[21–2]: For it is sayd comynly that he that mockqueth other shal be mocqued, **1484** *Aesop* 307[1–3]: Alle the sallary or payment of them that mokken other is for to be mocqued at the last. **1509** Barclay *Ship* I 213[5–7]: It also provyd full often is certayne That they that on mockes alway theyr myndes cast Shall of all other be mocked at the last. **1534** Heywood *Love* B4v[26–7]: For who so that mocketh shall surely stur This olde proverbe: mockum moccabitur, C1r[14–5]: Wherby I thought her owne tale lyke a bur Stack to her owne back, mockum moccabitur, C1v[18]: Wherwith I brought in moccum moccabitur, [21]: To gyve mock for mock, [25]. Apperson 420; *Oxford* 428; Tilley M1031. See **G491, S92.**

M613 **Mock** and mow
1509 Barclay *Ship* I 112[8]: They mocke and mowe at anothers small offence. **1532** More *Confutacion* 374 C[11–2]: And lyke the devils ape maketh mockes and mowes, 375 E[12]: To jest and mocke and mowe and rayle, 398 C[10–1]: To make him sporte, with mocking and mowing, **1533** *Apologye* 4[23–4]: The makynge of mockes and mowys, 169[1], *Confutacion* 562 A[13], 616 F[3], 618 C[2], 735 FG, 736 B[11–2]. Tilley M1030.

M614 A **Modicum** is more to allow (*praise*) so that Good Will be carver at the dais, *etc.*
c1475 Henryson *Fables* 11.236–8: Ane modicum is mair ffor till allow, Swa that gude will be kerver at the dais, Than thrawin vult and mony spycit mais. Cf. Tilley G338. See **D257, M700, P329.**

M615 As rotten as **Mold**
a1400 *Cursor* III 1528 F 27602: That within is rotin as molde.

M616 As black and dark as a **Mole**
1492 *Salomon and Marcolphus* 12[6]: In the ars blacke and derke lyke a molle.

M617 **Mona** (Anglesea) is the mother of Wales
a1387 Higden-Trevisa II 39[11–5]: In preisynge of this ilond Walsche men beeth i-woned to seie a proverbe and an olde sawe, *Mon mam Kembry,* that is to menynge in Englische *Mon moder of Wales.* For whan othere londes lakketh mete, that lond is so good that hit semeth that it wolde fynde corn i-now for alle the men of Wales. **a1447** Bokenham *Mappula* 13[24–6]: Ther is a comyn proverbe yn Walsshe, and hit is this: *Mon mam kimry,* That is to say on englyssh: Anglysseye modur of Walis. Apperson 11; *Oxford* 10; Tilley A248.

M618 Black **Monday**
1359 *Gild of St. Nicholas* in *English Gilds,* ed. Toulmin Smith (EETS 40, 1870) 97[7]: The secunde (*mornspeche*) schal be onblake monunday. **1435** *Chronicles of London* 13[13–4]: Wherfore, unto this day yt (*April 14, 1360*) ys caliyd blak Monday, and wolle be longe tyme here affter. **c1443** *Chronicle of London* 64[16–7]: Wherfore unto this day manye men callen it the blake Moneday. NED Monday 2. Cf. M. M. Mathews *Dictionary of Americanisms* (Chicago, 1951) Black 4(6).

M619 A **Monday's** handsel (*gift*) is great pain to children
c1475 *Rawlinson MS. D 328* 118.14: A mondayys hansell ys grete pane to chyddryn. Lunaris strena pueris est maxima pena. Walther II 780.14113. Cf. Apperson 444: New Year; NED Handsel 5.

M620 For **Money** men may find an advocate
c1480 *Contemplacioun* 193.184: Bot men for money may fynd ane advocat. Cf. Tilley M1065.

M621 Have **Money** in one's purse
1461 Paston III 300[9–11]: Withoute he have mony in hyse purse . . . ellys they wyll not sette by hem. Apperson 422:17; *Oxford* 429; Tilley M1090. See **M632.**

M622 Lady **Money** has all things under her buxomness (*obedience*)
a1430 Hoccleve *Roundel* II 36–7.2–3: I, lady moneie, of the world goddesse, That have al thyng undir my buxumnesse, 8–9, 14–5, 22–3. Cf. *Oxford* 430: Money will do anything, quote 1613.

M623 **Money** burns out the bottom of one's purse
1528 More *Heresyes* 195 B[5–7]: Having a littell wanton money, which hym thought brenned out the bottom of hys purs. Apperson 421:8;

Oxford 428; Taylor and Whiting 247–8; Tilley M1048.

M624 **Money** is like a conqueror over man
1509 Barclay *Ship* II 15[26]: Money over man is like a conquerour. See **G296.**

M625 The **Money** is not yet coined that I shall send
1470 Paston V 88[15–6]: Telle your brother that the mony is not yet cownyd that I xuld send hym for thersarsenet and damaske.

M626 **Money** makes marriage
c1495 *Arundel Vulgaria* 18.72: For nowadais money maketh mariage with sum menn rather then love or bewtye. Apperson 422; *Oxford* 430; Tilley M1074. See **M797.**

M627 **Money** makes the jolly palfreys leap and prance
a1500 Greene *Carols* 393.4: In the heyweyes ther joly palfreys Yt (*money*) makyght to lepe and praunce. Cf. Taylor and Whiting 248: Money makes the mare go.

M628 **Money** makes the man
a1500 Greene *Carols* 393.20: Yt ys allwayes sene nowadayes That money makythe the man. Apperson 422; *Oxford* 430; Tilley M1076. See **M362.**

M629 **Money** makes the merchant (chapman)
c1450 Idley 90.550: Ever monye maketh the marchaunte. **a1475** *Ludus Coventriae* 252.624–5: In old termys I have herd seyde That mony makyth schapman. **c1516** Skelton *Magnificence* 49.1574: Money maketh marchauntes, I tell you, over all. Apperson 422; Tilley M1078.

M630 **Money** (Pecunia) makes wrong right, *etc.*
1372 *Advocates MS.18.7.21* (John of Grimestone) f.14 in Owst *Literature* 317: Pecunia maket wrong rith, maket day niht, maket frend fo, maket wele wo. **c1500** *Everyman* 15–6.412–3: For it is sayd ever amonge That money maketh all ryght that is wronge. Tilley M1072, 1073. See **M494, 534, P124.**

M631 **Money** reigns
c1515 Barclay *Eclogues* 159.530: And money reygneth and doth all thing at will. Cf. Tilley H1060.

M632 Ready **Money** is the best ware (*varied*)
a1500 Greene *Carols* 393.8: At al tymys the best ware ys Ever redy money. **a1500** *O man more* 395.55–6: Trust nott a tappestere though she speke merelye, For a man may spede in all places for redy money. Jente 360. Cf. Tilley M1091, 1092. See **M621.**

M633 To **Money** all things obey
a1382 *WBible* Ecclesiastes x 19: To monee obeshen alle thingus. **c1390** Chaucer *CT* VII 1550[B2740]: Salomon seith that "alle thynges obeyen to moneye." **a1393** Gower *CA* II 409. 244–5: So that a man mai sothly telle That al the world to gold obeieth. **c1412** Hoccleve *Regement* 26.708–9: Fful soth fynde I the word of salomon, That to moneie obeien alle thinges. Apperson 421; Jente 67; *Oxford* 428; Smith 209; Tilley M1041a, 1052, T163. See **G296.**

M634 To pay (again) with the same **Money**
1525 Berners *Froissart* VI 76[32–3]: I shall paye them agayn with the same money, forged in the same forge, **1532** *Golden Boke* 336.7131–2: I wyll pay you with the same money. Apperson 487: coin; *Oxford* 491; Taylor and Whiting 76; Tilley C507.

M635 To piss **Money** on the walls
1471 Ripley *Compound* 155[25]: But as for Mony yt ys pyssyd on the walls.

M636 To spare **Money** no more than if it fell from the clouds
1523 Berners *Froissart* III 490[27–9]: The lordes . . . spared no more money than it had fallen fro the clowdes. Cf. Taylor and Whiting 248:8.

M637 Who has **Money** shall have men at need
c1450 Idley 92.687–8: Who that hath money shal have men at nede And frendis not a fewe to defende hym of his foo. Cf. Tilley M1082–3.

M638 Who has **Money** shall not fail to speed
a1500 *To yow, mastres* in *Rawlinson MS. C 813* 383.25–6: Who that hathe money, he shall not fayle At his desyre as well to spede. See **L80.**

M639 With **Money** the right goes forth
1481 Caxton *Reynard* 70[20–1]: Wyth money alleway the right goth forth.

M640 The **Monks** think it lawful to play when the abbot brings the dice
1509 Barclay *Ship* I 236[22–3]: The monkes thynke it lawfull for to play Whan that the Abbot bryngeth them the dyce. Jente 101. See **S348, W499.**

M641 Better is one **Month's** cheer than a churl's whole life
1546 Heywood *D* 86.194: Better is one monthes cheere, than a churles hole lyfe. Tilley M1108.

M642 For one **Month's** joy to bring a whole life's sorrow
1546 Heywood *D* 39.128: For one months joie to bryng hir hole lives sorow. See **H601, L274, W282, 606, Y14.**

M643 Move not your **Mood** too oft
a1400 *Proverbis of Wysdom* 245.66: Meve nott thy mode to ought, *(II)* 222.53: oft.

M644 To peck **Mood** (*i.e.*, change one's mind)
c1330 *Seven Sages A* 9.248: And sone sche gan to pekke mod. **c1412** Hoccleve *Regement* 156.4347: But or thei twynned thens, thei pekkid moode. NED Peck v.[1] 7.

M645 After a dropping (*misty*) **Moon** the weather oft clears
1420 Lydgate *Temple* 17.394–5: And oft also, aftir a dropping mone, The weddir clereth. Cf. Apperson 424: An old moon.

M646 As bright as the **Moon**
c1300 *South English Legendary* I 346.175: Hom thoghte is face brightore was thanne . . . mone. **c1502** *Lyfe of Joseph* 50.410: As bright as the mone that Illumyneth the nyght. **1509** Barclay *Ship* II 334[10]: Bryght as the mone. Taylor and Whiting 249.

M647 As changeable as the **Moon**
c1440 Scrope *Epistle* 22[2–3]: A foole is schawngeable as the moone. **a1449** Lydgate *Timor* in *MP* II 831.108: The wourld is chaungeable as the moone. **c1450** *Epistle of Othea* 28.19–20: The ffoole is chaungeable as the moone, butt the wyse man is stable. **a1500** *Fortune alas alas* 484.6: And art chaungeable eke as is the mone. Apperson 91; *Oxford* 88; Tilley M1111. See **M141, 652, 655, W526.**

M648 As dun as the **Moon** against the sun
a1400 Chestre *Launfal* 80.988–90: Than wer they wyth her also donne As ys the mone ayen the sonne, Aday whan hyt ys lyght. **a1475** *Landavall* 126.473–4: They to her were allso donn As the monelyght to the sonne. **a1500** *Lambewell* I 161.547–8: And there thé sate as dummbe As the moone is light from the sunn. See **S889.**

M649 As round as a **Moon**
a1460 *Towneley Plays* 125.278: As rownde as a moyn. Taylor *Comparisons* 69.

M650 As variant as the **Moon**
c1485 *Guiscardo* 50.215: More variaunt and flyttyng then ys the mutabyll mone. **a1500** Alcock *Sermo pro episcipo* B1[v][1.3–4]: Beynge as varyaunt as the mone. See **M662.**

M651 As wliti (*handsome*) as the **Moon** (*etc.*) (A number of single quotations are brought together here)
c1000 Aelfric *Homilies* I 444[1–2]: Maria is wlitigre ðonne se mona. **c1395** *WBible* Song of Solomon vi 9: Fair as the moone, chosun as the sunne. **a1420** Lydgate *Troy* II 519.4337–8: He shal hem (*women*) fynde stedefaste as the mone That is in point for to chaunge sone. **a1500** *Ragman Roll* 74.113: O constaunt womane, stabill as the mone.

M652 In the **Moon** is no stableness
a1449 Lydgate and Burgh *Secrees* 39.1208: Ffor in the moone is no stabylnesse. See **M647, 655.**

M653 The **Moon** is unlike the sun, *etc.*
a1437 *Kingis Quair* 76.110: Unlike the mone is to the sonne schene; Eke Januarye is (un)-like to May; Unlike the cukkow to the phylomene; Thair tabartis ar noght bothe maid of array; Unlike the crow is to the papejay; Unlike, in goldsmythis werk, a fischis eye To peres with perll, or maked be so heye.

M654 To bark at (against) the **Moon**
1402 *Daw Topias* 53[7–10]: But thou, as blynde Bayarde, Berkest at the mone, As an olde mylne dog When he bygynnith to dote. **1456** *Five Dogs of London* 190.6: Ffor ones that y barkyd a-geynys the mone. **1456** Paston III 105[25–7]: My felow Barker, as of such othyr berkers ayenst the mone, to make wysemen laugh at her foyle. **a1460** *Towneley Plays* 137.662: Can ye bark at the mone? **1520** Whittinton *Vulgaria* 72.4–5: They playe as the dogge doeth that barketh at the moon all nyght. Apperson 26; *Oxford* 22-3; Tilley M1123. See **B71.**

M655 To change like the **Moon** (*varied*)
c1395 *WBible* Ecclesiasticus xxvii 12: For whi a fool is chaungid as the moone. **a1400** *Romaunt B* 3778: And chaunge as the moone. **a1400** *Ware the Wheel* in *Pol. Rel. and Love Poems* 265.1–2: This wondir wel undir this trone, It changit ofte as dot the mone. **c1408** Lydgate *Reson* 2.47–8: After this Fortune sone, Which ofter changeth as the mone, 161.6162–8: Which in his sheeld, as yt ys kouthe, Bare a cressaunt Mone shene, To declare, thus I mene, That youthe in his grene age Varieth ofte of corage, Redy for to chaunge sone After the nature of the mone, **a1420** *Troy* III 622.1982. **1422** Yonge *Governaunce* 158.34–6: Salamon Sayth, "An holy man in wysdome abidyth as the Sonne,

And a foole chaungyth as the moone." **a1430** Lydgate *Pilgrimage* 521.19549–50: Than y, lykned to the moone, Ffolk wyl chaunge my name sone, **a1439** *Fall* II 339.364: Off chaunges braideth offter than the moone, III 824.38: Frenshep chaungeth as doth the cloudi moone, 1002.2938. **c1440** Charles of Orleans 137.4085–6: Me thynk y ledde a liif liik to the mone Now fulle now wane now round now chaungid this. **a1449** Lydgate *See Myche* in *MP* II 800.3–4: Lyke as the mone chaungith a-fore the pryme So faryth this worlde. **a1500** *Nut Brown Maid* 176.37–8. **1506** Hawes *Pastime* 83.2129, 155.4112. *Oxford* 88; Tilley M1111; Whiting *Scots* II 100. See **M647, 652, 662.**

M656 To (give) light like the **Moon**
a1000 *Vercelli Homilies* 87.178–9: He . . . lyht swa mone.

M657 (To imagine, cast) above (beyond) the **Moon**
c1422 Hoccleve *Complaint* 102.197–8: I may not lett a man to ymagine Ferre above the mone yf that hym lyst. **a1500** *Colyn Blowbol* 104.268: And wenith thir wittes be be yonde the mone. **c1516** Skelton *Magnificence* 8.224: That all is without Measure and fer beyonde the mone. **1546** Heywood *D* 25.36: Feare may force a man to cast beyonde the moone, **1555** *E* 180.191, **1556** *Spider* 422[3]: Blowing meate here (raw and roste) beyond the mone. Apperson 84; *Oxford* 81; Tilley M1114; Whiting *Drama* 355:717, *Scots* II 100.

M658 To move like the **Moon**
c1475 Henryson *Ressoning* 180.46: Quhen thi manheid sall move as the mone.

M659 To prove (make one believe that) the **Moon** is made of (a) green cheese
1528 More *Heresyes* 256 H[2–3]: Able to prove the mone made of greene cheese. **1546** Heywood *D* 86.218–9: Ye set circumquaques to make me beleve Or thinke, that the moone is made of a greene cheese. Apperson 425; *Oxford* 431; Taylor and Whiting 249; Tilley M1116; Whiting *Drama* 354:716.

M660 To shine like (the) **Moon**
a1400 Chestre *Launfal* 60.271–2: Hys eyen were carbonkeles bryght—As the mone the schon anyght. **a1475** *Landavall* 108.85–6: In his mouthe a carboucle, bright As the mone that shone light. **a1500** *Eger P* 272.970: It shone as Moone doth in the night. Whiting *Ballad* 30. See **M665.**

M661 To take the **Moon** where it sits
a1393 Gower *CA* II 71.1316–8: For also wel sche myhte seie, "Go tak the Mone ther it sit," As bringe that into my wit. Cf. Tilley M1124.

M662 To vary like the **Moon**
a1400 Wyclif *Sermons* II 177[22–4]: An unstable sikenesse, that varieth as the moone. For as the moone is modir of moiste thingis, so it hath unstable movyng. See **M650, 655.**

M663 To wax and wane like the **Moon**
a1200 *Ancrene* 87.14–5: The mone woneth and waxeth ne nis neaver studevest, and bitacneth for thi worltliche thinges, the beoth as the mone eaver ichange. **a1375** *All Other Love* in Brown *Lyrics XIV* 65.1–4: Al other love is lych the mone That wext and wanet as flour in plein, As flour that fayret and fawyt sone, As day that scwret and endt in rein. **c1375** William of Nassington *Poem on the Trinity* in Perry *Religious Pieces* 64.53–4: Of owre lyfe, that passes here sonne, And waxes and wanes als lyghte of the Monne. **c1380** Chaucer *HF* 2115–6: Somme to wexe and wane sone, As doth the faire white mone, **c1395** *CT* IV[E] 998: For lyk the moone ay wexe ye and wane. **a1400** *Trust Not* in *Pol. Rel. and Love Poems* 263.3–4: Worldes catel passet sone That wacset and wansit rit as te mone. **a1420** Lydgate *Troy* I 116.3510–1: To-day thei wexe and to-morwe wane, As doth the mone. **1509** Barclay *Ship* II 319[10]: Wexynge and waynynge lyke the mone.

M664 As clear as the **Moonlight**
a1400 ?Chaucer *Rom. A* 1010: And clere as the mone lyght. Svartengren 363.

M665 To shine like the **Moonlight**
c1390 Chaucer *CT* VII 879–80[B2069–70]: His brydel . . . shoon . . . as the moone light. See **M660.**

M666 **Moonshine** in the water
1468 Paston IV 305[20–1]: And put in hope of the moone shone in the water and I wot nat what. **1534** More *Comforte* 1184 A[2–5]: The priestes make folke fast, and put them to paine about the moone shene in the water, and doe but make folk foles. **1546** Heywood *D* 53.401: As waite againe for the mooneshine in the water, **1555** *E* 192.264. Apperson 426; *Oxford* 432; Tilley M1128.

M667 As black as a **Moor**
1485 Caxton *Charles* 123.19: Marpyn the theef as blacke as a moore, 191.22, **c1489** *Aymon* II 565.30–2: But soo was not ganellon for he was

soo angry for it, that he became as blacke as a moure. Tilley M1130.

M668 As bimodered (*covered with mud* [MED]) as a **Moorhen**
a1325 *On Consistory Courts* in Böddeker 111.58: Ant heo cometh bymodered as a morhen.

M669 As one speaks **More** the less he is believed
c900 *Old English Cato* 5.10–1: Swa mann mare specð, swa him læs manna gelefeð. See **L67, M773.**

M670 He that dispends **More** than he has is smitten to death without stroke
1474 Caxton *Chesse* 148[10–2]: And also hit is sayd that he that dispendith more than he hath with oute strook he is smyten to the deth. See **M672.**

M671 He that has **More** should be worshipped (worth) more
a1400 Wyclif *Sermons* II 31[4–5]: For it is a comune proverb, he that more hath, more shulde he be worshipid, 190–1: And so this is a fals principle that worldly men usen today,—ever the more that a man hath, ever the more worth he is. See **M265, 274.**

M672 He that spends **More** than he gets shall lead a beggar's life
a1475 *Good Wyfe Wold* 175.76: He that spendyth mor then he gettythe, a beggerrys lyfe he schall lede. Apperson 595:10. See **M670, T250.**

M673 If they had done **More** they had lost more
1525 Berners *Froissart* IV 177[29–30]: For if they had done more, more had they lost. Whiting *Froissart* 298:60.

M674 The **More** a man can (*knows*) the more he is worth
c1300 Robert of Gloucester II 544.7547: Vor the more that a man can the more wurthe he is.

M675 The **More** a man has the more burningly he asks
c1340 Rolle *Psalter* 97 (26.12): The mare that a man has the brennandere he askis. See **G305.**

M676 **More** and enough is no sore
c1458 *Knyghthode and Bataile* 43.1155–6: More and ynough to have, it is not soor, And spare wel, whil ther is aboundaunce.

M677 "**More** and more" is a song often sung
a1450 *Castle* 158.2716–7: "More and more," in many a place, Certys that song is oftyn songe, 159.2759, 2762, 2774.

M678 **More** behooves (*belongs*) to the plow
a1393 Gower *CA* III 452.2424–7: I wot and have it wel conceived, Hou that thi will is good ynowh; Bot mor behoveth to the plowh, Wher-of the lacketh, as I trowe. Apperson 503:6; *Oxford* 705; Tilley M1156; Whiting *Scots* II 112.

M679 The **Mo(re)** the merrier
c1380 *Pearl* 31.850: The mo the myryer, so God me blesse. **1546** Heywood *D* 82.65–6: The mo the merier, we all daie here and see. Ye, but the fewer the better fare. Apperson 428; *Oxford* 433; Taylor and Whiting 250; Tilley M1153; Whiting *Drama* 139.

M680 The **More** you seek the more you will find
c1450 *Merlin* I 139[17]: The more thow sechest the more shalt thow fynde. See **S136.**

M681 To do **More** than the priest spoke of on Sunday
1546 Heywood *D* 96.177–8: I woulde dooe more (quoth hee) Than the preest spake of on sonday. Apperson 512; Tilley M1161.

M682 To keep no **More** of the cat than her skin
c1450 *Douce MS.52* 50.74: I kepe no more but the skyn of the catt. **c1450** *Rylands MS.394* 100.12v.21: of the katte but the skynne. Apperson 89:74; *Oxford* 457; Tilley M1167. See **F600.**

M683 To lose **More** than one wins
c1450 *Merlin* II 196[27–8]: Full nygh hadde ye more loste than wonne, 246[19]. **1523** Berners *Froissart* II 497[6–7]: We may lose more than wyn. See **M707.**

M684 To say no **More** till the days be longer
1555 Heywood *E* 176.168: I wyll say no more, tyll the dayes be longer. Apperson 551; *Oxford* 563; Tilley M1142.

M685 To think **More** than one says (*varied*)
a1300 *Alisaunder* 415.7672: She thoughth more than she seide. **c1330** *Seven Sages A* 19.510: Sche thought wel more thanne she said, 82 B 1928: More he thowght than he sayd. **c1375** *St. Eustace* in Horstmann *Legenden 1881* 217.299: Litel he spak and thouhte more. **a1393** Gower *CA* II 93.2105–6: And to his tale an Ere he leide, And thoghte more than he seide. **a1400** *Ipomadon A* 8.190–2: No thyng he sayd, what so he thoughte, But stode stille and an-sweryd nought, But thynkyd ylka dell. **a1400** *King Edward* 970.599: He thoght more then he seyde. **c1400** *Triamour* 51.125. **1404** *Lerne say wele* in Kail 15.16. **a1425** *Metrical Paraphrase*

OT 82.16739: Sho toyght more then scho sayd. **a1445** *Carl* 133 B 225–6: "Sir," said Gawaine, "I sayd nought." "No, man," said the carle, "more thou thought," 138 A 377, 139 B 315–6. **a1450** *Partonope* 84.2702: He seyyth butte lytell, butte more thynckyth he. **a1450** *South English Legendary (Bodley)* 374.278: Ac he ne seyde but lyte, they he thought the more. **a1461** *John the Reeve* 561.101–2. **a1470** Malory II 488.31–2: And seyde but lytyll, but he thought the more. **c1475** *Why I Can't* 139.62: I seyde but lytylle and thowght the more. **c1477** Caxton *Jason* 171.37–8: Howe well she answerde not one word, wherfore she thoughte not the lasse. **a1500** *Clerk and the Husbandman* in Robbins 181.30: And qwer thay say lyttyll thai thynke moe. **a1500** *Eger H* 285.1664: Few words they said, but many thought. **c1522** Skelton *Speke* II 19.381: Some say but lityll, and thynke more in there thowghte. **1525** Berners *Froissart* V 73[5–6]: They . . . spake nothynge therof, but they thought the more, 153[9–10], 459[38–9]: But pacyentely suffred; howebeit he thought the more. **1546** Heywood *D* 63.63: I say little . . . but I thinke more. Apperson 551; *Oxford* 563; Taylor and Whiting 319; Tilley L367; Whiting *Scots* II 139, 161.

M686 Cloudy **Mornings** turn to clear afternoons
1546 Heywood *D* 98.254: Thus cloudy mornynges turne to cleere after noones. Apperson 103; *Oxford* 98; Tilley M1178. See **C315, M693.**

M687 A glad **Morning** is oft followed by a dark day
a1439 Lydgate *Fall* III 966–7.1695–8: But ofte it fallith, that a glad morwenyng, Whan Phebus sheweth his bemys cleer and briht, The day sumtyme, therupon folwyng, With sum dirk skie is clipsid of his liht. See **P166.**

M688 Many are jolly in the **Morning** and thole (*suffer*) death in the evening (*varied*)
a1300 *Alisaunder* 53.916–7: Many ben jolyf in the morowenyng And tholen deth in the evenyng. **1480** Caxton *Ovyde* 120[26–8]: Some ther ben that lawh in the mornyng And er the even com they complayne and wepe. Tilley M1176. Cf. Whiting *Drama* 302. See **F549.**

M689 As light as **Morning Star**
a900 *Old English Martyrology* 66.18–9: His eagan scinon swa leohte swa morgensteorra. **c970** *Blickling Homilies* 137[30]: Hit wæs þa swa leoht swa se mergenlica steorra. Cf. Svartengren 227.

M690 Suffer old **Morel** (*a dark colored horse*) to play
a1500 *Remedie of Love* CCCXXII[r][1.26]: O suffre yet olde Morell to plaie. (Let an old man frisk with women.) See **G473.**

M691 As fair as the bright **Morrow**
c1386 Chaucer *LGW* 1202: And she as fair as is the bryghte morwe.

M692 The glad **Morrow** sues (*follows*) the dark night
a1420 Lydgate *Troy* I 261.4092–3: For evene liche, as the glade morwe, Of kynde sweth the dirke, blake nyght.

M693 Of a full misty **Morrow** follows oft a merry summer's day
c1385 Chaucer *TC* iii 1060–4: For I have seyn, of a ful misty morwe Folowen ful ofte a myrie someris day; And after wynter foloweth grene May. Men sen alday, and reden ek in stories, That after sharpe shoures ben victories. *Oxford* 98; Skeat 182. Cf. Apperson 429; Tilley M1178. See **M686.**

M694 The shining **Morrow** has oft a stormy eve
a1440 Burgh *Cato* 310.279: The shynyng morwe hath ofte a stormy eve. See **E155.**

M695 A sweamful (*sad*) **Morrow** has a joyful evening
1449 Metham 75.2045: Thus hath this sqwemfful morw a joe-ful evynyng. See **B325, E161, 175.**

M696 To be like the bright **Morrow** of May
c1395 Chaucer *CT* IV[E] 1748: That she was lyk the brighte morwe of May.

M697 His **Morrow-sleep** shall be more lasting that has evilly drunk in the even
c1250 *Proverbs of Alfred* 100 T 260–4: And his morghe-sclep Sal ben muchil lestind(e) (*Maidstone* the werse) Werse the swo on even Yvele haved ydronken. MED drinken 3.

M698 To shine like the **Morrow Star**
1483 Caxton *Golden Legende* 225[v][2.30–1]: Whoos leves shone lyke to the morow sterre. Svartengren 227.

M699 A shining **Morrow-tide** betokens clear weather
c1400 *Three Kings* 2.22–3: A shynyng morowetyde bitokeneth a cleer wheder folowing.

M700 Better a **Morsel** of bread with joy than a houseful of delices with chiding (*varied*)
c1390 Chaucer *CT* X[I] 633: "Bettre is a morsel

of breed with joye than an hous ful of delices with chidynge," seith Salomon. **c1395** *WBible* Proverbs xvii 1: Betere is a drie mussel (**a1382:** morsel) with joye, than an hous ful of sacrifices with chidynge. **a1449** Lydgate *Fabules* in *MP* II 581.428–31: Salomon wryteth, howe hit ys bet by halfe A lompe of brede with rejoysyng, Then at festis to have a rostyd calfe With hevy chere, frownyng or grogyng. MED bettre 1c (b). See **A256, B412, C176, 178, D257, L387, 388, M614, P268, 329, 336, Q19, S916.**

M701 Fat **Morsels** and sweet make many (a) one to beg his bread
a1475 *Good Wyfe Wold* 175.75: Fatt mosellys and swett makyth mony on to begge ther brede.

M702 Not worth a **Morsel** of bread
c1475 *Mankind* 25.691: Yt ys not schapyn worth a morsell of brede.

M703 Backare (*stand back*), quoth **Mortimer** to his sow
1546 Heywood *D* 50.316: Nay, backare (quoth mortimer to his sow), **1555** *E* 181.194.1: Backare quoth Mortimer to his sow: se Mortimers sow speakth as good latin as he. Apperson 21; *Oxford* 18; Tilley M1183.

M704 He that **Most** takes has most charge (*varied*)
1402 *Jack Upland* in Skeat *Chaucerian* 197.214: Sith he that moost taketh, most charge he hath. **c1412** Hoccleve *Regement* 48.1310: Whoso moost hath, he moost of schal answere. Whiting *Scots* II 100–1.

M705 **Most** shall have that most may do
a1338 Mannyng *Chronicle A* I 102.2862: Bot most shal have, that most may do.

M706 Those that adventure **Most** win most
1525 Berners *Froissart* IV 305[2–4]: Some . . . moost adventured, and therby wan moost.

M707 To think to win **Most** and lose most
a1533 Berners *Arthur* 316[23–4]: They that had thought moost for to have wonne, I thynke hath nowe most loste. See **A104, M683, 774, 780.**

M708 As innumerable as **Motes** of the sun
a1475 *St. Birgitta* 98.7: Unnowmerable as motes of the sonne.

M709 As thick as **Motes** in (the) sun(-beam)
a1300 *Arthour and M.*[1] 255.9159–60: Also thicke the aruwe schoten, In sonne bem so doth the moten. **a1300** *Richard* 355.5439–40 (*var.*): Quarellys, arwes also thykke gan flye, As mootes in the soone that men myght se. **c1395** Chaucer *CT* III[D] 868: As thikke as motes in the sonne-beem. **a1400** *Scottish Legends* II 61.493–4: That thai fulfillit sa the are As motis ar in sownbeme fare. **c1400** *Laud Troy* I 202.6848–9: He falles hem thikker, than the motes In somertide fflyen In the sonne. **c1410** Lovelich *Merlin* II 383.14320–2: Men and hors . . . As thikke fallen . . . As that motes flen in the feld. **a1438** Kempe 88.8–9: As thykke in a maner as motys in the sunne. **c1440** *On Grace* in *Yorkshire Writers* I 309[2]: Ma thykkere and more glowande teres thene motes ere in the sonne. **c1450** *Owayne Miles* (*Brome*) 98.407–8: Fyndys stodyne on every syde As thyke as motys yn somer tyde, (*Auchinleck*) 106.120[5–6]: Never mot in sonne beme Thicker than the fendes yede. **c1500** *Melusine* 174.32–3: For there had ye seen arowes flee as thykk as motes in the sonne. **1515** Barclay *St. George* 67.1599: Sawe soules thycker than motes in the son. **1556** Heywood *Spider* 261[2]: They will marche on, as thick, as motes in the soon. Tilley M1192; Whiting *Scots* II 101.

M710 **Mote** (stalk, straw, festu) and beam (balk)
a900 Alfred *Gregory* (*Cotton*) 224.1–2: þu meaht gesion lytelne cið on ðines broður eagan, and ne meaht gefredan micelne beam on ðinum agnan. **c1000** *WSG* Matthew vii 3: To hwi gesihst þu þæt mot on þines broþor eagan, and þu ne gesyhst þone beam on þinum agenum eagan? Luke vi 41: þa egle on þines broþor eagan. **1340** *Ayenbite* 175[11–3]: Thet y-zyeth thet mot ine the othres eghe and ne yzyeth naght thane refter ine hire oghene eghe. **c1378** *Piers* B x 263–4: Why mevestow thi mode for a mote in thi brotheres eye, Sithen a beem in thine owne ablyndeth thi-selve? 277–8: Lewed men may likne yow thus, that the beem lithe in yowre eyghen, And the festu is fallen for yowre defaute. **c1390** Chaucer *CT* I[A] 3919–20: He kan wel in myn eye seen a stalke, But in his owene he kan nat seen a balke. **c1395** *Pierce* 6.140–2: Theire-as curteis Crist clereliche saide, "Whow myght-tou in thine brother eighe a bare mote loken, And in thyn owen eighe nought a bem toten?" **c1395** *WBible* Matthew vii 3: But what seest thou a litil mote in the ighe of thi brother, and seest not a beem in thine owne ighe? Luke vi 41. **a1400** Wyclif *Sermons* I 12[5–6]: That thei can see a mot in hir brother eye, but a beem in ther owen ighe thenke thei not oon. **c1400** *Vices and Virtues* 177.14–5: For thei seen wel a strawe in a-notherys eighe, but thei see not a schide in here owne. **1402** *Daw Topias* 95[14–7]: Bot thou accusist other men That han bot the mote In

the comparison Of alle your gret synnes. **a1415** Mirk *Festial* 86.31–2: And full eldyr seen a mote yn another manys ee that con not se a beem yn hor one. **c1415** *Middle English Sermons* 140.13–4: Cast avey first the bolke oute of thi eye, and than thou may cast oute the mote oute of thi brothers eye. **a1425** *Rule of St. Benet (1)* 5.34–5: In thi brothir ehe thu ses a stra, And noht a balke in thin aghen. **a1425** *WBible gloss* to Proverbs xxv 26: Of a festu he makith a beem. **a1439** Lydgate *Fall* III 790. 570–1: Of a smal mote ye can abraide me, But in your eye a beem ye cannat see, **a1449** *Exposition* in *MP* I 68.244–6: Can In myn eien nat seen a large beem, Though it spradde al abrood this Rewm, Can seen weell motys in other menhis sight. **c1449** Pecock *Repressor* I 3[25–8]. **a1450** Audelay 146.434–7: Fore a lytil mote ye con sone se In another mons ye then, Bot in your owne ye con not se Thagh ther be fallyn in ix or x. **a1450** *Myne awen dere* 169.623–6. **a1450** *Rule of St. Benet* (2) 59.401–4. **c1450** *Alphabet* I 155.26–9: And than he askid hym of the balke and the mote, what thai wer; and he told hym whatt thai war. And than he bad hym umthynk hym in his awn harte that this balk was his awn synys, and this litle mote was the synnys of the toder man. **1456** Hay *Governaunce* 156.22–4: That he se nocht (*sic*) a mote in his falowis eye, and nocht a grete balk in his awin eyne. **a1475** *Vision of Philibert* 24[5–6]: Fyrst take the pylere out of thyne ye, Or one me thou put anny defaute. **1481** Caxton *Reynard* 74[3–5], **1483** *Cato* D7r[5–7], **1484** *Royal Book* O4v[3–5]: For they see wel a lytel festue or a lytel mote in the eyen of other and beholde not a grete beme or blocke whyche is in theyr owen eyen. **1491** *Rule of St. Benet* (3) 119.24–6. **a1500** *Harley MS.2321* in *Rel. Ant.* I 207: Cast the beame out of thie owne eye, then thou maist see a mothe in another mans. **1509** Barclay *Ship* I 112[22–6]: He . . . may . . . be callyd a sote . . . Whiche in a nothers iye can spye a lytell mote And in his owne can nat fele nor espye A moche stycke. **1509** Watson *Ship* F3v[13–5]: Suche folkes spyeth well a lytell thorne in another mannes eye, but they se not a grete beme in theyr owne eye, H1r[4–5]. **1513** Douglas *Aeneid* II 17.499–500: Beis not ourstudyus to spy a mote in myne e, That in your awyn a ferry boyt can nocht se, IV 189.66: Quhilk in myne e fast staris a mote to spy. **1533** More *Confutacion* 646 E[1–3]: Take the beames out of your own eien . . . ere ye goe aboute to take the motes out of other mens. **1546** Heywood *D* 83.106–7: Ye can see a mote in an other mans iye, But ye can not see a balke in your owne. Apperson 430; MED balke 3(b); *Oxford* 435; Taylor and Whiting 18; Tilley M1191; Whiting *Scots* II 101. Cf. Smith 97, 100. See **B37.**

M711 Not help a **Mote**
c1390 *Sir Gawain* 68.2209: Hit helppes me not a mote.

M712 Not reck as much as a **Mote**
c1412 Hoccleve *Regement* 35.943: Nat wold I rekke as mochel as a mote.

M713 Not set a **Mote**
a1450 *St. Editha* 30.1320: Bot he set not by that leste a mote.

M714 To pick (out) a **Mote**
c1440 Charles of Orleans 171.5113: A ye my frend kan ye suche motis piik. **a1475** *Ludus Coventriae* 91.283: Blere myn ey and pyke out a mote.

M715 Not (a)vail a **Moth** (*or* ?Mote)
a1500 *Lay of Sorrow* 718.140: It valith nocht a moth.

M716 To melt away (*die*) like a **Moth**
c1390 *This World* in Brown *Lyrics XIV* 161.42: Mon melteth a-wey so deth a mouht.

M717 Abide, friend, your **Mother** bided till you were born
1546 Heywood *D* 97.239: But abyde freend, your mother bid till ye were borne. Tilley F682a.

M718 His **Mother** could not have known him
a1475 *Guy*[2] 311.10825–6: Noght hys modur, that hym bere, Kowde not have knowyn hym there. Taylor and Whiting 251.

M719 Many (ilka, every, each) (a) **Mother's** son (bairn, child)
a1225 *St. Marherete* (*Bodley*) 6.3: An of the moni moder-bern. **c1250** *Hendyng O* 197.33[4]: Mani modersone. **a1300** *Jacob and Joseph* 6.155: Mani a moder sone. **a1300** *Richard* 106.541, 295.4072, 301.4244: And with hym every modyr sone, 304.4308: And slowgh every modyr sone. **c1300** Robert of Gloucester I 387.5313: Ther was many moder child. **c1300** *South English Legendary* (*Laud*) 103.97: And thare schal mani a moder-child go to thi foule licame. **c1325** *Chronicle* 13.288. **c1380** *Cleanness* 49.1303: With moni a modey moder chylde mo then innoghe. **a1400** *Alexander C* 118.2098: For mekely ilka modire son. **a1400** *Firumbras* 50.1567: Many was the modyr sone. **a1400** *Guy*[3] 628.174: Many a moder

sone. **c1400** *Laud Troy* I 206.6989: But ther come many a moder barne. **a1425** Higden-Anon. Cont. VIII 483[26–7]: Lete us go and slee every moders son of theym. **a1425** *Metrical Paraphrase OT* 60.7769: Kyng David sayd what moder sun. **c1426** *Brut* II 435.17: And they weren, evyry modir sone, slayne. **c1440** *Prose Alexander* 17.20–1: And slewe tham ilke a moder son, 49.25–6. **c1443** *Chronicle of London* 36[9–10]: But the Normaunes were sclayn every modir sone, 116[18]. **a1447** Bokenham *Mappula* 30[7–8]: And slowe esche modris sonne. **c1450** *Chronicles of London* 138[28]: Be yolden every moderson un to the lordys above. **c1450** *Merlin* II 401[17]: Many a fre modres childe lay stiked. **c1450** *Robin Hood and the Monk* in Child III 98.24, 27. **1455** Paston III 26[36–7]: Every moder sone. **a1470** Malory II 621.32–3: For he castyth that we shall never ascape, modyrs sonne of us. **c1485** Malory I 77.30–1 (*var.*): And there were slayn many moders sones. **1519** Horman *Vulgaria* 370[17]: They were slayne every mothers sonne. Occidione occisi sunt, 375[33]: Omnes ad unum cesi sunt. Apperson 190–1; *Oxford* 435; Tilley M1202.

M720 Such **Mother** such child (daughter) (*varied*)
a1325 *Cursor* II 1080 CG 18857: O suilk a moder, wel slik a child. **c1395** *WBible* Ezekiel xvi 44–5: Lo! ech man that seith a proverbe comynli, schal take it to thee, and schal seie, As the modir, so and the doughtir of hir. **c1450** *Consail and Teiching* 73.253–4: Gud mothir child gud we presume Sa scho be kepyt fra Ill Custume. **c1450** *Ratis* 27.939–42: For comonly thai folow kynd And gretly to the modiris strind. Sen thar is bot the lyklyest Hald ay gud mothir dochtir best. **1474** Caxton *Chesse* 33[9–10]: For suche moder suche doughter comunely, **1483** *Cato* G4ᵛ[14–5]: For the doughters folowen ofte the condycyons and maners of the moders. Apperson 367; *Oxford* 435; Tilley M1199; Whiting *Scots* II 101. Cf. Jente 142. See **C89, D25, F80, L385.**

M721 To be **Mother-naked**
c1330 *Peniworth* 116.282: Thei we ben bothe modernaked. **c1390** *Talkyng* 44.28–9: Thou weore honged al mooder naked. **a1400** *Siege of Jerusalem* 19.346. **c1420** Wyntoun V 83.2747. **a1438** Kempe 190.20: Al modyr-nakyd as he was born. **c1450** Capgrave *Katharine* 358.608. **c1450** *How mankinde dooth* in Furnivall *Hymns* 58.11–2: I saw a child modir nakid, New born the modir fro. **1481** Caxton *Reynard* 22[23]. Whiting *Scots* II 101. See **B466.**

M722 (In one's) **Mother-tongue**
c1250 *Oure Fader* in *MLN* 49(1934) 236: Oracio dominica in materna lingua: Fader that hart in hevene. **c1378** ?Purvey *De Officio Pastorali* in Wyclif *EW* 430[4–5]: The comyns of engliyschmen knowen it best in ther modir tunge. **c1385** Usk 2.37–8: Suche wordes as we lerneden of our dames tonge. **c1395** *Arundel MS.254* in *WBible* I xiv, n.ᵏ[2.57]: The gospel in her modir tunge. **c1395** *WBible Prologue* I 59[9], [34]: here modir language, *Additional Prologue* to John [8]: in her modir tunge. **c1400** *Brut* II 315.18: Shold plede in her moder tunge. **c1400** *Lay Folks' Catechism* 15.236, 41.631. **c1400** *Office of Curates* in Wyclif *EW* 159[4]. **c1405** *Lollard Tract* in *Medium Ævum* 7(1938) 174.153, 160, 178.288: modir langage. **a1410** Love *Mirrour* 56[23–4]: The moder tonge of oure lady and alle Jewes. **a1415** *Lanterne* 18.23–4, 100.3–4: Englische, that is oure modir tunge. **1422** Yonge *Governaunce* 122.8: Youre modyr Englyshe tonge. **a1425** *Chester Plays* I 237.187. **c1440** Scrope *Epistle* 2[22]. **c1443** Pecock *Reule* 17[13]: in her modiris langage, 18[3, 7, 8, 11], 85[14], 87[31], 99[6]. **a1447** Bokenham *Mappula* 30[26, 31], 33[32]. **a1449** Lydgate and Burgh *Secrees* 51.1588. **c1449** Pecock *Repressor* I 9[5–6]: It were leerned of al the comon peple in hir modiris langage, [25–6], 47[4], 66[3]. **a1456** Shirley *Death of James* 29[10–1]: Oure moders Englisshe tong. **1479** Paston VI 6[6–7]: In modre tunge callyd Benett. **1481** Caxton *Mirror* 184[19–20]: This forsayd translacion in to our englissh and maternal tongue. **a1500** *Partenay* 224.6573: In our moder tonge, spoken in contre. **c1500** Betson *Treatyse* A2ʳ[5–6]. **c1500** Fabyan 476[16]. **1506** *Kalender* 169.3. **1509** Barclay *Ship* I 17[23–4], II 326[7]: In langage maternall. **1509** Fisher *Treatyse* 126.19. **1509** Watson *Ship* A1ʳ[20] (*the second of two A signatures*): Our maternall tongue of Englysshe. **1510** Copland *Apolyn* 2[18–9]: Our maternal Englysshe tongue. **1519** Horman *Vulgaria* 139[1]: He speketh well in his mothers tonge. Eloquens est in lingua vernacula: non materna. **c1520** *Terens* A1ʳ[3]. **1528** More *Heresyes* 154 D[17], 240 H[15], **1532** *Confutacion* 397 H[2], 415 G[11–2], 675 C[2], 761 C[14]. Taylor and Whiting 251; Whiting *Drama* 355:719, *Scots* II 101.

M723 **Mother-wit**
c1450 Idley 181.1336: All this they sey cometh of a verri modir wytt. **1528** More *Heresyes* 153 H[1–4]: One speciall thynge, without which all lernynge is halfe lame . . . a good mother wyt. **1556** Heywood *Spider* 33[2]: By mine ex-

perience and mother wit. Taylor and Whiting 251.

M724 Who **Mounts** higher than he should falls lower than he would
1484 Caxton *Aesop* 217[21–3]: For men sayn comynly who so mounteth hyher than he shold he falleth lower than he wold. Tilley M1211. See **C296.**

M725 As high as **Mountains**
a1533 Berners *Huon* 367.29–30: The waves . . . were as hye as mountaynes, 621.1. Whiting *NC* 447.

M726 A **Mountain** might be sooner (re)moved
1513 Bradshaw *St. Werburge* 37.852–4: A mountayne or hyll soner, leve ye me, Myght be remoeved agaynst the course of nature Than she for to graunte to suche worldly pleasure. See **M564, R161, S792, W24.**

M727 Beware of high **Mounting** for fear of over low descending
1493 *Tretyse of Love* 122.1–2: Beware of hye mountynge for fere of over lowe descendynge. See **C296.**

M728 After **Mourning** mirth is sweeter
c1485 *Guiscardo* 42.90–1: For evyr aftyr mornyng the myrthe ys the swetter, And aftyr gret sorow the joy shalbe the bettyr. See **P7, 225.**

M729 **Mourning** makes no mend (*varied*)
a1425 *Metrical Paraphrase OT* 73.8255–6: He bad all men be blyth Sen mowrnyng made no mende, 13.14255–6: Grett mornyng may not amend Wher no relefe may ryse. **a1450** *Partonope* 240.6236–7: Ye shende your-selfe, and ther-fore grette ffoly Hyt ys, sythe a-mendyd hyt may not be. **a1460** *Towneley Plays* 192.202: Mowr(n)yng, mary, may not amend. **a1500** *Coventry Plays* 65.1022: But mornyng ma nott ytt amend. Whiting *Drama* 284. See **C43, D337, G455, H134, K96, L52, R81, 87, S514, T160.**

M730 As drenkled (*drowned*) as a **Mouse**
a1450 *Castle* 168.3079–80: In pycke and ter, to grone and grenne, Thou schalt lye drenkelyd as a mous.

M731 As drunk(en) as a (any) **Mouse**
c1325 *Man in the Moon* in Brown *Lyrics XIII* 161.31: When that he is dronke ase a dreynt mous. **c1385** Chaucer *CT* I[A] 1261: We faren as he that dronke is as a mous, **c1395** III[D] 246: Thou comest hoom as dronken as a mous. **a1400** *Vespasian Psalter* in *Yorkshire Writers* II 243.106.27: Thai ere dreved and ere stired als dronkin mis. **a1430** Lydgate *Pilgrimage* 353.12998: Mad and dronke, as ys A mous. **a1500** *Colyn Blowbol* 98.141: That oft hath made (me) dronke as any mous, 103.243: And every man shalbe as drownke as any mous. **a1500** Greene *Carols* 401 A 4: Sum will be dronkyn as a mowse. **c1522** Skelton *Colyn* I 342.803. Apperson 166–7; *Oxford* 159; Tilley M1219; Whiting *Scots* II 101.

M732 As fearful as a **Mouse**
a1420 Lydgate *Troy* I 231.3024: Ferful for drede as a litel mows.

M733 As sure as a **Mouse** tied with a thread
1546 Heywood *D* 88.267–9: Every promise that thou therin dost utter Is as sure as . . . a mouse tied with a threede. Apperson 431; Tilley M1225.

M734 As weak as a **Mouse**
a1475 *Tree* 149.10: He is as weyke as a mouse.

M735 A hardy **Mouse** that breeds in the cat's ears (*varied*)
a1449 Lydgate *Order* in *MP* II 452.95–6: An hardy mous, that is bold to brede In cattys eris, that brood shal never the. **a1500** Hill 128.4: It is a sotill mowsse, that slepith in the cattis ere. **1522** Skelton *Why Come* II 50.753–6: Yet it is a wyly mouse That can bylde his dwellinge house Within the cattes eare Withouten drede or feare. **1546** Heywood *D* 76.193: A wyly mouse that should breede in the cats eare. Apperson 431; *Oxford* 54; Tilley M1231.

M736 **Mice** lake (*play*) where no bads (*cats*) are (*varied*)
a1400 *Alexander C* 98.1761–3: And maa thi lepis and thi laikis and quat the liste ellis, As ratons or rughe myse in a rowme chambre, Aboute in beddis or in bernys thare baddis ere nane. **c1440** *Prose Alexander* 21.20–4: Righte as a mouse crepeth oute of his hole, so thou ert cropen out of the lande of Sethym, wenynge wit a few rebawdes to conquere and optene the landes of Perse brade and lange, and to ryotte and playe the in thaym as myesse douse in the house whare na cattes ere. **c1470** *Harley MS.3362* in *Retrospective* 309[10] and Förster 201.10: The mows lordchypyth, ther a cat ys nawt. Mus debaccatur, ubi catus non dominatur. Apperson 89; Jente 276; *Oxford* 84; Smith 22; Tilley C175; Walther I 225.1967, II 1019.15760.

M737 The **Mouse** goes abroad where the cat is not lord
a1500 Hill 132.48: The mowse goth a-brode, wher the cat is not lorde, Mus devagatur, ubi

catus non dominatur. Apperson 431; *Oxford* 84; Tilley M1232.

M738 A **Mouse** in time may bite a cable in two **1546** Heywood *D* 84.146: A mouse in tyme, maie byte a two a gable (*for* cable). Apperson 430–1; *Oxford* 437; Tilley M1235.

M739 A **Mouse** that has but one hole is not worth a leek **c1395** Chaucer *CT* III[D] 572–4: I holde a mouses herte nat worth a leek That hath but oon hole for to sterte to, And if that faille, thanne is al ydo. Apperson 431; *Oxford* 437; Skeat 270; Tilley M1236.

M740 To be borne to ground like a **Mouse** **c1400** *Laud Troy* I 204.6917–8: Kyng Thelaman at that rescous Was born to grounde as a mous.

M741 To catch a **Mouse** in a cage is no mastery **c1400** *Beryn* 11.320: And also it is no mastry to cach a mouse in a cage. Cf. To shoot fish in a barrel.

M742 To cheep like a **Mouse** **a1513** Dunbar *Wowing* 53.55: The lamb than cheipit lyk a mows.

M743 To hide a **Mouse** **c1400** *Laud Troy* I 52.1757–8: Ther nys nought stondende an hous In al the toun to hide a mous.

M744 To slay (people) like **Mice** **c1400** *Laud Troy* I 235.7981: Ector hem sclow, as it were mys.

M745 What may the **Mouse** (do) against the cat? **a1393** Gower *CA* II 270.1643: What mai the Mous ayein the Cat?

M746 To creep into a **Mousehole** for fear **a1475** *Assembly of Gods* 57.1952–3: For feere . . . I wold have cropyn in a mouse hoole. Cf. Tilley M1244.

M747 To be taken in one's **Mousetrap** **c1500** *Our Sir John* in Robbins 20.13–5: Ser John ys taken In my mouse-trappe . . . He gropith so nyslye a-bought my lape. See **W530.**

M748 As red as the **Mouth** of a furnace **a1533** Berners *Huon* 427.18–9: His eyen . . . more redder than the mouthe of a fornays.

M749 Every **Mouth** says not truth **1484** Caxton *Ordre of Chyvalry* 55.8–9: For everyche mouth sayth not trouthe. See **B221.**

M750 He that keeps his **Mouth** keeps his soul **c1412** Hoccleve *Regement* 88.2431–2: He that his mouth kepith, Keepith his soule, as that the bookes teeche.

M751 In **Mouth** a lion, in heart a hare (sheep) **c1300** Robert of Gloucester II 665.9384: Is mouth is as a leon, is herte arn as an hare. **a1387** Higden-Trevisa VII 491[13–4]: In the mouth he is a lyoun, and in the herte an hare. **c1500** Fabyan 266[9]: In mowth he is a lyon, but in hart he is a shepe. See **L38.**

M752 An itching **Mouth** is a sign of kissing **c1390** Chaucer *CT* I[A] 3682–3: My mouth hath icched al this longe day; That is a signe of kissyng atte leeste.

M753 A lickerish **Mouth** must have a lickerish tail **c1395** Chaucer *CT* III[D] 464–6: And after wyn on Venus moste I thynke, For al so siker as cold engendreth hayl, A likerous mouth moste han a likerous tayl. Apperson 370; *Oxford* 364; Tilley T395.

M754 **Mouth** and heart agree (*varied*) **c1340** Rolle *Psalter* 228 (65.16): That .i. hafe in mouth .i. hafe in hert. **c1390** *Who says the Sooth* in Brown *Lyrics XIV* 152.9: Herte and mouth loke thei ben tweyne. **a1393** Gower *CA* II 4.61*–2*: A gentil herte his tunge stilleth, That it malice non distilleth, III 27.2923–5: For as men seith, Whan that a man schal make his feith, His herte and tunge moste acorde. **c1400** *Lay Folks' Catechism* 39.594–6: God commandys . . . that the herte and the mowth acorde togydre. **c1415** *Middle English Sermons* 62.34–5: Latt the herte and the tounge a-corde in hem. **a1420** Lydgate *Troy* I 89.2592–3: Myn hert(e) menyth as my tong(e) seith. **1422** Yonge *Governaunce* 187.16–7: Ffor hit is not fere fro the herte, that the mouthe Spekyth. **a1425** Mirk *Instructions* 2.24–5: And say thy serves wythowten hast, That mowthe and herte a-corden I-fere. **a1425** *Rule of St. Benet* (*1*) 19.18–9: And lokis, when ye sing, that yure herte acorde with yure voice. **1449** Metham 3.56: The mowth (schewyth) the hert. **1450** *Dicts* 36.11–2: The (mouth) shewith that the whiche is in the hert. **c1450** *Jacob's Well* 304.27–8: Of the gret coveytise of good, desyre in thin herte, spekyth thi mowth. **a1470** Malory II 897.29: Loke that your harte and youre mowth accorde. **a1470** Parker *Dives* VI^{r}[1.26–7]: The mouth bereth wytnesse to the herte. **c1475** *Rawlinson MS. D 328* 119.20: That the hert thynkyt the mowte spekyt. **1477** Rivers *Dictes* 24[3–4]: The mouth sheweth ofte what the hert thinketh. **1483** *Quatuor Sermones* 8[22–4]: In token that thou sayst wyth thy mouth thou sholdest say it wyth thyn herte, and not say one and thynke another. **1492** *Salomon and Marcolphus* 26[1–2]: He seyth trouthe that thinkyst wyth his herte as he spekyth wyth his mowth. **c1500** Newton 260.4: With hert and mothe accordynge in oon. **a1533** Berners *Arthur* 357[24]: That is had in the herte, is had in the mouth and speche. Apperson 295; MED herte 2b(b); *Oxford* 288; Tilley H334. See **M759, T383.**

M755 **Mouth** and heart do not agree (*varied*) **a1225** *Lambeth Homilies* 25[21]: He seith mid tha muthe thet nis naut in his heorte. **c1250** *Owl* 58.675–8: An sone mai a word misreke Thar muth shal ayen horte speke; An sone mai a word misstorte Thar muth shal speken ayen horte. **c1303** Mannyng *Handlyng* 93.2639–40: Who-so with hys mouthe, one, seys, And with hys herte thenketh outher weys. **c1340** Rolle *Psalter* 204 (57.1): Not ane in mouth another in hert. **a1350** *Ywain* 2.39–40: With the mowth men makes it hale, Bot trew trowth es nane in the tale. **c1350** *Gamelyn* 649.163–5: Thus seyde the knight to Gamelyn with mowthe, And thoughte eek of falsnes as he wel couthe. The knight thoughte on tresoun and Gamelyn on noon. **a1400** *Cloud* 102.5–6: Bitwix that prive pride in theire hertes with-inne and soche meek wordes with-outyn, the sely soule may ful sone sinke into sorow. **a1400** *Romaunt B* 2541–2: For they in herte cunne thenke o thyng, And seyn another in her spekyng. **c1415** *Middle English Sermons* 154.18–23: For it is wrytten, "Dum cor non orat, In vanum lingua laborat." That is to sey, "Ther the herte preyth not, the tonge trayveils in vayn:" ther-as the herte worshippes not, itt is but vaste that the tounge speketh. **a1420** Lydgate *Troy* I 67.1864: Whos herte acordeth ful selde with her tonge, **a1430** *Pilgrimage* 325.11926–8: The mouth dyverseth ffro the herte; But herte and mouth be bothen on: By dyvers pathys, in soth, they gon. **a1438** Kempe 115.21–2: Sche menyth not wyth hir hert as sche seyth with hir mowthe. **a1439** Lydgate *Fall* I 322.4375: Thouh mouth and herte departed wer on tweyne. **1449** Metham 27.737: But with ther mowth thei musyd one .j., and with ther hert anodyr. **a1450** Audelay 95.4–5: In mouth is hone swet wordis uchon; In hert is galle; in dede, tresoun, 144.365–6: Fore wyle hert worchipis noght, The tong foresoth labors in vayne. **a1450** *Gesta* 244[12–3]: Thow erte a foole, for wherto prayst thou by mouthe and not withe thyne herte? **a1450** *Partonope* 190.5049: Her hert ys full fer fro her worde. **c1450** *Ponthus* 7.31–2: Bot wold Gode that your hertt wer as your mouthe says. **a1470** Parker *Dives* M2^{v}[1.6–9]: Bilinguis and the double tonged man is he that sayth one thynge with his mouth, and thynketh an other in his herte. **1471** Caxton *Recuyell* I 40.9–10: And sayd to them with his mouth thynkyng contrary with his hert, 108.7–8: Sayng hyt with the mouth and not wyth the herte, **1480** *Ovyde* 46[28–9]: Take a kysse of her. Whyche I preyse not that whiche cometh of the mouth but that whyche cometh fro the hert is swete, **1483** *Cato* A4^{v}[19–21]: Suche as they say with theyr mowthe is al contraye to that whiche the herte thynketh, **1484** *Aesop* 72[14–6]: And thenne the nyghtyngale beganne to synge swetely not with the herte but with the throte onely. **1495** *Meditacyons of saynt Bernarde* D5^{r}[10–1]: I sayd one thynge with my mouthe: and I thought a nother wyth my herte. **a1500** *Deceit III* in Robbins 101.6: The mowthe seythe ane, the hert thinketh another. **a1500** *Imitatione* (*1*) 69.17–8: Somme hath me in mouthe, but litel is in the herte, 108.8–9: Many preche with the mouthe, but in livynge thei discorde fer therfro. **a1500** *Eger H* 299.1901–2: But a fair tale it may be shown, Another in the heart be known. **a1500** ?Ros *La Belle Dame* 311.389–90: A currish herte, a mouth that is curteys, Ful wel ye wot, they be not according. **1502** *Imitatione* (2) 199.29–30: Some ther be that bere me in mouthe . . . but lytell in herte. **c1505** Watson *Valentine* 217.21–3: Haufray and He(n)ry that same day said muche good of him with their mouthes, and with their hartes desyred his death. **1512** Copland *Helyas* A5^{r}[10–1]: All these wordes sayd she with mouthe, but not with herte. **a1513** Dunbar *None May Assure* 45.41–2: Fra everie mouthe fair wordis procedis; In everie harte deceptioun bredis. **1525** Berners *Froissart* IV 84[26–8]: Some pardoneth well by mouthe . . . but yet the hatered remayneth styll in their corages. Jente 14; MED herte 2b(b); Taylor and Whiting 178; Tilley W672; Whiting *Drama* 45, 96, *Scots* I 187, II 102. See **C174, H77, L376, 521, M570, S79, T383, W631.**

M756 One may not bless and curse with one **Mouth**
c1000 Aelfric *Homilies* II 36[6–7]: Ne magon we mid anum muðe bletsian and wyrian. Cf. Tilley M1258.

M757 One may not have a **Mouth** full of meal and also blow fire
c1025 *Durham Proverbs* 15.43: Ne mæg man muþ fulne melewes habban and eac fyr blawan. Non potest os ambo plenum ferrine et ignem sufflare. Note (p. 18) cfs. Singer I 58–9 and

Plautus *Mostellaria* 791: Simul flare sorbereque haud factu facilest.

M758 A parlous **Mouth** is worse than spear or lance
a1449 Lydgate *Order* in *MP* II 450.31: A perlous mouth is wers than spere or launce. See **T395, W640.**

M759 (To have) all in **Mouth** that (is) in mind
c1025 *Durham Proverbs* 11.12: Eall on muþe þæt on mode. Omne in ore quod in mente. See **M754.**

M760 To make a fair **Mouth**
c1350 *Good Wife E* 160.38: Laghe the might and faire mouth make.

M761 To make up one's **Mouth**
1546 Heywood *D* 52.377: To make up my mouthe. Apperson 393; *Oxford* 399; Tilley M1263; Whiting *Drama* 354:706–7.

M762 To seem to have crept out of one's **Mouth**
c1400 *Beryn* 97.3232: Be-hold thy sone! it semeth crope out of thy̆ mowith. Apperson 367; *Oxford* 368; Tilley M1246.

M763 To serve **Mouth** thankless
a1500 Kennedy 12.8 (*refrain*): That evir I schervit Mowth-thankless. Whiting *Scots* II 102.

M764 To speak as though he would creep into one's **Mouth**
1546 Heywood *D* 94.142: Ye speake now, as ye would creepe into my mouth. Apperson 594; *Oxford* 610; Tilley M1250.

M765 To stop one's **Mouth**
1546 Heywood *D* 69.114: But that shall not stop my mouth, ye maie well gesse, **1555** *E* 185.219: He shall not stop my mouth, no Nan I thinke that I beleve all the devils in hel stopth it nat. Tilley M1264.

M766 When the **Mouth** matheles (*speaks*) more than it should the ears shall hear it eft (*afterwards*)
a1250 *Proverbs of Alfred* 105 M 312–5: For hwanne muth matheleth More thanne he scolde, Than scollen his eren Eft it iheren. See **T397.**

M767 To make a **Mow** (*grimace*) on the moon
c1320 *Fasciculus Morum* in *Essays and Studies in Honor of Carleton Brown* (New York, 1940) 153[22–3]: Vel tu facies *a mowe on the mone*, hoc est, tu eris suspensus per collum immediate. **a1450** *York Plays* 358.285–6: Late hym hynge here stille, And make mowes on the mone, 361.77–8: Ya, late hym hyng, Full madly on the mone for to mowe, 79.

M768 To beat down as a **Mower** beats down grass
1471 Caxton *Recuyell* II 419.22–3: He bete doun the casteliens like as a mowar with a sithe bete doun the grasse in a medowe.

M769 As **Much** as one has (so) men will love (?praise) him
a1200 Lawman I 129.3055–6: Al swa muchel swa thu havest, Men the wllet luvien. See **G344, M265, 671.**

M770 He forgets **Much** that abides long
c1303 Mannyng *Handlyng* 353.11377–8: Seynt Bernard tharfore, to swych chyt, And seyth "moche forgyt, that longe abyt."

M771 He has done so **Much** with his two hands that he is come from the most to the least
1483 Caxton *Cato* G3v[11–3]: The comyn proverbe sayth, The same hath doon so moche by his two handes that he is come fro the moest unto the leste.

M772 He spares **Much** that has nought
c1450 *Douce MS.52* 55.124: He sparyth muche, that has nouhght. See **N145.**

M773 He that claps (speaks) **Much** lies oft (says not ever truth)
1402 Hoccleve *Letter of Cupid* 78.141–2: A foule thing ys of tonge to be lyght; For who so mychel clappeth gabbeth oft. **c1450** La Tour-Landry 17.26–7: And y praie you have not mani wordes, for who so usithe to speke moche, he saithe not ever trouthe. See **L67, M669.**

M774 He that embraces too **Much** distrains little
c1390 Chaucer *CT* VII 1215[B2405]: For the proverbe seith: "He that to muche embraceth, distreyneth litel." **c1390** ?Chaucer *Proverbs* 5–8: Of al this world the large compas Hit wol not in myn armes tweyne,—Whoso mochel wol embrace, Litel therof he shal distreyne. **c1430** Lydgate *Dance* 44.344: Who al embraceth litel schal restreyne. **1523** Berners *Froissart* II 162[20–1]: Ye have herde say, dyvers tymes, he that to moche enbraseth, holdeth the wekelyer. *Oxford* 262: grasp; Skeat 146; Tilley M1295. See **A91, M780.**

M775 He that has **Much** to tell the more shortly he ought to spell (*speak*)
a1325 *Cursor* II 490.8519–20: For he that mikel has for to tell The scortliker he aght to spell. See **P408.**

M776 He that makes too **Much** of little, it shall be long ere he have mickle
c1450 *Fyrst thou sal* 89.99–100: He that makes to myche of lytell It sal be long or he hafe mykell.

M777 He that owes **Much** and has nought, *etc.* (*varied*)
a1500 Hill 140.112: He that owith mych and hath nowght, And spendith mych, and gettith nowght, And lokith in his purse, and fyndith nowght, He may be right sory and say nowght. **a1500** *On Nought* in Robbins 81.1–4: He that spendes myche and getes nothing, And owthe myche and hathe nothing, And lokes in his porse and fyndes nothing, He may be sorye and saie nothing. Apperson 595; Brown-Robbins 1163; Tilley M1275. See **N145.**

M778 He that speaks **Much** must spill (*spoil*) some speech
a1500 *Counsels* in Brown *Lyrics XV* 284.36: Whoo speketh mykyll sum he most spylle. **a1500** *Proverbs of Salamon* 180.25.3: That spekyrus moche some speche he must spylle. *Oxford* 422; Tilley M916; Whiting *Scots* II 129.

M779 It costs not **Much** to behote (*promise*) and pay nought
a1449 Lydgate *Cok* in *MP* II 815.69–70: It costith nat mekyl to be hoote, And paye ryght nought whan the feyre is doon. See **P409, 411.**

M780 Look to win **Much,** lose all
1556 Heywood *Spider* 375[5]: Looking to win much, lease all. Cf. Tilley A192, M1295. See **A91, M707, 774.**

M781 **Much** he has that will (have) no more
c1450 *Douce MS.52* 51.84: Muche he has, that wylle no more. See **M792.**

M782 **Much** he leaves that keeps nothing for himself
c1000 Aelfric *Homilies* I 580[9]: Micel forlæt se ðe him sylfum nan ðing ne gehylt.

M783 **Much** in little
c1425 *St. Katherine of Sienna* 187.19: My wille is to conclude mykel in a litil. Tilley M1284. See **E49.**

M784 The **Much** (*great*) oft take shame of (*from*) the little
c1500 *Heartless Mistress* in Robbins 140.19–20: Ffor hit hath be seen of old tyme The moche of the lytyll taketh oft shame. See **E99.**

M785 **Much** rests to be done (abides behind) that a fool thinks
1484 Caxton *Aesop* 163[24–5]: Moche resteth to be done of that that a foole thynketh, **c1489** *Blanchardyn* 181.32–182.1: But it ys sayd often, in a comyn langage that "moche abydeth behynde that a fole thynketh." Tilley M1283. See **F448.**

M786 **Much** will have more
a1400 *Alexander C* 235.4397: Bot ay mekill wald have mare as many man spellis. **a1450** Audelay 13.83: Have thai never so mekyl mok he wyl have more. **a1450** *Castle* 79.88: Have he nevere so mykyl, gyt he wold have more. **c1450** *Douce MS.52* 49.65: Mykull wulle more. **c1450** *Rylands MS.394* 100.9. **a1500** *Proverbs of Salamon* 195.5.4: Nedeles moche wolde have more. Apperson 433; *Oxford* 438; Tilley M1287.

M787 Of **Much** they made more
a1500 *English Conquest* 41[15–6]: And as the maner is, of mych thay mad more. *Fama de magnis semper majore, vulgante.*

M788 Of too **Much** no man yelps (*boasts*)
a1393 Gower *CA* III 231.2391–2: To conne moche thing it helpeth, Bot of to mochel noman yelpeth. See **E123.**

M789 See **Much,** say little, and learn to suffer in time (do less)
a1449 Lydgate *See Myche* in *MP* II 800–1: See myche, say lytell, and lerne to soffar in tyme. **1546** Heywood *D* 50.313–4: I see muche, but I say little, and doo lesse, In this kinde of phisicke. Apperson 556; *Oxford* 570. See **H264.**

M790 They need **Much** that have much
897 Alfred *Boethius* 31.20–3: Se ealda cwide is swiðe soð þe mon gefyrn cwæð, þætte þa micles beðurfon þe micel agan willað and þa þurfon swiþe lytles þe maran ne wilniað þon genoges. **c1380** Chaucer *Boece* ii pr. v 119–21: And sooth it es that of many thynges han they nede, that many thynges han. **1410** Walton *Boethius* 97[3–4]: And this is sothe also that I schal seyn: Who so mychel hath, of mychel thing hath nede. **a1470** Parker *Dives* A2[v][2.2–3]: He that moche hath byhoveth moche. And he that hath lesse byhoveth lesse. Cf. Apperson 432: Much hath.

M791 Think **Much** and say nought
c1300 *Guy*[1] 260 A 4536: Gii thenketh michel, and nought no seyth. **a1449** Lydgate *Cok* in *MP* II 818.170: Thynk mekyl and sey nought. Apperson 551; *Oxford* 650. See **F436.**

M792 To have so **Much** that one can say ho

a1500 *Proverbs of Salamon* 188.73.7–8: I see full fewe that saumple lere Who hath so moche that can sey hoo. See **H398, M781.**

M793 Too **Much** of any thing is nought (*varied*) **a1440** Burgh *Cato* 313.424: To much is nouht of any maner thyng. **a1449** Lydgate *Stans Puer* in *MP* II 743.78–9: Be meek in mesour, nat hasty, but tretable; Over mekyll is nat worth in no thyng. **1480** Caxton *Ovyde* 9[36]: For overmoche is a vice. **a1500** *ABC of Aristotle* in F. J. Furnivall *Queene Elizabethes Achademy* (EETS ES 8, 1869) 66.38: For to moche of on thynge was never holsome. **1534** More *Comforte* 1184 D[17–8]: You wote wel to much is to much. **1546** Heywood *D* 69.115: To muche of one thyng is not good. Apperson 640–1; Jente 370; *Oxford* 665; Taylor and Whiting 253; Tilley T158.

M794 As vile as any **Muck** **c1350** *Mirror of Saint Edmund* in Perry *Religious Pieces* 17.21: Thou erte now vylere than any mukke.

M795 Every **Muck** must into mire **c1390** *Each Man* in Brown *Lyrics XIV* 142.80: For everi mok most in-to myre.

M796 **Muck** (*wealth*) and the mad man shall never meet **c1330** *Four Foes* in Brown *Lyrics XIV* 34.93–6: For al the craft that thou can, And al the wele thatow wan, The mock and the mad man No schul thai never mete.

M797 **Muck** (*wealth*) is now married and virtue set at nought **c1400** *Beryn* 28.844: Ffor muk is nowe I-maried, and vertu set at nought. See **M626.**

M798 The **Muck** of the world **a1393** Gower *CA* III 79.4854–5: But forto prinche and forto spare, Of worldes muk to gete encress. **1520** Whittinton *Vulgaria* 74.22–3: That maketh a man as a subjecte to the mukke of the worlde. **1546** Heywood *D* 53.403: To disdeygne me, who mucke of the worlde hoordth not. *Oxford* 438; Tilley M1298.

M799 To wither away like **Muck** upon mold **a1460** *Towneley Plays* 25.62–3: As muk apon mold I widder away.

M800 To be like a **Mule** **1509** Fisher *Treatyse* 38–9: They wyll contynue in it styll, and in no wyse go out of that waye, they be lyke to a mule. Taylor and Whiting 254.

M801 **Multitude** makes no victory (*varied*) **c1375** Barbour *Bruce* I 40.330–2: For multitud maiss na victory; As men has red in mony story, That few folk (oft has) wencusyt ma. **a1393** Gower *CA* III 154.7389–93: For in the multitude of men Is noght the strengthe, for with ten It hath ben sen in trew querele Ayein an hundred false dele, And had the betre of goddes grace. **c1395** *WBible* II Paralipomenon xxv 8: For if thou gessist that batels stonden in the myght of oost, the Lord schal make thee to be overcomun of enemyes, for it is of God for to helpe, and to turne in to flight, I Maccabees iii 19: For not in multitude of oost is the victorie of batel, but of hevene is strengthe. **a1400** *Arthur* 14.439–42: The Muchelnesse of Men sainfayle Ys nat victorie in Batayle; But after the wyll that in hevene ys, So the victorie falleth y-wys. **c1400** *Alexander Buik* I 20.627–8: Now be we Sparhalkis and thay Quailyeis, For multitude in fecht oft failyeis! **c1400** *Brut* I 288.5–8: So there itte was welle semyng Thatte with multitude is no scomfiting, Butt with God, fulle off mighte, Wham he will helpe in trewe ffighte. **c1421** Lydgate *Thebes* 180.4380–2: For though so the Comownerys be stronge With multitude and have no governaylle Of an hed, ful lytyl may avaylle, **a1439** *Fall* II 391.2227–8: But manli pryncis han this opynyoun: In multitude stondeth nat victorie, 573.3652–3: And in a feeld(e), pleynli to conclude, Victori alway stant nat in multitude, III 877.1926–32: My trust is hool, pleynli to conclude, Thou (*God*) shalt foorthre and fortune my viage, With litil folk ageyn gret multitude To make me have gracious passage, Aftir the proverbe of newe and old langage, How that thou maist and kanst thi poweer shewe Geyn multitude victorie with a fewe. **a1449** Lydgate and Burgh *Secrees* 69. 2162–3: Ffor good counseyl moore doth avaylle Than of pepil greet puissaunce in bataylle. **1456** Hay *Knychthede* 55.5–7: For oft tymes bataillis ar mare wonnyn be grace, na be force, and be wit and subtilitee na be multitude of armyt company, 12–3: For traist nocht that grete multitude makis grete victory, bot mekle erare, grete confusion. **c1458** *Knyghthode and Bataile* 12.300–1: Conflicte is not sure in multitude As in the myght, 39.1056–9: And ofte it hath be seid and is conclude, That oostis over grete be myscheved More of her owne excessif multitude Then of her foon. **c1470** *Wallace* 62.437: All fors in wer do nocht but governance. **1484** Caxton *Ordre of Chyvalry* 96.2–4: For many bataylles ben many tymes vanquysshed more by maystrye, by Wytte and Industrye, than by multytude of people of hors ne of good armours,

1489 *Fayttes* 99.9–10: And more helpeth vertue than multytude, And often is a rowme bettre than hys strength in a felde. **a1500** *Colkelbie* 294.426–7: Ffor multitude in negligence He seldin palme of victory. **a1500** *English Conquest* 23.6–8: Be ye wel undyrstond, That not wyth many men ne wyth grete Streynth, bot by ryght and trouth that man hath wyth hym, batalis doth overcome. **c1500** *Melusine* 128.21–3: Ne victorye also lyeth not in grette multitude of peuple but in good rule and ordynaunce. **1523** Berners *Froissart* I 370[9–10]: The vyctorie lyeth nat in the multitude of people, but wher as God wyll sende it. Apperson 229: Force; *Oxford* 219; Whiting *Scots* II 102. See **A25, 49, E202, F492, L381, M281, O51, W269, 418.**

M802 Where **Multitude** is there is truth
c1450 Capgrave *Katharine* 296.1077–8: Reson wil conclude that where multitude is, There is the truthe, a man may not mys. See **M309.**

M803 To play (say) **Mum**
1532 More *Confutacion* 412 H[11]: Yet would he play mumme, **1533** *Debellacyon* 992 C[2]: Saith not so much as mum. **1534** Heywood *Love* D4^{v}[20]: Stande and play mum. See **N172, W602.**

M804 Maugre one's **Mun** (*mouth*)
c1380 *Patience* 14.44: Much, maugre his mun, he mote nede suffer.

M805 What is sweet in your **Mun** give your fellow some
c1450 *Douce MS.52* 52.90: That, at is swete in thy mumme (*for* munne) Geve thy felawe summe. **c1450** *Rylands MS.394* 102.21–3: monne. Da partem socio quod sapit ore tuo. Walther I 589.4844.

M806 **Murder** cannot be hid (will out) (*varied*)
c1325 *Cursor* I 70.1083–4: For-thi men sais that to this tide Is naman that murth mai hide. **c1390** Chaucer *CT* VII 576[B1766]: Mordre wol out, certeyn, it wol nat faille, 3052[B4242]: Mordre wol out, that se we day by day, 3057 [B4247]: Mordre wol out, this my conclusioun. **a1393** Gower *CA* II 278.1920–1: Bot moerdre, which mai noght ben hedd, Sprong out to every mannes Ere. **c1400** *Beryn* 70.2292–3: For, wend how men (woll) wend, Ther may no man hele murdir, that it woll out atte last. **c1433** Lydgate *St. Edmund* 400.225–6: Moodre wil out, thouh it abide a while, Lyk his decert, he must receyve his meede, **a1439** *Fall* II 352.860–1: The Lord wil nat, which every thyng may see, Suffre moodre longe to be secre, 405.2741: But moordre will out, and al such fals tresoun. **c1450** *Brut* II 474.37–8: But God wold not so; for murdour woll com oute. **c1477** Caxton *Jason* 12.36: For murdre can not be hyd, **1481** *Reynard* 89[26–7]: Ffor murdre abydeth not hyd. **c1499** Skelton *Bowge* I 50.524: But that I drede mordre wolde come oute. Apperson 433–4; Jente 516; *Oxford* 439; Skeat 246; Taylor and Whiting 254–5; Tilley M1315. See **C454, D134, E23, 167, F611, L494, N170, S491, T165, 445, W237.**

M807 **Murder** cries for vengeance (*varied*)
a1439 Lydgate *Fall* II 526.1949–51: For moordre alway calleth to God of riht, Never cesyng, but bi contynuaunce, Up to the hevene to crie for vengaunce, 673.3144: Moordre crieth vengaunce day and niht, III 753.2932–3: Heer men may seen, what coostis that men weende, How moordre alwey requereth an evel eende, 917.3357: Moordre affor God requereth ay vengaunce.

M808 **Murder** is quit for murder
a1439 Lydgate *Fall* III 917.3372: Moordre quit for moordre, thei bothe lost her lyff.

M809 **Murder** will end with mischance
a1439 Lydgate *Fall* III 886.2275: Moordre of custum wil eende with myschaunce.

M810 As much as itwixt **Murk** and light
c1340 Rolle *Psalter* 358 (102.12): Als mykil as it is itwyx myrk and light, als fere he made us fra oure alde life.

M811 **Music** is sour when men groan for hunger
c1515 Barclay *Eclogues* 140.28: But soure is musike when men for hunger grone. Cf. Apperson 434: Music helps not the toothache; *Oxford* 440; Tilley M1320.

M812 To seek **Mussels** among froshes (*frogs*)
1484 Caxton *Royal Book* U4^{r}[9]: Lyke to hym that secheth muskles emonge frosshes. See *Vices and Virtues,* note p. 315.

M813 **Mutton** (is) good meat for a glutton
a1460 *Towneley Plays* 107.220–2: Moton Of an ewe that was roton, Good mete for a gloton. **c1516** Skelton *Magnificence* 70.2265–6: "Why, is there any store of rawe motton?" "Ye, in faythe; or ellys thou arte to great a glotton." Apperson 434; Tilley M1341.

N

Nail (1)

N1 As naked as my **Nail**
a1450 *Death and Life* 6.159: Shee was naked as my nayle. **1533** Heywood *Weather* D1v[36]: Thou myghtest go as naked as my nayle. Apperson 436; *Oxford* 442; Tilley N4.

N2 To blow on one's **Nails**
a1470 Malory III 1211.25–6: Untyll they have hunger and colde, and blow on their nayles.

Nail (2)

N3 As clear as the **Nail** in the fire
a1398(1495) Bartholomaeus-Trevisa S8r[1.4–5]: And clere as the nayle other fyre.

N4 As sharp as a **Nail**
a1430 Lydgate *Pilgrimage* 577.21632: And wyth hys pawnys, sharp as A nayl.

N5 Not worth a **Nail**
c1420 Wyntoun VI 292.348: Sa that nocht wantit worth a naill.

N6 One **Nail** drives out another
a1200 *Ancrene* 206.12–3: An neil driveth ut then other. **a1387** Higden-Trevisa VII 25[11–3]: Thanne the kyng drof out on nayle with another, and took wreche of a gyle by a gyle. **1555** Heywood *E* 164.111.2, 112: One nayle driveth out an other. Apperson 472; *Oxford* 441; Tilley N17; Whiting *Drama* 139. See **L547, O44, T141, V20, W168.**

N7 Set there a **Nail**
c1440 Charles of Orleans 13.354–5: To which he seide me nay sett there a nayle Speke me no more thereof.

N8 To drive in the **Nail**
c1400 *Beryn* 104.3464: Hym list to dryv in bet the nayll, til they wer fully cloyid.

N9 To hit (smite, strike) the **Nail** on the head
c1405 *Mum* 28.51–3: But ever he hitteth on the heed of the nayle-is ende, That the pure poynt pricketh on the sothe Til the foule flessh vomy for attre. **a1438** Kempe 152.27–8: I xal so smytyn the nayl on the hed. **a1500** *Eger H* 221.663: I strake the nail upon the head. **1508** (1519) Stanbridge *Vulgaria* 18.33: Thou hyttes the nayle on the heed. **c1520** *Terens* B2v[14]: Thou hyttist the nayle on the hed. **c1522** Skelton *Colyn* I 312.33–4: And yf that he hyt The nayle on the hede. **1528** More *Heresyes* 221 F[7]: Ye hyt the naile on the head. **1546** Heywood *D* 100.22: This hitteth the nayle on the hed. Apperson 435; *Oxford* 296; Taylor and Whiting 256–7; Tilley N16; Whiting *Drama* 349:625.

N10 As wicked to benim (*take away,* steal) one's good **Name** as his life (cattle [*property*])
c1390 Chaucer *CT* X[I] 566: For soothly, as wikke is to bynyme his good name as his lyf. **c1450** *Jacob's Well* 84.12–3: For it is werse to stelyn awey a mannys good name than his catell. Jente 719; *Oxford* 639.

N11 Evil **Name** is foul (evil) fame
c1450 *Good Wife L* 198.54–5: For he that cacchith to him an yvel name, It is to him a foule fame, **a1500** *N* 211.54–5: For gif thou have evill name, It will turne the to grame, **c1500** *T* 205.51–2: Evyll name Ys evell fame. Apperson 193.

N12 A good **Name** is worth (better than) gold (*varied*)
c1350 *Good Wife E* 164.81: God name is gold wrth. **c1395** *WBible* Proverbs xxii 1: Betere is a good name, than many richessis; for good grace is above silver and gold, Ecclesiastes vii 2: A good name is betere than preciouse oyne-

mentis. **a1400** Lavynham 15.23: Betere is a good name than many rychessys (Salomon). **a1430** Lydgate *Pilgrimage* 415.15405–12: "Ffor a good name (I dar expresse) Ys bet than gold or gret rychesse." "Thow mayse wel seyn yt off Resoun; Ffor, as the wyse Salomoun In hys proverbys bereth wytnesse, That gold, tresour, and gret Rychesse, A good name doth wel al surmounte, Who that lyst a-ryht acounte." **a1450** *Myne awen dere* 159.327–8: For a gode man (*read:* name) is mare to prays Than mykell golde, the wyse man says. **1450** *Dicts* 108.10–2: A good name is better than for to have goode, for good lesithe and a good name endurithe. **c1450** *Consail and Teiching* 77.406: Al riches passes gud renoune. **c1450** *Pilgrimage LM* 130[23–4]: For good name is more woorth than richesse . . . Salomon hath tauht it thee. **a1470** Parker *Dives* R1r[2.4–8]: As Salomon sayth . . . A good name is better than many rychesses. **a1475** *Tree* 127.14–5: Ffor better is a goode name than moche riches seyth salomon. **1477** Rivers *Dictes* 54[11–2]: Good renomme is bettir than richesse, for richesse wolbe loste and renomme wol laste, **1478** *Morale Proverbes* [4.15–6]: Better honneur is to have and a good name, Than tresor riche and more shal dure the fame. **1483** Caxton *Cato* E3v[20–1]: Salamon sayth that better is to acquyre a good name and good grace than golde or sylver. **a1500** *Eight Goodly Questions* 423[4]: And remember, that good name is gold worth. **a1500** *Good Wife N* 212.96–7: For wise men and old Sayne good name is worth gold. **1506** Barclay *Castell* E7v[17]: Good name is better than rychesse, **1509** *Ship* II 181[28]: A gode name: which better is than golde. **1519** Horman *Vulgaria* 429[7]: A good name or fame is better than golde. **1528** More *Heresyes* 218 G[5–6]: Better is good name then muche riches. Apperson 261; Smith 94; Tilley N22, R74; Whiting *Scots* II 102. See **G301, H447, R88, 122, W681.**

N13 A good **Name** lost is lost for ay
a1456 *Passe forth* clxxiv 21: A good name leste is leste for ay certain. See **E70, K94, M20, R82.**

N14 Good **Name** wins fele (*much*)
c1425 *Good Wife H* 161.36: Gode name fele wynneth.

N15 He is not dead whose good **Name** (renown) endures
1450 *Dicts* 268.23–4: Men say in a proverbe: he is not dede whos good name endurithe. **1477** Rivers *Dictes* 108[32–3]: It is sayde in a proverbe: he is not dede whoos renomme and fame lastith.

N16 Once shamed, hard to recure (*recover*) one's **Name** again
c1421 Lydgate *Thebes* 169.4126–7: For onys shamyd hard is to recure His name ageyn of what estat he be. Cf. Smith 61. See **R82.**

N17 One's good **Name** is joy and gladness to his friends
c1450 *Good Wife L* 201.133–4: Thi good name is to thi freendis Greet joie and gladnes.

N18 We love the **Name** that we are Christians and few (of) the virtues
a900 Alfred *Gregory* 5.6–8: þone naman anne we lufodon ðæt(te) we Cristne wæren, and swiðe feawe ða ðeawas. J. E. Cross in *MLR* 54(1959) 66.

N19 Well is him that has a good **Name**
a1400 *Proverbis of Wysdom* 244.12: Yea, well ys hym, that hath a gwod name. *Oxford* 56: Born.

N20 Whoso has a wicked (ill) **Name** is half hanged
a1450 *Always try to Say the Best* in Brown *Lyrics XIV* 193.51–2: For ho-so hath a wicked name Me semeth for sothe half hongid he is. **1546** Heywood *D* 80.74: He that hath an yll name, is halfe hangd. Apperson 324; *Oxford* 316; Tilley N25. See **S918.**

N21 To drink of that **Nap** (*cup*) (*i.e.*, death)
c1330 *Body and Soul* 34.157–60: Y nam the first, no worth the last, That hath ydronken of that nap; Nis non so kene that he is cast, The prodest arst may kepe his clap.

N22 When the **Nap** is rough it would be shorn
c1516 Skelton *Magnificence* 15.448: When the noppe is rughe, it wolde be shorne.

N23 As sweet as **Nard**
a1398(1495) Bartholomaeus-Trevisa L5v[1.19]: It smellyth swete as Nard. **c1516** Skelton *Magnificence* 73.2345: Your wordes be more sweter than ony precyous narde.

N24 **Nature** forms nothing in vain
1481 Caxton *Mirror* 44[11]: Nature fourmeth nothing in vayn. Tilley N43.

N25 **Nature** goes afore learning
a1492 *Salomon and Marcolphus* 18[4]: Nature goth afore lernyng. Cf. Smith 212; Tilley N47: Nature passes nurture.

N26 **Nature** is content with little
a1449 Lydgate *Fabules* in *MP* II 581.432: Nature ys content with full lytell thyng. Tilley N45.

N27 **Nature** loves nothing that is solitary
a1470 Tiptoft *Tullius* C8r[14–5]: Nature loveth nothynge that is solytary. Cf. Tilley N42.

N28 **Nature** loves variance
c1450 Capgrave *Katharine* 37.335–6: Ye may wete weel nature lovyth varyaunce, Somtyme men stodye, sumtyme thei daunce. See **M208.**

N29 **Nature** may not lie
c1489 Caxton *Aymon* II 424.12–3: As the fader oughte to love the childe, for nature maye not lie. **c1505** Watson *Valentine* 70.5–6: After the course of nature that can not lye.

N30 There **Nature** will not work, farewell physic!
c1385 Chaucer *CT* I[A] 2759–60: And certeinly, ther Nature wol nat wirche, Fare wel phisik! go ber the man to chirche! *Oxford* 497. See **K31, N32.**

N31 What **Nature** gives no man can take away
a1500 Hill 129.29: That natwre geweth, no man can tak awai. Apperson 437.

N32 Without **Nature** nothing may avail
c1450 Capgrave *Katharine* 318.1776: Withoute nature may no thyng avayle. See **N30.**

Naught, see **Nothing**

N33 One may mend three **Nays** with one yea
1549 Heywood *D* 46.155: Ye maie . . . mend three naies with one yee. Tilley N55.

N34 To nick (*nod*) with **Nay**
c1300 *Amis* 88.2188: No wold thai nick him with no nay. **a1325** *Cursor* I 232 CF 3917: Laban o leve tham nicked nai, 258 CF 4382: And has thou nicked me wit nay? II 382 CF 6604: Bot all ther-wit yee nik me nay, 934 CG 16376, III 1132 CFG 19773, 1416.24743, 1568.28923. **a1325** *Elde* in Heuser 170.1[3–4]: When eld me wol feld, Nykkest ther no nai. **c1325** *I Repent* 142.55. **a1375** *William* 133.4145. **c1390** *Sir Gawain* 22.706, 76.2471. **a1400** *Athelston* 82.503. **a1400** *Chevelere* 2.28. **a1400** *Eglamour* 9.129: He nytyde us never with naye. **a1400** *Perceval* 33.1024. **a1400** *Siege of Jerusalem* 6.89. **a1400** *Susan* 178.148. **a1450** Audelay 26.451: Nyk not this with nay. **a1460** *Towneley Plays* 323.571. **c1475** *Golagros* 5.115, 12.332. **a1500** *Alexander C* 79 Dublin 1460. **a1500** *Grene Knight* 76.489: But nicked her with nay. NED Nick v.[1] 2.

N35 To say **Nay** and take it (*varied*)
1506 Hawes *Pastime* 75.1938–9: Forsake her not, thought that she saye naye, A womans guyse is evermore to delaye. **1534** Heywood *Love* C3v[31]: Your payne is most if she say nay and take it, **1555** *E* 186.223: Say nay and take it. Apperson 391; *Oxford* 397; Tilley M34; Whiting *Drama* 264, *Scots* II 102.

N36 As great as a (any) **Neat**
a1350 *Ywain* 7.251–8.252: His hevyd, me thoght, was als grete Als of . . . a nete. **c1350** *Libeaus* 74 *var.* 134f: Or as grete as eny nete.

N37 As heavy as a **Neat**
c1300 *Havelok* 30.808: Al so hevi als a net, 38.1026.

N38 As thick as a **Neat**
c1475 *Guy*[1] 431 C 7762: He was thykker than a nete.

N39 One turns the **Neb** (*face*) blithely toward the thing one loves
a1200 *Ancrene* 129.27–9: Meturneth the neb blitheliche towart thing that me luveth, and frommard thing that me heateth. See **E207.**

N40 **Necessity** has never holiday
1440 Palladius 30.176: Necessite nath nevere halyday.

N41 **Necessity** oftentimes makes a man sell good cheap (*at a bargain*)
c1505 Watson *Valentine* 149.8–9: For necessyte maketh oftentymes a man sell good chepe. Cf. Tilley N63.

N42 As soon break his **Neck** as his fast in that house
1546 Heywood *D* 50.289–90: In that house . . . A man shall as soone breake his necke as his fast. Apperson 65; *Oxford* 62; Tilley N67.

N43 In the **Neck**
c1385 Usk 11.90–1: They have ofte me begyled; but ever, at the ende, it discendeth in their owne nekkes. **a1400** *Titus* 39.822–3: And ay they token it full light, But sithen it fell in her owne necke. **a1420** Wyntoun V 415.3535–6: Men sal (it) noucht weil mende agayne, For in the nek folowis the payne. **a1425** *Metrical Paraphrase OT* 92.17083–4: Bot ay whyls moyses prayd for pese, God sett ther noys in ther enmys nek (*var.* in theire awn nek). **a1460** *Towneley Plays* 384.555: And your synnes in youre nekkys. **a1500** *Court of Love* 414.186: And in your nek ye moot bere all the charge. **a1513** Dunbar *Rewl of Anis Self* 75.36: Bot dowt siclyk sall stryk the in the neck. **1513** Douglas *Aeneid* III 41.208: The charge lyis on thar nek. **1519** Horman *Vulgaria* 196[21]: He wyll never cease to be in my necke whyle he livethe. In me

servire non nisi cum morte desinet. **1528** More *Heresyes* 241 B[10–1]: The losse shoulde lye hole in his owne necke, **1533** *Answer* 1085 CD: He had lever laye it in the necke of the father of heaven, 1105 H[14–6]: Maketh al his wondering . . . fall in his owne necke, *Confutacion* 657 B[8–9]: The mischiefe shall falle in theyr own neckes, **1534** *Comforte* 1170 A[10–2]: And layde the lacke even where I found it, and that was even upon mine owne necke. Whiting *Drama* 362:836, *Scots* II 103. See **F555.**

N44 Extreme **Need** best proves (*tests*) a valiant courage
c1523 Barclay *Mirrour* 39[38]: Extreme nede best proveth a courage valiaunt.

N45 He that has **Need,** let him run
c1516 Skelton *Magnificence* 26.786: Tushe! he that hath nede, man, let hym rynne. See **N57.**

N46 In **Need** few friends and kinsmen are ready to help
1519 Horman *Vulgaria* 200[10]: In tyme of nede fewe frendys and kynsmen be redy to helpe. See **F634.**

N47 In the last **Need** all thing is common
a1470 Parker *Dives* R4[r][1.21–2]: For in the laste nede al thynge is comon. See **T98.**

N48 It is **Need** to take good heed
1519 Horman *Vulgaria* 76[19]: It is nede to take good hede. NED Need sb. 4a.

N49 The more the **Need** is high the more one needs to be sly
a1393 Gower *CA* III 441–2.2063–5: The more that the nede is hyh, The more it nedeth to be slyh To him which hath the nede on honde.

N50 **Need** has no cure
c1500 *Lyfe of Roberte* 255.919: Nede hath no cure. **1519** Horman *Vulgaria* 431[15]: Nede hath no cure if it be come to the uttermoste.

N51 **Need** has no law
c1378 *Piers* B xx 10: And Nede ne hath no lawe. **a1393** Gower *CA* II 332.1167: For as men sein, nede hath no lawe, III 388.75: Men sein that nede hath no lawe. **a1400** Wyclif *Sermons* II 181[22]: For sich nede hath no sich lawe. **1406** Hoccleve *Male Regle* 39.437: Neede hath no lawe as that the Clerkes trete. **a1450** *Partonope* 335.8267–8: But this is a full olde sawe: Nede hathe no maner of lawe. **c1450** *Jacob's Well* 206.30. **1460** *Battle of Northampton* in Robbins *Historical Poems* 214.127: Nede hathe no lawe, this all men say. **a1470** Parker *Dives* R4[r][1.24]. **c1475** Henryson *Fables* 28.731: For neid may haif na Law. **c1515** Barclay *Eclogues* 202.587. **c1522** Skelton *Colyn* I 344.864–5: But it is an olde sayd sawe, That nede hath no lawe. **1546** Heywood *D* 37.60, **1555** *E* 150.20. Apperson 438; *Oxford* 445; Tilley N76; Whiting *Drama* 233, 274. See **S299.**

N52 **Need** has no peer
c1390 Chaucer *CT* I[A] 4026: Nede has na peer. Skeat 231.

N53 **Need** makes a man travail (*work*)
a1500 *Proverbs of Salamon* 194.1.2–4: Nede makyth a man to travayle, The more travayle the more mede, So he do by goode counsayle.

N54 **Need** makes (a, the) old wife run (trot)
a1250 *Owl* 54.637–8: A vorbisne is of olde i(vu)rne, (Th)at node maketh old wif urne. **a1300** *Trinity MS. 0.2.45* 8(13): Neode makad heald wif eorne. Ut cito se portet vetule pes, cogit oportet. **c1470** *Harley MS.3362* f.3a in *Retrospective* 309[22]: Nede makyth an old wyf. **c1475** *Rawlinson MS. D 328* 124.72: Nede makyt a old wyfe to trotte. **a1500** *Harley MS.2321* in *Rel. Ant.* I 207: Need makes the old wife trott. **a1500** Hill 128.5: Nede makith the old wiff to trotte. **1546** Heywood *D* 99.37: Neede maketh the olde wife trot, **1555** *E* 160.91. Apperson 439; Jente 69; *Oxford* 446; Taylor and Whiting 259; Tilley N79; Whiting *Drama* 131, 137.

N55 **Need** makes a wild man full tame
c1450 Idley 93.726: Thus nede a wilde man maketh full tame.

N56 **Need** makes a wise man do evil
1492 *Salomon and Marcolphus* 12[10]: Nede makyth a right wyse man to do evyll.

N57 **Need** makes naked man run
a1500 *Miroure of Mans Salvacionne* 55[21]: Als nede makes naked man rynne. Apperson 439; *Oxford* 446; Tilley N77; Whiting *Scots* II 103. See **N45.**

N58 The **Need** of hunger may cause a man to break his oath
1481 Caxton *Reynard* 75[32]: The nede of hongre may cause a man to breke his oth, 76[16]: For the nede of hongre breketh oth alway.

N59 **Need** teaches many
c1025 *Durham Proverbs* 14.36: Seo nydþearf feala læreð. Necessitas plura docet.

N60 **Need** teaches wit
1519 Horman *Vulgaria* 83[1]: Nede taught hym wytte. Jente 71.

N61 **Needs** shall (must) that needs must (shall) **c1330** *Seven Sages A* 68.1597–8: O nedes he sschal, that nedes mot, Hit nis nowt mi wille, god hit wot. **a1393** Gower *CA* II 24.698: So soffre thei that nedes mote, 82.1714: Bot nede he mot that nede schal, 235.351–3: For it is seid thus overal, That nedes mot that nede schal Of that a lif doth after kinde, III 413.1020: Bot nede he mot, that nede schal. **a1500** *Additional MS.37075* 277.8: Nedys must that ned schall. **a1500** *Coventry Plays* 47.456: Then nedis muste thatt nedis schall, 68.1140. **a1500** *Jeaste* 208.43: Nedes must that nedes shall. *Oxford* 447.

N62 (Where) there is no **Need** gift has no meed (*merit*) **c1405** *Man, know thy self* in Kail 29.71: There nys no nede, gifte hath no mede.

N63 As bare as (a) **Needle** **c1415** *Middle English Sermons* 182.39: Thei shall make the as bare as nedill.

N64 As naked as a **Needle** **c1378** *Piers* B xii 162: And bothe naked as a nedle, xvii 56. **a1400** *Alexander C* 224.4026: And ay is naked (as) a nedill as natour tham schapis. **a1400** *Siege of Jerusalem* 20.361, 54.939. **a1470** Malory II 792.14: She was as naked as a nedyll. Apperson 436; *Oxford* 442; Tilley N94.

N65 As perceant as the point of a **Needle** **c1378** *Piers* B i 155: And portatyf and persant as the poynt of a nedle.

N66 As sharp as a **Needle** **a900** *Soul and Body* in *Exeter Book* 177.111–2: Gifer hatte se wyrm, þam þa geaflas beoð Nædle scearpran, *Vercelli Book* 58.116–7: Gifer hatte se wyrm, þe þa eaglas beoð Nædle scearpran. Apperson 561; Taylor and Whiting 259; Tilley N95.

N67 Not eat a **Needle** **a1460** *Towneley Plays* 123.233–4: I ete not a nedyll Thys moneth and more.

N68 Not give a **Needle** **a1300** *Arthour and M.*[1] 114.4012: He gave (*not*) a nedel of his fon. **a1400** *Ancrene* (*Recluse*) 55.13–4: I nolde noughth give a nedel for al her werk. **c1400** *Laud Troy* I 260.8828: He gaff of hem alle nought a nelde.

N69 Not worth a **Needle** **a1200** *Ancrene* 203.12: Ne beoth nawt wurth a nelde. **c1400** *Laud Troy* II 484.16448–9: That non of hem schal other mysdo Lastande the trewes a nedle worth. **c1400** *Plowman's Tale* 172.780: Such willers wit is nat worth a neld. **a1460** *Towneley Plays* 13.123: Then was myne not worth a neld. Apperson 457:24; *Oxford* 446.

N70 So near a **Needle** might narrowly (go) between **a1400** *Alexander C* 72.1370: So nere unethes at ane eld (Dublin: nedyll) might narowly betwene.

N71 To look for a **Needle** in a meadow **1532** More *Frith* in *Workes* 837 H[16–7]: To seke out one lyne in all hys bookes wer to go looke a nedle in a medow. Apperson 440; *Modern Language Forum* 24(1939) 77–80; *Oxford* 446–7; Taylor and Whiting 259–60; Tilley N97.

N72 As white as a **Neep** (*turnip*) **a1400** *Destruction of Troy* 100.3076: With nailes at the nether endes as a nepe white. **c1475** Henryson *Fables* 82.2395: Quhyte as ane Neip. Cf. Apperson 101: Clean.

N73 Not worth a withered **Neep** **c1475** Henryson *Fables* 81.2362: It will not wyn yow worth ane widderit neip.

N74 Blessed be the **Neighbor** that is ready to help at need **a1533** Berners *Arthur* 411[26–7]: Blyssed be the neighbour that is redy to helpe at nede. See **F634, N99.**

N75 Evil **Neighbor** makes evil morn **c1400** *Alexander Buik* II 120.391–2: For wyse men hes said beforne, "Evill nichtbour makes evill morne," IV 368–9.8819–21: Ane evill nichtbour had I thare! On this tyisday airly hes he Over tratourly wrethit me! Tilley N107. See **N77.**

N76 A good **Neighbor** is a fair jewel **a1300** *Alisaunder* 377.6993: Fair juel is gode neighboure.

N77 He that has a good **Neighbor** has a good morrow **c1450** *Merlin* II 434[17–8]: And therfore men seyn an olde sawe, who hath a goode neighbour hath goode morowe. **1489** Caxton *Doctrinal* D3^{v}[13–4]: Therfore it is cominly said, who that hath a good neyghbour hath good morow. **a1500** *Harley MS.116* in *Rel. Ant.* I 316: He that hath a good neyghboure hath a good morowe; He that hath a schrewyd wyfe hath much sorowe; He that fast spendyth must nede borowe; But whan he schal paye agen, then ys al the sorowe. Apperson 440; *Oxford* 254–5; Tilley N106. See **N75.**

N78 He that has a good **Neighbor** is relieved from great diseases (*troubles*)
c1450 Idley 95.878–9: Ffor he that hath a good neighboure is well relevyd Ffro diseases grete and myscheves harde.

N79 He that has evil **Neighbors** praises himself (*varied*)
1492 *Salomon and Marcolphus* 6[8–9]: He that hath evyll neighborys praysyth him self. **1509** Barclay *Ship* II 68[1–4]: But yet men olde . . . In theyr olde proverbes often comprehende That he that is amonge shrewyd neyghbours May his owne dedes laufully commende. Apperson 440; Jente 221; *Oxford* 447–8; Smith 217; Tilley N117. See **P349.**

N80 Let your **Neighbor** feel your friendship
a1400 *Proverbis of Wysdom* 244.23: Lete thy neyghburgh thy frendshep fele. **c1450** *Fyrst thou sal* 88.31.

N81 A near **Neighbor** is better than a far brother (*varied*)
c1390 *Proverbes of diverse profetes* 527.81–4: Of thi neighebor that neigh is to the Be thou tendre and have him in cherte; Ffor bettre is a neighebore neighe Then a brothur fer fro thin eighe. **c1395** *WBible* Proverbs xxvii 10: Betere is a neighbore nygh, than a brothir afer. **a1500** *Alexander-Cassamus* 76.551–4: Off straunge and fferre londys al day to late Come folkys, to helpe A man that ys yn nede; But the good neyghbour that dowellyth at youre gate Yow to sekour ffaste wyll he spede (French [p. 97]: Par gens d'estranges terres est on tart secoru). Apperson 437; *Oxford* 444; Tilley N110.

N82 The **Neighbor** that most may grieve (*harm*), make your friend
1414 *Lerne say wele* in Kail 15.33–6: Oo proverbe loke ye preve, Ye that wole to resoun bende: Look what neyghebore most may greve; By al way make hym thi frende.

N83 Of good **Neighbor** the wise makes shield
c1400 *Alexander Buik* II 175.2672: Of gud nichtbour the wyse makes sheild. **a1500** *Alexander-Cassamus* 76.555–7: Off a good neyghbour, wyth-owte ony drede, The wysse man al day makyth hym a schelde, Thus seyth the olde wyse and thus do ye, I rede (French [p. 97]: De bon voisin prochain fait saiges homs escu. Se tu ainsi le fais, bon conseil as creu). Cf. Jente 757.

N84 What may betide love your **Neighbor**
c1425 *Good Wife H* 171.178–9: For happe that may betide Love thi neybourgh the beside.

N85 When one sees his **Neighbor**('s house) burn he is busy to save himself (his own) (*varied*)
a1338 Mannyng *Chronicle A* II 570.16455–8: Of his long lyf can noman seye, That see his frend sodeynly deye; That sees his neighebur brenne hym by, To save hym self he ys bysy. **1456** Hay *Law* 174.18–9: It is na ferly, quhen a man seis his nychtbouris hous byrn, suppos he be rad for his awin. **a1500** *English Conquest* 39.10–1: As a man that seth his evyncrystyn his (*var.* neghbors) house brenne, he may dred the sparkys. **1519** Horman *Vulgaria* 184[21–2]: Whan my neybours house is a fyre: I can nat be out of thought for myn owne. Apperson 441; *Oxford* 447; Tilley N116, cf. M497; Whiting *Scots* II 104. See **F381, M63.**

N86 With your **Neighbor** make no debate
a1400 *Proverbis of Wysdom* 245.47–8: Ever more fle discord and hate, With thy neygbore make no debate. **c1450** *Fyrst thou sal* 88.57–8.

N87 To find the **Nest** but no ay (*egg*)
c1350 *Gamelyn* 660.610: Tho fond the scherreve nest, but non ay. **a1375** *William* 9.83: Than fond he nest and no neigh, for nought nas ther leved. Whiting *Drama* 291, *Scots* II 104. Cf. Taylor and Whiting 29:20. See **B303.**

N88 A **Net** is laid in vain before the eyes of birds
c1395 *WBible* Proverbs i 17: But a net is leid in veyn bifore the ighen of briddis, that han wengis. **1509** Barclay *Ship* I 197[1–3]: Who that to clerely layeth his net or snare Before the byrdes whome he by gyle wolde take Them playnly techyth of his gyle to be ware. Jente 589; *Oxford* 319; Tilley V3.

N89 The rough **Net** is not the best catcher of birds
1549 Heywood *D* 34.52: The rough net is not the best catcher of burdes. Apperson 539; *Oxford* 549; Tilley N129.

N90 To catch (find) without **Net**
c1385 Chaucer *TC* ii 583: That han swich oon ykaught withouten net, iv 1370–1: And I right now have founden al the gise, Withouten net, wherwith I shal hym hente. Whiting *Drama* 355:727.

N91 To fish before the **Net**
a1449 Lydgate *Order* in *MP* II 454.139: And he is a fool affore the net that ffissheth. **a1460** *Towneley Plays* 104.139: Ye fysh before the nett. **c1475** Henryson *Fables* 62.1763: And said, scho fischit lang befoir the Net. **c1522** Skelton *Speke* II 21.421: To fysshe afore the nette, and to

drawe polys. **1533** More *Apologye* 125–6: So judge before the profe and fishe before the nette. **1546** Heywood *D* 48.235: Yll fyshyng before the net, **1555** *E* 192.266. Apperson 217; *Oxford* 207; Tilley F335, N127; Whiting *Scots* II 104.

N92 To jet (*strut*) in a **Net** and believe oneself (un)perceived (*varied*)
c1475 *Mankind* 20.522–4: Ever I go invysybull; yt ys my jett; Ande be-for hys ey, thus I wyll hange my nett To blench hys syght, 33.869: Tytivilly, that goth invisibele, hynge hys nett be-fore my eye, 888: Beware of Titivilly with hys net. **1532** More *Confutacion* 421 D[9–11]: Wise people when thei daunce naked in a nette; believe that no manne see them, F[1–2]: I goe so bare daunsyng naked in a net, H[3–5], 647 D[5–6]: He went visible before us al naked in a nette. **1534** Heywood *Love* C1v[11–3]: Lyke as a foole myght have jettyd in a net, Belevyng hymselfe, save of hym selfe onely, To be perceyved of no lyvyng body. Apperson 134; *Oxford* 128; Tilley N130.

N93 As rough as a **Nettle**
c1430 ?Lydgate *Compleynt* 64.374: Now as the netyl row of hewe.

N94 Of a **Nettle** to have a rose (*varied*)
1471 Ripley *Compound* 158[15–6]: Wene they of a Nettyll to have a Rose, Or of an Elder an Apple swete. **a1500** Greene *Carols* 402.1: When nettuls in wynter bryng forth rosys red, And al maner of thorn trys ber fyggys naturally. See **G421, T223.**

N95 To meddle (*mix*) **Nettles** with rose flowers
a1449 Lydgate and Burgh *Secrees* 27.837: To medle netlys with soote Roose flours. Cf. Whiting *Scots* II 104.

N96 To piss on a **Nettle**
c1450 Fritz Heinrich *Ein mittelenglisches Medizinbuch* (Halle, 1896) 137–8: Take the urine of the seek, and caste hit on the rede netle, at even, while hit is warm, a noon as he pysseth, and come ageyn in to the morewynynge, and yef the netle be ded, hit is a sygne of deeth, and yef the netle be alyve, hit is a sygne of lyf. **1546** Heywood *D* 99.27–8: In no place could she sit hir selfe to settle, It seemed to him, she had pist on a nettle. Apperson 498; *Oxford* 502; Tilley N132.

N97 Change for no **New**
c1250 *Floris* 97.494–5: Ne chaunge luve for no newe, Ne lete the olde for no newe be. **c1300** *Amis* 17.382–4: Gete me frendes whare y may, Y no schal never bi night no day Chaunge him for no newe, 26.583–4. **c1375** Chaucer *Anel.* 218–9: Doth her observaunce Alwey til oon, and chaungeth for no newe, **c1386** *LGW* 1875. **a1400** Greene *Carols* 395.4. **a1420** Lydgate *Troy* I 260.4039–40, III 681.3988, 834.2163, **1420** *Temple* 42.999, 47.1128. **a1425** Greene *Carols* 451.6. **c1445** ?Lydgate *Kalendare* in *MP* I 371.232–3. **a1449** Lydgate *Freond* in *MP* II 757.86, *Gentlewoman's Lament* in *MP* II 419. 27–8. **a1450** *Castle* 99.726: I rede thee forsakyn hym for no newe. **a1450** *Generydes A* 175.5605–6. **a1450** *Myne awen dere* 154.175–6. **a1450** *Partonope* 48.1745–6, 72.2393–4. **a1450** *Pride of Life* in Waterhouse 92.130: I nil chong fer no new. **a1456** Earl of Warwick's *Virelai* in *PMLA* 22(1907) 606.37–8. **a1475** *Guy*[2] 4.122. **c1475** *Why I Can't* 139.46. **a1500** *Beauty of his Mistress III* in Robbins 128.57. **a1500** Greene *Carols* 455.2. **a1500** *Pledge of Loyalty* in Robbins 160.26–8. **a1500** *To his Mistress* in Robbins 191.42. **a1500** *Thoythis fre* in *MLN* 69(1954) 157.31. **a1500** *To his Mistress 'M'* in Robbins 194.3: I wil not change you for old ne newe, 195.24. **c1500** Greene *Carols* 346 *refrain:* An old saw hath be fownd trewe: 'Cast not away thyn old for newe.' **c1500** *So put yn fere* in Stevens *Music* 346.3[7]. **1506** Hawes *Pastime* 83.2124. **1509** Barclay *Ship* I 168[27–8]. Whiting *Drama* 235, *Scots* II 104. See **F650, O27.**

N98 **Newer** is truer
1546 Heywood *D* 68.69–70: Thy ryme . . . is muche elder then mine, But mine beyng newer is truer then thine. *Oxford* 451; Tilley N137.

N99 Look to your **Next** (*i.e.*, neighbor), he is good at need
c1250 *Proverbs of Alfred* 114 T 395–6: Ac loke thine nexte, He is ate nede god. See **N74.**

N100 The **Niggard** dispends as much as the large (*generous*)
1484 Caxton *Aesop* 166[3–5]: For hit is sayd comunly that as moche despendeth the nygard as the large, 170[24–5]: And therfore more despendeth the nygard than the large. Apperson 428; *Oxford* 115; Tilley M1151.

N101 After long **Night** daylight is comfortable
c1515 Barclay *Eclogues* 107.2: And after long night day light is comfortable. See **N108.**

N102 After the starry **Night** the gray morrow
c1440 Charles of Orleans 182.5437: Aftir the sterry nyght the morow gray.

N103 As dark as (any, the) **Night**
a1393 Gower *CA* III 386.16–7: Bot more derk

than eny nyht The peine schal ben endeles. **a1400** *Meditations* 25.920: And wex derker than the nyght. **1412** *God and man* in Kail 49.74: Sulpid in synne derk as nyght. **a1420** Lydgate *Troy* I 194.1724. **a1425** *Nicodemus* (*Additional*) 65.658, 67.675. **c1430** ?Lydgate *Compleynt* 64.366: Now derk as is the donne nyght. **a1450** *South English Legendary* (*Bodley*) 337.41: Bokus so derk as myste (?*for* nyghte, *rime:* myghte). **a1460** *Towneley Plays* 352.345. **a1500** *Stacyons of Rome* in *Pol. Rel. and Love Poems* 151.244. **1509** Fisher *Treatyse* 46.14–5: the. **a1513** Dunbar *Of the Passioun* 158.85: ony. **1513** Douglas *Aeneid* II 161.63, 195.20, III 56.50. Taylor and Whiting 262; Whiting *Scots* II 104.

N104 As murk as (the) **Night**
a1300 *Stacions of Rome,* ed. F. J. Furnivall (EETS 25, 1867) 7.194: Elles thou gost Merk as niht. **c1300** *Northern Homily Cycle* (*Edin. Coll. Phys.*) 98[25], 99[9]. **c1400** *Tundale* 13.219, 74.1273, 96.1689. **c1450** *Nicodemus* (*Sion*) 67.674. **c1475** Henryson *Orpheus* 139.303–4: A feir full streit, Myrk as the nycht. **1513** Douglas *Aeneid* II 119.88. Svartengren 239.

N105 As thester (*dark*) as the **Night**
a1300 *XI Pains* 150.121: The stude is thustrore thene the nyht, 153.225: Ho stondeth thustrur thane the nyht.

N106 The glad **Night** is worth a heavy morrow
c1385 Chaucer *Mars* 12: The glade nyght ys worth an hevy morowe!

N107 If **Night** were not one should not wit (*know*) what day is
c1378 *Piers* B xviii 206–7: If no nyghte ne were no man, as I leve, Shulde wite witerly what day is to mene. See **S943.**

N108 Next the dark **Night** the glad morrow (*varied*)
c1385 Chaucer *TC* i 951: And next the derke nyght the glade morwe. **a1393** Gower *CA* II 219.3315–6: And thus the woful nyhtes sorwe To joie is torned on the morwe. **a1400** *Orologium* 352.24–7: And righte as a derke nyghte goth tofore a brighte schinynge daye, and the colde scharpnesse of wynter goth byfore the likynge hete of somour, righte so tribulacyone comunly goth byfore bothe the inner and the utter coumforte of good soulles. **a1449** Lydgate *Fabula* in *MP* II 490.113–4: For, riht as afftir the blake nyht of sorwe Gladnesse folwith thoruh suyng of the day. **c1450** *Lover's Mass* 101–2: And after nyghtys dool and sorowe Ffolweth ofte a ful glade morowe Of Aventure. **1471** Caxton *Recuyell* II 473.1–2: Ther is no nyght so derke but that hit is surmounted wyth the day. **1532** Berners *Golden Boke* 257. 4606: After the nyght cometh the dewy mornyng. Skeat 154; Tilley N164; Whiting *Scots* II 104. See **M529, N101.**

N109 **Night** has rest
a1393 Gower *CA* III 152.7296: Bot for men sein that nyht hath reste. Tilley N175.

N110 As merry as (the, a) **Nightingale**
c1300 *Beves* 1.2–3: Is merier than the nightingale, that y schel singe. **c1390** Chaucer *CT* VII 833–4[B2023–4]: Yet listeth, lordes, to my tale, Murier than the nightyngale. **c1400** *Laud Troy* I 164.5548–51: So mery was nevere Nightyngale Syngand In no hasel-crop, . . . As Ayax was. **a1500** Greene *Carols* 343.3: An thou goo to the nale, As m(er)i as a nyghtyngale.

N111 Better to hear the **Nightingale** sing rather (*sooner*) than the cuckoo
c1400 ?Clanvowe *Cuckoo* in Skeat *Chaucerian* 349.46–50: But as I lay this other night wakinge, I thoghte how lovers had a tokeninge, And among hem it was a comune tale, That it were good to here the nightingale Rather than the lewde cukkow singe. Cf. Apperson 445; *Oxford* 452; Tilley N181. See **C603.**

N112 The **Nightingale** and the thorn
a1449 Lydgate *Nightingale* in *MP* I 222.10–1: Sauf upon a thorne The saame tyme I herde a Nightingale, 223.61–2: But thenk amonge upon the sharpe thorne Which prickethe hir brest with fyry remembraunce, 234.355–6: Where that ful lowd thamerous nightingale Upon a thorne is wont to calle and crye, *St. Petronilla* in *MP* I 158.123–6: And nightyngalys with amerous notys clere Salueth Esperus in hir armonye, The sharpe thorne towadre the partye Of hir herte, kepeth wakyr hir corage. **a1450** *As ofte as syghes* in *Archiv* 127 (1911) 324.42: And nyghtyngales with thorne undyr the brest. **a1500** *Squire* 36.801–2: The nightingale sitting on a thorne Shall synge you notes. **1513** Douglas *Aeneid* IV 142.61–2: Owtak the mery nychtgaill, Philomeyn, That on the thorn sat syngand fra the spleyn. Carol Maddison "Brave Prick Song," *MLN* 75(1960) 468–78; Tilley N183.

N113 To cry like a **Nightingale**
a1500 Greene *Carols* 344.6: And when thou syttyst at the ale, And cryyst lyk an nyghttyngale.

N114 To sing like a (any, the) **Nightingale**

c1390 Chaucer *CT* I[A] 3377: He syngeth, brokkynge as a nyghtyngale, **c1395** III[D] 458: And synge, ywis, as any nyghtyngale. **a1500** *Squire* 35.779–80: Lytle chyldren, great and smale, Shall syng, as doth the nyghtyngale. Taylor and Whiting 262.

N115 To sleep with open eye (like **Nightingales**)
c1387-95 Chaucer *CT* I[A] 9–10: And smale foweles maken melodye, That slepen al the nyght with open ye. **c1400** *Sowdone* 2.45–6: Whan lovers slepen withe opyn yghe, As Nightyngalis on grene tre. See **F577.**

N116 **Nimrod** was a strong hunter before God
c1000 Aelfric *Heptateuch* Genesis x 9: Be þam wæs gecweden bigword, swa swa Nemroth strang hunta ætforan Gode. **c1395** *WBible* Genesis x 9: Of hym a proverbe yede out, as Nemroth, a strong huntere bifore the Lord. Tilley N185.

N117 As long since as **Noah's** flood and seven years afore it
1529 More *Supplicacion* 311 H[9–10]: Sence almost as longe as Noyes floude and yet peradventure seven yere afore yt to.

N118 As bright as (of colors like) the new **Noble**
c1390 Chaucer *CT* I[A] 3255–6: Ful brighter was the shynyng of hir hewe Than in the Tour the noble yforged newe. **c1460** *Satirical Description* 199[3]: Of colourys like the noble newe. Svartengren 223.

N119 Beyond the **Nock**
1534 Heywood *Love* B3ᵛ[35]: She coulde and wolde do it beyonde the nock, E1ʳ[23]: Is not this a pang . . . beyonde the nock? Tilley N197.

N120 Such **Noise** that one uneath (*scarcely*) hears thunder
c1450 La Tour-Landry 9.3–4: Making suche noise that unnethe thei might have herde the thundre. *Oxford* 459.

N121 He is a **Noli** me tangere
c1475 *Mankind* 19.504–5: I xall spare master Woode of Fullburn; He ys a 'noli me tangere!' *Oxford* 460; Tilley N202.

N122 **Non** est inventus
c1475 *Mankind* 29.773–4: Ye must speke to the schryve for a 'cepe coppus,' Ellys ye must be fayn to retorn with 'non est inventus.' *Oxford* 460; Tilley N204.

N123 As right as **North** and south
a1425 *If One Only Knew* in Brown *Lyrics XV* 268.11–2: Stent as ryght as northe and sowthe.

N124 From the **North** shall come (be shown) all evil (*varied*)
a1338 Mannyng *Chronicle A* I 235.6703–4: Ffor by the northe ende comme alle tho That to the lond broughte werre or wo, 269.7659–60: Gyf hem lond y the north to lende,—Thy werre cometh evere in by that ende. **c1395** *WBible* Jeremiah i 14: Fro the north schal be schewid al yvel on alle the dwelleris of the lond. **a1450** *Gesta* 22[8–10]: By the Cite in the Northe is undirstond Hell, As it is wretin, *Pandetur omne malum,* This is to sey, fro the north shall be shewid all Ivell, 358[6]: All evels cometh out of the Northe. *Oxford* 461; Tilley N213. See **D163.**

N125 Maugre one's **Nose**
c1300 Robert of Gloucester I 148.2090: Maximian was suththe aslawe maugre is nose. Tilley S764; Whiting *Scots* II 105.

N126 To be plucked by the **Nose**
c1516 Skelton *Magnificence* 27.826: For Pryde hath plucked the by the nose. See **N130.**

N127 To have something cast in one's **Nose**
1509 Barclay *Ship* I 248[19–20]: That pore man that weddeth a ryche wyfe Cast in his nose shall styll hir bagges fynde.

N128 To hold one's **Nose** to the grindstone
1546 Heywood *D* 27.32: Hold their noses to grinstone, **1555** *E* 152.34: Thou canst hold my nose to the gryndstone. Apperson 452; *Oxford* 462; Taylor and Whiting 264; Tilley N218.

N129 To speak through (in) the **Nose**
c1390 Chaucer *CT* I[A] 4151: He yexeth, and he speketh thurgh the nose, IX[H] 61: He speketh in his nose. Tilley N242.

N130 To take one by the **Nose**
1451 Paston II 239[19–21]: Took them by the nose at every thred woord whiche myght weel by knowe for open parcialte. Cf. *Oxford* 46; Tilley N241. See **N126.**

N131 To wipe one's **Nose** with (upon) one's sleeve
1436 *Libelle* 24.452–5: And thus they wolde, if ye will so beleve, Wypen our nose with our owne sleve, Thow this proverbe be homly and undew, Yet be liklynesse it is for soth full trew. **1546** Heywood *D* 97.229: And make you wype your nose upon your sleeve. Apperson 695; *Oxford* 716; Tilley N243.

N132 Much **Note** (*work*) behooves him who shall hold (*keep*) house
c1350 *Good Wife E* 168.137: Michel note him

bihoveth that hus schal holden, **c1500** *T* 206.112: Meche besynesse behoveth hem that shall howse helden.

N133 Who shall sing so merry a **Note** as he that cannot change a groat?
1546 Heywood *D* 55.15–6: And who can syng so mery a note, As maie he, that can not chaunge a grote. Apperson 574; *Oxford* 592; Tilley N249.

Nothing and **Nought** are combined

N134 As good play for **Nought** as work for nought
1546 Heywood *D* 53.394: As good play for nought as woorke for nought, folke tell. Apperson 500; *Oxford* 504–5; Tilley N340.

N135 As good seek **Nought** as seek and find nought
1546 Heywood *D* 48.234: As good seeke nought . . . as seeke and finde nought. Apperson 556; Tilley N341.

N136 Deem **Nothing** suddenly
a1400 *Proverbis of Wysdom* 244.22: Ne deme no thyng sodenly. **c1450** *Fyrst thou sal* 91.166: to sodanly. See **D143, 344.**

N137 Deem **Nothing** that is in doubt till the truth is tried out
c1450 *Fyrst thou sal* 89.91–2: Deme no thinge that is in dowte, To the trewthe be tryed owte. See **J77.**

N138 Desire **Nothing** but that is moderate
1509 Barclay *Ship* II 275[7]: Desyrynge no thynge: but that is moderate. See **M451.**

N139 Dispraise **Nothing** that God sends you
c1450 *Fyrst thou sal* 90.121: Disprays no thynge that god the sent.

N140 Have **Nothing** and dread not
a1387 Higden-Trevisa I 413[2]: Have no thing and drede nought. Cf. Apperson 437: Naught is never in danger; *Oxford* 444; Taylor and Whiting 265:3; Tilley N331, 342. See **L395.**

N141 He hopes for **Nothing** that does not hope for home
c1025 *Durham Proverbs* 13.30: To nawihte ne hopað se to hame ne higeð. (G)audio caret cui non spes in mansione restat.

N142 He that had **Nought** has lost nought (*varied*)
a1393 Gower *CA* II 289.2322: He that noght hadde noght hath lore. **1555** Heywood *E* 161.94.2: Nought have, nought loose. Jente 238, 239; Tilley N331.

N143 He that has **Nought** is nought set by
a1500 Hill 132.40: He (that) hath nowght, ys nowght sett by. Apperson 459; Tilley N270.

N144 He that has **Nought** may give nought
a1470 Parker *Dives* K2ʳ[1.38–9]: He that nought have nought may gyve. Apperson 455:35; Jente 176; Tilley N337.

N145 He that has **Nought** shall always bide poor, *etc.* (*varied*)
1509 Barclay *Ship* I 100[27–8]: He that nought hathe, shall so alway byde pore, But he that over moche hath, yet shall have more. **1546** Heywood *D* 54–5.450–2: He that hath plentie of goodes shall have more, He that hath but a little, he shall have lesse. He that hath right nought, right nought shall possesse. Tilley P424. See **M772, 777.**

N146 He that undertakes **Nothing** achieves nothing (*varied*)
c1385 Chaucer *TC* ii 807–8: He which that nothing undertaketh, Nothyng n'acheveth, be hym looth or deere, v 783–4: "But for t'asay," he seyde, "it naught ne greveth; For he that naught n'asaieth, naught n'acheveth." **c1385** Usk 23.86–7: Who nothing undertaketh, and namely in my service, nothing acheveth. **a1393** Gower *CA* II 310.319–20: For who that noght dar undertake, Be riht he schal no profit take, 374.2694–5: For he which dar nothing beginne, I not what thing he scholde achieve. **1471** Caxton *Recuyell* II 464.17–8: That man that ne adventureth wynneth no thynge. **1523** Berners *Froissart* III 337[16–7]: He that never enterpriseth, lytell or nothynge atchyveth, 367[23–4]: He that nothyng adventureth nothynge getteth. **1546** Heywood *D* 48.232: Nought venter nought have, **1555** *E* 158.77. Apperson 454; *Oxford* 465; Skeat 164; Tilley N319, 320. Cf. Smith 51; Taylor and Whiting 265.

N147 He that will win **Nothing** must lose by skill (*reason*)
a1350 *Seven Sages C* 59.1745–6: For he that nothing win will, Nedely moste he lose bi scill.

N148 If you have **Nought** spend the less
a1400 *Romaunt B* 2274: And if thou have nought, spende the lesse.

N149 **Nothing** but is made soft and meek by large gifts
a1533 Berners *Arthur* 363[8–9]: There is nothynge but by large gyftes it is made softe and meke. See **G68, 82.**

N150 **Nought** can she do—what can she have then?

1549 Heywood *D* 38.100: Nought can she dooe, and what can she have than? Tilley N339.

N151 Nothing has its being of nought
c1380 Chaucer *Boece* V pr. i 42–5: For this sentence is verray and soth, that "no thing hath his beynge of naught," to the whiche sentence noon of thise oolde folk ne withseide nevere, **1385** *TC* ii 798: That erst was nothing, into nought it torneth. **1495** Fitzjames *Sermo* C1v (*by error* B1) [7–8]: Of noo thynge can noo thynge be made. Apperson 454–5; Jente 733; *Oxford* 462; Taylor and Whiting 265; Tilley N285; Whiting *Scots* II 105.

N152 Nothing has no savor
1546 Heywood *D* 32.60: But now I can smell, nothyng hath no saver, **1555** *E* 158.76. Apperson 453; *Oxford* 463; Tilley N260.

N153 Nought has nought pays
1456 Hay *Law* 233.2–3: For the law sais that Nocht has nocht payis. Apperson 455:35; Tilley N337.

N154 Nothing in earth (under the sun) is stable
a1449 Lydgate *Look* in *MP* II 766.29: Pleynly declare in erthe is no thyng stable. **1509** Fisher *Treatyse* 193.32–3: Noo thynge under the sonne is stable. See **N158, 161, T87, 101, 161, W671.**

N155 Nothing is commended but it be in measure
a1449 Lydgate *Mesure* in *MP* II 772–5.8: Nothyng commendyd but it in mesure be, 16, 24, *etc.* (*varied refrain*).

N156 Nothing is done while aught remains to do
1513 Douglas *Aeneid* III 65.152: Na thing is done quhil ocht remanys ado.

N157 Nothing is impossible to a stalwart nature (valiant heart)
a1400 Lanfranc 153.17: For ther is no thing unpossible to stalworthe nature. **1471** Caxton *Recuyell* I 276.29–30: Unto a vaylliant hert is no thynge Inpossible, II 328.1–2: Ther is no thynge Inpossible unto a valliant herte. **1506** Hawes *Pastime* 10.140: To a wyllynge herte is nought Impossyble. **1546** Heywood *D* 25.38: Nothing is impossible to a willyng hart. Apperson 454; *Oxford* 463; Tilley N299.

N158 Nothing lasts ever
1477 Paston V 278[8]: But no thyng lastyth evyr. **1513** More *Richard* 60 D[10]: But nothing lasteth alway. Smith 168. See **N154.**

N159 Nought lay down nought take up
1546 Heywood *D* 51.320: Nought lay downe, nought take up, **1555** *E* 197.297. Apperson 459; *Oxford* 465; Tilley N343.

N160 Nought may be disturbed that shall betide of necessity
c1385 Chaucer *TC* ii 622–3: For which, men seyn, may nought destourbed be That shal bityden of necessitee. See **A99.**

N161 Nothing may long continue here (*varied*)
897 Alfred *Boethius* 21.8–9: Eala þæt nanwuht nis fæste stondendes weorces a wuniende on worulde, **a900** *Lays of Boethius* 158.16–7: Eala þæt on eorðan auht fæstlices Weorces on worulde ne wunað æfre. **c1380** Chaucer *Boece* II m. iii 21–3: It is certeyn and establissched by lawe perdurable, that nothyng that is engendred nys stedfast ne stable. **1410** Walton *Boethius* 79.203[7–8]: There may nothing be kyndly perdurable That is engendred of thise elementes. **a1437** Lydgate *That Now is Hay* in *MP* II 810.33–4: Ther may nothynge here longe contynue For to endure in his freshenys. See **N154, T87.**

N162 Nothing which one loves seems difficult
a900 Alfred *Augustine* 26.9: Me ne þincð nanwiht hæfig ðes þe man lufað.

N163 Nothing will be got without it be dearly bought
1523 Berners *Froissart* II 200[12–3]: Ther is nothyng wyll be gote without it be derely bought. See **F58.**

N164 Nought will be nought
1509 Barclay *Ship* I 167[28]: And nought wyll be nought what so ever thou do. Tilley N344.

N165 Nought won by the one, nought won by the other
1546 Heywood *D* 51.322: Nought woon by the tone, nought won by the tother. Apperson 459; *Oxford* 465; Tilley N345.

N166 Nothing won through force and wrong may be used long
a1350 Castelford 70.21641–4: Nathing vonen thoru fors and wrang Mai be usede and maintend lang. He that thoru fors oght winnes and takes Unstable chosen to him he makes. Cf. *Oxford* 464; Tilley N321. See **F490, G342, T195.**

N167 One can lead **Nothing** from this life more than he brought (*varied*)
897 Alfred *Boethius* 60.31–2: Ne læt he his nanwuht of þis middanearde mid him mare þon he brohte hider, **a900** *Lays of Boethius* 173.9–11: Ne mot he þara hyrsta hionane lædan of ðisse worulde wuhte þon mare hordgestreona ðonne he hiðer brohte. **c1000** Aelfric *Lives* I

212.47: Ne miht ðu naht lædan of þysum life mid þe. **c1395** *WBible* I Timothy vi 7: For we broughten in no thing in to this world, and no doute, that we moun not bere awey ony thing. **c1440** *Daily Work* in *Yorkshire Writers* I 317 [40–2]: *Nichil aufert secum de universo labore suo,* that es thus mekill for to say: "Na thynge with hym he beris when he hythene weyndis, of all that he hase wonne with care and swynke." **c1450** *Jacob's Well* 118.7–9: Seynt Poule seyth, Ad Tymoth vj., Ryght nought we browghtyn in-to this world, and, wyth-oute dowte, nothyng schal we beryn out fro this world in oure ende. **c1450** *Secrete of Secretes* 14.16–8: Desire nought worldly thingis that are passyng and corruptible, but thynke that thou must leve alle and go hens nakid. **1483** *Quatuor Sermones* 33–4: For nakid thou camyst in to this world, And ageyn nakyd save a ragge, thou shalt goo out therof. **c1503** More *Early Poems* [15] B[9]: Remember nature sent the hyther bare. Brinton *Sermons* II 442[18–9]: Dicente poeta, Tecum nulla ferres, licet omnia solus haberes. Cf. Taylor and Whiting 365.

N168 Owe **Nought** and have nought is better at ease
c1450 *Fyrst thou sal* 89.79–80: Go awe noght and hafe noght is better at ese, Covetyce makes many man in yll disese. Cf. Tilley N254.

N169 There is **Nothing** but will serve for somewhat
c1495 *Arundel Vulgaria* 61.262: Ther is nothynge but it wyll serve for sumwhat, be it never so course. Lay hym upe ageynst another tyme. Apperson 455; *Oxford* 462; Tilley N327.

N170 There is **Nothing** may be hid that it is not kid (*known*) (*varied*)
a1350 *Seven Sages C* 10.283–4: For nathing mai ay unhid (*?for* unkid) be, Bot anely Goddes awin prevete. **a1393** Gower *CA* III 86.5123–4: Bot so wel may nothing ben hidd, That is nys ate laste kidd. **1471** Caxton *Recuyell* II 654.23–4: Yet ther is no thynge so secrete but otherwhile it is knowen. **1525** Berners *Froissart* IV 288[23]: There is lyghtely nothynge but that it is knowen, V 208[23–4]: Nothynge can be hydde if men putte to their dilygence to knowe. Tilley N330. See **M806.**

N171 There is **Nothing** said so soft that it comes not out at last
a1393 Gower *CA* III 9.2286–7: Bot ther is nothing seid so softe, That it ne comth out ate laste.

N172 To say **Nothing** but mum
c1522 Skelton *Colyn* I 346.907: Can say nothynge but mum. **1546** Heywood *D* 70.8: I will say nought but mum, and mum is counsell, **1555** *E* 185.218: Mum is counsell, 187.225: I wyll say nought but mum, **1556** *Spider* 192[21]: Flies may sai nought but mum. Tilley N279. See **M803, W602.**

N173 Where **Nothing** is a little does ease
1546 Heywood *D* 40.172: Where nothyng is, a little thyng dooth ease, **1555** *E* 161.93. Apperson 455; *Oxford* 463; Tilley N336.

N174 Where **Nothing** is the king must lose his right
1546 Heywood *D* 56.37: Where as nothing is, the kynge must lose his right. Apperson 455; *Oxford* 464; Tilley N338.

N175 Where **Nought** is to wed with, wise men flee the clog
1546 Heywood *D* 42.52: Where nought is to wed with, wise men flee the clog. Tilley N347.

N176 Who **Nothing** has can nothing get
a1513 Dunbar *To the King* 28.19: Quha na thing hes, can na thing gett. Whiting *Scots* II 105.

N177 Whoso does **Nought** serves nought
c1450 *Douce MS.52* 50.76: Who-so nought dois, nought servyth. Nil homini detur, qui nil sudans operetur. **c1450** *Rylands MS.394* 100.25.

N178 **Now** or never
c1225 *Horn* 65 C 1102: Com nu other nevre. **c1385** Chaucer *TC* iv 101: But now or nevere. **c1440** Charles of Orleans 30.882: O now or nevir make sum ordenaunce. **c1520** *Terens* C4r[6]: But now tyme is ells never. NED Now 8; Taylor and Whiting 266; Tilley N351.

N179 **Now** (this) now (that)
c1000 Aelfric *Homilies* I 184[2–3]: Hwilon we beoð hale, hwilon untrume; nu bliðe, and eft on micelre unblisse. **a1300** *Alisaunder* 375. 6982–7: Swiche chaunce the werlde kepeth—Now man leiggheth, now man wepeth! Now man is hool, now man is seek; Nys no day other ylyk. Noman that lyves hath borowe From evene libbe forto amorowe. **c1303** Mannyng *Handlyng* 108.3073–4: Now thou, and sythen y, So shal go, oure bayly, 121.3503–4: Now ys the floure whyte and rede, And now hyt ys bothe drye and dede. **c1330** *Four Foes* in Brown *Lyrics XIV* 32.21–3: Now kirt, now care. Now min, now mare, Now sounde, now sare, *etc.* **c1340** Rolle *Psalter* 476 (143.5): That now is

here, now a way. **1372** *Advocates MS.18.7.21* (John of Grimestone) f.10a in *JEGP* 20(1921) 274–5: Nu is up, nou is doun, Nou is frend, fo nou, Nou is out, nou is nout, Nou is al ago. **c1385** Chaucer *CT* I[A] 1531–3: As doon thise loveres in hir queynte geres, Now in the crope, now doun in the breres, Now up, now doun, as boket in a welle, *TC* ii 811: Now hoot, now cold. **c1385** Usk 39.47–9: Now is his soule here, now a thousand myle hence; now fer, now nygh, now hye, now lowe. **c1390** *This World* in Brown *Lyrics XIV* 160.3–4: Hit fareth as a foules fliht, Now is hit henne, now is hit here. **a1393** Gower *CA* II 20.569–70: Now hier now ther, now to now fro, Now up now down, this world goth so, 30.923–5: Right now the hyhe wyndes blowe, And anon after thei ben lowe, Now clowdy and now clier it is, 933–44: The See now ebbeth, now it floweth, The lond now welketh, now it groweth, Now be the Trees with leves grene, Now thei be bare and nothing sene, Now be the lusti somer floures, Now be the stormy wynter shoures, Now be the daies, now the nyhtes, So stant ther nothing al upryhtes, Now it is lyht, now it is derk; And thus stant al the worldes werk After the disposicioun Of man and his condicioun, III 433.1738: So goth this world, now wo, now wel. **a1400** *Cursor* III 1356 F 23719–21: For certis I, likkin hit to a quele Of our life the werldis wele, Now up now doun as fallis with chaunce. **a1400** *Pricke* 40.1432–4: Ofte chaunges the tymes here, als men wele wate, Als thus, now es arly, now es late, Now es day, now es nyght, *etc.* **c1400** *Remedy* in *Yorkshire Writers* II 110[21–2]: Now up now downe as wresteler be. **a1405** Lydgate *Black Knight* in *MP* II 401.458: Now up, now down, so rennyng is thy chaunce. **a1410** Love *Mirrour* 235[29–30]: Now hiderward and now thiderward: now ynne and now oute. **a1420** Lydgate *Troy* I 202.2002: Now up, now doun, in armys stant the glorie, **a1437** *That Now is Hay* in *MP* II 811–2: Nowe it is day, nowe it is nyght; Nowe it is fowlle, nowe it is feyre; Nowe it is derke, nowe it is lyght, *etc.*, 812.108: Now tryakle, nowe bytar galle, **a1439** *Fall* II 390.2192–6: What thyng mai heer floure in felicite, Or stonde stable be long contynuaunce In hih estatis outher in low degre? —Now flowe, now ebbe, now joie, now myschaunce, Afftir Fortune holdeth the ballaunce. **a1440** Burgh *Cato* 310.275–8: Sith manys liff is fulle of miserie, Whilom in mirthe and aftir in myscheef, Now in the vale, now in the mont on hihe; Now man is poore and eft richesse releffe. **c1440** Charles of Orleans 137.4089: Now wel now woo. **a1449** Lydgate *Fabula* in *MP* II 505.579: Now up, now doun, as doth a curraunt goute, 509.695–6: Now liht, now soory; now joiful, now in woo; Now cleer aloffte, now lowe in dirk(e)nesse, *Tyed* in *MP* II 834.53: Now six, now synk, now deny for my chaunce, 59: Now light, now hevy, now sorwe, now gladnes. **a1449** ?Lydgate *Pageant of Knowledge* in *MP* II 733.260: Now ebbe of povert, now flodys of ryches, 738.117. **a1450** *Barlam and Josaphat* (*South English Legendary*) 117.135–42: Triste me ne may To this false world: that chaungeth ech day: Nou ye seth the wedir is hoot and now cold, Now aman in his youthe is: and now he is old, Now aman is ryche: and now in povert I sete, Nou aman is in gret chele: and nou brenneth for hete, Now me is in gret wele: and now me is in wo; This world is unstedfast, ffor al thing faryth so. **a1450** *Generydes B* 95.2988: Now shynneth the sonne and (now) god sendith showrez. **a1450** *Goodly Balade* in Skeat *Chaucerian* 406.60: Now hot, now cold. **a1450** *Whan that phebus* in Sandison 124.43–7: Now myrth, now sorowe, now dolour, then gladnesse; Now better, now wursse, now plesure, then payne; Now to want, then to have, now love, then dysdayne; Now ebbe, now flodde, now corupte, now pure; Now hoote, now colde, now drowght, now rayne. **c1450** *As I me lend* in *Archiv* 107(1901) 50.17–9: Now wel now wo, now frend now foo, Now lef now thef, now in now out, Now cum now go, now to now froo. **c1450** Greene *Carols* 365.5: Now is joye, and now is blys; Now is balle and bitternesse; Now it is, and now it nys; Thus pasyt this word away. **c1450** Idley 91.605: Now above, now undre, as shippe undre saill, 627: Now sike, now hoole, now Joye, now doole, 104.1380–3: Ofte is seyn in a longe way Somtyme the wedir fresshe and faire of hewe, Now duste, now rayne, now sande, now clay, Now fresshe, now foule, now oolde, now newe, 145.2340: Now highe, now lowe, as ebbis and floodis. **a1460** *Towneley Plays* 120.125–6: Now in weyll, now in wo, And all thyng wrythys. **c1470** *Wallace* 59.336–40: Now want, now has; now loss, now can wyn; Now lycht, now sadd; now blisful, now in baill; In haist, now hurt; now sorouffull, now haill; Nowe weildand weyle; now calde weddyr, now hett; Nowe moist, now drowth; now waverand wynd, now weit. **c1475** Henryson *Fables* 101.2941–7: Now dolorus, now blyth as bird on breir; Now in fredome, now wrappit in distres; Now haill and sound, now deid and brocht on beir; Now pure as Job, now rowand in riches; Now gouins gay, now brats laid in pres; Now full as fitche, now hungrie as ane Hound; Now on the quheill, now wrappit to the ground, *Testament* 113.237–8: Now hait, now cauld, now blyith, now full of wo, Now grene as leif, now widderit and ago. **1478** Rivers *Morale Proverbes* [1.23–4]: Now preyse, now blame communely by usance Sheweth folye and noo maniere constance. **c1480** *Contemplacioun* 202.423–4: Now seike now hale now glad now in grevans Never in a stait to stand be condicioun. **1484** Caxton *Royal Book* H6v[4–6]: This is no thynge, but now wepe and anone laughe. Now is ease, now is he at mysease, now is he in angre, now is he in pees, now in Joye now in sorowe. **a1500** *Lover and the Advocate of Venus* in Robbins 172.96: Noght stedfast, but nowe up, nowe downe. **a1500** *Vanitas* in Brown *Lyrics XV* 238.2–4: Lo! how this werld is turnyd up and downe, Now wele, now wo, now tranquilyte, Now werre, now pese, and now rebilyoun. **1501** Douglas *Palice* 9.5–8: Thy transitorie plesance quhat availlis? Now thair, now heir, now hie and now devaillis, Now to, now fra, now law, now magnifyis, Now hait, now cauld, now lauchis, now bevaillis, *etc.* **a1508** Dunbar *Lament* 20.10–1: Now sound, now seik, now blith, now sary, Now dansand mery, now like to dee. **1509** Barclay *Ship* I 32[11]: Nowe up nowe downe, 128[8]: Now full nowe voyde as waters ebbe and flowe, 206[28]: Nowe up hye, now lowe in the dust. **a1513** Dunbar *Of the Warldis Vanitie* 151.19–23: Now day up bricht, now nycht als blak as sabill, Now eb, now flude, now freynd, now cruell fo; Now glaid, now said, now weill, now in to wo; Now cled in gold, dissolvit now in as; So dois this warld transitorie go. **1513** Douglas *Aeneid* II 193.34–5: Now dreid, now stryfe, now lufe, now wa, now play, Langeir in murnyng, now in melody. **c1516** Skelton *Magnificence* 79.2512–3: Now well, nowe wo, nowe hy, now lawe degre; Nowe ryche, nowe pore, nowe hole, nowe in dysease, *etc.* **1533** More *Apologye* 121[27–9]: Now up now downe, now fallynge by synne and now rysynge agayne by grace. **1546** Heywood *D* 62.105–6: Now in now out, now here now there, now sad, Now mery, now hie, now lowe, now good, now bad, **1556** *Spider* 424.16–7: The spider right now so hie: evin now so low. The flie right now at eb, evin now a flote. Rudolph E. Habenicht ed. John Heywood's *A Dialogue of Proverbs* (Berkeley, Cal., 1963) 210; Whiting *Scots* II 105. See **T350–5, 364.**

N180 The **Number** of fools is without end (*varied*)

c1390 Chaucer *CT* VII 1258[B2448]: Men shal alwey fynde a gretter nombre of fooles than of wise men. **c1395** *WBible* Ecclesiastes i 15: The noumbre of foolis is greet with outen ende. **c1450** *Speculum Christiani* (2) 208.31–2: *Ecclesiastes:* The nombre of foyles es endlez.

N181 As nice as a **Nun**

c1405 *Mum* 34.237: That thou ne art nycier than a nunne nyne-folde tyme.

N182 As nice as a **Nun's** hen

a1500 Greene *Carols* 401 B 1: Some (*women*) be nyse as a nonne hene. **1546** Heywood *D* 60.36: All in daliaunce, as nice as a nuns hen. Apperson 444; *Oxford* 451; Tilley N353.

N183 To be a **Nun** of the green coat

1506 Hawes *Pastime* 135.3530: Amonge the nunnes of the grene cote. Cf. NED Green lg; *Oxford* 266: To give a woman a green gown.

N184 As sweet as a **Nut**

a1500 *Inter Diabolus et Virgo* 444.18: What ys swetter than ys the nott? 445.38: Lowe ys swetter than ys the notte. Apperson 614; *Oxford* 635; Taylor and Whiting 266; Tilley N358.

N185 Knack (*crack*) me that **Nut**

1546 Heywood *D* 83.98: Knak me that nut. Apperson 460; *Oxford* 117; Tilley N359.

N186 Not give a **Nut**

c1300 *Havelok* 16.419: He ne yaf a note of hise othes.

N187 Not the nearer by a **Nut**

c1405 *Mum* 52.866: And nought the neer by a note.

N188 Not worth a **Nut**

c1300 *Havelok* 48.1332: Nouht the worth of one noute. **c1450** *Pilgrimage LM* 156[3–4]: To crye and braye shulde nouht be woorth to me a def note. **1562** Heywood *E* 230.3.6: Hers a freend for freendshyp, not woorth a crakt nut. Apperson 457:25; NED Deaf 6b.

N189 **Nut-brown**

a1325 *Cursor* II 1078.18833–4: His hare like to the nute brun, Quen it for ripnes fals dun, 1080.18846: Nute brun als i tald yow are. **a1500** *Nut Brown Maid* 175.20: Nutt-browne maide, 177[19], 183.162. Taylor and Whiting 266; Whiting *Ballad* 30, *Drama* 321:236.

N190 The **Nut** (kernel) is better than the shell (*varied*)

c1440 Scrope *Epistle to Othea* 53[8]: The nutte is better than the shelle. **c1450** *Epistle of Othea* 80.2: Ffor, lyke as better is the kernell then shyll, 8–9: As the kernell of a nutt excedythe in valew the schyll. **1532** Berners *Golden Boke* 419.10732–3: The nuttes ar very good, but the shales be to hard.

N191 One must break the **Nut** to have the kernel *(varied)*
a1225 *Lambeth Homilies* 79[13–4]: Nu hit iburd breke thas word, alse me breketh the nute for to habbene thene curnel. **a1396**(1494) Hilton *Scale* B7r[14–5]: He hath so wel gnawe on the bytter barke of the notte that he hath broken it, and fedeth him with the kyrnell, C2r[20–1]: They gnawe on the drye barke wythout, but the swete kernel of it, and the inly savour of it, may they not come to. **a1415** *Lanterne* 78.25–6: We must nede breke the nutt if we wole have the kirnel. **a1500** *Leconfield Proverbs* 493[16–7]: And yf ye wolde the swetnes have of the kyrnell, Be content to byte upon the harde shell. Apperson 177:25; *Oxford* 166–7; Tilley K19, N360.

N192 As sweet as **Nutmeg**
a1300 *Alisaunder* 27.427–8: His love is also swete, iwys, So note-muge.

N193 As bare as a **Nutshell**
c1450 Idley 197.2327–8: Ffor ye take fro the pouere that they shold by lieve, And make hym as baare as a note shelle.

N194 Not set a **Nutshell**
c1522 Skelton *Colyn* I 358.1227–8: We set not a nut shell The way to heven or to hell.

N195 Not worth a **Nutshell**
a1325 *Cursor* III 1362.23828: Thair spede es noght a (G: ne es worth a) nute-scell. **a1393** Gower *CA* II 316.566: Bot al nys worth a note schale. **a1529** Skelton *Against Venemous Tongues* I 135.4: And all is not worth a couple of nut shalis. *Oxford* 466; Tilley N366.

N196 The **Nutshell,** though it be hard and tough, holds the kernel
c1475 Henryson *Fables* 3.15–6: The nuttes schell, thocht it be hard and teuch, Haldis the kirnill, and is delectabill. Cf. Tilley N360.

O

O1 As round as an **O**
c1490 Ryman 222.3[2]: Heven and erthe rounde like an O. Whiting *NC* 452.

O2 As great as an **Oak** (*etc.*) (A number of single quotations are brought together here)
a1375 *Octavian* (*S*) 30.921–2: Guymerraunt, Greet as an ok. **c1395** Chaucer *CT* V[F] 158–9: Thurgh out his armure it wolde kerve and byte, Were it as thikke as is a branched ook. **c1450** Idley 138.1846: Thoughe it hadde be mighti as an oke.

O3 As hard as an **Oak** (board)
a1300 *Alisaunder* 341.6404–5: The face hii han playn and hard, Als it were an okes bord. **1480** Caxton *Ovyde* 131[9–10]: More harde than an Oke. Svartengren 260.

O4 As strong as an **Oak**
c1395 *WBible* Amos ii 9: He was strong as an ook. **a1475** *Guy*[2] 86.3004: Thogh he were as stronge as an noke. Svartengren 392; Whiting *Scots* II 105.

O5 As sturdy as an **Oak**
a1420 Lydgate *Troy* II 440.1594: Sturdy as an oke. Taylor *Comparisons* 79.

O6 Great **Oaks** fall for wind's strokes and small stand still
c1350 *Libeaus* 75.1351–3: I have y-sein grete okes Falle for windes strokes And smale stonde full stille. See **T464, W348.**

O7 An **Oak** comes of a little spire (*shoot*)
c1385 Chaucer *TC* ii 1335: An ook comth of a litel spir. Skeat 171. See **G418, K12.**

O8 An **Oak** falls all at once (*varied*)
c1385 Chaucer *TC* ii 1380–3: Thenk hereayeins: whan that the stordy ook, On which men hakketh ofte, for the nones, Receyved hath the happy fallyng strook, The greete sweigh doth it come al at ones. **c1385** Usk 135.99–101: So ofte must men on the oke smyte, til the happy dent have entred, whiche with the okes owne swaye maketh it to come al at ones. Apperson 272; *Oxford* 295.

O9 To fall down like an **Oak**
c1300 Robert of Gloucester I 297.4240: He vel adoun as a gret ok that binethe ykorve wer. **a1350** Castelford 93.22252–4: Als A grete ake thoru windes blaste, Louse rifen up so bi the rotes, This geante fel doune bifor his fotes.

O10 To stand like a great **Oak** (*etc.*) (A number of single quotations are brought together here)
a1350 Castelford 92.22237: Yia, ever he stod als A gret ake. **a1420** Lydgate *Troy* I 112.3390: And leied on him as men hewe on an oke, III 686.4178: But evere she sat stille as any oke. **a1425** *St. Robert* 65.742: Nay mare he mowed (*moved*) than dose an ake.

O11 While an **Oak** is a young spire (*shoot*) it may be wound into a withe (*halter*), *etc.*
1422 Yonge *Governaunce* 161.35–7: And whyle an hooke is a yonge Spyre, hit may be wonde into a wyth, but when hit is a wixen tree, an hundrid oxyn unneth hit may bowe. See **P251, W35, Y4.**

O12 To have an **Oar** in every man's boat (barge)
c1500 *Cock* 11[29]: In Cockes bote eche man had an ore. **1546** Heywood *D* 36.29: She must have an ore in every mans barge, **1555** *E* 180.189. Apperson 461; *Oxford* 467; Tilley O4; Whiting *Drama* 356:738.

O13 **Oath** done for strength (force) is no oath (*varied*)
c1300 Robert of Gloucester II 530.7344–5: Harald him sende word that folie it was to

truste To such oth as was ido mid strengthe as he wel wuste, 531.7351: Thervore nede oth isuore nede ibroke was. **1456** Hay *Law* 184.4–7: The law sais, Quod juramentum contra bonos mores compulsum non est servandum. That is to say that ane ath aganis gude custumes and gude thewis of gude men compellit is nocht to be haldin na kepit. **1481** Caxton *Reynard* 50[11–3]: I wente ones with a good man that said to me that a bydwongen oth or oth sworn for force was none oth, **1484** *Aesop* 47[1–3]: The thynge which is promysed by force and for drede is not to be hold, [18–9]: For the thyngs whiche are done by force have none fydelyte. **c1500** Fabyan 234[42–3]: A lewde othe myght and oughte to be broken, and specyally whan it is compelled to be sworne for nede or for drede. Jente 112; Tilley O7. See **C485, T197.**

O14 **Occupation** is the mother of virtue
a1439 Lydgate *Fall* I 230.1092: Modir of vertu is occupacyoun. See **I6, S392.**

O15 As good be **Occupied** as do nothing
c1516 Skelton *Magnificence* 23.692–3: As good to be occupyed as up and downe to trace And do nothynge. Cf. Tilley I7. See I7.

O16 To know what it is **O'clock**
c1522 Skelton *Colyn* I 319.219–20: To knowe whate ys a clocke Under her surfled smocke. *Oxford* 345; Tilley O10.

O17 As rich (happy) as **Octavian** (*varied*)
a1387 Higden-Trevisa II 21[21–2]: Riches that there (*England*) is an Yern wolde Octavian. **c1395** *WBible* III Kings iii 12 *gloss: And summe* weren richere as Octovyan. **c1400** *Seven Sages D* 26–7.822–6: In the tyme of octoviane That was ane mychti emprioure And lufit richess sa oure mesoure That gold and silver in hurd had he That uness It mycht noumerit be. **c1420** Wyntoun III 287.1091–4: Men oyssit for his worschep ay In til Rome a prowerb (*var.* commone proverb) say, Qwha happiar than Ottovian, Or qwha evir bettyr than Trajan? **a1449** Lydgate *Amor* in *MP* II 748.115: Passe Octovian or Cresus in riches. **1493** *Seven Wise Masters* 46[4–6]: In that tyme was an emperour named Octavyan, whiche in rychesse of golde and sylver exceded al other kynges and prynces, 82[1–2]: Octavianus themperour reygned in Rome ryghte ryche and coveytous, and above all thynges he loved golde. Whiting *Scots* II 106.

O18 **Odd** (Even) or even (odd)
a1325 *Erthe* 25.51–2: Loke thou lete, for oode ne for ewyne, Ffor tho byne the werkis that helpyne us to heyvyne. **a1400** *Scottish Legends* I 201.382–3: How dar thu thane for hod or ewyn Fra thi lorde tak hyre to the. **c1400** *Laud Troy* I 25.831–2: And swere me ther by that god Alle this to holde for even or od, 167.5666, 283. 9613–4, II 364.12349–51, 391.13284–5, 431. 14624: He scholde him scle for odde or evene, 531.18046–7. **a1425** *Metrical Paraphrase OT* 125.18273–4: He sayd that suld we never, Nauder for evyn ne ode. **a1450** *Castle* 121.1472: I schal not spare, for odde nor even. **c1450** *St. Cuthbert* 146.4957: Alle yone oste, bathe even and od. **a1460** *Towneley Plays* 101.20: Ffor even or for od I have mekyll tene. **1464** Hardyng 410[27–8]: The Scottes wyll ay do you the harme they may, And so they have full ofte with odde and even. **a1500** *Thre Prestis* 43.972: I sal hir never displeis for od nor evin. **a1513** Dunbar *Of Discretioun in Taking* 36.37: Than suld I tak bayth evin and od, *Devillis Inquest* 77.41–2: I forsak God, And all his werkis evin and od. MED even, adj. 15(c); NED Odd 2c.

O19 Great **Offence** requires great atonement
a1023 Wulfstan *Homilies* 268.23–4: We witan ful georne þæt to miclan bryce sceal micel bot nyde, and to miclan bryne wæter unlytel. See **W60.**

O20 Uncommitted (*unassigned*) **Office** oft annoys
c1380 Chaucer *PF* 518: For office uncommytted ofte anoyeth. Skeat 138. See **C447, S167.**

O21 As brown as **Oil**
a1425 *Mandeville* (*Egerton*) 79.5–6: Dyamaundes . . . broune as oile.

O22 As fat as **Oil**
a1475 *St. Birgitta* 20.35: Make not the sowle fatt as oyle.

O23 As nesh (*smooth*) as **Oil**
a1400 *Northern Verse Psalter* I 175 (54.22): Nesched als oyle his saghs bene (*var.* Smethe are mi sayes over oli). Apperson 582; *Oxford* 600; Taylor and Whiting 269; Tilley O25.

O24 To cast **Oil** in fire
c1390 Chaucer *CT* VI[C] 59–60: For wyn and youthe dooth Venus encresse, As men in fyr wol casten oille or greesse. Apperson 463; *Oxford* 469; Taylor and Whiting 269; Tilley O30; Whiting *Scots* II 106.

O25 To hold (bear) up **Oil**
a1387 Higden-Trevisa III 447[13–4]: A greet deel of hem that were at the feste hilde up the

kynges oyl. **c1390** *Suffer in Time* in Brown *Lyrics XIV* 202.74: And holde up 'oyl' by and by, *But thou say Sooth* 207.85: Hold up no monnus 'oyl', I rede (Note and glossary say 'oyl' is French 'yes'). **a1393** Gower *CA* III 292.2194–5: Bot holden up his oil and sein That al is wel, what evere he doth (Note [III 529] suggests 'oil' as French 'eye'), 303–4.2583–5: Prophetes false manye mo To bere up oil, and alle tho Affermen that which he hath told. **c1405** *Mum* 18.186: For braggynge and for bostynge and beringe uppon (?up of) oilles, 34.247: Easily for oyle, sire, and elles were I nyce, 35.271: And has housholde and hire to holde up thy oyles, 51.831: For alle was huyst in the halle sauf "holde up the oyles." Apperson 463.

O26 While there is **Oil** the lamp is lightly set afire
a1393 Gower *CA* III 461.2775–7: Whil ther is oyle forto fyre, The lampe is lyhtly set afyre, And is fulhard er it be queynt.

O27 Cast not away the **Old** until you are sure of the new (*varied*)
c1495 *Arundel Vulgaria* 80.335: Yete cast not away thyn olde by myne advyce tyll thou be sure of newe (*perhaps quite literal*). **a1500** *Cotton Galba E. ix.* f.66[b] in W. H. Hulme *Middle-English Harrowing of Hell* (EETS ES 100, 1907) xxv: He that casteth of the olde Before he know the newe, Maye weepe in the winter When frostes dooth inswe. All olde things ar not ill Where wise men doo weue; Som newe thinges are scharce good And that is trwe. See **F424, 650, N97, T132.**

O28 He that would be **Old** long should become old hastily
1481 *Tulle of Olde Age* 31[17–20]: I nevir consented to an olde proverbe . . . which amonyssheth and signifieth that thou becomyst olde hastli yf thou wilt long be olde. Apperson 464:11; *Oxford* 471; Tilley O34.

O29 Men may the **Old** (wise) atren (*outrun*) but not atrede (*outwit*) (*varied*)
c1250 *Proverbs of Alfred* 131 T 605–6: For the helder mon me mai of-riden Betere thenne of-reden. **c1385** Chaucer *CT* I[A] 2449: Men may the olde atrenne, and noght atrede, *TC* iv 1455–6: Youre syre is wys; and seyd is, out of drede "Men may the wyse atrenne, and naught atrede." **c1450** *Rylands MS.394* 107.20: Me may the olde over rynne but not over rede. Jente 525; Skeat 195.

O30 Not too **Old** to learn
c1515 Barclay *Eclogues* 71.538: Thou art not to olde for to lere. Cf. Taylor and Whiting 105:6.

O31 **Old** and cold
a1425 *Chester Plays* I 110.134: For I am both old and colde. *Oxford* 469.

O32 The **Olive** (branch) of peace
c1380 Chaucer *PF* 181: The olyve of pes. **a1398** (1495) Bartholomaeus-Trevisa R7[r][1.18–23]: (Olive) is a worthy tree and a tree of peas as he (Isadore) sayth ffor the story of the Romayns meanith that wythout braunches of olive noo messagers were sent to Rome to gete peas nother to profre peas to other men. **c1400** Mandeville *Travels* 7.3: For olyve betokneth pes. **a1475** *Guy*[2] 70.2446–8: A branche of olyfe in hys hande he bere That was a feyre tokenynge Of pees and of looveyng. **a1475** *Tree* 64.13–4: A braunche of an olyve tree; be the olyve is undirstonde pees. **1513** Douglas *Aeneid* III 129.48: In takyn of peax a branch of olyve tre, IV 13.2: Ambassatouris, with branch of olyve tre. **1518** Watson *Oliver* M2[r][24–5]: Berynge in his hande a braunche of Olyve is the sygne of peas. Taylor and Whiting 270.

O33 **Once** ought to suffice
c1408 Lydgate *Reson* 61.2313–6: Ne sholde nat, as semeth me, To oft(e) sythe rehersed be; For, by doctryne of the wyse, Oones ought y-nowgh suffise. Gavin Holt (*pseud.*) *Trail of the Skull* (London, [c1930]) 61: Once is enough for Santa Teresa.

O34 As fast as **One** goes another comes
1546 Heywood *D* 23.26: As fast as one goth an other comthe. *Oxford* 192; Tilley G161–2.

O35 **One** against all has seldom sovereignty
a1439 Lydgate *Fall* II 654.2482: Oon ageyn alle hath seelde sovereynte. Cf. Whiting *Drama* 188. See **M366.**

O36 **One** against two is not good to fight
c1350 *Libeaus* 32.548–9: Oon ageines two To fighte, that is nought good. See **T548.**

O37 **One** is two, friend is foe, will is woe
a1400 *Four Proverbs* in *Pol. Rel. and Love Poems* 251: On is two; Frend is foo; Wil is wo. Brown-Robbins 2167.

O38 **One** is worth a hundred and a hundred is not worth one
1523 Berners *Froissart* II 266[31–4]: For it is comonly sayde, that one is worthe a C. and a C. is nat worthe one . . . and . . . sometyme

it fortuneth, that by one man a hole countrey is saved. Apperson 472; *Oxford* 476; Tilley M354.

O39 **One** lost and two recovered
c1477 Caxton *Jason* 56.29–30: Have not ye ofte tymes herd saye that one lost and two recoverid.

O40 **One** may come and quit all
a1400 *Eglamour* 44.658–60: Slyke chans maye fall, That ane may come and quyte all, Be thou never so prest. Whiting *Scots* II 106–7. See **T308.**

O41 That **One** may not another may
1546 Heywood *D* 62.19: That one may not an other may. Tilley O62.

O42 That (which) pleases **One** smarts (*hurts*) another sorely
a1500 ?Ros *La Belle Dame* 313.454: That pleseth oon, another smerteth sore. Cf. Tilley M483. See **G104, 329, H653, M486.**

O43 To speak **One** and mean twain
a1420 Lydgate *Troy* III 704.4779: He spak but oon, and yit he ment(e) tweyne.

O44 When **One** is out another is in
a1500 *Clerk and the Nightingale I* in Robbins 174.64: When on is owt another is in. See **N6.**

O45 While **One** goes up another has a fall
a1420 Lydgate *Troy* I 202.2028: While on goth up, an-other hath a fal. See **B575, F512.**

O46 As sweet as any **Onion**
a1513 Dunbar *In Secreit Place* 55.53: My sowklar sweit as ony unyoun.

O47 Not worth an **Onion** (couple of onions)
1509 Barclay *Ship* I 63[27]: A yonge boy that is nat worth an onyon, 89[19]: Their purpose nat worth a cowpyll of onyons, **c1515** *Eclogues* 206.690: In valour scant worth a couple of onions. **1534** Heywood *Love* C2ʳ[3], **1556** *Spider* 106[4]. Apperson 458:38; Tilley O66.

O48 To pill (*peel*) one like an **Onion**
a1529 Skelton *Boke of Three Fooles* I 204[25–6]: They pill theim as an onion.

O49 When **Oportet** (*must*) comes in place *miserere* has no grace (*varied*)
c1378 *Piers* B x 439: For *qant OPORTET vyent en place yl ny ad que PATI.* **a1500** *My lefe chyld* in *Rel. Ant.* II 14[31–2]: And when *oportet* cums in plas, Thou knawys *miserere* has no gras. Note to *Piers* II 162–3.

O50 To take **Orders** of a good brand
c1330 *Otuel* 70.181–6: For yef ani of you so hardi be, That any strok munteth to me, Mahoun mi god ich here for-sake Yef he sschal evere ordres take, Of ani other bisschopes hond, Bot of Corsouze mi gode brond. See **P400.**

O51 **Ordinance** (*order*) in fight is better than strength
c1420 Wyntoun V 413–5.3528–30: Her by men may ensampil ta, That bettyr is ordynans in to feicht Sum tyme, than outhir strenythe or mycht. See **L381, M801.**

O52 Betwixt **Orkneys** and Ind
c1385 Chaucer *TC* v 971: As ben bitwixen Orkades and Inde.

O53 **Ossing** (*offering*) comes to bossing (*kissing*)
c1450 *Douce MS.52* 55.117: Ossyng comys to bossyng. **c1450** *Rylands MS.394* 104.18.7–9: Ossynge comes to bossinge. *Vulgus opinatur quod postmodum verificatur. Que predixerunt plures operata fuerunt.* Apperson 475; NED Osse 3; *Oxford* 479; Tilley O82.

O54 "God have mercy on our souls," said the holy **Oswald** as he fell
a900 Bede 188.16–8: Cwædon heo bi ðon þus in gydde: Drihten God miltsa þu sawlum ussa leoda, cwæð se halga Oswald, þa he on eorðan saag. **a900** *Old English Martyrology* 138.20–3: Oswald endade his lif in gebedes wordum þa hine mon sloh, ond þa he feol on eorðan, þa cwæð he: *"deus miserere animabus;"* he cwæð: "god, miltsa þu saulum." **c1000** Aelfric *Lives* II 136.161: And þus clypode (Oswald) on his fylle, "God gemiltsa urum sawlum!" **a1338** Mannyng *Chronicle A* II 560–1.16165–76: In his fallynge he seyde on hy, "Of alle our soules, Lord, have mercy!" That was the laste werde he seid, And fel doun, and ther he deyd. Of tho men that thys word herd, A byword in al the contre ferd, "God have our soules! quath Osewold." Thys byword was longe y-told, Thys they seide at ilka rage, And longe had they hit in usage: This word witnesseth wel seynt Bede, That longe was used in many lede. **a1387** Higden-Trevisa V 461[9–11]: And therfore yit hit is (a) bysawe, "God have mercy of soules, quoth Oswalde, and fil to the grounde." **a1425** Higden-Anon. V 461[8–10]: Wherefore hit is hade as a commune proverbe unto this tyme, "Oswaldus fallenge to therthe, seide, 'God have mercy on trewe sawles." A. H. Krappe *Science of Folk-Lore* (London, 1930) 149; B. J. Whiting "Earliest Recorded English Wellerism," *PQ* 15(1936) 310–1.

O55 Better that **Others** weep than yourself

c1385 Chaucer *TC* iv 591: Bet is that othere than thiselven wepe. See **C153.**

O56 To (a)venge one **Outrage** by another
c1390 Chaucer *CT* VII 1524–5[B2714–5]: And therfore me thynketh men oghten nat repreve me, though I putte me in a litel peril for to venge me, and though I do a greet excesse, that is to seyn, that I venge oon outrage by another. See **F491.**

O57 As the **Ouzel** (*blackbird*) whistles so answers the thrush
1492 *Salomon and Marcolphus* 10[21–2]: As the owsell whystelyth so answeryth the thrusshe.

O58 As hot as an **Oven**
c1395 *WBible* Hosea vii 7: Alle weren maad hoot as an ovene (**c1384:** fourneice). Taylor and Whiting 272.

O59 Do not yawn with (*against*) an **Oven**
c1250 *Owl* 28.289–92: Hit is a wise monne dome, And hi hit segget wel ilome, That me ne chide wit the gidie, Ne wit than ofne me ne yonie. Apperson 243; Jente 402; C. T. Onions in *Medium Ævum* 9(1940) 86–7; *Oxford* 233; Tilley G33.

O60 To see no more than in an **Oven**
a1500 *Partenay* 154.4453: No thyng he saw more then in a oven he.

O61 As red as an **Oven Mouth**
a1420 Lydgate *Troy* II 493.3446–7: Whos eyen eke, flawmynge also rede As the blase of an oven mouthe.

O62 **Overbusy** was never commendable (*varied*)
a1400 *Pricke* 31.1094–5: I hald that man noght witty, That about the world is over bysy. **a1500** *See Much* in Brown *Lyrics XV* 280.30: Over besy was (never) yit commend(able). Cf. *Oxford* 71: To be too busy; Tilley C621.

O63 That which is **Overdone** will not prove aright
c1395 Chaucer *CT* VIII[G] 645–6: That that is overdoon, it wol nat preeve Aright, as clerkes seyn; it is a vice. Apperson 640–1; *Oxford* 665; Skeat 283. See **M463, P383, T86.**

O64 He that **Overloads** himself is evilly strained
1484 Caxton *Aesop* 245[1–2]: He that over ladeth hym self is evylle strayned. See **F56, L413.**

O65 The **Overlooking** of the owner is better than hearing
1519 Horman *Vulgaria* 258[33–4]: The over-lokynge of the owner is better than the hyrynge by informacion. Cf. Taylor and Whiting 239; Tilley M733.

O66 Neither **Over-wish** nor over-purchase nor overbuild
1480 *Stonor Letters* II 98[27–30]: And of certen thynges I wold desire you and pray you in the name of God, that ye wolle not over wissh yow, ner owyr purches yow, ner owyr bild you; for these iii thynges wolle plucke a yongman ryth lowe.

O67 As crooknecked as an **Owl**
a1529 Skelton *Elynour* I 108.427: Crokenecked lyke an oule.

O68 As odious as an **Owl**
a1507 Dunbar *Epetaphe* 65.7: And he evir odious as an owle.

O69 **Owl** on stock and stock on owl, *etc.*
a1393 Gower *CA* II 242.585–7: Bot Oule on Stock and Stock on Oule; The more that a man defoule, Men witen wel which hath the werse. *Oxford* 482.

O70 The **Owl** to the stone and the stone to the owl but ever abides the silly owl
c1475 *Rawlinson MS. D 328* 120.39: The owle to the stone and the stone to the owle, but ever a-bydyth the sely owle. Seu bugo (*sic*) lapidi iactetur seu lapis ille ictus dampna gravis semper habebit avis.

O71 Stroke **Owl** and scrape owl and ever is owl owl
a1400 Bozon *Contes* 23[9–10]: Stroke oule and schrape oule and evere is oule oule. See **A228.**

O72 To cry like an **Owl**
a1300 *Tristrem* II 82.3032–3: As oule and stormes strong, So criestow on heye.

O73 To hide like an **Owl**
c1395 Chaucer *CT* III[D] 1081: And al day after hidde hym as an owle. Whiting *Scots* II 107.

O74 To know no more than the **Owl** of music
c1415 *Middle English Sermons* 194.13–4: Thoo he knowe no more ther-of than can the howle of musik. See **A227.**

O75 To look (be) like an **Owl**
c1400 *Plowman's Tale* 187.1270: And loked lovely as an owle. **a1450** *Castle* 149.2410: I loke lyke an howle. **a1450** *York Plays* 258.117–9: He lokis . . . like an nowele in a stok. **a1500** *Mocking Letter* in Robbins 219.6: Most fresch of contenaunce, evyn as an Oule. Whiting *Drama* 322:240.

O76 Own is own
c1250 *Hendyng O* 198.36: Owene is owene and other mannes edwyt (*shame, reproach*). **a1400** *Proverbis of Wysdom* 246.103: Own is own and othere men is edwyte. **1546** Heywood *D* 69.120: Alwaie owne is owne, **1555** *E* 187.227. Apperson 479; Kneuer 38–9; *Oxford* 482; Schleich 261–2; Singer III 133; Skeat 85. See **B505, T305.**

O77 As great as (an) **Ox**
c1350 *Libeaus* 74 *var.* 1344[c-d] : He is also grete, As is an ox. **c1385** Chaucer *TC* v 1469: For with a boor as gret as ox in stalle. Taylor *Comparisons* 16: big.

O78 Bind not the **Ox**'s mouth
a900 Alfred *Gregory* 105.7–8: Bi ðon wæs gecueden on ðære æ: Ne forbinden ge na ðæm ðyrstendum oxum ðone muð. **c1395** *WBible* Deuteronomy xxv 4: Thou schalt not bynde the mouth of the oxe tredynge thi fruytis in the corn floor, I Corinthians ix 9: For it is writun in the lawe of Moises, Thou schalt not bynde the mouth of the ox threischynge, I Timothy v 18: bridil. **a1400** *Pauline Epistles* I Corinthians ix 9: Thou schalt not bynde to the mouth of the oxe plowande, I Timothy v 18: brydele. **c1400** Paues 114 I Timothy v 18: For holy scripture seyth, Thou ne schalt noght bynde the mouth of the oxe that tyleth thi lond. **1533** More *Confutacion* 643 F[3–6]: Thou shall not bynde the mouth of the oxe as he goeth in the flowre and thresheth the corne. Tilley O113.

O79 The black **Ox** has not trod on his foot
1546 Heywood *D* 30.45: The blacke oxe had not trode on his nor hir foote, **1555** *E* 159.79: The blacke Oxe never trode on thy foote. Apperson 52; *Oxford* 48; Taylor and Whiting 273; Tilley O103; Whiting *Drama* 335:407, *Scots* II 107.

O80 Bring the **Ox** to the hall and he will to the stall
c1450 *Rylands MS.394* 92.11: Brynge the oxe to the halle ande he wolle to the stalle. *Oxford* 65: Bring a cow; Tilley C752.

O81 Now day to-morrow day, said the **Ox** that the hare chased
1492 *Salomon and Marcolphus* 13[15–6]: Now daye to morwe day, sayde the oxe that the hare chacyd.

O82 The **Ox** that draws backward shall be twice pricked
1492 *Salomon and Marcolphus* 7[17–8]: The ox that drawyth bacwarde shal be twyse prycked.

O83 Seldom dies his **Ox** that weeps for a cock
c1450 *Rylands MS.394* 92.6: Seldon dyeth his oxe that wepeth for a kok. **a1500** Hill 133.53: Selde dyeth the oxe that wepeth for the cok. Bos moritur rara qui gallo plorat amara. Apperson 479; Walther I 245.2153a.

O84 Three **Oxen** in (one) plow never draw well
a1450 *Boke of Curtasye* (*Sloane*) 307.285–8: Yf thou schalle on pilgrimage go, Be not the thryd felaw for wele ne wo; Thre oxen in plowgh may never wel drawe, Nother be craft, ryght, ne lawe. See **B433.**

O85 To be shut up like any **Ox** in stall
c1450 Idley 96.887: Thow shalt be shett up as ony oxe in stall.

O86 To call a black **Ox** "swan"
c1303 Mannyng *Handlyng* 145–6.4319–20: He ys no more crystyn man Than who so kallyth a blak oxe 'swan.' **c1450** Idley 174.972–3: Thow may well be called a crystyn man As a man use to name a blak oxe, swan.

O87 To ear (*plow*) with an **Ox** and an ass together
c1395 *WBible* Deuteronomy xxii 10: Thou schalt not ere with an oxe and asse togidere. **a1402** Trevisa *Dialogus* 12.14–5: Thanne ye ereth with an oxe and an asse ayenus youre Holy Writ. Apperson 504; *Oxford* 508; Tilley O109.

O88 To lead like an **Ox** by the horn
c1300 *Body and Soul* 51 L 413–4: Ye ledde me bi doune and dale, As an oxe bi the horn (*A*: As men doth ox bi the horn).

O89 To stand like **Ox** in stall
c1400 *Laud Troy* I 165.5603: Al that day stode as oxe in stalle.

O90 Two **Oxen** in one yoke draw (a)like
1492 *Salomon and Marcolphus* 12[2–3]: Two oxen in one yocke drawen lyke.

O91 Not the value of an **Oyster**
a1430 Lydgate *Pilgrimage* 357.13153–5: Ek I ne have noon avauntage Ffor to harme nor do damage—Nat the valu off An Oystre.

O92 Not worth an **Oyster**
c1387-95 Chaucer *CT* I[A] 182: But thilke text heeld he nat worth an oystre.

O93 A stopping (choking) **Oyster**
c1499 Skelton *Bowge* I 48.477: I have a stoppynge oyster in my poke. **1546** Heywood *D* 52.379–80: But therto deviseth to cast in my teeth, Checks and chokyng oysters, **1556** *Spider* 68[7]: A

meane wit maie deeme, it was a chokyng oister. Tilley O115. See **C240.**

O94 To drink to one's **Oysters**
1472 Paston V 138[14–7]: For and I had not delt ryght corteysly up on Holy Rood Day I had drownk to myn oystyrs, for yowng Heydon had reysyd as many men as he kowd mak in harneys to have holp Gornay. NED Oyster lc.

O95 Not worth an **Oystershell**
a1500 *Mischance Reigns* in Wright *Political Poems* II 239[15]: Alle be they not worth an oyster-schelle.

P

P1 The slower **Pace,** the further in running
a1449 Lydgate *Tyed* in *MP* II 833.24–5: The slowar paas, the further in rennynge; The more I renne, the more wey I lese. *Oxford* 281. See **H168.**

P2 As plain as a **Packstaff**
1533 More *Confutacion* 814 F[4–5]: So playne as a packe staffe. **1556** Heywood *Spider* 148[17]: You pacstaffe plaine: the ant crafty and close. Apperson 499; *Oxford* 503; Tilley P322.

P3 A **Pad** (*toad*) in the straw
1546 Heywood *D* 68.87: Or els this geare will breede a pad in the strawe, **1555** *E* 196.290. Apperson 481; *Oxford* 484; Tilley P9; Whiting *Drama* 356:750.

P4 To swell like a **Pad**
c1489 Caxton *Aymon* I 314.21: He swelled like a padde. Taylor and Whiting 376. See **T343.**

P5 To play one's **Pageant**
a1470 Malory II 748.7–8: I tolde you that thys day there wolde a knyght play his pageaunte, 759.29: Yondyr rydyth a knyght that playyth his pageauntes. **1483** ?Skelton *Kynge Edwarde* I 4.85: I have played my pageyond, now am I past. **c1505** Watson *Valentine* 51.17: You have taught me to play this pagent. **a1508** Dunbar *Lament* 21.46. **1509** *Fyftene Joyes* G4r[12]: How be it he hath sene suche pagentes playde. **c1515** Barclay *Eclogues* 112.141: With brauling they enter first pagiant to play. **c1516** Skelton *Magnificence* 17.505. **1528** More *Heresyes* 134 H[3–4]: Suche pageantes be played before all the towne, 271 GH: I never sawe any that more verely play that pageaunt than do thys kind of such preachers. **a1529** Skelton *Garnesche* I 127.37. **1529** More *Supplicacion* 297 C[10–1], 304 E[7], **1532** *Confutacion* 420 E[9], 605 D[16], 680 B[9–10]: This false pageaunt plaieth Tindal, *Frith* 842 F[1–3]: The young man playeth a very young wanton pageaunt, **1533** *Answer* 1041 A[13], C[13–4], **1534** *Comforte* 1222 F[9–11], *Correspondence* 504.58–9: Whan they had played their pageant and were gone out of the place. NED Pageant 1b.

P6 To get one's **Paiks** (*thrashing*)
a1508 Dunbar *Flyting* 7.70: How that thow, poysonit pelor, gat thy paikis. Whiting *Scots* II 108.

P7 After great **Pain** the joys are sweeter
1506 Hawes *Pastime* 91.2357: After grete payne the Joyes is the swetter. See **M728.**

P8 After **Pains** pleasure
c1523 Barclay *Mirrour* 26[9]: After paynes pleasure. See **B325, L70.**

P9 Better a short **Pain** than one that abides long
1509 Barclay *Ship* I 194[21]: Better a shorte payne, than that doth longe abyde. Whiting *Drama* 149. See **E205, L471.**

P10 Every **Pain** is good to flee
a1393 Gower *CA* III 442.2096–7: Of every lust thende is a peine, And every peine is good to fle.

P11 Small **Pain** (*effort*) has little hire (*reward*)
c1515 Barclay *Eclogues* 185.113: Small payne hath little hire. Cf. Smith 228.

P12 To take a **Pain** for a pleasure
1546 Heywood *D* 27.51: Take a peyne for a pleasure all wyse men can. *Oxford* 639.

P13 As white as **Paindemaine** (*white bread*)
c1390 Chaucer *CT* VII 725[B1915]: Whit was his face as payndemayn.

P14 Not worth a **Paindemaine**

c1422 Hoccleve *Dialog* 123.383: Thy conceit is nat worth a payndemayn.

P15 To show a fair **Pair** of heels
1546 Heywood *D* 81.34: But except hir maide shewe a fayre paire of heeles. Apperson 568; *Oxford* 586; Taylor and Whiting 274; Tilley P31.

P16 As wise as **Pallas**
c1390 Chaucer *CT* VI[C] 49: Though she were wis as Pallas.

P17 To win the **Palm**
c1000 Aelfric *Homilies* II 402[10]: Se palm is sige-beacen. **a1439** Lydgate *Fall* II 345.589: Thus Glad Povert hath the palme Iwonne, 350.796: Wan the palme off many gret victorie. Cf. Taylor and Whiting 275.

P18 **Palmers** (pilgrims) are liars (*varied*)
a1375 *Octavian* (S) 43.1365–8: Of other palmers he gan frayne Lesynges quaynte, As ech man behouyd, that ys yn payne, Hys tale paynte. **a1376** *Piers* A Prol. 46–9: Pilgrimes and palmers . . . Wenten forth in heore way with mony wyse tales, And hedden leve to lyghen al heore lyf aftir. **c1380** Chaucer *HF* 2121–4: And, Lord, this hous in alle tymes, Was ful of shipmen and pilgrimes, With scrippes bret-ful of lesinges, Entremedled with tydynges. **a1387** Higden-Trevisa I 225[18–9]: That piler pilgrims and palmers, that faste con lighe, clepeth it seint Petris corn hepe, 227[9]: Pilgryms ful of lesynges. **1509** Barclay *Ship* II 68[6–16]: Also I fynde that there thre sortes be Of people lyvynge, whiche may themselfe defende In lesynge, for they have auctoryte to lye, The first is pylgrymes that hath great wonders sene In strange countres, suche may say what they wyll Before tho men that hath nat also ben In those same places, and hath of them no skyll. The seconde ar men aged suche may bost theyr fyll Without repugnaunce. And men of hye degre Before theyr servauntis may playne say what they wyll, Yet ar they nought but folys if they lye. **c1545** Heywood *Four PP* A3[r–v]: For ye (*a Palmer*) may lye by aucthoryte, And all that hath wandred so farre That no man can be theyr controller. *Oxford* 668–9. See **J27, R185, S251.**

P19 As black as any (a) **Pan**
a1425 *Ipomadon B* 300.1647: An helme, as blak as any panne. **a1500** *How the Plowman Learned his Paternoster* in Hazlitt *EPP* I 214.130: Another black as a pan. **c1515** Barclay *Eclogues* 7.238: My head . . . blacke as any pan.

P20 Not count a **Pannier** full of herbs
c1395 Chaucer *CT* IV[E] 1568–9: I counte nat a panyer ful of herbes Of scole-termes.

P21 As thick as **Pap**
a1475 *Crafte of Lymnynge Bokys* in *Early English Miscellanies* (Warton Club, 1855) 87[15]: Temper hem with pysse thyk as pappe. Apperson 624: porridge.

P22 No **Pap** like mother's to nourish
a1500 *Partenay* 140.4041–2: To norish no pappe like moders never-mo, As beforn is said, ho many it purchas.

P23 As thin as **Paper**
a1399 *Forme of Cury* 73[12–3]: As thynne as Paper. Whiting *NC* 454.

P24 **Paper-white**
c1386 Chaucer *LGW* 1198: Upon a thikke palfrey, paper-whit. Taylor and Whiting 275.

P25 To play a **Parcel**
c1412 Hoccleve *Regement* 110.3055: In lordes courtes thou pleyest thi parcel. **c1443** Pecock *Reule* 267[25–6]: But certis if he wolde pleie this parcel withoute hope to have the faukun, thanne dide he undiscretely. NED Parcel 1f.

P26 **Parchment-dry**
1534 Heywood *Love* D1[v][20]: Parched perchment drye.

P27 To kiss the **Pardon-bowl** for the drink's sake
c1545 Heywood *Four PP* C2[v][12–3]: Suche is the payne that ye palmers take To kysse the pardon bowle for the drynke sake. See **C218, L37.**

P28 Not to part with the **Paring** of one's nails
1546 Heywood *D* 49.273: She will not part with the paryng of hir nayles. Apperson 483; *Oxford* 487; Tilley P52.

P29 Not to purpose (give) the **Paring** of a pear
c1405 *Mum* 42.522: This is not to pourpoos the pare of oon pere. **1532** More *Frith* in *Workes* 844 A[10–2]: I would not geve the paryng of a pere for his prayer. **1556** Heywood *Spider* 252[10]: Geve . . . not paring of a Pere.

P30 From hence to **Paris** (gates)
c1400 *Femina* 63[2]: Thanne alle the moulez fram henne to parys. **a1500** Medwall *Nature* C2[r][32–3]: I am spokyn of more than they all Hens to parys gatys. Tilley H429.

P31 The **Parish Priest** forgets that he was ever clerk (*varied*)
1533 Heywood *Johan* B3[v][41–2]: The olde pro-

verbe is treu, The parysshe preest forgetteth that ever he was clarke, **1546** *D* 48.224–5: For the paryshe priest forgetteth That ever he hath bene holy water clarke, **1555** *E* 153.48: The paryshe priest forgeth, he was paryshe clarke: And the person forgeth, he was parishe pryste. Apperson 512; *Oxford* 487; Tilley P56.

P32 As trim as a **Parrot**
1533 Heywood *Weather* C4v[23]: Then wolde we get (*jet*) the stretes trym as a parate.

P33 Speak **Parrot**
c1522 Skelton *Speke, Parrot* II 1–25. **1534** Heywood *Love* E1r[24]: Speke parot, I pray ye. Tilley P60.

P34 As tender as a **Parson's** leman
1546 Heywood *D* 38.99: It is as tender as a parsons lemman, **1555** *E* 189.238. Apperson 622; *Oxford* 647; Tilley P68.

P35 The big **Part** of her body is her bum
1546 Heywood *D* 36.36: And the bygge parte of hir bodie is hir bumme. Tilley P73.

P36 He that has lost **Part** oft by wrath loses all
1509 Barclay *Ship* I 184[14]: For he that part hath lost: by wrath oft lesyth all.

P37 To eat one's **Part** on Good Friday and fast never the worse
1546 Heywood *D* 46.163–4: He maie his parte on good fridaie eate, And fast never the wurs, for ought he shall geate. Apperson 258; *Oxford* 166; Tilley P75.

P38 To take one's **Part** as it comes
c1400 *Beryn* 37.1152: Take yeur part as it comyth, of roughe and eke of smoth. See **R220.**

P39 Praise at the **Parting**
a1450 *Gesta* 39[20]: Preyse at the parting. **a1460** *Towneley Plays* 108.267: Now prays at the partyng, 385.584: No, bot prase at the partyng, Ffor now mon ye fynde it. **c1475** *Rauf* 85.86. **c1497** Medwall *Fulgens* A4v[33]: And prayse at the parting evyn as ye fynde. **1520** Whittinton *Vulgaria* 100.22–3: He shall have no cause to prayse to his frendes at the partynge. Apperson 509; *Oxford* 515; Tilley P83; Whiting *Ballad* 24. See **B210, E81, 85, 158, H363, L254, P348, S715, T125.**

P40 As piping (*?wet and glossy*) as a **Partridge's** eye
c1475 Henryson *Fables* 74.2127: Pypand lyke ane Pertrik Ee.

P41 To flee as **Partridge** the falcon (sparhawk)
a1400 *Firumbras* 15.407: And made hem to fle on eche half as partrych the faucoun. **c1500** *Melusine* 175.4–5: His enemyes fled byfore hym as the partrych doth byfore the sperehauke.

P42 Judge not before the **Parties** are heard (*varied*)
1450 *Dicts* 134.9–10: Juge not without that the parties be herde. **a1471** Ashby *Policy* 36.758–64: Whan any man maketh suggestion Ayenst another for any grevance, Heerithe hym wele and make sad question How his tale may be had in assurance. But yeveth therto no trusty affiance, Until tyme that ye have herde the tother. Thaugh it seme sothe it may be founde other. **1481** Caxton *Reynard* 57[11]: Audi alteram partem. Here that other partye. **a1500** *Beves* 31 M 543–4: It fallid to geve no jugment, But bothe partyes were present. **1546** Heywood *D* 57.11: A man should here all partes, er he judge any, **1555** *E* 176.172: Here all parts, ere ye judge any, *Oxford* 286; Smith 161; Tilley M299, P87; Walther I 194.1708a. See **B268, J77, M412, T32.**

P43 The **Pass** of Alton
c1378 *Piers* B xiv 300–2: The sexte is a path of pees, ye, thorw the pas of Altoun Poverte myghte passe with-oute peril of robbynge, For there that poverte passeth pees folweth after. *Oxford* 488. See **M266.**

P44 **Pass-over** is an ease
c1395 Chaucer *CT* IV[E] 2115: Passe over is an ese, I sey namoore. **a1400** *Proverbis of Wysdom* 246.101: Passe over is an ese. **a1422** Lydgate *Life* 376.931, **a1449** *Fabula* in *MP* II 502.490. Apperson 608: Sufferance; *Oxford* 629. See **S859.**

P45 Too late to revoke what is **Past** (*varied*)
c1450 *Epistle of Othea* 81.7: Who revoketh that is past, to late calleth he. **c1450** Idley 130.1342: Ffor it is harde to calle ayen thyng that is paste. **1513** More *Richard* 39 F[3–4]: Thynges passed cannot be gaine called. **1523** Berners *Froissart* III 217[30–1]: That is past can nat be recovered. **1529** More *Supplicacion* 337 D[15–6]: That is passed and can not bee called agayn. **1546** Heywood *D* 37.82: But thinges past my hands, I can not call agein. *Oxford* 488; Tilley T203. See **D287, T198.**

P46 A little **Pasture** suffices a great bull
1474 Caxton *Chesse* 130[30–2]: Ye see comunly that a grete bole is suffisid wyth right a lityll pasture, And that a wood suffiseth to many olefauntes.

P47 It is evil **Patching** of that (which) is torn
c1516 Skelton *Magnificence* 15.447: It is evyll patchynge of that is torne.

P48 As sooth (true) as (the) **Paternoster**
1340 *Ayenbite* 71[24–5]: And thet is zoth ase paternoster, 77[22–3], 90[9]. **c1400** *Vices and Virtues* 69.17–8: And this is as soth as the pater noster, 76.1–2, 88.22. **c1450** *Alphabet* II 505.18–9: Als trew as the pater noster. **1484** Caxton *Royal Book* G2^{r}[15]: Trewe as the pater noster, G5^{v}[7], H4^{v}[7]. See **B281, C541, G399.**

P49 He may be in my **Paternoster,** but he shall never come in my creed
1546 Heywood *D* 96.195–6: He maie be in my Pater noster in deede, But be sure, he shall never come in my Creede, **1555** *E* 165.118. Apperson 485; *Oxford* 489; Tilley P96.

P50 A **Paternoster** while (*varied*)
c1300 *Guy*[1] 314 A 5826–7: In lasse while he hadde (him) y-slawe, Then men schold sigge a pater-noster. **a1376** *Piers* A v 192: He pissede a potel in a *pater-noster*-while. **c1425** Arderne *Fistula* 91.23–5: And late it stande stille without movyng by the space of a "pater noster" and "ave maria." **1448** Paston II 89[20]: And all thys was don, as men sey, in a Pater Noster wyle. **c1450** *Sche that Y love* in *Medium Ævum* 30(1961) 170[4]: Sche myght not be out of my thought a paternoster while. **1465** Leversege 27[12–3]: Within the seying of a paternoster. **1481** Caxton *Reynard* 85[10]: Er one myght saye his pater noster. **c1493** *Saint Katherin of Senis* 376.26: Made hyr rede in that book, as long tyme as a pater noster may be. **1528** More *Heresyes* 128 D[13–4]: In a Pater noster while, 132 C[14–5]. **1534** Heywood *Love* C3^{v}[28]: Then to say nay one Pater noster whyle. Apperson 485; Tilley P99; Whiting *Scots* II 108. See **C540.**

P51 All right **Paths** go one way
1492 *Salomon and Marcolphus* 12[24]: All reyght pathys goon to wardes oon weye.

P52 More than one **Path** leads to Rome (*varied*)
c1385 Chaucer *TC* ii 36–7: For every wight which that to Rome went Halt nat o path, or alwey o manere, **1391** *Astr.* Prol. 39–40: Right as diverse pathes leden diverse folk the righte way to Rome. Apperson 537; *Oxford* 545. See **W112.**

P53 Let **Patience** (*dock*) (and thyme) grow in your garden (*varied*)
1480 *Stonor Letters* II 99[2–6]: On thyng at is tolde me, that ye do make a fayre newe Garden; in the wiche I pray you for my sake to sette too herbis, the wiche ben, Paciens, Tyme: And that theis to herbis be put in the potage that ye ete, so ye may ete them dayly. **a1500** *Lay of Sorrow* 717.51–2: And forthir, In my garding quhare I sewe All peiciens, now fynd I nocht bot rewe. **1549** Heywood *D* 53.411: Let pacience growe in your gardein alwaie. Apperson 485; *Oxford* 489; Tilley P116, R198.

P54 **Patience** is a noble point, though it displease oft
c1380 *Patience* 13.1: Pacience is a poynt, thagh hit displese ofte, 32.531: That pacience is a nobel poynt, thagh hit displese ofte.

P55 **Patience** is a plaster (*varied*)
a1387 *Piers* C xx 89: And yut be plastred with pacience. **a1393** Gower *CA* II 242.613–5: If thou miht gete pacience, Which is the leche of alle offence, As tellen ous these olde wise. **a1500** *Att my begynning* in *Rawlinson MS. C 813* 323.31–2: Yff thou have troble or vexation, Take paciens to be thy phisition. **a1500** *MS. Marginalia* in Hoccleve I 224 n.[6]: A sufficyent salve for eache disease, The cheff revenge for cruell yre, Ys patyence, the present ease For to delaye eche flamy fyre. Apperson 485; *Oxford* 489; Tilley P107.

P56 **Patience** is a virtue
a1396(1494) Hilton *Scale* P8^{v}[15]: Yet this man hath the vertuw of pacyence. **a1400** *Cato* (*Copenhagen*) A4^{v}[23–4]: For pacience of grete vertu is Amonge alle thewis that been of pris. **a1425** *Contemplations* in *Yorkshire Writers* II 100[5]: The vertue of pacyence. **c1450** *Cato* (*Sidney*) 18.207–8: Pacience gretumli vertew is Among alle thewis, that ben of pris. **c1450** *Speculum Christiani* (2) 200.14–5: Gregorius: I trowe the vertu of pacyence be more than sygnes or myracles. **1483** Caxton *Cato* E1^{v}[23–4]: Pacyence is the grettest vertue of alle vertues. Apperson 485–6; *Oxford* 489; Smith 4; Taylor and Whiting 276–7; Tilley P109; Whiting *Scots* II 108. See **S861.**

P57 **Patience** is ?above all things
c1450 *Rules for Conduct* in Smith *Commonplace Book* 14[16]: For a-bethe all thyng ys nownyd pasyens.

P58 **Patience** is most of might (*varied*)
c900 *Old English Cato* 4.22: Geðyld byð mihtene mæst. **c1025** *Durham Proverbs* 10.1: Geþyld byð middes ea(des). Portio beatitudinis. **1450** *Dicts* 266.22: Pacience is a castelle inprenable. **1477** Rivers *Dictes* 53[1–2]: Pacience is a stronge castell.

P59 **Patience** makes a man peaceable
1490 Irlande *Meroure* 56.26–7: For it that makis maist a man peciabile is paciens, for a werray pacient man sustenis all thingis.

P60 **Patience** perforce
1504 W. Cornish *Tretyse* in *Archiv* 120(1908) 424.91: Pacyence perforce, content yew with wronge, 425.133. Apperson 486; *Oxford* 489; Tilley P111; Whiting *Drama* 190, *Scots* II 108.

P61 **Patience** vanquishes (overcomes, conquers) (*varied*)
c1378 *Piers* B xiv 52: For—*pacientes vincunt*. **c1385** Usk 89.58–9: Pacience in his soule overcometh and is nat overcomen. **a1393** Gower *CA* II 242.616–9: For whan noght elles mai suffise Be strengthe ne be mannes wit, Than pacience it oversit And overcomth it ate laste. **c1395** Chaucer *CT* V[F] 773–5: Pacience is an heigh vertu, certeyn, For it venquysseth, as thise clerkes seyn, Thynges that rigour sholde nevere atteyne. **a1425** Chauliac 26.33–4: For pacience overcometh malice, as it is seide in a-nother scripture. **a1439** Lydgate *Fall* I 38.1366–8: She (*Patience*) may be troublid, but overcome nevere; But for a tyme she may suffer werre, But atte ende she venquisshith evere. **1450** *Dicts* 80.10–1: Pacience and good bileeve in God makith a man to conquere. **1474** Caxton *Chesse* 144[19]: Pacience is a ryght noble maner to vaynquysshe, **1483** *Cato* E2[r][6]: Pacyence vaynquyssheth alle. **1506** Hawes *Pastime* 176.4702–3: For evermore the spyryte of pacyence Doth overcome the angry vyolence. Apperson 485; *Oxford* 490; Skeat 197; Walther III 730.20833f; Whiting *Drama* 190, *Scots* II 108. See **S865, T213.**

P62 As idle as **Paul's** knights
a1387 Higden-Trevisa I 349[19–20]: And woned by the see sides by assent of Irische men that were alwey idel as Poules knyghtes (Latin: De consensu Hiberniensium otio deditorum maritima loca occupantes, etc.).

P63 To wear **Paul's** steeple for a Turkey hat
1556 Heywood *Spider* 78[22–5]: For woulde I never so willingly will, To weare powles steeple for a turkey hat, Yet sins I might in deede, eate a hors mill, As soone as have powre, so to pranke with that.

P64 Good **Payment** is sometimes good confession
1474 Caxton *Chesse* 116[12–3]: For good payement is sometyme good confession. Cf. Chaucer *CT* I[A] 225–32.

P65 Better hold one's **Peace** than show one's nicety (*folly*)
c1380 Chaucer *PF* 571–2: Yit were it bet for the Han holde thy pes than shewed thy nycete.

P66 He that cannot hold his **Peace** is free to flite (*scold*)
1513 Douglas *Aeneid* II 107.20: Quha kan not hald thar peice ar fre to flyte. See **W258.**

P67 **Peace** is better than war (*varied*)
c1440 Lydgate *Debate* in *MP* II 556.399: Alwey consideryng that pees is bet than werre. **c1450** *Merlin* II 640[35–6]: Full good is it to have pees after the werre. **a1470** Malory III 1128.16–7: And bettir ys pees than evermore warre, 1212. 25–6: For better ys pees than allwayes warre. **a1475** *Seege of Troye* 201 H 1574[ab]: And, sir, better is in pees and rest to wende, Thanne leve in werre with-outyn end. **1556** Heywood *Spider* 346[24–5]: The worst peace: (as wise wightes sey:) Is better then is the best war. Tilley P153, 154. See **S69, W37.**

P68 **Peace** makes plenty (*varied*)
c1378 *Piers* B xiv 302: For there that poverte passeth pees folweth after. **a1425** *Trinity Coll. MS.602* in M. R. James *Catalogue* (Cambridge, 1901) II 95: Pees maketh plente, Plente makith pride, Pride makith plee, Plee makith povert, Povert makith pees. **1436** *Libelle* 55.1091: And power (*var.* poverte) causeth pease finall verily. **c1440** Lydgate *Debate* in *MP* II 558.456–65: Gyn first at pees which causith most richesse, And riches is the originall of pride, Pride causith, for lak of rihtwissnesse, Werre between rewmys, look, on every side, Hertis contrayre in pees can nat a-bide: Thus, fynally (whoo can considre and see,) Werre is cheff ground and cause of poverte. Povert bi werr brouht to disencrece, For lak of tresour than he can no more, Sauff only this he crieth aftir pees. Apperson 487–8; Brotanek 16–33; Brown-Robbins 2742; *Oxford* 492; Tilley P139. Cf. Whiting *Drama* 133. See **P394, T136, W42.**

P69 Such **Peace** that one could walk the land unmolested (*varied*)
a900 Bede 144.21–4: Is þæt sægd, ðæt in ða tid swa micel sib wære in Breotone æghwyder ymb, swa Eadwines rice wære, þeah þe a wiif wolde mid hire nicendum cilde, heo meahte gegan buton ælcere sceðenisse from sæ to sæ ofer eall þis ealond. **1087** *Peterborough Chronicle* I 220[12–5]: Betwyx oðrum þingum nis na to forgytane þæt gode frið þe he (*William I*) macode on þisan lande, swa þæt an man þe him sylf aht wære, mihte faran ofer his rice mid his bosum full goldes ungederad, **1135** I 263[10–2]: Pais he (*Henry I*) makede men and

dær. Wua sua bare his byrthen gold and sylvre, durste nan man sei to him naht bute god. **a1200** Lawman I 106.2512–3: Alch mon mihte faren yend hire lond, Thaih he bere raed gold, II 351–2.18486–9: He (*Uther*) sette grith, he sette frith, That aelc mon mihte faren with From londe to londe Theh he bere gold an ho(n)de, 485.21637–42: He (*Cador*) sette grit swithe god, That ther after longe stod, Theh aelc mon beere an honde Behghes (B: beghes) of golde, Ne durste navere gume nan Otherne ufele igreten. **c1300** *Guy*[1] 10.137–42: Thei a man bar an hundred pounde, Opon him, of gold y-grounde, The(r) nas man in al this londe That durst him do shame no schonde, That bireft him worth of a slo, So gode pais ther was tho. **c1300** *Havelok* 2–3.45–50: In that time a man that bore (Wel fifty pund, y wot, or more,) Of rede gold up-on his bac, In a male hwit or blac, Ne funde he non that him misseyde, N(e) hond on (him) with ivele leyde. **c1300** Robert of Gloucester II 554.7693–7: Thoru out al engelond he (*William I*) huld wel god pes Vor me mighte bere bi is daye and lede hardeliche Tresour aboute and other god over al aperteliche In wodes and in other studes so that no time nas Thet pes bet isusteined than bi his time was. **c1400** Mandeville *Travels* 131.4–7: This kyng (*the Cane of Cathay*) is so rightfull and of equytee in his doomes that men may go sykerlych thorghout all his contree and bere with him what him list, that noman schall ben hardy to robben him. **a1415** Mirk *Festial* 39.2–6: But yn a schort tyme, Thomas (*à Becket*) . . . made suche rest and pees throgh all the lond, that a man myght goo wher he wold unrobbet, wyth his good yn hys hond. **a1475** *Guy*[2] 4.103–6: He made pees, as he wolde: Yf a man were chargyd wyth golde, He schulde fynde no robber hym to reeve, That wolde take oght agenste hys leeve. **a1500** *Guy*[4] 14.117–22: All Englande, both towne and towre, That tyme he kept with such honour: For, had a man that eche stounde On him borne an hundered pounde, He should not have found no robbour To have robbed him of that treasour. Cf. C. W. Ceram (Kurt Marek) *Gods, Graves and Scholars* (New York, 1951) 271 (of Assurbanipal [668–626 B.C.] of Nineveh).

P70 Where **Peace** reigns no wight wot what war is
c1378 *Piers* B xviii 226: Wote no wighte what werre is there that pees regneth.

P71 As crank (*proud*) as a **Peacock**
a1500 Medwall *Nature* H1[r][21–2]: Here cometh Pryde, As crank as a pecok. Tilley P157.

P72 As fresh as **Peacock** feather
a1513 Dunbar *Of the Changes of Lyfe* 141.7–8: The seasoun, soft and fair, Com in als fresche as pako fedder.

P73 As orgulous (*proud*) as a **Peacock**
1480 Caxton *Ovyde* 131[10–1]: More orguyllous than a pecock whan he is preysed for hys fair taylle.

P74 The **Peacock** has fair feathers and foul feet (*varied*)
a1398(1495) Bartholomaeus-Trevisa B7[v][2.11–5]: And he (*the peacock*) wondryth of the fayrnes of his fethers . . . And thenne he lokyth to his fete and seeth the fowlenesse of his fete. **a1450** *Three Middle English Sermons* 63.432–6: We se wel, that the pekok whan a loketh abowte on his fair vetherus, his undirliche prowd and miche joie makis of hem, but whan a lokez doun and seith the vowlne(s) of feet, than a take gret sorw to him and wext hegeliche a-schamed of him-silf. **1471** Caxton *Recuyell* I 19.2–5: He was lyke unto the pecok that is proud of the fayr fethers diversly fair colourd wiche he spreded roound as a whele, and wyth all only loke of hys feet he leseth all his joye. **1532** More *Confutacion* 359 A[6–10]: Be not so ledde . . . with the beholdinge of a pecockes tayle but that ye regarde therwith hys fowle feete also. Apperson 488; *Oxford* 492; Tilley P158. See **F478.**

P75 To shine like the **Peacock**
a1513 Dunbar *Merle* 134.14: Quhois angell fedderis as the pacok schone.

P76 To stalk like a **Peacock**
a1393 Gower *CA* III 126.6498: He stalketh as a Pocok doth.

P77 As round as a **Pear**
a1400 *Destruction of Troy* 100.3080: With two propur pappes, as a peire rounde.

P78 Not appair (*impair*) a **Pear**
c1405 *Mum* 3.73: It shulde not apeire hem a peere.

P79 Not (a)vail a **Pear**
a1400 *Rowlande* 80.815: His armours ne vaylede noghte a pere. **c1412** Hoccleve *Regement* 5.103: That hys eres avayle hym nat a pere. **1504** Hawes *Example* Dd4[v][7]: Nor fortune without me avayleth not hym a pere.

P80 Not charge a **Pear**

a1400 *Susan* 276.246–7: And sythen to deth me be diht, I charge hit not a pere.

P81 Not count a **Pear**
c1420 Wyntoun III 60.773: Na I compt nocht na hurt a peire. **c1440** *Degrevant* 110.1712: We cownt tham noght at a pere. **c1450** Capgrave *Katharine* 133.907: And ye no man counte the valu of a pere. Whiting *Scots* II 109.

P82 Not dere (*harm*) a **Pear**
c1400 *Florence* 23.656–7: So tyte of lyvys were they done That all deryd not a pere. **c1400** *Laud Troy* I 57.1926–8: For thei may not a-geyns us dure . . . Nought the value of a pere.

P83 Not prize a **Pear**
c1420 Wyntoun III 61.769: Na I prysse na payne a pere.

P84 Not the worse by a **Pear**
c1440 *Degrevant* 24.363–4: Ffande he never ane slayne, Ne the worse by a pere.

P85 Not worth a **Pear**
a1300 *Alisaunder* 324 M 385: He ne hyld hit worth apere. **c1303** Mannyng *Handlyng* 28.769: For every gadlyng nat wurth a pere. **a1352** Minot 1.16: And al thaire pomp noght worth a pere. **c1380** *Ferumbras* 177.5721–2: Of thyne ne schalt thow lese noght The worthy of a pere. **c1412** Hoccleve *Regement* 84.2317. **c1450** Idley 120.762. **a1470** Malory II 934.11–2. **a1475** *Assembly of Gods* 18.596–7. Apperson 457–8; Tilley P161; Whiting *Scots* II 109.

P86 **Pears** without wine are venom
a1398(1495) Bartholomaeus-Trevisa S5v[1.8–10]: For as one sayth: Wythout wyne perys ben venym. Apperson 488; Tilley P159. See **A160, F691.**

P87 As precious as **Pearl**
a1349 Rolle *Meditatio* 43.10–1: Make me . . . precious as perle.

P88 As white as **Pearl**
1560 Heywood *E* 209.23.2: Thy here whyte as perle.

P89 Cast not **Pearls** before swine (*varied*)
c1000 *WSG* Matthew vii 6: Ne ge ne wurpen eowre meregrotu toforan eowrum swynon. **c1200** Orm I 256.7402–7: Heroffe seggth the Goddspellboc Thatt Crist himm sellf thuss seggde; Ne birrth the nohht nan halig thing Biforenn hundes werrpenn, Ne nohht ne birrth the to the swin Werrpenn marrgrotestaness. **a1225** *Lambeth Homilies* 135[8–10]: *Nolite spargere Margaritas ante porcos* . . . Ne sculen ge nawiht gimstones leggen swinen to mete. **1340** *Ayenbite* 152[35–6]: Huerof zayth ous god ine his spelle. Thet we ne thrauwe oure preciouse stones to-vore the zuyn. **a1376** *Piers* A xi 9–12: And seide, *noli mittere* margeriperles Among hogges that han hawes at heore wille; Thei don bot dravele theron, drof weore hem levere Then al the presciouse peerles that in paradys waxen. **c1395** *WBible* Isaiah Prol. III 224[14–5]: Lest hoeli (*thingis*) to dogges, and margarites to swyn thei yeeve, Matthew vii 6: Nethir caste ye youre margaritis bifore swyne. **a1400** Wyclif *Sermons* II 330[5–7]: And herfore biddith Crist in Matheu, that his disciplis gyve not holy thingis to houndis, ne scatere margarites amongis hogges. **c1400** *Speculum de Antichristo* in Wyclif *EW* 110[10–1]: And putten precious perlis to hoggis. **c1400** *Vices and Virtues* 151.33–5: Wher-for God seith to us in the gospel that we caste not oure riche and precious stones to-fore the swyn. **1402** *Daw Topias* 110[8–9]: And the presciouse perlis Ye strowun to hogges. **a1410** Lydgate *Churl* in *MP* II 479.253–6: Men shuld nat put a precious margarite As rubies, saphires or othir stonys ynde, Emeroudes, nor othir perlis whihte To fore rude swyn, that love draff of kynde. **c1445** Pecock *Donet* 160.5–6: Neithir caste ye youre margaritis bifore swyn. **c1450** *Epistle of Othea* 143.21–2: Perles among pesen is foly to strowe Before swyn and other bestes unresonable. **c1475** Henryson *Fables* 8.145–7: His hart wammillis wyse argument to heir, As dois ane Sow, to quhome men for the nanis, In hir draf troich wald saw precious stanis. **1484** Caxton *Royal Book* M7v[29–30]: Herof sayth God in the gospel, that we shold not caste the precyous stones tofore hogges. **1506** Hawes *Pastime* 41.925–6: But what avayleth evermore to sowe The precyous stones amonge gruntynge hogges. **1509** Barclay *Ship* II 257[19–20]: Cast precious stones or golde amonges swyne, And they had lever have dreggis, fylth or chaffe. **1546** Heywood *D* 93.101: But you to cast precious stones before hogs, **1555** *E* 159.86: Folly to cast. Apperson 488; *Oxford* 493; Taylor and Whiting 278; Tilley P165; Whiting *Drama* 357:760, *Scots* II 109.

P90 Not worth a **Pearl**
a1400 *Alexander C* 233.4330: Ne nevire toplight worth a perle to-ponyscht be-fore.

P91 A **Pearl** by the white pease is more of price
c1390 *Sir Gawain* 73.2364–5: As perle bi the

quite pese is of prys more, So is Gawayn . . . bi other gay knyghtes.

P92 White **Pearls** are oft found in black shells
a1449 Lydgate *Fabules* in *MP* II 567.26–7: Perlys whyte, clere and orientall Ben oft founde in muscle shellys blake. See **H3.**

P93 Not give two **Peascods**
a1475 *Assembly of Gods* 15.493–4: Yef hit shuld I wold nat yeve II pesecoddys.

P94 As full as **Pease**
c1475 Henryson *Fables* 101.2946 (*var.*): Now full as pease (*vars.* fitche, fysche).

P95 The greatness of a **Pease**
a1500 *Eger H* 239.947–8: Betwixt her een and eke her niese, There is the greatness of a piese.

P96 Not care a **Pease**
1506 Barclay *Castell* A5r[17]: I trowe she cared not a pease.

P97 (Not) count at a **Pease**
a1376 *Piers* A vii 155: And countede Pers at a peose. **1445** Claudian *Stilicho* 255.12: Othir rest is veyne, not cowntid at oo pease. Whiting *Scots* II 109.

P98 Not give a **Pease**
a1300 *Proprietates Mortis* in Brown *Lyrics XIII* 130.22: Off al this world ne gyffe ihic a pese. **c1380** *Ferumbras* 181.5847–8: Y nolde gyve a pyse, For cryst. **a1400** *Death* in *Rel. Ant.* I 65[12–3]: And of al this wordles b(l)isse Ne wold y geve a pese i-wis.

P99 Not set a **Pease**
a1387 *Piers* C x 345: I sette by pardon nat a peese. **c1440** Charles of Orleans 119.3556: By my liif y sette not here a pese. Apperson 457:26.

P100 Not the charge (*weight*) of a **Pease** (*etc.*) (A number of single quotations are brought together here)
a1400 *Alexander C* 13.403: Thare sall na chanche the chefe the charge of a pese, 136.2370: Loke quare it profet tham a peese all thaire proud strenth. **a1400** *Child* 319.371–2: Helpeth me not to the uttermost day The valure of a pese. **1402** *Daw Topias* 46[23–4]: Thi lewid prophecie I preise not at a peese. **c1450** G. R. Owst "A 15th Century Manuscript in St. Albans Abbey," *St. Albans and Hertfordshire Architectural and Archaeological Society: Transactions* (1924) 57[22]: Thei chargen not a pese, but laughen, and japen.

P101 Not worth a (half a) **Pease**
a1300 *Alisaunder* 311.5949: A pese nys worth thi riche sclaunder. **c1325** *Body and Soul* in Böddeker 243.241–2: Al this worldes blisse Nis nout worth a peose. **1374** Brinton *Sermons* I 156[10]: Al this werdlis blisse is nought worth a pese, II 337[26–7]. **c1390** *Who Says the Sooth* in Brown *Lyrics XIV* 152.3: His purpos I counte not worth a pese. **a1400** *Cambridge Univ. Lib. MS. Ii.iii.8* in Owst *Literature* 43[22]: Alle the worldis blisse ys nouth worthe a pese. **c1400** *Femina* 79[22]. **c1400** *Laud Troy* I 170.5769: His viser vayled not worth a pese. **c1400** *Plowman's Tale* 184.1163. **c1450** Greene *Carols* 405.5: Thou art not worght half a pese. **c1454** Pecock *Folewer* 115.13. **1556** Heywood *Spider* 101[25]: No dyffrence in othe, the woorth of a pease. Apperson 457:26; Tilley P135.

P102 The smaller **Peasen** the more to the pot, *etc.*
c1450 *Douce MS.52* 53.99: The smaller pesun, the more to pott; The fayrer woman, the more gylott. **c1450** *Rylands MS.394* 103.24–5. **c1470** *Harley MS.3362* f.7b: The smellere pesyn the mo to the pot, The fayrere womman the more gygelot or strumpet. **a1500** *Sloane MS.1210* in *Rel. Ant.* II 40: Tho smallere pese tho mo to the pott; The fayrere woman tho more gyglott. Quo graciles pisae plures offendimus ollae; Quo mage formosa mulier mage luxuriosa. Apperson 487; *Oxford* 493; Tilley P137.

P103 Who has many **Pease** may put the more in the pot
1546 Heywood *D* 26.15: Who hath many pease maie put the mo in the pot. Apperson 487; *Oxford* 493; Tilley P138.

P104 As much pity as a **Pedlar** has of cats
c1378 *Piers* B v 258–9: I have as moche pite of pore men as pedlere hath of cattes, That wolde kille hem, yf he cacche hem myghte, for coveitise of here skynnes. Skeat 108.

P105 The wretch (*poor*) **Pedlar** makes more noise to yeie (*call*) his soap than a rich mercer all his dearworth ware
a1200 *Ancrene* 36.25–7: The wrecche poure peoddere mare nurth he maketh to yeien is sape, then the riche mercer al his deorewurthe ware, 79.27–8: A Sapere the ne bereth bute sape and nelden yeiyeth hehe thet he bereth. A riche mercer geath forth al stille, **a1400** (*Recluse*) 69.25–7.

P106 Even **Peer** has no power into (*over*) his even peer
c1456 Pecock *Faith* 247[9–12]: But so it is that even peer hath not power into his even peer,

aftir the comoun wel allowid proverbe, neither the lasse worthi hath power over his worthier, cf. 279–80.

P107 Play (Jape, Bourd) with your **Peers**
a1300 *Richard* 97.357: With thy peres go and playe, 107.575: And pleye with hem that is thy pere. **c1450** *Foly of Fulys* 58.223–4: Thai hald evir faloschip with thar feris And plays thaim nocht bot with thar peris. **c1450** Idley 82.85: If thow shalt borde, Jape with thy peere. **a1500** *Poem on . . . Masonry* in James O. Halliwell *Early History of Freemasonry in England* (London, 1840) 38.769: Play thou not but with thy peres. **a1500** *Sone, y schal thee schewe* in Furnivall *Babees Book* 34.13: And whanne thou schalt boorde, bourde with thi peere. *Oxford* 506; Tilley P180; Whiting *Scots* II 109.

P108 As pale as a **Pellet**
a1376 *Piers* A v 61: As pale as a pelet. Svartengren 235.

P109 As swift as **Pellet** out of gun
c1380 Chaucer *HF* 1643–4: As swifte as pelet out of gonne, Whan fyr is in the poudre ronne. Svartengren 376.

P110 As proud as **Penniless**
a1460 *Towneley Plays* 374.236: As prowde as pennyles, his slefe has no poket. See **M267.**

P111 As like as any **Penny** is to another
a1300 *Alisaunder* 417.7686–7: It is thee als liche, my leve brother, Als any peny is another. **a1300** *Arthour and M.*[1] 183.6505–6: This Guenour was the other so liche, So pani is other, sikerliche. Cf. Taylor and Whiting 277: pea.

P112 As round as a **Penny**
a1450 *Agnus* 130.16: Rounde as a peny.

P113 Blessed be the **Penny** that brings home (saves) two
c1450 *Douce MS.52* 45.13: Blessyd be the peny, that bryngyth too home. **c1450** *Rylands MS.394* 96.6ᵛ.12. **a1500** Henley (Englished) 53[5–6]: For the wiseman seith, blessed be the i d. that savithe twayne (for the French see 24[29–30]). See **P123, 125.**

P114 He has laid down one **Penny** by mine
1546 Heywood *D* 50.318: He hath laied downe one peny by myne. Tilley P197.

P115 He has not one **Penny** to bless him
1546 Heywood *D* 90.62: He had not now one peny to blisse him. Apperson 123: cross; *Oxford* 119–20; Tilley C836. See **P450.**

P116 No **Penny** no paternoster
1546 Heywood *D* 96.199: No peny no Pater noster. Apperson 450; *Oxford* 458; Tilley P199.

P117 No **Penny** no ware, no cattle no care
a1400 *Gonville and Caius College Cambridge MS.261* f.234r in M. R. James *Catalogue* (Cambridge, 1907) I 317: Non peni, non ware; non catel, non care, Go, peni go.

P118 Not give a **Penny** (*etc.*) (A number of single quotations are brought together here)
1400 R. W. Chambers and M. Daunt *Book of London English, 1384–1425* (Oxford, 1931) 282[17–8]: Kyng herry yaf nowt of hem alle a peny. **c1400** *Alexander Buik* I 62.1945: He pryssit him nocht worth ane penny, III 308.6937: Thay pryse yow nocht with ane penny. **1480** Caxton *Ovyde* 47[33–4]: I preyse not only the worth of a peny havour, **1485** *Charles* 104.23–4: I shall not doubte ony paynym the valewe of a peny. **a1533** Berners *Arthur* 256[33–4]: I wyll not have therof the mountenaunce of a peny, *Huon* 411.16–7: (They) coude not hurte it of the value of a peny.

P119 Not to win one the **Penny**
c1382 Wyclif *De Pontificum* in *SEW* III 254[12]: But wel I woot that this bileve wynneth noght us the peny.

P120 Of two false **Pennies** the better may not be chosen
c1450 *Alphabet* I 200.7–8: Of ii fals penys the bettur may nott be chosyn. Cf. Tilley C358.

P121 **Pennies** make men free
a1338 Mannyng *Chronicle B* II 246[18]: Ther held thei long sojour, bot penies mad tham fre. (Perhaps quite literal.) *Oxford* 429–30; Whiting *Scots* II 109.

P122 A **Penny** for your thought
1522 More *Treatyce* 76 D[10–5]: It often happeth, that the very face sheweth the mind walking a pilgrimage, in such wise that not withoute som note and reproch of suche vagaraunte mind, other folk sodainly say to them: a peny for your thought. **1546** Heywood *D* 66.28: A peny for your thought. Apperson 489; *Oxford* 495; Taylor and Whiting 279; Tilley P203.

P123 The **Penny** is of rich mound (*value*) that saves the pound (*varied*)
a1300 *Alisaunder* 169.3023–4: The peny is of riche mounde that ysaveth the hole pounde. **c1400** *Beryn* 69.2243–4: Ffor there is a comyn byword, yf ye it herd havith; "Wele settith he his peny, that the pound (therby) savith." Ap-

person 490–1; Jente 682. Cf. *Oxford* 495: groat; Tilley P210. See **H344, P113.**

P124 **Penny** makes right of wrong
c1450 Greene *Carols* 392.1: Peny, of wrong he makyt ryght In every cuntre qwer he goo. See **M630.**

P125 A **Penny** spent by wise provision avails two
a1471 Ashby *Policy* 28.492–3: A peny spent bi wise provision Availith two in time seasonable. See **P113.**

P126 A **Penny** spent in season will save a pound
1457 Paston III 115[18]: For a peny yn seson spent wille safe a pounde.

P127 To think the **Penny** is mightier than God
c1340 Rolle *Psalter* 189 (51.7): He (that) thynkis the peny is myghtiere than god.

P128 Not appair (*harm*) a **Penny-brede** (*a space the breadth of a penny*)
c1350 *Alexander A* 169.1242: No myght apeire the place of a peny-brede. Cf. note p. 233.

P129 **Penny-man** is mickle in mind
a1450 *Castle* 156.2666: Peny-man is mekyl in mynde, 2671–4: Where-so I walke in londe or lede, Peny-man best may spede: He is a duke to don a dede Now in every place, 157.2678: In Penyman is al his trust. Cf. Robbins 50–5.

P130 Each **Pennyworth** of pleasure brings more than counterpoise of danger
1556 Heywood *Spider* 410[27–8]: Ech peniworth of pleasure: of such possest ware, Bringth more then counterpaise: of daunger and care. See **P265.**

P131 To give a **Pennyworth** for a penny
1475 Paston V 229[16–7]: Desyryng hym that he wyll geve yow a penyworthe for a peny. **a1500** Lady Anne Vernon in *An English Letter Book,* ed. Francis Bickley (London, 1925) 3[8–9]: And yef ye woll geve a penyworth for a peny ye shall have xx nobles at my commyng to London.

P132 If the **People** is poor the lord shall be unhappy (*unlucky*)
c1500 *Melusine* 112.19–20: For yf the peple is pouere the lord shal be unhappy.

P133 It is pain(ful) (hard) to please the **People**
c1400 Greene *Carols* 346.2: The peple to plese, ser, it is payn, Peraventure amonge twenti not twayn. **1449** Metham 3.54–5: For fulle herd yt ys, I knowe yt veryly, To plese the pepyl. See **M124.**

P134 The **People** are untrue (*varied*)
c1395 Chaucer *CT* IV[E] 995–1001: O stormy peple! unsad and evere untrewe! Ay undiscreet and chaungynge as a fane! Delitynge evere in rumbul that is newe, For lyk the moone ay wexe ye and wane! Ay ful of clappyng, deere ynough a jane! Youre doom is fals, youre constance yvele preeveth; A ful greet fool is he that on yow leeveth. **a1420** Lydgate *Troy* III 572.302–3: The trust of peple is feint and untrewe, Ay undiscrete and ful of doubilnes, *etc.* **c1450** Capgrave *Katharine* 267.180–1: Be this exaumple wyse men may weel leere To truste on the puple; for thei wil faile at nede. **1459** *Defence* 521[39–41]: Who so hathe rede in the olde storyes, he may be suffyciently informed of the grete varyablenes of the peple and of thyncertitude of thaire oppynions. **1495** Fitzjames *Sermo* D1[r][25–6]: Mobile vulgus, the Inconstaunt people. Cf. Tilley P225, 226. See **C392.**

P135 Such **People** such priest
a900 Alfred *Gregory* 133.6: Suelc ðæt folc bið, suelc bið se sacerd. **c1395** *WBible* Hosea iv 9: As the puple so the prest. **c1415** *Middle English Sermons* 118.6–8: It is not now to sey suche is the preest as the pepull is, but howe even as the werst of the peple is, so is the preeste now-a-daies. Apperson 367; *Oxford* 518; Tilley P583. See **J71, K56, M408.**

P136 Such **People** such usance (*custom*)
a1475 Ashby *Dicta* 49.153–4: Suche as people bene, suche is thair usance, After thair hertes thei make thair uttrance.

P137 Worse **People** worse laws
a1460 *Towneley Plays* 373.193–5: Sir, it is saide in old sawes—The longere that day dawes—"Wars pepill wars lawes."

P138 As black as **Pepper**
1555 Heywood *E* 184.212.2: Blacke like pepper.

P139 Though **Pepper** is black it has a good smack
c1450 *In Praise of Brunettes* in Robbins 31.17–9: Peper wyt-oute yt ys wel blac, Y-wys wyt-inne yt ys not so; Lat go the colur and tak the smac. **c1450** *Rylands MS.394* 105.28: Thawgh peper be blak, it hath a good smak. **c1470** *Harley MS.3362* f.5a: Thaw pepyr be blac . . . Est peper sapidum quamvis sit corpore nigrum. **a1500** *Additional MS.37075* 278.19: Thow pepyr be blacke hyt hathe a gode smake. **a1500** Hill 128.9, 130.17: Est piper nigrum, quod gratum prestat odorem. **1508**(1519) Stanbridge *Vulgaria*

23.1–2: Though peper be blacke it hathe a good smacke. Tamen si piper nig(ri) coloris sit bene sapit tamen. **1546** Heywood *D* 68.66: Pepper is blacke And hath a good smacke And every man doth it bye. Apperson 584: Snow; *Oxford* 496; Tilley S593. See **I44, S440.**

P140 To brew **Pepper**
a1400 *Romaunt C* 6028–30: Ladies shull hem such pepir brewe, If that they fall into her laas, That they for woo mowe seyn "allas!" NED Pepper 4.

P141 To have (take) **Pepper** in the nose
c1378 *Piers* B xv 197: And to pore peple han peper in the nose. **a1400** *Proverbis of Wysdom* 245.67: Have no peper yn thy nose. **1520** Whittinton *Vulgaria* 84.8–9: He may not forth with take peper in the nose. **1522** Skelton *Why Come* II 38.381: Take peper in the nose. **1546** Heywood *D* 69.112: He taketh pepper in the nose, **1555** *E* 184.212. Apperson 491; *Oxford* 496; Tilley P231.

P142 He that fears all **Perils** that fall shall let all fall
1546 Heywood *D* 25.33–4: All perils that fall maie, who fearth they fall shall, Shall so feare all thyng, that he shall let fall all. Cf. *Oxford* 219: Forecasts. See **T298.**

P143 He that loves **Peril** shall fall in peril (*varied*)
c1390 Chaucer *CT* VII 1671[B2861]: For Salomon seith, "He that loveth peril shal falle in peril." **c1395** *WBible* Ecclesiasticus iii 27: He that loveth perel, schal perische ther ynne. **a1410** Lydgate *Churl* in *MP* II 476.183: Whoo dredith no perel, in perel he shal falle.

P144 It is great **Peril** to abide where peril is
a1410 Lydgate *Churl* in *MP* II 476.194: Wher perel is, gret perel is tabide.

P145 **Peril** is drawn in with dretching (*delay*)
c1385 Chaucer *TC* iii 852–3: For, nece myn, thus writen clerkes wise, That peril is with drecchyng in ydrawe. Skeat 179; Whiting *Drama* 53. See **D157, T44.**

P146 To cast (foresee) **Peril**
1402 Hoccleve *Letter of Cupid* 81.215: They seyn, perylle to cast, ys avauntage. **a1420** Lydgate *Troy* I 120.3643–4: Who cast no pereil til that it be-falle, In-stede of sugre ofte tasteth galle. **a1450** *Consail and Teiching* 75.335–8: Forse a perell ore It cum For sudane cass is ay vylsum, And lichtlear hurtis that is fore-sen Na wnprowysytly cumyne had ben. **c1450** *Foly of Fulys* 64.435–6: Thai cast no perellis of before, Na lufys na forsicht, corn na store. Whiting *Drama* 42.

P147 Where great **Perils** lie there lies great honor
a1533 Berners *Huon* 56.33–57.1: Where as lyeth grete parelles there lieth grete honour.

P148 They tell of **Perown** that know full little of his manner
c1410 Lovelich *Grail* IV 301.885–6: Thus telleden they of Perown there That knewen ful lytel Of his Manere. See **R156.**

P149 Judge not a **Person** by his clothes
a1500 *O man more* 394.44–5: They be not best that goo most geye,—Juge not a person by his clothes. See **C312, H446.**

P150 A **Person** that cannot counsel himself is not worthy to help others
c1385 Usk 19–20.28–9: O, this is a worthy person to helpe other, that can not counsayle himselfe. Cf. Tilley P267. See **G353, T50.**

P151 To flee as one would **Pestilence**
1440 Palladius 29.150–1: But bareyn lond thou fle As pestilence. **c1450** *Alphabet* II 495.16: He fled hur as he wold hafe done pestelens. Cf. Whiting *Scots* II 110: Pest.

P152 Scantly worth a **Pet** (*fart*)
c1515 Barclay *Eclogues* 165.694: Though all their cunning be scantly worth a pet. See **F62.**

P153 Many a one speaks of **Peter** and John and thinks Judas in his heart
a1393 Gower *CA* II 53–4.655–7: For now aday is manyon Which spekth of Peter and of John And thenketh Judas in his herte. See **T189.**

P154 To rob **Peter** to pay Paul (*varied*)
c1382 Wyclif *Seven Werkys of Mercy* in *SEW* III 174[4–6]: Lord, hou schulde God approve that thou robbe Petur, and gif this robbere to Poule in the name of Crist? **c1450** *Jacob's Well* 138.19–20: To robbe Petyr, and yeve it Poule, it were non almesse but gret synne, 175.32–176.1: They robbyn seynt Petyr, and yevyn it seynt poule, 305.15–7: Thei robbyn seynt petyr and yevyn it seynt Poule, that is to seyne, thei getyn falsely here good of holy cherch. **c1515** Barclay *Eclogues* 47.1266: They robbe saint Peter therewith to cloth S. Powle. **1519** Horman *Vulgaria* 267[16]: Hit is no lyberalite to robbe Peter and enryche Paule. **1546** Heywood *D* 42.38: To rob Peter and paie Poule, **1555** *E* 150.19. Apperson 534; *Oxford* 545; Taylor and Whiting 281; Tilley P244.

P155 As fresh as a **Pheasant**
a1450 Spalding *Katherine* 158 xiv 7: And fresch as (a) fesaunt to hire fere than sche flytt.

P156 He that is still may be held a **Philosopher**
c1425 Arderne *Fistula* 6.38–9: Yif thou had bene stille thou had bene holden a philosophre. See **F441.**

P157 Farewell **Phip!** (*a sparrow's name*)
c1378 *Piers* B xi 41: "Yee, farewel, Phippe!" quod Fauntelte.

P158 As bright as **Phoebus**
a1422 Lydgate *Life* 355.626–7: The wheche brighter shon Than phebus dothe, in his large spere, **a1439** *Fall* III 820.1611: Briht as Phebus, wher thei dide appeere, **a1449** *Virtues* in *MP* I 94.158: Bryght as Phebus in hys mydday spere. **a1449** ?Lydgate *Pageant of Knowledge* in *MP* II 735.22. **1449** Metham 15.394. **1474** *Welcome to Prince Edward* in Robbins 117.23. **c1485** *Slaughter* (*Digby*) 20.492. **1504** Hawes *Example* Gg2r[7]. **1506** Barclay *Castell* B1r[7–8]: Her beaute full face shone as bryght As phebus doth in a may mornynge. **1511** Hawes *Comforte* B1v[13]. **1513** Bradshaw *St. Werburge* 120. 3329–30, 178.1388–9: Werburge appered . . . Bryghter than Phebus in his meridian spere. **1515** Barclay *St. George* 101.2544–5: The pryson shone more bryght Than phebus beamys agaynst a gyltyd tour, **c1515** *Eclogues* 170.836: Glistering as bright as Phebus orient. Whiting *Scots* II 110. See **S881.**

P159 As clear as **Phoebus**
c1433 Lydgate *St. Edmund* 431.1027: Conveied by an angel, as Phebus cler off lyht. **c1450** *When the son* 390.263: More clere then bemes of phebus shene. **c1500** *O beauteous braunche* in *Anglia* 72(1954) 402.8–9: Whos colour more clere ys . . . than Phebus in hys spere. See **S882.**

P160 As gay as **Phoebus**
c1502 *Lyfe of Joseph* 51.428: As gay as ever was phebus in his golde spere.

P161 **Phoebus** excels the stars (*varied*)
a1420 Lydgate *Troy* I 386–7.8471–3: For as Phebus with his bemys clere Amonge sterris, so dide he appere, Excellyng all, **a1439** *Fall* III 755.2983: In Phebus presence sterris lese her liht, 972.1878–80: So as Phebus passeth ech othir sterre, Riht so that kyngdam in comparisoun Passeth everi lond, 986.2350–1: Lik as Phebus passeth a litil sterre, Hiest upreised in his mydday speere. **1449** Metham 6.148–50: As Phebus in bryghtenes alle planetys excedyth, in general, Ryght so in beute Cleopes yche erthly creature Precellyd in fayrenes. **1506** Hawes *Pastime* 184.4909–10: As Phebus doth hye excell In bryghtnes truely the fayre sterres all. Whiting *Scots* II 110. See **S889.**

P162 **Phoebus** is most clear after clouds (*varied*)
a1439 Lydgate *Fall* I 188.6677–8: Like as whan cloudis ther blaknesse doun declyne, Phebus mor cleer doth with his bemys shyne, III 1002. 2949–50: As whan that it doth reyne, Phebus aftir sheweth mor cleernesse, **1439** *St. Albon* 160.1918–9: By ensample: as passed is the daungere Of stormy weders, Phebus is most clere.

P163 To be like **Phoebus** (in his sphere)
a1420 Lydgate *Troy* I 280.4741: Hir sonnysche her, liche Phebus in his spere, **1432** *Henry VI's Triumphal Entry* in *MP* II 634.109: Theyre heer dysplayed as Phebus in here spere, **c1433** *St. Edmund* 430.964: His sterryssh eyen lik Phebus off fresshnesse, **a1439** *Fall* I 295.3390: Hir her ontressid, lik Phebus in his speer.

P164 To glitter like **Phoebus**
1513 Bradshaw *St. Werburge* 61.1579: Glyterynge as Phebus. See **S895.**

P165 To shine like **Phoebus**
a1422 Lydgate *Life* 664.382: Shynyng as bright as phebus dothe in may, **1432** *Henry VI's Triumphal Entry* in *MP* II 635.157: Lyke Phebus bemys shone hire goldyn tresses, **a1439** *Fall* I 22.800: Hih as Phebus shynyth in his speer, III 975.1968–9, 1020.3565. **a1449** Lydgate and Burgh *Secrees* 5.136–7. **1501** Douglas *Palice* 3.15: A voice I hard preclair as Phebus schone, 55.7: Torris, quhilk like to Phebus schone. See **S897.**

P166 When **Phoebus** casts his light early, beware of rain
c1440 Lydgate *Debate* in *MP* II 563.572–5: A pronostik clerkis ber wittnesse: Beth war of Phebus that erly cast his liht, Of reyn, of storme, of myste or of derknesse Shal aftir folwe longe or it be nyht. Cf. Tilley S977, 978. See **M687.**

P167 He that lives by **Physic** shall starve (*die*) by physic
1340 *Ayenbite* 54[5–6]: Thet the ilke thet be fisike leveth: be fizike sterfth. **c1400** *Vices and Virtues* 51.6–7: And ofte it is seye, who-so lyveth bi phisike, bi phisike dieth.

P168 What should **Physic** do unless there were sickness?

c1475 *Court of Sapience* 138.372–4: What shuld Physyk, but yef that sekenes were? What nedeth salve, but yef there were a sore? What nedeth drynke where thryst hath no powere?

P169 The **Physician** promises health when he has no power
1492 *Salomon and Marcolphus* 6[2–3]: The phisician promysyth the seeke folke helthe whan he hath no power.

P170 **Physicians** hide their defaults (*errors*) under earth
1450 *Dicts* 66.16–9: And in his tyme ther was a peyntour that bi-come a fisician; (to) whome he saide: thow knewe wele that when thou were a peyntour men sawe at (ie) clerly thi defautes, bot nowe men may not se hem, for thei hide hem under erthe. **1477** Rivers *Dictes* 37[18–22]: He sawe a peyntour that was waxe a physicien, to whom he sayde, thou knowest that men might se at the eye the fawtes that thou didest in thy crafte, but nowe they may not be perceyved, for they ar hidde unther the erthe. Apperson 492; *Oxford* 498; Tilley D424.

P171 Maugre **Picard** and Breton
a1300 *Alisaunder* 309.5877–82: The kynges oost that withouten was Hadden aspyed al this cas, And broughtten gynnes to the walle—Hoven, shoven, and drowen alle, And, maugre Picard and Bretoun, Breken there the wal adoun. Note (II 135): "This expression is evidently idiomatic and perhaps proverbial; but I cannot trace it elsewhere."

P172 As whole (*healthy*) as any **Pickerel**
c1400 *Laud Troy* II 431.14627–8: For he is hol In flesch and fel, And as hole as any pykerel. See **F223, 228, P195, T485.**

P173 As jolly as a **Pie** (*magpie*)
c1390 Chaucer *CT* VII 209[B1399]: And forth she gooth as jolif as a pye, **c1395** III[D] 456: Stibourn and strong, and joly as a pye. *Oxford* 420: Merry.

P174 As merry as a **Pie**
1546 Heywood *D* 66.46: Mery as a pye. Apperson 413–4; *Oxford* 420; Tilley P281.

P175 As pilled (*bald*) as a **Pie** (*etc.*) (A number of single quotations are brought together here)
a1349 *Papelard Priest* 43.16: And callen me prust papelart, pilled as a pye. **c1390** Chaucer *CT* I[A] 3950: And she was proud, and peert as is a pye, **c1395** IV[E] 1848: And ful of jargon as a flekked pye, VIII[G] 565: He was of foom al flekked as a pye. **a1420** Lydgate *Troy* I 309.5755: And yit thei ben as chargaunt as a pye.

P176 Not too high for the **Pie** nor too low for the crow
1546 Heywood *D* 84.136: Not to hye for the pye, nor to lowe for the crowe, **1555** *E* 186.224. Apperson 455; *Oxford* 294; Tilley P283–4.

P177 Not worth a **Pie**(?)
a1400 *Rowlande* 91.1157: Your lawes are noghte worthe a pye. Notes (p. 156) give French: Ne valent une alie.

P178 The **Pie** betrays her birds by her chattering
1509 Barclay *Ship* I 107[6–7]: As the pye Betrays hir byrdes by hir chatrynge and crye, 109[22–3]: Let suche take example by the chatrynge pye. Which doth hyr nest and byrdes also betraye By hyr grete chatterynge. See **H343.**

P179 To chatter like a (the) **Pie**
c1475 *Why I Can't* 144.251: For whoso chateryt lyke a py. **a1500** Medwall *Nature* B1v[38]: That one chatreth lyke a pye. **a1508** Skelton *Phyllyp* I 63.397: The fleckyd pye to chatter. **1509** Barclay *Ship* I 145[10–1]: Styll grutchynge . . . lyke the chaterynge of the folysshe pye, II 4[8]: Sawynge theyr sede of chatrynge lyke the pye. Tilley P285; Whiting *Drama* 323:252.

P180 To patter like a **Pie**
a1450 *York Plays* 357.266: He patris like a py.

P181 To pipe like a **Pie**
a1425 *Chester Plays* I 150.428: Up as pie he piped.

P182 To preach (speak) like a **Pie**
a1400 Wyclif *Sermons* I 165[3–4]: For it is a foul thing that prestis speken as pies, and knowun not her owne vois more than doumbe beestis. **a1425** *Chester Plays* I 96.273: Popelard! thou preachest as a pie.

P183 A **Piece** of a kid is worth two of a cat
1549 Heywood *D* 87.253: A peece of a kyd is woorth two of a cat. Apperson 339; *Oxford* 499; Tilley P291.

P184 Not set a **Pie(s)-heel**
c1378 *Piers* B vii 194: I sette yowre patentes and yowre pardounz at one pies hele, **a1387** C x 345: Ich sette by pardon nat a peese nother a pye-hele.

Pig, see **Hog, Sow, Swine**

P185 Go in **Pig** and come out pike
1532 More *Confutacion* 395 EF: They will (do)

as lollardes dyd of late, that put a pygge into the water on good fryday, and sayd goe in pygge, and come oute pyke, and so when they had chaunged the name, they toke it for fishe and eate it.

P186 A **Pig** of one's own sow
c1525 ?Heywood *Gentlynes* 95.67: That is evyn a pyg of our own sow. **1546** Heywood *D* 81.38: A pyg of mine owne sow, **1555** *E* 177.178. Apperson 493; *Oxford* 499; Tilley P305.

P187 To buy a **Pig** in a poke
1546 Heywood *D* 97.234: Ye love not to bye the pyg in the poke, **1555** *E* 159.83. Apperson 494; *Oxford* 72–3; Taylor and Whiting 284; Tilley P304. See **C95, 102.**

P188 To lie like two **Pigs** in a sty
a1529 Skelton *Elynour* I 102.233–4: Than swetely together we ly, As two pygges in a sty.

P189 To have a **Pig** of the worse pannier
1533 Heywood *Johan* B4ᵛ[36]: And then had I a pyg in the woyrs panyer, **1546** *D* 101.44: He hath a pyg of the woorse panier. Apperson 493; *Oxford* 499; Tilley P301.

P190 To wallow (turn) like two **Pigs** in a poke
c1390 Chaucer *CT* I[A] 4278: They walwe as doon two pigges in a poke. **c1503** More *Early Poems* [4] B[14–5]: They turne and tumble, As pygges do in a poke. Skeat 301. See **D324.**

P191 To whine like **Pigs** in a poke
1562 Heywood *E* 247.100.22: Those rattes in those ragges whinde lyke pigges in a poke.

P192 When the **Pig** is proffered open (hold up) the poke
c1250 *Hendyng O* 195.23: Wen me bedeth the gris, opene the shet, **a1325** *C* 188–9.36: Wan man yevit the a pig, opin the powch. **c1450** *Douce MS.52* 54.114: When me profereth the pigge, open the pogh; For when he is an olde swyn, thow tyte hym nowghht. **c1450** *Rylands MS.394* 104.17ᵛ.24–5: For whan it is anolde swyn, he wol not com ther yn. **a1500** Hill 128.1: Whan I profir the pig, opin the poke. **1520** Whittinton *Vulgaria* 107.11–2: It is sayd comenly, whan the pygge is profered: open the poughen. **1546** Heywood *D* 22.16: Whan the pigge is proferd to holde up the poke. Apperson 495; Jente 95; Kneuer 69–70; *Oxford* 72–3; Schleich 263; Singer III 133–4; Tilley P308; Walther I 543.4516.

P193 As high as **Pig's-feet** (*i.e.*, very low)
c1475 Gregory *Chronicle* 190[17–9]: Save only they kepte (no) ordyr among them . . . for alle were as hyghe as pygysfete.

P194 As broad and flat as a **Pike** when it is splat (*split*)
c1400 *Laud Troy* II 413.14007–8: He layde him as brod and flat As is a pike when he is splat.

P195 As quart (*healthy*) as a **Pike**
a1400 *Moder of gresse* 171.286: And make hym qwart als pyk I say, 180.640–2: Rewe wil distroye venyme With outen mannes body and with Inne, And als a pike it makith hyme clene. See **F223, 228, P172, T485.**

P196 In **Pilate's** voice
c1390 Chaucer *CT* I[A] 3124: But in Pilates voys he gan to crie. **1546** Heywood *D* 36.54: Burst out in pilats voice, **1556** *Spider* 173[21]. *Oxford* 500; Tilley P323.

P197 To doubt (*fear*) no more than a **Pilch-clout**
a1300 *Richard* 428.6805–6: Here armure no more i ne doute Thenne it were a pylche-cloute.

P198 As thick as **Piles** (*spines*) on an urchin (*hedgehog*)
c1300 *South English Legendary* (*Laud*) 179.50: Heo (*arrows*) stikeden al-so thicke on him so yrichon deth of piles, 298.49: Ase ful ase is an Irchepil of piles al-a-boute.

P199 **Pilgrims** may go far but some tarage (*quality*) of whence they come bides
a1439 Lydgate *Fall* I 133.4772–4: Pilgrymes may gon ful ferr in ther passage, But I dar seyn, how ferr that ever thei go, Ther bit sum tarage off that that thei cam fro. See **A169, T465.**

P200 We are **Pilgrims** in this world (*varied*)
a1325 *Lollai litel child* in Brown *Lyrics XIV* 36.25–6: Child, thou ert a pilgrim in wikidnis ibor, Thou wandrest in this fals world, thou loke the bi-for. **c1390** Hilton *Mixed Life* (*Vernon*) in *Yorkshire Writers* I 281[11]: Seint Poul seith that as longe as we are in this bodi we are pilgrimes fro ure lord. **a1400** *Bonum Est* 86.9–10: Ffor hit is ordeynt for pilgrimus traveland in this lyf. **a1400** ?Wyclif *Of Weddid Men* in *SEW* III 197[29–31]: But thenk that thei ben gestis and pilgrimes in the world, and han not here a dwellynge-place for evere. **1407** *Epitaph of Thomas Palmer* in Thomas F. Ravenshaw *Antiente Epitaphes* (London, 1878) 5[4]: I ended thys worlde's pylgramage. **c1410** *Mirror of Sinners* in *Yorkshire Writers* II 438 [7–8]: Thow art but an outlawe, a gest, and a pilgrym heer in this wrecchide lyf. **a1415** *Lan-*

terne 85.32–86.1: Every citizen of the hevenli countre is a pilgrime of this world for al tyme of this present liif. **c1425** *Orcherd* 222.13, 252.7–8. **c1450** *Man ys dethys* in Brown *Register* I 470: Man is a pylgrym in is pasyng. **c1475** Henryson *Fables* 41.1111–2: The Meir is Men of gude conditioun As Pilgrymes Walkand in this wildernes. **1481** *Tulle of Olde Age* 92–3: I departe me from this presente life, as a walkyng weyfaryng man or as a voyagieng pilgryme departith from some lodgyngplace or an hostellrye for to come to his owne dwellyng house. **1483** Caxton *Cato* I6r[33–4]: The lyf of this world nys none other but a pylgremage. **1533** More *Confutacion* 616 D[6–10]: Yet them coumpte we stylle for vyagers and pylgrimes in the same pylgrimage that we bee towarde the same place of reste and wealth that we walke, **1534** *Comforte* 1238 A[1–3]: And in what countrye so ever we walk in this world, we be but as pilgrimes and wayfaryng men, *Passion* 1313 CD: Manne . . . is here but a pylgryme.

P201 The **Pilgrimage** of this life (*varied*)
c1340 Rolle *Psalter* 222 (64.1): Haly saules, that turnys fra pilgrymage of this life til endles gladnes, 437 (119.5): My pilgrimage in this warld is sa lange. **c1390** Chaucer *Truth* 17–8: Her is non hoom, her nis but wildernesse: Forth, pilgrim, forth! **c1395** *WBible* Ecclesiasticus xvi 9 *gloss:* Her liyf, which is a pilgrymage on erthe, 15 *gloss:* Present liyf, which liyf is seid the pilgrymage of man, Jeremiah xxxv 7: Ye lyve many daies on the face of erthe, in which ye goen in pilgrymage. **a1400** *Pricke* 38.1377–9: For we duelle here als aliens, To travail, here in the way, our lyms, Til our countré-warde, als pilgryms, 39.1394–5: This world es the way and passage, Thurgh whilk lyes our pilgrimage. **a1420** Lydgate *Troy* III 874.3570: For oure lyf here is but a pilgrymage, **c1421** *Thebes* 141.3418–9: And our lif her, who taketh hed ther-to, Is but an exile and a pilgrymage, **a1422** *Life* 626.550–3: And make us stronge and sure in our passage In this exile and parlous pylgrymage, Whiche our fomen of malice and of pryde Hath in this lyfe by-sett us on everysyde, **a1430** *Pilgrimage* 2.46: That yowre lyff her ys but a pylgrymage, **c1430** *Dance* 4.37: To schewe this worlde is but a pilgrimage, **a1439** *Fall* I 95.3464–5: Experience can teche in everi age, How this world heer is but a pilgrymage, III 721.1753: Transitoire been heer your pilgrymages, **a1449** *Testament* in *MP* I 344.394: Our dwellyng here is but a pilgrymage. **a1449** ?Lydgate *Pageant of Knowledge* in *MP* II 734.278–9: And thow shalt fynd this lyfe a pylgremage, In whyche ther ys no stedfast abydyng, 738.135–6. **1463** Ashby *Prisoner* 7.204–5: Thynke that thy lyfe here ys but pilgremage Towardes the hygh place celestiall. **1479** Rivers *Cordyal* 31.4–5: Senek seith in his boke of remedyes ayenst fortune That our lif is but a pilgrimage. **c1485** Caxton *St. Winifred* 303.34: The pylgremage of this lyf, **1487** *Book of Good Manners* G7r[3]: This present lyf is a right pylgremage. **1513** Bradshaw *St. Werburge* 58.1467: After this pylgrymage rewarded for to be. **1522** More *Treatyce* 88 D[1–3]: We be but going in pilgrimage, and have here no dwellyng place, **1528** *Heresyes* 181 C[11–2]: The pilgrymage of this shorte life. *Oxford* 365–6; R. M. Smith in *MLN* 65 (1950) 443–7; Tilley L249. See **W663.**

P202 As stable as a **Pillar**
a1449 Lydgate *St. Austin* in *MP* I 201.274: As ony pileer in our feith moost stable. **1484** Caxton *Royal Book* O7r[26–7]: Ferme and stable as is a pyler in the chirche.

P203 As stiff as a **Pillar**
c1425 *St. Katherine of Sienna* 193.2–3: But she, as a sadde piler, stode stiffe. Taylor and Whiting 285.

P204 As upright as a **Pillar**
c1300 *South English Legendary* (*Laud*) 50.108: (*A light*) ase apiler stonde uprighht. Cf. Svartengren 275.

P205 To stand like a **Pillar**
a1449 Lydgate *St. Thomas* in *MP* I 139.6: Stood as a peeler for hooly chirchis right.

P206 Not set the **Pilling** (*peeling, bark*) of a tree
a1400 *Rowlande* 94.1264–5: He sett the lawes of Cristyantee Nott at a pillynge of a tree.

P207 As sweet as **Piment** (*sweet wine*)
a1325 *Cursor* II 538.9356: Sco smelles better (FGT: Swettyr) then piment. **c1450** *Myroure of oure Ladye* 215[33]: Swetter than pyement.

P208 The nearer the **Pin** the better is the pudding
c1450 *Rylands MS.394* 94.22: The nerre the pynne the better is the puddynge. See **B444.**

P209 Not differ two **Pins**
1555 Heywood *E* 147.2.5: The meanyng herof, differth not twoo pins.

P210 Not give a **Pin**
a1300 *Alisaunder* 325.6136: He nolde give there-of a pynne.

P211 Not please of a **Pin**
1534 More *Comforte* 1158 E[2–3]: Not please hym of a pynne.

P212 Not set at a **Pin**
a1460 *Towneley Plays* 34.363–4: Thi felowship, Set I not at a pyn. Apperson 496; *Oxford* 78; Whiting *Drama* 358:772. See **P364.**

P213 Not worth a **Pin**
a1500 *Court of Love* 438.1078: Thow spekest not worth a pin. **1533** Heywood *Weather* C3v[17]: All our other gere not worth a pyn, **1556** *Spider* 399[27]: Without one penie cost: or one pins worth paine. Apperson 458; Tilley P334; Whiting *Drama* 358:772, *Scots* II 110. See **P365.**

P214 To hang by (be on) another **Pin**
c1408 Lydgate *Reson* 78.2952: They hangen by another pyn. **a1450** *Partonope* 348.8586–7: And yite your herte is on a-nother pyn. Ye have chose some new thinge. NED Pin sb.[1] 15.

P215 To hang on a jolly **Pin** (*varied*)
c1395 Chaucer *CT* IV[E] 1516: Youre herte hangeth on a joly pyn. **a1456** Sellyng *Evidens* 178.50: The younge manis herte stondithe on a joly pynne. **c1475** *Wisdom* 51.492: I woll sett my soule a mery pynne. **c1499** Skelton *Bowge* I 45.386: Plucke up thyne herte upon a mery pyne. **a1500** Medwall *Nature* C4r[4]: To set hys hart on a mery pyn, D2v[13]: Thys wyll set hym on a mery pyn. **a1500** *Myne hert is set* in *Archiv* 135(1916) 302.1: Myne hert is set upponne a lusty pynne. Apperson 415; NED Pin, sb.[1] 15; *Oxford* 421; Tilley P335; Whiting *Drama* 354:709.

P216 To hang on a slippery **Pin**
c1390 *Verses on the Earthquake of 1382* in Brown *Lyrics XIV* 188.79: Ur bagge hongeth on a sliper pyn.

P217 To hit the **Pin**
a1475 *Ludus Coventriae* 129.189: Now be myn trowth ye hytte the pynne. *Oxford* 96: cleave; Tilley P336.

P218 A **Pin's Head** or less
c1440 Charles of Orleans 180.5385–6: For myn hool hert of yowre the quantite As of a pynnys hed me yave or lasse. NED Pin sb.[1] 3c.

P219 At a **Pinch**
1489 Caxton *Fayttes* 63.24–5: And corageously at a pynche shal renne upon he(m). Apperson 497.

P220 To put one to a **Pinch**
1528 More *Heresyes* 164 G[5]: Ye put me nowe to a pynche. NED Pinch 4.

P221 As huge as a **Pipe** (*wine cask*)
a1500 *Partenay* 198.5773: Hys panche As A pipe hug and comerous.

P222 To dance after one's **Pipe**
1546 Heywood *D* 78.22: To daunce after her pipe, I am ny led. Tilley M488; Whiting *Drama* 358:773. See **W667.**

P223 He is a sorry **Piper** that when he begins cannot leave off
1478 *Stonor Letters* II 57[10–1]: I ffare lyke a sory pyper, whanne I begynne I can nat leve.

P224 **Piping** hot
c1390 Chaucer *CT* I[A] 3379: And wafres, pipyng hot out of the gleede. Apperson 498; NED Piping 3; Tilley P351.

P225 After a great **Pirrie** (*squall*) the weather seems more clear
1518 Nevill *Castell* 91.415: After a grete pery the wether semeth more clere. See **M728.**

P226 The **Pirrie** is blown that will ripen hereafter (*i.e.*, trouble is coming)
c1400 *Beryn* 41.1315–6: The pyry is I-blowe,—hop, Beryn, hop!—That ripe wol heraftir, and on thyn hede dropp.

P227 As angry as a **Pismire**
c1395 Chaucer *CT* III[D] 1825: He is as angry as a pissemyre. *Oxford* 11.

P228 The one cannot **Piss** but the other must let a fart
1546 Heywood *D* 72.66–7: My husband and he be so great, that the ton Can not pisse, but tother must let a fart. Tilley P354.

P229 Neither in the **Pistle** nor yet in the gospel
c1500 Fabyan 209[12–3]: To thyse narracions the herers may gyve credence as them lyketh; for they be nother in the pystle nor yet in the gospell.

P230 A shallow **Pit** cannot keep a hart or lion in cage
1515 Barclay *St. George* 92.2280–6: But an olde proverbe hath ben sayd comonly That a shalowe pyt can nat kepe in in cage An hart or lyon or lyke great beste savage. A spyders webbe can nat a dove inlace, None stoppith a Dam with a small febyl gate. Craft must be usyd and strenght in suche a case, And frawde agay(n)st fraude.

P231 To be on one's (the) **Pit's** brink

c1395 Chaucer *CT* IV[E] 1400–1: I am hoor and oold, And almoost, God woot, on my pittes brynke. **c1440** Charles of Orleans 27.798: Without an hert sechyng my pittis brynke. **a1450** *Barlam and Josaphat* (*South English Legendary*) 130.601: To the pittes brynke: wit the dede they wille go. **a1450** *Castle* 124.1584: Late men that arn on the pyttis brynke. See **D107.**

P232 To fall into the **Pit** (ditch, dike, lake) one digs (for another)
c900 *Paris Psalter* 12 (7.15): He adylf þone pytt, and he hine ontynð, and on þone ylcan befylð. **c1000** *Regius Psalter* 10 (7.16): Seað openude and adealf hine hreas on seað þone he worhte. **a1050** Defensor *Liber* 148[6–8]: Se þe pytt dylf nehstan on þæne he fealð; se þe sett stan nehstan he ætspyrnð on þam, and se þe grin oþrum legð he forwyrð on þam. **c1100** *Salisbury Psalter* 83 (7.16). **c1340** Rolle *Psalter* 27 (7.16): He fell in the pit that he made. **c1350** *Prose Psalter* 7 (7.16): He opened helle and dalf it, and fel in the diche that he made. **c1395** *WBible* Psalms vii 16: And he felde in to the dich which he made, lvi 7: Thei delveden a diche bifore my face; and thei felden doun in to it, Proverbs xxvi 27: He that delveth a diche, schal falle in to it, Ecclesiastes x 8, Ecclesiasticus xxvii 29. **a1400** *Ancrene* (*Recluse*) 136.22–3: Hii maden a grave and dalf it, and fel hem selven in the diche, that hii maden. **a1400** *Destruction of Troy* 370.11362–3: Hit is nedefull for noy, that neghis on hond, That thai droppe in the dike thai deghit have for us. **a1400** *Northern Verse Psalter* I 181 (56.7): Bi-for mi licham grove thai dike, And felle tham self thar inne ilike. **c1400** *Primer* 58[34–5]: He openyde a lake, and diggide it out; and he felde in-to the diche which he made. **1402** *Daw Topias* 85[5–6]. **a1420** Lydgate *Troy* I 354.7329–30: For in the dyche justly he is falle Whiche he made of malis for us alle, II 472.2728–9, III 708.4934–5. **1438** *Barlaam* 14.34–5: He was fall in the putte that he had made hym selff. **a1450** *Gesta* 326[14–5]: The stiward is fallyn in his owne diche. **1471** Caxton *Recuyell* II 654.14–5: Hyt shold not be ylle doon to make them falle in to the pytte that they have maad redy, **1484** *Aesop* 155[14–6]: Who so ever maketh the pytte redy for his brother, ofte it happeth that he hym self falleth in the same. **a1500** *Partenay* 136.3917. **1509** Barclay *Ship* II 40[5–6]: Makynge a pyt to others hurte and wo, Wherin hymselfe is destroyed at the last. **1509** Watson *Ship* Q3[r][22–4]. Tilley P356. See **B21, C640, D22, E180, F374, 555, G169, 490, M200, 284, 289, R166, S427, T17.**

P233 As black as (the, any) **Pitch**
a1300 *Alisaunder* 271.4904: That hii ben blak so pycches fom, 272.4964: Also blak so any pycche, 278.5181, 293.5591, 310.5938–9: any, 341.6406–7: Blake is her visage and lych, Als it were grounden pych. **a1300** *XI Pains* 149.77: Blakkure than the swarte pich. **c1300** *Guy*[1] 596 A 257.7. **c1303** Mannyng *Handlyng* 395. 12588. **c1350** *Libeaus* 73.1327, 76.1363. **c1380** *Ferumbras* 81.2461, 135.4329–30. **c1390** *God man and the devel* 354.969: eny. **c1390** *Northern Homily Cycle Narrationes* (*Vernon*) 301.95. **a1400** *How to hear Mass* 502.359. **a1400** *Ipomadon A* 176.6159. **c1400** *Tundale* 76.1308: ony. **c1410** Lovelich *Grail* II 289.437, 314.191–2, 363.396: Ony. **a1415** Mirk *Festial* 71.21–2, 85.25, 92.20, 97.3, 132.2: any, 238.6–7. **c1415** *Middle English Sermons* 176.38–9: anny. **a1420** Lydgate *Troy* I 272.4473, **1422** *Serpent* 61.6: eny. **a1425** *St. Robert* 63.694. **c1440** *St. Christopher* 464.827. **a1450** *South English Legendary* (*Bodley*) 322.538: eny. **a1450** *Three Middle English Sermons* 39.577: ani. **c1450** *Alphabet* II 351.20. **c1450** *De Claris Mulieribus* 36.725. **c1450** Idley 176.1091. **c1450** *Jacob's Well* 11.8. **c1450** *Owayne Miles* (*Cotton Caligula*) 118.405: any. **c1450** *St. Cuthbert* 206.7061: any. **c1450** *Way to Jerusalem* in S. Purchas *Hakluytus Posthumus* (Glasgow, 1905) VII 535[9]: any. **1465** Leversege 23[14]: any. **a1475** *Guy*[2] 243. 8461, 294.10241–2. **c1475** *Guy*[1] 431 C 7759: any. **1485** Caxton *Charles* 165.16–7: He is as blacke as pytche boylled, 167.22–3, 176.1, 233.18. **c1485** *Monk of Evesham* 57[10–1], 85[5]. **a1500** *Merchant and his Son* in Hazlitt *EPP* I 141.137: any. **a1500** *Trentals of Gregory* (*Harley 3810*) in *ESt* 40(1908–9) 356.61: any. **a1513** Dunbar *Devillis Inquest* 79.106. **1513** Douglas *Aeneid* II 230.56. **a1533** Berners *Arthur* 221[18, 30], 470[30]: any. Apperson 135; *Oxford* 47; Taylor and Whiting 287; Tilley P357.

P234 As dark as **Pitch**
c1390 Chaucer *CT* I[A] 3731: Derk was the nyght as pich. Apperson 135; Taylor and Whiting 287; Tilley P357; Whiting *Ballad* 30.

P235 As swart (*black*) as (the, any) **Pitch**
a1300 *Fiftene teknen* in Edmund Stengel *Codicem Manu Scriptum Digby 86* (Halle, 1871) 54.23: (*The sun*) Bicometh suartore then the pich **c1300** *Owayne Miles* (*Auchinleck*) 106.116 [6]. **c1330** *Rouland* 50.482–3: He loked lotheliche, And was swart as piche. **c1350** *Libeaus* 36.620. **a1500** *Almyghty god* in *Anglia* 3(1880) 545.99: any.

P236 He that touches **Pitch** shall be defouled (*varied*)
c1300 *Northern Homily Cycle* (*Edin. Coll. Phys.*) 111[5–8]: For qua sa nehe wit hend or slefes Hate molten pic, on thaim it clevis: Pik that cleves quen it is tan, Bisens deling wit wik man. **c1303** Mannyng *Handlyng* 212.6577–80: Seynt Poule seyth, that moche wote, "Who-so handlyth pycche wellyng hote, He shal have fylthe therof sumdeyl, Thogh he kepe hym never so weyl." **c1390** Chaucer *CT* X[I] 854: As whoso toucheth warm pych, it shent his fyngres. **c1395** *WBible* Ecclesiasticus xiii 1: He that touchith pitch, schal be defoulid of it. **a1398**(1495) Bartholomaeus-Trevisa S5r[1.26–7]: And (*pitch*) defoyllyth and smorchyth hondes that it towchyth. **c1400** *Satan and his Children* in Wyclif *EW* 218[10–1]: Therfore seith the wise man, he that handlith pich schal be foulid ther-of. **c1400** *Seven Deadly Sins* in Wyclif *SEW* III 167[12–3]: For hit is hard to touche tho picche and not be foulid therwith. **c1415** *Middle English Sermons* 235.36–8. **c1425** *Treatise on the Ten Commandments* in *SP* 6(1910) 28[24]: Ffor he that towchith picke is defouled of the picke. **a1439** Lydgate *Fall* I 131.4695–7: Be sentence off the wise, Who touchith pich, bassay men may see, It failith nat he shal defouled be. **a1450** *Three Middle English Sermons* 45.757–9. **c1450** Idley 83.167–8: He that waloweth amonge coole or piche, Ofte tymes it woll shewe suche, 193.2061–5. **c1515** Barclay *Eclogues* 102.1277: Or touche soft pitche and not his fingers file. **1534** More *Comforte* 1200 B[1–3]: It is a thing right hard, to touch pitch, and never fyle the fingers. Apperson 498; Jente 254; *Oxford* 667; Taylor and Whiting 287–8; Tilley P358; Whiting *Scots* II 111. See **F558, H88.**

P237 To cleave together like **Pitch**
a1400 *Pricke* 93.3424–5: For thai gadir on the saul ful thyk, And cleves togyder als dos pyk.

P238 **Pitch** and pay
c1405 *Mum* 73.1598: But shuld thay picche and paye at eche pleynte-is ende. **a1500** *Piers of Fullham* 9.206–7: Yt ys full hard bothe to pyche and paye: An empty purs may evyll accomptes yelde. Apperson 498; *Oxford* 502; Tilley P360.

P239 Small **Pitchers** have wide ears
1546 Heywood *D* 70.10: Avoyd your children. Small pitchers have wide eares. Apperson 372; Jente 147; *Oxford* 374; Tilley P363.

P240 Better to **Pity** than be pitied
1479 *Cely Papers* 14[18]: Hyt ys better to pyttye than be pyttyd. See **R230.**

P241 Peevish **Pity** mars the city
1556 Heywood *Spider* 326[20–1]: Or pevish pittie: Which (as thold saying sayith) marth the cittie. Apperson 229; *Oxford* 217; Tilley P366.

P242 **Pity** makes mercy pass right
c1386 Chaucer *LGW* F 161–2: Yet Pitee, thurgh his stronge gentil myght, Forgaf, and made Mercy passen Ryght. See **M508.**

P243 **Pity** runs soon in gentle heart (*varied*)
c1385 Chaucer *CT* I[A] 1761: For pitee renneth soone in gentil herte, *TC* i 898–900: That sith thy lady vertuous is al, So foloweth it that there is som pitee Amonges alle thise other in general, **c1386** *LGW* F 503: But pite renneth soone in gentil herte, 1078–9: Anon hire herte hath pite of his wo, And with that pite love com in also, **c1390** *CT* II[B] 660: As gentil herte is fulfild of pitee, **c1395** IV[E] 1986: Lo, pitee renneth soone in gentil herte, V[F] 479: Pitee renneth soone in gentil herte. **c1408** Lydgate *Reson* 181.6915–6: For pyte, who that kan adverte, Renneth sone in gentyl herte, **c1421** *Thebes* 140.3398: Only of pite which is in gentyl blood. **c1440** Charles of Orleans 132. 3929–30: A ladies hert forto want pite Hit is to fowle ageyne nature. **1509** *Fyftene Joyes* C7r[11]: A gentyll herte wolde pyte have and routhe. **a1533** Berners *Castell* B6v[20–3]: Gentyllwemen havyng noble hertes . . . ought naturally to have pyte. **1534** Heywood *Love* C2r[38–9]: For I have a mynde that every good face Hath ever some pyte of a pore mans case. Whiting *Drama* 288, *Scots* II 111. See **H273, M411.**

P244 Better seek a hundred **Places** away (from home) than suffer a hundred humiliations
c1025 *Durham Proverbs* 13.25: Selre byþ þæt man hund (?stowa) heona gesece þonne man hund hynþa geþolie. Melius centum adire locos quam centum perpati contumelias. Cf. R. Quirk in *MLR* 52(1957) 625.

P245 He that is in a sure **Place** is a fool to go from it
1484 Caxton *Aesop* 239[17–21]: For many tymes I have herd saye of my graunt moder, he that is wel meve not hym self, For he whiche is in a place wel sure is wel a fole to go fro hit, and to putte hym self in grete daunger and perylle. Apperson 674:2; Tilley F487. See **S297.**

P246 He that is parted in every **Place** is nowhere whole
c1385 Chaucer *TC* i 960–1: But he that parted is in everi place Is nowher hol, as writen clerkes wyse.

P247 A lowest **Place** is oft most sure and stable
1515 Barclay *St. George* 57.1271: A lowest place is oft moste sure and stable. See **H387, R191.**

P248 To sing **Placebo**
a1338 Mannyng *Chronicle B* II 247[1–2]: For gold and silver strong he gaf so grete plente, Bifor the kyng it song, *Placebo domine.* **1340** *Ayenbite* 60[29–30]: Thet huanne hi alle zingeth "Placebo," thet is to zigge: "Mi lhord zayth zoth, mi lhord deth wel." **c1390** Chaucer *CT* X[I] 617: Flateres been the develes chapelleyns, that syngen evere *Placebo,* **c1395** III[D] 2075: Syngeth *Placebo,* and "I shal, if I kan," IV[E] 1476: Of whiche that oon was cleped Placebo. **c1400** *Vices and Virtues* 58.15: Thei syngen alwey "Placebo." **a1430** Lydgate *Pilgrimage* 395.14654: My song to hem ys "placebo," 598.22417: Somme callen hir Placebo. **a1450** *Castle* 170.3125: Thi placebo I schal synge. **c1450** *Pilgrimage LM* 122[28–9]: I preyse hem ariht bothe in riht and in wrong in servinge hem of Placebo. **c1475** Henryson *Want of Wyse Men* 189.19: Quha can placebo, and noucht half dirige. **1481** Caxton *Reynard* 65[28]: Ther ben many that playe placebo, **1484** *Royal Book* F4ᵛ[30]: They synge alwaye the placebo of flaterye. **c1522** Skelton *Colyn* I 346.908–9: They occupye them so With syngyng *Placebo.* Apperson 573–4; *NQ* 210(1965) 17–8; *Oxford* 591–2; Tilley P378; Whiting *Scots* II 111. See **P264.**

P249 To graze on the **Plain**
1546 Heywood *D* 99.32: He turnde hir out at doores to grase on the playne. Apperson 269; *Oxford* 263; Tilley P380.

P250 Better freely give a **Plank** than be compelled to give a mart (*ox*)
c1475 Henryson *Fables* 78.2270–1: Far better is frelie ffor to giff ane plank Nor be compellit on force to giff ane mart. See **H344.**

P251 A green **Plant** may be plied with a man's fingers (*varied*)
c1400 *Beryn* 34.1062–6: A plant, whils it is grene, or it have dominacioun, A man may with his fyngirs ply it wher hym list, And make ther-of a shakill, a with(ey), or a twist; But let the plant(e) stond, and yeris ovir growe, Men shall nat, with both his hondis, unnethis make it bowe. **a1450** *Myne awen dere* 152.85–91: For als lange as a tre is yynge, Men may make it even to sprynge That walde hafe ben a croked tre Hadde noght men made it even to be. And righte thus will thy childer fare And thay be yynge withouten lare, Bathe ill and vicyous in all thynge. **a1470** Parker *Dives* K5ʳ[1.31–4]: Eccl. vii. Whyle a tree is a small sprynge it may be bowed as men wyll have it. But when it is full woxen it wyll not be bowed. **1487** Caxton *Book of Good Manners* D8ᵛ[9]: The rodde boweth whyle it is grene. **1509** Barclay *Ship* I 47[18–21]: A lytell twygge plyant is by kynde A bygger braunche is harde to bowe or wynde But suffer the braunche to a byg tre to growe And rather it shall brake than outher wynde or bowe. Apperson 38: Bend; *Oxford* 34; Tilley T632; Whiting *Drama* 120, *Scots* II 144. See **O11, W35, Y4.**

P252 One **Plaster** cannot heal all sores
1533 More *Debellacyon* 951 E[1–2]: One plaister can not heale all sores. Cf. Tilley S82.

P253 As hard as any **Plate**
a1420 Lydgate *Troy* I 20.306: And with skalys hard as any plate.

P254 To be beaten like a **Plate** upon a stith (*anvil*)
a1430 Lydgate *Pilgrimage* 207.7385–6: He was bete and hamryd wyth, As a plate up-on a styth.

Play, sb.

P255 After **Play** comes unride (*severe*) sorrows
a1460 *Towneley Plays* 100.11: Ffor after oure play com sorows unryde. See **J58.**

P256 He that is entered into a **Play** must needs assent to the play
c1395 Chaucer *CT* IV[E] 10–1: For what man that is entred in a pley, He nedes moot unto the pley assente. *Oxford* 505; Skeat 275.

P257 Sooth **Play** qued (*bad*) play (*varied*)
c1390 Chaucer *CT* I[A] 4357: But "sooth pley, quaad pley," as the Flemyng seith. **c1450** *Merlin* II 475[12–4]: And for that ever he (*Sir Kay*) wolde of custome borde of the sothe hym hated many a knyght for the shame that thei hadde of his wordes. **1546** Heywood *D* 89.27–8: It is yll jestyng on the soothe, Sooth bourd is no bourd, **1555** *E* 160.88: Sooth boorde, is no boorde: sooth boorde soundeth yll. Apperson 647:11; Jente 752; *Oxford* 604–5; *Revue Belge de Philologie et d'Histoire* 13(1934) 745–9; Skeat 238; Tilley B559.

P258 To play the common **Play**
a1450 *Partonope* 199.5265–6: For to have pleyed the comyn play Off wyche thes lovers have suche plesaunce. **c1450** *Merlin* II 508[34–5]: And fellen down on a grete bedde, and pleyde the comen pley.

P259 To teach one a new **Play** of Yule

a1460 *Towneley Plays* 239.344: We shall teche hym, I wote, a new play of yoyll. (Of the Buffetting)

Play, vb.

P260 He **Plays** best that wins
1555 Heywood *E* 187.230: He pleyth best that wins. Apperson 501; *Oxford* 506; Tilley P404.

P261 It is ill **Playing** with short daggers
1546 Heywood *D* 56.33: For though it be ill plaiyng with short daggers. Apperson 325; *Oxford* 506; Tilley P405.

P262 Long **Plea** is little avail
1454 Paston II 307[14–5]: I know the mater and that longe plee is litill avayll. See **P408.**

P263 After **Pleasance** oft trouble
a1508 Skelton *Phyllyp* I 62.368–9: Oft tyme after pleasaunce Trouble and grevaunce. See **J58, P265.**

P264 I will **Please,** what so betide
a1400 *Proverbis of Wysdom* 244.19–20: "I wyll please, what so betyde." If thow wylt please, lay truthe a syde. *Oxford* 506. See **P248.**

P265 After **Pleasure** comes pain (*varied*)
a1500 *Cotton Vespasian MS. A xxv* in *Rel. Ant.* I 323[2]: After plesur commethe payne. **1506** Hawes *Pastime* 175.4676–7: Thynke well quod she that in the worlde is none Whiche can have pleasure without wo and care. **1509** Barclay *Ship* I 39[21]: For often plesour endeth with sorowe and dolour, 80[21]: But this one pleasour was grounde of moche payne, II 319[23]: So after pleasour oft comys payne. **1513** Douglas *Aeneid* II 194.62: Sen erdly plesour endis oft with sorow, we se. **c1523** Barclay *Mirrour* 26[10]: So after great pleasour succedeth wo and payne. Apperson 3; Tilley P408. See **J58, P130, 263.**

P266 All present **Pleasure** is counted small
c1515 Barclay *Eclogues* 183–4.83–6: All pleasour present of men is counted small, Desire obtayned some counteth nought at all, What men hope after that seemeth great and deare, A(s) light by distaunce appeareth great and cleare.

P267 **Pleasure** seldom endures long
a1533 Berners *Castell* O4v[17]: Pleasour seldome endureth longe. See **W671.**

P268 What **Pleasure** in delicate feasts given with a glooming brow?
c1475 Henryson *Fables* 11.232–3: Quhat plesure is in ffeisitis delicate, The quhilkis ar gevin with ane glowmand brow? See **M700.**

P269 **Plenty** follows after need
1420 Lydgate *Temple* 17.416: And plenti gladli foloith after nede. See **J61.**

P270 **Plenty** is no dainty
c1300 *South English Legendary* (*Laud*) 307.266: For plente nis no deinte: ase we al day i-seot. **c1449** Pecock *Repressor* I 184[8]: Experience wole weel schewe that plente is no deinte. **1546** Heywood *D* 67.52: Plentie is no deintie. Apperson 502; *Oxford* 507; Tilley P425. See **C351.**

P271 Whoso of **Plenty** (wealth) will take no heed shall find default in time of need
a1400 *Proverbis of Wysdom* 247.159–60: Who of plente wyll take no hede, Shal fynd defawte yn tyme of nede. **c1450** *Fyrst thou sal* 89.85–6: Who so in welht takes no hede Sal fynde defawte in tyme of nede. **c1475** *Bodley MS.14526* f.55a in Brown-Robbins 4095: Who of plente wyll take no hede Shal fynde defawte . . . **a1500** Hill 139.1–2: Who so off welth takyth non hede, He shall fynd defawt in tyme of nede. **a1500** *Salamon seyth* in Person 52.25–6: fawte. *Oxford* 507; Whiting *Scots* II 151.

P272 The **Plover** lives on air
a1393 Gower *CA* III 192.943–4: And as the Plover doth of Eir I live. **1484** Caxton *Royal Book* F6r[8–11]: Thenne is he lyke the plovyer whyche lyveth of the wynde and of the ayer . . . And also to every colour that he seeth he chaungeth his sowne (?his owne). Cf. Tilley M226. See **C135.**

P273 Better the **Plow** lie still than to till after hunger
a1450 *Myne awen dere* 174.791–2: Wele better it ware the plugh lye styll Than efter honger for to tyll.

P274 To borrow another man's **Plow**
a1393 Gower *CA* III 353.4218–25: For whan a man mai redy finde His oghne wif, what scholde he seche In strange places to beseche To borwe an other mannes plouh, Whan he hath geere good ynouh Affaited at his oghne heste, And is to him wel more honeste Than other thing which is unknowe? See **C504.**

P275 To hold the **Plow**
1466 Paston IV 250[15–6]: They might not leve thereon, withought they shuld hold the plowe to the tayle. **1520** Whittinton *Vulgaria* 92.9–10: It is a synguler pleasur to me to se them come behynde and holde the plough.

P276 A **Plowman** should go no farther than his plow

c1515 Barclay *Eclogues* 169.792: What should a Ploughman go farther then his plough. Cf. Taylor and Whiting 75.

P277 It is not good to eat **Plums** with one's lord
1484 Caxton *Aesop* 11[1–2]: Men sayen that it is not good to ete plommes with his lord. Jente 669; Tilley C279.

P278 Not worth a (two) **Plum(s)**
c1348 Rolle *Form* in Allen *R. Rolle* 113.166–7: A litel delyte . . . that es noght worth a plowme. **1522** Skelton *Why Come* II 45.601: Ye rebads, nat worth two plummis.

P279 As still as a **Plump** (*clump*) of wood
a1470 Malory I 35.35: And stoode stylle as hit had be a plumpe of woode. NED Plump sb.[1].

P280 As proud as (a, any) **Po** (peacock, pohen)
a1325 *On Consistory Courts* in Böddeker 112.87: A pruest proud ase a po. **c1385** Chaucer *TC* i 210: And yet as proud a pekok kan he pulle, **c1390** *CT* I[A] 3926: As any pecok he was proud and gay. **c1390** *Deo Gracias II* in Brown *Lyrics XIV* 138.18: Another mon proudeth as doth a poo. **a1460** *Towneley Plays* 117.37: A swane as prowde as a po, 344.168: If that I prowde as pacok go. **c1500** Skelton *Womanhod* I 20.13: As proud a pohen, **a1508** *Phyllyp* I 64.438: The pecocke so prowde. **1513** Bradshaw *St. Werburge* 69.1805: Prowde as a Pecocke. **1556** Heywood *Spider* 198[8]: These prowd peacoks propertise. Apperson 514; *Oxford* 521; Taylor and Whiting 278; Tilley P157; Whiting *Drama* 322:245, *Scots* II 109.

P281 The first **Point** of hawking is to hold fast
1469 Paston V 22[25–6]: I purpose to use the fyrst poynt of hawkyng, to hold fast and I maye. **a1475** *Booke of Hawkyng* in *Rel. Ant.* I 296 [14–5]: The first (*term of hawking*) is holde fast when abatith. **1546** Heywood *D* 69.103: The fyrst point of haukyng is holde fast. Apperson 291; *Oxford* 283–4; Tilley P453.

P282 For a **Point** the Picard lost his eye
c1450 *Douce MS.52* 54.112: For a poynt the Picarde lost is ye. Uno pro puncto caruit Picardus ocello. **c1450** *Rylands MS.394* 104.19. Note (*Douce*) cfs. French *Faute d'un point Martin perdit son âne,* and queries an original *asello* for *ocello* in Latin.

P283 If a man is aggrieved in one **Point** he shall be relieved in another
c1390 Chaucer *CT* I[A] 4180–2: For, John, ther is a lawe that says thus, That gif a man in a point be agreved, That in another he sal be releved. See Robinson's note, p. 688. See **T339.**

P284 Not set a **Point**
1520 Whittinton *Vulgaria* 92.29: I set not a poynt what thou can laye to my charge.

P285 Not worth (the, a) **Point** (of a pin)
1556 Heywood *Spider* 409[14]: I take not the gift, worth the point of a pin, **1560** *E* 216.62.2: For he is not woorth a pointe. Apperson 458:29; Tilley P456. See **A71.**

P286 The **Point(ing)** of a preen (*pin*)
1445 *He michti Makar* in Felix J. H. Skene *Liber Pluscardensis* (*Historians of Scotland* 7 [Edinburgh, 1877]) 387[23]: Dyd nevir of plycth (*sin*) the pointyr of a preyn. **c1500** *King Hart* 89.27–8: That no man micht the poynting of ane prene Repreve.

P287 She has one **Point** of a good hawk, she is hardy
1546 Heywood *D* 69.102: She hath one poynt of a good hauke, she is hardie. Apperson 290; Tilley P454.

P288 As odious as **Poison**
c1475 Banester *Guiscardo* 18.292: Vhich wes to hym more odyouse then poysoune. Cf. Taylor and Whiting 290.

P289 **Poison** under sugar
a1420 Lydgate *Troy* I 26.515: The prevy poysoun under sugre cured. **1529** More *Supplicacion* 291 H[13–4]: Covering his poison under some tast of suger. See **C177, G12, H433, 440, V19.**

P290 As straight as any **Pole**
c1497 Medwall *Fulgens* E4^r[7]: I kyst it as strayght as ony pole, [14]: Of the holowe ashe as strayte as a pole.

P291 To stink like a **Polecat**
1533 Heywood *Johan* A2^r[3]: She shall stynke lyke a pole kat. Apperson 504; *Oxford* 621; Tilley P461.

P292 From the **Poor** turn never your face
a1400 *Proverbis of Wysdom* 245.83–4: If thou wylt have gwode grace, Fro the poere turne never thy face. **c1450** *Fyrst thou sal* 89.67–8. Cf. Tilley P471.

P293 He has well that gives to the **Poor** (*varied*)
c1350 *Good Wife E* 158.12: Wel hat that the pouere giveth, **c1425** *H* 159.12: Tresour he hath that pouere fedith, **c1450** *L* 197.12–3: Weel he proveth that the poore loveth, **c1500** *T* 203. 12–3: Well he tresoreth That the poore honowreth. Apperson 208. Cf. Tilley P471.

P294 He is not **Poor** that is happy
1525 Berners *Froissart* VI 65[8–9]: Therfore it

is an olde proverbe: He is nat poore that is happy. See **E120, P331.**

P295 If one is **Poor** his friends flee him (*varied*) **c1390** Chaucer *CT* II[B] 120–1: If thou be povre, thy brother hateth thee, And alle thy freendes fleen from thee, allas! VII 1559–60 [B2749–50]: And if thy fortune change that thou wexe povre, farewel freendshipe and felaweshipe; for thou shalt be alloone withouten any compaignye, but if it be the compaignye of povre folk. **a1400** ?Chaucer *Rom. A* 466–7: For pover thing, whereso it be, Is shamefast and dispised ay. **1509** Watson *Ship* Q1r[24]: The poore man hathe no frendes, S5r[5]: The poore man is hated of every body. **a1533** Berners *Arthur* 6[24–5]: Pore folkes hath but fewe frendes. *Oxford* 511; Skeat 243; Tilley P468. See **G348, M180, P301, 335, S109.**

P296 If the **Poor** (com)plain he wins but little **c1405** *Mum* 72–3.1575–9: And bringeth a bitter byworde a-brode among the peuple, And is in every cuntre but a comune tale That yf the pouer playne, though he plede ever And hurleth with his higher, hit happeth ofte-tyme That he wircheth al in waste and wynneth but a lite.

P297 Of the **Poor** men tell (*account*) little **c1300** *South English Legendary* (*Laud*) 288.15: Ech man tolde luyte of him—for of the povere Men wolleth so. Cf. Jente 107. See **M265.**

P298 The **Poor** and the rich are born and die in the same wise **a1393** Gower *CA* II 217.3246–9: The povere is bore as is the riche And deieth in the same wise, Upon the fol, upon the wise Siknesse and hele entrecomune. See **D101, K49, L448.**

P299 The **Poor** demands and begs ere he feels **1474** Caxton *Chesse* 148[9–10]: And therfore hit is sayd that the poure demandeth and beggeth er he felith.

P300 The **Poor** had no bread and yet he bought a hound **1492** *Salomon and Marcolphus* 10[9–10]: The pore had ne breed and yet he bought an hownde.

P301 The **Poor** has few to succor his party **a1449** Lydgate *Fabules* in *MP* II 575.242: The pore hathe few hys party to socour. See **G348, P295.**

P302 The **Poor** is hanged by the neck, a rich man by the purse **a1400** *Additional MS.41321* f.86 in Owst *Literature* 43[23–4]: As it is seide in olde proverbe—Pore be hangid bi the necke; a riche man bi the purs. See **B639, P448.**

P303 Some are now **Poor** that sometime were bold (wore gold) **c1425** *Good Wife H* 171.165: That now ben full pouer that sum tyme wer full bolde, **a1500** *N* 215.195: For some folk are now pore that somtime ware gold.

P304 As merry as a **Popinjay** **c1390** Chaucer *CT* VII 369[B1559]: And hoom he gooth, murie as a papejay. Svartengren 71.

P305 As proud as any **Popinjay** **a1508** *Freiris of Berwik* in Dunbar 186.142: Scho was als prowd as ony papingo.

P306 To sing like a **Popinjay** **c1395** Chaucer *CT* IV[E] 2322: Syngeth ful murier than the papejay. **a1430** Hoccleve *Roundel* II 38.20: And shee syngith ful lyk a papeJay.

P307 As sweet as resty (*rancid*) **Pork** **c1497** Medwall *Fulgens* C3v[3–4]: And her voyce is as doucett And as swete as resty porke.

P308 As fat as a **Pork-hog** **a1470** Malory I 295.3–4: He shall be as fatte . . . as a porke hog. Apperson 205; Tilley H483.

P309 To row to (arrive at, come to) (a) good (ill) **Port** **c1385** Chaucer *TC* i 969: For to good port hastow rowed. **1487** Caxton *Book of Good Manners* H3v[1–2]: They . . . shullen arryve at a good porte. **1509** Watson *Ship* T2v[2–3]: With grete payne may they come to gode porte. **a1533** Berners *Huon* 57.12: Ye be aryved at a good port, 74.7–8, 479.25–6: We be aryved at an yll port.

P310 Between this and **Portugal** **1481** Caxton *Reynard* 13[34]: Alle the hony that is bytwene this and portyngale.

P311 **Possession** takes no force of (*pays no heed to*) wrong or right **a1439** Lydgate *Fall* III 742.2527: Pocessioun take no fors of wrong or riht, 2534, 2541. Cf. Taylor and Whiting 292.

P312 As strong as a **Post** (*etc.*) (A number of single quotations are brought together here) **1340** *Ayenbite* 180[30–1]: Strang and stedevest ase a pos(t) ine his temple. **c1412** Hoccleve *Regement* 169.4695–6: As harde as is a post —A post? Nay, as a stoon—ben hertes now! **c1450** *Edward the Confessor Prose II* 111[4–5]: And so was Seynt Edward, hys yonger brother, left as post a-loon. **a1470** Malory I 196.23–4: And his pawys were as byg as a poste.

P313 From **Post** to pillar
a1475 *Assembly of Gods* 34.1147: Thus fro poost to pylour was he made to daunce. **c1515** Barclay *Eclogues* 117.273: From poste unto piller tossed. **1546** Heywood *D* 62.8: From post to pyller . . . I have beene tost, **1555** *E* 190.251. Apperson 496; *Oxford* 500; Taylor and Whiting 285; Tilley P328.

P314 To be like a **Post**
a1400 *Morte Arthure* 23.776: With yche a pawe as a poste.

P315 To kiss the **Post**
a1508 Skelton *Phyllyp* I 73.714–6: Troylus also hath lost On her moche love and cost, And now must kys the post. **c1515** Barclay *Eclogues* 91.1001: Shalt thou lose thy meat and kisse the post. Apperson 344; *Oxford* 340; Tilley P494.

P316 To play at **Post** and pillar
c1440 Charles of Orleans 162.4834: And there at post and piler did she play, 174.5203: For at the post and piler did thei play. See I xxxvii–viii and II 34, which suggest a children's game, but the context implies an adult modification, though still innocent.

P317 To preach to the (a) **Post**
c1450 *How mankinde dooth* in Furnivall *Hymns* 61.103: Good conscience, goo preche to the post. **1528** More *Heresyes* 287 A[5–7]: A man maye with as much fruite preache to a post, as reason with them, **1532** *Confutacion* 408 E[1–2]: It is nothing elles but to say a pater noster to a post, [11–2]. Cf. Taylor and Whiting 292: As deaf as a post; Tilley P491. See **S788, T519.**

P318 As dried as a **Pot**
a1400 *Northern Verse Psalter* I 61 (21.16): Dried als a pot might be Alle mi might with innen me.

P319 An earthen (glassen) **Pot** (vessel) should not fight with a cauldron
c1390 *Proverbes of diverse profetes* 526.73–4: Hit nis not worth an old Botoun An eorthene pot to fihte with a Caudron. **c1390** *Suffer in Time* in Brown *Lyrics XIV* 201.37–40: Hit is luytel worth, seith Socrates, A glasen pot is wayk and liht To puiten him self to fer in pres A-geynes a caudrun for to fiht. **c1395** *WBible* Ecclesiasticus xiii 3: What schal a cawdroun comyne (**a1382:** comune) to a pot? for whanne tho hirtlen hem silf togidere, *the pot* schal be brokun. **a1400** *Titus* 54.1159–60: The erthen vessell lasteth noght To hurtell with that of metall is wroght. Apperson 174; *Oxford* 164; Tilley P495. See **C553.**

P320 He that comes last to **Pot** is worst served (soonest wroth)
c1400 *Beryn* 101.3366–7: Fful soth is that byword, "to pot, who comyth last!" He worst is served. **a1500** Hill 132.42: He that commeth last to the pot, ys sonnest wrothe. **1546** Heywood *D* 98.18: He that commeth last to the pot, is soonest wroth. Apperson 351; *Oxford* 104; Tilley P496.

P321 Little **Pot** soon hot
1546 Heywood *D* 42.26: Little potte soone whot. Apperson 372; *Oxford* 374; Tilley P497.

P322 Neither **Pot** broken nor water spilt
1546 Heywood *D* 53.399: Neither pot broken, nor water spylt. Apperson 507; Tilley P499.

P323 The **Pot** goes so long to the water that (at last) it comes home broken
1340 *Ayenbite* 206[14–5]: Me couthe zigge: zuo longe geth thet pot to the wetere: thet hit comth to-broke hom. **c1400** *Vices and Virtues* 228.3–4: Men seien so longe goth the pott to the watre he cometh broke home. **c1412** Hoccleve *Regement* 160.4432–3: The pot so longe to the watir goth, That hoom it cometh at the laste y-broke. **c1450** *Douce MS.52* 52.88: The pot goth so longe to water, that he comyth broke home. **c1450** La Tour-Landry 82.17–9: And therfor it is a trew proverbe, that "the potte may goo so longe to water, that atte the laste it is broken," 90.18–9: And therfor, in olde Englisshe, it is saide that "so ofte goth the potte to water, that atte the laste it comithe broken home." **c1450** *Rylands MS.394* 102.8: The pot gos to the fyre ay tyl oon day. **a1460** *Towneley Plays* 126.317–9: Bot so long goys the pott to the water, men says, At last Comys it home broken. **1481** Caxton *Reynard* 67[15–8]: A pot may goo so longe to water that at the laste it cometh to broken hoom. I thynke your potte that so oft hath deceyved us shal now hastly be broken, **1484** *Royal Book* R4^{r}[18–9]: It is sayd that so longe gooth the potte to water, that at the laste it breketh. **1546** Heywood *D* 84.148–9: Yet lo, the pot so long to the water gothe, Tyll at the laste it comthe home broken. Apperson 498–9; Jente 42; Owst *Literature* 43; *Oxford* 502; Taylor and Whiting 288; Tilley P501.

P324 The **Pot** is easy to keep where the fat is overblown (*blown away*)
a1475 *Good Rule* in Brown *Lyrics XV* 265.59–60:

The pot is esy for to kepe Ther the fatte is over-blowe.

P325 A **Pot** that is well baked may best endure
1492 *Salomon and Marcolphus* 6[15–6]: A pot that is wele baken may best endure, and that clene is browyn that may they fayre drinken.

P326 To have the **Pot** by the steal (*handle*)
1402 Hoccleve *Letter of Cupid* 74.50–5: And whann this man the pot hath be the stele, And full is in his possessyon, With that woman kepeth he not to dele After. See **M206.**

P327 When the **Pot** boils the best remedy is to withdraw the fire
c1390 Chaucer *CT* X[I] 951: For certes, whan the pot boyleth strongly, the beste remedie is to withdrawe the fyr. See **B506.**

P328 A **Potful** of milk must be kept well from the cat
1492 *Salomon and Marcolphus* 6[12–3]: A potfull of mylke muste be kept wele from the katte. See **C109.**

P329 Better **Pottage** in charity than many delices with chiding (*varied*)
c1390 *Proverbes of diverse profetes* 535.193–6: Bettre is potage with-outen othur mes With charite and good(e) pes, Then mony delyces with chydyng—This is the wyse monnes saying. **a1500** *How the Wyse Man* 31.97–100: For bettyr hyt ys in reste and pees A messe of potage and no more, Then for to have a thousand messe Wyth grete dysese and anger sore. See **D257, M614, 700.**

P330 In a dirty **Pouch** a treasure often lies
c1025 *Durham Proverbs* 10.7: Oft on sotigum bylige searowa licgað. Sepe in file sacculo fulget aurum. See **H3.**

P331 Glad **Poverty** is an honest thing
c1395 Chaucer *CT* III[D] 1183–6: Glad poverte is an honest thyng, certeyn; This wole Senec and othere clerkes seyn. Whoso that halt hym payd of his poverte, I holde hym riche, al hadde he nat a sherte. See **P294.**

P332 Let him who tells of his **Poverty** beg before his friend
c1025 *Durham Proverbs* 10.5: Beforan his freonde biddeþ (*?for* bidde) se þe his wædle mæneþ. Postulet coram amico qui penuriam suam predicat.

P333 **Poverty** and patience are needs playferes (*playmates*)
c1380 *Patience* 14.45: Thus Poverte and Pacyence arn nedes play-feres.

P334 **Poverty** (de)parts (breaks) company (fellowship)
1406 Hoccleve *Male Regle* 29.133 Fy! Lak of coyn departith compaignie. **c1450** *Douce MS.52* 54.107: Poverte brekys companye. **c1450** *Rylands MS.394* 104.29: partes felshipe. **a1471** Ashby *Policy* 29.513–4: It hathe be, and yet is a comyn sawe, That Poverte departithe felaship. **1471** Paston V 122[6]: I may sey poverte partes feleschepe. **a1500** Hill 129.44: Powerte partith felishipe. **a1500** *Man, be war* in T. Wright *Songs and Carols* (PS 23, 1847) 34[3]: This wrat I oftyn, poverte partyth company. **1546** Heywood *D* 56.58: Povertie parteth felowship, **1555** *E* 190.249. Apperson 509; *Oxford* 514; Tilley P529. See **L507, P343.**

P335 **Poverty** has few friends (*varied*)
c1300 *Beves* 170.3593–4: For, whan a man is in poverte falle, He hath fewe frendes with alle. **a1400** *Romaunt B* 5456–62: Whanne they arn falle in poverte, And ben of good and catell bare; Thanne shulde they sen who freendis ware. For of an hundred, certeynly, Nor of a thousand full scarsly, Ne shal they fynde unnethis oon, Whanne poverte is comen upon. **c1450** *Proverbs of Good Counsel* 68.22: Poverte hathe but frendis fewe. **a1500** *Salamon seyth* in Person 52.24: Poverte hath but frendys few. Smith 234; Whiting *Drama* 84. See **G348, P295, 301, S109.**

P336 **Poverty** in surety is better than riches in fear (*varied*)
1477 Rivers *Dictes* 29[30–1]: Povertie in surete is better than richesse in fere. **1484** Caxton *Aesop* 17[1–3]: Better worthe is to lyve in poverte surely than to lyve rychely beyng ever in daunger. **1509** Barclay *Ship* I 188[13–4]: Better is povertye though it be harde to bere Than is a hye degre in jeopardy and fere. Tilley P525. See **M700.**

P337 **Poverty** is a possession that no wight will challenge
c1395 Chaucer *CT* III[D] 1199–1200: Poverte is this, although it seme alenge, Possessioun that no wight wol chalenge. See **W717.**

P338 **Poverty** is a spectacle (*means*) through which one sees his friends
c1395 Chaucer *CT* III[D] 1203–4: Poverte a spectacle is, as thynketh me, Thurgh which he may his verray freendes see. Jente 429. See **F634, 672.**

P339 **Poverty** is better than evil gotten richesse
1477 Rivers *Dictes* 54[20–1]: Povertee is better than evyll goten richesse.

P340 **Poverty** is hateful good
c1378 *Piers* B xiv 274: *"Pauperitas,"* quod Pacience, *"est odibile bonum."* **c1395** Chaucer *CT* III[D] 1195: Poverte is hateful good. See Robinson, p. 704.

P341 **Poverty** is mother of health
c1378 *Piers* B xiv 298: (Poverte) is moder of helthe. Apperson 508; *Oxford* 514; Tilley P528.

P342 Righteous **Poverty** may prevail against men of great avail (*worth*)
a1500 *Colkelbie* 302.185–7: Presome nevir bot povert may prewaill Be it rychtwiss aganis men of grit availl That ar nocht wyiss bot wranguss in thair deidis. See **R129.**

P343 Where **Poverty** is, all love is clearly past
c1520 Walter *Spectacle* B4ʳ[21]: Where poverty is, all love is clerely past. Cf. Tilley P531. See **L507, P334.**

P344 As thick as **Powder**
a1300 *Richard* 355.5439–40: Quarellys, arwes also thykke gan flye, As it were poudyr in the skye. **a1460** *Towneley Plays* 52.19–20: I shall thi seede multyply, As thyk as powder on erthe may ly. Svartengren 398.

P345 One must ever abow (*yield*) to him that has most **Power**
c1300 *South English Legendary* II 616.184: For evere me mot him abowe that hath mest power. See **B276.**

P346 **Power,** possession and richesse no man may set in sickerness
a1500 *Salamon seyth* in Person 52.11–2: Power, possessyon and rychesse No man may sette yn sykernesse.

P347 **Practice** in all touches the quick
1546 Heywood *D* 28.32–6: Practyse in all, above all toucheth the quicke. Proofe uppon practise, must take holde more sure, Than any reasonyng by gesse can procure. If ye bryng practise in place, without fablyng, I wyll banysh both haste and busy bablyng. Smith 236; Tilley P537a. See **L409, P358.**

P348 Each **Praise** is to be sung at the end
c1000 Aelfric *Homilies* I 56[27]: Aelc lof bið on ende gesungen. See **P39.**

P349 He must **Praise** himself since no man else will
c1450 *Douce MS.52* 49.60: I wyll prayse myselfe, syn no man ellys wyll. **c1450** *Rylands MS.394* 99.18. See **N79.**

P350 To **Praise** as one finds
a1449 Lydgate *Freond* in *MP* II 758.95: Preyse as thou fyndest in thyne opynioun. **c1497** Medwall *Fulgens* F6ᵛ[29]: I wyll prayse as I fynde. See **T16.**

P351 To **Praise** oneself is wrong (*varied*)
a1387 Higden-Trevisa VII 285[10–2]: For it is i-hated a man to make hymself curious in his owne preysinge. **c1395** *WBible* Proverbs xxvii 2: Another man, and not thi mouth preise thee; a straunger, and not thi lippis *preise thee.* **1450** *Dicts* 168.14–6: And thei askid him whate thing a man shulde not say though it were trouthe; he aunswered the preise of him-silve, 276.18–21. **1484** Caxton *Aesop* 229[1–2]: No fowler a thyng is to the man than with his mouth to preyse hym self. **c1523** Barclay *Mirrour* 76[12–4]: For this is a proverbe sounding to veritie, Of thy proper mouth thy laude is not laudable, But other mens prayse is greatly commendable. Smith 238; Tilley M476, P547; Whiting *Drama* 242. See **D155, M173.**

P352 To **Praise** to one's face
1483 *Vulgaria quedam abs Terencio* P5ᵛ[16]: I am ashamyd to prayse the to thy face. Cf. Taylor and Whiting 295.

P353 Great **Praisers** are commonly great lackers (*blamers*)
a1470 Parker *Dives* M2ᵛ[2.4–5]: For comonly grete praysers be grete lackers. See **L17, 562.**

P354 **Pray** for yourself, I am not sick
1549 Heywood *D* 85.159: Pray for your selfe, I am not sicke. Apperson 510; *Oxford* 516; Tilley P551.

P355 Much **Prayer** with little devotion
1546 Heywood *D* 96.197–8: Ave Maria (quoth he) how much mocion Here is to praiers, with how littell devocion. *Oxford* 516; Tilley P552.

P356 **Prayer** is (made) hardy (*bold*) with gifts
1481 Caxton *Reynard* 70[20]: The preyer is wyth yeftes hardy.

P357 A short **Prayer** pierces (thirls [*pierces*] wins) heaven
a1400 *Cloud* 75.5: It is wretyn that schort preier peersith heven. **a1470** Parker *Dives* E7ʳ[1.8–22]: It is a comon proverbe, that a shorte prayer thyrleth heven. Oracio brevis penetrat celum. . . . It is a comon proverbe of truantes, that soone be wery of theyr prayers, and have more haste to the taverne than to holy chirche, and have more lykynge in the worlde than in god. Nevertheles, yf it be well understande the proverbe is true, good and holy. **a1475** *Good Wyfe Wold* 175.84: A schort prayer

wynnythe heyvyn, the Pater Noster and an Ave. **c1475** *Mankind* 21.551: A schorte preyere thyrlyth hewyn: of thi preyere blyn. Apperson 567; Tilley P555.

P358 He **Preaches** that which he proves not
c1378 *Piers* B xiii 79: That he precheth he preveth nought. See **P347.**

P359 They **Preach** but do nothing as they preach
a1400 *Song against the Friars* in Wright *Political Poems* I 268[1–2]: Ful wysely can thai preche and say; Bot as thai preche no thing do thai. See **L463.**

P360 Except the **Preacher** himself live well, his predication helps never a deal
1533 Heywood *Pardoner* B3ᵛ[34–5]: For that except the precher hym selfe lyve well, His predycacyon wyll helpe never a dell. See **L463.**

P361 A **Preacher** should live perfectly and do as he teaches
a1450 Audelay 29.530–1: A prechur schuld lyve parfytly And do as he techys truly. Apperson 509. See **L463.**

P362 Many a (good) **Predication** (*sermon*) comes of evil intention
c1390 Chaucer *CT* VI[C] 407–8: For certes, many a predicacioun Comth ofte tyme of yvel entencioun. **a1400** *Romaunt B* 5763–4: For ofte good predicacioun Cometh of evel entencioun.

P363 Not count a **Preen** (*pin*)
c1470 *Wallace* 168.910: Off courtlynes thai cownt him nocht a preyne. Whiting *Scots* II 112.

P364 Not set a **Preen**
c1516 Skelton *Magnificence* 47.1489: I set not by the prowdest of them a prane, **1523** *Howe the Douty Duke* II 72.163–4: We set nat a prane By suche a dronken drane. Whiting *Drama* 359:787, *Scots* II 113. See **P212.**

P365 Not worth (half) a **Preen**
c1475 Henryson *Ressoning* 179.22: Nor of my pith may pair of wirth a prene (*var.* half a prene). **a1500** *Thre Prestis* 50.1191: To the thow thocht I was not worth ane prene. *Oxford* 500; Whiting *Drama* 359:787, *Scots* II 112–3. See **P213.**

P366 To put a **Preen** in one's eyes
a1200 *Ancrene* 45.5: The fikelere blent mon and put him preon i the ehe, **a1400** (*Recluse*) 36.18–9: Pryk, **a1500** (*Royal*) 11.20–1: prikes.

P367 Entre **Prendre** et pendre is but one letter
a1387 Higden-Trevisa VIII 231[1–3]: He (*St. Edmund Rich*) hated fongers of giftes, and seide on Frensche, "Entre prendre et pendre is but oon lettre alone." Latin (p. 230): Munerum acceptatores detestabatur, dicens Gallice, "Inter prendre et pendre unica dumtaxat distat iota."

P368 Great **Press** at market makes dear ware
c1395 Chaucer *CT* III[D] 521–3: With daunger oute we al oure chaffare; Greet prees at market maketh deere ware, And to greet cheep is holde at litel prys.

P369 **Press** has envy
a1439 Lydgate *Fall* II 533.2202–3: Hih clymbyng up is medlid with disdeyn: Pres hath envie, as it is ofte seyn.

P370 For **Price** nor prayer
a1500 *Disciplina Clericalis* 47[28]: For nothing price nor praier shal I syng. Cf. Taylor and Whiting 229: For love or money.

P371 He tines (*loses*) his **Price** (*honor*) that does faintise (*cowardice*) at the end
c1400 *Alexander Buik* I 78.2477–80: Bot he tynes his mekill prys That at the end dois fantys. Quha dois best at the ending, Thay have pryse and maist loving. See **E90, S163.**

P372 To give **Price** (prick) and prick (price)
c1495 *Arundel Vulgaria* 92.385: And such onn whom all menn gave price and pryke withoute comparicioun. **a1500** Medwall *Nature* F2ᵛ[42]: Now forsoth I gyve the pryk and pryse. NED Prick 20.

P373 As sharply as a **Prick**
a1396(1494) Hilton *Scale* C4ʳ[30]: It shal smyte upon thyne hert sharply as a prycke.

P374 To come to (drive nigh, be almost at, draw near) the **Prick**
c1390 Chaucer *CT* II[B] 119: Be war, therfore, er thou come to that prikke, 1029: There is no man koude brynge hire to that prikke. **c1400** *Laud Troy* I 196.6639–40: That he was dryven so ney the prikke, That he myght not his lippis likke. **c1422** Hoccleve *Lerne to Die* 209.847: Remembre or that he come to the prikke. **1431** Lydgate *Defence* in *MP* I 31.22–3: Constreyned was, and almost at the prikk Talefft hir song. **a1460** *Towneley Plays* 236.263: When it com to the pryk, 378.370: I trowd it drew nere the prik. **1528** More *Heresyes* 141 B[12–3]: This gere howe nere it goeth to the prik.

P375 To hit (shoot nigh) the **Prick**
c1400 *Sowdone* 65.2260: Thou kanste welle hit the prikke. **1546** Heywood *D* 28.31: Nowe

ye shoote nie the pricke. *Oxford* 296; Tilley P571.

P376 To set the **Prick**
c1412 Hoccleve *Regement* 20.528: Ther wold I fayne that were y-set the prikke.

P377 To spurn against the **Prick** (*varied*)
c1000 Aelfric *Homilies* I 390[9]: Derigendlic bið ðe þæt þu spurne ongean þa gade. **c1300** *South English Legendary* I 265.27: Ayen the prikke to wincy swuthe strong it is to the. **c1390** Chaucer *Truth* 11: Be war also to sporne ayeyns an al. **a1393** Gower *CA* II 229.116–7: And thus myn hand ayein the pricke I hurte and have do many day. **c1395** *WBible* Deeds of the Apostles, Prologue IV 507[24–5]: The apostlis, whom the Lord hadde chosun, that long tyme wynside ayen the pricke, ix 5: It is hard to thee, to kike ayens the pricke, xxii 7, xxvi 14. **a1400** *Cursor* III 1124 F 19625–8: Hit is to the ful harde and wik For to wirk a-gaine the prik, That is to say over might Againe thi lorde for to fight. **a1400** *Scottish Legends* I 44.542–3: For is it nocht hard to the Agane the brod thu for to prese? **c1400** *De Apostasia* in Wyclif *SEW* III 436[6]: It is to hard to kyke ayen the spore. **a1402** Trevisa *Dialogus* 23.14–5: Ye kiketh ayenus the prike of kynges. **c1425** Paues 146 (Acts 9.5): Hit es ful harde to the to kese (*vars.* kyse, kynse) agayne tho prikke, 192 (Acts 26.14): Hit es harde to the to kes (*vars.* kyce, kynse) agayne tho brodde (*var.* prikke). **a1430** Lydgate *Pilgrimage* 304.11136–9: And I kan wynse ageyn the prykke, As wylde coltys in Arras, Or as bayard out off the tras, Tyl I a lassh have off the whyppe, 390.14459: Hard ys to sporne ageyn an hal. **c1450** Idley 195.2212: Who sporneth ayenst a thorn, I holde hym madde. **c1450** *Pilgrimage LM* 120[8]: Men seyn he is not wys that hurteleth ayens a sharp poynt. **1471** Ripley *Compound* 132[10–1]: But hard hyt ys with thy bare foote to spurne, Agaynst a brodyke of Iyron or Stele new acuatte. **1483** Caxton *Golden Legende* 87^{v}[2.22–3]: It is harde to the to stryve ayenste the nalle or prycke. **1483** *Vulgaria quedam abs Terencio* Q2^{r}[14]: It is a foly to sporn ageyns the pryk. **c1485** *Conversion* 34.184: Yt ys hard to pryke a-gayns the spore. **1492** *Salomon and Marcolphus* 7[16]: It is hard to spurne agenst the sharp prykyl. **1513** More *Richard* 70 H[13–4]: I purpose not to spurne againste a prick. **1520** Whittinton *Vulgaria* 44.21: It is foly to spron agaynst the prycke. **1525** Berners *Froissart* V 54[18–9]: He spurneth agaynst the pricke. **1546** Heywood *D* 72.87: Foly it is to spourne against a pricke. Apperson 339; Jente 686; *Oxford* 333; Taylor and Whiting 296; Tilley B680, F433; Whiting *Drama* 351:659, *Scots* II 113. See **W20.**

P378 After **Pride** comes great reproof
a1400 *Ipomadon A* 29.941–3: It hathe byn sayd in lest of love, That aftur pryde comythe grette reprove, Of the wysest yet that was. See **P385.**

P379 Fie on **Pride** when men go naked
1562 Heywood *E* 233.28.1: Fie on pride when men go nakte. See **M267.**

P380 The higher in **Pride** the lower in pain
c1450 *Jacob's Well* 237.2: The heyghere in pride the lowere in peyne. See **C296.**

P381 In **Pride** and poverty is great penance (*pain*)
a1475 *Good Rule* in Brown *Lyrics XV* 264.37: In pryde and poverte is gret penaunce. Cf. Apperson 511; *Oxford* 517.

P382 The more **Pride** the more shame
a1500 *Proverbs of Salamon* 183.40.1: The more pryde the more schame.

P383 Overdone **Pride** works (makes) naked side
c1350 *Good Wife E* 164.104–5: Overdon pride Wirchet (*H* Makyth) nakede side, **a1500** *N* 215.196–7: Many folk for pride After weren a naked side. Apperson 512. See **O63, T86.**

P384 **Pride** brings many to woe (*varied*)
c1400 *Laud Troy* I 111.3749–51: I holde that power good every tyde That is with-oute the vice of pride, For offte it falles many to wo. **c1420** Wyntoun VI 229.6859–64: Swilk is casse of batalle, That pryde oftsyis wil gere fail That is apperande richt likly To do oft tymys succudry; Messurabil is gud to be, And heyr proffer of honest(e). **a1425** *Chester Plays* I 14.119–20: Therfore I warne the, Lucifere, This pride will turne to great distresse, 19.253: Ah! wicked pryde aye work thee wo! **c1485** *Conversion* 47.524–5: Who-so in pride beryth hym to hye, With mys(c)heff shalbe mekyd. Whiting *Scots* II 113.

P385 **Pride** goes before and shame comes after
a1400 *Proverbis of Wysdom* 244.11: Pryde goyth be fore, and after comythe shame. **a1400** *Tho oure lord god* 319[40–1]: For ever pride schent his frend by day other by nyghte, For pride goth ay by fore and schame cometh after. **c1400** *Additional MS.41321* f.101b in Owst *Literature* 42, n[11]: As it is seid in comen proverbe—Pride goth bifore, and schame cometh after. **c1420** Wyntoun VI 15.3965–70: Aulde men in thar prowerbe sayis (*var.* For wissmen

in ald proverbis sayis): "Pride gays before, and schaym alwayis Folowis this syne allssa fast, And it ourtakis at the last." Sa pride ourtane is oft withe skaythe, Or withe schaym, or than withe bathe. **a1440** Palladius 31.213–4: War arrogaunce in taking thyng on honde, Ffor aftir pride in scorn thou mayst assure. **c1450** *Douce MS.52* 56.135. **c1450** *Fyrst thou sal* 88.29. **c1450** Idley 140.2000: and shame cometh behynde. **c1450** *Jacob's Well* 70.12. **c1450** *Rylands MS.394* 107.23.1. **a1475** *Good Rule* in Brown *Lyrics XV* 265.71. **c1475** *Rawlinson MS. D 328* 119.22, 122.58. **c1475** *Thewis* 178.52: For eftyr prid oft folowis schame. **a1500** *Merita Missae* 153.170–1. **a1500** *Ryght as small flodes* 160.200: and shame cometh behynde. **a1500** Hill 128.17, 131.24. **1509** Barclay *Ship* II 164[21–2]: Therfore it is sayd (and true it is doutles) That pryde goth before, but shame do it ensue, 165[4], [12], [18–20], [27–8]. **a1529** Skelton *Garnesche* I 131.165. **1546** Heywood *D* 38.115, **1556** *Spider* 392[28]. Apperson 511; *Oxford* 518; Tilley P576; Whiting *Drama* 44. See **B413, P378, 391, 426.**

P386 Pride goes before sorrow
c1395 *WBible* Proverbs xvi 18: Pride goith bifore sorewe (**a1382:** contricioun); and the spirit schal be enhaunsid byfor fallyng. *Oxford* 518.

P387 Pride is man's bane
c1450 *Rylands MS.394* 110.ix: Allas pride is manys bane.

P388 Pride is the first seed of sorrow
a1400 Lavynham 5.29: Pride is the ferst seed of sorwe.

P389 Pride is the root of all evils (*varied*)
a1000 *Vercelli Homilies* 55.25–56.26: Ofer-hyȝd, sio is cwen eallra yfla. **c1000** Aelfric *Homilies* II 220[33–4]: Se eahteoða leahter is modignys. Se leahter is ord and ende ælces yfeles, *Lives* I 358.306–8: Seo eahteoðe leahter is superbia gehaten, þæt is on ænglisc modignyss gecweden, Seo is ord and ende ælcere synne, *Pastoral Letter* 204 O 151: Seo modiȝniss is ælces yfeles ord and ende. **c1000** *Ammonitio amici* in Napier 249.6–7: Seo modignyss ys ealra unþeawa anginn and ealra mægna hryre. **c1000** *Larspel* in Napier 245.12–3: Se forma is ælces yfeles ord, se is *superbia* gehaten. **c1200** *Vices and Virtues* (*Stowe*) 5.7–8: Superbia, that is, modinesse . . . was anginn of alle sennes. **a1225** *Lambeth Homilies* 103[33–4] (Aelfric's *Homily* as above): Superbia, thet is on englisc, modinesse. Heo is ord and ende of alle uvele. **a1333** Shoreham *Poems* 107.233–6: The ferste pryns hys prede, That ledeth thane flok, That of alle othere onlede Hys rote and eke stok. **1340** *Ayenbite* 16.11–2: The zenne of prede, vor thet wes the verste zenne and the aginninge of alle kueade. **c1340** Rolle *Psalter* 24 (7.3): Pride, the whilk is rote of all illes, 71 (18.14): Pride, that is bigynnynge and cheson of all synn. **a1393** Gower *CA* II 126.3309: Pride is the heved of alle Sinne. **c1395** *WBible* Ecclesiasticus x 15: Pride is the bigynnyng of al synne. **a1396**(1494) Hilton *Scale* H3ʳ[3–4]: As the wyse man sayth . . . The begynnyng of all maner of synne is pryde. **a1400** Lavynham 2.6: Pride he (*Seynt Gregory*) seyth is rote of alle vicys. **a1400** Wyclif *Sermons* I 43[18]: The rote of al this (*strife*) is pryde. **c1400** *Vices and Virtue* 11.14–5: Pride, for that was the first synne and bigynnyng of al evele. **a1410** Love *Mirrour* 82[12–3]: The bigynnynge of alle synne is pride. **c1415** *Middle English Sermons* 68.3: The begynnynge of every synne is pride. **a1422** Lydgate *Life* 611.341–3: O pryde, alas, o Rote of our distresse! Though thy boste above the skyes blowe Thy bildyng high shall be brought full lowe! **a1439** *Fall* I 37.1338–9: Ye that be wise, considreth how the roote Off vicis alle is pride. **a1450** *Desert* 60.97: Pryde was begynnyng of all ill. **c1450** Greene *Carols* 355.1: And pride is rot of every synne. **c1450** *Jacob's Well* 78.13: Pride is roote of alle synnes. **c1450** *Speculum Christiani* (2) 58.10–1: Bernardus: Pryde es be-gynnynge of al synne and cause of al undoynge. **1471** Caxton *Recuyell* II 556–7: For hit is so that of the synne of pryde growe alle other vyces. **a1475** *Tree* 3.12: The begynnyng of alle synne is pride. **c1475** Henryson *Thre Deid Pollis* 206.33: O wofull pryd, the rute of all distres. **c1475** *Wisdom* 53.530–1: Pryde, wyche ys a-geyn kynde, And of synnys hede. **1483** *Quatuor Sermones* 27[30–1]: This synne of pryde sayth saynt gregore is rote of alle evyl. **1489** Caxton *Doctrinal* K8ʳ[26]: Pryde whyche is rote of alle synnes. **a1500** Medwall *Nature* C3ᵛ[20]: Ye (*Pride*) be radix viciorum, Rote of all vertew, H4ᵛ[28]: The rote of all syn ys Pryde. **1504** Hawes *Example* Ccl ʳ[22–4]: Eschew also the synne of pryde, The moder and the fervent rote Of all the synnes. **1522** More *Treatyce* 82 G[10–1]: Pride, the mischievous mother of al maner vice, **1528** *Heresyes* 282 DE: For pryde is, as saynt Austine sayeth, the verye mother of all heresies, **1534** *Passion* 1273 B[4–7]: Pride . . . is . . . the heade and roote of all other sinnes. Tilley P578; Whiting *Scots* II 114. See **V7.**

P390 Pride makes its master rue (*varied*)

c1500 *Proper tretyse* 245[6]: Pride will make hys master commonly to rew. **a1533** Berners *Arthur* 95[5]: Pryde dooth oftentymes many harmes to his mayster, 96[5–6]: Pryde always overthroweth his maister. Cf. Tilley P581, quote 1721.

P391 **Pride** must needs have a shame
1528 More *Heresyes* 256 A[15–6]: Pride, as the proverbe is, must nedes have a shame. See **P385.**

P392 The **Pride** of the morning
a1475 *Talk of Ten Wives* 30[1–3]: I mett hym (*penis*) in the morowe tyde, When he was in his moste pryde, The lenghte of .iii. bene. Eric Partridge *Dictionary of Slang and Unconventional English* (5th ed., New York, 1962) 659. Cf. *Oxford* 518.

P393 **Pride** will have a fall (*varied*)
c1340 Rolle *Psalter* 438 (120.3): Pride kastis men doun. **a1393** Gower *CA* II 119.3065–6: That thogh it mounte for a throwe, It (*pride*) schal doun falle and overthrowe. **c1400** *Cleges* 41.96: Ffor fallyd was hys pride. **a1425** *Chester Plays* I 27.167–8: But pride cast me downe, I-wis, From heaven right to hell. **a1450** *Castle* 140. 2096–7: For, whanne Lucyfer to helle fyl, Pride, ther-of thou were chesun. **a1450** *Thorowowt a pales* in Dyboski 96.71: The syne of pryde will have a fall. **c1450** Hay *Alexander* 21[2.7–10]: And comounli befoir a gret mischance Thare cumis ane blythnes vithe ane arrogance, And thare vithe cumis ane velthful vantones vithe all, And comounlie sone efter cumis ane fall. **c1450** Holland *Howlat* 79.932–6: Thy pryde . . . approchis our hie Lyke Lucifer in estaite; And sen thow art so elate, As the Ewangelist wrait, Thow sal lawe be, 80.960–2: I may be sampill heir eft, That pryde never yit left His feir but a fall. **a1460** *Towneley Plays* 100–1.12–8: Ffor he that most may When he syttys in pryde, When it comys on assay is kesten downe wyde, This is seyn; When ryches is he, Then comys poverte, Hors-man Jak cope Walkys then, I weyn. **a1475** *Ludus Coventriae* 18.66–7: Thu lucyfere, ffor thi mekyl pryde I bydde the ffalle from hefne to helle. **c1475** Henryson *Fables* 24.593–4: Fy! puft up pryde, thow is full poysonabill; Quha favoris the on force man haif ane fall. **1509** Barclay *Ship* II 159[14]: Foule pryde wyll have a fall, [28]: Thus had his folysshe pryde a grevous fall, 161[28]: The pride in tham at last sholde have a fall, 163[6–7]: Thousandes are deceyved and brought to wofull fall By pryde. **1518** Nevill *Castell* 97.567: On cruell Cupyde your pryde wyll have a fall. **a1529** Skelton *Garnesche* I 131.158–9: I have red, and rede I xall, Inordynate pride wyll have a falle. **1546** Heywood *D* 38.114: Pryde wyll have a fall. Apperson 512; *Oxford* 518; Taylor and Whiting 296; Tilley P581; Whiting *Drama* 81, 158, *Scots* II 113. See **S341.**

P394 Privy **Pride** in peace is (a) nettle in arbor (*garden*)
a1338 Mannyng *Chronicle B* II 280[3–4] Exemplum (*in margin*): Prive pride in pes es nettille in herbere, The rose is myghtles, ther nettille spredis over fer. See **P68.**

P395 Through poor **Pride** many are shent (*ruined*)
c1400 *Alexander Buik* II 184.2960: Throw pure pryde ar mony shent. See **M267.**

P396 Young **Pride** is stanched (*ended*) soon
c1400 *Alexander Buik* I 76.2411–4: For, fra ane child be ston(a)yit, He sal be thairof sa mismayit That all his gude deid sal be done, For young pryde is stanshit sone.

P397 Do as the **Priest** says, but not as the priest does
c1000 Aelfric *Homilies* I 242[22–4]: And doð swa swa Crist tæhte, "Gif se lareow wel tæce and yfele bysnige, doð swa swa he tæcð, and na be ðam þe he bysnað," II 48–50: Gif se lareow riht tæce, do gehwa swa swa he tæcð; and gif he yfel bysnige, ne do ge na be his gebysnungum, ac doð swa swa he tæcð, 68[15]: Doð swa swa hi tæcað, and ne do ge swa swa hi doð. **c1450** *Douce MS.52* 53.101: Thow shall do, as the preste says, but not as the preste doos. **c1450** *Rylands MS.394* 103.3. **a1500** *Remedie of Love* CCCXXII^r[1.18–9]: He maie saie with our parishe prest, Doe as I saie, and not as I do. Tilley D394, F673. See **C514, L463.**

P398 Each **Priest** praises his own relics
c1450 *Rylands MS.394* 104.12: Eche preste preyseth his awgh relikes. *Oxford* 518.

P399 A **Priest's** child shall never be blessed
c1475 *Rawlinson MS. D 328* 124.75: A preste-ys chyld schall never be blessyd.

P400 To be one's **Priest**
a1300 *Richard* 350.5315–6: Hys lyff fforsothe nought longe lest, Ffor Kyng R. was his preeste. **a1400** *Guy*[5] xli[16]: Traytour . . . I sal be thy Prest. **a1400** *Ipomadon A* 93.3204–6: He sette syr Amfyon so hard, That never afterward He nede prest to asse. **a1450** *Generydes A* 121. 3856–8: That the Iren with the hawberk met Right ageyn the self brest; Wel nigh it had ben

his prest. **a1500** *Guy*[4] 145.4715–6: Lye there . . . evill mote thou thee! For my priest shalt thou never be! **c1505** Watson *Valentine* 76.34–5: If ony of them touched Orson . . . he should be his preest (French [p. 331]: La vie luy ostera). Tilley P587; Whiting *Scots* II 114. See **O50.**

P401 As proud as a **Prince**
c1300 *Amis* 22.495: As prince prout in pride, 58.1380, 61.1458, cf. 30.688. **c1350** *Libeaus* 48.861: As princes proude in pride, cf. 29.496, 46.822. **c1400** *Plowman's Tale* 179.999: He is as proud as prince in pall. Cf. Svartengren 67: princess.

P402 It is not lost that is lent to the **Prince**
c1458 *Knyghthode and Bataile* 42.1124: It loseth not, that to the prince is lent.

P403 Such **Prince** such household
1532 Berners *Golden Boke* 190.2345–6: And suche as the prince is, suche shalbe his householde. *Oxford* 519; Smith 242. See **C34, J71, L455, M408, P135.**

P404 To break **Priscian's** head
a1522 Skelton *Speke* II 9.176: Prisians hed broken now handy dandy. Apperson 513; *Oxford* 62; Tilley P595.

P405 **Prodigality** is the mother of poverty
a1393 Gower *CA* III 291.2162–3: Prodegalite, Which is the moder of poverte.

P406 Better to have more **Profit** and less honor
c1500 *Melusine* 238.8–9: And some saith that bettre is to have more of prouffyt and lasse honour. Tilley P598.

P407 Through proper (*private*) **Profit,** privy hate and young men's counsel Britain was lost
a1338 Mannyng *Chronicle* A II 506.14595–600: Of eighte that he (*Bede*) wrytes, y telle the thre, In stede of an autorite: Propre profit, and pryve hate, Yonge mennes conseil they toke algate; Ffor by all thyse thre they ches, And mest thorow thyse, Bretayne they les. (Not found in Bede or in any of Robert's sources.)

P408 Flee **Prolixity** (*varied*)
c1385 Chaucer *TC* ii 1564: But fle we now prolixitee best is, **c1395** *CT* V[F] 404–5: The savour passeth ever lenger the moore, For fulsomnesse of his prolixitee. **c1420** Wyntoun IV 127.1–3: Clerkys sayis that prolixite, That langsumnes may callit be, Genderis leth mar than delyte, 190.769–70: For all thar dedis to record Sall do prolixite and nocht conford. **c1502** *Lyfe of Joseph* 48.349–50: And this I knowe well, both in prose, ryme, and verse, Men love nat to rede an over longe thyng. See **M524, 582, 775, P262, S471, T159.**

P409 Great **Promise** small performance
1560 Heywood *E* 205.10.3: Great promise, small performance. Apperson 271; Smith 243; Tilley P602. See **B417, H371, M779.**

P410 Trust not in the **Promises** of lords
1471 Paston V 126[23–4]: Trost not mych up on promyses of lordis now a days. See **W374.**

P411 To be large in **Promisings** and small givers
1474 Caxton *Chesse* 70.24–5: They ben large in promysynges and smale gyvers. See **B414, 417, H371, M779.**

P412 By the **Proof** things are known
c1422 Hoccleve *Complaint* 102.200: But by the prefe bene thyng(e)s knowne and wiste.

P413 The **Proof** of all will be in the fine (*end*)
a1450 *Partonope* 439.10873: The prefe of all wole be in the fyn. See **E81.**

P414 **Proof** upon practice
1546 Heywood *D* 28.33–4: Proofe uppon practise, must take holde more sure, Than any reasonyng by gesse can procure. Tilley P609.

P415 All is not **Prophecy** that good men preach in pulpit
c1456 Pecock *Faith* 151[6–9]: It is not al trewe that bi holi men is in parchimyn ynkid, neither al is profecie that is of good men in pulpit prechid.

P416 A **Prophet** is not without honor save in his own country
c1000 *WSG* Matthew xiii 57: Nys nan witega butan wurþscype, buton on hys earde and on hys huse, Mark vi 4: Soðlice nis nan witega buton wurðscipe, buton on his eðele, and on his mægðe, and on his huse, Luke iv 24, John iv 44. **c1395** *WBible* Matthew xiii 57: A profete is not with oute worschip, but in his owen cuntre, and in his owen hous, Mark vi 4: That a profete is not without onoure, but in his owne cuntrey, and among his kynne, and in his hous, Luke iv 24, John iv 44. **c1400** *Pepysian Gospel* 18.28–30: For whi no prophete is so mychel honoured in his owen cuntree as he is in straunge cuntrees, 26.9–11: And Jesus . . . seide that prophetes weren over al honoured save in her owen cuntre, 44.9–11. **a1485** Malory I cxxiii.11–3 (Caxton's *Preface*): Sauf onelye it accordeth to the word of God, whyche sayth that no man is accept for a prophete in his owne contreye. **1487** Caxton *Book of Good Manners* G7[r][21–2]: Sayde Jhu Cryste that

noman is accepte for a prophete in his owen contreye. Jente 635; *Oxford* 520–1; Taylor and Whiting 297; Tilley M329–30.

P417 In **Prosperity** a man shall not know his friends
a1500 *MS. Marginalia* in Hoccleve I 199 n.[1]: In tyme of prosperitie, a man shall not knowe his frendes, and in adversitie an ennemye will not be hidde. See **A56.**

P418 In **Prosperity** men may find friends who are full unkind in adversity
c1500 *Everyman* 12.309–10: It is sayd in prosperyte men frendes may fynde, Whiche in adversytye be full unkynde. Apperson 514; *Oxford* 521; Tilley T301.

P419 In **Prosperity** remember adversity
a1500 *Leconfield Proverbs* 485[5–6]: In tyme of prosperite Remember adversite. Apperson 514; Tilley P610.

P420 **Prosperity** in earth is but a dream
1501 Douglas *Palice* 74.19: Prosperitie in eird is bot a dreme.

P421 **Prosperity** is blind
1406 Hoccleve *Male Regle* 26.33–4: But I have herd men seye longe ago, "Prosperitee is blynd and see ne may." See **P423.**

P422 **Prosperity** is transitory
1463 Ashby *Prisoner* 8.220: But transitory ys prosperyte. Whiting *Scots* II 114. See **W151, 671.**

P423 **Prosperity** makes us blind
1556 Heywood *Spider* 427[6]: Prosperite . . . makth us blinde. See **P421.**

P424 When temporal **Prosperity** is most flowing then is an ebb of adversity most to be dreaded
1422 Lydgate *Serpent* 55.20–2: Whan eny temperall prosperite is moste flowenge in felicite than is a sodeyn ebbe of adversite moste to be dradde. See **E41.**

P425 **Proteus** could change in every shape
a1400 *Romaunt C* 6319–20: For Protheus, that cowde hym chaunge In every shap, homly and straunge. *Oxford* 579; Tilley S285.

P426 He that is **Proud** is often shamed
c1340 Rolle *Psalter* 119 (33.5): Bot he that is proud shames ofte. See **P385.**

P427 Most **Proud** most fool
1556 Heywood *Spider* 198[10]: But most prowde, most foole, as flies proverbes conteine.

P428 None so **Proud** as he that is preferred to high estate out of poverty
a1449 Lydgate *Cok* in *MP* II 816.105–7: Is noon so proude, pompous in dignyte, As he that is so sodeynly preferryd To hih estaat, and out of poverte. See **C271.**

P429 **Prove** (Assay, Try) ere you purpose (plain, trust, trow, take, love, praise)
a1400 *Proverbis of Wysdom* 245.68: And preve well, ore thou purpose, (*II*) 222.46: Prove wel, or thou pleyn. **c1440** Scrope *Epistle of Othea* 81[4–5]: And Hermes seith that thou shuldest preve a man afore or that thou trost hym to gretely. **a1450** *Myne awen dere* 154.173–4: Tharfore I counseile the that thou Prove any person er thou trowe. **c1450** *Consail and Teiching* 76.357–8: And lipin nocht in a new-cumyne gest, Lat uthire hyme pruf ore thow hyme traist. **c1450** *Epistle of Othea* 110.1–2: Seyth the philosophre hermes: Prove the man or thu have grett truste in hym. **c1450** Greene *Carols* 338.3: Preve or ye take. **a1470** Tiptoft *Tullius* C7[r][17–8]: We may saye, when ye have preved, thenne love. **a1475** *Good Wyfe Wold* 175.59: Asay or ever thow trust. **1489** Caxton *Fayttes* 105.30–106.1: The teching of the wise that sayth prove the man or ye truste hym muche. **a1500** *Against Hasty Marriage, I* in Robbins 37.1: Prove or thow preyse yt. **a1500** *MS. Marginalia* in Hoccleve I 210 n.[1]: Try and then trust, quod bodyll. **1504** Hawes *Example* Aa5[v][13]: Prove or thou love. Apperson 651; *Oxford* 675; Tilley T595; Whiting *Scots* II 146. See **A232, F625, 658, K101, T204.**

P430 Long **Provision** makes sure possession
1525 Berners *Froissart* V 110[36–7]: It is sayd, longe provysion before, maketh sure possessyon.

P431 Pompous **Provision** comes not all of gluttony but sometimes of pride
1549 Heywood *D* 84.131–2: But pompous provision, comth not all, alway Of glottony, but of pryde sometyme, some say. *Oxford* 510; Tilley P617.

P432 There is a **Pudding** (*sausage*) in the pot
a1460 *Towneley Plays* 20.386–7: Harstow, boy? ther is a podyng in the pot; Take the that, boy, tak the that!

P433 To spring like a **Pudding** out of an arbalest (*crossbow*)
c1450 *Chaunce* 11.214–6: But soothe hyt is that slouthe Yow maystred hath and that is somedel routhe, Ffor out of Arwblaste as puddyng doth ye springe.

P434 To pinch at the payment of a **Pudding-prick**
c1516 Skelton *Magnificence* 66.2122: And pynche at the payment of a poddynge prycke. NED Pudding-prick.

P435 To come in **Pudding-time**
1546 Heywood *D* 97.224: This geare comth even in puddyng time. Apperson 516; *Oxford* 523; Tilley P634.

P436 The most **Puissant** is the first honored
c1505 Watson *Valentine* 285.2–3: Evermore the moost puyssaunt is the fyrste honoured. See **M265, 274.**

P437 To **Pull** (*pluck*) without scalding
a1400 *Romaunt C* 6820: Withoute scaldyng they hem pulle.

P438 One's **Purchase** is better than his rent (*varied*)
c1387-95 Chaucer *CT* I[A] 256: His purchas was wel bettre than his rente, **c1395** III[D] 1451: My purchas is th'effect of al my rente. **a1400** *Romaunt C* 6838: My purchace is bettir than my rente. **a1460** *Towneley Plays* 233.161–2: He gettis more by purches Then bi his fre rent. NED Purchase 4.

P439 As nice as (the) **Purse** (?*skin*) of an ay (*egg*)
c1440 Charles of Orleans 140.4193: Be nyse myn hert as purse is of an ay, 160.4779: What nys quod she as purse is of an ay. P. xlii: "Most probably points to some Kentish proverb;" note II 29: "as delicate as an eggshell."

P440 As round as (a) **Purse**
c1460 *Satirical Description* 200[4]: Here jowys been rownde as purs.

P441 Be it better, be it worse, do after him that bears the **Purse**
c1450 *Douce MS.52* 49.64: Do thow better, do thow worse, Do after hym, that beryth the purse. **c1475** *Rawlinson MS. D 328* 120.32: Be hit beter be hit werse folo hym that berit the pursse. **a1500** *Additional MS.37075* 278.21: Be hyt better, be hyt worse, folow hym that beryth the purse. **a1500** Hill 130.7. **1546** Heywood *D* 26.28: Dooe ye after him. Apperson 29; *Oxford* 25; Tilley P646.

P442 Gramercy mine own **Purse**
c1450 Greene *Carols* 390: Syng we alle, and sey we thus: "Gramersy myn owyn purs," **a1500** 391. **a1500** *A faythfull frende* in [Joseph Haslewood] *The Book Containing the Treastise of Hunting* (*1496*), *etc.* (London, 1810) E5v[21–2]: By this matere I saye in sawe, Ever gramercy myn owne purse. Cf. Claude M. Simpson *The British Broadside and its Music* (New Brunswick, N.J., 1966) pp. 262–3: *Gramercy Penny.*

P443 He shall never cut a **Purse**
1518 Watson *Oliver* H1v[9–10]: The knyght that he hathe smyten downe shal never cut no purse.

P444 Light **Purse** heavy heart
a1439 Lydgate *Fall* III 1014.3343: Herte hevy and purs lyght. Apperson 364–5; Tilley P659. See **P454.**

P445 One's **Purse** is his best (own) friend
a1450 *Castle* 152.2521–2: And thou schalt fynde, soth to sey, Thi purs schal be thi best(e) frende. **a1500** Greene *Carols* 391.1: In every plas qwere that I wende My pur(se) is my owne frende. Tilley P656.

P446 The (Thy) **Purse** is threadbare
1546 Heywood *D* 32.64: The purs is threede bare, **1555** *E* 192.269: Thy. Tilley P661.

P447 The **Purse** stole the money
c1475 Gregory *Chronicle* 214–5: But as for the mony, I wot not howe hit was departyd; I trowe the pursse stale the mony.

P448 To be hanged by the **Purse**
c1350 *Gamelyn* 667.885: He was hanged by the nekke and nought by the purs. **a1449** Lydgate *World* in *MP* II 846.81: The eraunt theef is hange be the purs. Whiting *Scots* II 114–5. See **B639, P302.**

P449 To be **Purse** sick and lack a physician
1546 Heywood *D* 50.307: For he is purs sicke, and lackth a phisicion. See **S328.**

P450 To find in one's **Purse** God's curse
c1450 *Pryd pryd wo* in *Proceedings of the Royal Irish Academy* 41(1932–3) Sec. C 207.11–2: He putth hys hand in hys powrs, *cum nichyll intus fuerat,* He ffownd none ther saw godeys cowrs, *hoc non sibi*(?) *deerat.* See **P115.**

P451 To give one's **Purse** a purgation
1546 Heywood *D* 50.304: Ye would, by my purs, geve me a purgacion. Apperson 517; Tilley P663.

P452 To line one's **Purse**
c1515 Barclay *Eclogues* 140.7–8: He had a pautner with purses manyfolde, And surely lined with silver and with golde. *Oxford* 370; Tilley P664.

P453 To ring in one's **Purse**
a1475 *Ludus Coventriae* 123.25–6: And loke ye

rynge wele in your purs, Ffor ellys your cawse may spede the wurs.

P454 When the **Purse** is heavy the heart is light
c1515 Barclay *Eclogues* 140.20: When purse is heavy oftetime the heart is light. Apperson 296; Tilley P655. See **P444.**

P455 Who will drink, unbuckle his **Purse**
a1500 *Additional MS.37075* 278.26: Who wull drynke, unbokyll hys purs.

P456 **Purse** penniless
a1449 Lydgate *Order* in *MP* II 452.103–4: A pore beggere for to be vengable, Purs Penylees in plees may never the, *Ryme* in *MP* II 794.74: A powche ful of straw, a prowde purs penyles. **a1460** *Towneley Plays* 101.32–3: I may syng With purs penneles.

Q

Q1 As still as a **Quail**
c1380 *Pearl* 39.1085: I stod as stylle as dased quayle.

Q2 To abide no more than the **Quail** abides the sparhawk
c1477 Caxton *Jason* 58.18–9: They wold nomore abide him thenne the quayle abideth the sperhauke.

Q3 To couch like a **Quail**
c1395 Chaucer *CT* IV[E] 1206: And thou shalt make hym couche as doth a quaille. *Oxford* 111.

Q4 To go (play) couch **Quail**
a1450 *Castle* 148.2386: I wyl gon cowche qwayl (*so MS.*). **c1522** Skelton *Speke* II 21.420: To lowre, to droupe, to knele, to stowpe, and to play cowche quale. **1533** More *Confutacion* 586 D[3–4]: And make them couch quaile. NED Couch-quail.

Q5 **Quaintise** (*cunning*) overcomes all things
a1338 Mannyng *Chronicle A* I 308.8798–802: Queyntise over-cometh alle thynge. Strengthe ys god wyth travaille; Ther strengthe ne may, sleyght wil availle; Sleyght and connyng doth many a chare, Begynneth thyng that strengthe ne dar. See **C615, L381.**

Q6 To ask after the **Quantity** rather than the quality
c1385 Usk 62.38–9: Commenly, suche asken rather after the quantitè than after the qualitè. Cf. Whiting *Scots* II 115.

Quarrel, sb.[1]

Q7 To fly (go, run) like a **Quarrel** out of arbalest (cross-bow)
a1300 *Arthour and M.*[1] 54.1848–9: Ac so quarel of alblast Thai flowen thider right anon. **a1300** *Richard* 218.2537–8: The galeye wente alsoo fast, As quarel out off the arweblast. **c1300** *Owayne Miles* (*Auchinleck*) 105.93: Into a stinkand river, That under the mounteyn ran o fer As quarel of alblast, 111.189: Thay flowe fram him as quarel of alblast. **1340** *Ayenbite* 71[13–5]: Al hit ys ywent wel rathre thanne . . . quarel of arblaste. **c1400** *Vices and Virtues* 69.5–7: Al is passed; ye, sonner than . . . a quarel of an arblawst. **c1450** *Merlin* II 533[11–2]: As quarell oute of arblast for swyftnesse of his horse. **1484** Caxton *Royal Book* G2^r[4–5]: Moche faster fledde fro us than . . . quarelles oute of a crosse bowe, **1485** *Charles* 157.26: It (*a river*) ranne lyke a quarel out of a crosbowe. See **A190.**

Quarrel, sb.[2]

Q8 False **Quarrel** comes to evil end
c1400 *Toulouse* 225.130–2: Soche grace god hym send, That false quarrel comes to evell end For oght, that may betyde. See **F51.**

Q9 In any **Quarrel** gold has most might
a1449 Lydgate *Cok* in *MP* II 816.100: In ony quarell gold hath ay moost myght. See **G296.**

Q10 To catch a **Quarrel** against absent folk
a1439 Lydgate *Fall* II 438.3925–7: For princis ofte, of furious hastynesse, Wil cachche a qu(a)rel, causeles in sentence, Ageyn folk absent, thouh ther be non offence. Apperson 1; *Oxford* 1; Tilley P86.

Q11 To pick a **Quarrel**
1449 Paston II 106[16–7]: The seyde parsone . . . hathe pekyd a qwarell to on Mastyr Recheforthe. **c1499** Skelton *Bowge* I 42.314: Fyrste pycke a quarell. **1519** Horman *Vulgaria* 188[1]: He begynneth to pyke or fyndeth a quarel of my wordes. Apperson 492–3; Tilley Q3.

Quarrel, vb.

Q12 Those do not **Quarrel** who are not together
c1025 *Durham Proverbs* 12.18: þa ne sacað þe

ætsamne ne beoð. Soli illi non contendunt qui in unum non conveniunt.

Q13 To have (give) the four **Quarters** of a knave
c1516 Skelton *Magnificence* 37.1166: Thou haste the four quarters of a knave, 70.2252: In faythe, I gyve the four quarters of a knave.

Q14 The **Quick** and the dead
c1300 Robert of Gloucester I 429.5877: Vor me halt evere mid the quike, the dede was sone stille, 467.6428: Vor the dede was voryite and the quike vor to paye. **c1300** *South English Legendary* I 113.92. **c1475** Henryson *Fables* 21.522: Let quik to quik, and deid ga to the deid. Apperson 375:38; *Oxford* 376; Tilley Q12.

Q15 To go near (touch one on) the **Quick**
a1470 Tiptoft *Tullius* A6[r][8–9]: I wil not go so nere the quycke as to saye that it may not be. **c1516** Skelton *Magnificence* 50.1611: As yf a man fortune to touche you on the quyke. **1546** Heywood *D* 28.32: Practyse is all, above all toucheth the quicke. Apperson 642; *Oxford* 667; Tilley Q13.

Q16 To wag like a **Quick-mire** (*quagmire*)
c1395 *Pierce* 9.226: That all wagged his fleche as a quyk myre.

Q17 As clear as **Quicksilver**
c1408 Lydgate *Reson* 4.123–4: And the wellys thanne appere As . . . quyk sylver clere.

Q18 To run like **Quicksilver**
a1420 Lydgate *Troy* I 215.2457–8: And the water, as I reherse can, Like quik-silver in his stremys ran.

Q19 Better is **Quiet** than riches with trouble
a1449 Lydgate *Fabules* in *MP* II 580.408: Better ys quyete, then troble with ryches. See **M700.**

Q20 **Quietness** is great richesse
c1545 Heywood *Four PP* C1[r][9–10]: And sure I thynke that quietnesse In any man is great rychesse. *Oxford* 529; Tilley Q15.

R

R1 **R** is the dog's letter
1509 Barclay *Ship* I 182[15–8]: This man malycious whiche troubled is with wrath Nought els soundeth but the hoorse letter R, Thoughe all be well, yet he none answere hath Save the dogges letter, glowmynge with nar nar. *Oxford* 530; Tilley R1.

R2 Who will change a **Rabbit** for a rat
1549 Heywood *D* 87.254: Who the divell will chaunge a rabet for a rat? Apperson 520; *Oxford* 530; Tilley R3.

R3 To run (hunt) about like a **Rache** (*hunting dog*)
a1393 Gower *CA* III 66.4387–8: With his brocours, that renne aboute Lich unto racches in a route. **1471** Ripley *Compound* 155[12]: They hunt about as doth a Rache.

R4 As swift as the **Rack** in the air
c1410 Lovelich *Grail* III 13.385–6: For the Schipe wente . . . Swiftere than the Rakke In the Eyr be kynd.

R5 At **Rack** and manger
c1378 Purvey *De Officio Pastorali* in Wyclif *EW* 435[6–8]: It is worse to have a womman with-ynne or with-oute at racke and at manger. Apperson 520; *Oxford* 530; Tilley R4.

R6 To play **Racket**
c1385 Chaucer *TC* iv 460: But kanstow pleyen raket, to and fro? **c1385** Usk 13.166–7: Ye wete wel . . . that I have not played raket, "nettil in, docke out," and with the wether-cocke waved. Apperson 500.

R7 **Radish** roots are good meat but they stink in the council
1492 *Salomon and Marcolphus* 8[21–3]: Salomon. The radissh rotys are good mete but they stynke in the Connsell. Mar. He that etyth Radyssh rotys coughyth above and undyr.

R8 As rude as a **Raft** (*rafter*)
c1425 *Avowynge* 69[18–9]: And aythir gripus a schafte, Was als rude as a rafte.

R9 **Ragman** (roll)
a1393 Gower *CA* III 451.2377–9: Venus, which stant withoute lawe In noncertein, bot as men drawe Of Rageman upon the chance. **c1395** *Pierce* 7.179–80: Ther is none heraud that hath halt swich a rolle, Right as a rageman hath rekned hem newe. **c1405** *Mum* 72.1565–6: There is a raggeman rolle that Ragenelle hymself Hath made of mayntennance. **c1450** *Bishop Boothe* in Wright *Political Poems* II 228[12]: And riken up the ragmanne of the hole rowte. **a1460** *Towneley Plays* 374.224: Here a roll of ragman of the rownde tabill. **a1500** *Ragman Roll* 68: Here begynnyth Ragmane roelle, 69[5]: Kynge Ragman bad me sowe in brede. **1523** Skelton *Garlande* I 420.1490: Apollo to rase out of her ragman rollis. **1532** More *Confutacion* 424 C[4–5]: I had rehersed up a Ragmans rol of a rable of heretikes, 653 E[12–3]: In all theyr whole raggemans rolle. **1533** Heywood *Pardoner* B3^{v}[24]: To publysh his ragman rolles with lyes. NED Ragman^{2} 3, Ragman's Roll; Whiting *Drama* 360:795.

R10 To shine like a newly smoothed **Rail** (*dress*)
a900 *Old English Martyrology* 206.26–7: Heo glytenode . . . swa . . . nigslicod hrægel. T. N. Toller *Supplement To An Anglo-Saxon Dictionary* (Oxford, 1921), *s.v.* Niw-slicod.

R11 After the **Rain** comes the fair weather
1484 Caxton *Aesop* 43[6–7]: And after the rayne cometh the fair weder. Apperson 520–1; Tilley R8. See **C315, D41.**

R12 As thick as **Rain**
a1300 *Richard* 244.2969–70: He gaderede his folk togedere, As thykke as rayn falles in wedere, 355.5439–40 (*var.*): Quarellys, arwes also thykke gan flye, As doth the rayne that falleth in the skye. **a1338** Mannyng *Chronicle A* I 240.6827: The arewes come so thykke so reyn. **a1400** *Alexander C* 228.4175–6: Than fell thar fra the firmament as it ware fell sparkis, Ropand doun o rede fire than any rayn thikire. **c1400** *Laud Troy* I 311.10555–6: The rayn fel nevere so thike on rise As Ector sclow his enemys. **c1400** *Plowman's Tale* 189.1345: His foules, that flewen as thycke as rayn. **c1450** Greene *Carols* 312.2: As dropys of reyn they comyn thikke, And every arwe with other gan mete. **c1450** *Merlin* II 211[28–9]: For ther sholde ye have sein knyghtes and sergeauntes falle as thikke as it hadde be reyn. **1481** Caxton *Godeffroy* 108. 36–7: They shotte so thycke upon our peple that there was never rayn . . . so like. **c1500** *Melusine* 367.23–4: There fell upon the kyng gret and pesaunt strokes, as thykk as rayn falleth fro the skye. **1513** Douglas *Aeneid* III 260.69–70: Terys, all invayn, Furth gettyng our hys chekis thyk as rayn. Svartengren 398–9. See **D411, H13.**

R13 As unimete (*immeasurable*) as **Rain** (rime [*hoar frost*])
a1200 Lawman III 140.28523–5: Folc unimete, Ridinde and ganninde, Swa the rim (*B* ren) falleth adune.

R14 He that dreads any **Rain** to sow shall have bare barns
c1385 Usk 23.84–5: He that dredeth any rayn, to sowe his cornes, he shal have than (bare) bernes. See **T298.**

R15 A little **Rain** lays a great wind (*varied*)
a1200 *Ancrene* 126.14–5: Eft me seith and soth hit is, that a muche wind alith with alute rein. **a1300** *Alisaunder* 75.1309–10: A grete storme is falle by a reyn—Sone wil he daunten thine meyn. **a1400** *Ancrene* (*Recluse*) 122.2: As men seth often, a litel rayn felleth a gret wynde. **c1430** Lydgate *Dance* 56.448: And wyndes grete gon doune with litel reyne. **1471** Caxton *Recuyell* II 461.10–1: But certayn, lyke as a small rayne abatyth or leyth doun a grete wynde. **1478** Rivers *Morale Proverbes* [4.10]: And litle reyne dooth a great wynd abate. **c1500** *Melusine* 247.33. **1506** Barclay *Castell* E5v[11–2]: We have oft sene grete wyndes blowe, And with a lytell rayne overcome. **a1533** Berners *Huon* 39.11–4: There is a comon proverbe the which hath begylyd many a man: it is sayd that a small rayne abatyth a grete wynd. **1533** Heywood *Weather* C1r[26]: Downe commeth the rayne and setteth the wynde at rest, D4r[7]: For plenty of rayne to set the wynde at rest. Apperson 521; Jente 786; *Oxford* 531; A. A. Prins in *English Studies* 29(1948) 146–50; Tilley R16.

R16 To rap on like **Rain**
a1508 Dunbar *Goldyn Targe* 117.195: The schour of arowis rappit on as rayn.

R17 To run down like **Rain**
a1400 *Ipomadon A* 160.5668–9: The blod ranne down fro his wondes wyde, As hit was droppus off rayne. **a1400** *Morte Arthure* 24.795: Rynnande on reede blode as rayne of the heven. **c1400** *Laud Troy* I 221.7502: The swot ran doun—so doth the rayn. **a1470** Malory II 625.33: The hote bloode ran downe as hit had bene rayne. Whiting *Scots* II 115.

R18 To trickle down like **Rain** (*etc.*) (A number of single quotations are brought together here)
c1390 Chaucer *CT* VII 674[B1864]: His salte teeris trikled doun as reyn. **a1400** *Song of "Sins"* in Brown *Lyrics XV* 230.17–8: And if thou schryve the of thi synnes Thei wasche a-way as dothe the rayne. **a1500** *Guy*[4] 212.7049: They smitten togither as rayne and thonder. **c1500** *Lyfe of Roberte* 246.704: As rayne the teares fell fro hys eyes. **a1513** Dunbar *Of the Warldis Instabilitie* 29.27: Purpos dois change as . . . rane.

R19 When the **Rain** rains and the goose winks, *etc.*
1523 Skelton *Garlande* I 418.1430–1: Yet whan the rayne rayneth and the gose wynkith, Lytill wotith the goslyng what the gose thynkith. Apperson 522; *Oxford* 531; Tilley R19.

R20 One may not reach the **Rainbow**
a1400 *Alexander C* 142.2466: And roomes noght at the ray(n)bowe that reche ye ne may (Latin [p. 302]: Ad altissima).

R21 To sit on the **Rainbow**
a1500 *Thre Prestis* 26.407: Than heyly to sit on the Rayne-bow.

R22 Of thin **Rain-showers** the earth is flooded
c1000 Aelfric *Homilies* II 466[7–8]: Oft of ðinnum ren-scurum flewð seo eorðe. See **D412.**

R23 As lean as a (any) **Rake**
c1387-95 Chaucer *CT* I[A] 287: As leene was his hors as is a rake. **a1475** *Lord, how shall I* in Dyboski 120.46: I wex as lene as any rake. **a1508** Skelton *Phyllyp* I 79.913: Leane as a rake.

1555 Heywood *E* 152.42.2: And yet art thou skyn and bone, leane as a rake. Apperson 356; *Oxford* 357; Tilley R22; Whiting *Scots* II 115.

R24 As rank (*strong*) as a **Rake**
c1450 Holland *Howlat* 54.216: Was dene rurale to reid, rank as a raike. NED Rake sb.[1] 1b.

R25 Not worth (avail) a **Rake-steel** (*rakehandle*)
c1395 Chaucer *CT* III[D] 949: But that tale is nat worth a rake-stele. **c1450** Capgrave *Katharine* 326.2009: Youre resons, lady, avayle not a rake-stele.

R26 As crooked as **Ram's** horns
a1500 *Guy*[4] 191.6308: His teeth crooked as rammes hornes. Apperson 122; Taylor and Whiting 303.

R27 As right as a **Ram's** horn (*varied*)
c1325 *Levedy a(n)d my love* in *Rel. Ant.* II 19[4]: As ryt as ramis orn. **c1400** *Beryn* 6.152: And a red (it) also right as (wolde) Rammys hornyd. **c1405** *Mum* 77.1725: And redith as right as the Ram is hornyd. **a1449** Lydgate *Ryght as a Rammes Horne* in *MP* II 461–4: Right as a rammes horne, 8, 16, 24, 32, 40, 48, 56. **a1500** *Additional MS.37075* 277.2: Hyt ys ryghth as a rameys horne. **1522** Skelton *Why Come* II 29.87: As ryght as a rammes horne, **c1522** *Colyn* I 357.1201: By the ryght of (*MS.* Be hyt ryghte as) a rambes horne, *Speke* II 24.498: So myche raggyd ryghte of a rammes horne. Apperson 531; *Oxford* 543; Taylor and Whiting 303; Tilley R28; Whiting *Scots* II 115. See **C18.**

R28 As riotous as **Rams**
a1513 Dunbar *To the Quene* 59.16: Sum, that war ryatous as rammis.

R29 A **Ram** draws back to push his enemy the harder (*varied*)
a1398(1495) Bartholomaeus-Trevisa Z1^{v}[1.30–2]: And for to pusshe his enmye the harder he (*a ram*) drawyth bakwarde and resyth and lepyth upwarde. **c1420** Wyntoun VI 219.6711–2: The ram oft gayis abak, That he the mair debait may mak. **c1450** *Merlin* I 142[13–4]: But it is grete nede a man to go bak to recover the better his leep. **c1500** *Melusine* 113.18–9: For alwayes wyse men goo abacke for to lepe the ferther. *Oxford* 535: Recoil; Tilley L369.

R30 To hurtle (rush) together like (two) **Rams**
a1470 Malory I 50.30–1: And so hurteled togydirs lyke too rammes that aythir felle to the erthe, 323.12–4: They toke their bere as hit had bene two rammys and horled togydyrs, 382.15–6, II 641.3–4: They russhed togydyrs with their shyldis lyke two . . . rammys.

R31 In **Rancor** without remedy is no avail
1456 *Five Dogs of London* 190.20: And yn rancur with-owte remedy ys none avayle. See **R81.**

R32 Oft **Rape** (*haste*) rues
c1250 *Hendyng O* 198–9.40: Ofte rape reweth. **c1300** *Amis* 29.656–7: Bithenk hou oft rape wil rewe And turn to grame wel grille. **a1325** *Hendyng C* 190.43: Oft and lome rake ful rewit. **a1393** Gower *CA* II 270.1625: Men sen alday that rape reweth. **a1400** *Proverbis of Wysdom* 244.40: Fore ofte rape rewythe at last. **1469** Paston V 11[23]: For oftyn tyme rape rueth, **1473** V 174[17–8]. Apperson 288; Kneuer 47–8; *Oxford* 533; Schleich 267–8; Singer III 135; Skeat 155. See **H159, R65, 90.**

R33 It may not help to **Rape** (*hasten*)
a1393 Gower *CA* II 271.1678: It mai noght helpe forto rape. See **H168.**

R34 To **Rape** (*seize*) and run
c1395 Chaucer *CT* VIII[G] 1422: But wasten al that ye may rape and renne. Apperson 524; Robinson's note p. 762.

R35 As mossy haired as a **Rat**
a1430 Lydgate *Pilgrimage* 371.13704: And moosy heryd as a raat.

R36 As pale as a drowned **Rat**
a1500 *Colyn Blowbol* 93.31: And pale of hew like a drowned ratte. Tilley M1237.

R37 To be like **Rats**
c1400 *Laud Troy* I 200.6786–7: That thei fflowen over the hors tayl Opon that playn, as it were two rattes, II 501.17019–20: Lay sprad with dede bodies, As it hadde ben rattis.

R38 The **Rather** (*sooner*) the liever (*better*)
1447 Shillingford 24[25]: The rather the levere. **c1475** *Mankind* 10.254: The sonner the lever. **1477** Paston V 288[29]: The soner the better. Taylor and Whiting 345; Tilley S641.

R39 To gnaw as any **Ratton** (*rat*) gnaws stockfish
a1438 Kempe 17.16–7: Thow xalt ben etyn and knawyn of the pepul of the world as any raton knawyth the stokfysch.

R40 To slay one like **Rattons** and mice
c1400 *Laud Troy* II 377.12797: Ye schal sle hem as ratons and mys.

R41 To **Rave** unrocked (*?excited*)
c1475 Henryson *Fables* 80.2346: Unroikit now ye raif. NED Unrocked; Whiting *Scots* II 115.

R42 As black as (a) **Raven**('s feather)
c1300 *South English Legendary* II 416.453:

That other del withinne blac as a reven is. **a1338** Mannyng *Chronicle B* II 295[17]: His stede was blak as raven. **c1385** Chaucer *CT* I[A] 2144: As any ravenes fethere it shoon for blak. Apperson 51; Taylor and Whiting 304.

R43 As swart (*black*) as a **Raven**
a1000 *Two Apocrypha* J 39[22–3]: Bið heo seofon siðum sweartre ðonne se hræfen, H 40: hwæren.

R44 Like **Ravens** to a carcass
c1000 Aelfric *Pastoral Letters* 133 Oz 182: Gaderiæð heom to þam lice, swa-swa gediȝe remnæs, þær-ðer heo hold iseoð, on holte oððe on feldæ. See **B430.**

R45 The **Raven** in its own nest will make defence against the falcon-gentle
a1420 Lydgate *Troy* I 333.6603–6: Like as the raven, with his fetheres blake, With-Inne his nest wil ofte tyme make Ageyn the faukon-gentil, of nature, Ful harde diffence. Cf. Tilley D465. See **C350, 567, F570, M207.**

R46 The **Raven** never eats its young birds
c1489 Caxton *Aymon* I 112.22: For never raven ete his yonge byrdes. Cf. Lean I 432: A raven always dines off a young one on Easter Sunday; Taylor and Whiting 106:25.

R47 The **Raven** says (sings, cries) *"Cras, cras"*
a1000 *Pseudo-Alcuin* 388.419–21: Ne ȝyf þu cwetst: *Cras, cras,* þæt is þæs hræfenes stefne. Se ræfen ne ȝercerde na to Noes arca, ac seo culfre cerde. **a1430** Lydgate *Pilgrimage* 374. 13809–12: Ffor I lernede, syth go fful long, The maner off the Ravenys song, Wych by delay (thys the cas) Ys wont to synge ay "craas, craas," 644.24052: Thaugh that he crye on the, "cras, cras," 645.24067–8: And I stonde in the same caas, Abyde, and synge alway "cras, cras." Walther I 424.3608.

R48 To gorge like a **Raven**
a1300 *Alisaunder* 293.5616: Alle gorg(ei)en as a ravene.

R49 When the **Raven** cries before the crow then may the husband ear (*plow*) and sow
a1500 Reginald M. Woolley *Catalogue of the Manuscripts of Lincoln Cathedral Chapter Library* (London, 1927) 90: Whan the Raven cryeth befor the crowe, Than may the husbonde ere and sowe. Whan the crowe cryeth befor the Raven, Than drawe Shippis in to the haven. Lean I 432.

R50 Neither **Raw** nor spun
a1333 Shoreham *Poems* 91.149–50: For wel to conne, and naugh(t) to don, Nys nather rawe ne y-sponne. NED Raw 2a.

R51 As carving (cutting) as a **Razor**
a1300 *Alisaunder* 349.6543: No rasoure so kervynde. **1340** *Ayenbite* 66[10–1]: The tonge more kervinde thanne rasour. **1484** Caxton *Royal Book* F7v[23–4]: Tongues more cuttyng than a rasour.

R52 As keen as a **Razor**
c1386 Chaucer *LGW* 2654: And out he caught a knyf, as rasour kene. **a1400** *Romaunt B* 1885–6: But though this arwe was kene grounde As ony rasour that is founde. *Oxford* 579.

R53 As sharp as (a, any) **Razor**
a1300 *Alisaunder* 351.6602–3: Hii han shuldren on the regge, Uche als sharp as rasoures egge. **c1300** *Owayne Miles* (*Auchinleck*) 106.121: a. **c1400** *Vices and Virtues* 64.2–3: Than ben here tonges scharper than any rasours. **c1410** Lovelich *Grail* II 290.454: As scharpe As A Rasowre bytyng ful wel. **c1450** *Jacob's Well* 154.14–5: a. **c1500** *Melusine* 283.2–3: a. **1519** Horman *Vulgaria* 400[18]. Apperson 561; Taylor and Whiting 305; Tilley R36; Whiting *Scots* II 116.

R54 With that above our **Reach** we have nothing to do
a1500 *MS. Marginalia* in Hoccleve I 192 n.[2]: So(crates) 27. What ys a-bove owre reche, We have no thing to do with all. See **F432, M47, 403, S620, T103.**

R55 A **Realm** that is divided may not stand
1464 Hardyng 180[15–6]: For where a realme or (a) cytee is devyded, It maye not stand, as late was verified. See **K62, V47.**

R56 They may **Reap** that sow
c1175 *Poema Morale* 170.22: Thanne hi mowe ripe thet hi er than siewe. See **S542.**

R57 He that refuses **Reason** reason shall go from him
c1450 *Ponthus* 89.21–2: And I have herd say "He that reson refuses, reson wolle goo fro hym; and so he myschevys wyllfully."

R58 **Reason** has no place where evil reigns
1525 Berners *Froissart* VI 265[39–40]: For reason, right, nor justyce hath no place nor audyence where as yvell reygneth.

R59 Where **Reason** cannot be heard pride must reign
1525 Berners *Froissart* VI 234[3–4]: Where as wyse reasone canne nat be herde, than pride muste reygne.

R60 Where no **Receivers** are no thieves are
1546 Heywood *D* 56.54: Where be no receivers, there be no theeves, **1555** *E* 157.69. Apperson 525; *Oxford* 458; Tilley R53. See **F42, H410, T73.**

R61 Even **Reckoning** makes long friends
1546 Heywood *D* 69.119: Even recknyng maketh longe freendes, **1555** *E* 185.216. Apperson 186; *Oxford* 176; Tilley R54.

R62 A right **Reckoning** comes of a small ragman (*list, contract*)
a1513 Dunbar *No Tressour* 149.37: Ane raknyng rycht cumis of ane ragment small.

R63 To give (have) a **Recumbentibus**
c1400 *Laud Troy* I 221.7491–3: He gaff the kyng Episcropus Suche a recumbentibus, He smot In-two bothe helme and mayle. **c1475** *Mankind* 17.439: I hade a schreude recumbentibus, but I fele no peyn, 18.489: Then speke to Mankynde for the recumbentibus of my jewellys. **1549** Heywood *D* 87.232: He would geve you a recumbentibus. *Oxford* 535; Tilley R58.

R64 From hence to the **Red Sea**
a1533 Berners *Huon* 172.6–7: Fro hense to the red see, 191.21.

R65 Better is **Rede** (*counsel*) than rap (*haste*, rese [*rush*])
a1220 Giraldus *Descriptio Kambriae* in *Opera* VI 188[8]: Betere is red thene rap. **c1250** *Hendyng O* 197.34: Betere is red then res. **c1350** *Royal MS.* in A. Chr. Thorn *Les Proverbes de Bon Enseignement de Nicole Bozon* (Lund, 1921) 9.20: Betere his red than res. Kneuer 68–9; Schleich 266; Singer III 135. See **R32, 90.**

R66 Cold **Rede** is quean (*woman*) rede (*varied*)
a1250 *Proverbs of Alfred* 118 C 441–2: Vor it seith in the led, Cold red is cwene red. **c1390** Chaucer *CT* VII 3256[B4446]: Wommennes conseils been ful ofte colde. Apperson 707:60; *Oxford* 726; Skeat 257. See **W532.**

R67 Hasty **Rede** forthinks (*is repented*) afterwards (*varied*)
1340 *Ayenbite* 184[3–4]: And another zuo zayth, thet hette socrates thet "of hastif red : hit vorthingth efte(r)ward." **c1400** *Vices and Virtues* 188.26–7: Sicrates (seith) that of hastyf counseil repenten hem men afterward. **1484** Caxton *Royal Book* O8ᵛ[27–8]: Socrates sayth that of hasty counceyl men repente hem after. See **H159, M357.**

R68 Short **Rede** good rede
1075 Roger of Wendover (d. 1236) *Chronica*, ed. H. O. Coxe (4 vols., London, 1841–2) II 18[4–5]: Schort red, god red, slea ye the bischop. Jente 447; *Oxford* 585.

R69 As unstable as the **Reed**
a1400 Wyclif *Sermons* II 189[12]: Seculers here, that weren unstable as the reed.

R70 A broken **Reed**
c1395 *WBible* IV Kings xviii 21: Whethir thou hopist in a staf of rehed and brokun, Isaiah xxxvi 6: Thou tristist on this brokun staf of rehed, Ezekiel xxix 6–7: Thou were a staf of rehed to the hous of Israel, whanne thei token the with hond, and thou were brokun. **a1500** *Imitatione* (*1*) 47.30–1: Truste not ner leene not upon a windy rede. **1502** *Imitatione* (*2*) 185.16–7: Be nat adherent ne put nat thy confidence in that thynge that is as an holowe stocke or a rede. **1534** More *Comforte* 1140 A[4–6]: As though you woulde cast awaye a strong staffe, and leane upon a rotten reede. Apperson 356; *Oxford* 66; Tilley R61. See **S594, 649, W249.**

R71 The **Reed** that bows will arise when the wind ceases (*varied*)
c1385 Chaucer *TC* ii 1387–9: And reed that boweth down for every blast, Ful lightly, cesse wynd, it wol aryse; But so nyl nought an ook, whan it is cast. **a1438** Kempe 1.19–22: And evyr sche was turned a-gen a-bak . . . lech un-to the reed-spyr whech boweth wyth every wynd and nevyr is stable les than no wynd bloweth. **a1450** *Rule of St. Benet* (*2*) 112.2278–80: Thinkand on hir awn frelte Lik to a rede in a forest, That bows with wind and wil not brest. **1556** Heywood *Spider* 288[8–11]: And like as we se the Oke: in stought storme of winde: Standing stiffe against the wynde: overthrowne, And the Reede: waving with the winde, still we finde: Saving it self, in all our blastes of winde blowne. *Oxford* 467; Skeat 149; Whiting *Drama* 262–3. See **T475.**

R72 To wag like a **Reed**
a1387 Higden-Trevisa VII 321[17]: Robard, waggynge as a reed, assented anon. Whiting *Scots* II 116.

R73 To wave like a **Reed**(-spire)
c1300 *Northern Homily Cycle* (*Edin. Coll. Phys.*) 40[24]: Yef he als red wald haf wevid, **c1390** *Narrationes* (*Vernon*) 244.67: Gif he wolde have weved as a Reode. **a1449** Lydgate *Testament* in *MP* I 353.653: Wawed with eche wynd, as doth a reedspere. **a1500** *Consideryng effectually* in Person 45.54: Like unto a Reede wavyng too and fro.

R74 Not to thole (*suffer, permit*) the **Reek** (*smoke*) to blow on one
a1500 *Thre Prestis* 16.228: His moder tholit nocht the reke on him to blaw. See **W323.**

R75 To fail (*vanish*) like **Reek** (*etc.*) (A number of single quotations are brought together here)
c1340 Rolle *Psalter* 134 (36.21): Fayland as reke thai sall fayle, 230 (67.2): As reke fails faile thai, 352 (101.4). **a1400** *Northern Verse Psalter* I 115 (36.20): Wanand als reke thai wane to noght, 207 (67.3), II 5 (101.4). **a1400** *Scottish Legends* II 158.229: Bot as a reke away he wat (*vanished*), 164.442: Bot fled as reke. **c1470** *Wallace* 158.579–80: The strang stour rais, as reik, upon thaim fast, Or myst, throuch sone, up to the clowdis past.

R76 To raise (a) **Reek**
a1450 *York Plays* 220.34: For thurgh his romour in this reme Hath raysede mekill reke. **a1460** *Towneley Plays* 372.168–9: She can rase up a reke If she be well nettyld. NED Reek sb.[1] 1c. See **S413.**

R77 To vanish like **Reek**
a1400 *Scottish Legends* II 113.511–2: And he away, as It ware reke, Wanyst, 117.646, 118.660, 675, 162.376–7: And (he), as he reke bene hade, Ful sodenely wanyste away. **1513** Douglas *Aeneid* II 232.138: Vanyst away as the reik in the ayr. Whiting *Scots* II 116. Cf. Taylor and Whiting 340. See **F699, S414.**

R77.1 Where there is **Reek** there is fire
1490 Irlande *Meroure* II 85.7–8: Quhar men seis mekle reik thai may knaw that thar is fyr. Tilley S569; Taylor and Whiting 340. See **F194.**

R78 To help with **Reel** and rock (*distaff*)
c1400 *Laud Troy* I 175.5939: Sche (*Fortune*) halpe him wel with Real and Rok.

R79 To harp on one **Refreit** (*refrain*)
a1500 Medwall *Nature* B3[v][19]: These .ii. folk harp both on refrayte. See **S839.**

R80 It is good to be purveyed of a **Remedy**
c1500 *Melusine* 92.10–1: But alwayes it is good to be purveyed of remedye.

R81 Where there is no **Remedy** it is folly to chide (*varied*)
c1390 Chaucer *CT* VII 427–9[B1617–9]: This marchant saugh ther was no remedie, And for to chide it nere but folie, Sith that the thyng may nat amended be. **c1450** Idley 171.770: Wher as is no remedie, ther is noo boote. **c1470** *Wallace* 367.1134–6: Litill reherss is our mekill off cair: And principaly quhar redempcioun is nayn, It helpys nocht to tell thar petous mayn. **c1485** *Burial and Resurrection* 209.1123–4: It is bot in vayn Thus remedilesse to mak compleyn. **1509** Barclay *Ship* II 179[1–2]: He is a Fole: and voyde of wyt certayne That mourneth for that whiche is past remedy. Whiting *Scots* II 116. See **D337, G455, L52, M729, R31, S514, T160, 179, 192, W381.**

R82 When **Renown** is lost it is late recovering of it
c1505 Watson *Valentine* 46.23–5: You know wel that renowne is dere, For whan it is lost be it by right or by wronge, it is late recoveringe of it. See **N13, 16.**

R83 To pay one his **Rent**
a1300 *Richard* 294.4055–6: Kyng R. hys ax in hond he hente And payde Sarezynys here rente. NED Rent sb.[1] 2a.

R84 To **Repent** too late
a1325 *Cursor* II 290.4958: Your repenting es now to late. **a1420** Lydgate *Troy* I 105.3151: List thou repente whan it is to late. **1481** Caxton *Reynard* 110[8–9]: That after they repente hem and thenne it is to(o) late. **a1500** ?Ros *La Belle Dame* 321.715–6: And, afterward if I shulde live in wo, Than to repent it were to late, I gesse. **c1500** Greene *Carols* 408.14: Then to repent yt ys to late. **c1500** *Melusine* 310.14–5: Over late is this repented. **1509** Barclay *Ship* I 225[7], 243[7]. **1511** Hawes *Comforte* B1[v][7]. **1518** Watson *Oliver* K1[v][29]. **a1533** Berners *Huon* 320.24–5. Tilley A211; Whiting *Ballad* 38, *Drama* 42, 156, 166, 225, 274. See **C448, R86, T158.**

R85 Beware of **Repentance** another day
c1500 *Wife Lapped* 185.124: And beware of repentaunce another day.

R86 **Repentance** is shown (comes) too late
1546 Heywood *D* 37.86: To late (quoth mine aunt) this repentance shewd is, **1556** *Spider* 342[24–5]: Which being now doone: and repented as soone, To late cumth that repentaunce: to avoyde thill. Apperson 528; *Oxford* 539; Tilley A211; Whiting *Scots* II 116–7. See **H134, R84.**

R87 **Repenting** may not avail
1471 Caxton *Recuyell* I 269.28–9: But that was for nought for the repentyng myght not avaylle. See **M729.**

R88 Good **Report** is best in every age
a1449 Lydgate *Haste* in *MP* II 764.135: Good

report is best in everi age. Cf. Tilley R85. See **N12.**

R89 Great **Reproof** follows little excess
a1420 Lydgate *Troy* I 345.7031: For litel excesse folweth gret reprefe.

R90 To rue one's **Rese** (*hasty action*)
a1325 *Cursor* I 254.4325: Reu his res than sal he sare. **a1338** Mannyng *Chronicle B* II 237[3]: The Walssh wer alle day slayn, now rewes tham ther res. **c1350** *Joseph* 16.491: That thorw him reowen no res. **c1400** *Roland* 117.370: Thoughe Roulond rew that rese. **c1425** *Avowynge* 68[16]: Him ruet alle his rees. NED Rese 3b. See **H159, R32, 65.**

R91 Every **Resemblance** delights (the) other
1477 Rivers *Dictes* 9[7]: Commonely every resemblance delyteth other. See **L272.**

R92 There is no **Resistence** (defence) where folk are drunk
a1439 Lydgate *Fall* I 307.3842–3: And wise men rehersen in sentence, Wher folk be dronke ther is no resistence, II 395.2379–80: For men mai knowe bi olde experience, In folkis dronke mai be no resistence, 573.3649–50: But it is said of old and is no fable, That no diffence is (in) dronk(e)nesse. See **C619, W494.**

R93 A little **Respite** sometimes speeds (*assists*)
a1450 *Generydes A* 167.5343–4: Litle respite at mych nede Falleth som tyme wele to spede.

R94 After long **Rest** comes sharp labor
1464 Hardyng 127[3–4]: But ever as next the valey is the hill, After long rest commeth sharpe labour. See **R96.**

R95 He is unwise that runs from **Rest** to jeopardy
1515 Barclay *St. George* 96.2386–7: He well may be callyd unwyse and fole hardy Which wylfully rennyth from rest to jeopardy. See **S297.**

R96 A little **Rest** engenders much labor
1450 *Dicts* 64.20: A litille rest engendrithe muche labour. See **R94.**

R97 With **Rest** and peace a man shall best increase
a1450 *Chronicle of London* 122[26–7]: With reste and pees, A man schal best encrees.

R98 A good **Retreat** is worth more than a foolish abiding
c1477 Caxton *Jason* 23.18–9: More is worth a good retrayte than a folisshe abydinge. Apperson 153: Discretion; *Oxford* 147; Tilley D354.

R99 More **Reverence** is given to wicked men for dread than to good men for love
a1400 *Scottish Legends* I 192.71–4: As men in proverbe sais, Mare reverens Is gewine always To vekyt men fore dred and dowte Thane to gudmen for luf al-owte. Cf. Tilley R105.

R100 Saving (Save) one's (your) **Reverence**
c1400 Mandeville *Travels* 123.22–3: But after my lytyll wytt it semeth me, savynge here reverence, that it is more. **1454** Paston II 317[8–9]: A fals harlot, sauf your reverens, one James Cook. **1455** *Rotuli Parliamentorum (1287–1503)* V 281[1.52–3]: The . . . defaime untruly, savyng youre reverence, leyed upon us. **1456** Paston III 106[21–2]: Save yowre reverens, Cristyfor sal(?) have swyche a maister, **1461** III 273[2–3]: And, Sir, as for the fals noise, sauf your reverence, that he leyth on me, **1468** IV 293–4. **1487** Caxton *Book of Good Manners* H3ᵛ[7–8]: Savyng the reverence of them that have wreton suche historyes. *Oxford* 562; Tilley R93.

R101 The **Reward** of sin is shame and sorrow
1464 Hardyng 302 *var.*[3]: The rewarde of synne is shame and sorowe observed. See **S338.**

R102 It may well **Rhyme** but it accords not (*varied*)
c1385 Usk 51.73–4: These thinges to-forn-sayd mowe wel, if men liste, ryme, trewly, they acorde nothing. **a1449** Lydgate *Ryme without Accord* in *MP* II 792–4.8: It may wele ryme, but it accordith nought, 16, 24, *etc.* **c1477** Caxton *Curtesye* 52.519–22: Goo, litle childe, and who doth you Appose, Seying, youre quaire kepeth non accordaunce, Tell (hym) as yite neyther of ryme ne prose Ye be experte. **a1500** *Sheep on the Green* in Robbins xxxviii[11]: Thys may ryme wel but hyt acorde nought. **c1500** *King Hart* 109.20: Suppois it ryme it acordis nocht all clene. **1523** Skelton *Garlande* I 410. 1210: It may wele ryme, but shroudly it doth accorde. **1546** Heywood *D* 53.404: It may ryme but it accordth not. Apperson 529; *Oxford* 540; Tilley R99; Whiting *Scots* II 117.

R103 **Rhyme** and reason (*variously contrasted*)
c1303 Mannyng *Handlyng* 272.8625–6: For foule englyssh, and feble ryme Seyde oute of resun many tyme. **c1325** *I Repent* 143.61–2: Richard, rote of resoun ryht, Rykening of rym ant ron. **c1385** Chaucer *TC* iii 90: His resons, as I may my rymes holde. **a1475** Russell *Boke* 199.1243: As for ryme or reson, the forewryter was not to blame. **c1475** Henryson *Aganis Haisty Credence* 215.23: Ryme as it may, thair

is na ressoun, *Want of Wyse Men* 191.61: But ryme or ressone all Is bot heble hable. **a1500** *Leconfield Proverbs* 493[14]: Regarde not the ryme but the reasone marke wele. **c1516** Skelton *Magnificence* 36.1151: It forseth not of the reason, so it kepe ryme, **a1529** *Garnesche* I 123.104–5: For reson can I non fynde Nor good ryme in yower mater, 127–8: In a felde of grene peson Ys ryme yet owte of reson. **1532** More *Confutacion* 495 C[7–10]: Save for the ryme I woulde not geve a rushe . . . for any reson. **1556** Heywood *E* 104.1: Ryme without reason, and reason without ryme. Apperson 529; *Oxford* 540; Taylor and Whiting 306; Tilley R98; Whiting *Drama* 360:799, *Scots* II 117.

R104 As red as **Rice** (*twig*)
c1350 *Libeaus* 125 *var.* 2220[c]: Hur rode was rede so rys.

R105 As white as **Rice**
a1475 *Lovely lordynges* in Halliwell *Early English Miscellanies* 4[24]: The creste blewe and whyte as rysse.

R106 To make the **Rice** blossom again (*i.e.*, improve the situation)
1481 Caxton *Reynard* 80[23]: She hath the rys doo blosme agayn.

R107 As long as I am reputed **Rich** I am saluted
a1500 *Harley MS.2321* in *Rel. Ant.* I 207: As long as I am riche reputed, With solem vyce I am saluted; But wealthe away once woorne, No one wyll say good morne. Tilley R103, cf. S307.

R108 If one is **Rich** he shall find a great number of fellows
c1390 Chaucer *CT* VII 1558[B2748]: Pamphilles seith . . . "if thou be right riche thou shalt fynde a greet nombre of felawes and freendes." **c1395** *WBible* Proverbs xiv 20: But many men ben frendis of riche men. *Oxford* 541; Smith 253; Tilley R103. See **M272, R115.**

R109 Make you not **Rich** of other man's thing
c1350 *Good Wife E* 168.147: Make the noght riche of other mannis thing. See **T217.**

R110 The **Rich** (is) preferred, the poor is culpable
a1449 Lydgate *Cok* in *MP* II 816.99–100: The ryche preferryd, the poore is ay cowpable. See **M265.**

R111 The **Rich** shall die as well as the poor
1474 Caxton *Chesse* 80[29–31]: For as well shall dye the ryche as the poure. See **D101, K49.**

R112 In **Richard** the devil's name
c1450 (c1335) Trevet 364.4–10 (f.75a, col. 2): Wherethorow be that grete crewelte that the men of the contre suffered soore had a proverbe among hem, and sayde whan theyre chyldren wept and wolde nat be styll, for to chastyse them whan they cryed, seyng thus, "Be styll for that devell Kyng Rychard." And of thys proverbe Englysshmen made a proverbe, "In the develles name Richard." Anglo-Norman in Notes p. 460: De ceo les Engleis empristrent un parole de ledenger, qant ils voleint reprover lour noyauntz, en disaunt en lour pateis, "In the develes name Richard."

R113 **Riches** are got with labor, held with fear and lost with grief
a1500 *Harley MS.2321* in *Rel. Ant.* I 208: Riches are gotten with labor, holden with feare, And lost with greyfe and excessive care. Apperson 530; Tilley R108.

R114 **Riches** gotten untruly cause conscience to be sorry
c1450 *Fyrst thou sal* 91.181–2: Rytches gettyn untrewly Causes conscience to be sory. See **G336.**

R115 **Riches** increase (make) friends
c1395 *WBible* Proverbs xix 4: Richessis encreessen ful many freendis. **c1415** *Middle English Sermons* 86.25–6: For as the wyse man seyth in is Proverbes, the iii chapitur, "Rychesse maketh frendes." **1546** Heywood *D* 27.33–4: And riches maie make Freends many ways. Jente 272. See **R108.**

R116 **Riches** make pens (*wings*)
c1395 *WBible* Proverbs xxiii 5: Richessis . . . schulen make to hem silf pennes, as of an egle, and tho schulen flee in to hevene. Apperson 530; *Oxford* 541; Tilley R111.

R117 **Riches** oft bring harm and ever fear
1546 Heywood *D* 55.12: Riches bringth oft harm, and ever feare. Jente 595; Smith 253; Tilley R109.

R118 Small **Riches** have most rest
c1515 Barclay *Eclogues* 136.765: Small riches hath most rest. See **B613.**

R119 Worldly **Riches** shall pass
c1412 Hoccleve *Regement* 47.1290–1: Worldly riches, have ay in thi memorye, Schal passe, al look it never on men so feire. Cf. Whiting *Drama* 116. See **C114, T449, W671.**

R120 Ill gotten **Richesse** comes to ill end (*varied*)
1506 Barclay *Castell* G2[v][14]: Rychesse yll goten cometh to yll ende. **1519** Horman *Vulgaria*

118[20]: Evyll goten ryches wyll never prove longe. **1525** Berners *Froissart* V 313[37–8]: That rychesse is nat good nor resonable that is yvell gotten. See **G345.**

R121 **Richesse** is mickle of power (has poustie [*power*])
a1338 Mannyng *Chronicle A* I 159.4557: Mikel is richesse of power. **a1400** *Romaunt C* 6484: But richesse hath pouste.

R122 There is no **Richesse** that may be compared to good fame
1456 Hay *Governaunce* 90.23–4: Thare is na richesse that may be comperit to gude fame and gude renoune. See **N12.**

R123 He **Rides** well that never fell
a1470 Malory II 516.5–6: And he rydyth well that never felle. Apperson 530; *Oxford* 543; Tilley R116.

R124 He **Rides** well that rides with his fellows
1492 *Salomon and Marcolphus* 13[6–7]: He rydyth well that ridyth wyth his felawes.

R125 Good **Riding** at two anchors
1549 Heywood *D* 93.81–2: Good ridyng at two ankers men have tolde, For if the tone faile, the tother maie holde. Apperson 262; *Oxford* 255; Smith 254; Tilley R119.

R126 **Riff** and (nor) raff
a1338 Mannyng *Chronicle B* I 38[26]: To Justy and Gudmund, thei tok alle riffe and raf, 111[2]: That noither he no hise suld chalange rif no raf, 151[16]: The Sarazins ilk man he slouh alle rif and raf, II 276[20], 277[6]. NED Riff[1].

R127 **Right** and the king ought to be as brothers
a1449 Lydgate and Burgh *Secrees* 65.2051: Ryght and the Kyng as brethryn owen to be.

R128 **Right** has no virtue
c1505 Watson *Valentine* 149.8: Ryght hath no vertue.

R129 **Right** makes the feeble (man) wight (*strong*)
c1375 Barbour *Bruce* I 21.510: And rycht mayss oft the feble wycht. **c1420** Wyntoun V 355. 2797–8: For I wate I haf richt; And richt oft makis the febil wicht. **a1450** *Generydes A* 172.5533–4: I have the right and he the wrong, Right maketh a feble man strong. Cf. Whiting *Drama* 167. See **P342.**

R130 To sell the **Right** of the first gendered child
c1395 *WBible* Genesis xxv 31: And Jacob seide to him, Sille to me the right of the first gendrid childe. *Oxford* 573; Tilley B403. See **H364.**

R131 As white as **Rime-frost**
c1250 *Genesis and Exodus* 95.3328: It lai thor, quit als a rim frost.

R132 As hard as a **Rind**
c1450 *When the son* 393.402: Not mannysshe rough hard as a rynde.

R133 As round as a **Ring**
a1400 *Destruction of Troy* 55.1635: Evyn round as a ryng richely wroght.

R134 A **Ring** of a rush (1)
c1449 Pecock *Repressor* I 166[4–11]: If a marchant or eny other man have myche nede forto bithenke upon a certeine erand . . . it is weel allowid and approved bi resoun that he make a ring of a rische and putte it on his fynger.

R135 A **Ring** of a rush (2)
1532 More *Frith* in *Workes* 835 B[6–7]: Gyve the bride . . . a proper ring of a rushe. **1546** Heywood *D* 23.33: I hoppyng without for a ryng of a rushe. Apperson 532; *Oxford* 543; Tilley R128.

R136 To become as well as a gold **Ring** in a swine's nose
a1400 *Ancrene* (*Recluse*) 97.1–2: And this draweth mychel to religioun And there it bicometh als wel as who so putt a gold ringe in a swynes nose. See **W486.**

R137 To come (hop) in (to, upon) the **Ring**
c1330 *Times of Edward II* 339.351: And whan theih comen to the ring, hoppe if hii kunne. **a1338** Mannyng *Chronicle B* II 305[20]: To the renge ere ye brouht, hop now if ye wille. **c1410** Lovelich *Merlin* I 11.373–4: And wiste wel be hire answeryng That sche scholde hoppen uppon hys rynge. **a1420** Lydgate *Troy* III 823.1781–2: O Ulixes, by ordre in my writyng, Thin aventures commen on the ring, **a1449** *Order of Fools* in *MP* II 450.25–6. **a1450** *Partonope* 456.11485: Now hoppe if he can, he is come to the ringe (*is fallen in love*). **a1500** *Alexander-Cassamus* 56.127: And yf y shal hoppe algate on lovys rynge.

R138 To lead (rule) the **Ring**
c1343 Rolle *Ego* in Allen *R. Rolle* 68.237: Bot suth than es it sayde that lufe ledes the ryng. **c1350** *Nominale* 9*.214: W. the ryng leduth for joye. **c1522** Skelton *Speke* II 7.132: He rulyth the ring.

R139 Whoso hops best at last shall have the **Ring**
a1500 Greene *Carols* 308.1: Thenkyst thou nothyng That whoso best hoppith at laste shal have the ryng? **1546** Heywood *D* 23.31–2: Where wooers hoppe in an out, long time may bryng Him that hoppeth best, at last to have the ryng. Tilley R130.

R140 After **Riot** (*excess*) soon comes evil fare
c1460 *To you beholders* 48.6: Ffor affter ryat sone cometh evyl fare.

R141 Every **Riot** must needs fall at last
a1393 Gower *CA* III 142.7131*–2*: Bot every riot ate laste Mot nedes falle and mai noght laste.

R142 **Ripe** and rotten (*varied*)
a1387 *Piers* C xiii 223: And that that rathest rypeth roteth most saunest. **c1390** Chaucer *CT* I[A] 3874–5: We olde men, I drede, so fare we: Til we be roten, kan we nat be rype. **c1450** Idley 136.1741: Ffor soone woll be rotyn that tymely is grene. **a1500** *O Mosy Quince* in Person 40.7: Ye be so rype ye wex almost rotyn. **1532** More *Frith* in *Workes* 841 EF: Many wittes waxe rotten ere they waxe rype. **1546** Heywood *D* 39.124: But soone rype soone rotten, **1556** *Spider* 450[6]: For feare of rotting: before riping began. Apperson 588; *Oxford* 604; Taylor and Whiting 307; Tilley R133; Whiting *Drama* 121, 165, 286, *Scots* II 117. See **F690, 694.**

R143 Whoso will **Rise** early shall be holy, healthy and seely (*happy*) (*varied*)
1496 ?Berners *Book of Hawking, etc.* (reproduced with . . . notices by Joseph Haslewood [London, 1810]) H1r[9–10]: As the olde englysshe proverbe sayth in this wise: who soo woll ryse erly shall be holy, helthy, and zely. **a1500** *Good Wife A* 220.165–6: Loke thou go to bed bytyme: Erly to ryse is fysyke fyne, *N* 215.180–1: So to bed betimes, at morne rise belive And so may thou better learne to thrive. Apperson 173; *Oxford* 164; Taylor and Whiting 21; Tilley B184. See **G259, S89.**

R144 A sudden **Rising** oft falls alow
1511 Hawes *Comforte* B2r[5]: A sodayne rysynge dooth oft fall alowe. See **C296.**

R145 As many as **Risoms** (*corn stalks*) in a rank field
a1400 *Alexander C* 180.3059–60: Thare fell as fele tham before of fotemen and othire, As risonis (*Dublin:* ressynnys) in a ranke fild quen riders it spillen.

R146 To romy (*roar*) like a rad **Rith** (*frightened ox*)
c1380 *Cleanness* 57.1543: And romyes as a rad ryth that rores for drede.

R147 In every **River** the worse fords the better fish
c900 *Old English Cato* 7.21–2: On ælcere ea swa wyrse fordes swa betere fisces.

R148 To have the **Rivers** run against the hill
1480 Caxton *Ovyde* 115[4–6]: The Ryvers shold rather renne ayenst the hylle that (*for* than) Ayax by hys wytte sholde . . . brynge Phylotes, 137[12–3]: Er that sholde falle the ryvers sholde renne ayenst the hylle.

R149 Cold **Roast** (1) (*i.e.*, hard times)
1406 Hoccleve *Male Regle* 36.363: And in thy cofre, pardee, is cold roost. **a1460** *Towneley Plays* 21.421: Yey, cold rost is at my masteres hame. NED Roast 2b.

R150 Cold **Roast** (2) (*i.e.*, stale news)
a1450 *Tottenham* 995.136: Thou spekis of cold rost. NED Roast 2b.

R151 To beshit the **Roast**
1546 Heywood *D* 90.70: He lookt lyke one that had beshyt the roste. See **B423.**

R152 To rule the **Roast**
a1500 *Carpenter's Tools* 85.176: My mayster yet shall reule the roste. **c1516** Skelton *Magnificence* 26.804: I rule moche of the rost, **1522** *Why Come* II 33.198: He ruleth all the roste, **c1522** *Colyn* I 350.1020–1: But at the playsure of one That ruleth the roste alone. **c1545** Heywood *Four PP* C1r[17]: Yf rychesse mygh(t) rule the roste, **1546** *D* 26.25: Than shalt thou rule the roste. Apperson 540; *Oxford* 551; Taylor and Whiting 308; Tilley R144; Whiting *Drama* 361:810, *Scots* II 117–8.

R153 To spoil the **Roast**
a1500 *Lover and the Advocate of Venus* in Robbins 170.52: Yur writyng afore spilt al the roste.

R154 He that **Robs** shall be robbed
1484 Caxton *Aesop* 60[4–6]: For he that robbeth shall be robbed. Juxta illud pellatores pillabuntur. See **G491.**

R155 Good even, good **Robin Hood**
1522 Skelton *Why Come* II 32.194: Good evyn, good Robyn Hood! Apperson 535; *Oxford* 251; Tilley E188.

R156 Many men speak of **Robin Hood** that never bent his bow (*varied*)

c1385 Chaucer *TC* ii 859–61: For swich manere folk, I gesse, Defamen Love, as nothing of him knowe. Thei speken, but thei benten nevere his bowe! **a1425** *MS. Ph marginal gloss:* of robyn hode, **c1450** *MS. H*[4]*:* Thei spekyn of robynhod but thei bente never his bowe [R. K. Root ed. *Troilus and Criseyde* (Princeton, 1926) 449]. **c1400–25** Legat *Sermon* 8.46–7: For mani, manime seith, spekith of Robyn Hood that schotte never in his bowe. **1402** *Daw Topias* 59[3–4]: And many men speken of Robyn Hood, and shotte nevere in his bowe. **1471** Ripley *Compound* 175[26–8]: For many man spekyth wyth wondreng: *Of Robyn Hode, and of his Bow, Whych never shot therin I trow.* **1546** Heywood *D* 78.14–5: But many a man speaketh of Robyn hood, That never shot in his bowe. Apperson 535; *Oxford* 611; Tilley R148; Whiting *Ballad* 24. See **A63, M33, 195, P148, W40.**

R157 A rhyme (song, jest, fable, tale) of **Robin Hood**
c1378 *Piers* B v 402: But I can rymes of Robyn Hood and Randolf erle of Chestre. **a1470** Parker *Dives* E4ʳ[2.33–6]: Lever to here a songe of Robynhode or of some rybaudrye than for to here masse or matynes. **1509** Barclay *Ship* I 72[14]: A folysshe yest of Robyn hode, II 155[27]: And all of fables and Jestis of Robyn hode, 331[17]: I wryte no Jest ne tale of Robyn hode, **c1515** *Eclogues* 166.720–1: Some mery fit Of mayde Marion, or els of Robin Hood. **1528** More *Heresyes* 243 B[4–6]: To handle holie scripture in more homely maner than a song of Robin hode, **1533** *Confutacion* 697 C[2–4]: If thei had told hym that a tale of Robyne hode had bene holye scrypture, D[3–4], 698 (*by error* 798) A[7–8]. **1546** Heywood *D* 94.138: Tales of Robin hood are good among fooles. Apperson 535–6; *Oxford* 643; Tilley T53; Whiting *Scots* II 118.

R158 As wise as **Robin Swine**
c1522 Skelton *Colyn* I 342.808: As wyse as Robyn swyne.

Rock (1)

R159 As dark as **Rock**
1501 Douglas *Palice* 8.17: Dark as rock.

R160 As stable as any **Rock**
a1422 Lydgate *Life* 360.706: In hert and will, as any Roche stable. Cf. Taylor and Whiting 308–9; Tilley R151.

R161 To move no more than a **Rock**
1513 Douglas *Aeneid* III 31.96–8: Moving na mair . . . Than scho had bene . . . a ferm rolk of Mont Marpesyane. Whiting *Scots* II 118. See **M564, 726, S792, W24.**

Rock (2)

R162 As sharp and small as **Rocks** (*distaffs*)
a1513 Dunbar *To the Quene* 60.23: With schinnis scharp and small lyk rockis.

R163 One's **Rock** is spun
c1450 *Rylands MS.394* 94.20–1: Good day my rokke ys sponne. Lux bona prestetur tibi nanque colus mea netur. Walther II 783.14137a.

R164 Thus rides the **Rock**
1546 Heywood *D* 92.77: Thus ryd the rocke, **1555** *E* 163.102: Thus rideth the rocke, if the rocke be ridyng, The spinsters thrift, is set a foote slidyng. *Oxford* 546; Tilley R150.

R165 To acore (*suffer*) the **Rod**
a1250 *Ancrene* (*Nero*) 26.2–3: Ase mon seith, thu schalt acorien the rode, that is, acorien his sunne.

R166 To be beaten with the **Rod** one makes for another
1484 Caxton *Aesop* 155[16–7]: And is beten with the same rodde that he maketh for other. See **P232, S652.**

R167 To be chastised without **Rod**
a1393 Gower *CA* III 226.2216–8: Thus was the king withoute rodd Chastised, and the queene excused Of that sche hadde ben accused. See **K91.**

R168 As light as a (the, any) **Roe**
c1390 *Deo Gracias II* in Brown *Lyrics XIV* 138.10: And liht to renne as is a Ro. **a1393** Gower *CA* II 376.2786–7: The Ro, which renneth on the Mor, Is thanne noght so lyht as I. **c1440** Charles of Orleans 46.1365: Forto ben glad and light as any roo. **a1450** *Tottenham* 994.129: the. **a1450** *York Plays* 281.262: Now than am I light as a roo. **a1475** *Ludus Coventriae* 327. 1640–1: Now hens we go As lyth as ro. **a1500** Greene *Carols* 396 *refrain:* any.

R169 As roless (*restless*) as the **Roe** (*etc.*) (A number of single quotations are brought together here)
a1325 *Labourers* in Brown *Lyrics XIII* 145.49–50: This world me wurcheth wo, Rooles ase the roo. **1372** *Christ's Three Songs* in Brown *Lyrics XIV* 92.9: Mi bodi is as red as ro. **c1390** Chaucer *CT* I[A] 4086: I is ful wight (*swift*), God waat, as is a raa. **1418** *Man, be warre* in Kail 64.110: And . . . recheles as a roo.

R170 As swift as the (any, a) **Roe**

c1330 *St. Margaret* 232.254: Sum wer swifter . . . than the ro. **a1375** *Octavian* (S) 43.1347–8: He ys swyftyr than ony roo Under lynde, 45.1417–8: Hyt ys swyfter than . . . ro, that renneth under lynde. **c1440** Charles of Orleans 198.5914: any. **a1449** Lydgate and Burgh *Secrees* 73.2302: the. **a1475** *Mergarete* 239.391: a. **a1500** *St. Margarete* B4v[13]: a. Tilley R158; Whiting *Scots* II 118.

R171 As wild as the (a, any) **Roe**
c1250 *Mater Salutaris* in Brown *Lyrics XIII* 22.11: Mi thoncc is wilde as is the ro. **a1300** *Alisaunder* 113.1989–90: Alisaundre . . . wilde so roo. **a1300** *Maximian* 99.226–7: Wilde ich wes her tho, Wildere then the ro. **c1325** *Old Man's Prayer* in Brown *Lyrics XIV* 4.27: the. **c1390** *Northern Homily Cycle Narrationes* (*Vernon*) 266.419: the. **1418** *Man, be warre* in Kail 64.110: a. **c1450** Idley 90.591: And as wilde as . . . a Roo in the fenne. **a1500** *Lay of Sorrow* 718.126: ony.

R172 To be befongen (*caught*) like a **Roe** with rope
c1000 *Corpus Christi Homily* (*St. Margaret*) in Assmann 172.71–2: Ic eam befangan . . . eal swa hra mid rape.

R173 To be inumen (*taken*) like a **Roe** in net
a1225 *St. Marherete* 8.9–10: Ase ra inumen i nette.

R174 To leap (up) like a **Roe**
c1325 *Sayings of St. Bernard* (*Laud*) 513.39: Thou lepest also a ro. **c1400** *Laud Troy* II 406.13770: He lepe up sone as a roo. Whiting *Scots* II 118.

R175 To run like any (a, the) **Roe**
a1400 *Childhood of Christ* in Horstmann *Sammlung* 107.466: Reny(n)g as faste as ony roo. **c1400** *Laud Troy* I 181.6127: He ran amonges hem as a roo, 267.9051–2: I trowe ther was nevere wilde ro That ran faster then his stede tho. **a1450** *Pride of Life* in Waterhouse 96.267–8: Mirth and solas he can make And ren so the ro.

R176 To skip like a **Roe**
a1300 *Les diz de seint bernard* in *Vernon* II 758.45: Thou skippest alse a ro. **a1325** *Cursor* II 1092.19080: That said that halt suld scep as ra.

R177 To start like a **Roe**
c1325 *Sayings of St. Bernard* 513.32–3: Nou art thou hevy, nou artou liht, Sturtynde as a Ro. **c1422** Hoccleve *Complaint* 100.128: For here and there forthe stirte I as a Roo.

R178 As dark as any **Roke** (*fog*)
1513 Douglas *Aeneid* IV 115.94–5: Swa heir the laithly odor raiss on hycht From the fyre blesis, dyrk as ony roik (*rime:* smoik).

R179 To be worth a **Roland** or an Oliver
1525 Berners *Froissart* IV 429[29–30]: Every man worth a Rowlande or an Olyvere.

R180 At (the court of) **Rome** all things are bought and sold (*varied*)
c1330 *Times of Edward II* 324.19–20: Voiz of clerk is sielde i-herd at the court of Rome; Ne were he nevere swich a clerk, silverles if he come. **a1338** Mannyng *Chronicle B* II 324[9–12]: He is folc (*for* fole) that affies in the courte of Rome, Comes a nother and bies, and fordos that dome. *Pur quante posse dare,* what thing and how mykelle, *Pur fare et defare,* Rome is now fulle fikelle. **a1387** Higden-Trevisa VII 183[1–3]: Wherfore he deserveth nevere for to gete his pal to Rome though al that byenge and sellynge wirk moche there. **c1400** *Apology* 12[12–4]: Opun and comyn fame traveylith, that in the court of Rome mai no man geyt no grace, but if it be bowt, nor ther is noon grauntid, but if it be for temporal meed. **c1500** Fabyan 227 [31–2]: But yet he never had the paule from Rome, though there be great sale that maketh many maistryes. **1509** Watson *Ship* Gg1r[10–1]: Rome is the rote of all the evylles of avaryce. *Oxford* 8; Tilley T164; Whiting *Scots* II 118.

R181 Better be at **Rome**
c1300 *Beves* 158.3381–2: That hem were beter at Rome, Thanne hii hadde hider icome. **a1400** *Perceval* 64.2015–6: Hym were better hafe bene at Rome, So every mote I thryfe. **a1425** *Chester Plays* II 298.418–9: Would God I hadd bene in Rome, When I the way hither nome.

R182 From hence to **Rome** (*varied*)
c1300 *Guy*[1] 364 A 6914: Hennes to Rome better nis nan. **c1300** *Havelok* 3.64: Was non so bold lond (?lord) to rome. **a1338** Mannyng *Chronicle B* II 254[1]: Fro Rome hiderward fayrer non was. **a1400** *Guy*[3] 627.113: Nis man bitwene this and Rome. **a1400** *Ipomadon A* 198.6960–2: There is no man fro hens to Roome, Mighte have done better, be my doome, Ne yett hens to Normandye. **a1400** *Scottish Legends* I 135.207: That thar ves nane sic in-to rome. **1436** *Libelle* 38.740–2: And well I wott that frome hens to Rome, And, as men sey, in alle Cristendome, There ys no grounde ne land to Yreland lyche. **a1500** *Partenay* 16.265–6: For A worthy man and vaillant he was As Any A-this-side Rome to purchas, 89.2468–9: And As that man non here more wurthy Was not

A-thys-side the romayns truly, 122.3472: Hys pere noght founde Athissid Rome truly. **a1500** *Thre Prestis* 33.645: And lyke to ane was nocht into Rome. **a1533** Berners *Huon* 609.20: Fro thense to Rome. **a1533** Heywood *Johan* B2v[1]: She is the erranst baud betwene this and Rome. Tilley H429; Whiting *Scots* II 118.

R183 **Rome** was not built in one day
1546 Heywood *D* 46.182–3: Rome was not built in one daie . . . and yet stood Till it was finisht, as some say, full faire, **1555** *E* 194.274. Apperson 537; Jente 152; *Oxford* 547–8; Taylor and Whiting 310; Tilley R163; Whiting *Scots* II 118.

R184 When at **Rome** do as (after) the doom
c1475 *Rawlinson MS. D 328* 122.57: Whan tho herd hat Rome Do so of ther the dome. Whan thu herd hels ware Do of ther as the dothe thare. Cum fueris Rome, Romane vivito more. Cum tu sis alibi vivito more loci. **a1500** Hill 130.6: Whan thou art at Rome, do after the dome; And whan thou art els wher, do as they do ther. Apperson 537; *Oxford* 547; Taylor and Whiting 310; Tilley R165; Walther I 497.4176. See **G493, W660.**

R185 A **Rome-runner** without a leasing (*lying*) fable (*i.e.*, an impossibility)
a1449 Lydgate *Ryme* in *MP* II 793.63: And take a Rome Renner without a lesyng fable. See **J27, P18, S251.**

R186 From thence unto **Roncesvalles**
c1475 *Golagros* 44.1313: Or all the renttis fra thyne unto Ronsiwall.

R187 To have one's **Roof** (house) on his nose (chin)
c1250 *Latemest Day* in Brown *Lyrics XIII* 47.29–30: Thin hus is sone ibuld ther thu salt wonien inne, Bothe the wirst (*for* firste) and the rouf sal liggen uppon thin chinne. **a1300** *Proprietates Mortis* in Brown *Lyrics XIII* 130.21–2: Thanne lyd min hus uppe min nose, Off al this world ne gyffe ihic a pese. **c1325** *Body and Soul* in Böddeker 243.239–42: When the flor is at thy rug, The rof ys at thy neose, Al this worldes blisse Nis nout worth a peose. **1374** Brinton *Sermons* I 156[9–10]: For whan the roof of thin hous lieth o thi nese, al this werdlis blisse is nought worth a pese, II 337[26–7]: For whan the roof of thy hous beth upon thy nese, all thys werdly blisse to the ne is worith a pese, 402 [30–1]: For whanne the roof of thi hous lyth on thi nese *et cetera.* **c1390** *Body and Soul* V 70.87–8: Thi boure is bult so cold in clay, The roof to resten on thi chyn. **a1400** *Cambridge Univ. Lib. MS. Ii.iii.8* f.166 in Owst *Literature* 43[21–2]: Whan the rofe of thyn hous lithe on thi nese, Alle the worldis blisse ys nouth worthe a pese.

R188 As rauk (*hoarse*) as **Rook**
c1475 Henryson *Testament* 120.443–5: My cleir voice . . . Is rawk as Ruik.

R189 To gape like a **Rook**
a1449 Lydgate *Order* in *MP* II 450.43: Gapeth as a rook.

R190 To roar like a **Rook**
a1300 *Cloisterer's Lament* in *Rel. Ant.* I 291[9]: I gowle au mi *grayel* and rore als a roke.

R191 In highest **Rooms** is greatest fear
1509 Barclay *Ship* II 318[21]: In hyest rowmes is greattest fere. See **E24, 149, 150, H385, 387, 609, K77, P247, S357, T434, 462, W302, 344.**

R192 Of an ill **Root** springs an ill tree
a1533 Berners *Arthur* 322[33]: Of an yll rote spryngeth an yll tre.

R193 **Root** and rind
a1338 Mannyng *Chronicle A* I 150.4285–6: Syn we ar comen alle of o kynde, And of o rote and of o rynde. **a1449** Lydgate *Fabula* in *MP* II 495.271–2: The(i) were ful besy to fynd out roote and rynde, Of what humour was causyd his dissese. **a1450** *Castle* 111.1138: Envye, thou arte rote and rynde. **a1500** Kennedy *Passion of Christ* 31.124: God hes the chosin to be baith rute and ryn.

R194 As meet as a **Rope** for a thief
1546 Heywood *D* 36.41–2: She is, to turne love to hate, or joye to greefe A paterne, as meete as a rope for a theefe. Apperson 538; *Oxford* 548; Tilley R169.

R195 Take not every **Rope**'s end with every man that hauls
a1475 *Good Wyfe Wold* 174.46: Take not every roppys end witt every man that hallys.

R196 As bright as **Rose**
a1450 *St. Katherine* (*Gibbs*) 41[28]: Thayr faces schone as bryght as roses. **c1500** Newton 264.25: Thay were as bright os . . . rose on brere.

R197 As fair as (the, a) **Rose**
c1386 Chaucer *LGW* 613: And she was fayr as is the rose in May. **a1400** *Destruction of Troy* 100.3057: The rede gomys, as a rose faire. **c1450** Capgrave *Katharine* 277.490: Tho wex she . . . fayre as the rose. **a1475** *Ludus Coventriae* 145.303: But fayr . . . as rose on thorn.

c1475 *Lamentation of Mary Magdalene* 414[35]: Fairer than rose. Svartengren 221.

R198 As fresh as (the, a, any) **Rose** (in May, on thorn)
c1390 *Song of Love* in Brown *Lyrics XIV* 180.95–6: Heo is of colour and beute As fresch as is the Rose In May. **c1395** Chaucer *CT* III[D] 448: I koude walke as fressh as is a rose. **a1400** *Destruction of Troy* 122.3771: Rede roicond in white, as the Roose fresshe. **a1420** Lydgate *Troy* II 558.5660: Beinge as freshe as any rose newe, III 580.585–6: the, 671.3640: any, 855. 2897: any, **a1422** *Life* 299.729: For she is fayre, and fresshe as Rose in May. **c1430** ?Lydgate *Compleynt* 64.373: Now as the rose, frosch and newe. **a1449** Lydgate *Mydsomer Rose* in *MP* II 784.104: Fressher than . . . ony somyr rose. **a1450** *O glorious virgyne* in Horstmann *Sammlung* 194.223: Made hire fresche as rose on thorne. **a1450** *Partonope* 195.5167: She was as freshe as the rose in maye. **c1450** Idley 163.250: ony. **c1450** La Tour-Landry 166.5–6: a. **1464** Hardyng 284[21]: Yonge, freshe . . . as the rose in Maye. **a1470** Parker *Dives* L8ʳ[1.27–8]: Fresshe as a rose in May, full lusty to the eye. **a1475** *Ludus Coventriae* 145.303: But . . . fresch as rose on thorn. **c1477** Caxton *Jason* 55.16–7: Your colour is fressh as roose in Maye. **a1500** *He said Ba-Bay* in Brown *Lyrics XV* 4–7.7: The virgine fresch as ros in may, 15, 22, *etc.* **a1500** *Now late me thought* 293[36]: Att all tymes fressh as rose in may. **1509** Barclay *Ship* II 16[22–3]: This prynce . . . Smellynge as the Rose ay freshe and redolent. Apperson 235; *Oxford* 225; Taylor and Whiting 312; Tilley R176.

R199 As red as (a, any, the) **Rose(s)**
a1250 *On God Ureison* in Brown *Lyrics XIII* 4.53: Heo beoth so read so rose. **c1325** *Annot* 137.11: Hire rode is ase rose that red is on rys. **c1325** *Maid of Ribbesdale* in Böddeker 156.35–6: And rode on eke, Ase rose when hit redes. **c1330** *Praise of Women* 291.47: White and rede so rose on riis. **a1350** *An Orison* in Brown *Lyrics XIV* 30.29: Ladi, flour of alle, so rose in erber red. **c1350** *Libeaus* 53.937. **c1350** *Proprium Sanctorum* 84.101: on Rys. **a1375** *William* 37.882. **c1385** Chaucer *TC* ii 1256, **c1386** *LGW* F 112. **c1390** *Castel of Love* 373.719: eny. **c1390** Chaucer *CT* VII 726[B1916]. **a1400** *Athelston* 69.71. **a1400** Chestre *Launfal* 79.937: As rose on rys her rode was red. **a1400** *Cursor* II 570 FGT 9927. **a1400** *Destruction of Troy* 297. 9129–30: Hir face . . . That was red as the Roses, richest of coloure. **a1400** *Firumbras* 23.692: any. **a1400** *Romaunt B* 2399. **a1400** *Susan* 78.212: the. **c1400** *Alexander Buik* II 209.3754–5: rose on rys. **1435** Misyn *Fire* 75.19. **c1435** Lydgate *St. George* in *MP* I 152. 194: any. **c1440** *Prose Alexander* 94.1–2. **c1440** *St. Christopher* 464.814–5: Till it was rede one ilke a syde Als rose es in the somers tyde. **a1450** *Death and Life* 3.66: Her rudd redder then the rose, that on the rise hangeth. **a1450** Macer 122.26: the. **a1450** *Partonope* 194 R 5157: the, 453.11381–2: Trapped in clothe of golde full fresshly, That is scarlete as rose was rede. **c1450** *Heil be thou, Marie* in Furnivall *Hymns* 6.12: As rose in eerbir so reed. **c1455** *Partonope* S 481.18. **a1475** Greene *Carols* 136 A 4: any. **a1475** *Landavall* 107.62: With ruddy, rede as rose, coloure, 125.435: As rose in May her rude was red. **a1475** *St. Birgitta* 68.13: a. **c1475** Henryson *Testament* 112.211. **c1477** Caxton *Jason* 156.1: a, **1481** *Mirror* 83.1–2: a, **c1489** *Blanchardyn* 64.16: a. **a1500** *Court of Love* 412.101, 436.1016–7. **a1500** *Eger P* 196.217: Her rud was red as rose in raine, 256.795. **a1500** *Gracious and Gay* in Robbins 144.11: roose yn may. **c1500** *Lady Bessy* 12[22]: rose in May. **c1500** *Melusine* 213.17–8: a. **c1500** *Smith* 325.295–6: Her rudde redder it is Than the rose is in rayne. **1509** Watson *Ship* Ee3ʳ[11]: Rede as two roses. **a1533** Berners *Castell* C3ʳ[18]: a, *Huon* 180.1–2: a. **1555** Heywood *E* 184.212.2: the. Apperson 526; *Oxford* 535; Taylor and Whiting 312; Tilley R177; Whiting *Scots* II 119.

R199a **Rose(y)-red**
c1000 *Old English Apollonius of Tyre,* ed. Peter Goolden (Oxford, 1958) 34.2: Apollonius mid rosan rude wæs eal oferbræded. **c1225** *Horn* 3 C 16: Rose red was his colur. **c1350** *Alexander A* 127.178. **c1350** *Libeaus* 90.1628. **c1380** Chaucer *CT* VIII[G] 254. **a1400** *Orologium* 388.35. **c1425** *ABC Poem* in *Pol. Rel. and Love Poems* 271.9. **a1450** *Partonope* 291.7399–400. **c1450** *When the son* 395.450: rosy reede. **a1500** *Alexander-Cassamus* 67.373: rosy red. **a1500** *Beauty of his Mistress III* in Robbins 126.16. **a1500** *Guy*[4] 13.75. **a1500** *Peterborough Lapidary* in *Lapidaries* 69[24]. Taylor and Whiting 312; Whiting *Ballad* 30–1.

R200 As ruddy as (a, the) **Rose**
c1200 *St. Juliana* 17.196–19.197: Rudi ase rose. **c1350** *Libeaus* 73.1321–2: For a lady of pris, Roddy as rose on rise. **c1378** *Piers* B xiii 99: As rody as a rose rubbed his chekes. **a1400** *Destruction of Troy* 99.3048: the, 129.3987: the. **a1400** *Meditations* 56.2124: Thou art rodier than rose on rys. **c1400-25** Legat *Sermon* 12.90–1.

a1450 *Partonope* 194.5157: the. **a1450** *Three Middle English Sermons* 43.715: a. **c1450** Capgrave *Katharine* 277.490: the. **c1450** La Tour-Landry 166.5–6: a. **a1475** *Assembly of Gods* 24.806: a. **a1475** *Guy*[2] 133.4656. **1485** Caxton *Charles* 90.12–3: rose in maye. **c1485** *Mary Magdalene* (*Digby*) 91.959: the. **a1500** *O my lady dere* in *Rawlinson MS. C 813* 331.118: a. **1506** Hawes *Pastime* 146.3858: a. **a1533** Berners *Arthur* 334[11–2]: a, 540[30]: a fresh rose, *Huon* 120.35–121.1: a, 451.18: a, 550.29: a **1534** Heywood *BS* 250.19: the. Tilley R177.

R201 As sweet as (any, the) **Rose**
a1400 *Meditations* 29.1081–2: Ihesu is swetter of savour than rose . . . or any other flour, 50.1900: That swetter is than rose in May. **1438** *Barlam and Josaphat* (*Vernon*) 220.395–6: A savour Swettur then eny Rose flour. **c1475** *Wisdom* 48.387–8: Hys laws to pursew, Ys swetter to me than sawoure of the rose. **a1500** *Beauty of his Mistress II* in Robbins 124.7: Swete as the roose that groeth on the rysse. **c1500** Newton 272.14: Fare-wele as swet as ros on hill. Taylor and Whiting 312; Tilley R178; Whiting *Scots* II 119.

R202 As wan as **Rose** unred (*etc.*) (A number of single quotations are brought together here)
a1325 *Cursor* III 1400 CG 24471: Thi face es wan as ros unrede. **c1350** *Libeaus* 53.955–6: Giffrouns lemman is clere, As rose in erbere. **a1400** ?Chaucer *Rom. A* 1015–6: As whyt as . . . rose in rys, Hir face. **1464** Hardyng 284[21]: Lusty as the rose in Maye. **a1533** Berners *Huon* 549.7–8: Her mouth as vermeyl as a rose.

R203 The fairest **Rose** takes soonest fading
c1475 *Thewis* 176.10: As farest ross takis sonest faidinge. Cf. *Oxford* 548–9; Tilley R180.

R204 **Rose**(s) and thorn(s)
a900 *Old English Martyrology* 160.11–2: He eardode in hæðenra midlene swa swa rose sio wyrt bið on þorna midlynæ. **a1420** Lydgate *Troy* III 652.2986–9: But as the thorn hid under the rose, Whos malys ay dareth by the rote, Though the flour a-bove be fayr and sote, That men the fraude under may nat se, **a1439** *Fall* I 2.57–8: Bi exaumple, as there is no rose Spryngyng in gardeyns, but ther be sum thorn, 111.3998–9: Thouh that roses at mydsomer be ful soote, Yit undirnethe is hid a ful sharp spyne, **a1449** *Look* in *MP* II 768.115: Sharp thornys hyd somtyme undir roosys, *St. Austin* in *MP* I 205.389: Cheese we the roosys, cast away the thorn, *Say the Best* in *MP* II 798.104–5: Resemblyng and braydyng on a rose, Outward fayre, and thorn in his entent. Apperson 451; *Oxford* 549; Tilley R182.

R205 The **Rose** is above all other flowers (*varied*)
c1330 *Praise of Women* 293.109–10: As over alle other floures Rose yrailed on riis. **c1395** *WBible* I Peter iii 3 *gloss* [IV 609]: Bi excellence, as a roose is seid the flour of flours. **a1400** *Destruction of Troy* 21–2.624–6: As the Roose in his Radness is Richest of floures, In the moneth of May when medowes are grene, So passis thi propurty perte wemen all. **a1420** Lydgate *Troy* I 89.2601–2: Passyng echon, me liste not for to glose, Amongis flouris as doth the rede rose, **1420** *Temple* 10–1.250–64: A ladi . . . (who) . . . as the rose in swetnes and odoure Surmounteth floures . . . Surmounteth al. **a1500** *Partenay* 4.106: As rose is above al floures most fine. **1513** Douglas *Aeneid* II 3.17–8: Lyke as the royss in June with hir sweit smell The maryguld or dasy doith excell. **a1533** Berners *Arthur* 376[29]: The rose is chefe of all floures. See **R227, S889.**

R206 The **Rose** springs from the brier (thorn) (*varied*)
a1200 *Ancrene* 142.9–10: Deale . . . breres rose blostmen? **c1300** Robert of Gloucester I 491. 6794–5: That as the rose springth of the brer that ssarp and kene is, Also com that clene maide of the luther man iwis. **a1325** *Cursor* II 538.9365–6: For als the rose es bred o thorn, Sua was maria o Juus born. **a1350** *Edward the Confessor* 11.299–302: Thet of holi lif and chaste was thet of hire father was bigete, As the rose cometh out of the brer as hit is of hire iwrite, For the rose springth out of the brer that so scharp and kene is, Also dude the clene maide of the lutherman iwis. **a1376** *Piers* A x 119–23: Riht as the rose that red is and swote, Out of a ragged roote and of rouwe breres Springeth and spredeth that spicers desyreth. Or as whete out of a weod waxeth uppon eorthe, So Dobest out of Dowel and Dobet doth springe. **a1400** *Orologium* 337.42–3: Trewe loveres take not myche fors of the thorne that bereth the rose, so that thei mowe have the roose that thei desyrene. **c1421** Lydgate *Thebes* 43.1016: Al be the Roose grow out of a thorn. **1447** Bokenham 2.44–5: No man the rose awey doth throwe Althow it growe up-on a thorn, 10.348–50: But ryht as of a ful sharp thorn Growyth a rose bothe fayr and good, So sprong Margrete of the hethene blood, 58.2115–6: But lych as oftyn off a full scharp thorn Flouris spryngyn fayre and delycious. **a1449** Lydgate *Look* in *MP* II 769.147–8: The holsome roser for al his soote

odouris, Growith on thornys prykyng sharp and keene. **a1449** Lydgate and Burgh *Secrees* 16.508–10: Takyng exaunple by two thynges in a Roose; Ffirst how the fflour greet swetnesse doth dispoose, Yit in the thorn men fynde greet sharpnesse. **a1450** *St. Katherine (Gibbs)* 7[25]: And ryght as the fayre and swoote rose spryngeth amonge the thornes. **a1450** *South English Legendary (Bodley)* 334.9–10: Ryght was this good childe of false kende I-come So is the swete rose of a charp thorn I-nome. **c1450** Capgrave *Katharine* 21.52–4: But ryght thus, wrot thei that were ful wys, Oute of the hard, thorny brymbyltre Groveth the fresh rose, as men may see, 29.201: Shulde this mayde sprynge as Rose oute of thorn, *Solace* 88[32–3]: So rede I he seith origen as thou I schuld gader roses fro thornes. **c1450** *Edward the Confessor Prose II* 113[9–10]: A good virgyn of an evil fader, lyke as a feir rose of swete savour cometh of a sharpe prikkyng thorne. **c1450** *Myroure of oure Ladye* 283[11–2]: The rose groweth amongest thornes and yet yt ys in yt selfe moste softe. **a1464** Capgrave *Chronicle* 128[20–1]: As a thorn bringith forth a rose, so sprang Ydani of Godwyn. **c1477** Caxton *Jason* 43.1: She is without peer as the rose among thornes, **1483** *Cato* E4ᵛ[32]: Oute of the thorne groweth the rose, *Golden Legende* 125ᵛ[1.21–2]: The rose that cometh of the thorne, 371ʳ[2.32–3]: Lyke as the fayr rose spryngeth among the breris and thornes. **a1496** *Rote or Myrour* I4ʳ[10]: The swete rose groweth on the sharpe thornes. **a1500** *Disciplina Clericalis* 21[5–6]: Roses spryngen on thornes nat for that they bien nat blasfemed. **a1500** *Peare of Provence* in *Pol. Rel. and Love Poems* 299[19–20]: He thouhtt upon the feyer lady and upon Arestotles proverbe, and said in this wise: "Sicut Rosa inter spinas, Sic amica inter filias." **c1505** Watson *Valentine* 163.22–4: For amongest a bus(sh)e of thornes is oftentymes founde a florysshed rose. **1510** Copland *Apolyn* 78[5–6]: The rose groweth amonge thornes and sharpe pryckes and is not of it self pryckynge. **1513** Bradshaw *St. Werburge* 33.724–5: Dothe not a royall rose from a brere procede, Passynge the stocke with pleasaunt dylectacyon? **1532** Berners *Golden Boke* 221.3332: What rose of thornes? See **F313.**

R207 To be like a **Rose** (*varied*)
c1300 *Havelok* 99.2918–21: The heu is swilk in hire ler So (is) the rose in roser, Hwan it is fayre sprad ut newe Ageyn the sunne briht and lewe. **c1325** *Lady, Have Ruth on Me* in Brown *Lyrics XIII* 140.32: Hire rode so rose on rys. **c1386** *St. Erkenwald* 7.91: With ronke rode as the rose. **a1400** ?Chaucer *Rom. A* 856–7: She semed lyk a rose newe Of colour. **a1400** Chestre *Launfal* 61.295–6: The rede rose, whan sche ys newe, Ayens her rode nes naught of hewe. **a1420** Lydgate *Troy* III 580.567–8: As quik of hewe To be-holde as any rose newe, **1420** *Temple* 43.1042–3: Right as the fressh rodi rose nwe Of hir coloure to wexin she bigan. **c1440** *Degrevant* 36.534: Hir rod as the rose on ryse. **a1449** Lydgate *St. Petronilla* in *MP* I 158.110: Lyke red roses ran doun hir chast blode. **a1450** *Castle* 137.2027: Rode as rose on rys I-rent. **a1475** *Landavall* 109.109–10: The rede rose whan it is newe To her rud is not of hewe. **c1475** Henryson *Orpheus* 140.354: Quhair is your rude as ross with cheikis quhyte. **1485** Caxton *Paris* 26.13–4: Alle hyr chere was coloured lyke a fresshe rose in the monthe of Maye. **a1500** *Alexander-Cassamus* 62.252: Her fresche face so rosy-hewed bright, 63.269: The face so whit, and rosy heue, 72.460–1: Hir face, W(h)ich that is coloured of rose and leleye lye. **a1500** *Catalogue of Delights* in Robbins 121.26: Her rudy is lyke the rose yn may. **a1500** *Quare* 196.39–40: Off coloure was sche lik unto the rose, Boith quhite and red ymeynt. **a1533** Berners *Huon* 549.5: Colouryd lyke the red rose. Whiting *Scots* II 119.

R208 To fade like a **Rose**
a1439 Lydgate *Fall* I 26.942: Al worldli welthe shal fadyn as a rose. **c1450** Idley 160.100: Ffor this pompis worlde woll fade as a rose. **c1475** Henryson *Fables* 56.1584–5: Richt as the Rois with froist and wynter weit Faidis, swa dois the warld.

R209 To shine like a **Rose**
c1000 Aelfric *Homilies* I 64[14]: Ge to lytelre hwile scinon swa rose, *Lives* II 362.114–5: Cyne-helmas . . . Scinende swa swa rose. **1513** Douglas *Aeneid* II 46.163: Hir nek schane lyke onto the royss in May.

R210 To stand on change like a midsummer **Rose**
a1449 Lydgate *As a Mydsomer Rose* in *MP* II 781–4.8: Al stant on chaung, lyke a mydsomyr rose, 16, 24, *etc.*

R211 To take one for a **Rose** that breeds a burr
1546 Heywood *D* 37.88: I toke hir for a rose, but she breedth a burre. Apperson 539; *Oxford* 665; Tilley R181.

R212 As blood-red as **Rose-flower**

a1400 *Meditations* 12.422: That is blod-red as rose-flour.

R213 As red as **Rose-flower**
a1400 *Meditations* 18.660: Red as rose-flour. **a1400** *Rowlande* 74.620: Hir rode red als rose floure. **c1400** *Toulouse* 228.200.

R214 As white as **Rose-flower**
a1400 *Meditations* 18.660: Whit . . . as rose-flour.

R215 Not give a **Rose-flower**
c1400 *Plowman's Tale* 171.751–2: Though all hir parish dye unshrive, They woll nat give a rose-flour.

R216 To pass like a **Rose-flower**
c1408 Lydgate *Reson* 163.6223–4: But passe, as dooth a Rose flour, Al unwarly with a shour.

R217 To shine like **Rose-flower**
c1390 *Northern Homily Cycle Narrationes* (*Vernon*) 300.41–2: Hir colour, That schyned as . . . Rose flour.

R218 To be like a red **Roser** (*rose-bush*)
a1400 *Meditations* 46.1752: His lippes lyk a red roser.

R219 The **Rother's** (*ox's*) bell, the hound's hoppe (*?bell*), the blashorn (*horn*), each is a melda (*informer*)
c950 *Edgar's Hundredgemot* in Liebermann I 194.8[B]: Hryðeres belle, hundes hoppe, blæshorn . . . ælc is melda geteald. Cf. II 287, *s.v.* Anzeiger, III 132–3. See **A250.**

R220 To take the **Rough** with the smooth
c1400 *Beryn* 37.1152: Take yeur part as it comyth, of roughe and eke of smoth. Apperson 539; *Oxford* 549. See **B324, P38, S945, T65, 127, W432, 657.**

R221 To dread as **Rouncy** does spur
c1300 *Havelok* 86.2568–9: For he him dredde swithe sore, So runci spore, and mikle more.

R222 To walk (run, prowl) at **Rover(s)**
1528 More *Heresyes* 228 C[14–5]: To walke at rovers, E[1]: ronne at rovers, **1533** *Confutacion* 554 D[5–6]: Like unbrideled coltes to runne out at rovers, 736 B[8–9]: runne oute at, 744 E[4–5]: runnyng at, 753 G[2]: runne out at, 786 E[7]: runne at, 810 E[8–9]: runne out at. **1546** Heywood *D* 42.37–8: Ye proule At rovers, 73.110: Leat not you toung roon at rover, 99.22: All the licour renne at rover. Apperson 541; *Oxford* 664; Tilley R194, T394.

R223 As red as any **Rowan**
a1400 *Eglamour* 40.608–9: I sall the gyffe a nobill stede, Es rede als any rone. NED Rone, sb.², Rowan¹; Whiting *Scots* II 119.

R224 As red as (the) **Ruby**
a1437 *Kingis Quair* 88.153[5]: Thair curall fynnis, as the ruby rede. **c1500** *King Hart* 97.10: As ruby reid. **a1503** Dunbar *Thrissil* 110.96: Reid of his cullour, as is the ruby glance, **a1508** *Goldyn Targe* 113.24: Throu bemes rede birnyng as ruby sperkis. MED adrop; Taylor *Comparisons* 68; Taylor and Whiting 313; Whiting *Scots* II 119.

R225 As round as **Ruby**
c1380 Chaucer *Rosemounde* 4: And lyke ruby ben your chekes rounde. Whiting *Scots* II 119.

R226 A royal **Ruby** may be closed in a poor sack
1430 Lydgate *St. Margarete* in *MP* I 174.13–4: A Royal Ruby in whiche ther is no lak, May closed ben in a ful pore sak. See **H3.**

R227 The **Ruby** has sovereignty over rich stones (*varied*)
a1405 Lydgate *Floure* in *MP* II 414.120–5: And as the ruby hath the soveraynte Of ryche stones and the regalye . . . Ryght so . . . She passeth al, **1420** *Temple* 10.259–61: And as the rubie bright Of al stones in beaute and in sight, As it is know, hath the regalie, **a1439** *Fall* II 424.3411–2: Gaff as gret brihtnesse As doth a rubi above ech other ston, **1439** *St. Albon* 116.298: As amonge stones the Ruby is moost shene. See **R205, S889.**

R228 As sweet as **Rue**
c1500 *Cock* 3[9]: For as swete was theyr brethe as . . . rewe.

R229 As bright as **Ruel-bone** (*ivory*)
c1330 *Gregorius* 169 A 994: Brighter than the rouwel bon. See **B441.**

R230 Better **Rule** than be ruled
1546 Heywood *D* 26.26: And better to rule, than be ruled by the rout, **1555** *E* 162.100: Better rule, then be rulde. Tilley R193. See **P240.**

R231 He **Rules** well that can guide himself well
a1513 Dunbar *Rewl of Anis Self* 75–6.8: He rewlis weill that weill him self can gyd, 16, 24, *etc.* See **M414.**

R232 In good **Rule** is mickle rest
c1450 *Fyrst thou sal* 88.45: In gode rewle is mykil reste.

R233 To bear no more **Rule** than a goose turd in the Thames
1546 Heywood *D* 79.57: Bearyng no more rule, than a goose turd in tems. Tilley R202.

R234 Common **Rumor** is oft truth
c1523 Barclay *Mirrour* 52[7]: And oft common rumour is truth I thee promise. See **M309.**

R235 He may ill **Run** that cannot go (*walk*)
1546 Heywood *D* 94.135: Men saie he maie yll renne, that can not go, **1555** *E* 165.114. Apperson 325; *Oxford* 553; Tilley R208. See **G179.**

R236 He may **Run** that shall read
c1395 *WBible* Habakkuk ii 2: Write thou the revelacioun, and make it pleyn on tablis, that he renne, that schal rede it. Tilley R211.

R237 He **Runs** far that never turns again
1546 Heywood *D* 91.22: He runth far, that never turnth againe, **1555** *E* 159.82, **1560** *E* 217.69.1: He goth farre that never doth turne him backe. Apperson 249:10; *Oxford* 553; Tilley R210.

R238 He that **Runs** fast may stumble on stones
c1450 Idley 91.621: He that renneth fast may stomble on stonys. See **H168.**

R239 Who best might **Run** best he sped
a1338 Mannyng *Chronicle A* I 178.5063–5: Ilk that ther myght fle, they fledde; That best myght renne, best he spedde, Bettere was fle, than worse abide. See **H510.**

R240 **Running** is not of swift men neither is battle of strong men
c1395 *WBible* Ecclesiastes ix 11: Rennyng is not of swift men, nethir batel *is* of stronge men. *Oxford* 530; Taylor and Whiting 301.

R241 As right as a **Rush**
a1400 ?Chaucer *Rom. A* 1701: The stalke was as rishe right. Cf. Svartengren 276: straight.

R242 As rough as a **Rush**
a1400 *Alexander C* 246.4726: Thai (*giants*) ware as rughe as a resche the bake and the sidis.

R243 Dear enough a **Rush**
c1385 Chaucer *TC* iii 1161: Noot I nought what, al deere ynough a rysshe.

R244 No more than a **Rush**
a1325 *Cursor* III 1228.21441: O ranscun namar than a ress (*vars.* risshe, rish).

R245 Not care a **Rush**
1509 *Fyftene Joyes* G5[v][30–1]: I Care not therof a rysshe. **1549** Heywood *D* 95.155: Care not a rushe. Taylor and Whiting 314; Tilley S917; Whiting *Drama* 361:812.

R246 Not count (at) a **Rush**
a1376 *Piers* A iii 137: Counteth hit not at a russche, **c1378** B xi 420: Of clergie ne of his conseil he counteth nought a rusche, **a1387** C xiii 196: Other for a confessour ykud that counteth nat a ruysshe.

R247 Not doubt the value of a **Rush** (*etc.*) (A number of single quotations are brought together here)
c1380 *Ferumbras* 4.124: Ne douteth he kyng ne Emperour the value of a ryssche. **a1393** Gower *CA* II 131.42: Thogh it availe hem noght a reisshe. **a1425** *St. Robert* 69.884: Myght noght chaunge hys chere a rysshe. **c1450** *St. Cuthbert* 177.6077: Noght harmed the valu of a resch. **a1500** *Eger H* 193.201: Mine harness helped not me a resh. **1532** More *Confutacion* 495 C[7–8]: I woulde not geve a rushe.

R248 Not regard a **Rush**
1534 More *Comforte* 1141 G[10–1]: I regarde him not a ryshe. Taylor and Whiting 314.

R249 Not set (at) a (three) **Rush(es)**
a1393 Gower *CA* II 378.2853: I sette slep noght at a risshe. **a1430** Hoccleve *Roundel* II 36–7.4: Nat sette by thy pleynte risshes three, 10, 16, 24. **a1450** *Generydes B* 54.1680: Of all his payne he wolde not sett a rissh. **a1450** *Partonope* 373. 9099: Of myn enemeys I wole not sette a risshe. **a1450** *St. Editha* 101.4537: That he set not by his lyff a rysshe. Whiting *Drama* 361:812.

R250 Not worth a (two) **Rush(es)**
a1349 *Papelard Priest* 45.77: Al my Rout ryot nys nout wor a ruch. **c1378** *Piers* A xi 17: Wisdam and wit nou is not worth a russche, **a1387** B iv 170: And yit yeve ye me nevere the worthe of a russhe. **c1425** Hoccleve *Jonathas* 222.193. **c1445** Pecock *Donet* 136.14–5: Bi eny argument which is worth a risch. **a1450** *Salutation* in Brown *Lyrics XV* 31.31. **c1450** Greene *Carols* 405.4. **a1471** Ashby *Policy* 39.837: Suche maner reule is nat worthe two Russhes. **a1475** *Ludus Coventriae* 28.391. **a1500** *Piers of Fullham* 3.20. **1532** More *Confutacion* 464 D[7]: Not worthe one ryshe, 486 H[9]: a, 722 H[3], 828 G[9–10], **1533** *Apologye* 26[28–9], *Debellacyon* 1012 F[9]. Apperson 458:39; Tilley S918.

R251 Only the value of a **Rush**
a1393 Gower *CA* III 74.4693–4: Than gete of him in hard or neisshe Only the value of a reysshe.

R252 Straw (*strew*) green **Rushes** for the stranger
1546 Heywood *D* 65.22: Greene rushes for this

straunger, strawe here (quoth she). Apperson 274; *Oxford* 626; Tilley R213.

R253 As red as **Rust**
a1400 Julian *Revelations* 199[10–1]: His hair was red as rust.

R254 It is hard to rub the **Rust** out of a cankered (*corroded*) sword
c1450 *Epistle of Othea* 136.17: Owte of a cankred sweerd is hard to rubbe the rust.

R255 **Rust** may not be scoured with rust
a1422 Lydgate *Life* 328.246–7: For Ruste with Rust, may nat scowrede be No foule with fylthe, may nat be puryfied.

S

S1 As black as **Sable**
a1393 Gower *CA* III 465.2904: A Peire of Bedes blak as Sable. **c1460** *Satirical Description* 204[2]. **a1500** *Scorn of Women* in Robbins 225.39: Were tornyd into ynke, blakkyr than sabyll. **a1513** Dunbar *Of the Warldis Vanitie* 151.19. **1513** Douglas *Aeneid* IV 89.99.

S1a **Sable-black**
c1475 Henryson *Testament* 112.221: The uther half Sabill black.

S2 As sad (*dark*) as **Sable**
c1480 *Contemplacioun* 203.457: With colour sad as sable.

S3 As black as a **Sack**
1483 Caxton *Golden Legende* 2^r[2.36–7]: The sonne shall be blacke as a sacke.

S4 It is a bad **Sack** that will abide no clouting
1546 Heywood *D* 66.12: It is a bad sacke that will abide no cloutyng. Apperson 325; *Oxford* 19; Tilley S6.

S5 An old **Sack** asks much patching
1546 Heywood *D* 64.84: An olde sacke axeth much patchyng. Apperson 466–7; *Oxford* 473; Tilley S8.

S6 The **Sack** of ambition is without bottom
c1523 Barclay *Mirrour* 64[47–9]: To beare of ambition the sacke insaciable, The sacke without bottome which never can say hoo, The moo they receyve, alway they gape for moo.

S7 To fare like torn **Sacks** (*etc.*) (A number of single quotations are brought together here)
c1400 *Laud Troy* I 192.6518: Ther aketons ferd as toren sekkes, 201.6824: And lefft hem ligge as a sak, II 436.14792: He teres the mayles as it were sekkes. **a1450** *Generydes A* 117.3722: Boistous bodies, as it wer a sak. **a1470** Malory II 594.10: But tumbeled adowne oute of his sadyll to the erthe as a sak. **c1489** Caxton *Aymon* I 238.27–8: And layed hym upon a lityll horse overhwarte like a sacke of corne.

S8 To be out of the **Saddle**
1549 Heywood *D* 95.150: Although I be ones out of the saddle cast. Tilley S18.

S9 Where **Saddles** lack better ride on a pad than on the horse bare-back
1549 Heywood *D* 40.173–4: Where saddles lacke Better ride on a pad, than on the horse bare backe. Apperson 542; *Oxford* 554; Tilley S19.

S10 **Safe** and sound
a1325 *Cursor* II 454.7867–8: Sauf and sond ai mot thou be To all the folk es under the. **a1375** *William* 93.2816: That he sauf was and sou(n)d fro the men a-schaped. **c1395** *WBible* Tobit viii 15: And foond hem saaf and sounde. **a1415** Mirk *Festial* 17.15: And soo he yede sonde and saf hys way. **a1437** *Kingis Quair* 92.165[4]: And set thame on agane full sauf and sound. **1483** Caxton *Golden Legende* 308^v [2.6]. **c1505** Watson *Valentine* 62.28, 110.36, 319.15–6. **a1533** Berners *Huon* 130.9–10. A. A. Prins *French Influence in English Phrasing* (Leiden, 1952) 252–3; Taylor and Whiting 315.

S11 As yellow as **Saffron**
c1330 *Seven Sages A* 4 B 101: His here was yelow as the safferon. **c1390** Chaucer *CT* VII 730[B1920]: His heer, his berd was lyk saffroun. **a1400** *Of erbis xxiiii* in *Anglia* 18 (1895–6) 320.521: Hys wyse is yelw lyk safroun. Svartengren 251; Whiting *NC* 469.

S12 To be like a **Saffron-bag**
a1508 Dunbar *Flyting* 10.171: Thy skolderit skin, hewd lyk ane saffrone bag. NED Saffron 6c; Whiting *Ballad* 25.

S13 As broad as a **Sail**
c1395 Chaucer *CT* III[D] 1687–8: A tayl Brodder than of a carryk is the sayl.

S14 To bear a low **Sail**
a1393 Gower *CA* II 55.704–5: Bot whanne he berth lowest the Seil, Thanne is he swiftest to beguile. **c1522** Skelton *Speke* II 21.422: He make(th) them . . . to bere a lowe sayle. NED Sail sb.[1] 3a.

S15 To hoist up **Sail**
1546 Heywood *D* 34.35: I will streight . . . hoyse up sail.

S16 One must ask **Saints** if it is fair in heaven
c1385 Chaucer *TC* ii 894–6: Men mosten axe at seyntes if it is Aught fair in hevene (why? for they kan telle), And axen fendes is it foul in helle.

S17 To look like a **Saint** and be worse than the devil
a1460 *Towneley Plays* 375.267–8: She lookys like a saynt, And wars then the deyle. **a1500** *O man more* 394.26: The many on ys develyshe and lokes lyke a saynt. Tilley S30.

S18 To speak like a **Saint** and work contrary
a1500 *Proverbs of Salamon* 186.62.1–2: Some men speken lyke a seynte, Full ofte contrarye the werke ys wrought.

S19 Young **Saint** old devil
a1400 *Qui Habitat* 9.2–3: And callen hem ypocrites or yong seyntes, olde develes. **c1415** *Middle English Sermons* 159.37–40: Itt is a comond proverbe bothe of clerkes and of laye men, "younge seynt, old dewell." And so thei arn disceyveyd. For often tymes sonere thou seyst a younge man die than an old man. **a1450** *Of the seven Ages* 484[7]: Yonge saynt alde devell is ane alde sawe. **a1470** Parker *Dives* C2v[1.17–21]: Dives: And yet it is a comon proverbe, yonge saynt olde devyll. Pauper: It is a synfull proverbe, to drawe men to synne fro vertue, fro god to the fende. **a1470** *Harley MS.3362* f.2a in *Retrospective* 309[1] and Förster 199.1. **a1500** *Additional MS.37075* 278.18. **a1513** Dunbar *Merle* 135.35: Of yung sanctis growis auld feyndis but faill. **1546** Heywood *D* 39.124, **1555** *E* 155.61. Apperson 720; *Oxford* 739; Tilley S33; Whiting *Drama* 220, *Scots* II 120. See **M253.**

S20 **St. George** to borrow
1511 Hawes *Comforte* A6v[25]: Good be my guyde, and saynt George unto borowe.

S21 As true as **St. John**
c1475 Henryson *Fables* 46.1270: Thocht he wer trew as ever wes sanct Johne.

S22 **St. John** to borrow
c1385 Chaucer *Mars* 9: Taketh your leve; and with seint John to borowe. **a1393** Gower *CA* III 40.3416: And tok himself seint John to borwe. **c1395** Chaucer *CT* V[F] 596: And took hym by the hond, Seint John to borwe. **a1405** Lydgate *Black Knight* in *MP* II 383.12: And Hope also, with Saint John to borowe, **a1420** *Troy* I 103. 3082: The(i) toke her leve, with seynt(e) John to borwe. **a1437** *Kingis Quair* 51.23[5]: With mony "fare wele" and "Sanct Johne to borowe." **a1500** *Colkelbie* 301.153: Than angrit scho sa and said sanct Johine to borrow. **1509** *Fyftene Joyes* C8r[8]: Than drynke they fast and saye saynt John to borowe. *Oxford* 557.

S23 To say **St. Julian's** paternoster
1518 Watson *Oliver* F4r[19–20]: But and ye had sayd Saynt Julyans pater noster ye had founde better lodgynge.

S24 As round as **St. Katherine's** wheel
1534 Heywood *Love* B3v[16–7]: Sent katheryns whele Was never so round as was her hele.

S25 As holy as **St. Paul**
1506 Barclay *Castell* E6r[18]: Were he as holy as was saynt poule.

S26 On **St. Valentine's** day every fowl chooses its make (*mate*)
c1380 Chaucer *PF* 309–10: For this was on seynt Valentynes day, Whan every foul cometh there to chese his make. **1477** Paston V 266[12–3]: Uppon Fryday is Sent Volentynes Day, and every brydde chesyth hym a make. Apperson 548; *Oxford* 559; Tilley S66.

S27 Old **Sakes** (*strifes*) come to new wandreth (*misery*)
a1325 *Cursor* I 288.4949–50: Now es us comen our ald sakes In to wandret new, and wrakes, **a1400** *F:* Wille light on us with harde wrakis, *G:* Into wandred sin and wrake, *T:* Now is comen oure aller sake Into woo synne and wrake.

S28 To pick a **Salad**
1520 Whittinton *Vulgaria* 37.28–9: He that laboureth no thynge holy but catcheth a patche of every thynge is mete t(o) pyke a salet. NED Salad 2c.

S29 Whoso buys evil (*not well*) shall make a sorry **Sale**
c1450 *Spurious Chaucerian line* in Manly-Rick-

ert V 437: For who so evel byeth shal make a sory sale. See **S173, W369.**

S30 From hence to **Salisbury**
c1515 Barclay *Eclogues* 136.763: From hence to Salisbury.

S31 To walk on **Salisbury Plain**
c1450 Capgrave *Katharine* 265.117–9: And therfore, er he deyed oute of this stryf, He stank on erthe as evere dede carayn—Lete hym goo walke on sarysbury playn. Cf. Tilley S73.

S32 As sweet as **Salmon**
a1430 Lydgate *Pilgrimage* 414.15365: Swettere than samoun.

S33 Foul **Salt** is good enough for foul butter
c1450 *Rylands MS.394* 92.19: Fowle salte is good inow for foule buttur.

S34 **Salt** and meal nourish many a brothel (*wretch*)
a1500 Hill 130.5: Salt and mele norissheth many a brothell. Cum sale farina nutritur plurima scurra.

S35 **Salt** saves cattle (*property*)
c1378 *Piers* B xv 421: Salt saveth catel, seggen this wyves.

S36 **Salt** seasons (gives savor to) all (meats)
1340 *Ayenbite* 242[19]: Vor ase thet zalt yefth smac to the mete. **a1400** *Scottish Legends* I 4.110: And as salt sesonis al. **c1400** *Vices and Virtues* 268.32: Right as the salt geveth savour to alle metes. Apperson 549; *Oxford* 560; Tilley S80.

S37 To be like **Salt** among quick (*live*) eels
a1387 Higden-Trevisa VII 479[2–3]: I am i-sette among men of court as salt among quyk elys.

S38 To be the **Salt** of the earth
c1000 Aelfric *Homilies* II 536[15–6]: Ge sind þære eorðan sealt. **c1000** *Ecclesiastical Institutes* II 402[13–4]: To us is gecweden þurh urne Drihten. Ge syndan eorðan sealt. **c1000** *WSG* Matthew v 13: Ge synt eorþan sealt; gyf þæt sealt awyrð on þam þe hit (*gesylt bið, hit*) ne mæg syððan to nahte. **c1395** *WBible* Matthew v 13: Ye ben salt of the erthe; that if the salt vanysche awey, whereynne schal it be saltid? **1528** More *Heresyes* 143 D[14]: Ye be the salt of the erth. Taylor and Whiting 316.

S39 To eat without **Salt** or bread
c1400 *Beryn* 37.1168: Yit wold she have I-ete his hert, with-out(e) salt or brede. Apperson 176:14; *Oxford* 166; Taylor and Whiting 316; Tilley S78.

S40 To lay **Salt** on a bird's tail
1533 More *Answer* 1108 GH: A man myghte send a child about with salt in his hand, and bidde him goe catch a byrde, by laying a little salte on her tayle, and when the byrde is flowen, coumfort hym then to goe catch another, and tell hym he hadde caughte that and it had tarried a little. **1556** Heywood *Spider* 59[14]: To go lay salt on an other flies taile. Apperson 549; *Oxford* 560; Taylor and Whiting 29, 316–7; Tilley B401.

S41 To soak like **Salt** into flesh
c1250 *Proverbs of Alfred* 98 T 256–7: Him suhth soreghe to, So deth the salit on fles.

S42 Lay a new **Salve** to an old sore
c1400 Gower *Peace* III 485.122: Ley to this olde sor a newe salve.

S43 Lay **Salve** to your own sore
c1522 Skelton *Colyn* I 330.482: Lay salve to your owne sore. See **C153, L171.**

S44 A little **Salve** may medicine a great sickness
1438 *Barlam and Josaphat* (*Northern*) 236.769–70: A litell salve, sir, suth it es, May medcyn a full grete sekenes. See **M159, 483, T113, 203.**

S45 The **Salve** comes too late to festered sores
a1439 Lydgate *Fall* III 1003.2996–7: To late kometh the salve and medecyne To festrid soris whan thei be incurable. See **C51, L168, M484.**

S46 To need no **Salve** (*i.e.*, be dead)
a1400 *Firumbras* 3.21: Ther-at Dorinydale doun glode ther nedyd no salve. **c1450** *Merlin* II 193[19–20]: Whom he a-raught a full stroke neded hym no salve, 624[33–4]: Smote hem so harde that thei metten that thei neded no salve. See **L176.**

S47 To see the **Salve** before the sore
a1393 Gower *CA* II 274.1801–3: Bot Nestor, which was old and hor, The salve sih tofore the sor, As he that was in conseil wys. See **D16.**

S48 As manly as **Samson**
a1500 *Lady of Pite* in *MLR* 49(1954) 292.69: Manly as Sampson.

S49 As mighty as **Samson**
1449 Metham 48.1302: Thow ye were as myghty as Sampson. Whiting *Drama* 325:280.

S50 As stiff (*firm*) as **Samson**
a1425 *Chester Plays* I 192.164: Stiffer then ever Sampson was.

S51 As strengthy as **Samson**
a1450 *Song of Mortality* in Brown *Lyrics XIV*

96.15: Strengthy and strang to wreke thi wrang als ever was sampson. **a1500** *Salamon sat and sayde* 291.25: And therto als strenthy als evyr was sampson.

S52 As strong as **Samson**
c1000 *Be rihtan cristendome* in Napier 146.31–147.1: And se hæfde Samsones strengðe, se wæs ealra eorðwarena strengest. **a1200** *Ancrene* 203.8: Samsones strengthe. **a1325** *Cursor* I 252.4298: Strenger than ever sampson was. **a1325** *Otuel and Roland* 138.2523: Thow were strong as sampson. **c1330** *Degare* 93.562. **1340** *Ayenbite* 204[13–4]. **c1390** Chaucer *CT* X[I] 955: But he be stronger than Sampson. **c1390** *Of clene Maydenhod* 465.19–20: And ther-to so strong to tere As in his tyme was Sampson. **a1400** *Torrent* 4.95. **a1400** *Pricke* 240.8931–2: And thare-with als mykelle strenthe had omang Als Sampson had, that was so strang, 243.9025. **a1400** ?Wyclif *Ten Commandments* in *SEW* III 88[4]. **c1400** *Vices and Virtues* 226.1. **c1410** *Mirror of Sinners* in *Yorkshire Writers* II 437[11–2]. **c1415** *Middle English Sermons* 68.6–7. **a1450** *Generydes A* 172.5536. **a1450** *Song of Mortality* in Brown *Lyrics XIV* 96.15: Strang to wreke thi wrang als ever was sampson. **c1450** *Pilgrimage LM* 106[31]. **1456** Hay *Law* 65.9: Sampson the wicht. **1484** Caxton *Royal Book* R3r[6–7], **1489** *Doctrinal* I4v[14], K3v[15–6]. **1493** *Tretyse of Love* 81.9–10: The strength of Sampson. **a1500** *Jeaste* 218.374. **a1500** Kennedy 26.18. **a1500** *Miroure of Mans Salvacionne* 145[16]. **c1500** *St. Anne* (3) 115.153: Who was strenger in his dayes than was sampson. **c1502** *Lyfe of Joseph* 50.411: Moche stronger than Sampson that had no pere. **1509** Watson *Ship* B8v[12]. **a1513** Dunbar *Of Manis Mortalitie* 149.10: Strong Sampsone. **a1533** Berners *Huon* 372.1–2: Yf ye were as strong and as great as ever was Sampson. Taylor *Comparisons* 79; Tilley S85; Whiting *Scots* II 120–1.

S53 As heavy as **Sand**
c1450 *Jacob's Well* 228.6: And thou art hevy as sande in slugnesse.

S54 As innumerable as the **Sands** (gravel) of the sea (*varied*)
c875 *Azarias* in *Exeter Book* 89.36–9: Swa unrime . . . Swa waroþa sond ymb sealt wæter. **a1325** *Cursor* I 142.2345–7: That naman suld cun sume ne neven . . . Namar then gravel in the see, 154–6.2570–1: Namar sal thou tham cun rede, than . . . sand in see. **a1382** *WBible* II Kings xvii 11: Unnoumbrable as the gravel (**c1395:** soond) of the see, III Kings iv 20: Unnoumbrable as the gravel (**c1395:** soond) of the see in multitude. **c1390** *Prikke of love* 271.99–103: Yif thou weore bounde for to telle In the see the smale gravelle, Or sterres in the ffirmament, Thow heddest gret neode, verrement, fforto a-vise the wonder wel. **c1395** *WBible* Judges vii 12: The camelis weren unnoumbrable as gravel that liggeth in the brenke of the see, Hosea i 10: The sones of Israel schal be as gravel of the see, which *gravel* is with out mesure, Hebrews xi 12: Ther ben borun . . . as gravel is at the see side out of noumbre, Apocalypse xx 7: Whos noumbre is as the gravel of the see. **a1400** *Orologium* 342.40–1: I have sinnede passynge the noumbre of the gravele of the see. **a1400** *Pauline Epistles* Hebrews xi 12: Ben manye born . . . as the gravelle innumerable that is att the se syde. **a1475** *Ludus Coventriae* 50.221–4: As sond in the se doth ebbe and flowe Hath cheselys many unnumerabyll So xal thi sede . . . Encres. **a1500** *Miroure of Mans Salvacionne* 54[16]: My synne passes in noumbre the gravell . . . in the see. Svartengren 397–8; Tilley S91.

S55 As many (thick) as the **Sands** (gravel) of the sea (*varied*)
897 Alfred *Boethius* 19.1–2: Swa fela welena swa þara sondcorna bið be þisum sæclifum. **c900** *Paris Psalter* 135 (138.16): Hi beoð ofer sandcorn sniome manige. **c1000** Aelfric *Homilies* I 536[30–1]: Heora getel is mare ðonne sand-ceosol, II 190[27–9]: On Egypta-landa, on ðam anum wæs corn, swa hit gecweden is, "Swa fela swa bið sand-ceosol on sæ," 576[28–30]: Him forgeaf ða God swa micelne wisdom, and snotornysse, and bradnysse heortan, swa swa sand-ceosol on sæ-strande. **a1300** *Alisaunder* 99.1739–40: And moo men with stronge bones Than ben in the cee gravel-stones. **c1340** Rolle *Psalter* 281 (77.31): And as gravel of the see foghils fethird. **c1395** *WBible* Psalms lxxvii 27: *He reinede* volatils fethered, as the gravel of the see, I Maccabees xi 1: The kyng of Egipt gaderide an oost, as gravel that is aboute the brynke of the see. **a1400** *Northern Verse Psalter* I 255 (77.27): Fogheles fethered, als sand of see. **c1425** *Speculum Sacerdotale* 222.21–2: A multitude of men as thicke as gravylle lythe in the see. **c1450** *Alphabet* I 57.27: I hafe synnyd ofter than ther is gravell in the see. **a1500** *Craft of Dying* in *Yorkshire Writers* II 409[47–8]: As many other synnes as be . . . gravell-stones in the stronde. Whiting *Ballad* 31, *Drama* 325:282.

S56 **Sandwich Haven** was decayed by Tenterden Steeple

1528 More *Heresyes* 277 H-278 C: Sandewyche haven . . . was . . . decayed . . . (*not by*) Goodwyn sands . . . (*but by*) tenterden steple, **1533** *Confutacion* 709 DE. Apperson 622; *Oxford* 647; Tilley T91.

S57 As clear as **Sapphire**
a1500 *Becket III* 267.196: Sche was cleer as saffer.

S58 As sad (*constant*) as a **Sapphire**
a1449 Lydgate and Burgh *Secrees* 34.1085: Sad as a Saphir and alwey of Oon hewe.

S59 A fair **Sapphire** set in a copper ring (is not commendable)
a1449 Lydgate *Look* in *MP* II 768.99: Nor (*is commendable*) a fayr saphir set in a copir ryng. See **D232.**

S60 **Sapience** is seen in old folk
c1475 *Court of Sapience* 130.160–1: Though I seme yong, full olde myn yerys bene; For Sapience in olde folk ys ay sene. See **F375, M255.**

S61 **Satan** transfigures himself into an angel of light
c1395 *WBible* II Corinthians xi 14: For Sathanas hym silf transfigurith hym in to an aungel of light. **c1450** Capgrave *Lives* 85.20–2: Therfor these neophites are for to prove, that Sathanas transfigur not him-self in-to an aungell of lith. Tilley D231.

S62 As soft as **Satin**
c1450 *When the son* 390.268: And softer hyt was then . . . satyn. Whiting *NC* 470.

S63 **Sauce** was found by gluttony
1519 Horman *Vulgaria* 238[11]: Sauce was founde by glottony. See **H642.**

S64 Sour **Sauce** is served before dainteous (*dainty*) meat
c1523 Barclay *Mirrour* 45[30]: The soure sauce is served before meat deynteous. See **M476.**

S65 Sweet **Sauce** begins to wax sour
1546 Heywood *D* 61.93: And whan she sawe sweete sauce began to waxe soure. *Oxford* 636; Tilley S97.

S66 To be served of the same **Sauce**
1523 Berners *Froissart* III 374[21–2]: They had bene served of the same sauce. Tilley S99.

S67 To eat **Sauce**
c1499 Skelton *Bowge* I 33.72–3: She sayde she trowed that I had eten sause; She asked yf ever I dranke of saucys cuppe, **c1516** *Magnificence* 44.1404: Ye have eten sauce, I trowe, at the Taylers Hall. Apperson 177; Tilley S100.

S68 As broad as a **Saucer**
a1350 *Seven Sages C* 106.3109–10: With eghen that war ful bright and clere, And brade ilkone als a sawsere. Cf. Taylor and Whiting 318–9: big. See **B58.**

S69 Better is **Saught** (*peace*) than unsib (*war*)
c1300 Lawman I 420 B 9844–5: Betere his sahte Thane onsibbe. Cf. Tilley S103. See **P67, W37.**

S70 As bitel (*sharp*) as a **Saw**
a1400 *Alexander C* 226.4096: A burly best with a bake as bedell as a saghe.

S71 As tattered as a **Saw**
c1395 *Pierce* 28.753: His teeth with toylinge of lether tatered as a sawe.

S72 To be like a **Saw**
c1440 *Prose Alexander* 74.34: His bakke lyk a sawe.

S73 Easier to **Say** (said) than to do (done) (*varied*)
1483 *Vulgaria quedam abs Terencio* Q3r[22]: Itt is esyere to say than to do. **a1500** ?Ros *La Belle Dame* 315.525–6: This your counsayl, by ought that I can see, Is better sayd than don. **1519** Horman *Vulgaria* 119[33]: It is lighter to commaunde or byd than do a thyng. **1546** Heywood *D* 77.238: That is . . . sooner said then doone. Apperson 543; *Oxford* 165, 458–9; Taylor and Whiting 319; Tilley S116, 117.

S74 If I **Say** it myself
a1450 *York Plays* 272.43–5: Ther is no lorde in this londe as I lere, In faith that hath a frendlyar feere, Than yhe me lorde, My-selffe yof I saye itt. (She is speaking of herself.) Tilley S114.

S75 Keep (*guard*) what you **Say**, to whom, of whom, how, why, where, when
c1400 *Vices and Virtues* 54.28–30: Yif thou wys be wil, six kepe thou whilke I the kenne: What thou seist, whom til, of whom, how, why, where, whenne. **a1500** *Think Before You Speak* in Brown *Lyrics XV* 282.57–60: Yf that thow wolte speke A-ryght, Ssyx thynggis thow moste observe then: What thow spekyst, and of what wyght, Whare, to wham, whye and whenne. **1509** Barclay *Ship* I 110[13–4]: A wyse man or he speke wyll be wyse and ware What (to whome) why (howe) whan and whare. A Taylor in *Proverbium* 1(1965) 1; *Vices and Virtues* lxii-lxiii.

S76 **Say** not all that you can (*know*)
a1400 *Proverbis of Wysdom* 245.60: Say not all, that thou kanne. **c1450** *Fyrst thou sal* 88.48. Tilley A202.

S77 **Say** well (the best) or be (hold you) still
a1400 *Proverbis of Wysdom (II)* 222.24: Say wel or be stylle. **c1450** *Bühler MS.21* in *Studies in Medieval Literature in Honor of Albert C. Baugh*, ed. MacEdward Leach (Philadelphia, 1961) 287: Sey the best or be stylle, Wyth thy tonge noman thou qwelle, Suffyr and have thy wylle. **c1450** *Cambridge Un. MS. Hh 4.11* in Robbins-Cutler 3079.2: Say the best and bere the softe, Ontaught tunge grevith ofte. **c1450** *Fyrst thou sal* 88.38, 89.103. **a1475** *As I stod* in Halliwell *Early English Miscellanies* 63–4[1]: Ewyre say wylle, or hold the styll, [10, 18, *etc.*]. **a1500** Hichecoke *This Worlde* 332.3–4: He that will noo wynde spille, Sey the best or hold hym stille. **c1500** Skelton *Comely Coystrowne* I 17.64: A proverbe of old, say well or be styll. Apperson 551–2; *Oxford* 563; Tilley S112. See **B273, S732, T369.**

S78 **Say** well, say little or say nought
1404 *Title* in Kail 14: Lerne say wele, say litel, or say noght.

S79 To **Say** well but think full ill
1506 Hawes *Pastime* 85.2173: For men saye well but they thynke full yll. **1556** Heywood *Spider* 230[7]: He sayd well: but he ment ill. See **L376, M755, W585, 620, 624.**

S80 When he has **Said** then has he done (*varied*)
a1300 *Alisaunder* 353.6620–1: It ne helpeth noughth al wel ysayed, Ac he was there-of yvel ypayed. **c1395** Chaucer *CT* V[F] 601: Whan he hath al wel seyd, thanne hath he doon. **c1440** Charles of Orleans 208.6216: And when thei have all seid then han thei doon. **c1500** *Everyman* 10.237–8: For he that wyll saye and nothynge do Is not worthy with good company to go. Whiting *Drama* 45. See **W599.**

S81 Who can **Say** better than he that can do worse?
c1395 Chaucer *CT* V[F] 600: Who kan sey bet than he, who kan do werse?

S82 Who will **Say** well must bethink well
a1300 *Trinity MS. O. 2.45* 8.12: Ho wle wel segge, he mot hine wel bi-thenche. Qui bene vult fari, bene debet premeditari.

S83 **Saying** and doing are two things
1525 Berners *Froissart* VI 300[36–7]: Bytwene sayenge and doyng is great difference. **1549** Heywood *D* 77.235: For they saie, saiyng and dooyng are two thinges, **1555** *E* 150.24. Apperson 552; *Oxford* 563; Tilley S119. See **W642.**

S84 Let (the) **Scabbed** claw
c1515 Barclay *Eclogues* 14.444: Let scabbed clawe, and gyly men be wroth, 108.41–2: And as for me, I no man discommende, If scabbed clawe, the truth shall me defende. See **G492.**

S85 Not give two **Scallions**
a1300 *Richard* 433.6903–4: For thy lyfe and thy barons He wyll not gyve two skalons.

S86 Not worth a **Scallion**
a1375 *Octavian* (S) 42.1313: He seyde, hy ner worth a scaloun.

S87 A little **Scar** (*breach*) upon a bank lets in the stream
a1393 Gower *CA* II 18.507–10: And ek fulofte a litel Skar Upon a Banke, er men be war, Let in the Strem, which with gret peine, If evere man it schal restreigne.

S88 **Scarborough** warning
1546 Heywood *D* 52.368: Scarbrough warnyng I had, **1555** *E* 194.279: I gave him scarborow warning, scarborow That warnyng cam short to bryng good harborow, **1557** *BS* 272–4.7: And take Scarborow warnynge everichone, 14, 21, *etc.* Apperson 552–3; *Oxford* 565; Tilley S128. See **L593.**

S89 If you will be a good **Scholar** arise early and worship the Trinity
a1500 Hill 129.1: A good scoler yf thou wilt be, A-rise erly and worship the trinite. See **G259, R143.**

S90 Diverse **Schools** make perfect clerks (*varied*)
c1395 Chaucer *CT* III[D] 44^{c-e} : Diverse scoles maken parfyt clerkes, And diverse practyk in many sondry werkes Maketh the werkman parfyt sekirly, IVE 1427–8: For sondry scoles maken sotile clerkis; Womman of manye scoles half a clerk is. *Oxford* 565. See **C479.**

S91 Be never too bold to chide against a **Scold** (*varied*)
c900 *Old English Cato* 3.23–4: Ne flit þu wið anwillne man ne wið ofer-spæcne. **c1250** *Proverbs of Alfred* 118 T 450–3: Be thu nevere to bold To chiden agen oni scold, Ne mid manie tales To chiden agen alle dwales. **c1390** *Cato* (*Vernon*) 565.149–50: Ageynes men ful of wordes Stryve thou riht nouht. **a1395** *WBible* Ecclesiasticus viii 4: Chide thou not with a man, a janglere, and leie thou not trees to in his fier.

a1400 *Cato* (*Copenhagen*) A2v[13–4]: Stryve nought with wordis be noo wys With hym that ful of wordis ys. **a1440** Burgh *Cato* 306.114–5: Ageyns the wordy folk ay ful of wynde Stryve nat atte all; it may the nat profite. **c1450** *Cato* (*Sidney*) 10.89–90: Mi leve sone, thou strive with worde in no wise With him, that ful of wordis ise. **a1475** *Cato* (*Rawlinson*) 11.91–2: Debate noght with wordys, and thou be wys, With him, that ful of wordys is. See **C165.**

S92 He that **Scorns** other men shall not go unscorned (*varied*)
c1425 Arderne *Fistula* 4.36–7: It is seid, "Deridens alios non inderisus abibit." "He that skorneth other men shal not go away unskorned." **a1439** Lydgate *Fall* II 345.600–2: For it was said(e) sithen go ful yore, He that rejoishith to scorne folk in veyn, Whan he wer lothest shal scorned been ageyne. Apperson 554. See **M612.**

S93 **Scorn** and hething (*derision*) go together
c1390 Chaucer *CT* I[A] 4110: Now are we dryve til hethyng and til scorn. **a1500** *Eger H* 259.1284: But scorn and heeding goes together. NED Hething.

S94 The **Scorner** shall be guerdoned (*rewarded*) ay with scorn
a1440 Burgh *Cato* 320.692: The skorner shal be guerdoned ay with scorne. See **G491.**

S95 As fell as any **Scorpion**
a1439 Lydgate *Fall* III 948.1034: Moor wood and fell than any scorpioun.

S96 The **Scorpion** flatters with its head when it will sting with its tail
a1200 *Ancrene* 107.28–2: Scorpiun is a cunnes wurm the haveth neb, as me seith, sumdeal ilich wummon and neddre is bihinden, Maketh feier semblant and fiketh mid te heaveth and stingeth mid te teile. **1340** *Ayenbite* 62[13–4]: Thes is the scorpioun thet maketh vayr mid the heavede and enveymeth mid the tayle. **c1395** Chaucer *CT* IV[E] 2057–9: O sodeyn hap! o thou Fortune unstable! Lyk to the scorpion so deceyvable, That flaterest with thyn heed whan thou wolt stynge. **c1395** *WBible* Ecclesiasticus xxvi 10 *gloss: A scorpioun;* that makith fair semelaunt with the face, and prickith with the tail; so a wickid womman drawith by flateryngis, and prickith til to deth. **a1400** *Vices and Virtues* 60.10–2: Thes ben like the scorpioun that maketh good semblaunt as with his visage, and envenymeth with his tail. **a1484** Caxton *Royal Book* F5v[22–3]: This is the scorpyon which blandyssheth wyth his face and prycketh wyth hys taylle. See **F5, L436, W488, 498.**

S97 To pay **Scot** (shot) (and lot)
c1100 *Munimenta Gildhallæ Londoniensis; Liber Albus,* ed. H. T. Riley (RS 1859) 128[18–9]: Quod cives Londoniarum sint quieti de Schot et Loth, et de Danegelde. **a1400** *Twelve Profits* in *Yorkshire Writers* II 58[42–3]: As when a pore mon drinkes in tho taverne and has not wherof he may paye his scott, byds dyng hym wel and let hym go. **1459** *Calendar of Ancient Records of Dublin,* ed. John T. Gilbert I(1889) 301[17–8]: Thay schall ber lot and schot with the citte. **1484** Caxton *Royal Book* E7v[31–2]: This is . . . the scott that is ofte payed for the synne of glotonye, S2r[13]. **1489** *English Gilds,* ed. Toulmin Smith (EETS 40, 1870) 189[6–7]: I shalbe redy at scott and lotte. **c1497** Medwall *Fulgens* A2r[6]: He that shall for the shott pay. **a1500** *Twelve Profits* (*Rawlinson*) in *Yorkshire Writers* II 404[47–9]: (As) it is used in som place that whan a pore man drynketh in a taverne and hath not wher-with to paye his scott, he asketh to be bettun and so to be delyverde. **1509** Watson *Ship* Gg3v[14–5]: And in peyenge the scotte wyll let hym go. **1519** Horman *Vulgaria* 241[7]: He loveth well to be at good fare: but he wyll pay no scotte. **c1520** *Terens* A4r[35]: But suppyd and payd his shot. **a1533** Berners *Arthur* 210[2]: And pay not for your shot or ye go, 491[30–1]: It shall behove theym to paye for theyr scotte, *Huon* 704.19: I wyll pay for my scot, 760.29–30, 761.16 (In the 1601 edition *scot* is changed to *shot*). **1534** More *Comforte* 1177 E[5–6]: And then lette Chrystes passion paye for all the scotte. **1546** Heywood *D* 54.435: The recknyng reckned he needs would pay the shot. Apperson 487; NED Scot sb.2 4, Shot sb.1 24; *Oxford* 491; Tilley S159, 398.

S98 **Scots** are full of guile (*varied*)
a1352 Minot 4.6: War yit with the Skottes for thai er ful of gile, 5.12, 18. **a1464** Capgrave *Chronicle* 202[1–2]: The Kyng, conseyvyng weel that the Scottis were evir ontrewe and ful of treson. **c1470** *Wallace* 338.168: "Yhe Scottis," thai said, "has evir yeit beyne fals." **c1475** Gregory *Chronicle* 224[20–3]: And the Schottys ben trewe hyt (*peace*) moste nedys contynu so longe, but hit ys harde for to tryste unto hem, for they byn levyr founde fulle of gyle and dyssayte. Apperson 202; *Oxford* 189; Tilley S154; Whiting *Scots* II 121. See **W195.**

S99 By **Scratching** and biting cats and dogs come together
1546 Heywood *D* 61.99–100: By scratchyng and bytyng Catts and dogs come together, by folkes recityng. Apperson 86:14; *Oxford* 568; Tilley S165.

S100 To run like a **Scut** (*hare*)
1523 Skelton *Garlande* I 386.632: He ran lyke a scut.

S101 **Scylla** and Charybdis
c1449 Lydgate and Burgh *Secrees* 50.1569–70: Thus atwen tweyne pereel of the see, Sylla and karybdys. **1532** Berners *Golden Boke* 304.6098–100: They . . . can not flee fro the perylle of Scilla without fallynge into Charibdis. **1534** More *Comforte* 1185 F[11–2]: And whyle he wold flye fro Silla drew him into Charibdis. *Oxford* 568; Taylor and Whiting 320–1; Tilley S169; Whiting *Scots* I 148.

S102 To cut as **Scythe** does grass
a1533 Berners *Arthur* 184[24–5]: He . . . cut them in peces as the sythe dooth the grasse.

S103 As deep as the **Sea**
a1000 *Vercelli Homilies* 130.220–2: His miht is . . . deopre þonne sae. **a1500** *Inter Diabolus et Virgo* 444.10: What ys dypper than ys the see? 445.30: Helle ys dypper than ys the see. Taylor and Whiting 321.

S104 As great as a **Sea**
c1390 *Charter of the Abbey* in *Yorkshire Writers* I 348[8]: Thi sorowe is as grete as a see.

S105 As haw (*dull blue*) as the **Sea**
1513 Douglas *Aeneid* III 28.53: Hys watry hewyt boyt, haw lyke the see. Cf. Svartengren 237: grey.

S106 As salt as any (the) **Sea**
c1380 *Cleanness* 38.984: Also salt as ani se. **c1500** *King Hart* 88.4: Salt as is the sey.

S107 As unstable as the **Sea**
c1450 *St. Cuthbert* 44.1489–92: Forthirmare, as wysemen wate, All this wriched warldely state, Is es unstabill as the se, In whilk na stabilnes may be. Cf. Whiting *Scots* II 122. See **W59.**

S108 In greatest **Seas** the tempest is sorest
c1515 Barclay *Eclogues* 136.766: In greatest seas moste sorest is tempest. Tilley S186.

S109 The **Sea** shall be dry when the poor man has a friend
1435 Misyn *Fire* 42.12–4: Now is trew the vers that is sayd: *pontus erit siccus cum pauper habebit amicum*, "the see sall be dry when the pore man has a frende." See **P295, 335.**

S110 To bring the **Sea** into a cup
c1445 Pecock *Donet* 177.3–5: Though I brynge not a greet book into a tretice, the see into a cuppe, or a mounteyn into an ynche, alle men muste holde me excusid. Cf. Tilley S183.

S111 To ebb and flow like the **Sea**
1404 *Lerne say wele* in Kail 14.1–2: As the see doth ebbe and flowe, So fareth the world hyder and thedere. **c1421** Lydgate *Thebes* 141.3421–3: Lich a See rennyng to and fro, Swyng an ebbe whan the flood is do, Lytil space abidyng at the fulle, **a1449** *Doublenesse* in *MP* II 439–40.33–6: The see eke, with his sterne wawes, Eche day floweth new ageyn, And by concourse of his lawes The ebbe foloweth, in certeyn. **a1450** *Gesta* 108[4–5]: As the see Ebbithe and Flowithe, so the worlde is now Riche, now pore, now hole, now seke. **1509** Barclay *Ship* II 319[8–9]: This worlde all hole goeth up and downe It ebbes and flowes lyke to the se. See **E42.**

S112 To teem (*empty*) the **Sea** by drops
1435 Misyn *Fire* 75.30–2: If I wald speke this Joy unabyll to be told, me semys to my self Als and I suld teym the see be droype and spar it all in a lityll hole of the erth. Tilley S183.

S113 To wood (*rage*) like the **Sea** (*etc.*) (A number of single quotations are brought together here)
a1393 Gower *CA* II 228.86: I wode as doth the wylde Se. **a1400** *Torrent* 6.147: He swellyd ase dothe the see. **1501** Douglas *Palice* 74.25: This warld walteris as dois the wallie sey.

S114 Under calm **Seas** are oft many perils
c1523 Barclay *Mirrour* 26[22]: Ofte under calme seas are perils many one. See **W70.**

S115 What needs the **Sea** to borrow of small rivers?
a1449 Lydgate *Fabules* in *MP* II 588.643–4: What nedith the see to borwe of smale rivers, Or a grete barne to borow of strait garners?

S116 While the **Sea** flows at Bordeaux it ebbs at some other place
1509 Barclay *Ship* I 128[15–6]: For whyle the Se floweth and is at Burdews hye, It as fast ebbeth at some other place.

S117 As fat as any **Seal**
c1420 Wyntoun II 273.48: The carl was fat as any selche (*var.* selghe). Taylor and Whiting 321.

S118 As round as a **Seal**
c1475 Henryson *Fables* 82.2395: Round als as ane seill.

S119 After fair **Season** oft falls sore tempest
c1523 Barclay *Mirrour* 20[28]: For after fayre season oft falleth sore tempest. See **C12, S121.**

S120 **Season** (*opportunity*) lost cannot be recovered
1478 Rivers *Morale Proverbes* [3.19–20]: Oon aughte to werke whil he hath liberte, For saison lost can not Recouvered be. See **T307.**

S121 The stormy **Season** follows merry days
c1422 Hoccleve *Lerne to Die* 189.294: The stormy seson folwith dayes merie. See **S119.**

S122 He that sits in the highest **Seat** holds the uppermost place
1492 *Salomon and Marcolphus* 9[12–3]: He that syttyth in the hyghest sete, he holdyth the uppermost place.

S123 Beware to whom you impart the **Secrets** of your mind
c1500 *Marginalia* in *Fitzwilliam Museum, Cambridge, McClean MS.132* in *Tree* xii: Beware to whome thou dost Impart the secarits of thy mind, for foules in ther fury will till all accoring to ther kinde. See **B304.**

S124 He is false that rehearses the **Secret** of his friend
1483 Caxton *Cato* E7v[21–2]: The proverbe sayth that he is false whiche reherseth and telleth the secrete of hys frende.

S125 **Secundum** usum (regula) Sarum
1388 *On the Times* in Wright *Political Poems* I 275[15–6]: They thynke it do welle, *Cum non sit regula Sarum.* **a1529** Skelton *Ware the Hauke* I 158.101–3: He hawked on this facion, *Tempore vesperarum, Sed non secundum Sarum.* Apperson 549–50; *Oxford* 569; Tilley S198; Whiting *Scots* II 121.

S126 As thick as **Sedges** in mire
c1400 *Laud Troy* I 150.5063–4: He was so laid with armes and legges Als thikke as mire with segges.

S127 **See** before ere you begin
c1450 Idley 87.390: Therfore see before or thou begynne, 96.912. See **L435.**

S128 **See** me and see me not
1546 Heywood *D* 74.126: See me, and see me not, the woorst part to flee, **1555** *E* 184.20. Apperson 556; *Oxford* 570; Tilley S203.

S129 Seldom **Seen** appals in love
a1439 Lydgate *Fall* II 407.2812: That seelde is seyn, in love doth appall.

S130 Seldom **Seen** soon forgotten
c1385 Chaucer *TC* iv 423–4: Or elles selde seynge of a wight, Don olde affeccious alle over-go. **a1390** *Seldom seen* 715–8.8: That selden I-seighe Is sone foryete, 16, *etc.* **a1400** *Proverbis of Wysdom* 244.25: Sele i-say ys sone fore-yete. **c1415** *Middle English Sermons* 77.31–2. **c1450** *Douce MS.52* 52.89. **c1450** *Rylands MS.394* 102.14. **c1460** *Ipomadon C* 326.36: For the wiseman saith: "Seldom seen, sone forgetyn." **c1470** *Harley MS.3362* f.2b in *Retrospective* 309[12] and Förster 201.12. **c1475** *Rawlinson MS. D 328* 118.13: Seld y-sey and sone y-fryt. **a1500** Hill 129.35. **a1500** *Pledge of Loyalty* in Robbins 160.16–20: She seith that she hath seyn it write That "seldyn seyn is sone for-geit." Yt is not so—Ffor yn good feith save only her I love no moo. **1546** Heywood *D* 41.15. Apperson 557; *Oxford* 572; Tilley S208. See **E213, 216, L536, S307.**

S131 To **See** (behold) and to be seen
c1395 Chaucer *CT* III[D] 552: And for to se, and eek for to be seye. **1513** Douglas *Aeneid* II 193.12: Ladeys desyris to behald and be seyn. **1532** Berners *Golden Boke* 175.1874–5: One thyng they (*women*) desire, that is to see, and to be sene. *Oxford* 569.

S132 To **See** as far come as nigh
1555 Heywood *E* 188.232: I have seene as far come as nie. Tilley S207.

S133 Who may not **See** stumbles the rather (*sooner*)
a1500 *Harley MS.1002* in *RES* NS 2(1951) 118: Who so may not se he stumble the rather, and he (*that*) hathe a nevyll wyfe he thryvythe the later. Cf. Tilley N171: He that runs in the night stumbles. See **M155.**

S134 To sow **Seed**
1451 Paston II 227[27–8]: Sir Thomas Todenhamys man and Heydonys sowyn this sedde all abowte the contre. NED Sow v.[1] 5a.

S135 To sow silver **Seed** (*to bribe*)
c1405 *Mum* 60.1147: Forto sowe silver seede.

S136 **Seek** and you shall find
c1000 *WSG* Matthew vii 7: Seceaþ, and ge hit findaþ, Luke xi 9. **c1395** *WBible* Matthew vii 7: Seke ye, and ye schulen fynde, Luke xi 9. **c1450** *Ladder* 109.11: Sych sekynge men may fynde. **1483** Caxton *Cato* D7r[17]: Therfore, sayth

Jhesu criste, seeke and ye shal fynde, **1484** *Royal Book* R5r[21]: Who so secheth, he fyndeth. **1534** Heywood *Love* C2r[10]: The olde seyng seyth, he that seketh shall fynde, **1546** *D* 37.63: He fyndth that seekes. Apperson 556; *Oxford* 571; Tilley F222, S213. See **A212, M680.**

S137 Worldly **Seeliness** (*happiness*) is meddled (*mixed*) with bitterness
c1385 Chaucer *TC* iii 813–5: "O God!" quod she, "so worldly selynesse, Which clerkes callen fals felicitee, Imedled is with many a bitternesse!" See **J59.**

S138 Under fair **Seeming** to have a false heart
1484 Caxton *Aesop* 116[14–5]: Whiche under fayre semynge have a fals herte. See **C174.**

S139 **Segging** (*saying, talk*) is good cope (*cheap*)
1546 Heywood *D* 94.125: The Ducheman saieth, that seggyng is good cope. *Oxford* 572; Taylor and Whiting 365: Talk (3); Tilley S215.

S140 To drink up **Seine**
a1400 *Romaunt B* 5709–10: He undirfongith a gret peyne, That undirtakith to drynke up Seyne. Cf. Tilley O9, S259.

S141 He is worth no **Sele** (*happiness*) that may feel no annoys
c1375 Barbour *Bruce* I 13.303–4: He thocht weill he wes worth na seyle, That mycht of nane anoyis feyle. See **L233, S943, W138, 143.**

S142 Rule your **Self** first
a1475 Ashby *Dicta* 47.98: Reule youre selfe first and than al other sone. See **M402.**

S143 **Self** do self have
a1400 *Proverbis of Wysdom* 244.37: Who so self do, self have. **c1500** *Wife Lapped* 194.235: Selfe doe selfe have. **1546** Heywood *D* 32.52. Apperson 557; Jente 787; *Oxford* 572; Tilley S217.

S144 **Self-will** does more harm than good
c1450 *Epistle of Othea* 119.4: Selfe-wyl moost comonly dothe mor harme then good.

S145 Every **Selth** (*happiness*) has unselth at the end
a1525 *English Conquest* 50.8–9: Every selth hath wnselth at the end. See **E80.**

S146 In **Semblance** is guile (*varied*)
a1393 Gower *CA* II 254.1045: In Semblant, as men sein, is guile. **1525** Berners *Froissart* IV 459[7]: In fayre semblauntes are grete decepcyons. See **A152.**

S147 Under **Semblance** of good oft sin is heled (*hidden*)
a1200 *Ancrene* 37.1–2: Under semblant of god is ofte ihulet sunne. See **A152.**

S148 As red as **Sendal**
a1533 Berners *Arthur* 202[20]: It blusshed as red as sendall. See **S312.**

Serpent, see **Adder**

S149 As angry as any **Serpent**
c1475 Henryson *Testament* 113.228: Angrie as ony Serpent vennemous.

S150 As bad as **Serpent**
c1421 Lydgate *Thebes* 43.1013: Wers than serpent.

S151 The eld (*old*) **Serpent**
c1395 *WBible* Apocalypse xx 2: The elde serpent, that is the devel and Sathanas. *Oxford* 473.

S152 No **Serpent** so cruel as a woman when she has caught an ire
c1395 Chaucer *CT* III[D] 2001–3: Ther nys, ywys, no serpent so cruel, Whan man tret on his tayl, ne half so fel, As womman is, whan she hath caught an ire.

S153 The **Serpent** (adder, snake, scorpion, lizard) in the grass (under flowers)
c1395 Chaucer *CT* III[D] 1994–5: War fro the serpent that so slily crepeth Under the gras, and styngeth subtilly, V[F] 512–3: Right as a serpent hit hym under floures Til he may seen his tyme for to byte. **c1408** Lydgate *Reson* 106.4022–4: But lowh under the freshe flours Ful covertly, who kan declare, Many serpent ther doth dare, **a1420** *Troy* I 17.185–6: Lyche an addre undre flouris fayre, For to his herte his tongue was contrarie, 18.209–11: His felle malys he gan to close and hide, Lyche a snake that is wont to glyde With his venym under fresche floures, 74.2091–2: For under floures depeint of stabilnes, The serpent dareth of newfongilnes, II 518.4281–2: serpent under floures, III 704.4766–7: serpent . . . undir floures, 717.5216–7: serpent . . . under floures, 797.845–7: serpent . . . under floures, **c1421** *Thebes* 74.1764–5: Liggyng in a-weyte, As a serpent forto undermyne, **a1422** *Life* 599.175–82: serpent undre floures, **a1430** *Pilgrimage* 408. 15158–61: serpent . . . under herbys, **a1439** *Fall* I 110.3961–3: serpent . . . under floures, 182.6434: serpent . . . under floures, II 336. 279–80: under . . . floures . . . The serpent, 544.2584–5: Under . . . flours . . . The serpent, 560.3163: Under flour(e)s . . . a serpent, III 911.3154: undir flours, a serpent, **a1449** *Look in MP* II 768.109–10: Undir flours . . . The serpent. **a1449** Lydgate and Burgh *Secrees*

49.1536: Wheer undir flourys restith the Scorpioun, 69.2191, 78.2455–6. **c1450** *Pilgrimage LM* 127[31]: I am the addere that holt him under the gras. **c1470** *Wallace* 292.1835–6: Wndyr cowart hyr malice hid perfyt, As a serpent watis hyr tym to byt. **a1475** *Vision of Philibert* 26[15–7]: But as a sarpent that creppyt under they roose, Lythe awayet, every tyme and houre, To sley the best that dare toche the floure. **c1500** Skelton *Dyvers Balettys* I 26.8: *Anguis sub viridi gramine saepe latet,* 27.15: Ware of the lesard lyeth lurkyng in the gras. **1509** Barclay *Ship* I 127[21]: For amonge swete herbes ofte lurkyth the serpent, II 40[27]: under flowres . . . the serpent, 323[21]: under floures . . . the serpent, **c1515** *Eclogues* 143.108: Oft under floures vile snakes have I founde. Apperson 583; *Oxford* 601; Taylor and Whiting 341; Tilley S585; Whiting *Scots* II 122.

S154 To be like a **Serpent** among eels (*a traitor*)
1481 Caxton *Godeffroy* 93.9: And was alway as the serpent emonge the elis. Cf. Tilley H89. See **H80.**

S155 To swell like a **Serpent**
c1503 More *Early Poems* [11] B[10]: Like any serpent she beginneth to swell.

S156 A full good **Servant** will crab (*provoke*) his master once
c1475 Henryson *Fables* 88.2580: Ane full gude servand will crab his Maister anis. Cf. *Oxford* 151: Dog is allowed.

S157 A good **Servant** must have good wages
c1500 *Lyfe of Roberte* 243.617: A good servaunte must have good wages. Apperson 262.

S158 He is worth little that makes his **Servant** master
c1450 *Fyrst thou sal* 88.27–8: He is litel worth and les gode can That makes his servande mayster and hymself man. See **H92.**

S159 In **Servants** is small trust
1509 Barclay *Ship* I 200[12]: In servauntis is small trust or confydence. See **S162.**

S160 It gains (*serves*) not for the **Servant** to dispute with the lord
c1500 *Lancelot* 4.121–2: It ganyth not, as I have harde Recorde, The servand for to disput with the lord. See **F427.**

S161 (A **Servant**) should have ass's ears, *etc.*
1506 Barclay *Castell* D2^{v}[19–26]: If that thou wylte thy mayster please, Thou must have these thre propretees, Fyrst must thou have an asses eares, With an hertes fete in all degrees, An hogges snoute and after these By suche meanes shall I declare . . . By them the better thou mayst fare. *Oxford* 574; Tilley S233.

S162 So many **Servants** so many thieves
c1450 Idley 103.1342–4: Senek seith a mervelous skille, That as many servantis as a man haase, So many theves be in his place, cf. 1315–6. *Oxford* 574–5; Tilley S242. See **S159.**

S163 Who **Serves** and does not full-serve loses his shipe (*wages,* hire)
1340 *Ayenbite* 33[21–2]: And me kan zigge: huo thet serveth and naght vol-serveth: his ssepe he lyest. **c1400** *Vices and Virtues* 29.7–9: Therfore it is seid, "Who-so serveth and ne serveth nought his terme, he lest his hure." "Quique sert et ne perlert son lower pert," dit ly fraunces. See **E90, P371, T104.**

S164 After good **Service** name (*reputation*) shall arise
c1450 *Good Wife L* 200.112–3: Aftir thi good servise Thi name schal arise.

S165 For long **Service** is no reward
a1513 Dunbar *None May Assure* 44.7: For lang service rewarde is none. Whiting *Scots* II 122. Cf. Tilley S254. See **S170.**

S166 No **Service** like to the king's
a1484 *Ther ne is dangyer* 19.9: Ne servyce lyke to the kyng soverayn. Apperson 452; *Oxford* 575–6; Tilley S251.

S167 Proffered (Bidden) **Service** stinks
c1395 Chaucer *CT* VIII[G] 1066–7: Ful sooth it is that swich profred servyse Stynketh, as witnessen thise olde wyse. **c1450** *Douce MS.52* 47.33: (B)odun servycys stynkys. **a1475** *Vision of Philibert* 22[2]: I se proferd serves stynkit. **1546** Heywood *D* 66.19, **1555** *E* 182.198. Apperson 513; Jente 123; *Oxford* 519; Skeat 285; Tilley S252. See **C447, O20.**

S168 **Service** (Labor) asks meed (reward)
a1393 Gower *CA* II 355.2023–4: Bot every labour axeth why Of som reward, III 290.2110: For every service axeth mede, 440.2012: The mede arist of the servise.

S169 **Service** is no heritage
c1412 Hoccleve *Regement* 31.841: Servyse, I wot wel, is non heritage. **c1450** *Consail and Teiching* 76.372: For heritage is na service. **c1450** Greene *Carols* 381 *refrain:* For servyse is non erytage. **1478** Rivers *Morale Proverbes* [7.1]: Service in court is noo seur heritaige. **c1495** *Arundel Vulgaria* 61.263. **a1500** *In a chambre* in Sandison 119–20.8, 16, *etc.* **c1500**

Fabyan 675[41–3]: (*There*) arose a proverbe amonge the Frenshemen, sayinge (Principibus obsequi hereditarium non esse;) the whiche is to meane, the servyce of prynces is nat heredytable. **1509** Barclay *Ship* I 106[14]: Thus worldly servyce is no sure herytage. Apperson 558–9; Jente 388; *Oxford* 575; Tilley S253.

S170 To trust in **Service** is no wisdom
c1450 Idley 161.144: It is noo wysdom in service to trast. See **S165.**

S171 **Set** and save if you will have (*varied*)
a1450 *Harley MS.2252* in *Archiv* 200(1963) 342: Sett and save yf thou wylt have, Waste and wante, lene and crave. **c1450** *Fyrst thou sal* 89.83–4: Set and sawe if thou wil hafe, Waste and want, leu (*for* len) and crafe. **a1500** *Harley MS.116* in *Rel. Ant.* I 316: Kype and save, and thou schalle have; Frest and leve, and thou schall crave; Walow and wast, and thou schalle want. Brown-Robbins 3088; Robbins-Cutler 3088.

S172 As sweet as any **Setwall**
c1390 Chaucer *CT* I[A] 3206–7: And he hymself as sweete as is . . . any cetewale.

S173 He that sells for **Seven** and buys for eleven, it is marvel if he ever thrive
1520 Whittinton *Vulgaria* 93.18–9: He that selleth for .vii. and byeth for a .xi., it is merveyle yf ever he thryve. See **S29, W369.**

S174 To go like a **Shade** (shadow)
1340 *Ayenbite* 71[13–4]: Al hit ys ywent wel rathre thanne ssed. **c1450** *When the son* 388. 185: Sum an hour lyke the shadowe wer ago. **1528** More *Heresyes* 116 A[2–3]: All which are now gone as a shadowe.

S175 Better to be in the **Shadow** than in the sunlight
a1533 Berners *Arthur* 89[26]: For it is better to be in the shadow than in the sonne light. See **G256.**

S176 One may not see his **Shadow** in wori (*turbid*) water
a1225 *Lambeth Homilies* 29[3–4]: Hu maht thu iseon thine sceadewe in worie watere?

S177 To be aghast of one's **Shadow** (*varied*)
1340 *Ayenbite* 179[17–8]: Zuich volk is y-lich the horse thet heth drede of his ssede. **c1400** *Vices and Virtues* 183.6–7: Suche men faren as an hors that is eschew, that is Agast of his owne schadewe. **c1425** *Orcherd* 207.28: A man maketh hym adred with his owne schadowe, 327.17: Beynge afeerd of her owne schadowe. **1484** Caxton *Royal Book* O6ᵛ[12–3]: The shough hors which is aferde of the shadow that he seeth. **1513** More *Richard* 49 (*for* 46) F[14–5]: Who maye lette her to feare her owne shadowe. **1556** Heywood *Spider* 264[16]: Makth you your owne shadowes to dread, 266[24–5]: The foole, or the infant, that his shadow spies: Wyll oftimes crie out in feare. Apperson 3; *Oxford* 3–4; Tilley S261; Whiting *NC* 472.

S178 To be (but) as a **Shadow**
c1100 *Instructions for Christians* 12.37: And eal þæt þu her sceawast hit is sceaduwa gelic. **a1200** *Ancrene* 99.17–8: Al the wa of this world nis bute schadewe of the wa of helle. **c1200** *Sawles Warde* (*Bodley*) 18.160: For al thet is on eorthe nis bute as a schadewe. **c1340** Rolle *Psalter* 418 (118.51): Proude mennys joy is noght bot as the shadow. **c1395** *WBible* I Paralipomenon xxix 15: Oure daies ben as schadewe on the erthe, Job viii 9. **1400** *Ancrene* (*Recluse*) 180.15: And al that nys bot as aschadewe to jesu cristes pyne. **1414** ?Brampton *Psalms* 32[17]. **a1420** Lydgate *Troy* III 802.1018: Liche a shadewe wast and transitorie. **c1460** Paston III 257[21–2]: But this joy is not stabill, but it is mutabill as a shadow. **c1523** Barclay *Mirrour* 19[36]: But this short life present as shadowe fugitive. Whiting *Scots* II 123.

S179 To bow (away) like a **Shadow**
c1350 *Prose Psalter* 122 (101.12): My daies boweden as shadow. **c1395** *WBible* Psalms ci 12: Mi daies boweden awei as a schadewe, cviii 23: I am takum awei as a schadowe, whanne it bowith awei. **c1400** *Primer* 41[18]: Mi daies bowiden awey as schadewe.

S180 To flee like (a, the) **Shadow** (shade)
a1200 *Trinity College Homilies* 175[25]: He is fleonde alse shadewe. **1340** *Ayenbite* 165[3–4]: Vor his lyf vlighth ase ssed. **c1395** *WBible* Job xiv 2: And fleeth as schadewe, and dwellith nevere perfitli in the same staat. **c1400** *Primer* 64[5–7]: a. **c1400** *Vices and Virtues* 165.4–5: the. **a1450** *Lessouns* in Kail 113.182. **a1450** *Pety Job* in Kail 131.308. **a1456** Sellyng *Evidens* 177.11: Youthe fledde als faste as shadow on the walle. **1479** Rivers *Cordyal* 35.18–9: a. **1484** Caxton *Royal Book* N6ᵛ[26].

S181 To follow one like his **Shadow**
c1422 Hoccleve *Complaint* 106.320–2: My wyckednesses evar followe me, As men may se the shadow a body swe, And in no maner I may them eschwe. Taylor and Whiting 323; Tilley S263. Cf. Whiting *Drama* 325:285.

S182 To glide away like the (a) **Shadow**
a1300 Thomas de Hales 69.32: Al so the schadewe

that glyt away. **c1455** *Speculum Misericordie* 946.219: a. **a1475** *Vision of Philibert* 37[8–9]: a. **1509** Fisher *Treatyse* 162.22–3: a. **a1513** Dunbar *Of Manis Mortalitie* 149.5–6: Lyk as ane schaddow in ane glas Hyne glydis all thy tyme that heir is. Whiting *Drama* 325:285.

S183 To hield (*sink*) like **Shadow**
c900 *Paris Psalter* 93 (108.23): Ic eom scuan gelic swyþe ahylded. **c1000** *Regius Psalter* 187 (101.12): Dagas mine swa swa scadu ahyldon, 211 (108.23): Swa swa scadu þonne heo ahyldeð alædd. **a1400** *Northern Verse Psalter* II 7 (101.12).

S184 To lose (*perish*) like a **Shadow** (*etc.*) (A number of single quotations are brought together here)
897 Alfred *Boethius* 63.26: Hi losiað swa swa sceadu. **1175** *Twelfth Century Homilies* 124.4–5: All that tofaraeth and toglit, swa swa monnes sceadu daeth. **a1400** *Northern Verse Psalter* II 159 (143.4): Als schadow forth-gane daies hisse. **1479** Rivers *Cordyal* 34.17: And fadeth as a shadowe. **1484** Caxton *Royal Book* G2r[3–4]: Departed and faylled as a shadowe.

S185 To pass like (the, a) **Shadow**
c1340 Rolle *Psalter* 15 (4.3): Thai passe as the shadow, 268 (74.1), 391–2 (108.22): the, 398 (111.9): the, 476 (143.5). **c1350** *Prose Psalter* 173 (143.5): Is daies passen as shadue. **c1390** Chaucer *CT* VII 8–9[B1198–9]: Swiche salu-taciouns and contenaunces Passen as dooth a shadwe upon the wal, X[I] 1068: And passen as a shadwe on the wal, **c1395** IV[E] 1315: That passen as a shadwe upon a wal. **c1395** *WBible* Psalms cxliii 4, Ecclesiastes vii 1, viii 13, xi 8 *gloss,* Wisdom ii 5: Forwhi oure tyme is the passyng of a schadewe, v 9. **a1400** *Orologium* 359.29–30: a. **a1400** *Pricke* 191.7071–2: a. **a1400** *Seven Penitential Psalms* in *Wheatley MS.* 46.633: My dayes passiden as schadow of light. **c1400** *Vices and Virtues* 69.5–8: a. **c1410** *Mirror of Sinners* in *Yorkshire Writers* II 436 [1–2]: a. **c1412** Hoccleve *Balade* I 67.12: a, **c1422** *Dialog* 120.275–6: Welthe of the world and longe and faire dayes, Passen as dooth the shadwe of a tree, *Lerne to Die* 185.199: a. **c1425** *Speculum Sacerdotale* 58.37–8: the. **1434** Misyn *Mending* 109.9–10. **a1470** Parker *Dives* X1v[2.13–4]: a, Y1v[1.40]: a, Y2v[1.10–1]: a shadewe at even, Y3r[1.37–8]: a. **1479** Rivers *Cordyal* 17.6–7: They be al past like a shadewe, 18.5–6: a, 25.22–3: a, 32.9: a. **1489** Caxton *Doctrinal* L5r[14–5]: a. **c1490** Ryman 255.4: a, 266.3: a. **a1500** *Ghostly Battle* in *Yorkshire Writers* II 428[37–8]: the. **a1500** *Imitatione* (*1*) 32.13–4: a. **a1500** Rolle *Mending* 33[14–5]: He shal dispise all thynges worldly the whiche passen as doeth the shadewe of the day. **1502** *Imitatione* (2) 173.34–5: a. **1509** Fisher *Treatyse* 162.15–6: a, **a1535** *Sermon . . . upon a good Friday* in *English Works* 392.33: a. Whiting *Drama* 325:285.

S186 To take **Shadow** and pursue wind (*varied*)
c1395 *WBible* Ecclesiasticus xxxiv 2: As he that takith (**a1382:** caccheth) schadewe, and pursueth wynd. **a1400** *Orologium* 379.31–2: Hee is aboute to clippe the wynde and folowe the schadowe the whiche trowith forto preyse me (*Wisdom-Christ*).

S187 To vanish away like a **Shadow**
1487 Caxton *Book of Good Manners* E6r[9–10]: Vanysshe awaye as dooth the shadowe. **1509** Fisher *Treatyse* 251.17–8: Vanysshe awaye as dooth a shadowe.

S188 As dry as a **Shaft**
c1385 Chaucer *CT* I[A] 1362: That lene he wex and drye as is a shaft.

S189 He loses his **Shaft** that shoots in the sand
1492 *Salomon and Marcolphus* 8[25]: He lesyth his shafte that shetyth in the sande.

S190 What **Shall** be shall be
1511 Hawes *Comforte* C1r[26]: The frenshe man sayth, that shall be shall be. **1546** Heywood *D* 60.63: That shalbe, shalbe, **1555** *E* 159.78. Apperson 560; Tilley M1331. See **D169, T167, 171.**

S191 It is no **Shame** to fall but to lie long
c1450 *Rylands MS.394* 93.10: It is no shame to fall, but to lye longe.

S192 It is no **Shame** to fall with hurt and arise with game
c1450 Idley 105.1420–1: Ffor in proverbe it is said: it is noo shame To falle with hurt and arise with game.

S193 Many think to avenge **Shame** (sorrow) and increase it (*varied*)
c1450 *Merlin* II 359[32–3]: But many a man weneth to a-venge his shame that it doth encrece, 419[14–5]: But some weneth to a-venge hym of his shame, and he doth it encrece, 496[23–5]: And therefore seith the wise man in reprof of soche. "Many oon weneth his shame to a-venge, and he it encreseth." **1471** Caxton *Recuyell* II 516.4–7: And to have in thy mynde that men saye comunely, Some man weneth to avenge hys sorowe And he encresyth hit. **a1500** *Partenay* 148.4260–3: Trowyng this instance,

Such supposse to venge ther huge shame perschance, Which ofte cressith hurt, men may wel it se, In sondry places conceyved may be. **c1500** *Melusine* 93.4–5: But as the proverbe saith, "Such weneth to avenge his shame that encreassith it." Tilley S279. See **A48, G468, I53, M200, S513, W718.**

S194 **Shame** elds (*is hardened by age*)
c1450 *Rylands MS.394* 103.16.11–2: Schame eldus. Tempore dilatus longo pudor inveteratus. MED elden v.(1) 4.

S195 **Shame** is as it is taken
1534 More *Comforte* 1253 B[10–2]: It is almoste in everye countrey becomen a common proverbe, that shame is as it is taken. **1546** Heywood *D* 33.26: Shame is as it is taken. Apperson 560; Tilley S274.

S196 **Shame** is past the shed (*parting*) of head
c1390 *Verses on the Earthquake of 1382* in Brown *Lyrics XIV* 188.67–8: We ben so ful of synne and slouthe, The schame is passed the sched of hed. **c1450** *Consail and Teiching* 68.67–8: And fra the schame be passit thar hed, Than war thaim fare bettir be ded. **a1500** *Lay of Sorrow* 718.117: So far hath schame the schede ourgone your hed. *Oxford* 578; Tilley S275; Whiting *Scots* II 123.

S197 **Shame** take him that shame thinks
1555 Heywood *E* 153.46: Shame take him that shame thinkth. Apperson 560; *Oxford* 314: I11; Tilley S277. See **G355, H373.**

S198 As loud as any **Shawm**
c1421 Lydgate *Thebes* 176.4298–9: And in Thebes loud as eny shalle, The Cry aroos. NED Shalle.

S199 All the **Sheaves** in the lathe (*barn*) must out late or rather (*sooner*)
c1380 Chaucer *HF* 2139–40: For al mot out, other late or rathe, Alle the sheves in the lathe.

S200 How shall good **Sheaf** be shorn of wicked grain?
1513 Douglas *Aeneid* II 147.14: Of wikkyt grayn quhou sal gude schaif beschorn? Cf. Tilley G405. See **T465.**

S201 To take as falls in the **Sheaf**
1555 Heywood *E* 185.217: I will take as falth in the sheafe. Apperson 617:21; Tilley S289.

S202 To be proud (make much) of one's painted **Sheath**
1520 Whittinton *Vulgaria* 105.8–9: He is not a lytle proude of his paynted sheythe, and loketh of a heyght. **1546** Heywood *D* 38.106: She maketh so much of hir peynted sheath, **1555** *E* 158.71: Thou makst much of thy peynted sheathe, and wylt do, It havynge not one good knyfe longyng therto. Apperson 356: Leaden sword; *Oxford* 400; Tilley S291.

S203 As bare as a new shorn **Sheep**
a1439 Lydgate *Fall* II 419.3261–2: To pile the peeple, as ye han herd toforn, Bare as a sheep that is but newe shorn. Tilley S299. See **S206.**

S204 As meek as (a) **Sheep**
a1400 *Scottish Legends* I 219.382: Als meke as thai schepe bene had. **1483** Caxton *Golden Legende* 322[r][1.39–41]: As meke and debonayr . . . as they had ben shepe or lambes. **1483** *Vulgaria quedam abs Terencio* P7[v][18–9]: I make hym as meke as a shepe. Cf. Taylor and Whiting 324: gentle. See **L31.**

S205 As mild as **Sheep**
a1200 *Trinity College Homilies* 195[12]: Milde alse shep. **c1200** Orm II 201.15946–7: Thatt shep iss all unnshathig der, And stille, and mec, and milde. See **L32.**

S206 As naked as a new shorn **Sheep**
c1450 Idley 187.1734: The soule was naked as a shepe new shore. Apperson 436; Tilley S299; Whiting *NC* 472. See **S203.**

S207 As rich as a new shorn **Sheep**
c1500 *Cock* 1[18]: As ryche as a newe shorne shepe. **1546** Heywood *D* 52.354. Apperson 529; *Oxford* 540; Tilley S295.

S208 As rough as a **Sheep**
c1300 *Beves* 47.997: Row he was also a schep. Cf. Apperson 520: Ragged.

S209 As soon comes a young **Sheep's** (lamb's) skin to the market as an old
1534 More *Comforte* 1172 E[7–10]: There is a very true proverbe, that as sone cometh a yonge shepes skin to the market as an olde. **1546** Heywood *D* 66.9–10: As soone goth the yonge lamskyn to the market As tholde yewes. Apperson 588; Jente 77; *Oxford* 604; Tilley L39. See **D98, M41, 385.**

S210 As still as (new shorn) **Sheep**
1447 Bokenham 185.6799: But stodyn as stylle as newe-shorn shepe. **1483** Caxton *Golden Legende* 200[v][1.16]: Stondynge stylle as a shepe.

S211 As tame as **Sheep** (*etc.*) (A number of single quotations are brought together here)
c1000 Aelfric *Homilies* II 492[21]: Sind þas

reðan tigres betwux eow swa tame swa scep, *Lives* II 284.1055: And heo, swa bilewite (*innocent*) swa scep. **c1390** *Visions of seynt poul* in *Vernon* I 257.219–20: So mony soules ther weore in hold, Uchon on othur, as schep in fold. **a1420** Lydgate *Troy* III 604.1385–6: Broke and disaraied, With-oute guyde, right as shepe dismayed. **c1450** *Merlin* II 640[3–4]: Thow art a-gein us as fooll hardy as the shepe a-gein the shepherd. See **L36.**

S212 As thick as **Sheep** in fold
c1400 *Sowdone* 84.2941: And mewe a-down as thikke as shepe in folde. **a1475** *Guy*[2] 156. 5447–8: The Lumbardes starte up full bolde As thycke as schepe do in folde. Whiting *Scots* II 123.

S213 As wise as a new shorn **Sheep**
c1500 *Lyfe of Roberte* 242.596: Ye be as wyse as a shepe newe shorne.

S214 He loves well **Sheep's** flesh (mutton) that wets his bread in wool
a1475 *Good Wyfe Wold* 174.35–6: The mon ys at the foll, That he wyll low ys scheppys flesche, that wettytt his bred in woll. **a1500** Hill 131.33: He loveth well moton, that weteth his bred in woll. **1546** Heywood *D* 75.159: He loveth well sheeps flesh, that wets his bred in the wul. Apperson 562; *Oxford* 393; Tilley M1339. See **M151.**

S215 Like **Sheep** opposed to wolves (*varied*)
a900 Bede 46.22–4: Forðon swa swa sceap from wulfum and wildeorum beoð fornumenne, swa þa earman ceasterwaran toslitene and fornumene wæron. **c1000** *Corpus Christi Homily* (*St. Margaret*) in Assmann 172.70–1: Ic eom gesett betweonen þisum folce, swa swa sceap betweonen wulfum. **a1300** *Alisaunder* 103.1819–20: Men dreden hym, on uche half, So . . . shep the wolf. **c1300** Robert of Gloucester I 156.2201–2: Ye ne conne bote fle Ase ssep to vore wolves. **a1400** *Arthur* 15.476–8: Agenst Arthour hadde no fusoun, No more than have twenty schep Agenst vyve wolfez greet. **a1400** *Scottish Leggends* II 50.127–8: That as a schepe ymang wlfis brath Beheld quha fyrst suld do hir scath. **c1400** *Alexander Buik* I 32.996–7: As scheip that for the wolf takis flicht, He led the folk before him was. **c1400** *Brut* I 285.28–30: The Scottis hade that day no more foisoun ne myght ageynes the Englisshe-men, than xx shepe shulde have ageyns v wolfes, 288.1–2: Ffor no nother wise dide thei stryve, Butt as .xx. shape among wolfes fyve. **a1415** Mirk *Festial* 175.29–30: Thai al fled from hym as schep from the wolfe. **a1420** Lydgate *Troy* II 448.1888: And like as schepe a-fore the wolf (to) fle. **c1450** *Jacob's Well* 74.25–6: Ferst thou semyst a scheep, and thanne thou schewyt the a wolfe. **c1450** *St. Cuthbert* 138.4693–4: And we to wolves as schepe er left, With outen hirde or helpe. **a1470** Malory I 216.2–4 (*Caxton's text*): And the Romayns and sarasyns fledde from hym as the sheep fro the wulf or fro the lyon. **1485** Caxton *Charles* 81.3–4: They ranne tofore hym as sheep tofore the wulf whiche is hongry. **1502** *Robert the Devil* B2ᵛ[14–6]: Every man fledde frome them lyke as the shepe fled frome the wolfe. Whiting *Scots* II 123.

S216 Old **Sheep** will oft infect the young
c1515 Barclay *Eclogues* 143.110–1: Infecte olde shepe with venim violent, And ofte be the yonge infected of the olde. See **B14, C347, D298.**

S217 One scabbed **Sheep** makes a foul flock (*varied*)
c1000 Aelfric *Homilies* I 124[32–3]: þylæs ðe an wannhal scep ealle ða eowde besmite. **a1400** Wyclif *Sermons* I 281[35–6]: For o leprous mai foule a flok, and a flok mai foule a more (*moor*). **a1425** *Rule of St. Benet* (*1*) 23.10–1: A wicke shep may spille al the flok. **a1440** *Spurious Chaucerian lines* in Manly-Rickert V 435: Even as a scabbed schepe in the folde, Alle a flocke wolle defyle, both yonge and olde. **a1450** *Rule of St. Benet* (2) 84.1331–2: For thurgh a schep that rote hase hent May many schep with rote be schent. **c1450** *Douce MS.52* 51.87: Oon scabbyd shepe makyth a fowle flock. **c1450** *Rylands MS.394* 102.6: shendith alle a flok. **c1460** *Take Good Heed* 206.12: For oon scabbed shepe may enfecte al a folde. **a1500** Hill 129.49: On skabbid shepe infectith all the folde. **1520** Whittinton *Vulgaria* 116.28–9: For one scabbed shepe (as they saye) marreth a hole flocke. Apperson 563; *Oxford* 564; Taylor and Whiting 324; Tilley S308; Whiting *Scots* II 123. Cf. Jente 329. See **A167, S280.**

S218 A **Sheep** in wolf's (fox's) clothing (skin)
c1350 *Smaller Vernon Collection* 30.248–9: Hit may bifalle, heo seide, parde, That undur wolves clothing a schep ther be. **1435** Misyn *Fire* 89.36–7: A scheep cled in foxis skyn. See **W474.**

S219 To bind like **Sheep**
c1200 Orm I 39.1187–9: Thatt mann himm band withth woghhe, Rihht all swa summ the shep onfoth Meoclig, thatt mann itt clippethth. **c1420** Wyntoun V 289.1894–5: And syne gert bynde thaim sickyrly As bundyn scheipe til Inglande.

S220 To come like **Sheep** out of the fold (*etc.*) (A number of single quotations are brought together here)
a1250 *Bestiary* 19.606–7: He to-gaddre gon o wolde, So sep that cumen ut of folde. **a1300** *Passion of Our Lord* in Morris *Old English Miscellany* 37.5: Al volk wes to-dreved, so schep beoth in the wolde. **c1300** Robert of Gloucester I 307.4371: And ye ssolleth hom mete and quelle as so mony ssep vor naght, II 665.9395: We ssolle as so monye ssep to drive al the route. **a1325** Bonaventura *Meditations* (*1*) 15.452: They renne about as herdles shepe. **a1393** Gower *CA* III 305.2656–8: I sih also The noble peple of Irahel Dispers as Schep upon an hell. **a1400** *Destruction of Troy* 45.1335: All shodurt (*scattered*) as shepe shont of his way. **c1400** *Brut* I 87.7–9: The Romaines . . . hade no more power ne strength to withstande ham, than xx shepe ayennes v. wolfes. **c1400** *Laud Troy* I 171.5808: The Gregeis died as schep In rot, 286.9694: Thei fel afftir him as hit were shepis. **c1400** Mandeville *Travels* 3.5–8: For a semblee of peple withouten a cheventeyn or a chief lord is as a flok of scheep withouten a schepp-erde the which departeth and desparpleth and wyten never whider to go. **a1420** Lydgate *Troy* I 140.4315: That liche to schepe wer forskatered wyde, III 785.430–1: And finally distroied, A(s) sely shepe. **c1420** Wyntoun III 42.511: And thare thai stekit thaim as scheip, 65.810. **c1460** *Satirical Description* 199[14]: Shoorn as a sheep with sherys keen. **1490** Caxton *Eneydos* 108.22–3: And nowe be we without pastoure, as the sheep that is habaundouned. **a1500** *Now late me thought* 286[21–2]: We wayled we wepte we fared as sheepe Whos herd was ded and lost us fro. **1509** Barclay *Ship* I 298[15]: Another bletyth lyke a shepe. **1520** Whittinton *Vulgaria* 117.11: And can noo moore good than a shepe.

S221 To flee like **Sheep**
a1300 *Richard* 447.7156: Thenne fledde the Sarezynes as they were scheep. **c1433** Lydgate *St. Edmund* 403.382: For they lik sheepe fledde out of his syht. **c1450** *Ponthus* 29.34. **1483** Caxton *Golden Legende* 143r[2.25–6]: They fled away lyke as sheep done fro wulves. **c1500** Fabyan 411[6]: They fledde before hym, as shepe before the wolfe, 531[2]. **1533** Berners *Huon* 188.9–10: (They) fled as the shepe doth fro the wolves, 748.12–3. Whiting *Scots* II 123. See **L43.**

S222 To follow like **Sheep**
a1470 Malory I 238.26: They folowed as shepe out of a folde. Taylor *Comparisons* 72; Whiting *NC* 472. See **L44.**

S223 To gather like **Sheep** in fold
a1475 *Guy*[2] 95.3312: He gedurd them, as shyp in folde. Whiting *Scots* II 123–4.

S224 To have **Sheep** graze under one's toe
1418 *Man, be warre* in Kail 62.45–6: For his mys-rulyng thou myght hyng, That shep myghte grese under thy to. Cf. *Oxford* 331: Keep sheep by moonlight.

S225 To know one from a **Sheep**
c1495 *Arundel Vulgaria* 12.49: I wyll never sytt agayn with the at on mease while I lyff, and I may know the from a shepe. Tilley S316.

S226 To lead like a **Sheep**
c1380 *Pearl* 29.801: As a schep to the slaght ther lad wats he. **c1395** *WBible* Psalms lxxix 2: That leedist forth Joseph as a scheep, Isaiah liii 7: As a scheep he schal be led to sleyng. **a1400** *Northern Verse Psalter* I 251 (77.21): Thou ledde als schepe thi folk on one, 267 (79.2): That ledes Josep als a schepe. **a1400** *Scottish Legends* I 287.71.

S227 To shed (*scatter*) like **Sheep** out of a fold
a1400 *Morte Arthure* 86.2922: Owte of the scheltrone they schede, as schepe of a folde. Whiting *Scots* II 123.

S228 To shred (*cut down*) like **Sheep** in (a) fold
a1400 *Le Morte A.* 77.2563: And shredde them downe as shepe in folde. **a1470** Malory III 1211.27: And shrede hem downe as shepe in a folde.

S229 To slay like **Sheep**
a1350 Castelford 121.23008: We sale tham now sla doune als schepe. **c1400** *Laud Troy* I 133. 4488: He sclow hem doun, as it were schepe. **c1420** Wyntoun III 43.508. **c1500** Fabyan 66[18–9]: The Brytons were slayne as shepe amonge wolvys.

S230 To stand like **Sheep**
c1433 Lydgate *St. Edmund* 403.340–1: For lik a sheepe they stood alone, unguyded, Withoute an hed, dispers and eek devyded. **c1450** *Ponthus* 29.16–8: The Saresyns . . . stode as shepe with-oute an herdman. See **L49.**

S231 To cast a **Sheep's Eye**
a1529 Skelton *Garnesche* I 121.54: When ye kyst a shepys ie. **1555** Heywood *E* 162.99: He cast a sheepes eye at her. Apperson 563; *Oxford* 580; Taylor and Whiting 325; Tilley S323.

S232 Scant worth a **Sheep's Pelt**
c1515 Barclay *Eclogues* 37.1030: Then is thy favour scant worth a shepes pelt.

S233 To go to **Sheep Wash** (*i.e.*, be killed)
c1443 *Chronicle of London* 112[26–8]: But the moste vengeaunce fell upon the proude Scottes; for there wente to schep wassh of them the same day mo thanne xvii[c] of cote armes be a countynge of herowdes.

S234 To be a **Sheet-anchor**
1528 More *Heresyes* 181 C[14–5]: Yet is this point their shote ancre, 195 F[9–10]: And thys was against the stone the very shote anker, **1529** *Supplicacion* 318 B[5–6], **1533** *Confutacion* 726 F[1–2]. **1546** Heywood *D* 27.50: Her substaunce is shoote anker, wherat I shoote, **1556** *Spider* 401[6]: I must make my shoote anker, [8], 412[19], 423[8]. NED Sheet-anchor b.

S235 As round as a **Shell**
c1475 Henryson *Fables* 82.2395 (*var.*): Als round as ane schell.

S236 Not (a)vail a **Shell**
c1400 *Laud Troy* I 213.7236: Here ropes vayled not of a schale.

S237 Not worth a **Shell**
a1400 *Cursor* III 1362 F 23828: Thaire speche is noght worth a shelle. **c1400** *Laud Troy* I 296.10053–4, II 436.14797. **c1450** Greene *Carols* 383.2: Ther is non man worght a schelle.

S238 To bring up from the **Shell**
1546 Heywood *D* 34.63–4: An aunte . . . who well (Sens my mother died) brought me up from the shell.

S239 To shoot at a **Shell** (*sexual sense*)
a1513 Dunbar *Ane His Awin Ennemy* 2.13: And schuttis syne at ane uncow schell. NED Shell sb.1 2b; Whiting *Scots* II 124.

S240 What a new **Shell** takes the old savors of (*varied*)
a1447 Bokenham *Mappula* 33[35–9]: Aftir the sentence of Oracius the poet, seyinge on this wyse: versus: Quo semel est imbuta recens servabit odorem testa diu et c.—That is to sey: syche savour as the newe shelle takithe, when hit is eldder hit kepythe, **1447** Bokenham 45.1649–50: For, as longe to-forne be a poete was tolde, What newe shelle taketh it savouryth olde. **1464** Hardyng 181[4–5]: For what savour a newe shell is taken with, When it is olde it tasteth of the same. **1509** Barclay *Ship* I 47[13–4]: But fyll an erthen pot first with yll lycoure And ever after it shall smell somwhat soure. **1520** Whittinton *Vulgaria* 110.15–6: I have red in Horace A pytcher wyll have a smatche longe after of the lyquoure that was fyrst put in it. **c1523** Barclay *Mirrour* 83[6–7]: Yet an earthen vessell is ever sweete or soure, And after still keepeth taste of the first licour. Horace, *Epistles* I.2.69–70: Quo semel est imbuta recens servabit odorem testa diu. See **C226, 525, 649, S262.**

S241 (Under a gentle **Shepherd**) the wolf shits wool (*varied*)
a1387 *Piers* C x 264: Thyne sheep are ner al shabbyd, the wolf shiteth woolle: *Sub molli pastore lupus lanam cacat, et grex In-custoditus dilaceratur eo.* **1492** *Salomon and Marcolphus* 12[18–9]: The shepherde that wakyth well, ther shall the wolf no wolle shyte. Walther V 163. 30542.

S242 Under a soft **Shepherd** the wolf has to-rent many a lamb
c1390 Chaucer *CT* VI[C] 101–2: Under a shepherde softe and necligent The wolf hath many a sheep and lamb torent. *Oxford* 723. Cf. Jente 40.

S243 Not worth a **Shide** (*piece of wood*)
c1330 *St. Katherine* 254 C 515: Thy stryvyng is nought wurth a schyde.

S244 To bring a **Shilling** to ninepence
1546 Heywood *D* 71.38: To bryng a shillyng to .ix. pens quickely. Apperson 564; *Oxford* 65; Tilley N194. See **M383.**

S245 As sooth as **Ships** sail over waters
a1500 *Thre Prestis* 49.1149: Als suith it is as ships saillis over watters.

S246 As swift as a **Ship**
a1450 *Castle* 129.1740–1: I go, I go, on grounde glad, Swyfter thanne schyp with rodyr!

S247 Like a steerless (*rudderless*) **Ship**
a1437 *Kingis Quair* 49.15[3–4]: Ryght as the schip that sailith stereles Upon the rok(kis) most to harmes hye. **c1450** Idley 89.532: They lieve in rest as shippe without Rother. Tilley S347.

S248 A **Ship** is more sicker in little water than in the deep sea (*varied*)
c900 *Old English Cato* 4.28–9: Unpleolucar man rowð mid lytle bate on lytle watere þone mid mycelan scipe on mycele wætere, (*Trinity College Cambridge*) in John M. Kemble *Dialogue of Salomon and Saturnus* (London, 1848)

262[1–3]: Beo gehalde on ðam ðe ðu hæbbe; unpleolicre hit bið on lytlum scipe and on lytlum wætere, ðonne on miclum scipe and on miclum wætre. **c1390** *Cato* (*Vernon*) 578.307–8: Schip is more siker in luitel water Then in the deope see. **a1400** *Cato* (*Copenhagen*) A5v[19–20]: For shepis that saylyn in esy floode, Comenly they comyn to goode, B4v[15–6]: For shippys ben sekerer by the lande Than in the tempest fer saylande. **a1440** Burgh *Cato* 313.429–30: For than is the ship in the see moste sur, What tyme the flode excedithe nat mesur. **a1475** *Cato* (*Rawlinson*) 23.256–7: Sykerer is the schyppe in esy flood, Than forthir forth in wawys wood. **1483** Caxton *Cato* E7v[5–7]: For the shyppe saylleth more surelye in a lytel ryvere than in a grete flode as in the se. See **S250, 655, 801.**

S249 A **Ship** or barge may be overladen
c1386 Chaucer *LGW* 621: For men may overlade a ship or barge. **a1420** Lydgate *Troy* III 571.288–9: Men with to moche may over-lade a barge, And nam(e)ly in tempest and in rage. See **B422, C16, T118, W6.**

S250 A **Ship** should never drown if it were kept in the haven
a1420 Lydgate *Troy* I 248.3610–4: For never schip schulde in pereil drown, . . . Yif it wer kepte in the havene stille. **c1520** Walter *Spectacle* D1r[20–1]: For the shyp sholde never by tempest spyll, Yf in the haven it contynued styll. Cf. Jente 188; *Oxford* 133; Tilley S345. See **S248.**

S251 **Shipmen** are liars
c1380 Chaucer *HF* 2121–4: And, Lord, this hous in alle tymes, Was ful of shipmen and pilgrimes, With scrippes bret-ful of lesinges, Entremedled with tydynges. See **D246, P18, R185.**

S252 **Shipmen** in peril are devout
1519 Horman *Vulgaria* 361[28]: Shypmen in parell be devout. Cf. Tilley V97.

S253 After the **Shipwreck** they dread the sea
a900 Alfred *Gregory* 403.12–3: Ðæt hie huru æfter ðæm scipgebroce him ða sæ ondræden. See **C201.**

S254 To din like the **Shipwright** on nail
a1300 *Alisaunder* 205.3659–60: That is dyned so righth, So on nayl dooth the ship-wrighth.

S255 To be nearer than one's **Shirt**
c1440 Charles of Orleans 93.2775: Which sat him nere than evyr sat him shert, 179.5364: As forto take yow nere me then my shert. See **C303.**

S256 To be **Shirted** nearer than one's skin
c1440 Charles of Orleans 17.493–4: The wofulle liif unto yow to biwray Which shertith me more nerre than doth my skyn. Cf. Apperson 437–8; *Oxford* 444; Taylor and Whiting 337; Tilley S356.

S257 A stepmother **Shive** (*slice of bread*)
1483 *Catholicon Anglicum* 361[2.9]: A stepmoder schyfe: *colirida.* NED Stepmother 1d. See **S720.**

S258 As black as any **Shoe**
c1410 Lovelich *Grail* III 42.106: And therto As blak As Ony Scho. Svartengren 242. See **S459.**

S259 Go clout (*mend*) your **Shoes**
a1460 *Towneley Plays* 33.353: Yei, noe, go cloute thi shone, the better will thai last. Whiting *Drama* 338:458, 356:742. Cf. Tilley S377.

S260 Not worth an old **Shoe**
c1395 Chaucer *CT* III[D] 707–8: The clerk, whan he is oold, and may noght do Of Venus werkes worth his olde sho. **a1500** *Carpenter's Tools* 85.182: It is not worthe an old sho. **1534** Heywood *Love* B4v[25]. Whiting *Drama* 362:834.

S261 Put your **Shoes** in your bosom for wearing
c1525 ?Heywood *Gentylnes* 98.184–5: Gentylmen? ye gentylmen? Jak heryng! Put your shone in your bosom for weryng! Whiting *Drama* 369:935.

S262 A **Shoe** holds its first form (*shape*)
1340 *Ayenbite* 220[23–4]: Zuiche fourme ase the sso takth ate ginnynge: he halt evremore ine thet stat. **c1400** *Vices and Virtues* 200.1–3: For a child wole ever-more holde his first forme and wone, as doth a scho, 244.23–4: And suche schap that a scho taketh on a foot at the first, he halt alwey. See **S240.**

S263 The **Shoe** will hold with the sole
1546 Heywood *D* 72.70: Folke say of olde, the shoe will holde with the sole, **1555** *E* 172.144. Apperson 565; *Oxford* 583; Tilley S371.

S264 They often do off his **Shoe** whose foot they would cut off
c1505 Watson *Valentine* 59.22–4: But it is sayd in a comyn proverbe, that they do the shoo often of, whom of they wolde cut of the foote. See note p. 331.

S265 To cast an old **Shoe** after one
1546 Heywood *D* 34.38: Nowe for good lucke, caste an olde shoe after mee. Tilley S372.

S266 To know best where one's **Shoe** wrings
c1395 Chaucer *CT* III[D] 491–4: For, God it woot, he sat ful ofte and song, Whan that his shoo ful bitterly hym wrong. Ther was no wight, save God and he, that wiste, In many wise, how soore I hym twiste, IV[E] 1553: But I woot best where wryngeth me my sho. **1546** Heywood *D* 74.138: My selfe can tell best, where my shooe doth wryng mee. Apperson 565; Jente 337; *Oxford* 583; Skeat 277; Taylor and Whiting 328–9; Tilley M129; Whiting *Drama* 39, *Scots* II 124. See **G186, M222.**

S267 To mistread one's **Shoe** (*varied*)
a1325 *People of Kildare* in Heuser 156.9[3]: Ofte mistredith ye (*nuns*) yur schone, yur fete beth ful tendre. **c1425** Hoccleve *Jonathas* 218.66: But swich oon as hath trode hir shoo amis. **c1450** *When the son* 388.169: Of xl yer maydens that never tred her sho amys. **c1475** *Thewis* 192.273: Quhen scho is tred hir scho one heill. **1563** Heywood *E* 232.21.1: My wyfe doth ever tread hir shooe a wry. Apperson 644; NED Tread v. 13b; Tilley S373; Whiting *Drama* 368:910, *Scots* II 124.

S268 To set as short as old **Shoes** (*i.e.*, treat rudely)
1532 More *Confutacion* 410 D[11–2]: Now if this made Tindal bolde to set Origene as short as his olde shone.

S269 To wear a **Shoe** on the hand and a glove on the foot
a1393 Gower *CA* II 14.356–9: Upon the hond to were a Schoo And sette upon the fot a Glove Acordeth noght to the behove Of resonable mannes us.

S270 Who is worse shod than the **Shoemaker's** wife?
1546 Heywood *D* 49.267–8: But who is wurs shod, than the shoemakers wyfe, With shops full of newe shoes all hir lyfe? **1555** *E* 194.277. Apperson 566; *Oxford* 432; Tilley S387.

S271 Short **Shooting** loses the game
1546 Heywood *D* 97.226: Short shootyng leeseth your game. Apperson 568; *Oxford* 585; Tilley S390.

S272 To set up **Shop** on Goodwin's Sands
1549 Heywood *D* 93.84: And so set up shop upon Goodwins sands. Apperson 265; *Oxford* 259; Tilley S393.

S273 To lean to the wrong **Shore**
1546 Heywood *D* 64.64: Ye leane . . . to the wrong shore. *Oxford* 357; Tilley S395.

S274 To spend one's **Shot**
1522 Skelton *Why Come* II 30.124: For we have spente our shot. See **B434.**

S275 As wholesome as a **Shoulder** of mutton for a sick horse
1546 Heywood *D* 86–7.224–6: Thou art, to be plaine, and not to flatter thee, As holsome a morsell for my comely cors, As a shoulder of mutton for a sicke hors. Apperson 568; *Oxford* 585; Tilley S399.

S276 To be **Shovel-footed**
a1400 *Morte Arthure* 33.1098: Schovell-fotede was that schalke.

S277 After sharp **Showers** (*battles*) are victories
c1385 Chaucer *TC* iii 1063–4: Men sen alday, and reden ek in stories, That after sharpe shoures ben victories. Skeat 182.

S278 After sharp **Showers** most sheen is the sun
c1378 *Piers* B xviii 409–12: After sharpe shoures . . . moste shene is the sonne; Is no weder warmer than after watery cloudes. Ne no love levere ne lever frendes, Than after werre and wo, whan Love and Pees be maistres. Apperson 604; Skeat 154. See **S734, 797.**

S279 As rife as a **Shower** of rain
a1300 *Floris* 76.73: With teres rive ase a scur of r(e)ne.

Shrew, sb.

S280 One **Shrew** in a court may shend (*ruin*) many a man (*varied*)
c1330 *Times of Edward II* 335.270: Ac o shrewe in a court many man may shende. **a1400** *Destruction of Troy* 409.12546–7: Oft-sythes men sayn, and sene is of olde, That all a company is cumbrit for a cursed shrewe. See **A167, S217.**

S281 A **Shrew** may get a right good child
c1398 W. Paris *Cristine* in Horstmann *Sammlung* 183.19: It was of hyme as of moo is: A sherew may gete a childe righte goode.

S282 Some **Shrew** is in every order
c1395 Chaucer *CT* VIII[G] 995: Of every ordre som shrewe is, pardee. Cf. Tilley F49.

S283 Two **Shrews** will accord (*varied*)
c1300 *South English Legendary* I 242.24: As tweie ssrewen acordeth sone at an luther rede, II 694.67–8: Vor they in al a contreye bote tweye schrewen nere Yut hii wolde felawes beo yif hii togadere were, 701.100: Vor twei schrewen wolleth beo freond thei noman elles nere. Cf. Tilley T121a.

S284 When all **Shrews** have dined change from foul weather to fair is oft inclined
1546 Heywood *D* 58.39–40: And when all shrews have dind, Chaunge from foule weather to faire is oft enclind. Apperson 568; *Oxford* 187; Tilley W218.

S285 Who deals with **Shrews** should work by advice (*varied*)
a1400 *Siege of Jerusalem* 50.866 (*var.*): It is good wurche be avys who schal dele with schrewys. **c1450** *Fyrst thou sal* 90.145–6: Who so is copyld with a schrewe Wyrk wysely and say bot fewe. **c1499** Skelton *Bowge* I 50.525: Who deleth with shrewes hath nede to loke aboute.

Shrew, vb.

S286 **Shrew** (*curse*) one, shrew other
a1400 Bozon *Contes* 78[1]: Schrewe on, schrewe other. See **G258.**

S287 As soft as any **Shrift**
c1386 Chaucer *LGW* 745: And with a soun as softe as any shryfte.

S288 **Shropshire** sharp shins
a1500 *Characteristics of Counties* in *Rel. Ant.* I 269[9]: Schropschir, my schinnes ben scharpe. Apperson 569; Tilley S340.

S289 **Shrovetide** comes once a year
1519 Horman *Vulgaria* 431[3]: Shroftyde cometh ones a yere and is full of sporte. Cf. Taylor and Whiting 69: Christmas.

S290 He **Shuns** (*keeps out of the way*) who knows himself foul (has misguilt)
c1250 *Owl* 22.233–6: A wis word, theh hit bo unclene, Is fele manne a-muthe imene, For Alured King hit seide and wrot: "He schunet that hine (vu)l wot." **a1400** *And Martha keped* in Horstmann *Sammlung* 163.24: For ever he schoneth that hath misgilt. See **G492, M326.**

S291 Not worth a **Shuttlecock**
1522 Skelton *Why Come* II 38.351: Nat worth a shyttel cocke.

S292 To sing **Si Dedero**
1381 *Jack Trewman* in Knighton II 139[22]: No man may come trewthe to, bot he syng si dedero. **a1400** *Harley MS.2316* in *Rel. Ant.* II 121[35–8]: Now goot falshed in everi flok, And trewthe is sperd under a lok; Now no man may comen ther to, But yef he singge *si dedero*, *Royal MS.17 B xvii* in *Yorkshire Writers* II 65[18–21]: Now gos gyle in ever-ilk flok, And treuthe is sperrid undre a lok; May no mon that lok undo, But if he syng si dedero. **a1449** Lydgate *Fabules* in *MP* II 577.327: *Si dedero* is now so mery a song. **a1450** *Castle* 103.881–2: Of Mankynde, getyth no man no good, But if he synge "si dedero." **a1450** *Summe maner* in *London Medieval Studies* 2(1951) 64.107: *Si dedero* was ther lessoun. **c1450** Idley 90.560: Thus must thou lerne to synge "Si dedero." *Rel. Ant.* II 6.

S293 **Sib** (*kinsman*) is dearest to each (*varied*)
c735 *Beowulf* 2600–1: Sibb' æfre ne mæg Wiht onwendan þam ðe wel þenceð. **c950** *Bodley MS. Auct. D 2.19* in Ker *Catalogue* 352[10]: Sibb is eghwæm leofost. See **B359.**

S294 As wise as **Sibyl**
a1500 *Croxton Sacrament* in Waterhouse 68.351: They hold hym wyser than ever was Syble sage.

S295 **Sice** (*six*) turns to ace
c1390 Chaucer *CT* VII 2661[B3851]: Thy sys Fortune hath turned into aas.

S296 He is wonder **Sick** that may let no man touch him
c1450 *Jacob's Well* 70.34–5: He is wonder syke that may lete no man towchyn hym.

S297 If you are **Sicker** put you not in dread (*varied*)
c1396 Chaucer *Bukton* 25–8: This lytel writ, proverbes, or figure I sende yow, take kepe of yt, I rede; Unwys is he that kan no wele endure. If thow be siker, put the nat in drede. **c1450** *Fyrst thou sal* 90.139–40: If thou be sykyr kepe thi place, Be war be tyme and take thi grace. Skeat 144. See **E32, P245, R95, S356, 668, W556.**

S298 After **Sickness** comes heal (*health*)
a1400 *Proverbis of Wysdom (II)* 222.34: After syknes cometh hele. See **B325.**

S299 **Sickness** has no law
a1420 Lydgate *Troy* I 370.7898: And for thei sawe that siknes hath no lawe. See **N51.**

S300 There is no **Sickness** but some succor is given
1489 Caxton *Fayttes* 168.25–6: For there is noo syknes but that som socoure is gyven therunto. Cf. Tilley S84.

S301 To be deaf on the better **Side** (*varied*)
c1450 Idley 90.567: When they list they be deiffe on the better side. **1555** Heywood *E* 163.107: I can not heare on that side, no trueth to tell: Of any side, thou couldst never yet heare well.

S302 To know on which **Side** one's bread is buttered

1546 Heywood *D* 88.264: I know on which syde my bread is buttred. Apperson 64; *Oxford* 346; Taylor and Whiting 332; Tilley S425.

S303 To rise on one's right **Side**
1546 Heywood *D* 67.56: You rose on your right syde here right. Apperson 532; *Oxford* 544; Taylor and Whiting 21–2; Tilley S426.

S304 As sib (*related*) as **Sieve** and riddle (*coarse sieve*)
a1500 *Thre Prestis* 28.476: I am to yow als sib as seif is to ane riddil. **a1508** Dunbar *Testament* 73.55–6: We weir als sib as seve and riddill, In una silva que creverunt. Apperson 570; *Oxford* 587; Tilley S434; Whiting *Scots* II 124.

S305 To keep as a **Sieve** keeps ale
a1393 Gower *CA* II 238.433–4: For as a Sive kepeth Ale, Riht so can Cheste kepe a tale. Cf. Taylor and Whiting 333.

S306 As swart as **Sigelwara** (*Ethiopians*)
a1000 *Two Apocrypha* H 40[2–4]: Se bið swa sweart swa . . . silharewa. J. R. R. Tolkien "Sigelwara Land," *Medium Ævum* 1(1932) 183–96, 3(1934) 95–111.

S307 Out of **Sight** out of mind (*varied*)
c1250 *Proverbs of Alfred* 122 T 487–8: For he that is ute bi-loken He is inne sone foryeten. **c1300** *South English Legendary* (*Laud*) 323.17–8: That heo ane hwyle nere Out of is sighte in othur stude: that heo fur-yite were. **c1385** Chaucer *TC* iv 423–4: Or elles selde seynge of a wight, Don olde affecciouns alle over-go. **c1400** Mandeville *Travels* 4.8–10: For thinges passed out of longe tyme from a mannes mynde or from his syght turnen sone in to foryetynge. **c1475** *Brome Abraham* in Waterhouse 44.201–2: For, be I onys ded and from yow goo, I schall be sone out of yowre mynd. **1518** Watson *Oliver* D3r[13–4]: And this notwithstandynge yf that he were ferre from his syghte yet he sholde not be longed from his herte. **1546** Heywood *D* 23.27: Out of sight of minde, **1555** *E* 151.32: Out of sight out of minde. Apperson 476; Jente 166; *Oxford* 480; Taylor and Whiting 333; Tilley S438; Whiting *Drama* 128, 140. See **A16, D72, E213, 216, H633, L536, M569, S130.**

S308 **Silence** is a great virtue
a1410 Love *Mirrour* 53[27]: Silence is a grete vertue. Cf. Apperson 594: Speech; Jente 800; *Oxford* 612; Taylor and Whiting 346. See **W587.**

S309 **Silence** overcomes (has the victory)
c1400 *Consilia Isidori* 369[34–5]: For by sylence thou schalte the sonner overcome. **a1420** Lydgate *Troy* III 724.5469–71: Silence, in soth, hath ofte in hasty strif Hadde of victorie a prerogatyf, And the palme of debatis wonne.

S310 As fine as **Silk**
c1500 *Lady Bessy* 47[9]: Hir faxe that was as fyne as silcke. Taylor and Whiting 334.

S311 As nesh (*soft*) as **Silk**
a1450 *Pety Job* in Kail 126.173–4: My bloode ys nessher than ys sylke, In reyny weder that sone woll fade.

S312 As red as **Silk**
a1400 *Floris* 79.366: And that other reed so sylk. See **S148.**

S313 As soft as (the, any) **Silk**
c1325 *Maid of Ribbesdale* in Böddeker 158.76: Eyther side soft ase sylk. **a1350** *Ywain* 83.3105: Of riche cloth soft als the sylk. **c1395** Chaucer *CT* V[F] 613: And strawe hir cage faire and softe as silk. **a1400** *Moder of gresse* 192.1090: Ther is a gres softe as sylke. **c1408** Lydgate *Reson* 44.1643: Of hir pappis softe as silke, **1420** *Temple* 24.540, **a1430** *Pilgrimage* 655.24466: any, **1420** *St. Margarete* in *MP* I 188.416, **a1439** *Fall* I 196.6943, II 556.3046, **a1449** *Fifteen Joys* in *MP* I 261.8: any. **a1450** *Partonope* 66.2237: eny. **c1450** *When the son* 390.268: And softer hyt was then opyn sylke. **c1455** *Partonope S* 487.235–6: In Armes hee klipte that womman free, Softe as selk hee gan hiere fynde. **1471** Ripley *Compound* 137[13]. **a1475** *Talk of Ten Wives* 31[23]: ony. **c1485** *Burial and Resurrection* 197.774: Your fleshe was soft os tender silke. **a1500** *Catalogue of Delights* in Robbins 121.30: any. **a1500** Medwall *Nature* D2r[38]. **a1500** *O Heavenly Star* in Brown *Lyrics XV* 206.8. **a1500** *St. Kateryne* 262.187: ony. **1506** Hawes *Pastime* 63.1590: ony. **a1508** Dunbar *Tretis* 87.96: Bot soft and soupill as the silk is his sary lume. **a1508** Skelton *Phyllyp* I 85.1119. Apperson 585; Taylor *Comparisons* 76; Tilley S449; Whiting *Drama* 325:290, *Scots* II 125.

S314 As sweet as **Silk**
a1400 *Cursor* III 1219 T 21296: And Jones hony swete as silke (CG: suilk, F: squilk).

S315 As white as (the) **Silk**
a1400 *Destruction of Troy* 129.3993: (Cassandra) as the silke white. **a1475** *Liber Cure Cocorum* 13[5]: Take flour of ryse, as whyte as sylke.

S316 One cannot make **Silk** of a goat's fleece
c1515 Barclay *Eclogues* 194.360: Nor (*can any*) make goodly silke of a gotes flece. Cf. Tilley P666. See **H484, L6, S976.**

S317 To be like **Silk**
a1400 *Destruction of Troy* 126.3899: Here huet on his hede as haspis of silke.

S318 To shine like **Silk**
a1475 *Seege of Troye* 199 H 1530g: Here lovely ffax shyned as selke.

S319 To be like **Silk Thread**
c1350 *Libeaus* 53.940: Her browes as selke threde.

S320 As bright as (any, the) **Silver**
c1300 *Guy*[1] 454 A 92.4: As bright as ani silver it was. **c1380** *Ferumbras* 39.988: Durendal, that schon so silver bright. **c1385** Chaucer *CT* I[A] 2608: Out goon the swerdes as the silver brighte. **a1393** Gower *CA* III 32.3110. **a1400** *Alexander C* 248.4808: the. **a1400** *Morte Arthure* 97.3282, 124.4215: ony. **a1400** *Scottish Legends* II 388.53–4. **c1410** Lovelich *Merlin* III 567.21285–6. **a1450** *Partonope* 158.4366. **c1450** *Merlin* II 260[28]: Hauberkes bright shynynge as fin silveir. **a1475** *Ludus Coventriae* 198.167. **a1500** *Take Erth of Erth* in Ashmole 273[30]. Tilley S453.

S320a **Silver-bright**
a1420 Lydgate *Troy* II 497.3569: Silver bright, with rounde perlys fyne, **a1439** *Fall* I 264.2273: Scales silver-briht. NED Silver 19.

S321 As clean as pured (*refined*) **Silver**
a1460 *Towneley Plays* 221.542–3: As cleyn . . . As puryd sylver.

S322 As fine as **Silver**
a1400 ?Chaucer *Rom. A* 1556–7: And eke the gravell, which that shoon Down in the botme as silver fyn.

S323 As white as **Silver**
c1440 *Prose Alexander* 94.15: Lefes whitt als sylver. Svartengren 232; Tilley S453.

S324 **Silver** is sweet
a1376 *Piers* A Prol. 83: Selver is swete.

S325 **Silver-sheen**
a1420 Lydgate *Troy* III 831.2055: With skalis silver shene, **c1421** *Thebes* 132.3219. Whiting *Scots* II 125.

S326 To be like **Silver**
c1380 *Pearl* 3.77: As bornyst sylver the lef on slydes.

S327 To be proved like **Silver**
897 Alfred *Boethius* 120.14–5: þa amered on ðæm heofonlican fyre, swa her bið seolfor. **c900** *Paris Psalter* 19 (65.9): Ure costade god clæne fyre Soðe dome, swa man seolfor deð, þonne man hit aseoðeð swyðe mid fyre. **c1000** *Regius Psalter* 116 (65.10): þu amyredest (*us*) swa swa amered bið seolfor. **c1100** *Salisbury Psalter* 161 (65.10). **c1350** *Prose Psalter* 76 (65.9): Thou assaid us with fur as silver is proved. **c1395** *WBible* Psalms lxv 10: Thou hast examyned us bi fier, as silver is examyned, Proverbs xvii 3: As silver is preved bi fier, and gold *is preved* bi a chymnei, so the Lord preveth hertis, xxvii 21: As silver is prevyd in a wellyng place, and gold *is preved* in a furneys; so a man is preved bi the mouth of preyseris. See **F180, G298, M522, S410.**

S328 To be **Silver** sick
c1475 Henryson *Fables* 71.2036: And ye ar silver seik, I wait richt weill. NED Silver 21; Tilley D620; Whiting *Scots* II 125. See **P449.**

S329 To shine like any **Silver**
a1470 Malory II 750.33: Hys shylde that shone lyke ony . . . sylver. Whiting *Scots* II 125.

S330 Where **Silver** fails dainties are oft seen in a pewter dish
a1449 Lydgate *Fabules* in *MP* II 567.17–8: Where sylver fayleth, in a pewter dyssh Ryall dentees byn oft tymes seyne. See **V24.**

S331 As bright as **Silver Wire**
c1400 *Laud Troy* I 134.4535–6: He toke his armes and his atyre, That were as bryght as silver wyre.

S332 **Simper** de cocket
a1529 Skelton *Elynour* I 96.54–5: And gray russet rocket, With symper the cocket. **1533** Heywood *Weather* D1r[31]: I saw you dally wyth your symper de cokket, **1546** *D* 32. *Oxford* 591; Tilley S462.

S333 Every **Sin** brings (tills [*draws*]) in another
c1400 *Seven Deadly Sins* in Wyclif *SEW* III 133[34]: Ffor everiche synne brynges in another. **a1450** *Castle* 108.1035: Thus Every synne tyllyth in other. See **M591, S340.**

S334 Forholen (*hidden*) **Sin** is like fire in the bosom
c1303 Mannyng *Handlyng* 390.12445–8: Ryght so fareth forholen synne, As fyre, bore bosum ynne; At the laste, hyt hym dereth, And brennyth that hym aboute bereth. See **F208.**

S335 Forsake **Sin** ere sin forsake you (*varied*)
a1000 *Pseudo-Alcuin* 388.421–2: Gyf þu þonne wylt don dædbote, þonne þu synegian ne miht, þonne forlæteð þe þine synnen, na þu heo.

c1175 *Poema Morale* 179.128–9: To late vorlet thet evele worc thet hit ne mai don na more. Senne let the and thu nah hoe thanne thu ne miht hi do more. **c1390** Chaucer *CT* VI[C] 286: Forsaketh synne, er synne yow forsake, X[I] 93: And therfore repentant folk, that stynte for to synne, and forlete synne er that synne forlete hem, hooly chirche holdeth hem siker of hire savacioun. **a1400** Lavynham 18.11–2: Thy synnys have forsake the and not thou thy synnys. **a1400** *Scottish Legends* II 70.39–42: For he that cesis nocht to syne Til that it lewis hyme, Sal nothyr haf thang no mede Til lef, quhen he ma do na dede. **c1415** *Middle English Sermons* 181.17–8: For-why he never forsoke lecherye to lechery forsoke hym. **a1450** Audelay 181.1–2: A! mon, yif thou wold savyd be Foresake thi syn or hit do the. **c1450** *Alphabet* I 22.3: At (*for* that) will not lefe syn or it lefe thaim. **c1450** *Fyrst thou sal* 91.174: Lefe thi syn ot (*for* or) the warld lefe the. **c1450** *Jacob's Well* 36. 18–9: I, synfull wrecche, lefte my synne, er my synne lefte me, 108.6: Tarye noght tyl thi synne hath forsake the. **c1450** *Of the seven Ages* 485 [22–3]: When thi syn has the forsake Than for thi bale thou aske heven blis. **c1450** *Ratis* 42. 1462–3: Syk men thar trepas lewis nocht Bot It lef thaim quhen thai na mocht. **a1500** *Thre Prestis* 51.1229: Thow leifs nocht sin quhill sin hes left the. **1502** *Wellcome MS.41* in S. A. J. Moorat *Catalogue of Western Manuscripts . . . in the Wellcome Historical Medical Library* (London, 1962) 27: Accipe that longeth to the, Redde to god that his shuld be, Fluge synne or it fle the, Thanne hevyn blysse your mede shalbe. **a1513** Dunbar *Maner of Passing* 169.69–70: Small merit is of synnes for to irke Quhen thow art ald and ma na wrangis wyrke. **1555** Heywood *E* 195.281: Leave it or it leave you, leave what folly, He can never leave it nor it him wholly. Whiting *Scots* II 125. See **W407.**

S336 If you think to do no **Sin,** do nothing that belongs thereto
a1475 *Good Wyfe Wold* 175.66: Men wyll sey so, "Yefe thou thenke to do no syne, do nothynge that longythe therto."

S337 It is a **Sin** to belie (lie on) the devil
1513 More *Richard* 57 C[8]: For sinne it wer to belie the devil. **1556** Heywood *Spider* 235[8]: Wyse flies saie: it is sin to lie on the devill. Apperson 144; *Oxford* 364; Tilley S470.

S338 Old **Sin** makes new shame
c1300 *Havelok* 83.2461: Old sinne makes newe shame. **a1333** Shoreham *Poems* 98.17–8: Senne maketh nywe schame, Thagh hy for-yete be. **a1393** Gower *CA* II 281.2033: Men sein, "Old Senne newe schame," III 377.5115–6: So that the comun clamour tolde The newe schame of Sennes olde. **a1450** *God of hefne, that sittest* 411.217–9: Ffor men seyen in olde speche, Grene wounde nys bote game, And ole synne maketh newe schame. **c1450** *Bishop Boothe* in Wright *Political Poems* II 226[14]: Shame sewith sone, whenne syn gooth byfore. **c1450** *Douce MS.52* 55.119: Olde synnys makyn new shamys. **c1450** *Fyrst thou sal* 90.117: Old syn makes newe schame. **c1450** *Rylands MS.364* 104.18.24: Elde. **1464** Hardyng 213[21]: Thus synnes olde, make shames come full newe. **c1475** *Rawlinson MS. D 328* 121.47. **c1500** *Melusine* 79.4–6: I now perceyve wel and see that the proverbe that is said commonly is trew, that is "that olde synne reneweth shame." Apperson 467; Jente 582; *Oxford* 473; Skeat 56; Tilley S471; Whiting *Scots* II 125. See **R101.**

S339 Old **Sins** will come out in green wax
c1450 Idley 92.665: Ffor olde synnes woll com out in grene wexe.

S340 One **Sin** will intermell (*intermingle*) with another
a1450 Quixley *Ballades* 47.293: Oon syn with another will entermelle. See **S333.**

S341 **Sin** has a fall
1509 Barclay *Ship* I 86[20]: For ever more all synne hath had a fall. See **P393.**

S342 **Sin** is fair without and foul within
a1500 *Trentals of Gregory* (*Edinburgh*) in *Anglia* 13(1890) 303.27–8: "Alas," he sayde, "alas for syn, So fayre with-out and fole with-in." See **A155.**

S343 **Sin** is not forgiven without restitution
a1387 *Piers* C vii 256–7: For the pope and alle hus penetauncers power hem faylleth, To a-soyle the of thy synnes *sine restitutione; Nunquam dimittitur peccatum nisi restituatur ablatum.* **c1450** Idley 144.2237–8: And also the synne is in no wyse foryeven Without restitucion, thoughe he therof be shreven, 150.2614–6: And the pope hymsilf may not dispence, Ffor ther availeth no penauns ne absolucion But if thow clierly make restitucioun. Walther III 248.17503; Whiting *Scots* II 125.

S344 **Sin** is sweet
a1445 *Carl* 140.410: For synn ys swete. Cf. Whiting *Scots* II 125.

S345 **Sin** returns ever upon its master

1484 Caxton *Aesop* 75[15–6]: For synne retorneth ever upon his mayster. See **D22, 342.**

S346 To do **Sin** is mannish, to persevere in sin is the work of the devil (*varied*)
c1390 Chaucer *CT* VII 1264[B2454]: The proverbe seith that "for to do synne is mannyssh, but certes for to persevere longe in synne is werk of the devel." **c1422** Hoccleve *Jereslaus's Wife* 167.783–4: Be nat abassht, it manly is to synne, but feendly is longe lye ther-ynne. **1487** *O thou most noble* 321[8–9]: For the doctor saieth it is naturall to synne, But diabolike to persevere therein. Apperson 572–3.

S347 To sink in one's own **Sin**
1546 Heywood *D* 39.150: Thou shalte sure sinke in thine own syn for us, **1555** *E* 189.240: He shall synke in his owne sinne, ye when he synkth, But he fleeeth in his owne sin yet me thinkth. Apperson 574; Tilley S468.

S348 When one bids you, it is no **Sin** to drink
c1470 *Harley MS.3362* f.3a in *Retrospective* 309[21]: Whan me byddyth the, yt ys no synne to drynke. See **M640, W499.**

S349 Let him that **Sings** worst begin first
1492 *Salomon and Marcolphus* 5[26–7]: He that singyth worst begynne furste.

S350 To **Sing** ill-a-hale
a1460 *Towneley Plays* 240.375: I may syng yllahayll. See **S469.**

S351 For one **Sinner** a hundred shall perish
a1500 *Partenay* 129.3685–6: Ye know what men sain moste, lo! comynly, For A synner perish shall An hundred, lo! See **A167.**

S352 Who dreads (neither) **Sire** nor dame shall aby (*pay for*) it
a1400 *Romaunt C* 5887–8: For who that dredith sire ne dame, Shal it abye in body or name. See **F78.**

S353 Three **Sisters**
a1405 Lydgate *Complaint* in *MP* II 402.487–8: Er I was borne, my destanye was sponne By Parcas sustren. **c1449** Pecock *Repressor* II 155[28–30]: This opinioun, that iii. sistris (whiche ben spiritis) comen to the cradilis of infantis, forto sette to the babe what schal bifalle to him. **c1475** Henryson *Orpheus* 145.505: Scho send hym doun unto the sistiris thre. *Oxford* 654; Tilley S490.

S354 To play "**Sister** me needs"
c1450 Capgrave *Lives* 31.12–5: The Manicheis held her skoles be nyth, and thedir cam both men and women, and all sodeynly aftir the lesson, the lith schuld be blow out and than schuld thei pley, as Wiclif disciples played, Sistir me nedith.

S355 Better **Sit** still than rise and fall (*varied*)
a1460 *Towneley Plays* 229.28: It is better syt still then rise up and fall. **a1500** *MS. Marginalia* in Hoccleve I 228 n. 9: Better hyt hys, seeten to abyde, Then hastly to clym, and hastly to clyde (glyde). **1546** Heywood *D* 73.102: Better syt styll than ryse and fall, **1555** *E* 183.204, **1556** *Spider* 385[2]: Wise flies saie: as good sit still: as rise and fall. Apperson 574; *Oxford* 41; Tilley S491. See **C296.**

S356 He that **Sits** well let him not move
1471 Caxton *Recuyell* II 516.8–9: The proverbe that sayth that he that sytteth well late hym not meve. Cf. Whiting *Scots* II 125–6. See **S297.**

S357 Who **Sits** highest is soonest overthrown (*varied*)
a1439 Lydgate *Fall* I 60.2163: For who sit hiest is sonest overthrowe, 94.3438–9: For who sit hiest, stant in jupartie, Undir daunger off Fortune lik to fall, 172.6089–90: For whan ye wene sitte hiest atte fulle, Than will she rathest your briht(e) fethres pulle, 283.2947: Whan ye sit hiest, your fal is most to dreede, **a1449** *Mydsomer Rose* in *MP* II 782.47: Who sittith hihest moost like to falle soone. *Oxford* 295; Whiting *Scots* I 188–9. See **R191.**

S358 To play **Sitisot** (*a game*)
c1300 *St. Alexius* 182.366: Som plaied with him sitti-sotte. **a1325** *Cursor* II 948 CG 16623: And wit him thai plaid sitisott (F: abobet, T: a bobet). MED abobbed.

S359 To set (cast) (all) at **Six** and seven (*varied*)
c1385 Chaucer *TC* iv 622: But manly sette the world on six and sevene. **a1400** *Morte Arthure* 63.2131: Thus he settez on seven with his sekyre knyghttez. **c1440** *Degrevant* 84.1294–6: Had my horse gane evyne, I sold haf sett alle on sevene Ffor Myldor the swete. **a1450** *Whan that phebus* in Sandison 124.27–8: Than sayth the worlde, "Set all at syxe and seven, Folowe thy lust and plesure." **a1460** *Towneley Plays* 101.38: By my wytt to fynde to cast the warld in seven, 169.128: I shall, and that in hy, set all on sex and seven. **c1475** *Golagros* 18.508–9: For thair is segis in yone sail wil set upone sevin, Or thay be wrangit, 23.668: With seymely scheildis to schew, thai set upone sevin. **c1495** *Arundel Vulgaria* 18.70: But settes all at sixe and sevyn. **1546** Heywood *D* 48.239–40: And sure I shall

Set all at sixe and seven, **1555** *E* 174.160. Apperson 575; *Oxford* 594; Taylor and Whiting 336; Tilley A208; Whiting *Scots* II 123, 126.

S360 Where one bids (*offers*) **Skill,** one ought to take skill
a1338 Mannyng *Chronicle B* I 184[19–20]: Ther men bedis skille, skille men ouh to take. Tho that wille not that tille, skille salle tham forsake. See **W275.**

S361 It is good to sleep in a whole **Skin**
c1475 Henryson *Fables* 38.1029–30: Me think it better To sleip in haill nor in ane hurt skyn. **1546** Heywood *D* 73.112: It is good slepyng in a whole skyn. Apperson 682–3; Jente 681; *Oxford* 596; Tilley S530; Whiting *Scots* II 126.

S362 To be but **Skin** and bone
c1450 *How mankinde dooth* in Furnivall *Hymns* 73.492: Me is lefte But skyn and boon. NED Skin 5b; *Oxford* 595.

S363 To be (fly) out of one's **Skin**
c1300 *South English Legendary* (*Laud*) 18.588: So sore werth the giu a-drad: that he werth neigh out of is felle. **a1425** *Chester Plays* I 165.135–6: He wold goe wood, by my faye, And fly out of his skin. Taylor and Whiting 337; Tilley S507: leap.

S364 To turn in one's **Skin**
c1422 Hoccleve *Complaint* 106.302–3: This troubly lyfe hathe all to longe enduryd, Not have I wyst how in my skynne to turne.

S365 When one looks on the outer **Skin** he knows little what is within
1509 Barclay *Ship* II 40[25–6]: For whan thou lokest upon the utter skyn Thou knowyst ful lytell what trust is within. See **A155.**

S366 Not worth three **Skips** of a pie (*magpie*)
1513 Skelton *Against the Scottes* I 185.100: Not worth thre skyppes of a pye. Tilley S512.

S367 To sit on one's **Skirts**
1546 Heywood *D* 27.32–3: And syt on theyr skurtes That erst sate on mine. Apperson 575; *Oxford* 593; Tilley S513.

S368 As bright as the **Sky**
1447 Bokenham 259.9543: And wyth myraclys bryhter than the skye. Svartengren 227.

S369 To pass like a **Sky** (*cloud*)
a1393 Gower *CA* II 340.1436–7: Sche passeth, as it were a Sky, Al clene out of this ladi sihte.

S370 It may be a **Slander** but it is no lie
1546 Heywood *D* 86.208: It maie be a sclaunder, but it is no lie. Apperson 577; *Oxford* 595; Tilley S520.

S371 **Slander** is no vassalage (*noble act*)
a1430 Lydgate *Pilgrimage* 291.10605–6: Record off ffolkys that be sage, "Sclaundere ys no vasselage."

S372 A **Slander** that is raised is evil to fell
c1350 *Good Wife E* 158.22: A sclandre that is reised is evil to stille. Apperson 577.

S373 He that **Slays** shall be slain (*varied*)
a1393 Gower *CA* II 292.2461–3: Thus was he slain that whilom slowh, And he which riche was ynowh This dai, tomorwe he hadde noght. **c1412** Hoccleve *Regement* 112.3115: Who-so that sleth, schal have the same chaunce. **a1500** *Eger H* 305.2004: Sir, he that slayes, he will be slain. **a1500** *Northern Passion* 57 H 568: Ffor he that slase he sall be slane. Tilley S525; Whiting *Scots* II 126. See **S405, 978.**

S374 Who that **Slays** (when) angry ought to be hanged when patient
1509 Barclay *Ship* I 185[13–4]: For who that one sleyth, angry and fervent Ought to be hangyd whan he is pacyent. Cf. Tilley M175. See **M103, S694.**

S375 Morning **Sleep** is golden
a1449 Lydgate *Dietary* in *MP* II 702.23–4: The morwe sleep, callid gyldene in sentence, Gretly helpith ayeen the mystis blake, 705.91: The golden sleep braidyng upon pryme. **c1450** Idley 173.911–2: And telleth hym that is the golden slepe: "And if thow arise now, it might do the harme."

S376 **Sleep** is most like to death (*varied*)
a900 *Salomon and Saturn* in *ASMP* 42.313: Slæp bið deaðe gelicost. **1481** *Tulle of Olde Age* 89[16–7]: Ther is nothyng so like the deth as is the slepe. **1519** Horman *Vulgaria* 48[18]: Slepe is a counterfette dethe. **1522** More *Treatyce* 80 F[10–2]: Among al wise men of old, it is agreed that slepe is the very ymage of death. *Oxford* 596; Smith 271; Tilley S526.

S377 **Sleep** is the nourice (*nurse*) of digestion
c1395 Chaucer *CT* V[F] 347: The norice of digestioun, the sleep. **a1449** Lydgate and Burgh *Secrees* 40.1261: Sleep is noryce of digestioun, 60.1892.

S378 A broken **Sleeve** holds the arm back (*varied*)
c1470 *Harley MS.3362* f.2b in *Retrospective* 309[15]: For my slefe y-broke . . . Pro manica fracta manus est mea sepe retracta. **a1500** Hill

132.51: For my brokyn sleve, men me refuce. Pro manica fracta, manus est mea sepe retracta. **1549** Heywood *D* 33.24: A broken sleeve holdth tharme backe. Apperson 69; *Oxford* 66; Tilley S531.

S379 To be dear of (*expensive at*) a riven (*torn*) **Sleeve**
1513 Douglas *Aeneid* III 1.24: Or cal on Sibil, deir of a revyn sleif. See **H453.**

S380 To hang on one's **Sleeve**
1546 Heywood *D* 70.29–30 (*var.*): Flattryng knaves and queans a sort, beyond the mark, Hang on his sleve. NED Sleeve 2c; Tilley S533.

S381 To have on (in) one's **Sleeve**
c1440 Charles of Orleans 133.3983–4: Madame y wold bi god alone How that myn hert were in yowre sleve, 146.4344–5: Which is the craft to make a keverkope To holde a two or thre so on his sleve. **c1522** Skelton *Speke* II 21.423: He careyth a kyng in hys sleve, yf all the worlde fayle. Tilley S534.

S382 To laugh in one's **Sleeve**
1546 Heywood *D* 75.168: To that I saide nought but laught in my sleeve. *Oxford* 352; Taylor and Whiting 338–9; Tilley S535; Whiting *Drama* 352:670, 364:856.

S383 To stuff one's **Sleeve** with flocks (*tufts of wool*) (*i.e.*, deceive)
1481 Caxton *Reynard* 56[27]: How can he stuffe the sleve wyth flockes.

S384 **Sleeveless** words (*varied*)
c1385 Usk 76.77: Not by slevelesse wordes of the people. **c1450** *Jacob's Well* 181.15–6: Summe in schryfte schal tarye the preest wyth sleveles talys. **a1500** *Burlesques* in *Rel. Ant.* I 83[43–4]: Y schall telle yow a sleveles reson. **1533** More *Confutacion* 790 H[15]: A very slevelesse aunswere. **1546** Heywood *D* 30.54: A sleeveles errande. Apperson 578; NED Sleeveless 2; *Oxford* 597; Tilley E180.

S385 As black as (any) **Sloe**
c1390 Chaucer *CT* I[A] 3246: And tho were bent and blake as any sloo. **a1400** ?Chaucer *Rom.* A 928: And blak as . . . ony slo. **a1400** *Torrent* 17.458: Ys fytte blac ase slon. **a1475** Greene *Carols* 136 A 5: Ivy hath berys as blake as any slo, B 2. **c1475** *Guy*[1] 31 C 506: Guy they fonde as blak as sloo. Apperson 51; Tilley S539; Whiting *Ballad* 31.

S386 Not a **Sloe**
c1300 *Havelok* 31.849: Of me, ne is me nouht a slo.

S387 Not avail a **Sloe**
c1475 *Guy*[1] 81 C 1414: That all his armes availled him not a sloo, 171 C 2936, 211 C 3638.

S388 Not give a **Sloe**
c1300 *Amis* 17.395: Sir, ther-of yive y nought a slo. **c1300** *Havelok* 68.2051. **c1330** *St. Katherine* 257.620. **a1500** *Orfeo* 30 H 328.

S389 Not (the) worth (of) a **Sloe**
c1250 *Prayer of Penitence* in Brown *Lyrics XIII* 56.18: This worldis blis nis wrd a slo, 58.28, 59.15. **a1300** *Arthour and M.*[1] 210.7498: Thou nart no god worth a slo. **a1300** *XI Pains* 154.274. **c1300** *Guy*[1] 10.141: That bireft him worth of a slo, 80 A 1414, 170 A 2936, 210 A 3638, 289 A 5076. **a1375** *Octavian* (S) 31.975. **c1380** *Ferumbras* 135.4338. **c1410** Lovelich *Merlin* I 75.2786: And no man to harmen the worth of a slo. **a1450** *South English Legendary* (*Bodley*) 415.26: Namore than we dredeth the the worth of a slo. Apperson 458.

S390 **Sloth** and delay oft cause much scathe (*harm*)
a1500 Bernardus *De Cura* 3.47–8: For it is sene and saide in sampylle batht, Slewthe and delay oft causis mekyll skatht. See **D157.**

S391 **Sloth** breeds a scab
1546 Heywood *D* 23.39: Sens we see slouth must breede a scab. Apperson 579; *Oxford* 597; Tilley S541.

S392 **Sloth** is the mother of vice (*varied*)
a1393 Gower *CA* II 392.3380–2: For Slowthe, which as Moder is The forthdrawere and the Norrice To man of many a dredful vice. **a1430** Lydgate *Pilgrimage* 280.10189–90: Tavoyde slouthe, cheff noryce And moder un-to every vyce, **a1449** *Fabules* in *MP* II 571.138: So of myschyef slouth ys chief maistresse, *Vertu* in *MP* II 838.83–4: Slouthe of vices is cheef porteresse, And a step-moodir to wysdam and science. **1478** Paston V 314[6–7]: For slouth ys the moder and norysher of all vices. **1506** Hawes *Pastime* 48.1147: Fy upon slouth the nouryssher of vyce. **1509** Barclay *Ship* II 185[6–7]: That damnable slouth is so corrupt a vyce That of his foule rote all yllys doth aryse. See **I6, O14.**

S393 When the **Slow** (*sluggard*) is full then the chare (*work*) is done
c1450 *Douce MS.52* 52.95: When the slowe is full, then the chare is done. Cum piger impletur, operis tunc finis habetur. **c1450** *Rylands MS.394* 103.28: Whan the slow is full, then ben his charres done. Walther I 517.4316.

S394 Often a **Sluggard** delays, *etc.*
757-786 *Proverb from Winfrid's Time* in *ASMP* 57: Oft dædlata dome foreldit, Sigistha gahuem, suuyltit thi ana. Notes (177): "Often a sluggard delays in his (pursuit of) glory, in each of victorious undertakings; therefore he dies alone."

S395 Always the nigh **Sly** makes the far lief (to be) loath (*varied*)
c1390 Chaucer *CT* I[A] 3391-3: Ful sooth is this proverbe, it is no lye, Men seyn right thus, "Alwey the nye slye Maketh the ferre leeve to be looth." **a1393** Gower *CA* II 277.1899-902: An old sawe is, "Who that is slyh In place where he mai be nyh, He makth the ferre Lieve loth": Of love and thus fulofte it goth. Apperson 438, 476; Skeat 226.

S396 He does **Small** (*little*) that boasts over greatly
c1458 *Knyghthode and Bataile* 59.1620-1: Avaunte not for colde nor for hete, For smale dooth that speketh over grete. See **B417, P409, 414.**

S397 Many **Small** make a great (*varied*)
c1303 Mannyng *Handlyng* 84.2366: For many smale maketh a grete. **c1390** Chaucer *CT* X[I] 362: For the proverbe seith that "manye smale maken a greet." **1465** Paston IV 135[27]: Many smale growe to a gret summe. **a1500** *Thre Prestis* 14.187-8: Quhill at the last of mony smallis couth mak This bony pedder a gud fut pak. **1546** Heywood *D* 47.194: Many small make a great, **1555** *E* 188.234. *Oxford* 406; Tilley S554.

S398 As bright as **Smaragd** (*emerald*)
a1500 *Court of Love* 430.788-9: And eke her yen ben bright and orient As is the smaragde.

S399 After stormy **Smarts** warm words bring lovers warm hearts
1534 Heywood *Love* B4v[34-5]: Swete harte, quoth I, after stormy colde smertes Warm wordes in warm lovers bryng lovers warm hartes. See **V9, W697.**

S400 Think not on **Smart** and you shall feel none
c1385 Chaucer *TC* iv 466: Thynk nat on smert, and thow shalt fele non.

S401 To **Smell** one out
1546 Heywood *D* 49.259: I smelde hir out, and had hir streight in the wynde, **1555** *E* 197.296. Tilley S558.

S402 **Smell-feasts** come uncalled
1519 Horman *Vulgaria* 120[8]: Smelle fyestes, lycke dysshes and franchars come uncalled.

S403 Better the last **Smile** than the first laughter
1549 Heywood *D* 95.148: Better is the last smyle, than the fyrst laughter. Apperson 43; *Oxford* 42; Tilley S560.

S404 One may **Smile** and hold him (*keep*) still and think guile
a1338 Mannyng *Chronicle B* I 185[13-4]: Philip held him stille, and bigan to smyle, Men sais that comes of ille, and thinkyng som gile. Cf. Shakespeare *Hamlet* I v 108. See **W535.**

S405 He that **Smites** shall be smitten
1483 *Quatuor Sermones* 10[24]: For he that smyteth shal be smyten. See **S373, 978.**

S406 **Smite** not too soon
c1390 Chaucer *CT* IX[H] 285: Smyt nat to soone, er that ye witen why. See **J77.**

S407 A hagher (*skillful*) **Smith** oft smiths a weak knife
a1200 *Ancrene* 31.2: Ofte a ful haher smith smeotheth a ful wac cnif. Apperson 581:1; *Oxford* 599.

S408 To beat as the **Smith** does with the hammer
c1300 *Havelok* 62.1876-7: And beten on him so doth the smith With the hamer on the stith.

S409 To lay on as the **Smith** does on the iron
a1300 *Arthour and M.*[1] 211.7519-20: Everich on other leyd with, So on the yren doth the smith.

S410 To try as the **Smith** does iron in the fire
c1475 *Mankind* 11.280-1: Lyke as the smyth trieth ern in the feer, So was he (*Job*) triede by Godis vysytacyon. See **F180, G298, M522, S327.**

S411 As unprofitable as **Smoke** for a man's eyes
1509 Barclay *Ship* II 185[22-3]: A slouthfull creature is as unprofytable As smoke or dust, is for a mannys iyen.

S412 The **Smoke** steres (*flavors*) the roast
a1500 Hill 131.26: I say with-owt boste that the smoke stereth the roste. Dico sine pompa, quod fumes violat ossa.

S413 To raise a **Smoke**
c1425 Hoccleve *Jonathas* 217.57-9: Sholde y a neewe smoke now up reyse, And y so mochil rered have or now By your sawe than were y nat to preise. **c1458** *Knyghthode and Bataile* 67.1837-8: And first with shot (*arrows*) provoke The adverse part, and on hem reyse a smoke. **c1499** Skelton *Bowge* I 48.479: But I am lothe

to reyse a smoke. **a1500** *How the Wyse Man* 32.119–20: For wemen in wrath they can noght hyde, But soone they can reyse a smoke (*var.* smokei rofe). See **R76.**

S414 To vanish like **Smoke** (*varied*)
897 Alfred *Boethius* 63.26–7: Hi losiað swa swa . . . smec, 117.17–8: Se yfla willa bið tostenced swaþær rec beforan fyre. **a900** *Old English Martyrology* 22.11–2: þonne glad þæt deofol ut . . . swa swa smyc, 180.7–8. **c900** *Paris Psalter* 86 (36.19): Beoð gedwæscte, swa ðer smec, 21 (67.2): Rece hi gelicast ricene geteoriað, 72 (101.3): Forðon dages mine gedroren syndan Smece gelice. **c1000** Aelfric *Lives* II 268.770: Se deofol þær-rihte for-dwan swa swa smic. **c1000** *Das angelsächsische Prosa-leben des hl. Guthlac,* ed. Paul Gonser, Anglistische Forschungen 27 (Heidelberg, 1909) 126.79–81: Se awyrigeda gast efne swa smic (*var.* rec) beforan his ansyne aidlode, 135.279–80, 137.20. **c1000** *Regius Psalter* 65 (36.20): Swa swa smic he geteorað, 118 (67.3). **c1100** *Salisbury Psalter* 125 (36.20): Swa smic aterat, 163 (67.3). **c1350** *Prose Psalter* 43 (36.21): Hii shul fail failand as smoke, 77 (67.2): Defailen hii, as smoke faileth, 121 (101.4). **c1395** *WBible* Psalms lxvii 3: As smoke falith, faile thei. **a1400** *Meditations* 58.2203: We vanyschon a(s) smoke a-way. **a1400** *Seven Penitential Psalms* in *Wheatley MS.* 43.569–70. **a1400** Wyclif *Sermons* II 365[8–9]. **c1400** *Primer* 41[5]: My daies han failid as smoke. **1414** ?Brampton *Psalms* 29[23–4]. **a1425** *St. Anthony* 121.30–1, 122.15: Alle hys enemys fle thai away as smoke. **c1450** *Lambeth Prose Legends* 343.25–6. **1479** Rivers *Cordyal* 35.16–7: Our yeres fayle and waste as the smoke, 67.6. **1484** Caxton *Royal Book* G2^r^[3–4]: Departed and faylled as . . . smoke, G7^v^[9–10], **1487** *Book of Good Manners* A8^r^[31–2]. **1496** *Myracles of our Lady* (London, de Worde, 1514) C5^r^[30–1]: Vanysshed awaye as a smoke dooth. **a1500** *Craft of Dying* in *Yorkshire Writers* II 420[24]: Faile thei as the smoke fayleth. **a1500** *Imitation* (*1*) 80.30–1: faile. **1502** *Imitatione* (2) 156.21, 157. 11–2, 208.14–6. **1509** Fisher *Treatyse* 146.1: wasted. Whiting *Drama* 326:294. See **F699, R77.**

S415 As slow as a **Snail**
c1440 *Prose Alexander* 74.35–75.1: Bot in his gangyng he was als slaw als a snyle. Taylor *Comparisons* 74; Tilley S579; Whiting *Scots* II 126.

S416 As swiftly as a **Snail**
a1500 *Ragman Roll* 71.49: To chirche as swyftly as a snayl ye hey. Cf. Whiting *Scots* II 126.

S417 As wrinkled as a **Snail** (*etc.*) (A number of single quotations are brought together here)
a1420 Lydgate *Troy* I 239.3313: Wrinkled double, like an hornyd snail. **a1450** *York Plays* 353.117–8: Nowe certis that schall I doo, Full suerly as a snayle. **1501** Douglas *Palice* 28.12: And in the deid als schairp as ony snaillis. **1533** Heywood *Johan* B1^v^[41]: Go and hye the as fast as a snayle.

S418 Not worth a **Snail**
c1400 *Laud Troy* I 202.6856–7: We are not worth a scnayle A-yeyn that man.

S419 To be afraid of a **Snail** (*varied*)
1340 *Ayenbite* 32[8–10]: Tho anlikneth than thet ne dar naght guo ine the pethe vor thane snegge thet sseaweth him his hornes. **c1400** *Vices and Virtues* 27.28–30: Thei beth like to hym that dar nought gon in the weye for the snayl that scheweth his hornes. **c1450** *Jacob's Well* 107.2–3: Thou faryst as he that dar noght entryn the cherch-yerd for the snayl that puttyth his horn oute ayens hym. **1484** Caxton *Royal Book* D5^v^[7–8]: They resemble hym that dare not entre in to the path or waye for fere of the snaylle that sheweth his hornes. Cf. *Thersites* (c1537) in F. J. Child *Four Old Plays* (Cambridge, Mass., 1848) 67–70.

S420 To drive a **Snail**
c1522 Skelton *Colyn* I 311.1–4: What can it avayle To dryve forth a snayle, Or to make a sayle Of an herynges tayle. **c1525** ?Heywood *Gentylnes* 123.992–3: In effect it shall no more avayle Than with a whyp to dryfe a snayle. Cf. *Oxford* 158: Drive a snail; Tilley S582.

S421 To hie like a **Snail**
1546 Heywood *D* 34.36: And thytherward hye me in haste lyke a snayle. *Oxford* 281; Tilley S583.

S422 To reel over and over like a **Snail**
c1400 *Laud Troy* I 199.6742–3: He smot Paris, that he doun reled Over and over, as were a snayl.

S423 To shrink like a **Snail**
a1475 *Ludus Coventriae* 198.148: Ffor If I went thus A-way and shrynkyd as a snayle.

S424 To sny (*move,* run) a **Snail's** pace
a1400 *Alexander C* 226.4095: Than snyghes thar, out of that snyth hill as with a snayles pas. **1555** Heywood *E* 187.226.2: Runnyng but a snayle pace. *Oxford* 600; Taylor and Whiting 340–1; Tilley S583.

S425 To start up like a **Snail**

a1450 *Tottenham* 996.177: He styrt up as a snayle.

S426 One **Snare** may take two birds
1532 Berners *Golden Boke* 169.1696–7: The proverbe sayth: One snare maye take two byrdes. Cf. Taylor and Whiting 29:21.

S427 To fall (be taken) in one's own **Snare** (grin [*snare*], net, panter [*net*], girn [*snare*], trap) (*varied*)
c900 *Paris Psalter* 16 (9.14): Heora fet synt gefangene mid þy ilcan gryne, þe hi me gehyd and gehealden hæfdon. **c1000** *Regius Psalter* 13 (9.16): On gryne þissum þe hy digledon gegripen is fot heora. **c1100** *Salisbury Psalter* 85 (9.16). **c1340** Rolle *Psalter* 123 (34.9): And in snare fall he in it, that is, in that ilk that he hid til me. **c1350** *Prose Psalter* 9 (9.16): In the gnares that the folk hid, is her fote taken. **c1390** *Psalterium b. Mariae* 71.501–2: Thei maden panters for othur men And fullen in to the same. **a1393** Gower *CA* III 21.2707–8: Thus he, whom gold hath overset, Was trapped in his oghne net. **c1395** *WBible* Psalms ix 16: In this snare, which thei hidden, the foot of hem is kaught. **a1400** *Northern Verse Psalter* I 23 (9.16): In this snare whilke thai hid swa Gripen es the fote of tha. **a1400** *Scottish Legends* I 391.619–20: And (sa) the traytoure, I of tel, In-to the gyrne he mad, syne fel. **c1400** *Beryn* 116.3893–4: Tyl he had us caught, even by the shyn, With his sotill wittis, in our owne gren. **1438** *Barlam and Josaphat* (*Northern*) 238.1007–9: Than nachore understode wele thare That he was takin in his awin snare, And fallen he was in his owin pit. **c1440** Scrope *Epistle to Othea* 86[24–7]: Hermes seith . . . "strech no snaris for to take men wythall . . . for at the last it will turne opon thiself." **c1450** *Epistle of Othea* 115.14: Ffor by that was sche take in hyr own snare. **a1471** *English Chronicle* 78[24–5]: But at seynt Albonys he fylle in to the same snare that he had ordeyned for theyme. **1481** Caxton *Reynard* 86[9–10]: The horse brought hym self in thraldom and was taken in his owne nette, **1483** *Golden Legende* 396r[1.5–6]: He was taken in hys owne snare. **1509** Barclay *Ship* II 40[7]: And some in theyr owne snarys ar taken fast. **1533** More *Answer* 1106 D (*by error* C) [11–2]: I am taken in mine own trap, 1108 A[8–9], 1109 D[13–4], E[6–7], F[1–2], G[4–5], 1115 A[6], *Confutacion* 568 D[10–1]: So caughte in a nette of hys owne makynge. Taylor and Whiting 381. See **G169, P232.**

S428 When you see others taken in the **Snare** beware
1509 Barclay *Ship* I 202[27–8]: Be ware, whan ye other se taken in the snare Let anothers peryll cause you to be ware. See **C161, W47.**

S429 Maugre one's **Snout**
a1338 Mannyng *Chronicle A* I 417.11935: And reve hym his regne, maugre his snoute.

S430 As blaght (*bleached, white*) as any **Snow**
a1400 *Alexander C* 84.1559–60: As blaght ere thaire wedis As any snyppand snawe that in the snape lightis, 252.4925: And as blaght was his berd as any bright snaw.

S431 As bright as **Snow**
970 *Blickling Homilies* 147[16–7]: And heo hæfde seofon siþum beorhtran saule þonne snaw. **c1300** *Beves* 24.521–2: So faire she was and bright of mod, Ase snow upon the rede blod. **1414** ?Brampton *Psalms* 24[1–2]: As snow, that fallyth in fyldes grene, Is . . . bryght.

S431a **Snow-bright**
a1500 *Childhood of Christ* in Horstmann *Altenglische Legenden 1875* 5.93: The sonne wax hot and snoughh brighht.

S432 As cold as (any) **Snow**
c1300 *South English Legendary* I 98.382: And caldore was thanne eny is other snou. **c1330** *Owayne Miles* in Horstmann *Altenglische Legenden 1875* 165.378: And caldore was then eny . . . snough. **c1390** *Gregorius* 140.1072: With herte cold as eny (C: the) snowe. **a1500** *Ghostly Battle* in *Yorkshire Writers* II 432[20–1]: any. Svartengren 315.

S433 As fordone (*destroyed*) as **Snow** in fire
c1385 Chaucer *TC* i 525: And thow fordon, as snow in fire is soone.

S434 As shire (*bright*) as **Snow**
a1400 *Cursor* II 996 FT 17371: That clothid was as snow shir.

S435 As thick as (the, any) **Snow**
a1200 Lawman III 94.27458–9: Flan al swa thicke Swa the snau adun valleth. **a1300** *Richard* 244.2969–70 (*var.*): He gaderede his folk togedere, As thykke as snowe falleth in wynter. **a1338** Mannyng *Chronicle A* II 470.13550–1: So thykke atones gon they fleye—Also thikke as snow (that) snew. **a1352** Minot 16.49: It semid with thaire schoting als it war snaw. **c1380** *Cleanness* 11.222: the. **c1400** *Alexander Buik* I 52.1648–9. **c1500** *Lady Bessy* 40[26–7]. **c1500** *Melusine* 230.31–2: Thenne bygan the shotte to be grete and thikk as snowe in the ayer. **1513** Douglas *Aeneid* IV 46.34–5: The dartis thik and fleand takyllys glydis, As doith the

schour of snaw. **1523** Berners *Froissart* I 298 [12–3], **1525** VI 221[16–7], **a1533** *Huon* 339.26–7: They . . . shot arrowes so thycke that it semed lyke snow, 389.13–5, 474.27–8, 664.19–21, 714.11–2. Svartengren 398; Whiting *Scots* II 127.

S436 As white as any driven **Snow**
c1300 *Guy*[1] 416 A 45.10–1: With white-hore heved and berd y-blowe, As white as ani driven snowe. **c1425** *Myrour of lewed men* 418.382: Ay is blaunched als whit as any dryven snawe. Taylor and Whiting 342; Tilley S591; Whiting *Ballad* 31.

S437 As white as (any, the) **Snow**
a900 *Old English Martyrology* 16.24–5: Paules sawle swa hwite swa snaw, 96.10–1, 120.27, 196.21–2. **c900** *Paris Psalter* 127 (50.8). **c970** *Blickling Homilies* 147[26–7]: Seo eadige Marie hæfde swa hwite saule swa snaw. **a1000** *Two Apocrypha* H 38–40. **c1000** Aelfric *Heptateuch* Numbers xii 10, *Homilies* I 222[31], *Lives* II 218.460–1: Heora lichaman wæron hwittran þonne snaw. **c1000** *Regius Psalter* 93 (50.9): Ofer snaw ic beo ablicen. **c1000** *WSG* Matthew xvii 2: And hys reaf wæron swa hwite swa snaw, xxviii 3, Mark ix 3. **c1100** *Salisbury Psalter* 147 (50.9). **c1200** *Vices and Virtues* (*Stowe*) 83.4: Hwittere thane ani snaw. **c1280** *Southern Passion* 66.1798. **a1300** *Richard* 106.555, 245.2995–6: the, 255.3212 (*var.*): Hys teeth whyte as snawe. **c1300** *Northern Homily Cycle* (*Edin. Coll. Phys.*) 143[4]. **c1300** *South English Legendary* I 285.189; eny, 287.253: eni, 301.293: eni, 318.82, II 592.64. **a1325** *Cursor* II 986 110°–1°, 1060. 18498. **c1330** *Horn Childe* 191.1048. **1340** *Ayenbite* 267[31]: the. **c1350** *Apocalypse* 7.14. **c1350** *Prose Psalter* 61 (50.8). **c1350** *Smaller Vernon Collection* 16.537. **a1387** Higden-Trevisa I 225[14–5]: eny, 261[6–7]: any. **c1390** *Northern Homily Cycle Narrationes* (*Vernon*) 301.111: eny. **c1390** *Psalm LI* in *Vernon* I 13.58: the. **c1395** *WBible* Numbers xii 10: Marie apperide whijt with lepre as snow, Psalms lxvii 15, Isaiah i 18, Lamentations iv 7, Daniel vii 9, Matthew xvii 2, Mark ix 2, Apocalypse i 14. **a1400** Bonaventura *Privity* in *Yorkshire Writers* I 213[34–5]: any, 218[22–3]: the. **a1400** ?Chaucer *Rom.* A 557–8: Hir throte, also whit of hewe As snowe on braunche snowed newe, 1214: But whit as snow yfallen newe. **a1400** Chestre *Launfal* 60.241: Har faces wer whyt as snow on downe, 61.292–3: Sche was as whyt as . . . snow that sneweth yn wynterys day. **a1400** *Cleansing* 11.12 (f.7^{v}), 61.9, 16 (f.39^{r}): the. **a1400** *Destruction of Troy* 99.3027–8: Hir forhed . . . Quitter to qweme then the white snaw. **a1400** *Ipomadon A* 90. 3095: any, 3103. **a1400** *Meditations* 23.841. **a1400** *Northern Verse Psalter* 163 (50.9). **a1400** *Scottish Legends* I 191.37, 419.590, II 149.886, 248.883: ony, 355.331: ony, 371.108. **a1400** *Seven Penitential Psalms* in *Wheatley MS.* 38.442: the. **a1400** Wyclif *Sermons* I 132[24], 267[14], II 58[3–4]: the. **c1400** *Beryn* 108.3613: eny. **c1400** *Brut* I 243.3, 9. **c1400** Mandeville *Travels* 139.28. **c1400** *Pepysian Gospel* 57.21–2: the, 102.10–1. **c1400** *Toulouse* 228.199. **c1400** *Tundale* 100.1748. **c1408** Lydgate *Reson* 142. 5423: any. **c1410** Lovelich *Grail* II 318.337, 365.460–1: ony, 371.131–2: ony, *Merlin* II 412. 15399–400: There nas nevere snow, that snew on grownde, Whittere thanne hire flesch. **1414** ?Brampton *Psalms* 24[1–2]. **a1415** Mirk *Festial* 132.2–3, 260.10. **a1420** Lydgate *Troy* III 683. 4075–7: That verrayly ther was no . . . snowe that flaketh fro Jubiteris tour Of whitnes fressher on to sene, **a1422** *Life* 436.105–6: And his clothyng like the lely floure Was whit in sothe, as snowe that fallith newe. **a1425** *St. Anthony* 126.43, 128.36. **a1425** *St. Robert* 74.1068: any. **c1425** *St. Mary Oignies* 156.16. **1430** Lydgate *Pilgrimage* 19.696, 519.19475, 579.21725: any, **c1433** *St. Edmund* 430.961–2. **1435** Misyn *Fire* 75.18–9. **a1437** *Kingis Quair* 64.67[3]: ony. **a1439** Lydgate *Fall* III 732.2142, **1439** *St. Albon* 136.536, 182.1188. **c1440** *Prose Alexander* 104. 27–8: any. **1447** Bokenham 64.2326–7, 120. 4393–4, 126.4620–2. **a1449** Lydgate *St. Gyle* in *MP* I 164.91. **a1450** *Legends of Mary* in *Anglia* 3(1880) 323.29. **a1450** *Lord that is* 214.135. **a1450** *York Plays* 188.97, 377.89. **c1450** *De Claris Mulieribus* 47.951. **c1450** *Edward the Confessor Prose I* 101[36]. **c1450** *Epistle of Othea* 78.21. **c1450** *Merlin* II 227[17], 575[8], 615[15–6]. **1456** Hay *Knychthede* 7.4: the, *Law* 284.5–6. **a1460** *Towneley Plays* 295.81. **a1470** Malory I 308.26: ony, II 877.24–5: ony, 990.18, 30–1: ony. **a1470** Parker *Dives* L5^{r}[2.8–9]. **a1475** *Asneth* 233.172: the, 248.527: the, 250.567: the, 256.734: the. **a1475** *Guy*[2] 16.539–41: any. **a1475** *Landavall* 109.105–6: She was white as . . . snowe that fallith yn wynterday. **a1475** *St. Birgitta* 68.12. **c1475** Henryson *Orpheus* 132.100: the. **1481** Caxton *Mirror* 84–5. **1483** *Catholicon Anglicum* 416[2.21]. **1483** Caxton *Golden Legende* 88^{r}[2.41–2]: the, 95^{v}[2.21], 117^{v}[2.37–8]: ony, 231^{r}[2.29], 311^{v}[2.29–30], 407^{r}[2.20]. **1483** *Quatuor Sermones* 44[16], [17–8]: ony. **1485** Caxton *Charles* 191.23–4. **c1485** *Monk of Evesham* 33[25]: the, 25[22]: the, 43[32]: the. **1489** Caxton *Fayttes* 290.17. **a1490** Ripley *Mistery* in Ashmole 384[18]. **1490** Irlande *Meroure* 81.27–8:

the. **1496** Alcock *Mons* B6v[13–4]. **a1500** *Court of Love* 430.799–800. **a1500** *Gregorius* 155 R 579. **a1500** *Lambeth Prose Legends* 323.29. **a1500** *Lamwell* 523.71: *Their faces as white* as snowe or (?on) downe. **a1500** *Miroure of Mans Salvacionne* 60[31]: the, 112[21]: the. **a1500** *Partenay* 100.2801–2: Unto hir navell shewing ther full white, like As is the snow A faire branche uppon. **1501** Douglas *Palice* 52.20: ony. **c1505** Watson *Valentine* 271.6. **1509** Fisher *Treatyse* 111.17, 20. **1513** Douglas *Aeneid* II 137.63, 158.19, III 211.87, IV 81.83–4: The quhilk stedis . . . Excedit far the snaw in cullour quhite. **a1533** Berners *Huon* 184.30, 239.33–4, 326.10–1, 332.2. **1533** Heywood *Weather* A2v[3]. Apperson 681; Taylor *Comparisons* 87–8; Taylor and Whiting 342; Tilley S591; Whiting *Drama* 326:297, *Scots* II 126–7.

S437a Snow-white
a900 *Old English Martyrology* 200.12–3: Snawhwit culfre. **c1000** Aelfric *Homilies* I 400[29]: Mid snaw-hwitum hreoflan beslagen, II 134[27]: On snaw-hwitum horse, *Lives* I 48.405: Snawhwitne hlaf, 394.164, II 362.114–5. **a1200** *Ancrene* 162.3–4: Snaw hwite schrudes. **a1200** Lawman II 608.24521. **a1200** *Trinity College Homilies* 115[6]. **c1200** *St. Katherine* (*Royal*) 120.2443. **a1225** *St. Marherete* 42.14. **a1290** *Seve dawes aren* in *Archiv* 52(1874) 37[1]. **c1300** Robert of Gloucester II 855.249. **c1330** *Orfeo* 14.145. **c1350** *Proprium Sanctorum* 93.148. **c1380** Chaucer *CT* VIII[G] 254, **c1385** *TC* iii 1250 (*var.*). **a1387** Higden-Trevisa I 239[18]. **c1390** Chaucer *CT* IX[H] 133. **a1393** Gower *CA* II 248.807. **c1395** Chaucer *CT* IV[E] 388. **c1410** Lovelich *Grail* IV 242.51. **c1445** ?Lydgate *Kalendare* in *MP* I 368.136. **1447** Bokenham 104.3812. **c1450** *When the son* 393.365: Snowysshe white, 395.448. **c1500** *O lady myne* in *Anglia* 72(1954) 410.76. **1513** Douglas *Aeneid* II 148.53, 179.106, III 43.91, 107.144, 166.112, IV 9.90, 150.13. **1546** Heywood *D* 68.76: A milke snow white . . . skyn. Taylor and Whiting 342; Whiting *Scots* II 127.

S438 Farewell all the **Snow** of fern (*former*) years!
c1385 Chaucer *TC* v 1176: Ye, fare wel al the snow of ferne yere! Skeat 203; Stevenson 1857.2.

S439 A good **Snow** is worth a dunging
a1450 *Song of the Three Children* in Wyclif *SEW* III 65[29–30]: Snow helpith to tempre the erthe; for a good snow is worth a dungyng, for it holdith heete withinne the erthe. Taylor and Whiting 342.

S440 Snow is white and lies in the dike, *etc.*
1546 Heywood *D* 68.65–8: Snow is white And lyeth in the dike And every man lets it lye. Pepper is blacke and hath a good smacke And every man doth it bye. Mylke . . . is white And lieth not in the dike But all men know it good meate. Inke is all blacke And hath an ill smacke No man will it drinke or eate. Apperson 584; *Oxford* 601; Tilley S593. See **I44, P139.**

S441 Snow makes a dunghill white
a1430 Lydgate *Pilgrimage* 392.14541–2: As Snowh (who that loke wel) Maketh whyht a ffoul dongel. **c1450** *Pilgrimage LM* 121[6]: The snow embelisheth and whiteth a dong hep with oute.

S442 To be like **Snow**
c1000 *Old English Nicodemus* 484.9–10: His reaf wæron swylce snaw. **a1300** *Richard* 364–5. 5627–9: As snowgh lygges on the mountaynes Behelyd were hylles and playnes With hawberkes bryghte. **c1390** *Robert* 12.251 (*var.*): Ther was never in yerthe snowe hyt lyke. **c1395** *WBible* Matthew xxviii 3: And hise clothis as snowe. **c1445** Lydgate *Miracles of St. Edmund* 442.189: Ek whan a dowe with snowych ffetherys whight.

S443 To be no more like than **Snow** and a crow
a1400 *Meditations* 21.757–8: He sholde ne lyknesse han I-knowe More than of snow and of a crowe.

S444 To fly away like any **Snow**
a1450 *Castle* 156.2642: It flyet a-wey, as any snow.

S445 To melt with (like) (the) **Snow**
c1303 Mannyng *Handlyng* 167.5052: Hys thryfte wyl melte away with snogh. **c1385** Chaucer *TC* iv 367: Gan as the snow ayeyn the sonne melte. **a1400** Chestre *Launfal* 73.740: Hyt malt as snow ayens the sunne. **c1500** *Lover's Farewell* in Robbins 209.16: My hert will melte as snowe in reyne. **1509** Watson *Ship* K6v[11]: They melte lyke snowe. Taylor and Whiting 342–3; Whiting *Scots* II 127.

S446 To shine like (the) **Snow**
c950 *Kentish Psalm* in *ASMP* 91.75: And eac ofer snawe self scinende. **c1000** Aelfric *Homilies* II 242[7]: His gewæda scinon on snawes hwitnysse, 322[11]: Hi beoð scinende on snawesh witnysse. **c1390** *Castel of Love* 373.721–2: With-Inne, the Castel is whit schinynge So the snowgh that is sneuwynge. **c1390** *Sir Gawain* 30.955–6:

Hir brest . . . Schon schyrer then snawe that schedes on hilles.

S447 To vanish like **Snow**
1509 Barclay *Ship* I 282[21]: Theyr hope vanyssheth as doth the snowe.

S448 To wanze (*waste*) away like **Snow**
c1400 *Alle owr mischevis* in *PMLA* 54(1939) 385.16: We wansin as the snowh away.

S449 As white as **Snow Down**
a1500 *Lambewell* 147.73: They had faces as white as snowdowne.

S450 As white as the **Snow-drift**
a1325 *Cursor* II 570.9932: That quitter es than snau drif (G: snau on drift).

S451 He shall have many **Snubs** that runs to town to burn tuns and tubs
a1349 *Papelard Priest* 44.69–70: He chal han mony snybbus That hay shall renne in to the toun to borne tonnes and tibbus.

S452 Two **Snuffs** are worth a candle
1509 Watson *Ship* U8^{r}[22–3]: Saying that two snuffes is worthe a candell. (*Of people who leave church for breakfast without hearing mass.*) See Aurelius Pompen *English Versions of the Ship of Fools* (London, 1925) 122.

S453 To shine like any **Soap**
a1513 Dunbar *Of ane Blak-Moir* 66.9: Scho shynes lyk ony saep.

S454 Not worth a pair of old gray **Socks**
a1508 Dunbar *Flyting* 9.144: Quhilk wes nocht worth ane pair of auld gray sox.

S455 Or (*before*) one can turn a **Sock**
c1516 Skelton *Magnificence* 42.1346: Trymme at her tayle or a man can turne a socke.

S456 As heavy as a **Sod**
a1460 *Towneley Plays* 101.21: As hevy as a sod, I grete with myne eene.

S457 He that is set on even **Soil** (*ground*) need not be hurt with any high fall
a1400 *Destruction of Troy* 69.2078–81: Ffor he that set is full sad on a soile evyn, And pight has his place on a playn ground, Hym thar not hede to be hurt with no hegh falle, Ne be lost thurgh his lip to the low erthe. See **E24, G479.**

S458 Better **Sold** than bought
1546 Heywood *D* 38.109: Myght bost you to be better solde then bought. Tilley S221. See **B637.**

S459 As black as any **Sole**
c1350 *Libeaus* 36 *var.* 619: That on was blak as any sole. See **S258.**

S460 As wise as **Solomon**
c1303 Mannyng *Handlyng* 142.4207: Who was wyser than Salamon? 256.8093: Thogh he were wyser than Salamon. **1340** *Ayenbite* 204[13–5]. **c1390** Chaucer *CT* X[I] 955. **c1390** *Of Clene Maydenhod* 465.22. **a1400** *Pricke* 241.8955–6: And that ilk ane moght als mykelle wisdom weld, Als Salamon had, that men swa wise held. **c1400** *Vices and Virtues* 226.2. **c1410** *Mirror of Sinners* in *Yorkshire Writers* II 437[11–2]. **c1415** *Middle English Sermons* 68.4–5. **a1425** *Chester Plays* II 382.276. **a1425** *Governance of Lordschipes* 41.17: The wit of Salamon. **a1449** Lydgate *Thoroughfare* in *MP* II 824.60. **a1450** *Song of Mortality* in Brown *Lyrics XIV* 96.13: War thou als wyse praysed in pryce als was salomon. **c1450** Idley 172.834. **1456** Hay *Law* 65.8: Salamon the wys. **1479** Rivers *Cordyal* 9.25–6: Where is the wyse Salomon? **1481** Caxton *Reynard* 78[18]: They were wyser than salamon Avycene or aristotiles, **1484** *Royal Book* R3^{r}[8], **1489** *Doctrinal* I4^{v}[14], K3^{v}[15]. **a1500** Kennedy 26.16. **a1500** *Miroure of Mans Salvacionne* 145[22]. **a1500** *Salamon sat and sayde* 291.24: War a man als wytty als evyr was salamon. **1509** Barclay *Ship* I 113[3–6]: Wyse as Salomon As holy as Poule, as Job als pacyent As sad as senecke, and as obedyent As Abraham, and as martyn vertuous. **1509** Watson *Ship* B8^{v}[11], Q1^{v}[5], Gg2^{v}[9]. **c1515** Barclay *Eclogues* 106.1366: Though I had riches and wit like Salomon. Taylor and Whiting 344; Tilley S609; Whiting *Scots* II 127.

S461 Here **Some** and there some
1546 Heywood *D* 47.194: Here some and there some, **1555** *E* 189.237. *Oxford* 293; Tilley S611.

S462 **Somewhat** is better than nothing
1546 Heywood *D* 40.176: Alwaie somwhat is better then nothyng, **1555** *E* 151.29: Some thyng is better then nothyng. Apperson 587; Jente 118; *Oxford* 603; Tilley S623.

S463 The **Son** oft bears the father's guilt
1456 *Five Dogs of London* 190.46: Offte beryth the sone the faderis gylte. See **F77.**

S464 The **Son** should not deem (*judge*) the father
c1300 *South English Legendary* II 644.1040: Hit is no lawe that the sone the fader ssolde deme.

S465 For his bare (*mere*) **Song** no man is long beloved or honored
c1250 *Owl* 50.569–74: Alured sede, that was wis: (He mighte wel, for soth hit is,) "Nis no man for is bare songe Lof ne w(u)rth noght suthe longe: Vor that is a forworthe man That bute singe noght ne can."

S466 One's **Song** is (To sing) "alas (and well-away)"
c1300 *Amis* 48.1104: "Allas" may be mi song! 76.1841. **c1300** *Guy*[1] 398 A 21.11, 400 A 23.3, 408 A 34.7, 410 A 37.10–2: And ther-fore now singen y may, "Allas the time and wayleway That mi moder me bare," 420 A 49.12: Y sing "allas," 502 A 143.3, 620 A 294.3. **a1325** *Flemish Insurrection* 120.111–2: The meste part of the lond bygon forte synge "Alas" ant "weylawo!" **a1325** *Owayne Miles* (*Auchinleck*) 104.81: That "Allas!" ever song. **c1380** *Ferumbras* 158.5117: "Alas!" and "welaway!" was ys song. **c1390** Chaucer *CT* I[A] 3398: synge, VII 118–9 [B1308–9]: For I may synge "allas and weylawey That I was born." **c1390** *Keep Well* in Brown *Lyrics XIV* 150.79: Leste thou synge this songe, "allas!". **c1390** *Robert* 46.305. **c1395** Chaucer *CT* IV[E] 1274: synge. **a1400** *Lightbern* in Horstmann *Sammlung* 142.329: sing. **a1400** *Romaunt B* 4104: synge. **a1400** *Rowlande* 86.1019. **c1400** *Brut* I 73.6–7, 204.31–2, 205.6. **c1400** *Laud Troy* II 448.15228: syng. **c1400** *Sowdone* 17.581: song (vb.), 74.2574. **a1425** *Arthour and M.*[2] 281.120: Syngand allas and weylawo. **a1425** *Bird with Four Feathers* in Brown *Lyrics XIV* 210.51. **a1426** Lydgate *Mumming at Hertford* in *MP* II 675.24: He with his rebecke may sing ful oft ellas, **a1449** *Bycorne* in *MP* II 435.59: We may wel sing and seyne allas! **a1450** Audelay 21.299: syngys, 48.71: Lest thou syng the sung alasse, 191.8: songyn. **a1450** *Body and Soul* 238 R 306: synge. **a1450** *Partonope* 239.6223–4, 257.6672, 296.7503. **a1450** *Pety Job* in Kail 141.642: synge. **a1450** *Seven Sages B* 41.1173. **a1450** *York Plays* 75.128. **c1450** *Epistle of Othea* 92.17: syng. **a1460** *Towneley Plays* 68.141, 270.406. **a1475** *Landavall* 107.49. **c1485** *Burial and Resurrection* 195.720. **c1500** *Wife Lapped* 214.838: sing. Whiting *Drama* 363:841.

S467 One's **Song** is (To sing) of woe
c1300 *Guy*[1] 20 A 320: Bot ever his song is wo and wi. **a1450** *Castle* 87.328: Of woful wo, man may synge. **c1475** *Guy*[1] 20 C 320: Bot evere is songe is woo with disporte.

S468 One's **Song** is sore sighing
a1460 *Towneley Plays* 271.429: Sore syghyng is my sang.

S469 One's **Song** is (To sing) "wellaway"
c1250 *Owl* 20.220: And al thi song is wailawai. **a1300** *Alisaunder* 61.1049: She wepeth and syngeth "weilaway!" **a1300** *Doomsday* in Brown *Lyrics XIII* 43.16: singen. **a1300** *Meidan Maregrete* 489.8: singet. **a1300** *Song of Sorrow* in Brown *Lyrics XIII* 122.20. **c1300** *Amis* 43.984, 76.1852, 86.2130. **c1300** *Guy*[1] 408 A 34.11. **c1300** *St. Alexius* 178.202: singe. **c1300** *South English Legendary* II 499.197: singe. **a1325** *Cursor* II 878.15367: sing. **a1325** *Flemish Insurrection* 116.8: singeth. **c1325** *Charter of Christ C* in *Vernon* II 651.424. **a1350** *Isumbras* 11.138, 51.654 (*var.*). **c1350** *Gamelyn* 650.197: singe. **c1350** *Gregorius* 58 C 298: Hire songe was wope and weilaway. **c1350** *Tower of Heaven* in Brown *Lyrics XIV* 66.7: singge. **c1385** Chaucer *TC* iv 1166. **c1390** *Castel of Love* 405.1708. **c1395** Chaucer *CT* III[D] 216: songen. **a1400** *Child* 317.191. **a1400** *Pricke* 67.2434, 198.7363: sing. **a1400** *Seven Penitential Psalms* in *Wheatley MS.* 38.462: syng. **a1400** *Torrent* 70.2007. **c1400** *Thomas of Erceldoune* 24.399*: syng. **c1400** *Tundale* 26.462. **a1410** *Prophecy* in Minot 106.81: sing. **a1420** Lydgate *Troy* I 256.3911. **a1422** *God that all this world* 219[17]. **a1425** *Celestin* in *Anglia* 1(1877–8) 69.65. **a1425** *Chester Plays* I 78.350. **a1425** *Nicodemus* (*Additional*) 105.1314: synge. **c1425** *Brut* II 376.19–20: songyn. **a1430** Lydgate *Pilgrimage* 526.19723: synge. **1448** John Piggot's *Memoranda* in C. L. Kingsford *English Historical Literature in the Fifteenth Century* (Oxford, 1913) 370[12]: synge. **a1450** *Partonope* 18.635, 249.6497. **a1450** *Seven Sages B* 47.1367: synge. **a1450** *South English Legendary* (*Bodley*) 415.60. **a1450** Greene *Carols* 356.3. **c1450** *Weddynge* 254.484. **a1475** *Ludus Coventriae* 176.245: synge, 225.8: syng, 374.29. **a1475** *Guy*[2] 155.5424: synge. **c1475** *Brome Abraham* in Waterhouse 45.234. **a1500** Basterfeld 368.63. **a1500** *Be thou pacient* in *Anglia* 78(1960) 420.72: syng. **a1500** *Beves* 71 M 1232. **a1500** *Guy*[4] 23.428: sing. **a1500** *It is my Father's Will* in Brown *Lyrics XV* 4.14. **a1500** *Lucky and Unlucky Days* in Robbins 68.34: syng. **a1500** *Maid hath Borne* in Brown *Lyrics XV* 113.27: synge. **a1500** *Theophilus* 8.21[5]: sayn. **c1500** Fabyan 260[37]: sange. **c1500** *Lady Bessy* 47[15]: synge. **1528** Skelton *Replycacion* I 211.78: syng. Whiting *Drama* 363:842, *Scots* II 153. See **S350.**

S470 One's **Song** is (To sing) "wellawo"
c1250 *Owl* 38.412: Thu singest a-winter wolawo. **a1300** *Lithir lok Sermon* 105[33–4]: Thanne mai(s)tu singin Wei-la-wei wo-la-wo. **c1380** *Ferumbras* 176.5682. **c1400** *Jesus Pleads* in Brown *Lyrics XIV* 226.36: synge. **a1450** *Castle* 143.2218: syngyn. **a1450** *Ffor thu art comen* in Homer G. Pfander *Popular Sermon of the Medieval Friar in England* (New York, 1937) 49[12].

S471 A short **Song** is good in ale

c1440 Charles of Orleans 104.3118: And for folk say short song is good in ale. See **P408.**

S472 To make no **Song** of one's thought
c1420 Wyntoun IV 283.1981: Off al his thoucht he made na sange.

S473 To sing a careful **Song** (of care)
a1460 *Towneley Plays* 232.129: Of care may thou syng, 244.55. **c1500** Greene *Carols* 152.10: A carefull songe now may I syng. Whiting *Drama* 363:841.

S474 To sing a new **Song**
1520 Whittinton *Vulgaria* 89.17–8: He hathe thaught me to synge a newe songe to daye.

S475 To sing a ruly (*sad*) **Song**
c1300 *Reinbrun* 659.86.9: Thow singest a reuly songe.

S476 To sing a sorry **Song** (*varied*)
c1400 *Laud Troy* II 346.11752–3: He wolde have taught him for to rede And to synge a sori sang. **a1425** *Chester Plays* II 322.118: He shall singe a sory song, 426.702: A sorrowfull songe, in fayth, shall he singe. **a1425** *Complaynt of Criste* in *Pol. Rel. and Love Poems* 219.434: A song of sorewe weel may I synge. **1436** *Libelle* 42.825: Leste a songe of sorow that wee synge. **a1500** *Coventry Plays* 59.847: Off sorro now schal be my songe. **a1500** *Lufaris Complaynt* 723.155: To syng the samyn sory sang thai sing. **a1500** *Miller of Abington* 116.448: Did often singe a sory songe.

S477 To sing an idle **Song**
c1380 *Ferumbras* 89.2753: Thow syngest an ydel songe.

S478 To sing another **Song**
a1393 Gower *CA* II 211.3012: Now schalt thou singe an other song. **c1450** *Pilgrimage LM* 82[1–2]: Resoun stinte not but song him of an oother song. **c1500** *Everyman* 16.414. **1528** More *Heresyes* 256 H[17–8]. **1533** Heywood *Pardoner* B4r[7]. *Oxford* 592; Taylor and Whiting 345; Tilley S637; Whiting *Drama* 363:843, *Scots* II 127.

S479 To sing one (the same) **Song**
1483 *Vulgaria quedam abs Terencio* A3v[13]: Thou syngeste alwey oon songe. **a1500** *Thre Prestis* 11.142: Wee al and sundrie sings the samin sang. Apperson 574; *Oxford* 592; Tilley S638; Whiting *Scots* II 127. See **C600.**

S480 As bitter as (the) **Soot**
a1325 *Flemish Insurrection* 121.134: Hit falleth the kyng of fraunce bittrore then the sote. **a1415** *Lanterne* 44.21–2: Haate as bittir as the soot. **a1447** Lichfield *Complaint* 514.200. Apperson 50; Svartengren 303.

S481 As black as (any) **Soot**
a1400 *Scottish Legends* I 220.440: As ony sut fere mare blake, II 59.428: ony. **a1415** Mirk *Festial* 238.8: Wyth a berde downe to his fete, blake as soote. **a1439** Greenacre's *Envoy* in Lydgate *Fall* III 1023.25. **c1450** *Epistle of Othea* 78.21. **a1475** *Assembly of Gods* 19.618. **a1533** Berners *Arthur* 41[12–3]. Apperson 51; Taylor and Whiting 345; Tilley S642.

S482 As sour as **Soot**
a1425 *Complaynt of Criste* in *Pol. Rel. and Love Poems* 210.336: They been to me as sowre as soote, 211.332.

S483 As sulped (*defiled*) as **Soot**
a1425 *St. Robert* 77.1152–3: My synnes to schew or to be seyn Are sulped as sute ys in my syght.

S484 As swart (*black*) as **Soot**
a900 *Old English Martyrology* 152.5–6: Wæs seo onsyn sweatre þonne hrum.

Sooth, see **Truth**

S485 All **Sooth** (truth) is not to be said (*varied*)
c1025 *Durham Proverbs* 12.19: Ne deah eall soþ asæd ne eall sar ætwiten. (N)onne namque vera dicende sunt. **c1385** Usk 32.57: By that al sothes be nat to sayne. **c1400** *Satan and his Priests* in Wyclif *EW* 270[24–5]: Sumtyme it harmeth men to seie the sothe out of covenable tyme. **1404** *Lerne say wele* in Kail 21.224: Alltymes nys not soth to say. **c1412** Hoccleve *Regement* 137.3794: Ffor alle soothes ben nought for to seie. **a1420** Lydgate *Troy* III 723.5455: Trouthes alle be nat for to seyn. **c1420** Wyntoun VI 386.1849–50: And in althynge ful suythe to say Is noucht speidful, na neidful ay. **a1450** *York Plays* 59.106: Bott all the soth is noght to sayne. **1450** *Dicts* 142.2–3: Alle trouthe is not good to say. **c1450** *Douce MS.52* 57.149: Alle the sothe, is not to be sayde. **c1450** *Rylands MS.394* 109.19: to seyn. **a1456** *Passe forth* clxxiv 10: Sey never al that which wolde the sothe seme. **a1475** *As I stod* in Halliwell *Early English Miscellanies* 63[11]: For soothe may not alle day be sayd. **a1475** *Tree* 10.1: Sumtyme it is lefful to hide a trewth. **1481** Caxton *Reynard* 65[26–7]: For who so sayth alway trouthe he may not now goo nowher thurgh the world. **c1497** Medwall *Fulgens* A4v[12]: Trouth may not be sayde alway. **1509** Barclay *Ship* II 325[14]: At eche season: trouthe ought nat to be sayde.

Apperson 650–1; *Oxford* 9; Taylor and Whiting 383; Tilley T594. Cf. Jente 282. See **S500.**

S486 It is suith (*very*) strong (*hard*) to fight against **Sooth**
a1250 *Owl* 58.667–8: An hit is suthe strong to fighte Ayen soth and ayen righte. See **S830.**

S487 Not all is **Sooth** nor all lies that men say
a1200 Lawman II 542 *A* 22975–6: Ne al soh ne al les That leod-scopes singeth, **c1300** *B:* Nis noht al soth ne al les That many men seggeth. See **B221, M309, 310.**

S488 One may say **Sooth** in game (*sport, jest*)
c1390 Chaucer *CT* I[A] 4354–5: But yet I pray thee, be nat wroth for game; A man may seye ful sooth in game and pley, VII 1964[B3154]: Ful ofte in game a sooth I have herd seye! **1533** More *Apologye* 194[23–4]: For as Horace sayeth, a man maye somtyme saye full soth in game. Horace *Satire* I i 24–5. Jente 432. Cf. Taylor and Whiting 413.

S489 **Sooth** is most sutel (*clear*)
c900 *Cotton Maxims* in *ASMP* 56.10: Soð bið switolost.

S490 The **Sooth** (truth) may not be hidden (*varied*)
a1393 Gower *CA* II 231.205: The sothe, which mai noght ben hid. **a1400** *Ipomadon A* 22.677: The sothe ys not to layne, 102.3545, 135.4702, 149.5196, 161.5617, 178.6222, 186.6531, 200. 7034, 203.7129, 209.7322, 230.8077, 231.8125: to hyde, 248.8711, 251.8810. **a1400** *Melayne* 5.141: The sothe is noghte to hyde. **a1400** *Quatrefoil* 9.270: The sothe es noghte for to layne. **c1400** *Florence* 54.1587: The sothe ys not to layne, 55.1617. **c1400** *St. Anne (1)* 58. 2220: Ffor soth es noght to layne. **1458** *Ship of State* in Robbins *Historical Poems* 193.56: The trouthe is not to hyde. **a1460** *Towneley Plays* 252.282: The trouth shuld no man layn, 317.376: The sothe is not to hyde. **a1471** Ashby *Policy* 26.436: The trouthe is not hid, ne never shalbe.

S491 **Sooth** (Truth) reveals itself (shall be seen) (*varied*)
c1025 *Durham Proverbs* 12.21: Soþ hit sylf acyþeð. Veritas seipsam semper declarat. **c1385** Chaucer *TC* v 1639–40: But natheles, men seyen that at the laste, For any thyng, men shal the soothe se. **a1393** Gower *CA* III 72.4604: For as the sothe mot be knowe. **a1400** Wyclif *Sermons* II 133[2–3]: For treuthe mut algatis be known, however false men hiden it. **c1400** *Beryn* 63.2037–8: Ffor, aftir comyn seying, "evir atte ende The trowith woll be previd, how so men evir trend." **c1400** *Seven Sages D* 42.1310: Suth will be sene. **1404** *Lerne say wele* in Kail 17–8.97–104: Though men in erthe trouthe hyde, On halle rof he wole be sayn. In botme of see he nyl not byde, But shewe in market, on the playn. And though trouthe a while be slayn, And dolven depe under clay, Yut he wole ryse to lyve agayn, And al the sothe he wole say. **c1421** Lydgate *Thebes* 115.2786: But at the ende the trouthe shal be sene, **a1422** *Life* 416.1491–3: For light wol oute, it may not be borne doune And so wil trouthe, have dominacion For any falsnesse, **1439** *St. Albon* 160.1915–7: Trouthe wyll out, magre fals envie, Ryghtwysenes may not be hyd, it is certayne, As for a tyme it may be over-layne. **1519** Horman *Vulgaria* 307[1]: The treuthe wyll appere in processe of tyme, 423[27]: Al wyll come out at the laste: though it be hyd now. Taylor and Whiting 384; Tilley T591. See **M806.**

S492 Whoso says the **Sooth** (truth) shall be shent (*ruined*)
c1390 *Who says the Sooth, he shall be Shent* in Brown *Lyrics XIV* 152–4.12: For hos seith the sothe, he schal be schent, 24, 36, *etc.*, cf. 205–8.12, 24, 36, *etc.* **a1439** Lydgate *Fall* II 397.2472: To seyn the sothe, a poore man mai be shent, **a1449** *Cok* in *MP* II 817.135: Whoo seith truthe offte he shall be shent. **c1475** Gregory *Chronicle* 203[31–2]: But *qui veritatem dicit caput fractum habebit, etc.* **c1450** *Douce MS.52* 57.148: Who-so ever sey sothe, he shal be of-shende. **c1450** *Fyrst thou sal* 90.122: Who so says the sothe is often schent. **c1450** *Rylands MS.394* 109.16. Cf. Jente 282. See **S496.**

S493 **Soothness** is steadfast
a1387 Higden-Trevisa VIII 157[13–4]: For the soothnes is stedefast and is streng in long tyme, but falnes i-feyned vanscheth awey in schort tyme.

S494 **Soothsaws** are loath to lords
c1412 Hoccleve *Regement* 106.2946–7: And, for soth sawes ben to lordes lothe, Noght wol he soth seyn, he hath made his oth. *Oxford* 605.

S495 **Soothsaws** are never the worse though mad men tell magel (*?false*) tales
c1387 Higden-Trevisa V 339[15–6]: Soth sawes beeth nevere the wors they madde men telle magel tales.

S496 To suffer for **Soothsaw**

a1400 *Romaunt C* 6128–30: But natheles, though thou beten be, Thou shalt not be the first that so Hath for sothsawe suffred woo. See **S492.**

S497 To be but **Sops** in ale
c1516 Skelton *Magnificence* 69.2233: These maters that ye move are but soppys in ale.

S498 To lie like a **Sop**
c1400 *Laud Troy* II 493.16728: That he lay ther as a sop.

S499 To set at a **Sop**
c1378 *Piers* B xiii 124: And sette alle sciences at a soppe save love one.

S500 Hold not all **Sore** (sooth) said nor atwite (*taunt, blame*) all sorrow
c1025 *Durham Proverbs* 12.19: Ne deah eall soþ asæd ne eall sar ætwiten. (N)onne namque vera dicende sunt. **a1220** Giraldus *Descriptio Kambriae* in *Opera* VI 188[7]: Ne halt nocht al sor (*var.* sel) isaid, ne al sorghe atwite. Latin (n.4): Non attinet omne malum suum alii revelare, nec omne alterius incommodum ei exprobrare. See **S485.**

S501 Not give a **Sore**(?)
a1425 *Seege of Troye* 124 L 1580: Y no geve a sore for heom alle.

S502 Of old **Sores** come grievous wounds (*varied*)
a1338 Mannyng *Chronicle A* I 44.1246–8: Oure olde skathes they wille make newe; And thus men seys, and ofte is founde, Of old sor cometh grevous wounde. **1509** Barclay *Ship* I 51[1]: An olde sore to hele is oft halfe incurable, 164[5]: In olde sores is grettest jeopardye, 193[28]: For in olde sorys is greatest jeopardy. Apperson 467; Tilley S649. See **H259.**

S503 One must show the **Sore** where the salve should be
c1405 *Mum* 36.316–7: That who-so were in wire and wold be y-easid Moste shewe the sore there the salve were. See **L173, M25.**

S504 The **Sore** may swell long ere the herb is grown
c1450 Capgrave *Katharine* 95.255–8: Every wysman as wel as I now knoweth The soor may swelle longe er the herbe Is growe or rype—a grete clerk of viterbe Seyde soo somtyme and wrote it in his booke. See **G437.**

S505 That **Sore** is hard to heal which breeds in the bone
1509 Barclay *Ship* I 44[19]: That sore is harde to hele that bredes in the bone. See **F273.**

S506 Where the **Sore** is the finger will be
a1450 *Partonope* 163.4480–4: For ther the sore ys, the fynger woll be, And where thy love is, thyne ey ys to se. For as thy ffynger drawethe to the sore, So wolle thyne eye ever-more, Drawe to that place that thou lovyste beste. Whiting *Scots* I 186–7. See **E207, T386.**

S507 After great **Sorrow** great grace (gladness)
a1475 *Ludus Coventriae* 67.117: Aftere grett sorwe . . . evyr gret grace growyht, 70.200: Aftere grett sorwe evyr grett gladnes is had. See **B325.**

S508 Be not too sad of your **Sorrow** or too glad of your joy
a1400 *Proverbis of Wysdom* 245.51–2: Off thy sorow be nott to sad, Of thy joy be not to glad. **c1450** *Fyrst thou sal* 88.11–2. *Oxford* 605.

S509 Better said (heard, hid) **Sorrow** than seen
a1400 *Amadace I* 28[6]: Bettur sayd soro thenne sene. **c1450** *Douce MS.52* 44.5: Better is herde sorow than seen. **c1450** *Rylands MS.394* 95.9. **a1500** *Amadace A* 244.28: Hyd sorro is better than sene.

S510 Better short **Sorrow** than long
a1400 *Titus* 170.3756: Better is short sorwe than longe.

S511 Every **Sorrow** will be assuaged (*varied*)
a1439 Lydgate *Fall* I 302.3634–5: But everi sorwe, be long continuaunce, At the laste it sumwhat must aswage. **c1489** Caxton *Blanchardyn* 133.4–5: Ther nys so grete sorowe, but that it may be forgoton at the laste. **c1500** *Melusine* 36.18–20: As it is wel trouth that there nys so grete a sorowe, but that within foure days it is somwhat peased. **c1500** *Three Kings' Sons* 46.24: There is no sorow nor mysfortune but it most passe. See **H285.**

S512 If you have **Sorrow** (care, woe) tell it not to your argh (*enemy*) but to your saddlebow (*varied*)
c1250 *Proverbs of Alfred* 94 T 217–8: Swich mon thu maist seien thi sor, He wolde thad thu hevedest mor, **a1300** 95 J 203–18: If thu havest seorewe, Ne seye thu hit nouht than arewe, Seye hit thine sadelbowe, And ryd the singinde forth. . . . Serewe if thu havest And the erewe hit wot, By-fore he the meneth, By-hynde he the teleth. Thu hit myht segge swych mon That the ful wel on. Wyth-ute echere ore, He on the muchele more. **a1500** Greene *Carols* p. 322 v5: The bryd seyde on his devys, "Thou mytyst telle sum man thi woo; He wol it were dublyd thryis: Thou wost wol lytil ho is thi foo." **a1500** *Salamon sat and sayde* 291.16–7: I tel the be-

ffore To swylkes may thou tel thi care thai wald it wer well more. See **C467, F366, M196.**

S513 Make not one **Sorrow** twain (*varied*)
a1410 Lydgate *Churl* in *MP* II 477.215–7: For who takith sorwe for losse in that degre, Rekne first his losse, and aftir rekne his peyne, Off oo sorwe, he makith sorwis twayne. **a1500** ?Ros *La Belle Dame* 308.300: Lesse harme it were, oon sorowful, than twayne. **1506** Hawes *Pastime* 66.1652: How of one sorowe ye do now make twayne. **1546** Heywood *D* 76.219: And reason saieth, make not two sorowes of one, **1555** *E* 152.41. Apperson 656; *Oxford* 680–1; Tilley S663. See **D4, 356, H140, L472, S193, T532.**

S514 **Sorrow** helps not (*varied*)
a1325 *Cursor* I 248.4205–6: Quat bote es soru, or mak mane O thing that covering has nane. **a1350** *Seven Sages C* 100.2929–30: What helpes it so to sorow the For thing that may noght mended be? **c1400** *Cleges* 42.127–8: Ye se wele, sir, it helpys noughht, To take sorow in your thoughht. **a1410** Lydgate *Churl* in *MP* II 477. 213–4: For tresour lost make nevir to grett sorwe, Which in no wise may recured be, 482.324–6: For thyng lost of sodeyn aventur, Thou sholdist nat make to mych sorwe, Whan thou seest thou maist it nat recur. **a1450** *Barlam and Josaphat* (*South English Legendary*) 124.395–6: Ne sorwe thu nought to sore: for thing that is lore, Yif it ne may be found: ne sorw thu nought ther fore. **1484** Caxton *Aesop* 270[21–2]: Take no sorowe of the thynge lost whiche may not be recovererd. **c1500** *Melusine* 24.1–3: And as me semeth it is grette symplenes to take ony sorowe or hevynes of suche thinges that may not helpe hyndre ne lette, 154.28–9: For that thing that may not be amended it is folye to make therof grete sorowe, 313.28–30: Thus to maynten and make suche sorowe of that thinge that may none other wyse be, and whiche may not be amended nor remedyed. **a1533** Berners *Huon* 55.26: Makyng of sorow can not avayle you. Cf. Apperson 126:6; *Oxford* 122; Tilley M939. See **D337, G455, L52, M729, R81.**

S515 **Sorrow** is at parting if laughter be at meeting (*varied*)
a1460 *Towneley Plays* 292.397: Thus sorow is at partyng at metyng if ther be laghter. **a1475** *Ludus Coventriae* 65.56: And tho that departe in sorwe god make ther metyng glad. Apperson 589; *Oxford* 605.

S516 **Sorrow** is ay meddled (*mixed*) with gladness
a1439 Lydgate *Fall* I 66.2406: Thus ay is sorwe medlid with gladnesse. See **J59.**

S517 **Sorrow** may not last ever
a1393 Gower *CA* III 191.886–7: Somtime I drawe into memoire Hou sorwe mai noght evere laste. See **D340, S798, W140.**

S518 **Sorrow** often comes soon and it is long or (*ere*) it pass
a1475 *Ludus Coventriae* 112.120–1: Ffor oftyn tyme sorwe comyth sone And longe it is or it pace.

S519 That **Sorrow** which follows felicity surmounts every sorrow
a1439 Lydgate *Fall* I 18.645–6: For thilke sorwe surmountith every sorwe, Which next folwith afftir felicite. See **W136.**

S520 To have **Sorrow** to one's sops
1546 Heywood *D* 89.26: I had sorow to my sops ynough be sure. Apperson 589; *Oxford* 605–6; Tilley S661.

S521 To sing of **Sorrow**
a1400 *Melayne* 23.696: Of sorowe now may thou synge. **c1400** *Sowdone* 61.2109: Or ellis I may singe of sorowe a songe, 69.2418. **a1425** *Chester Plays* II 436.240. **a1450** *Castle* 168.3062: Of sadde sorwe now may I synge. **a1475** *Ludus Coventriae* 171.67–8.

S522 To sup **Sorrow**
c1400 *Plowman's Tale* 182.1096: Hir servaunts sitte and soupe sorowe. Apperson 610.

S523 Who seeks **Sorrow** his be the receipt (is worthy) of it
a1500 ?Ros *La Belle Dame* 316.553: Who secheth sorowe, his be the receyt. **1509** Barclay *Ship* I 228[28]: He is worthy sorowe that wyll it alway seke. Apperson 556; *Oxford* 571.

S524 He is a **Sot** that is another man's friend better than his own
c1175 *Poema Morale* 171.30: Sot is thet is otheres mannes frend betre thanne his oghe. Apperson 227:71. See **C153.**

S525 A **Sot** in siege (*seat of power*) shall gar (*make*) states staver (*stagger*)
c1420 Wyntoun II 327.795–8: Thus in seige a sote to se, Or do a dowde in dignyte, Sal ger standande statis staver, And wil bathe wit and worschep waver.

S526 To love as one's (own) **Soul**
c1400 *Beryn* 81.2682: Saff a doughter, that he lovid (right) as his owne saal. **a1415** Mirk *Festial*

247.32: On sonne, the whech scho lovet as hur sowle. See **L252.**

S527 To reck (*care*) not if **Souls** go blackberrying (*varied*)
c1390 Chaucer *CT* VI[C] 405–6: I rekke nevere, whan that they been beryed, Though that hir soules goon a-blakeberyed. **c1450** Idley 128.1241: The soule shall goo grase in fieldis and in woodis, 188.1813: No force if the soule goo daunce with a taboure. See **B334.**

S528 When you see my **Soul** hang on the hedge, then hurl stones
1533 More *Confutacion* 657 A[12–4]: When thou seest my soule hange on the hedge, then hurle stones at it hardly and spare not. Tilley H362.

S529 After **Sour** sweet is a pleasant mess (*course*)
c1400 *Beryn* 110.3688: Ffor "aftir sour, when swete is com, it is a plesant mes."

S530 There are all **Sorts**
1556 Heywood *Spider* 201[1–3]: It is comonly said, and comonly sene, Where as any nomber of any sort be: Of all sortes there be, and evermore have bene. Tilley S666.

S531 **Southwark** ale
c1390 Chaucer *CT* I[A] 3139–40: And therfore if that I mysspeke or seye, Wyte it the ale of Southwerk, I you preye. *Oxford* 607; Tilley A107.

Sow, sb., see **Hog, Pig, Swine**

S532 As adrunken (*drowned*) as **Sows** (*etc.*) (A number of single quotations are brought together here)
a1290 *Seve dawes aren* in *Archiv* 52(1874) 36[1.40]: Adronken ase it were souwes. **c1387–95** Chaucer *CT* I[A] 552: His berd as any sowe . . . was reed, 555–6: A toft of herys, Reed as the brustles of a sowes erys. **c1400** *Laud Troy* I 206.6992: For he lay stille as a sowe. **a1500** *Beves* 118 M 2225: He was brysteled lyke a sowe. **c1515** Barclay *Eclogues* 65.373: A rustie ribaude more viler then a sowe.

S533 As meet as a **Sow** to bear a saddle
1546 Heywood *D* 60.44–5: As meete as a sowe To beare a saddle, **1555** *E* 196.288. Apperson 591; *Oxford* 608; Tilley S672; Whiting *Ballad* 36.

S534 **Sow-drunk**
1529 More *Supplicacion* 332 A[7–8]: Fell downe sowe drunke in the myre, BC: sowe drunken soule, **1533** *Confutacion* 591 F[8]: Waxe wanton or sowe dronke. Svartengren 204. See **S955.**

S535 The still **Sow** eats her meat (all the draff)
a1200 Serlo 204.54: The stille sue aet gruniende hire mete. **a1250** *Rawlinson MS. C 641* in *Zeitschrift für französische Sprache und Litteratur* 21(1899) 3.4: Si stille suge fret there grunninde mete. **c1450** *Rylands MS.394* 107.13: The stylle sowghe etus alle the draffe. **1546** Heywood *D* 38.121: The still sowe eats up all the draffe, **1555** *E* 171.142. Apperson 602; Jente 464; *Oxford* 620–1; Tilley S681.

S536 To grease the fat **Sow** in the arse
1549 Heywood *D* 48.245: What should we . . . grease the fat sow in thars. Apperson 591; Jente 496; *Oxford* 263; Tilley S682.

S537 To seethe a fat **Sow** in a pan
1509 Barclay *Ship* I 24[6–7]: Suche is as wyse a man As he that wolde seeth a quycke Sowe in a Pan. See Aurelius Pompen *English Versions of the Ship of Fools* (London, 1925) 294.

S538 To sing like a **Sow** in a slough
c1450 Idley 192.2040: As a sowe in a sloughe thy hede doithe synge.

S539 To slumber like a **Sow** in a slough
c1450 Idley 178.1198: And slombre not in foule synne as a sowe doith in a sloughe. Cf. Whiting *Scots* II 128: sleep.

S540 To take the wrong **Sow** by the ear
1546 Heywood *D* 92.65–6: Ye tooke . . . the wrong sow by theare. Apperson 715; *Oxford* 607; Taylor and Whiting 346; Tilley S685.

S541 To wallow like a **Sow** in a midden
a1400 *Scottish Legends* I 309.467–8: Ay valouand me in that syne, As sow a medynge dois vithine. Whiting *Scots* II 128.

Sow, vb.

S542 As one **Sows** so shall he reap (*varied*)
c800 Cynewulf *Christ* in *Exeter Book* 5.85–6: Swa eal manna bearn Sorgum sawað, swa eft ripað. **a900** Alfred *Gregory* 325.6: Se ðe lytel sæwð he lytel ripð. **a1050** Defensor *Liber* 156[9–10]: Paulus se apostol sæde se þe spærlice sæwð spærlice he eac g(e)ripð. **a1225** *Lambeth Homilies* 131[24–5]: *Qui parce seminat et cetera.* The mon thet lutel seweth he scal lutel maghe, 137[31–2]: Alswa we er seiden. *Qui parce seminat & cetera.* Aevric mon scal eft mowen bi tho the he nu saweth. **a1250** *Yc ou rede ye sitten stille* in *SP* 28(1931) 598.121–2: That lutel sowet lutel repet Ase in the boc tha apostel speket. **c1250** *Owl* 88.1037–42: Hit was iseid in olde laghe, An yet ilast thilke soth-saghe, That man shal erien an sowe, Thar he wenth after sum god mowe: For

he is wod that soweth his sed Thar never gras ne sprinth ne bled. **a1300** *Proverbs of Alfred* 79 J 78–9: Hwych so the mon soweth, Al swuch he schal mowe. **a1325** *Cursor* III 1566 C 28830–1: It was said sithen mani dais, "Qua littil saus, the lesse he mais." **c1330** *Praise of Women* 291.42–3: Hou schuld men ani corn repe, Ther no sede is souwe? **c1395** *WBible* II Corinthians ix 6: For Y seie this thing, he that sowith scarseli, schal also repe scarseli; and he that sowith in blessyngis, schal repe also of blessyngis, Galatians vi 8: For tho thingis that a man sowith, tho thingis he schal repe. **a1400** *Pauline Epistles* II Corinthians ix 6, Galatians vi 8. **1404** *Lerne say wele* in Kail 16.61–3: Ffor suche seed he doth sowe In stones, in thornes, and in clay, The same he schal repe and mowe. **c1415** *Middle English Sermons* 112.6–9: He that skarsely saweth, skarsely shall reepe . . . What that every man sawethe, that shall he repe. **a1425** *Cursor* III 1566 Cotton Galba 28830–1: And said it es thus in alde daws, "Who litill maws, the les he saws." **c1443** Pecock *Reule* 357[22–3]: Such as a man sowith, suche he schal reepe. **c1450** *God's Appeal* in Kail 86.21–3: For suche seed as thou dost sowe, Therof shal thyn hervest be, In hevene or helle to repe and mowe. **a1475** *Assembly of Gods* 37.1244–5: But suche as ye have sowe Must ye nedes reepe. **c1475** *Mankind* 7.175: But such as thei have sowyn, such xall thei repe. **c1480** *Contemplacioun* 196.265: Quhat seid men sawis sic corne thai mon neid scheire. **1492** *Salomon and Marcolphus* 13[9–10]: He that sowyth wyth skaerstye repyth skaersly. **1533** More *Confutacion* 743 H[12–3]: Whatsoever a man soweth, the same shall he repe. Apperson 591, 592; Jente 558; *Oxford* 608; Tilley S209, 210, 687; Whiting *Drama* 299, *Scots* II 128–9. See **C128, R56.**

S543 One **Sows** and another reaps
c1395 *WBible* John iv 37: For anothir is that sowith, and anothir that repith. Tilley S691.

S544 In **Space** comes grace
c1500 Newton 269.11–2: In space, Comes fortune and grace. **1546** Heywood *D* 25.22: In space comth grace, **1555** *E* 150.22. Apperson 592; *Oxford* 609; Tilley S697–8.

S545 As broad as a **Spade**
c1387–95 Chaucer *CT* I[A] 553: And therto brood, as though it were a spade.

S546 Between here and **Spain** (*varied*)
c1300 *Guy*[1] 110.1939: Anon to Speyne his better nis. **c1300** Robert of Gloucester I 275.3915: Ther nas bituene this and spayne no prince withoute al this. **a1533** Berners *Huon* 210.22: Fro thense in to Spayne.

S547 **Span-**(*chip-*)**new**
a1300 *Alisaunder* 227.4051: In spannewe knightten wede. **c1300** *Havelok* 36.968: And bouhte him clothes, al spannewe. **c1385** Chaucer *TC* iii 1665: This tale was ay span-newe to bygynne. **c1390** *Psalterium b. Mariae* 75.586: Al ur hele sponnewe. **1463–4** *Manners and Household Expenses of England* (RC, 1841) 160[4–6]: A new jakett of purpylle . . . and itt is spanne new. Apperson 595–6; *Oxford* 613; Tilley S748. Cf. Taylor and Whiting 346.

S548 As meek as a **Spaniel**
a1415 Mirk *Festial* 119.17–8: The lyon . . . fell downe to the knightes fete as meke as a spaynell.

S549 To fawn like a **Spaniel**
a1470 Malory II 912.34: The lyon wente allwey aboute hym fawnynge as a spaynell. *Oxford* 195; Tilley S704; Whiting *Scots* II 129.

S550 To leap on one like a **Spaniel**
c1395 Chaucer *CT* III[D] 267: For as a spaynel she wol on hym lepe.

S551 To make a **Spar** of a spindle
c1516 Skelton *Magnificence* 33.1036: Of a spyndell I wyll make a sparre. Tilley S756.

S552 Ever **Spare** and ever bare
1546 Heywood *D* 71.44: Ever spare and ever bare. Apperson 187; Tilley S706. See **S626.**

S553 He that will not **Spare** when he may shall not spend when he will
a1400 *Jug inscription in British Museum* in Joan Evans *English Art 1307–1461* (Oxford, 1949) 90: He that wyl not spare when he may he schal not spend when he wold. Cf. Tilley S707, 710. See **W275.**

S554 **Spare** to speak spare to speed (*varied*)
a1393 Gower *CA* II 71.1293: For specheles may noman spede, 313.439–40: Forthi, my Sone, if that thou spare To speke, lost is al thi fare. **c1405** *Mum* 29.86: And spare not to speke, spede yf thou mowe. **1420** Lydgate *Temple* 38.905: For specheles nothing maist thou spede. **c1440** Charles of Orleans 165.4942: Spare not to speke spede ye so or no. **c1445** ?Lydgate *Kalendare* in *MP* I 366.99: Who spareth to speke he spareth to spede. **a1450** Audelay 26.443–4: Who-so-ever sparys fore to speke, sparys for to spede, And he that spekys and spedys noght, he spellys the wynd, 446: Better is to speke and sped then hold hit in mynd. **c1450** *Douce MS.52* 46.27:

Who-so sparyth to speke, sparyth to spede. **c1495** *Arundel Vulgaria* 59.255: It is a comyn sayng, "spare speke, spare spede." **c1499** Skelton *Bowge* I 33.91: Who spareth to speke, in fayth he spareth to spede. **a1500** Hill 132.47: He that spareth to speke, ofte spareth to spede. **a1500** *Lincoln Cathedral Chapter MS.105 (4)* in Reginald M. Woolley *Catalogue of the Manuscripts of Lincoln Cathedral Chapter Library* (London, 1927) 68: Now to speke I will noght spare, Sen speche has made me for to spede. How schuld he wyte what my will ware Bot I wold neve my awn nede. He schall not cheven in his chafare That will bye and dare noght bede, Ne lenger lyfe with owten kare, Than all ever ilke worde take hede. **1506** Hawes *Pastime* 74.1891: Who spareth to speke he spareth to spede, 91.2351. **1546** Heywood *D* 48.232: Spare to speake spare to speede, **1555** *E* 179.188, 194.275. Apperson 593; *Oxford* 209; Tilley S709; Whiting *Scots* II 129–30. See **M276.**

S555 As prest (*active*) as a **Sparhawk**
c1378 *Piers* B vi 199: And what Pieres preyed hem to do, as prest as a sperhauke. Svartengren 122.

S556 To chase as the **Sparhawk** does the little birds
1480 Caxton *Ovyde* 89[24–5]: Chaced theym . . . as the sperhawke doth the lytil byrdes.

S557 To look like a **Sparhawk**
c1390 Chaucer *CT* VII 3457[B4647]: He loketh as a sperhauk with his yen.

S558 For **Sparing** a little cost one loses the coat for the hood
a1393 Gower *CA* III 77.4785–7: For sparinge of a litel cost Fulofte a man hath lost The large cote for the hod, 163.7716–8: And thus the Cote for the hod Largesse takth, and yit no Sinne He doth, hou so that evere he winne. Apperson 666; *Oxford* 387, cf. 691.

S559 Of a little **Spark** (sparkle) a great fire (*varied*)
c1300 *South English Legendary (Laud)* 474.425: Ake of(te) gret fuyr and eke stuyrne wext of a luytel spielde. **c1380** Chaucer *HF* 2077–80: And that encresing ever moo, As fyr ys wont to quyke and goo From a sparke spronge amys, Til al a citee brent up ys. **c1395** *WBible* Ecclesiasticus xi 34: Fier is encreessid of a sparcle. **a1398**(1495) Bartholomaeus-Trevisa &3ʳ[1.23–5]: For of a lytill sperkyll in an hepe of towe or of tyndyr cometh sodaynly a grete fyre. **a1400** *Destruction of Troy* 47–8.1426–31: A Proverbe. A word that is wrappid, and in wrath holdyn, May feston as a fyre with a fuerse lowe, Of a sparke unaspied, spred under askys, May feston up fyre to mony freike sorow; So lurkes with lordes of a light wrathe, That growes into gronnd harme, grevys full sore. **a1420** Lydgate *Troy* I 34.785–6: And of sparkys that ben of syght(e) smale, Is fire engendered that devoureth al. **1422** Yonge *Governaunce* 164.15–6: As a Sparke of fyre risyth an huge fyre able a realme to brente. **a1440** Burgh *Cato* 314.459: Off brondis smale be maad thes fires grete. **a1449** Lydgate *See Myche* in *MP* II 800.22–3: A lytell sparke ofte sette a tonne a-fyre But when it (brennythe), it is not lyghtely quent. **1450** *Dicts* 274.5: A litille sparke makithe lightly a (grete) fire. **c1450** *Douce MS.52* 48.55: Of a lytul sparkull comyth a grete fyre. **c1450** *Ladder* 109.2: Howe mych a fyre kendelyth of so litelle a sparkille. **c1450** *Rylands MS.394* 98.25. **c1470** *Harley MS.3362* f.4a in *Retrospective* 309[24]: Of a lytyl spark ys mad gret feer. **a1475** Ashby *Dicta* 61.426–7: For of a litle sparkel a grete fyre Comyth, displeasaunt to many a sire. **1483** Caxton *Cato* F1ʳ[9]: For a lytel sparcke of fyre kyndleth ofte a grete fyre. **a1500** *Additional MS.37075* 279.28: Of a lytyll sparkyll ther comyth a grett fyre. **a1500** Hill 130.15: Of a lytill sparkyll, commeth a gret fyre. **1509** Barclay *Ship* I 194[1–2]: A small sparcle often tyme doth augment It selfe: and groweth to flames peryllous. **1509** Watson *Ship* I3ᵛ[15–7]: The sparcle . . . encreaseth unto a grete flambe. **1528** More *Heresyes* 285 H[6–8]: The sparcle wel quenched ere it wer suffred to growe to over great a fyre. **1532** Berners *Golden Boke* 325.6779–80: With a lyttell sparcle, the house is sette a fyre. Apperson 593; Jente 731; Smith 274; Tilley S714. See **D413, E191, L402, W603.**

S560 To burn like **Spark** on gleed
c1300 *Guy*[1] 28.488: Y brenne so spark on glede. **c1330** *Tars* 38 A 194: Him thought, he brend so spark on glede.

S561 To leap like **Spark** out of gleed (*etc.*) (A number of single quotations are brought together here)
c1350 *Libeaus* 38.668–9: And lep out of the arsoun, As sperk doth out of glede. **a1400** *Alexander C* 174.2975: Sparis out spacly as sparke out of gledes. **a1420** Lydgate *Troy* III 695. 4459–60: Liche in twynklynge to the sparkis rede In grete fyres that abrod so sprede. **a1450** *Castle* 185.3603–4: As a sparke of fyre in the se, My mercy is synne quenchande. **1513** Douglas *Aeneid* III 207.67–8: Quhilkis, but abaid, alssone hess hym slane As spark of gleid wald in

the sey remane, IV 52.158: And furth scho sprent as spark of gleid.

S562 To spring like any **Spark** (sparkle) of (on) fire (gleed, flint)
a1200 Lawman II 478.21481–2: Cador sprong to horse, Swa spaerc him doh of fure, 565. 23507–8: He sprong forth an stede Swa sparc ded of fure. **c1300** *Guy*[1] 299 A 5464: And sprongen forth so spark on glede. **c1300** *Havelok* 4.91: That he ne sprong forth so sparke of glede. **a1325** *Otuel and Roland* 74.492: The fyr out sprang as spark of flynt, 103.1432: as sparcle of glede. **a1350** *Isumbras* 35.448 (*var.*): of flynte, 36.458: one glede. **c1350** *Octavian* (*NL*) 121.873–4: of glede, 153.1438: one glede. **c1390** *Tars* 38 V 188: as sparkle doth of glede. **a1400** *Cloud* 22.7–8: as sparcle fro the cole. **a1400** *Firumbras* 22.647: of glede, 51.1590: as sparcle doth of the fyre, 52.1622: as sparcle on fyre. **a1400** *Le Morte* A. 25.780: of glede, 83.2742: on glede, 84.2793: on glede. **c1400** *Laud Troy* II 418.14190: of glede. **c1400** *Sowdone* 7.205: As a sparkil of glede. **c1410** Lovelich *Merlin* II 226.8503–4: of fyre. **c1475** *Guy*[1] 473 C 8376–7: The mayles of her good hawberkis Sprongen owte as it were sperkis. **a1500** *English Conquest* 107.3–4: of fyre. **a1500** *King Arthur and King Cornwall* in Child I 287.67: of gleede. **a1500** *Octavian* (*NC*) 120.961–2: as sparkylle on glede, 124.1033–4, 152.1466. Whiting *Ballad* 31.

S563 As swift as **Sparkle** out of fire
c1410 Lovelich *Grail* IV 346.196: As swyft as Sparkle Owt Of fyre.

S564 Like **Sparkle** out of gleed
c1458 *Knyghthode and Bataile* 77.2102: And archerye, as sparkil out of glede.

S565 A small **Sparkle** may kindle love, but Severn may scantly quench it
c1515 Barclay *Eclogues* 57.175–6: For a small sparcle may kindle love certayne, But scantly Severne may quench it clene agayne.

S566 To fly (go, come) out as **Sparkle** (spark) of flint
a1325 *Otuel and Roland* 106.1515: That feer flye out as sparkyl of flynt, 116.1831. **c1380** *Ferumbras* 25.605: Of helmes and sheldes that fyr out went, so sparkes doth of brondes. **a1400** *Firumbras* 30.898–9: So that claryoun smote Ricer suche a dynt, That fyr flewe out as sparche of flynt, 52.1636: So come Roulond, as sparkyl doth of flynt. **a1450** *Generydes A* 288.9323–4: Aither smote hard dyntes, The sparkles flow out as doth on flyntes.

S567 To glide like **Sparkle** out of brand
c1390 Chaucer *CT* VII 904–5[B2094–5]: And forth upon his wey he glood As sparcle out of the bronde.

S568 To pass like **Sparkle** out of fire
c1410 Lovelich *Merlin* III 451.16839–40: For over the ryver they wylen desire To passen, as sparcle doth owt of fyre.

S569 To start like **Sparkle** out of (on) fire
a1400 *Firumbras* 19.541: A sarsin sterte forth as sparkyl doth on fyre. **a1475** *Guy*[1] 557 C 9954: He sterte forth as spekyll on fyre. **a1500** *Beves* 94 M [9–10]: Up he sterte also right As sperkyll oute of fire right.

S570 As hot and lecherous as a **Sparrow**
c1380 Chaucer *PF* 351: The sparwe, Venus sone, **c1387–95** *CT* I[A] 626: As hoot he was and lecherous as a sparwe. Svartengren 409; Tilley S715.

S571 To be befongen (*caught*) like **Sparrow** in net
c1000 *Corpus Christi Homily* (*St. Margaret*) in Assmann 172.71: Ic eam befangan eal swa spearwe on nette.

S572 To be taken like **Sparrows** with lime
c1400 *Laud Troy* I 229.7750–1: He slees the Gregeis, as men take sparwes With lym or net or lymyerdes.

S573 To chirk (*chirp*) like a **Sparrow**
c1395 Chaucer *CT* III[D] 1804–5: And chirketh as a sparwe With his lyppes.

S574 If you **Speak** well work so
c1025 *Durham Proverbs* 12.20: Gyf þu well sprece wyrc æfter swa. Bene loquere sic bene facias. See **W642.**

S575 It is dizzy (*foolish*) to **Speak** before one thinks
c900 *Old English Cato* 5.27: Hit byð dysig þæt man speca ær, þone he þænce. *Oxford* 205: First think.

S576 **Speak** or (*ere*) you smite, bark or you bite
a1500 *How shall y plece* in *Archiv* 106(1901) 274[14–5]: Speke or ye smyte, barke or ye byte, Hold yowr handes twayn. See **B44.**

S577 **Speak,** spend and speed
1381 *Jack Trewman* in Knighton II 139[23]: Speke, spende and spede, quoth Jon of Bathon. *Oxford* 611; Tilley S719. Cf. Whiting *Drama* 98.

S578 Those that **Speak** fair shall hear fair again

a1533 Berners *Arthur* 87[23]: They that speaketh fayre, fayre shal here agayne.

S579 To **Speak** as one finds
c1545 Heywood *Four PP* B4v[22]: Now speke all thre, evyn as ye fynde. Tilley S724.

S580 To **Speak** fair before but not behind (*varied*)
a900 *Homiletic Fragment* in *Vercelli Book* 59.3–6: Eorl oðerne mid æfþancum Ond mid teonwordum tæleð behindan, Spreceð fægere beforan, and þæt facen swa þeah Hafað in his heortan, hord unclæne. **a1415** Mirk *Festial* 112.18–9: Thus faryth moche pepull now-on-dayes that woll speke fayre befor a man, but bihynd thay woll sle hym wyth hor tong. **a1450** *Castle* 97.668–9: To speke fayre be-forn, and fowle be-hynde, Amongis men at mete and mele. **c1495** *Arundel Vulgaria* 60.260: Dobull tonguede felows which befor a manys face can speke fair and flater and behynde his bake doth say the worste. **1523** Skelton *Garlande* I 386.620: That speke fayre before the and shrewdly behynde. See **A90.**

S581 To **Speak** high and be low at the proof
c1489 Caxton *Aymon* I 161.1–3: And some of you speketh now hye, that whan the dede shall come to preeff, he shall be full lowe. Cf. Whiting *Drama* 188. See **B415, M367.**

S582 To **Speak** much and speed little
a1500 *English Conquest* 21.2–3: Mych they spoke of this, and lytyll thay Spede.

S583 To **Speak** other than one thinks
a1023 Wulfstan *Homilies* 189.120–2: To fela manna eac is nu on ðissere swicelan worulde þe ealswa to swyðe þurh hiwunge (*deceit*) eal oðer specað oþer hy þencað. **c1395** Chaucer *CT* III[D] 1568: The carl spak oo thing, but he thoghte another. **1402** Hoccleve *Letter of Cupid* 75.74: That spake so faire and falsly inward thoght. **1496** *The cyte is bond* in Mary D. Harris ed. *Coventry Leet Books* (EETS 135, 1908) 578[11–2]: We may speke feire and bid you good morowe, But luff with our hertes shull ye have non. **c1500** *Heartless Mistress* in Robbins 140.24: Ye speke fayre outward and feyneth withyn. **1523** Skelton *Garlande* I 392.759: For when he spekyth fayrest, then thynketh he moost yll. Tilley S725. Cf. Smith 275. See **F44, 50.**

S584 To **Speak** saves for truth is asleep (?)
c1475 *Rawlinson MS. D 328* 118.10: Speke savyth for trowyth ys a-slepe. Pacifice loquere quia veritas dormit in ede. Walther III 691. 20548.

S585 Whoso **Speaks** unwisely speaks too much
a1470 Parker *Dives* E7v[1.29–32]: It is a comon proverbe, that who so speketh unwysely and vaynely or in an evyll maner, he speketh to moche. Apperson 594.

S586 Each **Speaker** wishes a reply (to be heard)
c1000 *Royal MS.2 B v* in *Anglia* 2(1878–9) 373: Clipiendra gehwylc wolde, þæt him man oncwæde. Omnis invocans cupit audiri. **c1025** *Durham Proverbs* 14.39: Ciggendra gehwilc wile þæt hine man gehere. Omnis invocans cupit audiri.

S587 A great **Speaker** must be a liar
1532 Berners *Golden Boke* 153.1381: If he be a great speaker, he shall be a lyer. See **L67, W593.**

S588 A hasty **Speaker** falls in great damage
1509 Barclay *Ship* I 107[5]: A hasty speker falleth in great domage. See **S607, W592.**

S589 To be a fair **Speaker** and false thereunder
a1470 Malory II 595.2: For he was a fayre speker, and false thereundir. See **C174.**

S590 A great **Speaking** is seldom without fault
1512 Copland *Helyas* A6v[18–20]: The sage sayth. That a grete spekynge is seldon seen pronounced without to have ony faute. Wherby he sayth after, that that he never repented hym of to lytell speche. Cf. Tilley S728. See **L67.**

S591 Of ill advised **Speaking** comes harm
c1390 Chaucer *CT* IX[H] 335–7: My sone, of muchel spekyng yvele avysed, Ther lasse spekyng hadde ynough suffised, Comth muchel harm; thus was me toold and taught.

S592 As long as a **Spear**
c1475 Henryson *Testament* 110.161: And as ane speir als lang. **1513** Douglas *Aeneid* III 62.62: Gret ische schouchlis lang as ony speir.

S593 As sharp as (point of, any, a) **Spear**
c1387-95 Chaucer *CT* I[A] 113–4: A gay daggere Harneised wel and sharp as point of spere. **c1410** Lovelich *Grail* II 290.460: It was as scharpe As Ony spere, 409–10.159–60: Ony. **a1460** *Towneley Plays* 372.163: Thai ar sharp as a spere.

S594 A broken **Spear** is found false
c1400 *Roland* 107.9–10: Who so belevythe hym shall hym fals find, Right as A broken sper at the litill end. Cf. Tilley S805. See **R70, S649.**

S595 Buy (the) **Spear** from (your) side or bear (it there)
c1100 *Leges Edwardi Confessoris* in Liebermann

I 638–9: Emendationem faciat parentibus vel werram patiatur, unde Angli proverbium habebant (*var.* Parentibus occisi fiat emendatio, vel guerra eorum portetur): "Bugge (*var.* Begge) spere of side othe bere!" quod est dicere: "Lanceam eme de latere aut fer!" Cf. K. Malone in *A Literary History of England*, ed. Albert C. Baugh (New York, 1948) 43.

S596 The **Spear** of Achilles
c1395 Chaucer *CT* V[F] 238–40: And fille in speche of Thelophus the kyng, And of Achilles with his queynte spere, For he koude with it bothe heele and dere. *Oxford* 612; Tilley S731.

S597 To be a sure **Spear** at need
1520 Whittinton *Vulgaria* 98.14–5: Thou art a sure spere at nede that leves a man stykkynge in the breres.

S598 To smite like a **Spear**
a1400 *Ancrene* (*Recluse*) 44.15–6: That smott hym to the hert as a spere.

S599 That which is spoken in **Special** (*private*) spreads afar
a1400 *Destruction of Troy* 371.11373–6: But oftsythes hit is sene, and sum men hath feld, That spokyn is in speciall, spredes o fer. In yche company is comynly a claterer of mowthe, That no councell can kepe, ne no close talis.

S600 As clear as **Spectacle** (*something made of glass*)
a1449 Lydgate *St. Austin* in *MP* I 197.132: Feith of our lord wex moor cleer than spectacle.

S601 Beware of fair **Speech**
1449 Metham 14.365: And ever be-ware off fayre speche, fore many be ontrwe. See **T19.**

S602 Evil **Speeches** (words) destroy (corrupt) good thews (*customs*, manners) (*varied*)
c1395 *WBible* I Corinthians xv 33: For yvel spechis distrien good thewis. **a1400** *Pauline Epistles* I Corinthians xv 33: Forwhy evyl spechys corrumpyn goode manerys. **c1425** Arderne *Fistula* 5.18–9: And it is seid in another place, "Shrewed speche corrumpith gode maners." **c1425** *St. Mary Oignies* 163.12–3: For yvel to-gedir-spekynges harmeth good maners. **1447** Bokenham 251.9215–6: For, as seyth seynt poule, shrewyd talkyng Corumpyth good maners and good lyvyng. **c1450** Capgrave *Lives* 85.3–4: For evel speche often tyme appeyreth ful good maneres. **a1470** Parker *Dives* P6v[2.1–4]: For saynt Poule sayth . . . Wycked speche destroyed chastyte and good thewes. **1483** Caxton *Golden Legende* 50r[2.18–20]: Thapostle sayd: The evyll wordes corrupte the good maners, **1484** *Royal Book* R2v[13–4]: And saynt Poul sayth that the shreude wordes corrumpen good maners, S8r[3–5]: As sayth saynt Poul . . . The evyl wordes corrupten the good manners. **1509** Barclay *Ship* II 53[6–7]: For as the wyse man sayth in a parable Fowle wordes infectyth maners commendable. **1532** More *Confutacion* 409 AB: Evil woordes and sermons do corrupt and marre mens good maners, **1533** *Debellacyon* 960 AB: Evill communicacion corrupteth good maners. Apperson 193; *Oxford* 180; Taylor and Whiting 78; Tilley C558.

S603 Fair **Speech** (words) breaks never bone
a1400 *Ipomadon A* 3.7: Fayre speche brekyth never bone. **a1500** *Good Wife A* 217.43: Ne fayre wordes brake never bone. Apperson 200; *Oxford* 187; Tilley W789.

S604 Fair **Speech** has brought many a man above
a1393 Gower *CA* II 242.604–5: Fair speche hath ofte brought above Ful many a man, as it is knowe.

S605 Fair **Speech** makes many a good friend
c1280 *South English Legendary: OT History* 83.37–8: Faire speche . . . maketh many a good frend and holdeth hol many a bon. See **W584.**

S606 For too much **Speech** many a man has been spilled (*ruined*)
c1390 Chaucer *CT* IX[H] 325–8: My sone, ful ofte, for to muche speche Hath many a man been spilt, as clerkes teche; But for litel speche avysely Is no man shent, to speke generally.

S607 Hasty **Speech** engenders great damage
1509 Barclay *Ship* I 110[18]: For hasty speche ingendreth great damage. See **S588, W591.**

S608 In much **Speech** sin lacks not (*varied*)
a1382 *WBible* Proverbs x 19: In myche speche shal not lacke synne (**c1395:** Synne schal not faile in myche spekyng). **c1390** Chaucer *CT* IX[H] 338: In muchel speche synne wanteth naught. **c1412** Hoccleve *Regement* 88.2429: In mochil speche wantith not offence. **1491** *Rule of St. Benet* (3) 123.30–1: In moche speche, as it is writen, synne cann not be avoyded. **a1500** *Leconfield Proverbs* 485[35–6]: In many wordis is syn comonly, Speke litill and trewly. **1522** More *Treatyce* 76 A[3–4]: The scripture saith, in many wordes lacketh not sinne. See **L67, S612.**

S609 It is good to be soft of **Speech**
a1400 *Proverbis of Wysdom* 245.65: Off speche is gwode to be sought, (*II*) 222.51: soft. **c1450**

Fyrst thou sal 89.71–2: Of speche it is gode to be soft And mefe not thi mode to oft.

S610 The last **Speech** is better than the former
c1400 *Consilia Isidori* 373[15]: The laste speche (is) better then the former. See **W598.**

S611 Little **Speech** and much hearing conquers
a1475 Ashby *Dicta* 100.1259–60: So, in litil speche and right meche heryng, Many grete vertues is conquering. See **H264.**

S612 Much **Speech** is not without strife
c1390 *Proverbes of diverse profetes* 547.377–80: Muche speche nis not with-outen strif; Hose kepeth his tonge kepeth his lyf; He that his tonge can not holde, In cumpaygnye a schrewe is told. See **S608, W600.**

S613 Seldseen (*seldom*) **Speech** has much strength
a1200 *Ancrene* 42.1–2: And leornith yeorne her bi, hu seltsene speche haveth muche strengthe.

S614 To lose no more than one's **Speech** (word)
c1385 Chaucer *TC* v 798: I shal namore lesen but my speche. **a1513** Dunbar *Dream* 129.83: And he that askis nocht tynes bot his word.

S615 To teach someone to speak one's **Speech** (*i.e.,* conquer)
a1200 Lawman III 55.26542–4: Betere inc weoren inne Rome, For thus we eou scullen techen Ure Bruttisce speche, 68.26833–4: Nu is the wulle teche Bruttisce spaeche. **c1225** *Horn* 79 C 1367–8: We schulle the hundes teche To speken ure speche.

S616 Unadvised **Speech** causes repentance
a1439 Lydgate *Fall* I 176.6221: Spech onavised causeth repentaunce.

S617 Under fair **Speech** many vices are hid
c1385 Usk 55.48–9: And under colour of fayre speche many vices may be hid and conseled. See **W585.**

S618 Under fair **Speech** men may wry (*conceal*) treason (*varied*)
a1439 Lydgate *Fall* II 358.*var.:* But oft falleth as clerkes specefie Undre fair speche men may treson wrye. **c1450** Idley 97.950: Undre feire speche ofte is hidde treason. See **D122, M196, W623, 624.**

S619 The worst **Speech** is rathest (*soonest*) heard
a1393 Gower *CA* II 283.2120–2: Comunliche in every nede The worste speche is rathest herd And lieved, til it be ansuerd.

S620 No **Speed** to spend swink (*labor*) on thing which may not be brought to end
a1325 *Cursor* III 1192 CG 20857–8: It es na spede our suinc to spend, On thing we may noght bring til end. See **R54, T104.**

S621 **Speed** is small where haste is much
c1545 Heywood *Four PP* B1v[5]: That spede is small whan haste is muche. See **H167.**

S622 As burning as **Spelds** (*sparks*) of fire
c1300 *South English Legendary* I 99.411: Vleo up and doun al bernynge as spelden doth of fure.

S623 The best **Spent** is that lent for God's love
a1500 *Good Wife N* 210.12–3: For that is best I spende, That for Gods love I lend. See **E38.**

S624 The bolder to **Spend** the worse thriving
a1500 *Good Wife N* 214.160: The bolder to spend the worse thriving.

S625 He that fast **Spends** must needs borrow
a1500 *Harley MS.116* in *Rel. Ant.* I 316[15–6]: He that fast spendyth must nede borowe; But whan he schal paye ayen, then ys al the sorowe. *Oxford* 248. See **B467.**

S626 He that never **Spends** but always spares, commonly the worse he fares
a1461 *John the Reeve* 576.455–7: He that never spendeth but alway spareth, Comonlye oft the worsse he ffareth; Others will broake itt ffine. See **S552.**

S627 **Spend** not or (*ere*) you get it
a1400 *Proverbis of Wysdom* 245.76: Spend not, ore thou hit gete, (*II*) 223.62: Spend feyr, of thou mekil gete. Cf. Tilley S738. See **T250.**

S628 Scarce **Spending** scathes gentrice (*harms nobility*)
a1500 *Colkelbie* 296.486–7: Scarss spending skathis gentriss. Cf. Tilley S745. See **L447, M120.**

S629 As round as any **Sphere**
a1420 Lydgate *Troy* I 171.940: By compas cast, rounde as any spere, 276.4585.

S630 As sweet as any (the) **Spice**
a1300 Thomas de Hales 73.168: Thu ert swetture than eny spice. **a1333** Shoreham *Poems* 86.24: So swete so the spyce. **c1390** *Mary and the Cross* 613.57: Vertu swettore then spices. **a1415** Mirk *Festial* 223.19–20: any spices. **c1455** *Speculum Misericordie* 941.22. **c1500** Newton 270.20: My lovely lady swetter then spices.

S631 To creep with **Spiders** and fly with flies
1556 Heywood *Spider* 369[11–2]: Creeping with

spiders: at times when I lust, And flieng with flies: othertimes, evine as Just. See **H586.**

S632 Not worth a **Spill** (*splinter*)
c1300 *Becket I* 42.850: For hit nis noght worth a spille.

S633 A blithe **Spirit** makes a green age
1513 Douglas *Aeneid* II 193.20–1: So that the wyss tharof in proverb wrytis, "A blith spreit makis greyn and floryst age." Cf. Tilley H301.

S634 One's **Spirit** is where his affection is
a1400 Wyclif *Sermons* II 154[12–3]: And filosofris seien over, that mannys spirit is where evere his affecioun is. See **T451.**

S635 The **Spirit** is ready but the flesh is sick
c1000 *WSG* Matthew xxvi 41: Se gast is hræd, and þæt flæsc ys untrum. **c1395** *WBible* Matthew xxvi 41: The spirit is redi, but the fleisch is sijk. *Oxford* 614; Tilley S760. See **F272.**

S636 To have one's **Spirit** in his nose
c1400 *Seven Deadly Sins* in Wyclif *SEW* III 135[35–7]: And herfore biddes tho prophete to bewar with that man that hafs his spirit in his nose and hastly takes vengeaunce. Cf. Apperson 452: His nose will abide no jests; *Oxford* 462; Tilley N223.

S637 On the **Spleen** (*i.e.*, in jest)
1460 Paston III 209[22–4]: And at evyn drank to me, and made me good chere, half on the splene, &c. **a1500** *Nut Brown Maid* 185 (*Balliol MS.*) [5–6]: When men wille breke promyse, they speke The wordis on the splene (*var.* words upon the plaine).

S638 To drink like **Sponges** and old boots
1509 Watson *Ship* E1r[4–5]: Suche folkes drynketh lyke sponges and olde bootes, Q6r[29–30]: Bacchus servauntes, that drynketh wyne lyke sponges. Cf. NED Sponge sb.[1] 8; Svartengren 190.

S639 He must have a long **Spoon** that shall eat with a fiend (the devil)
c1395 Chaucer *CT* V[F]602–3: "Therfore bihoveth hire a ful long spoon That shal ete with a feend," thus herde I seye. **c1490** *Sloane MS.747* 203.17: He that wyll with the devyll ete, A longe spone must he gete. **a1500** *Harley MS.2321* in *Rel. Ant.* I 208[11–2]: He hath need of a long spoone that eateth with the Devill. **1546** Heywood *D* 75.190: He must have a long spoone, shall eate with the devill. Apperson 143–4; *Oxford* 382; Tilley S771; Whiting *Devil* 205–6.

S640 Not worth a **Spoon** (*splinter*)
c1300 *South English Legendary* I 18.62: That ne beoth noght worth a spone.

S641 To ming (*mix*) **Sport** with earnest
c1475 Henryson *Fables* 3.19–21: And Clerkis sayis it is richt profitabill Amangis ernist to ming ane merie sport, To light the spreit, and gar the tyme be schort. See **G21.**

S642 As a sharp **Spur** makes a horse run, so a yard (*rod*) makes a child learn
a1475 Symon *Lesson* 402.91–6: And as the wyse man sayth yn his boke Off proverbis and wysedomes, ho wol loke, "As a sharppe spore makyth an hors to renne Under a man that shold werre wynne, Ryght so a yerde may make a chyld To lerne welle hys lesson, and to be myld." See **Y1.**

S643 To win one's **Spurs**
1473 Paston V 199[13]: I pray yow wynne yowr sporys in hys mater. **a1475** *Assembly of Gods* 29.980: To wynne theyr spores they seyde they wold asay, 984. **1528** More *Heresyes* 239 A[14–5]: He should not winne his spurres, **1533** *Debellacyon* 1013 E[2–3]: He had well wonne his spurres. **1556** Heywood *Spider* 179[21]: Who shall here win boote, in winning here his spurs. Apperson 688; *Oxford* 711; Taylor and Whiting 349; Tilley S792.

S644 To **Spurn** (*trip*) rather than speed (*varied*)
c1420 Wyntoun IV 73.5073–4: He spurnyt oftar than he spede That blythtles byrde that braucht to bede, 185.683–4: Qwha God til greyf wil haf na dreide He sal oft spurn qwhen he sulde speide. **a1437** *Kingis Quhair* 98.186[6–7]: And quho that will noght for this prayer turn, Quhen thai wald faynest speid, that thai may spurn. **a1450** *York Plays* 422.15: I sporne ther I was wonte to spede. **c1450** *Foly of Fulys* 62.362: That garris thaim spwrn quhen thai suld speid. **c1475** *Golagros* 30.878–9: Oft in romanis I reid: Airly sporne, late speid. Whiting *Scots* II 130.

S645 As just as a **Square**
c1395 Chaucer *CT* III[D] 2090: Thou shalt me fynde as just as is a squyre. *Oxford* 329; Skeat 274.

S646 To start (*leap*) about like a **Squirrel**
a1400 *Grete ferly* 68.119–20: In no sted con thai rest ne duelle, But stirten about ay as a squyrelle. Svartengren 159, 378.

S647 As dry as a **Staff**
1523 Berners *Froissart* III 153[14–5]: All his body became as drie as a staffe.

S648 As stark (*stiff*) as a **Staff**
a1425 *Metrical Paraphrase OT* 33:10563–4:

Starke ase a stafe his arme con stand And wold not bow his body to.

S649 He that rests on a rotten **Staff** must fall
1502 *Imitatione* (2) 185.1–3: That persone that wyll rest or be supported of a dysceyvable or roton staffe muste of necessite fall therwith. Tilley S805. See **R70, S594.**

S650 A **Staff** and a wallet
1546 Heywood *D* 71.46: What sendth he? (saie I) a staffe and a wallet. Tilley S799.

S651 To drink with one's own **Staff** (*i.e.*, nothing)
a1425 *Arthour and M.*[2] 361.2045–6: And sware by the ruth, that god hem gave He shold drinke with his owne staffe. **c1500** *Arthour and M.*[3] 482.1932–3.

S652 To have (make) a **Staff** (yard, whip, wand, rod, hammer) for oneself (*varied*)
a1325 *Cursor* II 422.7231–2: That thai desire, thai sal it desire, thai sal it have, To thair aun heved a stave. **c1385** Chaucer *TC* i 740–2: For it is seyd, "man maketh ofte a yerde With which the maker is hymself ybeten In sondry manere," as thise wyse treten. **a1393** Gower *CA* II 229.120: And make unto miself a whippe. **c1400** *Alexander Buik* III 294.6487: I gadder the wande quhairof I fale. Or ai cuelli la verge dont je serai batus! **c1400** *Beryn* 41.1313–4: Ffor there nys beting half so sore, with staff nethir (with) swerd, As man to be (I-)bete(n) with his owne yerd, 71.2324–5: But nowe myne owne yerd Betith me to sore; the strokis been to hard. **c1450** *Alphabet* II 434.19–20: At he sulde be thus betyn with his awn staff. **c1450** Idley 85.287: And be not beten with thyn owne rodde. **c1450** La Tour-Landry 21.15–6: And that she had bete her selff with her owne staffe, 54.11–2: For many men for anger betithe hym selff with his owne staffe, 176.29–30: Every woman . . . may wel bete her self with her owne staf. **1450** *Dicts* 16.1–2: As he that sekithe, the rodde where-with he is beten. **a1475** *Hit is ful harde* in *MLN* 55(1940) 567.33: To thy self loke thou make not a whyppe. **1477** Rivers *Dictes* 14[10–1]: Leste ye resemble him that seketh a rod, to be betyn with all. **1484** Caxton *Aesop* 50[15–6]: And with the staf whiche he had made he was bete, 89[17–8]: For men ought not to gyve the staf by whiche they may be beten with, **c1489** *Aymon* I 97.10–1: And it is often sayd That men make often a rodde for theym selfe, II 428.29–30: I have made myself the rodde wherwith I am beten. **a1508** Dunbar *Tretis* 94.383–4: All thus enforsit he his fa and fortifyit in strenth, And maid a stalwart staff to strik him selfe doune. **1508**(1519) Stanbridge *Vulgaria* 23.9: He hath ordeyned a staffe for his owne heed. **1509** Watson *Ship* N1[v][21–2]: We forge a hammer for to breke our bodyes withall. **1513** Skelton *Against the Scottes* I 186.146: For your owne tayle ye made a rod. **1525** Berners *Froissart* VI 52[1–2]: The constable gadred the rodde wherwith hymselfe was beaten, 77[30–1]: The rodde is gadered wherwith they shall be shortely beaten and corrected. **1546** Heywood *D* 21.40: Haste proveth a rod made for his owne tayle. Apperson 536; Jente 504; *Oxford* 547,617; Tilley R153, S802; Whiting *Drama* 44, 129, *Scots* II 130, 149. See **E222, R166, T216.**

S653 To hold (live) at **Staff's** end
c1375 Chaucer *Anel.* 183–4: His newe lady holdeth him so narowe Up by the bridil, at the staves ende. **1546** Heywood *D* 51.335–6: I live here at staves end, Where I need not borowe, nor I will not. Apperson 599; Tilley S807.

S654 **Stafford** blue (*i.e.*, a beating)
a1460 *Towneley Plays* 29.200–1: Bot thou were worthi be cled in stafford blew; Ffor thou art alway adred. **a1500** *Ballad* in *Rel. Ant.* I 29[17]: And clothe here well yn Stafford blewe. Apperson 599; *Oxford* 617.

S655 It is safer to row by the **Staithe** (*shore*) than sail on the sea
c900 *Old English Cato* 6.17–8: Treowlicre hit is beo staðe to rowen, þonne ut on sæ to segeligen. See **S248, 801.**

S656 As still as **Stake**
a1325 *Cursor* II 434.7526: Bot thar he stod als still os stake. Svartengren 384; Tilley S809.

S657 He is bound at a **Stake** that may not do but as he is bidden
c1495 *Arundel Vulgaria* 46.198: But, as men say, he is bounde at a stake that may not do but as he is bidde. See **S664, W433.**

S658 It is an ill **Stake** that cannot stand one year in a hedge
1546 Heywood *D* 66.14–5: So it is an yll stake I have heard among, That can not stande one yere in a hedge. Apperson 325; *Oxford* 617; Tilley S811.

S659 **Stake** fast
c1450 *St. Cuthbert* 141.4768: He stode stak faste.

S660 To be driven to the **Stake**
c1421 Lydgate *Thebes* 152.3687–8: And thow art dryve so narowe to the stake That thow mayst nat moo delayes make.

S661 To dry like a **Stake**
c1450 *God Send Us Patience* in Brown *Lyrics XV* 234.29: Oure bonys wol drye as doth a stake.

S662 To have eaten a **Stake**
1546 Heywood *D* 45.137–8: How be it for any great courtesie he doth make, It seemth the gentill man hath eaten a stake. Apperson 177:31; *Oxford* 167; Tilley S810.

S663 To stand like (a) **Stake**
a1393 Gower *CA* III 172.191–2: Bot as it were a stake, I stonde. **a1500** *Degrevant* 69 C 1059–60: Hys helme shal be wel steled, That stond shal as stak.

S664 Who is attached to a **Stake** may go no further
1513 Douglas *Aeneid* II 11.297–8: Quha is attachit ontill a staik, we se, May go na ferthir bot wreil about that tre. Cf. Tilley B354. See **B102, S657.**

S665 It is a **Stale** (*trick*) to take the devil in a brake (*trap*)
a1529 Skelton *Elynour* I 105.324–5: It was a stale (*for* stare [Dyce]) to take The devyll in a brake.

S666 **Stale** (*theft*) loves no delay
c1000 Aelfric *Homilies* I 220[9]: Forðan ðe stalu ne lufað nane yldinge.

S667 As true as you **Stand** here
c1497 Medwall *Fulgens* C2r[2]: But it is as true as ye stond there. Taylor and Whiting 350; Tilley S818.

S668 He that **Stands** sure let him not stir (*varied*)
a1400 *Destruction of Troy* 69.2075–7: Hit is siker, for sothe, and a sagh comyn,—"He that stalworthly stondes, stir not too swithe, Lest he faile of his fotyng and a falle have." **a1420** Lydgate *Troy* I 197.1848–9: Nor the proverbe that techeth commounly, "He that stant sure, enhast hym not to meve." **c1420** Wyntoun VI 171.6074: Qwha standis weil, he sulde noucht stere. **1484** Caxton *Aesop* 233[20–2]: Therfore he whiche is and standeth wel sure ought to kepe hym soo that he falle not For to whiche is wel meve not hym self, 239[17–21]: For many tymes I have herd saye of my graunt moder he that is wel meve not hymself For he whiche is in a place wel sure is wel a fole to go fro hit and to putte hym self in grete daunger and perylle. Apperson 599. See **S297.**

S669 He that weens to **Stand** stithest (*firmest*) his fall is next
a1325 *Cursor* I 12.61–2: He that (s)titthest wenis at stand, Warre hym his fall is nexst his hand. See **F507, K4, M314, S915, T181.**

S670 If one **Stands** still he must needs fall
a1475 *Tree* 121.18–9: I seyde, stond not stille but be ever romyng, for outher thou must ascende or descende. Yif thou stonde still thou must nedis falle.

S671 None **Stands** so surely but otherwhile he falls (*varied*)
1481 Caxton *Reynard* 73[24–5]: Ther is none that stondeth so surely but otherwhyle he falleth or slydeth. **1509** Fisher *Henry VII* 286.24–6: Saynt Poule sayth: Qui stat videat ne cadat. He that standeth let him beware that he slydeth not, for the waye is slyppery. See **B275, H63, M45.**

S672 Long **Standing** and small offering make poor parsons
1546 Heywood *D* 97.241–2: Men saie . . . long standyng and small offring Maketh poore persons, **1555** *E* 197.291. Apperson 379; *Oxford* 382; Tilley S824.

S673 As bright as (the, any) **Star**(s)
a1300 *Maximian* 99.214–5: Mi ler that wes so bright Al so the sterre a-night. **c1300** *South English Legendary* (*Laud*) 15.499: This croiz is brightore to this world thane alle the steorrene beo. **a1349** Rolle *Meditatio* 42.28: Thi woundis ben brighter than sterris. **a1400** *Alexander C* 19.604: (*Eyes*) that ware as blyckenand bright as blesand sternes. **c1400** *Plowman's Tale* 178.969. **a1430** Lydgate *Pilgrimage* 342.12584: any. **c1430** ?Lydgate *Compleynt* 66.546–8: And for this ston may longe endure, In fer to brenne fayr and bryght, As sterrys in the wyntyr nyght. **a1450** *Generydes A* 176.5642–3: any. **a1475** *Asneth* 230.87: Fair of face, bright of ble, as sterre in the firmament. **a1500** *Court of Love* 411.82: All was as bright as sterres in winter been. **1506** Hawes *Pastime* 11.157: ony, 61.1511–2: ony, 88.2271: sterre refullgent, 141.3743: ony. **a1508** Dunbar *Goldyn Targe* 114.52: the stern of day. Svartengren 227; Taylor and Whiting 350; Whiting *Scots* II 131.

S674 As clear as a **Star**
1485 Caxton *Charles* 198.11–2: Eyen as clere as two sterres. **1493** *Tretyse of Love* 116.24: Was he as cleer as a full fayr sterre. **a1508** Dunbar *Goldyn Targe* 113.36: The stanneris clere as stern in frosty nycht. Svartengren 363; Whiting *Scots* II 131.

S675 As innumerable (*etc.*) as (the) **Stars**

c875 *Azarias* in *Exeter Book* 89.36–7: Swa unrime, Had to hebban swa heofonsteorran. **a893** Wærferth *Gregory* 55.9–11: Ic gemænifealde þin sæd swa swa heofones steoran. **897** Alfred *Boethius* 19.1–3: Swa fela welena swa . . . þara steorrena ðe þiostrum nihtum scinað. **c1000** Aelfric *Heptateuch* Genesis xxii 17: Ic ðe nu bletsige and ðinne ofspring(e) gemenigfylde swa swa steorran on heofonum, *Homilies* II 62[8–9]. **a1300** *Alisaunder* 99.1737–8: Ich have moo knighttes to werren Than ben in walken sterren. **c1325** *Way of Woman's Love* 163.29–31: Ase fele sythe and oft . . . As sterres beth in welkne. **c1380** Chaucer *Boece* II m. ii 5–7: As manye rychesses as ther schynen bryghte sterres in hevene on the sterry nyghtes, *HF* 1254: Moo than sterres ben in hevene. **c1395** *WBible* Genesis xxii 17: Y schal multiplie thi seed as the sterris of hevene, xxvi 4, Deuteronomy i 10: Ye ben ful many to dai, as the sterris of hevene, xxviii 62, II Esdras ix 23, Daniel iii 36, Romans iv 18, Hebrews xi 12. **a1400** *Alexander C* 213.3676: And tho ware strenkild with stanes as sterne o the hevyn. **a1400** *Pauline Epistles* Romans iv 18, Hebrews xi 12. **c1415** *Middle English Sermons* 114.2–3: Mo bodies gadered to-thethur than is sterres on heven or graweyll in the see. **a1425** *Chester Plays* I 82.450–1. **c1425** *Speculum Sacerdotale* 222.29–30: So grete a multitude that sterres of the hevene . . . was noght thicker. **1446** Lydgate *Nightingale*, ed. Otto Glaunig (EETS ES 80, 1900) 11.283–4. **a1450** *Benedictus* in Wyclif *SEW* III 58[15]. **a1475** *Ludus Coventriae* 50.217–8. **c1475** *Brome Abraham* in Waterhouse 51.392–4. **a1500** *Feast of All Souls* in *Archiv* 79(1887) 437.277–8: Also thyke semyd they As the sterres in the sky. **a1500** *From a Departing Lover* in Robbins 199.43–4: But ofte-tymes y grete you wel As sterris sitten on the skye. **a1500** *Sen that Eine* 106.80–3: So monye starris ar nocht in nichtis sein Nor in drawing colouris, Nor scipping froggis amid the medow grein As I thocht of dolouris. Svartengren 399; Whiting *Drama* 327:308, *Scots* II 131. See **S681.**

S676 As light as (the) **Stars**
a1000 *Vercelli Homilies* 130.220–2: His miht is . . . leohtre þonne heofones tungel. **a1400** *Ipomadon A* 70.2404–6: The pensell red there fore, . . . (was) lyghter then the sterres leme.

S677 As sheen as any **Star**
a1420 Lydgate *Troy* II 426.1094: The fire brast out, schene as any sterre.

S678 As steep (*brilliant*) as any (the) **Star**
c1200 *St. Katherine* (*Royal*) 81.1647–8: Of gimstanes steapre Then is eni steorre. **a1225** *St. Marherete* 20.25: His twa ehnen steareden steappre then the steoren. **c1380** *Pearl* 5.113–6: Stones stepe, . . . As stremande sternes, quen strothe-men slepe, Staren in welkyn in wynter nyght.

S679 Study not to handle the **Stars**
a1400 *Alexander C* 142.2480: Ye suld noght stody ne stem the sternes for to handill. Cf. Tilley S825.

S680 There are more **Stars** than a pair
c1380 Chaucer *PF* 595: There been mo sterres, God wot, than a payre! Apperson 216:20, 428; *Oxford* 618.

S681 To be able to name (number) no more than the **Stars** of heaven
a1325 *Cursor* I 142.2345–6: That naman suld cun sume ne neven Na mare then sterns of heven. **c1440** *Prose Alexander* 21.14–5: Thou myghte nerehand alsonne nommer the sternes of heven, as the folke of the empire of Perse. See **S675.**

S682 To give as great light as **Stars**
c1408 Lydgate *Reson* 27.1004–5: For they yaf as gret a lyght As sterris in the frosty nyght. **a1425** *St. Robert* 49.227–8: Hys lyffe to lele men gaffe great lyght Als doys a sterne apon a nyght.

S683 To glitter like **Stars** (*etc.*) (A number of single quotations are brought together here)
a1000 *Vercelli Homilies* 87.178: He glitenað swa steorra. **a1422** Lydgate *Life* 353.604–6: With fyre of love, brynnyng also bryght . . . As done the sterres, in the frosty nyght. **1447** Bokenham 19.695: Hys eyne glastryd as sterrys be nyht. **1485** Caxton *Charles* 90.15–6: Hyr eyen . . . sparklyng lyke ii sterres.

S684 To pry upon the **Stars** and fall in a pit
c1390 Chaucer *CT* I[A] 3457–61: So ferde another clerk with astromye; He walked in the feeldes, for to prye Upon the sterres, what ther sholde bifalle, Til he was in a marle-pit yfalle; He saugh nat that. Tilley S827.

S685 To shine like (the, a) **Star(s)**
c1000 Aelfric *Homilies* II 502[20]: Scinende swa swa tungel on soðre lare, *Pastoral Letters* 176.83 O: þa-þe ge-lærede beoð, hy scynað . . . swa-swa steorran. **c1000** Apuleius in Cockayne I 164[4–5]: þeos wyrt scineð on nihte swilce steorra on heofone. **c1000** *Ecclesiastical Institutes* II 414[9–10]: Hi scynað swa swa steorran in ecnysse. **c1300** *Sawles Warde* (*Bodley*) 30.287:

The schineth as doth steorren in the eche blissen. **1340** *Ayenbite* 267[27]: Ssyneth ase sterren. **a1400** *Destruction of Troy* 99.3035–6: Hir ene . . . Shynyng full shene as the shire sternys. **a1400** *Meditations* 52.1995–6: the. **a1400** *Scottish Legends* II 309.166–7: a. **a1415** Mirk *Festial* 17.3–4: a. **a1439** Lydgate *Fall* III 675.27–8: Whos brennyng eyen sparklyng of ther liht As doon sterris the frosti wyntres niht. **c1440** *Prose Alexander* 67.32–3: sternes. **1447** Bokenham 203.7450: sterrys. **a1450** *Hail, Star* in Brown *Lyrics XV* 36.6: a. **1485** Caxton *Charles* 32.17: sterres. **c1490** Ryman 317.10: *Sanctus Franciscus claruit*, As a sterre, in his live. **1501** Douglas *Palice* 18.7: sternis. **a1508** Dunbar *Goldyn Targe* 113.36: The stanneris clere as stern on frosty nycht. **1513** Douglas *Aeneid* IV 87.18: starris, 175.55–6: The crystall bemys of hir eyen twane, That as the brycht twynkland starnys schayn. Whiting *Scots* II 131.

S686 To twinkle like the (a) **Star(s)**
c1387-95 Chaucer *CT* I[A] 267–8: His eyen twynkled in his heed aryght, As doon the sterres in the frosty nyght. **1534** Heywood *BS* 250.15–6: Her beutye twinkleth like a starre, Within the frostye nyght.

S687 Ween not to sty (*ascend*) to the **Stars**
a1200 *Ancrene* 186.20–1: Ne wene nan with este stihen to heovene, **a1250** (*Nero*) 165.27: to the steorren. **a1250** *On Ureisun* in R. Morris *Old English Homilies, First Series* (EETS 34, 1868) 201[28–9]: Ne wene nomon to stihen with este to the steorren. **a1508** Dunbar *Flyting* 5.3: Quhilk hes thame self aboif the sternis styld. See **C320.**

S688 To **Stare** broad (*with open eyes*) but see not
a1420 Lydgate *Troy* III 860.3058: He stareth brode, but he may nat se. **c1500** *Series* in Brown *Lyrics XV* 270.29–30: Summe stare brode and may not se—Be many a clerk it faret so. Cf. Taylor and Whiting 32–3.

S689 As close as **Starlings**
c1450 *Merlin* II 260[33]: Thei hem renged clos on a sop (*troop*) as starlinges.

S690 To go together like **Starlings**
c1450 *Merlin* II 193[8]: And than thei yede to-geder as starlynges.

S691 The better (greater) **State** the more wisdom (behooves)
c1450 *Douce MS.52* 56.139: The better that thi state be, The better wysdom be-hovys the. **a1500** Hill 130.13: The grettir state, the more wisedom. Que status est melior, prudencia sit tibi maior.

S692 To move no more than a **Statue**
1513 Douglas *Aeneid* III 31.96–7: Moving na mair . . . Than scho had bene a statu of marbil stane. Svartengren 383–4; Taylor and Whiting 351. See **S775, 792.**

S693 He learned timely to **Steal** that could not say nay
a1460 *Towneley Plays* 133.524: He lernyd tymely to steyll that couth not say nay. *Oxford* 358; Tilley N53.

S694 Whoso **Steals** when he is drunk shall be hanged when he is fresh (*sober*)
c1475 *Rawlinson MS. D 328* 121.46: Ho so stelyth when he ys dronke he shall an-hanggyd when he ys fresch. Tilley M175: kills a man. See **D421, M103, S374.**

S695 It is ill **Stealing** from a thief
c1515 Barclay *Eclogues* 216.962: It is ill stealing from a thiefe. Apperson 473; Tilley S837.

S696 To run as swift as any **Steed**
c1300 *Guy*[1] 376.7164: And swifter ernend than ani stede.

S697 When the **Steed** is stolen make fast the stable door (*varied*)
a1393 Gower *CA* II 325.901–3: For whan the grete Stiede Is stole, thanne he taketh hiede, And makth the stable dore fast. **c1450** *Douce MS.52* 46.22: When the hors is stole, steke the stabull-dore. **c1450** *Rylands MS.394* 97.16. **c1475** *Rawlinson MS. D 328* 118.9: When the stede ys stole hit ys tyme to schette the stabell doyr. **1480** Caxton *Ovyde* 17[28–9]: It is a comyn proverbe and trouthe it is. Whan the hors is stolen, it is to late to shete the stable, **1484** *Aesop* 245[13–4]: It was not tyme to shette the stable whan the horses ben loste and gone. **c1490** *Sloane MS. 747* 204.19: Whan the stede ys stole, than shytte the stable dore. **a1500** Hill 128.23: Whan the stede is stolen, shit the stabill dore. **a1500** *Lay of Sorrow* 717.84–5: Bot all to late to stek the stable nowe; Begane I quhane the stede Is stollin away. **c1500** *King Hart* 107.25–6: The steid is stollin, steik the dure; lat se Quhat may avale; God wait! the stall is tume! **c1500** *Melusine* 97.8–9: And good it is to shette the stable before the hors be lost, 184.32–3: For good it is to shette the stable or ever the horses be lost. **c1505** Watson *Valentine* 46.16–8: For it is a comyn sayeng, that to late it is for to shyt the stable doore, whan the horse is loste. **1509** Barclay *Ship* I 76[17]: Whan the stede is stolyn

to shyt the stable dore. **1509** Watson *Ship* D3r[9–10]: The foole . . . shytteth the stable dore whan the horse is stolen. **1523** Skelton *Garlande* I 418.1435: When the stede is stolyn, spar the stable dur. **1525** Berners *Froissart* V 83[8–9]: Ye wyll close faste the stable whan the horse is loste, **a1533** *Huon* 311.15–6: Do as he doth that closyth the stable dore whan the horse is stollen. **1546** Heywood *D* 37.86–7: To late . . . Whan the steede is stolne shut the stable durre. Apperson 598–9; *Oxford* 587; Taylor and Whiting 109; Tilley S838; Whiting *Drama* 130, 144, 283, *Scots* II 131. Cf. Jente 15. See **B439, H608.**

S698 As firm as **Steel**
1480 Caxton *Ovyde* 185[30]: More ferme . . . than steel. Whiting *Scots* II 131.

S699 As hard as (any) **Steel**
c1175 *History of the Holy Rood-Tree*, ed. A. S. Napier (EETS 103, 1894) 24.36–26.1: þa wearð hit swa heard swylce hit stælen wære. **c1330** *Degare* 79.352(*var.*): And harder than stele, 354 (*var.*). **a1393** Gower *CA* II 25.733–5: As Stiel is hardest in his kynde Above alle othre that men finde Of Metals. **a1400** *Scottish Legends* I 267.408. **c1408** Lydgate *Reson* 32.1189. **c1410** Lovelich *Grail* II 290.453: ony, III 156.280. **a1430** Lydgate *Pilgrimage* 113.4275–6, **a1449** *Fabula* in *MP* II 494.234: any. **a1460** *Towneley Plays* 347.225, 348.258. **1480** Caxton *Ovyde* 185[30]. **c1500** *Lover's Farewell* in Robbins 213.128. **1509** Barclay *Ship* I 4[10]. **a1533** Berners *Arthur* 159[17–8]. Tilley S839; Whiting *NC* 481, *Scots* II 131.

S700 As sharp as **Steel**
1509 Watson *Ship* U6r[18–9]: A spere more sharper than stele. **a1533** Berners *Arthur* 170[23–4]: Teth . . . as sharp as stele. Taylor and Whiting 352.

S701 As stable as (any) **Steel**
a1325 *Cursor* III 1414.24708: And held thi stat ai stabil as stele. **a1449** Lydgate *Testament* in *MP* I 344.397: Lyke brotel glasse, not stable nor like stell. **a1460** *Towneley Plays* 197.70: Syn thou art stabyll as any steyll.

S702 As steadfast as **Steel**
a1350 *Nicodemus* (*Galba*) 38.261: This quest stedfast als stele. **a1450** *York Plays* 247.166.

S703 As stiff as **Steel**
c1375 *St. Matthew* 132.86: Was armed with scales stif als stele. **a1450** *How Man's Flesh* in Kail 93.124: Styffere than stel. **c1475** Henryson *Testament* 123.538. Tilley S839; Whiting *Scots* II 131.

S704 As stith (*strong*) and stark as **Steel**
c1400 *Alexander Buik* IV 364.8661: And was baith styth and stark as steill. Whiting *Scots* II 131.

S705 As strong as (any) **Steel**
c1330 *St. Katherine* 245.159: And that thyn herte be strong as steel. **a1333** Shoreham *Poems* 128.51: Thou ert the gate so stronge so stel. **a1338** Mannyng *Chronicle A* I 379.10851–2: any. **c1400** *Sowdone* 11.349. **a1425** *Templum Domini* 105.519. **a1475** *Wright's Chaste Wife*, ed. F. J. Furnivall (EETS 12, 1865) 3.82: eny. **1513** Douglas *Aeneid* III 41.211. Tilley S839; Whiting *NC* 481.

S706 As sure as (any) **Steel**
a1430 Lydgate *Pilgrimage* 214.7663: Ffor thys helm, surer than Stel, 218.7809: any. Tilley S840; Whiting *Drama* 327:309.

S707 As traist (*firm, sure*) as (the) **Steel**
1456 Hay *Law* 242.30: Traist as stele. **a1513** Dunbar *Of the Ladyis* 98.19: Trest as the steill. Whiting *Scots* II 131–2.

S708 As trist (*sure*) as (any) **Steel**
a1338 Mannyng *Chronicle A* I 39.1108: Gyf Brutus wold be tryst as stel, 171.4864: Tristiloker than ony stel. See **S712.**

S709 As true as (any, the) **Steel**
c1300 *Northern Homily Cycle* (*Edin. Coll. Phys.*) 167[4]: And wend that scho war treu als stele. **c1303** Mannyng *Handlyng* 83.2338: And to the dede was as trew as steyl. **c1330** *Horn Childe* 182.298. **a1338** Mannyng *Chronicle A* I 201.5718, *B* I 73[26]. **c1350** *Good Wife E* 164.80. **c1350** *Proprium Sanctorum* 106.84. **c1375** *St. Simon and St. Jude* in Horstmann *Legenden 1881* 139.139. **c1380** Chaucer *PF* 395: The wyse and worthi, secre, trewe as stel, **c1385** *TC* v 831, **c1386** *LGW* F 334: any, 2582. **c1390** *Song of Love* in Brown *Lyrics XIV* 180.70: eny. **c1390** *Verses on the Earthquake of 1382* in Brown *Lyrics XIV* 187.31. **a1393** Gower *CA* III 216.1814: eny. **c1395** Chaucer *CT* IV[E] 2426–7: As trewe as any steel I have a wyf. **a1400** *Dame Sirith* 5.95. **a1400** *Romaunt B* 5146: ony. **a1400** *Song of Mercy* in Brown *Lyrics XIV* 98.13: any. **a1400** *Torrent* 18.477. **c1400** *Florence* 11.301: any. **c1400** *Laud Troy* II 358.12145: any. **c1400** *Triamour* 48.17, 50.116: That ye ar trewe as stele on tree (*var.* [*Percy Folio Manuscript* II 84.104]: turtle on the tree). **c1408** Lydgate *Reson* 178.6802: any. **c1410** Lovelich *Grail* IV 289.452. **a1420** Lydgate *Troy* I 270.4400: any, 284.4874: any, II 538.4967, **1420** *Temple* 36.866:

eny, **c1421** *Thebes* 61.1450: eny. **c1422** Hoccleve *Dialog* 138.798. **a1425** *Metrical Paraphrase OT* 48.11096. **a1425** *Nicodemus (Additional)* 39.261. **c1440** *St. Christopher* 454.5: any. **a1450** *Castle* 96.618. **a1450** *Partonope* 168.4605, 462.11647, 465.11745. **a1450** *St. Etheldreda* 289.289: ony. **c1450** *Bi a forest* in Furnivall *Hymns* 96.51: ony. **c1450** *Good Wife L* 199.88. **c1450** *In Praise of Brunettes* in Robbins 31.22: any. **a1460** *Towneley Plays* 26.120, 123.226, 138.699. **1460** *In the day of faste* in *English Chronicle* 94[2]. **1464** Hardyng 407[5]: any. **c1470** *Wallace* 275.1274. **a1475** *Letter to his Mistress* in Robbins 196.12: anne. **a1475** *Sinner's Lament* in Anne L. Leonard *Zwei mittelenglische Geschichten aus der Hölle* (Zürich, 1891) 64.215: any. **a1475** *Vision of Philibert* 26[13]. **c1485** *Mary Magdalene (Digby)* 116.1637. **a1500** *Al tho that list* in *Bannatyne* IV 65.17. **a1500** *Christ's Resurrection* in *Archiv* 79(1887) 442.93. **a1500** *Eger H* 243.1003: the. **a1500** *Good Wife A* 219.95–6: Thofe that thei wer all trew As any stele that bereth hew. **a1500** Greene *Carols* 400 (*refrain*): Wemen be as trew as stele (*ironic*). **a1500** *Guy*[4] 102.3207–8. **a1500** *Merchant and his Son* in Hazlitt *EPP* I 146.194: any. **a1500** *Think Before You Speak* in Brown *Lyrics XV* 280.14: eny. **1504** Hawes *Example* Cc3[v][11]. **a1513** Dunbar *Welcome* 49.14: ony. **1557** Heywood *BS* 273.32. Apperson 647; *Oxford* 672; Taylor and Whiting 352; Tilley S840; Whiting *Drama* 327:309, *Scots* II 131.

S710 As trust (*trusty*) as (any) **Steel**
a1338 Mannyng *Chronicle B* I 60[24]: And his sonnes bothe tille him war trost als stele. **a1400** *Romaunt B* 5146: As trust . . . as ony stel.

S711 To endure better than the **Steel**
a1500 *Jeaste* 215.288: He endureth better than doth the steele.

S712 To trist (*trust*) as to the **Steel**
a1338 Mannyng *Chronicle A* II 488.14060: Til hym he tryste as to the stel. See **S708.**

S713 As great as any **Steer**
c1385 Chaucer *CT* I[A] 2148–9: White alauntz, Twenty and mo, as grete as any steer.

S714 To look like a wild **Steer**
c1422 Hoccleve *Complaint* 99.120–1: Men seyden, I loked as a wilde steer, And so my loke abowt I gan to throwe.

S715 Hery (*praise*) the **Steersman** but not before he comes safe to the hithe (*port*)
c1000 Aelfric *Homilies* II 560[22–3]: Hera ðone steorman, ac na swa-ðeah ærðan ðe he becume gesundful to þære hyðe. See **E81, 158, H363, P39.**

S716 **Stench** of garlic voids stench of dunghills (*varied*)
a1398(1495) Bartholomaeus-Trevisa JJ viii[r][1. 3–7]: And though noo good odoure be contrary to the other, yet some stenche is contrary to a nother stenche. For the stenche of Garlyk is contrari to the stenche of a dounghylle. **c1477** Norton *Ordinal* 71[20–3]: This olde opinion you maie teach your Brother, How noe good Odour is contrary to another; But it is not soe of stinking smells, For stinch of Garlick voydeth stinch of Dunghills. MED gar-lec 1 (c); Tilley S556.

S717 To be a **Stepchild** (-**son**)
c1410 Hoccleve *Balade* I 58.23: Let me no stepchyld been. **1520** Whittinton *Vulgaria* 55.30: He dealeth with me as hardely as I were his stepsone.

S718 To be a **Stepdame**
c1450 *Pilgrimage LM* 104[29–30]: She is more stepdame to pilgrimes than kyte to chekenes, 185[17]. **1532** Berners *Golden Boke* 209.2967–8: Stepdame to al foles.

S719 To be a **Stepfather**
c1300 *Northern Homily Cycle (Edin. Coll. Phys.)* 123[3–4]: Hir steffader cal I the Fend, For igain hir es he unhende. **c1383** *Grete Sentence* in Wyclif *SEW* III 335[16]: This weiward steffadris of mennus soulis. **c1489** Caxton *Aymon* I 83.16–7: It is no love of a natureill fader, but it is rigoure of a stepfader.

S720 To be a **Stepmother** (*varied*)
c1300 *Northern Homily Cycle (Edin. Coll. Phys.)* 123[10–2]: Hir stepmoder that dos hir wa, Hir stepmoder es fleys liking, That til hir stepfader wil hir bring. **c1300** *South English Legendary* I 110.10: For stepmoder is selde god. **c1330** *Seven Sages A* 9.249–50: And thoughte, so stepmoder doth In to falsenesse torne soth, 26. 679–80: Hit nis non hale To leve stepmoderes tale, 39.979–80. **a1375** *William* 10.130–2: Than studied sche stifly as stepmoderes wol alle To do dernly a despit to here stepchilderen; Fethli a-mong foure schore unnethe findestow on gode, 132.4099: And strived stifli with hire-self as stepmoderes wol alle. **1385** Usk 144.85–6: My dul wit is hindred by stepmoder of foryeting. **a1387** Higden-Trevisa I 5[12–3]: Forgetingnes all wey kypinge the craft of a stepdamme, he is enmy of mynde. **c1390** *Mary and the Cross* 613.62–3: Tre unkynde, thou schalt be kud; Mi

sone step-Moder, I the calle. **a1400** Gaytryge *Sermon* in Perry *Religious Pieces* 14.10: Step-modire and stamerynge agaynes gude thewes. **a1400** *Romaunt B* 5472–3: And plongeth hem in poverte, As a stepmoder envyous. **c1400** *Beryn* 40–1.1281–3: Ffor now, I am in certen, I have a Stepmodir: They been shrewis som,—ther been but few othir,—Vel fikil flaptaill, 72.2359–60. **c1408** Lydgate *Reson* 44.1647–9: Al thogh ful selde, as men may se, That stepmodres kynde be To children born out of wed-lok, **a1439** *Fall* I 65.2348: Lik a stepmooder avenged for to be, 134.4811, 217.642–4, II 330.29–30, 440.3980: Wil is a stepmoder of witt and of resoun, 477.150–1, 670.3047, III 687.477, **a1449** *Vertu* in *MP* II 838.83–4. **a1449** Lydgate and Burgh *Secrees* 21.664–5. **1480** Caxton *Ovyde* 38[16]: I am not to the as a bytter stepmoder, **c1483** *Dialogues* 33.2–3: She said that never stepfadre Ne stepmodre were good. **1483** *Quatuor Sermones* 35[27–8]: Ydelnesse . . . is . . . stepmoder to goodnes. **c1489** Caxton *Aymon* I 131.5–6: I am not a moder but a stepmoder. **c1500** ?Bradshaw *Radegunde* 4[16]. **c1515** Barclay *Eclogues* 186.154. NED Stepmother lc; Tilley H374. See **F520, S257.**

S721 From **Sterling** to Stranaver
a1513 Dunbar *Of a Dance* 60.13: To seik fra Sterling to Stranaver.

S722 Where a good **Steward** is seldom any riches want
a1500 *Good Wife A* 217.17–8: For wher that a gode stowerde is, Wantys seldom any ryches.

S723 As dry as a **Stick**
a1398(1495) Bartholomaeus-Trevisa Z1v[2.33–4]: And drye as is (*for* it) were a stycke. Svartengren 300; Taylor and Whiting 353.

S724 As stiff as a **Stick**
a1475 *Ludus Coventriae* 144.260: Styff as a stykke. Cf. Svartengren 263.

S725 As still as dry **Sticks**
c1375 *St. Andrew* in Horstmann *Legenden 1881* 7.230: Als dry stykkes than stode thai still.

S726 As thick as **Sticks** in a hedge (crow's nest)
a1300 *Alisaunder* 247.4431–2: The speres craketh also thicke So on hegge sere stykke. **a1300** *Arthour and M.*[1] 256.9171–4: Heveden, fet and armes ther Lay strewed everi wher Under stede fet so thicke, In crowes nest so dothe the sticke.

S727 The more **Sticks** the greater the fire
a1396(1494) Hilton *Scale* M2v (*by error* K2v) [16–7]: For the more styckes are layed to the fyre: the gretter is the fyre. See **W560.**

S728 Small **Sticks** burn first
c1303 Mannyng *Handlyng* 390.12436–7: Thou seest stykkes that are smale, They brenne fyrst, feyre and shyre. Apperson 373: Little; *Oxford* 375.

S729 With silver **Stick** one can grave gold
c1250 *Hendyng O* 194.15: Mid selvrene stikke me shal gold graven. Kneuer 66; Schleich 253–4; Singer III 128.

S730 To stumble at the **Stile**
a1352 Minot 4.87–8: The Scottes gaudes might no thing gain, For all thai stumbilde at that stile. NED Stile sb.[1] lb.

S731 You would be over the **Stile** ere you come to it
1528 More *Heresyes* 209 B[9–10]: We be now gone over the style or we come at it, **1533** *Confutacion* 666 G[2–3]: How he jugleth himself over the style ere he come at it. **1546** Heywood *D* 97.238: Ye would be over the style, er ye come at it. Apperson 602; *Oxford* 482; Tilley S856.

S732 Better wisely to be **Still** than foolishly to speak
1485 Caxton *Charles* 93.4–6: It is better a man wysely to be stylle than folysshly to speke. See **E177, S77.**

S733 He that holds him **Still** gives consent (*varied*)
c1384 Wyclif *Church and her Members* in *SEW* III 349[10–1]: For oo maner of consent is, whanne a man is stille and tellith not. **c1385** Usk 36.66–7: Lo eke an olde proverbe amonges many other: "He that is stille semeth as he graunted." **c1405** *Mum* 49.743–5: And also in cuntrey hit is a comune speche And is y-write in Latyne, lerne hit who-so wil: The reason is "qui tacet consentire videtur." **c1412** Hoccleve *Regement* 112.3092–4: Nat a worde dare he crake; And for he naght ne seith, he his assent yeveth therto, by mannes Jugement. **a1450** *Partonope* 467. 11783–4: This proverbe was seide full longe a-go: "Who so holdeth hym still dothe assent." **a1460** *Towneley Plays* 232.143–4: Et omnis qui tacet hic consentire videtur. **a1470** Parker *Dives* T7r[1.37–2.3]: For as the lawe sayth. Qui tacet consentire videtur. He that is styll and wyll not saye the treuthe whan he sholde saye it, he semeth that he consenteth to falsenesse. Apperson 571; Jente 297; *Oxford* 589; Taylor and Whiting 333; Tilley S446; Whiting *Scots* II 125.

S734 **Still** (*calm*) after storm

a1200 *Ancrene* 191.2–3: Thu laverd, the makest stille efter storm. *Oxford* 4. See **S278, 797.**

S735 To drop (run) like a **Stillatory**
c1395 Chaucer *CT* VIII[G] 580–1: His forheed dropped as a stillatorie, Were ful of plantayne and of paritorie. **1537** *Norfolk to Crumwell* in *State Papers Published Under the Authority of His Majesty's Commission, V: King Henry the Eighth, Part IV, cont.* (1836) 104[18–9]: My noose dothe contynewally ron like a styllitorie.

S736 As many as **Stitches** in a shirt
c1440 Charles of Orleans 107.3199: More joy then ther be stichis in my shert.

S737 As hard as a **Stithy**
1509 Watson *Ship* Aa4^r[10–1]: The herte also harde as a stedye. **a1533** Berners *Huon* 380.20–1: Yf his body were harder than a stethy of stele. Svartengren 260.

S738 As blind as (any) **Stock**
c1408 Lydgate *Reson* 141.5381: But is as blynde as stok. **a1450** *St. Editha* 80.3567–8: Bot they weron as blynd alle bothe y-wys As ever was ony stok.

S739 As dead as a **Stock**
c1300 *South English Legendary* II 589.102: He fel doun ded as a stok. **c1303** Mannyng *Handlyng* 34.940: And fyl hym self ded as a stok.

S740 As dry as a (any) **Stock**
c1303 Mannyng *Handlyng* 286.9107–8: But was as drye, with al the haunche, As of a stok were ryve a braunche. **c1450** Idley 209.345: Whych was drye as any stok or tre. See **T454.**

S741 As dumb as (a) **Stock**
a1420 Lydgate *Troy* I 301.5475: The ydole, doumbe as stok, **a1430** *Pilgrimage* 558.20921: But ys as dowmb as stok, **1439** *St. Albon* 150. 1380: Domme as a stocke. Whiting *Scots* II 132.

S742 As stiff as **Stock** (*etc.*) (A number of single quotations are brought together here)
a1300 *Arthour and M.*[1] 110.3855: Arthour on hors sat stef so stok, 223.7970. **c1408** Lydgate *Reson* 168.6411: But ben as deffe as stok, **a1420** *Troy* III 763.6786: Harder . . . than . . . stok. **c1425** *St. Elizabeth of Spalbek* 115.14: Alle-starke as a stok. **1439** Lydgate *St. Albon* 150.1387: Of tonge (mewet) as any stocke.

S743 Loath **Stock** (stake) stands long
c1450 *Rylands MS.394* 108.5: Loth stok longe stondes. Trunculus hostilis dat longo tempore vilis. **1546** Heywood *D* 66.13: The lothe stake standeth longe, **1555** *E* 193.271. Apperson 325: ill; *Oxford* 617; Tilley S812.

S744 Of cursed **Stock** comes unkind blood
c1421 Lydgate *Thebes* 43.1014: Of Cursid stok cometh unkynde blood. See **T465.**

S745 One might as well stir a **Stock** as a stone
a1450 *York Plays* 301.267: A man myght as wele stere a stokke as a stone.

S746 **Stock** still
c1475 *Golagros* 4.108: Stok still as ane stane. NED Stock still.

S747 To go no more than a **Stock**
c1300 *South English Legendary* (*Laud*) 34.28: That he ne mighhte non more thane a stok: a fot of that stude gon.

S748 To lie like a **Stock**
c1300 *South English Legendary* (*Laud*) 34.31: He liet him ligge thare ase astok. **1522** More *Treatyce* 80 D[4–5]: Lye specheles as a dead stock, F[8].

S749 Who lacks a **Stock** his gain is not worth a chip
1546 Heywood *D* 94.140: Who lackth a stocke, his gaine is not woorth a chip. Apperson 348; *Oxford* 347; Tilley S866.

S750 As wrinkled as a **Stockfish**
c1515 Barclay *Eclogues* 8.241: And as a stockfishe wrinkled is my skinne.

S751 A **Stockfish** bone gives a light in darkness (*i.e.*, don't count on looks)
a1449 Lydgate *Mydsomer Rose* in *MP* II 781.13: A stokfyssh boon in dirknesse yevith a light.

S752 A full **Stomach** may not be holy
c1450 La Tour-Landry 8.10–1: For a full stomake may not be holy and perfitly humble and devoute. Cf. Tilley B285. See **B243.**

S753 A full **Stomach** regards a honeycomb as nothing
a1500 *Leconfield Proverbs* 485[1–2]: A full stomake a honycome regardithe no thinge, But a sowre morsell is swete where hunger in constraynynge. See **F604, H643.**

S754 To take something sore at one's **Stomach** (*i.e.*, become annoyed)
1482 *Cely Papers* 131[6–7]: The wyche y understond ye taked sor at yowre stomak. NED Stomach 6. Cf. Tilley S874.

S755 All **Stones** that shine (of) color inde (*indigo*) are not sapphires
a1410 Lydgate *Churl* in *MP* II 481.307–8: Nor stoonys all bi natur, as I fynde, Be nat saphires that shewe colour ynde. See **G282.**

S756 As bare as (a) **Stone**
c1415 *Middle English Sermons* 182.39: Thei shall make the as bare as . . . stone. **c1440** *St. Christopher* 465.894: Als . . . bare als es a stane.

S757 As blind as (the, any, a) **Stone**
c1300 *South English Legendary* II 372.212: As blind as the ston. **a1330** *Legend of Mary* 501. 145: Yif thou be blinde as ani ston. **c1330** *Seven Sages A* 107.2349: He becam blind so ston, 207.1659: any, **a1350** *C* 89.2607: a. **c1375** *St. Anastasia* in Horstmann *Legenden 1881* 27.162: any. **c1375** *St. Cristine* in Horstmann *Legenden 1881* 96.296: any. **c1395** Chaucer *CT* IV[E] 2156: a. **a1400** *Romaunt B* 3703. **c1408** Lydgate *Reson* 141.5381. **a1425** *Hayle, bote of bale* in *Wheatley MS.* 8.77: any. **a1430** Lydgate *Pilgrimage* 264.9573: a, 270.9834: a. **a1450** *St. Editha* 80.3567–8: ony. **a1450** *St. Etheldreda* 305.1020: ony. **a1450** *York Plays* 212.356: any. **a1460** *Towneley Plays* 360.206: any.

S757a **Stone-blind**
a1400 *Scottish Legends* I 196.230: And to stane blynde gef als the sycht, 234.420: He worde stane-blynde in-to haste, II 342.1322. **1456** Hay *Law* 19.6–7. Taylor and Whiting 355; Whiting *Scots* II 133.

S758 As cold as (a, any) **Stone**
a1300 *Latemest Day* in Brown *Lyrics XIII* 47.21: Thenne liit the cleyclot cold alse an ston, 51.37. **c1300** *South English Legendary* I 21.80: This child ligge ded so cold so eny ston, (*Laud*) 183.80: a, 388.386: ani. **c1325** *Charter of Christ C* in *Vernon* II 641.124. **c1330** *Gregorius* 141 A 798: ani. **a1338** Mannyng *Chronicle B* I 56[24]: any. **1340** *Ayenbite* 242[14]: a. **1369** Chaucer *BD* 123. **c1400** *Vices and Virtues* 268.27: a. **a1420** Lydgate *Troy* I 267.4292–3: any, II 554.5533: any, **a1422** *Life* 456.384. **a1425** *Alexius* (*Laud* 463) 51.316. **a1437** *Kingis Quair* 74.103[4]. **a1450** *Partonope* 20.741: any. **c1450** *Owayne Miles* (*Cotton Caligula*) 117.316: ony. **1484** Caxton *Royal Book* T6ᵛ[5]: a. **a1500** *Knight of Curtesy* 3.66: any. **a1500** *Nut Brown Maid* 178[2]: any, 179.70: any. **1506** Barclay *Castell* A6ᵛ[14]: ony, **1509** *Ship* I 296[4], **1515** *St. George* 41.824. Apperson 106; Taylor and Whiting 355; Tilley S876; Whiting *Drama* 327:313, *Scots* II 132.

S759 As dead as (a, any, the) **Stone**
c1280 *Southern Passion* 18.498: Ar he lygge as ded as ston. **a1300** *Arthour and M.*[1] 98.3456. **a1300** *Meidan Maregrete* 493.149: The godes that tou levest on are dede ase a ston. **a1300** *Richard* 121.798: He fel doun ded as ony ston, 125.868: ony. **c1300** *Havelok* 89.2649: ani. **c1300** *St. Alexius* 185.512: a. **c1300** *South English Legendary* I 248.44, II 375.48: the, 706.238: a, (*Laud*) 368.48: any. **a1325** *Cursor* II 690 CG 12028, 1102.19258, III 1561.28661. **c1330** *Tars* 47 A 582: the. **a1338** Mannyng *Chronicle B* I 44[27]: any. **c1350** *Smaller Vernon Collection* 40.366: eny. **c1369** Chaucer *BD* 1300–1, **c1370** *Pity* 16: a. **a1393** Gower *CA* II 204.2741: eny. **c1395** Chaucer *CT* V[F] 474: a. **a1400** *Childhood of Christ* in Horstmann *Sammlung* 106.415: a. **a1400** *Cursor* II 962 FGT 16832. **a1400** *Destruction of Troy* 139.4281: a. **c1400** *Tundale* 6.106: one. **c1410** Lovelich *Grail* II 301.102: Ony, III 193.98, IV 284.278: Ony, *Merlin* III 677.25486: ony, 735.27714. **c1412** Hoccleve *Regement* 65.1804–5: Myn hert is also deed as is a stoon; Nay, ther I faile, a stoon no thyng ne felith, **c1422** *Lerne to Die* 205.714: a. **a1425** *Arthour and M.*[2] 336.1347: any. **a1425** *Blood of Hayles* in Horstmann *Legenden 1881* 277.140: a. **a1425** *Northern Passion* 142 CGg 55°: any. **a1430** Lydgate *Pilgrimage* 558.20927, **a1449** *Dan Joos* in *MP* I 313.68: a. **a1450** *Generydes A* 141.4528–9: a, 252.8151–2: a. **a1450** *Partonope* 352.8658: any. **a1450** *St. Editha* 44.1939: ony, 74.3319. **a1470** Malory I 208.19–20: a. **a1475** Banester *Guiscardo* 34.557. **a1500** *Alexius* (*Cotton*) 62.300: ony. **a1500** *Court of Love* 435.995. **a1500** *Eger H* 207.429: any. **c1500** *Arthour and M.*[3] 462.1286: any. Taylor and Whiting 355; Whiting *Scots* II 132.

S759a **Stone-dead**
a1300 *Arthour and M.*[1] 200 7116: Al so he stef and stan-ded were. **c1300** *Havelok* 60.1815: So that he stan-ded fel thor dune. **c1300** *South English Legendary* I 21.76, 161.26. **a1325** Bonaventura *Meditations* (*1*) 32.1030: Truly y am stonede (*var.* stone) dede for ay. **c1375** Barbour *Bruce* I 180.471. **a1400** *Morte Arthure* 112.3823. **a1400** *Scottish Legends* II 404.237, 406.276, 438.214, 222. **a1400** *Alexander Buik* I 37.1164, IV 387.9398, 394 *cont.* 9637. **c1400** *Beryn* 42.1341: Stan dede in swowe. **a1500** *Miracles of B.V.* in *PMLA* 38(1923) 362.25. Taylor and Whiting 355–6; Whiting *Drama* 327:313, *Scots* II 132.

S760 As deaf as (a) **Stone**
c1408 Lydgate *Reson* 168.6411: But ben as deffe as . . . ston. **a1467** *Musyng* in *Rawlinson MS. C 813* 326.55: A wretched prest as deeffe nere as a stoune. Taylor *Comparisons* 33; Tilley S877.

S761 As dull as **Stone**

a1513 Dunbar *Of Discretioun in Asking* 32.9: Sowld haif ane heirar dull as stane. Whiting *Scots* II 132.

S762 As dumb as (the, a, any) **Stone**
c1330 *St. Margaret* 229.162: Thine godes thatow levest on er dom so the ston. **c1330** *Seven Sages A* 198.504: To be dethe (*?for* deafe) and dome as a ston. **c1380** Chaucer *HF* 656: And, also domb as any stoon, **c1387-95** *CT* I[A] 774: a. **a1400** *Cursor* II 788 F 13739. **a1400** *Romaunt B* 2409: a. **c1400** *Gowther* 150.389: any. **c1412** Hoccleve *Regement* 54.1496–7. **a1420** Lydgate *Troy* I 301.5475, II 515.4177: any, III 671.3632: any, **1420** *Temple* 49.1184: eny. **a1425** *Blissed be thow, Baptist* in *Wheatley MS.* 17.70. **a1430** Lydgate *Pilgrimage* 558.20921, **a1449** *Fabula* in *MP* II 513.815: ony. **a1475** *Mergarete* 238. 258–9: any. Taylor and Whiting 356; Whiting *Ballad* 31.

S763 As hard as (the, any, a) **Stone(s)**
a800 Cynewulf *Elene* in *Vercelli Book* 81.565: Heo wæron stearce, stane heardran. **c1000** *Larspell* in Napier 234.20–1: And heo bið swa heard swa stan, 241.24–5. **c1200** Orm I 344. 9878–9: And haethen follkess herrte Iss harrd and starrc all allse stan, 346.9927: Thatt all iss harrd swa summ the stan, II 109.13326–40. **c1280** *Southern Passion* 59.1598: Whuch is thin heorte, hardour than eny ston? **c1300** *Beves* 125.2677: eni. **c1300** *South English Legendary* I 140.106: eny. **a1325** Bonaventura *Meditations (1)* 1.12. **c1330** *Degare* 80.362 (*var.*): His hed harder then the ston. **1340** *Ayenbite* 242[14]: Hit is hard . . . ase a ston. **a1349** Rolle *Meditations* in Allen *R. Rolle* 26.233–4, 239: the stonys. **c1375** *St. Matthew* 137.491. **c1375** William of Nassington *Poem on the Trinity* in Perry *Religious Pieces* 71.296: For my herte es hard als it ware stane. **c1386** Chaucer *LGW* 2554: any. **a1387** Higden-Trevisa I 261[3]. **c1390** *Talkyng* 18.6: eny. **c1395** Chaucer *CT* IV[E] 1990: any. **c1395** *WBible* Isaiah i 7: Y have set my face as a stoon maad hard, Jeremiah v 3: a. **a1400** Bonaventura *Privity* in *Yorkshire Writers* I 203[26]: the. **a1400** *Jhesu that hast* in Brown *Lyrics XIV* 114.5. **a1400** *Meditations* 31.1150: any, 36.1355. **a1400** Paues *Prologue* 9.15–6. **a1400** *Scottish Legends* I 403.22. **a1400** *Titus* 8.163: the. **a1400** Wyclif *Sermons* I 88[29], II 155[2]. **c1400** *Vices and Virtues* 268.27: a. **c1410** Lovelich *Grail* I 164.608. **c1412** Hoccleve *Regement* 169.4695–6: As harde as is a post—A post? Nay, as a stoon—ben hertes now! **a1415** Mirk *Festial* 112.28–9. **a1420** Lydgate *Troy* I 173.988: any, II 404.326: any, III 763.6786, **a1430** *Pilgrimage* 108.4105: any, 435.16216: eny, 582.21826: any, 583.21833: a, **c1430** *Dance* 2.1: a, **a1439** *Fall* II 330.63, **1439** *St. Albon* 182.1192: any. **c1440** Charles of Orleans 184.5499, 5507: eny, 5515: For ought y pray y fynde yow but a stoon, 5519: That y may fynde yow softer then a stoon, 200.5952: O hert more hard then roche of any stoon. **c1440** Scrope *Epistle* 31[18]: a. **a1449** Lydgate *Ave Maria!* in *MP* I 282.61: a, *Image of Pity* in *MP* I 297.2: the. **a1450** *God's Appeal* in Kail 86.27. **a1450** *How Man's Flesh* in Kail 93.124. **a1450** *Pety Job* in Kail 131.318: a. **a1450** *St. Editha* 39.1741: ony. **c1450** *De Claris Mulieribus* 36.735. **c1450** *Epistle of Othea* 38.25: a. **c1450** *In a noon tiid* in Furnivall *Hymns* 92.51. **c1450** *Jacob's Well* 280.15–6: a, 22–3: Here hertys ben hardere than stonys of gravel, 281.13, 282.21. **c1450** *Seege of Troye* 96 A 1215, 116 A 1463: the. **a1470** Malory II 895.25: the. **a1475** *Ludus Coventriae* 268.1054. **a1475** *St. Birgitta* 9.33–4: any. **c1475** Henryson *Fables* 50.1393. **1481** Caxton *Godeffroy* 152.3–4, **1483** *Golden Legende* 115ᵛ[1.7–8]: a, **1484** *Royal Book* T6ᵛ[5]: a. **c1485** *Burial and Resurrection* 207.1046, 217.1392. **c1489** Caxton *Aymon* II 347.26–7: a. **c1493** *St. Katherin of Senis* 98.4: ony. **a1500** *Good Wife N* 212.88, 215.188: the. **1509** Fisher *Treatyse* 177.2–3, 190.32–3. **1509** Watson *Ship* Dd1ᵛ[9–10]. **c1515** Barclay *Eclogues* 80.757: the. Apperson 284; *Oxford* 278; Taylor and Whiting 356; Tilley S878.

S763a **Stone-hard**
c1390 *Mary and the Cross* 618.222: Jewes stonhard in sinnes merk. NED Stone 19.

S764 As heavy as any (a) **Stone**
a1400 *Le Morte A.* 24.761: His herte was hevy as Any stone. **c1421** Lydgate *Thebes* 41.952: a. **a1425** *Daily Work* in *Yorkshire Writers* I 148[39]: a. **c1450** Capgrave *Katharine* 297. 1103–4: a. **a1470** Parker *Dives* R4ᵛ[2.26]: a. Whiting *Scots* II 132.

S765 As mute as a (any) **Stone**
c1408 Lydgate *Reson* 82.3081: Muet as hyt wer a stoon, 164.6267, **a1420** *Troy* III 863.3156, **c1421** *Thebes* 117.2844. **c1430** ?Lydgate *Compleynt* 59.50: But stonde mut as any stone. **1439** Lydgate *St. Albon* 150.1387: any.

S766 As naked as a **Stone**
c1440 *St. Christopher* 465.894: Als nakede . . . als es a stane. **a1450** *York Plays* 347.313: But naked as a stone be stedde. **c1450** Greene *Carols* 336.7.

S766a Stone-naked
a1400 *Meditations* 46.1762: He stand stan-naked lym and lith. **a1500** *Miroure of Mans Salvacionne* 77[11]: And ye tirved him stone naked. NED Stone 19.

S767 As sad (*firm*) as (any) **Stone**
c1422 Hoccleve *Dialog* 130.558–9: As sad as any stone His herte set is and nat change can. **a1425** Rolle *Psalter* 2.46: Every word is sad as stone. **c1425** *Speculum Sacerdotale* 33.1: For thow art Pete, *scilicet,* sadde as stone. Whiting *Scots* II 132.

S768 As sicker as (a) **Stone**
c1400 *Alexander Buik* I 10.303–4: Thairfor be we als sikker all As stane closit in castell wall. **1415** Hoccleve *Oldcastle* I 15.205: As siker as stoon, **c1422** *Lerne to Die* 198.529: They deemen stonde as siker as a stoon.

S769 As stable as (a, any, the) **Stone**
a1400 Wyclif *Sermons* I 129[27]: Stable as a stoon. **a1439** Lydgate *Fall* III 890.2397: In suich a mene stable as eny ston, **1439** *St. Albon* 144.1009: any, **a1449** *Benedic* in *MP* I 6.138: any, *Misericordias* in *MP* I 77.191: a, *Prayers* in *MP* I 123.70: a, *Procession* in *MP* I 39.123: the, *St. Ursula* in *MP* I 144.6: a. **a1450** *St. Editha* 95.4290: ony. **c1450** Capgrave *Katharine* 117.110: ony, 301.1251: the. **c1450** *Lover's Mass* 101[4]: Trewe of herte, stable as ston. **a1475** *St. Birgitta* 9.33–4: any.

S770 As steadfast as (the, any, a) **Stone(s)**
c1200 Orm II 170.15070–3: Forr Jesu Crist is wiss thurrh stan O fele bokess tacnedd, Forr Crist iss strang, and stedefasst, And findig, and unnfakenn. **a1325** *Cursor* II 372.6430: That held tham stedfastli (*G*: stedfast) als stan. **a1387** Higden-Trevisa II 369[2]: As stedfast as stones. **a1400** *Seven Penitential Psalms* in *Wheatley MS.* 49.723: To be stidefast as is the stoon. **a1425** *Blissed be thow, Baptist* in *Wheatley MS.* 15.21. **c1445** ?Lydgate *Kalendare* in *MP* I 373.281: any. **c1485** *Mary Magdalene* (*Digby*) 104.1291. **a1500** Richardoune in *Lapidaries* 60.7: Nat variable ne movyng, but as a stidefast stone, 14, 21, 42, 56. **a1500** *Throwe a towne* in Sandison 122.50: Trewe, stedfaste as stone yn wall.

S771 As stiff as (a) **Stone**
a1425 *Chester Plays* II 380.213: Then shall they after be stiffe as stonne. **a1450** *St. Editha* 67. 3013: Bot this schrene stode there stille as styff as stone. **c1450** *St. Cuthbert* 143.4854: a. **a1460** *Towneley Plays* 270.399. Svartengren 263.

S772 As still as (any, a, the) **Stone**
c1200 *St. Katherine* (*Royal*) 58.1253: Ah seten stille ase stan. **c1300** *Amis* 54.1273: That knight gan hove stille so ston, 93.2318(*var.*): He loked the dore as stylle as ston. **c1300** *Becket I* 52.1048: This holi man him wende forth, as stille as eni ston. **c1300** *Havelok* 34.928: Also stille als a ston, 66.1997: Ligge stille so doth the ston, 70.2109: the, 83.2475: the. **c1300** *South English Legendary* I 193.376: eni, 349.32: a, II 569.110. **c1303** Mannyng *Handlyng* 82. 2288, 200.6186: a. **a1325** *Cursor* II 402.6958, 696.12156, 740.12881, III 1232.21548, 1392. 24327. **a1325** *Otuel and Roland* 107.1542: ony. **c1330** *Degare* 82.384: a. **c1330** *Gregorius* 87 A 401. **c1330** *Otuel* 79.491, 113.1641–2: And also stille as a ston The squier lep to horse a non. **c1330** *Rouland* 51.525: ani. **c1330** *St. Margaret* 230.205: ani. **c1330** *Seven Sages A* 196.345: a. **c1330** *Tars* 48 A 635, 49 A 659. **a1338** Mannyng *Chronicle A* I 277.7885, *B* I 219[6]. **a1350** *Monologue of a Drunkard* in Robbins 106.10: any. **c1350** *Als y yod* in Thomas Wright ed. *Langtoft* (RS 47, 1868) II 454[9]: the. **c1350** *Gamelyn* 651.263, 655.395: eny, 423: ony. **a1375** *Octavian* (*S*) 7.185–6. **c1375** *St. Peter and St. Paul* 67.304, 78.174. **c1380** Chaucer *HF* 1605, **c1385** *TC* ii 600: any, 1494: any, iii 699, iv 354, v 1729, **c1386** *LGW* F 310: any. **c1386** *St. Erkenwald* 9.219: the. **a1387** Higden-Trevisa II 369[2]. **c1390** Chaucer *CT* I[A] 3472. **c1390** *Gregorius* 74.596. **c1390** *Maiden Mary* in Brown *Lyrics XIV* 183.68. **c1390** *Mercy Passes All Things* in Brown *Lyrics XIV* 125.16: eny. **c1390** *Miracles of Our Lady* 166.6. **c1390** *Sir Gawain* 71.2293: the. **c1390** *Tars* 47 V 543: a. **a1393** Gower *CA* II 84.1794: eny, 93.2104: eny, 153.846–7: eny. **c1395** Chaucer *CT* IV[E] 121, 1818, V[F] 171: any. **a1400** *Alexander C* 9.263: a, 233.4312: a. **a1400** *Ancrene* (*Recluse*) 58.4–5: a. **a1400** Chestre *Launfal* 63.357: any. **a1400** *Cursor* II 372 FT 6430: eny, 819 T 14279. **a1400** *How to Hear Mass* 493.9. 503.369. **a1400** *Ipomadon A* 104. 3617: anny, 187.6545: anny, 220.7704. **a1400** *Meditations* 14.524. **a1400** *Melayne* 16.472: any. **c1400** *Beryn* 21.653: ony, 98.3265. **c1400** *Laud Troy* II 361.12266: any, 533.18097. **c1400** *Sowdone* 73.2537. **c1400** *Thomas of Erceldoune* 12.233. **c1400** *Toulouse* 254.757: any. **c1405** *Mum* 49.755: a, 51.826: a. **c1410** Lovelich *Grail* II 297.713: A, 417.436: a, III 35.546: ony. **1410** Walton *Boethius* 48[15]. **a1420** Lydgate *Troy* I 230.2990: any, II 515.4177: any, **1420** *Temple* 29.689: eni, **c1421** *Thebes* 139.3388, **a1422** *Life* 585.390: any. **a1425** *Abide* in Brown *Lyrics XIV* 59.9. **a1425** *For Metyng of theves* in

Speculum 33(1958) 372.19: any (cf. *Speculum* 34(1959) 637.22). **a1425** *Metrical Paraphrase OT* 96.3340: a. **a1425** Mirk *Instructions* 24.777. **c1425** *St. Elizabeth of Spalbek* 112.28. **c1425** *Seven O's* in Brown *Lyrics XV* 90.18: any. **c1433** Lydgate *St. Edmund* 434.1212. **a1437** *Kingis Quair* 65.72[6]: any. **a1440** *De Miraculo Beate Marie* 504.75. **a1449** Lydgate *Fabula* in *MP* II 513.815: ony. **a1450** *Castle* 87.345, 127. 1700. **a1450** *Generydes A* 35.1118: any, 169. 5425. **a1450** *Northern Passion* 74 CDd 735: any. **a1450** *Partonope* 34.1282: any, 41.1525: a, 100. 3091: eny, 464.11705: any. **a1450** *St. Editha* 34.1527, 66.2949, 84.3777: ony, 95.4290: ony. **a1450** *St. Etheldreda* 305.1016: ony. **a1450** *Seven Sages B* 15.407: a, 16.427: a, 34.980, 37.1068–9: a, 47.1347: a, 1351, 66.1930: a, 98.2901–2. **a1450** *South English Legendary* (*Bodley*) 393.290. **a1450** *York Plays* 108.194, 146.4, 286.372: a, 303.311: a. **c1450** Capgrave *Katharine* 243.1190: the, 336.2301: ony. **c1450** *Childhood of Christ* in *Archiv* 74(1885) 334.524: any. **c1450** Greene *Carols* 236.5: ony. **c1450** Idley 148.2521: ony, 170.726: ony, 176.1103. **c1450** *Northern Passion* 154 A 231°–2°: a. **c1450** *Robin Hood and the Monk* in Child III 98.31: any. **c1450** *Three Kings of Cologne* in *Archiv* 129(1912) 57.287. **a1460** *Towneley Plays* 35.406, 39.525: a, 78.6, 222.561: any, 258.2: Stand as styll as stone in Wall, 327.60–1: He stud as still, that bright, As stone in wall. **a1475** *Guy*² 103.3585: a. **c1475** *Golagros* 4.108: ane. **1493** *Seven Wise Masters* 71[7]: a. **a1500** *Basyn* 49.127: any. **a1500** *Beves* 106[4]: eny. **a1500** *Chaucer's Dreme* in Speght's *Chaucer* 358ʳ[1.53]. **a1500** Greene *Carols* 399.2: a. **a1500** *Guy*⁴ 17.235: a, 105.3303. **a1500** *Our Lady's Imprecation* in Brown *Lyrics XV* 20.61: eny, 22.103. **a1500** *Prayer of the Holy Name* in Brown *Lyrics XV* 191.5: eny. **a1500** ?Ros *La Belle Dame* 319.656. **a1500** *Thoythis fre* in *MLN* 69(1954) 155.2: any. **c1500** *Lady Bessy* 29[30]: any, 47[19]: any. **c1500** *Lancelot* 31.1032: ony. **1513** Douglas *Aeneid* II 81.10. Apperson 602; Taylor and Whiting 356; Tilley S879; Whiting *Scots* II 133.

S772a Stone-still
a1200 *Ancrene* 212.12: Ye sitten with Marie stan stille ed godes fet. **a1338** Mannyng *Chronicle A* I 452.13034: And held Petron al ston(e) stille, *B* II 266[13]: Bot hold tham stone stille in pes at ther cuntre. **a1350** *Seven Sages C* 134.3994. **c1350** *Gamelyn* 646.67. **a1352** Minot 5.32. **c1390** *Sir Gawain* 8.242. **a1400** *Childhood of Christ* in Horstmann *Sammlung* 107.482. **a1400** *Hunting of the Hare* 281.42. **a1400** *Ipomadon A* 48.1603, 157.5488, 239.8416. **a1400** *Perceval* 27.841. **a1400** *Scottish Legends* I 21.491, 192.79, II 33.1143, 452.340, 456.481. **c1400** *Laud Troy* I 200.6788, 201.6819, 264.8949, II 503.17099–100. **c1400** *Scottish Troy* 276.1757. **c1420** Wyntoun V 342.2583, VI 328.741. **c1425** *St. Elizabeth of Spalbek* 115.36. **1449** Metham 60.1635. **a1450** *Seven Sages B* 59.1735. **a1450** *York Plays* 127.28, 248.175, 294.65, 300.243, 307.2, 337.2. **c1450** *Richard* 90.218 (*var.*). **a1460** *Towneley Plays* 78.12, 123.232, 125.280. **a1470** Malory I 164.17. **a1475** *Guy*² 288.10027. **a1500** *St. Anne* (*3*) 120.293. **1534** More *Comforte* 1181 H[4–5]. **1562** Heywood *E* 231.14.6. NED Stone-still; Whiting *Scots* II 133.

S773 As sure as **Stone**
c1450 Idley 109.44: With herte and thought as sure as stoone.

S774 As true as (a, any) **Stone**
a1300 *Tristrem* II 6.115: Rohand trewe so stan, 10.270. **a1325** *Cursor* III 1282 CFG 22409: And stabili agh we tru als stan. **c1350** *Good Wife E* 162.74 (*H*: the). **a1350** *Proprium Sanctorum* 105.30–1. **c1380** *Pearl* 30.822. **c1390** *Sir Gawain* p. viii[11]. **a1400** *Ipomadon A* 84.2903. **a1400** *Or Crist into cloudes* in *PMLA* 70(1955) 217.12: a. **a1400** *Romaunt B* 5248. **a1450** Audelay 12.59: ane, 205.18: To him thou art treu as ston in wal. **a1450** *Boke of Curtasye* (*Sloane*) 318.592: any. **a1460** *Towneley Plays* 38.515: Thou art trew for to trist as ston in the wall, 356.106: any. **c1475** *How a Merchant* 118.17, 119.53. **a1500** *Ballad* in *Rel. Ant.* I 28[18]. Whiting *Drama* 328:313, *Scots* II 133.

S775 As unmovable (unmoving) as a **Stone**
c1395 *WBible* Exodus xv 16: Be thei maad unmovable as a stoon. **a1425** *Mandeville* (*Egerton*) 56.13: Be thai unmouvand as a stane. See **S692.**

S776 As unstirrable as a **Stone** (*etc.*) (A number of single quotations are brought together here)
c1340 Rolle *Psalter* 506 (Song of Moses [I] 19): Made be thai unstirabil as a stane. **c1378** ?Purvey *De Officio Pastorali* in Wyclif *EW* 443[29]: Othere men ben drye as stoons. **a1400** *Destruction of Troy* 99.3035–7: Hir ene . . . Shynyng full shene as . . . any staring stone that stithe is of vertue, 129.3986: Hir ene flamyng fresshe, as any fyne stones. **c1408** Lydgate *Reson* 12.436: Bryghter than ston. **a1425** Mirk *Instructions* 21.653–4: That sacrament mote nede be done, Of a bysschope nede (?*needy*) as ston. **a1460** *Towneley Plays* 246.99: Truly as stone. **a1500** *Squire* 33.712: Nowe are ye pale as any stone. **1513** Douglas *Aeneid* IV 2.40: Voyd of curage,

and dolf (*dull*) as ony stane. **1556** Heywood *Spider* 148[18]: The ant scivile, you sturdy as the stone.

S777 He that throws a **Stone** on high it falls on his head
c1395 *WBible* Ecclesiasticus xxvii 28: If a man throwith a stoon an high, it schal falle on his heed. Tilley S889.

S778 A little **Stone** may gar welter (*cause to overturn*) a mickle wain
c1375 Barbour *Bruce* I 272.24–5: A litill stane oft, as men sayis, May ger weltir ane mekill wane. Apperson 373; Tilley S884. See **T137.**

S779 Of cold **Stone** men may smite fire
c1450 Idley 141.2070: Ffor of coolde stone men may smyte fire. Tilley F371.

S780 One may spit on a **Stone** so long that it will be wet at last
c1450 *Douce MS.52* 56.129: So long thou may, spitt on the ston, that hit wil be wet. **c1450** *Rylands MS.394* 107.8–9: So longe thu may, on the stone spete, That at the laste, it woll be wete. Tilley S887. See **D412.**

S781 To fall like (a) **Stone(s)**
a1300 *Meidan Maregrete* 495.216: Thou fal into helle, so ston deet into welle! **a1338** Mannyng *Chronicle B* II 305 [24]: To stand non ne degh, bot felle doun als stones. **c1375** Chaucer *Anel.* 170: To grounde ded she falleth as a ston, **c1390** *CT* II[B] 670: a. **a1398**(1495) Bartholomaeus-Trevisa A3^{v}[1.38]: a. **a1400** *Ipomadon A* 96.3318: a.

S782 To roast a **Stone**
1522 Skelton *Why Come* II 30.109: Or elles go rost a stone. **1546** Heywood *D* 63.43–4: I doo but roste a stone In warmyng hir. Apperson 533; *Oxford* 545; Tilley S892.

S783 To see no more than a **Stone**
a1350 *Edward the Confessor* 28.809: Ne mighte ise tho he a-woc no more than a ston. **a1430** Lydgate *Pilgrimage* 267.9697–8: Seyng cler he shold ha noon, Na mor than hath the colde ston.

S784 To sink like a **Stone**
c1330 *St. Margaret* 232.260: He sank into erthe, so ston in draught-welle. **c1410** Lovelich *Grail* III 113.289–90: Into the water they sonken . . . As thowgh it hadde ben . . . ston. **1483** Caxton *Golden Legende* 359^{v}[1.33–4]: Sanke doun to the bottom lyke a stone. Whiting *Ballad* 32.

S785 To spring (be sprung) of (a, the) **Stone**
c1225 *Horn* 59 C 1025–6: Horn him yede alone, Also he sprunge of stone. **c1300** Robert of Gloucester I 487.6721: As bar as wo seith of the kunde, as he sprong of the stone. **c1300** *South English Legendary* (*Laud* [*Cotton Jul. D ix*]) 396.106: Al naketh and bar of alle gode as ich sprong out of the stone. **a1350** *Edward the Confessor* 6.173–4: Tho was seint edward bileveth as ho seith alone, As bar as ho seith of the bende as he sprong out of the stone. **a1400** *Perceval* 34.1042–3: Than he rydes hym allane, Als he ware sprongen of a stane. **a1400** *Scottish Legends* II 82–3.472–5: Allace! allace! wa is me! That wyf has tynt and barnis fre, As thing wes sprongyn of the stan, Allace! I am ful wil of wane. **c1425** *Good Wife H* 169.159: But as bare as thou come from the harde ston. NED Stone 16e; *Oxford* 616. See **G477.**

S786 To stand like a **Stone**
a1000 *Judgement Day* in *ASMP* 63.174: And þær stænt astifad, stane gelicast. **a1400** *Awntyrs* 125.109: It stode als a stane. **a1400** *Cursor* II 889 T 15525–6: But I have preyed for thi feith: That hit stonde as stoon. **a1400** *Guy*[5] xxxiv[17]: Wot as a stan than stud tay stile. **a1450** *York Plays* 356.217: He made us stande as any stones.

S787 To drive (*break*) as **Stone** does the glass (*etc.*) (A number of single quotations are brought together here)
a1325 *Flemish Insurrection* 117.39: Al hem to dryven ase ston doth the glas. **c1350** *Libeaus* 55.988–90: This yinge, ferly frek Sit in his sadell steke As ston in castell wall. **c1395** *WBible* Exodus xv 5: Thei yeden doun in to the depthe as a stoon. **a1450** *Pride of Life* in Waterhouse 91.101–2: The cors that nere knewe of care, No more then stone in weye.

S788 What the **Stone** hears that shall the oak answer
1492 *Salomon and Marcolphus* 10[12]: What the stone heryth, that shall t(h)e oke answere. See **P317.**

S789 Better to bear the **Stone Barrow** than be matched with a wicked marrow (*mate*)
c1475 Henryson *Fables* 100.2915–7: To the wer better beir the stane barrow, For all thy dayis to delf quhill thow may dre, Than to be machit with ane wickit marrow.

S790 As cold as a **Stone-wall**
a1430 Lydgate *Pilgrimage* 272.9880: But ded and cold as a ston wal.

S791 As stable as a **Stone-wall**
a1449 Lydgate *St. Edmund* in *MP* I 126.63: Stable as a stoon wall.

S792 To move no more than a **Stone-wall**
a1533 Berners *Huon* 749.11–3: For all the stroke Croysant removed no more than tho he had stryken a stone walle. Whiting *Scots* II 133. See **M564, 726, R161, S692, W24.**

S793 To stand like (a) **Stone-wall**
c1000 Aelfric *Homilies* II 194[21–2]: And þæt wæter stod him on twa healfa swilce oðer stan-weall, *Judith* 105.104–5: Swa þæt þæt wæter astod swylce stanweallas Him on ælce healfe, *Treatise* in *Heptateuch* 30.348–50: And þæt wæter stod swilce stanweallas bufan heora heafdum. See **W25.**

S794 Between two **Stools** the man falls (*varied*)
1011 Byrhtferth *Manual,* ed. S. J. Crawford (EETS 177, 1929) 96.5–8: Se ðe sprycð on Frencisc and þæt ne can ariht gecweðan, se wyrcð *barbarolexin;* swylc he cweðe, *inter duo setles cadet homo,* þonne he sceolde cweðan, *inter duos sedes.* **a1393** Gower *CA* II 14.335–7: Bot it is seid and evere schal, Betwen tuo Stoles lyth the fal, Whan that men wenen best to sitte, 318.625–7: O fol of alle foles, Thou farst as he betwen tuo stoles That wolde sitte and goth to grounde. **a1500** Hill 129.31: Betwen two stolis, the ars goth to grwnd. **1546** Heywood *D* 23.38: While betweene two stooles, my tayle go to grounde, **1555** *E* 175.162. Apperson 656; *Oxford* 43; Taylor and Whiting 356; Tilley S900.

S795 A three-footed **Stool** fails a man at his most need
a1450 *Castle* 154.2599–600: Worldis wele is lyke a iii-foted stole; It faylyt a man at hys most nede.

S796 **Store** is no sore
c1458 *Knyghthode and Bataile* 10.261: An old proverbe is it: Stoor is not soor. **1471** Ripley *Compound* 186[7]: For wyse men done sey *store ys no sore.* **1546** Heywood *D* 26.14: The wise man saieth, store is no sore, **1555** *E* 155.59. Apperson 604; *Oxford* 623; Tilley S903.

S797 After **Storms** (tempest) the weather is often merry (*varied*)
c1385 Usk 23.87–8: After grete stormes the weder is often mery and smothe. **a1410** Love *Mirrour* 42[21–2]: Oure lord god after tempest sente softe and mery wedir. **a1420** Lydgate *Troy* I 261.4089: For after stormys Phebus brighter is, **1420** *Temple* 17.395–6: And whan the storme is done, The sonne shineth in his spere bright. **a1500** *Imitatione* (*1*) 49.32: After tempest cometh clerenes. **1502** *Imitatione* (*2*) 186.33: After the tempest the fayre wether. **1506** Barclay *Castell* D3^{v}[14]: After a storme the sonne doth shene, **c1523** *Mirrour* 45[27]: After sorest stormes moste clerest ayre we see. *Oxford* 4; Skeat 154, 182; Smith 278; Tilley S908. See **S278, 734.**

S798 There is no **Storm** (tempest) that lasts ever
a1420 Lydgate *Troy* I 261.4086–7: Ther is no storme that lasten evere, As clerkis wyse in bokis liste discerne, **c1421** *Thebes* 119.2876: Ther is no tempest may last evere in on. **a1500** *Colyn Blowbol* 99.152: Ther ys no storme ne tempest ay doth lest. **1523** Berners *Froissart* II 440[2–5]: They shall wery themselfe and all for nought: for oftentymes whan a storme or tempest ryseth in a countre, at last it wasteth away by itselfe. See **A75, B19, D340, M587, S517, W431.**

S799 **Stout** and rout (*i.e.,* entirely)
a1400 *Scottish Legends* II 269.351–3: Thane gert he his body bere al bare To bestis and foulis that fellon ware, Til ete hyme bath stout and rout. **c1450** *Alphabet* II 443.8: And all the cetie burn up stowte and rowte. NED Stoop and roop.

S800 To be **Strait-laced**
1546 Heywood *D* 47.209: He is so hy in thinstep, and so streight laste. Tilley S912.

S801 To sail by the **Strand** is sickerer than in the tempest
a1450 *Cato* (*Sidney*) 50.587–8: To seile is sekerer be the strande Than in the tempest fer seilande. See **S248, 655.**

S802 To seek (*put*) all faults on **Strangers**
c1450 *Foly of Fulys* 63.407–8: Thai goif one strangeris and thai keik, Ande al thar faltis one thaim thai seik. Jente 263. Cf. Whiting *NC* 482: Put the stranger near the danger.

S803 As thick as **Straw**
c1400 *Laud Troy* II 383.12995: The Peple lay as thikke as strawe.

S804 Not avail a **Straw**
c1380 Chaucer *HF* 362–3: Al hir compleynt ne al hir moone, Certeyn, avayleth hir not a stre. Whiting *Scots* II 134.

S805 Not care a **Straw**
1533 Heywood *Pardoner* B1^{r}[37]: I care nat for the an olde straw, **1556** *Spider* 123[3]: Thou needest not care for my will a straw. *Oxford* 78; Taylor and Whiting 357; Tilley S917; Whiting *Drama* 365:876, *Scots* II 134.

S806 Not costen (*cost*) a **Straw** (*etc.*) (A number

of single quotations are brought together here) **c1300** *South English Legendary* II 407.151: That necostnede worth a strau. **a1396**(1494) Hilton *Scale* Q2^{r-v}: Thei have no more likinge ne savour in havynge of hem than of a strawe. **a1400** *Alexander C* 122.2165: Than standis in stede noght of a stra all the store stedis. **c1400** *Alexander Buik* II 143.1652: It semis it deiris him nocht ane stra. **c1400** *Order of Priesthood* in Wyclif *EW* 172[26]: Thei chargen not a straw. **a1425** *Chester Plays* II 326.207: And I might not stirr one Stray. **1481** Caxton *Reynard* 30[9–10]: Alle shalle not helpe yow a strawe, **c1489** *Aymon* I 229.7–9: We sholde not doubte Charlemagne . . . of a strawe. **1513** Douglas *Aeneid* II 151.141: Syk luf dowe nocht a stra. **1532** More *Confutacion* 511 F[7–9]: Against makyng of any lawe, this texte serveth frere Barons a strawe. **1556** Heywood *Spider* 107[21]: None advauntage, to the value of a strawe.

S807 Not count three (a) **Straw(s)**
1369 Chaucer *BD* 718–9: For he ne counted nat thre strees Of noght that Fortune koude doo, 1237–8: God wot, she acounted nat a stree Of al my tale. **c1375** Barbour *Bruce* I 63.320: That I count nocht my lyff a stra. **c1420** Wyntoun IV 295.2169–70: I cowntyt noucht the tothir twa (Wicis) the walew of a stra. **1509** Barclay *Ship* II 124[19]: By his hye myght thou countest nat a strawe. **1513** Douglas *Aeneid* IV 135.22: Thy fervent wordis compt I not a stro. *Oxford* 78.

S808 Not dread a **Straw**
c1450 *Pilgrimage LM* 61[26–7]: Ther was no mortal werre ne tournament . . . that thei dredden a straw, 201[32]: I drede thee nouht a straw.

S809 Not esteem a **Straw**
1533 More *Debellacyon* 1010 D[3–7]: I would not esteme the babbeling . . . the mountenaunce of two strawes, **1534** *Comforte* 1257 C[8–9]: Esteme him not at a strawe.

S810 Not give a (two) **Straw(s)**
c1300 *Havelok* 12.315: Therof ne yaf he nouht a stra, 18.466. **c1300** *South English Legendary* I 318.79: He(o) ne yaf worth a stre(o). **c1380** *Ferumbras* 154.4975. **c1400** *Laud Troy* I 230. 7813–4: two strees. **c1450** *Epistle of Othea* 99.1–2. **a1500** *Fraternity* 204[4]. **a1500** *Guy*[4] 181.5953: A straw ne gave that dragon. **1533** Heywood *Johan* A4^{v}[13]. *Oxford* 624–5; Taylor and Whiting 357; Tilley S917.

S811 Not prize a **Straw**
c1375 Barbour *Bruce* I 155.505: He wald nocht priss his liff a stra. **c1400** *Alexander Buik* III 321.7359–60: Now prys I nocht the oist of Ynd The leist stra that men mycht find. Tilley S917.

S812 Not reck a **Straw**
1369 Chaucer *BD* 887: Algate she ne roughte of hem a stree. **a1475** *Assembly of Gods* 17.560: And yef I never do efte I rekke nat a strawe. Whiting *Scots* II 134.

S813 Not set a **Straw**
a1350 *Ywain* 71.2655: By his sare set he noght a stra. **c1390** Chaucer *CT* VII 3090[B4280]: I sette nat a straw by thy dremynges. **a1393** Gower *CA* II 347.1716: For al ne sette I at a stre, III 76.4735–6: I sette it at nomore acompte Than wolde a bare straw amonte. **a1450** *Myne awen dere* 169.638. **c1489** Caxton *Aymon* I 318.30–1. **a1500** *Imitatione (1)* 122.30–1. **c1500** *Everyman* 10.222. **c1500** *Lyfe of Roberte* 229. 264. **c1505** Watson *Valentine* 244.26–7. **1532** More *Confutacion* 375 D[1–2], **1533** *Debellacyon* 963 F[4–5]: Set I not .v. strawes. Whiting *Drama* 365:876.

S814 Not trine (*step*) over two (a) **Straw(s)**
a1450 *York Plays* 103.13: And may noght wele tryne over two strase. **1546** Heywood *D* 51.325–6: Where thou wilt not step over a straw, I thynke, To wyn me the woorth of one draught of drynke. Tilley S921.

S815 Not worth a **Straw**
c1300 *South English Legendary* I 17.44: That ne mowe the helpe worth a stre, 131.80, 324. 260. **c1350** *Libeaus* 27.449: Nis nought worth a stre. **c1369** Chaucer *BD* 671: I holde that wyssh nat worth a stree. **c1380** *Ferumbras* 74.2229. **c1390** Chaucer *CT* VII 1336[B2526], X[I] 601. **a1393** Gower *CA* II 244.666–7, 294. 2538, 429.997. **c1400** *Vices and Virtues* 85.5–6. **c1412** Hoccleve *Regement* 61.1669–70. **c1450** *Pilgrimage LM* 80[23–4]: And yit is not the vertu the lasse woorth bi a straw. **c1458** *Knyghthode and Bataile* 42.1135: And leve hym noght, or lite, unworth a stre. **a1475** Ashby *Dicta* 74.705. **a1475** Russell *Boke* 124.100. **c1489** Caxton *Aymon* I 107.3–4: Ye ben not worth an hanfull of strawe, 124.26–7. **a1500** *Coventry Plays* 61.896. **a1500** Greene *Carols* 380.5, 393.12. **c1500** Greene *Carols* 379.9. **c1500** *Melusine* 196.30–1. **c1500** *Smith* 322.22–3. **1509** Barclay *Ship* I 99[21], 105[25], 144[7], 249[25], II 48[4], 69[5], 325[10], **c1515** *Eclogues* 161.577. **c1516** Skelton *Magnificence* 43.1378. **c1523** Barclay *Mirrour* 16[28]. **1533** More *Debellacyon* 989 G[1–2]. **1556** Heywood *Spider* 198[15]: Not worth two strawse,

342[21]: No flie therby winner, the worth of a straw. Apperson 458; *Oxford* 624–5; Taylor and Whiting 357; Tilley S918; Whiting *Drama* 365:876, *Scots* II 134.

S816 A **Straw** for (it)
c1378 *Piers* B xiv 251: A strawe for the stuwes! **c1385** Chaucer *TC* v 362: A straw for alle swevenes signifiaunce! **c1395** *CT* IV[E] 1567: Straw for thy Senek, V[F] 695: Straw for youre gentillesse! VIII[G] 925: "Straw!" quod the thridde. **c1412** Hoccleve *Regement* 23.622: But straw unto hir reed! 51.1392, 68.1874: Ye straw! let be! 187.5191, **c1425** *Jonathas* 217.49: his wit. **a1475** *Ludus Coventriae* 222.377: thi tale. **c1497** Medwall *Fulgens* C4ᵛ[12]: your mockynge. **c1499** Skelton *Bowge* I 47.459: But, what, a strawe! **a1500** *Croxton Sacrament* in Waterhouse 61.125: talis. **c1500** *Be pes* in Stevens *Music* 339.1[3]: yeur tale. **c1500** Skelton *Manerly Margery* I 28.5: Tully valy, strawe, let be, I say! 10. **1506** Barclay *Castell* E1ᵛ[11]: A strawe, man, let her be despysed, **1509** *Ship* I 100[3]: cunnynge wysdome. **1513** Douglas *Aeneid* II 4.33: thys ignorant blabryng, III 170.41: Stra forto spek of gayt to gentill wight. **c1515** Barclay *Eclogues* 85.877: thy wisdome, 108.40: dreames, 196.398: fables. **c1516** Skelton *Magnificence* 18.549: Tushe, a strawe! 19.564, **1522** *Why Come* II 39.413: lawe canon, **c1522** *Colyn* I 322.296: Goddes curse. **c1523** Barclay *Mirrour* 18[10]: thy study. **c1525** ?Heywood *Gentylnes* 105.414: an halpeny, 418: thi councell! torde a fart! **a1529** Skelton *Elynour* I 112.535. **1532** More *Confutacion* 464 C[14]: all that. **1556** Heywood *E* 137.94.3: Straw for the, quoth the dawe. Tilley S917; Whiting *Drama* 365.876.

S817 To be had for a **Straw**
c1489 Caxton *Aymon* I 287.28–9: Nor that shall bye hym agen, though he myghte be had for a strawe.

S818 To draw the **Straw** before the cat (*varied*)
c1475 Henryson *Fables* 70.2010: Thow wenis to draw the stra befoir the cat! **1546** Heywood *D* 89.31: No plaiyng with a strawe before an olde cat. Apperson 87:39; *Oxford* 506; Tilley P406. See **F124.**

S819 To lay a **Straw**
c1475 Henryson *Orpheus* 137.241: Thairfoir of this mater a stray I lay. **c1515** Barclay *Eclogues* 218.1015: Have done nowe Faustus, lay here a straw and rest. **1546** Heywood *D* 68.86: And best we laie a strawe here. Apperson 354; Tilley S919; Whiting *Drama* 352:671, *Scots* II 134.

S820 To pick **Straws**
a1496 *Rote or Myrour* C6ʳ[7–8]: Rather to pycke strawes and clatter to his felawes than to lerne the lesson. Tilley S925.

S821 To play with (a) **Straw(s)**
c1200 *Vices and Virtues* (*Stowe*) 133.31–135.2: Ne lat hie (*Honestas*) nawht the hande pleighende mid stikke, ne mid strawe—nis that non god tocne of ripe manne, nis the hierte nauht yiet stedefast. **c1390** Chaucer *CT* IX[H] 44–5: I trowe that ye dronken han wyn ape, And that is whan men pleyen with a straw. **1479** *Cely Papers* 15[1]: He (*a horse*) ys hoyll, he wyll playe with a straw. **a1500** *Colyn Blowbol* 105.287: That one may make them play with strawes thre.

S822 To strip (pill [*peel*]) a **Straw**
1400 *Mede and muche thank* in Kail 7.25–6: I plese my lord at bed and bord, Though y do but strype a stre. **1522** Skelton *Why Come* II 35.262: They make us to pyll strawes. Tilley S923.

S823 To stumble at a **Straw** (*varied*)
1414 *Lerne say wele* in Kail 17.89–92: Many can stomble at a stre; They nyl not snapere at a style, And graunte purpos nay and yee, Though his thought be thens a myle. **1495** Fitzjames *Sermo* G4ᵛ[13–4]: Stomblynge atte a straawe And lepynge over a blocke. **a1500** *Colyn Blowbol* 105.307: And yet they wille stombile at a straw. **1546** Heywood *D* 93.78: Ye stumbled at a strawe, and lept over a blocke, **1555** *E* 171.143. Apperson 606; *Oxford* 627; Tilley S922; Whiting *Scots* II 133.

S824 To take the **Straw** and let (*leave*) the corn
a1400 *Romaunt C* 6353–4: But to what ordre that I am sworn, I take the strawe, and lete the corn. See **C428, F693.**

S825 To to-wend (*turn*) every **Straw**
a1200 *Ancrene* 166.25–7: A wummon the haveth ilosed hire nelde, other a sutere his eal, secheth hit ananriht, and towent euch strea, athet hit beo ifunden. NED Straw sb.[1] 9a. Cf. Taylor and Whiting 356:14.

S826 Too dear a **Straw**
a1450 *Always try to Say the Best* in Brown *Lyrics XIV* 193.57–8: I holde that dede to dere a stre, Don to do another fame.

S827 To be like **Strawberries**
a1500 *Beauty of his Mistress III* in Robbins 126.15: And your strawbery lyppes, 127.22: Your lyppes lyke the strawberye. Taylor and Whiting 358.

S828 To burst out (*etc.*) like a **Stream**
a1225 *St. Marherete* 14.5–6: Thet tet blod bearst ut and strac a-dun of hire bodi as streem deth of welle. **a1450** *Generydes A* 305.9858–9: The teres fel from hir visage As stremes doun out of a wel. **c1450** Capgrave *Katharine* 51.579: Grete alisaundre sprange of hym as strem oute of welle, 65.788–9: Bothe wit and wysdam oute of hir hert swelles (!), Evene as (the) strem renneth fro the welles. **c1500** Greene *Carols* 265.3: As stremes of a well the blode out sprong.

S829 To glide down like **Stream** of (*from*) the strand
a1400 *Song of Love-longing* in Brown *Lyrics XIV* 101.40: Als streme dose of the strande, his blode gan downe glyde.

S830 To row (strive) against the **Stream** (flood, sea) (*varied*)
a1300 *Proverbs of Alfred* 85 J 123–4: Strong (*T:* [S]orwe) hit is to reowe A-yeyn the séé that floweth (*T:* se-flod). **c1330** *On the King's Breaking* in Wright *Political Songs* 254–5: Whoso roweth agein the flod, Off sorwe he shal drinke; Also hit fareth bi the unsele, A man shal have litel hele Ther agein to swinke. **c1390** *Cato* (*Vernon*) 604.585: Ayeyn the strem ne strive thou nought. **a1393** Gower *CA* II 349.1780–1: Betre is to wayte upon the tyde Than rowe ayein the stremes stronge, 375.2729–31: Whanne he is falle in such a drem, Riht as a Schip ayein the Strem, He routeth with a slepi noise. **a1430** Lydgate *Pilgrimage* 301.10996–7: Lat hym wyth hys wyndes saylle, Ffrowardly ageyn the strem. **a1470** Malory II 619.5–6: Other ellys we rowe ayenste the streme. **a1475** *Turne up hur halter* in *Rel. Ant.* I 76[43]: Stryve ye never ageyn the streme. **c1475** *Wisdom* 51.491: I woll no more row a-geyn the floode. **a1500** *God wote grete cause* in *The Library,* 4th s. 15(1935) 318[10]: Hit ys harde a-yenst the streme to stryve. **c1500** Greene *Carols* 410.13: Ytt ys hard ayenst the strem to stryve. **1509** Barclay *Ship* II 32[7–8]: And nat . . . To stryve agaynst the streme, **c1523** *Mirrour* 66[27–8]: It is not lesse folly to strive agaynst kinde Then a shipman to strive agaynst both streme and winde. **1523** Skelton *Garlande* I 418.1432: He is not wyse ageyne the streme that stryvith. **1546** Heywood *D* 72.87–8: Foly it is . . . To stryve against the streme, **1555** *E* 183.203, **1556** *Spider* 363[3]: Against the streme, strife againe I will not make. Apperson 606; Jente 662; *Oxford* 627; Tilley S927; Whiting *Drama* 366:877, *Scots* II 134. See **S486, W332.**

S831 As common as the **Street**
a1393 Gower *CA* III 15.2497: Thus is he commun as the Strete. See **C64.**

S832 To beat the **Streets** (pavement)
a1352 Minot 5.25: The Skotte gase in Burghes and betes the stretes. **c1390** Chaucer *CT* I[A] 3936: He was a market-betere atte fulle. **c1400** *Curates* in Wyclif *EW* 152[5–6]: Thei fallen to nyse pleies . . . and beten the stretis. **c1400** *Priesthood* in Wyclif *EW* 166[25–6]: But bete stretis up and doun and synge and pleie as mynystrelis. **c1422** Hoccleve *Complaint* 102.185–6: A great fole I am, This pavyment a dayes thus to bete. MED beten 2b(b).

S833 No **Strength** (power) may (help) against rede (*counsel,* wisdom) (*varied*)
c1250 *Owl* 64–6.761–8: Vor soth hit is that seide Alured: "Ne mai no strengthe ayen red." Oft spet wel a lute liste, Thar muche strengthe sholde miste; Mid lutle strengthe, thurgh ginne, Castel and burgh me mai iwinne. Mid liste me mai walle(s) felle, An worpe of horsse knightes snelle, **a1300** 67 J 769–72: Vuel strengthe is lutel w(u)rth, Ac wisdom ne w(u)rth never unw(u)rth: Thu myht iseo thurh alle thing, That wisdom naveth non evening. **1340** *Ayenbite* 184[1–2]: Vor ase zayth the filozofe, "greate thinges byeth y-do naght be strengthe of bodie ne be armes, ac be guod red." **a1393** Gower *CA* II 66.1109–11: And therupon thei founde a weie, Wher strengthe myhte noght aweie, That sleihte scholde helpe thanne. **c1395** *WBible* Ecclesiastes ix 16: Wisdon is betere than strengthe. **c1400** *Vices and Virtues* 188.22–5: For, as the philsophre seith, grete thinges ben y-do not onliche bi strenkthe of armes ne of body, but bi good counseil and avisement. **c1450** Capgrave *Solace* 31[2–3]: Wisdam is mor of honour thann power. **c1450** *Epistle of Othea* 84.19–20: Ffor, as seyth seynt gregorye in the morales, that strengthe is noght wurthe, wher counceyll is nott. **a1464** Capgrave *Chronicle* 51[24–5]: And so the Kyng (*Alexander*) turnyd fro his purpose, seyng, "Evyr is wisdam above powere." Apperson 695:7; *Oxford* 716; Tilley W527. See **L381, S858.**

S834 To affy (*trust*) too much in **Strength** is folly (*varied*)
a1338 Mannyng *Chronicle A* I 431.12335–6: Ffor men seye, "hit is folye In strengthe to mikel for to affye." **c1450** *Epistle of Othea* 132.11: Who in strenthe put al is trust is soone confounde, 18–9: Therfor seyth plato: Who trusteth onely in strengthe is ofte overcome.

c1500 *Everyman* 28.827–8: He that trusteth in his strength She hym deceyveth at the length.

S835 As smooth as a **Strike** (*hank*) of flax
c1387-95 Chaucer *CT* I[A] 676: But smothe it heeng as dooth a strike of flex.

S836 As straight as a **Strike**
a1400 *Destruction of Troy* 99.3024: Streght as a strike.

S837 To **Strike** flat (*i.e.*, fail)
1475 *Stonor Letters* I 156[15–6]: But yt hys tolde me ye stryke flatte.

S838 Harp no more on that **String**
1555 Heywood *E* 161.97: Harpe no more on that strynge, **1556** *Spider* 97[8]. Tilley S934.

S839 To harp on one (that) **String**
c1385 Chaucer *TC* ii 1030–6: For though the beste harpour upon lyve Wolde on the beste sowned joly harpe That evere was, with alle his fyngres fyve, Touche ay o streng, or ay o werbul harpe, Were his nayles poynted nevere so sharpe, It sholde maken every wight to dulle, To here his glee, and of his strokes fulle. **1513** More *Richard* 49 G[8–10]: The Cardinall made a countinance to the tother Lord, that he should harp no more upon that string, **1528** *Heresyes* 244 AB: They that touche that poynt harpe upon the right string, **1529** *Supplicacion* 302 B[13–4]: For ever upon that stringe he harpeth, **1533** *Answer* 1093 B[8–9]: He harpeth upon the same string agayne, *Confutacion* 686 E[9–10]: Like a blind harper that harpeth all on one strynge. **1546** Heywood *D* 96.205: Harping on that stringe, **1556** *Spider* 317[16]: To se what bit we bite: or on what string we harp. Apperson 287; *Oxford* 280; Tilley S936; Whiting *Drama* 348:607. See **R79.**

S840 To harp on the **String** that gives no melody
1546 Heywood *D* 68.93: Ye harpe on the stryng, that geveth no melody. Apperson 287; *Oxford* 280; Tilley S935.

S841 To have two (many) **Strings** to one's bow
c1477 Caxton *Jason* 57.5–6: But that he have .ii. strenges on his bowe, 26–8: First as to the regarde for to have ii cordes or strenges on his bowe, that is to understande two ladyes, 58.5–6. **1525** Berners *Froissart* V 36[16]: We shall have two stryngges on our bowe. **1546** Heywood *D* 47.187: Ye have many stryngs to the bowe. Apperson 656; *Oxford* 681; Taylor and Whiting 358; Tilley S937.

S842 It is wicked (*harmful*) to **Strive** and have the worse
a1393 Gower *CA* II 270.1650–1: For this thei tellen that ben wise, Wicke is to stryve and have the werse, III 153.7353: Wicke is to stryve and have the worse.

S843 Better the first **Stroke** than the last dint
a1500 *Eger H* 277.1545–8: And in old stories he heard say, That both in earnest and in play, It were better who might it hint, Get the first strake nor the last dint.

S844 He that gives the first **Strokes** does not (win) the battle
c1500 *Melusine* 368.7–9: For he that gyveth the first strokes dooth not the batayll, but he that revengeth hym bryngeth it to effect.

S845 One should purvey (*foresee*) ere the **Stroke** fall where peril is
c1450 *Merlin* II 641[18–9]: Ffor oon ought to purveye er the stroke falle ther as is pereile. See **A183, W49.**

S846 **Strokes** fall upon the small and not the great
a1393 Gower *CA* II 16.425–8: And thus, how evere that thei tale, The strokes falle upon the smale, And upon othre that ben grete Hem lacketh herte forto bete. See **T70.**

S847 There is no **Stroke** but of the mastery (*victory*)
1471 Caxton *Recuyell* I 266.17: Men saye ther is no strook but of the maistre.

S848 To smite oneself with one's own **Stroke**
c1449 Pecock *Repressor* I 71[17]: For thanne he schulde smyte him silf with his owne stroke. See **D22, S950, T534, W711.**

S849 None is so **Strong** that he shall not pass (*die*)
a1300 *Alisaunder* 427.7829–30: So strong, so fair, nevere non nas, That he ne shal passe with "allas!"

S850 When two **Strong** (men) come together it is tough (*varied*)
c1300 Robert of Gloucester II 715.10605: Wan tueye stronge cometh to gadere it is somdel tou. **a1420** Lydgate *Troy* II 463.2408–10: As ful ofte it happeth, and is founde, Whan stronge doth mete with his parigal: Ther is no more, but every(ch) had a fal. Cf. Taylor and Whiting 161: Greek.

S851 As stiff as **Strucion** (*ostrich*)
a1500 Kennedy 26.26: As struttioun stif.

S852 As still as a **Stub**
c1390 *Sir Gawain* 71.2293–4: Bot stode stylle

as . . . a stubbe auther That ratheled is in roché grounde with rotes a hundreth.

S853 Be busy in **Study,** *etc.*
a1500 Hill 130.18: Besy in stody be thou, child, And in the hall, meke and mylde, And at the table, mery and glade And at bedde, softe and sadde.

S854 To be in (a) **Study**
a1338 Mannyng *Chronicle B* I 58[11]: Whan Edward perceyved, his herte was in studie. **c1385** Chaucer *CT* I[A] 1530: Into a studie he fil sodeynly. **a1470** Malory I 43.20–1: The kyng sat in a study. **a1475** *Ludus Coventriae* 207.225: In a colde stodye me thynkyth ye sytt. **a1533** Berners *Arthur* 200[19]: She stode in a stoudy, 331[31], 398[5–6]: In a sodayne study, 538[20], *Huon* 536.13–4. Apperson 70; *Oxford* 67; A. A. Prins *English Studies* 41(1960) 14–5; Taylor and Whiting 358; Tilley S945.

S855 As short as a **Stump**
c1450 Idley 159.46: It maketh hym a body short as a stompe.

S856 Whoso cannot be **Subject** cannot be sovereign
c1450 *Douce MS.52* 56.136: Who-so con not be suget, he con not be soverayn. **c1450** *Rylands MS.394* 107.23.5. Cf. Tilley S237. See **L443, M228, 407, T50.**

S857 If one is **Subtle** another is as false
c1450 *Fyrst thou sal* 88.21–2: Lerne this, my lefe brother, Als sotyl as thou, als fals is ane other. See **G491.**

S858 **Subtlety** in arms is worth more than strength
1489 Caxton *Fayttes* 168.26–7: And in armes is subtylyte mykel more worthe than is strengthe. Apperson 607; *Oxford* 628; Tilley S952. See **L381.**

S859 **Sufferance** does ease (*varied*)
a1393 Gower *CA* II 270.1639–40: Suffrance hath evere be the beste To wissen him that secheth reste. **a1420** Lydgate *Troy* I 146.82: Who best can suffre most schal have his ese. **a1440** Burgh *Cato* 311.310: "Suffraunce dothe ese," was seid full yore a-goo. **a1450** *Generydes A* 52.1669–72: He may not faile to have goode tide That can wel suffre and abide; for sofferaunce causeth oft certeyn A man his purpos to atteyn. **c1450** Idley 102.1286: Well y woote sufferaunce doth ease. **c1475** Gregory *Chronicle* 216[3]: But sufferens and fayr speche dyd them moche ese. **a1500** *Salamon seyth* in Person 52.15–6: Love to amende and feyne to please, Lothe to defende, sufferaunce doth ease. **1546** Heywood *D* 34.54: For of suffrance comth ease, **1555** *E* 153.43. Apperson 608; *Oxford* 629; Tilley S955. See **P44.**

S860 **Sufferance** in season will longest endure
c1450 Idley 153.2817: Sufferaunce in season woll longest endure. See **T310.**

S861 **Sufferance** is a virtue (*varied*)
c1378 *Piers* B xi 370–7: Suffraunce is a sovereygne vertue and a swyfte venjaunce. . . . Frenche men and fre men affeyteth thus her childerne, *Bele vertue est soffrance, mal dire est petyt venjance, Bel dire et bien soffrir fait lui soffrant a bien venir,* **a1387** C xiv 204: And so witnesseth the wyse and wysseth the Frenshe. **a1400** *Proverbis of Wysdom* 244.35–6: A fayre vertew is gwode suffrance: A fowle vyce is petite (*II* 221.20: Povert) venjawnce. **c1450** *Fyrst thou sal* 88.54: hasty vengeanc. **c1450** *Rules for Conduct* in Smith *Common-place Book* 14[6]: Vertu of vertuys ys in sufferans. **c1450** *St. Cuthbert* 5.145–7: Thar is na thing savours sa swete, To sighand saule hys bale to bete, As the vertu of sufferance. See **P56.**

S862 **Sufferance** is no quittance
1546 Heywood *D* 69.117: Suffrance is no quittance, **1555** *E* 185.214. Apperson 229: Forbearance; *Oxford* 219; Tilley F584.

S863 Well worth **Sufferance** which abates strife
a1400 Bozon *Contes* 20[16–7]: Wel wurth suffraunce that abates strif, And wo wurth hastinece that reves man his lif, 203[24–5].

S864 Without **Sufferance** may no man come to perfectness
c1400 *Vices and Virtues* 167.23–6: For with-oute suffraunce may no man ne womman come to parfightnesse; with-oute pacience ther hath no wight victorie, for who-so leseth suffraunce, he is overcome. Cf. *Ayenbite* 167[15–7]. See **S866.**

S865 The **Sufferant** (sufferance) overcomes
c1385 Chaucer *TC* iv 1584: Men seyn, "the suffrant overcomith," parde. **a1400** *Romaunt B* 3463–6: By sufferaunce, and wordis softe A man may overcome ofte Hym that aforn he hadde in drede, In bookis sothly as I rede. **1439** Lydgate *St. Albon* 112.88: Through meke sufferance he gate the victorie. **1489** Caxton *Fayttes* 192.31: But ought to overcome by suffraunce. Apperson 485: Patience (6); *Oxford* 172: Endures; Skeat 197. See **P61, T213, W264.**

S866 Easy **Suffering** shall bring a man to his desiring
a1500 Hichecoke *This Worlde* 333.45–6: Esy sufferyng and good abidynge Schall bryng a man to his desieryng. See **A10, S864.**

S867 Is he not rich that has **Suffisance?** (*varied*)
c1385 Usk 88.31–2: Is he nat riche that hath suffisaunce? **a1400** *Romaunt B* 5583–4: For suffisaunce all oonly Makith men to lyve richely. Apperson 530; *Oxford* 541. See **L394.**

S868 When you have **Suffisance** cease
c1523 Barclay *Mirrour* 25[29]: When thou hast suffisaunce ceasse and withdraw thy hand. See **E119.**

S869 **Suffolk** full of wiles, Norfolk full of guiles
a1500 *Characteristics of Counties* in *Rel. Ant.* I 269[19–20]: Suffolk, full of wiles; Norffolk, full of giles. Apperson 186: Essex; *Oxford* 176.

S870 As sweet as **Sugar**
c1378 *Piers* B xiv 312: No sugre is swettere. **c1408** Lydgate *Reson* 104.3944: Somtyme as any sugre soote. **c1485** *Mary Magdalene* (*Digby*) 132.2047: Swetter than sugur. **a1500** *Beauty of his Mistress III* in Robbins 126.5. **1509** Fisher *Treatyse* 227.23–4. Svartengren 306; Taylor and Whiting 359–60.

S871 **Sugar** and gall (poison, venom, bitterness, salt, saltpeter, ratsbane) (*varied*)
c1408 Lydgate *Reson* 89.3367–8: The sugre of hir drynkes all At the ende ys meynt with gall, 106.4047: Sugre and galle acorde nought, **a1410** *Churl* in *MP* II 476.180: Of sugre strowid, that hideth fals poisoun, **a1420** *Troy* I 79.2262: Can under sugre schrowden her poysoun, 203.2033–4: Schal with hir (*Fortune's*) sugre finde galle meynt, And hir hony ay with bitter spreynt, 239.3311: With sugre out-schad, and venym in the rote, II 518.4283: The sugre a-forn, the galle hid be-hynde, III 698.4582–3: For undre in secre The venym was, as sugre under galle, 701.4665: Under sugre yif ther be cured galle, 717.5220: Sugre in the crop, venym in the rote, 773.21: In-to her sugre galle of discordance, **1420** *Temple* 8.191–2: Allas that ever that it shuld(e) fal, So soote sugre Icoupled be with gal! 17.403–4: Ne no wight preiseth of sugre the swetnes, But thei afore have tasted bitternes, **a1422** *Life* 600.191: What can sugur undur galle faine? **1429** *Complaint* in *MP* II 611.60: With thayre sugre tempre galle, **a1430** *Pilgrimage* 1.25: And hyr sugre (ys) underspreynt wyth galle, 397.14704–5: In tast lyk sugre; but the galle Ys hyd, they may yt nat espye, **a1439** *Fall* I 7.243: Thei wil ther sugre tempre with no galle, 58.2112: His litil sugir temprid with moch gall, 94.3442: Summe folk han sugir, summe taste gall, 126.4536: Ther pompous sugre is meynt with bittir gall, 4543, 4550, 127.4557: Ay with hir sugre off custum tempre gall, 135.4828: Hid undir sugre, galle and fell poisoun, II 428.3575: For al hir sugir is meynt with bittirnesse, 547.2721: Outward sugre, inward bittirnesse, 615.1097: Under sugre can hide weel ther galle, **a1449** *Order* in *MP* II 450.30: Tonge spreynt with sugre, the galle kept secre, *Say the Best* in *MP* II 797.84–5: And tho tunges be most to wite That for suger yevyn gall. **a1449** Lydgate and Burgh *Secrees* 22.677: Ther sugre is soote, ther galle doth no good, 28.889: Be outward sugryd, and galle in existence. **c1450** *Bishop Boothe* in Wright *Political Poems* II 228[25]: But set under suger he shewithe hem galle. **a1500** *Court of Love* 424.542: And sugre strewe on gall. **a1500** *To yow, mastres* in *Rawlinson MS. C 813* 383.36: And under suger hyde bytter galle. **1513** Skelton *Against the Scottes* I 185.96: Know ye not suger and salt asonder? **1546** Heywood *D* 21.29: Whan time hath tournd white suger to white salte, 43.74: Whan sweete sugar should tourne to soure salte petur, 82.80: I have . . . for fyne suger, faire rats bane. Tilley S958. See **C177, G12, H433, 440, S948, T331.**

S872 **Suits** hang half a year at Westminster Hall, *etc.*
1562 Heywood *E* 207.12: Sutes hange halfe a yere at Westminster hall, At Tyburne, halfe an houres hangyng endeth all. Apperson 608; *Oxford* 630; Tilley S962.

S873 To set the **Sullow** (*plow*) before the oxen
1340 *Ayenbite* 243[9–10]: Ac moche volk of religion zetteth the zuolh be-vore the oksen. **a1400** *Vices and Virtues* 269.22–3: Many men and wommen of religion setten the ploughe to-fore the oxene. Apperson 503:5; *Oxford* 80; Tilley P434; Whiting *Scots* II 112. See **C60.**

S874 As hot as **Summer**
a1475 Russell *Boke* 167.742: As hoot as somer by his attyre. Cf. Svartengren 312.

S875 Hard is the **Summer** there the sun never shines
c1405 *Mum* 10.133–4: For well mowe ye wyttyn and so mowe we all, That harde is the somer ther sonne schyneth nevere.

S876 Next to **Summer** is winter
a1513 Dunbar *Of the Changes of Lyfe* 141.16: So nixt to summer winter bein. See **W372.**

S877 As bright as (any, the) **Summer's Day**
c1300 *Horn* 52 L 917–8: That feyre may Bryht so eny someres day. **c1390** *Castel of Love* 374.737–8: And feirore of liht Then the someres-day whon hee is briht. **c1400** *Emaré* 7.191–2: Aftyr the mayde fayr and gent, That was bryght as someres day, 14.438. **a1422** Lydgate *Life* 441.169–70: eny. **a1500** *St. Kateryne* 260.63–4: the. Apperson 68.

S878 As fair as the **Summer's Days**
a1500 *Lambewell* 157.418: Much fairer then the summers dayes, 160.510.

S879 As fresh as the **Summer's Day**
c1395 Chaucer *CT* IVE 1895–6: May, As fressh as is the brighte someres day.

S880 A (long) **Summer's Day**
a800 *Juliana* in *Exeter Book* 127.494–6: Ic asecgan ne mæg, þeah ic gesitte sumerlongne dæg, Eal þa earfeþu. **c1400** *Florence* 11.310–1: Thogh a man sate on a wyght palfreye All the longe somers day. **a1449** Lydgate *Fabula* in *MP* II 492.160–1: To rekken the fare and cours in thrifty wyse, A somerys day ne myht(e) nat suffise. **1528** More *Heresyes* 151 A[13–4]: As meke a simple soul, as a man should have sene in a somers daye. Cf. Apperson 256; Taylor and Whiting 360; Tilley S967.

S881 As bright as (the, any) **Sun** (*varied*)
a800 Cynewulf *Elene* in *Vercelli Book* 96–7.1109–10: þa cwom semninga sunnan beorhtra Lacende lig. **897** Alfred *Boethius* 112.15–6: ðа goodan scinað beorhtor þonne sunne. **a900** Bede 284.15–7: Wæs seo beorhtnes þæs onsendan leohtes mara, þon sunnan leoht bið æt middan dæge. **a1000** *Be Domes Dæge,* ed. H. Löhe (Bonn, 1907) 16.118: þonne sigel-beorht swegles brytta. **a1000** *Two Apocrypha* C 38–40: Oðer bið beorhtre þonne sunne, H 48: Heo bið swa beorht swa sunne, ꝥ 49. **c1000** *Old English Nicodemus* 512.17–9: And carinus and leuticus wæron þa færinga swa fægeres hywes swa seo sunne þonne he beorhtost scyneð. **c1100** *Elucidarium* in *English Miscellany Presented to Dr. Furnivall* (Oxford, 1901) 90[7–8]. **c1175** *Lambeth Homilies* 39[10–1]: tha, 139[11–2]: the. **a1200** *Ancrene* 23.22–3, 24.12, 74.5–6: the, 185.3: the, 208.28: the. **a1200** *Trinity College Homilies* 185[11–2]: se. **c1200** *St. Katherine* (*Royal*) 82.1665–6: the. **a1300** *Meidan Maregrete* 493.156: Ant scon ase britt so sonne abouten none. **a1300** *Richard* 84.75–6: the sunne thorwgh the glas. **c1300** *Guy*[1] 522 A 164.5: ani, 590 A 249.11–2: As bright as ani sonne it schon That glemes under schawe. **c1300** *South English Legendary* I 181.40: the, 227.187: the, 346.175, (*Laud*) 181.26: the, 371.162, 376.305. **c1303** Mannyng *Handlyng* 318.10199–200: the sunne ys, on days lyght, 10221–2: the. **a1325** *Cursor* III 1336.23394. **a1325** *Sarmun* in Heuser 95.199–200: the. **a1330** *Legend of Mary* 500.68–9. **c1330** *Orfeo* 15.152: the, 31.352: on somers day, 33.371–2: at none the sonne. **c1330** *St. Margaret* 233.331: ani. **c1340** Rolle *Psalter* 396 (111.2). **c1350** *Smaller Vernon Collection* 17.605–6: the. **c1370** *Theophilus* in *ESt* 1(1877) 55.706–7: the sun in someres tyde. **c1375** *All Saints* in Horstmann *Legenden 1881* 145.252–3: in the ayre. **c1380** *Ferumbras* 59.1695: the sonne on may. **c1380** *Pearl* 38.1055–6: bothe the sunne and mone. **c1390** *Alexius* (*Vernon*) 62.407–8. **c1390** *Gregorius* 168.1268: on Rouwel bon. **c1390** *Mournyng Song* in *Vernon* II 473.153, 474.198–9: in Southe. **c1390** *Of Clene Maydenhod* 468.123–4. **c1390** *Prayer to the Virgin* in *Vernon* II 738.109–10: the. **c1390** *Talkyng* 56.33: the. **a1400** *Alexander C* 192.3225: bemes of the son, 263.5262: the. **a1400** Bonaventura *Privity* in *Yorkshire Writers* I 218[22–3]: the. **a1400** *Eglamour* 42.637 (*var.*). **a1400** *Ipomadon A* 144.5021–2: that shynes throw glasse. **a1400** *Pricke* 169.6243, 235.8739, 246.9146–7: the. **a1400** *Scottish Legends* I 25.637–8: the, II 324.693–4: the. **c1400** *Elucidarium* 1–2: the. **c1400** *Scottish Troy* 225.472. **c1400** *Thomas of Erceldoune* 8.139–40: the. **c1400** *Tundale* 93.1621–2, 121.2097: the, 122.2119–20. **a1415** Mirk *Festial* 48.17: any, 28–9: the, 132.4–5: the, 174.21–2: any, 240.6–7: the, 249.3–5: the. **c1415** *Middle English Sermons* 113.38–9: the. **a1420** Lydgate *Troy* I 338.6780–1: the somer sonne, II 406.411: on someres day. **a1425** *All this before Jhesu* in Bowers *Three Middle English Religious Poems* 29.407. **a1425** *Chester Plays* II 389.41–2: the. **a1425** *Daily Work* in *Yorkshire Writers* I 147[42–3]: the. **c1425** *St. Mary Oignies* 156.16: the. **c1430** ?Lydgate *Compleynt* 64.371: the clere sonne. **c1433** Lydgate *St. Edmund* 425.675–7: Ther sholde a skye as any sonne bryht Dresse up his bemys to the sterrys cleere, Lyk Phebus tressyd in his mydday speere. **1435** Misyn *Fire* 97.16: the. **a1449** Lydgate *St. Gyle* in *MP* I 169.241–2: the. **a1449** Lydgate and Burgh *Secrees* 13.382: the. **a1450** Audelay 157.76: on somyr morowe. **a1450** *Death and Life* 3.65: the bright sonn, 4.99: the. **a1450** *St. Editha* 55.2451–2: the sonne in May. **c1450** *Alphabet* I 205.4–5: the. **c1450** Greene *Carols* 30.3: the, 125 A 8: in glas. **c1450** *Herkyns* in *Archiv* 85(1890) 48.56: the. **c1450** *Jacob's Well* 102.9: the. **c1450** *Owayne Miles* (*Cotton Caligula*)

119.543–4: ony. **a1456** *Stabat Mater* in Brown *Lyrics XV* 25.65–6: the sunne in the ffirmament. **a1460** *Towneley Plays* 4.88–9: the, 295.82: the, 352.347. **a1475** *St. Birgitta* 70.22: the, 90.29: the, 98.12–3: the. **1483** Caxton *Golden Legende* 85ʳ[2.10]: the, 382ᵛ[2.40]: the. **1496** Alcock *Mons* B6ᵛ[14–5]: the. **1496** *Myracles of our Lady* (London, de Worde, 1514) B1ᵛ[15–6]: the. **a1500** *Alexius* (*Cotton*) 62.301–2: the sonne on the daye lyght. **a1500** *Coventry Plays* 18.507–8: the sun in the meddis of the day. **a1500** *Farewell to his Mistress III* in Robbins 209.30: overhill. **a1500** Greene *Carols* 237 A 1: the, B 1: the. **a1500** *Merchant and his Son* in Hazlitt *EPP* I 148.233: any. **a1500** *Miroure of Mans Salvacionne* 149[32]: the. **a1500** *Orfeo* 32 H 358: ony. **a1500** *Take Erth of Erth* in Ashmole 270[13]: the. **c1500** Greene *Carols* 118.1: the. **1506** Barclay *Castell* E6ᵛ[15]: the. **1509** Fisher *Treatyse* 262.33: the. Svartengren 226–7; Taylor and Whiting 360; Whiting *Drama* 328:316, *Scots* II 135. See **P158, S899, 908, 910, 911.**

S882 As clear as (the, any, summer) **Sun**
c1300 *South English Legendary* I 325.294: He(o) ssinde as cler as the sonne, II 383.300: the, 384.302. **1340** *Ayenbite* 267[29]: the. **a1376** *Piers* A vi 75: the. **c1390** Chaucer *CT* X[I] 1078: the. **a1400** *Destruction of Troy* 272.8386: the. **a1400** *Pricke* 234.8709–10: Ffor ilk ane aungelle bi him-ane Salle clerer schyne than ever son schane. **c1400** *Tundale* 105.1839–40: ony. **a1420** Lydgate *Troy* I 113.3427–8: the somer sonne, **a1422** *Life* 267.284: For it was clever (?clerer) then the sonne bryght. **1447** Bokenham 49.1781: the. **a1449** Lydgate *Timor* in *MP* II 830.49–50: ony. **c1450** Trevet 369.9–10 (f.76ᵇ, col. 1): the. **1483** Caxton *Golden Legende* 171ʳ[2.6–7]: the. **1509** Fisher *Treatyse* 46.15: the. **1509** Watson *Ship* Ccl ʳ[18]: the. **1533** More *Confutacion* 721 A[1–2]: the. Apperson 101; Taylor and Whiting 360; Tilley S969; Whiting *Scots* II 135. See **P159, S901.**

S883 As fair as the **Sun**
c1000 *Old English Nicodemus* 512.17–8: And carinus and leuticus wæron . . . swa fægeres hywes swa seo sunne. **c1375** Chaucer *Anel.* 71–3: Anelida . . . That fairer was then is the sonne shene, **c1386** *LGW* 1004–6: the bryghte sonne.

S884 As glad (*bright*) as the **Sun** (*etc.*) (A number of single quotations are brought together here)
a750 *Riddles* in *Exeter Book* 242.3: Glædre þonne sunne. **c1000** Aelfric *Homilies* I 444[3]: Heo is gecoren (*fine*) swa swa sunne. **c1300** *Horn* 36 L 651: So whyt so the sonne. **c1300** *South English Legendary* I 152.119: And as wide him worth wo as the sonne ssineth aday. **1340** *Ayenbite* 84[22–4]: Maketh man . . . stedevest and lestinde ase the zonne thet alneway yernth and ne is nevre wery. **1399** Chaucer *Purse* 10–1: Or see your colour lyk the sonne bryght, That of yelownesse hadde never pere. **a1400** *Siege of Jerusalem* 6.102 (*var.*): As clene . . . as the sunne on the morwe whanne it furst schyneth. **1447** Bokenham 104.3801: Set ful of gemmys than the sunne moor lyht. **c1460** *Coronation II* in Brown *Lyrics XV* 71.57: Here face, moost splendaunt than the Sonne. **1471** Caxton *Recuyell* II 371.8–10: This desire . . . entryd in to his herte also sodeynly as the rayes of the sonne passe thurgh the glasse, **1483** *Golden Legende* 17ᵛ[2.8–9]: The eyen more shynynge than the sonne, 205ᵛ[1.9–10], 334ᵛ[1.2–3]. **a1500** *Miroure of Mans Salvacionne* 145[21]: Swiftere than is the sonne. **a1500** *Quare* 196.37–8: And als fresch in hir beautee and array As the bricht sonne at rising of the day.

S885 As hot as the **Sun**
a900 *Old English Martyrology* 38.6–7: Leoht of heofenum swa hat swa sunne bið on sumera. **c1000** Aelfric *Lives* I 250.197: Swa hat swa sunne scinende on sumere. **a1500** *Guy*[4] 25–6.523–4: The sonne, that is so hote above, Was never so hote, as is my love. **a1500** *Hymnal* in *Medieval Studies in Memory of Gertrude S. Loomis* (Paris, 1927) 484.76: As hote os sone shynyng at myddey.

S886 As sheen as the **Sun**
a1200 *Ancrene* 53.11–2: And habben him to leofmon that is thusent fald schenre then the sunne, 179.15–6: Schenre then the sunne, 185.17. **c1200** *Hali Meidenhad* 30.318–9, 56.593, 62.672: Ah schine ase sunne. **a1225** *St. Marherete* 44.16–7: schininde sunne, 54.2–3. **a1439** Lydgate *Fall* II 574.3683: any sonne sheene.

S887 As sicker as the **Sun** shines
c1449 Pecock *Repressor* I 89[31]: For, as sikir as the sunne schineth in somerys dai. Cf. Svartengren 360; Taylor and Whiting 360.

S888 As sooth as the **Sun** uprises
c1385 Chaucer *TC* iv 1443: For also soth as sonne uprist o-morwe. Cf. Taylor and Whiting 360.

S889 The **Sun** is brighter than all other stars (*varied*)
c1300 *South English Legendary* I 38.41: As amange alle other sterren the sonne brightore

is. **a1340** *Ayenbite* 81–2: This wyt paseth the wyttes of the worlde ase deth the zonne the brytnesse of the mone. **1369** Chaucer *BD* 821–6: That as the someres sonne bryght Ys fairer, clerer, and hath more lyght Than any other planete in heven, The moone, or the sterres seven, For al the world so hadde she Surmounted hem alle of beaute, **c1380** *PF* 298–301: A queene That, as of lyght the somer sonne shene Passeth the sterre, right so over mesure She fayrer was than any creature. **c1400** *Vices and Virtues* 80.19–21: This witt passeth the witt of this world as doth the sonne alle othere worldely lightes. **a1405** Lydgate *Floure* in *MP* II 414.113–9: As the somer sonne Passeth the sterre with his beames shene . . . My lady passeth . . . Al tho alyve to speke of womanhede. **c1410** Lovelich *Grail* II 388.127–8: So mochel schal he hem passen In alle degre Asse the sone the Mone doth. **1420** Lydgate *Temple* 10–1.250–64: A ladi . . . which right as the sonne Passeth the sterres . . . Surmounteth al, **a1422** *Life* 269.316–8: Passyde Ichone . . . Right as the sonne doth a litil sterre. **a1425** *Of Mynystris* in Wyclif *SEW* II 402[27–8]: For thei passen other preestis, as the sunne doith the moone. **c1433** Lydgate *St. Edmund* 397.41–2: Which passed hem in worthynesse as ferre As doth the sonne a verray litil sterre, **a1439** *Fall* I 227.995–6: For as a sterre in presence off the sunne Lesith his fresshnesse and his cleer(e) liht, III 901.2794–5: Among al kynges renommed and famous As a briht sonne set amyd the sterris, 1016.3415–6: As the gold-tressyd bryght(e) somyr sonne Passith othir sterrys with his beemys clere. **c1449** Pecock *Repressor* I 274[6–9]: For certis, how the sunne passith in cleernes, cheerte, and coumfort the moone, and as a greet torche passith a litil candel. **1471** Caxton *Recuyell* I 247.20–2: But hercules passyd And shone as ferre above hym as the sonne shyneth above the sterres, **c1477** *Jason* 26.10–1: Your resplendour is clere among the women as the sonne is among the sterres, **1484** *Royal Book* G8ʳ[7–8]: As the sonne passeth the clerenesse of the mone. **c1500** *Three Kings' Sons* 23.1–2: As the sonne passith the sterres, so passid this yong man othir folkes, 157.21–2: As the sonne in clerenesse passith the mone and the sterres, so they iii. ovir alle othir bare the brute of that feste, 185.40–186.1: But as the sonne passeth in beaute the sterres, so in beaute . . . passeth alle othir . . . Ioland. See **M648, P161, R205, 227.**

S890 The **Sun** is hotter after sharp showers

a1449 Lydgate *Guy* in *MP* II 519.81: The sonne is hatter affter sharpe schours. Cf. Whiting *Drama* 268.

S891 The **Sun** never tines (*loses*) its fairness though it shines on the muck-heap (*varied*)

c1303 Mannyng *Handlyng* 82.2299–302: The sunne, hys feyrnes never he tynes, Thogh hyt on the muk hepe shynes, But the muk ys the more stynkyngge There the sunne ys more shynyngge. **c1390** Chaucer *CT* X[I] 911: Hooly writ may nat been defouled, namoore than the sonne that shyneth on the mixne. **c1425** *Orcherd* 248.20–1: The sonne, that though it schyne upon a foule thing yit is it not therby defoulid. **c1450** Idley 148.2534–9: Whenne the sonne is feire and fresshe of hewe And shyneth on a mukehill stynkyng and oolde, The sonne in his cours is never the more untrue, But ever in his vertu like fresshe and newe; But the doungehill is the more unsavory and stynkyng alsoo That the might of the sonne hath over hym goo. Apperson 609; *Oxford* 631; Tilley S982.

S892 The **Sun's** light is never the worse though the bat flees from its bright beams

1513 Douglas *Aeneid* II 12.319–20: The sonnys lycht is never the wers, traste me, All thocht the bak hys brycht bemys doith fle. See **W84.**

S893 The **Sun** shines on the righteous and unrighteous alike

c1000 Aelfric *Homilies* I 406[28–30]: Se . . . Drihten, ðe læt scinan his sunnan ofer ða rihtwisan and unrihtwisan gelice, and sent renas and eorðlice wæstmas godum and yfelum. **c1000** *WSG* Matthew v 45: Se þe deð þæt hys sunne up aspringð ofer þa godan and ofer þa yfelan; and he læt rinan ofer þa rihtwisan and ofer þa unrihtwisan. **c1395** *WBible* Matthew v 45: Your fadir that is in hevenes, that makith his sunne to rise upon goode and yvele men, and reyneth on just men and unjuste. **a1450** Audelay 40.845–9: Take ensampil by the sunne ye syne here with syght. Wha may depreve him of his pouere and let his lyghtyng, That schenus apon a synful man as wele as on a ryght, Alse wele on fouele as on fayre without defouteryng, Alse wel apon a knave as apon a kyng? **1509** Fisher *Treatyse* 198.11–3: Whiche maketh his sonne to sprynge and shyne bothe upon good people and evyll. *Oxford* 631; Tilley S985.

S894 To drive as the **Sun** does mist (*etc.*) (A number of single quotations are brought together here)

a1300 *Arthour and M.*[1] 206.7364: We schul hem drive, so sonne doth mist. **c1340** Rolle

Psalter 410 (118.1): This psalme as sun brennand in mydday of ful light. **c1395** *Pierce* 5.122: With gaie glittering glas, glowing as the sonne. **a1400** *Alexander C* 263.5286: With stoute starand stanes that stremed as the son. **a1439** Lydgate *Fall* III 756.3017: That lik a sonne his fame spradde abrod. **1513** Douglas *Aeneid* III 265.79: Hys habyt as the scheyn son lemand lycht.

S895 To glitter like the **Sun**
a900 *Old English Martyrology* 206.26–7: Heo glytenode . . . swa scynende sunne. **c1385** Chaucer *CT* I[A] 2165–6: His crispe heer . . . was yelow, and glytered as the sonne. **c1390** *Sir Gawain* 19.604: That al glytered and glent as glem of the sunne. See **P164.**

S896 To melt as the **Sun** does snow
c1450 *Complaint Against Hope* 26.61: But ryght as the sonne grete snowes melte. **1509** Barclay *Ship* I 217[6–7]: Vayne pleasours, whiche shall sothly decay Lyke as the sone meltyth the snowe away.

S897 To shine like (the, any, a) **Sun**
a900 *Old English Martyrology* 56.20–1: Godes englas swa scinende swa sunne, 146.17–8: Heo nu scineð . . . swa swa sunne. **c1000** Aelfric *Homilies* I 466[12], II 242[6], *Lives* I 178.152: ðet hus eall scean swa swa sunne on dæg, 538.820–1, *Treatise* in *Heptateuch* 70.1194. **a1000** *Vercelli Homilies* 87.178–80: He . . . beorhtaþ swa sunna, þonne hio biorhtust bið scinende. **c1000** *Vercelli Homily 10* in Napier 265.15: þa soðfæstan scinað, swa sunne. **c1000** *WSG* Matthew xvii 2. **c1175** *Twelfth Century Homilies* 94.9, 112.5–6, 134.1–2. **c1200** *St. Juliana* 47.514–5: Hire nebscheaft schene as the sunne. **c1300** *Guy*[1] 454 A 92.5: The halle schon therof as sonne of glas. **c1300** *South English Legendary* I 52.165: the, 262.447: the. **c1340** Rolle *Psalter* 170 (46.4): the, 216 (61.7), 325 (88.36). **c1350** *Smaller Vernon Collection* 61.20. **c1380** *Pearl* 35.982. **c1390** *Castel of Love* 406.1807–8: the. **c1390** Chaucer *CT* VII 879 [B2069]: His brydel as the sonne shoon. **a1393** Gower *CA* III 220.1985: the. **c1395** Chaucer *CT* V[F] 170. **c1395** *WBible* Prologue I 47[17]: the, Judges v 31: the sunne . . . in his risyng, Matthew xvii 2: the, Apocalypse i 16: the. **a1400** Bonaventura *Privity* in *Yorkshire Writers* I 213[35]: the. **a1400** *Ipomadon A* 184.6465: the. **a1400** Wyclif *Sermons* I 143[7]: the, 185[1], II 58[3]: the, [6], [9]: the. **c1400** *Pepysian Gospel* 57.20–1: the. **c1400** *Thomas of Erceldoune* 2.47–8: the sonne on someres daye. **c1410** Lovelich *Grail* II 409.156–8: the sonne uppon the water whanne it is Glemerynge. **a1412** *God and Man* in Kail 49.75–6. **a1415** Mirk *Festial* 97.4–5: the, 223.19: the. **c1420** Page *Siege* 185.982: the. **c1425** Lydgate *Valentine* in *MP* I 308.94: any. **c1425** *Speculum Sacerdotale* 43.14–5: the, 227.23: the, 33–4: the. **a1430** Lydgate *Pilgrimage* 176.6719–20: any, **c1433** *St. Edmund* 388.675: an hevenly sonne, 419.277: any, **a1439** *Fall* II 563.3281: a, III 847.875: a, 894.2533: a. **a1445** *Carl* 132.281–2: anny. **1447** Bokenham 80.2909–10: the sunne in his degre. **a1450** *York Plays* 188.98: the. **a1450** Capgrave *Katharine* 225.884: the, 377.1177: the, *Lives* 136.25–6: the. **c1450** Greene *Carols* 124 B 3: the son dothe throwe the glas. **c1450** *Speculum Christiani* (2) 118.11–2: the. **1450** *Dicts* 184.18: the. **a1456** Hay *Law* 282.30–1: the. **a1475** *Seege of Troye* 203 H 1612l: the sonne bryght. **1483** Caxton *Golden Legende* 198[r][1.1]: the, 199[r] [1.16–7]: the. **1495** *Meditacyons of saynt Bernarde* B5[v][15]: the. **a1500** *Song of the Assumption* in Brown *Lyrics XV* 67.58. **1509** Barclay *Ship* II 289[6]: the. **a1533** Berners *Huon* 65.29: the. **1534** More *Comforte* 1258 E[4]: the. Whiting *Drama* 329:316, *Scots* II 135. See **P165, S906.**

S898 To win something as soon as (win) the **Sun** and moon from heaven
c1330 *Floris* (*Auchinleck*) 48.633–4: Hi scholde winne the mai so sone Ase from the hevene hegh the sonne and mone.

S899 As bright as (the, any) **Sunbeam**
c1000 Aelfric *Lives* II 192.42–3: Cristes rode breohtre þonne sunnan leoma. **a1300** *St. Eustace* in Horstmann *Legenden 1881* 212.43–4: The light of hevene and the glem, Brighttore then the sunne bem. **c1300** *South English Legendary* (*Laud*) 85.81–2: the, 480.624. **a1325** *Suete Jesu* in Brown *Lyrics XIV* 7.14: the. **c1325** *Maid of Ribbesdale* in Böddeker 155.7. **c1375** *St. Peter* in Horstmann *Legenden 1881* 103.41–2: the. **c1390** *Mayden, Modur, and comely Qween* 123.106: the. **a1400** *Ipomadon A* 70.2404–5: the. **a1400** *Laud Troy* II 457.15515–6: That yaff so bryght a gleme, As it hadde ben the sonne beme. **c1400** *Lay Folks' Catechism* 58.917–8: the. **a1415** Mirk *Festial* 233.2: the sonne beme When scho ys most schene. **a1425** *Alexius* (*Laud*) 64.439–40: the. **a1449** Lydgate *Letabundus* in *MP* I 49.26: the. **c1450** *Mary, Pray thy Son* in Brown *Lyrics XV* 33.18: the. **a1475** *Ludus Coventriae* 146.18: the, 162.317: the. **a1475** *St. Birgitta* 98.8: the. **c1490** Ryman 183.4: the. **a1500** *Against Adultery* 370.180: any. Whiting *Drama* 329:317. See **S881.**

S900 As clean as the **Sunbeam**
a1475 *St. Birgitta* 60.17–8: That spirite is so clene as the bemes of the sonne.

S901 As clear as the **Sunbeam**
1439 Lydgate *St. Albon* 136.553: Of all the signes, clere as the sonne beame. **c1490** Ryman 183.4: As the sonne beame as clere. See **S882.**

S902 As shire (*bright*) as **Sunbeam**
a1100 *Phoenix Homily* 147.10–1: His eagene twa . . . synden . . . swa scire swa suneleome.

S903 To be like a **Sunbeam** (*varied*)
a900 *Old English Martyrology* 90.5: His eagan wæron swelce sunnan leoma. **c1300** *Havelok* 22.591–2: Of hise mouth it stod a stem Als it were a sunnebem, 71.2122–3: the. **a1325** *Cursor* II 572.9945–6: That es o gretter light and leme Than somer dai es son bem.

S904 To flee like the **Sunbeam**
1513 Douglas *Aeneid* II 104.63: The figur fled as . . . the son beym, III 45.47.

S905 To leam (*gleam*) like a **Sunbeam**
a1445 *Carl* 142.424–5: Ovyr all the hall gan sche leme As hit wer a son-beme.

S906 To shine like the **Sunbeam**
a1100 *Phoenix Homily* 147.7: þonne scinð he swa sunne leome. **c1250** *Floris* 89.240: (*Shines*) as doth a day the sunne beme. **c1400** *Laud Troy* II 329.11172–3: In somer the sonne bem. **a1439** Lydgate *Fall* III 965.1643. **a1450** *Generydes A* 11.304. **c1450** *Speculum Christiani* (2) 50.12–4: sone-bemes. **c1475** *Guy*[1] 453 C 8098. **1501** Douglas *Palice* 74.23. See **S897.**

S907 He that hangs himself on **Sunday** shall still hang on Monday
1546 Heywood *D* 43.85–6: Well, he that hangth him selfe a sondaie (said hee) Shall hang still uncut downe a mondaie for mee. *Oxford* 276; Tilley S993.

S908 As bright as **Sun-gleam**
c1390 *Of Clene Maydenhod* 467.103–4: Ne nevere so briht sonne-gleme Then Mayden that is clene of thought. See **S881.**

S909 As swift as the **Sun-gleam**
a1200 *Ancrene* 88.21: Ye beon swifte ase the sunne gleam.

S910 As bright as the **Sunlight**
c1300 *South English Legendary* II 590.17: Tho sson is face brightore thanne the sonne light. **a1500** *Partenay* 78.2148–9: Ther bushinentes fayr resplendising, As the bryghty sune light and fayr shinyng. See **S881.**

S911 As bright as **Sunshine**
a1400 Rolle *All synnes* in Allen *R. Rolle* 39.22: Owre flesch wytt of mykel wyn and bryght as sonn schyne. See **S881.**

S912 **Sup** not much and late
a1400 *Proverbis of Wysdom* 245.79: Sope nott mych and late. **c1450** *Fyrst thou sal* 89.65: Sowp thou not to late. **a1500** *Diatorie* in Furnivall *Babees Book* 54.16: Use not to soupe late.

S913 A little **Supper** makes men light at morrow (*varied*)
a1449 Lydgate *Dietary* in *MP* II 704.60: A litill sopeer at morwe makith men liht. **a1500** Hill 129.2: Yf thow wilt be light, let thy soper be shorte. Cf. Tilley S1003.

S914 He that **Supplants** shall be supplanted
a1420 Lydgate *Troy* III 725.5499: And who supplaunteth shal supplaunted be. See **S978, V8.**

S915 In most **Surety** oft falls great peril
1489 Caxton *Fayttes* 51.26–7: For as the mayster sayth, in moost surete is ofte woned to fall grete peryll. See **S669, T181.**

S916 **Surety** in poverty is better than fear in riches
1450 *Dicts* 48.19: Suerte in poverte is better than fere in riches. See **M700.**

S917 There is no **Surfeit** where measure rules the feast
c1516 Skelton *Magnificence* 5.139: There is no surfet where Measure rulyth the feste. See **M453.**

S918 He that is once **Suspect** is half hanged
1402 *Daw Topias* 87[24–5]: Ffor who is oonis suspect, He is half honged. See **N20.**

S919 It behooves him that has no **Swain** to serve himself
c1390 Chaucer *CT* I[A] 4027–8: Hym boes serve hymself that has na swayn, Or elles he is a fool, as clerkes sayn. *Oxford* 574.

S920 He is no good **Swain** that lets (*puts off*) his journey for the rain
a1500 Hill 131.27: He is no good swayn that lettith his jorney for the rayn. Tilley S1022.

Swallow (1)

S921 As fast as a **Swallow**
c1410 Lovelich *Grail* III 62.813–4: The lytel vessel wente . . . as faste Away As Evere flew swalwe In the someris day.

S922 As gerish (*changeful*) as a **Swallow**
a1439 Lydgate *Fall* III 676.53: And as a swalwe gerissh of hir fliht.

S923 As swift as (any, a) **Swallow**
a1300 *Richard* 325.4835–6: On Favel of Cypre he sat ffalewe, Also swyfft as ony swalewe. **c1300** *Reinbrun* 661.91.1: Swift ase swalwe he com ride. **c1300** *South English Legendary* (*Laud*) 475.464–5: His schip bi-gan to go So blive . . . a(s) swaluwe swift. **c1380** *Ferumbras* 132.4231–2: That al so swyftlyche thanne yede, So swolwe doth on flyght. **c1400** *Laud Troy* I 157.5303–4: any, 202.6830–2: any. **c1405** *Mum* 67.1403: a. **c1408** Lydgate *Reson* 140.5356–7: any. **c1450** *De Claris Mulieribus* 52.1050. **a1475** *Mergarete* 239.392: a. **a1500** *Court of Love* 444.1298–9: And eke there nis no swallow swift, ne swan So wight of wing, ne half (so) yern can fly. Svartengren 378; Taylor and Whiting 361; Tilley S1023; Whiting *Scots* II 136.

S924 One **Swallow** makes not summer
1528 More *Heresyes* 128 H[14–5]: One swalow maketh not somer. **1546** Heywood *D* 74.143: One swalowe maketh not sommer. Apperson 612; *Oxford* 634; Taylor and Whiting 362; Tilley S1025.

S925 To glide forth like a **Swallow**
a1300 *Alisaunder* 213.3783: So a swalewe he gynneth forth glide.

S926 To go like a **Swallow**
c1489 Caxton *Aymon* I 258.30–1: Bayarde . . . went lyke a sualowe. Taylor and Whiting 362.

S927 To swing and sail about like a **Swallow**
c1450 Idley 173.903: And not to swyngge and saille aboute lyk a swalowe.

Swallow (2)

S928 The **Swallows** (*abysses*) of the sea and hell receive all
c1400 *Of Prelates* in Wyclif *EW* 97[29–30]: Thei may be wel licned to swolwis of the see and helle, that resceyven al that thei may and yelden not agen. Cf. Tilley S181.

S929 As fair and clean as **Swan's** feather
c1350 *Smaller Vernon Collection* 7.212–3: And then hire eghen wenten to geder, And feir and clene as swannes fether.

S930 As white as (the, any, a) **Swan**
a1300 *Maximian* 99.241: Levedies wiit so swan. **c1300** *Amis* 58.1359. **c1300** Robert of Gloucester II 831.13: Verst threo hundred steden so white so the swan. **c1325** *Alysoun* 139.27: the. **c1325** *Chronicle* 22.536: the. **c1330** *Horn Childe* 180.77: That er wer white so fether on swan. **c1330** *St. Katherine* 259.752: Here swyre was whyt as ony swan. **c1330** *Seven Sages A* 2 E 52. **c1330** *Tars* 33.12: As white as fether of swan. **a1350** *Seven Sages C* 3.78. **c1350** *Als y yod* in T. Wright *Langtoft* (RS 47, 1868) II 452[21]: any. **c1350** *Libeaus* 44.773, 81.1457. **c1350** *Smaller Vernon Collection* 42.45: swannes federe. **a1375** *Octavian* (S) 5.102, 19.554. **c1390** *Castel of Love* 398 *var.* 721–2: the swan when heo is swymbyng. **c1390** *Gregorius* 26.204: the fether of swan. **a1393** Gower *CA* II 247.797: eny. **a1400** *Eglamour* 42.637 (*var.*), 86.1284. **a1400** *King Edward* 962.365: any, **a1400** *Le Morte A.* 36.1141. **a1400** *Torrent* 27.759. **c1400** *Laud Troy* II 494.16761: swannes flawe. **c1400** *Sowdone* 79.2749. **c1400** *Thomas of Erceldoune* 5.68: any. **a1450** *Castle* 99.720. **c1450** *When the son* 393.401: swannys kynde. **c1455** *Partonope S* 482.37. **c1455** *Speculum Misericordie* 942.91: a. **a1470** Malory II 957.37: a. **a1475** *Ludus Coventriae* 56.166. **1480** Caxton *Ovyde* 131[6]: fethers of a Swan. **a1500** *Beves* 122 M 2308: any, 181 M 3601–2: any. **a1500** *Eger H* 309.2085. **a1508** Skelton *Phyllyp* I 84.1079: the. Svartengren 232; Whiting *Scots* II 136.

S930a **Swan-white**
a1387 *Piers* C xxi 215: Other swan-whit alle thynges. **c1475** *Guy*[1] 49 C 823: A Girfauk all swanne white. **a1508** Dunbar *Tretis* 90.243: Thai swanquhit of hewis. NED Swan-white.

S931 A black **Swan**
a1398(1495) Bartholomaeus-Trevisa B2[r][2.23–4]: For noo man fyndyth a blacke swanne. *Oxford* 49; Taylor and Whiting 362; Tilley S1027.

S932 The **Swan** sings before its death
c1375 Chaucer *Anel.* 346–7: But as the swan, I have herd seyd ful yore, Ayeins his deth shal singen his penaunce, **c1380** *PF* 342; The jelous swan, ayens his deth that syngeth, **c1386** *LGW* 1355–6: "Ryght so," quod she, "as that the white swan Ayens his deth begynnyth for to synge." **a1398**(1495) Bartholomaeus-Trevisa B2[v][1.15–20]: And whan she shall deye and that a fether is pyght in the brayne, thenne she syngyth. And agaynst the usage of other bestes in stede of gronyng the swanne syngyth, as Ambrose sayth. **c1408** Lydgate *Reson* 34.1247–8: So as the Swan, this is no nay, Syngeth to forn his fatal day, **1446** *Nightingale*, ed. Otto Glaunig (EETS ES 80, 1900) 1[2–3]: Lyke as the swan syngeth Afore his deth, **a1449** *Look* in *MP* II 766.26–8: The yelwe Swan . . . Ageyn his deth melodyously syngyng, His fatal notys pitous and lamentable. **1480** Caxton *Ovyde* 151[6–9]: She . . . murmured for sorow as a Swanne deyeng, whyche syngeth ayenst her deth, **1481**

Mirror 103[34]: The swanne syngeth ofte to fore her deth, **c1489** *Aymon* I 225.27–8: They were as the swan that syngeth that yere that he shal deye, II 511.3–4: I byleve that they ben as the swane is whan he shall deye. **1493** *Tretyse of Love* 112.7–8: The swann . . . that is of suche nature that whan she shall deye she singyth. **a1500** Kennedy 13.21–2: Rycht as the swan for sorrow singis Befoir hir deid ane littell space. Apperson 612–3; *Oxford* 634; Taylor and Whiting 362; Tilley S1028; Whiting *Drama* 366: 880, *Scots* II 136.

S933 The **Swan** sings in one note
c1450 Idley 86.348: Syngge in oo note as doith a swan. See **C600.**

S934 To be (not) like the **Swan**
a1325 *Cursor* II 996 CG 17371: His clething als the suan his suire. **a1500** *Lover's Mocking Reply* in Robbins 221.31: And yelow tethe not lyk to the swan.

S935 To deny that the **Swan** is white and the crow black
1529 More *Supplicacion* 324 D[6–8]: They . . . wil rather denye that the swan is whyte, and the crowe blacke. Whiting *Drama* 113.

S936 To walk (foot it) like a **Swan**
c1395 Chaucer *CT* III[D] 1930: Walkynge as a swan. **c1516** Skelton *Magnificence* 25.765: Yet thou fotys it lyke a swanne.

S937 To be like a **Swarm** of bees
1513 Bradshaw *St. Werburge* 137.172–4: Lyke a swarme of bees from dyvers nacion . . . Danes, Gotes, Norwayes. See **B177.**

S938 He that **Swears** craftily manswears (*swears falsely*) (*varied*)
c1400 *Scottish Troy* 245.590–3: Inne-to proverbe seyde ofte I-wyss: That he that swerys crafteley, Mansweris craftely for-thy. **c1415** *Middle English Sermons* 109.36–7: And therfore who that will gladely swere, gladely will be-gile. **c1450** *Consail and Teiching* 76.377–8: Suer nevir bot thow compellyt bee, For leif to suere is leif to lee. **c1458** *Knyghthode and Bataile* 43.1168–9: And where Me swereth ofte, it is deceptioun. **a1470** Parker *Dives* F8^{r}[2.14–5]: For comonly grete swerers and usaunt swerers ben full false. Apperson 613: He that will swear; *Oxford* 635; R. M. Smith in *MLN* 65(1950) 442–3; Tilley S1030. See **S954.**

S939 He that **Swears** till no man trust him, *etc.*
a1500 Hill 140.112: He that swerith till no man trist hym, And lyeth till no man beleve hym, And borowith till no man will lend hym, He may go ther no man knowith hym. Apperson 613.

S940 In the **Sweat** of one's face shall he eat bread (*varied*)
a1023 Abbo *Sermo de Cena Domini* in Wulfstan *Homilies* 368.29–30: On swate ðines andwlitan þu scealt ðines hlafes brucan, 370.86–7. **a1200** *Trinity College Homilies* 181[11]: On thine nebbes swote thu shalt thin bred noten. **a1382** *WBible* Genesis iii 19: In the swoot of thi chere, *or face,* thou shalt ete thi brede. **c1390** *Charter of the Abbey* in *Yorkshire Writers* I 344[14]: In swynke and in swete of thi visage thou schalt eten thi bred. **a1425** *Life of Adam and Eve* in *Wheatley MS.* 80.9–10: In the swoot of thi face or cheer thou schalt ete thi breed. **c1440** *Daily Work* in *Yorkshire Writers* I 313[39–40]: In swete of thi face thou sall ete thi brede. **1483** Caxton *Golden Legende* 236^{v}[2.11–3]: vysage. **a1500** Bernardus *De Cura* 15.357–8: Expendande ay thi wynnyng and rychess Be ewyne compenss to the swet of thi face. **1529** More *Supplicacion* 303 E[4–5]: Get their living in the swete of theire faces, **1534** *Passion* 1275 B[10–1]. *Modern Language Forum* 24(1939) 71; Tilley S1031.

S941 To drink one's own **Sweat**
a1393 Gower *CA* II 73.1390: Thus drinke I in myn oghne swot. See **D405.**

S942 After **Sweet** the sour comes (*varied*)
a1352 Minot 32.44: For first thai drank of the swete and sethin of the sowre. **a1393** Gower *CA* II 68.1190–1: Fulofte and thus the swete soureth, Whan it is knowe to the tast, III 197. 1127: That erst was swete is thanne sour. **c1400** *Beryn* 29.898: Aftir swete, the sour comyth, full offt, in many a plase. **c1405** *Mum* 57.1050: Whenne thay have soope the swete, the soure cometh aftre. **a1449** Lydgate *Fabula* in *MP* II 509.701–7: Who that wil entren to tamen of the sweete, He must as weel taken his aventure To taste in bittir, or he the vessel leete, And bothe ilich of strong herte endure; He may nat clense the thykke from the pure: Fo(r), who that wil swetnesse first abroche, He mot be war, or bittir wol approche. **c1475** *Court of Sapience* 138.369–70: And ryght as swete hath hys apryce by sowre, So by trespas Mercy hath all her myght. *Oxford* 635, 705–6; Taylor and Whiting 362; Whiting *Scots* II 136. See **M476.**

S943 He knows not **Sweet(ness)** that never tasted bitter(ness)
c1025 *Durham Proverbs* 13.29: Ne wat swetes ðanc se þe biteres ne onbyrgeð. Nescit suave diligere qui amarum non gustaverit. **c1385**

Chaucer *TC* i 638–9: For how myghte evere swetnesse han ben knowe To him that nevere tasted bitternesse? **a1500** *Thre Prestis* 16.226: Quhy suld he haf the sweit had nocht the sowre? **c1500** *King Hart* 109.13–4: Quha gustis sweit, and feld nevir of the sowre, Quhat can (he) say? How may he seasoun juge? Whiting *Scots* II 136. See **N107, S141, T110.**

S944 **Sweet** is sweeter after bitterness
1420 Lydgate *Temple* 52.1251: And swete is swettir eftir bitternes. See **B352, W153.**

S945 Take the **Sweet(ness)** with the sour
1509 Barclay *Ship* I 39[20]: Take ye in good worth the swetnes with the Sour. **1546** Heywood *D* 67.60: Take the sweete with the sowre. Apperson 614; *Oxford* 636; Tilley S1038. See **B324, R220.**

S946 For much **Sweetness** endure a little sour
1509 Barclay *Ship* I 196[18]: For moche swetnes, endure thou a lytell soure. Cf. Apperson 613–4; *Oxford* 137; Tilley S1035.

S947 The **Sweetness** of this world is mixed with bitterness (the sour)
897 Alfred *Boethius* 25.7–8: Wið swiðe monige biternesse is gemenged sio swetnes þisse worulde. **1509** Barclay *Ship* I 206[12–4]: For who in this worlde wyll come to avantage . . . Shall fynde the swetnes mengled with the sowre. See **J59.**

S948 **Sweetness** shall turn to gall
c1412 Hoccleve *Regement* 47.1299: Al that swetnesse tourne schal to gal. See **H433, S871.**

S949 **Swell** not that you burst not
1484 Caxton *Aesop* 61[18–9]: Wherfore men sayn comynly, Swelle not thy self to thende that thow breste not.

S950 To fall with one's own **Sweng** (*blow*)
c1250 *Owl* 108.1285–6: Go so hit go, at eche fenge Thu fallest mid thine ahene swenge. See **S848, T534, W711.**

S951 Of **Swevens** (*dreams*) one finds the contrary
c1400 *Beryn* 5.108: Ffor comynly of these swevenys the contrary men shul fynde. Apperson 164; *Oxford* 157; Taylor and Whiting 110–1; Tilley D588.

S952 **Swevens** (Dreams) are but vanities
c1348 Rolle *Form* in Allen *R. Rolle* 93.137–8: For whare many dremes er, thare er many vanitees. **c1390** Chaucer *CT* VII 2922[B4112]: Nothyng, God woot, but vanitee in sweven is, 3091[B4281]: For swevenes been but vanytees and japes. **a1393** Gower *CA* II 380.2918–21: A man mai finde of time ago That many a swevene hath be certein, Al be it so, that som men sein That swevenes ben of no credence. **a1400** ?Chaucer *Rom.* A 1–2: Many men sayn that in sweveninges Ther nys but fables and lesynges. **a1400** *Titus* 204.4516: Swevenes beth but a foles spelle. **a1450** *Gesta* (*second version*) 210[11–2]: Behold . . . what dremes ar, nought but vanyte and vayn! **c1450** Idley 114.384–7: Allso trowe thou not ony wyse in dremes, Ffor Clerkis seye it is ofte but vanyte That ebbeth and floweth as wilde stremes, That is not in certen ne never shall bee. **c1515** Barclay *Eclogues* 108.40: A strawe for dreames, they be but vanitie. Tilley D587. See **D387.**

S953 A **Swike** (*traitor*) beswikes himself
c1300 *South English Legendary* (*Laud*) 335.394: Thare he him-seolf, ase everech swyke doth, him-seolf he bi-swok!

S954 Who swears to be **Swike** becomes forsworn
a1400 *Destruction of Troy* 386.11832–3: But in proverbe hit is put with prise men of wit, "Who that sweyres to be swike, he forsworne worthes." Guido de Columnis *Historia Destructionis Troiae*, ed. Nathaniel E. Griffin (Cambridge, Mass., 1936) 231[23–4]: Quod verum est, licet in proverbio dictum sit: "Qui artificiose jurat, artificiose perjurat." See **S938.**

Swine, see **Hog, Pig, Sow**

S955 As drunk as (any) **Swine**
a1500 *Colyn Blowbol* 92.7: Till he was drounke as any swyne, 100.162: any. **1513** Douglas *Aeneid* III 187.28: Drunk as swyne, 192.20. **c1515** Barclay *Eclogues* 134.705. Apperson 167; Tilley S1042; Whiting *Scots* II 137. See **S534.**

S956 As full as **Swine**
1509 Barclay *Ship* II 328[9]: Theyr wombe to fede tyll they be full as swyne, **c1515** *Eclogues* 74.613. Cf. Whiting *Scots* II 137: fat.

S957 As rough as a **Swine**
a1425 *Arthour and M.*² 321.980: And rough as a swyn he wes. **1481** Caxton *Mirror* 84[33]: Peple ther ben that also Rowhe as swyne.

S958 As swollen as **Swine** (*etc.*) (A number of single quotations are brought together here)
a1400 *Siege of Jerusalem* 67.1145: S(ome) swallen (*vars.:* swonyng, swollyng, swellede, swellyn) as swyn. **a1425** *Chester Plays* II 341.264–5: All bemased in a sowne, As we had bene sticked swyne. **1509** Barclay *Ship* II 263[14]: Behave

they moche bestelyer than swyne. **1509** Watson *Ship* P1[r][27]: Lubryke as swyne.

S959 Every one feeds the fat **Swine** for the smear (*lard*)
a1325 *Hendyng C* 189–90.41: Ever man fedit the fat swine for the smere. Kneuer 51; *Oxford* 24; Schleich 271; Singer III 138. See **H403.**

S960 He should eat of the **Swine** that meddles among the bran
1492 *Salomon and Marcolphus* 8[8–9]: It is reson that he of the swyne ete that medlyth amonge te bren.

S961 "Now it is in the **Swine**'s judgement," said the churl (as he) sat on the boar's back
c1025 *Durham Proverbs* 11.10: Nu hit ys on swines dome, cwæþ se ceorl sæt on eofores hricge. Nunc in judicio porci dixit maritus sedens in apro.

S962 The **Swine** loves to lie in the fen (*varied*)
897 Alfred *Boethius* 115.6–10: He bið anlicost fettum swinum þe syle willað licgan on fulum solum, and næfre nellað aspyligan on hluttrum wætrum; ac þeah hi seldum hwonne beswemde weorðen, þonne sleað hi eft on ða solu and bewealwiað hi þæron. **c1000** Aelfric *Homilies* II 380[10–1]: Swa swa swyn deð, ðe cyrð to meoxe æfter his ðweale (*washing*). **a1225** *Lambeth Homilies* 81[13–4]: And (*he*) luveth his sunnen alse deth thet fette swin thet fule fen to liggen in. See **H567.**

S963 A **Swine** overfat is cause of his own bane
1549 Heywood *D* 84.129: A swyne over fatte is cause of his owne bane. Apperson 615; *Oxford* 637; Tilley S1043; Whiting *Scots* 136–7.

S964 To die like (a) **Swine**
c1420 Page *Siege* 182.918: And for defaute dyen lyke swyne. **a1425** Higden-Trevisa Cont. VIII 510[38–9]: Y dye in this wyse lyke a swyne. Whiting *Drama* 329:320.

S965 To fall like a (any) **Swine**
c1390 Chaucer *CT* VI[C] 556: Thou fallest as it were a styked swyn. **a1500** *Guy*[4] 96.2984: That dead he fell as any swyne. **1509** Watson *Ship* Dd5[r][28]: Fallynge in the fylthe and myre lyke swyne.

S966 To lie like (a) **Swine**
a1325 *Flemish Insurrection* 117.42: Hue leyghen y the stretes ystyked ase swyn. **c1330** *Otuel* 109.1502: That there he lay as a stiked swin. **c1400** *Laud Troy* II 388.13166: And lye here stynkyng as a swyne. **a1425** *Chester Plays* II 341.263–5: And lefte us lying, I wott near how! All be-mased in a sowne As we had bene sticked swyne. **c1470** *Wallace* 130.658: The Scottis all as swyne lyis droukyn thar. **a1533** Berners *Arthur* 484[4]. Whiting *Scots* II 137. See **H405.**

S967 To live like **Swine**
c1400 *Why Poor Priests* in Wyclif *EW* 253[18–9]: Thei lyven now as swyn in fleschly lustis. **c1515** Barclay *Eclogues* 207.726: Discorde and brauling and living like to swine.

S968 To rout (*snore*) like drunken **Swine** (*etc.*) (A number of single quotations are brought together here)
a1393 Gower *CA* III 136.6894–5: The servantz lich to drunke Swyn Begunne forto route faste. **a1400** *Cloud* 119.8: And wantounly weltre, as a swine in the myre. **c1400** *Laud Troy* I 169. 5707: He cleff Gregeis as men do swyn, 184. 6243–4: He cleve him doun by the chyn, As it hadde ben a lard swyn. **c1400** *Of Prelates* in Wyclif *EW* 62[32–3]: And bathe hem in lustis of synne as swyn in feen. **c1400** *Satan and his Children* in Wyclif *EW* 217[8–9]: To walwe in glotonye and drounkenesse as swyn in the feen. **a1450** *Castle* 110.1111–2: I schuld be stekyd as a swyne with a lothly launce. **a1470** Malory II 526.14–6: And they twenty knyghtes hylde them ever togydir as wylde swyne, and none wolde fayle other. **c1470** *Wallace* 151.349: Throuch full gluttre in swarff swappyt lik swyn. **c1489** Caxton *Aymon* II 505.5–6: And smote theim doun two and two at ones, as swynes. **a1500** *Partenay* 113.3215: He vomed And swatte, A swine resembling. See **H407.**

S969 To sit like a **Swine**
c1325 *On the Follies of Fashion* in Brown *Lyrics XIII* 133.23: He sitteth ase a slat (*baited*) swyn that hongeth is eren. **a1375** *Octavian* (S) 2.11–2: But as a swyn with lowryng cher All gronne he sytte.

S970 To sleep like (a, the) **Swine**
1340 *Ayenbite* 179[23–4]: He slepth ine his zenne, ase deth thet zuyn ine the wose. **c1390** Chaucer *CT* II[B] 745: Whil he sleep as a swyn. **c1390** *Mercy Passes All Things* in Brown *Lyrics XIV* 130.164: We slepe as swolle swyn in lake. **c1400** *Vices and Virtues* 183.14–5: He slepeth in his synne as the swyn that lith in a foule slowgh ful of gruttes. **c1410** Lovelich *Merlin* III 585.21970: Wherfore as swyn they lyn and Slepe. **a1439** Lydgate *Fall* II 395.2369: dronke swyn. **c1470** *Wallace* 151.357. **1481** Caxton *Mirror* 19[29]: the, **1484** *Royal Book* O6[v][18–9]: Slepeth in his synne lyke a swyn in the dunge.

1522 More *Treatyce* 97 A[16–7]: Lye down and slepe like a swine. Svartengren 168; Whiting *Scots* II 137. See **G467, H408.**

S971 To wallow like **Swine**
1340 *Ayenbite* 126[17–8]: We waleweth ase zuyn hyer benethe ine thise wose of thise wordle. Whiting *Drama* 329:320.

S972 When **Swine** are cunning in all points of music (*i.e.*, never)
a1500 Greene *Carols* 402.4: Whan swyn be conyng in al poyntes of musyke, And asses be docturs of every scyens. See **A227.**

S973 After **Swink** (*trouble*) comes joy
c1350 *Alexander B* 208.921: And aftur swaginge of swinc swithe cometh joie. See **J61.**

S974 As sharp as (a, any) **Sword**(s)
a1300 *Alisaunder* 347.6526: The horne is sharp als a swerd, 350 L 5336–7: sweordis egge. **c1390** *Psalterium b. Mariae* 71.499–500: swerd that kerveth Mayle. **c1395** *WBible* Proverbs v 4: a. **a1400** *Northern Verse Psalter* I 179 (56.5[6]): And thaire tunge scharp swerde es swa. **a1400** *Qui Habitat* 10.2: a. **c1400** Mandeville *Travels* 168.18–9: a. **a1440** Burgh *Cato* 306.102. **c1440** Charles of Orleans 213.6364: poynt of swerd. **c1440** *Prose Alexander* 74.34–5: a, 106.32–3: swerdes. **c1450** *Owayne Miles* (*Brome*) 98.416: ony. **1483** Caxton *Golden Legende* 200ʳ[2.35–6]: a. **a1500** *Court of Love* 424.544. **a1500** *Ghostly Battle* in *Yorkshire Writers* II 424[28]: any two-egede swerde. **c1500** Newton 265.11: any. **1509** *Fyftene Joyes* I8ᵛ[15]. Svartengren 256; Whiting *Scots* II 137.

S975 He that strikes with the **Sword** shall be served (stricken) with the scabbard
c1515 Barclay *Eclogues* 191.277–8: And therfore all suche as with the sworde do strike Feare to be served with the scaberd like. **1546** Heywood *D* 80.16–7: The proverbe saith, he that striketh with the swoorde, Shalbe strikyn with the scaberde. Apperson 615; *Oxford* 626; Tilley S1047.

S976 It is hard to make a two-handed **Sword** of a cow's tail
c1515 Barclay *Eclogues* 194.361–2: And harde is also to make withouten fayle A bright two hande sworde of a cowes tayle, **c1523** *Mirrour* 24[7]: None maketh twohande sworde of plyant cowes tayle. See **S316.**

S977 It is shrewd (*dangerous*) to jape (*jest*) with naked **Swords**
1508(1519) Stanbridge *Vulgaria* 20.12: It is shrewed to Jape with naked swerdes. Tilley J45. See **K88.**

S978 They that take the **Sword** shall perish by the sword (*varied*)
c1000 *WSG* Matthew xxvi 52: Witodlice ealle þa ðe swurd nymað, mid swurde hig forwurþað. **c1280** *Southern Passion* 42.1162: Who-so smyt with swerd he worth y-smyte with swerd also. **a1325** *Cursor* II 902.15801–2: He that smitand es wit suerd, O suerd sal ha the wite. **a1338** Mannyng *Chronicle B* II 339[13]: With suerd that smote, with suerd suld be smyten. **c1350** *Apocalypse* 101.10: That with swerd sleeth most be sleyn with swerd. **c1385** Usk 73.119–20: He that with swerde smyteth, with swerde shal be smitten. **c1395** *WBible* Matthew xxvi 52: For alle that taken swerd, schulen perische bi swerd. **a1400** Wyclif *Sermons* I 123[25–7]. **c1400** *Pepysian Gospel* 92.2–3. **c1400** *Plowman's Tale* 155.245–6. **a1425** *Chester Plays* II 278.342–3. **a1425** *Northern Passion* 56 CDd 569–70, 56 A 569–70: Wo so that with swerdis wyrkis bale He sall hafe the same dale, 57 H 569–70. **a1450** *York Plays* 259.148: For he that strikis with a swerd with a swerde schall be streken. **a1470** Parker *Dives* N3ᵛ[2.19–20]. **a1475** *Ludus Coventriae* 266.1000. Taylor and Whiting 363. See **E186, S373, 405, 914.**

S979 To have a (naked) **Sword** over one's head
897 Alfred *Boethius* 65.28–66.1: Eala, hwæt ðæt bið gesælig mon þe him ealne weg ne hangað nacod sweord ofer ðæ heafde be smale þræde, swa swa me git symle dyde. **1509** Fisher *Treatyse* 28.34–5: For truly over our hedes hangeth a swerde. **1511** Hawes *Comforte* B1ʳ[8–9]: By a sylken threde small as ony heere, Over I sawe hange a swerde full ponderous. *Oxford* 637: Damocles; Taylor and Whiting 363. See **H99, T244.**

S980 To pierce like a **Sword**
c1000 Aelfric *Homilies* I 444[31–2]: His ðrowung swa swa swurd þurhferde hire sawle. **a1325** Bonaventura *Meditations* 4.99: Thys voys as a swerd here hertes persed. **c1400** Paues 95 Hebrews 4.12: Goddes word is . . . more persynge than eny two-egged swerd.

S981 To rend the **Sword** out of the hands of Hercules
c1385 Usk 3.85–8: Who is thilke that wil not in scorne laughe, to here a dwarfe, or else halfe a man, say he wil rende out the swerde of Hercules handes, and also he shuld sette Hercules Gades a myle yet ferther. Whiting *Drama* 349:622.

T

T1 To touch one's **Tabard** (*i.e.*, pay him back) **c1400** *Beryn* 7.190: That I nol touch his taberd, somwhat of his care!

T2 To turn one's **Tabard** (tippet) **c1400** *Brut* I 273.8–10: Wherfore the Scottes, in despite of him (*Baliol*), callede him "Sir John Turnetabard," for cause that he wolde nought offende or trespasse ageynes Kyng Edward of Engeland. **1546** Heywood *D* 61.95: So turned they their typpets by way of exchaunge, **1555** *E* 156.68. Apperson 651–2; *Oxford* 676; Tilley T353.

T3 As plain (*flat*) as a **Table** **a1400** *Alexander C* 227.4138: Bot all as . . . playn as a playn table.

T4 As taut as any **Tabor** **c1395** Chaucer *CT* III[D] 2267–8: Thanne shal this cherl, with bely stif and toght As any tabour. **a1400** *Throw hys hond* in *Archiv* 166(1935) 196.15–6: Als touit als any tabour skynne, our lord lay tyght on tente. Our lord lay touyd in tente i-tyghth, no tabour tighht So toughht. Cf. Svartengren 259.

T5 To have (hold) **Tack** with **a1420** Lydgate *Troy* I 138.4258–9: Here lith on ded, ther a-nother wounded, So that thei myght with hem have no tak. **c1516** Skelton *Magnificence* 65.2084: A thousande pounde with Lyberte may holde no tacke. NED Tack sb.[1] 11a.

T6 To stand to one's **Tackling** **1532** More *Confutacion* 461 G[3–4]: He would honestlye stande to his tacklinge. **1562** Heywood *E* 244.86.1: Art thou in Newgate to stand to thy tacklyng? **1556** *Spider* 271[3]: Sticke to your takling. Tilley T7; Whiting *Drama* 365:871.

T7 **Tag** and rag **1556** Heywood *Spider* 218[5]: Tag and rag, like lions: raging now rage thay. Apperson 616; *Oxford* 638; Taylor and Whiting 364; Tilley T10.

T8 To be tickle of (under) the **Tail** (toe) **a1376** *Piers* A iii 126: Heo is tikel of hire tayl. **c1450** Greene *Carols* 403.4: And under the tayl they (*maidens*) ben ful tekyl. **a1475** *Ludus Coventriae* 126.63–4: Of hire tayle ofte tyme be lyght And rygh tekyl undyr the too. **c1475** *Prohemy of a Mariage* 31[10–1]: Canst thou no better come to holynesse, Than lese thiself al for a tikeltaylle. NED Tickle-tail.

T9 To be without **Tail** or head **1481** Caxton *Reynard* 65[10]: And leve theyr mater wythout tayl or heed. Cf. Taylor and Whiting 176:10. See **H244.**

T10 To have one's **Tail** cut (docked) **c1330** *Body and Soul* 26.40: Thi tayl is cutted the ful neighe. **1418** *Document* in R. W. Chambers and M. Daunt *Book of London English* (Oxford, 1931) 294[27–8]: Y wolde breke hys sege and make hem of Roon dokke hys tayle. **a1475** *Against the Lollards* in Wright *Political Poems* II 245[31–2]: By reson thei shul not long route, While the taile is docked of lollardie. MED dokken 1(b).

T11 To have one's **Tail** tagged (*i.e.*, to be in trouble) **a1500** *Thre Prestis* 45.1043: And I cum thair my tail it wil be taggit. See note, pp. 84–5.

T12 To keep at the **Tail** of an old dog **1485** Caxton *Charles* 121.17–9: Syr Admyral, byleve men another tyme: Alwaye atte tayl of an olde dogge kepe you. French (note, p. 260): Tousjours a la cue dung viel chien vous tenez.

T13 Stealing **Tailors** **1509** Barclay *Ship* II 307[3]: All stelyng taylers.

a1513 Dunbar *Sowtar* 123.17–8: For, quhill the greit sie flowis and ebbis, Telyouris will nevir be trew. Cf. *Oxford* 342: Knavery, 525: Put; Tilley K152, M957, T22; Whiting *Scots* II 137.

T14 Take it or leave it
1519 Horman *Vulgaria* 335[20]: Say or tell at a worde: What is the leste price, take it or leve it. Eloquere de stato precio. *Oxford* 640; Tilley T28.

T15 To **Take** as one finds
a1325 *Cursor* II 660.11517–8: Bot that thai faand, wit-uten wand Thai tok, and thanked godd his sand. **a1439** Lydgate *Fall* III 680.198: Men must at lepis take me as thei fynde. **a1470** Malory II 510.11: As I fynde the, I shall take the! III 1122.19: And therefore I woll take you as I fynde you. **c1475** Henryson *Testament* 124.566: Thairfoir, I reid, ye tak thame as ye find. **c1500** *Lady Bessy* 7[16]: I will him take as I him find. **c1516** Skelton *Magnificence* 45.1438–9: And so as ye se it wyll be no better, Take it in worthe such as ye fynde. Tilley T29; Whiting *Scots* II 138. See **P350.**

T16 To **Take** one as he means
1460 Paston III 216[15]: And take me as I mene. *Oxford* 641.

T17 To think to **Take** but to be taken
1525 Berners *Froissart* V 338[24–5]: We thought to take, but I feare we be taken. See **P232.**

T18 **Take Heed** is a fair thing
1546 Heywood *D* 89.42: Take heede is a faire thing. Apperson 617; *Oxford* 640; Tilley T33. See **A62.**

T19 Be not blind(ed) with fair **Tales**
a1500 *O man more* 394.34: With faire tales be nott thou blynde. See **S601, W584.**

T20 Beware of him that tells **Tales**
a1400 *Proverbis of Wysdom* 246.123–4: Be ware of hym, that tel-the talis, Lest thou have harme and be brought yn balis. *Oxford* 525: Put.

T21 Each **Tale** is ended as it has favor
a1449 Lydgate *World* in *MP* II 847.106–8: This proverbe present, Ech tale is endid, as it hath favour, For among many ech man seith his entent. **a1449** Lydgate and Burgh *Secrees* 51.1584–5: Me doth counforte a proverbe in myn entent; "Ech tale is endyd as it hath favour." Apperson 618.

T22 A false **Tale** is soon told
c1450 *Fyrst thou sal* 91.167: A fals tale is sone tolde.

T23 False **Tales** are better believed than good
a1500 *English Conquest* 103.9–10: As ofte maner is, that fals talys ben bettyr belewid, and lengyr thoght, than good.

T24 A flattering **Tale** is soon heard
1519 Horman *Vulgaria* 87[9]: A flaterynge tale is soone harde. See **M121.**

T25 A good **Tale** ill told is marred in the telling
1549 Heywood *D* 84.155: A good tale yll tolde, in the tellyng is marde. Apperson 262–3; *Oxford* 642; Tilley T38; Whiting *Scots* II 138.

T26 A good **Tale** twice told is the better
a1415 Mirk *Festial* 177.13–4: And thoghe a good tale be twys tolde, hit is the bettyr to lernen and forto undurstond. Apperson 618; *Oxford* 642; Tilley T39.

T27 Good **Tales** ill taken may make the teller smart
1556 Heywood *Spider* 325[19]: Good tales ill taken, may make the teller smart.

T28 One should not believe every fleying (*frightening*) **Tale**
c1495 *Arundel Vulgaria* 59.250: I have herde wyse men say many tymes that a mann sholde not beleve every fleynge tale.

T29 A **Tale** of a tub
1532 More *Confutacion* 371 H[1–2]: Ye shal find all his processe ther in a fayre tale of a tub, 576 B[13–4]. Apperson 618; *Oxford* 643; Tilley T45; Whiting *Drama* 368:913.

T30 A **Tale** that flies through many mouths catches many new feathers
1528 More *Heresyes* 238 B[7–9]: A tale that fleeth thorowe manye mouthes, catcheth manye newe fethers. Cf. Tilley T43.

T31 Thereby lies a **Tale**
a1500 *Assembly* 380.21: And therby lyth a tale. **1523** Skelton *Garlande* I 409.1200: Yet, thoughe I say it, thereby lyith a tale. *Oxford* 648; Tilley T48.

T32 To hear but the first **Tale**
c1516 Skelton *Magnificence* 24.742–3: I make them so fonde, That they wyll here no man but the fyrst tale. Cf. Apperson 473: One tale; *Oxford* 477: One tale is good; Tilley T42. See **P42.**

T33 To tell one a **Tale** and find him ears
1546 Heywood *D* 91.38: He must both tell you a tale, and fynde you eares. Apperson 621–2; *Oxford* 646; Tilley T41.

T34 To tell one another **Tale**
1481 Caxton *Reynard* 94[15–6]: I shal telle hym a nother tale. Tilley T49.

T35 To tell **Tales** out of school
1549 Heywood *D* 35.21: To tell tales out of schoole, that is hir great lust. Apperson 619; *Oxford* 643; Taylor and Whiting 365; Tilley T54.

T36 By merry **Talking** long time seems short
c1515 Barclay *Eclogues* 53.67–8: By mery talking long time seemeth short, In frendly speeche is solace and comfort. See **C394, 398.**

T37 Much **Talking** lets (*hinders*)
1484 Caxton *Aesop* 132[1]: Oftyme moche talkynge letteth, 133[1–3]: And therfor over moche talkyng letteth and to moche crowynge smarteth. See **L67.**

T38 As swart as **Tan**
a1508 Skelton *Phyllyp* I 79.910–1: With vysage wan, As swarte as tan. (NED does not have Tan before 1604.)

T39 As black as **Tar**
c1450 *De Claris Mulieribus* 36.725: Blakker than . . . tarr. Taylor and Whiting 366; Whiting *Scots* II 138.

T40 As bright as a **Tar-barrel**
a1513 Dunbar *Of Ane Blak-moir* 66.12: Schou blinkis als brycht as ane tar barrell.

T41 As small as **Tares**
a1300 *Arthour and M.*[1] 206.7353–4: Thei our folk tohewen waren To smale morsels, so beth taren.

T42 Not worth (set, count) a **Tare**
a1300 *Alisaunder* 313.5992–3: Al that we have wonne and wroughth Ne helde Ich worth a tare boughth. **c1350** *Proprium Sanctorum* 85.163: Hit is not worth a tare. **c1385** Chaucer *CT* I[A] 1570: Ne sette I nat the montance of a tare, **c1390** I[A] 4000: But therof sette the millere nat a tare, 4056: Of al hir art ne counte I noght a tare.

T43 As broad as a **Targe**
c1387-95 Chaucer *CT* I[A] 470–1: An hat As brood as is . . . a targe.

T44 In long **Tarrying** is noys (*harm*) (*varied*)
a1400 *Ipomadon* A 56.1880–1: In long tarying will come Grette noyse, and that we fynde! **c1450** Idley 103.1351: The longer taryeng, the more myscheve. **1457** Paston III 115[20–1]: Taryeng drawyth parell. **c1475** *Seyinges of wysemen* in *Archiv* 104(1900) 308[20–1]: In taryeng is oft full grete drede, Where a begynnyng causith vertued (*var.* vertuhede). **a1500** *Assembly* 393.418–20: The rather sped, the soner may we go. Gret cost alway ther is in tarying; And long to sewe, it is a wery thing. **1519** Horman *Vulgaria* 433[31]: Longe taryenge is hurtfull: whan nede is to hye. See **D157, 450, P145.**

T45 **Tarrying** tines (*loses*) thanks (*varied*)
c1475 Henryson *Fables* 78.2269: This tarying wyll tyne the all thy thank. **c1500** *Melusine* 111.28–9: For long taryeng quenchith moch the vertu of the yefte. Tilley T72. See **G76.**

T46 He that haunts **Taverns** forsakes his thrift
c1350 *Good Wife E* 160.50–1: That taverne hantet Is thrift forsaket, **a1500** *N* 211.61–2: For who the taverne usis His thrift he refusis. Apperson 620.

T47 **Tavern** boughs (bush) affect not the wine (*varied*)
a1430 Lydgate *Pilgrimage* 545.20415–24: And at tavernys (with-oute wene) Thys tooknys nor thys bowys grene, Thogh they shewe ffressh and ffayre, The wyn they mende nat, nor apeyre, Nor medle no thyng (thys the ffyn) Of the sale nor off the wyn, Nor hath nothyng to governe, Off the celer nor taverne: By hem ys no thyng do nor let; They be ther, but for markys set, 567.21258–66: Ryght as, off A taverner, The grene bussh that hangeth out, Ys a synge (yt ys no doute,) Outward, folkys for to telle, That with-Inne ys wyn to sell, And for al that, (I you ensure) Yt may falle off aventure, Ffor alle the bowes, rekne echon, That, with-Inne, wyn ys ther noon. *Oxford* 257–8. See **G35, W354.**

T48 The **Tavern** is the devil's schoolhouse
1340 *Ayenbite* 56[20–1]: The taverne ys the scole of the dyevle. **c1400** *Vices and Virtues* 53.29–30: The taverne is the develes scole house. **c1450** *Jacob's Well* 147.26–7: The taverne . . . may be clepyd the develys scolehous and the develys chapel.

T49 Those are stout and stern at the **Tavern** that turn their heels when strokes begin
a1300 *Richard* 286–7.3853–62: Whenne they sytte at the taverne, There they be stoute and sterne Bostfful wurdes ffor to crake, And off here dedes yelpyng to make . . . But whene they comen to the mystere, And see men begynne strokes dele, Anon they gynne to turne here hele. See **B415, F659, M367.**

T50 How shall he **Teach** another that cannot teach himself?
a1400 *Ancrene* (*Recluse*) 158.6–7: For hou schal

he techen another that can noughth techen hym selven? See **G353, M228, 407, P150, S856.**

T51 As fast as a **Tempest**
c1489 Caxton *Aymon* I 259.27: Cam ridyng upon bayarde as faste as tempest.

T52 To be like a **Tempest**
a1300 *Arthour and M.*[1] 188.6699–700: Thai arered a cri of more wonder Than tempest o fer or thonder.

T53 To come (on) like a **Tempest**
a1300 *Arthour and M.*[1] 167.5933–4: This thre and fourti com on hast, With norththen winde so doth tempast. **a1533** Berners *Huon* 292.16–7: The emperour came agaynst hym lyke the tempest, 300.22–3: They . . . cam togyther lyke the tempest.

T54 To drive in like a **Tempest**
c1450 *Merlin* II 209[20–1]: Than thei drive in a-monge hem as tempest of thunder.

T55 To fly like a **Tempest**
c1410 Lovelich *Merlin* II 383.14303–4: Thanne in they flyen as stordyly As evere dide tempest out of the sky.

T56 To run like (the) **Tempest**
1471 Caxton *Recuyell* I 147.26–7: And rennyng as tempeste passid by theyr arowes. **a1533** Berners *Huon* 186.25–6: Sorbryn came rynnynge lyke the tempest.

T57 As sharp as **Tenterhooks**
c1516 Skelton *Magnificence* 32.1002: Her naylys sharpe as tenter hokys.

T58 Homely **Terms** best express homely matter
1556 Heywood *E* 104.21: Homely matters, homly termes dooe best expresse. See **L68.**

T59 To give **Terns** (*double threes at dice*) and quernes (*fours*)
a1300 *Richard* 188.2019–21: Ternes and quernes (*var.* Termis and quermis; Strakes ynewe) he gave hym there, And sayd: "Syr, thus thou shalte lere To myssaye thy overhedlynge!" NED Tern sb.[2] B 1 (next example 1856), Querne (only example).

T60 **Testons** (*debased coins*) are gone to Oxford, *etc.*
1562 Heywood *E* 216.63–4: Testons be gone to Oxforde, god be their speede: To studie in Brasenose there to proceede. These Testons looke redde: how like you the same? Tis a tooken of grace: they blushe for shame. Tilley T92.

T61 **Text** and gloss (*varied*)
c1386 Chaucer *LGW* F 328: For in pleyn text, withouten nede of glose. **c1390** *Who says the Sooth* in Brown *Lyrics XIV* 152.15: To leve the tixt and take the glose. **a1400** *Romaunt C* 6555–6: And if men wolde ther-geyn appose The nakid text, and lete the glose. **a1420** Lydgate *Troy* I 24.414: The tixte was hyd, but no thing the glose. **c1450** Idley 90.573: Telleth hem the text and leevith the gloose, 125.1056: I telle you the texte, expowne ye the gloose!

T62 To pick a **Thank**
c1412 Hoccleve *Regement* 110.3048–9: But a thank to pike, His lordys wil and witte he justifieth, **c1422** *Jereslaus's Wife* 154.399: And so byhoveth a thank us to pyke. **1519** Horman *Vulgaria* 102[21]: Leve thy flaterynge wordes that goth aboute to pyke a thanke. NED Pick v.[1] 8b, Pickthank.

T63 So many **Thedes** (*countries*) so many thews (*customs*) (*varied*)
897 Alfred *Boethius* 43.21–3: Forþamþe þara ðeoda þeawas sint swiðe ungelice, and hiora gesetenessa swiðe mislica. **c900** *Maxims* in *Exeter Book* 157.17–8: Aelmihtig god, efenfela bega þeoda ond þeawa. **c1250** *Hendyng O* 191.3: Also fele thedes (*C* dedis), Also fele thewes. **c1385** Chaucer *TC* ii 28: In sondry londes, sondry ben usages, 42: Forthi men seyn, ecch contree hath his lawes. **c1385** Usk 22.43–4: Eke this countrè hath oon maner, and another countrè hath another, 47–8: Dyversitè of nation, dyversitè of lawe. **a1400** *Cleansing* 78.12–3 (f. 49[r]): For divers londes have divers customes, and to the comendable customes ye most obeye as to the lawe. **1523** Berners *Froissart* I 6[38]: Every nacion hath sondrie customes, **1525** IV 226[14–6]: For in suche maner the worlde is governed: for that is not in one countrey, is in another, and therby every thynge is knowen. Apperson 586; Jente 47; Kneuer 17–8; *Oxford* 113; Schleich 248–9; Singer III 125; Taylor and Whiting 82; Tilley C708, 711; Whiting *Drama* 229. See **H230.**

T64 Through **Thick** and thin
c1390 Chaucer *CT* I[A] 4066: And forth with "wehee," thurgh thikke and thurgh thenne. **a1420** Lydgate *Troy* I 214.2427–8: Or I was war, thorugh thikke and (thorugh) thinne, A ful gret hert I sawe a-fore me renne, **a1430** *Pilgrimage* 304.11134–5: Ffor I am ycallyd "youthe"; I passe bothe thorgh thynne and thykke. **1449** Metham 41.1108–10: And forth thru thyk and thyn He gan lepe; that nowdyr nettyl, busche, ner

thorn Myght hym let. **a1450** *Partonope* 17.627–8: Thoroughe thyke and thynne in that fforeste Ryghte faste they soghte, 279.7127–8: Through thick and thyn he hyed hym faste, Till al the fforest he was paste. **a1470** Malory II 588.19–20: He made his horse to ren and fledde as faste as he myght thorow thycke and thorow thynne, 685.1–2: When sir Bleoberys saw hym fle he felowed faste after thorow thycke and thorow thynne, 721.19. **a1500** *Kyng and the Hermyt* in Hazlitt *EPP* I 15.62–3: And chasyd hym ryght fast, Both thorow thyke and thine. **c1500** *Lo here is a ladde* in *MP* 14(1916) 7.42: The fawkoneres rennyng throw thykke and throwe thynne. **1519** Horman *Vulgaria* 246[15–6]: I have broughte a geldynge: that wyll bere me through thycke and thynne. Emi cantherium qui me per æqua et iniqua innoxie vehet, 379[31]: He ranne heedlynge through thycke and thynne. Per æqua et iniqua. Apperson 623; *Oxford* 648; Taylor and Whiting 368; Tilley T101; Whiting *Drama* 367:892.

T65 To take the **Thick** with the thin
a1449 Lydgate *Fabules* in *MP* II 576.280: Take, as hit falleth, the thyk with the thyn. Cf. Apperson 205: Fat; *Oxford* 641. See **R220.**

T66 As like as a **Thief** (is) to break into Newgate
1556 Heywood *Spider* 62[22–3]: I brake into this house now, quoth the flie, Like as a theefe doth breake into newgate.

T67 Deliver a **Thief** from the gallow(s) and he hates you after (*varied*)
c1300 *Beves* 58.1215–8: Thar fore hit is soth isaide And in me rime right wel ilaid: Delivre a thef fro the galwe, He the hateth after be alle halwe! **c1300** *Northern Homily Cycle* (*Edin. Coll. Phys.*) 167[5–8] Bot qua sa leses fra hinging Thef, or bringes up funding, Of nauther getes he mensc ne mede, Ne socour quen he havis nede. **c1400** *Florence* 43.1279–81: And toke hym downe that cursyd thefe That afturward dud hur grete grefe. Ther was nevyr no sawe sotheyr, 58.1708 ff. **a1439** Lydgate *Fall* III 762.3253–5: Who saveth a theef whan the rop is knet Aboute his nekke, as olde clerkis write, With sum fals tourn the bribour wil hym quite. **c1450** La Tour-Landry 201.1–2: He is wel a foole that saveth and respyteth ony theef fro the galhows. **1484** Caxton *Aesop* 15[5–7]: As men sayen comynly, yf ye kepe a man fro the galhows he shalle never love yow after. **a1500** *Beves* 58 M 969–71: This ys trewe, *by al halowes:* Delyver a theeff ffro the galoos, And he shall wayte the to rob or sloo. Apperson 550; *Oxford* 562; Taylor and Whiting 368; Tilley T109; Whiting *Drama* 300. See **F118.**

T68 The great **Thieves** punish the less (*varied*)
a1387 Higden-Trevisa III 357[5–7]: Zenocrates seygh oon i-lad to the honging, and lowh and sede, "the gretter theeves punscheth the lasse." **c1523** Barclay *Mirrour* 34[8–14]: What difference betwene a great thiefe and a small, . . . The small thiefe is judged, oft time the great is Judge. *Oxford* 265; Tilley T119. See **L456, M94, T77.**

T69 If one sues (*pursues*) a **Thief** he may be said to run with him
c1395 *WBible* Isaiah i 23 *gloss:* Lest it be seid of us, if thou suest a theef, thou rennedist with him.

T70 The little **Thief** is hanged but his resetter (*receiver*) is saved
c1450 *Alphabet* I 73.8–10: Ffor commonlie the lytle thieff is hanged, Bod his resettyr and his mayntynnuer is savid. Cf. Apperson 525; *Oxford* 534; Tilley R52. See **M23, S846, T74.**

T71 Murder not little **Thieves,** letting greater thieves go
c1523 Barclay *Mirrour* 33[36–7]: Murther not small thieves, letting greater thieves go Without execution, for feare, favour or mede. Jente 274; *Oxford* 375: Little. See **L106, T440.**

T72 One may better keep him from a **Thief** than from a liar
1450 *Dicts* 156.33–4: A(nd) yit a man may better kepe him from a thef than from a lier. Cf. Apperson 361: A liar is worse; *Oxford* 363; Tilley L218.

T73 There is no **Thief** without a louke (*accomplice*)
c1390 Chaucer *CT* I[A] 4415–7: And for ther is no theef withoute a lowke, That helpeth hym to wasten and to sowke Of that he brybe kan or borwe may. See **H410, M69, R60.**

T74 A **Thief** and his fellow should have one doom (*varied*)
c1303 Mannyng *Handlyng* 243.7623–6: Gyt sey men yn the olde lawe, That, of a thefe and hys felawe, O dome shul they bothe have, The toon ne tother shul men nat save, 346.11184–6: And the same seyth landes lawe, "That who so consenteth to a thefe, Evene peyne shul they have grefe." See **M23, T70.**

T75 A **Thief** must go in thester (*dark*) weather (*varied*)
c800 Cynewulf *Christ* in *Exeter Book* 27.871–2:

þeof þristlice, þe on þystre fareð, On sweartre niht. **c900** *Cotton Maxims* in *ASMP* 56.42: Þeof sceal gangan þyrstrum wederum. **a1398**(1495) Bartholomaeus-Trevisa Z1r[2.27–9]: (*Day*) is enmye to theves and makyth theim drede, for theves drede by daye. See **E184.**

T76 A **Thief** of venison can keep a forest best
c1390 Chaucer *CT* VI[C] 83–5: A theef of venysoun, that hath forlaft His likerousnesse and al his olde craft, Kan kepe a forest best of any man. Apperson 624; *Oxford* 472; Tilley D191.

T77 A **Thief** should not sit in judgment for theft
a1439 Lydgate *Fall* III 786.425–7: It sittith nat in no maner wise A theef for theffte to sitte in jugement; A lecherous man a lechour to chastise. See **T68.**

T78 A **Thief** that has done many a true man mischief goes at large
c1385 Chaucer *CT* I[A] 1325–7: Allas, I se a serpent or a theef, That many a trewe man hath doon mescheef, Goon at his large. Skeat 281.

T79 A **Thief** will not blin (*leave off*) till he hang by the chin
c1330 *Seven Sages A* 51.1265–6: For thef of steling wil nowt blinne, Til he honge bi the chinne. Cf. Jente 616.

T80 To be bound like a **Thief**
c1400 *Sowdone* 76.2656: That bounde was as a thefe fast.

T81 To dread as **Thief** does club
c1300 *Havelok* 76.2289: He dredden him so thef doth clubbe.

T82 To hang like a **Thief**
a1450 *Generydes A* 41.1307: He heng as high as any thefe. **a1450** *York Plays* 363.142: Hyngis as a theffe. **a1475** *Ludus Coventriae* 303.900–1: My swete sone . . . As a theff on cros doth honge.

T83 When **Thieves** fall out true men come to their good
1546 Heywood *D* 93.108: Whan theeves fall out, true men come to their goode, **1555** *E* 173.151. Apperson 625; *Oxford* 649; Tilley T122.

T84 As hollow as a **Thimble**
1506 *Kalender* 88.17: As holowe as a thymble.

T85 As round as a **Thimble**
a1500 *Carpenter's Tools* 80.18: I ame as rounde as a thymbyll.

T86 All overdone **Thing** deres (*harms*)
c1000 Aelfric *Lives* I 20.162–3: Hit is awryten, Omnia nimia nocent, þæt is ealle ofer-done þing dæriað. **c1175** *Twelfth Century Homilies* 90.27–8. **a1225** *Lambeth Homilies* 101[22–4]: (*O*)*mnia nimia nocent et temperancia mater virtutem dicitur*, thet is on englisc, alle ofer done thing denath (*for* deriath) and imetnesse is alre mihta moder. Walther III 584.19838. See **M463, O63, P383.**

T87 All **Thing** (Everything) has (must have) an end (*varied*)
c1385 Chaucer *CT* I[A] 2636: Som tyme an ende ther is of every dede, 3026: Thanne may ye se that al this thyng hath ende, *TC* iii 615: As every thyng hath ende, **c1386** *LGW* 651: Tyl at the laste, as every thyng hath ende. **c1390** *Against my Will* in Brown *Lyrics XIV* 134.19: For everi thing schal have an ende. **c1400** *Sowdone* 26.891: Al thinge moste have an ende. **c1425** *Avowynge* 88[16]: Iche ertheli thinke hase ende. **a1450** *Partonope* 447.11144: Ye wote wele of all thing moste be an ende. **a1500** *Chaucer's Dreme* in Speght's *Chaucer* 357r[2.52]. **a1500** *Man have mynd* 54.3. **c1500** Fabyan 554[38–9]: All operacion of man hath ende. **1509** Barclay *Ship* I 268[7]: All worldly thynges at last shall have an ende. **1509** Fisher *Treatyse* 197.33–4: All erthly thynges be mutable and shall have an ende. **1525** Berners *Froissart* IV 70[39–40]: Yet it cannat be alwayes thus; at last it must nedes have an ende, **1532** *Golden Boke* 261.4716–7: Al thingis hath an ende at last by deth, **a1533** *Huon* 74.23–4: All thynges creatyd in this mortall world must nedys have an ende. **1556** Heywood *Spider* 396[8–9]: As who seie: things most long after beginning: Yet must they (at last) nedlie cum to an ende. Apperson 8; *Oxford* 180; Skeat 224; Taylor and Whiting 369; Tilley E120. See **F92, L87, N154, 161, W431.**

T88 All **Thing** (Everything) has time (*varied*)
c1382 *WBible* Ecclesiastes iii 1: Alle thingus han time. **c1385** Chaucer *TC* ii 989: For every thing hath tyme, iii 855: Nece, alle thyng hath tyme, I dar avowe. **c1390** Hilton *Mixed Life* (*Vernon*) in *Yorkshire Writers* I 291[6–7]: *Omnia tempus habent:* Al thing hath tyme. **a1393** Gower *CA* III 149.7186–7: But tak this lore into thi wit, That alle thing hath time and stede. **c1395** Chaucer *CT* III[D] 1475: But alle thyng hath tyme, IV[E] 6: But Salomon seith "every thyng hath tyme," 1972: For alle thyng hath tyme, as seyn thise clerkes. **a1400** *Active and Contemplative Life* in Perry *English Prose Treatises* 43.4–5: The wyse man sayse, "*Omnis*

tempus habent." That es, "all thyngis hase tyme." **a1400** *Double Comminge* in *Yorkshire Writers* II 61[6]. **c1405** *Mum* 20.278. **a1430** Lydgate *Pilgrimage* 297.10863–4: Ech thyng (shortly for to ryme,) Muste duely have hys tyme. **a1437** *Kingis Quair* 82.133[1]: thus sais Ecclesiaste. **c1450** *Consail and Teiching* 76.353. **c1450** *Douce MS.52* 57.141. **c1450** *Rylands MS.394* 108.8. **a1475** *St. Birgitta* 72.34. **a1475** *Wright's Chaste Wife* (EETS 12, 1865) 2.26–7: As tyme comyth of alle thyng, (So seyth the profesye). **c1475** *Wisdom* 49.401: dew tymes. **1483** Caxton *Cato* E7r[24], G3r[6–7]: Al thynges have bothe theyr tyme and place. **1492** *Salomon and Marcolphus* 13[14]: Alle thynges have theyre seasons and tyme. **1509** Barclay *Ship* II 46[15]: For every thynge god hath a tyme purvayde. **1509** Fisher *Treatyse* 174.2. **a1529** Skelton *On Tyme* I 137.1–2: Ye may here now, in this ryme, How every thing must have a tyme, 8: All thynge hath tyme, who can for it provyde. Apperson 192; Jente 63; *Oxford* 180, 659; Smith 298; Tilley T314; Walther III 621.20086–7; Whiting *Scots* I 164. See **T313.**

T89 All **Thing** is gay that is green
1546 Heywood *D* 61.81: All thing is gay that is greene. Tilley T161. See **T117.**

T90 All **Thing** is proved and tried at the last
1515 Barclay *St. George* 102.2570: All thynge is provyd and tryed at the last. See **E81, T326.**

T91 All **Thing** is worse when it is worn (for the wearing)
c1516 Skelton *Magnificence* 15.451: All thynge is worse whan it is worne. **1546** Heywood *D* 61.83: All thyng is the woors for the wearyng. Tilley W207.

T92 All **Thing** may be suffered save wealth
1471 Caxton *Recuyell* II 516.10–1: Alle thynge may be suffryd save welthe. **1546** Heywood *D* 67.50: All thyng maie be suffred savyng welth. Tilley T171.

T93 All **Thing** may not be said at once
c1450 Capgrave *Katharine* 53.609: Alle thing may not be seyd at ones, as clerkys seyn.

T94 All **Thing** shows from whence it came
1549 Heywood *D* 44.91: Commenly all thyng shewth fro whens it camme. See **A169, E173.**

T95 All **Thing** that is sharp is short
1546 Heywood *D* 63.50: But all thing that is sharpe is short. Cf. Apperson 589: Sorrow for a husband is like a pain in the elbow, sharp and short.

T96 All **Thing** that seems sooth is not
a1400 *Romaunt C* 7544: It is nat al soth thyng that semeth. See **G282.**

T97 All **Things** are changeable
1456 Hay *Governaunce* 153.5: All thingis ar changeable. **1483** *Vulgaria quedam abs Terencio* A8r[23–4]: All thynges allter or chaung their tymes or all thyngis be chaungeable. Smith 23; Tilley C233.

T98 All **Things** are common among friends
1483 *Vulgaria quedam abs Terencio* P8v[21–2]: It is an olde byworde, all thyngis are common amonge frendys. *Oxford* 650; Smith 125; Tilley F729. See **N47.**

T99 All **Things** must go (pass) (*varied*)
c700 *Deor* in *Exeter Book* 178.7: þæs ofereode, þisses swa mæg, 13, 17, 20, 27, 42. **a1439** Lydgate *Fall* II 338.355–7: As flowe and ebbe al worldli thyng mut gon; For afftir flodis off Fortunys tyde, The ebbe folweth, and will no man abide. **a1449** ?Lydgate *Pageant of Knowledge* in *MP* II 733.268–9: All erthely thynges sodenly do passe Whyche may have here no seker abydyng, 738.125–6. **a1500** *Arundel MS.* in Robbins-Cutler 3823.5: All thinges schal passe save to love god aloone.

T100 All **Things** that are like will be understood (when) together
1481 *Tulle of Olde Age* 6[31–3]: Ffor aftir the auncient proverbe, all thyngys which be like of resemblant exsamples wold be undirstonde assemblyd and gaderd to gedyr. See **L272.**

T101 All worldly **Thing** has but a season
c1470 *Wallace* 48.9: All warldly thing has nocht bot a sesoune. Cf. Whiting *Drama* 270. See **C114, N154, T161.**

T102 Assay all **Thing** rather than fight
a1500 *English Conquest* 25[14–5]: As the Wysman Seyth, "Althynge we oghte to assay, radyr than fyght." Terence *Eunuchus* IV vii 19: Omnia prius experiri quam armis sapientem decet.

T103 Be not about to catch **Thing** that you may not latch (*grasp*)
1438 *Barlam and Josaphat* (*Vernon*) 221.439-40: The Brid seide, beo not aboute to cacche Thing that thou maist not lacche. See **R54, S620.**

T104 Begin not a **Thing** one may not end (achieve) (*varied*)
c1390 *Hou a man schal lyve parfytly* in *Vernon* I 244.885–6: Gret folye hit were to fo or ffrende, To be-ginne thing he may not ende. **a1393** Gower *CA* III 153.7346–7: Betre is to leve,

than beginne Thing which as mai noght ben achieved. **a1400** *Scottish Legends* II 277.197–8: Quhat ned the to begyne the thing That thu mycht nocht bring til ending. **1450** *Dicts* 92.26: Begynn no thing bot if thou may bring it to good ende. **a1475** *Mumming of the Seven Philosophers* in Robbins 111.34–5: That hyt ys foly a man suche to begyn which to performe hys wyttes be to thyn. **a1500** *Hunterian Mus. MS.320* 275: Yt ys ffolly a manne a thyng to begynne Wyche to perfform his wyttes be butt theynne. **1509** Watson *Ship* D8r[18–9]: It were better never to begynne a thynge than for to leve it unfynisshed. **1523** Berners *Froissart* III 234[25–7]: If we shulde begyn a thynge, the whiche we coulde nat acheve, we shulde never recover it agayne, **a1533** *Arthur* 161[8–10]: He ought not to be reputed neither for sage nor wise, that wyl take on hym suche a thyng that he cannot acheve. *Oxford* 41: Better never to begin; Tilley E115. See **B196, E90, S620, T106.**

T105 The best or worst **Thing** is the good or ill choosing (of a) good or ill wife
1546 Heywood *D* 21.19–20: The best or woorst thing to man for this lyfe, Is good or yll choosyng his good or yll wyfe. Tilley T123.

T106 Better not begin a **Thing** than leave (it) unended
1509 Barclay *Ship* I 176[7]: Than leve a thynge unendyd better nat begynne. See **E90, S163, T104.**

T107 Better tarry a **Thing,** then have it, *etc.*
c1545 Heywood *Four PP* A4r[28–9]: Yet better tary a thynge, then have it, Then go to sone and vaynly crave it.

T108 Borrowed **Thing** will home (again)
c1350 *Good Wife E* 168.149: Borewed thing wole hom. **a1400** *Proverbis of Wysdom* 244.31–2: Spend no man is gwode in vayn: Borowed thyng wyll home agayn. **1400** *Love god and drede* in Kail 2.38: And borwed thyng mot home ful nede. **c1450** *Fyrst thou sal* 88.51–2. **c1450** *Good Wife L* 202.175–6: For though thou borowe faste, It must hoome agen at laste. **c1450** *Proverbs of Good Counsel* 68.13–4. Apperson 61; Tilley T125.

T109 Common **Thing** is better (*varied*)
a1400 Wyclif *Sermons* I 165[1]: As comune thing is betere and bifore other thingis, 227[17–9]: But, as comun thing is ofte sothe, whanne the singuler is fals, so it fallith ofte tyme of comun witt and comune wille, II 195[11–2]: For of comoun thing and knowun shulden the comouns beste take ther witt. See **C351, D48.**

T110 Contrary **Things** are discoverings of each other (*varied*)
c1375 Barbour *Bruce* I 11.241–2: Thus contrar thingis evir-mar Discoweryngis off the tothir ar. **c1385** Chaucer *TC* i 637: By his contrarie is every thyng declared. **c1425** *Orcherd* 244.1–2: A contrarie is lightly knowe by his contrarie. **c1450** *De Claris Mulieribus* 9–10.162–6: Oon contrary evere shewyth anodyre: The daye is knowen clerere for the nyght; Swete and sowre —that on shewyth that odyre; Youthe by age, derkness is known by light; By vyce vertue, by wronge appereth right. **1490** Irlande *Meroure* II 54.29–31: Arestotill said and verite schawis, that a thing is richt weill knawin quhen the contrar of it is put besyd it And comperit to it, as the farnes of a lady or precius stane is better knawin quhen a foule thing is put besid it neir and comperit to it. Cf. Tilley C630. See **L383, S943, T111, W231.**

T111 Contrary **Things** may never accord (*varied*)
a1449 Lydgate *Cok* in *MP* II 814.46: Thynges contrarye may nevir accorde in oon, *Look* in *MP* II 768.97: Thynges contrary be nat accordyng. **a1475** *Ludus Coventriae* 99.64: Twey contraryes mow not to-gedyr dwelle. **1479** Rivers *Cordyal* 141.14–5: For nature wole not that two contraires be medled to gydre. Whiting *Drama* 138.

T112 Covet not **Thing** which you may not have (*varied*)
a1410 Lydgate *Churl* in *MP* II 482.331–2: I bad thou sholdist in no maner wyse, Coveite thyng which thou maist nat have. **1438** *Barlam and Josaphat* (*Northern*) 232.522: Ne yern noght that thou noght get may. **a1450** *Barlam and Josaphat* (*South English Legendary*) 124.397: Ne desire thu never that thing: that thu myght have nought.

T113 Dispraise not a little **Thing** (*varied*)
1450 *Dicts* 120.4–5: Dispreise not a litille thinge, for it may encrece. **a1500** *Colkelbie* 303.227–8: Ffor litill thing weill spendit may incres To he honour wirschep and gritt riches. See **M159, 483, S44, T203.**

T114 Do not evil **Things** that good may come
c1395 *WBible* Romans iii 8: And not . . . Do we yvele thingis, that gode thingis come. Tilley E203.

T115 Each **Thing** draws to its kind (*varied*)
c1395 Chaucer *CT* V[F] 607–9: I trowe he hadde thilke text in mynde, That "alle thyng, repeir-

ynge to his kynde, Gladeth hymself;" thus seyn men, as I gesse. **a1410** Lydgate *Churl* in *MP* II 479.260–2: Ech thing drawith un-to his semblable: Fissh in the see, bestis on the stronde, The eyr for fowlis of nature is covenable, **a1439** *Fall* I 133.4754: Everi thyng resortith to his kynde, **1439** *St. Albon* 127.9–11: Every thynge draweth to his nature Like as kynde gyveth hevenly influence For to disposen every creature, **a1449** *Every Thing* in *MP* II 801–8.8: Thus every thing drawethe to his semblable, 16, 24, *etc.*, *Ryme* in *MP* II 792.1–2: All thyng in kynde desirith thyng i-like, But the contrary hatis every thyng. **1450** *Dicts* 4.32: Comonly alle thingis desirith and sekithe his liknes. **a1475** Banester *Guiscardo* 34.581: Yche thing drawith unto hys similitude. See **L272.**

T116 Each **Thing** is best taken in its season
a1449 Lydgate *Haste* in *MP* II 762.73: Eche thyng is beeste take in his sesoun.

T117 Each **Thing** is fair when it is young
c1516 Skelton *Magnificence* 31.971: Eche thynge is fayre when it is yonge; all hayle, owle! Tilley T161. See **T89.**

T118 Each **Thing** must bow when it is overladen
a1439 Lydgate *Fall* I 126.4527: Ech thyng mut bowwe whan it is over-lade. See **B422, C16, S249, W6.**

T119 Fair **Things** are often found faken (*deceitful*)
c1475 Henryson *Fables* 97.2834: For fair thingis oftymis ar fundin faikin. *Oxford* 187; Tilley T198. See **F571.**

T120 Forbid us **Thing** and that we desire
c1395 Chaucer *CT* III[D] 519–20: Forbede us thyng, and that desiren we; Preesse on us faste, and thanne wol we fle. *Oxford* 219. See **L487, T162.**

T121 Four **Things** are never full (*varied*)
a1000 *Dialogue of Salomon and Saturnus*, ed. J. M. Kemble (London, 1848) 190.50: Saga me, hwæt syndon ða iiii þing ðe næfre fulle næron, ne næfre ne beoð. Ic ðe secge, an is eorðe, oðer is fyr, þridde is hell, feorðe is se gitsienda man worulde welena. **c1395** *WBible* Proverbs xxx 15–6: Thre thingis ben unable to be fillid, and the fourthe, that seith nevere, It suffisith; helle, and the mouth of the wombe, and the erthe which is nevere fillid with water; but fier seith nevere, It suffisith.

T122 Four **Things** cannot be kept close
1509 Barclay *Ship* I 199[22–8]: I fynde foure thynges whiche by (no) meanes can Be kept close, in secrete, one (?or) longe in prevetee: The firste is the counsell of a wytles man, The seconde a Cyte, whiche byldyd is a hye Upon a mountayne, the thyrde, we often se That to hyde his dedes a lover hath no skyll, The fourth is strawe or fethers on a wyndy hyll. **1509** Watson *Ship* K1[r][13–6]: There is foure thynges that can never be hydde, that is the waye, the secrete, of a man without wytte; a cyte that is edefyed upon a mountayne, and the folysshe conduyte of a man that is esprysed with love. (*Watson omits the fourth.*) See **C275.**

T123 Four **Things** make a man a fool
a1449 Lydgate *Four Things* in *MP* II 708.1–7: Ther beothe foure thinges that maketh man a fool. Honnour first putethe him in oultrage And aldernexst solytarye and sool. The secounde is unweldy crooked aage, Wymmen also bring men in dotage, And mighty wyne in many dyvers wyse Distempren folk wheche beon holden wyse, cf. 8–14, 709.15–21. Apperson 308:7.

T124 Four **Things** to be dread of every wise man
1486 ?Berners *Boke of St. Albans* F5[r]: Ther be iiii thynges principall to be drad of every wise man. The first is the curse of owre holy fader the pope. The secunde is thindignacion of a prince—Quia indignacion regis vel principis mors est. The thridde is the favor or the will of a Juge. The iiii. is Sclaunder and the mutacion of a comynalte. See **I39.**

T125 Haste not to praise **Things**
1450 *Dicts* 120.24–6: Haste the not to preise thingis to thou knowe wele that thei be worthi to be preised. See **E81, 158, H363, P39, S715.**

T126 He gladly believes that **Thing** that he would hear
1509 Barclay *Ship* II 29[28]: That thynge that he wolde here: he gladly doth beleve. See **M121, T24.**

T127 He that takes good **Thing** sometime must take ill
a1500 *Life of Holy Job* in *Archiv* 126(1911) 368.98: For be (?he) that takyth gode thyng sumtyme must take ill. Taylor and Whiting 14: Bad. See **R220.**

T128 High **Things** sometimes overheld (*fall over*) (*varied*)
a1400 *Alexander C* 32.725–8: For it was wont . . . as wyse men tellis, Full highe thingis overheldis to held other-quile. Slike as ere now

broght a-bofe nowe the bothum askis, And slike at left ere on lawe ere lift to the sternes. **1509** Barclay *Ship* I 128[6]: But somtyme hye, than after pore and lowe. See **F534.**

T129 It is hard to change elded (*old*) **Thing** **a1400** *Cursor* III 1500 F 26654–5: Of eldid thing ful wele we wate Harde hit is to chaunge the state. See **C645, D313, H513, T182.**

T130 It is hard to deem a **Thing** that is unknown
c1450 *Proverbs* in *Rel. Ant.* I 205[7–8]: A harde thynge hit is, y-wys, To deme a thynge that unknowen is. Apperson 284.

T131 It is hard to keep the **Thing** that each man would were his
a1325 *Cursor* I 178.2967–8: Bot herd it es to kepe, iwise, The thing that ilk man wald war his. See **C79.**

T132 It is not sicker (*safe*) to leave one good **Thing** till one sees a better
a1396(1494) Hilton *Scale* O4r[8–9]: It is not syker to a man to leve one good thynge utterly, tyll he see and fele a better. See **F424, O27, T157.**

T133 Lack (*blame*) not a **Thing** which you cannot amend
a1422 Lydgate *Life* 526.1370–1: Thyne hede is dulle on watir and on londe To lak thyng thou canste not a mende. See **T179.**

T134 Lend never that **Thing** that you need most
a1500 Hill 131.19: Lende never that thyng, that thow nedest moste. Apperson 360.

T135 Let all **Thing** pass that was
a1400 *Proverbis of Wysdom* 245.81–2: That wyll nott be, lete hit passe: Lete all thyng passe, that wasse.

T136 Little **Thing** grows with peace and great thing wites (*vanishes*) away with discord
c1475 *Court of Sapience* 139.389–91: For lytyll thyng, as clerkys can recorde, Wyth pease groweth, and gret thyng wyth discorde Wyteth awey. See **P68.**

T137 A little **Thing** may gar (*cause*) great harms arise
c1420 Wyntoun V 399.3320–2: Lo! how a litil thynge may gere Gret harmys rysse (*var.* Gret harme fall) on mony wisse, As men has seyn, and seis oft syis. Jente 732. See **S778.**

T138 Many **Things** would fall of men's thoughts were there no counter thoughts
1525 Berners *Froissart* IV 293[38–40]: It is often tymes sayd, Moche thynges sholde fall of mennes thoughtes yf there were no countre thoughtes there agaynst.

T139 Merry it is to look on (one's) own **Thing** (*varied*)
c1350 *Good Wife E* 162.63: Mirie is oune thing to loke (*H* kepe), **c1450** *L* 199.75–6: It is evermore a myrie thing A man to be served of his owne thing, **a1500** *N* 212.75: Mery is owne thing to see, **c1500** *T* 205.72–3: Meryer ys owne thyng on to loke Than any other mannys on to tote. Cf. Tilley M131. See **B505.**

T140 More **Things** belong to keep(ing) household than four bare legs in a bed
1549 Heywood *D* 32.41–2: In house to kepe housholde, whan folks wyll needes wed, Mo thyngs belong, than foure bare legs in a bed. Apperson 404; *Oxford* 409; Tilley M1146. See **F475.**

T141 New **Thing** drives old thing from its degree
a1450 *Of the sacrament* in Kail 104.29: Newe thyng dryveth old thyng fro his degre. See **L547, N6.**

T142 New **Thing** is sweet (*varied*)
c1386 Chaucer *LGW* 1077: To som folk ofte newe thyng is sote. **c1400** Mandeville *Travels* 209.25–6: For men seyn all weys that newe thinges and newe tydynges ben plesant to here. **a1420** Lydgate *Troy* III 572.300–1: Here men may se how it is natural Men to delite in thing(e) that is newe. **1450** *Dicts* 168.20–1: In al thingis that the whiche is newiste is best except love, for the elder it is the better it is. **1513** Douglas *Aeneid* IV 192.27: Begyn of new; al thing is gud onassayt. Apperson 444; *Oxford* 451; Tilley A125. See **M208.**

T143 New **Thing** likes (*is liked*), old thing loathes (*is loathed*)
c1470 *Harley MS.3362* f.2b in *Retrospective* 309[16]: Newe thyng lykyth, old thyng lothyth.

T144 No earthly **Thing** but sometime will fail
c1450 Idley 102.1271–4: Remembre and also have in mynde That non erthly thyng shalt thou fynde But somtyme woll faile moche or lite: Sauffe God aloone nothyng is perfite. See **M235, W671.**

T145 No good **Thing** bides long
c1515 Barclay *Eclogues* 16.520: No good thing bideth long.

T146 No new **Thing** under the sun

c1395 *WBible* Ecclesiastes i 10: No thing undir the sunne is newe. *Oxford* 464; Taylor and Whiting 369; Tilley T147. See **G494.**

T147 No worldly **Thing** so good but that it may do ungood
c1250 *Owl* 114.1363–5: For nis a-worlde thing so god, That ne mai do sum ungod, Yif me hit wule turne amis.

T148 Of a hasty **Thing** men may not preach or make tarrying
c1390 Chaucer *CT* I[A] 3545–6: This asketh haste, and of an hastif thyng Men may nat preche or maken tariyng. See **D157.**

T149 Of little **Thing** long thing oft lasts
c1300 Lawman I 400 B 9386–7: And ofte of lutel thing, Lang thing ilasteth.

T150 Of **Thing** loath begun often comes good end
c1385 Chaucer *TC* ii 1234–5: God woot, of thyng ful often looth bygonne Comth ende good. See **M589.**

T151 Of two **Things** one must take such as he finds or such as he brings
c1390 Chaucer *CT* I[A] 4129–30: I have herd seyd, "man sal taa of twa thynges Slyk as he fyndes, or taa slyk as he brynges." **a1400** *Trinity MS.1450* in Furnivall *Babees Book* 35: Hoo that comyght to an howse, Loke he be noo thyng dongerowse To take seche as he fyndyght; And yf he wolle not do soo, Reson A-greeght theretoo To take suche as he bryngyght. **a1450** *Wall Verses at Launceston Priory* 342: Who so comyth to any hows Ne be he nought dangerous: Tak that he fyndith, And but a wol do so Resone wolde accorde ther to, To take that he bryngith. Apperson 617:1; *Oxford* 642; Skeat 234.

T152 Of two **Things** to choose the worse is a great sin (*varied*)
a1300 Thomas de Hales 74.189–92: Ne doth he, mayde, on uvele dede, That may cheose of two that on, And he wile with-ute neode Take thet wurse, the betere let gon? **a1400** Wyclif *Sermons* I 28[36–8]: It is a greet synne of two thingis to chese the worse, whan a man may as freely have the betere as the worse. **a1420** Lydgate *Troy* III 701.4672–5: For every man is holden of prudence The wers to leve and the better take, Wysdam to swe and foly to forsake, And remedie to seke for his sore. See **E193.**

T153 Old **Things** should be loved
1464 Hardyng 32[7]: Old thinges shuld be loved. Cf. Tilley F321, 755.

T154 One grants lightly the **Thing** that cost nought
a1400 *Ipomadon A* 207.7251–3: He graunte hym lyghtly, and so he mowghte, The thyng, that never coste hym noughte, A fayre thyng in forty yere.

T155 One loves tenderly the **Thing** that is dear bought (*varied*)
a1400 *Romaunt B* 2738–9: A man loveth more tendirly The thyng that he hath bought most dere. **c1515** Watson *Valentine* 295.11: One loveth gladly the thyng that is dere bought. **c1520** Walter *Spectacle* B2^{v}[26]: A thynge harde wonne shall better be loved. See **F58.**

T156 One must forbear the **Thing** he may not have
c1505 Watson *Valentine* 149.6–8: One muste forbere and passe lyghtly of the thinge that they maye not have. See **T175.**

T157 One ought not leave for a vain **Thing** that which is certain
1484 Caxton *Aesop* 10[16–8]: For the love of a vayn thynge men ought not to leve that whiche is certeyn. See **F424, O27, T132.**

T158 Repent not of **Things** past
a1425 *Governance of Lordschipes* 63.3–4: Repent the noght of thinges passyd, for that ys a propirte to feble women. See **R84, T192.**

T159 Short **Thing** is more pleasing to be heard
c1420 Wyntoun V 149.25–6: Sen schort thynge is mare pleyssande, And to be herde is mare likande. See **P408.**

T160 Sorrow not for **Thing** lost that may not be found (*varied*)
1438 *Barlam and Josaphat* (*Northern*) 232.519–20: Man, murn thou noght on evyn ne morn For thing thou wate that thou haves lorn, (*Vernon*) 221.441–2: Ne for thing that is ilore Ne mai be founde serwe nought therfore. **c1450** *Alphabet* I 132.17–8: Make not sorow for that thyng that is verely loste and can never be requoverd. **1484** Caxton *Aesop* 270[21–2]: Take no sorowe of the thynge lost whiche may not be recovererd. **a1500** *Disciplina Clericalis* 48[2]: Ne sorowe thow nat of thynges lost. **1504** Hawes *Example* Ccl^{r}[1–2]: For a thynge lost without recover, Loke that thou never be to pensyfe. **a1533** Berners *Huon* 206.29: That thynge that can not be recoveryd must be left. Tilley T127. See **M729, R81, W381.**

T161 Temporal **Thing** lasts not ay (*varied*)
a1400 *Scottish Legends* I 123.504: For temporale thing lestis nocht ay. **c1450** *Verses on a Chained*

Horae in Robbins 87.9–10: But for-as-moche that noo thyng may endure That urthely ys, alwey, y trowe, certeyn. **a1533** Berners *Huon* 599.1: Every mortall thynge cannot alwayes endure. Whiting *Drama* 115, 270, *Scots* II 139. Cf. Tilley T177. See **C114, N154, T101, W671.**

T162 That **Thing** is desired more where there is contradiction
1480 Caxton *Ovyde* 20[23]: For comunly that thynge is desired more Where as is contradicion: than that thyng that is habandonned. See **C526, L487, T120, W549.**

T163 **Thing** done in the dark night is after known in day's light
a1393 Gower *CA* III 72.4597–600: Bot so prive mai be nothing, That it ne comth to knowleching; Thing don upon the derke nyht Is after knowe on daies liht. Apperson 156:40; Jente 541; *Oxford* 154; Tilley N179.

T164 A **Thing** foreseen is light to execute
a1475 Ashby *Dicts* 59.384: A thing foreseien is light texecute.

T165 **Thing** hid or stolen may not be long forholen (*concealed*)
c1330 *Seven Sages A* 8–9.235–8: Thing ihid ne thing istole, Ne mai nowt longe be for hole. Ne thing mai forhole be But Godes owen privete. See **M806.**

T166 **Thing** never begun has never end
c1500 *Melusine* 304.20–2: Thing never bygonne hath never ende. In every thing most be begynnyng, tofore the ende commeth. See **E164.**

T167 A **Thing** predestinate is hard to be broken
a1533 Berners *Arthur* 417[29]: A thynge predestynate is harde to be broken. Tilley F83. See **D169, S190, T171.**

T168 **Thing** that a man may not achieve at eve must abide till morrow
a1393 Gower *CA* II 270–1.1653–5: Thing that a man mai noght achieve, That mai noght wel be don at Eve, It mot abide til the morwe.

T169 **Thing** that is inome (*taken*) with strength may not be right
c1300 Robert of Gloucester I 283.4041: And thing that is mid strengthe inome, hou mighte it be mid righte? See **M534, T180.**

T170 A **Thing** that is long desired comes at the last
1483 *Quatuor Sermones* 53[28–9]: A thynge that is long desyred at the last it comyth. Apperson 379; *Oxford* 381.

T171 The **Thing** that is shaped (*destined*) for a man he may never flee (*varied*)
c1300 *South English Legendary* I 34.52: The thing that is a man yssape he ne may nevere vle(o). **c1385** Chaucer *CT* I[A]1466: Whan a thyng is shapen, it shal be. Apperson 560; *Oxford* 703. See **S190, T167.**

T172 **Thing** that may betide is for to doubt (*fear*)
c1425 *Good Wife H* 169.160: Thyng that may betyde is for to dowte. Apperson 129: Cured (2).

T173 **Thing** that may not be eschewed must be sued (*followed*) (*varied*)
c1408 Lydgate *Reson* 125.4757–8: For thyng that may nat be eschiwed Bot of force mot be sywed, **a1420** *Troy* I 236.3218–20: For thing ordeyned nedes moste be; The ordre of thinges with fate is so englued, For that schal falle may nat be eschewed, 238.3278–9: For that schal falle, as somme clerkis seyn, Ne may nat wel of men eschewed be. **1525** Berners *Froissart* VI 308[1–2]: That thynge that shall fall can nat be eschewed, 340[32–3]. *Oxford* 124: Cured. See **S190, T171.**

T174 The **Thing** that pleases is half sold
c1505 Watson *Valentine* 164.36–7: For it is said comonly that the thing that pleased one is halfe solde. See **M121.**

T175 **Thing** that will not be, let it be still (*varied*)
c1395 Chaucer *CT* IV[E] 1212g: But thyng that wol nat be, lat it be stille. **a1450** *Partonope* 354.8697–700: My counseylle is that never ye Thinke that thing that may not be, But lette it passe, it is the beste, And sette your herte in eace and reste. See **T156.**

T176 **Thing** to come is oft in adventure (*doubt*)
c1385 Chaucer *TC* i 784: Syn thyng to come is oft in aventure.

T177 **Thing** was never lost but it was had before
a1500 *Lover and the Advocate of Venus* in Robbins 170.35: Thyng was never lost but it wer had beforn. MED haven v. 1a(a) (g).

T178 The **Thing** which a fool thinks remains undone
c1505 Watson *Valentine* 16.12–3: It happeneth oftentymes that the thinge the whiche a foole thynketh remayneth undone. See **F448.**

T179 A **Thing** which cannot be amended must be borne (*varied*)
c1450 *Foly of Fulys* 57.199–200: Na tynis nocht

thar wyt to See The thing that may nocht mendyt bee. **c1489** Caxton *Aymon* I 202.17–8: A thyng that can not be amended, must be suffred and borne as well as men may, II 427.23–6: For that thyng that may not be amended men oughte to lete it passe in the best wyse; For it is shamfull to reherse that that is passed, 534.26–7. **a1500** *Partenay* 213.6222–3: Wisdom behovith to lete go and passe Which that men mow noght amend in no cas. **a1533** Berners *Arthur* 215[13–4]: A thynge the whiche can not be remedyed, must nedes be suffered in the best wyse that a man may. See **R81, T133, W381.**

T180 **Thing** which is begun with wrong may never stand well at end (*varied*)
a1393 Gower *CA* II 209–10.2954–7: Bot thing which is with wrong begonne Mai nevere stonde wel at ende; Wher Pride schal the bowe bende, He schet fulofte out of the weie. **c1505** Watson *Valentine* 270.30: For a thynge evyll begon can not have a good ende. **1525** Berners *Froissart* V 8[16–7]: Every thyng that turneth to yvell must have a begynning of yvell. See **B199, T169.**

T181 **Thing** which men ween to stand oft falls
a1393 Gower *CA* III 298.2390–1: For men sen ofte time falle Thing which men wende siker stonde. See **S669, 915.**

T182 **Things** used will not be refused (*varied*)
c1500 Greene *Carols* 419 A 23: For thyngis used Will not be refused. **1509** Fisher *Treatyse* 118.4–5: A thynge customably used is harde to be lefte. See **C646, T129, U8.**

T183 Three **Things** are avoid of mercy
1515 Barclay *St. George* 33.619–22: Thre maner thynges that be Avoyde of mercy: and very harde to stent, A comonte is one: whan the(y) in one assent, And fyre and water. *Oxford* 203; Tilley F254.

T184 Three **Things** are contrarious to good counsel
c1390 Chaucer *CT* VII 1121–2 [B2311–2]: And thanne shul ye dryve fro youre herte thre thynges that been contrariouse to good conseil; that is to seyn, ire, coveitise, and hastifnesse, 1246–7[B2436–7]. Apperson 10; *Oxford* 10.

T185 Three **Things** are hard to know
c1395 *WBible* Proverbs xxx 18–9: Thre thingis ben hard to me, and outirli Y knowe not the fourthe thing; the weye of an egle in hevene, the weie of a serpent on a stoon, the weie of a schip in the myddil of the see, and the weie of a man in yong wexynge age. **1486** ?Berners *Boke of St. Albans* F5v: Ther be iiii. thynges full harde for to knaw, Whyche way that thay will drawe: The first is the wayes of a yong man. The secunde the cours of a vessayll in the see. The thridde of an Edder or a serpent sprent. The iiii. of a fowle sittyng on any thyng. **a1500** Alcock *Sermo pro episcopo* A3r[2.6–18]: Thre thynges, sayth Salomon, ben harde to me to knowe, and the fourth utterly I knowe not. The flyght of the Egle in the ayer. The waye of the serpent on the erthe. The sayllynge of a shyppe in the see. But the fourth and moost hardest is to understande the waye of a man in his growynge age. **a1500** *Lansdowne MS. 762* in *Rel. Ant.* I 233[34–7]: There been thre thinges full harde to be knowen which waye they woll drawe. The first is of a birde sitting upon a bough. The second is of a vessell in the see. And the thirde is the waye of a yonge man. **1509** Barclay *Ship* II 7–8: I fynde in the worlde that there be thynges thre Right harde to knowe, the fourth that no man may Knowe nor perceyve, first, whan a byrde doth fle Alonge in the ayre; no man can spye hir way, The way of a Shyp in the se, thoughe it be day, Harde is to se whiche way the shyp hath gone; The thirde harde thynge as I have oft heard say Is the way of a serpent over a stone; But the fourth way that of all hardest is Of yonge man is, in youthes lustynes. A vycyous womans way is lyke to this. Apperson 630; *Oxford* 655; Tilley S349.

T186 Three **Things** cannot be called again
1509 Barclay *Ship* I 110[24–30]: In this world thou shalt fynde thynges thre Whiche ones past, can nat be callyd agayne. The firste is (tyme lost) by mannes symplycyte, The seconde (youth) revoked can nat be, The thyrde (a worde spoken) it gooth out in the wynde, And yet is the fourth, that is (virginyte), My forgetfull mynde, had lefte it nere behynde. See **M20, T307, W605, 639.**

T187 Three **Things** cause a man to flee from his own house (*varied*)
c1378 *Piers* B xvii 315–22: Thre thinges there ben that doth a man by strengthe Forto fleen his owne hous, as holywryt sheweth. That one is a wikked wyf that wil nought be chasted; Her fiere fleeth fro hyr for fere of her tonge. And if his hous be unhiled and reyne on his bedde, He seketh and seketh til he slepe drye. And whan smoke and smolder smyt in his syghte, It doth hym worse than his wyf or wete to slepe. **c1390** Chaucer *CT* VII 1086[B2276]: Of

which wommen men seyn that thre thynges dryven a man out of his hous,—that is to seyn, smoke, droppyng of reyn, and wikked wyves, X[I] 631: And therfore seith Salomon, "An hous that is uncovered and droppynge, and a chidynge wyf, been lyke," **c1395** III[D] 278–80: Thow seyst that droppyng houses, and eek smoke, And chidyng wyves maken men to flee Out of hir owene hous. **c1395** *WBible* Proverbs x 26: Smoke *noieth* the ighen, xix 13: And roofes droppynge contynueli is a womman ful of chiding, xxvii 15: Roovys droppynge in the dai of coold, and a womman ful of chidyng ben comparisond. **a1396**(1494) Hilton *Scale* E6ᵛ[11–3]: For whoo soo comyth untill his hous and fyndeth noo thyng therin but stynk and smoke and a chidyng wyf, he wolde soone renne out of it. **c1425** *St. Mary Oignies* 170.45–6: For, as Salamon seith: "there are three thinges that dryve a man fro home: smeke, droppynge rofe, and a wicked wyfe." **a1449** ?Lydgate *Evil Marriage* in *MP* II 459.89–91: But Salamon seith, ther be thynges thre, Shrewed wyfes, rayne, and smokes blake, Makith husbondes there howses to fforsake. **1492** *Salomon and Marcolphus* 9[24–5]: An angry housewyf, the smoke, the ratte and a broken plater, art often tymes unprofytable in an howse. **a1500** Greene *Carols* 409.4: In my hows ys swyche a smeke. Apperson 629–30; *Oxford* 655; Skeat 249; A. Taylor in *Hessische Blätter für Volkskunde* 24(1925) 130–46, *Proverb* 40, 50, 58, 160–4; Tilley H781, S574.

T188 Three **Things** trouble all this earth
c1395 Chaucer *CT* III[D] 362–7: Thou seydest eek that ther been thynges thre, The whiche thynges troublen al this erthe, And that no wight may endure the ferthe. O leeve sire shrewe, Jhesu shorte thy lyf! Yet prechestow and seyst an hateful wyf Yrekened is for oon of thise meschances. **c1395** *WBible* Proverbs xxx 21–3: The erthe is moved bi thre thingis, and the fourthe thing, which it may not susteyne; bi a servaunt, whanne he regneth; bi a fool, whanne he is fillid with mete; bi an hateful womman, whanne she is takun in matrymonye; and bi an handmaide, whanne sche is eir of hir ladi. **1509** Barclay *Ship* II 8[9–21]: Thre other thynges on erth I fynde certayne Whiche troubleth the grounde and also the see, The fourth nouther see nor londe may well sustayne. The firste is a churle that hath a bonde man be And so by fortune come unto hye degre. The seconde is a fole whan he is dronke and full. The thirde a wrathfull woman, full of cruelte: He that hir weddyth, hath a crowe to pull. Yet is the fourth wors and more elevate, That is a hande mayde lowe of hir lynage, Promotyd from a begger and so come to estate, Succedynge hir lady as heyr in herytage, Of suche procedeth moche malyce and outrage. **1509** Watson *Ship* P1ʳ[7–14]. See **H92.**

T189 To say (think) one **Thing** and think (say) the contrary (*varied*)
a1300 Lawman II 136 *B* 13415–8: And al the king lifde That Vortiger saide, Ac wolawo that nuste the king Of his thohte nothing. **c1340** Rolle *Psalter* 43 (10.2): When a fals man thynkis an and says a nother, to desaif him that he spekis with, 51 (13.3): That is he spekis noght ane and thynkis a nother. **a1420** Lydgate *Troy* II 518.4280: Thei can think oon, and a-nother seie. **c1450** Idley 151.2666–7: Thynke not oon thyng and sey the contrarie; Be never double of mowthe and herte. **c1450** Trevet 237.34–5 (f.48b, col.1): But that false woman thought other than she sayde. **1483** Caxton *Cato* D5ʳ[12–3]: For none ought to say one thynge and thynke the contrarye. See **P153, W631.**

T190 To seek for a **Thing** he would not find
1555 Heywood *E* 178.182: I seeke for a thyng wyfe, that I would not fynde. Tilley T135.

T191 To seek to find **Things** ere they be lost (*varied*)
a1449 Lydgate *Cok* in *MP* II 818.175: Tyl it be loost stoole thyng is nat sought. **1533** More *Confutacion* 595 FG: The comon people say among, that nothing can bee founden tyll it bee lost, saving that of a theefe they say in sport, he can finde a thinge ere it be lost, and so they prayse him in his cunning, that he can do such a maistry as no true man can. **1546** Heywood *D* 44.105–6: If ye seeke to fynde thynges, er they be lost, Ye shall fynde one daie you come to your cost. Tilley T182.

T192 To speak of **Thing** that is past is no remedy
a1500 *English Conquest* 141.8-9: Forto speke of thynge that is Paste, is no remedy. See **R81, T158, W381.**

T193 To speak (say) one **Thing** and do another
c1400 *Consilia Isidori* 371[33–4]: Speke not oo thinge and doo a nothere; sey not oo thinge and mene anothere. **1422** Yonge *Governaunce* 214.6–7: And Such ther bene had, that oone thynge sayne, and anothyr thynkes done. **a1425** *Governance of Lordschipes* 108.28–9: Many er swyche that oon sayen, and other-wayes doon. **1484** Caxton *Aesop* 119[12–3]: For one thynge

they saye and done another. **1506** *Kalender* 165.4–5: He shall say one and do another. Whiting *Scots* II 121. See **W642.**

T194 To take **Things** as they come
1509 Barclay *Ship* II 319[13–4]: But that man folowes hye wysdome Whiche takys thynges lyke as they come. **a1533** Berners *Castell* M4v[17–8]: But take every thynge as it commyth. **1546** Heywood *D* 25.40: To take all thinges as it comth, and be content. *Oxford* 642; Tilley T196.

T195 Violent **Thing** may not be eterne (*varied*)
a1420 Lydgate *Troy* I 261.4088: Thing violent may nat be eterne, **a1439** *Fall* I 302.3643. **c1443** Pecock *Reule* 124[25–6]: No thing that is violent and agens kynde is ever lastyng, **c1454** *Folower* 177.18–21: Also the philesofir seith: "No thing which is violent, that is to seie, out of right ordre and right joynt, schal dure for ever, but al such thing takith an eend." *Oxford* 464; Tilley N321; Whiting *Drama* 281. See **N166.**

T196 What **Thing** rests not cannot long endure
a1500 *MS. Marginalia* in Hoccleve I 187 n.[1]: Quod caret alterna requie, durabile non est. What thing restethe not now and then amonge, But still traveyleth, cannot endure longe. Walther IV 441.25741.

T197 When a **Thing** is done for doubt (*fear*) it comes oft the worse about
a1393 Gower *CA* III 320.3157–8: For whan a thing is do for doute, Fulofte it comth the worse aboute. See **C485, O13.**

T198 When a **Thing** is done it may be no other
a1420 Lydgate *Troy* III 821.1683: Whan thing is doon, it may be noon other. Apperson 625. See **D287, H134, P45, T199.**

T199 When a **Thing** is done there is no boot (*remedy*) (*varied*)
a1393 Gower *CA* III 395.339–40: Whan thing is do, ther is no bote, So suffren thei that suffre mote. **1509** *Fyftene Joyes* K2v[33]: But whan a thynge is done, what remedye? See **T198.**

T200 When a **Thing** is well begun it makes a good end
c1450 *How the Wyse Man* 35.7–8: And whanne a thing is weel bigunne, It makith a good eende at the laste. See **B204.**

T201 With a **Thing** corrupt a sound thing is destroyed
1509 Barclay *Ship* II 37[16–7]: For it is dayly provyd by experyence That with a thynge corrupt, a sounde thynge is distroyed. See **A167, C406.**

T202 With two **Things** one may not well mell: a young quean and an old wife
1500 *O man more* 394.29–30: Wythe (ii) thynges thow mayst nott well mell: That is to saye, a yonge quene and a olde wyffe.

T203 Without small **Things** greater may not stand
1513 More *Richard* 48 (*for* 45) C[11–2]: Sommetime withoute smal thinges greatter cannot stande. See **M159, 483, S44, T113.**

T204 **Think** ere you make fast
c1450 Greene *Carols* 338.3: Thenke or ye feste. See **K101, P429.**

T205 **Think** what you will but speak with the least
a1456 *Passe forth* clxxiii [3]: Thenke what thou wilt, but speke ay with the leeste. See **H264, T207.**

T206 To **Think** as one says
c1350 *Gamelyn* 654.367–8: And if it so be, And thou thenke as thou seyst, god yelde it thee!

T207 Whatever you **Think** say but lite (*little*)
a1400 *Proverbis of Wysdom* 246.104: What ever thu thynk, say but lyte. Cf. Whiting *Drama* 201. See **F436, T205.**

T208 One **Thirl** (*hole*) sinks the ship
a1325 *Cursor* III 1505.26846–7: A thirl (*F* hole) sinkes the schipp to grund, And oft man deies of a wond.

T209 As brethel (*fragile*) as **Thistle**
c1000 *Anglo-Saxon Charms* 210.19: Swa breþel seo, swa þystel.

T210 As sharp as a **Thistle**
a1460 *Towneley Plays* 119.101: As sharp as a thystyll.

T211 Better is **Tho** (*then, i.e.*, at some time) than no (*never*)
a1200 *Ancrene* 173.10: Betere is o thene no, **a1250** (*Nero*) 153.22: Betere is tho thene no, **a1300** (*Trinity*) 99.19–20: Miuuz vaut confession tardive ke nule, **a1300** (*Vitellius*) 242.37–243.2: Mes nepurquant mielz vaut ascune foiz qe jammes, **a1350** (*Merton*) 131.3–4: Nichilominus melius est tunc quam numquam. See **B274, L89.**

T212 Better **Thole** (*suffer*) sorely a while than mourn evermore
c1325 *Alysoun* 139.33–4: Betere is tholien whyle sore Then mournen evermore. See **T258.**

T213 He that **Tholes** (suffers) overcomes (*varied*) **c1450** *Consail and Teiching* 67.41: And quhay weill tholis al ourcummys. **1474** Caxton *Chesse* 144[20]: For he that suffreth overcometh. **1513** Douglas *Aeneid* II 230.81: All chance of forton tholand ourcummyn is. See **P61, S865.**

T214 Not worth a **Thong** **c1400** *Laud Troy* I 44.1469: He harmed him nought worth a thong.

T215 Not worthy to loose the **Thongs** of his shoes (*varied*) **c1000** *WSG* Matthew iii 11: ðæs gescy neom ic wyrðe to berenne, Mark i 7: Ne eom ic wyrðe þæt ic his sceona þwanga bugende uncnytte, Luke iii 16: Ic ne eom wyrþe þæt ic hys sceoþwang uncnytte, John i 27: unbinde. **a1200** *Trinity College Homilies* 137[32–3]: Ac ich nam noht ne forthen wurthe that ich uncnutte his sho thuong. **c1200** Orm II 6.10386–7: Thatt he ne wass nohht god inoh Cristess shothwang tunnbindenn, 7.10418–9, 87.12702–3. **c1300** *Northern Homily Cycle* (*Edin. Coll. Phys.*) 10[22–3]: That I me self es noht worthi To les the thuanges of his schon, 49[2–4]: The binding of his scho. **a1325** *Cursor* II 736 CGT 12822–3: O quam i am noght worthe to Lese the thuanges of his sco. **c1395** Chaucer *CT* V[F] 555; Ne were worthy unbokelen his galoche. **c1395** *WBible* Matthew iii 11: Whos schoon Y am not worthi to bere, Mark i 7: Y am not worthi to knele doun, and unlace his schoone, Luke iii 16: Of whom Y am not worthi to unbynde the lace of his schoon, John i 27: Y am not worthi to louse the thwong of his schoo. **a1400** *Scottish Legends* II 257–8. 1207–8: To quham I ame nocht worthi loute, Na of his schone the laise tak oute. **a1400** *Apology* 34[11–2]: Nether is no man worthi to opun the lasing of his scho. **a1400** Wyclif *Sermons* I 75[36–7]: And herfore seith Joon, that he is not worth to louse the thuong of Cristis shoo, II 280[7–8]. **c1425** *Evangelie* 587.833–4, 588.851–2. **c1425** Paues 159 Acts xiii 25: Of whom I am noghte worthi to lowse tho chausers (*var.* schoon) of hise fete. **c1450** La Tour-Landry 190.6–8: In trouthe he was not worthy to pulle of theyr shone and hosen fro theyr legges. **a1460** *Towneley Plays* 196. 49–50. **a1475** *Ludus Coventriae* 189.32: I am not worthy to on-bokyll his schon, 229.4. **1480** Caxton *Ovyde* 120[31–2]: A lord that a lytil afore had not be worthy to have taken of her hosyn and shoen, **1487** *Book of Good Manners* A7r[20–1]: And sayd hym self to be unworthy to touche the latchet of the shoo of Jhesu Cryst. Apperson 458–9; *Oxford* 734; Tilley L84.

T216 To carve a **Thong** of one's own skin **1419** *Remembraunce* in Kail 70.21–2: It is worthy he smerte and be wo, That of his owen skyn wole kerve a thong. See **S652.**

T217 To take broad **Thongs** of unbought (other men's) leather (*varied*) **c1250** *Hendyng O* 196.28: Of ounbiserewe (*C* 187.28: unbeswinke, *H* 296.216: un boht) huide me taketh (*H* kerveth) brod thwong. **c1400** *Vices and Virtues* 195.31–196.1: And maken of othere mennes lether brode thongges. **a1449** Lydgate *Fabules* in *MP* II 588.649–51: Lierne this proverbe, founde of old doctryne, "Suche as have no conscience of no maner wronges, Of other mennys ledir can kut ful large thonges." **1465** Paston IV 179[26]: For men cut large thongs here of other mens lether. **c1470** *Harley MS.3362* f.4b in *Retrospective* 309[30]: Of other mennys lethyr men makyt large laynerys. **1484** Caxton *Aesop* 220[25–6]: It is not honeste to make large thonges of other mennes leder. **c1490** *Sloane MS. 747* f.66a: Of anothyr mannes lyther man cuttyth longe thongs. **a1500** *Harley MS.2321* in *Rel. Ant.* I 207[2]: A large thonge of another mans hide. **a1500** Hill 132.44: Of an-other mannes ledder we cut a longe thonge. **1546** Heywood *D* 71.36: While they cut large thongs of other mens lether. Apperson 131; Jente 776; Kneuer 40; *Oxford* 126; Schleich 264; Singer III 134; Tilley T229. See **L62, R109.**

T218 As hard and tough as the **Thorn** **c1450** Capgrave *Katharine* 143.1041: Hir herte is hard and tough as is the thorn.

T219 As pricking as **Thorns** **1509** Barclay *Ship* II 6[19]: It is . . . pryckynge as thornes.

T220 As rough and rugged as **Thorns** **a1500** *Guy*[4] 191.6307: His head was rough and rugged as thornes.

T221 As sharp as (any, the) **Thorn** **c1350** *Proprium Sanctorum* 312.190: In to this world scharp as thorn. **a1400** *Awntyrs* 147.389: Als so scharpe als any thorne. **a1425** *St. Robert* 55.436. **a1430** Lydgate *Pilgrimage* 420.15595–6: any maner thorn. **c1440** Charles of Orleans 213.6364. **c1450** *Pilgrimage LM* 133[33]. **a1460** *Towneley Plays* 365.361. **a1475** *Vision of Philibert* 33[17]: any. **a1500** *Inter Diabolus et Virgo* 444.11: the, 445.31: the. **a1500** *Timor Mortis* in *MLR* 28(1933) 235[21]: the. **c1500** *So put yn fere* in Stevens *Music* 345.2[2]: Sharper than thorn, dyamond or steyll. Apperson 561; Tilley T230; Whiting *Ballad* 32.

T222 It is soon sharp that will be a **Thorn** (*varied*)
c1450 *Douce MS.*52 56.137: Hit is sone sharpe, that schal be a thorne. **c1450** *Epistle of Othea* 109.6–7: Hytt was an old soth saw or than thu were borne: He gynneth soone to prykke that wyll be a thorne. **a1500** *Coventry Plays* 56.748: Yt ys eyrly scharp thatt wol be thorne. **a1500** Hill 128.3: Sone hit sharpith, that thorn will be. **1523** Skelton *Garlande* I 418.1437: It is sone aspyed where the thorne prikkith. **1546** Heywood *D* 94.128: It pricketh betymes that will be a good thorne, **1555** *E* 164.109: that shalbe a sharpe thorne, **1556** *Spider* 43[19]: Thornes pricke yonge that shalbe sharpe, folke have tolde. Apperson 511; *Oxford* 164; Tilley T232; Whiting *Drama* 48, 49. See **E62.**

T223 **Thorns** do not bear figs (*varied*)
a1387 *Piers* C iii 28–9: For shal nevere brere bere beries as a vyne, Ne on croked kene thorne kynde fygys wexe. **a1430** Lydgate *Pilgrimage* 261.9460–1: Ffor yt were ageyn nature, A thorn to bern a Fygge soote. **c1450** *Pilgrimage LM* 90[20–1]: Riht as thornes mown not bere ne caste figes. See **G421, N94.**

T224 To catch a **Thorn**
c1385 Chaucer *TC* ii 1272–4: To God hope I, she hath now kaught a thorn, She shal nat pulle it out this nexte wyke. God sende mo swich thornes on to pike! **a1500** *Mocking Letter* in Robbins 220.32: Renne for your love tyl she had caught a thorn.

T225 To draw a **Thorn** out of one's heel and put it in another's
1402 *Daw Topias* 106[28–9]: Thou drawist a thorn out of thi hele, And puttist it in oure. Apperson 627; *Oxford* 523; Tilley T231.

T226 To put a **Thorn** in one's foot
c1400 *Testament of St. Francis* in Wyclif *EW* 50[16]: Thus thei putten a veyn thorn in his feet.

T227 To sit upon **Thorns**
1528 More *Heresyes* 234 D[11–3]: I long . . . and even syt on thornes, tyll I see that constitucion, E[4–5]: I cannot suffer to see you sytte so long on thornes, **1534** *Comforte* 1221 F[12–3]: He sat him thought on thornes, till he myghte here. **1546** Heywood *D* 39.126: While she was in this house she sat upon thornes. Tilley T239; Whiting *Drama* 364:849, 365:872.

T228 Not worth a **Thost** (*turd*)
a1450 *Castle* 149.2413: Al oure fare is not worth a thost. See **T526.**

T229 To set at a **Thost**
a1450 *Castle* 109.1067: And every man sette at a thost.

T230 As changeable as **Thought**
a1470 Parker *Dives* M6ʳ[2.37–8]: For ther is no thynge so chaungeable as thought.

T231 As hasty as a **Thought**
a1420 Lydgate *Troy* I 64.1764: By sodeyn chawnge, hasty as a thought.

T232 As quick as **Thought**
a1475 *Ludus Coventriae* 279.214: I am as whyt as thought. Apperson 518–9; NED Quick, a; Taylor and Whiting 370. See **M568.**

T233 As swift as (any, a) **Thought**
c1200 *Ancrene* 50–1.22–3: Alle theo in heovene schule beon ase swifte as is nu monnes thoht. **c1380** Chaucer *HF* 1924: And ever mo, as swyft as thought, **c1386** *LGW* 1195: And upon coursers, swift as any thought. **a1400** *Pricke* 214.7949–50: any. **a1400** *Romaunt B* 5024: any. **c1408** Lydgate *Reson* 183.6983–4: Ther ys in this worlde ryght noght Half so swyfte as ys a thoght, **a1430** *Pilgrimage* 170.6482: any, 337.12379: any. **a1475** *Tree* 7.10–1: a. **1501** Douglas *Palice* 41.27. Apperson 518–9; Taylor and Whiting 370; Tilley T240; Whiting *Scots* II 139.

T234 At a **Thought**
a1437 *Kingis Quair* 67.77[4–5]: Quhare sodaynly, as quho sais at a thoght, It opnyt. NED Thought[1] 3.

T235 Black **Thoughts** are hid under white words
a1437 *Kingis Quair* 83.136[4]: Thair thoughtis blak hid under wordis quhite. See **W627.**

T236 Of good **Thoughts** come good deeds
c1425 *Myrour of lewed men* 407.1–2: Who-so wele thinkes, wele may say, Ffor of gode thoghtes comes gode dedes ay.

T237 Short **Thoughts** and hasty speech make man most to err
1450 *Dicts* 276.7–9: Oon of the thingis that makithe man moost for to erre in his jugementis is short thought and hasti speche.

T238 **Thought** is free (has liberty)
a1393 Gower *CA* III 69.4485: I have herd seid that thoght is fre. **c1421** Lydgate *Thebes* 112.2700: Men seyn ful ofte how that thouht is fre, **a1449** *Cok* in *MP* II 818.173. **a1450** *Partonope* 440.10883–5: Therfore this proverbe is seide full truly: Thought to a man is ever ffre; What ever he luste thinke may he. **c1450** *Fortune in Life* in Smith *Common-place Book*

18.84: thus seyth the boke. **a1475** *As I stod* in Halliwell *Early English Miscellanies* 64[5]. **a1500** *Thoythis fre* in *MLN* 69(1954) 155.1: Thoythis fre, that lykis me. **a1508** Skelton *Phyllyp* I 88.1200–1: For thought hath lyberte, Thought is franke and fre. **1546** Heywood *D* 64.64: Thought is fre. Apperson 627; *Oxford* 652; Taylor and Whiting 370; Tilley T244; Whiting *Drama* 112, *Scots* II 139.

T239 To change like **Thought**
c1390 *Deo Gracias II* in Brown *Lyrics XIV* 138.5–6: And though hit greve, hit wol over go, As thought chaungeth, for such is graas.

T240 Where one's **Thought** is there is he
a1500 *Imitatione* (*1*) 127.4–5: Where my thoughte is, there am I, and where as my thought is, there I love. **1502** *Imitatione* (*2*) 242.2: There my thought and desyre is where that thyng is that I love. See **H302, T451.**

T241 Who skails (*scatters*) his **Thought,** in all things it is the less
c1420 Wyntoun V 329.2443–4: Qwha skalis his thoucht in syndrynes, In althynge it is the les. Cf. *Oxford* 683: Union; Tilley U11. See **H90, V47.**

T242 To beat as **Thrashers** do on wheat
c1400 *Laud Troy* I 275.9335–6: Echon on other ffaste doth bete, Ryght as threscheres doth on whete.

T243 As straight as a (any) **Thread**
c1500 *Order of Shoting* in *Retrospective Review* 1(1853) 208[10]: Stregh(t) as a threde. **1533** Heywood *Pardoner* A4[r][25]: Even to heven gatys, as strayght as any threde.

T244 To hang by a **Thread**
a1396(1494) Hilton *Scale* L3[r][22–5]: There is no thyng that holdeth hem fro the pytte of helle . . . but a bare syngyll threde of this bodily lyfe wherby they hange. **c1500** Fabyan 633–4: The . . . loveday hangyng by a smalle threde. Taylor and Whiting 370; Tilley T250. See **H99, S979.**

T245 To spin a (large, fair) **Thread**
a1300 *Alisaunder* 393.7244–5: He hath ysponnen on threde, That is ycome of yvel rede. **c1412** Hoccleve *Regement* 64.1762–3: This likerous dampnable errour, In this londe hath so large a threde I-sponne. **1546** Heywood *D* 26.22: And this threede fyner to spyn, 73.99: In beyng your owne foe, you spin a fayre threede, **1555** *E* 187.228, **1556** *Spider* 342[19]: What a threede this were spoon. Apperson 596; *Oxford* 614; Tilley T252; Whiting *Drama* 365:868.

T246 **Threat** is worth nought but there be deed
a1200 Lawman III 56.26555–6: Nis noht wurth thratte, Buten ther beo dede aet (?aec). Cf. Jente 103; Tilley T253.

T247 **Three** are wily: a fox, a friar, and a woman, *etc.*
a1500 in Thomas Wright *Songs and Carols* (PS 23, 1847) 4–5: Herfor, and therfor, and therfor I came, And for to preysse this praty woman. Ther wer iii wylly, 3 wyly ther wer: A fox, a fryyr, and a woman. Ther wer 3 angry, 3 angry ther wer: A wasp, a wesyll, and a woman. Ther wer 3 cheteryng, iii. cheteryng ther wer: A peye, a jaye, and a woman. Ther wer 3 wold be betyn, 3 wold be betyn ther wer: A myll, a stoke fysche, and a woman. **a1500** in Smith *Common-place Book* 12–3: Take iii claterars: a pie, a jai, a woman. Take iii lowrars: a ape, a owle, a woman. Take iii schrewys: a waspe, a wesill, a woman. Take iii angry: a frier, a fox, a woman. There be iiii thyngs take gret betyng: a stockfisch, a milston, a fedirbed, a wooman.

T248 **Three** may keep counsel if twain be away
a1500 *Ten Commandments of Love* in Robbins 166.49: For .3. may kepe counsell if twayn be away. **1546** Heywood *D* 70.6: Three maie kepe a counsayle, if two be away, **1555** *E* 193.273: twayne. Apperson 628; *Oxford* 330; Tilley T257. Cf. Whiting *Scots* II 140. See **T544.**

T249 **Three** to one is no vassalage (*brave deed*)
a1338 Mannyng *Chronicle A* I 431.12331–2: Me thynketh hit were no vasselage, Thre til on. Cf. Apperson 656–7; *Oxford* 681; Tilley T644.

T250 His **Thrift** waxes thin that spends more than he wins
c1350 *Good Wife E* 166.111–2: His thrift wexet thinne That spendet over that he winneth. Apperson 630; Tilley T260. See **M670, 672, S627.**

T251 One's **Thrift** is his friends' mirth
c1425 *Good Wife H* 172.202: Thi thrifte is thi frendis myrth. Apperson 630.

T252 **Thrift** and he are at a fray
1546 Heywood *D* 52.355: Howe be it whan thrift and you fell fyrst at a fray. Apperson 630; *Oxford* 655; Tilley T261.

T253 **Thrift** is sunk from those that are often drunk
c1450 *Good Wife L* 199.68–9: For tho that ben ofte drunke, Thrift is from hem sunke. Cf. Proverbs xxiii 21.

T254 When **Thrift** is in the town you are in the field

1546 Heywood *D* 92.70–2: Whan thrift is in the towne, ye be in the feelde. But contrary, you made that sence to sowne, Whan thrift was in the feelde, ye were in the towne. Apperson 630; *Oxford* 655; Tilley T262.

T255 **Thrildom** (*thraldom*) is war (*worse*) than death (*varied*)
c1375 Barbour *Bruce* I 12.269: And thryldome is weill wer than deid. **a1398**(1495) Bartholomaeus-Trevisa I6^r[1.29–30]: They (*Scots*) love nyghe as wel dethe as thraldom. **c1420** Wyntoun V 338.2551–2: And or we suld be in thrillage, Yit better de for oure heretage.

T256 Never to **Thrive** were too long a date
c1395 Chaucer *CT* VIII[G] 1411: Nevere to thryve were to long a date. Apperson 442; *Oxford* 449; Skeat 287. Cf. Tilley T263.

T257 The **Throat** well washed, the eyes love to wink
c1515 Barclay *Eclogues* 107.4: The throte wel washed, then love the eyn to wink. NED Wash v. 5c. See **B242, M477, V11.**

T258 Better to suffer a **Throw** (*time*) than be too wild and overthrown
a1393 Gower *CA* II 270.1637–8: Forthi betre is to soffre a throwe Than be to wilde and overthrowe. See **T212.**

T259 Not give a **Thrum** (*short thread*)
c1400 *Laud Troy* I 194.6566: But he yaff not ther-of a throme. NED Thrum sb.[2] 2.

T260 To bring one above the **Thumb**
1469 Paston V 31[8–9]: Thow thou can begyll the Dwk of Norffolk, and bryng hym abow the thombe as thow lyst. NED Thumb 5b.

T261 To get one's **Thumb** out of another's mouth (*i.e.*, escape)
1481 Caxton *Reynard* 49[35]: I have now goten my thombe out of his mouth. NED Thumb 5i.

T262 To hit on the **Thumbs**
1546 Heywood *D* 69.95: She hitteth me on the thombes. Apperson 302–3; *Oxford* 296; Tilley T274.

T263 To hold (keep) **Thumb** in fist
a1393 Gower *CA* II 143.468–70: Hire thombe sche holt in hire fest So clos withinne hire oghne hond, That there winneth noman lond. **c1450** *Douce MS.52* 53.98: Holde thy thombe in thi fyst, And kepe the welle fro "Had I wyst." **c1450** Idley 82.83: Kepe cloos all thyng as thombe in fiste. **c1450** *Rylands MS.394* 103.16^v.15–6. **a1500** Hichecoke *This Worlde* 332.11–2: Bende thi thombe yn thi fyste, And ever be ware of had y wiste. **a1500** *Urbanitatis* in Furnivall *Babees Book* 15.71–2: Close thyn honde yn thy feste, And kepe the welle from hadde-y-wyste. MED fist n. (1) 2(c).

T264 As black as **Thunder**
1483 Caxton *Golden Legende* 244^r[2.18–9]: An Ethyopyen more blacke than thonder. Apperson 52; Taylor and Whiting 371.

T265 As loud as (any) **Thunder(-clap)**
c1000 *Old English Nicodemus* 502.13: þær wæs stefen and gastlic hream swa hlud swa þunres slege. **c1380** Chaucer *HF* 1681: And north, as lowde as any thunder. **a1420** Lydgate *Troy* II 428.1166. **a1447** Bokenham *Mappula* 33[11]: In courtis and plees they ben as lowde as thundirclappis. Taylor and Whiting 371.

T266 As thick as **Thunder** (*etc.*) (A number of single quotations are brought together here)
a1300 *Richard* 355.5439–40 (*var.*): Quarellys, arwes also thykke gan flye, As it were thondyr in the skye. **a1393** Gower *CA* III 358.4401–2: Mor sodeinly than doth the thunder He cam. **c1408** Lydgate *Reson* 144.5486: More dredful than stroke of thonder, **a1420** *Troy* II 465.2466: Every stroke, grete as dent of thonder, **c1421** *Thebes* 177.4314–5: And the noyse, hydouser than thonder, Of gonne-shot. **c1450** *Merlin* II 210[15–6]: Thei com as faste as thunder so harde a-monge her enmyes, 386–7: A grete flame of fire as reade as thunder. **1513** Douglas *Aeneid* II 196.64: Als ferss as ony thundyr.

T267 Ere **Thunder** stints (*ceases*) comes a rain (*varied*)
c1395 Chaucer *CT* III[D] 732: Er that thonder stynte, comth a reyn! **1474** Caxton *Chesse* 143–4: He (*Socrates*) knewe well that after suche wynde and thonder sholde comen rayn and watre, **1489** *Doctrinal* B8^v[22–3]: I (*Seneca*) wyst wel that after thys thonder shold come rayne. Tilley T275.

T268 To be like (dent [*clap*] of) **Thunder(-blast)**
c1000 *Old English Nicodemus* 504.9–10: þær wæs geworden seo mycele stefen swylce þunres slege. **c1300** *Beves* 127.2737–8: A made a cri and a wonder, Ase hit were a dent of thonder. **c1300** *Guy*[1] 600 A 263.5–6: Bifor the stroke the fiir out went, As it were light of thonder. **c1300** Robert of Gloucester I 457.6282–3: As thonder that soun was, the sight as lighting, So that ech dunt thoghte light as it were and thondring. **a1325** *Cursor* II 1036.18075: Thar come a steven als thoner blast, 1038.18123–4:

And eft thar come a mikel steven, Als it a thoner war of heven. **c1350** *Libeaus* 107.1909–11: The dores and windowes alle Beten in the halle, As hit wer dent of thunder. **a1400** *Cursor* II 738 FGT 12872–3: The fader steyven ther thorou brast, Als hit ware a thonner-blast. **a1400** *Siege of Jerusalem* 30.531–2: Doust drof upon lofte, dymedyn alle aboute, As thonder and thicke rayn, throwolande in skyes. **c1400** *Laud Troy* I 156.5292: It was a strok lyke a thonder. **a1449** Lydgate *Guy* in *MP* II 531.382: Terryble strokys lyk the dent of thonder. **1471** Caxton *Recuyell* I 66.23–5: That of the noise and dene . . . hit semed as hit had ben thonder, **1485** *Charles* 79.16–7: And made grete bruyt emonge the other, For it semed as it had be thonder and tempeste. **a1533** Berners *Huon* 42.9–10: (*They*) dasht so to ther horses that it semed that the thounder had fallen fro heven. Whiting *Scots* II 140.

T269 To come (in) like **Thunder(-blast)**
a1470 Malory II 759.19–20: In cam sir Trystram as thundir, III 1109.10–2: He cam into the fylde . . . as hit had bene thunder. **a1475** *Ludus Coventriae* 289.531–2: As wylde fyre and thondyr blast He cam cryeng on to me.

T270 To come together like **Thunder**
a1470 Malory I 304.12–3: And com togydyrs as hit had bene thundir, 399.11: They cam togydir as thundir, 415.12–3, II 474.15–6, 531.31–2, III 1219.27–8.

T271 To din like **Thunder** (*etc.*) (A number of single quotations are brought together here)
a1300 *Alisaunder* 319 M 331–2: Sone they fondon and fought to geder As doth the thonder in rayne wedder. **a1300** *Arthour and M.*[1] 162.5739–40: Ther was swiche contek and wonder, That it dined so the thonder. **c1380** *Ferumbras* 26.631: Hure strokes fulle so styth and sare, thay schulde (*resounded*) so doth the thonder. **c1400** *Laud Troy* I 201.6809–10: Here speres brast al In-sunder, As it were a blast of thonder. **c1400** *Sowdone* 35.1207: He smote as doth the dinte of thondir. **c1410** Lovelich *Merlin* III 672.25328: Here hors togederis metten as thondir. **a1470** Malory II 486.22: They com rydyng togydirs as hit had bene thundir, 665.29–30: And than they hurled togydirs with her spearys as hit were thundir, III 1138.13–4: Dressed them togydir with spearys as thunder. **1513** Douglas *Aeneid* II 211.59–60: Nysus . . . start mair spedely Than . . . thundyr in the sky. **a1533** Berners *Arthur* 109[20–1]: He pricked forth his horse as rudely as though the thonder had dryven hym, 142 [25–6]: The stroke . . . dasht into the erth lyke thonder, *Huon* 187.18–9: He began to lepe and gambaud and galop as it had ben the thonder.

T272 To fare like **Thunder(-ing, -blast)**
a1350 Castelford 132.23287: So thoner he fore. **c1350** *Libeaus* 55.980–1: Har dentes ferde as thonder, That cometh out of the skie, 78.1394. **c1410** Lovelich *Merlin* II 380.14193, 383.14327–8: And swich a noyse amonges hem was, For lyk as thondring hit ferde in that plas, III 599.22510. **1513** Douglas *Aeneid* IV 119.86: Now, as the thundris blast, faris Enee.

T273 To go like (any, the) **Thunder**
a1513 Dunbar *Sowtar* 124.35–6: Ane rak of fartis, lyk ony thunner, Went fra him, blast for blast. **a1533** Berners *Arthur* 90[2]: Hys hors went like the thunder, 335[32–3]: They went togyther as though thunder had fallen fro heven. Taylor and Whiting 371.

T274 To roar like (the) **Thunder**
1485 Caxton *Charles* 157.27: (*The river*) rored lyke thundre. **1506** Hawes *Pastime* 180.4813: His seven hedes so rored lyke the thonder, 186.4943. Whiting *Scots* II 140.

T275 To rout (*roar*) like **Thunder**
a1300 *Richard* 305.4332: It routes as it were a thondyr. **1501** Douglas *Palice* 8.5: This laithlie flude rumland as thonder routit.

T276 To run (together) like **Thunder**
c1400 *Sowdone* 34.1167: To-geder thai ronnen as fire of thonder. **a1470** Malory I 356.34–357.1: They ran togedir as thundir. **c1500** *Melusine* 170.3–4: They rane upon theire enemys as thondre and tempeste. **a1533** Berners *Huon* 347.29–30: His horse . . . ranne lyke the thonder.

T277 To rush together like **Thunder**
a1470 Malory II 556.6: Than they russhed togydirs as hit had bene thundir. **a1533** Berners *Arthur* 80[5–6]: Than Arthur rusht forth so rudelye as thonder had fallen fro heaven.

T278 Winter **Thunder** never comes but the weather is unkind
c1300 *South English Legendary* II 420.559–60: Thare vore me seith that winter thonder me ssel selde god ise(o). For he nemai nevere come but that weder unkunde be(o). Cf. Apperson 694–5; *Oxford* 715; Tilley W514, 515.

T279 To drive like a **Thunder-din**
c1200 *St. Katherine* (*Royal*) 100.1997–8: And draf therto dunriht As an thunres dune.

T280 **Thursday** and Sunday are cousins

1483 Caxton *Golden Legende* 13r[1.18–21]: And therfore comenly the proverbe was, that the thursday and the sonday were cosyns. For thene that one was as solempne as that other. For context, see F. S. Ellis ed. *The Golden Legend* . . . by William Caxton (7 vols., London, 1900) I 53.

T281 To change like the **Tide**
c1390 Chaucer *CT* II[B] 1133–4: Joye of this world, for tyme wol nat abyde; Fro day to nyght it changeth as the tyde.

T282 He comes too soon that brings evil **Tidings**
c1505 Watson *Valentine* 194.23–4: To sone cometh he that bryngeth evil tydynges. Jente 406. Cf. Taylor and Whiting 261; Tilley N145.

T283 One may hear **Tidings** in a far country sooner than at home
c1450 Trevet 240.8–10 (f.49a, col.1): Ofte tymes in a ferre contre and straunge a man may oft tymes heere tidinges souner than at hoome at hys neyghbores house. Cf. Tilley C712.

T284 As cruel as (a) **Tiger**
c1385 Chaucer *CT* I[A] 1657: And as a crueel tigre was Arcite. **a1420** Lydgate *Troy* III 763. 6787–8: More cruel . . . than tigre, **a1439** *Fall* I 69.2514–5, II 540.2455–6, **1439** *St. Albon* 157.1726. Whiting *Scots* II 140.

T285 As eager (*fierce*) as a **Tiger**
c1395 Chaucer *CT* IV[E] 1198–9: And sklendre wyves, fieble as in bataille, Beth egre as is a tygre yond in Ynde. **1471** Caxton *Recuyell* I 157.22–3: Aygre as tygres, II 410.29–30.

T286 As fell as (any) **Tigers**
c1433 Lydgate *St. Edmund* 402.311: Be title of wil, as any tigres fel, **1439** *St. Albon* 166.276–7.

T287 As fierce as **Tiger(s)**
a1449 Lydgate *Fifteen Ooes* in *MP* I 242.130: Fersere than Tygrees, *Horns Away* in *MP* II 663.37–8: But arche wives . . . Fers as tygre ffor to make affray. Taylor and Whiting 373.

T288 As swift as a **Tiger** (*etc.*) (A number of single quotations are brought together here)
c1408 Lydgate *Reson* 183.6987–8: Swifter also of passage More than any Tigre rage, **a1420** *Troy* I 18.217: Dowble as a tygre slighly to compasse, II 423.991: Liche a tigre, gredy on his pray, 546.5246: More furious than tigre, III 803.1060: Wers than tigre or Cerberus the hounde, 846. 2577: And Pirrus tho, as any tigre wrothe, **c1421** *Thebes* 43.1013: Wers than . . . eny tigre wood, **a1430** *Pilgrimage* 365.13458: A. **a1500** Kennedy 26.26: As tigar tiranus.

T289 As terne (*fierce*) as **Tiger**
a1500 *Abuse of Women* in Robbins 226.15: Als terne as tygir. **a1508** Dunbar *Tretis* 91.261: Thought ye as tygris be terne. Whiting *Scots* II 140.

T290 As wood (*mad*) as (any) **Tiger**
a1420 Lydgate *Troy* II 547.5297–8: As wood As . . . tigre, III 601.1271, 686.4158–9: As wood As any tigre, 809.1264, **c1421** *Thebes* 37.867: eny, 175.4274, **c1433** *St. Edmund* 408.654: any. Whiting *Scots* II 140.

T291 To await as a **Tiger** for its prey (*etc.*) (A number of single quotations are brought together here)
a1393 Gower *CA* III 372.4943–5: His frendly speches he affaiteth, And as the Tigre his time awaiteth In hope forto cacche his preie. **a1420** Lydgate *Troy* I 139.4281–5: Hercules . . . Liche . . . a tigre in rage furious, Gan of newe hem of Troye assaile, 255.3857: Thei ran I-fere as tigres al unmylde, II 427.1142–3, 434.1394: Diffende hym silfe lik a tigre in Ynde, **a1439** *Fall* I 103.3732–3: And how the brethre mette a-mong the pres, Lich too tigres. **c1450** *Pilgrimage LM* 161[30–1]: I wole smite thee but thou flee fastere or go than a tigre. **a1500** *Quare* 211.557: (An)d birnyng as the tigir ay in hete.

T292 To be like a **Tiger**
a1420 Lydgate *Troy* III 765.6862–3: Like . . . a tigre, that can no routhe have, **c1421** *Thebes* 57.1356: In her fury lik Tygres. **c1489** Caxton *Blanchardyn* 88.32–4: Blanchardyn, lyke as . . . a tygre . . . that is broken loos from his boundes Heved upward his swerde. **1513** Douglas *Aeneid* III 217.15–6: Lyke as ane rageand wild tygyr onstabill Amang the febill bestis onfensabill. Whiting *Scots* II 141.

T293 To be like a **Tiger** that finds her whelps stolen
a1300 *Alisaunder* 107.1889–92: And so the tygre that fynt ystole Her whelpes oither forhole— Wyth mouth she brenneth beest and man, Bot she kever hem sone agan. **c1385** Chaucer *CT* I[A] 2626–8: Ther nas no tygre in the vale of Galgopheye, Whan that hir whelp is stole whan it is lite, So crueel on the hunte as is Arcite. Cf. Taylor and Whiting 19; Whiting *Drama* 119, 304:19. See **B103, L367.**

T294 To fall (on someone) like **Tigers**
a1420 Lydgate *Troy* II 453.2054–5: Everyche on other like tigers . . . Began to falle, **1439** *St. Albon* 181.1131–3: The paynyms, lyke tygrys . . . Fyllen upon the martyr.

T295 To fare like (a) **Tiger(s)**
a1420 Lydgate *Troy* II 465.2468–9: In her fight thei fare Like wode tigres, 543.5138–40: That like a tigre . . . That were deprived newly of hir praye, Right so firde he, III 678.3901–3: And like a tigre in his gredinesse, . . . That day she ferde, **1422** *Serpent* 51.17: And bothe twoo . . . ferden as Tigres. Whiting *Scots* II 141.

T296 To slay like (a) **Tiger(s)**
a1439 Lydgate *Fall* II 666.2905–7: For lik a tigre this tiraunt furious, Hir eldest sone, day of ther mariage, Born to been heir, he slouh of mortal rage, **1439** *St. Albon* 178.990–1: Lyke . . . tygrys of assent, They slough.

T297 To stand at defence like (a) **Tiger(s)**
a1420 Lydgate *Troy* III 644.2724: As a tigre stondeth at diffence, **1439** *St. Albon* 141.849–50: Agaynst hym so obstynate they stode Lyke . . . tygyrs in theyr rage.

T298 If **Tillmen** (*farmers*) took tent (*heed*) what would be tint (*lost*), corn should never be cast upon earth
a1400 *Destruction of Troy* 81.2462–5: Iff tylmen toke tent what shuld tynt worth, Of sede that is sawen, be sesyng of briddes, shuld never corne for care be caste uppon erthe: Ne never dede shuld be done but drese furth to noght. **c1400** *Laud Troy* I 74.2505–10: If it were so, Off eche a thynge that man schulde do, If thei caste that noght be-falle, nis no man of us nowher, bonde ne thralle, That any-thyng scholde be-gynne, fro drede That he scholde fayle or evel spede. **a1420** Lydgate *Troy* I 226.2857–62: For yif the plowman alwey cast a-forne, How many graynes in his feld of corne Schal be devourid of foulis ravynous, That he doth sowe in feldys plenteuous, Thanne schulde he never, in vale nor in pleyn, For cowardyse throwe abrod his greyne. **1471** Caxton *Recuyell* II 522.25–523.2: Yf in alle the werkys that men shold begynne, men shold avyse in all the particularytees and synguler thynges that myght happe or falle, ther shold never enterpryse ner no feet be doon ner maad by hardynes, yf the labourers shold leve to ere and sowe the lande for the seed that the birdes recuyelle and gadre, they shold never laboure. Cf. Jente 264: He that fears every twig should not hunt in the woods; *Oxford* 113; Smith 75; Tilley B737, C673, D571, L143. See **C311, F59, G438, M248, P142, R14, W65, 256, 304, 629.**

T299 As **Time** goes so must folk go
1484 Caxton *Aesop* 42[1–2]: Men say conynly that after that the tyme goth so must folke go. Cf. Tilley T343.

T300 As **Time** hurts (a) time cures (heals)
c1385 Chaucer *TC* v 350: As tyme hem hurt, a tyme doth hem cure. **c1385** Usk 135.94–6: Have I not seyd toforn this, as tyme hurteth, right so ayenward tyme heleth and rewardeth. *Oxford* 660.

T301 Consider three **Times,** that (which) is, was, and ever shall be
c1450 *Foly of Fulys* 59.281–2: Wysmen con-sidiris tymis thre, That is and was and evir sal bee. See **I63.**

T302 The hard **Time** (comes) after the soft
a1393 Gower *CA* II 252.979–80: It hath be sen and felt fulofte, The harde time after the softe. See **J58.**

T303 He that can abide his **Time** his will shall betide him (*varied*)
a1300 *Alisaunder* 29.463–4: He that can his tyme abide Al his wille hym shal bityde, 239. 4284–5. **a1437** *Kingis Quair* 82.133[2–3]: And wele is him that his tyme wil abit: Abyde thy time. See **A8, B318, W264.**

T304 He that does not prepare before his **Time** will be unprepared in his time
897 Alfred *Boethius* 67.11–2: Forðæm se ðe his ær tide ne tiolað, þonne bið his on tid untilad.

T305 In **Time** of need a man should aid him-(self) with his own
c1500 Fabyan 299[37]: In tyme of nede, it was good polycy for a man to ayde hym with his owne. See **O76.**

T306 Long **Time** slakes men's sorrow
1483 *Vulgaria quedam abs Terencio* O6v[8–9]: Longe tyme slaketh or taketh away mennys sorow, it is a comon seynge. Cf. Whiting *Drama* 287.

T307 Lost **Time** cannot be recovered (*varied*)
c1380 Chaucer *HF* 1257–8: For tyme ylost, this knowen ye, Be no way may recovered be, **c1385** *TC* iii 896: O tyme ilost, wel maistow corsen slouthe! iv 1283: For tyme ylost may nought recovered be, **c1390** *CT* II[B] 25–8: Wel kan Senec and many a philosophre Biwaillen tyme moore than gold in cofre; For "los of catel may recovered be, But los of tyme shendeth us," quod he. **a1393** Gower *CA* II 241.577–8: For noman mai his time lore Recovere, 341.1485–7: Men mai recovere lost of good, Bot so wys man yit nevere stod, Which mai recovere time lore. **a1400** *Romaunt B* 5121–4: Thy tyme thou shalt

biwepe sore, The whiche never thou maist restore; For tyme lost, as men may see, For nothyng may recovered be. **c1422** Hoccleve *Lerne to Die* 187.251–2: The tyme is past, the tyme is goon for ay; No man revoke or calle ageyn it may. **c1425** *St. Mary Oignies* 145.16–7: The harm of losse of tyme maye not be recuverid, nor dayes lost maye not be restoryd, as maye othere bodyly thinges that are loste. **a1449** Lydgate *Evil Marriage* in *MP* II 456 (*var.*): Take hede and lerne, thou lytell chylde, and se That tyme passed wyl not agayne retourne, *Testament* in *MP* I 338.248–50: Of myspent tyme a fole may weel compleyne, Thing impossible ageyn for to recure, Dayes lost in ydel no man may restreyne. **a1450** *In the ceson* in *Archiv* 167(1935) 34[15]: Ya now is to late tyme paste to call agayne. **1465** Paston IV 136[13–4]: A day lost in idyll can never be recoveryd. **a1475** *Tree* 15.20–1: Ther is none so gret a losse, as is the losse of tyme. A nother thing if it be loste may be founde a yen. A tyme lost may never be founde ayen. **c1490** Ryman 254.6[3–4]: For alle the tyme, that is forlore, May in no wyse be gote agayne. **a1500** *Alas! What rulythe* 267[3]: Alas! tyme past may not returne agayne. **a1500** *Imitatione* (*1*) 38.21–2: Tyme loste never cometh ayen. **a1500** *Trinity College* (*Dublin*) *MS.159* in *Speculum Christiani* xxxi: Loss Lous of goodes greveth me sore, But lous of hyme (*for* tyme) greveth me more, For lous of goodes they wyll restore, But lous of hyme (*for* tyme) comethe no more. **c1500** *Balliol MS.316B* in R. A. B. Mynors *Catalogue of the Manuscripts of Balliol College, Oxford* (Oxford, 1963) 334: Lost of goods greveth me full sor, But lost of good (*for* tyme) grevethe me moche mor. Recovery of goods es often tyms synn, And soo es the tym never recovered agen. **1502** *Imitatione* (2) 178.27–8: Tyme lost can nat be recovered. **1506** Barclay *Castell* A7^v[1–2]: Saynge that the tyme and space Ones lost coude not recovered be, D4^v[19–20]: But for the tyme passed I was dolent, Whiche lost coude not be called agayne, **1509** *Ship* I 153[8–9]: The tyme passeth as water in a ryvere, No mortall man can it revoke agayne. **1509** *Fyftene Joyes* A2^v[17]: For yeres passed may not retorne agayne. **1513** Bradshaw *St. Werburge* 11.76–7: For tyme evyl spende in labours vayne Is harde to be well recovered agayne. **1546** Heywood *D* 59.15: Tyme loste, again we can not wyn. Apperson 635; *Oxford* 660; Tilley T332. See **S120, T186.**

T308 One **Time** shall pay for all
1525 Berners *Froissart* IV 215[26]: And than one tyme they shall paye for all, 297[7–8]. Cf. Tilley T319. See **O40.**

T309 Remede (*remedy*) in **Time** and rue not all too late
a1513 Dunbar *Of the Warldis Vanitie* 150.5: Remeid in tyme and rew nocht all to lait. Whiting *Drama* 150, *Scots* II 142:13.

T310 Suffer in **Time** and that is best
c1390 *Suffer in Time* in Brown *Lyrics XIV* 200–2.12: But suffre in tyme, and that is best, 24, 36, 44, *etc.* See **S860.**

T311 Take **Time** when it comes (*varied*)
c1477 Caxton *Jason* 60.15–6: Certes the time muste be taken as hit cometh, is hit hard or softe. **1509** Watson *Ship* P1^v–2^r: The wise man . . . taketh the tyme as it cometh, be it ryche or pore. **a1529** Skelton *On Time* I 137.6–7: Tyme must be taken in season covenable; Take tyme when tyme is, for tyme is ay mutable. **1546** Heywood *D* 22.18: Take time whan time comth, lest time steale away, **1555** *E* 195.285. Apperson 634; *Oxford* 660; Tilley T312, 313; Whiting *Drama* 51, 139, 147, 283, 290, *Scots* II 141–2.

T312 Take **Time** when tide asks
a1400 *Destruction of Troy* 227–8.7067–9: He that tas not his tyme, when the tyde askes, But lettes it deuly over-dryve with delling to noght, Wite not his wirdis, thof hym woo happyn! See **A53.**

T313 There is a **Time** of love and a time of hatred
1438 *Barlam and Josaphat* (*Northern*) 238.955–8: Tyme es of luff in ilk a stede And tyme es als so of hatrede, Tyme es of pes and tyme of were, And all evyll tyme es for to forbere. **a1450** *Barlam and Josaphat* (*South English Legendary*) 139.917–20: Tyme to love it is, And tyme is to hate, that wot ech man I wis; Of werre ther is tyme, and of pes also; And that fallith to tyme, ech man aughte to do. See **T88.**

T314 There is a **Time** to sow and a time to reap
1483 Caxton *Cato* E7^r[23]: For there is tyme for to sowe and tyme for to repe.

T315 There is a **Time** to speak and a time to hold still
c1395 *WBible* Ecclesiastes iii 7: Tyme to be stille, and tyme to speke. **a1400** *Scottish Legends* II 142–3.645–50: As the wyse ecclesyastes Sais in his buk . . . That tyme is to hald men stil, And tyme als to speke with skyl. **1483** Caxton

Cato C6v[2–3]: There is one tyme for to speke and one tyme for to holde his pees, **1485** *Charles* 56.6–7: Thou knowest the comyn proverbe that sayth that there is a tyme of spekyng and tyme of beyng stylle. **1523** Berners *Froissart* III 77[26–7]: Ther is tyme to be styll, and tyme to speke. Apperson 634; Jente 684; *Oxford* 660; Tilley T316.

T316 There is a **Time** to spend and a time to spare
a1500 *Leconfield Proverbs* 486[4]: Tyme is to spende tyme is to spare. Tilley T315.

T317 The third **Time** throws best (is all the best)
a1350 *Seven Sages C* 70.2062: Men sais the thrid time thrawes best. **c1390** *Sir Gawain* 52.1680: Now "thrid tyme throwe best" thenk on the morne. **a1400** *Scottish Legends* I 94.1072–3: Anis yet we wil assay, And the thred tyme al-thire-beste. Apperson 626; *Oxford* 651; Taylor and Whiting 374; Tilley T319; Whiting *Scots* II 142.

T318 The **Time** (tide) abides no man
c1395 Chaucer *CT* IV[E] 118–9: For though we slepe, or wake, or rome, or ryde, Ay fleeth the tyme; it nyl no man abyde. **a1400** *Romaunt B* 5023–6: For present tyme abidith nought; It is more swift than any thought. So litel while it doth endure That ther nys compte ne mesure. **a1439** Lydgate *Fall* I 172.6081: The tide abit nat for no violence, II 407.2801–2: The tid abit nat for no maner man, Nor stynt his cours for no creature. **c1475** *Prohemy of a Mariage* 31[16]: The tide bitte no man. **a1500** *Piers of Fullham* 11.251: The tyde taryeth no lenger then hym lyste, 13.297–8: And eke, as I rehese can, The tide of love abidith no man. **c1500** *Everyman* 7.143: For wete you well the tyde abydeth no man. **c1500** *Farewell* in Brown *Lyrics XV* 237.29: The tide abidith no man. **a1529** Skelton *On Time* I 137.9: Byde for tyme who wyll, for tyme wyll no man byde. **1546** Heywood *D* 23.21: The tide tarieth no man, **1555** *E* 176.170. Apperson 633, 634; *Oxford* 658; Robbins-Cutler 765; Tilley T323; Whiting *Drama* 147, 148, *Scots* II 140.

T319 **Time** brings and time bears all things away
1532 Berners *Golden Boke* 231.3668–9: All this the time bringethe, and the time bereth away. See **G206.**

T320 **Time** changes all things
1480 Caxton *Ovyde* 18[33]: The tyme that alle thynge chaungeth. Cf. *Oxford* 659; Tilley T326; Whiting *Scots* II 141.

T321 **Time** is good in every thing
c1450 *Fyrst thou sal* 90.112: Tyme is gode in evre thinge.

T322 **Time** is precious
1340 *Ayenbite* 57[31–2]: Vor hy lyeseth thane time precious. **a1400** *Cloud* 20.6: For nothing is more precious than tyme. **c1400** *Vices and Virtues* 14.13: The precious tyme. **1479** Rivers *Cordyal* 60.9–11: Seynt Bernard compleyneth . . . seiyng. Ther is no thing more precious here than tyme. **a1500** *Imitatione* (*1*) 31.25: Now tyme is right preciose. **1502** *Imitatione* (*2*) 173.13: Nowe the tyme is very precious. Taylor and Whiting 374; Tilley N302; Whiting *Scots* II 142.

T323 **Time** is tickle
1546 Heywood *D* 23.27: Time is tickell, **1555** *E* 180.190. Apperson 635; *Oxford* 659; Tilley T331.

T324 A **Time** of cure is better than (one) of plaint
c1385 Chaucer *TC* iv 931: Bet is a tyme of cure ay than of pleynte. See **H616.**

T325 **Time** steals (passes, goes, flies)
c1390 Chaucer *CT* II[B] 19–24: Leseth no tyme, as ferforth as ye may. Lordynges, the tyme wasteth nyght and day, And steleth from us, what pryvely slepynge, And what thurgh necligence in oure wakynge, As dooth the streem that turneth nevere agayn, Descendynge fro the montaigne into playn. **a1400** ?Chaucer *Rom. A* 369–77: The tyme, that passeth nyght and day, And resteles travayleth ay, And steleth from us so prively That to us semeth sykerly That it in oon poynt dwelleth ever, And certes, it ne resteth never, But goth so faste, and passeth ay, That ther nys man that thynke may What tyme that now present is, 381–4: The tyme, that may not sojourne, But goth, and may never retourne, As watir that doun renneth ay, But never drope retourne may. **a1400** *Cursor* III 1193 T 20857–8: In short manere I shal you sey For tyme passeth faste awey. **c1450** Capgrave *Katharine* 93.223: Tyme gooth faste, it is ful lyght of lope. **1509** Barclay *Ship* I 153[8]: The tyme passeth as water in a ryvere, 165[17–8]: And passeth every houre Lyke to the water, II 114[14]: Our lyfe styll passyth as water of a flode. **1532** Berners *Golden Boke* 330.6927–8: The tyme fleeth with movyng of wynges. Apperson 634:17; Jente 208; *Oxford* 659; Smith 292; Taylor and Whiting 374; Tilley T327; Whiting *Drama* 137, 288, *Scots* II 141.

T326 **Time** tries truth out
a1500 *Alas! What rulythe* 268[40]: Truethe is well tried in tyme and space. **1529** More *Supplicacion* 299 B[7–8]: As time alway trieth out the trouth. **c1544** Heywood *BS* 264.24: Tyll tyme the trothe trye out, **1546** *D* 76.217–8: Tyme tryeth trouth in every doubt. And deeme the best, till time hath tryde the trouth out. Apperson 635; *Oxford* 660; Tilley T338; Whiting *Drama* 273, *Scots* II 141. See **T90.**

T327 **Time** well spent can never have lack
a1529 Skelton *On Tyme* I 138.23: For tyme well spent can never have lacke.

T328 To have **Time** (leisure) and place
c1385 Chaucer *TC* i 1063–4: And how he best myghte hire biseche of grace, And fynde a tyme therto, and a place, ii 1367–70: But tho that ben expert in love it seye, It is oon of the thynges forthereth most, A man to han a layser for to preye, And siker place his wo for to bywreye, **c1390** *CT* X[I] 354: And thanne wol he do it (*sin*), if he may have tyme and place. **1509** Barclay *Ship* II 157[10]: There is a tyme and place for every thynge. Taylor and Whiting 374:7.

T329 To lose one's **Time**
c1477 Caxton *Jason* 110.15–6: Wherfore they lost their tyme, 149.11, 197.10. See **T442.**

T330 To spend a **Time** to win a time is sometimes wit
c1385 Chaucer *TC* iv 1611–2: And thynketh wel, that somtyme it is wit To spende a tyme, a tyme for to wynne. See **L233.**

T331 When **Time** has turned white sugar to white salt
1546 Heywood *D* 21.29: Whan time hath tournd white suger to white salte. Apperson 635; *Oxford* 659; Tilley T341. See **S871.**

T332 As dry as **Tinder**
a1400 *Scottish Legends* II 434.72: Of wod dry as toundire. **1513** Douglas *Aeneid* III 77.78: Hait Torrida zona, dry as ony tundir. Tilley T344; Whiting *Scots* II 142.

T333 To burn like **Tinder**
a1425 *Chester Plays* II 397.282–4: Sea and water all shall Brenne Agaynst kynd, that mon may ken, Tinder as though it wear.

T334 To rot like **Tinder**
c1485 *Mary Magdalene* (*Digby*) 89.915: I xuld a-rottyt, as doth the tondyr.

T335 As thick as **Tines** in harrows
c1400 *Laud Troy* II 463.15723–4: Sclow hem thikkere with her arwes Than tyndes of tre stondis In harwes.

T336 To say with **Tinker,** "I trow, let amend"
c1475 *Wisdom* 60.755: They may sey with tenker, "I trow, lat a-mende."

T337 To have one's **Tippet** tipped (*i.e.,* be defeated)
a1338 Mannyng *Chronicle B* II 280[2]: For he has overhipped, his tippet is tipped, his tabard is tome.

T338 Little **Tit** (*titmouse*) all tail
1546 Heywood *D* 36.37: But little titte all tayle, I have heard er this. Apperson 373; *Oxford* 375; Tilley T355.

T339 **Tit** for tat
1546 Heywood *D* 69.97: Sens tyt for tat . . . on even hand is set, **1556** *Spider* 165[26], **1560** *E* 213.43.5. Apperson 635–6; *Oxford* 661; Taylor and Whiting 375; Tilley T356. See **P283.**

T340 To taunt one **Tit** over thumb
1546 Heywood *D* 69.96: Ye taunt me tyt over thumb. *Oxford* 644.

T341 As malicious as a **Toad**
1422 Yonge *Governaunce* 212.8: Malicious as a toode.

T342 As many **Toads** as breed in Ireland, *etc.*
c1515 Barclay *Eclogues* 215.939–44: As many todes as breede in Irelande, And as many Gripes as breede in Englande, As many Cuckowes as sing in January, And Nightingales as sing in February, And as many whales as swimmeth in the fen, So many be there in Cities of good men.

T343 To boll (*swell*) like a **Toad** (crapaud)
a1430 Lydgate *Pilgrimage* 421.15652: I bolle as any crepawd doth. **1546** Heywood *D* 49.254: She swelde lyke a tode, **1556** *Spider* 199[7]: This spiders breth makth me swell lyke a tode. Apperson 615; *Oxford* 636; Taylor and Whiting 376; Tilley T362; Whiting *Scots* II 142. See **P4.**

T344 The **Toad** (frog) said to the harrow, "Cursed be so many masters (lords)"
a1000 *Cotton Faustina MS. A x* in Ker *Catalogue* 194: þa tadda cw(æð) to þar eiþa, Forwurþa swa fola maistres. Ad traeam dixit, pereant tot, buffo, magistri. **a1400** Wyclif *Sermons* II 280[2–4]: So that Cristene men may seye, as the poete seith in proverbe,—the frogge seide to the harwe, cursid be so many lordis. Apperson 636; *Oxford* 229, 661; Taylor and Whiting 376; Tilley F764; Walther I 58.494, 249.2184–5.

T345 Whoso loves the **Toad** weens it is the moon
c1450 *Rylands MS.394* 92.1: Whoso loveth the toode, he wenyth yt is the mone. Bufonem cura, fiet te judice luna. Walther I 249.2187.

T346 As hot as (a) **Toast(s)**
a1450 *Harley Cook Book* in Thomas Austin *Two Fifteenth-Century Cookery-Books* (EETS 91, 1888) 12[21–2]: Serve forth alle hote as tostes. **1546** Heywood *D* 61.88: Hotte as a toste. Apperson 315; Taylor and Whiting 376; Tilley T363.

T347 Not worth a **Toast**
a1475 *Ludus Coventriae* 173.133: Ther is no lord lyke on lyve to me wurth a toost.

T348 Do **To-day** what you can do to-day (*varied*)
c970 *Blickling Homilies* 213[21–5]: Gemunde he þæt Drihten bebead on þæm godspelle, *de crastino non cogitare,* þæt se Godes man ne sceolde be þan morgendæge þencean, þylæs þæt wære þæt he þurh þæt ænig þara goda forylde, þe he þonne þy dæge gedon mihte, and ða weninge hweðer he eft þæs mergendæge gebidan moste. **c1390** Chaucer *CT* VII 1794–5 [B2984–5]: "Ther is an old proverbe," quod she, "seith that 'the goodnesse that thou mayst do this day, do it, and abide nat ne delaye it nat til to-morwe.'" **a1393** Gower *CA* II 301.7–9: Of that he mihte do now hier He tarieth al the longe yer, And everemore he seith, "Tomorwe." **a1398**(1495) Bartholomaeus-Trevisa b1v[2.16–7]: (*Angels*) done his hestes sodenly and in an instaunt, and put not of tyll on the morowe. **c1400** *Consilia Isidori* 372[34]: Tary not in puttynge-over tylle to the morowe. **1471** Caxton *Recuyell* I 64.21–3: Ffor that a man may do this day, late hym not put hit over tyll to morowe. **1509** Watson *Ship* H4v[1–2]: And tary not tyll to morowe syth that thou mayst do it to daye. Apperson 517; *Oxford* 526; Taylor and Whiting 377–8; Tilley T378.

T349 He **To-day,** I to-morrow
a1200 *Ancrene* 116.21–3: Ille hodie, ego cras . . . as he feol to dei, ich mei . . . to marhen, 143.6–7: Ille hodie, ego cras, that is, he to dei and ich to marhen. **c1425** *Orcherd* 226.37: Today thou, tomorowe I. Apperson 637; *Oxford* 312; Tilley T371; Walther II 343.11085a. See **T405.**

T350 Here **To-day,** gone to-morrow (*varied*)
a1325 *Cursor* I 10.56: To day it is, to moru away, III 1503.26768–9: And noght als neus (*F* trewes) that er tan, That ar to dai, to moru ar gan. **c1390** *Proverbes of diverse profetes* 530.127: To-day he is with the, to-morwe he flit. **c1390** *Think on Yesterday* in Brown *Lyrics XIV* 144.34: To-day is her, to-morwe a-way. *Oxford* 293; Taylor and Whiting 182; Tilley T368. See **H361, N179, T364.**

T351 **To-day** alive, to-morrow dead (*varied*)
c1000 Aelfric *Homilies* II 462[25–6]: ða wacan fugelas, þe nu to-dæg beoð, and beoð to-merigen to nahte awende, 464[12–3]: ða wyrta beoð nu to-dæg blowende on wynsumnysse, and to-merigen beoð forbærnde. **c1390** *Make Amends* in Brown *Lyrics XIV* 198.43–4: To-day yif thou be stout and gay, To-morn thou lyst ded bi the walle, 199.87: To-day artou lord, to-morn is thin heire. **c1395** *WBible* I Maccabees ii 62–3: And drede ye not the wordis of a man synnere, for the glorie of hym is tord and worm; to dai he is enhaunsid, and to morewe he schal not be foundun, for he is turnd in to his erthe, and his thought schal perische. **a1400** *Proverbis of Wysdom* 246.115–6: We shall dye, I nott, how son: To day a man, to morow non. **c1400** Gower *Peace* III 489.292: That now is up, to morwe is under grave. **1404** *Lerne say wele* in Kail 21.198: To-day is quyk, to-morwe is fay. **c1430** Lydgate *Dance* 48.360: Somme ben to dai that shul not be to morowe. **a1450** Audelay 165.26–7: To-day is fresche in his colour, To-morow he gyrdis to grownd. **a1450** *God of hefne, that sittest* 410.192–3: Thhaugh thou be now an horse heighe, Ar to morwe thou myght deye. **c1450** *Against Death* in Brown *Lyrics XV* 247.25–8: This day thocht thow were hail and feyr, As bern baldast, ore kyng with crowne, The morne thow may be brocht one beyr For al thi castalis, towre and towne. **c1450** Greene *Carols* 365.7: This day heyl, te morwe, perchaunce, We mown be ded and ley(d) in clay. **c1450** Idley 91.624–6: This day alyeve, to-morow in thy grave; This day a wyse man, to-morow but a foole; This day in worship, to-morow but a knave! 196.2289: This day alieve, to-morow thow goist henn. **a1500** Hill 129.34: This dai a man, to-morow non. **a1500** *Imitatione* (*1*) 30.10: This day a man is, and to morow he apperith not. **a1500** *Leconfield Proverbs* 476[32]: To day a man in golde to morow closyde in clay. **c1500** Greene *Carols* 374.1: Deth biddith, "Beware: this day a man, tomorow non." **1502** *Imitatione* (2) 172.18. **1509** Watson *Ship* S8r[18–9]: For yf we be hole to daye, we shall be deed to morowe. Apperson 636; *Oxford* 662; Tilley A109, M404; Whiting *Scots* II 143. See **K52, N179.**

T352 **To-day** in mirth and in woe to-morrow
a1420 Lydgate *Troy* II 516.4229: This day in myrthe and in wo to-morwe! See **N179.**

T353 **To-day** in office, to-morrow put out
a1500 *Salamon sat and sayde* 291.11–2: Thus this werld abowt, To day i am in offyce, to moru i am put owt. See **N179.**

T354 **To-day** is high (rich), to-morrow is low (poor)
c1303 Mannyng *Handlyng* 109.3100: To day ys hegh, te morwe ys lowe. **a1393** Gower *CA* II 291.2398–402: And natheles he that is riche This dai, tomorwe he mai be povere; And in contraire also recovere A povere man to gret richesse Men sen, 361.2216–9: For he that stant to day alofte And al the world hath in his wones, Tomorwe he falleth al at ones Out of richesse into poverte. See **N179.**

T355 **To-day** well, to-morrow all amiss, *etc.*
c1516 Skelton *Magnificence* 79–80.2536–46: To day it is well, to morowe it is all amysse; To day in delyte, to morowe bare of blysse; To day a lorde, to morowe ly in the duste: Thus in this worlde there is no erthly truste. To day fayre wether, to morowe a stormy rage; To day hote, to morowe outragyous colde; To day a yoman, to morowe made of page; To day in surety, to morowe bought and solde. To day mayster-fest, to morowe he hath no holde; To day a man, to morowe he lyeth in the duste: Thus in this worlde there is no erthly truste. See **N179.**

T356 To lake (*play with,* claw) one's **Toes**
a1400 *Siege of Jerusalem* 48.839–40: That manye renke out of Rome (by) rest(ing) of th(e) s(o)nne Was mychel lever a leche than layke myd his ton. **a1460** *Towneley Plays* 129.414: And dos bot lakys and clowse hir toose. MED clauen 2(b): ?be idle. See **T358.**

T357 To love someone's (least) **Toe** better than another's body
a1300 *Arthour and M.*[1] 60.2055–8: Merlin . . . loved better his litel to, Than al that other bodi tho. **c1489** Caxton *Aymon* I 286.7–8: For I love moche better the leest too of your fote, than all kyng yon my brother. See **H34.**

T358 To pick one's **Toes** (fingers)
c1300 *South English Legendary* II 404.68: Hom hadde betere be(o) atom and ipiked hore two. **c1516** Skelton *Magnificence* 39.1222–3: And teche them howe they sholde syt ydyll To pyke theyr fingers all the day longe. See **T356.**

T359 To turn the **Toe** to the heel
a1500 *Proverbs of Salamon* 181.28.5–6: They turne the too to the heele, And all that purpose they do lett. MED hele n. (3) 1(c).

T360 To turn up one's **Toe**
c1475 *Prohemy of a Mariage* 32[27–8]: But turn up too and caste his clook away, That is to sey she carethe nat thouhe he dey. NED Toe 5j.

T361 He that takes the **Toll** must take the charge
1456 Paston III 105[18–20]: He that takyth the tolle most take the charge, hyt ys hys negligence that wille take the labour more then he may awey.

T362 As wise as **Tom** (Jack) a thumb
c1522 Skelton *Colyn* I 322.284: As wyse as Tom a thrum (*var.* Jacke athrum). See **J1.**

T363 **Tom True-tongue** (Truth)
c1378 *Piers* B iii 320: Thanne worth Trew-tonge, a tidy man that tened me never, iv 17: And also Tomme Trew-tonge—telle-me-no-tales. **1533** More *Apologye* 181[8–10]: Good Tomme Treuth . . . weneth all the worlde knoweth how trewe his mater is. Apperson 638; NED Tom 7c; *Oxford* 663; Tilley T382.

T364 Farewell **To-morrow,** though it be sure to-day
a1420 Lydgate *Troy* II 519.4316: Far-wel to-morwe, though it be sure to-day! See **N179, T350.**

T365 **To-morrow** never comes
1523 Berners *Froissart* II 309[32–3]: It was sayde every day among them, we shall fight tomorowe, the whiche day came never. Apperson 637; *Oxford* 663; Tilley T379.

T366 Better hold one's **Tongue** than speak
c1380 Chaucer *PF* 514–6: But bet is that a wyghtes tonge reste Than entermeten hym of such doinge, Of which he neyther rede can ne synge, **c1390** *CT* VII 1219[B2409]: Bettre holde thy tonge stille than for to speke. **c1425** Hoccleve *Jonathas* 222.194–6: Bettre is, my tonge keepe than to wisshe That had kept cloos that is goon at large, And repentance is thyng that y moot charge. **1523** Berners *Froissart* III 52[33–4]: He sawe well it was better for hym to kepe his tonge than to speke. See **H133.**

T367 He is wise (discreet) that can refrain his **Tongue**
c1450 *Epistle of Othea* 63.6–7: And therfor seyth thus the poete Omer: He is full wyse that can refreygn hys tonge. **1477** Rivers *Dicts* 23[29–30]: He is discrete that can refrayne his tonge. Cf. Smith 258.

T368 Her **Tongue** runs on pattens (*wooden shoes*)
1546 Heywood *D* 81.27: Her tong ronth on patens, **1556** *E* 125.47.13: Hir tounge was

clappyng lyke a paten. Apperson 638; NED Patten 1c; *Oxford* 664; Tilley T387. See **T377.**

T369 Hold your **Tongue** and say the best (*varied*) **c1420** *Mazer inscriptions* in *Archaeologia* 50 (1877) 149: Hold yowre tunge and sey the best, and let yowre neyghbore sitte in rest. **c1450** *Cambridge University MS. Hh 411* in Robbins-Cutler 3079.2: Say the best and bere the softe, ontaught tunge grevith ofte. See **S77.**

T370 Hold your **Tongue** still and have all your will
c1250 *Tell me* in Brown *Lyrics XIII* 32.5–6: Hold thine tunke stille And hawe al thine wille.

T371 In the **Tongue** (of man) is life and death (*varied*)
a1200 *Ancrene* 39.6: Lif and death, seith Salomon, is i tunge honden. **a1382** *WBible* Proverbs xviii 21: Deth and lif in the hondis (**c1395:** ben in the werkis) of the tunge. **a1425** *Rule of St. Benet (1)* 10.34–5: In the pointe of the tunge es lif and ded. **1491** *Rule of St. Benet (3)* 123.31–2: Also in the power of the tongue is deth and lyfe. **a1500** *English Conquest* 47.33: For in manes tonge is oft lyfe and deth. See **T387, W635.**

T372 Keep your **Tongue** and be (at) peace
a1400 *Proverbis of Wysdom* 246.102: Hold thy tong and be pease. See **T374.**

T373 Keep (Hold) your **Tongue** and keep (hold) your friend
c1390 Chaucer *CT* IX[H] 319: My sone, keep wel thy tonge, and keep thy freend. **c1450** *Douce MS.52* 49.61: Holde thy tonge and holde thy frende. **c1450** Idley 86.335–6: Kepe thy tonge and kepe thy frende In every contree wher thou wende. **c1450** *Rylands MS.394* 99.23. **c1470** *Harley MS.3362* f.4a: Halt thy tunge and have thy frend. Jente 515; Whiting *Drama* 160.

T374 Keep your **Tongue** while you are in rest
1533 Heywood *Pardoner* B3[r][22–3]: I holde it best To kepe your tonge, while ye be in rest. See **T372.**

T375 Let your **Tongue** rest and you will not rue
c1325 *Worcester Cathedral MS. F 19* f.164[a] in Brown *Register* I 451[9]: And ther for let thy tonge rest, and the schal noght renne (*for* rewe), quod hendyng.

T376 One's own **Tongue** may be his foe
c1450 *How the Wyse Man* 36.27: Thin owne tunge may be thi foo. **c1500** Greene *Carols* 345.3: His tonge may be his most foo.

T377 Their **Tongues** go on wheels
a1450 *Partonope* 420.10125: Suche mennes tonges gone ever on wheles. Apperson 638; *Oxford* 664; Tilley T387. See **T368.**

T378 To affile (file) one's **Tongue**
c1385 Chaucer *TC* ii 1681: This Pandarus gan newe his tonge affile, **c1387-95** *CT* I[A] 712–3: He moste preche and wel affile his tonge To wynne silver. **a1393** Gower *CA* II 54.678–83: For whanne he hath his tunge affiled, With softe speche and with lesinge, . . . He wolde make a womman wene To gon upon the faire grene, Whan that sche falleth in the Mir. **a1400** *Romaunt B* 3812–4: His tunge was fyled sharp and squar, Poignaunt, and right kervyng, And wonder bitter in spekyng. **c1412** Hoccleve *Regement* 172.4772: And therto can so wel her tonge affyle. **a1439** Lydgate *Fall* III 1013.3329–30: The Frenssh unkouth compendyously compyled, To which language my tounge was nat affyled, **a1449** *Look* in *MP* II 770.169–70: Off every man, by repoort of language, Affile thy tunge of trewe affeccioun. **a1449** Lydgate and Burgh *Secrees* 7.217: His tounge ffyled, expert in al language. **a1533** Berners *Arthur* 477[12–3]: Thy tong is fayre fyled. MED affilen (a).

T379 To be gladder than **Tongue** can tell
a1500 *Beves* 131 M 2536: Than gladder was Bevys, than tunge coude tel.

T380 To have a still **Tongue** but a busy head
1562 Heywood *E* 244.83.16: Havyng a styll toung he had a besy head. *Oxford* 621; Tilley T401.

T381 To have two **Tongues**
c1395 *WBible* I Timothy iii 8: It bihoveth dekenes to be chast, not double tungid. **c1400** Paues 112 I Timothy iii 8: Dekenes also ben chaste and noght of two tunges. **c1450** *Jacob's Well* 263.18: Thou beryst too tungys in thin heved. **1484** Caxton *Aesop* 243[7–8]: For the felauship of the man whiche hath two tongues is nought. **1509** Barclay *Ship* I 105[17]: A dowble tunge with wordes lyke hony. See **F12.**

T382 To put one's **Tongue** in his purse
c1525 Heywood *Wit* 11[2]: That ye may now put your toong in your purs. Tilley T399.

T383 **Tongue** and heart (*variously contrasted*) **a900** *Homilectic Fragment* in *Vercelli Book* 60.24–30: Swa bioð gelice þa leasan man, þa ðe mid tungan treowa gehataþ Fægerum wordum, facenlice þencaþ, þonne hie æt nehstan nearwe beswicaþ, Hafað on gehatum hunigsmæccas, Smeðne sybcwide, and in siofan innan þurh deofles cræft dyrne wunde. **a1325** *Cursor* II 370.6399–400: For if thair tunges spac resun, Thair hertes ai war wit tresun. **1439** Lydgate *St. Albon* 178.953: Yet tonge and herte were of one assent. **1450** *Dicts* 240.2–3: If the tunge (seith) oo thinge, the hert thinkithe a-nother, 242.2–3: His tunge schewith as it liethe in his hert; and his wordis and his dedis be accordinge. **c1450** Idley 171.809: He hath a sugred tong and herte of bitter hate. **a1475** *Tree* 19.3–4: So that thi tonge be not in the queere and thin hert in the towne. **c1475** Henryson *Fables* 100.2922–3: Ane silkin toung, ane hart of crueltie, Smytis more sore than ony schot of arrow. **1477** Rivers *Dictes* 94[6–7]: Yf his tonge saith one, his herte thinketh another, 110[11–2]: It is convenient that the tonge and the hert to be of one opinion. **1492** *Salomon and Marcolphus* 24[19–20]: They speke wyth the tunge that they mene not wyth therte. Apperson 295:12; Tilley G194, H333, T391, W672. See **L376, M754, 755, V53, W631.**

T384 The **Tongue** breaks bone though itself has none

a1300 *Proverbs of Alfred* 119 J 464–5: For ofte tunge breketh bon, Theyh heo seolf nabbe non. **a1300** *Trinity MS. O.2.45* 6.5: Tunge bregth bon, thegh heo nabbe hire silf non. **c1325** *Hendyng H* 293.144: Tonge breketh bon, and nath hire selve non. **a1393** Gower *CA* II 238.463–5: For men sein that the harde bon, Althogh himselven have non, A tunge brekth it al to pieces. **c1395** *WBible* Proverbs xxv 15: A soft tonge schal breke hardnesse. **a1400** Wyclif *Sermons* II 44[9–10]: And so, sith tunge brekith boon, al if the tunge himsilf have noon. **a1449** Lydgate *Say the Best* in *MP* II 795–6.5–7: And men that bith most expert in prudens Seyn of old tyme, that "tong brekith boone" Of his nature, "though he hymself have none," 13–4, 20–1, *etc.* **a1450** *Myne awen dere* 160.356. **c1450** *Douce MS.52* 47.42: The tonge brekyth bon And hath hymselfe non. **c1450** Greene *Carols* 341.4: Wykkyd tunge. **c1450** *Rylands MS.394* 97.9. **1456** *Five Dogs of London* 190c. **c1470** *Harley MS.3362* f.2b in *Retrospective* 309:7 and Förster 200.7. **a1475** Ashby *Dicta* 64.489–90: The tonge breketh boon, thaugh he be tendre, And shethe (*for* sleeth) many men thaugh he be slendre. **a1500** *English Conquest* 47.33–4: And as hit is Sayd, Tonge brekyth bone, thegh hym-Selfe ne have non. **a1500** Hill 132.35: Tonge breketh bon wher bon he hathe non. **1509** Barclay *Ship* II 216[13–4]: Brekynge the bonys (god wot) of many one, Howbeit the tunge within it hath no bone. **a1529** Skelton *Against Venemous Tongues* I 134.16–7: Malicious tunges, though they have no bones, Are sharper then swordes, sturdier then stones. **1546** Heywood *D* 73.95: Toung breaketh bone, it selfe havyng none, **1555** *E* 179.187: and bone it hath none. Apperson 638; Kneuer 55–7; *Oxford* 663; Skeat 79; Tilley T403.

T385 A **Tongue** cuts friendship a-two

c1390 Chaucer *CT* IX[H] 340–2: Right as a swerd forkutteth and forkerveth An arm a-two, my deere sone, right so A tonge kutteth freendshipe al a-two. *Oxford* 664. See **T388.**

T386 The **Tongue** is ever there the tooth aches

c1450 *Douce MS.52* 44.6: Ever is my tonge, ther the toth akys. **c1450** *Rylands MS.394* 95.12: ther my tonge akes. **c1475** *Rawlinson MS. D 328* 123.64: Ever my tong ther my toth akythe. Apperson 639; *Oxford* 663; Tilley T404. See **E207, H278, S506.**

T387 A **Tongue** is man's best member and the worst

a1415 Mirk *Festial* 161.6–8: For a tonge ys the best membyr of a man whyll hit ys rewlet, and the worst when hyt ys out of rewle. Whiting *Drama* 187. See **T371, W635.**

T388 The **Tongue** is no edge-tool and yet it will cut

1546 Heywood *D* 36.34: Her tong is no edge toole, but yet it will cut. Apperson 639; *Oxford* 664; Tilley T405. See **T385.**

T389 The **Tongue** is nourice (*nurse*) of all blame

c1390 *Proverbes of diverse profetes* 540.273–6: The tonge is noryce of alle blame And mony mon putteth in uvel fame; Of al eveles hit is queene and ladi And fordoth both soule and bodi.

T390 The **Tongue** is short and long is its sentence

1440 Palladius 178.233: The tonge is short, and longe is his sentence.

T391 The **Tongue** of a discreet man is in his heart and the heart of a fool is in his tongue

1477 Rivers *Dictes* 115–6: The tonge of a discrete man is in his herte, and the herte of a foole is in his tonge. Apperson 698; *Oxford* 718; Tilley M602.

T392 The **Tongue** of an evil man is worse than a spear (*varied*)

1450 *Dicts* 40.6–8: Thei askid him whate was sharper than a spere; and he aunswerede: the tunge of oon eville man. **1484** Caxton *Aesop* 231[1–2]: Werse is the stroke of a tonge than the stroke of a spere. See **T385, 388, 395.**

T393 The **Tongue** of man may not be tamed
c1412 Hoccleve *Regement* 88.2439–43: But tonge of man, as it wel knowe and kid is, Nat may be tamed; o fy! man, for schame! Silence of tunge is wardein of good fame; And after repreef fissheth, clappeth, fouleth; The tunge of man, all the body defouleth.

T394 The **Tongue** speaks hastily and the hands work at leisure
1532 Berners *Golden Boke* 300.5986–7: Of custome the tonge speketh hastily, and the handes worke at leysure. See **W642.**

T395 **Tongues** are worse than swords (*varied*)
a1449 Lydgate *Say the Best* in *MP* II 795.26–7: For slaughtyr of sword doth not so grete offens As mordir of tonges, 799.158–60: For ther is neithir sword nor launce So whet to kerve with sharpnes, As tonges ful of doubylnes. **c1450** Idley 131.1406–7: Cursed tongis also sleith many oone, Moo than swerde, dagger, or knyffe, 133.1537–8: Ffor by croked tongis many a man is slayn, Brought in grete sorowe and endeles payn. **c1450** *Jacob's Well* 164.20–1: The tunge of the flaterere harmyth more than the swerd of the smytere. **1477** Rivers *Dictes* 25[23]: An evil tonge was sharper than a glayve. Jente 602; Smith 341. See **M758, T385, 388, 392, W640.**

T396 A venemous **Tongue** is more malicious than an adder (*varied*)
a1430 Lydgate *Pilgrimage* 215–6.7716–8: Ffor ther ys addere, nor serpent So dredful, nor malycyous, As ys A Tonge venymous, **a1439** *Fall* II 438.3932–3: But ther is no poisoun so weel expert nor prẹvid As is of tunges the hatful violence. *Oxford* 686: Venom; Tilley T407, V29.

T397 When the **Tongue** speaks more than it should, it shall hear when it will be loath (*varied*)
a1325 *Hendyng C* 189.37: Wan the tunge maket (?speket) more than he solde, Oft scel he hire, wan him lothe wolde. **c1325** *Worcester Cathedral Ms. F 19* f.164[a] in Brown *Register* I 451[6–8]: Wo so spekes of thyng that ys un-wreste, Thowgh it sem soft wenne he spekys moste, He schall hit heryn on lofte wenne he wenis lest. Kneuer 50; Schleich 270; Singer III 137–8. See **M766.**

T398 When your **Tongue** tickles let it walk at will
1546 Heywood *D* 29.50: When your tonge tickleth, at wyll let it walke.

T399 Who may stop every wicked **Tongue?**
c1385 Chaucer *TC* ii 804–5: And who may stoppen every wikked tonge, Or sown of belles whil that thei ben ronge? Cf. Tilley M618.

T400 Whoso has an evil **Tongue** ever speaks what is wrong
c1450 *Douce MS.52* 49.62: Who-so hath an evyll tonge, Ever he spekyth, that is wrong. **c1450** *Rylands MS.394* 99.3.

T401 Wicked **Tongue** is evil to steer
c1400 *Alexander Buik* II 211.3818: And said wicked toung was evill to steir.

T402 A wicked **Tongue** is worse than a fiend
c1390 Chaucer *CT* IX[H] 320: A wikked tonge is worse than a feend.

T403 Wicked **Tongue** never says well (will say amiss)
a1400 *Romaunt B* 3802: For Wikkid-Tunge seith never well. **a1449** Lydgate *Wicked Tunge* in *MP* II 839–44.7: A wicked tunge wille alwei sey a-mys, 14, 21, *etc. Oxford* 317.

T404 To be **Tongue-tied**
1546 Heywood *D* 74.127–8: Why thinke ye me so whyte lyverd (quoth shee) That I will be toung tyed? Tilley T416.

T405 His **Tonight** may be yours to-morrow
a1513 Dunbar *No Tressour* 148.5: His chance to nycht it may be thyne to morrow. Whiting *Scots* II 143. See **T349.**

T406 Maugre (In spite of) one's **Teeth**
a1300 *Alisaunder* 305.5831: And, maugre the teeth of hem alle. **c1300** *Guy*[1] 602 A 267.12: Right maugre al thin teth. **c1300** *South English Legendary* II 695.77. **c1378** *Piers* B xviii 81: Maugre his many tethe. **c1380** *Ferumbras* 23.567, 101.3202. **a1387** Higden-Trevisa III 161[4–5], VII 7[19], VIII 153[15], 315[11]. **a1400** *Cleansing* 179.6 (f.118[r]). **c1400** *Alexander Buik* IV 371.8900. **c1400** *Laud Troy* I 15.492, 93.3150, 148.5023, 232.7853, II 349.11848, 513.17425. **c1400** *Tundale* 36.637. **c1400** *Vices and Virtues* 67.8, 138.1. **a1402** Fitzralph's *Sermon* in Trevisa *Dialogus* 65.32. **1404** *Lerne say wele* in Kail 15.13. **a1425** *Arthour and M.*[2] 324.884. **a1425** *Chester Plays* II 323.143. **c1440** *Degrevant* 34.491. **1447** Bokenham 278.10219. **a1450** *Declaryng* in Kail 81.56. **a1450** *Gesta* 277[11]. **c1450** *Alphabet* I 140.5, 15, 214.2. **c1450** *Speculum Christiani* (2) 100.15–6: Magre in hys teethe. **c1489** Caxton *Aymon* I 109.13–4, 229.1. **a1500** *Gest of Robyn Hode* in Child III 67.225[4]: Maugre in theyr tethe. **a1500** Medwall *Nature* B1[v][40]. **c1503** More *Early Poems* [6] C[4], **c1505** *Picus* 11 H[3–4]. **1512** Copland *Helyas* I2[r][26]. **c1515** Barclay *Eclogues* 113.178. **1522**

Skelton *Why Come* II 55.939: In the spyght of his tethe. **1528** More *Heresyes* 184 G[10–1]: In despite of al their teth, 232 A[10], **1532** *Confutacion* 510 E[6], 576 D[9], 732 E[9–10], 802 D[16]: Spyght of theyr teeth. **a1533** Berners *Huon* 175.13: In the dyspyte of his teth. **1534** More *Comforte* 1168 G[10], 1249 E[2–3]: Spyte of oure teeth. Apperson 597; Taylor and Whiting 378; Tilley S764; Whiting *Drama* 367:904, *Scots* II 144. See **T418.**

T407 To be armed to the **Teeth**
c1300 *Beves* 172.3644: Al iarmede to the teth, 210.4485. **c1350** *Libeaus* 29.487: All y-armed into the teth. **c1380** *Ferumbras* 87.2707: They wern y-armed in-to the teth. NED Tooth 6.

T408 To cast (put, dash) in the **Teeth**
c1495 *Arundel Vulgaria* 80.335: Why doste thou rebuke me for that or cast it in my teth. **1519** Horman *Vulgaria* 110[24]: Why puttest thou that in my tethe. Cur hoc mihi exprobras. **1528** More *Heresyes* 245 EF: And dashe rashelye out holye scrypture in everye lewde felowes teeth, **1529** *Supplicacion* 336 C[4–5]: Cast in our teeth our olde love, **1534** *Comforte* 1229 E[13–4]. **1546** Heywood *D* 52.379–80: But therto deviseth to cast in my teeth, Checks and chokyng oysters. *Oxford* 81; Taylor and Whiting 378; Tilley T429.

T409 To have a sweet **Tooth**
a1393 Gower *CA* II 13.325–6: Delicacie his swete toth Hath fostred. *Oxford* 636; Taylor and Whiting 378; Tilley T420.

T410 To have a **Tooth** that follows yiverness (*avarice*, greediness)
c1200 Orm I 325.9317–8: Fra clake and sake, and fra thatt tothth Thatt follghhethth yiferrnesse, 355.10201–2: gredignesse.

T411 To have neither **Tooth** (tongue) nor tongue (tooth)
a1400 *Scottish Legends* I 474.560–2: This the wif sa abaysyt he mad That scho had nothir twng na tuht To say hyme that he sad nocht suth, II 449.257–8: Na man of ws had tuth na towng To conclud hir, 451.310–2: That nan in-to that place Agane hir suld haf tuth na tong Hir to resist.

T412 To have one's **Teeth** cold
1484 Caxton *Aesop* 53[4–6]: For suche weren fayre gownes and fayre gyrdels of gold that have theyr teeth cold at home, 123[16–8]: For he that werketh not ne doth no good shal have ofte at his teeth grete cold and lacke at his nede. NED Tooth 8a.

T413 To keep (hear) for one's own **Tooth**
c1395 Chaucer *CT* III[D] 449: But I wol kepe it for youre owene tooth. **1556** Heywood *Spider* 207[10]: Ech hoping to here a tale, for his own tooth. Whiting *Drama* 367:904.

T414 To lie throughout (amidward) the **Teeth**
c1280 *Southern Passion* 71.1958: He lyeth thorwout his teth. **c1300** *Guy*[1] 250.4385: Thou lexst amidward thi teth. NED Tooth 1c. See **H243.**

T415 To one's **Teeth**
1532 More *Confutacion* 379 BC: Tyndal dare say nay to hys teeth, 499 E[4–5]: Tel him wel and plainly to hys teth. **1556** Heywood *Spider* 162[28]: To the spiders teethes: anone, yle tell my minde. NED Tooth 6b; Taylor and Whiting 378; Whiting *Drama* 367:904.

T416 To stick in one's **Teeth**
1529 More *Supplicacion* 327 H[10–1]: Yet shal there styck in their teeth, the scrypture of the Machabees.

T417 **Tooth** and nail
1534 More *Comforte* 1250 D[8–10]: They would fayne kepe them as long as ever they mighte, even wyth tooth and nayle. Apperson 641; *Oxford* 200; Taylor and Whiting 378–9; Tilley T422; Whiting *Drama* 367:905, *Scots* II 144.

T418 Unthank in (*despite*) one's **Teeth**
c1200 *Hali Meidenhad* 66.709–10: Unthonc in his teth (*var.* unthonc hise teth). **c1200** *St. Juliana* 33.338: Telle the unthonc in his teth. NED Tooth 5. See **T406.**

T419 As soon drive a **Top** over a tiled house
1546 Heywood *D* 75.185–6: I shall as soone trie him or take him this waie, As dryve a top over a tyeld house, no naie. Apperson 641; *Oxford* 158; Tilley T438.

T420 From **Top** to (and) tail
c1400 *St. Anne* (*1*) 46.1781–2: The childre that of that doyng wyst Told hym fra top to tayle. **a1425** *Metrical Paraphrase OT* 87.8759–60: Th(i)s tale fro tope to tale He told them ylka word. **1438** *Barlam and Josaphat* (*Northern*) 228.141–2: And tolde to him fro top and taile Als thai had gyffen him in counsaile. **a1450** *York Plays* 299.193, 381.159. **c1450** *St. Cuthbert* 96.3276: Sho teld the tale fra tyle to topp. **a1460** *Towneley Plays* 298.162. NED Top sb.[1] 24a.

T421 From (the) **Top** to (the) toe(s) (nail)
c1200 *St. Juliana* 51.561–2: From the top to the tan. **c1300** *South English Legendary* I 152.118: Nou sorwe and sor him be(o) next fram toppe to the ho (*var.* to), 239.36: Ich ssel tor-

menti al thi body fram toppe to thin ho (*var.* the to). **1375** *Canticum de creatione* 316.551–2, 317.593: the. **c1390** *Mercy Passes All Things* in Brown *Lyrics XIV* 130.152–3. **c1395** *WBible* II Paralipomenon *Prologue* II 385[15–6]: I disputed with hym fro the top, as thei seyn, unto the laste nayl. **a1400** *Gast of Gy* 7.131. **a1400** *Scottish Legends* I 429.121–2, II 55.275–6. **a1425** *Bird with Four Feathers* in Brown *Lyrics XIV* 211.106. **a1425** *Dayes of the Mone* in *SP* 20(1923) 79[2.25–6]: the. **a1425** *Of alle the joyus* in Bowers *Three Middle English Religious Poems* 34.57. **a1450** *Castle* 95.615: I holde thee trewe ffro top to the too, 136.1986: Gere thee with geris fro toppe to the too. **a1460** *Towneley Plays* 396.95. **a1475** *Ludus Coventriae* 303.921–2. **c1489** Caxton *Blanchardyn* 139.35. **a1500** Basterfeld 368.82. **a1500** *Medicines* in Brown *Lyrics XV* 273.26: And traveld my body fro top to the too. **a1500** *Miroure of Mans Salvacionne* 75[12]: the. **1528** More *Heresyes* 235D[15–6]. **1556** Heywood *Spider* 325[2–3]: From top to toe, (as wo saie: hie, meane, and low.), So: from brim to botom. Taylor and Whiting 379; Tilley T436. See **C575, F468, H215.**

T422 To be in another's **Top**
1384 T. Usk *Appeal* in R. W. Chambers and M. Daunt *Book of London English 1384–1425* (Oxford, 1931) 28.170–1: I wot wel everi man sholde have be in others top. **c1500** Fabyan 249[3–4]: Leste he hadde brought all in his toppe atones. **1519** Horman *Vulgaria* 111[1]: He is ever in my toppe. Semper est mihi infestus, 190[26]: He hath sette every man in others toppe. Commisit omnes inter se, 201[14]: Every man is in my toppe. NED Top sb.[1] 22.

T423 To turn upon one's own **Top**
1532 More *Confutacion* 421 F[7–8]: (His) errours . . . turne upon his owne toppe.

T424 **Top** and tail (toe)
c1300 *Body and Soul* (*L*) 63.578: Bi top and tail he slongen hit. **c1303** Mannyng *Handlyng* 177.5416: Go to helle, bothe top and tayle, 279.8884. **c1380** Chaucer *HF* 879–80: And with thyne eres heren wel Top and tayl, and everydel. **c1390** *Make Amends* in Brown *Lyrics XIV* 197.21–2: Whon top and to to-gedre is knitte, Then schal thi proude wordes a-slake. **a1450** *York Plays* 352.114: And tugge hym to, by toppe and taile. NED Top sb.[1] 24a.

T425 **Top** (Tail) over tail (top)
a1300 *Richard* 314.4563–4: That he ne yede doun, saun ffayle, Off hys hors top over taylle. **c1330** *Degare* 94.577–8: Out of the sadel he him cast Tail over top right ate last. **a1375** *William* 92.2776. **c1375** Barbour *Bruce* I 179.455. **a1400** *Ipomadon A* 112.3881–2, 158.5500–1. **a1400** *Gowther* 154.473. **c1400** *Laud Troy* I 202.6840, 273.9261, II 493.16727: That he bar him tayl over top. **c1400** *Triamour* 66.821–2. **1449** Metham 5.117: That yt over-thrw the tempyl off Venus, top over tayle. **a1450** *Feest of Totenham* in Hazlitt *EPP* III 97.323–4. **a1461** *John the Reeve* 579.534. **1483** *Catholicon Anglicum* 390: Top over tayle: *precipitanter.* **a1500** *Richard* 93.1–2 (*var.*). **a1508** *Freiris of Berwik* in Dunbar 195.560. **1513** Douglas *Aeneid* III 89.9. NED Top sb.[1] 24d.

T426 As bright as **Topaz**
1513 Douglas *Aeneid* IV 68.37: Crysp haris, brycht as . . . topace.

T427 **Topsail**(s) over
a1300 *Richard* 442. *var.* after 7062: That he tumbled samfaile Top-saile over his hors-taile. **a1400** *Chevelere* 16.320: And eyther of hem topseyle tumbledde to the erthe. **a1400** *Destruction of Troy* 41.1219: Mony turnyt with tene topsayles over. **a1400** *Siege of Jerusalem* 71.1208 (*var.*): And over al where it hitte were they never so stronge, Topseyl over throwyd and in the dich fylln. NED Topsail c.

T428 To burn like any **Torch**
c1386 Chaucer *LGW* 2419: The se, by nyghte, as any torche it brende.

T429 To shine like **Torch-light**
c1410 Lovelich *Grail* IV 349.299–300: And Alwey hire tresses behinden hire was dyht, That weren schineng As torche lyht.

T430 **Tottenham** is turned French
1546 Heywood *D* 30.50: Their faces told toies, that Totnam was tournd frenche. Apperson 641–2; *Oxford* 666; Tilley T444.

T431 To make it **Tough**
a1300 *Arthour and M.*[1] 116.4077: Now thai han ymade it tough. **c1300** Robert of Gloucester II 712.10498: The king glosede her and ther and made it somdel tought. **a1325** *Otuel and Roland* 65.189–90: And y schall wete wel y-nowe Why thou makyst hyt sa towe. **c1325** *As I stod on a day* in *Rel. Ant.* II 20[5]. **c1330** *Body and Soul* 30.101–2: Thou that madest it so tough, Al thi bobaunce is now ystint. **c1330** *Otuel* 74.292–3. **c1330** *Peniworth* 117.329: Thus sche stroked his here and made it tough. **1369** Chaucer *BD* 531: He made hyt nouther towgh ne queynte. **c1380** *Ferumbras* 59.1716. **c1385** Chaucer *TC* ii 1025: As make it with thise argumentes tough,

iii 87: Al nere he malapert, or made it tough, v 101: If that I speke of love, or make it tough, **c1390** *CT* VII 377–9[B1567–9]: This marchant gan embrace His wyf al newe, and kiste hire on hir face, And up he gooth and maketh it ful tough. **c1390** *Miracles of Our Lady* 161.141. **c1390** *Thank God of all* in *Vernon* II 690.67: He wol Rore and make it touh. **c1390** *Who says the Sooth* in Brown *Lyrics XIV* 152.14: And uche mon maketh touh and queynte. **a1400** *King Edward* 975.787. **a1400** *Rowlande* 58.118. **a1400** *Siege of Jerusalem* 20.355: Tit tolden her tale, and wonder towe made. **c1400** *Beryn* 57.1830. **c1412** Hoccleve *Regement* 127.3516. **a1420** Lydgate *Troy* I 276.4603: With face pleyn he (*Ulysses*) coude make it towe. **a1425** *Metrical Paraphrase OT* 56.7613. **c1425** Hoccleve *Jonathas* 238.642: He thoghte nat to make it qweynte and tow. **c1440** Charles of Orleans 120.3584: To yelde me yow y kan not make it tow, 217.6475: Whi make ye towgh to com where ye shulde be? **c1450** Capgrave *Katharine* 303.1293. **c1475** *Golagros* 36.1069. **a1500** *Degrevant* 67 C 1027–8: Ffor he was gay and amorous, And made hyt so tow. **a1500** *Kyng and the Hermyt* in Hazlitt *EPP* I 24.308. **a1500** *Miller of Abington* 113.336. **a1500** *Ryght as small flodes* 157.139. **a1529** Skelton *Against Venemous Tongues* I 135.15–6. NED Tough 8; Whiting *Scots* II 144.

T432 To have more **Tow** (flax) on one's distaff (rock)
c1390 Chaucer *CT* I[A] 3774–5: He hadde moore tow on his distaf Than Gerveys knew. **c1412** Hoccleve *Regement* 45.1226–7: Tow on my distaf have I for to spynne, More, my fadir, than ye wot of yit, 53.1458: This is the tow that thou speke of ryght now. **a1460** *Towneley Plays* 128.389: I have tow on my rok more then ever I had. **1525** Berners *Froissart* V 436[26–7]: He shall have more flax to his dystaffe than he can well spynne. **1533** Heywood *Pardoner* B4v[25]: I have more tow on my dystaffe than I can well spyn, **1546** *D* 77.243–4: Some of them shall wyn More towe on their distaves, than they can well spyn. Apperson 642–3; *Oxford* 667; Tilley T450. See **Y5.**

T433 As firm as a **Tower**
1484 Caxton *Royal Book* K3r[28]: Ferme as a toure. Cf. Whiting *Scots* II 144.

T434 High **Towers** are cast low when the low cottages stand
c1450 *Tuta paupertas* in Person 53: Hiegh Towers by strong wyndes full lowe be cast When the lowe Cotages stand sure and fast. See **R191, T462, W344.**

T435 The higher **Tower** the more wind
a1200 *Ancrene* 117.10–1: For eaver se herre tur, se haveth mare windes. See **H387, T462.**

T436 It is eath (*easy*) to win the **Tower** that none weres (*defends*)
a1325 *Cursor* III 1358 C 23765–6: Eth es for to win wit heer, The ture that nan es bute to were. See **W27.**

T437 To dance another **Trace**
c1475 *Mankind* 20.521: I xall make hym to dawnce a-nother trace. NED Trace sb.[1] 3.

T438 A **Traitor** should not speed (*prosper*)
a1338 Mannyng *Chronicle A* II 492.14179–80: Hit was no wonder he hadde no grace, Ffor traitour scholde nought spede in place. See **T446.**

T439 **Traitors** may never have too much woe (sorrow)
a1350 *Edward the Confessor* 6.182: For me ne mai never traitors do to moche wo. **c1450** *Edward the Confessor Prose II* 111[10–1]: For traytours may nevir have to moche sorow. See **T446.**

T440 The less **Transgressor** has greatest punishment
c1523 Barclay *Mirrour* 33[23]: Or the lesse transgressour have greatest punishment. See **T71.**

T441 After **Travail** is need of rest
a1450 *Generydes A* 9.237: And aftre travaile, were nede of reste. See **L5.**

T442 To tine (lose, cast away) one's **Travail** (swink, labor, pain)
c1300 *Havelok* 29.770: Hise swink ne havede he nowht forlorn. **a1325** *Cursor* I 108.1741: Quen noe sagh his travail tint. **c1350** *Gamelyn* 652.301: That travail ys y-lore. **a1375** *William* 56.1560: Al that travaile he has tynt, 99.3015. **c1375** Barbour *Bruce* I 163.45. **c1378** *Piers* B xvii 246: Al thi laboure is loste, and al thi longe travaille. **c1380** *Ferumbras* 125.3991: Ac al hure travail a-way thay caste. **c1395** Chaucer *CT* VIII[G] 781: For lost is al oure labour and travaille. **a1400** *Dame Sirith* 7.134: Her thou lesest al thi swinke. **a1400** *Destruction of Troy* 319.9775. **a1400** *Ipomadon A* 124.4320: And yff I thus my travell loste. **a1400** *King Edward* 972.666: Thi travayle shal not be forlore. **a1400** *Morte Arthure* 105.3566. **a1400** *Romaunt B*

4452: Whiche leese her travel at the laste. **a1400** *Scottish Legends* I 447.207, II 21.708, 102.104, 158.238, 159.246. **c1400** *Laud Troy* I 282.9562: Certes he loste al his laboure, II 388.13162: For hit is but lorn travayle, 519.17623: And lese my travayle and lese my way, 526.17880: But lese oure speche and oure travayle. **a1420** Lydgate *Troy* III 865.3223: And sith, in soth, loste is my traveyl. **a1425** *Metrical Paraphrase OT* 29.10417. **1447** Bokenham 115.4201: labour . . . lore. **a1450** *Generydes B* 50.1548: lost . . . payn, 176.5516: lost my labour and my payn, 177.5543: lost his labour and his payn. **a1450** *Partonope* 309.7739: loste travayle, 351.8642: travayle lese. **c1450** *Alphabet* I 164.24: losis . . . labur. **c1450** *Merlin* I 23[11]: loste . . . travayle, 26[3]: lesith . . . traveyle. **c1450** *Weddynge* 253.436: laboure . . . lost, 254.478: lost . . . travaylle. **c1455** *Partonope S* 488.284: travaile . . . lost. **a1464** Capgrave *Chronicle* 291[28–9]: lost . . . laboure. **1465** Paston IV 158[36]: loose . . . labor. **a1471** Ashby *Policy* 32.617: lost . . . labour. **1471** Caxton *Recuyell* II 446.8–9: loste . . . labour and payne, **c1477** *Jason* 18.31–2: loste . . . payne, **1480** *Ovyde* 67[7–8]: lese . . . payn, 185[28]: losest . . . payne, **1481** *Reynard* 95[39]: payne loste. **c1485** *Monk of Evesham* 86[4–5]: loste . . . labur and besynes. **a1500** *Eger H* 339.2576. **c1500** Fabyan 100[47]: laboure loste, 381[26]: lost . . . labour, 563[48]: travayle lost. **1502** *Robert the Devil* D3r[14]: loste . . . laboure. **1504** Hawes *Example* Dd3r[5]: labour . . . lost in vayne. **c1505** Watson *Valentine* 96.35: lese . . . payne, 107.23: loste . . . payne, 164.21: lese . . . payne, 228.7: lost . . . payne, 229.10: loste . . . payne, 272.24: lesest . . . payne, **1518** *Oliver* G1r[13–4]: lese . . . payne. **1519** Horman *Vulgaria* 415[7]: lose . . . labour, 431[27]: lose . . . labour. **a1533** Berners *Huon* 757.17–8: lose . . . payne. **1533** More *Confutacion* 662 A[8]: leeseth . . . labour. Tilley L9. See **L11, T329, V1.**

T443 As true (try [*good*]) as **Treacle**
c1330 *Praise of Women* 295.188: Trewe as treacle er thai to fond. **c1350** *Alexander A* 128.198–9: Ne triacle in his taste so trie is too knowe, As that ladie.

T444 **Treachery** wends (*turns*) upon oneself
c1300 *South English Legendary* (*Laud*) 334.368: And symon Magus-is tricherie op-on him-sulf it gan i-wiende. See **G491.**

T445 Hid **Treason** shall be known (*varied*)
a1393 Gower *CA* II 209.2946–9: That it (*Treason*) nys lich the Sparke fyred Up in the Rof, which for a throwe Lith hidd, til whan the wyndes blowe It blaseth out on every side. **c1505** Watson *Valentine* 90.30–2: Treason that hathe ben hydde so longe, shalbe knowne manifestly before everi body. See **M806.**

T446 **Treason** has evil ending (*varied*)
a1300 *Alisaunder* 265.4723–4: For clerkes siggeth in her writyng Traisoun hath yvel endyng. **c1450** *Rawlinson Troye* 200.8–9: And alwey the ende of every treson and falsenes (turneth) to sorowe and myschef at the last. Skeat 59. See **T438, 439.**

T447 **Treason** is convenient (*suitable*) for treason
a1420 Lydgate *Troy* III 708.4915: Tresoun for tresoun is convenient. See **G491.**

T448 **Treason** returns ever to its master
c1505 Watson *Valentine* 43.33–4: Treason and falshode retourned ever to their maisters, 51.13–4: It is said com(m)enly the treason wil ever returne to his maister againe. See **D342.**

T449 All **Treasure** here is transitory
a1449 Lydgate *Benedic* in *MP* I 5.118: Al tresor here nys but transytorye. Cf. Whiting *Drama* 124. See **C114, R119.**

T450 **Treasure** has no tack (*endurance*)
a1450 *Castle* 166.2987–8: Tresor, tresor, it hathe no tak; It is other mens, olde and newe.

T451 Where the **Treasure** is the heart is
c1000 *WSG* Matthew vi 21: Witodlice þær ðin goldhord is, þær is ðin heorte, Luke xii 34. **c1200** *Vices and Virtues* (*Stowe*) 69.25: Thar the thin hord is, thaer is thin herte. **c1395** *WBible* Matthew vi 21: For where thi tresoure is, there also thin herte is, Luke xii 34. **c1425** *St. Mary Oignies* 146.15–6: Where hir tresoure was, there was hir herte, as Cryste seith. **c1450** *Ratis* 47.1660–1. **1483** Caxton *Golden Legende* 287 (*by error* 286) [2.19]. **1490** Irlande *Meroure* 29.24–6: For oft tymes men thinkis on the playis and the thingis that thar hert lufis—Mathei vi. **a1496** *Rote or Myrour* D4r[3–6]. **a1500** *Imitatione* (*1*) 127.8. **a1500** *Lambeth Prose Legends* 331.25–6. **1502** *Imitatione* (*2*) 242.4–5. **1509** Fisher *Treatyse* 29.30. **1522** More *Treatyce* 92 G[9–11], **1534** *Comforte* 1232 E[16–8]. Smith 300; Taylor and Whiting 381; Tilley T485. See **S634, T240.**

T452 A **Treasurer** for two years may lead a lord's life twenty years after
c1405 *Mum* 27.11–2: For two yere a tresorier twenty wyntre aftre May lyve a lord-is life, as leued men tellen.

T453 In long **Treaty** sometimes lies great falsehood
c1500 *Melusine* 113.18: For in long treatee lyeth somtyme grete falshed. See **L67.**

T454 As dry as a (any) **Tree**
a1325 Kildare *Swet Jesus* in Heuser 84.11[1–2]: The pouer man goth bifor the, Al idriid als a tre. **c1395** *WBible* Lamentations iv 8: The skyn . . . driede, and was maad as a tre. **c1400** *Seven Sages D* 47.1482. **a1500** *Eger P* 192.180: For blood as drye as any tree, *H* 201.316. Whiting *Scots* II 145. See **S740.**

T455 As dumb as a **Tree** (*etc.*) (A number of single quotations are brought together here)
c1390 Chaucer *CT* II[B] 1055: And she, for sorwe, as doumb stant as a tree. **a1400** *Scottish Legends* I 325.1005–6: Sa that I umquhyle wald be Hard frosyne as ony tre. **a1430** Lydgate *Pilgrimage* 558.20927: Ffor he ys ded as . . . tre. **c1450** *Alphabet* II 376.7: A man als hye as treis. **1484** Caxton *Royal Book* K3[r][28]: Roted as a tree.

T456 As lean as any (a) **Tree**
c1400 *Emaré* 12.365: She was wax lene as a tre. **c1420** Page *Siege* 186.1000: And were as lene as any treys. **c1450** *Brut* II 414.26. **a1508** Dunbar *Flyting* 10.182. Whiting *Scots* II 145.

T457 As stiff as **Tree**
c1300 *South English Legendary* II 546.95: Here armes . . . bicome as stif as treo. Whiting *Ballad* 32.

T458 As thick as **Trees**
c1400 *Laud Troy* I 225.7617–8: Then men myght se swordes drawe—Thikkere then trees by wode-schawe, 287.9741–2: For it is layd with dede bodies Thikkere than trees ar set In ris. Taylor and Whiting 381.

T459 As true as (the) **Tree**
c1350 *Good Wife E* 162.74: Thou thei weren also trewe so er was tre. **c1390** *Cristenemon and a Jew* in *Vernon* II 485.27–8: To his trouthe hedde he tiht, Trewe as the tre (*?the Cross*—NED Tree 4a).

T460 Great **Trees** sooner break than bow
c1523 Barclay *Mirrour* 24[14]: For sooner breake then bowe great trees of longe age. See **B484.**

T461 If in a green **Tree** they do these things, what will they do in the dry?
c1000 *WSG* Luke xxiii 31: For þam gif hig on grenum treowe þas þing doð, hwæt doð hig on þam drigean? **c1395** *WBible* Luke xxiii 31: For if in a greene tre thei don these thingis, what schal be don in a drie? *Oxford* 149.

T462 In highest **Trees** the force of winds is most advanced
1532 Berners *Golden Boke* 229.3605–6: In the mooste highest trees the force of wyndes is mooste advaunced. Tilley T509. See **H387, R191, T434, W344.**

T463 A low lying **Tree** grows least
c900 *Maxims* in *Exeter Book* 162.158: Licgende beam læsest groweð.

T464 Lowest **Trees** are most sure in stormy weather
1509 Barclay *Ship* I 188[8–10]: In stormy wyndes lowest trees ar most sure, And howsys surest whiche ar nat byldyd hye, Where as hye byldynges may no tempest endure. Cf. Tilley C208, T509; Whiting *Scots* II 144–5. See **O6.**

T465 Such **Tree** such fruit (*varied*)
c1000 *WSG* Matthew vii 17: Swa ælc god treow byrð gode wæstmas, and ælc yfel treow byrð yfele wæstmas. **c1300** *South English Legendary* (*Laud*) 282.166–7: For ore loverd seide, i-wis: "bi the fruyt man may i-seo hwat-manere treo it is." **a1325** *Cursor* I 10.33–8: Bot be the fruit may scilwis se, O quat vertu is ilka tre Of alkyn fruit that man schal fynd He fettes fro the rote his kynd. O gode pertre coms god peres, Wers tre, vers fruit it beres. **c1386** Chaucer *LGW* 2394–6: By preve as wel as by autorite, That wiked fruit cometh of a wiked tre, That may ye fynde, if that it like yow, **c1390** *CT* VII 1956[B3146]: Of fieble trees ther comen wrecched ympes, X[I] 115: And therfore oure Lord Jhesu Crist seith thus: "By the fruyt of hem shul ye knowen hem." **c1395** *WBible* Matthew vii 17: So every good tre makith good fruytis; but an yvel tre makith yvel fruytis. **a1400** *Cleansing* 17.7–8 (f.11[r]): Wicked fruyt springeth out of an evyl tre. **a1400** *Pricke* 19.658–9: Swilk als the tre es with bowes, Swilk es the fruyt that on it growes. **a1400** Wyclif *Sermons* I 21[14–5]: The word of Crist, that a good tree may not bere yvel fruyte, ne an yvel tree good fruyte, 166[34–5]. **c1400** *How Men ought to Obey Prelates* in Wyclif *EW* 35[30]: Cursed fruyt spryngith out of a cursed tree. **c1400** *Vices and Virtues* 21.33–4: Evele fruyght, and than knoweth men openly that the tree was never good. **1402** Hoccleve *Letter of Cupid* 79.176–7: A wikked tre, gode frute may noon forth bryng; For swiche the frute ys as that is the tre. **a1415** Mirk *Festial* 216.1–2: Thus God sayth hymself: "Of a good tre comythe good frute." **a1430** Lydgate *Pilgrimage* 261.

9457–9: For the ffrut (what-evere yt be) Bereth the tarage off the tre That yt kam fro, **c1433** *St. Edmund* 383.347: Good frut ay cometh fro trees that be goode, **a1439** *Fall* I 133.4771: As off the stok the frut hath his tarage, 206.246–7: Frut and apples taken ther tarage Wher thei first greuh off the same tree, II 471.5081–2: For, it is seid of ful old langage, Frut of sour trees take a sour tarage, III 969.1782: The frut also bert(h) of the tre witnesse, **1439** *St. Albon* 116.299: The tarage of trees by the frute is sene, **a1449** *Vertu* in *MP* II 835.17: Frut fet fro fer tarageth of the tre, *World* in *MP* II 844.18: Frute folwith the tarage of the tree. **1449** Metham 3.55: The (s)qwete frute schewyth the gentil tre. **c1449** Pecock *Repressor* II 321[21–2]: Aftir the sentence of Crist . . . *Such is the tre, which is the fruyt of the same tree.* **a1450** *Song of Moses* in Wyclif *SEW* III 38[30–1]: And thus yvele trees bringen forth yvel fruyt. **c1450** *Foly of Fulys* 54.73–6: Sa be thar werkis men may see That gud fruyt cumys ay of gude tre, Fore al mankind is knawin, I-wys, Be froyt that of hyme cumand Is. **c1450** *Jacob's Well* 74.26–7: Be the frute, men may knowe the tre. **c1450** *Pilgrimage LM* 90[19–20]: Riht it is that the tre bere swich fruyt as kynde techeth it. **c1475** *Rawlinson MS. D 328* 124.69: Sygge tre sygge frytte. **a1500** *Additional MS.37075* 278.25: A tre scheyth what frute comyth ofe. **a1500** Hill 128.18: Often times prowith the frwight after the stok that hit cometh off. **1509** Fisher *Treatyse* 185.12–3: An evyll tree may brynge forth no good fruyte. **c1515** Barclay *Eclogues* 151.321: So every tree hath fruit after his kinde. **1528** More *Heresyes* 263 GH: As Christ sayth . . . an evyll tre can not bring forth good frute. **1528** Skelton *Replycacion* I 214.156–7: For it is an auncyent brute, Suche apple tre, suche frute. Apperson 263, 607; *Oxford* 670; Taylor and Whiting 381; Tilley F777, T486, 494; Whiting *Scots* I 175, II 144. See **F309, I24, M82, P199, S200, 744, T472, W171.**

T466 To draw (congeal) like a **Tree** to rind
c1390 *Northern Homily Cycle Narrationes* (*Vernon*) 268.643: Thei drouh to hym as treo to Rynde. **c1450** Idley 100.1152: Congeled with hate as a tree to a rynde. Cf. Tilley B83.

T467 To fall like a (heavy) **Tree**
a1350 *Ywain* 67.2484–5: Bot fast unto the erth he fell, Als it had bene a hevy tre. **c1400** *Laud Troy* I 316.10719: He felde hem doun as hadde ben tres.

T468 To stand like a stalwart **Tree** (*etc.*) (A number of single quotations are brought together here)
c1300 *Northern Homily Cycle* (*Edin. Coll. Phys.*) 36[25–6]: Quen thai yed sain Jon to se, That stithe stod als stalworth tre. **c1330** *Orfeo* 43.508: He is y-clongen (*shrivelled*) al-so a tre. **a1400** *Scottish Legends* II 394.259–60: Bot scho mycht nocht steryt be Mare thane ware a rut-fast tre. **c1400** *Laud Troy* I 148.5025–6: He cleve hem with swordis egge, As man doth the tre with wegge.

T469 **Tree** and rind savor of one tarage (*taste*)
a1439 Lydgate *Fall* III 969.1781: Of oon tarage savoureth tre and rynde.

T470 The **Tree** crooks soon that will be a good cambrel (cammock [*bent stick*]) (*varied*)
a1400 *Titus* 206.4579: Ever hit is crokede (*var.:* But well sone hit is crokyd) that wil be wronge. **a1449** Lydgate *Vertu* in *MP* II 836.33–4: A yong braunch wol soone wexe wrong, Dis-poosyd of kynde for to been a crook. **a1475** *Good Wyfe Wold* 175.71–2: Al day men mey see, The tre crokothe son that good cambrel wyll be. **a1500** Hill 129.32: Son crokith the tre, that crokid will be. **c1523** Barclay *Mirrour* 24[10–1]: Soone crooketh the same tree that good camoke wilbe, As a common proverbe in youth I heard this sayde. **1546** Heywood *D* 94.129: Timely crooketh the tree, that will a good camok bee. Apperson 587–8; Jente 698; *Oxford* 119; Tilley T493. See **C17.**

T471 The **Tree** (oak) is feeble that falls at the first dent (stroke) (*varied*)
c1385 Usk 135.91–2: The tree is ful feble that at the firste dent falleth. **a1400** *Romaunt B* 3687–92: For no man at the firste strok Ne may nat felle down an ok; Nor of the reysyns have the wyn, Tyl grapes be rype, and wel afyn Be sore empressid, I you ensure, And drawen out of the pressure. **a1439** Lydgate *Fall* I 3.96–7: These ookis grete be nat doun ihewe First at a strok(e), but bi long processe. **1477** Paston V 266[18–9]: It is but a sympill oke, That (is) cut down at the first stroke, 269[20–2]: And I harde my lady sey, That it was a febill oke, That was kit down at the first stroke. **a1500** Hill 128.19: Hit is a febill tre that fallith at the first strok. **a1500** *O mercifull* in Stow *Chaucer* (1561) CCCXLIII[v][2.33]: It is a simple tree, that falleth with one stroke. **c1505** Watson *Valentine* 192.26–7: For at the first stroke with an axe the tree is not smyten downe. Apperson 461, 645; Jente 200; *Oxford* 466–7, 627; Tilley T496.

T472 A **Tree** is known by its fruit
c1000 *WSG* Matthew xii 33: Witodlice be þam wæstme byð þæt treow oncnawen, Luke vi 44: Ælc treow is be his wæstme oncnawen. **c1395** *WBible* Matthew xii 33: For a tree is knowun of the fruyt, Luke vi 44. **a1449** ?Lydgate *St. Anne* in *MP* I 130.5: Right as for the fruyte honoured is the tre. **1495** Fitzjames *Sermo* F2v[28]: Ye knowe the tree by the fruyte. **1513** Bradshaw *St. Werburge* 29.610–4: Every tree or plante is proved evydent Whyther good or evyll by experyence full sure, By the budde and fruyte and pleasaunt descent; A swete tree bryngeth forth by cours of nature Swete fruyte and delycyous in tast and verdure. **1528** More *Heresyes* 259 E[3–4]: As our saviour sayth ye shall knowe the tree by the frute. Apperson 645; Jente 93; *Oxford* 670; Smith 301; Taylor and Whiting 381; Tilley T497. See **T465.**

T473 The **Tree** is weak which cannot bide a blast
c1515 Barclay *Eclogues* 138.816: Weake is the tree which can not bide a blast.

T474 A **Tree** set in divers places will not bring forth fruit (*varied*)
c1385 Chaucer *TC* i 964–6: As plaunte a tree or herbe, in sondry wyse, And on the morwe pulle it up as blyve! No wonder is, though it may nevere thryve. **c1385** Usk 22.37–8: A tree ofte set in dyvers places wol nat by kynde endure to bringe forth frutes, 135.105–6: Every tree wel springeth, whan it is wel grounded and not often removed. **1496** Alcock *Mons* C6r[4–5]: A tree ofte transplantyd fro one place to a nother loseth his frute. Tilley T499.

T475 The **Tree** that bows to no wind is in most jeopardy in storms
1509 Barclay *Ship* II 213[1–2]: The tre that bowyth to no wynde that doth blowe In stormes and tempest is in moste jeoperdy. See **R71.**

T476 **Trees** departed from the rind may not thrive
a1439 Lydgate *Fall* III 912.3204: Trees may nat thryve departid fro the rynde.

T477 Where the **Tree** (stone) falls there it shall lie
c1395 *WBible* Ecclesiastes xi 3: If a tre fallith doun to the south, ether to the north, in what ever place it fallith doun, ther it schal be. **1522** More *Treatyse* 78 H[6–8]: As the Scrypture sayeth, wheresoever the stone falleth there shall it abyde. **1556** Heywood *Spider* 409[21]: And where the tree falth, theare lithe it: clarks say so. Apperson 644–5; *Oxford* 402: Man lives; Tilley M64, T503.

T478 As who says (Not so soon say) **Trey-Ace** (*a cast at dice*)
a1393 Gower *CA* II 116.2963: Al sodeinliche, as who seith treis. **c1400** *Laud Troy* I 263.8917–8: A man schuld not so sone say "trayse," As he fel ded and held his payse. **a1450** *Partonope* 212–3. 5607–10: To shyppe he gothe, and takethe the way Over the see streyghte to Bloys. Thyder he come as who seyethe treys (*vars.:* tryes, threys). Shorte tale to make, he yede to londe. NED Trey 1b, 3.

T479 At (In) a **Trice**
a1425 *Ipomadon B* 267.391–2: The howndis, that were of grete prise, Pluckid downe dere all at a tryse. **a1508** Skelton *Phyllyp* I 85.1130–3: To tell you what conceyte I had than in a tryce, The matter were to nyse. Tilley T517.

T480 To take one in a **Trip**
1546 Heywood *D* 65.34–5: And winke on me also hardly, if ye can Take me in any tryp. Tilley T526.

T481 As tender as a **Tripe** (*ironic*)
a1500 Greene *Carols* 401 B 4: And some (*women*) be tender as a tripe.

T482 True **Tristram**
c1380 Chaucer *Rosemounde* 20: That I am trewe Tristam the secounde. **a1400** *Thre Ages* 624: And sir Tristrem the trewe.

T483 **Troilus** the true
a1400 *Destruction of Troy* 49.1487: Was Troylus the true, tristy in wer, 127.3922, 198.6116: Troilus . . . truest of knyghtes, 233.7221: Troiell, the tru knight, 239.7387, 245.7563, 262.8070, 312.9590, 326.9991, 335.10274, 337.10322, 10344, 339.10395, 347.10656, 450.13776. **a1400** *Thre Ages* 326: Sir Troylus, a trewe knyghte. **a1425** *Chester Plays* I 142.245: Nowe comes Trowle (*a shepherd*) the trew. **1501** Douglas *Palice* 22.28: Trew Troilus, unfaithfull Cressida. Whiting *Scots* II 145.

T484 After **Trouble** hearts are made light
a1449 Lydgate *Guy* in *MP* II 520.85: Affter trouble hertys be maad lyght. See **B325.**

T485 As whole as any (a) **Trout**
a1325 *Cursor* II 470 CF 8150: That he was hale sume (*F* as) ani trote, 682.11884: Thou sal be hale sum (*vars.* as, als) ani trute. **c1516** Skelton *Magnificence* 51.1624: I am forthwith as hole as a troute. Apperson 590; *Oxford* 706; Tilley T536. See **F223, 228, P172, 195.**

T486 He that is **True** shall never rue
a1393 Gower *CA* III 286.1961–2: The proverbe is, who that is trewe, Him schal his while nevere rewe.

T487 As thundering as a **Trump**
c1385 Chaucer *CT* I[A] 2174: His voys was as a trompe thonderynge.

T488 To ring like a **Trumpet**
1513 Douglas *Aeneid* IV 163.68: Thy vocis soun, quhilk as a trumpet rang.

Trust, sb.

T489 Beware of **Trust** (*varied*)
a1425 *Deceit II* in Robbins 100.7–8: (W)herfore beware of trust, after my devise; (T)rust to thi-selfe and lerne to be wyse. **c1516** Skelton *Magnificence* 59.1885: And in theyr moste truste I make them overthrowe. Cf. Smith 302.

T490 Give not **Trust** to every word that you hear
c1450 *Alphabet* I 132.18–9: Gyff not truste unto everilk wurd at thou heris. See **M115, W629.**

T491 Hasty **Trust** oft fails fools
a1439 Lydgate *Fall* II 455.4520: But hasti trust doth foolis ofte faille. See **F448.**

T492 In **Trust** is treason (*varied*)
1460 Paston III 230[15–6]: Est vulgare proverbium "Accordyng to ryte reson that to oftyn it is in ceson, that in trust is gret treson." **a1475** *Good Wyfe Wold* 174.38: For oft in trust ys tressoun. **a1475** *Ludus Coventriae* 227.58. **c1475** *Mankind* 27.743. **a1500** *Wold God that men* 9[10]: Trost ys full of treson. **c1500** *Farewell* in Brown *Lyrics XV* 236.16: I have my dreme, in trust is moche treson. **1546** Heywood *D* 72.71. Apperson 648; *Oxford* 673; Tilley T549.

T493 Who trusts to **Trust** is ready to fall
a1425 *Deceit II* in Robbins 100.4: (W)ho trustith to truste ys redy for to falle.

Trust, vb.

T494 Where one **Trusts** he is beguiled
c1500 *Banished Lover* in Robbins 14.4: Ffor where I trusted I am begyld. See **E97.**

Truth, see **Sooth**

T495 Great is **Truth** and passes all other (things)
c1395 *WBible* III Esdras iv 41: Greet is treuthe, and it passith bifore alle othere. Tilley T579. See **T502, 505.**

T496 No **Truth** may be proved unassayed
1420 Lydgate *Temple* 51.1249: For un-assaied men may no trouthe preve.

T497 Set **Truth** before gold and silver
c1340 Rolle *Psalter* 204 (57.1): Ye sett trouth bifor gold and silvere. See **T502, 505.**

T498 There is more **Truth** in a hound than in some men
c1390 *Fy on a faint Friend* in Brown *Lyrics XIV* 156.51–2: Ther is more treuthe in an hounde Then in sum mon, I understonde.

T499 To tell **Truth** without sin
1546 Heywood *D* 39.137: If I maie (as they say) tell trouth without syn.

T500 **Truth** cannot feign (lie)
c1400 Gower *Peace* III 490.312: The trouthe can noght feine. **c1522** Skelton *Colyn* I 330.487: But trouth can never lye.

T501 **Truth** is best
c1390 *Truth is Best* in Brown *Lyrics XIV* 168–70.8: We schal wel fynde that treuthe is best, 16, 24, 32, *etc.* **1406** Hoccleve *Male Regle* 34.283: And yit is trouthe best at all assayes. **c1515** Barclay *Eclogues* 19.588: But to say truth is best.

T502 **Truth** is more than all the world
c1303 Mannyng *Handlyng* 98.2764: Trouthe ys more than alle the worlde. See **T495, 497.**

T503 **Truth** is plain
1546 Heywood *D* 61.97: That in plaine termes, plaine truth to you to utter. Smith 304; Tilley T593.

T504 **Truth** is the daughter of time
1532 Berners *Golden Boke* 105.69–70: Trouthe (the whiche accordynge to Aul. Gel. is doughter of the time). Apperson 650; *Oxford* 674; Tilley T580.

T505 **Truth** is triedest (*choicest*) treasure on earth
a1376 *Piers* A i 126: That treuthe is tresour triedest on eorthe. See **T495, 497, 502.**

T506 **Truth** may be bold in every place
a1500 *Alas! What rulythe* 268[39]: Truethe maye be bould in every place. Cf. Tilley T576.

T507 **Truth** may be troubled (gramed [*vexed*]) but never shamed
c1450 *Fyrst thou sal* 91.199–200: Trewthe may be trobyld Bot never sal be schamed. **a1475** Ashby *Dicta* 90.1056–7: For trouthe at longe shal never be shamed, Thaugh he be other while Ivyl gramed. Apperson 650; *Oxford* 674–5; Tilley T584. See **T510.**

T508 The **Truth** may not fail

1484 Caxton *Aesop* 261[6–7]: The trouthe may not faylle. Cf. Tilley T576, 579.

T509 Truth must stand (*varied*)
a1393 Gower *CA* II 15.369: For trowthe mot stonde ate laste, III 286.1957–60: The trouthe, hou so it evere come, Mai for nothing ben overcome; It mai wel soffre for a throwe, Bot ate laste it schal be knowe. **a1439** Lydgate *Fall* I 292.3297: But trouthe alway venquysshith at the eende. **c1450** Idley 90.598–9: Trouthe at last wol be shielde and fan And put forth falshede out at the gate. Apperson 651; *Oxford* 674, 675; Tilley T591.

T510 Truth never did its master shame
a1475 *Ludus Coventriae* 340.113: Trewth dyd nevyr his maystyr shame. **a1500** *Young Children's Book* 19.41–2: Treuth wy(l)t never his master schame, Yt kepys hym out offe synne and blame. Apperson 650; *Oxford* 674–5; Tilley T586. See **T507.**

T511 Truth overcomes all things
c1395 *WBible* III Esdras iii 12: Treuthe overcomith forsothe over alle thingis. Tilley T579. See **T513.**

T512 Truth (Soothfastness) seeks no herns (*corners*) (*varied*)
a1400 *Romaunt C* 6712: For sothfastnesse wole none hidyngis. **1401** *Treuth* in Kail 9.5: Trouthe secheth non hernes ther los is lamed. **1404** *Lerne say wele* in Kail 19.157: Ffor sothnes nevere hernes sought. **1414** *God save the kyng* in Kail 53.74: Trouthe secheth non hernes to shewe his speche. **c1475** *Court of Sapience* 134.263–4: Neyther hoole ne herne, the playne longeth to me (*Veryte* speaks, and there is a marginal note: *Veritas non querit angulos*). **1483** Caxton *Golden Legende* 101v[1.39–41]: For as saynt Jherom sayth, trouth seketh no corners. Apperson 650; Tilley T587; Whiting *Scots* II 128. See **L99.**

T513 Truth shall surmount
a1420 Lydgate *Troy* III 836.2216–7: Maugre who grucchith, trouth(e) shal surmounte,—I dar aferme—and bere a-weye the pris. Cf. Tilley T576, 579. See **T511.**

T514 The **Truth** tries the self
c1475 *Mankind* 31.831: The prowerbe seyth "the trewth tryith the sylfe." Apperson 651.

T515 Truth will not paint his words (*varied*)
a1393 Gower *CA* II 43.284: For trowthe hise wordes wol noght peinte. **1519** Horman *Vulgaria* 91[19]: Treuthe nedeth no peynted or colored termes. *Oxford* 675; Tilley T585.

T516 As full as a **Tun**
1546 Heywood *D* 54.423: Wherof I fed me as full as a tunne, **1555** *E* 181.193. Apperson 241; Tilley T598.

T517 As great as any (a) **Tun**
c1300 *Beves* 132.14: Hys myddyl was gret as a tunne. **a1400** *Eglamour* 52. *var.* after 774: Hys body gretter then a tonne. **a1430** Lydgate *Pilgrimage* 387.14330. **a1475** *Guy*[2] 195.6826: a. **a1500** *Beves* 128 M 2426. **1506** Hawes *Pastime* 194.5138. Cf. Whiting *Drama* 330:342.

T518 As large as **Tuns** (*etc.*) (A number of single quotations are brought together here)
c1421 Lydgate *Thebes* 114.2759–60: He sette many Gonnys, Grete and smale and some large as tonnys. **a1450** *York Plays* 430.127: Thanne was his toumbe tome (*empty*) as a tonne. **a1500** *Lover's Mocking Reply* in Robbins 222.38: Smal in the bely as a wyn toune. **c1515** Barclay *Eclogues* 166.724: Or buckishe Joly well stuffed as a ton.

T519 As well talk to a toom (*empty*) **Tun**
a1450 *York Plays* 264.249: Sir, we myght als wele talke Tille a tome tonne! See **P317, W26.**

T520 A full **Tun** will sound nothing (*i.e.*, make no sound)
a1400 *Stanzaic Life* 343.10113–6: The fyrst songe made no sowene After tho fyrst sowene doun comyng, As schawes bothe in tour and tone, A full tunne will sowen no thyng. See **V25.**

T521 To drink of another **Tun**
c1395 Chaucer *CT* III[D] 170–1: Thou shalt drynken of another tonne, Er that I go, shal savoure wors than ale.

T522 As foul as any **Turd**
1438 *Barlam and Josaphat* (*Vernon*) 224.708–10: The feirnes of that damysel and hire clothing Semed to him at o worde Ffoulore thenne then eny torde.

T523 The more one stirs a **Turd** (drit) the more it stinks (*varied*)
a1400 Wyclif *Sermons* I 89[10–1]: But dritte, yif stired more, is more unsavery. **1496** Alcock *Mons* B6r[6–8]: Ryght soo as a stynkinge dunghyll, the more that it is styred the more it savouryth. **1546** Heywood *D* 80.68: The more we stur a tourde, the wurs it will stynke. Jente 799; *Oxford* 621; Tilley T603.

T524 Not give a **Turd**
c1250 *Owl* 142.1686: A tort ne give ich for ow alle!

T525 Not set a stinking **Turd**

c1500 *Wife Lapped* 219.933: I set not by thee a stinking torde. Whiting *Drama* 368:914.

T526 Not worth a **Turd** (*varied*)
c1300 *Guy*[1] 212 A 3703–4: And thou, Mahoun, her alder lord, Thou nart nought worth a tord! **a1325** *Otuel and Roland* 100.1322: He sayde that oure god vas nought worth a tord. **c1390** Chaucer *CT* VII 930[B2120]: Thy drasty rymyng is nat worth a toord! **a1450** *Castle* 144.2227. **c1475** *Guy*[1] 213 C 3704: Thou art not worthe a mouse torde! **c1499** Skelton *Bowge* I 45.392. **a1500** *Carpenter's Tools* 83.110. **1519** Horman *Vulgaria* 425[29]: That reason is nat worth a pyggis turde. Ea ratio non aequat succerdam. Tilley T605. See **T228.**

T527 To fall down like a **Turd**
c1395 *WBible* Jeremiah ix 22: And the deed bodi of a man schal fal doun as a toord (**a1382:** drit) on the face of the cuntrei.

T528 To housel with a **Turd**
c1300 *Amis* 17. *var.* after 396: He that doyeth for a worthe, Howsele hym with a torde, Y ne yeve of thy nay.

T529 As bad as the **Turk**
1509 Barclay *Ship* II 138[4]: Wors than the turke.

T530 An evil **Turn** for another
a1400 Wyclif *Sermons* II 250[8–9]: For that worldly man is queynt, bothe in werres and other lyfe, that can yelde redely an yvel turne for another. **1509** Barclay *Ship* II 38[7]: One yll turne requyreth, another be thou sure, 39[19]: To one yll turne another doth belonge. *Oxford* 257; Tilley T617.

T531 An evil **Turn** is written in marble, a good turn in dust
1513 More *Richard* 57 E[9–11]: For men use if they have an evil turne, to write it in marble: and whoso doth us a good tourne, we write it in duste. Cf. Tilley T619.

T532 For every shrewd **Turn** to have twain
c1497 Medwall *Fulgens* D1[r][22]: For every shrewed turne he shall have twayne. See **S513.**

T533 One good **Turn** asks another (*varied*)
1340 *Ayenbite* 18[28–9]: Wel ssolde he thonki god: of alle his guode. Vor guodnesse: other as akseth. **a1400** *Speculum Christiani (1)* 99.4: Not yildand a gode dede for a nothir yif we may. **c1400** *Vices and Virtues* 14.4–5: For a good turne asketh a-nother, "Bounte autre requert," dit luy fraunseis. **a1450** *Generydes B* 182. 5698–700: And this I will remembre in my mende Eche creature of nature hym delitith, That on good turne another quytith. **c1450** *Epistle of Othea* 86.5–6: A good dede, of verrey ryght, another have wold Doon ageyn therfore. **c1450** *Rylands MS.394* 92.17: O good turne asket another. **1456** Hay *Law* 140.4–5: Sen a bountes askis ane othir be obligacioun naturale, 248.8–9: A gude requeris ane othir, and rycht sa, ane evill, be the commoun lawis. **c1475** Henryson *Fables* 55.1557: Cum help to quyte ane gude turne for ane uther. **c1475** *Rawlinson MS. D 328* 119.26. **1484** Caxton *Royal Book* C5[v][8]: For one bounte requyreth and asketh another, **1489** *Aymon* II 383.32–3: I knowe that one curtesie requyreth a nother. **1509** Fisher *Treatyse* 184.3–5: He that wyll remembre a good turne or benefeyte is worthy to have gentylnes and lyberalyte shewed to hym. **1519** Horman *Vulgaria* 172[9]: One good turne wyll have a nother, 177[27]: One good dede is quytte with a nother. **1549** Heywood *D* 51.321: One good tourne askth an other. Apperson 470–1; *Oxford* 257; Smith 307; Taylor and Whiting 386; Tilley T616; Whiting *Scots* II 146.

T534 To be cast with (in) one's own **Turn** (*wrestling trick*)
c1300 *Northern Homily Cycle (Edin. Coll. Phys.)* 83–4: Bot sinful man gers him oft schurne, And castis him wit his awen turne, Quen (he) him schrifes of his sin. **a1496** *Rote or Myrour* H1[v] [21–2]: And thus they gyve hym a falle in his owne tourne. **1555** Heywood *E* 186.220: He is cast in his owne turne. NED Turn 20; Whiting *Ballad* 36. See **S848, 950, W711.**

T535 To do a good **Turn** for an evil
c1450 *Robin Hood and the Monk* in Child III 100.77: I have done the a gode turne for an evyll, Quyte the whan thou may.

T536 To have a shrewd **Turn** for a good
c1495 *Arundel Vulgaria* 82.343: I se well nowe, yf a man do a goode turne he shall have a shrewde for it. Whiting *Drama* 39.

T537 To take one's **Turn**
c1393 Chaucer *Scogan* 42: Take every man hys turn, as for his tyme.

T538 **Turns** good or bad are quit though they be delayed
c1425 Hoccleve *Jonathas* 236.575–6: Tornes been qwit, al be they goode or badde, Sum-tyme, thogh they put been in delay.

T539 As chaste as a **Turtle**(-dove)
1456 Hay *Governaunce* 157.23: Sum chaste as a turtur dowe.

T540 As meek as a **Turtle**
c1450 *Secrete of Secretes* 35.18: Meek as a turtille.

T541 As simple as a **Turtle**
1480 Caxton *Ovyde* 98[6]: Symple to good folk as a Turtle.

T542 As true as a **Turtle** (*varied*)
c1325 *Annot* 137.22: To trewe tortle in a tour. **c1380** Chaucer *PF* 355: The wedded turtil, with hire herte trewe, 577: The turtle trewe, **c1390** *CT* I[A] 3706: That lik a turtel trewe is my moornynge. **c1390** *Salutacioun to ure lady* 135.43: Heil Tortul trustiest and trewe. **c1400** *Holy Meditaciun* in *PMLA* 54(1939) 379.17: Jesu in temple, as turtil trewe. **c1422** Hoccleve *Jereslaus's Wife* 141.48: As treewe as turtle that lakkith hir feere. **a1449** Lydgate *Our Lady* in *MP* I 258.78: O trest turtyl, trowest of al trewe. **a1450** *Behold Jesus* in Brown *Lyrics XV* 141.41: Trewe turtyl. **c1450** Holland *Howlat* 51.127–8: That was the Turtour trewest, Ferme, faithfull and fast, 52.135: The trewe Turtour, 57.287: The trewe Turtour and traist. **a1460** *Towneley Plays* 38.505–6: The dowfe is more gentill, her trust I untew, Like unto the turtill, for she is ay trew. **c1460** W. Huchen *Hymn* in *Pol. Rel. and Love Poems* 291.2: Turtill trew, flowre of women alle. **a1500** *Against Adultery* 370.152: The turtell trewe. **a1500** *Beauty of his Mistress II* in Robbins 124.8: As true as turtyll that syttes on a tree, *Beauty of his Mistress III* 126.11: Trew as turtyll on a tree. **a1500** *Court of Love* 415.234: Of hir, Anelida, true as turtill-dove. **a1500** Greene *Carols* 399.1: That women be trewe as tirtyll on tree. **a1500** *On a dere day* in Dyboski 84.10–2: A tyrtyll trew a-monge all tho, Sange this songe in sothfastnes: "Fortis ut mors dileccio." **a1500** *Thoythis fre* in *MLN* 69(1954) 157.29–30: Wald god gyf that ye war als trew As ever was turtyll dowff on tre. **a1500** *Triamour* (*P*) II 81.21: And as true as the turtle on tree, 84.104: You are as true as turtle on the tree. **a1500** *Verbum Caro* in Brown *Lyrics XV* 115.4: A tyrtull trew. **c1500** *Lover's Farewell* in Robbins 213.112: Ffarewell Turtill trewe triable. **c1500** Newton 270.40: Ye are as tru as a turtill-dove in true lovynge. **1506** *Kalender* 148.2: True as the tyrtyll dove. **a1508** Skelton *Phyllyp* I 65.465: With the turtyll most trew. Apperson 646; *Oxford* 671; Tilley T624; Whiting *Drama* 147, 252, 268, 331:345, *Scots* II 146.

T543 The **Turtle** as a symbol of fidelity in love
c1000 Aelfric *Homilies* I 142[12–5]: þa turtlan getacniað clænnysse: hi sind swa geworhte, gif hyra oðer oðerne forlyst, þonne ne secð seo cucu næfre hire oðerne gemacan, II 210[34]: Turtlan we offriað, gif we on clænnysse wuniað. **a1200** *Trinity College Homilies* 49[15–6]: Turtle ne wile habbe no make bute on, and after that non, and forthi it bitocneth the clenesse. **c1200** Orm I 42.1274–7: Forr turrtle ledethth charig lif, Thatt witt tu wel to sothe, Forr fra thatt hire make iss daed Ne kepethth sho nan otherr. **a1250** *Bestiary* 22.694–8: In boke is the turtres lif Writen o rime, wu lagelike Ge holdeth luve al hire lif time; Gef ge ones make haveth Fro him ne wile ge sithen (*etc.*). **c1300** *Northern Homily Cycle* (*Edin. Coll. Phys.*) 159[3–4]: For yef the turtel tin hir mak, Never mar wil scho other thac. **1340** *Ayenbite* 226[2–5]: Vor ase zayth the boc of kende of bestes, efter thet the turle heth ylore hare make: hi ne ssel nevremo habbe velaghrede mid othren, ac alneway hi is one and be-vlyght the velaghrede of othren. **c1390** *Alexius* (*Vernon*) 37.128–30: And seith that heo schal liven alone As turtul on the treo. Evermore with-outen Make. **c1395** Chaucer *CT* IV[E] 2080: Soul as the turtle that lost hath hire make. **a1398**(1495) Bartholomaeus-Trevisa B8^{v}[1.16–20]: The turture is a chaste birde . . . yf he lesyth his make he sekyth not company of other, but goth alone (*etc.*). **a1400** *Meditations* 47.1801–2: As turtel morneth for his make So don ful many for cristes sake. **a1400** *Scottish Legends* I 447.229–32: And thane scho sad, quhat-evir befel, That but mak ay suld scho dwel As turtur, til of hyre mak Hyre hapnyt confort for to tak. **c1400** *Alexius* (*Laud*) 40.422–6: Liik is my liif on to sene . . . the turtel that is for sorough lene, And tredeth on no gras grene, Sithen hire make is ded. **c1400** *Vices and Virtues* 250.22–6: For, as the bok seith of kyndes of bestes, after that the turtle hath loste here make, never after wole he holde felawschep with non other but ever-more is alone and fleth the companie of othere. **c1408** Lydgate *Reson* 179. 6853–62: A turtyl gave craftyly, To signefye that fynaly, With-out(e) Mutabilyte, That in Femynynyte Trouthe sholde lasten evere . . . And as a turtil from hir make Departeth by no maner weye In-to the tyme that he deye, **a1422** *Life* 653.232–4: He muste ensample of the Turtle take, And be well ware that he not varye But life sool whan he hathe lost his make. **a1425** *Alexius* (*Laud 463*) 31.163–6: Lemman, al for thi sake,—So doth the turtel for his make Whan he is y.-slawe,—Al myrthe I. wile forsake. **a1450** *As ofte as syghes* in *Archiv* 127(1911) 324.46: The trew(e) turtill mourneth for her make. **a1450** *Gesta* 312[1]: I shal be turtill in your

absence that hadde lost hire make. **a1450** *Lord, I long after Thee* in Brown *Lyrics XV* 182.1–3: Jhu, for the mourne I may As turtel that longeth bothe nyght and day For her love is gone hyr froo. **c1475** *Parting is Death* in Robbins 151.7: With the trew turtil all chaunge for-svering. **1481** Caxton *Mirror* 102[25–8]: Whan the Turtle hath loste her make whom she hath first knowen, never after wyl she have make, ne sytte upon grene tree, but fleeth emonge the (*for* dry) trees contynuelly bewayllyng her love, **1483** *Golden Legende* 93[r][2.16–8]: The turtle (*is*) naturelly chast: For whan she hath lost her make, she wyll never have other make, 344[r][1.9–12]: Make me . . . lyke to the turtle, whiche after she hath lost hir felaw wyll take none other, **1489** *Doctrinal* I7[v][23–6]: As sayen the maystres Naturiens in the book of nature of bestis, after that the turtle hath lost hys make he shal never after acompanye hym or her to another, but is alleway solytarye and fleeth the companye of other. **1493** *Seven Wise Masters* 131[1–2]: But as a turtyll douve she wolde for the love of her husbonde there abyde and dye. **a1500** *Court of Love* 446.1394–9: The turtill-dove said, "Welcom, welcom, May, Gladsom and light to loveres that ben trewe! . . . For, in gode sooth, of corage I pursue To serve my make till deth us must depart." **a1500** *Knight of Curtesy* 1.7–8: Chaste to her lorde, bothe day and nyght, As is the turtyll upon the tre. **a1500** *Sen that Eine* 103.18–21: Evin as men may the turtill trew persaif Once having loist hir feir On the dry brainche ay faytfull to the graif Bewayling perseveir. **a1508** Dunbar *Tretis* 91.262: And be as turtoris in your talk. For references, see **T542.**

T544 **Twain** is better than three in every counsel
a1400 *Romaunt B* 5257–60: For whanne he woot his secre thought, The thridde shal knowe therof right nought; For tweyne of noumbre is bet than thre In every counsell and secre. Apperson 655; *Oxford* 330. See **T248.**

T545 From **Tweed** into Kent
a1338 Mannyng *Chronicle B* II 279[1]: Inglond to destroye fro Tuede unto Kent. See **B260, D369.**

T546 To bring **Twenty-one** to nought
c1250 *Proverbs of Alfred* 132 T 631–3: So longe he vole be bi, He wole brinhin on and tuenti To nout, for sothe iche tellit the. See **A4.**

T547 In (the, a) **Twinkling** (twink) of an (the) eye
a900 Bede 136.3–4: Ac þæt bið an eagan bryhtm. **a1000** *Vercelli Homilies* 74.23–4: þincð him þeos woruld eft naht, butan swylce hwa his eaȝe be-priwe, 78.60: On anes eaȝan byrhtme. **c1000** Aelfric *Homilies* II 568[22–3]: On anre preowt-hwile. **c1303** Mannyng *Handlyng* 288.9179: And, as yn twynkelyng of an ye. **a1325** *Ypotis* in *PMLA* 31(1916) 121[35]: In space of twynglynge of thi eye. **c1325** *Sayings of St. Bernard* 521.191: Ac in twynklyng of an eighe. **c1340** Rolle *Psalter* 260 (72.19–20): the. **c1350** *Proprium Sanctorum* 302.302. **c1385** Chaucer *Mars* 222. **c1390** *Each Man* in Brown *Lyrics XIV* 141.63–4: With a. **c1390** *Prikke of Love* 286.671: a. **c1390** *Robert* 39.48, 47.343, 49.415. **a1393** Gower *CA* II 118.3033: And in a twinklinge of a lok, III 108.5935: a. **c1395** Chaucer *CT* IV[E] 37: a. **c1395** *WBible* I Corinthians xv 52. **a1396**(1494) Hilton *Scale* K1[r][20–1]: a. **a1400** *Pauline Epistles* I Corinthians xv 52: In a moment and in a smytyng of an eye. **a1400** *Pistle of Preier* 49.4–5: a. **a1400** *Pricke* 135.4976: Als in the space of an eghe twynklyng, 153.5651: Bot a short space als of a eghe twynklyng, 169.6261: Als short als an eghe twynkelyng, 209.7738: a, 214.7948: In a schort. **a1400** *Scottish Legends* II 64.594–5: And this merwale alson cane be As man mycht twinkil with his e. **c1400** *Beryn* 94.3107: In twynkelyng. **c1400** *Elucidarium* 5[9–10]: In twynkelinge of an yghe, that is to seie, al soone as thou maist opene thin yghe. **a1420** Lydgate *Troy* I 202.2026: with twynklyng, III 802.1016: with twyncling. **a1425** *Christ's Own Complaint* in *Pol. Rel. and Love Poems* 203.191: This world is an ighes twynkeling. **a1425** *Cur Mundus Militat* in Brown *Lyrics XIV* 238.24: in twinkeling. **1435** Misyn *Fire* 6.21–2: in twynkillyng. **a1437** *Kingis Quair* 91.163[7]: in twinklyng. **a1438** Kempe 16.37–8. **a1439** Lydgate *Fall* III 753.2915: With twynclyng. **1445** *Almanac* in *ESt* 10(1887) 35[7]. **a1447** Lichfield *Complaint* 510.59: In an eyes twynklyng. **1447** Bokenham 127.4635–6. **a1449** Lydgate *Ale-Seller* in *MP* II 431.41: in twynklyng. **a1450** Audelay 223.24–5: With the. **a1450** *Gesta* 177[9]: in twynkelynge. **a1450** *O ye al whilk* in *Archiv* 167(1935) 27[31]: with twynkillyng. **c1450** Idley 137.1796: with the. **c1450** *Lambeth Prose Legends* 345.31–2: in twynkeling, 346. 43–4. **c1460** *Robert of Cesyle* in Brotanek 38.71: with twynkeling. **a1470** Parker *Dives* B2[r][2.8–9]: a, Y3[r][1.28–9]: a. **1471** Ripley *Compound* 127[11]: In twynke of an Eye most sodenly. **a1475** *Promptorium* 494: Twynkelyng of the ey: *Connivencia.* **a1475** *Tree* 6.6–7: At the day of Jugement . . . shal be axid of the

every tyme of thi living how it hath be spendid, ye, unto the leest twynkeling of thin eighe. **1479** Rivers *Cordyal* 60.21–2: Accompte for the leest twynkylling of thyn eye and all the tyme of lyf, 68.9–10. **1483** Caxton *Cato* E5v[17]: a, [18]: a, *Golden Legende* 5v[1.24]: a. **c1485** *Monk of Evesham* 43[21]: the, 51[32–3]: In the space of a twynkelyng of an ye. **c1489** Caxton *Aymon* II 588.15: the. **1490** Irlande *Meroure* 140.16: And in a moment and twynklinge. **a1500** *Coventry Plays* 18.506: And with a twynke of myn iee. **a1500** *Disciplina* 57[30]: a, 59[14]. **a1500** *Ghostly Battle* in *Yorkshire Writers* II 433[30]: the. **1501** Douglas *Palice* 42.6: In twinkling. **1503** Dunbar *Thrissil* 110.85: in twynkling, **a1508** *Goldyn Targe* 118.235: In twynkling, **a1513** *Best To Be Blyth* 144.29: Heir is bot twynklyng of ane E. **c1545** Heywood *Four PP* D1r[9]: With the, **1556** *Spider* 29[4]: in twinklyng, 215[10–1]: With twynke, 218[1]: at twink, 424[13]: at twinke. Apperson 653; NED Twink sb.[1]; *Oxford* 678; Taylor and Whiting 388; Tilley T635; Whiting *Drama* 368:919, *Scots* II 146. See **E204, W365.**

T548 **Two** are stronger than one (*varied*)
c1390 Chaucer *CT* VI[C] 825: Two of us shul strenger be than oon. **c1395** *WBible* Ecclesiastes iv 9: Therfor it is betere, that tweyne be togidere than oon. **a1400** *Ipomadon A* 222. 7788–90: For ofte ys sayd be wyse of werre: Tow ageynst one man here, There in lyethe no chevalrye. **c1400** *Beryn* 18.542: Ffor wee too be stronge Inowgh with o man for to fighte. Jente 703; *Oxford* 681; Tilley T642. See **D332, O36.**

T549 **Two** have more wit than one
a1393 Gower *CA* II 63.1020–1: For he is on and thei ben tuo, and tuo han more wit then on. *Oxford* 680. See **H250.**

T550 When **Two** fight there shall be peace when one is vanquished
a1400 *Scottish Legends* I 14.259–60: For, quhene twa fechtis, pece sal be Quhen we the tane vincust se.

T551 To have a **Tyburn** check
c1516 Skelton *Magnificence* 29.910–1: A Tyborne checke Shall breke his necke.

T552 To hang like a **Tyke**
a1500 *Thou Sinful Man* in Brown *Lyrics XV* 152.47–9: Leid as an tyke, And theif-lyke, On gallowis to hyng. Taylor and Whiting 107:41. See **H574.**

T553 To steal away like a **Tyke**
a1400 *Melayne* 43.1325: Hase thou stollen a waye lyke a tyke.

U

U1 As good **Undone** as do it too soon
1546 Heywood *D* 77.258: As good undoone . . . as doo it to soone. Apperson 659; Tilley D393.

U2 **Ungirt** unblessed
c1477 Caxton *Curtesye* 44.454–5: Ungerde, unblesside, servyng at the table, Me semeth hym servaunt full pendable. Apperson 659; *Oxford* 682; Tilley U10.

U3 **Unhardy** is unseely (*unlucky*)
c1390 Chaucer *CT* I[A] 4210: "Unhardy is unseely," thus men sayth. Apperson 120; *Oxford* 465; Skeat 189. See **F519.**

U4 As fierce as a **Unicorn**
a1430 Lydgate *Pilgrimage* 353.13023–4: And whan with wyn ful ys myn horn, I am ffers as an unycorn. **c1450** *Pilgrimage LM* 158[28]: Whan the wyne is entred in to myn horn, thanne i am as feers as unicorn.

U5 **Unknown** unkissed
c1385 Chaucer *TC* i 809: Unknowe, unkist, and lost, that is unsought. **c1385** Usk 134.66–8: Who that traveyleth unwist, and coveyteth thing unknowe, unweting he shal be quyted, and with unknowe thing rewarded. **a1393** Gower *CA* II 143.467: For men sein unknowe unkest. **1402** *Daw Topias* 59[1–2]: On old Englis it is said, Unkissid is unknowun. **c1440** Charles of Orleans 22.642: Let me not goon as oon unknowe unbast. **c1500** Greene *Carols* 346.1: An old-said sawe, "Onknowen, onkyste." **1546** Heywood *D* 48.233: Unknowne unkyst, it is loste that is unsought, **1555** *E* 169.133. Apperson 659; Jente 570; *Oxford* 683; Smith 311; Tilley U14. See **L466.**

U6 **Unminded** unmoaned
1546 Heywood *D* 33.28: Unminded, unmoned. Apperson 659; *Oxford* 683; Tilley U16.

U7 As thick as an **Urchin's** piles (spines)
c1300 *South English Legendary* I 18.50: Hy stikede on him so thicke so irchon doth of pile, II 513.47–8: As ful as an illespyl (*var.* erchoun) is of pikes al aboute As ful he stikede of arewen. **c1400** *Brut* I 107.7–9: And made Archires to him schote with Arwes, til that his body stickede alse ful of Arwes as an hirchone is ful of prickes. **c1433** Lydgate *St. Edmund* 410.762–3: Made him with arwis of ther malis most wikke Rassemble an yrchoun fulfillid with spynys thikke.

U8 **Usage** (Wone, Use) makes (the) mastery ([a] master)
1340 *Ayenbite* 178[24–5]: Vor wone maketh maister. **a1387** Higden-Trevisa I 357[17–8]: Among hem longe usage and evel custume hath so longe i-dured, that it hath i-made the maistrie. **c1400** *Vices and Virtues* 182.1: Use maketh maistre. **1415** *Crowned King* in W. W. Skeat ed. *Vision of William concerning Piers the Plowman*, Part III (EETS 54, 1873) 529.124: Of all Artes under heven use is a maistre. **a1440** Burgh *Cato* 29.987–8: Use makithe maistrie; use konnyng therfore. Use helpethe art, and cure helpithe the witte. **c1450** *Ratis* 7.221–2: Fore nan may cum to his office But oyss that makis thir masteris wys. **1484** Caxton *Royal Book* O6r[16–7]: The usage maketh a mayster, **1487** *Book of Good Manners* F1v[7]: Usage maketh a maistre. **1546** Heywood *D* 62.20: Use maketh maistry, **1555** *E* 190.253, **1562** *E* 245.95.1. Apperson 509; *Oxford* 684; Smith 235; Tilley U24. See **C648, T182.**

U9 **Usage** perfects lore
c1450 *Cato* (*Sidney*) 46.538: For usage schal parfite ever thi lore. Cf. Taylor and Whiting 295: Practice.

U10 **Use** and custom cause all things to be bold
c1515 Barclay *Eclogues* 2.58: For use and custome causeth all thing be bolde.

V

V1 To travail (swink, labor) in **Vain** (idle)
c1000 Aelfric *Lives* I 294.167: þonne swince ge on idel, II 386.155: Ac he swuncon on idel. **c1340** Rolle *Psalter* 447 (128.7): No man blessys thaim that traveyls in vayn. **c1350** *Smaller Vernon Collection* 24.1000: And bad him travayle not in veyn. **c1375** Barbour *Bruce* I 176.376. **c1395** *WBible* Psalms cxxvi 1, Isaiah lxv 23, Philippians ii 16. **a1400** *Pauline Epistles* Philippians ii 16: For I hafe not . . . travelyd in voyde. **c1400** *Primer* 26[25–6]. **c1400** *Sowdone* 8.271: We laboure nowe alle in vayne. **c1400** *De Blasphemia* in Wyclif *SEW* III 423[26]. **a1410** Love *Mirrour* 167[16–7]. **c1422** Hoccleve *Jereslaus's Wife* 168.793: laboure. **a1425** *Metrical Paraphrase OT* 26.14703: labours. **c1425** *Orcherd* 114.7, 359.18. **c1425** *St. Elizabeth of Spalbek* 116.20. **1447** Bokenham 22.785: Laboure, 36.1312: labouren, 51.1847–8: Labouryde, 66.2423, 72.2615: labouryst. **a1450** *Gesta* 72[17], 158[24], 277[16–7]: laborist. **c1450** *Alphabet* II 296.23: labur, 340.12–3: labur. **c1475** Henryson *Fables* 65.1854: laubour. **c1477** Caxton *Jason* 188.31: laboured, **1480** *Ovyde* 79[14]: laboure, 185[27], **1483** *Golden Legende* 82^{v}[1.23]: laboured, 194^{v}[2.35–6]: laboured. **1483** *Vulgaria quedam abs Terencio* O8^{v}[20]: laboure. **1493** *Seven Wise Masters* 39[8–9]: laboure, 75[17]: laboure. **c1495** *Arundel Vulgaria* 24.98: labourede. **1495** *Medytacyons of saynt Bernarde* C4^{r}[25–6]: laboured. **a1500** *Imitatione (1)* 16.9–10: laborith. **a1500** *O glorius lady* in Rolf Kaiser *Medieval English* (Berlin, 1961) 509.44: labures. **c1500** Fabyan 206[17]. **1501** *Chronicles of London* 238[23]: labur is. **1502** *Imitatione (2)* 163.22–3: laboreth. **1509** Barclay *Ship* I 149[1]: laboreth. Tilley V5. See **L11, T442.**

V2 Next the **Valley** is the hill
c1385 Chaucer *TC* i 950: And next the valeye is the hil o-lofte. **1464** Hardyng 127[3–4]: But ever as next the valey is the hill, After long rest commeth sharpe labour.

V3 As changing as a **Vane**
c1395 Chaucer *CT* IV[E] 996: Chaungynge as a fane. **a1420** Lydgate *Troy* I 116.3509: The comoun peple chaungeth as a phane. *Oxford* 698.

V4 As variable as a **Vane**
1506 Barclay *Castell* E4^{v}[13–4]: Thus was my mynde as varyable As a fane stondynge in the wynde.

V5 To follow as a **Vane** does the wind (*etc.*) (A number of single quotations are brought together here)
1400 *Mede and muche thank* in Kail 8.57–8: I likne a gloser, in eche weder To folwe the wynd, as doth the fane. **1415** *Crowned King* in W. W. Skeat ed. *Vision of William concerning Piers the Plowman*, Part III (EETS 54, 1873) 528.111: For he that fareth as a faane, folowyng thy wille. **a1449** Lydgate *Fabula* in *MP* II 505.574: With wynd forwhirlyd as is a muaunt ffane. **c1458** *Knyghthode and Bataile* 62.1688: And longe on hem that whirleth as the fane. **a1513** Dunbar *Of the Warldis Instabilitie* 31.95: That evermore flytis lyk ane phane. **c1523** Barclay *Mirrour* 19[37]: And varying as fanes erect into the winde.

V6 To turn like a **Vane** (in, with the wind)
c1385 Usk 46.23: That stoundmele turneth as a phane. **c1408** Lydgate *Reson* 162.6180: They turne nat as doth a phane, **a1430** *Pilgrimage* 387.14324–5, **a1449** *Testament* in *MP* I 344.400: Lyke a phane, ay turnyng to and fro. **c1450** Idley 91.630: She turneth every waye as fane in the wynde. **c1475** *Mankind* 27.742: with the wynde. **a1500** *Lay of Sorrow* 718.129–30: Lycht

as a fayn, ay turnyt to and fro As stricht wynd gydith It to go. **a1500** *Lover and the Advocate of Venus* in Robbins 172.97: with the wynd. **c1500** *Melusine* 298.34–5: at al windes. Tilley V16.

V7 **Vanity** is mother of all evils (ills)
c1440 Scrope *Epistle* 19[8]: Vanite is modyr off all evelles, welle off all vices. **c1450** *Epistle of Othea* 25.5–6: Vanyte is moder of all ylle, welle off all vyces. See **P389.**

V8 **Vanquishers** ofttimes are vanquished
1471 Caxton *Recuyell* II 517.10–2: Ffor hit happeth ofte tymes that the vaynquers ben vaynquysshid of them that were vaynquysshid. See **B65, C157, F139, 533, S914, V32, W39.**

V9 The **Variance** of lovers is the renewing of love
1520 Whittinton *Vulgaria* 39.36–7: The variaunce of lovers (sayth Terence) is the renuynge of love. Amantium ire amoris redintegratio est. Apperson 202; Jente 467; *Oxford* 189; Smith 92; Tilley F40. See **S399, W697.**

V10 There may not go out of the **Vat** (vessel) but what is therein
1340 *Ayenbite* 203[33–4]: Vor ther ne may go oute of the vete: bote zuych ase ther is inne. **c1400** *Vices and Virtues* 225.17–8: For ther may no thing out of a vessel but suche as is ther-ynne.

V11 When the **Veins** are filled the body becomes heavy
c1375 Barbour *Bruce* I 168–9.173–5: For quhen the vanys filit ar, The body vorthis hevy evirmar; And to slepe drawis hevynes. Whiting *Scots* II 148. See **B242, M477, T257.**

V12 When **Veins** are replete the spirits will stir
c1400 *Beryn* 7–8.196–9: But then, as nature axith, (as these old wise Knowen wele,) when veynys been som-what replete, The spiritis wol stere, and also metis swete Causen offt(e) myrthis for to be I-mevid. See **B243, M469.**

V13 As soft as (any) **Velvet**
a1400 ?Chaucer *Rom. A* 1419–20: Sprang up the grass, as thicke yset And softe as any velvet. **a1405** Lydgate *Black Knight* in *MP* II 386.80: And softe as velvet the yonge gras, **a1420** *Troy* I 215.2450. Taylor and Whiting 391; Whiting *NC* 491.

V14 For each **Venom** treacle is made
a1420 Lydgate *Troy* III 673.3704–5: For eche venym maked is triacle, And every wo hath his remedie. Cf. Tilley R70, S84.

V15 There is no **Venom** so perilous as when it has a likeness of treacle
a1410 Lydgate *Churl* in *MP* II 476.181–2: Ther is no venym so perlious of sharppnesse, As whan it hath of triacle a liknesse. See **E97.**

V16 To flee something like **Venom** (poison)
1348 Rolle *Form* in Allen *R. Rolle* 117.32: And flees it as venym. **a1400** ?Wyclif *Of Dominion* in *EW* 285[17]: Fledde lordschipe as venym. **c1425** *Orcherd* 403.15: Sich oon fleeth his celle as he wolde fle venym. **1456** Hay *Governaunce* 109.2–3: Tharefore flee as poysone thaire venymous condicioun. Cf. Taylor and Whiting 290: Poison 3.

V17 To hide like **Venom** in a clout
c1450 Capgrave *Katharine* 371.1005–6: The sturdy herte in hym whiche was soo stoute, Was hid with langage as venym in a cloute.

V18 To spew (spit) one's **Venom** (atter)
a1200 *Ancrene* 47.15–6: The earre kimeth al openliche and seith uvel bi an other, and speoweth ut his atter. **c1390** Chaucer *CT* VI[C] 421–2: Thus spitte I out my venym under hewe Of hoolynesse. **c1450** *Myroure of oure Ladye* 205[2–3]: The enmy spued venym by a worde of lesyng. **1546** Heywood *D* 36.47: She would spit her venym. *Oxford* 614–5; Tilley V28. See **A237.**

V19 **Venom** and sugar (honey)
a1393 Gower *CA* III 24.2833–4: Whan venym melleth with the Sucre And mariage is mad for lucre. **a1500** *English Conquest* 115.1–2: Ever he shed Venym (*var.* attyr) undyr hony. See **C177, G12, H433, 440, P289, S871.**

V20 **Venom** fordoes (destroys) venom
c1378 *Piers* B xviii 152: For venym for-doth venym. **1532** Berners *Golden Boke* 423.10851–2: For one venyme oftentymes dystroyeth an other venym. Skeat 117; Tilley P457. See **N6.**

V21 **Venom** (Poison) is the doing (condition) of women
a1387 Higden-Trevisa VII 359[9–11]: Yif thou hast ordeyned venym, that is the doynge of wommen and nought of knyghtes. **c1420** Wyntoun IV 331.78–80: Or gif thou walde put me to dede Withe wenum, or withe scharpe poysson, That is a wiffis condiscion. Whiting *Scots* II 112.

V22 As clear as **Verre** (*glass*)
a1422 Lydgate *Life* 501.1018: In a closet more clere than verre.

V23 A leaking **Vessel** holds nothing

c1450 *Consail and Teiching* 76.381–2: As lekand weschell haldis no-thinge, Sa opin tung has na traistinge.

V24 **Vessels** of tree (*wood*) do service as well as those of gold
c1395 Chaucer *CT* III[D] 99–102: For wel ye knowe, a lord in his houshold, He nath nat every vessel al of gold; Somme been of tree, and doon hir lord servyse. God clepeth folk to hym in sondry wyse. **c1395** *WBible* II Timothy ii 20: But in a greet hous ben not oneli vessels of gold and of silver, but also of tree and of erthe; and so summen ben in to onour, and summe in to dispit. **a1400** *Pauline Epistles* II Timothy ii 20. See **S330.**

V25 A void **Vessel** makes a (great) sound
c1425 *Orcherd* 126.24–5: Thou woost wel that a voyde vessel yeveth a sown whanne it is touchid; whanne it is ful it dooth not so. **a1430** Lydgate *Pilgrimage* 428.15933–7: A voyde vessel, pype, or tonne, Whan the lycour ys out Ronne, Who smyt ther-on up or doun, Yt maketh outward a gret soun, Mor than to-forn, whan yt was ful. Apperson 182; *Oxford* 171; Taylor and Whiting 391; Tilley V36. See **T520.**

V26 Not give a **Vetch**
a1350 *Seege of Troye* 125.1580: I wyl not gyffe a fecche for hem alle. **c1400** *Laud Troy* I 60.2027: He seyde, he nolde yeve a fecche.

V27 Not worth two **Vetches** (a vetch)
c1385 Chaucer *TC* iii 936: This seyd by hem that ben nought worth two fecches. **a1400** *Laud Troy* I 221.7478: I holde the not worth a fecche.

V28 **Vetches** are menged (*mixed*) with noble seed
c1475 Henryson *Fables* 16.367–9: As fitchis myngit ar with nobill seid, Swa interminglit is adversitie With eirdlie joy. See **J59.**

V29 Every **Vice** applies (*joins*) to other
a1439 Lydgate *Fall* III 794.694–5: As every vice to othir doth applie,—Surfet and riot brouht in lecherie. Cf. Whiting *Scots* II 148.

V30 To hate the **Vice** (ill) and not the persons
1533 More *Apologye* 190[16–7]: I hate that vyce of theyrs and not theyr persones. **1556** Heywood *Spider* 440[22–4]: And such as be ill: yet maie we not hate: The persons, but the ill in the persons seene, This learned I of a preacher that preached late. *Oxford* 282; Smith 273; Tilley P238.

V31 Where **Vices** are gathered there is ever some mischance
c1475 *Wisdom* 61.769: Wer vycis be gederyde, ever ys sum myschance.

V32 A **Victor** is oft overcome by a vict (*one vanquished*)
a1400 *Destruction of Troy* 71.2144–5: Ffor ofte sith hit is sene, and in sere londes, That a victor of a victe is vile overcomyn. See **V8.**

V33 The **Victory** of word is no victory
a1460 *Dicts* (*Helmingham*) 279.29–30: The victorye of worde is no victorye, but the verrey victorye is in dedes. See **W642.**

V34 He that intends **Villainy,** it is no sin to quite him with the same
a1450 *Generydes B* 144.4528–9: He that entendith villany of shame, It is no synne to quyte hym with the same. See **B213, F52, 491, G487.**

V35 **Villainy** makes villein
a1400 *Romaunt B* 2181–2: For vilanye makith vilayn, And by his dedis a cherl is seyn. See **C258.**

V36 A **Villein's** sinful deeds make a churl
c1395 Chaucer *CT* III[D] 1158: For vileyns synful dedes make a cherl. MED dede 7.

V37 A **Villein's** subject, a boy's wife and a child's bird are hard bestead
c1523 Barclay *Mirrour* 67[36–8]: Amonge olde parables this often have I read, A vilayns subject, a jelous boyes wife, And a childes birde are wo and harde bested. See **C206, 261.**

V38 To praise the **Vine** before one tastes of the grape
1549 Heywood *D* 39.133: Ye praise the vyne, before ye tast of the grape. Apperson 510; *Oxford* 515; Tilley W493.

V39 As swift as any **Vire** (*crossbow bolt*)
c1500 *Lancelot* 32.1091: Goith to o knycht, als swift as ony vyre, 97.3288. **1513** Douglas *Aeneid* II 225.16: The virgyn sprent on swyftly as a vyre.

V40 To flee like a **Vire**
a1393 Gower *CA* II 134.150–2: And as a fyre Which fleth out of a myhti bowe, Aweie he fledde.

V41 The first **Virtue** is to keep the tongue (*varied*)
c1385 Chaucer *TC* iii 292–4: For which thise wise clerkes that ben dede Han evere yet proverbed to us yonge, That "firste vertu is to kepe tonge." **c1390** *Cato* (*Vernon*) 563.121–2: Kep thi tonge skilfulliche: The furste vertu forsothe hit is. **c1390** Chaucer *CT* IX[H] 332–4:

The firste vertu, sone, if thou wolt leere, Is to restreyne and kepe wel thy tonge; Thus lerne children whan that they been yonge. **a1400** *Cato* (*Copenhagen*) A2r[9–10]: The ferste vertu, my swete sone dere, That is to daunte thy tonge and stere. **a1400** *Romaunt C* 7505–9: Sir, the firste vertu, certayn, The greatest and moste soverayn That may be founde in any man, For havynge, or for wyt he can, That is his tonge to refrayne. **1422** Yonge *Governaunce* 188.19–23: Caton Sayth, . . . "Trow thou the Pryncipal vertue to refrayne thy tonge, For he is negh to god that can be still by reyson." **c1425** Arderne *Fistula* 8.24–6: For Caton seith, "Virtutem primum puta esse compescere linguam": The first vertu trow you to be to refreyne the tong. **a1440** Burgh *Cato* 305.65–6: The first of vertuys alle Is to be stille and keep thi tonge in mewe. **a1449** Lydgate *God* in *MP* I 30.93–5, *Say the Best* in *MP* II 797–8.92–5: Caton writith that good tung Of vertuous hath the first price, No man may stop whan thei be rong, Theis belles as in my devyce, *See Myche* in *MP* II 800.6–7, *Wicked Tunge* in *MP* II 844.129–31: The first vertu most plesyng to Jh(es)u Be the writyng and sentence of Catoun Is a good tonge, yn his oppynyoun. **a1450** *Myne awen dere* 160.347–8: Kepe wele thy tonge, whare-evere thou dwell: Of all vertues it is the well, 161.370: Kepe wele thy tonge, whare-evere thou ga. **c1450** *Proverbs of Good Counsel* 69.43–5: And yf thou wylte be owt of sorow and care, Hyt ys to kepe and Refrayne thi tonge, For this lernyth Chyldren when they be yonge. **a1475** Ashby *Dicta* 86.960–1. **a1500** *Quare* 206.401–2. Apperson 571; *Oxford* 439; Smith 258.

V42 One may learn **Virtue** of prudent folk
a1449 Lydgate *Vertu* in *MP* II 835.7–8: Byforn our dayes this proverbe provid was,—Of prudent folk men may vertu leere.

V43 To make (a) **Virtue** of necessity (a need)
c1385 Chaucer *CT* I[A] 3041–2: Thanne is it wysdom, as it thynketh me, To maken vertu of necessitee, *TC* iv 1586–7: Thus maketh vertu of necessite By pacience, **c1395** *CT* V[F] 593: That I made vertu of necessitee. **c1412** Hoccleve *Regement* 46.1252. **a1420** Lydgate *Troy* I 157.464. **1447** Bokenham 31.1125–6. **c1450** Capgrave *Lives* 86.19–20: So of nede thei mad vertue. **c1450** Trevet 169.14–5 (f.35a, col. 1): He made of necessyte wyll. **c1475** Henryson *Testament* 121.478: I counsall the mak vertew of ane neid. **1534** More *Comforte* 1148 F[1–2], 1228 H[5–6]. **a1550** Heywood *BS* 260.49, **1556** *Spider* 34[13]. Apperson 663; *Oxford* 688; Taylor and Whiting 392; Tilley V73; Whiting *Drama* 37, 40, 159, 266, *Scots* II 148.

V44 **Virtue** has no peer
1501 Douglas *Palice* 75.6: Remember than that vertew hes na peir. Cf. Smith 317; Tilley V78, 85.

V45 **Virtue** is in the midst (midward, middle)
c1400 Mandeville *Travels* 1.22–3: Virtus rerum in medio consistit, that is to seye: the vertue of thinges is in the myddes. **1456** Hay *Knychthede* 62.34–5: Vertu is ay in the mydwarde. **1484** Caxton *Ordre of Chyvalry* 56.16–57.1: Vertue and mesure abyde in the myddel of two extremytees. Tilley V80. See **M443, 455.**

V46 **Virtue** is oft hid under low degree
c1395 Chaucer *CT* IV[E] 425–7: And for he saugh that under low degree Was ofte vertu hid, the peple hym heelde A prudent man, and that is seyn ful seelde. See **H3.**

V47 **Virtue** (Thing) is stronger if it be gathered together (*varied*)
c1384 Wyclif *Church and her Members* in *SEW* III 341[22–5]: For as o virtu is strengere if it be gedrid, than if it be scatrid, so o malis is strenger whanne it be gederid in o persone, and it is of lesse strengthe whanne it is departid in manye. **c1395** Chaucer *CT* III[D] 1967–9: What is a ferthyng worth parted in twelve? Lo, ech thyng that is oned in himselve Is moore strong than whan it is toscatered. **a1439** Lydgate *Fall* II 623.1386: For thyng dissevered is menusid of his strengthe. **1484** Caxton *Aesop* 109[17–8]: For vertue whiche is unyed is better than vertue separate. **1521** Fisher *Sermon . . . agayn . . . luuther* in *English Works* 324.8–10: Quia omnis virtus unita fortior est, that is to say, For every vertue that is gadred togyder is more stronger. Cf. *Oxford* 683; Smith 310; Taylor and Whiting 390; Tilley U11. See **H90, R55, T241.**

V48 **Virtue** must have meed
a1400 *Proverbis of Wysdom* (*II*) 222.40: Vertue must have mede.

V49 Who sues (*follows*) **Virtue** shall lere (*learn*) virtue
a1449 Lydgate *Vertu* in *MP* II 835–8.16: W(h)o sueth vertu, vertu he shal leere, 24, 32, *etc.*

V50 Maugre one's **Visage**
c1440 Charles of Orleans 89.2648: Maugre my visage. **c1440** Lydgate *Debate* in *MP* II 557.431: To mete our e(n)myes magre ther visage. **a1470** Malory III 1189.3.

V51 A well favored **Vizor** on an ill favored face
1546 Heywood *D* 59.24–6: Many men wishte, for beautifyng that bryde, Hir waiste to be gyrde in, and for a boone grace, Some well favourd vysor, on hir yll favourd face. Tilley V92.

V52 The common **Voice** may not lie
a1393 Gower *CA* II 8.124: The comun vois, which mai noght lie. See **M309.**

V53 The **Voice** accords to the thought
c1340 Rolle *Psalter* 252 (70.25): In the whilke the voice acordis til the thoght. See **T383.**

V54 The **Voice** of the people is the voice of God
c1412 Hoccleve *Regement* 104.2886: Ffor peples vois is goddes voys, men seyne (Margin: Vox populi vox dei). **a1419** *Letter* in *MLR* 22(1927) 75[9]: Vox populi vox dei. **a1450** Audelay 12 (*between* 65 *and* 66): Vox populi vox Dei. **c1450** *Bishop Boothe* in Wright *Political Poems* II 227[25]: The voyse of the pepille is clepede *vox Dei*. **c1475** *Political Retrospect* in Wright *Political Poems* II 270[15]: The voyx of the peuple, the voix of Jhesu. Apperson 664; S. A. Gallacher in *PQ* 24(1945) 12–9; *Oxford* 688; Taylor and Whiting 392; Tilley V95.

W1 To be worthy one's **Wage**
a1425 *Metrical Paraphrase OT* 18.6243: Thei sayd he was well worthy his wage.

W2 To have more **Wages** than one craves (*i.e.*, to be defeated)
a1475 *Guy*[2] 289.10057–8: For of the they schall have More wageys then they wyll crave.

W3 To pay one his **Wages**
c1421 Lydgate *Thebes* 166.4039–40: And thus the devel for his old outrages, Lich his decert, paied hym his wages. **c1422** Hoccleve *Jereslaus's Wife* 165.725–6: God qwyte yow wole and your wages paye In swich(e) wyse that it yow shal affraye. **a1470** Malory I 311.6–7: Ryght sone shall mete the a knyght that shall pay the all thy wagys. **a1500** *Partenay* 84.2316–7: Iff Any demage don have in contre, Off ther wages thay truly payed be. **c1500** *Melusine* 247.33–4: And doubte you not but I shal pay them wel theire wages. See **H393.**

W4 **Wagging** (Turning) of a straw (rush)
c1385 Chaucer *TC* ii 1744–5: In titeryng, and pursuyte, and delayes, The folk devyne at waggyng of a stree. **a1393** Gower *CA* II 228.83–6: The more I am redy to wraththe, That for . . . the torninge of a stree I wode. **c1516** Skelton *Magnificence* 32.1015: Somtyme I laughe at waggynge of a straw. **1520** Whittinton *Vulgaria* 98.22–3: Suche cowardes . . . be aferde of every waggynge of a strawe. **1525** Berners *Froissart* IV 360[11–2]: Were redy for waggyng of a rysshe to make debate and stryfe. Apperson 665; *Oxford* 689; Tilley W5.

W5 As buxom (*pliable*) as a **Waile** (*?willow*)
c1500 *King Hart* 112.7: Thocht I be quhylum bowsum as ane waile.

W6 A great **Wain** may be overcharged
c1450 Idley 192.2034: Ffor somme tyme a grete wayne a man may overcharge. See **B422, C16, 52, S249, T118.**

W7 A **Wain** may (carry) no more than the fother (*load*)
c1450 *Rylands MS.394* 103.13: Wayne may no mor than the fouther. Justo plus onere plaustrum non debet habere. Walther II 664.13311.

W8 From **Wainfleet** (Lincolnshire) to Wales
1523 Skelton *Garlande* I 410.1218: Fynde no mo suche from Wanflete to Walis.

W9 The **Walking-staff** has caught warmth in your hand
1546 Heywood *D* 38.96: The walkyng staffe hath caught warmth in your hand. Apperson 665; Tilley W11.

W10 As close as any **Wall** (*etc.*) (A number of single quotations are brought together here)
a1420 Lydgate *Troy* III 631.2298: Al-be thei kepte hem clos as any wal, 842.2436: And he, ful sobre, stood stille as a wal, **a1439** *Fall* II 671.3081: He stood ay stable, upriht as a wall. **a1500** *Thre Prestis* 52.1249: Suppose thay be als wicht (*strong*) as ony wall.

W11 As constant as a **Wall**
c1395 Chaucer *CT* IV[E] 1047: And she ay . . . constant as a wal. **1420** Lydgate *Temple* 48.1153: Feithful in hert and constant as a walle, **a1422** *Life* 417.1509. Whiting *Scots* II 149.

W12 As pale as any **Wall**
1513 Douglas *Aeneid* II 182.56: Hir vissage wolx als pail as ony wall. Whiting *Scots* II 149.

W13 As sad (*firm*) as a **Wall**
c1395 Chaucer *CT* IV[E] 1047: And she ay sad . . . as a wal. **c1395** *WBible* Judith v 12: The watris weren maad sad as wallis.

W14 As stable as a **Wall**
a1400 Wyclif *Sermons* II 259[1–2]: The passing thourgh the Reed see and stondinge stable as a walle. **c1433** Lydgate *St. Edmund* 380.211: Stable, as a wal, of herte in thi constaunce, 420.390: Stable as a wal he stood in his degre.

W15 As steadfast as a **Wall**
a1400 *Romaunt B* 5250: And founde hym stedefast as a wall. **c1408** Lydgate *Reson* 162.6184: But stedfaster than ys a wal, **a1420** *Troy* III 836.2227, **a1439** *Fall* II 604.701, **1439** *St. Albon* 129.91.

W16 As stiff as any **Wall**
a1420 Lydgate *Troy* II 441.1634: But on his stede, stif as any wal. Whiting *Scots* II 149.

W17 As strong as a **Wall**
a1420 Lydgate *Troy* II 434.1389: He was so strong . . . as a wal. **a1513** Dunbar *No Tressour* 149.39: Strang as ony wall, *Tabill* 165.73: Nocht being strong as wall. Whiting *Scots* II 149.

W18 As sturdy as a **Wall**
a1420 Lydgate *Troy* I 133.4084: Duke Nestor firste, sturdy as a wal, 352.7270, II 434.1389, III 644.2733.

W19 One can (go) no further than the **Wall**
1478 Paston V 314[27–8]: I can no ferther then the walle. **1528** More *Heresyes* 187 D[14–6]: I am in this matter even at the harde wall, and se not how to go further. **1546** Heywood *D* 75.178–9: That deede without woords shall drive him to the wall. And further than the wall he can not go, **1555** *E* 169.129. Apperson 241; *Oxford* 231; Tilley W12.

W20 Spurn (Winch [*kick*]) (not) against the **Wall**
c1475 Henryson *Testament* 121.475–6: Quhy spurnis thow aganis the Wall, To sla thy self, and mend nathing at all? *Abbay Walk* 195.30: Spurn nocht thy fute aganis the wall. **1546** Heywood *D* 72.87–9: Foly it is . . . to winche or kicke Against the hard wall, **1555** *E* 191.254: Folly to spurne or kycke ageynst the harde wall, **1556** *Spider* 363[5]: I se what it is : to spurne against the wall. Whiting *Scots* II 149. See **C553, P377.**

W21 To be driven to the **Wall**
1529 More *Supplicacion* 319 E[10–1]: Drieven up to the harde walle, **1533** *Confutacion* 530 A[4–5]: He is drieven to the harde walle. **1546** Heywood *D* 75.178: That deede without woords shall drive him to the wall. Tilley W15.

W22 To beleave (*stand fast*) as a **Wall**
a1300 *Alisaunder* 131.2324: He bilaved so a walle. See **W25.**

W23 To hold like a **Wall**
a1338 Mannyng *Chronicle A* I 163.4657: Als a wal the scheltrom held.

W24 To remove no more than a strong **Wall**
a1533 Berners *Huon* 186.30–1: He removed no more for the stroke then it had ben a strong walle. See **M564, 726, R161, S792.**

W25 To stand like a **Wall**
c1175 *Lambeth Homilies* 141[6–8]: The see . . . ther stod a richt halve and a luft, alse an castel wal. **c1300** *South English Legendary* I 197.498: The lye of the vur stod up anhey as it a wal wer. **a1325** *Cursor* III 1482.26022: That stud bi-tuix us als a wal. **a1325** *XV Signa* in Heuser 104. 117–8: Al the see sal draw ifere, As a walle to stond upright. **c1390** *Castel of Love* 403. 1525–6: The furst day the see up ryse shall And stonden on hye as a wall. **c1390** *Corpus Christi* in *Vernon* I 169.25: The see stod up-riht as a wal. **c1400** *Alexander Buik* IV 404.9951–2: And stude on ilk syde as ane wall Quhill his men passed all. **a1415** Mirk *Festial* 2.31: Stondyng styll yn her styd, as hit wer a wall. **a1420** Lydgate *Troy* III 680.3946: For Grekis stood as a sturdy wal. **a1425** *Metrical Paraphrase OT* 55.1841: The watur stud upe ose a walle. **a1450** *South English Legendary* (*Bodley*) 310.168. **a1450** *York Plays* 90.379–80: On aythir syde the see sall stande, Tille we be wente, right as a wall. **c1450** *Myroure of oure Ladye* 35.26: The water stode up as a walle. **c1458** *Knyghthode and Bataile* 66.1815–6: These as a wal to make resistence Ay stille stode, 67.1824: For these stille abide as doth a wal. **a1460** *Towneley Plays* 76.390–1. Whiting *Drama* 331:350. See **S793, W22.**

W26 To take no more heed than the **Wall**
a1393 Gower *CA* III 431.1672–3: Bot he nomore than the wal Tok hiede of eny thing he herde. See **T519.**

W27 The **Walls** make not the strong castle
1489 Caxton *Fayttes* 143.14–6: For as a proverbe saith, The walles maken not the stronge castelles, but the deffense of good folke maketh hit imprenable. *Oxford* 419; Tilley M555. See **C70, T436.**

W28 Not a **Walsh-nut** (*walnut*) the wiser
c1405 *Mum* 37.349: But I was not the wiser by a Walsh note.

W29 As wise as **Waltham's** calf

c1522 Skelton *Colyn* I 342.811: As wyse as Waltoms calfe. **1546** Heywood *D* 65.14: And thinke me as wise as Walthams calfe. Apperson 696; *Oxford* 717; Tilley W22. See **C8.**

W30 As pliant as a **Wand**
a1420 Lydgate *Troy* I 215.2472: His slepy yerde, plyaunt as a wonde.

W31 As small as **Wands**
a1508 Dunbar *Goldyn Targe* 114.63: And mydlis small as wandis. Tilley W23; Whiting *Scots* II 149.

W32 As weak as the (any, a) **Wand**
a1400 *Seven Penitential Psalms* in *Wheatley MS.* 28.212: I wexe weyk as is the wonde. **a1450** *York Plays* 138.17: I waxe wayke as any wande. **c1475** Henryson *Ressoning* 179.13: ony. **a1513** Dunbar *To The Quene* 60.22: Ar nou maid waek lyk willing wandis. Whiting *Scots* II 149.

W33 As writhing (*bending*) as a **Wand**
c1300 *Body and Soul* 49 L 359: That ay was writhinde as a wond.

W34 To bow like a **Wand**
c1450 Idley 95.866: Be stronge in herte, bow not as a wande.

W35 Writhe (*twist*) the **Wand** while it is green
1464 Hardyng 181[17]: Wherfore writhe nowe (the wand while it) is grene. *Oxford* 653; Tilley W27; Whiting *Scots* II 149. See **O11, P251, Y4.**

W36 In the (wild) **Waniand** (wanion [*waning moon*])
a1352 Minot 31.25: It was in the waniand that thai furth went, 33.6: It was in the waniand that thai come thare. **a1450** *York Plays* 36.45: Whythir now in wilde waneand, 124.37: In the wanyand, 319.389: Nowe walkis on in the wanyand, 336.485: Furth in the wylde wanyand be walkand. **a1460** *Towneley Plays* 15.226: In the wenyand wist ye now at last, 129.405: Now walk in the Wenyand, 227.748, 290.339: Whistyll ye in the wenyande! 310.144. **1519** Horman *Vulgaria* 413[3]: Pycke the hens in the wanyon. Apage te in malam rem. NED Waniand, Wanion; Whiting *Drama* 369:939. See **C557.**

W37 After **War** peace is good (*varied*)
a1338 Mannyng *Chronicle A* I 406.11595–8: After werre, god ys pes; And after wo, the wele god ches; In pes ys don gret vasselage; Ffor love men doth gret outrage. **a1450** *Generydes B* 29.898: After this werr . . . god send us pece. Whiting *Drama* 268. See **B67, P67, S69.**

W38 Hard is the **War** where none escape (*varied*)
c1450 *Ponthus* 130.1–2: And harde is the werre, wher as noon escapes. **1546** Heywood *D* 54.434: A hard foughten feeld, where no man skapth unkyld. Apperson 285; *Oxford* 278; Tilley F207.

W39 In **War** some win and some lose (*varied*)
a1300 *Alisaunder* 93–5.1657–8: Men mote bothe wynne and lese—Chaunce ne lete(th) noman chese. **a1338** Mannyng *Chronicle* A I 225. 6399–400: Hit ys ther chaunce that werre bygynne, Umwhile to lese, umwhile to wynne, 335.9583–4: Hit ys custume that werre bygynne, Somme to lese, and somme to wynne. **c1375** Barbour *Bruce* I 312–3.373–4: For in punyeis (*combats*) is oft hapnyne Quhill for to vyne, and quhill to tyne. **c1400** *Alexander Buik* II 244. 4877–8: It fallis in weir quhilis to tyne, And for to wyn ane uthir syne. **c1400** Gower *Peace* III 489.290: The fortune of the werre is evere unknowe. **a1420** Lydgate *Troy* I 180.1245–6: And werre also stant in aventure, For ay of Marte dotous is the Ewre, 202.1995–6: By the chaunge and the variance Of werre and strif, that ever is in balance. **c1420** Wyntoun VI 117.5329–30: And qwhilis tuk, and qwhilis war tane; For ure of were is noucht ay ane. **a1439** Lydgate *Fall* II 597.441: Ther losse, ther wynnyng callid fortune of werre. **a1450** *Generydes B* 95.2989: This day was therys, A nother shalbe ourez. **c1450** *Merlin* I 184[27–8]: And some tyme he wan, and many tymes he loste, as is the fortune of werre, 188[19–20]. **1469** *Plumpton Correspondence* lxxiv[25]: The event of war is dubious (*modernized spellings*). **1471** Caxton *Recuyell* I 162.15–7: Warre gyveth this day victorie to oon and on the morn taketh hit away and gyveth hit to a nother And so putteth eche out, **1490** *Eneydos* 11.22–5: Knowyng to-fore that the advenements and adversitees of warre be doubtous, and under the honde of fortune, the whiche, after his mutabylite, gyveth vyctorye. **c1500** *King Hart* 111.4: For armes hes both happie tyme and chance. **1523** Berners *Froissart* II 265[14–6]: Some day wanne and some day loste, as the adventures of warre often tymes falleth, nowe up, nowe downe, **1525** IV 302[13–4]: So it goth by the warre. Tilley C223; Whiting *Drama* 39, 271, 284, 291, *Froissart* 308:227, *Scots* II 149–50. See **B65, F139, 533, V8, 32, W183.**

W40 Many cry "**War!** war!" who wot little to what war amounts
c1390 Chaucer *CT* VII 1038[B2228]: Ther is ful many a man that crieth "Werre! werre!" that woot ful litel what werre amounteth. Cf. Tilley W56, 57. See **R156.**

W41 **War** at the beginning has a great entering (entry)
c1390 Chaucer *CT* VII 1039–40[B2229–30]: Werre at his bigynnyng hath so greet an entryng and so large, that every wight may entre whan hym liketh, and lightly fynde werre; but certes what ende that shal therof bifalle, it is nat light to knowe. **a1533** Berners *Huon* 312.21–3: I have herd often tymes sayd that the entre into warre is large but the issuynge out ther of is very strayte. See **E131.**

W42 **War** is dreadful, virtuous peace is good
a1449 Lydgate *Praise of Peace* in *MP* II 791. 169–70: Al werre is dreedful, vertuous pees is good, Striff is hatful, pees douhtir of plesaunce. See **P68.**

W43 Be **Ware** and wise
c1450 *Foly of Fulys* 65.476: Be war and wyss.

W44 Be **Ware** betime
a1500 *How the Wyse Man* 29.41: Therfore, sone, be war be tyme. See **W46.**

W45 Be **Ware** ere you be woe (wreak)
1381 *John the Miller* in Charles Mackay *Collection of Songs and Ballads* (PS 4[1841]) 2[3–5]: Beware or be ye wo! Know your friend from your foe, Haveth ynough and saith hoe! **a1393** Gower *CA* II 65.1073–6: I finde a gret experience, Wherof to take an evidence Good is, and to be war also Of the peril, er him be wo. **a1400** *Harley MS.116* in Greene *Carols* p. 420: He ys wyse that can be ware er he be wo; He ys wyse that can do well and say also; He ys wyse that can ber yeve betwene frend and foo; He ys wys that hath inoghth and can say "Hoo"; He ys wyse that (hath) on wyffe and wol no moo. **a1400** *Harley MS.2316* in *Rel. Ant.* II 120[33–6]: He is wys that kan be war or him be wo; He is wys that lovet his frend and ek his fo; He is wys that havet i-now and kan seyn, "ho!" He is wys that kan don wel, and doeth al so. **a1400** *Hereford Cath. MS. O iv 14* in Brown *Register* I 446: Hee is wys that is ware here hym be wo; Hee is wys that con say wel and deth also; Hee is wys that hath ynowgh and kon say hoo. **a1400** *Proverbis of Wysdom* 245.62: And be ware, ore thou be wreke. **a1400** *Siege of Jerusalem* 64.1103–4: For he is wise, that is war, or hym wo hape, And with falsede a-fer is fairest to dele. **1418** *Man, be warre* in Kail 60–4.8: Eche man be war, er hym be wo, 16, 24, *etc.* **a1450** Audelay 11.42–3: He has wysdam and wyt, I tel yow trewly, That can be ware or he be wo, 140.218: In wele be ware or thou be wo, 182.1. **c1450** Greene *Carols* 338.3, 355 *refrain.* **c1475** Henryson *Fables* 63.1789: Wo is him can not bewar in tyme. **a1500** *Proverbs of Salamon* 179.18.1–2: That folowyth counseyle of hys frende He may be war or hym be woo. **a1500** *Who so off welth* in Dyboski 139.8: He ys wyse that ys ware or he harm fele. **c1500** *King Hart* 110.1. **1506** *Kalender* 66.14–5: But well were he that ware so wyse, That coude be ware or he be wo, 66.24. Tilley T291, W196; Whiting *Scots* II 142, 150. See **W145, 389.**

W46 It is good to be **Ware** afore
a1450 *Partonope* 125.3646: Hytt ys gode afore to be warys. See **W44, 392.**

W47 Who will not be **Ware** by other men, by him shall other men be corrected (*varied*)
c1395 Chaucer *CT* III[D] 180–3: Whoso that nyl be war by othere men, By hym shul othere men corrected be. The same wordes writeth Ptholomee; Rede in his Almageste, and take it there. **a1439** Lydgate *Fall* I 202.99–100: Who is nat war bi othres chastisyng, Othre bi hym shal chastised be. **c1450** Capgrave *Katharine* 149–51.1155–65: Ffor thus he wryteth, the Astronomer tholome: "Ho-so wil not doo as his neybour(s) werke, Ne wil not be war be hem whan thei doo amys, Of hym shul othere men bothe carpe and berke, And sey, beholde this man, loo he it is—Whether he doo weel or wheder he doo other-wys, He wyl non example of other men I-take, Exaumple to other men he shal be for that sake. Alle othere men shul be war by hym, Ffor thei shul see and fele in hemselve That his werkys were bothe deerke and dym." Skeat 263. See **C161, E197, F116, 449, L247, M170, 581, S428, W391.**

W48 To sit **Warm**
c1385 Chaucer *TC* iii 1630: Be naught to rakel, theigh thow sitte warme. **c1450** *How the Wyse Man* 40.113–4: And, sonne, if thou be weel at eese And warme amonge thi neighboris sitte.

W49 He that is **Warned** before is not beguiled (*varied*)
c1250 *Owl* 104.1223–6: For Alfred seide a wis word, Euch mon hit schulde legge on hord: "Yef thu isihst (er) he beo icume, His str(e)ncthe is him wel neh binume." **a1393** Gower *CA* III 297.2344–5: For him thar noght be reson pleigne, That warned is er him be wo. **c1425** Arderne *Fistula* 22.15: For he that is warned afore is noght bygiled, 30.8–9. **c1450** *Epistle of Othea* 134.17: He never is disceyved that warned is beforne. **a1471** Ashby *Policy* 37.770: He that is warned is not deceived. **a1475** *Turne up hur halter* in *Rel. Ant.* I 76[44]: If a man be warnyd

he ys wele at ese. **c1475** *Rawlinson MS. D 328* 120.33: He that ys fore-warnyd ys not be-gelide. **a1500** *Egerton MS.1995* in Robbins-Cutler 1152.5: He that is befor tyme warned, Litill or nowght is hurte or harmyd. **a1500** Hill 128.15: He that is warned beffore, is not begiled, 132.52: He that is warned ys half armed. **a1500** Medwall *Nature* F3ᵛ[2–3]: I am glad ye warn me thus in seson, I shalbe the better ware. **c1523** Barclay *Mirrour* 26[36]: One threatned (as is saide) halfe armed is and sure. **1546** Heywood *D* 80.73: Halfe warnd halfe armde. Apperson 230, 279; *Oxford* 220; Taylor and Whiting 144; Tilley H 54. See **M111, 305, 338, S845.**

W50 As angry as a **Wasp**
c1500 *Wife Lapped* 194.340: And as angry y wis as ever was waspe. **a1529** Skelton *Elynour* I 105.330: Angry as a waspy. **1546** Heywood *D* 42.28: Angry as a waspe. Apperson 668; *Oxford* 11; Tilley W76.

W51 As woe as a **Wasp**
c1420 Wyntoun V 345.2659–60: Fra he herde his men slayne swa, Was never in warlde a waspe (*vars.* wyf, wy) sa wa.

W52 As wroth as a **Wasp**
a1400 *Alexander C* 32.738: As wrath as (a) waspe. Apperson 668; *Oxford* 11.

W53 To sting like a **Wasp**
c1516 Skelton *Magnificence* 24.730: I stynge lyke a waspe.

W54 He that of **Waste** takes no heed shall want when he has need
a1500 *Hunterian Mus. MS.230* 175: He that of wast takys no hede, He schall wante whenne he hasse nede. Taylor and Whiting 394.

W55 Not (a)vail a **Wastel** (*loaf of bread*)
c1400 *Laud Troy* II 406.13796: But that vayled hem not a wastel. **c1450** Idley 96.885: All vaileth not worth a wastell.

W56 To bear **Wat's** pack
c1485 *Mary Magdalene* (*Digby*) 99.1154: For, be my feyth, thou (*a fat man*) beryst wattes pakke. **a1500** *Remedie of Love* CCCXXIIᵛ[2.22]: But wattes packe we bare all by and by (*are deceived*). Whiting *Scots* II 150.

W57 **Watch** (Ward) and ward (watch)
a1393 Gower *CA* III 8.2240–2: Thei gredily Ne maken thanne warde and wacche, Wher thei the profit mihten cacche. **1471** Caxton *Recuyell* I 94.1–2: Ye do kepe yow wyth good wacche and warde. **c1500** *Lady Bessy* 13[15]: Bid him lay away watch and ward. **1523** Berners *Froissart* III 434[10]: They stode styll kepynge watche and warde. NED Watch sb. 7.

W58 As mickle as **Water** in the sea (*varied*)
c1300 *Havelok* 78.2341–3: And of wyn, that men far fetes, Riht al so mikel and gret plenté So it were water of the se. **a1500** *Stations* 360. 359–64: There is more pardone, I telle the, Than is all the water in the se Or gresse or gravell onne the ground, Or sterrys be in the sky so rounde Or motys be in the sone, Sen the werld was fyrst begone. See **D409.**

W59 As unstable as (the) **Water**
a1400 Wyclif *Sermons* I 42[33–4]: So pride of worldly goodis, that ben unstable as the watir, 53[7], 92[19]: Thei weren unstable as water, II 10[22–3]: This Emperour . . . was unstable as watir. *Oxford* 683; Tilley W86. See **S107.**

W60 As **Water** quenches fire so alms quenches sin (*varied*)
c1000 Aelfric *Homilies* II 106[5–7]: Seo ælmysse ure synna lig adwæscte, swa swa hit awriten is, "Swa swa wæter adwæscð fyr, swa adwæscð seo ælmysse synna." **c1000** *Dominica Prima* in R. Morris *Old English Homilies, First Series* (EETS 34, 1868) 37–9: For þa boc seið, *Sicut aqua extinguit ignem, ita et elemosina extinguit peccatum.* Al swa þet water acwencheð þet fur, swa þe elmesse acwencheð þa sunne. **c1000** *Larspell* in Napier 238.3–6: Forðan hit is geræd and gecweden on halgum bocum, ðæt, swa swa wæter adwæsceð fyr, swa adwæsceð seo ælmesse þa synne. **c1303** Mannyng *Handlyng* 227. 7079–80: Almes fordoth alle wykkednes, And quenchyth synne. **c1395** *WBible* Ecclesiasticus iii 33: Watir quenchith fier brennynge, and almes ayenstondith synnes. **1483** Caxton *Golden Legende* 89ᵛ[1.34–6]: And almesse quenchyth synne as the water quencheth the fyre. **a1500** *Thre Prestis* 54.1319–20: For as thow seis watter dois slokkin fyre, Sa do I, Almos deid, the Judges ire. **c1500** ?Bradshaw *Radegunde* 10[16–7]: Suche frayle concupiscence of love entyre Soone seased as water quencheth the fyre. **1513** Bradshaw *St. Werburge* 73.1923–5: The naturall mocyon of his lascyvyte Was shortly slaked . . . By myracle, as water quencheth the fyre. **1533** More *Confutacion* 529 H[7–9]: As the water quencheth fyre, so doth almes dede avoyde sinne, 667 A[8–10]. Apperson 9; Whiting *Drama* 331:353. See **O19.**

W61 As weary as **Water** in wore (*?sandy shore*) (*etc.*) (A number of single quotations are brought together here)
a1325 *Alysoun* 139.30: Wery so water in wore.

a1387 Higden-Trevisa I 123[8]: Cleer as water. **c1390** *Mary and the Cross* 618.224: Softer then watur under serk, 227–9. **c1395** *WBible* Joshua vii 5: And the herte of the puple dredde, and was maad unstidefast at the licnesse of watir. **a1400** Wyclif *Sermons* II 139[15–6]: For wymmen ben freel as water, and taken souner printe of bileve. **c1400** *Tundale* 61.1049–50: Some of hem thai made as nesche (*soft*), As is the water, that is fresche.

W62 As welcome as **Water** into the ship
1520 Whittinton *Vulgaria* 88.18: He is as welcome to many of us as water into the shyppe. Apperson 669; *Oxford* 695; Tilley W89.

W63 Believe not still standing **Water**
1492 *Salomon and Marcolphus* 11[19–20]: The stylle standyng watyr and the man that spekyth but lytyll beleve thaym not. *Oxford* 43: Beware; Tilley M78. See **W70.**

W64 Foul **Water** will quench hot fire as soon as fair
1546 Heywood *D* 27.42: Foule water as soone as fayre, will quenche hot fyre. Apperson 232; *Oxford* 222; Tilley W92; Whiting *Scots* II 151.

W65 He that fears to take the **Water** shall never come over
1519 Horman *Vulgaria* 363[5–6]: If thou fere to take the water as longe as the see ebbeth and floweth thou shalt never come over. See **T298.**

W66 It is bad **Water** that cannot allay dust
c1515 Barclay *Eclogues* 78.705: It is bad water that can not allay dust. Cf. Jente 687.

W67 Like **Water** over the goose's back
1533 More *Confutacion* 756 D[13–6]: This tale . . . goeth fayre and smothe by a mannes eare, as the water goeth over the gooses backe, *Debellacyon* 962 G[1–2]: Yet goeth ever thys water over this gooses backe. Apperson 169: duck; *Oxford* 695: duck; Taylor and Whiting 395: duck.

W68 Much **Water** goes by the mill that the miller knows not of
1546 Heywood *D* 77.251–2: And thus though much water goeth by the myll, That the miller knowth not of. Apperson 417; *Oxford* 694; Tilley W99.

W69 Still **Water** oft breaks the staithe (*shore*)
c900 *Old English Cato* 6.16–7: Oft stille wæter staðe brecað. See **D412.**

W70 Still **Waters** run deep (*varied*)
c1390 *Cato* (*Vernon*) 604.579–80: Ther water is most deope, The lasse ther then steres he. **a1400** *Cato* (*Copenhagen*) B4v[7–8]: Ffor ful smothe watyr sumtyme is depe, And evyl to passe, who so wyl take kepe. **a1400** *Cato* (*Fairfax*) in *Cursor* III 1672.238–9: Ther the flode is deppist The water standis stillist. **a1410** Lydgate *Churl* in *MP* II 476.184: Smothe watres beth oft-sithis deepe, **a1439** *Fall* II 544.2586–7: In cristal watres that calm and smothe bee Arn pereillous pettis of decepcioun. **a1440** Burgh *Cato* 30.1050: In floodis stille is watir deep and hihe. **1532** Berners *Golden Boke* 325.6784–5: In depe stylle waters the pilote feareth more than in the greate hye wawes. Apperson 602–3; *Oxford* 621; Taylor and Whiting 394; Tilley W123. See **S114, W63.**

W71 Stolen **Waters** (drink) are (is) sweeter
a1382 *WBible* Proverbs ix 17: Stoln watris ben swettere, and hid bred more swete. **a1500** *Remedie of Love* CCCXXIIIv[2.22–8]: Moche swetter, she saith, and more acceptable Is drinke when it is stollen prively Than when it is taken in forme avowable, Bread hid and gotten jeoperdouslie Must nedes be swete, and semblablie Venison stolne is aie the swetter, The ferther the narower fet the better. Apperson 603; Jente 379; *Oxford* 622; Tilley B626, W131. See **M264.**

W72 There was no more **Water** than the ship drew
1546 Heywood *D* 90.58: There was no more water than the ship drew. Tilley W104.

W73 To burn **Waters**
c1405 *Mum* 71.1529–30: And braggeth and bosteth and wol brenne watiers, And rather renne in rede blode thenne a-rere oones. Cf. Taylor and Whiting 307–8: River.

W74 To fall down like **Water**
a1400 *Orologium* 360.14–5: We alle dyen, as water fallith downe into the erthe that turneth not ayen. **c1400** *Laud Troy* II 498.16912–3: Echon on other dong and thresched, That thei fel doun as water fro yse. **a1425** *Bird with Four Feathers* in Brown *Lyrics XIV* 215.215–6: It fel hym fro, and that scharply As dede the water owt of the flood.

W75 To find **Water** in the sea
1528 More *Heresyes* 220 G[1–3]: He that shoulde . . . studye for that, shoulde studye where to fynde water in the see. Tilley W113.

W76 To flow like **Water** (*etc.*) (A number of single quotations are brought together here)
a900 *Old English Martyrology* 114.24–5: þæt

blod fleow of hire þæm merwan lichoman swa wæter of æspringe. **c1250** *Genesis and Exodus* 29.1017–8: So malt that mete in hem to nogt, So a watres drope in a fier brogt. **a1300** *Maximian* 97.151: Ich walke as water in wore (*?sandy shore*). **c1340** Rolle *Psalter* 291 (78.3): Thai spilt thaire blode as watire. **c1380** *Pearl* 22.607–8: He laves hys gyftes as water of dyche, Other gotes of golf that never charde. **c1386** Chaucer *LGW* 851–2: The blod out of the wounde as brode sterte As water, whan the condit broken is. **c1390** *Sir Gawain* 68.2203: Hit wharred and whette, as water at a mulne. **c1395** *WBible* Hosea v 10: Y schal schede out on hem my wraththe as watir. **a1475** *Mergarete* 240.458–9: Tyll sche suete (*sweated*), flessch and fell, As it wer water oute of a well.

W77 To lay a **Water**
1402 *Daw Topias* 43[9–12]: But, Jak, though thi questions Semen to thee wyse, Yit lightly a lewid man Maye leyen hem a water. **c1412** Hoccleve *Regement* 41.1123–7: Men Yerne and desiren after muk so sore, That they good fame han leyd a watir yore, And rekken never how longe it ther stipe, Or thogh it drenche, so thei good may gripe. **1546** Heywood *D* 24.62–3: The proverbes, which I before them did lay, The triall thereof we will lay a water, **1555** *E* 166. 127: My matter is leyde a water, thats a false tale: Thy matters lie not in water, they lie in ale. Apperson 354; Tilley W108.

W78 To look to (see) one's **Water**
a1376 *Piers* A ii 199–200: This leornden this leches and lettres him senden For to wone with hem watres to loke. **a1387** Higden-Trevisa III 217[2–4]: I wolde a wiseman hadde (y-seie) his water, and i-held it in his throte they it were a galoun. **1546** Heywood *D* 50.302: By my faith you come to looke in my water. *Oxford* 384; Tilley W109.

W79 To run like **Water**
a1200 *St. Juliana* 67.722–3: This worlt went awei as the weater the eorneth. **a1300** *Arthour and M.*[1] 149.5295–6: That the blod ran in the valaie, So water out of a laie, 170.6055–8: For the blod . . . Ran . . . So water out of wel streme. **c1300** *Havelok* 61.1850–1: For the blod ran of his sides So water that fro the welle glides. **c1300** *South English Legendary* I 295.120: Bi stremes that blod orn adoun so water doth of welle, (*Laud*) 197.121: Strong fuyr thare can eornen out ase water doth of welle. **c1330** *St. Mergrete* 229.127: The blod ran of hir flesche, as water doth fram clive. **a1338** Mannyng *Chronicle A* II 484.13975: The blod ran ther as water stremes. **c1350** *Libeaus* 68.1217–8: As water doth of clive, Of him ran the blod. **a1400** *Morte Arthure* 17.540: No more (gyffes) of wyne than of watyre, That of the welle rynnys. **c1400** *Laud Troy* I 313.10612: The blod ran doun as water of welles. **a1410** Love *Mirrour* 20[26]: Bot renneth out as water. **1447** Bokenham 16.577–8: That lyk as watyr in a ryver So ran hyr blood owt plenteuously. **a1475** *Guy*[2] 337.11724: The blode ranne down, as watur on welle. **1481** Caxton *Godeffroy* 172.30–1: Lyke as water renneth in the see, cam fro alle partes grete rowtes and merveyllous plente of peple. **a1500** *St. Kateryne* 262.179–80: (*Blood*) rane downe on hur lyche Os watur dothe on the dyche.

W80 To waste (cast) **Water** in the Thames (sea) (*varied*)
c1378 *Piers* B xv 331–2: And who so filled a tonne of a fresshe ryver, And went forth with that water to woke (*dilute*) with Themese. **a1475** Ashby *Dicta* 92.1097–9: And who that to (un)nedy wolbe graunting, Is not accepted as for man witty, As wastyng water in the see, gilty. **1509** Barclay *Ship* I 166[3–5]: As great fole, as is that wytles wratche That wolde . . . in the se cast water, thynkynge it to augment. **1546** Heywood *D* 48.247–8: It is, to geve him, as muche almes or neede As cast water in tems. Apperson 84; *Oxford* 695; Tilley W106. See **F430.**

W81 To weep as one would writhe (*turn*) to **Water**
c1300 *St. Alexius* 187.570–1: With goulinge, and with rewfull grate, Als scho wald all to watir writhe (*var.* Scho fore als scho to water wald wryth). **a1350** *Ywain* 60.2235–6: Sum tyme, he saw, thai weped all Als thai wald to water fall, 79.2975–6. **c1385** Chaucer *TC* iii 115: And Pandare wep as he to water wolde. **a1393** Gower *CA* III 374.5018. **a1395** Chaucer *CT* V[F] 496. **a1420** Lydgate *Troy* I 257.3926, **c1433** *St. Edmund* 388.629.

W82 To wite (*go away*) like **Water**
c970 *Blickling Homilies* 59[19–20]: Ealle þa gewitað . . . swa swa wæteres stream. **c1300** *Northern Homily Cycle* (*Edin. Coll. Phys.*) 124[1–2]: That es at sai, til werldes play, That als water wites awai.

W83 **Water** and fire are contrarious (repugnant)
c1385 Usk 66–7.59–60: Water and fyr, that ben contrarious, mowen nat togider ben assembled.

c1523 Barclay *Mirrour* 24[39]: But are playne repugnaunt as water against fire. Tilley F246, W110. See **F183.**

W84 The **Water** shall not be blamed if a man drench (*drown*) himself
a1393 Gower *CA* III 355.4276–9: For if a man himself excite To drenche, and wol it noght forbere, The water schal no blame bere. What mai the gold, thogh men coveite? See **S892.**

W85 **Water** that stirs not (rests too much) stinks
a1200 *Ancrene* 216.19–20: Weater the ne stureth naw readliche stinketh. **1489** *Governayle* A7ʳ[2–3]: For why when water resteth to moche it stynketh. Cf. Tilley W103.

W86 **Water** through (in) a sieve (*varied*)
c1450 Idley 165.423: But lete it passe lightlie, as water thorow a seve. **c1475** *Rawlinson MS. D 328* 124.74: He that lurnyth with-out buckys drayt whater with a seyve. **c1475** *What Profiteth* in Brown *Lyrics XV* 288.1–2: Long wilbe, water in a welle to keche, A vessell made of yerdis that wil nat holde. **c1477** Norton *Ordinall* 17[1–2]: Else all their laboure shall them let and greive, As he that fetcheth Water in a Sive. **1509** Barclay *Ship* I 245[4]: It goeth through them as water trough a syve, **c1515** *Eclogues* 45.1231–2: And so such thinges which princes to thee geve, To thee be as sure as water in a sive. Apperson 669; *Oxford* 694–5; Tilley W111.

W87 Whoso is scalded with hot **Water** doubts (*fears*) hot water the more
c1400 *Vices and Virtues* 114.16–7: Who-so is y-scalded with hote watre, he dowteth the more hot watre. Cf. Tilley C163, 297. See **C201.**

W88 To stink like **Water-dogs**
a1300 *Alisaunder* 301.5762: And stynken as water-dogges.

W89 To fare like **Water-froth**
a1500 *For Old Acquaintance Sake* in Robbins 134.22: Hit farys as dothe the watter-frothe.

W90 As brown as the **Water-leech**
a1475 Russell *Boke* 176.874: His shon or slyppers as browne as is the watur-leche.

W91 The **Water-leech** has two daughters
c1395 *WBible* Proverbs xxx 15: The watir leche hath twei doughtris, seiynge, Brynge, bringe. *Oxford* 130.

W92 To clap like a **Water-mill**
c1400 *Beryn* 90.3005: Geffrey evir clappid, as doith a watir myll. See **M557.**

W93 As wrathful as **Waves** of the wild sea
a1500 *Alexander C* 189 Dublin 3167–8: Wrathfull . . . As wawes of the wild see when wynd thaim distrobles.

W94 To quap (*beat*) like the **Waves**
c1386 Chaucer *LGW* 865: And lik the wawes quappe gan hire herte. **a1420** Lydgate *Troy* I 93.2745: Amyd hir herte, quappyng as a wawe.

W95 To swim between two **Waves**
1523 Berners *Froissart* III 121[11–2]: Thus he swamme bitwene two waves, makyng himselfe newter, as nere as coulde. Whiting *Scots* II 151: Water (8).

W96 To walter (*surge*) like **Waves** in the wind
c1485 *Mary Magdalene* (*Digby*) 86.819: In woo I waltyr, as wawys In the wynd!

W97 As brockle (*brittle*) as **Wax**
c1300 *Northern Homily Cycle* (*Edin. Coll. Phys.*) 154[12]: For fleys es brokel als wax, and neys.

W98 As nesh (*soft*) as **Wax**
a1400 *Scottish Legends* I 104.265–6: And the stane, quhen he lad was ther, Wex nesch as it wax war.

W99 As tough as the **Wax**
a1500 *Eger H* 233.837: Teugh as the wax when it was wrought. **a1511** Guylforde *Pylgrymage* 54[10]: Toughe as wex.

W100 As treatable (easy) as **Wax**
1340 *Ayenbite* 94[32]: Tretable ase wex ymered. **c1400** *Vices and Virtues* 93.8: Esy as wex tempred. **1484** Caxton *Royal Book* H7ʳ[3–4]: Traytable lyke waxe chauffed. Cf. Tilley W135.

W101 As yellow as (any, the) **Wax**
a1300 *Alisaunder* 323.6112: And teeth hadden yelewe as wax, 343.6450: So yelough so wexe ben her visages. **c1330** *Degare* 106.785–6: Bothe his berd and his fax Was crisp an yhalew as ani wax. **c1350** *Libeaus* 10.139: His berd was yelow as wax. **c1387–95** Chaucer *CT* I[A] 675. **c1390** *God man and the devel* 335.247: the. **c1400** *Florence* 52.1543–4: the. **c1400** *Laud Troy* II 460.15616. **a1450** Macer 194.9. **a1500** *Inter Diabolus et Virgo* 444.21: the, 445.41: the.

W102 To burn like **Wax** (*etc.*) (A number of single quotations are brought together here)
a800 *Christ* in *Exeter Book* 30.988: Byrneth wæter swa weax. **a1050** Defensor *Liber* 169[3–4]: He byð toslopen (*dissolved*) swa wex fram ansyne fyres. **a1300** *Richard* 220.2577–8: Ffor non armour withstood his ax, No more than a knyff dos the wax, 253.3163–4, 431–2.6865–6: For theyr armure fared as waxe Ayenst Kynge

Rychardes axe. **c1300** *South English Legendary* II 525.290: Ac neschede (*became soft*) as wex aye(n) the fur. **c1375** *St. Thomas* in Horstmann *Legenden 1881* 23.232–4: The devyll and all that he in stode Was wastid all unto muk and myre, Right als wax wastes ogayns the fire. **c1395** Chaucer *CT* IV[E] 1429–30: But certeynly, a yong thyng may men gye, Right as men may warm wex with handes plye. **a1400** *Northern Verse Psalter* I 323 (96.5): Hilles als wax stremeden thai Fra face of Laverd. **c1408** Lydgate *Reson* 178.6816–7: For they be redy to and to Tobeye as wex. **c1450** *St. Cuthbert* 132.4479–80: The paynyms pride it sall expire, And dissolve as wax at fyre.

W103 To flee as **Wax** flees the fire
a1425 *St. Anthony* 122.15–6: As wax flees the fyre, so fle thai fro the syght of god. **1483** Caxton *Golden Legende* 279^r[2.31–3]: And flee from her lyke as waxe fleeth fro the face of fyre.

W104 To fleet (*dissolve*) like **Wax**
c1395 *WBible* Psalms lvii 9: As wexe that fletith awei, thei schulen be takun awei, lxvii 3: As wax fletith fro the face of fier, so perische synneris fro the face of God, xcvi 5: Hillis as wax fletiden doun fro the face of the Lord.

W105 To melt like **Wax**
a800 *Andreas* in *Vercelli Book* 34–5.1145–6: Het wæpen wera wexe gelicost On þam orlege eall formeltan. **a900** *Old English Martyrology* 180.7–8: þa gedwinon his drycræftas . . . swa swa . . . weax þonne hit for fyre gemelteð, 222.3–4: Ond þæt goldgeweorc todreas, swa swa weax gemylt æt fyre. **c900** *Paris Psalter* 10 (57.7): Swa weax melteð, gif hit byð wearmum neah Fyre gefæstnad, 21 (67.2): Swa fram fyre weax floweð and mylteð, Swa þa fyrenfullan frecne forweorðað. **c1000** Aelfric *Lives* II 424.409: And towende hi sona swa swa wex formylt. **c1000** *Larspell* in Napier 234.22–3: And heo mylteð swa wex æt fyre. **c1000** *Regius Psalter* 104 (57.9): Swa swa weax ȝemolten beoð afyrrede, 118 (67.3), 181 (96.5). **a1050** Defensor *Liber* 142[3–4]: On life yldryna ys gecweden swa swa fyr fornimð wex ealswa eac wæcce god geþancu wyrste. **c1100** *Salisbury Psalter* 153 (57.9): Swa wex þa mylt beoþ aferrode, 163 (67.3), 213 (96.5). **c1300** *South English Legendary* II 585.412: Ac bigonne al to multe awey ase wex deth ayen fure. **c1350** *Prose Psalter* 68 (57.8): The wicked shul ben wasted as wax that melteth, 77 (67.2), 118 (96.5). **c1375** *St. John* in Horstmann *Legenden 1881* 39.432–3. **a1396**(1494) Hilton *Scale* R1^v[27–8]. **a1400** *Northern Verse Psalter* I 61 (21.15), 183 (57.9), 207 (67.3). **a1400** *Scottish Legends* I 148.656: It meltit as It vax ware, 356.559–60, II 163.393–4. **c1400** *Tundale* 20.340: And molton as wax in a pan. **a1410** Love *Mirrour* 209[6–7]. **1449** Metham 48.1281–2. **a1475** *St. Birgitta* 9.36–7. **1483** Caxton *Golden Legende* 54^r[1.4], 196^r[1.22–3], 278^v[2.38–9], **1489** *Doctrinal* G6^r[11]. **1490** Irlande *Meroure* 146.7–9. **a1500** *Craft of Dying* in *Yorkshire Writers* II 420[24–5]. Tilley W137; Whiting *Scots* II 151.

W106 To run like **Wax**
c1340 Rolle *Psalter* 206 (57.8): And fall in till hell, as wax that rennys meltand at the fire, 230 (67.2). **c1380** *Ferumbras* 141.4557–8: As lightliche as hit had ibeo wax, ran the strok thanne of ys ax Chayne and tre thorghoute.

W107 To work (*be pliable*) like **Wax**
1546 Heywood *D* 78.19: At my wil I wend she should have wrought, like wax. Tilley W138.

W108 **Wax** is apt to take all things
c1495 *Arundel Vulgaria* 20.79: The myn(d) of a yong mann is as waxe, apte to take all thynge. Tilley W136.

W109 As old as the **Way**
a1393 Gower *CA* II 82.1711–3: His youthe schal be cast aweie Upon such on which as the weie Is old and lothly overal.

W110 But one **Way** leads to the prick (*target*)
a1400 Wyclif *Sermons* II 104[17–8]: As men may err fro the mark in many weies beside it, but o wey ledith to the pricke, as it is knowun comunli.

W111 Choose (Take) the better of the **Ways** (*varied*)
c1449 Pecock *Repressor* I 113[23–5]: Y wole and allowe rather that he go and chese the better of tho weies than the lasse good of tho weies. **c1477** Caxton *Jason* 48.26: And of two wayes to take the beste. **c1515** Barclay *Eclogues* 19.597–600: And he is a foole . . . Which choseth a place unto the same to go, And where divers wayes lead thither directly—He choseth the worst and most of jeopardie, 20.631: Of two wayes they use to leave the best, 106.1358–9: Els be they throwen in suche a blinde dotage, That of two wayes they chose moste jeopardous. **1525** Berners *Froissart* V 17[7–8]: A man ought of two or iii. wayes chose the best waye. See **E193, G357.**

W112 Divers **Ways** oft lead to one place
c1523 Barclay *Mirrour* 20[43]: Thou seest divers wayes oft leading to one place. See **P52, W121.**

W113 Go your **Way**, if you live long you shall find hard beds
1525 Berners *Froissart* IV 25[1–4]: We fynde nowe the olde sayenge of our fathers and mothers true, whane they wolde saye, Go your waye, and ye lyve long, ye shall fynde harde and poore beddes.

W114 The green (broad) **Way** to hell
a1200 *Ancrene* 98.20–2: Thenne dusie worldes men gath bi grene wei toward te wearitreo and to death of helle. **c1340** Rolle *Psalter* 29 (7.7): By the brad way thai ga till hell, 67 (17.46), 196 (54.11): Bi the brade way of covatis and lichery gas till hell, 478 (143.17), 483 (145.8): the brade wayes of synful.

W115 He that will go two **Ways** must either tear his arse or his breech
1492 *Salomon and Marcolphus* 11[27–8]: He that woll two weyes go muste eythre his ars or his breche tere. See **M227, W119.**

W116 In hard **Ways** men go softly
a1393 Gower *CA* II 270.1623–4: In harde weies men gon softe, And er thei clymbe avise hem ofte.

W117 The middle **Way** of measure is ever golden (*varied*)
a1200 *Ancrene* 172.6–7: The middel wei of meosure is eaver guldene. **c1200** *Sawles Warde* (*Bodley*) 6.49–50: Thet me meosure hat, the middel of twa uveles, 20.184: Is in euch worldlich thing the middel wei guldene. **a1393** Gower *CA* II 2.17–8: I wolde go the middel wei And wryte a bok betwen the tweie, III 162.7689–91: And thus betwen tomoche and lyte Largesce, which is noght to wyte, Halt evere forth the middel weie. **a1400** *Ancrene* (*Recluse*) 55.34–5: Thou most taken an evene weye in Mesure bitwixen hope and drede. **c1450** *Foly of Fulys* 55.133–4: Quharfor tyll hald the mydlyng vay Is best as I hard wysmen say. **1456** Hay *Governaunce* 81.3–4: In alde tymis amang wyse men, the mydlyn way was ay soucht to be haldin but repruf. **1483** Caxton *Cato* G8^{r}[14]: Thou oughtest to kepe the myddel waye, I3^{r}[15–6]: Hit is more sure for to holde the myddel way. **a1500** Bernardus *De Cura* 8.174: Off meswre ay he byddis the halde the gate. **a1500** Medwall *Nature* I2^{v}[29–30]: Take the myd way bytwyxt theym two And fle thextremytees. Apperson 255, 409–10; *Oxford* 250; Skeat 25; Whiting *Scots* II 97. Cf. Tilley M792. See **M439, 454.**

W118 No **Way** so sure as the plain
1484 *Ther ne is dangyer* 19.3: Ne so sure a way as is the playn. Tilley W163.

W119 One may not go two **Ways** at once
c1450 La Tour-Landry 7.19: For ye may not goe two waies atte onis. See **M227, W115.**

W120 Steadfast **Way** makes steadfast heart
c1385 Usk 60.117–8: Stedfast way maketh stedfast hert, with good hope in the ende.

W121 There be more **Ways** to the wood than one
1546 Heywood *D* 94.120: There be mo waies to the wood than one, **1555** *E* 163.105. Apperson 429; *Oxford* 696; Tilley W179; Whiting *Drama* 164. See **W112.**

W122 To go the **Way** of all earth
a1382 *WBible* Joshua xxiii 14: I to day goo into the weie of al erthe. Taylor and Whiting 396; Tilley W166.

W123 To go the **Way** of the world
c1450 *Speculum Christiani* (2) 142.5–6: Stronge to go the wey of worlde and feble to assaile the wey of commaundmentes of god. **1519** Horman *Vulgaria* 317[8]: Suche is the wey of the worlde: that &c. Ita comparatum est ut etc. Taylor and Whiting 396.

W124 To know which **Way** to the wood the hare goes
c1475 *Wisdom* 60.744–5: Wyche wey to the woode wyll the hare, They knewe, and they at rest sett als tyghte. Cf. Taylor and Whiting 60: Cat(47).

W125 To take the wrong **Way** to (the) wood
1546 Heywood *D* 92.66–7: Ye tooke The wrong way to wood. *Oxford* 736; Tilley W167.

W126 When you go by the **Way** beware where you throw (*MS.* drowe) (?stones)
c1470 *Harley MS.3362* f.2b in *Retrospective* 309[11] and Förster 201.11: Whan thou gest by the weyghe, be war where thou drowe . . . Pergens per vicum caveas jactare lapillum; Fortuitus jactus infert persepe periclum. Walther III 804.21362.

W127 He that hires **Wayfarers** builds on all sides
c1025 *Durham Proverbs* 14.32: Wide timbreð se þe wegferendum hyreð. Crebro struit qui viatoribus parat.

W128 The **Weaker** goes to the pot
1546 Heywood *D* 73.105–6: And where the small with the great, can not agree, The weaker goeth to the potte, **1562** *E* 197.292: The weaker goth

to the pot, ye, and god wot, Sum the weaker for ofte goyng to the pot. Apperson 507; *Oxford* 696; Tilley W183; Whiting *Drama* 346:578.

W129 The **Weaker** (feeblest) has the worse
c1400 *Alexander Buik* I 57.1782: The wakar sone the war can haif. **1481** Caxton *Reynard* 31[19–20]: Hit went with hem as it ofte doth the feblest hath the worst. **1546** Heywood *D* 35.6: But the weaker hath the wurs we all daie see, **1555** *E* 174.156: The weaker hath the woorse, in wrestlyng alway. Apperson 671; Jente 198; *Oxford* 696; Tilley W184. See **W131.**

W130 The **Weakest** goes to the wall
a1500 *Coventry Plays* 47.447: But the weykist gothe eyver to the walle. **1518** Nevill *Castell* 97.569: And amonge the waykest be put backe to the wall. Apperson 671; *Oxford* 697; Tilley W185; Whiting *Drama* 227, *Scots* II 151.

W131 The **Weakest** is cast beneath
c1390 *Suffer in Time* in Brown *Lyrics XIV* 201.41–2: The sothe al day is seene in siht, The weikest ay bi-neothe is cast. See **F110, W129.**

W132 After the **Weal** take the woe
a1400 *Le Morte A.* 56.1890–1: We shalle be of hertis good Aftyr the wele to take the wo. See **W432.**

W133 After **Weal** comes woe
a1400 *Alexander C* 242.4621: And eftir wele comys wa for so the werd askis. Tilley W188. See **J61.**

W134 He is unwise that can endure no **Weal**
c1396 Chaucer *Bukton* 27–8: Unwys is he that kan no wele endure. If thow be siker, put the nat in drede. Apperson 361: Let well; *Oxford* 360.

W135 He is well that has **Weal** after woe
a1450 *South English Legendary (Bodley)* 372.178: For wel is him alyve: that hath wele after wo.

W136 He is worse that is thrown from **Weal** than if he had known none
c1385 Chaucer *TC* iv 482–3: That hym is wors that is fro wele ythrowe, Than he hadde erst noon of that wele yknowe. See **S519.**

W137 He knows not what **Weal** is that never suffered woe
c1378 *Piers* B xviii 204–5: For no wighte wote what wel is that nevere wo suffred, Ne what is hote hunger that had nevere defaute. See **S141, W144.**

W138 It is worthy that he that may bear no **Weal** shall thole (*suffer*) woe
a1400 *Cursor* II 422 F 7311–2: For hit is worthi wele at qua May bere na wele salle thole the wa. **c1500** *Camb. Un. MS. Ff.5.47* in Robbins-Cutler 1162.5: He that may not suffre wele, with unskyle he pleynith hym thei he wo thole.

W139 Let no man trust too swith (*much*) to his **Weal**
c1250 *Owl* 108.1273–4: Ne truste no mon to his weole To swithe, thah he habbe veole. See **W141.**

W140 One **Weal** or one woe may not always endure
c1385 Usk 82.176–7: So that alway oon wele, as alway oon wo, may not endure. See **S517.**

W141 **Weal** beswikes (*betrays*) many a man
a1200 Lawman I 145.3411–4: Wela, weolla, wella, Hu thu bi-swikest monine mon; Thenne he the treowethe alre best on, Thenne bi-swikes tu heom. See **W139.**

W142 Whoso shall win **Weal** must find a waster
c1353 *Winner* 390: Who so wele schal wyn, a wastour moste he fynde. See note for German parallels.

W143 He is worthy no **Wealth** that may suffer no woe
c1385 Usk 18.153–4: For he is worthy no welthe, that may no wo suffer. Apperson 613–4; *Oxford* 734; Tilley W187. See **S141.**

W144 He wot not what **Wealth** is that never was sore
c1516 Skelton *Magnificence* 61.1971: He woteth not what Welth is that never was sore. See **W137.**

W145 In **Wealth** (weal) beware of woe (*varied*)
a1400 *Proverbis of Wysdom* 245.53–4: Fro foly ever kepe thy fare And yn welth all way be ware, (*II*) 222.38: wele *for* welth. **c1405** *Mum* 31.124: And in welthe to be ware ere that woo falle. **a1450** *Fyrst thou sal* 87.9–10: Man in thi wele bewar of woo Wele is he that can do soo. **c1450** *Camb. Un. MS. Hh.4.11* in Robbins-Cutler 1587.7: In wele be wyis and war or thou be wo; Though thou mow sle, yit do nothyng so. **c1450** *O wofull worlde* in *Guiscardo* xiii[25–6]: In wele beware the wysely, For fortune turneth sodenly. **c1450** *Proverbs of Good Counsel* 69.47: And ever in welth be ware of woo. **c1465** *As I fared* in Sandison 116.8: In thy most welth wysely beware, 16, *etc.* **a1500** Hill 139.5–6: In welth be ware of woo, what so the happes, And bere the evyn for drede of after-clappes. **1508**(1519)

Stanbridge *Vulgaria* 26.11: Be ware in welthe or thou be wo. **c1516** Skelton *Magnificence* 61.1974–5: Lo, suche is this worlde! I fynde it wryt, In Welth to beware; and that is Wyt, 67.2158–9: For to be wyse all men may lerne of me, In Welthe to beware of herde Adversyte, **a1529** *Garnesche* I 130.124: Wherfore in welthe beware of woo. Apperson 671; Tilley W196. See **W45.**

W146 **Wealth** after woe
c1350 *Alexander B* 208.919: To have welthe aftur wo, as the wor(l)d farus. See **B325.**

W147 **Wealth** can seldom suffer its estate in health
a1393 Gower *CA* II 26.786–8: In proverbe natheles Men sein, ful selden is that welthe Can soffre his oghne astat in helthe. Apperson 8.

W148 **Wealth** ebbs and flows as the flood
1463 Ashby *Prisoner* 7.185: Thus welth ebbeth and floweth as the flood.

W149 **Wealth** has a season
c1516 Skelton *Magnificence* 1.3: Be it erly or late, Welth hath a season.

W150 **Wealth** increases misrule
a1475 *Assembly of Gods* 48.1629–31: But oonly to shew the howe hit dothe apere That welthe, unbrydelyd dayly at thyne ey, Encreseth mysrewle and oft causyth foly.

W151 **Wealth** is full slipper (*undependable*)
c1412 Hoccleve *Regement* 33.903: Welth is ful slipir, be ware lest thou fall. Cf. Whiting *Drama* 85. See **P422, W189.**

W152 **Weapon** bodes (*betokens,* makes) peace
c1458 *Knyghthode and Bataile* 62.1692: Seyde ofte it is : the wepon bodeth peax. **c1475** *Rawlinson MS. D 328* 119.30: Wepyn bodyd pece. **a1500** Hill 128.13: Wepin makith pese diwers times. Apperson 671; Tilley W206. See **W638.**

W153 Fair **Weather** is worth more if there were stark storms before
897 Alfred *Boethius* 52.4–5: And eft smylte weder bið þy þancwyrðre gif hit hwene ær bið stearce stormas and norðanwindas and micle renas and snawas. See **S944.**

W154 Fair **Weather** oft wends (*turns*) to rain (*varied*)
a1250 *Death's Wither-Clench* in Brown *Lyrics XIII* 15.3: Fair weder ofte him went to rene. **c1400** *Alexius* (*Laud 622*) 73.1087–9: After fair weder falleth reyn, After wynnyng wep ageyn, And care is after kysse.

W155 To make fair **Weather**
1546 Heywood *D* 36.50a: Above all, with her I made fayre wether, 71.35: They can currifavell, and make faire wether. Taylor and Whiting 398; Tilley W221.

W156 **Weather** meet to set paddocks (*frogs*) abroad in
1546 Heywood *D* 58.37–8: We have had . . . Weather, meete to sette paddockes abroode in. *Oxford* 698; Tilley W222.

W157 As sad (*stable*) as **Weathercock** in wind
c1475 Henryson *Testament* 124.567: For thay ar sad as Widdercock in Wind.

W158 As unstable (stable) as a **Weathercock**
c1400 *Seven Deadly Sins* in Wyclif *SEW* III 165[10–2]: These men . . . ben unstable as wedircokkes, and wil turne with one foul wynde. **a1449** Lydgate *Freond* in *MP* II 757.71: As wethercok theire faites beo founde unstable. **a1500** *Mocking Letter* in Robbins 219[2]: As the wedyr cok he is stable.

W159 As wild as a **Weathercock**
a1425 *Heded as an ox* in *Nicodemus* xxv[7]: Wylled as a wedercoke.

W160 To be like a **Weathercock** (*varied*)
1340 *Ayenbite* 180[26–8]: Hi byeth ase the wedercoc thet is ope the steple, thet him went mid eche wynde. **c1370** Chaucer *Against Women Unconstant* 12–3: But, as a wedercok, that turneth his face With every wind, ye fare. **c1385** Usk 13.166–7: I have not . . . with the wethercocke waved. **c1400** *Vices and Virtues* 184.27–8: And therfore they faren as the wederkoc on a stepel, that turneth with alle wyndes. **1402** *Daw Topias* 50[17–8]: Wanderynge weder-cokkes, With every wynd waginge. **a1430** Lydgate *Pilgrimage* 387.14324–5: Turnynge as offte sythe aboute As . . . wheder-cok, **a1439** *Fall* III 679.147: Lik a wedircok my face ech day I tourne. **c1450** *Jacob's Well* 299. 28–9: Thei fayle, and faryn as a wedir kok, that turnyth wyth iche wynd. **c1475** *Magnificencia Ecclesie* in *PMLA* 24(1909) 693[29]: Lyke as the wedurcok ayenst yche wynde dothe m(?w)evyn. **1546** Heywood *D* 101.30: How like a wethercocke I have here varyed. Apperson 91; *Oxford* 698; Tilley W223; Whiting *Drama* 332:357, *Scots* II 152.

W161 To be like the **Weather-vane**
a1450 Audelay 215.26: And not in foundyng to be as the wederfane.

W162 It is better to **Wed** (wive, marry) than to burn

a900 Alfred *Gregory* 401.33–4: Forðæm hit is awriten ðæt hit sie betere ðæt mon gehiewige ðonne he birne. **a1340** *Ayenbite* 225[16–7]: Vor betere and more holy thing is to wyvi thanne him-zelve berne. **c1395** Chaucer *CT* III[D] 52: Bet is to be wedded than to brynne. **c1395** *WBible* I Corinthians vii 9: For it is betere to be weddid, than to be brent. **c1396** Chaucer *Bukton* 17–8: But yet, lest thow do worse, take a wyf; Bet ys to wedde than brenne in worse wise. **a1400** *Pauline Epistles* I Corinthians vii 9: For it is better to wedde then to brenne in *leccherye.* **c1400** *Vices and Virtues* 250.1–2: For bettre is hem to marye hem than brenne hem. **1484** Caxton *Royal Book* S5[v][23–4]: For better is to marye than to brenne them, **1489** *Doctrinal* D1[v][29–30]: For it is better for them to be maryed than to be brent. **1532** More *Confutacion* 463 C[4]: It is better to mary then to burne, D[10–1], 680 H[10–1]: Better it is to wedde then to burne. Tilley M692.

W163 Who **Weds** ere he be wise shall die ere he thrive
1549 Heywood *D* 31.32: Who wedth or he be wise shall die or he thrive, **1555** *E* 151.28. Apperson 672; Tilley W229.

W164 **Wedding** and hanging are destiny
1546 Heywood *D* 23.51–2: Be it far or nie, weddyng is desteny, And hangyng likewise, saith thet proverbe, sayd I, **1555** *E* 148.6: Weddyng and hangyng, are desteny I see. Apperson 403–4; *Oxford* 276; Tilley W232; Whiting *Drama* 189, 190, 222. See **D169.**

W165 **Wedding** is honorable
c1395 *WBible* Hebrews xiii 4: Wedding is in alle thingis onourable. *Oxford* 409.

W166 **Wedding** is the hardest band that any man may take on hand
c1375 Barbour *Bruce* I 12.266–9: For men may weile se, that ar wyss, That wedding is the hardest band That ony man may tak on hand. And thryldome is weill wer than deid. Whiting *Scots* I 135.

W167 **Wedding** would have good advisement
1463-7 Paston IV 291[20–1]: Me semez wedding wolde have goode avysement. See **A62.**

W168 One **Wedge** drives out another
1493 *Tretyse of Love* 112.34–5: For as men wyll and maye more easely dryve oute a wedge or a pyn of tree that is myssette by a-nother. Tilley W234. See **N6.**

W169 As wan as the **Weed**
c1475 Henryson *Fables* 84.2465: For verray wo woxe wanner nor the weid. Whiting *Scots* II 153.

W170 Evil **Weed** is soon grown (*varied*)
c1470 *Harley MS.3362* f.2a in *Retrospective* 309[5] and Förster 200.5: Ewyl weed ys sone y-growe. **1546** Heywood *D* 39.131: Ill weede growth fast . . . wherby the corne is lorne, **1555** *E* 189.239: Ill weede growth fast, it groweth fast in deede: The corne can scantly growe for the weede. Apperson 326; Jente 600; *Oxford* 317; Tilley W238.

W171 Of wicked **Weed** come no wholesome flowers
a1439 Lydgate *Fall* III 709.1307: Of wikked weed(e) come non holsum flours. See **T465.**

W172 To wallow (*wither*) like a (the) **Weed**
c1475 Henryson *Orpheus* 140.350: And walluid as the weid, *Thre Deid Pollis* 205.21: Holkit and how, and wallowit as the weid. **c1475** *Thewis* 182.94: And one the morne walowyt as a wed. Whiting *Scots* II 153.

W173 To waste away like **Weed**
c1375 *St. Laurence* in Horstmann *Legenden 1881* 109.149: It will noght wast oway als wede. **a1425** *Metrical Paraphrase OT* 33.14972: And sythyn as a wed wast away.

W174 The **Weed** overgrows the corn (*varied*)
c1330 *Seven Sages A* 48.1181: I se the wede waxe over the corn, **a1350** *C* 44.1281. **a1333** Shoreham *Poems* 31.871–2: As wed schel growen over the corn, Wythoute medicyne. **1439** Lydgate *St. Albon* 114.197–201: It hath ben sayn and writen here beforne By olde expert Poesy called doctrine: "(Withstond) pryncipIes, Leest above the corne The wede wex ayenst good graine to maligne," **a1449** *Amor* in *MP* II 746.52: Som tyme for lucre weede above the corn. **a1470** Malory I 306.1–2: To se suche a lad to macche you, as the wede growyth over the corne. **a1475** *Corruptions of the Times* in Wright *Political Poems* II 237[11–2]: Therfor every man may care, Lest the wade growe over the whete. **1546** Heywood *D* 39.132: For surely the weede overgroweth the corne. Apperson 672–3; *Oxford* 699; Tilley W242; Whiting *Scots* II 152.

W175 To be in by the **Week**
1546 Heywood *D* 86.201: Wherby this proverbe shewth the in by the weeke, **1555** *E* 155.60: *Of one in prison.* Thou art in by the weeke, nay syr I am here, Not in by the weeke, I am in by the yere. Tilley W244.

W176 To **Ween** one kens more than he knows

a1425 *Chester Plays* I 213.242: He wenes he kennes more then he knowes. **a1450** *York Plays* 159.90. **c1450** Trevet 238.35–6 (f.48b, col. 2): He weneth that he knowe more than he can. **a1460** *Towneley Plays* 188.64: He wenys he kens more then he knawys.

W177 **Weening** beguiles many a man
a1393 Gower *CA* II 89.1958: Wenyng beguileth many a man.

W178 To be worth one's **Weight** in gold (*varied*)
c1300 *Reinbrun* 636.15.10–1: And segge he hadde Reinbroun sold For is wighte of rede gold. **c1400** *Florence* 60.1789–90: So mekyll golde for hur he hyght That hyt passyd almoost hur weyght. **c1400** *Laud Troy* I 232.7859–60: He wold not for his weyghht of gold, That Achilles it (*horse*) hadde hold. **a1500** *Eger P* 290.1154: He is worth to her his waight in gold, 308.1228. **a1500** Medwall *Nature* C4v[32]: Ye ar worth thy weyght of gold, F3r[1]. **a1533** Berners *Arthur* 276[22–3]: Ye wold not go and seke to have it for your weyght of fyne golde. Apperson 714; *Oxford* 734; Taylor and Whiting 398; Tilley W253.

W179 If one may not change **Weird** (*fate*) it is best to thole (*suffer*) it.
c900 *Resignation* in *Exeter Book* 218.117–8: Giet biþ þæt selast, þonne mon him sylf ne mæg Wyrd onwendan, þæt he þonne wel þolige.

W180 **Weird** drives the world's things to the end
c1375 Barbour *Bruce* I 87.148–50: Bot werd, that to the end ay driffis The varldis thingis, sa thame travalit, That thai on twa halfis war assalit.

W181 **Weird** goes as it must
c735 *Beowulf* 455: Gæð a wyrd swa hio scel!

W182 **Weird** is strongest
c900 *Cotton Maxims* in *ASMP* 55.5: Wyrd byð swiðost.

W183 **Weird** of battle is wavering
c1420 Wyntoun III 39.450: For werde (*var.* ure) is waverande of bataille. See **B65, F533, W39.**

W184 **Weird** often changes
c1000 *Letter of Alexander* in *Three Old English Prose Texts* 11.2–3: Seo wyrd and sio hiow hie oft oncyrreð and on oþer hworfeð. See **F523.**

W185 **Weird** often saves a man when his courage avails
c735 *Beowulf* 572–3: Wyrd oft nereð Unfægne eorl, þonne his ellen deah! See **F519.**

W186 Such **Welcome** such farewell
1546 Heywood *D* 83.102: Such welcome, such farewell. *Oxford* 700; Tilley W256.

W187 To bid one **Welcome** over the fields
1546 Heywood *D* 50.300: Byddyng me welcome strangly over the feelds. Tilley W257.

W188 **Welcome** when you go
1546 Heywood *D* 82.74: Welcome when thou goest, thus is thine errand sped. *Oxford* 700; Tilley G475, W259.

W189 **Welfare** has no sickerness
a1500 *As I fared thorow* in Dyboski 88–9.8: Welfare hath no sykernes, 16, 24, *etc.* See **W151.**

W190 He has **Well** that deserves well
a1393 Gower *CA* III 439.1962: Thus hath he wel that wel deserveth. See **D165.**

W191 "It is far from **Well**," said he that heard wailing in hell
c1025 *Durham Proverbs* 15.44: Wide ne biþ wel, cwæþ se þe gehyrde on helle hriman. . . . ait qui audivit clamorem in inferno.

W192 Many **Wells** many buckets
1549 Heywood *D* 87.229: Well well (quoth she) many wels, many buckets. Apperson 400; *Oxford* 406; Tilley W264.

W193 To spring up like a **Well**
a1393 Gower *CA* II 237–8.427–34: That every thing which he can telle, It springeth up as doth a welle, Which mai non of his stremes hyde, Bot renneth out on every syde. So buillen up the foule sawes That Cheste wot of his felawes: For as a Sive kepeth Ale, Riht so can Cheste kepe a tale, 324.839–40: With teres, whiche, as of a welle The stremes, from hire yhen felle, III 374.5004–7: Riht as men sen a welle springe, With yhen fulle of wofull teres, . . . Sche wepte.

W194 He is blessed who may sit on his **Well-stool** and tell of his woe-stool
a1438 Kempe 82.5–7: The comown proverbe that men seyn, "He is wel blyssed that may sytten on hys wel-stool and tellyn of hys wo-stool."

W195 The **Welsh** ever love treachery (*varied*)
a1338 Mannyng *Chronicle A* I 247.7031–2: Fforteger was of the Walscherye, That evere lovede trycherye, *B* II 306[10–4]: Was never withouten gile Walsh man no Breton. . . . Saynt Bede sais it for lore, and I say it in ryme, Walsh man salle never more luf Inglis man no tyme. See **S98.**

W196 To make (use) a **Welshman's** hose
c1522 Skelton *Colyn* I 341.780–1: And make a Walshmans hose Of the texte and of the glose, **1523** *Garlande* I 411.1238–9: And after conveyauns as the world goos, It is no foly to use the Walshemannys hoos. *Oxford* 702; Whiting *Scots* II 153.

W197 As bitter as **Wermod** (*wormwood*)
a750 *Riddles* in *Exeter Book* 202.60–1: Swylce ic eom wraþre þonne wermod sy, þe her on hyrstum heasewe stondeþ. **c1395** *WBible* Proverbs v 4: The last thingis ben bittir as wormwod. **a1396**(1494) Hilton *Scale* N7[r][33]. **a1400** Wyclif *Sermons* I 89[6], 262[11]. **a1430** Lydgate *Pilgrimage* 342.12580–1: And he hath ek mor bytternesse Than any woormood growyng here, 421.15662. **a1500** *Remedie of Love* CCCXXII[v][1.21].

W198 As sour as **Wermod**
a1430 Lydgate *Pilgrimage* 421.15662: Mor sowr . . . than wormood. **c1450** *Pilgrimage LM* 134[14–5]. **c1500** *Remors* B1[r][8]: They be to me as souer as wormewode.

W199 To go **West**
a1500 *Man have mynd* 55.41–2: Women and mony wilsome wy As wynd or wattir ar gane west. NED West 1b(a).

W200 As fat as a **Whale**
c1395 Chaucer *CT* III[D] 1930: Fat as a whale. **a1513** ?Dunbar *General Satyre* 153.71: Sic fartingaillis on flaggis als fatt as quhailis.

W201 As great as a **Whale**
a1460 *Towneley Plays* 119.105: She is greatt as a whall.

W202 As blaght (*white*) as **Whale's-bone**
c1380 *Pearl* 8.212: Her ble more blaght then whalles bon.

W203 As white as (the, any) **Whale's-bone**
c1325 *Maid of Ribbesdale* in Böddeker 156.40: Hire teht aren white ase bon of whal. **c1325** *Wayle Whyt* in G. L. Brook *Harley Lyrics* (Manchester, 1948) 40.1: A wayle whyt ase whalles bon. **c1330** *Degare* 57.20 (*var.*): A doughter as whight as whales bone. **c1330** *St. Katherine* 248.282. **a1350** *Isumbras* 20.250. **c1353** *Winner* 181: Whitte als the whalles bone. **c1380** *Ferumbras* 80.2429. **a1400** *Destruction of Troy* 100.3055: (*Teeth*) qwyte and qwem as any qwalle bon. **a1400** *Eglamour* 45.680, 52–3.779–80, 60.892, 71.1052–3: Yowre nece . . . Es whytte as bone of qwalle. **a1400** *Torrent* 29.794. **c1400** *Emaré* 2.33. **c1400** *Toulouse* 235.358. **a1450** *St. Etheldreda* 298.688: A ston lay as whytte as whall. **c1455** *Partonope S* 481.17, 483.93–4. **1467** Paston IV 268[5]. **c1475** Henryson *Thre Deid Pollis* 206.29. **a1500** *Ballad* in *Rel. Ant.* I 28[15]. **a1500** *Beauty of his Mistress II* in Robbins 124.14, *III* 127.27. **a1500** *Squire* 27.537, 32.711. **c1500** *Smith* 324.219–20: She was whiter of lere Than bone is of whale, 328.529: She was whyte as a bone of whale. **1506** Hawes *Pastime* 64.1592. **a1513** Dunbar *In Secreit Place* 54.33. **1515** Barclay *St. George* 53.1150: A godly virgyne as whyte as bone of whall. Apperson 680; Tilley W279; Whiting *Scots* II 153. See **B443, E68, I68, R229.**

W204 To wit (know) **What** is what
a1350 *Ywain* 12.432: For wa I wist noght what was what. **c1422** Hoccleve *Dialog* 138.778: And elles woot I nevere what is what. **1522** Skelton *Why Come* II 60.1106: He said he knew what was what. Apperson 677–8; Taylor and Whiting 399; Tilley K178.

W205 **Wheat** and chaff
c1200 *St. Juliana* 71.775–6: Hwen drihtin o domes dei windweth his hweate and (weopth) thet dusti chef to hellene heate. **a1400** *Meditations* 48.1837: Whi dieth the whete under the chaf? **1401** *Treuth* in Kail 10.47: The whete fro the chaf ye tryghe. **1532** Berners *Golden Boke* 322.6693–4: To bye wheate without chaffe? See **C428, F693, S824.**

W206 The fifth **Wheel** to the cart
1513 Douglas *Aeneid* IV 144.117–8: As to the text accordyng never a deill, Mair than langis to the cart the fift quheill. Apperson 210; *Oxford* 200; Taylor and Whiting 399–400; Tilley W286.

W207 A shrewd **Wheel** cries more (*varied*)
c1450 *Pilgrimage LM* 123[1–3]: And i can with good oynture enoynte a shrewede wheel that cryeth that it shal crye more after and communeliche be the werse. **c1450** *Rylands MS.394* 106.20: Ever the worst spoke of the cart krakes. Apperson 713; *Oxford* 733; Tilley W287. See **C66.**

W208 To stand on another **Wheel**
a1393 Gower *CA* II 40.178: Mi world stod on an other whiel. See **W670.**

W209 To turn (wharve, trendle [*turn*]) like a **Wheel**
897 Alfred *Boethius* 57.31–2: Ac ælc gesceaft hwearfað on hire selfre swa swa hweol, *Lays of Boethius* 172.73–4. **c1200** Orm I 125.3640–3: Forr all thiss middellaerdess thing Ayy turr-

neththth her and wharrfeththth Nu upp, nu dun, swa summ the wheol, And nohht ne stannt itt stille. **1410** Walton *Boethius* 197[1]: And all his thoghtes trendlen as a whele. **c1450** *Foly of Fulys* 63.426: Bot tolterand, turnand as a quheill. **a1500** *How the Wyse Man* 33.157 (*var.*): Thys worlde hyt turnys evyn as a whele. **1509** Barclay *Ship* I 144[15]: One with his speche rounde tournynge lyke a whyle.

W210 Not worth a **Whelk**
c1500 *King Hart* 110.15: I compt not all your werkis wirth ane wilk.

W211 By the **Whelp** the lion is chastised
c1395 Chaucer *CT* V[F] 490–1: And for to maken othere be war by me, As by the whelp chasted is the leon. **a1439** Lydgate *Fall* I 6.211–2: Bi smale whelpis, as summe clerkis write, Chastised is the myhti fers leoun. **c1450** *Douce MS.52* 49.63: By the litul welpys me chastys the lyon. **a1450** *Rylands MS.394* 99.14. **a1470** Parker *Dives* Q6r[2.37–9]: And as the lyon is chastysed by betynge of the whelpe. **1481** Caxton *Mirror* 75[27–30]: And whan he that kepeth them (*lions*) bete and chastyseth a lytil dogge to fore them, they fere and doubte hym lyke as they knewe hym wel. Apperson 161; *Oxford* 27; Tilley D443. See **H4.**

W212 To be a **Whelp** of a shrewd hair
1519 Horman *Vulgaria* 106[13]: He is a whelpe of a shreude heare. Germen improbum.

W213 To rage (toddle) like a **Whelp**
c1387-95 Chaucer *CT* I[A] 257: And rage he koude, as it were right a whelp. **a1513** Dunbar *Wowing* 52.11: And todlit with hir lyk ane quhelp.

W214 The **Whelp** plays as long as the old hound will
c1450 *Rylands MS.394* 93.20: As longe pleyeth the whelpe, as the olde hounde wyll.

W215 While the **Whelp** plays the old dog grins
c1450 *Rylands MS.394* 93.5: While the welpe pleyes, the olde dog grennys. **a1500** Hill 132.41: Whan the whelpe gameth, the old dogge grenneth.

W216 To lie for the **Whetstone** (*varied*)
1418 *Proclamacio* in R. W. Chambers and M. Daunt *Book of London English 1384–1425* (Oxford, 1931) 95.29–32: He . . . shal stonde here upon the pillorye . . . with a Weston aboute hys necke in tokene of a Lyere. **c1450** *Chaunce* 10.173–5: This is your hap upon the whele yronne That ye may the wheston kepe and bere, Though al this londe at ones assembled were. **a1460** *Towneley Plays* 230.80–1: He lyes for the quetstone, I gyf hym the pryce. **c1500** Greene *Carols* 471 *refrain:* I will have the whetstone and I may. **1560** Heywood *E* 223. 98.1–2: Where doth Frances fabler now lie, Jane? At signe of the whetstone in double tunge lane. Apperson 679; *Oxford* 704; Tilley W298; Whiting *Drama* 370:942.

W217 A **Whetstone** makes sharp carving tools (*varied*)
c1385 Chaucer *TC* i 631–2: A wheston is no kervyng instrument, But yet it maketh sharppe kervyng tolis. **a1387** Higden-Trevisa I 13[9–10]: So saith the prophete Satiricus, "I fare as the wheston that maketh yren sharpe and kene." Apperson 679; *Oxford* 704; Tilley W299.

W218 As white as **Whey**
a1400 Lanfranc 67.14: Whight as whey.

W219 He loses his **While** (*time*) that does for the qued (*wicked*)
a1300 *Passion of Our Lord* in Morris *Old English Miscellany* 39.62: Me seyth his hwile he vor-leost that doth for the quede.

W220 In less **While** than a man may wink
a1400 *Pricke* 214.7935: Ffor in les while than a man may wynke. See **W365.**

W221 Stand a **While** and run a mile
c1450 *Rylands MS.394* 95.30: Stonde awhyle and rynne a myle. Tilley W300.

W222 Soft **Whispering** spreads not far
1556 Heywood *Spider* 316[12]: Softe wispring, not fer spreades.

W223 Not set a **Whistle**
c1475 *Prohemy of a Mariage* 27[13]: For he set not by his wrethe a whistel. **c1522** Skelton *Colyn* I 357.1187: They set not by us a whystell.

W224 Not worth a **Whistle**
c1522 Skelton *Colyn* I 320.238: Construe not worth a whystle. **1533** More *Confutacion* 581 A[13]: Not worth a whystle. Tilley W311.

W225 To wet one's **Whistle**
c1390 Chaucer *CT* I[A] 4155: So was hir joly whistle wel ywet. **a1460** *Towneley Plays* 119.103: Had She oones Wett Hyr Whystyll. **1519** Horman *Vulgaria* 158[16–7]: Yf I wete my mouthe or my whystyll: I shall gyve a crasshe or a fytte of myrthe. Si subbibero aliquid suave tinniam. Apperson 677; *Oxford* 703; Taylor and Whiting 401; Tilley W312.

W226 To **Whistle** (for something)

1513 More *Richard* 47 E[8–9]: There thei spende and bidde their creditours gooe whistle them. Taylor and Whiting 401; Tilley W313.

W227 As good never a **Whit** as never the better
1546 Heywood *D* 101.36: As good never a whit as never the better. Apperson 442; *Oxford* 448; Tilley W314.

W228 Set not a **Whit**
c1495 *Arundel Vulgaria* 27.111: He sett not a whitt be their woodenes. NED Whit sb.[1] 1.

W229 He that is **White** may cast scorns against a man of Ind
1509 Barclay *Ship* I 213[10–2]: And he that is whyte may well his scornes cast Agaynst a man of ynde, but no man ought to blame Anothers vyce whyle he usyth the same. **1509** Watson *Ship* K5v[9–10]: The crepyll lame and counterfet mocketh the ethyopyen. A. Pompen *English Versions of The Ship of Fools* (London, 1925) 78; Walther II 759.13964.

W230 **White** is token of cleanness (*purity*)
c1422 Lydgate *On Gloucester's Approaching Marriage* in *MP* II 605.110: The whyte also is tooken of clennesse, **a1449** *My Lady Dere* in *MP* II 423.99–100: And summe in token of clennesse, Weren whyte, takethe heed.

W231 **White** seems more by black (*varied*)
a1333 Shoreham *Poems* 148.541–6: Swythe fayr thyng hys that wyte, And ther by-syde blak a lyte, wel ydyght; The wyte hyt the vayrer maketh, And (hym) selve more hyt blaketh, And al hyt hyght. **c1385** Chaucer *TC* i 642–3: Eke whit by blak, by shame ek worthinesse, Ech set by other, more for other semeth. **c1385** Usk 35.47–8: Blacke and white, set togider, every for other more semeth; and so doth every thinges contrary in kynde, 97.75–9. **1420** Lydgate *Temple* 52.1250: For white is whitter, if it be set bi blak, **a1439** *Fall* III 755.2980–2: Too colours seyn that be contrarious, As whiht and blak; it may bee non othir, Ech in his kynde sheweth mor for othir. **a1500** *Corruptions of the Times* in Wright *Political Poems* II 241[9–10]: Wyghte is wyghte, gyf yt leyd to blake; And soote ys swettere aftur bytternesse. **1506** Hawes *Pastime* 57.1405: As whyte by blacke doth shyne more clerely. **1523** Skelton *Garlande* I 411.1237: The whyte apperyth the better for the black. Tilley B435. See **C366, L383, T110.**

W232 To be **White-livered**
1546 Heywood *D* 74.127: Why thinke ye me so whyte lyverd? NED White-livered; Tilley F180; Whiting *Drama* 370:945.

W233 There leaped a **Whiting**
1546 Heywood *D* 81.47: There lepte a whityng (quoth she) and lept in streite. Apperson 356–7; *Oxford* 357; Tilley W318.

W234 He that stretches further than his **Whittle** (*blanket*) will reach must stretch his feet in the straw (*varied*)
a1300 Henley *Husbandry* 4[6–8] Hom dit en reprover en engleys: Wo that stretchet fortherre than his wytel wyle reche, in the straue his fet he mot streche, **c1350** in *Ninth Report of the Royal Commission on Historical Manuscripts 1883* Part I, Appendix 75[2.62–4]: Hwo wille forthere hym streche Than his whitel wole reche, Ine the chaf he mot him strecche. **c1378** *Piers* B xiv 233: For whan he streyneth hym to streche the strawe is his schetes (*C* whitel). **c1470** *Harley MS.3362* f.4a: He that wyle further streche than hys schetyn wyl areche, in the straw he (s)chal hys feet seche. Apperson 605; *Oxford* 625; Robbins-Cutler 4113. Cf. Tilley A316.

W235 Hop **Whore,** pipe thief
1546 Heywood *D* 88.274: Where all thy pleasure is, hop hoore, pipe theefe. Apperson 309; *Oxford* 303; Tilley W320.

W236 The **Why** and the wherefore
1481 Caxton *Reynard* 113[22]: They knewe none other thyng why ne wherfore. Taylor and Whiting 401; Tilley W332.

W237 Though **Wickedness** be kept secre(t) it will be discovered
a1440 Burgh *Cato* 314.443–4: Thouh wykkydnesse for tyme be kept secre, Yitt att the laste will it discurid be. See **M806.**

W238 For fair **Wives** many lose their lives
c1450 *Rylands MS.394* 93.7: For feyre wyfes mony losyn her lyfes. See **W487.**

W239 A good **Wife** makes a good husband
1546 Heywood *D* 89.47: A good wife makth a good husbande (they saie). Apperson 264; *Oxford* 257; Tilley W351. See **H655.**

W240 A good **Wife** should not be kept in await (*watched*)
c1390 Chaucer *CT* IX[H] 148–54: A good wyf, that is clene of werk and thoght, Sholde nat been kept in noon awayt, certayn; And trewely, the labour is in vayn To kepe a shrewe, for it wol nat bee. This holde I for a verray nycetee,

To spille labour for to kepe wyves: Thus writen olde clerkes in hir lyves.

W241 He that has an evil **Wife** and loses her ought to be little sorrowful
c1505 Watson *Valentine* 247.3–4: For who that hath an evyll wyfe and leseth her, he ought to be lytell sorowful. Cf. Tilley W360.

W242 Never be so wood (*mad*) or so drunk as to tell your **Wife** your will (*varied*)
c1250 *Proverbs of Alfred* 102 T 281–4: Wurthu nevere swo wod Ne so drunken, That evere sai thu thi wif Al that thi wille be. **c1400** *Toulouse* 250.679: Womans tong ys evell to tryst. **c1500** *Lady Bessy* 10[4–6]: But it is hard to trust women, For many a man is brought into great woe, Through telling to women his privity. *Oxford* 647. Cf. Tilley W347a, 362. See **F426.**

W243 A nice **Wife** and a back door often make a rich man poor
c1450 *Proverbs of Good Counsel* 69.33–4: For a nyse wyfe, and A backe dore, Makyth oftyn tymus A ryche man pore. Apperson 199:9, 444; *Oxford* 451; Robbins-Cutler 81.5; Tilley W370.

W244 Old **Wives'** tales (*varied*)
c1395 *WBible* I Timothy iv 7: But eschewe thou uncovenable fablis, and elde (**c1384:** olde) wymmenus *fablis.* **a1500** *Colkelbie* 308.152: Quhich semys most to be a wyfis taill. **1509** Barclay *Ship* I 72[6]: The tales of an olde wyfe. **1528** More *Heresyes* 201 B[13–4]: He never found one olde wife so fonde to beleve him. Apperson 465; *Oxford* 473; Taylor and Whiting 402; Tilley W388; Whiting *Drama* 356:743, *Scots* II 154.

W245 Suffer your **Wife**'s tongue
c1395 Chaucer *CT* IV[E] 1377: Suffre thy wyves tonge, as Catoun bit. **a1400** *Cato* (*Copenhagen*) B1v[17–8]: Suffre thy wyvis tunge sum whyle, Thawgh she speke sum thyngis vile. **a1440** Burgh *Cato* 322.798–9: Thi wifis woord suffre and take in gree, Whan it availeth. **c1450** *Cato* (*Sidney*) 38.443–4: Suffre thi wife sum time, thow sche The speke wordis of perplexite.

W246 There is but one shrewd **Wife** but each man weens he has her
1528 More *Heresyes* 233 CD: There is but one shrewde wyfe in the worlde: but . . . everi man weneth he hath her. *Oxford* 257: Good; Tilley W374.

W247 Who has no **Wife** is no cuckold
c1390 Chaucer *CT* I[A] 3152: Who hath no wyf, he is no cokewold.

W248 A wicked **Wife** is ill to tame
c1450 *Fyrst thou sal* 90.118: A wykkyd wyfe is ill to tame.

W249 A **Wife** is full oft a broken post
c1475 *Prohemy of a Mariage* 29[24–5]: Ful ofte a wife is a broken poste, And he that lenethe may lihtly cache a fal. See **R70.**

W250 **Wives** are very unstable beasts
a1449 Lydgate *Evil Marriage* in *MP* II 459.92–3: Wyves been bestes very unstable In ther desires, which may not chaunged be.

W251 **Wives'** defence is worth little
c1400 *Alexander Buik* III 344.8104: For wyves defence is lytle worth! (French: Car deffensse de fenme ne vaut .ii. aus pelés!) See **W494.**

W252 **Wives** will hide their vices till they be fast (*i.e.* married)
c1395 Chaucer *CT* III[D] 282–4: Thow seyst we wyves wol oure vices hide Til we be fast, and thanne we wol hem shewe,—Wel may that be a proverbe of a shrewe!

W253 A young **Wife** and a harvest goose, much gaggle (*chatter*) with both
a1450 *Tribulations of Marriage* in Robbins 38.5–8: A yong wyf and an arvyst-gos Moche gagil with bothe; A man that hath ham yn his clos, Reste schal he wrothe. Apperson 719. See **W497.**

W254 It sits (*befits*) a woeful **Wight** to have a dreary fere (*companion*) (*varied*)
c1385 Chaucer *TC* i 12–4: For wel sit it, the sothe for to seyne, A woful wight to han a drery feere, And to a sorwful tale, a sory chere. **a1405** Lydgate *Black Knight* in *MP* II 390.183–6: For unto wo acordeth compleynyng, And delful chere unto hevynesse, To sorow also sighing and wepyng, And pitouse morenyng unto drerynesse, **a1420** *Troy* II 553.5453–4: For to a whight that is compleynynge, A drery fere is right wel sittynge, **a1439** *Fall* III 759.3144–5: To a glad mateer longeth a glad cheer, Men trete of wisdam with woordes of sadnesse, 764.3347–8: An hevy mateer requereth an hevy cheer; To a glad mateer longeth weel gladnesse. Cf. Taylor and Whiting 246: Misery.

W255 No **Wight** may come to worship but (*unless*) he endure pain (*varied*)
a1400 *Romaunt B* 2119–20: To worshipe no wight by aventure May come, but if he peyne endure. **1420** Lydgate *Temple* 17.398–9: Remembreth eke, hou never yit no wight Ne came to wirchip withoute some debate. See **L233, M236.**

W256 No **Wight** that dreads everything shall attain great thing(s)
c1450 *When the son* 390.240–1: Ther shal never wyght gret thing atteyne That dret every thing, but ay lyf in peyne. See **T298.**

W257 One should not woo a **Wight** in heaviness (*sorrow*)
c1385 Chaucer *TC* v 790–1: For wise folk in bookes it expresse, "Men shal nat wowe a wight in hevynesse."

W258 That **Wight** must speak that cannot hold his tongue
1513 Douglas *Aeneid* IV 193.36: That wight mon speke that can nocht hald hys tong. Apperson 357: Leave; *Oxford* 359–60; Tilley L168. See **P66.**

W259 A true **Wight** and a thief think not one (*alike*)
c1395 Chaucer *CT* V[F] 536–7: But sooth is seyd, goon sithen many a day, "A trewe wight and a theef thenken nat oon." Apperson 647:12; *Oxford* 672. See **F43.**

W260 As furious as a **Wild Cat**
a1500 *Colyn Blowbol* 93.30: He lokyd furyous as a wyld catt. Cf. Taylor and Whiting 402.

W261 As fearful as any **Wild-fire**
a1420 Lydgate *Troy* III 695.4456: Ferful of loke as any wylde fyre.

W262 To come like (the) **Wild-fire**
a1400 *Titus* 35.755–6: The dome shall come with grete ire, As a theef that steleth, or wilde-fuyre. **a1475** *Ludus Coventriae* 289.531–2: As wylde fyre and thondyr blast He cam cryeng on to me. **a1500** *Jeaste* 213.200–1: He came rydynge on a jolye coursyer, Dryvinge by leapes, as the wylde fyer. Taylor and Whiting 402.

Will, sb.

W263 He oftentimes wants his **Will** that thinks foolishly
a1533 Berners *Arthur* 263[11–3]: There is an olde prove(rb) that sayeth, oftentymes he wanteth of hys wyll that folysshely thynketh. See **F448.**

W264 Much of his **Will** abides (*remains*) that may thole (*suffer*) well (*varied*)
c1250 *Hendyng O* 199.41: Muchel of his wille abit, that wel may tholien, **c1325** *H* 298.248: Wel abit that wel may tholye. **a1400** *Proverbis of Wysdom* 246.100: Suffere and have thy will. **c1450** *Bühler MS. 21* in *Studies in Medieval Literature in Honor of Albert C. Baugh,* ed. MacEdward Leach (Philadelphia, 1961) 286[7–8]: And be meke and stylle, And thou shalt have alle thy wylle, 287[3]: Suffyr and have thy wylle. **c1450** Idley 84.192: Who can suffre, hath his desire. **a1500** *Counsels* in Brown *Lyrics XV* 283.21–4: Sum mene says that hyt ys soo, Who-so kone suffer, heyle, and hyde, May have hys wyll ofte tyme y-doo, And he wyll for the better A-byde. **a1500** *Good Wife N* 211.34: Suffer and have thy desire. Apperson 674–5; Jente 260; Kneuer 23–5; *Oxford* 25: Be still; Schleich 268; Singer III 135–6. See **B318, S865, T303.**

W265 A thraward (*perverse*) **Will** a thrawn (*distorted*) physiognomy
c1475 Henryson *Fables* 97.2830–3: "Ane thra-wart will, ane thrawin Phisnomy. The auld Proverb is witnes of this Lorum—*Distortum vultum sequitur distortio morum.*" "Na" (quod the Taid) "that Proverb is not trew." **a1508** Dunbar *Flyting* 8.81–2: Thocht I wald lie, thy frawart phisnomy Dois manifest thy malice to all men. Walther I 742.6026. See **M360.**

W266 To be wedded to one's **Will**
1513 More *Richard* 48 (*for* 45) G[9–13]: Never shal I . . . so wedde my selfe to myne own wyll, but that I shall bee readye to chaunge it uppon youre better advyses. **1546** Heywood *D* 101.45: I was wedded unto my wyll, **1562** *E* 149.12.2: Gill is wedded to wyll. *Oxford* 698; Tilley W392.

W267 To take the **Will** (intent) for the deed (*varied*)
a1400 *Scottish Legends* II 258.1223–4: And in thank tak my gud wil, Sene I no mare ma do thare til. **a1415** *Lanterne* 122.11–2: This wille is countid for a dede. **c1415** *Middle English Sermons* 201.27–8: God loketh more to herte and what mans will is than to the dede in itt-selfe. **a1425** *Contemplations* in *Yorkshire Writers* II 91[6–7]: God . . . receyveth that wyll as for dede, [22–3]: His good wyll shall be acounted before god as for dede. **a1438** Kempe 204.1–3: Thu xalt have the same mede and reward in Hevyn for this good willys and thes good desyrys as gyf thu haddist don hem in dede, 212.21–2: I receyve every good wyl as for dede. **1447** Bokenham 252.9268–71: God . . . Wych in every thyng more attendaunce Takyth to the entent than to the deed. **c1450** *Consail and Teiching* 74.294: The wyll Is reput for the deid. **c1475** *Wisdom* 43.221: Wyll, for dede oft ys take. **1489** Caxton *Doctrinal* D2^{v}[26]: For the wyll parfait is reputed for the dede. **c1500** *Melusine* 371.30–1: For in som cas the good wylle of a

man is accepted for the dede. **1519** Horman *Vulgaria* 179[28]: I prey you consider my good wyll, nat the thynge. **a1533** Berners *Castell* D3v[7–9]: Take . . . my desyre and not my power. **1533** More *Debellacyon* 959 D[1]: Taketh their willes for their dedes. Apperson 687; *Oxford* 709; Taylor and Whiting 402; Tilley W393. See **G83, I50, 51.**

W268 When **Will** oversties (*surmounts*) Wit, then Will and Wit are lost (*varied*)
c1250 *Will and Wit* in Brown *Lyrics XIII* 65.1–2: Hwenne-so wil wit oferstieth, Thenne is wil and wit for-lore. **a1400** in *Titus* xxvii: Whan wille over wyt wryes, Than gothe wille witt byforn. Mony a man to his harme hyes, Than hathe wille wit forlorn. **a1450** *Always try* in Brown *Lyrics XIV* 192.20: Let noght thi wille passe thi witte. **c1450** *Epistle of Othea* 92.11: Lett never thi wyll overcome thi wytte. **c1450** *Proverbs of Good Counsel* 69.39: Lett never thi wyll thi wytt over-lede. **a1500** *Eger H* 261.1305: Let not your will over-gang your wit. **a1500** *Sone, y schal thee schewe* in Furnivall *Babees Book* 34.7: Lete nevere thi wil thi witt over lede. **1513** Skelton *Against the Scottes* I 185.102: Your wyll than ran before your wyt. Whiting *Drama* 298. Cf. Apperson 699: Wit (10); *Oxford* 720. See **W408, 419.**

W269 **Will** has more might than force in battle
a1439 Lydgate *Fall* III 1014.3363: Wyl hath more myght than force hath in bataylle. See **M801.**

W270 **Will** is a good son and will is a shrewd boy
1546 Heywood *D* 45.133: Will is a good sonne, and will is a shrewde boy. *Oxford* 709.

W271 **Will** is a stepmother of wit and reason
a1439 Lydgate *Fall* II 440.3980: Wil is a step-mooder of witt and of resoun.

W272 **Will** is no law
c1440 Lydgate *Debate* in *MP* II 561.524–5: Will is no lawe whethir it be wrong or riht: Treuthe is put doun, the feeble is put to fliht.

W273 **Will** is no skill
c1450 *And ther for ye lordingis* in *MLR* 47(1952) 375.8: For wil is no skil with out good resoun. **c1516** Skelton *Magnificence* 6.148: But have ye not herde say that Wyll is no Skyll? **c1545** Heywood *Four PP* B2v[3]: What helpeth wyll where is no skyll?

W274 **Will** will have will though will win woe
1546 Heywood *D* 45.132: Wyll wyll have wyll, though will wo wyn. Apperson 687; *Oxford* 710; Tilley W397.

Will, vb.

W275 He that **Will** not when he may, may not when he will (*varied*)
a1000 *Pseudo-Alcuin* 388.430–3: Nu sceal ælc man efsten, þæt he to gode gecerre þa hwile þe he muge, þe-læste, gyf he nu nelle þa hwile þe he muge, eft þone he wyle, he ne mæig (Another *MS.*, c.14 only, in *Archiv* 122[1909] 259.49–51: Nu-þa sceal ælc mon, þæt he to Gode ʒe-cyrre þa hwile þe he mæʒe, þe læs, ʒif he nu nelle þa hwile þe he mæʒe, eft þonne he late wille, þæt he ne mæʒe). **c1175** *Poema Morale* 171.35: Thet wel ne deth the wile he mai, ne sal he thanne he wolde. **a1200** *Ancrene* 153.9–10: Hit is riht godes dom, that hwa ne deth hwen ha mei, ne schal ha hwen ha walde, 173.28–1: Ah ofte him liheth the wrench, that he ne mei hwen he wule, the nalde tha he mahte. **c1303** Mannyng *Handlyng* 159.4795–7: Hyt ys seyd al day, for thys skyl, "He that wyl nat whan he may, He shal nat, when he wyl." **a1325** *Cursor* III 1360.23815–6: For qua ne dos noght quen he mai, Quen he wald, men sal nick him nai. **a1325** *Hendyng C* 190–1.46: Wo se nel, wan he mai, he ne scel nouth, wan he wolde. **c1390** *Cato* (*Vernon*) 608.613–6: Tak what thing the profred is Whon thou maight redi have; He that nul not whon he may, Ofte hath not whon he wol crave. **a1393** Gower *CA* II 341.1498–501: Bot what Maiden hire esposaile Wol tarie, whan sche take mai, Sche schal per chance an other dai Be let, whan that hire lievest were. **a1400** *Ancrene* (*Recluse*) 160.15–7: For oft men seien on olde Englisch, he that wil noughth whan he may, he schal noughth whan he wolde. **a1400** *Ipomadon A* 135.4694–5: Foole, when thou myghte, thou wold not, Now thow wylt, now shalt thou not, 152.5287–8: But they, that woll not, when they maye, They shall not, when they wolde. **c1400** *Laud Troy* I 174.5901–6: For I have herd offte say, That he that wil not whan he may, When he wolde, he getis it noght, Then hit were ful faire be-sought, Som tyme as good hap nere, That comes not ones In sevene yere. **1422** Yonge *Governaunce* 161.30–3: A Poete Sayth, *Qui non wlt dum quid, Postea forte nequibit,* that is to say, "who so will not whan he may, he shal not when he wille." **a1430** Lydgate *Pilgrimage* 371.13691–3: But "who that wyl nat whan he may, He ys a fool, (yt is no nay,) And he ne shal nat whan he wolde." **c1450** *Camb. Univ. MS. Ee 4.37* f.2b in Brown-Robbins 1173: He that will not when he

may, When he will he shall have nay. **c1450** *Douce MS.52* 57.144: Who-so wylle not, when he may, He shall not, when he wylle. **c1450** *Jacob's Well* 22.9–11: Whanne I myghte have don penaunce, thanne wolde I noght, and now, thowgh I wolde, I may noght. **c1450** *Pilgrimage LM* 106[21–2]: He is a fool that doth not whan he may for he shal not when he wolde. **c1450** *Rylands MS.394* 108.17. **c1475** Henryson *Robene* 153.89–92: Robene, thow hes hard soung and say, In gestis and storeis auld, The man that will nocht quhen he may Sall haif nocht quhen he wald. **c1475** *Rawlinson MS. D 328* 117.3: He that wylnot whan he may a schall not whan he wyll. **1483** *Vulgaria quedam abs Terencio* O3r[20–2]: The condicyon or disposicyon of wymen is whan a man will, thei will not, And whan a man will not, than thei desyre moste. **1489** Caxton *Doctrinal* L10r[3–4]: He that wyl not whan he may he shall not whan he wold. **a1500** Marginal note in *Ludus Coventriae* xxxvi 151: Wee that will not when we paie (*for* maie), when we would we shall find nay. **a1500** *MS. Marginalia* in Hoccleve I 228 n.[9]: He that wyll not whan he maye, Whan he wolde, he shall have naye. **1546** Heywood *D* 22.1–2: He that will not whan he may, Whan he would, he shall have nay, 39.147–8: When we wold, ye wold not be our childe (quoth shee) Wherfore now whan ye wold, now will not wee, **1555** *E* 148.7. Apperson 292; Kneuer 48–9; *Oxford* 710; Schleich 268–9; Singer III 136–7; A. Taylor in *Studies in Old English Literature in Honor of Arthur G. Brodeur,* ed. Stanley B. Greenfield (Eugene, Oregon, 1963) 155–61; Tilley N54; Walther IV 227.24417; Whiting *Ballad* 24, *Scots* II 96. See **A53, F540, G359, S360, 553.**

W276 Who may not as he **Will** must as he may
1556 Heywood *Spider* 368[23]: Yet who maie not as he will, must as he maie. Whiting *Drama* 260.

W277 **Will** he nill he
c1200 *Hali Meidenhad* 40.434: Wullen ha, nullen ha, 44.464: Wulle ha, nulle ha. **c1250** *Hendyng O* 191.4[5]: Niltou, wiltou, 195.23[4]: Nilli, willi, 198.37[4]: Wille thei, nille thei. **a1300** *Alisaunder* 131.2313: Wil he, nyl he, ded he is. **c1300** *Beves* 161.3439: Wolde he, nolde he. **c1300** *Guy*[1] 34 A 578: Wiltow, niltow, 372 A 7109: Wille y so nille. **c1300** *Speculum Gy* 14.272: Wheither theih wolen, or theih nelle. **c1303** Mannyng *Handlyng* 266.8436: Wyltou, neltou. **a1325** *Cursor* III 1356.23728: Nil we, wil we (T: Wol we or nyl). **c1325** *Sayings of St. Bernard* 512.16: Woltou niltou. **c1330** *Orfeo* 15.154: Wold ich nold ich. **a1338** Mannyng *Chronicle A* I 136.3877: Wold he, ne wolde, 376.10772: Wold he, nold he. **c1340** Rolle *Psalter* 227 (65.10): Whedire we wild or we wild not. **1340** *Ayenbite* 139[21]: Wille he nolle he. **a1376** *Piers* A vii 144: Wol thou so nulle thou (B vi 158: Wiltow or neltow, C ix 153: Wolle thou, ne wolle thow). **a1387** Higden-Trevisa VIII 141[13]: Wilt thou nelt thou. **a1387** *Piers* C xxii 466: Wol he, nul he. **c1390** Chaucer *CT* II[B] 917: Wher-so she wolde or nolde. **a1400** *Alexander C* 10.301: Nyll he so will he. **a1400** *Ancrene* (*Recluse*) 51.17: Nyll he ne will he, 95.12: Nylle we ne wil we. **c1400** *Brut* I 79.24: Wolde he nolde he. **c1400** *Laud Troy* I 152.5142: Nolde or wolde—Troyle yede, II 517.17560: Wil thow, nele thow. **c1400** *Vices and Virtues* 184.25: Now thei willen, now thei nollen. **a1415** Mirk *Festial* 84.22. **a1425** *Ipomadon B* 296.1486: Wilthow, nyllthow. **a1425** *St. Robert* 53.370, 67.812. **c1425** Arderne *Fistula* 101.1. **c1425** *Foundation of St. Bartholomew's* 39.2. **c1425** *Orcherd* 34.22, 394.1. **c1425** *St. Mary Oignies* 163.37: Wolde deth or nolde. **c1440** *Prose Alexander* 88.22. **c1443** Pecock *Reule* 405[32–3]: Wole thei nyle thei, **c1445** *Donet* 148.10. **1447** Bokenham 251.9249: Wylt thou or nylt. **c1449** Pecock *Repressor* I 52[18], 98[31], II 428[32–3]. **c1450** Capgrave *Katharine* 111.521. **c1450** *Speculum Christiani* (2) 68.1. **a1470** Malory I 18.20, 398.33–4, II 593.31–2, 1003.6. **c1475** Gregory *Chronicle* 238[25–6]. **1480** Caxton *Ovyde* 126[22], **1483** *Golden Legende* 165r[1.38–9], **1484** *Royal Book* R6r[19], U1r[21]. **1489** *Governayle* A1v[22]. **c1493** *Saint Katherin of Senis* 50.33. **a1500** *Coventry Plays* 50.568. **a1500** *Disciplina Clericalis* 40[18]: Whether she wold or nold, 71[33]: Wold he nold he. Apperson 688; Taylor and Whiting 403; Tilley W401; Whiting *Drama* 370:948, *Scots* II 154–5. See **B453.**

W278 A **Willow** full of green leaves has many worms within
a1430 Lydgate *Pilgrimage* 409.15177–81: By exaumple, ys offte sene, Som whilwh ful off levys grene, Wych hath ful many werm with-Inne, That fro the herte wyl nat twynne Tyl they conswme yt everydel. **c1450** *Pilgrimage LM* 128[2–3]: Many a wilowh is ofte clothed with faire leves that is with inne al holowh and al ful of wormes. See **A155.**

W279 "Ware that!" quod **Wily**
c1475 *Wisdom* 55.606–7: To be fals, men report

yt game: Yt ys clepyde wysdom: "Ware that!" quod Wyly.

W280 **Wily** will beguile himself
c1475 Henryson *Fables* 69.1997 (*var.*): Wyly wil beguile himselfe. Apperson 501; *Oxford* 710; Tilley W406.

W281 Be your **Wimple** never so yellow you will go to bed as naked as you were born
a1300 *Cotton Cleopatra MS. C vi* in *Rel. Ant.* II 15: Ne be thi winpil nevere so jelu ne so stroutende, Ne thi faire tail so long ne so trailende, That tu ne schalt at evin al kuttid bilevin, And tou schalt to bedde gon so nakid as tou were (borin).

W282 It is little **Win** (*joy*) that makes the body smart
a1325 *Sir Simon Fraser* in Böddeker 131.167–8: Hit is lutel wunne, That maketh the body smerte. See **M642.**

W283 He that will **Win** must labor
1481 Caxton *Reynard* 27[26]: He that wil wynne he muste laboure and aventure. *Oxford* 465: Nothing venture. Cf. Jente 260.

W284 Lightly **Win** lightly tine (*lose*)
c1338 Mannyng *Chronicle A* I 158.4514: Lyghtli they wynne, lightly they tyne. See **C384, G52.**

W285 Whoso will not **Win** let him lose
c1450 *Rylands MS.394* 99.11.12: Who so woll not wynne, latte hym lose.

W286 **Win** whoso may, for all is for to sell
c1395 Chaucer *CT* III[D] 414: Wynne whoso may, for al is for to selle. Apperson 689.

W287 After mickle **Wind** the sun shines (*varied*)
a1200 *Ancrene* 126.14–6: Eft me seith and soth hit is, that a muche wind alith with alute rein, ant te sunne threfter schineth the schenre. **c1450** *Lover's Mass* 101[18–20]: Affter gret wynd and stormys kene, The glade sone with bemys shene May appere. A. A. Prins in *English Studies* 29(1948) 146–50. See **B325.**

W288 All this **Wind** shakes no corn
1546 Heywood *D* 46.174: All this winde shakes no corne. Apperson 690; *Oxford* 712; Tilley W410.

W289 As changeable as the **Wind**
c1400 *Chastising* 126.18–20: Her thoughtes bien ful chaungeable, now heere, now there, now so, now thus, liche to the wynde. **a1500** *Entierly belouvyd* in *Rawlinson MS. C 813* 368.19: For I am not changeable as the wynde. Taylor and Whiting 404:13; Tilley W412.

W290 As fast as the **Wind**
1509 Watson *Ship* H1v[8]: Renneth as faste as the wynde. **1525** Berners *Froissart* IV 207[28–9]: I came as fast as the wynde, or faster. Whiting *NC* 497.

W291 As fickle as the **Wind**
c1390 *Talkyng* 18.5: Fikelore then the wynt. Tilley W412.

W292 As fierce as **Wind**
1513 Douglas *Aeneid* IV 46.54: And to the toun spurris als ferss as wynd. Whiting *Scots* II 155.

W293 As light as (the) **Wind**
a1200 *Ancrene* 74.5: Lihtre then the wind is. **a1425** *Lyfe of Adam* in *Archiv* 74(1885) 345 [30–1]: The v partie was of the wynde: wher-of is made his breth; and ther-of he is light. **1509** Watson *Ship* U6v[13–4]: His mynde lyght as wynde. **c1523** Barclay *Mirrour* 21[5]: the, 67[15]. Tilley A90; Whiting *Ballad* 32.

W294 As swift as (the) **Wind**
c1300 *Guy*[1] 520 A 162.4–5: An ermine com of his mouthe Als swift als winde, that bloweth on clouthe. **c1330** *St. Mergrete* 232.254: Sum wer swifter than the winde. **a1439** Lydgate *Fall* I 120.4335: Swifft as the wynd in ther cours rennyng, III 731.2114. **c1477** Caxton *Jason* 73.7: the, **1480** *Ovyde* 149[6]. **a1500** *Inter Diabolus et Virgo* 444.19: the, 445.39: the. **1506** Hawes *Pastime* 16.317: the. **1513** Douglas *Aeneid* II 165.15, 207.158: the southt wynd, III 135.90: the, IV 124.95: the, 132.137. Tilley W411; Whiting *Scots* II 155.

W294a **Wind-swift**
a1300 *Names of the Hare* in *Rel. Ant.* I 133[33]: The wint-swifft. **1513** Douglas *Aeneid* III 52.100: The wynd swift hart he schot to ded.

W295 As unstable as the **Wind**
c1425 *Orcherd* 294.36: Thou art unstable and unstidefast as the wynd. **a1439** Lydgate *Fall* III 688.500: Now heer, now ther, as the wynd unstable. **c1440** *Daily Work* in *Yorkshire Writers* I 311[12–3]: Mannes lyfe es lykkynde to the wynde, that of all thynges es maste unstabill. **1506** Barclay *Castell* E4v[4]: That I unstable was as the wynde, **1509** *Ship* I 227[1]: These folys unstabyll as the wynde, II 71[12]. Whiting *Scots* II 155.

W296 As variable as (the) **Wind**
1480 Caxton *Ovyde* 131[15–6]: More varyable than wynde. **1509** Barclay *Ship* II 183[3]: A woman varyable as the wynde.

W297 As waste as **Wind**

c1375 *St. Agatha* 46.38: Youre hetinges waste als wind in rayne. **a1450** *York Plays* 157.16: I trowe oure wittis be waste as wynde.

W298 As wood (*mad*) and wild as **Wind** (*etc.*) (A number of single quotations are brought together here)
a1400 *Meditations* 13–4.485–8: The wode wynd that waketh on water, That maketh shippes to cleve and clater, So wod and wilde may not be As false Jewes weron the. **1410** Walton *Boethius* 121[20]: The firste seest thou fletyng as the wynde. **a1450** *Death and Life* 8.217: (As) wight as the wind that wappeth in the skye. **c1485** *Guiscardo* 80.723: Varyaunt as the wynd. **a1500** Bernardus *De Cura* 2.22: Ar febyle as the wynde. **a1500** Kennedy 26.21: Waldin (*pliant*) as wynd. **a1500** *Lay of Sorrow* 717.50: That bittirare ys nocht the northin wynd. **a1500** *Leconfield Proverbs* 497[14]: By vayne wordis unstedfast as the wynde. **1509** Watson *Ship* C2^{v}[15]: Some be movable as the wynde.

W299 As wroth as (the) **Wind**
a1325 *Erthe* 33.48: Erthe is as sone wroth as is the wynde. **c1350** *Smaller Vernon Collection* 88.1542: He wox al wroth as the wynde. **c1378** *Piers* B iii 328: Also wroth as the wynde wex Mede in a while. **c1380** *Patience* 28.410: the. **c1390** *Sir Gawain* 10.319: He wex as wroth as wynde. **a1400** *Athelston* 81.453. **a1400** *Destruction of Troy* 428.13091: the. **a1400** *Ipomadon A* 208.7292. **a1400** *Le Morte A.* 35.1144. **a1400** *Siege of Jerusalem* 44.78(*var.*): the. **c1400** *St. Anne (1)* 75.2878. **c1405** *Mum* 17.153: the. **a1425** *Metrical Paraphrase OT* 73.2502. **a1450** Audelay 46.995: And wry not fro Godis word as the wroth wynd. **a1475** *Ludus Coventriae* 7.217, 315.1280–1. **c1475** *Golagros* 26.770: the. Apperson 689; *Oxford* 736.

W300 Come **Wind** come rain come he never again
c1475 *Rawlinson MS. D 328* 124.73: Come wynde come reyne, come he never a-gayne. Ventus cum pluvia venient numquam retro-verte. Cf. Apperson 108:10; Tilley W414.

W301 Every **Wind** blows not the corn down
1546 Heywood *D* 94.117: Every wind blowth not downe the corne. Apperson 193; *Oxford* 712; Tilley W415.

W302 Great **Winds** blow in high courts
1484 Caxton *Curial* 5.26–7: The grete wyndes that blowe in hye courtes. Apperson 689; Tilley W450. See **H387, R191, W344.**

W303 The greatest **Wind** slakes at the last
c1515 Barclay *Eclogues* 124.466: The greatest winde yet slaketh at the last. Cf. Apperson 689:4.

W304 He that dreads the **Wind** sows seldom (not)
a900 Alfred *Gregory* 285.16–8: Salomon . . . cwæð: Se ðe him ealneg wind ondræt, he sæwð to s(e)ldon; and se ðe him ælc wolcn ondrædt, ne ripð se næfre. **c1395** *WBible* Ecclesiastes xi 4: He that aspieth the wynd, sowith not; and he that biholdith the cloudis, schal nevere repe. See **T298.**

W305 An ill **Wind** that blows no man to good
1546 Heywood *D* 94.116: An yll wynde that blowth no man to good, **a1550** *BS* 257.31, **1555** *E* 160.87, **1556** *E* 132.72.1: What winde can there blow, that doth not some man please? Apperson 326; *Oxford* 317–8; Taylor and Whiting 403; Tilley W421; Whiting *Drama* 152.

W306 Let this **Wind** overblow
1546 Heywood *D* 46.175: Let this wynde overblow, **1555** *E* 188.231: Let this winde overblow, when over blow This winde will over blow us first I trow. Apperson 690; Tilley W423.

W307 One may not weet (*know*) why every **Wind** turns
a1500 *Court of Love* 424.549: Men may not wete why turneth every wind.

W308 Stands (Is) the **Wind** in that door?
a1450 *Partonope* 444.11064: What! . . . stonte the wynde in that dore? **a1470** Malory I 360.6–7: Is the wynde in that dore? **1546** Heywood *D* 73.96: If the winde stande in that doore, it standth awry. Apperson 690; *Oxford* 712; Taylor and Whiting 404; Tilley W419; Whiting *Drama* 370:954.

W309 Stands the **Wind** so cold?
a1500 Medwall *Nature* F2^{v}[2]: A ha! standeth the wynd so cold? quod I. See **B341.**

W310 A sudden **Wind** shakes hasty (*early*) blossoms
a1449 Lydgate *Haste* in *MP* II 761.57: Hasty blosomes a sodeyne wynde doth (shake).

W311 There is no **Wind** so great but it (is) attempered
1471 Caxton *Recuyell* II 472–3: Ne ther is no wynde so grete ne so rygorous but hit attemperid. Tilley W413.

W312 To amble like (with) the **Wind**
a1500 *Robin Hood and the Potter* in Child III

113.75: Het hambellet as the weynde. **c1500** *King Hart* 91.6: That ambilit as the wynd. **1519** Horman *Vulgaria* 248[1]: I have an ambler: that ambleth with the wynde, 361[1]: The horse ambleth with the wynde. Whiting *Ballad* 32.

W313 To be but as (a, the) **Wind**
c1200 *St. Juliana* 67.724–5: Al nis but a leas wind thet we i this worlt livieth. **c1300** *Northern Homily Cycle* (*Edin. Coll. Phys.*) 36[13–4]: For werdes welthe and wa es winde, That makis werdes men ful blinde. **c1390** *Think on Yesterday* in Brown *Lyrics XIV* 144.52: This wrecched world nis but a wynde. **c1395** *WBible* Isaiah xli 29: Lo! alle men ben unjust, and her werkis ben wynd and veyn. **1410** *With god of love* in Kail 35.29–30: Man, thenke thy lyf is but a wynde; When that is blowen, thou art foryete. **a1420** Lydgate *Troy* III 570.240: It is but wynde, no thinge for to leve. **a1500** *To yow, mastres* in *Rawlinson MS. C 813* 383.19–20: For your love ys butt as the wynde,—Sum-tyme here and sumtyme there. **1509** Barclay *Ship* I 158[5]: Theyr maners lyke the wynde.

W314 To be clear in the **Wind**
c1385 Chaucer *TC* iii 526–7: Dredeles, it cler was in the wynd From every pie and every lette-game. **c1405** *Mum* 72.1552: Forto commenche a cause not cleere in the winde. NED Wind sb.[1] 20.

W315 To blow in the **Wind**
1509 Barclay *Ship* I 228[20–1]: But who that prayeth, and can nat as he ought, He bloweth in the wynde, and shall nat have his thought. Tilley W428. See **W332.**

W316 To blow with all **Winds**
1481 Caxton *Reynard* 97[17–8]: I pray yow here how he can blowe with alle wyndes.

W317 To bow to every **Wind**
1509 Barclay *Ship* II 212[27–8]: No man in Court shall nowe a lyvynge fynde Without that he can bowe to every wynde. See **C480.**

W318 To change like **Wind**
a1513 Dunbar *Of the Warldis Instabilitie* 29.27: Purpos dois change as wynd. Whiting *Scots* II 155.

W319 To fare like the **Wind**
a1350 *Ywain* 5.143: Bot word fares als dose the wind. **a1460** *Towneley Plays* 392.178–9: Thou farys as dothe the wynde; This warlde is wast and will away.

W320 To fight against the **Wind**
c1500 *Melusine* 107.1–3: For ye oweth to wete that wel fole is he that fighteth ayenst the wynd, wenyng to make hym be styll. Tilley W431.

W321 To fly like the **Wind**
a1200 Lawman II 191.14716–7: And Vortigerne the king Flaeh forth alse the wind. **c1380** *Ferumbras* 167.5383: Gweynes flegh forth so wynd and rayn. **a1440** Burgh *Cato* 306.128: Rumours newe, that flyen as the wynde.

W322 To gape after the **Wind**
c1503 More *Early Poems* [11] C[6]: To crouche and knele and gape after the wynde.

W323 To go in the **Wind**
c1460 *Dublin Abraham* in Waterhouse 29.110–1: Lat Isaac abide at home here, For I kept not he went in the wynde. Cf. Taylor and Whiting 404:15. See **R74.**

W324 To go like (the) **Wind**
c1378 *Piers* B xvii 350: And went away as wynde, C xx 332: the wynde. **c1475** *Prohemy of a Mariage* 45[14]: And hardly it shal away as wynde. **c1489** Caxton *Aymon* I 62.27–8: His horse Bayarde, that gooeth as the wynde. **a1500** *Man have mynd* 55.41–2: Women and mony wilsome wy As wynd or wattir ar gane west. Taylor and Whiting 404.

W325 To hang by the **Wind**
1475 Paston V 230[12–4]: Frendship may not hang by the wynde, nor for faire eyne, but causis must be shewid.

W326 To have one in the **Wind**
1546 Heywood *D* 49.259: I smelde hir out, and had hir streight in the wynde, **1555** *E* 194.276: I have him in the wynde. *Oxford* 711; Tilley W434.

W327 To hold (restrain the) **Wind**
c1395 *WBible* Proverbs xxvii 16: He that withholdith hir, as if he holdith wynd; and avoidith the oile of his right hond. **a1449** Lydgate *Doublenesse* in *MP* II 440.49–52: What man may the wynde restreyne, Or holde a snake by the tayle, Or a slepur eele constreyne That yt wil voyde, withoute fayle?

W328 (To know) how the **Wind** went (blew)
c1350 *Gamelyn* 662.703: To telle him tydinges how the wind was went. **1546** Heywood *D* 92.46: And knew, which waie the winde blewe, and will blow. Apperson 690; *Oxford* 345; Taylor and Whiting 404; Tilley W144.

W329 To lose (spill, waste) **Wind**
c1330 *Otuel* 71.216: That wind thou havest ilore.

a1352 Minot 6.33: The Skot in his wordes has wind for to spill. **a1400** *Destruction of Troy* 319.9788: But all thaire wordis thai wast, and thaire wynd alse. **a1450** *Descryvyng* in Kail 69.148: To preye to god, they waste here wynde. **a1450** *How Man's flesh* in Kail 90.56: To speke to here, my wynde y waste. **c1450** *Bi a forest* in Furnivall *Hymns* 97.55: Do way, mercy, thou spillist myche winde. **c1450** *How mankinde dooth* in Furnivall *Hymns* 64.207: In ydil oothis wasten thei her wynde, 67.281: Thou wastist thi wynde and spillist thi speche. **a1500** Hichecoke *This Worlde* 332.3–4: He that will noo wynde spille, Sey the best. **a1500** ?Ros *La Belle Dame* 324.795: Ye noy me sore, in wasting al this wynde. **a1500** *Thre Prestis* 49.1159: To ga to him I wait bot wind in waist. **c1516** Skelton *Magnificence* 44.1403: Wyll ye waste wynde and prate thus in vayne? **1523** *Garlande* I 384.565: But let us wast no wynde. **1546** Heywood *D* 65.41: Though I wast winde in vayne. Tilley B642; Whiting *Drama* 371:954. See **B525.**

W330 To pass (away) like (the) **Wind**
c1425 *Orcherd* 114.20–1: Thei passen awey as the wynd, 219.32. **1479** Rivers *Cordyal* 30.18: His lyf is passed as wynde. **1481** Caxton *Mirror* 183[14–5]: Ffor this world passeth fro tyme to tyme lyke as the wynde.

W331 To ride like the **Wind**
a1475 *Guy*[2] 126.4396: I rode awey, as dothe the wynde, 127.4424. Taylor and Whiting 405.

W332 To row (sail, strive) against (with) the **Wind**
c900 *Maxims* in *Exeter Book* 163.185: Werig scealc (*MS.* sceal se) wiþ winde roweþ. **1404** *Lerne say wele* in Kail 14.3–4: Ayen the wynd they sayle and rowe To gadre worldys gooddis to-gedere. **a1420** Lydgate *Troy* I 220.2618: And in her fere ageyn the wynd thei saille, III 771.7086–9: But like as he that gynneth for to saille Ageyn the wynde, whan the mast doth rive, Right so it were but in veyn to strive Ageyn the fate. **a1500** *Piers of Fullham* 13.302–4: Men rehercyn in there saw: Hard is to stryve with wynde or wawe, Whether it do ebbe or flowe. Whiting *Drama* 233. See **S830, W315.**

W333 To run like the **Wind**
1471 Caxton *Recuyell* I 144.23: An honderd men that ran as the wynde, 151.9–10: On horsback rennyng as the wynde, II 483.10–1: Renomee that renneth . . . as lightly as the wynde, **c1489** *Aymon* I 305.16–7, II 338.5. **1506** Hawes *Pastime* 11.160.

W334 To sow **Wind** and reap whirlwind
c1395 *WBible* Hosea viii 7: For thei schulen sowe wynd, and thei schulen repe whirlewynd. Apperson 592; *Oxford* 608; Taylor and Whiting 404; Tilley W437.

W335 To take **Wind** and tide with one
1546 Heywood *D* 46.175–6: A tyme I will spy, To take wynde and tyde with me, and spede therby. Tilley W429.

W336 To threst (*push*) like the **Wind** (*etc.*) (A number of single quotations are brought together here)
a1200 Lawman III 102.27643–4: Swulc hit the wind weore, He thraste to than fihte. **a1300** Thomas de Hales 68.13–4: Theos theines that her weren bolde Beoth aglyden so wyndes bles. **c1380** *Ferumbras* 55.1558: Sarasyns . . . that prikeath as wynd and rayn. **c1410** Lovelich *Grail* IV 262.769–70: As it hadde ben A wyndes blast These two Men thider Comen In hast. **a1420** Lydgate *Troy* I 67.1869: Is to and fro mevyng as a wynde, II 401.202: In Martis Ire as the wynde dothe blowe. **1435** Misyn *Fire* 88.3: As wynde my sorow vanischys. **a1500** *Death* in Brown *Lyrics XV* 257.17–8: Thynk this werld that wryched es Will wan o-way als wynde. **1513** Douglas *Aeneid* II 104.63: The figur fled as lycht wynd, III 45.47. **1525** Berners *Froissart* IV 456[31–2]: So these tydynges ranne abrode with the wynde, **a1533** *Arthur* 512[6]: Brayeng lyke the wynde.

W337 To turn like the **Wind**
a1400 *Alexander C* 265.5318: It (*wealth*) witis a-way at a wapp as the wynd turnes. **a1400** Wyclif *Sermons* I 21[15–6]: Thei may not turne as the wynd. **c1450** Idley 161.141–3: Ffor lordis woll now hate and now love, As the wynde turneth now Est and now Weste, Now heere, now there, now benethe, now above. **a1500** *Imitatione (1)* 40.14. **c1500** *Alone, alone* in Stevens *Music* 343.6[3]: Turnyng as the wynd. **1506** Barclay *Castell* G5[v][17]. **1506** Hawes *Pastime* 136.3559: But alway tornynge lyke a blast of wynde. **c1523** Barclay *Mirrour* 45[49]. Whiting *Drama* 332:366.

W338 To wane (*?vacillate*) with (as) the **Wind**
c1400 *Triamour* 53.245–6: And the knyght be there assente, Schulde wayne wyth the wynde. **a1415** *Lanterne* 52.1: Wanen aboute as the wynde.

W339 To wave like **Wind** (in water)
a1450 *Castle* 88.380: As wynde in watyr I wave. **a1513** Dunbar *None May Assure* 45.59: Quhais fals behechtis as wind hyne wavis.

W340 To waver like the **Wind**
a1450 *Whan that phebus* in Sandison 124.42: He wavers as the wynde and doth both gloyse and fayne. **c1475** Henryson *Fables* 75.2168–70: With that the Cadgear, wavering as the wind, Come rydand on the laid. **1546** Heywood *D* 62.104: But waveryng as the wynde, **1556** *E* 131.70.3. Apperson 670; *Oxford* 695; Tilley W412.

W341 To wend away like **Wind**('s blas [*blast*])
c1390 *Of clene Maydenhod* 465.30: Hit wendeth a-wey as wyndes bles. **a1450** *York Plays* 95.53–4: Thir wise wordis ware noght wroght in waste, To waffe and wende away als wynde. **c1475** Henryson *Abbay Walk* 195.12: Bot as the wind will wend away.

W342 To whistle after the **Wind**
c1500 *Cock* 12[24]: Some whysteled after the wynde. *Oxford* 705; Taylor and Whiting 405; Tilley W440.

W343 What **Wind** guides you here? (*varied*)
c1385 Chaucer *TC* ii 1104: What manere wyndes gydeth yow now here? **c1400** *Beryn* 51.1651: What manere wynd hath I-brought yewe here? (*perhaps literal*). **c1489** Caxton *Aymon* I 106.12–3: What wynde dryveth you hyther? 162.21: What wynde brought you hider? **1546** Heywood *D* 37.55: What wynde blowth ye hyther? Apperson 690; *Oxford* 711–2; Taylor and Whiting 404; Tilley W441.

W344 When northern **Winds** blow great houses are in trouble
1492 *Salomon and Marcolphus* 9[3–5]: Whann the northren wyndes blowe than ben the high howses in great trouble and daunger. See **H387, 606, R191, T434, 462, W302.**

W345 When the **Wind** is blowing north and south at once (*i.e.*, never)
c1412 Hoccleve *Regement* 135.3757–9: Lat us awayte wel whan the wynd south is And north at ones blowynge on the sky, And fynde swiche an hepe than hardily.

W346 Whenso (Howsoever) the **Wind** blows
a1450 *Castle* 153.2541–3: Certys, this ye wel knowe, It is good, whon-so the wynde blowe, A man to have sum-what of his owe. **a1475** *Tree* 46.5–6: No thing fering . . . of any adversite, how so ever the wynde blow.

W347 The **Wind** may turn
a1400 *Morte Arthure* 53.1788–9: So may the wynde weile turnne, I rewarde hym or ewyn. **1520** Whittinton *Vulgaria* 72.32–3: Sodaynly the wynde hathe tourned, so that he hath be wery of his parte.

W348 With great **Winds** fall great oaks
a1400 *Proverbis of Wysdom* 246.108: Wyth grete wyndis fallythe grete okis, (*II*) 224.98: good ookis. **c1450** *Fyrst thou sal* 89.88. See **O6.**

W349 To come in at the north **Window**
a1500 *Thre Prestis* 26.408–12: Thir Bishops cums in at the North window, And not in at the dur nor yit at the yet, Bot over Waine and Quheil in wil he get. And he cummis not in at the dur, Gods pleuch may never hald the fur. Apperson 692; *Oxford* 103; Taylor and Whiting 405; Tilley W456; Whiting *Scots* II 156. See **M299.**

W350 As clear as **Wine**
a1375 *Hermit* 175.246: Ther watyr was cler as wyne.

W351 As fair as **Wine**
c1395 Chaucer *CT* IV[E] 2142: How fairer been thy brestes than is wyn!

W352 As red as **Wine**
c1475 *Prohemy of a Mariage* 39[6]: Thyn eyene wax read as wyne. **a1500** *Peterborough Lapidary* in *Lapidaries* 69[23]: Red as . . . wyne. Whiting *Ballad* 32.

W352a **Wine-red**
a1200 *Trinity College Homilies* 213[14]: Winrede bruwes.

W353 Drink no **Wine** but of the well
a1425 *Metrical Paraphrase OT* 28.6627–8: Thei dranke no wyn bot of the well, Ne beyre bot of the reynnand beke. See **D427.**

W354 One knows not **Wine** by the hoops
c1450 *Pilgrimage LM* 128[1]: Men knowen nouht wyne bi the hoopes. Apperson 693:27; *Oxford* 713; Tilley W492. See **G35, T47, W361.**

W355 One loves not the **Wine** for the girths (*hoops*)
c1450 *Foly of Fulys* 55.117: Men lufys nocht for the gyrthis the wyne.

W356 Such **Wine** (liquor) yerns (*runs*) by the tap as is in the tun (vessel)
1340 *Ayenbite* 27[30–1]: Vor hit behoveth thet zuich wyn yerne by the teppe ase: ther is ine the tonne. **c1400** *Vices and Virtues* 23.11–2: For nedes suche licour as is in the tunne mote nedes come out at the faucetes hoole. **c1415** *Middle English Sermons* 300.17–8: For suche lycour as is wyth-inne, such comme(th) forthe. **1484** Caxton *Royal Book* D3ʳ[10–2]: For nedes

must suche wyne come oute of the tappe as is within the vessel.

W357 To spring out like **Wine** from a tun
1471 Caxton *Recuyell* II 586.25–7: And made the blood sprynge oute lyke as the wyn Renneth out of a tonne.

W358 **Wine** and women make wise men go backwards (fall into apostasy) (*varied*)
a1382 *WBible* Ecclesiasticus xix 2: Wyn and wymmen maken also wise men to go bacward, **c1395:** Wyn and wymmen maken to be apostataas, yhe, wise men. **1483** Caxton *Cato* I2r[5–7]: The wyse man sayth that by wyn and by wymmen comen many evyls and inconvenyents. **a1500** *Remedie of Love* CCCXXIII [1.31–2]: Wine and women into apostasie Cause wise men to fall. Apperson 693:9; *Oxford* 713; Tilley W474.

W359 **Wine** and youth increase Venus
c1390 Chaucer *CT* VI[C] 59–60: For wyn and youthe dooth Venus encresse, As men in fyr wol casten oille or greesse, 549: A lecherous thyng is wyn. *Oxford* 713; Skeat 258; Whiting *Scots* II 156. See **C125, G168.**

W360 **Wine** does wit (wisdom) away (*varied*)
a1393 Gower *CA* III 182.551–9: Men sein ther is non evidence, Wherof to knowe a difference Betwen the drunken and the wode, For thei be nevere nouther goode; For wher that wyn doth wit aweie, Wisdom hath lost the rihte weie, That he no maner vice dredeth; Nomore than a blind man thredeth His nedle be the Sonnes lyht. **c1412** Hoccleve *Regement* 138.3833–4: Thei (*wines*) birien wit, and forbeden scilence Of conseil. **a1425** *Metrical Paraphrase OT* 124.4347–9: When he of wyn was dronkyn wele, Then was hys wytt all wast away. **1450** *Dicts* 106.32–3: Wyne and wisdome may not be to-gader, for in some wise thei be contrarie. **c1450** *Douce MS.52* 52.96: Ofte drynke maketh thy wyttes renne. **c1450** *Rylands MS. 394* 103.2: makes thynne wytte. **1528** More *Heresyes* 243 B[2–3]: Whan the wyne wer in and the witte out. **1555** Heywood *E* 175.163: When ale is in, wyt is out. Apperson 164; Jente 3; *Oxford* 6; Smith 46; Taylor and Whiting 406; Tilley W471; Whiting *Drama* 134. See **D394, 421.**

W361 By the **Wine Hoop** men may see where the tavern is
a1475 *Good Wyfe Wold* 173.18: Be wyne hope men mey se wher the tawern ys. NED Hoop sb.[1] lb. See **W354.**

W362 To be like a **Wine-tun**
c1300 *Beves* 125.2673: His bodi ase a wintonne.

W363 To fly without **Wings** (feathers) (*varied*)
c1385 Chaucer *TC* iii 1263: Lo, his desir wol fle withouten wynges. **1509** Watson *Ship* C1v[14–5]: Lustye galauntes that wolde flee without wynges. **1523** Berners *Froissart* III 450[19–20]: The bysshoppe of Norwiche, who thought to have flyen or he had wynges, **1525** IV 200[17]: These calves that flye without wynges, V 148[12]: Yonge people, who wolde flye or they have wynges. **1549** Heywood *D* 45.144: He would fayne flee, but he wanteth fethers. Apperson 221; *Oxford* 211, 212; Smith 111; Tilley F164, 407; Whiting *Scots* I 166.

W364 Trust not your **Wing** to fly too high
1418 *Herrere degre* in Kail 62.47: To flighe to hyghe, treste not thy wyng. MED flien lb.

W365 As swift as one (eye) may **Wink**
a1325 *Cursor* I 28 C 341: Suiftliker then hee may wink, **a1400** F: Squyfter than any eye may wynke. Cf. Taylor and Whiting 406. See **T547, W220.**

W366 Better to **Wink** than to look
a1393 Gower *CA* II 46.383–4: For ofte, who that hiede toke, Betre is to winke than to loke. *Oxford* 715.

W367 He that **Winks** when he should see, God let him never thee (*thrive*)
c1390 Chaucer *CT* VII 3431–2 [B4621–2]: For he that wynketh, whan he sholde see, Al wilfully, God lat him nevere thee!

W368 **Winking** to drinking is always linking
c1545 Heywood *Four PP* B2r[19]: For wynkynge to drynkynge is alway lynkynge. See **B242.**

W369 Little **Winning** where men sell no dearer than they buy
c1495 *Arundel Vulgaria* 88.368: It is but a litell wynnynge (nay, nay, not a whitt) wher men sell no derer than they bye, but rather better Chepe. See **S29, 173.**

W370 To put (one's **Winning**) in one's eye and see never the worse
c1450 Idley 125.1067–9: I trowe ye nede not of ony grete malis To put in devocion—it woll in a litell purs, I trowe in youre eye and loke never the wers. **1546** Heywood *D* 51.333–4: At end I might put my winnyng in mine eye, And see never the woorse. Apperson 196; *Oxford* 8; Tilley W506; Whiting *Scots* I 165.

W371 Wrong **Winning** never did the winner good
c1450 *Consail and Teiching* 73.277–8: For wrang vyninge the vynnar to Dyd nevir gud na nevir sal do. See **G336.**

W372 After **Winter** follows May (*varied*)
c1385 Chaucer *TC* iii 1062: And after wynter foloweth grene May. **c1440** Charles of Orleans 182.5436: Aftir wyntir the veer with foylis grene. **a1449** Lydgate *Fabula* in *MP* II 490.117: And afftir wyntir sweth greene Maye, *Guy* in *MP* II 520.83: Affter wynter cometh May with fresshe fflours. **c1450** *Lover's Mass* 101[16–7]: And after wynter wyth hys shourys God send hem confort of May flourys. **a1500** *Imitatione* (*1*) 49.30–1: After wynter cometh somer. **1502** *Imitatione* (*2*) 186.32: After wynter foloweth somer. Skeat 182. See **S876.**

W373 **Winter** eats that summer gets
c1450 *Rylands MS.394* 92.9: Wyntur alle etus, that sommer be getus. **a1475** *Good Wyfe Wold* 175.77–8: Seyd hit ys be southe, "'Wynttor ettythe that somor gettyth' to olde men is unkoth." **c1475** *Rawlinson MS. D 328* 118.17: Whynter etyt that somer getyt. **a1500** Hill 128.14, 133.54. Apperson 694:10; *Oxford* 715; Tilley W510.

W374 **Winter's** weather, woman's thought and lord's love change oft (*varied*)
c1450 Greene *Carols* 381.2: Wynteris wether and wommanys thowt And lordis love schaungit oft. **a1500** *Hunterian Mus. MS.230* 175: A Lords purpose and a ladys thoughtt in a yer schevyth (*for* schangyth) full offte. Apperson 695; Tilley W673. See **L441, M297, P410.**

W375 As bright as drawn **Wire**
1506 Hawes *Pastime* 80.2037: Her heer was bryght as the drawen wyre.

W376 Better a **Wisdom** (purchased than one given free)
c1470 *Harley MS.3362* f.4a: Plus valet empta satis sapiencia quam data gratis. Betyr ys a wysdom (*no more*). Walther III 865.21792; Whiting *Scots* II 156. See **L519, W420.**

W377 He has **Wisdom** at will that can with angry heart be still (*varied*)
c1450 *Proverbs of Good Counsel* 69.37–8: He hathe wysdom at hys wyll That can with Angry harte be stylle. **1481** Caxton *Reynard* 110[4–5]: Therfore he is wyse that can in his angre mesure hym self and not be over hasty. **1549** Heywood *D* 53.409–10: He maie shewe wisdome at will, That with angry harte can holde his tongue styll. Apperson 695; *Oxford* 720: Wit; Tilley W553.

W378 It is great **Wisdom** sometime to feign folly
c1450 *Pilgrimage LM* 13–4: It is gret wysdom, what any man saye, sum time to feyne folye. Cf. Apperson 696:20; *Oxford* 718; Smith 112, 113; Tilley M428. See **F388, M346, 350.**

W379 It is great **Wisdom** to speak little
a1475 Ashby *Dicta* 85.939: Grete wisdam is, litil to speke. Apperson 571. See **H264.**

W380 It is no **Wisdom** to lie the more
c1470 *Harley MS.3362* f.4b: Hyt ys no wysdom to leghe the more.

W381 It is **Wisdom** to put in forgetting thing lost without recovering
c1390 *Proverbes of diverse profetes* 535.201–4: Hit is wisdam to putte in forgetyng Thing that is lost with-outen rekeveryng, And to suffre not grucchinde Thing that thou maight not amende. See **R81, T160, 179, 192.**

W382 It is **Wisdom** to suffer to win wealth
a1425 *Metrical Paraphrase OT* 28.6601–2: Yt is wysdom, os wysmen says, At suffer welth forto wyn.

W383 Of all **Wisdom** the most is measure
c1303 Mannyng *Handlyng* 211.6527–8: Of alle wysdom that shal dure, The most wysdom . . . ys "mesure." Skeat 25. See **M461.**

W384 They lack **Wisdom** that do not dread Fortune
1478 Rivers *Morale Proverbes* [2.25–6]: Wisdom thay lakke that fortune doo not drede, For many a wight to trouble dooth she lede.

W385 To have **Wisdom** at will
a1500 Greene *Carols* 332.3[1]: If thou have wysdom at thi wyll. Apperson 699:9; Tilley W552.

W386 Who weens himself wise, **Wisdom** wot him a fool
1562 Heywood *E* 203.1.7: Who weenth him selfe wise, wisdome wotth him a foole. Tilley W522.

W387 **Wisdom** shall never enter an evil willed (person)
c1475 *Rawlinson MS. D 328* 118.15: Wysdem schall never en-tre in to a newle (*for* an ewle) wyllyd.

W388 **Wisdom** stands not all by speech
c1450 *Proverbs of Good Counsel* 69.35: Wysdom stondyth not all by speche.

W389 **Wisdom** will be ware ere necessity comes **1449** Metham 50.1362: But wysdam wul to be ware, or ther come necessyte. See **W45.**

W390 Without **Wisdom** is weal (*wealth*) well unworth **a1300** *Proverbs of Alfred* 83 J 96–7: Wyth-ute wysdome Is weole wel unwurth. *Oxford* 716.

Wise, adj.

W391 He is **Wise** that can be ware by another's trespass (perils, harm) (*varied*) **c1408** Lydgate *Reson* 112.4244–51: He ys wyse that wyl be war And him self chastise kan By trespace of another man, Prudently to taken hede Of another mannys dede, The foly wisely to eschewe To fleen a-way and not to sewe, Where as he seeth yt be(t) to do (Notes II 121 give French: Car Il se fait Bon chastiier par aultrui fait). **c1475** *Additional MS.12195* in Robbins-Cutler 1137.3: He is wyse and happy that can be ware be an oder mannys harme. **c1475** *Rawlinson MS. D 328* 117.6: He ys wyse that can be-ware by other mans per-leys. **a1500** Hill 132.36: He is wysse, that can beware by an other manys harme. Tilley T291; Whiting *Drama* 236. See **C161, M170, W47, 400.**

W392 He is **Wise** that is (will be) ware **c1250** *Hendyng O* 199.45: Wis is that war is. **c1303** Mannyng *Handlyng* 256.8083–4: Yn a proverbe, telle men thys, "He wyys ys, that ware ys," 308.9884. **a1450** Audelay 44.949: I hold hym wyse that wyl be ware whan he has warnyng. Apperson 697:25; Kneuer 65–6; *Oxford* 718; Schleich 259–60; Tilley T291. See **W46.**

W393 He that seems the **Wisest** is most fool when it comes to the proof **c1395** Chaucer *CT* VIII[G] 967–9: He that semeth the wiseste, by Jhesus! Is moost fool, whan it cometh to the preef; And he that semeth trewest is a theef. See **C291.**

W394 One is never so **Wise** but he may be overseen (*mistaken*) **a1470** Malory II 516.4–5: And he was never so wyse but he myght be oversayne. Tilley M432.

W395 To be as **Wise** when one went as when one came **c1405** *Mum* 43.558: I was as wise whenne I wente as whenne I came to thaym. Cf. Tilley F460. See **C380, F392, G182, W413.**

W396 Whoso will call himself **Wise** makes him a fool **a1350** *Proprium Sanctorum* 108.81–2: Hose wys him-self calle wolle, A fol he maketh him atte fulle. Tilley C582.

W397 You are **Wise** enough if you keep you warm **1546** Heywood *D* 63.37: Ye are wyse inough . . . if ye keepe ye warme, **1555** *E* 169.131. Apperson 697; *Oxford* 717; Tilley K10.

Wise, sb.

W398 Learn of the **Wise,** the rather (*sooner*) you shall rise **c1450** *Fyrst thou sal* 88.25–6: Lerne of the wise, The rather thou salt ryse. See **C618.**

W399 Send the **Wise** and say nothing (*varied*) **c1390** Chaucer *CT* I[A] 3598: Men seyn thus, "sende the wise, and sey no thyng." **1461** Paston III 285[6–7]: Men sey, send a wiseman on thy erand, and sey litell to hym. Apperson 697; *Oxford* 717; Tilley M371. See **W588.**

W400 The **Wise** are chastised by the harm of fools **c1385** Chaucer *TC* iii 329: For wyse ben by foles harm chastised. Apperson 698:52; *Oxford* 40, 718; Skeat 176. See **C161, M340, W391.**

W401 The **Wise** must learn wit of the ignorant **c1515** Barclay *Eclogues* 9.284: The wise nowe must learne wit of the ignoraunt. See **M345.**

W402 One may not have by **Wishes** **a1471** Ashby *Policy* 39.835–7: Be wele ware that ye have not by wisshes, Wisshing that ye had doon or lefte suche thing, Suche maner reule is nat worthe two Russhes.

W403 **Wishers** and woulders are small (no good) householders **1508**(1519) Stanbridge *Vulgaria* 30.12: Wysshers and wolders be small hous holders. **1546** Heywood *D* 42.56: Wishers and wolders be no good householders. Apperson 699; *Oxford* 719; Tilley W539; Whiting *Scots* II 156–7. See **D261.**

W404 To fare like a **Wisp** afire **a1420** Lydgate *Troy* III 710.4984–6: For thei faren as a wisp a-fire: Whanne it brenneth brightest in his blase, Sodeinly it wasteth as a mase.

Wit, sb.

W405 Cheap **Wit** is better than wit bought overdear **a1500** *Proverbs of Salamon* 180.26.7–8: With grete cheep wytte thyn herte fylle Bettur than with wytt overdere boght.

W406 He eats by **Wit** that greets the eater **1492** *Salomon and Marcolphus* 8[6–7]: By wyt he etyth that gretyth the ether. Walter Hartmann *Salomon und Markolf* (Halle, 1934) 14.311–2, n.: Per ingenium manducat qui manducantem salutat.

W407 Leave **Wit** before it leaves you
1546 Heywood *D* 62.11–2: Except I shall seeme to leave my wit, Before it leave me, I must now leave it. Tilley W558. See **S335.**

W408 Let **Wit** pass (daunt) will
a1400 *Proverbis of Wysdom* (*II*) 221.23: Let thi witt passe thi wille. **c1450** *Consail and Teiching* 70.166: Bot set thi wyt thi will to dant. **c1450** *Fyrst thou sal* 87.5–6: Bot witt pas wylle Vyce wil vertewe spylle, 88.37. Cf. *Oxford* 720. See **W268.**

W409 Many **Wits** are better than a (*one*) man's wit (*varied*)
a1450 *Myne awen dere* 168.589–91: Many wittys better are Than a mans witte to declare Any mater, gode or yll. **1556** Heywood *E* 123.41.1: Two wittes are better then one. Apperson 655; *Oxford* 680; Tilley H281. See **H227.**

W410 One should have **Wit** when his neck is full of hair
1532 Berners *Golden Boke* 352.7675–6: Thou oughtest to have wyt, whan thy necke is full of heare. See **H23.**

W411 Tender **Wits** ween all they cannot understand is wile (*varied*)
c1385 Chaucer *TC* ii 271–2: For tendre wittes wenen al be wyle Thereas thei kan nought pleynly understonde, **a1395** *CT* V[F] 221–4: As lewed peple demeth comunly Of thynges that been maad moore subtilly Than they kan in hir lewednesse comprehende; They demen gladly to the badder ende. **c1495** *Arundel Vulgaria* 89.370: The conyngar a mann is, the more nede he hath to beware what eligance he useth to sum menn, for many tymes when thei cannot bolte oute the trewe sentence they interpretate to the worst that that thou writest of very lovyng mynde. **1533** More *Confutacion* 769 C[16–7]: But yet as folk be ready to deme the wurst.

W412 To be at one's **Wit's** end
c1378 *Piers* B xv 363: Astrymanes also aren at her wittes ende. **c1385** Chaucer *TC* iii 931: Right at my wittes ende. **a1475** *Assembly of Gods* 49.1665: When they were drevyn to her wyttes ende. **1481** Caxton *Reynard* 72[32]: He was at his wittes ende. **1508**(1519) Stanbridge *Vulgaria* 22.1. **1519** Horman *Vulgaria* 79[11], 436[4]. **1528** More *Heresyes* 215 F[1], **1533** *Confutacion* 627 G[16–7]. **1546** Heywood *D* 31.18. **1550** *Plumpton Correspondence* 254[12–3]. **1555** Heywood *E* 149.13, 234.33.4. Apperson 699; *Oxford* 721; Skeat 181; Tilley W575.

W413 To have one's **Wit** go out even as it came in
a1460 *Towneley Plays* 105.173: So gose youre wyttys owte evyn as It com In. See **F392, W395.**

W414 To have one's **Wit** in his heel
1406 Hoccleve *Male Regle* 32.231–2: The soothe of the condicion in hem bred, No more than hir wit were in hire heele.

W415 To have one's **Wit** in the wane
1562 Heywood *D* 84.130: His wit is in the wane. Tilley W555.

W416 To have **Wit** to make a ship be drowned
a1460 *Towneley Plays* 105.145: These wold by thare wytt make a shyp be drownde. Apperson 700; Tilley W572.

W417 **Wit** and wisdom is good warison (*wealth*)
c1250 *Hendyng O* 191.2: Wit and wisdom Is god wareisun. Apperson 699; Kneuer 20–1; *Oxford* 720; Schleich 248; Singer III 125. Cf. Jente 444.

W418 **Wit** is better than force or strength
1484 Caxton *Aesop* 102[1]: Wytte is better than force or strengthe. See **L381, M801.**

W419 **Wit** is more worthy than will
1450 *Dicts* 136.24–5: Witt is more worthi than will, for wit hath set the lord of tyme of the whiche wille wolde have the servaunt. See **W268.**

W420 **Wit** is worth nothing till it be dear bought (*varied*)
a1500 Medwall *Nature* I2ᵛ[20]: Wyt ys nothyng worth tyll yt be dere bought. **1546** Heywood *D* 31.21: Wit is never good tyll it be bought, **1555** *E* 149.14. Apperson 700; *Oxford* 58; Tilley W567; Whiting *Scots* II 156: Wisdom. See **G356, L519, W376.**

W421 The **Wit** (wisdom) of a woman is wonder(ful) to hear (*ironic*)
a1400 *Quartrefoil* 2.53–4: The witte of a woman es wonder to here, Es all thi sare syghynge to seke lufe trewe? **c1500** *Lady Bessy* 19[23]: Woman's wisdom is wondrous to hear, loe. Cf. Tilley W568.

W422 **Wits** of the people err full oft
c1400 *De Blasphemia* in Wyclif *SEW* III 408[23–4]: Wittes of tho puple erren ful ofte. See **C392.**

Wit, vb.

W423 Well were him that **Wist** to whom he might trust
c1450 *Douce MS.52* 46.30: Welle were hym, that (wist) to wham he myghht trist, And so were hym, that knew false fro the trewe. **c1475** *Rawlinson MS. D 328* 125.80: Well were hym that wyst to wam he myst tryst. **a1500** *Ashmole MS.1438* in William H. Black *Descriptive Catalogue of the Manuscripts* (Oxford, 1845) 1186[2.5–10]: Wel were hym that wyst To wham he moght trist Yn tyme off nede: Beter were he that knew The false fro the trew Clothyd yn oon wede. **a1500** *Royal MS. 17 B xlvii* in Brown *Register* I 366: Wele were him that wiste to whom he might trust, And so were he that knewe the fals from the trewe. Tilley M198.

W424 **Wit** ere you wend
a1475 *Good Wyfe Wold* 174.41: Wett or ever thou wende. See **L435.**

W425 Be such **Within** as you seem outward
a1450 *Declaryng* in Kail 83.118: Be suche withynne, as ye outward seme. See **A155, F3.**

W426 The **Withdrawal** of access slakes wantonness
a1400 *Scottish Legends* I 374.33–4: Fore be withdrawine of access Is slokit oft sic wantones. Whiting *Scots* I 130. See **E27.**

W427 Best **Witness** is he that sees
1440 Palladius 144.467: Best witnesse is that seeth.

W428 He that were **Witty** were seely (*happy*)
c1450 *Douce MS.52* 56.131: He, that were wytty, were sely. **c1450** *Rylands MS.394* 107.18.

W429 (All is for **Woe**) that the hen sings in the snow
c1250 *Owl* 38.413: Thu singest so doth hen a-snowe. **c1450** *Douce MS.52* 47.40: All hit is for wo, That the hen synges in (the) snowe. **c1450** *Rylands MS.394* 97.8^{v}.5.

W430 Every **Woe** by process must assuage
a1420 Lydgate *Troy* III 673.3702–3: For every wo by processe muste aswage, And overgon and wasten by myracle. See **B19, M587.**

W431 Every **Woe** must end at a term
a1420 Lydgate *Troy* I 157.458: And at a terme every wo mote ende. See **S798, T87.**

W432 To take the **Woe** with the weal
a1470 Malory III 1169.26: We woll take the woo with you as we have takyn the weale. Tilley W188. See **R220, W132.**

W433 **Woe** is a man that is bound
a1500 *Beves* 84 M [6–7]: "Lorde," said Beves in that stounde, "Woo ys a man, that is bound!" See **S657.**

W434 **Woe** is to him that is alone (*varied*)
a1200 *Ancrene* 129.4–6: For as Salomon seith . . . Wa eaver the ane, for hwen he falleth, naveth he hwa him areare. **c1385** Chaucer *TC* i 694–5: The wise seith, "Wo hym that is allone, For, and he falle, he hath non helpe to ryse." **a1393** Gower *CA* III 75.4705–6: So that al one he falleth ofte, Whan he best weneth stonde alofte. **c1395** *WBible* Ecclesiastes iv 10: Wo to hym that is aloone, for whanne he fallith, he hath noon reisynge him. **c1412** Hoccleve *Regement* 8.204–7: The boke seith thus—I redde it yore agon,—"Wo be to hym that list to ben allone! Ffor if he falle, helpe ne hath he non to ryse." *Oxford* 722; Skeat 151; Tilley W598.

W435 **Woe** to him that is unkind to his maker
1509 Barclay *Ship* I 284[14–5]: For we fynde in an olde sayde sawe, Wo is hym that to his maker is unkynde.

W436 **Woe** to the land where the child is king (*varied*)
a1200 Serlo 217.i: Thar the clild is kings and the iuerl is Alderman and the wale (*?foreigner*) is biscop, wa thene lede. **a1225** *Lambeth Homilies* 115[29–30]: For hit is awriten thet wa there þeode ther the king bith child. **c1303** Mannyng *Handlyng* 340.10975–6: But how seyth Salamon yn hys spellyng, "Wo the land, there chylde ys kyng!" **a1350** *Cambridge Un. MS. Gg i l* in *Chronicle* 107.618–24: Ke de enfaunt fet rey, e prelat de vileyn, e de clerc fet cunte, Dunke vet la terre a hunte. Wos maket of a clerc hurle, And prelate of a cheurle, And of a child maked king, Thanne is the londe undirling. **c1378** *Piers* B Prol. 189–91: For I herde my sire seyn, is sevene yere ypassed, There the catte is a kitoun the courte is ful elyng; That witnesseth holi-write, who-so wil it rede, Ve terre ubi puer rex est. **a1382** *WBible* Ecclesiastes x 16: Wo to thee, thou lond, whos king is a child, and whos princes erli eten. **a1398**(1495) Bartholomaeus-Trevisa N4^{r}[2.4–5]: Woo is the londe that hathe a chylde kynge. **c1440** Scrope *Epistle* 91[13–4]: An auctorite seith to this purpose that where a childe is kyng the londe ys onappy. **c1450** *Epistle of Othea* 121.8–10: And to the same intent seyth thus a philosophre: the lond is cursed wherof the governour is a chyld. **c1450** *Rylands MS.394* 102.15–6: There childe is kynge and clerke bysshop, And chorle reve all is greve.

1456 Hay *Law* 297.5–6: Thar to acordis wele haly writt, sayand, that unhapp cummys to thes lands of quhilk the king is a barne. **a1500** *Ancrene* (*Royal*) 17.32–3: Lust *ecclesiastes 10.* Seys Salamon, *ve tibi terra &c.* Who to the erthe of wom the kyng is a childe. **1509** Barclay *Ship* II 14[17–8]: But wo be that londe, whose crowne of royalte Is gyven to a childe. **1509** Watson *Ship* P2[r][3–4]: The londe where as is a yonge kynge or a prynce is not wel assured. **1513** More *Richard* 63 H[15–6]: Woe is that Realme, that hathe a chylde to theyre Kynge. Apperson 342–3; Jente 762; *Oxford* 338; Tilley W600.

W437 **Woe** to the man that has friends and no bread
1492 *Salomon and Marcolphus* 11[25]: Woo to that man that hath frendes and no breed.

W438 **Woe** worth the fruit (that) would put the tree to nought
a1513 Dunbar *In Prais of Wemen* 83.9: Wo wirth the fruct wald put the tre to nocht.

W439 As ferly (*suddenly*) as a **Wolf** (*etc.*) (A number of single quotations are brought together here)
c1000 Aelfric *Lives* II 316.39–40: And se foresæda hinguar færlice swa swa wulf On lande bestalcode and þa leode sloh. **a1300** *Alisaunder* 274.5022: Hii ben hore also a wolf. **c1395** *WBible* Habakkuk i 8: His horsis ben . . . swifter than eventyd wolvys. **1456** Hay *Governaunce* 157.18: Gredy as a wolf. **1506** Barclay *Castell* A4[v][15]: Lene as ony wolf ravysable.

W440 As ravenous as a **Wolf**
a1450 *Partonope* 82.2655–7: Agysor . . . thatt as a . . . wolffe ys ravennous. Cf. Taylor and Whiting 408: hungry.

W441 As wood (*mad*) as **Wolf**
a1338 Mannyng *Chronicle* A II 478.13795–8: Was nevere . . . wilde wolf . . . That was so wod, beste to byte, As Wawayn was. **1502** *Robert the Devil* B2[v][16]: As wode as wolves. Whiting *Scots* II 157.

W442 He is soon weary that plows with a **Wolf**
1492 *Salomon and Marcolphus* 8[20]: He is sone wery that plowyth wyth a wolf.

W443 He that scapes the **Wolf** meets the lion
1492 *Salomon and Marcolphus* 11[15–6]: He that skapyth t(h)e wolf metyth the lyon.

W444 It is hard to have the **Wolf** full and the wether whole
c1385 Chaucer *TC* iv 1373–6: Lo, Troilus, men seyn that hard it is The wolf ful, and the wether hool to have; This is to seyn, that men ful ofte, iwys, Mote spenden part the remenant for to save. Apperson 702.

W445 No more like than a **Wolf** to a lamb
c1300 Robert of Gloucester I 415.5680: No licchere is brother him nas, than wolf is a lomb.

W446 None ought to wear the **Wolf's** skin but he that will be like him
1484 Caxton *Aesop* 65[2–4]: For none ought to were on hym the skyn of the wulf but that he wyll be lyke to hym. Cf. Jente 210.

W447 One may not tear the **Wolf** out of his hide
a1400 *Romaunt C* 7311–5: I take youresilf to recorde heere, That men ne may in no manere Teren the wolf out of his hide, Til he be flayn, bak and side, Though men hym bete and al defile. Apperson 702:13; *Oxford* 723; Tilley W617.

W448 The she **Wolf** takes the lewdest (*vilest*) make (*mate*) (*varied*)
c1390 Chaucer CT IX[H] 183–6: A she-wolf hath also a vileyns kynde. The lewedeste wolf that she may fynde, Or leest of reputacioun, wol she take, In tyme whan hir lust to han a make. **c1410** Edward of York *Master* 31[21–5]: Therfore men seyn by yonde the see in somme contres, whan eny woman doth amys, that she is like to the wolf bicche, for she taketh hure to the worst and the foulest, And to the moost wrecch. **c1450** La Tour-Landry 82.9–10: But mani woman farithe as the femall of the wolff, that chesithe to her make the foulest wolff of all that ben in the wode.

W449 Speak of the **Wolf** and see his tail
a1533 Berners *Arthur* 377[14]: Whan one speketh of the wolfe lightly, he seeth his taile. Apperson 702:20; Tilley W608.

W450 Though you hood the **Wolf** to priest, ever are his ears to the grove-ward (*varied*)
a1250 Odo of Cheriton 195[15–7]: Thai thu W(o)lf hore hodi te preste, tho thu hym sette Salmes to lere, evere beth his geres to the grove-ward (*var.:* If al that the Wolf un to a preest worthe, and be set un to book psalmes to leere, yit his eye evere to the wodeward). **c1250** in Thomas Wright *Selection of Latin Stories* (PS 8, 1842) 55[21–4]: They thou the vulf hore hod to preste, They thou him to skole sette salmes to lerne, Hevere bet his geres to the grove grene. *Speculum* 9(1934) 219.n.[2]; R. M. Wilson

in *Leeds Studies in English and Kindred Languages* 6(1937) 44. See **E207.**

W451 To be (fall) in the **Wolf's** mouth
a1338 Mannyng *Chronicle B* I 38[23–4]: The lerid and the lewid, that wonned in the South, Sauh werre on ilk a side, thei wer in the woulfe's mouth, 42[24]: Than was Eilred in the wolfe's mouth. **a1420** Lydgate *Troy* III 824. 1814: He fil a-geyn in-to the wolves mouthe. NED Wolf 9g.

W452 To be like a **Wolf** (*varied*)
c1000 Aelfric *Homilies* II 404[25–7]: Hi sind . . . cristenra manna ehteras, and reaferas, swa swa reðe wulfas. **a1300** *Alisaunder* 183.3267–8: He hete his folk so a wode wolf Assailen hem on the cee half. **c1386** Chaucer *LGW* 1798–9: Ryght as a wolf that fynt a lomb alone, To whom shal she compleyne, or make mone? **c1400** *Brut* I 220.16–7: For o kynrede had no more pite of that other, than an hundred wolfes haveth on o shepe. **1439** Lydgate *St. Albon* 177.902–3: And lyke a wolfe in his cruell rage Stynt never. **a1470** Malory II 734.21–4: Kynge Arthure lykened . . . sir Gareth and sir Dynadan unto egir wolvis. **1479** Rivers *Cordyal* 56.24–5: Worse and more cursed than wolves. Whiting *Drama* 333:370, *Scots* II 157.

W453 To bear as the **Wolf** bears its prey (*varied*)
c1450 *Ponthus* 78.15: And bare hym as the wolfe beres his pray. **1485** Caxton *Charles* 221.25–6: And made nomore a-doo to bere hym, than dooth a wulf to bere a lytel lambe.

W454 To come like a **Wolf**
a1350 Castelford 7.19881–3: Kyng arthur herd how that baldulf Wald com opon him als a wulf, Bi nighter tal so dose A thef. **c1400** *Tundale* 8.136: As wilde wolves thai come rawmpand. **1485** Caxton *Charles* 136.17–8: And came ageynst hym as a wulf enraged, **1490** *Eneydos* 39.17–9: On that other syde cam upon theym Neptunus . . . as a wulfe enraged brayeng.

W455 To devour as **Wolves** do the lamb
c1475 *Lamentation of Mary Magdalene* 402[20–1]: Nevertheles ye devoured him with one assent, As hungry wolves doth the lambe innocent. **1515** Barclay *St. George* 104.2607: Redy as a wolfe a lambe for to devour. Whiting *Drama* 333:370.

W456 To fare like a **Wolf**
a1300 *Alisaunder* 123.2179–82: Alisaunder ferde on uche half Als it were an hungry wolf, Whan he cometh amonges shepe—With teeth and clowes he gynneth hem strepe. **c1380** *Ferumbras* 38.950–1: Als furde thay with that ilke hepe . . . As doth wolves among the shepe wan thay cometh hem to. **a1400** *Destruction of Troy* 333.10206–7: He fore with his fos in his felle angur, As a wolfe in his wodenes with wethurs in fold. **a1400** *Siege of Jerusalem* 62.1075: Wo wakned thycke, as wolves they ferde. **1447** Bokenham 93.3415–7: As raveynows wulvys be wone to do Among a flok of sheep, ryht evyn so Ferd these tyrauntys amoung this cumpany. **a1533** Berners *Arthur* 81[28–30]: Arthur . . . fared so amonge them as the wolfe doth among shepe.

W457 To go like **Wolves**
a1400 *Scottish Legends* I 250.39–40: Gais furth, I send you, I you tel, As wolfis amaung lammys unsel. **c1450** *Ponthus* 95.1–2: And as the wolfe goos oute of the wodd for hungre, so the xiii went oute of the cave. **1485** Caxton *Charles* 120.17: (They) goon . . . boystously as wulves hungry.

W458 To grin like **Wolves**
c1225 *Wohunge of Ure Laverd* 277[8–9]: Thai grennede for gladschipe euchan toward other as wode wulves that fainen of hare praie. **c1450** *Owayne Miles* (*Brome*) 95.46: They grenyd on hym as wolvys in wode. Taylor and Whiting 408.

W459 To howl like **Wolves**
c1000 Aelfric *Homilies* II 488[27–8]: Hi ðotorodon swilce oðre wulfas. Taylor and Whiting 408.

W460 To make a **Wolf** a pastor (*varied*)
1480 Caxton *Ovyde* 62[2]: The kynge made of a wolf a pastour. **a1500** *Partenay* 176.5116–7: Never trowed man for to se that houre A wolfe to become An herdly pastour. **1513** More *Richard* 45[*for* 44] F[16–7]: The lamb was betaken to the wolfe to kepe. **1556** Heywood *Spider* 430[10]: In no place: place a wolfe, the flocke to kepe. Apperson 702:17; *Oxford* 238–9, 723; Tilley W602; Whiting *Scots* II 157.

W461 To make of a **Wolf** a lamb
1447 Bokenham 89.3252–3: Wych hir husbond, a cruel man fyrst, lo, Made aftyr of a wulf a lambe to bene. **c1493** *Saint Katherin of Senis* 287.27–8: A lytell tyme after of a wolfe he was made a lambe and of a lyon a whelpe. See **L333.**

W462 To rese (*rush*) like (the) **Wolf**
a900 *Old English Martyrology* 170.24–6: Priscus . . . geræsde on þa fæmnan in cristenmonna midle, swa wulf geræseð on sceap in miclum ewede.

a1200 Lawman I 66.1544–7: Corineus heom rasde to, Swa the rimie (*B* wilde) wulf, Thane he wule on scheapen, Scathe werc wrchen.

W463 To run like a **Wolf**
a1393 Gower *CA* III 100.5632–3: And in a rage on hire he ran, Riht as a wolf which takth his preie. **c1500** *Melusine* 287.11–2: As a hongre wolf renneth upon sheep so dide he renne upon the enemyes of god.

W464 To rush like a **Wolf** (*etc.*) (A number of single quotations are brought together here)
a1200 Lawman II 421.20122–7: And he gon to rusien Swa the runie (*B* wode) wulf Thenne he cumeth of holte, Bi-honged mid snawe, And thencheth to biten Swulc deor (*B* seap) swa him liketh. **a1300** *Arthour and M.*[1] 115.4047–8: Ac, al so wolf the schip gan drive, Arthour smot hem after swithe. **a1300** *XI Pains* 149.85–6: Heo hire a-warieth (*worries*) al athrep Al so wulves doth the scep. **a1300** *Tristrem* II 30.1048–9: He faught with outen wene, So wolf, that wald wede. **c1300** *Beves* 118.2485–6: And be the right leg she him grep, Ase the wolf doth the schep. **a1338** Mannyng *Chronicle A* II 482.13897–8: As the wolf chaseth the schep, He dide the Romayns by-fore hym lep, 534.15379–80: Of prest ne clerk gaf they no kep, Namore than wolf doth of the schep. **a1350** *Libeaus* 26 *var.* 419–20: As wolfe that wolde awede (*go mad*), The mede of greet deray. **a1400** *Scottish Legends* I 217.312: Til thai as wolfis lowd can rare. **a1420** Lydgate *Troy* III 639.2549–50: Lyche a wolfe that is with hunger gnawe, Right so gan he ageyn his foon to drawe, **1439** *St. Albon* 154.1587: They fell upon hym as wolfes dispitous, 1615, 166.279–80: They kyll and slee of all conditions, As hungry wolfes in theyr beastiall rage. **1478** Rivers *Morale Proverbes* [5.17–8]: A cruel Juge . . . Stroyeth peuple as wolves doon the shepe. **1483** Caxton *Golden Legende* 318v [2.3–4]: And arage lyke wolves on shepe, **1485** *Charles* 175.17–8: The paynyms cryed and brayed as wulves enfamysshed, **c1489** *Aymon* II 515.24–7: Reynaude . . . shoved himself among the thickest, as a wolfe amonge a flocke of shepe. **c1505** Watson *Valentine* 288.29–30: Myllon . . . departed paynyms as the wolffe dothe the shepe. **a1533** Berners *Arthur* 470[3–4]: And laye on amonge his enemyes, as a wolfe dooth among lambes, 505[18–20].

W465 To slay like a **Wolf**
a1200 Lawman II 427.20268–9: Hu heo muwen Baldulf Slaen al se enne wulf. **a1300** *Alisaunder* 249.4463–4: Alisaunder . . . Sleeth doune-righth so dooth a raged wolf. **a1400** *Laud Troy* I 187.6333–4: And sclow hem bothe yonge and olde, As wolves don schep that ben In folde. **1439** Lydgate *St. Albon* 178.990–1: Lyke gredy wolfes . . . They slough.

W466 To spare no more than the **Wolf** does the sheep (*varied*)
c1400 *Brut* I 99.21–2: Thai ne sparede ham nomore than the wolfe doth the shepe, 220.16–7: Had no more pite . . . than an hundred wolfes haveth on o shepe.

W467 To to-draw (*pull apart*) as a **Wolf** (does) sheep
a1300 *Alisaunder* 137.2414–6: Hou Alisaunder, as a wolf That fele dawes had yfast The shep todraweth in the wast. **c1300** Robert of Gloucester I 385.5298–9: There hii barnde and robbede and that folc to grounde slowe, And as wolves among ssep reuliche hom to drowe. **c1300** *South English Legendary* II 447.132: Also fale wolves among lomb thare clene fleiss todrawe.

W468 To were (*keep*) the **Wolf** from the gate (door)
1464 Hardyng 181[19]: By whiche he maye the wolf werre frome the gate. **c1522** Skelton *Colyn* I 317.153–4: The wolfe from the dore To werryn and to kepe. **1546** Heywood *D* 85.172: To kepe the wolfe from the dur. Apperson 702; *Oxford* 331; Taylor and Whiting 408; Tilley W605.

W469 To yell like **Wolves**
c1300 *South English Legendary* II 454.156: As wolves wel soriliche hi yolle, 591.29. **c1400** *Brut* I 219.26: Yellynge as a wolfe.

W470 What the **Wolf** does pleases the wolfess
1492 *Salomon and Marcolphus* 11[8–9]: What the wolf doth that pleasyth the wolfesse.

W471 When a **Wolf** is sick she would have been a lamb
a1450 *Gesta* 271–2: Dum fero langorem, volo religionis amorem; Expers langoris, non sum memor huius amoris. Heu! cum languebat lupum, agnus esse volebat, Postquam convaluit, talis ut ante fuit. The exposicion of theise vers is this, While I suffre and am in sekenesse, I woll lede the life of religion, and of goode Rule, but while I was withoute such thraldom and sekenesse, not lovid I such life; and so it farith by me as it doith by a wolfe, for whenne she is syke, she wold have ben a lambe, but when she is Recoveryd, she is a shrewe as she was before. Walther I 809.6518. Cf. Taylor and Whiting 100:37.

W472 The **Wolf** and the avaricious man do no good till they be dead
1474 Caxton *Chesse* 109[1–4]: For the wolf doth never good tyll he be dede And thus it is sayd in proverbis of the wisemen that thavaricious man doth no good tyll that he be ded. Cf. Tilley D146. See **D74.**

W473 The **Wolf** eats the sheep, the great fish the small
1509 Barclay *Ship* I 101[1]: The wolfe etis the shepe, the great fysshe the small. See **F232.**

W474 A **Wolf** (fox) in a lamb's skin (*varied*)
c1000 Aelfric *Lives* I 328.120–2: Lease witegan þa ðe cumað to eow on sceape gelicnysse, And hi synd wiþ-innan reafigende wulfas. **c1000** *WSG* Matthew vii 15: Warniað eow fram leasum witegum, þa cumað to eow on sceapa gegyrelum, ac hig beoð innane reafigende wulfas. **a1200** *Ancrene* 36.8–9: For monie cumeth to ow ischrud mid lombes fleos, and beoth wedde wulves. **c1395** *WBible* Matthew vii 15: Be ye war of fals prophetis, that comen to you in clothingis of scheep, but withynneforth thei ben as wolves of raveyn. **a1400** *Romaunt C* 6259–62: Whoso took a wethers skyn, And wrapped a gredy wolf theryn, For he shulde go with lambis whyte, Wenest thou not he wolde hem bite? **a1400** *Scottish Legends* I 472.504–6: Bot yet he Wykyt wolfe wes withinne, And heylyt in a lameskine, II 135.378: Bot he is wolf in lamskine hyd. **a1400** Wyclif *Sermons* I 140[7–8]: Yvel wolvys ben religiouse, that Crist seith in Mathew's gospel, ben wolvys ravyshinge, alyif thei comen in sheepis clothis. **c1415** *Middle English Sermons* 295.22–3: Then comys forth a wulfe oute of lambes skynne. **c1425** *Orcherd* 286.17–8. **a1437** *Kingis Quair* 83.136[3]: Thair wolfis hertis, in lambis likness. **c1450** Idley 142.2195: Or a wolfe covered in a lambes cappe. **1451** Capgrave *Lives* 85.22: That the wolf do not on his bak a schepis wolle. **c1475** *Wisdom* 51.490. **1482** Higden-Trevisa Cont. VIII 535[40–1]: And under the habyte of a lambe hydynge wolvysshe cruelte. **1495** *Medytacyons of saynt Bernarde* D5^r[11–2]: I hydde my wulffyssh conscyence under a shepyssh skynne. **a1500** *Thre Prestis* 26.413–4: He is na Hird to keip thay sely sheip, Nocht bot ane Tod in ane Lambskin to creip. **a1508** Dunbar *Tretis* 95.423: As foxe in a lambis fleise fenye I my cheir. **1509** Barclay *Ship* II 7[11–2]: She is perchaunce A wolfe or gote within a Lammys skyn, 221[26–8]: And wolves ravysshynge full of unthryftynes Bere shepes skynnes showynge nat that they be Foxys within: shewynge out symplycyte, 323[22–3]: The wolfe or Foxe is hyd within the skyn Of the symple shepe, 327[6–7]: They shewe them outwarde as Lambes innocent, Lyke ravysshynge wolves yet ar they of intent. **a1513** Dunbar *Tydingis* 80.37: Sum in ane lambskin is ane tod. **c1523** Barclay *Mirrour* 31[9–11]: Then he which resembleth a sheepe forth in the skin, . . . He is in very deede a raging wolfe within. **1528** More *Heresyes* 281 H[4–7], 285 EF, **1533** *Debellacyon* 999 D[1–3], 1000 B[6–7, 9–10], 1002 D[5–8], 1003 H[6–7], 1004 A[5–6, 14–5], B[5–6], C[5–6], 1034 C[2–4], *Apologye* 154[8–11]: Which . . . poore men that can not apparell theyr speche wyth apparell of rethoryke, use comenly to call a woulfe in a lambes skynne, [18–9], *Confutacion* 763 F[13–5]. **1546** Heywood *D* 39.138: She is a wolfe in a lambes skyn. Apperson 701; *Oxford* 723; Taylor and Whiting 407–8; Tilley W614; Whiting *Drama* 333:370, *Scots* II 157. See **L46, S218.**

W475 The **Wolf** is in the tale
a1398(1495) Bartholomaeus-Trevisa ee4^r[2.14–9]: Churles spekyth of hym and meanyth that a man lesyth his voys yf the wulf seeth hym fyrste. Therfore to a man that is sodenly stylle and levyth to speke, it is sayde (Lupus est in fabula) the wulfe is in the tale. *Oxford* 722; Tilley W607.

W476 The **Wolf** is in the way
a1393 Gower *CA* II 310.327–8: Al is peril that he schal seie, Him thenkth the wolf is in the weie. See **L330.**

W477 A **Wolf** lives by the wind one month in the year
c1450 *Jacob's Well* 263.21–2: Thou faryst as a wolf, for he o monyth in the yere lyveth be the wynde. See **C135.**

W478 The **Wolf** never saw its father
c1410 Edward of York *Master* 31[30–1]: And that is the cause whi men say that the wolf seghe nevere his fadir.

W479 The **Wolf** takes no prey nigh the place where he nourishes his whelps
a1398(1495) Bartholomaeus-Trevisa ee4^v[2.25–8]: So that he (*the wolf*) takyth no proye of meete nyhe to the place where he norisheth his whelpes, But thenne he huntyth in places that ben feere thennes. Apperson 233:27; *Oxford* 223; Tilley F639.

W480 The **Wolf** that is taken either bites or shits
1492 *Salomon and Marcolphus* 12[11–2]: The

wolf that is takyn and set fast eythre he byyteth or shytyth.

W481 A **Wolf** will not change its skin
1474 Caxton *Chesse* 68[3–6]: Another sayd to vaspasian And a wolf shold sonner change his skyn and heer than thou sholdest chaunge thy lyf For the lenger thou lyvest the more thou coveytest. Cf. Taylor and Whiting 218; Tilley W617.

W482 To fight like a **Wolfess**
a1439 Lydgate *Fall* II 397.2456: This wromman fauht(e) lik a fell wolvesse.

W483 To shed blood like a **Wolfess**
a1439 Lydgate *Fall* II 541.2477–8: Wher lik a wolvesse, as auctours of hir write, To shede blood she gan hirsilff delite.

W484 All **Women** would be whores if men besought them (*varied*)
c1450 *Rylands MS.394* 100.12^v.3: Alle women wolden ben horis if men hem be sowten. **c1516** Skelton *Magnificence* 50.1586: Ye, for *omnis mulier meretrix si celari potest.* See **A231.**

W485 A clattering **Woman** may keep counsel of that thing she knows not
1519 Horman *Vulgaria* 436[1–2]: A claterynge woman may kepe only counsell of that thynge: the whiche she knoweth nat. Apperson 706:50; *Oxford* 723; Tilley W649. Cf. Whiting *Drama* 51. See **W534.**

W486 A fair **Woman** and a sot (*fool*) is like a gold bee (*ring*) in a sow's wroot (*nose*) (*varied*)
a1300 *Additional MS.33956* in Brown *Register* I 410: A gulden begh in a soghes wrot, A faire wyman and a sot. **c1390** Chaucer *CT* X[I] 155–6: Remembreth yow of the proverbe of Salomon. He seith: Likneth a fair wromman that is a fool of hire body lyk to a ryng of gold that were in the groyn of a soughe, **c1395** III[D] 784–5: A fair wromman, but she be chaast also, Is lyk a gold ryng in a sowes nose. **c1395** *WBible* Proverbs xi 22: A goldun sercle, *ether ryng,* in the nose thrillis of a sowe, a wromman fair and fool. **a1400** *Cambridge MS. Gg IV 32* in *Rel. Ant.* I 160[26–7]: Suo sit fairhed in wromman sot, Suo the geldene begh in suynes throt (MED bei le: Wrot). Whiting *Drama* 109. See **R136.**

W487 For **Women** and hounds is oft debate
a1400 *Proverbis of Wysdom* 246.112: Fore wymmen and howndis is ought (*for* oft) debate. Apperson 705:38; *Oxford* 725; Tilley W694. See **W238.**

W488 He that touches a **Woman** is like him that handles the scorpion
c1390 Chaucer *CT* X[I] 854: And therfore seith Salomon that "whoso toucheth and handleth a wromman, he fareth lyk hym that handleth the scorpioun that styngeth and sodeynly sleeth thurgh his envenymynge." **c1395** *WBible* Ecclesiasticus xxvii 10: A wickid wromman, he that holdith hir, is as he that takith a scorpioun. See **S96.**

W489 If a **Woman** does not chastise herself, with pain (*trouble*) may any other chastise her
c1505 Watson *Valentine* 249.1–3: Nowe it is sayd comenly and it is true that yf a woman do not chastise her selfe of her owne propre wyll wyth payne may any other chastise her.

W490 If a **Woman** is fair then is she young, if a priest is good then is he old
1528 More *Heresyes* 225 H[2–5]: They say that if a woman be fayre, than is she yonge, and if a prieste bee good, than he is olde, 227 G[8–10]: Yf the proverbe were true . . . that yf a prieste be good than he is olde.

W491 If (**Women**) spend it is unkend (*unknown*), their gear is none the less
a1513 Dunbar *Of the Ladyis* 98.31–2: Suppois thay spend, It is unkend, Thair geir is nocht the les. Whiting *Scots* I 176. See **C24.**

W492 Ilk (*each*) true **Woman** has a robe of gray marble stone
a1500 *Clerk and the Nightingale II* in Robbins 178.39–42: Clerk, ylk trew woman hath upon, With-owt any lesyng, A robbe of grey marbyl ston, And of gret cumpasyng.

W493 In **Woman** is no law
a1460 *Towneley Plays* 339.44–5: Wherfor in woman is no laghe, Ffor she is withoutten aghe. See **A247.**

W494 In **Women** vinolent is no defence
c1395 Chaucer *CT* III[D] 467–8: In wommen vinolent is no defence,—This knowen lecchours by experience. Cf. Tilley C901. See **C619, R92, W251.**

W495 Many a **Woman** sad in countenance has a merry heart
a1500 *O man more* 394.23–4: Doo nott ever beleve the womans compleynte,—Many in countenaunce ys sadde that hathe a mery harte. Cf. Tilley W672. See **F2, H292.**

W496 Nothing is feller than **Woman** when she will wend to evil
c1300 *South English Legendary* I 111.40: For

nothing nis fellor than womman wanne he(o) wol to uvel wende. Jente 603. Cf. *Oxford* 19: Bad woman.

W497 There **Women** are are many words, there geese are are many turds
a1450 *Castle* 156.2650–2: Ther wymmen arn, are many wordys: Lete hem gone hoppyn with here hakle! Ther ges sittyn, are many tordys. **c1450** *Douce MS.52* 50.69: There ben women, there ben wordis; There ben gese, there bene tordys. **c1450** *Rylands MS.394* 100.12.21–2. Apperson 705:30; Jente 279; *Oxford* 406; Tilley W687. See **E16, W253.**

W498 There **Women** make fairest semblant they will beguile
c1330 *Seven Sages A* 127.2713–6: Thou hast itawt me a newe ran, That i schal never leve wimman. For there thai make semblant fairest, Thai wil bigile the altherformest. See **S96.**

W499 To take a **Woman** by her own will is courteous theft
a1400 *Ipomadon A* 156.5439–41: But ofte I have hard saye, by skille, A woman to take be hyr own wille, Ys thefte of curtessy. See **M640, S348.**

W500 Two **Women** in one house, two cats and one mouse, *etc.*
c1417 *Lansdowne MS.762* in *Rel. Ant.* I 233 [38–41]: Two wymen in one howse, Two cattes and one mowce, Two dogges and one bone, Maye never accorde in one. **1486** ?Berners *Boke of St. Albans* F5v[21–2]: Too wyves in oon hous, too cattys and oon mous; Too dogges and oon boon: theis shall never accorde in oon. Apperson 657; *Oxford* 679; Tilley C186.

W501 Well travelled **Women** and well travelled horses were never good
c1417 *Lansdowne MS.762* in *Rel. Ant.* I 233[3–4]: Wele traveled wymen or wele traveled horsses were never good. **1486** ?Berners *Boke of St. Albans* F5r[11]. Cf. Tilley W633.

W502 When **Woman** is refused there is no bear so fell (*varied*)
a1400 *Scottish Legends* I 68.171–4: For quhen woman wald do sic myse With man, and refusit Is, Thar is no ber so fel no thra, Quhen hyr quhelpis ar tan hir fra, II 138–9.504–14: Quhen wemen settis hir likyne Of ony man, hyme to wyne In sic degre with hyr to syne, Gyf he ne wil consent hir til, Fra scho haf lattyn hym wit hir wil, Wes nevir lenx that schuttis fyre, Mare fulfillit of breth and yre, Quhen hir qwhelpis ar tan hir fra, To chas the takaris, thaim to sla, Than scho sal be to purches Il Til hyme that denyit hir wil. Whiting *Scots* II 158.

W503 When **Women** are masters they are evil to know
c1300 Robert of Gloucester II 670.9487: Wanne wimmen al maistres beth, hii beth uvel to knowe.

W504 When **Women** are well they cannot cease
a1450 *Partonope* 200.5281: When wymmen be well they can not cese (*R:* I can not sese).

W505 Who trusts **Woman** is deceived (*varied*)
a1425 *Chester Plays* I 34.349–52: Now all my kinde by me is kent, To flee womans intisement; Whoe trustes them in anye intent, Truly he is decayved. **a1425** *Metrical Paraphrase OT* 86.12479–80: Thus may men lyghtly lere Forto trow wemens tales (*ironic*). **a1439** Lydgate *Fall* I 154.5507–9: To truste so moche the mutabilite Off these women, which erli, late and soone Off ther nature braide upon the moone. **a1460** *Towneley Plays* 91.174–5: Now, who wold any woman trow? Certys, no man that can any goode, 338.29–34: And it is wretyn in oure law "Ther is no trust in womans saw, Ne trust faith to belefe; Ffor with thare quayntyse and thare gyle Can thay laghe and wepe som while, And yit nothyng theym grefe." **1484** Caxton *Aesop* 216[18–20]: And he is wel a fole that setteth his hope and truste in a woman, **1485** *Charles* 112.33–113.1: It is noo thynge covenable that . . . ye ought to truste in a woman, by cause of theyr mutabylte, 181.33–5: I have herde say longe sythe, that a man that trusteth in a woman, of thyng of Importaunce, is a moche fool. Cf. Jente 765. See **W532.**

W506 A **Woman** casts her shame away when she casts off her smock
c1395 Chaucer *CT* III[D] 782–3: He seyde, "a womman cast hir shame away, Whan she cast of hir smok." Walther II 959.15348. See **W521.**

W507 (A **Woman**) desired of many is kept with great pain
1532 Berners *Golden Boke* 245.4213–4: With great peyne it (*a pretty woman*) is kepte that is desired of many. See **C79, F501, T131.**

W508 **Woman** has an art more than the devil
c1450 *Merlin* II 418[27–8]: It is seide that woman hath an art more than the devell. **1534** More *Passion* 1273 DE: To bryng man to wo, the woman mai do more, then wyth al hys craft, the dyvell can do hymselfe. Cf. Tilley W648.

W509 A **Woman** has an over-foolish heart that makes acquaintance of a strange man
1480 Caxton *Ovyde* 138–9: There is a sayenge, and trouth it is, that a woman hath the herte over folysshe, that maketh her acqueyntance of a strange man. Cf. Chaucer *HF* 286–8 (also of Dido).

W510 A **Woman** has nine lives like a cat
1546 Heywood *D* 66.7: A woman hath nyne lyves lyke a cat, **1555** *E* 177.174. Apperson 703; *Oxford* 83; Tilley W652. Cf. Taylor and Whiting 58:4.

W511 A **Woman** is like an apple, rotten inwardly
a1460 *Towneley Plays* 338.35–43: In oure bookes thus fynde we wretyn, All manere of men well it wyttyn, Of women on this wyse: Till an appyll she is lyke—Withoutten faill ther is none slyke —In horde ther it lyse, Bot if a man assay it wittely, It is full roten inwardly At the colke within. See **A155.**

W512 **Woman** is man's woe
a1425 *Chester Plays* I 31.269–72: Yea, soothe said I (*Adam*) in prophesie, Whan thou (*Eve*) wast taken of my body, Mans woe thou woldest be witlie, Therfore thou wast so named. **1549** Heywood *D* 85.181–2: And what maryed I than? A woman. As who saith, wo to the man. Tilley W656.

W513 **Woman** is word-wood (*-mad*) and cannot wield (*control*) her tongue (*varied*)
a1300 *Proverbs of Alfred* 103 J 293–6: Wymmon is word-wod, And haveth tunge to swift; Theyh heo wel wolde, Ne may heo hi no-wiht welde. **c1390** *Gregorius* 84.661–2: Wommon is a wonder thing, Con heo nouht hire wordes lete. **a1400** *Quatrefoil* 10.292: Women are carp(and), it commes tham of kynde. **a1450** *Pride of Life* in Waterhouse 94.207–10: Ye, dam, thou hast wordis fale, Hit comith the of kinde; This nis bot women tale And that wol the ffinde. **1509** Barclay *Ship* I 109[26–8]: But touchynge wymen of them I wyll nought say They can nat speke, but ar as coy and styll As the horle wynde or clapper or (*for* of) a myll. Tilley W701.

W514 A **Woman's** wit is a subtle thing
a1533 Berners *Arthur* 377[9]: I se well it is a subtil thing of a womans wytte. Cf. *Oxford* 720; Tilley W568.

W515 **Woman's** words are but wind
a1500 *O man more* 394.35: Womans wordes thei be but as wynde. **1509** Barclay *Ship* II 5[11]: A womans wordes be but wynde. See **W643.**

W516 A **Woman** that takes gifts sells herself
c1450 La Tour-Landry 79.14–5: And therfor it is a true sawe, that a woman that takithe yeftes of ani man, sekith (*for* sellith) her selff. (Note [p. 255], French: Femme qui prent se vent.) Cf. Whiting *Drama* 163.

W517 A **Woman** that will not consent says that she has a scabbed arse
1492 *Salomon and Marcolphus* 8[17–8]: A woman that woll not consente, seyth that she hath a skabbyd arse.

W518 A **Woman** will be wroken (*revenged*) or burst
a1300 *Alisaunder* 77.1341–2: Wommanis hert is with the werst—She wil be wroken oither tobrest.

W519 A **Woman** will have her will (*varied*)
a1450 *Gesta* 30[5] second version: She wille in any wise have her owne wille. **c1460** *Dublin Abraham* in Waterhouse 31.197: Thi modre may not have hir wille all way. **c1475** *The hart lovyt* in Smith *Common-place Book* 11.4: The properte of a schrod qwen ys to have hyr wyll. **c1475** *Prohemy of a Mariage* 33[16]: So wommen have her wille, 36[1–2]: This is the wyle of the womman wyly, For she wol have hir wille at al hir lust, 44[2]: I se dame July must nedes haf hir wille. **1513** Douglas *Aeneid* III 119.88: Wifis wald have all thar will. Apperson 707: *Oxford* 726; Tilley W723; Whiting *Scots* II 158. See **M123, W539, 548.**

W520 A **Woman** will ofttimes do that she is not bid to do
a1500 Hill 132.39: A woman oftymes will do that she is not bede to do. Tilley W650. See **W549.**

W521 **Women** after misdoing can (*know*) no shame (*varied*)
a1300 *Alisaunder* 25.417–8: So dooth womman after mysdoyng, Ne can no shame ne no repentyng. **a1450** *Partonope* 235.6133–7: And seyde that all wemmen have A custome, and they sette hem to love, Off shame they ne recche ne of reprove, Be so that they mowe have here luste, For any thynge that be hadde moste. See **W506.**

W522 **Women** all follow the favor of Fortune
c1385 Chaucer *CT* I[A] 2681–2: For wommen, as to speken in comune, Thei folwen alle the favour of Fortune.

W523 **Women** are always ready
1534 Heywood *Love* D2r[12]: Men be not lyke women, alway redy.

W524 Women are fell and false
c1300 *South English Legendary* II 517.59–60: For ofte me saith and soth hit is, that this wymmen beoth Felle and false.

W525 Women are long bringing up and soon brought down
1533 Heywood *Weather* D1ʳ[11–2]: Oft tyme yt is sene, both in court and towne, Longe be women a bryngyng up, and sone brought down.

W526 Women are oft unstable (*varied*)
c1300 *South English Legendary* I 6.36: For unstable wymmen ofte beoth. **a1400** *Destruction of Troy* 15.443: Syn wemen are wilfull and there wit chaunges. **a1439** Lydgate *Fall* III 688.498–9: I am off maneres most chaungable, Off condiciouns verray femynyne. **1471** Caxton *Recuyell* II 606.5–6: O how sone is the purpos of a woman chaungid and torned, certes more sonner than a man can saie or thinke, **1485** *Charles* 116.33–117.1: Wymmen al day for lytel thynge ben chaunged and torned fro theyr thought, **c1489** *Blanchardyn* 130.7–9: For it is sayde of a custume, that the herte of a woman is mutable and inconstaunt, and not in purpos stedfast. **a1500** *English Conquest* 3.11–4: Roury . . . hadd a wel fayre woman to wyffe; and as men tellyth ofte, and sith hit is y-found, that some of them ben unstabill of hert, wherfore many harmys ben ofte-tymes. **c1505** Watson *Valentine* 156.12–3: The nature and wyll of women is varyable and lightely chaunged. **1513** Douglas *Aeneid* II 185.92: Variabill and changeand thyngis beyn wemen ay. Smith 337; Tilley W674; Whiting *Scots* II 159. See **M141, 647.**

W527 Women are one harm which may not be eschewed
1450 *Dicts* 70.29: Women is oon harme the whiche may not be eschewid. Cf. Tilley W703.

W528 Women are so full of fair words that men must needs agree
a1500 *Coventry Plays* 50.555–6: Soo full of feyre wordis these wemen be, That men thereto must nedis agre. See **W532.**

W529 Women are the confusion of man
c1390 Chaucer *CT* VII 1105–6[B2295–6]: Heere may ye se that if that wommen were nat goode, and hir conseils goode and profitable, oure Lord God of hevene wolde nevere han wroght hem, ne called hem help of man, but rather confusioun of man, 3164[B4354]: *Mulier est hominis confusio. Oxford* 723–4.

W530 Women are the devil's mousetraps
a1225 *Lambeth Homilies* 53[19]: Theos wimmen the thus luvieth (?livieth) beoth thes deofles musetoch iclepede. Cf. *Oxford* 725; Tilley W707. See **M747.**

W531 Women are wise in short advisement (*varied*)
c1385 Chaucer *TC* iv 936: Women ben wise in short avysement, 1261–3: I am a womman, as ful wel ye woot, And as I am avysed sodeynly, So wol I telle yow, whil it is hoot. **c1412** Hoccleve *Regement* 136.3781–2: Be-holde, of wommen here a noble wyle! In schort avisement, who can do bet? **1449** Metham 29.796: But redy womannys wytt ys yn soden casys off necessyte. **1474** Caxton *Chesse* 115[19–22]: And verily hit cometh of nature oftentymes to women to gyve counceyll shortly and unavysedly to thynges that ben in doute or perillous and nedeth hasty remedye. **c1485** *Guiscardo* 52.241–2: As oftyn tyme hyt fareth that wemen byn ryght wyse, And in a sodeyn case they byn ryght subtyle. Cf. *Oxford* 204; Tilley W668, 669, 670; Whiting *Scots* II 157. See **M166.**

W532 Women can deceive men (*varied*)
a1300 *Alisaunder* 417.7698–9: Ac noman ne may hym waite From thise wymmens dissaite. **c1380** *Ferumbras* 68.2013: Many ys the manlich man that thorw womman ys by-go. **c1390** *Sir Gawain* 74.2414–5: Bot hit is no ferly thagh a fole madde, And thurgh wyles of wymmen be wonen to sorghe. **a1400** *Scottish Legends* I 267.405–8: For weman are of brynnand wil Ay thare yarninge to fulfil And with wordis cane ryght wele Our-cum mene hard as stele. **c1400** *Beryn* 15.436–7: But who is, that a womman coud nat make his berd, And she were there-about, and set hir wit ther-to? **c1410** Lovelich *Grail* III 37.627–30: For that man Is born In non londe (As In My wit I undirstonde) That Kan be war of wommens wyle, So ful they ben of qweyntise and Gyle. **c1470** *Wallace* 226.1454–5: The suth weyll has beyn seyn, Wemen may tempt the wysest at is wrocht. **a1475** *Guy*^{2} 34.1165–6: I am not the furste nodur the laste, That thorowe a woman downe ys caste. **1481** Caxton *Reynard* 56[28–30]: I am not the fyrst that have been deceyved by wymmens counseyl by whiche many a grete hurte hath byfallen, **1485** *Charles* 91.34–5: And I remembre me now wel that oftymes by a woman I have knowen somme shamed and deceyved, 113.2–3: Ye knowe the trouthe how many have ben deceyved by wymmen. **a1500** *Guy*^{4} 52.1459–60: I ne am the fyrst ne the last, That women have in woe caste. See **R66, W505, 528.**

W533 Women can excuse them well

a1450 *York Plays* 107.162: Excuse tham wele there women can. Tilley W654.

W534 **Women** can keep no counsel (*varied*) **c1378** *Piers* B xix 157: For that that wommen witeth may noughte wel be conseille. **c1390** Chaucer *CT* VII 1084[B2274]: And as to youre fourthe resoun, ther ye seyn that the janglerie of wommen kan hyde thynges that they wot noght, as who seith that a womman kan nat hyde that she woot, **c1395** III[D] 950: Pardee, we wommen konne no thyng hele. **c1422** Hoccleve *Complaint* 96.32–5: I thowght I nolde it kepe cloos no more, Ne lett it in me for to olde and hore; And for to preve I cam of a woman, I brast oute on the morowe, and thus began, **c1425** *Jonathas* 222.192–3: Swich is wommannes inconstant nature, They can nat keepe conseil worth a risshe. **c1450** La Tour-Landry 204.2–3: For hit is not of newe, how that a woman can not kepe secretely that whiche men sayen to her in counceylle. **1474** Caxton *Chesse* 27 [19–20]: Wherfore it is a comyn proverbe that women can kepe no counceyle. **1525** Berners *Froissart* VI 47[18–20]: For chyldren and women naturally are harde to kepe counsayle of that thynge a man wolde have kepte secrete. *Oxford* 723; Whiting *Scots* II 159:9. See **W485.**

W535 **Women** can laugh and love not **c1450** *In Praise of Margaret the Queen* in Robbins 188–9.66–7: Hastow (*Lydgate*) not sayd eke that these women can Laugh and love nat? Parde, yt is not fair! **a1500** *Scorn of Women* in Robbins 224.26: Ffor they can lawgh and love nat—thys ys expresse. See **S404.**

W536 **Women** can (*know*) rede to help men at need (*varied*) **c1330** *Seven Sages A* 123.2647–8: He (thought) that wimmen couthe red To help men at her ned. **a1350** *Seven Sages C* 101.2955–6. **a1460** *Towneley Plays* 127.342: Yit a woman avyse helpys at the last. Cf. Apperson 704:15.

W537 **Women** can weep (and lie) at will (*varied*) **c1375** Barbour *Bruce* I 70–1.517–20: And that nane may but (anger) gret, Bot it be wemen, that can wet Thair chekys, quhen thaim list, with teris, The quethir weill oft thaim na thing deris. **a1420** Lydgate *Troy* III 672.3690–5: Allas! who seith wommen can nat wepe!—Yet dout(e)les thei have it of nature, Though it so be that thei no wo endure, Yit can thei feyne and salt(e) teris fynde, Plente y-nowe, of her owne kynde, And sorweles mornen and compleyne. **c1425** Hoccleve *Jonathas* 224.248–9: As sum womman othir whyle atte beste Can lye and weepe whan is hir lykyng. **a1438** Kempe 13.23–4: Mech pepul wend that sche mygth wepyn and leuyn whan sche wold. Smith 338; Tilley W716. See **D120.**

W538 **Women** can weep with one eye and laugh with the other (*varied*) **1369** Chaucer *BD* 633–4: She ys fals; and ever laughynge With oon eye. **a1400** *Destruction of Troy* 262.8055–9: Hit is a propertie aprevit, and put hom of kynd. To all wemen in the world, as the writ saythe, To be unstable and not stidfast, styrond of wille: Ffor yf the ton ee with teres trickell on hir chekes The tothur lurkes in lychernes, and laghes overthwert! **c1475** Henryson *Testament* 113.230–1: Thus variant scho was, quha list tak keip, With ane Eye lauch, and with the uther weip. **1492** *Salomon and Marcolphus* 24[15–7]: Whyllys a woman wepyth she laughyth wyth therte. They kan wepe wyth oon yie, and lawgh wyth the othyr. Apperson 126; *Oxford* 121; Tilley E248.

W539 **Women** desire to have sovereignty **c1395** Chaucer *CT* III[D] 1038–9: Wommen desiren to have sovereynetee As wel over hir housbond as hir love. **1464** Hardyng 26[1–2]: Note that wemen desyre of al thynges soveraynte, and, to my conceypt, more in this land then in any other. See **W519.**

W540 **Women** hate what their husbands love **c1395** Chaucer *CT* III[D] 780–1: They (*women*) been so wikked and contrarious, They haten that hir housbondes loven ay. **1513** More *Richard* 37 B[4–6]: As women commonly not of malice but of nature hate them whome theire housebandes love.

W541 **Women** in a house and eels in a poke can no more be closed in than the smoke of fire **c1450** Idley 207.160–1: For women in a howse and neyls in a poke Can no more be closyd then of fyer the smoke.

W542 **Women** in their hastiness will do that they repent after **a1470** Malory III 1047.18–20: And women in their hastynesse woll do oftyntymes that aftir hem sore repentith. Cf. Whiting *Scots* II 159:14. See **H158.**

W543 **Women** love no process (in wooing) **a1420** Lydgate *Troy* I 77–8.2218–23: For ne were Schame pleinly the wardeyne Of this wommen, by writyng of this olde, With-out assaut the castel were y-yolde; It were no nede a sege for to leyn: For in swyche case long trete were in veyne; For of nature thei love no processe. See **L481.**

W544 **Women's** prayer is well heard

a1400 Wyclif *Sermons* I 377[5]: For it is seid comunli that wymmens preier is wel herd.

W545 **Women** vanquish men in wicked counsel **c1390** Chaucer *CT* VII 1090[B2280]: Where as ye seyn that in wikked conseil wommen venquisshe men, 1094[B2284]: The philosophre that seith, "In wikked conseil wommen venquisshen hir housbondes." See **F119, M26.**

W546 **Women** weep for mood (*anger*) ofter than for any good **a1300** *Proverbs of Alfred* 117 J 429–34: Wymmon wepeth for mod Oftere than for eny god; And ofte lude and stille, For to vor-drye (T: wurchen) hire wille; Heo wepeth other-hwile For to do the gyle. *Oxford* 569, cf. 726.

W547 **Women** will be lightly wroth **a1350** *Seven Sages C* 37.1079–80: For wemen wil be ligh(t)ly wrath, And cownsail comunly to skath. See **C203.**

W548 **Women** will not forsake their purpose **c1375** *St. Mary Magdalen* in Horstmann *Legenden 1881* 85.346–8: And sore bigan scho forto grete —Als wemen wil noght sone forsake Thaire purpos that thai to wil take. **1447** Bokenham 162.5927–8: But not-for-than, as it is the guyse Of wummen, she nold hyr purpose lete. See **W519.**

W549 **Women** yearn what men forbid them (*varied*) **a1338** Mannyng *Chronicle A* I 22.639–40: Ffor out of wyt wommen yernes That men forbedes hure, and wernes. **c1395** Chaucer *CT* III[D] 517–20: Wayte what thyng we may nat lightly have, Ther-after wol we crie al day and crave. Forbede us thyng, and that desiren we; Preesse on us faste, and thanne wol we fle. **a1425** *Chester Plays* I 27.185–6: That woman is forbyd to doe, For any thinge therto will shoe. Tilley W650. See **L487, T162, W520.**

Womb, see **Belly**

W550 Better pleases a full **Womb** than fair clothes (*varied*) **c1450** *Douce MS.52* 57.143: Sonner plays fulle wombe then feyre clothis. Vestito melius venter sit (*for* scit) ludere plenus. **c1450** *Rylands MS.394* 108.12: Venter ovat plenus cicius quam veste serenus. **c1470** *Harley MS.3362* f.4a in *Retrospective* 309[25]: Betyr plesyth a ful wombe than a newe cote. Tilley W725.

W550.1 A full **Womb** makes no chaste soul **c1425** *Orcherd* 285.16: A ful wombe maketh no chast soule. See **W553.**

W551 A full **Womb** may lightly speak of hunger **c1175** *Poema Morale* 180–1.147–8: Lihtliche mai ful wombe speke of hungre and of festen; So mai of pine thet not wat is pine thet evre mo sel leste. Cf. Tilley B289. See **F697, G101, H149, 646.**

W552 Out of a full **Womb** the arse trumps **1492** *Salomon and Marcolphus* 12[2]: Out of a full wombe thars trompyth.

W553 A replete **Womb** soon afoams out into lechery **c1443** Pecock *Reule* 356[6–7]: For a replete wombe soone affometh out in to leccherie. See **B243, C125, W359, 550.1.**

W554 With full **Womb** to preach abstinence **a1449** Lydgate *Order* in *MP* II 454.161–2: With ful wombe they preche of abstynence, Ther botel fild with fressh wyn or good ale.

W555 A **Wonder** lasts but nine nights (days) (*varied*) **c1325** *In a fryht* in Böddeker 160.31–2: Sone thou woldest vachen an newe, Ant take an other with inne nyghe naht. **c1385** Chaucer *TC* iv 588: Ek wonder last but nyne nyght nevere in towne. **c1440** Charles of Orleans 208–9.6217–8: For this a wondir last but days nyne An oold proverbe is seid. **1546** Heywood *D* 61.65: This wonder (as wonders last) lasted nine daies, **1555** *E* 171.139: A woonder lasteth but .ix. daies. Apperson 446; *Oxford* 726; Taylor and Whiting 410; Tilley W728; Whiting *Scots* II 159.

W556 To **Wone** (*dwell*) where one is well (*varied*) **c1450** *Foly of Fulys* 63.425: Thai can nocht wone quhen thai ar veill. **a1500** *Thre Prestis* 48.1125–6: Thairfoir this tail is trew into al tyde, Quhair ane fairis weil the langer sould he byde. Whiting *Scots* II 153. See **S297.**

W557 **Wone** (*habit*) will have will (wone) or bide (dree [*endure*]) woe **c1250** *Hendyng O* 193.11: Wone wole wille haven other wo bide. **c1450** *Rylands MS.394* 100.8: Woon wolle won, or ellse woo dryve (*for* dree). Mos sibi vult morem, vel vult tolerare dolorem. Kneuer 58–9; Schleich 273; Singer III 140; Walther II 954.15310a.

W558 Better loose in **Wood** than bound in town **a1400** *Titus* 130.2865–6: For los (*var.* ofte) is better, as it is founde, In wode than in toun ybounde.

W559 He must needs walk in **Wood** that may not walk in town **c1350** *Gamelyn* 661.672: He moste needes walke in woode that may not walke in towne. See **M384.**

W560 The more **Wood** the more fire (*varied*)
c1385 Chaucer *TC* ii 1331–2: But as we may alday oureselven see, Thorugh more wode or col, the more fir. **a1400** *Ancrene* (*Recluse*) 155.30–1: And the mo brondes that ben on the fyre the hatter is the fyre. **c1400** *Consilia Isidori* 368[28–9]: Fyer by castynge-to of wode encreseth more and more; the more mater ys in the fyer, the more ys the flame. **c1425** *Orcherd* 47.28–9: And right as a sensible fier encreessith aftir that moore matere is put therto. **1450** *Dicts* 102.14–5: Thou farest like a fire; for the more wodde men puttithe ther-to, the hotter it is. **1534** More *Comforte* 1202 (*by error* 1124) G[7–9]: Covetice fareth like the fier: the more wood that cometh therto, the more fervent and the more gredy it is. Apperson 240–1. See **S727.**

W561 Not to see the **Wood** for the trees
1533 More *Confutacion* 741 H[2–3]: He can not see the wood for the trees. **1546** Heywood *D* 67.53: Ye can not see the wood for trees. Apperson 708; *Oxford* 570; Tilley W733.

W562 To look as (if) the **Wood** were full of thieves
c1395 Chaucer *CT* III[D] 2172–3: I se wel that som thyng ther is amys; Ye looken as the wode were full of thevys. *Oxford* 384.

W563 Wet (Green) **Wood** is hotter when well kindled than is (any) other
1450 *Dicts* 110.1–2: The fire of grete wete wodde is hotter whanne it is wele kindeled than other is. **1477** Rivers *Dictes* 54[35–6]: Grene wode is hotter than the other whan it is wel kyndeled. Apperson 274; *Oxford* 266; Tilley W735.

W564 As true as the **Woodbine**
c1390 *Salutacioun to ure lady* 136.59: Heil trewore then the wode-bynde.

W565 As wise as a **Woodcock** (*varied*)
a1425 *Heded as an ox* in *Nicodemus* xxv[6]: Witted (as) a wodkok. **1520** Whittinton *Vulgaria* 60.19–20: He hath . . . as many braynes as a wodcok. **1534** Heywood *Love* B2^r[6]: As wyse as a woodcock. Apperson 696; *Oxford* 717; Tilley W746; Whiting *Drama* 333:371, 371:959.

W566 A **Woodwall** (*woodpecker*) never bred a sparhawk
c1489 Caxton *Blanchardyn* 173.6–7: But men saye in a comyn langage that "never noo wodewoll (French: bruhier, 'buzzard') dyde brede a sperhawke." Apperson 709. See **F37.**

W567 As nesh (*soft*) as **Wool**
c1300 *South English Legendary* I 55.31: Lightloker me may thane harde ston make nesse as wolle.

W568 As soft as the **Wool**
c1390 Chaucer *CT* I[A] 3249: And softer than the wolle is of a wether. **a1450** *Castle* 149.2401: It is as softe a(s) wulle.

W569 As warm as **Wool**
c1475 Henryson *Fables* 15.358–9: Hir den, Als warme as woll. Tilley W751.

W570 As white as (any) **Wool**
c1000 Aelfric *Lives* II 12.176–7: þa loccas hire heafdes wæron swa hwite swa wull. **c1300** *South English Legendary* (*Laud*) 265.145: Hire her was hor and swithe hwijght as thei it were wolle. **c1350** *Apocalypse* 7.14. **c1395** *WBible* Isaiah i 18, Apocalypse i 14: His heeris weren whiit, as whiit wolle. **c1440** *Prose Alexander* 93.7–8: His berde and his heved ware als whitt als any wolle. Taylor and Whiting 411; Whiting *Scots* II 160.

W571 Evil spun **Wool** (yarn, web, weft) comes out evil (*varied*)
c1250 *Hendyng O* 198.37: Evere cometh out uvel sponnen wolle, bote if me hit withinne forbrenne, **a1325** *C* 189.39: Ever comith out lithre spon yerne, **c1325** *H* 298.272: Ever out cometh evel sponne web. **a1393** Gower *CA* III 231.2381–2: Bot lich to wolle is evele sponne, Who lest himself hath litel wonne. **a1440** *Spurious Chaucerian lines* in Manly-Rickert V 434–5: Evelle sponne wolle at the laste wolle come oute, They thou kepe it never as prevey in a lytelle cloute. **a1450** *Lernyng* in Kail 98.64: In helle is shewed evell-sponnen wyft. **c1450** *Douce MS.52* 47.31: Evyl spunnun yerne comyth evyll oute. **a1460** *Towneley Plays* 21.435: Ill spon weft ay comes foule out, 135.587: Ill spon weft, Iwys, ay commys foull owte. **a1500** *How the Wyse Man* 27.7–8: But jarne that ys ofte tyme evell spon, Evyll hyt cometh owt at the laste. Apperson 187, 325; Kneuer 45–7; *Oxford* 317; Schleich 266; Singer III 135; Tilley W249. See **E93.**

W572 Well spun **Wool** makes the cloth strong
c1400 Gower *Peace* III 490.299–301: Men sein the wolle, whanne it is wel sponne, Doth that the cloth is strong and profitable, And elles it mai nevere be durable.

W573 To go **Woolward**
a1333 Shoreham *Poems* 37.1023–4: Knewelyng, travayl, barvot go, Wolle-ward and wakynge. **c1378** *Piers* B xviii 1: Wolleward and weteshoed went I forth after. **c1400** *Brut* I 99.18: Wenten bare-fote and wolward. *Oxford* 728.

W574 After jangling **Words** comes "whist! peace! and be still!"
c1385 Usk 23.89–90: Thus, after jangling wordes, cometh "huissht! pees! and be stille!"

W575 Be not of many **Words** (*varied*)
c1350 *Good Wife E* 160.42–3: Be noght of mani wordes, ne swer thou noght to grete; Alle swiche maneres, douter, thou most lete. **a1400** *Proverbis of Wysdom* 246.117–8: A-vyse the well, what ever thu say, And have few wordis, I the pray. Tilley W798. Cf. Jente 456.

W576 Better is a **Word** before than three afterwards
a1400 *Firumbras* 21.608: Better ys a word by-fore thanne afterward thre. Apperson 710:3; Tilley W778.

W577 Better to give smooth **Words** than take sharp stripes
1556 Heywood *Spider* 363[1–2]: Better smoth woordes to geve: then smart stripes to take, Namelie where stripes win nought: and wordes maie win all. See **W615.**

W578 By folly (*foolish*) **Words** men may ken (*know*) a fool
c1303 Mannyng *Handlyng* 105.2967: By foly wurdys mow men a fole kenne. **1450** *Dicts* 22.22–3: Men knowith a foole bi his worde, and a wiseman bi his dedis. **1477** Rivers *Dictes* 17[16–7]: And saide the fole is knowen by his wordis and the wieseman by his werkis. Apperson 224:18. See **F401.**

W579 By the **Word** men know a wise man and by the look a fool
c1440 Scrope *Epistle* 55[23–4]: For a poyete seyth, "By the worde men knowyth a wyse man, and by the looke a foole." **c1450** *Epistle of Othea* 83.6–7: Ffor as seyth a sage phillosophre: By speche is the wyse man, and by the looke the foole knowen.

W580 Evil **Words** walk far
1513 More *Richard* 48(*for* 45) D[2–3]: Evyll woordes walke farre.

W581 Fair **Words** (speech) but no love (*varied*)
a1460 *Towneley Plays* 134.569: Ffare wordys may ther be bot luf is ther none. **a1470** Malory I 396.9–10: So aftir that, thoughe there were fayre speche, love was there none. **1509** Barclay *Ship* II 323[3]: The wordes fayre: but fals is theyr intent. Cf. Whiting *Scots* II 129. See **D122, F50, M196, S618, W624, 636.**

W582 Fair **Words** did fet (*fetch*) plenty gromwell seed (*very hard seeds*)
1546 Heywood *D* 61.70–1: Fayre woordes did fet, Gromelseede plentie. *Oxford* 187–8; Tilley W792.

W583 Fair **Words** hurt not the tongue
1549 Heywood *D* 34.51: It hurteth not the tounge to geve fayre wurdes. Apperson 200; *Oxford* 188; Tilley W793.

W584 Fair **Words** lead men against their mind (*varied*)
a1500 *Coventry Plays* 48.485–6: Loo! feyre wordis full ofte doth leyde Men cleyne agen there mynd. **c1500** *Lady Bessy* 7[12]: Your fair words shall never move my mind. See **S605, T19.**

W585 Fair **Words** without, hate within
a1500 *Proverbs of Salamon* 179.16.5–6: Wythowte fayre wordys faynte, Withynne ys hate and hyt were soght. Cf. Whiting *Scots* II 161:9. See **S79, 617.**

W586 Few **Words** and well set (*varied*)
c1420 Page *Siege* 174.767–9: Thynke with herte by-fore youre tunge, Leste youre wordys ben alle to longe. Speke but ffewe and welle hym set. **c1475** *Mankind* 5.102: Few wordis; few and well sett, 104: Many wordis, and schortely sett. **1484** Caxton *Aesop* 48[16–8]: Oftyme it happeth that of a fewe wordes evyll sette cometh a grete noyse and daunger. Jente 446; Tilley W799.

W587 Few **Words** show men wise
1556 Heywood *E* 138.95.1: Few woords shew men wise, wise men doe devise. Tilley W799. See **M260, 328, S308.**

W588 Few **Words** to the wise suffice
1463 *Stonor Letters* I 62[14]: Sapienti pauca. **1479-83** Paston VI 60[20–1]: I can nomore but *sapienti pauca*, etc. **a1513** Dunbar *Of Discretioun in Asking* 32.24: Few wordis may serve the wyis. **1546** Heywood *D* 84.150: Fewe woords to the wise suffice to be spoken, **1556** *Spider* 142[2–3]: Wherto all folke do know That unto the wise, few wordes at full suffise. Apperson 209, 710; *Oxford* 728; Taylor and Whiting 412; Tilley W781; Whiting *Scots* II 160. See **W399.**

W589 Give good **Word** for good deed
c1470 *Wallace* 338.164: Me think ye suld geyff gud word for gud deid.

W590 A good **Word** will weigh no more on the tongue than the worst
c1390 *Charity is no longer Cheer* in Brown *Lyrics XIV* 173.105–8: Certes, and ye loke ariht, A good word no more wol weye That hit lith on yor tonge as liht, As the worste that ye con seye. Cf. Apperson 264; Tilley W760.

W591 A hasty **Word** may be too sore bought
a1475 *Hit is ful harde* in *MLN* 55(1940) 567.31: An hasty worde may be to sore bought. See **S607.**

W592 He that is hasty at every **Word** for a medicine must eat his wife's turd

c1497 Medwall *Fulgens* C6v[29–30]: Ye, but he that is so hasty at every worde For a medsyn must ete his wyves torde. See **S588, 607.**

W593 In fele (*many*) **Words** are lies (*varied*) **a1400** *Ipomadon A* 69.2345–7: In fele wordis be reson ys lyes, And ay the moste man of price The leyste of them selff wille sayne! **a1410** Lydgate *Churl* in *MP* II 477.200: Mong many talis is many grett lesyng. **c1415** *Middle English Sermons* 333.31–2: And comonly where most faire wordes be spoken, ther is most falsehed. **1456** Hay *Governaunce* 156.18–9: Mekle speche may nocht all be trewe na honourable. **1483** Caxton *Cato* F4v[26–7]: Hit may not be but that in over many wordes ne been somme lesynges. **c1523** Barclay *Mirrour* 73[29–31]: Where man is . . . full of wordes, they can not all be true. **1556** Heywood *Spider* 191[25]: And so many woordes, so many lies. Jente 193. Cf. Apperson 400; Tilley W828; Whiting *Scots* II 129. See **D246, F379, L67, M184, S587, W607.**

W594 In fele (*many*) **Words** is oft lite (*little*) wisdom **a1440** Burgh *Cato* 306.118: In woordis fele is wisdom oft full lite. See **F379.**

W595 In few **Words** is courtesy **a1400** *Ipomadon A* 69.2339: In few wordes ys curtesye.

W596 In flattering **Words** lies guile **a1400** *Proverbis of Wysdom* 245.43: In flateryng wordis lyeth gyle. **c1450** *Fyrst thou sal* 88.55.

W597 In many **Words** much strength **a1200** *Ancrene* 106.5–6: Ye mote makien that wite ye, i moni word muche strengthe.

W598 The last **Word** binds the tale **a1325** *Sarmun* in Heuser 95.211: The last word bint the tale. **c1450** *Douce MS.52* 47.38: The last worde byndeth the tale. See **S610.**

W599 Many **Words** little matter **1533** Heywood *Weather* D2r[33]: Many wordes, lyttell mater, and to no purpose, **1556** *Spider* 294[16]. See **S80.**

W600 Many **Words** many buffets **1562** Heywood *D* 87.230: Many woords, many buffets. *Oxford* 406; Tilley W816. See **S612.**

W601 Many **Words** require much drink **c1515** Barclay *Eclogues* 107.3: And many wordes requireth much drinke. Tilley W818.

W602 No **Word** but mum **1523** Skelton *Garlande* I 406.1118: There was amonge them no worde then but mum. Taylor and Whiting 254; Tilley W767. See **M803, N172.**

W603 Of small **Words** waxes great conteck (*strife*) **c1390** *Cato* (*Vernon*) 580.327–8: Gret contex of smale wordes Waxeth ofte ful ryve. **a1400** *Cato* (*Copenhagen*) A6r[15–6]: Thurgh ful smale wordis ofte is seen to growe debate, dissese, and tene. **a1440** Burgh *Cato* 314.464–5: For this is sothe as God yaf the thi liffe: Off woordis small is bred ful muche striffe. See **S559.**

W604 One ill **Word** asks another **1546** Heywood *D* 34.49: One yll woord axeth an other. Apperson 471; *Oxford* 318; Tilley W770.

W605 One may not call his **Word** again (*varied*) **c1390** Chaucer *CT* IX[H] 353–8: But he that hath mysseyd, I dar wel sayn, He may by no wey clepe his word agayn. Thyng that is seyd is seyd, and forth it gooth, Though hym repente, or be hym nevere so looth. He is his thral to whom that he hath sayd A tale of which he is now yvele apayd. **a1420** Lydgate *Troy* III 640.2600–1: For like a wynde, that no man may areste, Fareth a word, discordaunt to the dede, **a1449** *Say the Best* in *MP* II 797.68–9: A word, when hit is onys i-spooke, May not be callid ayen of new. **1450** *Dicts* 96.22–3: A worde is in a mannes power to it be spoken; and whann it is said, it is out of his power. **c1450** La Tour-Landry 204.22–8: And in lyke wyse as the shafte is departed fro the bowe, must take her flyght and cours, and never cometh ageyne to the bowe tyll it have smyte somme thynge, soo is the word whiche yssued oute of the mouthe lyke it; for after that he is put out of the mouth, it may never be put in-to the mouthe ageyne, but that it shal be herd, be it good or evylle. **1477** Rivers *Dictes* 106[36–7]: I am mayster over my wordes or it be pronunced, but when it is spoken I am servaunt therto. **a1500** *Partenay* 124.3540: Such A word shal say, repent can not purchas. **1509** Barclay *Ship* I 108[26]: A worde ones spokyn revoked can nat be. **1523** Skelton *Garlande* I 384.567: Wordes be swordes, and hard to call ageine. Apperson 710:4; *Oxford* 728; Smith 339; Tilley W777; Whiting *Scots* II 161:13. See **T186, W625, 626, 639.**

W606 One may say a **Word** to-day that may be forthought (*regretted*) seven years after **c1450** *How the Wyse Man* 36.31–2: For thou myghte seie a word to day, That VII year after may be forthought. See **M642.**

W607 One may trust best to those that are of least **Words**
c1300 Robert of Gloucester I 63.859–60: Bi this tale me mai ise that men triwest we seth, And best me mai to hom truste that of lest wordes beth. Cf. Tilley W828. See **W593.**

W608 One **Word** spoken in sport requires another
1509 Barclay *Ship* II 35[1]: One worde in sporte spokyn, another lyke requyrys.

W609 One's **Word** is as true as his bond (*varied*)
1369 Chaucer *BD* 933–5: Ne lasse flaterynge in hir word, That purely hir symple record Was founde as trewe as any bond. **c1475** Henryson *Fables* 78.2282: His saw is ay als sickker as his Seill. Apperson 710; *Oxford* 300; Taylor and Whiting 413; Tilley M458.

W610 One's **Words** oft turn to his own shame
1509 Barclay *Ship* I 213[1]: Howbeit his wordes, oft turne to his owne shame. See **D342.**

W611 Painted **Words** hide a false intent
1509 Barclay *Ship* II 40[28]: So paynted wordes hydeth a fals intent.

W612 A short **Word** that first slides from man's tooth is commonly sooth
a1450 *Boke of Curtasye* (*Sloane*) 305.211–2: A schort worde is comynly sothe That fyrst slydes fro monnes tothe.

W613 Sore is **Word** and sore is work
c1250 *Hendyng O* 197.32: Sor is word and sor is werk, Sor is bite and sor is berk. Kneuer 59; Schleich 274; Singer III 140.

W614 Such is the **Word** such is the soul
c1400 *Consilia Isidori* 371[5–6]: And suche as the worde ys, suche ys the soule. Cf. Smith 214.

W615 Sweet **Words** refrain great ire
1483 Caxton *Cato* D8ᵛ[9]: Swete and frendely wordes refraynen grete yre, H3ʳ[18–9]: The comyn proverbe sayth that swete worde refrayneth grete yre. See **W577.**

W616 Sweet **Words** win more than rude dealing
1525 Berners *Froissart* VI 6[21–2]: Ye shall wyn more by swete and fayre wordes than by rude and frowarde dealynge. Cf. Taylor and Whiting 140–1.

W617 To be of bold **Word** at meat and coward in the field (*varied*)
c1300 Robert of Gloucester I 424.5803–4: Sire king, he sede, ech god mon, hit is vileynye To be of bold word atte mete and coward in the velde. **a1533** Berners *Arthur* 209[30–2]: Ye be one of the knightes that wyl menace and threten whan ye stand by the chymney warmyng you after souper, and in the mornynge all is forgoten. See **B415, F659, M367, S581, T49.**

W618 To be true with **Word** but feeble in faith
a1350 *Ywain* 2.37–8: With worde men makes it trew and stabil, Bot in thaire faith es noght bot fabil.

W619 To give two (three) **Words** for one
c1477 Caxton *Curtesye* 46.458: For every worde yevyng his maister tweyne. **1506** Hawes *Pastime* 135–6.3553–4: They wyll never lete Theyr tonges cease but gyve thre wordes for one.

W620 To greet with fair **Words** but think to do a wicked blink (*trick*)
c1303 Mannyng *Handlyng* 141.4180–2: Wyth feyre wurdys he shal the grete, But yn hys herte he shal thynke For to do the a wykked blynke. *Oxford* 202. See **S79, W624.**

W621 To have (be) nought but fair **Words**
a1387 Higden-Trevisa VII 321[18–9]: And hadde right nought but faire wordes. **a1400** *Morte Arthure* 86.2929: Thow arte feble and false and noghte bot faire wordes. Whiting *Drama* 241.

W622 To have one's **Word** fly before his wit
c1380 *Pearl* 11.294: Thy worde byfore thy wytte con fle. **1546** Heywood *D* 68.94: Your tounges run before your wits, **1555** *E* 187.226: Thy tongue runth before thy wit. Apperson 639; *Oxford* 664: Tongue; Tilley T412.

W623 Under fair **Words** is oft covered guile
a1440 Burgh *Cato* 309.234: Undir fair woordis ys ofte coverid gyle. See **S618.**

W624 Under soft (fair) **Words** to have (bear) privy venom
c1340 Rolle *Psalter* 467 (139.3): For undire soft touchynge of wordis, thai hafe pryve venym of snakis, that is, malice uncurabil in thaire hert. **1509** Barclay *Ship* II 41[8–10]: Under fayre wordes . . . Suche beryth venym. See **S79, 618, W581, 620.**

W625 When a **Word** is not said the bird is in the cage
1509 Barclay *Ship* I 110[19]: Whan a worde is nat sayd, the byrde is in the cage. *Oxford* 728. Cf. Tilley W776, 777. See **W605.**

W626 When a **Word** is spoken you are not its master but he that has heard it
1509 Barclay *Ship* I 110[21–2]: So whan thy worde is spokyn and out at large, Thou arte nat mayster, but he that hath it harde. **1509** Watson *Ship* Q3ʳ[10–2]: Speke not at aventure,

for whan the worde is departed out of the mouthe, they be subjectes unto the forsayd wordes. Apperson 710:10; *Oxford* 728; Tilley W776. See **W605, 637.**

W627 White **Words** (*i.e.*, insincere)
c1385 Chaucer *TC* iii 901: But feffe hym with a fewe wordes white, 1567: For al youre wordes white. **a1420** Lydgate *Troy* I 192.1661: With alle thi wordis white, II 518.4272: Hir wordis white, softe, and blaundyshynge, III 744.6160: Her feyned othes, nor her wordis whyte, 824.1796, **a1422** *Life* 286.557: With sugrede tonge, of many wordes whyte, 425.1625: And Tullyus, with all his wordys white (*in a favorable sense*). **a1437** *Kingis Quair* 83.136[4]. **c1475** Henryson *Fables* 24.601: To flatteraris with plesand wordis quhyte. **a1500** *Court of Love* 437.1042–3. **a1500** *Lay of Sorrow* 716.37. **a1500** *Miroure of Mans Salvacionne* 13[26]. **a1507** Dunbar *Dance* 121.48. **1513** Douglas *Aeneid* II 61.34: And hys dissemblit slekit wordis quhite. NED White a. 10; Whiting *Scots* II 161. See **T235, W611.**

W628 Who may (be)lieve in fair **Words?**
a1475 *Guy*[2] 90.3137–8: Who may leve anythynge In feyre wordys or feyre behetynge?

W629 Whoso will take heed of every **Word** shall never thrive
c1385 Chaucer *TC* v 757–9: For whoso wol of every word take hede, Or reulen hym by every wightes wit, Ne shal he nevere thryven, out of drede. See **M115, T298, 490.**

W630 A wicked **Word** may make great tinsel (*loss*) (*varied*)
c1420 Wyntoun VI 57.4524–5: A wickyt worde may qwhilis mak Ful gret tynsel, as it did here. **a1475** *Ludus Coventriae* 55.135–8: Wykkyd worde werkyht oftyn tyme grett ill, Be war ther fore of wykkyd langage. Wyckyd spech many on doth spyll, Therfore of spech beth not owt-rage. **1509** Watson *Ship* Bb7[r][28–9]: For the evyll wordes ben cause of many evylles.

W631 With **Word** and not with heart (*varied*)
c970 *Blickling Homilies* 69[24–5]: þis folc me weorþaþ mid wordum, and is þeah heora heorte feor fram me. **c1300** Lawman I 127 *B* 3017–8: Tho answerede heo mid worde, And noht mid heorte. **a1350** *Ywain* 5.143–4: Bot word fares als dose the wind, Bot if men it in hert bynd. **c1390** *Proverbes of diverse profetes* 539.257–60: Loke thou have nought to gret affyaunce In feire wordes and in cuntinaunce; Such mon parauntre profreth the to kis That in herte ha(te)the the, I-wis. **c1400** *Chastising* 129.4–5: Faire wordis thei shewen without, but the contrarie is in the herte. **c1415** *Middle English Sermons* 310.25–8: Vhat tyme the word of a mans mouthe acordeth not with the worde of is herte, than he bereth fals wittenes ayeyns is own herte and dampneth is own selfe. **a1439** Lydgate *Fall* I 323.4405: When woord and herte be contrarious. **1450** *Dicts* 14.12–4: And looke that your wordis divers and varie not fro the thought of your hert. See **L376, M570, 755, T189, 383.**

W632 **Word** and wind and man's mind are short but written letter dwells
c1395 *Camb. Univ. Lib. MS. Ii 6.26* in *WBible* I xiv, n.[k]: For it is a comoun sawe, and soth it is, Worde and wynde and mannes mynde is ful schort, but letter writen dwellith.

W633 **Word** has beguiled many a man
a1393 Gower *CA* III 275.1564: Word hath beguiled many a man. *Oxford* 188.

W634 **Word** is as wind, but dint (*blow*) is as devil
1456 Hay *Law* 271.21–2: For men sais commonly that word is as wynd, bot dynt is as devill. Tilley W834. See **W644.**

W635 **Word** is best and worst betwixt men (*varied*)
a1000 *Dialogue of Salomon and Saturnus,* ed. J. M. Kemble (London, 1848) 188.37: Word is betst and wyrst betwix mannum. **a1000** *Adrian and Ritheus, as above* 204.43: Saga me, hwæt bið betst and wyrst? Ic ðe secge, mannes word. See **L371, T371, 387.**

W636 The **Word** is gay but friendship is to seek
a1440 Burgh *Cato* 309.235: The woord is gay, but frenship is to seeche. See **W581.**

W637 **Word** is thrall
a1437 *Good Counsel* in *Kingis Quair,* ed. W. W. Skeat (STS, 1884) 51.15: Sen word is thrall, and thocht is only free. See **W626.**

W638 **Word** made never war's end, but sword ended the deed
1414 *Dede is worchyng* in Kail 59.127–8: With word of wynd, mad nevere werre ende, But dent of swerd endid the dede. See **W152.**

W639 A **Word** may never wend again
a1450 *Myne awen dere* 160.351–4: A worde may nevere agane wende: Thou kepe thy tonge and halde thy frende. A worde may nevere torne agayne If thou tharfore soulde be slane. See **T186, W605.**

W640 **Word** slays more than sword
a1200 *Ancrene* 39.4–5: Ma sleath word then sweord, **a1400** (*Recluse*) 32.13: For men saien: mo men slen with woorde than with knyf. Apperson 711; *Oxford* 729; Smith 341; Tilley W839; Whiting *Scots* II 160–1. See **M758, T395.**

W641 A **Word** with two visages
c1385 Chaucer *TC* v 898–9: That is to seyn, with double wordes slye, Swiche as men clepen a word with two visages. See **F8.**

W642 **Words** (Speech, Saws) and deeds (works) (*varied*)
c735 *Beowulf* 287–9: Æghwæþres sceal Scearp scyldwiga gescad witan, Worda ond worca, se þe wel þenceð. **c1000** Aelfric *Treatise* in *Heptateuch* 15.2: Se bið swiþe wis, se þe mid weorcum sprícð, 74.1257–8: Nu miht þu wel witan, þæt weorc sprecað swiþor þonne þa nacodan word, þe nabbað nane fremminge. **c1000** *Vercelli Homily 22* in *Festschrift für Lorenz Morsbach* (Halle, 1913) 145.7–9: Ac ðonne ðu hine ciȝst on þinum wordum, ne wið-sac ðu hine on þinum weorcum. **a1200** *Ancrene* 162. 16–7: Ah schulen the wordes beon ischawet efter the werkes. **a1250** *Bestiary* 19.592–5: He speken godcundhede, And wikke is here dede; Here dede is al uncuth With that speketh here muth. **c1250** *Proverbs of Alfred* 132 T 637–8: Ac nim the to a stable mon That word and dede bi-sette con. **c1300** Robert of Gloucester II 662.9326–7: In word he is god inou, and coward in dede, Slou to fighte and quic to fle, 9331: That muche wole segge and bihote, and lute ther to do, 665.9383: Mid word he thretneth muche and lute deth in dede, 706.10310: Ower dede ne may be no wors than ower word is. **a1338** Mannyng *Chronicle* A I 442.12653–4: Ther bostful wordes ar nought to seke, Ther dedes are nought worth a leke. **a1350** Castelford in Rolf Kaiser *Medieval English* (Berlin, 1961) 373. 537–8: This Edwarde als anens his lede Was wise of worde and fole in dede. **a1387** Higden-Trevisa VII 489[19]: When his word is i-saide he hath idoo his dede. **c1387–95** Chaucer *CT* I[A] 496–7: This noble ensample to his sheep he yaf, That first he wroghte, and afterward he taughte, **c1390** *Stedfastnesse* 4–5: That word and deed, as in conclusioun, Ben nothing lyk. **a1393** Gower *CA* II 17.450–1: Betwen the word and that thei werche Ther is a full gret difference, III 368.4778–80: It is . . . of non emprise To speke a word, bot of the dede, Therof it is to taken hiede. **a1400** *Romaunt C* 6360: Unlyk is my word to my dede, 7249: And that her wordis folowe her dede. **a1400** *Titus* 140.3116: Michell is bytwen worde and dede. **a1405** Lydgate *Floure* in *MP* II 416.209–10: For worde and dede, that she naught ne fal, Acorde in vertue and her werkes al, **a1420** *Troy* III 640.2600–1: For like a wynde, that no man may areste, Fareth a word, discordaunt to the dede. **a1425** *Metrical Paraphrase OT* 54.15724: Aftur thi dedes thi sawes persew. **c1425** Arderne *Fistula* 4.15–8: Wherfore seith a versifiour, "vincat opus verbum, minuit jactantia famam"; "lat werke overcome thi worde, for boste lesseneth gode lose." **1435** Misyn *Fire* 28.32–3: Noght has thou bott fayre sight and fayre worde, deyde has thou none. **a1439** Lydgate *Fall* I 323.4409–10: Lat never story afftir mor recorde, That woord and deede sholde in you discorde, **a1449** *Ballade* in *MP* II 380.31: Of whome that worde and thought acorde in deed. **a1449** Lydgate and Burgh *Secrees* 39.1223: Truste On the dede And nat in gay spechys, 1224: Leff woord and tak the dede. **1450** *Dicts* 8.14–6: A man schulde not jugee a man bi his wordis bot bi his dedis, for comonly wordis be voide bot bi dedis is knowen bothe harme and profite, 56.10–1: Preve . . . men bi their workis and not bi their wordes, 240.1–2: Ther is greet discorde bitwene his worde and his dede, 282.17–9: He is right a greete enmy of whome the deedis be feble and bittir and the wordes softe and curteise. **c1450** *Consail and Teiching* 71.195–6: Be nocht our-changabile in thi thocht That word and deid contrary nocht. **c1450** *Foly of Fulys* 54.71–2: Quharfore men suld do as thai say, That werk folow the word alway. **c1450** *Harley MS.2321* in Robbins-Cutler 1867.5: Let thy worke thy worde passe, for bost makyth thy fame lesse. **c1450** *In my yong age* in Furnivall *Hymns* 38.111: If her word and werk coorde not in fere. **c1450** *Merlin* II 486[33–4]: I preise not at a boton . . . the speche, but the dede be shewed. **1456** Hay *Governaunce* 89.33–4: A traist gude faithfull lord schawis in werk als wele as in word. **a1460** *Dicts* (*Helmingham*) 119.19–21: Worde withoute dede is lyke a grete habundaunce of watir that drowneth the men withoute doynge himself any proufite. **a1471** Ashby *Policy* 24.352–3: Say nat oon thyng and do the contrarie, Lete youre worde and dede be in accordance. **a1475** *Cato* (*Rawlinson*) 15.153: For wordis with-owte dede may lytil plesse. **1477** Rivers *Dictes* 94[5–6]: His dedes shal be moche discordaunt to his wordes. **1474** Caxton *Chesse* 103[28–30]: And that theyr dedes folowe theyr wordes. For he that sayth one thynge and doth another he condempneth hymself by his word. **a1483** Kay *Siege* [34.22–3]: To preve yf the dedys of the Rhodyans sholde accorde wyth

theyre grete wordes. **1483** *Vulgaria quedam abs Terencio* A6^r[19–20]: I wolde thou shuldist doo it in dede that thou promysed in wordys. **1484** Caxton *Aesop* 250–1: Many one ben frendes of wordes only but fewe ben in fayth or dede. **a1500** *Lovely Song of Wisdom* 196.20[5–6]: Whene worde and werke will not mete The caytefe hert recayreth agayne. **a1500** *Proverbs of Salamon* 195.7.5: If worde and werke cotrare be. **a1500** ?Ros *La Belle Dame* 309.340: The wordes preveth, as the workes sewe. **c1500** Fabyan 259[26]: If that his dede agayne his wordys preche. **c1500** *Morgan Lib. MS. M.722* in Robbins-Cutler 1439.8: If worde and ded agre, Your fyrnd (assured) wyll I be. **c1500** *Series* in Brown *Lyrics XV* 271.63: For that wurde and werke acordit not in fere. **1512** Copland *Helyas* A7^v[13–4]: Whose wordes were not accordaunte to her dedes. **a1513** Dunbar *Dunbar at Oxinfurde* 104.22: Giff to your sawis your deidis contrair be. **c1523** Barclay *Mirrour* 51[17]: That is when their wordes and workes well agree. **1532** Berners *Golden Boke* 129.628–9: Yf their plesant and well couched wordes agreed in effect with their warkes, 301.5999–6000: What nede wordes to our frendes, Whan we may succour them with workes? 344.7398–9: He that gyveth counsell with wordes, may remedy with workes, 396.9974–5: They that spake best wordes, are often taken with the worst dedes. **1556** Heywood *Spider* 430[27–8]: Whose deede and his thought repungnantlie varie, His woord and his thought jar likewise contrarie. Apperson 265, 710:7; Jente 202, 747; *Oxford* 135, 729; Tilley D333, W802, 820; Whiting *Scots* I 157, II 160. See **D133, 281, F89, H372, S83, 574, T193, 394, V33.**

W643 **Words** are (Word is) but wind (*varied*) **c1000** Aelfric *Lives* I 196.19: Eower word syndon winde gelice. **a1200** *Ancrene* 65.1: Hwet is word bute wind? **c1300** *South English Legendary* I 222.61: Word nis ayen hure bote wind. **a1350** *Ywain* 5.143: Bot word fares als dose the wind. **c1390** *Fy on a faint Friend* in Brown *Lyrics XIV* 155.4: With feire bi-heste and wordes as wynde. **a1393** Gower *CA* II 300.2768: For word is wynd. **c1398** W. Paris *Cristine* in Horstmann *Sammlung* 189.479–80: Thi wordis as wynde flyede too and froo, Bute strokes are sore ande evylle to byde. **a1400** *Ipomadon A* 222.7776–8: Wele I fynde, That many wordes wastes wynde, Inowghe of them I have. **a1400** *Scottish Legends* II 360.77. **1413** *God save the kyng* in Kail 52.51–2: For word of wynd lityl trespase; Non harm nys don, though word be spoken. **a1420** Lydgate *Troy* I 270.4383: Word is but wynde, and water that we wepe, III 777.138–9: How that he is, whan it commeth to nede, But word and wynd and sleighti compassyng, **1420** *Temple* 49.1183, **a1439** *Fall* III 1008.3165. **1447** Bokenham 229.8414–5: That alle youre wurdys, wych as wynd be, Youre thretys as flodys, youre hestys as reyn. **a1449** Lydgate *Freond* in *MP* II 757.69–70: But at the point, adieux, al nys but fable, Save worde and wynde conclusion of theire crede. **a1449** Lydgate and Burgh *Secrees* 39.1224. **a1450** *York Plays* 280.236. **c1450** *Foly of Fulys* 52.15–8: For word but writ as vynd ourgais And eftir that smal prefet mais, And wryt remanis and prentis in hart To thaim that sal cum eftirwart. **a1475** *Cato* (*Rawlinson*) 15.154–5: For fele wordis, thou schalt be told, Ful of wynd and noght goodly ben hold. **a1475** *St. Birgitta* 101.20. **a1500** *Imitatione* (*1*) 122.10–2: What are wordes but wordes (*?wynde*)? they fleeth by the ayre, but thei hurte not a stoon. **a1500** Medwall *Nature* B3^v[22]. **c1500** Greene *Carols* 443.3. **1502** *Imitatione* (2) 238.13–4: What be wordes but wynde that fleeth in the ayre without hurt of any stone. **1509** Barclay *Ship* I 207[16]. **1518** Nevill *Castell* 102.659: For as it is sayd wordes is nothynge but wynde. Apperson 710–1; *Oxford* 729; Tilley W833; Whiting *Drama* 184, 194, 283, 296, *Scots* II 161. See **W515.**

W644 **Words** I may suffer but stripes I may not **1520** Whittinton *Vulgaria* 107.16: Wordes I may suffre, but strypes I maye not awaye withal. Cf. Apperson 711:18; Tilley W834. See **W634.**

W645 The **Words** must be cousins to the deeds **897** Alfred *Boethius* 101.13–6: Ic gemunde nu ryhte þæs wisan Platones lara suma, hu he cwæð ðæt te se mon se ðe bispell secgan wolde, ne sceolde fon on to ungelic bispell ðære spræce þe he ðonne sprecan wolde. **c1380** Chaucer *Boece* iii pr. xii 205–7: The sentence of Plato that nedes the wordis moot be cosynes to the thinges of whiche thei speken, **c1387-95** *CT* I[A] 741–2: Eek Plato seith, whoso that kan hym rede, The wordes moote be cosyn to the dede, **c1390** IX[H] 207–10: The wise Plato seith, as ye may rede, The word moot nede accorde with the dede. If men shal telle proprely a thyng, The word moot cosyn be to the werkyng. **1410** Walton *Boethius* 206[10–2]. **a1500** Medwall *Nature* B3^r[40]: And let thy world (*for* word) be cousyn to thy dede. Apperson 368; *Oxford* 135. See **D133.**

Work, sb.

W646 He that begins his **Work** well wins a good end (*varied*) a1393 Gower *CA* II 6.86°–8: In proverbe I have herd seye That who that wel his werk begynneth The rather a good ende he wynneth. **a1500** *Thre Prestis* 4.62: The thing begwn is the sonere endit. Cf. Jente 133; Tilley B254. See **B204.**

W647 Ill **Work** brings a man to evil end
c1410 Lovelich *Merlin* I 8.283: For ille werk bryngeth a man to evele ende. See **D129, 137.**

W648 (On)looking **Works** are light (*easy*)
c1475 Henryson *Fables* 6.100–2: Thy cullour dois bot confort to the sicht, And that is not aneuch my wame to feid, For wyfis sayis, lukand werkis ar licht. **1513** Douglas *Aeneid* IV 191. 115–6: Yit have I hard oft said be men na clerkis, Tyll idyll folk full lycht beyn lukand warkis. Whiting *Scots* II 161.

W649 No **Work** may stand without groundwall (*foundation*)
a1325 *Cursor* I 14.125–6: Bot for-thi that na werc may stand Wit-outen grundwall to be lastand.

W650 To run to **Work** as if nine men held him
1546 Heywood *D* 51.345: Ye ren to woorke in haste as nine men helde ye. Apperson 250:29; *Oxford* 553; Tilley M608.

Work, vb.

W651 He that will not **Work** shall not eat (*varied*)
a1023 Wulfstan *Homilies* 193.41–3: Se apostol . . . cwæð: *Qui non vult operari nec manducet.* þæt is, se þe nyt beon nelle, he æniges godes ne abite. **a1375** *Octavian* (S) 22.675–6: Ech man behoveth to do som dede For hys sustynaunce. **c1395** *WBible* II Thessalonians iii 10: If ony man wole not worche, nethir ete he. **a1400** Paues 90 II Thessalonians iii 10: He that ne wol not trafaylen, ne ete he noght. **a1400** *Pauline Epistles* iii 10. **a1425** *St. Anthony* 117.28: Ffor he fonde wretyne: "Wo so workes not, not sal ete." **c1425** *St. Mary Oignies* 148.6. **a1450** *God of hefne, that sittest* 415.438–9: And ydel men that loth beth to swynke, The bok hem forbedeth mete and drinke. **a1470** Parker *Dives* S2ʳ[2.26–8]. **1509** Barclay *Ship* II 186[13–4]: And wryte doth testyfy That an Idell man to ete is nat worthy. **1509** Watson *Ship* Aa2ʳ[14–5]. *Oxford* 730; Taylor and Whiting 414; Tilley L10.

W652 No **Workman** may work both well and hastily
c1395 Chaucer *CT* IV[E] 1832–4: Ther nys no werkman, whatsoevere he be, That may bothe werke wel and hastily; This wol be doon at leyser parfitly. See **H168.**

W653 What is a **Workman** without his tools?
1546 Heywood *D* 94.137: For what is a woorkman, without his tooles? **1555** *E* 165.115. Apperson 711; *Oxford* 731; Tilley W859.

W654 The **Workman** is known by his works (*varied*)
c1385 Usk 3.69: The crafte of a werkman is shewed in the werke. **1481** Caxton *Mirror* 22[4–5]: Ffor by the werkys is the werkeman knowen, **1484** *Aesop* 121[23–4]: And therfore at the werke is knowen the best and most subtyle werker. **1509** Barclay *Ship* I 56[15]: By his warkes knowen is every creature. Tilley W860.

W655 The **Workman** is worthy of his hire (*varied*)
c1000 *WSG* Matthew x 10: Soþlice se wyrhta ys wyrþe hys metys, Luke x 7: Soðlice se wyrhta is his mede wyrðe. **c1395** Chaucer *CT* III[D] 1972–3: The hye God, that al this world hath wroght, Seith that the werkman worthy is his hyre. **c1395** *WBible* Matthew x 10: For a werkman is worthi his mete, Luke x 7: A werk man is worthi his hire, I Timothy v 18. **a1400** *Pauline Epistles* I Timothy v 18. **1400** *Mede and muche thank* in Kail 7.40: The trewe servant is worthy hys mede. **c1400** Paues 114 I Timothy v 18: A werkman is worthi his mede. **1410** *With god of love* in Kail 39.165: The werkman is worthy his mede. **c1430** Lydgate *Dance* 64.536: And to eche laboure due is the salarie. **1509** Fisher *Treatyse* 167.33–5: The werke man . . . is worthy to have his hyre, his rewarde. *Oxford* 347; Taylor and Whiting 212; Tilley L12.

W656 All the **World** goes by fair speech
a1500 Hill 130.11: All the world goth by fayre speche. Omnia mundana pertrancit pulcra loquela.

W657 He that will live in the **World** must suffer poverty as well as wealth (*varied*)
1525 Berners *Froissart* IV 25[14–6]: It behoveth them that wyll lyve in this worlde, thynkynge to have honoure, to suffre somtyme as well povertie as welth, VI 345[17–8]: He that wyll lyve in this worlde must endure somtyme trouble. See **R220.**

W658 It is a **World** to hear (see, look, consider)
a1450 *Generydes B* 71.2205: It was a world to here the sperys breke. **c1495** *Arundel Vulgaria* 3.9: It is a worlde to se, 24.100: It is a worlde to hunt the hare, 27.112: se, 39.164: se. **a1500** *Assembly* 397.539: loke on her visage. **1502** *Robert the Devil* D1ᵛ[17]: se. **1515** Barclay *St. George* 21.289: se. **c1520** *Terens* A7ʳ[22]. **c1523** Barclay *Mirrour* 65[29]: see. **1529** More *Sup-*

plicacion 300 H[6–7]: see, 325 F[16]: see, **1533** *Answer* 1090 F[11]: se, 1123 E[6]: consider, *Confutacion* 530 E[2]: see, 615 C[4–5]: see, 685 B[4–5], 796 E[9]: se, 802 H[5]: see, **1534** *Comforte* 1222 C[1]: see, *Passion* 1304 G[5–6]: marke and consider. **1534** Heywood *BS* 251.45: see. Apperson 711–2; *Oxford* 732; Tilley W878.

W659 Let the **World** pass (wag)
a1460 *Towneley Plays* 120.120: Whoso couthe take hede and lett the warld pas. **a1500** *Lady of Pite* in *MLR* 49(1954) 291.43: But Mastresse, as for my part let the world wag. **c1522** Skelton *Speke* II 6.90: But *moveature terra,* let the world wag. **c1525** ?Heywood *Gentylnes* 123.1010: I wyll let the world wagg. Apperson 360–1; *Oxford* 732; Taylor and Whiting 414; Tilley W879; Whiting *Drama* 371:963, *Scots* II 161. See **W668.**

W660 One must needs do as the **World** does
a1500 Medwall *Nature* B2v[35–6]: Also he must nedys do as the worlde doth That intendeth any whyle here to reygne, B4v[34–5]: Thynke that ye be here a worldly man, And must do as men that in the world dwell. See **R184.**

W661 Take the **World** as it would be (goes)
a1400 *Romaunt B* 5641: And taketh the world as it wolde be. **a1450** *Generydes A* 66.2108: Take the world nou as it gooth. **1519** Horman *Vulgaria* 89[12]: Thou muste take this worlde aworth as it goeth.

W662 This **World** is but a fair (cherry-fair)
1340 *Ayenbite* 76[22–3]: Vor this wordle is ase a fayre huer byeth manye fole chapmen. **c1385** Chaucer *TC* v 1840–1: And thynketh al nys but a faire This world. **c1390** *Make Amends* in Brown *Lyrics XIV* 199.85–6: This world nis but a chirie feire, Nou is hit in sesun, nou wol hit slake. **a1393** Gower *CA* II 17.454–5: For al is bot a chirie feire This worldes good, so as thei telle, III 191.890–1: And that endureth bot a throwe, Riht as it were a cherie feste. **c1400** *Vices and Virtues* 74.34–5: For this world fareth right as a feyre. **1401** *Treuth, reste, and pes* in Kail 14.145–6: The world is like a chery fayre, Ofte chaungeth all his thynges. **c1412** Hoccleve *Regement* 47.1289: This lyf, my sone, is but a chirie faire. **1445** Lydgate *Kalendare* in *MP* I 370.190: Lo, now tyme passith of chyrry fayre. **a1450** Audelay 20.280–1: Fore al the worchyp of this word hit wyl wype sone away; Hit falls and fadys forth, so doth a chere fayre. **c1450** Greene *Carols* 365.4: This word, lordynges, is but a farye; It faryt ryght as a neysche weye, That now is wet and now is dreye. **c1450** *How the Wyse Man* 41.143–4: Sonne, sette not bi this worldis weele, For it farith but as a cherifaire. **c1455** *Speculum Misericordie* 942.72: This worlde is but a cherie feyre. **c1465** *As I fared* in Sandison 116.22: For as a fayre this world doth fare. **c1475** *Mankind* 9.226–7: Remembur, my frende, the tyme of contynuance! So helpe me Gode! yt ys but a chery tyme! **a1500** Greene *Carols* 371.6: Thys world is butt a chery-fare. **a1500** *Lament of the Soul* in Brown *Lyrics XV* 251.22: No sertayne butt a chery fere full of woo. **c1500** *Farewell* in Brown *Lyrics XV* 236.8: This lyfe, I see, is but a cheyre feyre. **1506** *Kalender* 66.13: For thys worlde is but a chery fayre, 25, 67.3, 15, 27. **1520** Whittinton *Vulgaria* 82.10–1: Theyr tyme is but a chery feyre. MED cheri 2(a); NED Cherry-fair; Skeat 205.

W663 This **World** is but a thoroughfare full of woe (*varied*)
c1385 Chaucer *CT* I[A] 2847–8: This world nys but a thurghfare ful of wo, And we been pilgrymes, passynge to and fro. **a1439** Lydgate *Fall* I 22.795: How this world is a thoruhfare ful off woo, **a1449** *Thoroughfare* in *MP* II 822–8.6–8: To erthly pilgrymes that passen to and froo, Fortune shewith ay, by chaungyng hir see, How this world is a thurghfare ful of woo, 16, 24, *etc.*, 828.186–91: Remembre sothly that I the refreyd tooke, Of hym that was in makyng soverayne, My mayster Chaucier, chief poete of Bretayne, Whiche in his tragedyes made ful yore agoo, Declared triewly and list nat for to feyne, How this world is a thurghfare ful of woo. **1450** *Dicts* 84.23: This worlde is a passage for to go into the tother worlde, 156.13–4: This worlde is bot a house and a passage to go in-to the tother. **c1450** Idley 184.1563. **1458** Paston III 124[15–6]. **c1480** *Contemplacioun* 196.246–8: Thinkand this warld a throughfare full of wo, Quhat ever god send blyss him ay blythlie, As we war pilgrimis passand to and fro. **c1505** More *Picus* 26 C[3]: Thou seest this worlde is but a thorowefare. Cf. Apperson 712:15; *Oxford* 731; R. M. Smith in *MLN* 65(1950) 443–7; Tilley W883. See **P201.**

W664 This **World** is but a vanity
c1450 *Fortune in Life* in Smith *Common-place Book* 18.92: For the wor(l)d ys but a vanite. **c1450** *Fyrst thou sal* 90.109–10: Behold wele and see This warld is bot vanyte, 91.173: Trest to no wardes vanyte. **a1500** Hichecoke *This Worlde* 332.20, 333.50. **1504** Hawes *Example* Bb1r[10], Ee5v[16–7]. See **A92, E170.**

W665 Thus (How) goes (fares) the **World**

c1385 Chaucer *TC* v 1434: Thus goth the world. **a1393** Gower *CA* II 20.570: Now up now down, this world goth so, III 433.1738: So goth the world, now wo, now wel. **a1450** *Partonope* 379.9235: This is sene all day, and so gothe the worlde. **c1450** *Merlin* II 693[8]. **1456** Hay *Governaunce* 101.28. **1472** Paston V 139[14–5]: Send me word . . . how the world goethe, 141[16–7], 154[4–5]. **1481** Caxton *Reynard* 97[4–5]: Thus fareth the world that one goth up and another goth doun, 112[23–4]: fareth, **1484** *Aesop* 278[21–2]: For thus hit is of the world For when one cometh doune the other goth upward, **c1489** *Aymon* II 542.5–6. **a1533** Berners *Arthur* 343[25–6]: So goeth the worlde; some to pleasure, and some to anoyaunce, *Huon* 571.16. **1546** Heywood *D* 54.446. *Oxford* 731, 732; Whiting *Drama* 371:961.

W666 To have the **World** at will
a1387 *Piers* C xiii 227–8: That chaffaren as chapmen and chiden bote thei wynne, And haven the worlde at here wil other-wyse to lyve. Tilley W869.

W667 To hop (*dance*) while the **World** will pipe
c1390 Chaucer *CT* I[A] 3876: We hoppen alwey whil the world wol pype. **a1475** *Vision of Philibert* 25[4]: I wylle dance whylle the world wylle pype. **1546** Heywood *D* 78.22: That to daunce after her pipe, I am ny led. Apperson 134; Jente 557; *Oxford* 128–9; Tilley M488. See **P222.**

W668 To make the **World** wag
c1475 Henryson *Fables* 32.839–40: And thair he hard ane busteous Bugill blaw, Quhilk, as he thocht, maid all the warld to waig, *Testament* 111.195–6: Ane horne he blew, with mony bosteous brag, Quhilk all this warld with weir hes maid to wag. Whiting *Scots* II 161. See **W659.**

W669 To the **World's** end
a1350 *Ywain* 88.3310: Fra hethin to the werldes ende. **c1395** Chaucer *CT* III[D] 1454–5: Right so fare I, for ryde wolde I now Unto the worldes ende for a preye. **a1400** *Floris* 78.330: Thaugh it were to the worldes ende. **c1450** *Merlin* I 57[25–6]: A thinge as shall endure to the worldes ende. **c1485** *Mary Magdalene* (*Digby*) 75.544. **c1500** *King Hart* 112.16, 115.26. **1513** Douglas *Aeneid* IV 169.158. Tilley J78.

W670 The **World** runs (goes) on wheels
c1495 *Arundel Vulgaria* 2.1: But nowe the worlde rennyth upon another whele. **c1500** *Wife Lapped* 201.531: Nay, nay, deare mother, this world goeth on wheeles. **1546** Heywood *D* 81.33: The world runth on wheeles. Apperson 712; *Oxford* 731–2; Tilley W893. See **W208.**

W671 The **World's** bliss (joy) lasts but a while (*varied*)
a1300 *Richard* 153 *var.* 10–1: Lordynges, now thynkis in youre thoghte That the werldis blysse lastis bot a while. **a1300** Thomas de Hales 69.33–6: This world fareth hwilynde—Hwenne on cumeth an-other goth; That wes bi-fore nu is bihynde, That er was leof nu hit is loth. **c1340** Rolle *Psalter* 203 (56.9): All the joy of this warld is bot as the floure of the feld. **c1375** *Song of Love* in Brown *Lyrics XIV* 103.33–4: The joy that men hase sene es lyckend til the haye, That now es fayre and grene and now wytes awaye. **c1385** Chaucer *CT* I[A] 2777–9: What is this world? what asketh men to have? Now with his love, now in his colde grave Allone, withouten any compaignye, *TC* iii 1636–7: For worldly joie halt nought but by a wir. That preveth wel it brest al day so ofte, v 1748–9: Swich is this world, whoso it kan byholde: In ech estat is litel hertes reste, **c1390** *CT* I[A] 3428: This world is now ful tikel, sikerly, II[B] 1133–4: Joye of this world, for tyme wol nat abyde; Fro day to nyght it changeth as the tyde. **c1390** *God man and the devel* 343.566–8: Worldes wele is wonderful: Wel may I seyn, Lyk the se that floweth: And ebbeth a-geyn; Ther nis no sikernesse: In this worldes won. **c1390** *Northern Homily Cycle Narrationes* (*Vernon*) 266.434–8: Ffor i seo this world over gas, I seo this world is so chaungable, That nout that is ther Inne is stable: Ffor now is mon in gret pouste, And now pore and Meseise is he. **a1393** Gower *CA* II 377.2806: Ther mai no worldes joie laste, III 360.4472–3: And thenke hou ther be joies none Upon this Erthe mad to laste, 447.2259–64: I se the world stonde evere upon eschange, Nou wyndes loude, and nou the weder softe; I mai sen ek the grete mone change, And thing which nou is lowe is eft alofte; The dredfull werres into pes fulofte Thei torne. **c1395** Chaucer *CT* IV[E] 2055–6: But worldly joye may nat alwey dure To Januarie, ne to no creature. **a1400** *In Weal* in *Pol. Rel. and Love Poems* 256: In die bonorum non inmemor sis malorum. Yn time of wele thenk on thi wo, For the wele of this world wole sone go. **c1400** *Now all men* in Owst *Literature* 530[1–2]: Now all men mowe sen be me, That wor(l)dys Joye is vanyte. **c1412** Hoccleve *Regement* 3.47–9: Allas! wher is this worldis stabilnesse? Heer up, heer doun; heer honour, heer repreef; Now hool, now seek; now bounte, now myscheef, 26.705–7: O

lord! this world unstabyl is, and unsad, This world hunurith nat mannes persone Ffor him self, sone, but for good allone, 104.2866–7: And that this worldis joye is transitorie, And the trust on it slippir and fallible. **a1415** Mirk *Festial* 9.29: I se the well of thys world nys but a floure. **a1420** Lydgate *Troy* III 848.2638: In worldly Joie is no sikernesse. **c1422** Hoccleve *Complaint* 95.9–10: That stablenes in this worlde is there none; There is no thinge but chaunge and variaunce, 99.116–8: Who so that takethe hede ofte may se This worldis change and mutabilite In sondry wyse, *Dialog* 119.258–9: Whan al is doon al this worldes swetnesse At ende torneth in-to bittirnesse. **a1425** *Metrical Paraphrase OT* 75.16455–6: How that this werld wuns ever in were Fro wo to wele, fro wele to wo. **a1437** Lydgate *That Now is Hay* in *MP* II 809.1–6: Ther is full lytell sikernes Here in this worlde but transmutacion . . . Nowe ryche, now pore, now haut, now base, **a1439** *Fall* I 59.2152–3: What worldli joie may heer long endure, Or wher shal men now fynde stabilnesse? 83.3017: But who may truste on any worldli thyng! **a1449** *Amor* in *MP* II 747.81–2: The world unsure, fortune is variable, Booth right friendly founde in prosperite, *Deus* in *MP* I 11.43–4: All oder worldely weele y wyll dispice That floweth oft, and ebbeth as the floode, *Dietary* in *MP* II 706.152: No worldly joie lastith her but a while, *Fabula* in *MP* II 503.515: This world is ful chaungable, 505.582–3: But I knowe weel, who trustith on the (*world*) moost, Shal be deceyved, whan he to the hath neede, *Freond* in *MP* II 755.7: The worlde is divers, ffortune is chaungyng, *Testament* in *MP* I 336.205–6: The world unstable, now ebbe, nowe is flood, Ech thyng concludyng on mutabilite, *Thoroughfare* in *MP* II 826.128: Stabilnesse is founde in nothyng, *Timor* in *MP* II 831.108: The wourld is chaungeable as the moone, *Tyed with a Lyne* in *MP* II 834.57–9: The world unsure, contrary al stablenesse, Whos joye is meynt ay with adversite; Now light, now hevy, now sorwe, now gladnes, *World* in *MP* II 844–7.8: Exsperience shewith the wourld is varyable, 16, 24, *etc.* **a1449** Lydgate and Burgh *Secrees* 41.1288: Ffor worldly Joye lastith here but a whyle. **a1450** *Barlam and Josaphat* (*South English Legendary*) 117.135–42: Triste me ne may To this false world that chaungeth ech day . . . This world is unstedfast, ffor al thing faryth so, 125.437–8: Thu seyst that this world tornyth up so doun; Nou mon is in feld, and now he is in toun. **c1450** *Fyrst thou sal* 90.125: This warldis joyes passes sone, 135–6: Hafe done and com sone, For this warld is bot a blome. **c1450** Idley 161.152–4: This worlde is not stable in oon stacion; Now well, now woo, now Joye, now grevaunce: It is the worldis kynde thus to be in variaunce. **c1450** *Proverbs of Good Counsel* 69.25: This world ys mutabyll, so saythe sage. **a1460** *Towneley Plays* 100.10–1: Thus this Warld, as I say, farys on ylk syde, Ffor after oure play com sorows unryde. **c1460** *Take Good Heed* 206.14: For thei be double in wirking, as the worlde gos. **a1475** Ashby *Dicta* 54.258–9: So this world is not certeine ne stable, But whirlyng a bowte and mutable. **1481** Caxton *Godeffroy* 189.20–1: Thus goon the chaunges and mutacions of the world. **a1500** *Colkelbie* 295.440–3: Lo such is this warldis glore, Now law, now he, Nothing stable we se In this warld of variance. **a1500** *Harley MS. 2321* in *Rel. Ant.* I 208[13–4]: Put not in this world to much trust, The riches whereof will turne to dust. **a1500** *Leconfield Proverbs* 475[9–10]: In erthly thynges there is no surete, For unstabill and transitory they be, 480[18]: The worlde variethe every day. **a1500** *O man more* 395.54: The worlde is false and ever wasse. **a1500** *Wold God that men* 9[13–5]: Thys warlde ys varyabyll, Nothyng therin ys stable, Asay now ho so wyll. **c1500** Fabyan 281[28]: The worlde is transytory. **1504** Hawes *Example* Aa5^r[24]: This worlde is transytory, Ff2^r[18]. **a1513** Dunbar *None may Assure* 44–6.5: For in this warld may non assure, 10, 15, *etc.* **1513** Douglas *Aeneid* III 239.75: And how instabill was all warldis chance. **1515** Barclay *St. George* 60.1381: And erthly welth is frayle and transytory. **1523** Berners *Froissart* III 321[18]: The fortunes of the worlde are nothynge stable, **1525** VI 375[3–5]: This worlde is nothyng, the fortunes therof are marveylous, and somtyme tourne as well upon kinges and princes, as upon poore men. *Oxford* 731, 732; Tilley J90, W871, 897, 903; Whiting *Drama* 127, 163, *Scots* I 194, II 162. See **B154, C114, F108, G102, 156, 330, 338, N154, P267, 422, R119, T144, 161.**

W672 The **World** turns as a ball
a1400 *Proverbis of Wysdom* 244.33: The world turnythe, as a ball. **c1450** *Fyrst thou sal* 88.35. Tilley W901.

W673 As naked as a **Worm** (*varied*)
a1349 Rolle *Meditations* in Allen *R. Rolle* 21.55: Nakyd os a worm. **c1395** Chaucer *CT* IV[E] 880: Lat me nat lyk a worm go by the weye. **a1400** ?Chaucer *Rom.* A 454: For nakid as a worm was she. **a1475** *Ludus Coventriae* 25.291: I walke as werm with-outyn wede. **c1475** Gregory

Chronicle 211[3]: Nakyd as a worme. Apperson 436; *Oxford* 442.

W674 As vile as a **Worm**
1479 Rivers *Cordyal* 15.2: As vile as a worme.

W675 To be **Worm's** food (meat)
c1400 *Now all men* in Owst *Literature* 530[8]: To wyrmes mete now am I take. **c1430** Lydgate *Dance* 74.640: That wormes fode is fyne of owre lyvynge. **a1450** *In the seson* in *Archiv* 167 (1935) 30[3] *et passim:* Now turned to wormes mete and corrupcoun. **1479** Rivers *Cordyal* 12.19–20: And their flessh (is) delyvered for wormes mete, 18.25–6, 19.21–2, 23.11. **1483** *Quatuor Sermones* 28[17–8]: After thyn ende thou shalt be but wormys mete. **1484** Caxton *Royal Book* S1ʳ[8]: (*Man is*) mete to wormes after his deth, **1487** *Book of Good Manners* G7ᵛ[15]: A man is . . . wormes mete. **1495** *Medytacyons of saynt Bernarde* A8ᵛ[1]: Rotten caryon and meete to wormes, B1ʳ[2]: At the last meete to wormes to gnawe on, [14–5, 25], B1ᵛ[4–5]. **c1500** *O mortall mon* in Lydgate *Fall* IV 65: Remembr, mon, thow art but wormes mete. **1509** Watson *Ship* U1ʳ[13–4]: Your bodyes . . . the whiche is but wormes mete. Apperson 712.

W676 To have a wild **Worm** in one's head
a1500 Medwall *Nature* F2ᵛ[23]: The wylde worm ys com into hys hed. Cf. Tilley W907.

W677 To wend (*turn*) like a **Worm**
a1200 Lawman II 327.17912–3: That ofte he hine wende, Swulc hit a wurem weore.

W678 To wind (*writhe*) like a **Worm**
c1000 Aelfric *Homilies* I 414[17–8]: He wand þa swa swa wurm.

W679 Tread a **Worm** on the tail and it will turn again
1546 Heywood *D* 69.111: Tread a woorme on the tayle, and it must turne agayne, **1555** *E* 150.25. Apperson 712; *Oxford* 669; Taylor and Whiting 414–5; Tilley W909.

W680 One oft buys **Worship** dearly
c1400 *Alexander Buik* II 221 *cont.* 4147–8: For men worship byis oft dere, And purchessis pryse in places sere.

W681 **Worship** is better than the full womb
c1450 *Douce MS.52* 48.49: Better is worship then the full wombe. **c1450** *Rylands MS.394* 98.8. See **N12.**

W682 If the **Worst** fell we could have but a "nay"
1546 Heywood *D* 53.397: That if the woorst fell, we could have but a naie. Apperson 713; Tilley W916.

W683 Provide for the **Worst** while the best save(s) itself
1546 Heywood *D* 26.18: To provyde for the woorst, whyle the best it selfe save, **1555** *E* 191.260: Provyde for the woorst, the best wyll save it selfe. Apperson 515; *Oxford* 522; Tilley W913.

W684 The **Worst** is behind
1546 Heywood *D* 64.70: The woorst is behynd, **1555** *E* 170.138. Apperson 713; *Oxford* 733; Tilley W918. See **B265.**

W685 The **Worst** is ever for to doubt (*to be feared*)
c1400 Gower *Peace* III 485.138: For everemor the werste is forto doute. **a1500** Medwall *Nature* H1ʳ[8–9]: I dout and drede The wurst as wyse men do. Tilley W912.

W686 Hot **Worts** make hard crusts soft
c1450 *Rylands MS.394* 94.4.16: Hoote wortes make harde crustes nesche. Mollificant olera durissima fervida crusta. **a1500** *Burlesques* in *Rel. Ant.* I 82.II[1–3]: *Mollificant olera durissima crusta.* Fryndis this is to saye to your lewde undurstandyng, that hoote wortes (*erased*) crusstes makeyn sofft hard wortes. **a1500** Hill 132.37: Whote wortis make softe crustis. Apperson 315; Tilley W920; Walther II 913.15014a.

W687 No **Wort** grows that may ever uphold life
c1250 *Proverbs of Alfred* 88–90 T 161–4: Nis no wurt woxen On wode no on felde That evure mughe The lif up-helden.

W688 To hack as small as **Worts** to pot
c1450 Greene *Carols* 457.5: And yyt he hakkyt hem (*musical notes*) smallere than wortes to the pot. See **F270.**

W689 **Worthiness** after death is but a wind
a1420 Lydgate *Troy* III 618–9.1871–2: For worthines, after deth I-blowe, Is but a wynde, and lasteth but a throwe.

W690 **Worthiness** will not be had but it be oft sought
c1400 *Sowdone* 27.923–6: For worthynesse wole not be hadde, But it be ofte soughte, Ner knyghthode wole not be hadde, Tille it be dere boghte.

W691 One **Wot** (*knows*) what he wot though he make few words
1546 Heywood *D* 86.213: But I wot what I wot,

though I few woordes make. Apperson 714; *Oxford* 344; Tilley K173.

W692 Better the **Wounds** of him that loves than the kisses of him that hates (*varied*)
c1395 *WBible* Proverbs xxvii 6: Betere ben the woundis of hym that loveth, than the gileful cossis of hym that hatith. **c1523** Barclay *Mirrour* 21[41–2]: For much better it is, to bide a frendes anger then a foes kisse, 75[34–5]: Better to be blamed of frende that faythfull is, Then of a flattering foo to have Judas kisse, 78[17–9]: And certes it is better sharpe wordes and unkinde To suffer of a frende spoken for good intent, Then of a foo to have fayre speche and fraudulent. Apperson 238:9; Tilley F727. See **F628.**

W693 A fresh **Wound** is lighter to heal than a festered
1422 Yonge *Governaunce* 161.34–5: Lyghtyre is a fressh wounde to hele, than a festrid. Apperson 273: green; *Oxford* 266–7; Tilley W927; Whiting *Drama* 247, *Scots* II 162. See **W695.**

W694 A great **Wound** behooves (*needs*) a great leechdom
a900 Bede 350.20: Micel wund behofað micles læcedomes. Cf. Taylor and Whiting 103: Disease.

W695 A green **Wound** is but game
a1450 *God of hefne, that sittest* 411.217–9: Ffor men seyen in olde speche, Grene wounde nys bote game, And ole synne maketh newe schame. See **W693.**

W696 It is hard to heal a **Wound** that is oft broken
a1400 *Cleansing* 93.3–4 (f.58^v–59^r): Ffor harde hit is to heele a wounde that is ofte broken. **a1425** Mirk *Instructions* 45.1465–6: So ofter a wounde ys I-cot The worse to hele hyt nede be mot. **c1450** *Jacob's Well* 189.9–10: A wounde or a sore often hurte is ful hard to makyn hole. "Vulnus iteratum tardius sanatur. Kate O. Petersen *Sources of the Parson's Tale* (Radcliffe College Monographs 12, 1901) 26[1.7].

W697 After great **Wrath** love is the more
c1300 Robert of Gloucester I 92.1265–6: And god wole that men ofte be in wraththe and in sore, That after hor grete wraththe hor love be the more. See **A129, S399, V9.**

W698 He that will wreak (venge) him of every **Wrath,** the longer he lives the less he hath
c1450 *Fyrst thou sal* 88.19–20: He that wreke hym of evere wrathe, The langer he lyfes the les he hathe. **c1495** *Arundel Vulgaria* 59.250: He that wyl be vengyde on every wroth, the longer he lyveth the lesse he hath. **a1500** Hill 140.112: He that will venge every wreth, the longer he levith, the lesse he hath. Tilley W944. See **W718.**

W699 Never **Wrath** so great but a woman may appease it
a1533 Berners *Arthur* 435[23–4]: There was never so grete wrath, but a woman may appease it. See **M388.**

W700 When **Wrath** begins then comes umbraid (*upbraiding*)
a1338 Mannyng *Chronicle A* I 281.7999–8000: When wrathe bygynneth, then cometh umbreyd; Al that men wot, ys then forth seyd.

W701 When **Wrath** reigns reason cannot long abide
1509 Barclay *Ship* I 184[17–8]: For where that wrath doth rayne with his furours, There can no reason nor wysedome longe abyde, **c1515** *Eclogues* 160.563: When wrath is moved, then reason hath no might. See **I54, 62.**

W702 When **Wrath** walls (*boils*) within the heart there is no right doom
a1200 *Ancrene* 64.10–1: Hwil the heorte walleth inwith of wreaththe, nis ther na riht dom.

W703 **Wrath** benims (*takes away*) man's rede
c1250 *Owl* 80.940–1: An wiste wel on hire thohte, The wraththe binimeth monnes red. **c1390** *Cato* (*Vernon*) 577.299–300: Wraththe destruyeth monnes wit, Whon soth may not beo seiyene. Cf. *Oxford* 10: Anger and haste. See **I52.**

W704 **Wrath** has made many a worthy man be held for fools
c1450 *Merlin* II 500[28–9]: Wrath hath many a worthi man and wise made to be holde for foles, while the rage endureth. See **I54.**

W705 **Wrath** is a woodship (*madness*)
a1200 *Ancrene* 64.3–4: Ira furor brevis est. Wreaththe is a wodschipe, **a1400** (*Recluse*) 50.11–2: Wraththe is a wodeschip that turneth man in to beeste. Apperson 10; *Oxford* 10; Tilley A246; Walther II 600.12856, 602.12864. See **I54.**

W706 **Wrath** leads shame in a leash
1477 Rivers *Dictes* 59[18–9]: Wrath ledeth shame in a lese. See **I53.**

W707 **Wrath** said never well (*varied*)
a1393 Gower *CA* II 248.835: For Wraththe seide nevere wel. **c1450** *Fyrst thou sal* 89.104:

For wrethe says alway ylle. **1487** Paston VI 100[12–3]: But wrathe seyd never well. Smith 219; Tilley N307.

W708 After the **Wren** has veins men shall let her blood
c1350 *Good Wife E* 166.110: After the wrenne had veines thou schalt leten here blod. Apperson 714–5. Cf. Taylor and Whiting 34.

W709 Liever (*rather*) the **Wren** run about the shock (*group of sheaves*) than (know) fiddle playing or flute craft
a1325 *Le Traité de Walter de Bibbesworth,* ed. Annie Owen (Paris, 1929) 114, *var.* 755–8: Levere is the wrenne Abouten the scholke renne Than the fithel draut Other the floute craf (French: Car de alcies meuz vaut a restel Ki vironer en un beau trestel, Ki un beau treste de la viele).

W710 The **Wren** is our Lady's hen
a1508 Skelton *Phyllyp* I 69.600–1: To treade the prety wren That is our Ladyes hen. Tilley W936.

W711 To spurn (*trip*) with one's own **Wrench** (*trick*)
c1300 *South English Legendary* II 526.320: And atte laste hi schulle spurne mid here owe wrenche. See **S848, 950, T534.**

W712 For every **Wrenk** (*trick*) to have a wile
c1475 Henryson *Fables* 69.1987: For everie wrink, forsuith, thow hes ane wyle. NED Wrench sb.[1] Wrenk; Whiting *Scots* II 162.

W713 One may call him a **Wretch** (*miser*) that (com)plains and has enough
c1390 *Proverbes of diverse profetes* 532.153–6: A wrecche forsothe me may hym cal That pleyneth him and hath i-nough at al; Ffor though al the world were only his, He wolde seie he hedde nought, i-wis. See **C115, 488, E126, M53.**

W714 There is none so proud as a **Wretch** set in high estate
a1430 Lydgate *Fall* II 559.3151–5: Thus whan a wrech is set in hih estat, Or a begger brouht up to dignite, Ther is non so proud(e), pompous nor elat, Non si vengable nor ful of cruelte, Void of discrecioun, mercy and pite. See **B186, C271.**

W715 To (a) **Wretch** is consolation to have another fellow in his pain (*varied*)
c1385 Chaucer *TC* i 708–9: Men seyn, "to wrecche is consolacioun To have another felawe in hys peyne." **a1393** Gower *CA* II 137.260–4: For evere upon such aventure It is a confort, as men sein, To him the which is wo besein To sen an other in his peine, So that thei bothe mai compleigne. **c1395** Chaucer *CT* VIII[G] 746–8: For unto shrewes joye it is and ese To have hir felawes in peyne and disese. Thus was I ones lerned of a clerk. **c1440** Charles of Orleans 63.1855–7: For wrecchis whiche that are in thought heve As doth hit them a gret tranquyllite To have a felawe lyve with them in payne. **a1449** Lydgate *Evil Marriage* in *MP* II 457.20–1: Them-silf rejoysyng both at eve and morowe To have a ffelowe to lyve with them in sorowe. **1509** Barclay *Ship* II 236[26–8]: A prysoner lyenge longe in payne and wo Hath consolacion and great confort certayne To have many mo be partnes of his payne. Apperson 110; Jente 363; *Oxford* 106; Skeat 152; Smith 30, 265; Taylor and Whiting 246; Tilley C571.

W716 A **Wretch** draws to wretches
c1390 *God man and the devel* 333–4.187–8: A wrecche sone wol he ben, To wrecches he draweth, as alle men sen. See **L272.**

W717 Only **Wretchedness** has no enemy
1348 Rolle *Form* in Allen *R. Rolle* 102.190–1: For anely wretchednes has na enmy. See **M266, P337.**

W718 He that will wreak (*venge*) him of ilk (*every*) **Wrong** may not live in peace long
c1450 *Fyrst thou sal* 89.97–8: He that wil hym wreke of yll (*for* ylk) wronge May not lyf in pes longe. Cf. Smith 225, 345. See **I10, S193, W698.**

W719 Each **Wye** (*man*) may beware by wreak (*harm*) of another
a1400 *Morte Arthure* 113.3839: Iche a wy may be warre be wreke of another. See **M170.**

W720 As wroth as a **Wype** (*lapwing*)
a1425 *St. Robert* 62.675: Als wreth he wex als a wype. Cf. *Parlament of Byrdes* in Hazlitt *EPP* III 183.305: Thoughe thou be as hasty as a wype.

Y

Y1 He that spares the **Yard** (rod) hates his child (*varied*)
c1000 Aelfric *Homilies* II 324[32–3]: Se ðe sparað his gyrde, he hatað his cild; and se ðe hit lufað, he lærð hit anrædlice. **c1000** *Ecclesiastical Institutes* II 430[38–9]: Salomon cwæð: Seþe sparað þa gyrde, he hatað his bearn. **a1050** Defensor *Liber* 175[15–7]: Se þe sparað gyrde his he hatað suna his; se þe soðlice lufað hyne anrædlice lærð. **a1300** *Proverbs of Alfred* 99 J 245–50: The mon the spareth yeorde And yonge childe, And let hit arixlye, That he hit areche ne may, That him schal on ealde Sore reowe. **c1378** *Piers* B v 39–41: And Salamon seide the same that Sapience made, *Qui parcit virge, odit filium.* The Englich of this latyn is, who-so wil it knowe, Who-so spareth the sprynge spilleth his children. **c1395** *WBible* Proverbs xiii 24: He that sparith the yerde, hatith his sone, xxix 15: A yerde and chastisyng schal gyve wisdom; but a child, which is left to his wille, schendith his modir. **c1400** *Beryn* 34.1059–61: This mowe wee know(e) verely, by experience, That yerd(e) makith vertu and benevolence In Childhode for to growe, as previth Imaginacioun. **1422** Yonge *Governaunce* 161.37–9: Salamon sayth, *Qui parsit virge odit filium,* "who Sparith the yarde he hatyth the chylde." **a1449** Lydgate *Stans Puer* in *MP* II 744.91: Who spareth the yerde, al vertu set asyde. **c1450** Idley 179.1274: Therfore whoo lovyth the childe, he woll the rodde not spare. **a1470** Parker *Dives* K5^r^[2.3–4]: He that spareth the yerde hateth his sone, R5^r^[2.18–9]. **c1475** *Rawlinson MS. D 328* 125.79: Blesse be the rodde that chastyth the chyld. **c1475** Symon *Lesson* 402.89–90: And as men sayth that ben leryd, He hatyth the chyld that sparyth the rodde. **a1496** *Rote or Myrour* G6^r^[13–6]: Salomon . . . sayth . . . The fader whiche that loveth his childe, he beteth hym oftentymes. **a1500** *Good Wife N* 216.217–8: For gif thou love thy children wele Spare not the yard never a deale. **c1516** Skelton *Magnificence* 60.1928–30: For there is nothynge that more dyspleaseth God Than from theyr chyldren to spare the rod Of correccyon, but let them have theyr Wyll. **1529** More *Supplicacion* 326 F[6–8]: He that spareth the rod, saith holy writte, hateth the child. Apperson 592–3; *Oxford* 609; Taylor and Whiting 309; Tilley R155; Whiting *Drama* 196. See **B13, C200, 215, F74, L566, S642.**

Y2 Not give a **Yard**
c1400 *Laud Troy* I 285.9660: He yeves of hem not a yerd. NED Yard sb.[2] 1d.

Y3 To kiss the **Yard**
a1200 *Ancrene* 96.24–6: Thet deboneire child hwen hit is ibeaten, yef the feader hat hit, hit cusseth the yerde. *Oxford* 340; Tilley R156.

Y4 A **Yard** may grow so great that men may not writhe (*twist*) it
a1400 Wyclif *Sermons* I 278[26–7]: For as a yerde mai growe so greet, and be so stiff in his strengthe, that men shal not writhe it. See **O11, P251, W35.**

Y5 To have other **Yarn** on the reel
a1460 *Towneley Plays* 32.298: Ther is garn on the reyll other, my dame. See **T432.**

Y6 To speed one's **Yarn** (*i.e.,* succeed)
a1500 *Eger H* 295.1829–30: And asked at him how he had farn? Well, he did say, and sped my yarn.

Y7 (Neither) **Yea** nor nay
a1400 *Mede and muche thank* in Kail 7.27–8: And florische fayre my lordis word, And fede hem forth with nay and yee. **a1450** *Generydes A* 236.7639–40: (Clarionas) ful stil thoo lay,

And answerd nouthre yea nor nay. **a1450** *Generydes B* 101.3163–4: Of ther massag they praed them to say In all this mater playnly ye or nay, 109.3430: Say ye or nay, or ye go owt of this place. **a1450** *Partonope* 401.9692–3: They wole not swere never an othe But nay or yee, it is sothe. **a1470** Malory II 869.9: As to that he seyde nother yee nother nay. **1480** Caxton *Ovyde* 113[9–10]: Thoo was Ayax so abasshyd that he coud neyther saye ye nor naye. **1509** Barclay *Ship* II 213[5–6]: And he that can upholde his maysters lye With ye and nay. NED Yea B1,3; Burton Stevenson *Home Book of Proverbs, Maxims and Familiar Phrases* (New York, 1948) 2658.

Y8 The first **Year** wedlock is called play, *etc.* **c1475** *Prohemy of a Mariage* 45[1–5]: And ever thynk on this proverb trewe, Remembryng on age by ony weye, That veray dotage in olde age wol the sewe, That the first yere wedlokk is called pleye, The second dreye, and the thrid yere deye. Apperson 215.

Y9 It is a good **Year** when the hound gives to the raven
c1025 *Durham Proverbs* 10.6: God ger byþ þonne se hund þam hrefne gyfed. Bonus annus quando canis corvo exibet.

Y10 One may covet many a **Year** what may hastily appear
a1500 *Eger H* 305.2009–10: A man may covet many a year, That may right hastilie appear. Cf. Tilley H741. See **D56, H598.**

Y11 Seven **Years** (winters) (from 410 examples) **a893** Wærferth *Gregory* 197.23–4: Vii gær. **a900** Bede 176.10. **c1000** Aelfric *Lives* I 162.255. **a1200** Lawman I 101.2380, II 77.12032, III 153.28812. **c1225** *Horn* 7 C 96. **a1300** *Richard* 222.2617: sevene yer and more. **a1300** *Tristrem* II 4.48. **c1300** *Beves* 4.53: winter. **c1300** *Guy*[1] 368.7047: and more, 528 A 174.8: winter. **c1300** *Reinbrun* 632.4.2: winter and wel more. **c1300** *South English Legendary* I 187.209: This seve yer. **c1325** *Sayings of St. Bernard* 516.101: And thynken seven yer of a day. **c1330** *Horn Childe* 185.532: winter. **a1350** *Isumbras* 32.416: and more. **a1375** *Hermit* 173.117: These yerys sevene. **a1375** *Octavian* (S) 44.1386: and more. **a1375** *William* 15.206: winter, 170.5369: and more. **c1380** *Ferumbras* 9.269: and more. **c1385** Chaucer *CT* I[A] 1452: Thise seven yeer, **c1386** *LGW* 2120: This sevene yer. **c1390** *Northern Homily Cycle Narrationes* (*Vernon*) 304.395: winter. **c1390** *Sir Gawain* 43.1382: this. **a1400** *Alexander C* 92.1677: This sevyn wyntir. **a1400** *Amadace I* 27[6]: this. **al400** Chestre *Launfal* 72.678: More than thys. **a1400** *Ipomadon A* 16.479: this. **a1400** *King Edward* 966.475: this. **a1400** *Torrent* 3.65. **c1400** *Alexander Buik* IV 436.10981. **c1400** *Emaré* 26.816: fully. **c1400** *Thomas of Erceldoune* 17.286: and More. **c1405** *Mum* 59.1093: and sum dele more. **a1425** *Arthour and M.*[2] 359.1975–6. **a1425** *Chester Plays* I 120.406: this. **a1425** *St. Anthony* 134. 16–7: this. **c1425** *Avowynge* 91[29]: this. **a1438** Kempe 131.19. **c1450** *How the Wyse Man* 36.32. **a1470** Malory I 239.1: all this, II 517.22: thys, III 1065.17: thys. **1472** Paston V 131[25]: thys. **a1475** *Guy*[2] 193.6737: thys, 340.11842: more then. **a1475** *Herkons to my tale* in *Rel. Ant.* I 86[6]: this. **1480** *Cely Papers* 33[8]: thys. **1485** Caxton *Paris* 1.17: to gyder, **c1485** *St. Winifred* 299.31: The space of seven yere. **c1485** *Conversion* 31.107: Thys vii yere and more. **a1500** *Carpenter's Tools* 85.183: this. **a1500** *Eger H* 231.802: these. **a1500** *Gest of Robyn Hode* in Child III 73.346: this. **a1500** *Miller of Abington* 101.19: more than. **a1500** *Squire* 3.6: Fully the tyme of, 3.17: more than, 11.186: Till seven yere be comen and gone, 42.1000: this. **1502** *Robert the Devil* C7[r][20]: or there aboute. **c1505** Watson *Valentine* 188.4: the space of. **c1520** *Terens* D1[v][29]: this. **1520** Whittinton *Vulgaria* 103.3: this. **1528** More *Heresyes* 190 A[3]: Nor seven yere after neither. **a1533** Berners *Arthur* 102[25]: this, 392[31]: the space of. **1546** Heywood *D* 75.188: this. Apperson 559; Taylor and Whiting 416; Tilley Y25; Whiting *Drama* 362:827, *Scots* II 163.

Y12 To hang oneself after a hard **Year**
c1353 *Winner* 374: To hope aftir an harde yere, to honge thi-selven. Cf. Shakespeare *Macbeth* II iii 5; Joseph Hall *Virgidemiarum* in *Collected Poems,* ed. A. Davenport (Liverpool, 1949) 70.24–5 and note p. 223.

Y13 To trust of a good **Year**
1451 Paston II 210[18–9]: And so it semyth be here contenaunce that they trost of a good yere.

Y14 Woe worth seven **Years**' sorrow for seven nights' bliss
c1175 *Poema Morale* 180.142: Wo wurth sorghe seve yier vor sevenihte blisce! See **M642.**

Y15 **Yesterday** will not be called again (*varied*) **a1450** Audelay 85.118: Thus clepth agen yuster-day, 86.131: Thus yistyr-day thou clepe agayne. **c1516** Skelton *Magnificence* 63.2031: Yesterday wyll not be callyd agayne. **1546** Heywood *D* 91.16: It is to late to call again yesterdaie. Apperson 78; *Oxford* 737; Tilley Y31; Whiting *Scots* II 163.

Y16 Never to **Yield** (*pay*) and ever to crave make a man have few friends
1372 *Advocates MS.18.7.21* (John of Grimestone) f.32b in Robbins-Cutler 2289.5: Nevere to yelden and evere to craven Maket man fewe frendis to haven.

Y17 **Yield** or hang
1340 *Ayenbite* 31[1–2]: And hit behoveth yelde: other hongy, 218[13–5]: Thanne hit behoveth thet hi yelde: other thet hi hongi. Vor ase me zayth: "other yelde: other hongi." **c1400** *Vices and Virtues* 26.21–3: And it be-hoveth yelde or honge. "Rendre ou pendre," dit ly fraunceys, 241.31–3: Wher-of it bihoveth that thei yelden or be honged. For as the Frensche man seith, "Ou rendre ou pendre." **1484** Caxton *Royal Book* L7ᵛ[4]: For he must rendre or pendre, that is, hange.

Y18 To have the **Yoke** lie on one's neck
1501 Douglas *Palice* 54.13: I mon draw furth the yok lyis on my nek, **1513** *Aeneid* III 65.150: Thou mon draw furth, the yok lyis on thy nek.

Y19 As yellow as the **Yolk** of an ay (*egg*)
a1400 *Morte Arthure* 97.3283: The tother (*eye*) was yalowere then the yolke of a naye.

Y20 Tell the **Yolk** and put the white away
c1400 *Beryn* 24.731–2: Lepyng ovir no centence, as ferforth as I may, But telle yewe the yolke, and put the white a-way.

Y21 The **Yolk** cannot be without the white
1525 Berners *Froissart* IV 240[18–21]: The yolke of the egge can not be without the whyte, nor the whyte without the yolke, no more maye the clergy and the lordes be one without another.

Y22 Hence to **York**
c1397 Medwall *Fulgens* C3ᵛ[6–7]: But for that she hath no felow In syngynge hens to yorke. Cf. Tilley H429.

Y23 As you do when you are **Young** swilk (*such*) after will your living be
a1450 *Myne awen dere* 177.875–7: For as thou dose when thou art yonge, Swylke efter will be thy levynge Thurgh propryr use when thou art alde. See **Y32.**

Y24 Lere (*learn*) **Young** as you would elder be
a1450 *Myne awen dere* 177.883–4: Therfore, son, I commaunde the, Lere yonge as thou will elder be.

Y25 Nought **Young** worse old
1509 Barclay *Ship* I 41[7]: Nought yonge, wors olde, suche is my state.

Y26 You are **Young** enough to mend, but I am too old to see it
1546 Heywood *D* 91.23–4: Ye be yong enough to mende, I agree it, But I am . . . to old to see it. *Oxford* 738; Tilley A236.

Y27 **Young** wons (*is accustomed to*), old mones (*remembers*) (*varied*)
c1250 *Hendyng O* 192.5: Young woneth, Hold moneth. **c1303** Mannyng *Handlyng* 244.7671–3: Yn a proverbe of olde Englys Telle men and sothe hyt ys, "That yougthe wones, yn age mones." **c1325** *Hendyng H* 289.45: Whose yong lereth, olt he ne leseth. **c1400** *Vices and Virtues* 244.17–8: As men (seyne), "yonge woneth, olde moneth." Apperson 357, 720; Kneuer 19–20; *Oxford* 358, 740; Schleich 250; Singer III 126; Skeat 69. See **C210.**

Y28 After warm **Youth** comes cold age
c1450 Idley 81.28: After warme youthe cometh age coolde.

Y29 He that in **Youth** no virtue uses, in age all honor him refuses (*varied*)
a1400 *Proverbis of Wysdom* 244.9–10: Who that in youth no vertew usythe, In age all honowre hym refusythe. **c1450** *Proverbs of Good Counsel* 68.11–2: He that yn yowth no vertue wyll use, In Age all honour wyll hym Refuse. **c1450** *Royal MS.17 D xviii* f.99b in George F. Warner and J. P. Gilson *Catalogue* II(1921) 256: He that in yought to no vertew himselfe applieth, In age to amende him badd costome deniethe. **c1450** *Serve thy god* 262.27–8. **a1475** *Youth and Honour* in Robbins 81: He that in yowthe no vertu wyll yowes, In aege all honor shall hym refuse. **a1500** Hichecoke *This Worlde* 333.39–40. **a1500** Hill 140.3–4: He that in yowth no vertu will use, In age all honour shall refuce. **c1500** *MS. Marginalia* in Hoccleve I 169 n.[1]: He that in youth no verke will use, all . . . , 218, n.[1]: He that in yothe no vartue (?) well ues (*for* use), In age all honor will hym refuse. **a1500** *Young Children's Book* 17.3–4. Apperson 292; Brown-Robbins 1151; *Oxford* 740; Tilley Y37.

Y30 He that in **Youth** no virtue will learn shall go like a lubber and thrash in the barn
c1500 *Ashmole MS.1146* in W. H. Black *Descriptive . . . Catalogue* (Oxford, 1845) 1000[63–4]: He that in youth noe vertue will learne, Shall goe like a lubber and throshe in the bearne.

Y31 It is hard to overcome **Youth**

a1533 Berners *Arthur* 25[10]: It is a harde thynge to overcome youthe.

Y32 What **Youth** does age shows (*varied*)
c1000 Aelfric *Grammar,* ed. J. Zupitza (Berlin, 1880) 125.17–8: Eala gif ic rædde on jugoðe, þonne cuðe ic nu sum god. **c1303** Mannyng *Handlyng* 244.7667–8: For comunly, that men done yn yenkthe, Yn age haunte they hyt on lenkthe. **c1330** *Body and Soul* 46.357–8: Swiche as y lerd in mi youthe, Ich used, when that y was old. **c1400** *Beryn* 31.938: Ffor thing I-take in (youthe, is) hard to put away. **a1425** *Contemplations* in *Yorkshire Writers* II 83[32–4]: I rede that he that useth hym not to vertue(s) in his yonge age he shall not conne withstande vyces in his old age. **a1449** Lydgate *Haste* in *MP* II 764.154: Thyn(g)e take in youth hath good impression. **1450** *Dicts* 284.30–1: He that endurethe no thing in his youthe restith not in his age. **c1450** *Childhood of Christ* in *Archiv* 74(1885) 330.199–200: Whene he es olde, fulle mone hym falle, That in his youthe na gude wille lere. **c1450** Idley 81.22–5: I have herde saide in olde Romaunce, He that in youthe woll do his diligence To lerne, in age it woll hym avaunce To kepe hym fro alle indigence. **a1475** *Guy*[2] 25.871–4: He, that may do gode dede, He schulde hym force in yowthehede, So that he may, when he ys oolde, For a doghty man be tolde. **a1500** *Guy*[4] 44–5.1185–90: For, who so of pryce will be, In his youth travayle must he In dyvers landes to win pryse With his travayle, if he be wyse; In his age then may he have The more honour, so God me save. **a1500** *Hunterian Mus. MS.230* 175: Labur in youth qwylst helthe wyll last, So rest in age qwen strength is past. **a1500** *Leconfield Proverbs* 482[19–20]: As youthe is ordorid and accustomede in his yeris grene, So after warde in his olde age it shall be seane, 484[2]: For that is goten in youthe is harde to leve in age. **a1500** *Trinity College Oxford MS. Arch. 49* f.139b in Manly-Rickert I 540: He that in youth no gud kanne, In age selden ys thryfty man. **c1500** *Melusine* 193.1–4: And ye wote ynough, that who lerneth not his crafte in his yougthe, with grete peyne and hard shal be for hym to be a good werkeman in his old age. **1509** Barclay *Ship* II 43[6–7]: And he that in youth wyl nought for hym provyde In age must the paynes of povertye abyde. *Oxford* 313: Idle youth; Tilley Y38, 42. See **C210, 226, 524, L248, M181, 308, Y23.**

Y33 **Youth** and age are often at debate (*varied*)
c1390 Chaucer *CT* I[A] 3229–30: Men sholde wedden after hire estaat, For youthe and elde is often at debaat. **c1421** Lydgate *Thebes* 122.2963–4: Thus selde is seyne, the trouthe to termyne, That age and youthe drawe be o lyne. **a1460** *Towneley Plays* 91.170: It is ill cowpled of youth and elde. **1556** Heywood *E* 120.33.1: Age and youth together can seeld agree. Apperson 720; *Oxford* 739; Smith 346; Tilley Y43. See **B363, M254.**

Y34 **Youth** is frail
a1393 Gower *CA* III 408.834: Bot as men sein that frele is youthe.

Y35 **Youth** is reckless
c1400 *Beryn* 34.1052: Yowith is recheles. *Oxford* 740.

Y36 **Youth** seld takes heed of perils (*varied*)
1406 Hoccleve *Male Regle* 27.73–4: Ful seelde is seen that yowthe takith heede Of perils that been likly for to fall. **c1475** *Thewis* 183.99: And youthede can no perellis cast. *Oxford* 740; Tilley Y46.

Y37 **Youth** will to youth
a1475 Banester *Guiscardo* 34.579: Youth will to youth and lofe to lufe evermore. See **L272.**

Y38 As merry as **Yule** day
c1425 *Avowynge* 91[31–2]: For thay make als mirry chere, Als hit were yole day. Cf. Whiting *Drama* 338:455.

Y39 It is easy to cry **(Y)ule** at other men's cost
1549 Heywood *D* 45.120: It is easy to cry ule at other mens coste. Apperson 721; *Oxford* 122; Tilley Y53; Whiting *Scots* II 164.

Z

Z1 Have **Zeal** to yourself and then to your neighbor

a1500 *De Imitatione* (*1*) 43.9–10: Have therfore first zeel to thiself, and than maist thou have zeel to thi neighbore. **1502** *De Imitatione* (*2*) 182.1–2: Have first a zele and a respecte to thy selfe, and than thou mayst better attende to the dedes of other. See **C153.**

INDEX OF IMPORTANT WORDS

The purpose of this index is twofold: to make possible the identification of a saying in a form which differs from the lemma, and in some degree to facilitate thematic studies. Experience shows that an index of this kind cannot be altogether satisfactory. The shorter the index the less useful, the longer the index the less usable, and a happy medium between too little and too much is hard to achieve.

The index contains the important words in the lemmas, excluding the alphabetizing words but including the modern equivalents of obsolete words, and a selection of significant words from those quotations which differ markedly in phrasing from the lemmas. It is no doubt superfluous to observe that the same word may be important in one context and unimportant in another. Words from the lemmas and from the first three quotations in any entry are identified by the lemma numbers; for all other words the dates of the quotations are given in parentheses after the lemma numbers. Words from the quotations are listed only for first occurrence within an entry. In the index, words from the quotations are given, wherever possible, in the entry forms of the NED, and obsolete or unusual words are glossed if they have not already been glossed in a lemma.

If a word appears as more than one part of speech it is broken down grammatically, and homonyms are usually separated. When nouns occur in both singular and plural, no distinction is made in the index, save in the case of *man* and *woman*. If nouns are found only in the plural they are entered under the plural form, unless the words occur as another part of speech or unless the plural forms throw the words out of alphabetical order. All verb forms, except verbal nouns and verbal adjectives, are entered under the infinitive forms. Adjectives and adverbs appear under the positive forms unless the words appear only in the comparative or superlative, in which cases those forms are used. Expressions of worthlessness or contempt (see p. xvi) are grouped in the index under Not account, Not amend, and so forth, and the relatively few Wellerisms are brought together under that word.

A

B

C

D

E

F

G

I

J

K

N

Q

R

S

U

V

W

Y

INDEX OF PROPER NOUNS

This index contains all the proper nouns in the lemmas and the important proper nouns from the quotations. The few adjectives derived from proper nouns are included. In some cases it is impossible to determine the historical names, if any, which were intended.

References to the phrases which use place names to indicate inclusiveness or distance (see Introduction, p. xvi) are brought together here: A32, A34, A110, A134–5, B260, B554–5 B603, C6, C45, C63, C188, C410–1, C486, C579, D7, D160, D369–70, E101, F608, G448, H416, H631, I35–6, J25–6, J28, J56, K8–9, L112, L425–7, L595, O52, P30, P310, R64, R182, R186, S30, S546, S721, T545, W8, Y22.